THE MOTION PICTURE GUIDE

THIS VOLUME IS DEDICATED TO
JAMES CAGNEY
HUMPHREY BOGART
EDWARD G. ROBINSON

THE
MOTION PICTURE
GUIDE

E - G

1927-1983

Jay Robert Nash
Stanley Ralph Ross

CINEBOOKS, INC.

Chicago, 1986

Publishers of THE COMPLETE FILM RESOURCE CENTER

Publishers: Jay Robert Nash, Stanley Ralph Ross; **Editor-in-Chief:** Jay Robert Nash; **Executive Editor:** Stanley Ralph Ross; **Associate Publisher and Director of Development:** Kenneth H. Petchenik; **Senior Editor-in-Charge:** Jim McCormick; **Senior Editors:** David Tardy, Robert B. Connelly; **Production Editor:** William Leahy; **Associate Editors:** Oksana Lydia Dominguez, Jeffrey H. Wallenfeldt, Edie McCormick, Michaela Tuohy, Jeannette Hori, Tom Legge; **Contributing Editors:** James J. Mulay (Chief Contributing Editor), Daniel Curran, Michael Theobald, Arnie Bernstein, Phil Pantone, Brian Brock; **Assistant Editors:** Marla Dorfman, Kim O. Morgan, Susan Doll, Marla Antelis, Debra Schwieder, Susan Fisher, Donna Roth, Marla Kruglik, Kristina Marcy, Sarah von Fremd, Wendy Anderson; **Art Production and Book Design:** Cathy Anetsberger; **Research Staff:** Shelby Payne (Associate Editor and Chief Researcher), William C. Clogston, Tobi Elliott, Carol Pappas, Rosalyn Mathis, Millicent Mathis, Andrea Nash; **Business/Legal:** Judy Anetsberger.

Associate Publishers: Howard Grafman, Lynn Christian, James and Monica Vrettos, Antoinette Mailliard, Brent H. Nettle, Michael Callie, Constance Shea, Barbara Browne Cramer.

Editorial and Sales Offices: CINEBOOKS, 6135 N. Sheridan Road, Chicago, Illinois 60660.

Library of Congress Catalog Card Number: 85-071145
ISBN: 0-933997-00-0 THE MOTION PICTURE GUIDE (10 Vols.)
      0-933997-03-5 THE MOTION PICTURE GUIDE, Vol III (E-G)

Printed in the United States
First Edition
This volume contains 3,188 entries.

1 2 3 4 5 6 7 8 9 10

HOW TO USE INFORMATION IN THIS GUIDE

ALPHABETICAL ORDER

All entries have been arranged alphabetically throughout this and all subsequent volumes. In establishing alphabetical order, all articles (A, An, The) appear after the main title (AFFAIR TO REMEMBER, AN). In the case of foreign films the article precedes the main title (LES MISERABLES appears in the letter L) which makes, we feel, for easier access and uniformity. Contractions are grouped together and these will be followed by non-apostrophized words of the same letters. B.F.'s DAUGHTER is at the beginning of the letter B, not under BF.

TITLES

It is important to know what title you are seeking; use the *complete* title of the film. The film ADVENTURES OF ROBIN HOOD, THE, cannot be found under merely ROBIN HOOD. Many films are known under different titles and we have taken great pains to cross-reference these titles. (AKA, also known as) as well as alternate titles used in Great Britain (GB). In addition to the cross-reference title only entries, AKAs and alternate titles in Great Britain can be found in the title line for each entry. An alphabetically arranged comprehensive list of title changes appears in the Index volume (Vol. X).

RATINGS

We have rated each and every film at critical levels that include acting, directing, script, and technical achievement (or the sad lack of it). We have a *five-star* rating, unlike all other rating systems, to signify a film superbly made on every level, in short, a masterpiece. At the lowest end of the scale is *zero* and we mean it. The ratings are as follows: *zero* (not worth a glance), *(poor), **(fair), ***(good), ****(excellent), *****(masterpiece, and these are few and far between). Half-marks mean almost there but not quite.

YEAR OF RELEASE

We have used in all applicable instances the year of United States release. This sometimes means that a film released abroad may have a different date elsewhere than in these volumes but this is generally the date released in foreign countries, not in the U.S.

FOREIGN COUNTRY PRODUCTION

When possible, we have listed abbreviated names of the foreign countries originating the production of a film. This information will be found within the parenthesis containing the year of release. If no country is listed in this space, it is a U.S. production.

RUNNING TIME

A hotly debated category, we have opted to list the running time a film ran at the time of its initial U.S. release but we will usually mention in the text if the film was drastically cut and give the reasons why. We have attempted to be as accurate as possible by consulting the most reliable sources.

PRODUCING AND DISTRIBUTING COMPANIES

The producing and/or distributing company of every film is listed in abbreviated entries next to the running time in the title line (see abbreviations; for all those firms not abbreviated, the entire firm's name will be present).

COLOR OR BLACK-AND-WHITE

The use of color or black-and-white availability appears as c or bw following the producing/releasing company entry.

CASTS

Whenever possible, we give *the complete cast and the roles played* for each film and this is the case in 95% of all entries, the only encyclopedia to ever offer such comprehensive information in covering the entire field. The names of actors and actresses are in Roman lettering, the names of the roles each played in Italic inside parentheses.

SYNOPSIS

The in-depth synopsis for each entry (when such applies) offers the plot of each film, critical evaluation, anecdotal information on the production and its personnel, awards won when applicable and additional information dealing with the production's impact upon the public, its success or failure at the box office, its social significance, if any. Acting methods, technical innovations, script originality are detailed. We also cite other productions involving an entry's personnel for critical comparisons and to establish the style or genre of expertise of directors, writers, actors and technical people.

REMAKES AND SEQUELS

Information regarding films that have sequels, sequels themselves or direct remakes of films can be found at the very end of each synopsis.

DUBBING AND SUBTITLES

We will generally point out in the synopsis when a foreign film is dubbed in English, mostly when the dubbing is poor. When voices are dubbed, particularly when singers render vocals on songs mimed by stars, we generally point out these facts either in the cast/role listing or inside the synopsis. If a film is in a foreign language and subtitled, we signify the fact in a parenthetical statement at the end of each entry (In Italian, English subtitles).

CREDITS

The credits for the creative and technical personnel of a film are extensive and they include: p (producer, often executive producer); d (director); w (screenwriter, followed by adaptation, if any, and creator of original story, if any, and other sources such as authors for plays, articles, short stories, novels and non-fiction books); ph (cinematographer, followed by camera system and color process when applicable, i.e., Panavision, Technicolor); m (composer of musical score); ed (film editor); md (music director); art d (art director); set d (set decoration); cos (costumes); spec eff (special effects); ch (choreography); m/l (music and lyrics); stunts, makeup, and other credits when merited. When someone receives two or more credits in a single film the credits may be combined (p&d, John Ford) or the last name repeated in subsequent credits shared with another (d, John Ford; w, Ford, Dudley Nichols).

GENRES/SUBJECT

Each film is categorized for easy identification as to genre and/or subject and themes at the left-hand bottom of each entry. (Western, Prison Drama, Spy Drama, Romance, Musical, Comedy, War, Horror, Science-Fiction, Adventure, Biography, Historical Drama, Children's Film, Animated Feature, etc.) More specific subject and theme breakdowns will be found in the Index (Vol. X).

PR AND MPAA RATINGS

The Parental Recommendation provides parents having no knowledge of the style and content of each film with a guide; if a film has excessive violence, sex, strong language, it is so indicated. Otherwise, films specifically designed for young children are also indicated. The Parental Recommendation (**PR**) is to be found at the right-hand bottom of each entry, followed, when applicable, by the **MPAA** rating. The PR ratings are as follows: **AAA** (must for children); **AA** (good for children); **A** (acceptable for children); **C** (cautionary, some objectionable scenes); **O** (completely objectionable for children).

KEY TO ABBREVIATIONS

Foreign Countries:

Arg.	Argentina
Aus.	Australia
Aust.	Austria
Bel.	Belgium
Braz.	Brazil
Brit.	Great Britain (GB when used for alternate title)
Can.	Canada
Chi.	China
Czech.	Czechoslovakia
Den.	Denmark
E. Ger.	East Germany
Fin.	Finland
Fr.	France
Ger.	Germany (includes W. Germany)
Gr.	Greece
Hung.	Hungary
Ital.	Italy
Jap.	Japan
Mex.	Mexico
Neth.	Netherlands
Phil.	Philippines
Pol.	Poland
Rum.	Rumania
S.K.	South Korea
Span.	Spain
Swed.	Sweden

Key to Abbreviations (continued)

Switz.	Switzerland
Thai.	Thailand
USSR	Union of Soviet Socialist Republics
Yugo.	Yugoslavia

Production Companies, Studios and Distributors (U.S. and British)

AA	ALLIED ARTISTS
ABF	Associated British Films
AE	Avco Embassy
AEX	Associated Exhibitors
AH	Anglo-Hollandia
AIP	American International Pictures
AM	American
ANCH	Anchor Film Distributors
ANE	American National Enterprises
AP	Associated Producers
AP&D	Associated Producers & Distributors
ARC	Associated Releasing Corp.
Argosy	Argosy Productions
Arrow	Arrow Films
ART	Artcraft
Astra	Astra Films
AY	Aywon
BA	British Actors
B&C	British and Colonial Kinematograph Co.
BAN	Banner Films
BI	British Instructional
BIFD	B.I.F.D. Films
BIP	British International Pictures
BJP	Buck Jones Productions
BL	British Lion
Blackpool	Blackpool Productions
BLUE	Bluebird
BN	British National
BNF	British and Foreign Film
Boulting	Boulting Brothers (Brit.)
BP	British Photoplay Production
BPP	B.P. Productions
BRIT	Britannia Films
BRO	Broadwest
Bryanston	Bryantston Films (Brit.)
BS	Blue Streak
BUS	Bushey (Brit.)
BUT	Butchers Film Service
BV	Buena Vista (Walt Disney)
CAP	Capital Films
CC	Christie Comedy
CD	Continental Distributing
CHAD	Chadwick Pictures Corporation
CHES	Chesterfield
Cineguild	Cineguild
CL	Clarendon
CLIN	Clinton
COL	COLUMBIA
Colony	Colony Pictures
COM	Commonwealth
COMM	Commodore Pictures
COS	Cosmopolitan (Hearst)
DE	Dependable Exchange
DGP	Dorothy Gish Productions
Disney	Walt Disney Productions
DIST	Distinctive
DM	DeMille Productions
DOUB	Doubleday
EAL	Ealing Studios (Brit.)
ECF	East Coast Films
ECL	Eclectic
ED	Eldorado
EF	Eagle Films
EFF & EFF	E.F.F. & E.F.F. Comedy
EFI	English Films Inc.
EIFC	Export and Import Film Corp.
EL	Eagle-Lion
EM	Embassy Pictures Corp.

EMI	EMI Productions
EP	Enterprise Pictures
EPC	Equity Pictures Corp.
EQ	Equitable
EXCEL	Excellent
FA	Fine Arts
FC	Film Classics
FD	First Division
FN	First National
FOX	20TH CENTURY FOX (and Fox Productions)
FP	Famous Players (and Famous Players Lasky)
FRP	Frontroom Productions
Gainsborough	Gainsborough Productions
GAU	Gaumont (Brit.)
GEN	General
GFD	General Films Distributors
Goldwyn	Samuel Goldwyn Productions
GN	Grand National
GOTH	Gotham
Grafton	Grafton Films (Brit.)
H	Harma
HAE	Harma Associated Distributors
Hammer	Hammer Films (Brit.)
HD	Hagen and Double
HM	Hi Mark
HR	Hal Roach
IA	International Artists
ID	Ideal
IF	Independent Film Distributors (Brit.)
Imperator	Imperator Films (Brit.)
IP	Independent Pictures Corp.
IN	Invincible Films
INSP	Inspirational Pictures (Richard Barthelmess)
IV	Ivan Film
Javelin	Javelin Film Productions (Brit.)
JUR	Jury
KC	Kinema Club
KCB	Kay C. Booking
Knightsbridge	Knightsbridge Productions (Brit.)
Korda	Alexander Korda Productions (Brit.)
Ladd	Ladd Company Productions
LAS	Lasky Productions (Jesse L. Lasky)
LFP	London Films
LIP	London Independent Producers
Lorimar	Lorimar Productions
LUM	Lumis
Majestic	Majestic Films
Mascot	Mascot Films
Mayflowers	Mayflowers Productions (Brit.)
Metro	Metro
MFC	Mission Film Corporation
MG	Metro-Goldwyn
MGM	METRO-GOLDWYN-MAYER
MON	Monogram
MOR	Morante
MS	Mack Sennett
MUT	Mutual
N	National
NG	National General
NGP	National General Pictures (Alexander Korda, Brit.)
NW	New World
Orion	Orion Productions
Ortus	Ortus Productions (Brit.)
PAR	PARAMOUNT
Pascal	Gabriel Pascal Productions (Brit.)
PDC	Producers Distributors Corp.

Key to Abbreviations (continued)

PEER	Peerless
PWN	Peninsula Studios
PFC	Pacific Film Company
PG	Playgoers
PI	Pacific International
PIO	Pioneer Film Corp.
PM	Pall Mall
PP	Pro Patria
PRC	Producers Releasing Corporation
PRE	Preferred
QDC	Quality Distributing Corp.
RAY	Rayart
RAD	Radio Pictures
RANK	J. Arthur Rank (Brit.)
RBP	Rex Beach Pictures
REA	Real Art
REG	Regional Films
REN	Renown
REP	Republic
RF	Regal Films
RFD	R.F.D. Productions (Brit.)
RKO	RKO RADIO PICTURES
Rogell	Rogell
Romulus	Romulus Films (Brit.)
Royal	Royal
SB	Samuel Bronston
SCHUL	B.P. Schulberg Productions
SEL	Select
SELZ	Selznick International (David O. Selznick)
SF	Selznick Films
SL	Sol Lesser
SONO	Sonofilms
SP	Seven Pines Productions (Brit.)
SRP	St. Regis Pictures
STER	Sterling
STOLL	Stoll
SUN	Sunset
SYN	Syndicate Releasing Co.
SZ	Sam Zimbalist
TC	Two Cities (Brit.)
T/C	Trem-Carr
THI	Thomas H. Ince
TIF	Tiffany
TRA	Transatlantic Pictures
TRU	Truart
TS	Tiffany/Stahl
UA	UNITED ARTISTS
UNIV	UNIVERSAL (AND UNIVERSAL INTERNATIONAL)
Venture	Venture Distributors
VIT	Vitagraph
WAL	Waldorf
WB	WARNER BROTHERS (AND WARNER BROTHERS-SEVEN ARTS)
WEST	Westminster
WF	Woodfall Productions (Brit.)
WI	Wisteria
WORLD	World
WSHP	William S. Hart Productions
ZUKOR	Adolph Zukor Productions

Foreign

ABSF	AB Svensk Film Industries (Swed.)
Action	Action Films (Fr.)
ADP	Agnes Delahaie Productions (Fr.)
Agata	Agata Films (Span.)
Alter	Alter Films (Fr.)
Arch	Archway Film Distributors
Argos	Argos Films (Fr.)
Argui	Argui Films (Fr.)
Ariane	Les Films Ariane (Fr.)
Athos	Athos Films (Fr.)
Belga	Belga Films (Bel.)
Beta	Beta Films (Ger.)
CA	Cine-Alliance (Fr.)
Caddy	Caddy Films (Fr.)
CCFC	Compagnie Commerciale Francais Einematographique (Fr.)
CDD	Cino Del Duca (Ital.)
CEN	Les Films de Centaur (Fr.)
CFD	Czecheslovak Film Productions
CHAM	Champion (Ital.)
Cinegay	Cinegay Films (Ital.)
Cines	Cines Films (Ital.)
Cineriz	Cinerez Films (Ital.)
Citel	Citel Films (Switz.)
Como	Como Films (Fr.)
CON	Concordia (Fr.)
Corona	Corona Films (Fr.)
D	Documento Films (Ital.)
DD	Dino De Laurentiis (Ital.)
Dear	Dear Films (Ital.)
DIF	Discina International Films (Fr.)
DPR	Films du Palais-Royal (Fr.)
EX	Excelsa Films (Ital.)
FDP	Films du Pantheon (Fr.)
Fono	Fono Roma (Ital.)
FS	Filmsonor Productions (Fr.)
Gala	Fala Films (Ital.)
Galatea	Galatea Productions (Ital.)
Gamma	Gamma Films (Fr.)
Gemma	Gemma Cinematografica (Ital.)
GFD	General Film Distributors, Ltd. (Can.)
GP	General Productions (Fr.)
Gray	(Gray Films (Fr.)
IFD	Intercontinental Film Distributors
Janus	Janus Films (Ger.)
JMR	Macques Mage Releasing (Fr.)
LF	Les Louvre Films (Fr.)
LFM	Les Films Moliere (Fr.)
Lux	Lux Productions (Ital.)
Melville	Melville Productions (Fr.)
Midega	Midega Films (Span.)
NEF	N.E.F. La Nouvelle Edition Francaise (Fr.)
NFD	N.F.D. Productions (Ger.)
ONCIC	Office National pour le Commerce et L'Industrie Cinematographique (Fr.)
Ortus	Ortus Films (Can.)
PAC	Production Artistique Cinematographique (Fr.)
Pagnol	Marcel Pagnol Productions (Fr.)
Parc	Parc Films (Fr.)
Paris	Paris Films (Fr.)
Pathe	Pathe Films (Fr.)
PECF	Productions et Editions Cinematographique Francais (Fr.)
PF	Parafrench Releasing Co. (Fr.)
PIC	Produzione International Cinematografica (Ital.)
Ponti	Carlo Ponti Productions (Ital.)
RAC	Realisation d'Art Cinematographique (Fr.)
Regina	Regina Films (Fr.)
Renn	Renn Productions (Fr.)
SDFS	Societe des Films Sonores Tobis (Fr.)
SEDIF	Societe d'Exploitation ed de Distribution de Films (Fr.)
SFP	Societe Francais de Production (Fr.)
Sigma	Sigma Productions (Fr.)
SNE	Societe Nouvelle des Establishments (Fr.)
Titanus	Titanus Productions (Ital.)
TRC	Transcontinental Films (Fr.)
UDIF	U.D.I.F. Productions (Fr.)
UFA	Deutsche Universum-Film AG (Ger.)
UGC	Union Generale Cinematographique (Fr.)
Union	Union Films (Ger.)
Vera	Vera Productions (Fr.)

E

(NOTE: 1984 releases appear in Volume IX)

E.T. THE EXTRA-TERRESTRIAL**** (1982) 115m UNIV c

Dee Wallace *(Mary)*, Henry Thomas *(Elliott)*, Peter Coyote *(Keys)*, Robert MacNaughton *(Michael)*, Drew Barrymore *(Gertie)*, K.C. Martel *(Greg)*, Sean Frye *(Steve)*, Tom Howell *(Tyler)*, Erika Eleniak *(Pretty Girl)*, David O'Dell *(Schoolboy)*, Richard Swingler *(Science Teacher)*, Frank Toth *(Policeman)*, Robert Barton *(Ultra Sound Man)*, Michael Darrell *(Van Man)*, Milt Kogan *(Doctor)*, David Berkson, David Carlberg, Alexander Lampone, Rhoda Makoff, Robert Murphy, Richard Pesavento, Tom Sherry, Susan Cameron, Will Fowler, Jr., Barbara Hartnett, Di Ann Lampone, Mary Stein, Mitchell Suskin.

From the first moment anyone saw this film, there was never a doubt that it would be a hit but no one could guess it would become an all-time blockbuster. They didn't reckon with Spielberg's vision. Some have described it as the best picture Disney never made, and if Walt were alive, he would have been delighted to have been associated with it. It's partly autobiographical in that the young man, Thomas, suffers from having a father who departed to Mexico with another woman. (Spielberg himself was raised by his mother and stepfather, and probably missed his real father.) The story is a combination of *Peter Pan* and *The Bible* in that it uses the best of those two literary masterpieces as the core. Thomas, Robert MacNaughton, and Drew Barrymore live with mother Dee Wallace in a typical suburb quite like the one in Spielberg's POLTERGEIST. It so resembles the other household that one might think the two stories were happening side by side. Thomas finds E.T. a visitor from another planet similar to Tinker Bell—and decides to keep him. The rest of the story has to do with how the kids deal with the being, E.T.'s desire to get back to his planet, and how the children save the creature from the government types who want to keep him—against his will—on earth, not knowing that prolonged exposure to our air will kill him (as it will most people in Southern California's foul atmosphere). E.T. is captured by the authorities and is on his way to death when he is saved by a bunch of the kids. Next, a hair-raising BMX bike chase takes them out to where the creature has planned to meet his compatriots for the trip back; E.T. leaves and the picture ends. Now, that's the simple way of telling the story. The fun comes in the rich detail that Spielberg and associate producer/writer Melissa Mathison have devised. The odd little beast gets into all sorts of modern-day skirmishes. He puts a toy car into his mouth in much the same way that any infant might when trying out a new plaything. He gets drunk on beer, crushes the can, and throws it at the TV set while Tom and Jerry are up to their cartoon shenanigans. He learns some basic English and, in general, behaves like a youngster. Hence, he is totally understood by the kids in the picture as well as the kids in the audience. E.T. is like a little lost child whose parents can't find him at Disneyland. The conclusion; annunciation, redemption, and resurrection, is right out of the New Testament; E.T.'s glowing finger most resembles God touching Man on the Sistine Chapel ceiling. Whether or not Spielberg intended all of this symbolism doesn't actually matter. It is what the audiences read into the picture that counts. Despite all the first-rate acting and the excellent technical credits, the Movie Academy turned its collective back on E.T., perhaps more out of jealousy than anything else. Our main criticism was the feeling of constantly being manipulated by Spielberg, as if to say "let's have a laugh here, a thrill here, and a heart-tug there." There was something very studied about the whole experience, right down to the overblown John Williams score. It was sort of a young person's version of Spielberg's CLOSE ENCOUNTERS OF THE THIRD KIND; Dreyfuss could have been the 35-year-old version of Thomas. It's almost, but not quite, a classic.

p, Steven Spielberg, Kathleen Kennedy; d, Spielberg; w, Melissa Mathison; ph, Allen Daviau (Technicolor); m, John Williams; ed, Carol Littleton; prod d, James D. Bissell; set des, William Teegarden; set dec, Jackie Carr; cos, Deborah Scott; E.T. created by Carlo Rambaldi; spec vis eff, Industrial Light & Magic (Dennis Muren).

Fantasy **(PR:AAA MPAA:PR)**

EACH DAWN I DIE*½** (1939) 92m FN/WB bw

James Cagney *(Frank Ross)*, George Raft *("Hood" Stacey)*, Jane Bryan *(Joyce Conover)*, George Bancroft *(Warden John Armstrong)*, Maxie Rosenbloom *(Fargo Red)*, Stanley Ridges *(Muller)*, Alan Baxter *(Polecat Carlisle)*, Victor Jory *(W. J. Grayce)*, Willard Robertson *(Lang)*, Paul Hurst *(Garsky)*, John Wray *(Peter Kassock)*, Louis Jean Heydt *(Joe Lassiter)*, Ed Pawley *(Dale)*, Joe Downing *(Limpy Julien)*, Emma Dunn *(Mrs. Ross)*, Thurston Hall *(District Attorney Jesse Hanley)*, Clay Clement *(Attorney Lockhart)*, William Davidson *(Bill Mason)*, John Ridgely *(Jerry Poague, Reporter)*, John Harron *(Lew Keller, Reporter)*, Selmer Jackson *(Patterson)*, Robert Homans *(Mac the Guard)*, Harry Cording *(Temple)*, Abner Biberman *(Shake Edwards)*, Napoleon Simpson *(Mose)*, Cliff Saum, Tom Wilson, Al Lloyd, Jack Goodrich, Stuart Holmes, Alice Conners, Fern Barry *(Accident Witnesses)*, Maris Wrixon *(Girl in Car)*, Garland Smith, Arthur Gardner *(Men in Car)*, James Flavin *(Policeman)*, Charles Trowbridge *(Judge)*, Joe Sully *(Man Behind)*, Eddy Chandler *(Deputy)*, John Dilson *(Parole Board Member)*, Max Hoffman, Jr. *(Gate Guard)*, Henry Otho, Lee Phelps, Dick Rich, Jack C. Smith *(Guards)*, Walter Miller *(Turnkey)*, Fred Graham *(Guard in Cell)*, Wilfred Lucas *(Bailiff)*, Vera Lewis *(Jury Woman)*, Emmett Vogan *(Prosecutor)*, Earl Dwire *(Judge Crowder)*, Frank Mayo *(Telegraph Editor)*, Mack Gray *(Joe)*, Bob Perry *(Bud)*, Al Hill *(Johnny the Hood)*, Elliott Sullivan *(Convict)*, Chuck Hamilton *(Court Officer)*, John Conte *(Narrator)*, Nat Carr, Wedgewood Nowell, Jack Wise, Granville Bates.

As a pugnacious reporter, Cagney unearths evidence that will put some high-level politicians in jail. Before he can get his material into print he is abducted, knocked unconscious and put into a car, booze poured over him, and the car sent careening down the street where it runs over a man and kills him. The brutal frame works; Cagney is convicted of manslaughter and is sent to prison, where he befriends smooth crook Raft, a crime boss. On the train to the Big House, Raft smiles and jokingly asks Cagney to "write a piece about me. I like my name in the paper." At Rocky Point Prison Cagney repeatedly applies for parole, but is turned down again and again. He becomes so embittered that he throws in his lot with Raft, the very person he has despised as a reporter, helping Raft to escape on the promise that Raft will try to get evidence to clear him. Earlier Downing, an informer, was knifed while the prisoners watched a movie (WINGS OF THE NAVY, 1939). Raft, upon whom Downing informed, is rightly suspected of the killing; he is brought into court, as is Cagney, a witness. Cagney's testimony is never uttered. Raft makes a break for a window and dives three stories to land on the soft top of a waiting truck. He then rolls off to hop into a car that speeds away. Cagney at first waits patiently for Raft to obtain the freedom-bringing evidence but then despairs as the weeks pass; he is goaded into breaking rules that bring him before the warden, Bancroft, who insists he tell how Raft engineered his escape. Cagney refuses, and is told he will be thrown into solitary confinement. Spitting fire, Cagney shouts: "I'll get out if I have to kill every screw in the hole!" Bryan, who is Cagney's faithful girl friend and fellow reporter, goes to Raft's hideout and begs the underworld kingpin to keep his promise. Raft tells her that he believes Cagney almost ruined his escape and sneers under snake eyes: "Who ever did anything for me?" Cagney did, explains Bryan, and tells him how Cagney has gone into solitary confinement rather than inform on him. To repay the debt, Raft forces some hoodlums to pinpoint the criminal who framed Cagney, Wray, but then learns that Wray is at Rocky Point Prison, doing time for another offense. Raft suddenly turns himself in to Bancroft so he can bring Wray to the peculiar justice of the underworld. He vows that he'll break out again after squaring things anyway, that "no prison can hold me." During a wild prison riot and escape attempt, Raft compels Wray to confess, an admission which clears Cagney and is overheard by warden Bancroft. Raft then shoots Wray and dives into the yard ringed by guards, to die by machinegun fire. Cagney is released and rejoins his paper and Bryan, vowing to work for prison reform. Keighley's direction is sure and swift, as are Edeson's fluid cameras in this prison saga. Cagney and Raft give powerful and compassionate performances, with Raft emerging more memorable in some scenes, although it's Cagney's film all the way. Raft and Cagney were old pals when they met again for this film. Both had worked in vaudeville together and Cagney had persuaded Warner Bros. to give Raft a small part in TAXI (1932), just before Raft's star rose at Paramount. Studio executives thought at first to put either John Garfield or Fred MacMurray in the Raft part until Cagney insisted that Raft would be the only actor to do the hoodlum part justice. Cagney believed that Raft "was the only really tough man I knew in the business." Raft had, in his long and checkered career, been a rum-runner and bootlegger for NYC gangster Owney Madden, and he had picked up his mannerisms by observing such hoodlums as Joe Adonis. Cagney, one of the best hoofers of his day, thought Raft a great dancer and even ranked him with Fred Astaire. During the filming of EACH DAWN I DIE it was Cagney's great pleasure to introduce Astaire to Raft, but he had his apprehensions. Raft had a short fuse; any remark might set off his explosive temper, yet the two dancers got along famously and even planned to appear in a movie together, a musical never made. EACH DAWN I DIE was a blockbuster at the box office, even though it went over familiar prison yarn material, including the ever-used jute mill scene which Hollywood had been grinding out since films like THE CRIMINAL CODE (1931), but the script was tight and the acting electric, elevating the movie far beyond the average.

p, David Lewis; d, William Keighley; w, Norman Reilly Raine, Warren Duff, Charles Perry (based on the novel by Jerome Odlum); ph, Arthur Edeson; m, Max Steiner; ed, Thomas Richards; md, Leo Forbstein; art d, Max Parker; cos, Howard Shoup; makeup, Perc Westmore; tech adv, William Buckley.

Prison Drama **(PR:A MPAA:NR)**

EACH MAN FOR HIMSELF (SEE: RUTHLESS FOUR, THE, 1969, Ital./Ger.)

EADIE WAS A LADY** (1945) 67m COL bw

Ann Miller *(Eadie Allen/Edithea Alden)*, Joe Besser *("Professor" Diogenes Dingle)*, William Wright *(Tommy Foley)*, Jeff Donnell *(Pamela "Pepper" Parker)*, Jimmy Little *(Jimmy Tuttle)*, Marion Martin *(Rose Allure)*, Kathleen Howard *(Aunt Priscilla Alden)*, Tom Dugan *(Hannegan)*, Douglas Wood *(Dean Flint)*, George Meeker *(Caleb Van Horne, VIII)*, George Lessey *(Reverend Ames)*, Ida Moore *(Maid)*, Jack Cole *(Specialty Dancer)*, Hal McIntyre and his Orchestra.

Hard-to-believe drama starring Miller as a straitlaced girl's school student by day, who transforms herself into the top attraction at a steamy burlesque show at night. Besser stars as a comedian who has become a school teacher and Wright plays the owner of the club, the love interest for Miller. Songs include "Tabby The Cat" by Harold Dickinson, Howard Gibeling; "She's A Gypsy From Brooklyn" by L. Wolfe Gilbert, Ben Oakland; "Next Victory Day," "I'm Going To See My Baby" by Phil Moore; "Eadie Was A Lady" by Nacio Herb Brown, Buddy De Sylva, and Richard A. Whiting; "'Til You Came Along," and "Eadie's Back."

p, Michel Kraike; d, Arthur Dreifuss; w, Monte Brice; ph, Burnett Guffey; m, George Duning; ed, James Sweeney; md, M. W. Stoloff; art d, Carl Anderson; set d, Louis Diage; ch, Jack Cole; m/l, Saul Chaplin, Sammy Cahn, Phil Moore, L. Wolfe Gilbert, Ben Oakland, Howard Gibeling, Harold Dickinson, Buddy De Sylva, Nacio Herb Brown, Richard A. Whiting.

Musical **(PR:A MPAA:NR)**

EAGER BEAVERS (SEE: SWINGING BARMAIDS, THE, 1975)

EAGLE AND THE HAWK, THE*½** (1933) 72m PAR bw

Fredric March *(Jerry Young)*, Cary Grant *(Henry Crocker)*, Jack Oakie *(Mike Richards)*, Carole Lombard *(The Beautiful Lady)*, Sir Guy Standing *(Major*

Dunham), Forrester Harvey *(Hogan),* Kenneth Howell *(John Stevens),* Leyland Hodgson *(Kinsford),* Virginia Hammond *(Lady Erskine),* Crauford Kent *(General),* Douglas Scott *(Tommy Erskine),* Robert Manning *(Voss),* Adrienne D'Ambricourt *(Fifi),* Jacques Jou-Jerville *(French General's Aide),* Russell Scott *(Flight Sergeant),* Paul Cremonesi *(French General),* Yorke Sherwood *(Taxi Driver),* Lane Chandler, Dennis O'Keefe *(Fliers),* Olaf Hytten *(Story-Telling Officer).*

A vivid and unusual WW I film, THE EAGLE AND THE HAWK has March as the fearless leader of a British flying squadron who, at the film's opening, is already embittered by the slaughter in the skies. Grant arrives at his command post and shows his competitive anger by accusing March of keeping him from the front and glory. Of course, March *has* tried to prevent his former chums Grant and Oakie from going into combat, but for compassionate reasons. Nevertheless, a cynical rivalry between March and Grant ensues, even after Grant is assigned as March's observer, flying in the rear cockpit of the two-seater fighter to photograph enemy strongpoints and act as a rear machinegunner. Five men in the squadron have been killed; March's irritation and anger over the loss of life bubbles to the surface. He is ordered to take a ten-day leave and, in London, meets beautiful Lombard, who brings him back to affection. Upon his return, however, March learns that Grant, to win glory for himself, has flown off on a needless mission which causes the death of likable Oakie. Moreover, March discovers that the German ace he has just shot down, a long-standing opponent simply nicknamed Greentail, is nothing more than a beardless boy. He is sick to death of war and his world goes black. In a rage, March gets drunk, then delivers a searing denunciation against war in front of the entire squadron. Going to his room, March commits suicide. Grant finds his body and, out of the true respect he felt for the man (but never showed), he secretly places March in his plane, takes off, and, once in the air, swivels the machinegun about and riddles the body so that it will appear that March died heroically in combat. March is later buried in a hero's grave as Grant looks on. This film, with its fine aerial shots and exciting dogfights, was produced to compete with such popular war vehicles as THE DAWN PATROL and to also provide March with a project that would take him out of the drawing room and into adventure. March and Grant are terrific in their adversarial roles and Lombard, though shown briefly, is hauntingly effective. Standing, as the commander, is steadfast and authoritative.

d, Stuart Walker; w, Bogart Rogers, Seton I. Miller (based on the story by John Monk Saunders); ph, Harry Fishbeck.

War Drama   **(PR:C   MPAA:NR)**

EAGLE AND THE HAWK, THE**½   (1950) 103m PAR c
(AKA: SPREAD EAGLE)

John Payne *(Todd Croyden),* Rhonda Fleming *(Madeline Danzeeger),* Dennis O'Keefe *(Whitney Randolph),* Thomas Gomez *(Gen. Liguras),* Fred Clark *(Basil Danzeeger),* Frank Faylen *(Buck Hyatt),* Eduardo Noriega *(Roberto),* Grandon Rhodes *(Governor Lubbock),* Walter Reed *(Jones),* Margaret Martin.

Payne and O'Keefe form an uneasy alliance when sent by the government into Mexico to try to stop a planned invasion of Texas by Napoleon III's men, who are trying to install Maximillian as the emperor of Mexico. Payne and O'Keefe attempt to expose the fraud to the loyal followers of beloved Mexican patriot Juarez so that the Mexican people will rise and throw Napoleon III's army out. Lots of action and fabulous cinematography by James Wong Howe.

p, William H. Pine, William C. Thomas; d, Lewis R. Foster; w, Geoffrey Homes, Foster (based on the story "A Mission To General Houston" by Jess Arnold); ph, James Wong Howe (Technicolor); m, David Chudnow; ed, William Fox; art d, Lewis H. Creber.

Western   **(PR:A   MPAA:NR)**

EAGLE HAS LANDED, THE***   (1976, Brit.) 134m ITC Entertainment-
Assoc. General Films-Filmways Australasian/COL c

Michael Caine *(Col. Kurt Steiner),* Donald Sutherland *(Liam Devlin),* Robert Duvall *(Col. Max Radl),* Jenny Agutter *(Molly Prior),* Donald Pleasence *(Heinrich Himmler),* Anthony Quayle *(Admiral Wilhelm Canaris),* Jean Marsh *(Joanna Grey),* Sven Bertil Taube *(Capt. Ritter Neumann),* John Standing *(Father Philip Verecker),* Judy Geeson *(Pamela Verecker),* Treat Williams *(Capt. Harry Clark),* Larry Hagman *(Col. Clarence E. Pitts),* Siegfried Rauch *(Sgt. Brandt),* John Barrett *(Laker Armsby),* Leigh Dilley *(Winston Churchill/George Foster),* Maurice Roeves *(Maj. Corcoran),* Alexei Jawdokimov, Michael Byrne, Denis Lill, Leonie Thelen, Tim Barlow, Kate Binchy, David Gilliam, Asa Teeter, Terry Plummer, Jack McCulloch, Rick Parse, Richard Wren, Joachim Hansen, Keith Buckley, Jeff Conaway, Robert G. Reece.

Exciting WW II espionage drama starring Duvall as a Nazi colonel who, under direct orders from Heinrich Himmler (Pleasence), plots to kidnap Winston Churchill. To do this, Duvall hires English-hating Irishman Sutherland. Together with a 16-man task force led by another Nazi colonel, Caine, he parachutes into England and contacts enemy spy Marsh, who supplies them with the necessary information for Sutherland to execute his plan. Soon the plan starts to go haywire. Sutherland begins to fall in love with local girl Agutter, which leads to his making a series of mistakes in order to save the girl's life. Meanwhile, one of the Nazis tries to save the life of a child who is drowning. In the attempt, his outer clothing is torn, revealing his Nazi uniform underneath. These errors cause Agutter's sister, Geeson, to notify some American soldiers stationed nearby of the Germans' whereabouts. The Yanks corner the Nazis in a church. In the ensuing battle most of the Germans are killed, but Sutherland helps Caine escape before he opts to remain in the village with Agutter. Caine continues on the mission alone and eventually reaches Churchill. He shoots the British leader before being killed himself by the Prime Minister's guard. As it turns out, the British knew about the plot all along and had substituted a Churchill look-alike in place of the actual Prime Minister to bait the Nazis into the open.

p, Jack Winer, David Niven, Jr.; d, John Sturges; w, Tom Mankiewicz (based on a Jack Higgins novel); ph, Tony Richmond, Peter Allwork (Panavision, Eastmancolor); m, Lalo Schifrin; ed, Irene Lamb, Anne V. Coates; prod d, Peter Murton; art d, Charles Bishop; set d, Peter James; cos, Yvonne Blake; spec eff, Roy Whybrow; stunts, Gerry Crampton.

War   **Cas.**   **(PR:C   MPAA:PG)**

EAGLE IN A CAGE***   (1971, U.S./Yugo.) 97m Group W-Ramona/NGP c

John Gielgud *(Lord Sissal),* Ralph Richardson *(Sir Hudson Lowe),* Billie Whitelaw *(Mme. Bertrand),* Kenneth Haigh *(Napoleon Bonaparte),* Moses Gunn *(General Gourgaud),* Ferdy Mayne *(Count Bertrand),* Lee Montague *(Cipriani),* Georgina Hale *(Betty Balcombe),* Michael Williams *(Barry O'Meara),* Hugh Armstrong *(English Soldier),* Athol Coates *(Sentry).*

An outstanding cast is featured in this imaginative drama starring Haigh as the once-powerful Napoleon in his early days in exile on St. Helena. Haigh is superb as the defeated emperor who now dreams of rebuilding his empire, but deep down knows that it will probably never happen. There is a short period of optimism when British envoy Gielgud arrives and informs Haigh that Britain may help him escape his prison if he will agree to organize an attack on Prussia within six months. Haigh agrees to this deal, but he is stopped by the stomach cancer that would eventually consume him. Shot in Yugoslavia. Based on Lampell's Emmy-winning script for TV's "Hallmark Hall of Fame."

p, Millard Lampell; d, Fielder Cook; w, Lampell (based on his teleplay); ph, Frano Vodopivec (Eastmancolor); m, Marc Wilkson; ed, Max Benedict; art d, Vladmir Tadej; cos, David Walker.

Drama   **(PR:A   MPAA:PG)**

EAGLE OVER LONDON**   (1973, Ital.) 100m Cine Globe c
(AKA: EAGLES OVER LONDON)

Frederick Stafford, Van Johnson, Francisco Rabal, Evelyn Stewart, Luigi Pistilli, Renzo Palmer, Edy Biagetti, Luis Davila, Christian Hay, Jacques Berthier, Teresa Gimpera.

Nazi spies infiltrate British headquarters during the Battle of Britain. Cliche-ridden spy stuff. Notable as one of the very few late feature film appearances of 1940s bobby-soxer screen idol Van Johnson who, still boyish-looking, had—at the age of 57—been doing mostly dinner-theater and television work at the time.

p, Edmondo Amati; d, Enzo G. Castellari; ph, Alejandro Ulloa (Technicolor); m, Francesco De Masi.

Spy Drama   **(PR:C   MPAA:NR)**

EAGLE ROCK**   (1964, Brit.) 62m World Safari/CFF c

Pip Rolls *(Mark),* Christine Thomas *(Jean),* Stephen Morris *(Gavin),* Bryan Marsh *(Mr. MacGregor),* Jim Cameron *(Mr. McTavish),* Tony Paul *(Tony),* Colin Neal *(Hugh),* Nicholas Young *(Trevor).*

Rolls, a young student at the Adventure School at Dungeon Gyll, climbs a dangerous rock face to steal eggs from an eagle's nest and becomes trapped at the top. A rescue operation fetches him down safely in the inevitable climax. Decent children's adventure film with some nice color photography.

p,d&w, Henry Geddes (based on a story by Mary Cathcart Borer).

Children   **(PR:A   MPAA:NR)**

EAGLE SQUADRON***½   (1942) 109m UNIV bw

Robert Stack *(Chuck Brewer),* Diana Barrymore *(Anne Partridge),* John Loder *(Paddy Carson),* Eddie Albert *(Leckie),* Nigel Bruce *(McKinnon),* Leif Erickson *(Johnny Coe),* Edgar Barrier *(Wadislaw Borowsky),* Jon Hall *(Hank Starr),* Evelyn Ankers *(Nancy Mitchell),* Isobel Elsom *(Dame Elizabeth Whitby),* Alan Hale, Jr. *(Olesen),* Don Porter *(Ramsey),* Frederick Worlock *(Grenfall),* Stanley Ridges *(Air Minister),* Gene Reynolds *(The Kid),* Robert Warwick *(Bullock),* Clarence Straight *(Chandler),* Edmund Glover *(Meeker),* Gladys Cooper *(Aunt Emmeline),* Rhys Williams *(Sergeant Johns),* Paul Cavanagh *(Sir John),* Gavin Muir *(Severn),* Richard Fraser *(Lt. Jeffreys),* Richard Crane *(Griffith),* Howard Banks *(Barker),* Harold Landon *(Welch),* Todd Karns *(Meyers),* Charles King, Jr. *(Chubby),* Jill Esmond *(Phyllis),* Ian Wolfe *(Sir Charles Porter),* Alan Napier *(Black Watch Officer),* Harold de Becker *(Private Owen),* Donald Stuart *(Hoskins),* Carl Harbord *(Lubbock),* Charles Irwin *(Sir Benjamin Trask),* Olaf Hytten *(Day Controller),* Stanley Smith, Richard Davies *(R.A.F. Fliers),* Queenie Leonard *(Lankershire Blonde),* Ivan Simpson *(Simms),* John Burton *(Wing Commander),* Bruce Lester *(King),* Tom Stevenson *(Allison),* James Eagles *(Blind Patient),* James Seay *(Medical Officer),* Audrey Long *(Nurse),* Mary Carr *(Mother),* Peter Lawford *(Pilot),* Rex Lease *(German Soldier),* Tarquin Olivier *(Georgie),* William Severn *(Billy),* Linda Bieber *(A Little Girl),* Peggy Ann Garner *(Child),* Quentin Reynolds *(Narrator).*

Exciting and patriotic WW II air combat film follows Stack, Loder, Albert, Hall, Erickson and Barrier, American Volunteers fighting with the RAF before Pearl Harbor, chronicling their induction to an elite flying corps, their training, their air battles with the Nazi Luftwaffe, their brief romances with British women and some of their tragic deaths. Much of the film is focused on Stack and his love affair with Barrymore (John Barrymore's tragic-bound daughter), but splendid aerial photography, much of it documentary material supplied by British authorities, depicts actual combat. An exciting segment deals with a raid on the French coast where American pilots hijack a mysterious Nazi plane. Lubin's direction is as rapid as a staccato burst of gunfire from the wings of a Spitfire. All the performances are sound, often telling. Stack, Loder, and Hall are standouts in a rare film from Universal, one exceeding 100 minutes, which broke an unwritten rule on running time from the budget-minded studio.

p, Walter Wanger; d, Arthur Lubin; w, Norman Reilly Raine (based on a "Cosmopolitan" story by C.S. Forester); ph, Stanley Cortez; m, Frank Skinner; ed, Philip

Cahn; md, Charles Previn; art d, Jack Otterson, Alexander Golitzen; spec eff, John Fulton.

War Drama (PR:A MPAA:NR)

EAGLE WITH TWO HEADS*½ (1948, Fr.) 100m Vog bw

Edwige Feuillere (*The Queen*), Jean Marais (*Stanislas*), Sylvia Monfort (*Edith de Berg*), Jean Debucourt (*Felix de Willenstein*), Jacques Varennes (*Count de Foehn*), Abdallah (*Tony*), Gilles Queant (*Rudy*), Maurice Nasil (*Gentz*), Edward Stirling (*Adams*).

Filmmaker and poet Jean Cocteau brings his stage play to the screen, retaining Jean Marais in the lead role. His character, Stanislas, is an anarchist poet sent to assassinate the Queen, Feuillere. Instead, he falls in love with her; his passion for violence being supervened by a passion for love. The film, as in Cocteau's oeuvre, is film-poetry at its most pure. While his films have been judged by many as absurd or pretentious, director Jacques Rivette best defines Cocteau's work as "That which is never out of style, which is linked to neither fashion, nor style, but to a poverty turned to riches, limping turned to dance, in short to a happy destitution. The poet above all must reinvent simplicity . . ." While not as beautiful as ORPHEUS or BLOOD OF A POET, this practically unknown film should head any cinephiles list of films to see. (In French; English subtitles.)

p, George Danciger, Alexandre Mnouchkine; d&w, Jean Cocteau; ph, Christian Matraz; m, Georges Auric; art d, Christian Bernard.

Drama (PR:A MPAA:NR)

EAGLE'S BROOD, THE*½ (1936) 61m PAR bw

William Boyd (*Hopalong Cassidy*), Jimmy Ellison (*Johnny Nelson*), William Farnum (*El Toro*), George Hayes (*Spike*), Addison Richards (*Big Henry*), Joan Woodbury (*Dolores*), Dorothy Revier (*Dolly*), Paul Fix (*Steve*), Al Lydell (*Pop*), John Merton (*Ed*), George Mari (*Pablo*), Juan Torena (*Estaban*), Henry Sylvester (*Sheriff*), Frank Shannon.

Good early Hopalong Cassidy oater sees Boyd as a kindly sheriff who promises an aging outlaw who has saved his life that he will try to find his grandson. The townsfolk are outraged at the news and throw Boyd out of office. Boyd rides off in search of the boy who has been kidnaped by the villainous Richards. Climax sees Boyd and Richards struggling on a clifftop, and the boys from Bar 20 coming to the rescue. Well-paced and directed.

p, Harry Sherman; d, Howard Bretherton; w, Doris Schroeder, Harrison Jacobs (based on a story by Clarence E. Mulford); ph, Archie Stout; ed, Edward Schroeder; m/l, Sam H. Stept, Sidney Mitchell.

Western **Cas.** (PR:A MPAA:NR)

EAGLE'S WING (1979, Brit.) 104m Rank c

Martin Sheen (*Pike*), Sam Waterston (*White Bull*), Harvey Keitel (*Henry*), Stephane Audran (*The Widow*), Caroline Langrishe (*Judith*), John Castle (*The Priest*), Jorge Luke (*Red Sky*), Jose Carlos Ruiz (*Lame Wolf*), Manuel Ojeda (*Miguel*), Jorge Russek (*Gonzalo*), Pedro Damieari (*Jose*), Farnesio De Bernal (*Monk*), Cecelia Camacho (*Girl*), Claudio Brook (*Sanchez*), Julio Lucena (*Don Luis*), Enrique Lucero (*Shaman*).

Overly artsy and a bit pretentious British(?!) western starring Sheen as a city-bred trapper who is slowly educated in the ways of the wilderness as he battles Comanche chief Waterston over the capture of a magnificent, but elusive, white stallion. The whole thing is a rather obvious allegorical tale which sees white-man Sheen desiring the psyche and freedom of red-man Waterston. Nice try at a western by the British, but it is only held together by good performances from Sheen and Waterston. Screenplay writer John Briley went on to write GANDHI for which he won an Oscar.

p, Ben Arbeid; d, Anthony Harvey; w, John Briley (based on a story by Michael Syson); ph, Billy Williams; m, Marc Wilkinson; ed, Lesley Walker; prod d, Herbert Westbrook; cos, Tim Hutchinson.

Western (PR:A MPAA:PG)

EARL CARROLL SKETCHBOOK (1946) 90m REP bw
(GB: HATS OFF TO RHYTHM)

Constance Moore (*Pamela Thayer*), William Marshall (*Tyler Brice*), Bill Goodwin (*Richard Starling*), Johnny Coy (*Johnny*), Vera Vague (*Sherry Lane*), Edward Everett Horton (*Dr. Milo Edwards*), Hillary Brooke (*Lynn Stafford*), Dorothy Babb (*Lola*), Robert Homans (*Pop*).

Low-budget try at a big-budget musical by Republic Studios sees Moore as a singer and Marshall as her talented songwriter boy friend who has sold out to write radio jingles. This causes a strain on the relationship which requires much singing and dancing to make up. Songs include "Hittin' the Bottle," "I've Got a Right to Sing the Blues," Harold Arlen, Ted Koehler; "I've Never Forgotten," "I Was Silly, Headstrong and Impetuous," "What Makes You Beautiful, Beautiful?" "The Lady With a Mop," Sammy Cahn, Jule Styne.

p, Robert North; d, Albert S. Rogell; w, Frank Gill, Jr., Parke Levy (based on a story by Gill); ph, Jack Marta; ed, Richard L. Van Enger; md, Cy Feuer; spec eff, Howard and Theodore Lydecker; ch, Nick Castle; m/l, Jule Styne, Sammy Cahn, Harold Arlen, Ted Koehler.

Musical (PR:A MPAA:NR)

EARL CARROLL'S VANITIES (1945) 95m REP bw

Dennis O'Keefe (*Danny Baldwin*), Constance Moore (*Drina*), Eve Arden (*Tex Donnelly*), Otto Kruger (*Earl Carroll*), Alan Mowbray (*Grand Duke Paul*), Stephanie Bachelor (*Claire Elliott*), Pinky Lee (*Pinky Price*), Parkyakarkus (*Walter*), Leon Belasco (*Dashek*), Beverly Lloyd (*Cigarette Girl*), Edward Gargan (*Policeman*), Mary Forbes (*Queen Mother*), Tom Dugan (*Waiter in Club*), Chester Clute (*Mr. Weims*), Jimmy Alexander (*The Singer*), Tom London (*Doorman*), Robert Greig

(*Vance, the Butler*), Wilton Graff (*Mr. Thayer*), Tommy Ivo (*Tommy*), Lillane & Mario (*Dance Specialty*), Woody Herman and His Orchestra.

Kruger plays famed Broadway producer Earl Carroll, who is in search of a star for his new show. He discovers her in Moore, a visiting princess from a tiny European land who is in America trying to get a loan to bail out her principality's financial woes. O'Keefe is the romantic interest. Songs include: "Endlessly," Kim Gannon, Walter Kent, sung by Moore; "Apple Honey," Woody Herman; "Who Dat Up Dere?" Gannon, Kent; "Riverside Jive," Albert Newman; "Rockaby Boogie" and "You Beautiful Thing, You."

p, Albert J. Cohen; d, Joseph Santley; w, Frank Gill, Jr. (based on a story by Cortland Fitzsimmons); ph, Jack Marta; m, Walter Scharf; ed, Richard L. Van Enger; md, Albert Newman; art d, Russell Kimball, Frank Hotaling; ch, Sammy Lee.

Musical (PR:A MPAA:NR)

EARL OF CHICAGO, THE* (1940) 85m MGM bw

Robert Montgomery (*Silky Kilmount*), Edward Arnold (*Doc Ramsey*), Reginald Owen (*Gervase Gonwell*), Edmund Gwenn (*Munsey*), E.E. Clive (*Redwood*), Ronald Sinclair (*Gerald Kilmount*), Norma Varden (*Maureen Kilmount*), Halliwell Hobbes (*Lord Chancellor*), Ian Wolfe (*Reading Clerk*), Peter Godfrey (*Judson*), Billy Bevan (*Guide*), Rex Evans (*Vicar*), Charles Coleman (*Bishop*), Kenneth Hunter (*Lord Tyrmanell*), William Stack (*Coroner*), Miles Mander (*Attorney General*), Frederic Worlock (*Lord Elfie*), John Burton (*Clerk*), Art Berry, Sr. (*Seedman*), David Dunbar (*Plowman*), Harold Howard, Bob Corey (*Fishermen*), Henry Flynn (*Villager*), Vangie Beilby (*Old Maid*), Radford Allen (*Boy*), Crauford Kent (*Specialist*), Montague Shaw (*Doctor*), Ben Welden (*Driver*), Olaf Hytten (*Hodges*), Pierre Watkin (*Warden*), George Anderson (*Guard*), Nora Perry (*Receptionist*), William Haade (*Crapshooter*), Eddie Marr (*Offender*), Anthony Warde (*Salesman*), John Butler (*Slim*), Gladys Blake (*Silken Legs*), Lowden Adams (*Floor Waiter*), Alec Harford (*Mr. Dell*), Arthur Mulliner (*Mr. Brackton*), Barlowe Borland (*Fingal*), Alec Craig (*Son*), Billy Bevan (*Guide*), John Power (*Tourist*), Ivan Simpson (*Hargraves*), Barbara Bedford (*Doc's Secretary*), Tempe Pigott (*Mrs. Oades*), Ben Webster (*Gaffer*), Ellis Irving (*Russell*), Colin Kenny (*Sergeant*), Matthew Boulton (*Ickerton*), Paul England (*Chief Constable*), Boyd Irwin (*Presiding Magistrate*), Leonard Mudie (*Allington*), Halliwell Hobbes (*Lord High Chancellor*), David Clyde, B.J. Kelly (*Hangers-on*), Holmes Herbert (*Sergeant-at-Arms*), Ralph Stock (*Constable*), Leyton Lee (*Adjutant*), Gladden James (*Silky's Secretary*), Yvonne Severn (*Village Girl*), Harry Allen (*Mayer*), Colonel Ford (*Villager*), Frank Benson (*Sexton*), Jimmy Aubrey (*Cockney*), Frank Baker (*Policeman*), Forbes Murray (*Diplomat*), Robert Warwick (*Clerk at Parliament*), Zeffie Tilbury (*Old Lady*).

Another offbeat but gripping performance from Montgomery, who is a ruthless Chicago gangster suddenly informed that he has inherited an estate and title in England. The "dese, dems, and dose" hoodlum travels to England to pick up his "loot" but stays on in a vain attempt to take his place in the peerage. Gwenn is his patient valet and adviser in the ways of aristocratic manners and customs, none of which Montgomery masters as he fractures the language, inadvertantly insults nobles, and bumbles his way through a world he cannot understand. When he is betrayed in a scheme, his normal compunction to violence explodes, and he disposes of his antagonist. Later tried in the House of Lords where he admits his crime, he shouts: "He ratted on me!" Montgomery is sentenced to death. He goes to the scaffold at film's end, as downbeat a finale as Montgomery's fate in HERE COMES MR. JORDAN was upbeat. Arnold gives a powerful performance as an honest attorney sent to prison on a framed case. Director Thorpe keeps the film moving through comedic and dramatic scenes, and there are moments when Montgomery's personality turns almost as sinister as the unforgetable killer he played in NIGHT MUST FALL. Saville had produced only one other film in Hollywood up to this time, a programmer in 1930 for poverty-row studio Tiffany, but he had since gone on to head such British-produced blockbusters as THE CITADEL and GOODBYE, MR. CHIPS.

p, Victor Saville; d, Richard Thorpe; w, Lesser Samuels (based on a story by Brock Williams, Charles de Grandcourt, Gene Fowler); ph, Ray June; m, Werner R. Heymann; ed, Fred Sullivan; art d, Cedric Gibbons.

Comedy/Drama (PR:A MPAA:NR)

EARL OF PUDDLESTONE (1940) 67m REP bw

James Gleason (*Joe Higgins*), Lucille Gleason (*Lil Higgins*), Russell Gleason (*Sidney Higgins*), Harry Davenport (*Grandpa*), Lois Ranson (*Betty Higgins*), Tommy Ryan (*Tommy Higgins*), Eric Blore (*Horatio Bottomley*), Betty Blythe (*Mrs. Potter-Potter*), Forrester Harvey (*Tittington*), William Halligan (*Henry Potter-Potter*), Mary Ainslee (*Marian Potter-Potter*), William Brady (*Bill Connolly*), Ben Carter (*Homer*), James C. Morton (*Officer Brannigan*), Aubrey Mather (*Lord Stoke-Newington*), Mary Kenyon (*Judith*).

One of a series of low-budget family comedies from Republic intended to compete with similar big-studio successes, such as MGM's Andy Hardy series, starring Renaissance man Gleason, his wife, and his son. Earlier films in the series, beginning with THE HIGGINS FAMILY (1938), had been produced and directed by Gus Meins, but Meins' death the year of this release resulted in his input being uncredited by the studio. The series was halted briefly, then picked up again in 1941, but with Roscoe Karns and Ruth Donnelly replacing the elder Gleasons. The improbable plots, often played for slapstick, will be familiar to anyone weaned on TV situation comedies: the all-American family extricating itself from difficulties of its own making by means of unity and good fellowship. In this entry, daughter Ranson is snubbed by wealthy people. Grandpa Davenport invents imaginary titled relatives to combat the situation, but Ranson redeems herself on her own, demonstrating that democracy and simple family verities will always win in the end. The silly plot is partly redeemed by the acting of the talented Gleasons. This series entry had enough musical numbers to make it appear that the studio mavens were contemplating a switch to a musical-comedy format and were grooming singer-dancer Ranson for the lead. The metamorphosis never occurred; after two other films Ranson dropped out of sight, entering film biographer David Ragan's list of lost players. (See HIGGINS FAMILY series, Index.)

p&d Gus Meins; w, Val Burton, Ewart Adamson; ph, Jack Marta; ed, Ernest Nims; md, Cy Feuer.

Comedy **(PR:A MPAA:NR)**

EARLY AUTUMN✶✶ (1962, Jap.) 103m Toho/New Yorker c
(KOHAYAGAWA-KE NO AKI; AKA: LAST OF SUMMER; THE END OF SUMMER)

Ganjiro Nakamura (Manbei Kohayagawa), Setsuko Hara (Akiko), Yoko Tsukasa (Noriko), Michiyo Aratama (Fumiko), Yumi Shirakawa (Takako), Reiko Dan (Yuriko), Keiju Kobayashi (Hisao), Akira Takarada (Noriko's Boy Friend), Daisuke Kato (Yanosuke), Chieko Naniwa (Tsune Sasaki), Haruko Togo (Teruko), Haruko Sugimura, Hisaya Morishige, Chishu Ryu, Yuko Mochizuki.

Ozu is considered to be one of Japan's leading directors, but this film comes off as too melodramatic and seems more like a soap opera. Nakamura is the father of a family of three daughters and owns a sake brewery. He lets a son-in-law, Kobayashi, run the plant. Nakamura begins an affair with a woman who was once his mistress; she has a daughter believed to be fathered by Nakamura. One of his daughters discovers the relationship and tells him he is an unworthy father. He has a heart attack and everyone realizes how much they depend on him. Nakamura has another heart attack and dies when he goes to visit his mistress.

p, Sanezumi Fujimoto, Masakatsu Kaneko, Tadahiro Teramoto; d, Yasujiro Ozu; w, Kogo Noda, Ozu; ph, Asakazu Nakai (Tohoscope, Agfacolor); m, Toshiro Mayazumi; art d, Tomoo Shimogawara.

Drama **(PR:C MPAA:NR)**

EARLY BIRD, THE✶½ (1936, Brit.) 69m Crusade/PAR bw

Richard Hayward (Daniel Duff), Jimmy Mageean (Charlie Simpson), Charlotte Tedlie (Mrs. Gordon), Myrtle Adams (Lizzie), Nan Cullen (Mrs. Madill), Elma Hayward (Susan Duff), Terence Grainger (Archie Macready), Charles Fagan (Harold Gordon), Pat Noonan.

In an Irish village, puritanical Tedlie goes on a reforming binge, arousing the ire of the locals. Justice is served when the lady is sued for libel. Minor English comedy, mostly forgotten.

p, Victor M. Greene; d&w, Donovan Pedelty (based on a play by J. McGregor Douglas).

Comedy **(PR:A MPAA:NR)**

EARLY BIRD, THE✶✶ (1965, Brit.) 98m RANK c

Norman Wisdom (Norman Pitkin), Edward Chapman (Grimsdale), Jerry Desmonde (Hunter), Paddie O'Neill (Mrs. Hoskins), Bryan Pringle (Austin), Richard Vernon (Sir Roger), John Le Mesurier (Col. Foster), Peter Jeffrey (Fire Chief), Penny Morrell (Miss Curry), Marjie Lawrence (Woman in Negligee), Frank Thornton (Doctor), Dandy Nichols (Demented Woman), Harry Locke (Commissionaire), Michael Bilton (Nervous Man), Imogen Hassall (Sir Roger's Secretary), Nellie (Pitkin's Horse).

Popular British comic Wisdom stars in his first color movie as a milkman for a small, family-run dairy that is being taken over by a large monopoly. Not wanting this to happen, Wisdom takes on the combine and harrasses the owner of the firm by invading the businessman's garden and sabotaging his golf game. Most of the humor is slapstick, predictable, and only vaguely amusing.

p, Hugh Stewart; d, Robert Asher; w, Jack Davies, Norman Wisdom, Eddie Leslie, Henry Blyth; ph, Jack Asher (Eastmancolor); m, Ron Goodwin; ed, Gerry Hambling.

Comedy **(PR:A MPAA:NR)**

EARLY TO BED✶✶ (1933, Brit./Ger.) 83m UFA-GAU/W&F bw

Sonnie Hale (Helmut), Edmund Gwenn (Kruger), Fernand Graavey (Carl), Heather Angel (Grete), Donald Calthrop (Peschke), Lady Tree (Widow Seidelblast), Athene Seyler (Frau Weiser), Jillian Sande (Trude), Leslie Perrins (Meyer), Lewis Shaw (Wolf).

Another of the mass of musicals that poured out of UFA in the earliest days of sound. This one concerns a manicurist and a night waiter who fall in love, then realize that they are using the same apartment. Shot simultaneously in German and English.

p, Erich Pommer; d, Ludwig Berger; w, Robert Stevenson (based on a story by Hans Szekeley and Robert Liebmann).

Musical **(PR:A MPAA:NR)**

EARLY TO BED✶✶½ (1936) 75m PAR bw

Mary Boland (Tessie Weeks), Charlie Ruggles (Chester Beatty), George Barbier (Horace Stanton), Gail Patrick (Grace Stanton), Robert McWade (Burgess Frisbie), Lucien Littlefield (Mr. O'Leary), Colin Tapley (Doctor), Helen Flint (Mrs. Duvall), Rae Daggett (Miss Benson), William Wayne (Salesman), Eddie Borden (Salesman), Brooks Benedict (Craig), Tom Wilson (Joe), Sidney Blackmer (Rex Daniels), Arthur Hoyt (Smithers), Jane Gittleson (Mrs. Fosbinder), Billy Gilbert (Burger), Sarah Edwards (Miss Barton).

Ruggles and Boland are teamed in this comedy tale dealing with somnambulism. Ruggles plays a meek clerk who wanders around in his sleep. His sleepwalking soon gets him into trouble; he becomes involved with gangsters, which leads to a

false murder charge. Eventually, with the help of Boland, Ruggles clears himself and gets a promotion. Silly fun, but Ruggles and Boland make a good team.

p, Harlan Thompson; d, Norman McLeod; w, Arthur Kober (based on a story by Lucien Littlefield, Chandler Sprague); ph, Henry Sharp.

Comedy **(PR:A MPAA:NR)**

EARLY WORKS✶✶½ (1970, Yugo.) 87m Avala Film-Neoplanta Film/Grove Press bw (RANI RADOVI)

Milja Vujanovic (Yugoslavia), Bogdan Tirnanic (Dragisa), Cedomir Rodovic (Kruno), Marko Nikolic (Marko), Slobodan Aligrudic (Father), Zelimira Zujovic.

Using the character name Yugoslavia metaphorically, Vujanovic is a young politically idealistic reformer, who soon discovers that reality often interferes with romanticism. Using theoretical ideas set forth by Marx and Engels, she sets on her course to change the world. Showing her true belief in communism, she has three lovers, each of whom accompanies her on her journey to round up the proletariat. These peasants respond by beating her and her three lovers to a pulp, which sets the girl off in a mood in which she continuously derides her three men for their inabilities. They in turn decide they've had enough of the revolutionist and put her out of her misery. (In Croatian; English Subtitles)

d, Zelimar Zilnik; w, Zilnik, Branko Vucicevic; ph, Karpo Acimovic Godina; ed, Godina.

Political Drama **(PR:O MPAA:NR)**

EARRINGS OF MADAME DE . . ., THE✶✶ (1954, Fr.) 105m Franco-London Film Indus-Rizzoli/Arlan bw

Danielle Darrieux (Countess Louise de . . .), Charles Boyer (General Andre de . . .), Vittorio de Sica (Baron Fabrizio Donati), Mireille Perrey (Mme. de . . .'s Nurse), Jean Debucourt (Mon. Remy, the Jeweler), Serge Lecointe (Jerome, his Son), Lia di Leo (Lola, the General's Mistress), Jean Galland (M. de Bernac), Hubert Noel (Henri de Maleville), Leon Walther (Theater Manager), Madeleine Barbulee (Mme. de . . .'s Friend), Guy Favieres (Julien, the General's Valet).

A fairly standard romantic triangle with fabulous photography and some excellent work by the three stars. Critics were mixed in their assessment of the movie and it was not a great success at the wickets. Ophuls sets the movie in the Parisian *Belle Epoque* where Darrieux is a countess (no last name is ever given, hence the title and the credits) who sells her expensive diamond earrings, a wedding gift from husband Boyer, a general in the army. She tells him that she lost the valuable baubles the night they attended the opera. The newspapers dutifully report the loss of stones and jeweler Debucourt—who purchased them—returns them to Boyer, who pays for them again but does not tell his wife. Instead, he gives the earrings to his mistress, di Leo, who is going away to Constantinople. She loses the earrings gambling at the casino and they are later purchased by de Sica, a wealthy diplomat. Later, de Sica and Darrieux meet and fall in love. It goes without saying that he sends her the earrings as a token of his affection. Boyer discovers that Darrieux's usually harmless flirtations are quite serious in the case of de Sica. He sends her off to Italy and she suffers the pangs of separation until she and de Sica have a tryst. After returning to Paris, Darrieux claims that she's found the lost earrings and plans to wear them to a fancy affair. Boyer hits the ceiling and tells de Sica that Darrieux cannot accept the earrings. de Sica confronts Darrieux for the history of the trinkets and she eventually tells him what has transpired. de Sica is hurt by her duplicity and sells the earrings to Debucourt for the second time. Darrieux is hurt, angry, and not in the best of health. Hoping to revive her spirits, Boyer again buys the earrings from the jeweler and gives them to his ailing wife. She cries bitterly at the sight of them, as they remind her of the deep love she still carries for de Sica. Boyer now forces her to give the earrings to his niece. The young woman, who has just had a child, needs money and she sells the earrings to . . . you guessed it, Debucourt. He promptly goes to Boyer and offers them, but Boyer wants the earrings out of his sight. Darrieux hears that they are for sale so she sells some of her jewels to raise the money to buy them again. Boyer is now furious and challenges de Sica to a duel, if only to get the man out of his life. Darrieux pleads with de Sica to leave Paris with her, but he will not. The duel is fought, Boyer shoots de Sica, and Darrieux hears the shot and dies of a heart attack. The irony and coincidence are worthy of an O. Henry short story, and perhaps that's what this should have been, a much shorter story. It would be very tedious were it not for Ophuls' fluid camera. Very beautiful to look at, but ultimately a soap opera, and not a very good one at that.

p&d, Max Ophuls; w, Marcel Archard (adapted by Archard, Annette Wademant, Ophuls, from the novel by Louise de Vilmorin); ph, Christian Matras; m, Georges Van Parys (Oscar Strauss theme); ed, Boris Lewyn, set d, Jean D'Eaubonne.

Drama **(PR:C-O MPAA:NR)**

EARTH CRIES OUT, THE✶½ (1949, Ital.) 79m Lux bw (IL GRIDO DELLA TERRA)

Andrea Checcki (Arie), Marina Berti (Dina), Vivi Giol (Judith), Carlo Ninchi (Ship Captain), Luigi Tosi (David), Filippo Scelzo (Dr. Tannen), George Trent (George Birkemore).

A propagandistic picture which tells the tale of a boatful of Jews who leave Italy for the newly-formed Israel soon after the British pull-out. Interwoven into this semi-documentary treatment is an uninvolving story of three former friends who have gone their separate ways—one becoming a terrorist, one a British officer, and one a colonizer. The dubbing job is up to standard for Italian films, making it far superior to most countries at the time.

p, Albert Salvatori; d, Dullio Coletti; w, Lewis F. Gittier.

Drama **(PR:A MPAA:NR)**

EARTH DIES SCREAMING, THE**

(1964, Brit.) 62m Lippert/FOX bw

Willard Parker (Jeff Nolan), Virginia Field (Peggy Taggett), Dennis Price (Quinn Taggett), Vanda Godsell (Violet Courtland), Thorley Walters (Edgar Otis), David Spenser (Mel), Anna Palk (Lorna).

Test pilot Parker returns from a flight to discover that England has been wiped out. Robots have killed almost everyone just by touching them (they turn their corpses into zombies). With the help of a handful of survivors, Parker finds what is controlling the robots (aliens from another planet) and destroys the transmitting station.

p, Robert L. Lippert, Jack Parsons; d, Terence Fisher; w, Henry Cross, Harry Spalding; ph, Arthur Lowis; m, Elisabeth Lutyens; ed, Robert Winter; art d, George Provis; makeup, Harold Fletcher.

Science Fiction   **(PR:A   MPAA:NR)**

EARTH ENTRANCED***   (1970, Braz.) 110m Mapa Films/New Yorker bw (TERRA EM TRANSE)

Jardel Filho (Paulo Martins), Jose Lewgoy (Felipe Vieira), Glauce Rocha (Sara), Paulo Autran (Porfirio Diaz), Paulo Gracindo (Julio Fuentes), Danuza Leao (Silvia), Hugo Carvana (Alvaro), Zozimo Bulbul, Antonio Carnera, Emanuel Cavalcanti, Rafael de Carvalho, Mario Lago, Jose Marinho, Flavio Migliaccio, Francisco Milani, Paulo Cesar Pereio, Echio Reis, Thelma Reston, Ivan de Souza, Modesto de Souza, Jofre Soares, Mauricio do Valle, Darlene Gloria, Elisabeth Gasper, Irma Alvarez, Sonia Clara, Clovis Bornay.

The leading spokesman of the "cinema novo" movement from Brazil, Rocha, created this film about a man trapped in the middle of unstable and dishonest politics. Filho is the writer, shot at the beginning of the picture, who traces the events which have lead up to his present circumstance. He had abandoned a more rigid party leader in order to back the liberal candidate, a man who wins the election but does not fulfill the promises he made during his campaign. Disillusioned with the direction of his country's politics, Filho attempts to retire to his writing, but upon the insistence of his girl friend, Rocha, is right back in the middle of the turmoil. Filho's eventual downfall comes when he attempts to convince the country's leader to take a certain course and is then shot. Though criticized for a format that was not readily accessible to the general populace—which makes one question the validity of political filmmaking—EARTH ENTRANCED impressed enough people to win the International Film Critics Award at Cannes.

p, Zelito Viana; d&w, Glauber Rocha; ph, Luiz Carlos Barreto; m, Sergio Ricardo; ed, Eduardo Escorel; art d, Paulo Gil Soares; m/l, "Il Guaranay" Carlos Gomes; "Bachianas Brasileiras No. 3 & 6" Heitor Villa-Lobos; "Otello Overture" Giuseppe Verdi, (performed by Esdon Machado Quartet); "Samba Of The Favela De Rio," "Alue De Candomble Of Bahia."

Drama   **(PR:C   MPAA:NR)**

EARTH VS. THE FLYING SAUCERS***   (1956) 82m COL bw (AKA: INVASION OF THE FLYING SAUCERS)

Hugh Marlowe (Dr. Russell A. Marvin), Joan Taylor (Carol Marvin), Donald Curtis (Maj. Huglin), Morris Ankrum (Gen. Hanley), John Zaremba (Prof. Kanter), Tom Browne Henry (Adm. Enright), Grandon Rhodes (Gen. Edmunds), Larry Blake (Motorcycle Officer), Harry Lauter (Cutting), Charles Evans (Dr. Alberts), Clark Howat (Sgt. Nash), Frank Wilcox (Alfred Cassidy), Alan Reynolds (Maj. Kimberly).

A great sci-fi alien invasion film with outstanding special effects by Ray Harryhausen. Flying saucers arrive on Earth at an Army base, and, though they mean no harm, are greeted with gunfire. This sets the aliens off and they declare war, killing the soldiers and starting a large-scale invasion involving dozens of saucers. The aliens are winning the war until one is killed and the corpse is brought to scientist Marlowe for a post-mortem examination. Marlowe discovers that the aliens are highly sensitive to certain sound frequencies, which the earthlings then aim at the saucers, causing them to crash into many Washington, D.C. monuments. Among the landmarks spectacularly destroyed on screen via Harryhausen's magic: the Capitol, the Lincoln Memorial, and the Washington Monument. One of Harryhausen's most outstanding efforts.

p, Charles H. Schneer; d, Fred F. Sears; w, George Worthing Yates, Raymond T. Marcus (based on a story by Curt Siodmak, suggested by "Flying Saucers From Outer Space" by Maj. Donald E. Keyhoe); ph, Fred Jackman, Jr.; m, Mischa Bakaleinikoff; ed, Danny B. Landres; md, Bakaleinikoff; art d, Paul Palmentola; spec eff, Ray Harryhausen, Russ Kelley.

Science Fiction   **(PR:A   MPAA:NR)**

EARTH VS. THE SPIDER*   (1958) 73m Santa Rosa bw (AKA: THE SPIDER)

Ed Kemmer, June Kennedy, Gene Persson, Gene Roth, Hal Tory, Mickey Finn.

A very low-budget ripoff of Jack Arnold's TARANTULA, a spider that grows to enormous height and likes human flesh. After wrecking miniature towns, the spider is captured and put on display for tourists. It escapes and teenagers put the pest to rest. Don't get trapped in this web.

p&d, Bert I. Gordon; w, Lazio Gorog, George Worthing Yates; ph, Jack Marta.

Horror   **(PR:A   MPAA:NR)**

EARTHBOUND**½   (1940) 67m FOX bw

Warner Baxter (Nick Desborough), Andrea Leeds (Ellen Desborough), Lynn Bari (Linda Reynolds), Charley Grapewin (Mr. Whimser), Henry Wilcoxon (Jeffrey Reynolds), Elizabeth Patterson (Becky Tilden), Russell Hicks (Prosecutor), Christian Rub (Almette), Ian Wolfe (Motorcycle Officer), Lester Scharff (Detective), Reginald Sheffield (Defense Attorney), Pedro de Cordoba (Minister).

Remake of a 1920 silent film of the same title sees Baxter murdered by a former sweetheart and returning as a ghost because he cannot rest knowing that an innocent person is being convicted for the crime. His ghostly form comes to his widow, Leeds, and she helps him bring justice to murderer Bari. Idea is farfetched but it is carried off well.

p, Sol M. Wurtzel; d, Irving Pichel; w, John Howard Lawson, Samuel G. Engel (based on a story by Basil King) ph, Lucien Andriot; m, Alfred Newman; ed, Louis Loeffler.

Crime/Supernatural   **(PR:A   MPAA:NR)**

EARTHBOUND*   (1981) 94m Taft International c

Burl Ives (Ned Anderson), Christopher Connelly (Zef), Meredith MacRae (Lara), Joseph Campanella (Conrad), Todd Porter (Tommy), Marc Gilpin (Dalem), Elissa Leeds (Teva), John Schuck (Sheriff), Stuart Pankin (Sweeny), Joey Forman (Madden), Peter Isacksen (Willy), Doodles Weaver (Sterling), John Hansen (1st Rider), Tiger Thompson (Butch), Daryl Bingham (Pudge), Michael Witt (Snodgrass), April Gilpin (Bridgette), H.E.D. Redford (General), Michael Ruud (Coach), Mindy Dow (Rosie).

Moronic sci-fi "family" picture stars Connelly, MacRae, Marc Gilpin, and Leeds as a middle-class family of aliens whose spaceship crashes in midwestern America. Since they look fairly normal (except for their green chimpanzee, which eats light bulbs) the family is taken in by kindly innkeeper Ives. Hot on their trail however, is mean government man Campanella, who won't let the family mingle with earthlings. Luckily the clan members can make themselves invisible, thus staying one step ahead of the government. For dimwits only.

p, Michael Fisher; d, James Conway; w, Fisher; (Technicolor).

Science Fiction   **(PR:C   MPAA:PG)**

EARTHLING, THE*½   (1980) 97m Filmways-Roadshow/Earthlings c

William Holden (Patrick Foley), Ricky Schroder (Shawn Daley), Jack Thompson (Ross Daley), Olivia Hamnett (Bettina Daley), Alwyn Kurts (Christian Neilson), Redmond Phillips (Bobby Burns), Willie Fennell (R.C.), Ray Barnett (Parnell), Pat Evison (Meg Neilson), Jane Harders (Molly Ann Hogan), Allan Penney (Harlan), Walter Pym (Uncle), Harry Neilson (McGroaty), Tony Barry (Red).

Holden plays a man with terminal cancer who has returned to his native Australia to die. There, he comes across recently orphaned tot Schroder and teaches the boy what he knows about survival before he dies. The landscapes are beautiful, the script schmaltzy, and Schroder painfully selfconscious of his cuteness. Director Collinson himself was dying from cancer at the time.

p, Elliot Schick, John Strong; d, Peter Collinson; w, Lanny Cotler; ph, Don McAlpine (Panavision); m, Dick DeBenedictis; ed, Nick Beauman, Frank Morriss; prod d, Bob Hilditch; m/l, "Halfway Home," David Shire, Carol Connors.

Drama   **Cas.**   **(PR:C   MPAA:PG)**

EARTHQUAKE zero   (1974) 122m UNIV c

Charlton Heston (Graff), Ava Gardner (Remy Graff), George Kennedy (Patrolman Slade), Lorne Greene (Royce), Genevieve Bujold (Denise), Richard Roundtree (Miles), Marjoe Gortner (Jody), Barry Sullivan (Dr. Stockle), Lloyd Nolan (Dr. Vance), Victoria Principal (Rosa), Walter Matuschanskayasky (Matthau) (Drunk), Monica Lewis (Royce's Secretary), Gabriel Dell (Miles' Manager), Pedro Armendariz, Jr. (Slade's Partner), Lloyd Gough (Cameron), John Randolph (Mayor), Kip Niven (Assistant Seismologist), Scott Hylands (Assistant Dam Caretaker), Tiger Williams (Corry Marshall), Donald Moffat (Dr. Harvey Johnson), Jesse Vint (Buck), Alan Vint (Ralph), Lionel Johnston (Hank), John Elerick (Carl Reeds), John S. Ragin (Chief Inspector), George Murdock (Colonel), Donald Mantooth (Sid), Michael Richardson (Sandy), Alex A. Brown (Pool Player), Bob Cunningham (Dr. Frank Ames), John Dennis (Brawny Foreman), Gene Dynarski (Dam Caretaker), Bob Gravage (Farmer Mr. Griggs), H.B. Haggerty (Pool Player), Dave Morick (Technician), Inez Pedroza (Laura), Tim Herbert (Man), Debralee Scott (Newlywed).

Awful disaster movie which combined the worst elements of soap opera and special effects (bad matte paintings and the ridiculous "Sensurround") featuring an "all-star" cast that should have stayed home and waited for a real earthquake. Heston stars as a building executive who is married to boss Greene's bitchy daughter Gardner, and who also has a mistress, Bujold, whose husband was killed in a building accident on a construction site where Heston had assigned him. After too much of this drivel the earthquake hits, killing most of the cast. The highly touted "Sensurround" was nothing more than a low-frequency sound process that made the theater seem to rumble during the earthquake footage. The greatest effect it had was in drowning out the soundtracks in adjoining theaters in shopping mall complexes.

p&d, Mark Robson; w, George Fox, Mario Puzo; ph, Philip Lathrop (Panavision, Technicolor, Sensurround); m, John Williams; ed, Dorothy Spencer; prod d, Alexander Golitzen; art d, E. Preston Ames; set d, Frank McKelvy; cos, Burton Miller; spec eff, Frank Brendel, Jack McMasters, Glen Robinson, Albert Whitlock.

Disaster   **Cas.**   **(PR:A   MPAA:PG)**

EARTHWORM TRACTORS**½   (1936) 68m FN/WB bw

Joe E. Brown (Alexander Botts), June Travis (Mabel Johnson), Guy Kibbee (Sam Johnson), Dick Foran (Emmet McManus), Carol Hughes (Sally Blair), Gene Lockhart (George Healey), Olin Howlin (Mr. Blair), Joseph Crehan (Mr. Henderson), Sarah Edwards (Mrs. Blair), Charles Wilson (H.J. Russell), William Davidson (Mr. Jackson), Irving Bacon (Taxicab Driver), Stuart Holmes (The Doctor).

Brown stars as a super tractor salesman who talks traditional horse and-buggy lumberman Kibbee into buying Earthworm tractors. To prove his point, Brown moves Kibbee's house (which was to be transported to another part of town—hence had rollers already in place) with an Earthworm tractor, while the unsuspecting family sits down to dinner. Funny stuff, with a strong supporting cast.

p, Sam Bischoff; d, Raymond Enright; w, Richard Macaulay, Joe Traub, Hugh Cummings (based on the "Alexander Botts" stories by William Hazlett Upson); ph, Arthur Todd; ed, Doug Gould.

Comedy **(PR:A MPAA:NR)**

EASIEST WAY, THE½** (1931) 86m MGM bw

Constance Bennett *(Laura Murdock)*, Adolphe Menjou *(William Brockton)*, Robert Montgomery *(Johnny Madison)*, Anita Page *(Peg Murdock)*, Marjorie Rambeau *(Elfie St. Clair)*, J. Farrell MacDonald *(Ben Murdock)*, Clara Blandick *(Agnes Murdock)*, Clark Gable *(Nick Felici)*, Francis Palmer Tilton *(Artist)*, Charles Judels *(Gensler)*, Johnny Harron *(Chris Swobeda)*, Bill O'Brien *(Wales, the Butler)*, Hedda Hopper *(Clara Williams)*, Del Henderson *(Bud Williams)*, Lynton Brent *(Associate)*.

The title refers to "the easiest way" to go from poverty to riches—sleeping around. Based on a stage play that shocked audiences, this was the second time for this story, the first having been filmed in 1917 (Clara Kimball Young). Bennett is a poor but decent slum girl who works in a department store. She is discovered by MacDonald, who takes her away from the drab employment and gets her a job as a model in Menjou's modeling agency. Soon enough she becomes Menjou's mistress and is able to help her family with money received from the suave Adolphe (and was there ever anything else one could call him but "suave"?), but her new fortune is looked down upon by the family because it means a moral compromise. Page is Bennett's older sister and she marries Clark Gable, a laundryman. Page would take Bennett in no matter what she's done, but Gable, a prig, is against it. Bennett now falls for Montgomery, a rich Argentine, and he would marry her immediately but there is political unrest down in his country so he must hurry back to Buenos Aires and asks her to wait for him. Bennett is torn between her love for Montgomery and her arrangement with Menjou. She moves in with Menjou while Montgomery is gone. Upon his return, he is destroyed when learning of her living with Menjou so he gives her the air. Later, she and Menjou argue and he leaves her as well. The end of the film is different, depending on which print you see. In one, she is redeemed on Christmas Eve. In another, she becomes a pathetic and lonely prostitute. No question that the censorship of the day had something to do with that. This was Gable's second job, one of 13 in which he appeared in 1931.

d, Jack Conway; w, Edith Ellis (based on the play by Eugene Walter); ph, John Mescall; ed, Frank Sullivan; art d, Cedric Gibbons; cos, Rene Hubert.

Drama **(PR:C MPAA:NR)**

EAST CHINA SEA** (1969, Jap.) 105m Imamura/Nikkatsu c (HIGASHI SHINAKAI)

Masakazu Tamura *(Rokuro)*, Seizaburo Kawazu *(Ganaha)*, Yukie Kagawa *(Kana)*, Ryohei Uchida, Kin Omae, Toshinari Yamano, Takanobu Hozumi, Haruko Kato, Akemi Nara, Taiji Tonoyama, Nakajiro Tomida, Shoichi Kuwayama, Hirayoshi Aono, Shuntaro Tamamura, Yoshiyuki Nemoto, Michic Mori, Takumi Shinjo, Kanjuro Arashi, Tetsuya Watari.

Strange tale about a crew from a Japanese boat being led about by a gangster for purposes of giving the U.S. Air Force a target. Little do the crew know that they are actually to become "human" targets for a military bombardment.

d, Tadahiko Isomi; w, Isomi, Shohei Imamura (based on a story by Imamura); ph, Masahisa Himeda (NikkatsuScope, Fuji Color); m, Hajime Kaburagi.

Drama **(PR:C MPAA:NR)**

EAST END CHANT (SEE: LIMEHOUSE BLUES, 1934)

EAST IS WEST*½ (1930) 72m UNIV bw

Lupe Velez *(Ming Toy)*, Lew Ayres *(Billy Benson)*, Edward G. Robinson *(Charlie Yong)*, E. Alyn Warren *(Lo Sang Kee)*, Tetsu Komai *(Hop Toy)*, Henry Kolker *(Mr. Benson)*, Mary Forbes *(Mrs. Benson)*, Edgar Norton *(Thomas)*, Charles Middleton *(Dr. Fredericks)*, Jean Hersholt *(Man)*, Gordon "Wild Bill" Elliott.

This was the third version of this story which was based on an early play by Sam Shipman and John Hymer. A ship known as, believe it or not, 'the love boat' arrives in a Chinese port. It's filled with men looking for Asian wives. Ayres steps off the ship and straight into an auction of women! Velez has been put up for the highest bidder by her father. Ayres saves the girl. Warren, a gentle Chinese oldster, takes her to San Francisco where she immediately runs afoul of a local bluenose group. Alyn sells her to Robinson, a half-caste known as the Chop Suey King. Ayres kidnaps Velez and wants to marry her but that puts him in a dangerous position with his family, highly ranked socialites who are totally against that union. Velez then learns that she is not Chinese at all (she could have looked in the mirror in reel one to find *that* out) but was taken from her dead parents—murdered missionaries—and raised by a Chinese family. Once that is established, Robinson allows Velez to depart with Ayres and gives the young couple his blessings. Robinson was 37 when this was made and already playing characters much older than he was. He mugged and hammed up the part to the point of embarrassment. A typical movie of the period in that only one actual Asian (Komai) was allowed to play a Chinese, and he was Japanese! This was Ayres' fourth job in 1930, the same year he did the memorable ALL QUIET ON THE WESTERN FRONT, COMMON CLAY and THE DOORWAY TO HELL.

p, E.M. Asher; d, Monta Bell; w, Winifred Eaton Reeve, Tom Reed (based on the play by Samuel Shipman, John B. Hymer); ph, Jerry Ash; ed, Harry Marker; spec eff, Frank H. Booth.

Drama **(PR:C MPAA:NR)**

EAST LYNNE** (1931) 102 FOX bw

Ann Harding *(Lady Isabel)*, Clive Brook *(Capt. Levinson)*, Conrad Nagel *(Robert Carlyle)*, Cecilia Loftus *(Cornelia Carlyle)*, Beryl Mercer *(Joyce)*, O.P. Heggie *(Earl of Mount Severn)*, Flora Sheffield *(Barbara Hare)*, David Torrence *(Sir Richard Hare)*, J. Gunnis Davis *(Dodson)*, Ronald Cosbey *(William, as a Baby)*, Wally Albright *(William, as a Boy)*, Eric Mayne *(Doctor)*.

Fallen woman melodrama set in the 1870s and starring Harding as the tragic wife of the irascible Nagel, who tosses her out after the birth of their child on the advice of Harding's scheming sister, Loftus. Harding falls into the arms of dashing army captain Brook, but she is obsessed with regaining her child. The climax sees Harding finally at the crib of her baby, suddenly being struck blind, and then wandering off to her death over a cliff. Good cast rises above the extravagantly emotional and sentimental material. (Filmed as a silent)

d, Frank Lloyd; w, Bradley King, Tom Barry (based on the play by Mrs. Henry Wood); ph, John Seitz; m, Richard Fall; set d, Joseph Urban; ed, Margaret Clancy.

Drama **(PR:A MPAA:NR)**

EAST LYNNE ON THE WESTERN FRONT** (1931, Brit.) 85m GAU bw

Herbert Mundin *(Bob Cox/Lady Isobel)*, Mark Daly *(Maurice/Levison)*, Alf Goddard *(Ben/Cornelia)*, Hugh E. Wright *(Fred)*, Edwin Ellis *(Sam/Barbara Hare)*, Harold French *(Reggie Pitt)*, Blanche Adele *(Mimi)*, Wilfred Lawson *(Dick Webb/Carlyle)*, Escott Davies *(Joe/Little Willie)*, Roger Livesey *(Sandy)*, Philip Godfrey *(Jack/Hare)*, Norman Shelley, M. Borelli.

Fairly funny comedy set in 1915 France sees a group of bored soldiers behind the lines who decide to produce a burlesque version of the melodrama "East Lynne." To spice it up they add a few randy songs and chorus numbers, much to the dismay of recruited actor Lawson, who takes the whole thing seriously.

p, T.A. Welsh; d, George Pearson; w, Donovan Parsons, Mary Parsons (based on a story by Pearson, Welsh); ph, Percy Strong.

Comedy **(PR:A MPAA:NR)**

EAST MEETS WEST** (1936, Brit.) 74m GAU bw

George Arliss *(Sultan of Rungay)*, Lucie Mannheim *(Marguerite)*, Godfrey Tearle *(Sir Henry Mallory)*, Romney Brent *(Dr. Shagu)*, Ballard Berkeley *(Nazim)*, Ronald Ward *(Carter)*, Norma Varden *(Lady Mallory)*, John Laurie *(Dr. Ferguson)*, O.B. Clarence *(Osmin)*, Campbell Gullan *(Takasota)*, Eliot Makeham *(Goodsen)*, Peter Gawthorne *(Stanton)*, Stella Moya *(Suleeka)*, Ralph Truman *(Abdul)*, Patrick Barr *(O'Flaherty)*, Derek Elphinstone, Peter Croft.

Arliss plays a clever sultan of a small oriental country which contains a harbor desired by both England and Japan. He plays one country against the other and signs cash agreements with each, with both thinking they have walked off with an outstanding deal. Subplot involves the sultan's son getting involved with the wife of a crooked British official.

p, Haworth Bromley; d, Herbert Mason; w, Maude Howell, Edwin Greenwood (based on the play "The Lake of Life" by Greenwood); ph, Bernard Knowles; ed, Charles Frend.

Drama **(PR:A MPAA:NR)**

EAST OF BORNEO** (1931) 73m UNIV bw

Rose Hobart *(Linda Randolph)*, Charles Bickford *(Dr. Clark)*, Georges Renavent *(Prince of Marudu)*, Lupita Tovar *(Niela)*, Noble Johnson *(Osman)*.

Feisty wife Hobart braves the jungle and battles her way past snakes, pumas, crocodiles, monkeys, and tigers searching for her doctor husband, Bickford, who had run off into the jungle when he felt betrayed by her. She eventually finds him living comfortably as the court physician of Renavent in his jungle palace. Then a volcanic eruption climaxes their reunion. Silly but fun.

p, Carl Laemmle, Jr.; d, George Melford; w, Dale Van Every, Edwin H. Knopf (based on a story by Van Every); ph, George Robinson.

Adventure **Cas.** **(PR:A MPAA:NR)**

EAST OF EDEN***** (1955) 115m WB c

Julie Harris *(Abra)*, James Dean *(Cal Trask)*, Raymond Massey *(Adam Trask)*, Richard Davalos *(Aron Trask)*, Burl Ives *(Sam)*, Jo Van Fleet *(Kate)*, Albert Dekker *(Will)*, Lois Smith *(Ann)*, Harold Gordon *(Mr. Albrecht)*, Timothy Carey *(Joe)*, Mario Siletti *(Piscora)*, Lonny Chapman *(Roy)*, Nick Dennis *(Rantani)*.

This was Dean's screen debut and he burst like a thunderclap in the public's ears, not to mention staid Hollywood, which came to fear and admire the handsome, rebellious youth. In this haunting John Steinbeck tale Dean is the neurotic half of twin sons belonging to Bible-reading lettuce farmer Massey, whose vast acreage stretches through the rich Salinas Valley of California. Davalos, also making a powerful debut in films, is the well-adjusted, upstanding son who has a normal relationship with girl friend Harris and diligently pursues the development of his father's lands. His brother Dean is just the opposite, troubled and troublesome, challenging his father and all other authority, mistakenly believing that Davalos is loved and he is not, that his brother has everything and he has nothing. It is the Cain and Abel fable, circa 1917, and the rush from normality to destruction and tragedy is swift as Dean seeks to undo his brother as well as himself. To earn his father's blessings, Dean devises a scheme to plant special crops, while Massey banks on a new process of shipping his lettuce east, packing the cargo in ice. But the newly developed refrigeration process fails and the ice melts before the train gets over the Sierra Mountains. The crop is ruined and Massey's fortunes nosedive. So does his family. Dean has discovered that his real mother, long a ghost in the family closet, is alive and well-to-do, a successful madam operating a whorehouse in Monterey. It is she, Van Fleet, who advances him the money to produce the surprise crop to save his father's fortunes. When Dean goes to Massey to offer him money from his enterprise to supplant his losses, Massey rejects the money, learning how Dean made it and considering it tainted. After a confrontation, Massey is left paralyzed with a stroke. Full of anger, Dean leads Davalos to Van Fleet, causing his brother to be traumatized by the truth. Davalos later gets drunk and joins the army, going off to war full of hate. Harris, whom Dean has also managed to steal away from his brother, is left to deal with the self-destructive Dean. She has loved Davalos but is inexorably swept by sexual attraction to the lusty Dean. The overall theme of this powerful film was not lost on the creators of HUD and many another familiar production. Kazan's direction is masterful and all the principals give riveting performances, with Dean emerging as an overnight sensation, despite his early identification with the Brando style of "naturalistic" acting. Dean instantly became the symbol of America's disillusioned and disassociated youth; his fans and imitators became myriad, a cult following that lingered long after the actor's death in an auto accident a few years later at the tender age of 24. All the technical contributions are superlative, with Rosenman's score appropriately evocative and as nervous as the exploding energy of its star-crossed lead.

p&d, Elia Kazan; w, Paul Osborn (based on the novel by John Steinbeck); ph, Ted McCord (CinemaScope, Warner Color); m, Leonard Rosenman; ed, Owen Marks; art d, James Basevi, Malcolm Bert; set d, George James Hopkins; cos, Anna Hill Johnstone.

Drama					**Cas.**					**(PR:C-O MPAA:NR)**

EAST OF ELEPHANT ROCK*					(1976, Brit.) 92m
					Boyd's Company/Kendon c

Judi Bowker, Jeremy Kemp, John Hurt, Christopher Cazenove, Anton Rodgers, Vajira, Tariq Yunus.

Kemp is a civil servant in 1948 colonial Malaya who is shot by his mistress for having affairs with other women. Turgid melodrama, badly written and appallingly played.

p,d&w, Don Boyd; ph, Keith Goddard; m, Peter Skellern.

Drama					**Cas.**					**(PR:O MPAA:NR)**

EAST OF FIFTH AVE.*½					(1933) 74m COL bw

Wallace Ford (Vic), Dorothy Tree (Kitty), Mary Carlisle (Edna), Walter Connolly (Lawton), Willard Robertson (Dr. Morgan), Walter Byron (Baxter), Louise Carter (Mrs. Lawton), Lucien Littlefield (Gardner), Maude Eburne (Mrs. Conway), Harry Holman (Cronin), Fern Emmett (Lizzie).

Overwrought GRAND HOTEL-type melodrama concerning the lives of a group of people living together in a boarding house. Carlisle is a pregnant show girl dumped by her married boy friend, Ford, who has returned to his wife. She contemplates suicide but is talked out of it by a kindly elderly couple, Connolly and Carter, who turn the tables on her when they commit suicide themselves. Grim entertainment.

d, Al Rogell; w, Jo Swerling (based on a story by Lew Levenson); ph, Benjamin Kline; ed, Richard Cahoon.

Drama					**(PR:C MPAA:NR)**

EAST OF JAVA**					(1935) 72m UNIV bw

Charles Bickford (Bowers), Elizabeth Young (Ann), Frank Albertson (Larry), Leslie Fenton (Wong Bo), Siegfried Rumann (Muller), Jay Gilbuena (Lee), Clarence McNaughton (Sloppy Alf), Fraser Acosta (Malay), Clarence Muse (Johnson), Edgar Norton (Resident), Ivan Simpson (Bit), Ray Turner, Torben Meyer.

An Oriental ship with its cargo of dangerous animals runs aground on a deserted island. All the wild beasts escape and are a constant threat to the surviving passengers. One passenger, Bickford, is a criminal and he terrorizes the rest of the castaways, including the helpless captain, Fenton. One by one the survivors are attacked and killed by the lions and tigers, until even the evil Bickford meets his doom. Fast-paced and full of well-directed action scenes.

p, Paul Kohner; d, George Melford; w, Paul Perez, James Ashmore Creelman (based on the story "Tiger Island" by Gouverneur Morris); ph, Norbert Brodine, Daniel Hall; ed, Maurice Wright.

Drama					**(PR:A MPAA:NR)**

EAST OF KILIMANJARO**					(1962, Brit./Ital.) 75m Dudley Pictures
					International-Ameurope c (LA GRANDE CACCIA; GB: THE BIG SEARCH)

Marshall Thompson (Marsh Connors), Gaby Andre (Dr. Marie Avedon), Fausto Tozzi (Dr. Enrico Trino), Kris Aschan, Rolf Aschan (Themselves), Mike Robotham.

Freelance photographer Thompson goes on assignment in Africa, where an epidemic has hit the cattle in the region near Mount Kilimanjaro. He falls in love with Andre, a member of a scientific task force sent to control the epidemic. The scientists convince the Masai people that their cattle must be inoculated and big game hunter Kris Aschan is hired to catch other African wildlife. In the end, a vulture is found to be the carrier of the virus and Thompson leaves Andre realizing she'll be happier with doctor Tozzi.

p, Richard Goldstone, Edoardo Capolino; d, Arnold Belgard, Capolino; w, Belgard (based on a story by M. Levor, Goldstone, Daniel Mainwaring); ph, Edwin E. Olsen, Laurie Friedman; m, Alberico Vitalini; ed, Norma Suffern.

Adventure					**(PR:A MPAA:NR)**

EAST OF PICADILLY					(SEE: STRANGLER, THE, 1940)

EAST OF SHANGHAI					(SEE: RICH AND STRANGE, 1932, Brit.)

EAST OF SUDAN**					(1964, Brit.) 85m COL/BLC c

Anthony Quayle (Richard Baker), Sylvia Syms (Margaret Woodville), Derek Fowlds (Murchinson), Jenny Agutter (Asua), Johnny Sekka (Kimrasi), Harold Coyne (Maj. Harris), Joseph Layode (Gondoki), Ellario Pedro (Witch Doctor), Desmond Davies (Aide), Derek Bloomfield (2nd Major), Edward Ellis (Arab).

British adventure picture set in India during the 1880s tells of the efforts of the English to stamp out the slave trade against the Sudanese Moslems. When the Batash outpost is overrun, trooper Quayle and rookie lieutenant Fowlds help

pretty governess, Syms, and her charge, Agutter, to gain safety. Along the way the two soldiers are constantly at each other's throats, with the experienced Quayle becoming increasingly frustrated by the actions of his naive superior. After battling wild animals, tricky terrain, and Moslems, the two develop a grudging respect for each other. Quayle, of course, falls for Syms, and all turns out well when the team blows up an arsenal and saves a rag-tag group of British soldiers from certain death. Stock footage of the battle scenes from THE FOUR FEATHERS (1939) was used in making of this film.

p, Charles H. Schneer, Nathan Juran; d, Juran; w, Jud Kinberg; ph, Wilkie Cooper (Techniscope, Technicolor); m, Laurie Johnson; ed, Ernest Hosler.

Adventure					**(PR:A MPAA:NR)**

EAST OF SUMATRA**					(1953) 81m UNIV c

Jeff Chandler (Duke Mullane), Marilyn Maxwell (Lory Hale), Anthony Quinn (Kiang), Suzan Ball (Minyora), John Sutton (Daniel Catlin), Jay C. Flippen (Mac), Scatman Crothers (Baltimore), Aram Katcher (Atib), Antony Eustrel (Clyde), Eugene Iglesias (Paulo), Peter Graves (Cowboy), James Craven (Drake), John Warburton (Keith), Michael Dale (Co-Pilot), Gilchrist Stuart (Mr. Vickers), Charles Horvath (Corcoran), Earl Holliman (Cupid).

Chandler stars as the chief engineer of a tin-mining firm working the Island of Tunga. The company is owned by Sutton, who is engaged to Chandler's ex-girl friend, Maxwell. Chandler finds himself in hot water when his boss ignores his requests for food, and instead sends more mining supplies. This development does not please the ruler of the island, Quinn, who was promised the food in return for mining rights. Finding Chandler's slowness intolerable, Sutton arrives on the island with Maxwell in tow and demands that his chief engineer proceed with the mining, natives be damned. Sutton stirs up more trouble when he tries to get on Quinn's good side by accusing Chandler of romancing the ruler's fiancee, Ball. This sends Quinn into a frenzy and he destroys the mining crew's plane and supplies. Ball attempts to help the white folks off the island, but they are trapped by Quinn's warriors. Chandler is forced into a fight with Quinn and kills the ruler. Ball takes over the island and allows the crew to leave. Chandler and Maxwell are reunited, leaving Sutton to himself. Good cast and fast-paced direction by Boetticher.

p, Albert J. Cohen; d, Budd Boetticher; w, Frank Gill, Jr. (adapted by Jack Natteford, from a story by Louis L'Amour, Natteford); ph, Clifford Stine (Technicolor); ed, Virgil Vogel; art d, Bernard Herzbrun, Robert Boyle; m/l, "Strange Land," "Ballad To A Gypsy," Scatman Crothers.

Adventure					**(PR:A MPAA:NR)**

EAST OF THE RIVER**					(1940) 73m FN/WB bw

John Garfield (Joe Lorenzo), Brenda Marshall (Laurie Romayne), Marjorie Rambeau (Teresa Lorenzo), George Tobias (Tony), William Lundigan (Nick Lorenzo), Moroni Olsen (Judge Davis), Douglas Fowley (Cy Turner), Jack LaRue (Scarfi), Jack Carr ("No Neck" Griswold), Paul Guilfoyle (Balmy), Russell Hicks (Warden), Charles Foy (Customer), Ralph Volkie, Jimmy O'Gatty (Henchmen), Robert Homans (Patrolman Shanahan), Joe Conti (Joe As A Boy), O'Neill Nolan (Nick As A Boy).

Disappointing New York City saga shot on a badly constructed set on Warner Bros. back lot. Garfield's performance is overblown as the brother gone bad in a family run by a stereotypical Italian mother, Rambeau. With his adopted brother, Lundigan, the pair get into the usual boyhood mischief, but as they grow older their lives take different paths. Lundigan goes to college and Garfield gets out of San Quentin just in time to attend Lundigan's graduation ceremony. With girl friend, Marshall, in tow, Garfield arrives home and soon finds himself in trouble with the mob. Marshall and Lundigan fall in love and the couple announce their engagement, much to the dismay of Garfield. The climactic moment comes during the wedding ceremony when the mob shows up and Garfield stalls them long enough to hear the vows exchanged. Take-off of MANHATTAN MELODRAMA.

p, HarlanThompson; d, Alfred E. Green; w, Fred Niblo, Jr. (based on the story "Mama Ravioli" by John Fante, Ross E. Willis); ph, Sid Hickox; ed, Thomas Pratt.

Crime					**(PR:A MPAA:NR)**

EAST SIDE KIDS*					(1940) 62m MON bw

Leon Ames (Pat O'Day), Dennis Moore (Mileaway), Joyce Bryant (Molly), Vince Barnett (Whisper), Dave O'Brien (Knuckles), Richard Adams (Schmidt), Maxine Leslie (May), Sam Edwards (Pete), Robert Fiske (Cornwall), Jack Edwards (Algernon Wilkes), James Farley (Capt. Moran), Alden Chase (Joe), Fred Hoose (Mr. Wilkes), Eric Burtis (Eric), Eddie Brian (Mike), Frank Yaconelli (Tony), Hally Chester, Harris Berger, Frankie Burke, Donald Haines, David Durand (The East Side Kids).

Pretty poor (even by Dead End Kids' standards) dramatization of the bad urban conditions that drive boys into a life of crime. The usual bag of trite and predictable plot twists abound. Ames plays a former street-punk-turned-detective who helps the East Side Kids escape from a gang of counterfeiters they had hooked up with.

p, Sam Katzman; d, Robert F. Hill; w, Robert Lively; ph, Art Reed; m, Johnny Lange, Lew Porter; ed, Earl Turner.

Crime					**Cas.**					**(PR:A MPAA:NR)**

EAST SIDE KIDS MEET BELA LUGOSI, THE
					(SEE: GHOSTS ON THE LOOSE, 1943)

EAST SIDE OF HEAVEN**½					(1939) 85m UNIV bw

Bing Crosby (Danny), Joan Blondell (Mary), Mischa Auer (Nicky), Irene Hervey (Mona), Jerome Cowan (Claudius De Wolfe), Robert Kent (Cyrus Barrett, Jr.), C. Aubrey Smith (Barrett, Sr.), Jackie Gerlich (Bobbie), Douglas Wood (Fisher), Arthur Hoyt (Loftus), Brandon Hurst (Butler), Sandra Lee Henville (Baby Sandy), Raymond Parker (Messenger), Jack Powell (Happy Jack Powell), Jane Jones, Rose

Valyda, Helen Warner (Trio), J. Farrell MacDonald (Doorman), Russell Hicks (Winkle), Chester Clute (Phil), Phyllis Kennedy (Mamie), Clarence Wilson (Telegraph Operator), Joe King (Detective), Dorothy Christy (Mrs. Henry Smith), Wade Boteler (Detective), Jane Goude (Landlady), Emory Parnell (Doorman), Leleh Tyler (Woman), Edward Earle (Mr. Henry Smith), Frank Coghlan, Jr. (Messenger Boy), Harry Depp, Lloyd Ingraham (Executives), Lillian West (Nurse), Frank Moran (Workman), Billy Wayne (Garage Man), Mary Carr (Mrs. Travers).

Crosby stepped out of his Paramount contract for a loan-out to Universal and made an interesting deal on this picture; he put up his services and some of his own money to get a fifty-fifty deal with Universal on the profits. Whether that had something to do with the fact that Crosby was terrific in the lead, much better than in some of the Paramounters of the period, will never be known. In this movie he does the same kind of thing he did in 1938's PENNIES FROM HEAVEN in being tossed the responsibility of taking care of a child. Crosby and Blondell are engaged, but wedding plans must be shunted aside when Bing, a singing cab driver, has a baby given to him while the mother goes off to look for the father. Bing lives with Mischa Auer (absolutely first rate in a small but effective role) and the two men take care of the child until they learn that the wealthy grandpa, Smith, has the cops out looking for the baby, "Sandy." A whole bunch of contrived twists and turns follow until everything winds up for the best. Baby "Sandy" (a boy in the film) is really played by Sandra Lee Henville, a ten-month-old girl (at that age, who can tell the difference if they're wearing clothes?) who was quite remarkable in her reactions on camera. Bing croons to the tyke (tykette?) and his scenes with her are touching and lovely. Some very funny sequences and a host of forgettable songs: "Hang Your Heart On A Hickory Limb," "Sing A Song Of Sunbeams," "That Sly Old Gentleman," "East Side Of Heaven" (James V. Monaco, Johnny Burke), "My Melancholy Baby" (Ernie Burnett).

p, Herbert Polesie; d, David Butler; w, William Conselman (based on a story by Butler, Polesie); ph, George Robinson; ed, Irene Morra; md, Charles Previn; art d, Jack Otterson; set d, Russell A. Gausman.

Musical Comedy   **(PR:A   MPAA:NR)**

EAST SIDE SADIE**   (1929) 60m World Art Films bw

Bertina Golden, Jack Ellis, Boris Rosenthal, Lucia Backus Seger, Abe Sinkoff, John Halliday, Al Stanley, Maechivinko, Mark Schweid.

Golden is a Jewish sweatshop girl working feverishly to help her boy friend through college. He, however, gets involved with a professional matchmaker who sets him up with a rich woman. On the eve of his wedding to the wealthy vixen, Golden's brothers come and beat the stuffing out of him. He comes to his senses and returns to the girl who really loves him. This part-talking film has a few good songs and a fairly major cast.

d&w, Sidney M. Golden; ph, Frank Zucker; ed, Sam Citen.

Drama   **(PR:A   MPAA:NR)**

EAST SIDE, WEST SIDE*½   (1949) 108m MGM bw

Barbara Stanwyck (Jessie Bourne), James Mason (Brandon Bourne), Van Heflin (Mark Dwyer), Ava Gardner (Isabel Lorrison), Cyd Charisse (Rosa Senta), Nancy Davis (Helen Lee), Gale Sondergaard (Nora Kernan), William Conrad (Lt. Jacobi), Raymond Greenleaf (Horace Elcott Howland), Douglas Kennedy (Alec Dawning), Beverly Michaels (Felice Backett), William Frawley (Bill the Bartender), Lisa Golm (Josephine), Tom Powers (Owen Lee), Paula Raymond (Joan Peterson), Jimmy Horne, Geraldine Farmer, Maria Reachi (Guests), Wesley Bly (Club Attendant), Wheaton Chambers (Doorman), Rita Lynn, Stella Soldi (Sistine Wives), Peter Thompson (Jock Ardley), Stanley Orr (Bourne's Chauffeur), Stanley Waxman (John), Jack Gargan (Doorman), Tom P. Dillon (Dan the Old Policeman), Jewel Rose (Hat Check Girl), Sandra Spence (Cigaret Girl), Wilson Wood, Ralph Montgomery, Fred Hoose, Roger Moore, Betty Taylor (Reporters), Ernest Anderson (Redcap), Harry Strang (Fred the Doorman), Frank Meredith (Cop), Ferike Boros (Grandma Sistina).

High-gloss sudser based on Marcia Davenport's best-selling novel about love and life among the Park Aveneurotics. Gardner is a waitress-model who comes back to New York and hastens the marital decline of socialites Mason and Stanwyck who are on shaky ground already. Mason has been sort of keeping Gardner, and her appearance causes a large rift. Charisse saves Mason from embarrassment by doing him a good turn, and Stanwyck goes to her apartment to thank her. She learns that there's a party that night in honor of Heflin, a one-time policeman who went to war and is returning home as a hero. Stanwyck has known Heflin from afar ever since she was a little girl and she goes to the party without Mason, who was also invited but declined in favor of some urgent business. That urgent business was seeing Gardner. Mason does not come home until the next morning and Stanwyck is livid, although she had a marvelous time at the party the night before and discovered that she had more than a passing attraction for Heflin. Mason pleads to be forgiven and offers to take his wife on a vacation. Before they leave, Gardner prevails on Mason to divorce Stanwyck but Mason refuses. The couple are due to leave on a train and when Mason doesn't show up, Stanwyck calls Gardner's flat and Mason is there and tells her that Gardner has been murdered. Heflin is called upon and solves the foul deed (Mason is not the killer but to reveal who it is might spoil your fun, so we won't). Mason attempts to worm his way back into his wife's graces but she tells him to take a hike and it is presumed that she will eventually unite with Heflin. Stanwyck and Heflin are excellent, but Mason falls flat when he attempts to do an American accent. Nothing of great importance here other than it was the first film in which Nancy Davis (Helen Lee) appeared, although it was held up for release for quite a while. This was a "B" movie with an "A" cast and a few years later Davis married another "B" movie actor who eventually sought and gained political office. And if we have to tell you who he was, then you're in a lot of trouble. Look for William Conrad, while he still had a figure you could discern, as Lt. Jacobi. The producer was a former story department head and should have known better.

p, Voldemar Vetluguin; d, Mervyn LeRoy; w, Isobel Lennart (based on the novel by Marcia Davenport); ph, Charles Rosher; m, Miklos Rozsa; ed, Harold F. Kress; art d, Cedric Gibbons, Randall Duell; set d, Edwin B. Willis, Arthur Krams; cos, Helen Rose; spec eff, A. Arnold Gillespie.

Drama   **(PR:A-C   MPAA:NR)**

EASTER PARADE**   (1948) 107m MGM c

Judy Garland (Hannah Brown), Fred Astaire (Don Hewes), Peter Lawford (Jonathan Harrow III), Ann Miller (Nadine Hale), Jules Munshin (Francois), Clinton Sundberg (Mike the Bartender), Jeni LeGon (Essie), Richard Beavers (Singer), Dick Simmons (Al, Stage Manager for Ziegfeld), Jimmy Bates (Boy With Astaire in "Drum Crazy" Musical Number), Dee Turnell, Bobbie Priest, Patricia Jackson (Specialty Girls), Lola Albright, Joi Lansing (Hat Model Showgirls), Lynn and Jean Romer ("Delineator" Twins), Helene Heigh (Modiste), Wilson Wood (Marty), Peter Chong (Sam, Valet), Nolan Leary (Drug Store Clerk), Doris Kemper (Mary), Frank Mayo (Headwaiter), Benay Venuta (Bar Patron), Hector and His Pals—Carmi Tryon (Dog Act), Jimmy Dodd (Cabby), Robert Emmett O'Connor (Cop Who Gives Johnny A Ticket).

Delightful musical that is as light as a feather in its intent. Gene Kelly was supposed to have the lead but injured his ankle playing volleyball with some friends and so he suggested to Freed that they prevail on Astaire to come out of his 'retirement' and take the role. Astaire had announced he was done after BLUE SKIES but was obviously only waiting for someone to ask him, because he jumped at the opportunity. And how right he was. Ann Miller and Astaire are dance partners and when Miller is offered the lead in a new Ziegfeld extravaganza, she dumps him and leaves. Astaire is angry and wants to prove he can make a star out of anyone he chooses, so he opts for the least likely person he can find—a chorus girl, played by Garland. It's rough for Astaire because he is still very much enamored of Miller and carrying a torch larger than the Statue of Liberty's. He works hard at grooming Garland and they wind up strolling down Fifth Avenue during the Easter Parade, arm in arm and quite in love. The picture takes place in the year between Easter, 1911, and Easter, 1912, and the sets and costumes are quite authentic. Irving Berlin wrote 17 tunes (seven new, ten old) that appear in the film and Johnny Green and Roger Edens won an Oscar for their musical adaptation. Lawford scores as a playboy with designs on Garland and Miller. The production numbers are outstanding and the comedy is handled well by Jules Munshin. The musical-comedy form seems to have been made for the creative team of Freed (himself a songwriter), Walters, and all the writers. Berlin is acknowledged as one of America's musical geniuses (although born in Europe) and the incredible thing about his deceptively simple lyrics is that they were all written by a man to whom English was a second language! Making another appearance at the age of two and a half is Liza Minnelli in the final sequence. Liza later appeared with her mother on stage at the Palace Theater in New York when she was seven and achieved her first great success as "Flora, The Red Menace" for which she won a Tony. Songs: "Happy Easter," "Drum Crazy," "It Only Happens When I Dance With You," "Everybody's Doin' It Now," "I Want To Go Back To Michigan," "A Fella With an Umbrella," "I Love a Piano," "Snookey Ookums," "Ragtime Violin," "When the Midnight Choo-Choo Leaves for Alabam'," "Shaking the Blues Away," "Steppin' Out With My Baby," "A Couple of Swells," "The Girl On The Magazine Cover," "Better Luck Next Time," "Easter Parade," "Beautiful Faces Need Beautiful Clothes."

p, Arthur Freed; d, Charles Walters; w, Frances Goodrich, Albert Hackett, Sidney Sheldon, Guy Bolton (based on a story by Goodrich, Hackett); ph, Harry Stradling, Sr. (Technicolor); ed, Albert Akst; md, Johnny Green, Roger Green; art d, Cedric Gibbons, Jack Martin Smith; cos, Irene Valles; spec eff, Warren Newcombe; ch, Robert Alton; m/l, Irving Berlin; makeup, Jack Dawn.

Musical Comedy   **Cas.**   **(PR:AAA   MPAA:NR)**

EASTER SUNDAY   (SEE: BEING, THE, 1983)

EASY COME, EASY GO**   (1947) 77m PAR bw

Barry Fitzgerald (Martin L. Donovan), Diana Lynn (Connie Donovan), Sonny Tufts (Kevin O'Connor), Dick Foran (Dale Whipple), Frank McHugh (Carey), Allen Jenkins (Nick), John Litel (Tom Clancy), Arthur Shields (Mike Donovan), Frank Faylen (Boss), James Burke (Harry Weston), George Cleveland (Gilligan), Ida Moore (Angela Orange), Rhys Williams (Priest), Oscar Rudolph (Bookie), Lou Lubin (Tailor), Olin Howlin (Gas Man), Tom Fadden (Sanitation Man), Howard Freeman (Magistrate), Hobart Cavanaugh (Auto Repair Shop Manager), Byron Foulger (Sports Good Shop Owner), Rex Lease (Gambler), Chester Clute (Waiter), Crane Whitley (Prosecutor), Matt McHugh (Worker), Perc Launders (Bartender), Charles Sullivan (Cabbie), Stanley Price, Pat McVey (Gamblers), Stanley Andrews (Detective), James Flavin (Plainclothes Man), Polly Bailey (Housewife), Harry Hayden (Bank Teller), James Davies, James Cornell (Neighborhood Men).

Fitzgerald lends himself to Irish stereotyping in this drama about a likeable but shiftless, New York City Irishman with a penchant for the ponies. The whole film consists of Fitzgerald staying one step ahead of his creditors, nosing into his daughter's love life, and placing $2 bets at the track in the hopes that he will eventually hit the big numbers. The Irish come in for some amusing pokes in Fitzgerald's character, but they are scarcely offensive. Nothing much grows in this bit of the auld sod.

p, Kenneth Macgowan; d, John Farrow; w, Francis Edwards Faragoh, John McNulty, Anne Froelick (based on the "Third Avenue Stories" by McNulty); ph, Daniel L. Fapp; m, Roy Webb; ed, Thomas Scott; art d, Hans Dreier, Haldane Douglas; m/l, Ray Evans, Jay Livingston.

Drama   **Cas.**   **(PR:A   MPAA:NR)**

EASY COME, EASY GO** (1967) 95m PAR c

Elvis Presley *(Ted Jackson)*, Dodie Marshall *(Jo Symington)*, Pat Priest *(Dina Bishop)*, Pat Harrington *(Judd Whitman)*, Skip Ward *(Gil Carey)*, Frank McHugh *(Capt. Jack)*, Elaine Beckett *(Vicki)*, Shari Nims *(Mary)*, Sandy Kenyon *(Lt. Schwartz)*, Mickey Elley *(Lt. Whitehead)*, Read Morgan *(Lt. Tompkins)*, Elsa Lanchester *(Mme. Neherina)*, Diki Lerner *(Zoltan)*, Ed Griffith *(Cooper)*, Kay York *(Tanya)*, Robert Isenberg *(Artist)*.

Another mediocre Presley vehicle stars the rock 'n' roll idol as a Navy frogman who, with the help of yoga student-go-go dancer Marshall and washed-up nautical expert McHugh, uncovers a valuable cargo of gold from a sunken Spanish ship. As it turns out, the pieces-of-eight are only worth about $4,000 and Elvis-the-frogman graciously donates it to an arts center to impress Miss Marshall. Songs "Easy Come, Easy Go" (Sid Wayne, Ben Weisman), "The Love Machine" (Gerald Nelson, Chuck Taylor, Fred Burch), "Yoga Is As Yoga Goes," "Sing, You Children" (Nelson, Burch), "You Gotta Stop" (Bill Giant, Florence Kaye, Bernie Baum), "I'll Take Love" (Dee Fuller, Mark Barkan).

p, Hal B. Wallis; d, John Rich; w, Allen Weiss, Anthony Lawrence; ph, William Margulies (Technicolor); m, Joseph J. Lilley; ed, Archie Marshek; art d, Hal Pereira, Walter Tyler; set d, Robert R. Benton, Arthur Krams; spec eff, Paul K. Lerpae; ch, David Winters.

Musical **Cas.** **(PR:A MPAA:NR)**

EASY GO (SEE: FREE AND EASY, 1930)

EASY LIFE, THE*½** (1963, Ital.) 105m Fair-Incei-Sancro/EM bw (IL SORPASSO)

Vittorio Gassman *(Bruno Cortona)*, Jean-Louis Trintignant *(Roberto Mariani)*, Catherine Spaak *(Lilly, Bruno's Daughter)*, Luciana Angiolillo *(Bruno's Wife)*, Linda Sini *(Aunt Lidia)*, Corrado Olmi *(Alfredo)*, Claudio Gora *(Bibi, Lilly's Fiance)*, Franca Polesello, Edda Ferronao, Nando Angelini, Lilli Darelli, Bruno Simionato, Mila Stanic.

Gassman meets student Trintignant when the middle-aged jetsetter needs to use his phone. Gassman introduces the law student to the sybarite life of luxury and voluptuousness, and Trintignant is dazzled by the beautiful young sylphs who inhabit it, the dancing, and sailing on the Riviera. He loses all purpose and direction in life and is killed when Gassman wrecks his sports car. Gassman then realizes how shallow the life of a dissoulute middle-aged playboy is. An absorbing glimpse of decadence, with a beautiful Riviera background.

p, Mario Cecchi Gori; d, Dino Risi; w, Ettore Scola, Ruggero Maccari, Risi; ph, Alfio Contini; m, Riz Ortolani; ed, Maurizio Lucidi; art d, Ugo Pericoli.

Drama **(PR:C MPAA:NR)**

EASY LIFE, THE*** (1971, Fr.) 87m Films 13 c (LA VIE FACILE)

Henri Serre *(Albin)*, Michele Bonpart *(Elvire)*, Marianne Eggerikx *(Sister)*, Rufus *(Priest)*, Bernard Haller *(Mercenary)*, Grand Magic Circus.

On the way home, Serre runs into the circus and he picks up one of its girls, then gets rid of her when she rejects his advances. The circus sets up camp near Serre's home. On the rebound, he marries a local girl but the marriage goes sour due to Serre's brutality. The townsfolk have had enough of the circus people and the mayor attempts to throw them out, but Serre hires them to stage a big party for him and he hands out prizes to the villagers who attend, then he berates the citizens for accepting his gifts even though they know he has killed to earn the money. His two partners return during the party to get their share of the cash and in a gun battle one gunman is killed and Serre is murdered by the other. An insightful look into a man's efforts to impose a different meaning on his life, and the circus members who show him reality.

d, Francis Warin; w, Warin, Jerome Savary; ph, Georges Strouve (Eastmancolor); ed, Marie-Joseph Yoyotte.

Drama **(PR:C MPAA:NR)**

EASY LIVING*** (1937) 88m PAR bw

Jean Arthur *(Mary Smith)*, Edward Arnold *(J.B. Ball)*, Ray Milland *(John Ball, Jr.)*, Luis Alberni *(Mr. Louis Louis)*, Mary Nash *(Mrs. Ball)*, Franklin Pangborn *(Van Buren)*, Barlowe Borland *(Mr. Gurney)*, William Demarest *(Wallace Whistling)*, Andrew Tombes *(E.F. Hulgar)*, Esther Dale *(Lillian)*, Harlan Briggs *(Office Manager)*, William B. Davidson *(Mr. Hyde)*, Nora Cecil *(Miss Swerf)*, Robert Greig *(Butler)*, Vernon Dent, Edwin Stanley, Richard Barbee *(Partners)*, Marsha Hunt, Lee Bowman, Elisa Connor, Ethel Clayton, Gloria Williams, Nick Lukats *(Bits)*, Bennie Bartlett *(Newsboy)*, Jack Raymond, Adia Kuznetzoff *(Bums)*, Florence Dudley *(Cashier)*, Bob Murphy *(Automat Detective)*, Bernard Suss *(Man In Automat)*, Rex Moore *(Elevator Boy)*, John Marshall *(Osric)*, Dora Clement *(Saleslady)*, Hayden Stevenson *(Chauffeur)*, Arthur Hoyt, Hal Dawson *(Jewelers)*, Hector V. Sarno *(Armenian Rug Salesman)*, Gertrude Astor *(Saleswoman)*, Lee Phelps *(Hotel Detective)*, Hal Greene *(Bellhop)*, Jesse Graves *(Porter)*, Frances Morris *(Assistant Secretary)*, Sidney Bracy *(Chauffeur)*, Lois Clinton *(Brunette)*, Laura Treadwell *(Wife)*, Virginia Dabney *(Blonde)*, John Dilson *(Nervous Man)*, Forbes Murray *(Husband)*, John Picorri *(Oinest)*, Kathleen Hope Lewis, Helen Huntington *(Stenographers)*, Harold Entwistle *(Elevator Man)*, Dennis O'Keefe *(Office Manager)*, Robert Homans *(Private Guard)*, Stanley Andrews *(Captain)*, Leonid Snegoff *(Chef)*, Wilson Benge *(Butler)*, Harry Worth *(Hindu)*, George Cowl *(Bank President)*, Kate Price *(Laundress)*, Lu Miller, Amelia Falleur *(Housemaids)*, Don Brodie *(Auto Salesman)*, Florence Wix *(Woman In Hat Shop)*, Olaf Hytten, Francis Sayles *(Housemen)*, William Wagner *(Valet)*.

Screwball comedy written by Preston Sturges and starring Arthur as a poor office girl who, while riding on the top of a double-decker bus, is hit on the head with a fur coat flung out the penthouse terrace by angry Wall Street millionaire Arnold, who is arguing with his wife. Seeking to make his spouse jealous, Arnold tracks down the girl and insists she keep the coat and he buys her a hat to match. Arthur finally arrives at work and is fired due to her tardiness and suspicion over how she acquired the coat. Soon the news has spread on Wall Street that Arthur is Arnold's mistress and dozens of hotels and shops flock to her and give her anything she wishes. All she really wants is a cup of coffee and she meets and falls for the waiter, Milland, who happens to be Arnold's son. After many screwball misunderstandings and plot flips, Arthur and Milland finally connect. A great cast pushes the one-joke material through to a happy finish. Film was another great step upward for Jean Arthur as a comedienne.

p, Arthur Hornblow, Jr.; d, Mitchell Leisen; w, Preston Sturges (based on a story by Vera Caspary); ph, Ted Tetzlaff; m, Boris Morros; ed, Doane Harrison; md, Morros; art d, Hans Dreier, Ernst Fegte; cos, Travis Banton; spec eff, Faricot Edouart.

Comedy **(PR:A MPAA:NR)**

EASY LIVING½** (1949) 77m RKO bw

Victor Mature *(Pete Wilson)*, Lucille Ball *(Anne)*, Lizabeth Scott *(Liza Wilson)*, Sonny Tufts *(Tim McCarr)*, Lloyd Nolan *(Lenahan)*, Paul Stewart *(Argus)*, Jack Paar *(Scoop Spooner)*, Jeff Donnell *(Penny McCarr)*, Art Baker *(Howard Vollmer)*, Gordon Jones *(Bill Holloran)*, Don Beddoe *(Jaegar)*, Dick Erdman *(Buddy Morgan)*, William "Bill" Phillips *(Ozzie)*, Charles Lang *(Whitey)*, Kenny Washington *(Benny)*, Julia Dean *(Mrs. Belle Ryan)*, Everett Glass *(Virgil Ryan)*, James Backus *(Dr. Franklin)*, Robert Ellis *(Urchin)*, Steven Flagg *(Gilbert Vollmer)*, Alex Sharp *(Don)*, Russ Thorson *(Hunk Edwards)*, June Bright *(Billy Duane)*, Eddie Kotal *(Curley)*, Audrey Young *(Singer)*, The Los Angeles Rams *(Themselves)*, Dick Ryan *(Bartender)*, Steve Crandall *(Reporter)*, Ray George *(Referee)*, William Erwin, Carl Saxe *(Men)*, Robert Graham, Warren Schannon, Jackie Jackson, Alan Dinehart III *(Urchins)*, Erin Selwyn *(Nurse)*, Albin Robeling *(Chef)*, W.J. O'Brien, Gene Leslie *(Vendors)*.

Soap opera story of an aging star halfback for the New York Chiefs (Mature) who knows retirement is imminent. Adjusting to this fact is complicated by the constant nagging of his wife, Scott, and the disappearance of a college coaching job he had hoped for, which is taken from him by Tufts. To make matters worse, he discovers that he has a heart condition that forces him to retire earlier than expected. All along he is supported by team secretary Ball, who is in love with him from afar but contents herself with helping him through his difficulties. The brutal climax sees Mature finally slapping some sense into his wife. Disappointing effort from director Tourneur.

p, Robert Sparks; d, Jacques Tourneur; w, Charles Schnee (based on the story "Education of The Heart" by Irwin Shaw); ph, Harry J. Wild; m, Roy Webb; ed, Frederic Knudtson; md, Constantin Bakaleinikoff; art d, Albert S. D'Agostino, Alfred Herman; set d, Darrell Silvera, Harley Miller; cos, Edward Stevenson.

Drama **(PR:A MPAA:NR)**

EASY MILLIONS*½ (1933) 57m Freuler bw

Skeets Gallagher, Dorothy Burgess, Merna Kennedy, Johnny Arthur, Noah Beery, Bert Roach, Gay Seabrook, Pauline Garon, Ethel Wales, Arthur Hoyt, Walter Long, Henry Roquemore, Theodore Adams.

Badly written, played, and shot, this comedy sees Gallagher tell a pesty partner that he has inherited $1 million to discourage a risky business proposition. Soon the rumor has Gallagher collecting a sum three times that amount and he is besieged with problems, including engagements to three women.

d, Fred Newmayer; w, Jack Jevne (based on a story by Edgar Franklin); ph, Jules Cronjager; ed, Byron Robinson.

Comedy **(PR:A MPAA:NR)**

EASY MONEY** (1934, Brit.) 69m B&D/PAR British bw

Mary Newland *(Joan Letchworth)*, Gerald Rawlinson *(Jock Durant)*, George Carney *(Boggle)*, Lawrence Hanray *(Mr. Pim)*, Hubert Leslie *(Col. Hinckley)*, Harvey Braban *(Williams)*, Gladys Hamer *(Maggie)*, Rene Ray *(The Typist)*.

A bookmaker's assistant thwarts his boss' scheme to blackmail a wealthy old colonel by bringing out the "family ghost" to sink the plot. During the ghostly caper the clerk falls for the colonel's daughter, and comic doings end up in serious romance. Very English and very unfocused.

p&d, Redd Davis; w, Basil Mason (based on the play "The Ghosts of Mr. Pim" by Mason); ph, Geoffrey Faithfull.

Comedy **(PR:A MPAA:NR)**

EASY MONEY** (1936) 70m Invincible bw

Onslow Stevens *(Dan Adams)*, Kay Linaker *(Carol Carter)*, Noel Madison *("Duke" Trotti)*, Allen Vincent *(Eddie Adams)*, Barbara Barondess *(Tonia)*, Wallis Clark *(Mr. Curtis)*, Selmer Jackson *(Harrison)*, Robert Homans *(Sam Belden)*, Robert Graves *(Sillsby)*, John Kelly *(Carney)*, Alan Woods *(Chick)*, John Dilson *(Rusick)*, Robert Frazier, Broderick O'Farrell, Barbara Bedford, Dickie Walters, Betty Mack, Henry Herbert, Monte Vandergrift.

Tired drama sees a gangster murdered for trying to go straight. His death leads Stevens, his insurance investigator brother, on a trail that nets the gangster-killers jail sentences, including their crooked attorney. For crime film buffs mostly.

p, Maury M. Cohen; d, Phil Rosen; w, Arthur T. Horman (based on a story by Paul Perez, Ewart Adamson); ph, M.A. Andersen; ed, Roland D. Reed.

Crime **(PR:A MPAA:NR)**

EASY MONEY** (1948, Brit.) 94m EL-RANK/Gainsborough/GFD bw

Jack Warner *(Phillip Stafford)*, Marjorie Fielding *(Ruth Stafford)*, Yvonne Owen *(Carol Stafford)*, Jack Watling *(Dennis Stafford)*, Petula Clark *(Jackie Stafford)*, Mabel Constanduros *(Grandma)*, Meryvn Johns *(Herbert Atkins)*, Joan Young

(*Agnes Atkins*), Gordon McLeod (*Cameron*), Greta Gynt (*Pat Parsons*), Dennis Price (*Joe Henry*) , Bill Owen (*Mr. Lee*), Frederick Piper (*Martin*), Edward Rigby (*Teddy Ball*), Guy Rolfe (*Archie*), Raymond Lovell (*Mr. Cyprus*), Frank Cellier (*Orchestra Conductor*), David Tomlinson (*Martin*), Jack Raine (*Managing Director, Pools*), Maurice Denham (*Detective Inspector Kirby*), David Horne (*The Voice of Mr. Hessian*), Grey Blake (*Wilson*), Dennis Harkin (*1st Waiter*), John Blythe (*2nd Waiter*), Freddie Carpenter (*Dance Director*), Dancers from the London Casino, E.H.V. Emmett (*Commentary*).

Lackluster anthology film dealing with the trials and tribulations of four people trying to win the weekly $200,000 prize in the national football pool. First feature film produced by British documentary filmmaker Frank Bundy is pretty predictable, the forgotten ticket, the timid clerk, a seductress, the aging musician, all mixed up in a world of dreams.

p, A. Frank Bundy; d, Bernard Knowles; w, Muriel and Sydney Box (based on the play by Arnold Ridley); ph, John Asher, David Harcourt; ed, Vladimir Sagovsky.

Drama (PR:A MPAA:NR)

EASY MONEY*½ (1983) 100m Orion c

Rodney Dangerfield (*Monty*), Joe Pesci (*Nicky*), Geraldine Fitzgerald (*Mrs. Monahan*), Candy Azzara (*Rose*), Val Avery (*Louie*), Tom Noonan (*Paddy*), Taylor Negron (*Julio*), Lili Haydn (*Belinda*), Jeffrey Jones (*Clive*), Tom Ewell (*Scrappleton*), Jennifer Jason Leigh (*Allison*), Jeffrey Altman (*Bill*), David Vasquez (*Hector*), Kimberly McArthur (*Ginger*), Frank Simpson (*Fr. McIntyre*), Arch Johnson (*Vendor*), Dennis Blair (*Critic*), Steve Szucs (*Barfly*), Jennifer Dana Giangrasso (*Birthday Girl*), Mary Pat Gleason, Angela Pietropinto (*Party Mothers*), Carmen Bonifant (*Julio's Mother*), Pedro Ocampo (*Julio's Father*), Taylor Reed (*Fat Guy*), Peter Laurelli (*Fat Anthony*), Fiddle Viracola, John Scoletti, Filomena Spagnuolo, Peter D'Arcy, Polly Magaro, Rafael Cruz, Alfred De La Fuente, Harsh Nayyar, Sid Raymond, Jeff Gillen, Eric Van Valkenburg, Richard Van Valkenburg, John Delph, Walt Gorney, Jessica James, B. Constance Barry, Mary Wilshire, Gregor Roy, Milton Seaman, Wade Barnes, James Cahill, Ian Sullivan, Lisa McMillan, Andrea Coles, Jade Bari, McKenzie Allen, Richard Dow, Margot Avery.

Dangerfield is a laugh riot as a baby photographer with a rich mother-in-law who ostensibly dies and leaves him millions...all on the proviso that he thoroughly reform: no drinking, no smoking, and he must lose weight. From the lovable and laughable family man, Dangerfield turns into a grouchy, touchy jumble of quaking nerves, further vexed by a buxom next-door-neighbor with a penchant for topless sunbathing. Moreover, his daughter marries a sleazy Latin type and then immediately breaks up with him, causing him to slip in and out of Dangerfield's home to see his reluctant bride. Dangerfield's wife, Azzara, doesn't help matters by insisting that he stick to the letter of her mother's absurd will. Neither do his hard-drinking pals, headed by Pesci, who smoke, drink, and overeat in front of Dangerfield, driving him to bug-eyed jitters. In the end, Rodney wins the money by the deadline and gets all the respect he desires, learning that his mother-in-law, Fitzgerald, is very much alive. He still takes his simple pleasures in the basement of his mansion, where he joins Pesci and friends to guzzle beer in his T-shirt, smoke, gobble pizza, and play poker like a fiend. The action is fast and furious. Dangerfield is the whole show and he mugs his way to hilarity in almost every frame. Some of his scenes while attempting to photograph unruly children are absolutely side-splitting. Some occasional strong language has been gratuitously inserted.

p, John Nicolella; d, James Signorelli; w, Rodney Dangerfield, Michael Endler, P.J. O'Rourke, Dennis Blair; ph, Fred Schuler (Technicolor); m, Laurence Rosenthal; ed, Ronald Roose; prod d, Eugene Lee; cos, Joe Aulisi; m/l, "Easy Money," Billy Joel.

Comedy Cas. (PR:C-O MPAA:R)

EASY RICHES*½ (1938, Brit.) 67m GS Enterprises/RKO bw

George Carney (*Sam Miller*), Gus McNaughton (*Joe Hicks*), Marjorie Taylor (*Dorothy Hicks*), Tom Helmore (*Harry Miller*), Peter Gawthorne (*Stacey Lang*), Aubrey Mallalieu, Molly Hamley-Clifford, Michael Ripper.

A cement works owner and a brick factory owner, lifelong business rivals, join forces to expose a con man and his phony schemes for land developments. A happy romance between the families further unites the old warriors and by film's end all emotional barriers between them have fallen. An embarrassment of staleness.

p, A. George Smith; d, Maclean Rogers; w, John Hunter; ph, Geoffrey Faithfull.

Comedy (PR:A MPAA:NR)

EASY RIDER** (1969) 94m Pando-Raybert/COL c

Peter Fonda (*Wyatt*), Dennis Hopper (*Billy*), Antonio Mendoza (*Jesus*), Phil Spector (*Connection*), Mac Mashourian (*Bodyguard*), Warren Finnerty (*Rancher*), Tita Colorado (*Rancher's Wife*), Luke Askew (*Stranger*), Luana Anders (*Lisa*), Sabrina Scharf (*Sarah*), Sandy Wyeth (*Joanne*), Robert Walker, Jr. (*Jack*), Robert Ball, Carman Phillips, Ellie Walker, Michael Pataki (*Mimes*), Jack Nicholson (*George Hanson*), George Fowler, Jr. (*Guard*), Keith Green (*Sheriff*), Hayward Robillard (*Cat Man*), Arnold Hess, Jr. (*Deputy*), Buddy Causey, Jr., Duffy LaFont, Blase M. Dawson, Paul Guedry, Jr. (*Customers*), Suzie Ramagos, Elida Ann Hebert, Rose LeBlanc, Mary Kay Hebert, Cynthia Grezaffi, Colette Purpera (*Girls*), Toni Basil (*Mary*), Karen Black (*Karen*), Cathi Cozzi (*Dancing Girl*), Thea Salerno, Anne McLain, Beatriz Monteil, Marcia Bowman (*Hookers*), David C. Billodeau, Johnny David (*Pickup Truck*), Lea Marmer (*Madame*).

Fonda and Hopper made several motorcycle pictures before this one so they went to American International Pictures and hoped to secure the financing. They were turned down by the studio chiefs who felt that motorcycle pictures had had it in the marketplace. They later approached Columbia (with the team that used to produce "The Monkees" and later did HEAD) and secured just a few hundred thousand to make this little film. The result was a box office bonanza and new life

for former "B" movie actor Nicholson who received an Oscar nomination as Best Supporting Actor (but lost to Gig Young for THEY SHOOT HORSES, DON'T THEY?). The screenplay (by Hopper, Fonda, and Terry Southern, also nabbed a nomination and lost to BUTCH CASSIDY AND THE SUNDANCE KID) tells what is essentially a moralistic story of two men searching for an elusive freedom they can never attain. Fonda and Hopper are two seemingly scuzzy motorcyclists who make a dope deal with Spector (the famed rock and roll producer) in order to finance their trip. Fonda, called Captain America because of the stars and stripes on his cycle and jacket, stashes the money in his gas tank and they ride off, destination New Orleans. They hope to get there in time for Mardi Gras and a little fun. On the way, they are rebuffed at various motels because they look so weird to the squares who run the hostelries. They camp out, smoke some dope, talk almost unintelligibly to each other, and finally nod off in a cannabis cloud. They stop at a ranch to repair their bikes and have a lovely dinner with Finnerty and Colorado, then pick up a hitchhiker, Walker, Jr., and take him back to his commune where they pass a bit of time with some of the commune's women. Itching to hit the road, Hopper insists they leave. They ride to Texas where a local celebration is taking place with a large, squeaky-clean parade. They join in the procession and so infuriate the local gendarmes that they are arrested for "parading without a permit" and tossed into the clink. Now the picture suddenly shoots heavenward as they meet Nicholson, an alcoholic lawyer who specializes in civil rights cases. Nicholson is sanguine about being in jail, much preferring to suffer his hangovers there than to have to deal with his wealthy and often angry father. The trio become fast friends and Nicholson uses his connections to convince the authorities to forego the usual butch haircuts they apply to convicts, so Hopper and Fonda are spared that ignominy. Later, they invite Nicholson to join them and he reckons he just might, having always wanted to see The House Of Blue Lights bordello in the Crescent City. On their way to Louisiana, the men bed down off the road and they give Nicholson his first joint. Nicholson is very funny as he tells them his theory that Venusians have already landed on Earth and occupy several important posts. In the morning, they visit a small restaurant and the hostility on the part of the customers is so thick you can feel it pouring off the screen. That night, while camping out, they are beset by a group of rednecks who kill Nicholson and leave Hopper and Fonda badly beaten. Nicholson had wondered aloud, "This used to be a fine country. What went wrong?" Hopper and Fonda move on to New Orleans and decide to visit the brothel in honor of their dead pal, but neither the festive air of Fat Tuesday nor the hookers can bring them out of their depressions. They take Karen Black and Toni Basil, two of the whores, and go on an LSD trip in a nearby above-ground cemetery (Note: The LSD sequence was shot in 16mm and if the cemetery looks unusual with the crypts above ground, that's because New Orleans is actually built below the water table, and to dig six feet down would be to find mud. Therefore, people are buried in crypts and, when enough time passes, those bones are shoved to the rear and new bodies are put in. Not that this has much to do with the picture but we aim to educate as well as entertain.) The acid trip is a bad one so Fonda and Hopper bid ta-ta to the girls and take off again. On the road, they're passed by David and Billodeau in a pickup truck. The men point their shotguns at Hopper and Fonda, who respond by giving them the finger. Hopper is shot in the stomach and Fonda gets on his bike to try and find some medical help. But by that time, the pickup has made a U-turn and the men inside realize that they can't allow any witnesses to their crime, so they blow Fonda off the road, sending him and his motorcycle into a slow-motion death. Much has been written about EASY RIDER and almost every critic raved about the accurate depiction of life in these United States at that time. With such a success, one might have thought director Hopper would have established himself, but he was only allowed to make one more fictional picture, THE LAST MOVIE, which failed terribly. He also did a documentary, THE AMERICAN DREAMER, in which he appeared as himself. Fonda later directed THE HIRED HAND and WANDA NEVADA, neither of which had many viewers. Nicholson's performance was the standout and his character was the most realized in the movie. Knowing that Nicholson is also a writer, one wonders how much of the excellent dialog was in the script and how much was improvised or created by Nicholson. Black was appearing in her third feature (YOU'RE A BIG BOY, NOW and HARD CONTRACT preceding this) and impressed everyone with her work. The following year she worked with producer Schneider and Nicholson again in FIVE EASY PIECES, for which she secured an Oscar nomination. "Potent," "powerful," and "poignant" are some of the adjectives used to describe this landmark film that proved you don't need stars or a huge production to capture audiences. It was the beginning of a "small picture" revolution that may have contributed mightily to the art of movies for many years after. EASY RIDER was primitive in many ways, but there was no mistaking the talents or the intent of the people behind it, an indictment of the way things were and an attempt to alter them with art.

p, Peter Fonda; d, Dennis Hopper; w, Fonda, Hopper, Terry Southern; ph, Lazlo Kovacs (Technicolor); ed, Donn Cambern; art d, Jerry Kay; spec eff, Steve Karkus; m/l, "The Pusher," Hoyt Axton (sung by Steppenwolf), "Born to be Wild," Mars Bonfire (sung by Steppenwolf), "I Wasn't Born to Follow," Jerry Goffin, Carole King (sung by The Byrds), "The Weight," Jaime Robbie Robertson (The Band), "If You Want to Be a Bird," Antonia Duren (sung by The Holy Modal Rounders), "Don't Bogart Me," Elliot Ingber, Larry Waner (sung by Fraternity of Men), "If Six was Nine," Jimi Hendrix (sung by The Jimi Hendrix Experience), "Let's Turkey Trot," Goffin, Jack Keller (sung by Little Eva), "Kyrie Eleison," David Axelrod (sung by The Electric Prunes), "Flash, Bam, Pow" Mike Bloomfield (The Electric Flag), "It's Alright Ma (I'm Only Bleeding)," Bob Dylan (sung by Roger McGuinn), "Ballad of Easy Rider," Dylan, McGuinn (sung by McGuinn).

Drama Cas. (PR:O MPAA:R)

EASY TO LOOK AT (1945) 64m UNIV bw

Gloria Jean (*Judy*), Kirby Grant (*Tyler*), George Dolenz (*Antonio*), J. Edward Bromberg (*Gustav*), Eric Blore (*Billings*), Mildred Law (*Helene*), Leon Belasco (*Phillipe*), Maurice Cass (*Woolens*), Polly Bailey (*Landlady*), Jean Slemmon (*Stock

Girl), Grace Cunard (Tessie), Ida Moore (Sadie), Ethel Halls (Mary), Charles Wagenheim (Louie), Roy Darmour (Stage Manager), Pat Gleason (Doorman), Dick French (Orchestra Leader), Virginia Wicks (Girl), Paul Powers, Jack Davidson (Drunks), Myrtle Ferguson (Gardenia Gertie), Doug Carter (Taxi Driver), Eddie Cutler, Charles Teske (Dance Specialties), Delta Rhythm Boys.

Dull musical starring Jean as a young singer and budding costume designer who ventures off to New York in search of fame and fortune. She soon makes some inroads into the fashion business, but her career is shattered when she is accused of being a design thief. After many songs, histrionics, and romancing of Grant, Jean is cleared of all accusations and realizes her dream of being recognized in the fashion world. Songs: "Come Along My Heart," "Just For the Devil Of It," "That Does It," "Umbrella With a Silver Lining," "Swing Low Sweet Lariat" (Charles Newman, Arthur Altman) "Is You Is or Is You Ain't My Baby?" (Billy Austin, Louis Jordan).

p, Henry Blankfort; d, Ford Beebe; w, Blankfort; ph, Jerome Ash; ed, Saul A. Goodkind; md, H.J. Salter; art d, John B. Goodman, Robert Clatworthy.

Musical (PR:A MPAA:NR)

EASY TO LOVE★★ (1934) 62m WB bw

Genevieve Tobin (Carol), Adolphe Menjou (John), Mary Astor (Charlotte), Guy Kibbee (Justice of the Peace), Edward Everett Horton (Eric), Patricia Ellis (Janet), Hugh Herbert (Detective), Hobart Cavanaugh (Clerk), Robert Greig (Andrews), Harold Waldridge (Elevator Boy), Paul Kaye (Paul).

Menjou and Tobin play a middle-aged married couple whose marital bliss is jeopardized when Tobin catches Menjou in a clinch with a friend of the family, Astor. To get revenge, Tobin claims she has been having an affair with Astor's husband, Horton (she has not). The mess is settled when their daughter, Ellis, shocks the family back to reality by announcing her plans to run off with her boy friend, Kaye. Tired material is given a much-needed shot in the arm by a good cast and breathless direction.

p, Henry Blanke; d, William Keighley; w, Carl Erickson, Manuel Seff (based on the play by Thompson Buchanan, adapted by David Boehm); ph, Ernest Haller; ed, William Clemens; art d, Anton Grot; cos, Orry-Kelly; m/l, "Easy To Love," Irving Kahal, Sammy Fain.

Comedy (PR:A MPAA:NR)

EASY TO LOVE★★★ (1953) 96m MGM c

Esther Williams (Julie Hallerton), Van Johnson (Ray Lloyd), Tony Martin (Barry Gordon), John Bromfield (Hank), Edna Skinner (Nancy Parmel), King Donovan (Ben), Paul Bryar (Mr. Barnes), Carroll Baker (Clarice), Eddie Oliver (Band Leader), Benny Rubin (Oscar Levenson), Edward Clark (Gardener), June Whitley (Costume Designer), Emory Parnell (Mr. Huffnagel), David Newell (Makeup Man), Sondra Gould (Ben's Wife), Lillian Culver (Flora), Fenton Hamilton (Fat Man), Harriett Brest, Helen Dickson, Ann Luther, Maude Erickson, Peggy Remington, Violet Seton, Dorothy Vernon (Women Guests in Lobby), Richard Downing Pope, Bud Gaines (Tourists), Byron Kane, Reginald Simpson (Photographers), Joe Mell (Sleepy Waiter), Hal Berns (Melvin, The Pianist), Margaret Bert (Mrs. Huffnagel).

Nothing much in the plot department but some spectacular Busby Berkeley aquatic musical numbers should be enough to get anyone through this one. Williams loves her boss, Johnson, from afar, as she works for him as his secretary and the star of his aqua-show. He pays her no attention until she begins to romance swimming instructor Bromfield and crooner Martin and he realizes his deep-seated love for her. Major musical numbers have Williams swimming with a chimpanzee; with Bromfield in a beautiful, Technicolor, flower-strewn scene; and in an incredibly staged climax with dozens of motorboats towing water skiers. Berkeley made two more pictures, ROSEMARIE (1954) and Billy Rose's JUMBO (1962), neither of which had sequences that could match the finale of this one. Songs: "Easy To Love" (Cole Porter); "Coquette" (Carmen Lombardo, Johnny Green, Gus Kahn); "Beautiful Spring" (Paul Lincke); "That's What Rainy Day Is For," "Look Out! I'm Romantic," "Didja Ever" (Vic Mizzy, Mann Curtis).

p, Joe Pasternak; d, Charles Walters; w, Laslo Vadnay, William Roberts (based on a story by Vadnay); ph, Ray June (CinemaScope, Technicolor); ed, Gene Ruggiero; md, Lennie Hayton, George Stoll; musical numbers created and directed by Busby Berkeley; art d, Cedric Gibbons, Jack Martin Smith.

Musical (PR:A MPAA:NR)

EASY TO TAKE★★½ (1936) 66m PAR bw

Marsha Hunt (Donna Westlake), John Howard (Rodney Garfield), Eugene Pallette (Doc Kraft), Richard Carle (Judge Olney), Douglas Scott (Wilbur Westlake), Jan Duggan (Miss Higgie), Marilyn Knowldon (Gwen), Robert Greig (Judd), Carl Switzer (Kid Comic), Josephine Whittell, Charles Levinson, Billy Lee.

Fairly funny story starring Howard as kiddie show host Uncle Rodney, who becomes guardian of a bratty boy and trustee of an estate through the station, which thinks it would be good for publicity. His enthusiasm for the project soars when he meets the boy's sister, Hunt, but he soon learns that both are broke and he is stuck supporting them and keeping up the mansion. Howard's kiddie show finally lands a sponsor and he a sweetheart as all ends well.

p, Jack Cunningham; d, Glenn Tryon; w, Virginia Van Upp (based on a story by Wayne Kilbourne); ph, George Robinson; m, Gregory Stone; ed, Edward Dmytryk; md, Boris Morros.

Comedy (PR:A MPAA:NR)

EASY TO WED★★★ (1946) 109m MGM c

Van Johnson (Bill Stevens Chandler), Esther Williams (Connie Allenbury), Lucille Ball (Gladys Benton), Keenan Wynn (Warren Haggerty), Cecil Kellaway (J.B. Allenbury), Carlos Ramirez (Himself), Ben Blue (Spike Dolan), Ethel Smith (Herself), June Lockhart (Babs Norvell), Grant Mitchell (Homer Henshaw), Josephine

Whitell (Mrs. Burns Norvell), Paul Harvey (Farwood), Jonathan Hale (Hector Boswell), James Flavin (Joe), Celia Travers (Farwood's Secretary), Sybil Merritt (Receptionist), Sondra Rodgers (Attendant), Robert Emmett O'Connor (Taxi Driver), Katherine [Karin] Booth (Clerk), Dick Winslow (Orchestra Leader), George Calliga (Headwaiter), Tom Dugan (Waiter), Walter Soderling, Sarah Edwards (Mr. & Mrs. Dibson), Mitzie Uehlein, Mildred Sellers, Phyllis Graffeo, Kanza Omar, Louise Burnette, Katherine Denise (Girls at Pool), Charles Knight, Guy Bates Post, John Valentine (Butlers), Chavo de Leon, Nina Bara (Rumba Dancers), Milton Kibbee (Private Detective), Jack Shea (Lifeguard), Katherine Black (Masseuse), Joel Friedkin (Justice of the Peace), Charles Sullivan, Frank Hagney (Truck Drivers), Jean Porter (Frances), Fred Fisher, Alex Pollard (Waiters).

Musical remake of the 1936 Spencer Tracy, Jean Harlow classic LIBELED LADY, this time starring Williams as the rich playgirl who brings a massive lawsuit down on the head of newspaperman Wynn, who has printed an unflattering portrait of her lifestyle. To win the case, Wynn hires suave lover Johnson (a former employee of the newspaper) to persuade Williams to drop the charges. Of course everything goes haywire. Songs: "Easy To Wed" (Ted Duncan, Johnny Green), "Goosey-Lucy," "It Shouldn't Happen To A Duck" (Robert Franklin, Green); "Continental Polka," "Gonna Fall In Love With You" (Ralph Blane, Green), "Come Closer To Me" (Osvaldo Farres, Al Stewart).

p, Jack Cummings; d, Edward Buzzell; w, Dorothy Kingsley (adapted from the screenplay "Libeled Lady" by Maurine Watkins, Howard Emmett Rodgers, George Oppenheimer); ph, Harry Stradling (Technicolor); m, Johnny Green; ed, Blanche Sewell; md, Ted Duncan; art d, Cedric Gibbons, Hans Peters; set d, Edwin B. Willis, Jack Bonar; ch, Jack Donahue.

Musical (PR:A MPAA:NR)

EASY WAY (SEE: ROOM FOR ONE MORE, 1952)

EAT MY DUST!★★ (1976) 89m New World c

Ron Howard (Hoover), Christopher Norris (Darlene), Warren Kemmerling (Harry Niebold), Dave Madden (Big Bubba Jones), Robert Broyles (Bud), Evelyn Russel (Delores Westerby), Rance Howard (Deputy Clerk), Jessica Potter (Lallie), Charles Howerton (J.B.), Kathy O'Dare (Miranda), Brad David (Billy), Clint Howard (Georgie), Kedric Wolfe, John Thompson, Don Brodie, Harry Frazier, Mickey Fox, Pete Isacksen, W.L. Luckey, Paul Bartel, Lynn Brown, Margaret Fairchild, John J. Fox, John Kramer.

Sub-par Corman car-chase opus directed by Griffith, who penned such Corman classics as BUCKET OF BLOOD and LITTLE SHOP OF HORRORS. Howard plays the clean-cut but rowdy son of a small town sheriff, Kemmerling. The sheriff organizes a motorized posse to take off after his son and friend Norris who have stolen a racing car from professional driver Madden. The rest is a fun but mindless hour and a half of car wrecks that stretches across a few states. Look for veteran Corman director Paul Bartel in a walk-on part.

p, Roger Corman; d&w, Charles B. Griffith; ph, Eric Saarinen (Metrocolor); m, David Grisman; ed, Tina Hirsh; art d, Peter Jamison; stunts, Ronald Clark.

Action **Cas.** (PR:A MPAA:PG)

EATEN ALIVE★★ (1976) 90m Virgo International c
(AKA: DEATH TRAP; STARTLIGHT SLAUGHTER; HORROR HOTEL MASSACRE; LEGEND OF THE BAYOU)

Neville Brand, Mel Ferrer, Carolyn Jones, Marilyn Burns, William Finely, Stuart Whitman.

Brand is a psychopathic Louisiana hotel owner who kills anyone and everyone who registers or just stops by his place. He neatly kills them with his scythe or his alligator. Directed by Tobe Hooper (THE TEXAS CHAINSAW MASSACRE, POLTERGEIST), one of the masters in this genre.

p, Mardi Rustam; d, Tobe Hooper; w, Alvin Fast, Rustam.

Horror **Cas.** (PR:O MPAA:R)

EATING RAOUL zero (1982) 90m Bartel/FOX c

Mary Woronov (Mary Bland), Paul Bartel (Paul Bland), Robert Beltran (Raoul), Buck Henry (Mr. Leech), Richard Paul (Mr. Kray), Susan Saiger (Doris the Dominatrix), Ed Begley, Jr. (Hippy), Dan Barrows (Bobbie R.), Dick Blackburn (James), Ralph Brannen (Paco), Hamilton Camp (Mr. Peck), John Paragon (Sexshop Salesman), Edie McClurg (Susan), Allan Rich, Don Steele, Billy Curtis, Anna Mathias, John Shearin, Darcy Pulliam.

This so-called "black comedy" is a balloon without any air at all, inflated by the hot gases emitting from certain "new wave" or "inside" critics who wouldn't know a comedy from THE GRAPES OF WRATH. Woronov and Bartel are middle-class types who take to murdering swingers for their money to earn an income. They turn over the corpses to Beltran who, in turn, sells the bodies to a dog food concern. When he becomes bothersome, the married couple murder him and serve him as a meal—"We're having a friend for dinner." The whole thing is so amateurishly done, from its insipid acting by Woronov, Bartel, and Beltran to its seemingly directorless sequences that it becomes both an insult and a terrible waste of time to sit through this moronic tripe once. This is blind movie-making at its worst. Wrong-headed, pig-headed, and mindless, this independent film will mislead many another novice into believing its lack of technique is real technique, its nothing story is satiric, and its rotten acting is realistic. The only loss to be suffered at the destruction of every print of this miserable piece of garbage would be a bad taste in the mouth. The kind of people who find such non-films funny also roll in the aisles at the sight of bookburnings, torture, and genocide. (Sequel, BLAND AMBITION).

p, Anne Kimmel; d, Paul Bartel; w, Bartel, Richard Blackburn; ph, Gary Thieltges (Metrocolor); m, Arlon Ober; ed, Alan Toomayan; prod d, Robert Schulenberg.

Comedy **Cas.** (PR:O MPAA:R)

THE EAVESDROPPER   (1966, U.S./Arg.) 102m
Royal Films International bw (EL OJO DE LA CERRADURA)
Stathis Giallelis (*Martin Casals*), Janet Margolin (*Ines*), Lautaro Murua (*Hernan Ramallo*), Leonardo Favio (*Santos*), Nelly Meden (*Lola*), Ignacio de Soroa (*Ramon Casal*), Elena Cortesina (*Mariquita*).

Giallelis, a member of a fascist organization in Buenos Aires, goes into hiding when his group's activities are banned by the government. His hideaway is a hotel populated by Spanish exiles and actors. He overhears some of the Spaniards plotting the assassination of a visiting dictator he admires, not knowing it is only a play rehearsal. He gets word to the police, who learn that the Spaniards are innocent, but still they close down their theater. When the Spaniards discover that Giallelis turned them in, they kick him out of the hotel. Nothing much brisk or exciting about this one except the location shots of Buenos Aires, for those who care.

p, Paul M. Heller; d, Leopoldo Torre Nilsson; w, Beatriz Guido, Edmundo Eichelbaum, Joe Goldberg, Nilsson, Mabel Itzcovich (based on a story by Guido, Nilsson); ph, Alberto Etchebehere; m, Lopez Furst; ed, Jacinto Cascales; art d, Oscar Lagomarsino.

Drama   (PR:C   MPAA:NR)

EBB TIDE   (1932, Brit.) 74m PAR British bw/c
Dorothy "Chili" Bouchier (*Cassie*), Joan Barry (*Mary*), George Barraud (*Steve*), Vanda Greville (*Millie*), Alexander Field (*Barney*), Annie Esmond (*Landlady*), Merle Oberon (*Girl*), Anna Lee.

While his long-time sweetheart is doing time in prison, sailor Barraud falls hard for a shopgirl and marries her. Out of prison, the mistress plots to win him back but instead saves the wife, whom she sees the sailor really loves, from suicide. This was 21-year-old Merle Oberon's second feature appearance.

p, Walter Morosco; d, Arthur Rosson; w, Basil Mason, Reginald Denham (based on the novel *God Gave Me 20 Cents* by Dixie Wilson).

Drama   (PR:A   MPAA:NR)

EBB TIDE*   (1937) 91m PAR c
Oscar Homolka (*Capt. Therbecke*), Frances Farmer (*Faith Wishart*), Ray Milland (*Robert Herrick*), Lloyd Nolan (*Attwater*), Barry Fitzgerald (*Huish*), Charles Judels (*Port Doctor*), David Torrence (*Tapena Tom*), Lina Basquette (*Attwater's Servant*), Harry Field (*Tahiera*), George Piltz (*Sally Day*), Manuella Kalili (*Fiji Islander*), Jim Spencer (*Cook*), Arthur Allen, Joe Molina (*Native Sailors*), Sonny Chorre (*Attwater's Guard*), David Hope (*Sailor*), Leonard Sues (*Native Boy*), Inez Palange (*Native Woman*), Gloria Williams, Nancy Chaplin (*Women*), Jacques Vanaire (*Assistant Port Doctor*), Antrim Short, Don Wayson, Bob Haines (*Men*), Bernard Siegal (*Waiter*), Al Kikume (*Native Policeman*), Stella Francis (*Woman Tourist*), Olaf Hytten (*English Tourist*), Eugene Beday (*Port Officer*), Jack George (*Band Leader*), Jack Clark, Elizabeth Hartman (*Tourists*).

Off-beat adventure tale starring Homolka (in his first Hollywood role after leaving Gaumont-British in England), Fitzgerald, and Milland as aimless beachcombers hired by an island commission to remove a smallpox infected ship and its cargo from the island and sail it to Australia where it is to be destroyed. When they discover that the ship's cargo is champagne, they decide to sail the vessel to Peru where they can sell the liquor and the ship for a tidy profit. A monkey wrench is thrown in the works when Farmer, the daughter of the ship's dead captain, turns young Milland's head and he drops out of the plan. A typhoon nearly wrecks the ship and they are forced to anchor off an uncharted island run by the psychopathic Nolan, who kills Homolka and Fitzgerald with a Winchester in one hand and a Bible in the other, with Milland and Farmer going free. Fitzgerald steals the show as the salty vagrant. The novelette the film was based on was written by Robert Louis Stevenson and his stepson, Lloyd Osbourne, in Samoa, where Stevenson spent the last five years of his life. (Remade as ADVENTURE ISLAND.)

p, Lucien Hubbard; d, James Hogan; w, Bertram Milhauser (based on the novelette by Robert Louis Stevenson, Lloyd Osbourne); ph, Ray Rennahan, Leo Tover (Technicolor); m, Ralph Rainger, Leo Robin; ed, LeRoy Stone; cos, Edith Head; spec eff, Gordon Jennings.

Adventure   (PR:A MPAA:NR)

EBIRAH, HORROR OF THE DEEP
(SEE:GODZILLA VS THE SEA MONSTER, 1966, Jap.)

EBOLI*½   (1980, Ital.) 120m Franklin Media c
(AKA: CHRIST STOPPED AT EBOLI)
Gian Maria Volonte (*Carlo Levi*), Irene Papas (*Giulia*), Lea Massari.

Film rendition of the memoirs of Italian political prisoner Levi, banished to the harsh terrain of southern Italy during the mid-1930s. Meager in terms of plot, the film concentrates heavily upon Volonte's conception of the simple people who must struggle in order to create their bare sustenance. That which strikes Volonte's curiosity the most is the superstitious attitudes the peasants have toward medicine, especially since he is a doctor unable to practice his trade until a ban is lifted. Without really having too much force in terms of underlying themes, EBOLI is an insightful depiction of a people who seem almost stuck in time.

p, Franco Cristaldi, Nicola Carraro; d, Francesco Rosi; w, Rosi, Tonino Guerra, Raffaele La Capria (based on the book *Christ Stopped At Eboli* by Carlo Levi); ph, Pasqualino de Santis; m, Piero Piccioni; ed, Ruggero Mastroianni.

Drama   (PR:A   MPAA:NR)

ECHO, THE   (1964, Pol.) 90m Polski State bw (ECHO)
Wienczyslaw Glinski (*Henry*), Barbara Horawianka (*Wife*), Jacek Blawut (*Son*).

Plodding drama starring Glinski as a happily married man and a good father whose life is ruined when it is revealed that he collaborated with the Nazis during WW II.

Though he claims he did it only to save the life of another man, the man he saved has died and cannot corroborate his story. Because no one believes him, and his wife and child no longer respect him, he attempts suicide but fails even in that. Director Rozewicz is internationally known for his serious films, many of which he writes himself in collaboration with his brother, Tadeusz, a poet and playwright and a member of the Polish underground during the war. The film's photographer, Wojcik, is the gifted cameraman who shot, among other films, ASHES AND DIAMONDS.

d, Stanislaw Rozewicz; w, Tadeusz and Stanislaw Rozewicz; ph, Jerzy Wojcik; m, Wojeich Kilar.

Drama   (PR:C   MPAA:NR)

ECHO MURDERS, THE*½   (1945, Brit.) 80m BN-Strand/Anglo American bw
David Farrar (*Sexton Blake*), Dennis Price (*Dick Warren*), Pamela Stirling (*Stella Duncan*), Julien Mitchell (*James Duncan*), Dennis Arundell (*Rainsford*), Kynaston Reeves (*Beales*), Cyril Smith (*P.C. Smith*), Patric Curwen (*Dr. Grey*), Johnnie Schofield (*Purvis*), Paul Croft (*Marat*), Ferdy Mayne, Desmond Roberts, Danny Green, Tony Arpino, Vincent Holman, Howard Douglas, Billy Howard, Anders Timberg, Victor Weske, Gerald Pring, Noel Dainton, Charles Hersee, Olive Walter.

A SEXTON BLAKE series bummer out of England. Farrar, as detective Blake, goes sleuthing in Cornwall for a murderer and winds up tying that killing and another one to a bunch of Nazis who are trying to infiltrate the English coast, thus the "echo murders." Get it? This one is not a resounding success.

p, Louis H. Jackson; d&w, John Harlow (based on characters created by Harry Blyth); ph, James Wilson.

Crime   (PR:A   MPAA:NR)

ECHO OF A DREAM*   (1930, Ger.) 88m Haesike/Goldie bw (VERKLUNGENE TRAUME)
Hans Stuwe, Maly Delschaft, Eugene Rex, Harry Hardt.

Stuwe is the son of a Rumanian aristocrat who decides to take a peasant bride to strengthen the bloodline. He chooses Delschaft at a village celebration and takes her despite the fact that a priest who has long loved her is about to abjure his vows in order to marry the peasant lass. She is about to bear Stuwe's child when an old flame of his turns up, and Delschaft leaves to be reunited with the still faithful priest. Melodramatic and obvious, with poor performances and tunes that evaporate from the mind as soon as they end. Songs include: "Verklungene Traume," "Siehst De Wohl Das Kommt Davon," "Beim Tango Tanz Verliebt," and "Man Sich So Leicht."

d, Martin Berger.

Musical   (PR:A-C MPAA:NR)

ECHO OF BARBARA*½   (1961, Brit.) 58m
Independent Artists/RFD bw

Mervyn Johns (*Sam Roscoe*), Maureen Connell (*Paula Brown*), Paul Stassino (*Caledonia*), Ronald Hines (*Mike Roscoe*), Tom Bell (*Ben*), Brian Peck (*Ted*), Eddie Leslie (*Aide*), Beatrice Varley (*Mrs. Roscoe*).

Suspense-filled crime drama has Hines, the ne'er-do-well son of ex-convict Johns, recruiting stripper Connell to impersonate his long-lost sister in a ploy to get his father to reveal the hiding place of some loot. Above average for a British B movie.

p, Arthur Alcott; d, Sidney Hayers; w, John Kruse (based on a novel by Jonathan Burke).

Crime   (PR:C   MPAA:NR)

ECHO OF DIANA*½   (1963, Brit.) 61m But bw
Vincent Ball (*Bill Vernon*), Betty McDowall (*Joan Scott*), Geoffrey Toone (*Col. Justin*), Clare Owen (*Pam Jennings*), Peter Illing (*Kovali*), Raymond Adamson (*George*), Marianne Stone (*Miss Green*).

After McDowall's husband is murdered, reporters discover a ring of spies is behind the killing. Average espionage drama by a director who likes to churn out B thrillers and has a reputation for keeping them briskly paced.

p, John I. Phillips; d, Ernest Morris; w, Reginald Hearne.

Spy Drama   (PR:A-C MPAA:NR)

ECHOES   (1983) 89m Continental c
Richard Alfieri (*Michael Durant/Dream Michael*), Nathalie Nell (*Christine*), Ruth Roman (*Michael's Mother*), Gale Sondergaard (*Mrs. Edmunds*), Mercedes McCambridge (*Lillian Gerben*), Mike Kellin (*Sid Berman*), John Spencer (*Stephen*), Barbara Monte-Britton (*Dream Woman*), Duncan Quinn (*Dream Man*), Leonard Crofoot (*Danny*), Paul Joynt (*Ed*), Julie Burger (*Susan*), Sheila Coonan (*Rose*), Robin Karfo (*Sheila*), Ron Asher, Barry Eric (*Stage Managers*), Leib Lensky (*Backstage Doorman*), Raaf Baldwin (*Theater Doorman*), Damian Akhan (*Damian*), David M. Brezniak (*Art Student*), James Dunne (*Dancer Backstage*), Dennis Wayne (*Christine's Partner*), John Teitsort (*Robert*), Jan Winetsky (*Girl in Red Dress*), Joe Zaloom (*Truck Driver*).

Art student Alfieri's sanity begins to crumble when a recurring dream has his stillborn twin trying to kill him. An interesting premise that should have been much more entertaining.

p, George R. Nice, Valerie Y. Belsky; d, Arthur Allan Seidelman; w, Richard J. Anthony; ph, Hanania Baer; m, Gerard Bernard Cohen, Stephen Schwartz; ed, Dan Perry; art d, Neal Deluca; spec eff, Peter Kunz; ch, Dennis Wayne.

Fantasy   Cas.   (PR:O   MPAA:R)

ECHOES OF A SUMMER** (1976) 99m Cine Artists c (AKA: THE LAST CASTLE)

Richard Harris *(Eugene Striden)*, Lois Nettleton *(Ruth Striden)*, Geraldine Fitzgerald *(Sara)*, William Windom *(Dr. Hallett)*, Brad Savage *(Phillip Anding)*, Jodie Foster *(Deirdre Striden)*.

Routine tear-jerker starring Foster as a 12-year-old girl dying from a severe heart ailment and the effect her disease has on her family. The girl brings her parents, Harris and Nettleton, out of the depths of despair and teaches them to deal with her death through her tough example. Foster's performance keeps this drama from becoming totally maudlin.

p, Robert L. Joseph; d, Don Taylor; w, Joseph; ph, John Coquillon (Eastmancolor); m, Terry James; ed, Michael F. Anderson; art d, Jack MacAdams; m/l, "The Last Castle," Harris.

Drama **(PR:A MPAA:PG)**

ECHOES OF SILENCE** (1966) 76m Goldman bw

Miguel Chacour *(Miguel)*, Viraj Amonsin *(Viraj)*, Blanche Zelinka *(Blanche)*, Stasia Gelber *(Stasia)*, Jacquetta Lampson *(Jacquetta)*, Jean-Francois Gobbi *(Robert)*, Astrid Spiegel *(Astrid)*, Ellen Marcus, Maria Van Everett, Irwin Shapiro, John Pope, Bill Brach, Mactavish.

Low-budget independent film shot on 16mm and blown up to 35mm for theatrical release by producer, writer, director, photographer, editor Goldman. Loose plot deals with the ramblings of some drifters in Greenwich Village. It centers on one particular youth as we watch him try to pick up girls, fight off homosexual advances, and basically try to exist on the streets of New York. Only for those who like to suffer through somewhat pretentious, overlong, low-budget, pseudo-documentary "art" films.

d,w,ph&ed, Peter Emmanuel Goldman; m/l, Charles Mingus, Igor Stravinsky, Sergei Prokofiev, Pete Seeger.

Drama **(PR:C MPAA:NR)**

ECLIPSE*** (1962, Fr./Ital.) 123m Interopa Film-Cineriz-Paris-Films/Times Film bw (L'ECLISSE; L'ECLIPSE)

Monica Vitti *(Vittoria)*, Alain Delon *(Piero)*, Francisco Rabal *(Riccardo)*, Lilla Brignone *(Vittoria's Mother)*, Louis Seigner *(Ercoli)*, Rossana Rory *(Anita)*, Mirella Ricciardi *(Marta)*, Cyrus Elias *(Drunk)*.

Vitti leaves her boy friend of four years and then begins seeing Delon, a broker working for Vitti's mother. They fall in love, but both realize that they don't have much in common. They bury their fears by making love and decide that they will continue the relationship as long as it will last. The third in a series of similarly styled films from co-writer/director Antonioni, the others being L'AVVENTURA (1960)—which first brought him international acclaim—and LA NOTTE (1961), all starring the enigmatic heroine Vitti. The latter went on to become a truly international player, starring in films made in many countries.

p, Robert Hakim, Raymond Hakim; d, Michelangelo Antonioni; w, Antonioni, Tonino Guerra, Elio Bartolini, Ottiero Ottieri; ph, Gianni Di Venanzo; m, Giovanni Fusco; ed, Eraldo Da Roma; art d, Piero Poletto.

Drama **(PR:C MPAA:NR)**

ECSTASY*** (1940, Czech.) 82m Elekta/Jewel bw (EXTASE; EKSTASE) (AKA: SYMPHONY OF LOVE)

Hedy Kiesler [Lamarr] *(Eva)*, Jaromir Rogoz *(Emile)*, Aribert Mog *(Adam)*, Leopold Kramer *(Eva's Father)*.

This was undoubtedly the most notorious film of the early sound era, produced in Czechoslovakia in 1933 and not released generally in the U.S. until seven years later due to its controversial sex scenes which, by present standards, are as staid as the belly dances performed by "Fatima" in the nickelodian era. Kiesler (later Lamarr) is a child bride whose husband ignores her on her wedding night. She later, in frustration, has a sexual tryst in a hut with a roadway engineer. She is swimming when her horse wanders away carrying her clothes. She chases the horse and bumps into the engineer, who hands over her clothes like a gentleman. She arranges to go away with him, but leaves him after her former husband commits suicide. She later appears with a baby, the offspring of this illicit affair, happy and fulfilled. The story is a simple one but it is told through inventive techniques by director Machaty; one of his creative devices, showing the husband walking while being reflected in several mirrors, was lifted wholly by Orson Welles for CITIZEN KANE. Machaty, on the other hand, is clearly influenced by the Russian genius Eisenstein (who learned almost everything *he* knew from D.W. Griffith). Toward the end of ECSTASY, when Kiesler [Lamarr] is granted a divorce from her sexless husband, Machaty cuts to speeded up typewriters processing her papers, a scene duplicating Eisenstein's THE GENERAL LINE where bureaucratic office workers process the release of a tractor to petitioning farmers. The controversial scenes of ECSTASY, of course, are those showing Hedy bathing in the nude (she was 15 at the time) and later making love, but the love scenes were never anything more than head-and-shoulder shots recording the girl's "ecstactic" moments. It was always rumored that *somewhere* in the world prints existed showing Hedy in the altogether having explicit sex with her lover, but this was no more than a voyeuristic myth. The picture caused a stir in Europe long before America cast its suspicious eye on the film. (The normally reserved Pope Pius XII openly denounced the film, and Hitler's regime banned it from Germany.) Though it won the top award at the International Film Exposition in Venice in 1934, even the sophisticated capitals on the continent showed the film reluctantly because of its brief nudity. More frustrated was the German munitions magnate Fritz Mandl who later married Lamarr. He spent millions of dollars buying up what he thought to be every print of the film, but just as his minions would destroy a dozen prints, another dozen would pop up. When the elusive prints began to show up in the U.S., customs officials refused to admit them. (One U.S. marshal "accidentally" burned a print.) Several "edited" versions were admitted where Lamarr's nude scenes were cut down. One version inexplicably shows Hedy swimming with another unidentified woman, also nude. The film was seen widely and made quite a bit of money, especially after Lamarr became a top MGM star, following her debut in ALGIERS in 1938. U.S. exhibitor Samuel Cummins circumvented the censors when the film was prohibited on the grounds that it showed a married woman making love to another man. He had a special sequence inserted showing the girl writing (hands only) into her diary that "Adam and I were secretly married today" to justify the sex scene, later dubbing a voice claimed to be Lamarr's which states off camera, "I am so lonely. I must tell father we are married." These inserts were ridiculous because they did not work with the story continuity. Cummings went on to exploit the film with such sleazy slogans as, "The most whispered about film in the world," and "The stark naked truth of a woman's desire for love." Much was made of the real fact that Aribert Mog, who played the engineer in the film, was hopelessly in love with Hedy and that the love scenes were authentic. Fleeing Mandl, whom Hedy felt was controlling her life, she went to London, selling her jewels to finance her way. There an American press agent, Bob Ritchie, took her to see Louis B. Mayer, who was in London to sign up talent. She stood in front of the mogul, who sat in his suite with yes-men pouring heavy drinks. Mayer wore his hat and chomped on a cigar while sitting on a couch studying the young Hedy. In her book, *Ecstasy and Me*, Lamarr quoted the crude mogul as saying: "I saw ECSTASY. Never get away with that stuff in Hollywood. Never. A woman's ass is for her husband, not theatergoers. You're lovely, but I have the family point of view. I don't like what people would think about a girl who flits bare-assed around a screen." Lamarr protested, explaining that she was a serious actress, that she came from a good family and that ECSTASY was an artistic film, not a pornographic product. He smiled and patted her bottom, saying: "I know you would not make a vulgar picture intentionally. But in Hollywood, such accidents just don't happen. Not before the camera. We have an obligation to the audience—millions of families. We make clean pictures...and we like our stars to lead clean lives...If you like to make love...fornicate...with your leading men in the dressing room, that's your business, but in front of the camera, gentility. You hear, gentility." Mayer studied Lamarr, focusing on her breasts, telling her: "You have a bigger chest than I thought." He offered her $125-a-week contract and told her she'd have to get to America on her own hook. She walked out on him. But she had a plan in mind. Ritchie booked her passage on board the liner Mayer was taking back to America. She was being paid to escort a young violinist, Grisha Goluboff, whom Ritchie was also promoting. Though penniless, Hedy had kept some of the best gowns Mandl had bought her and she put on her finest on the last night of the voyage. She so impressed the mogul that Mayer gave her a $500-a-week contract for seven years. Lamarr also persuaded Mayer to give a contract to the boy violinist Goluboff. Even Machaty, who had worked with Erich von Stroheim in Hollywood during the 1920s, received an MGM contract, but he fared less well than Lamarr (Mayer ordered her name changed, because Kiesler sounded too much like "kiester," then a slang term meaning "buttocks"). Machaty was pushed into studio backwaters to grind out two-reel CRIME DOES NOT PAY shorts.

p, Franz Horky, Moriz Grunhut; Gustav Machaty; w, Machaty, Horky, Vitezslav Nezval, Jacques A. Koerpel; ph, Jan Stalich, Hans Androschin; m, Dr. Josef Becce; art d, Bohumil Hes; set d, Hosch.

Drama **Cas.** **(PR:O MPAA:NR)**

ECSTACY OF YOUNG LOVE*** (1936, Czech.) 75m Elekta/Metropolis bw (REKKA)

Vasa Jalovec *(Paul)*, Jarmila Berankova *(Pepi)*, Jar Vojta *(Paul's Father)*, Vojtova Mayerova *(Paul's Mother)*, J. Svitak *(The Poacher)*, Rudolf Deyl *(The Teacher)*.

Simplistic and touching tale in which a 17-year-old youth expresses his love for his poor girl friend by offering to get her the pair of shoes her parents cannot afford. Not as easy a task as it sounds because it requires the youth to catch and sell a large fish before being sent off to continue his education. The film is given a lyrical quality through this photography of the natural settings. (In Czechoslavakian; English subtitles).

d, J. Rovensky; w, Jan Snizek; m, Josef Dobes.

Drama **(PR:A MPAA:NR)**

EDDIE AND THE CRUISERS*½ (1983) 92m Aurora/EM c

Tom Berenger *(Frank)*, Michael Pare *(Eddie)*, Joe Pantoliano *(Doc)*, Matthew Laurance *(Sal)*, Helen Schneider *(Joann)*, David Wilson *(Kenny)*, Michael "Tunes" Antunes *(Wendell)*, Ellen Barkin *(Maggie)*, Kenny Vance *(Lew)*, John Stockwell *(Keith)*, Joe Cates *(Lois)*, Barry Sand *(Barry)*, Vebe Borge *(Gerry)*.

A lame, poorly structured film about an early 1960s rock star who mysteriously dies. A T.V. crew is headed by Barkin, who researches a documentary on Eddie Wilson and his band. Eddie died in an auto accident, but his body was never found. There are also the missing tapes of the last recording session. Barkin talks to people in the band and we flash back to the career of Eddie and the band. Kind of a rock 'n' roll CITIZEN KANE in form, but not in content. Pare as Eddie just doesn't work. He's a poor actor without any presence. The film bombed at the box office, then was a big hit when it came to cable. The soundtrack made the top-40 charts.

p, Joseph Brooks, Robert K. Lifton; d, Martin Davidson; w, Davidson, Arlene Davidson (adapted from the novel by P.F. Kluge); ph, Fred Murphy (Technicolor); m, John Cafferty; ed, Priscilla Nedd; art d, Gary Weist; set d, Chris Kelly.

Drama **Cas.** **(PR:C MPAA:PG)**

EDDIE CANTOR STORY, THE*½ (1953) 115m WB c

Keefe Brasselle *(Eddie Cantor)*, Marilyn Erskine *(Ida)*, Aline MacMahon *(Grandma Esther)*, Arthur Franz *(Harry Harris)*, Alex Gerry *(David Tobias)*, Greta Granstedt *(Rachel Tobias)*, Gerald Mohr *(Rocky)*, William Forrest *(Ziegfeld)*, Jackie Barnett *(Durante)*, Will Rogers, Jr. *(Will Rogers)*, Marie Windsor *(Cleo Abbott)*, Hal March

(Gus Edwards), Susan Odin (Ida, age 11), Owen Pritchard ("Boy" Harris), Douglas Evans (Leo Raymond), Ann Doran (Lillian Edwards), Richard Monda.

The picture begins and ends with Eddie and Ida Cantor coming to a screening room to see the picture that was made about them. They might have been wise to sue, as this is one of those can't-miss stories that missed. The major problem was Brasselle, who was absolutely the wrong choice for the role. His attempts at imitating Cantor could have been construed as libelous by a friendly judge as he bugs out his eyes, mugs horribly, and, in general, blows the whole thing with a caricature. Oddly enough, Brasselle was not a terrible actor, as he proved in A PLACE IN THE SUN (1951), THREE YOUNG TEXANS (1954), and IF YOU DON'T STOP IT, YOU'LL GO BLIND (1977), his last picture (he also co-directed). He was simply the wrong person to play the part. Cantor's life wasn't particularly dramatic, other than the fact that he neglected his wife and kids in favor of his career. When he suffered a heart attack, he realized what was important and spent the rest of his life doing good things for charity. Cantor became a star on Broadway in his early 20s by dint of sheer exuberance rather than a great singing voice. He segued into films, then to a successful radio show. He retired in 1952 after having won the hearts of millions with his work. Cantor's unique mannerisms were strictly for performance, but the creative powers here deemed that he should be shown to act that way at all times. It's almost as though a story of Groucho Marx would have him walking into his bathroom in a crouch and wearing a false mustache. Marilyn Erskine co-stars as Ida and does a good job in a not-terribly-interesting part. Will Rogers, Jr. plays his dad, and Jackie Barnett is Durante, but not much is made of their roles. Columnist Sidney ("But don't get me wrong, I love Hollywood") Skolsky produced and co-wrote this, and when you consider how Sidney used to criticize other movies, he should have turned some of that ire on himself when writing and casting this. The songs are all Cantor favorites: "Ida, Sweet As Apple Cider," Eddie Leonard, Eddie Munson; "Ma (He's Making Eyes At Me)," Sidney Clare, Con Conrad; "Margie," Benny Davis, Conrad, J. Russell Robinson; "You Must Have Been A Beautiful Baby," Johnny Mercer, Harry Warren; "Yes, We Have No Bananas," Frank Silver, Irving Cohn; "Making Whoopee," "Yes Sir, That's My Baby," Gus Kahn, Walter Donaldson; "Now's the Time to Fall In Love," Al Lewis, Al Sherman; "If You Knew Susie," Joseph Meyer, Buddy De Sylva; "How Ya Gonna Keep 'Em Down on the Farm," Donaldson, Sam M. Lewis, Joe Young; "Will You Love Me In December As You Do In May," James J. Walker, Ernest R. Ball; "Be My Little Baby Bumble Bee," Stanley Murphy, Henry I. Marshall; "Oh, You Beautiful Doll," A. Seymour Brown, Nat D. Ayer; "Bye, Bye, Blackbird," Mort Dixon, Ray Henderson; "If I Were a Millionaire," Will Cobb, Gus Edwards.

p, Sidney Skolsky; d, Alfred E. Green; w, Skolsky, Ted Sherdeman, Jerome Weidman (based on a story by Skolsky); ph, Edwin DuPar (Technicolor); ed, William Ziegler; md, Ray Heindorf; art d, Charles H. Clarke; ch, LeRoy Prinz.

Musical Biography　　　　　　**(PR:AA　MPAA:NR)**

EDDIE MACON'S RUN*　　　　　　(1983) 95m UNIV c

Kirk Douglas (Marzack), John Schneider (Eddie), Lee Purcell (Jilly), Leah Ayres (Chris), Lisa Dunsheath (Kay), Tom Noonan (Daryl), J.C. Quinn (Shorter), Gil Rogers (Logan), Jay O. Sanders (Rudy), Dan Anglin (Weigh Station), Nesbitt Blaisdell (Sheriff), Susan Bongard (Newscaster), Matthew Cowles (Ray), Bill DeWeese (Officer), Kenneth Allan Edgar, Vic Polizos (Desk Clerks), Dann Florek, J.T. Walsh (Men in Bar), Buddy Gilbert (Tucker), John Goodman (Hebert), Jim Gough (Judge), Nik Hagler (Partner), Lou Hancock (Woman), Loyd David Hart (Bartender), Ron Jackson (Police Partner), Matthew Kimbrough (Charlie), Billy Lynch (Announcer), Jerry McKnight (Billy Bob), Mark Margolis (Bar Owner), John L. Martin (Homer), Glenn H. Matthews, Matthew Meece, Ricardo Montemayor, Harry Murphy, Donald B. Nunley, Cynthia Piton, Gilbert Rendon, Brick Tripp, Woody Watson, Fernando E. Gutierrez, Javier A. Gutierrez.

Inane car-chase stuff has Schneider (in his first starring feature role after leaving TV's "The Dukes of Hazard") wrongly convicted of a crime and locked away. Of course, he escapes prison, and with lawman Douglas dogging his every move, tries to drive to Mexico. No depth at all, but it does move.

p, Louis J. Stroller; d&w, Jeff Kanew (based on the novel by James McLendon); ph, James A. Contner (Technicolor); m, Norton Buffalo; ed, Kanew; prod d, Bill Kenney.

Crime　　　　　**Cas.**　　　　　**(PR:A-C　MPAA:PG)**

EDDY DUCHIN STORY, THE**½　　　　　　(1956) 123m COL c

Tyrone Power (Eddy Duchin), Kim Novak (Marjorie Oelrichs), Victoria Shaw (Chiquita), James Whitmore (Lou Sherwood), Rex Thompson (Peter Duchin as a Boy), Mickey Maga (Peter at Age Five), Shepperd Strudwick (Mr. Wadsworth), Frieda Inescourt (Mrs. Wadsworth), Gloria Holden (Mrs. Duchin), Larry Keating (Leo Reisman), John Mylong (Mr. Duchin), Gregory Gaye (Philip), Warren Hsieh (Native Boy), Carlyle Mitchell (Doctor), Lois Kimbrell (Nurse), Richard Sternberg, Andy Smith (Peter's Friends), Ralph Gamble (Mayor Jimmy Walker), Richard Cutting (Captain), Richard Crane, Brad Trumbull (Seamen), Kirk Alyn, Richard Walsh (Young Men), Howard Price (Range Recorder Operator), Gloria Ann Simpson (Mrs. Rutledge), Oliver Cliff (Man), Joan Reynolds, Jacqueline Blanchard (Girls), Butler Hixson (Butler), Peter Norman (Waiter), Arline Anderson (Guest), Jack Albertson (Piano Tuner), Xavier Cugat (Himself).

A long and sad story about a man who was not very well known outside the haunts of New York Cafe Society. Power plays Duchin, son of a tailor, who arrives in New York City from Beantown, where he's just recently graduated as a pharmacist. Like so many children of immigrant parents, he was expected to have a "profession" before being able to attempt his avocation, the piano. It was "something to fall back on." He meets Kim Novak, a gorgeous and very wealthy socialite, and

she helps him get a job at the Central Park Casino with Keating (as Leo Reisman). His abilities are immediately recognized, and he soon gives up any thought of pill-pushing in favor of piano-playing. This new popularity causes him to have enough confidence to pop the question to Novak. Their marriage ends when Novak gives birth to son Peter and dies in the process. Duchin is devastated, and mistakenly blames the innocent boy for his mother's death. He gives the child to Novak's aunt and uncle, Inescourt and Strudwick, and goes off on a globe-girdling tour with his manager and best pal, James Whitmore. While serving as a Naval officer during WW II, he has a realization and, when he returns, he attempts to reconcile, but the boy will have none of it. Peter (Rex Thompson) is finally won over when Duchin approaches the boy through his nanny, Victoria Shaw, a British-born cutie with the unlikely name of Chiquita. Now back in the swing of things, Duchin's career takes a high ride until he discovers that he is dying of leukemia. Power marries Shaw for what remains of his life, and this very sad picture ends with an uplifting scene as the Duchins, pere et fils, sit at the piano for a last duet. Peter Duchin has gone on to become society's favorite and can be found jet-setting around the world wherever the rich and famous need a pianist. In the film, Carmen Cavallaro's playing served as Duchin's, and Power, though not a pianist, did an excellent job of faking it. If it weren't true, you wouldn't have believed it. A musical soap opera that almost manages to be very entertaining. Still, bring a box of tissues because if you don't cry during this movie then you must have had your tear ducts removed. Almost 30 songs are in the score, including: "What is This Thing Called Love?" Cole Porter; "Till We Meet Again," Ray Egan, Richard A. Whiting; "Blue Room," "Manhattan," Richard Rogers, Lorenz Hart; "The Man I Love," George and Ira Gershwin; "Brazil," Ary Barrosa, Bob Russell; "You're My Everything," Harry Warren, Mort Dixon, Joe Young; "La Vie En Rose," Edith Piaf, R.S. Louiguy; "Let's Fall In Love," Harold Arlen, Ted Koehler; "Shine On Harvest Moon," Jack Norworth, Nora Bayes; "It Must Be True," Gus Arnheim, Gordon Clifford, Harry Barris; "Exactly Like You," Dorothy Fields, Jimmy McHugh; "Dizzy Fingers," Zez Confrey; "I'll Take Romance," Oscar Hammerstein II, Ben Oakland; "Smiles," J. Will Callahan, Lee S. Roberts; "Shine," Cecil Mack, Lew Brown, Ford Dabney; "Sweet Sue," Will J. Harris, Victor Young; "Ain't She Sweet," Jack Yellen, Milton Ager; "April Showers," Buddy De Sylva, Louis Silver; "Three O'Clock In The Morning," Dorothy Terriss, Julian Robledo; "Nocturne in E-Flat Major," Frederic Chopin.

p, Jerry Wald; d, George Sidney; w, Samuel Taylor (from a story by Leo Katcher); ph, Harry Stradling, Sr. (Cinemascope, Technicolor); m, George Duning; ed, Viola Lawrence, Jack W. Ogilvie; md, Morris Stoloff; set d, William Kiernan, Robert Priestley; art d, Walter Holscher; cos, Jean Louis.

Musical Biography　　　　　　**(PR:A　MPAA:NR)**

EDEN CRIED*½　　　　　　(1967) 90m Alkoe Artists/CD c
　　　　　　(AKA: IN THE FALL OF '55 EDEN CRIED)

Carol Holland (Lorraine Parker), Tom Pace (Skip Garroway), Victor Izay.

Pace and Holland are Southern California high-school neighbors who begin to go out. While they are going to a dance, Skip is challenged to a drag race. The other driver is killed in the ensuing contest. Pace and Holland's parents won't allow the two to be with each other, but the teenagers continue to see each other on the sly and finally wed.

p, Shael Young, Charles Ellis; d&w, Fred Johnson.

Drama　　　　　　**(PR:A　MPAA:GP)**

EDGAR ALLAN POE'S CASTLE OF BLOOD
　　　　　　(SEE: CASTLE OF BLOOD, 1964, Ital./Fr.)

EDGAR ALLAN POE'S CONQUEROR WORM
　　　　　　(SEE: CONQUEROR WORM, 1968, Brit.)

EDGAR ALLAN POE'S "THE OBLONG BOX"
　　　　　　(SEE: OBLONG BOX, THE, 1969, Brit.)

EDGE, THE***　　　　　　(1968) 100m Blue Van-Alpha 60/Film-Makers bw

Jack Rader (Dan Rainer), Tom Griffin (Tom Eliot), Howard Loeb Babeuf (Bill Raskin), Jeff Weiss (Max Laing), Anne Waldman Warsch (Didi Stein), Sanford Cohen (Peter Stein), Paul Hultberg (Sinclair Davis), Catherine Merrill (Sally Kolka), Russell Parker (Michael Warren), Gerald Long (Gerry Toller), Theodora Bergery (Anne Davis), Randall Conrad (Randall Kates), Constance Ullman Long (Connie Barker), Susan Reiner (Girl In Bed), Robert Kramer (Mental Patient).

Interesting effort by the 1960s counter-culture at self-examination over a decade before John Sayles' THE RETURN OF THE SECAUCUS SEVEN and Lawrence Kasdan's THE BIG CHILL. Independent filmmaker Robert Kramer sees a group of disillusioned radicals who were once active in "New Left" cloistered together in an unnamed rural locale where they discuss the state of the world and how nothing has changed despite their efforts. With all their causes gone or failed, the people in the group must come to terms with starting their personal lives without the protests and marches that brought them together and gave them purpose. One of their number snaps and decides he will assassinate President Johnson as a last-ditch effort at significance, but the group is split on their feelings and reactions to this announcement. Some of them see the move as one of frustration and childishness, the others as a logical reaction to their feelings of increasing impotence. Not a perfect film by any means, but a fascinating—and grittier—companion piece to the other, later, more accessible and entertaining films by Sayles and Kasdan.

p, Robert Kramer, Robert Machover; d&w, Kramer; ph&ed, Machover.

Drama　　　　　　**(PR:C　MPAA:NR)**

EDGE OF DARKNESS*½   (1943) 120m WB bw

Erroll Flynn *(Gunnar Brogge)*, Ann Sheridan *(Karen Stensgard)*, Walter Huston *(Dr. Martin Stensgard)*, Nancy Coleman *(Katja)*, Helmut Dantine *(Capt. Koenig)*, Judith Anderson *(Gerd Bjarnesen)*, Ruth Gordon *(Anna Stensgard)*, John Beal *(Johann Stensgard)*, Morris Carnovsky *(Sixtus Andresen)*, Charles Dingle *(Kaspar Torgerson)*, Roman Bohnen *(Lars Malken)*, Richard Fraser *(Pastor Aalesen)*, Art Smith *(Knut Osterholm)*, Tom Fadden *(Hammer)*, Henry Brandon *(Major Ruck)*, Tonio Selwart *(Paul)*, Helene Thimig *(Frida)*, Frank Wilcox *(Jensen)*, Francis Pierlot *(Mortensen)*, Lottie Williams *(Mrs. Mortensen)*, Monte Blue *(Petersen)*, Dorothy Tree *(Solveig Brategaard)*, Virginia Christine *(Hulda)*, Henry Rowland *(Helmut)*, Kurt Katch *(German Captain)*, Kurt Kreuger *(German Aviator)*, Peter Van Eyck *(German Soldier)*, Vera Lewis *(Woman)*, Torben Meyer *(Clerk)*, Walt LaRue *(Villager-Patriot)*, William Edmunds *(Elderly Sailor)*, Vic Potel, Richard Kipling *(Men)*, Fred Giermann, Rolf Lindau, Peter Michael *(German Soldiers)*.

A Nazi patrol boat sails into a Norwegian port to discover that the whole German occupation force and the citizens of the town lie dead, apparently killed in a bloody battle for supremacy which ended with the Norwegian flag flying over the Nazi garrison. In flashback, we see the events leading up to the slaughter. Flynn is a Norwegian fisherman who is the leader of the local underground movement; Sheridan is his brave and loyal fiancee. Also in the movement are fiery innkeeper Anderson, whose husband was murdered by the Nazis, and Huston, a highly respected doctor. He and his meek wife Gordon have sired a weak and traitorous son, Beal, who along with businessman Dingle sells out to the Germans. The underground movement use passive resistance until finally shocking the Nazis with a dramatic show of firepower, provided by the British, well staged by veteran director Milestone. The shooting of EDGE OF DARKNESS was plagued with problems. During filming, Flynn was in the midst of his rape scandal, Sheridan was in the midst of divorcing her husband George Brent, and the location shooting in Monterey, California, was besieged by a heavy fog which made the shooting go over schedule, thus putting pressure on Anderson and Gordon, who were due to star on Broadway in "The Three Sisters." Despite all the problems, EDGE OF DARKNESS turned out to be a fine, compelling wartime drama filled with superb ensemble performances. Handsome Kurt Kreuger, who would go on to play ruthless Nazis in a spate of WW II films, made his debut in this production.

p, Henry Blanke; d, Lewis Milestone; w, Robert Rossen (based on the novel by William Woods); ph, Sid Hickox; m, Franz Waxman; ed, David Weisbart; art d, Robert Haas; set d, Julia Heron; montages, Don Siegel, James Leicester.

War   **(PR:A MPAA:NR)**

EDGE OF DIVORCE   (SEE: BACKGROUND, 1953, Brit.)

EDGE OF DOOM*   (1950) 99m Goldwyn/RKO bw
                                 (GB: STRONGER THAN FEAR)

Dana Andrews *(Father Roth)*, Farley Granger *(Martin Lynn)*, Joan Evans *(Rita Conroy)*, Robert Keith *(Mandel)*, Paul Stewart *(Craig)*, Mala Powers *(Julie)*, Adele Jergens *(Irene)*, Harold Vermilyea *(Father Kirkman)*, John Ridgely, Douglas Fowley *(Detectives)*, Mabel Paige *(Mrs. Pearson)*, Howland Chamberlain *(Mr. Murray)*, Houseley Stevenson, Sr. *(Mr. Stevenson)*, Jean Innes *(Mrs. Lally)*, Ellen Corby *(Mrs. Moore)*, Ray Teal *(Ned Moore)*, Mary Field *(Mary Jane Glennon)*, Virginia Brissac *(Mrs. Dennis)*, Frances Morris *(Mrs. Lynn)*.

A dark, gloomy, often depressing film, EDGE OF DOOM is nevertheless a powerful portrait of a mentally unbalanced youth, Granger, who, when his impoverished mother dies, begs the local priest, Vermilyea, for a lavish funeral mass. The narrow-minded priest refuses and, in a fit of rage, Granger crushes his skull with a heavy crucifix. He is almost identified by a witness but suspicion falls instead on Stewart, a petty crook living with moll Jergens, who was also seen in the neighborhood at the time of the priest's murder. Andrews is the priest who takes over the poor parish following Vermilyea's death. He launches his own investigation, which rankles detective Keith. He learns that Vermilyea had refused to bury Granger's father in hallowed ground after he committed suicide and that Granger had afterwards been hostile to the Catholic Church. Granger is found praying before his mother's body by Andrews, and confronted by the priest, he confesses the murder, saying he will go to the police if he is permitted to attend his mother's funeral, a request later granted by authorities. This raw drama was pummeled by critics when first released, which caused Goldwyn (who had paid $150,000 for the book rights) to withdraw the film and bring in Ben Hecht, the highest-paid screenwriter in the business, to fix up the script. The killing of a priest in films has always been sensitive material, as was the case with BOOMERANG, as well as priests dealing with murderers in or out of the confessional, such as Hitchcock's misfiring I CONFESS. Hecht wrote new, provocative dialog and reworked the story line so that the perspective was off killer Granger and on priest Andrews, who narrates the story from a softer angle. Charles Vidor, then doing preproduction work on HANS CHRISTIAN ANDERSEN, was pulled in to shoot additional scenes to conform to Hecht's rewrite; the overall additions lifted the film considerably out of the mediocre. Goldwyn, ever promotion-minded, had Granger, in one scene, flee his crime by running past a movie theater, its marquee clearly showing the title of another actual Goldwyn film, OUR VERY OWN, starring, of all people, Farley Granger!

p, Samuel Goldwyn; d, Mark Robson, with additional scenes by Charles Vidor; w, Philip Yordan, with additional scenes by Ben Hecht (based on the novel by Leo Brady); ph, Harry Stradling; m, Hugo Friedhofer; ed, Daniel Mandell; md, Emil Newman; art d, Richard Day; set d, Julia Heron; cos, Mary Wills; makeup, Blague Stephanoff.

Crime Drama   **(PR:C MPAA:NR)**

EDGE OF ETERNITY*   (1959) 81m Thunderbird COL c

Cornel Wilde *(Les Martin)*, Victoria Shaw *(Janice Kendon)*, Mickey Shaughnessy *(Scotty O'Brien)*, Edgar Buchanan *(Sheriff Edwards)*, Rian Garrick *(Bob Kendon)*,

Jack Elam *(Bill Ward)*, Alexander Lockwood *(Jim Kendon)*, Dabbs Greer *(Gas Station Attendant)*, Tom Fadden *(Eli)*, Wendell Holmes *(Sam Houghton)*, George Cisar *(The Dealer)*, Buzz Westcott *(Pilot)*, Ted Jacques *(Suds Reese)*, Paul Bailey *(Amphibian Pilot)*, John Roy *(Whitmore)*, George "Smokey" Ross *(Undersheriff)*, Hope Summers *(Motel Lady)*, John Ayres *(Coroner)*, Don Siegel *(Pipe Smoker at Motel Wearing a Neck Scarf)*.

Exciting modern-day western actioner directed by Don Siegel sees Wilde as a brave sheriff's deputy who is out to solve the murder of a gold-mine executive who had discovered his gold was being stolen and sold in Mexico for $50 an ounce instead of the $35 it would net in the U.S. When the culprit, Shaughnessy, discovers that Wilde is on his trail, he grabs Shaw as a hostage and drives off in a brand-new Thunderbird, headed for the Grand Canyon. Climax sees Wilde and Shaughnessy shooting it out in the yellow tram cars that span the magnificent canyon. Superb location photography by Burnett Guffey, and exciting direction by Siegel, help gloss over the rather weak script and make this film well worth watching.

p, Kendrick Sweet; d, Donald Siegel; w, Knut Swenson [Marion Hargrove], Richard Collins (story by Ben Markson, Swenson); ph, Burnett Guffey; m, Daniele Amfitheatrof; ed, Jerome Thoms; art d, Robert Peterson; set d, Frank A. Tuttle.

Western   **(PR:A MPAA:NR)**

EDGE OF FURY zero   (1958) 77m UA bw

Michael Higgins, Lois Holmes, Jean Allison, Doris Fesette, Malcolm Lee Beggs, Craig Kelly, John Harvey, Beatrice Furdeaux, Mary Elizabeth Boylan.

Sick low-budget grossness about a psychopathic young beachcomber, Higgins, who pretends to befriend a mother and two daughters living at their summer home. He talks the family into letting him rent the adjacent guest cottage, and then he slaughters the whole family.

P, Robert Gurney, Jr.; d, Irving Lerner, Gurney; w, Gurney, Ted Berkman (based on the novel *Wisteria Cottage* by Robert M. Coates); ph, Conrad Hall, Marvin Weinstein, Jack Couffer.

Crime   **(PR:O MPAA:NR)**

EDGE OF HELL**   (1956) 76m UNIV bw

Hugo Haas, Francesca de Scaffa, Ken Carlton, June Hammerstein, Jeffrey Stone, Syra Marti, Tracy Roberts, John Vosper, Tony Jochim, Julie Mitchum, Pat Goldin, Michael Mark, Tom Wilson, Sid Melton, William Kahn, Peter Bezbaz, Flip the dog.

Haas is a beggar with his trick performing dog, Flip. The two are hired to entertain at a wealthy child's birthday party, and Haas is offered $500 for his dog. He won't hear of it and later, when he can't provide for the dog anymore, Haas sells the dog for $20. The beggar is then beaten and robbed of his money, and when he learns that his dog has died, he joins Flip in heaven to perform for God.

p,d,&w, Hugo Haas; ph, Eddie Fitzgerald; m, Ernest Gold; ed, Robert Eisen; md, Gold; art d, Rudi Feld.

Drama   **(PR:A MPAA:NR)**

EDGE OF THE CITY**   (1957) 85m MGM bw
                                 (AKA: A MAN IS TEN FEET TALL)

John Cassavetes *(Axel North)*, Sidney Poitier *(Tommy Tyler)*, Jack Warden *(Charles Malik)*, Kathleen Maguire *(Ellen Wilson)*, Ruby Dee *(Lucy Tyler)*, Robert Simon *(Mr. Nordmann)*, Ruth White *(Mrs. Nordmann)*, William A. Lee *(Davis)*, Val Avery *(Brother)*, John Kellogg *(Detective)*, David Clarke *(Wallace)*, Estelle Hemsley *(Lucy's Mother)*, Charles Jordan *(Old Stevedore)*, Ralph Bell *(Nightboss)*.

The first film produced by David Susskind, directed by Martin Ritt and written by Robert Alan Aurthur, yields a grim and unrelenting tale of friendship and racism in the big city. Cassavetes plays a disenfranchised soldier who cannot return to his family because of the accidental death of his brother (for which he is blamed) who goes AWOL from the army and wanders into a job at a railroad yard in New York where he is befriended by black man Poitier. Through Poitier, Cassavetes learns to live again, but his happiness is shortlived when sadistic hiring boss Warden kills Poitier during a violent fight. When the police investigate the crime, Cassavetes follows the code of silence and keeps his mouth shut, but confronts Warden on his own. A good effort from all concerned.

p, David Susskind; d, Martin Ritt; w, Robert Alan Aurther (based on his teleplay *A Man Is Ten Feet Tall*); ph, Joseph Brun; m, Leonard Rosenman; ed, Sidney Meyers; art d, Richard Sylbert; cos, Anna Hill Johnstone.

Drama   **(PR:A MPAA:NR)**

EDGE OF THE WORLD, THE*   (1937, Brit.) 80m Rock Studios/Pax bw

Finlay Currie *(James Gray)*, Niall MacGinnis *(Andrew Gray)*, Grant Sutherland *(Cathechist)*, Campbell Robson *(The Laird)*, George Summers *(The Skipper)*, John Laurie *(Peter Manson)*, Belle Chrystall *(Ruth Manson)*, Eric Berry *(Robbie Manson)*, Kitty Kirwan *(Jean)*, Hamish Sutherland, Francesca Reidy, Michael Powell, and the people of the island of Foula.

This well-done Robert Flaherty-style quasi-documentary, beautifully photographed on the stark, desolate, rocky island of Foula in the Shetland chain, off the coast of Scotland, was writer-director Powell's first big success. The film's featured players and its secondary plot are mingled with the real occurrences of the island—here called Hirta, Nordic for death—and its fewer than 100 beleaguered inhabitants. The island's economy is dying, its waters fished out, its peat supplies nearly gone. Evacuation of the islanders to the mainland is urged by Berry over the opposition of his father Laurie and other islanders. Berry falls to his death during a test of courage with his friend MacGinnis, who is engaged to Berry's sister, Chrystall. The guilt-ridden MacGinnis departs from Hirta, leaving the pregnant Chrystall behind. Many months afterward, he returns to the island, just in time to save the life of his child. By this time, all the islanders have accepted the inevitable; driving their sheep and cows to the waiting boats, they depart. In a final gesture, old Laurie climbs a cliff to get a souvenir, a rare bird's egg. He falls to his death, emulating his son. Marvelous for the islanders' craggy faces and the faces of the island's crags, this is a grim but touching picture. The appropriate choral effects are done by the women of the Glasgow Orpheus Choir. Forty years later, the surviving cast and crew members returned to the island to shoot the documentary RETURN TO THE EDGE OF THE WORLD.

p, Joe Rock; d&w, Michael Powell; ph, Ernest Palmer, Skeets Kelly, Monty Berman; ed, Derek Twist; md, Cyril Ray.

Drama   **(PR:A   MPAA:NR)**

EDISON, THE MAN**   (1940) 104m MGM bw
Spencer Tracy (*Thomas Alva Edison*), Rita Johnson (*Mary Stilwell*), Lynne Overman (*Bunt Cavatt*), Charles Coburn (*Gen. Powell*), Gene Lockhart (*Mr. Taggart*), Henry Travers (*Ben Els*), Felix Bressart (*Michael Somon*), Peter Godfrey (*Ashton*), Frank Faylen (*Galbreath*), Byron Foulger (*Edwin Hall*), Guy D'Ennery (*Lundstrom*), Addison Richards (*Dr. Johnson*), Milton Parsons (*Acid Graham*), Arthur Aylsworth (*Bigelow*), Gene Reynolds (*Jimmy Price*), Grant Mitchell (*Shade*), Donald Douglas (*Jordan*), Harlan Briggs (*Bisbee*), Charles Trowbridge (*Clark*), Harold Minjir (*Blair*), George Meader (*Minister*), Charles Waldron (*Commissioner*), Charles Lane (*Lecturer*), Irving Bacon (*Sheriff*), Edward Earle (*Broker*), Joe Whitehead (*Man*), Emmett Vogan (*Secretary*), Tom Mahoney (*Policeman*), Bruce Mitchell (*Coachman*), Milton Kibbee (*Workman*), Nell Craig (*Woman*), Ann Gillis, Jay Ward, George Lessey, Paul Hurst.

MGM suddenly decided to go all out for Thomas Alva Edison in 1940, producing two films on his life. One of them was a surprising flop, YOUNG TOM EDISON with Mickey Rooney; EDISON, THE MAN was a much more lavish production, with Tracy giving a dynamic performance as the great inventor/humanitarian. The film opens as Tracy, at age 82, is about to be honored on the 50th anniversary of his invention of the incandescent light. He is being interviewed by two youths and begins to relate the story of his early manhood. The film goes into flashback to chronicle Edison's most productive years, from ages 25 to 35, when he produced the phonograph, the dictaphone, and the electric light. The film shows Tracy meeting Johnson, his future wife, during a rainstorm when she has trouble with her umbrella and he fixes it. They marry and have children, but the inventor quits his job with one firm to go on his own, inventing an early ticker-tape machine just to finance his expensive and exhaustive work on the electric light. This device he sells to financiers Coburn and Lockhart for $40,000. Following their agreement Coburn, inflating his own business acumen, informs Tracy that he and Lockhart were prepared to pay much more money for his invention. Tracy is not to be outdone; he tells Coburn that he was prepared to take much less than they paid. With his funds almost depleted, Tracy and his devoted staff finally produce a carbon-based incandescent light that burns and burns. He next announces that he will light New York City and sets about wiring Manhattan, given a contract with a six-month deadline to complete the task. With only hours to go, Tracy accomplishes the impossible, as did Edison, the great Wizard of Menlo Park. This is a fine film biography that relied upon facts instead of the kind of far-reaching fiction Fox insisted upon in mixing romance with fact in THE STORY OF ALEXANDER GRAHAM BELL (1939). Tracy went at the part like a monk reading scripture; he studied every known detail about the man, trying to capture his personality from rare films and books. He traveled to Menlo Park and stayed in the old laboratory, studying the inventor's notebooks. After weeks of saturating himself with Edison's persona he felt he understood the man, as well as admired him. He later stated: "Edison and I had at least one thing in common. We both had it pretty rough for awhile. There were times my pants were so thin I could sit on a dime and tell if it was heads or tails, but for Edison there wasn't even a dime to sit on." The Rooney film, released three months before EDISON, THE MAN, was a box office failure, Rooney's first, and MGM executives fretted that the same fate might befall the Tracy production. It didn't; the public responded well to this film, which was in no way intended as a sequel to YOUNG TOM EDISON, although common threads run through both films—Edison's minor deafness, his appetitie for milk and apple pie, his lack of a higher education, and his love of the song "Sweet Genevieve." Continuity of character was maintained by having scripters Schary, Butler, and Foote, who worked on YOUNG TOM EDISON, work with Jennings on the Tracy film.

p, John W. Considine, Jr., Orville O. Dull; d, Clarence Brown; w, Talbot Jennings, Bradbury Foote (based on a story by Dore Schary and Hugo Butler); ph Harold Rosson; m, Herbert Stothart; ed, Frederick Y. Smith; art d, Cedric Gibbons, John S. Detlie; set d, Edwin B. Willis; cos, Dolly Tree, Gile Steele; makeup, Jack Dawn; tech adv, William A. Simonds, Norman R. Speiden, the Edison Institute.

Biography   **(PR:AAA   MPAA:NR)**

EDUCATED EVANS**   (1936, Brit.) 86m WB-FN bw
Max Miller (*Evans*), Nancy O'Neil (*Mary*), Clarice Mayne (*Emily Hackitt*), Albert Whelan (*Sgt. Challoner*), Hal Walters (*Nobby*), George Merritt (*Joe Markham*), Julien Mitchell (*Arthur Hackitt*), Frederick Burtwell (*Hubert*), Anthony Shaw (*Lord Appleby*), Percy Walsh (*Capt. Reid*), Robert English (*Lord Brickett*), Arthur Westpayne.

Fast-paced comedy has Miller an upwardly mobile race track tout who takes a job as trainer for a man who has just inherited a stable, and later gets rich by betting on the wrong horse. One of a number of pictures extremely prolific director Beaudine made during a stay in England in the mid 1930s.

p, Irving Asher; d, William Beaudine; w, Frank Launder, Robert Edmunds (based on a novel by Edgar Wallace); ph, Basil Emmott.

Comedy   **(PR:A   MPAA:NR)**

EDUCATING FATHER**   (1936) 58m FOX bw
Jed Prouty (*John Jones*), Shirley Deane (*Bonnie Jones*), Dixie Dunbar (*Millicent*), Spring Byington (*Mrs. John Jones*), Kenneth Howell (*Jack Jones*), June Carlson

(*Lucy Jones*), George Ernest (*Roger Jones*), Florence Roberts (*Granny Jones*), William Mahan (*Bobby Jones*), Francis Ford (*Sheriff Hart*), Charles Tannen (*Jim Courtney*), J. Anthony Hughes (*Dick Harris*), David Newell (*Eddie Gordon*), Clarence H. Wilson (*Jess Boynton*), Johnathan Hale (*Fred Humphrey*), Erville Alderson (*Dr. Willoughby*).

The second in the series of Jones Family dramas. This one has father Prouty strongly disapproving of son Howell's ambitions to become a pilot, until the kid flies pop home in time from a far-away fishing trip to save the lease on the family-owned drug store. (See JONES FAMILY series, Index.)

p, Max Golden; d, James Tinling; w, Katherine Kavanaugh, Edward T. Lowe, John Patrick; ph, Daniel B. Clark; ed, Louis Loeffler; md, Samuel Kaylin.

Comedy/Drama   **(PR:A   MPAA:NR)**

EDUCATING RITA*½   (1983) 110m Acorn Pictures/COL c
Michael Caine (*Dr. Frank Bryant*), Julie Walters (*Rita*), Michael Williams (*Brian*), Maureen Lipman (*Trish*), Jeananne Crowley (*Julia*), Malcolm Douglas (*Denny*), Godfrey Quigley (*Rita's Father*), Dearbhla Molloy (*Elaine*), Pat Daly (*Bursar*), Kim Fortune (*Collins*), Philip Hurdwood (*Tiger*), Hilary Reynolds (*Lesley*), Jack Walsh (*Price*), Christopher Casson (*Professor*), Rosamund Burton (*Denise*), Marcus O'Higgins (*Marcus*), Mark Drew (Disco Manager), Gabrielle Reidy (*Barbara*), Des Nealon (*Invigilator*), Marie Conmee (*Customer in Hairdresser's*), Oliver Maguire (*Tutor*), Derry Power (*Photographer*), Alan Stanford (*Bistro Manager*), Gerry Sullivan (*Security Officer*), Patricia Jeffares (*Rita's Mother*), Maeve Germaine (*Sandra*), Liam Stack (*Sandra's Fiance*).

Walters is a married hairdresser who wants to become educated. She chooses alcoholic don Caine to be her tutor. Walters comes to realize that education is not the only thing a person needs, but through her determination she becomes her own person. Caine falls in love with her, but realizes that he has already given all he can to Walters, and that her needs do not include him. The film elegantly explores the teacher-student relationship along with class and gender separation. Walters' and Caine's performances are top notch.

p&d, Lewis Gilbert; w, Willy Russell (based on his play); ph, Frank Watts (Technicolor); m, David Hentschel; ed, Garth Craven; art d, Maurice Fowler.

Drama   **Cas.**   **(PR:A   MPAA:PG)**

EDUCATION OF SONNY CARSON, THE*½   (1974) 104m PAR c
Rony Clanton (*Sonny Carson*), Don Gordon (*Pigliani*), Joyce Walker (*Virginia*), Paul Benjamin (*Pops*), Thomas Hicks (*Young Sonny*), Mary Alice (*Moms*), Ram John Holder (*Preacher*), Jerry Bell (*Lil' Boy*), Ray Rainbow Johnson (*Benny*), Derrick Champ Ford (*Wolfe*), Roger Hill (*Lil' John*), Chris Forster (*Donovan*), George Miles (*Uncle Cal*), Jess Bolero (*Cousin Red*), B.T. Taylor (*Crazy*), Roger (D.A.) Davis (*Willie*), Eleanora Douglas (*Sally Jean*), Clifton Steere (*Psychiatrist*), Dennis Keir (*Western Union Boy*), Linda Hopkins (*Lil' Boy's Mother*), Mervyn Nelson (*Parole Board Chairman*), Prince Olafami, Ronnie Cole, Steve Sellers (*Supermarket Kids*), David Kerman (*Judge*), Ellerine Harding (*Funeral Singer*), Benny Diggs and the New York Community Choir, The Jolly Stompers, Tomahawks, Black Spades, Pure Hell, students of the Morningside High School.

Gritty ghetto story about the fall and rise of black youngster Clanton, who goes from participation in gangs and street robberies to crimes of a more serious nature. Eventually he is thrown in jail and given a rude awakening amidst the horrors of the penal institution, where he vows to forsake drugs and crime and rehabilitate himself. An uplifting exploitation film based on Sonny Carson's autobiography.

p, Irwin Yablans; d, Michael Campus; w, Fred Hudson (based on the book by Sonny Carson [Iwina Lmiri Abubadika]); ph, Ed Borwn (Panavision, Movielab Color); m, Coleridge-Taylor Perkinson; ed, Edward Warschilka, Harry Howard; art d, Manny Gerard; set d, Robert Drumheller; cos, Gene Coffin, Gregory Lecakin; stunts, Franklin Scott.

Drama   **(PR:C   MPAA:R)**

EDVARD MUNCH*   (1976, Norway/Swed.) 215m New Yorker-SR c
Geir Westby (*Edvard Munch*), Gro Fraas (*Fru Heiberg*), Johan Halsborg (*Dr. Christian Munch*), Lotte Teig (*Tante Karen Bjolstad*), Gro Jarto (*Laura Catherine Munch*), Rachel Pedersen (*Inger Munch*), Berit Rytter Hasle (*Laura Munch*), Gunnar Skjetne (*Peter Andreas Munch*), Kare Stormark (*Hans Jaeger*), Iselin Bast (*Dagny Juell*), Eli Ryg (*Oda Lasson*), Alf Kare Strindberg (*August Strindberg*), Eric Allum (*Edvard 1868*), Amund Berge (*Edvard 1875*), Kerstii Allum (*Sophie 1869*), Inger-Berit Oland (*Sophie 1875*), Susan Troldmyr (*Laura 1868*), Camilla Falk (*Laura 1875*), Ragnvald Caspari (*Peter 1868*), Erik Kristiansen (*Peter 1875*), Katja Pedersen (*Inger 1868*), Anne-Marie Daehli (*Inger 1875*).

The life of expressionist painter Munch is lovingly told in this lengthy film by director Watkins (THE WARGAME, PUNISHMENT PARK). Westby is the tortured genius, slowly slipping into madness as his paintings reflect more and more of his own inner turmoil. The cast is made up entirely of nonprofessionals, and they do an amazing job at recreating the atmosphere of Oslo at the close of the 19th century. Not for all audiences, and certainly not for the impatient, but an amazing biographical work, well worth seeing. (In Norwegian; English subtitles.)

d&w, Peter Watkins; ph, Odd Geir Saether; art d, Grethe Hajer; cos, Ada Skolmen.

Biography   **(PR:C   MPAA:NR)**

EDWARD AND CAROLINE*½   (1952, Fr.) 90m
                                                           U.G.C.-C.I.C.C/Commercial bw
Daniel Gelin (*Edward Mortier*), Anne Vernon (*Caroline Mortier*), Betty Stockfield (*Mme. de Barville*), Jean Toulout (*Mons. de Barville*), Jean Galland (*Beauchamp*), Jacques Francois (*Alain Beauchamp*), William Tubbs (*Borje*), Elina LaBourdette (*Florence Borje*), Gregoire Gromoff (*Igor*), Jean Marsac (*Guest*).

A delicate, fanciful romance which casts Gelin and Vernon as a pair of newlyweds whose love carries them through their occasional differences. Gelin, an aspiring concert pianist, finds his idyllic situation altered when he and his wife are invited to a ritzy party thrown by Vernon's uncle. The lovers' relationship stretches to an inevitable explosion, but a cheerful reconciliation ends the picture. Concerned less with plot (the script is incredibly sparse) than with creating two characters in the midst of a light-hearted romance, Becker succeeds in turning out a pleasant piece of entertainment. (In French; English subtitles.)

p, Robert Bossis; d, Jacques Becker; w, Becker, Annette Wademant; ph, Robert Lefebvre; m, Jean-Jacques Grunewald; ed, Marguerite Renoir; set d, Jacques Colombier; cos, Carven.

Romance   **(PR:A   MPAA:NR)**

EDWARD, MY SON*   (1949, U.S./Brit.) 112m MGM bw
Spencer Tracy (Arnold Boult), Deborah Kerr (Evelyn Boult), Ian Hunter (Dr. Larry Woodhope), Leueen MacGrath (Eileen Perrin), James Donald (Bronton), Mervyn Johns (Harry Simpkin), Harriette Johns (Phyllis Mayden), Felix Aylmer (Mr. Hanray), Walter Fitzgerald (Mr. Kedner), Tilsa Page (Betty Foxley), Ernest Jay (Walter Prothin), Colin Gordon (Ellerby), Julian D'Albie (Summers), Clement McCallin (Sgt. Kenyon).

Tracy is a business tycoon who not only dotes on his son Edward, never seen throughout the film, but who will destroy anyone or anything who gets in the spoiled young man's crooked way. Though outwardly affable, Tracy is as ruthless as a Banzai charge and, in protecting his son's fortunes, he drives two persons to suicide and even commits arson. When his wife, Kerr, tries to reform his evil ways, she is promptly put in her place. She begins drinking, so much so that it causes her death. The thoroughly corrupt son, who has abandoned his mistress after learning that she is pregnant, is killed in a plane crash (he is flying and showing off). Tracy is then found guilty of torching one of his establishments and is sent off to prison. Upon his release he tries to locate his grandson, but friends of the boy's mother refuse to let him see the child, fearing Tracy will corrupt him as he did the father. This powerful though somewhat dated drama saw great success on the London stage where Robert Morley starred as the corrupt businessman. It was felt that Morley would not have the box office appeal for the part, so it was given to Tracy who is really miscast, although he gave the role his all. Morley, who co-authored the play, was to say in his *Reluctant Autobiography*: "I used to be asked in those days whether I wouldn't have liked to play in the film myself, but I think I much preferred to sell it to Metro for Spence. A fine actor, he was criticized for his performance in the film because he played it too straight." Kerr gave a stunning performance which brought her the first of six Oscar nominations. In softening the British vehicle for Tracy's talents, scriptwriter Stewart changed his nationality from British to Canadian to excuse the American accent, and his sinister character was filed down at the edges to make him more palatable to viewers, all of which made an already complex story confusing.

p. Edwin C. Knopf; d, George Cukor; w, Donald Ogden Stewart (based on the play by Robert Morley and Noel Langley); ph, Freddie Young; m, John Woodridge; ed, Raymond Poulton; md, Sir Malcolm Sargent; art d, Alfred Junge; spec eff, Tom Howard.

Drama   **(PR:C   MPAA:NR)**

EEGAH!*   (1962) 90m Fairway-International Films c
Arch W. Hall, Jr. (Tom), Marilyn Manning (Roxy Miller), Richard Kiel (Eegah), William Watters [Arch W. Hall, Sr.] (Roxy's Father), Ray Dennis Steckler, Carolyn Brandt, Cash Flagg.

A terrible movie, made for little more than $15,000, which—due to its status among the "All-Time Worst"—has grossed a small fortune. The film deals with a giant cave man with prehistoric ways (Kiel, who plays Jaws in some of the James Bond movies), who kidnaps a young girl, and falls in love with her. Hall, Jr., the son of producer-director Hall, Sr., is the 16-year-old singer who saves the girl, Manning. Songs, including "Nobody Lives on the Brownsville Road," by Arch W. Hall, Jr., and The Archers, are performed as the police take care of the lumbering giant, Kiel.

p&d, Nicholas Merriwether [Arch W. Hall, Sr.]; w, Bob Wehling (based on a story by Merriwether); ph, Vilos Lapenieks (Eastmancolor); ed, Don Schneider.

Horror   **(PR:C   MPAA:NR)**

EERIE WORLD OF DR. JORDAN, THE
                                (SEE: SOMETHING WEIRD, 1967)

**EFFECT OF GAMMA RAYS ON MAN-IN-THE-
MOON MARIGOLDS, THE***   (1972) 100m FOX c
Joanne Woodward (Beatrice), Nell Potts (Matilda), Roberta Wallach (Ruth), Judith Lowry (Nanny Annie), Richard Venture (Floyd), Estelle Omens (Floyd's Wife), Carolyn Coates (Granny's Daughter), Will Hare (Junk Man), Jess Osuna (Sonny), David Spielberg (Mr. Goodman), Lynn Rogers (Miss Hanley), Ellen Dano (Janice Vickery), Roger Serbagi (Neighbor), John Lehne (Apartment Manager), Michael Kearney (Chris Burns), Dee Victor (Miss Wyant).

Woodward is superb in this film adaptation of Paul Zindel's Pulitzer Prize-winning play directed for the screen by her husband, Paul Newman. Woodward plays the embittered and overbearing widow and mother who is trying to raise her two somewhat strange and vastly different daughters, Wallach—daughter of players Eli Wallach and Anne Jackson—and Potts (Newman and Woodward's real-life daughter). Wallach is loud and outgoing while her sister Potts is withdrawn and shy. Woodward makes ends meet by boarding elderly people and making phone sales for a dance studio. She is spiteful and distrusting of all men, including Potts' science teacher Spielberg, whom she accuses of endangering her child's life by exposing her to gamma rays in order to grow marigolds for a school project (hence the title). Woodward's bitter outlook on life and grim proclamations regarding men slowly work their way into her daughters' consciousness, but the budding

marigolds are a symbol of hope that survives among the bleakness of their existence.

p&d, Paul Newman; w, Alvin Sargent (based on the play by Paul Zindel); ph, Adam Holender (DeLuxe Color); m, Maurice Jarre; ed, Evan Lottman; prod d, Gene Callahan; set d, Richard Merrell, cos, Anna Hill Johnstone.

Drama   **(PR:C   MPAA:PG)**

EFFECTS*½   (1980) 87m Image Works/International Harmony c
                              (AKA: THE MANIPULATOR)
John Harrison (Lacy), Susan Chapek (Celeste), Joseph Pilato (Dom), Bernard McKenna (Barney), Debra Gordon (Rita), Tom Savini (Nicky), Chuck Hoyes (Lobo), Blay Bahnsen (Scratch).

Low-budget horror movie about a wacko film director who is shooting a low-budget horror movie. Little does the cast and crew know that the director is really making a film about a film cast and crew that get murdered. Shot in Pittsburgh using some of George Romero's regular crew, including Tom Savini, who did the special make-up effects and has a small acting role.

p, John Harrison, Pasquale Buba; d & w, Dusty Nelson (based on a novel by William H. Mooney); ph, Carl Augenstein; ed, Buba; art d, Ellen Hopkins; spec eff, Tom Savini.

Horror   **(PR:O   MPAA:R)**

EFFI BRIEST**   (1974, Ger.) 140m Tango/Filverlag der Auroren bw
                              (AKA: FONTANE EFFI BRIEST)
Hanna Schygulla (Effi Briest), Wolfgang Schenck (Baron von Instetten), Ulli Lommel (Maj. Crampas), Lilo Pempeit (Frau Briest), Herbert Steinmetz (Herr Briest), Hark Bohm (Gieshuebler), Ursula Straetz (Roswitha), Irm Hermann (Johanna), Karl Scheydt (Kruse), Karl Heinz Boehm (Wuellersdorf), Rudolf Lenz (Rummschuettel), Andrea Schober (Annie), Barbara Valentin (Trippelli), Theo Tecklenburg (Pastor Niemeyer), Barbara Lass (Polish Cook), Eva Mattes (Hulda), Anndorthe Braker (Mrs. Pasche), Peter Gauhe (Dagobert).

One of the finest films of post-war Germany, EFFI BRIEST marked the 16th film in 5 years for the obsessive Fassbinder—his best until 1978's THE MARRIAGE OF MARIA BRAUN. The film tells the tragic tale of a 17-year-old girl (Schygulla) who is forced into a marriage to a much older count, Schenck, by her unloving parents. Her marriage is far from desirable, consisting mainly of bouts with loneliness in the count's house. She wanders into a relationship with Lommel and when it is later discovered (years after it has ended) Schenck kills her suitor in a duel. Schygulla loses the respect and friendship of her fellow socialites and family, as well as her husband. Schenck leaves her their child. Alone in life, Schygulla dies just one year later. An emotional powerhouse of a film which is carried on the shoulders of Schygulla, probably the finest actress working in Germany today. After years of association with the tyrannical Fassbinder, their partnership finally dissolved with this picture over money. Schygulla, however, found herself in high demand apart from Fassbinder (a fact none of the other Fassbinder "family" members can claim). Because of her talent and power as an actress and person she was able to remove herself from Fassbinder's directorial grip. It was quite a common sight to see him, in his ragged jeans, leather jacket, and scruffy beard, browbeat an actor into tears, reducing them to a pitiful soul dependent on his abuse. He would yell, scream and pout until he got his actors to do what he wanted and then simply say "Thanks" when the take was finished. Schygulla walked away from Fassbinder's phenomenal rise in the film world and would not return until THE MARRIAGE OF MARIA BRAUN in 1979. She also appeared, subsequently, in his BERLIN ALEX-ANDERPLATZ (a 15-hour mini-series for German television) and LILI MARLEEN.

d&w; Rainer Werner Fassbinder (based on the novel by Theodor Fontane); ph, Juergen Juerges Dietrich Lohmann; m, Camille St.-Saens; ed, Thea Eymes; art d, Kurt Raab; cos, Barbara Baum.

Drama   **(PR:O   MPAA:NR)**

EGG AND I, THE**   (1947) 108m UNIV bw
Claudette Colbert (Betty MacDonald), Fred MacMurray (Bob MacDonald), Marjorie Main (Ma Kettle), Louise Allbritton (Harriet Putnam), Percy Kilbride (Pa Kettle), Richard Long (Tom Kettle), Billy House (Billy Reed), Ida Moore (Old Lady), Donald MacBride (Mr. Henty), Samuel S. Hinds (Sheriff), Esther Dale (Mrs. Hicks), Elisabeth Risdon (Betty's Mother), John Berkes (Geoduck), Vic Potel (Crowbar), Fuzzy Knight (Cab Driver), Isabel O'Madigan (Mrs. Hick's Mother), Dorothy Vaughan (Maid), Sam McDaniel (Waiter), Jesse Graves (Porter), Herbert Heywood (Mailman), Joe Bernard (Pettingrew), Ralph Littlefield (Photographer), Jack Baxley (Judge), Carl Bennett (Attendant), Howard Mitchell (Announcer), George Lloyd (Farm Hand), Robert Cherry, Joe Hiser, Joe Recht, Sammy Schultz, Joe Ploski (Goons), Hector V. Sarno (Burlaga), Lou Mason (Bergheimer), Judith Bryant, Gloria Moore, Eugene Persson, Diane Florentine, George McDonald, Colleen Alpaugh, Teddy Infuhr, Robert Winans, Diane Graeff, Kathleen Mackey, Robert Beyers (Kettle Children), Nolan Leary (Announcer), Beatrice Roberts (Nurse), Bob Perry, William Norton Bailey, Polly Van Bailey, Vangie Beilby, Earl Bennett, Nella Spraugh (People at Social), Taylor Holmes, Nolan Leary.

Hilarious comedy where Colbert and MacMurray suddenly uproot themselves from city living after he decides that he can't stand the brokerage business. MacMurray buys a ramshackle farm, intending to raise chickens and live the leisure rural life. But it is one plaguing problem after another, which depletes the bank account, chiefly building and landscaping materials ordered by Kilbride, the most unhandy handyman on record (a role almost identical to the one he played in GEORGE WASHINGTON SLEPT HERE). Kilbride and his wife, Main, have so many children living on their tacky farm, adjacent to that of MacMurray and Colbert, that they can't even remember their names. (This was the first appearance of Kilbride and Main as Ma and Pa Kettle and they would go on playing these lovable dumb hick roles through a very successful series.) Just after the farm renovation is completed a fire destroys the house but neighbors prove they have a large collective heart and they contribute materials and soon restore the MacMurray-Colbert residence. Meanwhile, MacMurray becomes fascinated with the mechanized farm owned by Allbritton, a wealthy widow who blatantly flirts with him, trying to wreck his marriage and take him away from Colbert. Colbert becomes pregnant but before she can tell MacMurray he goes off to see a new device installed on Allbritton's estate. Colbert feels rejected and flees to her mother's home. MacMurray deluges her with letters but these are returned unopened. After her child is born, Colbert reconsiders and returns to show MacMurray their baby. She finds him living in Allbritton's house and verbally blasts him. He quietly tells her that he has purchased the home for her and the child. Colbert, contrite and embarrassed, asks MacMurray to forgive her which he has no trouble doing since he is deeply in love with her. THE EGG AND I has many a laugh-filled scene—Colbert attempting to carry water in a bottomless bucket, MacMurray beaming with pride as he chops down a bothersome tree which crashes down on the roof of the hen house—and the public loved it, returning $5.5 million to Universal's coffers. The studio bought the runaway bestselling novel by Betty MacDonald when it reached the million mark, paying $100,000 on account and giving the writer a percentage of the film, then a rare deal. Colbert is properly arch as the cultured city-bred lady trying to cope with eccentric rural life and MacMurray deftly deadpans his way through one disaster after another, proving he was not just another Hollywood goof. Main is superb as the tolerant Ma Kettle, playing mother earth with a littered floor, a part that earned her an Oscar nomination (she lost out to Celeste Holm for GENTLEMEN'S AGREEMENT). This sweet comedy was the second teaming of Colbert and MacMurray; they had appeared together in THE GILDED LILY 12 years earlier. Colbert looked as lovely and ageless then as she does at this writing.

p, Chester Erskine, Fred F. Finklehoffe; d, Erskine (based on the novel by Betty MacDonald); ph, Milton Krasner; m, Frank Skinner; ed, Russel Schoengarth; prod d, Bernard Herzbrun.

Comedy   **(PR:AAA   MPAA:NR)**

EGGHEAD'S ROBOT★★ (1970, Brit.) 90m Interfilm/Film Producer's Guild c

Keith Chegwin (Egghead Wentworth), Jeffrey Chegwin (Eric), Kathryn Dawe (Elspeth), Roy Kinnear (Park Keeper), Richard Wattis (Paul Wentworth), Patricia Routledge (Mrs. Wentworth).

Keith Chegwin uses his father's robot as his double for fights and tough situations. Keith's brother Jeffrey plays the robot in this enjoyable children's science-fiction film.

p, Cecil Musk; d, Milo Lewis; w, Leif Saxon; ph, Johnny Coquillon (Eastmancolor).

Science Fiction   **(PR:A   MPAA:NR)**

EGLANTINE★★★ (1972, Fr.) 90m Films Marquise-ORTF/CFDC-UGC-Sirius-Consortium Pathe c

Valentine Tessier (Eglantine), Claude Dauphine (Clement), Odile Versois (Marguerite), Micheline Luccioni (Yolanda), Jacques Francois (Edmond), Roger Carel (Ernest), Frederick (Leopold), Laure Jeanson (Pauline), Sylvia Barrouillet (Gilberte), Darling Legitimus (Lolo), Marco Perrin (Guillaume).

Lyrical film taking place in 1895 about an 11-year-old boy who is sent to his grandmother's house to stay—with his female cousins—for the summer. There he spends his vacation listening and learning about life, enraptured by his grandmother's stories. Tessier is wonderful as the octogenarian grandmother. A warm-hearted, beautiful film. This was actor Brialy's first directorial/co-writing effort, and an auspicious beginning it was. Actor Charrier also made his debut as producer on this lovely little film.

p, Jacques Charrier; d, Jean-Claude Brialy; w, Brialy, Eric Olivier; ph, Alain Derobe (Eastmancolor); m, Jean-Jacques Debout, Christian Chevalier; ed, Helene Arnai; art d, Jean-Marie Simon.

Drama   **(PR:A   MPAA:NR)**

EGON SCHIELE—EXCESS AND PUNISHMENT★★½   (1981, Ger.) 93m Gamma c

Mathieu Carriere (Egon Schiele), Jane Birkin (Vally), Nina Fallenstein (Tatjana), Christine Kaufmann, Kristina van Euck, Marcel Ophuls.

Strange, moody biography of Austrian painter Egon Schiele, one of the founders of expressionism. Carriere is fairly good as the tormented painter. Madly sketching pornographic nudes during a thoroughly depressing and humiliating stint of military service during WW I, his life is portrayed as a succession of humiliations as he is subjected to arrest for pornography, his sweetheart expires, his next tootsie Dear-Johns him; the only thing the audience is spared is his dog dying. After the war his paintings become all the rage, but before he can profit from this, he contacts a disease and dies. The cast members include director Marcel Ophuls (THE SORROW AND THE PITY, 1971), and international actresses Christine Kaufmann—one-time wife of actor Tony Curtis—and Jane Birkin, as well known in Europe as a chanteuse as she is a movie actress. A considerable number of uncredited pubescent females round out the cast. Electronic, spare soundtrack by Brian Eno is excellent. (In German; English subtitles.)

p, Dieter Geissler, Robert Russ; d, Herbert Vesely; w, Vesely, Leo Tichat; ph, Rudolf Blahacek; m, Brian Eno, Anton von Webern.

Biography   **(PR:O   MPAA:NR)**

EGYPT BY THREE★★   (1953) 76m Filmmakers bw

Ann Stanville (The Girl), Jackie Craven (The Wife), Paul Campbell (Knife Thrower), Abbas Fares (Caravan Sheik), Charles Fawcett (American Doctor), Mahmoud el Miligui (Egyptian Doctor), Hassan el Baroudi (Magician), Charles Mendick (Charlie), Eddie Constantine (Nick), Nabila Nouhy (Miriam), the Coptic Priests of the Church of Abu Sefen; narrated by Joseph Cotten.

Three separate tales of life on the Nile linked by narration spoken by Joseph Cotten. The first story deals with an affair between Stanville and her knife-thrower lover Campbell. When Campbell's wife, Craven, discovers her husband's infidelity, she refuses to clear him of a murder charge unless he vows never to see Stanville again. He agrees, but the viewer is left with the distinct impression that during an upcoming performance, Campbell may "accidentally" throw his knife into her and miss the target. The second tale deals with a cholera epidemic that threatens to end a caravan's trip to Mecca. The caravan's leader, Fares, saves the day by letting a carrier pigeon decide whether to continue. The pigeon flies west, homeward, rather than east to Mecca, allowing the troupe to stay in quarantine, while saving face. The third segment sees two American confidence men, Mendick and Constantine, trying to put one over on the locals by selling holy bread baked by the priests of the Church of Abu Sefen. Constantine sees no problem with selling the bread, while Mendick wants to use the loaves to smuggle stolen diamonds out of the country. In the end, the con men outwit themselves, and their good deeds outweigh their bad ones. All three stories are done well enough, but the material is nothing out of the ordinary and producer/director Stoloff's hope that the exotic locale might generate some excitement just doesn't pay off. Shortly after the film was released, Egypt's playboy king, Farouk I, was deposed by a military coup, leading to Egypt's emergence as a democracy. The resulting public interest in the locale didn't appear to help at the box office.

p&d, Victor Stoloff; w, Joseph Morheim, Fred Freiberger, Lou Morheim; ph, Nicholas Hayer.

Drama   **(PR:A   MPAA:NR)**

EGYPTIAN, THE★★   (1954) 140m FOX c

Jean Simmons (Merit), Victor Mature (Horemheb), Gene Tierney (Baketamon), Michael Wilding (Akhnaton), Bella Darvi (Nefer), Peter Ustinov (Kaptah), Edmond Purdom (Sinuhe), Judith Evelyn (Taia), Henry Daniell (Mikere), John Carradine (Grave Robber), Carl Benton Reid (Senmut), Tommy Rettig (Thoth), Anitra Stevens (Nefertiti), Donna Martell (Lady in Waiting), Mimi Gibson (Princess), Carmen De Lavallade (Dancer), Harry Thompson (Nubian), George Melford, Lawrence Ryle (Priests), Ian MacDonald (Ship's Captain), Michael Granger (Officer), Don Blackman (Nubian Prince), Mike Mazurki (Death House Foreman), Peter Reynolds (Sinuhe at Age Ten), Tyler McDuff (Cadet), Angela Clarke (Kipa), Edmund Cobb (Patient in Dispensary), George Chester (Nubian Guard), Michael Ansara (Hittite Commander), Harry Corden (Hittite Officer), Geraldine Bogdonovich (Tavern Waitress), Eglfshe Harout (Syrian at Nefer's), Tiger Joe Marsh, Karl Davis (Libyan Guards), Paul Salata (Egyptian Official), Joan Whinfield (Governess).

Long and tedious but lavishly-mounted spectacle that lost a great deal of money. Brando was penciled in to play the lead but bowed out and Fox contract player Edmund Purdom moved into the role. Zanuck was allegedly having an affair with Bella Darvi (her name, in fact, was a combination of his, Darryl, and his wife's, Virginia) and wanted her to be presented in a spectacular fashion. Purdom is a physician in pre-Christian times; Ustinov is his servant. Simmons is a tavern waitress who loves him and would like to marry him. Wilding is an epileptic Pharaoh who espouses the theory of one God and whose priests rankle at that and plan to assassinate him. While attending the Pharaoh, Purdom meets the Babylonian whore, Darvi, and has a brief affair with her. He is soon bored with her (as was Zanuck; she appeared in only seven films), and returns to Simmons, who is later killed for also being monotheistic. In the end, Purdom and Victor Mature, as the soldier who is to assume the mantle of leader after Wilding's death, play a tender scene as Wilding expires. Mature uttered the soon-to-be-forgotten line: "More wine, you waddling toad!" in this picture, and that was the best dialog. Ustinov was quoted as saying, "Being in this movie was like being on the set of 'Aida' and not being able to find the way out." Gene Tierney does a small bit as Purdom's half-sister but she, like Judith Evelyn, is wasted. A big, big movie and a big, big bore. Darvi left the States and went to Europe where she worked in a few films but finally, after three unsuccessful attempts, she took her own life in her Monaco apartment. Born in Poland, her real name was Bayla Wegier. She had been a heavy gambler, and it was evidently those debts that drove her to suicide.

p, Darryl F. Zanuck; d, Michael Curtiz; w, Philip Dunne, Casey Robinson (based on the novel by Mike Waltari); ph, Leon Shamroy (CinemaScope, DeLuxe Color); m, Alfred Newman, Bernard Herrmann; ed, Barbara McLean; md, Edward B. Powell; art d, Lyle Wheeler, George W. Davis; set d, Walter M. Scott, Paul S. Fox; cos, Charles LeMaire; ch, Stephen Papich; makeup, Ben Nye.

Historical Epic   **(PR:A-C   MPAA:NR)**

EIGER SANCTION, THE★★   (1975) 128m Malpaso/UNIV c

Clint Eastwood (Jonathan Hemlock), George Kennedy (Ben Bowman), Vonetta McGee (Jemima Brown), Jack Cassidy (Miles Mellough), Heidi Bruhl (Mrs. Montaigne), Thayer David (Dragon), Reiner Schoene (Freytag), Michael Grimm (Meyer), Jean-Pierre Bernard (Montaigne), Brenda Venus (George), Gregory Walcott (Pope), Candice Rialson (Art Student), Elaine Shore (Miss Cerberus), Dan Howard (Dewayne), Jack Kosslyn (Reporter), Walter Kraus (Kruger), Frank Redmond (Wormwood), Siegfried Wallach (Hotel Manager), Susan Morgan (Buns), Jack Frey (Cab Driver).

Having retired as an assassin for a secret organization, Eastwood leads a simple existence as an art history professor at a university. When an old friend is murdered, Eastwood is enticed into performing another "sanction" by organization head David, who promises Eastwood a painting by Pissarro if the assassination is successfully carried through. Eastwood flies to Europe and kills the man who murdered his old friend, thus getting revenge on the "other" organization. On the return flight, Eastwood flirts with and beds stewardess McGee, who is secretly working for David. In the morning, McGee steals Eastwood's savings. Infuriated, Eastwood returns to David's lair where the unscrupulous organization head blackmails Eastwood into performing one final "sanction," the assassination of the accomplice in the initial murder. The man's identity is not known, but he will be one of the three men attempting to scale the Eiger, a brutal mountain in the Swiss Alps. Eastwood, a famous climber, is forced into agreement, and prepares for the climb at old buddy Kennedy's Monument Valley climbing school and resort. Once there, Eastwood meets up with old enemy Cassidy, who attempts to kill Eastwood. Eastwood foils the plot and ditches Cassidy in the desert the next day. Eastwood flies off to the Eiger with Kennedy, who will be acting as the head of the ground crew during the climb. Once in Switzerland, Eastwood meets the three men who will be joining him on the expedition, one of whom will be Eastwood's victim. During the harsh and dangerous climb, Eastwood begins to suspect each member of the team. After all the men are killed during the dangerous trek, Eastwood realizes that Kennedy was the other man in on the murder. Near death himself, dangling on a thin rope over an icy abyss, Eastwood is saved by Kennedy, who assures him that he had no idea that their old friend was going to be murdered when he tagged along for the job. Eastwood, McGee and Kennedy renounce the organization and settle back for an idyllic drink in the Swiss countryside. As seen in the more recent FIREFOX as well as THE EIGER SANCTION, Eastwood is not very deft at creating an intriguing, exciting tale of international espionage. Unlike his brilliant work in directing westerns, Eastwood falls victim to stodgy pacing, ludicrous acting, and a lack of sense of pace or rhythm. THE EIGER SANCTION does, however, contain some brilliant, breathtaking mountaineering sequences in which Eastwood did his own stunt work. The icy, treacherous climb up the Eiger is depicted in brutally realistic, thrilling ways. Eastwood's impersonal style in the majority of the film, however, takes away the intense energy he can give a film when directing, as can be seen in THE OUTLAW JOSEY WALES, HONKYTONK MAN, and HIGH PLAINS DRIFTER.

p, Robert Daley; d, Clint Eastwood; w, Hal Dresner, Warren B. Murphy, Rod Whitaker (based on the novel by Trevanian); ph, Frank Stanley (Technicolor); m, John Williams; ed, Ferris Webster; art d, George Webb, Aurelio Crugnola; cos, Charles Waldo.

Spy Drama   **Cas.**   **(PR:C MPAA:R)**

8½****   (1963, Ital.) 140m EM bw
(OTTO E MEZZO; AKA: FEDERICO FELLINI'S 8½)

Marcello Mastroianni (*Guido Anselmi*), Claudia Cardinale (*Claudia*), Anouk Aimee (*Luisa Anselmi*), Sandra Milo (*Carla*), Rossella Falk (*Rossella*), Barbara Steele (*Gloria Morin*), Mario Pisu (*Mezzabotta*), Guido Alberti (*The Producer*), Madeleine LeBeau (*French Actress*), Jean Rougeul (*Writer*), Caterina Boratto (*Fashionable Woman*), Annibale Ninchi (*Anselmi's Father*), Giuditta Rissone (*Anselmi's Mother*), Ian Dallas (*Mindreader*), Eddra Gale (*La Saraghina*), Yvonne Casadei [*Jacqueline Bonbon*] (*Aging Dancer*), Annie Gorassini (*Producer's Girl Friend*), Tito Masini (*The Cardinal*), Eugene Walter (*The Journalist*), Gilda Dahlberg (*Journalist's Wife*), Hedy Vessel (*Model*), Nadine Sanders (*Airline Hostess*), Georgia Simmons (*Anselmi's Grandmother*), Hazel Rogers (*Negro Dancer*), Riccardo Guglielmi (*Guido as a Farm Boy*), Marco Gemini (*Guido as a Schoolboy*), Neil Robinson (*Agent for French Actor*), Mino Doro (*Claudia's Agent*), Mario Tarchetti (*Claudia's Press Agent*), Mary Indovino (*Maurice's Partner*), Mario Conocchia (*Director*), Cesarino Miceli Picardi (*Production Inspector*), Bruno Agostini (*Production Secretary*), Alberto Conocchia (*Production Manager*), John Stacy (*Accountant*), Mark Herron (*Luisa's Admirer*), Elisabeta Catalano (*Luisa's Sister*), Rossella Falk (*Luisa's Friend*), Francesco Rigamonti (*Enrico*), Matilda Calnan (*Older Journalist*), Alfredo de Lafeld, Sebastiano De Leandro (*Cardinal's Secretaries*), Frazier Rippy (*Lay Secretary*), Maria Tedeschi (*College Dean*), Maria Raimondi, Marisa Colomber (*Aunts*), Roberto Nicolisi (*Doctor*), Palma Mangini (*Aging Relative From the Country*), Roberta Valli (*Annoying Little Niece*), Eva Gioia, Dina De Santis (*Two Young Girls In Bed*), Olimpia Cavalli (*Miss Olympia*), Maria Antonietta Beluzzi (*Screen-Test Candidate for La Saraghina*), Polidor (*Clown in the Parade*), Elisabetta Cini, Luciana Sanseverino, Giulio Paradisi, Edward Fleming Moller, Valentina Lang, Annarosa Lattuada, Agnes Bonfanti, Flaminia Torlonia, Anna Caramini, Maria Wertmuller, Rossella Como (*Friend*).

Many filmmakers love nothing better than making films about making films. Sometimes it works (THE BAD AND THE BEAUTIFUL, 1952; DAY FOR NIGHT, 1973) and sometimes it sort of works (AFTER THE FOX, 1966). In the case of Federico Fellini's 8½, it works darn near perfectly. Many critics slammed Fellini for being self-indulgent in the making of this picture about making pictures, but *that* was the entire idea! Film directors are, by nature, self-indulgent, otherwise they wouldn't enjoy ordering people around the way they do and tossing out the script when it doesn't please them. The story of the film is about as close as anyone will be able to get to the inside of a human being's brain and how the creative process works. Mastroianni (in a thinly veiled characterization of Fellini) is a director coming off a big hit. He needs rest and goes to a spa-type hotel to regain his strength. While attempting to recuperate, his producer, Guido Alberti, won't let him be; he wants details from Mastroianni about the new sci-fi film for which they have committed. Hundreds of people are waiting in the wings for Mastroianni to get started. (It's similar to the way Charlie Chaplin used to keep everyone on salary while he went to his Beverly Hills home and mused for months until he came up with an idea he felt was worth filming.) Mastroianni finds himself creatively blocked and fending off the inquiries of his actors, reporters, and his pain-in-the-neck writer, Rougeul. Totally confused about what he wants to do next, Mastroianni begins to fantasize. We're never sure if he's actually recalling what has happened before or whether it is wishful thinking. He remembers his dead mother and father, a sequence wherein he watched a fat hooker dance on a beach, snippets of what it was like to be in a 1930s Catholic school, and a fantasy showing him controlling a horde of women with a whip. Now reality intrudes with the entrances of his wife, Aimee, and his mistress, Milo. He begins to examine his relationship with both women as well as with the others who invade his life. Claudia Cardinale arrives. She is an actress who personifies every woman he has ever dreamed of. His attitude toward Aimee is boredom, and he has the age-old "my wife doesn't understand me" quarrel with Milo. He thinks he may be able to find happiness with Cardinale but is shattered to learn that she is as dumb and

egotistical as she is succulent and desirable. This causes him to go even deeper into apathy and depression. He holds a press conference on the exterior set of a rocket ship which has been built for the as-yet-unwritten sci-fi film. The press barrages him with questions, none of which he can satisfactorily answer. He decides to forget about the sci-fi film and let the set disintegrate with time. He has one last fantasy in which he kills himself and that act frees him of his misgivings. A group of circus clowns arrives. With them is Mastroianni as a child, Guglielmi, playing a flute. Now a parade begins and it's everyone in his life; the living and the dead. They form a circle and start to dance as the picture ends. Phew! What does it all mean? Who knows? Everyone who's seen 8½ gets something different out of it and Fellini will only shrug if you ask him what it was all about. He'd made three short films and six full-length pictures when he did this. Searching for a title, he added up the total of his work and it came to 7½. This one made it 8½. It's a film about a crisis in a man's life, and Fellini is using the whole world as his psychiatrist. He bares more in this than any other filmmaker had until that time. (Bob Fosse may have eclipsed him for self-revelation with ALL THAT JAZZ.) There are two prints of this, one at 140m and one at 188m. See the shorter one if possible. Less is more in the case of 8½. Fellini has often annoyed and perplexed with his work, but as complex as this may be, the message he sends is clear; it isn't easy being a genius. (Note: One assistant director was Lina Wertmuller.)

p, Angela Rizzoli; d, Federico Fellini; w, Fellini, Tullio Pinelli, Ennio Flajano, Brunello Rondi (based on a story by Fellini and Flajano); ph, Gianni di Venanzo; m, Nino Rota; ed, Leo Catozzo, Adrianna Olasio; art & cos, Piero Gherardi; makeup, Otello Fava.

Drama   **Cas.**   **(PR:C MPAA:NR)**

EIGHT ARMS TO HOLD YOU   (SEE HELP!, 1965)

EIGHT BELLS**½   (1935) 69m COL bw

Ann Sothern (*Marg Walker*), Ralph Bellamy (*Steve Andrews*), John Buckler (*Roy Dale*), Catharine Doucet (*Aunt Susan*), Arthur Hohl (*Williams*), Charley Grapewin (*Grayson*), Franklin Pangborn (*Finch*), John Darrow (*Carl*).

Sothern smuggles herself aboard the ship commanded by Buckler, her fiance, but along the journey she falls in love with First Mate Bellamy, who resents Buckler for taking his command. Routine romantic drama.

p, J. G. Bachman; d, Roy William Neill; w, Ethel Hill, Bruce Manning (based on the play by Percy G. Mandley); ph, Joseph August; ed, Gene Havlick.

Drama   **(PR:A MPAA:NR)**

EIGHT GIRLS IN A BOAT**   (1932, Ger.) 81m Fanal/Terra bw
(ACHT MAEDLES IM BOOT)

Theodor Loos, Karin Hardt, Helmuth Klonka, Heinz Goedecke, Ali Ghito, Martha Ziegler, Hedwig Schlicter, Friedrich Ettel, F. W. Schroeder, Schromm, Katja Bennefeld, Hedi Heisig, Dora Thalmer, Sabine Peters, Gunni Dreyer, Dr. Mary Norden, Hedi Kirchner, Thea Dorree, Elfi Richsteiger, Helga Arndt, Ursula Schummat, Dolores de Padilla, Edna Gray.

Apparently made to exploit the success of the slightly earlier MAEDCHEN IN UNIFORM (1932), this part-musical film deals with a social problem in an authoritarian girls' school. After being assisted by her schoolmates with difficulties associated with her out-of-wedlock pregnancy, Hardt returns to the bosom of her family. The style and format were seen to be successful enough for Paramount to purchase the property and remake the film for release two years later. Songs include "A Day Without You Is a Day Without Happiness," by Arthur Rebner.

d, Ehrich Waschneck; w, Franz Winterstein (based on an idea by Helmut Brandis); ph, Fr. Behn-Grund; m, Arthur Rebner; set d, Alfred Junge.

Drama/Musical   **(PR:A MPAA:NR)**

EIGHT GIRLS IN A BOAT***   (1934) 85m PAR bw

Dorothy Wilson (*Christa Storm*), Douglas Montgomery (*David Perrin*), Kay Johnson (*Hanna*), Barbara Barondess (*Pickles*), Ferike Boros (*Frau Kruger*), Walter Connolly (*Storm*), James Bush (*Paul Lang*), Colin Campbell (*Smallman*), Peggy Montgomery (*Hortense*), Margaret Marquis (*Elizabeth*), Marjorie Cavalier (*Bobby*), Virginia Hall (*Mary*), Kay Hammond (*Katza*).

At a private girl's school in Switzerland, Wilson finds herself pregnant by Montgomery. He offers to marry her, but his father won't allow it, so the other girls decide to underwrite the child. When Montgomery's father has a change of heart and allows the marriage, the others are quite upset. Wilson's excellent performance makes this one worth watching today. The female supporting cast were the winners in a nationwide contest, with three girls from the East, two from the Midwest, and three from the West. (Remade from the German film of 1932.)

p, Charles R. Rogers; d, Richard Wallace; w, Casey Robinson, Arthur Rebner (based on an original story by Helmut Brandis and Lewis Foster); ph, Gilbert Warrenton; m, Arthur Rebner, Harold Lewis; lyrics, Sam Coslow.

Drama   **(PR:C MPAA:NR)**

EIGHT IRON MEN**½   (1952) 80m COL bw

Bonar Colleano (*Colucci*), Arthur Franz (*Carter*), Lee Marvin (*Mooney*), Richard Kiley (*Coke*), Nick Dennis (*Sapiros*), James Griffith (*Ferguson*), Dick Moore (*Muller*), George Cooper (*Small*), Barney Phillips (*Capt. Trelawney*), Robert Nichols (*Walsh*), Richard Grayson (*Lt. Crane*), Douglas Henderson (*Hunter*), Mary Castle (*Girl*), David McMahon (*Cafferty*).

An infantry squad is trapped in a bombed-out house while outside one of their buddies is pinned down in a hole in the rain by a machine gun. The men talk of rescuing him, but one attempt after another fails until Colleano, who up to this time has been thinking about women, goes out and gets the job done. Good performances, above-average war drama.

p, Stanley Kramer; d, Edward Dmytryk; w, Harry Brown (based on his play "A Sound Of Hunting"); ph, Roy Hunt; m, Leith Stevens; ed, Aaron Stell, md, Morris Stoloff; set d, James Crowe.

War   (PR:C   MPAA:NR)

EIGHT O'CLOCK WALK*½** (1954, Brit.) 87m British Aviation/BL bw

Richard Attenborough (Tom Manning), Cathy O'Donnell (Jill Manning), Derek Farr (Peter Tanner), Ian Hunter (Geoffrey Tanner), Maurice Denham (Horace Clifford), Bruce Seton (D.C.I.); Harry Welchman (Justice Harrington); Kynaston Reeves (Mr. Munro), Lilly Kann (Mrs. Zunz), Eithne Dunne (Mrs. Evans), Cheryl Molineaux (Irene Evans), Totti Truman Taylor (Miss Ribden-White), Robert Adair (Mr. Pettigrew); Grace Arnold (Mrs. Higgs), David Hannaford (Ernie Higgs), Sally Stephens (Edith Higgs), Vernon Kelso, Robert Sydney, Max Brimmell, Humphrey Morton, Arthur Hewlett, Philip King, Jean St. Clair, Enid Hewitt, Noel Dyson, Dorothy Darke, Bartlett Mullins, Sue Thackeray.

Attenborough is a taxi driver who is tricked by a little girl on April Fools day, leading him to playfully chase her. Later the girl's murdered body is found and witnesses and circumstantial evidence all point to Attenborough. Defense Attorney Farr stands by his client and when he sees witness Denham offering candy to a child he realizes that he is the killer. He breaks Denham down on the witness stand and manages to get a confession. Good courtroom drama, with Attenborough very good as an innocent man caught in the wheels of justice.

p, George King; d, Lance Comfort; w, Katherine Strueby, Guy Morgan (based on a story by Jack Roffey, Gordon Harbord); ph, Brendan Stafford; m, George Melachrino; ed, Francis Bieber.

Drama   (PR:A   MPAA:NR)

EIGHT ON THE LAM* (1967) 107m Hope Enterprise/UA c
(GB: EIGHT ON THE RUN)

Bob Hope (Henry Dimsdale), Phyllis Diller (Golda), Jonathan Winters (Jasper Lynch), Shirley Eaton (Ellie Barton), Jill St. John (Monica Day), Stacey Maxwell (Linda), Kevin Brody (Steve), Robert Hope (Mike), Glenn Gilger (Andy), Avis Hope (Dana), Debi Storm (Lois), Michael Freeman (Mark), Austin Willis (Mr. Pomeroy), Peter Leeds (Marty).

Wretched Hope vehicle has him taking off with his family and maid (Diller) when he is accused of embezzling from the bank where he works. They are pursued by Winters until it is revealed that Willis, Hope's boss, took the money. Hope isn't funny, Winters misses the mark completely, and watching Diller is like scratching your fingernails down a blackboard. A comedy to be avoided.

p, Bill Lawrence; d, George Marshall; w, Albert E. Lewin, Burt Styler, Bob Fisher, Arthur Marx (based on a story by Fisher and Marx); ph, Alan Stenvold (DeLuxe Color); m, George Romanis; ed, Grant Whytock; art d, Walter Simonds; set d, Raymond Paul.

Comedy   (PR:A   MPAA:NR)

EIGHTEEN AND ANXIOUS*½ (1957) 93m AB-PT/Rep bw
(AKA: NO GREATER SIN)

Mary Webster (Judy), William Campbell (Pete), Martha Scott (Lottie Graham), Jackie Loughery (Ava), Jim Backus (Harvey Graham), Ron Hagerthy (Danny), Jackie Coogan (Eager), Damian O'Flynn (Mr. Bayne), Katherine Barrett (Mrs. Bayne), Charlotte Wynters (Mrs. Warren), Yvonne Craig (Gloria), Joyce Andre (1st Girl), Slick Slavin (Morty), Benny Rubin (Guest).

Webster is a girl secretly married to a young man who is subsequently killed drag racing. When she later has the youth's baby, she is unable to prove she was married and, anyway, she refuses to care for the baby, preferring to make a play for jazz trumpeter Campbell. He takes her to Las Vegas but when she realizes he has no intention of marrying her, she leaves, ending up married to disc jockey Hagerthy. Routine teen exploitation picture, later re-released as part of a birth-of-a-baby film.

p, Edmond Chevie; d, Joe Parker; w, Dale and Katherine Eunson; ph, Sam Leavitt; m, Leith Stevens; ed, Douglas Stewart; m/l, Phil Tuminello.

Drama   (PR:C   MPAA:NR)

EIGHTEEN IN THE SUN* (1964, Ital.) 85m
Dino De Laurentis Cinematografica/Goldstone Film Enterprises c
(DICIOTTENNI AL SOLE; AKA: BEACH PARTY ITALIAN STYLE)

Catherine Spaak (Nicole Molino), Lisa Gastoni (Frances), Gianni Garko (Nicola Molino), Spiros Focas (Johnny), Fabrizio Capucci (Matthew), Giampiero Littera (Carlo), Stelvio Rosi (George), Oliviero Prunas (Bruno), Luisa Mattioli (Jeannie), Franco Giacobini (Commissar), Gabriele Antonini (Louie), Eleonora Morana (Maggie), Loris Bazzocchi (Gino), Paolo De Bellis.

Spaak is a young Frenchwoman and Garko is a young Italian male, and they find themselves booked into the same hotelroom on the Mediterranean island of Ischia. (They have the same last names.) Garko promises that he won't try anything and Spaak makes sure by making him sleep on the balcony. The two fight back and forth until—yup—they fall in love.

p, Isidoro Broggi; d, Camillo Mastrocinque; w, Franco Castellano Pipolo; ph, Riccardo Pallottini (Panoramic Wide-screen, Eastmancolor); m, Ennio Morricone.

Comedy   (PR:C   MPAA:NR)

18 MINUTES* (1935, Brit.) 88m Allied/Pathe-Vogue bw

Gregory Ratoff (Nikita), John Loder (Trelawney), Benita Hume (Lady Phyllis Pilcott), Katherine Sergava (Lida), Richard Bennett (Korn), Hugh Wakefield (Lord Pilcott), Paul Graetz (Pietro), Carl Harbord (Jacques), Rosamund Barnes (Lida as a Child), Hal Gordon, Margaret Yarde.

Lion tamer Ratoff hears that a rival tamer has been killed by one of his lionesses so he purchases the killer animal and adopts the man's daughter (Barnes, soon to grow into Sergava). As the girl grows up he becomes jealous of the attention other men are paying to her so he tells her that she will marry him. They are married but soon she falls in love with Loder, a magician who is replacing Ratoff as the chief attraction at the circus. Ratoff plans to face the killer lioness with his hands cuffed behind him in an attempt to regain his stature but just as he is about to enter the cage he learns of the affair between Sergava and Loder. Despite the pleas of his faithful dresser he enters the cage and turns his back to the animal, which immediately seizes the opportunity and kills him. Interesting drama, way above average for British films of the time.

p, Gregory Ratoff; d, Monty Banks; w, Fred Thompson (based on a story by Ratoff); ph, Geoffrey Faithfull, John J. Cox.

Drama   (PR:A   MPAA:NR)

1812* (1944, USSR) 95m Mosfilm/Artkino bw (AKA: KUTUZOV)

Alexei Dykki (Prince Kutuzov), Sergei Mezhinsky (Napoleon), Nikolai Okhlopkov (Gen. Barclay de Tolly), S. Zakariadze (Gen. Bagration), V. Gotovzev (Gen. Beningsen), E. Kaluzhski (Marshal Berthier), A. Stephanov (Marshal Ney), N. Timchenko (Alexander I), E. Brilling, A. Poliakov, N. Ruzhov, S. Blinnikov, B. Chirkov, I. Skuratov, G. Terkhov, Sergei Kournakoff (Narrator).

Just as the Russians were turning the tide against the German invasion, this film, a dramatization of the life and career of the general who defeated Napoleon, went into production at the Moscow Film Studios—one of the first productions there since the city was evacuated in the face of the German Army the year before. The film is a straightforward biography, heavy on the patriotism and propaganda. It is well worth seeing for the grand battle scenes, including one at Borodino shot on the 131st anniversary of the event. (Narration in English.)

d, Vladimir Petrov; w, Vsevolod Solovyov; ph, Mikhail Gindin; m, Yuri Shaporin; prod d, Vladimir Yegorov.

Biography/Historical Epic   (PR:A   MPAA:NR)

EIGHTH DAY OF THE WEEK, THE*½** (1959, Pol./Ger.) 84m
Film Polski-C.C.C./Continental bw/c (OSMY DZIEM TYGODNIA)

Sonja Ziemann (Agnieshka), Zbigniew Cybulski (Peter), Ilse Steppat (Mother), Bum Krueger (Father), Tadeusz Lomnicki (Gregor), Emil Karewicz (Zawadzki), Jan Swiderski (Journalist), Zbigniew Wojcik (Painter), Barbara Polomska (Elisabeth).

Cybulski and Ziemann are a young Polish couple unable to be alone together because of the critical housing shortage in Warsaw. Caught up in the depressing world of Socialist regulation and restriction they somehow manage to transcend their surroundings and find true love with one another. An unusual Polish-West German co-production, the Polish government refused to allow Polish-language prints to leave the country (presumably because they show the Polish Communist experience to be unrelentingly grim and dehumanizing) so most prints in circulation are in German. The performances are superb and Ford's direction is up to his highest standards. This classic Eastern European film is a must-see. (In German; English subtitles.)

d, Alexander Ford; w, Marek Hlasko, Ford (based on the novel by Hlasko); ph, Jerzy Lipman.

Drama   (PR:C-O   MPAA:NR)

80 STEPS TO JONAH* (1969) 108m Motion Pictures International-
El Tigre/WB c

Wayne Newton (Mark Jonah Winters), Jo Van Fleet (Nonna), Keenan Wynn (Barney Glover), Diana Ewing (Tracy), Slim Pickens (Scott), R. G. Armstrong (Mackray), Brandon Cruz (Little Joe), Erin Moran (Kim), Teddy Quinn (Richard), Michele Tobin (Cathy), Susan Mathews (Velma), Lily Martens (Nina), Ira Augustain (Pepe), Butch Patrick (Brian), Dennis Cross (Maxon) Frank Schuller (Whitney), James Bacon (Hobo), Jackie Kahane (Jackie Kahane), Mickey Rooney (Wilfred Bashford), Sal Mineo (Jerry Taggart), Coby Denton (Wilks), Joe Conley (Jenkins), Fred Dale, Don Hamilton (Sheriffs), Holger Bendixen (Fisherman), Lord Nelson (Ralph), Bertha (A Lamb).

A sappy story about a man, Newton, on the run from the police because he is thought to be a car thief. He ends up at a camp for blind children that is run by Van Fleet. She mistakes Newton for the handyman she was expecting, and Newton becomes beloved by the kids and Van Fleet. The police track him down, but he's cleared of charges when a drunk verifies Newton's story, and he returns to the camp. A sugar-coated film with no surprises.

p&d, Gerd Oswald; w, Fredric Louis Fox (based on a story by Fox and Oswald); ph, Joseph La Shelle (Technicolor); m, George Shearing; ed, Tony DiMarco; art d, Howard Hollander; m/l, "My World," "If I Could Be to You," "Tender Loving Care" (Wayne Newton, Don Vincent), "It's Such A Lonely Time of the Year" (Al Gorgoni, Chip Taylor).

Drama   (PR:A   MPAA:G)

80,000 SUSPECTS* (1963, Brit.) 113m RANK bw

Claire Bloom (Julie Monks), Richard Johnson (Steven Monks), Yolande Donlan (Ruth Preston), Cyril Cusack (Father Maguire), Michael Goodliffe (Clifford Preston), Mervyn Johns (Buckridge), Kay Walsh (Matron), Norman Bird (Mr. Davis), Basil Dignam (Medical Officer), Andrew Crawford (Dr. Rudding), Ray Barrett (Health Inspector Bennett), Norman Chappell (Welford), Arthur Christiansen (Mr. Gracey), Vanda Godsell (Mrs. Davis), Ursula Howells (Joanna Druten), Jill Curzon (Nurse Jill), Bruce Lewis (TV Reporter).

When a smallpox epidemic breaks out in Bath, England, doctor Johnson heads the search for the carrier while trying to keep together his marriage with nurse Bloom. Eventually the search narrows down to the dipsomaniacal, nymphomaniacal wife of an associate. Frequently gripping thanks to documentary style, location shooting in Bath, and decent performances.

p, Val Guest, Frank Sherwin Green; d&w, Guest (based on the novel *The Pillars of Midnight* by Elleston Trevor); ph, Arthur Grant; m, Stanley Black; ed, Bill Lenny.

Drama **(PR:C MPAA:NR)**

EL**** (1955, Mex.) 100m Tepeyac/Omnifilms bw
(AKA: EL, THIS STRANGE PASSION TORMENTS)

Arturo De Cordova *(Francisco)*, Delia Garces *(Gloria)*, Luis Beristain *(Raoul)*, Manuel Donde *(Pablo)*, Martinez Baena *(Padre Velasco)*, Fernando Casanova *(Beltran)*, Aurora Walker *(Mother)*, Rafael Banquells *(Ricardo)*.

A fascinating study of a married man's obsession that his wife is unfaithful. The middle-aged De Cordova is a church-goer who has abstained from sex his entire life. While helping the local priest wash the feet of parishioners, he notices the delicate feet of a woman. He looks up to see Garces, a hauntingly beautiful woman with whom he becomes instantly enamored. He leads a desperate search for her and upon finding her, lures her away from her architect lover. They marry, but on their wedding night he interrogates her about an acquaintance of hers, confronting her with raging jealousy. He accuses the man of being one of Garces' previous lovers and believes that the man is spying on them. To dismiss his paranoia, he pokes a sewing-needle through the door's keyhole in hopes of jabbing out the voyeur's eyeball. He swings from passionate desire for her, to unbearable jealousy. Objections are raised by Garces' mother and the local pastor. In a blind rage, De Cordova tries to strangle the priest, thinking he is the subject of the church's mockery. After many years, De Cordova is visited in a monastery by Garces, now married and with a child. On the surface De Cordova seems to have overcome his "strange passion," but as he walks away in a familiarly maddening zig-zag fashion we are sure that he is just as obsessed as before. One of Bunuel's finest films of his Mexican period (second only to THE YOUNG AND THE DAMNED), EL is a fine example of his indictment of religious repression. Surprisingly, the film was battered by the Cannes Film Fest crowd which consisted of hundreds of war veterans who were in attendance for a film about Georges Clemenceau.

p, Oscar Dancigers; d, Luis Bunuel; w, Bunuel, Luis Alcoriza (based on the novel *Pensamientos* by Mercedes Pinto); ph, Gabriel Figueroa; m, Hernandez Breton; ed, Carlos Savage; set d, Edward Fitzgerald.

Drama **(PR:C-O MPAA:NR)**

EL ALAMEIN** (1954) 66m COL bw

Scott Brady *(Banning)*, Edward Ashley *(Capt. Harbison)*, Robin Hughes *(Sgt. Alf Law)*, Rita Moreno *(Jara)*, Michael Pate *(Sgt. McQueen)*, Peter Brocco *(Selim)*, Peter Mamakos *(Corp. Singh Das)*, Ray Page *(Nazi Pilot)*, Benny Rubin *(Egyptian Driver)*, Henry Rowland *(Nazi Officer)*.

Brady, a civilian delivering tanks to the British soldiers at the front, becomes trapped with a small group of men at a desert oasis the Afrika Korps is using as a fuel dump. They hold off the German onslaught until help arrives, then blow up the gasoline. Routine WW II heroics.

p, Wallace MacDonald; d, Fred F. Sears; w, Herbert Purdum, Horace McCoy, George Worthing Yates (based on a story by Purdum); ph, Henry Freulich; ed, Richard Fantl; art d, Edward L. Ilou.

War **(PR:A-C MPAA:NR)**

EL BRUTO (SEE: BRUTE, THE 1952, Mex.)

EL CID*** (1961, U.S./Ital.) 180m Bronston-Rank/AA c

Sophia Loren *(Chimene)*, Charlton Heston *(Rodrigo Diaz de Bivar/El Cid)*, John Fraser *(King Alfonso)*, Raf Vallone *(Count Ordonez)*, Genevieve Page *(Queen Urraca)*, Gary Raymond *(King Sancho)*, Herbert Lom *(Ben Yussef)*, Massimo Serata *(Fanez)*, Douglas Wilmer *(Moutamin)*, Frank Thring *(Al Kadir)*, Hurd Hatfield *(Count Arias)*, Ralph Truman *(King Ferdinand)*, Andrew Cruickshank *(Count Gomez)*, Michael Hordern *(Don Diego)*, Carlo Giustini *(Bermudez)*, Christopher Rhodes *(Don Martin)*, Gerard Tichy *(King Ramirez)*, Fausto Tozzi *(Dolfos)*, Tullio Carminati *(Priest)*, Barbara Everest *(Mother Superior)*, Franco Fantasia.

This is a very colorful historical pageant recounting the legendary exploits of Spain's heroic Rodrigo Diaz de Bivar, better known as El Cid. Heston, no stranger to epic, plays the title role and Loren, his fiancee, is estranged from him early on when he kills her father, Gomez, after the old man accuses the knight of treason at court. They are married but never enjoy a wedding night; she plots against Heston and when her intrigues come to naught she enters a convent. Spain is no sooner cleared of Moors by the battling Heston than its kingdom is divided with the death of Truman (King Ferdinand) whose offspring take to war against each other over the spoils. Loren by then has taken Heston to her bed. Children are produced and the family retreats to a monastery while Heston lays siege to Valencia, the last outpost of the usurpers. He is killed by an arrow from the battlement but his troops mount his dead body on a horse and he leads a posthumous charge against the defenders who panic at the sight of what they believe is an immortal knight. Lom, the usurper, is killed when his men stampede over him and Heston is hailed as Spain's greatest hero. The spectacle and grandeur of 11th-century Spain is fully chronicled here and the photography is spectacular, as are the battle scenes, but the story is muddled and Heston might as well have been Steve Reeves for all the inane dialog he utters from a shallow and uninteresting script. Loren is not required to act and doesn't, merely displays as much of her large, voluptuous body as the period costuming will permit. Mann is an on-and-off director and here he is off by miles. Aside from the amazing battle scenes where half of the Spanish army was employed, the film is sluggish and directionless. Heston and Loren sort of grunt and grumble in each other's directions as unlikely and unappealing lovers. Mann had insisted on making this film with only two superstars. Heston agreed immediately but the director had to chase Loren all around Rome to get her to agree to play the Spanish noblewomen, a role she had turned down twice, saying: "I just don't see myself in the part." Neither did anyone else. The film oozes history, and this is because the Spanish historian Don Ramon Menendez Pidal was used as a consultant by writers Frank and Yordan, as well as composer Rozsa and art directors Colasanti and Moore, and that is its problem. The film becomes a history lesson more than telling a dramatic tale. Krasker's photography is a standout; he had long established his brilliance with such films as Olivier's HENRY V and this film was no exception to his achievements. Another standout in this film was Hollywood's finest stuntman, Yakima Canutt, who brilliantly staged the siege of Valencia scenes, using the ancient walled city of Pensacola, and 5,000 troops of the Spanish army. (A Moorish battle fleet of 35 perfectly reconstructed lifesize ships was employed.) Bronston spent untold millions on this film, lavishing $150,000 on medieval art objects, $40,000 on jewelry. The producer looked over the Cathedral at Burgos but was unhappy with its modern-day renovations so he ordered an exact reproduction built. Heston, who later admitted that he was in "the best shape of my entire career" during this film, performed strenuous stunts and an impressive duel, after training long and hard with European fencing master Enzo Musemeci Greco. The film, a sort of Spanish IVANHOE, is basically drawn from ALEXANDER NEVSKY but nowhere approaches the Eisenstein masterpiece. From the looks of it, EL CID is a huge Spanish bell swinging ponderously in a high cathedral tower. But there is no resounding gong, only a tinkle or two.

p, Samuel Bronston, Anthony Mann; d, Mann; w, Philip Yordan, Fredric M. Frank; ph, Robert Krasker (Super Technirama, Technicolor); m, Miklos Rozsa; ed, Robert Lawrence; art d & cos, Veniero Colesanti, John Moore; makeup, Mario Van Riel; stunts second-unit d, Yakima Canutt; spec eff, Alex Weldone, Jack Erickson.

Adventure/Historical Drama **Cas.** **(PR:A MPAA:NR)**

EL CONDOR* (1970) 102m Carthay Continental/NG c

Jim Brown *(Luke)*, Lee Van Cleef *(Jaroo)*, Patrick O'Neal *(Chavez)*, Mariana Hill *(Claudine)*, Iron Eyes Cody *(Santana)*, Imogen Hassall *(Dolores)*, Elisha Cook, Jr. *(Old Convict)*, Gustavo Rojo *(Col. Aguinaldo)*, Florencio Amarilla *(Aguila)*, Julio Pena *(Gen. Hernandez)*, Angel Del Pozo *(Lieutenant)*, Patricio Santiago *(Julio)*, John Clark *(Prison Guard Captain)*, Raul Medoza Castro *(Indian)*, Rafael Albaicin *(Officer)*, George Ross *(Guard for Convicts)*, Ricardo Palacios *(Chief Mexican Bandit)*, Charles Stalnaker, Carlos Bravo, Dan Van Husen *(Bandits)*, Peter Lenahan, Art Larkin, Per Barclay *(Convicts)*.

Brown and Van Cleef team up to rob the treasure hidden away in a Mexican fortress commanded by O'Neal. Considerable carnage ensues, at the end of which Brown is left with Hill among smoking ruins and bleeding bodies. An attempt by Americans to make an Italian western, this is convincing evidence of the foolishness of such an undertaking.

p, Andre de Toth; d, John Guillermin; w, Larry Cohen, Steven Carabatsos (based on a story by Carabatsos); ph, Henri Persin (Technicolor); m, Maurice Jarre; ed, William Ziegler, Walter Hannemann; art d, Julio Molina Juanes.

Western **(PR:O MPAA:R)**

EL DIABLO RIDES* (1939) 57m Metropolitan bw

Bob Steele, Claire Rochelle, Kit Guard, Carleton Young, Ted Adams, Robert Walker, Bob Robinson, Hal Carey.

Tired horse opera has Steele winning Rochelle's heart on the range after besting bad guys Young and Adams. Poor script and worse direction make this one a rough canter.

p, Harry S. Webb; d, Ira Webb; w, Carl Krusada (based on a story by Harry Gordon); ph, Eddie Kull.

Western **(PR:A MPAA:NR)**

EL DORADO*** (1967) 125M PAR c

John Wayne *(Cole Thornton)*, Robert Mitchum *(J. P. Harrah)*, James Caan *(Alan Bourdillon Traherne, called Mississippi)*, Charlene Holt *(Maudie)*, Michele Carey *(Joey MacDonald)*, Arthur Hunnicutt *(Bull Harris)*, R. G. Armstrong *(Kevin MacDonald)*, Edward Asner *(Bart Jason)*, Paul Fix *(Doc Miller)*, Christopher George *(Nelse McLeod)*, Johnny Crawford *(Luke MacDonald)*, Robert Donner *(Milt)*, John Gabriel *(Pedro)*, Mariana Ghane *(Maria)*, Robert Rothwell *(Saul MacDonald)*, Adam Roarke *(Matt MacDonald)*, Chuck Courtney *(Jared MacDonald)*, Anne Newman *(Saul's Wife)*, Diane Strom *(Matt's Wife)*, Victoria George *(Jared's Wife)*, Olaf Wieghorst *(Swedish Gunsmith)*, Anthony Rogers *(Dr. Donovan)*, Dean Smith *(Charlie Hagan)*, William Albert Henry *(Sheriff Bill Moreland)*, Don Collier *(Deputy Joe Braddock)*, Jim Davis *(Jason's Foreman)*, Nacho Galindo *(Mexican Saloonkeeper)*, John Mitchum *(Bartender, Jason's Saloon)*, Rosa Truich *(Rosa)*, Ralph Volkie, Danny Sands, Buzz Henry, Deen Pettinger, Lee Powell, Enrique Contreras, Riley Hill, John Strachen, Mike Letz, Betty Graham, Richard Andrade, Ruben Moreno, Robert Shelton, Linda Dangcil, Myrna MacMurray, Bonnie Charyl Josephson, Joe Garcio, Christopher West, Frank Leyva, Charlita, Rodolfo Hoyos, Chuck Roberson.

John Wayne is a gunfighter (so what else is new?) who rides into the small town of El Dorado and renews his friendship with Mitchum, now the sheriff of the town. Asner, a wealthy cattle baron, has sent for Wayne and intends to put him to work but Wayne declines the job when he learns that his duties include driving a family off their land, land that Asner needs for the water. As Wayne leaves the saloon where he and Mitchum are lathering their tonsils, Wayne runs into Holt, his former girl friend and now the current girl friend of Mitchum. Armstrong heads the family that Asner wants to drive out and he issues orders to his son, Johnny Crawford, to fire a warning shot if Wayne appears. They all know that Wayne has been hired by Asner but they don't know that he is turning down the job. Crawford falls asleep at his watch and awakens to see Wayne, and fires a few wild shots. Wayne's response is swift and decisive as he fires back and wounds the young man. The pain is so intense that Crawford kills himself! Wayne brings the body back to the family's ranch house where Armstrong is with his other three sons, Rothwell, Roarke,

Courtney. When daughter Michele Carey sees her dead brother, she tries to shoot Wayne but is stopped by the others. She leaves and waits in ambush on the road near a creek. She shoots Wayne in the back and the bullet is too close to the spine for local sawbones Fix to fix. Wayne is taken to Mitchum's house to rest up and Carey, now aware that her brother did himself in, comes to apologize to Wayne. When he's recovered his strength, Wayne departs. Almost a year later, Wayne is sitting in a bar near the Mexican border. A few tables away, some gunslingers are playing poker when Caan walks in, confronts one of the players and accuses him of being the last of four men who killed an old miner. Caan doesn't have a six gun but goes after the man with a knife. When Donner pulls a gun to shoot Caan, he is shot by Wayne. George, leader of the card-players has been sitting and watching. He offers Wayne a job. George and his men are about to go into the employ of Asner. Wayne says "no thanks." Later, Wayne arrives in El Dorado and finds Mitchum in an alcoholic haze and too incapacitated to handle his lawman duties. Three of George's hoods wound Armstrong while he's visiting at Holt's establishment. A shaky Mitchum, Wayne, Caan and Mitchum's old deputy, Hunnicutt, go after George and Asner and their minions. A long gun battle ensues and all of George's men are shot. Mitchum collars Asner who tries to persuade George to aid him but George apparently refuses, and agrees to leave town the following day. At noon, George and his battered gang leave, in full view of the town. But later, under cover of darkness, they come back and begin shooting up Mitchum's office and wound Mitchum in the leg. Next day, Wayne and Caan are chasing one of the criminals when the bullet lodged near Wayne's spine acts up and his hand becomes partially paralyzed. At the same time, Caan is whacked over the head. George offers Mitchum a hostage swap: Wayne and Caan for Asner, and Mitchum accepts. Carey appears and tells the newly-released Wayne and Caan that George is holding Rothwell and will kill him unless Armstrong agrees to sign over the water rights to Asner. The crippled quartet of Mitchum (on crutches), Wayne (still partially paralyzed and unable to shoot a revolver), headachy Caan, and Hunnicutt, carrying a bow and arrow, go after the villains, who are holed up in Holt's saloon. After a prolonged battle, the criminals are defeated, Caan decides to settle down with Carey, Mitchum is suddenly sober, and Wayne thinks it's about time for him to re-court Holt. EL DORADO was part of the inadvertent trilogy with RIO BRAVO, and RIO LOBO. The stories were similar, probably because the director of all three was Hawks and the screenwriter was Brackett. In each case, it was the story of a man assembling a rag-tag gang and taking on the ruthless family that ruled those parts. Hawks liked being surrounded with pals and it's interesting to see how many of his westerns have the same basic characters. Using RED RIVER, RIO BRAVO, EL DORADO and RIO LOBO, Wayne starrers all, the second leads were John Ireland, Dean Martin, Mitchum, and Jorge Rivero. There was always a young man and they were, in the order of the films, Montgomery Clift, Rick Nelson, Caan, Chris Mitchum. The old man's character was Brennan (twice), Hunnicutt, and Jack Elam. Hawks must have felt that the audiences didn't much care what the actual plots were as long as the Duke could mosey from here to there, shoot a few crooks and show his general heroism. EL DORADO had a nice balance of action to humor, although one never felt they were spoofing the western genre. Instead, we watched a movie where the protagonists had a healthy respect for a hearty laugh. It was relaxed, amiable and, except for some very out-of-place violence (Johnny Crawford's suicide, the only scene from the book that remained intact), good fun.

p&d, Howard Hawks; w, Leigh Brackett (based on the novel *The Stars in Their Courses* by Harry Brown); ph, Harold Rosson (Technicolor); m, Nelson Riddle; ed, John Woodcock; art d, Carl Anderson, Hal Pereira; set d, Robert Benton, Ray Moyers; cos, Edith Head; spec eff, Paul K. Lerpae; proc ph, Farciot Edouart.

Western   **Cas.**   **(PR:A-C   MPAA:NR)**

EL DORADO PASS＊½   (1949) 55m COL bw

Charles Starrett *(The Durango Kid)*, Smiley Burnette *(Smiley Burnette)*, Elena Verdugo *(Dolores)*, Steve Darrell *(Page)*, Rory Mallinson *(Sheriff Tom Wright)*, Ted Mapes *(Dodd)*, Stanley Blystone *(Barlow)*, Shorty Thompson and His Saddle Rockin' Rhythm.

Starrett is falsely accused of robbing a stagecoach so he does what all falsely accused heroes do—he breaks jail and finds the real culprits, this time bandits led by Darrell. Nothing noteworthy in this entry in THE DURANGO KID series.

p, Colbert Clark; d, Ray Nazarro; w, Earle Snell; ph, Rex Wimpy; ed, Burton Kramer.

Western   **(PR:A   MPAA:NR)**

EL GRECO＊＊   (1966, Ital., Fr.) 95m c
Produzione Artistiche Internazionale-Arco/Films du Siecle/FOX

Mel Ferrer *(El Greco)*, Rosanna Schiaffino *(Jeronima de las Cuevas)*, Franco Giacobini *(Francisco)*, Renzo Giovampietro *(Fra Felix)*, Mario Feliciani *(Cardinal Nino de Guevara)*, Nino Crisman *(Don Diego of Castile)*, Adolfo Celi *(Don Miguel de las Cuevas)*, Angel Aranda *(Don Luis)*, Gabriella Giorgelli *(Maria)*, Rosy Di Pietro *(Isabel)*, Rossana Martini *(Zaida)*, Giulio Donnini *(Pignatelli)*, Andrea Bosic *(The Prosecutor)*, Giuliano Farnese *(Master of Arms)*, Ontanoni *(Leoni)*, Fernando Rey *(King Philip II)*, Rafael Rivelles *(Marquis of Villena)*, John Karlsen *(Prosecutor)*, Bruno Scipioni *(Officer)*, Franco Fantasia *(Fencing Master)*, Maria Marchi *(Mother Superior)*, John Francis Lane *(De Agueda)*.

Cretan painter Ferrer goes to 16th-century Spain, becomes famous, has a one-sided affair with Schiaffino, and avoids being burned at the stake by the Spanish Inquisition. Dull biopic is enlivened only by actual locations in Toledo, Spain.

p, Mel Ferrer; d, Luciano Salce; w, Guy Elmes, Massimo Franciosa, Luigi Magni, Salce (based on a story by Elmes); ed, Fred Burnley; ph, Leonida Barboni (CinemaScope, DeLuxe Color); cos, Danilo Donati.

Biography   **(PR:A   MPAA:NR)**

EL PASO＊＊   (1949) 91m PAR bw
John Payne *(Clayton Fletcher)*, Gail Russel *(Susan Jeffers)*, Sterling Hayden *(Burt Donner)*, George "Gabby" Hayes *(Pesky)*, Dick Foran *(Sheriff La Farge)*, Henry Hull *(Judge Jeffers)*, Mary Beth Hughes *(Stage Coach Nellie)*, Eduardo Noriega *(Nacho Vasquez)*, H. B. Warner *(Judge Fletcher)*, Catherine Craig *(Mrs. John Elkins)*, Arthur Space *(John Elkins)*, Bobby Ellis *(Jack Elkins)*, Peggy McIntyre *(Mary 'Lizbeth Fletcher)*, Chief Yowlachi *(Piute Pete)*, Steven Geray *(Mexican Joe)*, Lawrence Tibbett, Jr. *(Denton)*.

Payne is a young lawyer on the frontier who is forced to take up a gun when threatened by bad guys. Routine western, barely above B status, but with an interesting cast of studio players not usually found in oaters.

p, William Pine, William Thomas; d&w, Lewis R. Foster. (based on a story by J. Robert Bren, Gladys Atwater); ph, Ellis W. Carter; ed, Howard Smith; md, David Chudnow; art d, Lewis H. Creber.

Western   **(PR:A   MPAA:NR)**

EL PASO KID, THE＊＊   (1946) 54m REP bw
Sunset Carson, Marie Harmon, Hank Patterson, Edmund Cobb, Robert Filmer, Wheaton Chambers, John Carpenter, Tex Terry, Zon Murray, Bob Wilke, Edward Cassidy, Post Park, Charlie Sullivan.

Carson is a member of a holdup gang who breaks away from the rest after they refuse to treat the wounds sustained by fellow robber Patterson during a stage-coach job. He and Patterson strike out on their own, attempting to take away a stagecoach their former comrades are robbing. While Patterson pins down the robbers from the rocks above, Carson chases and stops the runaway stage. All this is observed by Harmon, the Sheriff's daughter, who thinks the men are do-gooders and escorts them into town, hailing them as heroes. The men are given jobs by the stage line, and while Patterson wants to go straight, Carson is just biding his time for the one big job that he can retire on. When his old gang come to rob the office he's guarding, his past comes to light, but he redeems himself by leading the posse to the bandits' roost and capturing the leader. He and Patterson are pardoned, and Carson marries Harmon. Slightly above average program oater, with the mild curiosity of the hero being of dubious integrity throughout.

p, Bennett Cohen; d, Thomas Carr; w, Norman Sheldon; ph, Edgar Lyons, ed, William P. Thompson, md, Raoul Kraushaar; art d, Fred A. Ritter.

Western   **(PR:A   MPAA:NR)**

EL PASO STAMPEDE＊   (1953) 53m REP bw
Allan "Rocky" Lane *(Allan "Rocky" Lane)*, Black Jack *(His Stallion)*, Eddy Waller *(Nugget Clark)*, Phyllis Coates *(Alice Clark)*, Stephen Chase *(Mason Ransey)*, Roy Barcroft *(Floyd Garnett)*, Edward Clark *(Josh Bailey)*, Tom Monroe *(Marty)*, Stanley Andrews *(Marshal Banning)*, William Tannen *(Joe)*, John Hamilton *(Rancher)*.

Rustlers led by town dentist Chase are stealing cattle intended to feed U.S. troops fighting the Spanish in Cuba. Government agent Lane teams up with grain merchant Waller to clear up the problem. Lane's last "Rocky" Lane western for Republic, and a poor end to an otherwise not bad series.

p, Rudy Ralston; d, Harry Keller; w, Arthur Orloff; ph, John MacBurnie; m, Stanley Wilson; ed, Tony Martinelli; art d, Frank Arrigo.

Western   **(PR:A   MPAA:NR)**

EL TOPO＊   (1971, Mex.) 123m Producciones Panicas/ABKCO c

Alexandro Jodorowsky *(El Topo)*, Mara Lorenzio *(Mara)*, Paula Romo *(Woman in Black)*, Jacqueline Luis *(Small Woman)*, David Silva *(Colonel)*, Hector Martinez *(1st Master)*, Juan Jose Gurrola *(2nd Master)*, Victor Fosado *(3rd Master)*, Agustin Isunza *(4th Master)*, Brontis Jodorowsky *(Brontis as a Child)*, Robert John *(Brontis as a Man)*, Jose Antonio Alcarz *(Sheriff)*, Felipe Diazgarza *(Deputy)*, Julien De Meriche *(Priest)*.

The mass of indecipherable symbolic images, combined with the obvious self-indulgence on the part of a writer-director-star Jodorowsky, make what could have been an entertaining western into one of the most pretentious pieces ever to hit the cinema. The plot is a basic one, gunfighter avenges the death of his wife, then spurred on by a woman seeks to prove himself the best by defeating other master gunfighters. Jodorowsky, as the gunfighter, manages to kill the masters through deceitful methods, rather than through the conventional means. This same method of deceit eventually leads to Jodorowsky's intense feeling of guilt, and he retraces his steps in the hope of finding enlightenment. He finds it, but first must go through a resurrection, blatantly symbolic of Christ's own death. The pacing and action sequences are staged in a manner reminiscent of a spaghetti western, and are quite good, but the allegories are too much and too many. At the time of its release the film managed to attract a large cult following, but in retrospect the elements that made it a cult film don't hold up, making it an almost laughable piece of allegory. (English and Spanish with subtitles.)

p, Roberto Viskin; d,w&m, Alexandro Jodorowsky; ph, Raphael Corkidi (Eastmancolor); ed, Frederico Landeros.

Western   **(PR:O   MPAA:NR)**

ELDER BROTHER, THE＊   (1937, Brit.) 67m Triangle/PAR bw
John Stuart *(Ronald Bellairs)*, Marjorie Taylor *(Susan Woodward)*, Basil Langton *(Hugo Bellairs)*, Stella Bonheur *(Lady Hobbs)*, Hilary Pritchard *(Sir Frederick Hobbs)*, Claude Horton *(Doctor)*, Fred Withers, Cecil Bevan.

A man confesses to the murder of a married woman his brother was having an affair with. Routine drawing-room melodrama.

p, George King; d, Frederick Hayward; w, Dorothy Greenhill (based on a novel by Anthony Gibbs).

Drama   **(PR:A   MPAA:NR)**

ELECTRA**   (1962, Gr.) 110m Finos Films/Lopert Pictures bw

Irene Papas (Electra), Aleka Katselli (Clytemnestra), Yannis Fertis (Orestes), Theano Ioannidou (Chorus Leader), Notis Peryalis (Electra's Husband), Takis Emmanouel (Pylades), Phoebus Rhazis (Aegisthus), Manos Katrakis (The Tutor), Theodore Demetriou (Agamemnon), Elsie Pittas (Electra as a Girl), Pierre Ampeles (Orestes as a Boy), Eleni Karpeta, Kitty Arseni, Eleni Marki, Eleni Marinou, Anna Stavridou, Rota Logapoulou, Elli Trigonopoulou, Liza Koundouri, A. Gregoriades, D. Kallas, T. Exarchos, M. Sakellarios, Elly Vozikiadou (Chrysothemis).

Adapted from Euripides' "Elecktra," in which a brother and sister plot to kill their mother. Motive? Mother was responsible in part for their father's murder. The classic roles are classically played, especially by Papas, and the elemental tragedy is not badly translated to film.

p,d&w, Michael Cacoyannis (based on Euripides' "Elecktra"); ph, Walter Lassally; m, Mikis Theodorakis; ed, L. Antonakis; art d, Spyros Vassilou.

Drama   (PR:A MPAA:NR)

ELECTRA GLIDE IN BLUE**   (1973) 106m UA c

Robert Blake (John Wintergreen), Billy "Green" Bush (Zipper Davis), Mitchell Ryan (Harve Poole), Jeannine Riley (Jolene), Elisha Cook (Willie), Royal Dano (Coroner), David Wolinski (Bus Driver), Peter Cetera (Bob Zemko), Terry Kath (Killer), Lee Loughnane (Pig Man), Walter Parazaider (Loose Lips), Joe Samsil (Sgt. Ryker), Jason Clark (L.A. Detective), Michael Butler (Truck Driver), Susan Forristal, Lucy Angle Guercio (Ice Cream Girls), Melissa Green (Zemko's Girlfriend), Jim Gilmore (Detective), Bob Zemko (The Beard), Madura (Rock Group at Concert), Rebecca Kapp (Cop's Girlfriend), Jim Gilmore, Percy Curtis, John Scovern, Herb Sells, Lew Burch (Detectives), Gary Nichamin (Hospital Attendant), J.N. Roberts (Belly Flop), Pam Kath (Commune Girl), Steve Fagin, Jim Wright, Michael Phillips (Commune Guys), Jane Ferris (Policewoman), Adrienne Hayes, Susan Hail (Bike Girls), Michelle Powers (Waitress), George Dockstader (Police Car Driver), Kate Hall, Brett Kaufman, Gary Guercio (Children), Chester Grimes, Bob Ott, Jeff Ramsey, Bob Mayon, Dick Karie, Doug Burns, Jerry Brutsche, Scott Dockstader, Rock Walker, Ron Rondell, Mickey Alzola, Alan Gibbs.

Blake is an Arizona motorcycle cop (mounted on a Harley-Davidson Electra Glide) investigating a murder and trying to become a detective, but constantly harassed by the system. Violent and harsh and not entirely successful, but the final shot of Blake shotgunned off his bike and left sitting up dead in the middle of the highway is unforgettable.

p&d, James William Guercio; w, Robert Boris, Michael Butler (based on a story by Rupert Hitzig and Boris); ph, Conrad Hall (Panavision, DeLuxe Color); ed, Jim Benson, Jerry Greenberg, John F. Link III; art d, Tom Wilkes; set d, Jim Walker; cos, Rita Riggs; spec eff, Candy Flanagin, Joe Lombardi; m/l, "Tell Me," Guercio (sung by Terry Kath), "Most of All," Alan Freed, Harvey Fuqua (sung by The Marcels), "Meadow Mountain Top," "Song of Sad Bottles," Mark Spoelstra (sung by Spoelstra), "Free from the Devil," Alan De Carlo (sung by Madura), stunts, Bud Ekins, Jerry Brutsche.

Crime Drama   (PR:C MPAA:PG)

ELECTRIC HORSEMAN, THE**½   (1979) 120m COL/UNIV c

Robert Redford (Sonny Steele), Jane Fonda (Hallie Martin), Valerie Perrine (Charlotta), Willie Nelson (Wendell), John Saxon (Hunt Sears), Nicholas Coster (Fitzgerald), Allan Arbus (Danny), Wilford Brimley (Farmer), Will Hare (Gus), Basil Hoffman (Toland), Timothy Scott (Leroy), James B. Sikking (Dietrich), James Kline (Tommy), Frank Speiser (Bernie), Quinn Redeker (Bud Broderick), Lois Areno (Joanna Camden), Sarah Harris (Lucinda), Tasha Zemrus (Louise), James Novak (Dennis).

Generally-mild, modern comedy-western that owes a lot to LONELY ARE THE BRAVE in its concept of a cowboy who is anachronistic. Unusual in the sense that it was made by Columbia and Universal (just a few films have been so large or convoluted in their contracts that they needed two studios; THE TOWERING INFERNO is another, made by WB and Fox). THE ELECTRIC HORSEMAN pulls up lame early in the race. Redford is five-time cowboy champion of all the rodeos. He's hired by a huge food conglomerate to rep their cereal. Head of the company is John Saxon who looks at Redford as nothing more or less than a piece of meat for hire. After a while, Redford gets bored being the "special attraction" at supermarket openings and various other insulting appearances. He's ordered to Las Vegas to be part of a declassé stage revue where he will ride on stage in a neon suit astride a $12 million horse owned by the company for which he works. Fonda, in the role of the reporter she played a few months later in her own production of THE CHINA SYNDROME, needles Redford at a press conference and intimates that he probably has never even eaten the cereal he tub-thumps for. Later, Redford tells Saxon how much he hates what he's doing and Saxon reminds him that he is making more money doing far less dangerous work than he has ever done before. Redford begins rehearsing with the expensive animal, Rising Star, and a bond is established between man and horse. When Redford learns that Rising Star has been doped heavily with tranquilizers in order to calm him for the stage appearance, Redford resents what they are doing to this magnificent beast and horsenaps him, taking him into the desert. Saxon calls the cops and hundreds of officers are dispatched to bring the horse back alive; Redford doesn't matter. Fonda is able to track down Redford (how the others miss him is uncanny) as she desperately wants an exclusive on this story. Redford says he's going to ride the horse to Utah, then let him loose to find his own way. As they trek together, Redford and Fonda fall in love. She notifies her home office of what he intends and the story races across America, with everyone rooting for Redford and Rising Star to make it to Utah before the accursed conglomerate gets them. Saxon now discovers that cereal sales have soared to new levels and Redford is beloved by one and all for his selfless deed. Charges are dropped and Saxon makes a press appearance where he backs up Redford for what he's doing. Redford frees the horse in a picturesque Utah valley and the film concludes. This was the third

teaming of Redford and Fonda (THE CHASE, BAREFOOT IN THE PARK) but was something far short of what might have been. A predictable script is what brought this down. The lofty intentions of showing a reconstituted alcoholic fighting against a monolithic conglomerate with the aid of a woman who, at first, is there for personal gain but later learns to love him, are all there. It is the realization that falls apart. Willie Nelson is super as Redford's manager and proves that he can do more than just write and sing wonderfully. Valerie Perrine, as Redford's former wife, is not given enough to do. Saxon brings excellent dimension to a role that might have been a caricature. Saxon has aged well (albeit losing his hair), and developed into a fine actor after doing many dumb roles in his youth. The picture looks wonderful but hasn't enough substance to merit a higher rating. In the hands of less experienced makers, it would have been "nice work, for a beginner," but we've come to expect much more from Lumet and Stark, et al.

p, Ray Stark; d, Sidney Pollack; w, Robert Garland (based on a screenplay by Garland and Paul Gaer and a story by Shelly Burton); ph, Owen Roizman (Panavision, Technicolor); m, Dave Grusin; ed, Sheldon Kahn; art d, J. Dennis Washington; set d, Mary Swanson; cos, Bernie Pollack; prod d, Stephen Grimes; spec eff, Augie Lohman.

Western/Comedy   Cas.   (PR:A-C MPAA:PG)

ELECTRONIC MONSTER, THE***½   (1960, Brit.) 72m
Anglo-Amalgamated/COL bw
(GB: ESCAPEMENT; AKA: THE ELECTRIC MONSTER)

Ron Cameron (Jeff Keenan), Mary Murphy (Ruth Vance), Meredith Edwards (Dr. Maxwell), Peter Illing (Paul Zakon), Carl Jaffe (Dr. Hoff), Kay Callard (Laura Maxwell), Carl Duering (Blore), Roberta Huby (Verna Berteaux), Felix Felton (Commissaire), Larry Cross (Brad Somers), Carlo Borelli (Signore Kallini), John McCarthy (Claude Denver), Jacques Cey (French Doctor), Armande Guinle (French Farmer), Malou Pantera (Receptionist), Pat Clavin (Receptionist), Alan Gifford (Wayne).

Looking into the mysterious death of a Hollywood star, insurance investigator Cameron discovers an exclusive therapy center where people who want to get away from life for a time are hypnotized, then put in morgue-style drawers to dream for up to six weeks. However, Dr. Illing is using an electronic device to alter the dreams, enabling him to bend the sleepers to his will. An intriguing feature in that it was among the first to examine the possibilities of psychological manipulation and brainwashing.

p, Alec C. Snowden; d, Montgomery Tully; w, Charles Eric Maine, J. MacLaren-Ross (based on the novel Escapement by Maine); ph, Bert Mason; m, Richard Taylor; ed, Geoffrey Muller; art d, Wilfred Arnold.

Science Fiction   (PR:C MPAA:NR)

ELEPHANT BOY***   (1937, Brit.) 91m LEP/UA bw

Sabu (Toomai), Walter Hudd (Petersen), Allan Jeayes (Machua Appa), W. E. Holloway (Father), Bruce Gordon (Rham Lahl), D. J. Williams (Hunter), Wilfrid Hyde-White (Commissioner), Iravatha (Kala Nag).

When first released, this almost-documentary excited everyone who saw it. Although it has not aged well, there is still a great deal of merit to the story, the style and the stars and any young person seeing it cannot fail to love it. Basically simple, ELEPHANT BOY tells the story of Sabu, a young man from a family of four generations of mahouts (elephant handlers). His father is killed and the elephant he rode (and his father and grandfather before him) is given to another driver, over Sabu's pleadings. The new driver is a mean type who doesn't like the elephant and proceeds to treat him harshly. His behavior is rewarded by response on the elephant's part that results in a few broken bones. A death sentence is pronounced on the pachyderm (they think he must have gone crazy and become a rogue elephant) and Sabu steals him late one night. The elephant and Sabu live happily in the jungle (not unlike THE ELECTRIC HORSEMAN's Redford and Rising Star in the Nevada desert) until Sabu discovers a herd of wild elephants that have been the object of an extensive search by the British authorities. Some action, some laughs, a lot of heart. Sabu had actually been a stable worker in the home of a wealthy Indian. Born in Mysore, he was discovered by documentarian Flaherty and cast in this film. He played in several of this type of movies before his untimely death of a heart attack in 1963. He had not yet turned 40 but still looked in his 20s.

p, Alexander Korda; d, Robert Flaherty, Zoltan Korda; w, John Collier, Akos Tolnay, Marcia de Silva (based on the Rudyard Kipling novel Toomai of the Elephants); ph, Osmond Borradaile; m, John Greenwood; ed, William Hornbeck, Charles Crichton; prod d, Vincent Korda; md, Muir Mathieson.

Jungle Drama   (PR:AA MPAA:NR)

ELEPHANT CALLED SLOWLY, AN**   (1970, Brit.) 91m
Morning Star/American Continental c

Virginia McKenna (Ginny), Bill Travers (Bill), George Adamson (Himself), Vinay Inambar (Mr. Mophagee), Joab Collins (Henry), Ali Twaha (Mutiso), Raffles Harman.

McKenna and Travers go to Kenya to house-sit for a friend. The two become quick pals with a few elephants, one of them the title character Slowly. They also visit their neighbor Adamson, and his lions (from the film BORN FREE). The couple meet a lot of animals, most of them surprisingly tame for being in the wilds of Africa. More of a travelog then a dramatic film.

p&w, Bill Travers, James Hill; d, Hill; ph, Simon Trevor (Eastmancolor, Movielab); m, Bert Kaempfert; Howard Blake, ed, Andrew Borthwick; md, Blake; m/l, "A Swingin' Affair," "Market Day," "Happy Trumpeter," "Arikaan Beat," "Tootie Flute," Kaempfert.

Adventure   (PR:A MPAA:G)

ELEPHANT GUN** (1959, Brit.) 92m RANK/Lopert c (GB: NOR THE MOON BY NIGHT)

Belinda Lee *(Alice Lang)*, Michael Craig *(Rusty Miller)*, Patrick McGoohan *(Andrew Miller)*, Anna Gaylor *(Thea Boryslawski)*, Eric Pohlmann *(Anton Boryslawski)*, Pamela Stirling *(Mrs. Boryslawski)*, Lionel Ngakane *(Nimrod)*, Joan Brickhill *(Harriet Carver)*, Ben Heydenrych *(Sergeant Van Wyck)*, Alfred Kumalo *(Chief)*, Doreen Hlantie *(Oasis)*, John Withers *(Sandy)*, Ken Oelofse *(Jan)*, Gordon MacPherson *(Tom)*.

Lee plays a young woman who cares for her sick mum. The only other thing in her life is a pen pal in Africa. When her mother kicks off, Lee heads off to meet her correspondent. Arriving in the Dark Continent she finds her pen pal (McGoohan) is busy chasing elephants, so she settles for his brother, played by Craig. The film ends happily for all, and in the interim there are confrontations between man and beast including lions, cobras and elephants. Lee has it somewhat easier than the men, contending only with the likes of a porcupine. The direction gives the weak script somewhat of a humorous flair. McGoohan and Craig's performances are the straight-laced macho variety found in jungle pictures while Lee manages to squeal on cue. It's really a silly and stupid picture, but redeemed by some interesting animal photography.

p, John Stafford; d, Ken Annakin; w, Guy Elmes (based on the novel by Joy Packer); ph, Harry Waxman (Eastmancolor); m, James Bernard; ed, Alfred Roome; md, John Hollingsworth; art d, John Howell.

Action/Romance (PR:A MPAA:NR)

ELEPHANT MAN, THE**** (1980, Brit.) 125m PAR bw

Anthony Hopkins *(Dr. Frederick Treves)*, John Hurt *(John Merrick)*, Anne Bancroft *(Mrs. Kendal)*, John Gielgud *(Carr Gomm)*, Wendy Hiller *(Mothershead)*, Freddie Jones *(Bytes)*, Michael Elphick *(Night Porter)*, Hannah Gordon *(Mrs. Treves)*, Helen Ryan *(Princess Alex)*, John Standing *(Fox)*, Dexter Fletcher *(Bytes' Boy)*, Lesley Dunlop *(Nora)*, Phoebe Nicholls *(Merrick's Mother)*, Pat Gorman *(Fairground Bobby)*, Claire Davenport *(Fat Lady)*, Orla Pederson *(Skeleton Man)*, Patsy Smart *(Distraught Woman)*, Frederick Treves *(Alderman)*, Stromboli *(Fire Eater)*, Richard Hunter *(Hodges)*, James Cormack *(Pierce)*, Robert Bush *(Messenger)*, Roy Evans *(Cabbie)*, Joan Rhodes *(Cook)*, Nula Conwell *(Nurse)*, Tony London *(Porter)*, Alfie Curtis *(Milkman)*, Bernadette Milnes, Brenda Kemper *(Fighting Women)*, Carole Harrison *(Tart)*, Hugh Manning *(Broadneck)*, Dennis Burgess *(1st Committeeman)*, Fanny Carby *(Mrs. Kendal's Dresser)*, Morgan Sheppard *(Man in Pub)*, Kathleen Byron *(Lady Waddington)*, Gerald Case *(Lord Waddington)*, David Ryall *(Man with Whores)*, Deirdre Costello, Pauline Quirke *(Whores)*, Kenny Baker *(Plumed Dwarf)*, Chris Greener *(Giant)*, Marcus Powell, Gilda Cohen *(Midgets)*, Lisa and Teri Scoble *(Siamese Twins)*, Eiji Kusuhara *(Japanese Bleeder)*, Robert Day *(Little John)*, Patricia Hodge *(Screaming Woman)*, Tommy Wright, Peter Davidson *(Bobbies)*, John Rapley *(King in Panto)*, Hugh Spight *(Puss in Panto)*, Teresa Codling *(Princess in Panto)*, Marion Betzold *(Principal Boy)*, Beryl Hicks *(Fairy)*, Victor Kravchenko *(Lion/Coachman)*, Florenzio Morgado, Caroline Haigh *(Trees)*, Janie Kells, Michele Amas, Penny Wright, Lucie Alford *(Horses)*.

There are many oddities about this black and white film, beyond the fact that it's based on a true story and hews closely to that bizarre tale. Produced by Mel Brooks' company and made in England, it combines British and American actors in a screenplay culled from factual material and having nothing at all to do with the hit play of the same name. There was a bit of noise about lawsuits when the film was released because of the prior play but what the producers and playwright of that original production did not realize was that the story was real and there was no way to copyright anything beyond their interpretation of it, thereby leaving any other version unprotected. Nominated for eight Oscars, it won none in the wake of the victories by COAL MINER'S DAUGHTER, TESS, ORDINARY PEOPLE, and FAME. John Hurt is Merrick, victim of a hideous disease that causes his head to be huge and grotesquely deformed and doesn't enable him to speak clearly due to the malformation inside his mouth. Merrick had been sold to a carnival as a young boy and lived as a freak until found by Dr. Treves (Hopkins) and brought to a hospital where he could be studied. The press gets hold of the news and visiting Hurt in the hospital becomes *the* thing to do for royalty as well as society. So even in virtual seclusion, Hurt is still a freak. Subtly done on all levels, the film shows Hopkins' character to be on dilemma's horns: Is he doing this for medicine or to raise himself higher in society with his discovery? The real elephant man died young when he could no longer support his head with his shoulders and the windpipe closed when he fell asleep in his bed. He was in his 20s. Cult director Lynch (ERASERHEAD) does a wonderful job in evoking 19th-century England. Freddie Francis's black and white photography is flawless as are all technical credits. The picture dwells a bit too long on soul-searching and psychological reasons when it might have done better to just get on with it and let the audience determine what it wanted to. Bancroft (Mel Brooks' wife) is the actress who befriended the elephant man but the role is not what the stage part was and any bite has been removed. On stage, the actress was sexually aroused by being in Merrick's presence. Here, it's all Bancroft can do to keep from yawning. Freddie Jones is excellent as Hurt's "owner," a carny man of the lowest stature. Rather than expose the ugly face at once, the script calls for gradual revelations so that by the time we see the entire face, it can be swallowed without revulsion. Hurt is brilliant in conveying emotions even while hampered by the inability to use his face or even much of his voice. A tour de force from one of the world's finest actors, but one of the worst judges of material. Otherwise, why would he have taken such rotten jobs as THE SHOUT, HEAVEN'S GATE and PARTNERS?

p, Jonathan Sanger; d, David Lynch; w, Christopher DeVore, Eric Bergren, Lynch (based on *The Elephant Man: A Study In Human Dignity* by Ashley Montagu and *The Elephant Man and Other Reminiscences* by Sir Frederick Treves); ph, Freddie Francis (Panavision); m, John Morris, Samuel Barber; ed, Anne V. Coates; prod d, Stuart Craig; art d, Bob Cartwright; set d, Hugh Scaife; cos, Patricia Norris; ex p, Stuart Cornfeld.

Biography Cas. (PR:A-C MPAA:PG)

ELEPHANT STAMPEDE*½ (1951) 70m MON bw

Johnny Sheffield *(Bomba)*, Donna Martell *(Lola)*, Edith Evanson *(Miss Banks)*, Martin Wilkins *(Chief Nagala)*, John Kellogg *(Bob Warren)*, Myron Healey *(Joe Collins)*, Leonard Mudie *(Andy Barnes)*, Guy Kingsford *(Mark Phillips)*.

Hunters Kellogg and Healey are about to make off with a cache of ivory the natives want to give to missionary Evanson, but Bomba the Jungle Boy, Sheffield, calls on his elephant friends to trample them to death. African adventure is strictly kid stuff. (See BOMBA series, Index.)

p, Walter Mirisch; d&w, Ford Beebe; ph, William Sickner; ed, William Austin; spec eff, Max Luttenberg.

Adventure (PR:A MPAA:NR)

ELEPHANT WALK*½** (1954) 102m PAR c

Elizabeth Taylor *(Ruth Wiley)*, Dana Andrews *(Dick Carver)*, Peter Finch *(John Wiley)*, Abraham Sofaer *(Appuhamy)*, Abner Biberman *(Dr. Pereira)*, Noel Drayton *(Atkinson)*, Rosalind Ivan *(Mrs. Lakin)*, Barry Bernard *(Strawson)*, Philip Tonge *(Ralph)*, Edward Ashley *(Gregory)*, Leo Britt *(Chisholm)*, Mylee Haulani *(Rayna)*, Jack Raine *(Norbert)*, Victor Millan *(Koru, Servant)*, Norma Varden *(Mrs. Beezely)*, Carlos Rivero *(Car Servant)*, Delmar Costello *(Native Patient)*, Satini Pualioa *(Foreman)*, Vivien Leigh *(Ruth Wiley in the Ceylon Long Shots)*, The Madhyma Lanka Mandala Dancers *(Themselves)*, Henry Carr, William Bengal Alwis, Reginald Lal Singh, Charles Heard, Rodd Redwing, Adolfo Ornelas, Leslie Sketchley.

Taylor is radiant as the new bride Finch brings home to the ancestral plantation in exotic Ceylon. She is surrounded by menacing jungles and soon becomes a woman living in a doll's house, her husband more concerned with drinking with cronies and honoring the memory of his dead, tyrannical father than attending to her emotional and sexual needs. Handsome American overseer Andrews enters the picture and she soon falls in love with him but before the two can run off, a devastating plague of cholera breaks out and Taylor ministers to the sick. Worse, the elephants who have been tooting and bellowing throughout the film, threatening to crash through the walls of Finch's palatial estate—it was built spitefully and intentionally by his father in the middle of their ancient pathway—finally come stampeding into the mansion, destroying the walls, the fine manor house, and reclaiming their old right of way. Though the production values of this film are superior and the direction is swift, the acting is less than energetic. Finch ambles about like an inebriated oaf, not the decisive master of a great plantation. Andrews is charming but shallow, and Taylor's talent is limited to knitting her pretty eyebrows for the heavy dramatic scenes. The elephant stampede is impressive and a game of polo played on bicycles is fun, but the best acting is performed by supporting players—Sofaer as a truculent major-domo and Biberman as a patient and understanding doctor. This film was originally planned for Laurence Olivier and his then wife, Vivien Leigh. He bowed out and was replaced by Finch but Leigh actually began the movie, then grew ill after a month's production and was replaced by Taylor, although Leigh can still be viewed in some long shots. Leigh traveled to the on-location site in Ceylon but the heat brought on an attack of her recurrent tuberculosis and caused her incessant insomnia; she continued for two weeks at the Paramount lot, then collapsed with a nervous breakdown. In desperation producer Asher borrowed Taylor from MGM, paying that studio $150,000 for her services, plus $3,500 for each day of overtime. More than two dozen dresses designed by Edith Head for Leigh had to be let out for the more fulsome Taylor. The beautiful Elizabeth suffered one of her first in-production tragedies in ELEPHANT WALK. A wind machine malfunctioned and a steel splinter flew into her eye; she was hospitalized and almost lost the sight of one eye. The lush Grigg cinematography and rich Waxman score enhance an otherwise lightweight movie.

p, Irving Asher; d, William Dieterle; w, John Lee Mahin (based on the novel by Robert Standish); ph, Loyal Griggs (Technicolor); m, Franz Maxman; ed, George Tomasini; art d, Hal Pereira, Joseph MacMillan Johnson; set d, Sam Comer, Grace Gregory; cos, Edith Head; ch, Ram Gopal; spec eff, John P. Fulton, Paul Lerpae; process ph, Farciot Edouart.

Romance/Adventure (PR:A MPAA:NR)

11 HARROWHOUSE** (1974, Brit.) 95m FOX c (AKA: ANYTHING FOR LOVE)

Charles Grodin *(Chesser)*, Candice Bergen *(Maren)*, John Gielgud *(Meecham)*, Trevor Howard *(Clyde Massey)*, James Mason *(Watts)*, Peter Vaughan *(Coglin)*, Helen Cherry *(Lady Bolding)*, Jack Watson *(Miller)*, Jack Watling *(Fitzmaurice)*, Cyril Shaps *(Wildenstein)*, Leon Greene *(Toland)*, Joe Powell *(Hickey)*, Peter Forbes Robertson *(Hotel Manager)*, David Rowlands *(Club Manager)*, Richard Montez *(2nd Manager)*, Gilbert France *(Croupier)*, Warwick Sims *(Maren's Friend)*, Rory McDonald *(Rich Young Man)*, Clive Morton *(Sir Harold)*, Larry Cross *(Whitman)*, Glynn Edwards, John Bindon *(Security Officers)*, Jimmy Gardner *(Man in Snack Bar)*, Donald Tandy, Trevor T. Smith *(Men in Vault)*.

Millionaire Howard hires diamond merchant Grodin to rob the vault of a diamond cartel run by Gielgud. The vault is guarded by an elaborate security system headed by Vaughan. Grodin enlists Bergen, his girl friend, and Mason, a disgruntled employee, to help in the heist, which is effected by running a vacuum hose into the vault and sucking out the gems. Back at Howard's estate, the millionaire sics his henchmen on the robbers in order to keep all the haul for himself, and after a long chase over the estate they manage to escape thanks to Cherry, Howard's lady companion, who is sexually attracted to Bergen. Unconvincing, contrived heist film has a terrific supporting cast utterly wasted.

p, Elliot Kastner; d, Aram Avakian; w, Jeffrey Bloom (from an adaptation by Charles Grodin of a novel by Gerald A. Browne); ph, Arthur Ibbetson (Panavision,

DeLuxe Color); m, Michael J. Lewis; ed, Anne V. Coates; art d, Peter Mullins; set d, Jack Stephens; cos, Anthony Mendleson.

Crime (PR:C MPAA:PG)

ELEVENTH COMMANDMENT*½ (1933) 66m Allied Pictures bw

Marian Marsh, Theodore Von Eltz, Alan Hale, Marie Prevost, Ethel Wales, Gloria Shea, Arthur Hoyt, William V. Mong, Lee Moran, Lyman Williams.

An inferior melodrama about a young girl in love whose adoration for a handsome young fellow is met with opposition by her stepfather. The nasty old man tries his best to break the lovers up, but as we've come to expect, love prevails.

d, George Melford; w, Adele Buffington, Kurt Kempler (based on the story by Brandon Fleming); ph, Harry Neumann; ed, Mildred Johnston.

Drama (PR:A MPAA:NR)

ELI ELI*½ (1940) 86m Cinema Service bw

Esther Field, Lazar Freed, Irving Jacobson, Mae Schoenfeld, Muni Serebroff, Rose Greenfield, Max Badin, Paula Lubelska, Eddie Friedlander, Isidor Frankel, Herman Rosen.

Yiddish Language tear-jerker has Field and Freed as aging parents forsaken by their children. Up to modest standards of Yiddish cinema and an old, tragic theme in Yiddish theater. (In Yiddish; English subtitles.)

d, Josef Selden; w, Isidor Frankel; md, Sholom Secunda.

Drama (PR:A MPAA:NR)

ELIMINATOR, THE (SEE: DANGER ROUTE, 1968)

ELINOR NORTON*½ (1935) 71m FOX bw

Claire Trevor (Elinor Norton), Gilbert Roland (Rene Alba), Henrietta Crosman (Christine Somers), Hugh Williams (Tony Norton), Norman Foster (Bill Carroll), Theodore von Eltz, Guy Usher (Army Officers), Cora Sue Collins (Betty).

Trevor is the apex of a romantic triangle. While her husband, Williams, is off fighting WW I, Trevor succumbs to the advances of South American coffee baron Roland. Williams returns home shell-shocked and jealous and Trevor takes him out West to a ranch to cure him. Roland follows his love and the men become friends while Roland helps Williams back to health only to tell him that he is running away with Trevor. Slow-moving and boring, and generally unlikable characters do not help.

p, Sol M. Wurtzel; d, Hamilton MacFadden; w, Rose Franken, Philip Klein (based on the novel The State vs. Elinor Norton by Mary Roberts Rinehart); ph, George Schneiderman; ed, Paul Weatherwax.

Drama (PR:A MPAA:NR)

ELISABETH OF AUSTRIA**½ (1931, Ger.) 110m
Gottschalk/Tobis Forenfilm bw (ELISABETH VON OESTERREICH)

Lil Dagover (Elisabeth of Austria), Maria Solveg (Fanny Angerer), Paul Otto (Franz Joseph), Ekkehard Arend (Crown Prince Rudolph), Gert Pilary (Princess Stephanie), Charlotte Ander (Mary Vetsera), Ida Perry (Archduchess Sophie), Ludwig Stoessel (Bratfisch), Sergius Sax (Crown Prince Ludwig), Ida Wuest (Jolanda Szoerek).

Dagover is a regent suffering through a forced political marriage, the suicides of both her son and her lover, and finally her assassination by an anarchist. Lavishly shot in Austrian locations, the film is almost too complex to follow without a knowledge of 19th-century Central European politics. Lil Dagover is best remembered today as the sleepwalker's victim in THE CABINET OF DOCTOR CALIGARI.

d, Adolf Trotz; w, G. C. Claren, A. Lantz, A. Shirokauer; ph, Frederik Fuglsang; md, Felix Guenther; ch, Jan Trojanswoki.

Biography (PR:A MPAA:NR)

ELIZA COMES TO STAY*½ (1936, Brit.) 75m Twickenham bw

Betty Balfour (Eliza Vandan), Seymour Hicks (Sandy Verrall), Oscar Asche (Herbert), Ellis Jeffreys (Lady Elizabeth), Nelson Keys (Sir Gregory), A. R. Whatmore (Monty Jordan), Vera Bogetti (Vera Laurence), Ben Webster, Diana Ward, Agnes Imlay, Billy Worth, Donald Burr.

Orphan Balfour comes to live with aging bachelor Hicks, who had been expecting an infant, and falls in love with him. Tedious pre-WW I comedy was updated by putting everyone in modern dress.

p, Julius Hagen; d, Henry Edwards; w, H. Fowler Mear (based on a play by H. V. Esmond); ph, Sydney Blythe, William Luff.

Comedy (PR:A MPAA:NR)

ELIZA FRASER***½ (1976, Aus.) 130m Hexagon/Roadshow c

John Castle (Capt. Rory McBryde), Abigail (Buxom Girl), Gerard Kennedy (Martin Cameron), Arna-Maria Winchester (Mrs. Cameron), Noel Ferrier (Capt. James Fraser), Carole Skinner (Mrs. Shortland), Charles Tingwell (Duncan Fraser), Vicki Bray (Mrs. Annie Fraser), Susannah York (Eliza Fraser), John Waters (David Bracefell), Martin Harris (John Graham), Trevor Howard (Capt. Foster Fyans), Leon Lissek (Sergeant), Graham Matherick (Flogger), Dennis Miller (Fyan's Cook), Bruce Spence (Bruce Mclver), John Frawley (Brown), Gus Mercurio (Darge), Bill Hunter (Youlden), Sean Scully (Elliott), Serge Lazareff (Doyle), Martin Phelan (Stone), John Cobley (Hodge), Lindsay Rouchsey (Euenmundi), George Mallaby (Lt. Otter), Ingrid Mason (Mrs. Otter), Alan Finney (Sideshow Spruiker), David Phillips (First Mate).

Ferrier and York are shipwrecked along the Australian coast, captured by aborigines, and held for some time before being rescued. Based on a true incident (the real Eliza Fraser supported herself for years luridly embroidering her tale in

front of crowds at county fairs), the film plays it for laughs and succeeds very well. The entire cast is excellent, with Ferrier a standout.

p&d, Tim Burstall; w, David Williamson; ph, Robin Copping, Dan Burstall (Eastmancolor); m, Bruce Smeaton; ed, Edward McQueen-Mason; art d, Leslie Binns; spec eff, Graham Matherick.

Drama/Comedy (PR:C MPAA:NR)

ELIZABETH OF ENGLAND (SEE: DRAKE THE PIRATE, 1935, Brit.)

ELIZABETH OF LADYMEAD*½ (1949, Brit.) 97m Imperadio/BL c

Anna Neagle (Beth/Elizabeth/Betty/Liz), Hugh Williams (John, 1946), Bernard Lee (John, 1903), Michael Laurence (John, 1919), Nicholas Phipps (John, 1854), Hilda Bayley (Mother, 1946), Isabel Jeans (Mother, 1903), Catherine Paul (Mother, 1854), Jack Allen (Maj. Wrigley, 1946), Ken Warrington (Maj. Wrigley, 1919), Michael Shepley (Maj. Wrigley, 1903), Claude Bailey (Maj. Wrigley, 1854), Norman Pierce, Edgar Norfolk, Edie Martin.

Neagle plays four generations of wives who discover independence while their husbands are off fighting a war. The stories are interesting at first, but by war No. 4 the film becomes pretty dull. Nice to look at, with lavish settings.

p&d, Herbert Wilcox; w, Frank Harvey, Nicholas Phipps (based on the play by Harvey); ph, Max Greene, Robert Walker, Ken Gray (Technicolor); m, Robert Farnon.

Drama (PR:A MPAA:NR)

ELIZABETH THE QUEEN
(SEE: PRIVATE LIVES OF ELIZABETH AND ESSEX, THE, 1939)

ELIZA'S HOROSCOPE** (1975, Can.) 120m O-Zali c

Elizabeth Moorman (Eliza), Tom Lee Jones (Tommy), Lila Kedrova (Lila), Rose Quong (Chinese Astrologer), Richard Manuel (Bearded Composer).

Odd, muddled film deals with Moorman's search for a rich husband after Chinese fortune teller Quong tells her that she will find one. A series of weird incidents follows, at the end of which she still hasn't found her man. Almost hallucinatory at times and the point is anyone's guess.

p,d,w&ed, Gordon Sheppard; ph, Jean Boffety, Paul Van Der Linden, Michel Brault.

Drama (PR:O MPAA:NR)

ELLERY QUEEN AND THE MURDER RING** (1941) 70m COL bw

Ralph Bellamy (Ellery Queen), Margaret Lindsay (Nikki Porter), Charley Grapewin (Inspector Queen), Mona Barrie (Miss Tracy), Paul Hurst (Page), James Burke (Sgt. Velie), George Zucco (Dr. Janney), Blanche Yurka (Mrs. Stack), Tom Dugan (Thomas), Leon Ames (John Stack), Jean Fenwick (Alice Stack), Olin Howland (Dr. Williams), Dennis Moore (Dr. Dunn), Charlotte Wynters (Miss Fox), Pierre Watkin.

Bellamy helps father Grapewin solve a murder in a hospital in this Ellery Queen mystery. More comedy than mystery here, with Hurst and Dugan a pair of funny hit men. (See ELLERY QUEEN series, Index.)

p, Larry Darmour; d, James Hogan; w, Eric Taylor, Gertrude Purcell (based on a story by Ellery Queen); ph, James S. Brown, Jr.; m, Lee Zahler; ed, Dwight Caldwell; art d, Hiecke.

Mystery/Comedy (PR:A MPAA:NR)

ELLERY QUEEN AND THE PERFECT CRIME* (1941) 67m COL bw

Ralph Bellamy (Ellery Queen), Margaret Lindsay (Nikki Porter), Charley Grapewin (Inspector Queen), Spring Byington (Carlotta Emerson), H. B. Warner (Ray Jardin), James Burke (Sgt. Velie), Douglas Dumbrille (John Mathews), John Beal (Walter Mathews), Linda Hayes (Marian Jardin), Sidney Blackmer (Anthony Rhodes), Walter Kingsford (Henry), Honorable Wu (Lee), Charles Lane (Dr. Prouty).

Clumsy series entry has Bellamy discovering the murderer of an unscrupulous utilities promoter who sells shady stocks. The crime is neatly solved by Bellamy and so isn't perfect at all, and the film is a waste of time except for an able supporting cast. (See ELLERY QUEEN series, Index.)

p, Larry Darmour; d, James Hogan; w, Eric Taylor (based on a story by Ellery Queen); ph, James S. Brown, Jr.; m, Lee Zahler; ed, Dwight Caldwell.

Mystery/Comedy (PR:A MPAA:NR)

ELLERY QUEEN, MASTER DETECTIVE** (1940) 58m COL bw

Ralph Bellamy (Ellery Queen), Margaret Lindsay (Nikki Porter), Charley Grapewin (Inspector Queen), James Burke (Sgt. Velie), Michael Whalen (Dr. James Rogers), Marsha Hunt (Barbara Braun), Fred Niblo (John Braun), Charles Lane (Dr. Prouty), Ann Shoemaker (Lydia Braun), Marian Martin (Cornelia), Douglas Fowley (Rocky Taylor), Morgan Wallace (Zachary), Byron Foulger (Amos), Katherine DeMille (Valerie Norris), Lee Phelps (Flynn), Jack Rice.

The kickoff to the bleak nine-picture Ellery Queen series (with four different Ellery Queens) has Bellamy catching the killer of millionaire Niblo at a health spa. A bad start to a bad series except for the inspired touch of having Bellamy meet Lindsay, who promises to become his secretary. (See ELLERY QUEEN series, Index.)

p, Larry Darmour; d, Kurt Neumann; w, Eric Taylor (based on a story by Ellery Queen); ph, James S. Brown, Jr.; ed, Dwight Caldwell.

Mystery/Comedy (PR:A MPAA:NR)

ELLERY QUEEN'S PENTHOUSE MYSTERY** (1941) 69m COL bw

Ralph Bellamy (Ellery Queen), Margaret Lindsay (Nikki Porter), Charley Grapewin (Inspector Queen), Anna May Wong (Lois Ling), James Burke (Sgt. Velie), Eduardo Ciannelli (Count Brett), Frank Albertson (Sanders), Ann Doran (Sheila Cobb), Noel

Madison (*Gordon Cobb*), Charles Lane (*Doc Prouty*), Russell Hicks (*Walsh*), Tom Dugan (*McGrath*), Mantan Moreland (*Roy*), Theodore Von Eltz (*Jim Ritter*).

Mystery writer Bellamy helps his police inspector father (Grapewin) solve the robbery and murder of a Chinese vaudeville performer who was smuggling jewels into the U.S. Above average for the series, but that's not saying much. (See ELLERY QUEEN series, Index.)

p, Larry Darmour; d, James Hogan; w, Eric Taylor (from a story by Ellery Queen); ph, James S. Brown, Jr.; m, Lee Zahler; ed, Dwight Caldwell.

Mystery/Comedy   **(PR:A   MPAA:NR)**

ELMER AND ELSIE**   (1934) 65m PAR bw

George Bancroft (*Elmer Beebe*), Frances Fuller (*Elsie Beebe*), Roscoe Karns (*Rocky Cott*), George Barbier (*John Kincaid*), Nella Walker (*Mrs. Eva Kincaid*), Charles Sellon (*George Simpson*), Helena Phillips Evans (*Ma Simpson*), Ruth Clifford (*Mamie*), Albert Conti (*Barlotti*), Floyce Brown (*Anna*), Vera Stedman (*Blanche*), Helene Lynch (*Ruby*), Marie Wells (*Mabel*), Tom Dempsey (*Joe*), Eddie Baker (*Evans*), Duke York (*Smith*), William Robyns (*Al*), Alf P. James (*Postman*).

Whatever punch and humor the original Kaufman-Connelly play had in 1922 was pretty much lost by this time. Bancroft is a truck driver constantly dominated by his wife, Fuller. Bancroft is cast against type here and despite his best efforts fails completely to carry the role off.

p, Louis D. Lighton; d, Gilbert Pratt; w, Humphrey Pearson (from the play "To The Ladies" by George S. Kaufman and Marc Connelly); ph, William Meller; ed, Richard Currier.

Comedy   **(PR:A   MPAA:NR)**

ELMER GANTRY****   (1960) 146m UA c

Burt Lancaster (*Elmer Gantry*), Jean Simmons (*Sister Sharon Falconer*), Arthur Kennedy (*Jim Lefferts*), Shirley Jones (*Lulu Bains*), Dean Jagger (*William L. Morgan*), Patti Page (*Sister Rachel*), Edward Andrews (*George Babbitt*), John McIntire (*Rev. Pengilly*), Joe Maross (*Pete*), Everett Glass (*Rev. Brown*), Michael Whalen (*Rev. Phillips*), Hugh Marlowe (*Rev. Garrison*), Philip Ober (*Rev. Planck*), Wendell Holmes (*Rev. Ulrich*), Barry Kelly (*Capt. Holt*), Rex Ingram (*Preacher*), Jean Willes, Sally Fraser (*Prostitutes*).

Lancaster is remarkable in one of his finest roles (an Oscar winner), utterly captivating as the lustful, ambitious charlatan created in Sinclair Lewis' powerful novel. And he is drunk at the opening of the film as in the book, roaring drunk, trying to cadge drinks while selling his own brand of gobbledygook scripture. With his brilliant gift of oratory, the self-ordained zealot encounters evangelist Simmons, in a profile lifted directly from Aimee Semple McPherson, as was Lewis' intent. At first Simmons sees Lancaster for the opportunistic skirt-chaser he is, but he pumps up her vanity and is allowed to join her entourage. Together they become famous and rich, until Simmons can build her huge seaside temple. She is in love with Lancaster, who is in love with life and every woman he meets, as he had once been with a preacher's daughter, Jones, now turned prostitute after his deflowering and desertion of her. In revenge, she compromises him in her room while photographers lurk outside, taking pictures. These later appear in the press and cause Lancaster and Simmons to be shunned by most of their fanatical flock. Simmons by then is convinced that she has the power to cure an illness or deformity through divine intervention. While attempting to conduct a revival meeting, a fire breaks out in her temple and she dies in the flames. Lancaster delivers her eulogy and moves off to new adventure. Some minor changes were made by director Brooks who also wrote the script. Gantry is no longer the ordained minister fallen from grace as pictured in the novel, but a traveling salesman who uses the name of "Jesus" in his sales pitch. Kennedy, as his empathic friend, is not another seminary dropout but a cynical, savvy newsman a la H. L. Mencken, yet the characterizations remain intact. Brooks later sarcastically commented that "ELMER GANTRY is the story of man who wants what everyone is supposed to want—money, sex, and religion. He's the All-American boy." All of the acting is above average, even that of Page, a pop singer, and the script is both literate and ironic. Just to watch Lancaster go into his love-and-religion monolog is a wonder to behold, hearing those dulcet lines: "Love is like the morning and the evening star . . ." (Lancaster's portrayal is certainly drawn from the acrobatic evangelist Billy Sunday, particularly when making his "slide to God," duplicating Sunday's slide up and down ramps, using the expertise Sunday gleaned when playing professional baseball.) Jones is a standout as the memory-haunted floozy and won an Oscar for her role. In this pre-MPAA-rated era United Artists thought it prudent to publicly advise exhibitors to admit no one under 16 to see this film as some of the scenes and lines were of an adult nature. Daring for the day, ELMER GANTRY is now just great drama on film.

p, Bernard Smith; d&w, Richard Brooks (based on the novel by Sinclair Lewis); ph, John Alton; m, Andre Previn; ed, Marge Fowler; cos, Dorothy Jenkins.

Drama   **Cas.**   **(PR:C   MPAA:NR)**

ELMER THE GREAT***   (1933) 64m WB/FN bw

Joe E. Brown (*Elmer*), Patricia Ellis (*Nellie*), Frank McHugh (*High-Hips Healy*), Claire Dodd (*Evelyn*), Preston Foster (*Walker*), Russell Hopton (*Whitey*), Sterling Holloway (*Nick*), Emma Dunn (*Mrs. Kane*), Charles Wilson (*Bull McWade*), Jessie Ralph (*Sarah Crosby*), Douglas Dumbrille (*Stillman*), Charles Delaney (*Johnny Abbott*), Berton Churchill (*Col. Moffitt*), J. Carrol Naish (*Jerry*), Gene Morgan (*Noonan*), Lloyd Neal.

Likable baseball comedy stars Brown as a home-run hitter who beats both gangsters and cheating pitchers to win the World Series for the Cubs against the Yankees. Brown's acting is no great shakes, but his mugging comedy talents provide many a laugh and he can play baseball, having done so professionally before going into show biz. The Ring Lardner-George M. Cohan play was first filmed in 1929 as FAST COMPANY.

p, Ray Griffith; d, Mervyn LeRoy; w, Tom Geraghty (based on a play by Ring Lardner and George M. Cohan); ph, Arthur Todd; ed, Thomas Pratt.

Comedy   **(PR:A   MPAA:NR)**

ELOPEMENT**   (1951) 82m FOX bw

Clifton Webb (*Howard Osborne*), Anne Francis (*Jake Osborne*), Charles Bickford (*Tom Reagan*), William Lundigan (*Matt Reagan*), Reginald Gardiner (*Roger Evans*), Evelyn Varden (*Millie Reagan*), Margalo Gillmore (*Claire Osborne*), Tommy Rettig (*Daniel Reagan*), J. Farrell MacDonald (*Mr. Simpson*), Julia Dean (*Mrs. Simpson*), Howard Price (*Pinky*), William Bouchey (*Dr. Brenner*), Maude Wallace (*Mrs. Brenner*), Selmer Jackson (*Dr. Halsey*), Norman Leavitt (*Clerk*), Doris Kemper (*Pinkie's Mother*), Frank Ferguson (*Pinkie's Father*), Michael Ross (*Sid*), Parley Baer (*Charlie*), Robert Foulk (*Bert*).

Industrial designer Webb wants his daughter (Francis) to follow in his footsteps, but on her graduation from college she elopes with psychology professor Lundigan. Both families are infuriated and take off after the pair, intending to get the wedding annulled. They start out at each other's throats but soon become friends. When they catch up to the lovers they find them on the verge of breaking up, so both families pitch in to keep them together. Webb's performance keeps the shallow story from falling apart.

p, Fred Kohlmar; d, Henry Koster; w, Bess Taffel; ph, Joseph La Shelle; m, Cyril J. Mockridge; ed, William B. Murphy; md, Lionel Newman; art d, Lyle Wheeler, Richard Irvine; spec eff, Fred Sersen.

Comedy   **(PR:A   MPAA:NR)**

ELUSIVE CORPORAL, THE***½   (1963, Fr.) 108m
Pathe-Cinema/Union bw (LE CAPORAL EPINGLE)

Jean-Pierre Cassel (*The Corporal*), Claude Brasseur (*Pater*), Claude Rich (*Ballochet*), Jean Carmet (*Emile*), Mario David (*Caruso*), Philippe Castelli (*Electrician*), Jacques Jouanneau (*Penche-a-Gauche*), Conny Froboess (*Erika*), Raymond Jourdan (*Dupieu*), O. E. Hasse (*Drunk on the Train*), Guy Bedos (*Stutterer*), Gerard Darrieu (*Cross-Eyed Man*), Sacha Briquet (*Escaping "Woman" Prisoner*), Lucien Raimbourg (*Station Guard*), Francois Darbon (*French Soldier Married to German Peasant*), Elisabeth Marcus, Elisabeth Stiepl, Helmut Janatsch.

Cassel, The Corporal, is accompanied by friends Brasseur and Rich in an escape attempt from a German prison in 1940. They are caught and sent to a detention center where Rich is separated from the other two. The Corporal and Brasseur again try an escape, but the try is aborted. Eventually The Corporal is reunited with Rich, though he is no longer paired with Brasseur, who has had enough of trying to escape. After getting a toothache, The Corporal meets and falls in love with the daughter of a German dentist. He again tries unsuccessfully to escape. Finally, by the sixth attempt, he gets away and is safely reunited with Brasseur in Paris, where they vow to aid the Resistance. Renoir has again dealt with prisoners-of-war, which he so brilliantly addressed in THE GRAND ILLUSION. This has, however, been compared more closely to THE LOWER DEPTHS in its reduction of the characters to their barest existence. When the picture was released, Renoir loudly protested cuts which were made in the newsreel segments, which were invaluable, the director felt, to the theme of liberty. An early collaboration with Charles Spaak (THE GRAND ILLUSION) on the script was abandoned.

p, J. W. Beyer; d, Jean Renoir; w, Renoir, Guy Lefranc; ph, Georges Leclerc; m, Joseph Kosma; ed, Renee Lichtig; art d, Wolf Witzemann; set d, Eugene Herrly; cos, Witzemann.

War/Drama/Comedy   **Cas.**   **(PR:A   MPAA:NR)**

ELUSIVE PIMPERNEL, THE
(SEE: FIGHTING PIMPERNEL, THE, 1950)

ELVIRA MADIGAN****   (1967, Swed.) 90m Europa-Janco/Cinema V c

Pia Degermark (*Elvira*), Thommy Berggren (*Sixten Sparre*), Lennart Malmer (*Friend*), Nina Widerberg (*Little Girl*), Cleo Jensen (*Cook*).

A retelling of a famous love affair in 19th-century Sweden, this is the story of a tight-rope performer (Degermark) and an army lieutenant (Berggren) who deserts his family to "find a new freedom" for himself with Degermark. Their joys and tribulations along the star-crossed path they have chosen for themselves are beautifully photographed by Jorgen Persson, and director Bo Widerberg deliberately shuns any hint of Hollywood-type sentimentality as the lovers go on denying the realities of life to their inevitable doom. Additional music by Mozart and Vivaldi is ideally suited to film.

d,w&ed, Bo Widerberg (based on a ballad by Johan Lindstrom Saxon); ph, Jorgen Persson; m, Ulf Bjorlin.

Drama   **Cas.**   **(PR:O   MPAA:NR)**

ELVIS! ELVIS!**   (1977, Swed.) 101m
Moviemakers-Swedish Film Institute-Sandrews c

Lele Dorazio (*Elvis*), Lena-Pia Bernhardsson (*Elvis's Mother*), Fred Gunnarsson (*Elvis's Father*), Elisaveta (*Elvis's Grandmother*), Allan Edwall (*Elvis's Grandfather*).

Sporadically charming and occasionally touching story of an intelligent 7-year-old boy, Dorazio, whose mother is completely devoted to the "King of Rock'n'Roll," to the point of naming her son after him. The boy understands most everything and everybody around him, but is not understood by anyone except his grandparents. Based on a series of stories by Gripe about a real boy named Elvis Karlsson.

p, Bert Sundberg; d, Kay Pollak; w, Maria Gripe, Pollak; ph, Mikhael Salomon, Torbjoern Andersson (Eastmancolor); m, Ralph Lundsten; ed, Lasse Lundberg.

Drama   **(PR:A   MPAA:NR)**

EMBALMER, THE zero   (1966, Ital.) 83m
Gondola/Europix-Consolidated bw (IL MOSTRO DI VENEZIA)

Maureen Brown, Gin Mart, Elmo Caruso, Viki Castillo, Luciano Gasper, Anita
Todesco, Alcide Gazzotto, Alba Brotto, Carlo Russo, Antonio Grossi, Jack Judd,
Paola Vaccari, Maria Rosa Vizzina, Gaetano Dell'Era, Pietro Walter, Roberto
Contero, Francesco Bagarrini.

A stupid Italian horror film tells about a madman in Venice who embalms his
female victims. Sometimes he parades around in a monk's shroud and when he
goes hunting for his beautiful victims he puts on scuba gear and swims up and
down the canals of Venice. A newspaperman finally tracks down the fiend and
puts an end to the mess.

p, Christian Marvel, Walter Manley; d, Dino Tavella; w, Tavella, G. Muretta; ph,
Mario Parapetti; m, Marcello Gigante; art d, Giuseppe Ranieri.

Horror   (PR:C MPAA:NR)

EMBARRASSING MOMENTS½**   (1930) 60m UNIV bw

Reginald Denny (Thaddeus Cruikshank), Merna Kennedy (Marion Fuller), Otis
Harlan (Adam Fuller), William Austin (Jasper Hickson), Virginia Sale (Aunt
Prudence), Greta Granstedt (Betty Black), Mary Foy (Mrs. Hickson).

Kennedy is engaged to marry vain dandy Austin, and she doesn't want to go
through with it. She invents a name and claims to be married, but Denny, whose
name it is, shows up and wrecks the plan but wins the girl from the fop. Harlan is
very entertaining as Kennedy's self-important and easily annoyed father.

d, William James Craft; w, Earle Snell, Gladys Lehman (based on a story by Snell);
ph, Arthur Todd; ed, Duncan Mansfield.

Comedy   (PR:A MPAA:NR)

EMBARRASSING MOMENTS*½   (1934) 67m UNIV bw

Chester Morris (Jerry Randolph), Marion Nixon (Jane), Walter Woolf [King] (Paul),
John Wray (Slug), Alan Mowbray (Ahearn), Huntley Gordon (Runyon), George
Stone (Louie), Henry Armetta (Morganza), Gay Seabrook (Miss Dodd), Herman
Bing (Bartender), Virginia Sale (Mother), Jane Darwell (Mrs. Stuckelberger),
Charles Wilson (Attorney), John T. Murray (Lawyer), Lois January (Tipsy Girl),
Christian Frank, Carl Miller (Men), Charles E. Coleman (Bit).

Morris is a practical joker who is taught a lesson when one of his victims pretends
to commit suicide. A few funny moments, but overall the plot line is weak.

d, Edward Laemmle; w, Gladys Unger, Dickson Morgan, Charles Logue (based on
a story by Wiliam Anthony McGuire); ph, Charles Stumar; m/l, "What a Fool Am
I," "I Won't Talk about Tomorrow," Eddie Ward, C. Waggner.

Comedy   (PR:A MPAA:NR)

EMBASSY½**   (1972, Brit.) 90m Hemdale c

Richard Roundtree (Shannon), Chuck Connors (Kesten), Marie-Jose Nat (Laure),
Ray Milland (Ambassador), Broderick Crawford (Dunninger), Max von Sydow
(Gorenko), David Bauer (Kadish), Larry Cross (Gamble), David Healy (Phelan),
Karl Held (Rylands), Sarah Marshall (Miss Harding), Dee Pollack (Stacey), Afif
Boulos (Foreign Minister), Leila Buheiry (Leila), Gail Clymer (Switchboard Oper-
ator), Edmond Rannania (1st Man in Black), Mounir Massari (Michel el Fahdi),
Saladin Nader (Roger), David Parker (Tuler), Dean Turner (Clem Gelber), Peter
Smith (Cypher Clerk).

Von Sydow is a Soviet defector under asylum at the U.S. embassy in Beirut. Air
Force colonel Connors, in reality a Russian spy, infiltrates the embassy and
wounds Von Sydow. He is captured, escapes, is recaptured, escapes again, and is
captured yet again. So-so espionage thriller, with Von Sydow typically fine, but it is
Connors' performance as a killer that stands out.

p, Mel Ferrer; d, Gordon Hessler; w, William Fairchild, John Bird (based on a novel
by Stephen Coulter); ph, Raoul Coutard; m, Jonathan Hodge; ed, Willy Kemplen;
prod d, John Howell; art d, Maurice Labaye Fanykovy; set d, Klary Confalonieri;
prod d, John Howell; m/l, "Somebody Stop This Madness," Biddu.

Spy Drama   (PR:C MPAA:NR)

EMBEZZLED HEAVEN   (1959,Ger.) 92m Rhombus/UFA c
(DER VERUNTREUTE HIMMEL)

Annie Rosar (Teta Linek), Hans Holt (Chaplain Seydel), Victor de Kowa (Theo),
Vilma Degischer (Livia Argan), Fred Liewehr (Leopold Argan), Kurt Meisel
(Mojmir), Kai Fischer (Mascha), Rudolf Vogel (Kompert), Lotte Lang (Frau Linek),
Jane Tilden (Frau Fleissig), Christine Kaufmann (Doris), Edith Elmay (Elli), Ulla
Moritz (Mizzi), Kurt Keintel (Pastor of Hustopec), Fritz Muliar (Fasching), Pope Pius
XII.

Rosar is a cook who saves all her money to give to her nephew, Meisel, so he can
study for the priesthood, in hopes that this will guarantee her a place in heaven.
Meisel, however, is much more interested in pursuing a life of vice, and when the
old woman discovers that her money has gone to bad ends, she embarks on a
pilgrimage to Rome. In a nicely done crowd sequence in which documentary
footage of Pope Pius XII is intercut with shots of Rosar, she feels her sins lifted,
then dies happily. Mediocre adaptation of this Franz Werfel novel will interest
those who want to see the Pope in what is almost a full-fledged part. Others will be
bored. (Dubbed in English.)

d&w, Ernst Marischka; ph, Bruno Mondi (Agfacolor); m, Anton Profes.

Drama   (PR:A MPAA:NR)

EMBEZZLER, THE*½   (1954, Brit.) 61m Kenilworth/GFD bw

Charles Victor (Henry Paulson), Zena Marshall (Mrs. Forrest), Cyril Chamberlain
(Johnson), Leslie Weston (Piggott), Avice Landone (Miss Ackroyd), Peggy Mount
(Mrs. Larkin), Michael Gregson (Dr. Forrest), Frank Forsyth (Inspector Gale), Pat-
rick Jordan, Martin Wyldeck, Olive Kirby, Tony Lennon, Chris Bank, Lesley Carol

[Carol Lesley], Phyllis Morris, Sam Kydd, Alastair Hunter, Dennis Chinnery,
Ronnie Stevens, Ian Fleming, Michael Craig.

Marshall, the wife of a doctor, befriends a bank clerk embezzler who is in flight
from the bank after his guilt is exposed. Learning that Marshall is being
blackmailed by a former lover, the bank clerk saves her and loses his own life.

p, Robert S. Baker, Monty Berman; d&w, John Gilling; ph, Jonah Jones.

Crime   (PR:A MPAA:NR)

EMBRACEABLE YOU½**   (1948) 79m WB bw

Dane Clark (Eddie), Geraldine Brooks (Marie), S. Z. Sakall (Sammy), Wallace Ford
(Ferria), Richard Rober (Sig Ketch), Lina Romay (Libby), Douglas Kennedy (Dr.
Wirth), Mary Stuart (Miss Purdy), Philip Van Zandt (Matt), Rod Rogers (Bernie).

While driving a killer from the murder scene, Clark runs over Brooks. Detective
Ford is sure of Clark's guilt but is unable to prove it, so he forces him to care for the
girl, who will die soon from a blood clot caused by the accident. Clark falls in love
with her and begins blackmailing the killer in the getaway car for the money to
care for her. The tearjerker climax has him marrying Brooks, who promptly dies.
Sentimental, but not too bad.

p, Saul Elkins; d, Felix Jacoves; w, Edna Anhalt (based on the story "Sunburst" by
Dietrich V. Hanneken, Aleck Block); ph, Carl Gutherie; m, William Lava; ed,
Thomas Reilly.

Drama   (PR:A MPAA:NR)

EMBRACERS, THE*   (1966) 65m Yucca/Joseph Brenner bw
(AKA: THE GREAT DREAM; NOW)

Lois Adams (The Girl), Gary Graver (The Boy), Billy Rhodes (The Drunken Man),
R.J. Gristak (The Strange Man), John Romeyn (The Boy on the Beach), Bert Byers,
Robert Parr, Tony Tsavidis, Robert Huard (The "Keepers"), Murray Bolen.

Adams is seduced on the beach by a young man, who then takes her into his
Hollywood living quarters because she is homeless. There, four of the young man's
friends rape her while the young man is away; Adams finally escapes them. She
meets a struggling actor. They fall in love; the four thugs find them and beat up the
actor and rape Adams again. Mishap upon mishap follows the girl and the actor
until finally the actor decides he has had enough of Hollywood and goes home
without the girl. As a story of disillusion and loneliness, this one is unrelenting on
making its points. An almost wholly negative film experience.

p,d&w, Gary Graver; ph, John Willheim; m, Les McCann.

Drama   (PR:C MPAA:NR)

EMBRYO*   (1976) 108m Cine Artists c

Rock Hudson (Dr. Paul Holliston), Diane Ladd (Martha), Barbara Carrera (Victoria),
Roddy McDowall (Riley), Ann Schedeen (Helen), John Elerick (Gordon), Jack
Colvin (Dr. Winston), Vincent Bagetta (Collier), Joyce Spitz (Trainer), Dick Win-
slowe (Forbes), Lina Raymond (Janet Novak), Dr. Joyce Brothers (Herself).

Hudson grows beautiful Carrera in a test tube and uses tapes to program her into a
superintelligent superlover, but soon she begins to deteriorate and Hudson ends
up killing her, crying as he clutches her withered corpse. Film starts out interestingly, but rapidly degenerates into idiocy.

p, Arnold H. Orgolini, Anita Doohan; d, Ralph Nelson; w, Jack W. Thomas,
Doohan (based on a story by Thomas); ph, Fred Koenekamp (DeLuxe Color); m,
Gil Melle; ed, John Martinelli; art d, Joe Alves; set d, Phil Abramson.

Science Fiction   **Cas.**   (PR:C MPAA:PG)

EMERGENCY! 1953   (SEE: HUNDRED HOUR HUNT, 1953)

EMERGENCY**   (1962, Brit.) 63m But bw

Glyn Houston (Inspector Harris), Zena Walker (Joan Bell), Dermot Walsh (John
Bell), Colin Tapley (Dr. Lloyd), Garard Green (Prof. Graham), Anthony Dawes (Sgt.
Phillips), Edward Ogden (Tommy Day), Helen Forrest (Mrs. Day).

A little girl is dying and only a transfusion of a rare blood type can save her. A
search is started for a soccer player, a fugitive killer, and a traitor, each known to
have the requisite blood type. Competent though dull remake of HUNDRED
HOUR HUNT (1953).

p&d, Francis Searle; w, Don Nicholl, James O'Connolly (based on a story by Lewis
Gilbert, Vernon Harris).

Drama   (PR:A MPAA:NR)

EMERGENCY CALL**   (1933) 70m RKO bw

Bill Boyd (Joe Bradley), Wynne Gibson (Mabel Weenie), William Gargan (Steve
Brennan), Betty Furness (Alice Averill), Reginald Mason (Dr. Averill), Edwin
Maxwell (Tom Rourke), George E. Stone (Sammie Jacobs), Merna Kennedy (File
Clerk), Ruth Fellows (Mildred), Jane Darwell (Head Nurse), Arthur Hoyt (Male
Secretary), Oscar Apfel, Paul Fix, Alberta Vaughn, Helen Lynch, Gertrude Sut-
ton, Larry Schoebel, Cyril Ring.

Racketeers have taken over the hospital where Boyd is a surgeon and Gargan his
driver. Nurse Gibson shoots the gang leader and Gargan ends up murdered,
leaving Boyd to carry on the fight. Boyd and Gargan were teamed a number of
times and this is by far the best of the lot.

p, Sam Jaffe; d, Edward Cahn; w, John B. Clymer, Joseph L. Mankiewicz (based
on a story by Clymer, James Ewens); ph, Roy Hunt; ed, William Hamilton; set d,
Van Nest Polglase, Al Herman.

Crime   (PR:A MPAA:NR)

EMERGENCY CALL, 1953   (SEE: HUNDRED HOUR HUNT, 1953)

EMERGENCY HOSPITAL**½ (1956) 62m UA bw

Margaret Lindsay (*Janet Carey*), Walter Reed (*Sgt. Arnold*), Byron Palmer (*Ben Caldwell*), Rita Johnson (*Norma Mullen*), John Archer (*Dr. Ellis*), Jim Stapleton (*Jimmy Arnold*), Peg LaCentra (*Fran Richards*), Frank Fenton (*Edward Northrop*), George Cisar (*Mr. Fanmorn*), Tito Vuolo (*Ramon*), Mary Carver (*Ann Banks*), Joy Lee (*Mitsi*), Vera Francis (*Vera Winston*), Maxine Gates (*Sylvia Tetlow*), Robert Keys (*Flaherty*), Jan Englund (*Marie Johnson*), Mark Lowell (*Harry Johnson*), William "Red" Murphy (*Will Teeter*), George Sawaya (*Jack Larson*), Gary Gray (*Earl Fanmorn*), Rhodes Reason (*Ross*), William Boyet (*Traffic Officer*), Saul Martell (*Robert Wilson*), John Merrick (*Alverson*).

Episodic film deals with one night in Los Angeles' Emergency Hospital. Chief story deals with doctor Lindsay turning down the marriage proposal of wealthy Palmer because of his speed-demon driving habits. She has a change of heart when she learns he wrecked his expensive sports car rather than hit a crippled motorcyclist. One incident flows smoothly into another at a nice clip through the film's 62 minutes.

p, Howard W. Koch; d, Lee Sholem; w, Don Martin; ph, William Margulies; m, Paul Dunlap; ed, John F. Schreyer; cos, Wesley V. Jefferies.

Drama (PR:A MPAA:NR)

EMERGENCY LANDING* (1941) 67m PRC bw

Forrest Tucker (*Jerry*), Carol Hughes (*Betty*), Evelyn Brent (*Maude*), Emmett Vogan (*Doc*), William Halligan (*Lambert*), George Sherwood (*Jones*), Joaquin Edwards (*Pedro*), I. Stanford Jolley (*Karl*), Stanley Price (*Otto*), Jack Lescoulie (*North*), Paul Scott (*Colonel*).

Tucker is a test pilot and Vogan the designer of a radio-controlled plane which crashes on its first test. While the pair try to figure out the problem they have to contend with, spoiled rich girl Hughes appears on the scene and thankfully so, providing whatever interest this super low-budget film may have.

p, Jed Buell; w, William Beaudine; w, Martin Mooney; ph, Jack Greenhalgh; ed, Robert Crandall.

Drama (PR:A MPAA:NR)

EMERGENCY SQUAD** (1940) 58m PAR bw

William Henry (*Pete Barton*), Louise Campbell (*Betty Bryant*), Richard Denning (*Dan Barton*), Robert Paige (*Chester Miller*), Anthony Quinn (*Nick Buller*), John Miljan (*Slade Wiley*), John Marston (*Lt. Murdock*), Joseph Crehan (*Editor Joyce*), Catherine Proctor (*Emily*), James Seay (*Slim*), Walter Tetley (*Matt*), Lillian Elliott (*Landlady*), Jack Kennedy (*Callahan*), Weldon Heyburn (*Lennie*), Kenneth Duncan (*Jack*), Jimmie Dundee (*Jimmy*), Stanley Blystone (*Mack*), Wilfred Roberts (*Wally*), Barbara Barondess (*Ada*), Henry Blair (*Ada's Son*), Pat O'Malley (*Fire Captain*), Darryl Hickman (*Bob*), Zeffie Tilbury (*Mrs. Cobb*).

Campbell is a young reporter whose boss (Crehan) tells her to get a front page scoop. She tags along with Emergency Squad drivers Henry and Denning while they stage a rescue at a burning chemical plant. Later, while investigating a series of accidents at a tunnel project, she learns that contractor Miljan and racketeer Quinn are involved. They take her on a tour of the project timed to end just before another explosion in order to divert suspicion from themselves, but a sudden cave-in traps them in the tunnel with only ten minutes before the bomb is to go off. Henry and Denning stage a last-minute rescue but one of them is killed, leaving Campbell in the arms of the other. Routine B stuff.

p, Stuart Walker; d, Edward Dmytryk; w, Garnett Weston, Stuart Palmer (based on a story by Robert Musel, Michael Raymond); ph, Stuart Thompson; m, Boris Morros; ed, Everett Douglas; art d, Hans Dreier, Franz Bachelin.

Drama (PR:A MPAA:NR)

EMERGENCY WARD (SEE: CAREY TREATMENT, THE, 1962)

EMERGENCY WEDDING** (1950) 78m COL bw

Larry Parks (*Peter Kirk*), Barbara Hale (*Helen Hunt*), Willard Parker (*Vandemer*), Una Merkel (*Emma*), Alan Reed (*Tony*), Eduard Franz (*Dr. Helmer*), Irving Bacon (*Filbert*), Don Beddoe (*Forbish*), Jim Backus (*Ed Hamley*), Teru Shimada (*Ho*), Myron Welton (*Freddie*), Ian Wolfe (*Dr. White*), Helen Spring (*Miss Toomey*), Greg McClure (*Richard Andrews*), Queenie Smith (*Rose*), Jerry Mickelsen (*Newsboy*), George Meader (*Motel Manager*), Dorothy Vaughn (*Woman Patient*), Boyd Davis, Sydney Mason, Pierre Watkin (*Doctors*), Lucille Shamburger, Arthur Howard, Virginia Cruzon, Grace Burns, Elsa Peterson (*Bits*), Cosmo Sardo (*Headwaiter*), Joe Palma, Frank Arnold (*Waiters*), Wilson Benge (*Frederick, the Butler*), Myron Healey, Mike Lally, Warren Mace, Shirley Ballard, Jean Willes, Mary Emery (*Guests*), Thomas F. Martin (*Bartender*), Stephen Chase (*Kirk*), Thomas Patrick McCormick (*Baby*), Billy Nelson (*Cab Driver*), James O'Gatty (*Pedestrian*), Ted Jordan (*Orderly*), William E. Green (*Chairman*), James Conaty, James Carlisle (*Committee Men*), Bobby Johnson (*Sammy*), Vivian Mason (*Kitty*), Kathleen O'Malley (*Mabel*), Louise Kane (*Switchboard Girl*), Harry Harvey (*Dr. Wilson*), William Forrest (*Personnel Director*), Frank Cady (*Mr. Hoff*), Ann Tyrrell (*Miss Nielson*), Simon "Stuffy" Singer (*Little Boy*), Paul Bradley, John Kascier, Richard LaMarr (*Barbers*), Elizabeth Flournoy (*Saleswoman*), Mary Newton (*Governess*), Ruth Wareen (*Shopper*), Virginia Cruzon (*Dignified Woman*), Muriel Maddox (*Mrs. Crain*), Marjorie Stapp (*Mrs. Young*), Beverly Crane (*Mrs. Hayes*), Ted Stanhope, Henry Sylvester (*Clerks*).

Hale is a doctor married to rich playboy Parks. He thinks she is spending too much time with her male patients and makes a fool of himself trying to prove her guilt, which leads her to leave him. But then he puts up the money for a new hospital and she comes back to him. A remake of YOU BELONG TO ME, which was much better.

p, Nat Perrin; d, Edward Buzzell; w, Perrin, Claude Binyon (based on a story by Dalton Trumbo); ph, Burnett Guffey; m, Werner R. Heymann; ed, Al Clark; md, Morris Stoloff; art d, Carl Anderson.

Drama (PR:A MPAA:NR)

EMIGRANTS, THE**** (1972, Swed.) 151m Filindustri Svensk/WB c (UTVANDRARNA)

Max von Sydow (*Karl Oskar*), Liv Ullmann (*Kristina*), Eddie Axberg (*Robert*), Svenolof Bern (*Nils*), Aina Alfredsson (*Marta*), Allan Edwall (*Danjel*), Monica Zetterlund (*Ulrika*), Pierre Lindstedt (*Arvid*), Hans Alfredson (*Jonas Petter*), Ulla Smidje (*Danjel's Wife*), Eva-Lena Zetterlund (*Ulrika's Daughter*), Gustaf Faringborg (*Vicar*), Ake Fridell (*Aron*), Agneta Prytz (*Fina Kajsa*), Halvar Bjork (*Anders, Her Son*), Arnold Alfredsson (*Kyrkvarden*), Bror Englund (*Mans Jakob*), Tom C. Fouts (*Patter Jackson*), Goran Lundin (*1st Mate*), Peter Hoimark (*2nd Mate*), Erik Johansson (*Capt. Lorentz*), Staffan Liljander (*Landborg*), Ditte, Lasse, and Pelle Martinsson, Annika Nyhammar, Yvonne Oppstedt, Linn Ullmann (*Children*).

An engaging, well-crafted film about a group of Swedish peasants who migrate to America in the mid-19th century. One of the best films to show the tribulations, bravery, and faith the people had who helped build this country. The film is split into three parts: their leaving Sweden, the voyage over, and the journey to Minnesota. Acting is superb by all cast members, but some might be put off by the film's pace. The tone is very lyrical and the photography (by director Troell) gives an added dimension. Sequel is THE NEW LAND.

p, Bengt Forslund; d, Jan Troell; w, Troell, Forslund (adapted from the novels of Vilhelm Moberg); ph, Troell (Technicolor); m, Erik Nordgren; ed, Troell; art d, P.A. Lundgren, Berndt Fritiof; cos, Ulla-Britt Soderlund.

Drama (PR:A MPAA:PG)

EMIL*** (1938, Brit.) 63m Wainwright/GAU bw (GB: EMIL AND THE DETECTIVES)

George Hayes (*Man in Bowler Hat*), Mary Glynne (*Mrs. Blake*), John Williams (*Emil Blake*), Clare Greet (*Grandmother*), George Merritt (*PC*), Marion Foster (*Polly*), Donald Pittman (*Gussy*), Bobby Rietti (*Professor*), John Singer (*Tuesday*), Derek Blomfield (*Jerry*), Ricky Hyland (*Flying Stag*), Roy McBane.

Little Williams is given drugged candy by Hayes, who then lifts the boy's money. Williams gets some other children together and they track the thief down, recovering the money and collecting a reward from the police. So-so telling of a classic German children's tale, released in 1935 in England.

p, Richard Wainwright; d, Milton Rosmer; w, Cyrus Brooks, Margaret Carter, Frank Launder (based on the novel *Emil Und Die Detektiven* by Erich Kastner and a screenplay by Billy Wilder); ph, Mutz Greenbaum; ed, C. Heck.

Crime/Children (PR:AA MPAA:NR)

EMIL AND THE DETECTIVE***½ (1931, Ger.) 73m Ufa bw (EMIL UND DIE DETEKTIVE)

Rolf Wenkhaus (*Emil*), Fritz Rasp (*Man with the Derby*), Kaethe Haack (*Mrs. Tischbein*), Olga Engl (*Grandmother*), Inge Landgut (*Pony Huetchen*), Hans Schaufuss (*Gustav the Hoop*), Hans Richter (*Flying Stag*), Hans Loehr (*Dienstag*), Ernst-Eberhard Reling (*Gerald*), Rudolf Biebrach, Hubert Schmitz, Waldemar Kapezyk.

Wenkhaus, as Emil, is going to Berlin to visit his grandmother, but on the train he is doped and robbed by Rasp. He recovers in time to see the man leave and follows him all over, eventually picking up more children to help him. They catch the thief and the police give Emil 1,000 marks and a plane ride home, where the mayor and town band give him a hero's welcome. This first filmization of Erich Kastner's children's novel is by far the best and most exciting and does not condescend to its juvenile audience. (In German.)

p, Guenther Stapenhorst; d, Gerhard Lamprecht; w, Billy Wilder (based on the novel *Emil Und Die Detektiven* by Erich Kastner); ph, Werner Brandes; m, Schmidt-Boelcke.

Crime/Children (PR:AA MPAA:NR)

EMIL AND THE DETECTIVES** (1964) 99m BV c

Walter Slezak (*Baron*), Bryan Russell (*Emil*), Roger Mobley (*Gustav*), Heinz Schubert (*Grundeis*), Peter Ehrlich (*Muller*), Cindy Cassel (*Pony*), Elsa Wagner (*Nana*), Wolfgang Volz (*Stucke*), Eva-Ingeborg Scholz (*Frau Tischbein*), Franz Nicklisch (*Desk Sergeant*), Brian Richardson (*Professor*), David Petrychka (*Dienstag*), Robert Swann (*Hermann*), Ann Noland (*Frieda*), Ron Johnson (*Rudolf*), Rick Johnson (*Hans*), Paul Glawton (*Traffic Policeman*), Gerhard Retschy (*Officer Kiessling*), Viktor Hospach (*Newsstand Proprietor*), Konrad Thoms (*Waiter*), Egon Vogel (*Dispatcher*), Gert Wiedenhofen (*Policeman*), Georg Rebentisch (*Bus Driver*), Rolf Rolphs (*Butler*), Roswitha Habedank (*Parlor Maid*).

The sixth version of Erich Kastner's novel (two by the Germans, one each by the British, Japanese, and Brazilians) gets the full Disney treatment, pumped up and pasteurized until it barely resembles its source. This time Russell is the robbed Emil, enlisting a crowd of kids to help him catch pickpocket Schubert. The photography of a still bombed-out Berlin is excellent, as is Schubert, a fine pantomimic comedian.

p, Walt Disney; d, Peter Tewksbury; w, A.J. Carothers (based on the novel *Emil Und Die Detektiven* by Erich Kastner); ph, Gunther Senftleben (Technicolor); m, Heinz Schreiter; ed, Thomas Stanford, Cotton Warburton; cos, Leo Bei, Josef Wanke.

Crime/Children (PR:AA MPAA:NR)

EMILY* (1976, Brit.) 84m Emily c

Koo Stark (*Emily*), Sarah Brackett (*Margaret*), Victor Spinetti (*Richard*), Jane Hayden (*Rachel*), Constantin de Goguel (*Rupert*), Ina Skriver (*Augustine*), Richard

Oldfield (James), David Auker (Billy), Jeremy Child (Gerald), Jeannie Collings (Rosalind), Jack Haig (Taxi Driver), Pamela Cundell (Mrs. Prince).

Sleazy flim has Stark returning from finishing school in 1928 to a sexual awakening. The film is nicely shot but Stark disrobes for the flimsiest of reasons, providing more visual interest, which is a definite advantage in a film where nobody shows any talent for acting. Rod McKuen contributes a typically wretched soundtrack.

p, Christopher Neame; d, Henry Herbert; w, Anthony Morris; ph, Jack Hildyard; m, Rod McKuen; ed, Keith Palmer; art d, Jacquimine Charott-Lodwidge.

Drama   **Cas.**   **(PR:O   MPAA:NR)**

EMILY   (SEE: AMERICANIZATION OF EMILY, THE, 1964)

EMMA*½**   (1932) 70m MGM bw

Marie Dressler (Emma Thatcher), Richard Cromwell (Ronnie Smith), Jean Hersholt (Mr. Smith), Myrna Loy (Isabelle), John Miljan (District Attorney), Purnell B. Pratt (Haskins), Leila Bennett (Matilda), Barbara Kent (Gypsy), Kathryn Crawford (Sue), George Meeker (Bill), Dale Fuller (Maid), Wilfred Noy (Drake), Andre Cheron (Count Pierre), Dawn O'Day (Girl), Dorothy Peterson (Woman).

Dressler is hired by Hersholt as a nanny for his large family and over the next 20 years she becomes an integral part of the household, finally marrying him. Hersholt dies and leaves his fortune to his wife, but Loy and the other children try to break the will, and when that fails accuse Dressler of murdering their father. A long trial follows. Dressler is eventually acquitted and she renounces the children who now want her back. She leaves and finds another family to work for. Film frequently threatens to sink into sentimentality, but Dressler marvelously keeps it together. This was Loy's first appearance as an MGM contract player after Irving Thalberg spotted her in SKYLINE.

d, Clarence Brown; w, Leonard Praskins, Zelda Sears (based on a story by Frances Marion); ph, Oliver T. Marsh; ed, William Levanway; art d, Cedric Gibbons.

Drama   **(PR:A   MPAA:NR)**

EMMA MAE**   (1976) 100m Pro-International c

Jerri Hayes (Emma Mae), Ernest Williams II (Jesse), Charles David Brooks III (Zeke), Eddie Allen (James), Robert Slaughter (Devo), Malik Carter (Big Daddy), Teri Taylor (Dara), Leopoldo Mandeville (Chay), Gammy Burdett (Daisy), Eddy Dyer (Huari), Synthia James (Ulika), Jewell Williams (Maddie), Laetitia Burdett (Melik).

Hayes is a poor naive black country girl who comes to the big city and grows up fast. She falls in love with gang leader Williams, who robs and abandons her and gets beaten up by her later for it. Film ends with Hayes a tough, independent woman.

p,d&w, Jamaa Fanaka; ph, Stephen Posey (Metrocolor); m, H.B. Barnum; ed, Robert Fitzgerald; art d, Adel Mazen; cos, Stephanie A. Bell, Beverly Ventriss, Marva Farmer.

Drama   **(PR:O   MPAA:R)**

EMPEROR AND A GENERAL, THE*½**   (1968, Jap.) 158m Toho bw
(NIPPON NO ICHIBAN NAGAI HI; NIHON NO ICHIBAN NAGAI HI)

Toshiro Mifune (War Minister Anami), So Yamamura (Navy Minister), Chishu Ryu (Prime Minister), Seiji Miyaguchi (Foreign Minister), Takashi Shimura (Information Chief), Toshio Kurosawa (Maj. Hatanaka), Shogo Shimada (Imperial Commander Mori), Susumu Fujita (Col. Haga), Yunosuke Ito (Maj. Gen. Nonaka), Daisuke Kato (Yabe of NHK), Jun Tazaki (Col. Kosono), Michiyo Aratama (Yuriko Hara), Nobuo Nakamura (Lord Kido), Kenjiro Ishiyama (Gen. Tanaka), Keiju Kobayashi (Chamberlain Tokugawa), Yuzo Kayama (Tateno of NHK), Koshiro Matsumoto (Emperor Hirohito), Rokko Toura, Yoshio Kosugi, Ushio Akashi, Takeshi Kato, Akihiko Hirata, Tadao Nakamaru, Ryuji Kita, Eisei Amamoto, Makoto Sato, Ichiro Nakaya, Koji Mitsui, Yoshio Tsuchiya.

Mifune is Japan's War Minister during WW II and tries to stop Emperor Hirohito from broadcasting the declaration of surrender to the Japanese people. Mifune gathers other officers together who want to continue the war. They kill the commander of the Imperial Guards and take over the palace to prevent the broadcast. Ishiyama's soldiers stop the coup and Mifune commits suicide. Based on real incidents in 1945.

d, Kihachi Okamoto; w, Shinobu Hashimoto (based on a novel by Soichi Oya); ph, Hiroshi Murai (Tohoscope, Technicolor); m, Masaru Sato; art d, Iwao Akune.

War   **(PR:O   MPAA:NR)**

EMPEROR AND THE GOLEM, THE**   (1955, Czech.) 110m
Czechoslovak State/Artkino c

Jan Werich (The Emperor/The Baker), Marie Vasova (Countess Strada), Natasa Gollova (Kathy), Jiri Plashy (Kelley), Frantisek Cerny, Bohus Zahorsky, Zdenek Stepanek, Frantisek Filiposky.

Overlong story of baker Werich who manages to assume the identity of an emperor and have a great time with the ladies at court before doing good for the people of the country. Good fantasy cut together from two films: THE EMPEROR'S BAKER and THE BAKER'S EMPEROR.

d, Martin Fric; w, Fric, Jan Werich, Jiri Brdecka (based on a story by Werich, Brdecka); ph, Jan Stallich, Bohumil Haba (Sovcolor); m, Julius Kalas; ed, Jan Kohout; set d, Jan Zasvorka; cos, Jiri Trnka.

Fantasy   **(PR:A   MPAA:NR)**

EMPEROR AND THE NIGHTINGALE, THE**   (1949, Czech.)
71m Czech State bw (CISARUV SLAVIK).

Jaromir Sobotoa (The Boy), Helena Patockova (The Girl).

A small boy, kept in seclusion by his two aunts in their large house, watches a pretty girl play outside and longs to be her friend. He gets sick and dreams that his dolls come to life. He becomes the Emperor of China but soon is bored. A nightingale sings a song of freedom to him and he awakens and joins the girl playing in the woods. An animated children's film with Boris Karloff doing the narration for the English version.

d, Milos Makovec (live action) and Jiri Trnka (animation); w, Trnka, Jiri Brdecka (based on a story by Hans Christian Andersen); ph, Ferdinand Pecenka (Agfacolor); m, Vaclav Trajan; narration, Boris Karloff; English narrative, Phyllis McGinley.

Children   **(PR:AA   MPAA:NR)**

EMPEROR JONES, THE**   (1933) 80m Krimsky-Cochran/UA bw

Paul Robeson (Brutus Jones), Dudley Digges (Smithers), Frank Wilson (Jeff), Fredi Washington (Undine), Ruby Elzy (Dolly), George Haymid Stamper (Lem), Jackie Mayble (Marcella), Blueboy O'Connor (Treasurer), Brandon Evans (Carrington), Taylor Gordon (Stick-Man).

A realistic, fascinating production of the brooding O'Neill play has Robeson in his most forceful and memorable role. He has just become a railroad porter and the film opens to show him before a mirror, admiring himself in his new uniform, then follows him into a Baptist church where his rich baritone booms out a moving hymn. His ego inflated, Robeson swaggers away from his fiancee and takes liberties with his best friend's girl, then deserts her and gets into a desperate crap game where he stabs his friend Wilson to death. Though he pleads innocence, claiming that the killing was accidental, he is sent to a chain gang for life. He escapes after murdering the warden and later works as a stoker on board a freighter. Off Haiti, Robeson jumps ship, swimming ashore. There he meets Digges, an unscrupulous trader who uses him as a bully boy to keep the natives in line. He is so successful and feared by the natives that he becomes rich as Digges' partner. As a joke, Robeson loads his gun with blanks and tells the gullible natives to shoot him. When he survives he is hailed as immortal. Robeson tells the astonished natives that only a silver bullet can kill him. In a short time he has run off the king and delared himself emperor, ruling the land with an iron fist. The tyrant is overthrown by a revolution; Robeson flees to the jungle where he has secreted supplies and riches. But everywhere he is greeted with scenes from his wicked past, until, haunted by visions of his dark acts, he becomes hopelessly lost. He shrinks into the thick underbrush. Every noise heralds the approach of his enemies, he thinks, and he withdraws the silver bullet, holding it up before his gaze. "Don't she shine pretty?" he says ironically, and slips it into the chamber of his pistol, a moment before committing suicide. Playwright O'Neill was easily convinced by director Murphy, who had adapted DRACULA for the screen, to bring this explosive drama to film. Murphy then convinced apprentice producers Krimsky and Cochran to put up the necessary funding and brought in William C. DeMille to supervise production. The brilliant art director Herman Rosse persuaded DeMille (whose older brother, Cecil, reportedly staged some of the scenes in the film) to cancel the planned location shooting in Haiti, and said he could recreate a more menacing jungle under controlled production circumstances in the old sound stages of the Eastern Service Studios in Long Island, N.Y. (formerly occupied by Paramount Publix Studio), and Rosse delivered, providing grimly realistic sets which elevate the overall look and feel of this film. Rosse was one of the most imaginative and creative persons working in films during the early 1930s. After immigrating from Holland he worked as a book illustrator in Chicago (his drawings in Ben Hecht's original editions of 1001 Afternoons in Chicago are astoundingly surreal). He earned fame as a muralist and architect and his sets and artwork for DRACULA, FRANKENSTEIN, MURDERS IN THE RUE MORGUE, and RESURRECTION were masterpieces of the grotesque. He would also win an Oscar for his work in THE KING OF JAZZ, 1929. Rosse's designs would be imitated and copied outright by many others but his elaborate sets often created headaches for cameramen. In THE EMPEROR JONES, the superb cinematographer Haller had to shoot around myriad mirrors, drapes, and columns set up by Rosse, and, in the jungle sequences, around and through dense foliage Rosse had created. The only exterior scenes are those depicting the chain gang where Robeson toils; these were shot in a stone quarry outside Westchester, N.Y. Robeson is, of course, the whole film, well supported by the sleazy Digges (the only white actor in an otherwise all black cast). His powerful presence, particularly through his wonderful, mellifluous voice, dominates each scene. He sings, "Now Let Me Fly," "I'm Travelin'," and "Water Boy," the last becoming something of a popular hit. There was never any doubt about Robeson playing the role of the vainglorious Jones; he had been appearing in O'Neill's "All God's Children Got Wings" to rave reviews in England just before going into the production of THE EMPEROR JONES. The film made him an international star and he traveled to the USSR where he embraced communism. He was later denounced by Manning Johnson, a former member of the Communist Party and one-time friend of Robeson's. Before HUAC Johnson stated that Robeson came to believe he was the "Emperor Jones." He has delusions of grandeur. He wants to be a black Stalin among Negroes." The actor-singer became a cause celebre but most producers boycotted him during the witchhunts of the early 1950s. He died in obscurity in 1976 in Philadelphia at age 77.

p, John Krimsky, Gifford Cochran, William C. DeMille; d, Dudley Murphy; w, DuBose Heyward (based on the play by Eugene O'Neill); ph, Ernest Haller; m, Rosamond Johnson; md, Frank Tours; art d & set d, Herman Rosse.

Drama   **Cas.**   **(PR:C   MPAA:NR)**

EMPEROR OF PERU
(SEE: ODYSSEY IN THE PACIFIC, 1981, Can./Fr.)

EMPEROR OF THE NORTH POLE*** (1973) 132m Inter-Hemisphere/FOX c (AKA: EMPEROR OF THE NORTH)

Lee Marvin *(A No. 1)*, Ernest Borgnine *(Shack)*, Keith Carradine *(Cigaret)*, Charles Tyner *(Cracker)*, Malcolm Atterbury *(Hogger)*, Simon Oakland *(Policeman)*, Harry Caesar *(Coaly)*, Hal Baylor *(Yardman's Helper)*, Matt Clark *(Yardlet)*, Elisha Cook *(Gray Cat)*, Joe di Reda *(Dinger)*, Liam Dunn *(Smile)*, Diane Dye *(Prudence)*, Robert Foulk *(Conductor)*, James Goodwin *(Fakir)*, Ray Guth *(Preacher)*, Sid Haig *(Grease Tail)*, Karl Lukas *(Pokey Stiff)*, Edward McNally *(Yard Clerk)*, John Steadman *(Stew Bum)*, Vic Tayback *(Yardman)*, Dave Willock *(Groundhog)*.

Grim and hardscrabble as a hobo's life, this film documents Marvin and Carradine in their bumming travels, particularly their attempt to ride the one freight train controlled by the meanest cop on the rails, Borgnine. Marvin is superb as the No. 1 hobo of all time, the most ingenious railrider in the history of tramping. Young drifter Carradine intends to become more famous than the man he most admires, Marvin, so he, too, boards the Borgnine train as it chugs northward, vying for the title of Emperor of the North Pole by surviving Borgnine's sadistic attacks. Borgnine beats both Marvin and Carradine mercilessly with iron rods, chains, and fists in his attempt to remove them from his train. But in the end it is Marvin who survives, with Carradine thrown from the train. Borgnine and Marvin battle to the death in an obsessive, unrealistic finale that proves Marvin is, indeed, "king of the hoboes." Aldrich's direction is tight and faster than the freight train running through his frames and the Biroc lensing captures breathtaking scenery, but the story is about as probable as an honest election in Chicago. Well pictured are the vast hobo camps that dotted the rural landscape of America during the Depression-torn time of the early 1930s. The film was shot on location in Oregon and along the rails of the Oregon, Pacific & Eastern Railway.

p, Stan Hough; d, Robert Aldrich; w, Christopher Knopf; ph, Joseph Biroc (DeLuxe Color); m, Frank DeVol; ed, Michael Luciano; art d, Jack Martin Smith; m/l, DeVol, Hal David.

Drama/Adventure (PR:C MPAA:PG)

EMPEROR WALTZ, THE*** (1948) 105m PAR c

Bing Crosby *(Virgil Smith)*, Joan Fontaine *(Johanna Franziska Von Stultzenberg)*, Roland Culver *(Baron Holenia)*, Richard Haydn *(Emperor Franz Josef)*, Lucile Watson *(Princess)*, Sig Rumann *(Dr. Zwieback)*, Julia Dean *(Archduchess Stephanie)*, Harold Vermilyea *(Chamberlain)*, Roberta Jonay *(Chambermaid)*, John Goldsworthy *(Obersthofmeister)*, Doris Dowling *(Tyrolean Girl)*, James Vincent *(Abbe)*, Harry Allen *(Gamekeeper)*, Frank Elliot *(Von Usedon)*, Paul de Corday *(Officer)*, Jack Gargan *(Master of Ceremonies)*, Cyril Delevanti *(Diplomat)*, Frank Corsaro *(Marquess)*, Bert Prival *(Chauffeur)*, Alma Macrorie *(Proprietor of Tyrolean Inn)*, Gerald Mohr *(Marques Alonso)*.

Charming but essentially featherweight musical from the brains of Billy Wilder and Charles Brackett, two of the best screenwriters ever. In this film ostensibly set in Franz Josef's Austria (but actually shot in Canada's Jasper National Park), Bing Crosby, a silver-tongued U.S. salesman arrives. He's selling phonographs and wants to convince the Austrian royal family to use his machine so the rest of the country may follow suit and he can make a million schillings (that's what they use in Austria). He secures an audience with Richard Haydn (Franz Josef) but when he enters with the device the security guards mistake it for a bomb and toss him out. He tries again and attempts softening Fontaine, Haydn's niece, in the hopes that she will be able to get him another date with the Emperor. She is pleasant enough to him but lets him know, in no uncertain terms, that he is far below her station in the caste system and there is no way that she could see him socially. Crosby reluctantly accepts that, then learns that his pet dog is also attempting romance with Fontaine's pet and the two animals have been at each other's throats. Fontaine wants to calm her dog so she brings it to meet Crosby's animal and the two eventually begin to happily sniff each other. Almost the same thing happens when Crosby drops his smug cocky attitude and Fontaine loses her snobbish airs. A couple of plot ploys later, the two are in love and we fade out happily. It sounds hokey and it is, but the dialog is so witty and the tunes so tuneful that we can forgive the basic inanity of the story. Funnier than most pictures of this ilk. Songs: "The Emperor's Waltz" (Johann Strauss, Johnny Burke), "Friendly Mountains" (Swiss airs, Burke), "Get Yourself a Phonograph" (James Van Heusen, Burke), "The Kiss in Your Eyes" (Richard Heuberger, Burke), "I Kiss Your Hand, Madame" (Ralph Erwin, Sam M. Lewis, Joe Young, Fritz Rotter), "The Whistler and His Dog" (Arthur Pryor).

p, Charles Brackett; d, Billy Wilder; w, Brackett, Wilder; ph, George Barnes (Technicolor); m, Victor Young; ed, Doane Harrison; art d, Hans Dreier, Franz Bachelin; set d, Sam Comer, Paul Huldschinsky; cos, Edith Head, Gile Steele; spec eff, Gordon Jennings; ch, Billy Daniels.

Musical Comedy (PR:AA MPAA:NR)

EMPEROR'S CANDLESTICKS, THE** (1937) 92m MGM bw

William Powell *(Wolensky)*, Luise Rainer *(Countess Muranova)*, Frank Morgan *(Col. Baron Suroff)*, Maureen O'Sullivan *(Maria)*, Henry Stephenson *(Prince Johann)*, Robert Young *(Grand Duke Peter)*, Douglas Dumbrille *(Korun)*, Bernadene Hayes *(Mitzi)*, Donald Kirke *(Antone)*, Charles Waldron *(Dr. Malcher)*, Barnett Parker *(Rudolph)*, Frank Reicher *(Pavloff)*, Paul Porcasi *(Santuzzi)*, Bert Roach *(Porter)*, E.E. Clive *(Auctioneer)*, Spencer Charters *(Usher)*, Ian Wolfe *(Leon)*, Theodore von Eltz *(Adjutant)*, Mitchell Lewis *(Plainclothesman)*, Egon Brecher *(Chief of Police)*, Erville Alderson *(Conductor)*, Clarence H. Wilson *(Stationmaster)*, Emma Dunn *(Housekeeper)*, Lionel Pape *(Sugar Daddy)*, Maude Turner Gordon *(Concierge)*, Rollo Lloyd *(Jailer)*, Frank Conroy *(Col. Radoff)*, William Stack *(Czar)*, Ramsay Hill, Olaf Hytten *(Conspirators)*, Torben Meyer *(Train Announcer)*, Davison Clark, Harvey Clark *(Conductors)*, King Baggott *(Customs Official)*, George Davis *(Waiter)*, Russ Powell *(Coachman)*, Clarice Sherry *(Blonde)*, Frank Lawson *(Prince Johann's Butler)*, Leonard Carey *(Valet to Walensky)*, Mariska Aldrich *(Ugly Woman)*, John Picorri *(Italian Ambassador)*, Roland Varno *(Czar's Officer)*, Cyril Thornton, Vernon Downing, Bruce Mitchell, Agostino Borgato, Carole Landis.

Powell and Rainer are rival spies in pre-World War I Eastern Europe. Both hide important documents in a pair of candlesticks, and when they are stolen they chase around the continent trying to recover them. Extravagant production can't save this bloated star vehicle. Carole Landis in a bit part was marking her first year in films; she was 18 years old.

p, John W. Considine, Jr.; d, George Fitzmaurice; w, Monckton Hoffe, Harold Goldman (based on a novel by Baroness Orczy); ph, Harold Rosson; m, Franz Waxman; ed, Conrad A. Nervig; art d, Cedric Gibbons.

Drama (PR:A MPAA:NR)

EMPIRE OF NIGHT, THE*** (1963, Fr.) 90m UFA/Comacico bw (L'EMPIRE DE LA NUIT)

Eddie Constantine *(Eddie)*, Elga Andersen *(Widow)*, Genevieve Grad *(Girl)*, Harold Nicholas *(Sidekick)*, Michel De Re *(Melchior)*.

European cult figure Constantine is a nightclub singer foiling an attempt by racketeers to take over a string of clubs. Complex, entertaining crime drama.

p, Jacques Roitfeld; d, Pierre Grimblat; w, Frederic Dard, Grimblat; ph, Michel Kelber; ed, Albert Jurgenson.

Crime (PR:C MPAA:NR)

EMPIRE OF THE ANTS* (1977) 89m AIP c

Joan Collins *(Marilyn Fryser)*, Robert Lansing *(Dan Stokely)*, John David Carson *(Joe Morrison)*, Albert Salmi *(Sheriff Kincade)*, Jacqueline Scott *(Margaret Ellis)*, Pamela Shoop *(Coreen Bradford)*, Robert Pine *(Larry Graham)*, Edward Power *(Charlie Pearson)*, Brooke Palance *(Christine Graham)*, Tom Fadden *(Sam Russell)*, Irene Tedrow *(Velma Thompson)*, Harry Holcombe *(Harry Thompson)*, Jack Kosslyn *(Thomas Lawson)*, Ilse Earl *(Mary Lawson)*, Janie Gavin *(Ginny)*, Norman Franklin *(Anson Parker)*, Florence McGee *(Phoebe Russell)*, Mike Armstrong *(Jim)*, Jim Wheelus *(Crewman)*, Tom Ford *(Pete)*, Charles Red *(Taxi Driver)*, Mark and Hugh Hooker *(Stuntmen)*.

Collins is a crooked real estate agent trying to sell a group of suckers lots on an island used as a nuclear waste dump. Soon they are menaced by giant mutant ants superimposed on footage behind them. Laughable exploitation film results in a complete waste of time and talent.

p&d, Bert I. Gordon; w, Jack Turley (based on a screen story by Gordon and a story by H.G. Wells); ph, Reginald Morris (Movielab Color); m, Dana Kaproff; ed, Michael Luciano; prod d, Charles Rosen; set d, Anthony C. Montenaro; cos, Joanne Haas; spec eff, Roy Downey, Gordon.

Science Fiction Cas. (PR:C MPAA:NR)

EMPIRE STRIKES BACK, THE*½** (1980) 124m FOX c

Mark Hamill *(Luke Skywalker)*, Harrison Ford *(Han Solo)*, Carrie Fisher *(Princess Leia)*, Billy Dee Williams *(Lando Calrissian)*, Anthony Daniels *(C-3PO)*, David Prowse *(Darth Vader)*, Peter Mayhew *(Chewbacca)*, Kenny Baker *(R2-D2)*, Frank Oz *(Yoda)*, Alec Guinness *(Ben Kenobi)*, Jeremy Bulloch *(Boba Fett)*, John Hollis *(Lando's Aide)*, Jack Purvis *(Chief Ugnaught)*, Des Webb *(Snow Creature)*, Kathryn Mullen *(Performing Assistant for Yoda)*, Clive Revill *(Voice of Emperor)*, Kenneth Colley *(Adm. Piett)*, Julian Glover *(Gen. Veers)*, Michael Sheard *(Adm. Ozzel)*, Michael Culver *(Capt. Needa)*, John Dicks, Milton Johns, Mark Jones, Oliver Maguire, Robin Scoby *(Officers)*, Bruce Boa *(Gen. Rieekan)*, Christopher Malcolm *(Zev)*, Dennis Lawson *(Wedge)*, Richard Oldfield *(Hobbie)*, John Morton *(Dak)*, Ian Liston *(Janson)*, John Ratzenberger *(Maj. Derlin)*, Jack McKenzie *(Deck Lieutenant)*, Jerry Harte *(Head Controller)*, Norman Chancer, Norwich Duff, Ray Hassett, Brigitte Kahn, Burnell Tucker *(Officers)*.

Second of the STAR WARS trilogy failed to engender excitement, sympathy, or anything near the enthusiasm of the ones that preceded and followed it. More than $30 million was lavished on this script written by old-timer Brackett and newcomer Kasdan, and Lucas may have made a great mistake entrusting this to director Kershner, who has a history of turkeys second only to Richard Fleischer and Arthur Hiller (STAKE-OUT ON DOPE STREET, THE FACE IN THE RAIN, LOVING, UP THE SANDBOX, S*P*Y*S). Add that to a cardboard script and what you have is a great disappointment for all those who found STAR WARS so refreshing. Darth Vader (Prowse) is, once again, attempting to take over the universe. The rebel forces are on the ice planet Hoth and Prowse sends his troops to wipe them out. In the process Hamill searches for and finds Yoda, a wise little creature they say was patterned after the face of Pulitzer prize-winning author Theodore White. Ford and Mayhew (Chewbacca) flee their tormentors in the best sequence, an asteroid belt chase. The final showdown is the laser duel between Hamill and Prowse, but not before we've seen some wonderful special effects, including shootouts, aerial dogfights, and huge new mechanical devices. But with all this, the movie is far more metallic than human. Many might argue that this was the most mythic of the three, filled with underlying philosophy. We felt it was the weakest and might have been greatly improved if Lucas had paid closer attention to it rather than handing over the reins to others. James Earl Jones was Vader's voice again, and the creator of Miss Piggy, Frank Oz, was Yoda. If we'd not seen STAR WARS and CLOSE ENCOUNTERS OF THE THIRD KIND already, this might have been impressive. As it was, it wasn't. Nominated for three Oscars, won one plus a special achievement award. Some location shooting in Norway. Sequel: RETURN OF THE JEDI.

p, Gary Kurtz; d, Irvin Kershner; w, Leigh Brackett, Lawrence Kasdan (based on a story by George Lucas); ph, Peter Suschitzy (Panavision, DeLuxe Color); m, John Williams; ed, Paul Hirsch; prod d, Norman Reynolds; art d, Leslie Dilley, Harry

Lange, Alan Tomkins; set d, Michael Ford; cos, John Mollo; spec eff, Brian Johnson, Richard Edlund, Dennis Muren, Bruce Nicholson.

Fantasy **Cas.** **(PR:A MPAA:PG)**

EMPLOYEE'S ENTRANCE***½ (1933) 74m FN/WB bw

Warren William (Kurt Anderson), Loretta Young (Madeline), Wallace Ford (Martin West), Alice White (Polly), Albert Gran (Ross), Allen Jenkins (Sweeney), Marjorie Gateson (Mrs. Hickox), Hale Hamilton (Monroe), Ruth Donnelly (Miss Hall), Zita Moulton (Marion), Frank Reicher (Garfinkle), Berton Churchill (Bradford), Charles Sellon (Higgins), Helen Mann (Josie), H.C. Bradley (Meek), Frank McGlynn (The Editor), Sam Godfrey (The Man), Edward McWade (An Employee), Henry Stockbridge (Meek), Neal Dodd (Minister), Muriel Gordon (Girl).

William is a ruthless department store manager whose dictatorial personality extends to his personal life as well. Young is the wife of one of his employees whom he falls for before finally getting the punishment he deserves. A bravura performance by William, and solid support by Young and White (as a blonde flirt). Briskly written by Robert Presnell and excellently directed by veteran craftsman Roy Del Ruth.

p, Lucien Hubbard; d, Roy Del Ruth; w, Robert Presnell (based on a play by David Boehm); ph, Barney McGill; art d, Robert Hayes.

Drama **(PR:A MPAA:NR)**

EMPRESS AND I, THE*** (1933, Ger.) UFA bw
(ICH UND DIE KAISERIN)

German cast: Mady Christians, Conrad Veidt, Lilian Harvey, Heinz Ruhmann, Friedel Schuster, Hubert V. Meyerinck, Julius Falkenstein; English cast: Mady Christians, Charles Boyer, Lilian Harvey, Maurice Evans, Friedel Schuster, Ernest Thesiger, Huntley Wright.

Complex musical has Harvey, the Empress' hairdresser, confused for the Empress by a delirious nobleman. Much confusion and singing ensues before it's all sorted out. Well done by veteran director Pommer with two separate casts, one for German, the other for English-speaking audiences. Director Hollander, also a composer, wrote many of the songs Marlene Dietrich made famous, and set designer Robert Herlth's ideas strongly influenced German "expressionism" in art (THE CABINET OF DR. CALIGARI is the best example of the movement in films). The writer for THE EMPRESS AND I, Reisch, later won an Oscar for his script on the film TITANIC.

p, Erich Pommer; d, Friedrich Hollander; w, Walter Reisch, Robert Liebmann (based on an idea by Felix Salten); ph, Friedel Behn-Grun; m, Franz Wachsmann [Franz Waxman]; set d, Robert Herlth, Walter Rohrig; m/l, Hollander.

Musical **(PR:A MPAA:NR)**

EMPRESS WU** (1965, Hong Kong) 120m Shaw Brothers c (WU-HOU)

Li Li-hua (Wu Tse-tien), Chao Lei (Emperor Kao Tsung), Lo Chi (Prince Hsuan), Chang Chung-wen (Empress Wang), Yen Chaun (Hsu Yiuking), Lo Wei (Pei Yen), Cheung Ying-tsai (Chang Chong-chung), Paul Chang Chung (Chang Yi-tse), Ting Ning (Shang Kuan Wan-erh).

A biographical film about a Chinese empress, Wu Tse-tien, who ruled during the T'ang dynasty, the "Golden Age" of Chinese civilization (AD 618-906). Despite the flowering of literature, science, the arts, and the introduction of foreign religions, Wu ruthlessly murdered a vast number of people, including her own sons, to keep herself on the throne. By film's end she has died and a parade of those she murdered passes before her.

p, Run Run Shaw, Runme Shaw; d, Li Han-hsiang; w, Wang Yueh-ting.

Biography/Drama **(PR:A MPAA:NR)**

EMPTY CANVAS, THE* (1964, Fr./Ital.) 118m EM bw
(LA NOIA: L'ENNUI ET SA DIVERSION, L'EROTISME)

Bette Davis (Dino's Mother), Horst Buchholz (Dino), Catherine Spaak (Cecilia), Isa Miranda (Cecilia's Mother), Lea Padovani (Balestrieri's Widow), Daniela Rocca (Rita), Georges Wilson (Cecilia's Father), Leonida Repaci (Balestrieri), Luigi Giuliani (Luciani), Dany Paris (Nun), Daniela Calvino, Micaela Dazzi (Prostitutes), Marcella Rovena (Tenant), Amos Davoli (Barman), Edoardo Nevola (Waiter), Jole Mauro (Cashier), Mario Lanfranchi (Police Officer).

Buchholz is a talentless artist in love with model Spaak. He brings her to the family estate to meet his mother, Davis, and to impress her with his wealth. She refuses to marry him but offers to be his mistress until someone she likes better comes along. He tries to change her mind by covering her nude body with money, when suddenly Davis walks in. The mother surveys the strange tableau and coolly leaves. When Spaak later goes on a holiday with a rival of Buchholz, he suffers a breakdown. Davis helps him through it and finally he is well enough to paint, announcing that he can do something worthwhile because he now knows that life is not an empty canvas. A bad, pompous film, though Davis is fun to watch.

p, Carlo Ponti; d, Damiano Damiani; w, Damiani, Tonino Guerra, Ugo Liberatore (based on the novel La Noia by Alberto Moravia); ph, Roberto Gerardi; m, Luis Enriquez Bacalova; ed, Renzo Lucidi; md, Bacalova; art d, Carlo Egidi; set d, Dario Michell.

Drama **(PR:O MPAA:NR)**

EMPTY HOLSTERS*½ (1937) 62m WB bw

Dick Foran (Clay Brent), Pat Walthall (Judy Ware), Emmett Vogan (Ace Cain), Anderson Lawlor (Buck Govern), Glenn Strange (Tex Roberts), Wilfred Lucas (John Ware), Tom Brower (Dad Brent), George Chesebro (Cutter Smith), Charles Lemoyne (Tom Raines), Edmund Cobb (Cal Hardin), J.P. McGowan (Billy O'Neill), Milton Kibbee (Jim Hall), Earl Dwire (Doctor), Henry Otho (Jerry), Gordon Hart, Addison Richards, Merrill McCormack, Ben Corbett, Art Mix, Artie Ortego.

Foran is framed for a stage holdup and sent to prison for five years. Upon his return, the sheriff forbids him to wear a gun, but he manages to see justice is done anyway. Plenty of gunplay and Foran's tenor voice singing two songs is pleasant to listen to.

p, Bryan Foy; d, B. Reeves Eason; w, John T. Neville (based on a story by Ed Earl Repp); ph, Ted McCord; ed, Clarence Kolster; m/l, "Old Corral," "I Gotta Get Back to My Gal," M.K. Jerome, Jack Scholl.

Western **Cas.** **(PR:A MPAA:NR)**

EMPTY SADDLES** (1937) 65m UNIV bw

Buck Jones (Buck Devlin), Louise Brooks (Boots Boone), Harvey Clark (Swap Boone), Charles Middleton (Cim White), Frank Campeau (Kit Kress), Lloyd Ingraham (Jim Grant), Claire Rochelle (Madge Grant), Gertrude Astor (Eloise Hayes), Niles Welch (Jasper Kade), Mary Mersch (Mrs. Mills), Ruth Cherrington (Mrs. Hilton), Oliver Eckhart (Mr. Hilton), Robert Adair (Ezra Biggers), Charles LeMoyne (Mace), Ben Corbett (Vegas), Buck Moulton (Sam), Earl Askam, William Lawrence, "Silver."

Routine Jones oater has him putting a stop to a range war between cattlemen and sheepmen. Notable as one of the few talkie appearances of Louise Brooks, an idol of film cultists when her early silent films were rediscovered in the mid-1950s. EMPTY SADDLES represented one of her vain attempts at a comeback after her retirement from the screen in 1931.

p, Buck Jones; d, Lesley Selander; w, Frances Guihan (based on a story by Cherry Wilson); ph, Allan Thompson, H. Kirkpatrick.

Western **(PR:A MPAA:NR)**

EMPTY STAR, THE** (1962, Mex.) 107m
Produccions Corsa/Azteca c (LA ESTRELLA VACIA)

Maria Felix (Olga Lang), Ignacio Lopez Tarso (Luis), Enrique Rambal (Rodrigo), Carlos Lopez Moctezuma (Federico), Ramon Gay (Raul), Carlos Navarro, Rita Macedo, Wolf Rubinsky, Tito Junco, Jose Luis Jimenez, Mauricio Garces, Rosa Elena Durgel.

A power-wielding film actress is killed in a plane crash and the men in her life try to piece together some reason for her unhappiness. We see how she went from her small town, where she modeled in a dress shop to pay for her acting lessons, to meeting the director of a theater group who leads her to a contact at a Mexican film studio. Men come and go as her fame grows and she becomes rich, and then she realizes how empty her life has become. She takes a plane to Europe to start anew, but the plane crash ends her life.

p&d, Emilio Gomez Muriel; w, Julio Alejandro de Castro (based on a novel by Luis Spota); ph, Gabriel Figueroa; m, Gustavo Cesar Carrion; ed, Jorge Bustos; art d, Jesus Bracho; cos, Balenciaga, Jean Patou.

Drama **(PR:A MPAA:NR)**

ENCHANTED APRIL* (1935) 66m RKO bw

Ann Harding (Lotty Wilkins), Frank Morgan (Mellersh Wilkins), Katharine Alexander (Rose Arbuthnot), Reginald Owen (Henry Arbuthnot), Jane Baxter (Lady Caroline), Ralph Forbes (Beppo Briggs), Jessie Ralph (Mrs. Fisher), Charles Judels (Domenico), Rafaela Ottiano (Francesca).

Four women, Harding, Alexander, Ralph, and Baxter, take an Italian villa for a vacation from their various romantic troubles. Assorted husbands and lovers turn up in this mishmash of comedy and melodrama. The whole thing flopped completely and helped put the final skids on the career of Ann Harding, whose public was becoming tired of her typecast slot as the noble lady always making tearjerking sacrifices.

p, Kenneth MacGowan; d, Harry Beaumont; w, Samuel Hoffenstein, Ray Harris (based on a novel by "Elizabeth" [Mary Annette Beauchamp Russell] and a play by Kane Campbell); ph, Edward Cronjager; ed, George Hively.

Drama/Comedy **(PR:A MPAA:NR)**

ENCHANTED COTTAGE, THE***** (1945) 91m RKO bw

Dorothy McGuire (Laura), Robert Young (Oliver), Herbert Marshall (John Hillgrave), Mildred Natwick (Abigail Minnett), Spring Byington (Violet Price), Richard Gaines (Frederick), Hillary Brooke (Beatrice), Alec Englander (Danny), Mary Worth (Mrs. Stanton), Josephine Whittell (Canteen Manager), Robert Clarke (Marine), Eden Nicholas (Soldier).

This sensitive and touching film, based on the classic romance play by Pinero, is beautifully enacted by McGuire and Young as the uncommon lovers. Young is the embittered, disfigured WW I veteran who is obsessed with suicide, the only alternative, he feels, to coping with an ugliness that repels everyone. He meets McGuire, whose looks are decidedly plain, a girl no one would look at twice. They marry and move into seclusion inside a small New England cottage, shutting off communication with the rest of the world. (The cottage they rent is all that's left of a great estate which had been burned in a raging fire years earlier. It is a honeymoon cottage where scores of lovers who have carved their initials on the windowpanes have found happiness; its owner, Natwick, knows well the legend of its wonderful spell.) Slowly a small miracle occurs. Young regains his handsome countenance and McGuire blossoms into a beautiful young woman. It is, of course, the love they feel for each other that has brought about the astounding transformation, images that are momentarily shattered by mindless friends who point out their actual ugliness. Outside reality intrudes into their visions of each other but this is only transitory as they quickly realize that they perceive each other through the eyes of love and they recapture each other's beauty. Though cruelly attacked by unthinking critics when this talkie remake was first released, the story is truly beautiful and is wonderfully written. Young and McGuire underplay roles that would have become more histrionic in less able hands. Pinero's intent, to write about the triumph of love over adversity, is fully appreciated today as it was in its original 1922 stage production and silent filming in 1924, starring Richard Barthelmess and May McAvoy. The 1945 remake improves the story with subtle makeup, a stirring score by Webb, innovative lensing by Tetzlaff and a literate script by Mankiewicz and Bodeen. Cromwell's direction is first rate and supporting players Marshall and Natwick are outstanding. This unforgettable fable is a timeless story for lovers, no matter their shape or form, for here it is proven that beauty is absolutely in the eye of the beholder, that the true image of love is etched in the human heart.

p, Harriet Parsons; d, John Cromwell; w, De Witt Bodeen, Herman J. Mankiewicz (based on the play by Sir Arthur Wing Pinero); ph, Ted Tetzlaff; m, Roy Webb; ed, Joseph Noriega; md, C. Bakaleinikoff; art d, Albert S. D'Agostino, Carroll Clark; set d, Darrell Silvera, Harley Miller; spec eff, Vernon L. Walker.

Romance   (PR:A   MPAA:NR)

ENCHANTED FOREST, THE***½   (1945) 82m PRC c

Edmund Lowe (*Steven Blaine*), Brenda Joyce (*Anne*), Billy Severn (*Jackie*), Harry Davenport (*Old John*), John Litel (*Henderson*), Clancy Cooper (*Gilson*), "Jim" the Crow (*Blackie*).

Davenport is an old hermit who lives in the forest communing with the animals. While moving deeper into the woods to escape the inroads made by loggers, he teaches little Severn about nature. Charming children's film will please adults, too. PRC put an impressive amount of money and care into this one, and it is easily one of its most ambitious efforts.

p, Jack Schwartz; d, Lew Landers; w, Robert Lee Johnson, John Lebar, Lou Brock (based on a story by Lebar); ph, Marcel LePleard (Cinecolor); m, Albert Hay Malotte; ed, Roy Livingston; art d, Frank Sylos.

Children   (PR:AAA   MPAA:NR)

ENCHANTED ISLAND**   (1958) 93m Waverly/WB c

Dana Andrews (*Abner Bedford*), Jane Powell (*Fayaway*), Don Dubbins (*Tom*), Arthur Shields (*Jimmy Dooley*), Ted de Corsia (*Capt. Vangs*), Friedrich Ledebur (*Mehevi*), Augustin Fernandez (*Kory Kory*), Francisco Reiguera (*Medicine Man*), Les Hellman (*1st Mate Moore*), Eddie Saenz, Dale Van Sickel, Paul Stader (*Sailors*).

Andrews and Dubbins are a pair of 19th-century whalers who jump ship on a tropical island inhabited by cannibals. Dubbins apparently is eaten, but Andrews takes up with the chief's daughter, Powell, and avoids a similar fate. They escape the island and return to the ship Andrews had previously left, and captain de Corsia, instead of hanging Andrews as he had threatened, makes him first mate, but Powell is harpooned by the enraged tribal medicine man and the film is unclear at the end whether she's dead or not. Mangled adaptation of Herman Melville's *Typee*.

p, Benedict Bogeaus; d, Allan Dwan; w, James Liecester, Harold Jacob Smith (based on the novel *Typee* by Herman Melville); ph, George Stahl (Technicolor); m, Raul LaVista; ed, Leicester; m/l, "Enchanted Island," Robert Allen.

Drama   (PR:A   MPAA:NR)

ENCHANTED VALLEY, THE**   (1948) 77m EL c

Alan Curtis (*Johnny*), Anne Gwynne (*Midge*), Charley Grapewin (*Grandpa*), Donn Gift (*Timmy*), Joseph Crehan (*Chief Scott*), Joseph Devlin (*Buggsy*), Al Le Rue (*Pretty Boy*), John Bleifer (*Menelli*), Rocky Cameron (*Constable*), Jerry Riggio (*Gangster*).

Gift is a crippled boy who lives in the woods with grandpa Grapewin. Their idyllic existence is interrupted by the arrival of armed robbers Curtis and Devlin, and moll Gwynne. Under the gentle influence of Gift, the criminals reform. Mediocre programmer.

p, Jack Schwartz; d, Robert Emmett Tansey; w, Frances Kavanaugh; ph, Ernie Miller (Cinecolor); m, David Chudnow; ed, George McGuire; animal trainers, Byron Nelson, Curley Twiford, Earl Johnson.

Drama   (PR:A   MPAA:NR)

ENCHANTING SHADOW, THE**   (1965, Hong Kong) 85m
                                          Shaw Brothers c (CHIN NU YU HUN)

Betty Loh Tih (*Hsiao Chien*), Chao Lei (*Ning*), Yang Chih-ching (*Yen*), Marguerite Tong Jo-ching (*Lo Mu*), Li Kuo-hua.

Lei is a student who finds the temple he goes to haunted by witches and ghosts. He resists the ghost of the beautiful Tih, who tries to seduce him, and thus saves his life. Finally, he overcomes the sorceress who haunts the temple and brings Tih back to life. Interesting fantasy from the Far East.

p, Run Run Shaw; d, Li Han-hsiang; w, Wang Yueh-ting; ph, Ho Lu-ying (Eastmancolor); m, Chi Hsiang-tang; ed, Chan Chi-jui.

Fantasy   (PR:A   MPAA:NR)

ENCHANTMENT***   (1948) 102m RKO bw

David Niven (*Gen. Sir Roland Dane*), Teresa Wright (*Lark Ingoldsby*), Evelyn Keyes (*Grizel Dane*), Farley Granger (*Pilot Pax Masterson*), Jayne Meadows (*Selina Dane*), Leo G. Carroll (*Proutie*), Philip Friend (*Pelham Dane*), Shepperd Strudwick (*Marchese del Laudi*), Henry Stephenson (*Gen. Fitzgerald*), Colin Keith-Johnston (*The Eye*), Gigi Perreau (*Lark as a Child*), Peter Miles (*Rollo as a Child*), Sherlee Collier (*Selina as a Child*), Warwick Gregson (*Pelham as a Child*), Marjorie Rhodes (*Mrs. Sampson*), Edmond Breon (*Uncle Bunny*), Gerald Oliver Smith (*Willoughby*), Melville Cooper (*Jeweler*), Dennis McCarthy (*Lance Corporal*), Gaylord Pendleton (*RAF Officer*), Matthew Boulton (*Air Raid Warden*), Robin Hughes (*Corporal*), William Johnstone (*Narrator*).

Slow-moving love story that marks one of the rare Goldwyn pictures that lacked a central driving force. It was Gregg Toland's last photographic job before his death,

and the look of the film far outweighs the content. Fifty years in the life of a London home is the theme. The address is 99 Wiltshire Place and the action, such as it is, occurs between 1894 and 1944. Teresa Wright is an orphan taken into the house to be a sister to Meadows, Niven, and Friend. When their father dies, Meadows' hatred for Wright emerges. Wright is in love with Niven, but he's not certain if he shares that love for her. Who *is* certain is brother Friend and wealthy Italian Strudwick. Meadows wishes Wright would run off with Strudwick and stay out of her hair, but Wright has her own ideas. Eventually, Niven and Wright decide to wed and tell Meadows. She is irate and convinces Niven's military boss, Stephenson, to send him off to India. According to the rules, officers may *not* take their wives to India, so now Wright must wait several years until Niven completes his service. Niven must make a decision and hesitates just a moment too long. Wright is furious and exits, to Meadows' delight. Niven says he'll never come into 99 Wiltshire Place as long as she lives and throws the latch key on the floor, then turns on his heel. Wright goes to Italy with Strudwick and no one, except Meadows, is happy. Half a century later, Niven returns to the old, dark house. He's served all those years and is a retired general. His one remaining friend and aide is his equally ancient butler, Leo G. Carroll. It's the middle of WW II and Niven's American granddaughter is Evelyn Keyes, an ambulance driver. Niven is crusty, grouchy, and eventually accepts her after a disastrous first meeting. Wright's nephew is Farley Granger, a Canadian pilot in London for the duration. Keyes and Granger fall in love and he would like to marry but she is more pragmatic and says they must wait until after the war is ended. Niven recognizes the lost opportunity he had for happiness so many years ago and tells his niece that love is a rare and unique thing and must be grabbed, like the brass ring on a merry-go-round, whenever one can reach for it. It may never happen again. Keyes immediately rushes out into the street to find Granger. An air raid is taking place and a bomb hits the house and destroys it and Niven and Carroll. The picture ends. Phew! Not a lot of laughs and a lack of fulfillment is what hurts this movie more than anything else. The direction was excellent and John Patrick's dialog was eminently believable but, in the end, one wants to see lovers unite and happiness prevail.

p, Samuel Goldwyn; d, Irving Reis; w, John Patrick (from Rumer Godden's novel *Take Three Tenses*); ph, Gregg Toland; m, Hugo Friedhofer; ed, Daniel Mandell; art d, George Jenkins; set d, Julia Heron; md, Emil Newman; cos, Mary Wills; ch, Billy Daniels.

Drama/Romance   (PR:A   MPAA:NR)

ENCORE***   (1951, Brit.) 89m RANK-PAR GFD bw

The Ant and the Grasshopper: Nigel Patrick (*Tom Ramsey*), Roland Culver (*George Ramsey*), Alison Leggatt (*Freda Ramsey*), Charles Victor (*Mr. Bateman*), Peter Graves (*Philip Cronshaw*), Margaret Vyner (*Gertrude Wilmot*), Margaret Withers (*Mrs. Bateman*), Dorothy Bramhall (*Secretary*), Patricia Raine (*Office Girl*), Campbell Cotts (*Club Member*), Michael Trubshaw (*Ascot Man*); Winter Cruise: Kay Walsh (*Miss Reid*), Noel Purcell (*Captain*), Ronald Squire (*Doctor*), John Laurie (*Engineer*), Jacques Francois (*Pierre*), John Horsley (*Mate*), Joan Harben (*Miss Price*); Gigolo and Gigolette: Glynis Johns (*Stella Cotman*), Terence Morgan (*Syd Cotman*), David Hutcheson (*Sandy Wescott*), Charles Goldner (*Paco Espinal*), Mary Merrall (*Flora Penezzi*), Heather Thatcher (*Eva Barrett*), Daphne Barker (*Countess*), Martin Miller (*Carlo Penezzi*), Guido Lorraine (*Russian Prince*), Ferdy Mayne, Guy du Monceau, John Boxer.

An anthology of three W. Somerset Maugham stories. The first, "The Ant and the Grasshopper," deals with a man (Patrick) constantly borrowing money from his brother, but finally marrying a rich woman and buying the family estate his brother had sold. In the second episode, "Winter Cruise," Walsh is a spinster on a cargo ship cruise whose constant chattering threatens to drive everyone crazy. The crew elects porter Francois to engage her in an affair to get her to shut up. In the third story, "Gigolo and Gigolette," Morgan is a high-dive artist whose wife (Johns) gambles away their savings trying to win enough for him to give up the dangerous act. All three episodes are engaging and well done, with good performances by all involved. Quite entertaining.

p, Anthony Darnborough; d, Harold French, Pat Jackson, Anthony Pelissier; w, T.E.B. Clarke, Arthur Macrae, Eric Ambler (based on short stories of the same titles by W. Somerset Maugham); ph, Desmond Dickinson; m, Richard Addinsell; ed, Alfred Roome.

Drama/Comedy   (PR:A   MPAA:NR)

ENCOUNTERS IN SALZBURG**½   (1964, Ger.) 100m
                                          Paris Inter Productions bw

Curt Jurgens (*Hans Wilke, General Director*), Nadia Gray (*Felicitas, His Wife*), Victor de Kowa (*Bernhard von Wangen*), Walter Giller (*Kroener, Insurance Agent*), Daniele Gaubert (*Manuela*), Paul Dahlke (*Insurance Director*), Marte Harell (*Fraulein Niederalt, Secretary*).

Wealthy industrialist Jurgens travels to Salzburg to visit a friend who is playing the role of "Death" in the city's annual production of "Everyman," the medieval morality play. He meets Gaubert and makes her his mistress, and then suffers a heart attack. The film ambitiously tries to parallel the play with the industrialist's life, but the whole thing comes off as muddled. The photographer, Georg Krause, worked with Stanley Kubrick on PATHS OF GLORY. (In German; English subtitles.)

p, Peter Bamberger; d, Max Friedman; w, Thomas Muenster; ph, Georg Kraus; m, Peter Thomas.

Drama   (PR:C   MPAA:NR)

ENCOUNTER WITH THE UNKNOWN*½   (1973) 87m
                                          Centronics International/Libert c

Rosie Holotick, Gary Brockette, Gene Ross, Annabelle Weenick, Bob Ginnaven, August Sehven, Kevin Kieberly, Rod Serling (*Narrator*).

Rod Serling of TV's "The Twilight Zone" steps in to do some of the narration in this series of three very cheaply made stories of that "zone." One story tells about three teenagers who are cursed; another is about a ghost that haunts a bridge; and the last reveals a mysterious hole in a farmer's field. The cheapie quality of the whole thing is betrayed by the use of some of the same footage repeatedly in each segment, and the fact that the dialog was dubbed in after the shooting.

p, Joe Glass; d, Harry Thomason.

Horror   **Cas.**   **(PR:C MPAA:PG)**

END, THE**   (1978) 100m UA c

Burt Reynolds (Sonny Lawson), Dom De Luise (Marlon Borunki), Sally Field (Mary Ellen), Strother Martin (Dr. Kling), David Steinberg (Marty Lieberman), Joanne Woodward (Jessica), Norman Fell (Dr. Krugman), Myrna Loy (Maureen Lawson), Kristy McNichol (Julie Lawson), Pat O'Brien (Ben Lawson), Robby Benson (The Priest), Carl Reiner (Dr. Maneet), Louise Letourneau (Receptionist), Bill Ewing (Hearse Driver), Robert Rothwell (Limousine Driver), Harry Caesar (Hospital Orderly), James Best (Pacemaker Patient), Peter Gonzales (Latin Lover), Connie Fleming (Girl Dancer), Janice Carroll (Ballet Teacher), Ken Johnson (Whistling Lunatic), Frank McRae (Tall Male Nurse), Alfie Wise (Short Male Nurse), Jock Mahoney (Old Man), Edward Albrecht (Insurance Man), Jerry Fujikawa (Gardner), Patrick Moody (Old Man's Son), Carolyn Martin (Old Man's Daughter-In-Law), Queenie Smith (Old Lady In Car), Jean Ann Coulter (Driving Teacher).

Reynolds learns that he will die in three months from a rare blood disease. He goes to church for his first confession in 20 years, and all novice priest Benson can say is "Wow!" He tries to commit suicide and fails, waking up in an insane asylum. He enlists fellow patient De Luise to kill him and the rest of the film is a burlesque of his repeated attempts to die. Eventually, Reynolds decides that he wants to live, even if only for a few months. The film veers wildly from decent black comedy to dumb slapstick and director Reynolds seems unsure of his own intentions, but in a few places this film is quite funny, although De Luise and all the scenes he's in are unbearable.

p, Lawrence Gordon; d, Burt Reynolds; w, Jerry Belson; ph, Bobby Byrne (DeLuxe Color); m, Paul Williams; ed, Donn Cambern; prod d, Jan Scott; set d, John Franco, Jr.; cos, Norman Salling; spec eff, Cliff Wenger, Carol Wenger; stunts, Hal Needham.

Comedy   **Cas.**   **(PR:O MPAA:NR)**

END OF A DAY, THE***   (1939, Fr.) 94m Regina/Pax bw
                                              (LA FIN DU JOUR)

Victor Francen (Maryn), Louis Jouvet (St. Clair), Michel Simon (Cabrissade), Madeleine Ozeray (Jeannette), Arthur Devere (Director), Gabrielle Dorziat (Mme. Chabert), Aquilliere (Mr. Lucien), Joffre (Mr. Philemon), Mme. Lherbay (Mme. Philemon), Jean Coquelin (Delormel), Pierre Magnier (Mr. Laroche), Granval (Deaubonne), Jean Ayme (Victor), Tony Jacquot (Pierre), Gaby Andreu (Danielle), Gaston Modot (Innkeeper).

Life in an actors' retirement home is given a sentimental treatment by Duvivier in this tale of the home's despairing, partly admirable-partly pathetic cast of characters. As the home suffers from a severe financial burden, the characters carry their own burdens about the past: Frances, whose overly intellectual approach rarely moved his audiences; Jouvet and his former fame as a sex symbol; and the sorrowful Simon, who is determined to keep people from learning that he was merely an understudy. The fine script and the performances of the three chief actors highlight this poignant memory of the past. (In French; English subtitles.)

d, Julien Duvivier; w, Duvivier, Charles Spaak; ph, Christian Matras; m, Maurice Jaubert.

Drama   **(PR:A MPAA:NR)**

END OF A PRIEST**   (1970, Czech.) 82m Barrandov/Grove Press bw
                                              (FARARUV KONEC)

Vlastimil Brodsky (Sexton), Jana Brejchova (Majka), Jan Libicek (Village Teacher), Zdena Skvorecka (Anna), Jaroslav Satoransky (Tonik), Vladimir Valenta (Farmer), Helena Ruzickova (Farmer's Wife), Josefa Pedhlatova (Granny), Martin Ruzek (White Bishop), Gueye Cheick (Black Bishop).

Brodsky, the bell ringer and grave digger for a church, impersonates a priest until an athiest schoolmaster and a Communist discover his true identity. They try to unmask him by fixing him up with a whore. But Brodsky finds out about the plot and sets the barn, where the tryst was to be held, on fire, killing a poor hobo who had been hiding inside. Now the cops are after him, but he is killed when he falls off the church roof. Director Schorm is known as the "spiritual authority" of the internationally acclaimed Czech "new wave" and is acknowledged to be its leading director. Brejchova is Czechoslovakia's most popular and best-known screen actress.

d, Evald Schorm; w, Schorm, Josef Skvorecky (based on a novel by Skvorecky); ph, Jaromir Sofr; m, Jan Klusak; art d, Jindrich Goetz.

Comedy/Drama   **(PR:C MPAA:NR)**

END OF AUGUST, THE*   (1982) 105m Quartet c

Sally Sharp (Edna), Lilia Skala (Mlle. Reisz), David Marshall Grant (Robert), Kathleen Widdoes (Adele), Paul Roebling (Leonce), Paul Shenar (Arobin), John McLiam (Colonel), Mark Linn-Baker (Victor), Patricia Barry (Mrs. Merriman), Roy Poole (Dr. Mandalet), Patricia Falkenhain (Mme. Lebrun), William Meisle (Alphonse), Miles Mutchler (Farival), Adrian Boyes (Roaul), Andrews Chambers (Etienne), Brown Wallace (Merriman), Jenna Worthen (Grandmother), Sally Maloney (Nurse), Robert Harper (Joe), Saundra Santiago (Mariequiuta).

A boring period piece on the frustration a married woman faces in trying to become her own person in turn-of-the-century New Orleans. It seems that more

attention was put on set design and costumery than in developing a story that would grab and hold a filmgoer's interest, which says little for the four writers employed on the screenplay.

p, Warren Jacobson, Sally Sharp; d, Bob Graham; w, Eula Seaton, Leon Heller, Anna Thomas, Gregory Nava (based on the novel The Awakening by Kate Chopin); ph, Bob Elswit; m, Shirley Walker; ed, Jay Lash Cassidy; prod d, Jacobson, Erin Jo Jurow, Fred Baldwin; art d, Joe Wertheimer; cos, David Loveless, Bob Anton.

Drama   **(PR:C-O MPAA:PG)**

END OF AUGUST AT THE HOTEL OZONE, THE**   (1967, Czech.)
            85m Czechoslovak Army Film Studios/New Line Cinema bw
                                    (KONEC SRPNA V HOTELU OZON)

Ondrej Jariabek (Old Man), Beta Ponicanova (Old Woman), Magda Seidlerova (Barbara), Hana Vitkova (Theresa), Jana Novakova (Clara), Vanda Kalinova (Judith), Natalie Maslovova (Magdalen), Irina Lzicarova (Anna), Jitka Horejsi (Martha), Alena Lippertova (Eva).

Nine women roam the countryside for food and other human beings after the end of WW II, hoping to find men so they can restart the human race. The women are led by an old woman, and they travel on foot and on horseback. They meet an old man after they kill his cow and, overwhelmed at meeting other humans, the old man invites them to his place. They have dinner and the young women are amazed by his phonograph (his only record is "Beer Barrel Polka"). The older woman dies during the night and the other women, preparing to leave the next day, kill the old man when he won't give them his phonograph. A bleak example of Czech film-making in the late 1960s.

d, Jan Schmidt; w, Pavel Juracek; ph, Jiri Macak; m, Jan Klusak; ed, Miroslav Hajek.

Science Fiction   **(PR:C MPAA:NR)**

END OF BELLE, THE   (SEE: PASSION OF SLOW FIRE, THE, 1962, Fr.)

END OF DESIRE**   (1962 Fr./Ital.) 86m
            Agnes Delahaie-Nepi/Continental c (UNE VIE; UNA VITA; AKA: ONE LIFE)
Maria Schell (Jeanne Dandieu), Christian Marquand (Julien de la mare), Pascale Petit (Rosalie), Ivan Desny (Fourcheville), Antonella Lualdi (Ghilberte Fourcheville), Marie-Helene Daste (Mme. Dandieu), Louis Arbessier (Dandieu), Michel de Slubicki (Paul), Andree Tainsy (Ludivine), Gerard Darrieu (Fisherman).

Schell discovers that her husband, Marquand, married her to pay off his debts and that he's having an affair with the maid. Her love is strong enough to look beyond these facts, but grows shaky when the maid becomes pregnant with her husband's child. Marquand then begins an affair with Lualdi and when her husband, Desny, discovers this, he kills them. A French period piece melodrama that moves at a very slow pace. (In French; English subtitles.)

p, Agnes Delahaie, Annie Dorfman; d, Alexandre Astruc; w, Roland Laudenbach, Astruc (based on Guy de Maupassant's Une Vie); ph, Claude Renoir (Eastmancolor); m, Roman Vlad; ed, Claudine Bouche; art d, Paul Bertrand; cos, Lucilla; English subtitles; Herman G. Weinberg.

Drama   **(PR:A MPAA:NR)**

END OF INNOCENCE**** (1960, Arg.) 76m Argentine Sono/Kingsley bw
Elsa Daniel (Ana), Lautaro Murua (Pablo), Guillermo Battaglia (Castro), Jordana Fain (Nana), Berta Ortegosa (Senora Castro), Barbara Mujica (Vicenta), Alejandro Rey (Julian), Lili Gacel (Julietta).

Daniel is a rich Argentine girl who leads a sheltered existence on her father's estate until she is raped by her father's best friend. The plot, however, is just an excuse for an analysis of class structure and politics in 1920s Argentina. An excellent film, for which Daniel won a best actress award at the Cannes Film Festival. (In Spanish; English subtitles.)

d, Leopoldo Torre Nilsson; w, Beatriz Guido, Nilsson, Martin Rodriguez Mentasti (based on the novel House of the Angel by Guido); ph, Anibal Gonzalez Paz; m, Juan Carlos Paz.

Drama   **(PR:O MPAA:NR)**

END OF MRS. CHENEY**½   (1963, Ger.) 96m Roxy/Europa bw
                                              (FRAU CHENEY'S ENDE)

Lilli Palmer (Mrs. Cheney), Carlos Thompson (Artur Dilling), Martin Held (Charles), Francoise Rosay (Mme. Ebley), Maria Sebaldt (Helene), Wolfgang Kieling (Dimanche), Willy Birgel.

Palmer is a widow who moonlights as a jewel thief on the Riviera. All goes well until she meets and falls in love with Thompson and goes straight. Routine script redeemed by Palmer's performance. Hans-Martin Majewski, who wrote the music for the film, wrote operettas and cabaret tunes after WW II and became one of the busiest musicians on the German film scene. His operetta and cabaret work undoubtedly lay behind the unusual musical ideas and instrumentation for which he is known.

p, Luggi Waldleitner; d, Franz Josef Wild; w, Johanna Sibelius, Eberhard Keindorff (based on a comedy by Frederick Lonsdale); ph, Gunther Anders; m, Hans-Martin Majewski.

Comedy   **(PR:A MPAA:NR)**

END OF SUMMER, THE   (SEE: EARLY AUTUMN, 1962, Jap.)

END OF THE AFFAIR, THE**   (1955, Brit.) 107m COL bw

Deborah Kerr (Sarah Miles), Van Johnson (Maurice Bendrix), John Mills (Albert Parkis), Peter Cushing (Henry Miles), Michael Goodliffe (Smythe), Stephen Murray (Father Crompton), Charles Goldner (Savage), Nora Swinburne (Mrs. Bertram),

Frederick Leister (Dr. Collingwood), Mary Williams (Maid), O'Donovan Shiell (Doctor), Elsie Wagstaff (Bendrix Landlady), Christopher Warbey (Lancelot Parkis), Nan Munro (Mrs. Tomkins), Joyce Carey (Miss Palmer), Josephine Wilson (Miss Smythe), Shela Ward (Old Woman), Stanley Rose (Fireman), Mary Reed, Margaret Holmes, John H. Watson (Guests).

Kerr and Johnson are having an affair in wartime London. When a bomb injures Johnson, Kerr prays, promising God that she will leave him and return to her husband if he recovers. Johnson does recover, and Kerr keeps her word, though she endures a long battle with her conscience to do so. Tedious and overlong, with Kerr and Johnson totally mismatched.

p, David Lewis; d, Edward Dmytryk; w, Lenore Coffee (based on a novel by Graham Greene); ph, Wilkie Cooper; m, Benjamin Frankel; ed, Alan Osbiston; md, Frankel; art d, Don Ashton; cos, Julia Squire.

Drama (PR:A MPAA:NR)

END OF THE GAME**½ (1976, Ger./Ital.) 106m FOX c
(AKA: GETTING AWAY WITH MURDER)

Jon Voight (Walter Tschantz), Jacqueline Bisset (Anna Crawley), Martin Ritt (Hans Barlach), Robert Shaw (Richard Gastmann), Helmut Qualtinger (Von Schwendi), Gabriele Ferzetti (Dr. Lutz), Rita Calderoni (Nadine), Friedrich Duerrenmatt (Friedrich), Willy Huegli (Clenin), Norbert Schiller (Dr. Hungertobel), Guido Cerniglia (Coroner), Margarethe Schell von Noe (Mrs. Schoenler), Otto Ryser (Blatter), Rudolf Hunsperger, Edy Hubacher (Guards), Pinchas Zukerman (Violinist), Lil Dagover (Mrs. Gastman), Toni Roth (Old Lady), Wieland Liebske (Taxi Driver), Anton Netzer (Dr. Schallert), Kathrin Brunner (Cleaning girl).

Veteran police inspector Ritt is tenacious in his efforts to nail the man who 30 years before killed the woman both men loved, but now Ritt is dying. His new assistant, Voight, brings fresh life and new methods into the case, which includes an investigation into the murder of Ritt's previous assistant, Sutherland, who Ritt believes was also killed by the man he is after. A further facet of the strange story finds Bissett also attempting to solve the assistant's murder. Swiss playwright Duerrenmatt, who collaborated on the script, is known for his treatment of the bizarre and his authority over the filming of this story is evident in the layers of confusion spread over it until the denouement.

p, Maximillian Schell, Arlene Sellers; d, Schell; w, Friedrich Duerrenmatt, Bo Goldmann, Schell (based on the novel The Judge and His Hangman by Duerrenmatt); ph, Ennio Guarnieri, Robert Gerardi, Klaus Koenig (DeLuxe Color); ed, Dagmar Hirtz; art d, Mario Garbuglia.

Mystery (PR:C-O MPAA:PG)

END OF THE LINE, THE* (1959, Brit.) 64m Fortress/Eros/Balsam bw

Alan Baxter (Mike Selby), Barbara Shelley (Liliane Crawford), Ferdy Mayne (Edwards), Jennifer Jayne (Ann Bruce), Arthur Gomez (John Crawford), Geoffrey Hibbert (Max Perrin), Jack Melford (Inspector Gates), Marianne Braun (Desk Clerk), Charles Clay, Stella Bonheur, Maxwell Foster, Charles Cameron, Harry Taub, Colin Rix, Sheldon Allen, Barbara Cochran, Joe Wadham.

Baxter, an American writer in London, is prodded by mistress Shelley to rob her husband, a fence for stolen jewelry. The robbery is successful but the victim is later found dead and a blackmailer threatens Baxter. He decides to turn himself in to the police, then learns that the whole thing has been a plot between Shelley and Mayne, the victim's partner. Unbelievable crime drama with another of those American actor leads British B movies seem so fond of.

p, Guido Coen; d, Charles Saunders; w, Paul Erickson; ph, Walter J. Harvey; m, Edwin Astley.

Crime (PR:A-C MPAA:NR)

END OF THE RIVER, THE** (1947, Brit.) 83m Rank-Archers/GFD bw

Sabu (Manoel), Bibi Ferreira (Teresa), Esmond Knight (Dantos), Robert Douglas (Mr. Jones), Antoinette Cellier (Conceicao), Torin Thatcher (Lisboa), Orlando Martins (Harrigan), Raymond Lovell (Col. Porpino), James Hayter (Chico), Nicolette Bernard (Dona Serafina), Maurice Denham (Defense), Alan Wheatley (Irygogen), Charles Hawtrey (Raphael), Zena Marshall (Sante), Dennis Arundell (Continho), Milton Rosmer (Judge), Minto Cato (Dona Paula), Eva Hudson (Maria Gonsalves), Peter Illing (The Ship's Agent), Nino Rossini (Feliciano), Basil Appleby (Ship's Officer), Milo Sperber (Ze), Andrea Malandrinos (Officer of the India Protection Society), Arthur Goullet (The Pedlar), Russell Napier (Padre).

Sabu is a South American Indian brought out of the jungle to stand trial for murder. Flashbacks show him getting mixed up with revolutionaries. A confusing, mediocre film shot in Brazil, with little to recommend it to audiences elsewhere.

p, Michael Powell, Emeric Pressburger; d, Derek Twist; w, Wolfgang Wilhelm (based on a novel by Desmond Holdridge); ph, Christopher G. Challis; m, Lambert Williamson; ed, Brereton Porter; md, Muir Mathieson; art d, Fred Pusey.

Drama (PR:A MPAA:NR)

END OF THE ROAD, THE**½ (1936, Brit.) 72m FOX bw

Harry Lauder (John MacGregor), Ruth Haven (Sheila MacGregor), Ethel Glendinning (Jean MacGregor), Bruce Seton (Donald Carson), Margaret Moffatt (Maggie), Campbell Gullan (David), Vera Lennox (Flo), Tully Comber (Alan Cameron), Johnny Schofield.

So-so comedy about a traveling minstrel (Lauder) who keeps on trouping despite the death of his daughter and the loss of his life savings. Lauder is a good showman and he gets to sing all the songs that made him famous in Britain (and got him knighted), but that's about all there is here.

p, John Findlay; d, Alex Bryce; w, Edward Dryhurst; ph, Jack Parker.

Musical Comedy (PR:A MPAA:NR)

END OF THE ROAD** (1944) 61m REP bw

Edward Norris (Robert Kirby), John Abbott (Chris Martin), June Storey (Kitty McDougal), Jonathan Hale (Gregory McCune), Pierre Watkin (District Attorney), Ted Hecht (Walter Gribbon), Kenne Duncan (Al Herman), Eddy Fields (Joe Ferrari), Ferris Taylor (Drake), Emmett Vogan (Mannenburg), Charles Williams (Jordan), Edward Van Sloan (Judge).

Norris is a mystery writer who believes in the innocence of a man convicted of murder. He arranges a series of incidents that upset Abbott, the real killer, and, in the process clears the innocent man. Slightly interesting crime drama, with Abbott very good as the crazed killer.

p&d, George Blair; w, Denison Clift, Gertrude Walker (from a New Yorker magazine article by Alva Johnston); ph, William Bradford; m, Richard Sherwin; ed, Arthur Roberts; art d, Fred A. Ritter.

Crime (PR:A MPAA:NR)

END OF THE ROAD, THE*** (1954, Brit.) 76m BL/Group 3 bw

Edward Chapman (Works Manager), George Merritt (Timekeeper), Eugene Leary (Old Worker), Finlay Currie (Old "Mick-Mack"), Edie Martin (Gloomy Gertie), Duncan Lamont (Barney), David Hannaford (Barney Wee), Naomi Chance (Molly), Gordon Whiting (Young Kennie), Pauline Winter (Personnel Manager), Michael Bird (Builder), Tony Kilshawe (Manager), Hilda Fenemore (Madge), Herbert C. Walton, Claude Bonser, Kenneth Henry, Sam Kydd, Hugh Munro, Bert Sims, John Baker, Ewen Solon, Edward Malin.

Sentimental drama has Currie, a forcibly retired electroplater, forced to move in with his son. His daughter-in-law threatens to leave unless the old man is institutionalized, and at one point he wanders off into the night but his little grandson follows him and brings him back. Finally he solves a problem in a smelting vat at his old plant and in gratitude they give him a job as timekeeper.

p, Alfred Shaughnessy; d, Wolf Rilla; w, James Forsyth, Geoffrey Orme (from a radio play by Forsyth); ph, Arthur Grant; m, John Addison; ed, Bernard Gribble.

Drama (PR:A MPAA:NR)

END OF THE TRAIL***½ (1932) 61m COL bw

Tim McCoy, Luana Walter, Wheeler Oakman, Wally Albright, Lafe McKee, Wade Boteler, Chief White Eagle.

One of the only early sound westerns that gives a fair portrayal of the American Indian. McCoy plays an Army officer who is sympathetic to the Indian cause and is framed into a court-martial. He's charged with selling guns to the Indians, but the real criminal is Oakman. Thrown out of the Army McCoy loses all his friends; his son, Albright, and best friend, Boteler, are killed. McCoy is wounded in the end just as he has arranged an agreement between the Indians and the government. Originally, McCoy was then supposed to be killed, but Columbia felt this too depressing an ending and shot another in which he recovers. The film was shot entirely on location in Lander, Wyoming, and contains many then-authentic scenes of Indian life. This footage shows the American Indians not as brute savages, but as a people with a distinctive lifestyle and culture. McCoy had almost complete control of the project.

p, Irving Briskin; d, D. Ross Lederman; w, Stuart Anthony; ph, Benjamin Kline; ed, Otto Meyer.

Western (PR:A MPAA:NR)

END OF THE TRAIL*** (1936) 72m COL bw

Jack Holt (Dale Brittenham), Louise Henry (Belle Pearson), Douglass Dumbrille (Bill Mason), Guinn "Big Boy" Williams (Bob Hildreth), George McKay (Ben Parker), Gene Morgan (Cheyenne), John McGuire (Larry Pearson), Edward LeSaint (Jim Watrous), Frank Shannon (Sheriff Anderson), Erle C. Kenton (Theodore Roosevelt), Hank Bell, Art Mix, Blackie Whiteford, Blackjack Ward, Edgar Dearing.

Interesting, intelligent western has Holt a veteran of the Spanish-American war who is unable to find work and so turns to rustling. He is about to give up the outlaw life when the younger brother of his sweetheart (Henry) is shot. Holt kills the killer and is arrested by his best friend and rival for Henry, Sheriff Williams. Justice takes its course and Holt walks to the gallows leaving his heartbroken friend and sobbing sweetheart behind. Director Kenton has a brief cameo as Teddy Roosevelt.

p, Irving Briskin; d, Erle C. Kenton; w, Harold Shumate (from the novel Outlaws of Palouse by Zane Grey); ph, John Stumar; ed, Al Clark.

Western (PR:A MPAA:NR)

END OF THE WORLD, THE* (1930, Fr.) 91m L'Ecran d'Art bw
(LA FIN DU MONDE)

Abel Gance, Victor Francen, Georges Colin, Colette Darfeuil, Sylvia Grenade, Samson Fainsilber, Jean d'Yd, Wanda Vangen, Jeanne Brindeau, Philippe Hersent.

A dismal film directed by the man who did the French silent version of NAPOLEON (1926). Two brothers, one a religious madman (Gance) and the other a scientist (Francen), try to save the world's soul as a comet approaches earth. They preach a fascist-like dogma, which goes unheeded, in any case, because as the comet relentlessly advances to destroy earth, everyone jumps into orgies. A silly film and one that Gance was fired from after shooting because of the mess. (French; English subtitles, 1934.)

p, V. Ivanoff; d, Abel Gance; w, Gance, Andre Lang (based on a story by Camille Flammarion); ph, Jules Kruger, Nicolas Rudakov, Roger Hubert, Forster; m, Ondes Martenot, Michel Michelet; ed, Mme. Bruyere; art d, Lazare Meerson, Jean Perrier.

Science Fiction (PR:A MPAA:NR)

END OF THE WORLD, THE, 1962
(SEE: PANIC IN YEAR ZERO!, 1962)

END OF THE WORLD* (1977) 86m Irwin Yablans Co./Charles Band c

Christopher Lee, Sue Lyon, Kirk Scott, Lew Ayres, Macdonald Carey, Dean Jagger.

Lee is an alien masquerading as a priest; he heads a convent full of nun/aliens who plan to destroy the world. Lyon and Scott are scientists who discover the scheme, but instead of saving the earth they let Lee destroy it and go back with him to the planet Utopia. They should have taken this film with them.

p, Charles Band; d, John Hayes; w, Frank Ray Perelli; ph, John Huneck (DeLuxe Color).

| Science Fiction | Cas. | (PR:C MPAA:PG) |

END OF THE WORLD (in Our Usual Bed in a Night Full of Rain), THE*½ (1978, Ital.) 104m Liberty/WB c

Giancarlo Giannini (Paolo), Candice Bergen (Lizzy), Anne Byrne, Flora Carabella, Mario Scarpetta, Alice Colombo, Michael Tucker, Lucio Amelio, Anita Paltrinieri, Giuliana Carnescecchi, Agneso De Dunoto, Anny Papa, Alice Colombo Oxman, Massimo Wertmuller (Friends).

Made in English with Wertmuller's usual Italian crew, this is saved from being a total bore by the acting of Bergen and Giannini. Bergen is an American photographer and Giannini is an Italian journalist. They meet at a festival when Bergen, an ardent feminist, attempts to break up a fight between an Italian couple. When her Samaritanism threatens to get her into trouble, Giannini helps her escape then tries to seduce her but is rebuffed and goes off, shrugging his shoulders at the insanity of American women. "How could she resist me?" is his attitude. Bergen and Giannini meet again in San Francisco, fall in love, marry and spend the remainder of the picture arguing. He is a Communist but with expensive tastes and she, as previously stated, is an Equal Rights Advocate. In other words, as compatible as licorice and mayonnaise. Talky, often silly and almost always ponderous, the film shows none of the brilliance Ms. Wertmuller promised in THE SEDUCTION OF MIMI, SEVEN BEAUTIES, and SWEPT AWAY. A former assistant director to Fellini, Wertmuller decided to cancel the rest of her deal with Warner's after the cruel reviews for this. She'd had a multi-picture agreement but felt that she was an independent who needed more creative freedom. It didn't help and her next two films also took nose dives.

p, Gil Shiva; d&w, Lina Wertmuller; ph, Giuseppe Rotunno (Technicolor); m, G. B. Pergolesi, Roberto DeSimone; ed, Franco Fraticelli; art d, Enrico Job; set d, Gianni Giovagnoni; cos, Benito Persico; ex p, Harry Colombo.

| Drama | | (PR:C MPAA:R) |

END PLAY*** (1975, Aus.) 110m Roadshow/Hexagon c

George Mallaby (Robert Gifford), John Waters (Mark Gifford), Ken Goodlet (Supt. Cheadle), Robert Hewett (Sgt. Robinson), Delvane Delaney (Janine Talbort), Kevin Miles (Charlie Bricknall), Charles Tingwell (Dr. Fairburn), Walter Pym (Stanley Lipton), Sheila Florance (Mavis Lipton), Adrian Wright (Andrew Gifford), Belinda Giblin (Margaret Gifford).

Mallaby and Waters are brothers, Waters a merchant seaman and Mallaby a wheelchair-confined paraplegic with only a few months to live. Both become suspects in a series of blonde hitchhiker murders in the area, and each seems to be trying to cover up for the other—or diverting suspicion from himself. Well directed and acted Aussie suspense film.

p,d&w, Tim Burstall (from a novel by Russell Braddon); ph, Robin Copping; ed, David Bilcock; art d, Bill Hutchinson.

| Crime | | (PR:C MPAA:NR) |

ENDANGERED SPECIES zero (1982) 97m MGM/UA c

Robert Urich (Ruben Castle), JoBeth Williams (Harriet Purdue), Paul Dooley (Joe Hiatt), Hoyt Axton (Ben Morgan), Peter Coyote (Steele), Marin Kanter (Mackenzie Castle), Gailard Sartain (Mayor), Dan Hedaya (Peck), Harry Carey, Jr. (Dr. Emmer), John Considine (Burnside), Margery Bond (Judy), Joseph G. Medalis (Lawyer), Patrick Houser (Chester), Alvin Crow (Deputy Wayne), Ned Dowd (Deputy Bobby), Kent Rizley (Deputy Ray), Heather Menzies (Susan), Michelle Davison (Mrs. Haskins), Henry G. Sanders (Dr. Ross), Vernon Weddle (Varney).

Conspiracy theory trash with Urich a New York detective visiting out west and looking into a wave of cattle mutilations, where organs seem to have been surgically removed. He turns up a germ warfare research project involving the CIA, unscrupulous businessmen, corrupt politicians and crazed Vietnam veterans. The conspiracy plot makes no sense whatsoever and the amateurish performances don't help.

p, Carolyn Pfeiffer; d, Alan Rudolph; w, Rudolph, John Binder (from a story by Judson Klinger and Richards Woods); ph, Paul Lohmann (Metrocolor); m, Gary Wright; ed, Tom Walls; prod d, Trevor Williams; set d, R. Chris Westlund; spec eff, Jonnie Burke, Steve Galich.

| Drama | Cas. | (PR:O MPAA:R) |

ENDLESS LOVE zero (1981) 115m UNIV c

Brooke Shields (Jade), Martin Hewitt (David), Shirley Knight (Anne), Don Murray (Hugh), Richard Kiley (Arthur), Beatrice Straight (Rose), Jimmy Spader (Keith), Ian Ziering (Sammy), Tom Cruise (Billy), Jeffrey B. Versalle (Stuart), Jami Gertz (Patty), Maria Todd (Girl Friend), Douglas Alan-Mann (Teacher in Museum), Steve Calicchio (Weaver), Robert Kahn (Gene), Jeremy Bar-Illan (Jeremy), Scott Cushman (Gabe), David Willis (Walter), Barry Pruitt, Amy Whitman, Kenneth Cory, Teri Shields, Sylvia Short, Ethelmae Mason, Anna Berger, Joan Glasco, Mark Hopson Arnold, Kathy Bernard, Philip Lenkowsky, Arthur Epstein, Leonard H. Pass, Lawrence Sellars, Ron Perkins, Gilbert Stafford, Marvin Foster, Millidge Mosley, Willie Wenger, Ruth Last, Walt Gorney, Robert Altman, Lee Kimball, George Kyle, Duffy Puccini, Martin Pinckney.

Seventeen-year-old Hewitt and 15-year-old Shields fall in love. Shields' father (Murray) tolerates it for a time, but when Hewitt very nearly moves into Shields' bedroom, he puts his foot down and banishes the boy from the house for a month. Hewitt determines to redeem himself by setting the house on fire and then rescuing the family. The arson, however, gets out of control and the house burns to the ground and Hewitt is sent off to jail for a couple of years. Upon his release he is forbidden to see Shields, but after unintentionally bringing about the death of her father he gets to see her for a few moments before the cops drag him off again. Scott Spencer's intelligent, realistic novel is watered down until here it's just another teen sex film. The graphic sex scenes that were at the core of the book are reduced to picture-perfect set pieces, and the film is slow beyond belief. Shields' acting ability extends little beyond looking both pretty and vacuous.

p, Dyson Lovell; d, Franco Zeffirelli; w, Judith Rascoe (from the novel by Scott Spencer); ph, David Watkin (Technicolor); m, Jonathan Tunick; ed, Michael J. Sheridan; prod d, Ed Wittstein; art d, Ed Pisoni; set d, Alan Hicks; cos, Kristi Zea.

| Drama | Cas. | (PR:O MPAA:R) |

ENDLESS NIGHT, THE**½ (1963, Ger.) 84m Atlas-Film bw
(DIE ENDLOSE NACHT)

Karin Huebner (Lisa), Harald Leipnitz (Wolfgang Spitz), Paul Esser (J. M. Schreiber), Louise Martini (Mascha), Wolfgang Spier (Dr. Achtel), Werner Peters (Herbert), Hannelore Eisner (Silvia Stoessl).

Bad weather closes Berlin's Tempelhof airport and strands a number of travellers. Their stories, overwhelmingly dealing with sex in one form or another, make up the bulk of this intriguing film, shot on location in the airport waiting room without any prepared script. The film is talky at times, as might be expected from the lack of script, but the stories are, all in all, pretty interesting.

p,d&w, Will Tremper; ph, Hans Jura; m, Peter Thomas; ed, Susanne Paschen.

| Drama | | (PR:C MPAA:NR) |

ENDLESS NIGHT** (1971, Brit.) 99m BL c
(AKA: AGATHA CHRISTIE'S ENDLESS NIGHT)

Hayley Mills, Hywel Bennet, George Sanders, Britt Ekland, Per Oscarsson, Lois Maxwell, Peter Bowles.

Wealthy American girl Mills ventures to England, buys a beautiful country home, and marries a chauffeur. Her life is progressing swimmingly—then it ends. She is murdered. Though the characters never really take hold in this film based on an Agatha Christie novel, there are some suspenseful moments that leave audiences grabbing their seats.

d&w, Sidney Gilliate (based on a novel by Agatha Christie); ph, Harry Waxman (Eastmancolor); m, Bernard Herrmann.

| Suspense | Cas. | (PR:C MPAA:NR) |

ENDSTATION 13 SAHARA
(SEE: STATION SIX-SAHARA, 1964, Brit./Ger.)

ENEMIES OF PROGRESS**½ (1934, USSR) 80m Rosfilm/Amkino bw

Livanov (Ataman Annenkov), Gardin (General Janen), Taskin (Pereferitsin), Youdin (Ivan), Trakhtina (Daughter), Kostrichkin.

Livanov is a brilliant Czarist general who continues to fight the Communists even after all other resistance in Russia has stopped. He tries to enlist the peasants to help him, but they refuse, so he turns to a policy of terror until they rise up and with the help of the reds throw the general into China. Good action sequences and photography. This was the first Russian film to be seen in the United States after the U.S. officially recognized the U.S.S.R.

d&w, Nicolai Beresnyev; ph, Sigayev; m, Astradantsev.

| Drama | | (PR:A MPAA:NR) |

ENEMIES OF THE LAW* (1931) 69m Independent bw

Mary Nolan (Florence Vinton), Johnny Walker (Larry Marsh), Lou Tellegen (Eddie Swan), Harold Healy (Jack), Alan Brooks (Lefty), Dewey Robinson (Tony Catello), John Dunsmuir (The Big Shot), Danny Hardin (Joey Regan), Bert West (Babe Ricardo), Gordon Westcott (Blackie), Barry Townley, Doe Green.

Pretty bad low-budget gangster flick with Nolan a female cop fighting the baddies. Cliche after cliche in the story, low production values, hysterical overacting—in fact, virtually a catalog of every bad thing a crime movie can be.

p, S.S. Krellberg; d, Lawrence C. Windom; w, C.R. Jones; ph, Frank Zucker; ed, Russell Shields.

| Crime | | (PR:A MPAA:NR) |

ENEMY, THE (SEE: HELL IN THE PACIFIC, 1968)

ENEMY AGENT**½ (1940) 61m UNIV bw

Richard Cromwell (Jimmy Saunders), Helen Vinson (Irene Hunter), Robert Armstrong (Gordon), Marjorie Reynolds (Peggy O'Reilly), Jack Arnold (Lester Taylor), Russell Hicks (Lyman Scott), Philip Dorn (Dr. Jeffrey Arnold), Jack LaRue (Alex), Bradley Page (Francis), Abner Biberman (Baronoff), Luis Alberni (A. Calteroni), Jack Carson (Ralph), Milburn Stone (Meeker), Henry Victor (Karl, Butler), Charles Williams (Restaurant Patron), Harry Tyler (Patron), Eddy Waller (Cell Mate), Charles Wilson (Chief), Robert Homans (Doorman), Vic Potel (George, The Garageman), Gaylord [Steve] Pendleton (Mickey), Netta Packer (Landlady), Jean

De Briac, Lloyd Igraham *(Barbers)*, Peter Potter *(Bob)*, Ernie Adams *(Janitor)*, Dick Rush *(Jailer)*, Polly Bailey *(Woman)*, Nick Copeland *(Waiter)*, *Chuck Morrison (Policeman)*, Charles Sullivan *(Lender)*, Jessie Mae Jackson *(Young Girl)*, Brooks Benedict *(Head Waiter)*, James Craig *(Drunken College Boy)*.

Enemy agents plant blueprints to a secret bombsight on draftsman Cromwell when G-men close in. Then they turn around and kidnap him to recover the prints. Thanks to undercover agent Vinson, however, the G-men arrive just in the nick of time dressed as college boys, and literally tackle the spies. Unpretentious but fun B programmer, with footage taken from Universal's 1937 serial, "Radio Patrol."

p, Ben Pivar; d, Lew Landers; w, Edmund L. Hartman, Sam Robins (from a story by Robins); ph, Jerome Ash; ed, Ted Kent.

Spy Drama **(PR:A MPAA:NR)**

ENEMY AGENTS MEET ELLERY QUEEN* (1942) 64m COL bw

William Gargan *(Ellery Queen)*, Margaret Lindsay *(Nikki Porter)*, Charley Grapewin *(Inspector Richard Queen)*, Gale Sondergaard *(Mrs. Van Dorn)*, Gilbert Roland *(Paul Gillette)*, Sig Ruman *(Heinrich)*, James Burke *(Sgt. Velie)*, Ernest Dorian *(Morse)*, Felix Basch *(Helm)*, Minor Watson *(Commodore Lang)*, John Hamilton *(Commissioner Bracken)*, James Seay *(Sgt. Stevens)*, Louis [Ludwig] Donath *(Reece)*, Dick Wessel *(Sailor)*.

The last of the dismal Ellery Queen series, its plot given away in the title. The film ends with mobs of sailors and marines rushing in to beat the stuffing out of Nazi spies. A fittingly inauspicious end to a mercifully brief series. (See ELLERY QUEEN series, Index.)

p, Larry Darmour; d, James Hogan; w, Eric Taylor (based on a story by Ellery Queen (Manfred Lee and Frederic Dannay)); ph, James S. Brown, Jr.; m, Lee Zahler; ed, Dwight Caldwell.

Mystery **(PR:A MPAA:NR)**

ENEMY BELOW, THE**** (1957) 98m FOX c

Robert Mitchum *(Capt. Murrell)*, Curt Jurgens *(Von Stolberg)*, Al Hedison *(Lt. Ware)*, Theodore Bikel *(Schwaffer)*, Russell Collins *(Doctor)*, Kurt Kreuger *(Von Holem)*, Frank Albertson *(C.P.O. Crain)*, Biff Elliot *(Quartermaster)*, Alan Dexter *(Mackeson)*, Doug McClure *(Ensign Merry)*, Jeff Daley *(Corky)*, David Blair *(Ellis)*, Joe di Reda *(Robbins)*, Ralph Manza *(Lt. Bonelli)*, Ted Perritt *(Messenger)*, Jimmy Bayes *(Quiroga)*, Arthur La Ral *(Kunz)*, Frank Obershall *(Braun)*, Robert Boon *(Chief Engineer)*, Werner Reichow *(Mueller)*, Peter Dane *(Andrews, Radio Operator)*, Ronnie Rondell *(American Sailor)*, Lee J. Winters *(Striker)*, David Post *(Lewis)*, Ralph Reed *(Fireman)*, Maurice Donner *(Cook)*, Jack Kramer *(German Sailor)*, Robert Whiteside *(Torpedo Officer)*, Dan Tann, Dale Cummings, Sasha Harden, Michael McHale, Joe Brooks, Thomas Beyl, Richard Elmore, Vincent Deadrick, Dan Nelson, Roger Cornwell.

Here is an absorbing war film which comes down not to two battling countries and their ships but to two men in a deadly chess game of wit and cunning. Mitchum is the war-weary captain of a destroyer escort and Jurgens, in his American film debut, is the captain of a German U-Boat, both on the prowl for each other in the North Atlantic during WW II. Right from the first moment the tension mounts as the sonar operator on board Mitchum's ship, the *Haines*, picks up an underwater signal and Jurgens' submarine is identified. Mitchum begins tracking him. Jurgens, also a war-fatigued veteran, is on a desperate mission to rendezvous with a wolf pack and will not deviate from his course. But no matter his clever maneuvers, Mitchum stays on his tail, running ahead to drop depth charges, then falling back to track. Mitchum is relentless but Jurgens is shrewd and dauntless in this see-saw battle, the sub getting the worst of it, but capable of retaliating by firing its torpedoes if Mitchum's ship ever turns the wrong way. The German crew shows its courage by loudly singing some old WW I songs with the volume of its intercom playing the records turned up so that the American crew can hear them; this display of bravado fails to stir Mitchum's respect. At one point he remarks to his executive officer Hedison, "I don't want to know the man I'm trying to destroy." Jurgens is equally dedicated to his task of eliminating his enemy, as well as accomplishing his mission. His sub is pounded for days and nights as the two vessels play deadly cat-and-mouse games. Jurgens finally takes his submarine to the bottom and rests on the ocean floor, playing dead. The pressure against the sub is terrific; leaks spout everywhere and the German crew becomes jumpy, thinking the hull may be crushed any second. Jurgens gives his second-in-command, Bikel, a knowing smile and says, "They build them good in Germany, eh, Heinie?" But no ship can forever take the beating Mitchum administers so, in a desperate gamble, following the pattern of the depth charges his opponent has been dropping, Jurgens reverses his course, brings up his sub, and sends two torpedoes into the destroyer which is turning just as Jurgens figured it would. The destroyer is mortally wounded, but still has power. Mitchum plays possum, starting fires on deck and pretending his ship is dead in the water. The sub surfaces to finish off the American ship with its deck guns only to see the destroyer get up steam and race toward it, ramming it. The sub begins to sink, a detonator on a timing device set to blow both ships up in minutes. The Germans abandon ship as do the Americans but Jurgens and Mitchum remain on board their vessels, saluting each other. Jurgens goes back for his wounded friend, Bikel, and Mitchum helps both men escape their burning submarine, all three going into the water before the ships explode. Mitchum and Jurgens are seen together on board an American rescue ship following Bikel's burial at sea. They speak briefly, not as friends but as worthy opponents who have played out their hands to the last card. THE ENEMY BELOW is expertly helmed by actor-turned-director Powell who builds suspense and excitement scene by scene, giving as much necessary attention to the mechanics of war as to his principal actors. He quickly establishes his characters and then moves on to the deadliest game. Mitchum underplays his role and his reserved, almost stoic nature, perfectly suits his part. Jurgens is extremely sympathetic and powerful as the old WW I submariner who hates the Nazis and is fighting for ancient concepts of the fatherland. This was one of the first films to portray the WW II enemy with some understanding, if not outright empathy, and the portrait was accepted by the public, although box office returns barely covered the budget. Here is a fascinating look at war that is impartial, almost clinical; a brilliant perception by Powell that displays his many-sided talents.

p&d, Dick Powell; w, Wendell Mayes (based on the novel by D.A. Rayner); ph, Harold Rosson (CinemaScope, DeLuxe Color); m, Leigh Harline; ed, Stuart Gilmore; md, Lionel Newman; art d, Lyle R. Wheeler, Albert Hogsett; spec eff, L.B. Abbott.

War Drama **(PR:A MPAA:NR)**

ENEMY FROM SPACE*½** (1957, Brit.) 84m Hammer/UA (GB: QUATERMASS II)

Brian Donlevy *(Quatermass)*, John Longden *(Inspector Lomax)*, Sydney James *(Jimmy Hall)*, Bryan Forbes *(Marsh)*, William Franklyn *(Brand)*, Vera Day *(Sheila)*, Charles Lloyd Pack *(Dawson)*, Tom Chatto *(Broadhead)*, John Van Eyssen *(The P.R.O.)*, Percy Herbert *(Gorman)*, Michael Ripper *(Ernie)*, John Rae *(McLeod)*, Marianne Stone *(Secretary)*, Ronald Wilson *(Young Man)*, Jane Aird *(Mrs. McLeod)*, Betty Impey *(Kelly)*, Lloyd Lamble *(Inspector)*, John Stuart *(Commissioner)*, Gilbert Davis *(Banker)*, Joyce Adams *(Woman MP)*, Edwin Richfield *(Peterson)*, Howard Williams *(Michaels)*, Philip Baird, Robert Raikes *(Laboratory Assistants)*, John Fabian *(Intern)*, George Merritt *(Super)*, Arthur Blake *(Constable)*, Michael Balfour *(Harry)*, Jan Holden.

Doctor Quatermass learns of a strange meteorite shower in a nearby community and when he goes to investigate he finds the whole area cordoned off by the authorities—and a strange collection of pressure domes. It turns out that the meteorites have brought tiny organisms from space that have taken over human bodies and are building the pressure domes to house the host of aliens waiting out in space. Donlevy discovers that the aliens have also taken over a number of government officials and the Commissioner of Scotland Yard. Finally he rallies the townspeople, disgruntled because they aren't getting the jobs at what they believe to be a government construction project, to attack the domes and pump in air to kill the aliens. This, the second film in the Quatermass trilogy, is definitely the best, very similar to INVASION OF THE BODY SNATCHERS released the previous year. If anything, ENEMY FROM SPACE, is even more paranoid than Siegel's film as the conspiracy to take over the earth reaches into the highest levels of the government. One of the best science fiction films ever to come from Britain. Sequel: THE CREEPING UNKNOWN, FIVE MILLION YEARS TO EARTH.

p, Anthony Hinds; d, Val Guest; w, Guest, Nigel Kneale (based on Kneale's TV series); ph, Gerald Gibbs; m, James Bernard; ed, James Needs; art d, Bernard Robinson; spec eff, Les Bowie.

Science Fiction **(PR:A MPAA:NR)**

ENEMY GENERAL, THE** (1960) 75m Sam Katzman/COL bw

Van Johnson *(Lemaire)*, Jean-Pierre Aumont *(Durand)*, Dany Carrel *(Lisette)*, John Van Dreelen *(Gen. Bruger)*, Francoise Prevost *(Nicole)*, Hubert Noel *(Claude)*, Jacques Marin *(Marceau)*, Gerard Landry *(Navarre)*, Edward Fleming *(Sgt. Allen)*, Paul Bonifas *(Mayor)*, Paul Muller *(Maj. Zughoff)*.

Johnson is an O.S.S. agent during WW II who is sent to help a German general, Dreelen, escape occupied France to London. Dreelen killed Johnson's girl friend, Carrel, and eleven other French hostages. Johnson is given a hard time by the French underground and must battle his own feelings as he escorts the general out of France. When he finally realizes that the general is a plant for Nazi counter-espionage, he kills Dreelen.

p, Sam Katzman; d, George Sherman; w, Dan Pepper, Burt Picard (adapted from a story by Pepper); ph, Basil Emmott; m, Mischa Bakaleinikoff; ed, Gordon Pilkington, Edward Bryant; art d, Gaston Medin,

War **(PR:A MPAA:NR)**

ENEMY OF THE LAW** (1945) 59m PRC bw

Tex Ritter, Dave O'Brien, Guy Wilkerson, Kay Hughes, Jack Ingram, Charles King, Frank Ellis, Kermit Maynard, Henry Hall, Karl Hackett, Edward Cassidy, Ben Corbett.

In this entry in the Texas Rangers series, the trio is sent after a gang of terrorists threatening the frontier. Standard saddle stuff interspersed with songs.

p, Arthur Alexander; d&w, Harry Fraser; ph, Jack Greenhaigh; ed, Holbrook Todd; md, Lee Zahler.

Western **(PR:A MPAA:NR)**

ENEMY OF THE PEOPLE, AN** (1978) 103m First Artists-Solar/WB c

Steve McQueen *(Dr. Thomas Stockmann)*, Charles Durning *(Peter Stockmann)*, Bibi Andersson *(Catherine Stockmann)*, Eric Christmas *(Morten Kiil)*, Michael Cristofer *(Houstad)*, Richard A. Dysart *(Aslaksen)*, Michael Higgins *(Billing)*, Richard Bradford *(Captain Forster)*, Ham Larsen *(Morten Stockmann)*, John Levin *(Ejlif Stockmann)*, Robin Pearson Rose *(Petra Stockmann)*.

McQueen is the town doctor who discovers that waste from the tannery is contaminating the water in the recently opened hot springs the town hopes will bring in tourist revenue. He ignores the advice of his brother (Durning), the mayor, to keep his findings to himself; instead, he publicizes them and ends up an outcast, his practice gone and his family splintered. McQueen is totally miscast, and in the scenes with Durning completely acted off the screen. McQueen was also executive producer.

p&d, George Schaefer; w, Alexander Jacobs (from an adaptation by Arthur Miller of a play by Henrik Ibsen); ph, Paul Lohmann (Metrocolor); m, Leonard Rosenman; ed, Sheldon Kahn; prod d, Eugene Lourie; set d, Anthony Mondello; cos, Noel Taylor.

Drama **(PR:A MPAA:G)**

ENEMY OF THE POLICE* (1933, Brit.) 51m WB-FN bw

John Stuart *(John Meakin)*, Viola Keats *(Preston)*, A. Bromley Davenport *(Sir Lemuel Tapleigh)*, Margaret Yarde *(Lady Tapleigh)*, Violet Farebrother *(Lady Salterton)*, Ernest Sefton *(Slingsby)*, Winifred Oughton *(Martha Teavle)*, Alf Goddard *(Gallagher)*, Molly Fisher *(Ann)*, Hal Walters *(Bagshaw)*, Nora Brenon.

Feeble, unfunny comedy has Stuart, the head of a reform society, arrested as a criminal and brainwashed into seeing the error of his ways.

p, Irving Asher; d, George King.

Comedy **(PR:A MPAA:NR)**

ENEMY OF WOMEN** (1944) 86m MON bw (AKA: THE PRIVATE LIFE OF PAUL JOSEPH GOEBBELS)

Claudia Drake *(Maria Brandt)*, Paul Andor *(Paul Joseph Goebbels)*, Donald Woods *(Dr. Hans Traeger)*, H.B. Warner *(Col. Brandt)*, Sigrid Gurie *(Madga Quandt)*, Ralph Morgan *(Mr. Quandt)*, Gloria Stuart *(Bertha)*, Robert Barrat *(Wallburg)*, Beryl Wallace *(Jenny Hartmann)*, Byron Foulger *(Krause)*, Lester Dorr *(Hanussen)*, Craig Whitley *(Hanke)*, Charles Halton *(Uncle Hugo)*, Marian Sais *(Mrs. Bendler)*.

Strange, offbeat biography of Nazi propaganda minister Goebbels, played with monotone and cold-fish stare by Andor who is shown as a struggling playwright in his youth. He is rejected by Drake, a novice actress, and this so incenses the lustful, vindictive Andor that he spends the rest of his twisted life (or the duration of the movie) trying to get even with her. During the so-called "Night of the Long Knives" (when top Nazis purged their ranks of enemies), Andor orders the death of Warner, Drake's father, among others on his "hit" list. Drake flees the Nazi scourge to marry Woods in Vienna but the long arm of the Nazis and Andor reaches out to ruin her life. She winds up in Berlin and is killed during an air raid, Andor wandering through the ruins of her death site. This is a weak effort by all concerned, a film produced by Minneapolis theater owner W.R. Frank, and haphazardly directed by Zeisler. Though it purports to show the inside life of the insidious Goebbels, little real research is in evidence other than headlines-of-the-day information. Andor and Drake are positively awful and the script is idiotic. Gurie, whom Samuel Goldwyn, had tried to make a superstar a few years earlier in such films as THE ADVENTURES OF MARCO POLO, has no more than a minor role here in a Poverty Row production seldom seen, such had her star faded. The producers undoubtedly felt that the film's title would entice female patrons, but it didn't. Fleischer's stylish, expensive sets belie a Monogram production and provide the only noteworthy elements in an otherwise dull programmer.

p, W.R. Frank, Fred W. Kane; d, Alfred Zeisler; w, Zeisler, Herbert O. Phillips; ph, John Alton; m, Arthur Guttman; ed, Douglas W. Bagler; art d, Stanley Fleischer.

War/Biography **(PR:C MPAA:NR)**

ENEMY, THE SEA, THE (SEE: MY ENEMY, THE SEA, 1964)

ENFORCER, THE**** (1951) 87m United States Pictures/WB bw (GB: MURDER, INC.)

Humphrey Bogart *(Martin Ferguson)*, Zero Mostel *(Big Babe Lazich)*, Ted De Corsia *(Joseph Rico)*, Everett Sloane *(Albert Mendoza)*, Roy Roberts *(Capt. Frank Nelson)*, Lawrence Tolan *(Duke Malloy)*, King Donovan *(Sgt. Whitlow)*, Bob Steele *(Herman)*, Adelaide Klein *(Olga Kirshen)*, Don Beddoe *(Thomas O'Hara)*, Tito Vuolo *(Tony Vetto)*, John Kellogg *(Vince)*, Jack Lambert *(Philadelphia Tom Zaca)*, Patricia Joiner *(Teresa Davis/Angela Vetto)*, Susan Cabot *(Nina Lombardo)*, Mario Siletti *(Louis the Barber)*, Alan Foster *(Shorty)*, Harry Wilson *(B.J.)*, Pete Kellett, Barry Reagan *(Interns)*, Dan Riss *(Mayor)*, Art Dupuis *(Keeper)*, Bud Wolfe *(Fireman)*, Creighton Hale *(Clerk)*, Patricia Hayes *(Teenager)*, Robert Strong *(Secretary)*, Mike Lally *(Detective)*, George Meader *(Medical Examiner)*, Ralph Dunn *(Sergeant)*, Perc Launders *(Police Sergeant)*, Tom Dillon *(Policeman)*, John Maxwell *(Doctor)*, Howard Mitchell *(Chief)*, Brick Sullivan *(Police Chauffeur)*, Greta Granstedt *(Mrs. Lazick)*, Louis Lettieri *(Boy)*, Monte Pittman *(Intern)*, Chuck Hamilton, Jay Morley *(Policemen)*, Richard Bartell *(Clerk)*, Karen Kester *(Nina as a Child)*, Eula Guy *(Landlady)*.

One of the first films to deal directly with nationwide organized crime, THE ENFORCER pulls no punches in telling its grim but fascinating story. De Corsia, head of the syndicate's professional murder squad, has been brought into protective custody, after agreeing to testify against crime czar Sloane. Bogart, who is the district attorney, has spent years building his case against Sloane and now, with De Corsia's testimony, he will be able to send him to the electric chair for mass murder. De Corsia is terrified that nothing can save his life from Sloane and his killers. In an attempt to escape, De Corsia knocks out a guard, slips out a bathroom window, and tries to walk along a narrow ledge so he can leap to the fire escape of an adjoining building. Bogart rushes into the room and leans out the window, telling De Corsia he can't make it, to come back along the ledge; when De Corsia reaches out for him he slips and falls to his death and with him goes Bogart's case. Bogart begins to think back, going over his many bound pages of testimony and reports, thinking back to when a young hoodlum, Tolan, walked into a precinct headquarters to report murdering his girl friend, Cabot. In flashback we see Tolan take police to a rural spot where an empty grave yields no body. Tolan later commits suicide in his cell, yet his testimony implicates a bevy of hoodlums whom Bogart and his aides, Roberts, Donovan, etc., track down. One, Lambert, is found in a lunatic asylum, crazily salivating his answers to Bogart's queries from a shock treatment table. Another, Mostel, is found hiding in a church. Another is found burning in a basement furnace. Mostel talks when Bogart threatens to prosecute his innocent wife as an accessory, and he relates how he joined the murder troop and how contracts were awarded killers for "hits," a troop built on killing where the killers, having no motivation, easily escape detection. Sloane's story is related in the tapes made by De Corsia, who describes how Sloane built the organization from his first killing for which he was paid $500, the murder of a restaurant owner. De Corsia is shown accompanying Sloane to the restaurant and watching in horror as Sloane murders the owner. A man and his little daughter enter just as the killers depart and De Corsia starts to break into a run. Sloane stops him, saying: "Walk . . . run and someone runs after you." Killers on Sloane's payroll later murder the man who witnessed Sloane's murder but the girl is not found until years later by Tolan. Her body is subsequently turned up in a swamp with dozens more, the burial site of the gang's victims. With the heat on, the murder troop takes to cover but other killers from distant cities track it down, killing them so they will never testify against Sloane. In a flash-forward, Bogart, with only a few hours before going to trial without his star witness, finds a discrepancy in testimony and the statistics of Tolan's murdered girl friend. The little girl who had witnessed the killing had blue eyes and Tolan's girl had brown eyes. Bogart realizes that the gang has killed the wrong girl and that the real witness is still alive. He also realizes that Cabot is the murdered girl's roommate, not the real witness, Joiner. By then Sloane, too, realizes his men have killed the wrong girl and, even from his cell, he is able to order Joiner killed by out-of-town hit man Steele. Now it becomes a race to see who can get to Joiner first. In a clever ruse, Bogart reaches her first on the street and when Steele tries to shoot him and her, Bogart guns him down. It is left to the viewer to speculate whether or not Sloane will be convicted and pay for his horrific crimes. The film is taken straight out of the newspaper headlines of a decade earlier, chronicling Murder, Inc. De Corsia's character is wholly based on the notorious informer Abe "Kid Twist" Reles, who exposed Murder, Inc., and either fell or was pushed from his hotel room in the Half Moon Hotel in Coney Island, falling many floors to his death in 1942. Sloane's part is that of the sinister Louis "Lepke" Buchalter, head of Murder, Inc., who went to the electric chair in 1944. Bogart plays the crusading district attorney, Burton B. Turkus, the man who exposed the killer-for-hire organization. This powerful crime drama is shot in stark black and white by Burks. Windust's crisp, quick directing was aided considerably by veteran helmsman Walsh. Though uncredited, Walsh's sure imprint is to be found everywhere as he establishes the semi-documentary approach which proved so successful in WHITE HEAT. Rackin's script is tough, even brutal, in depicting the slaughterhouse deeds of the worst gang of killers ever to intimidate America. Advance publicity blurbs alerted viewers about what to expect as Bogart "matched himself against a nationwide network of killers-for-hire . . . and tore apart the evil dynasty that peddled murder for a price." Bogart appears infrequently as the many stories in flashbacks are told, but his solid, restrained performance is the linking element to this classic *film noir* tale. He is nothing less than superb. Bogart had been so impressed with the chilling performance by Steele in THE BIG SLEEP that he specifically asked executives to cast him in the role of the calculating out-of-town killer in THE ENFORCER. All of the supporting players are chillingly effective, particularly Sloane, a master at playing sinister roles. De Corsia is a terrifying, snarling hoodlum, as are Tolan, Kellogg and Lambert. Mostel gives a wild, histrionic performance as an obese would-be killer, more hanger-on than hanger-in, a bald-headed, pop-eyed slob afraid of his own shadow.

p, Milton Sperling; d, Bretaigne Windust and (uncredited) Raoul Walsh; w, Martin Rackin; ph, Robert Burks; m, David Buttolph; ed, Fred Allen; art d, Charles H. Clarke; set d, William Kuehl.

Crime Drama **(PR:C MPAA:NR)**

ENFORCER, THE** (1976) 96m Malpaso/WB c

Clint Eastwood *(Harry Callahan)*, Tyne Daly *(Kate Moore)*, Bradford Dillman *(Capt. McKay)*, Harry Guardino *(Lt. Bressler)*, DeVeren Bookwalter *(Bobby Maxwell)*, John Mitchum *(DiGeorgia)*, John Crawford *(The Mayor)*, Albert Popwell *(Big Ed)*.

Eastwood is at it again as Dirty Harry, a San Francisco cop who enjoys taking the law into his own hands and exposing the corrupt elements of his own police force. He is teamed with Daly, after his regular sidekick Mitchum is stabbed by a pimp turned terrorist. Eastwood at first resents Daly and their confrontations are tough but he later falls in love with her. Eastwood and Daly uncover a terrorist organization which has been amassing ammunition and explosives; this group abducts the mayor of San Francisco, Crawford, and holds him for a huge ransom. Eastwood goes undercover, pretending to be a tourist visiting a nude massage parlor, then visiting a black militant headquarters and other unsavory sites of the city to turn up evidence leading to the terrorist ring. He and Daly finally learn that Crawford is being held on deserted Alcatraz Island and they attempt to free him, Daly being shot to death in a hail of machine gun fire. Eastwood manages to kill the culprits, free Crawford, and reject offers of rewards, remaining deadly stoic to the end. Improbable as are all the Dirty Harry films, THE ENFORCER, is crammed with action and spilling over with violence. The lensing is fine but the gore is repugnant, as is Daly's obnoxious overacting. She is about as appealing as a fireplug with legs. Daly's whining Eastern accent, her forced delivery and mannish postures dismiss her as a serious actress, let alone a romantic lead. She possesses a grating, annoying personality that detracts from any believability in her role; a hopeless miscasting. Eastwood just goes through the motions, as usual, which is the best his myriad fans can expect. Dillman, as the oafish police superior, is wasted. This third in the Dirty Harry films, originally entitled DIRTY HARRY III, is slow-paced and basically dull, yet it culled $24 million at the box office. Sequel: SUDDEN IMPACT. (See DIRTY HARRY series, Index.)

p, Robert Daley; d, James Fargo; w, Stirling Silliphant, Dean Reisner (based on characters created by Harry Julian Fink and R.M. Fink); ph, Charles W. Short (Panavision, DeLuxe Color); m, Jerry Fielding; ed, Joel Cox, Ferris Webster, art d, Allen E. Smith; stunts, Wayne Van Horn.

Crime **Cas.** **(PR:O MPAA:R)**

ENGAGEMENT ITALIANO** (1966, Fr./Ital.) 85m Archimede/Film-France/Cinema/Productions-Incom/Centro Cinematografico bw (Ital.: LA RAGAZZA IN PRESTITO)

Rossano Brazzi *(Mario)*, Annie Girardot *(Clara)*, Tony Anthony *(Franco)*, Marisa Merlini *(Regina)*, Giuditta Rissone, Silla Bettini, Nino Dal Fabbro, Giorgio Tedeschi, Cesarina Gherardi, Renzo Palmer.

Brazzi is a middleaged playboy who inherits his father's furrier business. The company is run by his father's mistress, Merlini, so Brazzi spends his time with his friends. His fiancee, Girardot, becomes pregnant, but he won't marry her. She leaves him for Brazzi's best friend, Anthony, and one by one Brazzi finds that all his friends have left him. The aging playboy ends up with his father's mistress who's had an eye on him for some time.

p, Pietro Notarianni; d&w, Alfredo Giannetti; ph, Enzo Scrafin; m, Armando Trovajoli.

Comedy Drama   **(PR:A MPAA:NR)**

ENGLAND MADE ME***½   (1973, Brit.) 100m Cine Globe/Hemdale c

Peter Finch (Eric Krogh), Michael York (Anthony Farrant), Hildegard Neil (Kate Farrant), Michael Hordern (F. Minty), Joss Ackland (Haller), Tessa Wyatt (Liz Davidge), Michael Sheard (Fromm), Bill Baskiville (Stein), Demeter Bitenc (Reichminister), Mira Nikolic (Nikki), Vladimir Bacic (Hartmann), Maja Papadopulo (Nightclub Singer), Vladan Zivkovic (Heinrich), Cvetka Cupar (Maria).

York is an idealistic young Englishman on his way home from the Far East who passes through Nazi Germany and runs into corrupt, decadent industrialist Finch. Scrupulously accurate and well acted adaptation of Graham Greene's first novel.

p, Jack Levin; d, Peter Duffell; w, Desmond Cory, Duffell (from a novel by Graham Greene); ph, Ray Parslow (Panavision, Eastmancolor); m, John Scott; ed, Malcolm Cooke; prod d, Tony Woollard; art d, Peter Young; cos, John Furniss.

Drama   **(PR:C MPAA:PG)**

ENGLISH WITHOUT TEARS   (SEE: HER MAN GILBY, 1948, Brit.)

ENGLISHMAN'S HOME, AN
      (SEE: MAD MEN OF EUROPE, 1939, Brit.)

ENIGMA*½   (1983) 101m Filmcrest International/Embassy c

Martin Sheen (Alex Holbeck), Sam Neill (Dimitri Vasilkov), Brigette Fossey (Karen), Derek Jacobi (Kurt Limmer), Michel Lonsdale (Bodley), Frank Finlay (Canarsky), David Baxt (Melton), Kevin McNally (Bruno), Michael Williams (Hirsch), Warren Clarke (Konstantin).

Sheen is an East German defector who has worked for Radio Free Europe recruited by the CIA to return to East Berlin to steal a coded microprocessor in order to save five dissidents living in the west from assassination by the KGB. Once behind the Iron Curtain, Sheen looks up Fossey, his old girl friend, and enlists her help. Neill is a rising young KGB man trying to make his name by catching Sheen. Complex and not very convincing, with Sheen's performance consisting of little more than a funny accent.

p, Peter Shaw, Ben Arbeid, Andre Perqament; d, Jeannot Szwarc; w, John Briley (from the novel Enigma Sacrifice by Michael Barak); ph, Jean Louis Picavet; m, Marc Wilkinson, Douglas Gamley; ed, Peter Weatherley, Peter Culverwell; art d, Francois Comtet, Marc Frederix.

Spy Drama   **Cas.**   **(PR:C MPAA:NR)**

ENJO***   (1959, Jap.) 96m Daiei bw
(AKA: FLAME OF TORMENT; CONFLAGRATION)

Raizo Ichigawa, Ttasuya Nakadai, Ganjiro Nakamura, Yoko Uraji, Michiyo Aratama, Tamao Nakamura, Yoichi Funaki, Kinzo Shin, Tanie Kitabayashi.

Calculating and distancing study of a young religious fanatic and his desire to keep his beloved temple from being dirtied by the presence of impure forces wishing to take advantage of the temple. This leads him to a ritualized burning of the sacred building, followed by his own suicide. This adaptation from the novel by Mishima—one of Japan's most famous authors, noted for his tales of obsessed individuals—is brilliant in detailing the events which lead up to this youth's final experience. Excellent black and white, wide-screen photography by Miyagawa, the same man responsible for the cinematography on the much-heralded RASHOMON.

d, Kon Ichikawa; w, Natto Wada, Keiji Hasebe (based on the novel The Temple Of The Golden Pavillion by Yukio Mishima); ph, Kazuo Miyagawa; m, Toshio Mayuzumi.

Drama   **(PR:O MPAA:NR)**

ENLIGHTEN THY DAUGHTER*   (1934) 75m Exploitation Pictures bw

Herbert Rawlinson (Dr. Richard Stevens), Beth Barton (Ruth Stevens), Charles Eaton (David Stevens), Claire Whitney (Alice Stevens), Edmund MacDonald (Gerald Winthrop), Russell Hicks (Daniel Stevens), Ara Gerald (Ethel Stevens), Miriam Battista (Lillian Stevens), Jack Arnold (Stanley Jordan), Eunice Reed (Margie), Wesley Barry (Wes), Audrey Maple (Mrs. Crosby), Lillian Walker (Mrs Grainger), Robert Emmett Keane (Dr. Palmer).

Slow-moving melodrama in which two daughters of two men meet very different fates. One, daughter of a dedicated reformer who neglects her, gets pregnant and commits suicide. In the other family, the father, a doctor, gives his daughter lots of love, so she grows up happily. Moralistic and trite, with amateur production values, this is a remake of a 1917 silent produced by Ivan Abramson.

p, Robert Mintz; d, John Varley; w, Arthur Hoerl, Bob Lively, Betty Laidlaw (based on a story by Ivan Abramson); ph, William E. Miller, Nicholas J. Rogalli; m, Lou Herscher; ed, Patricia Rooney.

Drama   **(PR:A MPAA:NR)**

ENOUGH ROPE**   (1966, Fr./Ital./Ger.) 104m
International Productions-Cocinor-Les Films; Marceau-Sancro;
Film-Galatea-Corona Filmproduktion/Artixo bw
(LE MEURTRIER; L'OMICIDA; DER MORDER; AKA: THE MURDERER)

Marina Vlady (Ellie), Robert Hossein (Corby), Maurice Ronet (Walter Saccard), Yvonne Furneaux (Clara Saccard), Paulette Dubost (Helen Kimmel), Gert Frobe (Melchior Kimmel), Harry Mayen (Tony), Jacques Monod (Police Commissioner), Clara Gansard.

An unhappily married architect, Ronet, becomes interested in Frobe's trial for the murder of his wife, and begins to collect newspaper clippings on the trial. Frobe is acquitted, but Ronet still believes him guilty. He visits Frobe and becomes even more convinced that Frobe murdered his wife. Then Ronet's wife is found dead in a ravine and Frobe assumes that Ronet committed the crime and begins blackmailing him. The police find the murder-trial newspaper clippings in Ronet's home and then, because Frobe believes Ronet is trying to ruin him, he murders the architect.

d, Claude Autant-Lara; w, Pierre Bost, Jean Aurenche (based on the novel The Blunderer by Patricia Highsmith); ph, Jacques Natteau (Franscope); m, Rene Cloerez; ed, Madeleine Gug; art d, Max Douy.

Murder Mystery   **(PR:A MPAA:NR)**

ENSIGN PULVER**½   (1964) 104m WB c

Robert Walker, Jr. (Ensign Pulver), Burl Ives (Captain), Walter Matthau (Doc), Tommy Sands (Bruno), Millie Perkins (Scotty), Kay Medford (Head Nurse), Larry Hagman (Billings), Gerald S. O'Loughlin (LaSueur), Sal Papa (Gabrowski), Al Freeman, Jr. (Taru), James Farentino (Insigna), James Coco (Skouras), Don Dorrell (Payne), Peter L. Marshall (Carney), Robert Matek (Stretch), Diana Sands (Mila), Joseph Marr (Dowdy), Jack Nicholson (Dolan).

Walker takes the Jack Lemmon role in this sequel to MISTER ROBERTS. The USS Reluctant roams the South Pacific in the waning days of World War II, dropping cargo at obscure island bases. The ship is ruled over by the tyrannical Ives, and most of the comedy revolves around his excesses and the men's dissatisfaction. Walker entertains ambitions of becoming a doctor and ship's doctor Matthau is his mentor. When a storm washes Ives overboard, Walker goes out to rescue him, but it's not until morning that they are missed. The pair drift in a rubber raft until they wash up on an island. Ives gets appendicitis and Walker has to operate, getting his instructions over the radio from Matthau back on the ship. Vastly inferior to its predecessor, with Walker no Lemmon and Ives no Cagney. Best reason to see this is to see a number of future stars (Hagman, Farentino, Coco, Sands, Nicholson, et al.) as youngsters.

p&d, Joshua Logan; w, Logan, Peter S. Feibleman (based on characters in play by Logan and Thomas Heggen, from the novel by Heggen); ph, Charles Lawton (Panavision, Technicolor); m, George Duning; ed, William Reynolds; art d, Leo K. Kuter; cos, Dorothy Jeakins.

Comedy   **Cas.**   **(PR:A MPAA:NR)**

ENTENTE CORDIALE***   (1939, Fr.) 95m Flora Films bw

Victor Francen (Edouard VII), Gaby Morlay (Queen Victoria), Andre Lefaur (Lord Clayton), Marcelle Praince (Lady Clayton), Jeanine Darcey (Sylvia Clayton), Jacques Gretillat (Deputy Roussel), Pierre Richard Willm (Capt. Roussel), Bernard Lancret (Jean Roussel), Arlette Marchal (Queen Alexandra), Jean Galland (Lord Kitchener), Jean d'Yd (Joseph Chamberlain), Jean Toulout (Lord Salisbury), Jean Perrier (President Loubet), Jean Worms (Theophile Delcasse), Jacques Baumer (Clemenceau), Jacques Catelain (The Prince Consort), Zizani (Paul Cambon), Andre Roanne (Lord Balfour), Aime Clariond (Russian Ambassador), Seigner (German Ambassador), Juny Astor, Ginette Gaubert (The Actresses), Carine Nelson (Marjorie, Lady of Honor to the Queen), Nita Raya (Music Hall Star), Dorville (Coachman), Abel Tarride (Maitre d'Hotel), Pierre Labry (Journalist), Gildes (Secretary), Brochard (Valet), Sinoel (Concierge).

Giant cast acts out the history of Franco-British diplomacy beginning during the reign of Queen Victoria and continuing to WW I. Well acted all the way through, this was most likely made to remind the British of their lasting friendship with France in the face of impending German attack.

p, Max Glass; d, Marcel l'Herbier; w, Steve Passeur, Abel Hermant, Glass (based on Edward VII and His Times by Andre Maurois); ph, Ted Pahle, Marc Fossard; m, Darius Milhaud; cos, Boris Bilinsky.

Historical Drama   **(PR:A MPAA:NR)**

ENTER ARSENE LUPIN**   (1944) 72m UNIV bw

Charles Korvin (Arsene Lupin), Ella Raines (Stacie), J. Carrol Naish (Ganimard), George Dolenz (Dubose), Gale Sondergaard (Bessie Seagrave), Miles Mander (Charles Seagrave), Leyland Hodgson (Constable Ryder), Tom Pilkington (Pollett), Lillian Bronson (Wheeler), Holmes Herbert (Jobson), Charles LaTorre (Inspector Cogswell), Gerald Hamer (Doc Marling), Ed Cooper (Cartwright), Art Foster (Superintendent), Clyde Kenny (Beckwith), Alphonse Martell (Conductor).

Korvin is a French jewel thief who robs a huge emerald from Raines aboard a train. Later he falls in love with her and so follows her to England. There he returns the jewel and discovers that cousin Sondergaard is planning to murder her for her inheritance. In between a few more heists, he manages to save her life, although it results in his capture by Naish. Not very well scripted, and Korvin comes off as a second-rate Charles Boyer, though the supporting cast does a good job. (See ARSENE LUPIN series, Index.)

p&d, Ford Beebe; w, Bertram Millhauser (based on characters created by Maurice LeBlanc, Frank de Croisset); ph, Hal Mohr; m, Milton Rosen; ed, Saul A. Goodkind; md, Rosen; art d, John B. Goodman, Abraham Grossman.

Crime   **(PR:A MPAA:NR)**

ENTER INSPECTOR DUVAL**   (1961, Brit.) 64m
Bill&Michael Luckwell/COL bw

Anton Diffring (Inspector Duval), Diane Hart (Jackie), Mark Singleton (Inspector Wilson), Charles Mitchell (Brossier), Aiden Grennell (Mark Sinclair), Susan Hallinan (Doreen), Charles Roberts (Charley).

Diffring, a French police detective, lends his support to a Scotland Yard investigation into the murder of a socialite during a jewel theft. Diffring has ulterior motives. They're not very interesting.

p, Bill Luckwell, Jock MacGregor; d, Max Varnel; w, J. Henry Piperno (based on a story by Jacques Monteux).

Crime   **(PR:A-C   MPAA:NR)**

ENTER LAUGHING***½   (1967) 112m COL c

Jose Ferrer (*Mr. Marlowe*), Shelley Winters (*Mrs. Kolowitz*), Elaine May (*Angela*), Jack Gilford (*Mr. Foreman*), Reni Santoni (*David Kolowitz*), Janet Margolin (*Wanda*), David Opatoshu (*Mr. Kolowitz*), Michael J. Pollard (*Marvin*), Don Rickles (*Harry Hamburger*), Richard Deacon (*Pike*), Nancy Kovack (*Miss B.*), Herbie Faye (*Mr. Schoenbaum*), Rob Reiner (*Clark Baxter*), Danny Stein (*Spencer Reynolds*), Milton Frome (*Policeman*), Lillian Adams (*Theatregoer*), Mantan Moreland (*Subway Rider*), Patrick Campbell (*Butler*), Peter Brocco (*Lawyer Peabody*).

Stage-struck Santoni leaves his job as a machinist's apprentice and gets work at a decrepit theater run by Ferrer, a drunken old ham. Winters, Santoni's mother, objects to his choice of careers, wanting her son to go to school and become a druggist. Based on Carl Reiner's recollections of his beginnings, the Broadway play made a star out of Alan Arkin, but Santoni is hopeless in the lead, lacking both the charm and the wit to pull it off.

p, Carl Reiner, Joseph Stein; d, Reiner; w, Stein, Reiner (from a play by Stein); ph, Joseph Biroc (PatheColor); m, Quincy Jones; ed, Charles Nelson.

Comedy   **(PR:A   MPAA:NR)**

ENTER MADAME**½   (1935) 81m PAR bw

Elissa Landi (*Lisa Della Robbia*), Cary Grant (*Gerald Fitzgerald*), Lynne Overman (*Mr. Farnum*), Sharon Lynne (*Flora Preston*), Michelette Burani (*Bice*), Paul Porcasi (*Archimede*), Adrian Rosley (*The Doctor*), Cecilia Parker (*Aline Chalmers*), Frank Albertson (*John Fitzgerald*), Wilfred Hari (*Tamamoto*), Torben Meyer (*Carlson*), Harold Berquist (*Bjorgenson*), Diana Lewis (*Operator*), Richard Bonelli (*Scarpia on Stage*), Matt McHugh (*Reporter*), Nina Koshetz (*dubbed Landi's singing*), Wallis Clark, Fred Malatesta, Tonly Merlo, Dick Kline, Gino Corrado, Diana Lewis, Frank G. Dunn, Mildred Boothe, Jack Byron, Richard Bonelli, Bud Galea.

Grant falls in love with and marries Landi, an opera star. He finds himself reduced to just another member of her entourage as they tour Europe, and finally, sick of it, he returns to New York City and files for divorce. Lynne is waiting in the States to marry him as soon as the divorce is final, but Landi decides not to give him up so easily. Rushing back, she invites Grant and Lynne to a performance, and while singing an aria, she recaptures Grant's heart for a happy ending. Pleasant domestic comedy with some classy music dubbed over Landi's mouthing.

p, A. Benjamin Glaser; d, Elliott Nugent; w, Charles Brackett, Gladys Lehman (from a play by Gilda Varesi Archibald and Dorothea Donn-Byrne); ph, Theodor Sparkuhl, William Mellor; art d, Hans Dreier, Ernst Fegte; cos, Travis Banton.

Comedy   **(PR:A   MPAA:NR)**

ENTER THE DRAGON***   (1973) 98m Concord/WB c

Bruce Lee (*Lee*), John Saxon (*Roper*), Jim Kelly (*Williams*), Shih Kien (*Han*), Bob Wall (*Oharra*), Ahna Capri (*Tania*), Angela Mao Ying (*Su-Lin*), Betty Chung (*Mei Ling*), Geoffrey Weeks (*Braithwaite*), Yang Sze (*Bolo*), Peter Archer (*Parsons*).

Lee is recruited by government agent Weeks to enter a martial arts contest on the island fortress of Kien, who is believed to be involved in drug smuggling and prostitution. Lee agrees because he knows that Kien's right-hand man, Wall, is responsible for his sister's death (she committed suicide rather than be raped by him). On the island he meets Saxon and Kelly, ex-army buddies from the U.S., on the run, respectively, from the Mob and the Law. Lee tries to infiltrate Kien's underground chamber but fails, beating up a number of guards in the process. The next morning Kien orders the men who let the intruder escape to fight Sze, who kills them all easily. Kien tries to get Kelly to tell him who the intruder was, but he refuses. Kien kills him with an iron claw. Lee is pitted against Wall in the competition and kills him. Kien tries to recruit Saxon to work for him, but when Saxon sees that Kien has killed Kelly, his friend, he refuses. Lee manages to enter the underground chamber and collect the evidence of Kien's guilt, but on the way out, after defeating hundreds of guards, he is trapped between two steel doors. Kien orders Saxon to fight Lee, but he refuses. So Kien pits Saxon in a fight to the death with the huge Sze. The women Kien keeps imprisoned escape and attack. After a vicious fight Saxon kills Sze. Lee chases Kien into his hiding place, a room of mirrors. Kien uses his iron claw to cut Lee badly, but Lee defeats him by impaling him on a spear. By far the best of the Kung Fu genre, despite some major differences from the bulk of them attributable to U.S., rather than Hong Kong, production. Lee proves why he is still the dominant legend in the genre more than 12 years after his death. During one fight scene, Lee performed a flying kick so fast it couldn't be captured on film at 24 frames a second. The cameraman had to film the sequence in slow motion to get it to look like it wasn't faked. Nobody shows much evidence of acting ability, and the script is full of holes. Non-stop action is what these are about, and that's what you get here.

p, Fred Weintraub, Paul Heller; d, Robert Clouse; w, Michael Allin; ph, Gilbert Hubbs (Technicolor); m, Lalo Schifrin; ed, Kurt Hirshler, George Watters; art d, James Wong Sun.

Martial Arts   **Cas.**   **(PR:O   MPAA:R)**

ENTER THE NINJA*   (1982) 99m Golan-Globus/Cannon c

Franco Nero (*Cole*), Susan George (*Mary-Ann Landers*), Sho Kosugi (*Hasegawa*), Alex Courtney (*Frank Landers*), Will Hare (*Dollars*), Zachi Noy (*The Hook*), Constantin de Goguel (*Parker*), Dale Ishimoto (*Komori*), Christopher George (*Charles Venarius*), Jonee Gamboa, Leo Martinez, Ken Metcalfe, Subas Herrero, Alan

Amiel, Bob Jones, Derek Webster, Doug Ivan, Jack Turner, Konrad Waalkes, James Gaines, Don Gordon, Isolde Winter, Lucy Bush.

After graduating from Ninja school, Nero goes to Manila to help ex-mercenary buddy Courtney save his jungle plantation from bad guys led by limp-wristed Christopher George, who imports his own Ninja (Kosugi). Dumb and dull. Sequel: REVENGE OF THE NINJA.

p, Judd Bernard, Yoram Globus; d, Menahem Golan; w, Dick Desmond, Golan, Bernard; ph, David Gurfinkel; m, W. Michael Lewis, Laurin Rinder; ed, Mark Goldblatt; stunt/fight ch, Mike Stone.

Martial Arts   **Cas.**   **(PR:O   MPAA:R)**

ENTERTAINER, THE****   (1960, Brit.) 96m Woodfall/Bryanston-BL bw

Laurence Olivier (*Archie Rice*), Brenda de Banzie (*Phoebe Rice*), Joan Plowright (*Jean*), Roger Livesey (*Billy*), Alan Bates (*Frank*), Daniel Massey (*Graham*), Albert Finney (*Mick Rice*), Miriam Karlin (*Soubrette*), Shirley Ann Field (*Tina*), Thora Hird (*Mrs. Lapford*), Tony Longridge (*Mr. Lapford*), Mcdonald Hobley (*Film Star*), Charles Gray (*Columnist*), Angie & Debbie Dean (*Sisters Alhambra*), Geoffrey Toone (*Hubbard*), James Culliford (*Cobber Carson*), Gilbert Davis (*Brother Bill*), Anthony Oliver (*Interviewer*), Jo Linden (*Gloria*), Mercia Turner (*Britannia*), Vicky Travers (*Other Nude*), Beryl & Bobo (*Trampoline Act*), Herman & Constance Welles (*Scots Singers*), The Clippers (*Rock 'n' Roll Trio*), Max Bacon (*Charlie Klein*), George Doonan (*Eddie Trimmer*).

"Life is a beastly mess," states the great Olivier in this superb drama of the seedy music hall life. He is a third-rate vaudevillian whose song and dance routines are crusty, unappealing, and decidedly boring. He appears in a broken-down music hall, once so popular with British audiences, playing to an almost deserted house. Olivier's home life is as shabby as his stage career. His wife, De Banzie, is a shrewish alcoholic who nags him constantly about his failures. His father, Livesey, a once famous entertainer, is dying, yet Olivier prevails upon him to back just one more tawdry musical revue. Only Plowright, his protective daughter who has given up her own life and career, tries to meet Olivier's emotional needs. But he is an incorrigible liar and self-promoter whose raging ego demands he be admired by one and all. To that end he even cheats on his wife with a witless beauty contestant to enhance his coffers and self-esteem. His sons, Bates and Finney, see Olivier for what he is but accord him superficial respect. The seamy life, his own hammy cliches, his frightful desperation to consider himself a "star," is summed up in his cheap little act and the grim makeup he dons as a guise behind which to hide, presenting a face overly colored so that his eyes appear sunken, his skin pallid, a grotesque gargoyle of a face. But Olivier cannot delude himself forever; when Livesey pathetically dies in the wings, knowing his son is a dismal failure, Olivier recognizes his own miserable character, telling Plowright that he is "dead behind the eyes." Olivier's world comes tumbling down finally onto the garbage heap he has built up through a life of self-deception, sneaky schemes, and ruthless unconcern for those who love him. This depressing but fascinating film is another Olivier tour de force; the actor, whom many consider the greatest thespian of this age, is compelling and unforgettable in a flawless performance that earned him an Oscar nomination (he lost out to Burt Lancaster for ELMER GANTRY). He was later to shock critics and public alike by stating that the role in THE ENTERTAINER, which he had perfected on the London stage, really reflected his own personality. He told an interviewer that "it had the advantage of being a complete break from the other sort of work and that made it much more refreshing than tormenting oneself through these punishing roles of Shakespeare. I have an affinity with Archie Rice. It's what I really am. I'm not like Hamlet." Plowright, brilliant as the daughter in her screen debut, would become Olivier's wife a year after completing THE ENTERTAINER. The rest of the magnificent cast is stunning, even in small roles. Scripters Osborne and Kneale present a penetrating but utterly dyspeptic script, one where Osborne's much vaunted "grim realism" (LOOK BACK IN ANGER) has no knockout punch. Richardson's direction of this unhappy little gem gives off the appropriate dull glimmer and is both economical and inventive. THE ENTERTAINER was remade in 1975 with Jack Lemmon in the title role, but Lemmon faced an uphill battle against the hovering image Olivier had so well etched in the minds of viewers.

p, Harry Saltzman; d, Tony Richardson; w, John Osborne, Nigel Kneale (based on Osborne's play); ph, Oswald Morris; m, John Addison; ed, Alan Osbiston; art d, Ralph Brinton, Ted Marshall; cos, Barbara Gillette; makeup, Tony Sforzini.

Drama   **(PR:A   MPAA:NR)**

ENTERTAINER, THE***½   (1975) 105m Stigwood/Seven Keys c

Jack Lemmon (*Archie Rice*), Ray Bolger (*Billy Rice*), Sada Thompson (*Phoebe Rice*), Tyne Daly (*Jean Rice*), Michael Cristofer (*Frank Rice*), Annette O'Toole (*Bambi Pasko*), Mitch Ryan (*Mr. Pasko*), Allyn Ann McLerie (*Mrs. Pasko*), Rita O'Connor (*Lilly*), Dick O'Neill (*Charlie*), Leanne Johnson (*Charlene*), Alan De Witt (*Bakery Clerk*).

Originally made as a television special, this was later released as a feature but fell short of the Olivier version on most levels. The location and time have been switched to accommodate the American accents. Elliott Baker adapted the hit play by John Osborne and it now takes place in an American seaside resort in 1944. Lemmon is a middle-aged vaudevillian who never made it and is struggling to get laughs. His father, Bolger (making his first film appearance in ten years), is a star but Lemmon will never be more than a second banana, if that. He's a mean man in many ways, neglects his wife, Thompson, and son, Cristofer (now a successful playwright). His act is a hodgepodge of old jokes and feeble attempts at off-color humor. Lemmon agrees to emcee a beauty contest to pick up some much-needed money (his eldest daughter, from his first marriage, Daly, is an army nurse home for some R & R and his eldest son is also due home). He meets O'Toole, one of the contestants. She's younger than his daughter but he seduces her when he learns that her father, Ryan, is wealthy and her mother, McLerie, wants her daughter to make it big in show business. Lemmon persuades Ryan to back a new show that will feature O'Toole. They don't know that Lemmon is married until Bolger spills the beans. Lemmon now has a host of outstanding bad checks he must cover for a show that will never happen. Needing money more than ever, Lemmon prevails on his father to help out and the two men do a routine in the theater. It's a smash. Bolger now tries some dancing alone, has a heart attack and dies. At almost the same moment, Lemmon learns that his eldest son has died in a car accident. Lemmon is left on stage alone, a pitiable figure. Lemmon is marvelous but the picture doesn't have the bite of the original and suffered from the transposition to U.S. shores. A parallel would be to take something uniquely American like *Tom Sawyer* and put it into the mouths of Liverpudlians. Several songs by Marvin Hamlisch and some deliberately awful Ron Field choreography fail to elevate this beyond a very good TV special. John Avildsen (ROCKY) was penciled in to direct but was replaced by TV director Donald Wrye at the last moment. Wrye does some fine work for the little tube but needs more seasoning for the big screen, although since this was originally made for TV, he obviously soars above most of his peers. Musical numbers danced to by Lemmon are "The Only Way To Go," "Bend Over Backwards" (with chorus), and "Can't Stop Horsing Around" (with Bolger).

p, Beryl Vertue, Marvin Hamlisch; d, Donald Wrye; w, Elliott Baker (from play by John Osborne); ph, Jim Crabe (uncredited color); m, Hamlisch (lyrics, Robert Joseph); ed, Ralph Winters; art d, Bob Mackichan; set d, Sam Jones; cos, Marie Brown, Dick Bruno; ch, Ron Field; theme music, Tim Rice.

Drama (PR:A-C MPAA:NR)

ENTERTAINING MR. SLOANE*½** (1970, Brit.) 94m Canterbury/Anglo-Amalgamated/Warner Pathe c

Beryl Reid (*Kath*), Peter McEnery (*Mr. Sloane*), Harry Andrews (*Ed*), Alan Webb (*Dada Kemp*).

Garishly dressed and licking a popsicle while observing a funeral, heavy, grotesque Reid spots young, handsome, blonde McEnery soaking up the sun on a nearby tombstone. She asks him to move into her home, and there sets about seducing him while her brother (Andrews), a latent homosexual, entertains similar notions. Their father (Webb), a retired gravedigger, recognizes McEnery as the man who had killed his former boss, a pornographer. Webb accuses McEnery of murder and McEnery calmly kicks him to death. Reid—now pregnant—and Andrews threaten to tell the police what happened unless McEnery swears eternal allegiance to them. While their father lies in funereal state, Andrews tears the Bible from his hands and performs a marriage ceremony between his sister and the lodger; then Reid takes the Bible and weds her brother to McEnery. A grotesque black comedy taken from Joe Orton's play, which won the London Drama Critics Best Play award in 1964, but which folded after only 13 performances on Broadway, ENTERTAINING MR. SLOANE is full of morbid humor and offensive touches. That is, the film is a delight, constantly going out of its way to shock whenever possible, and the tiny cast is uniformly splendid, with Reid a standout. Not a film for all tastes, but a fine one, nonetheless.

p, Douglas Kentish; d, Douglas Hickox; w, Clive Exton (from play by Joe Orton); ph, Wolfgang Suschitzky (Technicolor); m, Georgie Fame; ed, John Trumper; prod d, Michael Seymour; cos, Emma Porteous.

Comedy **Cas.** (PR:O MPAA:NR)

ENTITY, THE½** (1982) 125m Belleport Investors/FOX c

Barbara Hershey (*Carla Moran*), Ron Silver (*Phil Schneidermann*), David Labisoa (*Billy*), George Coe (*Dr. Weber*), Margaret Blye (*Cindy Nash*), Jacqueline Brooks (*Dr. Cooley*), Richard Brestoff (*Gene Kraft*), Michael Alldredge (*George Nash*), Raymond Singer (*Joe Mehan*), Allan Rich (*Dr. Walcott*), Natasha Ryan (*Julie*), Melanie Gaffin (*Kim*), Alex Rocco (*Jerry Anderson*), Sully Boyar (*Mr. Reisz*), Tom Stern (*Woody Browne*), Curt Lowens (*Dr. Wilkes*), Paula Victor (*Dr. Chevalier*), Lee Wilkof (*Dr. L. Hase*), Deborah Stevenson, Mark Weiner (*Interns*), Lisa Gurley (*Receptionist*), Chris Howell (*Guard*), Renee Neimark (*Nurse*), John Branagan, Daniel Furie, Amy Kirkpatric, Todd Kutches, Pauline Lomas (*Students*).

Hershey is a suburban single mother repeatedly assaulted and raped by an invisible presence. She tries to convince herself that it's just a hysterical reaction to childhood traumas, but eventually psychiatry fails and parapsychology wins as a big, scary thing makes an appearance. Allegedly based on a true story, the film somehow succeeds in creating an effectively frightening atmosphere despite a laughable script. Hershey's performance and Furie's intelligent direction redeem this far above the level of the material.

p, Harold Schneider; d, Sidney J. Furie; w, Frank DeFelitta (from his novel); ph, Stephen H. Burum (Technicolor); m, Charles Bernstein; ed, Frank J. Urioste; prod d, Charles Rosen; spec eff, Joe Lombardi.

Horror **Cas.** (PR:O MPAA:R)

ENTRE NOUS* (1983, Fr.) 110m MGM-UA c (COUP DE FOUDRE)

Miou Miou (*Madeleine*), Isabelle Huppert (*Lena*), Jean-Pierre Bacri (*Costa*), Guy Marchand (*Michel*), Robin Renucci (*Raymond*), Jacques Airic (*Monsieur Vernier*), Jacqueline Doyen (*Madame Vernier*), Patricia Champane (*Florence*), Saga Blanchard (*Sophie*), Guillaume LeGuellec (*Rene*), Christine Pascal (*Sarah*), Anne Levy, Dominique Lavanant, Francois Cluzet, Gerard Chambre, Jacques Blal, Bernard Cazassus, Anne Fabien, Jean-Claude de Goros, Denis Lavant, Sonia Pfirmann, Pascal Pistacio, Serge Ruben, Niels Tavernier.

A semi-autobiographical account from French director Diane Kurys in which Huppert and Miou, two of Europe's top actresses, share the billing as friends whose relationship survives through turmoil created by one of their husbands. The picture centers on Miou, who—never having fully recovered from the death of her first husband—puts an end to her marriage to the narcissistic Bacri. Kurys portrays a powerful bond between Miou and Huppert, a bond rarely portrayed on the screen. While ENTRE NOUS (which, oddly, is the U.S. release title) is a better-

than-average picture, it wouldn't seem to deserve all of the acclaim it received, not to mention its 1983 Academy Award nomination for Best Foreign Film.

p, Ariel Zeitoun; d&w, Diane Kurys (from the book by Kurys, Olivier Cohen); ph, Bernard Lutic (CinemaScope); m, Luis Bacalov; ed, Joele Van Effenterre; prod d, Jacques Bufnoir.

Drama **Cas.** (PR:C MPAA:NR)

EPILOGUE* (1967, Den.) 93m Bent Christensen Filmproduktion/Gold Star Pictures bw

Erno Muller (*Martin*), Maud Berthelsen (*Lis*), Buster Larsen (*Gorm*), Preben Neergaard (*Officer*), Jorn Jeppesen (*Fabian*), Paul Hagen (*Photographer*), Morten Grunwald (*Ivan*), Kirsten Rolfes, Claus Neilsen, Birger Jensen.

Muller returns to Copenhagen after a 17-year stay in Kenya as a coffee planter. He starts a relationship with Berthelsen who is about half his age. She can't understand his fixation with death and his haunting memories of WW II. Muller, who had participated in the murder of a Nazi collaborator in WW II, is ultimately killed by the other men who murdered the Nazi collaborator.

p, Bent Christensen; d, Henning Carlsen; w, Leif Panduro; ph, Henning Kristiansen; m, Krzysztof Komeda; ed, Maj Soya; art d, Steini Sveinbjornsson.

Drama (PR:A MPAA:NR)

EPISODE* (1937, Aust.) 99m Metropolis bw

Paula Wesseley (*Valerie Gaertner*), Karl Ludwig Diehl (*Kinz*), Otto Tressler (*Torresani*), Erika von Wagner (*Frau Torresani*), Wolf Dieter Tressler (*Eugen Torresani*), Hans Jurgel Tressler (*Toni Torresani*), Friedl Czepa (*Mizzi*).

Viennese romantic comedy has Wesseley as a young girl who tries to find some way to support herself and her aged mother. She meets art dealer Tressler who agrees to help her financially, and though the girl believes he wants something in return, his motives are strictly charitable. It is just as well because at his house she meets Diehl, an ex-officer working as tutor to Tressler's two sons. A lot of predictable confusion reigns until the art dealer's wife, von Wagner, sorts it all out. Competent, but indistinguishable from most other films set in old Vienna. (In German; English subtitles.)

p, Gregor Rabinowicz; d&w, Walter Reisch; ph, Harry Stradling; m, Willi Schmidt-Gentner.

Comedy (PR:A MPAA:NR)

EQUINOX* (1970) 82m Tonylyn/VIP c

Edward Connell Skip Shimer (*Dave*), Barbara Hewitt (*Susan*), Frank Boers, Jr. (*Jim*), Robin Christopher Robin Snider (*Vicki*), Jack Woods (*Asmodeus*), Jim Phillips (*Reporter*), Fritz Leiber (*Dr. Waterman*), Patrick Burke (*Branson*), Jim Duran (*Orderly*), Norville Brooks, Irving L. Lichenstein.

Four teenagers go to a state forest to look for a missing scientist (Leiber), where they find a strange book of incantations from ancient Persia discovered by Leiber. Forest ranger Asmodeus, actually king of the demons, threatens them with a series of giant monsters to try to recover the book. People disappear, castles appear, and a dimensional barrier sucks them in. Told in a disjointed form, and frequently confusing, the film does contain some fine moments of terror. Basically an amateur film shot in 16mm in 1967, co-producer Harris added scenes for its release, comprising more than half of the final footage. By far the best parts are the special effects, stop-motion models of a giant apelike monster, and a winged demon that rival anything done by Ray Harryhausen and Willis O'Brien. Justly regarded as a minor classic of American horror films.

p, Dennis Muren, Jack H. Harris; d&w, Jack Woods (from a story by Mark Thomas McGee); ph, Mike Hoover (DeLuxe Color); m, John Caper; ed, John Joyce; spec eff, David Allen, Jim Danforth, Muren; makeup, Robynne Hoover.

Horror **Cas.** (PR:C-O MPAA:NR)

"EQUUS"* (1977) 137m UA c

Richard Burton (*Dr. Martin Dysart*), Peter Firth (*Alan Strang*), Colin Blakely (*Frank Strang*), Joan Plowright (*Dora Strang*), Harry Andrews (*Harry Dalton*), Eileen Atkins (*Magistrate Hesther Saloman*), Jenny Agutter (*Jill Mason*), John Wyman (*The Horseman*), Kate Reid (*Margaret Dysart*), Ken James (*Mr. Pearce*), Elva Mai Hoover (*Miss Raintree*), James Hurdle (*Mr. Davies*), Karen Pearson (*Mary*), David Gardner (*Dr. Bennett*), Patrick Brymer (*Hospital Patient*), Sheldon Rybowski (*First Child*), Sufi Bukhari (*Second Child*), Anita Van Hezewyck (*Horse Trainer*), Mark Parr (*Clown*), Frazier Mohawk (*Ringmaster*).

One of Burton's best-ever performances but he lost an Oscar to Richard Dreyfuss for THE GOODBYE GIRL in 1977. Shaffer adapted his own gripping play about a young man, Firth, who is driven to blinding horses. Burton is the psychiatrist who realizes that Firth's religious fervor is the key to the mystery. His mother, Joan Plowright, has supplied the confused youth with a thwarted view of life and the result is his behavior. Judge Atkins appoints Burton to get to the bottom of the reasons for Firth's deeds and Burton learns much about himself in the process. This is as close to a real psychiatrist-patient relationship as you are ever to see in movies. Burton is sensational as he begins to take stock of his own life in the pressure-cooker of his work with Firth. Shaffer (who also wrote AMADEUS, THE ROYAL HUNT OF THE SUN, and others) is the twin brother of Anthony Shaffer (SLEUTH, THE WICKER MAN, FRENZY) so who says there is nothing to genetics when it comes to talent? Lumet does his best with what is still a filmed play. Shaffer's words are brilliant and incisive but the film could have done with a few less of them. The horses were handled by veteran Yakima Cannutt and the scenes in which they are blinded is so frightening that animal lovers across the world were incensed and had to be assuaged. There was no actual damage done to the steeds although the photography almost caused disbelief by its excellence.

p, Lester Persky, Elliott Kastner; d, Sidney Lumet; w, Peter Shaffer (from his play); ph, Oswald Morris (DeLuxe Color); m, Richard Rodney Bennett; ed, John

Victor-Smith; prod d, Tony Walton; art d, Simon Holland; set d, Gerry Holmes; cos, Walton, Patti Unger, Brenda Dabbs; horse wranglers, Yakima Canutt, John Vanderpas, Doug Doner.

Drama   (PR:C-O   MPAA:R)

ERASERHEAD***   (1978) 90m AFI/Libra bw

John Nance (Henry Spencer), Charlotte Stewart (Mary X), Allen Joseph (Mr. X), Jeanne Bates (Mrs. X), Judith Anna Roberts (Girl Across the Hall), Laurel Near (Lady in the Radiator), V. Phipps-Wilson (Landlady), Jack Fisk (Man in the Planet), Jean Lange (Grandmother).

David Lynch's film ERASERHEAD is described by its creator as a "dream of dark and troubling things," and it is, possibly, cinema's only true nightmare, disturbing, repulsive, hilarious, frightening, sensitive, challenging. ERASERHEAD is filled with thousands of haunting, nightmarish images, its characters existing in an utterly strange world. Its "plot" is almost impossible to follow. A young man, Nance, living in a dilapidated apartment building in an industrialized city learns that his girl friend, Stewart, is pregnant. Leaving his room (that seems to be inhabited by sperm-like creatures), he visits Stewart and her parents, a hyperactive father with a passion for synthetic meat, and a mother obsessed with her daughter's sexuality. Grandmother sits in the kitchen, stone-like. Maybe dead. Stewart moves in with Nance and they begin to take care of their "baby," a deformed, constantly crying mass of tissue and bandages that looks like a skinned lamb. The infant is repulsive, yet fascinating and also sad. Its constant whining drives Stewart out of the apartment and Nance is left alone with the baby. Accidentally killing it, he is thrown into the nightmare world that has existed on the fringes of his "real" world since the beginning of the film. After a series of weird trials and tribulations (which cause him at one point to lose his head), Nance is united with the Lady in the Radiator (a bleached blonde), a frighteningly "cute" woman with monstrous apple dumpling cheeks, who brings him into a calm world by singing "In heaven, everything is fine." ERASERHEAD is not simply a film about a man who has nasty dreams. It shows that the "dark and troubling things" that we like to repress inhabit dresser drawers, or live behind the radiator, or under the bed. They are part of the environment. There is no separation between what is dreamed and what is real, no foggy dissolves, no waking-up scenes, no escape. A former painter, Lynch is interested in allowing richly textured things, objects, and people to inhabit the film frame, creating compositions that strike the viewer with weird power. ERASERHEAD is very popular on the cult midnight-movie circuit, its gross elements enticing bored college students initially, and its mysterious qualities bringing them back again and again to a very dark dream.

p,d&w, David Lynch; ph, Frederick Elms, Herbert Cardwell; m, Fats Waller; ed, Lynch; art d, Lynch; m/l, "Lady in the Radiator," Peter Ivers.

Horror   **Cas.**   (PR:O   MPAA:NR)

ERASMUS WITH FRECKLES   (SEE: DEAR BRIGITTE, 1965)

ERIC SOYA'S "17"**   (1967, Den.) 87m
Palladium/Peppercorn-Wormser c (SYTTEN; AKA: SEVENTEEN)

Ole Soltoft (Jacob Petersen), Ghita Norby (Vibeke), Lily Broberg (Miss Rosegod), Ole Monty (Jacob's Uncle), Bodil Steen (Jacob's Aunt), Hass Christensen (Prof. Petersen), Susanne Heinrich (Hansigne), Lise Rosendahl (Sophie), Hugo Herrestrup (Knud), Jorgen Kiil (Dr. Irving Mogensen), David Ingolf (Pharmacist), Annie Birgit Garde (Girl on Train), Arthur Jensen, Jytte Abildstrom, Henry Nielsen, Valso Holm, Jens Jensen.

ERIC SOYA'S "17" half humorously and quite sensitively charts a teenager's initiation into sex, and the outcome leaves the shy young man somewhat of a rake, in keeping with the Danes' often witty outlook on themselves. Soltoft is aware of his budding interest in sex, and finds the family maid willing to teach him about it, but he is scared off. Later, at his uncle's cottage, he falls in love with a cousin and they make love. When the girl returns to college, he carries on with his uncle's maid, then his housekeeper, and continues his education on the train back home, when he seduces a fellow passenger. At home, the all too willing maid is waiting for him.

d, Annelise Meineche; w, Bob Ramsing (based on the novel Sytten; Erindringer Og Refleksioner by Carl Eric Soya); ph, Ole Lytken (Eastmancolor); m, Ole Hoyer; ed, Edith Schlussel; art d, Otto Lund, Herbi Gartner.

Comedy Drama   (PR:O   MPAA:NR)

ERIK THE CONQUEROR*½   (1963, Fr./Ital.) 90m
Galatea-Criterion-Societe Cinematographique Lyre/AIP c
(GLI INVASORI; LA RUEE DES VIKINGS; AKA: FURY OF THE VIKINGS)

Cameron Mitchell (Iron), Giorgio Ardisson (Erik, Duke of Helfort), Andrea Checchi (Gunnar), Francoise Christophe (Queen Alice), Ellen Kessler (Daja), Alice Kessler (Rama), Folco Lulli (Aello), Franco Giacobini (Rustichello), Joe Robinson (Iron's Rival), Raffaele Badassarre (Blak), Enzo Doria (Bennet), Franco Ressel (King Lotar), Livia Contardi (Hadda), Jean-Jacques Delbo.

An account of the English-Viking battles in the 10th century finds a Viking raised from babyhood by the British fighting his brother, a leader of the invaders. They finally unite when they recognize each other, and turn on the counselor to Queen Alice, who had betrayed her to the Vikings. One brother is killed and so is the counselor, and the British and Vikings unite to defeat the rascal's troops. A so-so effort on an epic topic.

d, Mario Bava; w, Oreste Biancoli, Bava, Piero Peirotti; ph, Ubaldo Terzano, Bava (Dyaliscope, Technicolor); m, Roberto Nicolosi; ed, Mario Serandrei; art d, Giorgio Giovannini; set d, Giuseppe Tavazzi; cos, Tina Grani; ch, Leo Coleman.

Action   (PR:C   MPAA:NR)

ERNEST HEMINGWAY'S ADVENTURES OF A YOUNG MAN*
(SEE: ADVENTURES OF A YOUNG MAN, 1962)

ERNEST HEMINGWAY'S THE KILLERS, 1964*
(SEE: KILLERS, THE, 1964)

ERNESTO*   (1979, Ital.) 98m Ciesi-Cinematografica/Spectrafilm c

Martin Halm (Ernesto), Michele Placido (Ilio), Virna Lisi (Mother), Turo Ferro, Lara Wendel, Gisela Hann, Francisco Marso, Stefano Madia, Miranda Nocelli, Conchita Velasco, Renato Salvatori.

Halm is a Jewish boy who begins a homosexual relationship with a worker at his uncle's factory in Trieste at the turn of the century. He subjugates and discards the lover and then discovers he likes heterosexuality, too, after visiting a prostitute. He meets a rich pair of mixed twins and is attracted to both. The families arrange a marriage between Halm and the girl, and Halm accepts conventional sexuality. The film has pretensions toward a serious analysis of sex roles and class differences, but it comes off as a soft-focus sex film, from Samperi, the King of Italian soft-focus sex films. (In Italian; English subtitles.)

p, Jose Frade; d, Salvatore Samperi; w, Barbara Alberti, Amadeo Paganini, Samperi (based on the novel Ernesto by Umberto Saba); ph, Camillo Bazzoni (Technicolor); m, Carmelo Bernaola; ed, Sergio Montanari; prod d, Rzio Altieri; cos, Cristiana Lafayette.

Drama   (PR:O   MPAA:R)

EROICA***   (1966, Pol.) 82m Kadr Film Unit/Ameripol Enterprise bw
(AKA: HEROISM)

Scherzo Alla Pollaca: Edward Dziewonski (Dzidzius), Barbara Polomska (Zosia), Leon Niemczyk (Lt. Kolya), Ignacy Machowski (Major), Kazimierz Opalinski (Colonel); Ostinato Lugubre: Jozef Nowak (Kurzawa), Roman Klosowski (Szpakowski), Mariusz Dmochowski (Korwin-Makowski), Bogumil Kobiela (Dabecki), Wojciech Siemion (Marianek), Kazimierz Rudzki (Turek), Jozef Kostecki (Zak), Henryk Bak (Krygier), Tadeusz Lomnicki (Zawistowski).

This film is made up of two segments on WW II. The first, "Scherzo Alla Pollaca," is about a married Polish man who decides to be a black marketeer when the Nazis invade. He accidentally gets involved in the Polish underground and decides to drop his way of life to join the underground. The second segment, "Ostinato Lugubre," is about Polish inmates in a Nazi concentration camp whose spirits are kept high because they believe one Pole has escaped from the camp. A prisoner commits suicide and the inmates discover the body of the man they thought had escaped. To keep the legend going, they cremate him in an oil burner. Munk, the director, was a leader of the highly talented group of directors who emerged as the "Polish film school" in the 1950s with his trademark a bitter irony which is uniquely Polish. His death in a car crash in 1961 was a blow to Polish film art. Other gifted production people on EROICA were the scriptwriter, Stawinski, a popular novelist also associated with the "Polish film school;" and the film's photographer, Wojcik, who worked as the second cameraman on the great Polish films KANAL and THE REAL END OF THE GREAT WAR.

p, Stanislaw Adler; d, Andrzej Munk; w, Jerzy Stefan Stawinski; ph, Jerzy Wojcik; m, Jan Krenz; ed, Jadwiga Zaicek; art d, Jan Grandys.

War Drama   (PR:C   MPAA:NR)

EROTIQUE*½   (1969, Fr.) 85 m Paris Inter/VIP, Goldstone c
(TRAQUENARDS: TRAQUENARDS EROTIQUES)

Anna Gael (Agnes), Hans Meyer (Varen), Roland Lesaffre (Bob), Claude Charney (Claude), Robert Lombard (Georges Corbeaux), Anne Renate (Leda), Dominique Erlanger (Olga), Charles Dalin (Francky Corbeaux), Jean Droze (Paul), Nadia Vasil (Solange).

A French crime melodrama about a couple, Meyer and Lesaffre, who get involved with a white slave trader. They are also being pursued by the Corbeaux brothers, who kill Lesaffre while Meyer kills one of the brothers. Meyer's friend, Gael, tries to help but she's captured and the remaining brother kills Meyer. Gael is about to be sold into slavery when her boy friend, Charney, arrives with the police. A melodramatic mash that offers little to make it tasty.

p, Joel Lifschutz; d, Jean-Francois Davy; w, Michel Levine, Davy; ph, Daniel Lacambre (Eastmancolor); m, Jack Arel.

Crime   (PR:C   MPAA:NR)

ERRAND BOY, THE½** (1961) 92m PAR bw

Jerry Lewis *(Morty S. Tashman)*, Brian Donlevy *(Mr. T.P.)*, Dick Wesson *(The A.D.)*, Howard McNear *(Dexter Sneak)*, Felicia Atkins *(Serina)*, Kathleen Freeman *(Mrs. T.P.)*, Mary and Paul Ritts *(Themselves)*, Isobel Elsom *(Irma Paramutual)*, Fritz Feld *(Foreign Director)*, Iris Adrian *(Great Actress)*, Renee Taylor *(Miss Giles)*, Stanley Adams *(Grumpy)*, Sig Ruman *(Baron Elston Carteblanche)*, Doodles Weaver *(Man on Scaffold)*, Kenneth MacDonald *(Mr. Fumble)*, Joey Forman *(Jedson)*, Dave Landfield *(Lance)*, Del Moore *(M.C.)*, Rita Hayes *(Singer)*, Pat Dahl *(Miss Carson)*, Mike Mazurki *(Blonde "Movie Siren")*, Dan Blocker, Lorne Greene, Michael Landon, Pernell Roberts *(Guest Stars)*, Murray Alper, Phil Arnold, Richard Bakalyan, Donald Barry, Bellfontevro, John Benson, Joe Besser, Jan Bradley, Sue Casey, Connie Cezon, Harry Cheshire, Booth Colman, Theodora Davitt, Jean Engstrom, Judy Erwin, Milton Frome, Barry Gray, Daryn Hinton, Bob Hopkins, Judy Howard, Robert Ivers, Hank Ladd, Frances Lax, Barry Livingston, Sally Mansfield, Mickey Manners, Quinn O'Hara, Snub Pollard, Sherwood Price, Hal Rand, Tony Regan, Caroline Richter, Sheila Rogers, Mike Ross, Benny Rubin, Frank Scannell, Jeanne Taylor, Mary Treen, Herb Vigran, William Wellman, Jr., Dick Winslow.

Lewis performs his juvenile antics in Hollywood this time, and a vast number of movie faces are there to help him. Forget a plot line, but for fans of Lewis, this is one of his best.

p, Ernest D. Glucksman; d, Jerry Lewis; w, Lewis, Bill Richmond; ph, W. Wallace Kelley; m, Walter Scharf; ed, Stanley E. Johnson; art d, Hal Pereira, Arthur Lonergan; set d, Sam Comer, Ed Pine; cos, Edith Head; ch, Nick Castle; m/l, Lou Y. Brown, Richmond, Lewis.

Comedy **(PR:A MPAA:NR)**

ESCAPADE*½ (1932) 63m CHES bw

Anthony Bushell *(Phillip Whitney)*, Sally Blane *(Kay Whitney)*, Thomas Jackson *(Bennie)*, Jameson Thomas *(John Whitney)*, Walter Long *(Gympy McLane)*, Carmelita Geraghty *(Mildred)*, Phillips Smalley *(Wally Hines)*, David Mir *(Poet)*.

On his release from prison, Bushell goes to the home of his brother, a prosecutor who knows nothing about his stretch in the pen. He begins an affair with Blane, his brother's wife, and tries to protect the prosecutor from his former cellmate, who intends to kill the man who put him away. In the final shootout, Bushell and his former cellmate both die, and the brother never finds out about the affair. Low-budget crime melodrama has nothing of interest.

p, Maury M. Cohen, George R. Batcheller; d, Richard Thorpe; w, E. T. Lowe; ph, M.A. Anderson.

Crime **(PR:A MPAA:NR)**

ESCAPADE*½** (1935) 93m MGM bw

William Powell *(Fritz)*, Luise Rainer *(Leopoldine)*, Frank Morgan *(Karl)*, Virginia Bruce *(Gerta)*, Reginald Owen *(Paul)*, Mady Christians *(Anita)*, Laura Hope Crews *(Countess)*, Henry Travers *(Concierge)*, Mathilda Comont *(Carmen)*, Charles Chrysler *(Doorman)*, Will Stanton, Billy Gilbert *(Singers)*, Bess Flowers, Jean Fenwick, Vessie Farrell, Monya Andre, Lita Chevret *(Guests)*, Mary MacLaren *(Nurse)*, Scott Mattraw *(Cab Driver)*, Lillian Irene *(Maid)*, Michael S. Visaroff *(Doorman)*, Mahlon Hamilton *(Announcer)*, Tom Ricketts *(Old Dandy)*, Charles Requa *(Young Dandy)*.

Charming light comedy set in turn-of-the-century Vienna. Powell is an artist who falls for sweet, innocent Rainer. Comic complications revolve around a nude sketch of married lady Bruce which accidentally gets published, and her husband, Morgan, thinks the drawing is of his brother's fiancee (Christians). Originally intended as a William Powell-Myrna Loy vehicle, Loy walked out at the last minute in a salary dispute. Rather than give up the picture, MGM brought in Rainer, who had been waiting around the lot for the right part for her American debut. She stole the picture from its more established performers, and at the end Powell stepped out of character to tell the audience about Luise Rainer and the big plans MGM had for her.

p, Bernard H. Hyman; d, Robert Z. Leonard; w, Herman J. Mankiewicz (based on an Austrian film, MASKERADE, written by Walter Reisch); ph, Ernest Haller; m, Bronislaw Kaper, Walter Jurmann; ed, Tom Held; m/l, Gus Kahn, Harold Adamson, Jurmann, Kaper.

Comedy **(PR:A MPAA:NR)**

ESCAPADE½** (1955, Brit.) 88m Eros bw

John Mills *(John Hampden)*, Yvonne Mitchell *(Stella Hampden)*, Alastair Sim *(Dr. Skillingsworth)*, Marie Lohr *(Mrs. Hampden)*, Colin Gordon *(Deeson)*, Jeremy Spenser *(Daventry)*, Andrew Ray *(Max Hampden)*, Peter Asher *(Johnny Hampden)*, Nicky Edmett *(Paton)*, Christopher Ridley *(Potter)*, Sean Barrett *(Warren)*, Sonia Williams *(Miss Betts)*, Mark Dignam *(Sykes)*, Kit Terrington *(Smith)*, Colin Freear *(Young Skilly)*, Stephen Abbott *(Parsons)*, Anne Allen *(Miss Lunt)*, John Rae *(Curly)*.

The sons of a pacifist writer (Ray and Asher) get a petition pleading for world peace together at their school, signed by students all over the country, then steal an airplane to fly to Vienna to present it to the four powers occupying Germany. Okay comedy with a message, but the play was better.

p, Daniel M. Angel, Hannah Weinstein; d, Philip Leacock; w, Gilbert Holland (based on a play by Roger MacDougall); ph, Eric Cross; m, Bruce Montgomery; ed, John Trumper.

Comedy **(PR:A MPAA:NR)**

ESCAPADE IN JAPAN** (1957) 90m UNIV-RKO c

Teresa Wright *(Mary Saunders)*, Cameron Mitchell *(Dick Saunders)*, Jon Provost *(Tony Saunders)*, Roger Nakagawa *(Hiko)*, Philip Ober *(Lt. Col. Hargrave)*, Kuniko Miyake *(Michiko)*, Susumu Fujita *(Kei Tanaka)*, Katsuhiko Haida *(Capt. Hibino)*, Tatsuo Saito *(Mr. Fushimi)*, Hideko Koshikawa *(Dekko-San)*, Ureo Egawa *(Chief of Kyoto Police)*, Frank Tokunaga *(Farmer)*, Ayako Hidaka *(Farmer's Wife)*, Clint Eastwood *(Dumbo)*.

Little Provost is flying to Japan to join his parents when his plane is forced down in the ocean. Saved by fishermen, he is taken to the home of one of them. When the fisherman's son (Nakagawa) hears his father mention the police, he and Provost run away to look for Provost's parents. A series of adventures follow, such as a night in a geisha house, before the two are located in a pagoda. Routine children's fare handled with a light touch and photographed in lovely Japanese locations. Clint Eastwood, in a small role as a serviceman named "Dumbo," was making his second movie for RKO.

p&d, Arthur Lubin; w, Winston Miller; ph, William Snyder (Technirama, Technicolor); m, Max Steiner; art d, George W. Davis, Walter Holscher.

Adventure **Cas.** **(PR:A MPAA:NR)**

ESCAPE** (1930, Brit.) 70m Associated Talking Pictures/RKO bw

Sir Gerald du Maurier *(Capt. Matt Denant)*, Edna Best *(Shingled Lady)*, Gordon Harker *(Convict)*, Horace Hodges *(Gentleman)*, Madeleine Carroll *(Dora)*, Mabel Poulton *(Girl of the Town)*, Lewis Casson *(Farmer)*, Ian Hunter *(Detective)*, Austin Trevor *(Parson)*, Marie Ney, *(Grace)*, Felix Aylmer *(Governor)*, Ben Field *(Captain)*, Fred Groves *(Shopkeeper)*, Nigel Bruce *(Constable)*, S.J. Warmington *(Warder)*, Phyllis Konstam *(Wife)*, Ann Casson *(Girl)*, George Curzon *(Constable)*, Jean Cadell, David Hawthorne, H. St. Barbe West, Eric Cowley, Edward Addison, Lawrence Baskcomb.

Du Maurier (father of novelist Daphne) is a WW I hero who accidentally kills a reprehensible detective during a brawl over a street girl. Sentenced to five years of hard labor, he endures as long as he humanly can and then escapes. Several women shelter him and help him avoid capture, but finally he surrenders while hiding in a church, rather than have the pastor lie about his presence. RKO's first attempt at overseas production was this John Galsworthy character study of a man driven outside the law, and the kindly people who help him.

p&d, Basil Dean; w, Dean, John Galsworthy (based on a play by Galsworthy); ph, Jack Mackenzie, Robert G. Martin; ed, Milner Kitchin.

Drama **(PR:A MPAA:NR)**

ESCAPE, THE½** (1939) 58m FOX bw

Kane Richmond *(Eddie Farrell)*, Amanda Duff *(Juli Peronni)*, June Gale *(Annie Qualen)*, Edward Norris *(Louie Peronni)*, Henry Armetta *(Guiseppi Peronni)*, Frank Reicher *(Dr. Shumaker)*, Scotty Beckett *(Willie Rogers)*, Leona Roberts *(Aunt Mamie Qualen)*, Rex Downing *(Tommy Rogers)*, Jimmy Butler *(Jim Rogers)*, Roger McGee *(Swat)*, Richard Lane *(David Clifford)*, Jack Carson *(Chet Warren)*, Matt McHugh *(Pete)*, Helen Ericson *(Helen Gardner)*.

Reporter Carson covers the funeral of a gangster and learns the redeeming story of his life. He is told the story by doctor Reicher, who starts it with the gangster (Norris) being released from prison. Norris' father (Armetta) begs him to go straight, but the son pulls off a warehouse heist instead. Armetta turns him in and Norris' pals kidnap the district attorney's daughter to spring him. It turns out that the girl is actually the daughter of Norris and Gale, put up for adoption years before. With the help of Richmond, a childhood friend and cop, Norris escapes and frees his daughter, though at the cost of his own life. Superior direction by Cortez lifts an ordinary tale through its hackneyed paces to a swift and action-filled finale.

p, Sol M. Wurtzel; d, Ricardo Cortez; w, Robert Ellis, Helen Logan; ph, Edward Cronjager; m, Samuel Kaylin; ed, Fred Allen.

Crime **(PR:A MPAA:NR)**

ESCAPE*** (1940) 104m MGM bw (AKA: WHEN THE DOOR OPENED)

Norma Shearer *(Countess Von Treck)*, Robert Taylor *(Mark Preysing)*, Conrad Veidt *(Gen. Kurt Von Kolb)*, Alla Nazimova *(Emmy Ritter)*, Felix Bressart *(Fritz Keller)*, Albert Bassermann *(Dr. Arthur Henning)*, Philip Dorn *(Dr. Ditten)*, Bonita Granville *(Ursula)*, Edgar Barrier *(Commissioner)*, Elsa Basserman *(Frau Henning)*, Blanche Yurka *(Nurse)*, Lisa Golm *(Anne)*.

Taylor is an American traveling to Germany to locate his mother, Nazimova, a once-famous stage actress who had returned to the Fatherland to sell her late husband's estate. He befriends Shearer, a German-American who runs a girl's finishing school and who is having an affair with Veidt, a German general prone to dizzy spells. Taylor learns that his mother is in a concentration camp, condemned to death for the capital crime of attempting to smuggle money out of the country. Shearer finds herself falling in love with the charming American and decides to help him, introducing him to Dorn, the anti-Nazi doctor in the concentration camp where Nazimova resides. Dorn gives Nazimova a drug that induces a death-like state and her body is released to Taylor. As mother and son near the border a snowstorm cuts off their escape and Taylor takes the comatose Nazimova to Shearer's remote mountain estate. Shearer is moved by their plight and deceives Veidt, who arrives moments after Taylor and Nazimova get aboard a plane with a fake passport for Nazimova, arranged by Shearer. He learns of the plan and tries to warn officials but is struck down by another spell and Shearer makes certain that the plane is not stopped. ESCAPE is packed with suspense and Shearer, Taylor, and Veidt give arresting, restrained performances, although the scripters were certainly not fully aware of the real nature of Hitler's concentration camps when writing the story. That Nazimova could find any way in which to survive, let alone a camp physician who would work against the regime and on her behalf, is beyond plausibility. Shearer fans think she gave one of her best efforts in ESCAPE, one of the first anti-Nazi films from MGM. Hitler banned the film from Germany. He threatened to ban all MGM films if another movie depicted the Fatherland in such critical light. MGM next produced the anti-Nazi film THE MORTAL STORM and the ban was put into effect. The great silent film star Nazimova returned to the screen in a powerful performance in this, her debut in talking pictures. Ironically, this actress was at the zenith of her career in 1917-18 when performing in anti-

German films during WW I, notably WAR BRIDES. This was also the American debut of the distinguished actor Veidt, who had established a 20-year career in European films, beginning as the sonambulist in THE CABINET OF DR. CALIGARI. LeRoy's direction is tightly constructed and fluid and all the technical personnel perform well.

p&d, Mervyn LeRoy; w, Arch Oboler, Marguerite Roberts (based on the novel by Ethel Vance); ph, Robert Planck; ed, George Boemier; art d, Cedric Gibbons; cos, Adrian.

Drama/Suspense **(PR:A MPAA:NR)**

ESCAPE*** (1948, Brit.) 79m FOX bw

Rex Harrison (Matt Denant), Peggy Cummins (Dora Winton), William Hartnell (Inspector Harris), Betty Ann Davies (Girl), Norman Wooland (Parson), Jill Esmond (Grace Winton), Frederick Piper (Convict), Cyril Cusack (Rogers), Marjorie Rhodes (Mrs. Pinkem), John Slater (Salesman), Frank Pettingell (Village Constable), Frederick Leister (Judge), Maurice Denham (Crown), George Woodbridge (Farmer Browning), Stuart Lindsell (Sir James), Michael Golden (Plain Clothes Man), Walter Hudd (Defense Counsel), Jacqueline Clarke (Phyllis), Frank Tickle (Mr. Pinkem), Peter Croft (Titch), Ian Russell (Car Driver), Patrick Troughton (Shepherd), Cyril Smith (Policeman).

An oddball but engrossing film has Harrison as an ex-WW II air force ace, talking to a prostitute in Hyde Park when a policeman interrupts, roughly treating the girl. Harrison shoves the cop away in a scuffle and the officer is accidentally killed when he freakishly hits his head. Harrison is put on trial and then sent to prison for three years. One fog-bound night Harrison flees Dartmoor Prison and is taken in by Cummins, who feeds and clothes him. Harrison vows he will never return to prison but Cummins persuades him to surrender after he takes refuge in a church and can't bear to have the parson, Wooland, lie to protect him. He walks out to the police knowing that Cummins will be waiting for him. This was a remake of the 1930 British release and a decided improvement of the Galsworthy story, particularly because of the dynamic talent of Harrison and top-drawer support from a fine cast. Mankiewicz's adroit direction and Young's imaginative lensing brought the story up to date and made it a taut thriller.

p, William Perlberg; d, Joseph L. Mankiewicz; w, Philip Dunne (based on the novel by John Galsworthy); ph, Frederick A. Young; m, William Alwyn; ed, Alan L. Jaggs, K. Heeley-Ray; md, Muir Mathieson; art d, Vetchinsky.

Suspense/Thriller **(PR:A MPAA:NR)**

ESCAPE ARTIST, THE**½ (1982) 93m Zoetrope/Orion-WB c

Raul Julia (Stu Quinones), Griffin O'Neal (Danny Masters), Desiderio Arnaz (Mayor Quinones), Teri Garr (Arlene), Joan Hackett (Aunt Sybil), Gabriel Dell (Uncle Burke), John P. Ryan (Vernon), Elizabeth Daily (Sandra), M. Emmet Walsh (Fritz), Jackie Coogan (Magic Shop Owner), Hal Williams (Cop at Mayor's Office), Helen Page Camp (Neighbor), David Clennon (Newspaper Editor), Harry Caesar (Sax Player), Huntz Hall (Turnkey), Harry Anderson (Harry Masters), George Brengel (Water Commissioner), Carlin Glynn (Treasurer's Secretary), Isabel Cooley (Secretary at Newspaper Office), Tom Signorelli (Mailbox Cop), George Cantero (Jail Trustee), Harry Cohn (Jailmate), James Howard (Cop at Bridal Shop), R. Wayne Kruse, Margaret Ladd (Reporters), Tom Mahoney (M.C.), G. K. Marshall (Drummer), Doug McGrath (Photographer), Susi Sherman (Woman at Club).

O'Neal, the son of the "greatest escape artist since Houdini," is trying to follow in his father's footsteps. He lifts the wallet of Julia, a corrupt mayor's son, who then sends goons and threats against the boy. Finally O'Neal gets even with Julia and his father (Arnaz). A simple story is lost in the film's complex structure and only when O'Neal and Julia are on screen together does it come to life. Deschanel's directorial debut, after he acted as director of photography on THE BLACK STALLION and BEING THERE, lacks the visual style he showed earlier.

p, Doug Claybourne, Buck Houghton; d, Caleb Deschanel; w, Mellissa Mathison, Stephen Zito (based on a novel by David Wagoner); ph, Stephen H. Burum (Technicolor); m, Georges Delerue; ed, Arthur Schmidt; prod d, Dean Tavoularis; art d, Angelo Graham, James Murakami; set d, George R. Nelson; cos, Gloria Gresham.

Drama **(PR:C MPAA:PG)**

ESCAPE BY NIGHT*½ (1937) 67m REP bw

William Hall (Nick), Anne Nagel (Linda), Dean Jagger (Capper Regan), Steffi Duna (Jo), Ward Bond (Spudsy), Murray Alper (Red), Charles Waldron (Pop), George Meeker (Fred), Bill (Seeing Eye Dog), Anthony Warde, Ralph Sanford, Arthur Aylesworth, Wallis Clark, John Dilson.

A bunch of gangsters, hiding out from the law at an isolated farm, are overawed by the simple virtues of rural life and their affection for old, blind Waldron and his Seeing Eye dog, Bill. When the gang's chief summons them to come out of hiding, they turn him in to the law. As sweetly sticky as a jar of jam.

p, Harold Shumate; d, Hamilton McFadden; w, Shumate; ph, Edward Snyder; ed, Murray Seldeen, W. Donn Hayes; md, Alberto Colombo; art d, John Victor Mackay.

Drama **(PR:A MPAA:NR)**

ESCAPE BY NIGHT** (1954, Brit.) 79m Tempean/Eros bw

Bonar Colleano (Tom Buchan), Andrew Ray (Joey Weston), Sidney James (Gino Rossi), Ted Ray (Mr. Weston), Simone Silva (Rosetta Mantania), Patrick Barr (Inspector Frampton), Peter Sinclair (MacNaughton), Avice Landone (Mrs. Weston), Ronald Adam (Tallboy), Eric Berry, Martin Benson, Ronan O'Casey.

Hard-boiled reporter Colleano goes after racket boss James, matching wits with him constantly. Finally, wise to what is going on, James takes Colleano prisoner and goes gunning for moll Silva, whom he suspects of informing on him. Colleano

escapes and saves Silva's life, and James is cut down in a hail of police bullets. Plot moves fast enough to make viewers forget the plot holes.

p, Robert Baker, Monty Berman; d&w, John Gilling; ph, Berman.

Crime **(PR:A-C MPAA:NR)**

ESCAPE BY NIGHT** (1965, Brit.) 75m Eternal/AA bw (GB: CLASH BY NIGHT)

Terence Longdon (Martin Lord), Jennifer Jayne (Nita Lord), Harry Fowler (Doug Roberts), Peter Sallis (Victor Lush), Alan Wheatley (Ronald Grey-Simmons), Vanda Godsell (Mrs. Grey-Simmons), Arthur Lovegrove (Ernie Peel), Hilda Fenemore (Mrs. Peel), Mark Dignam (Sydney Selwyn), John Arnatt (Inspector Croft), Richard Carpenter (Danny Watts), Stanley Meadows (George Brett), Robert Brown (Mawsley), Tom Bowman (Bart Rennison), Ray Austin (The Intruder).

Gangsters hijack a busload of prisoners to free their boss (Bowman). Surrounded in a barn, they pour paraffin over the thatched roof and threaten to set it afire. Low-budget British prison-break story with some fine characterizations at the cost of action, the barn-burning scene at the end providing most of that.

p, Maurice J. Wilson; d, Montgomery Tully; w, Wilson, Tully (based on a novel Clash By Night by Rupert Croft-Brooke); ph, Geoffrey Faithful, Alan McCabe; m, John Veale; ed, Maurice Rootes; md, Philip Martell; art d, Frank White.

Crime Drama **(PR:C MPAA:NR)**

ESCAPE DANGEROUS*½ (1947, Brit.) 62m DS Films/H&S bw

Beresford Egan (Dr. Belhomme), Mary "Marianne" Stone (Jacqueline Fabre), Lily Lapidus (Mme. Angeline), Daphne Day (Blanche de Vigny), Peter Noble (Michel), Humberston Wright (Aristide Fabre).

During the French Revolution, doctor Egan helps aristocrats sought by the mob to escape for a fee, then turns them in for another fee. Stuffy costume drama, with Egan's demise at the end predictable from the first frame.

p, John Denny, Digby Smith; d, Smith; w, Oswell Blakeston.

Drama **(PR:A MPAA:NR)**

ESCAPE FROM ALCATRAZ***½ (1979) 112m PAR c

Clint Eastwood (Frank Morris), Patrick McGoohan (Warden), Roberts Blossom (Doc), Jack Thibeau (Clarence Anglin), Fred Ward (John Anglin), Paul Benjamin (English), Larry Hankin (Charley Butts), Bruce M. Fischer (Wolf), Frank Ronzio (Litmus), Fred Stuthman (Johnson), David Cryer (Wagner), Madison Arnold (Zimmerman), Blair Burrows (Fight Guard), Bob Balhatchet (Medical Assistant), Matthew J. Locricchio (Exam Guard), Don Michaelian (Beck), Ray K. Goman (Cellblock Captain), Jason Ronard (Bobs), Ed Vasgersian, Ron Vernan, Stephen Bradley, Garry Goodrow, Dan Leegant, John Garabedian, Donald Siegel, Denis Berkfeldt, Jim Haynie, Tony Dario, Fritz Manes, Dana Derfus, Don Cummins, Gordon Handforth, John Scanlon, Don Watters, Lloyd Nelson, George Orrison, Gary F. Warren, Joe Whipp, Terry Wills, Robert Irvine, Joseph Knowland, James Collier, R. J. Ganzert, Robert Hirschfeld, Dale Alvarez, Sheldner Feldner, Danny Glover, Carl Lumby, Patrick Valentino, Glenn Wright, Gilbert Thomas, Jr., Eugene W. Jackson.

The escape-proof "Rock" was designed in the early 1930s to hold the most infamous, incorrigible, and escape-prone inmates in the federal prison system. Located in the dead center of shark-infested, evil-currented San Francisco Bay, Alcatraz was considered by J. Edgar Hoover and other federal executives to be the only American prison from which no inmate could ever escape. Hoover, as with so many of his notions, was wrong about that. In 1962 Frank Morris and the Anglin brothers made good their escape from the prison that had once held Al Capone, Doc Barker, Alvin "Creepy" Karpis, Blackie Audett, Volney Davis, John Paul Chase, and a host of other bad men. Their bodies were never found; authorities concluded the escapees drowned but many others felt they made good their escape and are living out their lives under assumed identities. But what mattered most was that they were able to get off of Alcatraz and reach distant Angel Island before vanishing forever, and that was reason enough to close down the maximum federal prison. This film is the story of that escape, convincingly enacted by Eastwood as mastermind Morris, a taciturn, calculating, and absolutely nerveless miscreant. Upon Eastwood's arrival at Alcatraz he is met by vain, smug McGoohan, the warden, who tells him that he can forget about escaping from "The Rock"; it has never been done and never will be done. But as an inmate who has escaped from other prisons, Eastwood's attitude remains unchanged. He befriends Ronzio, an ancient prisoner with a pet mouse; Benjamin, a black inmate serving time for murder; and Blossom, a long-termer who paints in his cell. Others are not so friendly, especially Fischer, a gargantuan prisoner who tries to stab Eastwood to death in a knife fight in the middle of the yard. Both men are thrown into solitary and Fischer vows vengeance. Eastwood returns to the general population to meet the newly arrived Anglin brothers, Thibeau and Ward, whom he has known in other prisons. They and Butts, another inmate, persuade him to try to escape. Meanwhile, Blossom chops off his fingers in the prison workshop after McGoohan sadistically discontinues his painting privileges (he had painted a cartoon-like canvas which made McGoohan look like an idiot). Using makeshift tools, Eastwood and the others chisel the ancient wall away from the ventilation grills in their cells and are able to wriggle through these tiny openings to a shaft leading to the roof of their cell block. On the big night of their escape, the men, except for Butts who cannot squeeze through the opening in time, make it to the roof, let themselves down outside the wall and into the icy waters of San Francisco Bay, using makeshift water wings to swim away. McGoohan and other officials later find some of their personal effects on distant Angel Island but never recover the bodies as they predicted they would do. The pace of this film is a bit slow, but Siegel's deliberate, sparse helmsmanship works to the benefit of a film where time is all his characters have. He was an old hand at the genre, having directed RIOT IN CELL BLOCK 11 in 1954. Surprisingly, there are few hysterical moments in this film and little real violence, except for the gratuitous finger-chopping scene.

Much care was taken to duplicate the actual Morris-Anglin escape, including the meticulous reconstruction by the prisoners of their own heads, made from paste and plaster and hair from the prison barber shop then placed in their bunks so that they barely protruded from covers when patroling guards checked their cells, believing the dummy heads to be real. The production marked the second time Eastwood worked with director Siegel (DIRTY HARRY in 1971) and it caused many a headache. More than 15 miles of cable had to be laid for electricity and tons of equipment and materials used in reconstructing the crumbling cell blocks had to be brought piecemeal to the island from San Francisco. It took several months just to get federal permission to use the place. The producers agreed to leave their improvements on the island and did, which presently benefits the 800,000 tourists visiting Alcatraz each year. This film was both a critical and box office success, gleaning almost $22 million the first time around.

p&d, Don Siegel; w, Richard Tuggle (based on the book by J. Campbell Bruce); ph, Bruce Surtees (Panavision, DeLuxe Color); ed, Ferris Webster; prod d, Allen Smith; set d, Edward J. McDonald.

Prison Drama   Cas.   **(PR:C MPAA:PG)**

ESCAPE FROM CRIME**   (1942) 51m WB bw

Richard Travis (*Red O'Hara*), Julie Bishop (*Molly O'Hara*), Jackie C. Gleason (*Convict*), Frank Wilcox (*Cornell*), Rex Williams (*Slim Dugan*), Wade Boteler (*Lt. "Biff" Malone*), Charles Wilson (*Reardon*), Paul Fix (*Dude Merrill*), Ruth Ford (*Myrt*), John Hamilton (*Rafferty*), Ann Corcoran (*Belle Mason*), Ben Taggart (*Warden Kirby*).

Travis is an ex-convict newspaper photographer who is persecuted by a suspicious detective and only wins a pardon after putting away his old gang. A young Jackie Gleason makes a brief appearance carrying a mysterious middle initial, which, it can be supposed, was a carryover from his earlier high-faluting idea to continue on as a composer, arranger, and conductor, which had already won him some fame. A remake of PICTURE SNATCHER (1933), with James Cagney.

p, William Jacobs; d, D. Ross Lederman; w, Raymond L. Schrock (based on the story "Picture Snatchers" by Danny Ahearn); ph, James Van Trees; ed, Doug Gould; art d, Stanley Fleischer.

Crime Drama   **(PR:A MPAA:NR)**

ESCAPE FROM DEVIL'S ISLAND**   (1935) 64m COL bw

Victor Jory (*Dario*), Florence Rice (*Johanna*), Norman Foster (*Andre*), Stanley Andrews (*Steve*), Daniel Haynes (*Djikki*), Herbert Heywood (*Bouillon*), Frank Lackteen (*Python*), Arthur Aylesworth (*Commandante*), Noble Johnson (*Bisco*).

Jory and Foster effect an escape from the "inescapable" French penal colony, but because of bickering over Rice fail to rendezvous with the ship that will carry them to freedom in Venezuela. Mediocre programmer once again portraying the miserable human conditions in the infamous French colony.

d, Albert Rogell; w, Earle Snell, Fred Niblo, Jr. (based on a story by Fred De Gresac); ph, John Stumar; ed, Otto Meyer.

Crime Drama   **(PR:A MPAA:NR)**

ESCAPE FROM EAST BERLIN**½   (1962) 89m MGM bw
(AKA: TUNNEL 28)

Don Murray (*Kurt Schroeder*), Christine Kaufmann (*Erika Jurgens*), Werner Klemperer (*Brunner*), Ingrid Van Bergen (*Ingeborg Schroeder*), Karl Schell (*Maj. Eckhardt*), Kai Fischer (*Heidi*), Bruno Fritz (*Uncle Albrecht*), Alfred Balthoff (*Klussendorf*), Horst Janson (*Gunther Jurgens*), Edith Schultze-Westrum (*Mother Schroeder*), Anita Kupsch (*Bambi*), Kurt Waitzmann (*Prof. Jurgens*), Helma Seitz (*Frau Jurgens*), Ronald Dehne (*Helmut*), Arne Elsholtz (*Lemke*), George Bastian (*Tillerman*), Waltraut Runze-Waitzmann (*Marga Wegener*), Bruno W. Pantell (*Moeller*), Kate Jaenicke (*Rosa*), Christian Bottcher (*Fritz*), Maria Tober (*Marga*).

Murray is a young East Berliner who digs a tunnel under the wall and leads 27 fellow freedom-seekers to safety. Murray is fine but no tension is maintained because the outcome is inevitable. The film was based on a true incident, but was multiplied many times over in the early dark days of the Berlin wall.

p, Walter Wood; d, Robert Siodmak; w, Gabrielle Upton, Peter Berneis, Millard Lampell (based on a story by Upton, Berneis); ph, Georg Krause; m, Hans-Martin Majewski; ed, Maurice Wright; art d, Ted Haworth, Dieter Bartels; spec eff, Augie Lohman.

Drama   **(PR:A MPAA:NR)**

ESCAPE FROM FORT BRAVO***   (1953) 98m MGM c

William Holden (*Capt. Roper*), Eleanor Parker (*Carla Forester*), John Forsythe (*Capt. John Marsh*), William Demarest (*Campbell*), William Campbell (*Cabot Young*), Polly Bergen (*Alice Owens*), Richard Anderson (*Lt. Beecher*), Carl Benton Reid (*Col. Owens*), John Lupton (*Bailey*), Howard McNear (*Watson*), Alex Montoya (*Chavez*), Forrest Lewis (*Dr. Miller*), Fred Graham (*Jones*), William Newell (*Symore*), Frank Matts (*Kiowa Indian*), Charles Stevens (*Eilota*), Michael Dugan (*Sims*), Valerie Vernon (*Girl in Bar*), Phil Rich (*Barman*), Glenn Strange (*Sgt. Compton*), Harry Cheshire (*Chaplain*), Eloise Hardt (*Girl*), Richard P. Beedle (*Confederate Lieutenant*).

Holden's first movie at MGM features him as a captain in the Union Army who watches over a stockade filled with Confederate rebels. The place is Arizona, the time 1863, right in the middle of the war between the states. Holden is a martinet who treats all prisoners like dirt and his fellows also hate him because he doesn't treat them much better. He brings escaped prisoner Lupton back to the prison with a noose around the young man's neck to show any of the others that the same fate awaits them if they dare attempt to flee. His commanding officer, Reid, takes Holden to task and his compatriots will have nothing to do with him as a result of his cruel attitudes. Holden feels that discipline must be maintained and he defends his behavior. Parker arrives at the fort to attend the wedding of Reid's daughter,

Bergen, who is to marry officer Anderson. She is, in reality, a southern agent whose job it is to break out Forsythe, leader of the rebels, and his pals. She begins to seduce Holden and learns that he is not as bad as she thought. Like turns to love, but her first order of business is her job. She breaks the rebs out and departs with them in the still of night. Holden soon pursues and eventually catches up with them. He engages in a hand-to-hand battle with Forsythe (who is also in love with Parker). Holden leads the captured men back to the fort but they are waylaid by hostile Indians and trapped in an untenable position. Lupton grabs a stray horse and escapes the area, thereby being called a deserter. The Indians send hundreds of arrows at the soldiers and many are hurt. Forsythe prevails on Holden to escape, and he reveals that Parker is in love with him, even though she is zealous in her duty and belief in the Gray cause. Holden tries a ploy; he walks out to the Indians and says he is the only survivor. The Indians fall for this until he opens fire on them. Holden is hit and it appears he is a goner when Lupton arrives with a horde of Blues from the fort. They are saved, except for Forsythe, who expires. It's an old story and we've seen it before many times, but this version is several notches higher due to Sturges' excellent direction and a literate script by Fenton. Michael Pate, a well-known actor in this kind of movie, co-authored the story. A couple of songs serve as melodic counterpoint to the near nonstop action. Western fans will enjoy it more than others.

p, Nicholas Nayfack; d, John Sturges; w, Frank Fenton (based on a story by Michael Pate, Phillip Rock); ph, Robert Surtees (Ansco Color); m, Jeff Alexander; ed, George Boemler; art d, Cedric Gibbons, Malcolm Brown; set d, Edwin B. Willis, Ralph Hurst; cos, Helen Rose; spec eff, Warren Newcombe; m/l, "Soothe My Lonely Heart," Jeff Alexander; "Yellow Stripes," Stan Jones.

Western   **(PR:A MPAA:NR)**

ESCAPE FROM HELL ISLAND
(SEE: MAN IN THE WATER, THE, 1964)

ESCAPE FROM HONG KONG***   (1942) 60m UNIV bw

Leo Carrillo (*Pancho*), Andy Devine (*Blimp*), Marjorie Lord (*Valerie Hale*), Don Terry (*Rusty*), Gilbert Emery (*Maj. Crossley*), Leyland Hodgson (*Maj. Reeves*), Frank Puglia (*Kosura*), Chester Gan (*Yamota*), Frank Kelly (*Sergeant*), Paul Dubov (*Franz Schuler*).

Terry, Devine, and Carrillo have a sharpshooting act in a Hong Kong vaudeville show. Terry gets involved with British counter-espionage agent Lord and ends up exposing a spy in the ranks of British intelligence. The group escapes in a speedboat on Dec. 7, 1941, when the Japanese attack Hong Kong. Fast-paced action programmer is a lot of fun but little else. Terry sings "Where the Prairie Meets the Sky."

p, Marshall Grant; d, William Nigh; w, Roy Chanslor; ph, Woody Bredell; m/l, Milton Rosen, Everett Carter; ed, Maurice Wright; md, Charles Previn; art d, Jack Otterson.

Spy Drama   **(PR:A MPAA:NR)**

ESCAPE FROM NEW YORK**½   (1981) 99m AE c

Kurt Russell (*Snake Plissken*), Lee Van Cleef (*Bob Hauk*), Ernest Borgnine (*Cabby*), Donald Pleasence (*The President*), Isaac Hayes (*Duke of New York*), Season Hubley (*Girl in Chock Full O'Nuts*), Harry Dean Stanton (*Brain*), Adrienne Barbeau (*Maggie*), Tom Atkins (*Rehme*), Charles Cyphers (*Secretary of State*).

A futuristic thriller set in the year 1997 finds an ex-war hero and now a convict, Russell, sent to rescue the President of the U.S. whose plane has crashed in New York City, which by now has become a fortress walling in untold numbers of criminals and madmen. He goes forth into fights, narrow escapes, white-knuckle adventures against every form of loony, to a climactic chase across a mined bridge with the President, Pleasence, to safety. Weak scripting and uneven pacing mar another entry by director Carpenter, maker of HALLOWEEN and ASSAULT ON PRECINCT 13.

p, Debra Hill, Larry Franco; d, John Carpenter; w, Carpenter, Nick Castle; ph, Dean Cundey (Panavision, Metrocolor); m, John Carpenter, Alan Howorth; ed, Todd Ramsay; prod d, Joe Alves; set d, Claudia; cos, Stephen Loomis.

Action/Thriller   Cas.   **(PR:O MPAA:R)**

ESCAPE FROM RED ROCK**½   (1958) 75m FOX bw

Brian Donlevy (*Bronc Grierson*), Eilene Janssen (*Janie Acker*), Gary Murray (*Cal Bowman*), Jay C. Flippen (*John Costaine*), William Phipps (*Arky Shanks*), Myron Healey (*Joe Skinner*), Nesdon Booth (*Pete Archer*), Daniel White (*Farris*), Andre Adoree (*Guard*), Courtland Shepard (*Boyce*), Tina Menard (*Maria Chavez*), Natividad Vacio (*Miguel Chavez*), Zon Murray (*Krug*), Rick Vallin (*Judd*), Ed Hinton (*Tarrant*), Frosty Royce (*Coach Driver/Double*), Frank Richards (*Price*), Linda Dangell (*Elena Chavez*), Eumenio Blanco (*Mayor*), Elena Davinci (*Antonia Chavez*), Hank Patterson (*Grover*), Eileene Stevens (*Mrs. Donnely*), Frank Marlowe (*Manager*), Joe Becker (*Clerk*), Dick Crockett (*Krug Henchie*), Roydon Clark, Sailor Vincent (*Doubles*), Bud Osborne, Adamson Twins, Al Baffert, Vincent Padula.

Rancher Murray is forced to participate in a robbery when an outlaw chief, Donlevy, threatens to let Murray's crooked brother die of wounds from a previous job. After the holdup, Murray flees with Janssen toward Mexico, getting married along the way. In Indian country they find a cabin whose occupants have been killed by Apaches, leaving only a baby. The posse sent to pick up Murray on a murder charge stemming from the robbery learn that he is innocent and save him and his bride from another attack by the Indians. Despite top billing, Donlevy has a small part, but his appearances are the best thing in this okay oater.

p, Bernard Glasser; d&w, Edward Bernds; ph, Brydon Baker (Regalscope); m, Les Baxter; ed, John F. Link; art d, Rudi Feld.

Western   **(PR:A MPAA:NR)**

## ESCAPE FROM SAN QUENTIN**						(1957) 81m COL bw

Johnny Desmond (*Mike Gilbert*), Merry Anders (*Robbie*), Richard Devon (*Roy Gruber*), Roy Engel (*Hap Graham*), William Bryant (*Richie*), Ken Christy (*Curly Gruber*), Larry Blake (*Mack*), Don Devlin (*Piggy*), Victor Millan (*Mendez*), John Merrick (*Sampson*), Norman Fredric (*Jerry*), Barry Brooks (*Georgie*), Lennie Smith (*Bud*).

Recording star Johnny Desmond plays a convict who breaks out of prison along with Devon and Engel. While Devon tries to contact his father to get the loot he had stashed before going in, Desmond takes up with Anders, the sister of his wife who is divorcing him. Engel is shot dead by cops and Desmond and Devon are back in the pen at the finale. Strictly routine fare. Desmond sings "Lonely Lament."

p, Sam Katzman; d, Fred F. Sears; w, Raymond T. Marcus; ph, Benjamin H. Kline; m, Laurindo Almenda; ed, Saul H. Goodkind; art d, Paul Palmentola; m/l, Johnny Desmond.

**Crime Drama						(PR:A MPAA:NR)**

## ESCAPE FROM TERROR**						(1960) 70m Paladium/Googan-Rogers c

Jackie Coogan (*MVD Agent Petrov*), Mona Knox (*Kathe Solotkin*), Mike Stokey (*Paul Martin*), Lynn Merrick (*Lee Brooks*), Gabriel Dell (*MVD Col. Touchenko*), Erick Erichsen (*The Boy*).

Coogan is a Soviet agent who's pursuing Americans Knox and Stokey. The duo meet night club singer Merrick, who helps them get to safety in Copenhagen. Coogan follows them but finds he rather likes the freedoms of the West. He decides to remain, which sets off the wrath of his superior Dell (an ex-member of the Dead End Kids). It leads to a semi-thrilling climax in what amounts to a middle-budgeted espionage adventure. The story's not bad but the results are clearly hampered by the budget.

p, Egon C. Nielsen; d, Jackie Coogan, George Coogan; w, James Barnett; ph (Eastmancolor).

**Spy Thriller						(PR:A MPAA:NR)**

ESCAPE FROM THE DARK (SEE: LITTLEST HORSE THIEVES, 1977)

## ESCAPE FROM THE PLANET OF THE APES**½						(1971) 97m APJAC/FOX c

Roddy McDowall (*Cornelius*), Kim Hunter (*Zira*), Bradford Dillman (*Dr. Lewis Dixon*), Natalie Trundy (*Dr. Stephanie Branton*), Eric Braeden (*Dr. Otto Hasslein*), William Windom (*The President*), Sal Mineo (*Milo*), Albert Salmi (*E-1*), Jason Evers (*E-2*), John Randolph (*Chairman*), Harry Lauter (*Gen. Winthrop*), M. Emmet Walsh (*Aide*), Roy E. Glenn, Sr. (*Lawyer*), Peter Forster (*Cardinal*), Norman Burton (*Army Officer*), William Woodson (*Naval Officer*), Tom Lowell (*Orderly*), Gene Whittington (*Marine Captain*), Donald Elson (*Curator*), Bill Bonds (*TV Newscaster*), Army Archerd (*Referee*), James Bacon (*Gen. Faulkner*), Ricardo Montalban (*Armando*), John Alderman (*Corporal*), Steve Roberts (*Gen. Brody*).

The third episode in the Apes series has apes McDowall, Hunter, and Mineo escaping their exploding world in the spaceship Charlton Heston left behind in the first film. They arrive in Los Angeles in the 20th century and are treated as research animals until they reveal their powers of speech. Soon the government is after a now-pregnant Hunter because they fear her child will lead the apes to conquer the humans, and presidential advisor Braeden is leading the chase. The apes find shelter with a friendly circus owner (Montalban), and he takes and hides the child when the authorities catch up with and kill McDowall and Hunter. The film ends with a cute baby chimp shouting "Mama! Mama! MAMA!" The least interesting of the Apes films simply because it takes place in the human world of 1971. (See PLANET OF THE APES series, Index.)

p, Arthur P. Jacobs; d, Don Taylor; w, Paul Dehn (based on characters created by Pierre Boulle); ph, Joseph Biroc (Panavision, DeLuxe Color); m, Jerry Goldsmith; ed, Marion Rothman; art d, Jack Martin Smith, William Creber; set d, Walter M. Scott, Stuart A. Reiss; spec eff, Howard A. Anderson Co.; makeup, John Chambers, Dan Striepeke.

**Science Fiction						(PR:C MPAA:NR)**

## ESCAPE FROM THE SEA*						(1968, Brit.) 57m Wallace/CFF c

Paul Martin (*Mat*), Simon Milton (*Chris Oakley*), Nicky Broadway (*Robbie*), Alison Glennie (*Jane Oakley*), Larry Hamilton (*Pen*), Fabienne Symons (*Meg*), Peggy Sinclair (*Mrs. Oakley*), Chief Petty Officer Fairfield (*CPO Scott*).

Predictable children's film has Coast Guardsmen coming to the rescue of children stranded near the Cornish coast. Even the youngest viewers will swear they've seen it before.

p, A. Frank Bundy; d&w, Peter Seabourne (based on a story by Frank Wells); ph (Eastmancolor).

**Children						(PR:AA MPAA:NR)**

## ESCAPE FROM YESTERDAY**½						(1939, Fr.) 88m Societe Nouvelle de Production/J.H. Hoffberg bw (LA BANDERA)

Jean Gabin (*Pierre Gilleth*), Annabella (*Aischa La Siaoui*), Robert Le Vigan (*Fernando Lucas*), Pierre Renoir (*Capt. Weller*), Aimos (*Marcel Mulot*), Margo Lion (*Planche a Plain*), Gaston Modot (*Muller*), Reine Paulet (*Rosita*).

This film is more interesting for the presence of Duvivier's definitive style—an impressive blend of low-key moodiness and subtle camera movement—than for the rather common story of heroism in North Africa. Gabin plays a man fleeing France for a murder he has committed, by hooking up with the Spanish Foreign Legion. Police informer Le Vigan is unwilling to give up his pursuit of Gabin, following him all the way to the most remote regions of North Africa, where the fugitive has found temporary asylum and a chance to court the hand of the Arab beauty Annabella. The bond that has kept a tie between pursuer and pursued, one

that evolved from a lustiness in conquering the hardships of the desert, is given its final expression when the two join hands in order to fight off invading Arabs. For some reason this picture was dedicated to General Francisco Franco who at the time of release in France was a commander in the Legion.

d, Julien Duvivier; w, Duvivier, Charles Spaak (based on the novel by Pierre Mac Orlan); ph, Jules Kruger, Marc Fossard; m, Jean Wiener, Roland Manuel; ed, Marthe Poncin; art d, Jacques.

**Drama						(PR:A MPAA:NR)**

## ESCAPE FROM ZAHRAIN**						(1962) 92m PAR c

Yul Brynner (*Sharif*), Sal Mineo (*Ahmed*), Jack Warden (*Huston*), Madlyn Rhue (*Laila*), Anthony Caruso (*Tahar*), Jay Novello (*Hassan*), Leonard Strong (*Ambulance Driver*), James Mason (*Johnson*), Vladimir Sokoloff.

Student radicals free revolutionary leader Brynner from police custody and, along with student leader Mineo and American convict Warden, they hijack an ambulance containing Rhue and drive it across the desert with the police in pursuit. Unspectacular desert chase film with Mason making a brief cameo as a garage mechanic.

p&d, Ronald Neame; w, Robin Estridge (based on the novel by Michael Barrett); ph, Ellsworth Fredricks (Panavision, Technicolor); m, Lyn Murray; ed, Eda Warren; art d, Eddie Imazu, Hal Pereira; set d, Frank R. McKelvy; spec eff, John P. Fulton.

**Adventure						(PR:A MPAA:NR)**

## ESCAPE IN THE DESERT**½						(1945) 79m WB bw

Jean Sullivan (*Jane*), Philip Dorn (*Philip Artveld*), Irene Manning (*Mrs. Lora Tedder*), Helmut Dantine (*Capt. Becker*), Alan Hale (*Dr. Orville Tedder*), Samuel S. Hinds (*Gramp*), Bill Kennedy (*Hank Albright*), Kurt Kreuger (*Lt. Von Kleist*), Rudolph Anders (*Hoffman*), Hans Schumm (*Klaus*), Blayney Lewis (*Danny, 10 years old*).

Remake of THE PETRIFIED FOREST has Dutch flier Dorn hitchhiking across America on his way to duty in the Pacific area and meeting with Sullivan in a lonely desert diner. Soon the place is invaded by Nazis led by Dantine, who have escaped a desert POW compound. Lots of heavy propaganda slows down the action.

p, Alex Gottlieb; d, Edward A. Blatt; w, Thomas Job (based on an adaptation by Marvin Borowsky of the play "The Petrified Forest" by Robert E. Sherwood); ph, Robert Burks; m, Adolph Deutsch; ed, Owen Marks; md, Leo F. Forbstein; art d, John Hughes; spec eff, Willard Van Enger.

**Crime						(PR:A MPAA:NR)**

## ESCAPE IN THE FOG**						(1945) 65m COL bw

Nina Foch, William Wright, Otto Kruger, Konstantin Shayne, Ivan Triesault, Ernie Adams, Mary Newton, Ralph Dunn, John Tyrell, Charles Jordan, Noel Cravet, John H. Elliott.

A forgettable programmer which would have been forgotten by now had director Boetticher not changed his name to Budd and gone on to helm a number of praised westerns in the 1950s starring Randolph Scott. This minor entry, however, offers no clue to his talent. It tells the story of a nurse whose premonitions of seeing a man murdered soon materialize. She sets out on a desperate search for the doomed man to warn him of the impending danger.

p, Wallace MacDonald; d, Oscar Boetticher, Jr. [Budd Boetticher]; w, Aubrey Wisberg; ph, George Meehan; ed, Jerome Thoms; art d, Joseph Kish.

**Crime Drama						(PR:A MPAA:NR)**

## ESCAPE IN THE SUN**½						(1956, Brit.) 86m Phoenix/PAR c

John Bentley (*Jim Harrison*), Martin Boddey (*Michael O'Dell*), Vera Fusek, Alan Tarlton, Frankie Vaughan.

Shades of THE MOST DANGEROUS GAME are felt in this lively adventure film with a millionaire, Boddey, who tries to track down and kill his wife and her lover. Bentley, a hunter, dislikes the idea of being thought of as game and manages to kill Boddey by the finale. One of a handful of pictures that Breakston made in Africa. Before trying his hand at direction, Breakston appeared as a teenager in many of the ANDY HARDY film series.

p, George Breakston, John R. Carter; d&w, Breakston; ph, Bernard Davies (Eastmancolor).

**Adventure						(PR:A MPAA:NR)**

## ESCAPE LIBRE						(SEE: BACKFIRE, 1965, Fr.)

ESCAPE ME NEVER*½ (1935, Brit.) 93m British and Dominions/UA bw

Elisabeth Bergner (*Gemma Jones*), Hugh Sinclair (*Sebastian Sanger*), Griffith Jones (*Caryl Sanger*), Penelope Dudley-Ward (*Fenella McClean*), Irene Vanbrugh (*Mrs. McClean*), Leon Quartermaine (*Mr. McClean*), Lyn Harding (*Heinrich*), Rosalinde Fuller (*Teremtcherva*).

Bergner is a thoroughly likable flirt and sleep-arounder who, before she can save herself, becomes an unwed mother facing the lethal facts of life. She is taken in by a bounder of a composer who marries her, though actually he is in love with his brother's fiancee, Dudley-Ward. The stage play was a roaring success, the film much less so, although Bergner's transition from pretty vamp to helpless mother is an acting treasure.

p, Herbert Wilcox; d, Paul Czinner; w, Carl Zuckmayer, Robert J. Cullen (based on a play by Margaret Kennedy); ph, F. A. Young; m, William Walton; ed, David Lean.

**Drama						(PR:A MPAA:NR)**

ESCAPE ME NEVER**½   (1947) 101m WB bw

Erroll Flynn (Sebastian Dubrok), Ida Lupino (Gemma Smith), Eleanor Parker (Fenella MacLean), Gig Young (Caryl Dubrok), Reginald Denny (Ivor MacLean), Isobel Elsom (Mrs. MacLean), Albert Basserman (Prof. Heinrich), Ludwig Stossel (Mr. Steinach), Milada Mladova (Natrova), George Zoritch (Dancer), Helene Thimig (Landlady), Frank Puglia (Guide), Frank Reicher (Priest), Doris Lloyd (Mrs. Cooper), Anthony Caruso (Dino), Ivan Triesault (Choreographer), Jack Ford (Double for Albert Basserman), Alfredo Sabato, Mario Siletti (Gondoliers), Hector Sarno (Waiter), George Humber (Vendor), Robert St. Angelo (Burly Servant), Leon Lenoir (Butler), Angela Greene (Girl), Helen Pender, Joan Winfield (Girls), Leonard Mudie (Doctor), Corps de Ballet (Ballet Sequence).

Parker suspects her fiance, Young, of having an affair with widow Lupino, the mother of an infant son. Actually, Young's brother, Flynn, a poor composer, is taking care of Lupino and the child, and when he goes to explain the matter to Parker, he falls in love with her. He agrees to marry Lupino, however, and plans to sit down and write a ballet inspired in him by Parker. Soon he leaves Lupino for Parker, and Lupino's baby dies the night his ballet opens. Flynn goes back to Lupino and promises eternal loyalty. Pretty weepy material and not at all Flynn's type of role. An excellent ballet sequence, "Primavera," was written by one-time child prodigy composer Erich Wolfgang Korngold, who also wrote the arresting score for the film.

p, Henry Blanke; d, Peter Godfrey; w, Thomas Williamson (based on the novel *The Fool of the Family* by Margaret Kennedy and the play "Escape Me Never" by Kennedy); ph, Sol Polito; m, Erich Wolfgang Korngold; ed, Clarence Kolster; art d, Carl Jules Weyl; set d, Fred M. MacLean; ballet cos, Travilla; cos, Bernard Newman; spec eff, Harry Barndollar, Willard Van Enger; ch, LeRoy Prinz; makeup, Perc Westmore.

Drama   (PR:A   MPAA:NR)

ESCAPE ROUTE   (SEE: I'LL GET YOU, 1952, Brit.)

ESCAPE TO ATHENA**

(1979, Brit.) 125m Grade/Associated Film Distribution c

Roger Moore (Maj. Otto Hecht), Telly Savalas (Zeno), David Niven (Prof. Blake), Claudia Cardinale (Eleana), Richard Roundtree (Nat), Stefanie Powers (Dottie), Sonny Bono (Rotelli), Elliott Gould (Charlie), Anthony Valentine (Volkmann), Sigi Rauch (Braun), Michael Sheard (Mann), Richard Wren (Reistoffer), Philip Locke (Vogel), Steve Ubels (Lantz), Elena Secota (Brothel Girl).

Big-name war movie has Gould, Niven, Bono, etc., escaping from a Greek POW camp run by good-German Moore. They hitch up with partisans led by Savalas to save some ancient treasures from the Nazis. Horror of horrors, though, it lacks suspense, certainly the ingredient a mixture like this must have to taste like noodles, not unleavened bread.

p, David Niven, Jr., Jack Wiener; d, George P. Cosmatos; w, Richard S. Lochte, Edward Anhalt (based on an original story by Lochte and Cosmatos); ph, Gil Taylor (Panavision); m, Lalo Schifrin; ed, Ralph Kemplen; prod d, Michael Stringer; art d, John Graysmark; cos, Yvonne Blake.

War   Cas.   (PR:C   MPAA:PG)

ESCAPE TO BERLIN**   (1962, U.S./Switz./Ger.) 80m Stun Film/Herts
Lion International bw (FLUCHT NACH BERLIN; AKA: THE CAPTIVES)

Christian Doermer (Claus Baade), Susanne Korda (Doris Lange), Narziss Sokatscheff (Hermann Gueden), Gerda Blisse, S. Kubitzky.

Another story of an escape from gloomy East Germany. This one has Doermer, a government worker trying to collectivize some farmland, fighting a balking farmer, Sokatscheff. Sokatscheff decides he has had enough of the Democratic Republic and, with the help of a Swiss journalist, Korda, and with Doermer in tow, who has fallen out with his bosses, they escape over the border. A pedestrian effort at best by director Will Tremper, a one-time Berlin police reporter who is much concerned with social themes.

d,w&ed, Will Tremper; ph, Gunter Haase, Gerd von Bonin; m, Peter Thomas.

Drama   (PR:A   MPAA:NR)

ESCAPE TO BURMA**   (1955) 86m RKO c

Robert Ryan (Jim Brecan), Barbara Stanwyck (Gwen Moore), David Farrar (Cardigan), Murvyn Vye (Mekash), Robert Warwick (Sawbwa), Reginald Denny (Commissioner), Lisa Montell (Andora), Peter Coe (Guard Captain), Anthony Numkena (Kasha), Alex Montoya (Dacoit), Robert Cabal (Kumat), Lal Chand Mehra (Pookan), William Benegal Raw (John Mansfield (Sergeant), Gavin Muir (Astrologer), Roger (The Leopard), Neil (The Chimpanzee), Emma (Kartoum, the Elephant), Little Babe, Tessie, Marge, Judy, Mary (Elephants), Pete Kooy, Bob Corby, Polly Burson, Billy Cartledge, Neyle Morrow, Wayne Van Horn, Henry Escalante, Sharon Lee, Jackie Loughery, Gloria Marshall, Paul Fierro, John Dodsworth, Billy Wilkerson, Carl Mathews, Tom Humphrey, Riley Sunrise, George Deere, Art Felix, Joe Milan, Leo McMahon, Artie Ortejo, Manuel Ybarra, Jose Saenz, Kuka Tuitama, Rocky Barry, Joe Ferrante, Wag Bessing, Jimmy Van Horne, Tim Nelson.

On the run through the jungle from a murder he didn't commit, Ryan stumbles across a plantation owned by Stanwyck. They begin a torrid affair interrupted by the appearance of policeman Farrar. A long chase through more jungle ensues, complete with tigers, bandits, and henchmen of the father of the man he is supposed to have killed. Finally, as if by magic, a witness turns up who clears Ryan and he and Stanwyck return to the jungle plantation. Second-rate jungle chase film shot in an animal world compound in California.

p, Benedict E. Bogeaus; d, Allan Dwan; w, Talbot Jennings, Hobart Donavan (based on the story "Bow Tamely to Me" by Kenneth Perkins); ph, John Alton (Superscope, Technicolor); m, Louis Forbes; ed, James Leicester; art d, Van Nest Polglase; set d, Fay Babcock; cos, Gwen Wakeling, Lucille Southern,; spec eff, Lee Savitz; animal trainers, Wally Ross, Bert Pettus, Larry White, Mel Koontz.

Adventure   (PR:A   MPAA:NR)

ESCAPE TO DANGER*½   (1943, Brit.) 92m RKO bw

Eric Portman (Arthur Lawrence), Ann Dvorak (Joan Grahame), Karel Stepanek (Franz von Brinkman), Ronald Ward (Rupert Chessman), Ronald Adam (George Merrick), Lilly Kann (Karin Moeller), David Peel (Lt. Peter Leighton), Felix Aylmer (Sir Alfred Horton), Brefni O'Rorke (Security Officer), A. E. Matthews (Sir Thomas Leighton), Charles Victor (PO Flanagan), Marjorie Rhodes (Mrs. Pickles), Frederick Cooper (Goesta), Ivor Barnard (Henry Waud), George Merritt (Works Manager), Anthony Shaw (Lisbon Attache), Hay Petrie, John Ruddock, Richard George, D'Oyley John, James Pirrie, Ian Fleming, George Woodbridge, Norman Whitcomb.

Danish double-agent Dvorak, whose real allegiance is to the Allies, is sent to England by the Nazis to steal the plans for the invasion of Europe. Followed and exposed by English agent Portman, she participates in a scheme to lure the German navy out of port with false information on how to sink the invasion barges and then destroy it. The plot works, but Dvorak is killed. WW II espionage tale was timely for its day but was dated.

p, William Sistrom; d, Victor Hanbury, Lance Comfort, Mutz Greenbaum, w, Wolfgang Wilhelm, Jack Whittingham (based on a story by Patrick Kirwan) ph, Guy Green.

Spy Drama   (PR:A   MPAA:NR)

ESCAPE TO GLORY*½ (1940) 70m COL bw (AKA: SUBMARINE ZONE)

Pat O'Brien (Mike Farrough), Constance Bennett (Christine Blaine), John Halliday (John Morgan), Melville Cooper (Penney), Alan Baxter (Larry Perrin), Edgar Buchanan (Charles Atterbee), Marjorie Gateson (Mrs. Winslow), Francis Pierlot (Prof. Mudge), Jessie Busley (Mrs. Mudge), Stanley Logan (Capt. Hollister), Frank Sully (Tommy Malone), Erwin Kalser (Dr. Behrens), Don Beddoe (Chief Engineer), Leslie Dennison (1st Mate), Bruce Bennett (Lieutenant), Olaf Hytten (Agent), Frank Baker, Arthur Mulliner (Detectives), Jimmie Kilgannon (Sailor), Arno Frey (Submarine Gunner), Bert Kennedy (Stand-in for Pat O'Brien), Kay Smith (Stand-in for Constance Bennett).

A collection of 1940s characters going home from England on a freighter react to the news about the outbreak of war. Despite the machinations of German doctor Kalser, heroic actions by some of the passengers manage to sink a U-boat. The coming clouds of war hang heavy over this B picture and provide a sense of how it was then.

p, Sam Bischoff; d, John Brahm; w, P.J. Wolfson (based on a story by Sidney Biddell, Fredric Frank); ph, Franz Planer; ed, Al Clark; md, M.W. Stoloff.

War Drama   (PR:A   MPAA:NR)

ESCAPE TO PARADISE*½   (1939) 60m RKO bw

Bobby Breen (Roberto), Kent Taylor (Fleming), Maria Shelton (Juanita), Joyce Compton (Penelope Carter), Pedro de Cordoba (Don Miguel), Robert O. Davis (Alexander Komac), Rosina Galli (Duenna), Frank Yaconelli (Manuel), Anna Demetrio (Senora Ramos).

Singer Breen made a series of films for RKO and this is the last of them. He is a South American motorcycle-taxi driver guiding gringo tourist Taylor. After fixing Taylor up with Senorita Shelton he gets him into trouble by buying the dried leaves of mate plant in his name. Happy end has Taylor making a fortune in the export of the leaves and winning Shelton. Breen sings a number of tunes, "Tra-La-La," "Rhythm of the Rio," "Ay, Ay, Ay" among them.

p, Barney Briskin; d, Erle C. Kenton; w, Weldon Melick (based on a story by Ian Hunter and Herbert C. Lewis); ph, Charles Schoenbaum; ed, Arthur Hilton; md, Victor Young; m/l, Nilo Menendez, Edward Cherkose.

Musical/Comedy   (PR:A   MPAA:NR)

ESCAPE TO THE SUN**   (1972, Fr./Ger./Israel) 105m Noah Films-
Comacico-SL Films/Cinevision c (HABRICHA EL HASHEMESH)

Laurence Harvey (Maj. Kirsanov), Josephine Chaplin (Nina Kaplan), John Ireland (Jacob Kagan), Lila Kedrova (Sarah Kaplan), Jack Hawkins (Baburin), Yuda Barkan (Yasha Bazarov), Yehuda Efroni (Romek), Peter Capell (Prof. Abramoviz), Gila Almagor (The Judge), Clive Revill (The Drunk).

Soviet Jews Barkan and Chaplin wish to emigrate but are forbidden to do so by the KGB. In desperation they become involved in a scheme to hijack a jetliner and fly it to freedom, but KGB man Harvey learns of the plot and foils it, capturing all the would-be escapers except Barkan and Chaplin, who flee across the frozen steppes. Barkan dies of an infected wound and Chaplin is captured by Harvey and taken to face trial. ESCAPE TO THE SUN is a melodramatic and badly acted and directed attempt by Israeli schlockmeister Golan to exploit a serious issue. The presence of some highly talented actors fails to help, as all show an alarming stiffness in every move.

p&d, Menahem Golan; w, Golan, Joseph Gross (based on a story by Uri Dan); ph, David Garfinkel; m, Dov Seltzer; ed, Fred Srp.

Drama   Cas.   (PR:C   MPAA:PG)

ESCAPE TO WITCH MOUNTAIN**½   (1975) 97m BV c

Eddie Albert (Jason), Ray Milland (Aristotle Bolt), Donald Pleasence (Deranian), Kim Richards (Tia), Ike Eisenmann (Tony), Walter Barnes (Sheriff Purdy), Reta Shaw (Mrs. Grindley), Denver Pyle (Uncle Bene), Alfred Ryder (Astrologer), Lawrence Montaigne (Ubermann), Terry Wilson (Biff Jenkins), George Chandler (Grocer), Dermott Downs (Truck), Shepherd Sanders (Guru), Don Brodie (Gasoline Attendant), Paul Sorenson (Sgt. Foss), Alfred Rossi (Policeman No. 3), Tiger Joe Marsh (Lorko), Harry Holcombe (Capt. Malone), Sam Edwards (Mate), Dan

Seymour (Psychic), Eugene Daniels (Cort), Al Dunlap (Deputy), Rex Holman, Tony Giorgio (Hunters).

Richards and Eisenmann are a pair of orphaned alien children with psychic powers but suffering from amnesia. Evil tycoon Milland wants to use them toward his own nefarious ends, but kindly Albert saves them in his camper, which takes to the air in the climax. Could have been a decent science fiction film, but instead it's just another Disney helping of homily and sentiment. Sequel: RETURN FROM WITCH MOUNTAIN.

p, Jerome Courtland; d, John Hough; w, Robert Malcolm Young (based on a book by Alexander Key); ph, Frank Phillips (Technicolor); ed, Johnny Mandell; ed, Robert Stafford; art d, John Mansbridge, Al Roelofs; set d, Hal Gausman; cos, Chuck Keehne, Emily Sundby; spec eff, Art Cruickshank.

Science Fiction	Cas.	(PR:AA MPAA:G)

ESCAPE 2000*   (1983, Aus.) 80m Filmco/New World c
                                   (AKA: TURKEY SHOOT)

Steve Railsback (Paul), Olivia Hussey (Chris), Noel Ferrier (Mallory), Carmen Duncan (Jennifer), Lynda Stoner (Rita), Michael Craig (Thatcher), Roger Ward (Ritter), Michael Petrovich (Tito), Gus Mercurio (Red), Steve Rackmann (Alph), John Ley (Dodge), Marina Finaly (Melinda), John Godden (Andy), Bill Young (Griff).

Apparently unhinged from too many viewings of THE MOST DANGEROUS GAME, the Australian government takes convicts and releases them in a dense jungle, then hunts them down for sport. Incredibly blood-soaked, largely to divert attention from a script the producers must have got real cheap.

p, Anthony I. Giannane, William Fayman; d, Brian Trenchard-Smith; w, Jon George, Neill Hicks (based on a story by George Schenck, Robert Williams, David Lawrence); ph, John McClean; m, Brian May; ed, Alan Lake; prod d, Bernard Hides; cos, Aphrodite Kondos.

Science Fiction	Cas.	(PR:O MPAA:R)

ESCAPED FROM DARTMOOR**   (1930, Brit.) 77m
                                   British Instructional—Swedish Biograph/PP bw
                                   (GB: A COTTAGE ON DARTMOOR)

Nora Baring (Sally), Uno Henning (Joe), Hans Schlettow (Harry), Judd Green (Customer).

Bloody melodrama has Henning, a barber, tortured by jealousy when pretty manicurist Baring starts paying too much attention to a customer, Schlettow. He finally resorts to the razor to rid himself of his unwanted rival. Some interesting effects and direction, with only a few minutes of dialog coming from the screen when the principals go to see a talking picture. Sound was synched in Berlin.

p, H. Bruce Woolfe; d&w Anthony Asquith (based on a story by Herbert Price); ph, S. Rodwell, M. Lindblom; m, William Hodgdon; song, "My Woman."

Crime		(PR:C MPAA:NR)

ESCORT FOR HIRE*½   (1960, Brit.) 66m Danziger/MGM c

June Thorburn (Terry), Peter Murray (Buzz), Noel Trevarthan (Steve), Jan Holden (Elizabeth), Peter Butterworth (Inspector Bruce), Mary Laura Wood (Barbara), Derek Blomfield (Jack), Jill Melford (Nadia), Guy Middleton (Arthur), Patricia Plunkett (Eldon Baker).

Down-on-his-luck actor Trevarthan takes a job as an escort, but finds himself framed for murder when a rich client turns up dead. Routine British crime melodrama with the limited attraction of Technicolor to enhance it.

p, Brian Taylor; d, Godfrey Grayson; w, Mark Grantham; ph, (Technicolor).

Crime		(PR:A-C MPAA:NR)

ESCORT WEST*½**   (1959) 75m UA bw

Victor Mature (Ben Lassiter), Elaine Stewart (Beth Drury), Faith Domergue (Martha Drury), Reba Waters (Abbey Lassiter), Noah Beery, Jr. (Jamison), Leo Gordon (Vogel), Rex Ingram (Nelson), John Hubbard (Lt. Weeks), Harry Carey, Jr. (Travis), Slim Pickens (Wheeler), Roy Barcroft (Doyle), William Ching (Capt. Poole), Ken Curtis (Burch), Claire Dubrey (Mrs. Fenniman), Syd Saylor (Elwood), X. Brands (Tago), Chuck Hayward, Charles Soldani (Indians).

Mature is an ex-Confederate officer traveling west with his daughter, Waters. He meets sisters Stewart and Domergue being escorted by Union troops after they survived an Indian attack. He falls for Stewart in spite of her sister's hatred of the South, and finally leads them to safety. An interesting B western.

p, Robert E. Morrison, Nate H. Edwards; d, Francis D. Lyon; w, Leo Gordon, Fred Hartsook (based on a story by Steven Hayes); ph, William Clothier; m, Henry Vars; ed, Otto Ludwig; art d, Alfred Ybarra; set d, Mowbray Berkeley; cos, Elmer Ellsworth, Neva Rames; spec eff, David Koehler.

Western		(PR:A MPAA:NR)

ESPIONAGE**   (1937) 66m MGM bw

Edmund Lowe (Kenneth), Madge Evans (Patricia), Paul Lukas (Kronsky), Ketti Gallian (Sonia), Skeets Gallagher (Brown), Frank Reicher (Von Cram), William Gilbert (Turk), Robert Graves (Duval), Leonid Kinskey (Burgos), Mitchell Lewis (Sondheim), Charles Trowbridge (Doyle), Barnett Parker (Cordell), Nita Pike (Fleurette), Juan Torena (South American), George Sorel (Maitre d'Hotel), Gaston Glass (La Forge), Egon Brecher (Chief of Police), Max Lucke (Foreign Civilian), Michael S. Visaroff (Foreign Spy), Carlos J. de Valdez (Foreign Officer), Guy d'Ennery, Gordon de Main, Gennaro Curci, Ramsey Mill, Jack Chefe, Walter Bonn, Russell Hicks (Bits), Albert Pollet (French Waiter), Lita Chevret (French Secretary), Jacques Vanaire, Andre Cheron (French Inspectors), Christian J. Frank (French Guard), Eugene Beday (French Gateman), Fered Malatesta (French Pickpocket), Paul Weigel (French Telegraph Man), Carrie Daumery (French Flower

Woman), Gino Corrado (Musician), Leo White (Barber), Francesco Maran (Train Guard), Eugene Borden (Doctor), Sven Borg (Masseuse), William von Brincken (Legation Officer), Jean Perry, Robert du Couedic, Albert Moriene (Waiters), Betty Blythe (Passenger), Charles Williams (Simmons), Otto Fries (Driver), George Davis (Bartender), Herbert Corthell (Police Judge), Torben Meyer (Police Inspector), Barbara Leonard (German Telephone Operator).

Evans and Lowe are a pair of rival reporters who fall in love aboard a Paris-Basle train while tracking down a munitions baron, Lukas. After getting implicated in and then cleared of a plot to kill Lukas, the pair end up professing true love on a bicycle built for two after Lukas himself falls in love and renounces munitions for more peaceful manufacturing items. A yawner calling a suspension of all belief.

p, Harry Rapf; d, Kurt Neumann; w, Manuel Seff, Leonard Lee, Ainsworth Morgan (based on a play by Walter Hackett); ph, Ray June; ed, W. Donn Hayes.

Drama		(PR:A MPAA:NR)

ESPIONAGE AGENT* *½**   (1939) 74m WB bw

Joel McCrea (Barry Corvall), Brenda Marshall (Brenda Ballard), Jeffrey Lynn (Lowell Warrington), George Bancroft (Dudley Garrett), Stanley Ridges (Hamilton Peyton), James Stephenson (Dr. Rader), Howard Hickman (Walter Forbes), Nana Bryant (Mrs. Corvall), Robert O. Davis (Paul Strawn), Hans von Twardowsky (Dr. Helm), Addison Richards (Bruce Corvall), Edwin Stanley (Secretary of State), William Hopper, Glenn Langan (Students), Lionel Royce (Hoffmeyer), Henry Victor (Foreign Official), Lucien Prival (Decker), Lloyd Ingraham (Woodrow Wilson), Chris Martin (Tunisian Guard), Stuart Holmes, John Harron, Fern Barry, Al Lloyd, Eddie Graham, Sally Sage, Alice Connors (Americans), Fred Vogeding, Arno Frey (Men), Sarah Edwards, Lois Chenney, Lottie Williams (Women), Louis Adlon (Youth), Vera Lewis (Militant Woman), Dorothy Vaughan (Stout Woman), Sidney Bracy (Steward), Alex Melesh (Headwaiter), George Irving (Elderly Official), Emmett Bogan, William Worthington, Selmer Jackson (Instructors), John Hamilton (Code Room Instructor), Rolf Lindau (Foreign Agent), Egon Brecher (Detective Larson), Nella Walker (Mrs. Peyton), Jean De Briac (Waiter), Henry Von Zynda (Guard), Billy McClain (Manservant), Winifred Harris (Lady Ashford), Frederick Lindsley (Announcer), Eddie Acuff (Taxi Driver).

State Department agent McCrea teams up with Marshall to steal the evidence of Nazi espionage in the U.S. off a train somewhere in Europe. A pallid imitation of CONFESSIONS OF A NAZI SPY has only a few moments of interest today, although its on-target topicality in its time gave it good box office appeal.

p, Lou Edelman; d, Lloyd Bacon; w, Warren Duff, Michael Fessier, Frank Donaghue (based on the story "Career Man" by Robert Henry Buckner); ph, Charles Rosher; ed, Ralph Dawson.

Spy Drama		(PR:A MPAA:NR)

ESTHER AND THE KING*   (1960, U.S./Ital.) 110m FOX c

Joan Collins (Esther), Richard Egan (King Ahasuerus), Denis O'Dea (Mordecai), Sergio Fantoni (Haman), Rick Battaglia (Simon), Renato Baldini (Klydrathes), Gabriele Tinti (Samual), Rosalba Neri (Keresh), Robert Buchanan (Hegai), Daniella Rocca (Queen Vashti), Folco Lulli (Tobiah).

A biblical epic with Collins the Jewish girl Esther who marries Persian king Egan in order to make him stop his oppression against the Jews, which she manages to do over two torturous hours. A leaden-weighted insult to the biblical story of Esther with Collins leading the mishmash by acting without a shred of conviction.

p&d, Raoul Walsh; w, Walsh, Michael Elkins; ph, Mario Bava (CinemaScope, Technicolor); m, Francesco Lavagnino, Roberto Nicolosi; ed, Jerry Webb; art d, Giulio Giovannini.

Drama		(PR:A MPAA:NR)

ESTHER WATERS *½**   (1948, Brit.) 108m Rank-Wessex/GFD bw

Kathleen Ryan (Esther Waters), Dirk Bogarde (William Latch), Cyril Cusack (Fred Parsons), Ivor Barnard (Mr. Randall), Fay Compton (Mrs. Barfield), Mary Clare (Mrs. Latch), Julian d'Albie (Mr. Barfield), Morland Graham (Mr. Ketley), Shelagh Fraser (Margaret Gale), Margaret Withers (Miss Grover), Lalage Lewis (Miss Peggy), George Hayes (Journeyman), Alex Parker (Fred Archer), Pauline Mameson (Hospital Nurse), Margaret Diamond, Joseph Dillon, Philip Ashley, Harry Ross, Billy Rees, Fred Lane, Nuna Davey, Barbara Shaw.

Ryan is a virgin made pregnant by Bogarde, a footman in the household where Ryan is a maid. He offers to marry her but at the last minute vanishes with another girl. After years of wandering about trying to scrape together a living for her son, she meets Bogarde again, now a prosperous bookie. They marry and live happily for a while, but Bogarde, now ill, bets their life's savings on a horse and dies, never knowing that his horse lost and his widow and orphan are again reduced to poverty. A well-done but melancholy costume drama from the book by the Irish playwright and critic George Moore, a co-founder of the theater group that led to the famous Abbey Theatre.

p, Ian Dalrymple; d, Peter Proud, Dalrymple; w, Michael Gordon, William Rose, Gerard Tyrrell (based on a novel by George Moore); ph, C. Pennington-Richards, H.E. Fowle; m, Gordon Jacob; ed, Brereton Porter; art d, Fred Pusey.

Drama		(PR:C MPAA:NR)

ETERNAL FEMININE, THE*½   (1931, Brit.) 82m Starcraft/PAR bw

Guy Newall (Sir Charles Winthrop), Doria March (Yvonne de la Roche), Jill Esmond Moore (Claire Lee), Garry Marsh (Arthur Williams), Terence de Marney (Michael Winthrop), Madge Snell (Lady Winthrop), Arthur Varney (Al Peters).

Actress March leaves the stage when she marries aristocrat de Marney, but when he is injured in an auto accident she takes a job in a show backed by Newall, her husband's brother. Static comedy all but forgotten today.

p&d, Arthur Varney; w, Varney, Hugh Broadbridge, Brock Williams (based on a story by Varney).

Comedy (PR:A MPAA:NR)

ETERNAL HUSBAND, THE (1946, Fr.) 90m Alcina bw
(L'HOMME AU CHAPEAU ROND)

Raimu (Nicolas Pavlovitch), Aime Clariond (Michel), Lucy Valnor (Lisa), Gisele Casadesus (Marie), Louis Seigner (The Father), Jane Marken (The Mother), Micheline Boudet (Neighbor), Helena Manson (Agathe), Arlette Mery (Mathilde).

Raimu, a widower, discovers through his wife's letters that she had a lover and that their child was fathered by him. To get revenge, he gives the child to the real father, Clariond, but it dies and both men suffer for it. Raimu wants to kill Clariond, but can't bring himself to do it, and so he just wanders off. A densely atmospheric film that translates Dostoyevsky's novella very well. For Raimu (born Jules Muraire), called "the greatest actor that ever lived" by Orson Welles," this would be his last film. He died in Paris the year the movie came out, at 63 years of age.

d, Pierre Billon; w, Charles Spaak, Pierre Brive, Billon (based on the novella by Fyodor Dostoyevsky); ph, Nicolas Toporkoff; m, Maurice Thiriet; ed, Germaine Artus.

Drama (PR:C MPAA:NR)

ETERNAL LOVE* (1960, Ger.) 95m Casino c

Barbara Ruetting (Ursula Diewen), Claus Holm (Uwe Karsten Alslev), Katharina Mayberg (Martha Detleffsen), Herbert Huebner (Ernst Diewen), Carola Hoehn, Hans Quest, Wolfgang Lukschy, Guenther Lueders, Kaethe Itter, Franz Schafheitlin, Lotte Brackebusch, Josef Sieber, Carsta Loeck, Richard Drosten, Kaethe Haack, Heidi Bruehl, Claus-Dieter Schmoller.

Weepy melodrama sees Ruetting suffering mightily as she learns that her fiance has fathered her best friend's child. When she goes to the country and finds a new love, schoolmaster Holm, local gossip turns against her and she again flees, but she returns to Holm when she learns that he has been badly burned saving a drunk in a fire. They are married and for a short time happy, then Ruetting succumbs to diphtheria while caring for a friend's stricken child. The film fades as she and Holm vow the title of this forgotten import. (In German; English subtitles.)

d, Hans Deppe; w, (based on a novel by Felicitas Rose); ph, Fritz Arno Wagner (Eastmancolor); md, Heinrich Riethmueller.

Drama (PR:A MPAA:NR)

ETERNAL MASK, THE** (1937, Swiss) 74m Progress Films bw

Peter Petersen (Prof. Tscherko), Mathias Wieman (Dr. Dumartin), Olga Tschechowa (Mme. Negar), Tom Kraa (Dr. Wendt), Thekla Ahrens (Sister Anna), Franz Schafheitlin (Mons. Negar).

An eerie, psychological drama that evokes memories of the early German Expressionist films (THE CABINET OF DR. CALIGARI, METROPOLIS). Weiman is a young physician who believes he has concocted a cure for meningitis but medicine being what it is, he is ordered not to try it out by the hospital chief at the facility where he works. One of his patients is terminal with the disease and Weiman thinks that anything would be better than the man's death, so he injects the serum against orders. At first, the patient seems to be improving, then takes a bad turn and dies. When authorities reason that Weiman gave the man the serum against orders, they chastize him and he leaves the hospital and begins a hegira around the city. Now a sequence begins whereby we are never certain what is real and what is fantasy. The sets commence to subtly change as Weiman feels his life as a doctor is over. He haunts the streets and everything around him becomes increasingly stylistic as he goes deeper into psychotic depression. He throws himself off a bridge and plunges into a river. After he's rescued, he is almost totally incapacitated and lives his life solely within his mind, running down mental corridors, hiding behind mental doorways, but never actually moving. The hospital chief discovers that Weiman's serum actually does work and he must now approach Weiman because he is the only person who knows the formula. Now starts a sequence of events whereby they must bring Weiman back through illusion into reality. If this film were only technique, it would remain a cinematic exercise and little more. But the power of the story is a combination of sympathy for Weiman connected to the vision of director Hochbaum and the screenplay of Lapaire. The English subtitles leave much to be desired but, even if one knows no German, the picture is so visual that it could have been shown silently with much effect. In three words, Schizophrenia On Screen. Sometimes jerky, sometimes agonizingly slow, THE ETERNAL MASK builds to a satisfying conclusion and the entire experience is unforgettable. (In German; English subtitles.)

d, Werner Hochbaum; w, Leo Lapaire (based on his novel); ph, Oscar Schnirch; , Anton Profes; art d, Hans Jacoby.

Psychological Drama (PR:A-C MPAA:NR)

ETERNAL MELODIES* (1948, Ital.) 93m E.N.I.C./Grand bw

Gino Cervi (Mozart), Conchita Montenegro (Aloisia W. Lange), Luisella Beghi (Costanza Weber Mozart); Maria Jacobini (Anna Maria Mozart), Jone Salinas (Nannina Mozart), Margherita Bagni (Signora Weber), Paolo Stoppa (Haibl), Lauro Gazzolo (Deiner), Luigi Pavese (Leopoldo Mozart), Carlo Barbetti (Mozart as a Child).

Highly fictionalized, dull biography of Wolfgang Amadeus Mozart, focusing on his relationship with sisters Beghi and Bangni, one of whom he loves, the other of whom he marries. A thick layering of misinformation about the great composer's life and loves, saccharine, which he would have hated, and, ultimately, lifeless. The music is Mozart's, and that is wonderful.

p, G. Amato; d, Carmine Gallone; w, Guido Cantini, Gallone (based on a story by Ernest Marischka); ph, Brizzi; ed, Nicola Lazzari; md, Ricci; set d, Florine.

Biography (PR:A MPAA:NR)

ETERNAL RETURN, THE*½ (1943, Fr.) 100m Discina bw
(L'ETERNEL RETOUR; GB: LOVE ETERNAL)

Jean Marais (Patrice), Madeleine Sologne (Nathalie I), Jean Murat (Marc), Yvonne de Bray (Gertrude), Pierre Pieral (Achille), Jean d'Yd (Amedee), Junie Astor (Nathalie II), Roland Toutain (Lionel), Jeanne Market (Anne), Alexandre Rignault (Morolt).

A modernized version of the Tristan and Isolde legend which has Marais falling in love with two characters named Nathalie (Sologne and Astor). Thinking that Nathalie I (Sologne) doesn't love him, Marais proposes to Nathalie II (Astor). He tries to see Sologne once more before his marriage, trying to get her attention by signaling to her bedroom window. There is no answer. Unknown to Marais, she has switched bedrooms. Marais is shot by evil dwarf Pieral and flees into the woods where he dies. Sologne rushes to her lover's side, and already frail and weak, lies next to him and also dies. While the film is directed by Jean Delannoy, who is mediocre at best, the credit deservedly belongs to scriptwriter Jean Cocteau. Although he had won praise 13 years earlier with THE BLOOD OF A POET. Thinking that the painter-poet-playwright didn't gain real status in the cinema until this picture. Everything in it bears his mark, from the magical love potion to the idea of life continuing after death. It also marks the beginning of Cocteau's association with Marais, casting him later in BEAUTY AND THE BEAST, and ORPHEUS. For their parts in THE ETERNAL RETURN Cocteau insisted that Marais and Sologne dye their hair blonde to accentuate their Celtic heritage. Film critics, however, took this as a reference to Nazism and the Aryan nation, especially since the picture was made during the Occupation. Initially Michele Morgan was to play Sologne's part, but instead left France to work in the States. Pieral adds a demonic touch to the film with his portrayal of the dwarf. His hateful presence, from the opening scene in which he kills a dog to his shooting of Marais in the finale, becomes an essential part of the picture's atmosphere. Marais does, however, have a second dog, Moulouk, which was his own pet in real life. Significant French cinema in which a first-rate script is handled by a second-rate director.

p, Andre Paulve; d, Jean Delannoy; w, Jean Cocteau; ph, Roger Hubert; m, Georges Auric; ed, Suzanne Fauvel; set d, Georges Wakhevitch.

Romance/Fantasy (PR:A MPAA:NR)

ETERNAL SEA, THE*½ (1955) 103m REP bw

Sterling Hayden (Rear Adm. John M. Hoskins), Alexis Smith (Sue Hoskins), Dean Jagger (Vice Adm. Thomas L. Semple), Ben Cooper (Zuggy), Virginia Grey (Dorothy Buracker), Hayden Rorke (Capt. William Buracker), Douglas Kennedy (Capt. Walter Riley), Louis Jean Heydt (Capt. Walter F. Rodee), Richard Crane (Lt. Johnson), Morris Ankrum (Adm. Arthur Dewey Struble), Frank Ferguson (Adm. "L.D."), John Maxwell (Adm. William F. Halsey).

Interesting biography picture has Hayden a Navy officer who continues to command a carrier despite the fact that his leg was blown off in a Japanese attack on his carrier Princeton early in WW II. He then fought to stay on active duty when carrier-borne jet aircraft came along. Lots of exciting footage of carrier plane landings and takeoffs, and a nicely balanced view between sentiment and reality of the women the carrier men leave behind. Still a good look-see for anybody interested in airplanes and the men who fly them.

p, Herbert J. Yates; d, John H. Auer; w, Allen Rivkin (based on a story by William Wister Haines); ph, John L. Russell, Jr.; m, Elmer Bernstein; ed, Fred Allen; cos, Adele Palmer; art d, Frank Hotaling; tech advisors, Lt. Joseph D. Adkins, USN, Lt. Col. Edward R. Kendel, USAF.

Biography (PR:A MPAA:NR)

ETERNAL SUMMER* (1961) 80m Viscaya bw

Gwen DeCastro (Kay Holden), Jeff Brown (Ed Holden), Ron Corsi (Roy Gibson), Maggie Chamberlain (Rose), Yanka Mann (Billie), William Mayer (Jack Todd), Dave Dundon (Belser), Thora Randall (Model), Ed Thomas (Policeman).

Dull domestic drama has DeCastro and Brown's marriage disintegrating after 8 years in the Miami suburbs. Producer Van Hearn concocted this very predictable script.

p, J. Van Hearn; d, Larry Wolk; w, Van Hearn; ph, Lloyd Beckworth, Max Landow; ed, Marian Kley; ch, Corky Newton.

Drama (PR:A MPAA:NR)

ETERNAL WALTZ, THE* (1959, Ger.) 97m
A.C.W. Tetting-Transocean/Bakros International c
(EWIGER WALZER)

Bernhard Wicki (Johann Strauss), Hilde Krahl (Henriette Treffz), Annemarie Dueringer (Adele), Friedl Loor (Maria Geistinger), Lis Van Essen (Olga), Willy Trenk-Trebitsch (Leibrock), Hans Putz (Alexander Girardi), Ulrich Bettac (Director Steiner), Leonard Steckel (Baron Carlo Todesco), Michael Toost (Baron Victor Todesco), Eduard Strauss, Jr. (Eduard Strauss), Josef Hendrichs (Josef Strauss), Elizabeth Newman (Mother Strauss), Maria Eis (Princess Metternich), Gert Froebe (Gawrinoff), Ellen Hille (Anastasia), Claus Biderstaedt (Gregor), Eric Frey (Emperor Franz Josef), Harry Hardt (Prof. Billroth), Arnulf Schroeder (Jacques Offenbach), Herman Thimig (Haslinger).

A biographical sketch of famed composer Johann Strauss was a bit too heavy in dishing out the sentiment, without really getting into the forces that make a great artist create. Soundtrack, staging and sets are excellent—with Verhoeven handling the contrived situations well—otherwise viewers would probably walk away disappointed.

d, Paul Verhoeven; w, Alexander Rix, Friedrich Schreyvogel.

Biographical Drama (PR:A MPAA:NR)

ETERNALLY YOURS**   (1939) 99m UA bw

Loretta Young (Anita Halstead), David Niven (Tony Halstead/The Great Arturo), Hugh Herbert (Benton), Billie Burke (Aunt Abby), C. Aubrey Smith (Bishop Hubert Peabody), Raymond Walburn (Harley Bingham), ZaSu Pitts (Carrie Bingham), Broderick Crawford (Don Barnes), Virginia Field (Lola De Vere), Eve Arden (Gloria), Ralph Graves (Mr. Morrissey), Lionel Pape (Mr. Howard), Walter Sande (Ralph), Leyland Hodgson (Capt. Vickers), Fred Keating (Master of Ceremonies), The Kettering Triplets (Gloria's Baby), Hillary Brooke (Blonde on Stage), Mary Field (Isabell, the Maid), Herman the Rabbit (Himself), Frank Jaquet (Doctor), Paul Le Paul (Butler), May Beatty (Dowager), Ralph Norwood (Waiter), Tay Garnett (Pilot), Eleanor Stewart, Evelyn Woodbury, Patricia Stillman, Doreen McKay, Luana Walters (Girls at Shower), Jack Perrin, Broderick O'Farrell (Ship's Officers), George Cathrey (Officer), Granville Bates (Ship Captain), Franklin Parker (Croupier), Billy Wayne (Stage Manager), Douglas Wood (Phillips), Dennie Moore (Waitress), Edwin Stanley (Mr. Jones, Lawyer), John Rice, Claude Payton (Scotland Yard Men on Plane), Larry Harris, Dickie Jackson (Boy Boxers), Jack Greene, Dick Allen (Detectives), Walter James (Police Official), Al Hill (Heckler).

Young leaves her society sweetheart, Crawford, for an exciting magician, Niven. They marry and after a few years of traveling, Young realizes that what she really wants is a home of her own and a man to care for. Realizing that Niven is never going to give her that, she divorces him during a South America tour and returns to Crawford. Mediocre drama helped by an excellent supporting cast, and just the type of film late 1930s audiences consumed by the ton.

p, Walter Wanger; d, Tay Garnett; w, Gene Towne, Graham Baker, John Meehan; ph, Merritt Gerstad, Ray Binger; m, Werner Janssen; ed, Dorothy Spencer; art d, Alexander Golitzen.

Drama   **Cas.**   **(PR:A   MPAA:NR)**

ETERNITY OF LOVE***   (1961, Jap.) 100m Takarazuka/Toho c
(WAKARETE IKIRU TOKI MO)

Yoko Tsukasa (Michi), Tadao Takashima, Kiyoshi Kodama, Keiju Kobayashi, Hiroshi Akutagawa, Seizaburo Kawazu, Kinuyo Tanaka, Ikio Sawamura, Kenzo Tamu, Kin Sugai, Asao Koike, Chikako Hosokawa.

An adolescent love relationship that ends sourly precipitates a downhill slide for Tsukasa in this gloomy example of post-war Japanese filmmaking. Tsukasa, a high school student, marries a teacher after he ruins her relationship with a college student. Soon he is beating her and she runs away. Meeting up with a Korean, she achieves a little peace, but her husband appears and gets her fired from her job. She next marries another student, and he is drafted to serve in the waning days of WW II, meeting his death in a sea disaster and leaving Tsukasa with a baby and to survive on the black market. Not much sunlight filters through this dreary tale, but Japanese locales are interesting.

d, Hiromichi Horikawa; w, Zenzo Matsuyama, Toshiro Ide, Horikawa; ph, Asakazu Nakai (Tohoscope, Eastmancolor); m, Yasushi Akutagawa.

Drama   **(PR:C MPAA:NR)**

EUREKA**   (1983, Brit.) 129m UA c

Gene Hackman (Jack McCann), Theresa Russell (Tracy), Rutger Hauer (Maillot van Horn), Jane Lapotaire (Helen McCann), Ed Lauter (Perkins), Mickey Rourke (Aurelio), Joe Pesci (Mayakofsky), Helena Kallianiotis (Frieda), Corin Redgrave (Worsley), James Faulkner (Roger), Tim Scott (Webb), Cavan Kendall, Joe Spinell, Frank Pesce, Michael Scott Addis, Norman Beaton, Emrys James, Ann Thornton, Emma Relph, John Vine, Tim Van Rellim, Ellis Dale, Lloyd Berry, Tom Heaton, Geri Dawson, Annie Kidder, Ian Tracey, Brad Sakiyama, Sandra Friesen, Raimund Stamm, Suzette Collins, Tommy Lane.

Hackman is a wealthy man whose life lost its meaning when he gained his wealth. He lives on an isolated island, constantly afraid of someone taking his money. Finally he is killed by hit men sent by Pesci, whose request to build a gambling resort on Hackman's island was refused. Full of the lush, confusing images one comes to expect in a Roeg film, with all the self-indulgent meaninglessness one also comes to expect from him.

p, Jeremy Thomas; d, Nicolas Roeg; w, Paul Mayersberg (based on the book Who Killed Sir Harry Oakes? by Marshall Houts); ph, Alex Thomson (Technicolor); m, Stanley Myers; ed, Tony Lawson; prod d, Michael Seymour; art d, John Beard.

Drama   **(PR:O MPAA:NR)**

EUREKA STOCKADE   (SEE: MASSACRE HILL, 1948, Brit.)

EUROPE 51   (SEE: GREATEST LOVE, THE, 1951, Ital.)

EUROPEANS, THE**   (1979, Brit.) 90m Levitt-Pickman c

Lee Remick (Eugenia), Robin Ellis (Robert Acton), Wesley Addy (Mr. Wentworth), Tim Choate (Clifford Wentworth), Lisa Eichhorn (Gertrude Wentworth), Nancy New (Charlotte Wentworth), Kristin Griffith (Lizzie Acton), Helen Stenborg (Mrs. Acton), Norman Snow (Mr. Brand), Tim Woodward (Felix), Gedda Petry (Augustine).

Remick is a European-raised American who returns to her stuffy Boston relatives along with her brother, Ellis, a bohemian painter. Based on the 1878 novel by Henry James, and therefore fraught with seriousness, it comes off as boredom.

p, Ismail Merchant; d, James Ivory; w, Ruth Prawer Jhabvala (from a novel by Henry James); ph, Larry Pizer; m, Richard Robbins; ed, Humphrey Dixon; art d, Jeremiah Rusconi; cos, Judy Morcroft.

Drama   **Cas.**   **(PR:A   MPAA:NR)**

EVA***   (1962, Fr./Ital.) 100m Rank/Paris Film-Interopa bw
(AKA: EVA THE DEVIL'S WOMAN)

Jeanne Moreau (Eva), Stanley Baker (Tyvian), Virna Lisi (Francesca), Giorgio Albertazzi (Braneo Maloni), James Villiers (Arthur McCormick), Riccardo Garrone (Michele), Lisa Gastoni (The Redhead), Checco Rissone (Pieri), Enzo Fiermonte (Enzo), Nona Medici (Ann Maria), Alex Revides (The Greek), John Pepper (Little Boy), Roberto Paoletti, Van Eicken, Evi Rigano, Ignazio Dolce, Peggy Guggenheim, Gilda Dahlberg, Joseph Losey, Vittorio De Sica.

Writer Baker meets a prostitute, Moreau, and quickly becomes infatuated with her, fatally as it turns out. He abandons his fiancee, Lisi, and spends all his money on Moreau, but she taunts and leaves him. He marries Lisi but betrays her on their honeymoon when he sees Moreau again, and Lisi, finding out about the betrayal, kills herself. The smitten writer goes on seeing Moreau and at one point tries to kill her to erase her image from his mind. Finally he discards her entirely, and Baker, abandoned and broke, sinks down into poverty and loneliness. A grim drama rides the back of this broken-down horse of a story.

p, Robert Hakim, Raymond Hakim; d, Joseph Losey; w, Hugo Butler, Evan Jones (based on the novel Eve by James Hadley Chase); ph, Gianni di Venanzo; m, Michel Legrand; ed, Reginald Beck, Franca Silvi; md, Carlo Savina; art d, Richard MacDonald, Luigi Scaccianoce; cos, Pierre Cardin; m/l, "Adam and Eve," Michel Legrand (sung by Tony Middleton); "Willow Weep for Me," Ann Rondel (sung by Billie Holiday); "Loveless Love," W.C. Handy (sung by Holiday).

Drama   **(PR:O MPAA:NR)**

EVANGELINE**   (1929) 87m UA bw

Dolores Del Rio (Evangeline), Roland Drew (Gabriel), Alec B. Francis (Father Felician), Donald Reed (Baptiste), Paul McAllister (Benedict Bellefontaine), James Marcus (Basil), George Marion, Sr. (Rene LeBlanc), Bobby Mack (Michael), Lou Payne (Governor General), Lee Shumway (Col. Winslow).

Longfellow's poem about the trials of the exiled Arcadians is the subject of this early talker. The only line of dialog (excepting songs) comes at the end of the film when Del Rio's lover dies in her arms after a long separation. Several good songs, one of them written by Al Jolson and Billy Rose.

p&d, Edwin Carewe; w, Finis Fox (based on the poem by Hendry Wadsworth Longfellow); ph, R.B. Kurrle, Al M. Green.

Musical Drama   **(PR:A MPAA:NR)**

EVE*   (1968, Brit./Span.) 97m Udastex Films-Ada-Hispamer/COM c
(EVA EN LA SELVA; GB: THE FACE OF EVE)

Robert Walker, Jr. (Mike Yates), Celeste Yarnall (Eve), Herbert Lom (Diego), Fred Clark (John Burke), Christopher Lee (Col. Stuart), Jean Caffarel (Pepe), Rosenda Monteros (Conchita), Maria Rohm (Anna), Ricardo Diaz (Bruno).

American pilot Walker crashes in an upper Amazon jungle and is saved by Yarnall, who is worshipped as a goddess by the jungle natives. The news of the heroic rescue lets loose a volley of evil shots: a showman wants her for his freak show; the natives want to kill her for helping a white man; an explorer, her grandfather, wants to shut her up. In the end Yarnall shakes her head at all the noise and confusion and returns to her jungle home. Very poorly done story of a Tarzaness.

p, Harry Alan Towers; d, Jeremy Summers, Robert Lynn; w, Peter Welbeck [Harry Alan Towers]; ph, Manuel Merino (Eastmancolor); m, Malcolm Lockyer; ed, Allan Morrison; art d, Santiago Ontanon.

Adventure   **(PR:A MPAA:NR)**

EVE KNEW HER APPLES**   (1945) 64m COL bw

Ann Miller (Eve Porter), William Wright (Ward Williams), Robert Williams (Steve Ormand), Ray Walker (George McGrew), Charles D. Brown (Joe Gordon), John Eldredge (Walter W. Walters II), Eddie Bruce (Roberts), Frank Jaquet (Doctor), Betty Hill (Maid), Jessie Arnold (Mrs. Green), Boyd Davis (Mr. Birch), Abe Dinovitch (Wrestler), Al Hill (1st Officer on Motorcycle), Syd Salor (2nd Officer on Motorcycle), Mary Rowland (Janice), Almeda Fowler (Matron of Honor), Si Jenks (Landlord), Hank Bell (Mr. Green), Dick Rush (Sheriff), Minta Durfee (Landlady), Jack Rice (Hotel Clerk), Tom Hanlon (Announcer), Harry Semels (Tony), John Tyrrell (Reporter), George Ford, Dick Thorne (Rewrite Men).

One of several takeoffs on IT HAPPENED ONE NIGHT, this mildly amusing program musical is more a pale reflection than an homage. Oddly enough, it gives Miller a chance to display her vocal talents (never her strongest suit) rather than her legs. She sings five songs, but never dances. Miller plays a famous radio singing star who gets fed up with the fast pace and wants a rest. She runs away from her money and fame by hiding out in the trunk of a car. The car, of course, belongs to enterprising reporter Wright, who's eager for a good story. The story follows the same sort of complications and mistaken identities of its more esteemed relation. Songs: "Someone to Love," "An Hour Never Passes," "I've Waited a Lifetime," "I'll Remember April" (Jimmy Kennedy, Edward Brandt, Bob Warren, Gene de Paul, Don Raye, Pat Johnston). Sir Lancelot wrote and sang "Vita-Vim Flakes Calypso Song." This same gifted singer/composer later proved colorfully effective as a soulful singer among the doomed prisoners of BRUTE FORCE.

p, Wallace McDonald; d, Will Jason; w, E. Edwin Moran (based on a story by Rian James); ph, Burnett Guffey; ed, Jerome Thoms; art d, Carl Anderson; set d, Louis Diage.

Musical   **(PR:A MPAA:NR)**

EVE OF ST. MARK, THE***   (1944) 96m FOX bw

Anne Baxter (Janet Feller), William Eythe (Pvt. Quizz West), Michael O'Shea (Pvt. Thomas Mulveray), Vincent Price (Pvt. Francis Marion), Ruth Nelson (Nell West), Ray Collins (Deckman West), Stanley Prager (Pvt. Glinka), Henry Morgan (Pvt. Shevlin), Robert Bailey (Cpl. Tate), Joann Dolan (Lill Bird), Toni Favor (Sal Bird),

George Matthews *(Sgt. Ruby)*, John Archer *(Pvt. Carter)*, Dickie Moore *(Zip West)*, Joven E. Rola *(Pepita)*, Harry Shannon *(Chaplain)*, David Essex *(Guide)*, Arthur Hohl *(Sheep Wagon Driver)*, Roger Clark *(The Captain)*, Jimmy Clark *(Neil West)*, Murray Alper *(Sgt. Kriven)*, Reed Hadley *(Radio Voice)*, Blake Edwards *(Soldier)*, Milton Kibbee *(Peter Peller)*, Buddy Yarus *(Polinski)*.

Maxwell Anderson's Broadway hit adapted somewhat successfully by George Seaton and John Stahl. About a cadre of American soldiers who train and go off to fight in the Phillipines in WW II, the picture evoked the disastrous news headlines of the Corregidor march and the battles of Wake Island and Guam. Many soldiers were missing in action and THE EVE OF ST. MARK served to give the folks at home hope that they would be rescued. Eythe is the young hayseed who is in love with Baxter. When he goes overseas, her letters keep him on an even keel. Since the play was essentially a small-set drama, Seaton and Stahl attempted to open it up somewhat but it suffers from its stagebound birth. Price, in an unusual "good guy" role, plays a Shakespeare-spouting Southerner. A few of the Broadway players come to the screen, notably Michael O'Shea (known as Eddie O'Shea on the Great White Way), who had already scored heavily in JACK LONDON. The idea behind the film was to show what our boys were going through, but it was light on action and heavy on dialog (albeit Anderson and Seaton's dialog was witty, trenchant, and truthful). It was not a great success but did much to promote morale on the home front. In the play, the men in the squad don't make it and the realistic effect was devastating. Fox opted for a hopeful ending so we are never certain whether they are rescued, but there is a glimmer of hope at the fade out.

p, William Perlberg; d, John M. Stahl; w, George Seaton (based on the play by Maxwell Anderson); ph, Joseph La Shelle; m, Cyril J. Mockridge; ed, Louis Sackin; md, Emil Newman; art d, James Basevi, Russell Spencer; spec eff, Fred Sersen.

War Drama **(PR:A-C MPAA:NR)**

EVE WANTS TO SLEEP*** (1961, Pol.) 98m Syrena Film Unit./Film Polski bw (EWA CHCE SPAC)

Barbara Lass [Kwiatowska] *(Eve)*, Stanislaw Mikulski *(Peter)*, Ludwik Benoit *(Safecracker)*, Zygmunt Zintel *(Police Chief)*, W. Turowski *(Professor)*, Stefan Bartik *(Captain)*, Roman Klosowski *(His Pupil)*, E. Wichura *(Sergeant)*, B. Rachwalska *(Matron)*, Jarema Stepowski *(Cafe Owner)*, Maria Kaniewska *(Cashier)*, W. Oto-Suski *(Undertaker)*, Waclaw Kowalski *(Arsenal Supervisor)*, Stanislaw Milski *(School Janitor)*, Gustaw Lutkiewicz.

Lass is a 16-year-old who arrives at a technical school a day too soon. The school's dorms are closed and she has no money. During her attempts to find a place to sleep she meets safecrackers, thieves, and gets arrested. She discovers that the town is very strange and there seems no distinction between the police and criminals because they help each other. The police and a group of thieves Lass gets entangled with plan a jewel theft. It seems as though everyone in the town gets involved and things become so wild that the camera crew is thrown in front of the camera. A crazy and entertaining farcical comedy made by a director noted for his fast, taut style. (In Polish; English subtitles.)

p, Wieslaw Mincer; d, Tadeusz Chmielewski; w, Chmielewski, Andrzej Czekalski; ph, Stefan Matyjaszkiewicz, Josef Stawiski; m, Henryk Czyz; ed, Janina Niedzwiecka, Lena Deptula; art d, Roman Mann, Adam Nowakowski; English subtitles, Noelle Gillmor.

Comedy **(PR:A MPAA:NR)**

EVEL KNIEVEL½** (1971) 90m Fanfare c

George Hamilton *(Evel Knievel)*, Sue Lyon *(Linda)*, Bert Freed *(Doc Kincaid)*, Rod Cameron *(Charlie Kresson)*, Dub Taylor *(Turquoise Smith)*, Ron Masak *(Pete)*, Hal Baylor *(Sheriff)*, Betty Bronson *(House Mother)*, Sylvia Hayes *(Grandma)*, Mary Peters *(Marge)*, Judy Baldwin, Kathy Baumann, Jayne Melon, Cassie Solomon *(Sorority Girls)*, Ben Bentley, Ten Henningsen *(Men in Bar)*, Alana Collins, Ellen Tucker *(Nurses)*, Jan Davis, Inga Nielson *(Showgirls)*, Lee De Broux, Robert B. Williams *(Wranglers)*, Roger Edington *(Bartender)*, Frank Ellis *(Rodeo Clown)*, Paul Sorrenson, John Garwood *(Guards)*, Richard Ford Grayling *(Soundman)*, Mary Grover *(Girl in Ontario)*, Bob Harris *(Policeman)*, John Haymer *(Rodeo Cook)*, Randee Jensen *(Bathtub Girl)*, Ski Kirkwell, Howard Larson *(Miners)*, Frank Loverede *(Newsman)*, Trish Mahoney *(Girl at Rodeo)*, John Dale McCutchan *(Evel, age 12)*, Cliff Medaugh *(Bill, the Banker)*, Eveline Micone *(Girl Friend)*, Irwin W. Moseley *(Janitor)*, Henry Olek *(Bill Jennings)*, Barbara Parsons *(Girl at Pond)*, Ralph Schmidt *(Plumber)*, Pat Setzer *(Little Cowboy)*, Mike Shak *(Anesthetist)*, Joey Viera *(Truck Driver)*, Liv Von Linden *(Girl Photographer)*, John Yates *(Photographer)*.

Cartoon mentality biography of the man who jumps over cars with a motorcycle. Hamilton portrays Knievel from his early days in Butte, Montana, to a rodeo owned by Taylor, where he gets his start, to the jump over the fountain at Caesar's Palace that almost kills him, Hamilton swaggers and struts through a bad script and makes it worth watching for camp value if nothing else.

p, George Hamilton; d, Marvin Chomsky; w, Alan Caillou, John Milius (based on a story by Caillou); ph, David Walsh (Metrocolor); m, Pat Williams; ed, Jack McSweeney; art d, Norman Houle; set d, Bob Nelson; spec eff, Tim Smyth, Barry Bedig; cos, Arnold Lipin; m/l, "I Do What I Please," Williams, Bradford Craig; stunts, Everett Creach.

Biography **Cas.** **(PR: A MPAA: PG)**

EVELYN PRENTICE½** (1934) 78m MGM bw

Myrna Loy *(Evelyn Prentice)*, William Powell *(John Prentice)*, Una Merkel *(Amy Drexel)*, Harvey Stephens *(Lawrence Kennard)*, Isabel Jewell *(Judith Wilson)*, Rosalind Russell *(Nancy Harrison)*, Henry Wadsworth *(Chester Wylie)*, Edward Brophy *(Eddie Delaney)*, Cora Sue Collins *(Dorothy Prentice)*, Jessie Ralph *(Mrs. Blake)*, Perry Ivins *(Dr. Gillette)*, Sam Flint *(Dr. Lyons)*, Pat O'Malley *(Det. Pat Thompson)*, J.P. McGowan *(Det. Mack Clark)*, Jack Mulhall *(Gregory)*, Wilbur Mack, Garry Owen, Phil Tead *(Reporters)*, Herman Bing *(Klein, the Antique Dealer)*, Samuel S. Hinds *(Newton)*, Georgia Caine *(Mrs. Newton)*, John Hyams *(Mr. Humphreys)*, Howard Hickman *(Mr. Whitlock)*, Sam McDaniel *(Porter)*, Billy Gilbert *(Barney, the Cafe Owner)*, Crauford Kent *(Guest)*, Clarence Hummel Wilson *(Public Defender)*, Mariska Aldrich *(Matron)*, Francis McDonald *(Charles, the Chauffeur)*, Jack Mack *(Albert, the Butler)*, Milton Owen *(Waiter)*, Richard Tucker *(Mr. Dillingham)*, Frank Conroy *(District Attorney Farley)*, Sherry Hall *(Court Clerk)*, Stanley Andrews *(Judge)*, Matty Roubert *(Newsboy)*, Ruth Warren *(Miss Meade, John Prentice's Secretary)*, Bob Perry *(Juryman)*, Larry Steers *(Diner/Extra)*.

Combination mystery-soap opera that pairs Loy and Powell for the third time but the results are not nearly so powerful as the earlier THIN MAN outings. Powell and Loy are again married, but this time Powell is a rakehell attorney with a roving eye. On an out-of-town jaunt, he has an affair with Rosalind Russell (in her movie debut). When Loy learns of that, she seeks solace with "poet" Harvey Stephens who has been making a big play for her. Loy makes the error of sending Stephens some incriminating letters but soon understands that she's still in love with her husband and the Stephens relationship must be terminated. Powell returns home and Loy accepts him. They plan a second honeymoon abroad and will take their daughter, Collins. Stephens asks Loy to visit his flat on a phony matter, then tells her that unless she coughs up $15,000 he will show Powell the letters she wrote. There is a revolver nearby so Loy picks it up and threatens Stephens unless he hands over the letters. He does, but hits her with his free hand and the gun fires as she is sent reeling against the wall. Stephens is hit by a bullet and falls to the floor. Loy races out of his residence just as his mistress, Jewell, enters. Jewell is found with the body later and accused of being the killer. Filled with guilt, Loy convinces Powell that they should defer the trip to Europe and that he should take up Jewell's defense. In a highly charged courtroom scene, Loy can take it no longer. She stands and shouts that Jewell is innocent and that she, Loy, is the actual killer. Powell is stunned but believes his wife is innocent so he begins a cross-examination in his best sophisticated style and gets Jewell to admit that the shot that killed Stephens was, in fact, fired by her. After the trial, Loy and Powell take Collins and depart on their European trip. The picture was adapted from a 1933 novel that was much steamier and tougher. Due to censorship, Coffee's screenplay had to be softened to make it palatable for the bluenoses. As it was, ten minutes was snipped from the film and we'll never know what they were about as all parties concerned aren't talking. Beautifully mounted and photographed, it was an unusual enterprise in that Loy and Powell were hardly the perfect couple—he being a philanderer and she playing a role that caused her to jettison her usually logical mind in favor of raw emotion. Whatever laughs are in the movie are gleaned by Una Merkel as Loy's pal. Merkel's career began in silents with D.W. Griffith (WAY DOWN EAST, 1920) and continued for five decades. Her busiest years were the 1930s when she appeared in almost 40 films, including DESTRY RIDES AGAIN, RIFFRAFF, 42ND STREET, and the original MALTESE FALCON (1931). EVELYN PRENTICE, would be remade poorly in 1939 as STRONGER THAN DESIRE with Walter Pidgeon and Virginia Bruce in the Powell-Loy roles.

p, John W. Considine, Jr.; d, William K. Howard; w, Lenore Coffee (based on the novel by W.E. Woodward); ph, Charles G. Clarke; m, Oscar Raclin; ed, Frank Hull; art d, Cedric Gibbons, Arnold Gillespie, Edwin B. Willis; cos. Dolly Tree.

Mystery **(PR:C MPAA:NR)**

EVENINGS FOR SALE** (1932) 61m PAR bw

Herbert Marshall *(Count von Degenthal)*, Sari Maritza *(Lela Fischer)*, Charlie Ruggles *(Bimfel)*, Mary Boland *(Jennie Kent)*, George Barbier *(Heinrich Fischer)*, Bert Roach *(Otto Volk)*, Lucien Littlefield *(Schwenk)*, Clay Clement *(Von Trask)*, Arnold Korff *(Richter)*, Freeman Wood, Reginald Barlow, Lillian Elliott, Grace Hayle, Reginald Pasch, Fred Sullivan, Jacques Jou-Jerville.

Down-on-his-luck Viennese nobleman Marshall contemplates suicide but undertakes the life of a gigolo instead. Then he meets title-struck Yankee widow Boland and by various blandishments and with her help regains his feet and pride. A handsomely produced little nothing performed well by Marshall and Boland.

d, Stuart Walker; w, S.K. Lauren, Agnes Brand Leahy (based on the story "Widow's Evening" by I.A.R. Wylie); ph, Harry Fischbeck.

Comedy **(PR:A MPAA:NR)**

EVENSONG½** (1934, Brit.) 83m GAU/FOX bw

Evelyn Laye *(Irela)*, Fritz Kortner *(Kober)*, Alice Delysia *(Mme. Valmond)*, Carl Esmond *(Archduke Theodore)*, Emlyn Williams *(George Murray)*, Muriel Aked *(Tremlowe)*, Patrick O'Moore *(Bob McNeil)*, Dennis Val Norton *(Sovino)*, Arthur Sinclair *(Pa McNeil)*, Browning Mummery *(Solo Tenor)*, Conchita Supervia *(Baba)*.

Laye is an Irish opera singer whose career rises and falls over the course of the film. Kortner is her manager, who always forbade his prima donna romance, depriving her of the happiness she might have found with Esmond. The final scene has the aging diva with the burned-out voice upstaged by a young singer. She then returns to her dressing room to listen to her old records, and dies. A tragic story competently acted and told.

p, Michael Balcon; d, Victor Saville; w, Edward Knoblock, Dorothy Farnum (based on a play by Knoblock and Beverley Nichols written from the novel by Nichols); ph, Mutz Greenbaum; m, M. Spoliansky; ed, Otto Ludwig; m/l, Knoblock, Spoliansky.

Musical Drama **(PR:A MPAA:NR)**

EVENT, AN*** (1970, Yugo.) 93m Jadran Film c (DOGADJAJ)

Pavle Vujisic *(Grandfather)*, Serdjo Mimica *(Grandson)*, Boris Dvornik *(Gamekeeper)*, Fabijan Sovagovic *(Friend)*, Neda Spasojevic *(Gamekeeper's Wife)*, Marina Nemet *(Girl)*, Fahro Konjhodzic, Zdenka Hersak, Lena Politeo, Stevo Vujatovic.

A farmer and his grandson set off to a fair to sell their horse in this dark tale from the pen of the great Russian short story writer Anton Chekhov. Going through the forest they are chased by a hungry wolf, but they make the ferry safely that is to take them into town. On the boat, the captain tells them to beware of a gamekeeper and his family. The pair sell their horse and set out for home again, but in the forest they are chased by the gamekeeper. Exhausted, the old farmer gives the profits from the horse sale to his grandson and tells him to flee. The boy does, right into the cabin of the gamekeeper.

d, Vatroslav Mimica; w, Zeljko Senecic, Mimica, Kruno Quien (based on a story by Anton Chekhov); ph, Frano Vodopivec (Movielab); ed, Katja Majer; art d, Zeljko Senecic;

Drama   (PR:C MPAA:NR)

EVENTS**½   (1970) 84m Grove Press c

Ryan Listman (Ryan), Joy Wener (Joy), Frank Cavestani (Frank), Marsha Rossa (Marsha), Lee Roscoe (Lee), Greer St. John (Greer), Kristen Steen (Kristen), Myron "Butch" Ogelsby (Butch), Malissa Corragio (Malissa), Louise Violet (Louise), Eddie Keegan (Eddie), Robert Altman (Bob).

Listman is a young filmmaker who rounds up a group of his friends to make a pornographic film. This in turn will provide the money for his real interest, a film about Lenny Bruce. Intriguing low-budget underground feature suffers from some technical problems, but nonetheless it makes an honest effort to explore the emotions of the actors and actresses as they confront the experience of making sex before the cameras.

p,d&w, Fred Baker; ph, Stephen Bower, Baker; m, Eric Gale; ed, Bernard Hajdenberg; m/l, Charlie Smalls.

Drama   (PR:O MPAA:R)

EVER IN MY HEART**½   (1933) 70m WB bw

Barbara Stanwyck (Mary), Otto Kruger (Hugo), Ralph Bellamy (Jeff), Ruth Donnelly (Lizzie), Frank Albertson (Sam), George Cooper (Lefty), Nella Walker (Martha Sewell), Florence Roberts (Eunice), Laura Hope Crews (Grandma), Ronnie Crosby (Teddy), Harry Beresford (Eli), Clara Blandick (Anna), Donald Meek (Storekeeper), Elizabeth Patterson (Clara), Wallace Clark (Enoch Sewell), Frank Reicher (Dr. Hoffman), Virginia Howell (Serena), George Renavent, Ethel Wales, Claire DuBrey, Willard Robertson.

In 1909, much to the disapproval of her parents, Stanwyck marries German-American professor Kruger. They live happily until the outbreak of WW I, when Kruger joins the Army but is really a spy for the Germans. Stanwyck is torn between her love for him and her patriotism, with patriotism winning out as she poisons him before he can send his information to Berlin. Stanwyck then poisons herself, ending the film on a distressingly downbeat note. Stanwyck pulls out all the stops in this one and looks thoroughly distressed by her predicament.

p, Robert Presnell; d, Archie Mayo; w, Bertram Milhauser (based on a story by Beulah Marie Dix and Milhauser); ph, Arthur Todd; ed, Owen Marks; art d, Anton Grot; cos, Earl Luick.

Drama   (PR:C MPAA:NR)

EVER SINCE EVE**   (1934) 75m FOX bw

George O'Brien (Neil Rogers), Mary Brian (Elizabeth Vandegrift), Herbert Mundin (Horace Saunders), Betty Blythe (Mrs. Vandergrift), Roger Imhof (Dave Martin), Russell Simpson (Jim Wood), George Meeker (Philip Baxter).

O'Brien is a young heir from the country who comes to New York with two elderly guardians and falls in love with Brian. He marries her but soon discovers that she is only interested in his fortune. He leaves her but then returns sometime later and finds that she has a baby and really does love him. Good snoozing fare if insomnia is a problem.

d, George Marshall; w, Henry Johnson, Stuart Anthony (based on the play "The Heir to Hoorah" by Paul Armstrong); ph, Arthur Miller; md, Samuel Kaylin.

Comedy   (PR:A MPAA:NR)

EVER SINCE EVE**   (1937) 77m Cosmopolitan/WB bw

Marion Davies (Marge Winton), Robert Montgomery (Freddy Matthews), Frank McHugh (Mabel De Craven/Mike McGillicuddy), Patsy Kelly (Sadie Day), Louise Fazenda (Abigail Belldon), Barton MacLane (Al McCoy), Marcia Ralston (Camille Lansing), Carol Hughes (Manicurist), Frederick Clark (Alonzo), Mary Treen (Employment Clerk), Anderson Lawler (Hotel Clerk), Charles Foy (Bellboy), Arthur Hoyt (Hotel Manager), Spencer Charters (Mike, Hotel Porter), Charles Trowbridge (Doctor), Frank Faylen (Bandit Leader), Jack Mower (Policeman), Harry Hayden (Mason, League President), Harry C. Bradley (League Manager), Robert Homans (Sergeant), Don Downen (Office Boy), John T. Murray (Lowell), Pierre Watkin (Barton), William B. Davidson (Henderson), Florence Gill (Annie, Cleaning Lady), Dorothy Thompson (Hula Dancer), Frank Orth (Waiter), Gertrude Sutton (Homely Girl), Minerva Urecal (Reception Clerk), Don Barclay, Hal Neiman (Neighbors), Pat West (Neighbor with Water), Huey White, Al Herman (Taxi Drivers), Don Turner, Allen Cavens (Doormen), Jerry Mandy (Italian Barber), Frank Otto (Another Barber), Dudley Dickerson (Bootblack), Ferris Taylor (Elderly Gentleman), Rebecca Wassem (Maid), Joseph Romantini (Maitre D'Hotel), Etta McDaniel (Black Maid), Henry Otho (Bandit), Jerry Fletcher (Bellboy), Frank Shannon (Desk Sergeant), Pat O'Malley (Officer), Edward Price (Reporter), Wendell Niles (Police Announcer), Spec O'Donnell (Newsboy), The Theodores (Dance Team), Bess Flowers (Dance Extra), Claudia Simmons, Fern Barry, Perc Teeple, Sam Rice, Jack Wise (Pedestrians).

The end of Marion Davies' strange career is marked by EVER SINCE EVE, an unfunny comedy where she plays a beautiful stenographer whose attraction for men is so alarming it's sufficient reason to don horn rim spectacles and tweed suits to escape them. She takes a job as secretary to writer Montgomery to help him make the deadline set by gruff publisher Fazenda. Love, of course, blossoms when Montgomery sees Davies without her de-glamorizing gear. It all resolves itself after

a while and everyone is happy. An insipid comedy that not even Warner's entire stock of comedy character actors could save. Songs: "Wreaths Of Flowers" (Hoopii Haaia), "Ever Since Eve" (M.K. Jerome, Jack Scholl), "Shine on Harvest Moon" (Jack Norworth, Nora Bayes).

p, Hal B. Wallis; d, Lloyd Bacon; w, Lawrence Riley, Earl Baldwin, Lillie Hayward (based on a story by Gene Baker, Margaret Lee); ph, George Barnes; ed, William Holmes; md, Leo B. Forbstein; art d, Robert Haas.

Comedy   (PR:A MPAA:NR)

EVER SINCE VENUS***   (1944) 74m COL bw

Ina Ray Hutton (Herself), Hugh Herbert (P.G. Grimble), Ann Savage (Janet Wilson), Billy Gilbert (Tiny Lewis), Glenda Farrell (Babs Cartwright), Ross Hunter (Bradley Miller), Alan Mowbray (J. Webster Hackett), Margaret Gateson (Maud Hackett), Thurston Hall (Edgar Pomeroy), Fritz Feld (Michele), Dudley Dickerson (Clarence), Stewart Foster (Himself), Bill Shawn, Carol Adams, Doreen Mulvey (Dancers), Eddie Borden (Waiter), Muni Seroff (Pierre), Paul Conrad (Radio Announcer), Ralph Dunn (Policeman), Bertha Priestly (Fat Girl), P.J. Kelly (Watchman), Charles Jordan (Bartender), Kernan Cripps (Waiter), Isabel Withers (Miss Murray), Pat Hogan (Salesgirl), Mary Gordon (Mrs. Murphy), Jack Carr (Customer), Byron Foulger (Henley, the Druggist), Chester Clute (Milquetoast Customer), Harry Depp (Taylor), Jack Rice (Butler), Ann Loos (Messenger).

Hunter invents a nonstaining lipstick (named Rosebud) and tries to get a booth in the American Beauty Association Show. Cosmetic king Mowbray tells him it will cost $1,000, because Mowbray doesn't want anyone to threaten a big sale of his to Hall. Hunter's friend, Gilbert, wins the beauty show theme song contest and the prize money pays for the booth. Hunter sells his lipstick to Hall and Mowbray tells the buyer that Hunter has no one to manufacture the product. Mowbray offers to buy Hunter out for $5,000 and that's when Herbert, who has been at the show incognito, offers Hunter his factory. An enjoyable B musical comedy. Songs include: "Wedding Of the Samba and the Boogie" (Bernie Wayne, Ben Raleigh), "Glamour For Sale" (Lester Lee, Harry Harris), "Rosebud, I Love You," "Do I Need You?" (Sammy Cahn, Saul Chaplin).

d, Arthur Dreifuss; w, McElbert Moore, Dreifuss; ph, Benjamin Kline; ed, Otto Meyer; art d, Lionel Banks, Cary Odell; ch, Jack Boyle.

Musical   (PR:A MPAA:NR)

EVERGREEN***   (1934, Brit.) 82m GAU bw

Jessie Matthews (Harriet Green), Sonnie Hale (Leslie Benn), Betty Balfour (Maudie), Barry Mackay (Tommy Thompson), Ivor MacLaren (Marquis of Staines), Hartley Power (Treadwell), Patrick Ludlow (Lord Shropshire), Betty Shale (Mrs. Hawkes), Marjorie Brooks (Herself), Richard Murdoch, Buddy Bradley Dancers.

In 1909 London, Matthews is a star of the musical stage. On the eve of her marriage to a marquis, her old lover, long thought dead, turns up and demands blackmail. Matthews puts her little daughter in the care of a loyal maid and drops out of sight. Twenty-five years pass and Matthews' daughter auditions for a spot in the chorus line and is spotted by her mother's old understudy. She is made up to look older and then passed off to the public as a "remarkably preserved" Matthews, Sr. Complications ensue when she falls in love with a young hoofer who claims to be her son. Matthews was a—perhaps the—major star of the British Musical Comedy and EVERGREEN marks her at the peak of her powers and popularity. Fred Astaire, who had just completed FLYING DOWN TO RIO and was currently appearing on the London Stage in "The Gay Divorcee" wanted to co-star opposite Matthews in this one, but RKO wouldn't allow it. Songs include: "Over My Shoulder," "When You've Got a Little Springtime in Your Heart," "Daddy Wouldn't Buy Me A Bow-Wow" (Harry Woods), "Dancing on the Ceiling," "Dear, Dear" (Richard Rodgers, Lorenz Hart).

p, Michael Balcon; d, Victor Saville; w, Emlyn Williams, Marjorie Gaffney (based on a play by Benn W. Levy); ph, Glen MacWilliams; m, Benn Levy, Larry Hart; ed, Ian Dalrymple.

Musical   Cas.   (PR:A MPAA:NR)

EVERY BASTARD A KING**½   (1968, Israel) 100m CD c
(KOL MAMZER MELECH; AKA: EVERY MAN A KING)

Pier Angeli (Eileen), William Berger (Roy Hemmings), Oded Kotler (Raphi Cohen), Yehoram Gaon (Yehoram), Ori Levy (Foreign Office Man), Reuven Morgan (Photographer), Tami Tsifroni (Woman Officer), Moshe Yanai (Yossi), Ariela Shavid, Meir Levy, Edith Astruc, Dvora Dotan, Zecharia Manzur, Yaacov Levy, Aviva Paz, Edward Shurush, A.A. Wolf, Michael Brant, Yaacov Bukman, Nili Keinan, The Hagadash Trio.

Loosely based on a true story, this film tells the story of Kotler, who, on the eve of the Six-Day War, tried to fly his small plane to Cairo to plead for peace with Gamal Abdel Nasser. He is forced down over the Sinai, and the outbreak of the war finds him unable to get back to join the Israeli army. Not especially funny or poignant, emotions it strives for, but there is a 20-minute tank battle staged with British-built Israeli tanks and captured Russian-built Egyptian tanks that is highly exciting. Actual films of the Israeli-Arab war are included in the picture.

p, A. Deshe, Haim Topol; d, Uri Zohar; w, Zohar, Eli Tavor; ph, David Gurfinkel (Movielab Color); m, Michel Colombier; ed, Anna Gurit; set d, Zeev Lichter; spec eff, Yaacov Noyman.

Comedy/Drama   (PR:C MPAA:NR)

EVERY DAY IS A HOLIDAY**   (1966, Span.) 76m Guion Films/
                                                    COL c (CABRIOLA)

Marisol (Chica), Angel Peralta (Himself), Rafael de Cordova (Dancer), Jose Marco Davo (Impresario), Pedro Maria Sanchez (Manolo), Vala Cliffton (Femme Fatale), Jesus Guzman (Salesman), Jose Sepulveda (Gypsy), Francisco Camiras (Servant),

Jose Maria Labernie (Hotel Employee), Luis Barbero (Employee at Bullring), Toni Canal (Boy), Jack Gaskins (American Father), Juan Ramon Torremocha.

Marisol is a girl who masquerades as a boy so she can become a bullfighter. She trains hard to impress her idol, Peralta. He is impressed with her skills and finds her work at smalltown bullrings. When she sees Peralta with another woman she becomes outraged and the bullring manager realizes she is a woman. He persuades her to dress in a gypsy costume and when Peralta sees her dance he takes her up on his horse to ride with him in a parade through the streets.

p, Manuel J. Goyanes; d, Mel Ferrer; w, Ferrer, Jose Maria Palacio (based on a story by Ferrer); ph, Antonio L. Ballesteros (Eastmancolor); m, Augusto Alguero; ed, Rosa Terregrosa; art d, Enrique Alarcon; m/l, Augusto Alguero, Jose Torregrosa, Antonio Guijarro.

Comedy/Drama   (PR:A   MPAA:NR)

EVERY DAY'S A HOLIDAY**   (1938) 80m PAR bw

Mae West (Peaches O'Day/Mlle. Fifi), Edmund Lowe (Capt. Jim McCarey), Charles Butterworth (Larmadou Graves), Charles Winninger (Van Reigble Van Pelter Van Doon III), Walter Catlett (Nifty Bailey), Lloyd Nolan (Honest John Quade), Louis Armstrong (Band Leader), George Rector (Himself), Herman Bing (Fritz Krausmeyer), Roger Imhof (Trigger Mike), Chester Conklin (Cabby), Lucian Prival (Danny the Dip), Adrian Morris (Asst. Police Commissioner), Francis MacDonald, John Indrisano (Henchmen), Irving Bacon, Allan Rogers, Otto Fries, John "Skins" Miller (Quartet), Dick Elliott (Bar Patron), James C. Morton (Bartender), Edgar Dearing (Cop at Store Window), Johnny Arthur, William Austin (Extras), Weldon Heyburn, Ferdinand Munier, Herbert Rawlinson (New Year's Eve Party Guests).

West's last film for Paramount—a studio she had earlier saved—was doomed from the outset. In 1938—the year of the picture's release—she drew so much outraged publicity from a radio appearance with Edgar Bergen and Charlie McCarthy on the Chase & Sanborn Hour that the decent-minded throughout the country were ready to pounce if she so much as asked for cream in her coffee. Unfortunately for moviegoers, with this one she gave them no reason to pounce. The only woman in the cast (in a script she wrote herself), she plays a year-1900 confidence woman who impersonates a French singer in order to elude the cops. In the process, she gets rid of the bad cops and helps put a reform mayor in office. So alert for offense was the Hays Office, however, that it deleted lines such as "I wouldn't even lift my veil for that guy," which didn't leave West with much to say. Songs include "Jubilee" (Stanley Adams, Hoagy Carmichael), "Fifi" and "Flutter by, Little Butterfly" (Sam Coslow), "Every Day's a Holiday" and "Along the Broadway Trail" (Coslow, Barry Trivers).

p, Emanuel Cohen; d, A. Edward Sutherland; w, Mae West; ph, Karl Struss; ed, Ray Curtiss; md, LeRoy Prinz; art d, Wiard Ihnen; cos, Basia Bassett; gowns, Schiaparelli.

Comedy   (PR:A   MPAA:NR)

EVERY DAY'S A HOLIDAY, 1954
                                                     (SEE: GOLD OF NAPLES, 1954, Ital.)

EVERY DAY'S A HOLIDAY, 1965
                                                     (SEE: SEASIDE SWINGERS, 1965, Brit.)

EVERY GIRL SHOULD BE MARRIED**½   (1948) 84m RKO bw

Cary Grant (Dr. Madison Brown), Franchot Tone (Roger Sanford), Diana Lynn (Julie Hudson), Betsy Drake (Anabel Sims), Alan Mowbray (Mr. Spitzer), Elisabeth Risdon (Mary Nolan), Richard Gaines (Sam McNutt), Harry Hayden (Gogarty), Chick Chandler (Soda Clerk), Leon Belasco (Violinist), Fred Essler (Pierre), Anna Q. Nilsson (Saleslady), Charmienne Harker (Miss King), Marjorie Walker, Alvina Temin, Rosalie Coughenour, Joan Lybrook (Models), Louise Franklin (Elevator Girl), Dan Foster (Cigar Store Clerk), Gwyn Shipmen (Mother), Arnolda Brown, Jean Andren (Customers), Elaine Riley (Young Lady), Lois Hall, Pat Hall (Girls), Carol Hughes (Girl at Counter), Claire DuBrey (Mrs. Willoughby), Helen Brown (Dignified Woman), Kate Lawson (Large Woman), Anne Nagel (Woman), James Griffith (Insurance Salesman), Al Rhein (Photographer), Joe Granby (Louis, the Barber), Selmer Jackson (Clergyman).

Drake made her debut in this film and took most of the notices as she burst on the screen with an insouciant quality that had seldom been seen before (and with a bubbly-voiced, cue-jumping delivery duplicated by Joanne Woodward). One year later, she married co-star Grant. She's a clerk in a large urban department store who sets her sights on pediatrician Grant and decides that he is the man for her. With great patience, she begins learning all she can about Grant: his college life, his eating habits, his bachelor haunts, and even his favorite color (blue). Armed with this information, she begins her campaign to make him her husband. Grant is hip to it all and successfully resists all her Machiavellian tactics. Several ploys fail, including the use of Tone, her boss at the store, as a subject of jealousy. In the end, she hires an actor to pose as an old beau who is coming to take her back to her little town. Grant finally bites (as he did in real life) and succumbs to Oscar Wilde's theory that "We are attracted to those who are attracted to us." Funny lines but slightly overdone direction by Hartman. In the hands of Hawks, it could have been better but even adequate Cary Grant is better than no Cary Grant at all. Feminists and men who dislike aggressive women will not love this movie but it was right for its time and still packs a punch.

p&d, Don Hartman; w, Stephen Morehouse Avery, Hartman (based on story by Eleanor Harris); ph, George S. Diskant; m, Leigh Harline; ed, Harry Marker; md, Constantine Bakaleinikoff; art d, Albert S. D'Agostino, Carroll Clark, set d, Darrell Silvera, William Stevens; cos. Irene Sharaff; spec eff, Russell Cully; ex p, Dore Schary.

Comedy   Cas.   (PR:A   MPAA:NR)

EVERY HOME SHOULD HAVE ONE
                                                     (SEE: THINK DIRTY, 1970, Brit.)

EVERY LITTLE CROOK AND NANNY*½   (1972) 92m MGM c

Lynn Redgrave (Miss Poole, Nanny), Victor Mature (Carmine Ganucci), Paul Sand (Benny Napkins), Maggie Byle (Stella), Austin Pendleton (Luther), John Astin (Garbugli), Dom DeLuise (Azzecca), Louise Sorel (Marie), Phillip Graves (Lewis Ganucci), Lou Cutell (Landruncola), Leopoldo Trieste (Truffatore), Pat Morita (Nonaka), Phil Foster (Lt. Bozzaris), Pat Harrington (Willie Shakespeare), Severn Darden (Dominick), Katharine Victory (Jeanette Kay), Mina Kolb (Ida), Bebe Ouie (Sarah), Lee Kafafian (Bobby), Sally Marr (Ida's Mother).

Redgrave's dancing school is taken over for a betting parlor by gangster Mature's goons, so she gets herself hired on as nanny for Mature's son, then absconds with him. But because all this happens in the first 15 minutes of this film, and very little happens in the remaining 77 minutes, this is a boring movie—unless you're a fan of Victor Mature. This was his first film since he retired in 1960, and he seems to be enjoying himself.

p, Leonard J. Ackerman; d, Cy Howard; w, Howard, Jonathan Axelrod, Robert Klane (based on a novel by Ed McBain [Evan Hunter]); ph, Philip Lathrop (Metrocolor); m, Fred Karlin; ed, Henry Berman; prod d, Philip Jefferies; set d, James I. Berkey; m/l, "Big Ben," Karlin, Tylwyth Kymry.

Comedy   (PR:C   MPAA:PG)

EVERY MAN A KING   (SEE: EVERY BASTARD A KING, 1968, Israel)

EVERY MAN FOR HIMSELF***   (1980, Fr.) 87m
                 Sonimage-Sara-MK2-Saga/Zoetrope/New Yorker c
                 (SAUVE QUI PEUT/LA VIE; AKA: SLOW MOTION)

Isabelle Huppert (Isabelle Riviere), Jacques Dutronc (Paul Godard), Nathalie Baye (Denise Rimbaud), Roland Amstutz (2nd Costumer), Anna Baldaccini (Isabelle's Sister), Fred Personne (1st Costumer), Nicole Jaquet (Woman), Dore DeRosa (Elevator Attendant), Monique Barscha (Opera Singer), Cecile Tanner (Paul's Daughter), Roger Jendly (2nd Guy), Michel Cassagne (Piaget), Paule Muret (Paul's Ex-wife), Catherine Freiburghaus (Farm Girl), Bernard Cazassus (1st Guy), Eric Desfosses (Character), Nicole Wicht (Woman), Claude Champion (Stranger), Gerard Battaz (Motorcyclist), Angelo Napoli (Italian Fiance), Marie-Luce Felber (Coach).

Godard marks his return to commercial cinema after years of Marxist and television films with a picture that delves into the familiar Godardian themes of money, prostitution, and the relationship between sound and image. For the first time since 1972's TOUT VA BIEN, (with Yves Montand and Jane Fonda) Godard decided to use stars in his films, casting Huppert as an expensive Swiss prostitute who answers to men's fantasies and fetishes. Her clients' desires to control her (especially in one bizarrely funny office sex scene where she and three others engage in a "sex chain") are paralleled by Godard's manipulation and control of the soundtrack in relation to the visuals. The SLOW MOTION part of the title comes from stretch-printing/freeze-framing of a recurring woman's image. Godard's desire to use big name "stars" began to coincide with his choice of subject matter, particularly in the projected THE STORY, which was to be shot at Coppola's Zoetrope Studios with Robert DeNiro, Diane Keaton, and Marlon Brando. A gangster film about Hollywood, THE STORY never made it past the script stage.

p, Alain Sarde, Jean-Luc Godard; d, Godard; w, Jean-Claude Carriere, Anne Marie Mieville; ph, William Lubtchansky, Renato Berta; m, Gabriel Yared; ed, Mieville, Godard; art d, Romain Goupil.

Drama   Cas.   (PR:O   MPAA:NR)

EVERY MAN FOR HIMSELF AND GOD AGAINST ALL***½
                 (1975, Ger.) 110m ZDF/Cine International-Cinema 5 c
                 (JEDER FUR SICH UND GOTT GEGEN ALLE;
                 AKA: THE MYSTERY OF KASPAR HAUSER)

Bruno S. (Kaspar), Walter Ladengast (Daimer), Brigitte Mira (Kathe), Hans Musaus (Unknown Man), Willy Semmelrogge (Circus Director), Michael Kroecher (Lord Stanhope), Henry van Lyck (Captain).

The winner of the Grand Jury Award at the 1975 Cannes Film Festival helped to give director-writer Werner Herzog a world-wide reputation, as well as prove that a thriving film industry existed in Germany waiting to be appreciated by people of other lands, especially America. Based on the discovery of child genius Kaspar Hauser in the early 1800s, Bruno S. is a young man isolated from virtually any contact with human beings suddenly thrust in the middle of a town square and forced to adapt to society. Where this strange man came from remains a mystery to the town's people, whose authorities make note of his every move in an attempt to discover his identity and the cause of his odd behavior. Eventually Bruno S. learns to talk, making prosaic statements about the nature of man and society that have an impact akin to quotes from great philosophical thinkers. As mysteriously as Bruno S. came into the small community he also leaves, being killed one evening by an unseen assailant. A doctor does an autopsy on Bruno and comes up with the conslusion that his behavior was a result of some form of mental deformity, not even questioning the impact of rigid social and ethical codes. (In German; English subtitles.)

p,d&w, Werner Herzog; ph, Jorge Schmidt-Reitwein (Eastmancolor); m, Albinoni Pachelbel, Orlando Di Lasso; ed, Beate Mainka-Jellinghaus.

Biography/Drama   Cas.   (PR:A   MPAA:NR)

EVERY NIGHT AT EIGHT**½   (1935) 80m PAR bw

George Raft ("Tops" Cardona), Alice Faye (Dixie Dean), Patsy Kelly (Daphne O'Connor), Frances Langford (Susan Moore), Jimmie Hollywood, Henry Taylor, Eddie Bartel (Three Radio Rogues), Harry Barris (Snorky), Walter Catlett (Col.

Bayes, Master of Ceremonies), Dillon Ober *(Trick Drummer)*, Florence Gill *(Henrietta, the Chicken Lady)*, Eddy Conrad *(Italian Singer)*, Charles Forsyth *(Sound Effects Man)*, Herman Bing *(Joe Schmidt)*, Boothe Howard *(Martin)*, John H. Dilson *(Huxley)*, Florence Roberts *(Mrs. Murgatroyd)*, Louise Larabee, Louise McNames *(New Employees)*, Herb Ashley *(Piano Mover)*, Louise Carver *(Mrs. Snyder)*, Richard Powell *(Fresh Sailor)*, Lynton Brent *(Mail Sorter)*, Phyllis Crane, Gertie Green *(Telephone Operators)*, Nina Gilbert *(Chief Operator)*, Eddie Fetherston *(Photo Layout Man-Gold Strike Cigarettes)*, Harry Holman *(Jacksonville Colonel)*, Claude Allister *(Rich Bore)*, Stephen Chase *("Barrymore")*, Bud Flanagan [Dennis O'Keefe] *(Extra)*.

Amiable musical comedy that packs a lot of story and music into just 80 minutes. The Swanee sisters (Faye, Langford and an unusually-well-dressed Kelly) work at Huxley's Mint Julep Co. and have just impressed all the employees with their act at the company show. They decide to pursue their career and use their boss' Dictaphone machine to make a recording. Caught in the act, they are summarily dismissed from the company, then locked out of their rooms when they can't pay the rent. A billboard on the side of a truck is a bolt from the blue; it advertises an amateur radio show (not unlike Major Bowes Original Amateur Hour). They go on the show and are in the midst of their song when Langford faints from hunger and the contest is won by Raft, who leads a band. Raft feels sorry for the trio and invites them to join his orchestra. They have an engagement at a nightclub and do well enough but it's still not the Big Time. Eventually, they are hired to do a show for the same company that fired them and they are thrust into another world. The girls dress up in fine furs, gowns and baubles but they are so busy working for Raft that they feel their lives are not their own. By this time, Langford and Raft are goony about each other but that doesn't stop the trio from attending an elegant yacht party with a bunch of society types. Soon enough, the girls realize that they are out of their league and they rush back to the radio station where they join in with Raft for the show. The movie ends with Langford and Raft goo-goo-eyeing each other. The best comedy sequence is the satire on the amateur show with some funny stuff by Gill doing bird calls to opera. Gorgeous costumes and some popular songs highlight the proceedings. Songs: "I Feel a Song Comin' On" (George Oppenheimer, Dorothy Fields, Jimmy McHugh), "Take It Easy," "Speaking Confidentially," "I'm in the Mood for Love," "Every Night at Eight" (Fields, McHugh), and "Then You've Never Been Blue" (Ted Fiorito, Joe Young, Sam Lewis, Frances Langford).

p, Walter Wanger; d, Raoul Walsh; w, Gene Towne, Graham Baker, Bert Hanlon, (based on "Three On A Mike," a short story by Stanley Garvey); ph, James Van Trees; ed, W. Donn Hayes; art d, Alexander Tobuloff; cos, Helen Taylor.

Musical Comedy (PR:A MPAA:NR)

EVERY SATURDAY NIGHT** (1936) 60m FOX bw

June Lang *(Bonnie Evers)*, Thomas Beck *(Clark Newall)*, Jed Prouty *(Mr. Evers)*, Spring Byington *(Mrs. Evers)*, Florence Roberts *(Granny Evers)*, Kenneth Howell *(Jack Evers)*, George Ernest *(Roger Evers)*, June Carlson *(Lucy Evers)*, Paul Stanton *(Mr. Newall)*, Paxton Sisters *(Themselves)*, William Mahan *(Bobby Evers)*, Kay Hughes *(Patty Newall)*, Phyllis Fraser *(Millicent)*, Fred Wallace *(Jed)*, Oscar Apfel *(Mr. Dayton)*.

In this, the first of the Jones Family series, the Prouty-Byington-led clan is known as "Evers." But no matter, it's the same homespun humor they dispense under the name of Jones. There's no plot, really, just a string of children passing back and forth before their parents' bewildered eyes. Guaranteed safe. (See JONES FAMILY series, Index.)

p, Max Golden; d, James Tinling; w, Edward Eliscu (based on a play by Katharine Kavanaugh); ph, Joseph August; ed, Fred Allen; md, Samuel Kaylin.

Comedy (PR:A MPAA:NR)

EVERY SPARROW MUST FALL* (1964) 82m Jay Gee/Distributors c

Robert Shea, Frank Salmonese.

A mad electronics expert develops a gadget that will kill everyone in the world. Fortunately the world is saved when the sister of a man he drove to suicide poisons him before he can activate his gizmo. An inane mess.

p, James J. Gannon; d, Ronald R. Budsan; m, Joseph A. Kroculick; ed, Lee Jacobs.

Drama (PR:C MPAA:NR)

EVERY WHICH WAY BUT LOOSE½** (1978) 119m Malpaso/WB c

Clint Eastwood *(Philo Beddoe)*, Sondra Locke *(Lynn Halsey-Taylor)*, Geoffrey Lewis *(Orville)*, Beverly D'Angelo *(Echo)*, Ruth Gordon *(Ma)*, Clyde *(Himself)*.

Eastwood had been warned by his associates not to make this picture but he did and his share of the profits are reputed to be in excess of $15,000,000! So much for associates. Eastwood is a trucker who picks up money by challenging the toughest men in every area to bare-knuckle bouts. In an early match, he's won a huge, 11-year-old orangutan (Clyde) that he now travels with. His other driving partner is thick-witted Lewis. On a pub-crawling evening, they meet Locke, a C&W singer and Eastwood falls for her (which he did in real life, using her in many movies, much to the detriment of the movies) and thinks that the two of them can establish a life together. She is flighty and departs before anything can be established. Determined not to let her walk out of his life, Eastwood decides to catch up with her. Along the way, he has a few fights and makes enemies of two lawmen as well as a rag-tag Hell's Angels-type band. In the course of the film, Eastwood bests the lawmen and the motorcyclists several times (a few times too often, actually). Later, they encounter D'Angelo, a hitchhiker, and take her aboard. She is a former fruit-stand vendor and an excellent shot—something that comes in handy later when an eagle eye is needed. They meet Locke again and she says she's sorry for walking out on Eastwood. The relationship begins again but Locke has not changed colors; her feelings for Eastwood are mild and she much prefers her old boy friend. He allows her to leave and fights one last fight against a town tough. Although he knows he can beat the old clown, he realizes that this means a lot to the beer-bellied guy so he throws the fight, thus keeping the braggart's local image intact. At the fade out, Eastwood is driving off and passes the battered lawmen and motorcyclists. Ruth Gordon has the best lines as Eastwood's 80-year-old mother but most of the huge laughs are at the antics of Clyde, an incredible animal with near-human abilities. Lots of cars are crashed, lots of blood is shed, Eastwood doesn't say much and everyone has what appears to be a good time. The sequel was ANY WHICH WAY YOU CAN and if you didn't see the title of the movie, it would be hard to know which one you were watching. There's no accounting for the success of this over the failure of Eastwood's infinitely superior BRONCO BILLY. The year 1978 was the year of "heavy" pictures, with THE DEER HUNTER, COMING HOME and MIDNIGHT EXPRESS. Perhaps people just wanted to sit back, eat some popcorn and have a good old evening of cheers and laughter. In another year this might not have done as well. Songs: "Every Which Way But Loose," "I'll Wake You up When I Get Home" (Steve Dorff, M. Brown), "Coca-Cola Cowboy" (S. Pinkard, I. Dain, S. Atchley, Dorff), "Behind Closed Doors" (K. O'Dell), "Ain't Love Good Tonight!" (G. Skerov, R. Cate, G. Howe), "Send Me Down to Tucson" (C. Crofford, T. Garrett), "Don't Say You Don't Love Me No More" (P. Everly, J. Paige), "Honkytonk Fever," "Monkey See, Monkey Do" (Crofford, Garrett), "I Can't Say No to a Truck-drivin' Man" (Crofford), "I Seek the Night" (Locke), and "Red Eye Special" (S. Collins, Pinkard, Garrett).

p, Robert Daley; d, James Fargo; w, Jeremy Joe Kronsberg; ph, Rexford Metz (DeLuxe Color); ed, Ferris Webster, Joel Cox; art d, Elayne Ceder; set d, Robert De Vestel; stunt co-ord, Wayne Van Horn; cos, Glenn Wright; boxing inst, Al Silvani.

Action/Comedy Cas. (PR:C MPAA:PG)

EVERYBODY DANCE** (1936, Brit.) 74m Gainsborough/GAU bw

Cicely Courtneidge *(Lady Kate)*, Ernest Truex *(Wilbur Spurgeon)*, Charles Reisner, Jr. *(Tony Spurgeon)*, Billie de la Volta *(Shirley Spurgeon)*, Percy Parsons *(Josiah Spurgeon)*, Alma Taylor *(Rosemary Spurgeon)*, Peter Gawthorne *(Sir Rowland Morton)*, Helen Haye *(Lady Morton)*, Kathleen Harrison *(Lucy)*, Bruce Winston *(Pierre)*, C. Denier Warren *(Dan Fleming)*, Janet Johnson *(Lilian)*.

Courtneidge is a nightclub singer who, when her sister dies, suddenly finds herself saddled with two children. She leaves the stage to raise the children on a farm, but her avaricious manager tries to have her declared incompetent. Courtneidge does what she can, but is ultimately dragged under by the muddled, sentimental script and tedious musical numbers.

p, Michael Balcon; d, Charles Reisner; w, Stafford Dickens, Ralph Spence, Leslie Arliss; ph, Arthur Crabtree.

Musical (PR:A MPAA:NR)

EVERYBODY DOES IT*** (1949) 98m FOX bw

Paul Douglas *(Leonard Borland)*, Linda Darnell *(Cecil Carver)*, Celeste Holm *(Doris Borland)*, Charles Coburn *(Maj. Blair)*, Millard Mitchell *(Mike Craig)*, Lucille Watson *(Mrs. Blair)*, John Hoyt *(Wilkins)*, Leon Belasco *(Hugo)*, George Tobias *(Rossi)*, Tito Vuolo *(Makeup Man)*, Geraldine Wall *(Carol)*, Ruth Gillette *(Mrs. Craig)*, Gilbert Russell *(Chamberlain)*, John Ford *(High Priest)*, Aubrey Mather *(Mr. Hertz)*, Phyllis Morris *(Mrs. Hertz)*, John Goldsworthy *(Butler)*, Ruth Clifford *(Nurse)*, Robert Emmett Keane *(Hotel Manager)*, Kay Bell *(Angelo)*, John Burton *(Mr. Murray)*, William Pullen *(Bank Teller)*, Jack Chefe *(Hairdresser)*, Erik Rolf *(Dr. Walker)*, Ed Max *(Cleary)*, Jerry Miley *(Orderly)*, Billy Graeff, Jr. *(Bellboy)*, Dudley Dickerson *(Pullman Porter)*, William Griffith *(Makeup Man)*, Mabel Smaney *(Wardrobe Woman)*, Jane Hamilton *(Secretary)*, Mae Marsh *(Housekeeper)*, Joe Gilbert *(Man)*, Bruce Kellogg *(Guard)*, Larry Fielder *(Call Boy)*, Fred Libby *(Guard)*, George Davis *(French Singer)*, Sid Marion *(Props)*, Joan Douglas.

Businessman Douglas indulges his wife Holm's operatic pretensions, but when her debut bombs, he is discovered to have a magnificent baritone voice himself. He is a hit in a series of recitals, but when he's put in an opera, his awkwardness reduces the show to a shambles. He returns home humbled. Pretty good.

p, Nunnally Johnson; d, Edmund Goulding; w, Johnson (based on a story by James M. Cain); ph, Joseph La Shelle; m, Mario Castelnuovo-Tedesco; ed, Robert Fritch; md, Alfred Newman, art d, Lyle Wheeler, Richard Irvine.

Comedy (PR:A MPAA:NR)

EVERYBODY GO HOME!** (1962, Fr./Ital.) 105m
Dino De Laurentiis Cinematografica-Orsay/Davis-Royal Films bw
(TUTTI A CASA; LA GRANDE PAGAILLE)

Alberto Sordi *(Alberto Innocenzi)*, Martin Balsam *(Cpl. Fornaciari)*, Serge Reggiani *(Pvt. Ceccarelli)*, Nino Castelnuovo *(Young Codegato)*, Mario Feliciani *(Capt. Passerin)*, Didi Perego *("Available" Girl)*, Carla Gravina *(Silvia Modena)*, Jole Mauro *(Maria Fornaciari)*, Alex Nicol *(American Paratrooper)*, Eduardo De Filippo *(Innoncenzi's Father)*, Mino Doro *(Maj. Nocella)*, Claudio Gora *(Colonel)*, Vincenzo Musolino *(1st Fascist)*, Mac Ronay *(Evaristo Brisigoni)*, Mario Frera *(2nd Fascist)*, Silla Bettini *(Lt. Di Fazio)*.

A group of Italian soldiers hear that an armistice has been declared during WW II and all the men, except Sordi and Reggiani, desert. Sordi and Reggiani begin their journey back to the main Italian forces. Along the way partisan fighters try to get the two to join them and more soldiers join the two. One soldier, Balsam, is arrested by the Italian Fascists because his family hid an American paratrooper. The Germans make Sordi and Reggiani work on a road gang. They're attacked by the partisans and Sordi escapes and Reggiani is killed during the fighting. Sordi realizes that he can't escape the war and joins the partisians.

p, Dino De Laurentiis; d, Luigi Comencini; w, Comencini and Marcello Fondato; ph, Carlo Carlini, Gastone Di Giovanni; m Francesco Lavagnino; ed, Nino Baragli; art d, Carlo Egidi.

War Comedy   **(PR:A   MPAA:NR)**

EVERYBODY SING**   (1938) 80m MGM bw

Allan Jones (*Ricky Saboni*), Fanny Brice (*Olga Chekaloff*), Judy Garland (*Judy Bellaire*), Reginald Owen (*Hillary Bellaire*), Billie Burke (*Diana Bellaire*), Reginald Gardiner (*Jerrold Hope*), Lynne Carver (*Sylvia Bellaire*), Monty Woolley (*John Fleming*), Adia Kuznetzoff (*Boris*), Henry Armetta (*Signor Vittorino*), Micheletta Burani (*Madame Le Brouchette*), Mary Forbes (*Miss Colvin*).

Garland is the baby of a family of theater performers, and the whole family is down on its luck. Garland and her older sister, Carver, get kicked out of boarding school because Judy likes to sing Mendelssohn to a swing beat. At home, Judy does one of those let's-put-on-a-show routines (something that would be over-used in later films) and gets the family back on their feet. Brice plays the maid, but she doesn't get enough screen time to show her talents. Songs include, "Swing, Mr. Mendelssohn, Swing," "The One I Love," "Down on Melody Farm," "The Show Must Go On," "I Wanna Swing," "Never Was There Such a Perfect Day" (Gus Kahn, Bronislau Kaper, Walter Jurmann), "Quainty Dainty Me," "Why? Because," "Snooks" (Bert Kalmar, Harry Ruby), "Cosi Cosa" (Ned Washington, Kaper, Jurmann), "Swing Low, Sweet Chariot" (traditional, arranged by Roger Edens).

p, Harry Rapf; d, Edwin L. Marin; w, Florence Ryerson, Edgar Allen Woolf (additional dialog by James Gruen); ph, Joseph Ruttenberg; ed, William S. Gray; md, Dr. William Axt.

Musical   **(PR:A   MPAA:NR)**

EVERYBODY'S BABY**   (1939) 61m FOX bw

Jed Prouty (*John Jones*), Shirley Deane (*Bonnie Thompson*), Spring Byington (*Mrs. John Jones*), Russell Gleason (*Herbert Thompson*), Ken Howell (*Jack Jones*), George Ernest (*Roger Jones*), June Carlson (*Lucy Jones*), Florence Roberts (*Granny Jones*), Billy Mahan (*Bobby Jones*), Reginald Denny (*Dr. Pilcoff*), Robert Allen (*Dick Lane*), Claire Du Brey (*Nurse Cordell*), Marvin Stephens (*Tommy McGuire*), Hattie McDaniel (*Hattie*), Arthur Loft (*Chief Kelly*), Howard Hickman (*Dr. Jenkins*).

Another harmless Jones family film. This time young mother Deane wants to follow the teachings of corrupt pediatrician Denny. After a while the men of the town prove he's a fraud and chase him out of town. Nothing worth staying up late to see. (See JONES FAMILY series, Index.)

p, John Stone; d, Malcolm St. Clair; w, Karen De Wolf, Robert Chapin, Frances Hyland, Albert Ray (based on a story by Hilda Stone and Betty Reinhardt and the characters created by Katherine Kavanaugh); ph, Edward Snyder; ed, Norman Colbert; md, Samuel Kaylon.

Comedy   **(PR:A   MPAA:NR)**

EVERYBODY'S DANCIN'**   (1950) 65m Lippert bw

Spade Cooley (*Himself*), Richard Lane (*Colonel*), Barbara Woodell (*Mama Berne*), Ginny Jackson (*Ginny*), Hal Derwin (*Bill*), James Millican (*Papa Berne*), Lyle Talbot (*Contractor*), Michael Whalen (*Mr. Lansberg*), Sid Melton (*Agent*), Tex Cromer (*Himself*), Bobby Hyatt (*Donald*), Sons of the Pioneers, Chuy Reyes and Orchestra, Flying Taylors, the Great Velardi, Medians, Adele Jergens, Roddy McDowall, Jimmy "Shamrock" Ellison, Russ "Lucky" Hayden.

West Coast TV and CW personality Cooley more or less plays himself here, stepping in to help an old friend save his dance hall by booking in swing bands and a small circus. The musical numbers are far and away the best things here, and they include: "Foolish Tears" sung by Ginny Jackson; "Oblivious" by Hal Derwin; "Deep Freeze Dinah" sung by Tex Cromer; "I Shook" by Les Anderson; and Chuy Reyes and his Orchestra performing "Rhumba Boogie."

p, Bob Nunes; d, Will Jason; w, Dorothy Raison (based on a story by Nunes, Spade Cooley); ph, Benjamin Kline; ed, Edward Mann; md, Albert Glasser.

Musical   **(PR:A   MPAA:NR)**

EVERYBODY'S DOING IT**   (1938) 66m RKO bw

Preston Foster (*Bruce*), Sally Eilers (*Penny*), Cecil Kellaway (*Beyers*), Lorraine Krueger (*Bubbles*), William Brisbane (*Willy*), Richard Lane (*Dovers*), Guinn ["Big Boy"] Williams (*Softy*), Arthur Lake (*Waldo*), Sally Ward (*Gus*), Frank M. Thomas (*Bartender*), Herbert Evans (*Butler*).

So-so comedy made to capitalize on the craze for picture puzzles sweeping America at the time. Foster is a whiskey-swigging ad man with a penchant for inventing puzzles. When he goes on a bender without leaving the answers to a nationwide breakfast cereal contest, co-worker Eilers is sent out after him. She finds him and takes him to a health farm to dry out, but gangsters who want the answers kidnap him. Nothing original here. Lorraine Krueger tap dances and tries to sing "Put Your Heart in Your Feet and Dance" (Hal Borne, Mort Greene).

p, William Sistrom; d, Christy Cabanne; w, J. Robert Bren, Edmund Joseph, Harry Segall (based on a story by George Beck); ph, Nicholas Musuraca, Paul Vogel; ed, Ted Chessman; md, Frank Tours; art d, Van Nest Polglase, Field M. Gray.

Comedy   **(PR:A   MPAA:NR)**

EVERYBODY'S HOBBY*½   (1939) 56m FN/WB bw

Irene Rich (*Mrs. Leslie*), Henry O'Neill (*Tom Leslie*), Jackie Moran (*Robert Leslie*), Aldrich Bowker (*Uncle Bert Leslie*), Jean Sharon (*Evelyn Leslie*), John Ridgely (*Morgan*), Peggy Stewart (*Bunny*), Frederic Tozero (*Hatfield*), Albert Morin (*Ramon Castillo*), Nat Carr (*Jim Blake*), Sidney Bracy (*Terris*), Jack Mower (*Capt. Ogden*), Don Rowan (*Murphy*), Jackie Morrow (*Chuck*).

More family-oriented comedy from Warner's. This time papa O'Neill loses his job as managing editor of the hometown newspaper when a big syndicate takes it over. He becomes involved in photography while the rest of his family pursue their own hobbies. All come in handy when a forest fire threatens them, son Moran using his shortwave to call for help, and O'Neill using his telephoto lens to take a picture of the man who sets it. Innocuous if uninvolving.

p, Bryan Foy; d, William McGann; w, Kenneth Gamet, William W. Brockway (based on the story "The Hobby Family" by Brockway); ph, Sid Hickox; ed, Frank Magee.

Comedy   **(PR:A   MPAA:NR)**

EVERYBODY'S OLD MAN**   (1936) 82m FOX bw

Irvin S. Cobb (*William Franklin*), Rochelle Hudson (*Cynthia Sampson*), Johnny Downs (*Tommy Sampson*), Norman Foster (*Ronald Franklin*), Alan Dinehart (*Frederick Gillespie*), Sara Haden (*Susan Franklin*), Donald Meek (*Finney*), Warren Hymer (*Mike Murphy*), Charles Coleman (*Mansfield*), Maurice Cass, Ramsey Hill, John Miltern, Walter Walker, Frederick Burton, Hal K. Dawson, Delma Byron, Hilda Vaughn.

When tough old businessman Cobb learns of the death of his competitor and former partner, he takes a year off to think his life through, finding time to help his friend's children straighten out their lives. Cobb was a talented character actor, but his skill alone can't save this.

p, Bogart Rogers; d, James Flood; w, Patterson McNutt, A.E. Thomas (based on a story by Edgar Franklin); ph, Barney McGill; ed, Lloyd Nosler; md, David Buttolph; art d, Mark-Lee Kirk.

Comedy   **(PR:A   MPAA:NR)**

EVERYMAN'S LAW*½   (1936) 62m Principal/Supreme bw

Johnny Mack Brown (*The Dog Town Kid*), Beth Marion (*Marian*), Frank Campeau (*Gibbs*), Roger Gray (*Lobo Kid*), Lloyd Ingraham (*Morgan*), John Beck (*Pike*), Horace Murphy (*Sheriff Bradley*), Dick Alexander (*Barber*), Slim Whitaker (*Pete*).

Brown is an undercover Ranger who turns on his two villainous cohorts to help Marion save her ranch. You've seen this one before.

p, A.W. Hackel; d, Albert Ray; w, Earle Snell; ph, Jack Greenhaigh; ed, L.R. Brown.

Western   Cas.   **(PR:A   MPAA:NR)**

EVERYTHING BUT THE TRUTH**   (1956) 83m UNIV c

Maureen O'Hara (*Joan Madison*), John Forsythe (*Ernie Miller*), Tim Hovey (*Willie Taylor*), Frank Faylen (*Mac*), Les Tremayne (*Lawrence Everett*), Philip Bourneuf (*Mayor Parker*), Paul Birch (*Sen. Winter*), Addison Richards (*Roger Connolly*), Barry Atwater (*Arthur Taylor*), Jeanette Nolan (*Miss Adelaide Dabney*), Roxanne Arlen (*Blonde*), Ray Walker (*Doctor*), Howard Negley (*Chairman of School Board*), Bill Walker (*Waiter*), Elizabeth Flournoy (*Salesgirl*), Don Dillaway (*Official*), Ken Osmund (*Orrin Cunningham*), Bill Anders (*Passenger*), Dorothy Abbott (*Hostess*), Arnold Ishii (*Japanese Reporter*), Gertrude Astor (*Bit*).

Orphan Hovey lives with his uncle Atwater and is taught by schoolteacher O'Hara to always tell the truth. When Hovey tells the truth about Atwater's paying $10,000 to the mayor in a crooked real estate deal, lots of tedious complications ensue. Designed for the family trade.

p, Howard Christie; d, Jerry Hopper; w, Herb Meadow; ph, Maury Gertsman (Eastmancolor); ed, Sherman Todd; md, Milton Rosen; art d, Alexander Golitzen, Bill Newberry.

Comedy   **(PR:AA   MPAA:NR)**

EVERYTHING HAPPENS AT NIGHT**½   (1939) 76m FOX bw

Sonja Henie (*Louise Favers [Norden]*), Ray Milland (*Geoffrey Thompson*), Robert Cummings (*Ken Morgan*), Maurice Moscovich (*Dr. Hugo Norden*), Leonid Kinskey (*Groder*), Alan Dinehart (*Fred Sherwood*), Fritz Feld (*Gendarme*), Jody Gilbert (*Hilda*), Victor Varconi (*Cavas*), William Edmunds (*Hotel Clerk*), Michael Visaroff (*Otto, the Woodcutter*), Christian Rub (*Telegrapher*), Frank Reicher (*Becher, the Pharmacist*), John Bleifer, Adolph Milar (*Sled Drivers*), Lester Mathews (*Philip*), Russ Powell (*Hilda's Papa*), George Davis (*Bellhop*), Paul Porcasi (*Bartender*), Eleanor Weselhoeft (*Woodcutter's Wife*), Ferdinand Munier (*Conductor*), Rolfe Sedan (*Felicien, the Waiter*), Louis Mercier (*Taxi Driver*), Eugene Borden (*Waiter*), Jeanne Lafayette (*Brunette*), Nick Kobliansky (*Doorman*), Albert Conti (*Maitre d'Hotel*), Martha Bamattre (*Pharmacist's Wife*), Glen Cavender (*Guide*), Torben Meyer (*Station Master*), Joseph De Stefani (*Norden Servant*), Georges Renavent (*Gendarme on Dock*), Jean Del Val (*Gendarme*), Holmes Herbert (*Featherstonebaugh*), Roger Imhof (*Judge*), Wolfgang Zilgzer (*Dock Lounger*).

Working on tips that a political commentator thought assassinated was living in Switzerland, rival reporters Milland and Cummings discover him, but both fall in love with his daughter (Henie). Torn between the woman they love and the story of a lifetime, Cummings gets the girl and Milland gets the exclusive. Henie does her thing on the ice a few times, but this film was designed to expand her image as a serious actress. It didn't do that, but it did make money, largely on the strength of her name.

p, Darryl F. Zanuck; d, Irving Cummings; w, Art Arthur, Robert Herari; ph, Edward Cronjager; ed, Walter Thompson; md, Cyril J. Mockridge; skating numbers staged by Nick Castle.

Drama   **(PR:A   MPAA:NR)**

EVERYTHING HAPPENS TO ME**   (1938, Brit.) 82m FN-WB bw

Max Miller (*Charles Cromwell*), Dorthy "Chili" Bouchier (*Sally Green*), H. F. Maltby (*Arthur Gusty*), Frederick Burtwell (*Norman Prodder*), Norma Varden (*Mrs. Prodder*), Winifred Izard (*Mrs. Gusty*), Adin Weeks (*Johnny*), Ivor Barnard (*Martin*),

Nell Emerald (Matron), Allan Jeayes, Martita Hunt, Eliot Makeham, Hal Walters, Phyllis Monkman, Sam Wilkinson, Roy Emerton.

Miller is a cleaner salesman-turned-electioneer who shifts his loyalties from corrupt orphanage operator Maltby to henpecked Burtwell. Easy to take comedy with some funny moments.

p, Jerome Jackson; d, Roy William Neill; w, Austin Melford, John Dighton; ph, Basil Emmott.

Comedy   (PR:A MPAA:NR)

EVERYTHING I HAVE IS YOURS**½   (1952) 91m MGM c

Marge Champion (Pamela Hubbard), Gower Champion (Chuck Hubbard), Dennis O'Keefe (Alec Tackabury), Monica Lewis (Sybil Meriden), Dean Miller (Monty Dunstan), Eduard Franz (Phil Meisner), John Gallaudet (Ed Holly), Diane Cassidy, Elaine Stewart (Showgirls), Jonathan Cott (Freddie), Robert Burton (Dr. Charles), Jean Fenwick (Mrs. Tirson), Mimi Gibson (Pamela, age 3½), Wilson Wood (Roy Tirson).

The real-life husband and wife dance team of Marge and Gower Champion play a husband and wife dance team in a stunning bit of original casting. While he dallies with Lewis, she remains at home with the baby daydreaming about dancing with her husband. They can't act very well, but they can and do dance. Songs include: "Derry Down Dilly" by Johnny Green and Johnny Mercer; "Like Monday Follows Sunday" by Green, Clifford Grey, Rex Newman, Douglas Furber; "17,000 Telephone Poles" by Saul Chaplin; "Serenade For a New Baby" by Green; "My Heart Skips a Beat" by Bob Wright, Chet Forrest, and Walter Donaldson; and "Everything I Have Is Yours" by Harold Adamson and Burton Lane.

p, George Wells; d, Robert Z. Leonard; w, Wells; ph, William V. Skall (Technicolor), ed, Adrienne Fazan; md, David Rose; art d, Cedric Gibbons, Randall Duell; set d, Edwin B. Willis, Jacques Mapes; ch, Gower Champion, Nick Castle.

Musical   (PR:A MPAA:NR)

EVERYTHING IN LIFE*½   (1936, Brit.) 70m Tudor/COL bw

Gitta Alpar (Rita Bonya), Neil Hamilton (Geoffrey Loring), Lawrence Grossmith (Lewis Radford), H.F. Maltby (Sir Algernon Spindle), Gerald Barry (Vere Ponsonby), Dorothy Boyd (Miss Winstone), Wyn Weaver (William Tewkes), Clarissa Selwyn (Matilda Tewkes), Bruce Winston (Franz Graumann), Vera Bogetti (Carolyn Dexter), John Deverell (Johns), Oliver Gordon, Rosalind Rose, Judy Hallatt, Henry Ford.

Alpar, an opera singer, shucks stardom and its pressures. She falls in love with struggling composer Hamilton without his knowing her identity. She backs his new show, and still without his realizing who she is, stars in it. Enjoyable, if often confusing musical comedy.

p, Marquis of Ely; d, J. Elder Wills; w, James E. Lewis; m, Hans May.

Musical   (PR:A MPAA:NR)

EVERYTHING IS RHYTHM**   (1940, Brit.) 65m Astor/ABDF bw

Harry Roy (Harry Wade), Princess Pearl [Pearl Vyner Brooke] (Princess Paula), Dorothy Boyd (Grethe), Clarissa Selwyn (Miss Mimms), Robert English (The Duke), Gerald Barry (Count Rudolph), Phyllis Thackeray (Lucy), Bill Currie (George), Agnes Brantford (Mrs. Wade), Sid Crossley (The Waiter), Ivor Moreton, Davy Kaye, Robert English, Johnnie Nit, Mabel Mercer, Harry Roy's Band.

Released in England in 1936, this Ruritanian musical romance has Princess Pearl (allegedly the genuine article) falling in love with bandleader Roy. Her ministers don't approve of this and try to sabotage the proceedings, but love will out, and by the conclusion they're in a clinch. Pretty silly, but some of the songs are good. They include: "Sky High Honeymoon," "You're the Last Word in Love," "Black Minnie's Got the Blues," "Internationale," "Man of My Dreams," and "Make Some Music," all by Cyril Ray and Jack Meskill, and "Life is Empty Without Love," "No Words, No Anything" and "Cheerful Blues" by Harry Roy.

p, Joe Rock; d, Alfred Goulding; w, Syd Courtenay, Jack Byrd, Stanley Hayes (based on a story by Tom Geraghty); ph, Ernest Palmer; ed, Samuel Simmonds.

Musical   (PR:A MPAA:NR)

EVERYTHING IS THUNDER***   (1936, Brit.) 76m GAU bw

Constance Bennett (Anna von Stucknadel), Douglass Montgomery (Hugh McGrath), Oscar Homolka (Schenck Goertz), Roy Emerton (Kostner), Frederick Lloyd (Muller), Peggy Simpson (Mitzi), George Merritt (Webber), Robert Atkins (Adjutant), Terence Downing (Spicer), Clifford Bartlett (Glendhill), Albert Chevalier (McKenzie), H.F. Maltby (Burgomaster), Norman Pierce (Hans), Frederick Piper (Denker).

Canadian officer Montgomery escapes from a German POW camp during WW I. Prostitute Bennett helps him flee across the border to Holland at the cost of her own life, taken by her lover/detective, Homolka. Fairly suspenseful and moody.

p, S. C. Balcon; d, Milton Rosmer; w, Marian Dix, J.O.C. Orton (based on a novel by Jocelyn Hardy); ph, G. Krampf; ed, C. Saunders.

Drama   (PR:A MPAA:NR)

EVERYTHING OKAY*   (1936, Brit.) 79m City/AP&D bw
(GB: ON TOP OF THE WORLD)

Betty Fields (Betty Schofield), Frank Pettingell (Albert Hicks), Leslie Bradley (Jimmy Priestley), Ben Field (Old Harry), Charles Sewell (Mr. Preston), Eileen Latham (Anne), Wally Patch (Cardsharper), Fewlass Llewellyn (Soames).

Fields is a factory girl in grimy Lancashire who inherits a string of greyhounds when her father dies. She sells all but the best, using its race winnings to finance a soup kitchen when the factory workers go out on strike. Weak vehicle that was supposed to make a star out of Fields, the younger sister of talented comedienne Gracie Fields.

p, Basil Humphreys; d, Redd Davis; w, Evelyn Barrie (based on a story by H.B. Parkinson).

Comedy   (PR:A MPAA:NR)

EVERYTHING YOU ALWAYS WANTED TO KNOW ABOUT SEX, BUT WE'RE AFRAID TO ASK**½   (1972) 87m UA c

Woody Allen (Victor, Fabrizio, Fool and Sperm), John Carradine (Dr. Bernardo), Lou Jacobi (Sam), Louise Lasser (Gina), Anthony Quayle (The King), Tony Randall (Operator), Lynn Redgrave (The Queen), Burt Reynolds (Switchboard), Gene Wilder (Dr. Ross), Jack Barry (Himself), Erin Fleming (The Girl), Elaine Giftos (Mrs. Ross), Toni Holt (Herself), Robert Q. Lewis (Himself), Heather MacRae (Helen), Sidney Miller (George), Pamela Mason (Herself), Regis Philbin (Himself), Titos Vandis (Milos), Stanley Adams (Stomach Operator), Oscar Beregi (Brain Control), Alan Caillou (Fool's Father), Dort Clark (Sheriff), Geoffrey Holder (Sorcerer), Jay Robinson (Priest), Ref Sanchez (Igor), Baruch Lumet (Rabbi Baumel), Robert Walden (Sperm), H.E. West (Bernard Jaffe), Don Chuy, Tom Mack (Football Players), Inga Neilson (Royal Executioner).

Woody Allen took on more than any human being could do when he attempted to adapt the best-seller, Everything You Always Wanted to Know About Sex and We're Afraid to Ask. It was a non-fiction book, so Allen did what anyone would have done; he threw it out and started from the top. Seven segments make up this melange—some of them work, some of them are dreadful. It was Allen's sixth screenplay and his third directorial assignment and one of his weakest efforts. When Allen appears in a segment, it works, as in "Do Aphrodisiacs Work?" He plays a court jester to Anthony Quayle's king. He gives the queen an aphrodisiac and then can't open her chastity belt. Lots of Shakespearean references in this, one of the better ones. Gene Wilder stars in "What Is Sodomy?" as a man in love with a sheep who is caught making love to the animal by his wife and her divorce attorneys. The best piece is an Antonioni take-off with Allen and Lasser in "Why Some Women Have Trouble Reaching Orgasm." You could sell this bit as a short and it stands on its own. In "Are Transvestites Homosexuals?" Lou Jacobi is an old Jewish businessman who likes to dress up in drag and has to escape when visiting the house of his daughter's fiance. In "What Happens During Ejaculation?" Tony Randall stars as the operator who sends Allen out as Sperm No. 2 only to be encountered by a 400-foot diaphragm. Jack Barry satirizes himself in "What's My Perversion?" as the host of a kinky TV show and the weakest of the bunch stars John Carradine with Allen and MacCrae as a young couple visiting a sexual clinic in a Karloff-type house. It winds up with them all being chased by a mammoth breast across the countryside. The film was filled with lively humor and Wilder, as a psychiatrist who scoffs at his patient's love affair with a sheep (until he meets the sheep himself), does some of his best acting. It's filled with cameos (see cast list) and the stories read better than they play. Despite all of the sex antics, it's cute and off-color rather than being totally obscene. Worth watching but only on cable tv because the network censors will never let it play the way it was done.

p, Charles H. Joffe; d&w, Woody Allen (based on the book by Dr. David Reuben); ph, David M. Walsh (DeLuxe Color); m, Mundell Lowe; ed, James T. Heckert, Eric Albertson; prod d, Dale Hennesy; set d, Marvin March.

Comedy   Cas.   (PR:O MPAA:R)

EVERYTHING'S DUCKY zero   (1961) 80m COL bw

Mickey Rooney (Beetle McKay), Buddy Hackett (Adm. John Paul Jones), Jackie Cooper (Lt. Parmell), Joanie Sommers (Nina Lloyd), Roland Winters (Capt. Lewis Bollinger), Elizabeth McRae (Susie Penrose), Gene Blakely (Lt. Cmdr. Kemp), Gordon Jones (Chief Conroy), Richard Deacon (Dr. Deckham), James Millhollin (George Imhoff), Jimmy Cross (Misanthropist), Robert B. Williams (Duck Hunter), King Calder (Frank), Ellie Kent (Nurse), William Hellinger (Corpsman), Ann Morell (Wave), George Sawaya (Simmons), Dick Winslow (Froehlich), Alvy Moore (Jim Lipscott), Harold Kennedy (Mr. Johnson).

Appallingly stupid comedy with Rooney and Hackett an idiotic pair of sailors entrusted with a talking duck which has memorized a top-secret rocket-guidance system. After a while the film comes to a rather abrupt halt with the trio trapped in a space capsule in orbit around the earth. It's amazing that any movie this bad, this incompetent, this insultingly half-witted could have been released by a major studio. But here it is. Walker Edmiston supplies the voice of the duck, for which no less than seven stand-ins were used. Songs: "Everything's Ducky," "Moonlight Music," "Scuttlebutt Walk" (Harold Spina).

p, Red Doff; d, Don Taylor; w, John Fenton Murray, Benedict Freedman; ph, Carl Guthrie; m, Bernard Green; ed, Richard K. Brockway.

Comedy   (PR:A MPAA:NR)

EVERYTHING'S ON ICE**   (1939) 65m RKO bw

Irene Dare (Irene), Roscoe Karns (Felix Miller), Edgar Kennedy (Joe Barton), Lynne Roberts (Jane Barton), Eric Linden (Leopold Eddington), Mary Hart (Elsie Barton), Bobby Watson (French), George Meeker (Harrison Gregg), Mary Currier (Miss Tillifer), Maxine Stewart (Hat Check Girl), Wade Boteler (White).

Six-year-old figure-skating sensation Dare plays a six-year-old figure-skating sensation in this dull musical. She is hauled off to Florida and exploited by her nasty uncle Karns. When Dare skates she's nice enough, but she can't act, and the direction and script do nothing to help. Songs: "Birth of a Snowbird" (Victor Young, Paul Webster), "Everything's on Ice," "Georgie Porgie" (Milton Drake, Fred Stryker).

p, Sol Lesser; d, Erle C. Kenton; w, Adrian Landis, Sherman Lowe; ph, Russell Metty; ed, Arthur Hilton; md, Lud Gluskin; ch & ice numbers staged by Dave Gould.

Drama   (PR:A MPAA:NR)

EVERYTHING'S ROSIE** (1931) 60m RAD bw

Robert Woolsey *(Dr. J. Dockweiler Droop)*, Anita Louise *(Rosie)*, John Darrow *(Billy Lowe)*, Florence Roberts *(Mrs. Lowe)*, Frank Beal *(Mr. Lowe)*, Alfred P. James *(Oberdoff)*, Lita Chevret *(Miss Van Dorn)*, Clifford Dempsey *(Sheriff)*.

Woolsey was always the funnier in his vaudeville act with Bert Wheeler, and in their films together, but he's a bit too much undiluted here as a medicine show hawker who adopts a little girl. When she grows up into Louise, he embarrasses her in front of her fiance's parents. Woolsey, who died in 1938, is undeservedly forgotten today, but he can't carry a picture alone, as he is asked to do here.

d, Clyde Bruckman; w, Tim Whelan, Ralph Spence, Al Boasberg (based on a story by Boasberg); ph, Nick Musuraca.

Comedy (PR:A MPAA:NR)

EVICTORS, THE zero (1979) 92m AIP c

Vic Morrow *(Jake)*, Michael Parks *(Ben)*, Jessica Harper *(Ruth)*, Sue Anne Langdon *(Olie)*, Dennis Fimple *(Bumford)*, Bill Thurman *(Preacher)*, Jimmy Clem *(Buckner)*, Harry Thomasson *(Wheeler)*, Twyla Taylor *(Mrs. Bumford)*, Glen Roberts *(Dwayne)*.

Worthless exploitation junk has Morrow, a deranged real estate agent, knocking off the prospective buyers of a supposedly haunted house located back in the boonies. Just awful.

p&d, Charles B. Pierce; w, Pierce, Garry Rusoff, Paul Fisk; ph, Chuck Bryant (Panavision, Movielab Color); m, Jaime Mendoza-Nava; ed, Shirak Khojayan.

Horror Cas. (PR:O MPAA:PG)

EVIDENCE** (1929) 79m WB bw

Pauline Frederick *(Myra Stanhope)*, William Courtenay *(Cyril Wimborne)*, Conway Tearle *(Harold Courtenay)*, Lowell Sherman *(Norman Pollock)*, Alec B. Francis *(Harbison)*, Freddie Burke Frederick *(Kenyon Wimborne)*, Madeline Seymour *(Mrs. Debenham)*, Ivan Simpson *(Peabody)*, Myrna Loy *(Native Girl)*, Lionel Belmore *(Innkeeper)*.

Falsely accused of adultery, Frederick is divorced by her husband (Courtenay) and forbidden ever to see her son again. Six years later she is recognized in a park by her son and taken home. Courtenay once again throws her into the street. Finally, a rejected suitor commits suicide and leaves a note confessing that he had deceived Courtenay so that he might have had her for himself. Courtenay begs forgiveness and Frederick, of course, grants it. Myrna Loy has another of those native girl parts her career was so encumbered by before it took off. Song: "Little Cavalier" by M.K. Jerome and Al Dubin.

d, John G. Adolfi; w, J. Grubb Alexander (based on the play "Divorce Evidence" by J. Du Rocher MacPherson); ph, Barney McGill; ed, Robert Crandall.

Drama (PR:A MPAA:NR)

EVIL, THE** (1978) 89m New World c

Richard Crenna *(C.J.)*, Joanna Pettet *(Caroline)*, Andrew Prine *(Raymond)*, Cassie Yates *(Mary)*, Lynne Moody *(Felicia)*, Victor Buono *(The Devil)*, George O'Hanlon, Jr. *(Pete)*, Mary Louise Weller *(Laurie)*, Robert Viharo *(Dwight)*, Milton Selzer *(Realtor)*, Galen Thompson *(Vargas)*, Emory Souza *(Demon)*.

Psychologist Crenna and wife Pettet rent a haunted house, and, when strange things start to happen, they invite a group of students to help investigate. A trapdoor discovered in the cellar releases a nasty force that engulfs all of them while it disposes of them one by one. It's all pretty intelligently done, and Victor Buono is sublime as the Devil himself, although his concluding scene has been cut out of some prints.

p, Ed Carlin; d, Gus Trikonis; w, Donald G. Thompson; ph, Mario Di Leo (Movielab Color); m, Johnny Harris; ed, Jack Kirshner; art d, Peter Jamison; cos, Barbara Andrews, James Alvarez.

Horror (PR:O MPAA:R)

EVIL COME, EVIL GO (SEE: YELLOW CANARY, THE, 1963)

EVIL DEAD, THE***½ (1983) 85m Renaissance/New Line c

Bruce Campbell *(Ash)*, Ellen Sandweiss *(Cheryl)*, Betsy Baker *(Linda)*, Hal Delrich *(Scott)*, Sarah York *(Shelly)*.

Five teenagers take shelter in an abandoned cabin deep in the woods. Inside they find a strange book and a cassette tape explaining that the book is an ancient Sumerian Book of the Dead. The tape translates some of the incantations in the book, and giant demons are unleashed in the woods. One by one the teenagers are taken over by the demons, until only Campbell is left to fight evil. Shot in 16mm on a tiny budget, the film is definitely limited technically, but because of good, creative filmmaking it is nonetheless a masterpiece of recent American horror. Thoroughly shocking and spooky, with enough black humor to keep it all from getting too oppressive. Takeoff of NIGHT OF THE LIVING DEAD, THE HOUSE ON HAUNTED HILL as well as a host of others.

p, Robert G. Tapert; d&w, Sam Raimi; ph, Tim Philo, Joshua M. Becker (Du Art Color); m, Joe LoDuca; ed, Edna Ruth Paul; spec eff, Bar Pierce; makeup, Tom Sullivan.

Horror Cas. (PR:O MPAA:NR)

EVIL EYE** (1964 Ital.) 92m Galatea-Coronet/AIP bw (LA RAGAZZA CHE SAPEVA TROPPO)

Leticia Roman *(Nora Dralston)*, John Saxon *(Dr. Marcello Bassi)*, Valentina Cortese *(Laura Terrani)*, Dante Di Paolo *(Landini)*, Robert Buchanan *(Dr. Alessi)*, Gianni Di Benedetto *(Prof. Terrani)*, Jim Dolen, Virginia Doro, Chana Coubert, Peggy Nathan, Marta Melecco, Lucia Modugno, John Stacy, Milo Quesada, Tiberio Murgia, Titti Tomaino, Pini Lido, Dafydd Havard.

Roman, an American visiting her aunt in Rome, finds her suffering from a heart attack. While seeking a doctor, Saxon, she is attacked and knocked out and, upon awakening in a hospital, she remembers that before she fell unconscious she had seen a woman being stabbed. Doctor Saxon, however, doesn't believe her, and she returns to her aunt's house to find that her aunt has died, and she learns that there have been other murders in the neighborhood. She begins to suspect Di Benedetto, who lives in the house with his wife, Cortese, but the killer turns out to be the wife. A well-paced mystery that runs out of steam at the end.

d, Mario Bava; w, Ennio De Concini, Eliana De Sabata, Franco Prosperi, Enzo Corbucci, Mino Guerrini, Mario Bava; ph, Bava; m, Les Baxter; ed, Mario Serandrei; art d, Giorgio Giovannini; set d, Luigi D'Andria.

Mystery (PR:A MPAA:NR)

EVIL GUN (SEE: DAY OF THE EVIL GUN, 1968)

EVIL IN THE DEEP (SEE: TREASURE OF JAMAICA REEF, THE, 1974)

EVIL MIND (SEE: CLAIRVOYANT, THE, 1935)

EVIL OF FRANKENSTEIN, THE*½ (1964, Brit.) 84m Hammer/UNIV c

Peter Cushing *(Baron Frankenstein)*, Peter Woodthorpe *(Zoltan)*, Sandor Eles *(Hans)*, Kiwi Kingston *(The Creature)*, Katy Wild-Rena *(Beggar Girl)*, David Hutcheson *(Burgomaster)*, Duncan Lamont *(Chief of Police)*, James Maxwell *(Priest)*, Caron Gardner *(Burgomaster's Wife)*, Howard Goorney *(Drunk)*, Timothy Bateson *(Hypnotized Man)*, Alister Williamson *(Landlord)*, Tony Arpino *(Bodysnatcher)*, Frank Forsyth *(Manservant)*, Kenneth Cove *(Cure)*, Michelle Scott *(Little Girl)*, Anthony Blackshaw *(Burly Constable)*, David Conville *(Young Constable)*, Steven Geray *(Dr. Sergado)*, William Phipps *(Rena's Father)*, Maria Palmer *(Rena's Mother)*, Tracy Stratford *(Rena as a Child)*, Patrick Horgan *(David Carrell)*, Derek Martin, Robert Flynn, Anthony Poole, James Garfield *(Roustabouts)*.

The old masters-of-the-monsters, Universal, teamed with Hammer in a series of remakes of the great. So, for Hammer's third foray into the Frankenstein family tree, the monster dips into Universal's treasure lode and looks like Boris Karloff. Cushing finds his creature frozen in an ice cave. He thaws him out and enlists the help of hypnotist Woodthorpe to control him. Woodthorpe, instead, uses the monster to wreak havoc on his enemies. At the end the poor peasants of Karlstaad take up torches and farm implements once more to put an end to the strange goings on up at the castle. Hammer did more to revive the horror film than anyone between WW II and the present. This one did not contribute much. Sequel to REVENGE OF FRANKENSTEIN and FRANKENSTEIN CREATED WOMEN.

p, Anthony Hinds; d, Freddie Francis; w, John Elder; ph, John Wilcox (Eastmancolor); m, Don Banks; ed, James Needs; art d, Don Mingaye; spec eff, Les Bowie; makeup, Roy Ashton.

Horror (PR:A MPAA:NR)

EVIL UNDER THE SUN** (1982, Brit.) 102m EMI/UNIV c

Peter Ustinov *(Hercule Poirot)*, Colin Blakely *(Sir Horace Blatt)*, Jane Birkin *(Christine Redfern)*, Nicholas Clay *(Patrick Redfern)*, Maggie Smith *(Daphne Castle)*, Roddy McDowall *(Rex Brewster)*, Sylvia Miles *(Myra Gardener)*, James Mason *(Odell Gardener)*, Denis Quilley *(Kenneth Marshall)*, Diana Rigg *(Arlena Marshall)*, Emily Hone *(Linda Marshall)*, John Alderson *(Police Sergeant)*, Paul Antrim *(Police Inspector)*, Cyril Conway *(Police Surgeon)*, Barbara Hicks *(Flewitt's Secretary)*, Richard Vernon *(Flewitt)*, Robert Dorning *(Concierge)*, Dimitri Andreas *(Gino)*.

Agatha Christie defies coherent filming. The only one of her novels ever to work out well on the big screen was AND THEN THERE WERE NONE. This tedious star vehicle does nothing to change her luck. People gather at an isolated island retreat. Most have reason to hate bitchy stage star Rigg and so she turns up dead halfway through the running time. Then Ustinov plods his way through the alibis, working it all out and revealing the solution in the traditional way of having all the suspects in the same room. Still, it is strewn with talent and backed with some nice Cole Porter tunes.

p, John Brabourne, Richard Goodwin; d, Guy Hamilton; w, Anthony Shaffer (based on the novel by Agatha Christie); ph, Christopher Challis (Technicolor); m, Cole Porter; ed, Richard Marden; prod d, Elliot Scott; cos, Anthony Powell.

Mystery Cas. (PR:A MPAA:PG)

EVILSPEAK*½ (1982) 89m Leisure Investment-Coronet/Moreno c

Clint Howard *(Coopersmith)*, R. G. Armstrong *(Sarge)*, Charles Tyner *(Col. Kinkaid)*, Joseph Cortese *(Rev. Jameson)*, Claude Earl Jones *(Coach)*, Lynn Hancock *(Miss Freidermyer)*, Lenny Montana *(Jake)*, Don Stark, Hamilton Camp.

Military school cadet Howard, constantly tormented by his school mates, discovers a secret book of black magic and wires it through his computer to get even with the cadets who are baiting him. Among his weapons are a swarm of razor-toothed swine which finally run rampant over the drill and athletic fields. An absurdity, certainly, but it has its trance-inducing moments.

p, Sylvio Tabet, Eric Weston; d, Weston; w, Joseph Garofalo, Weston; ph, Irv Goodnoff; m, Roger Kellaway; art d, George Costello; spec eff, Harry Woolman, John Carter.

Horror Cas. (PR:O MPAA:R)

EX-BAD BOY** (1931) 76m UNIV bw

Robert Armstrong *(Chester Binney)*, Jean Arthur *(Ethel Simmons)*, Jason Robards *(Roger Shields)*, Spencer Charters *(Henry Simmons)*, Grayce Hampton *(Mrs. Simmons)*, Lola Lane *(Letta Lardo)*, George Brent *(Donald Swift)*, Mary Doran *(Sadie Bloom)*, Tony Stakenau *(Trainer)*, Eddie Kane *(Theater Manager)*, Eddie Hearn *(Assistant Manager)*.

Hick Armstrong pretends to be a city slicker with a shady past in order to get small-town queen Arthur. Robards, as her father, does his best to put a stop to it. Not bad, and a chance to see Jean Arthur at her prettiest.

d, Vin Moore; w, Dale Van Every, Fred Niblo, Jr. (based on the play "The Whole Town's Talking" by Anita Loos and John Emerson); ph, Jerome Ash.

Comedy (PR:A MPAA:NR)

EX-CHAMP** (1939) 72m UNIV bw (GB: GOLDEN GLOVES)

Victor McLaglen (Gunner Grey), Tom Brown (Bob Hill), Nan Grey (Joan Grey), William Frawley (Mushy Harrington), Constance Moore (Doris Courtney), Donald Briggs (Jeff Grey), Samuel S. Hinds (Commissioner Nash), Marc Lawrence (Bill Corsley), Thurston Hall (Mr. Courtney), Charles Halton (Trilby), Kid Chissel (Olson).

McLaglen is the ex-boxing champ, reduced to being a doorman at a nightclub, while his ambitious son works his way up Wall Street and prepares to marry a banker's daughter. In his spare time McLaglen trains a promising young welterweight (Brown). Briggs, the son, gets into trouble for embezzling some funds, but his father tries to put it right by instructing his fighter to throw the fight, while he bets heavily on the opponent, Chissell. Sidekick Frawley saves the day, though, by betting an even larger sum on Brown, who naturally wins. Pleasant enough, but no more.

p, Burt Kelly; d, Phil Rosen; w, Alex Gottlieb, Edmund L. Hartmann (based on a story by Gordon Kahn); ph, Elwood Bredell; ed, Bernard Burton.

Comedy (PR:A MPAA:NR)

EX-FLAME* (1931) 68m Liberty/TIF bw

Neil Hamilton (Sir Carlyle Austin), Marian Nixon (Lady Catherine Austin), Norman Kerry (Beaumont Winthrop), Judith Barrie (Barbara Lacy), Roland Drew (Umberto), Joan Standing (Kilmer), Snub Pollard (Boggins), May Beatty (Lady Harriet), Lorimer Johnson (Col. Lacy), Jose Bohr (Argentinian), Cornelius Keefe (Keith), Joseph North (Wilkins), Charles Crockett (Parson), Little Billie Haggerty (Austin Child), Louis Armstrong and His Jazz Band.

Thoroughly muddled melodrama based on the ancient boo-and-hiss stage play "East Lynne" about English aristocrats having affairs, getting divorces, and fighting for custody of the children. This one is not as good as it could be—in fact, it's pretty bad.

d, Victor Halperin; w, George, Draney, Herbert Farjeon (based on the play "East Lynne" by Mrs. Henry Wood); ph, Ernest Miller; ed, Donn Hales.

Drama (PR:A MPAA:NR)

EX-LADY*½ (1933) 56m WB bw

Bette Davis (Helen Bauer), Gene Raymond (Don Peterson), Frank McHugh (Hugo Van Hugh), Monroe Owsley (Nick Malvyn), Claire Dodd (Iris Van Hugh), Kay Strozzi (Peggy Smith), Ferdinand Gottschalk (Mr. Smith), Alphonse Ethier (Father), Bodil Rosing (Mother), Gay Seabrook (Girl), Ynez (Rhumba Dancer).

Advertising writer Raymond is in love with Davis and wants to marry her. She however, is a liberated woman who thinks that living together is a superior arrangement. The two begin a prosperous ad agency that falters after a couple of years. He begins to pay close attention to client Strozzi and Davis becomes jealous. She begins an affair with Owsley. Caught in a compromising position by Raymond, Davis professes her innocence and confesses that she was only trying to make him jealous. Reconciled, the two decide that marriage is the way to go. Lame little melodrama notable chiefly for being the first film to have Bette Davis' name above the title. EX-LADY is a remake of the Barbara Stanwyck vehicle—her sixth film—ILLICIT (1931). It seems remarkable that two up-and-coming young actresses such as Davis and Stanwyck should have starred in essentially the same story with so little time elapsing between releases. This film was one of the final ones made by Warner Bros. under the aegis of then-production chief Darryl F. Zanuck. That same year, Zanuck resigned to form his own production company, 20th Century Pictures—which, the following year, merged with Fox to become 20th Century-Fox.

p, Lucien Hubbard; d, Robert Florey; w, David Boehm (story by Edith Fitzgerald, Robert Riskin); ph, Tony Gaudio; ed, Harold McLernon; art d, Jack Okey; cos, Orry-Kelly.

Drama (PR:A MPAA:NR)

EX-MRS. BRADFORD, THE*½ (1936) 80m RKO bw

William Powell (Dr. Lawrence Bradford), Jean Arthur (Paula Bradford), James Gleason (Inspector Corrigan), Eric Blore (Stokes), Robert Armstrong (Nick Martel), Lila Lee (Miss Prentiss), Grant Mitchell (Mr. Summers), Erin O'Brien-Moore (Mrs. Summers), Ralph Morgan (Mr. Hutchins), Lucille Gleason (Mrs. Hutchins), Frank M. Thomas (Salsbury), Frank Reicher (Henry Strand), Charles Richman (Turf Club President), John Sheehan (Murphy), Paul Fix (Lou Pender), Johnny Arthur (Frankenstein Process Server), Spencer Charters (Coroner), James Donlan (Cabby), Dorothy Granger (Receptionist), Stanley Blystone (Police Radio Operator), Sid Saylor (Detective), Rollo Lloyd (Landlord), Charles McMurphy (Cop), Sam Hayes (Race Announcer), Edward McWade (Minister—on Film), John Dilson (Analyst).

Two of the brightest stars of comedy in the 1930s were teamed for this enjoyable screwball romp. Powell is a doctor slowly falling in love with his ex-wife while investigating a murder that eventually leads to him. Arthur is the ex, a mystery-story writer, saving Powell by presenting the police with some new evidence to clear him. Very good, and unjustly neglected today. A top-grossing film the year of its release to a public hungry for more of THE THIN MAN-style comedy-mysteries.

p, Edward Kaufman; d, Stephen Roberts; w, Anthony Veiller (based on a story by James Edward Grant); ph, J. Roy Hunt; ed, Arthur Roberts; md, Roy Webb.

Comedy/Mystery Cas. (PR:A MPAA:NR)

EXCALIBUR** (1981) 140m Orion/WB c

Nigel Terry (King Arthur), Nicol Williamson (Merlin), Nicholas Clay (Lancelot), Helen Mirren (Morgana), Cherie Lunghi (Guenevere), Paul Geoffrey (Perceval), Robert Addie (Mordred), Gabriel Byrne (Uther), Keith Buckley (Uryens), Katrine Boorman (Igrayne), Liam Neeson (Gawain), Corin Redgrave (Cornwall), Niall O'Brien, Patrick Stewart, Clive Swift, Ciarin Hinds, Liam O'Callaghan, Michael Muldoon, Mannix Flynn, Garrett Keogh, Emmet Bergin, Barbara Byrne, Brid Brennan, Kay McLaren, Eammon Kelly.

Here is a grand but brooding fantasy depicting the Arthurian legend from the young king's anonymous background to his rise as supreme ruler of ancient England. Background of Excalibur, the magical sword wielded by Arthur, is well established as the warriors preceding his era are shown in factional warfare. Terry is excellent as the naive, trusting, and altruistic Arthur, and Williamson chews up medieval forests and castles as the rhetoric-spewing wizard and magician supreme who exhausts his life and other-world talents on Arthur's behalf. The most fascinating aspects of this lengthy filmic legend are those dealing with the mythical Camelot and the lust-laden betrayal of Arthur by his lovely queen Guenevere, Lunghi, and his heart-bound friend Lancelot, Clay. Addie, as the evil Mordred, and Mirren, as Morgana, are very effective. Outstanding is Geoffrey as the Holy Grail questing knight, Sir Perceval, who is rewarded with the dazzling sight of his quest before returning along the death path that had claimed scores of other knights seeking the same elusive goal. It is also Geoffrey who finds his cherished king dying and, at his request, hurls the great Excalibur into the pristine lake where the female arm of the lady of the lake catches it, salutes its owner for a final time, then disappears beneath the still waters to await another valiant king. This is an absolutely compelling film streaming out of the mind of director Boorman and it presents a raw age of lumbering knights, smudged with grime, bearded and barbaric, their world dimly lit and full of slithering dragons, mesmerizing magic, and the struggle between good and evil, Christianity and paganism. Boorman somehow managed to pack Malory's tale into a splendid film full of eye-popping scenes, one that moves as quick as a sword slash, although the violence will shock any young viewer. The makeup and costuming, particularly the feudal iron coated knights, bring to mind the medieval warriors in ALEXANDER NEVSKY. Jones' score is eerie and inspiring. The script is as faithful to this most popular of legends as it can be. EXCALIBUR, was filmed in rustic Ireland which gives the feeling of timelessness, a land not unaccustomed to magic, if not outright sorcery.

p&d, John Boorman; w, Rospo Pallenberg, Boorman (based on the novel Le Morte D'Arthur by Thomas Malory); ph, Alex Thomson (Technicolor); m, Trevor Jones; ed, John Merritt; prod d, Anthony Pratt; art d, Tim Hutchinson; cos, Bob Ringwood; spec eff, Peter Hutchinson, Alan Whibley; armor, Terry English.

Action/Fantasy Cas. (PR:C-O MPAA:R)

EXCESS BAGGAGE* (1933, Brit.) 59m Real Art/RAD bw

Claud Allister (Col. Murgatroyd, RSVP), Frank Pettingell (Gen. Booster, SOS), Sydney Fairbrother (Miss Toop), Rene Ray (Angela Murgatroyd), Gerald Rawlinson (Clive Wrayne), Viola Compton (Martha Murgatroyd), O.B. Clarence (Lord Grebe), Maud Gill (Duchess of Dillwater), Finlay Currie (Inspector Toucan), Minnie Rayner, Ruth Taylor, Charles Groves.

While hunting a ghost, Allister thinks he has accidentally shot his superior. Panicking, he packs the body into a trunk and prepares to dump it in a river, but it becomes confused with Gill's trunk and she takes the soon-to-revive officer into the allegedly haunted house at which she is staying. Fair British B comedy.

p, Julius Hagen; d, Redd Davis; w, H. Fowler Mear (based on the novel by H.M. Raleigh); ph, Sydney Blythe.

Comedy (PR:A MPAA:NR)

EXCLUSIVE*½ (1937) 73m PAR bw

Fred MacMurray (Ralph Houston), Frances Farmer (Vina Swain), Charlie Ruggles (Tod Swain), Lloyd Nolan (Charles Gillette), Fay Holden (Mrs. Swain), Ralph Morgan (Horace Mitchell), Edward H. Robins (Col. Bogardus), Harlan Briggs (Springer), Willard Robertson (Mr. Franklin), Horace MacMahon (Beak), William Mansell (Formby), Steve [Gaylord] Pendleton (Elliott), Chester Clute (Garner), Irving Bacon (Dr. Boomgarten), Frank Bruno (Lollipop), Bennie Bartlett (Boy), James Blakely (Mr. Walton), Sam Hayes (Radio Announcer), Ann Marsters (Reporter), John Kelly (Cab Driver), Gertrude Simpson, Ricca Allen, Ethel Clayton, Gloria Williams (Bits), Richard Allen, Edward Hearn, Jack Daley, Dick Rush (Policemen), Mariska Aldrich (Policewoman), Ray Turner (Bellboy), Joseph De Stephani (Foreman), Edward Churchill (Advertising Manager), Harry Hayden (City Editor), Mack Gray (Secretary), Frances Morris (Beak's Wife), Billy Lee (Beak's Child), Oscar Hendrian (Janitor), Jack Chapin (Reed), Billy Arnold (Reporter), Bill Franey (News Vendor), R. E. Milasch (Gangster), Max Davidson (Tailor).

Crusading editor MacMurray exposes corrupt politicians who are trying to strong-arm a department store owner into line. Decent newspaper yarn with a good cast. The second year of stardom for the gorgeous, bright, multitalented, but ultimately tragic Farmer, who was being groomed by Paramount moguls for superstardom.

p, Benjamin Glazer; d, Alexander Hall; w, John C. Moffitt, Sidney Salkow, Rian James (story by Moffitt); ph, William Mellor; ed, Paul Weatherwax.

Drama (PR:A MPAA:NR)

EXCLUSIVE STORY* (1936) 76m MGM bw

Franchot Tone (Dick Barton), Madge Evans (Ann Devlin), Stuart Erwin (Tim Higgins), Joseph Calleia (Ace Acello), Robert Barrat (Werther), J. Farrell MacDonald (Michael Devlin), Louise Henry (Tess), Margaret Irving (Mrs. Higgins),

Wade Boteler *(O'Neil)*, Charles Trowbridge *(James Witherspoon, Sr.)*, William Henry *(James Witherspoon, Jr.)*, Raymond Hatton *(City Editor)*, J. Carrol Naish *(Comos)*.

Forgettable newspaper drama with crusading reporter Erwin helping kindly storekeeper MacDonald keep out of the hands of numbers racketeers. This film exploited the topical theme of the Harlem numbers racket being taken over by organized crime, a Hearst newspaper headliner of the day, and also included a far-fetched side plot involving a steamship disaster resembling the *Morro Castle* conflagration two years earlier. Calleia's gangster is the best thing here.

p, Lucien Hubbard; d, George B. Seitz; w, Michael Fessier (based on a story by Martin Mooney); ph, Lester White; ed, Conrad A. Nervig.

Drama **(PR:A MPAA:NR)**

EXCUSE MY DUST*½** (1951) 82m MGM c

Red Skelton *(Joe Belden)*, Sally Forrest *(Liz Bullitt)*, Macdonald Carey *(Cyrus Random, Jr.)*, William Demarest *(Harvey Bullitt)*, Monica Lewis *(Daisy Lou Shultzer)*, Raymond Walburn *(Mayor Fred Haskell)*, Jane Darwell *(Mrs. Belden)*, Lillian Bronson *(Mrs. Matilda Bullitt)*, Guy Anderson *(Ben Parrot)*, Paul Harvey *(Cyrus Random, Sr.)*, Marjorie Wood *(Mrs. Random, Sr.)*, Lee Scott *(Horace Antler)*, Alex Gerry *(Mr. Antler)*, Jim Hayward *(Nick Tosca)*, Will Wright *(Race Judge)*, Sheree North *(Club Member)*, Ed Peil, Sr. *(2nd Man)*.

Fast-mugging Skelton is a live wire laugh producer in this turn-of-the-century tale. He is an eccentric inventor forever tinkering with gadgets and gizmos, much to the chagrin of neighbors and relatives. Pretty, petite Forrest loves his extravagant ways but her father, Demarest, just thinks he's a looney (and he is for the most part). Moreover, Demarest owns a livery stable and the mere thought of Red's proposed horseless carriage drives him into a rage. Woven expertly into this very funny film are some delightful numbers, including a period dance piece that cleverly segues into the modern era when the participants imagine what it will be like 50 years hence. Beyond his clownish foibles and fumblings, the great Skelton manages to win Forrest and create a steam engine that wins the big cross-country race, an hilarious finish, earning the $5,000 prize money to finance future contraptions for which the world is waiting with sweaty anticipation. (Forrest's singing voice is dubbed by Gloria Grey.) This is a delightful comedy loaded with entertaining tunes which include "Spring Is Sprung," "Lorelei Brown," "That's For The Children," "Get A Horse," "Going Steady," and "I'd Like To Take You Out Dreaming" (Arthur Schwartz, Dorothy Fields).

p, Jack Cummings; d, Roy Rowland; w, George Wells; ph, Alfred Gilks (Technicolor); ed, Irvine Warburton; md, George Stoll; art d, Cedric Gibbons, Randall Duell; ch, Hermes Pan.

Musical/Comedy **(PR:AAA MPAA:NR)**

EXCUSE MY GLOVE*½ (1936, Brit.) 75m Alexander/ABF bw

Len Harvey *(Don Carter)*, Archie Pitt *(Bill Adams)*, Betty Ann Davies *(Ann Haydon)*, Olive Blakeney *(Aunt Fanny Stafford)*, Wally Patch *(Hurricane Harry)*, Ronald Shiner *(Perky Pat)*, Arthur Finn *(Madigan)*, Vera Bogetti *(Lucille)*, Bobbie Comber *(Bivex)*, Don McCorkindale, Tommy Farr, Jimmy Wilde, Bombadier Billy Wells, Gunner Moir, Benny Caplan, Dave McCleave, Frank Hough, George Daly, Harry Mizler, Ted Broadribb, Matt Wells, Johnny Rice, Jimmy Butler, Maurice Strickland, Syd Hull, John McAdam, Pancho Villar, Andre Lenglet, Moss De Young.

Boxer Harvey was packaged into this so-so film as a mild-mannered glass collector whose talent for the ring is recognized by a fairground proprietor. He is built into a champion despite a rival manager's attempts to prevent it. British fight fans of the time recognized a number of their favorite pugilists in supporting roles.

p, R. Howard Alexander, Joe Rock; d, Redd Davis; w, Val Valentine, Katherine Strueby (based on a story by Alexander); ph, Jack Wilson.

Drama **(PR:A MPAA:NR)**

EXECUTIONER, THE*½ (1970, Brit.) 111m COL c

George Peppard *(John Shay)*, Joan Collins *(Sarah Booth)*, Judy Geeson *(Polly Bendel)*, Oscar Homolka *(Racovsky)*, Charles Gray *(Vaughan Jones)*, Nigel Patrick *(Col. Scott)*, Keith Michell *(Adam Booth)*, George Baker *(Philip Crawford)*, Alexander Scourby *(Prof. Parker)*, Peter Bull *(Butterfield)*, Ernest Clark *(Roper)*, Peter Dynely *(Balkov)*, Gisela Dali *(Anna)*.

Peppard is a British spy out to prove that a former associate (Michell) was a Soviet spy. It's all very talky, and Wanamaker's idea of direction is to prolong everything as much as possible.

p, Charles H. Schneer; d, Sam Wanamaker; w, Jack Pulman (based on a story by Gordon McDonell); ph, Denys Coop (Panavision, Technicolor); m, Ron Goodwin; ed, Roy Watts; art d, Edward Marshall; cos, Yvonne Caffin; makeup, Trevor Crole-Rees.

Spy Drama **(PR:C MPAA:PG)**

EXECUTIVE ACTION½** (1973) 91m NG c

Burt Lancaster *(Farrington)*, Robert Ryan *(Foster)*, Will Geer *(Ferguson)*, Gilbert Green *(Paulitz)*, John Anderson *(Halliday)*, Paul Carr *(Gunman Chris)*, Colby Chester *(Tim)*, Ed Lauter *(Operation Chief Team A)*, Walter Brooke *(Smythe)*, Sidney Clute *(Depository Clerk)*, Deanna Darrin *(Stripper)*, Lloyd Gough *(McCadden)*, Richard Hurst *(Used Car Salesman)*, Robert Karnes *(Man at Rifle Range)*, James MacColl *(Oswald Imposter)*, Joaquin Martinez *(Art Mendoza)*, Dick Miller, Hunter Von Leer, John Brascia *(Riflemen Team B)*, Oscar Orcini *(Jack Ruby)*, Tom Peters *(Sergeant)*, Paul Sorenson *(Officer Brown)*, Sandy Ward *(Policeman)*, William Watson *(Technician Team B)*, Richard Bull, Lee Delano *(Gunmen Team A)*, Ed Kemmer.

Lancaster, Ryan, and Geer are leaders of the military-industrial complex who sit in a room and conspire to kill John F. Kennedy. Most of the action takes place on newsreels but the main plot is just a contrivance, albeit one that does make a turgid point or two. Dogmatic, sophomoric drivel not enhanced by grim Kennedy assassination newsreel.

p, Edward Lewis; d, David Miller; w, Dalton Trumbo (from a story by Donald Freed, Mark Lane); ph, Robert Steadman; m, Randy Edelman; ed, George Grenville, Irving Lerner; art d, Kirk Axtell.

Drama **Cas.** **(PR:C MPAA:PG)**

EXECUTIVE SUITE***** (1954) 104m MGM bw

William Holden *(McDonald Walling)*, June Allyson *(Mary Blemond Walling)*, Barbara Stanwyck *(Julia O. Tredway)*, Fredric March *(Loren Phineas Shaw)*, Walter Pidgeon *(Frederick Y. Alderson)*, Shelley Winters *(Eva Bardeman)*, Paul Douglas *(Josiah Walter Dudley)*, Louis Calhern *(George Nyle Caswell)*, Dean Jagger *(Jesse W. Grimm)*, Nina Foch *(Erica Martin)*, Tim Considine *(Mike Walling)*, William Phipps *(Bill Lundeen)*, Lucille Knoch *(Mrs. George Nyle Caswell)*, Mary Adams *(Sara Asenath Grimm)*, Virginia Brissac *(Edith Alderson)*, Edgar Stehli *(Julius Steigel)*, Harry Shannon *(Ed Benedeck)*, Charles Wagenheim *(Luigi Cassoni)*, Virginia Eiler *(Western Union Operator)*, Jonathan Cott *(Cop)*, Robin Camp *(Mailroom Boy)*, Ray Mansfield *(Alderson's Secretary)*, A. Cameron Grant, Bert Davidson *(Salesmen)*, May McAvoy *(Grimm's Secretary)*, Willis Bouchey, John Doucette *(Morgue Officials)*, Esther Michelson, Gus Schilling *(News Dealers)*, Abe Dinovitch *(Cab Driver)*, Faith Geer *(Stork Club Hat Check Girl)*, Mimi Doyle *(Telephone Operator)*, Mary Alan Hokanson *(Nurse)*, Paul Bryar *(Stork Club Waiter)*, John Banner *(Enrique, Stork Club Waiter Captain)*, Raoul Freeman *(Avery Bullard)*, Bob Carson *(Lee Ormond)*, John Hedloe *(Reporter)*, Wilson Wood *(Airport Clerk)*, Mike Lally *(Spectator at Ball Game)*, Phil Chambers *(Toll Station Attendant)*, Matt Moore *(Servant)*, Carl Saxe, Dick Landry *(Workers)*, Kazi Orzazewaki *(Liz)*, Burt Mustin *(Sam Teal)*, Helen Brown *(Miss Clark)*, John McKee *(Umpire)*, Ann Tyrell *(Shaw's Secretary)*, Chet Huntley *(Narrator/Tredway)*.

A spectacular array of superstars make up the cast in this excellent business drama. When the owner of a gigantic furniture firm dies there ensues a series of power plays among the company's executives, all vying for the top position. The jockeying vice presidents are March, Douglas, Pidgeon, Calhern and a junior executive, Holden. Surveying the candidates for the presidential position is Stanwyck, daughter of the founder of the manufacturing firm and mistress to the recently departed company head. She is also the chief stockholder so her decision will tip the scales. March is ruthless in his quest for the top position, blackmailing Douglas into supporting him by threatening to expose an extramarital affair and using the same tactics on Calhern when he learns that he has attempted to make profits on side deals. The only executive not actively contending for the presidency is Holden, who is only concerned with living the good life with his wife, Allyson, and son, Considine. At a crucial meeting Holden gives a compassionate speech about the firm and the lofty ideals it must uphold in practicing ethical business procedures. Stanwyck, moved by his eloquence, votes for his presidency and the rest of the board members fall into line. EXECUTIVE SUITE is brilliantly directed by Wise and his intercutting among the many characters clearly unifies the story and action instead of fragmenting the tale. The roles played by the leads are believable and the drama fairly drips from a sparkling, witty, and provocative script. Holden, March, Douglas, Stanwyck, Calhern, Jagger, Foch, and Pidgeon are riveting in their parts, even though some are only on camera occasionally, like Stanwyck. She was later to state of her small role: "Size has never bothered me. If it had, I would not have done EXECUTIVE SUITE. I liked the role and I wanted to do it, no matter how short it was. I think I worked all of seven days." Holden, still building a great career, was almost in awe of the grand cast. "Everybody was so good—so on his toes"—he was quoted as saying, "that when you went in there in the morning you had to put on your best. It was a great experience." This was the first time Stanwyck had worked with Holden in 15 years, their previous appearance together being GOLDEN BOY. March later praised Holden's performance as the young idealist but critics universally and accurately singled March out as the most impressive in the awesome cast; his obsessive villain hasn't a single virtue, only the relentless drive to win at all costs while mouthing the predictable rationale that he is merely practicing "good business." Power business and high finance are the focal points here, fascinating American audiences for the first time. Foch, as the suicidal secretary to the deceased boss, won an Oscar nomination as Best Supporting Actress but lost out to Eva Marie Saint of ON THE WATERFRONT. Allyson, still playing the sticky-sweet housewife role, finished her MGM contract with this entry, which the studio successfully patterned after its 1930s all-star movies DINNER AT EIGHT and GRAND HOTEL. The magic, thanks to Houseman's tasteful production, still worked. The cast cost MGM a hefty amount for that day, about $700,000 for the top leads, with another $500,000 to cover the entire production. (Wise only received $30,000 for his directorial chore, according to Houseman's autobiography, *Front and Center*.) This was also one of the first major films to eschew a continuous musical score, Houseman electing to incorporate the sounds of business throughout, such as the bells of a Wall Street clock as the cast names roll up on the screen. A miserable remake of this film by CBS-TV aired in an anemic series in 1976 and thankfully died a quick death. PATTERNS (1956) is a much better version and more faithful to the original.

p, John Houseman; d, Robert Wise; w, Ernest Lehman (based on the novel by Cameron Hawley); ph, George Folsey; ed, Ralph E. Winters; art d, Cedric Gibbons, Edward Carfagno; set d, Edwin B. Willis, Emile Kuri; cos, Helen Rose; makeup, William Tuttle; spec eff, A. Arnold Gillespie.

Drama **(PR:A MPAA:NR)**

EXILE, THE* (1931) 93m Frank Schiffman bw

Eunice Brooks, Stanley Morrell, Katherine Noisette, Nora Newsome, Charles Moore, George Randol, A.B. Comatheire, Carl Mahon, Lou Vernon, Celeste Coles, Louise Cook, Roland Holder, Donald Heywood's Band, Leonard Harper's Chorus.

Oscar Micheaux was the grand showman of the early black cinema and this is one of his typical works. The plot is largely an excuse for some fantastic musical numbers, but for what it's worth, Morrell is in love with a girl who decides she wants to turn her mansion into a bordello. He leaves her and goes west, where he falls in love with a white girl, only to find she has Negro blood. Much more interesting as a cultural artifact than as a movie; chances are no prints remain.

p, Frank Schiffman; d&w, Oscar Micheaux (based on his story, *The Conquest*).

Musical/Drama **(PR:C-O MPAA:NR)**

EXILE, THE** (1947) 94m UNIV bw

Maria Montez *(The Countess)*, Paula Croset [Paula Corday] *(Katie)*, Henry Daniell *(Col. Ingram)*, Nigel Bruce *(Sir Edward Hyde)*, Robert Coote *(Pinner)*, Otto Waldis *(Jan)*, Eldon Gorst *(Seymour)*, Milton A. Owen *(Wilcox)*, Colin Keith-Johnston *(Capt. Bristol)*, Ben H. Wright *(Milbanke)*, Colin Kenny *(Ross)*, Peter Shaw *(Higson)*, Will Stanton *(Tucket)*, C.S. Ramsey-Hill *(Cavalier Officer)*, Gordon Clark *(Cavalier Guard)*, Lumsden Hare *(Roundhead General)*, Lester Matthews *(Robbins)*, Thomas P. Dillon *(Jasper)*, William Trenk *(Footman)*, Fred Cavens *(Coachman)*, Alla Dunn *(Marie)*, Torben Meyer *(Sea Captain)*, Grayce Hampton *(1st Court Lady)*, Mary Forbes *(2nd Court Lady)*, Charles Stevens *(Painter)*, Douglas Fairbanks, Jr. *(Charles Stuart)*, James Logan *(Thurber)*, Art Foster *(Jessup)*, Harry Cording, Bruce Riley *(Roundheads)*, Erich Von Schilling, Garry Watson, Joe Ploski, Lillian Castle *(Servants)*, Reginald Sheffield *(Commanding Officer)*, Colin Campbell *(Old Secretary)*, James Craven, Leonard Carey, Pat O'Moore *(Cavaliers)*, Lotte Stein *(Fat Dutch Woman)*, Michael Mark *(Drunk)*, Edwin August *(Burger)*, David Cavendish *(Pigeon Keeper)*, Norbert Schiller *(Messenger)*, John Meredith *(Trumpeter)*, Richard Abbott *(Dutch Berger)*, Keith Hitchcock *(Military Man)*, Daniel de Jonghe *(Working Man)*, Charles Knight *(Ingram's Aide)*, Edith Clinton *(Cavalier's Wife)*, Perc Launders *(Guitar Player)*, Mary Bye *(Waitress)*, Sheldon Jett, Frank Austin, Jack Curtis *(Card Players)*, Pat Griffin *(Small Boy)*, Eddie Cregar *(Young Boy)*, Joseph Kamaryt *(Man at Inn)*, Elinore Vandivere *(Woman)*, Diane Stewart *(Girl)*.

Fairbanks, Jr.'s second stint as a movie producer—and his first as a writer—was an ambitious attempt to dramatize the tale of the restoration of Charles II to the throne of England. An avowed Anglophile, Fairbanks, Jr. had a strong sense of the history of his adoptive land (he was born in New York City). Unfortunately, the drama and excitement of the pursuit of Charles Stuart—Fairbanks, Jr.—after his return from self-imposed exile in Holland by Oliver Cromwell's bowl-tressed Puritans is dampened by the producer-author-star's insistence on a walking pace for the story. Much of the film is consumed by Fairbanks, Jr.'s trysting with the luscious Croset—later Paula Corday—in her first starring role as a Royalist who conceals the fugitive king on her estate. Despite a strong supporting cast and an interesting concept, the film is dull. It is graced to some extent by the fluid sepia-toned visuals characteristic of director Ophuls in his first completed American directorial effort (he was fired from his initial directing job by Howard Hughes).

p, Douglas Fairbanks, Jr.; d, Max Ophuls; w, Fairbanks, Jr. (from the novel *His Majesty, the King* by Cosmo Hamilton); ph, Frank F. Planer; m, Frank Skinner; ed, Ted J. Kent; art d, Bernard Herzbrun, Hilyard Brown; set d, Howard Bay; spec eff, David Horsley.

Drama **(PR:A MPAA:NR)**

EXILE EXPRESS½** (1939) 70m United Players/GN bw

Anna Sten *(Nadine Nikolas)*, Alan Marshal *(Steve Reynolds)*, Jerome Cowan *(Paul Brandt)*, Jed Prouty *(Hanley)*, Walter Catlett *(Gus)*, Stanley Fields *(Tony Kassan)*, Leonid Kinskey *(David)*, Irving Pichel *(Victor)*, Harry Davenport *(Dr. Hite)*, Addison Richards *(Purnell)*, Feodor Chaliapin, Jr. *(Kaishevsky)*, Spencer Charters *(Justice of Peace)*, Byron Foulger *(Serge)*, Etienne Girardot *(Caretaker)*, Don Brodie *(Mullins)*, Henry Roquemore *(Constable)*, Maude Eburne *(Mrs. Smith)*, Vince Barnett *(Deputy)*, Charles Richman *(Judge)*.

Sten is a laboratory assistant trying to escape from the men who killed her scientist-boss aboard an indeterminate European night train. They want her to fill in part of a missing formula that was destroyed by acid. The Stanislavsky-trained Sten was given free reign to overact by her then-husband, producer Frenke, thoroughly justifying her industry-wide cognomen, "Goldwyn's Folly." A good supporting cast saves this one from derailing.

p, Eugene Frenke; d, Otis Garrett; w, Edwin Justus Mayer, Ethel LaBlanche; m, George Parrish; ed, Robert Bishoff; art d, Ralph Berger; ch, Buddy Harak.

Drama **(PR:A MPAA:NR)**

EXILED TO SHANGHAI½** (1937) 65m REP bw

Wallace Ford *(Ted Young)*, June Travis *(Nancy Jones)*, Dean Jagger *(Fred Sears)*, William Bakewell *(Andy)*, Arthur Lake *(Bud)*, Jonathan Hale *(J.B. Willet)*, William Harrigan *(Powell)*, Sarah Padden *(Aunt Jane)*, Syd Saylor *(Maloney)*, Charles Trowbridge *(Walters)*, Johnny Arthur *(Poppolas)*, Maurice Cass *(Hotel Manager)*, Minerva Urecal *(Claire)*, Sally Payne *(Mabel)*.

Republic programmer has Ford and Jagger a couple of newsreel men. Ford invents some kind of television system that revolutionizes the business. No one is exiled. Shanghai is never mentioned. Good fun, though.

p, Armand Schaefer; d, Nick Grinde; w, Wellyn Totman (based on his story); ph, Ernest Miller; ed, Howard O'Neill.

Drama **(PR:A MPAA:NR)**

EXILES, THE½** (1966) 72m MacKenzie/Pathe Contemporary bw

Yvonne Williams *(Yvonne)*, Homer Nish *(Homer)*, Tommy Reynolds *(Tommy)*.

Intriguing, serious-minded drama about the plight of young reservation-raised American Indians in the big city (Los Angeles). Interesting independent feature which debuted at the Venice Film Festival.

p,d&w, Kent MacKenzie; ph, Erik Daarstad, Robert Kaufman, John Merril; m, Anthony Hilder, The Revels, Robert Hafner, Eddie Sunrise; ed, Warren Brown, Thomas Conrad, Thomas Miller, Beth Pattrick, MacKenzie, Daarstad.

Drama **(PR:C MPAA:NR)**

EXIT THE DRAGON, ENTER THE TIGER* (1977, Hong Kong) 84m Hong Kong Alpha/Dimension c

David Lee [Lee Shaio Lung] *(Bruce Li/Bruce Lee)*, Lung Fei, Ma Chi Chiang, San Moo, An Ping, Chang Sing Yee, Tsao Shao Jung.

Lee decides to investigate the mysterious death of his friend and teacher Bruce Lee and runs into a gang of drug smugglers who killed the master when he refused to act as a courier for them. After his girl friend is gang-raped and his best friend killed, Lee meets the head of the gang on the shores of Kowloon Bay and beats him to death after a long fight. A styleless, tedious martial arts opus, one of a spate of films capitalizing on the mystery surrounding the death of the only star the genre produced. (Dubbed in English.)

p, Jimmy Shaw, R.P. Shah; d, Lee Tse Nam; w, Hugo Grimaldi (based on the Cantonese language script by Chang Shun Yee); ph, Yip Chin Biu; m, Chow Fook Leung.

Martial Arts **Cas.** **(PR:O MPAA:R)**

EXODUS**** (1960) 212m Preminger/UA c

Paul Newman *(Ari Ben Gannan)*, Eva Marie Saint *(Kitty Fremont)*, Ralph Richardson *(Gen. Sutherland)*, Peter Lawford *(Maj. Caldwell)*, Lee J. Cobb *(Barak Ben Canaan)*, Sal Mineo *(Dov Landau)*, John Derek *(Taha)*, Hugh Griffith *(Mandria)*, Gregory Ratoff *(Lakavitch)*, Felix Aylmer *(Dr. Lieberman)*, David Opatoshu *(Akiva)*, Jill Haworth *(Karen)*, Marius Goring *(Von Storch)*, Alexandra Stewart *(Jordana)*, Michael Wager *(David)*, Martin Benson *(Mordekai)*, Paul Stevens *(Reuben)*, Betty Walker *(Sarah)*, Martin Miller *(Dr. Odenheim)*, Victor Madden *(Sergeant)*, George Maharis *(Yaov)*, John Crawford *(Hank)*, Samuel Segal *(Proprietor)*, Dahn Ben Amotz *(Uzi)*, Ralph Truman *(Colonel)*, Peter Madden *(Dr. Clement)*, Joseph Furst *(Avidan)*, Paul Stassino *(Driver)*, Marc Burns *(Lt. O'Hara)*, Esther Reichstadt *(Mrs. Hirshberg)*, Zeporah Peled *(Mrs. Frankel)*, Philo Hauser *(Novak)*.

A stirring and heroic film that beautifully chronicles Israel's struggle for independence in 1947 when most of the world left the infant nation naked in a manger ringed with hostile bayonets, albeit the U.S. was the first country to acknowledge its existence. Newman, as the young Hagannah leader, is the focal point of this epic which engulfs his angry love affair with Saint who adopts a homeless Jewish girl, Haworth. Other episodes dealing with Mineo, as a devout Irgun fighter, the peace-seeking Cobb as an elder, and his brother, the destruction-bent Opatoshu, graphically show how each faction built the nation while fending off attacks from many Arab countries bent on suffocating the new country. Then there is the internecine struggle between the moderate Hagannah and the terrorist-prone Irgun, an ideological battle within the larger struggle to survive. Interspersed throughout are segments dealing with the migration of European Jews to the new land, the ragged survivors of Nazi death camps on board the vessel *Exodus*, blockaded in a Cyprus harbor by British warships. At first Newman threatens to blow up the ship, then he sets in motion a hunger strike embraced by all of its 611 pathetic passengers. The British finally relent and allow the ship to sail to Palestine. The second segment deals with the struggle of the Jews in Palestine to gain partition, and the third segment profiles the main characters in post-partition Palestine as the Jews fight to stay alive as a nation. The entire cast renders stunning performances and many a scene becomes unforgettable in the careful telling, including the blowing up of the King David Hotel, the capture of Irgun leaders Opatoshu, Mineo, and others, their clever rescue by Newman while impersonating a British officer (not unlike a similar scene from SWORD IN THE DESERT which earlier dealt with the birth of Israel, and the bold announcement of independence). Preminger masterfully dealt with the enormous crowd scenes and detailed with meticulous care the historical events portrayed in the bestselling Uris novel. In attempting to deal with an enormous body of work some development of character was inevitably lost, but what remains in this film is excellent, despite the carping of some critics that Newman was too restrained. (Had he been more histrionic he would have been condemned for extravagance.) Haworth's premature death and burial alongside Newman's boyhood friend Derek, a sympathetic Arab who dies for the Jewish cause, is particularly poignant, and Newman's speech about continuing the fight at the finale is moving. The film could not be perfect because it could not say enough, show enough, be enough in equating itself to the titanic events and unforgettable characters it profiles. Yet it was the best Preminger could provide and, as is, the film is a landmark achievement even though Uris denounced Preminger after the film's completion. Uris had originally been sought as the screenwriter but the director felt he had no feel for dialog and dismissed him. (This was a recurrent Preminger problem; he had first thought to have Chicago author Nelson Algren write the screenplay for THE MAN WITH THE GOLDEN ARM but personality conflicts got in the way of that arrangement.) There were also arguments against the film by governing heads of Israel where it was shot on location, as well as leaders of the terrorists groups, so Preminger had to face external pressure as well as criticism from within the production. In the end Preminger did it his way, which was superb, later admitting: "I think that my picture . . . is much closer to the truth, and to the historic facts, than is the book. It also avoids propaganda. It's an American picture, after all, that tries to tell the story, giving both sides a chance to plead their side." His production values are flawless and, though overlong, the story is told with dazzling perception. Gold's score has since become a classic of its kind. More than $4 million went into the production but its returns at the box office were many times that then-staggering amount. Of particular note in the supporting cast were Ralph Richardson and Peter Lawford, both playing British officers. Richardson, though always defending the British position of referee between Jew and Arab, is definitely sympathetic to the cause of Israel while Lawford's cultivated manners cannot shroud his deep-seated anti-Semitism.

p&d, Otto Preminger; w, Dalton Trumbo (based on the novel by Leon Uris); ph, Sam Leavitt (Super Panavision 70, Technicolor); m, Ernest Gold; ed, Louis R. Loeffler; art d, Richard Day, Bill Hutchinson; set d, Dario Simoni; cos, Joe King, May Walding, Margo Slater, Rudi Gernreich, Hope Bryce; makeup, George Lane; spec eff, Win Ryder.

Drama/Historical Epic　　　**Cas.**　　　**(PR:C　MPAA:NR)**

EXORCISM AT MIDNIGHT*　　　(1966, Brit. revised 1973, U.S.)
Gibralter-Protelco/Independent International bw (tinted) (AKA: NAKED EVIL)
Anthony Ainley (Dick Alderson), Basil Dignam (Benson), Suzanne Neve (Janet), Richard Coleman (Hollis), Ronald Bridges (Wilkins), George A. Saunders (Danny), Carmen Munroe (Beverley), Brylo Ford (Amazon), Dan Jackson (Lloyd), Pearl Prescod (Landlady); (1973 version only) Lawrence Tierney.

Coleman is a detective investigating a series of murders that seem to stem from a West Indian witch doctor. An old servant is the witch doctor casting his spells from deep in a hidden basement. The film was re-released in 1973 to attract some of the huge audience from THE EXORCIST. New scenes were shot with American actors in a tinted process called MultiColor.

p,d&w, Stanley Goulder (based on the play *The Obi* by John Manship White); ph, Geoffrey Faithfull; m, Bernard Ebbinghouse; art d, George Provis, Dennis Pavitt.

Horror　　　　　　　**(PR:C-O　MPAA:NR)**

EXORCISM'S DAUGHTER zero　　(1974, Span.) 93m Howard Mahler/
National Forum c (AKA: HOUSE OF INSANE WOMEN)
Amelia Gade, Francisco Rabal, Espartaco Santoni.

Rabal runs an asylum and finds that Gade went insane because her mother died while being exorcised. You won't die or go insane watching this film but it sure will seem like it.

d&w, Rafael Morena Alba.

Horror　　　　　　　**(PR:O　MPAA:R)**

EXORCIST, THE****　　　(1973) 121m WB c
Ellyn Burstyn (Mrs. MacNeil), Max von Sydow (Father Merrin), Jason Miller (Father Karras), Lee J. Cobb (Lt. Kinderman), Jack MacGowran (Burke), Kitty Winn (Sharon), Linda Blair (Regan), Vasiliki Maliaros (Mother Karras), Wallace Rooney (Bishop), Titos Vandis (Karras's Uncle), Rev. William O'Malley (Father Dyer), Mercedes McCambridge (Voice of the Demon).

A truly terrifying film version of the bestselling Blatty novel is far superior to the book in condensing sheer horror into two hours of nerve-jangling scenes. Attacked is a 12-year-old child, Blair, whose inexplicable fits and strange behavior cause her mother, Burstyn, a famous stage actress with no specific religious convictions, to seek medical help. Doctors examining the child can pinpoint no physical or psychiatric ailment and cryptically suggest to Burstyn that she seek religious counsel. Instead, Burstyn returns Blair home where she becomes more and more violent, attacking her mother, having to be tied to her bed, and becoming emaciated, not being able to keep food in her stomach. In desperation Burstyn asks the help of young priest Miller. The priest's own life has become a shambles and his faith has been weakened; he rejects his own mother's plight and those of his impoverished parishioners. En route to Burstyn's stylish, expensive home, Miller passes a derelict, oblivious to his plea of "Can you help a former altar boy, Father?" Upon witnessing the child, her face contorted, her body racked with convulsions, bloodless, screaming out vile oaths, Miller informs Burstyn that Blair is possessed of a devil and a priest with special gifts, von Sydow, can exorcise the demon. Von Sydow arrives in the middle of a fog-bound night and, with Miller, confronts the dark spirit residing in Blair. There is a monstrous battle as the child's voice changes into many voices, speaking many languages, shrieking and growling oaths and obscenities. At one chilling point the voice duplicates that of Miller's mother and the Irish brogue of the parishioner Miller had met on the street, mockingly stating: "Can you help a former altar boy, Father?" Von Sydow attempts to administer the lengthy exorcism, while the demon spits out green slime into his face, the child's body bucks, then levitates, her head turning full circle, the bedroom becoming icy cold. Again and again the priests attempt to drive out the demon but it's too much for the elderly von Sydow; he drops dead of a heart attack. Miller continues the religious rite and manages to bring the devil forth but the beast enters his own body. With a last act of consciousness, Miller, to destroy the monster, hurls himself out of the window and falls to his death. Blair is saved at the cost of two lives. Blatty's runaway bestseller was based upon a reported exorcism in 1949 and uses the Catholic ritual of driving out a devil as reprinted in the *Rituale Romanum* in 1947. The film, directed by the gifted Friedkin, is a masterpiece of special effects, one of the most frightening films ever made, and it became one of the five highest grossing movies with more than $82 million returned at the box office, against a $10 million budget. Coupled with the horrendous transformation of a sweet child to a vile demon is a bone-chilling score and makeup that would scare Bela Lugosi. McCambridge's deep moans, rasping taunts, all amplified, turn the blood to ice water. (Blair did not enact the vomitting scenes; these were performed by Eileen Smith who later sued to have proper credit.) This one is certainly not for young viewers nor anyone with a heart condition.

p&w, William Peter Blatty; d, William Friedkin (based on Blatty's novel); ph, Own Roizman, Billy Williams (Metrocolor); m, Jack Nitzche; ed, Norman Gay, Jordan Leondopoulos, Evan Lottman, Bud Smith; prod d, Bill Malley; set d, Jerry Wunderlich; spec makeup eff, Dick Smith, Rick Baker.

Horror　　　**Cas.**　　　**(PR:O　MPAA:R)**

EXORCIST II: THE HERETIC*　　(1977) 117m WB c
Linda Blair (Regan), Richard Burton (Father Lamont), Louise Fletcher (Dr. Gene Tuskin), Max von Sydow (Father Merrin), Kitty Winn (Sharon), Paul Henreid (The Cardinal), James Earl Jones (Older Kokumo), Ned Beatty (Edwards), Belinda Beatty (Liz), Rose Portillo (Spanish Girl), Barbara Cason (Mr. Phalor), Tiffany Kinney (Deaf Girl), Joey Green (Young Kokumo), Fiseha Dimetros (Young Monk), Ken Renard (Abbot), Hank Garrett (Conductor), Larry Goldman (Accident Victim), Bill Grant (Taxi Driver), Shane Butterworth, Joely Adams (Tuskin Children).

Soporific, sluggish, and silly is this forced sequel to its blockbuster original. Blair, now 18, is again possessed by the demon Pazuzu but this time is treated by child psychologist Fletcher, a wan version of Ellyn Burstyn (the two have strikingly similar appearances but their acting abilities differ drastically, the former being an accomplished thespian, the latter a deadpan actress with a monotone delivery, no animation, and the personality of a long deceased herring). Fletcher, using Burton as a replacement for von Sydow (although Max is shown in flashback, even though he perished in the original, THE EXORCIST), hooks the heretical priest up to a mind processing machine of her own invention, with Blair at the other end to produce some scary visual scenes. But for the most part the devil possession is so lamely constructed by Boorman (who, oddly, was able to turn out brilliant films such as EXCALIBUR) as to present arrant absurdity, which caused audiences to actually laugh at the first-run showings. Called back for editing, no one was able to fix up this miserable exploitation of the original. Disjointed, mindless, and without cohesion, this film flings scenes of no significance at the viewer. At one point Beatty, appearing briefly as a pilot, flies Burton across some primitive spots of Africa and Burton tells him that he has taken the same trip before—on the back of a bug! "I flew with Pazuzu. It's difficult to explain. I was under hypnosis." Would that the viewer had been allowed the same privilege. Burton is later swarmed to death by demon locusts in Blair's deserted house. Fletcher concludes the film by removing the electrodes from Blair's head, idiotically stating: "I understand now. But the world won't." The world just didn't care. This shabby sequel hardly made back its $11 million pricetag which is easy enough to understand; the production was possessed . . . of bad taste.

p, John Boorman, Richard Lederer; d, Boorman; w, William Goodhart (based on characters created by William Peter Blatty); ph, William A. Fraker (Technicolor); m, Ennio Morricone; ed, Tom Priestley; prod d, Richard Macdonald; art d, Jack Collins; set d, John Austin; cos, Robert de Mora; spec eff, Albert J. Whitlock, Van der Veer, Chuck Gaspar, Wayne Edgar, Jim Blount, Jeff Jarvis, Roy Kelly.

Horror　　　**Cas.**　　　**(PR:O　MPAA:R)**

EXOTIC ONES, THE zero　　　(1968) 60m Ormond Organization bw
Ron Ormond, June Ormond.

Total obscurity from prolific exploitation director Ormond. This time he's got a pot-smoking monster wandering New Orleans' French Quarter mangling strippers. From the man responsible for FORTY ACRE FEUD and a number of other films designed for the southeastern drive-in circuit, most of them starring himself and wife June. (Posing a stripper as a victim, of course, allows for plenty of flashing of flesh; at least some desperately needed humor might have been produced if the victims were plumbers or electricians. Who knows? A whole new filmic school might have been created such as "The Baggy Pants Wave.")

p, d&w, Ron Ormond.

Horror　　　　　　　**(PR:O　MPAA:NR)**

EXPENSIVE HUSBANDS**½　　(1937) 62m WB bw
Patric Knowles (Prince Rupert), Beverly Roberts (Laurine Lynne), Allyn Joslyn (Joe Craig), Gordon Oliver (Ricky Preston), Eula Guy (Trommy), Robert C. Fischer (Joseph), Fritz Feld (Herr Meyer), Vladimir Sokoloff (Andrew Brenner), John Butler (Savage), Ann Codee (Maria), George Humbert (Giovanni), Otto Fries (Franz).

Roberts is an up-and-coming young film actress who marries impoverished prince Knowles while in Europe. The resultant publicity makes her a star, but before long Knowles turns up in Hollywood, running up huge bills in her name. He returns to Austria and she goes after him, only to find that he has now come into his inheritance and that his spending binge was just a test of her love. Not bad at all.

p&d, Bobby Connolly; w, Lillie Hayward, Jean Negulesco, Jay Brennan (from a story by Kyrill de Shishmareff); ph, James Van Trees; ed, Lou Hesse; art d, Hugh Reticker; m/l, M.K. Jerome, Jack Scholl.

Comedy　　　　　　　**(PR:A　MPAA:NR)**

EXPENSIVE WOMEN*　　　(1931) 62m WB bw
Dolores Costello (Constance Newton), Warren William (Neil Hartley), Anthony Bushell (Arthur Raymond), Joe Donahue (Bobby Brandon), H.B. Warner (Melville Raymond), Polly Walter (Molly Lane), Allan Lane, Morgan Wallace (Young Men), Mae Madison (Irene), Adele Watson (Martha), William House (George Allison).

Insipid melodrama about Costello going from one man to another, finding the one she wants is already married, getting another one killed by the first in a fit of jealousy, and finally settling on a third. Costello broke a two-year retirement for this one. She needn't have bothered.

d, Hobart Henley; w, Harvey Thew, Raymond Griffith (based on the novel *Passionate Sonata* by Wilson Collison); ph, William Rees; ed, Desmond O'Brien.

Drama　　　　　　　**(PR:C　MPAA:NR)**

EXPERIENCE PREFERRED . . . BUT NOT ESSENTIAL***½
(1983, Brit.) 80m Enigma/Goldwyn c
Elizabeth Edmonds (Annie), Sue Wallace (Mavis), Geraldine Griffith (Doreen), Karen Meagher (Paula), Maggie Wilkinson (Arlene), Ron Bain (Mike), Alun Lewis (Hywel), Robert Blythe (Ivan), Roy Heather (Wally), Peter Doran (Dai), Arwen Holm (Helen), Sion Tudor Owen (Nin), Robert Gwilym (Gareth), Mostyn Evans (Now), Paul Haley (Howard), Margo Jenkins (Mrs. Howard), Jerry Brooke (M.C.).

Very good film about Edmonds finding love with a cook at a small Welsh hotel in 1962. Her relative happiness is contrasted with the desperate search for love of everyone else. Excellent early 1960s period sets, costumes, and music makes this a joy for nostalgia buffs. The film is the second of a series of three from the talented British producers, all of them dealing with youthful romance. Originally produced for British television. Not to be missed.

p, Chris Griffen; d, Peter Duffell; w, June Roberts; ph, Phil Meheux; m, John Scott; ed, John Shirley; art d, Jane Martin; cos, Tudor George.

Drama **Cas.** **(PR:C MPAA:PG)**

EXPERIMENT ALCATRAZ** (1950) 58m Crystal/RKO bw

John Howard *(Dr. Ross Williams)*, Joan Dixon *(Joan McKenna)*, Walter Kingsford *(Dr. Finlay)*, Lynne Carter *(Ethel Ganz)*, Robert Shayne *(Barry Morgan)*, Kim Spalding *(Duke Shaw)*, Sam Scar *(Eddie Ganz)*, Kenneth MacDonald *(Col. Harris)*, Dick Cogan *(Dan Staley)*, Frank Cady *(Max Henry)*, Byron Foulger *(Jim Carlton)*, Ralph Peters *(Bartender)*, Lewis Martin *(Asst. District Attorney)*, Harry Lauter *(Richard)*, Raymond Largay *(Warden Keaton)*.

Howard is a doctor testing a radioactive drug on convicts in return for pardons should they survive. One of the men appears to go nuts and kills another inmate, and the experiment is threatened. Howard can't find any reason for his drug to have had such an effect, so he digs around and discovers that the dead man had a fortune hidden away that the killer, Shayne, wanted. Howard gets himself murdered for his troubles, but his experiment is vindicated. Okay programmer.

p&d, Edward L. Cahn; w, Orville H. Hampton (from a story by George W. George and George F. Slavin); ph, Jackson J. Rose; m, Irving Gertz; ed, Philip Cahn; art d, Boris Leven.

Drama **(PR:A MPAA:NR)**

EXPERIMENT IN TERROR*** (1962) 123m COL bw (AKA: GRIP OF FEAR)

Glenn Ford *(John Ripley)*, Lee Remick *(Kelly Sherwood)*, Stefanie Powers *(Toby)*, Roy Poole *(Brad)*, Ned Glass *(Popcorn)*, Anita Loo *(Lisa)*, Patricia Huston *(Nancy)*, Ross Martin *(Red Lynch)*, Gilbert Green *(Special Agent)*, Clifton James *(Capt. Moreno)*, William Bryant *(Chuck)*, Dick Crockett *(F.B.I. Agent)*, James Lanphier *(Landlord)*, Sidney Miller *(Drunk)*, Sherry O'Neil *(Edna)*, Mari Lynn *(Penny)*, Harvey Evans *(Dave)*, William Sharon *(Raymond Burkhardt)*, Warren Hsieh *(Joey Soong)*, Clarence Lung *(Attorney Yung)*, Frederic Downs *(Welk)*, Fred Coby, Kelly McCormick, Bill Neff, Richard Norris, Kenny Jackson, James Callahan, David Tomack, Ken Wales *(F.B.I. Agents)*, Edward Mallory *(Dick)*, Judee Morton *(Louella)*, Ray Kellogg *(Man at Ballpark)*, Claire Griswold *(Peggy)*, Fay McKenzie *(Hospital Superintendent)*, Audrey Swanson *(Nurse)*, Mario Cimino *(Cook)*, Helen Jay *(Waitress)*, Beal Wong *(Pastor)*, Tommy H. Lee *(Chinese Waiter)*, Barbara Collentine *(Janie)*, George Moorman *(Radio Man)*, William Remick *(Coroner)*, Bob Carraher *(Police Lieutenant)*, Gil Perkins *(Taxi Driver)*, Mike Foran *(Danny)*, Bob Dempsey *(Helicopter Pilot)*, Mary Ellen Popel *(Secretary)*, Robert Coffey *(Announcer)*, Russ Whiteman *(T.V. Director)*, Karen Norris *(Saleswoman)*, Peggy Patten *(Housekeeper)*, Al Avalon *(Man Who Picked Up Kelly)*.

Ford is a rugged but by-the-book FBI agent called into an extortion case involving Remick. She is a bank teller who has been accosted in her garage by a man shrouded in darkness. In an asthmatic voice he tells her to steal $100,000 from her bank or she and her sister will meet a dire fate. Remick is told by Ford to play along with the culprit while he plants agents in the bank and throughout the neighborhood where Remick and her sister, Powers, live. Through informants and through the extortionist's asthmatic condition, Ford is able to identify Martin. The price of the information is high, as many of the informants are later found murdered by Martin. As the dragnet tightens about him, Martin abducts Powers and holds her as ransom for the $100,000. Remick, following Ford's instructions, takes the money from the bank and meets with the killer at Candlestick Park during a baseball game. Just as he is about to flee a bevy of planted FBI agents jump up from their seats, and shoot it out with him, killing him. Powers is found safe and Remick looks upon Ford as more than just her protector at film's end. Filmed on location in San Francisco, EXPERIMENT IN TERROR offers rich lensing of cable cars, magnificent bridges, and the inherent attractions of one of the most beautiful cities in the world, the site for many another crime film (THE LINEUP, DIRTY HARRY, HELL ON FRISCO BAY). Enhancing the sinister sounds of Martin's rasping deliveries is an autoharp composer Mancini worked into his chilling score, one that echoes the psychopath's eerie voice. Martin's physical oddity makes him all the more menacing, a *film noir* device that worked with Alan Ladd in THIS GUN FOR HIRE (a deformed wrist, a hairlip in the Grahame Greene novel), Richard Widmark in KISS OF DEATH (a maniacal giggle), Everett Sloane in THE LADY FROM SHANGHAI (a lurching limp), William Talman in THE HITCHHIKER (an eye that never closes). Edwards' direction is effective although he relies too heavily on overhead and boom shots to show his action scenes.

p&d, Blake Edwards; w, Gordon Gordon, Mildred Gordon (based on their novel *Operation Terror*); ph, Philip Lathrop; m, Henry Mancini; ed, Patrick McCormack; art d, Robert Peterson; set d, James M. Crowe; makeup, Ben Lane.

Crime Drama **(PR:C MPAA:NR)**

EXPERIMENT PERILOUS*½** (1944) 90m RKO bw

Hedy Lamarr *(Allida Bedereaux)*, George Brent *(Dr. Huntington Bailey)*, Paul Lukas *(Nick Bedereaux)*, Albert Dekker *(Claghorne)*, Carl Esmond *(John Maitland)*, Olive Blakeney *(Cissie Bedereaux)*, George N. Neise *(Alec Gregory)*, Margaret Wycherly *(Maggie)*, Stephanie Bachelor *(Elaine)*, Mary Servoss *(Miss Wilson)*, Julia Dean *(Deria)*, William Post, Jr. *(D.A. MacDonald)*, Billy Ward *(Alec, age 5)*, Alan Ward *(Shoes)*, Nolan Leary *(Bellhop)*, Larry Wheat *(Caterer)*, Sam McDaniel *(Porter)*, Edward Clark *(Train Steward)*, Joel Friedkin *(Brakeman)*, Broderick O'Farrell *(Frank)*, Jack Deery *(Doorman)*, Almeda Fowler *(Clerk)*, John Elliott *(Telephone Operator)*, Charles McMurphy *(Cop)*, Michael Orr *(Nick, age 3)*, Peggy Miller *(Cissie, age 8)*, Evelyn Falke *(Cissie, age 5)*, Janet Clark *(Deria as a Girl)*, Georges Renavent, Adrienne D'Ambricourt *(Voice Instructors)*, John Mylong *(Nick, Sr.)*, Perc Launders *(Ambulance Man)*, Michael Visaroff *(Ballet Master)*.

Psychiatrist Brent meets and falls in love with Lamarr, who is married to insane philanthropist Lukas. Lamarr lives in constant fear of Lukas and when Brent comes to take her away from him he fills the house with gas and threatens to blow them all up. The men struggle, Lamarr and her young son escape, and Brent escapes just as the house explodes. Just another melodrama as scripted, but in the hands of horror-and-fantasy director Tourneur and with excellent performances by all the principals, a minor classic.

p, Warren Duff, Robert Fellows; d, Jacques Tourneur; w, Duff (based on the novel by Margaret Carpenter); ph, Tony Gaudio; m, Roy Webb; ed, Ralph Dawson; md, C. Bakaleinikoff; art d, Albert S. D'Agostino, Jack Okey; set d, Darrell Silvera, Claude Carpenter; cos, Leah Rhodes, Edward Stevenson; spec eff, Vernon L. Walker.

Drama **(PR:A MPAA:NR)**

EXPERT, THE** (1932) 65m WB bw

Charles "Chic" Sale *(Grandpa Minick, The Expert)*, Dickie Moore *(Dickie)*, Lois Wilson *(Nettie Minick)*, Earle Foxe *(Fred Minick)*, Ralf Harolde *(Crowley)*, Adrienne Dore *(Sadie)*, Walter Catlett *(Al)*, Noel Francis *(Daisy)*, May Boley *(Mrs. Smallbridge)*, Dorothy Wolbert *(Annie)*, Louise Beavers *(Lulu)*, Ben Holmes *(Price)*, William Robyns *(Briggs)*, Charles Evans *(Dietenhofer)*, Clara Blandick *(Mrs. Crackenwald)*, Zita Moulton *(Miss Lippincott)*, Elsa Peterson *(Miss Stack)*.

Old Sale comes to live with his son and makes friends with orphan-next-door Moore. Sale is talented, but he can't hold his ground against a script this hapless. The story line would have been more meaningful to audiences a half-century or so later on, with the aging of the population of the developed countries. The plight of an isolated elderly man caught between the frying pan of his grown children and the fire of the old folks' home—or worse—became a too-familiar one in the 1980s. This film was remade in 1939 with the title NO PLACE TO GO.

d, Archie Mayo; w, Julian Josephson, Maude Howell (based on a stage play by Edna Ferber and George S. Kaufman, and the story "Old Man Minick" by Ferber); ph, Bob Kurrie; ed, Jim Gibbon.

Comedy **(PR:A MPAA:NR)**

EXPERT'S OPINION*½ (1935, Brit.) 71m British and Dominions/PAR British bw

Lucille Lisle *(Marian Steele)*, Leslie Perrins *(Richard Steele)*, Molly Fisher *(Kay Frost)*, Franklyn Bellamy *(Keller)*, Kim Peacock *(Desmond Carter)*, John Kevan *(Jay Frost)*, Lawrence Hanray *(Coroner)*, Lawrence Anderson.

Incoherent thriller has Perrins a ballistics expert who testifies at trials, forced to take the stand when his wife (Lisle) is accused of murder. It turns out that the man she killed was a spy looking for secret plans of Perrins' design for an anti-aircraft gun.

p, Anthony Havelock-Allen; d, Ivar Campell; w, Campbell, Sheila Campbell (based on a story by Guillan Hopper).

Crime **(PR:A MPAA:NR)**

EXPLOSION** (1969, Can.) 96m Meridian/AIP c (AKA: THE BLAST)

Don Stroud *(Richie Kovacs)*, Gordon Thomson *(Alan Evans)*, Michele Chicoine *(Doris Randolph)*, Cec Linder *(Mr. Evans)*, Robin Ward *(Peter Evans)*, Ted Stidder *(Timms)*, Murray Matheson *(Owner of Jaguar)*, Ann Sears *(Jaguar Owner's Wife)*, Sherry Mitchell *(Susan)*, Olga Kaya *(Valerie)*, Harry Saunders *(Inspector Kelso)*, Richard Conte *(Dr. Philip Neal)*.

Thomson is an American draft dodger living in Canada who goes crazy when he hears his brother has been killed in Vietnam. He teams with Stroud to steal a car and kills a couple of people before the cops get him. Tries to be profound, but it comes off contrived.

p, Julian Roffman; d, Jules Bricken; w, Bricken, Alene Bricken (from a story by Robert Hartford-Davies and J. Bricken); ph, Joseph Brun; m, Sol Kaplan; ed, Tony Lower; art d, Bruce Grimes; cos, Ilse Richter; makeup, Phyllis Newman.

Drama **Cas.** **(PR:O MPAA:NR)**

EXPLOSIVE GENERATION, THE** (1961) 89m Vega/UA bw

William Shatner *(Peter Gifford)*, Lee Kinsolving *(Dan Carlyle)*, Patty McCormack *(Janet Sommers)*, Billy Gray *(Bobby Herman, Jr.)*, Virginia Field *(Mrs. Sommers)*, Phillip Terry *(Mr. Carlyle)*, Hanna Landy *(Mrs. Carlyle)*, Edwart Platt *(Mr. Morton)*, Suzi Carnell *(Marge Ryker)*, Jocelyn Brando *(Mrs. Ryker)*, Beau Bridges *(Mark)*, Peter Virgo, Jr. *(George)*, Bruce Kerner *(Stephen)*, Peter Virgo, Sr. *(Dean of Men)*, Mark Lowell *(Printing Teacher)*, Judee Morton *(Charlene)*, Jan Norris *(Terry)*, Stafford Repp *(Police Captain)*, Vito Scotti *(Custodian)*, Anne Dore *(The Girl)*, Michael Gibbs *(Substitute Teacher)*, Ronnie Kelman, Lee Harris, Jim D'Arcy *(Basketball Players)*, Steve Dunne *(Bobby Herman, Sr.)*, Arch Johnson *(Mr. Sommers)*.

Shatner is a high-school teacher fired for teaching sex education. The students protest with a silence strike that climaxes in an eerily silent basketball game. All works out well when the parents of one student learn that she did not sleep with her boy friend. Shatner gets his job back shortly thereafter. Shows its budget limitations at every turn, but interesting nonetheless.

p, Stanley Colbert; d, Buzz Kulik; w, Joseph Landon; ph, Floyd Crosby; m, Hal Borne; ed, Melvin Shapiro; cos, Alexis Davidoff; makeup, Ted Coodley.

Drama **(PR:C MPAA:NR)**

EXPOSED*½ (1932) 65m Eagle/IN bw

William Collier, Jr., Barbara Kent, Raymond Hatton, Bobby "Wheezer" Hutchins, Walter McGrail, Jack Quinn, Roy Stewart, Billy Engels.

Muddled, low-budget gangster stuff with Collier a young doctor forced to work for the mob, but stooling to the cops. To add interest there's a baby, a pretty nurse, and a car chase. Unfortunately, none of these can add anything to this loser.

d, Albert Herman; w, Mauri Grashin.

Crime **(PR:A MPAA:NR)**

EXPOSED* (1938) 63m UNIV bw

Glenda Farrell *(Click Stewart)*, Otto Kruger *(William Reardon)*, Herbert Mundin *(Skippy)*, David Oliver *(Tim)*, Lorraine Krueger *(Betty Clarke)*, Charles D. Brown *(Steve Conway)*, Bernard Nedell *(Mike Romero)*, Richard Lane *(Tony Mitchell)*, Eddie Anderson *(William)*, Maurice Cass *(Aloysius J. Meggs)*, John Kelley *(Boxer)*, John Butler *(Wendell)*, James Blaine *(Joe)*, Dorothy Arnold, Frances Robinson, Irving Bacon, Al St. John, Matt McHugh.

Kruger is an ex-District Attorney turned skid-row bum because he sent an innocent man to the chair. He is uncovered in a flophouse by news photographer Farrell, who helps him sober up, make restitution to the daughter of the innocent man, and break up a ring of racketeers. Substandard even for a B picture.

p, Max H. Golden; d, Harold Schuster; w, Charles Kaufman, Franklin Coen (from *Candid Camera Girl* by George Bilson); ph, Stanley Cortez; ed, Maurice Wright.

Drama **(PR:A MPAA:NR)**

EXPOSED** (1947) 59m REP bw

Adele Mara *(Belinda Prentice)*, Robert Scott *(William Foreman, III)*, Adrian Booth *(Judith)*, Robert Armstrong *(Inspector Prentice)*, William Haade *(Iggy Broty)*, Bob Steele *(Chicago)*, Harry Shannon *(Severance)*, Charles Evans *(Jonathan Lowell)*, Joyce Compton *(Emmy)*, Russell Hicks *(Col. Bentry)*, Paul E. Burns *(Prof. Ordson)*, Colin Campbell *(Dr. Richard)*, Edward Gargan *(Big Mac)*, Mary Gordon *(Miss Keets)*, Patricia Knox *(Waitress)*.

Mara is a lady private eye trying to finger the killer of her client. Nothing to remember, and no big names, but nicely done.

p, William J. O'Sullivan; d, George Blair; w, Royal K. Cole, Charles Moran (based on a story by Moran); ph, William Bradford; m, Ernest Gold; ed, Irving M. Schoenberg; art d, James Sullivan.

Crime Drama **(PR:A MPAA:NR)**

EXPOSED*** (1983) 100m MGM/UA c

Nastassia Kinski *(Elizabeth Carlson)*, Rudolf Nureyev *(Daniel Jelline)*, Harvey Keitel *(Rivas)*, Ian McShane *(Greg Miller)*, Bibi Andersson *(Margaret)*, Ron Randell *(Curt)*, Pierre Clementi *(Vic)*, Dov Gottesfeld *(Marcel)*, James Russo *(Nick)*, Marion Varella *(Bridgit)*, Murray Moston *(Hotel Manager)*, Stephanie Farrow *(Waitress)*, Daisy Carrington *(Daisy)*, Carl Lee *(Duke)*, Mariana Magnasco *(Maya)*, Miguel Pinero, Jeff Silverman, Ray Sawhill, Michel Delahaye *(Men in Street)*, Brian Hamill *(Store Manager)*, Tony Sirico, Jr. *(Thief)*, Geoffrey Carey, Dennis McGovern *(Waiters)*, Patrick Baker *(Skip)*, Emil Tchakarov *(Conductor)*, Madeleine De Blonay *(Katia)*, Jacques Preyer, Vincent Lascoumes *(French Cabbies)*, Jurgen Straub *(Hans)*, Irving Buchman *(Makeup Man)*, Anthony Cortino *(Hairdresser)*, Marcela Moore *(Hostess)*, James Toback *(Leo Boscovitch)*.

Kinski leaves her Wisconsin home and travels to the big city to become a concert pianist or, failing that, a top model. Discovered as a waitress, she becomes a top model and before long falls in love with Nureyev, a concert violinist and zealous anti-terrorist. Kinski follows him to Paris and gets inveigled into a plot to bring international terrorist Keitel to the surface. Like a piece of expensive candy, if you chew on this film too long, it disintegrates. Look at it as attractive people doing odd and interesting things in strange and wonderful places.

p,d&w, James Toback; ph, Henri Decae (Metrocolor); m, Georges Delerue; ed, Robert Lawrence, Annie Charvein; prod d, Brian Eatwell; art d, Robert Luchaire; set d, John Godfrey, Carlos Conti; cos, Aude Bronson-Howard.

Drama **Cas.** **(PR:O MPAA:R)**

EXPRESSO BONGO*½ (1959, Brit.) 111m CD bw

Laurence Harvey *(Johnny Jackson)*, Sylvia Syms *(Maisie King)*, Yolande Donlan *(Dixie Collins)*, Cliff Richard *(Bongo Herbert)*, Meier Tzelniker *(Mayer)*, Ambrosine Philpotts *(Lady Rosemary)*, Eric Pohlmann *(Leon)*, Gilbert Harding *(Himself)*, Hermione Baddeley *(Penelope)*, Reginald Beckwith *(Rev. Tobias Craven)*, Wilfrid Lawson *(Mr. Rudge)*, Martin Miller *(Kakky)*, Avis Bunnage *(Mrs. Rudge)*, Barry Lowe *(Beast Burns)*, Kenneth Griffith *(Charlie)*, Susan Hampshire *(Cynthia)*, Peter Myers *(Her Boy Friend)*, Susan Burnet *(Edna Rudge)*, Lisa Peake *(Chinese Rose)*, Patricia Lewis *(Woman Columnist)*, Wolf Mankowitz *(Sandwich Man)*, Norma Parnell, Roy Everson, Copeland Lawrence, Katherine Keeton, Christine Phillips, Sylvia Steele, Paula Barry, Rita Burke, Maureen O'Connor, Patty Dalton, Pamela Morris, Esma Cannon.

Cliff Richard's Top of the Pops career got its start with this musical about life on the low side in London's Soho area, with its stripper clubs and coin-op emporiums. He is discovered playing at the Tom Tom Club by sleazy promoter Harvey and turned into a teen idol. He remains a good boy, though, singing religious songs to his mother and eventually breaking his contract with Harvey. Skillfully done, but Richard is insufferably nice. The fast-talking Harvey does a terrific job as the upwardly striving would-be impresario, reprising—in a scuzzy manner—the characterization that brought him such success in ROOM AT THE TOP a year earlier. Songs include "Nausea," "Shrine On the Second Floor," and "I've Never Had It So Good."

p, John Pennington, Val Guest; d, Guest; w, Wolf Mankowitz (based on a play by Mankowitz and Julian More); ph, John Wilcox (Dyaliscope); art d, Tony Masters; cos, Beatrice Dawson; m/l, Julian More, Monty Norman, David Henneker, Robert Farnon, Guest, Norrie Paramor, Paddy Roberts, Bunny Lewis; ch, Kenneth MacMillan.

Musical **(PR:C MPAA:NR)**

EXTERMINATING ANGEL, THE**** (1967, Mex.) 91m Uninci-S.A. Films 59/Altura bw (EL ANGEL EXTERMINADOR)

Silvia Pinal *(Letitia, the Walkyrie)*, Jacqueline Andere *(Senora Alicia Roc)*, Jose Baviera *(Leandro)*, Augusto Benedico *(Doctor)*, Luis Beristain *(Christian)*, Antonio Bravo *(Russell)*, Claudio Brook *(Majordomo)*, Cesar Del Campo *(Colonel)*, Lucy Gallardo *(Lucia)*, Rosa Elena Durgel *(Silvia)*, Enrico Garcia Alvarez *(Senor Roc)*, Ofelia Guilmain *(Juana Avila)*, Nadia Haro Oliva *(Ana Maynar)*, Javier Loya *(Francisco Avila)*, Angel Merino *(Lucas)*, Javier Masse *(Eduardo)*, Ofelia Montesco *(Beatriz)*, Patricia Moran *(Rita)*, Patricia De Morelos *(Blanca)*, Bertha Moss *(Leonora)*, Enrique Rambal *(Nobile)*, Tito Junco *(Raul)*, Pancho Cordova, Luis Lomeli, Guillermo Alvarez Bianchi, Elodia Hernandez, Eric del Castillo, Chel Lopez, David Hayyad Cohen, Florencio Castello.

A skillfully pointed blitzkrieg on the bourgeois from the master of iconoclastic assault, Luis Bunuel. An allegory about the savage interiors of a group of upper-class dinner guests who discover that they cannot leave the room they are in. Days and days pass, their well-mannered facades torn down by the animalistic qualities that they harbor inside themselves. One guest (Bravo) dies and is irreverently stuffed into a cupboard; a pair of lovers (Masse, Montesco) commit suicide; a believer in witchcraft (Oliva) hallucinates and brings forth demons; an incestuous brother and sister (Loya, Guilmain) steal morphine from a cancer-ridden guest. They even contemplate cannibalism—a fine way for the rich to act. When they finally do get out of the room they head for a nearby cathedral. Again they are trapped, this time for what may be an eternity. The theme of entrapment in a Hell of our own making—one fashioned largely of social conventions and traditions—is a familiar one in literature (Jean-Paul Sartre's *No Exit*, the *Don Juan in Hell* sequence from George Bernard Shaw's *Man and Superman*, for example), but it has never been more successfully rendered in visual terms. Bunuel's subjective, surreal imagery had not been so outspoken since L'AGE D'OR 37 years previously. Bunuel, like no other director, has continually exploded in the faces of the bourgeois with the swiftest of blows, and in THE EXTERMINATING ANGEL he is in top form. His elegant kicks in the crotch to the upper-crust have not lost their potency from his first short UN CHIEN ANDALOU (1929) to his Academy Award-winning DISCREET CHARM OF THE BOURGEOISIE (1972).

p, Gustavo Alatriste; d, Luis Bunuel; w, Bunuel, Luis Alcoriza (based on the play *Los naufragos de la Calle de la Providentia* by Jose Bergamin); ph, Gabriel Figueroa; m, Alessandro Scarlatti, Pietro Domenico Paradisi, traditional Gregorian chants of the *Te Deum*; ed, Carlos Savage; md, Raul Lavista; art d, Jesus Bracho; cos, Georgette Somohano; spec eff, Juan Munoz Ravelo; makeup, Armando Meyer.

Satire/Allegory **Cas.** **(PR:O MPAA:NR)**

EXTERMINATOR, THE zero (1980) 101m Interstar/AE c

Christopher George *(Det. James Dalton)*, Samantha Eggar *(Dr. Megan Stewart)*, Robert Ginty *(John Eastland)*, Steve James *(Michael Jefferson)*, Tony Di Benedetto *(Chicken Pimp)*, Dick Boccelli *(Gino)*, Patrick Farrelly *(CIA Agent)*, Michele Harrell *(Maria)*, David Lipman *(State Senator)*, Cindy Wilks *(Candy)*, Dennis Boutsikaris *(Frankie)*.

Ginty is a demented Vietnam veteran who arranges gruesome deaths for street criminals. George is the cop out to catch him. Both wind up murdered by the CIA. Perhaps the most wretched genre of all was the brief spate of vigilante-justice movies in the late 1970s. This is certainly one of the worst offerings. Take-off of DEATH WISH. A film to avoid.

p, Mark Buntzman; d&w, James Glickenhaus; ph, Robert M. Baldwin; m, Joe Renzetti; ed, Corky O'Hare; spec eff, Tom Brumberger.

Crime Drama **Cas.** **(PR:O MPAA:R)**

EXTERMINATORS, THE* (1965 Fr.) 95m C.F.F. c (COPLAN FX 18 CASSE TOUT; AKA: FX-SUPERSPY)

Richard Wyler *(Coplan)*, Gil Delamere, Jany Clair, Valeria Ciangotini, Robert Manuel, Maria Rosa Rodriguez, Jacques Dacqmine, Robert Favart.

Wyler is a secret agent on a mission to learn what happened to a pair of top German nuclear physicists who vanished. Aided by a pair of Israeli agents, he uncovers a secret organization building an Intercontinental Ballistic Missile targeted at New York City in a plot to provoke WW III. Gallic spy stuff with little to recommend it.

p, Jean Maumy; d, Ricardo Freda; w, Claude Maroel Richard (based on the novel *Stop Coplan* by Paul Kenny); ph, Henri Persin; m, Michel Magne; ed, Reny Lichtig; art d, Jacques Mawart.

Spy Drama **(PR:A-C MPAA:NR)**

EXTORTION* (1938) 57m COL bw

Scott Colton *(Larry Campbell)*, Mary Russell *(Betty Tisdelle)*, Thurston Hall *(Prof. Tisdelle)*, Arthur Loft *(Inspector Corrigan)*, Gene Morgan *(Flashlight)*, Frank C. Wilson *(Craig Banning)*, Ann Doran *(Margie Blake)*, J. Farrell MacDonald *(Coach Pearson)*, George Offerman, Jr. *(Soupy Pettit)*, Nick Lukats *(Roy Jennings)*, Roland Got *(Kong Lee)*, Albert Van Dekker *(Jeffrey Thompson)*, Ruth Hilliard *(Babs)*.

Fourth-rate campus whodunit concerns the murder of an unpopular proctor (Van Dekker). Physics professor Hall is suspected, but school paper editor Colton figures out who really did it. A forgotten film today, and deservedly so.

d, Lambert Hillyer; w, Earl Felton; ph, Benjamin Kline; ed, Gene Havlick.

Mystery/Comedy **(PR:A MPAA:NR)**

EXTRA DAY, THE*½ (1956, Brit.) 83m BL c

Richard Basehart *(Joe Blake)*, Simone Simon *(Michele Blanchard)*, George Baker *(Steven Marlow)*, Josephine Griffin *(Toni Howard)*, Colin Gordon *(Sir George Howard)*, Laurence Naismith *(Kurt Vorn)*, Charles Victor *(Bert)*, Sidney James *(Barney West)*, Joan Hickson *(Mrs. West)*, David Hannaford *(Buster West)*, Olga

Lindo *(Mrs. Bliss)*, Philip Ray *(Mr. Bliss)*, Jill Bennett *(Susan)*, John Humphrey *(Guy)*, Dennis Lotis *(Ronnie Baker)*, Meier Tzelniker *(Lou Skeat)*, Beryl Reid *(Beryl)*, Shani Wallis *(Shirley)*, Bryan Forbes *(Harry)*, Doreen Dawn *(Beauty Queen)*, Eddie Byrne *(Robin)*, Patrick Cargill, Peter Coke, Tommy Clegg, Hugh Dempster, Gerald Harper, Frank Williams, Elizabeth Wright, Jessie Evans.

Basehart is an assistant director sent out to find five extras needed for retakes of some lost scenes from a film starring Simon. All of the five have their own little story to tell; the whole affair grows tedious very quickly, despite its clever in-industry gimmick.

p, E.M. Smedley-Aston; d&w, William Fairchild; ph, Arthur Grant (Eastmancolor); m, Philip Green; ed, Bernard Gribble.

Drama **(PR:A MPAA:NR)**

EXTRAORDINARY SEAMAN, THE zero (1969) 79m MGM c

David Niven *(Lt. Comdr. Finchhaven)*, Faye Dunaway *(Jennifer Winslow)*, Alan Alda *(Lt. [JG] Morton Krim)*, Mickey Rooney *(Cook [3C] W.W.J. Oglethorpe)*, Jack Carter *(Gunner's Mate Orville Toole)*, Juano Hernandez *(Ali Shar)*, Manu Tupou *(Seaman [1C] Lightfoot Star)*, Barry Kelly *(Adm. Barnwell)*, Leonard O. Smith, Richard Guizon, John Cochran *(Dyaks)*, Jerry Fujikawa *(Adm. Shimagoshi)*, NEWSREEL FOOTAGE: Bess Truman, Dorothy Lamour, Erroll Flynn, Winston Churchill, Adolf Hitler, Joseph Stalin, Douglas MacArthur.

Dull wartime comedy has Alda, Rooney, Carter, and Tupou washed up out of the ocean during WW II to find a British gunboat commanded by Niven. After another half hour of running time, we find out that Niven is actually a ghost who drowned 30 years earlier in a drunken stupor (shades of THE FLYING DUTCHMAN). Now he wanders the seas trying to redeem himself. MGM tried to pad this one by adding about 10 minutes of newsreel footage and titles lifted from Winston Churchill's memoirs (i.e., *Their Finest Hours, The Hinge of Fate,* etc.). Such a dog that the studio withheld it almost two years before they slipped it into circulation. Public response was so bad the film was quickly withdrawn.

p, Edward Lewis, John H. Cushingham; d, John Frankenheimer; w, Philip Rock, Hal Dresner (based on a story by Rock); ph, Lionel Lindon (Panavision, Metrocolor); m. Maurice Jarre; ed, Fredric Steinkamp; art d, George W. Davis, Edward Carfagno; set d, Henry Milton Rice, Henry Grace, Hugh Hunt; cos, Frank Roberts; spec eff, J. McMillan Johnson; makeup, William Tuttle, Lewis Sweeney.

Comedy **(PR:A MPAA:G)**

EXTRAVAGANCE* (1930) 60m TIF bw

Owen Moore *(Jim Hamilton)*, June Collyer *(Alice Kendall)*, Lloyd Hughes *(Fred Garlan)*, Dorothy Christy *(Esther Hamilton)*, Jameson Thomas *(Morrell)*, Nella Walker *(Mrs. Kendall)*, Robert Agnew *(Billy)*, Gwen Lee *(Sally)*, Martha Mattox, Arthur Hoyt *(Guests)*, Addie McPhail, Joan Standing, Lawrence Baskcomb, Davis Hawthorne.

Thomas in his first American role is the amorous British cad who almost breaks up the happy marriage of Hughes and Collyer because of a misunderstanding over Collyer's extravagant purchase of a sable coat. The similar experience revealed by the older wife, Christy, results in her husband's (Moore) suicide. A well-written and well-directed piece.

d, Phil Rosen; w, Adele Buffington, Frances Hyland, Rosen (based on a story by A. P. Younger); ph, Max Dupont; ed, Charles K. Harris.

Drama **(PR:A MPAA:NR)**

EYE CREATURES, THE zero (1965) 80m AIP-TV c

John Ashley, Cynthia Hull, Warren Hammack, Chet David.

An alien attempt to conquer the Earth is foiled by teen-ager Ashley and his girl friend. This low-budget feature was shot in a few days and is missing such basic items as establishing shots. What isn't confusing is merely tiresome.

p&d, Larry Buchanan; w, (based [uncredited] on the book *The Cosmic Frame* by Paul W. Fairman); ph, Ralph K. Johnson.

Science Fiction **(PR:A-C MPAA:NR)**

EYE FOR AN EYE, AN½** (1966) 92m Circle/EM c

Robert Lansing *(Talion)*, Pat Wayne *(Benny)*, Slim Pickens *(Ike Slant)*, Gloria Talbott *(Bri Quince)*, Paul Fix *(Quince)*, Strother Martin *(Trumbull)*, Henry Wills *(Charles)*, Jerry Gatlin *(Jonas)*, Rance Howard *(Harry)*, Clint Howard *(Jo-Hi)*.

Decent western has Lansing teaming up with bounty hunter Wayne to catch Pickens and his gang, responsible for the deaths of his wife and child. In a gunfight Lansing is wounded in his gun hand, Wayne is creased in the skull and blinded, and Pickens gets away. Lansing agrees to be the eyes for Wayne's gun, and together they set out again after Pickens. A second gunfight follows, leaving Wayne and Pickens dead, and Lansing to ride off into the sunset. *Spaghetti Americani,* a Sergio Leone clone right down to the whistled theme behind the titles, but well directed and photographed.

p, Carroll Case; d, Michael Moore; w, Bing Russell, Sumner Williams; ph, Lucien Ballard (Pathecolor); m, Raoul Kraushaar; ed, William Austin; art d, Al Roelofs; set d, Chuck Pierce; cos, Tony Scarano, Aida Swenson.

Western **(PR:C MPAA:NR)**

EYE FOR AN EYE, AN*½ (1981) 106m Adams Apple-Wescom Barber International/AE c

Chuck Norris *(Sean Kane)*, Christopher Lee *(Morgan Canfield)*, Richard Roundtree *(Capt. Stevens)*, Matt Clark *(Tom McCoy)*, Mako *(James Chan)*, Maggie Cooper *(Heather Sullivan)*, Rosalind Chao *(Linda Chan)*, Toru Tanaka *(Giant)*, Stuart Pankin *(Nicky La Belle)*, Terry Kiser *(Davie Pierce)*, Mel Novak *(Montoya)*, Richard Prieto *(Stark)*, Sam Hiona *(Ambler)*, Dorothy Dells *(Cab Driver)*, Dov Gottesfeld *(Doctor)*, J.E. Freeman *(Tow Truck Dude)*, Joe Bellan *(Truck Driver)*, Daniel Forest *(VW Driver)*, Joseph DeNicola *(Parlor Manager)*, Jeff Bannister *(Man on Walkie-Talkie)*; Robert Behling *(Coroner)*, Edsel Fung *(Proprietor)*, Harry Wong *(Shop Owner)*, Nancy Fish, Gary T. New, Joe Lerer, Michael Christy *(Reporters)*, Earl Nichols *(Officer Ed)*, Don Pike *(Watcher)*, Tim Culbertson *(Policeman)*.

Martial arts mediocrity has Norris quitting the San Francisco police in order to avenge the murder of his partner by an Oriental drug syndicate. If you've seen one of these, you've seen them all. Christopher Lee looks quite uncomfortable.

p, Frank Capra, Jr.; d, Steve Carver,; w, William Gray, James Bruner (story by Bruner); ph, Roger Shearman (CFI Color); m, William Goldstein; ed, Anthony Redman; prod d, Sandy Veneziano; art d, Vance Lorenzini.

Martial Arts **Cas.** **(PR:O MPAA:R)**

EYE OF THE CAT*½ (1969) 102m Joseph H. Schenck Enterprises/UNIV c

Michael Sarrazin *(Wylie)*, Gayle Hunnicutt *(Kassia)*, Eleanor Parker *(Aunt Danny)*, Tim Henry *(Luke)*, Laurence Naismith *(Dr. Mills)*, Jeniffer Leak *(Poor Dear)*, Linden Chiles *(Bendetto)*, Mark Herron *(Bellemondo)*, Annabelle Garth *(Socialite)*, Tullia *(The Cat)*.

Cosmetologist Hunnicutt conspires with heir Sarrazin to murder rich aunt Parker. Parker plans to leave her fortune to the slew of cats she keeps around the house, and before Sarrazin can set himself up in the household he has to convince her to get rid of them all (he has a terrible aversion to them since one tried to suck out his breath when he was a baby). Later, when the pair try to carry out their scheme, the cats reappear to scare the bejeezus out of Sarrazin. Goody-goody nephew Henry is then revealed to have been in collusion with the avaricious Hunnicutt all along, the two of them having planned to kill Sarrazin after he kills Parker, then share the fortune. The plot is full of holes you could drive a truck through, and the whole thing doesn't live up to its terrific opening credit sequence.

p, Bernard Schwartz, Philip Hazelton; d, David Lowell Rich; w, Joseph Stefano; ph, Russell Metty, Ellsworth Fredricks (Technicolor); m, Lalo Schifrin; ed, J. Terry Williams; art d, Alexander Golitzen, William D. DeCinces; set d, John McCarthy, John Austin; cos, Edith Head; makeup, Bud Westmore; cat trainer, Ray Berwick.

Horror **(PR:C MPAA:M)**

EYE OF THE DEVIL** (1967, Brit.) 89m Filmways/MGM bw (AKA: 13)

Deborah Kerr *(Catherine de Montfaucon)*, David Niven *(Philippe de Montfaucon)*, Donald Pleasence *(Pere Dominic)*, Edward Mulhare *(Jean-Claude Ibert)*, Flora Robson *(Countess Estell)*, Emlyn Williams *(Alain de Montfaucon)*, Sharon Tate *(Odile)*, David Hemmings *(Christian de Caray)*, John Le Mesurier *(Dr. Monnet)*, Suky Appleby *(Antoinette de Montfaucon)*, Donald Bisset *(Rennard)*, Robert Duncan *(Jacques de Montfaucon)*, Michael Miller *(Grandec)*, Pauline Letts.

When the crop fails for the third straight year, wealthy vineyard owner Niven agrees to an ancient ritual wherein his life will be sacrificed to assure a good harvest in the future. Kerr, as his wife, is understandably less than enthusiastic, but by the time she can put a stop to it, it's too late. At picture's end, heir Duncan and local priest Pleasence exchange a knowing glance, suggesting that the youthful marquis has also accepted his family's heritage—and the fate that awaits him. It's all treated very seriously, which may be the major flaw here. In production for years, the movie was set back when Kim Novak was injured and replaced by Kerr, necessitating retakes of a number of scenes. The behind-the-scenes creatives also played musical chairs. Scripting was initially done by Terry Southern who was replaced by the credited writers. Director Thompson's predecessors were Michael Anderson, Sidney J. Furie, and Arthur Hiller.

p, Martin Ransohoff, John Calley; d, J. Lee Thompson; w, Robin Estridge, Dennis Murphy (based on the novel *Day of the Arrow* by Philip Loraine); ph, Erwin Hillier; m, Gary McFarland; ed, Ernest Walter; art d, Elliot Scott; cos, Julie Harris, John Furness.

Horror **(PR:C MPAA:NR)**

EYE OF THE NEEDLE, THE** (1965, Ital./Fr.) 97m MEC Cinematografica-Les Films Agiman/Eldorado bw (LA SMANIA ANDOSSO)

Vittorio Gassman *(Lawyer Mazzaro)*, Annette Stroyberg *(Rosaria)*, Gerard Blain *(Toto)*, Nino Castelnuovo *(Nicola)*, Gino Cervi *(Lawyer D'Angelo)*, Mariangela Giordano *(Carmelina)*, Ernesto Calindri *(Don Salvatore)*, Leopoldo Trieste *(Don Calo)*, Umberto Spadaro *(Don Luigino)*, Ignazio Balzamo *(Don Nene)*, Alfredo Varelli *(Police Brigadier)*, Carla Calo *(Za Santa)*, Rina Franchetti *(Za Rita)*, Enrichetta Medin.

Blain and Castelnuovo are a pair of Sicilian bachelors who seduce—or rape—virgin Stroyberg and get into trouble with shotgun-toting papa Spadaro; and with the local carabinieri. Broad Italian comedy tries to make some points about Sicilian society, but they're too scattered and incoherent to make an impression.

p, Aldo Calamara, Achille Filo Della Torre, Otello Cocchi; d, Marcello Andrei; w, Giuseppe Mangioni, Alberto Bevilacqua, William Demby, Andrei (based on a story by Giuseppe Berto, Dante Troisi); ph, Riccardo Pallottini; m, Carlo Rustichelli.

Comedy **(PR:C MPAA:NR)**

EYE OF THE NEEDLE*½** (1981) 111m Kings Road/UA c

Donald Sutherland *(Faber)*, Stephen MacKenna *(Lieutenant)*, Philip Martin Brown *(Billy Parkin)*, Kate Nelligan *(Lucy)*, Christopher Cazenove *(David)*, George Belbin *(Lucy's Father)*, Faith Brook *(Lucy's Mother)*, Barbara Graley *(Constable)*, Arthur Lovegrove *(Peterson)*, Colin Rix *(Oliphant)*, Barbara Ewing *(Mrs. Garden)*, Chris Jenkinson *(German SS Officer)*, William Merrow *(German Radio Operator)*, Patrick Connor *(Insp. Harris)*, David Hayman *(Canter)*, Ian Bannen *(Godliman)*, Rupert Frazer *(Muller)*, Jonathan Nicholas Haley *(Joe)*, Alex McCrindle *(Tom)*, John Bennett *(Kleinmann)*, Alan Surtees *(Col. Terry)*, Bill Fraser *(Mr. Porter)*, Sam Kydd, John Paul, Stephen Phillips, Richard Graydon, Michael Mellinger, Don

Fellows, Stuart Harwood, Rik Mayall, Rory Edwards, Ellis Dale, Michael Joseph, John Rees, John Grieve, Bruce White, David Ashton, Bill Nighy.

As a ruthless, dedicated Nazi spy there is nothing to recommend Sutherland to humanity in this espionage thriller, yet he turns in a masterful performance while knifing those who get in his way. Sutherland has been planted as a low-level worker in the British railway system in 1940. When his landlady discovers him working with a short-wave radio, he quietly walks up to her and stabs her to death, then departs. At the same time newlyweds Nelligan and Cazenove are shown being married and racing off to their honeymoon in a sports car only to have a terrible accident from which Cazenove, an RAF commander, is paralyzed from the waist down for life. It is suddenly four years later and the Allies are about to launch the D-Day invasion. Sutherland is by now one of the top Nazi spies in England and his mission is to determine the location of a secret air base. After photographing row after row of dummy planes, he realizes that the fake airfield means the Allies intend to land at Normandy, and that this base is a ruse to make the Germans believe an air armada will spearhead the attack elsewhere. He is discovered by two British home guardsmen whom he coldly murders, then flees, taking his revealing photos with him. Sutherland must rendezvous with a German U-boat off the aptly named Isle of Storms, a remote, isolated dot of craggy land linked to the outside world only through a short-wave radio. En route, on board a train heading north, Sutherland is tracked by CID men led by MacKenna. He knifes Brown and jumps the speeding train, making his way by stolen bicycle and hitchhiking to the northern isles where he steals a small tugboat and reaches the Isle of Storms in a raging blow which wrecks his boat. He is taken in by Nelligan and Cazenove. He makes love to the sex-starved Nelligan who falls in love with him and he later kills Cazenove in a fierce struggle after the ex-Spitfire pilot gets on to him. When Nelligan finds the crumpled body of her husband tossed onto the rocks at water's edge and learns Sutherland is a spy, she flees her home with her child, barricading herself in another remote house which has a short-wave set. She has made up her mind to opt for country instead of love. Sutherland arrives and begins battering down the windows and doors to stop her from contacting British authorities. She stabs him, but he overpowers her and rushes to the radio to contact the German submarine nearby. Nelligan short-circuits the electrical system by jamming her soaking hand into a light socket. Sutherland then tries to flee, running to the shore to get into a rowboat and get out to sea where the sub will pick him up. Nelligan runs after him with an ancient gun, shooting him several times just as he shoves off. He falls into the boat dead, his secret about the Allied invasion dying with him. Beyond Sutherland's riveting performance, the sensuous Nelligan turns in a fine job of acting, as does Cazenove. The script, direction, and lensing are done in the old tradition of spy thrillers out of the 1940s, even including an old score by Rozsa from THE KILLERS. The story pattern and characters smack of THE DAY OF THE JACKEL and a 1939 minor espionage classic, THE SPY IN BLACK but the film remains intriguing and suspense-filled. There are touches of Fritz Lang, Alfred Hitchcock, and Anatole Litvak throughout, but these reminescent tidbits only enhance the overall production.

p, Stephen Friedman; d, Richard Marquand; w, Stanley Mann (based on the novel by Ken Follett); ph, Alan Hume (Technicolor); m, Miklos Rozsa; ed, Sean Barton; prod d, Wilfred Shingleton; art d, Bert Davey, John Hoesli; set d, Hugh Scaife; cos, John Bloomfield.

Spy Drama **Cas.** **(PR:C-O MPAA:R)**

EYE WITNESS** (1950, Brit.) 104m Coronado/WB bw (YOUR WITNESS)

Robert Montgomery *(Adam Heyward)*, Leslie Banks *(Col. Summerfield)*, Felix Aylmer *(Judge)*, Patricia [Cutts] Wayne *(Alex Summerfield)*, Andrew Cruickshank *(Sir Adrian Horth, K.C.)*, Harcourt Williams *(Beamish)*, Jenny Laird *(Mary Baxter)*, Michael Ripper *(Sam Baxter)*, Ann [Susan] Stephens *(Ann "Sandy" Summerfield)*, Wylie Watson *(Widgery)*, James Hayter *(Prouty)*, Noel Howlett *(Martin Foxglove, K.C.)*, John Sharp *(P.C. Hawkins)*, Shelagh Fraser *(Ellen Foster)*, Philip Dale *(Jim Foster)*, Hal Osmond *(Taxi Driver)*, Lyonel Watts *(Vicar)*, Derick Penley *(Clerk of Assize)*, Eric Chitty *(Judge's Clerk)*, Ruth Lee *(Miss Hubert)*, Stanley Baker *(Sgt. Bannoch)*, Richard Wattis.

American lawyer Montgomery goes to England to try to clear an old friend accused of murder (Ripper). He is unable to find the woman with whom Ripper spent the night of the killing, but with the help of a book of poems, he deduces her identity and her courtroom testimony frees Ripper. Routine crime melodrama with another of the American heroes British audiences seem to like.

p, Joan Harrison, David E. Rose; d, Robert Montgomery; w, Ian McClellan Hunter, Hugo Butler, William Douglas Home (based on a story by Butler); ph, Gerald Gibbs; m, Malcolm Arnold; ed, Leto Carruthers; art d, Ralph Brinton.

Crime **(PR:A-C MPAA:NR)**

EYEBALL zero (1978, Ital.) 91m Brenner c (GATTO ROSSI IN UN LABIRINTO DO VETRO)

John Richardson, Martine Brochard, Ines Pelegrin, Silvia Solar, George Rigaud.

Worthless Italian crime drama with a title and advertising campaign that make it seem like a horror film. A mad killer is on the loose, and this one's gimmick (all mad killers in movies have a gimmick) is that he likes to gouge out the eyes of his victims.

p, Joseph Brenner; d, Umberto Lenzi; w, Felix Tusell.

Crime **(PR:O MPAA:R)**

EYES IN THE NIGHT*** (1942) 80m MGM bw

Edward Arnold *(Capt. Duncan Maclain)*, Ann Harding *(Norma Lawry)*, Donna Reed *(Barbara Lawry)*, Allen Jenkins *(Marty)*, John Emery *(Paul Gerente)*, Horace McNally [Stephen NcNally] *(Gabriel Hoffman)*, Katherine Emery *(Cheli Scott)*, Reginald Denny *(Stephen Lawry)*, Rosemary DeCamp *(Vera Hoffman)*, Stanely C. Ridges *(Hansen)*, Barry Nelson *(Busch)*, Steve Geray *(Anderson)*, Erik Rolf *(Boyd)*, Reginald Sheffield *(Victor)*, Ivan Miller *(Herman)*, Milburn Stone *(Pete)*, Mantan Moreland *(Alistair)*, Cliff Danielson *(Boy)*, Frances Rafferty *(Girl)*, Edward Kilroy *(Pilot)*, John Butler *(Driver)*, William Nye *(Hugo)*, Frank Thomas *(Police Lieutenant)*, Marie Windsor *(Actress)*, Cliff Danielson, Fred Walburn, Robert Winkler, Walter Tetley *(Boys)*, Friday the Dog.

A B-thriller with a standard story line, this film nonetheless features a novel gimmick: Its hero, Arnold, plays a blind, middle-aged private detective led by a seeing-eye dog. Arnold is sought out by an old friend, Harding, whose young stepdaughter (Reed) is involved with an older self-centered actor (Emery). There is no love lost between Harding and Reed, partly due to the fact Emery and Harding were, at one time, lovers. When Reed later discovers the actor murdered in his apartment—and Harding standing nearby—she automatically holds her stepmother responsible for the crime. A subplot involving a group of Nazi agents' search for a WW II-related secret formula unfolds as Arnold sets out to solve Emery's murder. Highlights of the film include the return of Harding to the screen after a five-year absence. Reed, who would later become known for her portrayal of a sugary sweet TV mom, is convincing as the willful, precocious stepdaughter.

p, Jack Chertok; d, Fred Zinnemann; w, Guy Trosper, Howard Emmett Rogers (based on the novel *Odor of Violets* by Baynard Kendrick); ph, Robert Planck, Charles Lawton; ed, Ralph Winters; art d, Cedric Gibbons.

Mystery **(PR:A MPAA:NR)**

EYES OF A STRANGER zero (1980) 85m Georgetown/WB c

Lauren Tewes *(Jane)*, Jennifer Jason Leigh *(Tracy)*, John DiSanti *(Stanley Herbert)*, Peter DuPre *(David)*, Gwen Lewis *(Debbie)*, Kitty Lunn *(Annette)*, Timothy Hawkins *(Jeff)*, Ted Richert *(Roger)*, Toni Crabtree *(Mona)*, Bob Small *(Dr. Bob)*, Stella Rivera *(Dancer)*, Dan Fitzgerald *(Bartender)*, Jose Bahamande *(Jimmy)*, Luke Halpin *(Tape Editor)*, Rhonda Flynn *(Woman in Car)*, Tony Federico *(Man in Car)*, Alan Lee *(Photographer)*, Amy Krug *(Young Jane)*, Tabbetha Tracey *(Young Tracy)*, Sarah Hutcheson *(Friend)*, Jilian Lindig *(Mother)*, George DeVries *(Father)*, Melvin Pape *(Doctor)*, Robert Goodman *(Crewman)*, Pat Warren *(Susan)*, Kathy Suergiu *(Karen)*, Madeline Curtis *(Nurse)*, Richard Allen *(News Director)*, Herb Goldstein, Sonia Zomina *(Elderly Couple)*, Michael de Silva *(Technical Director)*, Joe Friedman *(Movie Patron)*.

Tewes is a TV newswoman trying to protect her sister from the homicidal crazy next door (DiSanti). Another slasher movie with a big cast promoting the sexual pervert thing that scares women half to death. TV-created Tewes is as awful as the film.

p, Ronald Zerra; d, Ken Wiederhorn; w, Mark Jackson, Eric L. Bloom; ph, Mini Rojas (Technicolor); m, Richard Einhorn; ed, Rick Shaine; art d, Jessica Sack.

Horror **Cas.** **(PR:O MPAA:R)**

EYES OF ANNIE JONES, THE** (1963, Brit.) 73m Parroch-McCallum-AP/FOX bw

Richard Conte *(David Wheeler)*, Francesca Annis *(Annie Jones)*, Joyce Carey *(Aunt Helen)*, Myrtle Reed *(Carol Wheeler)*, Shay Gorman *(Lucas)*, Victor Brooks *(Police Sergeant Henry)*, Jean Lodge *(Geraldine Wheeler)*, Alan Haines *(Constable Marlowe)*, Mara Purcell *(Orphanage Matron)*, Mark Digman *(Orphanage Director)*, Patricia McCarron *(Miss Crossley, Secretary)*, Max Bacon *(Pubkeeper Hoskins)*, Barbara Leake *(Margaret)*.

When a wealthy Englishwoman is discovered missing, her aunt has a girl, Annis, from the local orphanage, try to find her. Annis is supposed to have extrasensory perception and the woman's brother, Conte, and the local cab driver, Gorman, fear that she will lead the police to the murdered body. Conte prevents the girl from revealing anything, pays off Gorman for murdering his sister, and this is witnessed by the police. Gorman is chased by the police, crashes, and confesses. No bang, just mildly interesting.

p, Jack Parsons, Neil McCallum; d, Reginald LeBorg; w, Louis Vittes (based on a story by Henry Slesar); ph, Peter Hennessy; m, Buxton Orr; ed, Robert Winter; art d, George Provis; set d, Andrew Campbell.

Mystery **(PR:A MPAA:NR)**

EYES OF FATE** (1933, Brit.) 67m Sound City/UNIV bw

Allan Jeayes *(Knocker)*, Valerie Hobson *(Rene)*, Terence de Marney *(Edgar)*, Faith Bennett *(Betty)*, Nellie Bowman *(Mrs. Knocker)*, O.B. Charence *(Mr. Oliver)*, Tony Halfpenny *(George)*, Edwin Ellis *(Jefferson)*, Hugh Rene, John Herring, May Hallatt, Edmund Cozens.

Jeayes is a bookie who is given the next day's newspaper. He uses its racing results to win a fortune at the track, then, unsurprisingly, reads his own obituary. Not entirely successful, but the inspiration for several better films on the same theme.

p, Norman Loudon; d, Ivar Campbell; w, Holloway Horn.

Fantasy **(PR:A MPAA:NR)**

EYES OF HELL (SEE: MASK, THE, 1961, U.S./Can.)

EYES OF LAURA MARS** (1978) 104m COL c

Faye Dunaway *(Laura Mars)*, Tommy Lee Jones *(John Neville)*, Brad Dourif *(Tommy Ludlow)*, Rene Auberjonois *(Donald Phelps)*, Raul Julia *(Michael Reisler)*, Frank Adonis *(Sal Volpe)*, Lisa Taylor *(Michele)*, Darlanne Fluegel *(Lulu)*, Rose Gregorio *(Elaine Cassell)*, Bill Boggs *(Himself)*, Steve Marachuk *(Robert)*, Meg Mundy *(Doris Spenser)*, Marilyn Meyers *(Sheila Weissman)*, Gary Bayer, Mitchell Edmonds *(Reporters)*, Michael Tucker *(Bert)*, Jeff Niki, Toshi Matsuo *(Photo Assistants)*, John E. Allen *(Billy T)*, Dallas Edward Hayes *(Douglas)*, Paula Lawrence *(Aunt Caroline)*, Joey R. Mills *(Makeup Person)*, John Sahag *(Hairdresser)*, Hector Troy *(Cab Driver)*, Anna Anderson, Deborah Beck, Jim Devine, Hanny Friedman, Winnie Hollman, Patty Oja, Donna Palmer, Sterling St. Jacques, Rita Tellone,

Kari Page (Models), John Randolph Jones, Al Joseph, Gerald Kline, Sal Richards, Tom Degidon (Policemen).

Though a polished production, this occult thriller fails to thrill and is long predictable before the end of the first reel. Dunaway is a fashion photographer who suddenly develops the telepathic vision to see her beautiful subjects gruesomely murdered, a slaughterhouse soothsayer who cannot, until the last minute, determine the identity of the killer because he is so close to her emotionally. Ther are so many disjointed scenes in accordance with a roaming, whirring hand-held camera in Dunaway's hands that the haphazard plot is hard to follow. This disorganization passes for suspense and the red herrings are so blatant as to make many scenes laughable. Dunaway and the rest of the cast are allowed to overact, overreact, and generally tear up the on-location sites in the Big Apple. Jones, as the police lieutenant, is miscast and is wholly unbelievable, carrying no authority with a character he obviously misunderstands. All of these miserable failures in a major film are, of course, director Kershner's responsibility.

p, Jon Peters; d, Irvin Kershner; w, John Carpenter, David Zelag Goodman; ph, Victor J. Kemper (Panavision, Metrocolor); m, Arite Kane; ed, Michael Kahn; prod d, Gene Callahan; art d, Robert Gundlach; set d, John Godfrey; cos, Theoni V. Aldredge; stunts, Alex Stevens; m/l, "Prisoner" Karen Lawrence, John DeSautels (sung by Barbra Streisand).

Crime   Cas.   (PR:O   MPAA:R)

EYES OF TEXAS***   (1948) 71m REP c

Roy Rogers (Himself), Lynne Roberts (Fanny Thatcher), Andy Devine (Cookie Bullfincher), Nana Bryant (Hattie Waters), Roy Barcroft (Vic Rabin), Danny Morton (Frank Dennis), Francis Ford (Thaddeus Cameron), Pascale Perry (Pete), Stanley Blystone (Sheriff), Bob Nolan and the Sons of the Pioneers.

Top quality Rogers vehicle has him a U.S. Marshal on the trail of lawyer Bryant, who is after a land package and uses a trained dog pack to do her killing to get it. Grim and fast moving, qualities one doesn't expect from Rogers.

p, Edward J. White; d, William Witney; w, Sloan Nibley; ph, Jack Marta (Trucolor); ed, Tony Martinelli; md, Morton Scott; art d, Frank Hotaling.

Western   (PR:A   MPAA:NR)

EYES OF THE AMARYLLIS, THE*½   (1982) 94m c

Ruth Ford, Martha Byrne, Jonathan Bolt, Guy Boyd, Katharine Houghton.

Tedious drama has Byrne going to visit her grandmother on Nantucket Island and finding the old woman (Ford) waiting for her long-dead husband to send her a sign. A decent premise totally wasted.

d, Frederick King Keller (based on a story by Natalie Babbitt).

Drama   (PR:A-C   MPAA:NR)

EYES OF THE UNDERWORLD*   (1943) 61m UNIV bw

Richard Dix (Richard Bryan), Wendy Barrie (Betty Standing), Lon Chaney, Jr. (Benny), Lloyd Corrigan (J.C. Thomas), Don Porter (Edward Jason), Billy Lee (Mickey Bryan), Marc Lawrence (Gordon Finch), Edward Pawley (Lance Merlin), Joseph Crehan (Kirby), Wade Boteler (Sgt. Clancy), Gaylord Steve Pendleton (Hub Gelsey), Mike Raffetto (District Attorney).

Dix is a police chief trying to keep his own prison record a secret. When he busts a car theft ring, one of the crooks recognizes him from prison and tries to blackmail him. Dix resigns rather than compromise his office, then he goes after the bad guys. Below grade programmer.

p, Ben Pivar; d, Roy William Neill; w, Michael L. Simmons, Arthur Strawn (based on a story by Maxwell Shane); ph, George Robinson; ed, Frank Gross; md, Hans J. Salter; art d, George Otterson.

Crime   (PR:A   MPAA:NR)

EYES OF THE WORLD, THE   (1930) 78m INSP/UA bw

Eulalie Jenson (Mrs. Rutledge), Hugh Huntley (James Rutledge), Myra Hubert (Myra), Florence Roberts (Maid), Una Merkel (Sybil), Nance O'Neil (Myra), John Holland (Aaron King), Fern Andra (Mrs. Taine), Hugh Huntley (James Rutledge), Frederic Burt (Conrad La Grange), Brandon Hurst (Mr. Taine), William Jeffrey (Bryan Oakley).

Crude hillbilly melodrama has Holland an artist who takes to the hills for solitude and inspiration, but falls for the lovely Merkel when he spys her skinny-dipping. Long takes of a typewriter with a barely legible sheet of paper explain the action. King became one of the most consistently talented directors in Hollywood, but he shows little of his later abilities in this awful effort.

p, Sol Lesser; d, Henry King; w, Clarke Silvernail, N. Brewster Morse (based on a novel by Harold Bell Wright); ph, Ray June, John Fulton; ed, Lloyd Nosler.

Drama   (PR:C   MPAA:NR)

EYES THAT KILL*½   (1947, Brit.) 55m Condor/But bw

Robert Berkeley (Martin Bormann), Sandra Dorne (Joan), William Price (Maj. Redway).

Nazi Party secretary Berkeley escapes Hitler's bunker in the closing hours of the Battle of Berlin and makes his way to England, where he sets up an organization called "The Eyes That Kill" and goes about using it to establish the Fourth Reich on the still-smoldering remains of the Third. MI5 man Price makes the world safe for democracy by dispatching the war criminal. Pure conjecture.

p, Harry Goodman; d&w, Richard M. Grey (based on a story by Warwick Charlton); ph, Ray Densham; ed, Cynthia Henry; art d, Edward Steward.

Crime   (PR:A   MPAA:NR)

EYES, THE MOUTH, THE**½   (1982, Ital./Fr.) 100m RAI TV-Triumph/GAU c

Lou Castel (Giovanni), Angela Molina (Vanda), Emanuelle Riva (Mother), Michel Piccol (Nigi), Antonio Piovanelli (Father), Gianpaolo Saccarola (Agostino), Viviana Toni (Adele), Antonio Petrocelli (Doctor).

Castel attends the funeral of his brother and winds up falling in love with the same girl his brother had committed suicide over. Fraught with political overtones and undercurrents, the film survives despite them. Look for the segment where Castel and Molina go to see the movie FIST IN HIS POCKET. Director Bellocchio directed Castel in that movie. (In Italian; English subtitles.)

p, Enzo Porcelli, Enea Ferrario; d, Marco Bellocchio; w, Bellocchio, Vincenzo Cerami; ph, Giuseppe Lanci (Eastmancolor); m, Nicola Piovani; ed, Sergio Nuti.

Drama   Cas.   (PR:O   MPAA:R)

EYES, THE SEA AND A BALL**½   (1968 Jap.) 115m Takarazuka-Kinoshita/Toho c (NATSUKA SHIKI FUE YA TAIKO)

Yosuke Natsuki, Mayumi Ozora, Kumeko Urabe, Kamatari Fujiwara, Yoichiro Takahashi.

Natsuki goes off to a remote island to teach after a friend commits suicide. The children he teaches are not interested in learning; their parents are fishermen who find no use for education. Natsuki introduces volleyball to them and this sparks their interest. The kids win the island tournament and go on to win the national chamionship. Natsuki gets married and breaks his promise to his wife and stays on the island. The kids and parents have now found a reason for the teacher and for education. A Japanese moral tale about pride and how to regain self-esteem.

d&w, Keisuke Kinoshita; ph, Hiroyuki Kusuda (Tohoscope); m, Chuji Kinoshita.

Drama   (PR:A   MPAA:NR)

EYES WITHOUT A FACE
                    (SEE: HORROR CHAMBER OF DR. FAUSTUS, 1960, Fr./Ital.)

EYEWITNESS**   (1956, Brit.) 82m Rank bw

Donald Sinden (Wade), Muriel Pavlow (Lucy Church), Belinda Lee (Penny), Michael Craig (Jay Church), Nigel Stock (Barney), Susan Beaumont (Probationer Nurse), David Knight (Mike), Ada Reeve (Mrs. Hudson), Avice Landone (Night Sister), Richard Wattis (Anesthetist), George Woodbridge (Patrolman), Gillian Harrison (Molly), Nicholas Parsons (House Surgeon), Leslie Dwyer (Henry Cammon), Anna Turner (Mrs. Hays), Anthony Oliver (Podge), John Stuart (Chief Constable), Allan Cuthbertson (Detective Inspector), Harry Taub (Sugdon), Charles Victor (Sergeant), Martin Boddey, Thomas Heathcote, Lionel Jeffries.

Sinden and Stock are a pair of thieves witnessed in the act by Pavlow, who is run over by a bus as she flees the robbery scene. The two try to get into the hospital to kill her, but are continuously foiled. Finally a conscience-stricken Stock kills Sinden to keep him from murdering Pavlow. A nice little thriller by the Sydney and Muriel Box team.

p, Sydney Box; d, Muriel Box; w, Janet Green; ph, Reginald Wyler; m, Bruce Montgomery; ed, Jean Barker.

Crime   (PR:A   MPAA:NR)

EYEWITNESS, 1970   (SEE: SUDDEN TERROR, 1970, Brit.)

EYEWITNESS***   (1981) 108m FOX c (GB: THE JANITOR)

William Hurt (Daryll Deever), Sigourney Weaver (Tony Sokolow), Christopher Plummer (Joseph), James Woods (Aldo), Irene Worth (Mrs. Sokolow), Kenneth McMillan (Mr. Deever), Pamela Reed (Linda), Albert Paulsen (Mr. Sokolow), Sharon Goldman (Israeli Woman), Steven Hill (Lt. Jacobs), Morgan Freeman (Lt. Black), Alice Drummond (Mrs. Deever), Chao-Li Chi (Mr. Long), Keone Young (His Son), Dennis Sakamoto, Henry Yuk (Vietnamese), Mikhail Bogin (Shlomo), Moshe Geffen (Cantor), Jo Davidon (Man at Concert), Bill Mazer (Sports Announcer), John Roland (Anchorman), James Ray Weeks (T.V. Producer), Milton Zane, Richard Murphy, Dow McKeever, Joe Breedlove, Kimmy Wong, Alex Rosa, Mark Burns, Iris Whitney.

Improbable but exciting thriller has Hurt as a janitor who is infatuated with big-time TV newscaster Weaver. He videotapes her nightly news reports and fantasizes about some day meeting her. The opportunity comes in less than romantic circumstances. A murder occurs in Hurt's building and, when Weaver arrives to interview the building's residents, Hurt feeds her a cryptic line about knowing something she should know about the killing. Of course, he knows nothing but he strings her along until bedding her. By that time she has a momentary emotional tie to him and he, by virtue of blabbering about the killing, has placed himself in jeopardy. The real culprits, including the suave and calculating Plummer, go after janitor Hurt. Some wild action takes place, one gruesome scene dealing with an attack on Hurt's dog. The janitor survives but his affair with cultured, rich, snobbish Weaver does not. The whole thing is a dream wish conjured by writer Tesich who was a janitor, and was in love with a New York City TV newscaster lady. He, more than any viewer, must have enjoyed watching this impossible film. Yates, however, takes a wobbly story and makes much more out of it, driving the tale and his characters at a hectic pace and providing some truly unnerving moments. Since this is a 1980s film, the usual gratuitous sex scenes and the mandatory producer's obscenities are present to mar more frames than necessary. Hurt is terrific and Weaver nice to look at but boring to listen to; veteran Plummer grips his scenes with a small but taut performance. A standout character role as Hurt's invalid father is rendered by McMillan. EYEWITNESS is a traditional story of the boy who cried wolf but here the hounds attack his best friend, neurotic Woods, who seldom plays anything other than unbalanced types and vies with Michael Moriarity in the loony-bin department of current offbeat films.

p&d, Peter Yates; w, Steve Tesich; ph, Matthew F. Leonetti (Technicolor); m, Stanley Silverman; ed, Cynthia Scheider; prod d, Philip Rosenberg; cos, Hillary Rosenfeld.

Crime Drama   Cas.   (PR:O   MPAA:R)

F

F.I.S.T.★★★   (1978) 145m UA c

Sylvester Stallone (Johnny Kovak), Rod Steiger (Sen. Madison), Peter Boyle (Max Graham), Melinda Dillon (Anna Zerinkas), David Huffman (Abe Belkin), Tony Lo Bianco (Babe Milano), Kevin Conway (Vince Doyle), Cassie Yates (Molly), Peter Donat (Arthur St. Claire), Henry Wilcoxon (Win Talbot), John Lehne (Gant), Richard Herd (Mike Monahan), Elena Karam (Mrs. Zerinkas), Ken Kercheval (Bernie Marr), Tony Mockus (Tom Higgins), Brian Dennehy (Frank Vasko), James Karen (Andrews).

Stallone likes to depart from his customary muscle image from time to time. Often it fails (RHINESTONE, PARADISE ALLEY) and sometimes he succeeds, as in this interesting but somewhat flawed drama of a Hoffa-like trade union leader. He's a serious and moral young man who is corrupted by the machinations of the labor movement as he rises higher and higher and eventually assumes the mantle of boss in the Federation Of Inter-State Truckers (F.I.S.T., in case you were wondering where the title sprang from). Based on a series of articles by Joe Eszterhas, it details the story of a trucker's rise to heights never dreamed of. The picture begins in the late 1930s and follows Stallone and his best friend, Huffman, as young truckers working for Wilcoxon. They begin organizing the unaffiliated drivers in the company for Herd, the union representative. Management hoodlums arrange for Herd's death, which sends Stallone into bad company. He joins forces with gangster Conway to fight fire with fire. With Conway as a partner, it isn't long before the mobsters move in, led by Tony Lo Bianco. Two secondary stories are taking place which only serve to weigh down the main thrust; Stallone and Dillon fall in love, as do Huffman and Yates. Flash forward to the 1950s and Stallone uses some blackmail to oust international union leader Boyle, who then runs into Steiger, a senator who talks out of both sides of his mouth. In the third act, Stallone is kidnaped and we don't know if he will wind up on top or in a cement block. The core of the story is that Stallone's morality wanes as his prestige and power rise. He has given in to the corrupting forces around him, albeit for a worthwhile reason, but he wonders if that was justified and the question is never answered. At 145 minutes it is far too long. This was the kind of socio-crime drama that ran 80 minutes in the 1930s when Cagney and Robinson were making them. Beautiful photography from Kovacs and an excellent acting job by Stallone. It was not a big hit and may not have even covered the cost of prints and advertising. Stallone has since decided to stick to what "the people want to see" and made some ROCKY sequels as well as two RAMBO films that have grossed millions. Conti, who was a starving composer newly arrived from Rome when Stallone tapped him for the first ROCKY, has since gone on to great success. Born in Rhode Island, he couldn't get any work in the U.S. so he went to Italy and did several small jobs before deciding to make a last try at the big time. Huffman, making his film debut, was superb and would have gone on to a great career were his life not cut short by a stabbing in San Diego where he was appearing in a play in early 1985. Peter Donat does his usual good work but has never gotten the big break he deserves. His CYRANO, for ACT in San Francisco, was broadcast by Public Television and may have been the definitive portrayal, perhaps even better than Ferrer's. Donat played Rostand's hero as a creaky swordsman at the end of his days, living only for the thought of Roxanne (Marsha Mason). If it comes to your area on TV, cancel everything else to watch it.

p&d, Norman Jewison; w, Joe Eszterhas, Sylvester Stallone (based on articles by Eszterhas); ph, Laszlo Kovacs (Technicolor); m, Bill Conti; ed, Graeme Clifford, Tony Gibbs; prod d, Richard MacDonald; art d, Angelo Graham; set d, George Bob Nelson; cos, Anthea Sylbert, Thalia Phillips, Tony Scarano.

Drama   **Cas.**   (PR:A-C MPAA:PG)

F.J. HOLDEN, THE★★½   (1977, Aus.) 105m FJ Films/Greater Union c

Paul Couzens (Kevin), Eva Dickinson (Anne), Carl Stever (Bob), Gary Waddell (Deadlegs), Colin Yarwood (Brian), Graham Rouse (Police Sergeant).

Young lad Couzens, raised in a working class neighborhood, saves enough cash to buy a souped-up car. The script focuses on the gratification he gets from his wheels, as well as the cavalier treatment he gives his girl friend, Dickinson, until she rebels. Picturesque photography of suburban Australia from cameraman Gribble.

p&d, Michael Thornhill; w, Terry Larsen; ph, David Gribble (Panavision); m, Jim Manzie; ed, Max Lemon; art d, Lissa Coote, Monte Fleguth.

Drama   (PR:O MPAA:NR)

F MAN★★   (1936) 63m PAR bw

Jack Haley (Johnny Dime), William Frawley (Hogan), Grace Bradley (Evelyn), Adrienne Marden (Molly Carter), Onslow Stevens (Mr. Shaw), Franklin Parker (Craig), Norman Willis (Jerry), Edward McWade (Mr. Whitney), Robert Middlemass (Cartwright), Walter Johnson (Dougherty), Spencer Charters (Sheriff).

Haley is a bothersome soda jerk (they call them "fountain engineers" today) who persistently pesters federal agents about becoming a "G-man." Tired of his antics, they jokingly make him an "F-man," which leads to more zaniness. The bumbling kid endangers a real agent, but proves his worth when he captures a thug with a water pistol. A fine comic performance from Haley, who later shone as "The Tinman" in THE WIZARD OF OZ.

p, Val Paul; d, Edward F. Cline; w, Eddie Welch, Henry Johnson, Paul Gerard Smith (based on a story by Richard Connell); ph, Leo Tovar; ed, Paul Weatherwax; art d, Hans Dreier, Earl Hedrick.

Comedy   (PR:A MPAA:NR)

F.P. 1★★½   (1933, Brit.) 74m GAU/FOX bw

Leslie Fenton (Capt. Droste), Conrad Veidt (Maj. Ellisen), Jill Esmond (Claire), George Merritt (Lubin), Donald Calthrop (Photographer), Warwick Ward (1st Officer), Dr. Philip Manning (Doctor), Nicholas Hannen (Matthias), William Freshman (Konrad), Alexander Field, Francis L. Sullivan (Sailors), Will Van Allen.

The English version of the story about a "floating platform" in the middle of the Atlantic that becomes a target of unscrupulous men. Filmed at the same time as the German version, in Germany, it never measured up although its cast was much better box office than that of the Berliners.

p, Erich Pommer; d, Karl Hartl; w, Walter Reisch, Kurt Siodmak, Robert Stevenson, Peter Macfarlane (based on a story by Reisch, Siodmak); ph, Fritz Thiery; m, Rowland Leigh, Donovan Parsons.

Drama   (PR:A MPAA:NR)

F.P. 1 DOESN'T ANSWER★★★   (1933, Ger.) 109m UFA bw
(F.P. 1 ANTWORTET NICHT)

Hans Alberg (Ellissen), Sybille Schmitz (Claire), Paul Hartmann (Droste), Peter Lorre (Johnny), Hermann Speelmans (Damsky), Paul Westermeier (Shipbuilder), Arthur Peiser (Man with Toothache), Gustav Puttjer (Man with High Voice), Georg August Koch (1st Officer), Hans Schneider (2nd Officer), Werner Schott (Matthias), Erik Ode (Konrad), Philip Manning (Doctor), Georg John (Machinist), Rudolf Platte (Radio Operator), Friedrich Gnas (Radio Operator at Shipyard).

Hans Albers, Germany's No. 1 matinee idol, carries this fine UFA film. It concerns a pilot's efforts to save an "island"—F.P. 1 (Floating Platform 1) in the mid-Atlantic. He succeeds in getting an airplane hanger built on the island, but learns it is endangered when his fickle lover tells him of a radio message she overheard. He saves F.P. 1 from a traitor and, instead of staying with his one-time gal, he flies off alone. The charming Albers was able to fill theaters all across Germany, and was the major reason for the picture's success. Lorre made four more films in Germany before he exiled himself to France, England, and finally the U.S. when the Nazis came to power. (In German.)

p, Erich Pommer; d, Karl Hartl; w, Walter Reisch (based on a story by Kurt Siodmak); ph, Gunther Rittau, Konstantin Tschet, Otto Baecker; m, Allan Gray; ed, Willy Zeyn, Jr.; art d, Erich Kettelhut; spec eff, Konstantin Tschetwerikow; m/l, Allan Gray.

Drama   (PR:A MPAA:NR)

FABIAN OF THE YARD★★   (1954, Brit.) 75m Beauchamp/Eros bw

Bruce Seton (Superintendent Fabian), Richard Pearson, Gwen Cherrill, Viola Lyel, Diana Beaumont, Howard Connell, Sarah Churchill, Victor Maddern, Margaret Boyd, Malcolm Kindell, Ann Hanslip, Jack Crowley, James Raglan.

This trilogy of Scotland Yard mysteries has supersleuth Seton faced with a truck driver who strangles a hitchhiker, a blackmailed actress, and a group of IRA terrorists who plan to detonate a bomb in Piccadilly. By the finale Seton, once again, proves the efficiency of the Yard.

p, Anthony Beauchamp; d, Beauchamp, Edward Thompson; w, Rex Rienits, John Davenport (based on the book by Robert Fabian); ph, Hilton Craig.

Crime   (PR:A MPAA:NR)

FABIOLA★★½   (1951, Ital.) 96m UA bw

Michele Morgan (Fabiola), Henri Vidal (Rhual), Michel Simon (Fabius), Gino Cervi (Quadratus), Elisa Cegani (Sira), Massimo Gerotti (Sebastian), Louis Salou (Fulvius).

The Emperor Constantine is marching toward Rome to establish it as a Christian city, but those loyal to the old gods are stepping up their persecution of the Christians so there won't be any left when Constantine arrives. The plot, after translating and dubbing, doesn't make much sense, but the film is filled with scenes of Christians being beheaded, burned at the stake, and thrown to the lions. Good performances by Morgan, as the daughter of a senator who supports the Christians, and Henri Vidal, as the gladiator and secret emissary of Constantine whom she loves. The success of this film paved the way for the onslaught of Italian costume epics in the 1950s and 1960s. (Dubbed into English.)

p, Salvo d'Angelo; d, Alessandro Blasetti; w, Blasetti, Marc Connelly, Fred Pressburger, Forrest Izard (based on the novel by Nicholas Wiseman); ph, Osvaldo Civirani; m, Enso Masetti; set d, Veniero Colasanti, Arnaldo Fischin.

Historical Drama   (PR:A-C MPAA:NR)

FABLE, A★★½   (1971) 80m MFR c (AKA: THE SLAVE)

Al Freeman, Jr. (Leader), Hildy Brooks (Wife), James Patterson (Husband).

Director Freeman stars as a black radical who enters the home of his white ex-wife and holds her, her husband, and two daughters at gunpoint. His fine performance culminates when he shoots the husband, and then dynamites the house. An extremely dated picture of racial tensions which still has power.

p, Victor Ramos, Jr.; d, Al Freeman, Jr.; w, LeRoi Jones (based on his play "The Slave"); ph, Bruce Sparks; ed, George Bowers.

Drama   (PR:O MPAA:NR)

FABULOUS ADVENTURES OF MARCO POLO, THE
(SEE: MARCO THE MAGNIFICENT, 1964, Fr./Ital./Yugo./Egypt)

FABULOUS BARON MUNCHAUSEN, THE
(SEE: BARON MUNCHAUSEN, 1962, Czech.)

FABULOUS DORSEYS, THE★★½   (1947) 88m UA bw

Tommy Dorsey (Himself), Jimmy Dorsey (Himself), Janet Blair (Jane Howard), Paul Whiteman (Himself), William Lundigan (Bob Burton), Sara Allgood (Mrs. Dorsey), Arthur Shields (Mr. Dorsey), James Flavin (Gorman), William Bakewell (Eddie), Dave Willock (Foggy), Bobby Warde (Young Tommy), Buz Buckley

(Young Jimmy), Ann Carter (Young Jane), Tom Dugan (Waiter), Jack Searl (Joe), James Taggart (Phil), Hal K. Dawson (Artie), Sherry Sherwood (Herself), Edward Clark (Hotel Clerk), Andrew Tombes (De Witt), Jack Roper (Radio Station Attendant), Charlie Barnet, Henry Busse, Mike Pingatore, Ziggy Elman, Bob Eberly, Helen O'Connell, Art Tatum, Stuart Foster, Ray Bauduc, Tommy Dorsey's Orchestra, Jimmy Dorsey's Orchestra.

A biography of the famed big band brothers Tommy and Jimmy Dorsey which roots itself in the formative role of their father, Shields. Beginning in their home town in Pennsylvania, dad is seen encouraging the young Dorseys to play. Music was the only thing that could carry them out of their grimy steel town. The death of their father brings the two rival brothers together in a charity performance and from there they go on to musical history. Songs: "At Sundown" (Walter Donaldson), "I'll Never Say Never Again" (Harry Woods), "To Me" (Allie Wrubel, Don George), "Green Eyes" (Nilo Menendez, Adolfo Utrera, E. Rivera, Eddie Woods), "Dorsey Concerto" (Leo Shuken, Ray Bauduc), "Art's Blues" (Art Tatum), "Everybody's Doin' It" (Irving Berlin), "Marie" (Berlin), "The Object Of My Affection" (Pinky Tomlin, Coy Poe, Jimmie Grier), "Runnin' Wild" (Joe Grey, Leo Wood, A. Harrington Gibbs), "When You And I Were Young, Maggie" (James Austin Butterfield, George W. Johnson), "Waitin' At The Gate For Katy" (Richard Whiting, Gus Kahn).

p, Charles R. Rogers [John W. Rogers]; d, Alfred E. Green; w, Richard English, Art Arthur, Curtis Kenyon; ph, James Van Trees; ed, George Arthur; md, Louis Forbes; spec eff, Alfred Schmid; ch, Charles Baron.

Musical   **Cas.**   **(PR:A   MPAA:NR)**

FABULOUS SENORITA, THE*½   (1952) 80m REP bw

Estelita (Estelita Rodriguez), Robert Clarke (Jerry Taylor), Nestor Paiva (Jose Rodriguez), Marvin Kaplan (Clifford Van Kunkle), Rita Moreno (Manuela Rodriguez), Leon Belasco (Senor Gonzales), Tito Renaldo (Pedro Sanchez), Tom Powers (Delaney), Emory Parnell (Dean Bradshaw), Olin Howlin (Justice of the Peace), Vito Scotti (Estaban), Martin Garralaga (Police Captain), Nita Del Rey (Felice).

The spicy Estelita is wasted in this feeble tale of the daughter of a Cuban businessman who is fixed to marry a wealthy banker's son. Instead, she falls in love with a romantic college professor whom she hooks by playing the fake roles of identical twins. Poor scripting deals this a fatal blow.

d, R.G. Springsteen; w, Charles E. Roberts, Jack Townley (based on a story by Townley, Charles R. Marion); ph, Jack Marta; m, Stanley Wilson; ed, Tony Martinelli; art d, Al Ybarra.

Comedy   **(PR:A   MPAA:NR)**

FABULOUS SUZANNE, THE**   (1946) 70m REP bw

Barbara Britton (Suzanne), Rudy Vallee (Hendrick Courtney, Jr.), Otto Kruger (Hendrick Courtney, Sr.), Richard Denning (Rex), Bill Henry (William Harris), Veda Ann Borg (Mary), Irene Agay (Ginette), Grady Sutton (Marstenson), Frank Darien (Mr. Tuttle), Harry Tyler (Lawyer), Eddie Fields (Hamburger Man), Al Hammer (The Little Man).

A very plain picture stuck in a state of lethargy. Fabulous Suzanne the waitress (Britton) has uncanny luck with the horses. She simply jabs a pin into a racing form and picks the winning filly. She leaves her quaint job in a pie shop and hauls off to the Big Apple ready to try her hand in the stock market. All Wall Street holds for her are countless men interested in courting her. She begins to long for the sincerity of her home town and makes the trek back. A yawner in which Rudy Vallee croons "A Couple Of Years Ago."

p&d, Steve Sekely; w, Tedwell Chapman, Randall Faye (based on a story by Chapman, William Bowers); ph, Henry Sharpe; m, Arthur Lange; ed, John Hoffman; art d, Frank Sylos; m/l, Bert Reisfeld, Larry Stewart.

Comedy   **(PR:A   MPAA:NR)**

FABULOUS TEXAN, THE**   (1947) 97m REP bw

William Elliott (Jim McWade), John Carroll (John Wesley Barker), Catherine McLeod (Alice Sharp), Albert Dekker (Gibson Hart), Andy Devine (Elihu), Patricia Knight (Josie Allen), Ruth Donnelly (Utopia Mills), Johnny Sands (Bud Clayton), Harry Davenport (Reverend Barker), Robert H. Barrat (Dr. Sharp), Douglass Dumbrille (Luke Roland), Reed Hadley (Jessup), Roy Barcroft (Standifer), Russell Simpson (Wade Clayton), James Brown (Shep Clayton), Jim Davis (Sam Bass), George Beban (Dick Clayton), John Miles (Sim Clayton), Robert Coleman, Tommy Kelly, Frank Ferguson, Glenn Strange, Selmer Jackson, Harry V. Cheshire, John Hamilton, Harry Woods, Karl Hackett, Ed Cassidy, Pierre Watkin, Tristram Coffin, Stanley Andrews, Olin Howlin, Kenneth MacDonald, Edythe Elliott, Crane Whitley, Jack Ingram, Ted Mapes, Pierce Lyden, Al Ferguson, Ethan Laidlaw, Franklyn Farnum, Ray Teal.

An overblown western about the adventures of two Confederate officers, Elliott and Carroll, who make their way back to their Texas homes. What they find is the Lone Star state crawling with lecherous carpetbaggers and corrupt officials. Carroll is forced into the hills after avenging his father's murder—killing a town officer. He is soon joined by buddy Elliott. They leave their shared love, McLeod, behind when they are pursued by vigilantes. They split up, but only Elliott survives, returning to the lawfully restored town and settling down with McLeod. In a bizarre wrap-up, a widowed and elderly McLeod pontificates on her late husband, Elliott, while standing before a statue of him.

p, Edmund Grainger; d, Edward Ludwig; w, Lawrence Hazard, Horace McCoy (based on a story by Hal Long); ph, Reggie Lanning; m, Anthony Collins; ed, Richard L. Van Enger.

Western   **(PR:A   MPAA:NR)**

FABULOUS WORLD OF JULES VERNE, THE***   (1961, Czech.) 83m Ceskoslovensky/WB bw (VYNALEZ ZKAZY)

Louis Tock [Lubor Tokos] (Simon Hart), Ernest Navara [Arnost Navratil] (Prof. Roche), Milo Holl [Miroslav Holub] (Artigas), Francis Sherr [Frantisek Slegr] (Pirate Captain), Van Kissling [Vaclav Kyzlink] (Serke), Jane Zalata [Jana Zatloukalova] (Jana).

A poetic recreation of the mystical atmosphere found in Jules Verne's novels, particularly The Deadly Invention. By mixing live action and 19th century engravings which accompanied the novels, the animators have come up with a technique they tagged "Mystimation." The acceptably thin plot concerns the pirate kidnaping of a genius scientist in order to harness his knowledge of explosives. The remarkable visual style draws much from the early works of film magician Georges Melies. Originally released in 1958 in Czechoslovakia, producer Levine brought the film to the States, tagged on a pointless introduction by Hugh Downs, and took the liberty of Americanizing the names of the cast and crew.

p, Joseph E. Levine; d, Karel Zeman; w, Zeman, Francis Gross, Milan Vacca (based on the novels of Jules Verne); ph, George Taran, B.S. Piccard, Anthony Hora; m, Sydney Fox; ed, Zdenik Stehlik; md, Frank Belfin; art d, Zep Kopal; spec eff, George Taran; anim, Ernest Marchand, Henry Liss, Francis Kramm.

Fantasy   **Cas.**   **(PR:AA   MPAA:NR)**

FACE, THE   (SEE: MAGICIAN, THE, 1958, Swed.)

FACE AT THE WINDOW, THE**   (1932, Brit.) 52m REA/RKO bw

Raymond Massey (Paul le Gros), Isla Bevan (Marie de Brisson), Claude Hulbert (Peter Pomeroy), Eric Maturin (Count Fournal), Henry Mollison (Lucien Courtier), A. Bromley Davenport (Gaston de Brisson), Harold Meade (Dr. Renard), Dennis Wyndham (Lafonde), Charles Groves (Jacques), Berenoff and Charlot.

Massey is a Parisian detective who fakes the revival of a dead man in order to expose a count as a bank robber. A minor film for Massey.

p, Julius Hagen; d, Leslie Hiscott; w, H. Fowler Mear (based on a play by F. Brooke Warren).

Crime   **(PR:C   MPAA:NR)**

FACE AT THE WINDOW, THE**   (1939, Brit.) 65m Pennant/BL bw

Tod Slaughter (Chevalier del Gardo), Marjorie Taylor (Cecile de Brisson), John Warwick (Lucien Cortier), Leonard Henry (Gaston), Aubrey Mallalieu (De Brisson), Robert Adair (Inspector Guffert), Wallace Evennett (Prof. le Blanc), Kay Lewis (Babette), Margaret Yarde (Le Pinan), Harry Terry (The Face), Billy Shine.

Slaughter and his deformed brother work together to terrorize Paris, using their activities as a cover for a bank robbery. A police trap exposes the pair, but Slaughter escapes, apparently drowning in the Seine. Sensational melodrama typical of Slaughter.

p&d, George King; w, A.R. Rawlinson, Randall Faye (based on a play by F. Brooke Warren); ph, Hone Glendinning.

Crime   **Cas.**   **(PR:C   MPAA:NR)**

FACE BEHIND THE MASK, THE**·½   (1941) 69m COL bw

Peter Lorre (Janos Szabo), Evelyn Keyes (Helen Williams), Don Beddoe (Jim O'Hara), George E. Stone (Dinky), John Tyrell (Watts), Stanley Brown (Harry), Al Seymour (Benson), James Seay (Jeff), Warren Ashe (Johnson), Charles Wilson (Chief O'Brien), George McKay (Terry Finnegan), Ben Taggart (Dr. Jones), Mary Currier (Nurse Kritzer), Sarah Edwards (Mrs. Perkins), Frank Reicher (Dr. Cheever), Ralph Peters (Cook), Al Hill (Horton), Walter Soderling (Harris), Lee Prather (Immigration Officer), David Oliver (Steward), John Dilson (Anderson), Joel Friedkin (Mr. Perkins), Lee Phelps (Brown), Sam Ash (Mike Cary), Ed Stanley (Dr. Beckett), Claire Rochelle (Nurse Bailey), Walter Merrill (Joe), Victor Travers (Man), Almeda Fowler, Bessie Wade (Women), Harry Strang (Clerk Stimson), Al Bridge (Horgan), Lee Shumway (Policeman), Jack Gardner (Man at Fire), Eddie Foster (City Slicker), Chuck Hamilton (Gas Station Attendant), Billy Lally (Wilson), Al Rhein, Ernie Adams.

Lorre plays a Hungarian immigrant who is hideously burned in the face and dons an equally awful mask. To cover the cost of his expressionless false face, he regrettably gets mixed up in the mob. He soon falls in love with a blind girl, Keyes, who is accidentally killed in a car bomb meant for Lorre. A stylish film about human suffering which was poorly received upon its release, though it was re-released two years later. As expected with the drink and drug addicted Lorre, Director Florey, who was given only 24 days to complete this film and MEET BOSTON BLACKIE, had endless difficulties with the actor, who used drugs to justify what he termed "silly dialog" and to endure the uncomfortable facial makeup.

p, Wallace McDonald; d, Robert Florey; w, Allen Vincent, Paul Jarrico (based on a story by Arthur Levinson and a radio play by Thomas Edward O'Connell); ph, Franz A. Planer; ed, Charles Nelson; md, M.W. Stoloff; art d, Lionel Banks.

Drama/Horror   **(PR:C   MPAA:NR)**

FACE BEHIND THE SCAR**   (1940, Brit.) 63m Premier-Stafford/Film Alliance bw (GB: RETURN OF A STRANGER)

Griffith Jones (James Martin), Rosalyn Boulter (Carol), Ellis Jeffreys (Lady Wall), Athole Stewart (Sir Patrick Wall), Cecil Ramage (John Forbes), Constance Godridge (Esme), Sylvia Marriott (Mary), James Harcourt (Johnson), Harold Scott (Peters).

A fair British yarn about chemist Jones and his love interest, Boulter. A murder charge is tagged on him and he flees to South Africa where he quickly moves to the top of the medical profession. An explosion in the laboratory disfigures his face, leaving him scarred. Thinking he cannot be identified he returns to London to find his girl married. His scar isn't as bad as he thought and he is identified, but all goes well in the finale. Originally released in England in 1937, and later re-issued in 1950.

p, John Stafford; d, W. Victor Hanbury; w, Akos Tolnay, Reginald Long (based on a story by Tolnay and a play by Rudolph Lothar); ph, James Wilson.

Crime   **(PR:A MPAA:NR)**

FACE IN THE CROWD, A****   (1957) 125m WB bw

Andy Griffith (*Lonesome Rhodes*), Patricia Neal (*Marcia Jeffries*), Anthony Franciosa (*Joey Kiely*), Walter Matthau (*Mel Miller*), Lee Remick (*Betty Lou Fleckum*), Percy Waram (*Colonel Hollister*), Rod Brasfield (*Beanie*), Charles Irving (*Mr. Luffler*), Howard Smith (*J.B. Jeffries*), Paul McGrath (*Macey*), Kay Medford (*First Mrs. Rhodes*), Alexander Kirkland (*Jim Collier*), Marshall Nielan (*Sen. Fuller*), Big Jeff Bess (*Sheriff Hosmer*), Henry Sharp (*Abe Steiner*), Willie Feibel (*1st Printer*), Larry Casazza (*2nd Printer*).

An unforgettable screen debut for Griffith as a cracker barrel philosopher Neal finds and puts on her local TV station in Arkansas. His down home wit and backwater jokes soon find widespread audiences until one of the state's largest stations picks up his show, then a network, until his face is seen throughout the land and his condescending wisdom begins to affect a broadbase America. Neal and her assistant Matthau soon realize that good old "Lonesome Rhodes" is not the kindly rural savant they think him to be. Even though corporate TV executives make jokes behind his back, Griffith is a shrewd, power-mad flim-flammer, cynical and hateful at the core. He begins to use his power by boosting certain firms and politicians in return for later promises of money and power. He then makes a deal with a presidential hopeful and pushes his image, expecting a bonanza of riches, prestige and influential position once the man is elected. When off camera, Griffith reveals his true nature, obnoxious, insulting and venomous. Just as he is on the brink of total success, Neal, who has by this time become his secret lover, opts for truth and turns on the TV superstar's microphone when he thinks it's off, and, while grinning at his millions of viewers, he is heard to call them stupid suckers, "slobs," pawns in his hands. In a few seconds, Griffith's shooting star explodes. He is finished as the great "Aw shucks" American philosopher a la Will Rogers and is sent back to the oblivion of his birth, disgraced, exposed, instantly forgotten, as is his affair with Neal. It is the end of a Frankenstein monster created by the TV media. The Kazan-Schulberg combine so effective in ON THE WATERFRONT again proved its ability to produce a penetrating and terrifying portrait of raw humanity. Griffith, who had made a name for himself on Broadway with "No Time for Sergeants," skyrocketed to fame with this film, capturing the kind of vicious but fascinating character he himself would take some time to live down, as reluctant in later years to talk about this role as Robert Mitchum was to discuss his role of the maniacal killer in NIGHT OF THE HUNTER. Neal is superb as the outwardly tough lady TV producer but love-vulnerable female snared by the hillbilly philosopher. Matthau plays his cynical newsman to the hilt.

p&d, Elia Kazan; w, Budd Schulberg (based on his short story "The Arkansas Traveler"); ph, Harry Stradling, Gayne Rescher; m, Tom Glazer; cos, Anna Hill Johnstone; m/l, Glazer, Schulberg.

Drama   **Cas.**   **(PR:C MPAA:NR)**

FACE IN THE FOG, A**   (1936) 66m Victory bw

June Collyer (*Jean Monroe*), Lloyd Hughes (*Frank Gordon*), Lawrence Gray (*Peter Fortune*), Al St. John (*Elmer*), Jack Mulhall (*Reardon*), Jack Cowell (*Wilson*), John Elliott (*Davis*), Sam Flint (*Harrison*), Forrest Taylor (*Cromwell*), Edward Cassidy (*Detective*), Robert Williams (*Policeman*).

A low-budget programmer with Collyer and Hughes a pair of newspaper employees out to solve a mysterious string of murders that are threatening the cast of a play called "Satan's Bride." With the help of dimwitted photographer St. John, Collyer and Hughes begin collecting clues. Also investigating the killings is Gray, a playwright whose interest in mysteries gives him some added insight. After a few more corpses are chalked up to the "Fiend," as the murderous hunchback is called, Hughes discovers that Gray is actually the killer in disguise. Things look dim for Hughes but just as he is about to be killed St. John shows up with the police in tow. A captivating picture if you can look past the meager production values.

p, Sam Katzman; d, Bob Hill; w, Al Martin (based on the novel *The Great Mono Miracle* by Peter B. Kyne); ph, Bill Hyer; ed, Earl Turner; set d, Fred Preble.

Mystery   **(PR:A MPAA:NR)**

FACE IN THE NIGHT   (SEE: MENACE IN THE NIGHT, 1956, Brit.)

FACE IN THE RAIN, A**½   (1963) 81m EM bw

Rory Calhoun (*Rand*), Marina Berti (*Anna*), Niall McGinnis (*Klaus*), Massimo Giuliani (*Paolo*), Danny Ryais, Peter Zander.

A fine wartime picture places American spy Calhoun in German-occupied Italy. He is hidden in the home of an underground contact whose wife Berti demands that he leave. It turns out that she is having an affair with a German officer who is searching for Calhoun. Sheltered in the attic by Berti's son, Calhoun is accidentally spotted by Berti and the German when they unexpectedly arrive home. Nazi troops chase him as he scampers across rain-drenched tile roofs, and also chase Berti who they believe has been harboring a spy. To save face, the officer-lover shoots and kills Berti. An intriguing plot which is restrained by mediocre performances and direction.

p, John Calley; d, Irvin Kershner; w, Hugo Butler, Jean Rouverol (based on a story by Guy Elmes); ph, Haskell Wexler; m, Richard Markowitz; ed, Melvin Sloan; art d, Sergio Canevari.

War Drama   **(PR:A MPAA:NR)**

FACE IN THE SKY**   (1933) 68m FOX bw

Spencer Tracy (*Joe Buck*), Marian Nixon (*Madge*), Stuart Erwin (*Lucky*), Sam Hardy (*Triplett the Great*), Lila Lee (*Sharon Hadley*), Sarah Padden (*Ma Brown*),

Frank McGlynn, Jr. (*Jim Brown*), Russell Simpson (*Pa Brown*), Billy Platt (*Midget*), Guy Usher (*Albert Preston*).

Tracy and Erwin are sign painters traveling through New England who decide to use Nixon's sweet smile as a model for their work. She soon finds her face literally on the broad side of a barn. Before long, Tracy and Nixon get hitched, but the new wife is left behind as he and his partner travel to New York City for a big job. He is challenged to paint a huge sign and again uses his face as the inspiration. Without knowing his whereabouts, Nixon sets out to find him and, in a city of many millions, miraculously finds him on day one.

d, Harry Lachman; w, Humphrey Pearson (based on a story by Myles Connolly); ph, Lee Garmes; m, Peter Brunelli, R.H. Bassett, Hugo Friedhofer, J.S. Zamecnik; ed, Ralph Dietrich; md, Louis De Francesco; set d, William Darling; cos, David Cox.

Romance   **(PR:A MPAA:NR)**

FACE OF A FUGITIVE**   (1959) 80m COL c

Fred MacMurray (*Jim Larson/Ray Kincaid*), Lin McCarthy (*Mark Riley*), Dorothy Green (*Ellen Bailey*), Alan Baxter (*Reed Williams*), Myrna Fahey (*Janet*), James Coburn (*Purdy*), Francis De Sales (*Allison*), Gina Gillespie (*Alice Bailey*), Ron Hayes (*Danny*), Paul Burns (*Jake*), Buzz Henry (*Burton*), John Milford (*Haley*), James Gavin (*Stockton*), Hal K. Dawson (*Stableman*), Stanley Farrar (*Eakins*), Rankin Mansfield (*Minister*), Harrison Lewis (*Bartender*).

MacMurray is a bank robber on the lam who is accused of killing a deputy, who actually was slain by MacMurray's brother. He hides in a neighboring town and falls in love with the sheriff's sister. MacMurray soon becomes pals with the sheriff, who doubles as a lawyer, because the sheriff reminds him of his brother. He is defended by the sheriff, but, alas, justice has its way. James Coburn is wonderfully nasty as he harasses the lawyer-sheriff.

p, David Heilweil; d, Paul Wendkos; w, David T. Chantler, Daniel B. Ullman (based on a story "Long Gone" by Peter Dawson); ph, Wilfrid M. Cline (Eastmancolor); m, Jerald Goldsmith; ed, Jerome Thoms; art d, Robert Peterson; set d, Louis Diage, Bill Calvert.

Western   **(PR:A MPAA:NR)**

FACE OF A STRANGER**   (1964, Brit.) 56m Merton Park/AA bw

Jeremy Kemp (*Vince Howard*), Bernard Archard (*Michael Forrest*), Rosemary Leach (*Mary Bell*), Philip Locke (*John Bell*), Elizabeth Begley, Jean Marsh, Mike Pratt, Keith Smith.

Yet another of the long series of Edgar Wallace mysteries turned out by the Merton Park studios between 1960 and 1963. In this, the 26th offering, an ex-convict, just released from jail, pretends to be his still incarcerated cellmate and goes to live with the man's blind wife, planning to learn the hiding place of his cellmate's loot. Interesting programmer.

p, Jack Greenwood; d, John Moxey; w, John Sansom (based on a novel by Edgar Wallace).

Crime   **(PR:A-C MPAA:NR)**

FACE OF ANOTHER, THE*½   (1967, Jap.) 124m
                Teshigahara-Tokyo Eiga/Toho bw (TANIN NO KAO)

Tatsuya Nakadai (*Okuyama*), Machiko Kyo (*His Wife*), Kyoko Kishida (*His Nurse*), Mikijiro Hira (*His Doctor*), Eiji Okada, Miki Irie, Minoru Chiaki, Etsuko Ichihara, Hideka Muranatsu, Yoshie Minami, Shinobu Itomi, Hisashi Igawa.

Nakadai is an industrialist whose face is severely burned in a factory accident. A plastic surgeon creates a mask for him and when his wife tries to seduce him he accuses her of adultery. She leaves him saying she knew it was him. Nakadai drives himself crazy, rapes a woman, and kills the plastic surgeon who created his misery. Unrelentingly bleak story of a crisis of identity.

d, Hiroshi Teshigahara; w, Kobo Abe; ph, Hiroshi Segawa; m, Toru Takemitsu.

Drama   **(PR:O MPAA:NR)**

FACE OF EVE, THE   (SEE: EVE, 1969, Brit.)

FACE OF EVIL   (SEE: DOCTOR BLOOD'S COFFIN, 1961, Brit.)

FACE OF FEAR   (SEE: PEEPING TOM, 1960, Brit.)

FACE OF FEAR, 1964   (SEE: FACE OF TERROR, 1964, Span.)

FACE OF FIRE**   (1959, U.S./Brit.) 79m AA bw

Cameron Mitchell (*Ned Trescott*), James Whitmore (*Monk Johnson*), Bettye Ackerman (*Grace Trescott*), Royal Dano (*Jake Winter*), Miko Oscard (*Jimmie Trescott*), Robert Simon (*The Judge*), Richard Erdman (*Al Williams*), Howard Smith (*Sheriff Nolan*), Lois Maxwell (*Ethel Winter*), Jill Donahue (*Bella Kovac*).

Whitmore's talents are barely employed as he rescues a young boy from a raging inferno, and in turn is grossly disfigured. Once adored by the townsfolk, Whitmore's ordeal mentally disfigures him as well. His bitter treatment by his neighbors nearly causes murderous results. An oddly interesting adaptation of Stephen Crane's story which was wrongly promoted as a horror picture.

p, Albert Band, Louis Garfinkle; d, Band; w, Garfinkle (based on the story "The Monster" by Stephen Crane); ph, Edward Vorkapich; m, Erik Nordgren; ed, Ingemar Ejve; art d, Vorkapich.

Drama   **(PR:C MPAA:NR)**

FACE OF FU MANCHU, THE**½ (1965, Brit.) 96m Hallam/Seven Arts c

Christopher Lee (*Fu Manchu*), Nigel Green (*Nayland Smith*), James Robertson Justice (*Sir Charles Fortesque*), Howard Marion-Crawford (*Dr. Walter Petrie*), Tsai Chin (*Lin Tang*), Joachim Fuchsberger (*Carl Jansen*), Karin Dor (*Maria*), Walter

Rilla (Prof. Muller), Harry Brogan (Prof. Gaskell), Poulet Tu (Lotus), Peter Mossbacher (Hanumon), Edwin Richfield (Mandarin), Archie O'Sullivan, Eric Young, Deborah Du' Lacey.

As Fu frequently claims, "The world has not heard the last of Fu Manchu," and indeed it hasn't—for the first time since the 1940 serial, DRUMS OF FU MANCHU, the Chinese arch-villain is back on the screen with Lee in the lead. Lee invents a lethal gas which ends all life in a small English village, and then hides out under the Thames with his daughter. Green, as the do-gooder, puts an end to Lee's terrorizing in a crafty explosion. Filmed in Dublin. Sequel: THE BRIDES OF FU MANCHU followed in 1966.

p, Harry Alan Towers, Oliver Unger; d, Don Sharp; w, Peter Welbeck [Towers] (based on the character created by Sax Rohmer); ph, Ernest Steward (Techniscope, Technicolor); m, Christopher Whelen; ed, John Trumper; art d, Frank White.

Horror (PR:O MPAA:NR)

FACE OF MARBLE, THE½ (1946) 72m MON bw

John Carradine (Prof. Randolph), Claudia Drake (Elaine), Robert Shayne (David Cochran), Maris Wrixon (Linda), Willie Best (Shadrach), Thomas E. Jackson (Inspector Norton), Rosa Rey (Marika), Neal Burns (Jeff), Donald Kern, Allan Ray (Photographers).

Carradine is a brain surgeon who revives the dead and, curiously, a Great Dane. He gets caught when a failed experiment turns a sailor into marble. Some people will believe anything. The only worthwhile aspect is Carradine's strong performance.

p, Jeffrey Bernerd; d, William Beaudine; w, Michael Jacoby (based on a story by William Thiele and Edmund Hartman); ph, Harry Neumann; ed, William Austin; md, Edward Kay.

Horror (PR:A MPAA:NR)

FACE OF TERROR* (1964, Span.) 81m Documento Film/Cinema-Video International-Futuramic Releasing Corp. bw
(LA CARA DEL TERROR; AKA: FACE OF FEAR)

Lisa Gaye (Norma), Fernando Rey (Dr. Charles Taylor), Virgilio Texeira (Playboy), Conchita Cuetos (Almas), Gerard Tichy (Sanitarium Head), Carlos Casaravilla, Emilio Rodriguez, Angel Menendez, Paul Pisget.

Rey is a plastic surgeon who gives a beautiful face to a mentally disturbed woman, played by Gaye. There's just one catch: she needs a special lotion for her new face to stay in place. The transformed woman becomes extremely paranoid about her past as an inmate of an insane asylum, leading her to murder the man who gives her a job. Rey tries to restrain her but she escapes and marries a rich man. On her honeymoon Gaye runs out of the stay-beautiful lotion and metamorphoses back to her old face. Her horrified husband flees when getting a gander at her hideous countenance but she runs him over with a car. Returning to Rey's laboratory to acquire more of the precious lotion, Gaye struggles with the doctor's assistant (Cuetos) then falls to her death, landing, to no one's surprise, with her face in the remainder of the lotion. For a brief period this type of film enjoyed a mini-genre in Spain. Reportedly, an American version with the same cast but produced by Jack Leroy Miles and directed by William J. Hole was put through an intense ordeal with the censoring shears, making the possibilities for a good film even more remote. All in all, a complete loss of face.

p, Gustavo Quintana; d, Isidoro Martinez Ferry; w, Monroe Manning; ph, Jose Fernandez Aguayo; m, Jose Buenagu, Miguel Asins-Arbo; ed, Jose Antonio Rojo; art d, Sigfrido Burman.

Horror (PR:C MPAA:NR)

FACE OF THE SCREAMING WEREWOLF* (1959, Mex.) 60m Diana/Associated Distributors Pictures bw
(LA CASA DEL TERROR; AKA: HOUSE OF TERROR)

Lon Chaney, Jr. (Mummy/Werewolf), Landa Varle, Raymond Gaylord, D. W. Baron, German "Tin Tan" Valdes, Yerye Beirute, Agustin Fernandez, Consuelo Guerrero de Luna, Oscar Ortiz de Pinedo.

A scientist tries to revive a mummy but what he gets is Chaney, Jr., in werewolf makeup. Chaney then goes on to work mayhem on the community before he dies in a fire. Somehow lost in the dubbing shuffle for U.S. release was the comedy, with which the Mexican version is replete.

p, Jerry Warren (English version); d, Gilberto Martinez Solares, Warren; w, Solares, Juan Garcia, Fernando de Fuentes; ph, Raul Martinez Solares; m, Luis Hernandez Breton; ed, Carlos Savage; art d, Jorge Fernandez.

Horror (PR:A MPAA:NR)

FACE ON THE BARROOM FLOOR, THE* (1932) 65m IN bw

Dulcie Cooper (Mary Bronson), Bramwell Fletcher (Bill Bronson), Alice Ward (Mrs. Grove), Phillips Smalley (Grove), Walter Miller (Sam Turner), Maurice Black (Vanzetti), Eddie Fetherstone (Slick), Patricia Wing (Secretary).

Bearing only the title similarity, this picture has nothing to do with the 1923 silent. It is, instead, a view of prohibition, focusing on the downhill tumble of a thirsty bank clerk. Pretty dry fare for an audience.

p, Aubrey Kennedy; d, Bert Bracken; w, Bracken, Barry Barringer (based on a story by Kennedy); ph, Bob Kline.

Drama (PR:A MPAA:NR)

FACE TO FACE* (1952) 89m RKO bw

The Secret Sharer: James Mason (Captain), Gene Lockhart (Capt. Archbold), Michael Pate (Swimmer), Albert Sharpe (1st Mate), Sean McClory (2nd Mate), Alec Harford (Ship's Cook); The Bride Comes To Yellow Sky: Robert Preston (Sheriff),

Marjorie Steele (Bride), Minor Watson (Bad Man), Dan Seymour (Drummer), Olive Carey (Saloon Keeper), James Agee (Prisoner).

A feature length film comprised of two short story adaptations, Joseph Conrad's "The Secret Sharer," and Stephen Crane's "The Bride Comes To Yellow Sky." The connection between the two stories comes in the film's title, as in both shorts a figure of authority is confronted with problematic characters. In "The Secret Sharer," James Mason is a rookie sea captain who discovers that a fugitive has swum aboard his vessel and he must mete out justice to him. In "The Bride Comes To Yellow Sky," Preston is a sheriff who is threatened by a gun-toting old-timer who is still bent on the law of the gunfighter. From James Agee's screenplay, the latter is similar in ideology to John Ford's 1959 THE MAN WHO SHOT LIBERTY VALANCE. Steele was the wife of millionaire producer Huntington Hartford.

p, Huntington Hartford; d, John Brahm, Bretaigne Windust; w, Aeneas MacKenzie, James Agee (based on stories by Joseph Conrad and Stephen Crane); ph, Karl Struss, George Diskant; m, Hugo Friedhofer; ed, Otto Meyer; art d, Edward Ilou; set d, Clarence Steenson.

Drama (PR:A MPAA:NR)

FACE TO FACE* (1967, Ital.) 110m P.E.A./Arturo Gonzales c
(FACCIA A FACCIA)

Gian-Maria Volonte, Tomas Milian, William Berger, Jolanda Modio, Carole Andre, Gianni Rizzo.

Volonte is a professor of history, recuperating in the American Southwest from tuberculosis. There he meets bad man Milian and becomes fascinated by him. He uses his intellect to help the outlaw in crime and rapidly descends to violence so pointless that Milian allows him to take the role of leader. Finally Milian kills his violent oppressor. A bit of European history strangely transplanted to the American southwest, the picture is almost a perfect representation of Italy's fascination and final oppression by Adolf Hitler's Germany.

p, Alberto Grimaldi; d&w, Sergio Sollima; ph, Rafael Pacheco (CinemaScope).

Western (PR:O MPAA:NR)

FACE TO FACE** (1976, Swed.) 136m De Laurentiis/PAR c

Liv Ullmann (Dr. Jenny Isaksson), Erland Josephson (Dr. Tomas Jacobi), Gunnar Bjornstrand (Grandpa), Aino Taube-Henrikson (Grandma), Kari Sylwan (Maria), Siv Ruud (Mrs. Elizabeth Wankel), Sven Lindberg (Dr. Erik Isaksson), Tore Segelcke (The Lady), Ulf Johansson (Dr. Helmuth Wankel), Kristina Adolphson (Veronica), Gosta Ekman (Mikael Stromberg), Kabi Laratei (Concert Pianist).

What a shame that we had to see this heavily edited version in the U.S. Bergman originally filmed FACE TO FACE for television in a four-part series—the same thing he did for SCENES FROM A MARRIAGE (1973)—and the liberal TV codes of Sweden made it easy to broadcast. Faced with the impossibility of getting it onto U.S. television, he edited it to a length where it could be distributed as a movie. Despite the snipping, it remains one of the best of its psychological genre. Bergman adores women and it shows in every frame, just as De Palma's disdain for women shows in his films. Ullmann is a psychiatrist who is spending a vacation at her grandparents' home in the country. She is married to Lindberg but he is away so she goes alone. The house is gloomy and she soon begins experiencing hallucinations of an old woman. This leads to depression and a feeling that she cannot do anything to help herself. She is desperate to have some enjoyment on this holiday so she attends a party thrown by her over-age swinger friend, Ruud. At the gala, she encounters Josephson, a doctor who is handsome, charming, and very captivated by Ullmann. She tells him straightaway that she's married but that doesn't deter him one whit. He takes her back to his place for a nightcap, then attempts to bed her but she declines. A few days later, Josephson's persistence pays off and they are in bed together when she suddenly sits up and is thrown into an unprovoked fit of hysteria. Her screams and tears appear to be bottomless but Josephson manages to stanch them both. The next day, feeling somewhat relieved for having gone through the mental flames the night before, she appears to be all right but the old woman appears again, this time a mirror of her grandmother. Ullmann cannot take it any longer and downs a handful of sleeping pills in a shocking suicide attempt. Falling into the sleep that precedes death, she dreams of her late parents and various other people in her past. She is now dressed as Red Riding Hood and the sequence is both symbolic and surrealistic. In her dream, she chastises her parents for making her the neurotic she is (much the same way Ullmann attacked Ingrid Bergman in the babbling AUTUMN SONATA). Raised in an unbending atmosphere, this strict background did much to chain her thinking. She wakes to find herself in a hospital, having been rescued by Josephson before the barbiturates took their final, deadly effect. Her recovery is long and difficult and she has one more relapse in which she realizes, in a flash, why she is the way she is. Her mother was a Swedish Eva Braun and her grandmother and mother often engaged in drawn-out arguments which resulted in the grandmother's face assuming a malevolent expression. Once this is gleaned, Ullmann decides to go home and attempt to resume a normal existence. It's Ullmann's picture from the start to finish as she goes through a panoply of emotions seldom seen in U.S. cinema. Whether it is the actress or the truly literate screenplay (by Bergman) or his direction, we can never be sure. What we can be certain of is that this portrayal must rank as one of the greatest ever in foreign films. Despite all of the above as well as Nykvist's accustomed brilliance behind the camera, the movie was overlooked by the Academy in favor of much lesser fare. All supporting roles are excellent, including an unbilled bit by Bergman's daughter as Ullmann's unresponsive daughter. (In Swedish; English subtitles.)

pd&w, Ingmar Bergman; ph, Sven Nykvist (Eastmancolor); m, Wolfgang Amadeus Mozart; ed, Siv Lundgren; prod d, Anne Hagegard; set d, Peter Krupenin.

Drama (PR:O MPAA:R)

FACE TO THE WIND (SEE: COUNT YOUR BULLETS, 1972)

FACELESS MAN, THE (SEE: COUNTERFEIT KILLER, THE, 1968)

FACELESS MEN, THE (SEE: INCIDENT AT PHANTOM HILL, 1966)

FACELESS MONSTERS (SEE: NIGHTMARE CASTLE, 1966, Ital.)

FACES* (1934, Brit.) 68m British and Dominions/PAR bw

Anna Lee (*Madeleine Pelham*), Harold French (*Ted*), Walter Sondes (*Dick Morris*), Moore Marriott (*Robert Pelham*), Kate Saxon (*Mrs. Pelham*), Beryl de Querton (*Amy Amor*), Noel Shannon (*Alphonse*), Olive Sloane (*Lady Wallingford*), Madeleine Seymour, Peter Northcote, Mary Gaskell.

Boring little melodrama has Lee a beautician seeking to improve her station in life. She dumps boy friend, French, to become the mistress of a wealthy man, but changes her mind when she learns that the man's wife is one of her best and most likable customers.

p, Herbert Wilcox; d, Sidney Morgan; w, Joan Wentworth Wood (based on a play by Patrick Ludlow, Walter Sondes).

Drama **(PR:A MPAA:NR)**

FACES** (1968) 130m CD bw

John Marley (*Richard Forst*), Gena Rowlands (*Jeannie Rapp*), Lynn Carlin (*Maria Forst*), Fred Draper (*Freddie*), Seymour Cassel (*Chet*), Val Avery (*McCarthy*), Dorothy Gulliver (*Florence*), Joanne Moore Jordan (*Louise*), Darlene Conley (*Billy Mae*), Gene Darfler (*Jackson*), Elizabeth Deering (*Stella*), Dave Mazzie, Julie Gambol, James Bridges.

Often called one of the most important American films of the 1960s, FACES is an elementary story of husband and wife, disenchanted after 14 years of marriage, who drift apart. Marley, the husband, spends an evening with a prostitute, Rowland, while Carlin, his wife, and her girl friends go out looking for love. She finds it in the form of aging hippie Cassel, whom she takes home to bed. The illusion that comes with night is gone the following morning, sending Carlin to the medicine cabinet looking for a permanent way out. Cassel saves her from suicide and leaves before Marley returns home. The original cut ran nearly six hours, making it an inevitable victim of the splicing block. Unfortunately, that version exists only in the form of a published script. In a sense, this film can be seen as a reaction to Cassavetes' previous directorial outing, A CHILD IS WAITING, which he disowned after it was recut by producer Stanley Kramer. Cassavetes became wary of the major companies and turned independent. As with all indie features, he experienced the good with the bad with this one, spending nearly two years in the editing process battling synchronization problems. Upon its release the film was hailed by most critics but tepidly received by the movie goers. Though it is often a tedious viewing experience, its improvisational and documentary techniques are rewarding. Marley took the Best Actor award at the Venice Fest; Carlin (a "nonacting" secretary) received a Best Supporting Actress nomination from the Academy Awards, as did Cassel in the Best Supporting Actor category, and Cassavetes in the Best Screenplay category.

p, Maurice McEndree; d&w, John Cassavetes; ph, Al Ruban; m, Jack Ackerman; ed, McEndree, Ruban, Cassavetes; md, Ackerman; art d, Phedon Papamichael; m/l, "Never Felt Like This Before," Charles Smalls.

Drama **(PR:O MPAA:NR)**

FACES IN THE DARK*½ (1960, Brit.) 85m RANK bw

John Gregson (*Richard Hammond*), Mai Zetterling (*Christiane Hammond*), Michael Denison (*David Merton*), John Ireland (*Max Hammond*), Tony Wright (*Clem*), Nanette Newman (*Janet*), Rowland Bartrop (*French Doctor*), Colette Bartrop (*1st Nun Nurse*), John Serret (*French Surgeon*), Valerie Taylor (*Miss Hopkins*), Joyce Marlow.

Gregson is a light bulb manufacturer who is blinded in an explosive experiment on the day that his wife Zetterling is preparing to leave him. Sensing that she should tend to him, she stays, but before long Gregson's increasing self-pity and madness send her back to her lover, Denison. Gregson soon gets the bright idea that the duo are planning to murder him, though in the finale it is they who lose out. Has some pot-holes but the chilling climax is smooth as glass.

p, Jon Penington; d, David Eady; w, Ephraim Kogan, John Tully (based on the novel by Pierre Boileau, Thomas Narcejac); ph, Ken Hodges; m, Edwin Astley; ed, Oswald Hafenrichter; art d, Tony Masters; set d, Maurice Fowler.

Crime **(PR:A MPAA:NR)**

FACES IN THE FOG* (1944) 71m REP bw

Jane Withers (*Mary Elliott*), Paul Kelly (*Tom Elliott*), Lee Patrick (*Cora Elliott*), John Litel (*Dr. Mason*), Eric Sinclair (*Joe Mason*), Dorothy Peterson (*Mrs. Mason*), Gertrude Michael (*Nora Brooks*), H.B. Warner (*Defense Attorney Rankin*), Richard Byron (*Mike*), Roger Clark (*Sgt. O'Donnell*), Adele Mara (*Gertrude*), Bob Stebbins (*Les Elliott*), Charles Trowbridge (*Mr. White*), Helen Talbot (*Alice*), Joel McGinnis (*Danny*), Tom London (*Auto Court Manager*), Emmett Vogan (*Capt. Roberts*).

Sinclair and Withers are young lovers who secretly marry after Withers' innocent involvement in a hit-and-run accident. Sinclair takes the blame and gets expelled from school. Wither's angry dad shoots Sinclair, but at the trial his daughter perjures herself to save her father's hide. Everything ends happily as the kids take a belated honeymoon. Parents step on the soap box in this one, but the potential juvenile delinquents have their innings, too.

p, Herman Millakowsky; d, John English; w, Jack Townley; ph, Reggie Lanning; ed, Tony Martinelli; md, Richard Cherwin; art d, Frank Hotaling.

Drama **(PR:A MPAA:NR)**

FACING THE MUSIC*½ (1933, Brit.) 70m Wardour/BI bw

Stanley Lupino (*Jack Foley*), Jose Collins (*Mme. Calvini*), Nancy Brown (*Mme. Rivers*), Nancy Burne (*Nina Carson*), Doris Woodall (*Mme. D'Ava*), Lester Matthews (*Becker*), Dennis Hoey (*Capradossi*), Morris Harvey (*De Breen*), Hal Gordon (*Sim*), Charles Gerrard, Ian Wilson, Darroll Richards, Nancy Neale.

A stiff opera-oriented production using "Faust" as a backdrop. Opera buff Lupino falls madly in love with Burne, a beauty he sees in the audience. Various situations, including an attempted heist of the singer's jewels, make it difficult for boy to meet girl.

p, John Maxwell; d, Harry Hughes; w, Clifford Grey, Frank Launder, Stanley Lupino (based on a story by Grey, Sidney Gilliat); ph, Walter Harvey, Bryan Langley.

Musical/Romance **(PR:A MPAA:NR)**

FACING THE MUSIC* (1941, Brit.) 79m BUT bw

Bunny Doyle (*Wilfred Hollebone*), Betty Driver (*Mary Matthews*), H.F. Maltby (*Mr. Bulger*), Dorothy [Chili] Bouchier (*Anna Braun*), Wally Patch (*Briggs*), Gus McNaughton (*Illusionist*), Ruby Miller (*Gloria Lynn*), Eliot Makeham (*Secretary*), Gordon McLeod (*Mr. Kelly*), Ronald Chesney, Paddy Drew, Aubrey Mallalieu, Gerald Rex, Kenneth Henry, Eric Clavering, Dorothy Dewhurst, Rita Grant, Jacy Vyvyan, Bryan Herbert, Paul Martin, John Slater, Marjorie Day, Norah Gordon, Vi Kaley, Percival Mackey's Band.

Doyle is a bumbling munitions worker put in charge of a dummy plant to fool Nazi saboteurs. The Germans attack and are captured and Doyle, a hero, finds he has some value at last. Not a good, deep laugh to be found here.

p&d, Maclean Rogers; w, Rogers, Kathleen Butler; ph, Stephen Dade.

Comedy **(PR:A MPAA:NR)**

FACTS OF LIFE, THE (SEE: QUARTET, 1949, Brit.)

FACTS OF LIFE, THE*½ (1960) 103m UA bw

Bob Hope (*Larry Gilbert*), Lucille Ball (*Kitty Weaver*), Ruth Hussey (*Mary Gilbert*), Don DeFore (*Jack Weaver*), Louis Nye (*Charles Busbee*), Philip Ober (*Doc Mason*), Marianne Stewart (*Connie Mason*), Peter Leeds (*Thompson*), Hollis Irving (*Myrtle Busbee*), William Lanteau (*Airline Clerk*), Robert F. Simon (*Motel Clerk*), Louise Beavers (*Gussie*), Mike Mazurki (*Man in Motel Room*).

A typical showing of Hope and Ball's outrageous comedy which, in this picture is chiefly bedroom humor. The pair both leave their respective spouses in suburbia and run into each other's arms. The bedroom-hopping, as funny as it is, seems predictable. Eydie Gorme and Steve Lawrence blurt a Johnny Mercer tune over Saul Bass' fine credits. An Academy Award nominee for Best Cinematography and Best Screenplay and Academy Award winner in Best Costume category for Edith Head's creations.

p, Norman Panama, Melvin Frank; d, Frank; w, Panama, Frank; ph, Charles Lang, Jr.; m, Leigh Harline; ed, Frank Bracht; art d, J. Macmillan Johnson, Kenneth A. Reid; cos, Edith Head.

Comedy **(PR:A MPAA:NR)**

FACTS OF LOVE* (1949, Brit.) 83m Oxford bw
(GB: 29 ACACIA AVENUE)

Gordon Harker (*Mr. Robinson*), Betty Balfour (*Mrs. Robinson*), Jimmy Hanley (*Peter*), Carla Lehmann (*Fay*), Hubert Gregg (*Michael*), Jill Evans (*Joan*), Henry Kendall (*Mr. Wilson*), Dinah Sheridan (*Pepper*), Megs Jenkins (*Shirley*), Noele Gordon (*Mrs. Wilson*), Guy Middleton (*Gerald*), Aubrey Mallalieu (*Martin*).

A lot of sly and racy humor fills this marital comedy concerning a middle-aged couple and their marriage-bound son and daughter. Most of the laughs come from the son's courting of both a farm girl and a married socialite. Originally released in 1945 in England.

p, Sydney Box; d, Henry Cass; w, Muriel Box, Sydney Box (based on the play "29 Acacia Avenue" by Denis and Mabel Constanduros); ph, Ernest Palmer, Nigel Duke; ed, Julian Wintle; md, Muir Mathieson; art d, James Carter.

Comedy **(PR:A MPAA:NR)**

FACTS OF MURDER, THE*½ (1965, Ital.) 110m Riama Cinematografica/Seven Arts bw (UN MALEDETTO IMBROGLIO)

Pietro Germi (*Inspector Ciccio Ingravallo*), Claudia Cardinale (*Assuntina*), Eleonora Rossi Drago (*Liliana Banducci*), Claudio Gora (*Remo Banducci*), Franco Fabrizi (*Valdarena*), Nino Castelnuovo (*Diomede*), Cristina Gajoni (*Virgina*), Saro Urzi (*Detective Saro*), Ildebrando Santafe (*Anzaloni*), Gianni Giori Musy (*Retalli*), Toni Ucci (*Thief*), Peppino De Martino (*Dr. Fumi*), Rosolino Bua (*Priest*), Silla Bettini (*Oreste*), Vincenzo Tocci (*Filone*), Antonio Acqua (*The General*), Renato Terra (*Marchetti*), Nanda De Santis, Loretta Capitoli, Attilio Martella, Rina Mascetti, Pietro Tordi, Leandro Marini, Vittorio Scarabello, Antonio Gradoli, Maria Saccenti, April Hennessy, Vinicio Ricchi, Elsa Canevazzi, Claudia Fabiani.

Germi is a police inspector investigating the murder of a wealthy homosexual. His main suspect is Castelnuovo, an electrician who has a solid alibi. Germi goes through many suspects but everything keeps pointing at Castelnuovo. Everyone he meets seems to be sleazier then the next, a pimp, a Fascist, a bogus doctor, and a mistress. When socialite Drago is murdered, Germi then has enough on the electrician to make an arrest. An imbroglio indeed.

p, Giuseppe Amato; d, Pietro Germi; w, Alfredo Giannetti, Germi, Ennio De Concini (adapted from a novel by Carlo Emilio Gadda); ph, Leonida Barboni; m, Carlo Rustichelli; ed, Roberto Cinquini; art d, Carlo Egidi.

Crime **(PR:O MPAA:NR)**

FADE TO BLACK* (1980) 100m American Cinema c

Dennis Christopher (*Eric Binford*), Linda Kerridge (*Marilyn*), Tim Thomerson (*Dr. Moriarty*), Morgan Paull (*Gary*), Hennen Chambers (*Bart*), Marya Small (*Doreen*), Eve Brent Ashe (*Aunt Stella*), Bob Drew (*Rev. Shick*), Gwynn Gilford (*Anne*), John Steadman (*Sam*), Mickey Rourke (*Richie*), Melinda Fee (*Talk Show Hostess*), Jane K. Wiley (*Gofer*), Peter Horton (*Joey*), Norman Burton (*Marty*), James Luisi (*Gallagher*), Anita Converse (*Dee Dee*), Marcie Barkin (*Stacy*), Gilbert Lawrence Kahn (*Counterman*), Al Tafoya (*Newscaster*), Bruce Reed (*Franco*).

A demented movie fanatic spends his time romancing Kerridge—who looks like Marilyn Monroe—and killing people. Eric Binford, played by Christopher, lives and kills for the movies. Dressed up as one of his favorite screen idols, he murders in their style. The weak, overly violent narrative is intercut with portions of the films and stars he loves—Cagney in WHITE HEAT, Widmark in KISS OF DEATH, Lugosi in DRACULA, Karloff in THE MUMMY, William Boyd as Hopalong Cassidy. It never really goes anywhere beyond a gimmick, failing, as did DEAD MEN DON'T WEAR PLAID, to provide insight into the character.

p, George Braunstein, Ron Hamady; d&w, Vernon Zimmerman; ph, Alex Phillips, Jr.; ed, Howard Kunin; set d, Robert E. Lowy; spec eff, James Wayne.

Horror **Cas.** **(PR:O MPAA:R)**

FAHRENHEIT 451*** (1966, Brit.) 112m Anglo Enterprise-Vineyard-Rank/UNIV c

Oskar Werner *(Montag)*, Julie Christie *(Linda/Clarisse)*, Cyril Cusack *(Captain)*, Anton Diffring) *(Fabian)*, Jeremy Spenser *(Man with Apple)*, Bee Duffell *(Book Woman)*, Gillian Lewis *(T.V. Announcer)*, Anne Bell *(Doris)*, Caroline Hunt *(Helen)*, Anna Palk *(Jackie)*, Roma Milne *(Neighbor)*, Alex Scott *(Henry Brulard)*, Dennis Gilmore *(Martian Chronicles)*, Fred & Frank Cox *(Pride & Prejudice)*, Michael Balfour *(Machiavelli's Prince)*, Judith Drynan *(Plato's Dialogues)*, David Glover *(Pickwick Papers)*, Yvonne Blake *(Jewish Question)*, John Rae *(Weir of Hermiston)*, Gillian Aldam *(Judoka Woman)*, Arthur Cox, Eric Mason *(Male Nurses)*, Noel Davis, Donald Pickering *(TV Announcers)*, Michael Mundell *(Stoneman)*, Chris Williams *(Black)*, Edward Kaye *(Judoka Man)*, Mark Lester, Kevin Elder *(Small Boys)*, Joan Francis *(Bar Telephonist)*, Tom Watson *(Sgt. Instructor)*, Earl Younger *(Nephew of "The Weir of Hermiston")*.

Ray Bradbury's novels do not always translate well on the screen, the vignette-glutted ILLUSTRATED MAN (1969) being a case in point. Yet pantheon director Truffaut manages a top job in putting FAHRENHEIT 451 (the temperature at which paper burns) through its paces even though the story still bogs down his genius. Werner, in a compassionless futuristic society, is a fireman who routinely helps to burn books with other firemen. Once heroic firefighters, the warped totalitarian regime that rules them now insists that they hunt down secret libraries and burn the contents to suppress any free thought. Christie is Werner's listless wife, completely absorbed with viewing wall-size TV shows dictating mindless pursuits. Lonely, isolated and retaining a deadly ounce of curiosity, Werner meets a book-loving lady (Christie again in another hair style) and is easily converted to the underground philosophy of the "book people" who spend their lives memorizing great literary works so they won't be lost to the world (including one of Bradbury's own works, *The Martian Chronicles*). Further committing Werner to the book people is when he witnesses an old lady willing to die in the fire set upon her books rather than live without them. It is really at this point, when taking one of her books, that Werner steps beyond the control of the regime, particularly embodied by the cold, unfeeling fire commander, Cusack, who is utterly dedicated to destroying every book in the world. It is Cusack who suspects Werner of becoming an avid book reader and, with the help of Christie the wife who informs on her husband, uncovers his cache of tomes, burning them. In a rage, Werner incinerates some of the firemen and flees to the wilds where he joins Christie the rebel as a permanent exile, his job being to memorize the works of Edgar Allan Poe. Oddly, there is little science fiction in this futuristic movie with only a few techniques to suggest a scientifically advanced society—TV walls, a monorail system, a few futuristic fire engines and cars. The best thing about this Bradbury tale is Truffaut's brilliant direction, notably the startling dream sequence. This was Truffaut's first color film, first English-speaking film, and his only directorial chore in science fiction, although he later played the French scientist in CLOSE ENCOUNTERS OF THE THIRD KIND. Truffaut spent five years writing the script for this film.

p, Lewis Allen; d, Francois Truffaut; w, Truffaut, Jean Louis Richard, David Rudkin, Helen Scott (based on the novel by Ray Bradbury); ph, Nicolas Roeg (Technicolor); m, Bernard Herrmann; ed, Thom Noble; prod d, Tony Walton; art d, Syd Cain; cos, Walton; spec eff, Charles Staffell, Bowie Films.

Science Fiction **(PR:C MPAA:NR)**

FAIL SAFE**** (1964) 111m COL bw

Dan O'Herlihy *(Gen. Black)*, Walter Matthau *(Groeteschele)*, Frank Overton *(Gen. Bogan)*, Edward Binns *(Col. Grady)*, Fritz Weaver *(Col. Cascio)*, Henry Fonda *(The President)*, Larry Hagman *(Buck)*, William Hansen *(Secretary Swenson)*, Russell Hardie *(Gen. Stark)*, Russell Collins *(Knapp)*, Sorrell Booke *(Cong. Raskob)*, Nancy Berg *(Ilsa Wolfe)*, John Connell *(Thomas)*, Frank Simpson *(Sullivan)*, Hildy Parks *(Betty Black)*, Janet Ward *(Mrs. Grady)*, Dom DeLuise *(Sgt. Collins)*, Dana Elcar *(Foster)*, Stuart Germain *(Mr. Cascio)*, Louise Larabee *(Mrs. Cascio)*, Frieda Altman *(Jennie)*.

What those who logically dread—an accidental Armageddon—came to pass in Lumet's chilling, terrifying FAIL SAFE. The catastrophe begins when a squadron of SAC bombers heads for Moscow to drop its nuclear bombs through a faulty transmission of orders which cannot be normally reversed. The U.S. military tries everything but the bombers fly beyond "fail safe" and President Fonda is alerted. He goes to his bomb-proof concrete bunker deep beneath the White House where, in a simple, sterile room he attempts to inform Russian leaders of the terrible blunder being made. Meanwhile, the president's cabinet and advisers meet in the War Room, keeping him informed of the fast-developing events, channeling messages from Omaha command center. Overall Air Force commander Overton sends fighters after the bombers but they run out of fuel and crash into the Alaskan seas, their crews doomed to freezing death. Fonda then asks Omaha to pass to Russian military leaders the methods by which the U.S. bombers can be shot down. One officer, Weaver, who is embarrassed by his poverty background and has an overpowering sense of superiority, attempts to take over Omaha command, knocking Overton off his feet and announcing that the U.S. is being betrayed. He is overpowered. Overton regains command and finally compels a sergeant, DeLuise, to give the Russians the needed information. The bombers are shot down one by one by guided missiles but one plane piloted by tough, shrewd Binns, manages to evade the Russian attack and head for Moscow. Fonda meanwhile negotiates to the breaking point in trying to deal with the Russians who are about to launch a counter-strike, using a nervous interpreter (Hagman) to relay his sensitive messages. In the war room power-mad scientist Matthau urges all-out war, now that the U.S. has the momentary upper hand, but cooler heads, notably O'Herlihy, prevail. Fonda, realizing that nothing can stop Binns and his crew from hitting Moscow, orders his friend O'Herlihy into the air with orders to drop an A-bomb on New York City to show the Russians that the U.S. strike was accidental. Both bombs drop on each city with life in NYC shown coming to a split-second halt in a series of devastating zooming freeze-frames of activity. All the leads give masterful performances, with Fonda rendering an excrutiatingly restrained role in a claustrophobic atmosphere similar to that in 12 ANGRY MEN, also directed by Lumet, whose quick intercutting and inventive set-ups make the most of tight physical confines. Overton, O'Herlihy, Weaver and Matthau are postively riveting in their good-and-evil roles. This film suffered drastically when it ran afoul of Stanley Kubrick's comedic DR. STRANGELOVE which followed the identical story but was played for blatant black humor. Kubrick went to Columbia's top brass and threatened a law suit of plagiarism since his film was based on Peter George's earlier but almost unknown novel *Red Alert*. Since Columbia was distributing both DR. STRANGELOVE and FAIL SAFE, it appeased Kubrick by releasing his film first and, of course, that cult classic captured the lion's share of the viewing audience, leaving FAIL SAFE to appear as a serious, almost dreary replay of the same story some months later, a cruel happenstance that injured an otherwise fine film. The novel caused a sensation when it first appeared but authors Burdick and Wheeler found that Hollywood bidders abruptly vanished when rumors began to fly about that President Johnson did not want the story put on film. (Fonda later claimed that he had inside information to the contrary.) Yet Lumet and Youngstein discounted the rumors and went ahead with production immediately after securing the rights. Their dedication to the story is evident in every frame. Worthy of additional kudos is Hirschfeld's stark black-and white cinematography and the tight editing by Rosenblum.

p, Max E. Youngstein; d, Sidney Lumet; w, Walter Bernstein (based on the novel by Eugene Burdick and Harvey Wheeler); ph, Gerald Hirschfeld; ed, Ralph Rosenblum; art d, Albert Brenner; set d, J.C. Delaney; cos, Anna Hill Johnstone; spec eff, Storyboard, Inc.; makeup, Harry Buchman.

Drama **Cas.** **(PR:C MPAA:NR)**

FAIR EXCHANGE½** (1936, Brit.) 63m WB bw

Patric Knowles *(Tony Meredith)*, Roscoe Ates *(Elmer Goodge)*, Isla Bevan *(Elsie Randall)*, Raymond Lovell *(Sir Reeves Willoughby)*, Cecil Humphreys *(Matthew Randall)*, Louis Goodrich *(James Meredith)*, Morland Graham *(Dr. Franz Schmidt)*.

In order to strip his son of any ambitions as a detective, a criminologist stages the theft of a picture. Ironically, the son upstages dad by proving there really was a burglary and he goes on to solve it.

p, Irving Asher; d, Ralph Ince; w, Brock Williams, Russell Medcraft; ph, Basil Emmott.

Comedy **(PR:A MPAA:NR)**

FAIR WARNING½** (1931) 62m FOX bw

George O'Brien *(Whistlin' Dan Barry)*, Louise Huntington *(Kate Cumberland)*, Mitchell Harris *(Jim Silent)*, George Brent *(Les Haines)*, Nat Pendleton *(Purvis)*, John Sheehan *(Kelduff)*, Erwin Connelly *(Morgan)*, Willard Robertson *(Tex Calder)*, Alphonz Ethier *(Mr. Cumberland)*, Ernest Adams *(Jordan)*.

Better-than-average oater based on a Max Brand novel. It was filmed once as a silent in 1921 but this is the superior version. Not much dialog, just wall-to-wall action with lots of gunplay, chases, and brawls. Brent does a small role in one of his earliest efforts (his third picture). Pendleton provides what little smiles there are but the center of the story is the nonstop pace, well-directed by Werker. Brent was born in Ireland where he took a very active role in the activities during "The Troubles." This caused him to be a marked man and he had to escape to Canada where he took up acting. While still in his 20s, he started his own acting company and had a successful career on the stage before making his way to the U.S. and a career as a suave leading man in many films. That polish may have also been the reason for his having been married half a dozen times, with Ruth Chatterton and Ann Sheridan among his wives.

d, Alfred L. Werker; w, Ernest L. Pascal (based on the novel *The Untamed* by Max Brand); ph, Ross Fisher; ed, Ralph Dietrich.

Western **(PR:A MPAA:NR)**

FAIR WARNING** (1937) 70m FOX bw

J. Edward Bromberg *(Matthew Jericho)*, Betty Furness *(Kay Farnham)*, John Howard Payne *(Jim Preston)*, Victor Kilian *(Sam)*, Billy Burrud *(Malcolm Berkhardt)*, Gavin Muir *(Herbert Willett)*, Gloria Roy *(Grace Hamilton)*, Andrew Tombes *(J.C. Farnham)*, Ivan Lebedeff *(Count Andre Lukacha)*, John Eldredge *(Dr. Galt)*, Julius Tannen *(Mr. Taylor)*, Paul McVey *(Mr. Berkhardt)*, Lelah Taylor *(Mrs. Berkhardt)*, Lydia Knott *(Miss Willoughby)*.

A fair oater set in a Death Valley winter resort with sheriff Bromberg investigating the murder of a wealthy mine owner. By employing the aid of a young chemical whiz, Burrud, they track down the guilty party. Nice little western mystery with chemical hijinks adding to the interest.

p, Sol M. Wurtzel; d, Norman Foster; w, Foster (based on a story by Philip Wylie); ph, Sidney Wagner; ed, Louis Loeffler; md, Samuel Kaylin.

Western/Mystery **(PR:A MPAA:NR)**

FAIR WIND TO JAVA½** (1953) 92m REP c

Fred MacMurray *(Capt. Boll)*, Vera Ralston *(Kim Kim)*, Robert Douglas *(St. Ebenezer/Pulo Besar)*, Victor McLaglen *(O'Brien)*, John Russell *(Flint)*, Buddy Baer

(King), Claude Jarman, Jr. (Chess), Grant Withers (Jason Blue), Howard Petrie (Reeder), Paul Fix (Wilson), William Murphy (Ahab), Sujata (Dancer), Philip Ahn (Gusti), Stephan Bekassy (Lieutenant), Keye Luke (Pidada), John Halloran, Howard Chuman, Mailoa Kalili, Al Kikume (Guards), Blackie Whiteford, Chuck Hayward (Sailors), Richard Reeves (Hoppo Two), Virginia Brissac (Bintang).

MacMurray is an honest trader trying to amass his fortune in the Dutch East Indies. He comes across a diamond fortune and buys Ralston, a Javanese dancer. Later to make things legal, he marries her. The antagonist is Douglas who is cast both as a backstabbing pirate and as an honest Dutchman trying to get his hands on the stones. MacMurray in his admirable way continues on to make his fortune, even though the diamonds are lost to the sea when a volcano erupts. Songs include "Bound For the Open Sea" and "Darling Nelly Gray."

p&d, Joseph Kane; w, Richard Tregaskis (based on the novel by Garland Roark); ph, Jack Marta (Trucolor); m, Victor Young; ed, Richard L. Van Enger; art d, Frank Arrigo; spec eff, Howard and Theodore Lydecker.

Adventure **(PR:A MPAA:NR)**

FAITHFUL✭✭ (1936, Brit.) 78m WB-FN/WB bw

Jean Muir (Marilyn Koster), Gene Gerrard (Danny Reeves), Hans Sonker (Carl Koster), Dorothy [Chili] Bouchier (Pamela Carson), Margaret Yarde (Mrs. Kemp).

Minor musical has Muir and Sonker a pair of music conservatory students who elope to London. With her support, he becomes a popular nightclub singer, but then has an affair with high society girl Bouchier. Muir decides to leave her husband, but the two are reconciled by impresario Gerrard, who has secretly loved Muir all the time.

p, Irving Asher; d, Paul L. Stein; w, Brock Williams; ph, Basil Emmott.

Musical **(PR:A MPAA:NR)**

FAITHFUL CITY✭✭½ (1952, Israel) 86m Molodeth/RKO bw

Jamie Smith (Sam), Ben Josef (Davidei), John Slater (Ezra), Rachel Markus (Sarah), Dina Peskin (Anna), Israel Hanin (Max), Juda Levi (Jean), Amnon Lifshitz (Willy).

An occasionally insightful tale of a group of Jewish children orphaned during the war who have come to idolize Smith, the American who befriends them. When the picture concentrates on the children's conversations or captures their innocent gazes (the cast is made up mostly of non-professionals) it is most successful. The melodramatic punch of having Smith battle the Arabs and save a water supply truck, however, never feels fully satisfying. Though produced in Israel the picture is spoken with English dialog.

p,d&w, Joseph Leytes; ph, G. Gibbs; m, Eduard Ben Michael; ed, J.D. Guthridge; md, Muir Mathieson; art d, R. Simm.

Drama **(PR:A MPAA:NR)**

FAITHFUL HEART✭ (1933, Brit.) 82m Helber/GAU bw
(GB: THE FAITHFUL HEART)

Herbert Marshall (Waverly Ango), Edna Best (Blackie), Mignon O'Doherty (Miss Gattiscombe), Lawrence Hanray (Major Ango), Anne Grey (Diana), Athole Stewart (Sir Gilbert Oughterson).

Tame British picture poorly dubbed with American voices, even for Marshall's. Story concerns a girl who finds the father who long ago deserted her mother. The visit stirs up past emotions and memories, causing the wealthy father to break off his engagement to a woman who will not accept his past. Directing is obviously a big fault in making this one a dud.

p, Michael Balcon; d, Victor Saville; w, Angus MacPhail, Robert Stevenson, Lajos Biro, Saville (based on a play by Monckton Hoffe); ph, Mutz Greenbaum.

Drama **(PR:A MPAA:NR)**

FAITHFUL HEARTS (SEE: FAITHFUL HEART, 1933, Brit.)

FAITHFUL IN MY FASHION✭✭✭ (1946) 81m MGM bw

Donna Reed (Jean Kendrick), Tom Drake (Jeff Compton), Edward Everett Horton (Hiram Dilworthy), Spring Byington (Miss Swanson), Sig Ruman (Prof. Boris Riminoffsky), Harry Davenport (Great Grandpa), William "Bill" Phillips (1st Barfly), Margaret Hamilton (Miss Applegate), Hobart Cavanaugh (Mr. Wilson), Warner Anderson (Walter Medcraft), Connie Gilchrist (Mrs. Murphy), Fred Essler (Nikolai), Wilson Wood (Mr. Stute), Jack Overman (2nd Barfly).

Soldier Drake returns home on a two-week furlough to spend some time with his girl, Reed, who has given her heart away to another. Her co-workers convince her to play innocent for the two weeks and not mention her other love. She heeds their advice, but soon falls back in love with Drake. He, however, finds out the truth. They sort out the mess, as expected, and all is forgiven. A likable mixture of laughs and sobs.

p, Lionel Houser; d, Sidney Salkow; w, Houser; ph, Charles Salerno, Jr.; m, Nathaniel Shilkret; ed, Irvine Warburton; art d, Cedric Gibbons, Harry McAffee.

Romantic Comedy **(PR:A MPAA:NR)**

FAITHLESS✭✭ (1932) 75m MGM bw

Tallulah Bankhead (Carol Morgan), Robert Montgomery (Bill Wade), Hugh Herbert (Mr. Blainey), Maurice Murphy (Anthony Wade), Louise Closser Hale (Landlady), Anna Appel (Another Landlady), Lawrence Grant (Mr. Ledyard), Henry Kolker (Mr. Carter), Sterling Holloway (Photographer), Phil Tead (Reporter), Jack Clifford (Truck Driver), Ben Taggert (Officer Clancy).

A depression-era soap which sees the glamorous Bankhead going from riches to rags while also breaking up and reuniting with Montgomery. The cast performs fine in a film which couldn't have been very amusing to the post-crash audience until the very end, when Montgomery gets a $70-a-week job (did anybody make that much then?).

d, Harry Beaumont; w, Carey Wilson (based on the story "Tinfoil" by Mildred Cram); ph, Oliver T. Marsh; ed, Hugh Wynn.

Drama **(PR:A MPAA:NR)**

FAKE, THE✭✭ (1953, Brit.) 81m Pax/UA bw

Dennis O'Keefe (Paul Mitchell), Coleen Gray (Mary Mason), Hugh Williams (Sir Richard Aldingham), Guy Middleton (Smith), John Laurie (Henry Mason), Eliot Makeham (Pavement Artist), Gerald Case (Peter Randall), Seymour Green (Weston), Stanley van Beers (Cartwright), Dora Bryan (Barmaid), Ellen Pollock (Miss Fossett), Philip Ray (Bearded Tramp), Morris Sweden (Pettigrew), Michael Ward (Art Salesman), Arnold Bell (Police Inspector), Clifford Buckton (Lodging House Keeper), Marianne Noelle (Girl Student), Leslie Phillips (Boy Student), Billie Whitelaw (Waitress), Beatrice Kane (Schoolteacher), Guy Deghy (Stranger), Tommy Clegg (1st Thug), John Wadham (2nd Thug), Frank Atkinson, Johnny Schofield, Leonard Sharpe (Tate Gallery Attendants).

O'Keefe is an American guarding a U.S. art exhibit in London with special care, especially because Leonardo da Vinci's "Madonna and Child" is part of the show. A recent flurry of art thefts has the exhibitors concerned, and, as expected, the Da Vinci is swiped, with a fake left in its place. The watchful O'Keefe follows the burglars as they unsuspectingly lead him to the private gallery of the wealthy villain. Technical aspects on fake paintings are fascinating.

p, Steven Pallos; d, Godfrey Grayson; w, Patrick Kirwan, Bridget Boland (based on a story by James Daplyn); ph, Cedric Williams; ed, Charles Hasse; art d, Dennis Wereford.

Crime **(PR:A MPAA:NR)**

FAKERS, THE (SEE: HELL'S BLOODY DEVILS, 1970)

FAKE'S PROGRESS✭ (1950, Brit.) 52m Falcon Films/Arrow bw

Lou Cass (Clerk), Harry Nova (Spiv), Harry Secombe, Humphrey Lestocq (Commentators).

The action it almost totally silent in this feeble comedy as clerk Cass and greasy swell Nova embark on a disastrous series of money-making schemes. An independent attempt to make a comedy in the form of the early silents was doomed from the outset, but it did pave the way for wordless comedies like MR. HULOT'S HOLIDAY.

p, Hilary Long; d, Ken Fairbairn; w, Long, Fairbairn; ph, Alan Blowey.

Comedy **(PR:A MPAA:NR)**

FALCON AND THE CO-EDS, THE✭✭✭ (1943) 67m RKO bw

Tom Conway (Tom Lawrence/The Falcon), Jean Brooks (Vicky Gaines), Rita Corday (Marguerita Serena), Amelita Ward (Jane Harris), Isabel Jewell (Mary Phoebus), George Givot (Dr. Anatole Graelich), Cliff Clark (Timothy Donovan), Ed Gargan (Bates), Barbara Brown (Miss Keyes), Juanita Alvarez, Ruth Alvarez, Nancy McCullum (The Ughs), Patti Brill (Beanie Smith), Olin Howlin (Goodwillie), Ian Wolfe (Eustace L. Harley), Margie Stewart (Pam), Margaret Landry (Sarey Ann), Carole Gallagher (Elsie), Barbara Lynn (Mildred), Mary Halsey (Telephone Operator), Perc Launders (Garage Man), Elaine Riley (Ellen), Dorothy Maloney [Malone], Julia Hopkins, Dorothy Kelly (Co-eds), Dorothy Christy (Maya Harris), Anne O'Neal (Miss Hicks), Ruth Cherrington (Dowager), Rosemary LaPlanche, Barbara Coleman, Daun Kennedy.

One of the best of the Falcon series has the debonaire Conway, surrounded by the tender-aged gals of the Bluecliff School, called in to investigate the murder of a professor, a scandal the school wants to avoid. Upon his arrival the murder rate rises and he follows the clues to the killer. Future Academy Award winner Dorothy Malone, here billed as "Maloney," has a bit as one of the chatty co-eds. Brightened by some fine oceanside photography, a rarity for the film noir days. It has often been pointed out that rarely has a movie star been accompanied by so many beautiful women in one film as Conway was in the FALCON AND THE CO-EDS. The reason, most certainly, was because when the film was made many male stars were in the services or in Washington, and there were, for the first and only time in Hollywood history, an absolute plethora of beauties on hand looking for work and scripts were developed to utilize them. (See THE FALCON series, Index.)

p, Maurice Geraghty; d, William Clemens; w, Ardel Wray, Gerald Geraghty (based on an original story by Wray from the character created by Michael Arlen); ph, Roy Hunt; ed, Theron Warth; md, C. Bakaleinikoff; art d, Albert S. D'Agostino; spec eff, Vernon L. Walker.

Crime Mystery **(PR:A MPAA:NR)**

FALCON FIGHTERS, THE✭✭
(1970, Jap.) 100m Daiei Motion Picture Co. c
(RIKUGUN HAYABUSA SENTOTAI)

Makoto Sato (Lt. Takeo Kato), Shiho Fujimura (His Wife), Sei Hiraizumi (2nd Lt. Kihara), Kojiro Hongo (2nd Lt. Ando), Jun Fujimaki (Cho Eishun), Yoko Namikawa (Keiko), Akio Hasegawa, Ken Utsui.

Sato is a flight instructor in the newly formed Japanese air force. His two best pilots are Hiraizumi and Fujimaki, a Chinese officer studying in Japan. Years later, when war breaks out between Japan and China, Fujimaki shoots down Hiraizumi in northern China. Sato challenges his former student to an air duel and shoots him down. He is deeply troubled by the incident and carries his torment into the war against the Allies in the Pacific. Later, he is shot down over the Bay of Bengal. An interesting look at some behind-the-scenes flying by the Japanese during WW II.

d, Mitsuo Murayama; w, Katsuya Suzaki; ph, Kimio Watanabe (Daieiscope, Fujicolor); m, Seitaro Omori; art d, Koichi Takahashi; spec eff, Noriaki Yuasa.

War **(PR:C MPAA:NR)**

FALCON IN DANGER, THE½** (1943) 69m RKO bw

Tom Conway *(Falcon)*, Jean Brooks *(Iris Fairchild)*, Elaine Shepard *(Nancy Palmer)*, Amelita Ward *(Bonnie Caldwell)*, Cliff Clark *(Inspector Timothy Donovan)*, Ed Gargan *(Bates)*, Clarence Kolb *(Stanley Harris Palmer)*, Felix Basch *(Morley)*, Richard Davies *(Ken Gibson)*, Richard Martin *(Georgie Morley)*, Erford Gage *(Evan Morley)*, Eddie Dunn *(Grimes)*, Bruce Edwards *(Mechanic)*, Joan Barclay *(Hysterical Girl)*, Jack Mulhall *(Casino Manager)*, Russell Wade.

With Ward as the Falcon's love interest, the supersleuth tries to track down two industrialists who disappeared along with their $100,000 from a small passenger plane while in the air. The Falcon's snooping tells him the answer revolves around a subversive plot against the government. The first of three Falcon pictures directed by Clemens. (See THE FALCON series, Index.)

p, Maurice Geraghty; d, William Clemens; w, Fred Niblo, Jr., Craig Rice (based on the character created by Michael Arlen); ph, Frank Redman; ed, George Crone; md, C. Bakaleinikoff; art d, Albert S. D'Agostino, Walter E. Keller.

Crime **(PR:A MPAA:NR)**

FALCON IN HOLLYWOOD, THE½** (1944) 66m RKO bw

Tom Conway *(Falcon)*, Barbara Hale *(Peggy Callahan)*, Rita Corday *(Lili D'Allio)*, Jean Brooks *(Roxanna)*, Veda Ann Borg *(Billie)*, Konstantin Shayne *(Alec Hoffman)*, John Abbott *(Martin Dwyer)*, Emory Parnell *(Inspector McBride)*, Frank Jenks *(Lt. Higgins)*, Sheldon Leonard *(Louie)*, Walter Soderling *(Ed Johnson)*, Useff Ali *(Nagari)*, Carl Kent *(Art Director)*, Gwen Crawford, Patti Brill *(Secretaries)*, Bryant Washburn, Sammy Blum *(Actors' Agents)*, Nancy Marlowe *(Mail Clerk)*, Chris Drake *(Assistant Cameraman)*, George De Normand *(Truck Driver)*, Jimmy Jordan *(Operator)*, Perc Launders *(Zoltan)*, Jacques Lory *(Musician)*, Wheaton Chambers, Bert Moorhouse *(Men)*, Chester Clute *(Hotel Manager)*, Chili Williams *(Blonde)*, Margie Stewart, Greta Christiansen *(Girls)*, Robert Clarke *(Perc Saunders)*.

The Falcon takes a vacation hop to the glamour city and, of course, gets involved in a murder case. Slain is a former actor whose wife, the studio's fashion designer, has been having an affair with a director. The film takes place on RKO's back lot, allowing for a tourist's eye view of the studio. (See THE FALCON series, Index.)

p, Maurice Geraghty; d, Gordon Douglas; w, Gerald Geraghty (based on the character created by Michael Arlen); ph, Nicholas Musuraca; ed, Gene Milford; md, C. Bakaleinikoff; art d, Albert D'Agostino, L.O. Croxton.

Crime **Cas.** **(PR:A MPAA:NR)**

FALCON IN MEXICO, THE*** (1944) 70m RKO bw

Tom Conway *(Falcon)*, Mona Maris *(Raquel)*, Martha MacVicar [Vickers] *(Barbara Wade)*, Nestor Paiva *(Manuel Romero)*, Mary Currier *(Paula Dudley)*, Cecilia Callejo *(Dolores Ybarra)*, Emory Parnell *(James Winthrop Hughes/Lucky Diamond)*, Joseph Vitale *(Anton)*, Pedro de Cordoba *(Don Carlos Ybarra)*, Fernando Alvarado *(Pancho Romero)*, Bryant Washburn *(Humphrey Wade)*, George Lewis *(Mexican Detective)*, Julian Rivero *(Mexican Doctor)*, Juanita and Ruth Alvarez *(Singers)*.

New paintings from a supposedly dead artist surface in New York City, arousing the suspicions of the Falcon and the artist's daughter. After a gallery owner is killed, Conway and MacVicar travel to Mexico City to unearth the mystery. It all comes to light in a small town inn where dancer Maris fills in the missing pieces. Some wonderful exterior footage, supposedly from Orson Welles' aborted RKO documentary, IT'S ALL TRUE. (See THE FALCON series, Index.)

p, Maurice Geraghty; d, William Berke; w, George Worthing Yates, Gerald Geraghty (based on a character created by Michael Arlen); ph, Frank Redman; ed, Joseph Noriega; md, C. Bakaleinikoff; art d, Albert S. D'Agostino; spec eff, Vernon L. Walker; m/l, "Negrita No Me Dejes," Aaron Gonzales.

Crime **Cas.** **(PR:A MPAA:NR)**

FALCON IN SAN FRANCISCO, THE** (1945) 66m RKO bw

Tom Conway *(Falcon)*, Rita Corday *(Joan Marshall)*, Edward S. Brophy *(Goldie Locke)*, Sharyn Moffett *(Annie Marshall)*, Faye Helm *(Doreen Temple)*, Robert Armstrong *(De Forrest Marshall)*, Carl Kent *(Rickey)*, George Holmes *(Dalman)*, John Mylong *(Peter Vantine)*, Edmund Cobb *(Cop)*, Myrna Dell *(Beautiful Girl)*, Esther Howard *(Mrs. Peabody)*.

The Falcon investigates a silk-smuggling operation in the "city by the bay" with his pal Goldie Locke, played by the recognizable character actor Brophy. Conway's interaction with his befriended tot, Moffett, is the brightest spot in this poorly scripted addition to the series. The tiredness of the production could account for the fact that only one Falcon picture was filmed in 1945. (See THE FALCON series, Index.)

p, Maurice Geraghty; d, Joseph H. Lewis; w, Robert Kent, Ben Markson (based on an original story by Kent from the character created by Michael Arlen); ph, Virgil Miller, William Sickner; ed, Ernie Leadlay; md, C. Bakaleinikoff.

Crime **(PR:A MPAA:NR)**

FALCON OUT WEST, THE½** (1944) 64 RKO bw

Tom Conway *(Falcon)*, Carole Gallagher *(Vanessa)*, Barbara Hale *(Marion)*, Joan Barclay *(Mrs. Irwin)*, Cliff Clark *(Inspector Donovan)*, Ed Gargan *(Bates)*, Minor Watson *(Caldwell)*, Don Douglas *(Hayden)*, Lyle Talbot *(Tex)*, Lee Trent *(Dusty)*, Perc Launders *(Red)*, Wheaton Chambers *(Sheriff)*, Lawrence Tierney *(Orchestra Leader)*, Chief Thunderbird *(Eagle Feather)*, Tom Burton *(Photographer)*, Steve Winston *(Caldwell Cowboy)*, Harry Clay *(Hall)*, Robert Anderson *(Wally Waldron)*, Edmund Glover *(Frank Daley)*, Mary Halsey *(Cissy)*, Daun Kennedy *(Gloria)*, Rosemary La Planche *(Mary)*, Chef Milani *(Manager)*, Elaine Riley *(Cigarette Girl)*, Shirley O'Hara, Patti Brill *(Hat Check Girls)*, Michael St. Angel *(Man)*, Eddie Clark *(Coroner)*, Joe Cody *(Toni)*, Bert Roach *(Charlie)*, Norman Willis *(Callahan)*, Kernan Cripps *(Murphy)*, Slim Whittaker *(Cowboy)*, William Nestell *(Chef)*, Zedra Conde *(Carlita)*, Norman Mayes *(Pullman Porter)*.

Dusty Texas serves as the backdrop for this whodunit, as The Falcon shadows the fiancee of a murdered Lone Star playboy. After the Texan dies in a New York night club, it is discovered that he was slipped some rattlesnake venom. On the trail, the Falcon is kidnaped and nearly killed, but he escapes and solves the mystery. (See THE FALCON series, Index.)

p, Maurice Geraghty; d, William Clemens; w, Billy Jones, Morton Grant (based on the character created by Michael Arlen); ph, Barry Wild; m, Roy Webb; ed, Gene Milford; md, C. Bakaleinikoff; art d, Albert S. D'Agostino, Alfred Herman; dialog d, Donald Dillaway; cos, Renie.

Crime/Western **(PR:A MPAA:NR)**

FALCON STRIKES BACK, THE½** (1943) 63m RKO bw

Tom Conway *(Falcon)*, Harriet Hilliard *(Gwynne Gregory)*, Jane Randolph *(Marcia Brooks)*, Edgar Kennedy *(Smiley Dugan)*, Cliff Edwards *(Goldie)*, Rita Corday *(Mia Bruger)*, Erford Gage *(Rickey Davis)*, Wynne Gibson *(Mrs. Lipton)*, Richard Loo *(Jerry)*, Andre Charlot *(Bruno Steffen)*, Cliff Clark *(Inspector Timothy Donovan)*, Ed Gargan *(Bates)*, Byron Foulger *(Argyle)*, Frank Faylen *(Cecil)*, Jack Norton *(Hobo)*, Joan Barclay.

The Falcon is wrongly accused of murdering a banker and stealing some war bonds. Trailed by the law, he escapes to the mountains and holes up in a vacation lodge. It is here he discovers a war bond racket and, as expected, he ropes the band of evil-doers. This was Conway's first solo outing as the title crime fighter. (See THE FALCON series, Index.)

p, Maurice Geraghty, d, Edward Dmytryk; w, Edward Dein, Gerald Geraghty, (story by Stuart Palmer, based on the character created by Michael Arlen); ph, Jack MacKenzie; ed, George Crone; md, C. Bakaleinikoff; art d, Albert S. D'Agostino, Walter E. Keller.

Crime **(PR:A MPAA:NR)**

FALCON TAKES OVER, THE*** (1942) 62m RKO bw

George Sanders *(Falcon)*, Lynn Bari *(Ann Riordan)*, James Gleason *(Inspector Mike O'Hara)*, Allen Jenkins *(Goldie Locke)*, Helen Gilbert *(Diana Kenyon)*, Ward Bond *(Moose Malloy)*, Ed Gargan *(Bates)*, Anne Revere *(Jessie Florian)*, George Cleveland *(Jerry)*, Harry Shannon *(Grimes)*, Hans Conried *(Lindsey Marriot)*, Mickey Simpson *(Bartender)*, Selmer Jackson *(Laird Burnett)*, Turhan Bey *(Jules Amthor)*, Charlie Hall *(Lovie, Swan Club Waiter)*.

The third in the Falcon series which was, this time, based on the Raymond Chandler novel *Farewell, My Lovely*. Sanders is cast as the Falcon, which is nothing more than a transposed Philip Marlowe. After an ex-wrestler is released from jail, he sets out to find his long lost girl friend, leaving a path of dead bodies behind. Sanders and lovely lady reporter Bari try their best to crack the case. They are led to a gambling operation, whereupon Bari gets her story and Sanders gets the reporter, Remade by RKO in 1945 with Dick Powell as Marlowe, as MURDER MY SWEET, and again in 1975 with Robert Mitchum in the role, under the original title of FAREWELL, MY LOVELY. (See THE FALCON series, Index.)

p, Howard Benedict; d, Irving Reis; w, Lynn Root, Frank Fenton (based on the character created by Michael Arlen, and the novel *Farewell, My Lovely* by Raymond Chandler); ph, George Robinson; ed, Harry Marker; md, C. Bakaleinikoff; art d, Albert S. D'Agostino, F.M. Gray.

Crime **Cas.** **(PR:A MPAA:NR)**

FALCON'S ADVENTURE, THE½** (1946) 61m RKO bw

Tom Conway *(Falcon)*, Madge Meredith *(Louisa Braganza)*, Edward S. Brophy *(Goldie Locke)*, Robert Warwick *(Kenneth Sutton)*, Myrna Dell *(Doris Blanding)*, Steve Brodie *(Benny)*, Ian Wolfe *(Denison)*, Carol Forman *(Helen)*, Joseph Crehan *(Inspector Cavanaugh)*, Phil Warren *(Mike Geary)*, Tony Barrett *(Paolo)*, Harry Harvey *(Duncan)*, Jason Robards *(Lt. Evans)*, Dave Sharpe *(Crew Member)*.

The noble and daring Falcon rescues Meredith from a gang of kidnapers who are after her father's formula for synthetic diamonds. When the scientist is killed, the police blame the Falcon, forcing the pair to flee to Florida. Once they arrive there another murder occurs, making the Falcon look even guiltier. The police, however, are proven wrong as the super-sleuth rounds up the real culprits. This film marked the final appearance for Conway as the Falcon. He went on to continue crime-solving on the radio as Sherlock Holmes and The Saint. Actually the last picture in the Falcon series, though three lower-quality ripoffs followed. (See THE FALCON series, Index.)

p, Herman Schlom; d, William Berke; w, Aubrey Wisberg, Robert E. Kent; ph, Harry Wild, Frank Redman; m, Paul Sawtell; ed, Marvin Coil; art d, Albert D'Agostino, W.E. Keller; spec. eff, Russell A. Cully.

Crime **Cas.** **(PR:A MPAA:NR)**

FALCON'S ALIBI, THE*** (1946) 63m RKO bw

Tom Conway *(Falcon)*, Rita Corday *(Joan Meredith)*, Vince Barnett *(Goldie Locke)*, Jane Greer *(Lola Carpenter)*, Elisha Cook, Jr. *(Nick)*, Emory Parnell *(Metcalf)*, Al Bridge *(Inspector Blake)*, Esther Howard *(Gloria Peabody)*, Jean Brooks *(Baroness Lena)*, Myrna Dell *(Girl with Falcon)*, Paul Brooks *(Alex)*, Jason Robards *(Beaumont)*, Morgan Wallace *(Bender)*, Lucien Prival *(Baron)*, Edmund Cobb *(Detective Williams)*, Betty Gillette *(Elevator Operator)*, Forbes Murray *(Mr. Thompson)*, Alphonse Martel *(Louie)*, Edward Clark *(Coroner)*, Bonnie Blair *(Telephone Operator)*, Nan Leslie *(Girl)*, Bob Alden *(Bellhop)*, Joe La Barba, Eddie Borden *(Men)*, Mike Lally, Jack Stoney *(Thugs)*, George Holmes *(Man)*, Harry Harvey *(Race Fan)*, Alf Haugen *(Doorman)*.

In a plot similar to the series entry, THE GAY FALCON, Conway is hired to guard a rich woman's jewels by her secretary, who is fearful that she will be blamed if they are stolen. They are soon fingered and Conway is on the corpse-paved trail of the thief. Typically, Conway is suspected, but proves his innocence by providing the police with the murderer. Elisha Cook, Jr. (the shifty-eyed hood in THE

MALTESE FALCON) is well cast as a crazed DJ who does the deed while playing a tape of his show in his absence. (See THE FALCON series, Index.)

p, William Berke; d, Ray McCarey; w, Paul Yawitz (from a story by Dane Lussior, Manny Seff); ph, Frank Redman; ed, Philip Martin, Jr.; md, C. Bakaleinikoff; art d, Albert S. D'Agostino, Lucius Croxton.

Crime (PR:A MPAA:NR)

FALCON'S BROTHER, THE* (1942) 63m RKO bw

George Sanders (Gay Lawrence), Tom Conway (Tom Lawrence), Jane Randolph (Marcie Brooks), Don Barclay (Lefty), Cliff Clark (Donovan), Ed Gargan (Bates), Eddie Dunn (Grimes), Charlotte Wynters (Arlette), James Newill (Paul Harrington), Keye Luke (Jerry), Amanda Varela (Carmela), George Lewis (Valdez), Gwili Andre (Diane Medford), Mary Halsey (Miss Ross), Andre Charlot (Savitski), Charles Arnt (Pat Moffett), Richard Martin (Steamship Official), Kay Aldredge (Victory Gown Model/Spanish Girl), John Dilson (Ship's Officer).

The Falcon brothers, Gay (Sanders) and Tom (Conway), team up to crack a gang of Nazi saboteurs. Sanders is informed that brother Conway has been killed, but upon viewing the corpse realizes that the Nazis got the wrong man. The pair travel to South America where Sanders is killed while protecting a government official. Conway assumes the Falcon's role and continues on in his brother's crime-fighting footsteps. Intended as a way to get Sander's out of a role he didn't like, RKO officials teamed him with real life brother Conway with the intent of wrapping up the series. Conway, however, reached such a high level of popularity that they suited him up as the Falcon nine more times. (See THE FALCON series, Index.)

p, Maurice Geraghty; d, Stanley Logan; w, Stuart Palmer, Craig Rice (based on the character created by Michael Arlen); ph, Russell Metty; m, Roy Webb; ed, Mark Robson; md, C. Bakaleinikoff; art d, Albert S. D'Agostino, Walter E. Keller.

Crime **Cas.** (PR:A MPAA:NR)

FALL GIRL, THE (SEE: LISETTE, 1963)

FALL GUY, THE (1930) 66m RKO bw
(GB: TRUST YOUR WIFE)

Jack Mulhall (Johnny Quinlan), Mae Clarke (Bertha Quinlan), Ned Sparks (Dan Walsh), Pat O'Malley (Charles Newton), Tom Jackson ("Nifty" Herman), Wynne Gibson (Lottie Quinlan), Ann Brody (Mrs. Bercowich), Elmer Ballard ("Hutch"), Alan Roscoe (Det. Keefe).

Naive drug clerk Mulhall befriends a mobster who plants a cache of drugs on his person. Mulhall is then nabbed by the cops, but is smart enough to con the guilty one into a confession. Supporting Mulhall is Mae Clarke, who is best remembered for a smaller role, when James Cagney pushed a grapefruit in her face in PUBLIC ENEMY.

p, William Le Baron; d, A. Leslie Pearce; w, Tim Whelan (based on a play by George Abbott, James Gleason); ph, Leo Tover; ed, Archie Marshek.

Crime/Comedy (PR:A MPAA:NR)

FALL GUY½ (1947) 64m MON bw

Clifford Penn (Tom Cochrane), Teala Loring (Lois Walter), Robert Armstrong (Mac McLaine), Virginia Dale (Marie), Elisha Cook, Jr. (Joe), Douglas Fowley (Shannon), Charles Arnt (Uncle Jim Grossett), Harry Strang (Taylor), Iris Adrian (Mrs. Sindell), John Harmon (Mr. Sindell), John Bleifer (Clerk), Lou Lubin (Benny), Christian Rub (Swede), George Backus (Police Physician), Jack Overman (Mike), Theodore Gottlieb (Inmate), Franklin Dix, Monty Ford, Wally Walker (Men), Katherine Marlowe, Edna Harris, Marlyn Gladstone (Women), Bob Carleton (Pianist)

Penn is a nice guy with a problem. He's been arrested for a murder on a night he cannot remember. Unfortunately all the evidence, including his possession of the bloody knife used in the murder, points directly at him. Armstrong, his policeman buddy, frees Penn and together they piece together what little information they have. It is discovered that Penn has been framed by his uncle (Arnt) who didn't like Penn dating his ward (Loring). The dead woman has also been Arnt's mistress and was blackmailing him. Mad with jealousy over Loring, and eager to get rid of his mistress, Arnt had fixed Penn with a powerful narcotic and created the scene to make Penn look guilty. Arnt is arrested, with Penn and Loring happily reunited.

p, Walter Mirisch; d, Reginald LeBorg; w, Jerry Warner; John O'Dea (based on the short story "Cocaine" by Cornell Woolrich); ph, Mack Stenger; ed, William Austin; md, Edward J. Kay; art d, Dave Milton, set d, Vin Taylor; spec eff, Augie Lehman.

Crime/Mystery (PR:C MPAA:NR)

FALL GUY, THE (SEE: FALLGUY, THE, 1962)

FALL OF EVE, THE (1929) 67m COL bw

Patsy Ruth Miller (Eve Grant), Ford Sterling (Mr. Mack), Gertrude Astor (Mrs. Ford), Arthur Rankin (Tom Ford, Jr.), Jed Prouty (Tom Ford, Sr.), Betty Farrington (Mrs. Mack), Fred Kelsey (Cop), Hank Mann (Bob White).

An energetic farce which has a businessman trying to secure a deal with his client by taking him to a ritzy nightclub with Miller in tow as his female escort. The client's wife insists on tagging along, thereby causing Miller to be passed off as the businessman's wife. Meanwhile the businessman's real wife is listening to a radio broadcast from the nightclub when she hears a song request placed by her husband and Miller. Her suspicions are aroused and she heads for the club where the situation goes from one zany twist to another. If one can get past the primitive sound recording the film may bring out a laugh or two.

d, Frank Strayer; w, Gladys Lehman, Fred Hatton, Fanny Hatton (based on the story by John Emerson, Anita Loos); ph, Teddy Tetzlaff; ed, Gene Havlick.

Comedy (PR:A MPAA:NR)

FALL OF ROME, THE** (1963, Ital.) 89 Atlantica Cinematografica/ Medallion c (IL CROLLO DI ROMA)

Carl Mohner (Marcus), Loredana Nusciak (Svetla), Ida Galli (Licia), Andrea Aureli (Rako), Piero Palermini (Valerio), Giancarlo Sbragia (Giunio), Nando Tamberlani (Matteo), Maria Grazia Buccella (Xenia), Laura Rocca (Madre Tullio), Jim Dolen (Caius), Riccardo Ricci (Tullio), Mimmo Maggio, Roberto Bettoni, Nando Poggi, Claudio Scarchilli, Renato Terra, Joe Pollini.

Mohner is a Roman centurion and Christian when Sbragia takes the throne after Emperor Constantine's death. Sbragia wants all Christians put to death, and Mohner hides out in the camp of the barbarians. Mohner goes back to Rome and into the arena as a gladiator and defeats three men to win the Christians their freedom. Mohner is sent back into the arena and an earthquake takes place, killing Sbragia and most of the Roman population, and Mohner escapes to preach the gospel. More Roman history from the font of it all.

p, Marco Vicario; d, Anthony Dawson [Antonio Margheriti]; w, Margheriti, Gianni Astolfi, Mauro Mancini; ph, Riccardo Pallottini; m, Riz Ortolani; ed, Renato Cinquini.

Historical Epic (PR:C MPAA:NR)

FALL OF THE HOUSE OF USHER, THE* (1952, Brit.) 70m GIB/Vigilant bw

Kay Tendeter (Lord Roderick Usher), Gwendoline Watford (Lady Usher), Irving Steen (Jonathan), Lucy Pavey (The Hag), Vernon Charles (Dr. Cordwell), Gavin Lee (The Butler), Tony Powell-Bristow (Richard), Connie Goodwin (Louise), Robert Wolard (Greville), Keith Lorraine (George).

An Edgar Allan Poe adaptation crippled by a bloodless script and tired direction. Supposedly Tendeter is horrified when his sister returns from the great beyond, leaving him with nothing but a blazing abode.

p&d, Ivan Barnett; w, Kenneth Thompson, Dorothy Catt (based on the story by Edgar Allan Poe); ph, Barnett; m, De Wolfe.

Horror (PR:C MPAA:NR)

FALL OF THE HOUSE OF USHER, THE (SEE: HOUSE OF USHER, 1960)

FALL OF THE HOUSE OF USHER, THE* (1980) 101m Sunn Classic c

Martin Landau (Roderick Usher), Ray Walston (Thaddeus), Charlene Tilton (Jennifer), Dimitra Arliss (Madeline), Robert Hays (Jonathan).

Forgettable adaptation of the Edgar Allan Poe story. Landau and Walston hit a low point in their respective careers with this film, while Tilton and Hays were just getting on the way. This was atypical of Sunn Classic fare, which usually leaned towards family and docudrama films. Filmed in Salt Lake City.

p, Charles E. Sellier, Jr.; d, James L. Conway; w, Stephen Lord (based on the story by Edgar Allan Poe); ph, (Technicolor).

Horror **Cas.** (PR:O MPAA:PG)

FALL OF THE ROMAN EMPIRE, THE*½ (1964) 188m Bronston-Roma/PAR c

Sophia Loren (Lucilla), Stephen Boyd (Livius), Alec Guinness (Marcus Aurelius), James Mason (Timonides), Christopher Plummer (Commodus), Anthony Quayle (Verulus), John Ireland (Ballomar), Mel Ferrer (Cleander), Omar Sharif (Sohamus), Eric Porter (Julianus), Douglas Wilmer (Niger), Peter Damon (Claudius), Andrew Keir (Polybius), George Murcell (Victorinus), Lena von Martens (Helva), Gabriella Licudi (Tauna), Rafael Luis Calvo (Lentulus), Norman Wooland (Virgilianus), Virgilio Texera (Marcellus), Michael Gwynn (Cornelius), Guy Rolfe (Marius), Finlay Currie (Caecina).

An overlong, sometimes engrossing spectacle that attempts to chronicle the bloody transitional period following the death of Marcus Aurelius (Guinness). Philosopher-emperor Guinness calls a meeting of his family clan and supporters at his fortress in Germany. He confides to daughter Loren that he intends to make his adopted son, Boyd, the new emperor upon his death, instead of his legal heir, Plummer. Blind soothsayer Ferrer, who is one of Plummer's cronies, overhears Guinness and poisons him. Following Guinness' death Loren tells Boyd of the dead emperor's wishes, but he spurns the throne and allows the strutting Plummer to become Rome's new Caesar. The empire begins to erode as Plummer's sense of power and ego inflate. Although Boyd and Mason are able to institute some small reforms, little they do can stem the mounting revolt against Plummer's tyrannical ways. Loren marries Sharif who is later killed by Plummer's legions invading his Armenian territory. She then returns to Rome with Boyd where Plummer has gone berserk, declaring himself a god, as did so many vainglorious emperors before him. He murders anyone who stands in his way, including the humanitarian Mason. When he learns that Quayle, his old gladiatorial tutor, is really his father, Plummer has Quayle killed. Realizing that Loren has a stronger tie to the throne, Plummer orders her death, too, in an agonizing end where she is staked out in the arena and is about to be burned to death. Boyd arrives as the flames begin to lick at her pretty toes and saves Loren at the last minute. He then draws his sword against Plummer; the battle between them is bloody and to the death, with good guy Boyd triumphant. Boyd is heralded as the rightful heir of the emperor, but, with Loren in his arms, he turns his back once more on the glorious title (a more modest and self-effacing hero you will never see). As the lovers depart, the power-crazed Plummer aides begin bidding fortunes for the right to become emperor. THE FALL OF THE ROMAN EMPIRE, for all its sumptuous sets, wall-to-wall armies, and exciting action, is as vacuous as an arena without lions. No orderly history is presented here, even though the much-vaunted historian Will Durant was consultant on the production, but rather a hodge-podge of suspicious facts, events, and personalities are thrown willy-nilly into the story which is fragmentary and often so threadbare that it hardly exists. Whenever there is a lull, director Mann throws the bosomy, sensual Loren at the viewer in some provocative bedroom pose. Her thick accent brutalizes her lines as horrendously as the pagan punishments administered to the hapless Christians in the arena. Of course, she considered her part a challenge, when realizing that Guinness would momentarily play opposite her. She is quoted as saying that she was frightened of the great British actor: "After all, he has a title." She got over that, visiting Guinness at his home during the production. "We used to do the Twist together," Loren later bubbled. "He did it very well." Guinness has a very small part in the film and was obviously used for star value. He sleepwalks through his role, as does Mason, both British stalwarts seeming to shrug at their parts in this fuzzy epic. Boyd's performance as the heroic and noble Roman is typically devoid of emotion, another jaw-jutting granite performance. Only Plummer is fascinating as the eccentric, wholly unpredictable despot. Producer Bronson had lavished fortunes on such enormous films as EL CID (1961) and KING OF KINGS (1961) but he opened all the floodgates with this one, pouring more than $20 million into this beautiful but soggy Roman tale. He lost more than $18 million which caused him to collapse his production facilities in Spain and abandon his wholesale rental of an otherwise unoccupied Spanish army. Only Fox's disastrous CLEOPATRA, released the year before, exceeded this financial catastrophe. Mann excused his failure by stating that the film's story was "defeatist" and therefore he could not be upbeat about it.

p, Samuel Bronston; d, Anthony Mann; w, Ben Barzman, Basilio Franchina, Philip Yordan; ph, Robert Krasker (Ultra-Panavision 70, Technicolor); m, Dimitri Tiomkin; ed, Robert Lawrence; prod d, Veniero Colasanti, John Moore; set d, Colasanti, Moore; cos, Gloria Mussetta; spec eff, Alex Weldon; makeup, Mario Van Riel; historical consultant, Will Durant.

Historical Epic **Cas.** **(PR:O MPAA:NR)**

FALLEN ANGEL*½** (1945) 98m FOX bw

Alice Faye *(June Mills)*, Dana Andrews *(Eric Stanton)*, Linda Darnell *(Stella)*, Charles Bickford *(Mark Judd)*, Anne Revere *(Clara Mills)*, Bruce Cabot *(Dave Atkins)*, John Carradine *(Prof. Madley)*, Percy Kilbride *(Pop)*, Olin Howlin *(Joe Ellis)*, Hal Taliaferro *(Johnson)*, Mira McKinney *(Mrs. Judd)*, Gus Glassmire, Jimmy Conlin *(Hotel Clerks)*, Leila McIntyre *(Bank Clerk)*, Garry Owen *(Waiter)*, Horace Murphy *(Sheriff)*, Martha Wentworth *(Maid)*, Paul Palmer *(Detective)*, Paul Burns *(Newsman)*, Herb Ashley *(Plain Clothes Man)*, Stymie Beard *(Shoe Shine Boy)*, Chick Collins, William Haade *(Bus Drivers)*, Dorothy Adams *(Store Keeper)*, Harry Strang *(Policeman)*, Max Wagner *(Bartender)*.

Taut and twisty crime yarn has impoverished press agent Andrews thrown off a San Francisco bound bus for lack of a fare, landing in Walton, a small coastal community. He connives a bed for the night with Howlin, an advance man for medium Carradine, promising to build up Carradine's act and bring in a large crowd. Hired, he meets Faye, a wealthy but reclusive young woman, learning her background. Later he visits a diner where svelte waitress Darnell captures his eye. Carradine delivers his "spook lecture," revealing some town secrets, including that of Faye and sister Revere, with the help of Andrews' inside information. Carradine and Howlin leave for San Francisco, having paid Andrews a handsome sum for beefing up their show. Andrews, however, is so smitten with Darnell that he stays behind. The sultry, scheming waitress wants no part of him unless he suddenly inherits Fort Knox. To appease her greedy ambitions, Andrews tells her he will marry the lovesick Faye, get her money and then divorce her, so they can be together. After the nuptials, Andrews deserts Faye. The next day Darnell's body is found and the investigation into her murder is conducted by retired cop Bickford, who had been a regular visitor to the diner where she worked. He tries to beat a confession out of shifty Cabot, a one-time Darnell beau, then turns the heat on Andrews. With the loyal Faye in tow, Andrews flees to San Francisco and draws his wife's money from the bank. He has her wait for him in a hotel room, saying he's going to clear his own name. After Andrews vanishes, Faye is arrested. Andrews appears in Walton just as police are about to charge Faye with Darnell's killing. He confronts the brutal Bickford in the diner where he forces the one-time detective to admit that he had loved Darnell from afar and was driven nearly mad at the sight of seeing her with Cabot and other men (she had been two-timing Andrews all the while he worked away at bilking Faye on her behalf). He could no longer stand it, Bickford admits, and killed the vixen. (Here the viewer is presented with the oddball plot of having the investigating detective really searching for himself!) Andrews and Faye reunite and try to make a go of their marriage. Director Preminger hoped to have another LAURA with this film but it fell short due to some loose ends in the script and disjointed points of view as the director sometimes shifts the focus of the story erratically from one character to another, a blatant red herring to mislead the viewer from guessing the killer's identity. The overall mood, lighting, and pace of the film, nevertheless, is top, hardboiled *film noir*. Bickford, as the quiet, always watching cop who routinely visits the diner, sips his coffee, plays one song ("Slowly," sung by Faye), then leaves, is a gem of restraint. Faye, who had been a Fox super star for many years, had been promised a meaty and significant part; she had rejected almost three dozen scripts before accepting the lead in FALLEN ANGEL but her role was slowly chiseled away by Preminger, who played up Darnell during the production, giving her more and more scenes. Faye felt that some of her best scenes had been chopped and considered herself betrayed. "I was terribly upset," Faye was later quoted. "I felt the film had been ruined, and, feeling utterly at a loss, I left the studio. I didn't even go to my dressing room to collect my personal belongings." Faye retired on the spot, so bitter that it would be 16 years before she returned to the screen.

p&d, Otto Preminger; w, Harry Kleiner (based on the novel by Marty Holland); ph, Joseph LaShelle; m, David Raksin; ed, Harry Reynolds; md, Emil Newman; art d, Lyle Wheeler, Leland Fuller; set d, Thomas Little, Helen Hansard; cos, Bonnie Cashin; spec eff, Fred Sersen; m/l, "Slowly," Raksin, Kermit Goell; makeup, Ben Nye.

Crime Drama **Cas.** **(PR:A MPAA:NR)**

FALLEN IDOL, THE***** (1949, Brit.) 94m London Film/BL bw (AKA: THE LOST ILLUSION)

Ralph Richardson *(Baines)*, Michele Morgan *(Julie)*, Bobby Henrey *(Felipe)*, Sonia Dresdel *(Mrs. Baines)*, Denis O'Dea *(Inspector Crowe)*, Walter Fitzgerald *(Dr. Fenton)*, Karel Stepanek *(1st Secretary)*, Joan Young *(Mrs. Barrow)*, Dandy Nichols *(Mrs. Patterson)*, Bernard Lee *(Detective Hart)*, Jack Hawkins *(Detective Lake)*, Geoffrey Keen *(Detective Davis)*, Hay Petrie *(Clockwinder)*, James Hayter *(Perry)*, John Ruddock *(Dr. Wilson)*, Dora Bryan *(Rose)*, Torin Thatcher *(Policeman "A")*, *George Woodbridge (Police Sergeant)*, Gerard Heinz *(Ambassador)*, Nora Gordon *(Waitress)*, Ethel Coleridge *(Housekeeper)*, Ralph Norman, James Swan *(Policemen)*.

A beautifully directed thriller, THE FALLEN IDOL is set in a foreign embassy inside London. The ambassador departs and leaves his precocious, imaginative son, Henrey, with butler Richardson and Richardson's housekeeper wife, Dresdel. The boy idolizes kindly, considerate Richardson and rightly dislikes his shrewish, vicious wife. Richardson and embassy typist Morgan have been having an affair and Henrey overhears them agreeing to end their affair. This information is later wheedled out of Henrey by Dresdel, who later has a violent argument with her husband. In her jealous rage, Dresdel accidentally falls down a flight of stairs to her death, a loud demise heard but not wholly witnessed by the boy. When police begin a routine investigation, Henrey, fearful that his idol Richardson will be arrested (he believes him to be guilty but justified in his actions), obviously withholds information from detectives led by Hawkins. In doing so, he ironically prevents Richardson from clearing himself. Only through Richardson's special understanding of the boy is he able to have Henrey finally reveal the truth necessary to save him from the gallows. Richardson is superb as the innocent butler (in Greene's short story, the man is guilty of murder and the idolizing boy accidentally betrays him while trying to cover up the facts). His tender treatment of Henrey, his cultured bearing, and his gentlemanly demeanor is in evidence in every frame, conveying the supreme nobility of being willing to accept guilt for a crime he did not commit rather than see a web of tangled evidence snare his true love, Morgan. This French actress is equally moving as the devoted, undemanding mistress. Henrey is nothing short of wonderful in his arresting portrayal of glee, fear, joy, and childish frustration at not being able to save the one person dear to him. It was director Reed's handling of Henrey that earned him the reputation of being a great "children's director," beyond being a great director, a talent proven again in the marvelous performance he drew from Mark Lester in OLIVER! (1968). Reed's secret in directing children was simple. Knowing these gifted amateurs remember and deliver their lines well but flub repeatedly the cues from professionals, he would have the adult actors render lines, then conduct a separate take with the child, cueing the child himself, to achieve a natural response, later dubbing the child's line into the scene. Reed had already established himself prior to this production with such hair-raising thrillers as NIGHT TRAIN TO MUNICH (1940) and ODD MAN OUT (1947). Following THE FALLEN IDOL, Reed would create one of the most provocative films of the post WW II era, THE THIRD MAN (1949). In 1948, the year of British release, THE FALLEN IDOL received the Best British Film award.

p, David O. Selznick, Carol Reed; d, Reed; w, Graham Greene, Lesley Storm, William Templeton (based on the short story "The Basement Room" by Greene); ph, Georges Perinal; m, William Alwyn; ed, Oswald Haffenrichter; md, Dr. Hubert Clifford; prod d, Vincent Korda, James Sawyer, John Hawkesworth; spec eff, W. Percy Day; cos, Ivy Baker; makeup, Dorrie Hamilton.

Mystery/Thriller **Cas.** **(PR:A MPAA:NR)**

FALLEN SPARROW, THE*½** (1943) 94m RKO bw

John Garfield *(Kit)*, Maureen O'Hara *(Toni Donne)*, Walter Slezak *(Dr. Skaas)*, Patricia Morison *(Barby Taviton)*, Martha O'Driscoll *(Whitney Hamilton)*, Bruce Edwards *(Ab Parker)*, John Banner *(Anton)*, John Miljan *(Insp. Tobin)*, Sam Goldenberg *(Prince Francois)*, Hugh Beaumont *(Otto Skaas)*, Bruce Edwards *(Ab Parker)*, George Lloyd *(Sgt. Moore)*, Russ Powell *(Priest)*, James Farley *(Bartender)*, Lee Phelps *(Cop)*, Charles Lung *(Carlo)*, Rosina Galli *(Mama)*, Marty Faust *(Chef, Carlo's Cafe)*, Lillian West *(Receptionist)*, Miles Mander *(Dr. Gudmundson)*, Edith Evanson *(Nurse)*, Bud Geary *(Cab Caller)*, William Edmunds *(Papa)*, Stella Le Saint *(Woman in Street)*, Nestor Paiva *(Jake)*, Jack Carr *(Danny)*, Jane Woodworth, Patti Brill, Margie Stewart, Margaret Landry, Mary Halsey *(Bits)*, Andre Charlot *(Pete)*, Eric Wilton *(Butler)*, Erford Gage *(Roman)*, Joe King *(Desk Sergeant)*, Al Rhein *(Man)*, Fely Franquelli *(Gypsy Dancer)*, Mike Lally *(Taxi Driver)*, Rita Gould *(Dot)*, Sam Goldenberg *(Prince Francois de Namur)*, Billy Mitchell *(Porter)*, Babe Green, George Sherwood *(G-Men)*, Russell Wade *(Flower Clerk)*, Stanley Price *(Caterer)*.

In a powerhouse, riveting performance, Garfield portrays a fear-haunted veteran of the Spanish Civil War who has returned to the U.S. As a member of the Lincoln Brigade that had fought the fascists for three years, he was captured and tortured in a Franco concentration camp. He was driven half mad with brutal punishment as Gestapo agents attempted to get him to reveal where he had hidden the battle flag captured from one of Hitler's elite regiments. Back in the States the Nazis are still relentless, hounding him and using a bevy of beauteous women (O'Hara, Morison, and O'Driscoll) to worm the information from him. Moreover, Nazi agent Slezak, who has murdered a Garfield pal who had originally received the flag, attempts to drive Garfield insane so that he will reveal the hiding place of the hated banner. O'Hara is forced by Slezak into luring Garfield to a house filled with Nazi agents but Garfield destroys his tormentors and manages to escape to freedom with O'Hara in tow. O'Hara is completely miscast here as a femme fatale but the limping Slezak renders a sinister portrait halfway between Peter Lorre and Sidney Greenstreet, practicing psychological warfare on the mentally disturbed Garfield. This film attempted to take sides but comes up short in condemning Franco's fascist regime for arcane political reasons. Franco, during WW II, had declared neutrality and was later a strong U.S. ally, but his repressive Falangist government was no friend to freedom. Garfield himself elected to play this role, while on loan-out to RKO from Warner Bros., having been a supporter of the lost Loyalist cause in 1936-1939. Director Wallace sets a brisk pace but lets Garfield carry the entire burden of a character plagued by anguished memories. It's a haunting film but, like Garfield's stellar career, has the feeling of being unfinished.

p, Robert Fellows; d, Richard Wallace; w, Warren Duff (based on the novel by Dorothy B. Hughes); ph, Nicholas Musuraca; m, Roy Webb; ed, Robert Wise; prod d, Van Nest Polglase; md, C. Bakaleinikoff; art d, Albert D'Agostino, Mark Lee Kirk; spec eff, Vernon L. Walker.

Spy Drama/Mystery **(PR:C MPAA:NR)**

FALLGUY*½ (1962) 64m Harling Productions/International Films bw
(AKA: THE FALL GUY)

Ed Dugan (Sonny Martin), George Andre (Carl Tamin), Lou Gartner (Police Chief), Don Alderette (Sam Johnson), Madeline Frances (June Johnson), Wes Carlson, Fabian Dean.

Dugan is a teenager who witnesses a gangland killing of a racket boss. He goes to the police, but the police chief is involved in the mob and tries to frame the murder on Dugan. The teenager flees and hides on skid row while a professional killer tries to track him down. He goes to Frances's house and tells her that her father is in the mob. While they look for evidence, the gangsters close in on Dugan and a gunfight breaks out. Dugan and Frances are wounded and the mobsters kill each other.

p&d, Donn Harling; w, Richard Adams, George Mitchell; ph, Villis Lapenicks; m, Jaime Mendoza-Nava; ed, Ron Honthaner.

Crime **(PR:A MPAA:NR)**

FALLING FOR YOU** (1933, Brit.) 88m Gainsborough/W&F bw

Jack Hulbert (Jack Hazleden), Cicely Courtneidge (Minnie Tucker), Tamara Desni (Sondra van Heyden), Garry Marsh (Archduke Carl), Alfred Drayton (Editor), Ivor McLaren (Sweep), Tonie Edgar Bruce (Aunt Alice), O.B. Clarence (Trubshawe), Morton Selten (Caldicott), Leo Sheffield (Butler), Lillimor Schmidt, Gwyneth Lloyd.

Hulbert and Courtneidge are reporters for rival papers trying to get the scoop on an heiress who has vanished. They trace her to Switzerland, where Hulbert falls in love with her. He rescues her from marriage to an aristocrat and lets Courtneidge write the big story. Okay comedy features Hulbert singing three songs and dancing on skis.

p, Michael Balcon; d, Jack Hulbert, Robert Stevenson; w, Hulbert, Sidney Gilliat, Stevenson, Douglas Furber, Claude Hulbert; ph, Bernard Knowles; m/l, Vivian Ellis, Furber.

Comedy **(PR:A MPAA:NR)**

FALLING IN LOVE (SEE: TROUBLE AHEAD, 1936)

FALLING IN LOVE AGAIN*½ (1980) 103m O.T.A./International Picture Show of Atlanta c

Elliott Gould (Harry Lewis), Susannah York (Sue Lewis), Stuart Paul (Pompadour/Young Harry), Michelle Pfieffer (Sue Wellington), Kay Ballard (Mrs. Lewis), Robert Hackman (Mr. Lewis), Steven Paul (Stan the Con), Todd Helper (Alan Childs), Herb Rudley (Mr. Wellington), Marion McCargo (Mrs. Wellington), Bonnie Paul (Hilary Lewis).

Gould, traveling cross-country with his wife and children on his way to a high school reunion, flashes back to the days of his youth. The standard midlife crisis is the center of his maudlin recollections, which focus on his then unattainable wife, York. Practically a family production, it was produced, directed, and written by 21-year-old Paul, who in place of talent was blessed with energy. A poorly constructed film which proves the adage that one must live films before one can make them. One fails to understand why the young Paul would consider making a film about two middle-aged characters he cannot possibly understand or empathize with. Paul went on to the considerably less successful adaptation of Kurt Vonnegut's SLAPSTICK with Jerry Lewis.

p&d, Steven Paul; w, Paul, Susannah York, Ted Allan; ph, Michael Mileham, Dick Bush, Wolfgang Suschitzky; m, Michel Legrand; ed, Bud Smith, Doug Jackson, Jacqueline Cambas; m/l, Legrand, Sammy Cahn, Carol Connors, Dennis Lambert.

Romantic Comedy **Cas.** **(PR:C MPAA:PG)**

FALSE COLORS** (1943) 64m UA bw

William Boyd (Hopalong Cassidy), Andy Clyde (California Carlson), Jimmy Rogers (Himself), Tom Seidel (Bud Lawton/Kit Mayer), Claudia Drake (Faith Lawton), Douglass Dumbrille (Mark Foster), Bob Mitchum (Rip Austin), Glenn Strange (Sonora), Pierce Lyden (Lefty), Roy Barcroft (Sheriff Clem Martin), Sam Flint (Judge Stevens), Earle Hodgins (Lawyer Jay Griffin), Elmer Jerome (Jed Stevers), Tom London (Townsman), Dan White (Bar Spectator), George Morrell (Denton Townsman).

The 49th Hopalong Cassiday western has Boyd and gang up against the evil Dumbrille. To secure water rights, the baddie kills off the heirs to a cattle ranch and substitutes an imposter. Will Rogers' son Jimmy is cast as the kid sidekick. Mitchum again appears in a supporting role. (See HOPALONG CASSIDY series, Index).

p, Harry Sherman; d, George Archainbaud; w, Bennett Cohen, (based on characters created by Clarence E. Mulford); ph, Russell Harlan; ed, Fred Berger; art d, Ralph Berger.

Western **Cas.** **(PR:A MPAA:NR)**

FALSE EVIDENCE** (1937, Brit.) 71m Crusade/PAR bw

Gwenllian Gill (Judy Endale), George Pembroke (John Massiter), Michael Hogarth (Gerald Wickham), Daphne Raglan (Annabelle Stirling), George Pughe (Tom Vanderlam), Francis Roberts (Inspector Jones), Langley Howard (Julius Wickham),

Ralph Michael (Police Constable Barlow), Dempsey Stuart, Ben Williams, Terry Conlin.

Hogarth is accused of the murder of his uncle, but Gill, his ex-fiancee and daughter of the murdered man, proves that it was Raglan and her gang of thieves that did the killing. Hogarth is shot, Raglan is strangled, and the gang leader dies in a fall out a window, all in the closing minutes. Interesting story, but the cast lacks the expertise to pull it off.

p, Victor M. Greene; d&w, Donovan Pedelty (based on the novel I'll Never Tell by Roy Vickers).

Crime **(PR:A-C MPAA:NR)**

FALSE FACE (SEE: SCALPEL, 1976)

FALSE FACES*½ (1932) 73m KBS/Worldwide bw

Lowell Sherman (Dr. Silas Brenton), Peggy Shannon (Elsie Fryer), Lila Lee (Georgia Rand), Berton Churchill (Dr. J.B. Parker), David Landau (McCullough), Harold Waldridge (Jimmy), Geneva Mitchell (Florence Day), Oscar Apfel (Fineberg), Miriam Seegar (Lottie Nation), Joyce Compton (Dottie Nation), Nance O'Neil (Mrs. Finn), Edward Martindel (Mr. Jonathan Day), Purnell Pratt (Jefferson Howe).

A Chicago plastic surgeon, Sherman, who normally restricts his work to faces, accidentally causes a patient to lose her legs. Needless to say, she sues. In court, facing the loss of her case, she shoots and kills the doctor. A strange soap unintentionally filled with black humor and intentionally dominated by its director, who took over the leading role.

d, Lowell Sherman; w, Kubec Glasmon, Llewellyn Hughes; ph, R.O. Binger, Theodore McCord, ed, Rose Loewinger.

Drama **(PR:A MPAA:NR)**

FALSE FACES* (1943) 58m REP bw

Stanley Ridges (Stanley Harding), Bill Henry (Don Westcott), Rex Williams (Craig Harding), Veda Ann Borg (Joyce Ford), Janet Shaw (Diana), Joseph Crehan (Capt. O'Brien), Chester Clute (Manager), John Maxwell (Stewart), Dick Wessel (Mallory), Billy Nelson (Jimmy), Nicodemus (Mac), Etta McDaniel (Magnolia).

Ridges is a district attorney whose son Williams is wrongly accused of a nightclub singer's murder. The D.A., sure of his son's innocence, presses the case and is able to point a guilty finger at hotel manager Clute. A whodunit without the suspense. Penned by Curt Siodmak, who also wrote THE WOLF MAN (1941), I WALKED WITH A ZOMBIE (1943), and THE BEAST WITH FIVE FINGERS (1946).

p&d, George Sherman; w, Curt Siodmak; ph, William Bradford; ed, Arthur Roberts; md, Morton Scott; art d, Russell Kimball.

Crime **(PR:A MPAA:NR)**

FALSE MADONNA* (1932) 70m PAR bw

Kay Francis (Tina), William "Stage" Boyd (Marcy), Conway Tearle (Grant Arnold), John Breeden (Phillip Bellows), Marjorie Gateson (Rose), Charles D. Brown (Peter), Almeda Fowler (Mrs. Swanson).

A couple of cheats, one of them a phoney doctor, aid a sick woman traveling on a train. When she dies, the shady Francis poses as the woman in order to collect a hefty sum of money. She soon grows fond of the dead woman's blind son and turns her back on the cash. An attorney gets suspicious. When the disillusioned boy has a fatal heart attack, the implausible finale has Francis and the attorney wed. (William "Stage" Boyd (1890-1935) is not the Hopalong Cassidy Boyd.)

d, Stuart Walker; w, Arthur Kober, Ray Harris (based on May Eddington's story "The Heart Is Young"); ph, Henry Sharp.

Drama **(PR:A MPAA:NR)**

FALSE PARADISE** (1948) 60m UA bw

William Boyd (Hopalong Cassidy), Andy Clyde (California Carlson), Rand Brooks (Lucky Jenkins), Joel Friedkin, Elaine Riley, Kenneth MacDonald, Don Haggerty, Cliff Clark, Dick Alexander, William Norton Bailey, Zon Murray, George Eldridge.

Boyd and his cheery sidekicks get into a scrap with a banker who is trying to cheat some decent folk out of their silver-rich land. Boyd learns that the banker is in cahoots with an outlaw gang and brings them all to justice. (See HOPALONG CASSIDY series, Index).

p, Lewis J. Rachmil; d, George Archainbaud; w, Doris Schroeder, Harrison Jacobs; ph, Mark Stengler; m, Ralph Stanley; ed, Fred W. Berger; art d, Jerome Pycha, Jr.

Western **(PR:A MPAA:NR)**

FALSE PRETENSES*½ (1935) 67m CHES/FD bw

Irene Ware (Mary Beekman), Sidney Blackmer (Kenneth Alden), Russell Hopton (Pat Brennan), Betty Compson (Clarissa), Edward Gargan (Mike O'Reilly), Herbert Clifton (Bleven), Lucy Beaumont (Clara), John Piccori, Dot Farley, William Humphries, Wilson Benge, Al Thompson, Jack Shutta, Frank O'Connor.

Pauper-ette Ware, a waitress, devises a scheme with millionaire Blackmer to work her way up the social ladder. Watchable performances marred by insipid direction.

p, George R. Batcheller; d, Charles Lamont; w, Ewart Adamson (based on a story by Betty Burbridge entitled "Suicide Bridge"); ph, M.A. Anderson; ed, Roland D. Reed.

Comedy **(PR:A MPAA:NR)**

FALSE RAPTURE*½ (1941) 61m Film Alliance bw
(AKA: SECRETS OF SIN)

Otto Kruger (Petrov), Mary Maguire (Tania), Walter Rilla (Roudine), John Wood (Karlo), Marie Wright (Miss Brown).

A classical story, which takes place in pre-war Russia, about a headwaiter who hides his profession from his daughter. She eventually discovers his presumably low line of work as he simultaneously makes the even more interesting discovery that his daughter is getting it on in one of the restaurant's private dining rooms with the moneybags who has promised to lend him the money he needs to purchase the premises. A technical embarrassment which is mercilessly slow.

p, Walter C. Mycroft; d, Herbert Brenon; w, Dudley Leslie; ph, Gunther Krampf; ed, Lionel Tomlinson.

Drama (PR:A MPAA:NR)

FALSE WITNESS (SEE: ZIGZAG, 1970)

FALSTAFF (SEE: CHIMES AT MIDNIGHT, 1967, Span./Switz.)

FAME** (1936, Brit.) 67m GFD bw

Sydney Howard (Oswald Bertwhistle), Muriel Aked (Mrs. Bertwhistle), Miki Hood (Joan Riley), Brian Lawrence (Douglas Cameron), Herbert Lomas (Rumbold Wakefield), Guy Middleton (Lester Cordwell), H.F. Maltby (The Mayor), Frank Pettingell (Reuben Pendleton), Frederick Piper (Press Representative), Arthur Finn (Film Director), Sydney Fairbrother (Train Passenger), Maire O'Neill (Mrs. Docker), Geraldine Hislop (Film Star), Russell Thorndike (Judge), Henry Victor (Actor), Geraldo and His Orchestra.

Moderately entertaining comedy about department store floorwalker Oswald Bertwhistle, Howard, and his humorous escapades after winning a contest to become a film actor.

p, Herbert Wilcox; d, Leslie Hiscott; w, Michael Barringer, R.P. Weston, Bert Lee, Jack Marks (based on a story by John Harding, William Hargreaves); ph, Orford St. John or F.A. Young (sources disagree).

Comedy (PR:A MPAA:NR)

FAME**½ (1980) 134m MGM/UA c

Eddie Barth (Angelo), Irene Cara (Coco), Lee Curreri (Bruno), Laura Dean (Lisa), Antonia Franceschi (Hilary), Boyd Gaines (Michael), Albert Hague (Shorofsky), Tresa Hughes (Mrs. Finsecker), Steve Inwood (Francois Lafete), Paul McCrane (Montgomery), Anne Meara (Mrs. Sherwood), Joanna Merlin (Miss Berg), Barry Miller (Ralph), Jim Moody (Farrell), Gene Anthony Ray (Leroy), Maureen Teefy (Doris), Debbie Allen (Lydia), Richard Belzer, Frank Bongiorno, Bill Britten, Eric Brockington, Nicholas Bunin, Cindy Canuelas, Nora Controne, Mbewe Escobar, Gennady Filimonov, Victor Fischbarg, Penny Frank, Willie Henry, Jr., Steven Hollander, Sang Kim, Darrell Kirkman, Judith L'Heureux, Ted Lambert, Nancy Lee, Sara Malament, James Manis, Carol Massenberg, Isaac Mizrahi, Raquel Mondin, Alba Oms, Frank Oteri, Traci Parnell, Sal Piro, Leslie Quickley, Ray Ramirez, Loris Sallahian, Ilse Sass, Dawn Steinberg, Jonathan Strasser, Yvette Torres, Frank X. Vitolo, Stefanie Zimmerman.

The sheer joyful exuberance of this picture is almost enough to recommend it, though that is all it has going for it. Parker's heavy-handed direction takes a glorified look at the life of students attending Manhattan's High School of Performing Arts. Told in five episodes—auditions and each academic year—it focuses on a half-dozen characters: Cara, a gifted singer; McCrane, a confused gay actor; Ray, an illiterate dancer; Curreri, a synthesizer player; Miller, an ashamed closet Puerto Rican; and Meara, the tough English teacher. Parker's interest lies mainly in lavish production numbers (as in THE WALL), instead of concentrating on more intimate subtleties, turning it into an episode of "Solid Gold." Cara, who shines as Coco, is the only one of the talented bunch to actually experience fame, racking up a couple of AM hit singles. Most revealing is that the real-life school refused to let the film crew inside the building, leading one to believe that they too disapproved of the sensationalism. The subject's treatment was best suited for the television show it launched. The Academy Award winning score includes such tunes as "Red Light," "Fame," "I Sing The Body Electric" Michael Gore, Dean Pitchford; "Dogs In The Yard" Dominic Bugatti, Frank Musker; "Hot Lunch Jam" Gore, Robert F. Colesberry, Lesley Gore; "Out Here On My Own" Michael Gore, Lesley Gore; "Is It OK If I Call You Mine?" Paul McCrane.

p, David DeSilva, Alan Marshall; d, Alan Parker; w, Christopher Gore; ph, Michael Seresin (Metrocolor); m, Michael Gore; ed, Gerry Hambling; prod d, Geoffrey Kirkland; art d, Ed Wittstein; set d, George DeTitta; cos, Kristi Zea; ch, Louis Falco.

Musical Drama Cas. (PR:C MPAA:PG)

FAME IS THE SPUR**½ (1947, Brit.) 116m Two Cities/GFD bw

Michael Redgrave (Hamer Radshaw), Rosamund John (Ann Radshaw), Bernard Miles (Tom Hanaway), High Burden (Arnold Ryerson), Jean Shepheard (Mrs. Radshaw), Guy Verney (Grandpa), Percy Walsh (Suddaby), Carla Lehmann (Lady Lettice), Seymour Hicks (Old Buck), David Tomlinson (Lord Liskeard), Marjorie Fielding (Aunt Lizzie), Milton Rosmer (Magistrate), Wylie Watson (Pendelton), Anthony Wager (Boy Hamer), Brian Weske (Boy Ryerson), Gerald Fox (Boy Hannaway), Charles Wood (Dai).

Loosely based on the life of labor leader Ramsay MacDonald, the adaptation of the "faction" novel (a mixture of fiction and fact), by Howard Spring, doesn't quite hold together but it does provide an interesting, albeit lengthy, look at the reasons why Labor and Conservatives often clash in Great Britain. Redgrave is a young man from the hard-hit northern area who decides to devote his life to benefit his fellow laborers. A sword picked up by his grandfather, one used to slash workers at the Battle of Peterloo in 1819, is his Excalibur. He becomes the British version of Willie Stark as he rouses the rabble with rhetoric and finally winds up in Parliament as a Labor M.P. Soon enough, he is seduced by the trappings of power and when Labor takes over the government, the transformation is complete. His wife, John, is the one person who sees through his veneer but loves him anyhow. She is an interesting character, an early Equal Rights advocate, and she pays the

penalty for her position by spending some time in the slammer. Redgrave begins sacrificing all his principles to keep his lofty position and, in the end, he is rejected by a wise electorate and finally accepts a peerage. He becomes Lord Radshaw, an old fool who is barely able to express himself; the very kind of person he preached against in reel one. He attempts to lift his trademark sword while addressing a huge banquet, but it is rusted in its scabbard, a symbol of how his great dreams must have rusted as well. Bernard Miles (Hanaway) does excellently as a shrewd plutocrat. Oddly enough, his life culminated in his becoming a life peer as well. He was made Lord Miles in 1979 for his dedication to British theater. (He originated the modern Mermaid Theatre.) Look hard for light comedian David Tomlinson in a small role as Lord Liskeard. Tomlinson's greatest U.S. successes were in Disney's MARY POPPINS and BEDKNOBS AND BROOMSTICKS.

p, John Boulting; d, Roy Boulting; w, Nigel Balchin (based on the novel by Howard Spring); ph, Gunther Krampf, Harry Waxman, Richard S. Pavey; m, John Wooldridge; ed, Richard Best; md, Hans May; art d, John Howell; cos, Honoria Plesch; makeup, Tony Sforzini.

Drama Cas. (PR:A MPAA:NR)

FAME STREET*½ (1932) 60m MON bw (AKA: POLICE COURT)

Henry B. Walthall (Nat Barry), Leon Janney (Junior Barry), Aileen Pringle (Diana McCormick), King Baggott (Henry Field), Lionel Belmore ("Uncle" Al Furman), Al St. John (Skid) Edmund Breese (Judge Robert Webster).

This early cinema industry self-examination film edges into melodrama of a type archaic even in its time. The plot deals with a failing former film star, Walthall, who has become an alcoholic and, in his career's perigee, is hauled before a magistrate, Breese, on charges of public intoxication. His son, Janney, makes an impassioned plea on his behalf; he is freed, albeit with a stern warning to sin no more. Unable to find employment within an industry the production schedules of which he has too often hindered, the aging actor reverts to the sauce. Son Janney, ever empathic, procures for dad Walthall a small part in a movie in which he himself, following father's footsteps, plays a role. Walthall, impressed by the lad's faith and devotion, straightens out sufficiently to play his best scene, expiring due to liver damage just at the final "cut". But, it's a take! Oddly, the picture proved portentous: Walthall, best known for his role of the Little Colonel in D. W. Griffith's THE BIRTH OF A NATION (1915) died in the midst of production of his last film, CHINA CLIPPER (1936).

p, I. E. Chadwick; d, Louis King; w, Stuart Anthony; ph, Archie Stout; ed, Charles Hunt.

Drama (PR:A MPAA:NR)

FAMILY, THE** (1974, Fr./Ital.) 109m Fono Roma-Unidis & Universal France/International Co-productions & EDP Films Inc. c (GB: VIOLENT CITY; CITTA VIOLENTA)

Charles Bronson (Jeff), Jill Ireland (Vanessa), Michel Constantin (Killain), Telly Savalas (Weber), Umberto Orsini (Steve), George Savalas (Shapiro), Ray Sanders (Black Prisoner), Benjamin Lev (Young Prisoner), Peter Dane (Television M.C.).

Bronson is a hit man in New Orleans. His girl friend (Bronson's real wife Ireland) double-crosses him. Sex, car crashes, and violent gunplay ensue. Bronson has revenge on Ireland and Orsini in the end. The top-billed players all die. THE FAMILY was made in 1970 but not released in the United States until 1974, capitalizing on the sudden fame of Bronson and Savalas. Shot on location in Rome and New Orleans, the film was poorly made; English dubbing further detracted from the plot for American audiences. Lina Wertmuller, who was to become a noted director in the 1970s, shares screenwriting credit.

p, Arrigo Colombo, Giorgio Papi; d, Sergio Sollima; w, Sauro Scavolini, Gianfranco Calligarich, Lina Wertmuller, Sollima (based on a story by Dino Maiuri, Massimo De Rita); ph, Aldo Tonti (Techniscope, Technicolor); m, Ennio Morricone; ed, Nino Baragli; art d, Francesco Bronzi.

Crime Cas. (PR:O MPAA:R)

FAMILY AFFAIR, A*** (1937) 67m MGM bw

Lionel Barrymore (Judge Hardy), Mickey Rooney (Andy Hardy), Cecilia Parker (Marian Hardy), Eric Linden (Wayne Trenton), Charley Grapewin (Frank Redmond), Spring Byington (Mrs. Hardy), Julie Haydon (Joan Hardy), Sara Haden (Aunt Milly), Allen Vincent (Bill Martin), Margaret Marquis (Polly), Selmer Jackson (Hoyt Wells), Harlan Briggs (Oscar Stubbins).

MGM hit on something big with this picture, the first in the Andy Hardy series. Employing most of the members of AH, WILDERNESS, they cast Barrymore as Judge Hardy and Rooney as his puppyish son Andy. As usual, Rooney is up in arms over that "swell gal," Polly, here played by Marquis. Critics of the time of release felt that this film might score as part of a double bill, but studio moguls were apparently unaware of the monster they had unleashed, which spawned a series totaling 15 movies from 1937 through 1946. In the second of the series, YOU'RE ONLY YOUNG ONCE (1938), Lewis Stone took over from Barrymore, who was suffering from the disease that was to cripple him, and in an entracte announced the birth of the series. (See HARDY FAMILY series, Index.)

p, Lucien Hubbard, Samuel Marx; d, George B. Seitz; w, Kay Van Riper (from Aurania Rouverol's play "Skidding"); ph, Lester White; m, David Snell; ed, George Boemler.

Comedy (PR:AAA MPAA:NR)

FAMILY AFFAIR** (1954, Brit.) 81m Hammer/Exclusive bw (GB: LIFE WITH THE LYONS)

Bebe Daniels (Bebe Lyon), Ben Lyon (Ben Lyon), Barbara Lyon (Barbara Lyon), Richard Lyon (Richard), Horace Percival (Mr. Wimple), Molly Weir (Aggie), Hugh Morton (Mr. Hemingway), Arthur Hill (Slim Cassidy), Doris Rogers (Florrie Wainwright), Gwen Lewis (Mrs. Wimple), Belinda Lee (Violet Hemingway).

Ben Lyon and Bebe Daniels were major stars of the silent era. They married and emigrated to England, where, with their children, they became major radio celebrities in the 1940s and 1950s. This is their first feature, showing the family's misadventures in trying to get a landlord to sign the lease on their new apartment. His reluctance is natural in light of the total havoc the family seems to bring with them everywhere they go. Followed the same year by THE LYONS IN PARIS.

p, Robert Dunbar; d, Val Guest; w, Dunbar, Guest (based on a radio series by Bebe Daniels, Bob Block, Bill Harding); ph, Walter Harvey.

Comedy (PR:A MPAA:NR)

FAMILY DIARY** (1963 Ital.) 115m Titanus/MGM c (CRONACA FAMILIARE)

Marcello Mastroianni *(Enrico)* Jacques Perrin, *(Lorenzo)*, Sylvie *(Grandmother)*, Salvo Randone *(Salocchi)*, Valerie Ciangottini *(Enzina)*, Serena Vergano *(Hospital Nun)*.

A sappy story of twin brothers, Mastroianni and Perrin, who are separated when their mother and father die. Perrin is adopted by a butler and Mastroianni is reared by their grandmother. Perrin is spoiled, living the life style of the rich. When the butler's employer dies, Perrin finds himself unable to make a living. The brothers are reunited and Mastroianni tries to help his brother, but Perrin is plagued by problems. He becomes sick, is taken to a hospital in Rome, and dies before his brother can take him to see his wife and child. A heavy melodrama that is carried by the performances of the two leads.

p, Goffredo Lombardo; d, Valerio Zurlini; w, Zurlini, Mario Missiroli (based on Vasco Pratolini's story "Cronaca Familiare"); ph, Giuseppe Rotunno (Technicolor); m, Goffredo Petrassi; ed, Mario Serandrei; art d, Flavio Mogherini; cos, Gaia Romanini.

Drama (PR:A MPAA:NR)

FAMILY DOCTOR (SEE: RX MURDER, 1958, Brit.)

FAMILY HONEYMOON½** (1948) 90m UNIV bw

Claudette Colbert *(Katie Armstrong Jordan)*, Fred MacMurray *(Grant Jordan)*, Rita Johnson *(Minna Fenster)*, Gigi Perreau *(Zoe)*, Jimmy Hunt *(Charlie)*, Peter Miles *(Abner)*, Lillian Bronson *(Aunt Jo)*, Hattie McDaniel *(Phyllis)*, Chill Wills *(Fred)*, Catherine Doucet *(Mrs. Abercrombie)*, Paul Harvey *(Richard Fenster)*, Irving Bacon *(Mrs. Webb)*, Chick Chandler *(Taxi Driver)*, Frank Jenks *(Gas Station Attendant)*, Wally Brown *(Tom Roscoe)*, Holmes Herbert *(Rev. Miller)*, John Gallaudet *(Prof. Pickering)*, Wilton Graff *(Dr. Wilson)*, Fay Baker *(Fran Wilson)*, O.Z. Whitehead *(Jess)*, Lorin Raker *(Hotel Clerk)*, Sarah Edwards *(Mrs. Carp)*, Anne Nagel *(Irene Bartlett)*, Lois Austin *(Louise Pickering)*, Beatrice Roberts *(Belle)*, William Norton Bailey *(Todd)*, Frank MacGregor *(Saunders)*, Barbara Challis, Lois Hall, Denise Kay *(Girls)*, Frank Orth *(Candy Butcher)*, Harry Hayden *(Railroad Conductor)*, Almira Sessions *(Maid)*, Constance Purdy *(Helen Hockinson)*, Minerva Urecal *(Mrs. Webb)*, Syd Saylor *(Station Master)*, Joel Fluellen *(Waiter)*, Smoki Whitfield *(Porter)*, Jay Silverheels *(Elevator Boy)*, Harold Goodwin *(Guide)*, Nick Thompson *(Indian Buck)*, Herbert Heywood *(Station Agent)*, Edmund Cobb *(Stage Driver)*, Richard Dumas, Carl Vernell, Bill Murphy *(Boys)*, Tom Chatterton *(Stewart)*, John O'Connor *(Intern)*, Ella Ethridge *(Woman)*, Edward Short *(Red Cap)*, Vangie Beilby *(Woman Passenger)*, Snub Pollard *(Man Passenger)*, Heinie Conklin *(Man on Train)*.

The only reason this wasn't an ABC Television movie is that ABC wasn't making TV movies back in 1948 when this was lensed. Light as cotton candy, it's basically a one-joke premise, and the title tells it all. Colbert and MacMurray were reteamed after their success in THE EGG AND I, but this one is a souffle that falls flat more than it rises. Colbert is the widowed mother of Perreau, Hunt, and Miles, three aggressive and often annoying kids. She agrees to marry MacMurray, a university professor, and they plan a lovely, leisurely honeymoon. When Colbert's sister, Bronson, suffers an accident, there's no one to leave the children with so the whole family embarks on a Family Honeymoon. They are on their way to the Grand Canyon, and several predictable events occur. The kids are left behind when they get off the train by mistake, and they wind up at the farmhouse of Irving Bacon. Colbert and MacMurray must stay the night at the Bacon place, but she sleeps with the kids and he has to stay with the ranch hand. They take a day coach and finally make it to the Grand Canyon only to find that MacMurray's old flame, Johnson, is a guest at the same inn. Colbert is jealous, and if that weren't enough, she has to put up with her trio of snide brats, all of whom refer to their new stepfather as "that man." Colbert and MacMurray hardly have a moment to spend with each other. His patience wears out and he spanks the kids, something the audience has been hoping for from the moment the children marched on screen. An argument ensues and they go back home separately. Johnson is already back and she arranges a welcome-home party, mainly to embarrass Colbert. Colbert realizes that her kids will eventually grow up and leave and she wants to spend the rest of her life with MacMurray so she uses her wiles to effect a reconciliation. The two of them march into the party arm in arm, a happy couple. They pretend to be surprised; the picture ends with everyone, except vamp Johnson, happy. A nice enough picture, but it fails on a few levels; some Hawksian lunacy might have helped, but just a touch of the sexual frustration that would have been felt by the couple in real life would have been appreciated. It just didn't go far enough, although second-time director Binyon kept the pace lively. Binyon had an interesting background—he once wrote for the show business trade paper "Variety" where it is said that he penned the famous 1929 Crash headline: "Wall Street Lays An Egg." His screenwriting credits include HOLIDAY INN (1942), INCENDIARY BLONDE (1945), PEPE (1960), NORTH TO ALASKA (1960), and THE SAXON CHARM (1948), a savage look at a predatory Broadway producer said to be based upon Jed Harris.

p, John Beck, Z. Wayne Griffin; d, Claude Binyon; w, Dane Lussier (based on the novel by Homer Croy); ph, William Daniels; m, Frank Skinner; ed, Milton Carruth; art d, Bernard Herzbrun, Richard H. Riedel; set d, Al Fields, Russell A. Gausman; md, Milton Schwarzwald; cos, Orry-Kelly; spec eff, David S. Horsley; makeup, Bud Westmore.

Comedy (PR:A MPAA:NR)

FAMILY HONOR*½ (1973) 96m Rocinante/Cinerama c

Anthony Page, Vera Visconti, James Reyes.

Page is a young cop who remains faithful to the code of his family and avenges the death of his father at the hands of the mob. He sets out on the mission and pits himself alone against organized crime. A cops vs. the mob story seen endlessly in television series, and, in fact, another series was made from this story.

p, Louis Pastore; d, Clark Worswick; w, Pastore.

Crime (PR:O MPAA:R)

FAMILY JEWELS, THE½** (1965) 98m PAR c

Jerry Lewis *(Willard Woodward/"Bugs" Peyton/Capt. Eddie Peyton/James Peyton/Skylock Peyton/Julius Peyton/Everett Peyton)*, Sebastian Cabot *(Dr. Matson)*, Donna Butterworth *(Donna Peyton)*, Gene Baylos *(Clown)*, Milton Frome *(Pilot)*, Herbie Faye *(Joe)*, Marjorie Bennett, Frances Lax, Ellen Corby, Renie Riano, Jesslyn Fax *(Plane Passengers)*, Robert Strauss *(Pool Hall Owner)*, Jay Adler, Neil Hamilton *(Attorneys)*, John Lawrence, Francine York, John Hubbard, Michael Ross, John Macchia, Douglas Deane, Maurice Kelly, Gary Lewis and The Playboys *(In-Flight Film Clip)*, Anne Baxter.

Despite the suggestive title, this film could hardly be termed gonadic, save for the fact that, like other Lewis vehicles, its production required a good measure of gall. Depending on your sentiments about Jerry Lewis, the film is either Nirvana or a vicious nightmare. The spunky Lewis produced, directed, wrote, and acted in seven roles in this nutty comedy. Nine-year-old Butterworth, who happens to be one of the most annoying child actors in the history of cinema, inherits $30 million and must decide which uncle she wants as her guardian. She has a big choice—Lewis times seven. If a case is to be made for Lewis' comic genius, this could well be the deciding factor.

p&d, Jerry Lewis; w, Lewis, Bill Richmond; ph, W. Wallace Kelley (Technicolor); m, Pete King; ed, Arthur P. Schmidt, John Woodcock; art d, Hal Pereira, Jack Poplin; set d, Sam Comer, Robert R. Benton; cos, Edith Head; spec eff, Paul K. Lerpac.

Comedy (PR:A MPAA:NR)

FAMILY LIFE½** (1971, Brit.) 105m Kestrel/MGM-EMI c (GB: WEDNESDAY'S CHILD)

Sandy Ratcliff *(Janice)*, Bill Dean *(Baildon)*, Grace Cave *(Mrs. Baildon)*, Malcolm Tierney *(Tim)*, Hilary Martyn *(Barbara)*, Michael Riddall *(Dr. Donaldson)*, Alan MacNaughton *(Carswell)*, Johnny Gee *(Man in Garden)*.

An overt social statement about Ratcliff's rebellion against her repressive parents. After she gets pregnant, mom and dad (Cave and Dean) arrange for an abortion in an attempt to retain control of their daughter's liberated life style. One evening she returns home too late, and finds herself locked out of the house. She seeks refuge with her boy friend, but by now her parents are completely fed up. She is sent off to a shrink, then to group therapy, and finally shock treatments which reduce her to a psychiatry-class case-study. Photographed in documentary style, it now looks like an indulgent and clinical exercise in parental finger-pointing, too quick to place blame at mom and dad's doorstep. Originally made for television, it was the recipient of a special award at the 1972 Berlin Film Fest. It is saved only by its exceptional performances.

p, Tony Garnett; d, Ken Loach; w, David Mercer; ph, Charles Stewart (Technicolor); m, Marc Wilkinson; ed, Roy Watts; art d, William McCrow.

Drama Cas. (PR:O MPAA:NR)

FAMILY NEXT DOOR, THE* (1939) 60m UNIV bw

Hugh Herbert *(George Pierce)*, Joy Hodges *(Laura)*, Eddie Quillan *(Sammy)*, Ruth Donnelly *(Mrs. Pierce)*, Juanita Quigley *(Susan)*, Bennie Bartlett *(Rufus)*, Spooks, the Dog *(Baby)*, Frances Robinson *(Jane Hughes)*, Tom Beck *(Bill Trevis)*, James Bush *(Harold Waner)*, Cecil Cunningham *(Cora Stewart)*, Lillian Yarbo *(Blossom)*, Dorothy Arnold, Stanley Hughes.

Plumber Herbert continually fails to fulfill his family's aspirations, so his wife (Donnelly) begins investing in real estate. Lame comedy intended for the family trade. Universal's nabobs may have been trying for a series comparable to MGM's HARDY FAMILY or Fox's JONES FAMILY. They tail-ended the trend with this silliness, and it never happened.

p, Max H. Golden; d, Joseph Santley; w, Mortimer Offner; ph, Milton Krasner; ed, Frank Gross; md, Charles Previn; art d, Jack Otterson.

Comedy (PR:A MPAA:NR)

FAMILY PLOT*½** (1976) 120m UNIV c

Karen Black *(Fran)*, Bruce Dern *(Lumley)*, Barbara Harris *(Blanche)*, William Devane *(Adamson)*, Ed Lauter *(Maloney)*, Cathleen Nesbitt *(Julia Rainbird)*, Katherine Helmond *(Mrs. Maloney)*, Warren J. Kemmerling *(Grandison)*, Edith Atwater *(Mrs. Clay)*, William Prince *(Bishop)*, Nicholas Colasanto *(Constantine)*, Marge Redmond *(Vera Hannagan)*, John Lehne *(Andy Bush)*, Charles Tyner *(Wheeler)*, Alexander Lockwood *(Parson)*, Martin West *(Sanger)*, Louise Lorimer, Kate Murtagh, Clint Young, Alfred Hitchcock.

Hitchcock was in less than top form here. Perhaps it was the material, or it might have been the cast. It was his final production which marked a half century of movie-making that began with THE PLEASURE GARDEN. Hitchcock and Ernest Lehman united again (they did NORTH BY NORTHWEST, 1959) but the results were just a shade disappointing. A mild heart attack stopped matters a bit but once Hitchcock's pacemaker was installed, he went back to work in the traditional quiet but intense fashion. With more comedy than usual, FAMILY PLOT begins with a phony seance run by seer Barbara Harris for ancient Nesbitt. Harris is partnered with Dern; they are a conning, cunning couple who specialize in bilking believers. Dern is a crackerjack investigator, and makes certain he has all the facts. When he feeds them to Harris, she appears to have true psychic powers. Nesbitt gave her sister's baby away forty years ago and is now having bad dreams about it. She is a rich woman, and wants to find her long-lost nephew and give him all her money. Meanwhile, lost nephew Devane and Black are a kidnaping duo who insist that the ransoms be paid in diamonds (Devane's cover work is as a jeweler). They've just nabbed Colasanto, a wealthy Greek shipping czar. Two stories are told in parallel fashion as both couples go after the Nesbitt fortune. Devane nabs Harris and puts her into a secret room in his house, but she is saved by Dern. Together, they put Black and Devane in the room. The final scenes are a combination of suspense and comedy. All the characters were well-drawn and Devane, in particular, is one of the most heinous villains ever seen in a Hitchcock film. He's so oily that you could put him in your crankcase. Dern is a strangely appealing villain, sort of a dumb galoot whom you can't help but like. Barbara Harris has never been put to a test the way Hitchcock did it, and she comes through beautifully in a funny and sometimes vulnerable role. Karen Black has the least-defined part, but she does the best with what she has. Colasanto went on to TV success on the series "Cheers" before his death in 1985. He had a second career as a TV director and distinguished himself in that capacity as well. A multi-talented man who will be missed. So, with such good performances and a witty script, plus Hitchcock's eye for detail, why wasn't this a big winner? *Quien sabe?* Perhaps the whole was not equal to the sum of all its parts. The original casting for Adamson was Roy Thinnes, but he was replaced early by Devane, a wise choice. It's too bad that Hitchcock's last film was not up to most of his others, but even fair Hitchcock is ten times better than all of the new directors who keep ripping him off and calling it homage.

p&d, Alfred Hitchcock; w, Ernest Lehman (from the novel *The Rainbird Pattern* by Victor Canning); ph, Leonard South (Technicolor); m, John Williams; ed, J. Terry Williams; art d, Henry Bumstead; set d, James W. Payne; cos, Edith Head; spec eff, Frank Brendel, Albert Whitlock.

Suspense/Mystery **Cas.** **(PR:C MPAA:PG)**

FAMILY SECRET, THE*** (1951) 85m Santana/COL bw

John Derek *(David Clark)*, Lee J. Cobb *(Howard Clark)*, Jody Lawrance *(Lee Pearson)*, Erin O'Brien-Moore *(Ellen Clark)*, Santos Ortega *(George Redman)*, Henry O'Neill *(Donald Muir)*, Carl Benton Reid *(Dr. Reynolds)*, Peggy Converse *(Sybil Bradley)*, Jean Alexander *(Vera Stone)*, Dorothy Tree *(Marie Elsnore)*, Raymond Greenleaf *(Mr. Sims)*, Onslow Stevens *(Judge)*, Elizabeth Flournoy *(Cora French)*, Bill Walker *(Larry)*, Frances E. Williams *(Bertha)*, Mary Alan Hokanson *(Miss Martin)*, Whit Bissell *(Joe Elsnore)*.

An intriguing premise which gets lost in an excess of plot. Derek accidentally kills his best friend, but since there were no witnesses he fails to inform the police. He tells only his family, who differ in opinion on what to do. His father, impeccably portrayed by Cobb, insists he confesses the incident, while mom, O'Brien-Moore, wants to keep it quiet. Dad buckles under family pressure and opts to keep his mouth shut. Plot becomes implausible when Cobb is called on to perform lawyer duties for the innocent man accused of the crime. Eventually, Derek's guilt forces him to confess, leading to a stint in the slammer.

p, Robert Lord; d, Henry Levin; w, Francis Cockrell, Andrew Solt (based on a story by Marie Baumer, James Cavanagh); ph, Burnett Guffey; m, George Duning; ed, Al Clark; md, Morris Stoloff; art d, George Brooks.

Crime **(PR:A MPAA:NR)**

FAMILY WAY, THE*½** (1966, Brit.) 114m BL/WB c

Hayley Mills *(Jenny Piper)*, Hywel Bennett *(Arthur Fitton)*, John Mills *(Ezra Fitton)*, Marjorie Rhodes *(Lucy Fitton)*, Avril Angers *(Liz Piper)*, John Comer *(Leslie Piper)*, Wilfred Pickles *(Uncle Fred)*, Barry Foster *(Joe Thompson)*, Liz Fraser *(Molly Thompson)*, Andrew Bradford *(Eddie)*, Thorley Walters *(The Vicar)*, Colin Gordon *(Mr. Hutton, Travel Agent)*, Robin Parkinson *(Mr. Phillips)*, Ruth Trouncer *(Marriage Counsellor)*, Harry Locke *(Mr. Stubbs)*, Maureen O'Reilly *(Miss Hunt)*, Lesley Daine *(Dora)*, Hazel Bainbridge *(Mrs. Bell)*, Murray Head *(Geoffrey Fitton)*, Ruth Gower *(Mrs. Pike)*, Diana Coupland *(Mrs. Rose)*, Fanny Carby *(Mrs. Stone)*, Helen Booth *(Mrs. Lee)*, Margaret Lacey *(Mrs. Harris)*.

Hayley Mills comes of age in this frank marital comedy which co-stars Bennett as her newlywed husband. The film begins on the day of their much-awaited wedding, capped off with a practical joke that sends their bed collapsing to the floor as they are about to consummate their relationship. Their desire to become former virgins is again ruined when their honeymoon plans fall through, forcing them to stay with their folks. Eventually the deed is done in a tactful and gentle scene. The especially stark script makes no attempts to portray the ex-Disney star as a fluffy-pure newlywed. Fine support comes from Mills' real-life father, John Mills, as well as Rhodes, who is brilliant as his understanding wife. Although it seems harmless and sweet now, upon release this picture caused many mouths to hang open. The 20-year-old role model was to be seen smoking, drinking, swearing, and prancing around bare-bottomed in one scene. To many, the darling Hayley had gone too far. Their disillusionment was made even greater when news leaked out that she had fallen in love with 53-year-old director Roy Boulting. Scandal erupted and the gossip columns had a field day, especially because the elder Mills was present on the set, the romance going on under his very nose. The lovebirds, however, made it legal in 1971. Fine score by Beatle Paul McCartney.

p, John Boulting; d, Roy Boulting; w, Bill Naughton, Roy Boulting, Jeffrey Dell (from Naughton's play *All In Good Time*); ph, Harry Waxman (Eastmancolor); m, Paul McCartney; ed, Ernest Hosler; art d, Alan Withy; cos, Bridget Sellers; makeup, Trevor Crole-Rees.

Drama **(PR:O MPAA:NR)**

FAMOUS FERGUSON CASE, THE* (1932) 80m FN-WB bw

Joan Blondell *(Maizie Dickson)*, Tom Brown *(Bruce Foster)*, Adrienne Dore *(Tony Martin)*, Walter Miller *(Cedric Works)*, Leslie Fenton *(Perrin)*, Vivienne Osborne *(Mrs. Marcia Ferguson)*, J. Carroll Naish *(Claude Wright)*, Purnell Pratt *(George M. Ferguson)*, Kenneth Thomson *(Bob Parks)*, Grant Mitchell *(Martin Collins)*, Leon [Ames] Waycoff *(Judd Brooks)*, Clarence Wilson *(County Attorney)*, Bert Hanlon *(Eddie Klein)*, Mike Donlin *(Photographer)*, Russell Hopton *(Rusty Calahan)*, Miriam Seegar *(Mrs. Brooks)*, Willard Robertson *(Sheriff)*, George Meeker *(Jigger Bolton)*, Russell Simpson *(Craig)*, Fred Burton *(Bridges)*, Spencer Charters *(Fire Chief)*.

A yawner which looks at the role of yellow journalists during the anything-but-famous title case. The talkative Brown delivers monologue after monologue about placing the sensationalized murder case on the front page.

d, Lloyd Bacon; w, Courtney Terrett, Harvey Thew (based on the story "Circulation" by Terrett, Granville Moore); ph, Dev Jennings; ed, Howard Bretherton.

Crime **(PR:A MPAA:NR)**

FAN, THE** (1949) 79m FOX bw (GB: LADY WINDERMERE'S FAN)

Jeanne Crain *(Lady Windermere)*, Madeleine Carroll *(Mrs. Erlynne)*, George Sanders *(Lord Darlington)*, Richard Greene *(Lord Windermere)*, Martita Hunt *(Duchess of Berwick)*, John Sutton *(Cecil Graham)*, Hugh Dempster *(Lord Augustus Lorton)*, Richard Ney *(Mr. Hopper)*, Virginia McDowall *(Lady Agatha)*, Hugh Murray *(Dawson)*, Frank Elliott *(Jeweler)*, John Burton *(Hoskins)*, Trevor Ward *(Auctioneer)*, Patricia Walker *(American Girl)*, Eric Noonan *(Underwood)*, Winifred Harris *(Maid)*, Alphonse Martell *(Philippe)*, Felippa Rock *(Rosalie)*, Colin Campbell *(Tailor)*, Terry Kilburn *(Messenger)*, Tempe Pigott *(Mrs. Rudge)*, George Beranger *(Philippe's Assistant)*.

Another of the many examples of the adage "If you can't do it better, don't remake it." Oscar Wilde's famous play "Lady Windermere's Fan" had been brought to the silver screen by Ernst Lubitsch in 1925. Preminger's version, despite a strong cast, was bowdlerized by the scripters into a soapy mess. Preminger later confessed his mistake, stating that he hated the film during production, and that whatever he did to it was wrong. The story centers on the self-imposition of the notorious, aging, but still beautiful Carroll into the otherwise happy, patrician existence of youthful, wealthy nobleman Greene and his lovely but prudish and judgmental young wife, Crain. When Crain discovers that Greene has given financial assistance to adventuress Carroll—indeed, has been supporting her in the grand manner—she opts to run off with supercad Sanders, who has ardently pressed his attentions on her. Carroll, discovering Crain's intent, follows her to Sanders' apartments, admonishing her not to repeat the mistake that she, herself, had made, one which resulted in her ostracism from polite society. Deviating from Wilde's classic, she reveals—in a manner which might sell soapsuds—that she is Crain's long-lost mother. As the two women speak, they hear Sanders, Greene, and Dempster enter, and quickly conceal themselves. Greene, discovering Crain's distinctive fan, demands to search the premises. The men fight, the ladies escape, but Carroll later returns, compromising her already tarnished honor, claiming that it was she who had left the fan, which she had picked up by mistake. Carroll, having made the mandatory maternal sacrifice, then departs for the Continent, once again a social pariah. Greene and Crain live into a happy dotage until, in an anachronistic departure from period, they are blown to bits in the blitz of WW II, a surprising termination. The original play, of course, ended with the moralizing Lady Windermere, chastened by her experience, more accepting of human frailty, more forgiving, but still ignorant of her maternal heritage. As is too often the case with filmed classics, dialog was sacrificed to further a perverted plot. Wilde's witty aphorisms were excised, and with them went any merit the film might have had. Had Preminger and the scripters adhered to the original, this movie of a classic might have been a movie classic. THE IMPORTANCE OF BEING EARNEST (1952) demonstrated that Wilde's wordy works *can* be successfully brought to the screen.

p&d, Otto Preminger; w, Walter Reisch, Dorothy Parker, Ross Evans (based on the play "Lady Windermere's Fan" by Oscar Wilde); ph, Joseph La Shelle; m, Daniele Amfitheatrof; ed, Louis Loeffler; md, Alfred Newman; art d, Lyle R. Wheeler, Leland Fuller; set d, Thomas Little, Paul S. Fox; cos, Charles Le Maire, Rene Hubert; spec eff, Fred Sersen.

Drama **(PR:A MPAA:NR)**

FAN, THE** (1981) 95m Filmways/PAR c

Lauren Bacall *(Sally Ross)*, James Garner *(Jake Berman)*, Maureen Stapleton *(Belle Goldman)*, Hector Elizondo *(Ralph Andrews)*, Michael Biehn *(Douglas Breen)*, Anna Maria Horsford *(Emily Stolz)*, Kurt Johnson *(David Branum)*, Feiga Martinez *(Elsa)*, Reed Jones *(Choreographer)*, Kaiulani Lee *(Douglas' Sister)*, Charles Blackwell *(John Vetta)*, Dwight Schultz *(Director)*, Dana Delany *(Saleswoman)*, Terence Marinan *(Young Man in Bar)*, Lesley Rogers *(Heidi)*, Parker McCormick *(Hilda)*, Robert Weil *(Pop)*, Ed Crowley *(Caretaker)*, Gail Benedict *(Assistant Choreographer)*, D. David Lewis *(Pianist)*, Griffin Dunne *(Production Assistant)*, Themi Sapountzakis *(Markham)*, Jean DeBaer *(Stage Manager)*, Liz Smith *(Herself)*, Haru Aki, Rene Ceballos, Clif DeRaita, Edyie Fleming, Linda Haberman, Sergio Lopez-Cal, Jamie Patterson, Justin Ross, Stephanie Williams, Jim Wolfe *(Dancers)*, Thomas Saccio *(Prop Man)*, Victoria Vanderkloot *(Pen Thief)*, James Ogden *(Drummer)*, Terri Duhaime *(Nurse)*, Donna Mitchell *(Hostess)*, Hector Osorio *(Doughnut Vendor)*, Lionel Pina *(Customer)*, Miriam Phillips *(Woman on Steps)*, Jack R. Marks, George Peters *(Doormen)*, Esther Benson, Eric Van Valkenburg, Ann Pearl Gary, Madeline Moroff, Leo Schaff *(Fans)*, James Bryson, J. Nesbit Clark, Tim Elliott, Paul Hummel, Jacob Laufer *(Stagehands)*.

Lots of good talent is mostly wasted in a highly predictable plot that we've seen before and will, no doubt, see again. Does life imitate art, or is it the other way around? In this case, art came first as Bob Randall's novel was released quite some time before, and the picture had been finished months ahead of the tragedy that took place outside New York's Dakota Apartments when Mark David Chapman took the life of John Lennon. Bacall is a famous star who is loved by a fan, Biehn. He tries to get in touch with her but can't get close as Bacall's secretary, Stapleton, keeps everyone from her boss. Garner is Bacall's ex-husband. They have parted on good terms, so she is in touch with him more than split people usually are. Biehn's love turns to hate when he can't get past Stapleton, so he kills the faithful factotum. The rest of the film is what you might expect: an obsession that turns violent. Lots of gore and lots of wasted words. Bacall is set up to be a lovely person who is totally innocent and knows nothing of the letters and other communications from Biehn; she is understandably shocked when blood begins to flow. It's a B movie with an A cast. No amount of good acting or directing (this was commercials director Bianchi's first feature effort and he did well enough) will triumph over what is a cliched story.

p, Robert Stigwood; d, Edward Bianchi; w, John Hartwell, Priscilla Chapman (based on the novel by Bob Randall); ph, Dick Bush (Technicolor); m, Pino Donaggio; ed, Alan Heim; prod d, Santo Loquasto; art d, Paul Eads; cos, Jeffrey Kurland, Tom McKinley; m/l, Marvin Hamlisch, Tim Rice; ch, Arlene Phillips.

Suspense/Thriller   **Cas.**   **(PR:C-O   MPAA:R)**

FANATIC   (SEE: DIE! DIE! MY DARLING, 1965, Brit.)

FANCY BAGGAGE**   (1929) 71m WB bw

Audrey Ferris (Naomi Iverson), Myrna Loy (Myrna), George Fawcett (Iverson), Hallam Cooley (Dickey), Wallace MacDonald (Ernest Hardin), Eddie Gribbon (Steve), Burr McIntosh (Austin), Edmund Breese (John Hardin), Virginia Sale.

Fawcett receives a long prison sentence for illegal stock manipulations, and is keeping his silence about the involvement of his one-time business partner, Breese. Ferris decides to vindicate her father and sneaks onto Breese's yacht in hope of getting Breese to confess. Instead, she meets Breese's son, MacDonald, and falls in love. But she becomes involved with a rum runner and MacDonald must rescue her. Eventually all is resolved: Breese and Fawcett reconcile and the young couple is given their blessing. Despite her high billing, Loy is given little more to do than stand around, wear fancy clothing, and look pretty. At the time, and for many years after, Loy was firmly typecast as a vamp; her comedic talents came to light later. This was not her first talkie; she had a small role in the first talkie, THE JAZZ SINGER (1927). The film is a myriad of loose ends and unbelievable coincidences. The dialog is poorly recorded.

d, John G. Adolfi; w, C. Graham Baker, James A. Starr (based on a story by Jerome Kingston); ph, William Reis; ed, Owen Marks.

Drama   **(PR:A   MPAA:NR)**

FANCY PANTS**½   (1950) 92m PAR c

Bob Hope (Humphrey), Lucille Ball (Agatha Floud), Bruce Cabot (Cart Belknap), Jack Kirkwood (Mike Floud), Lea Penman (Effie Floud), Hugh French (George Van-Basingwell), Eric Blore (Sir Wimbley), John Alexander (Teddy Roosevelt), Joseph Vitale (Wampum), Norma Varden (Lady Maude), Virginia Kelly (Rosalind), Colin Keith-Johnston (Twombley), Joe Wong (Wong), Robin Hughes (Cyril), Percy Helton (Maj. Fogarty), Hope Sanberry (Millie), Grace Gillern Albertson (Dolly), Oliver Blake (Mr. Andrews), Chester Conklin (Guest), Edgar Dearing (Mr. Jones), Alva Marie Lacy (Daisy), Ida Moore (Betsy, Bessie), Ethel Wales (Mrs. Wilkins), Jean Ruth (Miss Wilkins), Jimmie Dundee, Bob Kortman (Henchmen), Major Sam Harris (Umpire), Gilchrist Stuart (Wicket Keeper), Charles Cooley (Man), Olaf Hytten (Stage Manager), Alex Frazer (Stagehand), Almira Sessions (Belle), Howard Petrie, Ray Bennett (Secret Service Men), Harry Martin (Englishman), Gilbert Alonzo, David Alvarado, Robert Dominguez, Vincent Garcia, Henry Mirelez, Alfred Nunez (Indian Boys), Hank Bell (Barfly).

An occasionally side-splitting Hope-Ball comedy which has Hope cast as a fake British lord. Ball is introduced to him in England and invites him back to her New Mexico home. Once in the southwest, he continues putting on the false airs, fooling even the visiting Teddy Roosevelt. The expected occurs when Ball's jealous beau unfurls the disguise. A remake of Leo McCarey's RUGGLES OF RED GAP (1935). Includes the songs "Fancy Pants" and "Home Cookin'."

p, Robert L. Welch; d, George Marshall; w, Edmund Hartman, Robert O'Brien (based on the story Ruggles of Red Gap by Harry Leon Wilson); ph, Charles B. Lang, Jr. (Technicolor); m, Van Cleave; ed, Archie Marshek; art d, Hans Dreier, Earl Hedrick; m/l, Jay Livingston, Ray Evans.

Musical Comedy   **(PR:A   MPAA:NR)**

FANDANGO**   (1970) 79m Tivoli Productions/Clover Films c

James Whitworth (Dan Murphy), Shawn Devereaux (Mona DeLyse), Sebastian Gregory (Muck Mulligan), Jay Scott (Billy Busby), Marland Proctor (Sissy Sam), Donna Stanley (Pauline), Neola Graef (Joy), Paul Harper (Greaser), John Dennis, Bonnie Cooper, Miller Pettit, Frank Teichman, Wendy Sweeney, Maxine DeVille France, Jeff Latham, Jeannie Anderson, Roger Gentry, Jim Feazell, Paul Brunton, Beverly Fredericks, Gene Connor, Ray Saniger, Byron Wardlow, Jerry Seay, Earl Newell, Allison Racy Young.

Whitworth takes a group of men up into the mountains to set up a gold mining camp. The camp is harassed by Gregory's band of outlaws, and there is a constant food shortage. When the men become restless for women, Whitworth and a couple of the miners go into town to round up some whores. They go to the Fandango Saloon where Whitworth knows the madam. The miners get into a gunfight with the outlaws both while in town and before and after the prostitutes leave the camp. The madam kills the leader of the gang, which ends one problem for the miners.

p, Henning Schellerup, Paul Hipp; d&w, John Hayes; ph, Paul Hipp (Eastmancolor); m, Mario Toscana.

Western   **Cas.**   **(PR:O   MPAA:NR)**

FANFAN THE TULIP**   (1952, Fr.) 104m Les Films Ariane-Filmsonor-Amato/Lopert bw (AKA: SOLDIER IN LOVE)

Gerard Philipe (Fanfan the Tulip), Gina Lollobrigida (Adeline), Noel Roquevert (Fier-A-Bras), Olivier Hussenot (Tranche "Samson"), Marcel Herrand (Louis XV), Jean-Marc Tennberg (Lebel), Jean Paredes (Capt. La Houlette), Henri Rollan (Marshall of France), Nerio Bernardi (Sgt. La Franchise), Genevieve Page (La Pompadour), Sylvie Pelayo (Henriette de France), Georgette Anys (Mrs. Samson), Hiram Sherman (English Commentary).

Charming, witty satire of Errol Flynn swashbucklers features Gerard Philipe as a 17th-century swordsman with tongue firmly planted in cheek. He's being forced into a shotgun (or saber) wedding and escapes the clutches of the woman by joining the king's army. A bogus soothsayer examines his palm and predicts he will one day marry the king's daughter and establish himself as one of France's greatest heroes. Riding along the road one day, he spies a coach being attacked by criminals. He cuts the band of malfeasants, cuts them to bits with his swordplay, and then learns that Madame Pompadour (Page) and the king's daughter, Gina Lollobrigida, are in the coach. A kiss is his payment. Next thing you know, Philipe and his pals win the war and he is offered the hand of lovely Gina as well as the hand of yet another beauty. Along the way, there are several swordfights, a mock sentence of death, a raid on a convent, and the eventual awarding of a commission from the king. Forget any rhyme or reason to the script and just enjoy all the derring-do. There's English narration lovingly spoken by veteran actor Hiram Sherman, so there is no mistaking what's happening, even if your French is non-existent. It's a subtle anti-war piece, and shows the futility of combat without banging you over the head with any moral judgments. Philipe made many movies in a brief career that ended when he had a heart attack at age 36. He'll best be remembered for DEVIL IN THE FLESH (1947), THE SEVEN DEADLY SINS (1952) and BEAUTIES OF THE NIGHT (1952). In his short life, he appeared in more than 30 films as well as directing himself in his screenplay for BOLD ADVENTURE (1956).

p&d, Christian-Jaque; w, Henri Jeanson, Christian-Jaque, Rene Wheeler (based on a story by Wheeler, Rene Fallet); ph, Christian Matras; m, Georges Van Parys, Maurice Thiriet; ed, Jean Desagneaux.

Comedy/Adventure   **(PR:A   MPAA:NR)**

FANGELSE   (SEE: DEVIL'S WANTON, THE, 1959)

FANGS OF THE ARCTIC**   (1953) 62m MON bw

Kirby Grant, Lorna Hansen, Warren Douglas, Leonard Penn, Richard Avonde, Robert Sherman, John Close, Phil Tead, Roy Gordon, Kit Carson, Chinook the Dog.

Brave and loyal mountie Grant gets some canine assistance from Chinook in his search for a gang of unlawful trappers. His chase is given the added Northwest Territory obstacle of blinding snowstorms, but Chinook lends a paw and saves the day.

p, Lindsley Parsons; d, Rex Bailey; w, Bill Raynor, Warren Douglas (based on a story by James Oliver Curwood); ph, William Sickner; art d, David Milton.

Adventure   **(PR:A   MPAA:NR)**

FANGS OF THE WILD**   (1954) 72m Lippert bw (AKA: FOLLOW THE HUNTER)

Charles Chaplin, Jr. (Roger), Onslow Stevens (Jim), Margia Dean (Linda), Freddy Ridgeway (Tad), Phil Tead (Mac), Robert Stevenson (Deputy Sheriff), Buck, the Wonder Dog (Shep).

A young boy, Ridgeway, witnesses a murder at his father's hunting lodge, but no one believes him. The killer, Chaplin, said the murder was a hunting accident, and the explanation satisfies deputy sheriff Stevenson and Ridgeway's father, Stevens. Chaplin, though, gets nervous and tries to kill the only witness to his crime. The young boy is saved by his dog, Buck, after a climactic chase in the mountains. Heavily melodramatic and moves at a snail-like pace.

p, Robert L. Lippert Jr.; d, William Claxton; w, Orville Hampton (adapted from a story by Claxton); ph, Paul Ivano; m, Paul Dunlap; ed, Monica Collingwood.

Adventure   **(PR:A   MPAA:NR)**

FANNY**½   (1948, Fr.) 125m Pagnol/Siritzky International bw

Raimu (Cesar Olivier), Orane Demazis (Fanny), Pierre Fresnay (Marius), Fernard Charpin (Honore Panisse), Alida Rouffe (Honorine Cabanis), Robert Vattier (M. Brun), Auguste Mouries Felix Escartefigue), Milly Mathis (Aunt Claudine Foulon), Maupi (Chauffeur), Edouard Delmont (Dr. Felicien Venelle).

When Marcel Pagnol learned that Paramount had the audacity to hire another writer to rewrite his screenplay for TOPAZE without even notifying him, he became determined to control his own works as much as he could. He went into an agreement with a distribution company and hired director Marc Allegret to helm his play adaptations. Pagnol's plays were successfully made into such films as THE BAKER'S WIFE and THE WELL-DIGGER'S DAUGHTER and the characters in FANNY were first seen in the play and film MARIUS. Harry Baur played the part of Cesar in the stage version of FANNY but Raimu moved back in for the film. It picks up right where the first finished with Pierre Fresnay departing for the sea. Raimu tosses Orane Demazis (reprising her role as Fanny) over his shoulder as she swooned and fainted when Fresnay left. Demazis is brought back to consciousness. She tells Raimu that his son has fallen prey to the call of the sea and is now aboard the Malaisie and will explore the world. Raimu tries very hard to say "no matter," but the fact that he hasn't heard from Fresnay for three weeks gnaws at him. Then a letter arrives and Raimu smiles. Meanwhile, Charpin, the sailmaker, wants Demazis to marry him. When she discovers she's enceinte by Fresnay, she prays for his return so he can marry her and give the child a name. Raimu's wife, Rouffe, learns that Fanny is expecting and wants her to leave instantly. Demazis faints and

Rouffe, a mother in her own right, suddenly becomes maternal as she realizes that Demazis has a grandchild inside her. Still, she advises Demazis to marry Charpin, if only to save face. Demazis goes to Charpin and tells him that she is pregnant with Fresnay's child but that does not deter the wealthy widower. His late wife was barren and the thought of fatherhood is pleasing. All he asks is that she agree that he will be the father with no mention of Fresnay. Raimu tells Demazis that Fresnay's letter indicates that he'll be returning in about two years. Charpin tells Raimu that it doesn't make a difference, Demazis has agreed to marry him. The two men argue and then Demazis arrives to tell Raimu that she and Charpin have an imminent wedding planned. At first, Raimu thinks that Demazis is two-timing his son but when he learns that she's pregnant, he relents and allows himself to be named godfather. There is an agreement to name the child after Raimu and Fresnay. Demazis and Charpin marry and have a son on Easter morning. Raimu conceals the fact that Demazis is married and a mother in all his letters to Fresnay. Fresnay comes home for a brief visit just after Charpin has apparently gone off to Paris on a trip. Fresnay learns of Demazis' situation and goes to see her. She tells him that Charpin is asleep in the bedroom and he berates her for not waiting for him. Mouriès, a pal of Charpin, arrives from the station with flowers sent by the latter and Fresnay, now understanding that she's lied, realizes that the child must be his own. They look at each other passionately and kiss. Then Raimu arrives and parts them. Raimu is adamant about Fresnay not compromising Demazis. A few moments later, Charpin walks in. He's decided not to take the trip after all, being unable to leave his beloved wife and child. Here is the scene Charpin has feared all along, a confrontation with Fresnay. This final scene is powerful, with Demazis admitting that she loves Fresnay, but she will never leave Charpin. The child may not be physically his, but surely it is his child in every other way. Raimu must perform a reluctant deed now. He tells his son that there is no longer any room for him in Demazis's heart and that it would be much better for all concerned if the young man went back to sea. Fresnay exits as Fanny breaks down and cries and the picture ends. FANNY was filmed in 1932, but MGM bought remake rights and prevented the original film's release for 16 years. The story was done again in 1954 as a musical, then remade in 1961, and it still stands up today. Pagnol wrote a warm, touching tale and it has been a success wherever it has played as the situation is totally truthful and knows no nàtion's bounds. The same things could happen anywhere and that is Pagnol's genius. Other remakes include an Italian version, directed by Almirante in 1933 and a German version starring the great Emil Jannings as Cesar. It was done again as PORT OF SEVEN SEAS (1938) with Wallace Beery and Frank Morgan, and will probably have two or three more versions before the 20th century ends.

p, Marcel Pagnol; d, Marc Allegret; w, Pagnol (from his play); ph, Nicolas Toporkoff, Andre Dantan, Roger Hubert, Georges Benoit, Coutelain; m, Vincent Scotto; ed, Raymond Lamy; Eng. titles, H.G. Weinberg.

Drama (PR:A-C MPAA:NR)

FANNY*** (1961) 133m Mansfield/WB c

Leslie Caron (*Fanny*), Maurice Chevalier (*Panisse*), Charles Boyer (*Cesar*), Horst Buchholz (*Marius*), Baccaloni (*Escartifique*), Lionel Jeffries (*Monsieur Brun*), Raymond Bussieres (*Admiral*), Victor Francen (*Louis Panisse*), Georgette Anys (*Honorine*), Joel Flateau (*Cesario*).

This version contains the final story in Pagnol's Marseilles trilogy. There was MARIUS, then FANNY and finally, CESAR and if you look at the synopsis provided in the original French version, you'll see that the story ends as Marius goes back to sea, leaving Fanny with Panisse, her husband, and the son that Marius fathered, now acknowledged to be Panisse's. This remake goes over the same territory earlier indicated, then continues beyond it. Nine years pass and Marius (now played by Horst Buchholz) is working as a garageman in a nearby town, having given up his passion for the sea and the need to sail to the "isles beneath the wind." The aged Panisse is played by Chevalier and the grandfather by Boyer. A pal takes the child, now nine (Flateau) to visit Buchholz, who is overcome by the sight of the boy. As this happens, Caron arrives and tells her long-lost love that Chevalier is dying and has dictated a letter from his deathbed that it is his sincere desire for Buchholz and Caron to marry as soon as they can after his death. Thus blessed, the lovers unite and the picture concludes. This version is essentially the same as the Joshua Logan/Harold Rome musical, with the songs omitted. Why they deleted the lovely score is a mystery, as it contained some of Rome's best music. In fact, Harry Sukman used that music as the basis for his film score, and received an "adaptation" credit rather than the usual "music by."

p&d, Joshua Logan; w, Julius J. Epstein (from the play by Logan and S.N. Behrman, based on the play "Fanny" and the "Marseilles Trilogy" by Marcel Pagnol); ph, Jack Cardiff (Technicolor); m, Harry Sukman adaptation of the score by Harold Rome; md, Morris Stoloff; ed, William H. Reynolds; art d, Rino Mondellini; set d, Robert Turlure; cos, Anne-Marie Marchand.

Drama **Cas.** (PR:A-C MPAA:NR)

FANNY AND ALEXANDER**** (1983, Swed./Fr./Ger.) 188m AB Cinematograph-Swedish Film Institute-Swedish TV One-Gaumont-Persona Film-Tobis Filmkunst/Embassy c (FANNY OCH ALEXANDER)

Gunn Wallgren (*Widow/Grandmother Helena Ekdahl*), Boerje Ahlstedt (*Her Son, Prof. Carl Ekdahl*), Christina Schollin (*Lydia Ekdahl, His Wife*), Allan Edwall (*Helena's Son Oscar, Actor*), Ewa Froeling (*Oscar's Wife Emilie*), Pernilla Allwin (*Their Daughter Fanny, 8*), Bertil Guve (*Their Son, Alexander, 10*), Jarl Kulle (*Helena's Son Carl-Gustav*), Mona Malm (*His Wife, Alma*), Pernilla Wallgren (*His Mistress, Helena's Maid Maj*), Anna Bergman (*Hanna Schwarz*), Gunnar Bjoernstrand (*Filip Landahl*), Jan Malmsjoe (*Bishop Edvard Vergerus*), Marianne Aminoff (*His Mother Blenda*), Kerstin Tidelius (*His Sister Henrietta*), Harriet Andersson (*Justina, Kitchen Maid*), Erland Josephson (*Isak Jacobi*), Stina Ekblad (*Ismael*), Mats Bergman (*Aron*), Licka Sjoman, Per Mattson, Sune Mangs, Ake Lagergren, Tore

Karte, Kerstin Karte, Marianne Karlbeck, Maud Hyttenberg-Bartoletti, Heinz Hopf, Gus Dahlstrom, Sven Erik Jacobsen, Hugo Hasslo, Lars-Owe Carlberg, Nils Brand, Marrit Olsson, Marianne Neilson, Hans Henrik Lerfeldt, Mona Andersson, Harriet Andersson, Inga Alenius, Gunn Wallgren, Emilie Werko, Hans Straat, Gosta Pruzelius, Lena Olin, Kabi Laretei, Svea Holst, Olle Hilding, Sonya Hedenbratt, Eva Von Hanno, Maria Granlund, Majlis Granlund, Patricia Gelin, Siv Ericks.

Steering away from heavy metaphysical questions and the state of Man's psyche Ingmar Bergman created a film of magical proportions based on childhood memories at the turn of the century. FANNY AND ALEXANDER begins with a Christmas celebration by Ekdahl family members, their large family home being the meeting ground for a merry celebration by both family members and servants who dance about unaware of any form of social restraint. Late that night, the ten-year-old Alexander is put to sleep by the buxom maid, who apologizes for being unable to spend the night with him because she has other obligations, these being to service his Uncle Carl, a married man with children of his own and the owner of a restaurant who loves the sensual life. His wife is completely aware of his pleasure seeking adventures, but does nothing to stop them. The synthetic image of a happy, innocent life is quickly shattered when Alexander's acting father suffers a heart attack and dies. The widow (Froeling) is seen in a crying jag when her beloved husband passes from this world; an understanding reverend arrives to calm her down. Froeling marries this man of the cloth, taking her two young children Fanny and Alexander away from the happy family into the cold, strict world of the preacher. Living in a place void of any physical luxuries or beauty to which he has grown accustomed, Alexander is forced to endure in a virtual hell. His new father takes pleasure in beating the boy for committing the most innocent of childhood pranks, while he is also required to do chores reserved for servants. Grandmother Wallgren becomes aware of the nightmare her grandchildren are forced to live with and arranges for her Jewish friend and lover to have the children kidnaped. Then, in the most magical moment of this film, Alexander is able to have his hated step-father burned to a crisp. He goes into the basement of the Jewish man's house to encounter the son that has been kept locked up because of powers which must be kept under control. The two make the reverend's home go up in flames; Froeling and her children are now able to return to the warmth and happiness of the family. Not only did Bergman manage to capture the flavor and atmosphere of the 1907 Swedish town, he also expertly revealed events as seen through the eyes of a child. Without making any wordy dissertations on doctrines, Bergman made powerful statements against oppressive religious zealots. The results are quite frightening and far superior to the lengthy speeches and depressing anxiety that fill many of the earlier Bergman films. FANNY AND ALEXANDER is a magical film and will likely be an achievement for which Bergman will be most remembered.

d&w, Ingmar Bergman; ph, Sven Nykvist (Eastmancolor); m, Daniel Bell, Benjamin Britten, Frans Helmerson, Robert Schumson, Marianne Jacobs; ed, Sylvia Ingemarsson; art d, Anna Asp; set d, Jacob Tigerskiold; cos, Marik Vos.

Drama **Cas.** (PR:C-O MPAA:R)

FANNY BY GASLIGHT (SEE: MAN OF EVIL, 1944, Brit.)

FANNY FOLEY HERSELF*½ (1931) 73m RKO c (GB: TOP OF THE BILL)

Edna May Oliver (*Fanny Foley*), Hobart Bosworth (*Seely*), Helen Chandler (*Lenore*), John Darrow (*Teddy*), Rochelle Hudson (*Carmen*), Florence Roberts (*Lucy*), Robert Emmett O'Connor (*Burns*), Harry O. Stubbs (*Crosby*).

Veteran character actress Oliver was hired by RKO to rival Marie Dressler, but her film debut as a star falls flat, not a fault of hers, but that of the director and writers. Oliver is a vaudeville performer with two daughters and a wealthy father-in-law who wants to take the daughters away from their theater life style. The direction swings from drama to broad comedy without logic. In one scene, Oliver parachutes from a plane to check on her newly married daughter. RKO went all-out on this one, apparently hoping to launch a series. The two-color technicolor process, in which red and green images were superimposed on the screen by a special prismatic projector, was costly both in production and projection, and was little used except for selected segments of feature films of the time.

p, John E. Burch; d, Melville Brown; w, Carey Wilson and Benard Schubert (adapted from a story by Juliet Wilbur Tompkins); ph, Ray Rennahan (two-color Technicolor).

Comedy (PR:A MPAA:NR)

FANNY HILL: MEMOIRS OF A WOMAN OF PLEASURE zero (1965) 104m Famous Players/Favorite Films bw

Miriam Hopkins (*Mrs. Maude Brown*), Letitia Roman (*Fanny Hill*), Walter Giller (*Hemingway*), Alex D'Arcy (*Admiral*), Helmut Weiss (*Mr. Dinklespieler*), Chris Howland (*Mr. Norbert*), Ulli Lommel (*Charles*), Cara Garnett (*Phoebe*), Karin Evans (*Martha*), Syra Marty (*Hortense*), Albert Zugsmith (*Grand Duke*), Christiane Schmidtmer (*Fiona*), Heide Hansen (*Fenella*), Erica Ericson (*Emily*), Patricia Huston (*Amanda*), Marshall Raynor (*Johnny*), Hilda Sessack (*Mrs. Snow*), Billy Frick (*Percival*), Jurgen Nesbach (*James*), Herbert Knippenberg (*Mudge*), Susanne Hsiao (*Lotus Blossom*), Renate Hutte (*Niece*), Ellen Velero (*Girl*).

Russ Meyer (VIXEN, SUPER VIXEN) directed this sexploitation fare adapted from John Cleland's novel. Cheap and tasteless aren't adjectivally adequate to describe this garbage production. Roman is Fanny, a country girl who goes to London, loses her virginity, and finds herself in a brothel. Hopkins, who starred in the 1932 version of DR. JEKYLL AND MR. HYDE, is the helpful Madam. In the end, Fanny marries the sailor she loves. It is a very watered-down version of the erotic novel, with barren directing from Meyer. Production values are slipshod, with careless editing (shots don't match), poor dubbing, and lame narration.

p, Albert Zugsmith; d, Russ Meyer; w, Robert Hill (adapted from the novel by John Cleland); ph, Heinz Holscher; m, Erwin Halletz; ed, Alfred Arp.

Drama   **(PR:O   MPAA:NR)**

FAN'S NOTES, A**   (1972, Can.) 90m Coquihala/WB c

Jerry Orbach (Fred), Patricia Collins (Patience), Burgess Meredith (Mr. Blue), Rosemary Murphy (Moms), Conrad Bain (Poppy), Julia Robinson (Bunny Sue).

Orbach is an aspiring Canadian writer visiting the United States. Not only is he struggling to write, but trying to fit into the shoes of his star-football-player father. The title derives from Orbach's realization that he'll never be on the playing field, either as a writer or anything else. He is stuck in the stands watching. But, Orbach has another problem—he's become impotent with his sexually demanding American girl friend. The broad humor pulls the hero into self-pity too often to enjoy his trials and tribulations.

d, Eric Till; w, William Kinsolving (based on a book by Frederick Earl Exley); ph, Harry Makin; m, Ron Collier.

Comedy   **(PR:C   MPAA:NR)**

FANTASIA*****   (1940) 120m Disney/RKO c

Deems Taylor (Himself), Leopold Stokowski and the Philadelphia Symphony Orchestra (Themselves), Mickey Mouse [Animation] (Sorcerer's Apprentice).

The most impressive piece of animation ever to come out of the Disney studios was this revolutionary integration of great works of classical music and wonderfully imaginative animated visuals running the gamut from dancing hippos to the purely abstract. The film opens with the musicians in silhouette taking their places and tuning their instruments, yellow light beaming out of each piece as it begins to play. Narrator Taylor walks onto the stage and tells the audience about the three types of music: that which paints a picture, music that tells a story, and music for music's sake, "absolute music." In this last category is the first segment: J.S. Bach's "Toccata and Fugue in D Minor" is illustrated with swirling abstracts, strings across the sky being played with a floating bow, finally coming to rest on the figure of Stokowski, conducting the orchestra. Next is Tchaikovsky's "Nutcracker Suite," each of its segments illustrated by different forms dancing, starting with fairies and moving through mushrooms, flower petals, fish, and finally ending up with thistles and orchids doing "The Cossack Dance." The next segment is the most famous, the wonderful "Sorcerer's Apprentice" by Paul Dukas starring Mickey Mouse. When the old sorcerer goes to bed, apprentice Mickey tires of carrying buckets of water back and forth to scrub the floor, so he tries on the conjurer's tall conical hat (which glows slightly to show the magic stored there) and commands a broom to grow arms and legs and carry buckets of water. As Mickey watches the broom tirelessly fetching buckets he nods off, awakening from his dreams to find the room half filled with water. He feverishly tries to stop the broom, but it will not obey any command. Mickey grabs an axe and chops the broom to pieces, but each piece grows arms and legs and continues to fetch water, although now they are completely submerged. The sorcerer appears at the top of the stairs and with a wave of his hand restores the room. With the slightest trace of suppressed amusement he retrieves his broom from the sheepish Mickey, then gives the mouse a swat across the backside with it. Stravinsky's "Rite of Spring" is the next piece, illustrated with scenes of the birth of the planet, the rise of life, the growth, then the decline and extinction of the dinosaurs, the destruction of that world, and the rebirth of our world. The next episode provoked the most controversy, most of it from stuffed-shirt music critics who couldn't stand seeing Beethoven's "Pastoral Symphony" illustrated with a cartoon Bacchus, nymphs, centaurs, and the like. "The Dance of the Hours" by Ponchielli is the next segment, ostriches, hippos, crocodiles, and elephants doing a lively ballet in a great hall. Their stomping makes the walls shake and the heavy door crumble. The finale is Mussorgsky's "Night on Bald Mountain" segueing into "Ava Maria" by Schubert. Spirits rise from a graveyard and fly through the night to the top of Bald Mountain, where Tchernobog, the Black God, waits for them to do him honors. The spirits and flames swirl around him surrealistically, as the evil one revels (the figure was pantomimed by Bela Lugosi in front of the Disney artists). The dawn breaks, church bells ring, and as the spirits return to their rest, Tchernobog is driven back into the mountain. "Ave Maria" spreads over the countryside with the light. Originally intended as a short, "The Sorcerer's Apprentice" is the piece that brought Disney and Stokowski together. Disney had been looking for a piece of music that already had a story to go with it to do another "Silly Symphony." He decided on "Apprentice" and brought Stokowski to the studio to direct the studio musicians (it is the only segment not performed by the Philadelphia Orchestra). When the piece was finished in 1938, it had run way over budget and Disney knew that the only way he could make his money back was to incorporate the segment into a feature. The film began to appear in limited roadshow engagements in 1940, but due to difficulties in getting the materials for the sound system that had to be installed in each theater because of the outbreak of the war, it was not until 1942 that it began to get any kind of general release, and it was not for many years that it made back its heavy investment. In the late 1960s the film became a cult film for druggies, some of whom believed wholeheartedly that the entire Disney staff must have been high. Art Babbitt, the artist responsible for the dancing mushroom sequence, said "Yes, it is true. I myself was addicted to Ex-Lax and Feenamint." One segment that did not appear in the final film was Debussy's "Clair de Lune" although the animation did turn up years later with new music written for it in MAKE MINE MUSIC (1946).

p, Walt Disney; "Tocatta and Fugue in D Minor" by Johann Sebastian Bach: d, Samuel Armstrong; story development, Lee Blair, Elmer Plummer, Phil Dike; art d, Robert Cormack; animators, Cy Young, Art Palmer, Daniel MacManus, George Rowley, Edwin Aardal, Joshua Meador, Cornett Wood; background paintings, Joe Stanley, John Hench, Nino Carbe; "The Nutcracker Suite" by Peter Ilich Tchaikovsky: d, Samuel Armstrong; story development, Sylvia Moberly-Holland, Norman Wright, Albert Heath, Bianca Majolie, Graham Heid; character designers, John Walbridge, Elmer Plummer, Ethel Kulsar, Art d, Robert Cormack, Al Zinnen,

Curtiss D. Perkins, Arthur Byram, Bruce Bushman; animators, Arthur Babbitt, Les Clark, Don Lusk, Cy Young, Robert Stokes; background paintings, John Hench, Ethel Kulsar, Nino Carbe; "The Sorcerer's Apprentice" by Paul Dukas: d, James Algar; story development, Perce Pearce, Carl Fallberg; art d, Tom Codrick, Charles Philippi, Zack Schwartz; animation supervision, Fred Moore, Vladimir Tytla; animators, Les Clark, Riley Thompson, Marvin Woodward, Preston Blair, Edward Love, Ugo D'Orsi, George Rowley. Cornett Wood; background paintings, Claude Coats, Stan Spohn, Albert Dempster, Eric Hansen; "The Rite of Spring" by Igor Stravinsky; d, Bill Roberts, Paul Satterfield; story development and research, William Martin, Leo Thiele, Robert Sterner, John Fraser McLeish; art d, MacLaren Stewart, Dick Kelsey, John Hubley; animation supervision, Wolfgang Reitherman, Joshua Meador; animators, Philip Duncan, John McManus, Paul Busch, Art Palmer, Don Tobin, Edwin Aardal, Paul B. Kossoff; background paintings, Ed Starr, Brice Mack, Edward Levitt; special camera effects, Gail Papineau, Leonard Pickey; "Pastoral Symphony" by Ludwig van Beethoven: d, Hamilton Luske, Jim Handley, Ford Beebe; story development, Otto Englander, Webb Smith, Erdman Penner, Joseph Sabo, Bill Peet, George Stallings; character design, James Bodrero, John P. Miller, Lorna S. Soderstrom; art d, Hugh Hennessy, Kenneth Anderson, J. Gordon Legg, Herbert Ryman, Yale Gracey, Lance Nolley; animation supervision, Fred Moore, Ward Kimball, Eric Larson, Arthur Babbitt, Oliver M. Johnston, Jr., Don Towsley; animators, Berny Wolf, Jack Campbell, John Bradbury, James Moore, Milt Neil, Bill Justice, John Elliotte, Walt Kelly, Don Lusk, Lynn Karp, Murray McLennan, Robert W. Youngquist, Harry Hamsel; background paintings, Claude Coats, Ray Huffine, W. Richard Anthony, Arthur Riley, Gerald Nevius, Roy Forkum. "Dance of the Hours" by Amilcare Ponchielli: d, T. Hee, Norman Ferguson; character design, Martin Provensen, James Bodrero, Duke Russell, Earl Hurd; art d, Kendall O'Connor, Harold Doughty, Ernest Nordli; animation supervision, Norman Ferguson; animators, John Lounsbery, Howard Swift, Preston Blair, Hugh Fraser, Harvey Toombs, Norman Tate, Hicks Lokey, Art Elliott, Grant Simmons, Ray Patterson, Franklin Grundeen; background paintings, Albert Dempster, Charles Conner; "Night on Bald Mountain" by Modest Mussorgsky and "Ave Maria" by Franz Schubert: d, Wilfred Jackson; story development, Campbell Grant, Arthur Heinemann, Phil Dike; art d, Kay Nielsen, Terrell Stapp, Charles Payzant, Thor Putnam; animation supervision, Vladimir Tytla; animators, John McManus, William N. Shull, Robert W. Carlson, Jr., Lester Novros, Don Patterson; background paintings, Merle Cox, Ray Lockrem, Robert Storms, W. Richard Anthony; special animation effects, Joshua Meador, Miles E. Pike, John F. Reed, Daniel MacManus; special camera effects, Gail Papineau, Leonard Pickley; special lyrics for "Ave Maria" by Rachel Field; "Ave Maria" chorus directed by Charles Henderson; soloist, Julietta Novis.

Animation/Children   **(PR:AAA   MPAA:NR)**

FANTASIES zero   (1981) 81m Joseph Brenner c
                                        (AKA: AND ONCE UPON A LOVE)

Bo Derek (Anastasia), Peter Hooten (Damir), Anna Alexiadis (Mayor), Pheacton Gheorghitais (Photographer), Constantine Beladames (Godfather), Nicos Paschalidis (Priest), Therese Bohlin (Model), Boucci Simma (Beautifuloni), Vienneula Koussefhane (Saleslady).

This is John and Bo Derek's first collaboration, shot in 1973, but not released until after the Dereks' TARZAN, THE APE MAN in 1981. An incredibly immature filming of the story of a brother and sister (Hooten and Derek), who return to their Greek island home and begin to realize that they are falling in love with each other. Luckily, the mayor of the island (Alexiadis) remembers that the two had come from different families, and so worries of incest can be forgotten. The two lovers then get the villagers together to rebuild their home to attract tourists. There is also a sub-plot that concentrates on Bo's bathing habits. These are the "fantasies" of the title. When Hooten and Derek marry, the groom presents his wife with an ancient bath tub dug up from the ruins. It is one of John Derek's fantasies that he is a filmmaker.

p, Kevin Casselman; d,w&ph, John Derek; m, Jeff Silverman; ed, Bret Weston.

Drama   **(PR:O   MPAA:R)**

FANTASM zero   (1976, Aus.) 85m Filmways Australasian c

John Bluthal, Dee Dee Levitt, Maria Arnold, Bill Margold, Gretchen Gayle, Rene Bond, Al Williams, Con Covert, Mara Lutra, Uschi Digart, Maria Welton, John Holmes, Mary Gavin, Gene Allan Poe, Robert Savage, Kirby Hall, Shayne, Sue Doloria, Al Ward, Clement St. George, Serena.

A pseudo-documentary-style Australian film about women's "most common" sexual fantasies. An actor playing a sexologist and researcher presents the ten hot dreams females have: group sex, rape, incestuous relationship, religious sexual encounter, lesbian affair, S&M, and a couple others not nearly so exciting—even. The research for this film must have been done via a porno magazine subscription.

p, Anthony I. Ginnane; d, Richard Franklin; w, Ross Dimsey (from an idea by Ginnane); ph, Vincent Monton; ed, Tony Patterson.

Drama   **(PR:O   MPAA:NR)**

FANTASTIC COMEDY, A**½ (1975, Rum.) 90m Casa De Filme Cinci c

Dem Radulescu, Cornel Coman, Vasilia Tastaman, George Mihaita, Horea Popescu.

An uneasy mix of light-hearted fun and disturbing psycho-drama. A FANTASTIC COMEDY tells two stories: the first is a humorous story about a robot sent to Earth to search for new sources of energy his home planet needs. The second tells of a boy exiled in outer space in a cruel experiment intent on creating the perfect human being. This is an incongruous mix, though certainly an interesting idea with high production qualities. Popescu-Gopo was a noted animator before turning to feature film.

d&w, Ion Popescu-Gopo; ph, Grigore Ionescu, Stefan Horvath.

Comedy/Drama   **(PR:C   MPAA:NR)**

FANTASTIC INVASION OF THE PLANET EARTH, THE
(SEE: BUBBLE, THE, 1966)

FANTASTIC INVENTION, THE   (SEE: FABULOUS WORLD OF JULES
VERNE, THE, 1958, Czech.)

FANTASTIC PLANET*   (1973, Fr./Czech.) 71m Les Films Armorial/
Service De Recherche Ortif/Ceskoslovensky Film Export c
(LA PLANETE SAUVAGE)

Voices: Barry Bostwick, Marvin Miller, Olan Soule, Cynthia Alder, Nora Heflin,
Hal Smith, Mark Gruner, Monika Ramirez, Janet Waldo.

A story for social justice told as animated science fiction feature. Draggs, the 39-
foot-tall inhabitants of the planet Yagam, keep the tiny Oms as pets. The Oms
have evolved from humans who came to Yagam long ago. One Om, Terr, is
accidentally educated by the Draggs and returns to unite his people. The Oms
ultimately achieve equality with the Draggs. Simple story but terrific animation.
This film has a minor cult following.

p, Simon Damiani, Andre Valio-Cavaglione; d, Rene Laloux; w, Laloux, Roland
Topor (from the novel *Oms en Serie* by Stefan Wul); ph, Lubomir Rejthar, Boris
Baromykin; chief animators, Josef Kabrt, Josef Vana, Jindrick Barta, Zdena
Bartova, Bohumil Sedja, Zdenek Sob, Karel Strebl, Jiri Vokoum; m, Alain
Goroguer.

Science Fiction   **(PR:A   MPAA:NR)**

FANTASTIC THREE, THE*   (1967, Ital./Ger./Fr./Yugo.) 94m
Cinesecolo/Parnass Film/FFp/Avala Film
(I FANTASTICI TRE SUPERMAN)

Tony Kendal [Luciano Stella], Brad Harris, Nick Jordan, Joscen Brockmann,
Sabine Sun, Bettina Busch.

Good silly fun involving Stella and Jordan as a pair of robbers who team up with
FBI agent Harris to pursue ace bad guy Brockmann. Lots of acrobatics and
clowning (the two robbers wear Superman suits!). Don't miss "the Universal
Reproducer," Brockmann's secret weapon.

p, Italo Martinenghi, Aldo Addobbati; d, Frank Kramer [aka Gianfranco Parolini];
w, Kramer, Marcello Coscia; ph,Fransceso Izzarelli.

Comedy   **(PR:A   MPAA:NR)**

FANTASTIC VOYAGE*   (1966) 100m FOX c
(AKA: MICROSCOPIA; STRANGE JOURNEY)

Stephen Boyd (*Grant*), Raquel Welch (*Cora Peterson*), Edmond O'Brien (*Gen.
Carter*), Donald Pleasence (*Dr. Michaels*), Arthur O'Connell (*Col. Donald Reid*),
William Redfield (*Capt. Bill Owens*), Arthur Kennedy (*Dr. Duval*), Jean Del Val (*Jan
Benes*), Barry Coe (*Communications Aide*), Ken Scott (*Secret Serviceman*), Shelby
Grant (*Nurse*), James Brolin (*Technician*), Brendan Fitzgerald (*Wireless Operator*).

A medical crew (Boyd, Welch, Redfield, Kennedy, and Pleasence) and a submarine are miniaturized to remove a blood clot in the brain of a defecting scientist
from Czechoslovakia. The defector was shot, causing the clot, during his escape,
which was aided by agent Boyd. Once shrunk, and inside the body, the crew must
not only fight white corpuscles, but the heart and lungs make their traveling
rougher. Early on, it becomes apparent that one of the crew members is a double
agent and doesn't want to see the mission completed. After a red-herring and
slowing plot pace, the saboteur is killed by hungry corpuscles, the clot is broken
up, and the crew escapes through the patient's tear duct, seconds before they
regain their normal size. The special effects—traveling through the body's blood
stream and past the different organs, which become another world for the
characters and viewers—is the fantastic part of this film. Smokers note the black
spots on the patient's lungs. One of the more visual science fiction films.

p, Saul David; d, Richard Fleischer; w, Harry Kleiner, David Duncan (adapted
from the novel by Otto Klement and Jay Lewis Bixby); ph, Ernest Laszlo
(CinemaScope, DeLuxe Color); m, Leonard Rosenman; ed, William B. Murphy;
spec eff, L. B. Abbott, Art Cruikshank, Emil Kosa, Jr.

Science Fiction   **Cas.**   **(PR:A   MPAA:NR)**

FANTASTICA*½   (1980, Can./Fr.) 104m E.I. Productions/GAU c

Carole Laure (*Lorca*), Lewis Furey (*Paul*), Serge Reggiani (*Euclide*), Claudine
Auger (*Johanna*), John Vernon (*Jim*), Denise Filiatrault (*Emma*), Claude Blanchard
(*Hector*), Michel Labelle (*Louis*).

Actress Laure is in a traveling musical revue and having an affair with the show's
director, creator and lyricist, Furey. She falls in love with an older ecological
activist, Reggiani. When he becomes frightened by his own feelings, he takes off,
and the actress continues his ecological fight to keep a factory from being built on a
virgin forest and stream. This almost does in the revue and the industrialists win
out in the end. Very uneven film that can't make up its mind what it's about.

d&w, Gilles Carl; ph, Francois Protat; m/l, Lewis Furey; ed, Hughes Darmois; art
d, Jocelyn Joly; ch, Larry Gradus.

Drama   **(PR:C-O   MPAA:NR)**

FANTOMAS*   (1966, Fr./Ital.) 104m Lopert c (FANTOMAS CONTRO
SCOTLAND YARD; AKA: FANTOMAS)

Jean Marais (*Fantomas, Fandor*), Louis De Funes (*Commissioner Juve*), Mylene
Demongeot (*Helene*), Marie-Helene Arnaud (*Lady Beltham*), Jacques Dynam
(*Juve's Assistant*), Robert Dalban (*Newspaper Editor*), Christian Toma (*Chief
Inspector*), Hugues Wanner, Michel Duplaix, Andree Tainsy, Henri Attal, Pierre
Collet, Rudy Lenoir, Jean Minisini, Bernard Musson, Dominique Zardi, Francoise
Christophe, Jean Roger Caussimon, Andre Dumas, Henri Serre.

One of three FANTOMAS films made by the same team. Marais plays a dual role:
Fantomas, the super criminal, and Fandor, a newspaper reporter who says
Fantomas is a creation of the police to explain unsolved crimes. Naturally this
infuriates Fantomas. Having a metal face has forced him to become a master of
disguise so he even the score by disguising himself as Fandor and the police
commissioner (De Funes) for his next series of crimes.

p, Paul Cadeac, Alain Poire; d, Andre Hunebelle; w, Jean Halain, Pierre Foucaud
(based on the "Fantomas" novels by Marcel Allain, Pierre Souvestre); ph, Marcel
Grignon; m, Michel Magne; ed, Jean Feyte; art d, Paul-Louis Boutie.

Crime/Comedy   **(PR:AA   MPAA:NR)**

FANTOMAS STRIKES BACK**   (1965, Fr./Ital.) 94m SNEG-
PAC/Victory c (FANTOMAS SE DECHAINE)

Jean Marais (*Fantomas, Fandor*), Louis De Funes (*Commissioner Juve*), Mylene
Demongeot (*Helene*), Jacques Dynam (*Juve's Assistant*), Robert Dalban (*Newspaper Editor*), Albert Dagnat.

A lesser effort in the FANTOMAS series. Marais as the super criminal kidnaps a
group of scientists. His plan is to have them create a mind-controlling ray. De
Funes is the police commissioner who stops Marais from carrying out his evil plans
but not before the villain escapes in his aerial car. Stylish sets (Marais' hideout is an
elaborate affair inside a volcano), but basically a tedious film.

p, Alain Poire, Paul Cadeac; d, Andre Hunebelle; w, Jean Halain, Pierre Foucaud;
ph, Raymond Lemoigne (CinemaScope).

Comedy/Crime   **(PR:A   MPAA:NR)**

FAR COUNTRY, THE**   (1955) 96m UNIV c

James Stewart (*Jeff*), Ruth Roman (*Ronda*), Corinne Calvet (*Renee*), Walter Bren-
nan (*Ben*), John McIntire (*Mr. Gannon*), Jay C. Flippen (*Rube*), Henry [Harry]
Morgan (*Ketchum*), Steve Brodie (*Ives*), Royal Dano (*Luke*), Gregg Barton
(*Rounds*), Chubby Johnson (*Dusty*), Eddy C. Waller (*Yukon Sam*), Robert Foulk
(*Kingman*), Eugene Borden (*Doc Vallon*), Allan Ray (*Bosun*), Connie Gilchrist
(*Hominy*), Bob Wilke (*Madden*), Jack Elam (*Newberry*), Kathleen Freeman (*Grits*),
Guy Wilkerson (*Tanana Pete*), Paul Bryar (*Sheriff*), Edwin Parker (*Carson*), Ange-
line Engler (*Mrs. Kingman*), Andy Brennan (*Man*), Gregg Barton (*Rounds*), Connie
Van (*Molasses*), Stuart Randall (*Capt. Benson*), Jack Williams (*Shep*), William J.
Williams (*Gant*), Chuck Roberson (*Latigo*), Damian O'Flynn (*Second Mate*), Don C.
Harvey (*Tom Kane*), John Halloran (*Bartender*), Carl Harbaugh (*Sourdough*),
Charles Sweetlove (*Porcupine Smith*), John Doucette, Robert Bice, Paul Savage,
James W. Horan, Gerard Baril, Ted Kemp, John Mackin, Dick Taylor, Dick
Dickinson (*Miners*), Ted Mapes, Len McDonald, Jack Dixon (*Deputies*), Marjorie
Stapp, Gene Holland (*Girls*).

Stewart and Brennan are partners set to bring a herd of cattle up to Canada from
Wyoming and sell them for a fortune in the gold-boom towns. They arrive in the
town of Skagway, where the self-proclaimed law man, McIntire, takes the herd
from them. Stewart steals his cattle back, and goes to the town of Dawson. The
saloon keeper, Roman, befriends Stewart and helps him against McIntire and his
men, who are out to get the herd back. McIntire's men kill Brennan, and Roman is
killed while enroute to warn Stewart. Stewart, a man who ordinarily likes to keep
to his own affairs, is aroused enough to avenge his friend's death by killing
McIntire. This was the fifth collaboration between producer Rosenberg, director
Mann, and Stewart. THE FAR COUNTRY is one of the most entertaining and
original westerns to come out of the 1950s, and this is due to Stewart's flawless
performance, Mann's strong and thoughtful direction and the well written script by
Chase. The cinematography of the Canadian wilderness is beautiful. (McIntire's
role is based on the notorious con man "Soapy Smith").

p, Aaron Rosenberg; d, Anthony Mann; w, Borden Chase; ph, William Daniels
(Technicolor); m, Joseph Gershenson; ed, Russell Schoengarth; art d, Bernard
Harzbrun, Alexander Golitzen.

Western   **(PR:A   MPAA:NR)**

FAR FROM DALLAS**   (1972, Fr.) 95m Rainbow Production/J.P. Faure c

Daniel Gelin (*Jean*), Alexandra Stewart (*Wife*), Philippe Rouleau (*Regis*), Matt
Carney (*Turner*), Robert Vattier (*Inspector*).

A French thriller with the over-used conspiracy theory of President Kennedy's
assassination as an axis. A reporter comes home to learn that a friend might have
been killed by two gunmen in an American car. He begins to search for his friend,
and after being shot at and beaten up, gets closer to the truth. He finds that the
European Mafia and the French secret police may have been involved in some
manner. He meets an American, who tells the reporter he is wasting his time
because there are too many elements, and too many walls to break through to find
the truth. The reporter realizes that he could never penetrate the maze of collusion
and cover-ups and gives up his search. A small thriller with all the cliched elements
of political thrillers: corrupt politicians, government agencies covering things up,
and crime organizations that are in cahoots with the government.

d, Philippe Toledano; w, Toledano, Nicole Aufay; ph, Jean Bourdelon
(Eastmancolor); ed, Isabelle Rafferly.

Thriller   **(PR:C   MPAA:NR)**

FAR FROM THE MADDING CROWD*½   (1967, Brit.) 168m MGM c

Julie Christie (*Bathsheba Everdene*), Terence Stamp (*Sgt. Troy*), Peter Finch
(*William Boldwood*), Alan Bates (*Gabriel Oak*), Prunella Ransome (*Fanny Robin*),
Fiona Walker (*Liddy*), Paul Dawkins (*Henery Fray*), Andrew Robertson (*Andrew
Randle*), John Barrett (*Joseph Poorgrass*), Julian Somers (*Jan Coggan*), Pauline
Melville (*Mrs. Tall*), Vincent Harding (*Mark Clark*), Lawrence Carter (*Laban Tall*),
Margaret Lacey (*Maryann Money*), Harriet Harper (*Temperance*), Denise Coffey
(*Soberness*), Brian Rawlinson (*Matthew Moon*), Freddie Jones (*Cainy Ball*), John
Carrie (*Pennyways*), Marie Hopps (*Mrs. Coggan*), Owen Berry (*Old Smallbury*),
Michael Beint (*Laborer*), Alison Leggatt (*Mrs. Hurst*), Victor Stone (*Billy Smallbury*),

Peter Stone (Teddy Coggan), Walter Gale (Jacob Smallbury), Jonathan Newth (Gentleman at Cockfight), Derek Ware (Corporal), John Donegal (Sailor), Peggy Ann Clifford (Fat Lady at Circus), Noel Henkel (Circus Manager), Bryan Mosley (Barker), David Swarbrick (Fiddler at Barn Dance), Julius Alba (Gentleman at Party), Leslie Anderson, Keith Hooper (Boldwood's Laborers), Frank Duncan, Hugh Walker (Farmers at Corn Exchange).

Director Schlesinger makes the best of a script that adheres to Thomas Hardy's novel almost page for page. Christie is in love with (and feels superior to) three men, Stamp, Finch and Bates. Christie inherits a farm and Bates, a soldier, finally wins her love. A very predictable story—set in 1874—that Schlesinger struggles to keep fresh and moving. The actors themselves have a difficult time with the one-dimensional characters, but at times are able to breath life into them. Nicolas Roeg's cinematography is stunning.

p, Joseph Janni; d, John Schlesinger; w, Frederic Raphael (adapted from the novel by Thomas Hardy); ph, Nicolas Roeg (Metrocolor); m, Richard Rodney Bennett; ed, Malcolm Cooke; md, Marcus Dods; art d, Roy Smith; set d, Peter James; cos, Alan Barrett.

Drama   **(PA:A   MPAA:NR)**

FAR FRONTIER, THE**   (1949) 67m REP c

Roy Rogers (Roy Rogers), Gail Davis (Susan Hathaway), Andy Devine (Judge Cookie Bullflacher), Francis Ford (Alf Sharper), Roy Barcroft (Bart Carroll), Clayton Moore (Tom Sharper), Robert Strange (Willis Newcomb), Holly Bane (Rocco), Lane Bradford (Butch), John Bagni (Rollins), Clarence Straight (Defendant), Edmund Cobb (Sheriff), Foy Willing and the Riders of the Purple Sage, Trigger the Horse, Tom London.

Rogers helps the border patrol round up wanted criminals who are being smuggled across from Mexico. A friend of Rogers on the patrol is kidnaped by the smugglers and is forced to aid in a bank robbery. This is when Roy and Trigger step in. A passel of cowboy songs by Rogers and the Riders of the Purple Sage, equine tricks by Trigger.

p, Edward J. White; d, William Witney; w, Sloan Nibley; ph, Jack Marta (Trucolor); m, Dale Butts; ed, Tony Martinelli; art d, Frank Hotaling.

Western   **Cas.**   **(PR:A   MPAA:NR)**

FAR HORIZONS, THE***½   (1955) 108m PAR c

(AKA: THE UNTAMED WEST)

Fred MacMurray (Meriwether Lewis), Charlton Heston (Bill Clark), Donna Reed (Sacajawea), Barbara Hale (Julia Hancock), William Demarest (Sergeant Gass), Alan Reed (Charboneau), Eduardo Noriega (Cameahwait), Larry Pennell (Wild Eagle), Argentina Brunetti (Old Crone), Julia Montoya (Crow Woman), Ralph Moody (Le Borgne), Herbert Heyes (President Jefferson), Lester Matthews (Mr. Hancock), Helen Wallace (Mrs. Hancock), Walter Reed (Cruzatte), Bill Phipps, Tom Monroe, LeRoy Johnson, Joe Canutt, Bob Herron, Herman Scharff, Al Wyatt, Voltaire Perkins, Vernon Rich, Bill Walker, Margarita Martin, Frank Fowler, Fran Bennett.

Solid historical adventure film that excitingly, if not accurately, depicts the explorations of Lewis and Clark (1803-06) as well as deeply profiling the widely divergent partners who trekked from St. Louis to the great northwest to reach the Pacific Ocean. Heston is the tough military officer Clark who will not compromise with the elements or the Indians, while MacMurray portrays the taciturn, scientific Lewis, the great cartographer who placed loyalty to mission above human consideration. Reed, in her traditional role of Indian maiden, is the legendary Sacajawea who led the intrepid explorers to their far destination. To give internal conflict to this filmic expedition the writers have Heston and MacMurray at odds almost from the beginning. They both compete for Hale's affections, with Heston winning before they journey into the unknown, leaving MacMurray resentful. MacMurray becomes further vexed when his truculent partner receives the love of Reed. Interspersed between the bickering rivalry are Indian attacks, river hazards, brutal weather, seemingly insurmountable mountains, and impregnable wilderness. After completing their heroic tasks, assigned by Heyes (as President Jefferson), the explorers return to Washington, D.C., with Reed at their sides. Though she loves Heston, Reed leaves him, realizing that she could never adapt to civilization, returning to her wilds in the Far West. Great liberties were taken with the true characters here but the film is based upon a novel and even so provides a great deal of entertainment and visual reward as director Mate, a former cinematographer, records a stunning panorama of the American West. Overlong, a bit too wordy, with a Salter score that sometimes deafens, THE FAR HORIZONS nevertheless is worth the trip.

p, William H. Pine, William C. Thomas; d, Rudolph Mate; w, Winston Miller, Edmund H. North (based on the novel Sacajawea of the Shoshones by Della Gould Emmons); ph, Daniel L. Fapp (VistaVision, Technicolor); m, Hans Salter; ed, Frank Bracht; art d, Hal Pereira, Earl Hedrick; cos, Edith Head.

Adventure/Historical Epic   **(PR:A   MPAA:NR)**

FAR SHORE, THE*** (1976, Can.) 104m Far Shore/Bauer International c

Celine Lomez (Eulalia Turner), Frank Moore (Tom McLeod), Lawrence Benedict (Ross Turner), Sean McCann (Cluny), Charlotte Blunt (Mary McEwan), Susan Petrie (Kate), Jean Carignan (Fiddler).

A fictionalized account of Canadian painter, Tom Thomson, a member of Canada's famed Group of Seven. A love affair develops between the painter, Moore, and a married woman, Lomez. The husband, Benedict, discovers his wife's affair and confides in his friend, McCann, about the situation. McCann, out of loyalty, kills the lovers before the husband can stop him. A well executed low-budget Canadian production, and the first feature by avant-garde filmmaker Joyce Wieland.

p, Joyce Wieland, Judy Steed; d, Wieland; w, Brian Barney (adapted from a story by Wieland); ph, Richard Leiterman (Kodacolor); m, Douglas Pringle; ed, George Appelby, Brian French; prod d, Anne Pritchard.

Drama   **(PA:O   MPAA:NR)**

FARARUV KONEC   (SEE: END OF A PRIEST, 1970, Czech.)

FAREWELL AGAIN   (SEE: TROOPSHIP, 1937, Brit.)

FAREWELL, DOVES*½   (1962, USSR) 82m
Yalta Film Studio/Artkino Pictures bw (PROSHCHAYTE)

Aleksey Loktev (Gena), Svetlana Savyolova (Tanya), Valentina Telegina (Mariya Yefimovna), Sergey Plotnikov (Maksim Petrovich), A. Nikolayeva, P. Postnikova, A. Maksimova, A. Sumarokov, V. Pridayevich, Leonid Gallis, G. Ignatyeva, S. Kramarov, P. Vesklyarov, V. Teslya, Valentin Bryleyev, Olya Narovchatova, Ye. Anufriyev, V. Savinykh, Ye. Kovalenko, V. Tvoruzhek, V. Dibrov, I. Markevich.

Soviet political dogma aimed at the country's young adults. Loktev is an apprentice gas worker and raises pigeons. He gets a girl friend who is surprised he's not part of the Komsomol youth group. His boss takes tips from customers. Through his hard work Loktev is able to discourage his boss' actions. He tells his girl friend that he'll go to the meeting of the youth group and on the way he puts out a fire. He joins the Komsomol and frees his pigeons because they are old enough to fend for themselves. (This is a symbolic act? Nyet?)

d&w, Yakov Segel; ph, V. Ilyenko; m, M. Fradkin; ed, L. Rodionova; art d, L. Georgiyev, V. Levental.

Drama   **(PR:A   MPAA:NR)**

FAREWELL, FRIEND***   (1968, Fr./Ital.) 115m Greenwich Film
Productions/Medusa Distribuzione c (ADIEU L'AMI)

Alain Delon (Dino Barran), Charles Bronson (Franz Propp), Olga Georges-Picot (Isabelle Manue), Brigitte Fossey (Dominique "Waterloo" Austerlitz), Bernard Fresson (Inspector Antoine Meloutis), Michel Barcet (Inspector Muratti), Marianna Falk (Catherine), Andre Dumas (Personnel Director), Ellen Bahl (Martha), Lisette Lebon (Gilberte), Catherine Sola (Nurse), Steve Eckardt (Big Man), Guy Delorme (Man from Neuilly).

A good chemistry between Delon and Bronson in this one. After being discharged from the French Army, American mercenary Bronson and French doctor Delon form a criminal partnership. Georges-Picot and Fossey are two attractive con artists looking for someone to frame for their own robbery. They fool the two men into thinking they'll be taking home 200 million francs. Instead Bronson and Delon find themselves trapped in an underground vault for three days. The two women are killed in a shoot-out and Delon is cleared of all charges. Bronson is not as fortunate, however. Arrested for an earlier crime, he honors a pact made with Delon: neither will admit knowing the other. Some problems with the plot but otherwise intriguing. A poorly dubbed English version was shelved and not released in America until Bronson was a popular star in the States.

p, Serge Silberman; d, Jean Herman; w, Sebastian Japrisot; ph, Jean-Jacques Tarbes (Eastmancolor); m, Francoise de Roubaix; ed, Helene Plemiannikov; art d, Jacques Dugied; set d, Tanine Autre.

Crime   **(PR:O   MPAA:NR)**

FAREWELL, MY BELOVED**   (1969, Jap.) 93m Shochiku Co. c
(WAKARE)

Kazuo Funaki (Makito), Mayumi Ozora (Yuko), Ken Ogata (Tadayuki), Nana Ozaki (Yumiko).

A Japanese melodrama that takes place during WW II. A young student falls in love with the widow of naval officer, but she is strongly attached to his memory. The student joins the naval academy and learns that the woman is going to marry her dead husband's best friend. This man is assigned to a Kamikaze unit and after the war the young man tells the woman that her second husband was assigned as a Kamikaze because he married her. This news leads the woman to commit suicide.

d, Hideo Oba; w, Genyo Takahashi; ph, Hiroyuki Nagaoka (GrandScope, Eastmancolor); m, Chuji Kinoshita; art d, Tadataka Yoshino.

Drama   **(PR:O   MPAA:NR)**

FAREWELL, MY LOVELY, 1944 (SEE: MURDER, MY SWEET, 1944)

FAREWELL, MY LOVELY***   (1975) 97m EK-ITC/AE c

Robert Mitchum (Phillip Marlowe), Charlotte Rampling (Mrs. Velma Grayle), John Ireland (Lt. Nulty), Sylvia Miles (Mrs. Jessie Florian), Jack O'Halloran (Moose Malloy), Anthony Zerbe (Laird Burnette), Harry Dean Stanton (Billy Rolfe), Jim Thompson (Judge Grayle), John O'Leary (Lindsay Marriott), Kate Murtagh (Frances Amthor), Walter McGinn (Tommy Ray), Jimmy Archer (Georgie), Joe Spinell (Nick), Sylvester Stallone (Kelly/Jonnie), Burton Gilliam (Cowboy), Ted Gehring (Roy), Logan Ramsey (Commissioner), Margie Hall (Woman), Jack Bernardi (Louis Levine), Ben Ohta (Patron in Pool Hall), Jerry Fujikawa (Fence), Richard Kennedy, John O'Neill, Mark Allen (Detectives), Andrew Harris (Mulatto Child), Napoleon Whiting (Hotel Clerk), John Eames (Butler), Rainbeaux Smith (Doris), Stu Gilliam (1st Man), Roosevelt Pratt (2nd Man), Dino Washington (Bouncer), Harry Caesar (Bartender), Bill Gentry (Hood), Cory B. Shiozaki (Waiter), Noelle Worth (Girl), Wally Berns (Father), Lola Mason (Mother), Joan Shawlee (Woman in Ballroom), Edra Gale (Singer), Karen Gaston (Prostitute).

This affectionate period film set in the early 1940s beautifully depicts the seamy side of Los Angeles and the backways followed by Mitchum as the intrepid private eye Marlowe who, in the summer of 1941, is hired by giant thug O'Halloran, recently released from prison. He wants Mitchum to find his old girl friend; in search of this elusive femme fatale, Mitchum runs up against a series of murders. The first occurs when he accompanies O'Leary to a rendezvous where he plans to buy back a jade necklace stolen from Rampling, later Mitchum's client. Mitchum is blackjacked and O'Leary murdered, the cash he was carrying for the purchase taken. Plunging into an investigation that has now produced his anger at being victimized, Mitchum visits the widow, Miles, of a nightclub owner where O'Halloran's girl once worked, but her drunken remarks lead to a seeming dead end. Rampling and her wealthy husband then hire the detective to find O'Leary's killer. Mitchum's inquiries bring thugs to his seedy office; he is kidnaped and taken to the notorious brothel run by obese, vicious Murtagh whom he slugs. Murtagh's goons, including Stallone, overpower Mitchum and drug him. He manages to snap out of momentary hallucinations and escape while madam Murtagh is murdered in a brawl. Drunken widow Miles is later found murdered but Mitchum by then has enough information to piece the puzzle together. He is about to be arrested for the Miles murder by one-time friend cop Ireland but the cop gives him a break, allowing him to follow his leads to a gambling ship, agreeing to take a launch full of cops on his trail after he gets aboard. Once on board the ship Mitchum confronts gambler Zerbe and his mistress Rampling who turns out to be the long-lost girl O'Halloran is seeking. Mitchum learns that Rampling had been a one-time call girl for Murtagh and when his investigation closed in on the bestial madam, she and Zerbe had Murtagh killed, along with Miles and others who might disclose Rampling's true identity. O'Halloran, who has accompanied Mitchum, then learns that Rampling had no intention of freeing him from prison where he was doing time for a robbery she had committed. He makes a move toward her and Rampling shoots him. Mitchum then shoots Rampling as Ireland and his police scramble aboard. Messy, but mostly explained, Mitchum had wrapped up another case, leaving a bevy of bodies in the famous Marlowe wake. FAREWELL, MY LOVELY is a good period film, with excellent mood scenes and striking sets, costumes, and props, its color diffused to make way for those all-important *film noir* shadows, the same kind of atmospherics photographer Alonzo had created for the memorable CHINATOWN. Yet Mitchum is a bit too weary even for the dog-tired detective, often appearing to sleepwalk through his tough-guy scenes. Rampling oozes sex and sensuality but somehow manages to be unconvincing as the scheming menace author Chandler so accurately profiled in his novel. This film was made twice before, once in 1942 as a vehicle for George Sanders in RKO's THE FALCON TAKES OVER, a poor programmer and the third entry of the grade-B detective series, and the superb MURDER, MY SWEET (1945), which is the best of the lot with Dick Powell giving a bravura, unequaled performance as *the definitive* Philip Marlowe, even beyond Humphrey Bogart's wonderful interpretation in THE BIG SLEEP (1946). Mitchum's bones are too full of winter, his hooded eyes not alert enough for danger; he is mostly phlegmatic, almost lethargic, exuding the kind of sardonic attitude that actually burlesques his character, one lamely profiled as he recites in narration fatigue, not intrigue. Mitchum's appeal here has nothing to do with Marlowe or Chandler, but with Mitchum's own cult image and mythic persona. Beyond the untidy story, there is Mitchum to observe and ponder, and these days that's almost enough. Other performances, including Rampling's, are merely perfunctory, as if the actors realized they were essaying characters too firmly entrenched by stars of another decade. Miles received an Oscar nomination for her role as the alcoholic widow. Murtagh, as the beefy lesbian madam, is a repulsive caricature never envisioned by Chandler. The muscle-brained Moose Malloy enacted by O'Halloran has only size in his role, nothing sinister, nothing pitiful. The always off-beat Ireland is obviously along for the ride. Songs include "Sunday" (Jule Styne, Ned Miller, Chester Cohn, Bennie Krueger); "I've Heard That Song Before (Styne, Sammy Cahn).

p, George Pappas, Jerry Bruckheimer; d, Dick Richards; w, David Zelag Goodman (based on the novel by Raymond Chandler); ph, John A. Alonzo (Panavision, Fujicolor); m, David Shire; ed, Walter Thompson, Joel Cox; prod d, Dean Tavoularis; art d, Angelo Graham; set d, Bob Nelson; cos, Tony Scarano; spec eff, Chuck Gaspar; makeup, Frank Westmore.

Mystery/Thriller   **Cas.**   **(PR:C-O MPAA:R)**

FAREWELL PERFORMANCE*   (1963, Brit.) 73m Sevenay/RFD bw

David Kernan (*Ray Baron*), Delphi Lawrence (*Janice Marlon*), Frederick Jaeger (*Paul Warner*), Derek Francis (*Supt. Raven*), Alfred Burke (*Marlon*), John Kelland (*Mitch*), Toni Gilpin (*Carol*), James Copeland (*Andrews*), Ron Parry (*Dennis*), The Tornadoes, Heinz, Tommy Devel and Partner, Chad Carson

Lawrence is the wife of animal trainer Burke, trying to figure out who poisoned her pop star lover. Cheap British exploitation item best forgotten.

p, J.P. O'Connolly; d, Robert Tronson; w, Aileen Burke, Leone Stuart, O'Connolly.

Crime/Musical   **(PR:A-C MPAA:NR)**

FAREWELL TO ARMS, A**   (1932) 90m PAR bw

Helen Hayes (*Catherine Barkley*), Gary Cooper (*Lt. Frederic Henry*), Adolph Menjou (*Maj. Rinaldi*), Mary Philips (*Helen Ferguson*), Jack LaRue (*The Priest*), Blanche Frederici (*Head Nurse*), Henry Armetta (*Bonello*), George Humbert (*Piani*), Fred Malatesta (*Manera*), Mary Forbes (*Miss Van Campen*), Tom Ricketts (*Count Greffi*), Robert Cauterio (*Gordoni*), Gilbert Emery (*British Major*), Peggy Cunningham (*Molly*), Agostino Borgato (*Giulio*), Paul Porcasi (*Inn Keeper*), Alice Adair (*Cafe Girl*).

A mannered and restrained love story and the first Hemingway tale to reach the screen, A FAREWELL TO ARMS has Cooper as the adventuresome American serving in the Italian ambulance corps (as did Hemingway). Cooper returns from the front lines to be greeted by Menjou, his superior and close friend. The womanizing Menjou delightfully tells Cooper about the arrival of some nurses at the local hospital, extolling the beauty of one English volunteer, Hayes. That night Cooper gets tipsy at a local saloon, and, when staggering outside, following a bombardment of the town by Austrian guns, spies a woman standing in the shadows. He makes some crude overtures to her, believing she is a streetwalker. When she steps into the light following the bombardment, Cooper sees she is a nurse and mumbles his apologies. The next day Menjou introduces them formally and they laugh lightheartedly. A courtship develops and quickly deepens, which

distrubs the jealous Menjou. When Cooper returns to the front, Menjou transfers Hayes to Milan to keep her from seeing his young protege. Cooper is wounded during a night attack at the front while aiding wounded troops and is carried back to the field hospital where Menjou performs an operation on his leg. Ashamed of his jealousy, Menjou orders the youth to the Milan hospital where he knows Hayes will be with him. In Milan, the bedridden Cooper is attended day and night by Hayes but the couple's lovemaking ends when Cooper mends and is once more ordered to the front. Pregnant, Hayes leaves Italy and goes to Switzerland to await the birth of their child. Cooper's letters to her never get through and Hayes' missives to him are waylaid by the avuncular Menjou, who thinks it best he stop the affair. Cooper, desperate, joins the massive Italian retreat south from the mountains where the Austrians have broken through. He is almost shot as a deserter when military police begin pulling from the streaming horde all officers and executing them out of hand for allowing the retreat. Cooper dives into a river and swims to safety, then makes his way to Milan to find Hayes. He learns she is in Switzerland and goes to her, crossing a storm-tossed lake. He finds his child born dead and Hayes apparently dying. At the news of the war's ends, with bells tolling in the town, Hayes seems to rally, embracing her lover from her hospital bed and the viewer is left to wonder about her survival. Hemingway, who wrote the novel in 1930, was upset at the film's ambiguous ending, one implying that Hayes might survive and that there would be happiness ahead when he clearly indicated in his narrative that the nurse died. (He was not alone in criticizing the film; the Italian ambassador to the U.S. protested the showing of the executions in the film.) But American audiences thronged to see this tender love story, paying $1.65 at the box office for first-run viewings, a hefty amount in 1932. Borzage's direction is masterful, placing emphasis on the love story and downplaying the war, but the epic scenes he does permit are sweeping, loaded with armies of extras moving through enormous period sets smacking of war-torn reality. The famous retreat from Caporetto is captured in Lang's UFA-like montage, showing the disintegration of an army and the destruction of a generation, achieved in overlapping stark black and white scenes. These scenes were unfortunately reduced to blurry black frames by the 1950s when reissue prints, taken from poorly made 16mm prints, were run through art houses, and barely survive today. Some prints, reissued in 1938, retain the complete running time and are in mint condition, but after Selznick Studios bought the rights to the film, from 10 to 20 minutes were chopped from the film, notably the love scenes, to place emphasis on the war action, and this harmed Borzage's delicate continuity. He was a unique director who had the ability to control sentiment without having his scenes become mawkish, as witnessed in such great love stories as SEVENTH HEAVEN, THREE COMRADES, FLIRTATION WALK, I'VE ALWAYS LOVED YOU, and many others. Ruth Chatterton was originally slated to play the star-crossed nurse but Hayes was signed at the last minute. The first lady of American theater was never more appealing in a role tailor-made for her sensitive abilities. Menjou is at his manipulative best, a rascal with a heart. Cooper's performance electrified the public and critics alike, for here he displayed a depth of feeling never before shown. Unlike Hayes, who split her efforts between movies and Broadway plays (and never became the boxoffice star her talents would normally command), Cooper went on to become one of America's most beloved actors, placing among the high ratings of the *Motion Picture Herald* poll of exhibitors for 18 years (1936 to 1958), a record surpassed only by Bing Crosby and John Wayne. All the supporting players for this version of A FAREWELL TO ARMS performed well. LaRue, noted for his gangster roles of the early 1930s, was exceptional as the sympathetic priest. Hemingway's basic story and dialog is kept much intact in this production, despite the so-called happy ending that produced the author's "disgust." The story itself was wholly drawn from his own experiences in Italy as an ambulance driver and his love affair with a British nurse who rejected his offers of marriage. He returned to the U.S. as "the most wounded man" of WW I. A bomb had gone off in the Italian/Austrian front lines while he was handing out chocolate bars to Italian troops and thousands of tiny shrapnel fragments were embedded in his body, as well as blowing off part of a knee. It was while he was recuperating that he met Agnes von Kurowsky, the nurse and great love of his life. Throughout the remainder of Hemingway's life he discovered small bits of steel from the blast working their ways to the surface, through his fingers, and around his neck and jaw (which later caused him to grow his famous beard). A FAREWELL TO ARMS saw two more versions, a revamped production in 1950 with William Holden, Nancy Olsen, and Frank Lovejoy entitled FORCE OF ARMS, and the disastrous 1957 remake with Rock Hudson and Jennifer Jones.

d, Frank Borzage; w, Benjamin Glazer, Oliver H. P. Garrett (based on the novel by Ernest Hemingway); ph, Charles Lang; m, Ralph Rainger, John Leipold, Bernhard Kaun, Paul Marquardt, Herman Hand, W. Franke Harling; ed, Otho Lovering; art d, Hans Dreier, Roland Anderson; cos, Travis Banton; tech adv, Charles Griffin, Dr. Jardini.

Romance/War Drama   **Cas.**   **(PR:A MPAA:NR)**

FAREWELL TO ARMS, A½**   (1957) 152m Selznick/FOX c

Rock Hudson (*Lt. Frederick Henry*), Jennifer Jones (*Nurse Catherine Barkley*), Vittorio De Sica (*Maj. Alessandro Rinaldi*), Alberto Sordi (*Father Galli*), Mercedes McCambridge (*Miss Van Campen*), Oscar Homolka (*Dr. Emerich*), Elaine Stritch (*Helen Ferguson*), Leopoldo Trieste (*Passini*), Franco Interlenghi (*Aymo*), Georges Brehat (*Capt. Bassi*), Memmo Carotenuto (*Nino*), Victor Francen (*Col. Valentini*), Joan Shawlee (*Nurse*), Guido Martufi (*Boy Scout*), Umberto Spadaro (*Barber*), Umberto Sacripanti (*Ambulance Driver*), Albert D'Amario (*Arrested Officer*), Giacomo Rossi Stuart, Carlo Pedersoli (*Carabinieres*), Alex Revides (*Carabiniere Officer*), Franco Mancinelli (*Captain at Outpost*), Patrick Crean (*Medical Lieutenant*), Guidarino Guidi (*Civilian Doctor*), Diana King (*Hospital Receptionist*), Clelia Matania (*Hair Dresser*), Eduard Linkers (*Lt. Zimmerman*), Johanna Hofer (*Mrs. Zimmerman*), Luigi Barzini (*Court-Martial Colonel*), Carlo Licari (*Racetrack Announcer*), Angiolo Galassi (*Firing Squad Commander*), Carlo Hintermann, Tiberio Mitri (*Diners*), Peter Illing (*Milan Hotel Clerk*), Sam Levine (*Swiss Sergeant*),

Eva Kotthaus *(Delivery Room Nurse),* Gisella Mathews *(Nurse in Catherine's Room),* Vittorio Jannitti.

An overblown Hollywood extravaganza that was universally condemned when first released and one that hasn't improved with age, this third and final version of the Hemingway classic romance story has Jennifer Jones, wife of producer Selznick, as the doomed nurse, Catherine Barkley, and the ponderous Hudson as her lover. This epic was the bow-out production for the dynamic David O. Selznick who openly stated that this heavily funded film was a special vehicle for his wife, Jones, and his sheer Hollywood ego insisted she play the role of a young nurse when it was apparent to audiences and critics alike that the 38-year-old actress was long past her prime as a youthful beauty. In the familiar Hemingway story she meets and falls in love with ambulance driver Hudson, gets pregnant, and delivers a dead child, dying herself a few hours later while Hudson coments: "Poor kid! Maybe this is the price you pay for sleeping together." The price Selznick paid was in excess of $5 million for this box office bomb. He himself contributed to the film's horrible demise by constantly interfering with the production, deluging director John Huston (later replaced by Charles Vidor) with contradicting memos on how to shoot the film almost frame by frame. Huston later stated that the film was "a debacle . . . an unhappy experience for everyone connected with it." The only virtue of this hollow epic is the stupendous color photography taken in the Italian Alps by Portalupi and Morris, breathtaking, panoramic shots, along with a well-managed segment dealing with the Caporetto retreat. De Sica, as the wily Maj. Rinaldi, gives an inspired performance but it's not enough to offset the flagrant overacting by Jones and the wooden portrayal by Hudson. This nepotistic catastrophe was really well-written by veteran scriptwriter Hecht (who knew Hemingway when they were young reporters in Chicago just after WW I), but his lines are so badly mangled by the leads that little of the terse Hemingway-Hecht dialog manages to impact. Jones would later go on to ruin another literary classic, TENDER IS THE NIGHT (1962), by Scott Fitzgerald, attempting to play a young neurotic playgirl at age 43. Here it was a case of the boss' wife flitting about in an unrestrained performance while everyone looked away in embarrassment and the boss dropped millions to indulge himself and his wife, then foisted this mess upon a public that expected much more from the man who gave the world GONE WITH THE WIND (1939). Selznick did not like the 1932 version of A FAREWELL TO ARMS; he called it "a critic's pet," and intended to not only reshape the film to his own perspective but have Hecht rewrite its meaning, which angered Hecht. Moreover, he quibbled constantly with Huston, pointing out to this director (as quoted from *Memo From David O. Selznick)* that "you are getting a fabulous amount of money—$250,000—to direct a single motion picture. You are not entitled, therefore, to the privileges of an artist with an investment." Huston told Selznick that his manipulating of him and the story and letting Jones go full blast into her unbelievable histrionics, made him feel like a "prostitute." Countered Selznick: "Maybe my way of making pictures is not your way, but it's the only way I know . . . my family . . . is even more important than A FAREWELL TO ARMS." Selznick must have realized he had brutalized a fine story and wrote Hemingway a long, windy letter, begging recognition for the film, then almost asking Hemingway to like him, apologizing to Hemingway for not standing up years earlier when Hemingway's wife Mary walked into a Cuban cafe where Selznick was concentrating on learning a Mexican version of canasta!

p, David O. Selznick; d, Charles Vidor; w, Ben Hecht (based on the novel by Ernest Hemingway); ph, Piero Portalupi, Oswald Morris (CinemaScope, DeLuxe Color); m, Mario Nascimbene; ed, Gerard J. Wilson, John M. Foley; md, Franco Ferrara; art d, Mario Garbuglia.

Romance/War Drama (PR:C MPAA:NR)

FAREWELL TO CINDERELLA⋆⋆ (1937, Brit.) 64m RKO bw

Anne Pichon *(Margaret),* John Robinson *(Stephen Morley),* Arthur Rees *(Uncle William),* Glennis Lorimer *(Betty Temperley),* Sebastian Smith *(Andy Weir),* Ivor Barnard *(Mr. Temperley),* Margaret Damer *(Mrs. Temperley),* Ena Grossmith *(Emily)*

An Australian uncle (Rees) plays fairy godmother and helps his niece overcome drudgery and her large family to win the affections of an artist. Not much magic.

p, A. George Smith; d, Maclean Rogers; w, Rogers, Kathleen Butler, H.F. Maltby (based on a story by Arthur Richardson); ph, Geoffrey Faithfull.

Romance (PR:A MPAA:NR)

FAREWELL TO LOVE⋆⋆½ (1931, Brit.) 96m STER bw
(GB: CITY OF SONG)

Jan Kiepura *(Giovanni Cavallone),* Betty Stockfield *(Claire Winter),* Hugh Wakefield *(Hon. Roddy Fielding),* Heather Angel *(Carmela),* Francesco Maldacea *(Chi),* Philip Easton *(John Barlow),* Miles Malleson *(Doorman).*

Financed by Germans, starring a Pole and with a supporting cast of British and Italians, directed by a Neapolitan, with photography and art direction by Germans, FAREWELL TO LOVE is a prime example of The Brotherhood Of Movie Makers —except it just doesn't quite make it. Betty Stockfield is a wide-eyed British lass traveling in Naples where she meets and falls in love with her guide, Kiepura. She learns that he has a terrific tenor voice, so she takes him back to Jolly Olde to get him some serious vocal training. Being the handsome devil that he is, Kiepura breaks many hearts and one of his ladies is understandably miffed when he wends his way to England. He is an immediate sensation at a private party and booked to play the opera house the following evening. Meanwhile, Kiepura is very jealous of the way Stockfield flirts with other men. Then he learns that his opera debut is being financed and that he is not actually earning money from people who are flocking to the theater to see him. This infuriates his frail ego and he attacks Stockfield's friends, most of whom were backing the concert. They decide to cancel it and Kiepura goes back to Naples to sing to his sweetie. Scarcely enough plot to sustain 96 minutes, it does have some good moments, though, and Kiepura's voice is pleasant enough. Miles Malleson, a legendary British playwright

and actor, wrote the dismal dialog for this. Malleson is one of those people you always recognize but whose names are hard to place. Think of the reverend Chasuble in THE IMPORTANCE OF BEING EARNEST or the executioner in KIND HEARTS AND CORONETS and you might recall him.

p, Isadore Schlesinger; d, Carmine Gallone; w, Miles Malleson, Hans Szekley (based on a story by C.H. Dand).

Drama (PR:A MPAA:NR)

FARGO⋆⋆ (1952) 69m Silvermine/MON bw

Bill Elliott, Phyllis Coates, Myron Healey, Fuzzy Knight, Jack Ingram, Arthur Space, Robert Wilke, Terry Frost, Robert Bray, Denver Pyle, Tim Ryan, Florence Lake, Stanley Andrews, Richard Reeves, Eugene Roth, Stanford Jolley, Stanley Price, House Peters, Jr.

Elliott, still wearing his guns reversed in their holsters (the first movie cowboy to do so) stars in this hard-hitting oater as the brother of a murdered rancher who died at the hands of angry cattle drivers. To keep the cattle drivers honest, Elliott puts up a barbed wire fence around his Fargo ranch and brings law to the territory. Tough, well made oater.

p, Vincent M. Fennelly; d, Lewis D. Collins; w, Joseph Poland, Jack DeWitt; ph, Ernest Miller (Sepiatone); m, Raoul Kraushaar; ed, Sam Fields; art d, David Milton.

Western (PR:A MPAA:NR)

FARGO, 1964 (SEE: WILD SEED, 1964)

FARGO EXPRESS⋆½ (1933) 61m KBS Productions bw

Ken Maynard, Helen Mack, Roy Stewart, William Desmond, Paul Fix, Jack Rockwell, Claude Payton, Joe Rickson, Bud "Tarzan" McClure, Hank Bell.

Mack's kid brother Fix is arrested for robbing the stage after being identified by his distinctive horse. Maynard's mad for Mack and will do anything he can to win her affections, including capturing a similar looking wild horse and repeating the robbery to clear Fix's name. Lot's of action but pretty silly stuff.

p, Burt Kelly, Sam Bischoff, William Saal; d, Alan James; w, James, Earle Snell; ph, Ted McCord.

Western Cas. (PR:A MPAA:NR)

FARGO KID, THE⋆⋆ (1941) 63m RKO bw

Tim Holt *(Fargo Kid),* Ray Whitley *(Johnny),* Emmett Lynn *(Whopper),* Jane Drummond *(Jennie),* Cyrus W. Kendall *(Kane),* Ernie Adams *(Bush),* Paul Fix *(Mallory),* Paul Scardon *(Winters),* Glenn Strange *(Sheriff),* Mary McLaren *(Sarah),* Dick Hogan, Carl Stockdale, Harry Harvey, Lee Phelps.

This movie is a remake of MAN IN THE ROUGH (1928) and THE CHEYENNE KID (1933), with Holt in the title role. He meets a well known professional gun in the desert and nabs the shooter's horse. Holt goes into a nearby town, and is mistaken for the gunman. When hs sees the crooked doings of two mining bosses, he plays the shooter to clean up the town. An average B western, and the second in the Tim Holt series. Songs: "Crazy Ole Trails," "Twilight on the Prairie" (Ray Whitley, Fred Rose).

p, Bert Gilroy; d, Edward Killy; w, Morton Grant, Arthur V. Jones (story by W.C. Tuttle); ph, Harry Wild; m, Paul Sawtell; ed, Frederick Knudtson.

Western (PR:A MPAA:NR)

FARM GIRL (SEE: FARMER'S OTHER DAUGHTER, THE, 1965)

FARMER, THE zero (1977) 97m FIA-Cinema-Milway/COL c

Gary Conway *(Kyle Martin),* Angel Tompkins *(Betty),* Michael Dante *(Johnny O),* George Memmoli *(Passini),* Timothy Scott *(Weasel),* Jack Waltzer *(Doc Valentine),* Ken Renard *(Gumshoe),* John Popwell *(Conners),* Stratton Leopold *(Laundry Sam),* Sonny Shroyer *(Corrigan),* Eric Weston *(Lopie),* Don Payne *(Mr. Moore),* Bill Moses *(Bank Representative),* Ray Tatum *(Soldier),* Laura Whyte *(Waitress),* Wayne Stewart *(Sergeant),* Ray McIver *(Train Bartender),* Lewell Akins *(Conductor),* Louis C. Pessolano *(Bartender),* Dave Craig *(2nd Soldier),* Judge Parker, Saturday Session *(Banjo Players).*

A violent revenge film about a WW II veteran, Conway, who tries to start a farm. When he's unable to make the mortgage payments, he goes to a local mobster, Dante, for help. Conway is contracted to kill a few thugs and that he does with plenty of gore and bullets. A totally negative film of violence that barely avoided an X rating.

p, Gary Conway; d, David Berlatsky; w, Janice Colson-Dodge, John Carmody, Patrick Regan, George Fargo, (based on a story by Fargo); ph, Irv Goodnoff (Panavision, CFI Color); m, Hugo Montenegro; ed, Richard Weber; art d, Charlie Hughes; cos, Vickie Sanchez; m/l, "The American Dreamer," "Outside the Law," Gene Clark (sung by Clark), "There's Only Me and You," Jack Segal (sung by Irv Goodnoff).

Action (PR:O MPAA:R)

FARMER IN THE DELL, THE⋆⋆ (1936) 67m RKO bw

Fred Stone *(Pa Boyer),* Jean Parker *(Adie Boyer),* Esther Dale *(Ma Boyer),* Moroni Olsen *(Chester Hart),* Frank Albertson *(Davy Davenport),* Maxine Jennings *(Maud Durant),* Ray Mayer *(Spike),* Lucille Ball *(Gloria),* Rafael Corio *(Nicky Ranovitch),* Frank Jenks *(Crosby),* Spencer Charters *(Milkman),* John Beck, Tony Martin.

The starring role was initially slotted for Will Rogers, who died in a plane crash before production started. The producers tried to force Stone into a Will Rogers mold, but he doesn't fit, in a movie that doesn't work. An Iowa farm family lives peacefully until Ma decides they're moving to Hollywood so the daughter can become a star. Father is the one who becomes a film actor. Ma plays the pushy stage mother, and almost ruins her daughter's love life. Father quickly whisks his family back to a normal life on the farm. A few laughs, but all too predictable.

p, Robert Sisk; d, Ben Holmes; w, Sam Mintz, John Grey (based on the novel by Phil Stong); ph, Nick Musuraca; ed, Geo. Hively.

Comedy **(PR:A MPAA:NR)**

FARMER TAKES A WIFE, THE*** (1935) 94m FOX bw

Janet Gaynor *(Molly Larkins)*, Henry Fonda *(Dan Harrow)*, Charles Bickford *(Jotham Klore)*, Slim Summerville *(Fortune Friendly)*, Andy Devine *(Elmer Otway)*, Roger Imhof *(Sam Weaver)*, Jane Withers *(Della)*, Margaret Hamilton *(Lucy Gurget)*, Siegfried Rumann *(Blacksmith)*, John Qualen *(Sol Tinker)*, Kitty Kelly *(Ivy)*, Robert Glecker *(Freight Agent)*, Louis Mason *(Barfly)*, Zeffie Tilbury *(Old Lady)*, Dick Foran *(Lansing)*, Max Davidson *(Seller)*, Mitchell Lewis *(Man in Office)*, Wade Boteler *(Show Fan)*, James Burtis *(Sailor)*, Chief Thundercloud *(Chief)*, Jim Thorpe, Iron Eyes Cody *(Indians)*, Esther Howard *(Cook)*, J. M. Kerrigan *(Angus)*, Irving Bacon *(Man on Bridge)*, Stanley Blystone *(Worker)*, DeWitt Jennings *(Agent)*, Billy Benedict *(Boy)*, Frederick Burton *(Butterfield)*, Robert Warwick, Frank Melton, Lee Kohlmar, J. Farrell MacDonald, Philip Cooper, Robert Adair, Lilyan Irene, Bert Hanlon.

This was Fonda's first screen role, recreating the role he performed on Broadway. Fonda was not the first choice for the role; Gary Cooper and Joel McCrea were offered it first, but both were committed to other projects. The story is set in the New York farm lands of the 1850s when the Erie Canal was the major transportation route and the railroads were just beginning to grow. Farmers and Canal workers were always at odds because of their differing lifestyles. Fonda is a young man who takes work on a boat to earn money for a farm. The boat's cook, Gaynor, falls in love with him even though she sees farmers as weak and boring. Fonda wins a boat in a lottery, and Gaynor leaves Bickford's boat to join Fonda. Fonda's and Gaynor's relationship begins to stall when Gaynor realizes Fonda really is going to be a farmer. Bickford, mad at Fonda for taking Gaynor away from his boat, goes after him and Fonda runs from the big man. When Gaynor hears this, she leaves. When Fonda finds out that people are ridiculing him because of his cowardice, he challenges Bickford and beats him up. As Fonda plows his fields at the end of the film, Gaynor comes running and becomes his wife. An enjoyable film and a shining intro for Fonda.

p, Winfield R. Sheehan; d, Victor Fleming; w, Edwin Burke (adapted from the play by Frank B. Elser and Marc Connelly and the novel *Rome Haul* by Walter D. Edmonds); ph, John F. Seitz; md, Oscar Bradley; ed, Harold Shuster.

Drama **(PR:A MPAA:NR)**

FARMER TAKES A WIFE, THE** (1953) 80m FOX c

Betty Grable *(Molly)*, Dale Robertson *(Daniel Harrow)*, Thelma Ritter *(Lucy Cashdollar)*, John Carroll *(Jotham Klore)*, Eddie Foy, Jr. *(Fortune Friendly)*, Charlotte Austin *(Pearl)*, Kathleen Crowley *(Susanna)*, Merry Anders *(Hannah)*, Donna Lee Hickey *(Eva)*, Noreen Michaels *(Amy)*, Ruth Hall *(Abbie)*, William Pullen *(John)*, Juanita Evers *(Miss Kranz)*, Mort Mills *(Floyd)*, Lee Turnbull *(Andy)*, Gwen Verdon *(Abigail)*, Howard Negley *(Gov. Fish)*, Joanne Jordan *(Boatwife)*, Gene Roth *(Ethan McCarthy)*, Mel Pogue *(Abner Green)*, May Wynn *(Eva)*, Gordon Nelson *(Race Official)*, Ralph Sanford *(Quack)*, Don Garrett *(Cab Driver)*, Jack Harris *(Militia Officer)*, Kermit Maynard, Ted Jordan *(Drivers)*, Lee Phelps *(Bartender)*, Donald Kerr *(Jacob)*, Martin Deane, Bobby Hyatt, Brad Mora *(Boys)*, Ed Hinton, Max Wagner, John Close, Fred Aldrich, Paul Kruger, Ralph Montgomery *(Boaters)*, Fred Graham, Jack Stoney, John Butler, Emile Meyer, Wesley Hurdman.

The re-makers of the 1935 film, starring Henry Fonda and Janet Gaynor, made a critical mistake in turning the story into a musical. Grable plays the role of the boat cook who falls in love with a struggling farmer, Robertson. Set in the 1850s, the musical has numbers lacking luster and the acting is worse. Why can't Hollywood leave well enough alone? Songs include: "We're In Business," "On the Erie Canal," "We're Doing It For The Natives in Jamaica," "When I Close My Door," "Today I Love Everybody," "Somethin' Real Special," "With The Sun Warm Upon Me," and "Can You Spell Schenectady" (Harold Arlen, Dorothy Fields).

p, Frank P. Rosenberg; d, Henry Levin; w, Walter Bullock, Sally Benson, Joseph Fields (adapted from the play by Frank B. Elser and Marc Connelly and the novel *Rome Haul* by Walter D. Edmonds); ph, Arthur E. Arling (Technicolor); m, Cyril Mockridge; ed, Louis Loeffler; ch, Jack Cole.

Musical **(PR:A MPAA:NR)**

FARMER'S DAUGHTER, THE½** (1940) 60m PAR bw

Martha Raye *(Patience Bingham)*, Charlie Ruggles *(Nicksie North)*, Richard Denning *(Dennis Crane)*, Gertrude Michael *(Clarice Sheldon)*, William Frawley *(Scoop Trimble)*, Inez Courtney *(Emily French)*, William Demarest *(Victor Walsh)*, Jack Norton *(Shimmy Conway)*, William Duncan *(Tom Bingham)*, Ann Shoemaker *(Mrs. Bingham)*, Benny Baker *(Monk Gordon)*, Tom Dugan *(Forbes)*, Lorraine Krueger *(Valerie)*, Betty McLaughlin *(Dorinda)*, Anne Harrison *(Rosalie)*, Pat West *(Chuck Stevens)*, Darryl Hickman *(Billy Bingham)*, John Hartley *(Barney Bingham)*, Etta McDaniel *(Anna)*, Grace Hayle *(Torsavitch)*, Si Jenks *(Farmer)*, Wanda McKay, Jane Webb *(Cashiers)*, John "Skins" Miller *(Carpenter)*, George McKay *(Process Server)*, Nick Moro *(Sound Effects Man)*, Janet Waldo *(Switchboard Operator)*.

A millionaire, who wants to get his acting girl friend out of his hair, puts up the money for a play to be produced in a small farm town. When opening night comes, the star gets sick and the farmer's daughter, who has learned all the lines, saves the show. Film has few laughs, and the director must have thought Raye was at her funniest when falling down.

p, William C. Thomas; d, James Hogan; w, Lewis R. Foster (adapted from the story by Delmer Daves); ph, Leo Tover; ed, Archie Marshek; m/l Frank Loesser, Frederick Hollander.

Comedy **(PR:A MPAA:NR)**

FARMER'S DAUGHTER, THE*½** (1947) 96m RKO bw

Loretta Young *(Katrin Holstrom)*, Joseph Cotten *(Glenn Morley)*, Ethel Barrymore *(Mrs. Morley)*, Charles Bickford *(Clancy)*, Rose Hobart *(Virginia)*, Rhys Williams *(Adolph)*, Harry Davenport *(Dr. Mathew Sutven)*, Tom Powers *(Nordick)*, William Harrigan *(Ward Hughes)*, Lex Barker *(Olaf Holstrom)*, Harry Shannon *(Mr. Holstrom)*, Keith Andes *(Sven Holstrom)*, Thurston Hall *(Wilbur Johnson)*, Art Baker *(A. J. Finley)*, Don Beddoe *(Einar)*, James [Arness] Aurness *(Peter Holstrom)*, Anna Q. Nilsson *(Mrs. Holstrom)*, Sven Hugo Borg *(Dr. Mattsen)*, John Gallaudet *(Van)*, William B. Davidson *(Eckers)*, Charles McGraw *(Fisher)*, Jason Robards *(Night Editor)*, Cy Kendall *(Sweeney)*, Frank Ferguson *(Matternack)*, William Bakewell *(Windor)*, Charles Lane *(Jackson, Reporter)*, Douglas Evans *(Silbey, Politician)*, Robert Clarke *(Assistant Announcer)*, Bess Flowers *(Woman)*.

The difficulty that Young had in sustaining the necessary Swedish accent to make this story work didn't seem to matter a smidgeon when it came to the Oscar votes. Young nabbed the Academy Award for her delightful performance, a mixture of farce and reality that smacked of Capra without directly imitating any of his films. Young is what the title says, a fármer's daughter. She leaves the confines of life in the slow lane and makes her way to the big city where she hopes to secure work as a nurse. On her journey, she is bilked of her savings and must take a job as a maid. She finds employment in the palatial mansion of Cotten and his powerful mother, Barrymore. Cotten is a congressman and Barrymore is the power behind the city's political thrones and when Young arrives, they are knee deep in a battle over the election of another congressman. Young is one of the first liberated women of the 1940s in movies as she openly expresses displeasure at the candidate chosen by Cotten and Barrymore. She is the perfect maid in almost every way: she cooks divinely, she can give a great massage and she makes herself quite useful in the household under the tutelage of butler Bickford (who received an Oscar nomination as best supporting actor but lost to Edmund Gwenn's Santa Claus in MIRACLE ON 34TH STREET). Cotten takes Young to a rally and is stunned as she stands up and publicly disagrees with the candidate's rhetoric. It becomes a cause celebre and is heavily covered by the media. In a Hollywood credibility leap, Young is nominated by the rival party. The bad guys in Cotten's party do their best to defeat her and go so far as to manufacture a morals rap against her the day before the election. Cotten is appalled by their tactics and rallies to Young's defense. The picture winds up with Young winning the election as well as securing Cotten for a lifetime running mate. Funny, satiric and often reeking of backroom boys' cigar smoke, THE FARMER'S DAUGHTER was a winning comedy-romance that was welcomed by 1947 audiences who had only a few humorous pictures from which to choose that year (MIRACLE ON 34TH STREET, THE BISHOP'S WIFE, SONG OF THE SOUTH and THE BACHELOR AND THE BOBBY-SOXER were about it). Look hard for James Arness, Lex Barker and Keith Andes in small roles that hardly foreshadowed their later successes.

p, Dore Schary; d, H.C. Potter; w, Allen Rivkin, Laura Kerr (from the play "Hulda, Daughter Of Parliament" by Juhni Tervataa); ph, Milton Krasner; m, Leigh Harline; ed, Harry Marker.

Comedy **Cas.** **(PR:AA MPAA:NR)**

FARMER'S OTHER DAUGHTER, THE** (1965) 84m United Producers Releasing Organization c (AKA: FARM GIRL)

Judy Pennebaker *(June)*, Bill Michael *(Jim Huckleberry)*, William Guhl *(Cyrus B. Barksnapper)*, Harry Lovejoy *(Horace Jefferson Brown)*, Jean Bennett *(Ma Jefferson Brown)*, Norman Hartweg *(Cyrus, Jr.)*, Janice Evan *(Elsie)*, Jack Barbour *(Sheriff)*, Robert Adamson *(Deputy)*, Joseph Sharon *(Cedric)*, Norman Fields *(Government Man)*, Lyle Gordon *(Mayor)*, Marci Stone *(Government Girl)*, Clarence White, Roland White, Roger Bush, Donavan Cotton, Richard Greene, Ernest Ashworth, Billy Ray Latham.

Lovejoy is a poor farmer who lives with his daughter, Pennebaker. Traveling salesman Michael helps Lovejoy get rid of the sheriff and is taken to the family bosom. Pennebaker falls in love with him and the salesman gets the girls in the area to wear his bathing suits at the Fourth of July beauty contest. At the contest the bathing suits disintegrate and Michael just avoids being lynched. The town boss is after Lovejoy's farm and so the farmer applies for farm aid from the government. He gets foreign aid instead. A slap-stick rural comedy.

p, William Norton, Paul Leder; d, John Hayes; w, Norton; ph, Paul Hipp; m, Victor Pierce; ed, Bob Brebor; set d, Ray Storey.

Comedy **(PR:A MPAA:NR)**

FARMER'S WIFE, THE*½ (1941, Brit.) 78m Pathe bw

Basil Sydney *(Samuel Sweetland)*, Wilfrid Lawson *(Churdles Ash)*, Nora Swinburne *(Araminta Grey)*, Patricia Roc *(Sibley)*, Michael Wilding *(Richard Coaker)*, Bunty Payne *(Petronell)*, Enid Stamp Taylor *(Mary Hearne)*, Betty Warren *(Louisa Windeatt)*, Viola Lyel *(Thirza Tapper)*, Edward Rigby *(Tom Gurney)*, Kenneth Griffith *(George Smerdon)*, A. Bromley Davenport *(Henry Coaker)*, Jimmy Godden *(Sergeant)*, Gilbert Gunn *(Pianist)*, James Harcourt *(Valiant Dunnybrigg)*, Mark Daly *(P. C. Chave)*, Davina Craig *(Susie)*.

Sydney is a farmer trying to find a wife, but his efforts are rewarded with few laughs in this talky comedy. He tries for the hand of three well-bred women with no luck, and finally realizes it's the housekeeper he's in love with. A British comedy that is a little too stiff.

p, Walter C. Mycroft; d, Norman Lee, Leslie Arliss; w, Lee, Arliss and J.E. Hunter (adapted from the play by Eden Philpotts); ph, Claude Friese-Greene.

Comedy **(PR:A MPAA:NR)**

FASCINATION*½ (1931, Brit.) 70m BIP bw

Madeleine Carroll *(Gwenda Farrell)*, Carl Harbord *(Larry Maitland)*, Dorothy Bartlam *(Vera Maitland)*, Kay Hammond *(Kay)*, Kenneth Kove *(Bertie)*, Louis Goodrich *(Col. Farrington)*, Roland Culver *(Ronnie)*, Freddie Bartholomew *(Child)*, Merle Oberon *(Extra)*, Allison Van Dyke, John Kove.

Harbord is a devoted husband but falls for actress Carroll. His wife finds out about his affair and gets together with Carroll to talk everything out. Wife and mistress kiss and husband decides he should go back to his wife.

p, Clayton Hutton; d, Miles Mander; w, Victor Kendall (adapted from the play by Eliot Crawshay-Williams); ph, W. Winterstein, Horace Wheddon).

Drama　　　　　　　　　　　　　**(PR:A　MPAA:NR)**

FASCIST, THE*　　　　　　　(1965, Ital.) 102m Dino De Laruentiis Cinematografica/EM bw (II FEDERALE)

Ugo Tognazzi (Primo Arcovazzi), Georges Wilson (Professor Bonafe), Stefania Sandrelli (Lisa), Mireille Granelli (Rita), Gianrico Tedeschi (Baldacci), Elsa Vazzoler (Baldacci's Wife), Franco Giacobini, Renzo Palmer, Gianni Agus, Luciano Salce.

Tognazzi is a hardline fascist ordered by Italy's Fascist High Command to capture a professor, Wilson, who's an anti-fascist. Tognazzi tracks him down and the two go through a series of comic incidents on the way to Rome. When they arrive in the city the American army has taken over and Tognazzi is almost shot, but the professor saves him by giving him his clothes to wear. An intelligent comedy drama with some funny scenes and good acting by Tognazzi and Wilson.

p, Isidoro Broggi, Renato Libassi; d, Luciano Salce; w, Salce, Pipolo, Franco Castellano (adapted from a story by Pipolo and Castellano); ph, Erico Menczer; m, Ennio Morricone.

Comedy　　　　　　　　　　　　**(PR:A　MPAA:NR)**

FASHION HOUSE OF DEATH
　　　　　　　　(SEE: BLOOD AND BLACK LACE, 1965, Ital.)

FASHION MODEL½　　　　　　(1945) 59m MON bw

Robert Lowery (Danny O'Brien), Marjorie Weaver (Peggy Rooney), Tim Ryan (O'Hara), Lorna Gray (Yvonne), Dorothy Christy (Mme. Celeste), Dewey Robinson (Grogan), Sally Yarnell (Marie), Jack Norton (Shiftless), Harry Depp (Harvey Van Alyn), Nell Craig (Jessica), Edward Keane (Duval), John Valentine (Davis), Cedric Stevens (Jeffries).

A well done B comedy murder mystery. Lowery is a stockboy in a clothes factory and the main suspect in the murder of two people. A model and the owner of the factory are killed, and Lowery's girl friend, Weaver, discovers the real murderer and saves her boy friend. Light but entertaining.

p, William Strohbach; d, William Beaudine; w, Tim Ryan, Victor Hammond (adapted from a story by Hammond); ph, Harry Neumann; ed, Dan Milner, William Austin, md, Edward J. Kay.

Comedy　　　　　　　　　　　　**(PR:A　MPAA:NR)**

FASHIONS IN LOVE**　　　　　(1929) 70m PAR bw

Adolphe Menjou, Fay Compton, John Miljan, Robert Wayne, Joan Standing, Russell Powell, Billie Bennett, Jacques Vanaire, Miriam Seeger.

Menjou takes his first talking role in FASHIONS IN LOVE as a concert pianist fond of women other than his wife. After a performance one evening he meets a lady and plans a weekend retreat at a mountain cottage. Menjou's wife is informed of his extracurricular romance and heads for the resort with the other woman's husband in tow. The romantic pairings become increasingly confused and tangled until they finally decide to remain with their respective spouses. Besides hearing Menjou speak, the audience was also treated to his delivery of the film's theme song and a piano performance.

d, Victor Schertzinger; w, L. Long.

Comedy/Romance　　　　　　**(PR:A-C　MPAA:NR)**

FASHIONS OF 1934*½　　　(1934) 80m FN bw (AKA: FASHIONS)

William Powell (Sherwood Nash), Bette Davis (Lynn Mason), Frank McHugh (Snap), Verree Teasdale (Grand Duchess Alix, [Mabel McGuire]), Reginald Owen (Oscar Baroque), Henry O'Neill (Duryea), Philip Reed (Jimmy), Hugh Herbert (Joe Ward), Gordon Westcott (Harry Brent), Dorothy Burgess (Glenda), Etienne Girardot (Glass), William Burress (Feldman), George Humbert (Glass Caponelli), Hobart Cavanaugh (Mons. Gautier), Nella Walker (Mrs. Van Tyle), Spencer Charters (Telephone Man), Frank Darien (Jules), Harry Beresford (Bookseller), Helen Freeman (Mme. Margot), Tibby (Scotch Terrier), Sam McDaniel (Cleaning Man), Lee Phelps (Desk Clerk), Arthur Treacher (Butler), Martin Kosleck (Dance Director), Jane Darwell (Dowager), Georges Renavant (Fashion Salon Owner), Eric Wilton (2nd Butler), Laura Treadwell (Woman), Juliet Ware (Girl).

Powell is a fashion designer who has a reputation for ripping off well known designers' creations and selling them as his own. The fashion world is becoming wise to his way, and none of his spies in Paris can get in to see the fashions of the French designers. Powell goes himself, taking his assistants, Davis and McHugh, the latter having a miniature camera in the head of his cane. In Paris, they meet a California feather merchant, Humbert, who is trying to get designers to use more feathers in their designs. They also meet a struggling songwriter, Reed, and Powell's former girl friend, Teasdale. Teasdale is posing as a Russian noblewoman, and is engaged to Paris' most famous fashion designer, Owen. Powell blackmails his former girl friend into a showing of her fiance's latest designs. At the showing, Powell and company are caught red-handed. Powell threatens to expose Teasdale in the newspaper, and the designer suggests that Powell use his designs, the feathers, and songwriter's music and put on a show. Show's a hit, and Powell proposes to Davis and thinks about going legit. A fast-paced musical comedy with magnificent choreography by Busby Berkeley. Songs: "Spin a Little Web of Dreams," "Broken Melody" (Irving Kahal, Sammy Fain).

p, Henry Blanke; d, William Dieterle; w, F. Hugh Herbert, Gene Markey, Kathryn Scola, Carl Erickson (adapted from a story by Harry Collins and Warren Duff); ph, William Rees; md, Leo F. Forbstein; ed, Jack Killifer; art d, Jack Okey, Willy Pogany; ch, Busby Berkeley; gowns, Orry-Kelly.

Musical　　　　**Cas.**　　　　**(PR:A　MPAA:NR)**

FAST AND FURIOUS*½　　　(1939) 70m MGM bw

Franchot Tone (Joel Sloane), Ann Sothern (Garda Sloane), Ruth Hussey (Lily Cole), Lee Bowman (Mike Stevens), Allyn Joslyn (Ted Bentley), John Miljan (Erie Bartell), Bernard Nedell (Ed Connors), Mary Beth Hughes (Jerry Lawrence), Cliff Clark (Sam Travers), James Burke (Claney), Frank Orth (Capt. Burke), Margaret Roach (Emmy Lou), Gladys Blake (Miss Brooklyn), Granville Bates (Chief Miller).

The last entry in Metro's "fast" mystery series starred Tone and Sothern as the book-dealing couple who double as detectives. Tone is trying to find the murderer at a sea-side beauty pageant. His friend Joslyn is jailed, and Tone is trying to clear Joslyn's name when there is a second murder. Tone has also been named a judge in the pageant and Sothern is not too happy. Clues are found, narrow escapes performed and the murderer is unmasked. An entertaining comedy/mystery directed by Busby Berkeley. (See FAST COMPANY and FAST AND LOOSE.)

p, Frederick Stephani; d, Busby Berkeley; w, Harry Kurnitz; ph, Ray June; ed, Elmo Veron.

Mystery/Comedy　　　　　　**(PR:A　MPAA:NR)**

FAST AND LOOSE*　　　　　(1930) 70m PAR bw

Miriam Hopkins (Marion Lenox), Carole Lombard (Alice O'Neil), Frank Morgan (Bronson Lenox), Charles Starrett (Henry Morgan), Henry Wadsworth (Bertie Lenox), Winifred Harris (Carrie Lenox), Herbert Yost (George Grafton), David Hutcheson (Lord Rockingham), Ilka Chase (Millie Montgomery), Hershell Mayall (Judge Summers).

An uneven comedy about a rich boy, Wadsworth, wanting to marry a showgirl, Lombard, and his sister, Hopkins, getting engaged to a mechanic. Their mother and father can't believe their choices and try to talk them out of their plans. When the showgirl and mechanic are the ones to nix the wedding plans, the rich parents have a change of heart, and everyone gets back together for a double wedding. A comedy that lost the humor somewhere among its lines. It was Hopkins' first film.

d, Fred Newmeyer; w, Doris Anderson, Jack Kirkland, Preston Sturges (adapted from the play The Best People by David Gray and Avery Hopwood); ph, William Steiner.

Comedy　　　　　　　　　　　　**(PR:A　MPAA:NR)**

FAST AND LOOSE**　　　　　(1939) 78m MGM bw

Robert Montgomery (Joel Sloane), Rosalind Russell (Garda Sloane), Reginald Owen (Vincent Charlton), Ralph Morgan (Nicholas Torrent), Etienne Girardot (Christopher Gates), Alan Dinehart (Dave Hillard), Jo Ann Sayers (Christina Torrent), Joan Marsh (Bobby Neville), Anthony Allan [John Hubbard] (Phil Sergeant), Tom Collins (Gerald Torrent), Sidney Blackmer (Lucky Nolan), Ian Wolfe (Wilkes).

Montgomery and Russell take over the helm in this fast-mystery series. Montgomery, the book dealer and amateur detective, tries to find missing rare editions of library tycoon, Morgan. Russell, always suspicious of her husband's doings, helps to complicate the situation. Action and laughs come at a fast clip in this enjoyable mystery. (See FAST COMPANY and FAST AND FURIOUS.)

p, Fredrick Stephani; d, Edwin L. Marin; w, Harry Kurnitz; ph, George Folsey; ed, Elmo Veron.

Comedy/Mystery　　　　　　**(PR:A　MPAA:NR)**

FAST AND LOOSE*　　　　　(1954, Brit.) 75m Group/GFD bw

Stanley Holloway (Mr. Crabb), Kay Kendall (Carol), Brian Reece (Peter), Charles Victor (Lumper), June Thorburn (Barbara), Reginald Beckwith (Tripp-Johnson), Vida Hope (Gladys), Joan Young (Mrs. Gullett), Fabia Drake (Mrs. Crabb), Dora Bryan (Rawlings), Aubrey Mather (Noony), Toke Townley (Alfred), Alexander Gauge, Eliot Makeham, John Warren.

After missing a train, Reece must spend the night at an inn, not knowing that his beautiful former fiancee (Kendall) is staying there, too. In the morning both their spouses turn up and are naturally full of suspicion. Unfunny remake of A CUCKOO IN THE NEST (1933).

p, Teddy Baird; d, Gordon Parry; w, A.R. Rawlinson, Ben Travers (based on the play "A Cuckoo In The Nest" by Travers); ph, Jack Asher.

Comedy　　　　　　　　　　　　**(PR:A　MPAA:NR)**

FAST AND SEXY**　　　　　　(1960, Fr./Ital.) 99m COL c

Gina Lollobrigida (Anna), Dale Robertson (Raffaele), Vittorio De Sica (Priest), Amadeo Nazzari (Ciccone), Renzo Cesana (Baron), Peppino de Filippo (Mayor-Pharmacist), Carla Macelloni, Gabriella Pallotti, Luigi De Filippo, Mario Girotti, Clelia Matania, Augusta Ciolli, Gigi Reder, Marco Tulli, Carlo Rizzo, Ruth Wolner, Molly Robinson.

An Italian boy meets girl production. Sexpot Lollobrigida goes back to her Italian village from New York, and begins to date the local men. The one man she wants, Robertson, isn't interested. After some comical situations, Lollobrigida gets her man and it comes as no surprise. Neither is the shabby dubbing in this lame excuse to parade busty Gina about in scanties.

p, Milko Skofic; d, Reginald Denham; w, E.M. Margdonna, Lucianna Corda, Joseph Stefano; ph, Giuseppe Rotunna (Technirama, Technicolor); m, Alssandro Cicognini, Vittorio De Sica; ed, Eraldo Da Roma; art d, Gastone Medin.

Comedy　　　　　　　　　　　　**(PR:A　MPAA:NR)**

FAST AND THE FURIOUS, THE**　　(1954) 73m Palo Alto/American Releasing Corp. bw

John Ireland (Frank Webster), Dorothy Malone (Connie Adair), Bruce Carlisle (Faber), Marshall Bradford (Race Official), Jean Howell (Sally), Larry Thor (Police Sergeant), Robin Morse (Gas Station Attendant), Bruno VeSota (Truck Driver), Iris Adrian (Waitress).

Corman produced and wrote this low-budget production, which was distributed by American Releasing Corporation, (later AIP). Ireland is on the run from a framed murder charge and meets Malone at a truck stop cafe. He takes Malone's Jaguar with her in it, and enters the Pebble Beach road race to get across the border to freedom. During the race, Malone and Ireland fall for each other, and when Ireland runs another driver off the road, he decides to go back and clear his name.

p, Roger Corman; d, John Ireland, Edwards Sampson; w, Jerome Odlum, Jean Howell (adapted from a story by Corman); ph, Floyd Crosby; m, Alexander Gerens; ed, Sampson.

Crime　　　　　　　　　　　　**(PR:A　MPAA:NR)**

FAST BREAK*½ (1979) 107m COL c

Gabriel Kaplan (David Greene), Harold Sylvester (D.C.), Michael Warren (Preacher), Bernard King (Hustler), Reb Brown (Bull), Mavis Washington (Swish), Bert Remsen (Bo Winnegar), Randee Heller (Jan), John Chappell (Alton Gutkas), Rhonda Bates (Enid Cadwallader-Gutkas), K Callan (Ms. Tidwell), Marty Zagon (Henry), Richard Brestoff (Howard), Connie Sawyer (Lottie), Doria Cook (Snooty Girl), James Jeter (Officer Wedgeview), Steve Conte (Man on Bus), Larry Farmer (Beaton), Craig Impleman (Hollis), Charles Penland (Larry), Jim Spillane (Krebbs), Le Tari (Thompson), Oscar Williams (Norman), Marty Gorowitz (Frenchie), Bob Levine (Bum), John McCurry (Hal), Jack Smight (Dibber), Jackie Sule (Polly), Laurence Fishburne III (Street Kid).

Kaplan's screen debut and more or less it's a re-hash of his TV character from "Welcome Back Kotter." He takes a group of New York City street basketball players to a Nevada college that has hired him to coach. It takes time for the urban players to adjust and one in the group turns out to be a woman, who posed as a male to play at the school. The climactic big game ends predictably. A couple of good laughs, but mostly uninspired stuff with Kaplan standing around demanding that others tell him he's as funny as the laughtrack on his idiotic TV show. He isn't.

p, Stephen Friedman; d, Jack Smight; w, Sandor Stern (from a story by Marc Kaplan); ph, Charles Correll (Metrocolor); m, David Shire, James di Pasquale; ed, Frank J. Urioste; art d, Norman Baron.

Comedy   **Cas.**   **(PR:A MPAA:PG)**

FAST BULLETS** (1936) 59m Reliable Pictures bw

Tom Tyler (Tom), Rex Lease (Jimmy), Margaret Nearing (Joan), Al Bridge (Travis), Bill Gould (Drummond), Bob Walker (Frank), James Aubrey (Jake), Slim Whitaker (Pat), Charles King, Lew Meehan, Nelson McDowell, Jack Evans.

Tyler and Lease are Texas Rangers out to get a group of contraband runners. Nearing is kidnaped by the bad guys and is rescued by the rangers off a runaway wagon. Most original piece from this B oater is when the Rangers use two dummies on horses to divert the bad guy's attention. Pliny Goodfriend's cinematography is the best element of the production.

p, Bernard R. Ray; d, Henri Samuels [Harry S. Webb]; w, Jay J. Bryan, Carl Krusada, Rose Gordon; ph, Pliny Goodfriend; ed, Fred Bain.

Western   **(PA:A MPAA:NR)**

FAST CHARLIE . . . THE MOONBEAM RIDER* (1979) 99m UNIV c
(AKA: FAST CHARLIE AND THE MOONBEAM)

David Carradine (Charlie Swattle), Brenda Vaccaro (Grace Wolf), L.Q. Jones (Floyd Bevins), R.G. Armstrong (Al Barber), Terry Kiser (Lester Neal), Jesse Vint (Calvin Hawk), Noble Willingham (Pop Bauer), Whit Clay (Wesley Wolf III), Ralph James (Sheriff), Bill Hartman (Young Man), Stephen Ferry (Cannonball McCall).

Carradine is a WW I vet who dreams of winning the first transcontinental motorcycle race. He hires his war buddies, men whom Carradine ran out on when the Germans attacked. (He had a message to deliver.) He also picks up Vaccaro and her son for the race. Vaccaro and Carradine become romantic about each other and Carradine wins the race. A shoddy production, and the only important race is to the end credits.

p, Roger Corman, Saul Krugman; d, Steve Carver; w, Michael Gleason (adapted from story by Ed Spielman and Howard Friedlander); ph, William Birch; m, Stu Phillips; ed, Tony Redman, Eric Orner; art d, Bill Sandell, Michael Riva, set d, Margie Fritz.

Action/Adventure   **(PR:C MPAA:PG)**

FAST COMPANIONS** (1932) 71m UNIV bw

Tom Brown (Marty Black), James Gleason (Silk Henley), Maureen O'Sullivan (Sally), Andy Devine (Information Kid), Mickey Rooney (Midge).

Brown is a crooked jockey working with Gleason at throwing races at small town tracks. Brown mends his ways when he falls for O'Sullivan, a boardinghouse proprietess. This film contains enough laughs and action to make it enjoyable.

d, Kurt Neumann; w, Earle Snell, C.J. Marks (adapted from a story by Gerald Beaumont and Charles Logue); ph, Arthur Edeson.

Comedy/Drama   **(PR:A MPAA:NR)**

FAST COMPANY** (1929) 70m FP-PAR bw

Evelyn Brent (Evelyn Corey), Jack Oakie (Elmer Kane), Richard "Skeets" Gallagher (Bert Wade), Sam Hardy (Dave Walker), Arthur Housman (Barney Barlow), Gwen Lee (Rosie La Clerq), Chester Conklin (C. of C. President), E. H. Calvert (Platt), Eugenie Besserer (Mrs. Kane), Bert Rome (Hank Gordon), Irish Meusel, Arnold "Jigger" Statz, Truck Hannah, Gus Sanberg, Ivan Olson, Wal Wally Rehg, Jack Adams, George Boehler, Howard Burkett, Red Rollings, Frank Greene, Lez Smith (Themselves, Baseball Players).

Oakie is the home run-hitting hayseed who singlehandedly defeats gangsters in this okay comedy. Remade just four years later as ELMER THE GREAT.

d, A. Edward Sutherland; w, Florence Ryerson, Patrick Kearney, Walton Butterfield, Joseph L. Mankiewicz (based on the play "Elmer The Great" by George M. Cohan and Ring Lardner).

Comedy   **(PR:A MPAA:NR)**

FAST COMPANY** (1938) 73m MGM bw

Melvyn Douglas (Joel Sloane), Florence Rice (Garda Sloane), Claire Dodd (Julia Thorne), Shepperd Strudwick (Ned Morgan), Louis Calhern (Elias Z. Bannerman), Nat Pendleton (Paul Torison), Douglass Drumbrille (Arnold Stamper), Mary Howard (Leah Brockler), George Zucco (Otto Brockler), Minor Watson (Steve Langner), Donald Douglas (Lt. James Flanner), Dwight Frye (Sidney Wheeler), Thurston Hall (District Attorney MacMillan), Horace McMahon (Danny Scolado), Roger Converse (Assistant District Attorney Byers), Natalie Garson (Mildred), Henry Sylvester (Auctioneer), Edward Hearn (Policeman), James B. Carson (Safe Expert), Ronnie Rondell (Taxi Driver), Jack Foss (Attendant), Barbara Bedford (Secretary).

Theater distributors at the time complained about the period of time between THIN MAN movies so MGM started a trilogy featuring a husband and wife team of amateur detectives, of which this is the first. In each film different actors played the starring roles (Robert Montgomery and Rosalind Russell in FAST AND LOOSE, 1939, and Franchot Tone and Ann Sothern in FAST AND FURIOUS, 1939). Douglas is Sloane this first time around, with Rice as his wife. Douglas plays the sleuth, spotting bogus and stolen first edition books, collecting the reward money from insurance companies. When there is a murder, Douglas searches for and finds the killer.

p, Frederick Stephani; d, Edward Buzzell; w, Marco Page (Harry Kurnitz) and Harold Tarshis (adapted from a story by Page-Kurnitz); ph, Clyde DeVinna; m, Dr. William Axt; ed, Frederick Y. Smith; art d, Cedric Gibbons.

Mystery/Comedy   **(PA:A MPAA:NR)**

FAST COMPANY** (1953) 67m MGM bw

Howard Keel (Rick Grayton), Polly Bergen (Carol Maldon), Marjorie Main (Ma Parkson), Nina Foch (Mercedes Bellway), Robert Burton (Dave Sandring), Carol Nugent ("Jigger" Parkson), Joaquin Garay (Manuel Morales), Horace MacMahon ("Two-Pair" Buford), Sig Arno ("Hungry"), Iron Eyes Cody (Ben Iron Mountain), Perry Sheehan, Pat Golding, Jonathan Cott, Benny Burt, Jack Kruschen, Paul Brinegar, Jess Kirkpatrick, Lou Smith.

Bergen has a relative who died and left her a race horse. The horse is now in the care of Keel, who is keeping the horse at a losing pace in hopes Bergen will sell the animal to him at a cheap price. Bergen keeps her horse, and when she gets fleeced by track sharpies, Keel steps in—and a relationship starts. Foch, a very wealthy woman, steps between them for awhile, but Keel and Bergen patch things up in the end. A light comedy.

p, Henry Berman; d, John Sturges; w, William Roberts, Don Mankiewicz (adapted from a story by Eustace Cockrell); ph, Harold Lipstein; md, Alberto Colombo; ed, Joseph Dervim; art d, Cedric Gibbons, Leonid Vasian.

Comedy   **(PR:A MPAA:NR)**

FAST LADY, THE** (1963, Brit.) 95m RANK c

James Robertson Justice (Charles Chingford), Leslie Phillips (Freddy Fox), Stanley Baxter (Murdoch Troon), Kathleen Harrison (Mrs. Staggers), Julie Christie (Claire Chingford), Eric Barker (Wentworth), Allan Cuthbertson (Bodley), Oliver Johnston (Bulmer), Esma Cannon (Lady), Dick Emery (Shingler), Derek Guyler (Dr. Blake), Victor Brooks (Policeman), Terence Alexander (Policeman on Motorcycle), Danny Green, Michael Balfour, Eddie Leslie (Bandits), Clive Dunn (Old Gentleman), Campbell Singer (Kingscombe), Trevor Reid (Examiner), Eddie Gray, Fred Emney, Frankie Howerd, Raymond Baxter, Graham Hill, John Boister, Bill Fraser.

Baxter is a Scottish civil servant who wants to learn to drive a Bentley sports car so he can properly impress his girl friend's wealthy father. Most of the story concerns Baxter learning the rules of the road. There is a Keystone Kop-like car chase between Baxter and a gang of bank robbers. The comedy is very broad and, from scene to scene, unrelated.

p, Julian Wintle, Leslie Parkyn; d, Ken Annakin; w, Jack Davies, Henry Blyth (from a story by Keble Howard); ph, Reg Wyer (Eastmancolor); m, Norrie Paramor; ed, Ralph Sheldon.

Comedy   **(PR:A MPAA:NR)**

FAST LIFE*½ (1929) 80m FN-WB bw

Douglas Fairbanks, Jr., Loretta Young, William Holden, Chester Morris, Ray Hallor, John St. Polis, Purnell Pratt, Frank Sheridan.

A dismal courtroom drama which has Fairbanks getting sent to death row for the murder of man who fancied his wife, Young. Although it is quite clear that Fairbanks is innocent, he is condemned to death by the unbelieving jury. In the proverbial nick of time Fairbanks is saved from his fatal trip to the electric chair by the discovery that the murder was actually committed by the son of governor Holden. A happy ending for lovers Fairbanks and Young, but the governor is stricken with grief when his son kills himself. Ill-conceived dialog and illogical situations undermine any strengths the film may show. Holden, who died in 1932 and is not to be confused with the modern-day leading man, at one point remarks: "This has been an awful ordeal for all of us," a comment viewers laughingly interpreted as being directed at this film.

d, John Francis Dillon; w, John F. Goodrich (based on a play by Samuel Shipman, John B. Hymer); m/l, "Since I Found You," Ray Perkins.

Drama   **(PR:A MPAA:NR)**

FAST LIFE*½ (1932) 82m MGM bw

William Haines (Sandy), Madge Evans (Shirley), Conrad Nagel (Burton), Arthur Byron (Jameson), Cliff Edwards (Bumpy), Warburton Gamble (Halstead), Kenneth Thomson (Mr. Williams), Albert Gran (Van Vrinken), Ben Hendricks (Sherman).

Haines, after two more B quickies following this, ended his career in films to become an internationally renowned interior decorator. Here he invents a new speedboat motor and gets the shipbuilder's daughter when his boat wins a big motor race that saves the father's company from bankruptcy. Some good boat races, but rather dull stuff.

d, Harry Pollard; w, Byron Morgan, Ralph Spence (adapted from the story "Let's Go" by E. J. Rath); ph, Harold Wenstrom; ed, Hugh Wynn.

Drama   **(PA:A MPAA:NR)**

FAST ON THE DRAW* (1950) 57m Lippert bw

Jimmy Ellison (Shamrock), Russ Hayden (Lucky), Raymond Hatton (Colonel), Fuzzy Knight (Deacon), Betty [Julie] Adams (Ann), Tom Tyler (Bandit Leader), George Lewis (Pedro), John Cason (Tex), Stanley Price (Carter), Stephen Carr, Dennis Moore, George Chesebro, Bud Osborne, I. Stanford Jolley, Roy Butler, Judith Webster, Cliff Taylor, Helen Gibson, Eugene Lay, Fraser McMinn, James Van Horn, Bud Hooker.

Rodeo star Ellison has a fear of guns because his father was a gun-blazing sheriff. When Ellison's friend is wounded by outlaws, he overcomes his phobia and—guns blazing—nabs the criminals. A sub-standard B-western.

p, Ron Ormond; d, Thomas Carr; w, Ormond, Maurice Tombragel; ph, Ernest Miller; ed, Hugh Winn; md, Walter Greene; art d, Fred Preble.

Western (PR:A MPAA:NR)

FAST TIMES AT RIDGEMONT HIGH**½ (1982) 92m UNIV c

Sean Penn (*Jeff Spicoli*), Jennifer Jason Leigh (*Stacy Hamilton*), Judge Reinhold (*Brad Hamilton*), Robert Romanus (*Mike Damone*), Brian Backer (*Mark "Rat" Ratner*), Phoebe Cates (*Linda Barrett*), Ray Walston (*Mr. Hand*), Scott Thomson (*Arnold*), Vincent Schiavelli (*Mr. Vargas*), Amanda Wyss (*Lisa*), Ron Johnson), Forest Whitaker (*Charles Jefferson*), Kelli Maroney (*Cindy*), Tom Nolan (*Dennis Taylor*), Blair Ashleigh (*Pat Bernardo*), Eric Stoltz (*Stoner Bud*), Stanley Davis, Jr. (*Jefferson's Brother*), James Russo (*Robber*), James Bershad (*Greg*), Nicholas Coppola (*Brad's Bud*), Reginald H. Farmer (*Vice Principal*), Anthony Edwards (*Stoner Bud*), Pamela Springsteen (*Dina Phillips*), Stuart Cornfield (*Pirate King*), Sonny Davis (*Businessman*), Michael Wyle (*Brad's Bud*), David F. Price (*Desmond*), Patrick Brennan (*Curtis Spicoli*), Julie Guilmette, Shelly O'Neill (*Pizza Waitresses*), Stu Nahan (*Himself*), Duane Tucker (*Dr. Brandt*), Martin Brest (*Dr. Miller*), Douglas Brian Martin, Steven M. Martin (*Twins*), Taylor Negron (*Himself*), Kenny Lawrence, John Hollander, Ricky Redlich (*Customers*), Nancy Wilson (*Girl in Car*), Virginia Peters (*Waitress*), Laurie Hendricks (*Nurse*), Lois Brandt (*Mrs. O'Rourke*), Ellen Fenwick (*Stacy's Mom*), Cherie Effron, Suzanne Marie Fava (*Girls*), Lana Clarkson (*Mrs. Vargas*), Roy Holmer Wallack (*Santa Claus*), Ava Lazar, Lorie Sutton (*Playmates*).

FAST TIMES is the adaptation of Cameron Crowe's book which he researched by going back to high school for a year to chronicle the lives of a group of California teen-agers. The movie has lost most of the book's sensitive portrayal of these students, replacing it with naked bodies. The main focus of the film is a brother and sister, Leigh and Reinhold. Reinhold is a popular senior and Leigh is an innocent freshman. Leigh, through the experienced senior, Cates, gets an all-too-quick introduction to men and sex, and Reinhold sees his popularity falter when he is fired from his job at a fast-food restaurant. Other characters in the film are Backer, who has a crush on Leigh, but is shy and awkward with her, leading her to believe he doesn't like her. Romanus is Backer's slick friend who pretends to be more worldly than he is. Backer and Leigh have a quick encounter and when Leigh realizes she is pregnant, he is not able to face her and take her to the abortion clinic. The experience of having an abortion is shrugged off as if it were simply a shopping trip. Director Heckerling at times presents a very insightful view into the trials and tribulations of growing up, but the unnecessary nudity detracts from her efforts. Penn steals the show in a relatively small role as a pot-smoking surfer, and the relationship between him and teacher Walston is right on target. This might have been a very special film, but isn't.

p, Art Linson, Irving Azoff; d, Amy Heckerling; w, Cameron Crowe (adapted from Crowe's book); ph, Matthew R. Leonetti (Technicolor); m, Joe Walsh; ed, Eric Jenkins; art d, Dan Lomino.

Comedy **Cas.** (PR:O MPAA:R)

FAST-WALKING*½ (1982) 115m Lorimar/Pickman Film c

James Woods (*Fast-Walking Miniver*), Tim McIntire (*Wasco*), Kay Lenz (*Moke*), Robert Hooks (*William Galliot*), M. Emmet Walsh (*Sgt. Sanger*), Timothy Agoglia Carey (*Bullet*), Susan Tyrrell (*Evie*), Charles Weldon (*Jackson*), John Friedrich (*Squeeze*), Sandy Ward (*Warden Riker*), Lance Le Gault (*Lt. Barnes*), Deborah White (*Elaine*), Helen Page Camp (*Lady in Visitor's Room*), Sydney Lassick (*Ted*).

Woods is a pot-smoking, sharp-shooting prison guard who on the side brings in johns to Tyrrell's whore house. He is caught between a scheme by his cousin to kill a black militant prisoner and helping the black man escape for $50,000. A very cynical film in which the racial conflicts are never fully developed in a realistic light.

p&d, James B. Harris; w, Harris (based on the novel *The Rap* by Ernest Brawley); ph, King Baggot (Metrocolor); m, Lalo Schifrin; ed, Douglas Stewart; art d, Richard Haman.

Drama **Cas.** (PR:O MPAA:R)

FAST WORKERS* (1933) MGM 67m bw

John Gilbert (*Gunner Smith*), Robert Armstrong (*Bucker Reilly*), Mae Clarke (*Mary*), Muriel Kirkland (*Millie*), Vince Barnett (*Spike*), Sterling Holloway (*Pinky Magoo*), Virginia Cherrill, Muriel Evans, Guy Usher, Warner Richmond, Robert Burns.

The "Great Lover" John Gilbert's last picture for MGM; three years later he was dead of alcoholism. Gilbert and Armstrong are construction workers and friends. Armstrong plans to marry one of the many girls Gilbert has cavorted with and this causes a lot of problems that aren't worth sitting through. Scriptwriter of this near-potboiler was the distinguished Laurence Stallings who ironically had written Gilbert's greatest smash hit of the silent era, THE BIG PARADE.

d, Tod Browning; w, Laurence Stallings (adapted from the play "Rivets" by John W. McDermott); ph, Peverell Marley; ed, Ben Lewis.

Drama (PR:A MPAA:NR)

FASTEST GUITAR ALIVE, THE* (1967) 87m MGM bw

Roy Orbison (*Johnny*), Sammy Jackson (*Steve*), Maggie Pierce (*Flo*), Joan Freeman (*Sue*), Lyle Bettger (*Charlie*), John Doucette (*Sheriff Max Cooper*), Patricia Donahue (*Stella*), Ben Cooper (*Rink*), Ben Lessy (*Indian Chief*), Douglas Kennedy (*Joe*), Len Hendry (*Deputy*), Iron Eyes Cody (*1st Indian*), Sam the Sham (*1st Expressman*), Wilda Taylor (*Emily*), Victoria Carroll (*Margie*), Maria Korda (*Tanya*), Poupee Camin (*Carmen*).

C&W singer Orbison's fans should avoid his screen debut film so as not to ruin their image of him. He is a Confederate spy who steals a Union shipment of gold from

San Francisco with partner Jackson. When they head back from their mission, the war ends and they are now criminals. They team up with Pierce and Freeman, two dance hall girls, as they try to escape from a band of renegades. Orbison uses his shotgun guitar (that's right), to save the day. Mindless dribble, but Orbison sings eight songs, seven of which he wrote with Bill Dees. Songs: "Pistolero," "Good Time Party," "Whirlwind," "Rollin' On," "River," "Medicine Man," "The Fastest Guitar Alive" (Roy Orbison, Bill Dees), "Snuggle Huggle" (Fred Karger).

p, Sam Katzman; d, Michael Moore; w, Robert E. Kent; ph, W. Wallace Kelley (Metrocolor); m, Fred Karger; ed, Ben Lewis; art d, George W. Davis, Merrill Pye; set d, Henry Grace, Joseph J. Stone.

Western/Comedy (PR:A MPAA:NR)

FASTEST GUN, THE (SEE: QUICK GUN, THE, 1964)

FASTEST GUN ALIVE**½ (1956) 89m MGM bw

Glenn Ford (*George Temple*), Jeanne Crain (*Dora Temple*), Broderick Crawford (*Vinnie Harold*), Russ Tamblyn (*Eric Doolittle*), Allyn Joslyn (*Harvey Maxwell*), Leif Erickson (*Lou Glover*), John Dehner (*Taylor Swope*), Noah Beery, Jr. (*Dink Wells*), J.M. Kerrigan (*Kevin McGovern*), Rhys Williams (*Brian Tibbs*), Virginia Gregg (*Rose Tibbs*), Chubby Johnson (*Frank Stringer*), John Doucette (*Ben Buddy*), William "Bill" Phillips (*Lars Toomey*), Christopher Olsen (*Bobby Tibbs*), Paul Birch (*Sheriff Bill Toledo*), Florenz Ames (*Joe Fenwick*), Joseph Sweeney (*Reverend*), Addison Richards (*Doc Jennings*), Michael Dugan (*Clement Farley*), Glenn Strange (*Sheriff*), Earle Hodgins (*Medicine Man*), Bud Osborne (*Rancher*), Dub Taylor.

Ford is a storekeeper who tries to live down his father's reputation as a quick gun. When he gets drunk, Ford shows his talent with a pistol and this gets back to Crawford. Crawford thinks he himself is the top gun and forces the reluctant Ford to a showdown. After the showdown, the townspeople dig two graves, one marked for Crawford, the other for Ford—so that Ford can live out the rest of his life in peace. Tamblyn does a nicely choreographed acrobatic dance number before it is all over.

p, Clarence Greene; d, Russell Rouse; w, Frank D. Gilroy, Rouse (based on Gilroy's teleplay "The Last Notch"); ph, George J. Folsey; m, Andre Previn; ed, Ferris Webster, Harry V. Knapp; art d, Cedric Gibbons, Merrill Pye; ch, Alex Romero.

Western (PR:A MPAA:NR)

FAT ANGELS*½ (1980, U.S./Span.) 92m Impala-Mambru Movies c

Farnham Scott (*Mike*), January Stevens (*Mary*), Jack Aaron (*Frank*), Amy Steel (*Alison*), Robert Reynolds (*Jackie*), B. Constance Barry, Peter Bogyo, Nina David, Sanford Seeger, Robert Caus.

An innocent treatment of the loneliness, mainly when it comes to relations with the opposite sex, which seems inevitable with overweight people. Scott is the easy going and fun-loving piano player whose addiction to candy has made him quite overweight and lonely. He attempts to solve this problem by striking up a relationship via the mail with a hefty woman living down in Florida. This correspondence seems to fulfill some of Scott's needs, but the woman's trip to New York causes havoc because neither wants to show the other what they look like. Humor tends a bit too much toward slapstick, which would be okay except that neither of these obese actors is very appealing.

d, Manuel Summers; w, Summers, Chumey Chumez, Leon Tchaso, Joe Gonzalez (based on a story by Summers); ph, Mauel Rojas (Eastmancolor); m, Bob Dorough; ed, Gloria Pineyro; set d, Ramiro Gomez.

Comedy (PR:C MPAA:NR)

FAT CITY**** (1972) 100m COL c

Stacy Keach (*Tully*), Jeff Bridges (*Ernie*), Susan Tyrrell (*Oma*), Candy Clark (*Faye*), Nicholas Colasanto (*Ruben*), Art Aragon (*Babe*), Curtis Cokes (*Earl*), Sixto Rodriguez (*Lucero*), Billy Walker (*Wes*), Wayne Mahan (*Buford*), Ruben Navarro (*Fuentes*).

This was John Huston's first film in the U.S. since THE MISFITS and it's one of his best. Stacy Keach is a washed-up, alcoholic boxer living in a small California town. He tries for a comeback with the help of Bridges, but fails and goes back to his drinking. Tyrell is the woman who lives with him while her black boy friend is in jail. She has a hard time fitting into society because of her relationship with a black man. A sad and powerful character study of a boxer who has seen his last fight, and the people he develops relationships with who are also living on the short end of the stick, people who have been defeated but still dream. Powerful performances from Keach, Bridges, and Tyrell.

p, Ray Stark; d, John Huston; w, Leonard Gardner (based on his novel); ph, Conrad Hall (Eastmancolor); m, Marvin Hamlisch; ed, Marguerite Booth; prod d, Richard Sylbert; set d, Morris Hoffman; cos, Dorothy Jeakins; spec eff, Paul Stewart; m/l, "Help Me Make It Through the Night," Kris Kristofferson (sung by Kristofferson).

Drama (PR:C MPAA:PG)

FAT MAN, THE** (1951) 77m UNIV bw

J. Scott Smart (*Brad Runyan*), Julie London (*Pat Boyd*), Rock Hudson (*Roy Clark*), Clinton Sundberg (*Bill Norton*), Jayne Meadows (*Jane Adams*), John Russell (*Gene Gordon*), Jerome Cowan (*Detective Stark*), Emmett Kelly (*Ed Deets*), Lucille Barkley (*Lola Gordon*), Teddy Hart (*Shifty*), Robert Osterloh (*Chuck Fletcher*), Harry Lewis (*Happy Stevens*), Marvin Kaplan (*Pinkie*), Ken Niles (*Dr. Bromley*), Ed Max (*Murray*), Bob Roark (*Tony*), Mary Young (*Saleswoman*), Tristram Coffin (*Missing Persons Officer*), Peter Brocco (*Clerk*), Tom Keene (*Mac*), Shimen Ruskin (*Louie*), Harry Tyler (*Landlord*), Robert Jordan (*Bellhop*), Gertrude Graner (*Mother*), Guy Wilkerson (*Justice of the Peace*), George Wallace (*Carl*), Cheerio Meredith (*Scrubwoman*), Art Lind, Everett Hart, Abe Goldstein (*Clowns*), Jack Chefe (*Chef*), Eric Alden (*Guard*).

This is the adaptation of the radio series "The Fat Man," with Smart bringing his radio character to the screen. Smart is a rotund gourmet detective trying to solve the murders of a dentist and his nurse. He finds clues from New York to Los Angeles, and the main suspect is a circus clown, Emmett Kelly (in a film debut for the great big-top clown), until the Fat Man reveals Rock Hudson as the real killer.

p, Aubrey Schenck; d, William Castle; w, Harry Essex, Leonard Lee (based on a story by Lee); ph, Irving Glassberg; md, Joseph Gershenson; ed, Edward Curtiss; art d, Bernard Herzbrun, Richard H. Riedel.

Murder/Mystery **(PR:A MPAA:NR)**

FAT SPY* (1966) 75m Philip/Magna c

Phyllis Diller (Camille), Jack E. Leonard (Irving/Herman), Brian Donlevy (Wellington), Jayne Mansfield (Junior), Jordan Christopher (Frankie), The Wild Ones (Themselves), Johnny Tillotson (Dodo), Lauree Berger (Nanette), Lou Nelson (The Sikh), Toni Lee Shelly (Mermaid), Penny Roman (Secretary), Adam Keefe (Special Voice), Chuck Alden, Tommy Graves, Linda Harrison, Deborah White, Tracy Vance, Eddie Wright, Tommy Trick, Toni Turner, Jill Bleidner, Jeanette Taylor (Treasure Hunters).

Diller, Leonard, and Christopher make their screen debuts in this no laugh comedy about the aformentioned stars seeking the fountain of youth on a Florida island. On that island, they find a bunch of pop singing teen-agers and the top-heavy Mansfield. A waste of time, talent, and celluloid.

p, Everett Rosenthal; d, Joseph Cates; w, Matthew Andrews; ph, Joseph Brun; m, Al Kasha, Joel Hirshhorn, Hans Hunter; ed, Barry Malkin; cos, Lilli Pearlman; m/l, "Wild Way Of Living," "People Sure Act Funny," Chuck Alden, Jordan Christopher.

Comedy **(PR:A MPAA:NR)**

FATAL DESIRE** (1953) 106m Excelsa/Ultra c
(AKA: CAVALLERIA RUSTICANA)

Anthony Quinn (Alfio), Kerima (Lola), May Britt (Santuzza), Ettore Manni (Turiddu), Umberto Spadaro (Uncle Brasi), Grazia Spadaro (Aunt Camilla), Virginia Balestrieri (Mamma Lucia), Tito Gobbi (Voice).

A melodramatic Italian love story filled with deceit, adultery, and vendettas. Quinn's wife, Kerima, is compelled to have an affair with her former sweetheart, Manni, who has just returned after five years in the army. She resists at first, and the spurned Manni finds his way into the arms of Britt. Unsatisfied, Manni sneaks into Kermia's house one night after Quinn has gone to work, and the affair begins. Britt is outraged at this turn of events and informs Quinn of his wife's infidelity. Quinn swears revenge and kills Manni in a duel with Sicilian knives. Originally shot in color (80m) and in 3-D, it was released in the U.S. in 1963 in black and white (106m).

p, Carlo Ponti; d, Carmine Gallone; w, Mario Monicelli, Basilio Franchina, Francesco De Feo, Art Cohn, Gallone (based on the novel by Giovanni Verga and opera by Pietro Mascagni); ph, Karl Struss, Riccardo Pallottini (3-D, Ferraniacolor); ed, Rolando Benedetti; md, Oliviero De Fabritiis; art d, Gastone Medin.

Drama **(PR:C MPAA:NR)**

FATAL HOUR, THE** (1937, Brit.) 65m B&D-PAR British bw

Edward Rigby (Cready), Moira Reed (Mary Denston), Moore Marriott (Dixon), Dick Hunter (Peter), Derek Gorst (James West), D.J. Williams (Evangelist), J.H. Lockwood (Sir George Bell), Ernest Sefton (Pat), Douglas Vine, Cyril Hillier.

Rigby is seemingly the innocuous proprietor of an antique shop, but when a plot to blow up a scientist with a time bomb concealed in a clock sold by the dealer fails, he is revealed to be the boss of a spy ring. A good performance by Rigby can only help the mediocre story so much.

p, Anthony Havelock-Allan; d, George Pearson; w, Ralph Neale, Gerald Elliott (based on the novel The Clock by Cicely Frazer-Simpson).

Spy Drama **(PR:A MPAA:NR)**

FATAL HOUR, THE** (1940) 67m MON bw

Boris Karloff (James Lee Wong), Grant Withers (Capt. Street), Marjorie Reynolds (Robbie Logan), Charles Trowbridge (Forbes), John Hamilton (Belden, Sr.), Craig Reynolds (Belden, Jr.), Jack Kennedy (Mike), Lita Chevret (Tanya), Frank Puglia (Hardway), Stanford Jolley (Soapy), Jason Robards (Griswold), Pauline Drake (Bessie).

Police sergeant Withers can't dig up a clue in his best friend's murder so he enlists Karloff's aid. The murdered detective was working on a smuggling case and Karloff is able to round up a jeweler and a nightclub owner as two of the suspects. When three more murders are committed, Karloff finally captures the real killer with the help of reporter Reynolds. Karloff gets the only raves in this feeble effort.

p, William T. Lackey; d, William Nigh; w, Scott Darling, Joseph West (based on the "James Lee Wong" stories by Hugh Riley); ph, Harry Neumann; ed, Russell Schoengrath.

Murder/Mystery **(PR:A MPAA:NR)**

FATAL LADY* (1936) 75m PAR bw

Mary Ellis (Marion Stuart/Marla Delasano/Malevo), Walter Pidgeon (David Roberts), Ruth Donnelly (Melba York), Norman Foster (Phillip Roberts), Guy Bates Post (Feodor Glinka), John Halliday (Romero Fontes), Alan Mowbray (Uberto Malla), Samuel Hinds (Guili Ruffano), Edgar Kennedy (Rudy), Albert Conti (Headwaiter), Irene Franklin (Russian Countess), Jean Rouverol (Anita), Frank Puglia (Felipe), Frederick Roland (Anita's Father), Laura Treadwell (Anita's Mother), Robert Graves (French Guide), Harry Depp, Frank Hammond, Lucille Ward, Fern Emmett (American Tourists), George Davis, Don Brodie (French Waiters), Ward Bond (American Stage Manager), Edward Van Sloan (French

Surete), Russell Hicks (American Opera House Manager), Russ Bell, Henry Oliver (Cab Drivers).

Ellis is brought in by New York police on suspicion of murder on the night of her operatic debut. The trauma of the interrogation causes laryngitis. In disgrace, she goes to South America where she is courted by Foster and Mowbray. When Mowbray is killed as he and Ellis sing, she is again under suspicion. She proves her innocence, and when Foster is killed Post is unmasked as the killer who murdered for music. A poorly plotted murder mystery with too many holes and contrivances to be enjoyed.

p, Walter Wanger; d, Edward Ludwig; w, Samuel Ornitz, Horace McCoy (based on a story by Harry Segall); ph, Leon Shamroy; m/l, Sam Coslow, Victor Young.

Murder/Mystery **(PA:A MPAA:NR)**

FATAL NIGHT, THE** (1948, Brit.) 50m Anglofilm/COL bw

Lester Ferguson (Puce), Jean Short (Geraldine), Leslie Armstrong (Cyril), Brenda Hogan (Julia), Patrick Macnee (Tony), Aubrey Mallalieu (Yokel).

Ferguson takes up a dare by two Englishmen to stay in a haunted house. Settling down with a candle, a gun, and a thriller about two Victorian sisters who are killed in a ghost-ridden house, he reads and falls asleep to dream about the sisters. Waking up startled, he sees a ghost, fires at it, and faints. Scene shifts. Much later, the two Englishmen meet Ferguson who had vanished. They explained that the ghost was a ruse and the gun he had used contained blanks. Ferguson, enraged, suddenly attacks one of them and just then attendants from a nearby insane asylum arrive to take him back from where he had just escaped.

p&d, Mario Zampi; w, Gerald Butler, Kathleen Connors (based on the story "The Gentleman from America" by Michael Arlen); ph, Cedric Williams; m, Stanley Black; ed, Giullo Zampi.

Drama **(PA:A MPAA:NR)**

FATAL WITNESS, THE* (1945) 69m REP bw

Evelyn Ankers (Priscilla Ames), Richard Fraser (Inspector Trent), George Leigh (John Bedford), Barbara Everest (Lady Ferguson), Barry Bernard (Scoggins), Frederick Worlock (Sir Humphrey Mung), Virginia Farmer (Martha), Colin Campbell (Sir Malcolm Hewitt), Crauford Kent (Butler), Peggy Jackson (Gracie Hallet).

A lame murder mystery where the murderer is unmasked halfway through the picture. A man is slain and a Scotland Yard inspector, who falls in love with the victim's niece, nabs the killer.

p, Rudolph E. Abel; d, Lesley Selander; w, Jerry Sackheim, Cleve F. Adams (based on a story by Rupert Croft-Cooke); ph, Bud Thackery; ed, Ralph Dixon.

Murder/Mystery **(PA:A MPAA:NR)**

FATE IS THE HUNTER* (1964) 106m FOX bw

Glenn Ford (McBane), Nancy Kwan (Sally Fraser), Rod Taylor (Capt. Jack Savage), Suzanne Pleshette (Martha Webster), Jane Russell (Herself), Wally Cox (Bundy), Nehemiah Persoff (Ben Sawyer), Mark Stevens (Mickey Doolan), Max Showalter (Crawford), Howard St. John (Hutchins), Robert Wilke (Stillman), Bert Freed (Dillon), Dort Clark (Wilson), Mary Wickes (Mrs. Llewelyn), Robert F. Simon (Proctor), Constance Towers (Peg Burke), Dorothy Malone (Lisa Bond), Peter Ford (Attendant), Harold Goodwin (Art Baldwin), Marianna Case (D'Arcy), Pauline Myers (Mother), John Hubbard (Robbins), Joseph Hoover (Newsman), Richard Walsh (Radio Newscaster), Kort Falkenburg, Joe Scott (Controllers), Rusty Lane (Supervisor), Morgan Len Justin (TV Camera Crewman), George Dockstader (Policeman), James Secrest (Orderly), Marshall Reed, Paul Lukather, Ralph Thomas, Rusty Burrell, Robert Doggan, John Stevens (Reporters), Kem Dibbs, Robert Adler (FBI Men), Evadne Baker (Secretary), Angela Dawson (Child), Stanley Adams (Bartender), Francois Andre, David BeDell (Technicians), Iris Adrian (Ad-Libber), Jim Boles (Passenger), Harry Swoger (Airport Employee), Pitt Herbert.

Ford is a flight director for a commercial airline, and personally investigates a crash that killed 53 people. The pilot of the plane (Taylor), was a wartime friend of his and, knowing he was one of the best, Ford sets out to clear his name. With the surviving stewardess, Pleshette, he re-enacts the fatal crash and discovers that a short circuit caused the disaster. Director Nelson uses flashbacks well to develop the character of the dead pilot and events leading to the crash. Pleshette overacts as usual but Ford is terrific.

p, Aaron Rosenberg; d, Ralph Nelson; w, Harold Medford (based on the novel by Ernest K. Gann); ph, Milton Krasner (CinemaScope); m, Jerry Goldsmith; ed, Robert Simpson; art d, Jack Martin Smith, Hilyard Brown; set d, Walter M. Scott, Stuart A. Reiss; cos, Moss Mabry; spec eff, L.B. Abbott, Emil Kosa, Jr.; m/l, "Fate Is the Hunter," Jerry Goldsmith, Don Wolf; "No Love, No Nothin'," Harry Warren, Leo Robin (sung by Jane Russell).

Drama **(PR:A MPAA:NR)**

FATE TAKES A HAND**½ (1962, Brit.) 72m Danziger/MGM bw

Ronald Howard (Tony), Christina Gregg (Karon), Basil Dignam (Wheeler), Jack Watson (Bulldog), Peter Butterworth (Ronnie), Mary Laura Wood (Sandra), Noel Trevarthen (Bob), Sheila Whittingham (Jenny), Valentine Dyall (Wilson).

A bag of mail stolen 15 years before is recovered, and the effect of the late letters delivered to the recipients makes for five delightful little tales. Good performances all the way around.

p, Brian Taylor; d, Max Varnel; w, Brian Clemens.

Drama **(PR:A MPAA:NR)**

FATHER* (1967, Hung.) 95m Mafilm/CD bw (APA)

Andras Balint (Tako), Miklos Gabor (Father), Klari Tolnay (Mother), Daniel Erdelyi (Tako, as a Child), Kati Solyom (Anni), Zsuzsa Rathonyi (Mother, as a Young

Woman), Rita Bekes, Judit Halasz, Anna Nagy, Zsuzsa Balogh, Judit Zsolnai, Terez Nagy, Ila Loth, Geza Partos, Bela Asztalos, Geza Boszormenyi, Lajos Pozsar, Andras Kozak, Ervin Csomak, Gyula Koltai, Gyorgy Kezdi, Jozsef Madaras, Laszlo Balogh, Ilona Petenyi, Laszlo Sztano, Matyas Eorsi, Gabi Bertha, Karoly Versits, Gyozo Orgon, Istvan Raits, Gabor Algacs, Laszlo Bakos, Istvan Balogh, Elek Daniel, Gabor Eross, Maria Egri, Robert Foldeak, Tibor Fulop, Laszlo Haraszti, Laszlone Haraszti, Pal Hetenyi, Peter Huszti, Erzsebet Horeszku, Istvan Kardos, Tibor Kovacs Toth, Laszlo Kurucsai, Erzsi Lados, Antal Meszaros, Gyula Nagymarosi, Jozefa Orvos-Toth, Karolyne Ohler, Janos Rubleszky, Zsuzsa Pajzs, Aniko Safar, Ida Simenfalvy, Jozsef Szentirmai, Matyas Vargha, Sandorne Varnagy, Klara Zakarias.

Erdelyi plays a Hungarian boy who, after his father is killed at the end of WW II, conjures up a fantasy of what his father must have been like. In the boy's imagination he was a brave resistance fighter and a glorious hero. Erdelyi's tales of his father's bravery naturally lead to his own leadership among his schoolmates. As he gets older, Balint (who now assumes the role) finds that the stories of his father's heroism attract women who are enthralled by the tales of adventure. In 1956, during the Hungarian uprising, Balint meets and falls in love with a Jewish girl, Solyom. Together they work as extras on a movie set portraying Jewish refugees from Hitler's Germany. The experience shakes Balint into an understanding of the reality of Solyom's heritage, and creates an interest in the reality of his own. Upon investigation, Balint discovers that his father was an average man and never a hero. Finally deciding he can live without the myth of his father, Balint swims out into the sea and cleanses the legend from his mind.

d, Istvan Szabo; w, Janos Hersko (based on a story by Szabo); ph, Sandor Sara; m, Janos Gonda; ed, Janos Rozsa; cos, Erzsebet Mialkovszky.

Drama Cas. (PR:A MPAA:NR)

FATHER AND SON** (1929) 67m COL bw

Jack Holt *(Frank Fields)*, Dorothy Revier *(Grace Moore)*, Mickey McBan (Jimmy Fields), Helene Chadwick *(Mary White)*, Wheeler Oakman *(Anton Lebau)*.

One of the few early talkies that is unmistakably dependent on the sound format, FATHER AND SON has Holt a widower and loving father to 10-year-old McBan. When the youngster's birthday comes along McBan receives a phonograph recorder which becomes an integral element of the plot. Holt takes a trip to Paris and falls in love with Revier, a shady countess who keeps her dark side hidden away. McBan, however, suspects Revier and shuts her out when she removes a portrait of his dead mother. He is scolded for his negative attitude by Holt and retreats to his room to record an apology on disc for his father. In the meantime Revier's former lover comes to the house and kills her. Holt is accused of the crime but the boy tries to take the blame. During the trial the judge requests the record as evidence, plays it, hears the shot, and clears both father and son of any involvement in the killing. Interesting only for its innovative use of sound, FATHER AND SON offers little else of interest.

d, Erle C. Kenton; w, Frederic Hatton, Fanny Hatton (based on a story by Elmer Harris); ph, Teddy Tetzlaff; m, Constantine Bakaleinikoff.

Drama (PR:A MPAA:NR)

FATHER AND SON*½ (1934, Brit.) 48m BN/WB bw

Edmund Gwenn *(John Bolton)*, Esmond Knight *(Michael Bolton)*, James Finlayson *(Bildad)*, Charles Carson *(Colin Bolton)*, Daphne Courtney *(Emily Yates)*, O.B. Clarence *(Tom Yates)*, Margaret Yarde *(Victoria)*, Roland Culver *(Vincent)*.

Thinking his ex-convict father has fallen back to his old ways, a bank clerk takes blame for a theft. The father was innocent after all, and this snippet of a film comes to an end.

p, Irving Asher; d, Monty Banks; w, Randall Faye (based on the novel *Barber John's Boy* by Ben Ames Williams).

Crime (PR:A MPAA:NR)

FATHER BROWN (SEE: DETECTIVE, THE, 1954, Brit.)

FATHER BROWN, DETECTIVE** (1935) 67m PAR bw

Walter Connolly *(Father Brown)*, Paul Lukas *(Flambeau)*, Gertrude Michael *(Evelyn Fischer)*, Robert Loraine *(Inspector Valentine)*, Halliwell Hobbes *(Sir Leopold Fischer)*, Una O'Connor *(Mrs. Boggs)*, E.E. Clive *(Sergeant)*, Bunny Beatty, Robert Adair, Gwenllian Gill, King Baggott, Eldred Tilbury.

Lukas steals a diamond cross from Connolly's church to impress Michael, who he had met during a gambling raid. The priest goes on the trail and catches Lukas, who repents but eludes the police. Connolly is suspected by the police and church of losing his mind for forgiving the thief, but Lukas turns himself in to prove that Connolly was correct in trying to reform him.

p, Edward Sedgwick; w, Henry Myers, C. Gardner Sullivan (based on a story by Gilbert K. Chesterton); ph, Theodor Sparkuhl; ed, James Smith.

Mystery/Comedy (PR:A MPAA:NR)

FATHER CAME TOO** (1964, Brit.) 93m Rank c

James Robertson Justice *(Sir Beverley Grant)*, Leslie Phillips *(Roddy Chipfield)*, Stanley Baxter *(Dexter Munro)*, Sally Smith *(Juliet Munro)*, Ronnie Barke *(Josh)*, James Villiers *(Benzil Bulstrode)*, Raymond Huntley *(Mr. Wedgewood)*, Geoffrey Dunn *(Mr. Trumper)*, Anita Sharp Bolster *(Mrs. Trumper)*, Barbara Roscoe *(Lana)*, Cardew Robinson *(Fire Officer)*, Vanda Hudson *(Neil Gwynne)*, Eric Barker *(Mr. Gallagher)*, Fred Emney *(Sir Francis Drake)*, Kennedy Cope *(Ron)*, Peter Jones *(Charles II)*, Terry Scott *(Executioner)*, Hugh Lloyd *(Mary, Queen of Scots)*, Timothy Bateson *(Wally)*, Philip Locke *(Stan)*, Julian Orchard *(Bath Salesman)*, Sydney Bromley *(Lang)*, Clifford Earl *(Police Motorcyclist)*, Nicky Henson *(Motorcyclist)*, Arthur Mullard *(Traffic Warden)*, Joseph Brady *(Guy Fawkes)*, Vanda Hudson *(Nell Gwynne)*, John Bluthal *(Robert the Bruce)*, Patrick Newell *(King Harold)*.

A broad British comedy about newlyweds who buy a rundown cottage to get away from the bride's father. The house is so dilapidated that they are forced to enlist the father and an inept builder to get it in shape. In the end, it catches on fire and the fire brigade ruins a local historical pageant getting to it too late to help. A "Mr. Fixit" nightmare with occasional snickers instead of belly laughs.

p, Julian Wintle, Leslie Parkyn; d, Peter Graham Scott; w, Jack Davies, Henry Blyth; ph, Reg Wyer (Eastmancolor); m, Norrie Paramor; ed, Tom Priestley; art d, Harry Pottle.

Comedy (PR:A MPAA:NR)

FATHER GOOSE*½** (1964) 115m UNIV c
(GRAND MECHANT LOUP APPELLE)

Cary Grant *(Walter Eckland)*, Leslie Caron *(Catherine Freneau)*, Trevor Howard *(Commodore Frank Houghton)*, Jack Good *(Lt. Stebbins)*, Verina Greenlaw *(Christine)*, Pip Sparke *(Anne)*, Jennifer Berrington *(Harriet)*, Stephanie Berrington *(Elizabeth)*, Laurelle Felsette *(Angelique)*, Nicole Felsette *(Dominique)*, Sharyl Locke *(Jenny)*, Simon Scott *(Submarine Captain)*, John Napier *(Submarine Executive)*, Richard Lupino *(Radioman)*, Alex Finlayson *(Doctor)*, Peter Forster *(Chaplain)*, Don Spruance *(Navigator)*, Ken Swofford *(Helmsman)*.

Despite heavy trade advertising and a large promotional campaign, FATHER GOOSE only secured one Oscar (Best Screenplay) but was a fair-to-middling success with audiences in a year that featured such blockbusters as MY FAIR LADY, TOPKAPI, ZORBA THE GREEK, MARY POPPINS, GOLDFINGER, THE UNSINKABLE MOLLY BROWN, and YESTERDAY, TODAY AND TOMORROW. Grant doffs his accustomed suavity in favor of a role as a drunken beachcomber-type who is spending WW II on a small tropical island watching for Japanese planes and reporting said air activity via his short-wave radio. Trevor Howard is an Australian navy man who prevails on Grant to take up the war cudgels and Grant only accepts when his motor launch is rendered inoperative because of a crash with an Australian gunboat. Howard has a huge store of booze but will only dole it out to Grant if Grant does what is desired: reports on the Japanese. On another island, some 40 miles away, another plane-watcher is stranded and Grant sets out to rescue him in a tiny dinghy. Once there, he discovers Leslie Caron and a septet of young girls who have been stranded when the plane taking them from New Guinea dropped them off because the pilot was ordered to rescue the crew of a downed bomber. Now Grant, a woman-hater not unlike Bogart in THE AFRICAN QUEEN, must take care of these women. Caron is very prissy (not unlike Hepburn in the picture named above). The resultant complications are mostly telegraphed but done so well that we don't care. It all ends in a too-fast conclusion with a questionable drunk scene, the marriage of Grant and Caron by a chaplain, and a bit of Grant's heroics as he draws the fire of a Japanese boat offshore so an American sub can nail the enemy ship. Well-directed by Nelson, it was just a bit too hodge-podgy with an attempt to use every war gag ever done before. As is the case of so many Hollywood collaborations, the two screenwriters met for the first time on the stage when they accepted their Oscars. Tarloff, a Lincoln High School graduate from Brooklyn, and Stone (who had just finished writing CHARADE and went on to be a Tony winner for his Broadway books for musicals) worked separately on the screenplay and a Writers Guild Arbitration ordered the shared credit. They were both amazed at their awards after noting their competition. The man who sang the title song was Digby Wolfe, a British-Australian comic and singer who later went on to be the head writer on "Laugh-In." Pleasant and fast-moving, it just misses being a comedy classic but stands up well 20 years later when compared to many of the mindless comedies released in the 1980s. The title refers to the code name of Grant, "Mother Goose," when reporting the Japanese air movements. Grant never did another scuzzy role after that, making just one more film, WALK, DON'T RUN, and then retiring and staying in retirement to grow old gracefully and enjoy the fruits of a career which began in 1917 as a song and dance man with an acrobatic troupe. For a while, Grant worked as a lifeguard at Coney Island, where ironically, screenwriter Tarloff was born and raised in the early 1920s.

p, Robert Arthur; d, Ralph Nelson; w, Frank Tarloff, Peter Stone (based on the story "A Place Of Dragons" by S.H. Barnett); ph, Charles Lang, Jr. (Technicolor); m, Cy Coleman; ed, Ted J. Kent; md, Joseph Gershenson; art d, Alexander Golitzen, Henry Bumstead; set d, George Milo, John McCarthy; cos, Ray Aghayan; m/l "Pass Me By," Coleman, Caroline Leigh (sung by Digby Wolfe); makeup, Bud Westmore.

War Comedy Cas. (PR:AAA MPAA:NR)

FATHER IS A BACHELOR*½ (1950) 83m COL bw

William Holden *(Johnny Rutledge)*, Coleen Gray *(Prudence Millett)*, Mary Jane Saunders *(May Chalotte)*, Charles Winninger *(Prof. Mordecai Ford)*, Stuart Erwin *(Pudge Barnham)*, Clinton Sundberg *(Plato Cassin)*, Gary Gray *(Jan Chalotte)*, Sig Ruman *(Jericho Schlosser)*, Billy Gray *(Feb Chalotte)*, Lloyd Corrigan *(Judge Millett)*, Frederic Tozere *(Jeffrey Gilland, Sr.)*, Peggy Converse *(Genevieve Cassin)*, Arthur Space *(Lucius Staley)*, Warren Farlow *(March)*, Wayne Farlow *(April)*, Tommy Ivo *(Jeffrey Gilland, Jr.)*, Hank Worden *(Finnegan)*, Dooley Wilson *(Blue)*, William Tannen *(Willis)*, Ruby Dandridge *(Maid)*, Thomas Kingston *(Bit)*, Al Thompson *(Court Clerk)*, Eddy Waller *(White)*.

Holden, a tramp who would rather fish than work, is in cahoots with Winninger, owner of a medicine show. When the show goes out of business, Holden happily goes off to fish. His idyll is disrupted when five orphans adopt him and rehabilitate him into a hard-working man. Uninspired film with a script heavy in sentimentality, and six musical numbers that aren't worth singing. Too mushy for words. Holden, six months later, appeared in the magnificent SUNSET BOULEVARD.

p, S. Sylvan Simon; d, Norman Foster, Abby Berlin; w, James Edward Grant, Aleen Leslie (based on a story by Grant); ph, Burnett Guffey; m, Arthur Morton; ed, Jerome Thoms; md, Morris Stoloff; art d, Carl Anderson.

Musical (PR:A MPAA:NR)

FATHER IS A PRINCE** (1940) 59m FN/WB bw

Nana Bryant (Mrs. Bower), Grant Mitchell (Bower), John Litel (Dr. Stone), George Reeves (Gary), Jan Clayton (Connie), Lee Patrick (Aunt), Pierre Watkin (Mr. Lee), Billy Dawson, Richard Clayton, John Ridgely, Frank Wilcox, Vera Lewis, Frank Ferguson, Mary Currier, Frank Orth.

Mitchell drives his family crazy with his penny-pinching ways. He refuses to pay his taxes, and yanks out electric lights so bills won't be so high. When he meets the family of his daughter's future husband, he almost ends the wedding plans with his tantrums. Bryant struggles to keep the family and herself from falling apart in this sometimes rough look at how parsimony can stunt a family's joy in life.

d, Noel Smith; w, Robert E. Kent (based on the play "Big Hearted Herbert" by Sophie Kerr Underwood and Anna S. Richardson); ph, Ted McCord; ed, Frank Magee; art d, Charles Novi.

Drama (PR:A MPAA:NR)

FATHER MAKES GOOD** (1950) 61m MON bw

Raymond Walburn (Henry Latham), Walter Catlett (Mayor Colton), Barbara Brown (Mrs. Latham), Gary Gray (David Latham), George Nokes (Georgie Colton), Mary Stuart, Olin Howlin, Robert Emmett Keane, Brett King, Pat Collins, Mary Field, William Hudson, Margaret Brayton, Lois Austin, Gertrude Astor, Everett Glass, Paul E. Burns, Francis Ford, Hal Price, Jack Kirkwood.

Outraged over a new tax on milk, amiable comedian Walburn buys himself a cow and produces his own, letting the jokes and merriment stream out. Only a minor comedy for the veteran rapscallion of many a Hollywood film, and one in a series he did for Monogram. (See HENRY LATHAM series, Index.)

p, Peter Scully; d, Jean Yarbrough; w, D.D. Beauchamp; ph, William Sickner; md, Edward Kay; art d, Dave Milton.

Comedy (PR:A MPAA:NR)

FATHER O'FLYNN*½ (1938, Irish) 66m But/Hoffberg bw

Tom Burke (Father O'Flynn), Jean Adrienne (Macushlah), Robert Chisholm (Nigel), Henry Oscar (Westmacott), Ralph Truman (Fawcett), Denis O'Neil (Flannigan), Dorothy Vernon (Bridget O'Loveley), Johnny Schofield (Cassidy), Billy Holland (Muldoon), Ethel Revnell & Gracie West, Stanley Kirkby, Sherman Fisher Girls, Louis Goodrich, Esme Lewis, Robert Hobbs, Clifford Buckton, Ian Wilson.

An Irish production about a young girl, Adrienne, adopted by a priest, Burke, when her father is jailed. She is in love with a young man, and when her father is released he tries to break up their relationship. The singing doesn't help this melodrama whose appeal outside of Ireland is small at best.

p, Wilfred Noy; d, Noy, Walter Tennyson; songs: "Ave Maria" (sung by Burke), "Macushla," "Let's Fall In Love," "Father O'Flynn," "I Know Two Bright Eyes."

Musical (PR:A MPAA:NR)

FATHER OF A SOLDIER*½** (1966, USSR) 83m Gruziya/Artkino bw (OTETS SOLDATA; AKA: A SOLDIER'S FATHER)

Sergei Zakariadze (The Father), Vladimir Privaltsev (Nikolay), Keto Bochorishvili (Arkadiy), A. Nazarov, A. Lebedev, V. Kolokoltsev, Yu. Drozdov, I. Kosykh, Vitya Kosykh, V. Uralskiy, V. Pitsek, P. Lyubeshkin, T. Sapozhnikova, I. Barmin, I. Vykhodtseva, R. Vild An, B. Goginava, V. Zharikov, V. Kulik, G. Kobakhidze, I. Kokrashvili, I. Kvitayshvili, Yelena Maksimova, R. Muratov, V. Mizin, I. Nizharadze, L. Zgvauri, A. Startsev, F. Stepun.

In the closing days of WW II Georgian farmer Zakariadze, upon learning that his son, a soldier, has been wounded in battle, travels on a long journey to see him in the hospital. Along the way he is deeply disturbed to see the battle scars that have destroyed the once lush landscape. At the hospital, he is shocked to learn that his son has been returned to his tank unit. Zakariadze is determined to see his boy and continues his quest. After being caught in the middle of a battle, Zakariadze decides that he, too, will join the army, but his love of the land forces him to halt an attack on German vineyards by Soviet tanks. Eventually he meets up with his son, but the boy is caught in enemy fire and dies in his father's arms. Ruggedly masculine veteran actor Zakariadze was a famous Russian footballer in the 1920s before he went on the stage. He added another facet to his career in the 1960s when he became a member of the Politburo.

d, Revas Chkheidze; w, Suliko Zhgenti, Chkheidze; ph, Lev Sukhov, A. Filipashvili, L. Namgalashvili; m, Sulkhan Tsintsadze; ed, Vasiliy Dolenko; art d, Z. Medzmariashvili, N. Kazbegi; spec eff, O. Magakyan, R. Vashadze.

War (PR:C MPAA:NR)

FATHER OF THE BRIDE*½** (1950) 92m MGM bw

Spencer Tracy (Stanley T. Banks), Joan Bennett (Ellie Banks), Elizabeth Taylor (Kay Banks), Don Taylor (Buckley Dunstan), Billie Burke (Doris Dunstan), Leo G. Carroll (Mr. Massoula), Moroni Olsen (Herbert Dunstan), Melville Cooper (Mr. Tringle), Taylor Holmes (Warner), Paul Harvey (Rev. Galsworthy), Frank Orth (Joe), Rusty Tamblyn (Tommy Banks), Tom Irish (Ben Banks), Marietta Canty (Delilah), Willard Waterman (Dixon), Nancy Valentine (Elise), Mary Jane Smith (Effie), Jacqueline Duval (Peg), Fay Baker (Miss Bellamy), Frank Hyers (Duffy), Chris Drake, Floyd Taylor, Don Anderson, William Mahon, Walter Kelly, Peter Thompson, Carleton Carpenter (Ushers), Lucille Barnes, Erin Selwyn, Janet Fay, Wendy Waldron (Bridesmaids), Douglas Phillips, Stuart Holmes, Anne Kunde (Bits in Dream Sequence), Fred Santley, Philo McCullough, Harry Stanton, Lucille Curtis, Estelle Ettere, Peggy Leon, Betty Farrington (Guests), Lillian Bronson (School Teacher), Aileen Carlyle (Woman), Thomas Browne Henry (Stranger), Mickey Golden, Gene Coogan (Barmen), Lee Phelps (Motor Cop), Patricia Miller (Wispy Girl), Frank Richards (Truck Driver), William Haade, Jeff York (Policemen), Dewey

Robinson, Ed Gargan, Ralph Peters, Dick Wessel, Dick Alexander, Joe Brown, Jr., Jim Hayward, Gil Perkins (Movers), Brad Hatton (Florist), John Welsh (Western Union Boy), William Phillips (Foreman of Movers).

Tracy, the picture and the screenplay all garnered Oscar nominations but lost out to Jose Ferrer's CYRANO DE BERGERAC, ALL ABOUT EVE, and Joseph Mankiewicz's screenplay for ALL ABOUT EVE. This is one of the most believable comedies to come out of that era at MGM, and anyone who has ever been married, been the parents of children about to get married, has been to a wedding, or is contemplating getting married will indentify with this. Tracy is a superb farceur as he portrays the father of Taylor, a sweet young thing who is marrying Don Taylor (no relation). The movie begins as an exhausted Tracy looks over the debris and chaos in his home, the result of the wedding. He turns to the audience and begins to relate the tale. The problems of marrying off a daughter are legion; the heart-to-heart talk with the suitor, meeting the in-laws, selecting the honeymoon site, and all of the financial havoc wreaked on any Father Of The Bride. It's a satiric look at the American Family, circa 1950, and not much has changed in suburbia. Under less sure hands than veteran Minnelli's, this could have disintegrated into slapstick but the script by Goodrich and Hackett was witty, intelligent, and incisive. Likable is the key word here. One might have wanted a bit more tension that was honestly motivated but that's a nit-pick. Joan Bennett is excellent as Tracy's wife in her first film for MGM. All supporting roles are well done with special kudos to Olsen and Burke as the parents of the groom. Don Taylor gave up acting in favor of directing in later years with such screen credits as ESCAPE FROM THE PLANET OF THE APES, THE ISLAND OF DR. MOREAU, and DAMIEN, OMEN II. As an actor he appeared in such diverse films as WINGED VICTORY (repeating his Broadway role), THE NAKED CITY, I'LL CRY TOMORROW, and RIDE THE HIGH IRON. In a tiny bit, look for Bondsman Roger Moore. Sequel: FATHER'S LITTLE DIVIDEND.

p, Pandro S. Berman; d, Vincente Minnelli; w, Francis Goodrich, Albert Hackett (based on the novel by Edward Streeter); ph, John Alton; m, Adolph Deutsch; ed, Ferris Webster; art d, Cedric Gibbons, Leonid Vasian; set d, Edwin B. Willis, Keogh Gleason; cos, Helen Rose, Walter Plunkett.

Comedy (PR:AA MPAA:NR)

FATHER STEPS OUT** (1937, Brit.) 64m RKO bw

George Carney (Joe Hardcastle), Dinah Sheridan (Helen Hardcastle), Bruce Seton (Johnnie Miller), Vivienne Chatterton (Mrs. Hardcastle), Basil Langton (Philip Fitzwilliam), Peter Gawthorne (Mr. Fitzwilliam), Zillah Bateman (Mrs. Fitzwilliam), Elizabeth Kent (Joan), Isobel Scaife (Alice).

Some sharp-talking con artists swindle a cheese manufacturer out of a bundle, but his brainy chauffeur helps him make it back by hoodwinking the sharpies. Before this breezy little number is over the chauffeur gets his just desserts when he marries the boss's daughter.

p, George Smith; d, Maclean Rogers; w, Kathleen Butler; ph, Geoffrey Faithfull.

Comedy (PR:A MPAA:NR)

FATHER TAKES A WIFE*½ (1941) 80m RKO bw

Adolphe Menjou (Fredric Osborne, Sr.), Gloria Swanson (Leslie Collier), John Howard (Fredric Osborne, Jr.), Desi Arnaz (Carlos), Helen Broderick (Aunt Julie), Florence Rice (Enid), Neil Hamilton (Vincent Stewart), Grady Sutton (Tailor), George Meader (Henderson), Mary Treen (Secretary), Ruth Dietrich (Miss Patterson), Frank Reicher (Captain), Grant Withers (Judge Waters), Pierre Watkin (Mr. Fowler), Georgie Choper (Agnes, the Maid), Teddy Peterson, Lorna Dunn, Mary Arden (Secretaries), George Murray (Tailor), Frank Jaquet (Innkeeper), Netta Packer (Innkeeper's Wife), Edythe Elliott (Mrs. Plant), William Dudley (Mr. Porter), Lois Austin (Mrs. Sturgis), Jerry Storm (Stage Manager), Cliff Bragdon (Taxi Driver), Dorothy Vernon (Sewing Woman), William Gould (Ship Captain), Cally Cairns (Cigarette Girl), Broderick O'Farrell (Junior's Butler), Ruth Dwyer (Nurse).

In Swanson's return to the screen after a seven-year hiatus, she marries Menjou, a shipping magnate, and they honeymoon aboard a cruise ship. But it's no smooth sail. Stowaway Arnaz plays marriage counselor, and helps the two get on smoother waters. Weak direction, and a script void of humor, sinks this film. RKO's publicity department pulled out all the stops for this one, broadly advertising that "there's glamour on the screen again because Gloria's back." No one seemed to care if the faded flickering image of the silent era with the bee-stung lips returned or not. Swanson blamed the failure for this film on director Hively, later stating that his experience was limited because he "had never been out of Pomona." (The film grossed only a little more than $100,000.)

p, Lee Marcus; d, Jack Hively; w, Dorothy and Herbert Fields; ph, Robert de Grasse; m, Roy Webb; ed, George Hively.

Comedy (PR:A MPAA:NR)

FATHER TAKES THE AIR*½** (1951) 60m MON bw

Raymond Walburn (Henry Latham), Walter Catlett (Mayor Colton), Gary Gray (David Latham), Florence Bates (Minerva Bobbin), Barbara Brown (Mrs. Latham), M'Liss McClure (Barbara Latham), James Brown (Bob), George Nokes (Georgie Colton), Carl Milletaire (Bennett), Tom Dugan (Benny), Billy Bletcher (Haggarly), Maxine Semon (Miss Wells), Don Hicks (Twitchell), Joan Valerie (Blonde).

Walburn's daughter, McClure, takes over a flying school when the owner is recalled for service in the military. Her father and his pal, the mayor, pitch in to help, reliving their flying experiences in WW I. Their tomfoolery ends when a bank robber takes over the plane Walburn and the mayor are flying, but it runs out of gas and the cops nab the crook when the plane crash lands. Light stuff but well done. (See HENRY LATHAM series, Index.)

p, Peter Scully; d, Frank McDonald; w, D.D. Beauchamp; ph, William Sickner; ed, Carlton Sand.

Comedy (PR:A MPAA:NR)

FATHER WAS A FULLBACK★★½   (1949) 84m FOX bw

Fred MacMurray (George Cooper), Maureen O'Hara (Elizabeth Cooper), Betty Lynn (Connie Cooper), Rudy Vallee (Mr. Jessop), Thelma Ritter (Geraldine), Natalie Wood (Ellen Cooper), James [Jim] Backus (Prof. Sullivan), Richard Tyler (Joe Burch), Buddy Martin (Cheerleader), Mickey McCardle (Jones), John McKee (Cy), Charles J. Flynn (Policeman), William Self (Willie), Joe Haworth (Reporter), Gwenn Fields (Daphne), Gilbert Barnett (Stinky Parker), Tommy Bernard (Delivery Boy), Mike Mahoney (Sailor), Tom Hanlon (Radio Announcer), Pat Kane (Bellhop), Forbes Murray (College President), Fred Dale, Lee MacGregor (Cheerleaders), Don Hicks (Bill), Wilson Wood, Rodney Bell, Don Barclay (Grandstand Coaches), Bill Radobich (Football Player), Harry Carter, Bob Adler (Grandstand Bits), Bob Patten (Manager), Bess Flowers (Woman), Louise Lorimer (Mrs. Jones), Ruth Clifford (Neighbor).

MacMurray is the football coach of a losing state college team, bringing the alumni and administration down on his back. At home, he has two daughters with growing pains who cause dad problems. O'Hara is the wife and mother who helps her husband iron out the problems. MacMurray isn't able to produce the winning game the alumni wants, but he sees to it that his teen-age daughter, Lynn, gets a boy friend. A light, surprisingly human comedy.

p, Fred Kohlmar; d, John M. Stahl; w, Aleen Leslie, Casey Robinson, Mary Loos, Richard Sale (based on a play by Clifford Goldsmith); ph, Lloyd Ahern; m, Cyril Mockridge; ed, J. Watson Webb, Jr.; md, Lionel Newman; art d, Lyle Wheeler, Chester Gore; set d, Thomas Little, Stuart Reiss; cos, Kay Nelson; spec eff, Fred Sersen.

Comedy   **(PR:A MPAA:NR)**

FATHERS AND SONS★★   (1960, USSR) 100m Lenfilm/Artkino c

Victor Avdiushko (Yevgeni Bazarov), Alla Larionova (Anna Sergeyevna Odintsova), Eduard Martsevich (Arkadi Kirsonov), Alexei Konsovsky (Nikolai Petrovich Kirsonov), Bruno Freindlich (Pavel Petrovich Kirsonov), Nikolai Sergeyev (Vasili Ivanovich Bazarov), Yekaterina Alexandrovskaya (Arina Vailievna Kirsonov), Isolda Izvitskaya (Fenechka).

A Russsian adaptation of the classic Ivan Turgenev novel about fathers and sons and their widely divergent values in a changing world. Avdiushko is the central character, a nihilistic young doctor with modern ideas, who is stuck in a Russian hinterland hardly out of the middle ages. Martsevich is the hero's best friend, scion of an aristocratic family determined to defend its privileges. Largely static, filled with long speeches in Russian, the film works better in its English subtitles, on the level of simple reading matter, than it does as an entertaining feature film. (In Russian; English subtitles.)

p&d, Adolph Bergunker, Natalia Rashevskaya; w, Alexander Vitov, Rashevskaya (based on the novel Fathers and Sons by Ivan Turgenev); m, V. Pushkov.

Drama   **(PR:A MPAA:NR)**

FATHER'S DILEMMA★★★   (1952, Ital.) 88m Franco-London bw

Aldo Fabrizi (Mr. Carloni), Gaby Morlay (Mrs. Carloni), Adrianna Mazzotti (Carloni's Daughter), Ludmilla Dudarova (The Pretty Neighbor), Enrico Viarisio (Man in the Derby), Jean Tissier (Man in the Taxi), Lucien Baroux (The Archbishop), Laura Gazzolo (Carloni's Maid), Max Elloy (Limping Man), Ernesto Almirante (Italian Patriot).

An Italian comedy and an award winner at the 1950 Venice Film Festival. Fabrizi, the priest in OPEN CITY, is a father searching for his daughter's communion dress. The hunt through the city holds the majority of laughs. He's harassed by a traffic cop, his car breaks down, and he can't get a taxi. Finding the dress, he takes a bus, ends up in a fight, and ruins the dress. Fabrizi tries to buy a neighbor girl's dress and pleads to have the communion time pushed back. Unknown to him, his daughter already has a new dress.

p, Salvo D'Angelo; d, Alessandro Blasetti; w, Cesare Zavattini; ph, Mario Craveri; m, B. Gigognini.

Comedy   **(PR:A MPAA:NR)**

FATHER'S DOING FINE★★   (1952, Brit.) 83m Marble Arch/ABP c

Richard Attenborough (Dougall), Heather Thatcher (Lady Buckering), Noel Purcell (Shaughnessy), George Thorpe (Dr. Drew), Diane Hart (Doreen), Susan Stephen (Bicky), Mary Germaine (Gerda), Virginia McKenna (Catherine), Jack Watling (Clifford Magill), Peter Hammond (Roly), Brain Worth (Wilfred), Sidney James (Taxi Driver), Ambrosine Phillpotts, Harry Locke, Jonathan Field, Wensley Pithey.

Fast moving, barely plotted comedy centers on eccentric widow Thatcher and her four equally daft daughters coping with a string of comic complications. Attenborough is the nervous husband of one pregnant daughter. Unpretentious entertainment.

p, Victor Skutezky; d, Henry Cass; w, Anne Burnaby (based on the play "Little Lambs Eat Ivy" by Noel Langley); ph, Erwin Hillier (Technicolor).

Comedy   **(PR:A MPAA:NR)**

FATHER'S LITTLE DIVIDEND★★★   (1951) 82m MGM bw

Spencer Tracy (Stanley Banks), Joan Bennett (Ellie Banks), Elizabeth Taylor (Kay Dunstan), Don Taylor (Buckley Dunstan), Billie Burke (Doris Dunstan), Moroni Olsen (Herbert Dunstan), Richard Rober (Police Sergeant), Marietta Canty (Delilah), Rusty Tamblyn (Tommy Banks), Tom Irish (Ben Banks), Hayden Rorke (Dr. Andrew Nordell), Paul Harvey (Rev. Galsworthy), Frank Faylen (Policeman), Beverly Thompson (Nurse), Dabbs Greer (Taxi Driver), Robert B. Williams (Officer), Frank Sully (Diaper Man), James Menzies (Mike), Thomas Menzies (Red), Harry Hines (Old Man), Nancy Valentine, Wendy Waldron (Bridesmaids), Lon Poff (Elderly Man on Porch), George Bruggeman (Gym Instructor), Donald Clark (The Dividend).

A rare Hollywood occurence took place with this movie; it was that most unusual item, a sequel that is almost as good as the original. Everyone reprises in this; the stars, the writers, the director, and the producer, everyone but the music writer. This time, Tracy seems to have it made. His daughter is married, his two sons, Tamblyn and Irish, are at school, and now he can settle down with wife Bennett and they can enjoy each other's company. Then Taylor announces that she is pregnant and Tracy goes through the roof. He does not approve of such a quick family but eventually accepts the inevitability of the event. The usual problems evolve between the young couple as well as the two prospective sets of grandparents and the funniest piece is when the grandson (Donald Clark) erupts in squalls of tears whenever Tracy gets near him. Hollywood loves nothing better than putting a star next to a baby (Cooper, Crosby, and even Grant have all been placed in this scene-stealing predicament) and Tracy makes the best of it as he baby-talks the child and becomes the adoring grandpa he swore he'd never be. Taylor was divorcing her first husband (hotel heir Nicky Hilton) at the time and the resultant publicity helped the picture's grosses. Goodrich and Hackett do their usual splendid job making the most of a thin story line and filling it out with good situations and fast, funny dialog. They were a very versatile husband-wife screenwriting team when one considers they also wrote the screenplays for THE DIARY OF ANNE FRANK, A CERTAIN SMILE, SEVEN BRIDES FOR SEVEN BROTHERS, LADY IN THE DARK, and EASTER PARADE, among their many credits. Hackett, the son of actress Florence Hackett and brother of actor Raymond Hackett, is nine years younger than wife Goodrich, whose second husband (Hackett is her third) was historian Hendrik Willem Van Loon. Sequel to FATHER OF THE BRIDE.

p, Pandro S. Berman; d, Vincente Minnelli; w, Francis Goodrich, Albert Hackett (based on characters created by Edward Streeter); ph, John Alton; m, Albert Sendrey; ed, Ferris Webster; md, Georgie Stoll; art d, Cedric Gibbons, Leonid Vasian; set d, Edwin Willis, Keogh Gleason; cos, Helen Rose.

Comedy   Cas.   **(PR:AA MPAA:NR)**

FATHER'S SON★★   (1931) 76m WB-FN bw

Leon Janney (Bill Emory), Lewis Stone (William Emory), Irene Rich (Ruth Emory), John Halliday (Dr. Franklin), Robert Dandridge, George Reed, Mickey Bennett, Gertrude Howard, Bertha Mann, Grover Liggon.

Janney is a troublesome youngster, and his father, Stone, gets most of the grief. Rich is his understanding mother, and Halliday is the doctor who befriends the boy and brings him back home when he runs away. Typical adventures that Booth Tarkington (Penrod) puts his boys through. Thoroughly enjoyable.

d, William Beaudine; w, Hope Loring (based on a story "Old Fathers and Young Sons" by Booth Tarkington); ph, Art Miller.

Drama   **(PR:A MPAA:NR)**

FATHER'S SON★   (1941) 57m WB bw

John Litel (William Emory), Frieda Inescort (Ruth Emory), Billy Dawson (Bill Emory), Christian Rub (Lunk Nelson), Bernice Pilot (Della), Phillip Hurlie (Vestibule), Sammy McKim (Junior Stewart), Sonny Bupp (Berrien Sweeney), Scotty Beckett (Danny), Myra Marsh (Mrs. Stewart), John Dilson (Tex), George Lloyd (Gus), Inez Gay (Mrs. Sweeney).

A poor remake of the 1931 film adaptation of Booth Tarkington's story. Litel and Inescort are the parents of a mischievous young boy, Dawson. Through his pranks, the boy splits up his parents. He gets them back together by faking his own kidnaping.

d, D. Ross Lederman; w, Fred Niblo, Jr. (adapted from a story by Booth Tarkington); ph, Allen G. Siegler; ed, Frank Magee.

Drama   **(PR:A MPAA:NR)**

FATHER'S WILD GAME★½   (1950) 61m MON bw

Raymond Walburn (Henry Latham), Walter Catlett (Mayor Colton), Gary Gray (David Latham), Barbara Brown (Mrs. Latham), M'liss McClure (Barbara Latham), George Nokes (Georgie Colton), Jane Darwell, Fred Libby, Roscoe Ates, Ralph Sanford, Emmett Vogan, Maxine Semon, Doris Kemper, Ann Tyrell.

Another entry in Walburn's series finds him again the cheapskate, taking up hunting rather than pay the rising prices at the butcher shop. Nothing special here except another chance to see a professional funnyman in action. (See HENRY LATHAM series, Index.)

p, Peter Scully; d, Herbert I. Leeds; w, D.D. Beachamp (based on the short story "A Hunting We Will Go" by Beauchamp); ph, Karl Struss; ed, Carlo Lodato; md, Edward Kay; art d, David Milton.

Comedy   **(PR:A MPAA:NR)**

FATHOM★   (1967) 104m FOX c

Tony Franciosa (Peter Merriweather), Raquel Welch (Fathom Harvill), Ronald Fraser (Douglas Campbell), Greta Chi (Jo-May Soon), Richard Briers (Timothy), Tom Adams (Mike), Clive Revill (Mr. Trivers), Reg Lye (Mr. Trivers), Ann Lancaster (Mrs. Trivers), Elizabeth Ercy (Ulla), Tutte Lemkow (Mehmed).

A foreign agent spoof with Welch a parachutist who is hired to help find a nuclear triggering device lost in the Mediterranean. In Spain, she gets tangled up with "Chinese agent" Franciosa, but he turns out to be a detective, and the A-device is actually priceless jewelry stolen in China. A confusing little story, not helped along by a problem of identities as to who is a good guy, and who is bad.

p, John Kohn; d, Leslie H. Martinson; w, Lorenzo Semple, Jr. (based on the novel by Larry Forrester); ph, Douglas Slocombe (CinemaScope, DeLuxe Color); m, John Dankworth; ed, Max Benedict; art d, Maurice Carter; set d, Alan Cassie; m/l, "Theme From Fathom," Dankworth.

Action/Adventure   **(PR:A MPAA:NR)**

FATSO* (1980) 94m Brooksfilms/FOX bw

Dom DeLuise *(Dominick DiNapoli)*, Anne Bancroft *(Antoinette)*, Ron Carey *(Frankie)*, Candice Azzara *(Lydia)*, Michael Lombard *(Charlie)*, Sal Viscuso *(Vito)*, Delia Salvi *(Ida Rendino)*, Robert Costanzo *(Johnny)*, Estelle Riener *(Mrs. Goodman)*, Richard Karron *(Sonny)*.

DeLuise and Bancroft are two overweight New Yorkers trying to lose their fat. They are members of the Chubby Checkers, whose members make sure their fellow fat fighters have no food close to their mouths. The film is thin on genuine humor. It marked the first picture directed and written by the talented actress and former dancer Bancroft.

p, Stuart Cornfield; d&w, Anne Bancroft; ph, Brianne Murphy (DeLuxe Color); m, Joe Renzetti; ed, Glenn Farr; prod d, Peter Wooley; set d, Linda DeScenna; cos, Patricia Norris.

Comedy **(PR:A MPAA:PG)**

FATTY FINN** (1980, Aus.) 91m Children's Film/Hoyts c

Ben Oxenbould *(Fatty Finn)*, Bert Newton *(Mr. Finn)*, Noni Hazelhurst *(Mrs. Finn)*, Gerard Kennedy *(Tiger Murphy)*, Greg Kelly *(Bruiser Murphy)*, Lorraine Bayly *(Maggie McGrath)*, Henri Szeps *(Mr. Zilch)*, Frank Wilson *(Lord Mayor)*, Peter Carroll *(Teacher)*, Ross Higgins *(Radio Announcer)*.

A popular Australian comic strip is the inspiration for this limited appeal item. Oxenbould is the title pudge, caught in the middle of a street gang war in Depression-era Sydney. Mostly dull except to those familiar with the cartoon, and that audience is almost entirely Down Under.

p, Brian Rosen; d, Maurice Murphy; w, Bob Ellis, Chris McGill (based on an idea by Ellis); ph, John Seale (Eastmancolor); m, Graham Bond, Rory O'Donohue; ed, Bob Gibson.

Comedy **(PR:A-C MPAA:NR)**

FAUSSES INGENUES (SEE: RED LIPS, 1964, Fr./Ital.)

FAUST½** (1963, Ger.) 121m Divina/Walter Traut c

Will Quadflieg *(Faust)*, Gustaf Grundgens *(Mephisto)*, Ella Buchi *(Gretchen)*, Elisabeth Flickenschildt *(Marthe)*, Hermann Schomberg *(Theater Director)*, Eduard Marks *(Wagner)*, Max Eckard *(Valentin)*, Uwe Friedrichsen *(Pupil)*, Heinz Reincke *(Frosch)*, Hans Irle *(Altmayer)*, F.C. Beckhaus *(Brander)*, K.H. Wupper *(Siebel)*, Heidi Leupolt, Gustl Busch.

Another filmed performance of Johann Wolfgang von Goethe's 1808 classic drama about the old scholar who yearns to comprehend all knowledge and experience, but finds that to do so he must sell his soul to the devil. Filmed during a performance at the Hamburg Deutsches Schauspielhaus, directed by Gustaf Grundgens.

d, Peter Gorski (based on Johann Wolfgang von Goethe's drama); ph, Gunther Anders; m, Mark Lothar; ed, Walter Boos; art d, Werner Achmann; set d, Theo Otto; cos, Otto, Claudia Herberg.

Drama **(PR:A MPAA:NR)**

FAUST* (1964) 100m Kalmer bw

Robert Towner *(Faust)*, Judy Peters *(Margaret)*, Roban Cody *(Bolus)*.

A modern version of Goethe's *Faust*, with Towner as a young magician who wants to perform real magic, not illusions. Mephistopheles is a psychiatrist, Cody, who makes the legendary deal with Faust. A low-budget mess that couldn't afford actors who knew their craft.

p, Calvin Floyd; d&w, Michael Suman; ph, Tony Forsberg; m, Gordon Zahler.

Drama **(PR:A MPAA:NR)**

FBI CODE 98* (1964) 94m WB bw

Jack Kelly *(Robert P. Cannon)*, Ray Danton *(Fred Vitale)*, Andrew Duggan *(Alan W. Nichols)*, Phillip Carey *(Inspector Leroy Gifford)*, William Reynolds *(Special Agent Edward P. Fox)*, Peggy McCay *(Deborah Cannon)*, Kathleen Crowley *(Marian Nichols)*, Merry Anders *(Grace McLean)*, Jack Cassidy *(Walter Macklin)*, Vaughn Taylor *(Joseph Petersen)*, Eddie Ryder *(Lloyd Kinsel)*, Ken Lynch *(SAC Gibson White)*, Charles Cooper *(Special Agent Bernard Lyons)*, Paul Comi *(Special Agent Philip Vaccaro)*, Robert Hogan *(Timothy Farrell)*, Laura Shelton *(Anita Davidson)*, Robert Ridgely *(Carl Rush)*, Francis De Sales *(Assistant Director)*, William Quinn *(Special Agent Alan Woodward)*, Ross Elliott *(Special Agent Vernon Lockhart)*, William Woodson *(Narrator)*.

Originally intended as a TV special, this film would not have fared any better there. Pure FBI propaganda with a narration that goes on interminably about the Bureau's successful techniques. Agents track down an angered employee of an electronics company, who likes to plant bombs. The biggest bomb is the film itself.

p, Stanley Niss; d, Leslie H. Martinson; w, Niss (based on the story "Headquarters: FBI" by Niss); ph, Robert Hoffman; m, Max Steiner; ed, Leo H. Shreve; art d, William Campbell; set d, William Stevens.

Crime **(PR:A MPAA:NR)**

FBI CONTRO DR. MABUSE (SEE: RETURN OF DR. MABUSE, THE, 1961, Fr./Ital./Ger.)

FBI GIRL*½ (1951) 74m Lippert bw

Cesar Romero *(Glen Stedman)*, George Brent *(Jeff Donley)*, Audrey Totter *(Shirley Wayne)*, Tom Drake *(Carl Chercourt)*, Raymond Burr *(Blake)*, Raymond Greenleaf *(Gov. Owen Grisby)*, Tom Noonan, Pete Marshall *(Television Act)*, Margia Dean *(Natalie Craig)*, Alexander Pope *(George Denton)*, Richard Monoham *(Donald)*, Don Garner *(Paul Craig)*, Jan Kayne *(Doris)*, Walter Coy *(Priest)*, Byron Foulger *(Morgue Attendant)*, Joel Marston *(Hotel Clerk)*, Marie Blake *(Landlady)*.

The FBI captures a murderer and breaks up a crime ring. Totter is the FBI girl, working in the identification division. Romero and Brent use her to capture killer Burr. All the technology of the time is used to catch the criminals.

p&d, William Berke; w, Richard Landau, Dwight Babcock (based on a story by Rupert Hughes); ph, Jack Greenhaigh; m, Darrell Calker; ed, Phil Cahn; art d, F. Paul Sylos.

Crime **(PR:A MPAA:NR)**

FBI STORY, THE*** (1959) 149m WB c

James Stewart *(Chip Hardesty)*, Vera Miles *(Lucy Hardesty)*, Murray Hamilton *(Sam Crandall)*, Larry Pennell *(George Crandall)*, Nick Adams *(John Graham)*, Diane Jergens *(Jennie as an Adult)*, Jean Willes *(Anna Sage)*, Joyce Taylor *(Anne as an Adult)*, Victor Millan *(Mario)*, Parley Baer *(Harry Dakins)*, Fay Roope *(McCutcheon)*, Ed Prentiss *(U.S. Marshal)*, Robert Gist *(Medicine Salesman)*, Buzz Martin *(Mike as an Adult)*, Kenneth Mayer *(Casket Salesman)*, Paul Genge *(Suspect)*, Ann Doran *(Mrs. Ballard)*, Forest Taylor *(Wedding Minister)*, Scott Peters *(John Dillinger)*, William Phipps *(Baby Face Nelson)*.

Good production values and a solid performance by Stewart lift this overlong film out of the doldrums, although it is essentially an FBI propaganda film, extolling the virtues of one man's public image, the despotic J. Edgar Hoover, through the heroic actions of his underlings. The film opens with Stewart slaving away in a backwater bureau office in 1924. (It was then known as the Bureau of Investigation, was poorly organized, and run haphazardly by one-time private eye, William J. Burns.) His wife, Miles, wants Stewart to quit his job and become a lawyer so they can better themselves. Stewart goes to Washington, D.C., to resign, but, upon meeting the new chief, Hoover, and being inspired by his plans for a modern FBI, he decides to stay with the organization. While he and Miles produce children and move from one bureau to another, Stewart battles the forces of evil in episodic segments, first taking on the sinister Ku Klu Klan in the South during the late 1920s, then solving a brutal murder of an Osage Indian by sharpers bilking oil rights during the oil boom in Oklahoma. All of the infamous gangsters of the early 1930s—Ma Barker and her sons, Baby Face Nelson (who shoots Stewart's partner, Hamilton), and John Dillinger are paraded before the viewer in brief shootouts. Stewart next deals with Nazi agents during WW II and then Communist spies during the Cold War period, while struggling to maintain his family; at one point Miles leaves him but returns, realizing that he is dedicated to his work. It's a good portrait of the kind of unsung agent who did the dirty work for Hoover, and there were many of these truly heroic men, even though the facts are glossed over, or even changed to suit the story line. LeRoy, an old hand at crime-and-cops films (I AM A FUGITIVE FROM A CHAIN GANG, 1932), does a creditable job rehashing familiar territory, and Steiner's score is top notch. A tableau of old myths worth watching if only for the visual rewards.

p&d, Mervyn LeRoy; w, Richard L. Breen, John Twist (based on the book by Don Whitehead); ph, Joseph Biroc (Technicolor); m, Max Steiner; ed, Philip W. Anderson; art d, John Beckman; set d, Ralph S. Hurst; cos, Adele Palmer; makeup, Gordon Bau.

Crime **(PR:C MPAA:NR)**

FEAR*** (1946) 68m MON bw (AKA: SUSPENSE)

Warren William *(Capt. Burke)*, Anne Gwynne *(Eileen)*, Peter Cookson *(Larry Crain)*, James Cardwell *(Ben)*, Nestor Paiva *(Schaefer)*, Francis Pierlot *(Prof. Morton Stanley)*, Johnny Strong *(John)*, William Moss *(Al)*, Darren McGavin *(Chuck)*, Henry Clay *(Steve)*, Almira Sessions *(Mrs. Williams)*, Ernie Adams *(Painter)*, Charles Calvert *(Doc)*, Fairfax Burger *(Magician)*, Cedric Stevens *(Man)*, Bubbles Hecht *(Woman)*, Lee Lasses White *(Janitor)*, Ken Broeker *(Uniformed Officer)*, Carl Leviness *(Tailor)*, Dewey Robinson *(Bartender)*, Brick Sullivan *(Policeman)*, Jack Richardson, Winnie Nard, Phyllis Ayres, Hy Jason *(Pedestrians)*, Chester Conklin *(Switchman)*.

A clever little thriller where Cookson, a medical student running out of money, pawns his last few possessions with Pierlot, one of his professors, a mean-minded, avaricious individual, to pay his tuition. When he learns that his small scholarship has been cut off, Cookson comes to believe that Pierlot is behind it all, and kills the professor. Cookson is sloppy in his work and forgets to retrieve his money, leaving clues behind for police. A short time later he meets Gwynne and falls in love. Then he earns $1,000 from an academic magazine publishing his article which advocates supremacy of the intellect. The school's faculty is so impressed that Cookson's scholarship is reinstated. William, heading the detectives investigating Pierlot's murder, begins to suspect Cookson, particularly after the young man offers to help police and unwittingly aids them by dropping hints about the killer's identity. When William turns the spotlight on Cookson, the student accuses him of persecuting him. Paranoid, Cookson confesses the crime to sweetheart Gwynne but before he turns himself in, William tells him that another has admitted killing Pierlot. Cookson prepares to flee with Gwynne but is run over by a car and killed. Just at that moment, Cookson wakes up; the entire story has been a nightmare. Pierlot, the victim in his fearful dream, arrives to advance him money and inform him that he has persuaded the school to continue his scholarship. Reality is proved better than the machinations of the subconscious when, a few minutes later, Cookson meets the girl of his dream, Gwynne, and begins romancing her for real. Though much is drawn for this story from the evil exploits of Richard Loeb who murdered Bobbie Franks in Chicago in 1924 with Nathan Leopold, the twists and turns of this well-written and directed film will keep the viewer fascinated. All the production values are above standard, especially for Poverty Row's Monogram Studios.

p, Lindsley Parsons; d, Alfred Zeisler; w, Zeisler, Dennis Cooper; ph, Jackson Rose; ed, Ace Herman; art d, Dave Milton; set d, Charles Thompson, Vin Taylor; spec eff, Bob Clark.

Crime Drama **(PR:C MPAA:NR)**

FEAR*** (1956, Ger.) 91m Minerva Films bw (ANGST)

Ingrid Bergman (*Irene Wagner*), Mathias Wieman (*Professor Wagner*), Kurt Kreuger (*Heinz Baumann*), Elsie Aulinger (*Housekeeper*).

Bergman is the bored wife of factory owner Wiemann. Though she still has great affection for her husband, she takes a lover. But the lover's former mistress appears and begins blackmailing Bergman. Rather than risk scandal, Bergman pays the mistress large sums of money. It is finally revealed that Wiemann is behind the blackmail. Bergman tries suicide but her husband stops her and the two reconcile. One of Rossellini's lesser works, though Bergman is magnificent, keeping the film from turning into melodrama. Her first German-language picture in 16 years.

p. Jochen Genzow; d, Roberto Rossellini; w, Rossellini, Sergio Amidei, Franz Graf Treuberg (from the novel *Der Angst* by Stefan Zweig); ph, Peter Heller; m, Renzo Rossellini.

Drama **Cas.** **(PR:O MPAA:NR)**

FEAR, THE** (1967, Gr.) 102m Trans-Lux bw (HO FOVOS)

Elli Fotiou (*Chryssa*), Elena Nathanael (*Anna*), Mary Chronopoulou (*Mrs. Kanalis*), Anestis Vlachos (*Anestis Kanalis*), Spiros Focas (*Nikos*), Alexis Damianos (*Dimitri Kanalis*).

A grim drama about a disturbed family led by Damianos, a wealthy, middle-aged farmer who ignores his second wife for his gambling and whoring habits. No better is his son, Vlachos, a sexually perverted boy whose deviate attentions become focused on the family's deaf-mute maid, Fotiou. His stepsister, Nathanael, returns home from school hoping to marry a young engineer, Focas, but his family is despised by Damianos. Unfortunately, Vlachos is driven into a sexual frenzy when he sees Nathanael and Focas make love, which leads him to assault and accidentally kill Fotiou. He tries to hide the body in a hayloft, but it is discovered by the family. Damianos decides to sink the corpse into the lake and tell the police that the maid has disappeared. Nathanael confronts her father with her suspicions and blackmails him into allowing the marriage. As the family celebrates the union, a fisherman discovers the body of the maid.

p, Theophanis A. Damaskinos, Viktor G. Michaelides; d&w, Kostas Manoussakis; ph, Nikos Gardelis; m, Yannis Markopoulos; ed, George Chaoulis.

Crime **(PR:O MPAA:NR)**

FEAR AND DESIRE*** (1953) 68m Kubrick/Joseph Burstyn bw

Frank Silvera (*Mac*), Kenneth Harp (*Lt. Corby*), Paul Mazursky (*Sidney*), Steve Coit (*Fletcher*), Virginia Leith (*Girl*), David Allen (*Narrator*).

Stanley Kubrick's first film, produced when he was 22-years-old on a budget of $40,000. Not only did he produce and direct, but he also shot and edited this story of four soldiers caught behind enemy lines in an abstract war. Trying to move back to their own side, they kill a couple of enemy soldiers and capture a young woman. Mazursky is left to guard her as Silvera, Harp and Coit go to a river to build a raft. Wanting to seduce the girl, Mazursky unties her from a tree, and when she runs away he kills her, then goes insane. Returning from the river, the three soldiers discover an enemy outpost holding a general and his aid. Silvera draws enemy fire as Harp and Coit attack the outpost, kill the general, and the four escape in an enemy plane. Most promising first effort by Kubrick.

p&d, Stanley Kubrick; w, Howard O. Sackler, Kubrick; ph, Kubrick; m, Gerald Fried; ed, Kubrick.

War **(PR:C MPAA:NR)**

FEAR CHAMBER, THE* (1968, US/Mex.) 87m Azteca c (LA CAMARA DEL TERROR)

Boris Karloff, Yerye Beirut, Julissa Santanon, Carlos East.

One of the rarely-seen last efforts of Boris Karloff. His scenes were shot in Los Angeles and then cut into the rest of the film, which was shot in Mexico. Here he plays a scientist who is stricken with a rare disease after experimenting with a "living rock," takes to bed, and is never seen again. His assistants continue his work—whatever it may have been—by taking the blood of young women and feeding it to the rock.

p, Louis Enrique Veragara; d, Juan Ibanez, Jack Hill; w, Hill.

Horror **(PR:C MPAA:NR)**

FEAR EATS THE SOUL*** (1974, Ger.) 94m Tango Film-Filmverlag der Autorn/New Yorker c (AKA: ALI—FEAR EATS THE SOUL)

Brigitte Mira (*Emmi*), El Hedi Ben Salem (*Ali*), Barbara Valentin (*Barbara*), Irm Hermann (*Krista*), Peter Gauhe (*Bruno*), Karl Scheydt (*Albert*), Rainer Werner Fassbinder (*Eugen*), Marquard Bohm (*Gruber*), Walter Sedlmayer (*Angermayer*), Doris Mattes (*Mrs. Angermeyer*), Liselotte Eder (*Mrs. Munchmeyer*), Gusti Kreissl (*Paula*).

Excellent serious drama by the prolific, if short-lived, Fassbinder. Mira is a widowed cleaning lady, lonely and neglected, who begins an affair with a similarly neglected and lonely Moroccan mechanic (Salem). Over the objections of her appalled family and friends, she marries him. No longer lonely, she begins to change, eventually becoming as prejudiced and self-centered as her friends. One of the German director's most thought-provoking films. (In German; English subtitles.)

p,d&w, Rainer Werner Fassbinder; ph, Jurgen Jurges; ed, Thea Eymes.

Drama **(PR:O MPAA:NR)**

FEAR IN THE NIGHT*** (1947) 71m PAR bw

Paul Kelly (*Cliff Herlihy*), De Forest Kelley (*Vince Grayson*), Ann Doran (*Lil Herlihy*), Kay Scott (*Betty Winters*), Robert Emmett Keane (*Lewis Belnap*), Jeff York (*Torrence*), Charles Victor (*Capt. Warner*), Janet Warren (*Mrs. Belnap*), Michael

Harvey (*Bob Clune*), John Harmon (*Mr. Bilyou*), Gladys Blake (*Bank Clerk*), Stanley Farrar (*Patron*), Julia Faye (*Mrs. Tracey-Lytton*), Dick Keane (*Mr. Kern*), Joey Ray (*Contractor*), Chris Drake (*Elevator Operator*), Loyette Thomas (*Waitress*), Jack Collins, Leander de Cordoba (*Men*).

Kelley enters a completely mirrored room, as if sleepwalking, and witnesses a man cutting into a safe with a torch, a woman (Warren) standing over him. The man with the torch turns and attacks Kelley who grabs an electric drill from the woman and drives this into the man's heart, killing him. The woman slips out a door while Kelley drags the body into a closet, slamming the door and locking it, clutching the key and a button from the man's suitcoat, then escapes through another mirrored door. The next morning Kelley awakens with the key and the button in his hand, convinced his terrible experience was real, not a nightmare. He goes to his friend Paul Kelly, a police detective, and explains what happened. Kelly does not believe his friend but humors him by saying he will look into the matter. Later, when Kelly, his wife Doran, accompanied by Kelley and his girl friend Scott, are driving through a storm, they take refuge in a mansion where the mirrored room is found. Its eccentric owner, Keane, gives them shelter. Kelly, after some investigation, comes to believe that his friend indeed has committed a murder but he delays arresting him until he gathers more evidence. Meanwhile, the rich Keane explains that his wife has been killed in an auto accident recently and all attend the funeral. Kelley believes Keane has hypnotized him to produce the murderous dream and re-enters the mirrored room where Keane does hypnotize him, compelling him to write a confession that he has killed Warren to cover up the fact that Keane himself had done the awful deed. But Paul Kelly is wise to the scheme and has wired the mirrored room. Before Kelley can commit suicide, detective Kelly intervenes and pursues Keane, who crashes his own car and dies. The plot is complex and the clues to the real killer unfold slowly and cleverly. Shane directs his own story with a brisk pace and inventive setups. He later remade the film in 1956 as NIGHTMARE but it lacked the verve and suspense of the original.

p, William H. Pine, William C. Thomas; d, Maxwell Shane (based on the short story "Nightmare" by William Irish [Cornell Woolrich]); ph, Jack Greenhalgh; m, Rudy Schrager; ed, Howard Smith; art d, F. Paul Sylos; set d, Elias H. Reif.

Crime/Drama **(PR:C-O MPAA:NR)**

FEAR IN THE NIGHT* (1972, Brit.) 85m Hammer/International c

Peter Cushing (*Michael Carmichael*), Joan Collins (*Molly Carmichael*), Ralph Bates (*Robert Heller*), Judy Geeson (*Peggy Heller*), James Cossins (*Doctor*), Gillian Lind (*Mrs. Beamish*), John Brown (*1st Policeman*), Brian Grellis (*2nd Policeman*).

Cushing is the one-armed headmaster of a private school whose wife, Collins, and a young teacher, Bates, conspire to drive Bates' wife insane so that she will kill Cushing. Far-fetched to say the least. Collins is awful.

p&d, Jimmy Sangster; w, Sangster, Michael Syson; ph, Arthur Grant; ed, Peter Weatherley.

Drama **Cas.** **(PR:C MPAA:R)**

FEAR IS THE KEY** (1973) 105m KLK/PAR c

Barry Newman (*John Talbot*), Suzy Kendall (*Sarah Ruthven*), John Vernon (*Vyland*), Dolph Sweet (*Jablonski*), Ben Kingsley (*Royale*), Ray McAnally (*Ruthven*), Peter Marinker (*Larry*), Elliott Sullivan (*Judge Mollison*), Roland Brand (*Deputy*), Tony Anholt (*FBI Man*).

Newman, a sea salvage expert, witnesses the murder of his wife and son, and follows the police to intercept the killers. To get in cahoots with the criminals, Newman fakes the murder of a cop, and kidnaps Kendall, an oil heiress. He captures his wife's killers in a mini-sub and cuts off their oxygen supply to get a confession. Ben Kingsley, who went on to fame in *GANDHI*, made his film debut in FEAR IS THE KEY and did not work in films until GANDHI.

p, Alan Ladd, Jr., Jay Kanter; d, Michael Tuchner; w, Robert Carrington (adapted from the novel by Alistair MacLean); ph, Alex Thomson (Panavision, Technicolor); m, Roy Budd; ed, Ray Lovejoy; art d, Sidney Cain, Maurice Carter.

Action/Suspense **(PR:C MPAA:NR)**

FEAR NO EVIL** (1981) 99m Avco Embassy c

Stefan Arngrim (*Andrew*), Elizabeth Hoffman (*Mikhail/Margaret Buchanan*), Kathleen Rowe McAllen (*Gabrielle/Hulie*), Frank Birney (*Father Daly*), Daniel Eden (*Tony*), Jack Holland (*Rafael/Father Damon*), Barry Cooper (*Mr. Williams*), Alice Sachs (*Mrs. Williams*), Paul Haber (*Mark*), Roslyn Gugino (*Marie*), Richard Jay Silverthorn (*Lucifer*).

A fantasy horror film about a high school student, Arngrim, who is the Antichrist. An old woman and young girl are angels sent to destroy him. None of them know their missions, and when they finally realize them, mayhem explodes. Arngrim calls up a horde of zombies during a local passion play. An odd, but promising first feature from 27-year-old La Loggia.

p, Frank and Charles M. La Loggia; d&w, Frank La Loggia; ph, Fred Goodich (CFI Color); m, F. La Loggia, David Spear; ed, Edna Ruth Paul.

Horror **Cas.** **(PR:O MPAA:R)**

FEAR NO MORE** (1961) 80m Scaramouche/Sutton bw

Jacques Bergerac (*Paul Colbert*), Mala Powers (*Sharon Carlin*), John Harding (*Milo Seymour*), Helena Nash (*Irene Maddox*), John Baer (*Keith Burgess*), Ann Carroll (*Denise Colbert*), Robert Karnes (*Joe Brady*), Peter Brocco (*Steve Cresca*), Peter Virgo, Jr. (*Duke Maddox*), Gregory Irvin (*Chris Colbert*).

Powers plays a young woman who is framed for murder when she is sent on a train to San Francisco (from Los Angeles) on business by her boss, Harding. She is knocked unconscious in her sleeping compartment, only to waken next to the corpse of a woman who had been sharing the compartment. Police detective Karnes takes Powers off the train, but she escapes and is picked up on the road by Bergerac. The friendly motorist accompanies the distraught woman into her home where she discovers the dead body of her friend Baer, an alcoholic writer whom she had let use her apartment for the weekend. Shaken, she tells Bergerac of the events of the last few hours and admits that she had once been a patient in a mental hospital. Smelling a rat, Bergerac takes Powers back to her boss Harding who denies he even sent her to San Francisco. Eventually it is revealed that Harding had murdered his wife and planted the body with former mental patient Powers so that it would look like she had become a homicidal maniac. Harding kidnaps Powers and takes her to the mountains to kill her (and make it appear to be a suicide), but Bergerac follows and rescues the innocent girl.

p, Bernard Wiesen, Earl Durham; d, Wiesen; w, Robert Bloomfield; ph, Ernest Haller; m, Paul Glass; ed, John Bushelman; art d, Gibson Holley.

Mystery   **(PR:C   MPAA:NR)**

FEAR SHIP, THE*   (1933, Brit.) 66m Associated Sound/PAR bw

Cyril McLaglen (Capt. Petrie), Dorothy Bartlam (Ivy Bywater), Edmund Willard (Jack Arkwright), William Holmes (Capt. Bywater), John Blake (Buckeye), Hal Booth.

McLaglen is a sailor who saves a schooner from disaster and wins the owner's daughter (Bartlam) along the way. Good photography may keep audiences from falling asleep.

p,d,&w, James Steven Edwards (based on the novel The Second Mate by R.F.W. Rees).

Adventure   **(PR:A   MPAA:NR)**

FEAR STRIKES OUT****   (1957) 100m PAR bw

Anthony Perkins (Jimmy Piersall), Karl Malden (John Piersall), Norma Moore (Mary Teevan), Adam Williams (Dr. Brown), Peter J. Votrian (Jimmy Piersall as a Boy), Perry Wilson (Mrs. John Piersall), Dennis McMullen (Phil), Gail Land (Alice), Brian Hutton (Bernie Sherwill), Bart Burns (Joe Cronin), Rand Harper (Radio Announcer), Howard Price (Bill Tracy), George Pembroke (Umpire), Morgan Jones (Sandy Allen), Bing Russell, James McNally, Edward Byrnes, Ralph Montgomery, Robert Victor Stern, June Jocelyn, Wade Cagle, Courtland Shepard, Heather Hopper, Mary Benoit, Don Brodie, Richard Bull, Gere Craft, John Benson, Eric Alden, Don McGuire, Marilyn Malloy.

Perkins portrays Jimmy Piersall in a true story about a young man relentlessly pushed by his father to make it into major league baseball. When he does make the Boston Red Sox, he breaks down. He is admitted to Westborough State Hospital, and gradually recovers under the supervision of Williams and goes back to play the outfield for the Red Sox, superlatively. Perkins and Malden are also superlative playing as father and son in this compelling film.

p, Alan Pakula; d, Robert Mulligan; w, Ted Berkman, Raphael Blau (based on the autobiography by James A. Piersall, with Albert S. Hirshberg); ph, Haskell Boggs; m, Elmer Bernstein; ed, Aaron Stell; c, Edith Head; spec eff, John B. Fulton.

Drama   **(PR:C   MPAA:NR)**

FEARLESS FAGAN***   (1952) 79m MGM bw

Janet Leigh (Abby Ames), Carleton Carpenter (Pvt. Floyd Hilston), Keenan Wynn (Sgt. Kellwin), Richard Anderson (Capt. Daniels), Ellen Corby (Mrs. Ardley), Barbara Ruick (Nurse), John Call (Mr. Ardley), Robert Burton (Owen Gillman), Wilton Graff (Col. Horne), Parley Baer (Emil Tauchnitz), Jonathan Cott (Cpl. Geft).

Carpenter is a young man, who is drafted into the army. He has a problem, a pet lion that has grown up with him; the two have a very strong bond. Not wanting to sell his pet to a cruel circus trainer, Carpenter asks his sergeant, Wynn, to help him find Fagan a home. The sergeant thinks it's a joke until the lion gets out of its cage and the Army is forced to send out search parties for it. With the help of Army publicity, the soldier is able to find a good home for his pet. But, Fagan gets out of his cage again and causes havoc during troop maneuvers. An enjoyable family comedy, intelligently written, and well paced.

p, Edwin H. Knopf; d, Stanley Donen; w, Charles Lederer (adapted by Frederick Hazlitt Brennan from a story by Sidney Franklin, Jr., and Eldon W. Griffiths); ph, Harold Lipstein; ed, George White; spec eff, A. Arnold Gillespie.

Comedy   **(PR:AA   MPAA:NR)**

FEARLESS FRANK**½   (1967) 83m Jericho Film/AIP c
                                                      (AKA: FRANK'S GREATEST ADVENTURE)

Jon Voight (Frank/False Frank)), Monique Van Vooren (Plethora), Severn Darden (Doctor/Claude), Joan Darling (Lois), Lou Gilbert (Boss), Ben Carruthers (The Cat), David Steinberg (The Rat), Ken Nordine (The Stranger), Nelson Algren (Needles), David Fisher (Screwnose), Anthony Holland (Alfred).

An interesting comedy, independently made in Chicago, that marked Phil Kaufman's first solo effort as director. He'd previously co-directed the offbeat GOLDSTEIN, another independently produced Chicago effort. Utilizing the talents of several Second City comic actors, it's the story of Voight, a rube, who comes to Chicago, gets shot by some mobsters, and awakens to find that he has the powers of Superman. Sexy Van Vooren spoofs the bombshells of gangster movies and Darden does the first of what was to be many mad scientists on his resume. Joan Darling, who has since become a successful TV director after an improvisational career that also saw her as part of "The Premise" (the same group that spawned director James Frawley—THE MUPPET MOVIE (1979)), is cute but doesn't get much of a chance to stretch herself. Author Nelson Algren (THE MAN WITH THE GOLDEN ARM (1955) among others) does well as Needles. An impressive first movie for many of the talents involved and the expression "better luck, next time" really came to pass in many of the careers. Ben Carruthers, who got his start understudying Lou Gossett in Broadway's "Take A Giant Step" in the 1950s, is excellent as The Cat. David Steinberg proves he has no talent as The Rat. Technical credits are not as good as the intentions. With some more money, this could have been a big winner in 1967.

p,d,&w, Phil Kaufman; ph, Bill Butler (Movielab Color); m, Meyer Kupferman; ed, Aram Boyajian, Luke Bennett.

Satire   **(PR:A-C   MPAA:G)**

FEARLESS VAMPIRE KILLERS, OR PARDON ME BUT YOUR TEETH ARE IN MY NECK, THE***½   (1967) 91m MGM c
                                                      (GB: DANCE OF THE VAMPIRES)

Jack MacGowran (Prof. Abronsius), Roman Polanski (Alfred), Alfie Bass (Shagal), Jessie Robins (Mrs. Shagal), Sharon Tate (Sarah Shagal), Ferdy Mayne (Count Von Krolock), Iain Quarrier (Herbert Von Krolock), Terry Downes (Koukol), Fiona Lewis (Maid), Ronald Lacey (Idiot), Sydney Bromley (Driver), Andreas Malandrinos, Otto Di Amant, Matthew Walters (Woodcutters).

Polanski's spoof on the vampire legend has the director as the assistant of an old vampire hunter, MacGowran. The pair goes to Slovania where a ball for a colony of vampires is being held. There is a Jewish vampire, who isn't affected by a crucifix, a hunchback vampire, and a homosexual vampire. Tate is kidnapped by the Count, and is saved by Polanski and MacGowran. Unknown to them, she's a vampire and gives the bite to Polanski. Shot in the Italian Alps, the cinematography is striking. MGM, against Polanski's wishes, cut 20 minutes out and put in an animated title sequence.

p, Gene Gutowski; d, Roman Polanski; w, Gerard Brach, Polanski; ph, Douglas Slocombe; m, Christopher Komeda; ed, Alastair McIntyre; ch, Tutte Lemkow.

Comedy   **(PR:C   MPAA:NR)**

FEARMAKERS, THE***   (1958) 83m UA bw

Dana Andrews (Alan Eaton), Dick Foran (Jim McGinnis), Mel Torme (Barney Bond), Marilee Earle (Lorraine Dennis), Kelly Thordsen (Harold Loder), Joel Marsion (Rodney Hillyer), Veda Ann Borg (Vivian Loder), Robert Fortier (Col. Buchane), Roy Gordon (Senator Walder).

Andrews is a Korean War vet who had been brainwashed as a prisoner of war. Arriving back home in Washington, D.C., he discovers that his public relations-opinion research firm is being run by communists. His partner was killed in a mysterious accident and his firm is now promoting communist-backed organizations. It is also fixing polls to swing public opinion their way. Tourneur's fresh direction keeps the film from becoming just anti-red propaganda.

p, Martin Lancer; d, Jacques Tourneur; w, Elliot West, Chris Appley (adapted from a novel by Darwin L. Teilhet); ph, Sam Leavitt; m, Irving Gertz; ed, J.R. Whittridge.

Drama   **(PR:A   MPAA:NR)**

FEAST OF FLESH   (SEE: NIGHT OF THE LIVING DEAD, 1968)

FEATHER, THE*   (1929, Brit.) 88m Strand/UA bw

Jameson Thomas (Roger Dalton), Vera Flory (Mavis Cottrell), Randle Ayrton (Rizzio), Mary Clare (Mrs. Dalton), W. Cronin Wilson (Mr. Cottrell), James Reardon (Quint), Charles Paton (Professor Vivian), Irene Tripod (Mrs. Higgins), Grace Lane (Nun).

Thomas is an insurance agent stuck in a stale relationship who falls for aspiring opera singer Flory. In order to pay for her to take lessons in Rome, he steals money from his insurance firm. A weak romancer more concerned with exploiting its opera soundtrack than with providing a believable situation.

p, Julius Hagen; d,&w, Leslie Hiscott (based on a novel by C.M. Matheson); ph, Basil Emmott.

Romance   **(PR:A   MPAA:NR)**

FEATHER IN HER HAT, A*½   (1935) 72m COL bw

Pauline Lord (Clarissa Phipps), Basil Rathbone (Capt. Courtney), Louis Hayward (Richard Orland), Billie Burke (Julia Trent Anders), Wendy Barrie (Pauline Anders), Victor Varconi (Paul Anders), Nydia Westman (Emily Judson), Thurston Hall (Sir Elroyd Joyce), Nana Bryant (Lady Drake), J.M. Kerrigan (Pobjoy), David Niven (Leo Cartwright), Lawrence Grant (Dr. Phillips), Doris Lloyd (Liz Vining), John Rogers (Henry Vining), Leonard Mudie (Orator), Harry Allen (Alf), E. E. Clive (Higgins, Pub Owner), Ottola Nesmith (Susan), Tempe Pigott (Katy), Lois Lindsey (Woman), Leyland Hodgson (Leading Man), Olaf Hytten (Taxi Driver), Doreen Munroe (Mrs. Pobjoy), Gil Perkins (Ticket Taker), Vivian Patterson (Nurse), Wilson Benge, James May (Butchers), Major Sam Harris, Lorimer Johnston (Men).

Lord is a loving mother, who tells her son that he isn't hers. She does this so the boy will be able to climb out of their poor surroundings. He goes on to become a playwright and his mother sells her store to produce his first play. At the end of the film, the mother reveals—surprise—that she lied about her son's birthright. A plodding, unreal melodrama.

p, Everett Riskin; d, Alfred Santell; w, Lawrence Hazard (adapted from a story by I.A.R. Wylie); ph, Joseph Walker; ed, Viola Lawrence.

Drama   **(PR:A   MPAA:NR)**

FEATHER YOUR NEST**   (1937, Brit.) 86m ATP/ABFD bw

George Formby (Willie), Polly Ward (Mary Taylor), Enid Stamp-Taylor (Daphne Randall), Val Rosing (Rex Randall), Davy Burnaby (Sir Martin), Jack Barty (Mr. Chester), Clifford Heatherley (Valet), Frederick Burtwell (Murgatroyd), Ethel Coleridge (Mrs. Taylor), Jimmy Godden (Mr. Higgins), Moore Marriott (Mr. Jenkins), Syd Crossley (Police Constable), Frank Perfitt (Manager), Frederick Piper, Mike Johnson, The Three Rhythm Sisters.

Formby is a clumsy worker at a record factory who accidentally breaks an irreplaceable master disc. To cover up his mistake, he replaces the broken record with one of his own voice. Naturally enough, the record is released and becomes a big hit. Not one of Formby's best films, but mildly enjoyable, nonetheless. One of a number of films American director (and notorious hack) Beaudine made in England in the mid-1930s. Formby sings "Leaning on a Lamppost," which actually did become a hit.

p, Basil Dean; d, William Beaudine; w, Austin Melford, Robert Edmunds, Anthony Kimmins (based on a story by Ivar and Sheila Campbell); ph, Ronald Neame.

Comedy (PR:A MPAA:NR)

FEATHERED SERPENT, THE*½ (1934, Brit.) 72m
GS Enterprises/COL bw

Enid Stamp-Taylor (Ella Crewe), Tom Helmore (Peter Dewin), D.A. Clarke-Smith (Joe Farmer), Moore Marriott (Harry Hugg), Molly Fisher (Daphne Olroyd), Vincent Holman (Inspector Clarke), Evelyn Roberts (Leicester Crewe), Iris Baker (Paula Ricks), O.B. Clarence (George Beale).

Yet another crime drama based on an Edgar Wallace novel, this one has Stamp-Taylor an actress suspected in the murder of a fence. Things look grim for her until reporter Helmore starts looking into the case, soon finding the evidence to prove her innocent.

p, A. George Smith; d, Maclean Rogers; w, Rogers, Kathleen Butler (based on a novel by Edgar Wallace); ph, Geoffrey Faithfull.

Crime (PR:A MPAA:NR)

FEATHERED SERPENT, THE (1948) 68m MON bw

Roland Winters (Charlie Chan), Keye Luke (Lee Chan), Victor Sen Yung (Tommy Chan), Mantan Moreland (Birmingham), Robert Livingston (John Stanley), Martin Garralaga (Pedro), Nils Asther (Prof. Paul Evans), Carol Forman (Sonia Cabot), Beverly Jons (Joan Farnsworth), George J. Lewis (Capt. Juan), Leslie Dennison (Prof. Farnsworth), Jay Silverheels (Diego), Juan Duvan, Frank Leyva, Milton Ross, Fred Crodova, Erville Alderson, Charles Stevens.

One of the most unrewarding and uninteresting Chan programmers has Charlie solve a series of killings over some priceless antiques. Moreland provides the usual mugging laughs while two Chan offspring, Luke and Yung, play at being their famous father. (See CHARLIE CHAN series, Index.)

p, James S. Burkett; d, William Beaudine; w, Oliver Drake; ph, William Sickner; ed, Ace Herman; md, Edward Kay.

Crime (PR:A MPAA:NR)

FEDERAL AGENT*½ (1936) 60m REP bw

William Boyd (Bob), Charles A. Browne (Mullins), Irene Ware (Helen), George Cooper (Wilson), Lentia Lace (Vilma), Don Alvarado (Recard).

Boyd is a federal agent chasing after foreign spies. Seems they've killed Boyd's friend, and want a new chemical explosive. A tedious crime film entangled in cliches.

d, Sam Newfield; w, Barry Barringer; ph, Harry Forbes; ed, Charles Hunt.

Crime (PR:A MPAA:NR)

FEDERAL AGENT AT LARGE*½ (1950) 60m REP bw

Dorothy Patrick (Solitare), Robert Rockwell (Dr. Ross Carrington), Kent Taylor (Matt Reedy), Estelita Rodriguez (Lopita), Thurston Hall ("Big Bill" Dixon), Frank Puglia (Angelo "Angel" Badillo), Roy Barcroft (Nels Berger), Denver Pyle ("Jumpy" Jordan), Jonathan Hale (Goodwin), Robert Kent (Monahan), Kenneth MacDonald (Captain), Sonia Darrin (Mildred), Frank McFarland (Duke Warren), John McGuire (Customs Officer).

Taylor is a treasury agent trying to break a gold smuggling ring on the Mexican border. They smuggle the gold in Aztec pottery and Taylor goes undercover as a mobster to infiltrate the gang. Patrick is the female gangleader who falls for the T-agent and turns in her gang.

p, Stephan Auer; d, George Blair; w, Albert DeMond; ph, John MacBurnie; m, Stanley Wilson; ed, Arthur Roberts.

Crime (PR:A MPAA:NR)

FEDERAL BULLETS** (1937) 61m MON bw

Milburn Stone (Tommy), Zeffie Tilbury (Mrs. Crippen), Terry Walker (Milly), Selmer Jackson (Harker), William Harrigan (Chief Inspector), Mattie Fain (Barber John), Lyle Moraine (Pete), Warner Richmond (Burke), Eddie Phillips (Durkin), Betty Compson (Sue), Helen MacKellar (Mrs. Thompson), John Merton (Manny Goe).

The FBI cracks a fake philanthropic organization which is in actuality a front for a crime ring headed by a tough old lady, Tilbury. A lot of gun battles and action in this crime film.

p, Lon Young; d, Karl Brown; w, Brown (adapted from a story by Maj. George F. Eliot); ph, Gilbert Warrenton.

Crime (PR:A MPAA:NR)

FEDERAL FUGITIVES*½ (1941) 63m PRC bw

Neil Hamilton (Capt. Madison), Doris Day (Rita), Victor Varconi (Dr. Kaskell), Charles Wilson (Bruce Lane), George Carleton (Henry Gregory), Lyle Latell (Chuck), Frank Shannon (Col. Hammond), Betty Blythe (Marcia), Gerald Oliver Smith (Hobbs), Frank Moran (Ox).

Hamilton is on the trail of war-time saboteurs. The foreign spies want to make sure the United States isn't able to re-arm. A gorgeous female spy falls in love with Hamilton and saves him from a poison pill. A low-budget production and a rehash of many better spy films.

p, George R. Batcheller; d, William Beaudine; w, Martin Mooney; ph, Arthur Martinelli; m, Albert Colombo; ed, Guy Thayer.

Spy Drama (PR:A MPAA:NR)

FEDERAL MAN** (1950) 67m EL bw

William Henry (Sherrin), Pamela Blake (Mrs. Palmer), Robert Shayne (Stuart), Lyle Talbot (Johnson), George Eldredge (Brandon), Movita Castaneda (Lolita), John Laurenz (Rodriguez), William Edwards (Mr. Palmer), Lori Irving (Betty Herbert), Ben Moselle (Mack), Dennis Moore (Harry), Noel Cravat (Rocky), Paul Hoffman (George), Joseph Turkel (Sneeze), Bill Lester, Carlos Schipa.

A documentary-style crime film about the federal narcotics agency. Agents are killed, and Henry is the one sent to track down the dope ring that committed the murder. His investigation takes him to Mexico and with the help of the agency's scientific devices, he breaks the ring.

p, Jack Schwartz; d, Robert Tansey; w, Sam Neuman, Nat Tanchuck; ph, Clark Ramsey; m, Darrel Calker; ed, Reg Browne.

Crime (PR:A MPAA:NR)

FEDERAL MAN-HUNT*½** (1939) 64m REP bw

Robert Livingston (Bill), June Travis (Anne), John Gallaudet (Rennick), Ben Welden (Goldie), Horace MacMahon (Soapy), Charles Halton (Lauber), Gene Morgan (Hawlings), Matt McHugh (Kilgore), Sybil Harris (Mrs. Banning), Jerry Tucker (Scoop), Margaret Mann (Mrs. Ganter), Frank Conklin (Beeber).

An innovative prison break film. Criminals escape from Alcatraz by arranging a bogus wedding in the prison chapel. Things move swiftly and the convicts are caught when the hero smashes his car in the getaway plane. The script brings things in at new angles and makes this a very watchable B-crime picture.

p, Armand Schaefer; d, Nick Grinde; w, Maxwell Shane (adapted from a story by Sam Fuller, William Lively); ph, Ernest Miller; ed, Murray Seldeen.

Crime (PR:A MPAA:NR)

FEDERICO FELLINI'S 8½ (SEE: 8½, 1963, Ital.)

FEDORA* (1946, Ital.) 97m Variety Films bw

Luisa Ferida (Fedora), Amadeo Nazzari (Loris), Osvaldo Valenti (Vladimir), Rina Morelli (Olga), Sandro Ruffini (De Cirieux), Memo Benassi (Prince Tariskine), Augusto Marcacci (Gretch), Annibale Betrone (Boroff), Guido Celano (Cirille).

Ferida plays the title role in Sardou's famous tragedy. Valenti is a count who is killed before he weds Ferida. She then falls in love with Nazzari, a Russian painter. Mastrocinque directing is strong, with excellent cinematography from La Torre. (In Italian; English subtitles.)

d, Camille Mastrocinque; w, Antonio Rossi (adapted from a play by Victorien Sardou); ph, Giuseppe La Torre; m, Umberto Giordano.

Drama (PR:A MPAA:NR)

FEDORA** (1978, Ger./Fr.) 110m Gevial Rialto/UA c

William Holden (Barry Detweiler), Marthe Keller (Fedora), Jose Ferrer (Dr. Vando), Hildegard Knef (Neff) (Countess Sobryanski), Frances Sternhagen (Miss Balfour), Mario Adorf (Hotel Manager), Hans Jaray (Count Sobryanski), Gottfried John (Kritos), Michael York (Himself), Henry Fonda (Himself), Panos Papadopulos (Barkeeper), Elma Karlowa (Maid), Christoph Kunzer (Clerk), Stephen Collins, (Barry at 25).

This FEDORA is on the same line as Wilder's SUNSET BOULEVARD, but does not come close to the 1950 classic. Holden is a director who hasn't had a movie in years. He goes to a Mediterranean island, where a Greta Garbo-like reclusive actress is living, to persuade her to be in his new film project. She commits suicide, though, as Leo Tolstoy's Anna Karenina did, by throwing herself under a train. (Holden wanted to do a film version of the Tolstoy story.) The director discovers that it was the reclusive actresses' daughter who killed herself. She had been posing as her mother so people would believe her mother still had her youthful beauty.

p&d, Billy Wilder; w, I.A.L. Diamond, Wilder (adapted from the novel Crowned Heads by Thomas Tryon); ph, Gerry Fisher (Eastmancolor); m, Miklos Rozsa; ed, Stefan Arsten; art d, Robert Andre, cos, Charlotte Flemming.

Drama (PR:C MPAA:PG)

FEEDBACK* (1979) 90m Feedback Company c

Bill Doukas (Rick Dawson), Myriam Gibril (Gabrielle), Denise Gordon (Eve), Taylor Mead (Judge), Louis Walden (Jerry).

Doukas is a true artist in his first feature; writing, producing, directing, and acting in this independent film that was partially funded by the American Film Institute. Doukas bites off far too much however, and this story of political conspiracy falls into melodrama and the climactic court room scene is unrealistic to the point of being laughable. Doukas is a low life living in New York with two women and he gets a criminal indictment. He then spends most of the film trying to get out of it, going to lawyers, a priest, a psychiatrist, and hoods who cut off one of his fingers. Watergate-type paranoia runs through this film, but is only examined in a comic book light.

p,d&w, Bill Doukas; ph, Oliver Wood (Movielab Color), m, Jake Stern; ed, Carol Hayward.

Thriller (PR:C MPAA:NR)

FEELIN' GOOD* (1966) 85m Pike c

Travis Pike (Ted), Patricia Ewing (Karen), Judi Reeve (Judi), Leslie Burnham (Elaine), Ron Stafford (Danny), Frank Dolan (Landlord), Brenda Nichols, The Montclairs, The Brattle Street East.

Counterculture musical drama starring Pike (who was something of an auteur on this picture by producing, directing, photographing and co-writing) as a returning soldier (from soft duty in Germany, not Vietnam) who is greeted by his girl friend Ewing and her friends Reeve and a rock band called The Brattle Street East. Trouble occurs for the lovers when Ewing's roommate Burnham takes Pike for a ride in her sports car. Along the way the car breaks down and it takes several hours to get home. Angered, Ewing kicks the both of them out. Eventually the couple patches things up, listen to a lot of rock and roll music and blissfully spend the rest of the film dancing and "feeling good." Songs: "Feelin' Good," "Come Back Home," "I Beg Your Pardon," "Ute Ute," "Don't Hurt Me Again," "It Isn't Right," "The Way I Need You," "Watch Out, Woman," (Travis Pike); "Summertime" (George Gershwin); "Ride the Rainbow" (Brenda Nichols); "Bad Dream" (Arthur Korb).

p,d,&ph, James A. Pike (Eastmancolor); w, Pike, Mildred Maffei; m, Arthur Korb.

Drama/Musical (PR:A MPAA:NR)

FEMMES D'UN ETE (SEE: LOVE ON THE RIVIERA, 1964, Fr./Ital.)

FEET FIRST★★★ (1930) 93m Harold Lloyd Corp. bw

Harold Lloyd (Harold Horne), Robert McWade (John Tanner), Lillianne Leighton (Mrs. Tanner), Barbara Kent (Mary), Alec Francis (Old Timer), Noah Young (Ship's Officer), Henry Hall (Endicott), Arthur Housman (Drunken Clubman), Sleep 'n' Eat (Willie Best) (Janitor), Noah Beery (Shoe Store Bit), Buster Phelps (Little Boy), Leo Willis (Truck Driver), Nick Copeland (Man Arguing with Friend), James Finlayson (A Painter).

Silent comic Lloyd makes a successful transition into sound pictures with his second talkie. He's a shoe salesman and finds himself dangling from skyscrapers once again. On a cruise, Lloyd falls in love with Kent, who thinks he's a rich businessman. The rest of the film revolves around his attempts to hide his true identity. In one of the best sequences, to his horror, Lloyd finds a magazine that has an article about him in it and he buys all the copies, throwing them overboard. But the wind scatters them around the decks.

d, Clyde Bruckman; w, Felix Adler, Lex Neal, Paul Gerard Smith (based on a story by John Grey, Alfred A. Cohn, Bruckman); ph, Walter Lundin, Henry Kohler; ed, Bernard Burton.

Comedy (PR:A MPAA:NR)

FEET OF CLAY★ (1960, Brit.) 55m Danziger/UA bw

Vincent Ball (David Kyle), Wendy Williams (Fay), Hilda Fenemore (Mrs. Clarke), Robert Cawdron (Saunders), Brian Smith (Jimmy), Angela Douglas (Diana), Jack Melford (Soames).

Ball, a lawyer working on a case, discovers that a probation officer is the man behind a drug smuggling operation. Muddy crime drama.

p, Brian Taylor; d, Frank Marshall; w, Mark Grantham.

Crime (PR:A MPAA:NR)

FELLER NEEDS A FRIEND★½ (1932) 72m COS bw

Jackie Cooper (Eddie Randall), Chic Sale (Uncle Jonas), Ralph Graves (Mr. Randall), Dorothy Peterson (Mrs. Randall), Andy Shuford (Froggie), Helen Parrish (Diana), Oscar Apfel (Doctor).

Cooper is a crippled child, whose well-meaning parents hamper the young boy's maturing. His nephew is brought in as a playmate, and bullies him. His self-esteem falls even lower when his uncle's awkward attempts to help backfire. An outrageously melodramatic tear-jerker.

d, Harry Pollard; w, Sylvia Thalberg, Frank Butler (adapted from the novel Limpy by William Johnson); ph, Harold Rosson; ed, William Levenway.

Drama (PR:A MPAA:NR)

FELLINI SATYRICON★★★★ (1969, Fr./Ital.) 128m P.E.A.-Les Productions Artistes Associes/UA c (AKA: SATYRICON)

Martin Potter (Encolpius), Hiram Keller (Ascyltus), Max Born (Giton), Capucine (Tryphaena), Salvo Randone (Eumolpus), Magali Noel (Fortunata), Alain Cuny (Lichas), Lucia Bose (Suicide Wife), Tanya Lopert (Caesar), Gordon Mitchell (Robber), Fanfulla (Vernacchio), Mario Romagnoli (Trimalchio), Donyale Luna (Oenothea), Giuseppe Sanvitale (Habinnas), Hylette Adolphe (Oriental Slave Girl), Joseph Wheeler (Suicide Husband), Genius [Eugenio Mastropietro] (Cinedo), Danica La Loggia (Scintilla), Antonia Pietrosi (Widow of Ephesus), Wolfgang Hillinger (Soldier at Tomb), Elio Gigante (Owner of Garden of Delights), Sibilla Sedat (Nymphomaniac), Lorenzo Piani (Her Husband), Luigi Zerbinati (Her Slave), Vittorio Vittori (Notary), Carlo Giordana (Captain of Ship), Marcello DiFolco (Proconsul), Luigi Montefiori (Minotaur), Elisa Mainardi (Ariadne), Suleiman Ali Nashnush (Tryphaena's Attendant), Luigi Battaglia (Transvestite), Tania Duckworth (Brothel Girl), Maria De Sisti (Fat Woman), Il Moro, Elizabetta Moscatelli, Antonia Mirio.

The bizarre characters and situations which filled the films of Fellini since his early VARIETY LIGHTS found their ultimate expression in this dreamlike and near hallucinatory depiction of ancient Rome. Based on the first century novel by Petronius Arbiter (with added inspiration from other writings from the same period) all the glamour and honor associated with the early Romans has been stripped away in this film to expose a society in which the concept of morality has virtually no significance. Fellini's desire was not to criticize ancient Rome, nor was it to set the history books straight. Rather, he found the perfect setting with which to parallel the moral decay of the youth culture in the late 1960s. Potter and Keller are two students whose adventures are an excuse for a threadbare plot which holds the extraordinary spectacle together. Their sole aim being the pursuit of their selfish hedonistic desires, they are perfect examples of modern students who abandon their books to sojourn across Europe in search of far-out excitements. It is here that Fellini drops any resemblance to realism and enters into a dreamy display that is both sickening and frightening, but remains thoroughly fascinating. We are first introduced to Potter and Keller as they are fighting over the favors of Born, a pretty, effeminate boy who takes up with Keller, leaving Potter to journey forth on his own. The two friends are later reunited after Potter indulges in a drunken orgy given by a poet and is then taken prisoner aboard a ship run by Cuny and Capucine, working in the name of Caesar to find

possible concubines. Keller also is aboard this ship and the two escape when a revolt against Caesar allows them the chance. Continuing on their journey together they enter a villa where an honorable Roman couple has just committed suicide out of an inability to retain their values in a culture where they have no significance. An extremely sensual Ethiopian slave who has been left behind entertains the two youths before they hook up with a thief in a scheme to steal Hermaphrodite (an asexual albino infant with healing powers) from the cavern where it is worshipped as a divinity. This sickly looking creature dies in the care of Potter and Keller when they attempt to carry it across the desert. Potter then finds himself forced to fight the mythical Minotaur, which actually turns out to be a man with a bull-like mask who sets the youth free after he gets down on his hands and knees. Given the reward of a beautiful woman, Potter discovers that he has become impotent and then travels to a place known as "The Garden of Delights" to find a cure. The sadistic methods used do little to cure him, so he seeks out a witch on the advice of the elderly poet who had acted as his guide. After this meeting, he rejoins Keller to find him dying from wounds he received in a fight. Left alone, Potter then comes upon the sea and the boat which had belonged to his poet friend, who is now also dead. As in other Fellini productions, many of the actors were chosen not so much for acting abilities as for how their looks fit into the director's scheme of things. Neither Potter nor Keller had any real acting experience, the first being a refined-looking Englishman and his co-star a rowdy American, but both were possessed of the good looks necessary for their characters. Though decked out in Roman garb, these two remained identifiable as the modern youths Fellini found so offensive. The color photography is all accomplished with artificial light sources, which enhance a surreal quality. Apparently, another film adaptation of Petronius' book around the same time as Fellini's version was made but did not have much international success after the Italian government considered it too obscene to be shown at theaters.

p, Alberto Grimaldi, d, Federico Fellini; w, Fellini, Bernardino Zapponi, Brunello Rondi (based on the play "Satyricon" by Petronius Arbiter); ph, Giuseppe Rotunno (Panavision, DeLuxe Color); m, Nino Rota; Ilhan Mimaroglu, Tod Dockstader, Andrew Rudin; ed, Ruggero Mastroianni; prod d, Danilo Donati; art d, Luigi Scaccianoce, Giorgio Giovannini; cos, Donati; spec eff, Adriano Pischiutta; makeup, Rino Carboni.

Historical Drama (PR:C-O MPAA:NR)

FELLINI'S CASANOVA (SEE: CASANOVA, 1976, Ital.)

FELLINI'S ROMA (SEE: ROMA, 1972, Ital.)

FEMALE★★ (1933) 65m WB bw

Ruth Chatterton (Alison Drake), George Brent (Jim Thorne), Philip Reed (Claybourne), Ruth Donnelly (Miss Frothingham), Johnny Mack Brown (Cooper), Lois Wilson (Harriet), Gavin Gordon (Briggs), Ferdinand Gottschalk (Pettigrew), Rafaela Ottiano (Della), Kenneth Thomson (Red), Huey White (Puggy), Douglass Dumbrille (Mumford), Walter Walker (Jarratt), Charles Wilson (Falihee), Edward Cooper (Butler), Spencer Charters (Tom), Sterling Holloway, Laura Hope Crews, Robert Warwick.

Chatterton is the head of an auto factory and likes to wine, dine and bed the office men. She always gives them the strictly business line the next day at the office until Brent comes along. Chatterton falls in love with him so hard that she makes him the boss of the company. She admits to him that it's a man's job, after all. A fine example of chauvinistic filmmaking.

d, Michael Curtiz, William Dieterle; w, Gene Markey, Kathryn Scola (adapted from a story by Donald Henderson Clark); ph, Sid Hickox; ed, Jack Killifer; art d, Jack Okey; cos, Orry-Kelly.

Drama (PR:A MPAA:NR)

FEMALE, THE★★ (1960, Fr.) 100m Gray-Dear-Progefi-Pathe/Pather c (LA FEMME ET LE PAUTIN; AKA: THE WOMAN AND THE PUPPET)

Brigitte Bardot (Eva), Antonio Vilar (Don Mateo), Dario Moreno (Arababijan), Michel Roux (Albert), Jacques Mauclair (Marchand), Espanita Cortez (Maria), Jess Hahn (Sydney), Daniel Ivernal (Berthier).

Basically a B.B. vehicle which takes the voluptuous blonde to Seville where she drives the local men crazy with lustful desires. One of them goes so far as to throw all his money and family away to pursue the girl, not obtaining his goal until he is looked upon as a total fool by the rest of the population. Not one of Bardot's better efforts, her body being the center of everyone's attention, including the camera's.

d, Julien Duvivier; w, Jean Aurenche, Albert Valentin, Marcel Achard (based on the novel by Pierre Louys); ph, Roger Hubert (Eastmancolor); m, Jean Weiner; ed, Jacqueline Sadoul.

Drama (PR:C MPAA:NR)

FEMALE ANIMAL, THE★½ (1958) 92m UNIV bw

Hedy Lamarr (Vanessa Windsor), Jane Powell (Penny Windsor), Jan Sterling (Lily Frayne), George Nader (Chris Farley), Jerry Paris (Hank Lopez), Gregg Palmer (Piggy), Mabel Albertson (Irma Jones), James Gleason (Tom Maloney), Richard H. Cutting (Dr. John Ramsay), Ann Doran (Nurse), Yvonne Peattie (Hairdresser), Casey Adams (Charlie Grant), Douglas Evans (The Director), Aram Katcher (Mischa Boroff), Almira Sessions (Landlady), Isabel Dawn (Masseuse), Richard Avonde (Lily's Gigolo), Laurie Mitchell (Manicurist), Walter Kelly (Motion Picture Assistant Director), Bob Wegner (Coffee-Wagon Attendant).

This was Lamarr's last film before she went into retirement, and not a very good finale. Lamarr is a movie star who is saved from a falling light by extra Nader. She gives him a job as caretaker of her beach house, which starts an affair. Trouble starts when Nader falls for Powell, who turns out to be Lamarr's adopted daughter. Lamarr brings in a good performance considering the material, but her co-stars fall way below par.

p, Albert Zugsmith; d, Harry Keller; w, Robert Hill (adapted from a story by Zugsmith); ph, Russell Metty (CinemaScope); m, Hans J. Salter; ed, Milton Carruth; md, Joseph Gershenson; art d, Alexander Golitzen, Robert Clatworthy; cos, Bill Thomas.

Drama   **(PR:A MPAA:NR)**

FEMALE BUNCH, THE zero   (1969) 86m Dalia/Gilbreth c
(AKA: A TIME TO RUN)

Jenifer Bishop (Grace), Russ Tamblyn (Russ), Lon Chaney, Jr. (Monty), Nesa Renet (Sandy), Jeoffrey Land (Jim), Regina Carrol (Waitress), Don Epperson (Singer), John Cardos (Mexican Farmer), Albert Cole (Barkeep), A'Lesha Lee, William Bonner, Jackie Taylor, Lesley MacRae, Bobby Clark.

A group of women living on a ranch all have one thing in common: they are man haters! So what happens when the dashing and seductive Tamblyn happens along? Chaney is a hired hand cum dope dealer in what was to be his last released film. This sordid little feature was shot partly on the Charles Manson ranch shortly after his arrest for mass cult murders in Beverly Hills, California; and location shots in Utah and Nevada.

p, Ralph Nussbaum; d, Al Adamson, John Cardos; w, Jale Lockwood, Brent Nimrod (based on a story by Nussbaum); ph, Paul Glickman; m, Jaime Mendoza; ed, George Goncharoff, Nimrod; m/l, "Two Lonely People," John Gay (sung by Bruce Powers).

Drama   **Cas.**   **(PR:O MPAA:R)**

FEMALE BUTCHER, THE zero (1972, Ital./Span.) 87m Film Ventures c
(CEREMONIA SANGRIENTA; AKA: LEGEND OF BLOOD CASTLE; BLOOD CEREMONY)

Lucia Bose (Countess Elizabeth Bathory), Ewa Aulin.

Yet another unimaginative horror drama about an old countess who stays eternally young by bathing in the blood of nubile virgins.

p, Jose Maria Sonzalez Sinde; d, Jorge Grau; w, Juan Tabar, Sandro Contenenza.

Horror   **(PR:O MPAA:R)**

FEMALE FIENDS½   (1958, Brit.) 69m
Merton Park/Anglo-Amalgamated bw
(GB: THE STRANGE AWAKENING)

Lex Barker (Peter Chance), Carole Mathews (Selena Friend), Lisa Gastoni (Marny Friend), Nora Swinburne (Mrs. Friend), Peter Dyneley (Dr. Rene Normand), Joe Robinson (Sven), Malou Pantera (Isabella), Richard Molinas (Louis), John Serret (Commissaire Sagain), Stanley Maxted (Mr. Moffat), Monica Grey (Iris Chance), Yvonne Andre (Nun), Raf De La Torre (Mr. Petheridge).

A suspenseful picture set in France which casts Barker as a tourist who becomes a pawn in a money-making scheme organized by Swinburne. Upon giving hitchhiker Molinas a ride, Barker is left unconscious on the roadside. He is brought back to Swinburne's house without any identification or memory of his past. She plans to use him as an heir to a fortune her now-dead husband was to receive. Barker catches on to the ruse and brings justice to all involved.

p, Alec Snowden; d, Montgomery Tully; w, J. McLaren Ross (based on the novel Puzzle For Fiends by Patrick Quentin); ph, Philip Grindrod.

Crime   **(PR:A MPAA:NR)**

FEMALE FUGITIVE   (1938) Mono 60m bw

Evelyn Venable (Peggy Mallory), Craig Reynolds (Jim Mallory), Reed Hadley (Bruce Dunning), John Kelly (Red), Charlotte Treadway (Mrs. Bannister), Reginald Sheffield (Doctor), Rafael Bennett (Burke), John Merton (Mort), Emmett Vogan (Leonard), Lee Phelps (Roberts), Martha Tibbetts (Claire Bannister).

Venable is the wife of a truck hijacker, and she unknowingly gets involved in his crimes. She goes on the run with the help of Kelly, a chauffeur, then falls in love with artist Hadley. Her husband is killed and she is cleared of any wrongdoing. Fair crime yarn.

p, E. B. Derr; d, William Nigh; w, John T. Neville, Bennett R. Cohen (based on a story by Cohen); ph, Arthur Martinelli.

Crime Drama   **(PR:A MPAA:NR)**

FEMALE JUNGLE, THE   (1955) 70M AIP
(AKA: THE HANGOVER)

Lawrence Tierney (Sgt. Stevens), John Carradine (Claude Almstead), Jayne Mansfield (Candy Price), Burt Kaiser (Alec Voe), Kathleen Crowley (Peggy Voe), James Kodl (Joe), Rex Thorsen (Sgt. Duane), Jack Hill (Capt. Kroger), Bruce Carlisle (Chuck), Connie Cezon (Connie), Robert Davis (George), Gordon Urquhart (Larry Jackson), Bill Layne (Heckler), Bruno Ve Sota (Frank), Jean Lewis (Monica Madison).

Police sergeant Tierney takes on the case of a murdered film actress. He was off duty and found drunk at the scene of the crime. He goes through bedrooms and back alleys and everything seems to point to the man who had helped her career, Carradine. When nymphomaniac Mansfield is murdered—in her first film role—Tierney nabs Kaiser as the murderer, however. This low-budget production (Mansfield got $150 for her role) took two weeks to film, and looks it.

p, Burt Kaiser; d, Bruno Ve Sota; w, Kaiser, Ve Sota; ph, Elwood Bredell, ed, Carl Pingitore.

Crime   **(PR:C MPAA:NR)**

FEMALE ON THE BEACH   (1955) 97m UNIV bw

Joan Crawford (Lynn Markham), Jeff Chandler (Drummond Hall), Jan Sterling (Amy Rawlinson), Cecil Kellaway (Osbert Sorenson), Natalie Schafer (Queenie Sorenson), Charles Drake (Lt. Galley), Judith Evelyn (Eloise Crandall), Stuart Randall (Frankovitch), Marjorie Bennett (Mrs. Murchison), Romo Vincent (Pete Gomez), Nan Boardman (Mrs. Gomez), Jack Reitzen (Boat Attendant), Jim Ryland (Cop), Helene Heigh (Cleaning Woman), Judy Pine (Woman at Beach), Ed Fury (Roddy).

One of the first things that knowledgeable producers do when working with writers is the establishment of some likable or, at least, identifiable characters as the protagonists. That's not the case here, as Crawford, Chandler and Sterling provide the audience with people who are hardly the kind one might want to have dinner with. Crawford is the widow of a Las Vegas gambler and she's come to Balboa, California, to take occupancy of a beach house she's never seen. Sterling is the female realtor and her behavior is, at best, quirky. Chandler is a well-tanned beach bum who walks around the house as though he has a proprietary interest in it. The former lessor, Evelyn, died when she was pushed or fell from a balcony but no one is sure. Detective Drake appears from time to time and lets Crawford know that a mystery surrounds Evelyn's death. Crawford spots Chandler for what he is, a handsome man living by his wits and making the most out of his rugged good looks. Chandler works with card sharps Kellaway and Schafer and they earn their keep by bilking unsuspecting players into high stakes games. Despite her brains telling her to stay away, Crawford eventually falls for Chandler, then finds the late Evelyn's diary which tells of Chandler's activities with his partners and the fact that she'd been set up for a fraudulent card game. Crawford attempts to sever the relationship but the physicality is overpowering and she is putty in his muscular arms. Sterling is also in love with Chandler and would like to see Crawford out of the way. Drake warns Crawford, but it's of no use and she marries Chandler. On their honeymoon night, several very contrived events occur and Crawford has the distinct impression that Chandler did, in fact, murder Evelyn and that she is next on his murderous list. In the end, the revelation is that Sterling killed the first woman and is responsible for the circumstances which took place on the first night of the Crawford/Chandler marriage. Everyone overacts in this with the exception of Kellaway, Schafer and Drake. Crawford is the most guilty of the emoters and the gnawing sound in the background was her chewing up the scenery, the props and probably starting on the camera equipment by the time the picture mercifully ends.

p, Albert Zugsmith; d, Joseph Pevney; w, Robert Hill, Richard Alan Simmons (from the play "The Besieged Heart" by Hill); ph, Charles Lang; ed, Russell Schoengarth; md, Joseph Gershenson; art d, Alexander Golitzen, Robert Clatworthy; cos, Sheila O'Brien.

Crime Drama   **(PR:A-C MPAA:NR)**

FEMALE PRINCE, THE   (1966, Hong Kong) 105m Shaw Brothers bw

Ivy Ling Po, Fang Yin, Li Chang, Chin Feng, Chin Han, Chiang Kuang-chao.

Po flees a marriage her parents have arranged to a local rich man. Dressed as a male, she goes to the city searching for her brother, but through a series of mistakes, she ends up engaged to marry the daughter of the Emperor. The Shaw brothers had limited success with this sort of costume epic of old China before they discovered the martial arts films that would make them major figures in Far Eastern film.

p, Run Run Shaw; d, Chou See-loke; w, Chang Chek.

Historical Drama   **(PR:C MPAA:NR)**

FEMALE PRISONER, THE   (SEE: LA PRISONNIERE, 1968, Fr.)

FEMALE RESPONSE, THE   (1972) 88m Trans-American c

Raina Barrett (Leona), Jacque Lynn Colton (Rosalie), Michaela Hope (Sandy), Jennifer Welles (Andrea), Gena Wheeler (Victoria), Marjorie Hirsch (Marjorie), Roz Kelly (Gilda), Lawrie Driscoll (Karl), Edmund Donnelly (Mark), Todd Everett (Gary), Richard Wilkins (Tom), Phyllis MacBride (Rachel), Suzy Mann (Ramona), Curtis Carlson (Alex), Herb Streicher (Max), Anthony Scott Craig (Caller), Richard Lipton (Leland).

A weak sexploitation film about Barrett, a columnist, who gets fired for writing dirty articles. She starts a sex seminar and five women sign up for the course. The film tries to show the female perspective on sexuality, but misses the target completely.

p, Richard Lipton; d, Tim Kincaid; w, Kincaid, David Newburge; ph, Arthur D. Marks (Eastmancolor); m, Bill Reynolds; ed, Graham Place, Arthur Marks.

Drama   **(PR:O MPAA:R)**

FEMALE TRAP, THE   (SEE: NAME OF THE GAME IS KILL, THE, 1968)

FEMALE TROUBLE   (1975) 95m New Line Cinema c

Divine (Dawn Davenport/Earl Peterson), David Lochary (Donald Dasher), Mary Vivian Pearce (Donna Dasher), Mink Stole (Taffy Davenport), Edith Massey (Ida Nelson), Cookie Mueller (Concetta), Susan Walsh (Chiclett), Michael Potter (Gater), Ed Peranio (Wink), Paul Swift (Butterfly), George Figgs (Dribbles), Susan Lowe (Vikki), George Hulse (Teacher), Roland Hertz (Dawn's Father), Betty Woods (Dawn's Mother), Hilary Taylor (Taffy as Child), Channing Wilroy (Prosecutor), Seymour Avigdor (Defense Lawyer), Elizabeth Coffey (Earnestine).

John Waters' films are not for everyone and FEMALE TROUBLE is no exception. Making a cult form of bad taste, Waters has cast in PINK FLAMINGOS everyone from Edith Massey to transvestite Divine in this $25,000 production. Divine builds to a life of crime when she gets out of high school: She is raped, gives birth to a kid that kills her father, marries a beautician, locks her mother-in-law in a bird cage, and opens her own night club. She has a unique act, that of shooting members of the audience with a gun. For all her sins, the 300-pound transvestite dies in the electric chair. A midnight movie with a trashy offbeat sense of humor.

p,d,w,&ph, John Waters; ed, Charles Roggero.

Comedy   **Cas.**   **(PR:O MPAA:NR)**

FEMININE TOUCH, THE***   (1941) 96m MGM bw

Rosalind Russell (*Julie Hathaway*), Don Ameche (*John Hathaway*), Kay Francis (*Nellie Woods*), Van Heflin (*Elliott Morgan*), Donald Meek (*Capt. Makepeace Liveright*), Gordon Jones (*Rubber-Legs Ryan*), Henry Daniell (*Shelley Mason*), Sidney Blackmer (*Freddie Bond*), Grant Mitchell (*Dean Hutchinson*), David Clyde (*Brighton*).

An intelligent comedy that uses screwball humor to advantage. Russell is married to professor Ameche, who's fired when he won't pass the school's All-American tackle. They go to New York, and Russell becomes an assistant to publisher Heflin. Heflin falls in love with Russell, while she suspects co-worker Francis is going after her husband. Hilarious situations arise and Francis pairs off with Heflin and Russell's and Ameche's marriage stays intact.

p, Joseph L. Mankiewicz; d, W.S. Van Dyke, II; w, George Oppenheimer, Edmund L. Hartmann, Ogden Nash; ph, Ray June; m, Franz Waxman; ed, Albert Akst; art d, Cedric Gibbons; spec eff, Warren Newcombe.

Comedy   **(PR:A MPAA:NR)**

FEMININE TOUCH, THE**   (SEE: GENTLE TOUCH, THE, 1956, Brit.)

FEMMINA**   (1968 Fr./Ital./Ger.) 97m GAU/Hillgold c

(SAUTERELLE; LA GRANDE SAUTERELLE; EIN MADCHEN WIC DAS MEER)

Mireille Darc (*Salene*), Hardy Kruger (*Carl*), Maurice Biraud (*Alfred*), Venantino Venantini (*Vladimir*), Francis Blanche (*Gedeon*), Georges Geret (*Marco*), Pepe Abded (*Grubert*), Pierre Massimi (*Le Voyou*), Margot Trooger, Mino Doro.

Kruger plays a small-time thief who, while traveling in Beirut, falls in with old friend Biraud and decides to participate in a scheme to rob high-stakes gambler Abded of his winnings. Kruger also meets lovely lady Darc and when he learns that his arch-enemy, Geret, is on his trail, he runs off to the mountains with her. When he telephones Biraud, he learns that Geret has decided not to kill him and has joined the robbery scheme. Kruger returns to Beirut but decides not to go through with the robbery. He goes to the casino and after informing Geret and Biraud that Abded has won big that night, leaves them to their fate (they are killed in the robbery attempt) and goes off to start a new life with Darc. Limp crime yarn filmed on location in Paris and Lebanon.

p&d, Georges Launter; w, Vahe Katcha, Michel Audiard; ph, Maurice Fellous (Eastmancolor); m, Bernard Gerard; ed, Michele David.

Crime   **(PR:C MPAA:R)**

FEMMINE DI LUSSO   (SEE: LOVE, THE ITALIAN WAY, 1964, Ital.)

FENCE RIDERS*   (1950) 57m MON bw

Whip Wilson (*Himself*), Andy Clyde (*Winks*), Reno Browne (*Jean*), Myron Healey (*Crogan*), Riley Hill (*Hutch*), Ed Cassidy (*Sheriff*), Frank McCarroll (*Pete*), George DeNormand (*Joe*), Holly Bane (*Gus*), Carl Mathews (*Ted*).

A dead horse of a western, with Wilson and Clyde as partners. They aid a female ranch owner in ridding the home spread of rustlers. In between, Wilson is accused of murder and jailed, but escapes to drag the story on.

p&d, Wallace Fox; w, Elliot Gibbons; ph, Harry Neumann; ed, John C. Fuller; md, Edward Kay.

Drama   **(PR:A MPAA:NR)**

FERNANDEL THE DRESSMAKER**½   (1957, Fr.)

84m Cite Films/Union Film Distributors bw

Fernandel (*Fernand*), Suzy Delair (*Adrienne*), Francoise Fabian (*Sophie*), Georges Chamarat (*Maitre Plaisant*), Pasquali (*Picafos*), Robert Destain (*Zwertas*), Andre Bervil (*Apollini*), Robert Pizani (*The Baron*).

So-so vehicle for the French comic finds him a cutter at a men's tailor shop, but wanting to become a high-fashion dress designer. When an old friend dies and leaves her interest in a failing dress firm to Fernandel, he has his chance, but first he must rid himself of his effeminate, cheating partners. Fair entertainment, but a far remove from Fernandel's best work.

p, Jacques Bar; d, Jean Boyer; w, Gerard Carlier, Serge Veber (based on an adaptation by Boyer and Jean Manse); ph, Charles Svin; m, Paul Misraki.

Comedy   **(PR:A MPAA:NR)**

FEROCIOUS PAL*   (1934) 54m Principal bw

Harry Dunkinson, Henry Roquemore, Nelson McDowell, Ruth Sullivan, Gene Tolar, Robert Manning, Tom London Grace Wood, Ed Cecil, "Kazan."

FEROCIOUS PAL stars Kazan, one of the not-so-familiar wonder dogs of Hollywood. Nothing but a boy and his dog story, the action takes place in Oregon sheep country. Kazan gets a reputation as a sheep killer but his owner, Tolar, knows that the dog would not harm even a flea. About as engrossing as watching a TV test pattern.

p, Sol Lesser; d, Spencer Gordon Bennett; w, Joseph Anthony Roach; ph, Ed Kull

Juvenile   **(PR:AAA MPAA:NR)**

FERRY ACROSS THE MERSEY**   (1964, Brit.) 88m UA bw

Gerry Marsden (*Gerry*), Fred Marsden (*Fred*), Les Chadwick (*Chad*), Les Maguire (*Les*), Julie Samuel (*Dodie*), Eric Barker (*Col. Dawson*), Deryck Guiler (*Trasler*), George A. Cooper (*Mr. Lumsden*), Patricia Lawrence (*Miss Kneave*), Mona Washbourne (*Aunt Lil*), Mischa de la Motte (*Dawson's Butler*), T.P. McKenna (*Hanson*), Margaret Nolan (*Norah*), Andy Ho (*Chinese Restaurant Manager*), Donald Gee, Bernard Sharper (*Dawson's Chauffeur*), Keith Smith (*Dawson's Chauffeur*), Cilla Black, The Fourmost, Jimmy Savile, Earl Royce and the Olympics, The Blackwells, The Black Knights.

Not wanting to be outdone by those upstarts The Beatles, who had just done a film called A HARD DAY'S NIGHT, rival British pop band Gerry and the Pacemakers, who also played the Liverpool circuit, cranked out this cheap imitation. Welcomed home by their screaming fans after a successful American tour, the leader of Gerry and the Pacemakers, Gerry Marsden, has a flashback which shows us how the band got its start. The boys met when enrolled as art students (isn't this how *all* British invasion bands met?) and they formed a rock 'n' roll band. Only scraping by on the money they made from the Cavern, the boys are lucky enough to meet a helpful young girl who introduces them to a manager. Before they know it, they're playing regularly and they win first place in the European Beat competition. The rest, as they say, is history. Other, now long forgotten, Liverpool bands make musical guest appearances and the Pacemakers perform their short-lived hits "Ferry Across the Mersey" and "It's Gonna Be All Right."

p, Michael Holden; d, Jeremy Summers; w, David Franden (based on a story by Tony Warren); ph, Gilbert Taylor; ed, John Victor Smith; md, George Martin; m/l, Gerry Marsden.

Musical   **(PR:A MPAA:NR)**

FERRY TO HONG KONG**   (1959, Brit.) 113m Rank c

Curt Jurgens (*Mark Conrad*), Orson Welles (*Capt. Hart*), Sylvia Syms (*Liz Ferrers*), Jeremy Spenser (*Miguel Henriques*), Noel Purcell (*Joe Skinner*), Margaret Withers (*Miss Carter*), John Wallace (*Police Inspector*), Roy Chiao Hung (*Johnny Sing-Up*), Shelley Shen (*Foo Soo*), Louis Seto (*Tommy Cheng*), Milton Reid (*Yen*), Ronald Decent (*Portuguese Major*), Don Carlos (*Archdeacon*), Nick Kendall (*2nd Police Inspector*), Kwan Shan Lam (*1st Guardian*).

Welles once again puts in an embarrassing performance that makes one run to the reference books to see if he is indeed the same man who directed and starred in CITIZEN KANE. This film is a tired adventure yarn featuring the rotund ham as the captain of a ferry boat which makes trips between Hong Kong and Macao. Jurgens plays an aimless derelict from Austria who was kicked out of his home country and is now wandering about looking for action. The action he finds gets him banned from both Hong Kong *and* Macao, so he spends most of his time shuttling back and forth on Welles' boat, much to the captain's dismay. Jurgens, however, is content to stay on board because it is the first place he has planted roots in for quite some time. Welles soon becomes fed up with the exile's presence and the two men soon develop a healthy hatred for each other. Eventually things work out for the best when Jurgens tries like hell to save the ship from sinking in a storm. The ship survives the storm, but slowly sinks as it pulls back into Hong Kong harbor. Seeing that the man he thought was a useless rummy has gained some pride and self-respect from the experience, Welles decides that Jurgens is all right after all. As a young man of high-school age, Welles had accompanied his father, an embarrassing alcoholic, on a long voyage to the Orient, and no doubt he contributed this personal memory—as was his custom—to the script of this film.

p, George Maynard; d&w, Lewis Gilbert; w, Vernon Harris; ph, Otto Heller (Cinemascope, DeLuxe Color); m, Ken Jones; ed, Peter Hunt.

Adventure   **Cas.**   **(PR:A MPAA:NR)**

FEUD MAKER*½   (1938) 55m REP bw

Bob Steele (*Texas Ryan*), Marion Weldon (*Sally Harbison*), Karl Hackett (*Rand Lassiter*), Frank Ball (*Harbison*), Budd Buster (*Cowlick Conners*), Lew Meehan (*Jake*), Roger Williams (*Sheriff Manton*), Forrest Taylor (*Marshal*), Jack C. Smith (*Nelson*), Steve Clark (*Mark*), Lloyd Ingraham (*Hank Younger*), Sherry Tansey, Wally West, Tex Palmer.

Steele is the hero in this film, of course, trying to stop the feud between the nasties and the cowmen. Hackett plays an all-around louse who falsely befriends each side, while plotting to buy up the land for pennies when both sides have killed each other off. Hackett's plan is figured by Steele, who bides his time until he can confront him. The climax sees the long-awaited showdown, with predictable results.

p, A.W. Hackel; d, Sam Newfield; w, George H. Plympton (story by Harry F. Olmsted); ph, Robert Cline; ed, Roy Claire.

Western   **(PR:A MPAA:NR)**

FEUD OF THE RANGE*½   (1939) 55m Metropolitan bw

Bob Steele (*Bob Gray*), Richard Cramer (*Tom Gray*), Gertrude Messinger (*Madge Allen*), Frank La Rue (*Harvey Allen*), Jean Cranford (*Helen Wilson*), Robert Burns (*Dad Wilson*), Budd Buster (*Happy*), Jack Ingram (*Baxton*), Charles King (*Dirk*), Duke R. Lee (*Sheriff*), Denver Dixon, Carl Mathews.

A poor, low budget Bob Steele western using a lot of stock and double footage to avoid costs. The film is about a badman who starts a range war so that he can cheaply buy the land from the survivors after driving them out of the valley, and then sell that land at a nice profit to the railroad, which is making its way to the valley.

p&d, Harry S. Webb; w, Carl Krusada.

Western   **Cas.**   **(PR:A MPAA:NR)**

FEUD OF THE TRAIL*   (1938) 58m MON bw

Tom Tyler, Marlene Wood, Milburn Morante, Roger Williams, Lafe McKee, Jim Corey, Dick Alexander, Vane Calvert, Slim Whitaker, Colin Chase, Francis Walker.

A blah sagebrush tale, FEUD OF THE TRAIL has Tyler playing a good sheriff as well as the outlaw he is hunting down. The evil Tyler knows about a gold deposit on his father's ranch. So bad-guy Tyler and his three cohorts, Whittaker, Alexander, and Williams, try to buy out the old man's property. Having no success, they rob Pops and on the way to the bank meet the good Tyler. The good Tyler kills his evil duplicate and returns to his father's ranch in triumph.

p, Sam Katzman; d, Robert Hill; w, Basil Dickey; ph, Bill Hyer; ed, Holbrook Todd.

Western   **(PR:A   MPAA:NR)**

FEUD OF THE WEST*   (1936) 62m Diversion bw

Hoot Gibson (Whitey), Joan Barclay (Molly), Buzz Barton (Six-Bits), Reed Howes (Bart Hunter), Robert Kortman (Hawk Decker), Edward Cassidy (Walters), Nelson McDowell (Wild Horse Henderson), Lew Meehan, Bob McKenzie, Allen Greer, Roger Williams.

This vehicle for famous B-western cowboy Gibson has him as a rodeo performer mixed up in a feud between a group of ranchers and horse rustlers. Four nearly unexplained shootings add to the suspense of the film.

p, Walter Futter; d, Harry Fraser; w, Phil Dunham (story by Russell A. Bankson, adaptation by Walton T. Farrar, Roger Allman); ph, Ted McCord; ed, Carl Himm.

Western   **Cas.**   **(PR:A   MPAA:NR)**

FEUDIN' FOOLS*   (1952) 63m MON bw

Leo Gorcey (Slip), Huntz Hall (Sach), Bennie Bartlett (Butch), David Gorcey (Chuck), Bernard Gorcey (Louie), Paul Wexler (Luke Smith), Oliver Blake (Clem Smith), Bob Easton (Caleb Smith), O.Z. Whitehead (Yancy Smith), Anne Kimbell (Ellie Mae), Dorothy Ford (Tiny Smith), Lyle Talbot (Big Jim), Fuzzy Knight (Traps), Russell Simpson (Grandpa Smith), Arthur Space (Mr. Thompson), Bob Bray, Bob Keyes (Private Detectives), Leo "Ukie" Sherin (Pinky), Benny Baker (Corky).

Lackluster BOWERY BOYS entry which sees Hall inheriting a farm in Kentucky. The gang decide to go there and soon find themselves in the middle of a feud between the Smiths and the Joneses. Luckily the Smiths come to the rescue when bank robbers arrive at the door of the Joneses and force the clan to tend to their wounds. The boys loudly address the robbers as "Joneses" and the Smiths come running with their guns, accidentally capturing the criminals. (See BOWERY BOYS series, Index.)

p, Jerry Thomas; d, William Beaudine; w, Bert Lawrence, Tim Ryan; ph, Marcel Le Picard; ed, William Austin; md, Edward Kay; art d, Dave Milton.

Comedy   **(PR:A   MPAA:NR)**

FEUDIN', FUSSIN' AND A-FIGHTIN'**½   (1948) 78m UNIV bw

Donald O'Connor (Wilbur McMurty), Marjorie Main (Maribel Matthews), Percy Kilbride (Billy Caswell), Penny Edwards (Libby Matthews), Joe Besser (Sharkey Dolan), Harry Shannon (Chauncey), Fred Kohler, Jr. (Emory Tuttle), Howland Chamberlin (Doc Overholt), Edmund Cobb (Stage Driver), Joel Friedkin (Stage Passenger), I. Stanford Jolley (Guard), Louis DaPron (Specialty), Charles Middleton (Citizen), Kenneth MacDonald, Herbert Heywood (Judges), Harry Brown (Man in Tree), Arthur Miles, Gene Stutenroth (Big Men), Roy Butler, Bill Sundholm, Monte Montague (Men in Cafe), Francis Ford, Tommy Coats (Checkers), Francis Williams (Citizen at Dance), the Sportsmen Quartet.

In this pleasant backwoods musical, O'Connor shows his tap dancing prowess. The film stars O'Connor as a traveling salesman selling his wares as he passes through the town of Rimrock. Because O'Connor proves to be swift of foot, the villagers kidnap him in order to persuade O'Connor to be their representative in an annual foot-race with their rival village. O'Connor displays his tap dancing skills in two numbers, "S'posing" (Andy Razaf, Paul Denniker), and "Me and My Shadow" (Al Jolson, Billy Rose, Dave Dryor). The title number was written by Al Dubin and Burton Lane.

p, Leonard Goldstein; d, George Sherman; w, D.D. Beauchamp; ph, Irving Glassberg; m, Leith Stevens; ed, Edward Curtiss; art d, Bernard Herzbrun, Frank A. Richards.

Musical/Comedy   **(PR:A   MPAA:NR)**

FEVER HEAT*   (1968) 109m Heartland/PAR c

Nick Adams (Ace Jones), Jeannine Riley (Sandy Richards), Norman Alden (Herbert Herpgruve), Vaughn Taylor (Toad Taplinger), Daxson Thomas (Ronnie Richards), Robert Broyles (Loren Peale), Al Ruscio, Walt Reno, Jr., Skip Nelson, Ron Foreman, Mary Walker, Alvin Meyer, Dwayne Bacon, Arthur Greco, Sharon Baum, Robert McClelland, Art Breese, Gail Miller, Dick Davis, Lon Parsons, John Doughten, Jack Thompson.

Filmed in Iowa, this cheapie uses locals for the crowd scenes and lacks excitement or thrills. An undeveloped plot has Adams running a garage he had only stopped at to repair his truck. The owner of the garage, Riley, inherited it from her husband, who was killed in an auto race. Riley falls for Adams, who tries to take over the local track. Adams finds it is not easy running a race track, and a couple of his friends are killed in a race due to sabotage. In the end, Adams sees that he has been wrong to strive for race track czardom and decides to settle down with the widow and her garage.

p&d, Russell S. Doughten, Jr.; w, Henry Gregor Felsen (based on the novel by Angus Vicker); ph, Gary Young (Techniscope, Technicolor); m, Jaimie Mendoza-Nova; ed, Thomas Boutross.

Action   **(PR:A   MPAA:NR)**

FEVER IN THE BLOOD, A**   (1961) 117m WB bw

Efrem Zimbalist, Jr. (Judge Leland Hoffman), Angie Dickinson (Cathy Simon), Jack Kelly (Dan Callahan), Don Ameche (Senator A.S. Simon), Ray Danton (Marker), Herbert Marshall (Governor Thornwall), Andra Martin (Laura Mayberry), Jesse White (Mickey Beers), Rhodes Reason (Walter Thornwall), Robert Colbert (Thomas Morely), Carroll O'Connor (Matt Keenan), Parley Baer (Bosworth), Saundra Edwards (Lucy Callahan), June Blair (Paula Thornwall).

Due to lack of excitement, this complicated satirical, political/judicial film falls a bit flat. The three main characters, the senator, Ameche, the judge, Zimbalist, Jr., and the shady district attorney, Kelly, all have hopes of becoming governor. Each

of their careers is jeopardized by a murder case that they become involved in. In the end, Ameche dies of a heart attack, the voters discover that Kelly is really a louse, and Zimbalist, Jr. wins by a landslide. Dickinson is mere leg dressing, as usual.

p, Roy Huggins; d, Vincent Sherman; w, Huggins, Harry Kleiner (from novel by William Pearson); ph, J. Peverell Marley; m, Ernest Gold; ed, William Ziegler; art d, Malcolm Bert; set d, George James Hopkins; cos, Howard Shoup.

Comedy   **(PR:A   MPAA:NR)**

FEW BULLETS MORE, A** (1968, Ital./Span.) 85m RAF/Golden Eagle c
(E DIVENNE IL PIU SPIETATO BANDITO DEL SUD; EL HOMBRE QUE MATO A BILLY EL NINO)

Peter Lee Lawrence (Billy Bonney), Fausto Tozzi (Pat Garrett), Diane Zura [Dianik Zurakowska] (Helen Tunstill), Gloria Milland (Billy's Mother), Carlos Casaravilla, Antonio Pica, Enrique Avila, Orlando Baralla, Paco Sanz, Luis Rivera, Barta Barri, Alfonso Rojas, Luis Prendes, Tomas Blanco, Luis Induni, Jose Canalejas.

Fairly accurate telling of the Pat Garrett/Billy the Kid story, this time by the Italians (the film's title was an obvious attempt to capitalize on the success of the Sergio Leone/Clint Eastwood westerns). The "Kid" (Lawrence) and Garrett's (Tozzi) paths cross in their youth and they become friends. Eventually, after Lawrence has developed an infamous reputation as a robber and killer, Garrett, now a lawman, must track him down and bring him to justice. When Tozzi finally tracks Lawrence down he is able to convince the young killer to change his ways, but it is too late and soon after the kid is gunned down by a rival (in real life, Garrett killed the Kid). Though Tozzi didn't pull the trigger, he is accused of the killing and the blame follows him the rest of his life.

p, Silvio Battistini; d, Julio Buchs; w, Federico de Urrutia, Buchs (based on a story by Buchs, Jose Mallorqui, de Urrutia, Carlo Veo); ph, Miguel F. Mila (Eastmancolor); m, Gianni Ferrio; ed, Magdalena Pulido; art d, Francesco Calabrese; set d, Vazquez Brothers.

Western   **(PR:A   MPAA:G)**

FFOLKES*½   (1980, Brit.) 99m UNIV c
(GB: NORTH SEA HIJACK; AKA: ASSAULT FORCE)

Roger Moore (ffolkes), James Mason (Admiral Brinsden), Anthony Perkins (Kramer), Michael Parks (Shulman), David Hedison (King), Jack Watson (Olafsen), George Baker (Fletcher), Jeremy Clyde (Tipping), David Wood (Herring), Faith Brook (Prime Minister), Lea Brodie (Sanna), Anthony Pullen Shaw (Ackerman), Philip O'Brien (Webb), John Westbrook (Dawnay), Jennifer Hilary (Sarah), John Lee (Phillips), Brook Williams (Helicopter Pilot), Tim Bentinck (Harris), Saburo Kimura (Saburo), Eiji Kusuhara (Eiji), David Landbury (Eriksen), Alastair Llewellyn, Sean Arnold, Eric Mason, Thane Bettany, George Leach, Richard Graydon, Mathias Kilroy, Angela Thorne, Martin Matthews, Lindsay Campbell, Jonathan Nutt, Robert Swan, William Abney.

FFOLKES is the strange name of Moore, who is a super frogman attempting to save a British oil rig from destruction. Perkins, once again playing a deranged bad guy, has stolen a ship, the "Esther," and is demanding a ransom, or he will use the stolen ship to destroy the oil rig, "Ruth," and a production platform, "Jennifer." Moore and his frogmen must capture the "Esther" and bring Perkins to justice. Mason plays a stuffy admiral who helps Moore get ready for his mission. British screen writer, Jack Davies, wrote this screenplay based on his own novel.

p, Elliott Kastner; d, Andrew V. McLaglen; w, Jack Davies (based on his novel, Esther, Ruth and Jennifer); ph, Tony Imi (Technicolor); m, Michael J. Lewis; ed, Alan Strachan; art d, Bert Davey; set d, Simon Wakefield; spec. eff., John Richardson.

Adventure/Action   **Cas.**   **(PR:C   MPAA:PG)**

FIANCES, THE**   (1964, Ital.) 84m
Titanus Sicilia-Ventidue Dicembre-SEC/Janus bw (I FIDANZATI)

Carlo Cabrini (Giovanni), Anna Canzi (Liliana).

Cabrini accepts a welding job in Sicily that will take him away from his fiancee, Canzi, for 18 months. He looks forward to the separation because their long courtship has taken their once happy relationship to a point of habit and indifference. Though only in Sicily for a few weeks, Cabrini grows tired of its arid landscape and longs for contact with his home and Canzi. He sends a postcard to her and finally puts into words what is in his heart, restoring the relationship.

p, Goffredo Lombardo; d&w, Ermanno Olmi; ph, Lamberto Caimi; m, Gianni Ferrio; ed, Carla Colombo; art d, Ettore Lombardi.

Romance   **(PR:A   MPAA:NR)**

FIASCO IN MILAN**   (1963, Fr./Ital.) 104m Titanus-Vides-SGC/Avion-
Trans-Universe-Jerand bw (HOLD-UP A LA MILANAISE; AUDACE COLPO DEI SOLITI IGNOTI)

Vittorio Gassman (Peppe), Renato Salvatori (Mario Angeletti), Vicky Ludovisi (Floriana), Carlo Pisacane (Capannelle), Claudia Cardinale (Carmela Nicosia), Nino Manfredi (Ugo Nardi), Riccardo Garrone (The Milanese), Tiberio Murgia (Ferribotte), Gianni Bonagura (Accountant), Gastone Moschin, Mario Feliciani.

Italian crime-comedy starring Gassman as the bumbling leader of a gang of thieves who plan to steal a suitcase full of money from a high-stakes soccer pool. After a series of misadventures (where the suitcase finds its way into the possession of several people) Gassman finally retrieves the money only to abandon it in a park when the police arrest him for jaywalking.

p, Franco Cristaldi; d, Nanni Loy; w, Age & Scarpelli, Loy; ph, Roberto Gerardi; m, Piero Umiliani; ed, Mario Serandrei; art d, Carlo Egidi.

Crime/Comedy   **(PR:A   MPAA:NR)**

FICKLE FINGER OF FATE, THE**½   (1967, Span./U.S.) 91m PRC c
(EL DEDO DEL DESTINO; AKA: THE CUPS OF SAN SEBASTIAN)

Tab Hunter (*Jerry*), Luis Prendes (*Winkle*), Gustavo Rojo (*Estrala*), Fernando Hilbeck (*Fuentes*), Ralph Brown (*Jaffe*), Pedro Maria Sanchez (*Paco*), Elsa Skolinstad (*Inger*), Patty Sheppard (*Pilar*), Alejandra Nilo (*Maria*), Andrea Lascelles (*Maika*), May Heatherly (*Jane*), Katia Losser.

A good little comedy thriller made in Spain with U.S. support. Hunter plays an American engineer working in Madrid. Upon finishing his assignment he is stopped from leaving when an unusual candlestick is found in his luggage. The candlestick, one of a pair known as "The Fickle Fingers of Fate," is a priceless church art object. Because of a suspected luggage switch, Hunter is detained in Madrid until a solution to the theft is found. Hunter attempts to help find the missing candlestick, suspecting five beauty contest winners, which leads him to a murder, a kidnaping, and the eventual capture of the real criminal.

p, Sidney Pink, Jose Lopez Moreno; d, Richard Rush; w, Aurelio Lopez Monis, Jim Henaghan; ph, Antonio Macasoli (Eastmancolor); m, Gregorio Garcia Segura; ed, John Horvath; set d, Luis Arguello.

Comedy/Crime   **(PR:A   MPAA:NR)**

FIDDLER ON THE ROOF***½   (1971) 180m Mirisch/UA c

Chaim Topol (*Tevye*), Norma Crane (*Golde*), Leonard Frey (*Motel*), Molly Picon (*Yente*), Paul Mann (*Lazar Wolf*), Rosalind Harris (*Tzeitel*), Michele Marsh (*Hodel*), Neva Small (*Chava*), [Paul] Michael Glaser (*Perchik*), Raymond Lovelock (*Fyedka*), Elaine Edwards (*Shprintze*), Candy Bonstein (*Bielke*), Shimen Ruskin (*Mordcha*), Zvee Scooler (*Rabbi*), Louis Zorich (*Constable*), Alfie Scopp (*Avram*), Howard Goorney (*Nachum*), Barry Dennen (*Mendel*), Vernon Dobtcheff (*Russian Official*), Ruth Madoc (*Fruma Sarah*), Patience Collier (*Grandma Tzeitel*), Tutte Lemkow (*Fiddler*), Stella Courtney (*Shandel*), Jacob Kalich (*Yankel*), Brian Coburn (*Beri*), George Little (*Hone*), Stanley Fleet (*Farcel*), Arnold Diamond (*Moishe*), Marika Rivera (*Rifka*), Mark Malicz (*Ezekial*), Aharan Ipale (*Sheftel*), Roger Lloyd Pack (*Sexton*), Vladimir Medar (*Priest*), Alfred Maron (*Previous Rabbi*), Otto Diamant (*Yussel*), Hazel Wright (*Rebecca*), Carl Jaffe (*Isaac*), Miki Iveria (*Bess*), Hilda Kriseman (*Zelda*), Sarah Cohen (*Bashe*), Susan Sloman (*Nechama*), Cyril Bass, A. Haverstock, Leo Wright, C.C. Bilham, M. Winter, H. Krein (*Village Band Members*), Ivan Baptie, Michael Ingleton, Ken Robson, Bob Stevenson, Roy Durbin, Jody Hall, Barry Lines, Adam Scott, Lou Zamprogna, Albin Pahernik (*Jewish Male Dancers*), Ina Claire, Karen Trent, Tanya Bayona, Petra Siniawski (*Jewish Female Dancers*), Peter Johnston, Larry Bianco, Walter Cartier, Rene Sartoris, Donald MacLennan, Guy Lutman, Sammy Bayes (*Russian Dancers*).

Scenarist Joseph Stein stayed close to his original Broadway book and all of the great songs were present but the picture was too thick and the photography so dim that one wished to reach out and raise the 'brightness' level so we could see what was happening. One of the longest-running plays in Broadway history becomes one of the longest movies in movie history. Chaim Topol, who played the role of Tevye in London, was chosen over Zero Mostel, who originated the part. Topol is a much younger man and it can only be assumed that the producers felt Mostel was too fat and sloppy to cause any hearts to flutter in the audience. The scene is pre-revolutionary Russia where a hardy band of Jews do their best to live in harmony with the Cossacks surrounding them. Tevye is a milkman with five daughters and just about no money to bestow on them for dowries. Based on several stories by Sholem Aleichem (a pseudonym meaning a greeting in Hebrew), FIDDLER ON THE ROOF is the story of Tevye, his long-suffering wife Golde (Norma Crane), and their older, very different daughters, Marsh, Harris, and Small. Each of the girls chooses a husband and Tevye is furious for various reasons. One marries a gentile, one marries out of love and without the traditional services of the town's matchmaker (Picon), and one marries a radical who is arrested and sent to Siberia. Under all this pressure, Tevye talks to his God as though speaking to a friend and the effect is lovely. Meanwhile, the Czar would like the Jews out of there and the local policeman, Dobtcheff, has to tell Tevye that a 'spontaneous demonstration' is going to take place. It does, and the wedding of Frey and Harris is raided at the end of act one. Act two is very brief and wraps up Tevye's feelings about the daughter who married Lovelock, the gentile. At first, he'd mourned for her as dead, the way Orthodox Jews do when a relative passes on. It's symbolic and the worst thing a parent can do to a child. In the end, he realizes that times are changing and he must change with them so he accepts her back into his life. The movie is filled with authentic touches of what it was like in those days and anyone who remembers their grandparents talking about it will identify with the experiences. The songs are the same as on the stage with such hits as "Sunrise, Sunset' (Topol, Crane), "If I were A Rich Man" (Topol), "Do You Love Me?" (Topol, Crane), "Matchmaker, Matchmaker" (Harris, Small, Edwards, Bonstein, Marsh) and all the others that served to make this one of the most tuneful scores ever. The picture fails in its editing, the darkness of the photography, and the poor choices of shots in all the dance numbers. On stage, it was magical and one could see the spectacle of choreography. But Jewison's selection of cuts was misguided and the result was a great loss of the joy and elan seen on stage. The Fiddler signifies the plight of the Jewish people in that their lives were as precarious as that of a Fiddler On The Roof. Tutte Lemkow, the well-known British actor and choreographer, was the Fiddler with the music being dubbed by Isaac Stern. The play was a hit in more than 30 different countries, thus proving the universality of the story. The biggest surprise was its acceptance in Japan where the audience felt it was truly Japanese. Odd as that may sound, it really isn't once you consider the theme: a deeply religious man is at war with his daughters whom he feels no longer respect age and tradition. He fights his own deep-seated beliefs and eventually succumbs to the love of his family. It could have happened in a Kurosawa movie just as easily as this. Jewison's direction is strangely cool. Perhaps it might have been better if they'd gotten a Jewish director to helm it (Jewison is not), someone with the blood of Anatevka in his veins. Despite all of the detriments, this is still a memorable movie as well as an instructional one. Other than some of the Yiddish films made in the 1920s and 1930s or even HESTER STREET, this is as close as anyone will come to knowing what it was like to be in that place at that time. Topol's career never did take off and this was, at this writing, his greatest role. No one else in the cast was made any appreciable impact on films. Oscars for Morris, Williams, and sound engineers David Hildyard and Gordon McCallum. Nominations for Picture, Topol, Frey, Jewison. Other songs: "Tradition," "Sabbath Prayer," "To Life," "Miracle of Miracles," "Tevye's Dream," "Bottle Dance," "Far From the Home I Love," "Anatevka," "Wedding Celebration," "Chava Ballet," (Jerry Bock, Sheldon Harnick).

p&d, Norman Jewison; w, Joseph Stein (from the book of the musical, based on stories by Sholem Aleichem); ph, Oswald Morris (Panavision 70, Technicolor); ed, Anthony Gibbs, Robert Lawrence; md, John Williams; art d, Michael Stringer; set d, Peter Lamont; cos, Elizabeth Haffenden, Joan Bridge; ch, Tom Abbott, Sammy Bayes.

Musical Comedy   **Cas.**   **(PR:AAA   MPAA:G)**

FIDDLERS THREE*½   (1944, Brit.) 88m EAL bw

Tommy Trinder (*Tommy*), Frances Day (*Poppaea*), Sonnie Hale (*Professor*), Francis L. Sullivan (*Nero*), Diana Decker (*Lydia*), Elisabeth Welch (*Thora*), Mary Clare (*Volumnia*), Ernest Milton (*Titus*), Frederick Piper (*Auctioneer*), Robert Wyndham (*Lionkeeper*), Russell Thorndike (*High Priest*), Danny Green (*Lictor*), James Robertson Justice (*Centurion*), Alec Mango, Kay Kendall, Frank Tickle.

When a thunderstorm threatens to douse sailors-on-leave Trinder and Hale and a Wren (Decker), they take cover under the altar stone at Stonehenge. The stone is struck by lightning and the trio are zapped back to ancient Rome. At first they impress emperor Sullivan with their predictions of the future, but soon they are in serious enough trouble to be thrown to the lions. Just as they are about to become cat food, lightning strikes again and they are returned to wartime England. Boring costume comedy notable only for the debut of Scottish actor James Robertson Justice, a naturalist and a journalist before taking to the screen, who would give memorable performances in a number of otherwise unmemorable films.

p, Robert Hamer; d, Harry Watt; w, Watt, Diana Morgan, Angus Macphail; ph, Wilkie Cooper; ed, Eily Boland.

Comedy   **(PR:A   MPAA:NR)**

FIDDLIN' BUCKAROO, THE*½   (1934) 65m UNIV bw

Ken Maynard, Gloria Shea, Fred Kohler, Frank Rice, Jack Rockwell, Joe Girard, Jack Mower, Slim Whitaker, Al Bridge, Bob Kortman, Bob McKenzie, Hank Bell, Frank Ellis, Roy Bucko, Buck Bucko, Bud McClure, Pascale Perry, Tarzan the horse.

One of several movies Maynard directed and produced himself, and only interesting for his use of music. The heroine, Shea, sings one song, the bandits, led by Kohler, sing another, and Maynard warbles his way throughout. Maynard plays a government agent, disguised as a musical ventriloquist named Fiddlin', who is hunting down Kohler and his gang. Kohler's gang robs the town and Maynard is mistakenly accused of the crime. However, Maynard skips out of jail, captures Kohler's gang, and frees the kidnaped Shea for a happy ending.

p&d, Ken Maynard; w, Nate Gatzert; ph, Ted McCord.

Western   **(PR:A   MPAA:NR)**

FIDELIO**½   (1961, Aust.) 90m Akkord/Brandon bw

Richard Holm (*Florestan*), Claude Nollier (*Leonore/Fidelio*), Erwin Gross (*Don Fernando*), Hannes Schiel (*Don Pizzarro*), George Wieter (*Rocco*), Sonja Schoner (*Marcellina*), Fritz Berger (*Jaquino*), Michael Tellering (*1st Prisoner*), Harry Payer (*2nd Prisoner*), Vienna State Opera Chorus.

A film adaptation of Ludwig van Beethoven's classic opera set in Spain. Filmed in 1955, but not released until 1961. The performance includes a second version of Beethoven's "Leonore" Overture. (In German; English subtitles)

d, Walter Felsenstein; w, Felsenstein, Hanns Eisler (based on the opera by Ludwig van Beethoven and other music by Pierre Gaveaux, libretto by Jean Nicolas Bouilly); ph, Nicholas Hayer, Hannes Fuchs, Viktor Meihsl, Walter Tuch; m, Beethoven; set d, Rochus Gliese, Leo Metzenbauer; md, Erich Bertel; English subtitles, Herman G. Weinberg.

Opera   **(PR:A   MPAA:NR)**

FIDELIO**½   (1970, Ger.) 119m Polyphon c

Hans Sotin (*Don Fernando*), Theo Adam (*Don Pizarro*), Richard Cassilly (*Florestan*), Anja Silja (*Leonore/Fidelio*), Ernst Wiemann (*Rocco*), Lucia Popp (*Marcellina*), Erwin Wohlfahrt (*Jaquino*), Kurt Marschner, William Workman (*Prisoners*).

Another film version of Beethoven's famous opera produced for West German television and shown theatrically in America. The performance includes a second version of Beethoven's "Leonore" Overture. (In German)

p, Rolf Liebermann; d, Joachim Hess; w, Joseph Sonnleithner, Georg Friedrich Treitschke (based on the opera by Ludwig van Beethoven and other music by Pierre Gaveaux, libretto by Jean Nicolas Bouilly); ph, Hannes Schindler (Eastmancolor); m, Beethoven; art d, Wilhelm Reinking, set d, Ita Maximovna.

Opera   **(PR:A   MPAA:NR)**

FIELDS OF HONOR   (SEE: SHENANDOAH,1965)

FIEND*   (1980) 93m Cinema Enterprises c

Don Leifert (*Eric*), Richard Nelson (*Gary*), Elaine White (*Marsha*), George Stover (*Dennis*), Greg Dohler (*Scotty*), Del Winans (*Jimmy*), Kim Dohler (*Kristy*), Pam Merenda (*Jane*), Anne Fritch (*Katie*), Steve Vertlieb (*Announcer*), Steve Frith (*Man in Cemetery*), Denise Grzybowski (*Kristy's Friend*), Debbie Vogel (*Helen Weiss*), Richard Geiwitz (*Fred*), Lydia Vuynovich (*Girl in Cemetery*), Tom Griffith (*Man With Beard*), Barbara Shuman (*Woman With Dog*), Anna Dorbert (*Woman With*

Groceries), Phil De Flavis (Father At Academy), Dannielle De Flavis (Daughter At Academy).

An unimpressive horror venture which introduces the "fiend"—a bug-like monster that lives off the dead, turning the corpses into killing machines capable of extracting energy from the living. Leifert becomes the unlucky recipient of a fiend and carries on gothic rituals in his cellar. The story is crippled by implausibilities and the skimpy makeup effects are even worse.

d&w, Don Dohler; ph, Dohler, Richard Geiwitz; m, Paul Woznicki; ed, Dohler; set d, Mark Supensky; spec eff, David W. Renwick; makeup, Supensky.

Science-Fiction/Horror   Cas.   (PR:O   MPAA:NR)

FIEND OF DOPE ISLAND*½   (1961) 76m Essanjay bw

Bruce Bennett (Charlie Davis), Robert Bray (David), Tania Velia (Glory La Verne), Ralph Rodriguez (Naru), Miguel Angel Alvarez (Capt. Fred), Edmundo Rivera Alvarez (Paco), Ruth Fernandez (Tula), Molly Odell (Mahla), Milton Steifel, Yvonne Peck, Tito Enriquez, Eddie Ortiz, Baby Gonzalez, Russel Torres, Amos Rivera.

Silly actioner starring Bennett as the self-proclaimed "baron" of a Caribbean island which he rules with an iron fist. Living off of his dealings in black-market arms and marijuana, Bennett builds an empire, but he is lonely. He instructs Alvarez, his loyal gun runner, to procure a nubile young white woman for his pleasure. Soon Alvarez returns and brings with him Velia, a nightclub entertainer. Velia catches on to Bennett's criminal dealings quickly and seeks to leave the island with his lieutenant, Bray, with whom she's fallen in love. The pair unite to sabotage Bennett's operation and end his tyranny.

p, J. Harold Odell; d, Nate Watt; w, Bruce Bennett, Mark Carabel (based on a story by Watt); ph, Gayne Rescher; m, James Peterson; ed, James Gaffney; m/l, "Hold Me Forever," Ken Darby.

Crime   (PR:C   MPAA:NR)

FIEND WHO WALKED THE WEST, THE**   (1958) 101m FOX bw

Hugh O'Brian (Dan Hardy), Robert Evans (Felix Griffin), Dolores Michaels (May), Linda Cristal (Ellen Hardy), Stephen McNally (Emmett), Edward Andrews (Judge Parker), Ron Ely (Dyer), Ken Scott (Finney), Emile Meyer (Ames), Gregory Morton (Gage), Shari Lee Bernath (Janie).

O'Brian plays a man sharing a jail cell with crazed psychopath Evans after he was caught robbing a bank to bail himself out of financial trouble. Stupidly, he tells Evans that he stashed the money and only his partner knows the location. Soon after, Evans is released and goes on a brutal rampage to get the money. Shocking brutality is depicted as Evans does everything from feeding ground glass to an unfortunate victim to forcing the miscarriage of a pregnant woman. The authorities allow O'Brian to escape so that he can track down the savage Evans, which he does. The big showdown ends in a barroom from which Evans does not exit. Loosely based on the Ben Hecht-Charles Lederer scripted film noir classic KISS OF DEATH (1946) that helped to establish Richard Widmark's name, THE FIEND WHO WALKED THE WEST fails because it wallows in graphic, horrible brutality while failing to provide any insight into Evans' disturbing character.

p, Herbert B. Swope, Jr.; d, Gordon Douglas; w, Harry Brown, Philip Yordan (based on a story by Eleazar Lipsky from a screenplay by Ben Hecht, Charles Lederer); ph, Joe MacDonald (CinemaScope); m, Leon Klatzkin; ed, Hugh S. Fowler; art d, Lyle R. Wheeler, Walter M. Simonds; cos, Adele Balkan; spec eff, L.B. Abbott.

Western   (PR:O   MPAA:NR)

FIEND WITH THE SYNTHETIC BRAIN
(SEE: BLOOD OF GHASTLY HORROR, 1965)

FIEND WITHOUT A FACE***   (1958) 74m MGM bw

Marshall Thompson (Maj. Jeff Cummings), Terence Kilburn (Capt. Chester), Michael Balfour (Sgt. Kasper), Gil Winfield (Dr. Warren), Shane Cordell (Nurse), Stanley Maxted (Col. Butler), James Dyrenforth (Mayor Hawkins), Kim Parker (Barbara), Kerrigan Prescott (Atomic Engineer), Kynaston Reeves (Prof. Walgate), Peter Madden (Dr. Bradley), R. Meadows White (Ben Adams), Lala Loyd (Amelia Adams), Robert MacKenzie (Gibbons), Launce Maraschal (Melville).

A top horror/sci-fi film with a good plot and a lot of gruesome special effects and gore. The story takes place on an isolated U.S.-Canadian air base-radar station in Canada's north woods. A scientist, Thompson, is using the base's atomic power to try to materialize people's thoughts. The experiment gets out of hand when his bad thoughts take the form of huge floating brains, and start killing people by sucking out their brains and spinal cords (it's not as silly as it sounds). The brains use their spinal cords to propel themselves through the air. Several of the brains are shot by soldiers in a closeup showing plenty of deflating brains and blood. Thompson finally diffuses the monsters by shutting off the base's atomic power. The film was directed by Crabtree, a former cinematographer who had an earlier success with the film, HORRORS OF THE BLACK MUSEUM. The special effects for the "Brains" were created by a team of Austrians and it is their work that distinguishes this effort.

p, John Croydon; d, Arthur Crabtree; w, Herbert J. Leder (based on a story by Amelia Reynolds Long); ph, Lionel Banes; m, Buxton Orr; ed, R.Q. McNaughton; md, Frederic Lewis; spec eff, Puppel Nordhoff, Peter Nielsen.

Horror/Science Fiction   Cas.   (PR:C-O   MPAA:NR)

FIENDISH GHOULS, THE   (SEE: MANIA, 1960, Brit.)

FIENDISH PLOT OF DR. FU MANCHU, THE*   (1980) 98m Orion c

Peter Sellers (Fu Manchu/Nayland Smith), Helen Mirren (Alice Rage), David Tomlinson (Sir Roger Avery), Sid Caesar (Joe Capone), Simon Williams (Robert Townsend), Steve Franken (Pete Williams), Stratford Johns (Ismail), John LeMesurier

(Perkins), John Sharp (Sir Nules Thudd), Clement Harari (Dr. Wretch), Lee Kwan-Young (Tong), Burt Kwouk (Fu's Servant), Clive Dunn (Keeper Of The Keys), David Powers (Bedser), Grace Coyle (Queen Mary), Rene Aranda (King George V), Iska Khan (Fu's Sergeant), Jaqueline Fogt (Woman Dignitary), Katia Chenko (Tour Guide), Marc Wilkinson (Conductor), George Hilsden (Newsvendor), John Taylor (Sellers' Double), John Tan, Philip Tan, Serge Julien, Johns Rajohnson, Pralith Jngam Oeurn, Lim Bun Song.

Peter Sellers' last film and a sad end to a distinguished career. The plot, set in the 1930s, has Sellers trying to steal the crown jewels and a vital ingredient for a youth restorative tonic. He also portrays his long-time enemy Nayland Smith. There is much running around after the gems, and in the end he gets the tonic, too. He also does an Elvis Presley impersonation with a song entitled "Rock Fu."

p, Zev Braun, Lelan Nolan; d, Piers Haggard, w, Jim Moloney, Rudy Dochtermann (based on the character created by Sax Rohmer); ph, Jean Tournier (Technicolor); m, Marc Wilkinson; prod d, Alex Trauner; ed, Russell Lloyd; cos, John Bloomfield; ch, Barry Collins.

Comedy   Cas.   (PR:C   MPAA:PG)

FIENDS, THE   (SEE: DIABOLIQUE, 1955, Fr.)

FIERCEST HEART, THE**   (1961) 91m FOX c

Stuart Whitman (Bates), Juliet Prowse (Francina), Ken Scott (Harry Carter), Raymond Massey (Willem), Geraldine Fitzgerald (Tante Maria), Rafer Johnson (Nzobo), Michael David (Barent), Eduard Franz (Hugo Bauman), Rachel Stephens (Sarah), Dennis Holmes (Peter), Edward Platt (Madrigo), Alan Caillou (Maj. Adrian), Hari Rhodes (Hendrik), Katherine Henryk (Mrs. Adrian), Oscar Beregi (Klaas).

Boers are searching for their promised land in this film, set in 1837, in South Africa. Whitman has escaped from a British army stockade, and he joins up with some Boer farmers. The farmers have a couple of small fights with some Zulu warriors. Prowse is Whitman's love interest and the daughter of the Boer leader. Olympic decathlon champ Rafer Johnson does a good job in this role.

p&d, George Sherman; w, Edmund H. North (based on the novel by Stuart Cloete); ph, Ellis W. Carter (CinemaScope, DeLuxe Color); m, Irving Gertz; ed, Richard Billings; art d, Duncan Cramer, George Van Marter; set d, Walter M. Scott, Stuart A. Reiss; ch, Roy Fitzell.

Adventure   (PR:A   MPAA:NR)

FIERY SPUR   (SEE: HOT SPUR, 1968)

FIESTA**   (1947) 104m MGM c

Esther Williams (Maria Morales), Akim Tamiroff (Chato Vasquez), Ricardo Montalban (Mario Morales), John Carroll (Jose "Pepe" Ortega), Mary Astor (Senora Morales), Cyd Charisse (Conchita), Fortunio Bonanova (Antonio Morales), Hugo Haas (Maximino Contreras), Jean Van (Maria Morales as a Child), Joey Preston (Mario Morales as a Child), Frank Puglia (Doctor), Los Bocheros (The Basque Singers), Alan Napier (Tourist), Alex Montoya (Vaquero), Rosa Rey (Housekeeper), Nacho Galindo (Proprietor), Robert Emmett O'Connor (Bus Driver), Soledad Jimenez (Nurse), Rudy Rama (Photographer), Jose Portugal (Reporter), Ben Welden, Dewey Robinson (Cops).

FIESTA offered leading roles for the first time to Montalban and Charisse. This musical, about a pair of twins, was shot on location in Mexico. A retired matador, Bonanova, and his wife, Astor, are the parents. Bonanova wants Montalban to become a matador. Montalban is more interested in music, and wants to be a composer. Williams has also developed matador skills and disguises herself as her brother. She goes into the ring so she can save the family from disgrace, and so her brother will not be thought of as a coward. She is discovered and the shocked Bonanova finally allows Montalban to study music. Charisse is the love interest for Montalban and the two sing and dance together. There are several colorful musical sequences, including Aaron Copland's "El Salon Mexico," retitled "Fantasia Mexican," doubling as the wonderful composition piece supposedly written by Montalban. Other songs: "La Bamba" (Luis Martinez Serrano), "La Luna Enamorada" (Angel Ortiz De Villajos), "Miriano" (Bolanos Recio, Leocadio Martinez Durango), "Romeria Vasca" (Los Bocheros).

p, Jack Cummings; d, Richard Thorpe; w, George Bruce, Lester Cole; ph, Sidney Wagner, Charles Rosher, Wilfrid M. Cline (Technicolor); m, Johnny Green; ed, Blanche Sewell; art d, Cedric Gibbons, William Ferrari; ch, Eugene Loring.

Musical   Cas.   (PR:A   MPAA:NR)

15 FROM ROM   (SEE: OPIATE '67, 1967, Fr./Ital.)

FIFTEEN MAIDEN LANE*   (1936) 63m FOX bw

Claire Trevor (Jane Martin), Cesar Romero (Frank Peyton), Douglas Fowley (Nick Shelby), Lloyd Nolan (Detective Walsh), Lester Matthews (Gilbert Lockhart), Robert McWade (John Graves), Ralf Harolde (Tony), Russell Hicks (Judge Graham), Holmes Herbert (Harold Anderson).

Romero plays a suave and unscrupulous jewel thief and Trevor plays an insurance detective who joins his gang when she goes undercover to bust up his operations. Romero stages a fake holdup and murder so he can test Trevor's honor among thieves. Romero calls in some fake police to see if Trevor will squeal. Trevor steals some of her own jewels, hoping it will lead her to the mastermind of the outfit. With police detective Nolan, she slaps the cuffs on the entire gang. Outraged, Romero shoots Trevor.

p, Sol M. Wurtzel; d, Allan Dwan; w, Lou Breslow, David Silverstein, John Patrick (based on a story by Paul Burger); ph, John Seitz; ed, Alex Troffey.

Crime   (PR:A   MPAA:NR)

FIFTEEN WIVES* (1934) 68m IN bw

Conway Tearle *(Inspector Dawes)*, Natalie Moorhead *(Carol Manning)*, Raymond Hatton *(Sgt. Mead)*, Noel Francis *(Ruby Cotton)*, John Wray *(Jason Getty)*, Margaret Dumont *(Sybilla Crum)*, Ralf Harolde *(The Electric Voice)*, Oscar Apfel *(District Attorney)*, Robert Frazer *(Chemist)*, Harry Bradley *(Hotel Manager)*, Lew Kelly *(Hotel Detective)*, Clarence Brown *(Head Porter)*, "Slickem" *(Porter)*, Alex Pollette *(Thompson)*, Alameda Fowler *(Nurse)*, John Elliott *(Doctor)*, Sidney Bracy *(Butler)*, Dickie Jones *(Boy)*, Hal Price *(Detective)*, Lynton Brent *(Reporter)*.

A below-par murder mystery that begins with a dead man in a hotel room. It is uncertain how he died; the police assume he was murdered. Police inspector Tearle finds that the man was a bigamist and had been married 15 times. Film features three of the wives, one of whom Tearle falls for.

p, Maury M. Cohen; d, Frank R. Strayer; w, Charles Beiden, Frederick Stephani; ph, M.A. Andersen; ed, Roland Reed; art d, Edward S. Jewell.

Mystery **(PR:A MPAA:NR)**

FIFTH AVENUE GIRL½** (1939) 82m RKO bw

Ginger Rogers *(Mary Grey)*, Walter Connolly *(Mr. Borden)*, Verree Teasdale *(Mrs. Martha Borden)*, James Ellison *(Mike)*, Tim Holt *(Tim Borden)*, Kathryn Adams *(Katherine Borden)*, Franklin Pangborn *(Higgins)*, Ferike Boros *(Olga)*, Louis Calgern *(Dr. Kessler)*, Theodore Von Eltz *(Terwilliger)*, Alexander D'Arcy *(Maitre D'Hotel)*, Bess Flowers *(Woman in Nightclub)*, Jack Carson *(Sailor In Park)*, Charles Lane, Harlan Briggs *(Labor Representatives)*, Roy Gordon *(Board Member)*, Manda Lane, Mildred Coles, Larry McGrath, Robert Emmett Keane, Kerman Cripps, Louis King, Dick Hogan, Earl Richards, Philip Warren, Dell Henderson, Cornelius Keefe, Bob Perry, Dorothy Dilly, Lionel Pape, Max Wagner, Kenny Williams, George Rosener, Aaron Gonzalez and his Tango-Rumba Band.

Amiable trifle featuring Ginger Rogers in a nonsinging role as an unemployed but happy young woman hired by unhappy millionaire Connolly, who wants her to pose as his mistress. Connolly has been overlooked by his family on his birthday and wears a long face as he meets Rogers in Central Park. He takes her out to a night spot, then back to his Fifth Avenue mansion where she poses as a money-hungry girl who is mad for the old reprobate. Wife Teasdale, daughter Adams, and son Holt are understandably annoyed and all ends well when they realize how they have neglected Connolly. Adams falls for their socialist chauffeur (Ellison) and Holt eventually takes an interest in the family business (prior to that he was only a polo-playing playboy) and then in Rogers. Ginger is excellent and gives good fun to the words supplied by screenwriter Scott. She makes it seem effortless and that is the key to comedy. The moment it becomes labored (as in Spielberg's 1985 GOONIES, directed by Richard Donner), it begins to feel leaden. It's sort of the distaff version of MY MAN GODFREY but not quite as frantic or as fast. Slightly dated in motivation, if you can make believe you're in 1939, you'll enjoy it a bit more. Pangborn does his usual good job as a prissy counterpoint to the very sensuous Rogers.

p&d, Gregory La Cava; w, Allan Scott; ph, Robert DeGrasse; m, Robert Russell Bennett; ed, Robert Wise, William Hamilton; art d, Van Nest Polglase, Perry Ferguson; set d, Darrell Silvera; cos, Howard Greer; m/l, "Tropicana," Aaron Gonzalez.

Comedy **Cas.** **(PR:A MPAA:NR)**

FIFTH FLOOR, THE* (1980) 87m Hickmar/Film Ventures International c

Bo Hopkins *(Carl)*, Dianne Hull *(Kelly McIntire)*, Patti D'Arbanville *(Cathy Burke)*, Sharon Farrell *(Melanie)*, Mel Ferrer *(Dr. Coleman)*, Julie Adams *(Nurse)*, John David Carson *(Ronnie Denton)*, Patti Brooks *(Disco Singer)*, Robert Englund *(Benny)*.

Hull, a disco dancer, takes some strong drugs by mistake. She goes crazy and is locked up on the fifth floor of a psycho ward. Hopkins, a crazy attendant, tries to rape her. Ferrer, the head doctor, does little to help as Hull is constantly being threatened by her surroundings, and her only thought is of escape. Hopkins finally gets his just reward with a pair of scissors in the stomach.

p&d, Howard Avedis; w, Meyer Dolinsky (based on a story by Avedis, Marlene Schmidt); ph, Dan Pearl; m, Casablanca Records and Filmworks; ed, Stanford Allen.

Drama/Exploitation **Cas.** **(PR:O MPAA:R)**

FIFTH HORSEMAN IS FEAR, THE*** (1968, Czech.) 100m Barrandov/Sigma III bw (. . . A PATY JEZDEC JE STRACH)

Miroslav Machacek *(Dr. Braun)*, Olga Scheinpflugova *(Music Teacher)*, Jiri Adamira *(Mr. Vesely)*, Ilja Prachar *(Sidlak)*, Josef Vinklar *(Mr. Fanta)*, Zdenka Prochazkova *(Mrs. Vesely)*, Slavka Budinova *(Mrs. Wiener)*, Alexandra Myskova *(Singer)*, Jiri Vrstala *(Police Inspector)*, Jana Pracharova *(Sidlak's Wife)*, Tomas Hadl *(Honzik)*, Eva Svobodova *(Porter's Wife)*, Karel Novacek *(Panek)*, Cestmir Randa *(Dr. Wiener)*, Iva Janzurova *(Anicka)*, Jana Brezkova *(Girl in Nightclub)*, Ruzena Preislerova *(Lowyova)*, Stepanka Cittova *(Coatroom Attendant)*, Ota Sattler *(Musician)*, Frantisek Chocholaty *(Nightclub Attendant)*, Helena Ruzickova *(Masseuse)*, Ivo Gubel *(Chief Physician)*, Anny Freyova, Arnost Vrana *(Musicians)*, Lida Matouskova *(Nurse)*, Zdenek Hodr *(Roubicek)*, Bohuslav Dodek *(Ruzicka)*, Ladislav Potmesil *(Vendor)*, Helena Pejskova *(2nd Girl)*, Eva Rohanova *(Dancer)*, Karel Smid *(Deranged Man)*, Roman Hemala, Milan Mach, Mirko Musil, Jiri Pleskot *(Husbands)*, Jiri Ostermann.

Grim war-time drama set in Nazi Germany stars Machacek as a Jewish doctor no longer allowed to practice medicine. He contents himself with a job working in a warehouse until a fellow tenant asks him to remove a bullet from the wound of a political fugitive. Machacek hesitantly agrees to perform the operation, but he must find morphine with which to keep his patient quiet. After a long search he finds the drug and returns to perform the operation. Forced to hide his patient in the boarding house attic when the police arrive, he is shocked to discover that one of the other tenants has informed the Nazis of his activities and soon he is hauled into jail. Machacek confesses his "crime" and takes poison, killing himself. The police then force the other tenants to file past the doctor's body and they are all stricken with guilt and cannot look at him, save for one woman who closes the dead man's eyes.

p, Carlo Ponti; d, Zbynek Brynych; w, Brynych, Jan Kalis, Milan Nejedly, Ester Krumbachova, Ota Koval (based on a story by Hana Belohradska, Brynych, adapted by Vera Kalabova, Radovan Kalina); ph, Jan Kalis; ed, Miroslav Hajek; art d, Nejedly.

Drama/War **(PR:C MPAA:NR)**

FIFTH MUSKETEER, THE (SEE: BEHIND THE IRON MASK, 1978, Aust.)

FIFTY FATHOMS DEEP*½ (1931) 65m COL bw

Jack Holt *(Tim Burke)*, Richard Cromwell *(Pinky)*, Loretta Sayers *(Myra)*, Mary Doran *(Florine)*, Wallace MacDonald *(Mate)*, Christine Montt, Henry Mowbray.

Set on the high seas, this film tells the story of a woman who drives a deep wedge between two good friends, Holt, an experienced older diver, and Cromwell, a student diver and protege of Holt. They are turned against one another when a fortune hunter, Sayers, marries Cromwell. Sayers then leaves Cromwell to run off with a rich yachtsman. An accident occurs on the rich man's yacht while Sayers is aboard, and it is up to Holt's salvage crew to reach the scuttled yacht before it sinks. While diving on the sinking yacht, Holt's foot becomes trapped between iron beams. The crew wants to abandon him and go back to port as a storm brews, but Cromwell puts the past behind him and cuts Holt loose with an underwater blow torch. Sayers' drowned corpse is viewed briefly by the two men, a sign that their bad past is gone.

d, R. William Neill; w, Dorothy Howell, Roy Chanslor (based on a story by Howell); ph, Joseph Walker; ed, Gene Havlick.

Adventure **(PR:A MPAA:NR)**

55 DAYS AT PEKING*** (1963) 150m Bronston Prod./AA c

Charlton Heston *(Maj. Matt Lewis)*, Ava Gardner *(Baroness Natalie Ivanoff)*, David Niven *(Sir Arthur Robertson)*, Flora Robson *(Dowager Empress Tzu Hsi)*, John Ireland *(Sgt. Harry)*, Harry Andrews *(Father de Bearn)*, Leo Genn *(Gen. Jung-Lu)*, Robert Helpmann *(Prince Tuan)*, Icchizo Itami *(Col. Shiba)*, Kurt Kasznar *(Baron Sergei Ivanoff)*, Philippe Leroy *(Julliard)*, Paul Lukas *(Dr. Steinfeldt)*, Lynne Sue Moon *(Teresa)*, Elizabeth Sellars *(Lady Sarah Robertson)*, Massimo Serato *(Garibaldi)*, Jacques Sernas *(Maj. Bobrinski)*, Jerome Thor *(Lt. Andy Marshall)*, Geoffrey Bayldon *(Smythe)*, Joseph Furst *(Capt. Hanselman)*, Walter Gotell *(Capt. Hoffman)*, Alfred Lynch *(Gerald)*, Martin Miller *(Hugo Bergmann)*, Eric Pohlmann *(Baron von Meck)*, Alfredo Mayo *(Spanish Minister)*, Conchita Montes *(Mme. Gaumaire)*, Jose Nieto *(Italian Minister)*, Aram Stephan *(Gaumaire)*, Robert Urquhart *(Capt. Hanley)*, Felix Defauce *(Dutch Minister)*, Andre Esterhazy *(Austrian Minister)*, Carlos Casaravilla *(Japanese Minister)*, Fernando Sancho *(Belgian Minister)*, Michael Chow *(Chiang)*, Mitchell Kowal *(U.S. Marine)*, Ronald Brittain *(Sgt. Britten)*, Mervyn Johns *(Clergyman)*, Nicholas Ray *(American Minister)*, Kenji Takako, Dong Kingman, Soong Ling, Stephen Young, Andy Ho, John A. Tinn, John Moulder-Brown.

Another Bronston historical adventure epic stars that man of epics, Heston, a U.S. Marine major, commanding American troops in Peking, China in 1900. When terrorist Boxers murder the German ambassador and demand that all "foreign devils" leave China, Niven, the British ambassador, urges everyone to make a stand inside the international compound while reinforcements are sent for; the representatives of eleven nations agree and Heston is placed at the head of their small military units. Meanwhile the sinister dowager Empress Tzu Hsi (Robson), connives with the Boxers whom she secretly supports, aiding their siege of the international settlement by having imperial troops join them. She is particularly vexed at Heston for having prevented her deportation of Gardner, a titled Russian of dubious virtue whose husband has committed suicide. As the siege lengthens, the Europeans become more desperate. Food and medical supplies dwindle, ammunition begins to run out, and the numbers of the defending troops diminish. In a humanitarian act, Gardner sells some priceless jewels and purchases medicine and food, smuggling these supplies into the old walled settlement, but she is mortally wounded. The defenders linger but their situation appears hopeless until, on August 14, 1900, fifty-five days after the siege has begun, the troops of eleven nations stream to the rescue and lift the siege. Heston is his usual forceful self in this historical opus and Gardner, as his vampy lover, convincing. But Niven quietly steals the show as the witty, clever British ambassador. Robson is superb as the scheming, half-mad empress and good support comes from Lukas, Ireland, Genn, Andrews, and a precocious child, Lynne Sue Moon, playing an orphan adopted by Heston at the last moment in a stirring scene. Though ponderous, the film presents plenty of action and the reconstructed 1900 Peking sets by Colasanti and Moore are marvels to behold. Tiomkin's score is terrific. Director Nicholas Ray, a Hollywood maverick loaded with talent, did not want to direct this Bronston opus but undertook the job for need of funds. He was much more at home with dramatic chores involving limited casts such as IN A LONELY PLACE (1950), KNOCK ON ANY DOOR (1949), and REBEL WITHOUT A CAUSE (1955). Crowd scenes and battle footage were never his specialties and when it came time to film these scenes for 55 DAYS AT PEKING Ray grew suddenly ill. Andrew Marton, who was uncredited, undertook to direct these spectacular scenes (staged for him by famed stuntman Yakima Canutt) and they remain the stunning highlights of an otherwise spotty film. This picture was one of a succession of films that producer Bronston made in Spain, where production costs were minimal. This was the first of his Spanish-made epics to lose money, but others soon followed, including FALL OF THE ROMAN EMPIRE (1964) and CIRCUS WORLD (1964), with John Wayne.

p, Samuel Bronston; d, Nicholas Ray (2nd unit, Andrew Marton, Noel Howard); w, Philip Yordan, Bernard Gordon, Robert Hamer; ph, Jack Hildyard, Milton Krasner (Super Technirama 70, Panavision, Technicolor); m, Dimitri Tiomkin; ed, Robert Lawrence; md, Tiomkin; prod d, Veniero Colasanti, John Moore; set d, Colasanti, Moore; cos, Colasanti, Moore; spec eff, Alex Weldon; m/l, "So Little Time," Tiomkin, Paul Francis Webster.

Historical Epic   Cas.   (PR:A   MPAA:NR)

FIFTY MILLION FRENCHMEN**   (1931) 68m WB c

William Gaxton (*Jack Forbes*), Olsen & Johnson (*Simon & Peter*), John Halliday (*Michael Cummings*), Helen Broderick (*Violet*), Claudia Dell (*Looloo Carroll*), Lester Crawford (*Billy Baxter*), Charles Judels (*Pernasse*), Carmelita Geraghty (*Marcelle Dubrey*), Nat Carr (*Jewish Tourist*), Vera Gordon (*His Wife*), Norman Phillips, Jr. (*Their Son*), Bela Lugosi (*Magician Who Loses His Clothes*).

Gaxton bets $50,000 he can win the heart of Dell in two weeks without spending a franc. Olsen and Johnson are hired to make sure his plans are foiled. Despite a great cast (many repeating their original Broadway roles) the film is a disappointment. Deciding that musicals were box office poison, Warner Bros. cut out Cole Porter's songs from FIFTY MILLION FRENCHMEN, using them as background music instead. (The songs later appeared in a two-reel short, PAREE, PAREE, featuring Bob Hope.) Be sure to watch for a pre-DRACULA Lugosi as a bearded magician. Cast members Helen Broderick and Lester Crawford are the parents of Broderick (ALL THE KING'S MEN) Crawford.

d, Lloyd Bacon; w, Joseph Jackson, Al Boasberg, Eddie Welch (based on the stage musical by Cole Porter and Herbert Fields); ph, Dev Jennings (Technicolor); m, Porter; ed, Robert Crandall.

Comedy   (PR:AA   MPAA:NR)

FIFTY ROADS TO TOWN***   (1937) 80m FOX bw

Don Ameche (*Peter Nostrand*), Ann Sothern (*Millicent Kendall*), Slim Summerville (*Edwin Henry*), Jane Darwell (*Mrs. Henry*), John Qualen (*Sheriff Daw*), Douglas Fowley (*Dutch Nelson*), Allan Lane (*Leroy Smedley*), Alan Dinehart (*Tycoon Jerome Q. Kendall*), Stepin Fetchit (*Percy*), Paul Hurst (*Tom*), Spencer Charters (*George Hession*), De Witt Jennings (*Capt. Galloway*), Bradley Page (*Pinelli*), Oscar Apfel (*Smorgen*), John Hamilton, Russell Hicks, Arthur Aylesworth, Jim Toney.

Sothern's running away from her father so she can elope; Ameche's running away from testifying against friends in a sticky divorce case; and Fowley's a gangster running from the law. They all end up in a snowbound cabin with only one bed and a can of caviar. An amusing if unlikely premise that is well done. Sothern and Ameche have a nice duet. Good light-hearted escapism.

p, Raymond Griffith; d, Norman Taurog; w, George Marion, Jr., William Conselman (based on a story by Louis Frederick Nebel); ph, Joseph H. August; ed, Hansen Fritch; md, David Buttolph; art d, Rudolph Sternad; m/l, Mack Gordon, Harry Revel.

Comedy   (PR:A   MPAA:NR)

52ND STREET*   (1937) 80m UA bw

Ian Hunter (*Rufus Rondell*), Leo Carrillo (*Fiorello Zamarelli*), Pat Paterson (*Margaret Rondell*), Ella Logan (*Betty*), ZaSu Pitts (*Letitia Rondell*), Dorothy Peterson (*Adela Rondell*), Sid Silvers (*Sid*), Marla Shelton (*Evelyn Macy*), Jack White (*Jack*), Collette Lyons (*Minnie*), Roman Bohnen (*Lawyer*), Wade Boteler (*Butler*), Al Shean (*Klauber*), Jack Adair (*Porky*), Kenny Baker (*Benjamin Zamarelli*), Georgie Taps, Dorothy Saulter, Maurice Rocco, Al Norman, Jerry Colonna, Pat Harrington.

A boring musical telling of the metamorphosis of the New York street, from a quiet residential neighborhood to a wild red-light district filled with nightclubs. Taking place in the years from 1912 to 1937, the story also concerns the soap opera saga of a brother and two sisters who live on the street. The brother doesn't talk to his sisters for many years because the brother married an actress, and in 1912 high society looked down upon stage performers. Songs: "I Still Love To Kiss You Goodnight," "Nothing Can Stop Me Now," "I'd Like to See Some Mo' of Samoa," "Don't Save Your Love for a Rainy Day," "52nd Street," "23 Skiddoo," "Let Down Your Hair and Sing," "We Love the South" (Walter Bullock, Harold Spina).

p, Walter Wanger; d, Harold Young; w, Grover Jones, Sid Silvers; ph, George Schneiderman; m, Walter Bullock, Harold Spina; ed, Otho Lovering, William Reynolds; md, Alfred Newman; ch, Danny Dare.

Musical   (PR:A   MPAA:NR)

FIFTY-SHILLING BOXER**   (1937, Brit.) 74m RKO bw

Bruce Seton (*Jack Foster*), Nancy O'Neil (*Moira Regan*), Moore Marriott (*Tim Regan*), Eve Gray (*Miriam Steele*), Charles Oliver (*Jim Pollett*), Aubrey Mallalieu (*Charles Day*), Michael Ripper.

Seton clowns around in this one as he dreams of leaving the circus and becoming a great boxer. This ambition gets sidetracked when he is spotted in a cheap fight and offered the role of a fighter in a film. After an imbroglio on the set, he gets fired as an actor but hired as a fighter, and so the wheels spins to a poor B ending.

p, George Smith; d, Maclean Rogers; w, Guy Fletcher; ph, Geoffrey Faithfull.

Sport Drama   (PR:A   MPAA:NR)

50,000 B.C. (BEFORE CLOTHING)*   (1963) 75m Biolane/Waldorf-Sam Lake-American Film Distributing c (AKA: NUDES ON THE ROCKS)

Charlie Robinson, Hedi Leonore, Mila Milo, The Cavegirls, Eddie Carmel, Paul Lavert and his Swinging Cavemen.

Dumb "naughty" comedy starring Robinson as an ex-burlesque comedian who stumbles into his neighbor's time machine and ends up back in the title year. There he is seized by unfriendly cavemen and sentenced to death by the king. Luckily, the queen saves him but he soon falls into trouble again by trying to seduce an

"untouchable" maiden. Soon a farce-like trial begins and the whole thing begins to remind Robinson of the vaudeville routines he once performed. Robinson redeems himself and rises to be the new "king," but by accident he falls into the time machine and is transported back to present day America where he desperately tries to get back to 50,000 B.C.

p, Herbert Lannard; d, Warner Rose; m, Martin Roman.

Comedy   (PR:O   MPAA:NR)

52 MILES TO MIDNIGHT   (SEE: HOT RODS TO HELL, 1967)

52 MILES TO TERROR   (SEE: HOT RODS TO HELL, 1967)

FIGHT FOR ROME**½   (1969, Ger./Rum.) 99m Constantin Film c (KAMPF UM ROM (PART I))

Laurence Harvey (*Celhegus*), Orson Welles (*Justinian*), Sylva Koscina (*Theodora*), Honor Blackman (*Amalaswintha*), Robert Hoffmann (*Totila*), Harriet Andersson (*Mathaswintha*), Michael Dunn (*Narses*), Ingrid Brett (*Julia*), Lang Jeffries (*Belisar*).

A joint German and Rumanian attempt at producing a sword-and-spear epic, using a big name cast and magnificent sets. Set in 526 A.D. during the decline of the Roman Empire, the story concerns the many struggling forces vying for pieces of that rapidly disintegrating domain. The subject is so enormous that director Siodmak has a little too many things going on at once. He does a credible job, but the film tends to get bogged down by its huge story structure.

p, Arthur Brauner; d, Robert Siodmak; w, Ladislas Fodor (based on a book by Felix Dahn); ph, Richard Angst (Eastmancolor); m, Riz Ortolani; ed, Alfred Srp; set d, E. Schomer, C. Simionescu.

Historical Epic   (PR:A   MPAA:NR)

FIGHT FOR THE GLORY*½   (1970, Jap.) 85m Shochiku c (EILO ENO KUROHYO)

Kensaku Morita (*Goro Matsunaga*), Miyoko Akaza (*Misa*), Yuuki Meguro (*Yuri Komiwama*), Chishu Ryu (*Yonoshin*), Shuji Sano (*Prof. Kanzaki*), Etsuko Ikuta (*Yukiko*), Yuko Enatsu (*Naomi*), Akuko Motoyama, Yoshiyuki Hosokawa, Taro Nanshu, Zaizu Ichiro, Akemi Kita, Mitsuko Takahashi, Miyoshi Kaneko, Jun Kashima, Nana Ozaki, Etsuko Nami, Mikiko Hirota.

Maudlin Japanese drama starring Meguro as the maniacal captain of a university soccer team who alienates his teammates by his stringent training measures. One day he is informed by the school that he has been selected to study in Germany for three years, which leaves him torn between his desire to go on the trip, and the fact that he will not see his girl friend for a long time. In addition, he had promised his grandfather that he would take over the family brewery if the team lost its final match. Teammate Morita learns that the soccer team has run out of funds and he challenges Meguro's grandfather to a fencing match. If the older man loses, he will fund the team. Morita wins, the team has money, but Meguro injures his leg during practice. Though the team makes a valiant effort, they lose the match. Morita admits that Meguro was right about the harder training methods and the grandfather allows Meguro to go to Germany.

p, Kiyoshi Higuchi; d, Hirokazu Ichimura; w, Shiro Ishimori; ph, Masao Kosugi (Shochiku Grandscope/Eastmancolor); m, Hirooki Ogawa; ed, Shizu Ozaka; art d, Chiyoo Umeda.

Drama   (PR:C   MPAA:NR)

FIGHT FOR YOUR LADY*   (1937) 67m RKO bw

John Boles (*Robert Densmore*), Jack Oakie (*Ham Hamilton*), Ida Lupino (*Marietta*), Margot Grahame (*Marcia Trent*), Gordon Jones (*Mike Scanlon*), Erik Rhodes (*Spadissimo*), Billy Gilbert (*Boris*), Paul Guilfoyle (*Jimmy Trask*), Georges Renavent (*Joris*), Charles Judels (*Felix Janos*), Maude Eburne (*Nadya*), Charles Coleman (*Butler*), Forrester Harvey (*Referee*), Ward Bond, Pat Flaherty (*Wrestlers*), Torben Meyer (*Hungarian Police Officer*), Gino Corrado (*Waiter*), Sidney Bracy (*Servant*), Major Sam Harris (*Fight Spectator*).

A mediocre musical farce stars Lupino as a ventriloquist in a Budapest night club. Oakie, an American wrestling trainer in Hungary, befriends an American singer, Boles, who also works at the club. When Boles is dumped by Grahame, the rough and tough Oakie decides to help him with his love life. Boles makes a bad move by trying to romance Lupino, who is married to Rhodes, an expert sword fighter who has already skewered more than forty men in duels. Lupino sings the theme song, "Blame it on the Danube" (Harry Akst, Frank Loesser).

p, Albert Lewis; d, Ben Stoloff; w, Ernest Pagano, Harry Segall, Harold Kusell (based on a story by Isabel Leighton and Jean Negulesco); ph, Jack MacKenzie; m, Harry Akst, Frank Loesser; ed, George Crone; md, Frank Tours; art d, Van Nest Polglase.

Musical   (PR:A   MPAA:NR)

FIGHT FOR YOUR LIFE Zero   (1977) 89m William Mishkin c

William Sanderson, Robert Judd, Catherine Peppers, Lela Small, Reginald Bythewood, Daniel Faraldo, Peter Yoshida, Bonni Martin, William Cargill, Richard A. Rubin, David Dewlow, Ramon Saunders, Nick Mariano.

A vile low-budget film that couldn't have found a receptive audience even during the height of tough blaxploitation films. It tells the story of three escaped convicts who brutalize a black minister and his family. After bloodshed and vile acts, the convicts decide to use the minister's house as a hideout. The convicts consist of a deranged white man who forces the minister into calling him "Massa," a barbarous oriental, and a knife-wielding chicano. Throughout the majority of the film, the convicts are allowed to have their way with the innocent family, committing a whole slew of barbaric acts upon them. However, in the last part the scene changes as the black family captures the convicts and commit similar atrocities upon their former torturers in a bloody sequence. Some feeble attempts are made to explain the white leader's hatred of blacks in a psychological manner, but it doesn't come off properly, and the meaning is lost.

p, William Mishkin, Robert A. Endelson; d, Endelson; w, Straw Weisman; ph, Lloyd Freidus; m, Jeff Slevin; ed, Endelson.

| Crime | Cas. | (PR:O MPAA:R) |

FIGHT TO THE FINISH, A**   (1937) 58m COL bw

Don Terry (Duke Mallory), Rosalind Keith (Ellen Ames), George McKay (Spudsy), Ward Bond (Eddie Hawkins), Wade Boteler (A.K. McDonald), Lucille Lund (Mabel), Ivan Miller (Capt. Jameson), Thomas Chatterton (Mayberry), Frank Sheridan (Warden), Harold Goodwin (Henry).

A fast-moving film about a taxi war between two cab companies. Terry is the hero, a man doublecrossed by Bond, who set him up on a murder charge to get his job as fleet superintendent of the largest cab company in the city. On his release from prison, Terry discovers that it was Bond who framed him. Terry gathers together some of his old taxi driver friends, and forms a rival cab company. The police become involved when a full-fledged taxi war begins. In the end, Bond gets his just desserts, while Terry gets Keith and the stronger cab company.

p, Ralph Cohn; d, C.C. Coleman, Jr.; w, Harold Shumate; ph, George Meehan; ed, Dick Fantl.

| Drama | | (PR:A MPAA:NR) |

FIGHT TO THE LAST**   (1938, Chi.) 54m Chinese Film Co./Garrison bw

Kao Chan-Fei (Brig. Gen Tsefang), Lily Lee (Tsefang's Wife), Yeh Ping (Siping, Tsefang's Sister), C. Jen (Son of Tsefang), L. Tu (Father of Tsefang), F.K. Ho (Japanese Commander), P. Wong (Man Servant), F. Ling (Chinese Traitor), T.S. He (Japanese Captain).

A rare Chinese film about the strife and indignities China endured under the attacks by Japan. The horrors inflicted upon the civilians are detailed throughout the film. The story concerns a Chinese general fighting on the front lines. His home is captured by the Japanese, and his family is murdered. On receiving the news of its capture and the death of his family, he turns the guns on his home. (In Chinese; English subtitles.)

d, Y.C. Cheng; ph, W.L. Woo; m, C.R. Sheng.

| War | | (PR:C MPAA:NR) |

FIGHTER, THE**½   (1952) 78m UA bw
(AKA: THE FIRST TIME)

Richard Conte (Filipe Rivera), Vanessa Brown (Kathy), Lee J. Cobb (Durango), Frank Silvera (Paulino), Roberta Haynes (Nevis), Hugh Sanders (Roberts), Claire Carleton (Stella), Martin Garralaga (Luis), Argentina Brunetti (Maria), Rudolfo Hoyos, Jr. (Alvarado), Margaret Padilla (Elba), Paul Fierro (Fierro), Rico Alaniz (Carlos), Paul Marion (Rivas), Robert Wells (Tex).

Conte, a Mexican who joins patriots trying to overthrow the dictator Diaz, falls for one of the other workers, Brown. Through a flashback we see how Conte's family, sweetheart, and village were destroyed by Diaz's soldiers. Conte becomes a boxer to help raise money for the cause, and decides to fight a top contender in a large purse battle. He wins the fight and uses the money to buy arms for a guerrilla leader, Cobb. A fair adaptation of Jack London's story "The Mexican."

p, Alex Gottlieb; d, Herbert Kline; w, Aben Kandel, Kline (based on the short story "The Mexican" by Jack London); ph, James Wong Howe; m, Vicente Gomez; ed, Edward Mann; m/l, Victor Cordero.

| Drama | | (PR:A MPAA:NR) |

FIGHTER ATTACK**½   (1953) 80m AA c

Sterling Hayden (Steve), J. Carrol Naish (Bruno), Joy Page (Nina), Kenneth Tobey (George), Anthony Caruso (Aldo), Frank DeKova (Benedetto), Paul Fierro (Don Gaetano), Maurice Jara (Ettore), Tony Dante (Mario), David Leonard (Father Paola), James Flavin (Col. Allison), Harry Lauter (Lt. Duncan), John Fontaine (Lt. Gross), David Bond (Priest), Louis Lettieri (Boy), Joel Marston.

A good WW II film that takes place in Italy in 1944. It revolves around the missions of an air base in Corsica and attempts to destroy a Nazi supply dump. Once the dump is eliminated the Allies can start their offensive. Squadron leader Hayden stays for this extra mission, though he has completed his tour of duty, and gets shot down. He is rescued by Page, a worker in the Italian underground, and taken to her leader, Naish. Hayden destroys the dump with the help of the underground and the air base pilots. He makes it back to the base in Corsica and at war's end is reunited with Page.

p, William Calihan, Jr.; d, Lesley Selander; w, Simon Wincelberg; ph, Harry Neumann (Cinecolor); m, Marlin Skiles; ed, Stanley Rabjohn, Lester A. Swanson; m/l, "Nina," Skiles, Sol Meyer.

| War | | (PR:A MPAA:NR) |

FIGHTER SQUADRON***½   (1948) 96m WB c

Edmond O'Brien (Maj. Ed Hardin), Robert Stack (Capt. Stu Hamilton), John Rodney (Col. Bill Brickley), Tom D'Andrea (Sgt. Dolan), Henry Hull (Brig. Gen. Mike McCready), James Holden (Tennessee), Walter Reed (Capt. Duke Chappell), Shepperd Strudwick (Brig. Gen. M. Gilbert), Arthur Space (Maj. Sanford), Jack Larson (Shorty), William McLean (Wilbur), Mickey McCardle (Jacobs), George Backus, Joel Allen (Sentries), Gilchrist Stuart, Elliott Dare, Guy Kingsford (English Photographers), Bill Cabanne (Control Tower Operator), Robert Manning (Bomber Pilot), John Morgan (Gunner), Dick Paxton (Turret Gunner), George Adrian (German Pilot), Harry McKim (Ball Turret Gunner), Patricia Northrop (Blonde Girl), John McGuire (Maj. Duncan), Rock Hudson, Don Phillips (Lieutenants), Jack Grant (Projectionist), Carl Harbaugh (Cockney), Willy Wickerhauser, Geza Remy

(German Pilots), Charles Lind (Beagle Operator), Jeff Richards (Captain), William Yetter, Jr., John Royce (German Radio Operators), Hallene Hill (Old Lady), Jean Fenwick (Lady Woodbine).

Action expert Walsh provides a stirring account of U.S. fighter pilots battling the Luftwaffe in 1943-44 when WW II hung in the balance over England and France. O'Brien is magnificent as the leader of the small squadron, trying to hold on to his own nerves as well as those of his men, leading sortie after sortie against vastly superior numbers. Interlacing the fragmentary profiles of O'Brien's crew is a good deal of color combat footage, superbly edited by Nyby. Quiet, pensive Stack is equally absorbing as O'Brien's protege and intended successor, while veteran actors Hull and Strudwick take up the unrewarding chores of the big brass obligated to send men into the air to their deaths. A haunting mood pervades this film and when looking back upon the genuine heroes it profiles one cannot forget the sacrifice such men made. The script does not eschew cliches but then again there are no cliches in a man's struggle to stay alive inside a war bent on claiming his life. In FIGHTER SQUADRON the planes fall one by one and the lives are claimed and new pilots arrive, hoping they will not join their predecessors but readily stepping into the shoes of their fate. Steiner's score contains the dynamic force of a propeller whining upward to flight velocity, and the lensing by Hickox and Cline is awesome. This was Rock Hudson's first picture. The inexperienced Hudson, who had never acted before, required 38 takes before his one-line scene could be canned.

p, Seton I. Miller; d, Raoul Walsh; w, Miller, Martin Rackin; ph, Sid Hickox, Wilfred M. Cline (Technicolor); m, Max Steiner; ed, Chris Nyby; md, Ray Heindorf; art d, Ted Smith; set d, Lyle B. Reifsnider; spec eff, John Holden, Roy Davidson, H.F. Koenekamp; makeup, Perc Westmore, Norman Pringle.

| War Drama | | (PR:A MPAA:NR) |

FIGHTING BACK**   (1948) 61m FOX bw

Paul Langton (Nick Sanders), Jean Rogers (June Sanders), Gary Gray (Jimmy Sanders), Joe Sawyer (Sgt. Scudder), Morris Ankrum (Mr. Higby), John Kellogg (Sam Lang), Dorothy Christy (Mrs. Higby), Tommy Ivo (Larry Higby), Lela Tyler (Mrs. Winkle), Pierre Watkin (Colonel), Daisy (Snuffy).

FIGHTING BACK sees convict Langton gaining his freedom by serving in the military during WW II. After being released, he gets a job from a manufacturer, Ankrum. Things are smooth for Langton as a law-abiding citizen until an old friend shows up. The crooked friend's performing dog, Daisy, steals Ankrum's wife's bracelet, and Langton is blamed. In the end the dog reveals the actual crook and Langton is saved.

p, Sol M. Wurtzel; d, Malcolm St. Clair; w, John Stone; ph, Benjamin Kline; m, Darrell Calker; ed, William F. Claxton; md, David Chudnow.

| Drama | | (PR:A MPAA:NR) |

FIGHTING BACK**   (SEE: DEATH VENGEANCE, 1982)

FIGHTING BACK**½   (1983, Brit.) 101m
Samson-Adams Packer Film/Enterprise c

Lewis Fitz-Gerald, Paul Smith, Kris McQuade, Robyn Nevin, Caroline Gillmer, Wyn Roberts, Ben Gabriel, Rob Steele, Ray Bennett, Derek Barnes, Don Reid, Gillian Jones, Maurie Fields, Anne Haddy, Michael Cove, Michael Smith, Stephen Gray, David Godden, Robert Beaven, Joe Rawson, Stephanie Wishart, Leanne Ellis.

An idealistic teacher reaches out and helps a disturbed, angry student in this grim picture of one aspect of life at a run-down school. A well-meaning attempt to depict a teacher's sacrifice, and success, sinks under the weight of its own good intentions.

p, Sue Milliken, Tom Jeffrey; d, Michael Caulfield; w, Michael Cove, Jeffrey (based on the book Tom by John Embling); ph, John Seale (Eastmancolor); m, Colin Stead; ed, Ron Williams; art d, Christopher Webster.

| Drama | | (PR:C MPAA:NR) |

FIGHTING BILL CARSON*½   (1945) 51m PRC bw

Buster Crabbe, Al "Fuzzy" St. John, Lorraine Miller, Kay Hughes, I. Stanford Jolley, Kermit Maynard, Bob Cason, Budd Buster, Bud Osborne, Charles King.

Riding to the rescue of a young lady in a stage holdup, Buster and Fuzzy don't figure out until later that she is actually a member of the gang. They use her to set a trap that captures the rest of the robbers. Routine saddle heroics from Poverty Row.

p, Sigmund Neufeld; d, Sam Newfield; w, Louis Rousseau; ph, Jack Greenhalgh; ed, Holbrook N. Todd; md, Frank Sanucci.

| Western | | (PR:A MPAA:NR) |

FIGHTING BILL FARGO**   (1942) 57m UNIV bw

Johnny Mack Brown (Bill), Fuzzy Knight (Grubby), Jeanne Kelly [Jean Brooks] (Linda), Kenneth Harlan (Hackett), Nell O'Day (Julie), Ted Adams (Vic Savage), James Blaine (Cash Scanlon), Al Bridge (Houston), Joseph Eggerton (Judge), Bob Kortman, Earle Hodgins, Tex Palmer, Harry Tenbrook, Kermit Maynard, Blackie Whiteford, Merrill McCormack, Bud Osborne, Eddie Dean Trio.

An above average B western has Brown, with sidekick Knight, returning home after a jail term, to restart his father's newspaper business. Brown gets caught up in the sheriff's election, and his father's old partner, who had been helping to rig the election, decides to go straight. The partner tells Brown all he knows only to be killed later by his former gang. Before he dies the partner takes a picture of his killer. This photo turns up just before the election and implicates the crooked sheriff and his gang, leading to their ouster.

p, Will Cowan; d, Ray Taylor; w, Paul Franklin, Arthur V. Jones, Dorcas Cochran (based on a story by Franklin); ph, Charles Van Enger; m, Milton Rosen, Everett Carter; md, H.J. Salter.

Western (PR:A MPAA:NR)

FIGHTING BUCKAROO, THE*½ (1943) 58m COL bw

Charles Starrett (*Steve Harrison*), Kay Harris (*Carol Comstock*), Arthur Hunnicutt (*Arkansas*), Stanley Brown (*Dan McBride*), Ernest Tubb (*Ernie*), Wheeler Oakman (*Sam Thacher*), Forrest Taylor (*Mark Comstock*), Robert Stevens (*Fletch Thacher*), Norma Jean Wooters (*Buckshot*), Roy Butler (*Sheriff*), Lane Bradford, Johnny Luther's Ranch Boys.

This oater tells the oft-told tale of the lone hero, Starrett, riding into town to clear his buddy's (Brown) name. Brown has been framed by the president of the local cattlemen's association, who makes it appear that Brown is the head of a group of rustlers. Brown's prison term, served for trumped-up larceny charges, does not help Starrett prove his innocence. The daughter of the president, Harris, is in love with Brown and eventually helps Starrett prove that her father is the real leader of the rustlers.

p, Jack Fier; d, William Berke; w, Luci Ward; ph, Benjamin Kline; ed, William Claxton, art d, Lionel Banks.

Western (PR:A MPAA:NR)

FIGHTING CABALLERO*½ (1935) 59m Merrick/Superior bw

Rex Lease, Dorothy Gulliver, Earl Douglas, George Chesebro, Robert Walker, Wally Wales [Hal Taliaferro], Milburn Morante, George Morrell, Pinky Barnes, Carl Mathews, Barney Furey, Franklyn Farnum, Marty Joyce, Paul Ellis.

Lease cleans up a western town with the aid of his Rough Rider pals when they learn that a mine owner is being harassed by outlaws. With the usual exchange of gunfire, Lease is able to bring in the bad guys, enabling the miner to pull more silver out of the earth.

p, Louis Weiss; d, Elmer Clifton; w, Clifton, George M. Merrick.

Western (PR:A MPAA:NR)

FIGHTING CARAVANS** (1931) 91m PAR bw
(AKA: BLAZING ARROWS)

Gary Cooper (*Clint Belmet*), Lily Damita (*Felice*), Ernest Torrence (*Bill Jackson*), Fred Kohler (*Lee Murdock*), Tully Marshall (*Jim Bridger*), Eugene Pallette (*Seth Higgins*), Roy Stewart (*Couch*), May Boley (*Jane*), James Farley (*Amos*), James Marcus (*The Blacksmith*), Eve Southern (*Faith*), Donald Mackenzie (*Gus*), Syd Saylor (*Charlie*), E. Alyn Warren (*Barlow*), Frank Campeau (*Jeff Moffitt*), Charles Winninger (*Marshal*), Frank Hagney (*The Renegade*), Jane Darwell (*Pioneer Woman*), Irving Bacon (*Barfly*), Harry Semels (*Brawler*), Iron Eyes Cody (*Indian after Firewater*), Merrill McCormick (*Townsman*), Tiny Sandford (*Man at Wagon Train*), Chief Big Tree (*Indian at Opening Scene*).

A disappointing big budget western which claimed to be based on Zane Grey's 1929 novel, but resembles the 1923 silent western, THE COVERED WAGON. One of Cooper's early films, he plays the protege of Torrence and Marshall, a couple of wagon train scouts. Prior to leaving Missouri with a cross-country train, Cooper is tossed in jail on a disturbing the peace charge. A French girl, Damita, who is crossing the country alone, joins the caravan and is persuaded by Torrence and Marshall to pose as Cooper's wife so the sheriff will release him. Meanwhile, a member of the train, Kohler, plots an Indian attack. Cooper and Damita strike up a romance, which Torrence and Marshall immediately attempt to break up so they won't lose Cooper to marriage. While the caravan is crossing a river, the Indians attack. The raid takes the lives of both Torrence and Marshall, as well as the evil Kohler. Cooper throws kerosene on the river and sets it ablaze to ward off the attackers. Their journey continues, with only Cooper left to carry on. This production was so big it had two directors, two cinematographers, and nine musical score composers. There was so much unused footage left over from the film that it was used for background in the 1934 Randolph Scott film, WAGON WHEELS.

d, Otto Brower, David Burton; w, Edward E. Paramore, Jr., Keene Thompson, Agnes Brand Leahy (based on a novel by Zane Grey); ph, Lee Garmes, Henry Gerrard, m, John Leipold, Oscar Potoker, Emil Bierman, Max Bergunker, Emil Hilb, Herman Hand, Karl Hajos, Sigmund Krumgold, A. Cousminer; ed, William Shea; art d, Robert Odell.

Western Cas. (PR:A MPAA:NR)

FIGHTING CHAMP* (1933) 57m MON bw

Bob Steele, Arletta Duncan, George Hayes, Charles King, Lafe McKee, Kit Guard, George Chesebro, Frank Ball, Henry Rocquemore, Hank Bell.

This film is a mixture of bad boxing and a bad western. Steele, besides doing a lot of riding and shooting, steps into the boxing ring where he unconvincingly takes on all comers. Guard is a big-headed fighter who ends up firing his manager for bribing an opponent to lay down in the ring.

p, Trem Carr; d, J.P. McCarthy; w, Wellyn Totman; ph, Archie Stout.

Western (PR:A MPAA:NR)

FIGHTING CHANCE, THE* (1955) 70m REP bw

Rod Cameron, Julie London, Ben Cooper, Taylor Holmes, Howard Wendell, Mel Welles, Bob Steele, Paul Birch, Carl Milletaire, Rodolfo Hoyos, Jr., John Damler, Sam Scar.

London is the girl who causes a rift between a horse trainer and a jockey in this routine B feature. Nothing you haven't seen before and nothing you will want to see again.

p, Herbert J. Yates; d, William Witney; w, Houston Branch (based on a story by Robert Blees); ph, Bud Thackery; ed, Irving Schoenberg; md, R. Dale Butts; art d, Frank Arrigo; cos, Adele Palmer.

Drama (PR:A MPAA:NR)

FIGHTING COAST GUARD** (1951) 86m REP bw

Brian Donlevy (*Cmdr. McFarland*), Forrest Tucker (*Bill Rourk*), Ella Raines (*Louise Ryan*), John Russell (*Barney Walker*), Richard Jaeckel (*Tony Jessup*), William Murphy (*Sandy Jessup*), Martin Milner (*Al Prescott*), Steve Brodie (*Red Toon*), Hugh O'Brian (*Tom Peterson*), Tom Powers (*Adm. Ryan*), Jack Pennick (*Coast Guardsman*), Olin Howlin (*Desk Clerk*), Damian O'Flynn (*Capt. Adair*), Morris Ankrum (*Navy Captain*), James Flavin (*Cmdr. Rogers*), Roy Roberts (*Capt. Gibbs*), Sandra Spence (*Muriel*), Eric Pedersen (*Civilian Wrestler*), and Sons of the Pioneers.

More a recruiting picture for the Coast Guard than a serious narrative, this film highlights the Guard's beach operations in WW II. Film follows a group of shipyard workers, spurred on by the attack on Pearl Harbor, who join the Coast Guard's officer training program. Shipyard boss Tucker is tricked into joining the Guard by worker Russell. The result is Tucker failing officer training, but he is given a bos'n rating and he and his pals go off to fight. The group sees action in all major battles in the South Pacific. Actual wartime footage was used for the beachhead landings.

p&d, Joseph Kane; w, Kenneth Gamet (story by Charles Marquis Warren); ph, Reggie Lanning; m, David Buttolph; ed, Arthur Roberts.

War (PR:A MPAA:NR)

FIGHTING CODE, THE*½ (1934) 64m COL bw

Buck Jones, Diane Sinclair, Ward Bond, Dick Alexander, Louis Natheaux, Alf James, Erville Alderson, Niles Welch, Gertrude Howard, Bob Kortman, Charles Brinkley, Buck Moulton.

Jones plays a wandering do-gooder who discovers the murderer of Sinclair's father through a lot of snooping, riding, and fighting. Mystery angle gives an interesting twist to this otherwise routine western.

d&w, Lambert Hillyer; ph, Al Siegler; ed, Clarence Kolster.

Western (PR:A MPAA:NR)

FIGHTING COWBOY*½ (1933) 58m California Motion Picture Enterprises/Superior Talking Pictures bw

Buffalo Bill, Jr., Genee Boutell, Allen Holbrook, William Ryno, Marin Sais, Tom Palky, Bart Carre, Jack Evans, Boris Bullock, Ken Broeker, Betty Butler, Hamilton Steele, Clyde McClary, Ernest Scott, Bud Baxter, Jack Bronston.

A generic oater which is about as inventive as its drab title. Buffalo Bill, Jr. saves a tungsten miner from ruin when a fellow miner gets greedy and enlists the help of some iniquitous outlaws.

p, Victor Adamson; d, Denver Dixon [Adamson]; w, L.V. Jefferson.

Western (PR:A MPAA:NR)

FIGHTING DEPUTY, THE* (1937) 60m Spectrum bw

Fred Scott, Al St. John, Marjorie Beebe, Eddie Holden, Charles King, Frank LaRue, Lafe McKee, Phoebe Logan, Sherry Tansey, Jack C. Smith, Jack Evans, Chick Hannon, "White King."

Scott is a deputy who drives a hard bargain when dealing with the criminal type. He toughens up to put an end to a raging gang war that's affecting the inhabitants of a hard-working community.

p, Jed Buell; d, Sam Newfield; w, William Lively (based on a story by Bennett Cohen).

Western (PR:A MPAA:NR)

FIGHTING FATHER DUNNE** (1948) 92m RKO bw

Pat O'Brien (*Father Dunne*), Darryl Hickman (*Matt Davis*), Charles Kemper (*Emmett Mulvey*), Una O'Connor (*Miss O'Rourke*), Arthur Shields (*Mr. O'Donnell*), Harry Shannon (*John Lee*), Joe Sawyer (*Steve Davis*), Anna Q. Nilsson (*Mrs. Knudson*), Donn Gift (*Jimmy*), Myrna Dell (*Paula*), Ruth Donnelly (*Kate Mulvey*), Jim Nolan (*Danny Briggs*), Billy Cummings (*Tony*), Billy Gray (*Chip*), Eric Roberts (*Monk*), Gene Collins (*Lefty*), Lester Matthews (*Archbishop*), Griff Barnett (*Governor*), Jason Robards, Sr. (*Bonin*), Rudy Whistler (*Soloist*), Don Haggerty (*Blake*), Ricky Berger (*Boy*), Paul Dunn (*Harry*), Buddy Roosevelt (*Pedestrian*), Raymond Burr (*Prosecuting Attorney*), Emmett Vogan (*Defense Attorney*), Ellen Corby (*Colpeck's Secretary*), Frank Ferguson (*Colpeck*), Phillip Morris (*Prison Guard*), Harry Hayden (*Mr. Dunfee*), Robert Clarke, Robert Bray (*Priests*), Ralph Dunn, Chuck Flynn (*Workmen*).

It's a tossup as to who played more priests: O'Brien or Barry Fitzgerald. In this one, O'Brien is the priest who oversees a bunch of tough newsboys in St. Louis, sometime in the early 1900s. Meant to be an uplifting and spiritual film, it does not do a thing for viewers. Based on a true story, it attempts to be pious and succeeds only in being pedantic. Hickman is good as a young boy who goes for religion just before he is due to be executed for a murder he didn't mean to happen.

p, Jack J. Gross, Phil L. Ryan; d, Ted Tetzlaff; w, Frank Davis, Martin Rackin (from a story by William Rankin); ph, George E. Diskant; m, Roy Webb; ed, Frederic Kundtson; md, C. Bakaleinikoff; art d, Albert S. D'Agostino, Walter E. Keller.

Biography (PR:A MPAA:NR)

FIGHTING FOOL, THE* (1932) 57m COL bw

Tim McCoy (*Tim Collins*), Marceline Day (*Judith*), William V. Mong (*Uncle John Lyman*), Robert Ellis (*Crip Mason*), Arthur Rankin (*Bud Collins*), Dorothy Granger (*Nina*), Harry Todd (*Hoppy*), Bob Kortman (*Dutch Charley*), Ethel Wales (*Aunt Jane*), Mary Carr.

In this average western McCoy plays a sheriff who seems to be constantly riding in pursuit of an outlaw named "The Shadow." Love sparks between McCoy and Day. However, when trying to get information on "The Shadow" from a dance hall girl, Granger, Day becomes jealous. McCoy makes up with Day, just in time to capture "The Shadow," who turns out to be McCoy's brother.

d, Lambert Hillyer; w, Frank Howard Clark; ph, Benjamin Kline; ed, Otto Meyer.

Western **(PR:A MPAA:NR)**

FIGHTING FOOLS** (1949) 89m MON bw

Leo Gorcey (Slip), Huntz Hall (Sach), Gabriel Dell (Gabe Moreno), Frankie Darro (Johnny Higgins), Billy Benedict (Whitey), David Gorcey (Chuck), Benny Bartlett (Butch), Lyle Talbot (Blinky Harris), Teddy Infuhr (Boomer Higgins), Bernard Gorcey (Louie), Dorothy Vaughan (Mrs. Higgins), Ben Welden (Lefty Conlon), Evelyn Eaton (Bunny Talbot), Bert Conway (Dynamite Carson), Paul Maxey (Editor), Robert Wolcott (Jimmy Higgins), Bill Cartledge (Joey Prince), Anthony Warde (Marty), Ralph Peters (Beef), Stanley Andrews (Commissioner), Bert Hanlon (Dorgan), Marty Mason (Needles), Eddie Gribbon (Highball), Sam Hayes (Bill Radar), Frank Moran (Goon), Tom Kennedy (Rosemeyer, Guard), Bud Gorman (Call Boy), Roland Dupree (Young Man in Sweetshop), Johnny Duncan (Fighter in Gym), Mike Pat Donovan (Pete), Joe Gray, Larry Anzalone, Johnny Kern, Al Bayne (Fighters), Jack Mower (Fight Announcer), Charlie Sullivan, Jimmy O'Garty, Gene Delmont, John Indrisano (Referees), Sammy LaMarr, Benny Goldberg (Fighters in Montage), Eddie Rio (Handler), Carl Sklover (Knockdown Timekeeper), Joe Greb (Ad Libber).

Gorcey and sidekick Hall once more lead the Bowery Boys through this so-so prizefighting comedy. After a pal is killed in the ring, Gorcey and the gang want to clean out the mobsters, who are moving in on the action. Darro, the dead fighter's brother and a boxer turned alcoholic, is persuaded to return to the ring to avenge his brother's death. Mob tricks hamper the boys, but Darro ends up winning the championship. There are a lot of fight scenes, but the ring is no match for the humor of the Bowery Boys. (See BOWERY BOYS series, Index.)

p, Jan Grippo; d, Reginald Le Borg; w, Edmond Seward, Gerald Schnitzer, Bert Lawrence; ph, William Sickner; ed, William Austin; md, Edward Kay; art d, Dave Milton.

Comedy **(PR:A MPAA:NR)**

FIGHTING FRONTIER**½ (1943) 57m RKO bw

Tim Holt (Kit), Cliff Edwards (Ike), Ann Summers (Jeannie), Eddie Dew (Walton), William Gould (Slocum), Davison Clark (Judge Halverson), Slim Whitaker (Sheriff Logan), Tom London (Snap), Monte Montague (Pete), Jack Rockwell (Ira), Bud Osborne, Russell Wade.

This better than average oater features Holt posing as an outlaw to get the goods on a gang of villains. Comedy and action mix well as Holt is imprisoned and almost hung for his trouble. Eventually he catches the leader of the marauders, and goes off to repair his trouble with his girl who thought all the time he had become a crook.

p, Bert Gilroy; d, Lambert Hillyer; w, J. Benton Cheney, Norton S. Parker (based on a story by Bernard McConville); ph, Jack Greenhalgh; ed, Les Millbrook; md, Paul Sawtell; art d, Albert S. D'Agostino, Walter E. Keller; m/l, "On the Outlaw Trail," "The Edwards and the Drews," Fred Rose, Ray Whitley.

Western **(PR:AA MPAA:NR)**

FIGHTING FURY (SEE: OUTLAW'S HIGHWAY, 1935)

FIGHTING GENTLEMAN, THE* (1932) 69m Monarch/Freuler bw

William Collier, Jr. (Jack Duncan), Josephine Dunn (Jeanette Larkin), Natalie Moorhead (Violet Reed), Crauford Kent (Claude Morgan), Lee Moran (Mr. Hurley), Pat O'Malley (Dot Moran), James J. Jeffries (Referee), Hughie Owen, Mildred Rogers, Peggy Graves, Paty O'Flynn, Duke Lee.

Popular leading man Collier, Jr., is a mechanic who aspires to the prize fight ring. He gets knocked out in the first round of a fight with a young up-and-comer and determines to develop himself, so he goes into training for a rematch. This time he kayos his foe and he and his manager realize he has a great future before him. However, money and fame lead him into high living, and at picture's end he has wound up back in the garage, licked clean.

d, Fred Newmeyer; w, Edward Sinclair, F. McGrew Willis; ph, Edward Kull; ed, Fred Bain.

Sport Drama **(PR:A MPAA:NR)**

FIGHTING GRINGO, THE**½ (1939) 59m RKO bw

George O'Brien (Wade Barton), Lupita Tovar (Nita), Lucio Villegas (Don Aliso), William Royle (Ben Wallace), Glenn Strange (Rance Potter), Slim Whitaker (Monty), Le Roy Mason (John Courtney), Mary Field (Sandra Courtney), Martin Garralaga, Dick Botiller, Bill Cody, Cactus Mack, Chris-Pin Martin, Ben Corbett, Forrest Taylor, Hank Bell.

A well-made western in the best tradition of the O'Brien series of films. O'Brien leads a group of do-gooders looking for trouble and finding it with a Mexican rancher who is falsely accused of murder. The cowpokes clear the rancher's name, save his ranch, and O'Brien has just enough time to romance the rancher's daughter, Tovar. Packed with action.

p, Bert Gilroy; d, David Howard; w, Oliver Drake; ph, Harry Wild; ed, Frederic Knudtson.

Western **(PR:A MPAA:NR)**

FIGHTING GUARDSMAN, THE** (1945) 84m COL bw

Willard Parker (Roland), Anita Louise (Amelie de Montrevel), Janis Carter (Christine Roualt), John Loder (Sir John Tanley), Edgar Buchanan (Pepe), George Macready (Gaston de Montrevel), Lloyd Corrigan (King Louis XVI), Elisabeth Risdon (Mme. de Montrevel), Ian Wolfe (Berton), Ray Teal (Albert), Victor Kilian (Montebar), Charles Halton (Hyperion Picot), Maurice Tauzin (Edouard), Charles Waldron (Abbe).

An artistic period piece set in France during the reign of Louis XVI, this film is based on Alexandre Dumas' Companions of Jehu. The Robin Hood-type hero, Parker is a baron who believes that most of his contemporaries are crooked. He bands together a group of revolutionaries, robs the king's tax collectors, and then distributes the loot to the poor. The plot is complicated by Parker's love for Louise, who is an aristocrat. Because of his passion for her, Parker must frequently prove his mettle to his men, and ultimately loses their respect when he spares the life of Louise's brother, Macready, in a duel. Parker's romance with Louise is saved as the French Revolution starts, clearing up many of the social problems he fought against.

p, Michel Kraike; d, Henry Levin; w, Franz Spencer, Edward Dein (based on the novel Companions of Jehu by Alexandre Dumas); ph, Burnett Guffey; m, Paul Sawtell; ed, Viola Lawrence; md, M.W. Stoloff; art d, Stephen Goosson, Walter Holscher.

Historical Drama **(PR:A MPAA:NR)**

FIGHTING HERO* (1934) 55m Reliable/William Steiner bw

Tom Tyler, Renee Borden, Edward Hearn, Dick Bottler, Ralph Lewis, Murdock McQuarrie, Nelson McDowell, Tom London, George Chesebro, Rosa Rosanova, J.P. MacGowan, Lew Meehan, Jimmy Aubrey.

An average fast-moving western, with Tyler an express company detective camouflaged as an outlaw to capture a gang of bandits. Tyler plays Robin Hood as he distributes some of the bandit's crooked money to the needy and falls for a Mexican woman who befriends him. He also rescues a girl falsely accused of murder. Two years before this film was made, former stuntman Tyler's career as a popular western hero took a 180-degree turn when director William S. Van Dyke, after testing scores of handsome actors and athletes, tested him to play the first talking Tarzan. Van Dyke thought he was the best so far, but temporarily held out for somebody with a bigger physique. That turned out to be the greatest swimmer of the half century, Johnny Weissmuller, even though, much to everybody's surprise, Johnny's voice was strangely high-pitched.

p, Bernard B. Bray; d, Harry S. Webb; w, Rose Gordon, Carl Krusada (based on a story by C.E. Roberts); ph, J. Henry Kruse; ed, Fred Bain.

Western **(PR:A MPAA:NR)**

FIGHTING KENTUCKIAN, THE*** (1949) 100m John Wayne/REP bw

John Wayne (John Breen), Vera Ralston (Fleurette DeMarchand), Philip Dorn (Col. Georges Geraud), Oliver Hardy (Willie Paine), Marie Windsor (Ann Logan), John Howard (Blake Randolph), Hugo Haas (Gen. Paul DeMarchand), Grant Withers (George Hayden), Odette Myrtil (Mme. DeMarchand), Paul Fix (Beau Merritt), Mae Marsh (Sister Hattie), Jack Pennick (Capt. Dan Carroll), Mickey Simpson (Jacques), Fred Graham (Carter Ward), Mabelle Koenig (Marie), Shy Waggner, Crystal White (Friends), Hank Worden (Announcer of Wrestling Contest), Charles Cane (Band Leader), Cliff Lyons, Chuck Roberson (Drivers).

Wayne, who produced this box-office winner for Republic, is a member of a Kentucky regiment returning from New Orleans where Andrew Jackson has beaten the British Army. In Mobile, Alabama he meets lovely Vera Ralston (wife of Republic Studio boss Herbert J. Yates), and stays behind with sidekick Hardy. Ralston is the daughter of Haas, a French general who had fought with Napoleon and has led an exiled contingent of Frenchmen to settle at Demopolis, occupying four townships; the industrious, peace-bent French have made homes in the rich wilderness, land coveted by Howard and Withers. Wayne resigns from his regiment and begins to woo Ralston but Haas quietly informs him that she must marry one of her own kind. Wayne won't take no for an answer and tries to obtain work, discovering Howard's plot to take over the French lands while pretending to be a surveyor. He is jailed but his cell door is left open so that he can be shot by Withers while escaping. Through a ruse, Howard is killed instead by his partner Withers, who then leads a full-scale attack with his riverboat cutthroats against the French settlement. Wayne aids the Frenchmen but they are hopelessly outnumbered. Just when the river men appear to break through, Hardy, who has gone for help, arrives with Wayne's regiment of Kentucky riflemen who make short work of the river men and polish off Withers and his cronies, too. Wayne receives Haas' undying gratitude and the hand of his daughter Ralston while the Kentuckians continue their journey northward to home. The action is brisk and Wayne is a one-man army battling evil. Withers, of course, is the evil one, a man you love to hate. Howard, who had competed for Ralston's hand, does good work as the good-bad guy and Hardy provides a lot of laughs as the bumbling sidekick in one of his few roles without Stan Laurel. Ralston does her usual overacting but Haas is moving and convincing as the French officer with only memories of glory, a far cry from the murky film noir B-productions which he produced and appeared in with such blonde vamps as Cleo Moore. Dorn excels as the noble one-armed second-in-command to Haas and Fix, a pal of Wayne's—who appeared in most of the Duke's films—plays a Withers henchman at his backstabbing best. Though a formula film, Waggner's direction is top-notch, aided greatly by the sharp lensing of master cinematographer Garmes.

p, John Wayne; d&w, George Waggner; ph, Lee Garmes; m, George Antheil; ed, Richard L. Van Enger; art d, James Sullivan; cos, Adele Palmer; spec eff, Howard and Theodore Lydecker; makeup, Bob Mark, Webb Overlander, Don Cash, Cecil Holland.

Adventure **Cas.** **(PR:A MPAA:NR)**

FIGHTING LAWMAN, THE** (1953) 71m Westwood/AA bw

Wayne Morris, Virginia Grey, John Kellogg, Harry Lauter, John Pickard, Rick Vallin, Myron Healey, Dick Rich.

Grey is a cowgirl out to steal the loot from a gang of robbers, with sheriff Morris close behind. Weak oater was typical of films once-popular Morris was cast in after he returned from WW II as a Navy flying hero.

p, Vincent M. Fennelly; d, Thomas Carr; w, Dan Ullman; ph, Gilbert Warrenton; m, Raoul Kraushaar; ed, Sam Fields.

Western   **(PR:A   MPAA:NR)**

FIGHTING LEGION, THE*½   (1930) 74m UNIV bw

Ken Maynard (*Dave Hayes*), Dorothy Dwan (*Molly Williams*), Ernie Adams (*Jack Bowie*), Stanley Blystone (*Burl Edwards*), Frank Rice (*Cloudy Jones*), Harry Todd (*Dad Williams*), Bob Walker (*Tom Dawson*), Jack Fowler (*John Blake*), Les Bates (*Fred Hook*), Bill Nestelle (*Ed Hook*), Charles Whitaker (*Red Hook*), Tarzan the Horse.

One of the first sound oaters to use the new medium to its fullest potential, FIGHTING LEGION demonstrates cowboy star Maynard's foresight by his incorporation of music and singing into the western as well as the standard atmospheric devices of thundering hoofbeats, gunshots, and tough-guy dialog. The story, however, is painfully typical. Maynard rides off in search of the murderer of his brother, a Texas Ranger. He eventually locates the scoundrel, Adams, and the film ends with the inevitable showdown at midnight on Main Street.

p, Ken Maynard; d, Harry J. Brown; w, Bennett Cohen, Leslie Mason; ph, Ted McCord; ed, Fred Allen.

Western   **(PR:A   MPAA:NR)**

FIGHTING MAD*   (1939) 54m Criterion Pictures bw

James Newill (*Renfrew*), Sally Blane (*Ann*), Benny Rubin (*Benny*), Dave O'Brien (*Kelly*), Milburn Stone (*Cardigan*), Walter Long (*Frenchy*), Warner Richmond (*Trigger*), Ted Adams (*Leon*), Chief Thundercloud (*Indian*), Ole Olson (*Joe*), Horace Murphy (*Smith*).

Another in the "Renfrew of the Mounties" series, this one based on the Laurie Yorke Erskine story, "Renfrew Rides Again." Newill plays the singing mountie. The story involves Blane, who has fallen in with a gang of thieves who loot in the U.S. and take the booty back to Canada. Blane, fearful of both the police and the gang, hides the money. Newill takes to Blane and proves that she is just a victim by capturing the real crooks. (See RENFREW series, Index.)

p, Phillip Krasne; d, Sam Newfield; w, George Rosener, John Rathmell (based on the novel *Renfrew Rides Again* by Laurie Yorke Erskine); ph, Jack Greenhalgh; ed, Roy Luby; m/l, Jack Brooks, Betty Laidlaw, Robert Lively.

Adventure   **(PR:A   MPAA:NR)**

FIGHTING MAD**½   (1948) 74m MON bw

Leon Errol (*Knobby Walsh*), Joe Kirkwood (*Joe Palooka*), Elyse Knox (*Anne Howe*), John Hubbard (*Charles Kennedy*), Patricia Dane (*Iris March*), Charles Cane (*George Wendell*), Wally Vernon (*Archie Stone*), Frank Hyers (*Ralph*), Jack Shea (*Jeff Lundy*), Jack Roper (*Waldo*), Horace McMahon (*Looie*), Jack Overman (*Truck Driver*), Eddie Gribbon (*Scranton*), Sarah Padden (*Mom Palooka*), Michael Mark (*Pop Palooka*), Evelynne Smith (*Truck Driver's Wife*), Geneva Gray (*Hat Check Girl*), Johnny Indrisano (*Referee*), Frank Reicher (*Dr. MacKenzie*), Jay Norris (*Stevie*), Paul Scardon (*Dr. Burman*), Virginia Belmont (*Nurse*), Larry Steers (*Dr. Gray*), Robert Conway, Herb Vigran (*Reporters*), Dewey Robinson (*Fighter*), Emil Sitka (*Photographer*), Murray Leonard (*Arthur Wild*), Robert C. McCracken (*Fight Announcer*), Cy Kendall (*Commissioner*), Bill McLean (*Water Boy*), Jack Mower (*Cop*), Paul Bryar (*Detective*), Sammy Wolfe (*Bookmaker*), Reid Kilpatrick (*Radio Announcer*), Ted Pavelec (*Sparring Partner*).

Joe Palooka is brought to the screen in this boxing film. Palooka, played by Kirkwood, goes blind due to a fight injury. He regains his eyesight through an operation, but the doctors tell him not to fight for at least a year. Kirkwood's manager, Errol, has bought heavyweight Cane to remain active while Kirkwood heals. But gamblers are using Errol's fighter to fix their fights. Kirkwood decides to go back into the ring to save his manager from dishonor. Risking his eyesight, Kirkwood wins in a well-staged fight sequence. (See JOE PALOOKA series, Index.)

p, Hal E. Chester; d, Reginald LeBorg; w, John Bright, Monte F. Collins (based on a story by Ralph S. Lewis, Bernard D. Shamberg); ph, William Sickner; ed, Roy Livingston; md, Edward J. Kay; art d, Dave Milton; set d, Raymond Boltz, Jr.

Sport Drama   **(PR:A   MPAA:NR)**

FIGHTING MAD*   (1957, Brit.) 53m Border/New Realm bw

Joe Robinson (*Muscles Tanner*), Adrienne Scott (*Paula*), Beckett Bould (*Uncle Jake*), Jack Taylor (*Walker*), Colin Cleminson.

Robinson quits boxing and moves to Canada after killing two men in the ring. There he helps his uncle, Bould, whose oil claim is being blocked by evil lumber barons. The bad guys try to kill Robinson, but he survives. With a name like "Muscles" it's not difficult to figure out what Robinson does to the crooks. Weak entertainment, crudely done.

p, Edwin J. Fancey; d, Denis Kavanagh; w, Jennifer Wyatt; ph, Hal Morey.

Crime   **(PR:A-C   MPAA:NR)**

FIGHTING MAD**½   (1976) 90m FOX c

Peter Fonda (*Tom*), Lynn Lowry (*Lorene*), John Doucette (*Jeff*), Philip Carey (*Pierce*), Scott Glenn (*Charlie*), Kathleen Miller (*Carolee*), Harry Northup (*Sheriff*), Ted Markland (*Hal*), Gino Franco (*Dylan*), Noble Willingham (*Senator*).

Fonda fights back against a coal mining magnate who's trying to buy the family property. When Fonda discovers a plot to kill two members of his family he carries his case to an indifferent sheriff. Frustrated, he takes the law into his own hands. There's nothing new in the story but Demme's spirited direction augments the material.

p, Roger Corman, Evelyn Purcell; d, Jonathan Demme; w, Demme; ph, Michael Watkins (Deluxe Color); m, Bruce Langhorne; ed, Anthony Magro; stunts, Allan Wyatt.

Drama   **(PR:C   MPAA:R)**

FIGHTING MAN OF THE PLAINS**   (1949) 94m FOX c

Randolph Scott (*Jim Dancer*), Bill Williams (*Johnny Tancred*), Victor Jory (*Dave Oldham*), Jane Nigh (*Florence Peel*), Douglas Kennedy (*Ken Vedder*), Joan Taylor (*Evelyn Slocum*), Berry Kroeger (*Cliff Bailey*), Rhys Williams (*Chandler Leach*), Barry Kelley (*Slocum*), James Todd (*Hobson*), Paul Fix (*Yancey*), James Millican (*Cummings*), Burk Symon (*Meeker*), Dale Robertson (*Jesse James*), Herbert Rawlinson (*Lawyer*), J. Farrell MacDonald (*Partridge*), Harry Cheshire (*Lanyard*), James Griffith (*Quantrell*), Tony Hughes (*Kerrigan*), John Hamilton (*Currier*), John Halloran (*Harmer*), Cliff Clark (*Travers*), Anthony Jochim (*Holz*), James Harrison (*Slattery*), Matt Willis (*Ferryman*).

Fair western with Scott as an outlaw who assumes the mantle of the detective who captures him when the man is accidentally killed. Once free, he comes to the town of Lanyard where Kelley is a rich rancher fencing off land for planting and irking the railroad people as well as the cattlemen. Once he arrives, Scott is acknowledged to be the new marshal. In this unfamiliar capacity he soon excels and finds that he likes it better inside the law than outside. Jane Nigh is the brief romantic interest and she and Scott are planning to make it legal when he's recognized as being a criminal and brought to the gibbet for a necktie party. Dale Robertson, as Jesse James, rides in to rescue Scott and all is forgiven. Jory is particularly good as a gambler who makes Scott a pal and helps him when he can. Jory was born in Alaska in the early 1900s and was the boxing and wrestling champion in the U.S. Coast Guard before going on the stage in 1929 and then into movies in 1932 (PRIDE OF THE LEGION).

p, Nat Holt; d, Edwin L. Marin; w, Frank Gruber; ph, Fred Jackman, Jr. (Cinecolor); m, Paul Sawtell; ed, Philip Martin; art d, George Van Marter.

Western   **(PR:A   MPAA:NR)**

FIGHTING MARSHAL, THE**   (1932) 58m COL bw

Tim McCoy, Dorothy Gulliver, Mary Carr, Matthew Betz, Pat O'Malley, Edward Le Saint, Lafe McKee, W.A. Howell, Dick Dickinson, Bob Perry, Harry Todd, Ethan Laidlaw, Lee Shumway, Black-Jack Ward, Blackie Whiteford.

Film opens with popular cowboy actor McCoy, a recently escaped convict who was serving time for a crime he did not commit. While headed for a new town where no one has seen him before, he finds the body of a dead marshal, takes his identity, and masquerades as the town's new marshal. The town just happens to be the same place where the two men who committed the crime he was arrested for live. McCoy's convict friend who helped him to escape shows up and discloses everything before he dies.

d, Ross Lederman; w, Frank Howard Clark; ph, Benjamin Kline; ed, Otto Meyer.

Western   **(PR:AA   MPAA:NR)**

FIGHTING O'FLYNN, THE***   (1949) 91m UNIV bw
(AKA: THE O'FLYNN)

Douglas Fairbanks, Jr. (*The O'Flynn*), Helena Carter (*Lady Benedetta*), Richard Greene (*Lord Sedgemouth*), Patricia Medina (*Fancy Free*), Arthur Shields (*Dooley*), J.M. Kerrigan (*Timothy*), Ludwig Donath (*Hendrigg*), Lumsden Hare (*The Viceroy*), Otto Waldis (*Gen. Van Dronk*), Henry Brandon (*Lt. Carpe*), Pat O'Moore (*Maj. Steele*), Tom Moore (*Tavernkeeper*), Leslie Denison (*Colonel*), James Craven (*Subaltern*), Harry Cording (*Pat*), John Doucette (*Jack*).

Unbuckle your swash and let the blarney fly as Fairbanks plays a rip-snorting Irish leader in the time of Napoleon. There was worry that The Little Corporal would attempt to take over Erin, and Fairbanks, equally adroit with a sabre, rapier, shillelagh, or a kiss, does a splendid job in what is almost, but not quite, a satire of Errol Flynn and even Fairbanks himself in THE CORSICAN BROTHERS. Fairbanks is traveling to a castle he has inherited when he rescues Carter, daughter of Viceroy Hare, as her coach is being waylaid. Fairbanks leaps from horse to horse, roof to roof, heart to heart, and saves Ireland from the duplicity of Greene, who is Hare's assistant and in Napoleon's employ. Very enjoyable nonsense with lots of derring-do from Fairbanks in the kind of role his dad used to play.

p, Douglas Fairbanks, Jr.; d, Arthur Pierson; w, Fairbanks, Robert Thoeren (based on the novel *The O'Flynn* by Justin Huntly McCarthy); ph, Arthur Edeson; m, Frank Skinner; ed, Russell Schoengarth; md, Milton Schwarzwald; art d, Bernard Herzbrun; spec eff, David S. Horsley.

Adventure   **(PR:A   MPAA:NR)**

FIGHTING PARSON, THE*   (1933) 66m Allied bw

Hoot Gibson, Marceline Day, Ethel Wales, Robert Frazer, Stanley Blystone, Skeeter Bill Robbins, Charles King, Jules Cowan, Phil Dunham, Frank Nelson.

Townspeople mistake wanderer Gibson for a preacher for their revival meeting in this oater. Reversing the "good-guy-pretends-to-be-a-bad-guy-to-catch-criminals" approach, Gibson willingly takes on the position. Weak script is only somewhat saved by the lead character and a landslide sequence. One of the eleven westerns Gibson made for Allied after Universal dropped his contract in 1931, fearing the unprofitability of sound westerns, and, like the rest, sadly lacking in good production techniques.

d, Harry Frazer; w, Ed Weston; ph, M.H. Hoffman, Jr.

Western   **(PR:A   MPAA:NR)**

FIGHTING PIMPERNEL, THE**½   (1950, Brit.) 109m BL c
(GB: THE ELUSIVE PIMPERNEL)

David Niven (*Sir Percy Blakeney*), Margaret Leighton (*Marguerite Blakeney*), Jack Hawkins (*Prince of Wales*), Cyril Cusack (*Chauvelin*), Robert Coote (*Sir Andrew Ffoulkes*), Edmond Audran (*Armand St. Juste*), Danielle Godet (*Suzanne de*

Tournai), Arlette Marchal (Comtesse de Tournai), Gerard Nery (Philippe de Tournai), Charles Victor (Col. Winterbottom), David Hutcheson (Lord Anthony Dewhurst), Eugene Deckers (Capt. Merieres), John Longden (Abbot), Arthur Wontner (Lord Grenville), David Oxley (Capt. Duroc), Raymond Rollett (Bibot), Philip Stainton (Jellyband), Robert Griffiths (Trubshaw), George de Warfaz (Baron), Jane Gill Davies (Lady Grenville), Richard George (Sir John Coke), Cherry Cottrell (Lady Coke), John Fitzgerald (Sir Michael Travers), Patrick Macnee (Hon. John Bristow), Terence Alexander (Duke of Dorset), Tommy Duggan (Earl of Sligo), John Fitchen (Nigel Seymour), John Hewitt (Maj. Pretty), Hugh Kelly (Mr. Fitzdrummond), Richard Nairne (Beau Pepys), Sally Newland, Peter Copley.

Lackluster telling of the story of the English aristocrat who assumes a number of disguises to rescue nobles from the French Revolution guillotine. Niven tries hard in the title role, but is overwhelmed by the leisurely pacing and Technicolor effects. (Remake of THE SCARLET PIMPERNEL.)

p, Samuel Goldwyn, Alexander Korda; d&w, Michael Powell, Emeric Pressburger (based on the novel *The Scarlet Pimpernel* by Baroness Orczy); ph, Christopher Challis (Technicolor); m, Brian Easdale; ed, Charles Poulton; prod d, Hein Heckroth; set d, Arthur Lawson, Joseph Bato; spec eff, W. Percy Day.

Adventure (PR:A MPAA:NR)

FIGHTING PIONEERS** (1935) 54m Resolute bw

Rex Bell (Lt. Bentley), Ruth Mix (Wa-No-Na), Buzz Barton ("Splinters"), Stanley Blystone (Hadley), Earl Dwire (Sgt. Luke), John Elliott, Roger Williams, Guate Mozin, Chief Standing Bear, Chuck Morrison, Chief Thunder Cloud.

Mix, after the death of her father, leads her tribe against the Federals in this story of Indians fighting soldiers. Conspiracy ensues as a scheming sergeant and the fort's storekeeper sell rifles to the Indians. Breezy, likable Bell, an Army lieutenant, is suspected of being behind the nefarious scheme until he catches the real crooks. Another of the four gun-blazers Rex made for Resolute and featuring Tom Mix's daughter, Ruth, which remain even today among the unique cowboy pictures in spite of their low-grade quality, on the strength of Bell's presence, and because he always provided pleasant memories in his sage-brushers.

p, Al Mannon; d, Harry Fraser, w, Fraser, Chuck Roberts; ph, Robert Cline; ed, Logan Pierson.

Western (PR:A MPAA:NR)

FIGHTING PLAYBOY zero (1937) 50m Northern Films bw

Nick Stuart (Don), Lucille Browne (Connie), James Magrath (Pettray), Robert Webb (Gillis), Michael Heppell (Rennie), C. Middleton Evans (Maclean), A. Legge Willis (Wainright), A. McNeil (John), Reginald Hincks (Bill).

Stuart is a playboy who is cut off by his father because he is having too much fun with the family funds. Stuart then goes to the Canadian north woods and there proves himself by making a fortune and finding a bride. A quickie best forgotten quickly.

p, Kenneth J. Bishop; d, Robert F. Hill; w, Arthur Hoerl (based on the story "The Crimson West" by Alex Phillip); ph, William J. Beckway.

Western (PR:A MPAA:NR)

FIGHTING PRINCE OF DONEGAL, THE** (1966, Brit.) 110m BV c

Peter McEnery (Hugh O'Donnell), Susan Hampshire (Kathleen MacSweeney), Tom Adams (Henry O'Neill), Gordon Jackson (Capt. Leeds), Andrew Keir (Lord MacSweeney, Clan Leader), Maurice Roeves (Martin, Prison Boy), Donal McCann (Sean O'Toole, Prisoner), Richard Leech (Phelim O'Toole, O'Neill Clan Leader), Peter Jeffrey (Troop Sergeant), Marie Kean (Mother), Bill Owen (1st Officer Powell), Peggy Marshall (Princess Ineen), Fidelma Murphy (Moire), Maire O'Neill, Maire Ni Ghrainne (Moire's Sisters), Norman Wooland (Sir John Perrott), John Forbes-Robertson, Patrick Holt, Robert Cawdron, Roger Croucher, Keith McConnell, Inigo Jackson, Peter Cranwell.

An inferior fictional piece of the 11th-century Irish-British political scene, produced by Walt Disney and based on Robert T. Reilly's historical novel, *Red Hugh, Prince of Donegal.* The story is about McEnery, a young Irish prince who becomes leader of his people after an escape from capture by the British. Jackson, leader of the British troops in Ireland, retaliates by kidnaping the prince's mother and true love. McEnery faces up to the British and recaptures the castle.

p, Walt Disney, Bill Anderson; d, Michael O'Herlihy; w, Robert Westerby (based on book *Red Hugh, Prince of Donegal* by Robert T. Reilly); ph, Arthur Ibbetson (Technicolor); m, George Bruns; ed, Peter Boita; art d, Maurice Carter; set d, David Ffolkes; cos, Hugh Anthony Mendleson; spec eff, Peter Ellenshaw.

Juvenile/Adventure (PR:AAA MPAA:NR)

FIGHTING RANGER, THE**½ (1934) 60m COL bw

Buck Jones (Jim), Dorothy Revier (Tonita), Frank Rice (Thunder), Bradley Page (Cougar), Ward Bond (Dave), Mozelle Brittone (Rose), Paddy O'Flynn (Bob), Art Mix (Kelso), Frank LaRue (Pegleg Barnes), John Wallace (Capt. Wilkes), Denver Dixon, Art Smith, Bud Osborne, Lew Meehan, Jim Corey, Steve Clemente, Frank Ellis, Silver the Horse.

Basically a remake of Jones' earlier film, BORDER LAW (1931), Jones and his sidekick Rice leave Texas to track down his brother's killer. Jones finds the killer in Mexico and takes vengeance after the usual gun fights, riding, and fist fights. Another of the sixty one films Jones, the most loved and respected of all film cowboys, made between 1932 and 1938, and every one a moneymaker.

p, Irving Briskin; d, George B. Seitz; w, Harry Hoyt; ph, Sid Wagner; ed, Leon Barsha.

Western (PR:A MPAA:NR)

FIGHTING RANGER, THE*½ (1948) 57m MON bw

Johnny Mack Brown, Raymond Hatton, Christine Larson, Marshall Reed, Eddie Parker, Charlie Hughes, I. Stanford Jolley, Milburn Morante, Steve Clark, Bob Woodward, Peter Perkins.

Oater star Brown travels down the well-trodden trail of Western plots as he takes the role of a law-abiding ranger who, with fellow badge-carrier Hatton, leads a pursuit of an outlaw gang. The action-packed finale has Brown once again emerging victorious.

p, Barney Sarecky; d, Lambert Hillyer; w, Ronald Davidson.

Western (PR:A MPAA:NR)

FIGHTING REDHEAD, THE** (1950) 55m EL c

Jim Bannon (Red Ryder), Don Kay Reynolds (Little Beaver), Emmet Lynn (Buckskin), Marin Sais (Duchess), Peggy Stewart (Sheila), John Hart (Faro), Lane Bradford (Windy), Forrest Taylor (O'Connor), Lee Roberts (Goldie), Bob Duncan (Sheriff), Sandy Sanders (Joe), Billy Hammond (Evans), "Spooky" Reynolds (Mary).

The last film in the short lived "Red Rider" series based on the comic strip. The film has Hart as a cattle rustling murderer, uncovered by Taylor, who is then also killed by Hart. Stewart, Taylor's daughter, attempts to avenge her father's death, but has no success until Bannon, the hero, arrives. After the failure of the series, Bannon took on supporting roles in various film genres, and then drifted into TV work. (See RED RYDER series, Index)

p, Jerry Thomas; d, Lewis D. Collins; w, Paul Franklin, Thomas (based on the comic strip, "Red Ryder"); ph, Gilbert Warrenton; m, Darrell Calker, David Chudnow; ed, Joseph P. Gluck.

Western (PR:A MPAA:NR)

FIGHTING RENEGADE** (1939) 54m Victory bw

Tim McCoy (Lightning Bill Carson/El Puma), Joyce Bryant (Marian Willis), Ben Corbett (Magpie), Ted Adams (Link Benson), Budd Buster (Old Dobie), Dave O'Brien (Jerry Leonard), Forrest Taylor (Prof. Lucius Lloyd), Reed Howes (Sheriff), John Elliott (Prospector), Carl Matthews.

McCoy gets tangled in some complicated identity changes and murder charges on an expedition into Mexico in search of an Indian burial ground. Wrongfully accused of being the murderer of the leader of the first expedition, he disguises himself as El Puma, a feared Mexican bandit, when a second expedition arrives to continue the search. The leader of that expedition, Taylor, is knifed and the killer, Adams, blames it on El Puma. McCoy is accused of two murders. After a search for the relics and the murderer by McCoy, Adams, the sheriff, and his deputies, the killer is found and justice is served. The usual thing livened with some beautiful outdoor camerawork.

p, Sam Katzman; d, Sam Newfield; w, William Lively; ph, Art Reed; ed, Holbrook Todd.

Western Cas. (PR:AA MPAA:NR)

FIGHTING ROOKIE, THE* (1934) 67m Mayfair bw

Jack LaRue, Matthew Betz, Ada Ince, DeWitt Jennings, Arthur Belasco, Thomas Brewer.

A tough young cop is disgraced by the mob only making him tougher. He fights back and brings law and order down upon the gangsters' regime. A weak programmer with little punch.

d, Spencer Gordon Bennett; w, George Morgan (based on the story by Homer King Gordon); ph, James S. Brown, Jr.; ed, Fred Bain.

Crime Drama (PR:A MPAA:NR)

FIGHTING SEABEES, THE*** (1944) 100m REP bw

John Wayne (Wedge Donovan), Susan Hayward (Constance Chesley), Dennis O'Keefe (Lt. Comdr. Robert Yarrow), William Frawley (Eddie Powers), Leonid Kinskey (Johnny Novasky), J. M. Kerrigan (Sawyer Collins), Grant Withers (Whanger Spreckles), Paul Fix (Ding Jacobs), Ben Welden (Yump Lumkin), William Forrest (Lt. Kerrick), Addison Richards (Captain Joyce), Jay Norris (Joe Brick), Duncan Renaldo (Juan).

A rousing propaganda film, one of the most popular during WW II, has the swaggering Wayne as the head of a construction company working for the Navy on a remote Pacific island, building fortifications and an airstrip. Hayward, in one of her better early-starring roles, is a news correspondent who falls in love with Wayne, who will have nothing to do with her. Navy commander O'Keefe, in love with Hayward, is at odds with the Duke over his unorthodox ways and because he forsakes Hayward's affections. When the Japanese invade the island, Wayne ignores O'Keefe's orders to have his men take refuge; enraged when some of his workers are machinegunned by strafing Zeros, Wayne orders his men armed, and they attack the Japanese shock troops. A slaughter ensues with the construction workers mowed down by professional troops. O'Keefe's carefully drawn plans at an ambush are fouled up by the interference of Wayne's men. The Japanese are finally destroyed but the price is high. Hayward, thinking Wayne wounded or dead, searches the battlefield for him and is severely wounded by a Japanese soldier playing dead (one of the typical Japanese tricks Americans learned to despise). Before doctors operate on her, she begs Wayne to tell her she loves him. Thinking she is dying, Wayne blurts it out (like a drill sergeant barking a command). But Hayward recovers and believes she will finally land Wayne. Meanwhile, O'Keefe is about to have Wayne thrown out of his Navy contract, if not the Pacific altogether. But the Duke sees the errors of his ways and apologizes, realizing that his judgment has been faulty. He and O'Keefe journey to Washington where Richards puts together a new Navy unit with Wayne and O'Keefe at its head, the Seabees. All of Wayne's workers are enlisted, along with the phalanxes of construction men Wayne recruits. They are quickly but rigorously trained and then sent to another island. As they build their airstrip, the Japanese pick them off from hiding (behind rocks, from holes beneath the ground, while perched in palm trees). Wayne can stand it no longer. Again, he disobeys orders and leads his men in a sweep of the island, leaving the oil tanks undefended. O'Keefe and a handful of men try to stem a large Japanese counter-attack. When Wayne hears that O'Keefe' forces are being pressed hard, he leads his men back wading into the enemy. (It was in this film that Wayne got the reputation of being able to destroy legions of enemy troopers. At one point he kills five Japanese soldiers with gun butt, bayonet, and bare hands, then grabs a machine gun to destroy a whole line of charging enemy troopers. This is easily accomplished since the enemy is profiled as buck-toothed, squinty-eyed, with glasses the thickness of telescopes, and standing no higher than Baby Leroy.) Just as the enemy is about to make a breakthrough, Wayne mounts a bulldozer laden with dynamite and purposely drives it into an oil tank, blowing up the enemy and himself. He is later given a posthumous citation in the States while Hayward and O'Keefe, united at the end, look on proudly. It's all very hokey, but it's as action-packed as the best of the serials, and Wayne's male supremacist role is both funny and awesome as he fends off pesky female Hayward. In this most expensive Republic film to date, Hayward excels as the lovestruck newslady. (This would be her third and last film for a studio that could no longer afford salary demands commensurate with her enormous popularity.) On board ship while heading for the first island, Hayward stands with Wayne at the rail, looking out to sea and poetically saying: "Watching a ship's wake always makes me think of things that time puts behind us forever—hopes, dreams, illusions. What does it make you think about?" Replies Wayne: "If they changed the pitch of that propeller, they'd get a couple of more knots out of this tub!" Flares Hayward: "I thought I caught you being human for once. Don't you have anything under that thick hide of yours but cylinders and a carburetor?" He shrugs: "A sparkplug maybe." Even though she's hopelessly in love with Wayne, she considers him "a hotheaded ape with a hair-trigger temper." Of course, that's why she loves him. Who wouldn't? Director Ludwig handles the action well and Scharf's exceptional score earned him an Oscar nomination.

p, Albert J. Cohen; d, Edward Ludwig, Howard Lydecker; w, Borden Chase, Aeneas MacKenzie (based on a story by Chase); ph, William Bradford; m, Walter Scharf; ed, Richard Van Enger; art d, Duncan Cramer; spec eff, Theodore Lydecker.

War Drama **Cas.** **(PR:C MPAA:NR)**

FIGHTING SHADOWS*½ (1935) 58m COL bw

Tim McCoy, Robert Allen, Geneva Mitchell, Ward Bond, Si Jenks, Otto Hoffman, Edward J. LeSaint, Bud Osborne, Alan Sears, Ethan Laidlaw.

McCoy takes the lead role as a courageous, hard-riding lawman who rids his Western town of an unscrupulous bandit gang, once again making it safe for the locals. Highlighted by some fine trick riding—a skill for which McCoy was known. The same year, McCoy gave the public a thrill as a rider for Ringling Bros. Circus, a feat also shared by fellow oater star Tom Mix a few years earlier.

d, David Selman; w, Ford Beebe; ph, George Meehan; ed, Gene Milford.

Western **(PR:A MPAA:NR)**

FIGHTING SHERIFF, THE* (1931) 65m Beverly/COL bw

Buck Jones, Loretta Sayers, Robert Ellis, Harlan Knight, Paul Fix, Lillian Worth, Nena Quartero, Clarence Muse, Lilliane Leighton, Tom Bay, Silver the Horse.

Sayers, a society debutante, is thrown together with Jones, a rough and tumble cowboy. The two dislike each other's lifestyles, but after a series of typical Western happenings, the two fall in love. Jones was making about $300 a week at this time, working for Sol Lesser's Beverly Productions, a steep drop from what he had formerly been making at Fox. But with the slump in westerns in the early 1930s he was lucky to be making anything.

p, Sol Lesser; d, Louis King; w, Stuart Anthony; ph, Teddy Tetzlaff.

Western **(PR:A MPAA:NR)**

FIGHTING 69TH, THE***** (1940) 90m WB bw

James Cagney *(Jerry Plunkett)*, Pat O'Brien *(Father Duffy)*, George Brent *(Wild Bill Donovan)*, Jeffrey Lynn *(Joyce Kilmer)*, Alan Hale *(Sgt. Big Mike Wynn)*, Frank McHugh *("Crepe Hanger" Burke)*, Dennis Morgan *(Lt. Ames)*, William Lundigan *(Timmy Wynn)*, Dick Foran *(John Wynn)*, Guinn "Big Boy" Williams *(Paddy Dolan)*, Henry O'Neill *(The Colonel)*, John Litel *(Capt. Mangan)*, Sammy Cohen *(Mike Murphy)*, Harvey Stephens *(Maj. Anderson)*, William Hopper *(Pvt. Turner)*, Tom Dugan *(Pvt. McManus)*, George Reeves *(Jack O'Keefe)*, Charles Trowbridge *(Chaplain Holmes)*, Frank Wilcox *(Lt. Norman)*, Herbert Anderson *(Casey)*, J. Anthony Hughes *(Healey)*, Frank Mayo *(Capt. Bootz)*, John Harron *(Carroll)*, George Kilgen *(Ryan)*, Richard Clayton *(Tierney)*, Edward Dew *(Regan)*, Wilfred Lucas, Joseph Crehan, Emmett Vogan *(Doctors)*, Frank Sully *(Sergeant)*, James Flavin *(Supply Sergeant)*, George O'Hanlon *(Eddie)*, Jack Perrin *(Major)*, Trevor Bardette, John Arledge, Frank Melton, Edmund Glover *(Alabama Men)*, Edgar Edwards *(Engineer Officer)*, Ralph Dunn *(Medical Captain)*, Arno Frey, Roland Varno *(German Officers)*, Layne Ireland *(Hefferman)*, Elmo Murray *(O'Brien)*, Jacques Lory *(Waiter)*, Frank Coghlan, Jr. *(Jimmy)*, Frank Faylen *(Engineer Sergeant)*, Jerry Fletcher *(Telephonist)*, Byron Nelson, Sol Gorss *(Soldiers)*, Jack Boyle, Jr. *(Chuck)*, Creighton Hale, Benny Rubin, Eddie Acuff, Jack Mower, Nat Carr, Jack Wise.

One of the great, patriotic WW II films, THE FIGHTING 69TH offers Cagney in a tour de force role of a wisecracking, swaggering would-be hero from Brooklyn who joins the all-Irish 69th New York regiment (later the 165th Infantry, incorporated into the Rainbow Division). He is a street corner brawler who could care less about the illustrious military history embodied in the old 69th. He encounters O'Brien, famous Father Duffy, the regimental chaplain, thinking he is no more than another enlisted man at Camp Mills, N.Y. After the two help to break up a brawl between the 69th men and 4th Alabama regiment which has come to join them, Cagney learns O'Brien's true identity. He regards O'Brien with disdain, telling him, "I don't go in for that Holy Joe stuff." Throughout his training, he defies his superiors, from tough old sergeant Hale to commander Brent, playing the true-to-life part of Col. William "Wild Bill" Donovan, a famed fighter and later head of OSS, the first modern U.S. spy service. Following his training, which Cagney thinks is a waste of time, the regiments are shipped to France. As the men march toward the trenches, Cagney's obnoxious braggadocio increases. He speaks openly of tearing into "those Heinies," and carries the packs and rifles of exhausted soldiers. When Cagney gets into the trenches and witnesses the slaughter inflicted upon his regiment by the Germans, he panics and sends up a star shell to pick off some German snipers. By doing so, Cagney has given away his regiment's position and an incredible barrage devastates the American trenches, killing scores. Cagney cringes in fear, then runs for cover. Dugouts collapse and scores more are killed. O'Brien finds Cagney and tries to quiet him but Cagney is unreachable, gripped by overwhelming fear. Later, when sent on patrol, he spots the enemy approaching and begins to run, stopped by some of his own men. When he cries out, the Germans are alerted and open fire, killing scores of doughboys, including Morgan and Lundigan, Hale's brothers, along with Lynn, playing the part of the poet Joyce Kilmer. (Kilmer was really killed while going for a drink of water in a dugout which suddenly received a direct hit by a single shell sent into the American lines by a randomly firing German battery.) Under arrest to face court martial for cowardice, Cagney is sent to a makeshift prison adjacent to the hospital in the town. O'Brien goes to Brent following Cagney's conviction and sentence of death to beg for his life. Brent is adamant, labeling Cagney a "bully, a braggart, and a coward," and refuses to grant a reprieve. On the eve of his execution, Cagney suddenly hears a massive German bombardment and cowers inside the locked storefront where he is held prisoner. A bomb hits the building, collapsing a wall opening on to the hospital area. Cagney watches as the wounded doughboys begin to panic and O'Brien, moving courageously among the, calms them, then has them join with him in prayer. When O'Brien looks up, he sees Cagney on his knees, praying. The condemned Cagney then stands up and nods knowingly to O'Brien. He dashes outside and quickly makes his way to the front lines where the 69th is being slaughtered in a frontal attack against strong German positions, held up by streams of barbed wire. Cagney grabs a mortar and, with the help of the wounded Hale, sends one shell after another into the wire, blowing holes so wide into it that the 69th men are able to pour through and take the German positions. A German soldier, however, sends a well-aimed grenade into Cagney's foxhole and, to save Hale's life, he falls on it, the blast mortally wounding him. He is taken to a field hospital where O'Brien administers the last rites. Brent arrives and looks down on Cagney, saying, "And I thought this man was a coward." Hale, standing nearby, grunts: "Coward, sir. From now on, every time I hear the name Plunkett, I'll stand to attention and salute!" Cagney dies a hero's death and, in a final and stirring montage showing the regiment's "lost generation" of soldiers parading by, O'Brien gives a moving prayer that these men will not be forgotten. THE FIGHTING 69TH was an enormous hit with the public despite the lack of a single woman in the story (Priscilla Lane was originally cast to play a-girl-at-home part but was dropped). The wise marketing by Warner Bros. rightly assumed that the U.S. public, close to entering WW II, would respond well to a solid patriotic film and with the consummate actor Cagney, a terrific supporting cast, and Keighley's inspired direction, it couldn't and didn't miss. The script by Niblo, Raine, and Franklin is both funny and touching, dealing with a host of characters—Guinn "Big Boy" Williams, Frank McHugh, Tom Dugan, Sammy Cohen—who people the film with color and drama. O'Brien is superb as the heroic Father Duffy (whose noble statue still stands in Manhattan's Times Square). He considered this among his finest roles, although he knew his job would be harder playing across from Cagney. O'Brien later remarked that "Jimmy can steal a scene by lifting an eyebrow." The film was lavished with sets of epic proportions; Warners spent a fortune recreating Camp Mills, French villages, and spectacular battlefields, as well as using armies of extras, turning over the studio's entire Calabasas Ranch for the massive production. The film premiered in New York and Father Duffy attended, shaking hands with Cagney, O'Brien, Brent, and every actor sent to attend, Irish all, an event that prompted tens of thousands more to flock to see the film. One of the great Warner cinematographers, Gaudio, excelled here; this was his kind of film, plenty of action for his always fluid cameras. Warners beat rival studios MGM and Fox to the punch with this marvelous production. Fox was attempting to borrow Spencer Tracy from MGM for a film it was planning, tentatively entitled FATHER DUFFY OF THE FIGHTING 69TH. When Warners launched its Cagney film, Fox abandoned its own version. There are no dull moments in this film, a fact emphasized by Cagney himself when reporters gathered on the set. One reporter asked the acting dynamo what was going to happen next. Incredulous, Cagney retorted: "Are you really that interested?"

p, Jack L. Warner; d, William Keighley; w, Norman Reilly Raine, Fred Niblo, Jr., Dean Franklin; ph, Tony Gaudio; m, Adolph Deutsch; ed, Owen Marks; md, Leo F. Forbstein; art d, Ted Smith; spec eff, Byron Haskin, Rex Wimpy; makeup, Perc Westmore.

War Drama **(PR:A MPAA:NR)**

FIGHTING STALLION, THE* (1950) 63m EL bw

Bill Edwards *(Lon Evans)*, Doris Merrick *(Jeanne Barton)*, Forrest Taylor *(Martin Evans)*, Don Harvey *(Cmdr. Patrick)*, Robert Carson *(Tom Adams)*, Concha Ybarra *(Nantee)*, Rocky Camron *(Lem)*, William Merrill McCormick *(Yancy)*, John Carpenter *(Chuck)*, Maria Hart *(Dude)*.

Edwards is a war veteran who trains a seeing-eye horse after he finds out he is losing his eyesight. The horse is thought to be mean and of bad blood, but Edwards shows that the animal is good-tempered and docile once trained. A lot of footage was wasted on this tame production.

p, Jack Schwarz, Robert Tansey; d, Tansey; w, Frances Kavanaugh (based on a story by George P. Slavin); ph, Clark Ramsey; m, Edward Paul; ed, Reg Browne.

Western **(PR:A MPAA:NR)**

FIGHTING STOCK   (1935, Brit.) 68m Gainsborough/GAU bw

Tom Walls (*Sir Donald Rowley*), Ralph Lynn (*Sidney*), J. Robertson Hare (*Duck*), Marie Lohr (*Barbara Rivers*), Lesley Wareing (*Eileen Rivers*), Veronica Rose (*Diana Rivers*), Herbert Lomas (*Murlow*), Hubert Harben (*Mr. Rivers*), Mary Jerrold (*Emmie*), Sybil Grove (*Mrs. Peacock*), Norah Howard (*Ada*), Margaret Davidge, Peggy Simpson (*Maids*).

Walls and nephew Lynn rent a cottage and collide with neighbor Harben over fishing rights. The situation deteriorates further when Lynn takes up with Wareing, Harben's stepdaughter. All are reconciled when Walls and Lynn save Rose, Harben's niece, from blackmailer Lomas. Middling British comedy.

p, Michael Balcon; d, Tom Walls; w, Ben Travers; ph, Philip Tannura.

Comedy   (PR:A   MPAA:NR)

FIGHTING SULLIVANS, THE   (SEE: SULLIVANS, THE, 1944)

FIGHTING TEXAN   (1937) 58m Ambassador bw

Kermit Maynard (*Glenn*), Elaine Shepard (*Judy*), Frank LaRue (*Walton*), Budd Buster (*Old Timer*), Ed Cassidy (*Hadley*), Murdock McQuarrie (*Slim*), Bruce Mitchell (*Sheriff*), Art Miles (*Carter*), Frank McCormack (*Bart*).

Kermit Maynard buys a troubled ranch with a partner and, when the partner is shot, is suspected of having done the deed to get the ranch for himself. The rest of the film follows Maynard's search for the culprit and the clearing of his name. Kermit, the lesser known brother of Ken Maynard, could outride his famous brother but lacked the charisma (and the horse Tarzan) his brother had. He began in films as a double for Ken and other cowboy stars.

p, Maurice Conn; d, Charles Abbott; w, Joseph O'Donnell, (based on an original story by James Oliver Curwood); ph, Jack Greenhalgh; ed, Glen Glenn.

Western   (PR:A   MPAA:NR)

FIGHTING TEXANS   (1933) 60m MON bw

Rex Bell (*Randolph Graves*), Luana Walters (*Joan Carver*), Betty Mack (*Rita Walsh*), Gordon DeMain (*Julian Nash*), Lafe McKee (*Sheriff Carver*), Al Bridge (*Gus Durkin*), George Nash (*Albert*), George Hayes (*Old Man Martin*), Wally Wales (*Pete*), Yakima Canutt (*Hank*), Anne Howard (*Mrs. Whimple*).

Bell, a young Texas oil salesman, persuades an entire town to invest in an oil well that the bankers are sure will be nothing but a dry hole. The bankers are, of course, flabbergasted and dismayed when the well is a gusher and the whole town gets rich.

p, Trem Carr; d, Armand Schaefer; w, Wellyn Totman, Charles Roberts; ph, Archie Stout.

Western   (PR:A   MPAA:NR)

FIGHTING THOROUGHBREDS½   (1939) 65m REP bw

Ralph Byrd (*Ben Marshall*), Mary Carlisle (*Marian*), Robert Allen (*Greg*), George Hayes (*Gramp*), Marvin Stephens (*Hefty*), Charles Wilson (*Bogart*), Kenne Duncan (*Brady*), Victor Kilian (*Wilson*), Eddie Brian (*Colton*).

A neat horse race story that mixes a Kentucky feud and a good romantic conflict with fast action on the track when a Kentucky Derby winner sires a colt belonging to impecunious Carlisle and her grandfather, who have incurred the wrath of the derby winner's owner, Wilson. Of course, the colt grows up to have dirt smarts and makes off with the purses at several minor tracks. When the big day comes (the derby, naturally), the smart nag is entered along with (who else?) a horse belonging to Wilson, who gets his comeuppance at the finish line.

p, Armand Schaefer; d, Sidney Salkow; w, Wellyn Totman, Franklyn Coen (based on a story by Clarence E. Marks, Robert Wyler); ph, Jack Marta; m, Cy Feuer; ed, Ernest Nims.

Drama   (PR:A   MPAA:NR)

FIGHTING THRU   (1931) 61m TIF bw (AKA: CALIFORNIA IN 1878)

Ken Maynard (*Dan Barton*), Jeanette Loff (*Alice Madden*), Wallace MacDonald (*Tennessee Malden*), Carmelita Geraghty (*Queenie*), William L. Thorne (*Ace*), Charles L. King (*Fox Tyson*), Fred Burns (*Sheriff*), Bill Nestell, Tommy Bay, John [Jack] Fowler, Charles Baldra, Art Mix, Jack Kirk, Bud McClure, Jim Corey, Tarzan the Horse.

Ken Maynard's first all-talking western was not one of his better outings, although as always his spectacular horsemanship was there. When his partner is murdered, the killers accuse Maynard. The dead man's sister, Loff, is convinced by the real killers that Maynard is to blame and nearly gives all of her inheritance to them. A late confession saves her money, clears Maynard, and he and Loff clinch at the end.

p, Phil Goldstone; d, William Nigh; w, Jack Natteford; ph, Arthur Reed; ed, Earl Turner.

Western   **Cas.**   (PR:A   MPAA:NR)

FIGHTING TROOPER, THE   (1935) 63m Ambassador bw

Kermit Maynard (*Burke*), Barbara Worth (*Diane*), Leroy Mason (*La Farge*), Charlie Delaney (*Blackie*), Robert Frazer (*Hatfield*), Walter Miller (*Sgt. Leyton*), Joseph W. Girard (*Inspector O'Keefe*), George Regas, George Chesebro, Charles King, Artie Ortego, Lafe McKee, Milburn Morante, Gordon DeMain, Nelson McDowell, George Morrell, Merrill McCormack.

Kermit Maynard makes his long-delayed transition into sound in this story of a novice Northwest Mountie who goes undercover as a trapper to catch the man who killed one of his comrades. Good stunts, all done by Maynard himself, but boring romance.

p, Maurice Conn; d, Ray Taylor; w, Forrest Sheldon (based on the James Oliver Curwood story "Footprints"); ph, Edgar Lyons; ed, Ted Bellinger.

Western   **Cas.**   (PR:A   MPAA:NR)

FIGHTING TROUBLE   (1956) 61m AA bw

Huntz Hall (*Sach*), Stanley Clements (*Duke*), Adele Jergens (*Mae*), Joseph Downing (*Handsome Hal*), Queenie Smith (*Mrs. Kelly*), John Bleifer (*Bates*), Thomas B. Henry (*Arbo*), David Gorcey (*Chuck*), Laurie Mitchell (*Dolly*), Danny Welton (*Butch*), Charles Williams (*Smith*), Clegg Hoty (*McBride*), William Boyett (*Conroy*), Tim Ryan (*Vance*), Michael Ross (*Evans*), Benny Burt (*Max Kling*), Ann Griffith (*Hawaiian Girl*), Rick Vallin (*Vic*).

A late entry in the BOWERY BOYS series sees Hall and Clements working as freelance photographers for the *New York Morning Blade*. They photograph notorious gangster Henry for the paper by posing as interior decorators, but in their haste ruin the negative. Desperate to get another picture, Hall disguises himself as one of the mobster's Chicago connections and smuggles a camera into his nightclub. After a series of mistaken identity jokes, Hall receives counterfeit money from the hood which gives the police enough evidence to bust up the operation. (See BOWERY BOYS series, Index.)

p, Ben Schwalb; d, George Blair; w, Elwood Ulman; ph, Harry Neumann; ed, William Austin; md, Buddy Bregman; art d, David Milton; set d, Joseph Kish.

Comedy   (PR:A   MPAA:NR)

FIGHTING VALLEY   (1943) 60m PRC bw

Dave [Tex] O'Brien (*Tex Wyatt*), Jim Newill (*Jim Steele*), Guy Wilkerson ("*Panhandle*" *Perkins*), Patti McCarty (*Joan Manning*), John Merton (*Dan Wakely*), Robert Bice (*Paul Jackson*), Stanley Price (*Tucson Jones*), Mary McLaren (*Ma Donovan*), John Elliott (*Frank Burke*), Charles King (*Slim*), Dan White, Carl Mathews, Curley Dresden, Jimmy Aubrey, Jess Cavin.

One of the Oliver Drake "Texas Rangers" series, the film stars O'Brien (in a mid-career actioner), Newill, and Wilkerson as Rangers out to break up a crime ring in the ore smelting business. A large company's efforts to swallow up smaller firms are aided by Bice, who convinces his fiancee, McCarty, to play along for his own personal gain. Later in his career O'Brien turned from the movies to TV directing, and also wrote comedy material for Red Skelton.

p, Alfred Stern, Arthur Alexander; d&w, Oliver Drake; ph, Ira Morgan; ed, Charles Hinkle, Jr.

Western   (PR:A   MPAA:NR)

FIGHTING VIGILANTES, THE   (1947) 61m EL bw

Al "Lash" LaRue (*Cheyenne*), Al "Fuzzy" St. John (*Fuzzy*), Jennifer Holt (*Abby*), George Chesebro (*Price Taylor*), Lee Morgan (*Sheriff*), Marshall Reed (*Check*), Carl Mathews (*Shanks*), Russell Arms (*Trippler*), Steve Clark (*Frank Jackson*), John Elliot (*Old Man*), Felice Richmond (*Old Woman*).

This average western stars LaRue as a U.S. Marshal trying to wipe out a terrorizing food distributor who is eliminating his competition in foul ways. Holt (the daughter of the rugged film hero Jack Holt) is a girl held up by the bandits, who later joins her father, Clark, in forming a citizen's group called "The Vigilantes." The villains are caught, prices go down, and everyone can eat without fear once again. Another low-budget production in the brief film career of LaRue, known as "Lash" because of the long bullwhip he used to humble his enemies.

p, Jerry Thomas; d, Ray Taylor; w, Robert Churchill; ph, Ernest Miller; m, Walter Greene; ed, Hugh Winn.

Western   (PR:A   MPAA:NR)

FIGHTING WILDCATS, THE   (1957, Brit.) 75m Winwell/REP bw
                                          (GB: WEST OF SUEZ)

Keefe Brasselle (*Brett Manders*), Kay Callard (*Pat*), Karel Stepanek (*Langford*), Maya Koumani (*Men Hassa*), Bruce Seton (*Maj. Osborne*), Harry Fowler (*Tommy*), Ursula Howells (*Eileen*), Richard Shaw (*Cross*), Sheldon Lawrence (*Jeff*), Alex Gallier.

American mercenary Brasselle is hired by Stepanek to blow up a visiting Arab dignitary. The plot is foiled after a gun battle, and Brasselle's girl friend sacrifices her life to save the Arab. Stricken with grief over her death, Brasselle goes gunning for Stepanek. They kill each other in an exchange of gunfire. Okay suspense story with a dull romantic subplot.

p, Kay Luckwell, Derek Winn; d, Arthur Crabtree; w, Norman Hudis (based on a story by Lance Z. Hargreaves and Hudis); ph, Jimmy Harvey; ed, Peter Mayhew; md, Wilfred Burns; art d, John Stoll.

Crime   (PR:A-C   MPAA:NR)

FIGHTING YOUTH   (1935) 80m UNIV bw

Charles Farrell (*Larry Davis*), June Martel (*Betty Wilson*), Andy Devine (*Cy Kipp*), J. Farrell MacDonald (*Coach Parker*), Ann Sheridan (*Carol*), Eddie Nugent (*Tonetti*), Herman Bing (*Luigi*), Phyllis Fraser (*Dodo*), Alden Chase (*Markoff*), Glenn Boles (*Paul*), Charles Wilson (*Bull Stevens*).

Radical youths have decided that the nation's favorite team sport, college football, should go, so they draft temptress and future "Oomph Girl" Sheridan to seduce star player Farrell into dumping his loyal girl friend and taking up the wild life. His football abilities stagger of course. However, the pendulum swings back when Farrell, out of shape from his defiant behavior, rushes back in the final three minutes of the season's last game to make two touchdowns and win the championship. Undercover G-Man Nugent (posing as a college student) chases down the radical group to return the school to the status quo.

p, Fred S. Meyer; d, Hamilton Macfadden; w, Henry Johnson, Florabel Muir, Macfadden (based on a story by Stanley Meyer); ph, Eddie Snyder.

Sports Drama   (PR:A   MPAA:NR)

FIGURES IN A LANDSCAPE**

(1970, Brit.) 95m
Cinecrest-Cinema Center Films/NG c

Robert Shaw (MacConnachie), Malcolm McDowell (Ansell), Pamela Brown (Widow), Henry Woolf, (Helicopter Pilot), Christopher Malcolm (Helicopter 1st Observer), Andrew Bradford, Roger Lloyd Pack, Warwick Sims, Robert East, Tariq Younus (Soldiers).

Not even director Losey, who successfully adapted the oblique works of Harold Pinter for the screen, could breathe much life into this dull allegorical tale starring Shaw and McDowell as two escaped prisoners from an unnamed prison, running for their lives through an unnamed desert, being chased by a helicopter directed by an unnamed authority. Shaw represents instinct, while McDowell is symbolic of rational thought. That's about it. The men run; the chopper pursues. They run some more; they are buzzed by the chopper. They find a rifle, the helicopter arrives, and Shaw kills one of the men inside. They run again and then hide in a cane field. Their pursuers set fire to it and they are saved by farmers who flood the field. Just shy of friendly territory, the helicopter, after plenty of unused opportunities, shoots them dead. Good performances, good photography, and good locations surprisingly do not a good movie make.

p, John Kohn; d, Joseph Losey; w, Robert Shaw (based on the novel by Barry England); ph, Henri Alekan (Panavision, Eastmancolor); m, Richard Rodney Bennett; ed, Reginald Beck; md, Marcus Dods; art d, Fernando Gonzalez, Ted Tester; cos, Susan Yelland; spec eff, Manolo Baquero.

Action/Drama (PR:C MPAA:GP)

FILE OF THE GOLDEN GOOSE, THE**½

(1969, Brit.) 105m UA c

Yul Brynner (Peter Novak), Charles Gray (Nick Harrison, "The Owl"), Edward Woodward (Peter Thompson), John Barrie (Sloane), Adrienne Corri (Tina Dell), Bernard Archard (Collins), Karel Stepanek (Mueller), Walter Gotell (Leeds), Graham Crowden (Smythe), Geoffrey Reed (Martin), Ken Jones (Stroud), Janet Rossini (Debbie), Joe Cornelius (Grodie), Denis Shaw (Vance), Ray Marioni (Croupier), Philip Anthony (Laboratory Technician), Ivor Dean (Reynolds), Hugh McDermott (Moss), Hilary Dwyer (Anne), Anita Prynne (Genevieve), Paddy Webster (Mary), Illario Pedro (Bongo Player), Anthony Jacobs (Firenzo).

Brisk crime drama starring Brynner as a U.S. Treasury agent who combines forces with Scotland Yard detective Woodward to bust up a counterfeit gang known only as the Golden Goose. The pair join the gang to gather inside information about its operation, but soon Brynner suspects that Woodward has gone over to the other side when he and gang member Gray suggest the three go into business for themselves. Brynner is proved mistaken when Gray tricks Woodward into revealing his true identity and kills him. Gray in turn is killed by the gang for acting independently. Brynner (whose cover has not been blown) is then taken to the crime boss' headquarters. There, one of the gang members discovers his identity and promises to turn state's evidence. This is overheard and the man is killed. Brynner kills the man's murderer and with the help of men from Scotland Yard, smashes the counterfeit ring.

p, David E. Rose; d, Sam Wanamaker; w, John C. Higgins, James B. Gordon (based on a story by Higgins); ph, Ken Hodges (DeLuxe Color); m, Harry Robinson; ed, Oswald Hafenrichter; md, Philip Martell; art d, George Provis.

Crime Drama (PR:C MPAA:NR)

FILE ON THELMA JORDAN, THE***½

(1950) 100m PAR bw
(AKA:THELMA JORDAN)

Barbara Stanwyck (Thelma Jordan), Wendell Corey (Cleve Marshall), Paul Kelly (Miles Scott), Joan Tetzel (Pamela Marshall), Stanley Ridges (Kingsley Willis), Richard Rober (Tony Laredo), Minor Watson (Judge Calvin Blackwell), Barry Kelly (District Attorney Pierce), Laura Elliott (Dolly), Basil Ruysdael (Judge Hancock), Jane Novak (Mrs. Blackwell), Gertrude W. Hoffman (Aunt Vera Edwards), Harry Antrim (Sidney), Kate Lawson (Clara), Theresa Harris (Esther), Byron Barr (McCarty), Geraldine Wall (Matron), Jonathan Corey (Timmy Marshall), Robin Corey (Joan Marshall), Garry Owen (Bailiff), Clancy Cooper (Chase), Stephen Robert (Jury Foreman), Ottola Nesmith (Mrs. Asher), Stan Johnson (Young Melvin Pierce), Virginia Hunter (Secretary to the District Attorney), Nolan Leary (Court Clerk), Rodney Bell (Withers), Dorothy Klewer, Michael Ann Barrett, Fairy Cunningham, Geraldine Jordan, Lynn Whitney, Dot Farley (Women Prisoners), Lee Phelps (Chauffeur), Kenneth Tobey (Police Photographer), Tony Merrill, Eric Alden, Jack Roberts, Howard Gardiner, Jerry James, Bill Meader, Nick Cravat (Reporters), Lew Harvey (Court Reporter), Bill Hawes (Spectator), Jim Davies (Bailiff), Gertrude Astor (Juror), Caroline Fitzharris (Cook's Daughter), John Cortay (Deputy Sheriff), Ethel Bryant (Woman Deputy), William Hamel, Harry Templeton (Newsmen), Sam McDaniel (Porter), Lynn Whitney, Dot Farley (Women Prisoners), Ezelle Poule, Lorna Jordon (Women), Mary Gordon (Charwoman), Eddie Parks (Proprietor).

Stanwyck approaches assistant district attorney Corey after office hours one night to discuss attempted break-ins at the home of her wealthy aunt. Corey falls in love with her and, despite his marriage, they have an affair. Stanwyck tells Corey that she is married to Rober, but doesn't want to see him anymore. One night Corey finds himself through a chain of circumstances at the home of Stanwyck's aunt. There he finds the woman dead, the safe looted, and Stanwyck cleaning up the scene of the crime. She explains that she is removing evidence of Rober's guilt. Corey tells her to go to bed and pretend to sleep while he escapes across the grounds ahead of the police. Stanwyck is arrested for the murder and Corey is assigned to prosecute. He pays for her lawyer and has her acquitted. She prepares to leave with Rober and tells Corey that their affair has been a setup from the start. Rober knocks out Corey and drives away with Stanwyck, who is overwhelmed by guilt and causes the car to crash through a guardrail and down a cliff. Before she dies, Stanwyck confesses her guilt, but does not implicate Corey as the man seen running away from the scene of the crime. Corey himself tells his partner what he has done and walks off, another life ruined. Similar to several

other Stanwyck roles (especially DOUBLE INDEMNITY (1944) and THE STRANGE LOVE OF MARTHA IVERS (1946)), here she once again takes an innocent man and uses him for her own ends. Not one of director Siodmak's best efforts, the film is nonetheless beautifully crafted in his usual precise manner.

p, Hal B. Wallis; d, Robert Siodmak; w, Ketti Frings (based on a story by Marty Holland); ph, George Barnes; m, Victor Young; ed, Warren Low; art d, Hans Dreier, Earl Hedrick; set d, Sam Comer, Bertram Granger; cos, Edith Head; spec eff, Gordon Jennings; makeup, Wally Westmore, R. Ewing, J. Stinton.

Crime (PR:A-C MPAA:NR)

FILE 113*

(1932) 53m AP bw

Lew Cody (Mons. Gaston Le Coq), Mary Nolan (Mlle. Adoree), Clara Kimball Young (Mme. Fauvel), George E. Stone (Verduet), William Collier, Jr. (Prosper Botomy), June Clyde (Madeline), Herbert Bunston (Fauvel), Roy D'Arcy (De Clameran), Irving Bacon (Lagors), Harry Cording (Michele), Crauford Kent (Ottoman).

Loosely based on the famous story by the pioneer who popularized the detective story in France, Emile Gaboriau, memorable detective Monsieur Le Coq (Lew Cody) performs nimbly in solving a bank robbery complicated by a blackmail plot, all in time to keep a date with an actress. Published in 1883, an old-fashioned air to the story's structure still clings to it in the filming.

p, M.S. Hoffman; d, Chester M. Franklin; w, J. Francis Natteford, (based on the novel by Emile Gaboriau); ph, Tom Galligan, Harry Neuman.

Crime (PR:A MPAA:NR)

FILES FROM SCOTLAND YARD*½

(1951, Brit.) 57m
Parthian/IFD bw

John Harvey (Jim Hardy), Moira Lister (Joanna Goring), Louise Hampton (Agatha Steele), Reginald Purdell (Inspector Gower), Dora Bryan (Minnie Robinson), Ben Williams.

Anthology film consisting of three short stories dramatized from authentic Scotland Yard cases. The stories are: "The Lady's Companion," "The Telephone," and "The Interrogation." Mediocre filler item was the precursor to a whole series of "Scotland Yard" short features to come.

p, Henry Hobhouse; d, Anthony Squire.

Crime (PR:A MPAA:NR)

FILM WITHOUT A NAME**

(1950, Ger.) 79m Camera Film bw

Hildegarde Neff (Christine), Willy Fritsch (The Actor), Hans Sohnker (Martin), Irene von Meyendorff (Angelika), Fritz Odemar (The Author), Peter Hamel (The Director), Erich Ponto (Herr Schichtholz), Carsta Lock (Frau Schichtholz), Annamarie Holtz (Viktoria Luise), Fritz Wagner (Jochen), Kate Pontow (Helene), Carl Voscherau (Fleming).

The first German film to be produced in the British zone after WW II, the story, related in flashbacks, is of a maid whose employer falls in love with her. They separate and later reunite. The charm of this film stems from the way the story is told. Screenwriter Odemar, while attempting to create a new script, sees a couple walking along the street. This prompts him to imagine their life story which is intercut with actor Fritsch relating his own interpretation of the tale. (In German; English subtitles.)

d, Rudolph Jugert; w, Helmut Kautner, Ellen Fechner, Jugert; ph, Igor Oberberg; m, Bernhard Eichhorn; English titles, Edward L. Kingsley.

Comedy (PR:A MPAA:NR)

FINAL APPOINTMENT*½

(1954, Brit.) 61m ACT Films/Monarch bw

John Bentley (Mike Billings), Eleanor Summerfield (Jenny Drew), Hubert Gregg (Hartnell), Jean Lodge (Laura Robens), Sam Kydd (Vickery), Meredith Edwards (Tom Martin), Liam Redmond (Inspector Corcoran), Charles Farrell (Percy), Peter Bathurst, Arthur Lowe.

Feeble comedy thriller with Bentley a reporter and Summerfield his irksome assistant. Together they investigate the murders of a number of ex-soldiers, all killed on successive July 10ths. They learn that the victims were all participants in a wartime court-martial and eventually uncover the killer, the victim of an injustice at the court-martial who has been impersonating his brother. A sequel entitled STOLEN ASSIGNMENT that continued the adventures of Bentley and Summerfield was released in 1955 and was even weaker than this one.

p, Francis Searle; d, Terence Fisher; w, Kenneth R. Hayles (based on a story by Sidney Nelson and Maurice Harrison); ph, Jonah Jones.

Crime (PR:A MPAA:NR)

FINAL ASSIGNMENT*

(1980, Can.) 101m Persephone/Inter Ocean c

Genevieve Bujold (Nicole Thomson), Michael York (Lyosha Petrov), Burgess Meredith (Zak), Colleen Dewhurst (Dr. Valentine Ulanova), Alexandra Stewart (Sam O'Donnell), Richard Gabourie (Bowen).

This misguided attempt pits Canadian TV journalist Bujold against the entire Russian KGB. While in the Soviet Union covering disarmament treaty talks between Canada and Russia, she falls upon some horrible Russian experiments using steroids on children. She attempts to smuggle a videotape of the experiments, along with the Russian daughter of scientist Dewhurst, who is badly in need of a stateside brain operation, out of the country. Gifted Meredith stars as a Jewish fur merchant, in Russia on a buying trip, who helps Bujold. Shot in Montreal, the exteriors are quite unconvincing. The Canadian location for the filming was not a strange one for sensitive Bujold; she was born in Montreal and made both her stage and motion picture debuts in Canadian productions.

p, Lawrence Hertzog, Gail Thomson; d, Paul Almond; w, Marc Rosen; ph, John Coquillon; m, Peter Germyn; ed, Debbie Karin.

Drama **Cas.** (PR:C MPAA:PG)

FINAL CHAPTER—WALKING TALL zero   (1977) 112m AIP c

Bo Svenson (*Buford Pusser*), Margaret Blye (*Luan*), Forrest Tucker (*Grandpa Pusser*), Lurene Tuttle (*Grandma Pusser*), Morgan Woodward (*The Boss*), Libby Boone (*Pusser's Secretary*), Leif Garrett (*Mike Pusser*), Dawn Lyn (*Dwana Pusser*), Bruce Glover (*Pusser's Deputy*), Taylor Lacher (*Martin French*), Sandy McPeak (*Lloyd Tatum*), Logan Ramsey (*John Witter*), Robert Phillips (*Johnny*), Clay Tanner (*O.Q. Teal*), David Adams (*Robbie Teal*), Vance Davis (*Aaron*), H. B. Haggerty (*Bulo*), John Malloy (*Producer*).

Just like the producers of FRIDAY THE 13TH—THE FINAL CHAPTER (who promised to stop inflicting their drivel on the public and then reneged on the deal) this was not the FINAL CHAPTER of the WALKING TALL series. It was, as far as the movie houses were concerned, but after this turkey a television pilot and a series continued the saga (kind of a prequel because Pusser was already dead). Sheriff Pusser was the big, strapping redneck who grabbed a big stick and beat the hell out of the ever-present mobsters who continually corrupted his fair city. This one is pretty much the same, except that in FINAL CHAPTER Pusser (Svenson) is offered a movie role from the producers of WALKING TALL who want him to star in the sequel, PART 2, WALKING TALL as himself. He signs on, everything looks peachy, and then the big 'ol sheriff gets himself killed in a mysterious car wreck. Beat that with a big stick.

p, Charles A. Pratt; d, Jack Starrett; w, Howard B. Kreitsek, Samuel A. Peeples; ph, Robert B. Hauser (Deluxe Color); m, Walter Scharf; ed, Housely Stevenson; art d, Joe Altadonna; cos, Michael W. Hoffman, Chris Zamiara; stunt coordinator, Paul Nuckles.

Exploitation   **(PR:O   MPAA:R)**

FINAL CHORD, THE**   (1936, Ger.) 101m UFA bw
(SCHLUSSAKKORD; AKA: NINTH SYMPHONY)

Willy Birgel (*Garvenberg, the Conductor*), Lil Dagover (*Charlotte, his Wife*), Maria von Tasnady (*Hanna*), Theodor Loos (*Dr. Obereit*), Maria Koppenhofer (*Housekeeper*), Albert Lippert (*Clairvoyant*), Kurt Meisel (*Foolish Count*), Erich Ponto (*Chairman of the Assizes*), Peter Bosse, Hella Graf, Paul Otto, Alexander Engel, Eva Tinschmann, Walter Werner, Carl Auen, Erich Bartels, Johannes Bergfeld, Ursula Deinert, Peter Elsholtz, Robert Forsch, Liselotte Koster, Richard Ludwig, Odette Orsy, Hermann Pfeiffer, Ernst Sattler, Walter Steinweg, Bruno Ziener.

Contrived story about an impoverished mother, von Tasnady, who gives up her child for adoption in order to go to America with her husband. The child is adopted by an orchestra conductor, Birgel, and his wife, Dagover. After her husband commits suicide, von Tasnady returns to Germany and gets herself employed as the child's nurse. Dagover, feeling guilty over her numerous affairs, kills herself. Birgel and von Tasnady are accused of murder but are exonerated and marry at the film's end.

p, Bruno Duday; d, Detlef Sierck; w, Sierck, Kurt Heuser; ph, Robert Baberske; m, Kurt Schroder, with parts of Ludwig van Beethoven's "Ninth Symphony," Petr Illich Tchaikovsky's "Nutcracker Suite," and George Frederick Handel's "Judas," played by the Berliner Solistenvereinigung under the direction of the Berliner Staatsoper; ed, Milo Harbich; set d, Erich Kettelhut.

Drama   **(PR:C   MPAA:NR)**

FINAL COLUMN, THE*   (1955, Brit.) 51m Danzigers/PAR bw

Ron Randell, John Longden, Jeannette Sterke, Christopher Lee, Kay Callard, Laurence Naismith, Sandra Dorne, Brian Worth, Robert Sansom.

A couple of worthless tales of murder plans gone wrong, the first telling of a man who plots to kill both himself and the blackmailer who loves his daughter. Before he can carry out the killing, the police burst in and save the day. In the second, less substantial episode, a doctor hypnotizes the chap who's having an affair with his wife. The plan is to have the lover break into the wife's room and she, thinking he is an intruder, will shoot him. Everything goes well until she realizes the doctor masterminded the whole scheme and she turns her murderous rage on him.

p, Edward Danziger, Harry Lee Danziger; d, David Macdonald; w, James Eastwood, Paul Tabori; ph, Jimmy Wilson.

Crime Drama   **(PR:A   MPAA:NR)**

FINAL COMEDOWN, THE**   (1972) 84m New World c

Billy Dee Williams (*Johnny Johnson*), Raymond St. Jacques (*Imir*), D'Urville Martin (*Billy Joe Ashley*), R.G. Armstrong (*Mr. Freeman*), Celia Kaye (*Rene Freeman*), Pamela Jones (*Luanna*), Maidie Norman (*Mrs. Johnson*), Morris Erby (*Mr. Johnson*), Billy Durkin (*Michael Freeman*), Edmund Cambridge (*Dr. Smalls*).

Williams is a black youth increasingly frustrated by racism who finally goes over the edge into radicalism when he is turned down for a job that is given to a less qualified white man. Under the influence of some white radicals, he becomes convinced that violent revolution is the solution. He joins with St. Jacques and Martin in a plan to rise up against the police, but when white and black alike fail to support the revolt, it collapses and the men are cornered in an alley where a bloody shootout claims all their lives, as well as a goodly number of police lives. Director Williams received a grant from the American Film Institute for this debut feature, a mediocre piece that seldom rises above its unimaginative direction and soap-operatic plot to talk about the issues at the heart of the film.

p,d&w, Oscar Williams; ph, William B. Caplan (Metrocolor); m, Wade Marcus; ed, Bick Van Enger, Jr.

Crime   **(PR:O   MPAA:R)**

FINAL CONFLICT, THE*   (1981) 108m FOX c

Sam Neill (*Damien Thorn*), Rossano Brazzi (*Father DeCarlo*), Don Gordon (*Harvey Dean*), Lisa Harrow (*Kate Reynolds*), Barnaby Holm (*Peter Reynolds*), Mason Adams (*President*), Robert Arden (*American Ambassador*), Tommy Duggan

(*Brother Matteus*), Leueen Willoughby (*Barbara*), Louis Mahoney (*Brother Paulo*), Marc Boyle (*Brother Benito*), Richard Oldfield (*Brother Simeon*), Milos Kirek (*Brother Martin*), Tony Vogel (*Brother Antonio*), Arwen Holm (*Carol*), Hugh Moxey (*Manservant*), William Fox, John Baskcomb (*Diplomats*), Norman Bird (*Dr. Philmore*), Marc Smith (*Press Officer*), Arnold Diamond (*Astronomer*), Eric Richard (*Astronomer's Technician*), Richard Williams (*Vicar*), Stephen Turner (*Stigwell*), Al Matthews (*Workman*), Larry Martyn, Frank Coda, Harry Littlewood (*Orators*), Hazel Court.

The third installment in the saga of Damien the Antichrist sees the Devil's kid grown up and doing well as the head of Thorn Industries. Now played by Neill (who takes himself too seriously), Damien is just about ready to take over the world for his papa. But Neill is disturbed to learn that a child has been born when three stars join in the night sky. He sends his minions out to kill every baby born on that night. Meanwhile, rugged monk Brazzi has found those handy daggers (the same ones unsuccessfully used on Damien in OMEN's I & II) and drafts six of his bravest brothers to take one dagger each and try to assassinate Neill. The monks are no match for Neill and they die in a variety of ways. One slips, falls, hooks his foot in a rope and swings upside down on a television stage wrapped in burning plastic in full view of the folks at home, another is eaten by a bunch of beagles, etc. At the same time, all over the world, babies are being killed in an equally sick and disgusting manner (steam irons seem to be the favored method). In the end, the Almighty finally puts an end to Damien and that's that.

p, Harvey Bernhard; d, Graham Baker; w, Andrew Birkin (based on characters created by Dave Seltzer); ph, Robert Paynter, Phil Meheux (Panavision; DeLuxe Color); m, Jerry Goldsmith; ed, Alan Strachan; prod d, Herbert Westbrook; art d, Martin Atkinson.

Horror   **Cas.**   **(PR:O   MPAA:NR)**

FINAL COUNTDOWN, THE**   (1980) 104m UA c

Kirk Douglas (*Capt. Matthew Yelland*), Martin Sheen (*Warren Lasky*), Katharine Ross (*Laurel Scott*), James Farentino (*Cmdr. Richard Owens*), Ron O'Neal (*Cmdr. Dan Thurman*), Charles Durning (*Senator Chapman*), Victor Mohica (*Black Cloud*), James C. Lawrence (*Lt. Perry*), Soon-Teck Oh (*Simura*), Joe Lowry (*Cmdr. Damon*), Alvin Ing (*Kajima*), Mark Thomas (*Cpl. Kullman*), Harold Bergman (*Bellman*), Dan Fitzgerald (*Navy Doctor*), Lloyd Kaufman (*Lt. Cmdr. Kaufman*), Peter Douglas (*Quartermaster*), Phil Philbin (*Admiral*), Ted Riehert, George Warren, Gary Morgan, Robert Goodman, Richard Liberty, Neil Ronco, William Couch, Jack McDermott, Masayuki Yamazuki, Orwin Harvey, Colby Smith, George H. Strohsahl, Jr., Ronald R. Stoops, Kenneth J. Jaskolski, Sergei M. Kowalchik, Jake Dennis, Jim Toone.

America's finest nuclear-powered aircraft carrier, the U.S.S. Nimitz, is thrown through a time warp from 1980 to Pearl Harbor, December 7, 1941. Will the crew intervene? Will the course of history be changed forever? Sheen is a hapless observer aboard ship, Durning's a senator who sees political implications within the situation, and Douglas (whose production company was responsible for THE FINAL COUNTDOWN) goes on and on about ethics, history, and other biggies. Some military machismo displayed seems to reflect the mood of the country at the time of the film's release.

p, Peter Vincent Douglas; d, Don Taylor; w, David Ambrose, Gerry Davis, Thomas Hunter, Peter Powell; ph, Victor J. Kemper (Panavision, Technicolor); m, John Scott; ed, Robert K. Lambert; prod d, Fernando Carrere; cos, Ray Summers.

Fantasy/Adventure   **Cas.**   **(PR:C   MPAA:PG)**

FINAL CUT, THE**   (1980, Aus.) 82m Wilgar/GUO c

Louis Brown (*Chris*), David Clendenning (*Dominic*), Jennifer Cluff (*Sarah*), Narelle Johnson (*Yvette*), Carmen J. McCall (*Julie/Lyn*), Thaddeus Smith (*Mick*).

The first Australian feature film to be made and funded in Queensland concerns actor/entrepreneur Clendenning arriving back in Queensland after a successful show-business career abroad. Reporter Brown and his girl friend Cluff manage to follow him around his yacht and penthouse to do a story on him. They discover some good dirt in Clendenning's past, finding that he had dealings in porno films, and quite possibly snuff films. Full of nudity and sex sequences, the film ventures far away from the plot's earlier promise.

p, Mike Williams; d, Ross Dimsey; w, Jonathan Dawson, Dimsey (based on an original idea by Dawson); ph, Ron Johanson (Eastmancolor); m, Howard Davidson; ed, Tony Patterson.

Drama   **(PR:O   MPAA:NR)**

FINAL EDITION**   (1932) 66m COL bw

Pat O'Brien (*Sam Bradshaw*), Mae Clarke (*Anne Woodman*), Mary Doran (*Patsy King*), Bradley Page (*Sid Malvern*), Morgan Wallace (*Neil Selby*), James Donlan (*Freddie*), Phil Tead (*Dan Cameron*), Wallis Clark (*Jim Conroy*), Bertha Mann (*Mrs. Conroy*).

A well-made crime story, Clarke is the girl reporter who is going after the head of the syndicate, Wallace, who controls the dirty money in town. A new police commissioner gets the goods on him, so Wallace's men murder the commissioner and steal the evidence. Clarke gets friendly with Wallace's right-hand man, Page, outsmarting them both and nearly getting herself killed in the process, but ends up with the evidence and the best story of her life. Clarke, famed for having had a grapefruit pushed into her kisser by James Cagney in THE PUBLIC ENEMY (1931), had real-life played a feature role in the newspaper story that spawned this one and a host of others, THE FRONT PAGE (1931). Pat O'Brien also starred in the latter film, reprising his role of tough editor in this one.

d, Howard Higgin; w, Dorothy Howell (based on a story by Roy Chanslor); ph, Benjamin Kline; ed, Jack Dennis.

Crime   **(PR:A   MPAA:NR)**

FINAL EXAM zero   (1981) 90m Bedford/AE c

Cecile Bagdadi (Courtney), Joel S. Rice (Radish), Ralph Brown (Wildman), Deanna Robbins (Lisa), Sherry Willis-Burch (Janet), John Fallon (Mark), Terry W. Farren (Pledge), Sam Kilman (Sheriff), Don Hepner (Dr. Reynolds), Jerry Rushing (Coach), Timothy L. Raynor (Killer).

Barely a passing grade to this latest entrance to the horror film genre, set on a college campus. There isn't enough gore for someone with a real lust for blood, rendering the film totally pointless. The movie tries to develop the characters, and finding that they are too boring to live, the hope that someone will hurry up and kill them is the only thing that sustains any interest. The maniac kills just about everyone, leaving a large amount of unexpected housing open to next semester's students.

p, John L. Chambliss, Myron Meisel; d&w, Jimmy Huston; ph, Darrell Cathcart (DeLuxe Color); m, Gary Scott; ed, John O'Connor.

Horror   **Cas.**   **(PR:O   MPAA:R)**

FINAL HOUR, THE*   (1936) 57m COL bw

Ralph Bellamy (John Vickery), Marguerite Churchill (Flo Russell), John Gallaudet (Red McLarnen), George McKay (Charlie), Elisabeth Risdon (Fortune Teller), Marc Lawrence (Mike Magellon), Lina Basquette (Belle).

Film features Bellamy as a drunken lawyer who straightens up to defend Churchill, falsely accused of larceny and murder. He helps her beat the charges with the assistance of his street-people friends, and the two fall in love.

d, D. Ross Lederman; w, Harold Shumate; ph, Lucien Ballard; ed, John Rawlins.

Drama   **(PR:A   MPAA:NR)**

FINAL OPTION, THE* (1983, Brit.) 125m Richmond Light Horse/MGM c
(GB: WHO DARES WINS)

Lewis Collins (Capt. Skellen), Judy Davis (Frankie), Richard Widmark (Secretary of State), Robert Webber (Gen. Potter), Edward Woodward (Cmdr. Powell), Tony Doyle (Col. Hadley), John Duttine (Rod), Kenneth Griffith (Bishop Crick), Rosalind Lloyd (Jenny), Ingrid Pitt (Helga), Norman Rodway (Ryan), Maurice Roeves (Maj. Steele), Patrick Allen (Police Commissioner), Bob Sherman (Capt. Hagen), Albert Fortell (Capt. Freund), Mark Ryan (Mac), Aharon Ipale (Malek), Paul Freeman (Sir Richard), Allan Mitchell (Harkness), Richard Coleman (Martin), Nigel Humphries (Sgt. Pope), Stephen Bent (Neil), Martyn Jacobs (Policeman), Raymond Brody (Bank Manager), Andrew McLachlan (Immigration Officer), Peter Geddes (Butler), Jon Morrison (Dennis), Ziggy Byfield (Baker), Michael Forest (Pickley), Don Fellows (Ambassador Franklin), Meg Davies (Mary), Anna Ford, Bill Hamilton.

Collins is a Special Air Services man, Britain's answer to U.S. Army Rangers, who goes undercover to infiltrate a gang of international terrorists planning to take over the U.S. embassy in London. Some recognizable faces in the cast, but the story is ludicrous. Widmark is barely on screen, despite third billing.

p, Euan Lloyd; d, Ian Sharp; w, Reginald Rose (based on the novel The Tiptoe Boys by George Markstein); ph, Phil Meheux; m, Roy Budd, Jerry Donahue, Marc Donahue; ed, John Grover; prod d, Syd Cain; art d, Mo Cain; ch, Anthony Van Laast.

Adventure Drama   **Cas.**   **(PR:O   MPAA:R)**

FINAL PROGRAMME, THE
(SEE: LAST DAYS OF MAN ON EARTH, THE, 1973, Brit.)

FINAL RECKONING, THE*   (1932, Brit.) 64m Equity British bw

James Benton (Bill Williams), Margaret Delane (Violet Williams), Will Marriott (Arthur Harding), Bessie Richards (Mrs. Williams), Thomas Moss.

One of the last silents made in England, diehard independent producer Argyle was finally forced to add sound to this film prior to release. He needn't have bothered, as the film is a dull, melodramatic work barely more sophisticated than an old two-reeler. Benton is the son of a mine owner driven to attempt to murder a miner he thinks is having an affair with his wife.

p,d&w, John F. Argyle.

Crime   **(PR:A   MPAA:NR)**

FINAL TERROR, THE*   (1983) 84m Comworld-Watershed-Roth c
(GB: CAMPSITE MASSACRE, AKA:
BUMP IN THE NIGHT; THE FOREST PRIMEVAL)

John Friedrich (Zorich), Rachel Ward (Margaret), Adrian Zmed (Cerone), Darryl Hannah (Windy), Joe Pantoliano (Eggar), Ernest Harden, Jr. (Hines), Mark Metcalf (Mike), Lewis Smith (Boone), Cindy Harrell (Melanie), Akosua Busia (Vanessa), Irene Sanders (Sammie), Richard Jacobs (Morgan), Donna Pinder (Mrs. Morgan).

Teen-age campers in the redwood forest die one-by-one at the hands of a deranged woman. The only reason to watch this is to see soon-to-be-stars Zmed, Hannah, and Ward deal the bloody deaths.

p, Joe Roth; d, Andrew Davis; w, Jon George, Neill Hicks, Ronald Shusett; ph, A. Davidescu; m, Susan Justin; ed, Paul Rubell, Erica Flaum, Hannah Washonig; art d, Aleka Corwin; cos, Sue Miller; spec eff, Ken Myers.

Horror   **Cas.**   **(PR:O   MPAA:R)**

FINAL TEST, THE**   (1953, Brit.) 91m ACT Films/GFD bw

Jack Warner (Sam Palmer), Robert Morley (Alexander Whitehead), Brenda Bruce (Cora), Ray Jackson (Reggie Palmer), George Relph (Syd Thompson), Adrianne Allen (Aunt Ethel), Stanley Maxted (Senator), Joan Swinstead (Miss Fanshawe), Richard Bebb (Frank Weller), Valentine Dyall (Man In Black), Len Hutton (Frank Jarvis), Denis Compton, Alec Bedser, Godfrey Evans, Jim Laker, Cyril Washbrook (Cricket Players), Audrey White, Richard Wattis.

A good British comedy that deals with a favorite religion, cricket. The story is about a famed English player, Warner, who is playing the last few games of his

career. His son Jackson, who writes poetry, disappoints his father by missing his second-to-last game. Intending to be at the final game, he is unexpectedly invited to the home of a very famous poet, Morley. It seems that Jackson will miss his father's final game, but it turns out that Morley is a cricket fan, and when he hears about Jackson's dad being on the team, he insists that they go to the final game. All works out well in the end.

p, R. J. Minney; d, Anthony Asquith; w, Terence Rattigan (based on his TV play); ph, Bill McLeod; m, Benjamin Frankel; ed, Helga Cranston; art d, R. Holmes-Paul.

Comedy/Sport   **(PR:A   MPAA:NR)**

FINAL WAR, THE**   (1960, Jap.) 77m
New Toei/Sam Lake Enterprises, bw
(DAI SANJI SEKAI TAISEN; YOUJU ICHI JIKAN NO KYOFU;
41 JIKAN NO KYOFU; AKA: WORLD WAR III BREAKS OUT)

Tatsuo Umemiya, Yoshiko Mita, Yayoi Furusato, Noribumi Fujishima, Yukiko Nikaido, Michiko Hoshi.

When the United States accidentally sets off a nuclear bomb over South Korea, a conflict begins which escalates into an all-out nuclear war between the U.S. and the Soviet Union. The battle begins in Tokyo and spreads world-wide. At the war's end, Argentina is the only country left. A sub-plot dealing with a dying journalist's search for his lover among the ruins is effectively handled. This frighteningly realistic premise is all the more poignant considering that Japan is the only country ever to suffer nuclear holocaust.

d, Shigeaki Hidaka; w, Hisataka Kai, T. Yasumi, Takeshi Kimura; ph, Tadashi Arakami (ToeiScope).

Drama   **(PR:C   MPAA:NR)**

FINALLY SUNDAY   (SEE: CONFIDENTIALLY YOURS, 1983, Fr.)

FINCHE DURA LA TEMPESTA   (SEE: TORPEDO BAY, 1963, Fr.)

FIND THE BLACKMAILER*   (1943) 55m WB bw

Jerome Cowan (D. L. Trees), Faye Emerson (Mona Vance), Gene Lockhart (John M. Rhodes), Marjorie Hoshelle (Pandora Pines), Robert Kent (Harper), Wade Boteler (Detective Cramer), John Harmon (Ray Hicky), Bradley Page (Farrell), Lou Lubin (Olen), Ralph Peters (Coleman).

In a mild takeoff on THE MALTESE FALCON, private eye Cowan is hired by a mayoral candidate, Lockhart, to find a talking blackbird that can incriminate the candidate in a murder. The story then takes several twists and turns, ending up with all the ends tied neatly together.

p, William Jacobs; d, D. Ross Lederman; w, Robert E. Kent (from the story "Blackmail With Feathers" by G.T. Fleming-Roberts); ph, James Van Trees; ed, Harold McLernon; art d, Charles Novi.

Crime   **(PR:A   MPAA:NR)**

FIND THE LADY*   (1936, Brit.) 70m FOX bw

Jack Melford (Schemer Doyle), Althea Henley (Venus Doyle), George Sanders (Curly Randall), Viola Compton (Lady Waldron), Violet Loxley (Vilma Waldron), Dorothy Vernon, Eric Pavitt, Jack [John] Warwick, Nancy Pawley, Vera Martyn, Angela Litolff, Bombardier Billy Wells, Cecil Bishop, David Keir, George Lane, Philip Ray, Billy Shine, Ben Williams, Paul Neville.

Melford and Henley are a team of American confidence tricksters who come to England with a phony faith-healing scheme. Henley falls in love with an impoverished young man who is in turn in love with a daughter of the aristocracy. Henley helps him win her in this mild comedy of interest only for the presence of George Sanders in one of his earliest roles.

p, John Findlay; d, Roland Gillett; w, Gillett, Edward Dryhurst (based on the play "The Fakers" by Tod Waller); ph, Stanley Grant.

Comedy   **(PR:A   MPAA:NR)**

FIND THE LADY**   (1956, Brit.) 56m Major/RFD bw

Donald Houston (Bill), Beverley Brooks (June Weston), Mervyn Johns (Hurst), Kay Callard (Rita), Maurice Kaufmann (Nicky), Edwin Richfield (Max), Moray Watson (Jimmy), Ferdy Mayne (Tony Del Roma), Anne Heywood (Receptionist), John Drake, Edgar Driver, Nigel Green, Enid Lorimer.

Model Brooks goes to visit her godmother in the country, but finds she has vanished. She convinces doctor Houston to help her look for the old woman, but ends up captured by the same gang of robbers who have kidnaped the godmother. They are hiding out at her house and using it as a base of operations, but Houston arrives on the scene with a squad of police and justice prevails. Allegedly a comedy-thriller, the thriller part works much better than the comedy part.

p, John Temple-Smith, Francis Edge; d, Charles Saunders; w, Kenneth R. Hayles (based on a story by Paul Erickson, Dermot Palmer); ph, Brendan J. Stafford.

Crime Comedy   **(PR:A   MPAA:NR)**

FIND THE WITNESS*   (1937) 55m COL bw

Charles Quigley (Larry McGill), Rosalind Keith (Linda Mason), Henry Mollison (Rudolph Mordini), Rita LaRoy (Rita Calmette), James Conlin (Swifty Mullins), Charles Wilson (Charley Blair), Wade Boteler (Inspector Collins), Harry Depp (Dr. Rice), Edward Earle (Mr. Quinn), Alyce Ardell (Louise).

A lame news-reporter-who-is-a-detective film. The story has a magician murdering his wife and a couple other people, while doing a magic act at a seaside resort. His act consists of him having himself sealed in a box and then dropped in the ocean. The reporter proves to the inept police that the magician has a deep-sea diver pull the box to land. The magician would then get out of the box and commit the murders.

p, Ralph Cohn; d, David Selman; w, Grace Neville, Fred Niblo, Jr. (based on a story by Richard Sale); ph, Virgil Miller; ed, William Lyon.

Crime/Mystery   **(PR:A   MPAA:NR)**

FINDERS KEEPERS**   (1951) 75m UNIV bw

Tom Ewell *(Tiger Kipps)*, Julia Adams *(Sue Kipps)*, Evelyn Varden *(Ma Kipps)*, Dusty Henley *(Tiger Kipps, Jr.)*, Harold Vermilyea *(Mr. Fitzpatrick)*, Douglas Fowley *(Frankie)*, Richard Reeves *(Joey)*, Jack Elam *(Eddie)*, Herbert Anderson *(Hotel Clerk)*, Harvey Lembeck, Madge Blake.

A childish comedy without much to laugh at. A cute idea, but there is not enough spunk to pull it off. Henley, a two year old, finds some hidden loot left by bank robbers. Dad, Ewell, out on parole and grandma, Varden, go crazy when they see Henley bringing home the money in his wagon. The kid can't tell them where, how or from whom he got the money. Varden wants to keep the money, but Mom, Adams, wants Ewell to burn the dough so he won't get into trouble with the parole board. Ewell decides to turn it over to the police, unbeknownst to his family. When the robbers return for their money, they kidnap Henley but Henley grabs Grandma's gun and shoots the crooks. This was one of Western heavy Elam's early city-crook roles, and one of beach-blanket comic villain Lembeck's first features.

p, Leonard Goldstein; d, Frederick de Cordova; w, Richard Morris; ph, Carl E. Guthrie; m, Hans Salter; ed, Milton Carruth; art d, Bernard Hertzbrun, Richard Reide.

Comedy   **(PR:AA   MPAA:NR)**

FINDERS KEEPERS**   (1966, Brit.) 94m Interstate/UA c

Cliff Richard *(Cliff)*, Bruce Welch, Hank B. Marvin, Brian Bennett, John Rostill *(The Shadows)*, Robert Morley *(Colonel Roberts)*, Peggy Mount *(Mrs. Bragg)*, Viviane Ventura *(Emilia)*, Graham Stark *(Burke)*, John Le Mesurier *(Mr. X)*, Robert Hutton *(Commander)*, Gordan Ruttan *(Junior Officer)*, Ellen Pollock *(Grandma)*, Ernest Clark *(Air Marshal)*, Burnell Tucker *(Pilot)*, George Roderick *(Priest)*, Bill Mitchell *(G.I. Guard)*, Ronnie Brodie *(Drunk)*.

This musical comedy tells of a mini-bomb that is dropped, by accident, from an American plane near a town in Spain. A singing group, Cliff Richards and the Shadows, arrives at a hotel in the town only to find it empty. The bomb has scared everyone away, and the singers have no audience. The group searches for the bomb in an effort to return it to the U.S. troops, who are also looking for it. Foreign spy Le Mesurier blackmails the owner of the hotel, Morley, to look for the bomb, for the gain of Le Mesurier's nation. The three search parties are constantly bumping into each other. Richard and The Shadows sing several tunes, cutting in to an interruptable story line.

p, George H. Brown; d, Sidney Hayers; w, Michael Pertwee (story by Brown); ph, Alan Hume (Eastmancolor); ed, Tristam Cones; cos, Cynthia Tingye; ch, Malcolm Clare, Hugh Lambert; m/l, The Shadows.

Musical/Comedy   **(PR:A   MPAA:NR)**

FINDERS KEEPERS, LOVERS WEEPERS*   (1968) 71m
                                                            Eve Productions c

Anne Chapman *(Kelly)*, Paul Lockwood *(Paul)*, Gordon Wescourt *(Ray)*, Duncan McLeod *(Cal)*, Robert Rudelson *(Feeny)*, Lavelle Roby *(Claire)*, Jan Sinclair *(Christiana)*, Joey Duprez *(Joy)*, Nick Wolcuff *(Nick)*, Pam Collins, Vickie Roberts, John Furlong, Michael Roberts.

Realizing that her husband Lockwood and tramp Roby have been having a long-standing affair, Chapman is induced to join bartender Wescourt for a "swim" in his pool. In the meantime, Roby aids a plan to set up Lockwood's go-go bar for a robbery by luring him away to her place. Chapman, Wescourt, Lockwood, and Roby all return to the bar as it is being held up. The crooks then play the victims off each other by telling of their infidelities, and threatening to rape Chapman unless the safe is opened. End sees robbers killed by Lockwood, but not before Roby is murdered and Wescourt is knifed.

p&d, Russ Meyer; w, Richard Zachary (based on a story by Meyer); ph, Meyer (Eastmancolor); m, Igo Kantor; ed, Meyer, Richard Brummer.

Exploitation   **Cas.**   **(PR:O   MPAA:NR)**

FINE FEATHERS*   (1937, Brit.) 68m BL bw

Renee Houston *(Teenie McPherson)*, Donald Stewart *(Jim)*, Francis L. Sullivan *(Hugo Steinway)*, Robb Wilton *(Tim McPherson)*, Jack Hobbs *(Felix)*, Marcelle Rogez *(Mme. Barescon)*, Henry Victor *(Gibbons)*, Stella Arbenina *(Elizabeth)*.

Lame musical has Houston a Scottish shopgirl posing as the mistress of a Ruritanian prince to help an American oil man get drilling rights in the prince's country. Not much of interest here.

p, Herbert Smith; d, Leslie Hiscott; w, Michael Barringer.

Musical   **(PR:A   MPAA:NR)**

FINE MADNESS, A**½   (1966) 104m Pan Arts/WB c

Sean Connery *(Samson Shillitoe)*, Joanne Woodward *(Rhoda)*, Jean Seberg *(Lydia West)*, Patrick O'Neal *(Dr. Oliver West)*, Colleen Dewhurst *(Dr. Vera Kropotkin)*, Clive Revill *(Dr. Menken)*, Werner Peters *(Dr. Vorbeck)*, John Fiedler *(Daniel K. Papp)*, Kay Medford *(Mrs. Fish)*, Jackie Coogan *(Mr. Fitzgerald)*, Zohra Lampert *(Mrs. Tupperman)*, Sorrell Booke *(Leonard Tupperman)*, Sue Anne Langdon *(Miss Walnicki)*, Bibi Osterwald *(Mrs. Fitzgerald)*, Mabel Albertson *(Chairwoman)*, Gerald S. O'Loughlin *(Chester Quirk)*, James Millhollin *(Rollie Butter)*, Jon Lormer *(Dr. Huddleson)*, Harry Bellaver *(Knocker)*, Ayllene Gibbons *(Clubwoman)*, Bernie Meyer, Richard Castellano, Renee Taylor.

An off-beat attempt to document the view of poet Connery, who is frustrated in his attempts to compose a masterpiece. He dislikes women, being considerate only to his second wife, Woodward. Late alimony payments set him off, causing him to have a nervous breakdown. He tries to get help, and ends up with a lobotomy. Director Kershner demonstrates fine visual talents in his use of New York locations.

p, Jerome Hellman; d, Irvin Kershner; w, Elliott Baker (based on his novel); ph, Ted McCord (Technicolor); m, John Addison; ed, William Ziegler; cos, Ann Roth.

Drama   **(PR:C   MPAA:NR)**

FINE PAIR, A**   (1969, Ital.) 88m Cinema Center/NG (UNA COPPIA
                            TRANQUILLA; AKA: RUBA AL PROSSIMO TUO)

Rock Hudson *(Capt. Mike Harmon)*, Claudia Cardinale *(Esmeralda Marini)*, Tomas Milian *(Roger)*, Leon Askin *(Chief Wellman)*, Ellen Corby *(Mrs. Walker)*, Walter Giller *(Franz)*, Guido Alberti *(Uncle Camillo)*, Peter Dane *(Albert Kinsky)*, Vittorio Campanella, Gianni Carnago, Raniero Dorascienzi, Andrea Hesterasy, Umberto Fantoni, Aldo Formisano, Adrianao Fraticelli.

Italian policeman's daughter Cardinale—*en deshabille* sufficiently that the film's title seems descriptive of her—visits New York City to seek the assistance of police captain Hudson, who once worked with her late father, in returning some stolen gems to their rightful owners. She explains that she had gotten involved with an international jewel thief, but is now repentant. The two fly to Austria, where Hudson seeks out the local police authorities and persuades them to afford him the professional courtesy of explaining the sophisticated electronic surveillance system installed in the burglary victims' villa. He and Cardinale subvert the system and enter the villa, opening the safe and returning the gems. However, Cardinale has actually seized the real gems—never stolen in the first place—and substituted the fakes she had shown Hudson. She then attempts to involve him in another similar scheme, whereupon he discloses that he had been wise to her from the beginning but, loving both Cardinale and the thrill of criminal adventure, he has elected to be her partner. Cardinale turns contrite, averring that she prefers a peaceful life as a policeman's wife, but Hudson turns reciprocal trickster and snares her into continuing their adrenaline-rush criminal career. Like many another heist-caper film, this one suffers from apparently having had critical parts of the plot left on the cutting-room floor, a fatal flaw. The English dubbing is poor, and Cardinale's body language is far more understandable than her verbalizing.

p, Leo L. Fuchs; d, Francesco Maselli; w, Maselli, Luisa Montagnana, Larry Gelbart, Virgil C. Leone (story by Montagnana); ph, Alfio Contini (Panavision, Technicolor); m, Ennio Morricone; ed, Nicoletta Nardi; art d, Luciano Puccini; set d, Gabriele D'Angelo; cos, Enrico Sabbatini; makeup, Pier Antonio Mecacci, Mark Reedall.

Crime   **(PR:C   MPAA:M)**

FINGER MAN*   (1955) 81m AA bw

Frank Lovejoy *(Casey Martin)*, Forrest Tucker *(Dutch Becker)*, Peggie Castle *(Gladys Baker)*, Timothy Carey *(Lou Terpe)*, John Cliff *(Cooper)*, William Leicester *(Rogers)*, Glenn Gordon *(Carlos Armor)*, John Close *(Walters)*, Hugh Sanders *(Mr. Burns)*, Evelynne Eaton *(Lucille)*, Charles Maxwell *(Amory)*, Lewis Charles *(Lefty Stern)*.

A ho-hum crime film starring Lovejoy as a recidivist ex-convict criminal captured by the Bureau of Internal Revenue. Lovejoy chooses to help the Feds put syndicate head Tucker in jail over spending time there himself. Ex-mob girl Castle tries to help her beau Lovejoy, causing her own death and nearly eliminating him as well. In the end, the crooks get what's coming to them. Veteran character actor and acting teacher Carey does his usual fine job as Forrest's psychotic henchman; he specialized in these persona to such an extent that filmgoers must wonder whether he was capable of playing a *compos mentis* role.

p, Lindsley Parsons; d, Harold Schuster; w, Warren Douglas (based on a story by Morris Lipsius, John Lardner); ph, William Sickner; m, Paul Dunlap; ed, Maurice Wright.

Crime   **(PR:A   MPAA:NR)**

FINGER OF GUILT**½   (1956, Brit.) 85m Anglo-Guild-Merton Park/RKO
                          bw (GB: THE INTIMATE STRANGER)

Richard Basehart *(Reggie Wilson)*, Mary Murphy *(Evelyn Stewart)*, Constance Cummings *(Kay Wallace)*, Roger Livesey *(Ben Case)*, Faith Brook *(Lesley Wilson)*, Mervyn Johns *(Ernest Chapple)*, Vernon Greeves *(George Mearns)*, Andre Mikhelson *(Steve Vadney)*, David Lodge *(Police Sergeant Brown)*, Basil Dignam *(Doctor Gray)*, Grace Denbeigh-Russell *(Mrs. Lynton)*, Jay Denyer, Katherine Page, Frederick Steger, Wilfrid Downing, Edna Landor, Jack Stewart, Michael Ward.

Another cinema-industry introspection film, this time from filmmakers who had reason to introspect. Director Losey and writer Koch were two of the talented industry people disenfranchised and self-exiled during the blacklistings of the McCarthy era. Both worked under pseudonyms; the U.S. release even credited producer Snowden with direction in this instance. The film deals with Basehart an American expatriate—like the writer and director—a former Hollywood film editor, now a producer in a large London-based studio. Vengeful studio intrigue has him doubting his own sanity and threatening his career and his marriage to Brook, whose father, Livesey, is the studio chief. The threat comes from a series of intensely personal letters penned by Murphy which suggest an intimacy and knowledge of Basehart's business affairs that could only come through close acquaintance. The problem is that the lady is unknown to Basehart, who already has enough trouble in the form of Cummings, the demanding prima donna of his current production. Since the coals of Basehart's despair stem from Newcastle, he and suspicious wife Brook travel there to confront Murphy. Her convincing performance as his sometime paramour causes Brook to leave him. Suspecting himself of amnesiac dualism, Basehart desperately explores the matter further. The mystery is resolved when Murphy is proved to have been receiving intelligence about him from Johns, his predecessor at the studio, who initiated the scheme to discredit Basehart in the hope of redeeming himself in the eyes of

Livesey. Basehart and Brook are reconnected; his job is secure; schemer Johns gets the FINGER OF GUILT in the end.

p, Alec Snowden; d, [Joseph Losey] Joseph Walton; w, Howard Koch [Peter Howard] (based on his novel *Pay the Piper*); ph, Gerald Gibbs; m, Trevor Duncan; ed, Geoffrey Muller; md, Richard Taylor; art d, Wilfred Arnold; cos, Alice McLaren.

Drama **(PR:A MPAA:NR)**

FINGER ON THE TRIGGER** (1965, US/Span.) 87m Comet/AA c (EL DEDO EN EL GATILLO)

Rory Calhoun *(Larry Winton)*, James Philbrook *(Adam Hyde)*, Todd Martin *(Hillstrom)*, Silvia Solar *(Violet)*, Brad Talbot *(Fred)*, Leo Anchoriz *(Ed Bannister)*, Jorge Rigaud *(Benton)*, Eric Chapman *(McKay)*, Benny Dues *(O'Brien)*, Axel Anderson *(McNamara)*, Tito Garcia *(Zubarri)*, Willie P. Elie *(Mike Daly)*, John Clarke *(Numitah)*, Antonio Molino Rojo *(Benham)*, Juan Antonio Peral *(Tom Sharpe)*, German Grech *(Delmer)*, Fernando Bilbao *(Mayer)*, Sebastian Cavalier *(Slim)*.

Competent oater starring Calhoun as the leader of a band of ex-Union soldiers looking to homestead in New Mexico soon after the Civil War. When they arrive at Fort Grant they find that it has been taken over by renegade Confederates who are awaiting a shipment of golden horseshoes. The Union soldiers find the gold in a ghost town called Southernville. When the fort is attacked by Indians, the rival sides combine, melt down the gold for shell casings, and drive the Indians off.

p&d, Sidney Pink; w, Luis de los Arcos, Pink; ph, Antonio Macasoli, Miguel Barquero (Techniscope, Technicolor); m, Jose Sola; ed, Margarita Ochoa; art d, Patrick Corcoran; set d, Edward Bennett; cos, Vicky; makeup, Joe Echovar; spec eff Tony Molina.

Western **(PR:A MPAA:NR)**

FINGER POINTS, THE*** (1931) 90m FN-WB bw

Richard Barthelmess *(Breckenridge Lee)*, Fay Wray *(Marcia Collins)*, Regis Toomey *(Breezy Russell)*, Clark Gable *(Louis Blanco)*, Robert Elliott *(City Editor)*, Oscar Apfel *(Managing Editor)*, Robert Gleckler *(Larry Hayes)*, Mickey Bennett *(Office Boy)*, Herman Krumpfel *(Tailor)*, J. Carrol Naish *(Voice)*, Noel Madison *(Larry Hays)*.

A hard-hitting early gangster talkie, THE FINGER POINTS is lifted wholly out of the headlines of the day. Barthelmess is a young southern reporter who goes to work for a big city newspaper and is given a crime beat. He is contacted to suppress a story about bigshot gangster Gable and, where his co-workers laugh at the idea, he seriously entertains the "hush money" offered him. He soon succumbs to the gangland bribes which make him rich far beyond his $35-a-week salary. Girl reporter Wray, in love with Barthelmess, begs him to give up the "blood money" but the young reporter is now a hardened, cynical type and can't turn down the heavy cash Gable funnels to him for continued suppression of news stories concerning his crime cartel. When Gable orders two rival gangsters murdered, the story gets past Barthelmess, despite Gable's instructions to "bury it." The published story brings police "heat" down on Gable and his minions and the crime czar reacts in a frenzy, believing Barthelmess has betrayed him. He "fingers" the young reporter for his hired killers and Barthelmess is gunned down by machinegunners. The film blatantly profiles the murder of real-life *Chicago Tribune* reporter Alfred "Jake" Lingle, venal newsman on Al Capone's payroll, murdered on June 9, 1930 at Scarface's orders, after leaking information on Capone operations to rival gangster George "Bugs" Moran. Barthelmess, of course, is Lingle and Gable is Capone in the film. Gable was borrowed from MGM for this uncompromising gangster opus and he is convincing as the brutal crime boss. Barthelmess was a silent screen star who had peaked in D.W. Griffith's WAY DOWN EAST (1920). His career slid downward as the talkie era deepened due to his mannerisms of acting style that dated him and a voice delivery that always seemed unsure of whether he was responding to verbal cues or title cards as used in the silent movies. His last important part would be, ironically, as a washed up pilot in Howard Hawks' ONLY ANGELS HAVE WINGS (1939). THE FINGER POINTS was produced in the fashion of LITTLE CAESAR (1930), which is no surprise since one of its scriptwriters, W.R. Burnett, was the author of that landmark gangster book and film, a Chicago scribe who knew well the Lingle-Capone story.

d, John Francis Dillon; w, Robert Lord (based on a story by John Monk Saunders, W.R. Burnett); ph, Ernest Haller; ed, Leroy Stone.

Crime Drama **(PR:C MPAA:NR)**

FINGERMAN, THE*** (1963, Fr.) 108m Rome-Paris-Champion/Lux bw (LE DOULOS; AKA: THE STOOLIE)

Jean-Paul Belmondo *(Silien)*, Serge Reggiani *(Maurice)*, Monique Hennessy *(Therese)*, Rene Lefevre *(Gilbert)*, Jean Desailly *(Inspector)*, Michel Piccoli *(Leader)*, Carl Studer *(Kern)*.

Like all Melville's films, THE FINGERMAN pays homage to the American gangster films of the 1930s and 1940s, while still remaining distinctly Parisian. Belmondo stars as the title informer who, it appears, goes to the police with information on jewel thief and murderer Reggiani. To get revenge, Reggiani sets a trap for the informer, but it turns out that Belmondo was actually working for, not against, the thief. With inspector Desailly on their track, both men are killed in Reggiani's trap. Melville's most obvious homages in this picture are to John Huston's ASPHALT JUNGLE and Rouben Mamoulian's CITY STREETS, the police headquarters of which was copied exactly.

d&w, Jean-Pierre Melville (based on the novel by Pierre Lesou); ph, Nicolas Hayer; ed, Monique Bonnot.

Crime **(PR:C MPAA:NR)**

FINGERPRINTS DON'T LIE* (1951) 67m Lippert bw

Richard Travis *(James Stover)*, Sheila Ryan *(Carolyn Palmer)*, Sid Melton *(Hypo Dorton)*, Tom Neal *(Prosecutor)*, Margia Dean *(Nadine Connell)*, Lyle Talbot *(Lieut. Grayson)*, Michael Whalen *(Frank Kelso)*, Richard Emory *(Paul Moody)*, Rory Mallinson *(Brad Evans)*, George Eldredge *(King Sullivan)*, Dee Tatum *(Connie Duval)*, Karl Davis *(Rod Barenger)*, Syra Marty *(Syra)*, Forbes Murray *(Edwin Monroe)*, Zon Murray *(Forrest Taylor)*, Roy Butler *(Bailiff)*.

An unoriginal crime film, involving a man charged with a small-town mayor's murder. The fingerprints which are the main evidence against the man turn out to be forged. In the end, we find the police commissioner was the one who had the motive and the know-how to kill the mayor and fake the prints. A product of the prolific producer-director brother team of Neufeld/Newfield, the giants of the poverty-row studio programmer pictures. Director Newfield cranked out 88 films in a seven-year period during one phase of his long career.

p, Sigmund Neufeld; d, Sam Newfield; w, Orville Hampton (based on a story by Rupert Hughes); ph, Jack Greenhalgh; m, Dudley Chambers; ed, Harry Reynolds.

Crime **(PR:A MPAA:NR)**

FINGERS** (1940, Brit.) 69m FN/WB bw

Clifford Evans *(Fingers)*, Leonora Corbett *(Bonita Grant)*, Esmond Knight *(Sid Harris)*, Edward Rigby *(Sam Bromley)*, Elizabeth Scott *(Meg)*, Roland Culver *(Hugo Allen)*, Reginald Purdell *(Creeper)*, Joss Ambler *(Inspector)*, Peter Cotes.

Simple-minded drama has Evans a noted jewelry fence in London's East End who chucks his life of working-class crime for socialite Corbett. He eventually realizes his error and leaves her, returning to the slums and the girl who really loves him (Scott).

p, A.M. Salomon; d, Herbert Mason; w, Brock Williams; ph, Basil Emmott.

Crime **(PR:A MPAA:NR)**

FINGERS*** (1978) 90m Brut c

Harvey Keitel *(Jimmy Angelelli)*, Tisa Farrow *(Carol)*, Jim Brown *(Deems)*, Michael V. Gazzo *(Ben Angelelli)*, Marian Seldes *(Mother)*, Carole Francis *(Christa)*, Georgette Muir *(Anita)*, Danny Aiello *(Butch)*, Dominick Chianese *(Arthur Fox)*, Anthony Siroco *(Riccamonza)*, Tanya Roberts *(Julie)*, Ed Marinaro *(Gino)*, Zack Norman *(Cop)*, Murray Mosten *(Dr. Fry)*, Jane Elder *(Esther)*, Lenny Montana *(Luchino)*, Frank Pesche *(Raymond)*.

A very interesting, but fairly flawed psychological drama starring Keitel (in one of his best performances in a film filled with good performances) as the son of Mafia chieftain Gazzo (who wants his boy to be in the family business) who really wants to fulfill his ambition as a concert pianist. The dichotomy between what he feels his father wants and what he wants for himself creates a disturbing tension in Keitel that makes him seem about to explode. While all this is engrossing, director/screenwriter Toback tends to muddle things up by introducing *too many* psychological sketches and the film begins to lose its dramatic focus. FINGERS was screenwriter Toback's directorial debut. His next two films were LOVE AND MONEY, 1982 (which barely got released), and EXPOSED, 1983 (which is awful).

p, George Barrie; d&w, James Toback; ph, Mike Chapman (Eastmancolor); ed, Robert Lawrence; prod d, Gene Rudolf; set d, Fred Weiler; cos, Albert Wolsky.

Drama **(PR:O MPAA:R)**

FINGERS AT THE WINDOW*** (1942) 79m MGM bw

Lew Ayres *(Oliver Duffy)*, Laraine Day *(Edwina Brown)*, Basil Rathbone *(Dr. H. Santelle)*, Walter Kingsford *(Dr. Cromwell)*, Miles Mander *(Dr. Kurt Immelman)*, Charles D. Brown *(Inspector Gallagher)*, Cliff Clark *(Lieutenant Allison)*, James Flavin *(Lieutenant Schaeffer)*, Russell Gleason *(Ogilvie)*, William Tannen *(Devlan)*, Mark Daniels *(Hagney)*, Bert Roach *(Krum)*, Russell Hicks *(Dr. Chandley)*, Charles Wagenheim *(Fred Bixley)*, Robert Homans *(Officer O'Garrity)*.

A real thriller which sees the patients of an insane asylum turned into ax murderers by psychotic Rathbone. Day, a victim of an attack, is saved at the last minute by actor-turned-sleuth Ayres. Ayres proceeds to expose Rathbone and his victims. This was the last film for Ayres until after WW II. Ayres was shipped off to the Medical Corps after announcing that he was a conscientious objector. Americans ensconced in "the last refuge of the scoundrel"—jingoistic wartime superpatriotism—were loath to accept Ayres as a legitimate cinema hero following the disclosure of what many regarded as his "cowardice." Studio moguls apparently expected to make much of the co-stardom of Ayres and Day in this thriller; as written, their roles possessed some of the ambiance of the William Powell/Myrna Loy team of the popular THE THIN MAN (1934) and it sequels. Ayres and Day had achieved wide public acceptance in YOUNG DOCTOR KILDARE (1938), and went on to make a successful series with the same characters. An expectation of a similar result in the mystery genre seemed legitimate, and might have come to pass, save for the unfortunate coincidence of Ayres' untimely announcement. This film was prolific screenwriter Lederer's first directorial effort, and his last for some years.

p, Irving Starr; d, Charles Lederer; w, Rose Caylor, Lawrence P. Bachmann (based on a story by Caylor); ph, Harry Stradling, Charles Lawton; m, Bronislau Kaper; ed, George Boemler; art d, Cedric Gibbons.

Mystery Horror **(PR:C MPAA:NR)**

FINIAN'S RAINBOW½** (1968) 145m WB/Seven Arts c

Fred Astaire *(Finian McLonergan)*, Petula Clark *(Sharon McLonergan)*, Tommy Steele *(Og the Leprechaun)*, Don Francks *(Woody Mahoney)*, Keenan Wynn *(Judge Rawkins)*, Barbara Hancock *(Susan the Silent)*, Al Freeman, Jr. *(Howard)*, Ronald Colby *(Buzz Collins)*, Dolph Sweet *(Sheriff)*, Wright King *(District Attorney)*, Louis Silas *(Henry)*, Brenda Arnau *(Sharecropper)*, Avon Long, Roy Glenn, Jester Hairston *(Passion Pilgrim Gospeleers)*.

Astaire, aging but as full of pep as a man in his thirties, arrives in Rainbow Valley, Missitucky, U.S.A., with his daughter Clark in tow, fleeing an angry leprechaun, Steele, from whom he has stolen a crock of gold in the Old Sod. Astaire discards his usual sophisticated mold here for the image of a naive, rather simple-minded Irish immigrant who believes that America's riches grow out of the ground through the gold buried at Ft. Knox. He therefore buries his stolen crock of gold to await further riches. Clark gets involved with Francks, a down-and-out sharecropper who is about to lose his farm to a wicked landgrabbing, bigoted sheriff, Wynn. Astaire loans him the money to pay off Wynn but the sheriff is still a thorn in their sides. He is inveigled into a scheme whereby one of three wishes are granted by Steele, the leprechaun who has arrived from Ireland to reclaim his gold. Wynn's wish backfires and he is turned into a black; he soon learns the evils of racism in hilarious first-hand adventures. Steele's love for Hancock turns him into a human and Clark overcomes the stigma of being a witch so that she can settle down happily with Francks, leaving her wandering, whimsical father, Astaire, to bid a sad farewell as he continues his journey into fancy and new lands. This delightful comedy, peppered with memorable tunes, was a smash hit on Broadway in 1947, running for 725 performances, but it suffers a bit from the heavy directorial hand of Coppola who was out of his element; the GODFATHER movies later proved him perfect for *film noir.* He did, however, bring the budget in for under $4 million, which surprised studio moguls, achieving this small miracle by having the cast rehearse for five weeks prior to any principal shooting, and then completing the film in seven weeks. Sets, costumes, and orchestration for this production are outstanding. Astaire, however, is not given the space nor attention in this film as in his major musical comedies; he once stated that the film was his "biggest disappointment" (Coppola called it "a disaster"). In the stage version, Finian had only a few dance and song bits and the part was necessarily enlarged for Astaire's enormous talents, yet these numbers appear to be the patch jobs they are. Coppola tried to rewrite most of the stage play which was better left alone, and even presumed to tell Hermes Pan (Astaire's long-time choreographer who was signed to the film at the dancer's insistence) how to stage his numbers. When seeing the dances, Coppola pronouced them "abysmal" in true David O. Selznick style, and then went on to stage the dance pieces himself, ignoring even Astaire's advice. Pan, who was fired midway through the filming by the director, considered Coppola "a real pain. He knew very little about dancing and musicals. . . These schoolboys who studied at UCLA think they're geniuses, but there is a lot they don't understand." Coppola was 29 years old when given this, his first big-time feature assignment, and he was clearly over his head, although he did inherit a film already cast and structured. He proved himself, nevertheless, a clod thumping through a genre for which he had no sensitivity, no imagination, no workable creative ideas. Coppola could no more be effective with this production than Bela Lugosi would have been directing THE SOUND OF MUSIC. *He* was the "disaster" that befell FINIAN'S RAINBOW. Songs include: "How Are Things In Glocca Morra?" "Look To The Rainbow," "That Old Devil Moon," "If This Isn't Love," "Something Sort Of Grandish," "The Be-Gat," "This Time Of year," "The Great Come And Get It Day," "When I'm Not Near The Girl I Love," "When The Idle Poor Become The Idle Rich," and the "Rain Dance Ballet" (Burton Lane, E.Y. Harburg).

p, Joseph Landon; d, Francis Ford Coppola; w, E.Y. Harburg, Fred Saidy (based on their play); ph, Philip Lathrop (Panavision, Technicolor); m, Burton Lane; ed, Melvin Shapiro; md, Ray Heindorf; prod d, Hilyard Brown; set d, William L. Kuehl, Philip Abramson; cos, Dorothy Jeakins; ch, Hermes Pan; makeup, Gordon Bau.

Musical/Comedy/Fantasy Cas. (PR:A MPAA:NR)

FINISHING SCHOOL*½ (1934) 70m RKO bw

Frances Dee *(Virginia Radcliffe)*, Billie Burke *(Mrs. Radcliff)*, Ginger Rogers *(Pony)*, Bruce Cabot *(MacFarland)*, John Halliday *(Mr. Radcliff)*, Beulah Bondi *(Miss Van Alstyn)*, Sara Haden *(Miss Fisher)*, Marjorie Lytell *(Ruth)*, Adalyn Doyle *(Madeline)*, Dawn O'Day [Anne Shirley] *(Billie)*, Rose Coghlan *(Miss Garland)*, Ann Cameron *(Miss Schmidt)*, Claire Myers, Susanne Thompson, Edith Vale *(Girls)*, Caroline Rankin *(Miss Weber)*, Jack Norton *(Drunk)*, Joan Barclay *(Short Girl)*, Helen Freeman *(Dr. Hewitt)*, Jane Darwell *(Maud, Head Nurse)*, Irene Franklin, Florence Roberts, John David Horsley, Eddie Baker.

Another girls' school pranks-to-pregnancy picture stemming from the successes of MAEDCHEN IN UNIFORM (1932) and EIGHT GIRLS IN A BOAT (1934), with comedy, pathos, bathos, and a few songs. This one bombed badly at the time of its release despite a strong cast and the presence of Rogers who, as the sophisticated, wise-cracking roommate of poor-little-rich-girl heroine Dee, got the scene-stealing role and played it brilliantly. Rogers' espoused philosophy—get away with whatever you can, just don't get caught—attunes well with that of the principal of the exclusive school, Bondi, and her pedantic minions, who wish above all else to avoid scandal. Dee's unhappiness—she contemplates suicide—is justified in conventional sociological terms by the inept foster-parenting of the snobbish school's staff and by her relative abandonment by her disinterested father, Halliday, and her social-climbing mother, Burke. Dee's depression is allayed somewhat by the jolly camaraderie of her schoolmates and by her interest in Cabot, a hospital intern and part-time waiter, and an unlikely choice as the juvenile (he might have been either hero or heavy from his appearance and charisma in virtually any role he played). The uneven direction was probably the result of the limited experience of co-directors Tuchock and Nicholls, who had, respectively, been a screenwriter and a film editor. Following the romance and the mandatory pregnancy, all ends well, with Dee wedding the poor-but-honest Cabot and finding a chance for lower-middle-class happiness.

p, Merian C. Cooper; d, Wanda Tuchock, George Nicholls; Jr.; w, Tuchock, Laird Doyle (based on a story by David Hempstead and on the play "These Days" by Katherine Clugston); ph, J. Roy Hunt; md, Max Steiner; ed, Arthur Schmidt; art d, Van Nest Polglase, Al D'Agostino; cos, Walter Plunkett; makeup, Mel Burns.

Drama (PR:A MPAA:NR)

FINN AND HATTIE** (1931) 77m PAR bw

Leon Errol *(Finley P. Haddock)*, Mitzi Green *(Mildred Haddock)*, ZaSu Pitts *(Mrs. Haddock)*, Jackie Searl *(Sidney)*, Lilyan Tashman *(The Princess)*, Mack Swain *(Frenchman with Beard)*, Regis Toomey *(Collins)*, Harry Beresford *(Street Cleaner)*.

Child actors steal this film from the adults and make it a juvenile comedy. Green, a child with the IQ of Einstein, spends her time getting her cousin, Searl, into trouble. Errol takes his wife, Pitts, daughter Green, and nephew Searl on a voyage to Paris. Green does terrible things to Searl; she pushes him over the boat, shoves him down an air shaft, and pokes his head into a fishbowl. Green spends the remainder of her time helping her father get out of the trouble he keeps getting into with confidence trickster Toomey and vamp Tashman.

d, Norman Taurog, Norman McLeod; w, Sam Mintz, Joseph L. Mankiewicz (from *Mr. and Mrs. Haddock Abroad* by Donald Ogden Stewart); ph, Dev Jennings.

Comedy (PR:A MPAA:NR)

FINNEGANS WAKE*** (1965) 92m Expanding Cinema/Grove Press bw (AKA: PASSAGES FROM "FINNEGANS WAKE"; PASSAGES FROM JAMES JOYCE'S "FINNEGANS WAKE")

Martin J. Kelly *(Finnegan/H.C. Earwicker)*, Jane Reilly *(Anna Livia Plurabelle, ALP)*, Peter Haskell *(Shem)*, Page Johnson *(Shaun)*, John V. Kelleher *(Commentator)*, Ray Flanagan *(Young Shem)*, Maura Pryor *(Young Iseult)*, Jo Jo Slavin *(Young Shaun)*, Luke J. O'Malley *(Accordion Player)*, Joseph Alderham, Ray Allan, Virginia Blue, Sean Brancato, Joan Campbell, Paddy Croft, Leonard Frey, Eileen Koch, Joe Maher, Janis Markhouse, Kevin O'Leary, Herbert Prah, Jan Thompson, Virginia J. Wallace, Carmen P. Zavick *(Celebrants)*.

An ambitious and all-in-all successful independent undertaking, this first filming of the great literary wordsmith, Irish expatriate poet-punster James Joyce's last work was a labor of dedicated love. The filmmakers drew on the important resources available, such as the James Joyce Society, to ensure as authentic a rendition possible of word-coiner Joyce's witty, much-studied philosophical fantasy. Melding animation and stock footage with live action and location shots, the film recounts the history of humanity in Joyce's vision, through the medium of Dublin publican Kelly's vision of his own death, and the keening, hard-drinking celebrants attending his wake. A cognizant corpse, the coffined Kelly participates in the ceremony, casting himself in many mental roles as his wife Reilly and two sons, Haskell and Johnson, enact the appropriate supporting figures, along with the other riotous mourners. At cock's crow, Finnegan—Kelly—awakens from his dream of his demise with enhanced self-awareness. Considering the impossibility of translating what is essentially a literary mind game into filmic terms, the picture is a triumph.

p&d, Mary Ellen Bute; w, Bute, Ted Nemeth, Jr., Romana Javitz (based on the play "Finnegans Wake, a Dramatization in Six Scenes of the Book of James Joyce" by Mary Manning and the novel by James Joyce); ph, Nemeth; m, Elliot Kaplan; ed, Bute, Yoshio Kishi, Paul Ronder, Thelma Schoonmaker, Catherine Pichonnier.

Drama (PR:A MPAA:NR)

FINNEY½** (1969) 72m Gold Coast bw/c

Robert Kilcullen *(Jim Finney)*, Bill Levinson *(Billy Freeman)*, Joan Sundstrom *(Joyce Finney)*, Anthony Mockus, Dick Stanwood, Richy Hill, Dwight Lawrence, Jerry Kaufherr.

After being forcibly retired from the Chicago Bears, defensive tackle Kilcullen is offered a job as a defensive coach. He turns it down to pursue a career as an artist, but his paintings, all of football themes, are not accepted by the art world. Rejected, he throws his canvases into the Chicago River. His wife, whose career as a singer is rapidly moving, leaves him. Depressed and with no one to turn to, he writes her a letter, receiving a publicity photo as his only reply. Film is relayed mostly in color football flashback sequences, with occasional returns to the black-and-white present of Kilcullen as a bartender. This was Hare's premiere feature film, and the acting debut of each of the three leads. A well-photographed and directed, but ultimately depressing, independent effort.

p,d,w,&ed, Bill Hare; ph, Jack Richards; m, Dick Reynolds, Les Hooper, Eli Wolf.

Drama (PR:A MPAA:NR)

FINO A FARTI MALE** (1969, Fr./Ital.) 86m Les Films Number One-Poste Parisien-Franco Riganti/Sigma III c (AKA: ADELAIDE)

Ingrid Thulin *(Elisabeth Hermann)*, Jacques Sorel *(Frederic Cournot)*, Sylvie Fennec *(Adelaide Hermann)*, Jacques Portet *(Potier)*, Jean-Pierre Bernard *(Christian)*, Faith Brook *(Governess)*, Joelle Bernard *(Janine)*, Simone Gusin, Cynthia Grenier, Robert Higgins.

Engineer Sorel becomes the love interest of the recently widowed Thulin and her daughter Fennec in this confusing tale of a love triangle. The mother and Sorel marry, Sorel's affair with the daughter kept on the side and with the complete knowledge of Thulin. She eventually tires of having to share her new husband, and asks Sorel to get Fennec out of the way. Digging up Portet, a possible suitor for Fennec, Sorel discovers he can't bear parting from the girl. He gets into a fight with the new man that ends in his receiving a serious injury. Forced to remain in his bed, both mother and daughter nurse him lovingly, enclosing themselves in their own little world of passion as they watch over the wounded man in their mansion. A suggestive ending has several officials coming to the mansion to give Sorel recognition for his engineering feats, but arriving just in time to hear three gunshots being fired. Apparently the confusion in passion was a bit too much for these three people, as it also gets to be with the audience. Portrayals are cold and distant, seldom rising to the level supposedly being felt by the three players. (In French; English subtitles.)

p, Felix Garas, Pierre Kalfon; d, Jean-Daniel Simon; w, Jean-Pierre Petrolacci, Simon (based on the novel *Adelaide* by Joseph Arthur de Gobineau); ph, Patrice

Pouget (Eastmancolor); m, Pierre Vassilu; ed, Brigitte Dornes; art d, Claude Pignot.

Drama (PR:O MPAA:R)

FIRE AND ICE*½ (1983) 81m Producer Sales Organization/FOX c

MODELS/VOICES: Randy Norton/William Ostrander *(Larn)*, Cynthia Leake/Maggie Roswell *(Teegra)*, Steve Sandor *(Darkwolf)*, Sean Hannon/Stephen Mendel *(Nekron)*, Leo Gordon *(Jarol)*, William Ostrander *(Taro)*, Ellen O'Neill/Susan Tyrrell *(Juliana)*, Elizabeth Lloyd Shaw *(Roleil)*, Mickey Morton *(Otwa)*, Tamarah Park/Clare Nono *(Tutor)*, Big Yank *(Monga)*, Greg Elam *(Pako)*, Holly Frazetta *(Subhuman Priestess)*, Alan Koss *(Envoy)*, Hans Howes *(Defender Captain)*, James Bridges, Shane Callan, Archie Hamilton, Michael Kelloff, Dale Park, Douglas Payton *(Subhumans)*.

As in his two previous films, LORD OF THE RINGS (1978) and AMERICAN POP (1981), Bakshi employed "rotoscope," using live models as the armatures for the animated characters. This seventh of his animated films exploited the current popularity of his co-producer, comic-book and poster artist Frank Frazetta, he of the heroic figures and Gustav Dore-like composition. The plot is basic good-vs-evil in a mythic prehistoric time, with a land peopled by monstrous non-people, subhuman creatures consigned to *apartheid*, and the consignors, the blue-eyed muscle boys and voluptuous, lightly clad women. Their major weapons are glaciers, invoked and mobilized by powerful wizard Nekron. The childish narrative, doubtless inspired by a spate of similar simplicities such as CONAN THE BARBARIAN (1982), is marred by poor story continuity and terrible transitions.

p, Ralph Bakshi, Frank Frazetta; d, Bakshi; w, Roy Thomas, Gerry Conway (based on a story and characters by Bakshi, Frazetta); ph, (live) Francis Grumman (Deluxe Color); m, William Kraft; ed, A. David Marshall.

Fantasy/Animation Cas. (PR:C MPAA:PG)

FIRE DOWN BELOW½** (1957, U.S./Brit.) 116m Warwick/COL c

Rita Hayworth *(Irena)*, Robert Mitchum *(Felix)*, Jack Lemmon *(Tony)*, Herbert Lom *(Harbor Master)*, Bonar Colleano *(Lt. Sellars)*, Bernard Lee *(Dr. Sam)*, Edric Conner *(Jimmy Jean)*, Peter Illing *(Captain)*, Joan Miller *(Mrs. Canaday)*, Anthony Newley *(Miguel)*, Eric Pohlmann *(Hotel Owner)*, Vivian Matalon, Gordon Tanner, Maurice Kaufmann *(U.S. Sailors)*, Lionel Murton *(American)*, Murray Kash *(Bartender)*, Maya Koumani *(Waitress)*, Philip Baird *(Young Man)*, Keith Banks *(Drunken Young Man)*, Dean Moster, Greta Remin, Lorna Wood, Barbara Lane, Brian Blades, Gina Chare, Shirley Rus *(Dancers)*, Stretch Cox Troupe *(Limbo Dancers)*, Anatole Smirnoff, Terry Shelton, Robert Nelson.

Small time smugglers Mitchum and Lemmon pick up transient tramp Hayworth, taking her along on their small boat through the West Indies so she can get a passport in Santa Nada (not on any real map) where no questions are asked. Lemmon falls for the sexy Hayworth against the warnings of seasoned Mitchum. She herself bemoans her own damaged goods by laconically telling Lemmon: "I'm not good for you, no good for anyone. Armies have marched over me." But Lemmon likes his ladies a little used up and his infatuation grows to jealous love when it is apparent that Hayworth and Mitchum are inexorably drawn together like a wad of hot wax and a pair of brand new dentures. But Lemmon won't give up on Rita and this leads to a confrontation between him and Mitchum. Jealousy seeps from Mitchum's craw, too, and he goes off in a huff, later informing police of Lemmon's smuggling operation. As the Coast Guard moves in, Lemmon escapes, then signs on board a freighter heading for Mitchum's island hideout where he and wornout Hayworth are making whoopee, intending to murder his former partner for stealing the half-eaten tomato. A dense fog, however, causes the freighter to strike another ship, resulting in heavy damage where Lemmon is pinned in the wreckage of a hold while the ship slowly begins to sink. The cargo around him is about to blow up and it's only a matter of scant hours before Lemmon enters Davy Jones' locker. Mitchum hears the news and boards the doomed ship, goes into the hold, and frees his former pal. Lemmon comes to his senses and wishes Mitchum and Hayworth good luck with each other. This is a tired love triangle that provides laughs in all the wrong places, even though Parrish's direction is good and the pace is brisk, with excellent photography from Dickinson. Shaw's script is not only corny but is peppered with cliches, profiling Hayworth in a reprise of her prositute role in MISS SADIE THOMPSON (1953). Hayworth does a hip-grinding, thigh flaunting dance number similar to the bit in that earlier movie; here she is not the love interest but the sex object, as in so many of her later films. Everybody but simon-pure Lemmon labels her a tart, even Mitchum who winds up with her. At one point Mitchum kisses her and when she doesn't respond, he carps, "I'm proud—I don't make love to the dead." This was Hayworth's first film in four years but it brought in heavy box office receipts, mostly due to the current publicity about her volatile divorce from Dick Haymes and some stormy affairs. Furthering the appeal of FIRE DOWN BELOW was the image projected of her in THE BAREFOOT CONTESSA (1954), despite the loud denials of that film's producer, Joseph L. Mankiewicz, that the film was based on Hayworth's tempestuous life. Mitchum saunters through the film in the usual somnambulistic state with his traditional flat-voiced delivery and all the enthusiasm of a stuffed bear. At best, he is indifferent to the script, his fellow actors, and the lush on-location sites of Trinidad and Tobago (where Mitchum also worked in HEAVEN KNOWS, MR. ALLISON, 1957). Lemmon brings the production some high voltage energy and is the best thing about it. He even composed the "Harmonica Theme" for the film about which he later commented: "To date I've made something like seventeen dollars in royalties from it." FIRE DOWN BELOW, though it has some exciting moments, is just another love triangle with a few corners missing, hyped up in an exotic setting and an ad campaign that blared FIRE DOWN BELOW was "Spontaneous combustion! Hayworth sizzles! Mitchum explodes! Lemmon burns!" They were all, of course, blowing smoke.

p, Irving Allen, Albert R. Broccoli; d, Robert Parrish; w, Irwin Shaw (based on the novel by Max Catto); ph, Desmond Dickinson (CinemaScope,Technicolor); m, Arthur Banjamin; ed, Jack Slade; md, Muir Mathieson; art d, Syd Cain; set d, John Box; cos, Balmain, Bermans; spec eff, Cliff Richardson; ch, Tutte Lemkow; m/l, "Fire Down Below," Lester Lee, Jack Washington (sung by Jeri Southern).

Adventure/Drama (PR:C MPAA:NR)

FIRE HAS BEEN ARRANGED, A** (1935, Brit.) 70m Twickenham bw

Bud Flanagan *(Bud)*, Chesney Allen *(Ches)*, Mary Lawson *(Betty)*, Robb Wilton *(Oswald)*, Harold French *(Toby)*, C. Denier Warren *(Shuffle)*, Alastair Sim *(Cutte)*, Hal Walters *(Hal)*, The Buddy Bradley Girls *(Shopgirls)*.

Comedy team Flanagan and Allen play a pair of convicts just released after ten years in prison. They return to the site where they had buried their loot, but find the whole area developed and a shop on the exact spot where the jewels were buried. The managers of the store have been having a difficult time, so they are quite willing to help the two ex-cons burn the establishment to the ground. Unfortunately for crookdom, the lady who is the legitimate legatee of the lad from whom they lifted the loot bags the booty before the burning. Acceptable entertainment.

p, Julius Hagen; d, Leslie Hiscott; w, H. Fowler Mear, Michael Barringer (based on a story by Mear, James Carter); ph, Sydney Blythe.

Comedy (PR:A MPAA:NR)

FIRE IN THE FLESH** (1964, Fr.) 80m Societe Francais des Films-Alfred Rode/Pacemaker c (LA FILLE DE FEU)

Claudine Dupuis *(Fern Heldt)*, Erno Crisa *(Larry Gordon)*, Yoko Tani *(Yulie, the Captain's Girl)*, Bill Marshall *(Stork)*, Allan Lamaire [Hugo Del Carril] *(Ortiz)*, Robert Dupont [Armand Mestral] *(Captain Le Guen)*, Raymond Souplex *(Professor Theodore Heldt)*, Albert Dinan *(Captain)*.

While on a scientific expedition to an uncharted island in the South Seas, a professor (Souplex), his daughter Dupuis, and his assistant, Crisa, find themselves shipwrecked and alone. Ten years later, after Souplex dies, Dupuis and Crisa decide to "marry." Fearing he may lose Dupuis if they are returned to civilization, Crisa fails to light a signal fire when he spots a ship on the horizon. Nevertheless, the ship, which carries a crew of international smugglers, docks on the island. When the smugglers discover Crisa and Dupuis they decide to kill Crisa and take Dupuis with them. Desperate, Crisa leads the men to a cache of valuable pearls and a gunfight ensues between the greedy criminals. Back on the ship, Dupont, the captain, fears that they will be caught in an oncoming typhoon and goes ashore in search of the men. He finds the bodies and no sign of Crisa, and informs Dupuis that he has probably been killed. As the ship sails away, Dupuis spots Crisa standing on a cliff. She loyally dives overboard and swims back to the island to stay with her "husband."

p&d, Alfred Rode; w, Jean-Pierre Marchand, Claude Desailly, Louis Martin (based on the novel by John D. Fellow); ph, Jean Isnard (Agfacolor); m, Paul Bonneau; ed, Paul Cayatte; art d, Claude Bouxin.

Drama (PR:A MPAA:NR)

FIRE IN THE STONE, THE½** (1983, Aus.) 96m South Australian Film Corp. c

Paul Smith *(Ernie)*, Linda Hartley *(Sophie)*, Theo Pertsinidis *(Nick)*, Andrew Gaston *(Willie)*, Alan Cassell *(Robbie)*, Ray Meagher *(Dosh)*.

Okay kids' fare from Australia concerns the efforts of three teenagers who live in a small opal mining town to recover some gems stolen by one of the miners. The boys, one black and two white, learn more about themselves and each other during the adventure and eventually retrieve the gems. Originally distributed to schools before being shown on Australian television.

p, Pamela Vanneck; d, Gary Conway; w, Graeme Koestveld (based on the novel by Colin Thiele); ph, Ross Berryman; ed, Philip Reid; art d, Derek Mills.

Drama/Children (PR:AA MPAA:NR)

FIRE IN THE STRAW*** (1943), Fr.) 89m Carl Laemmle bw (LE FEU DE PAILLE)

Lucien Baroux *(Antoine Vautier)*, Orane Demazis *(Jeanne Vautier)*, Jean Fuller *(Christian Vautier)*, Jeanne Helbling *(Monica)*, Aimos *(Gueretrain)*, Gaby Basset, Henri Nassiet, Jeanne Fusier-Gir.

A thespian father watches his young son rise to fame in motion pictures as his own career falters. The boy's popularity at the box office is brief, and he discovers what his father already knows, that acting is an arduous career. A bittersweet story, with skillfully created characters. FIRE IN THE STRAW was completed before the Nazi occupation of France in 1940, and in its U.S. release was touted as the last film to be exported from Free France. Expatriate producer/director Benoit-Levy had been living and teaching in New York City for three years when the film opened there.

p&d, Jean Benoit-Levy; w, Benoit-Levy, Henry Troyat (based on Troyat's novel *Grandeur Nature*); ph, Marcel Lucien; ed, Darlowe.

Drama (PR:A MPAA:NR)

FIRE MAIDENS FROM OUTER SPACE** (1956, Brit.) 80m Criterion/Eros bw (AKA: FIRE MAIDENS OF OUTER SPACE)

Anthony Dexter *(Luther Blair)*, Susan Shaw *(Hestia)*, Paul Carpenter *(Larson)*, Harry Fowler *(Sydney Stanhope)*, Jacqueline Curtiss *(Duessa)*, Sydney Tafler *(Dr. Higgins)*, Owen Berry *(Prasus)*, Rodney Diak *(Anderson)*, Maya Koumani, Jan Holden, Kim Parker *(Fire Maidens)*.

Dexter is a space captain who discovers escaped remnants of the lost civilization of Atlantis on the thirteenth moon of Jupiter. It just so happens that this population is entirely female, with the exception of elderly sage Berry and a voyeuristic monster. They decide to return to earth with the idea of reviving Atlantis, but this plan is done in when the moon monster kills Berry and kidnaps one of the scantily clad maidens. The crew saves her from the beast and returns to earth with one of the maidens. They promise to return for the others in the near future. This picture proves that the English can be just as cheap and hokey as their colonial cousins. Borodin's theme music sounds only when the lens is on the cavorting maidens, suggesting that one of them may tote a ghetto blaster. Hero Dexter briefly flamed as the star of VALENTINO (1951) and THE BRIGAND (1952).

p, George Fowler; d&w, Cy Roth; ph, Ian Struthers; m, "Polovtsian Dances" by Alexander Porphyrievich Borodin, from "Prince Igor," the opera by Borodin et al; ed, A. C. T. Clair, Lito Carruthers; art d, Scott MacGregor; makeup, Roy Ashton.

Science Fiction **(PR:A MPAA:NR)**

FIRE OVER AFRICA** (1954, Brit.) 84m Film Locations/COL c (GB: MALAGA)

Maureen O'Hara *(Joanna Dane)*, Macdonald Carey *(Van Logan)*, Binnie Barnes *(Frisco)*, Guy Middleton *(Soames Howard)*, Hugh McDermott *(Richard Farrell)*, James Lilburn *(Danny Boy)*, Harry Lane *(Augie)*, Leonard Sachs *(Paul Dupont)*, Ferdy Mayne *(Mustapha)*, Eric Corrie *(Pebbles)*, Bruce Beeby *(Potts)*, Gerard Tichy *(Cronkhite)*, Derek Sydney *(Signor Amato)*, Jacques Cey *(Monsieur Ducloir)*, Mike Brendall *(Rodrigo)*, Meinhart Maur *(Jakie)*.

A ludicrous North African adventure with O'Hara as a secret agent sent to the Dark Continent to uncover a smuggling ring. She was suggested by a fellow American agent working with foreign law enforcement. His reason for choosing her was that she's a female, and he'd be the only one to know her identity to keep leaks from springing. Good idea, but he's killed and no one has a clue of who O'Hara is at her arrival. Agent O'Hara deals with the situation, and is able to break the smuggling ring with the help of co-agent Carey, initially thought to be one of the gang, and heart-of-gold saloonkeeper Barnes (wife of co-producer Frankovitch, a fortuitous bit of nepotism, as hers is easily the best performance). The location shots in Tangier are lovely, but Carey is no *Pepe le Moko*, nor is O'Hara a *Gaby*. The highly predictable script detracts from any possible enjoyment of the action.

p, Colin Lesslie, M.J. Frankovitch [Montagu Marks]; d, Richard Sale; w, Robert Westerby; ph, Christopher Challis (Technicolor); m, Benjamin Frankel; ed, A.S. Bates; art d, Vincent Korda, Wilfred Shingleton.

Action/Adventure **(PR:A MPAA:NR)**

FIRE OVER ENGLAND**** (1937, Brit.) 92m Mayflower-Pendennis-Korda-London Films/UA bw

Laurence Olivier *(Michael Ingolby)*, Flora Robson *(Queen Elizabeth)*, Leslie Banks *(Earl of Leicester)*, Raymond Massey *(Philip of Spain)*, Vivien Leigh *(Cynthia)*, Tamara Desni *(Elena)*, Morton Selten *(Burleigh)*, Lyn Harding *(Sir Richard)*, George Thirlwell *(Gregory)*, Henry Oscar *(Spanish Ambassador)*, Robert Rendell *(Don Miguel)*, Robert Newton *(Don Pedro)*, Donald Calthrop *(Don Escobal)*, Charles Carson *(Admiral Valdez)*, James Mason *(Hillary Vane)*, Herbert Lomas *(Richard Ingolby)*, Lawrence Hanray *(French Ambassador)*, Roy Russell *(Cooper)*, Howard Douglas *(Lord Amberley)*, Cecil Mainwaring *(Illingworth)*, Francis de Wolfe *(Tarleton)*, Graham Cheswright *(Maddison)*, A. Corney Grain *(Hatton)*, Evelyn Ankers.

A rare film that succeeds superbly in two genres, as a swashbuckling epic and as a historical drama. That finest of actors, Olivier, is a young British naval officer whose father is burned to death as a heretic in the Spanish Inquisition. He seeks revenge and finds his opportunity in the court of the tempestuous Queen Elizabeth I, embodied wholly by Robson. She knows she is surrounded by traitors in league with her arch enemy, Philip of Spain (Massey), who plans to invade England. When Olivier offers to go to Spain, infiltrate Massey's court, and learn the identity of the English informants and the date of the invasion, Robson clutches the opportunity. She is also romantically inclined toward the handsome and dashing officer and a little vexed at the attentions he shows his childhood sweetheart and her lady-in-waiting, Leigh. Yet Olivier goes off with her blessings. In Spain, through noblewoman Desni, who loves him, and Rendell, an artistocrat who admires him, Olivier learns of Massey's plans for an Armada, along with the identities of the villains in Elizabeth's own court. He just barely manages to escape back to England after several harrowing adventures. There he exposes the traitors and helps lead the British ships into battle against the Spanish Armada, which is destroyed. For his valiant efforts, Olivier is not only knighted by grateful queen Robson, but wins the hand of the lovely Leigh. Tasteful in every way, Korda's production is typically lavish and historically accurate in detail, save for the Olivier role which is apochryphal. Robson is simply marvelous as Elizabeth, a demanding, reclusive, reservedly kind monarch, a role she plays to perfection and would repeat three years later in the stupendous THE SEA HAWK (1940) with Erroll Flynn. Olivier is ebullient and athletic in the role of the dashing officer and Leigh was never lovelier; this was their first film together (they would make only three films together) and the meeting produced an affair that deepened over the fourteen weeks of production. Both were married at the time and it would be four years before painful divorces allowed them to wed. British movie mogul Alexander Korda admired the directorial abilities of Howard, and, after seeing Howard's THE POWER AND THE GLORY, hired him to helm this expensive production. Howard brought the talented cinematographer Howe with him from the U.S., and his camerawork greatly contributed to the fluid look of the film, with marvelous action sequences that intercut to the Armada battle of convincing models in the Denham Studio tank. A host of versatile supporting players adds to the depth of FIRE OVER ENGLAND, not the least of whom is Massey as the darkly brooding, expansionist Philip. Banks, the faithful Leicester, and Selten as the queen's treasurer are also standouts. In a brief scene, Olivier is shown weeping over his father's remains, which caused jeers in some theaters during the U.S. release. This scene, about a minute, was cut in some prints, UA distributing executives believing that tears from a swashbuckler were unsuitable to his part. Portions of the miniature battle scenes were later used in 1939's THE LION HAS WINGS.

p, Erich Pommer (for Alexander Korda); d, William K. Howard; w, Clemence Dane, Sergei Nolbandov (based on the novel by A.E.W. Mason); ph, James Wong Howe; m, Richard Addinsell; ed, John Dennis; md, Muir Mathieson; art d, Lazare Meerson; set d, Meerson; cos, Rene Hubert; spec eff, Ned Mann, Lawrence Butler, Edward Cohen.

Historical Epic **Cas.** **(PR:A MPAA:NR)**

FIRE RAISERS, THE** (1933, Brit.) 77m GAU/W&F bw

Leslie Banks *(Jim Bronson)*, Anne Grey *(Arden Brent)*, Carol Goodner *(Helen Vaughan)*, Frank Cellier *(Brent)*, Francis L. Sullivan *(Stedman)*, Laurence Anderson *(Twist)*, Joyce Kirby *(Polly)*, Henry Caine *(Bates)*, George Merritt *(Sonners)*.

Banks is an insurance assessor who almost turns crooked and joins an arson-for-hire gang. A crisis of conscience keeps him on the straight and narrow and he turns his almost-associates in to the police. Early, minor Powell, but interesting anyway.

p, Jerome Jackson; d, Michael Powell; w, Jackson, Powell.

Crime **(PR:A MPAA:NR)**

FIRE SALE* (1977) 88m FOX c

Alan Arkin *(Ezra Fikus)*, Rob Reiner *(Russel Fikus)*, Vincent Gardenia *(Benny Fikus)*, Anjanette Comer *(Marion Fikus)*, Kay Medford *(Ruth Fikus)*, Barbara Dana *(Virginia)*, Sid Caesar *(Zabbar)*, Alex Rocco *(Al)*, Byron Stewart *(Captain)*, Oliver Clark *(Blossom)*, Richard Libertini, MacIntyre Dixon *(Painters)*, Augusta Dabney *(Mrs. Cooper)*, Don Keefer *(Banker)*, Bill Henderson *(Psychiatrist)*, John Horn *(Louis)*, Sally K. Marr *(Jackie)*, Speedy Zapata *(Janitor)*, Kimelle Anderson *(Nurse)*, Selma Archerd *(Ellie)*, Bob Leslie *(Van Driver)*, John Hudkins *(Wheelchair Patient)*, Viola Harris *(Helen)*, Marvin Worth *(Milton)*, Bill Bogert *(Insurance Doctor)*, William Prince *(Mr. Cooper)*, Mickey Gilbert *(Fireman)*.

When this picture is good, it's mildly funny. When it's bad, which is more often than when it's good, it is just abysmal. Gardenia owns a failing department store where son Reiner is his assistant, one who acts like a whipped dog. Other son Arkin long ago left to become a basketball coach. Arkin is married to Comer, who wants a child. Arkin wants a winning team, so he adopts black teen-ager Stewart in an attempt to satisfy both their needs. Nutty uncle Sid Caesar, a WW II veteran, is brought in to burn down the store. Caesar has been told by Gardenia it is a Nazi headquarters in the hope that he will torch the place so they can collect the fire insurance. Basically a picture about totally unlovable people, it misses on many levels; not the least is Arkin's direction. Nepotism reared its head as Arkin cast his wife, Dana, in the role of Virginia. They thought it was "black humor" but they should realize that black humor usually refers to movies that aren't funny to anyone except the makers. Producer Marvin Worth, a former performer, does a small bit and the most controlled acting is by Alex Rocco. Otherwise, it's as strained as a hernia.

p, Marvin Worth; d, Alan Arkin; w, Robert Klane (based on his novel); ph, Ralph Woolsey (DeLuxe Color); m, Dave Grusin; ed, Richard Halsey; prod d, James H. Spencer; set d, Dennis Peeples; cos, Norman Burza, Lynn Bernay; spec eff, Logan Frazee; stunts, Mickey Gilbert.

Comedy **(PR:A-C MPAA:PG)**

FIRE WITHIN, THE*** (1964, Fr./Ital.) 110m Nouvelles Editions-Arco/Governor bw (LE FEU FOLLET; FUOCO FATUO)

Maurice Ronet *(Alain Leroy)*, Lena Skerla *(Lydia)*, Yvonne Clech *(Mademoiselle Farnoux)*, Hubert Deschamps *(d'Avereau)*, Jean-Paul Moulinot *(Dr. La Barbinais)*, Mona Dol *(Madame La Barbinais)*, Jeanne Moreau *(Jeanne)*, Alexandra Stewart *(Solange)*, Pierre Moncorbier *(Moraire)*, Rene Dupuy *(Charlie)*, Bernard Tiphaine *(Milou)*, Bernard Noel *(Dubourg)*, Ursula Kubler *(Fanny)*, Alain Mottet *(Urcel)*, Francois Gragnon *(Francois Minville)*, Romain Bouteille *(Jerome Minville)*, Jacques Sereys *(Cyrille Lavaud)*, Claude Deschamps *(Maria)*, Toni Taffin *(Brancion)*, Henri Serre *(Frederic)*, Vera Valdez, J. Wells, Claude Deleusse, Madeleine Declercq, Michele Mahaut.

Ronet is an alcoholic writer who no longer sees any choice for himself except suicide. When he proves impotent in an encounter with a friend (Skerla) of his estranged wife she takes him back to the sanitorium from which he has just been discharged. He tells the doctor that he is awash with anxiety, but the doctor only recommends that he telephone his wife and tell her everything is fine. Ronet begins reading a book, cuts out a picture of Marilyn Monroe and several obituaries, and keeps a diary in which he has targeted July 23 as the date of his suicide. He travels to Paris to visit some old friends, but he is unable or unwilling to communicate with them. He returns to the sanitorium the next day, July 23, finishes his book, then calmly shoots himself through the heart. On the screen appears Ronet's reason for his act: "I kill myself because you have not loved me, because I haven't loved you. I kill myself because the bonds between us were loose, and to tighten those bonds. I will leave an indelible stain on you." Generally regarded as Malle's best work, THE FIRE WITHIN is a somber study of a man gradually cutting himself off from everything until there is no more reason to remain alive. Malle adapted the story from a 1931 novel by Pierre Drieu La Rochelle which fictionalized the suicide of surrealist writer Jacques Rigaut in 1929. La Rochelle, who collaborated with the German occupiers in World War II, himself committed suicide in 1945. A commercial failure, Malle himself best summed up why: "It is such a harsh subject and it's such a depressing movie."

p, Alain Queffeleah; d&w, Louis Malle (based on the novel *La Feu Follet* by Pierre Drieu La Rochelle); ph, Ghislain Cloquet; m, Erik Satie; ed, Suzanne Baron, Monique Nana; art d, Bernard Evein.

Drama **(PR:O MPAA:NR)**

FIREBALL, THE** (1950) 83m Thor/FOX bw

Mickey Rooney *(Johnny Casar)*, Pat O'Brien *(Father O'Hara)*, Beverly Tyler *(Mary Reeves)*, James Brown *(Allen)*, Marilyn Monroe *(Polly)*, Ralph Dumke *(Bruno)*, Bert

Begley *(Shilling)*, Milburn Stone *(Jeff Davis)*, Sam Flint *(Dr. Barton)*, John Hedloe *(Ullman)*, Glenn Corbett *(Mack Miller)*.

Roller derby was just getting started in the late 1940s and Hollywood was quick to jump on the bandwagon. Rooney escapes from an orphanage run by priest (you guessed it) Pat O'Brien. After getting a job in a small restaurant he meets Tyler, a skater, who teaches him how to don the skates and roll around the track. He eventually has a few match races with Corbett; he loses regularly until Tyler tells him how to win and he does. Later, Rooney joins a roller derby team and again runs into O'Brien who admits that he knew where the kid was all the time but allowed him to go it on his own. Rooney soon becomes a crowd favorite and his ego grows to ten times the size of his diminutive body. He forgets about being a team player and just concentrates on his own success. He meets Marilyn Monroe, sort of a derby groupie, who cares about him because he is a star, not because he is a person. Now tragedy strikes and he is knocked for a loop by polio. Tyler helps him back to health; he goes back to work feeling better, but still as cocky and self-centered as before. He eventually realizes the folly of his selfish ways and allows his teammates to score some points. Once that's done, Tyler and O'Brien welcome him back with open arms. Roller derby was later handled better in DERBY (1971) and KANSAS CITY BOMBER (1972) but Rooney is a joy to watch in everything he does and carries the film, challenging us to love him despite his attitude. This was Monroe's ninth film, and it wasn't for another couple of years that she caught fire in NIAGARA (1953) and GENTLEMEN PREFER BLONDES (1953).

p, Bert Friedlob; d, Tay Garnett; w, Garnett, Horace McCoy; ph, Lester White; m, Victor Young; ed, Frank Sullivan; art d, Van Nest Polglase.

Sports/Drama (PR:A MPAA:NR)

FIREBALL 500** (1966) 91m AIP c

Frankie Avalon *(Dave)*, Annette Funicello *(Jane)*, Fabian *(Leander)*, Chill Wills *(Big Jaw)*, Harvey Lembeck *(Charlie Bigg)*, Julie Parrish *(Martha)*, Doug Henderson *(Hastings)*, Baynes Barron *(Bronson)*, Mike Nader *(Joey)*, Ed Garner *(Herman)*, Vin Scully, Sandy Reed *(Announcers)*, Sue Hamilton *(Farmer's Daughter)*, Renie Riano *(Herman's Wife)*, Len Lesser *(Man in Garage)*, Billy Beck *(Jobber)*, Tex Armstrong *(Herman's Friend)*, Mary Hughes, Patti Chandler, Karla Conway, Hedy Scott, Sallie Sachse, Jo Collins, Maria McBane, Linda Bent *(Leander Fans)*, The Don Randi Trio Plus One, The Carole Lombard Singers.

Avalon and Fabian are race car drivers chasing Funicello when not driving. Bootleggers trick Avalon into carrying their contraband during a cross-country race. Director Asher, who started the 1960s' surfing movie craze, pulls out an above-average teen-age fare with FIREBALL 500. Avalon and Funicello are even able to find time to sing between car crashes and checkered flags. Songs include the title tune, "Fireball 500," "Country Carnival," "Step Right Up," "My Way That Gets Me My Way," "A Chance Like That," "Turn Around, You'll Know Where To Find Me."

p, Burt Topper, James H. Nicholson, Samuel Z. Arkoff; d, William Asher; w, Asher, Leo Townsend; ph, Floyd Crosby (Panavision, Pathecolor); m, Les Baxter; ed, Fred Feitshans, Eve Newman; md, Al Simms; art d, Daniel Haller; set d, Harry Reif; cos, Richard Bruno; spec eff, Frank DeMarco; m/l, Guy Hemric, Jerry Styner; makeup, Ted Cooley.

Action (PR:A MPAA:NR)

FIREBALL JUNGLE** (1968) 96m Americana c (AKA: JUNGLE TERROR)

Alan Mixon *(Cateye Meares)*, John Russell *(Nero Sagittarius)*, Lon Chaney, Jr. *(Sammy, Junkyard Owner)*, Randy Kirby *(Steve Cullen)*, Chuck Daniel *(Marty)*, Nancy Donohue *(Ann Tracey)*, Vicki Nunis *(Judy)*, Billy Blueriver, Tiny Kennedy, Babs Beatty, Joie Chitwood, Ed Wisner, Candy Stebbins, Andrew Martinez, Pat Rast, Sharon Cramer, James LaRue, Black Star, Bruce Atkins, Bruce Roberts, Linda Roberts, Dohle Rast, Kathy Roberts, Ronnie Bell, Bobby Rast, Edward Thompson, Herman the Wonder Dog.

Mobster Russell and his sidekick Mixon put their muscle on the Southern stock-car racing circuit and *nobody* is going to stop them! Lots of cars are destroyed in the process, with some stunt driving by famed stock-car driver Joie Chitwood. Shot in and around Tampa, Florida. Lots of automobile crashes, and an interesting opportunity to see Chaney, Jr. go up in flames.

p, G. B. Roberts; d, Jose Priete [Joseph Prieto]; w, Harry Whittington; ph, Clifford Poland (Eastmancolor); ed, John Dalton; set d, Ralph L. Brown; sp eff, Doug Hobart; m/l, Tiny Kennedy.

Crime/Action (PR:C MPAA:NR)

FIREBIRD, THE*½ (1934) 75m WB bw

Verree Teasdale *(Carola Pointer)*, Ricardo Cortez *(Herman Brandt)*, Lionel Atwill *(John Pointer)*, Anita Louise *(Mariette)*, C. Aubrey Smith *(Police Inspector)*, Dorothy Tree *(Jolan)*, Hobart Cavanaugh *(Emile)*, Robert Barrat *(Halasz)*, Russell Hicks *(Stage Manager)*, Spencer Charters *(Max)*, Etienne Girardot *(Professor Peterson)*, Florence Fair *(Thelma)*, Nan Gray *(Alice Von Attern)*, Helen Trenholme *(Mlle. Mousquet)*, Hal K. Dawson *(Assistant Stage Manager)*.

Initial suspense is well managed in this mystery drama dealing with the murder of a Viennese bounder, Cortez, a self-adoring mime actor whose avocation is the seduction of a succession of ladies. The plot unfolds through the medium of the family in the flat above the actor's own, diplomat Atwill, wife Teasdale, and daughter Louise. Their perceptions of their downstairs neighbor are conditioned in part by his frequent renditions of the same music, selections from Stravinsky's "The Firebird," long and loudly played. Teasdale's antithesis to the music, which she views as vulgar, suggests that she may object too much, to some suspicious end. Is she the current conquest of the cad, signaled by the melodic theme that the coast is clear for another romantic—if illicit—liaison? The lilting strains of the theme music sound again. Dissolve to the doorway of the dressing-gowned deceiver. Greeting his unrevealed inamorata, he ushers her into his pit of passion. End of actor; the final curtain descends for now-corpse Cortez, as we discover with the visit of police inspector Smith to the suspects upstairs. Whodunit? Who wrote the finale to the philanderer? A trysting Teasdale? An outraged Atwill? A lustful Louise? In a disappointing denouement, deductive details disclose the dame who did the deadly deed, a disillusioned darling of the dastard.

p, Gilbert Miller; w, Charles Kenyon, Jeffrey Dell (based on a play by Lajos Zilahy); ph, Ernest Haller; m, Igor Stravinsky; ed, Ralph Dawson; art d, Anton Grot.

Mystery (PR:A MPAA:NR)

FIREBIRD 2015 AD*½ (1981) 97m Mara c

Darren McGavin, Doug McClure, George Toulatos, Mary Beth Rubens, Alex Diakun, R.C. Wisden.

For car lovers only, FIREBIRD 2015 AD is set in a not too distant future in which gasoline is a rare commodity. An agency, the Department of Vehicular Control, is set up to destroy autos owned by private citizens. The only condition is that the owners themselves must not be injured. Diakun, a DVC driver, takes things a little too far and goes on a murderous rampage. The fast, tire-squealing pace will hold interest for a while, but a lack of intelligence and technical know-how acts as a disadvantage. This could have found a following, but instead it runs out of gas long before its 97 minutes have expired.

p, Merritt White; d, David Robertson; w, Barry Pearson, Biff McGuire, Maurice Hurley; ph, Robert Fresco; m, Paul Hoffert, Lawrence Shragge, Brenda Hoffert, art d, Richard Hudolin, Don Zacharias; spec eff, Neil Trifunovich, Gary Paller.

Science Fiction Cas. (PR:O MPAA:NR)

FIREBRAND, THE** (1962) 63m AP/FOX bw

Kent Taylor *(Maj. Tim Bancroft)*, Valentin De Vargas *(Joaquin Murieta)*, Lisa Montell *(Clarita Vasconcelos)*, Joe Raciti *(Jack Garcia)*, Chubby Johnson *(Tampico)*, Barbara Mansell *(Cassie)*, Allen Jaffe *(Torres)*, Troy Melton *(Walker)*, Fred Krone *(Dickens)*, Sid Haig *(Diego)*, Felix Locher *(Ramirez)*, Jerry Summers *(Rafael Vasconcelos)*, Tom Daly, I. Stanford Jolley, Pat Lawless.

Loosely based on the lawless life of legendary Joaquin Murieta, the Hispanic Robin Hood of California in the mid-1800s, this film offers a sympathetic view of the plight of the Spanish-speaking long-time residents of the area during the invasion of the gold-hungry gringos. De Vargas is the dashing don whose derring-do delights the dispossessed. When Summers, brother of his lady love, Montell, is wounded, De Vargas offers to release his captive, bounty hunter Johnson, in payment for doctoring the lad. Against his conscience, Johnson is later pressed by Ranger chief Taylor—whose gold-shipment stewardship has been violated by De Vargas' band—to lead him to the outlaw encampment. In a surprise attack, the Rangers butcher the inhabitants, including Summers. The absent De Vargas, hearing of the tragedy while in a *cantina*, goes wild and gets arrested. Ignorant of the importance of their catch, the arresting deputies let him go free. Assembling the remnants of his band, De Vargas assaults Taylor's Ranger group and captures him. After some introspection, De Vargas elects to settle for shaming his opponent rather than killing him. He sends Taylor back to town bound and lashed to his horse. De Vargas and his merry men then make haste for Sonora and safety, his sweetheart as his side.

p&d, Maury Dexter; w, Harry Spalding; ph, Floyd Crosby (CinemaScope); m, Richard La Salle; ed, Jodie Copelan; set d, Harry Reif; cos, Ray Summers; makeup, Harry Ross.

Western (PR:C MPAA:NR)

FIREBRAND JORDAN* (1930) 55m National Players/Big Four bw (AKA: FIREBRAND JOHNSON)

Lane Chandler *(Firebrand Jordan)*, Yakima Canutt *(Red Carson)*, Aline Goodwin *(Joan Howe)*, Tom London *(Ed Burns)*, Frank Yaconelli *(Tony)*, Cliff Lyons *(Pete)*, Fred Harvey *(Judd Howe)*, Alfred Hewston *(Ah Sing)*, Lew Meehan *(Spike)*, Marguerite Ainslee *(Peggy Howe)*, Sheldon Lewis *(David Hampton)*.

A horse opera that's almost really an opera. Lots of songs and vain attempts at action, but this is a smeller from the start. Ho-hum attempts at comedy fall flatter than cowpats on the prairie. Canutt, born Enos Edward Canutt, is the only good thing about this, but his voice never really made the transition to talkies, so he took up second unit directing and stunt work and eventually won an Oscar for his work as a stuntman, a special award given to him in 1966 when he was 71 years old. Chandler spent most of his life in Westerns and began his career in 1927 with OPEN RANGE. He also appeared in films as diverse as LAURA (1944), PRIDE OF THE YANKEES (1942), and SAMSON AND DELILAH (1949). But everyone associated with this particular film wishes it would just go away.

p, F. E. Douglas, Henry Taylor; d, Alvin J. Neitz [Alan James]; w, Carl Krusada; ph, William Nobles.

Western (PR:A MPAA:NR)

FIREBRANDS OF ARIZONA** (1944) 55m REP bw

Smiley Burnette *(Beefsteak Discoe/Frog Millhouse)*, Sunset Carson *(Himself)*, Peggy Stewart *(Poppy Calhoun)*, Earle Hodgins *(Sheriff Hoag)*, Roy Barcroft *(Deputy Ike)*, Rex Lease *(Deputy Sheriff)*, Tom London *(Wagon Driver)*, Jack Kirk *(Memphis)*, Bud Geary *(Slugs)*, Bob Wilke *(Deputy Sheriff)*, Leroy Mason *(Bailey)*, Fred Toones *(Charlie)*, Pierce Lyden *(Gopher)*, Budd Buster *(Printer)*, Bob Burns *(Stage Driver)*, Jack O'Shea *(Ranch Hand)*, Hank Bell *(Townsman)*, Frank Ellis, Frank McCarroll *(Outlaws)*, Jess Cavan, Bob Woodward *(Townsmen)*, Charles Morton *(Stunt Double)*.

Confusion reigns in the West as hypochondriacal sidekick Burnette is mistaken for a notorious robber with a $66,000 price on his head. While the good Burnette languishes in jail, the bad one tries to hold up the stage bringing the reward money. Carson foils the attempt, but by the time he's managed to convince the sheriff of what's going on, the robber has kidnaped his double out of jail and taken his place so he can steal the reward money in the safe. More mistaken identities fill this one out until Carson figures out who's who. The bad Burnette is taken away to be hanged, and the good one is cured of his imaginary afflictions. Perhaps the most interesting moment of the film occurs when Burnette the good and Burnette the bad, fighting, knock each other out. In an unusual departure from the code of the western film, this was the third of a string of four pictures featuring the nominal sidekick, the popular Burnette, top-billed over Carson, the hero. Paradoxically, Carson—born Michael Harrison—had been sent to acting school to lose his Plainview, Texas accent during the early 1940s when he was a roommate of struggling young actors Alan Ladd and Rory Calhoun, before he settled into his Republic Studios western niche. Burnette had long been a popular comic-relief character, having been Gene Autry's constant filmic companion since 1934.

p, Louis Gray; d, Lesley Selander; w, Randall Faye; ph, Bud Thackery; ed, Harry Keller; md, Joseph Dubin; art d, Frank Hotaling.

Western **(PR:A MPAA:NR)**

FIRECHASERS, THE* (1970, Brit.) 101m ITC/RFD c

Chad Everett *(Quentin Barnaby)*, Anjanette Comer *(Toby Collins)*, Keith Barron *(Jim Maxwell)*, Joanne Dainton *(Valerie Chrane)*, Rupert Davies *(Prentice)*, James Hayter *(Inspector Herman)*, Robert Flemyng *(Carlton)*, Roy Kinnear *(Roscoe)*, Allan Cuthbertson *(Jarvis)*, John Loder *(Routledge)*.

Journalist Comer teams up with insurance investigator Everett to capture an arsonist. So-so entertainment.

p, Julian Wintle; d, Sidney Hayers; w, Philip Levine; ph, (Eastmancolor).

Crime **(PR:C MPAA:NR)**

FIRECRACKER zero (1981) 83m New World Pictures c

Jillian Kesner *(Susanne Carter)*, Darby Hinton *(Chuck Donner)*, Ken Metcalfe *(Erik)*, Chanda Romero *(Malow)*, Tony Ferrar *(Tony)*, Reymond King *(Rey)*, Vic Diaz *(Grip)*, Pete Cooper *(Pete)*.

Metcalfe, as scriptwriter, must have thought it clever to have a woman get her clothes ripped off every other scene, then do kung-fu in the nude. Rapists, other assailants, and her knife-wielding lover all participate in disrobing Kesner as she searches for her sister in the Philippines. In the climactic martial arts battle, to give the story a twist, Kesner fights with all her clothes on.

p, Syed Kechico; d, Cirio Santiago; w, Ken Metcalfe; ph, Don Jones.

Martial Arts **Cas.** **(PR:O MPAA:R)**

FIRECREEK** (1968) 104m WB c

James Stewart *(Johnny Cobb)*, Henry Fonda *(Larkin)*, Inger Stevens *(Evelyn)*, Gary Lockwood *(Earl)*, Dean Jagger *(Whittier)*, Ed Begley *(Preacher Broyles)*, Jay C. Flippen *(Mr. Pittman)*, Jack Elam *(Norman)*, James Best *(Drew)*, Barbara Luna *(Meli)*, Jacqueline Scott *(Henrietta Cobb)*, Brooke Bundy *(Leah)*, J. Robert Porter *(Arthur)*, Morgan Woodward *(Willard)*, John Qualen *(Hall)*, Louise Latham *(Dulcie)*, Athena Lorde *(Mrs. Littlejohn)*, Harry "Slim" Duncan *(Fyte)*, Kevin Tate *(Aaron)*, Christopher Shea *(Franklin)*.

FIRECREEK is a senior citizen version of HIGH NOON in that it features Stewart as a sort of free-lance sheriff who has to defend his small burg against a bunch of hoodlums who are returning from the range wars in Missouri. Fonda, Lockwood, Best, Woodward, and Elam arrive in the town of Firecreek and decide to stay there for some R & R while Fonda heals from a wound. Stewart, who lives outside of the village, leaves his pregnant wife, Scott, and comes into Firecreek to keep an eye on the freebooters. Fonda is resting at the boarding house run by Flippen and casting an eye on Flippen's daughter, Stevens. Meanwhile, his pals are making mincemeat out of the quiet town, breaking up the church services run by Begley, the local preacher. Stewart, a non-violent type like Cooper in HIGH NOON, attempts to talk some sense into the rowdies but it's no use. Best tries to rape Luna, an Indian woman, and Porter, a dim-witted stable boy, kills the man. Stewart jails Porter, more for his own safety than for the crime. Stewart returns to his farm to be there for the birth of his child and while he's away, the other criminals force the townsfolk to go to a wake for Best and then cold-bloodedly lynch Porter. The killers sense that there is no one in the town who will stand up to them and they fully expect to take it over entirely. Stewart grabs for his Peacemaker and shoots Woodward, Elam, and Lockwood but Fonda, in an unaccustomed villain's role, shoots Stewart badly enough to render him inoperative. Just as he's about to kill Stewart, Stevens puts a rifle bullet through him. There are only short bursts of action in between nearly endless talkieness in the Clements' script. Despite a huge cast of very competent actors, the film misses the mark and you'll be hard-pressed to remember anything about this movie within minutes after seeing it. The odd part of this is that the producers were truly Western veterans, having been involved in TV's long-running "Gunsmoke" series. This appears to be a TV film with movie names featured in it.

p, Philip Leacock, John Mantley; d, Vincent McEveety; w, Calvin Clements; ph, William Clothier (Panavision, Technicolor); m, Alfred Newman; ed, William Ziegler; art d, Howard Hollander; set d, William L. Kuehl; cos, Yvonne Wood.

Western **(PR:C MPAA:NR)**

FIRED WIFE* (1943) 75m UNIV bw

Louise Allbritton *(Tig Callahan)*, Diana Barrymore *(Eve)*, Robert Paige *(Hank Dunne)*, Walter Abel *(Chris McClelland)*, George Dolenz *(Oscar Blix)*, Rex Ingram *(Charles)*, Richard Lane *(Tracey)*, Samuel S. Hinds *(Justice of the Peace)*, Walter Catlett *(Judge)*, Alan Dinehart, Ernest Truex.

Allbritton, the assistant to a Broadway producer, must keep her marriage to Paige secret in order to keep her job. Bland farce reworks ground long barren of laughs, and only Allbritton's just-competent performance keeps the film from being a total loss.

p, Alex Gottlieb; d, Charles Lamont; w, Michael Fessier, Ernest Pagano (based on a story by Hagar Wilde); ph, Paul Ivano; m, Frank Skinner; ed, Paul Landres; md, Charles Previn; art d, John B. Goodman, Martin Obzina.

Comedy **(PR:A MPAA:NR)**

FIREFLY, THE** (1937) 140m MGM bw

Jeanette MacDonald *(Nina Maria Azara)*, Allan Jones *(Don Diego Manrique de Lara)*, Warren William *(Col. deRougemont)*, Douglass Dumbrille *(Marquis DeMelito)*, Leonard Penn *(Etienne)*, Billy Gilbert *(Innkeeper)*, Belle Mitchell *(Lola)*, Tom Rutherford *(King Ferdinand)*, Henry Daniell *(Gen. Savary)*, George Zucco *(St. Clair)*, Ian Wolfe *(Izquierdo)*, Manuel Alvarez Maciste *(Coach Driver)*, Robert Spindola *(Coach Driver's Son)*, Zeni Vatori *(Waiter in Cafe)*, Frank Puglia *(Pablo)*, John Picorri *(Cafe Proprietor)*, James B. Carson *(Smiling Waiter)*, Milton Watson *(French Officer)*, Peter DuRey *(Officer)*, Maurice Black *(Pigeon Vendor)*, Maurice Cass *(Strawberry Vendor)*, Sam Appel *(Fruit Vendor)*, Rolfe Sedan *(Hat Vendor)*, Mabel Colcord *(Vendor)*, Inez Palange *(Flower Vendor)*, Theodore von Eltz *(Capt. Pierlot)*, Pedro de Cordoba *(Spanish General)*, Monya Andre *(Civilian Wife)*, Frank Campeau *(Beggar)*, Stanley Price *(Napoleon)*, Guy D'Ennery *(Spanish General)*, Robert Wilbur *(Dying Soldier)*, Sidney Bracy *(Secretay)*, Roy Harris [Riley Hill] *(Lieutenant)*, Eugene Borden *(Captain)*, Jean Perry *(Major)*, Corbett Morris *(Duval)*, Ralph Byrd *(French Lieutenant)*, Eddie Phillips *(Captain)*, Bentley Hewett *(Major)*, Donald Reed, William Crowell, Drew Demorest, Lester Dorr, Hooper Atchley, John Merton, Ramsey Hill, Anthony Pawley *(French Officers)*, Frank Yaconelli, Harry Semels, Charles Townsend, Frederic MacKaye, Roger Drake, Jacques Lory, Alan Curtis *(French Soldiers)*, Paul Sutton *(Spanish Civilian)*, Capt. Fernando Garcia *(Napoleonic Officer)*, Soledad Gonzales *(Extra)*, Robert Z. Leonard, Albertina Rasch *(Bayonne Cafe Extras)*, Dennis O'Keefe, Ray Bennett *(Soldiers in Bayonne Cafe)*, Karl Hackett *(Bit Spaniard)*, Boyd Gilbert *(Aide)*, Russ Powell *(Stablehand)*, Lane Chandler *(Captain of Guards)*, Agostino Borgat *(Peasant)*, Joe North, Colin Kenny, Brandon Hurst, Pat Somerset *(English Generals)*, Matthew Boulton *(Duke of Wellington)*, Edward Keane *(Chief of Staff)*, Victor Adams *(Jail Guard)*, Harry Worth *(Adjutant, Secret Service)*, Lew Harvey *(Officer)*, Jason Robards, Sr. *(Spanish Patriot)*, David Tihmar *(Madrid Cafe Dancer)*.

Somewhat long and unsatisfying lensing of the 1912 Rudolf Friml operetta which starred Emma Trentini and Henry Vogel in the Broadway version. It was supposed to take place in the Pyrenees but was almost totally shot on the MGM lot, with location work done at Lone Pine, California, at the foot of the Sierras. MacDonald is "Mosca del Fuego" (firefly), a singer in a cafe in Madrid; the year is 1808. Penn is her long-time beau but she'd like to get rid of him, so she begins coyly eyeing Jones, a rich young Spaniard. Singing is her cover job but she is actually a secret agent working for Dumbrille who is King Ferdinand's (Rutherford) advisor. Napoleon, whom you may recall was going to invade Ireland in THE FIGHTING O'FLYNN, is also planning to take over Spain and MacDonald's job is to uncover his plans. She gets friendly with William, a Napoleon confidante and colonel in his army. She tries to enlist Jones then learns he is also in the Little Corporal's employ and his job is to keep his eye on her. She blows her assignment and Rutherford is forced to leave, with Napoleon's brother taking over the throne. Five years pass and the British arrive and join forces with the Spanish. MacDonald meets William again and is soon unmasked as a spy by Jones. She is sentenced to death and Jones comes to see her, very contrite about turning her in but his loyalty to his country triumphed over his love for her. Wellington (Boulton) arrives and takes over the town before she is executed. Jones is wounded and the combined armies of the English and Spanish retake Spain. Later, she finds Jones wounded and recovering in a hospital. Now that there is no war, and they are free to fall in love, they ride away together. MacDonald wanted to rid herself of co-star Nelson Eddy and do a solo shot, but Jones distinguished himself and took the reviews with his rendition of the hit song "The Donkey Serenade" (lyrics by Bob Wright and Chet Forrest). Many other songs, but none as famous as the aforementioned. MacDonald surprised everyone by some excellent dancing to complement her glorious voice. In one tune, "When a Maid Comes Knocking At Your Heart" (lyrics by Otto Harbach), MacDonald played her own piano accompaniment, another talent that most people didn't realize she had. A lavish production with what seems like thousands of extras, it was, ultimately, a tuneful bore. A very young Dennis O'Keefe can be seen as a French Soldier. This was just after he changed his name from Bud Flanagan. Songs: "Giannina Mia" (lyrics by Harbach), "Love Is Like a Firefly," "English March," "A Woman's Kiss" (lyrics by Wright and Forrest), "He Who Loves and Runs Away" (lyrics by Gus Kahn), "Sympathy" (lyrics by Kahn and Harbach), "When a Maid Comes Knocking At Your Heart," and "When The Wine Is Full of Fire."

p, Hunt Stromberg; d, Robert Z. Leonard; w, Frances Goodrich, Albert Hackett, Ogden Nash (from the musical book by Otto Harbach); ph, Oliver T. Marsh (Sepia); m, Rudolf Friml; ed, Robert J. Kern; md, Herbert Stothart; art d, Cedric Gibbons; cos, Adrian; gowns, Adrian.

Musical **(PR:A MPAA:NR)**

FIREFOX*½** (1982) 137m WB c

Clint Eastwood *(Mitchell Gant)*, Freddie Jones *(Kenneth Aubrey)*, David Huffman *(Buckholz)*, Warren Clarke *(Pavel Upenskoy)*, Ronald Lacey *(Semelovsky)*, Kenneth Colley *(Col. Kontarsky)*, Klaus Lowitsch *(Gen. Vladimirov)*, Nigel Hawthorne *(Pyote Baranovich)*, Stefan Schnabel *(First Secretary)*, Thomas Hill *(Gen. Brown)*, Clive Merrison *(Maj. Lanyev)*, Kai Wulff *(Lt. Col. Voskov)*, Dimitra Arliss *(Natalia)*, Austin Willis *(Walters)*, Michael Currie *(Capt. Seerbacker)*, James Staley *(Lt. Comdr. Fleischer)*, Ward Costello *(Gen. Rogers)*, Alan Tilvern *(Air Marshall Kutuzov)*, Oliver Cotton *(Dmitri Priabin)*, Bernard Behrens *(William Saltonstall)*, Richard Derr *(Adm. Curtin)*, Woody Eney *(Maj. Dietz)*, Bernard Erhard *(KGB Guard)*, Hugh Fraser *(Police Inspector Tortyev)*, David Gant *(KGB Official)*, John Grillo *(Customs Officer)*, Czeslaw Grocholski, Barrie Houghton, Neil Hunt, Vincent J. Isaacs, Alexei Jawdokimov, Wolf Kahler, Eugene Lipinski, Phillip Littell, Curt Lowens, Lev Mailer, Fritz Manes, David Meyers, Alfredo Michelson, Zenno

Nahayevsky, George Orrison, Tony Papenfuss, Oliver Pierre, Grisha Plotkin, George Pravda, John Ratzenberger, Alex Rodine, Lance Rosen, Eugene Scherer, Warrick Sims, Mike Spero, Malcolm Storry, Chris Winfield, John Yates, Alexander Zale, Igor Zatsepin, Konstantin Zlatev.

Eastwood is a top pilot called out of retirement and sent to Russia to steal a new super-fighter that can run rings around anything we have and whose weapon systems are thought controlled, but only if you're thinking in Russian. Eastwood goes off to England for training and is eventually smuggled into the Soviet Union. Narrowly avoiding hordes of suspicious bureaucrats and too-inept-to-be-real KGB men, he steals the plane and flies it back home, two similar fighters in hot pursuit. Eastwood manages to lose them long enough to land on the polar ice cap where an American submarine is waiting to refuel him, then he takes off again and, after a few anxious moments when the weapons won't work because he's not thinking in Russian, he blows the Reds out of the sky. Apart from the flying sequences, which are spectacular though largely derivative of STAR WARS, this is one of Eastwood's least satisfying films. Way overlong (it's more than an hour before he even starts on his mission) and hard to take seriously, the film nevertheless tapped a vein in Americans who wanted to see the Russians beaten by a real American hero. This same audience would make RED DAWN (1984), and others great successes a couple of years later. Eastwood's direction of the action scenes is confident enough, but he is still unable to deal with deep psychological motivations in the characters he plays. The legions of Eastwood fans ignored all this film's shortcomings and added it to the long list of his box-office successes. The 52-year-old Eastwood was getting a little craggy-looking for such adventures; he was reported to have undertaken a radical dietary regimen in an effort to regain his youthful appearance and physical abilities at about this time.

p&d, Clint Eastwood; w, Alex Lasker, Wendell Wellman (based on the novel by Craig Thomas); ph, Bruce Surtees (Panavision, DeLuxe Color); m, Maurice Jarre; ed, Ferris Webster, Ron Spang; art d, John Graysmark, Elayne Ceder; set d, Ernie Bishop; spec eff, Robert Shepherd, Roger Dorney, Al Miller, John Dykstra.

Action   **Cas.**   **(PR:C   MPAA:PG)**

FIREMAN, SAVE MY CHILD*   (1932) 67m WB-FN bw

Joe E. Brown (Joe Grant), Evalyn Knapp (Sally Toby), Lillian Bond (June), George Meeker (Stevens), Guy Kibbee (Pop), George Ernest (Mascot for St. Louis Team), Ben Hendricks, Jr. (Larkin), Virginia Sale (Miss Gallop), Frank Shallenbach (Pitcher), Richard Carle (Dan Toby), Louis Robinson (Trainer), Curtis Benton (Radio Announcer).

Brown is a firefighter in a small Kansas town, and also a baseball sensation. His pitching talents are so good, in fact, that he gets a starting rotation slot with the St. Louis Cardinals. But Brown is lackadaisical about his big league job, and puts most of his energy into creating a new type of fire extinguisher. A well written very funny story, ending with the comedian putting out the fire he started to demonstrate his (dud) fire extinguisher, then saving the Cards in the World Series.

d, Lloyd Bacon; w, Bacon, Robert Lord, Ray Enright, Arthur Caesar; ph, Sol Polito; ed, George Marks.

Comedy   **(PR:A   MPAA:NR)**

FIREMAN SAVE MY CHILD*   (1954) 79m UNIV bw

Spike Jones (Lt. McGinty), His City Slickers (Firemen), Buddy Hackett (Smokey), Hugh O'Brian (Smitty), Tom Brown (Capt. Bill Peters), Adele Jergens (Harry's Wife), George Cleveland (Chief Rorty), Willis Bouchey (Mayor), Henry Kulky (Harry), Harry Cheshire (Commissioner Spencer), Madge Blake (Mayor's Wife), Tristram Coffin (Tucker), John Cliff (Crane).

Spike Jones stars in this comedy about a turn-of-the-century San Francisco fire department, and the slapstick comedy and avalanche pace clearly bear the stamp of Jones' musical comedy style. The fire station is being motorized, and Jones and the boys have a hard time making the transition from their horse-drawn wagon. Hackett is the rookie firefighter, whose fire extinguisher patent is stolen, and the whole company chases the crooks through the city. Bud Abbott and Lou Costello were originally slated to star in this production, but withdrew when Costello became ill. Though it has the same title, the film has no resemblance to the 1932 comedy starring Joe E. Brown.

p, Howard Christie; d, Leslie Goodwins; w, Lee Loeb, John Grant; ph, Clifford Stine; m, Joseph Gershenson; ed, Russell Schoengrath.

Comedy   **(PR:A   MPAA:NR)**

FIREMAN'S BALL, THE*½   (1968, Czech.) 73m
                                                      Barrandov/Cinema V c
                                                      (HORI MA PANENKO)

Vaclav Stockel (Fire Brigade Commander), Josef Svet (Old Man), Josef Kolb (Josef), Jan Vostrcil (Committee Chairman), Frantisek Debelka (1st Committee Member), Josef Sebanek (2nd Committee Member), Karel Valnoha (3rd Committee Member), Josef Rehorek (4th Committee Member), Marie Jezkova (Josef's Wife), Anina Lipoldva, Alena Kvetova, Mila Zelena (Beauty Queen Candidates), Vratislav Cermak, Vaclav Novotny, Frantisek Reinstein, Frantisek Paska, Stanislav Holubec, Josef Kutalek, Ladislav Adam, Jiri Libal, Antonin Blazejovsky, Stanislav Ditrich, Jarmila Kucharova, Marie Slivova, Hana Hanusova, Hana Kuberova.

Hilarious black comedy from Czech director Milos Forman and screenwriter Ivan Passer before both left Czechoslovakia for America and Hollywood where their films would once again be critically acclaimed. (Forman went on to direct ONE FLEW OVER THE CUCKOO'S NEST, HAIR, RAGTIME, AMADEUS. Passer directed the vastly underappreciated CUTTER'S WAY.) THE FIREMAN'S BALL is a bizarre farce that uses a small, local event—in this case a retirement ball and a beauty contest—to analyze larger social and political problems. Promised the presentation of a ceremonial hatchet at a ball given upon his retirement, a cancer-stricken, 86-year-old retired commander of a fire brigade sits helplessly as all hell breaks loose around him. A beauty contest organized as part of the evening's events fizzles when the contestants, barely a beauty among them, refuse to come out of the bathroom, despite the firemen's best efforts to coax them out. The tension is broken by an alarm which tears the fire company away from the festivities and to a fire that is destroying another old man's home. Unfortunately, the fire truck sinks into the snow and is unable to function, forcing the firemen to watch helplessly as the house burns to the ground. To console the houseless old man, the firemen give him free raffle tickets to their ball, but the raffle prizes, and the tickets, are then stolen. Embarrassed, the master-of-ceremonies turns out the lights and encourages the thief to return the stolen items under cover of darkness. When the lights go back on, it is the raffle's director who is caught returning a stolen item. He suffers a heart attack and must be carried off by the firemen. The hall empties, leaving the guest of honor to discover that the case that holds his ceremonial fire-hatchet is empty, his retirement gift having been purloined also. The New York Times reported that 40,000 Czech firemen resigned when the government released the film in their homeland—then Forman let it be known the film might be allegorical and they returned to their posts. (In Czechoslovakian; English subtitles.)

d, Milos Forman; w, Forman, Ivan Passer, Jaroslav Papousek; ph, Miroslav Ondricek (Eastmancolor); m, Karel Mares; ed, Miroslav Hajek.

Farce   **Cas.**   **(PR:C   MPAA:NR)**

FIREPOWER*½   (1979, Brit.) 104m Associated Film Distribution c

Sophia Loren (Adele Tasca), James Coburn (Jerry Fanon/Eddie), O.J. Simpson (Catlett), Eli Wallach (Sal Hyman), Anthony Franciosa (Dr. Felix), George Grizzard (Gelhorn), Vincent Gardenia (Frank Hull), Fred Stuthman (Halpin), Richard Caldicot (Calman), Frank Singuineau (Manley Reckford), George Touliatos (Stegner), Andrew Duncan (Cooper), Hank Garrett (Oscar), Billy Barty (Dominic Carbone), Conrad Roberts (Lestor), Jake La Motta (Nickel Sam), Vincent Beck (Trilling), Dominic Chianese (Dis Orlov), Paul D'Amato (Tagua), Paul Garcia (Vito Tasca), Richard Roberts (Dr. Ivo Tasca), Thurman Scott (Policeman), William Trotman (Pathologist), Victor Argo (Anders), Owen Hollander (Sweezy), J. C. Quinn (Dunn), Chris Gampel (Senator), Paula Lawrence (Bejewelled Woman), Victor Mature (Harold Everett).

An action thriller devoid of originality. Loren, believing that her chemist husband was killed by a wealthy industrialist, pulls hitman Coburn out of retirement. Coburn enlists the help of Simpson, and they start shooting and blowing things up. Plot gets foggy with too many double-crosses and killings to care about anything but the locations.

p&d, Michael Winner; w, Gerald Wilson; ph, Robert Paynter, Dick Kratina, Richard Kline (Technicolor); m, Gato Barbieri; ed, Arnold Crust; Ms. Loren's gowns, Per Spook of Paris.

Thriller   **Cas.**   **(PR:O   MPAA:R)**

FIRES OF FATE*   (1932, Brit.) 70m BIP/Powers bw

Lester Matthews (Lt. Col. Egerton), Dorothy Bartlam (Kay Byrne), Kathleen O'Regan (Nora Belmont), Donald Calthrop (Sir William Royden), Jack Raine (Filbert Frayne), Garry Marsh (Capt. Archer), Clifford Heatherley (Abdullah), Jean Cadell (Miss Byrne), Hubert Harben (Rev. Mark Royden), Arthur Chesney (Mr. Braddell).

This story of a man's travels in Egypt (the man, Matthews has only one year to live) falls deeply into melodrama. The doomed Matthews is kidnaped along with a group of tourists, and they are rescued by Egypt's Camel Corps. In the end, Matthews discovers his illness has reversed itself, so naturally he proposes to his girl friend.

p&d, Norman Walker; w, Dion Titherage (adapted from A. Conan Doyle's novel The Tragedy of Korosko); ph, Claude Friese-Green; ed, A. E. Bates.

Adventure   **(PR:A   MPAA:NR)**

FIRES ON THE PLAIN*   (1962, Jap.) 105m Daiei/Harrison bw
                                                                           (NOBI)

Eiji Funakoshi (Tamura), Osamu Takizawa (Yasuda), Mickey Curtis (Nagamatsu), Mantaro Ushio (Sergeant), Kyu Sazanka (Army Surgeon), Yoshihiro Hamaguchi (Officer), Asao Sano, Masaya Tsukida, Hikaru Hoshi (Soldiers).

Grim, intense Japanese war drama starring Funakoshi as a soldier condemned to wander a battle-scarred landscape in the closing days of WW II. Separated from his unit and rejected by the hospital because of his tuberculosis, Funakoshi flees the advancing Americans and is forced to hide in the jungle where he encounters all manner of death, disease, and horror. Eventually he meets another small group of displaced soldiers and together the men try to find food and shelter. Suddenly American tanks appear and most of the group are killed. Funakoshi survives, however, and crazed with starvation and illness, he stumbles across a camp occupied by Takizawa and Curtis. The men's basic distrust of each other reaches a fever pitch when Curtis ambushes and kills Takizawa and begins to feed off his body. When Funakoshi discovers this, he shoots Curtis. Almost dead from starvation, Funakoshi stumbles to the distant American camp to surrender, only to be caught and killed in the crossfire from some farmers. A strong allegorical treatment of the war and Japan's self-destruction from director Ichikawa.

p, Masaichi Nagata; d, Kon Ichikawa; w, Natto Wada; ph, Setsuo Kobayashi; m, Yashushi Akutagawa; ed, Hiroaki Fujii, Ichikawa; art d, Tokuji Shibata.

War   **Cas.**   **(PR:O   MPAA:NR)**

FIRETRAP, THE*½   (1935) 63m Empire bw

Norman Foster, Evalyn Knapp, Sidney Blackmer, Oscar Apfel, Ben Alexander, Herbert Corthell, Arthur Houseman.

Routine crime programmer has a pair of arsonists who push their insurance fraud scheme too far and attract the law. Of little interest and no significance.

p, Larry Darmour; d, Burt Lynwood; w, Charles Francis Royal; ph, Bert Longnecker; ed, Earl Turner.

Crime   **(PR:A MPAA:NR)**

FIRM MAN, THE**   (1975, Aus.) 91m Australian Film Institute c

Peter Cummins (Gerald Baxter), Eileen Chapman (Melissa Baxter), Peter Carmody, Chris McQuade, Max Gillies, Bruce Spence.

An exercise in tedium from Australia has Cummins working for a corporation known simply and ominously as "The Firm." Strange things happen. His wife has an affair with an old friend, and Cummins has visions. If it all adds up to anything, the audience isn't clued in to it. Little more than a student film.

p,d,&w, John Dunigan; ph, Sasha Trikojus.

Drama   **(PR:C MPAA:NR)**

FIRST A GIRL**½   (1935, Brit.) 94m Gaumont-British bw

Jessie Matthews (Elizabeth), Sonnie Hale (Victor), Griffith Jones (Robert), Anna Lee (Princess), Alfred Drayton (McIntosh), Constance Godridge (Darryl), Martita Hunt (Seraphina), Eddie Gray (Goose Trainer), Donald Stewart (Singer).

Matthews is a delivery girl for a dressmaker sent to drop off some costumes at a local theater. There, she meets a female impersonator who has contracted laryngitis, and he gets her to take his place on stage. She's a success and begins touring Europe masquerading as a man, with Hale as her manager. A wealthy princess, Lee, and her boy friend suspect Matthews' real gender and go to great lengths, on a yacht trip, to uncover the truth. Blake Edwards successfully re-made this in 1982 as VICTOR/VICTORIA. Songs: "Everything's in Rhythm with My Heart," "Written all over My Face," "Half-and-Half," "Say the Word and It's Yours," "Little Silkworm," and "Wiggle My Ears" (Maurice Sigler, Al Goodhart, Al Horrman).

p, Michael Balcon; d, Victor Saville; w, Marjorie Gaffney (from the play "Victor/Victoria" by Reinhold Schunzel); ph, Glen MacWilliams; md, Louis Levy.

Comedy   **(PR:A MPAA:NR)**

FIRST AID*   (1931) 60m Ralph Like/Sono Art-World Wide bw

Grant Withers, Marjorie Beebe, Wheeler Oakman, Donald Keith, William Desmond, Paul Panzer, Ernie Adams, George Chesebro, Harry Shutan, Billy Gilbert, Stuart Hall.

An implausible story about a doctor who's abducted by thieves. The crooks want him to operate on a wounded member of the gang who knows the location of some hidden jewelry. The doc sends messages to police through his prescriptions, but it takes a while for the cops to catch on. Once freed, the doctor asks the police to let the wounded thief go because Doc wants to marry the thief's sister. The cops see nothing wrong with that request.

p, Ralph Like; d, Staurt Paton; w, Michael L. Simmons; ph, Jules Cronjager.

Crime/Drama   **(PR:A MPAA:NR)**

FIRST AND THE LAST, THE   (SEE: 21 DAYS, 1937, Brit.)

FIRST BABY**   (1936) 74m FOX bw

Johnny Downs (Johnny Ellis), Shirley Deane (Trudy Wells), Dixie Dunbar (Maude Holbrook), Jane Darwell (Mrs. Ellis), Marjorie Gateson (Mrs. Wells), Gene Lockhart (Mr. Ellis), Taylor Holmes (Mr. Wells), Willard Robertson (Dr. Clarke), Hattie McDaniel (Dora).

Downs marries Deane, and, being too poor to afford a house of their own, the two move in with Deane's parents. Downs' mother-in-law causes the couple all kinds of grief until her grandchild falls ill and brings the family together.

p, John Stone; d, Lewis Seiler; w, Lamar Trotti; m, John W. Green, Edward Heyman; ph, Barney, McGill; ed, Al DeGaetano.

Drama   **(PR:A MPAA:NR)**

FIRST BLOOD zero   (1982) 97m Orion c

Sylvester Stallone (Rambo), Richard Crenna (Trautman), Brian Dennehy (Teasle), David Caruso (Mitch), Jack Starrett (Galt), Michael Talbott (Balford), David Crowley (Shingleton), Chris Mulkey (Ward), Don Mackay (Preston), Alf Humphreys (Lester), John McLiam (Orval), Bill McKinney (Kern), Chuck Tamburro (Pilot), Bruce Barbour (Cathcart), Craig Huston (Radio Operator), Patrick Stack (Lt. Morgan), Dan Woznow (Boy), Mike Winlaw (TV Reporter), Peter Lonstrup (Attendant), Raimund Stamm, Stephen Dimopoulos, Robert Metcalfe (Guardsmen), Gary Hetherington, Alex Kliner, R.G. Miller (Hunters).

Rocky with a rapid-fire weapon going off in his hands is what this mindless, ultra-violent film is all about, as Stallone mumbles his soporific way through a carnage-torn Northwest community that has treated him with disrespect. He is a vagabond Vietnam vet who is run out of a small town by bullyboy sheriff Dennehy. When he returns he is arrested, roughed up, and maltreated by the local cops. He goes berserk, escapes, and causes the death of a pursuing officer. A posse is greeted in the dense woodlands and mountainous terrain with reprisals from what is later described by Crenna as "a killing machine," one of the last indefatigable Green Berets who slew whole armies of the Viet Cong enemy and has resorted to the kind of warfare he was trained to wage. When he turns back the cops, the Army enters the picture and platoons of men assault his mountain stronghold. When they think they've blown him up in an old mining shaft where he has taken refuge, the hunt is called off. Crenna doesn't believe he's dead; he's a colonel arriving from the East to appeal to Stallone to give up, and he later warns Dennehy that no one will capture Stallone; he's almost proud of stating that this social misfit has won the Congressional Medal of Honor and conveys the distorted notion that such an award somehow excuses his one-man war. Stallone does survive and manages to take over a military truck loaded with automatic weapons. He drives back into the town and blows it to pieces, riddling the place and scattering the forces of law and order. Only Crenna quells the violent rampage in a final appeal as his old military

commander to obey an order—which he does, stepping outside to view his carnage and await a sequel to this socially irresponsible film. Even more savage than Stallone and this horrendous panorama of senseless destruction are the producers of such claptrap, employing the tired cliche of the betrayed Vietnam veteran as an excuse to parade a sadistic-masochistic theme without any redeeming virtues. Stallone's character is never developed, his motivations are at best vague, and the story line seems as if it were drawn from Hitler's Mein Kampf. The box office success of this bloody, mindless mess gave birth to yet another abortion, RAMBO.

p, Buzz Feitshans; d, Ted Kotcheff; w, Michael Kozoll, William Sackheim, Q. Moonblood (based on the novel by David Morrell); ph, Andrew Laszlo (Panavision, Technicolor); m, Jerry Goldsmith; ed, Tom Noble, Joan Chapman; prod d, Wolf Kroeger; art d, Stephane Reichel; cos, Tom Bronson.

Action   **Cas.**   **(PR:O MPAA:R)**

FIRST COMES COURAGE**½   (1943) 88m COL bw

Merle Oberon (Nicole Larsen), Brian Aherne (Captain Allan Lowell), Carl Esmond (Maj. Paul Dichter), Fritz Leiber (Dr. Aanrud), Erville Alderson (Soren), Erik Rolf (Ole), Reinhold Schunzel (Col. Kurt Von Elser), Isobel Elsom (Rose Linstrom), William Martin (Dichter's Chauffeur), Richard Ryen (Dr. Hoff), Lewis Wilson (Dr. Kleinich), John H. Elliott (Norwegian Patient), Greta Granstedt (Girl Assistant), William Phillips (Aanrud's Assistant), Peitro Sosso (Janitor), Conrad Binyon (Small Boy), Arno Frey (Sergeant), Eric Feldary, Henry Rowland (Privates), Hans von Morhart (German Guard), Ethel Griffies (Nurse), Walter Thiel (Orderly), John Royce (German Orderly), Frederick Brunn (German Guard), Lloyd Ingraham (Old Norwegian), Duke Louis Adlon (Nazi Lieutenant), Niels Bagge (Thorsten), Rex Williams, Otto Reichow (Young Nazi Officers), Hans Von Twardowski (Nazi Captain), Fern Emmett (Dress Designer), Robert McKenzie (Justice of the Peace), Guy Kingsford (Sub Commander), Louis Jean Heydt (Norwegian), George O'Flaherty, Emerson Fisher-Smith (Cipher Experts), Nelson Leigh (Blake), Tom Stevenson (Blakeley), Miles Mander (Col. Wallace), Evan Thomas (Ship's Captain), Larry Parks (Capt. Langdon), Marten Lamont (Lieutenant Colonel), Byron Foulger (Norwegian Shopkeeper), Rolf Lindau (Jr. Officer), Charles Irwin (Capt. Lungden), Paul Langton, Gordon Clark (Commandos), Sven-Hugo Borg (Schmidt), Paul Power, Leslie Denison (English Officers), J. Pat Moriarity (Irish Top Sgt.).

Oberon is a member of the Norwegian underground romancing a Nazi major to obtain vital war information in this 1943 mid-WW II film. Aherne, a British commando captain, is sent to Norway on a secret mission, and meets Oberon. Turns out they had a love affair going before the war. Aherne is captured by the Germans and Oberon aids in his rescue, the captain pleads with her to leave for England with him, but she stays to continue her work.

p, Harry Joe Brown; d, Dorothy Arzner; w, Lewis Meltzer, Melvin Levy, George Sklar (from the novel by Elliott Arnold, The Commandos); ph, Joseph Walker; m, Ernst Toch; ed, Viola Lawrence; md, M. W. Stoloff; art d, Lionel Banks, Rudolph Sternad; set d, Fay Babcock.

War   **(PR:A MPAA:NR)**

FIRST DEADLY SIN, THE*½   (1980) 112m Filmways Pictures c

Frank Sinatra (Edward Delaney), Faye Dunaway (Barbara Delaney), David Dukes (Daniel Blank), George Coe (Dr. Bernardi), Brenda Vaccaro (Monica Gilbert), Martin Gabel (Christopher Langley), Joe Spinell (Doorman), Jeffrey DeMunn (Sgt. Fernandez), Anthony Zerbe (Capt. Broughton), James Whitmore (Dr. Sanford Ferguson), Fred Fuster (Delivery Man).

Sinatra's first film after a ten-year hiatus is not spectacular, to say the least. He's a detective a few weeks away from retirement, who takes on the case of a random murderer. Besides tracking the killer, he visits his sick wife, Dunaway, in the hospital. Dunaway's talent is wasted lying abed pincushioned with tubing. The killer, Sinatra discovers, likes to use a mountain-climbing ice ax on his victims. The film drags; the book it's based on didn't. Pity for Frank.

p, George Pappas, Mark Shanker; d, Brian G. Hutton; w, Mann Rubin (based on the novel by Lawrence Sanders); ph, Jack Priestley (Movielab Color); m, Gordon Jenkins; ed, Eric Albertson; art d, Woody Mackintosh.

Thriller   **Cas.**   **(PR:O MPAA:R)**

FIRST FAMILY zero   (1980) 104m WB c

Bob Newhart (President Manfred Link), Gilda Radner (Gloria Link), Fred Willard (Presidential Assistant Feebleman), Richard Benjamin (Press Secretary Bunthorne), Bob Dishy (Vice President Shockley), Madeline Kahn (Mrs. Link), Julius Harris (Ambassador Longo), Harvey Korman (Ambassador Spender), Maurice Sherbanee (Arab Delegate), Austin Pendleton (Alexander Grade), Dudley Knight (Secretary of Defense Springfield), Lou Felder (Secretary of State Reigie), Buck Henry (Father Sandstone), John Hancock (President Mazai Kalundra), Rip Torn (General Dumpston).

Buck Henry's debut as a director is a resounding failure. It is also mystifying how the writer of THE GRADUATE could come up with such inept, cretinous balderdash. A satirical story of a U.S. president and family would seem to be a likely target for Henry but a further miss would be hard to find. Newhart is the president, with daughter Radner struggling to lose her virginity. She is kidnaped in Africa by a tribe that wants to sacrifice her. Daddy comes in to save the day by making a deal where the Africans will get white Americans as slaves. The story and situations are illogical and far-fetched, the humor juvenile and stupid. In any race, FIRST FAMILY comes in dead last.

p, Daniel Melnick; d&w, Buck Henry; ph, Fred J. Koenekamp (Technicolor); m, John Philip Sousa; ed, Stu Linder.

Comedy   **Cas.**   **(PR:O MPAA:R)**

FIRST GENTLEMAN, THE   (SEE: AFFAIRS OF A ROGUE, 1948, Brit.)

FIRST GREAT TRAIN ROBBERY, THE (SEE: GREAT TRAIN ROBBERY, 1978, Brit.)

FIRST HUNDRED YEARS (SEE: FIRST ONE HUNDRED YEARS, 1938)

FIRST LADY*** (1937) 82m WB bw

Kay Francis *(Lucy Chase Wayne)*, Anita Louise *(Emmy Page)*, Verree Teasdale *(Irene Hibbard)*, Preston Foster *(Stephen Wayne)*, Walter Connolly *(Carter Hibbard)*, Victor Jory *(Senator Keane)*, Louise Fazenda *(Mrs. Greevey)*, Marjorie Gateson *(Sophie Prescott)*, Marjorie Rambeau *(Belle Hardwick)*, Eric Stanley *(Tom Hardwick)*, Henry O'Neill *(George Mason)*, Lucille Webster Gleason *(Mrs. Ives)*, Sara Haden *(Mrs. Mason)*, Harry Davenport *(Charles)*, Gregory Gaye *(Gregoravitch)*, Olaf Hytten *(Bleacker)*, Jackie Morrow *(Boy)*, Jack Mower *(Halloran)*, Elizabeth Dunne, Lillian Harmer *(Women)*, Joseph Romantini *(Senor Ortega)*, Robert Cummings, Sr., Wedgewood Nowell *(Men)*.

This film adaption of George S. Kaufman's and Katharine Dayton's 1935 Broadway stage play loses none of the wit of the original, but much of the pizzazz. Francis is the granddaughter of a former President and the wife of the Secretary of State, whom she is pushing for the Presidency. Her friend, Teasdale, the wife of a Supreme Court Justice, is the individual who almost gets into the Oval Office.

p, Hal B. Wallis; d, Stanley Logan; w, Rowland Leigh (from the play by George S. Kaufman and Katharine Dayton); ph, Sid Hickox; m, Leo F. Forbstein; ed, Ralph Dawson; art d, Max Parker.

Comedy **(PR:A MPAA:NR)**

FIRST LEGION, THE*** (1951) 86m UA bw

Charles Boyer *(Father Marc Arnoux)*, William Demarest *(Monsignor Michael Carey)*, Lyle Bettger *(Dr. Peter Morrell)*, Barbara Rush *(Terry Gilmartin)*, Leo G. Carroll *(Fr. Paul Duquesne)*, Walter Hampden *(Fr. Edward Quarterman)*, Wesley Addy *(Fr. John Fulton)*, Taylor Holmes *(Fr. Keene)*, H.B. Warner *(Fr. Jose Sierra)*, George Zucco *(Fr. Robert Stuart)*, John McGuire *(Fr. Tom Rawleigh)*, Clifford Brooke *(Lay Brother)*, Dorothy Adams *(Mrs. Dunn)*, Molly Lamont *(Mrs. Gilmartin)*, Queenie Smith *(Henrietta)*, Jacqueline DeWitt *(Nurse)*, Bill Edwards *(Joe)*.

The beginning of Sirk's film is a character study of the differing priests at St. Gregory seminary. Boyer is the head of the seminary and an ex-criminal lawyer, and Addy was a concert pianist struggling between the priesthood and his music. Demarest is the Monsignor inclined to challenge the Jesuit's faith at every opportunity. The film moves on to the "miracle" and the repercussions that follow. Bedridden priest, Warner, suddenly finds that he has regained the use of his legs. Skeptical, Boyer discovers that an agnostic town doctor, Bettger, used the power of suggestion to enable Walker to walk. The film ends with the true miracle of crippled Rush rising from her wheelchair. This end comes as somewhat of a letdown of a very engaging film. Sirk examines themes that reappear in most of his works; religion and the foggy dividing line between the rational and irrational.

p&d, Douglas Sirk; w, Emmett Lavery; ph, Robert DeGrasse; m, Hans Sommer; ed, Francis D. Lyon.

Drama **(PR:A MPAA:NR)**

FIRST LOVE½** (1939) 84m UNIV bw

Deanna Durbin *(Constance Harding)*, Robert Stack *(Ted Drake)*, Eugene Pallette *(James Clinton)*, Helen Parrish *(Barbara Clinton)*, Lewis Howard *(Walter Clinton)*, Leatrice Joy *(Grace Clinton)*, June Storey *(Wilma van Everett)*, Frank Jenks *(Mike)*, Kathleen Howard *(Miss Wiggins)*, Thurston Hall *(Mr. Drake)*, Marcia Mae Jones *(Maria Parker)*, Samuel S. Hinds *(Mr. Parker)*, Doris Lloyd *(Mrs. Parker)*, Charles Coleman *(George)*, Jack Mulhall *(Chauffeur)*, Mary Treen *(Barbara's Maid)*, Dorothy Vaughan *(Mrs. Clinton's Maid)*, Lucille Ward *(Cook)*.

Durbin, a major box-office star in the late 1930s, made headlines (no joke) with FIRST LOVE by getting her first screen kiss in the film. Aside from that, FIRST LOVE is not too memorable. Durbin is an orphan adopted by a rich, uncaring family. Returning from school, she is snubbed by relatives, who try to prevent her from going to the gala ball. With the help of the servants, she goes and meets Prince Charming, Stack, and he gives her that monumental kiss. Film debut for Robert Stack. Songs: "Sympathy," "A Change of Heart," "Deserted" (Ralph Freed, Frank Skinner); "Spring in My Heart" (lyrics, Freed); "Amapola" (Albert Ganse, Joseph M. LaCalle); "Home Sweet Home" (John Howard Payne, Sir Henry Bishop); "One Fine Day" (from Puccini's "Madame Butterfly").

p, Joe Pasternak; d, Henry Koster; w, Bruce Manning, Lionel Houser; ph, Joseph Valentine; m, Frank Skinner; ed, Bernard Burton; md, Charles Previn; art d, Jack Otterson.

Romance **(PR:A MPAA:NR)**

FIRST LOVE½** (1970, Ger./Switz.) 92m UMC c (ERSTE LIEBE)

John Moulder Brown *(Alexander)*, Dominique Sanda *(Sinaida)*, Maximilian Schell *(Father)*, Valentina Cortese *(Mother)*, Marcus Goring *(Dr. Lushin)*, Dandy Nichols *(Princess Zasekina)*, Richard Warwick *(Lt. Belouzorov)*, Keith Bell *(Count Malevsky)*, Johannes Schaaf *(Nirmatsky)*, John Osborne *(Maidanov)*.

A 16-year-old European boy falls in love with a 21-year-old girl, who toys with his feelings. This experience matures the boy to manhood. (The boy's father has been committing adultery with the girl.) The story unfolds against the backdrop of the growing threat of war in Europe. This was actor Schell's first directorial effort.

p, Maximilian Schell, Barry Levinson; d, Schell; w, Schell, John Gould (based on a story by Ivan Turgenev); ph, Sven Nykvist (Eastmancolor); m, Mark London; ed, Dagmar Hirtz.

Romance **Cas.** **(PR:C-O MPAA:NR)**

FIRST LOVE* (1977) 91m PAR c

William Katt *(Elgin Smith)*, Susan Dey *(Caroline)*, John Heard *(David)*, Beverly D'Angelo *(Shelley)*, Robert Loggia *(John March)*, Tom Lacy *(Prof. Oxtan)*, Swoosie Kurtz *(Marsha)*, June Barrett *(Felicia)*, Patrick O'Hara *(Zookeeper)*, Judy Kerr *(Secretary)*, Jenny Hill *(Girl in Bar)*, Virginia Leith *(Mrs. March)*, Billy Beck *(Cafeteria Boss)*.

A melodramatic film about a romance between two college students, Katt and Dey. The film's principals come off as if they were in their late thirties not early twenties. Actress Darling's directorial debut.

p, Lawrence Thurman, David Foster; d, Joan Darling; w, Jane Stanton Hitchcock, David Freeman (based on the story "Sentimental Education" by Harold Brodkey); ph, Bobby Byrne (Metrocolor); m, Joel Sill; ed, Frank Morriss; prod d, Robert Luthardt.

Romance **Cas.** **(PR:O MPAA:R)**

FIRST MAN INTO SPACE½** (1959, Brit.) 77m Anglo Amalgamated/MGM bw (AKA: SATELLITE OF BLOOD)

Marshall Thompson *(Commander C.E. Prescott)*, Marla Landi *(Tia Francesca)*, Bill Edwards *(Lt. Dan Prescott)*, Robert Ayres *(Capt. Ben Richards)*, Bill Nagy *(Wilson)*, Carl Jaffe *(Dr. Paul von Essen)*, Roger Delgado *(Mexican Consul)*, John McLaren *(State Dept. Official)*, Richard Shaw *(Witney)*, Bill Nick *(Clancy)*, Chuck Keyser, John Fabian, Spencer Teakle *(Control Room Officials)*, Michael Bell *(State Trooper)*, Helen Forrest *(Secretary)*, Rowland Brand *(Truck Driver)*, Barry Shawzin *(Mexican Farmer)*, Mark Sheldon *(Doctor)*, Sheree Winton *(Nurse)*, Franklin Fox *(C.P.O.)*, Laurence Taylor *(Shore Patrolman)*.

A British production about an American astronaut, who returns to Earth covered with a slime-like meteor dust and with a cosmic organism inside him. The creature takes over the spaceman's body; it needs human blood to live. After a couple of killings and a break-in at a blood bank, the astronaut's scientist brother kills the creature *and* his brother in a decompression chamber. A scary and well done S.F. exploitation film set in Arizona but shot in England.

p, John Croydon, Charles F. Vetter, Jr.; d, Robert Day; w, John C. Cooper, Lance Z. Hargreaves (adapted from a story by Wyott Ordung); ph, Geoffrey Faithfull; m, Buxton Orr; ed, Peter Mayhew.

Science Fiction **(PR:A MPAA:NR)**

FIRST MEN IN THE MOON** (1964, Brit.) 102m Ameran/COL c

Edward Judd *(Arnold Bedford)*, Lionel Jeffries *(Cavor)*, Martha Hyer *(Kate Callender)*, Eric Chitty *(Gibbs)*, Betty McDowall *(Maggie)*, Miles Malleson *(Registrar)*, Lawrence Herder *(Glushkov)*, Gladys Henson *(Matron)*, Marne Maitland *(Dr. Tok)*, Hugh McDermott *(Challis)*, Gordon Robinson *(Martin)*, Sean Kelly *(Col. Rice)*, John Murray Scott *(Nevsky)*, Paul Carpenter, Huw Thomas *(Announcers)*.

An enjoyable science fiction film adapted from H.G. Wells' novel. An 1899 British crew land on the moon and are attacked by Ray Harryhausen's creations. Director Juran also directed ATTACK OF THE 50-FOOT WOMAN, using the name Nathan Hertz, and also shared an Oscar for his design of John Ford's HOW GREEN WAS MY VALLEY.

p, Charles H. Schneer; d, Nathan Juran; w, Nigel Kneale, Jan Read (based on the novel by H.G. Wells); ph, Wilkie Cooper (Technicolor); m, Laurie Johnson; ed, Maurice Rootes; spec eff, Ray Harryhausen.

Science Fiction **(PR:A MPAA:NR)**

FIRST MARINES (SEE: TRIPOLI, 1950)

FIRST MRS. FRASER, THE** (1932, Brit.) 95m Sterling bw

Henry Ainley *(James Fraser)*, Joan Barry *(Elsie Fraser)*, Dorothy Dix *(Janet Fraser)*, Harold Huth *(Mario)*, Richard Cooper *(Lord Larne)*, Hargrave Pawson *(Ninian Fraser)*, Henry Hewitt *(Philip Logan)*, Arnold Riches *(George)*, Gibb McLaughlin *(Butler)*, Ivan Brandt *(Murdo Fraser)*, Millicent Wolf *(Mabel)*, Oriel Ross *(Connie)*, Eileen Peel *(Ellen Fraser)*, Naunton Wayne, Frances Day, Yvette, Noel Leyland, Edgar K. Bruce, Ellen Pollock, Billy Cotton and His Band, The Gaucho Tango Orchestra.

Mediocre musical soap opera has Barry wanting to divorce husband Ainley so she can marry her aristocratic lover, but Dix, Ainley's still-loving first wife, acquires evidence of Barry's dalliances and a divorce finds Barry the guilty party and Dix and Ainley reunited.

p, Louis Zimmerman; d, Sinclair Hill; w, Leslie Howard Gordon (based on a play by St. John Irvine).

Musical/Drama **(PR:A MPAA:NR)**

FIRST MONDAY IN OCTOBER½** (1981) 98m PAR c

Walter Matthau *(Dan Snow)*, Jill Clayburgh *(Ruth Loomis)*, Barnard Hughes *(Chief Justice Crawford)*, Jan Sterling *(Christine Snow)*, James Stephens *(Mason Woods)*, Joshua Bryant *(Bill Russell)*, Wiley Harker *(Justice Harold Webb)*, F. J. O'Neil *(Justice Waldo Thompson)*, Charles Lampkin *(Justice Josiah Clewes)*, Lew Palter *(Justice Benjamin Halperin)*, Richard McMurray *(Justice Richard Carey)*, Herb Vigran *(Justice Ambrose Quincy)*, Edmund Stoiber *(Committee Chairman)*, Noble Willingham *(Nebraska Attorney)*, Richard McKenzie *(Hostile Senator)*, Ann Doran *(Storekeeper)*, Dallas Alinder *(Norman)*, Olive Dunbar *(Ms. Radabaugh)*, Hugh Gillin *(Southern Senator)*, James E. Brodhead *(Court Marshall)*, Arthur Adams, Sig Frohlich *(Custodians)*, Nick Angotti *(Plaintiff's Attorney)*, Jeanne Joe *(Waitress)*, Christopher Tenney *(Robinson)*, Richard Balin *(Photographer)*, Martin Agronsky *(TV Commentator)*, Bob Sherman, Ray Colbert *(Senators)*, Carol Coggin *(Attorney)*, Kenneth DuMain *(Guard)*, Stanley Lawrence *(Court Guard)*, Dick Winslow *(Barber)*, Joe Terry, Sandy Chapin *(Clerks)*, Dudley Knight *(Assistant Manager)*, Edwin M. Adams *(Clergyman)*, Ronnie Thomas *(Firing Party Commander)*, Jeff Scheulen *(Ambulance Attendant)*, Jordan Charney *(Doctor)*, Mary Munday *(Head Nurse)*, Bebe Drake-Massey *(Nurse)*, Richard de Angeles *(News Producer)*, Jim Vanko *(Chief Ranger)*, Dale House *(Pilot)*, William G. Clark, Wendy E. Taylor *(Cab Drivers)*.

Sometimes entertaining comedy where grumpy, old-but-liberal Supreme Court Justice Matthau resists the appointment of the first lady justice, Clayburgh, to his august company. The exchanges between them are mildly amusing but their combative encounters grow tiresome after the first half-hour and then the film bogs down into an investigation by both judges into the shady dealings of Clayburgh's deceased tycoon husband. It's all reminiscent of the great Tracy-Hepburn films, but nowhere near the wit and wonder of those marvelous movies. Neame's direction is slow-paced, even lazy in spots, as if he had his mind on making another movie or that this one just didn't interest him too much. Matthau loafs about like some cracker-barrel philosopher whose time is better served on his office couch than behind the bench. Clayburgh merely mouths generalities and platitudes. Both are fairly forgettable. Shortly after this film's release, President Reagan appointed the first woman to the U.S. Supreme Court, but the timeliness of his action did not bolster box office returns of this production. Henry Fonda played Matthau's role in the stage version. The co-producer of the film was actress Martha Scott.

p, Paul Heller, Martha Scott; d, Ronald Neame; w, Jerome Lawrence, Robert E. Lee (based on their play); ph, Fred J. Koenekamp (Panavision, Metrocolor); m, Ian Fraser; ed, Peter E. Berger; prod d, Philip M. Jefferies; art d, John V. Cartwright; set d, Beverli Egan, Geoff Hubbard, Robert de Vestel, Ernie Biship.

Comedy/Drama   **Cas.**   **(PR:O MPAA:NR)**

FIRST NIGHT*   (1937, Brit.) 69m Crusade/PAR bw

Jack Livesey (*Richard Garnet*), Rani Waller (*Judith Armstrong*), Sunday Wilshin (*Rosalind Faber*), Ernest Mainwaring (*Henry Armstrong*), Margaret Damer (*Elaine Armstrong*), Ann Wilton (*Ivy*), Felix Erwin (*Patterson Luke*).

Understanding young producer Livesey helps plain, shy Waller overcome her personal problems to become a successful playwright. Nothing remotely of interest here.

p, Victor M. Greene; d&w, Donovan Pedelty (based on a play by Sheila Donisthorpe).

Drama   **(PR:A MPAA:NR)**

FIRST NUDIE MUSICAL, THE*   (1976) 90m PAR c

Stephen Nathan (*Harry Schechter*), Cindy Williams (*Rosie*), Bruce Kimmel (*John Smithee*), Leslie Ackerman (*Susie*), Alan Abelew (*George Brenner*), Diana Canova (*Juanita*), Alexandra Morgan (*Mary La Rue*), Frank Doubleday (*Arvin*), Kathleen Hietala (*Eunice*), Art Marino (*Eddie*), Hy Pyke (*Benny*), Greg Finley (*Jimmy*), Herb Graham (*Frankie*), Rene Hall (*Dick Davis*), Susan Stewart (*Joy Full*), Artie Shafer (*Actor*), Jerry Hoffman (*Schlong*), Wade Crookham (*Mr. "Orgasm"*), Nancy Chadwick (*Lesbian*), John Kirby (*Bad Actor*), Vern Joyce (*Assistant Director*), Jan Praise (*Cameraman*), Eileen Ramsey (*Brenda*), Jane Ralston (*Buck & Wing Girl*), Claude Spence (*Old Man Schechter*), Chris Corso (*Pervert*), Alison Cohen (*Jane*), Susan Gelb (*Tapper*), Kathryn Kimmel (*The Hand*), Nancy Bleier, Susan Underwood, Cindy Ashley, Jane Ralston, Jeff Greenberg, Susan Buckner, Diana Vance, Lauren Lucas, Lloyd Gordon, Kathy Wigglet, Chris Malott, Alana Reed, Joe Blum, Rick Nickerson (*Dancers*).

A humorous concept, perhaps, but as a film it's unable to develop the basic idea. To save his sinking exploitation film production company, Nathan—on the advice of his secretary—sets out to make the title musical. The script is episodic, depending on gimmicks and one-liners to keep things moving. Songs like "Let 'Em Eat Cake (And I'll Eat You)" and "Perversions" are passably funny, but can't substain a ninety-minute film. The film does have a sizeable cult following. The humor, of course, isn't for everyone. Songs (music and lyrics by Bruce Kimmel), "The First Nudie Musical," "The Lights and the Smiles" (sung by Annette O'Toole) "Orgasm," "Lesbian Butch Dyke," "Dancing Dildos," "Perversion," "Honey, What Ya Doin' Tonight," "Let 'Em Eat Cake," "I Don't Have to Hide Anymore," "Where Is a Man" (sung by Valerie Gillett).

p, Jack Reeves; d, Mark Haggard, Bruce Kimmel; w, Kimmel; ph, Douglas H. Knapp (DeLuxe Color); m, Kimmel; ed, Allen Peluso; md, Kimmel; art d, Tom Rassmussen; set d, Timothy J. Bloch; cos, Rassmussen; ch, Lloyd Gordon.

Musical/Comedy   **Cas.**   **(PR:O MPAA:R)**

FIRST OF THE FEW, THE   (SEE: SPITFIRE, 1942, Brit.)

FIRST OFFENCE**   (1936, Brit.) 66m Gainsborough/GAU bw
(AKA: BAD BLOOD)

John Mills (*Johnnie Penrose*), Lilli Palmer (*Jeanette*), Bernard Nedell (*The Boss*), Michael Andre (*Michel*), H.G. Stoker (*Dr. Penrose*), Jean Wall (*The Zebra*), Paul Velsa (*Peanuts*), Maupi (*Man in Panama*), Judy Kelly (*Girl in Garage*), George Malkine.

Mills, spoiled son of wealthy doctor Stoker, is so upset when his father refuses to buy him a car that he travels to France and joins a gang of car thieves led by Nedell. When Stoker arrives to rescue his son from the police, the two are reconciled. Some good chase scenes highlight this otherwise routine crime drama partly shot in France.

p, Michael Balcon; d, Herbert Mason; w, Austin Melford (based on a story by Stafford Dickens); ph, Arthur Crabtree.

Crime   **(PR:A MPAA:NR)**

FIRST OFFENDERS½**   (1939) 63m COL bw

Walter Abel (*Gregory Stone*), Beverly Roberts (*Susan Kent*), Iris Meredity (*Mary Kent*), Johnny Downs (*Fred Gray*), Diana Lewis (*Ann Blakeley*), John Hamilton (*Sheriff Slavin*), Forbes Murray (*Mr. Wentworth*), Pierre Watkin (*Mr. Blakeley*), John Tyrell (*Lew Haskell*), George Offerman, Jr. (*Skinny*), Robert Sterling (*Nick*), Warren Douglas (*Tom*), Michael Conroy (*Tony*), Donald Barry (*Art*).

Abel is an idealistic district attorney who quits to run a farm where city boys can learn a trade, rather than criminal habits. One teen-ager the attorney sent up the river seeks revenge, but Abel and his farm reform him.

d, Frank McDonald; w, Walter Wise (from a story by J. Edward Slavin); ph, Henry Freulich; m, M.W. Stoloff; ed, James Sweeney.

Drama   **(PR:A MPAA:NR)**

FIRST 100 YEARS, THE*½   (1938) 75m MGM bw

Robert Montgomery (*David Conway*), Virginia Bruce (*Lynn Conway*), Warren Williams (*Harry Borden*), Binnie Barnes (*Claudia Weston*), Alan Dinehart (*Samuel Z. Walker*), Harry Davenport (*Uncle Dawson*), Nydia Westman (*Midge*), Donald Briggs (*William Regan*), Jonathan Hale (*Judge Parker*), E. E. Clive (*Chester Blascomb*), Lee Bowman (*George Wallace*), Torben Meyer (*Karl*), Bodil Rosing (*Martha*), Irving Bacon (*Wilkins*), Priscilla Lawson (*Mary Brown*), Rex Evans (*Reggie*), Edgar Dearing (*Policeman*), Eleanor Lynn (*Receptionist*), Jean Fenwick (*Miss Moffat*), Wally Maher, Harry Strang, Monte Vandergrift (*Workmen*), Roger Converse (*Young Actor*), Barbara Bedford (*Sadie*), Frederick Clark (*Ito*), Roger Moore (*Ship's Steward*), Lane Chandler (*Doorman*).

Bruce is a career woman in New York, married to Montgomery. She must decide if she should give up her well-paying job to live with her husband in New Bedford, Mass., on his $15,000-a-year salary. A light comedy with somewhat dated themes.

p, Norman Krasna; d, Richard Thorpe; w, Melville Baker (from a story by Krasna); ph, Joseph Ruttenberg; m, Dr. William Axt; ed, Conrad A. Nervig; art d, Cedric Gibbons.

Comedy   **(PR:A MPAA:NR)**

FIRST REBEL, THE   (SEE: ALLEGHENY UPRISING, 1939)

FIRST SPACESHIP ON VENUS***   (1960, Ger./Pol.) 80m
Centrala/Crown International c
(DER SCHWEIGENDE STERN; MILCZACA GWIAZDA)

Yoko Tani (*Sumiko Ogimura*), Oldrich Lukes (*Harringway*), Ignacy Machowski (*Orloff*), Julius Ongewe (*Talua*), Michal Postnikow (*Durand*), Kurt Rackelmann (*Sikarna*), Gunther Simon (*Brinkman*), Tang-Hua-Ta (*Tchen Yu*), Lucyna Winnicka (*Joan Moran*).

A multi-national team of astronauts is sent to explore Venus. They find that the Venus population, planning to invade Earth, had destroyed itself, thanks to nuclear weapons. A critically acclaimed science fiction film with a clear anti-nuclear statement and superb special effects. Fifty minutes of the original 130 minutes of footage was cut from the American release.

p, Newton P. Jacobs, Paul Schreibman, Edmund Goldman; d, Kurt Maetzig; w, Maetzig, J. Barckhausen, J. Fathke, W. Kohlhaase, G. Reisch, G. Rucker, A. Stenbock-Fermor (from novel *Astronauci [Planet of Death]* by Stanislaw Lem); ph, Joachim Hasler (Agfacolor); m, Gordon Zahler; ed, Lena Neumann; spec eff, Vera Kunstmann, Jan Olejniczak, Helmut Grewald.

Science Fiction   **Cas.**   **(PR:A MPAA:NR)**

FIRST START**   (1953, Pol.) 140m Film Folski/Artkino bw

Leopold Nowak (*Tomek Spojda*), Jadwige Chejnacka (*Spojdzina*), Adam Mikolajewski (*Spojda*), Janus Jaron (*Studzinski*), Jerzy Pietraszkiewiez (*Goracz*), Wladyslaw Woznik (*Commander*), Wladyslaw Walter (*Stypula*), Anna Rosiak (*Hania*), Bohdan Niewinowski (*Jurek*), Stanislaw Mikulski (*Franek*), Wiesla Wilk (*Ryszard*).

Nowak enters the Polish government's airplane glider school and flunks his class because he doesn't like to study. He's kicked out of the school, even though he has the most potential and talent. He proves his worth by piloting a lost glider, and is reinstated at the school. (In Polish; English subtitles.)

d, Leonard Buczkowski; w, Ludwik Starski; m, Rusinek B. Brok; ph, Felike Srednicki.

Drama   **(PR:A MPAA:NR)**

FIRST TASTE OF LOVE**   (1962, Fr.) 80m International Thanos/Altura bw
(LES NYMPHETTES)

Christian Pezey (*Lucien*), Colette Descombes (*Joelle*), Claude Arnold (*Mireille*), Jacques Perrin (*Philippe*), Adrienne Servantie (*The Mother*), Mario Pilar (*Mario*), Corrado Guarducci (*The Producer*), Rene Rozan (*The Priest*), Michele Dumontier (*Marianne*), Marc Halford (*Marc*), Marie-Therese Navaret (*Claire*), Daniel Lorieux (*Jean-Loup*), Alain Dumoulin, Colette Colas, Mathilda Sides, Colette Andre, Christine Kerl, Catherine Candida, Pierre Chantarel.

Pezey plays an engineering student who is shocked to discover that his long-time girlfriend Arnold has been seeing an older man, Pilar. Distraught, Pezey wanders the streets of Paris and meets Descombes, a street-wise teenager who makes her living by doing a striptease act in a sleazy nightclub. The couple fall in love, but when Arnold learns of the romance, she attempts to split them up. Her efforts fail, leaving her stuck with Pilar, while Pezey and Descombes continue their by-now blissful relationship.

p,d&w, Henry Zaphiratos; w, Zaphiratos, Bernard Chesnais, Roland Guinier du Vignaud; ph, Roger Duculot; m, Louiguy; ed, Armand Psenny; art d, Roger Bar.

Drama   **(PR:C MPAA:NR)**

FIRST TEXAN, THE**   (1956) 82m AA c

Joel McCrea (*Sam Houston*), Felicia Farr (*Katherine*), Jeff Morrow (*Bowie*), Wallace Ford (*Delaney*), Abraham Sofaer (*Don Carlos*), Jody McCrea (*Baker*), Chubby Johnson (*Deaf Smith*), Dayton Lummis (*Austin*), Rodolfo Hoyas (*Cos*), William Hopper (*Travis*), Roy Roberts (*Sherman*), David Silva (*Santa Ana*), Frank Puglia (*Pepe*), Salvador Baguez (*Veramendi*), James Griffith (*Crockett*), Nelson Leigh (*Hockley*), Carl Benton Reid (*Andrew Jackson*), Scott Douglas, William Phipps.

An antiseptic film biography of Sam Houston. McCrea plays Houston and the film moves slowly until the historic Battle of San Jacinto. The film follows Houston from young man to President of the Republic of Texas, but it is a superficial portrait.

p, Walter Mirisch; d, Byron Haskin; w, Daniel B. Ullman; ph, Wilfrid Cline (CinemaScope, Technicolor); m, Roy Webb; ed, George White.

Western **(PR:A MPAA:NR)**

FIRST TIME, THE** (1952) 89m COL bw

Robert Cummings *(Joe Bennet)*, Barbara Hale *(Betsey Bennet)*, Bill Goodwin *(Mel Gilbert)*, Jeff Donnell *(Donna Gilbert)*, Carl Benton Reid *(Andrew Bennet)*, Mona Barrie *(Cassie Mayhew)*, Kathleen Comegys *(Florence Bennet)*, Paul Harvey *(Leeming)*, Cora Witherspoon *(Miss Salisbury)*, Bea Benaderet *(Mrs. Potter)*.

A domestic comedy with Cummings and Hale as first-time parents. They find that raising a child costs more than they expected, in more ways than financial, as was to be expected.

p, Harold Hecht; d, Frank Tashlin; w, Tashlin, Jean Rouverol, Hugh Butler, Dane Lussier (adapted from a story by Rouverol and Butler); ph, Ernest Laszlo; m, Frederick Hollander; ed, Viola Lawrence; md, Morris Stoloff.

Comedy **(PR:A MPAA:NR)**

FIRST TIME, THE* (1969) 90m UA c
(GB: YOU DON'T NEED PAJAMAS AT ROSIE'S; AKA: THE BEGINNERS THREE; THE BEGINNERS; THEY DON'T WEAR PAJAMAS AT ROSIE'S)

Jacqueline Bisset *(Anna)*, Wes Stern *(Kenny)*, Rick Kelman *(Mike)*, Wink Roberts *(Tommy)*, Gerard Parkes *(Charles)*, Sharon Acker *(Pamela)*, Cosette Lee *(Grandmother)*, Vincent Marino *(Frankie)*, Eric Lane *(Joe)*, Murray Westgate *(Customs Officer)*, Leslie Yeo *(Bartender)*, Guy Sanvido *(Stranger)*, William Barringer *(Elevator Man)*, Gail Carrington *(Blonde in Hot-Rod)*, Sharon Masters, Rhondi Polango *(Go-Go Girls)*.

An innocuous teen-age comedy with Stern spending the summer with his grandparents in Buffalo and writing fictitious letters back home to two friends, Kelman and Roberts. One letter is about a visit to a Canadian bordello called "Rosie's." Kelman and Roberts, on their way to summer camp, stop to see their friend, hoping to go to Rosie's. Stern tries to talk them out of it, since he has no idea where Rosie's is (he had heard two men talk about the bordello, and that was the basis for his letter). They cross the border, and meet Bisset in an abandoned house Stern says is Rosie's. Thinking Bisset, who has no passport, is a call girl, they help her cross into the states. Their ulterior motives account for the film's title.

p, Roger Smith, Alan Carr; d, James Neilson; w, Jo Heims, Smith (adapted from a story by Bernard Bassey); ph, Ernest Laszlo (Deluxe Color); m, Kenyon Hopkins; ed, Henry Molin; art d, Trevor Williams.

Comedy **(PR:C MPAA:M)**

FIRST TIME, THE*** (1978, Fr.) 85m EDP c

Alaine Cohen *(Claude)*, Charles Denner *(Claude's Father)*, Zorica Lozic *(Claude's Mother)*, Delphine Levy *(Arlette)*, Claude Lubicki *(Rene)*, Philippe Teboul *(Bernard)*, Jerome Loeb *(Sammy)*, Bruno Resenter *(Loulou)*, Daniele Schneider *(Carole)*, Maryse Raymond *(Bernadette)*, Carine Riviere *(Irene)*, Daniele Minazzoli *(Nathalie)*, Roland Blanche *(Robert)*, Joel Moskowitz *(Cousin Leon)*.

The second installment in Berri's series of autobiographical films starring Cohen (the first was THE TWO OF US) finds the young hero on the edge of sexual initiation and quite worried about it. Charming comedy bears comparison with Truffaut's Antoine Doinel films. (In French; English subtitles.)

p, Raymond Danon; d&w, Claude Berri; ph, Jean Cesar Chiabaut; m, Rene Urtreger; ed, Dominique Daudon; art d, Alexander Trauner; cos, Mic Cheminal.

Comedy **(PR:O MPAA:NR)**

FIRST TIME, THE** (1983) 95m New Line Cinema c

Tim Choate *(Charlie)*, Krista Errickson *(Dana)*, Marshall Efron *(Prof. Rand)*, Wendy Fulton *(Wendy)*, Raymond Patterson *(Ron)*, Wallace Shawn *(Prof. Goldfarb)*, Wendie Jo Sperber *(Eileen)*, Cathryn Daman *(Gloria)*, Jane Badler *(Karen)*, Bradley Bliss *(Melanie)*, Eva Charney *(Polly)*, Bill Randolph *(Rick)*, Rex Robbins *(Leon)*, Robert Trebor *(Joel)*, Larry "Bud" Melman [DeForest].

Choate finds college tough going when he can't score with the girl of his dreams and his aspirations of becoming a filmmaker are challenged by esoteric film teacher Shawn. Choate's black roommate, Patterson, tries to teach him his rap on women, but it doesn't fit. Psych. professor Efron counsels the young man, helping him lose his virginity in what turns out to be part of a research project. In the end, Choate hooks up with fellow film student and outsider Fulton and wins top honors at the school's film festival. Director Loventhal and producer Irvin were assistants on Brian DePalma's HOME MOVIES and DePalma was creative consultant on this picture. The humor at times becomes downright silly.

p, Sam Irvin; d, Charlie Loventhal; w, Loventhal, Susan Weiser-Finley, and W. Franklin Finley; ph, Steve Fierberg (TVC Color); m, Lanny Meyers; ed, Stanley Vogel; art d, Tom Surgal.

Comedy **Cas.** **(PR:O MPAA:R)**

FIRST TO FIGHT*** (1967) 97m WB c

Chad Everett *(Jack Connell)*, Marilyn Devin *(Peggy Sanford)*, Dean Jagger *(Lt. Col. Baseman)*, Bobby Troup *(Lt. Overman)*, Claude Akins *(Capt. Mason)*, Gene Hackman *(Sgt. Tweed)*, James Best *(Sgt. Carnavan)*, Norman Alden *(Sgt. Schmidtmer)*, Bobs Watson *(Sgt. Maypole)*, Ken Swofford *(O'Brien)*, Ray Reese *(Hawkins)*, Garry Goodgion *(Karl)*, Robert Austin *(Adams)*, Clint Ritchie *(Sgt. Slater)*, Stephen Roberts *(President F.D. Roosevelt)*.

Action packed WW II film has Everett as a tough-as-nails Marine, "Shanghai Jack" Connell, whose position on Guadacanal is almost overrun by swarms of Japanese until Everett gets behind a machinegun. He mows down the phalanxes of Japanese for which he wins the Congressional Medal of Honor. Returned to the U.S. to promote the sale of war bonds, he meets, falls in love, and marries Devin. She at first resists him, frightened of committing herself to another serviceman after her fiance has been killed in the war. The couple settle down on a Marine base. She gets pregnant and he trains recruits but he is haunted by the thought that he is shirking his duties, that he should rejoin his buddies on the battlefield in the Pacific. But once sent to a front-line company as an officer, he finds he cannot take command and suspects that he has lost his nerve. Hackman, a loud-mouth sergeant, goads him into taking command and he again proves himself heroic. Everett is good in his stoic role and Devin is believable as the reluctant wife. Jagger, as Everett's commander, is outstanding, as is the impressive cinematography by Wellman and Steiner's moving score which encompasses the "As Time Goes By" theme song from CASABLANCA (1942) (which Everett and Devin view in one scene). Character actor Conrad produced this film at the height of the Vietnam War, no doubt thinking it would instill a patriotic fervor in recruits for that hopeless conflict. Shot at Camp Pendleton at Oceanside, California, and some battle scenes filmed in the San Fernando Valley.

p, William Conrad; d, Christian Nyby; w, Gene L. Coon; ph, Harold Wellman (Panavision, Technicolor); m, Fred Steiner; ed, George Rohrs; art d, Art Loel; set d, Hal Overell; makeup, Gordon Bau; tech adv, Major Fred A. Kraus.

War Drama **(PR:C MPAA:NR)**

FIRST TRAVELING SALESLADY, THE* (1956) 92m RKO c

Ginger Rogers *(Rose Gillray)*, Barry Nelson *(Charles Masters)*, Carol Channing *(Molly Wade)*, David Brian *(James Carter)*, James Arness *(Joel Kingdon)*, Clint Eastwood *(Jack Rice)*, Robert Simon *(Cal)*, Frank Wilcox *(Marshall Duncan)*, Daniel M. White *(Sheriff)*, Harry Cheshire *(Judge Benson)*, John Eldridge *(Greavy)*, Robert Hinkle *(Pete)*, Jack Rice *(Dowling)*, Kate Drain Lawson *(Annie Peachpit)*, Edward Cassidy *(Theodore Roosevelt)*, Fred Essler *(Schlessinger)*, Bill Hale *(Sheriff's Deputy)*, Lovyss Bradley *(Mrs. Bronson)*, Nora Bush *(Mrs. Pruett)*, Ann Kunde *(Mrs. Cobb)*, Janette Miller, Kathy Marlowe, Lynn Noe, Joan Tyler *(Models)*, Hans Herbert *(Night Clerk)*, Robert Easton *(Young Cowboy)*, Belle Mitchell *(Emily)*, Ian Murray *(Prince of Wales)*, Roy Darmour, Peter Croydon, Al Cavens, Paul Bradley, Hal Taggart *(Men)*, Gilmore Bush *(1st Salesman)*, John Connors *(2nd Salesman)*, Lester Dorr, Frank Scannell, Paul Keast *(Salesmen)*, Mauritz Hugo, Julius Evans, Stanley Farrar, Charles Tannen *(Buyers)*, Hank Patterson *(1st Cowhand)*, Britt Wood *(2nd Cowhand)*, James Stone, Cactus Mack, Deacon Moor, Lane Chandler *(Ranchers)*, Chalky Williams *(Spectator)*, George Barrows *(Meat Packer)*, George Baxter *(Headwaiter)*, George Brand *(Telegraph Operator)*, Tris Coffin *(Day Hotel Clark)*, Theron Jackson *(Bellhop)*, Herbert Deans *(Secretary)*, William Fawcett, Casey MacGregor *(Old-timers)*, William Forrest *(Supreme Court Justice)*, Jim Hayward *(Sam)*, Earl Hodgins *(Veterinarian)*, Johnny Lee *(Amos)*, Pierce Lyden *(Official)*, Tony Roux *(Mexican in Courtroom)*, Clarence Muse *(Amos)*.

Rogers is a Gay Nineties corset designer who goes west to sell barbed wire with her secretary, Channing, in one of the last films from RKO studios. Nothing memorable about this film except it was the first role of any substance for Clint Eastwood, playing Channing's boy friend. He had his contract dropped by Universal and picked up by RKO, who ran his credit as "introducing Clint Eastwood." Songs: "A Corset Can Do a Lot for a Lady," "The First Traveling Saleslady."

p, Arthur Lubin; d, Lubin; w, Stephen Longstreet, Devery Freeman; ph, William Snyder (Technicolor); m, Irving Gertz, Hal Levy; ed, Otto Ludwig; art d, Albert S. D'Agostino; set d, Darrell Silvera.

Comedy **(PR:A MPAA:PG)**

FIRST WIFE (SEE: WIVES AND LOVERS, 1963)

FIRST YANK INTO TOKYO** (1945) 82m RKO bw
(GB: MASK OF FURY)

Tom Neal *(Major Ross)*, Barbara Hale *(Abby Drake)*, Marc Cramer *(Jardine)*, Richard Loo *(Col. Okanura)*, Keye Luke *(Haan-soo)*, Leonard Strong *(Major Nogira)*, Benson Fong *(Capt. Tanahe)*, Clarence Lung *(Maj. Ichibo)*, Keye Chang *(Capt. Sato)*, Michael St. Angel *(Capt. Andrew Kent)*, Bruce Edwards *(Capt. Harris)*, Albert Law *(Japanese Pilot)*, Gerald Pierce *(Waist Gunner)*, Harry Anderson *(Sub Commander)*, Ralph Stein *(Bellhop)*, Russell Hicks *(Col. Thompson)*, Wallis Clark *(Dr. Langley)*, John Hamilton *(Dr. Stacey)*, Selmer Jackson *(Col. Blaine)*, Joseph Kim *(Sgt. Osami)*, Paul Fung *(Capt. Yamanashi)*, Bob Chinn, Chet Verovan *(Japanese Soldiers)*, Bo Ching *(Dancer)*, Eddie Luke *(Ling Wan)*, Peter Chong *(Dr. Kai Koon)*, George Lee *(Chinese Captain)*, Edmund Glover, Robert Clarke, Johnny Strong, Eden Nicholas, Jimmy Jordan *(Prisoners)*, Artarne Wong, Larry Wong *(Koreans)*, Dorothy Curtis, Gwen Crawford, Betty Gillette, Frances Haldern, Ione Reed, Aline Goodwins, Noreen Lee, Bobby La Salle *(Nurses)*, Thomas Quon Woo, Weaver Levy, George Chung, Spencer Chan, James Leong *(Bits)*, Richard Wang, Tommy Lee *(Japanese Sentries)*.

A strange one, this film, where Neal is a super patriotic American pilot who has been raised in Japan and agrees to return to Nippon to obtain weaponry information from a captive scientist, Cramer. The suicidal mission doesn't frighten Neal. His sweetheart, Hale, is dead and he now only wishes to die serving his country. Plastic surgeons give him a fighting chance before he parachutes into Japan, drastically altering his features so that he is completely Orientalized and telling him that he cannot reverse the image through future plastic surgery. Once in Japan, Neal discovers that Hale is very much alive, a nurse taken prisoner who is now in love with another prisoner, American serviceman, St. Angel. Neal nevertheless follows his orders and obtains the vital information; to do so he encounters and outwits several unsavory Japanese officers, including the insidious Strong who specializes in filching army funds. Loo is his true adversary, a wily intelligence colonel with whom Neal had actually gone to college, one who remembers every quirk of his school chum. Loo even goes so far as to run newsreel footage showing Neal on the gridiron to illustrate his nervous traits, all to determine if Neal is really his one-time Caucasion friend. At the last minute Neal sacrifices his life, fending off attacking Japanese as Hale and St. Angel escape. Since this film was finished just as the A-bomb was dropped on Japan, the producers went back to the cameras and changed Neal's assignment to obtaining vital A-bomb information. In a new and incredulous ending, a narrator explains how Neal gave up his life so the A-bomb could be perfected! Pathe newsreel footage was then tacked on, showing nuclear explosions, thus making this the first Hollywood feature to deal with the A-bomb. Neal does a fine job with an impossible role but Hale is only a beautiful prop. It is the slippery Loo who gives an outstanding and memorable performance as the hateful enemy, the kind of role this Hawaiian-born actor brought to uneasy perfection.

p, J. Robert Bren; d, Gordon Douglas; w, Bren (based on a story by Bren and Gladys Atwater); ph, Harry J. Wild; m, Leigh Harline; ed, Philip Martin, Jr.; md, C. Bakaleinikoff; art d, Albert S. D'Agostino, Walter Keller; set d, Darrell Silvera, Charles Nields; tech adv, R. Andrew Smith.

War Drama (PR:C MPAA:NR)

FIRST YEAR, THE **½ (1932) 80m FOX c

Janet Gaynor (*Grace Livingston*), Charles Farrell (*Tommy Tucker*), Minna Gombell (*Mrs. Barstow*), Leila Bennett (*Hattie*), Dudley Digges (*Dr. Anderson*), Robert McWade (*Fred Livingston*), George Meeker (*Dick Loring*), Maude Eburne (*Emily Livingston*), Henry Kolker (*Pete Barstow*), Elda Vokel (*Helen*).

Gaynor and Farrell, major box office draws at the time, are newlyweds who move to a small country town. Gaynor becomes dissatisfied by the easygoing ways of her husband, and begins to fall for the advances of an old boy friend. Farrell has bought some property and sets up a sale to the railroad. He invites the buyers to a dinner which turns into a disaster, sending Gaynor scurrying back to her parents. After patching things up with the railroad men and completing the sale, he goes to his wife and saves their marriage. Similar treatment appeared in UP POPS THE DEVIL (1931) and a marvelous dining room scene was almost wholly lifted and perfected by director George Stevens in ALICE ADAMS (1935).

d, William K. Howard; w, Lynn Starling (adapted from a play by Frank Craven); ph, Hal Mohr; ed, Jack Murray.

Drama (PA:A MPAA:NR)

FISH HAWK* (1981, Can.) 95m AE c

Will Sampson (*Fish Hawk*), Charlie Fields (*Corby*), Geoffrey Bowes (*Towsack*), Mary Pirie (*Sarah*), Don Francks (*Deut*), Chris Wiggins (*Marcus*), Kay Hawtrey (*Mary*), Mavor Moore (*Joke*).

Tedious children's film stars Sampson as a drunken Indian trying to clean up his act for the sake of a young farm boy who looks up to him. Even kids will see through this Oh-so-nice movie.

p, Jon Slan; d, Donald Shebib; w, Blanche Hanalis (based on a novel by Mitchell Jayne); ph, Rene Verzier; m, Samuel Matlofsky; ed, Ron Wisman.

Children Cas. (PR:AA MPAA:G)

FISH THAT SAVED PITTSBURGH, THE* (1979) 104m UA c

Julius Erving (*Moses Guthrie*), Jonathan Winters (*H.S./Halsey Tilson*), Meadowlark Lemon (*Rev. Grady Jackson*), Jack Kehoe (*Setshot*), Kareem Abdul-Jabbar (*Himself*), Margaret Avery (*Toby Millman*), James Bond III (*Tyrone Millman*), Michael V. Gazzo ("*Harry the Trainer*"), Peter Isacksen ("*Driftwood*"), Nicholas Pryor (*George Brockington*), M. Emmet Walsh (*Wally Cantrell*), Stockard Channing (*Mona Mondieu*), Flip Wilson (*Coach "Jock" Delaney*), Marvin Albert (*Himself*), George Von Benko (*P.A. Announcer*), Debra Allen (*Ola*), Damian Austin (*Man Ordering*), Alfred Beard, Jr. (*Himself*), Dee Dee Bridgewater (*Brandy*), Alix Elias (*Michelle*), Julius J. Carry, III, Jerry Chambers, Malek Abdul Mansour, The Spinners, The Sylvers.

A basketball film that fails because of a nonexistent storyline, with the humor and plot running dry after the first 15 minutes. A losing Pittsburgh NBA team has all but one player quit the team. Erving is the only one to stay, and astrologer Channing and Bond get players that are happy with Dr. J's astrological sign (Pisces).

p, Gary Stromberg, David Dashev; d, Gilbert Moses; w, Jaison Starkes, Edmond Stevens (adapted from a story by Stromberg and Dashev); ph, Frank Stanley (Technicolor); m, Thom Bell; ed, Frank Mazzola, Arthur Schmidt, Bud Friedgen, Jr.; art d, Herbert Spencer Deverill; ch, Debra Allen.

Comedy Cas. (PA:A MPAA:PG)

FISHERMAN'S WHARF*½ (1939) 72m RKO bw

Bobby Breen (*Tony*), Leo Carrillo (*Carlo*), Henry Armetta (*Beppo*), Lee Patrick (*Stella*), Rosina Galli (*Angelina*), Tommy Bupp (*Rudolph*), George Humbert (*Pietro*), Leon Belasco (*Luigi*), Pua Lani, Leonard Kibrick, Jackie Salling, Ronnie Paige, Milo Marchetti, Jr. (*Tony's Gang*), Slicker the Seal.

Breen is an orphan adopted by a San Francisco fisherman, Carrillo. He runs away when Carrillo's widowed sister-in-law, Patrick, moves in with her brat son. Carrillo sets up a massive search and finally patches things up with his adopted singing son. Songs: "Fisherman's Chantey" (William Howe, Harlan Myers), "Sell Your Cares for a Song," (Charles Newman, Victor Young), "Blue Italian Waters" (Paul Francis Webster, Frank Churchill).

p, Sol Lesser; d, Bernard Vorhaus; w, Bernard Schubert, Ian McLellan Hunter, Herbert Clyde Lewis; ph, Charles Schoenbaum; ed, Arthur Hilton.

Drama (PR:AA MPAA:NR)

FIST IN HIS POCKET** (1968, Ital.) 105m Peppercorn-Wormser bw
(I PUGNI IN TASCA;
AKA: FISTS IN THE POCKET)

Lou Castel (*Alessandro*), Paola Pitagora (*Giulia*), Marino Mase (*Augusto*), Liliana Gerace (*Mother*), Pier Luigi Troglio (*Leone*), Jennie MacNeil (*Lucia*), Mauro Martini (*The Boy*), Gianni Schicchi (*Tonino*), Alfredo Filippazzi (*Doctor*), Gianfranco Cella (*Young Man at the Party*), Celestina Bellocchio (*Young Woman at the Party*),

Stefania Troglio (*Chambermaid*), Irene Agnelli (*Bruna*), Sandra Bergamini, Lella Bertante.

Sick but fascinating little drama about a family of crazed epileptics and their blind mother whose problems stifle the life of the one healthy member of the family, Mase, who wants to marry but feels that he cannot as long as his family is around to haunt him. His younger brother, Castel, feels guilty and wants to help Mase rid himself of their problems, so he decides to kill off the rest of the family so that Mase can use the inheritance to begin a new life. After doing the dirty deeds, Castel goes to his room, listens to a series of operatic arias and then has a severe epileptic seizure with no one around to help him except Pitagora, who won't.

p, Ezio Passadore; d&w, Marco Bellocchio; ph, Alberto Marrama; m, Ennio Morricone; ed, Aurelio Mangiarotti; art d, Gisella Longo.

Drama (PR:O MPAA:NR)

FIST OF FEAR, TOUCH OF DEATH zero (1980) 90m Aquarius Releasing Inc. c

Fred Williamson, Ron Van Clief, Adolph Caesar, Aaron Banks, Bill Louis, Teruyuki Higa, Gail Turner, Richard Barathy, Hollywood Browde, Louis Neglia, Cydra Karlyn, Annett Bronson, Ron Harvey, John Flood, film clips of Bruce Lee.

Another kung-fu film cashing in on the late Bruce Lee. Old film clips have been pieced together to tell the supposed story of Lee's childhood with bogus interviews.

p, Terry Levene; d, Matthew Mallinson; w, Ron Harvey (adapted from a story by Harvey and Mallinson); ph, John Hazard; m, Keith Mansfield; ed, Mallinson, Jeffrey Brown.

Kung Fu Cas. (PR:O MPAA:R)

FIST OF FURY (SEE: FISTS OF FURY, 1972, CHI.)

FISTFUL OF CHOPSTICKS, A (SEE: THEY CALL ME BRUCE, 1982)

FISTFUL OF DOLLARS, A* (1964, Ital./Ger./Span.) 100m Jolly Film/UA c (PER UN PUGNO DI DOLLARI)

Clint Eastwood (*The Man with No Name*), Marianna Koch (*Marisol*), John Wells [Gian Maria Volonte] (*Ramon Rojo*), Pepe Calvo (*Silvanito*), Wolfgang Lukschy (*John Baxter*), Sieghardt Rupp (*Esteban Rojo*), Antonio Prieto (*Benito Rojo*), Margarita Lozano (*Consuela Baxter*), Daniel Martin (*Julian*), Carol Brown [Bruno Carotentuto] (*Antonio Baxter*), Benito Stefanelli (*Rubio*), Richard Stuyvesant [Mario Brega] (*Chico*), Josef Egger (*Piripero*), Antonio Vica, Raf Baldassare, Johannes Siedel, Carla Calo.

A landmark Western that established the Clint Eastwood persona and revitalized a genre whose time had just about run out. The plot is deceptively simple—and is lifted from Japanese director Akira Kurosawa's 1961 classic YOJIMBO (as John Sturges' western THE MAGNIFICENT SEVEN had been taken from Kurosawa's masterpiece THE SEVEN SAMURAI (1954)). Eastwood, as the mysterious Man with No Name, rides into a small town embroiled in a struggle for power between two families. Eastwood hires himself out as a mercenary, first to one faction and then to the other, with no regard for honor or morality. He plays both sides against the middle, collecting his money, until he eventually destroys both, leaving the town to the bartender, coffin-maker, and bell ringer as he rides off into the desert from whence he came. The plot is simple and the Italian performances overblown (almost operatic), but Leone revitalizes the Western through a unique and complex visual style. The film is full of brilliant spatial relationships (extreme close-ups in the foreground, with detailed compositions visible in the background, punctuated by head-banging tight close-ups) combined with Ennio Morricone's vastly creative musical score full of grunts, wails, groans, and bizarre-sounding instruments that come together to give a wholly original perspective of the West and its myths. Leone originally wanted Henry Fonda to play an older Man with No Name, but couldn't afford him. His next choices were James Coburn and then Charles Bronson, but it was a young Clint Eastwood (who wanted to get out of the TV series "Rawhide") who eventually landed the part. Eastwood had a heavy hand in the interpretation of his role, stripping his part of most of its dialog. His character is wholly amoral, a mystery man with no past who relies on his skill with a gun and his cleverness. (Eastwood's character is shown to be surprisingly smart, using violence only when necessary.) This image, which he would hone to perfection in the subsequent Leone movies (FOR A FEW DOLLARS MORE and THE GOOD, THE BAD, AND THE UGLY) turned Eastwood into an almost mythical, incredibly popular, last-of-the-movie-stars performer, an image that the actor continues to examine and sometimes criticize (especially in the films where he directs himself). Though far from perfected in this film, Leone's style would mature through his next two films and peak with his masterpiece ONCE UPON A TIME IN THE WEST in 1969.

p, Arrigo Colombo, Giorgio Papi; d, Sergio Leone; w, Leone, Duccio Tessari, Victor A. Catena, G. Schock (based on the film YOJIMBO by Akira Kurosawa); ph, Jack Dalmas [Massimo Dallamano] (Techniscope, Technicolor); m, Ennio Morricone; ed, Roberto Cinquini.

Western Cas. (PR:C MPAA:NR)

FISTFUL OF DYNAMITE, A (SEE: DUCK, YOU SUCKER, 1972, Ital.)

FISTS OF FURY** (1973, Chi.) 103m NGP c
(AKA:THE BIG BOSS)

Bruce Lee (*Cheng*), Maria Yi (*Mei*), Han Ying Chieh (*Mi*), Tony Liu (*Mi's Son*), Malalene (*Prostitute*), Paul Tien (*Chen*), Miao Ke Hsiu (*Yuan*), Li Quinn, Chin Shan, Li Hua Sze, Robert Baker.

Lee is a kung-fu student out to avenge his boxing master's murder. He uncovers Japanese gangsters smuggling drugs, who killed the master when he discovered their doings. Comic book style story is only saved by Lee's amazing athletic and martial arts ability.

p, Raymond Chow; d&w, Lo Wei; ph, Chen Ching-chu; m, Ku Chih-hui; ed, Chang Ching-chu.

Martial Arts **Cas.** **(PR:O MPAA:R)**

FIT FOR A KING** (1937) 73m RKO bw

Joe E. Brown *(Virgil Jones)*, Helen Mack *(Jane Hamilton)*, Paul Kelly *(Briggs)*, Harry Davenport *(Archduke Julio)*, Halliwell Hobbes, *(Count Strunsky)*, John Qualen *(Otto)*, Donald Briggs *(Prince Michael)*, Frank Reicher *(Kurtz)*, Russell Hicks *(Mr. Hardwick)*, Charles Trowbridge *(Mr. Marshall)*.

Brown is a cub reporter on his uncle's newspaper, who is assigned to cover an aged archduke. He falls in love with the crown princess and uncovers a plot to murder her and her father. In a slapstick chase with automobiles, motorcycles, bicycles and Brown on a haycart, which falls apart, the assassination is thwarted and Brown gets the princess, now a queen.

p, David L. Loew; d, Edward Sedgwick; w, Richard Flournoy; ph, Paul Vogel; m, Arthur Morton; ed, Jack Ogilvie.

Comedy **(PR:A MPAA:NR)**

FITZCARRALDO**** (1982) 157m New World Pictures c

Klaus Kinski *(Brian Sweeney Fitzgerald/Fitzcarraldo)*, Claudia Cardinale *(Molly)*, Jose Lewgoy *(Don Aquilino)*, Miguel Angel Fuentes *(Cholo the Mechanic)*, Paul Hittscher *(Captain Orinoco Paul)*, Huerequeque Enrique Bohorquez *(Huerqueque the Cook)*, Grande Othelo *(Station Master)*, Peter Berling *(Opera Manager)*, David Perez Espinosa *(Chief of the Campa Indians)*, Milton Nascimento *(Black Man at Opera House)*, Rui Polanah *(Rubber Baron)*, Salvador Godinez *(Old Missionary)*, Dieter Milz *(Young Missionary)*, Bill Rose *(Notary)*, Leoncio Bueno *(Prison Guard)*, Ceriano Luchetti, Costante Moret, Dimiter Petkov, Jean-Claude Dreyfuss, Mietta Sighele, Lourdes Magalhaes, Isabel Jimines de Cisneros, Liborio Simonella, Jesus Goiri, Christian Mantilla *(Soloists in Opera Sequences)*, and the Ashininka-Campa Indians and their chiefs Miguel, Nicolas and Pascal Camaiteri Fernandez, the Campas Indians and their chief David Perez Espinosa, and the Machiguengas.

In a modern masterpiece, Kinski dreams of bringing opera and his avatar Caruso to the South American jungle. But with limited funding he must figure out how to finance the opera house. Deciding to capitalize on South America's rubber industry, Kinski sets out for a hidden forest of rubber trees that is well protected by rapids. However there is an alternative river on the other side of a small group of mountains. In order to get there, Kinski hires local natives to pull his steamship over the mountain: 320 tons up a 40-degree incline. The hauling of the boat is the heart of the film and no camera trickery is used. This is a real steamship being hauled over a real mountain. The seeming insurmountability of this labor and Kinski's determination to see it through parallels the story of FITZCARRALDO. Like Kinski's dream in the film, director Herzog's dream of making the film was an all-encompassing passion which to achieve he had to overcome incredible factors. The lead was originally played by Jason Robards, Jr. who dropped out after catching a jungle illness. Kinski, who had worked with Herzog in South America on AGUIRRE, THE WRATH OF GOD, was finally hired to play the lead. Numerous accidents and technical problems, along with a border skirmish that forced the production to move 1,500 miles to a new location, failed to discourage Herzog. "If I should abandon this film I should be a man without dreams. . . I live my life or end my life with this project," he said. FITZCARRALDO is a highly personal film, as much about the man who made it as it is about its ostensible subject. An interesting companion piece to FITZCARRALDO is BURDEN OF DREAMS, a documentary about Herzog and the making of this film.

p, Werner Herzog, Lucki Stipetic; d&w, Herzog; ph, Thomas Mauch; m, Popol Vuh; ed, Beate Mainka-Jellinghaus; art d, Henning von Gierke, Ulrich Bergfelder; cos, Gisela Storch.

Drama **Cas.** **(PR:C MPAA:NR)**

FITZWILLY** (1967) 102m UA c
(GB: FITZWILLY STRIKES BACK)

Dick Van Dyke *(Fitzwilliam)*, Barbara Feldon *(Juliet Nowell)*, Edith Evans *(Victoria Woodworth)*, John McGiver *(Albert)*, Harry Townes *(Mr. Nowell)*, John Fiedler *(Mr. Dunne)*, Norman Fell *(Oderblatz)*, Cecil Kellaway *(Buckmaster)*, Stephen Strimpell *(Byron Casey)*, Anne Seymour *(Grimsby)*, Helen Kleeb *(Mrs. Mortimer)*, Sam Waterston *(Oliver)*, Paul Reed *(Prettikin)*, Albert Carrier *(Pierre)*, Nelson Olmsted *(Simmons)*, Dennis Cooney *(Adams)*, Noam Pitlik *(Charles)*, Antony Eustrel *(Garland)*, Laurence Naismith *(Cotty)*, Karen Norris *(Kitty)*, Patience Cleveland *(Dolly)*, Lew Brown *(Frank)*, Monroe Arnold *(Goldfarb)*, Bob Williams *(Ryan)*, Billy Halop *(Restaurant Owner)*.

Van Dyke is the butler to elderly Evans, who isn't as wealthy as she thinks. To keep the illusion that she is, Van Dyke and the rest of the servants pull off a score of robberies. A mediocre comedy not helped by uninspired direction.

p, Walter Mirisch; d, Delbert Mann; w, Isobel Lennart (adapted from the novel *A Garden Of Cucumbers* by Poyntz Tyler); ph, Joseph Biroc (Panavision, DeLuxe Color); m, Johnny Williams; ed, Ralph Winters; art d, Robert F. Boyle; m/l, Alan and Marilyn Bergman.

Comedy **(PA:A MPAA:NR)**

FIVE** (1951) 93m COL bw

William Phipps *(Michael)*, Susan Douglas *(Roseanne)*, James Anderson *(Eric)*, Charles Lampkin *(Charles)*, Earl Lee *(Barnstaple)*.

Five people have survived a nuclear holocaust and live in a Frank Lloyd Wright-designed cliff house. A pregnant woman, a black doorman, a bank cashier, a frustrated idealist, and a mountain climber are the five survivors. They begin to die from radiation poisoning, and the black man is murdered so that there will be less competition for the one woman. The woman's baby dies when she and the murderer go into the city to search for her husband. The murderer dies of radiation, and the woman, Douglas, goes back to the house to start a new world with the surviving male, Phipps. An oversimplified and heavy-handed end-of-the-world film.

p,d&w, Arch Oboler; ph, Louis Clyde Stoumen, Sid Lubow; m, Henry Russell; ed, John Hoffman.

Drama **(PR:C MPAA:NR)**

FIVE AGAINST THE HOUSE*** (1955) 84m COL bw

Guy Madison *(Al Mercer)*, Kim Novak *(Kay Greylek)*, Brian Keith *(Brick)*, Alvy Moore *(Roy)*, William Conrad *(Eric Berg)*, Kerwin Mathews *(Ronnie)*, Jack Dimond *(Francis Spieglebauer)*, Jean Willes *(Virginia)*, John Zaremba *(Robert Fenton)*, George Brand *(Jack Roper)*, Mark Hanna *(Brad Lacey)*, Carroll McComas *(Mrs. Valent)*, Hugh Sanders *(Pat Winters)*.

Five college students, led by Madison, work out the perfect plan to rob a Reno casino, more as a joke or intellectual feat until Keith, who is heavily in debt and becoming mentally unbalanced, compels the group to go through with the crazy scheme. First Mathews works out the intricate plan to rob the real-life Harold's Club just to see if it will work, then he inveigles Madison and his lounge singer girl friend Novak into the scheme. Then psycho ex-GI Keith and student Moore, who thinks it's all a lark, join the group. Midway through the caper Madison is able to outwit Keith and talk him into surrendering to authorities. All in the cast are merely props to Keith's mentally askew character, a performance that is worth the whole film. Karlson's direction is top-drawer, in keeping with his superb film noir reputation. Silliphant's script is taut and literate, as well as accurate in portraying the follies of 1950s youth.

p, Stirling Silliphant; d, Phil Karlson; w, Silliphant, William Bowers, John Barnwell (based on a story by Jack Finney); ph, Lester White; m, George Duning; ed, Jerome Thoms; md, M.W. Stoloff; art d, Robert Peterson; set d, Frank Tuttle; cos, Jean Louis.

Crime Drama **(PR:C MPAA:NR)**

FIVE AND TEN**½ (1931) 88m COS/MGM bw
(AKA: DAUGHTER OF LUXURY)

Irene Rich *(Jenny Rarick)*, Marion Davies *(Jennifer)*, Leslie Howard *(Berry)*, Richard Bennett *(John Rarick)*, Kent Douglass *(Avery)*, Mary Duncan *(Muriel)*, Lee Beranger *(Leslie)*, Arthur Housman *(Piggy)*, George Irving *(Brooks)*, Halliwell Hobbes *(Hopkins)*, Charles Giblyn *(Dennison)*, Henry Armetta *(Taxi Driver)*, Ruth Selwyn *(Midge)*.

Davies becomes extremely wealthy because of her chain of five-and-dime stores, and is chased after by Howard. She rejects him, but when he marries, Davies wrecks the marriage. Sumptuous production lacks a solid story, but Howard is a standout.

d, Robert Z. Leonard; w, A.P. Younger, Edith Fitzgerald (adapted from the novel by Fannie Hurst); ph, George Barnes; ed, Margaret Booth.

Drama **(PR:A MPAA:NR)**

FIVE ANGLES ON MURDER**½ (1950, Brit.) 88m Javelin/GFD bw
(GB: THE WOMAN IN QUESTION)

Jean Kent *(Astra)*, Dirk Bogarde *(Bob Baker)*, John McCallum *(Murray)*, Susan Shaw *(Catherine)*, Hermione Baddeley *(Mrs. Finch)*, Charles Victor *(Pollard)*, Duncan MacRae *(Supt. Lodge)*, Lana Morris *(Lana)*, Joe Linnane *(Inspector Butler)*, Vida Hope *(Shirley)*, Bobbie Scroggins *(Alfie Finch)*, Duncan Lamont *(Barney)*, Anthony Dawson *(Wilson)*, Albert Chevalier *(Gunter)*, John Boxer, Julian d'Albie, Richard Pearson, Richard Dunn, John Martin, Ian Fleming, Josephine Middleton, Everley Gregg, Helen Goss, Nora Gordon, Merle Tottenham, Tom Macauley.

Fairground fortuneteller Kent is murdered, and police investigating the case get five different views of the victim through interviews with people who knew her. Finally police superintendant MacRae deduces the killer, mild-mannered shopkeeper Victor. A good idea that sputters out quickly.

p, Teddy Baird; d, Anthony Asquith; w, John Cresswell; ph, Desmond Dickinson; m, John Wooldridge; ed, John D. Guthridge; art d, Carmen Dillon.

Crime **(PR:A MPAA:NR)**

FIVE ASHORE IN SINGAPORE
(SEE: SINGAPORE, SINGAPORE, 1968)

FIVE BLOODY GRAVES (SEE: GUN RIDERS, 1970)

FIVE BOLD WOMEN** (1960) 82m Citation c

Jeff Morrow *(Kirk Reed)*, Merry Anders *(The Missouri Lady)*, Jim Ross *(The Missouri Kid)*, Irish McCalla *(Big Pearl)*, Guinn "Big Boy" Williams *(Big Foot)*, Kathy Marlowe *(Faro Kitty)*, Dee Carroll *(Crazy Hannah)*, Lucita Blain *(Maria The Knife)*, Robert Caffey, George Kramer.

Morrow is a U.S. Marshal who travels across Texas to bring five female murderers to prison. En route, however, Morrow and the gals must ward off the usual Indian attacks, battle the overpowering elements, and even control their romantic urges. By the finale a couple of the ladies, including leader Anders, become the victims of an Indian attack.

p, Jim Ross, Glenn H. McCarthy; d, Jorge Lopez-Portillo; w, Mortimer Braus, Jack Pollexfen; ph, (Eastmancolor).

Western **(PR:A MPAA:NR)**

FIVE BRANDED WOMEN***½ (1960) 100m PAR bw

Barbara Bel Geddes *(Marja)*, Silvana Mangano *(Jovanka)*, Vera Miles *(Daniza)*, Jeanne Moreau *(Ljuba)*, Carla Gravina *(Mira)*, Richard Basehart *(Capt. Reinhardt)*, Harry Guardino *(Branco)*, Steve Forrest *(Sgt. Keller)*, Alex Nicol *(Svenko)*, Pietro Germi *(Partisan Commander)*, Romolo Valli *(Mirko)*, Van Heflin *(Velko)*, Sid Clute

(Milan), Teresa Pellati *(Boja)*, Guido Celano, Franca Dominici, Gerard Herter, Aldo Silvani, Tiberio Mitri, Giacomo Rossi Stuart, Carlo Hinterman, Gerard Landry, Erwin Strahl, Bob Cunningham, Tonio Selwart, Vera Fusek, Nona Medici, Lina Rogers, Cyrus Elias.

A compelling story of the Yugoslavian underground's fight against the Nazis. (The five "branded" women have their heads shaved because of fraternization with the enemy.) The horrors of war and the toll it exacts from the people caught up in it are illuminated effectively through Ritt's direction and Perilli's screenplay.

p, Dino DeLaurentiis; d, Martin Ritt; w, Ivo Perilli (adapted from novel by Ugo Pirro); ph, Giuseppe Rotunno; m, Francesco Lavagnino; ed, Jerry Webb.

Drama **(PR:C MPAA:NR)**

FIVE CAME BACK½** (1939) 75m RKO bw

Chester Morris *(Bill)*, Lucille Ball *(Peggy)*, Wendy Barrie *(Alice Melhorne)*, John Carradine *(Crimp)*, Allen Jenkins *(Peter)*, Joseph Calleia *(Vasquez)*, C. Aubrey Smith *(Prof. Henry Spengler)*, Kent Taylor *(Joe)*, Patric Knowles *(Judson Ellis)*, Elisabeth Risdon *(Martha Spengler)*, Casey Johnson *(Tommy)*, Dick Hogan *(Larry)*.

A clipper plane crashes in a South American jungle with 12 passengers on board. The pilot and co-pilot struggle to repair the plane as conflicts between passengers flare up. They also have a tribe of headhunters to worry about. When the plane is fixed, only five can go back; the rest must stay and face the unfriendly natives. Remade as BACK FROM ETERNITY in 1956 by the same director.

p, Robert Sisk; d, John Farrow; w, Jerry Cady, Dalton Trumbo, Nathaniel West (adapted from a story by Richard Carroll); ph, Nicholas Musuraca; m, Roy Webb; ed, Harry Marker; art d, Van Nest Polglase.

Drama **Cas.** **(PR:A MPAA:NR)**

FIVE CARD STUD** (1968) 101m PAR c

Dean Martin *(Van Morgan)*, Robert Mitchum *(Rev. Rudd)*, Inger Stevens *(Lily Langford)*, Roddy McDowall *(Nick Evers)*, Katherine Justice *(Nora Evers)*, John Anderson *(Marshal Dana)*, Ruth Springford *(Mama Malone)*, Yaphet Kotto *(Little George)*, Denver Pyle *(Sig Evers)*, Bill Fletcher *(Joe Hurley)*, Whit Bissell *(Dr. Cooper)*, Ted De Corsia *(Eldon Bates)*, Don Collier *(Rowan)*, Roy Jenson *(Mace Jones)*, Boyd "Red" Morgan *(Fred Carson)*, George Rowbotham *(Stoney)*, Jerry Gatlin *(Stranger)*, Louise Lorimer *(Mrs. Wells)*, Hope Summers *(Woman Customer)*, Chuck Hayward *(O'Hara)*, Robert Hoy.

Five men lynch a card cheat and subsequently each is mysteriously knocked off. Martin, who tried to stop the hanging, sets out with gun-toting preacher Mitchum to find the murderer. A flat western that nosedives when the killer is unmasked halfway through the film.

p, Hal B. Wallis; d, Henry Hathaway; w, Marguerite Roberts (adapted from Ray Gaulden's novel); ph, Daniel L. Fapp (Technicolor); m, Maurice Jarre; ed, Warren Low; prod d, Walter Tyler.

Western **(PR:C MPAA:NR)**

FIVE DAYS (SEE: PAID TO KILL, 1954, Brit.)

FIVE DAYS FROM HOME*½ (1978) 108m UNIV c

George Peppard *(T. M. Pryor)*, Neville Brand *(Inspector Markley)*, Sherry Boucher *(Wanda Dulac)*, Victor Campos *(Jose Stover)*, Robert Donner *(Baldwin)*, Ronnie Claire Edwards *(Marian)*, Jessie Lee Fulton *(Mrs. Peabody)*, William Larsen *(J. J. Bester)*, Robert Magruder *(The Colonel)*, Savannah Smith *(Georgie Haskin)*, Don Wyse *(Howie)*, Ralph Story *(TV Newsman)*.

A bland thriller with Peppard, an ex-cop who killed his wife's lover, escaping from prison with only six days left to serve. He breaks out to see his seriously ill son. In his journey to his son, he encounters an assortment of characters, but among them Smith is the only stand-out. Brand is the ruthless lawman pursuing Peppard.

p&d, George Peppard; w, William Moore; ph, Harvey Genkins (CFI Color); m, Bill Conti; ed, Samuel E. Beetley; m/l, Norman Gimbel.

Action/Drama **(PR:C MPAA:PG)**

FIVE DAYS ONE SUMMER* (1982) 108m Ladd Company/WB c

Sean Connery *(Douglas)*, Betsy Brantley *(Kate)*, Lambert Wilson *(Johann)*, Jennifer Hilary *(Sarah)*, Isabel Dean *(Kate's Mother)*, Gerard Buhr *(Brendel)*, Anna Massey *(Jennifer Pierce)*, Sheila Reid *(Gillian Pierce)*, Georges Claisse *(Dieter)*, Kathy Marothy *(Dieter's Wife)*, Terry Kingley *(Georg)*, Emilie Lihou *(Old Woman)*, Alfred Schmidhauser *(Martin)*, Jerry Brouwer *(Van Royen)*, Alexander John *(MacLean)*, Robert Dietl *(Station Master)*, Gunther Clemens *(Guide)*, Michael Burrell *(Horse Taxi Driver)*, Skil Kaiser-Passini *(Eva)*, Marc Duret, Francois Caron, Benoist Ferreux *(French Students)*.

A disastrous disappointment from the acclaimed director of HIGH NOON and FROM HERE TO ETERNITY. Connery is on a Swiss Alps vacation in 1932 with a young woman, Brantley, he says is his wife. It turns out that she is his niece, who has had a crush on him since childhood. Connery goes on a dangerous mountain climb with a young Swiss guide, Wilson. Brantley has become attracted to him, also, and during the climb Connery flashbacks to reveal the true nature of his and Brantley's relationship. The film is lifeless, and that seems surprising since Zinnemann had been wanting to do the film for 40 years.

p&d, Fred Zinnemann; w, Michael Austin (based in part on Kay Boyle's short story, "Maiden Maiden"); ph, Giuseppe Rotunno (Technicolor); m, Elmer Bernstein; ed, Stuart Baird; ch, D'Dee.

Drama **Cas.** **(PR:A MPAA:PG)**

FIVE EASY PIECES***** (1970) 96m BBS/COL c

Jack Nicholson *(Robert Eroica Dupea)*, Karen Black *(Rayette Dipesto)*, Billy "Green" Bush *(Elton)*, Fannie Flagg *(Stoney)*, Sally Ann Struthers *(Betty)*, Marlena MacGuire *(Twinky)*, Richard Stahl *(Recording Engineer)*, Lois Smith *(Partita Dupea)*, Helena Kallianiotes *(Palm Apodaca)*, Toni Basil *(Terry Grouse)*, Lorna Thayer *(Waitress)*, Susan Anspach *(Catherine Van Ost)*, Ralph Waite *(Carl Fidelio Dupea)*, William Challee *(Nicholas Dupea)*, John Ryan *(Spicer)*, Irene Dailey *(Samia Glavia)*.

A wonderful film from the same people who brought us the incredibly successful EASY RIDER and the terribly disappointing HEAD. Instead of continuing in the free-wheeling tradition of EASY RIDER, director Rafelson decided to attack a much more conservative topic in an equally conservative fashion and the results were superb. (The title, incidentally, refers to a practice book seen on any youngster's piano.) Quality and care are in every frame, with none of the gimmickry or camera trickery so many directors were guilty of during this period. Nicholson is Robert Eroica Dupea, a roughneck in a California oil field. He's working with his best friend Bush and they spend most of their off-time downing beers, bowling, and just hanging out. Nicholson is from a family of musicians and he is a brilliant classical pianist who has given up the 88 keys in favor of another life. When Black, his witless waitress girl friend, announces that she's pregnant, he leaves his job and heads for Los Angeles to visit with Smith, his sister, who is also a pianist and about to record an album. Smith tells Nicholson that their father, Challee, has suffered a pair of strokes back at their home on Puget Sound and it might be nice if he visits the old man before death plays its coda on their father's life. When he tells Black of his northbound intentions, she convinces him to take her. They bid Bush and his wife Flagg goodbye and begin the drive to Washington. On the road, they pick up two lesbians, Kallianiotes and Basil, an ecological maniac and a neatness freak. Their incessant rhetorical chatter begins to irk Nicholson. In the funniest scene in the picture, the four of them walk into a typical roadside coffee shop where Nicholson orders a very simple meal but the waitress will allow no substitutions. All he wants is toast with his breakfast and he finally asks for "a chicken salad sandwich on toast, but throw the chicken away and I'll pay for the sandwich." One thing leads to another and a brouhaha occurs with Nicholson flying off the handle and all of them being tossed out of the diner. After dropping off the two women hitch-hikers, Nicholson parks Black in a motel and goes on to the family home. The surroundings are even drearier than he recalls after being away three years. Challee is in a wheelchair and unable to speak so Nicholson doesn't know if he's getting through to the old man. His brother, Waite, is a violinist affianced to Anspach, a pianist. Although they are apparently very unalike, Nicholson and Anspach are physically attracted to each other and when Waite leaves temporarily, the two of them make love in her room. She is a gentle soul and Nicholson is bubbling rage and yet they cannot keep away from each other. Black, who is, at best, sweet but cotton-headed, arrives at the family home. The others welcome her as cordially as they can but she is very out of place. (She can't, for example, believe there's no television set in the living room.) Nicholson attempts to convince Anspach to run away with him but they both know it won't work. In a touching scene, he explains to his ailing father why he's given up his music and attempts to apologize for his wastrel existence, then breaks into tears. When Dailey, a snobbish family acquaintance, makes fun of Black, Nicholson springs to her defense. Later, he discovers his father's burly male nurse massaging his semi-nude sister, Smith. Enraged, he picks a fight with the muscle-bound nurse and gets knocked on his keester for his efforts. Now, he exits with Black, stops at a gas station—and abandons her, his car and all of his possessions to jump aboard a truck on its way to Alaska and, perhaps, a new start for a life that seems to be filled with nothing but endings. The film grossed less than $10 million first time around, but everyone who saw FIVE EASY PIECES had to have been moved by it. Nicholson was supremely convincing in the role, and every supporting role, down to the smart-alec waitress, Thayer, was exquisitely cast. It's a perfect portrait of a man between life-styles, careers, and totally out of his element wherever he goes. But instead of reaching for the 1960s rebelliousness so often seen in minor movies, Rafelson and screenwriter Joyce (a pseudonym for Carol Eastman) opted for a unique telling of what might have been a tiresome film in other hands. There is more character study than story, and there is no compelling tension to the tale, other than the excellence of the players. Possibly one cares about Nicholson and the others but without the deep-down gut-wrenching that might have been evinced with some minor alterations, but that's just a quibble about an otherwise satisfying film. The search for a person's identity has seldom been better shown. In a small role as Betty, look for Sally Struthers (when she was still using her middle name and before she achieved nationwide fame on TV's "All In The Family"). Karen Black adds one more unusual portrait to her gallery of excellent performances. She has never been afraid to look ugly, to sweat, to do anything to convince us that she is who we think she is on screen. She won the 1970 New York Film Critics award for this role as well as an Oscar nomination. The picture, the script, and Nicholson were also nominated but failed to win because of the PATTON sweep that year. Deceptively simple, it's one of the most complex pictures of the 1970s.

p, Bob Rafelson, Richard Wechsler; d, Rafelson; w, Adrien Joyce [Carol Eastman] (from a story by Joyce and Bob Rafelson); ph, Laszlo Kovacs (Movielab Color); m, Bach, Mozart, Chopin; ed, Gerald Shepard, Christopher Holmes; int des, Toby Rafelson; cos, Bucky Rous; m/l, Billy Sherill, Tammy Wynette, Bobby Braddock, Merle Kilgore, Sonny Williams, Claude Putnam, Jr., H. Cochran; piano solo, Pearl Kaufman.

Drama **(PR:C-O MPAA:R)**

FIVE FINGER EXERCISE*½ (1962) 108m COL bw

Rosalind Russell *(Louise Harrington)*, Jack Hawkins *(Stanley Harrington)*, Maximilian Schell *(Walter)*, Richard Beymer *(Philip Harrington)*, Annette Gorman *(Pamela Harrington)*, Lana Wood *(Mary)*, Todd Armstrong *(Tony Blake)*, Terry Huntington *(Helen)*, William Quinn *(Salesman)*, Kathy West *(Alice)*, Valora Noland *(Girl)*, Mary Benoit *(Woman)*, Bart Conrad *(Announcer)*, Karen Parker, Jeannine Riley *(Girls)*.

A contrived melodrama adapted from a hit play, this film has Russell as the pseudo-intellectual mother, Hawkins as the rude, intolerant businessman father, Beymer as a mama's boy, and Gorman as the high-spirited daughter. This

California family takes in a German refugee, Schell, as a tutor, who tries to become part of the family, but Russell doesn't like how he goes about it. Feeling increasingly alienated, the German tries to take his life, and this action—somehow, for unexplained reasons—brings everyone together.

p, Fredrick Brisson; d, Daniel Mann; w, Frances Goodrich, Albert Hackett (adapted from a play by Peter Shaffer); ph, Harry Stradling; m, Jerome Moross; ed, William A. Lyon; Ms. Russell's gowns, Orry-Kelly.

Drama **(PR:A MPAA:NR)**

FIVE FINGERS**** (1952) 108m FOX bw (AKA: OPERATION CICERO)

James Mason *(Cicero)*, Danielle Darrieux *(Anna)*, Michael Rennie *(George Travers)*, Walter Hampden *(Sir Frederic)*, Oscar Karlweis *(Moyzisch)*, Herbert Berghof *(Col. von Richter)*, John Wengraf *(Von Papen)*, A. Ben Astar *(Siebert)*, Roger Plowden *(MacFadden)*, Michael Pate *(Morrison)*, Ivan Triesault *(Steuben)*, Hannelore Axman *(Von Papen's Secretary)*, David Wolfe *(Da Costa)*, Larry Dobkin *(Santos)*, Nestor Paiva *(Turkish Ambassador)*, Antonio Filauri *(Italian Ambassador)*, Richard Loo *(Japanese Ambassador)*, Keith McConnell *(Johnson)*, Jeroma Moshan *(Char Woman)*, Alberto Morin *(Butler)*, Stuart Hall *(British Military Attache)*, Otto Waldis *(Pullman Porter)*, Frank Hemingway *(Narrator)*, Leo Mostovoy *(Spectator)*, Sadik Tarlan, Eghiche Harout *(Men)*, Konstantin Shayne *(Proprietor)*, Marc Snow *(Banker)*, Martin Garralaga *(Butler)*, Lumsden Hare, Stanley Logan *(M.P.s)*, Lester Mathews *(Under Secretary)*, Salvador Baguez *(Ship's Captain)*, Faith Kruger *(German Singer)*, John Sutton *(Narrator)*.

Mason is a valet working for the British Ambassador in Ankara who goes into the espionage business after learning of the top secret documents passing through ambassador Hampden's office safe. He begins photocopying the important papers and selling these to the Germans under the pseudonym of "Cicero," receiving huge payments in return. Using a down-and-out but attractive noblewoman, Darrieux, as a front, he sets her up in a sumptuous mansion and there meets with German agents to negotiate more purchases of secret papers. The Germans keep buying, particularly after Wengraf, playing the real Von Papen, thinks the documents are genuine, although the German high command considers Cicero's secrets too incredible to accept, even the real time and date of the invasion of Europe. The Germans are afraid, however, to shut off the flow of information, and they keep purchasing Cicero's documents. The British finally discover a leak in the embassy, and Rennie leads a team of agents to unearth the spy. Just before they arrest Mason, he flees with a fortune in what he later realizes is counterfeit money. The Germans have double-crossed him and most of his hazardous work has been for nothing. With no fortune left to him, exiled in a strange land (Rio), Darrieux adds the final failure by leaving him. Mankiewicz's direction is almost flawless as he holds suspense from beginning to end, superbly aided by the quick cameras of cinematographer Brodine. The script by Wilson is tight and fascinating. Cicero really existed and he managed to sell German intelligence 35 top secret documents. Oddly, the Nazis never acted on one of them. Mason is a suave wonder to behold as the shifty, ever-on-the-alert Albanian valet who outwitted British intelligence. Mankiewicz is not credited with any scriptwriting, but he did add much dialog and even some jokes to the screenplay.

p, Otto Lang; d, Joseph L. Mankiewicz; w, Michael Wilson (based on the book *Operation Cicero* by L. C. Moyzisch); ph, Norbert Brodine; m, Bernard Herrmann; ed, James B. Clark; art d, Lyle Wheeler, George W. Davis; spec eff, Fred Sersen.

Thriller/Spy Drama **(PR:A MPAA:NR)**

FIVE FINGERS OF DEATH* (1973, Hong Kong) 104m Shaw Brothers/WB c (AKA: HAND OF DEATH)

Lo Lieh *(Chao Chi-hao)*, Wang Ping *(Sung)*, Wang Chin-Feng *(Yen)*, Nan-Kung Hsun *(Han)*, Tien Feng *(Meng)*, Chao Hsiung *(Okada)*, Tung Lin *(Meng)*.

Lieh is a student at a martial arts academy who is given the secret of the "Iron Fist," which allows him to win the national karate tournament, as well as defeat the evil karate experts who want to stop him. Routine martial arts stuff, but this is the one that first became a hit in the United States and opened the floodgates for all those to follow.

p, Run Run Shaw; d, Cheng Chang Ho; w, Chiang Yang; ph, Wang Yunglung (DeLuxe Color).

Martial Arts **(PR:O MPAA:R)**

FIVE GATES TO HELL*** (1959) 98m FOX bw

Neville Brand *(Chen Pamok)*, Benson Fong *(Gung Sa)*, Ken Scott *(Dr. John Richter)*, John Morley *(Dr. Jacques Minelle)*, Dolores Michaels *(Athena)*, Patricia Owens *(Joy)*, Gerry Gaylor *(Greta)*, Nobu McCarthy *(Chioko)*, Greta Chi *(Yoette)*, Nancy Kulp *(Susette)*, Linda Wong *(Ming Cha)*, Irish McCalla *(Sister Magdelana)*, Shirley Knight *(Sister Maria)*.

Two doctors, seven nurses, and a nun are abducted by guerillas in Vietnam during the French involvement there (Indochina) in the 1950s. They're taken captive to use their skills to save a dying war-lord. The women are also given to the soldiers for sexual pleasure. They are unable to save the war-lord and when the guerillas are away on a raid, the doctors and nurses make an escape attempt. Both doctors and several of the women are killed, as are most of their guards. Clavell brings a sensitivity to the film that in other hands might have become just another war melodrama (Clavell spent five years as a prisoner of war in the Pacific during WW II). Oriental customs and thinking are portrayed insightfully, and Clavell also suggests that women are stronger and more organized than men.

p,d,&w, James Clavell; ph, Sam Leavitt (CinemaScope); m, Paul Dunlap; ed, Harry Gerstud; art d, Lyle R. Wheeler, John Mansbridge.

War **(PR:O MPAA:NR)**

FIVE GIANTS FROM TEXAS** (1966, Ital./Span.) 101m Miro Cinematografica/P.C. Balcazar (I CINQUE DELLA VENDETTA)

Guy Madison, Monica Randall, Vidal Molino, Molina Rojo, Vassili Karamesinis, Giovanni Cianfriglia.

Madison is an American defending the land he snatched from Mexican peasants and bandidos. Madison was one of the first Americans to leave Hollywood for cheap European films, eventually ending up in spaghetti westerns such as this.

p, Roberto Capitani, Aldo Ricci; d, Aldo Florio; w, Alfonso Balcazar, Joe Antonio de la Loma Hernandez; ph, Victor Montreal.

Western **(PR:C MPAA:NR)**

FIVE GOLDEN DRAGONS½** (1967, Brit.) 70m WB-Pathe/Anglo Amalgamated c

Robert Cummings *(Bob Mitchell)*, Rupert Davies *(Comm. Sanders)*, Margaret Lee *(Magda)*, Maria Perschy *(Margret)*, Klaus Kinski *(Gert)*, Brian Donlevy *(Dragon)*, Dan Duryea *(Dragon)*, Christopher Lee *(Dragon)*, George Raft *(Dragon)*, Maria Rohm *(Ingrid)*, Sieghardt Rupp *(Peterson)*.

Oriental intrigue for Cummings; he's a member of the American jet set visiting Hong Kong. Regrettably, no one has told him about Christopher Lee's group of baddies, the Five Golden Dragons. Lee's about to make his last sales pitch to the Mafia when Cummings gets involved. Lots of action and murder. Don't miss Raft's cameo in a kimono.

p, Harry Alan Towers; d, Jeremy Summers; w, Peter Welbeck [Towers]; ph, John von Kotze (CinemaScope, Technicolor); m, Malcolm Lockyer; ed, Donald J. Cohen; m/l, Lockyer, Hal Shaper, Sid Colin.

Action/Drama **(PR:O MPAA:NR)**

FIVE GOLDEN HOURS½** (1961, Brit.) 89m Anglofilm/COL

Ernie Kovacs *(Aldo Bondi)*, Cyd Charisse *(Baronessa Sandra)*, George Sanders *(Mr. Bing)*, Kay Hammond *(Martha)*, Dennis Price *(Raphael)*, Clelia Matania *(Rosalia)*, John LeMesurier *(Dr. Alfieri)*, Finlay Currie *(Fr. Superior)*, Reginald Beckwith *(Brother Geronimo)*, Avice Landone *(Beatrice)*, Sydney Tafler *(Alfredo)*, Martin Benson *(Enrico)*, Bruno Barnabe *(Cesare)*, Ron Moody *(Gabrielle)*, Leonard Sachs *(Mr. Morini)*, Marianne Stone *(Tina)*, Gordon Phillott *(Old Monk)*, Georgina Cookson *(Lady Passenger)*, Hy Hazell, Joy Shelton *(Lady Guests)*, Maya Fabio *(Aldo's Nurse)*.

Kovacs, whose real niche was pioneering TV comedy, has his hands full trying to keep this weak script from collapsing. He's a professional mourner and pallbearer who takes advantage of wealthy widows. When he falls in love with sexy Charisse, a broke baroness, he collects money from three other widows to try to double it for her. Charisse disappears with the money, however, and to avoid explaining what happened, Kovacs tries to knock off the widows. When that fails, he pretends to be crazy. He finds Charisse and marries her; she has an eye on his fortune and untimely death. Sanders gives a rare performance as a fellow fake lunatic in the asylum where Kovacs schemes his way to fortune.

p&d, Mario Zampi; w, Hans Wilhelm; ph, Christopher Challis; m, Stanley Black; ed, Bill Lewthwaite; art d, Ivan King.

Comedy **(PR:A MPAA:NR)**

FIVE GRAVES TO CAIRO**** (1943) 96m PAR bw

Franchot Tone *(John J. Bramble)*, Anne Baxter *(Mouche)*, Akim Tamiroff *(Farid)*, Erich von Stroheim *(Field Marshal Rommel)*, Peter Van Eyck *(Lt. Schwegler)*, Fortunio Bonanova *(Gen. Sebastiano)*, Konstantin Shayne *(Maj. von Buelow)*, Fred Nurney *(Maj. Lamprecht)*, Miles Mander *(British Colonel)*, Leslie Denison *(British Captain)*, Ian Keith *(British Captain)*, Bud Geary *(English Tank Commander)*, Frederick Giermann *(German Sergeant)*, Bill Mussetter *(Schwegler, Body Guard)*, John Royce *(German Technician)*, Otto Reichow *(German Engineer)*, Clyde Jackman *(Rommel's Orderly)*, Sam Waagenaar *(Rommel's Orderly)*, Peter F.U. Pohlney *(German Soldier)*, John Erickson *(1st Soldier)*, Philip Ahn *(2nd Soldier)*, Hans Maebus *(3rd Soldier)*, Roger Creed *(4th Soldier)*.

This is a witty and tense WW II espionage film with a superlative performance from Tone as a British enlisted man stranded in a desert town which suddenly fills up with German troops. Tone assumes the role of a dead servant at the hotel run by Tamiroff and Baxter. Housekeeper Baxter is a French woman deeply resentful of the British for leaving behind French troops, including her brother, at Dunkirk, when they evacuated their troops in 1940. She reluctantly allows Tone to assume his false identity while the hotel is suddenly taken over by headquarters troops heralding the arrival of Germany's most daring military leader, Field Marshal Erwin Rommel, played to the hilt as a brutal Hun by von Stroheim. Tone hobbles about on a shoe especially built for the club-footed servant who is buried under the rubble of a bomb explosion in the hotel's basement. He quickly realizes, when von Stroheim's aide, Van Eyck, approaches him and reads from a notebook, that his impersonation is even more hazardous than he envisioned, and that the dead man was really a Nazi spy who had been supplying von Stroheim with information. Tone manages to convince the Germans, and the strutting von Stroheim, that he is indeed, a spy in their employ, and he is instructed to go to Cairo to prepare for von Stroheim's entry with his victorious armies. A group of British soldiers are brought as prisoners to the hotel and Tone makes contact with the commanding officer, Mander, who orders him to find out what he can from von Stroheim regarding his battle plans, particularly where his huge caches of supplies are hidden, by which he fuels, arms, and feeds his fast-moving Africa Corps as it moves toward Cairo. Von Stroheim has already played the genial host with his British prisoners, taunting his enemies with his ability to strike with lightning speed, seemingly able to have his tanks move with the aid of an invisible supply line. Tone busies himself with unearthing the secret while Baxter plays up to Van Eyck, then Von Stroheim, trying to persuade them to contact authorities in Berlin and have her brother released from a concentration camp. Van Eyck merely toys with her, but von Stroheim rejects her plea out of hand. Then Tone discovers the clever secret of the hidden supplies, but he is about to be exposed as an imposter by Van Eyck who finds the real servant's body in the basement during an air raid. Tone and Van Eyck race about the hotel during the raid, exchanging gunfire until Van Eyck is killed. Tone is then sent on his way by von Stroheim, who later learns of Van Eyck's murder. He confronts Tamiroff and Baxter. The girl is about to give Tone away but takes the blame for the killing, lambasting von Stroheim and the Nazis in a defiant speech. Tone makes it back to British lines, turning over his information to superiors. After the British counter-attack at El Alamein, Tone fights along with them in a tank, finally returning to the little desert town. He learns from Tamiroff that Baxter is dead, executed for killing Van Eyck. Tone places a parasol on Baxter's grave, one he had bought for her in Cairo, promising her that all the Germans will be driven out of the desert. He then hurries to catch up with his tank column. The dialog in FIVE GRAVES TO CAIRO is exceptional, crackling through almost every frame in this first production where the electric writing team of Wilder and Brackett, who had collaborated on many fine scripts, became a director-producer team. The results are stunning, particularly with Seitz's lensing. Rozsa's music, however moving, seems to be almost a direct lift from Max Steiner's brilliant score for SAHARA, 1943. The polished and urbane Tone was never better than in this suspenseful cat-and-mouse war drama, as are Baxter and the sluggish but lovable Tamiroff. Van Eyck is properly sleazy as the conniving Nazi aide and Bonanova is a standout as an opera-loving Italian general. Von Stroheim is simply marvelous as a sneering, arrogant Rommel. Wilder opens his scene with a close-up on the back of his heavily-creased neck bursting over a high military collar, a play on von Stroheim's own silent films where von Stroheim similarly profiled the evil Huns of WW I.

p, Charles Brackett; d, Billy Wilder; w, Brackett, Wilder (based on a play "Hotel Imperial" by Lajos Biro); ph, John F. Seitz; m, Miklos Rozsa; ed, Doane Harrison; art d, Hans Dreier, Ernst Fegte; set d, Bertram Granger; cos, Edith Head.

War Drama (PR:A MPAA:NR)

FIVE GUNS TO TOMBSTONE½ (1961) 71m UA bw

James Brown (Billy Wade), John Wilder (Ted Wade), Walter Coy (Ike Garvey), Robert Karnes (Matt Wade), Joe Haworth (Hoke), Quent Sondergaard (Hank), Boyd Morgan (Hoagie), Jon Locke (Kolloway), Della Sharman (Arlene), Jeff DeBenning, Gregg Palmer, Willis Bouchey, John Eldredge, Brad Trumbull, Willis Robards, Jerry Todd, Boyd Stockman, Al Wyatt, Bob Woodward.

Brown is a retired gunslinger whose brother, Karnes, escapes from prison and is hired for a bank heist he gets Brown involved. Brown goes undercover for the authorities and foils the heist. Lots of action, and that's all.

p, Robert E. Kent; d, Edward L. Cahn; w, Richard Schayer, Jack DeWitt (adapted from a story by Arthur Orloff); ph, Maury Gertsman; m, Paul Sawtell; ed, Bernard Small; art d, Serge Krizman.

Western (PR:A MPAA:NR)

FIVE GUNS WEST** (1955) 78m American Releasing Corp. c

John Lund (Govern Sturges), Dorothy Malone (Shalee), Michael "Touch" Connors (Hale Clinton), Bob Campbell (John Candy), Jonathan Haze (Billy Candy), Paul Birch (J.C. Haggard), James Stone (Uncle Mime), Jack Ingram (Jethro), Larry Thor (Confederate Captain).

Corman's first directorial effort has Lund as a Confederate officer who leads a band of prisoners after a shipment of Union gold. They're also gunning for traitor Ingram, who's on the same stagecoach. Marketed for the drive-in crowd and similar to the B-westerns of Republic.

p&d, Roger Corman; w, R. Wright Campbell; ph, Floyd Crosby (Pathe Color); ed, Ronald Sinclair; md, Buddy Bregman.

Western (PR:A MPAA:NR)

FIVE LITTLE PEPPERS AND HOW THEY GREW** (1939) 58m COL bw

Edith Fellows (Polly Pepper), Clarence Kolb (Mr. King), Dorothy Peterson (Mrs. Pepper), Ronald Sinclair (Jasper), Charles Peck (Ben Pepper), Tommy Bond (Joey Pepper), Jimmy Leake (Davie Pepper), Dorothy Ann Seese (Phronsie Pepper), Leonard Carey (Martin), Bruce Bennett (Chauffeur), Paul Everton (Townsend), George Lloyd (Truck Driver), Edward Le Saint (Dr. Emery), Linda Winters [Dorothy Comingore] (Nurse), Harry Hayden (Dr. Spence), Betty Roadman (Cook), Bessie Wade (Asst. Cook), Harry Bernard (Caretaker), Maurice Costello (Hart), Flo Campbell (Woman).

Routine family film about Mrs. Pepper and her five kids. Mom works at a factory, while the oldest Pepper, Fellows, takes care of the clan. She becomes friends with Sinclair, a rich boy who sneaks over to play with the Peppers. When the youngest Pepper gets the measles, Sinclair and his grandfather, Kolb, are stuck in the quarantined house. Fellows collapses from too much work, and Kolb moves the whole family to his mansion. Things get even brighter when it's discovered that Fellows has inherited controlling shares in a mine that Kolb wants to buy. (See FIVE LITTLE PEPPERS series, Index.)

p, Jack Fier; d, Charles Barton; w, Nathalie Bucknall, Jefferson Parker (based on the novel Five Little Peppers and How They Grew by Margaret Sidney); ph, Henry Freulich; ed, James Sweeney.

Comedy/Drama (PR:AA MPAA:NR)

FIVE LITTLE PEPPERS AT HOME½ (1940) 67m COL bw

Edith Fellows (Polly Pepper), Dorothy Ann Seese (Phronsie), Clarence Kolb (Mr. King), Dorothy Peterson (Mrs. Pepper), Ronald Sinclair (Jasper), Charles Peck (Ben), Tommy Bond (Joey), Bobby Larson (Davie), Rex Evans (Martin), Herbert Rawlinson (Decker), Laura Treadwell (Aunt Martha), Spencer Charters (Mr. Shomer), Bruce Bennett (King's Chauffeur), Jack Rice (Bainbridge), Edward Le Saint (Dr. Emery), Ann Doran (Nurse), Paul Everton (Townsend), John Dilson

(Daniels), Joe DeStefani (Hart), Richard Fiske (Wilcox Chauffeur), Tom London (Miner), Sam Ash (Hartley), Marin Sais (Neighbor Woman).

Continues where FIVE LITTLE PEPPERS left off, but far less entertaining. Ma Pepper (Peterson) and Mr. King (Kolb) struggle to keep from going bankrupt, with all the little Peppers helping out. A little excitement emerges when the children become briefly trapped in a copper mine cave-in. (See FIVE LITTLE PEPPERS series, Index.)

d, Charles Barton; w, Harry Sauber (adapted from the novel Five Little Peppers and How They Grew by Margaret Sidney); ph, Allen G. Siegler; m, M. W. Stoloff; ed, Viola Lawrence.

Comedy/Drama (PR:AA MPAA:NR)

FIVE LITTLE PEPPERS IN TROUBLE* (1940) 63m COL bw

Edith Fellows (Polly), Dorothy Ann Seese (Phronsie), Dorothy Peterson (Mrs. Pepper), Pierre Watkin (Mr. King), Ronald Sinclair (Jasper), Charles Peck (Ben), Tommy Bond (Joey), Bobby Larson (Davie), Rex Evans (Martin), Kathleen Howard (Mrs. Wilcox), Mary Currier (Mrs. Lansdowne), Helen Brown (Miss Roland), Betty Jane Graham (May), Shirley Mills (June), Shirley Jean Rickert (Kiki), Antonia Oland (Pam), Rita Quigley (Peggy), Beverly Michaelson (Dorothy), Judy Lynn (Betty), Bess Flowers (Miss Roberts), Reginald Simpson (Mr. Corman), Carlton Griffin (Mr. Barnes), Sue Ann Burnett (Madeline), Fred Mercer (Tim), Billy Lechner (Tom), Ruth Robinson (Miss Simpson), Robert Carson (King's Chauffeur), Eddie Laughton (Wilcox's Chauffeur), Ann Barlow (Cynthia).

The main trouble with this film is that there exists no reason for it. In this third and worst of the Pepper series, the Pepper kids and Jasper (Sinclair) are sent to boarding school and cause a lot of predictable problems. (See FIVE LITTLE PEPPERS series, Index.)

d, Charles Barton; w, Harry Rebuas (adapted from the novel Five Little Peppers and How They Grew by Margaret Sidney); ph, Benjamin Kline; ed, Robert Fantl.

Comedy/Drama (PR:A MPAA:NR)

FIVE MAN ARMY, THE** (1970, Ital.) 105m Tiger Film/MGM c (UN ESERCITO DI 5 UOMINI)

Peter Graves (Dutchman), James Daly (Augustus), Bud Spencer (Mesito), Tetsuro Tamba (Samurai), Nino Castelnuovo (Luis Dominguez), Daniela Giordano (Maria), Claudio Gora (Manuel Estaban), Annabella Andreoli (Perla), Carlo Alighiero (Gutierrez), Jack Stuart (Mexican Officer), Marc Lawrence (Carnival Barker), Jose Torres (Mexican Spy), Marino Mase (Train Engineer).

During the 1914 Mexican Revolution four men rescue a comrade. With their collective knowledge of samurai, dynamite, and train robbing, they set off to rob an evil general's $500,000 railway gold shipment. It's sort of a DIRTY DOZEN or MAGNIFICENT SEVEN for the spaghetti western fan: a predictable script and lackluster direction backed with Hollywood stars.

p, Italo Zingarelli; d, Don Taylor; w, Dario Argento, Marc Richards; ph, Enzo Barboni (Metrocolor); m, Ennio Morricone; ed, Sergio Montanari; art d, Enzo Bulgarelli; set d, Ennio Michettoni; cos, Bulgarelli, Luciano Sagoni.

Western (PR:C MPAA:GP)

FIVE MILES TO MIDNIGHT* (1963, U.S./Fr./Ital.) 110m Filmsonor-Dear Film/UA bw

Sophia Loren (Lisa Macklin), Anthony Perkins (Robert Macklin), Gig Young (David Barnes), Jean-Pierre Aumont (Alan Stewart), Yolande Turner (Barbara Ford), Tommy Norden (Johnny), Mathilde Casadesus (Mme. Duval de Concierge), Billy Kearns (Capt. Wade), Barbara Nicot (Mrs. Wade), Louis Falavigna (Pharmacist), Elina Labourdette (Mme. Lafont), Regine (Regine), Pascale Roberts (Streetwalker), Sophie Real (Housemaid), Jean Ozenne (Mons. Babasse), Clement Harari (Mons. Schmidt), Nicolas Vogel (Eric Ostrum), Giselle Preville (Mrs. Harrington), Jean Hebey (Nikandros), Yves Brainville (Mons. Dompier), Guy Laroche (Guy Laroche), Jacques Marin, Jacqueline Porel.

Tawdry little melodrama has sexy Sophia marrying neurotic Perkins, a jealous, paranoid American youth. When he catches her doing a hip-grinding, butt-bouncing Twist in front of salivating nightclubbers in a Paris bistro, Perkins explodes and slaps her. Before he departs on a business trip, Loren tells Perkins she never wants to see him again. She is later horrified when learning that his plane has crashed and all on board are killed. Returning home, her horror changes to shock when she finds Perkins waiting for her—dirty, bruised, and desperate with a scheme to defraud the airline. He intends to collect $120,000 in coverage he took out before takeoff and tells Loren he plans to play dead. She will collect the money for him, he tells her, and then he will be out of her life. Loren seeks advice from Aumont and Young, two journalists she has been seeing, but they are of little help. Her life is made more complicated by insurance investigators plaguing her and Perkins' volatile behavior as he remains in hiding. Finally, she collects and the pair drive to the Belgium border. Here Perkins tells Loren that he never had any intention of giving up his exhibitionist wife, that she will stay with him for life. Loren panics and runs him over in her car, then returns to Young who calls police to set this mess right. This was a sorry disappointment for the gifted director Litvak and none of the plot works, the leads being too lightweight to carry the heavy tale. Loren shows her animal attractiveness and more or less babies Perkins who acts like a motherless child in her fleshy embrace. Beyond that, the acting is miserable. Loren lumbers about with a stare to replace emotional reaction to events and Perkins twitches through his role like a person going through electric shock treatment. The two were paired for this dismal drama after their appearance in DESIRE UNDER THE ELMS (1958) and that film didn't work either. Five minutes were deleted from the U.S. release of this film, which was shot in Paris.

p&d, Anatole Litvak; w, Peter Viertel, Hugh Wheeler; ph, Henri Alekan; m, Mikis Theodorakis; ed, Bert Bates; art d, Alexander Trauner; cos, Guy Laroche.

Drama (PR:O MPAA:NR)

FIVE MILLION YEARS TO EARTH✶✶✶½ (1968, Brit.) 98m Hammer-Seven Arts/FOX c
(GB: QUATERMASS AND THE PIT)

James Donald (*Dr. Matthew Roney*), Andrew Keir (*Prof. Bernard Quatermass*), Barbara Shelley (*Barbara Judd*), Julian Glover (*Col. Breen*), Duncan Lamont (*Sladden*), Bryan Marshall (*Capt. Potter*), Peter Copley (*Howell*), Edwin Richfield (*Minister*), Grant Taylor (*Sgt. Ellis*), Maurice Good (*Sgt. Cleghorn*), Robert Morris (*Watson*), Sheila Steafel (*Journalist*), Hugh Futcher (*Sapper West*), Thomas Heathcote (*Vicar*), Keith Marsh (*Johnson*), James Culliford (*Cpl. Gibson*), Bee Duffell (*Miss Dobson*), Hugh Morton (*Elderly Journalist*), Noel Howlett (*Abbey Librarian*), Hugh Manning (*Pub Customer*), June Ellis (*Blonde*), Roger Avon (*Electrician*), Brian Peck (*Technical Officer*), John Graham (*Inspector*), Charles Lamb (*Newsvendor*).

The third and best of the Quatermass films. The other two are THE CREEPING UNKNOWN and ENEMY FROM SPACE. In this, an alien spaceship is unearthed during construction work in a London subway. At first, it's thought to be an undetonated bomb from WW II, but then the scientists realize it's a Martian spacecraft that is protected by a mental energy. They tap into the energy and discover that the aliens started the evolution process to make better slaves out of apes. The Martians died and man was left on his own. The scientists also find a device inside the craft that incites violence in people, and they accidentally let loose a destructive monster on London, which one of the scientists destroys, but at the cost of his own life. This film was followed by QUATERMASS CONCLUSION.

p, Anthony Nelson-Keys; d, Roy Ward Baker; w, Nigel Kneale; ph, Arthur Grant (Deluxe Color); m, Tristram Cary; ed, James Needs, Spencer Reeve; art d, Bernard Robinson.

Science Fiction (PR:A MPAA:NR)

FIVE MINUTES TO LIVE✶✶ (1961) 80m Sutton bw
(AKA: DOOR-TO-DOOR MANIAC)

Johnny Cash (*Johnny Cabot*), Donald Woods (*Ken Wilson*), Cay Forester (*Nancy Wilson*), Pamela Mason (*Ellen*), Midge Ware (*Doris*), Vic Tayback (*Fred*), Ronnie Howard (*Bobby*), Merle Travis (*Max*), Howard Wright (*Pop*), Norma Varden (*Priscilla*).

Johnny Cash made his debut in a starring role in this trite exploitation film. Cash plays a cool-headed murderer, who mugs, then holds hostage the wife of a bank president, Forester. No problem except that bank executive, Woods, is seeing another woman, Mason, and planning to dump Forester anyway. Tayback is Cash's partner in crime while Ronnie Howard is his precocious son. The screenplay is by M.K. Forester, which happens to be the pen name for Cay Forester, the victim of the tale.

p, James Ellsworth; d, Bill Karn; w, M.K. Forester, Robert Joseph (based on a story by Palmer Thompson); ph, Carl Guthrie; m, Gene Kauer; ed, Donald Nosseck; art d, Edwin Shields; set d, Harry Reif; m/l, "Five Minutes to Live," "I've Come To Kill," Johnny Cash, sung by Cash.

Crime **Cas.** (PR:C MPAA:NR)

5 MINUTES TO LOVE (SEE: ROTTEN APPLE, THE, 1963)

FIVE OF A KIND✶½ (1938) 83m FOX bw

Jean Hersholt (*Dr. John Luke*), Claire Trevor (*Christine Nelson*), Cesar Romero (*Duke Lester*), Slim Summerville (*Jim Ogden*), Henry Wilcoxon (*Dr. Scott Williams*), Inez Courtney (*Libby Long*), John Qualen (*Asa Wyatt*), Jane Darwell (*Mrs. Waldron*), Pauline Moore (*Eleanor Kingsley*), John Russell (*Dickie*), Andrew Tombes (*Dr. Bruno*), David Torrence (*Sir Basil Crawford*), Marion Byron (*Nurse Corday*), Hamilton MacFadden (*Andrew Gordon*), Spencer Charters (*Rev. Matthew Brand*), Charles D. Brown (*Editor Crane*), Dionne Quintuplets (*Themselves*).

This was the third of the Dionne Quint screen appearances. With no story to follow, the Quints (at 4½ years of age) dance, sing, and look cute and huggable, but are only on the screen for 18 minutes. The remaining 65 minutes are devoid of entertainment.

p, Sol M. Wurtzel; d, Herbert I. Leeds; w, Lou Breslow, John Patrick; ph, Daniel B. Clark; m, Samuel Kaylin; ed, Fred Allen; art d, Bernard Herzbrun, Chester Gore.

Comedy (PR:AA MPAA:NR)

FIVE OF THE JAZZBAND (SEE: JAZZBAND FIVE, 1932)

FIVE ON THE BLACK HAND SIDE✶✶✶½ (1973) 96m UA c

Clarice Tayler (*Mrs. Brooks*), Leonard Jackson (*Mr. Brooks*), Virginia Capers (*Ruby*), Glynn Turman (*Gideon*), D'Urville Martin (*Booker T*), Richard Williams (*Preston*), Sonny Jim (*Sweetmeat*), Ja'Net Dubois (*Stormy Monday*), Bonnie Banfield (*Gail*), Frankie Crocker (*Rolls Royce*), Tchaka Almoravids (*Fun Loving*), Carl Mikal Franklin (*Marvin*), Godfrey Cambridge, Cal Wilson, Philomena Nowlin, Brenda Sutton, Douglas Johnson, Ronald Warden, Jean Taylor, Rudy Joe Ringo, Fred Daniel Scott, Imamu Sukuma, Kwasi Badu.

A comedy about a black middle-class family living in the Watts section of L.A. Taylor is the wife and mother who becomes fed up with her husband's tyrannical rule. Their three children assimilate to the new black consciousness and so does Taylor. Before her daughter's wedding, she gets an Afro and hands hubby a list of demands. He must sign agreement to them or it's goodbye.

p, Brock Peters, Michael Tolan; d, Oscar Williams; w, Charlie L. Russell (based on his play); ph, Gene Polito (DeLuxe Color); m, H.B. Barnum; ed, Michael Economou.

Comedy (PR:A MPAA:PG)

FIVE PENNIES, THE✶✶✶ (1959) 117m PAR c

Danny Kaye (*Loring "Red" Nichols*), Barbara Bel Geddes (*Bobbie Meredith*), Louis Armstrong (*Himself*), Bob Crosby (*Wil Paradise*), Harry Guardino (*Tony Valani*), Susan Gordon (*Dorothy Nichols at 6*), Tuesday Weld (*Dorothy at 12-14*), Valerie Allen (*Tommye Eden*), Ray Anthony (*Jimmy Dorsey*), Shelley Manne (*Dave Tough*), Bobby Troup (*Arthur Schutt*), Ray Daly (*Glenn Miller*).

A schmaltz-laden biopic, THE FIVE PENNIES is nevertheless a jazz lover's movie loaded with good old Dixieland, epitomized by Kaye playing the talented Nichols who migrates from southern obscurity to big city music where his cornet is heard and most appreciated during the 1920s. Kaye gets a job with Crosby's band and soon becomes a virtuoso on the horn. He meets singer Bel Geddes (her vocals are dubbed by Eileen Wilson) and they marry, having a baby girl. Kaye and Crosby begin to argue over the popular ballads of the day he is compelled to play; his nonconformist ways finally get him fired. With Guardino managing his new group, "The Five Pennies," Kaye becomes a great jazz sensation, one of the leading advocates of Dixieland. At the height of his popularity, Kaye begins ignoring his family, compelling his wife and child, Gordon, to travel the country by bus with the band, ignoring homelife and the child's schooling. Then Gordon is stricken with polio which devastates Kaye to the point where he quits music altogether and takes a job in a Los Angeles shipyard. He slavishly devotes his life to making a good home for his little family and curing his daughter's disease. She grows to a teenager, Weld, and unearths her father's old records. She and Bel Geddes encourage Kaye to make an appearance at a small West Coast club and it first seems that he is a bust, but then the place fills up with his old cronies, including jazz greats of his 1920s era, not the least of whom is the superlative Louis "Satchmo" Armstrong. He is a hit and has a great comeback, joyous to see his daughter overcome her affliction. THE FIVE PENNIES is solid entertainment and Kaye is believable as the ambitious jazzman who learns his lessons on a hard scale. The script is a bit maudlin, even mawkish in spots, but the 25 tunes that pepper the production uplift the film considerably. Bel Geddes, later a star in TV's "Dallas," is very good as the loyal wife and Weld in her first film at age 15, playing a 13-year-old, shows an early and promising talent. Some of the 1920s jam sessions shown are great highlights. Songs include: "Good Night Sleep Tight," "The Five Pennies," "Battle Hymn of the Republic," "When the Saints Go Marching In," "The Music Goes 'Round and Around," "Jingle Bells," "Carnival of Venice," and "Paradise." Sylvia Fine, associate producer for the film and Kaye's wife, contributed four of her own songs to the production, including "Lullaby in Ragtime" and "Follow the Leader."

p, Jack Rose; d, Melville Shavelson; w, Shavelson, Rose (based on a story by Robert Smith, suggested by the life of Loring "Red" Nichols); ph, Daniel L. Fapp (VistaVision, Technicolor); m, Leith Stevens; ed, Frank P. Keller; art d, Hal Pereira, Tambi Larsen; spec eff, John P. Fulton.

Musical/Biography (PR:A MPAA:NR)

FIVE POUND MAN, THE✶½ (1937, Brit.) 76m Fox British bw

Judy Gunn (*Margaret Fenton*), Edwin Styles (*Richard Fordyce*), Frank Allenby (*Claud Fenton*), Charles Bannister (*Eustace Grant*), Esma Cannon (*Lucy*), G. H. Mulcaster (*Sinclair*), Paul Blake (*Bennett*), Norman Wooland (*Lodge Keeper*), David Arnold.

Styles is an unemployed ex-convict drifting around England looking for the gang who framed him on a counterfeiting charge. At a charity auction he sells his services as a butler for five pounds. Bought by Gunn, it turns out that the five-pound note she paid for is a fake. He confronts her father (Allenby) with his discovery, and accuses him of being the man responsible for his jail sentence. Allenby promptly and honorably kills himself to avoid jail and end the film. Allegedly a comedy, but how funny can a suicide climax be? Mercifully forgotten today.

p&d, Albert Parker; w, David Evans; ph, Stanley Grant.

Comedy (PR:C MPAA:NR)

5 SINNERS✶✶ (1961, Ger.) 80m Rex Film-Bloemer and Co./Astor Pictures bw (DAS NACHTLOKAL ZUM SILBERMOND; AKA: THE SINNERS)

Marina Petrowa (*Magali*), Pero Alexander (*Jussuf*), Jurg Holl (*Christian "Whiskey" Peters*), Marisa Mell (*Liliane*), Loni von Friedl (*Inge*), Renate Rohm (*Doris*), Aina Capell (*Gerda*), Rolf Olsen (*Police Commissioner Elam*), Gerdina Gordon (*Vera*), Raoul Letzer, Guido Wieland, Erica Schramm, Peter Preses, Heinrich Trimbur, Wolf Harnisch, Angeles Durand, Camillo Felgen, The Nielsen Brothers.

This cheaply made from Germany concentrates on the sleazy happenings in a Turkish nightclub, which includes being the front for a gang of jewel thieves, among other things. Petrowa is the woman who runs the place in a sadistic fashion, keeping her gangland-type activities secret from the other employees. But dancer-stripper Mell gets wind of what's happening and through the aid of an admiring bouncer sees that her boss and gang receive what's coming to them. Picture has a pessimistic form of fatalism reminiscent of Hollywood film noir of the late 1940s and early 1950s.

p, Ernest Muller, August Rieger; d, Wolfgang Gluck; w, Peter Loos, Rieger, Gluck; ph, Walter Tuch; m, Carl Niessen; ed, Eleonore Kunze; art d, Felix Smetana.

Crime (PR:C-O MPAA:NR)

FIVE STAR FINAL✶✶✶ (1931) 89m FN-WB bw
(AKA: ONE FATAL HOUR)

Edward G. Robinson (*Randall*), Marian Marsh (*Jenny Townsend*), H.B. Warner (*Michael Townsend*), Anthony Bushell (*Philip Weeks*), George E. Stone (*Ziggie Feinstein*), Frances Starr (*Nancy Voorhees Townsend*), Ona Munson (*Kitty Carmody*), Boris Karloff ("*Reverend" Vernon Isopod*), Robert Elliott (*Brannegan*), Aline MacMahon (*Miss Taylor*), Purnell Pratt (*French*), David Torrence (*Weeks*), Oscar Apfel (*Hinchecliffe*), Gladys Lloyd (*Miss Edwards*), Evelyn Walsh Hall (*Mrs. Weeks*), Harold Waldridge (*Arthur Goldberg*), Polly Walters (*Telephone Operator*), James Donlin (*Reporter*), Frank Darien (*Schwartz*).

This is an offbeat but fascinating film which pillories the transgressions of the muckraking tabloids so popular in the 1920s. Apfel is the uncaring, circulation-lusting publisher of the New York *Gazette*, a notorious scandal sheet, who hires Robinson, a hard-working, slightly scrupulous editor, telling him to dust off a 20-year-old murder case by infiltrating the family involved and obtaining background information. To accomplish this unsavory job, Robinson reluctantly hires Karloff, a slimy, sneaky scandalmongering reporter who pretends to be a priest while ingratiating himself to Warner and Starr; it is Starr on whom Karloff concentrates as she had been convicted of manslaughter after slaying her betraying lover two decades earlier. He digs up enough additional scandal for a shocking expose. When the story hits, Starr is overcome with shame and shock, as is her consoling husband, Warner; they both commit suicide which drives their frantic daughter, Marsh, whose life has also been ruined by the story, to arrive at the newspaper and to attempt to kill publisher Apfel. Robinson stops her but, in disgust at what his paper has done, turns around and verbally blasts his boss in one of the greatest resignation speeches in the history of film, threatening to kill Apfel himself if the stories continue, then he walks out for the film's finish. Although banality creeps into the tearjerker, Robinson's bravura role as the conscience-stricken editor, the workings of the tabloid office, and Karloff's incredibly repulsive character (he had been a divinity student defrocked for drunkenness) is utterly captivating. Robinson employs a symbolic habit of washing his hands after every dirty deed he performs for Apfel, but only with water poured into a basin in his office, using soap in the final scene before resigning. Warner and Starr are excellent as the victims, as is Marsh, the horrified daughter. A standout is Munson as a hardened picture chaser for Apfel's tabloid, one without pity or compassion, unlike the kind-hearted madam she was later to play to perfection in GONE WITH THE WIND (1939). Good, too, are the cynical, heartless newspaper types portrayed by Stone and MacMahon. Apfel is properly detestable as the ruthless newspaper publisher, a character closely resembling the publisher of the old New York *Mirror*. This film was based on a successful London-based play, "Late Night Final," written by Louis Weitzenkorn, one time managing editor of Bernarr MacFadden's scandal sheet, the New York *Evening Graphic*, which peddled wild scandal and rumor as news during the 1920s. Weitzenkorn, like the Robinson character, quit the tabloid in disgust and later took his revenge with his hard-hitting play. *Film Daily* selected FIVE STAR FINAL as one of the 10 best movies of 1931, a production that boosted Robinson's career and got him out of typecast gangster roles he created too well for himself in LITTLE CAESAR (1930). This film, was released the same year as THE FRONT PAGE, both of them establishing the traditions which would be profiled into cliches in many a newspaper movie to come. Remade in 1936 as TWO AGAINST THE WORLD.

d, Mervyn LeRoy; w, Byron Morgan, Robert Lord (based on a play by Louis Weitzenkorn); ph, Sol Polito; ed, Frank Ware; md, Leo Forbstein; art d, Jack Okey.

Crime Drama **(PR:C MPAA:NR)**

FIVE STEPS TO DANGER** (1957) 80m UA bw

Ruth Roman *(Ann Nicholson)*, Sterling Hayden *(John Emmett)*, Werner Klemperer *(Dr. Simmons)*, Richard Gaines *(Dean Brant)*, Charles Davis *(Kirk)*, Jeanne Cooper *(Helen Bethke)*, Peter Hansen *(Karl Plesser)*, John Mitchum *(Deputy)*, John Merrick *(Sheriff)*, Karl Lindt *(Kissell)*.

Hayden's car breaks down on the way to a fishing spot and Roman picks him up. She is enroute to drop coded information to a scientist. Unknown to both of them, they are being stalked by communist spies who want the coded info. The commies don't get it.

p,d&w, Henry S. Kesler (adapted from a story by Donald Hamilton); ph, Kenneth Peach; m, Paul Sawtell; ed, Aaron Stell; art d, Rudi Feld.

Thriller **(PR:A MPAA:NR)**

FIVE THE HARD WAY** (1969) 82m Fantascope/Crown International c (AKA: THE SIDEHACKERS)

Ross Hagen *(Rommel)*, Diane McBain *(Rita)*, Michael Pataki *(J.C.)*, Claire Polan *(Paisley)*, Richard Merrifield *(Luke)*, Edward Parrish *(Nero)*, Michael Graham *(Cooch)*, Hoke Howell *(Crapout)*, Robert Tessier *(Jake)*, Eric Lidberg *(Tork)*, Erik Cord *(Dirty John)*, Toni Moss *(Lois)*, Diane Tessier *(Debbie)*, Joey Tessier *(Billy)*, Warren Hammack, Irv Ross *(Mechanics)*, Tony Lorea *(Announcer)*.

Hagen is a three-wheel competition motorcyclist (sidehacker) who meets cyclist Pataki at a weekend competition. Pataki's girl friend gets the hots for Hagen, but he turns her down. She tells her boy friend that Hagen raped her, so Pataki and his buddies beat him up and rape and kill his fiancee, McBain. Hagen recovers and wreaks his revenge.

p, Jon Hall, Ross Hagen; d, Gus Trikonis; w, Tony Huston, Larry Billman (from a story by Billman); ph, Hall (Eastmancolor); m, Mike Curb, Jerry Stynerv, Guy Hemric; ed, Pat Somerset.

Action/Drama **(PR:O MPAA:R)**

5,000 FINGERS OF DR. T, THE**** (1953) 89m COL c

Peter Lind Hayes *(Zabladowski)*, Mary Healy *(Mrs. Collins)*, Hans Conried *(Dr. Terwilliker)*, Tommy Rettig *(Bart)*, John Heasley *(Uncle Whitney)*, Robert Heasley *(Uncle Judson)*, Noel Cravat *(Sgt. Lunk)*, Henry Kulky *(Stroogo)*.

In this surrealistic children's film (co-written by Ted Geisel, better known as Dr. Seuss), Rettig is a young boy who would rather play baseball than take his piano lessons with his teacher Dr. Terwilliker. The boy dreams he's being chased by weird creatures with butterfly nets through a land of fog, cylinders, and odd-shaped mounds. He stumbles upon the castle of Dr. T, who runs a piano school for 500 captive boys. In the dungeon Dr. T keeps creatures who have grown green and moldy, put there for playing instruments other than the piano. The prisoners have built musical instruments out of odd materials and, in the best sequence of the film, perform a strange ballet. Rettig, with the help of Hayes, fights off two men on rollerskates who are connected by their beards. They also build a bomb that absorbs sound waves, and help Rettig's mother escape from Dr. T's bizarre world. Songs: "The Kid's Song," "Ten Happy Fingers," "Get Together Weather," "Dream Stuff," "The Dressing Song, (My Do-Me-Do-Duds)," "Dungeon Elevator," "Hypnotic Duel," and "Victorious" (Ted Geisel).

p, Stanley Kramer; d, Roy Rowland; w, Ted Geisel [Dr. Seuss], Allan Scott; ph, Franz Planer (Technicolor); m, Frederick Hollander; ed, Al Clark; md, Morris Stoloff; prod d, Rudolph Sternad; art d, Cary Odell; ch, Eugene Loring.

Fantasy/Musical **(PR:AAA MPAA:NR)**

FIVE TO ONE*½ (1963, Brit.) 56m Merton Park/AA bw

Lee Montague *(Larry Hart)*, Ingrid Hafner *(Pat Dunn)*, John Thaw *(Alan Roper)*, Brian McDermott *(John Lea)*, Ewan Roberts *(Deighton)*, Heller Toren *(Mai Hart)*, Jack Watson *(Inspector Davis)*, Richard Clarke *(Lucas)*.

Another of the Edgar Wallace second features out of England in the early 1960s, this one concerns a betting parlor robbery scheme that goes disastrously wrong. Not one of the series best, but still watchable. After a single, highly successful run on British television, reruns were banned as being "without merit."

p, Jack Greenwood; d, Gordon Flemyng; w, Roger Marshall (based on the story "Thief In The Night" by Edgar Wallace).

Crime **(PR:C MPAA:NR)**

FIVE WEEKS IN A BALLOON** (1962) 102m FOX c

Red Buttons *(Donald O'Shay)*, Fabian *(Jacques)*, Barbara Eden *(Susan Gale)*, Cedric Hardwicke *(Fergusson)*, Peter Lorre *(Ahmed)*, Richard Haydn *(Sir Henry Vining)*, Barbara Luna *(Makia)*, Billy Gilbert *(Sultan-Auctioneer)*, Herbert Marshall *(Prime Minister)*, Reginald Owen *(Consul)*, Henry Daniell *(Sheik Ageiba)*, Mike Mazurki *(Slave Captain)*, Alan Caillou *(Inspector)*, Ben Astar *(Myanga)*, Raymond Bailey *(Randolph)*, Chester the Chimp *("The Duchess")*.

A comical adaptation of Jules Verne's first novel, a story about a team of 19th-century Britons crossing Africa in a balloon. They want to plant the Union Jack on unclaimed land in West Africa. Hardwicke leads the expedition, with reporter Buttons, scientist Haydn, and his assistant, Fabian, on board. They rescue Eden from a drunken sultan, and give lovable slave trader Lorre a ride, too. Producer and director Allen would move to TV, then in the 1970s start the inane and poorly-researched disaster film craze.

p&d, Irwin Allen; w, Charles Bennett, Allen, Albert Gail (adapted from Jules Verne's novel); ph, Winton Hoch (CinemaScope, DeLuxe Color); m, Paul Sawtell; ed, George Boemler; art d, Jack Martin Smith, Alfred Ybarra; set d, Walter M. Scott, Stuart A. Reiss, Norman Rockett.

Comedy/Adventure **Cas.** **(PR:A MPAA:NR)**

FIVE WILD GIRLS*½ (1966, Fr.) 95m American Film Distributing bw (CINQ FILLES EN FURIE; AKA: FIVE WILD KIDS)

French Cast: Marc Bonseignour, Madeleine Constant, Nicole Merouze, Denyse Roland, Marie-France Mignal, Michel Monfort, Colette Regis, Maria Tamar; American Cast: Jacqueline Wolff *(Isabel)*, Jeannie Peterson *(Sylvia)*, Felicia Andrews *(Jenny)*, Anna Marie Shaw *(Agnes)*, Susann Flynn *(Gladys)*, Josell Como *(Grandmother)*, Fred Thompson *(Blackie)*, Michael Jameson *(George)*.

Vile drama detailing the efforts of three obnoxious sisters and their two equally reprehensible cousins who descend like vultures on a small village to claim a fortune hidden by their grandfather before his death (despite the fact that their grandmother swore never to reveal the location of the treasure). Eventually the women learn where the fortune is hidden and converge on the spot only to find nothing of value.

d, Max Pecas; w, Louis Soulanes, Maurice Cury, Robert Topart, Pecas; ph, Roger Duculot; m, Georges Garvarentz.

Drama **(PR:O MPAA:NR)**

FIXATION (SEE: SHE-MAN, THE, 1967)

FIXED BAYONETS*** (1951) 92m FOX bw

Richard Basehart *(Cpl. Denno)*, Gene Evans *(Sgt. Rock)*, Michael O'Shea *(Sgt. Lonergan)*, Richard Hylton *(Wheeler)*, Craig Hill *(Lt. Gibbs)*, Skip Homeier *(Whitey)*, Henry Kulky *(Vogl)*, Richard Monohan *(Walowicz)*, Paul Richards *(Ramirez)*, Tony Kent *(Mainotes)*, Don Orlando *(Borcellino)*, Patrick Fitzgibbon *(Paddy)*, Neyle Morrow *(Medic)*, George Wesley *(Griff)*, Mel Pogue *(Bulcheck)*, George Conrad *(Zablocki)*, David Wolfson *(Bigmouth)*, Buddy Thorpe *(Husky Doggie)*, Al Negbo *(Lean Doggie)*, Wyott Ordung *(Fitz)*, Pat Hogan *(Jonesy)*, James Dean *(GI)*, John Doucette *(GI)*, Bill Hickman, Kayne Shew.

Relentless but engrossing study of a platoon of men during the Korean War, FIXED BAYONETS offers a fine cast and excellent direction by director Fuller, a war film specialist (STEEL HELMET, 1951, THE BIG RED ONE, 1980). Basehart is an intellectual, refined soldier who operates well when being ordered to his battle chores but when his superiors, Evans, O'Shea, and Hill are picked off one by one in a rear guard action atop snowy mountaintops, Basehart finds himself in a dilemma. He must take command and be responsible for the lives and deaths of others. He almost falters but at the last minute takes a firm hand and saves a near hopeless situation. Remnants of the platoon survive under his leadership and rejoin their retreating regiment. There is nothing glamorous about this film, as Fuller documents the mental and physical strain the infantryman must undergo, a grimy, bone-weary situation where hope comes down to the ability to wield the cold steel of a bayonet. Basehart is excellent as the introspective soldier and Evans and O'Shea are terrific as the seasoned veterans who take as routine the rear-guard order to lay down their lives if necessary to save their comrades. This film had particular box office appeal in that it was released while the Allies and North Koreans-Chinese were conducting peace talks. Though the story for the film was based on a novel by John Brophy, another source was also cited, according to director Fuller: "This was an original, but Darryl Zanuck decided to credit also an old film 20th made, THE IMMORTAL SERGEANT (1943), because it dealt with a timid soldier. The stories have nothing in common whatsoever." The realistic sets were all photographed beautifully by master cinematographer Ballard on Stage 8 of the Fox Studio where art directors Wheeler and Patrick, and set decorators Little and Rhode superbly recreated the Korean terrain ravaged by war.

p, Jules Buck; d&w, Samuel Fuller (based on a novel by John Brophy); ph, Lucien Ballard; m, Roy Webb; ed, Nick De Maggio; md, Lionel Newman; art d, Lyle Wheeler, George Patrick; set d, Thomas Little, Fred J. Rhode; cos, Charles Le Maire; spec eff, Fred Sersen; tech adv, Capt. Raymond Harvey.

War Drama (PR:A MPAA:NR)

FIXER, THE*½ (1968) 130m MGM c

Alan Bates (*Yakov Bok*), Dirk Bogarde (*Bibikov*), Georgia Brown (*Marfa Golov*), Hugh Griffith (*Lebedev*), Elizabeth Hartman (*Zinaida*), Ian Holm (*Grubeshov*), David Opatoshu (*Latke*), David Warner (*Count Odoevsky*), Carol White (*Raisl*), George Murcell (*Deputy Warden*), Murray Melvin (*Priest*), Peter Jeffrey (*Berezhinsky*), Michael Goodliffe (*Ostrovsky*), Thomas Heathcote (*Proshko*), Mike Pratt (*Father Anastasy*), Stanley Meadows (*Gronfein*), Francis De Wolff (*Warden*), David Lodge (*Zhitnyak*), William Hutt (*The Czar*), Roy Sone (*Akimytch*), Alfie Bass (*Potseikin*), Michael Balfour (*Boatman*), Danny Green (*The Giggler*), Helen Dowling (*Black Page*), Norbert Viszlay (*Zhenia*).

Bates is a Jew in turn-of-the-century Czarist Russia. Anti-Semitism is rampant and Bates is accused of killing a young boy. Never formally charged, he is put through physical and mental torture to confess his crime. Bates refuses and his case becomes news worldwide. Bogarde is the government lawyer trying to help Bates out of his plight. Frankenheimer's direction is strong in this unrelentingly brutal film.

p, Edward Lewis; d, John Frankenheimer; w, Dalton Trumbo (from the novel by Bernard Malamud); ph, Marcel Grignon (Metrocolor); m, Maurice Jarre; ed, Henry Berman; art d, Bela Zeichan.

Drama (PR:O MPAA:M)

FIXER DUGAN* (1939) 68m RKO bw (GB: DOUBLE DARING)

Lee Tracy (*Charlie Dugan*), Virginia Weidler (*Terry*), Peggy Shannon (*Adgie Modeno*), Bradley Page (*Owner Barvin*), William Edmunds (*Smiley*), Edward Gargan (*Jake*), Jack Arnold (*Darlow*), Rita LaRoy (*Patsy*), Irene Franklin (*Jane*), John Dilson (*Steve*), Edythe Elliott (*Mrs. Fletcher*).

Tracy is a circus fixer, a diplomat of sorts, patching up problems the Barvin circus has with patrons and the law. His smooth talking also takes care of internal problems. A fixer is most needed for the filming itself.

p, Cliff Reid; d, Lew Landers; w, Bert Granet, Paul Yawitz (adapted from a play by H.C. Potter); ph, J. Roy Hunt; ed, Henry Berman.

Drama (PR:A MPAA:NR)

FLAG LIEUTENANT, THE* (1932, Brit.) 80m British & Dominions/GAU bw

Henry Edwards (*Lt. Dicky Lascelles*), Anna Neagle (*Hermione Wynne*), Joyce Bland (*Mrs. Cameron*), Peter Gawthorne (*Maj. Thesiger*), Louis Goodrich (*Adm. Wynne*), Sam Livesey (*Col. McLeod*), Michael Hogan (*Lt. Palliser*), O.B. Clarence (*Gen. Gough-Bogle*), Abraham Sofaer (*Meheti Salos*), Peter Northcote (*Midshipman Lee*), Tully Comber (*Midshipman Hood*).

A British naval lieutenant performs a deed of bravery during a battle against a Chinese fort, but he lets his best friend take the credit. The friend is promoted and the lieutenant is branded a coward. Another officer realizes what the lieutenant did and everything is straightened out. An heroic effort by director-actor Edwards.

p, Herbert Wilcox; d, Henry Edwards; w, Joan Wentworth Wood (based on the play by W.P. Drury, Leo Tover); ph, Stanley Rodwell.

Drama (PR:A MPAA:NR)

FLAME, THE*½ (1948) 96m REP bw

John Carroll (*George MacAllister*), Vera Ralston (*Carlotta Novak*), Robert Paige (*Barry MacAllister*), Broderick Crawford (*Ernie Hicks*), Henry Travers (*Dr. Mitchell*), Blanche Yurka (*Aunt Margaret*), Constance Dowling (*Helen Anderson*), Hattie McDaniel (*Celia*), Victor Sen Yung (*Chang*), Harry V. Cheshire (*Minister*), John Miljan, Garry Owen (*Detectives*), Eddie Dunn (*Police Officer*), Vince Barnett (*Stage Door Attendant*), Hal K. Dawson (*Telegraph Clerk*), Jeff Corey (*Stranger*), Ashley Cowan (*Page Boy*), Cyril Ring (*Mr. Moffett*), Howard Mitchell (*Doorman*), Martha Holliday (*Check Girl*), John Albright (*Youth*), John Treback (*Waiter*).

A contrived melodrama with Carroll plotting to get his sick brother's fortune. The brother, Paige, is only supposed to live for a couple of months, so Carroll has his girl friend, Ralston, marry him to inherit the money. She falls in love with Paige and nurses him back to health. A blackmailer steps onto the scene and threatens to reveal Ralston's original intentions. Carroll, trying to redeem himself, gets in a fatal shootout with the blackmailer.

p&d, John H. Auer; w, Lawrence Kimble (based on a story by Robert T. Shannon); ph, Reggie Lanning; m, Heinz Roemheld; ed, Richard L. Van Enger; md, Cy Feuer; art d, Gano Chittenden; song, "Love Me Or Leave Me" (sung by Constance Dowling).

Crime/Drama (PR:A MPAA:NR)

FLAME* (1975, Brit.) 75m VPS-Goodtimes c

Noddy Holder (*Stoker*), Jim Lea (*Paul*), Dave Hill (*Barry*), Don Powell (*Charlie*), Tom Conti (*Seymour*), Johnny Shannon (*Harding*), Alan Lake (*Daniels*), Sara Clee (*Angie*), Anthony Allen (*Russell*), Tommy Vance (*Ricky Storm*), Rosko (*Himself*), John Dicks (*Lenny*), Michael Coles (*Roy Priest*), Nina Thomas (*Julie*), Patrick Connor (*Foreman*), A.J. Brown (*Chairman*), Barrie Houghton (*Ron*), Jimmy Gardner (*Charlie's Dad*), Sheila Raynor (*Charlie's Mum*).

Behind the scenes of the rock music business with the British rock band Slade in starring roles. The band moves from playing bars to the big time through clever marketing. The band members become disillusioned with the lives they lead and break up. Nothing new to be seen, but the Slade group all turn in glowing performances and are a quite likable quartet.

p, Gavrik Losey; d, Richard Loncraine; w, Andrew Birkin; ph, Peter Hannen (Technicolor); m, Noddy Holder, Jimmy Lea; ed, Mike Bradsell; art d, Brian Morris.

Drama (PA:C MPAA:NR)

FLAME AND THE ARROW, THE*½ (1950) 89m WB c

Burt Lancaster (*Dardo*), Virginia Mayo (*Anne*), Robert Douglas (*Alessandro*), Aline MacMahon (*Nonna Bartoli*), Frank Allenby (*Ulrich*), Nick Cravat (*Piccolo*), Lynne Baggett (*Francesca*), Gordon Gebert (*Rudi*), Norman Lloyd (*Troubadour*), Victor Kilian (*Apothecary*), Francis Pierlot (*Papa Pietro*), Robin Hughes (*Skinner*).

The first of the two costume swashbucklers Lancaster starred in for the production company he formed with Harold Hecht. Lancaster is a Lombard mountain man in medieval Italy whose wife has left him with their son to become the mistress of Allenby, commander of the Hessian mercenaries who occupy the region. When she decides she wants her son back, Allenby sends soldiers to kidnap the boy. Lancaster is wounded fighting them, but when he recovers he kidnaps Allenby's niece, Mayo. She falls in love with her captor while Allenby's men search for child. Allenby announces that he will hang a number of hostages if Lancaster does not return Mayo and surrender himself, so he does, finding himself imprisoned under sentence of death. Some of his friends manage to slip him into a special harness that lets him appear to be hanged, and, after duping the guards, he is smuggled to safety. He and his cohorts return later disguised as a troop of acrobats and after a marvelous show of tumbling they attack the guards and capture the castle. One of Lancaster's most enjoyable vehicles, THE FLAME AND THE ARROW was what finally established him as a leading man and not just another *film noir* tough guy. Lancaster did all his own stunts (apart from a few fight scenes where he was doubled by Don Turner), many of them alongside Cravat, Lancaster's partner in a circus acrobatic act in the late 1930s, playing his mute sidekick here. To publicize the film they went on tour, performing some of the acrobatics from the film. Well-directed by Tourneur, the film is lightweight but never veers into self-parody (unlike THE CRIMSON PIRATE two years later). Many of the sets were left over from THE ADVENTURES OF ROBIN HOOD (1938) and another Errol Flynn epic, THE ADVENTURES OF DON JUAN (1948).

p, Frank Ross, Harold Hecht; d, Jacques Tourneur; w, Waldo Salt (based on his story "The Hawk and the Arrow"); ph, Ernest Haller (Technicolor); m, Max Steiner; ed, Alan Crosland, Jr.; art d, Edward Carrere.

Adventure (PR:A MPAA:NR)

FLAME AND THE FLESH* (1954) 104m MGM c

Lana Turner (*Madeline*), Pier Angeli (*Lisa*), Carlos Thompson (*Nino*), Bonar Colleano (*Ciccio*), Charles Goldner (*Mondari*), Peter Illing (*Peppe*), Rosalie Crutchley (*Francesca*), Marne Maitland (*Filiberto*), Eric Pohlmann (*Marina Proprietor*), Catherina Ferraz (*Dressmaker*), Alex de Gallier (*Playboy*).

They tried their best to emulate the sexy Italian neo-realistic pictures that were coming out at this time, but the production code and the color lensing worked against their intentions and the result was a disappointment both critically and at the box office. Based very faintly on the novel by Auguste Bailly, the picture was made once before in French as NAPLES AU BAISER DE DEU in 1937 and didn't fare any better than this remake. That one starred Viviane Romance, Mireille Balin, and Tino Rossi, none of whom became household words, even in France. Turner is hurled out of her apartment in Naples and is picked up by Colleano, a kind musician. He feeds her and gives her a place to stay but she rewards him by taking up with his roommate, Thompson, a handsome singer. She comes on very strong and he finally succumbs to her amorous onslaught. Colleano still thinks he can make an honest woman of her but she'll have none of that and steals Thompson away from his fiancee, Angeli, just before they are due to be married. Turner and Thompson move in together but the bloom wears off the rose quickly as he loses singing job after job when the customers pay too much attention to his woman. Eventually, Turner realizes that she is the wrong woman for Thompson and sends him back to Angeli in Naples. The picture ends as the very steamy Turner walks the streets, looking for her next adventure. The biggest problem here was that Brooks, in one of his first assignments, didn't ride herd on the Helen Deutsch script and it seemed to go everywhere at once and go nowhere. Turner was a brunette and that was a mistake. It's like bobbing Streisand's nose or putting a blonde wig on Yul Brynner. This was Turner's first film made in Europe and it was shot partially on location in Naples, with interiors completed at MGM's Elstree Studios in London. Colleano was only thirty four when he died in 1958 after a fourteen year career in British films. His real name was Bonar Sullivan but he looked very Italian and took his name from the circus act he toured with from the age of five, the Colleanos. He was a good actor and always believable, even in this thankless role. Thompson gave up acting for production, married Lilli Palmer, and moved to Switzerland. Born in Buenos Aires of German parents, his real name is Juan Carlos Mundanschaffter, so it's not difficult to see why he became Carlos Thompson.

p, Joe Pasternak; d, Richard Brooks; w, Helen Deutsch (based on the novel by Auguste Bailly); ph, Christopher Challis (Technicolor); m, Nicholas Brodszky; ed, Ray Poulton, Albert Akst; md, George Stoll; art d, Alfred Junge; m/l, "Languida," "By Candlelight," "Then I Loved," Brodszky, Jack Lawrence.

Drama (PR:C MPAA:NR)

FLAME BARRIER, THE**½   (1958) 70m UA bw
(AKA: IT FELL FROM THE FLAME BARRIER)

Arthur Franz (Dave Hollister), Kathleen Crowley (Carol Dahlmann), Robert Brown (Matt Hollister), Vincent Padula (Julio), Rodd Redwing (Waumi), Kaz Oran (Tispe), Grace Matthews (Mexican Girl), Pilar Del Rey (Indian Girl), Larry Duran (Bearer), Bernie Gozier (Wounded Indian), Roberto Contreras (Village Indian).

A satellite crashes in the Yucatan jungle and Franz goes after it. The satellite is covered with B-movie-grade protoplasm that sears human flesh from the bone. Brown and Padula are hired by Franz's wife (Crowley) to find her husband. Some good jungle sequences. This is typical post-Sputnik film fare that played to the fear of the times.

p, Arthur Gardner, Jules V. Levy; d, Paul Landres; w, Pat Fielder, George Worthing Yates (based on a story by Yates); ph, Jack McKenzie; ed, Jerry Young; art d, James Vance.

Science Fiction   **(PR:C   MPAA:NR)**

FLAME IN THE HEATHER*   (1935, Brit.) 66m Crusade/PAR bw

Gwenllian Gill (Alison), Barry Clifton (Col. Stafford), Bruce Seton (Murray), Richard Hayward (Fassiefern), Ben Williams (Rushton), Kenneth McLaglen (Donald), Rani Waller (Myrat), Francis de Wolff (Hawley), Donald Robertson, Margaret Duncan, Honor Magee, Jock Rae.

Laughable costume epic has Clifton as an intrepid English officer who sneaks into Scotland during the Jacobite Rebellion of 1745 to do some spying. He is taken in by the Cameron Clan, and falls in love with the daughter of the house, Gill. After saving her life, the lovers ride back to England. Cheaply made and awful.

p, Victor M. Greene; d&w, Donovan Pedelty (based on the novel The Fiery Cross by Esson Maule).

Historical Drama   **(PR:A   MPAA:NR)**

FLAME IN THE STREETS***   (1961, Brit.)
93m Somerset-RANK/Atlantic c

John Mills (Jacko Palmer), Sylvia Syms (Kathie Palmer), Brenda de Banzie (Nell Palmer), Earl Cameron (Gabriel Gomez), Johnny Sekka (Peter Lincoln), Ann Lynn (Judy Gomez), Wilfrid Brambell (Mr. Palmer), Meredith Edwards (Harry Mitchell), Newton Blick (Visser), Glyn Houston (Hugh Davies), Cyril Chamberlain (James Dowell), Michael Wynne (Les), Dan Jackson (Jubilee), Gretchen Franklin (Mrs. Bingham), Harry Baird (Billy).

Mills is a union boss who prevents a strike because of a black foreman. He tells union members that the color of a man's skin isn't important. At home he finds that his daughter is in love with a Jamaican and he and his wife in the end are forced to face the situation squarely and together.

p, Roy Baker, Jack Hanbury; d, Baker; w, Ted Willis (based on the play "Hot Summer Night" by Willis); ph, Christopher Challis (CinemaScope, DeLuxe Color); m, Philip Green; ed, Roger Cherrill; md, Green; art d, Alex Vetchinsky.

Drama   **(PR:A   MPAA:NR)**

FLAME OF ARABY**   (1951) 77m UNIV c

Maureen O'Hara (Tanya), Jeff Chandler (Tamerlane), Maxwell Reed (Medina), Susan Cabot (Clio), Lon Chaney, Jr. (Borka), Buddy Baer (Hakim), Richard Egan (Capt. Fezil), Royal Dano (Basra), Dewey Martin (Yak), Neville Brand (Kral), Henry Brandon (Mallik), Judith Braun (Calu), Tony Barr (Malat), Frederic Berest (Ibid), Cindy Garner (Elaine), Norene Michaels (Zara), Richard Hale (King Chandra), Virginia Brissac (Alhena), Dorothy Ford (Naja), William Tannen (Captain of Guards), Andre Charlot, Joe Kamaryt (Physicians), Lillian Ten Eyck (Elaine's Mother), Leon Charles (Huntsman), Chuck Hamilton (Ayub), Barry Brooks (Guard).

Bedouin Chandler hunts for the fastest black stallion in the Tunisian desert. Also after the horse is princess O'Hara, who wants the steed to beat the horse of two brutal brothers so as not to have to marry one of them. Chandler finds the horse and wins O'Hara and the climactic race. Light diversion in the company of fiery redhead O'Hara. The evil brothers are delightfully played by Chaney and Baer, the latter a one-time giant real-life boxer whose brother Max had once been heavyweight champ of the world and who also turned to clownish acting in his fading years.

p, Leonard Goldstein; d, Charles Lamont; w, Gerald Drayson Adams; ph, Russell Metty (Technicolor); ed, Ted J. Kent; md, Joseph Gershenson; art d, Bernard Herzbrun.

Adventure/Drama   **(PR:A   MPAA:NR)**

FLAME OF CALCUTTA**   (1953) 70m COL c

Denise Darcel (Suzanne Roget), Patric Knowles (Capt. Keith Lambert), Paul Cavanagh (Lord Robert Clive), George Keymas (Prince Jehan), Joseph Mell (Jowal), Ted Thorpe (Rana Singh), Leonard Penn (Nadir), Gregory Gay (Amir Khasid), Edward Clark (Pandit Bandar), Robin Hughes (Lt. Bob Ramsey), Sujata, Asoka (Dancers).

India circa 1760 is the backdrop for this melodrama. Darcel, the sensuous top-heavy daughter of a slain French official, assumes the title of "The Flame" and wages a guerrilla war on villain prince Keymas, who has vowed to blow out "The Flame" and get rid of the British East India Co. British officer Knowles falls in love with Darcel, and together they finish off Keymas. A breezy romp back through history with a license to change the facts at will.

p, Sam Katzman; d, Seymour Friedman; w, Robert E. Kent (based on a story by Sol Shor); ph, Henry Freulich, Ray Cory (Technicolor); m, Mischa Bakaleinikoff; ed, Jerome Thoms; art d, Paul Palmentola.

Adventure/Drama   **(PR:A   MPAA:NR)**

FLAME OF LOVE, THE*   (1930, Brit.) 74m British International bw

Anna May Wong (Hai Tang), John Longden (Lt. Boris), George Schnell (Grand Duke), Percy Standing (Col. Moravjev), Mona Goya (Yvette), J. Ley-On (Wang Hu), Fred Schwartz (Birnbaum).

Wong's brother, Ley-On, shoots a Russian grand duke in the arm when the duke gets fresh with her in this pre-Revolutionary Russia musical. Ley-On is given a death sentence for the crime, but Wong, a cabaret singer, tricks the duke with a come-hither ploy which effectively gets her and her brother kicked out of the country when she tells the duke she prefers the exit to the bed. A weak flame at best. This was one of several British and German films Wong, who had achieved international fame, made while on a lecture tour of Europe.

p, Richard Eichberg; d, Eichberg, Walter Summers; w, Monckton Hoffe, Ludwig Wolff; ph, Henry Gartner; ed, Emile De Rulle.

Drama   **(PR:A   MPAA:NR)**

FLAME OF NEW ORLEANS, THE**½   (1941) 78m UNIV bw

Marlene Dietrich (Claire Ledeux), Bruce Cabot (Robert Latour), Roland Young (Charles Giraud), Mischa Auer (Zolotov), Andy Devine (1st Sailor), Frank Jenks (2nd Sailor), Eddie Quillan (3rd Sailor), Joe Devlin (4th Sailor), Laura Hope Crews (Auntie), Franklin Pangborn (Bellows), Theresa Harris (Clementine), Clarence Muse (Samuel), Melville Cooper (Brother-in-Law), Anne Revere (Sister), Bob Evans (Williams), Emily Fitzroy, Virginia Sale, Dorothy Adams (Cousins), Anthony Marlowe, Gitta Alpar (Opera Singers), Gus Schilling (Clerk), Bess Flowers (Woman Guest), Reed Hadley (Man), Shemp Howard (Waiter), Frank Sully (Waterfront Waiter), Mary Treen (Woman at Ball), Rex Evans (Giraud's Butler).

This picture was assaulted by the critics when it was originally released but that was unfair and it looks good on a new viewing. It was French director Rene Clair's first U.S. film and he was hamstrung by censorship so he was unable to do the little things that brought him to America in the first place. Dietrich is a golddigger in the Crescent City, circa 1841. She's come from Europe to marry the richest man in New Orleans and assumes the role of a wealthy noblewoman in order to worm her way into society. The picture begins as we see a gorgeous wedding gown floating down the Mississippi and we flash back to learn what's happened to Dietrich who was to wear that dress on her wedding day. Once arrived in New Orleans, she pretends to faint in the box next to rich Roland Young at the opera. Naturally, he leaps to her side to help. After the performance, Young instructs his butler, Muse, to follow Dietrich's maid, Harris. He learns that Dietrich will be in the park on the following day. While she's riding in the park, Cabot, a tough but lovable sea captain, sees his pet monkey wrap his tail around Dietrich's carriage underbelly and he stops the vehicle. Dietrich bids the driver to go on but Cabot turns the carriage on its side, gets his monkey, and disappears. Dietrich thought it was part of Young's plot to waylay her and she feigns anger, never realizing that the incident was purely accidental. Later, Young comes to call on her and overhears some of her materialistic dialog in the other room. Thinking quickly, Harris assures Young that the words are not from Dietrich but from her "cousin." Young invites Dietrich to a party where she again encounters Cabot and his monkey. Cabot takes an immediate liking to her but she informs him she is to become Young's wife as soon as his ancient aunt, Crews, approves. There's a swanky party and Dietrich sings for the assemblage but is shocked to see Auer, a Russian from her notorious European past. Dietrich convinces Young that Auer is referring to her "cousin," a true trollop who is, at this moment, performing in a sleazy New Orleans waterfront dive known as the Oyster Bed Cafe. Young and his pal, Cooper, go to the cafe to see the wanton woman with Auer and Pangborn. She convinces them she is who she is. Later, Cabot is at the cafe and wonders how it is that two "cousins" can look so much alike. Unknown to Dietrich, Young and Cabot trail Dietrich to her residence and now know the truth. Young strikes a bargain with Cabot and gives him money if he'll take the "cousin" away on his boat. Cabot agrees. She joins him on the boat the night before her wedding and, the next day, at the ceremony, Cabot arrives. She faints and then disappears. She cannot be found anywhere and the picture ends with the dress enigmatically floating down Ol' Man River. Dietrich is very funny in the scene where Crews explains the "facts of life" to her and she sits there wide-eyed as the most virginal bride could be. It might have been better suited for Mae West than for Dietrich, but there was enough subtlety to make it worth a second look. The costumes are resplendent, the production is lush, and just to hear Dietrich sing "Sweet As The Blush Of May" is worth watching the rest of the film. Good comedy from Devine, Quillan, and Jenks as rough sailors in the Oyster Bed Cafe.

p, Joe Pasternak; d, Rene Clair; w, Norman Krasna; ph, Rudolph Mate; m, Frank Skinner; ed, Frank Gross; md, Charles Previn; art d, Jack Otterson, Martin Obzina, Russell A. Gausman; cos, Rene Hubert; m/l, "Sweet as the Blush of May" (sung by Dietrich), "Salt O' the Sea" (sung by the ship's crew), "Oh, Joyous Day" (sung by chorus), Previn, Sam Lerner.

Comedy   **(PR:A-C   MPAA:NR)**

FLAME OF SACRAMENTO   (SEE: IN OLD SACRAMENTO, 1946)

FLAME OF STAMBOUL*½   (1957) 68m COL bw

Richard Denning (Larry Wilson), Lisa Ferraday (Lynette Garay), Norman Lloyd (Baracca), Nestor Paiva (Willie), George Zucco (The Voice), Donald Randolph (Hassan), Peter Mamakos (Pierre), Paul Marion (Ahmed Raschin), Peter Brocco (Sadik Raschin).

Denning is a U.S. intelligence agent chasing "The Voice," Zucco, who is after Suez Canal defense plans. The criminal uses Oriental dancer Ferraday to distract the high-ranking Egyptian holding the papers. Denning foils the plot and brings the villains to justice. Fast-paced action thriller.

p, Wallace MacDonald; d, Ray Nazarro; w, Daniel B. Ullman; ph, Philip Tannura; m, Ross DiMaggio; ed, James Sweeney; md, DiMaggio; art d, Caru Odell.

Spy Drama   **(PR:A   MPAA:NR)**

FLAME OF THE BARBARY COAST** (1945) 91m REP bw

John Wayne (Duke Fergus), Ann Dvorak (Flaxen Tarry), Joseph Schildkraut (Tito Morell), William Frawley (Smooth Wylie), Virginia Grey (Rita Dane), Russell Hicks (Cyrus Danver), Jack Norton (Byline Conners), Paul Fix (Calico Jim), Manart Kippen (Dr. Gorman), Eve Lynne (Martha), Marc Lawrence (Disko), Butterfly McQueen (Beulah), Rex Lease (Headwaiter), Hank Bell (Cabby), Al Murphy (Horseshoe Brown), Adele Mara (Marie), Emmett Vogan (Rita's Agent).

Wayne is a Montana cattleman who falls in love with Dvorak on San Francisco's Barbary Coast. She helps him win a large sum of money on the gambling tables. He then loses it to a card cheat, Schildkraut. The Duke goes back to Montana and learns cards from an ace gambler. Returning to Frisco, he cleans up and opens his own gambling saloon. Dvorak is hired as the entertainment. The 1906 earthquake destroys Wayne's place and when Dvorak recovers from her injuries they leave for Montana. A lame script that a cast of healthy actors could not put on its feet, although Schildkraut makes a fine effort.

p&d, Joseph Kane; w, Borden Chase (based on a story by Prescott Chaplin); ph, Robert de Grasse; m, Morton Scott; md, Richard L. Van Enger; art d, Gano Chittenden; spec eff, Howard Lydecker, Theodore Lydecker; ch, Larry Ceballos; m/l, "Have a Heart," "Baby Blue Eyes," Jack Elliott (sung by Dvorak).

Western   Cas.   (PR:A   MPAA:NR)

FLAME OF THE ISLANDS*½ (1955) 90m REP c

Yvonne De Carlo (Rosalind Dee), Howard Duff (Doug Duryea), Zachary Scott (Wade Evans), Kurt Kasznar (Cyril Mace), Barbara O'Neil (Mrs. Duryea), James Arness (Kelly Rand), Frieda Inescort (Mrs. Hammond), Lester Matthews (Gus), Donald Curtis (Johnny), Nick Stewart (Willie), John Pickard (Parks), Leslie Denison (Foster Williams), Peter Adams (Clint Johnson).

DeCarlo gets her hands on some cash in a not-so-legitimate fashion and joins with Kasznar and Scott in starting a gambling club in the Bahamas. She is the hostess and signer, and revives her affair with old flame Duff. He gets involved with gangsters wanting control of the club, and Arness arrives to save the day.

p&d, Edward Ludwig; w, Bruce Manning (based on a story by Adele Comandini); ph, Bud Thackery (TruColor); m, Sonny Burke, Jack Elliott; ed, Richard L. Van Enger; md, Nelson Riddle; m/l, "Bahama Mama," "Take It Or Leave It," Burke, Elliott (sung by De Carlo).

Drama   (PR:A   MPAA:NR)

FLAME OF THE WEST*** (1945) 71m MON bw
(AKA: FLAMING FRONTIER)

Johnny Mack Brown (John Poore), Raymond Hatton (Add), Joan Woodbury (Poppy), Douglas Dumbrille (Nightlander), Lynne Carver (Abbie Compton), Harry Woods (Wisdon), John Merton (Compton), Riley Hill (Midland), Steve Clark (Hendricks), Bud Osborne (Pircell), Jack Rockwell (Knott), Raphael Bennett (Rocky), Tom Quinn (Ed), Jack Ingram (Slick), Pee Wee King and His Golden West Cowboys.

Brown drops his series character, Nevada John McKenzie, and plays a pacifist doctor, forced to use violence when the sheriff is murdered by outlaws. Doctor Brown goes after them with guns blazing in a terrific action-packed production. Considered to be Brown's best Western. Director Hillyer worked with W.S. Hart in the silent era.

p, Scott R. Dunlap; d, Lambert Hillyer; w, Adele Buffington; ph, Harry Neumann; ed, Dan Milner; md, Frank Sanucci; art d, E. R. Hickson.

Western   (PR:A   MPAA:NR)

FLAME OF TORMENT (SEE: ENJO, 1958, Jap.)

FLAME OF YOUTH* (1949) 60m REP bw

Barbara Fuller (Lila Coletti), Ray McDonald (Bill Crawford), Danni Nolan (Jerry Briggs), Tony Barrett (Deke Edwards), Carol Brannon (Catherine Briggs), Anita Carrell (Barb Spranklin), Michael Carr (Cicero Coletti), Don Beddoe (George Briggs), Denver Pyle (Lefty), Willard Waterman (Steve Miller), Arthur Walsh (Hector), Kathryn Lang (Miss O'Brien), Maurice Doner (Loomis), Stephen Chase (Charles Howard), Charles Flynn (Jim Bennet), Audrey Farr (Waitress).

A group of high school students makes money by stealing automobile accessories and operating nickel-and-dime handbooks. The worst of the group gets gunned down and the rest realize crime isn't the life for them. Heavy-handed and boring picture.

p, Lou Brock; d, R.G. Springsteen; w, Robert Libott, Frank Burt, Bradford Ropes (adapted from a story by Albert DeMond); ph, John MacBurnie; m, Stanley Wilson; ed, Robert Leeds; art d, Frank Hotaling.

Crime   (PR:A   MPAA:NR)

FLAME OVER INDIA*** (1960, Brit.) 130m RANK—RFD/FOX c
(AKA: NORTH WEST FRONTIER)

Kenneth More (Capt. Scott), Lauren Bacall (Catherine Wyatt), Herbert Lom (Van Leyden), Wilfrid Hyde White (Bridie), I.S. Johar (Gupta), Ursula Jeans (Lady Wyndham), Ian Hunter (Sir John Wyndham), Eugene Deckers (Peters), Jack Gwillim (Brig Ames), Govind Raja Ross (Prince Kishnan), Frank Olegario (Maharaja), Moultrie Kelsall, Lionel Murton, S. M. Asgaralli, S.S. Chowdhry, Jaron Yalton, Homi Bode, Ronald Cardew, Basil Hoskins.

This beautifully photographed film starts with a Moslem siege of a British fortress town in rural India. The main thrust of the film is to get the Maharaja's son away from the trouble spot. More commandeers an old train with colorful I.S. Johar as the feisty engineer, and, along with a number of other people, escapes from the fort; the fugitives have a number of wild adventures along the way, including dealing with traitor Lom in their midst. A very enjoyable film, loaded with action, suspense and excellent thesping, especially from Bacall and More who have a

tempestuous relationship, and Hyde White as a charming Englishman with the manners of a Victorian gentleman.

p, Marcel Hellman; d, J. Lee Thompson; w, Robin Estridge; ph, Geoffrey Unsworth (CinemaScope, DeLuxe Color); m, Mischa Spoliansky; cos, Yvonne Caffin.

Adventure   (PR:A   MPAA:NR)

FLAME OVER VIETNAM**½ (1967, Span./Ger.) 88m
Westside International-UFA/PRC bw

Elena Barrios (Sister Paula), Jose Nieto (Lazlo), Manolo Moran (Brother Bartholomew), Nicolas Perchicot (Father Elias), Rosita Palomar (Selma), Felix Dafauce (Ellison), Maria Martin (Angela), Vicente P. Avila (Driver).

War drama set in Vietnam during the disastrous French occupation finds Nieto as a wounded gunrunner who is nursed back to health by a nun, Barrios. Later he helps the nun and a band of orphans she is shepherding escape from a Vietminh concentration camp and, while lifting the last of the orphans onto an escape plane he has chartered, he is killed. A moving story of self-sacrifice in a country where such actions are legion.

p, Sidney Pink; d, Joe Lacy [Jose Maria Elorrieta]; w, Ralph Salvia [Rafael Salvia], Lacy, John Hart (based on a story by Salvia); ph, Miguel F. Mila; m, Fernando Garcia Morcillo; ed, Felix Suarez; m/l, "Mon Amour, Mon Amour," Genaro Camilo Murillo (sung by Maria Martin).

War   (PR:A   MPAA:NR)

FLAME WITHIN, THE** (1935) 72m MGM bw

Ann Harding (Mary White), Herbert Marshall (Gordon Phillips), Maureen O'Sullivan (Lillian Belton), Louis Hayward (Jack Kerry), Henry Stephenson (Jock Frazier), Margaret Seddon (Mrs. Grenfell), George Hassel (Rigby), Eily Malyon (Murdock), Claudelle Kaye (Nurse Carter).

Harding is a psychiatrist who becomes deeply involved with her patients. She helps a male patient fight alcoholism, and also the girl who loves him. The girl tries to commit suicide because of her failing relationship and Harding pulls them back together leaving Harding a little the worse for the wear. A good case history illuminating the old saw that a psychiatrist should never get too close to a client.

p,d&w, Edmund Goulding; ph, James Wong Howe; m, Jerome Kern; ed, Blanche Sewell.

Drama   (PR:C   MPAA:NR)

FLAMES*½ (1932) 64m MON bw

Johnny Mack Brown (Charlie), Noel Francis (Pat), George Cooper (Fishy), Marjorie Beebe (Gertie), Richard Tucker (Garson), Russell Simpson (Jake), Kit Guard (Pete).

Brown is a well-dressed fireman chasing after Francis, and so is her new boss. Brown warns her that the building she lives in is a fire trap, and when it does go up in flames Francis realizes Brown is the man for her. In all the film's smoke there isn't much fire.

d, Karl Brown; w, Brown, I.E. Chadwick.

Drama   (PR:A   MPAA:NR)

FLAMING BULLETS** (1945) 55m PRC bw

Tex Ritter, Dave O'Brien, Guy Wilkerson, Charles King, Patricia Knox, I. Stanford Jolley, Bob Duncan, Bud Osborne, Kermit Maynard, Dick Alexander, Dan White.

The last of the Texas Rangers series has the trio breaking up a gang that breaks men out of jail, then kills them for the reward money. Finally one of the heroes gets himself locked up so the criminals will break him out. Okay action scenes, but the series was visibly on its last legs.

p, Arthur Alexander; d&w, Harry Fraser; ph, Robert Cline; ed, Holbrook N. Todd.

Western   (PR:A   MPAA:NR)

FLAMING DESIRE (SEE: SMALL HOURS, THE, 1962)

FLAMING FEATHER**½ (1951) 79m PAR c

Sterling Hayden (Tex McCloud), Forrest Tucker (Lt. Tom Blaine), Barbara Rush (Nora Logan), Arleen Whelan (Carolina), Carol Thurston (Turquoise), Edgar Buchanan (Sgt. O'Rourke), Victor Jory (Lucky Lee), Richard Arlen (Showdown Calhoun), Ian MacDonald (Tombstone Jack), George Cleveland (Doc Fallon), Bob Kortman (Lafe), Ethan Laidlaw (Ed Poke), Don Dunning, Paul Burns, Ray Teal, Nacho Galindo, Frank Lackteen, Gene Lewis, Larry McGrath, Herman Nowlin, Bryan Hightower, Donald Kerr.

Rancher Hayden is attacked by a band of renegade Indians led by a mysterious outlaw. He goes after them, and so does cavalry officer Tucker. Jory is the mysterious outlaw posing as a wealthy landowner, and Rush, in one of her first feature roles, plans to marry him because he saved her from the Indians.

p, Nat Holt; d, Ray Enright; w, Gerald Drayson Adams, Frank Gruber; ph, Ray Rennahan (Technicolor); m, Paul Sawtell; ed, Elmo Billings; art d, John Goodman.

Western   (PR:A   MPAA:NR)

FLAMING FRONTIER* (1958, Can.) 70m Regal/FOX bw

Bruce Bennett (Capt. Jim Hewson), Jim Davis (Col. Hugh Carver), Don Garrard (Sgt. Haggerty), Paisley Maxwell (Felice Carver), Cecil Linder (Capt. Dan Carver), Peter Humphreys (Sgt. Emundson), Ben Lennick (Jeff Baxter), Larry Solway (Chief Little Crow), Bill Walsh (Gen. Dunn), Larry Mann (Bradford), Mike Fitzgerald (Maj. Franklin), Bob Vanstone (Capt. Carver's Sentry), Shane Rimmer (Running Bear), Charles Kehoe (Soldier), Brandon Dillon (Store Clerk), Jeffrey Alexander (Army Doctor), Daryl Masters (Man), Allen Chrysler (Capt. Leech), Dave Wright (2nd Clerk).

Bennett is a halfbreed officer in the U.S. Cavalry who manages to keep the Indians and the Army from fighting. Downright bad oater, the last film by veteran B movie director Newfield.

p&d, Sam Newfield; w, Louis Stevens; ph, Frederick Ford (RegalScope); m, John Bath; ed, Douglas Robertson; md, Bath; art d, Tom Kemp.

Western (PR:A MPAA:NR)

FLAMING FRONTIER½ (1968, Ger./Yugo.) 92m Rialto-Jadran/WB c

Stewart Granger (Old Surehand), Pierre Brice (Winnetou), Larry Pennell (The General), Letitia Roman (Judith), Mario Girotti (Toby), Erik Schumann (Captain Miller), Wolfgang Lukschy (Judge Edwards), Paddy Fox (Old Wabble), Aleksandar Gavric, Voja Miric, Dusan Janicijevic, Dusan Antonijevic, Vladimir Hedar, Hermina Pipinic, Jelena Jovanovic, Bata Zivojinovic.

This German-Yugoslavian production was one of the many European westerns flooding American theaters in the late 1960s. Granger is a frontiersman whose guns and fast-talking prevent a war between settlers as he tracks down his brother's killer. One of the films Granger did as a free-lance actor after he left MGM.

p, Horst Wendlandt, Preben Phillipsen; d, Alfred Vohrer; w, Fred Denger (based on a story by Karl May); ph, Karl Loeb (Ultrascope, Eastmancolor); m, Martin Boettcher; ed, Hermann Haller; art d, Vladimir Tadej; cos, Irms Pauli; spec eff, Erwin Lange.

Western (PR:A MPAA:NR)

FLAMING FURY** (1949) 59m REP bw

Roy Roberts (Capt. Taplinger), George Cooper (Russ Haines), David Wolfe (Tony Polacheck), Billy Wayne (Berkeley), Peter Brocco (E.V. Wessman), Ransom Sherman (Mr. Hollingworth), Paul Marion (Sam Polacheck), Celia Lovsky (Bertha Polacheck), Cliff Clark (Rollins), Jimmie Dodd (Kenneth Bender), G. Pat Collins (Battalion Chief), Bob Purcell (Deputy Fire Chief).

A documentary style melodrama about the Los Angeles Fire Department's arson squad. The boys are chasing down a gang of crooks who are setting fires to hide their crimes. Cooper is the rookie assigned to go undercover as one of the bad guys. He finds that the gang is headed by a mother, who uses her canaries to decide whether to start a fire. Nicely paced look behind the scenes of a big city problem.

p, Sidney Picker; d, George Blair; w, John K. Butler; ph, John MacBurnie; ed, Tony Martinelli; art d, Frank Hotaling.

Crime (PR:A MPAA:NR)

FLAMING GOLD* (1934) 54m RKO bw

Bill Boyd (Dan Manton), Pat O'Brien (Ben Lear), Mae Clarke (Claire Arnold), Rollo Lloyd (Banning), Helen Ware (Tess).

A large oil company comes down hard on O'Brien and Boyd, two wildcatters in Mexico, it wants to drive out of the desert for reasons only tycoons know. Instead, after a zigzag story course, the pair gets their faces blackened as oil streams out in a gush from their well. No lamps will get lighted from this piece of the oil scene.

p, Merian C. Cooper; d, Ralph Ince; w, Malcolm Stuart Boylan, John Goodrich (based on a story by Houston Branch); ph, Charles Rosher; ed, George Crone; art d, Earl Wolcott.

Drama (PR:A MPAA:NR)

FLAMING GUNS½ (1933) 57m UNIV bw

Tom Mix, Ruth Hall, William Farnum, George Hackathorne, Clarence Wilson, Bud Osborne, Duke Lee, Pee Wee Holmes, Jimmy Shannon, William Steele, Walter Patterson, Fred Burns, Slim Whitaker, Clyde Kinney, Tony, Jr.

Cowboy Mix falls in love with banker's daughter Hall. When her parents disapprove, the lovers elope to Mexico. Not one of the star's more satisfactory efforts.

d, Arthur Rosson; w, Jack Cunningham (based on a story by Peter B. Kyne); ph, Jerry Ash; ed, Phil Cahn.

Western **Cas.** (PR:A MPAA:NR)

FLAMING LEAD½ (1939) 57m Colony bw

Ken Maynard (Clark), Eleanor Stewart (Kay), Walter Long (Greeley), Tom London (Daggett), Ralph Peters (Panhandle), Carleton Young (Hank), Reed Howes (Tex), Dave O'Brien (Gordon), Bob Terry (Larry), Kenne Duncan (Larry), Ethan Allen (Sheriff), Joyce Rogers (Gertie), John Merton, Carl Mathews.

Maynard works in a nightclub doing cowboy tricks in this late career outing, and hard-drinking O'Brien hires him to work on his ranch. He wants Maynard to act as half-owner, so he can get an Army horse contract. Maynard had lost much of his appeal by now, and younger cowboys were taking over the range.

p, Max Alexander, Arthur Alexander; d, Sam Newfield; w, Joseph O'Donnell; ph, Art Reed; ed, Holbrook Todd.

Western **Cas.** (PR:A MPAA:NR)

FLAMING SIGNAL** (1933) 64m IN bw

Marceline Day (Sally James), John David Horsley (Jim Robbins), Carmelita Geraghty (Molly), Noah Beery (Otto von Krantz), Henry B. Walthall (The Reverend Mr. James), Mischa Auer (Manu), Francisco Alonso (Taku), Janne Olmes (Rari), Flash (The Dog).

An abundance of action was provided in this adventure saga in which Horsley plays a risk-taking pilot forced to crash near a small island in the Pacific. His entrance coincides with native unrest against the few whites on the island, sparked by the unscrupulous dealings of opportunist Beery. This German trader has shown little respect for the locals, who eventually explode when Beery attempts to take advantage of a local beauty, venting their anger against the other whites on the island. Horsely does everything possible to save the missionary and his daughter (Day), but only the girl is able to reach safety with the pilot, while all the others are killed in the uproar. Flash, Horsley's dog, is instrumental in providing the heroics. This animal and Horsely are equally forced in their deliveries, though a strong

supporting cast helped to ease this problem, as did the non-stop action and fast pace.

p, William Berke; d, C.E. Roberts, George Jeske; w, Roberts, Thomas Hughes (based on a story by William G. Storer); md, Abe Meyer; set d, F.W. Widdowson.

Adventure **Cas.** (PR:A MPAA:NR)

FLAMING STAR** ½ (1960) 92m FOX c

Elvis Presley (Pacer Burton), Barbara Eden (Roslyn Pierce), Steve Forrest (Clint Burton), Dolores Del Rio (Neddy Burton), John McIntire (Pa Burton), Rudolph Acosta (Buffalo Horn), Karl Swenson (Dred Pierce), Ford Rainey (Doc Phillips), Richard Jaeckel (Angus Pierce), Anne Benton (Dorothy Howard), L.Q. Jones (Tom Howard), Douglas Dick (Will Howard), Tom Reese (Jute), Marian Goldina (Ph' Sha Knay), Monte Burkhart (Ben Ford), Ted Jacques (Hornsby), Rodd Redwing (Indian Brave), Perry Lopez (Two Moons), Sharon Bercutt (Bird's Wing), Ray Beltran (Indian), Barbara Beaird (Dottie Phillips), Virginia Christine (Mrs. Phillips), Griswold Green, Tom Allen, Guy Way, Joe Brooks, William Herrin (Men at Crossing), The Jordanaires (Vocal Accompaniment).

This was Presley's best film, far superior to the moronic material he was usually saddled with. He plays an Indian half-breed, who must chose between his white father, McIntire, and his Kiowa mother, Del Rio. Despite his parents' attempts to remain neutral, Del Rio is killed by a white man and McIntire is later killed in an Indian raid. Presley has joined the Indians and Forrest, his brother, tries to avenge McIntire's death by attacking the Indians singlehandedly. He ambushes and kills the chief, but is severely wounded. Presley ties his brother to a horse and sends him off to safety while staving off the marauding tribe. Eden tends to Forrest's wounds and tries to keep him in bed, but he struggles off to help Presley. When he makes it to the streets, he can only watch as the mortally wounded Presley rides off into the mountains to die. A violent Western of racial prejudice that focuses on the consequences rather than the causes. Siegel's crafty direction shapes this film into a standout Western, and proves that, with an intelligent script, Presley could give a forcible acting performance. The film was refreshingly absent of the record peddling emphasis so predominant in other Presley vehicles (there isn't a song sung after the first ten minutes). The script was originally written for Marlon Brando by Johnson, then rewritten for Presley by Huffaker. The studio cut ten minutes from the original film. This film ranks up there with Presley's JAILHOUSE ROCK. Classic Elvis!

p, David Weisbart; d, Don Siegel; w, Clair Huffaker, Nunnally Johnson (adapted from the novel by Huffaker); ph, Charles G. Clarke (CinemaScope, DeLuxe Color); m, Cyril J. Mockridge; ed, Hugh S. Fowler; art d, Duncan Cramer, Walter M. Simonds; set d, Walter M. Scott, Gustav Berntsen; cos, Adele Balken; ch, Josephine Earl; m/l, "Flaming Star," "A Cane and a High Starched Collar," Sherman Edwards, Sid Wayne (sung by Presley).

Western **Cas.** (PR:C-O MPAA:NR)

FLAMING TEEN-AGE, THE* (1956) 67m Truman bw

Noel Reyburn, Ethel Barrett, Jerry Frank, Shirley Holmes.

An episodic pseudo-documentary on the evils of alcohol and drugs. First part has a father take his son out to the bars to show him the evils of alcohol. The last segment is an alleged true story of a dope addict who becomes an evangelist. Cheap and exploitative.

p&d, Ervin S. Yeaworth, Charles Edwards; w, Jean Yeaworth, Ethel Barrett; ph, John Ayling; art d, Bill Jersey.

Drama (PR:A MPAA:NR)

FLAMINGO AFFAIR, THE* (1948, Brit.) 58m Inspiration/GN bw
(AKA: BLONDE FOR DANGER)

Denis Webb (Dick Tarleton), Colette Melville (Paula Danvers), Arthur Chesney (Roberts), Eddie Matthews (Eddie Williams), Michael Anthony (Reynolds), Geoffrey Wilmer (Schultz), Hilary Trent (Maid), Charmain Innes (Singer), Pamela Fisher, Stephane Grappelly and his Quintet, Eugene Pini and His Tango Orchestra.

Discharged from the commandos at the end of the war, Webb takes a job in a garage and falls in love with Melville, a blonde with black-market connections. She convinces him to rob the safe in his office, but conscience keeps him honest. An appearance by jazz violinist Stephane Grappelly is the only reason to watch this clinker.

p&d, Horace Shepherd; w, Maurice Moisiewitsch; ph, Freddie Ford.

Crime (PR:A MPAA:NR)

FLAMINGO ROAD** (1949) 94m WB bw

Joan Crawford (Lane Bellamy), Zachary Scott (Fielding Carlisle), Sydney Greenstreet (Titus Semple), David Brian (Dan Reynolds), Gladys George (Lute-Mae Sanders), Virginia Huston (Annabelle Weldon), Fred Clark (Doc Waterson), Gertrude Michael (Millie), Alice White (Gracie), Sam McDaniel (Boatright), Tito Vuolo (Pete Ladas), Dick Ryan, Pat Gleason (Barkers), Tristram Coffin (Ed Parker), Dale Robertson (Tunis Simms), Iris Adrian (Blanche), Carol Brewster, Sunny Knight (Waitresses), Lester Kimmel (Lawyer), Frank Scannell (Man), Sam McKim (Bellboy), Pierre Watkin (Senator).

A Crawford vehicle all the way, FLAMINGO ROAD profiles a woman many times wronged who struggles to reach her destination, happiness. Crawford is a dancer in a carnival sideshow, a cooch wiggler who catches the eye of Scott, a charming but weak-willed deputy to tyrant sheriff Greenstreet. When the show folds and she is stranded, Scott gets Crawford a job as a waitress. Greenstreet, who considers Scott his political protege and a controllable candidate for state senator, does not want to see his plans upset by some scheming female. He frames Crawford on a phony prostitution charge and she is sent to prison. Greenstreet goes on to arrange a "politically correct" marriage for Scott with socialite Huston. After serving a prison term, Crawford returns to the southern town bent on revenge. George gives her a job as a hostess in a road house and here Crawford meets political boss

Brian, who falls in love with her and later marries her. Through Crawford's machinations, Brian becomes a reformer and goes into head-to-head battle with Greenstreet over the state's political machine, wrecking his candidates' chances of re-election. One of these is the spineless Scott, who goes to Crawford to beg for support. When she refuses, he commits suicide. Not missing any opportunities, Greenstreet uses his protege's death to scandalize Brian and Crawford. Incensed, Crawford goes to Greenstreet and the two struggle with a gun she has brought along. It goes off and the corrupt sheriff is killed. Crawford is again arrested and jailed but Brian appears and offers his support, so it looks like there is a glimmer of hope for the unlucky Crawford. The actress does a commendable job in a role that demands much; she is both tough and sensitive when needed, playing well against Scott, the weakling, and Brian, the strong man, her best scenes being those where the thoroughly malignant Greenstreet tests her strength. When Jack Warner offered Crawford FLAMINGO ROAD, she demanded that it be rewritten. Warner ordered it rewritten. Still she was not satisfied. Warner threw in Curtiz for direction, fine production mounting, and excellent supporting players, and Crawford finally acquiesced.

p, Jerry Wald; d, Michael Curtiz; w, Robert Wilder, Edmund H. North (based on the play by Wilder and Sally Wilder); ph, Ted McCord; m, Max Steiner; ed, Folmar Blangsted; md, Ray Heindorf; art d, Leo K. Kuter; set d, Howard Winterbottom; cos, Travilla; makeup, Perc Westmore.

Drama (PR:C MPAA:NR)

FLANAGAN BOY, THE (SEE: BAD BLONDE, 1953, Brit.)

FLANNELFOOT* (1953, Brit.) 74m E.J. Fancey/New Realm bw

Ronald Howard (Sgt. Fitzgerald), Mary Germaine (Kathleen Fraser), Jack Watling (Frank Mitchell), Gene Anderson (Rene Wexford), Ronald Adam (Inspector Duggan), Adrienne Scott (Cynthia Leyland), Graham Stark (Ginger), Kim Peacock, Vanda Godsell, Edwin Richfield, Ronald Leigh-Hunt.

Ace crime reporter Watling tries to discover the identity of a notorious jewel thief, but his informant is murdered. At a house party, Watling helps detective Adam expose the criminal. Routine crime drama manages to maintain some suspense, but otherwise it is not very good.

p, E.J. Fancey; d, Maclean Rogers; w, Carl Heck (based on a story by Jack Henry); ph, Geoffrey Faithfull.

Crime (PR:A MPAA:NR)

FLAP zero (1970) 107m WB c (GB: THE LAST WARRIOR; AKA: NOBODY LOVES A DRUNKEN INDIAN, NOBODY LOVES A FLAPPING EAGLE)

Anthony Quinn (Flapping Eagle), Claude Akins (Lobo), Tony Bill (Eleven Snowflake), Victor Jory (Wounded Bear Mr. Smith), Don Collier (Mike Lyons), Victor French (Rafferty), Rodolfo Acosta (Storekeep), Anthony Caruso (Silver Dollar), Shelley Winters (Dorothy Bluebell), Susana Miranda (Ann Looking Deer), William Mims (Steve Gray), Rudi Diaz (Larry Standing Elk), Pedro Regas (She'll-Be-Back-Pretty-Soon), J. Edward McKinley (Harris), Robert Cleaves (Gus Kirk), John War Eagle (Luke Wolf).

Quinn is an alcoholic Indian who starts a P.R. campaign for Indian rights. His girl friend is a madame, Winters, and he's in a continuing feud with the police sergeant, French. Quinn begins destroying bulldozers and hijacking trains, and he lassos a police helicopter, justifying everything by old Indian treaties. A ludicrous comedy which does nothing for the cause of the American Indian. Warner Bros. kept the film in a vault for 18 months before releasing it, and it's too bad it didn't have a chance to decay. FLAP got its just rewards, though, by becoming a $6-million flop.

p, Jerry Adler; d, Carol Reed; w, Clair Huffaker (based on the novel Nobody Loves a Drunken Indian by Huffaker); ph, Fred J. Koenekamp (Panavision, Technicolor); m, Marvin Hamlisch; ed, Frank Bracht; prod d, Art Loel; art d, Mort Rabinowitz; set d, Ralph S. Hurst; m/l, "If Nobody Loves," Marvin Hamlisch, Estelle Levitt (sung by Kenny Rogers and the First Edition).

Comedy (PR:A MPAA:GP)

FLAREUP ** (1969) 96m MGM c (AKA: FLARE UP, FLARE-UP)

Raquel Welch (Michele), James Stacy (Joe Brodnek), Luke Askew (Alan Morris), Don Chastain (Lieutenant Manion), Ron Rifkin ("Sailor"), Jean Byron (Jerri Benton), Kay Peters (Lee), Pat Delany (Iris), Sandra Giles (Nikki), Joe Billings (Lloyd Seibert), Carol-Jean Thompson (Jackie), Mary Wilcox (Tora), Carl Byrd (Sgt. Newcomb), Steve Conte (Lt. Franklin), Tom Fadden (Mr. Willows), Michael Rougas (Dr. Connors), David Moses (Technician), Will J. White (Sgt. Stafford), Doug Rowe (Gas Station Attendant), Gordon Jump (Security Guard), Ike Williams (Policeman), The Gazzarri Dancers.

Welch dances at a Las Vegas night spot with two other women. One is divorced and her ex-husband kills her and goes after her two friends, whom he blames for putting ideas in his wife's head. When the second woman is killed, Welch goes to dance in a Los Angeles bar called The Loser. There, she starts a romance with parking attendant Stacy. The killer follows and at the end is killed. Welch comes through royally in this suspense-filled drama, albeit her hip-grinding dance numbers are more suggestive than artistic.

p, Leon Fromkess; d, James Neilson; w, Mark Rodgers; ph, Andrew J. McIntyre (Metrocolor); m, Lex Baxter; ed, Aaron Stell; md, Baxter; art d, Frank Sylos; set d, Ralph Sylos; m/l, "Flareup," Baxter, Lenny Adelson.

Thriller (PR:O MPAA:M)

FLASH AND THE FIRECAT* (1976) 89m Sebastian c

Roger Davis (Firecat), Tricia Sembera (Flash), Dub Taylor (Sheriff), Richard Kiel (Investigator), Joan Shawlee (Rose), Philip Burns, Tracy Sebastian.

Low budget exploitation item has Davis and Sembera riding around in their dune buggy planning the big job and staying ahead of sheriff Taylor. Nothing worthwhile here.

p,d&w, Ferd and Beverley Sebastian; ph, (Movielab Color).

Crime Cas. (PR:C MPAA:PG)

FLASH GORDON** (1936) 97m UNIV bw
(AKA: ROCKET SHIP, SPACESHIP TO THE UNKNOWN, SPACE SOLDIERS, ATOMIC ROCKETSHIP)

Larry "Buster" Crabbe (Flash Gordon), Jean Rogers (Dale Arden), Charles Middleton (Ming the Merciless), Priscilla Lawson (Princess Aura), John Lipson (King Vultan), Richard Alexander (Prince Barin), Frank Shannon (Dr. Zarkov), Duke York, Jr. (King Kala), Earl Askam (Officer Torch), George Cleveland (Prof. Hensley), Theodore Lorch (High Priest), House Peters, Jr. (Shark Man), James Pierce (King Thun), Muriel Goodspeed (Zona), Richard Tucker (Flash Gordon, Sr.), Fred Kohler, Jr., Lane Chandler, Al Ferguson, Glenn Strange (Soldiers).

The one, the only, the original, and the best. This started as a thirteen part serial shown week by week in movie houses during the 1930s. Taken from the King Features comic strip, Flash Gordon (Olympic hero Crabbe) and his companion, Dr. Zarkov (Shannon), along with sweetheart Dale Arden (Rogers) blast off to planet Mongo, trying to stop it from a collision course with Earth. There Crabbe encounters evil Ming the Merciless (Middleton of bald head and cruel mustache) along with assorted hawk men, shark men, dinosaurs, horned gorillas, giant lobsters, space ships on none too subtle wires, and some nifty costumes. There's a great love triangle with Middleton lusting wantonly for Rogers, while Princess Aura (Lawson), Middleton's outer space daughter, has a heavy crush on Crabbe. The music and some sets were borrowed from THE BRIDE OF FRANKENSTEIN released a year earlier. Great fun and not to be missed.

p, Henry MacRae; d, Frederick Stephani; w, Stephani, George Plympton, Basil Dickey, Ella O'Neill (based on the comic strip by Alex Raymond); ph, Jerry Ash, Richard Fryer; m, Franz Waxman (from THE BRIDE OF FRANKENSTEIN); art d, Ralph Berger; spec eff, Norman Drewes.

Science Fiction/Adventure Cas. (PR:AAA MPAA:NR)

FLASH GORDON ** (1980) 110m UNIV c

Sam J. Jones (Flash Gordon), Melody Anderson (Dale Arden), Topol (Dr. Hans Zarkov), Max von Sydow (Emperor Ming), Ornella Muti (Princess Aura), Timothy Dalton (Prince Barin), Brian Blessed (Prince Vultan), Peter Wyngarde (Klytus), Mariangela Melato (Kala), John Osborne (Arborian Priest), Richard O'Brien (Fico), John Hallam (Luro), Philip Stone (Zogi, the High Priest), Suzanne Danielle (Serving Girl), William Hootkins (Munson), Bobbie Brown (Hedonia), Ted Carroll (Biro), Adrienne Kronenberg (Vultan's Daughter), Stanley Lebor (Mongon Doctor), John Morton, Burnell Tucker (Airline Pilots), Robbie Coltrane (Man At Airport), Peter Duncan (Young Treeman), Ken Sicklen (Treeman), Tessa, Vanetia Spicer (Hawkwomen), Francis Mugham (Wounded Hawkman), Paul Bentall (Klytus' Pilot), Oliver MacGreevey (Klytus' Observer No. 1), John Hollis (Klytus' Observer No. 2), Tony Scannell (Ming's Officer), Leon Greene (Colonel in Battle Control Room), Graeme Crowther (Battle Room Controller), David Neal (Captain of Ming's Air Force), Deep Roy (Princess Aura's Pet), Sally Nicholson (Queen of Azuria), Doretta Dunkler (Queen of Frigia), Colin Taylor (King of Frigia), George Harris (Prince of Ardentia), Miranda Riley (Frigian Girl), Andrew Bradford, Bertram Adams, Terry Forrestal, Mike Potter, John Sullivan, John Lees, Eddie Stacy, Roy Scammell (Hawkmen), Robert Goody, Peter S. James, Steven Payne, Daniel Venn, Max Alford, Anthony Olivier, Stephen Calcutt, Stuart Blake, Nigel Jeffcoat, Jim Carter (Azurdian Men), Trevor Ward, Alva Shelley, Joe Iles, Nik Abraham, Glen Whittier, Leonard Hay (Ardentian Men), Jamalia, Sunanka, Jil Lamb, Karen Johnson (Ming's Serving Girls), Kathy Marquis, Kathy September, Sophie, Glenna Forster Jones (Sandmoon Girls), Rosanne Romine, Sneh, Shaka, Magda, Linda, Viva, Camella, Frances Ward, Beverly Andrews, Kerry Loy Baylis (Cytherian Girls), Lorraine Paul, Carolyn Evans, Ruthie Barnett, Celeste, Tina Thomas (Aquarian Girls), Racquel, Fai, Gina (Ming's Exotic Girls), Eddie Powell, Chris Webb, John Gallant, Les Crawford, Peter Brace, Terry Richards (Ming's Brutes), Kenny Baker, Malcolm Dixon, Mike Edmonds, Tiny Ross, John Ghavan, Rusty Goffe, Mike Cottrell, Peter Burrows, Richard Jones, John Lummis (Dwarfs), Michelle Mildwater, Marie Green, Imogen Claire, Kay Zimmerman, Stephen Brigden, Ken Robertson, Fred Warder, Lionel Guyett.

The only good thing about this pseudo-camp version of the classic 1936 serial is the impressive production design by Danilo Donati. Jones as the title character has to rank as one of the all-time worst casting choices. DeLaurentiis discovered him on the TV show "The Dating Game," and his lines had to be dubbed by another actor. This time around Flash is a football quarterback saving the world from Emperor Ming, Von Sydow. Semple's script seems to poke more fun at the audience's intelligence than at the story itself. Kids will enjoy this, but anyone over ten years old, forget it.

p, Dino DeLaurentiis; d, Mike Hodges; w, Lorenzo Semple, Jr., Michael Allin (based on characters created by Alex Raymond); ph, Gil Taylor (Todd-AO, Technicolor); m, Howard Blake; ed, Malcolm Cooke; prod d, Danilo Donati; art d, John Graysmark; set d, Donati; cos, Donati; spec eff, George Gibbs, Richard Conway (models and skies), Derek Botel (flying).

Science Fiction/Fantasy Cas. (PR:AA MPAA:PG)

FLASH THE SHEEPDOG* (1967, Brit.) 58m
International Film Associates/CFF c

Earl Younger (Tom Stokes), Ross Campbell (Dougie), Alex Allan (Andra), Victor Carin (Uncle John), Margaret Greig (Elspeth), David Hanley (Ian), John Short (Jimmie), Marjorie Thompson (Aunt Meg).

Feeble children's film has Younger an orphan in Scotland who trains a sheepdog owned by his uncle to be a prizewinner at dog trials. An insipid story that seems to be the plot of most children's films, plus almost nonexistent production values add up to a disappointment for old and young alike.

p, J.B. Holmes; d&w, Laurence Henson (based on a novel by Kathleen Fidler); ph (Eastmancolor).

Children (PR:AA MPAA:NR)

FLASHDANCE* (1983) 96m Polygram/PAR c

Jennifer Beals (Alex Owens), Michael Nouri (Nick Hurley), Lilia Skala (Hanna Long), Sunny Johnson (Jeanie Szabo), Kyle T. Heffner (Richie), Lee Ving (Johnny C), Ron Karabatsos (Jake Mawby), Belinda Bauer (Katie Hurley), Malcolm Danare (Cecil), Phil Bruns (Frank Szabo), Micole Mercurio (Rosemary Szabo), Lucy Lee Flippin (Secretary), Don Brockett (Pete), Cynthia Rhodes (Tina Tech), Durga McBroom (Heels), Stacy Pickren (Margo), Liz Sagal (Sunny), Norman Scott (Norm-ski), Marc Lemberger (Mr. Freeze), Wayne Frost (Frosty Freeze), Kenneth Gabbert (Prince Ken Swift), Richard Colon (Crazy Legs), Larry John Meyers, David Dimanna (Welders), Helen Dexter, Mark Anthony Moschello, Debra Gordon (Dancers at Repertory), Erika Leslie (Blonde Skater), Jim McCardle, Ernie Tate (Ice-Rink Officials), Bettina Birnbaum, Deirdre L. Cowden (Strippers), Colin Hamilton (Maitre d'), Tony de Santis (Waiter), Marjean Dennis (Woman in Restaurant), Bob Harks (Priest), Ann Muffly (Woman at Hanna Long's), Hank Crowell (Racquetball Player), Frank Tomasello (Harry), Marine Jahan (Dancer for Beals).

One of the most successful movies of 1983, this is a piece of glossy fluff. Beals stars as an 18-year-old welder in a Pittsburgh steel mill who moonlights as a dancer in a bar her co-workers frequent. She is having an affair with her boss (Nouri) and he uses his influence to help her achieve her dream—to be a ballerina. A film almost wholly without depth or plausibility but carried off with great style. Director Lyne did television commercials before this and that reliance on slick cutting and sumptuous visuals is the cornerstone of his work here. The most common reaction to the film was the feeling of having sat through a long rock video, with Beals (and a lot of stand-in Marine Jahan) doing frenzied underwater dances to the latest rock 'n' roll, exposing as much flesh as the "R" rating would permit. Several hit records came off the soundtrack album, and one of them, "Flashdance—What a Feeling," sung by Irene Cara, won the Academy Award for Best Original Song.

p, Don Simpson, Jerry Bruckheimer; d, Adrian Lyne; w, Tom Hedley, Joe Esterhas (based on a story by Hedley); ph, Don Peterman (Movielab Color); m, Giorgio Moroder; ed, Bud Smith, Walt Mulconery; prod d, Charles Rosen; set d, Marvin March; cos, Michael Kaplan; ch, Jeffrey Hornaday.

Drama Cas. (PR:O MPAA:R)

FLASHING GUNS* (1947) 57m MON bw

Johnny Mack Brown (Johnny), Raymond Hatton (Shelby), Jan Bryant (Ann), Douglas Evans (Longden), James E. Logan (Ainsworth), Ted Adams (Ripley), Edmund Cobb (Sheriff), Norman Jolley (Foley), Ken Adams (Dishpan), Gary Garrett (Duke), Ray Jones (Stirrup), Jack O'Shea (Sagebrush), Steve Clark (Cannon), Frank LaRue (Judge), Jack Rockwell (Cassidy).

One-time Rose Bowl football hero Brown struggles to help out a heavily mortgaged rancher, Hatton. A corrupt banker aligned with gamblers wants the ranch at any price. Brown uses his six shooters to get rid of most of the bad guys and digs up enough dirt to put the banker behind bars, and Hatton keeps his ranch. Made in the heyday of Brown's reign as one of the top moneymaking cowboys in motion pictures.

p, Barney A. Sarecky; d, Lambert Hillyer; w, Frank H. Young; ph, Harry Neumann; ed, Fred Maguire; md, Edward J. Kay.

Western (PR:A MPAA:NR)

FLAT TOP* (1952) 83m MON/AA c

Sterling Hayden (Dan Collier), Richard Carlson (Joe Rodgers), Bill Phipps (Red Kelley), John Bromfield ("Snakehips" MacKay), Keith Larsen (Barney Smith), William Schallert (Longfellow), Todd Karns (Judge), Phyllis Coates (Dorothy), Dave Willock (Willie), Walter Coy (Commander).

Hayden is the commanding officer of an air group aboard an aircraft carrier during WW II. He runs a tight group, knowing that is how to keep his pilots alive. The men don't like it but once the war is over they realize he was right. Entertaining picture with plenty of actual combat scenes taken during the war.

p, Walter Mirisch; d, Lesley Selander; w, Steve Fisher; ph, Harry Neumann (Cinecolor); m, Marlin Skiles; ed, William Austin; art d, David Milton.

War Cas. (PR:A MPAA:NR)

FLAT TWO* (1962, Brit.) 60m Merton Park/AA bw

John le Mesurier (Warden), Jack Watling (Frank Leamington), Bernard Archard (Inspector Trainer), Barry Keegan (Charles Berry), Ann Bell (Susan), Campbell (Hurley Brown), Charles Lloyd Pack (Miller), David Bauer (Emil Louba).

The attorney defending an architect accused of killing a professional gambler is finally forced to confess that he himself is the murderer. Another of the Edgar Wallace revival series of the early 1960s produced by Jack Greenwood. With TV ultimately in mind, the series tended to overcondense Wallace's twisting, surprise-filled stories, to their detriment for big screen showing.

p, Jack Greenwood; d, Alan Cooke; w, Lindsay Galloway (based on the novel by Edgar Wallace).

Crime (PR:A-C MPAA:NR)

FLAVOR OF GREEN TEA OVER RICE, THE (SEE: TEA AND RICE, 1973, Jap.)

FLAW, THE* (1933, Brit.) 67m PAR bw

Henry Kendall (John Millway), Eric Maturin (James Kelver), Phyllis Clare (Laura Kelver), Eve Gray (Irene Nelson), Douglas Payne (Inspector Barnes), Sydney Seaward (Sergeant), Vera Gerald (Mrs. Mamby), Elsie Irving, E.A. Williams.

A man plans the perfect crime, the poisoning of another. Once he has administered the dose, he explains his scheme to the victim, who points up a flaw in the plan. The killer is so upset and confused that the victim gets him to swallow the lethal substance. The would-be murderer dies, and the intended victim lives to save his own life. Nicely constructed thriller.

p, Patrick K. Heale; d, Norman Walker; w, Brandon Fleming.

Crime (PR:A MPAA:NR)

FLAW, THE*½ (1955, Brit.) 61m Cybex/Renown bw

John Bentley (Paul Oliveri), Donald Houston (John Millway), Rona Anderson (Monica Oliveri), Tonia Berne (Vera), Doris Yorke (Mrs. Bower), J. Trevor Davies (Sir George Bentham), Cecilia Cavendish (Lady Bentham), Vera Mechechnie, Ann Sullivan, June Dawson, Langley Howard, Gerry Levy, Herbert St. John, Christine Bocca, Derek Barnard, Andrew Leigh, Eric Aubrey.

Race car driver Bentley plans to murder his heiress wife, but her lawyer (Houston), who loves her, finds out about it. Bentley poisons the meddler, then outlines his entire plan to kill both of them. Houston turns out to have been faking his symptoms, and after a fight aboard a yacht, Bentley falls in the ocean and drowns. Remake of the 1933 version doesn't have anything going for it that the original didn't do first.

p, Geoffrey Goodhart, Brandon Fleming; d, Terence Fisher; w, Fleming; ph, Cedric Williams.

Crime (PR:A MPAA:NR)

FLAXY MARTIN½** (1949) 86m WB bw

Virginia Mayo (Flaxy Martin), Zachary Scott (Walter Colby), Dorothy Malone (Nora Carson), Tom D'Andrea (Sam Malko), Helen Westcott (Peggy), Douglas Kennedy (Hap Richie), Elisha Cook, Jr., (Roper), Jack Overman (Caesar), Douglas Fowley, Buddy Roosevelt, Monte Blue (Detectives), Frances Morris (Woman Witness), Jack Cheatham (Police Operator), George Sherwood (Police Officer), Ed Dearing, Ed Parker (Motorcycle Cops), George Magrill (Court Officer), Rose Plummer (Court Spectator), Fred Kelsey (Watchman), John Elliott (Judge Edward R. McVey), Lee Phelps (Guard), Marjorie Bennett (Neighbor).

Scott is a mob lawyer who falls in love with gun moll Mayo. When his conscience starts bothering him, he dumps Mayo and tries to break his ties with the mob. The hoods frame him for murder and he is sent to prison. He escapes and meets and falls in love with Malone. To straighten his life out, Scott nails the real crooks and goes back to jail on a new and shorter sentence. A formula thriller with a few high spots, with Scott taking a break from his usual sleek scoundrel roles to assume a sympathetic one.

p, Saul Elkins; d, Richard Bare; w, David Lang (based on a story "Smart Money" by Lang); ph, Carl Guthrie; m, William Lava; ed, Frank Magee; art d, Ted Smith.

Crime (PR:A MPAA:NR)

FLEA IN HER EAR, A½** (1968, Fr.) 95m FOX c

Rex Harrison (Victor Chandebisse/Poche), Rosemary Harris (Gabrielle Chandebisse), Louis Jourdan (Henri), Rachel Roberts (Suzanne), John Williams (Dr. Finache), Gregoire Aslan (Max), Edward Hardwicke (Pierre), Georges Descrieres (Don Carlos), Isla Blair (Antoinette), Frank Thornton (Charles), Victor Sen Yung (Oke Saki), Laurence Badie (Eugenie), Dominique Davray (Olympe), Olivier Hussenot (Uncle Louis), Estella Blain (Defendant), Moustache (Fat Man), David Horne (Prosecutor), Roger Carel (Taxi Driver).

Harris is convinced that her attorney husband, Harrison, is fooling around with another woman (or women) because he never has any energy left for her at home. To catch him in the act, she sets up a rendezvous with Harrison at a hotel exclusively used for extra-marital affairs. She meets a good number of lovers, jealous husbands, and a faithful husband. A cheerful little thing frothing over with naughtiness.

p, Fred Kohlmar; d, Jacques Charon; w, John Mortimer (based on the play by Georges Feydeau); ph, Charles Lang (Panavision, Deluxe Color); m, Bronislaw Kaper; ed, Walter Thompson; prod d, Alexander Trauner; md, Lionel Newman; art d, Auguste Capelier; set d, Maurice Barnathan, Pierre Charron; cos, Andre Levasseur; spec eff, Robert MacDonald; m/l, "A Flea In Her Ear," Kaper, Sammy Cahn (sung by Claudine Longet).

Comedy (PR:C MPAA:NR)

FLEDGLINGS* (1965, Brit.) 72m Unlimited/Contemporary bw

Julia White (Julia), Mike Ross (Mike), Iain Quarrier (Iain), Victor Lowndes (Reev Passmore).

Tedium runs rampant as seedy filmmakers Ross and Quarrier try to get model White to sleep with the American producer who might give them money for their next project. Not even spicy, just a worthless hour or so in Chelsea.

p,d&w, Norman Thaddeus Vane.

Drama (PR:O MPAA:NR)

FLEET'S IN, THE* (1942) 93m PAR bw

Dorothy Lamour (The Countess), William Holden (Casey Kirby), Eddie Bracken (Barney Waters), Betty Hutton (Bessie Day), Cass Daley (Cissie), Gil Lamb (Spike), Leif Erickson (Jake), Betty Jane Rhodes (Diana Golden), Lorraine and Rognan (Dance Team), Jack Norton (Kellogg), Jimmy Dorsey and his Band with Helen

O'Connell and Bob Eberly, Barbara Britton (*Eileen Wright*), Harry Barris (*PeeWee*), Dave Willock, Rod Cameron (*Sailors*), Stanley Andrews (*Commander*), Chester Clute (*Minister*), Roy Atwell (*Arthur*), Robert Warwick (*Adm. Wright*), Charlie Williams (*Photographer*), Oscar Smith (*Valet*), Lyle Latell (*Drunk*), Hal Dawson (*Diana's Manager*), Fred Santley (*Waiter*), Phyllis Ruth (*Hazel*), Elinor Troy, Alice Weaver, Louise LaPlanche, Laurie Douglas, Judith Gibson, Lynda Grey, Alaine Brandes, Katherine Booth (*Swingland Hostesses*), Jimmy Dundee, Jack Chapin.

A pleasant trifle but most notable for the debuts of two of the most dynamic women on screen, Betty Hutton and Cass Daley, both of whom were skin-stretched over enthusiasm. This was released after director-songwriter Schertz-inger's death and served to lighten the heavy wartime mood of the country. It's as typical a war musical as could be devised and is actually just a paper-thin story line surrounded by several set pieces that almost become a filmed vaudeville show. Based on the Broadway offering "Sailor Beware!," it was first filmed in 1930 as TRUE TO THE NAVY with Clara Bow, then again in 1936 as LADY BE CAREFUL with Lew Ayres and Mary Carlisle, and again in 1961 with Martin and Lewis as SAILOR BEWARE. Dorothy Lamour, thankfully unsaronged, is known as the Countess of Swingland. She entertains at that club and is known far and wide for her coolness toward tars, gobs, or anyone who wears bell-bottom trousers. There seems to be no one who can get to her as she appears to be Miss Aloof of 1942 the moment she steps off the stage. Holden is a painfully-shy sailor who has achieved a misrepresented reputation of being a ladies' man. His pals make bets that he can kiss the icy Lamour in public and that's about the plot. Hutton is Lamour's roommate and she has a relationship with Bracken. Daley is the admiral's daughter and you don't believe one frame of what's happening for one second but it really matters not. It was right for the time and provided welcome relief from Hitler's encroachments in Europe and Tojo's in the Far East. Not a great deal of production value and only one or two songs that anyone recalls these days. The tunes include "Arthur Murray Taught Me Dancing In A Hurry" (sung by Hutton), "I Remember You," "Build A Better Mousetrap" (sung by Hutton), "It's Somebody Else's Moon," "The Fleet's In," "Why Doesn't Anything Happen To Me?" "Tomorrow You Belong To Uncle Sam," "When You Hear The Time Signal," (Johnny Mercer, Victor Schertzinger), "Tangerine" (Frank Loesser, Schertzinger). The plot is mostly secondary to the music, which is almost secondary to the performances.

p, Paul Jones; d, Victor Schertzinger; w, Walter DeLeon, Ralph Spence, Sid Silvers (based on the play "Sailor Beware!" by Kenyon Nicholson, Charles Robinson and a story by Monte Brice, J. Walter Ruben); ph, William Mellor; ed, Paul Weatherwax.

Musical/Comedy   **(PR:AA   MPAA:NR)**

FLEMISH FARM, THE★★½   (1943, Brit.) 82m TC/GFD bw

Clive Brook (*Maj. Lessart*), Clifford Evans (*Jean Duclos*), Jane Baxter (*Tresha*), Philip Friend (*Fernard Matagne*), Brefni O'Rorke (*Minister*), Wylie Watson (*Farmer*), Ronald Squire (*Hardwicke*), Mary Jerrold (*Mme. Duclos*), Charles Compton (*Ledoux*), Richard George (*Scheldheimer*), Lili Kahn (*Farm Wife*), Irene Handl (*Frau*).

Allegedly based on an actual incident which happened during WW II. Belgian airman goes back to his Nazi-occupied country to retrieve the flag of the Belgian air force he and a pal had buried before escaping the country. Good production and telling of an heroic action, but a mite too long.

p, Sydney Box; d, Jeffrey Dell; w, Jeffrey Dell, Jill Craigie Dell; ph, Eric Cross; m, Ralph Vaughan Williams.

War Drama   **(PR:A   MPAA:NR)**

FLESH★★★   (1932) 95m MGM bw

Wallace Beery (*Polikai*), Karen Morley (*Lora*), Ricardo Cortez (*Nicky*), Jean Hersholt (*Mr. Herman*), John Miljan (*Joe Willard*), Vince Barnett (*Waiter*), Herman Bing (*Pepi*), Greta Meyer (*Mrs. Herman*), Ed Brophy (*Dolan*), Ward Bond, Nat Pendleton.

There have been many movies made about wrestling since this effort by John Ford but none have come close to the feeling generated by the actors. At best, it's an unattractive subject but Beery manages a performance that touches the heart in this first MGM film by Ford after a lengthy sojourn at Fox. Beery is a sweet-natured wrestler in Germany. He never takes advantage of his opponents, just defeats them and then worries if he's hurt them (much like Slapsie Maxie Rosenbloom was in real-life boxing). Sexy Morley is in prison and when she's released, she contacts Beery and gets him to pay for Cortez's release from prison. She tells Beery that Cortez is her "brother" when he is, in fact, her lover. She gets pregnant by Cortez who strolls the minute he knows of her condition. Beery and Morley get married and come to the U.S. where he becomes a champion. He takes the title the same night Morley gives birth to the baby fathered by Cortez. Cortez gets in touch with them and becomes Beery's matchmaker and attempts to convince him to throw matches. When Beery sees Cortez raise his hand to Morley, he kills him, then goes on to win a match he was supposed to lose. Beery is arrested and tossed in jail where, in a touching scene, Morley declares her love for him as they look at each other through the bars. The three leads are excellent in demanding roles. Beery must be lovable while tossing 200-pounders around a ring, Morley has to make us like her despite her duplicity, and Cortez has to play a despicable cad and still convince us that he has enough charm to cause Morley to be obsessed with him. We don't know how long Beery will serve in jail but, in the end, we hope it won't be too long and that he and Morley can resume their lives together. It was a different kind of CHAMP for Beery and he was totally believable in his German dialect, the same one he used that same year in GRAND HOTEL. Cortez was hardly the Latin lover they played him up to be. Born Jacob Krantz in Vienna, he came to the U.S. at the age of three and was raised in Coney Island. Maybe it's the sea air that does it, or the fact that the extreme poverty caused the kids of the area to try that much harder. How else can one explain the success of Neil Diamond, Neil Sedaka,

Herschel Bernardi, Mimi Benzell, Louis Gossett, Harvey Keitel, Mel Brooks . . . the list goes on and on.

d, John Ford; w, Moss Hart, Leonard Praskins, Edgar Allen Woolf (from a story by Edmund Goulding); ph, Arthur Edeson; ed, William S. Gray.

Drama   **(PR:C   MPAA:NR)**

FLESH AND BLOOD★★★   (1951, Brit.) 102m BL bw

Richard Todd (*Charles Cameron/Sutherland*), Glynis Johns (*Katherine*), Joan Greenwood (*Wilhelmina Cameron*), Andre Morell (*Dr. Marshall*), Freda Jackson (*Mrs. Hannah*), James Hayter (*Sir Douglas Manley*), George Cole (*John Hannah*), Ursula Howells (*Harriet Marshall*), Ronald Howard (*Purley*), Walter Fitzgerald (*Dr. Cooper*), Muriel Aked (*Mrs. Walker*), Michael Hordern (*Webster*), Helen Christie (*Minnie Arnott*), Lilly Kann (*Patrick Macnee*), Molly Weir, Hugh Dempster, Betty Paul, Alexander Gauge, Peter MacDonnell, Hector MacGregor, Archie Duncan, Anna Canitano, John Kelly, Joan Heal, Nina Parry, Billy Newsbury, Sally Owen, William Chappell, Jock McKay, Fred Johnson, John Vere.

A plodding melodrama telling three stories all connected by thin hairs. A sick medical student dies in a Glasgow slum, and leaves an expecting fiancee. She dies, also, leaving her brother to take care of the baby girl. The daughter grows up and has an affair with a lab assistant. When he threatens to ruin her wedding, she poisons him, and the wedding ceremony goes as planned. She has a son, and then commits suicide because of her past crime. Her son goes on to discover a vaccine for a deadly disease. Cast handles the complexities of this rambling saga quite well.

p, Anatole de Grunwald; d, Anthony Kimmins; w, De Grunwald (based on the play "A Sleeping Clergyman" by James Bridie); ph, Otto Heller; ed, G. Turney-Smith; m, Charles Williams; ed, G. Turner-Smith.

Drama   **(PR:C   MPAA:NR)**

FLESH AND BLOOD SHOW, THE★   (1974, Brit.) 91m Entertainment
                                                      Ventures c (AKA: ASYLUM OF THE INSANE)

Ray Brooks, Jenny Hanley, Robin Askwith, David Howey, Penny Meredith, Luan Peters, Patrick Barr.

Actors and actresses don't have to die on stage: they're killed at the audition by a hooded murderer. Blood and gore with some sex thrown in as well. This is one of the few 3-D horror films released during the spate of bad 3-D and 3-D sex films that were popular in the early 1970s.

p&d, Pete Walker; w, Alfred Shaunghnessy.

Horror   **Cas.**   **(PR:O   MPAA:R)**

FLESH AND FANTASY★★★   (1943) 92m UNIV bw

Edward G. Robinson (*Marshall Tyler*), Charles Boyer (*Paul Gaspar*), Barbara Stanwyck (*Joan Stanley*), Betty Field (*Henrietta*), Robert Cummings (*Michael*), Thomas Mitchell (*Septimus Podgers*), Charles Winninger (*King Lamarr*), Anna Lee (*Rowena*), Dame May Whitty (*Lady Pamela Hardwick*), C. Aubrey Smith (*Dean of Chichester*), Robert Benchley (*Doakes*), Edgar Barrier (*Stranger*), David Hoffman (*Davis*), Mary Forbes (*Lady Thomas*), Ian Wolfe (*Librarian*), Doris Lloyd (*Mrs. Caxton*), June Lang (*Angel*), Grace McDonald (*Equestrienne*), Joseph Crehan (*Acrobat/Detective*), Arthur Loft, Lee Phelps (*Detectives*), James Craven (*Radio Announcer*), Marjorie Lord (*Justine*), Eddie Acuff (*Policeman*), Peter Lawford (*Pierrot*), Frank Mitchell (*Acrobat*), Lane Chandler (*Acrobat/Satan*), Gil Patrick (*Death*), Paul Bryar, George Lewis (*Harlequins*), Clinton Rosemond (*Old Negro*), Charles Halton (*Old Man Prospector*), Jacqueline Dalya (*Angel*), Leyland Hodgson (*Cop*), Edward Fielding (*Sir Thomas*), Heather Thatcher (*Lady Flora*), Clarence Muse (*Jeff*), Jack Gardner (*Gunman*), Neara Sanders, Beatrice Barrett (*Chorus Girls*), Frank Arnold (*Clown*), Carl Vernell, Phil Warren, Sandra Morgan (*Neighbors*), Harold DeBecker (*Clerk*), Anita Sharp Bolster, Ferdinand Munier (*Relatives*), Bruce Lester (*Young Man*), Harry Stubbs (*Proprietor*), Olaf Hytten (*Chemist*), Marcel Dalio (*Clown*), Jerry Maren, Jeanette Fern (*Midgets*), Mary Ann Hyde (*Gaspar's Assistant*), Con Colleano (*Gaspar's Double*), Eddie Kane (*Immigration Officer*).

This trio of separate stories was an attempt to recreate the success of the similar TALES OF MANHATTAN. It was not as fortunate at the box office. There were four stories originally planned by the producers but the last was dropped and later turned up as DESTINY with Gloria Jean. They added some footage and released it as a second feature a year after this one. Segmented films have not fared well with the notable exceptions being TRIO, QUARTET, and one or two others. Benchley and Hoffman are sitting around their club one night, discussing dreams and elements of the supernatural. Their conversation is what keys the three stories. In the first, Field is a plain-faced dressmaker who is angry at the visage that God handed her. She doesn't know that beauty comes from within and if she would shed her bitter attitude, it might cause her to become beautiful. Mardi Gras in New Orleans is about to begin and she is handed a face mask to wear during the galas of Fat Tuesday. The man is mysterious and masked as well and he assures her that wearing the mask will change her life, if she is willing to jettison the envy and hatred that gnaws at her. She meets handsome Cummings, a frustrated attorney, and their romance flourishes that night. She is fearful of removing the mask, despite his pleadings. When she does, it make no difference to Cummings who has fallen in love with the woman behind the mask and the face. Beauty is in the eyes of the beholder and Cummings beholds a gorgeous woman in Field. In the second episode, Robinson pooh-poohs the prediction by seer Mitchell that he will commit a murder. They are at a fashionable party and Robinson publicly puts Mitchell down as a charlatan. But the thought eats at him and he wonders if there is anything to palm reading. Eventually, Robinson decides to actually murder and fails in two attempts, then finally strangles Mitchell and fulfills the prediction. In the third, and weakest of the episodes, Boyer is a circus aerialist who performs without a net while under the influence of alcohol. Boyer has a dream of Stanwyck being seated in the audience when he falls to his death. He eventually meets her on a sea voyage to America and learns she is a jewel thief. Another dream tells him that she is to be arrested and we're never sure what happens at the end of the segment. Boyer also produced the film but might have paid more attention to the script for his section. The stars are what makes this work and Robinson is particularly good in his role. It is essentially three one-act plays and ultimately fails to sustain deep interest. When you can walk out after any given section of a film, the film is in trouble. In a very small bit, look for Lawford in the third segment. It was co-photographed by Stanley Cortez, brother of Ricardo. Benchley had virtually no opportunity to display his wry wit. They might have been wise to let him have a go at rewriting the script to add some lightness to some otherwise dreary goings-on.

p, Julien Duvivier, Charles Boyer; d, Duvivier; w, Ernest Pascal, Samuel Hoffenstein, Ellis St. Joseph (based on stories by St. Joseph, Laslo Vadnay, and "Lord Arthur Saville's Crime" [second segment] by Oscar Wilde); ph, Stanley Cortez, Paul Ivano; m, Alexandre Tansman; ed, Arthur Hilton; md, Charles Previn; art d, Robert Boyle, John B. Goodman, Richard Riedel; set d, Russell A. Gausman, E.R. Robinson; cos, Vera West, Edith Head (Stanwyck's costumes only).

Drama (PR:A-C MPAA:NR)

FLESH AND FLAME (SEE: NIGHT OF THE QUARTER MOON, 1959)

FLESH AND FURY*** (1952) 82m UNIV bw

Tony Curtis (*Paul Callan*), Jan Sterling (*Sonya Bartow*), Mona Freeman (*Ann Hollis*), Wallace Ford (*Jack Richardson*), Connie Gilchrist (*Mrs. Richardson*), Katherine Locke (*Mrs. Hollis*), Joe Gray (*Cliff*), Ron Hargrave (*Al Logan*), Harry Guardino (*Lou Callan*), Harry Shannon (*Mike Callan*), Harry Raven (*Murph*), Ted Stanhope (*Whitey*), Louis Jean Heydt (*Andy Randolph*), Nella Walker (*Mrs. Hackett*), Ken Patterson (*Dr. Lester*), Virginia Gregg (*Claire*), Grace Hayle (*Mrs. Bien*), Frank Wilcox (*Businessman*), Harry Cheshire (*Dr. Gundling*), Tommy Farrell (*Rocky*), George Eldredge (*Dr. Buell*), Bruce Richardson (*Burns*), Beatrice Gray (*Mother*), Edwin Parker (*Man*), Sam Pierce (*Nash*), Karl "Killer" Davis (*Broadway Character*), Ed Hinton (*Cop*), Sally Yarnell (*Bit*), Ed Hinkle (*Student*), Bryan Forbes (*Fighter*), Lucille Curtis (*Maid*).

Curtis is a deaf mute prizefighter quickly moving up in the boxing world. Sterling hooks onto him, seeing for herself a free meal ticket. Journalist Freeman comes along, falls in love with the boxer, and helps him get an operation to restore his hearing, which he loses during the title match but regains when he dumps Sterling for Freeman. Good values all around and some wry social comments along the way.

p, Leonard Goldstein; d, Joseph Pevney; w, Bernard Gordon (based on a story by William Alland), ph, Irving Glassberg; m, Hans J. Salter; ed, Virgil Vogel; art d, Bernard Herzbrun, Emrich Nicholson.

Sports Drama (PR:A MPAA:NR)

FLESH AND THE FIENDS, THE (SEE: MANIA, 1959, Brit.)

FLESH AND THE SPUR* (1957) 78m AIP c

John Agar (*Luke/Matthew Random*), Maria English (*Willow*), Touch [Michael] Connors (*Stacy*), Raymond Hatton (*Windy*), Maria Monay (*Lola*), Joyce Meadows (*Rena*), Kenne Duncan (*Tanner*), Frank Lackteen (*Indian Chief*), Mel Gaines (*Blackie*), Michael Harris (*Deputy Marshal*), Eddie Kafafian (*Bud*), Richard Alexander (*Bartender*), Kermit Maynard, Bud Osborne, Buddy Roosevelt (*Outlaws*).

An empty western cowritten by Corman regular Charles B. Griffith. The uneventful plot has the young Agar on a search for the murderer of his twin brother. Along the way he teams up with Connors, only to learn that he is the killer.

p, Alex Gordon; d, Edward L. Cahn; w, Charles B. Griffith, Mark Hanna; ph, Frederick E. West (Eastmancolor); m, Ronald Stein; ed, Ronald Sinclair; m/l, "Flesh and the Spur," Ross Bagdasarian.

Western (PR:C MPAA:NR)

FLESH AND THE WOMAN** (1954, Fr./Ital.) 95m Cinedis/Dominant c (LE GRAND JEU; AKA: THE BIG GAME)

Gina Lollobrigida (*Helena/Sylvia*), Arletty (*Blanche*), Jean-Claude Pascal (*Pierre*), Raymond Pellegrin (*Mario*), Peter Van Eyck (*Fred*), Temerson (*Noblet*), Jean Hebey (*Brigadier*).

Typical genre picture about attorney Pascal joining the French Foreign Legion to forget mistress Lollobrigida. One day he sees a local beauty who is his former mistress' double. An amnesia victim, she knows little about her past life and Pascal tries to rekindle what once was with this new-found woman. The old mistress turns up and sends the double away. Film ends with Pascal returning to the Legion once more. The photography does wonders with the scenery and Lollobrigida but can't help the cliches and coincidences within the story. The direction is competent but the stereotyped characters are given little room to develop. The Foreign Legion scenes serve merely as decoration. FLESH AND THE DEVIL marked an insignificant return to Europe for director Siodmak, who left France with the coming of the Nazis back in 1936. Most memorable from his sojourn to the U.S. was the gripping THE KILLERS (1946).

d, Robert Siodmak; w, Charles Spaak (based on "Le Grand Jeu" by Spaak and Jacques Feyder); ph, Michel Felber (Eastmancolor); m, George Van Parys, Maurice Thiriet; ed, V. Mercantan.

Drama (PR:O MPAA:NR)

FLESH EATERS, THE**½ (1964) 92m Vulcan/Cinema bw

Martin Kosleck (*Peter Bartell*), Rita Morley (*Laura Winters*), Byron Sanders (*Grant Murdock*), Ray Tudor (*Omar*), Barbara Wilkin (*Jan Letterman*).

An alcoholic film queen (Morley) and her secretary crash-land on an island inhabited by a mad scientist (Kosleck). He's working with tiny sea creatures who can devour human flesh in a matter of moments. The sea creatures were created by scratching the film stock with pins. Original viewers of THE FLESH EATERS were handed a packet of "instant blood" to protect themselves during the film. The ending is a great surprise.

p, Jack and Terry Curtis, Arnold Drake; d, J. Curtis; w, Drake; ph, Carson Davidson; m, Julian Stein; ed, Radley Metzger, Frank Forest; spec eff, Ray Benson.

Horror (PR:O MPAA:NR)

FLESH FEAST** (1970) 72m Viking/Cine World c

Veronica Lake (*Dr. Elaine Frederick*), Phil Philbin (*Ed Casey*), Heather Hughes (*Kristine*), Martha Mischon, Yanka Mann, Dian Wilhite, Chris Martell.

Lake is a Miami Beach plastic surgeon who just happens to be a former mental patient. This could explain why she chooses a somewhat radical form for restoring youth. Maggots (real ones raised especially for the film) eat away old skin tissue before Lake works her medical wonders. Things proceed nicely until she discovers that her newest patient is Adolf Hitler! Lake's mother, a victim of Nazi concentration camps, is gleefully avenged as Hitler is munched on by a myriad of maggots. Mercifully, this is not one of Lake's most remembered performances, though it was her final film. Filmed in Florida.

p, Veronica Lake, Brad F. Ginter; d, Ginter; w, Ginter, Thomas Casey; ph, Casey, Andy Romanoff; prod d, Harry Kerwin; spec eff, Doug Hobart.

Horror (PR:O MPAA:R)

FLESH IS WEAK, THE* (1957, Brit.) 88m Eros bw

John Derek (*Tony Giani*), Milly Vitale (*Marissa Cooper*), William Franklyn (*Lloyd Buxton*), Martin Benson (*Angelo Giani*), Freda Jackson (*Trixie*), Norman Wooland (*Inspector Kingcombe*), Harold Lang (*Henry*), Patricia Jessel (*Millie*), John Paul (*Sgt. Franks*), Denis Shaw (*Saradine*), Joe Robinson (*Lofty*), Roger Snowden (*Benny*), Patricia Plunkett (*Doris Newma*), Vera Day (*Edna*), Shirley Ann Field (*Susan*), Charles Lloyd Pack (*Salvi*).

Vitale is the stereotype innocent country girl who visits big city London and becomes a hooker. She has an affair with a pimp and goes to jail in a frame-up. A do-gooding journalist convinces her to talk, putting her beau behind bars. The backers thought the film could succeed as both a social commentary and an entertaining drama, instead it is a mediocre bucket of sleaze.

p, Raymond Stross; d, Don Chaffey; w, Leigh Vance; ph, Stephen Dade; m, Tristam Cary.

Drama (PR:O MPAA:NR)

FLESH MERCHANT, THE* (1956) 90m Joseph Brenner Associates bw

Joy Reynolds (*Nancy*), Mariko Perri (*Perrini*), Lisa Rack (*Paula*), Guy Manford (*Sogel*).

A cheap, cheesy, attempt to make a provocative study of the operations of a couple of prostitutes. The script is one cliche after another, leaving only the sexy mannequins to arrest the viewers' attentions (obviously the makers' original intent). Odds are that anyone but an extremely desperate individual would immediately be put to sleep.

p&d, W. Merle Connell; w, Peter Perry, Jr., Jay M. Kude.

Crime (PR:O MPAA:NR)

FLICK (SEE: DR. FRANKENSTEIN ON CAMPUS, 1970, Can.)

FLIGHT*** (1929) 116m COL bw

Jack Holt (*Panama Williams*), Ralph Graves (*Lefty Phelps*), Lila Lee (*Elinor*), Alan Roscoe (*Major*), Harold Goodwin (*Steve Roberts*), Jimmy De La Cruze (*Lobo*), Bill Williams, Jerry Jerome.

Strong-jawed Holt and rival Graves are Marine Corps fliers in Nicaragua battling for the love of Lee. Soap opera cliches are made tolerable by wonderful aerial sequences. In Capra's autobiography, *The Name Above The Title*, he recalls that during the shooting of one scene where Holt was supposed to stand up in the back seat of the open biplane and fire his machine gun, Holt froze and would only shake his head back and forth despite Capra's frantic gestures from another plane. Finally, disgusted, they returned to base and Capra saw why Holt refused to stand up. He had been playing with his parachute and it accidentally popped open. He had pushed himself down as hard as he could on the chute and refused to budge. Had he stood up, the chute would have caught the air and jerked him out of the plane to almost certain death. After that, they tied a red ribbon to Holt's ripcord to keep him from repeating his mistake. Capra persuaded the Marine Corps to extend full cooperation. He was given the use of nine Curtis fighter bombers with full crews and the Marine base at North Island near San Diego was thrown open to Capra and his film crew. Two of the pilots performing astounding stunts for FLIGHT included Bill Williams and Jerry Jerome, both later generals in the Corps.

d, Frank Capra; w, Howard J. Green, Capra (based on a story by Ralph Graves); ph, Elmer Dyer, Joe Novak, Joseph Walker; ed, Maurice Wright, Gene Milford, Ben Pivar.

Aviation Drama (PR:A MPAA:NR)

FLIGHT*½ (1960) 72m San Francisco/COL bw

Efrain Ramirez (*Pepe*), Ester Cortez (*Mother*), Maria Gonzales (*Sister*), Endrew Cortez (*Brother*), Ed Smith (*Old Man*), Susan Jane Darby (*Young Girl*), Richard Crommie, Edward O'Brien, Barnaby Conrad (*Hunters*).

A desperate Mexican youth is sent fleeing to the mountains after killing a drunk in a California bar. The police chase him, and have an easy time of doing him in. The approach is stark and realistic, though the result leaves much emotional fulfillment to be desired.

d, Louis Bispo; w, Barnaby Conrad (based on a story by John Steinbeck); ph, Verne Carlson; m, Laurindo Almeida.

Drama   **(PR:C MPAA:NR)**

FLIGHT ANGELS*   (1940) 74m FN/WB bw

Virginia Bruce (Mary), Dennis Morgan (Chick), Wayne Morris (Artie), Ralph Bellamy (Graves), Jane Wyman (Nan), John Litel (Doc), Margot Stevenson (Rita), Dorothea Kent (Mabel), John Ridgely (Lt. Parsons), Lucille Fairbanks (Thelma), Maris Wrixon (Bonny), Carol Hughes (Texas), Mary Anderson (Daisy), DeWolfe [William] Hopper (Lefty), Jan Clayton (Jane), Marilyn [Lynn] Merrick (Peggy), Phyllis Hamilton (Phyllis), Nell O'Day (Sue), Elizabeth Sifton (Dora), Ferris Taylor (Mr. Kimball), Richard Elliott (Mr. Rutledge), Natalie Moorhead (Miss Mason), Leona Roberts (Mrs. Hutchinson), John Arledge (Mr. Perry), Janet Shaw (Mrs. Perry), Grace Stafford (Buxton), Victor Zimmerman (Capt. Brady), Jean O'Donnell (Grace), Peter Ashley (Joe), Peggy Keyes (Stewardess), Creighton Hale (Attendant), Dutch Hendrian (Mechanic), Rosella Towne (Student), Addison Richards, Tony Hughes (Officers).

The ups and downs of airline romance are highlighted in this early soap on the lives of stewardesses and pilots. Pilot Morgan does his best to become Bruce's beau, while copilot Morris fends off some vampish moves from Wyman. Ground this one.

p, Edmund Grainger; d, Lewis Seiler; w, Maurice Leo (based on a story by Jerry Wald, Richard Macauley); ph, William O'Connell; ed, James Gibbon.

Drama   **(PR:A MPAA:NR)**

FLIGHT AT MIDNIGHT**   (1939) 66m REP bw

Phil Regan (Spinner), Jean Parker (Maxine), Col. Roscoe Turner (Himself), Robert Armstrong (Jim Brennan), Noah Beery, Jr. (Torpy), Harlan Briggs (Pop), Helen Lynd (Josephine), Barbara Pepper (Mildred), Harry Hayden (Neary), Raymond Bailey (Bill Hawks).

Regan is a footloose mail pilot who sets his sights on airline hostess Parker. He is shunned when, due to his carelessness, his airplane mechanic pal is killed. For his penance, Regan saves Parker's life when the plane she's in nearly hits some high tension wires. Turner, who had little to do in the film but play himself, was the crack speed pilot in the 1930s who went on to become a distinguished aviation expert.

p, Armand Schaefer; d, Sidney Salkow; w, Eliot Gibbons (based on a story by Daniel Moore, Hugh King); ph, Ernest Miller; ed, William Morgan; md, Cy Feuer; m/l, "I thought I'd Never Fall In Love," Ralph Freed, Burton Lane (sung by Regan).

Aviation Drama   **(PR:A MPAA:NR)**

FLIGHT COMMAND***   (1940) 113m Frank Borzage/MGM bw

Robert Taylor (Ensign Alan Drake), Ruth Hussey (Lorna Gary), Walter Pidgeon (Squadron Cdr. Bill Gary), Paul Kelly (Lt. Cdr. Dusty Rhodes), Shepperd Strudwick (Lt. Jerry Banning), Red Skelton (Lt. "Mugger" Martin), Nat Pendleton (C.P.O. "Spike" Knowles), Dick Purcell (Lt. "Stitchy" Payne), William Tannen (Lt. Freddy Townsend), William Stelling (Lt. Bush), Stanley Smith (Lt. Frost), Addison Richards (Vice-Admiral), Donald Douglas (First Duty Officer), Pat Flaherty (Second Duty Officer), Forbes Murray (Captain), Marsha Hunt (Claire), Lee Tung-Foo (Jung), John Hamilton (Pensacola Commander), Gaylord [Steve] Pendleton (Enlisted Man), Jack Luden (Hell Cat), Dick Wessel (Big Sailor), Reed Hadley (Admiral's Aide).

Action-packed "war" movie that was made before we went to war, so there is no actual fighting, just a lot of superb flying footage, flag-waving, and sort of a softening-up process of American audiences for the eventual moment when we would take up arms against the Axis. Navy Squadron Eight is based at San Diego. They've been nicknamed The Hellcats because of their excellent skills and discipline in the air. Commander Pidgeon is admired by his men, as is his beauteous wife, Ruth Hussey. One of the squadron dies during training and is replaced by Taylor, a self-assured Pensacola cadet who is under the mistaken impression that this group always requests its replacements. He soon becomes anathema to the others and wonders why, since he was asked for. Then he learns that wasn't the case at all. Hussey accepts Taylor and they become pals. The men, who adore her, begin to relent when they see she enjoys his company. Strudwick is Hussey's brother, who is killed when he tries out a "flying-blind" device in a dense fog. Hussey is devastated. Taylor begins to work on the device in an attempt to make it feasible for use in the Naval Air Force. The Hussey-Taylor friendship develops into something more, and she is convinced that she loves him, but Taylor is a gentleman and holds back. The squadron senses Taylor's and Hussey's burgeoning affair and demands he resign. That's rescinded when Taylor risks his life to save Pidgeon. Eventually, Hussey returns to her husband and all is forgiven. Taylor becomes part of the squadron and the film concludes. The Navy gave its cooperation to the film's crew, and it smacks of authenticity from the opening titles to the fadeout. FLIGHT COMMAND was the first of many films about the war and one of the best when you realize that there was no actual enemy to fight and no beaches to take. This was Red Skelton's second film. He played one of the fliers in the squadron and gave absolutely no indication that he would later become MGM's number-one comedian. A fine script by Wells Root and Commander Harvey Haislip. The latter, no doubt, supplied much of the reality in the training sequences while leaving the love story to veteran Root.

p, J. Walter Ruben; d. Frank Borzage; w, Wells Root, Cdr. Harvey Haislip (based on a story by Haislip, John Sutherland); ph, Harold Rosson; m, Franz Waxman; ed, Robert J. Kern; art d, Cedric Gibbons; set d, Edwin B. Willis; cos, Dolly Tree, Giles Steele; spec eff, Arnold Gillespie; m/l "Eyes of the Fleet," Lt. Cdr. J. V. McElduff; tech adv. Cdr. Morton Seligman.

Aviation Drama   **(PR:A MPAA:NR)**

FLIGHT FOR FREEDOM***   (1943) 101m RKO bw

Rosalind Russell (Toni Carter), Fred MacMurray (Randy Britton), Herbert Marshall (Paul Turner), Eduardo Ciannelli (Johnny Salvini), Walter Kingsford (Adm. Graves), Damian O'Flynn (Pete), Jack Carr (Bill), Matt McHugh (Mac), Richard Loo (Mr. Yokahata), Charles Lung, Bud McTaggart, Don Dillaway, Eddie Dew (Flyers), Jack Cheatham (Doorman), Frank Mills (Cab Driver), Ed Agresti (Headwaiter), Paul Stanton (Airport Official), Ann Summers (Woman at Airport), Stanley Andrews (Prosperous Gent), Gerald Pierce (Bellhop), Ernie Alexander (Drunk), Tom Dugan (Bartender), Buddy Williams (Black Waiter), Martin Ashe (Collins), Hugh Beaumont (Flight Instructor), Mary Treen (Newspaper Woman), Clarence Straight (Petty Officer), Kathleen Ellis, Isabelle LaMal (Telephone Operators), Forbes Murray (Capt. Knowles), Shirley Lew (Mrs. Yokahata), Byron Shores (George Lake), James Eagles (Charlie), Theodore Von Eltz (Cdr. George), William Forrest (Vice-Consul).

Russell is a pretty young woman enthralled with flying who learns her tricks of the aviation trade from Marshall, her devoted instructor. Marshall cautions Russell early on to never fall in love with flyers, because "they live at 10,000 feet." But after her first solo flight, Russell bumps into MacMurray and does exactly that. He's a hotshot pilot who is amused by her ambitions as well as being competitive with those aims. Russell and MacMurray have a brief affair and then she's off flying in the cross-country Bendix race. Next she breaks the Los Angeles-to-New York record, then announces she will fly around the world and break that record, too. MacMurray is rarely seen through the middle of the film as Russell goes about her frantic aviatrix business, but he meets up with her just before her last venture ends in disaster. At that time the U.S. Navy approaches Russell and asks her to fly over the mandated islands in the Pacific to photograph secret military installations created by the Japanese, this in 1937, four years before Pearl Harbor. Moreover, she is asked to crash her plane near these islands so the Navy can conduct a widespread search for her and gather further information about Japanese operations. Russell patriotically agrees and does crash in the Pacific and the Navy ostensibly gets its vital information while the world honors the dead aviatrix as a heroine. Of course the film is based upon the life, times, and disappearance of Amelia Earhart, as well as flyer Jacqueline Cochran, wife of RKO studio head Floyd Odlum who took a special interest in this film. Earhart's widower, George Palmer Putnam, allowed FLIGHT FOR FREEDOM to use his vanished wife's career as long as her name was not used; he was paid, according to one report, $7,500 for the privilege. Russell is good in her heroic role but Marshall and MacMurray are merely love interest props. Director Mendes does a commendable job of moving the story along and Garmes' photography is excellent. Ironically, Katharine Hepburn appeared in a prophetic film, CHRISTOPHER STRONG, in 1933 which closely profiled Earhart's career and strange fate.

p, David Hempstead; d, Lothar Mendes; w, Oliver H.P. Garrett, S.K. Lauren, Jane Murfin (based on a story by Horace McCoy); ph, Lee Garmes; m, Roy Webb; ed, Roland Gross; md, C. Bakaleinikoff; art d, Albert S. D'Agostino, Carroll Clark; set d, Darrell Silvera, Harley Miller; spec eff, Vernon L. Walker.

Adventure   **(PR:A MPAA:NR)**

FLIGHT FROM ASHIYA**   (1964, U.S./Jap.) 102m Daiei-Harold Hecht/UA c (ASHIYA KARA NO HIKO)

Yul Brynner (Sgt. Mike Takashima), Richard Widmark (Col. Glenn Stevenson), George Chakiris (Lt. John Gregg), Suzy Parker (Lucille Carroll), Shirley Knight (Caroline Gordon), Daniele Gaubert (Leila), Eiko Taki (Tomiko), Joe de Reda (Sgt. Randy Smith), Mitsuhiro Sugiyama (Japanese Boy Charlie), E.S. Ince (Capt. Walter Mound), Andrew Hughes (Dr. Horton).

Filmed entirely in Japan and surrounding waters, this Japanese-American co-production has some fine special effects, created by the resourceful host-country craftsmen. Effects are about all this maudlin adventure/love drama possesses; even consummate actor Widmark (with the meatiest role) seems as wooden as a ginkgo tree. The tale deals with three members—Widmark, Brynner, and Chakiris—of a U.S. Air Force rescue team during a storm-tossed rescue mission at sea. Chakiris has turned coward, the result—flashback—of a failed rescue mission when his helicopter precipitated an avalanche, wiping out the nominal rescuees. Brynner, of Polish/Japanese extraction, has lost his zest for life since—flashback—the death of his Algerian sweetheart, Gaubert, in a North African bridge-demolition wartime foul-up. Team leader Widmark thinks the Nipponese, including half of Brynner, should ride in the rear of the aircraft because—flashback—his wife, Knight, and infant child died in a Japanese prison camp. Loath to risk his aircraft and crew for a handful of Japanese survivors on fragile rafts in the raging waters below, Widmark finally recalls his dead bride's final injunction to him—eschew hatred—and opts to save the survivors. He effects this rescue, oddly, by having the half-Japanese Brynner parachute into the storm with supplies for the victims. So long, sucker? No, indeed; Widmark and Chakiris land the amphibian and pick everyone up. Widmark is injured during the landing in order to give Chakiris a chance to overcome his fear of flying and ferry the folks back to the base at Ashiya, where the pokerfaced Parker awaits him. The film is notable only for having at least one flashback inside a flashback.

p, Harold Hecht; d, Michael Anderson; w, Elliott Arnold, Waldo Salt (based on Arnold's novel); ph, Joseph MacDonald, Burnett Guffey (Panavision, Eastmancolor); m, Frank Cordell; ed, Gordon Pilkington; prod d, Eugene Lourie; art d, Tomoo Shimogawara.

Aviation Drama   **(PR:A MPAA:NR)**

FLIGHT FROM DESTINY***½   (1941) 73m WB bw

Geraldine Fitzgerald (Betty Farroway), Thomas Mitchell (Prof. Henry Todhunter), Jeffrey Lynn (Michael Farroway), James Stephenson (Dr. Lawrence Stevens), Mona Maris (Ketti Moret), Jonathan Hale (District Attorney), David Bruce (Saunders), Thurston Hall (Dean Somers), Mary Gordon (Martha), John Eldredge (Peterson), Hardie Albright (Ferrera), William Forrest (Prentiss), Weldon Heyburn (Brooks), DeWolf [William] Hopper (Travin), Alexander Lockwood (Conway), Frank Reicher (Edvaard Kreindling), Willie Best (George), Libby Taylor (Maid).

Mitchell—a college professor with only three months to live—asks the advice of some younger university members on how to spend his final days. One suggests that he murder someone who is escaping legal justice. Mitchell contemplates the idea and chooses to eliminate Maris, a scheming wench who thrives on ruining the lives and marriages of others, including former students Fitzgerald and Lynn. He succeeds in killing her, but turns himself in upon the realization of his ill ideology. An exceptional offering on the effect of imminent death on the human condition.

p, Jack L. Warner, Edmund Grainger; d, Vincent Sherman; w, Barry Trivers (based on the story and play *Trial and Error* by Anthony Berkeley); ph, James Van Trees; m, Heinz Roomheld; ed, Thomas Richards; md, Leo F. Forbstein; art d, Esdras Hartley.

Drama   **(PR:A   MPAA:NR)**

FLIGHT FROM FOLLY*½   (1945, Brit.) 94m WB bw

Pat Kirkwood (*Sue Brown*), Hugh Sinclair (*Clinton Gray*), Sydney Howard (*Dr. Wylie*), Marian Spencer (*Harriet*), Tamara Desni (*Nina*), A.E. Matthews (*Neville*), Jean Gillie (*Millicent*), Leslie Bradley (*Bomber*), Charles Goldner (*Ramon*), Mildred Shay, Edmundo Ros and his Band, Halamar & Konarski.

Destitute showgirl Kirkwood, in desperate financial straits, impersonates a nurse hoping to find remunerative employment. She is sent to care for Sinclair, a talented—but hypochondriacal and alcoholic—show-business composer, whose outrageous behavior has induced his wife to depart for Majorca. Composer and pseudo-nurse travel to the tuneful island in the hope of effecting a reunion; but the magic and the music of Majorca work their wiles; neurotic Sinclair is rejuvenated and reclaimed, discovering that his hireling Kirkwood is his one true love.

p&d, Herbert Mason; w, Basil Woon, Lesley Storm, Katherine Strueby (based on a story by Edmund Goulding); ph, Otto Heller.

Musical   **(PR:A   MPAA:NR)**

FLIGHT FROM GLORY***½   (1937) 66m RKO bw

Chester Morris (*Smith*), Whitney Bourne (*Lee Wilson*), Onslow Stevens (*Ellis*), Van Heflin (*George Wilson*), Richard Lane (*Hanson*), Paul Guilfoyle (*Jones*), Solly Ward (*Itzky*), Douglas Walton (*Hilton*), Walter Miller (*Old Timer*), Rita LaRoy (*Molly*), Pasha Khan (*Pepi*).

A remarkable low-budget production from the talented cast, crew, and writers, with a plot anticipating and paralleling that of Howard Hawks' ONLY ANGELS HAVE WINGS (1939) and Henri-Georges Clouzot's THE WAGES OF FEAR (1953), later remade by William Friedkin as SORCERER (1977). A group of self-exiled pariahs, pilots all, have accepted the dangerous job of flying supplies from a central base camp to isolated mines, using antiquated aircraft to power them over the rugged Andean mountains. Sequestered by boss Stevens in their austere, womanless compound—virtually a company town; their earnings quickly disappear, used for their own needs, and the occupants are enslaved by debt—their potentially volatile existence is held in check through the quiet strength of chief pilot Morris, who watches them fly to ultimate death, one by one. As replacements arrive, the attrition continues. One day, Heflin—unlicensed as a pilot for an infraction that resulted in a death—drops in from the skies with Bourne, his lovely young wife, the only woman worthy of fantasy to have been seen by the group in years. With difficulty, Morris restrains the tinderbox situation her presence represents, falling in love with her in the process. The brash but weak Heflin shows signs of breaking up; Morris shoulders the added responsibility of attempting to keep him alive. In a final effort at redemption, Heflin take the pitiless Stevens on a terminal flight, ramming his plane into an Andean peak. Morris and Bourne escape the confines of the camp.

p, Robert Sisk; d, Lew Landers [Louis Friedlander]; w, David Silverstein, John Twist (based on a story by Robert D. Andrews); ph, Nicholas Musuraca; ed, Harry Marker; spec eff, Vernon L. Walker.

Aviation Drama   **(PR:A   MPAA:NR)**

FLIGHT FROM SINGAPORE*½   (1962, Brit.) 74m President/PAR bw

Patrick Allan (*John Scott*), Patrick Holt (*Squadron Leader Hill*), William Abney (*Flight Lt. Bob Elliott*), Harry Fowler (*Sgt. Brooks*), Denis Holmes (*Smithy*), Jane Jordan Rogers (*Cleo*), Rosemary Dorken (*Joan Elliott*).

An intrepid air crew transporting desperately needed blood over the jungles of Malaya finds itself forced down into the bush. Nothing you haven't seen before, but an okay time waster.

p, James Mellor; d&w, Dudley Birch.

Aviation Drama   **(PR:A   MPAA:NR)**

FLIGHT FROM TERROR   (SEE: SATAN NEVER SLEEPS, 1962)

FLIGHT FROM VIENNA**   (1956, Brit.) 58m New Realm bw

John Bentley (*Capt. Lawson*), Theodore Bikel (*Kosice*), Adrienne Scott, Carina Helm, Donald Gray.

Bikel, an important figure in the Hungarian government, defects to the West and asks asylum. To prove his loyalty and sincerity, he is made to return to Hungary and bring out a scientist who also wishes to defect. Safely back in England, an attempt is made to assassinate Bikel. His life is saved and he is given asylum at last. Decent cold war drama mostly carried by Bikel's skillful performance.

p, E.J. Fancey; d&w, Denis Kavanagh; ph, Hal Morey.

Drama   **Cas.**   **(PR:A   MPAA:NR)**

FLIGHT INTO NOWHERE**½   (1938) 65m COL bw

Jack Holt (*Jim Horne*), Jacqueline [Julie Bishop] Wells (*Joan Hammond*), Dick Purcell (*Bill Kellogg*), James Burke (*Ike Matthews*), Karen Sorrell (*L-Ana*), Fritz Leiber (*Ti-Ana*), Howard Hickman (*Howard Hammond*), Robert Fiske (*Dr. Butler*), Hector Sarno (*Vincente*).

Hot-shot flyer Purcell breaks the rules once too often and is grounded, even though he is married to the boss' niece. Being young and foolish, he steals a plane, but ends up crashing in an uncharted jungle region. A search party is sent out and he is found living with an Incan tribe and married to one of the native girls. Offbeat, but entertaining.

d, Lewis D. Collins; w, Jefferson Parker, Gordon Rigby (based on a story by William Bloom, Clarence Jay Schneider); ph, James S. Brown, Jr.; ed, Dwight Caldwell.

Aviation Drama   **(PR:A   MPAA:NR)**

FLIGHT LIEUTENANT**   (1942) 80m COL bw

Pat O'Brien (*Sam Doyle*), Glenn Ford (*Danny Doyle*), Evelyn Keyes (*Susie Thompson*), Jonathan Hale (*Sanford*), Minor Watson (*Major Thompson*), Frank Puglia (*Father Carlos*), Edward Pawley (*Larsen*), Gregory Gaye (*Becker*), Clancy Cooper (*Scanlon*), Trevor Bardette (*Carey*), Marcel Dalio (*Faulet*), John Gallaudet (*Jackson*), Larry Parks (*Sandy Roth*), Lloyd Bridges (*Bill Robinson*), Hugh Beaumont (*John McGinnis*), Douglas Croft (*Danny Doyle, as a Boy*), Ralph Simone (*Bartender*), Ferdinand Munier (*Photographer*), Robert Frazer (*Captain Hall*), William Forrest (*Captain*), George Neise (*Radio Operator*), Crauford Kent (*Company Official*), Sidney Kibrick (*Pudgy*).

Commonplace aviator picture about a jungle plane crash in which the pilot survives and the co-pilot doesn't. The survivor goes into exile, leaving his son to be raised as an air corps cadet. The cohesive performance is Ford's, as the son who meets and falls in love with the co-pilot's daughter. The unconvincing finale has dad re-entering the service as a private, while the son has worked his way up to lieutenant. Dad sacrifices his own life when he volunteers to test a new plane, in place of his son. Of course dad is playing martyr, and the plane takes a fatal tumble. Inept cutting and poor transitions further demolish a film with a plot aged enough to have applied to chariot testing.

p, B.P. Schulberg; d, Sidney Salkow; w, Michael Blankfort (based on a story by Richard Carroll, Betty Hopkins); ph, Franz F. Planer; m, Werner R. Heymann; ed, Charles Nelson; md, M. W. Stoloff; art d, Lionel Banks.

Aviation Drama   **(PR:A   MPAA:NR)**

FLIGHT NURSE*½   (1953) 90m REP bw

Joan Leslie (*Lt. Polly Davis*), Forrest Tucker (*Capt. Bill Eaton*), Arthur Franz (*Capt. Mike Barnes*), Jeff Donnell (*Lt. Ann Phillips*), Ben Cooper (*Pfc. Marvin Judd*), James Holden (*Sgt. Frank Swan*), Kristine Miller (*Lt. Kit Ramsey*), Maria Palmer (*Capt. Martha Ackerman*), Richard Simmons (*Lt. Tommy Metcalf*), James Brown (*Flight Engineer*), Hal Baylor (*Sgt. Jimmy Case*).

Painfully contrived tale of an Air Force nurse on the front lines during the Korean War. A love-triangle and some anti-Communist preachiness only add extra weight to the already sluggish script. Included is the poem, "The Nurse's Prayer," by Edith A. Aynes.

p, Herbert J. Yates; d, Allan Dwan; w, Alan LeMay; ph, Reggie Lanning; m, Victor Young; ed, Fred Allen; art d, James Sullivan.

War Drama   **(PR:A   MPAA:NR)**

FLIGHT OF THE DOVES***   (1971) 101m COL c

Ron Moody (*Hawk Dove*), Jack Wild (*Finn Dove*), Dorothy McGuire (*Granny O'Flaherty*), Stanley Holloway (*Judge Liffy*), Helen Raye (*Derval Dove*), William Rushton (*Tobias Cromwell*), Dana (*Sheila*), John Molloy (*Mickser*), Barry Keegan (*Powder*), Brendan O'Reilly (*Michael*), Emmett Bergin (*Paddy*), Noel Purcell (*Rabbi*), Nial O'Brian (*Joe*), Ronnie Walsh (*Inspector Town*), Brenda Cauldwell (*Club Manager*), Thomas Hickey (*Garda Pat Flynn*), Tom Irwin, Joe Cahill, Clara Mullen, Des Keogh.

An engaging family picture which follows the adventures of a pair of adorable youngsters who are running away from their cruel British stepfather to the security of their Irish grandmother. Ron Moody—the putative heir to a fortune if the kids fail to survive—is superb as he tries to track the tots, who are beneficiaries to the grandfather's will. Especially entertaining for the younger set. The terribly contrived production numbers are sometimes embarrassing to adults. Shot on location in Ireland, with an international cast, two of whom may be familiar to American audiences: Moody and Wild were, respectively, Fagin and The Artful Dodger in the film version of the musical OLIVER! (1968). Songs include "The Far Off Place," Roy Budd, Brendan O'Dbuil, "You Don't Have To Be Irish To Be Irish," Budd.

p&d, Ralph Nelson; w, Frank Gabrielson, Nelson (based on a book by Walter Macken); ph, Harry Waxman; m, Roy Budd; ed, John Jympson; art d, Frank Arrigo; cos, Ted Parvin; makeup, Mark Reedall.

Drama/Children   **(PR:AA   MPAA:G)**

FLIGHT OF THE EAGLE**½
                                     (1983, Swed.) 141m Summit Feature Distributors c

Max von Sydow (*Salomon August Andree*), Goran Stangertz (*Nils Strindberg*), Sverre Anker Ousdal (*Knut Fraenkel*), Clement Harari (*Lachambre*), Eva von Hanno (*Guril Linder*), Lotta Larsson (*Anna Charlier*), Jon-Olof Strandberg (*Nils Ekholm*), Henric Holmberg (*GVE Svedenborg*), Mimi Pollak (*Mina Andree*), Cornelis Vreswijk (*Lundstrom*), Ulla Sjoblem (*Andree's Sister*), Ingvar Kjellson (*Alfred Nobel*), Brunno Serwing (*Oscar II*), Ake Whilney (*The Captain*), Knut Husebo (*Nansen*).

Hauntingly beautiful photography of the Arctic is the highlight of this film, based on the ill-fated Andree expedition of 1897. Von Sydow is the explorer, attempting to fly a balloon to the North Pole but crashing, and dying while trying to make it back to civilization. The last half, with three men struggling across the icy wastes and ultimately succumbing, tends to drag, but the film is well worth viewing. Nominated for an Academy Award for best foreign-language film. The plot has strong similarities to THE RED TENT (1971) where Sean Connery as Roald

Amundsen and Peter Finch as General Nobile re-enact an actual 1928 event, a tragic event in which Amundsen lost his life while trying to rescue a downed dirigible. (In Swedish; English subtitles.)

p, Goran Setterberg; d, Jan Troell; w, Georg Oddner, Ian Rakoff, Klaus Rifbjerg, Troell (based on a novel by Per Olof Sundman); ph, Troell; m, Hans Erik Philip; ed, Troell; art d, Ulf Axen.

Adventure/Drama   Cas.   **(PR:A-C   MPAA:NR)**

FLIGHT OF THE LOST BALLOON zero

(1961) 91m Woolner Bros.-AIP c

Mala Powers (Ellen), Marshall Thompson (Dr. Faraday), James Lanphier (Hindu), Douglas Kennedy (Sir Hubert), Robert Gillette (Sir Adam), Felippe Birriel (Gelan), A.J. Valentine (Giles), Blanquita Romero (The Malkia), Jackie Donoro (Native Dancer).

A quickie rip-off of the popular AROUND THE WORLD IN 80 DAYS (1956) with a low-cost cast, this period piece features Thompson in the unflappable David Niven role. Theater patrons were advised upon entering the lobby that the wild, erratic flight of the title balloon, as depicted on the screen, might require them to consume anti-nausea pills. The thought was a sound one, but for reasons other than those stated by the promoters. Playing the comic villain is Lanphier, in what is basically the Cantinflas part, an acquisitive Hindu who journeys to Victorian London to persuade the directors of the Geographic Society to mount a rescue mission to save famed explorer Kennedy, a captive in a secret dungeon on the Nile River. It is all part of a diabolical plot; Lanphier is, in truth, Kennedy's captor, hoping to force from the latter's lips the location of Cleopatra's entombed treasures. Thompson elects to lead the rescue team, joined by Kennedy's fiancee, the luscious Powers, and the sinister Hindu, Lanphier. Setting out in the basket of a balloon, the intrepid adventurers are beset by peril with every vagrant gust of wind, the top-hatted Thompson meeting every challenge with phlegmatic British imperturbability. Upon the ultimate arrival of the trio at the dungeon, the curvaceous Powers is the attractive victim of unspeakable tortures, Lanphier's method of wringing Kennedy's secret from his hitherto mute mouth. Kennedy, as greedy as his captor, keeps his own counsel even as the callipygian cutie is stretched on the rack. But wait! As the horrible Hindu savors the suffering of his sweet victim, our hero loosens his bonds and saves the unfortunate duo. Hoist by his own petard, explorer Kennedy dies attempting to cram the treasure into the balloon's basket. The noble Thompson and the nubile Powers take off for home, jettisoning the jewels to lighten the load save only for one diamond, to be fitted into an engagement ring for Powers, who compensates for the burden by tossing Tompson's topper into the turbulence. With decent dialog and effects, and a dash of real wit, this adventure romp, with some location sequences in Puerto Rico, might have been in a class with the later INDIANA JONES series (see Index). Alas, it lacked *panache*.

p, Bernard Woolner, d&w, Nathan Juran; ph, Jacques Marquette (SpectraScope, Eastmancolor); m, Hal Borne; ed, Rex Lipton.

Drama   **(PR:C   MPAA:NR)**

FLIGHT OF THE PHOENIX, THE****

(1965) 149m FOX c

James Stewart (Frank Towns), Richard Attenborough (Lew Moran), Peter Finch (Capt. Harris), Hardy Kruger (Heinrich Dorfmann), Ernest Borgnine (Trucker Cobb), Ian Bannen (Crow), Ronald Fraser (Sgt. Watson), Christian Marquand (Dr. Renaud), Dan Duryea (Standish), George Kennedy (Bellamy), Gabriele Tinti (Gabriele), Alex Montoya (Carlos), Peter Bravos (Tasso), William Aldrich (Bill), Barrie Chase (Farida), Stanley Ralph Ross (Arab Singer).

Here is a riveting film of survival where Stewart and supporting players give power-packed performances as downed pilots and passengers awaiting death in the Sahara desert. Stewart assumes the blame for the crash landing, although it's clearly the fault of the inept navigator, Attenborough, whose alcoholism has led to errors that forced the plane down. The men await rescue in the broiling sun, conserving their water and thinking of their own comforts. Finch, a British officer, announces he will go in search of help from a passing caravan. He is warned that the Arabs may be hostile but he believes he will prevail upon their better instincts. His sergeant, Fraser, a dough-faced, surly coward, refuses to accompany Finch and is replaced by Montoya. They are discovered murdered the next day, the Arabs having slit their throats and robbed them. All seems hopeless until Kruger announces that he believes he can design a new single-engined plane from the wreck, one that will actually fly them all out. The men slave away at constructing this new plane, dubbed the "Phoenix," which miraculously manages to take flight with the survivors strapped to the wings and Stewart at the controls, flying them to safety. Stewart is superb as the pilot whose authority is finally usurped by the scientifically methodical Kruger, whom he grows to resent. One of the great scenes in this excellent film occurs when Stewart learns that Kruger has never designed any craft bigger than a model airplane. Finch is convincing as the stoic British officer and Borgnine, Marquand, and Duryea give fine portrayals as stranded men. Barrie Chase, a sensuous dancer, does a mirage shimmy to the song"Desert Sands" (Stanley Ralph Ross). Aldrich's direction is sharp and well-paced and his script is absorbing and realistic. Veteran stunt pilot Paul Mantz was killed during the making of this film while on location near Yuma, Arizona and, in the closing credits, the production is dedicated to his memory.

p&d, Robert Aldrich; w, Lukas Heller (based on a novel by Elleston Trevor); ph, Joseph Biroc (DeLuxe Color); m, Frank De Vol; ed, Michael Luciano; art d, William Glasgow; set d, Lucien Hafley; cos, Norma Koch; sp eff, L. B. Abbott, Howard Lydecker; m/l, "Senza Fine," Gino Paoli (sung by Connie Francis); makeup, Ben Nye.

Adventure   **(PR:C   MPAA:NR)**

FLIGHT OF THE SANDPIPER, THE

(SEE: SANDPIPER, THE, 1965)

FLIGHT THAT DISAPPEARED, THE**½

(1961) 71m UA bw (AKA: THE FLIGHT THAT VANISHED)

Craig Hill (Tom Endicott), Paula Raymond (Marcia Paxton), Dayton Lummis (Dr. Morris), Gregory Morton (Examiner), John Bryant (Hank Norton), Addison Richards (Sage), Nancy Hale (Barbara Nielsen), Bernadette Hale (Joan Agnew), Harvey Stephens (Walter Cooper), Brad Trumbull (Jack Peters), Meg Wyllie (Helen Cooper), Francis De Sales (Manson), Carl Princi (Announcer), Eden Hartford (Miss Ford), Ed Stoddard (O'Connor), Roy Engel (Jamison), Jerry James (Ray Houser), Jack Mann (Garrett), Stephen Ellsworth Crowley (ATC Official), Joe Haworth (Radio Operator).

Science-fiction rears its socially conscious head in this commendable no-nuke message. Three top scientists traveling by plane to a presidential meeting at the Pentagon are mysteriously transmitted to another dimension. They are kept captive by the future generations of earth, who try to deter them from presenting plans for the development of an ultimate bomb. A minor pacifist film which becomes more relevant with time.

p, Robert E. Kent; d, Reginald LeBorg; w, Ralph Hart, Judith Hart, Owen Harris; ph, Gilbert Warrenton; m, Richard LaSalle; ed, Kenneth Crane; set d, Morris Hoffman; cos, Sabine Manela, Jerry Bos; spec eff, Barney Wolff; makeup, Harry Thomas.

Science Fiction   **(PR:A   MPAA:NR)**

FLIGHT TO FAME**

(1938) 67m COL bw

Charles Farrell (Capt. Lawrence), Jacqueline Wells [Julie Bishop] (Barbara), Hugh Sothern (Fisk), Alexander D'Arcy (Perez), Jason Robards (Muller), Charles D. Brown (Major Loy), Addison Richards (Colonel), Frederick Burton (General), Selmer Jackson (Peabody), Reed Howes (Curran).

Columbia pulled the death ray out of the closet for this formulated flier pic. Robards plays a crazed aerial ace who steals the weapon and kills off all the pilots who harassed him during the war. Farrell and inventor's daughter Wells discover his plan and pull the plug on his ray gun. Of historical importance only as an early example of the cinematography of the brilliant Lucien Ballard, who went on to gain fame as Sam Peckinpah's cameraman.

d, C.C. Coleman, Jr.; w, Michael Simmons; ph, Lucien Ballard; ed, James Sweeney.

Science Fiction/Drama   **(PR:A   MPAA:NR)**

FLIGHT TO FURY**½

(1966, U.S./Phil.) 62m Lippert/FOX bw (CORDILLERA)

Dewey Martin (Joe Gaines), Fay Spain (Destiny Cooper), Jack Nicholson (Jay Wickham), Jacqueline Hellman (Gloria Walsh), Vic Diaz (Lorgren), Joseph Estrada (Garuda), John Hackett (Al Ross), Juliet Prado (Lei Ling), Jennings Sturgeon (Bearded Man), Lucien Pan (Police Inspector).

Tight, grim little drama directed by Monte Hellman, written by and starring Jack Nicholson. Martin plays a world adventurer who meets up with evil American Nicholson in Southeast Asia. Nicholson murders a young woman in search of a cache of valuable diamonds (unbeknownst to Martin) and soon the two are on a passenger plane en route to the Philippines with Nicholson still searching for the diamonds. The plane crash-lands in the jungle and the man carrying the diamonds, Hackett, is seriously wounded. Before he dies, Hackett passes the diamonds to Martin, who is unaware that they really belong to Diaz, another passenger. Diaz grabs the gems at gunpoint, but the survivors are besieged by natives who imprison them. The group escapes and Nicholson kills Diaz for the diamonds, then flees into the underbrush. Martin pursues and wounds him with a gunshot. Dying, Nicholson throws the diamonds into a river and then shoots himself before he can be recaptured, leaving Martin alone to face the wrath of the natives. This collaborative effort was filmed simultaneously in Tagalog for its local release, these scenes being directed by Eddie Romero. A prior collaboration of Nicholson and Hellman, shot in the same Philippine locations and with some of the same players, was BACK DOOR TO HELL (1964).

p, Fred Roos; d, Monte Hellman; w, Jack Nicholson (based on a story by Hellman, Roos); ph, Mike Accion.

Crime/Drama   **(PR:C   MPAA:NR)**

FLIGHT TO HONG KONG**½

(1956) 88m UA bw

Rory Calhoun (Tony Dumont), Barbara Rush (Pamela Vincent), Dolores Donlon (Jean Blake), Soo Yong (Mama Lin), Pat Conway (Nicco), Werner Klemperer (Bendesh), Mel Welles (Boris), Paul Picerni (Quisto), Aram Katcher (Lobero), Rhodes Reason (Bob Denham), Bob Hopkins (Cappy), Timothy Carey (Lagarto), Carleton Young (Cmdr. Larabee), Aaron Saxon (Sargas), Noel Cravat (Gantz), Guy Prescott (Pondry), Barry Brook (Andaras), George Barrows (Janvoort), Booth Coleman (Maxler), Ralph Smiley (Boussard), Paul Brinegar (Carstairs).

Calhoun is a syndicate boss in Hong Kong who divides his day between adorable novelist Rush, the equally irresistible Donlon, and his plan to steal and smuggle $1 million worth of a maharajah's jewels. Not only does he two-time the ladies, but he tries the same trick with the mob. Calhoun discovers, all too soon, that one mustn't mess with the mob. Luckily for him, the Hong Kong police get to him before it's too late.

p&d, Joseph M. Newman; w, Leo Townsend, Edward G. O'Callaghan (based on a story by Newman, O'Callaghan, Gustave Field); ph, Ellis W. Carter; m, Monty Kelly; ed, Ralph Dawson; art d, Serge Krizman; cos, Fay Moore, Tommy Thompson.

Crime   **(PR:C   MPAA:NR)**

FLIGHT TO MARS** (1951) 71m MON c

Marguerite Chapman *(Alita)*, Cameron Mitchell *(Steve)*, Arthur Franz *(Jim)*, Virginia Huston *(Carol)*, John Litel *(Dr. Lane)*, Richard Gaines *(Prof. Jackson)*, Morris Ankrum *(Ikron)*, Lucille Barkley *(Terris)*, Robert H. Barrat *(Tillamar)*, Edward Earle *(Justin)*, William Forrest *(Gen. Archer)*.

On its last legs, Monogram released this picture on the coattails of the highly successful DESTINATION MOON (1950). The chief difference is that this time color is used—a first for sci-fi films. A group of scientists crash-land on the red planet and are held prisoner. The Martians plan to copy the U.S. spacecraft and build their own invasion fleet. Of course there is a love-stricken Martian girl who aids the Earthlings in their escape.

p, Walter Mirisch; d, Lesley Selander; w, Arthur Strawn; ph, Harry Neumann (Cinecolor); m, Marlin Skiles; ed, Richard Heermance; art d, David Milton; spec eff, Irving Block, Jack Cosgrove.

Science-fiction Cas. (PR:A MPAA:NR)

FLIGHT TO NOWHERE zero (1946) 75m Golden Gate/Screen Guild bw

Alan Curtis *(Hobe Carrington)*, Evelyn Ankers *(Kathie Forrest)*, Micheline Cheirel *(Countess Marie/Dolly Lorraine)*, Jack Holt *(Bob Donovan)*, Jerome Cowan *(Gerald Porter)*, Inez Cooper *(Irene Allison)*, Hoot Gibson *(Sheriff Bradley)*, John Craven, Roland Varno, Michael Visaroff, Gordon Richards.

This bottom-of-the-barrel film starts before the credits with a Korean courier being killed for a map showing uranium deposits on a South Pacific island. Curtis is a former intelligence agent who is now a charter pilot and is reluctantly persuaded by Holt, a federal agent, to help solve the case. The pilot takes a group of people (a fraudulent countess, her secretary, and the secretary's brother, a mining engineer, etc.) by plane to a hotel in Death Valley. Here the hero gets clobbered on the head a couple of times, two people are murdered, and the map is passed around from one person to another. Gibson is the local western sheriff. Eventually, this muddled state of affairs gets straightened out and Curtis ends up with Ankers.

p, William B. David; d, William Rowland; w, Arthur V. Jones; m, Carl Hoefle; ph, Marcel Le Picard; ed, Greg Tallas.

Spy Drama/Western (PR:C MPAA:NR)

FLIGHT TO TANGIER*** (1953) 80m PAR c

Joan Fontaine *(Susan)*, Jack Palance *(Gil Walker)*, Corinne Calvet *(Nicole)*, Robert Douglas *(Danzar)*, Marcel Dalio *(Gogo)*, Jeff Morrow *(Col. Wier)*, Richard Shannon *(Lt. Luzon)*, Murray Matheson *(Franz Kovac)*, John Doucette *(Tirera)*, John Pickard *(Hank Brady)*, James Anderson *(Dullah)*, Don Dunning, Eric Alden *(Moroccans)*, Bob Templeton *(Luzon's Policeman)*, Peter Coe *(Hanrah)*, Madeleine Holmes *(Rosario)*, John Wengraf *(Kalferez)*, Otto Waldis *(Wisil)*, Jerry Paris *(Policeman in Car)*, Rene Chatenay, Albert D'Arno, Anthony De Mario *(Policemen)*, Karin Vengay *(Greek Girl)*, Pilar Del Ray *(Spanish Girl)*, Josette Deegan *(French Girl)*, Mark Hanna *(Corporal at Airport)*, Rodric Redwing *(Police Orderly)*.

This time it's Tangier that serves as the centerpiece for violent underworld goings-on. Fontaine, Palance, and Calvet are all lined up against Douglas on the search for $3 million coming in from the Iron Curtain. Also dipping its hand in is the FBI. A wide and intriguing array of characters nicely texture the frame. Shot in Technicolor and in three dimensions for those exhibitors who wanted to charge extra for the Polaroids, and released also in 2-D, with choice of regular dimensions or wide-screen, this one covered all the bases technically.

p, Nat Holt; d&w, Charles Marquis Warren; ph, Ray Rennahan (3-D, Technicolor); m, Paul Sawtell; ed, Frank Bracht; art d, Hal Pereira, John Goodman.

Drama (PR:A MPAA:NR)

FLIM-FLAM MAN, THE*** (1967) 104m FOX c
(GB: ONE BORN EVERY MINUTE)

George C. Scott *(Mordecai)*, Sue Lyon *(Bonnie Lee Packard)*, Michael Sarrazin *(Curley)*, Harry Morgan *(Sheriff Slade)*, Jack Albertson *(Mr. Packard)*, Alice Ghostley *(Mrs. Packard)*, Albert Salmi *(Deputy Meshaw)*, Slim Pickens *(Jarvis Bates)*, Strother Martin *(Lovick)*, George Mitchell *(Tetter)*, Woodrow Parfrey *(Supermarket Manager)*, Jay Ose *(2nd Fertilizer Man)*, Raymond Guth *(1st Fertilizer Man)*, Jesse L. Baker *(Doodle Powell)*.

Incorrigible, glib, and packing around a bag of ancient confidence tricks, Scott is fascinating as a bumbling flimflam artist who refuses to abandon his larcenous trade. He takes on a pupil, Sarrazin, who has deserted from the army, teaching him methods of bilking his fellow man. Sarrazin is an apt student, successfully working bunco games with small-town people until meeting and falling hopelessly in love with Lyon, and then trying to reform the old man. Scott will have none of it and in one scam involving a stolen car, the flimflammer goes berserk and wrecks half the town in his escape attempt. He is jailed but later freed by Sarrazin who pretends to have enough dynamite to blow up the jail. After Scott escapes, and watches from hiding, Sarrazin is arrested, then released when authorities realize he meant no real harm. "Thank you, son," whispers Scott and he races off to hop a freight train and continue his errant ways. Scott mugs and twitches his charming way through a fascinating performance that must carry the lightweight, wholly ridiculous story which is further muddled by the amateur talent of Sarrazin. Further color is added by Scott's irate victims, notably Martin and Pickens, two Southern slickers taken to the cleaners out of their own greedy ways. Kershner's direction is slighly above average, working hard to save an episodic and less than inventive script. There are more than a few laughs provided by Scott, but the action is pure slapstick. Goldsmith's score is outstanding.

p, Lawrence Turman; d, Irvin Kershner; w, William Rose; ph, Charles Lang (Panavision, DeLuxe Color); m, Jerry Goldsmith; ed, Robert Swink; art d, Jack Martin Smith, Robert E. Smith, Lewis Creber; set d, Walter M. Scott, John Sturtevant; cos, Dorothy Jeakins; spec eff, L. B. Abbott, Art Cruickshank, Emil Kosa, Jr.; makeup, Ben Nye.

Comedy Cas. (PR:A MPAA:NR)

FLIPPER*½** (1963) 87m MGM c

Chuck Connors *(Porter Ricks)*, Luke Halpin *(Sandy Ricks)*, Connie Scott *(Kim Parker)*, Jane Rose *(Hettie White)*, Joe Higgins *(Mr. L. C. Porett)*, Robertson White *(Mr. Abrams)*, George Applewhite *(Sheriff Rogers)*, Kathleen Maguire *(Martha Ricks)*, Mitzi *(Flipper)*.

One cannot take a critical stance for or against a dolphin, nor does one really want to. Tot Halpin nurses Flipper back to health after a pesty spear is removed from the sea mammal's back. Dad, fisherman Connors, acts with animal consciousness and insists that the critter be released from its fish-pen tank and returned to its natural home. Halpin is naturally upset at the news, but his faith is restored when Flipper comes back and saves the lad from sharks, displaying the obligatory underwater antics. Granted, this film strikes at a formula, but it does so with such success that it feels fresh. Highly recommended for the kids.

p, Ivan Tors; d, James B. Clark; w, Arthur Weiss (based on a story by Ricou Browning, Jack Cowden); ph, Lamar Boren, Joseph Brun (Metrocolor); m, Henry Vars; ed, Warren Adams; m/l, "Flipper," "By" Dunham, Vars.

Drama/Children (PR:AAA MPAA:NR)

FLIPPER'S NEW ADVENTURE*** (1964) 92m MGM c
(AKA: FLIPPER AND THE PIRATES)

Luke Halpin *(Sandy)*, Pamela Franklin *(Penny)*, Helen Cherry *(Julia)*, Tom Helmore *(Sir Halsey Hopewell)*, Francesca Annis *(Gwen)*, Brian Kelly *(Porter Ricks)*, Joe Higgins *(L.C. Porett)*, Lloyd Battista *(Gill)*, Gordon Dilworth *(Sea Captain)*, Courtney Brown, William Cooley *(Convicts)*, Dan Chandler *(Coast Guard Commander)*, Ricou Browning *(Dr. Clark Burton)*, Robert Baldwin, Ric O'Feldman *(Veterinarians)*, Susie *(Flipper)*.

Nothing is lost in this dolphin sequel which takes Halpin and his finned friend to a remote island in the Bahamas. The duo complicates the plot of a gang holding a wealthy British family captive. Flipper performs his usual ocean acrobatics for Halpin and his new girl friend Franklin. This film's hero, as in the original, became the object of many children's heartfelt fantasies. Also cast was Brian Kelly, who took the role of Flipper's pal in the subsequent television series.

p, Ivan Tors; d, Leon Benson; w, Art Arthur (based on a story by Ivan Tors, and from characters created by Ricou Browning, Jack Cowden); ph, Lamar Boren (Metrocolor); m, Henry Vars; ed, Warren Adams, Charles Craft; m/l, "Imagine," "It's A Cotton Candy World," and "Flipper," "By" Dunham, Henry Vars.

Drama/Children (PR:AAA MPAA:NR)

FLIRTATION WALK*** (1934) 95m FN-WB bw

Dick Powell *(Dick "Canary" Dorcy)*, Ruby Keeler *(Kit Fitts)*, Pat O'Brien *(Sgt. Scrapper Thornhill)*, Ross Alexander *(Oskie)*, John Arledge *(Spike)*, John Eldredge *(Lt. Robert Biddle)*, Henry O'Neill *(Gen. Jack Fitts)*, Guinn "Big Boy" Williams *(Sleepy)*, Frederick Burton *(Gen. Paul Landacre)*, John Darrow *(Chase)*, Glen Boles *(Eight Ball)*, University of Southern California and Army Polo Teams *(Polo Players)*, Lt. Joe Cummins *(Cadet)*, Gertrude Keeler *(Dancer)*, Col. Tim Lonergan *(General)*, Tyrone Power, Jr., Carlyle Blackwell, Jr., Dick Winslow *(Cadets)*, Maude Turner Gordon *(Dowager)*, Frances Lee *(Blonde)*, Avis Johnson *(Redhead)*, Mary Russell *(Girl)*, William J. Worthington *(Civilian)*, Cliff Saum, Paul Fix *(Soldiers)*, Sol Bright *(Native Leader)*, Emmett Vogan *(Officer)*, Frank Dawson *(Butler)*, Sol Hoopii and his Native Orchestra.

FLIRTATION WALK was the quintessential West Point musical. Sixteen years later it was sort-of remade as THE WEST POINT STORY with James Cagney and Doris Day. Powell is an army private in Hawaii (where much of this was actually filmed. The studio spared no expense and took the cast and crew to the Islands (and West Point) rather than re-dress Santa Monica or Malibu as had so often been done before) where he falls in love with General Henry O'Neill's daughter, Keeler, after they take a moonlit ride along the ocean. The only problem is that she's engaged to Eldredge, a lieutenant. When he discovers the two of them in each other's arms, Eldredge commands Powell to return to his barracks. Powell wants to avoid a *cause celebre* at any cost so he plans to desert, rather than put Keeler in a bad light. She, on the other hand, wants to protect *him* so she fibs that the evening was nothing more than a passing fancy and she doesn't care a whit about Powell. He believes that (hey, it's a movie and we have to suspend disbelief, right?) and decides to move up in life, enter West Point, and become an officer (he is already a gentleman). Powell's best friend is O'Brien, a grizzled sergeant who urges Powell to take the step. Dissolve, and it's three years later. Powell has established himself as a top cadet as well as the man who writes, produces, directs, and stars in the annual musical. O'Neill is made superintendent at West Point and Keeler, who is still engaged to Eldredge, arrives as well. Powell is very cold to her but can't stay away very long (the whole picture is under one hundred minutes, and who has time to play games at this breakneck pace?). Keeler becomes his leading lady in the Academy play. She arrives late for the first rehearsal and they have a bit of a spat (much of the dialog is witty, trenchant and free of cliches) that, to an untrained eye, might indicate enmity but since we know they'll wind up together, the secondary texture of the scene is sexual tension. The show is a hit, Eldredge realizes that Keeler and Powell were meant for each other (as they were in so many films), and bids them happiness. At the fade, O'Brien, who is on leave from Shanghai, is in the reviewing stand with Keeler as Powell and the others march by. Tough O'Brien has tears of pride flow from his eyes in a turnabout from his usual wise-cracking characterization, a nice moment. Keeler and Powell decide to get married and the film ends. Tyrone Power (when he still attached the 'junior' to his name) is seen as a cadet for just a fleeting moment. His son, actually Tyrone Power, the third, is now using the 'junior' in his screen credits. Dick Winslow, another cadet, now makes a living in Southern California as a musician and one-man band. Ross Alexander, Powell's roommate, was a bright young light comedian whom the studio was grooming for bigger things, but his career took a nosedive after this film; he wound up in several "B" movies (HOT MONEY (1936), I MARRIED A DOCTOR (1936), SHIPMATES FOREVER (1935) and eventually committed suicide before he was 31 years old. No great songs in the Wrubel-Dixon score, which included "Flirtation Walk," "When Do We Eat?" "I See Two Lovers," and "Mr. and Mrs. Is The Name" (Allie Wrubel, Mort Dixon). Keeler, in an attempt to rid herself of her image, barely dances at all, a loss for the viewer.

p, Robert Lord; d, Frank Borzage; w, Delmer Daves (based on a story by Lou Edelman, Daves); ph, Sol Polito, George Barnes; ed, William Holmes; md, Leo F. Forbstein; art d, Jack Okey; cos, Orry-Kelly; ch, Bobby Connolly.

Musical/Comedy   **(PR:AA MPAA:NR)**

FLIRTING WIDOW, THE**   (1930) 70m FN-WB bw

Dorothy Mackaill (Celia), Basil Rathbone (Col. Smith), Leila Hyams (Evelyn), William Austin (James Raleigh), Claude Gillingwater (Faraday), Emily Fitzroy (Aunt Ida), Flora Bramley (Phyllis), Anthony Bushell (Bobby), Wilfred Noy (Martin).

This breezy film has eldest sister Mackaill—at Father Gillingwater's insistence—trying to avoid being the first of her sibling trio to walk down the aisle. She concocts a scheme around a supposedly fictional character named Col. Smith, who ironically turns out to really exist—Rathbone—leading to zany results.

d, William A. Seiter; w, John F. Goodrich (based on the play "Green Stockings" by Alfred Edward Woodley Mason); ph, Sid Hickox; ed, Goodrich.

Comedy   **(PR:A MPAA:NR)**

FLIRTING WITH DANGER**½   (1935) 69m MON bw

Robert Armstrong (Bob Owens), William Cagney (Lucky Davis), Edgar Kennedy (Jimmie Pierson), Marion Burns (Mary Leslie), Maria Alba (Rosita), William von Brincken (Von Kruger), Ernest Hilliard (Dawson), Gino Corrado (Capt. Garcia), Guy Usher (Fenton).

Armstrong, Kennedy, and Cagney are a trio of bumbling explosives men in this comical, but tedious, film. After accidentally producing explosion after explosion on the job, the three get sent to South America on assignment. Below the border things get even crazier when they mistake an independence-day fireworks display for a violent political overthrow. The comedy is effective, but there isn't enough of it to justify even a 69-minute film. William Cagney is James Cagney's brother. He had a brief acting career and then became a producer of his brother's films.

d, Vin Moore; w, Albert E. DeMond, Norman S. Hall (based on a story by George Bertholon); ph, Archie Stout; ed, Carl Pierson.

Comedy   **(PR:A MPAA:NR)**

FLIRTING WITH FATE*½   (1938) 70m MGM bw

Joe E. Brown (Dixon), Leo Carrillo (Sancho), Beverly Roberts (Patricia), Wynne Gibson (Bertha), Steffi Duna (Carlita), Charles Judels (Garcia), Stanley Fields (Fernando), Leonid Kinskey (Lopez), Chris Martin (Solado), Inez Palange (Senora Lopez), Irene Franklin (Hattie), Jay Novello (Del Valle), George Humbert (Del Rio), Lew Kelly (Herbie), Philip Trent (Larry), Ann Hovey (Ida), Dick Botiller (Renaldo), Carlos Villerias (Captain).

A forgettable comedy about a vaudeville troupe travelling through South America with Brown heading the way. After blowing their big chance and feeling that he let down his performers, Brown decides to kill himself so the troupe can collect his life insurance. Carrillo, the Paraguayan *bandido* insulted by Brown in his lust for lifelessness, is entertaining as he ignores the little loudmouth's affronts. One would think that Duna's off-key warbling on "El Bandellero" and "Mate" would be enough to do in anyone. This was the first independent film to be released by MGM, a policy switch which may have resulted from producer Loew's family connection with the company, rather than with the picture's intrinsic merit.

p, David L. Loew; d, Frank McDonald; w, Joseph Moncure March, Ethel La Blanche, Charlie Melson, Harry Clork (from a story by A. Dorian Otvos, Dan Jarrett); ph, George Schneiderman; m, Walter G. Samuels, Charles Newman; ed, Robert O. Crandall.

Comedy   **(PR:A MPAA:NR)**

FLITTERWOCHEN IN DER HOLLE   (SEE: ISLE OF SIN, 1964)

FLOATING DUTCHMAN, THE** (1953, Brit.) 76m Merton Park/AA bw

Dermot Walsh (Alexander James), Sydney Tafler (Victor Skinner), Mary Germaine (Rose Reid), Guy Verney (Snow White), Hugh Morton (Inspector Cathie), James Raglan (Mr. Wynn), Nicolas Bentley (Collis), Arnold Marle (Otto), Derek Blomfield (Philip Reid), Orest Olaff, Ian Wilson, Walter Horsbrugh, Frank Hawkins, Lindsay Hooper, Marjorie Gresley, Ken Midwood, Kathleen Page, Anna Turner, Howard Lang, John Cunningham, Jack Sands.

Detective Walsh infiltrates a jewel theft ring to catch thief Tafler and find the killer of a Dutch jeweler whose body was found bobbing in the Thames. Below average crime drama.

p, W.H. Williams; d&w, Vernon Sewell (based on a novel by Nicolas Bentley); ph, Joe Ambor.

Crime   **(PR:A MPAA:NR)**

FLOATING WEEDS**½   (1970, Jap.) 119m Daiei/Altura c
(UKIGUSA; AKA: DUCKWEED STORY, THE; DRIFTING WEEDS)

Ganjiro Nakamura (Komajuro), Haruko Sugimura (Oyoshi), Hiroshi Kawaguchi (Kiyoshi), Machiko Kyo (Sumiko), Ayako Wakao (Kayo), Koji Mitsui (Kichinosuke), Mutsuko Sakura, Mantaro Ushio, Haruo Tanaka, Hitomi Nozoe, Chishu Ryu.

Nakamura leads a traveling theater troupe to a seaside village, where he runs into his ex-mistress, Sugimura, and his illegitimate son, Kawaguchi. Instead of staying with his fellow thespians, he lavishes attention on his son, who believes Nakamura is his uncle. Jealous of his suddenly shifted devotion, Kyo, Nakamura's current mistress, arranges to have one of the troupe's actresses, Wakao, seduce the son. The two fall in love and the short-on-cash troupe breaks up. Nakamuro jilts

Sugimura for the second time, continuing his dalliance with Kyo. A subpar film from Japan's great director, Ozu. Called the "most Japanese of Japanese directors," Ozu has consistently gone unrecognized outside his homeland. FLOATING WEEDS, for example, was not shown elsewhere until eleven years after its Japanese release in 1959. Paradoxically, the Japanese hesitate to send Ozu's films to the West for fear of poor reviews, but when they are praised the Japanese are baffled by outside appreciation of something "truly Japanese." The outstanding Kyo also starred in the two classic Japanese films RASHOMON (Akira Kurosawa) and UGETSU (Kenji Mizoguchi).

d, Yasujiro Ozu; w, Ozu, Kogo Noda (based on a story by Ozu and the film UKIGUSA MONOGATARI, screenplay by Tadeo Ikeda); ph, Kazuo Miyagawa (Daiei Color); m, Takanobu Saito.

Drama   **(PR:A MPAA:NR)**

FLOOD, THE*   (1931) 65m COL bw

Eleanor Boardman, Monte Blue, Frank Sheridan, William V. Mong, Violet Barlowe, Eddie Tamblyn, Arthur Hoyt, Ethel Wales, Buddy Ray, Ethan Allen, David Newell.

Varicose-vein plot of young girl torn between the man she loves and the man she married. Set against the background of a faltering dam, this contrived story is further bogged down by lackluster direction. When the flood comes it looks more like a leaky faucet than Biblical wrath.

d, James Tinling; w, John Thomas Neville (based on a story by Neville); ph, John Stumar; ed, Gene Milford.

Drama   **(PR:A MPAA:NR)**

FLOOD, THE*   (1963, Brit.) 58m AB-Pathe/CFF bw

Waveney Lee (Clarissa Weathersfield), Christopher Ellis (Robin), Frank Knight (Reg), Jonathan Bergman (Bill Brasted), Ian Ellis (Charles), Leslie Hart (Ernie), Richard Leech, Daphne Anderson, Russell Waters.

Rising flood waters threaten six farm children, but they are rescued in the inevitable nick of time. Another insipid, unimaginative children's film that any child with a brain in his head will find unbearable.

p, Terry Ashwood; d, Frederic Goode; w, Jean Scott Rogers (based on a story by Frank Wells).

Children   **(PR:AA MPAA:NR)**

FLOOD TIDE**   (1935, Brit.) 63m RA/RKO bw

George Carney (Captain Bill Buckett), Peggy Novak (Mabel), Leslie Hatton (Ted Salter), Janice Adair (Betty Buckett), Wilson Coleman (Ben Salter), Minnie Rayner (Sarah Salter), Mark Daly (Scotty), Edgar Driver (Titch), Wilfred Benson, William Fazan, Bertram Dench.

Carney is a lock keeper's son and an officer. Novak's a bargeman's daughter. They meet, fall in love, and get married, after the usual hemming and hawing. Hohum.

p, Julius Hagen; d, John Baxter; w, Ernest Anson Dyer.

Romance   **(PR:A MPAA:NR)**

FLOOD TIDE**   (1958) 82m UNIV bw

George Nader (Steve Martin), Cornell Borchers (Anne Gordon), Michel Ray (David Gordon), Judson Pratt (Harvey Thornwald), Joanna Moore (Barbara Brooks), Charles E. Arnt (Mr. Appleby), Russ Conway (Bill Holleran), John Morley (Detective Lieutenant), John Maxwell (John Brighton), Carl Benson (District Attorney), Della Malzarn (Beverly), Hugh Lawrence (Charlie).

Ray, cast as a disturbed and crippled youngster, is insanely jealous of his mother's relationship with Nader, a well-meaning neighbor. Most of the screen time is devoted to Nader's efforts to win the boy over. Nader gets him to admit that he lied during a trial which sent an innocent man to prison. Sad, but strangely intriguing.

p, Robert Arthur; d, Abner Biberman; w, Dorothy Cooper (based on a story by Barry Trivers); ph, Arthur E. Arling (CinemaScope); m, Henry Mancini, William Lava; ed, Ted J. Kent; art d, Art Golitzen, Bill Newberry; cos, Bill Thomas.

Drama   **(PR:C MPAA:NR)**

FLOODS OF FEAR***   (1958, Brit.) 84m RANK/UNIV bw

Howard Keel (Donovan), Anne Heywood (Elizabeth Matthews), Cyril Cusack (Peebles), Harry H. Corbett (Sharkey), John Crawford (Jack Murphy), Eddie Byrne (Sheriff), John Phillips (Dr. Matthews), Mark Baker (Fatchman), James Dyrenforth (Mayor), Jack Lester (Businessman), Peter Madden (Banker), John Kingsley Poynter (Deputy Sheriff), Gordon Tanner (Lt. Colonel), Robert MacKenzie (Police Captain), Vivian Matalon, Gordon Sterne, Bill Edwards, Graydon Gould, Kevin Scott, Ed Devereaux.

Keel, an innocent man convicted of murder, escapes with a fellow con during a flood, and befriends the marooned Heywood. Initially she is frightened by his threats to kill the man who framed him, but gathers enough courage to contact the police and inform them of his innocence. Heywood is a joy to watch as she stands up to the impending aquatic doom.

p, Sydney Box; d, Charles Crichton; w, Vivienne Knight, Crichton (based on the novel by John and Ward Hawkins); ph, Christopher Challis; m, Alan Rawsthorne; ed, Peter Bezencenet; art d, Cedric Dawe.

Drama   **(PR:A MPAA:NR)**

FLOODTIDE*½   (1949, Brit.) 90m Aquila/GFD bw

Gordon Jackson (David Shields), Rona Anderson (Mary Anstruther), John Laurie (Joe Drummond), Jack Lambert (Anstruther), Jimmy Logan (Tim Brogan), Janet Brown (Rosie), Elizabeth Sellars (Judy), Ian MacLean (Sir John), Archie Duncan (Charlie Campbell), James Woodburn (John Shields), Molly Weir (Mrs. MacTavish),

Ian Wallace *(First Director)*, Alexander Archdale *(Second Director)*, Grace Garvin *(Mrs. MacCrea)*, Alastair Hunter *(Dick Crawford)*, Kitty Kirwan *(Granny Shields)*, Peter Illing *(Senor Aranha)*, Gordon McLeod *(Pursey)*, Norah Gordon, Molly Urquhart, Sam Kydd, James Fraser, Arthur Lowe, Hugh Munro.

An uneventful romance between a shipyard apprentice and the boss' daughter is picturesquely placed against a dockside atmosphere. The film traces the lad's rise to power until he finally achieves a powerful company post. A forgettable plot with an impressive setting.

p, Donald B. Wilson; d, Frederick Wilson; w, George Blake, Donald B. Wilson, Frederick Wilson; ph, George Stretton, Bill Allan, Arthur Ibbetson.

Drama/Romance (PR:A MPAA:NR)

FLORENTINE DAGGER, THE*** (1935) 70m WB bw

Donald Woods *(Cesare)*, Margaret Lindsay *(Florence Ballau)*, C. Aubrey Smith *(Dr. Lytton)*, Henry O'Neill *(Victor Ballau)*, Robert Barrat *(The Captain)*, Florence Fair *(Teresa)*, Egon Brecher *(Karl)*, Frank Reicher *(Von Stein)*, Rafaela Ottiano *(Lili Salvatore)*, Eily Malyon *(Fredericks)*, Paul Porcasi *(Antonio)*, Charles Judels *(Salvatore)*, Henry Kolker *(Auctioneer)*, Herman Bing *(The Baker)*.

Woods is a descendant of the renaissance Borgias. After visiting his ancestral castle in Italy, he becomes a successful playwright but also comes to believe that he has inherent killer instincts. Enter Lindsay, whom Woods selects to play the femme fatale in his new hit play, believing her to be another Lucretia Borgia. A murder occurs and Woods, Lindsay, and even the psychiatrist treating Woods (Smith) are equal suspects. An above-average whodunit with many clever twists and turns. The Ben Hecht novel upon which this film is based is better than the movie, one where the author detailed three suspects with dual personalities, a theme not fully developed in the film. Woods and Lindsay are fine, and Smith, that venerable British character actor, brightens every scene he plays. Florey directs with lightning speed, as was his special trait.

d, Robert Florey; w, Tom Reed, Brown Holmes (based on the novel by Ben Hecht); ph, Arthur Todd; ed, Thomas Pratt.

Mystery (PR:A MPAA:NR)

FLORIAN** (1940) 91m MGM bw

Robert Young *(Anton)*, Helen Gilbert *(Diana)*, Charles Coburn *(Hofer)*, Lee Bowman *(Oliver)*, Reginald Owen *(Emperor Franz Josef)*, Lucile Watson *(Countess)*, Irina Baronova *(Trina)*, Rand Brooks *(Victor)*, S.Z. Sakall *(Max)*, William B. Davidson *(Franz Ferdinand)*, George Lloyd *(Borelli)*, George Irving *(Bantry)*, Charles Judels *(Editor)*, Dick Elliott *(Auctioneer)*, Adrian Morris *(Ernst)*, Jack Joyce *(Ringmaster)*, Morgan Conway *(Kingston)*, Charles Brown *(New York Police Lieutenant)*, Frank Orth *(Detective)*, John Russell *(Andy At Age Six)*, Walter Bonn, George Rosener *(Inspectors of Riding School)*, Jack Luden, Ellis Irving *(Swiss Officers)*, Alex Pollard *(Butler)*, Mary Forbes *(Grandmother)*, Joe Yule *(Barker)*, Henry Brandon *(Groom)*, Earle Hodgins *(Concession Owner)*, Constantine Romanoff *(Russian)*, Hillary Brooke, Caroline Frasher, Winifred Lynn *(Horsewomen)*.

Proof that an animal alone cannot carry a picture. Florian, a beautiful white Lippizan stallion is the fondly groomed companion of stable boy Young. Time passes and the boy/horse relationship goes through a variety of strains. After saving Young's life at war, the critter is shipped to the U.S. to pull a junk cart. A tearful New York reunion takes place as the pair is joined by Young's love, Gilbert. The beautiful Florian and the film's opening in Austria respond poetically to the camera, as does a cameo by ballerina Baronova.

p, Winfield Sheehan; d, Edwin L. Marin; w, Noel Langley, James Kevin McGuinness, Geza Herczeg (based on a novel by Felix Salten); ph, Karl Freund; m, Franz Waxman; ed, Frank Hull; art d, Cedric Gibbons; ch, Ernst Matray.

Drama/Children (PR:AAA MPAA:NR)

FLORIDA SPECIAL½** (1936) 68m PAR bw

Jack Oakie *(Bangs Carter)*, Sally Eilers *(Jerry Quinn)*, Kent Taylor *(Wally Tucker)*, Frances Drake *(Marina Landon)*, J. Farrell MacDonald *(Harrigan)*, Sam Hearn *(Schlepperman)*, Dewey Robinson *(Skeets)*, Claude Gillingwater *(Simeon Stafford)*, Clyde Dilson *(Louie)*, Dwight Frye *(Jenkins)*, Sidney Blackmer *(Jack Macklyn)*, Matthew Betz *(Herman)*, Harry C. Bradley *(Conductor)*, Jack Heller *(Singer)*, Jean Bary *(Violet)*, Sam Flint *(Doctor)*, Stanley Andrews, Mack Grey.

Gillingwater is a witty millionaire travelling to Florida via rail with $1,000,000 in diamonds. Knowing that a gang of thieves is on board he disguises himself as an invalid with an ice bag on his head. Consciously playing on the pun, Gillingwater hides the diamonds in the bag and circulates a phony cache for the thieves. Justice reigns as the train pulls into a station full of waiting police. Heller croons "It's You I'm Talking About."

p, Albert Lewis; d, Ralph Murphy; w, David Boehm, Marguerite Roberts, Laura Perelman, S. J. Perelman (based on a story "Recreation Car" by Clarence Buddington Kelland); ph, Leo Tovar; ed, James Smith; m/l, Mack Gordon, Harry Revel.

Comedy/Crime (PR:A MPAA:NR)

FLORODORA GIRL, THE½** (1930) 73m MGM bw/c
(GB: THE GAY NINETIES)

Marion Davies *(Daisy)*, Lawrence Gray *(Jack)*, Walter Catlett *(De Boer)*, Louis John Bartels *(Hemingway)*, Ilka Chase *(Fanny)*, Vivian Oakland *(Maud)*, Jed Prouty *(Old Man Dell)*, Claud Allister *(Rumblesham)*, Sam Hardy *(Fontaine)*, Nance O'Neil *(Mrs. Vibart)*, Robert Bolder *(Commodore)*, Jane Keithly *(Constance)*, Maude Turner Gordon *(Mrs. Caraway)*, George Chandler *(Georgie Smith)*, Anita Louise, Mary Jane Irving *(Vibart Children)*.

Set during the 1900s, Marion Davies is genuinely funny as a shy Florodora gal who eventually falls under the spell of a loving millionaire. The plot isn't that far removed from Davies' own encounters as William Randolph Hearst's celebrated mistress. Intriguing mainly for Davies' name, it contains such tunes as "My Kind Of Man," "Pass The Beer And Pretzels," "Swingin' In The Lane," and a dazzling Technicolor stage sequence of "Tell Me Pretty Maiden" by Owen Hall and Leslie Stuart.

d, Harry Beaumont; w, Gene Markey, Ralph Spence, Al Boasberg, Robert Hopkins (based on a story by Markey); ph, Oliver T. March; ed, Carl L. Pierson; m/l, Herbert Stothart, Clifford Grey, Andy Rice.

Musical (PR:A MPAA:NR)

FLOWER DRUM SONG** (1961) 133m Hunter-Fields/UNIV c

Nancy Kwan *(Linda Low)*, James Shigeta *(Wang Ta)*, Juanita Hall *(Auntie [Madame Liang])*, Jack Soo *(Sammy Fong)*, Miyoshi Umeki *(Mei Li)*, Benson Fong *(Wang Chi-Yang)*, Reiko Sato *(Helen Chao)*, Patrick Adiarte *(Wang San)*, Kam Tong *(Dr. Li)*, Victor Sen Yung *(Frankie Wing)*, Soo Yung *(Madame Fong)*, Ching Wah Lee *(Professor)*, James Hong *(Headwaiter)*, Spencer Chan *(Dr. Chon)*, Arthur Song *(Dr. Fong)*, Weaver Levy *(Policeman)*, Herman Rudin *(Holdup Man)*, Cherylene Lee, Virginia Lee *(San's Girlfriends)*, Virginia Grey *(TV Heroine)*, Paul Sorensen *(TV Sheriff)*, Ward Ramsey *(Great White Hunter)*, Laurette Luez *(Mexican Girl)*, Robert Kino *(Bank Manager)*, Beal Wong *(Tailor)*, Jon Fong *(Square Dance Caller)*, Willard Lee, Frank Kumagai *(Tradesmen)*.

The smash Rodgers-Hammerstein Broadway hit was only adequately adapted in this overblown Hunter production. Perhaps the cloying sweetness of the story played better in the small confines of a stage but when it was enlarged, it bordered on heavy diabetic doses of sugarcoated pap. Umeki (who is Japanese) plays a Hong Kong arrival in San Francisco. She has had a marriage arranged for her to nightclub boniface Soo (himself a Japanese, despite the Chinese name. It was shortened during the war for obvious reasons) whom she has never met. Soo is a rakehell, almost an Asian version of Nathan Detroit, and he has a longstanding relationship with Kwan, a singer at his club. Kwan wants to marry Soo but he is fending her off. Umeki is FOB (fresh off the boat) and she meets the handsomest young man in Chinatown, Shigeta (also Japanese). They fall in love and the picture ends very quickly in a double wedding ceremony not unlike the one that concluded GUYS AND DOLLS. Chinese movie-goers were less than happy about their portrayal, an almost condescending look at their lifestyles. Hall, Umeki and Soo came from the Broadway show and Soo later played the role in a "tab" version of the show at a Las Vegas hotel where it ran almost two years to large audiences. The abridged version played quicker and better than the original and Soo was magnificent in the role. Not too many memorable tunes in the score but a pleasant-enough picture, if you're willing to overlook the cliched treatment of the script. The hits were "I Enjoy Being A Girl," "Don't Marry Me," "Grant Avenue," "You Are Beautiful," and "A Hundred Million Miracles." Some of the other tunes include "Fan Tan Fanny," "Chop Suey," "The Other Generation," "I Am Going To Like It Here," and "Love Look Away." (Richard Rogers, Oscar Hammerstein II).

p, Ross Hunter (in association with Joseph Fields); d, Henry Koster; w, Fields (based on the novel by C.Y. Lee and the Broadway musical book by Fields); ph, Russell Metty (Panavision, Technicolor); m, Richard Rodgers; ed, Milton Carruth; md, Alfred Newman; art d, Alexander Golitzen, Joseph Wright; cos, Irene Sharaff; ch, Hermes Pan.

Musical Comedy (PR:A MPAA:NR)

FLOWER THIEF, THE* (1962) 70m Film-Makers/Cinema Guild bw

Taylor Mead *(Flower Thief)*, Philip McKenna, Ella Henry, Linda Evanoff, Turk Leclair, Dick Stevenson, Bob Kaufman, Heinz Ellsworth, Barry Clark, Mickey, Ted, Eric Nord.

An early counter-culture "art" film shot in 16mm in San Francisco off and on between the years 1959-60. Mead stars as a homosexual beatnik who carries a teddy bear, an American flag and, of course, a flower around the city getting into a series of disconnected incidents. He eventually picks up a guy at an amusement park and they walk off into the sea. The soundtrack includes excerpts from *Alice In Wonderland*. Pretentious and archaic.

p,d,w,&ed, Ron Rice; m, Claude Debussy (various selections).

Drama (PR:O MPAA:NR)

FLOWERS FOR THE MAN IN THE MOON** (1975, Ger.) 83m Defa c
(BLUMEN FUER DEN MANN IM MOND)

Jutta Wachowiak, Stefan Lisewski, Dieter Franke, Sven Grothe, Astrid Heinz, Dirk Foerster, Yvonne Diessner.

The son of a famous vegetable gardener and agriculture co-op chairman wants to make working on the moon more enjoyable by planting a flower garden. With the help of a test pilot and a biology expert named Professor Vitamin he creates a hybrid flower that will successfully bloom on the moon. Supposedly a children's film, but too moralistic and heavy handed for its own good.

d, Rolf Losansky; w, Losansky, Irmgard Speitel, Ulrich Speitel; ph, Helmut Grewald.

Fantasy (PR:A MPAA:NR)

FLOWING GOLD½** (1940) 82m WB bw

John Garfield *(Johnny Blake)*, Frances Farmer *(Linda Chalmers)*, Pat O'Brien *(Hap O'Connor)*, Raymond Walburn *(Wildcat Chalmers)*, Cliff Edwards *(Hot Rocks)*, Tom Kennedy *(Petunia)*, Granville Bates *(Charles Hammond)*, Jody Gilbert *(Tillie)*, Edward Pawley *(Collins)*, Frank Mayo *(Mike Branigan)*, William Marshall *(Joe)*, Sol Gross *(Luke)*, Virginia Sale *(Nurse)*, John Alexander *(Sheriff)*.

Garfield is a drifter, distrusting, embittered, and on the run from the law, who enters a mud-rutted oil town. O'Brien befriends this aimless one and gives him a job bossing his oil well drilling. There's frantic little time since the lease on the well will run out soon. In their haste, the drillers have several accidents, one of which results in O'Brien breaking a leg. Fugitive Garfield takes over and brings in the gusher; then he and Farmer, a street-wise gal as hardened as he, decide to face the murder charge Garfield has been evading. Beyond Garfield's dynamic persona, this is just another routine film for him, one with a fairly predictable plot. FLOWING GOLD was turned out quickly by Warner Bros. to take advantage of the enormous popularity generated by MGM's BOOM TOWN (1940). This was O'Brien's last film for Warners, made just after he completed the successful KNUTE ROCKNE, ALL AMERICAN. When Jack Warner refused to give him a raise at the end of his contract, O'Brien walked out. Their final exchange was blunt. "You'll be back, Pat,"snorted Warner. "Anytime, Jack. You know my terms." "You an artist or a banker?" sneered Warner. "For you, I'm a moneymaker," retorted O'Brien as he walked out of Warner's office. The film was also a nadir for Garfield who was repeatedly denied the meaty roles he requested. Garfield told Jack Warner he wanted the lead in THE ADVENTURES OF MARTIN EDEN (1942) and got another no, this part going to Glenn Ford. He then asked for the lead in JACK LONDON (1943) and got a no, the part going to Michael O'Shea. In desperation, Garfield sent a note to Warner upon which he printed in large bold red letters: "PAROLE ME!" But he stayed in the old Warner Bros. cell of melodramatic roles until he decided to leave the studio and strike out on his own. Frances Farmer's tale concerning this film was even more tragic. Her part in FLOWING GOLD was originally slated for Ann Sheridan but she turned it down, despite the fact that Warners threatened her with suspension. Then Olivia de Havilland refused the part and Garfield begged the front office to give the role to Farmer who had recently returned from New York where her volatile temperament had gotten her kicked out of the Group Theater and the production of Hemingway's "The Fifth Column." Farmer was having an increasingly hard time getting roles. Her snarling, vicious attitude—she was a real hard case who had made only one significant appearance, as a hardcase, in COME AND GET IT (1936)—had put her on everyone's "don't touch" list. Garfield prevailed and Warners gave her the role in FLOWING GOLD but refused to give her a long-term contract. Her notorious vagrancy charge followed and then agonizing years in mental institutions where she was lobotomized. She reemerged in the late 1950s as a nightclub singer and appeared in a low-budget programmer, THE PARTY CRASHERS (1958). Before her death, Farmer announced to the world that she had a torrid affair with Garfield during the making of FLOWING GOLD, one of the few women in this talented actor's life to ever make public Garfield's wide-ranging womanizing.

p, William Jacobs; d, Alfred Green; w, Kenneth Gamet (based on the story by Rex Beach); ph, Sid Hickox; ed, James Gibbon; spec eff, Byron Haskin, Willard Van Enger.

Adventure/Drama **(PR:A MPAA:NR)**

FLUCHT NACH BERLIN (SEE: ESCAPE TO BERLIN, 1962, Ger.)

FLUFFY½** (1965) 92m UNIV c

Tony Randall *(Daniel Potter)*, Shirley Jones *(Janice)*, Edward Andrews *(Griswald)*, Howard Morris *(Sweeney)*, Ernest Truex *(Claridge)*, Jim Backus *(Sergeant)*, Frank Faylen *(Catfish)*, Celia Kaye *(Sally Brighton)*, Dick Sargent *(Tommy)*, Adam Roarke *(Bob Brighton)*, Whit Bissell *(Dr. Braden)*, Harriet MacGibbon *(Mrs. Claridge)*, Jim Boles *(Pete)*, Parley Baer *(Police Captain)*, Connie Gilchrist *(Maid)*, Stuart Randall *(State Trooper)*, Sammee Tong *(Cook)*, Barry O'Hara *(Fireman No. 2)*, Sam Gilman *(Policeman)*, Milton Frome *(Tweedy Physicist)*, Doodles Weaver *(Yokel)*.

The title serves as the perfect adjective for this silly Disneyesque piece of entertainment. Randall is a scientist who has domesticated Fluffy, a lion, to prove that even the wildest of animals can be kept as pets if they are trained properly. Needless to say, the mere sight of a lion sends people into a panic, including the police. Randall hides out in a hotel where Jones falls in love with both lion and master. Other notables in the cast are Backus as the police sergeant, and Sargent of TV's "Bewitched." Children will enjoy it.

p, Gordon Kay; d, Earl Bellamy; w, Samuel Roeca; ph, Clifford Stine (Eastmancolor); m, Irving Gertz; ed, Russell F. Schoengarth; art d, Alexander Golitzen, Walter Simonds; cos, Rosemary O'Dell.

Comedy **(PR:AAA MPAA:NR)**

FLY, THE*½** (1958) 94m FOX c

Al "David" Hedison *(Andre)*, Patricia Owens *(Helene)*, Vincent Price *(Francois)*, Herbert Marshall *(Insp. Charas)*, Kathleen Freeman *(Emma)*, Betty Lou Gerson *(Nurse Andersone)*, Charles Herbert *(Philippe)*, Eugene Borden *(Dr. Ejoute)*, Torben Meyer *(Gaston)*, Harry Carter *(Orderly)*, Charles Tannen *(Doctor)*, Franz Roehn *(Police Doctor)*, Arthur Dulac *(French Waiter)*.

This enormously successful horror picture casts Hedison as an obsessed scientist fiddling around with a matter-transmitting device. After zapping guinea pigs from dimension to dimension, he decides to put it to the ultimate test and enters the machine himself. He fatefully pulls the switch, but fails to notice the presence of a pesty housefly also in the machine. That little nuisance proves to be a gross inconvenience as Hedison, now fly-headed, emerges from his experiment. Buzzing somewhere around the house is the fly, sporting Hedison's mug. The scientist tries to hide his disgustingly fuzzy head from wife Owens by sticking it under a napkin (?!) Owens soon grasps that the slurping and buzzing sounds being emitted from her husband are problem signs. She tries to recapture the Hedison-headed fly but cannot, resulting in the scientist's increasing madness. Mercifully she smashes her husband's skull in a gigantic steam press. This is where the film opens, Owens relaying all this information to police investigators. The surprising success of this film is hard to fathom. Endless plot loopholes,cannot deter the audience or lessen the film's popularity. Why doesn't the examining doctor notice that the crushed man had the head of a fly? Why, if the scientist has the head of the housefly, can he still think like a human? These and other questions are destined to go unanswered. The film takes on a disturbing morality in its vivid ending. When Price, Hedison's brother, walks by a spider web, he notices the presence of a captured fly, though he fails to hear the childlike cry for help coming from its miniature Hedison head. He watches as the spider approaches the wriggling fly and, when the sight gets unbearable, Price puts his fly-brother out of his misery by smashing him and the spider with a rock. Again poor Hedison gets his head crushed. The film is both fun and frightening, but can also be viewed (however naive its intentions) as a commercialized techno-version of Franz Kafka's existential allegory *Metamorphosis*. Its success led to two less inspired sequels, THE RETURN OF THE FLY and CURSE OF THE FLY. The original version was scripted by James Clavell, who went on to do the highly successful TV mini-series SHOGUN.

p&d, Kurt Neumann; w, James Clavell (from a story by George Langelaan); ph, Karl Struss (CinemaScope, DeLuxe Color); m, Paul Sawtell; ed, Merrill G. White; art d, Lyle R. Wheeler, Theobald Holsopple; spec eff, Lyle B. Abbott.

Horror/Science Fiction **Cas.** **(PR:O MPAA:NR)**

FLY-AWAY BABY½** (1937) 60m WB bw (AKA: THE ADVENTURES OF TORCHY BLANE)

Glenda Farrell *(Torchy Blane)*, Barton MacLane *(Steve McBride)*, Gordon Oliver *(Lucien "Sonny" Croy)*, Hugh O'Connell *(Hughie Sprague)*, Marcia Ralston *(Ila Sayre)*, Tom Kennedy *(Gahagan)*, Joseph King *(Guy Allister)*, Raymond Hatton *(Maxie)*, Gordon Hart *(Sills)*, Anderson Lawler *(Torey)*, Harry Davenport *(Col. Higgam)*, Emmett Vogan *(Clifford Vance)*, George Guhl *(Desk Sergeant)*.

Reporter Torchy Blane (Farrell), sets out to impress her fiance police lieutenant by investigating a celebrated murder case. On a tip, she takes to the air along with two rival tabloid writers and, en route, discovers that one of them is the killer. Farrell performs better than average in an entertaining, but forgettable, role.

d, Frank McDonald; w, Don Ryan, Kenneth Gamet (from an idea by Dorothy Kilgallen); ph, Warren Lynch; ed, Doug Gould.

Crime **(PR:A MPAA:NR)**

FLY AWAY PETER½** (1948, Brit.) 60m Production Facilities/GFD bw

Frederick Piper *(Mr. Hapgood)*, Kathleen Boutall *(Mrs. Hapgood)*, Margaret Barton *(Myra Hapgood)*, Patrick Holt *(John Neilson)*, Elspet Gray *(Phyllis Hapgood)*, Peter Hammond *(George Harris)*, Nigel Buchanan *(Arthur Hapgood)*, John Singer *(Ted Hapgood)*, Josephine Stuart *(Dandy)*, Sam Kydd.

Bouthall plays a mother who tries to keep her children from growing up and leaving home. When her youngest daughter remains only as a sacrifice to accommodate her, she realizes her mistake and encourages the daughter to fly the roost. Formula heart-tugger, but appealing.

p, Henry Passmore; d, Charles Saunders; w, Arthur Reid (based on a play by A.P. Dearsley); ph, Roy Fogwell.

Drama **(PR:A MPAA:NR)**

FLY BY NIGHT*** (1942) 74m PAR bw (GB: SECRETS OF G32)

Nancy Kelly *(Pat Lindsey)*, Richard Carlson *(Jeff Burton)*, Albert Basserman *(Dr. Storm)*, Martin Kosleck *(George Taylor)*, Nestor Paiva *(Grube)*, Walter Kingsford *(Heydt)*, Edward Gargan *(Charlie Prescott)*, Mary Gordon *(Ma Prescott)*, Oscar O'Shea *(Pa Prescott)*, Miles Mander *(Prof. Langner)*, Michael Morris *(John Prescott)*, Arthur Loft *(Insp. Karns)*, John Butler *(Jenks)*, John Dilson *(Tracy)*, Cy Kendall *(Dahlig)*.

A fine little *film noir* with young inventor Carlson in the spotlight, as the wrongly accused murderer of a kidnaped inventor. With aid from dame Kelly, he escapes from the law so he can prove his innocence. Exciting chase sequences and stylish photography overcome a boggling, complicated plot.

p, Sol C. Siegel; d, Robert Siodmak; w, Jay Dratler, F. Hugh Herbert (based on a story by Ben Roberts, Sidney Sheldon); ph, John Seitz; ed, Arthur Schmidt.

Crime **(PR:A MPAA:NR)**

FLY NOW, PAY LATER zero (1969) 75m Cintex bw

Charlotte Rouse *(Sally)*, Shep Wild *(Man in Snow)*, O.K. Baime *(Nephew)*, Simone Renard *(Sandra)*, Cherie Walters *(Joan)*, Ronald Arunde *(Alan)*, George Wilson *(Richard Fleetwood)*, Judy Caine *(Beth)*, Misty *(Carole)*, Imano Kutt *(Man With Dagger)*, Rip Thonger *(Man With Whip)*, Emile Nitrate *(Passive Man)*, Morris Towne *(Fatim)*, B.S. Kroul *(Abdul)*, A. Pismo Clamm *(Uncle)*, Myron Mogul, IV *(Man in Front of Shop)*.

Vile crime/sexploitation drama starring Wilson as a tough detective hired to find a host of stewardesses who have mysteriously disappeared while flying the Morocco route. As it turns out, the women have been kidnaped by a sadistic gang of drug-runners and exposed to the gamut of humiliating and degrading behavior (including lesbian sex, bondage, whippings, and massive amounts of drug taking of the gang's product, "khelp"). All are killed except Winters, whom Wilson rescues in the nick of time. Thoroughly disgusting and tasteless.

p&d, B. H. Dial; w, Gillian Vastlake, Basta Laparola (from story by Vastlake); ph, Dial; m, A. Pismo Clamm; ed, Jacques Chein-Lit; set d, Viva Lamano.

Crime **(PR:O MPAA:NR)**

FLY, RAVEN, FLY (SEE: DESERT RAVEN, THE, 1965)

FLYING BLIND** (1941) 69m PAR bw

Richard Arlen *(Jim Clark)*, Jean Parker *(Shirley Brooks)*, Nils Asther *(Eric Karolek)*, Marie Wilson *(Veronica)*, Roger Pryor *(Rocky Drake)*, Eddie Quillan *(Riley)*, Dick Purcell *(Bob Fuller)*, Grady Sutton *(Chester Gimble)*, Kay Sutton *(Miss Danila)*.

Average aerial melodrama which has Arlen piloting honeymooners to and from Los Angeles and Las Vegas, with Parker and mechanic buddy Quillan. Halfway into the pic the trio gets involved in an unbelievable turn of events involving foreign agents and their plans to secure aircraft blueprints. No surprises here.

p, William H. Pine, William C. Thomas; d, Frank McDonald; w, Maxwell Shane, Richard Murphy; ph, Fred Jackman, Jr.; m, Dmitri Tiomkin; ed, Robert Crandall; art d, F. Paul Silos.

Aviation Drama/Adventure **Cas.** **(PR:A MPAA:NR)**

FLYING CADETS*½ (1941) 60m UNIV bw

William Gargan *(Trip)*, Edmund Lowe *(Rocky)*, Peggy Moran *(Kitty)*, Frank Albertson *(Bob Ames)*, Frankie Thomas *(Adams)*, Roy Harris *(Barnes)*, Charles Williams *(Mr. Prim)*, John Maxwell *(Mr. Taylor)*, George Melford *(Conductor)*, Arch Hendricks *(Colonel)*, Louise Lorimer *(Mary)*.

This yarn barely gets off the ground with the story of a spry young flier who wants to start a training school almost as much as he wants to sell the government his aircraft plans. Not much to offer except Air Force propaganda, which neatly coincided with America's involvement in WW II.

p, Paul Malvern; d, Erle C. Kenton; w, Joseph West, Roy Chanslor, Stanley Rubin; ph, John W. Boyle; ed, Otto Ludwig; art d, Jack Otterson.

Aviation Drama (PR:A MPAA:NR)

FLYING DEUCES, THE½** (1939) 67m RKO bw

Stan Laurel *(Stan)*, Oliver Hardy *(Ollie)*, Jean Parker *(Georgette)*, Reginald Gardiner *(Francois)*, Charles Middleton *(Commandant)*, Jean Del Val *(Sergeant)*, Clem Wilenchick, Crane Whitley *(Corporal)*, James Finlayson *(Jailer)*, Rychard Cramer *(Truck Driver)*, Michael Visaroff *(Innkeeper)*, Monica Bannister, Bonnie Bannon, Mary Jane Carey, Christine Cabanne *(Georgette's Girl Friends)*, Frank Clarke *(Pilot)*, Eddie Borden, Sam Lufkin *(Legionnaires Knocked Out by Corks)*, Kit Guard, Billy Engle, Jack Chefe *(Other Legionnaires)*.

Not one of the great duo's best efforts but even so-so Laurel and Hardy is better than none at all. Based loosely on a French farce film, THE TWO ACES, the film has Laurel and Hardy as two Iowa fishmongers visiting Paris on holiday when Hardy meets and falls hard for a waitress, Parker. After she jilts him, Hardy is disconsolate and plans to jump into the Seine. Laurel is quite ready to help Hardy in his quest for drowning but is understandably reluctant to join him in the cold river. Gardiner, a French Foreign Legionnaire, talks Hardy out of it and convinces them to join the famous fighting force. Once in the service, Hardy finds it difficult to forget Parker because she is married to Gardiner. A series of mishaps and an attempt at deserting have the boys sentenced to be shot at dawn. They escape from the prison in an airplane and go on a mad ride through the skies until the plane crashes and Hardy is reincarnated as a horse with Laurel being totally unscathed. Not too many bright spots other than a brief scene with Laurel plucking a prison bed spring the way Harpo Marx might have. Hardy sings "Shine On, Harvest Moon" while Laurel does a brief soft shoe. Laurel came by his dancing ability and some of his acrobatics in his years with Fred Karno's knockabout vaudeville troupe in England where he understudied Charlie Chaplin. One of the two co-writers of the film was baby-faced Langdon who was in between pictures as an actor. In a small role as the prison jailer was the delightful silent veteran Finlayson who could get more laughs with a squint than most people with a page full of dialog.

p, Boris Morros; d, A. Edward Sutherland; w, Ralph Spence, Alfred Schiller, Charles Rogers, Harry Langdon; ph, Art Lloyd; m, John Leopold, Leo Shuken; ed, Jack Dennis; md, Edward Paul; art d, Boris Leven; aer ph, Elmer Dyer; spec eff, Howard Anderson; tech adv, Frank Clarke.

Comedy Cas. (PR:AAA MPAA:NR)

FLYING DEVILS** (1933) 60m RKO bw (GB: THE FLYING CIRCUS)

Arline Judge *(Ann Hardy)*, Bruce Cabot *(Ace Murray)*, Eric Linden *(Bud Murray)*, Ralph Bellamy *(Speed Hardy)*, Cliff Edwards *("Screwy" Edwards)*, June Brewster *(Girl Friend)*, Frank LaRue *(Kearns)*.

An aerial act's "double chute jump" brings together circus folks Linden and Judge, the latter being inconveniently wed to Bellamy. When Linden's eldest brother learns of Bellamy's plan of vengeance he arranges an airplane collision, which cuts the number of cast members in half. With Bellamy eliminated, the path is paved for the lovebirds to carry on. This plane picture was a very plain picture, but smooth direction adds some fuel.

p, David Lewis; d, Russell Birdwell; w, Byron Morgan, Louis Stevens (based on a story by Stevens); ph, Nick Musuraca; ed, Arthur Roberts.

Aviation Drama (PR:A MPAA:NR)

FLYING DOCTOR, THE* (1936, Aus.) 87m GFD bw

Charles Farrell *(Sandy Nelson)*, Mary Maguire *(Jenny Rutherford)*, James Raglan *(Dr. John Vaughn)*, Joe Valli *(Dodger Green)*, Margaret Vyner *(Betty Webb)*, Eric Colman *(Geoffrey Webb)*, Tom Lurich *(Blotch Burns)*, Maudie Edwards *(Phyllis)*, Phyllip Lytton *(Dr. Rutherford)*, Andrew Beresford *(Mr. Rutherford)*, Katie Towers *(Mrs. O'Toole)*, Phil Smith *(Barman Joe)*, Jack Clarke *(Pop Schnitzel)*, Don Bradman *(Himself)*.

The unadventurous adventures of the Flying Medical Association's work via helicopter in Australia is outlined in this rambling, unpolished drama. Under-budgeted bomb that failed to deliver on initial buildup.

p&d, Miles Mander; w, J.O.C. Orton (based on a story by Robert Waldron); ph, Derick Williams; m, Alfred Lawrence, Willy Redstone.

Adventure (PR:A MPAA:NR)

FLYING DOWN TO RIO**** (1933) 89m RKO bw-c

Dolores Del Rio *(Belinha de Rezende)*, Gene Raymond *(Roger Bond)*, Raoul Roulien *(Julio Rubeiro)*, Ginger Rogers *(Honey Hale)*, Fred Astaire *(Fred Ayres)*, Blanche Frederici *(Dona Elena)*, Walter Walker *(Senor de Rezende)*, Etta Moten *(Black Singer)*, Roy D'Arcy, Maurice Black, Armand Kaliz *(The Three Greeks)*, Paul Porcasi *(Mayor)*, Reginald Barlow *(Banker)*, Eric Blore *(Butterbass the Headwaiter)*, Franklin Pangborn *(Hammersmith the Hotel Manager)*, Luis Alberni *(Carioca Casino Manager)*, Jack Goode, Jack Rice, Eddie Borden *(Yankee Clippers)*, Alice Gentle *(Concert Singer)*, Ray Cooke *(Banjo Player)*, Wallace MacDonald *(Pilot Who Performs Marriage)*, Gino Corrado *(Messenger)*, Lucille Browne, Mary Kornman *(Belinha's Friends)*, Clarence Muse *(Caddy in Haiti)*, Harry Semels *(Sign Poster)*, Movita Castaneda *(Singer)*, Martha LaVenture *(Dancer)*, The Brazilian Turunas, The American Clippers Band *(Band)*, Sidney Bracey *(Rodriguez the Chauffeur)*, Harry Bowen *(Airport Mechanic)*, Manuel Paris *(Extra at Aviators' Club)*, Adrian Rosley *(Club Manager)*, Howard Wilson, Margaret Mearing, Betty Furness, Francisco Maran, Helen Collins, Carol Tevis, Eddie Tamblyn, Alice Ardell, Rafael Alvir, Barbara Sheldon, Douglas Williams, Alma Travers, Juan Duval, Eddie Boland, Julian Rivero, Pedro Regas.

This was the slam-bang musical that introduced the greatest song and dance team the movies have ever known, Astaire and Rogers, and, although it is sheer fluff and piffle, it's pure Hollywood magic, packed with extraordinary dance numbers and unforgettable tunes. There's hardly a plot at all. Raymond, a smooth bandleader, has eyes for sultry, sexy Del Rio. He doubles as a pilot and offers to fly her down to Rio so she can join her singing troupe. Through a ruse Raymond pretends to have engine trouble en route and lands on a deserted island where he pitches woo but remains a gentleman. She discovers his plane intact and insists they resume their journey. Upon arriving in Rio, Raymond learns that Roulien, the tenor of the group, is Del Rio's fiance. Del Rio must ultimately choose between her two admirers and her back-and-forth decisions consume most of the movie, with Roulien gallantly bowing out in favor of Raymond when he learns that Del Rio is mad about the blond boy. The willy-nilly story of the leads provides mere background to a musical romp which glories in the fantastic. The musical numbers open up with Rogers, scantily clad, doing a bandstand number, "Music Makes Me." After several false starts, "Orchids in the Moonlight" is finally completely sung by Roulien to Del Rio (shown in a color tint). The most spectacular number, "Flying Down to Rio," occurs on squadrons of double-winged planes; upon the wings of these planes are perched scores of bathing beauties doing daredevil dances and acrobatic sequences sure to compel anyone suffering from vertigo to swoon. The bizarre numbers were staged by Dave Gould in the Busby Berkeley tradition, an incredible finale captioned by Roulien's exit from Del Rio's life by a high dive out of one of the airplanes, but he lands safely thanks to the handy parachute he's brought along. In the middle of the film is the memorable "Carioca," a dance Astaire and Rogers witness as armies of hoofers move to the lively music. Captivated by the music, Astaire says to Rogers, who is standing nearby: "I'd like to try this just once—come on," and pulls her onto the dance floor. At that moment the famous team made history, almost as a casual, offhanded thought to the near plotless film. Astaire and Rogers only make two appearances in the "Carioca" number, but their steps are unbelievably electrifying as they follow the moves created by Hermes Pan, who (uncredited) assisted Gould in the choreographic chores. The dance is also executed by 40 white dancers and 10 blacks (to capture the mixed racial makeup of Rio; Negro singer Etta Moten, who sang the haunting "My Forgotten Man" in GOLD DIGGERS OF 1933, is only one of three singers belting out this song). It's really a fast tango patterned after the Maxixe, which had been introduced into U.S. cafe society by Vernon and Irene Castle before WW I. Pan designed the to-and-fro movement shift from pelvis to pelvis to forehead to forehead, with Astaire and Rogers doing a complete turn while keeping their heads touching. This dance was continued by scores of partners and waves of chorus lines in various forms, constituting the longest dance number on record in film history, almost 18 minutes in the original running time. No one but a few grumpy critics complained about its length; this dance became a nationwide craze following the movie with tens of thousands paying dance studios to teach them the steps. Astaire briefly solos, displaying that winning combination of dance, half tap, half ballroom—all style. In fact, this is one of the few films where he actually repeats a few steps; in the future every step Astaire would take would have a meaning all its own, as befitting this genius of innovation. The great dancer would later remark: "I thought Ginger and I looked all right together, but I was under the impression that we weren't doing anything particularly outstanding." It's true that the fourth and fifth-starred team were not before the cameras dancing for all that long in FLYING DOWN TO RIO, but it was enough to make Astaire and Rogers overnight superstars, and the studio knew it from the first moment, which is why the film ends with the dynamic duo on screen and not its top-billed stars. Astaire had appeared in only one film before this, DANCING LADY, in a brief dancing sequence with Joan Crawford, but Rogers was a seasoned Hollywood veteran by the time she stepped onto that "Carioca" set with Fred, having appeared in 19 features and four shorts but only two were musicals, 42ND STREET (1933) and GOLD DIGGERS OF 1933. Only through the emotional notion of another did Rogers ever get this opportunity; her part was originally given to Dorothy Jordan, but Miss Jordan quit at the last minute to marry the movie's executive producer, Merian C. Cooper, and fate and fame awaited Ginger instead. The film was a blockbuster, one that filled RKO's coffers to the brim and brought that studio back from the brink of bankruptcy where it had been teetering in this, the worst year of the Great Depression. RKO picked a winner from the start, using Vincent Youman's most dazzling score. This was the composer's last score before moving to Denver with incurable tuberculosis; he would die there in 1946. The selection for this film came in a roundabout manner. David O. Selznick had left RKO as head of production and was replaced by Cooper, hardly a man inclined toward musicals; Cooper was an adventurer who had spent a great deal of time in the wilds of South America and was obsessed with aviation. Knowing this, producer Lou Brock talked Cooper into making a film that appealed to his two chief interests, South America, in particular Rio de Janiero, and aviation. So enthralled was Cooper with FLYING DOWN TO RIO that, as a member of the board of directors of Pan American Airways, he ordered dozens of the large Sikorsky clipper planes of his airline to be used in the production and launched an advertising campaign for the movie, thinking it would promote South American plane travel. It is on the wings of Pan Am's planes that every available chorine in Hollywood is festooned and anchored in the "Flying Down to Rio" sequences which were shot on location and also over Malibu Beach, California. Another bit of self-promotion included Del Rio and Raymond firing off countless radiograms to Rio to announce their impending arrival. It was not by accident that these scenes were included in FLYING DOWN TO RIO; RKO was affiliated with RCA Communications, which specialized in radiograms and, with RKO, owned the famed Radio City Music Hall. Everything about this wonderful production was lavish, from its stunning art deco sets to its armies of dancing choruses. With this film RKO re-entered the musical field and the sure-fire team of Astaire and Rogers would return the studio to solvency and wealth within a few years, one musical blockbuster following another—THE GAY DIVORCEE (1934), ROBERTA (1935), TOP HAT (1935), FOLLOW THE FLEET (1936), SWING TIME (1936), SHALL WE DANCE (1937)—all because Fred got so intrigued with a South American ditty he had to "try this just once."

p, Lou Brock (for Merian C. Cooper); d, Thornton Freeland; w, Cyril Hume, H.W. Hanemann, Erwin Gelsey (based on a play by Anne Caldwell from an original story by Brock); ph, J. Roy Hunt; m, Vincent Youmans; ed, Jack Kitchin; md, Max Steiner; art d, Van Nest Polglase, Carroll Clark; cos, Walter Plunkett; spec eff, Vern Walker; ch, Dave Gould; m/l, Youmans, Edward Eliscu, Gus Kahn.

Musical (PR:A MPAA:NR)

FLYING EYE, THE**½** (1955, Brit.) 53m British Films/BL-Children's Film Foundation bw

David Hannaford (Bunstuffer), Julia Lockwood (Angela), Harcourt Williams (Professor), Ivan Craig (Mayer), Geoffrey Sumner (Col. Audacious).

Sumner and youthful sidekick Hannaford invent a model airplane with a television camera in it, then use it to save a secret formula from enemy spies. A rarity, a children's film with a sense of fun to it, and one that adults should enjoy as well.

p, William Weedon; d, William C. Hammond; w, Hammond, Ken Hughes, Darrell Catling (based on a novel by John Newton Chance); ph, Hone Glendinning.

Children (PR:AA MPAA:NR)

FLYING FIFTY-FIVE*** (1939, Brit.) 72m Admiral/RKO bw

Derrick de Marney (Bill Urquhart), Nancy Burne (Stella Barrington), Marius Goring (Charles Barrington), John Warwick (Jebson), Peter Gawthorne (Jonas Urquhart), D.A. Clarke-Smith (Jacques Gregory), Amy Veness (Aunt Eliza), Ronald Shiner (Scrubby Oaks), Billy Bray (Cheerful), Francesca Bahrle (Clare), Hay Plumb, John Bryning, Basil McGrail, Victor Wark, Terence Conlin, John Miller, Norman Pierce.

De Marney is an amateur jockey who quarrels with his father and hooks up with Burne, a rival racehorse owner. He enters the big race on a horse that only allows him behind the reigns. Ignoring a blackmail threat to throw the race, de Marney wins on a technicality and weds Burne. Send it to the glue factory.

p, Victor M. Greene; d, Reginald Denham; w, Greene, Vernon Clancey, Kenneth Horne (based on the novel by Edgar Wallace); ph, Ernest Palmer.

Crime (PR:A MPAA:NR)

FLYING FISTS, THE*½** (1938) 63m Victory bw

Herman Brix [Bruce Bennett] (Hal Donovan), Jeanne Martel (Kay Conrad), Fuzzy Knight (Spider), J. Farrell MacDonald (Kay's Father), Guinn Williams (Slug Cassidy), Dickie Jones (Dickie), Charles Williams (Meggs).

Brix takes to the ring earning fame and fortune with his fists until he falls in love with a lass who doesn't take kindly to the sport. She whistles a different tune, however, when her dad is in financial straits. Brix returns to the ring, battling not only his opponent, but the thugs who fixed the match. The dialog makes one think that the writer himself is a bit punch-drunk.

d, Bob Hill; w, Basil Dickey (based on a story by Rock Hawkey); ph, Bill Hyer.

Sports Drama (PR:A MPAA:NR)

FLYING FONTAINES, THE**½** (1959) 73m COL c

Michael Callan (Rick Rias), Evy Norlund (Suzanne Fontaine), Joan Evans (Jan), Rian Garrick (Bill Rand), Joe de Santis (Roberto Rias), Roger Perry (Paul Fontaine), John van Dreelen (Victor Fontaine) Jeanne Manet (Michele), Barbara Kelley (Margie), Dorothy Johnson (Sally), Pierre Watkin (Doctor), Murray Parker (Ring Announcer), William Quinn (Al Bartlett).

Back under the Big Top, aerial artist Callan returns from the war only to find his gal now married to the troupe's catcher, Perry. He turns his affections to the younger Norlund and she also rejects him. While practicing his high wire act, Callan seriously injures himself, but once on the sickbed everything shapes up and Norlund agrees to be his girl. Unfortunately all subtlety is lost in the epical atmosphere of the Big Top. Norlund is a lovely sight, entering the movie world after a stint as Miss Denmark.

p, Sam Katzman; d, George Sherman; w, Donn Mullally, Lee Ewin; ph, Fred Jackman (Eastmancolor); m, Mischa Bakaleinikoff; ed, Saul A. Goodkind; art d, Paul Palmentola.

Drama (PR:A MPAA:NR)

FLYING FOOL**** (1929) 73m Pathe bw

William Boyd, Marie Prevost, Russell Gleason, Tom O'Brien.

It's brother versus brother in the battle to romance sexy nightclub singer Prevost. It's easy to see why, as this hot songstress is really something, with the ability to change personalities according to partner. As the more manly and worldly of the two, Boyd naturally wins the battle. A walk-through for Boyd, though given a script that breathes life into the story with its zesty dialogue.

d, Taylor Garnett; w, James Gleason (based on the story by Elliott Clawson); ph, Arthur Miller.

Comedy (PR:A MPAA:NR)

FLYING FOOL, THE**½** (1931, Brit.) 65m BI/Wardour bw

Henry Kendall (Vincent Floyd), Benita Hume (Marion Lee), Wallace Geoffrey (Michael Marlowe), Martin Walker (Jim Lancer) Ursula Jeans (Morella Arlen), Barbara Gott (Mme. Charron), Charles Farrell (Ponder), Syd Crossley (Hicks).

A breezy airplane drama hinting at comedy which follows the adventures of an amateur sleuth on the trail of gang of sky-bound jewel thieves. Most memorable is

the ending chase which has an airplane pursuing a car along winding mountainside roads.

d&w, Walter Summers (from a play by Arnold Ridley and Bernard Merivale); ph, Claude Friese-Greene, Stanley Rodwell, J. Rosenthal, James Wilson, A.L. Fisher; ed, J.W. Stockvis.

Aviation Comedy/Drama (PR:A MPAA:NR)

FLYING FORTRESS*½** (1942, Brit.) 110 WB bw

Richard Greene (Jim Spence, Jr.), Carla Lehmann (Sydney Kelly), Betty Stockfield (Lady Deborah Ottershaw), Donald Stewart (Sky Kelly), Charles Heslop (Harrington), Sydney King (Lord Ottershaw), Basil Radford (Capt. Wilkenson), Joss Ambler (Sheepshead), Edward Rigby (Dan Billings), Billy Hartnell (Drunk Taxi-driver), John Stuart (Captain Harvey), Percy Parsons (Coroner), Gerry Wilmot (Control Tower Operator), Frank Wilcox (Judge), Robert Beatty (Connor, Scandal Photographer), John Slater (Air Raid Warden), John Boxer, Peter Croft, Tommy Duggan, Hubert Gregg, Andrea Malandrinos.

A tediously long look at a rich playboy pilot's decision to become a hero. The film begins with hung-over millionaire Greene checking out the planes in an airplane hanger, shifts to some footage of bombings in London, and then shows the eager American entering the RAF. The film drags for an eternity during the first half, but moves more quickly once they get him across the Atlantic. He displays his heroism when he climbs onto the wing of his plane in mid-air and does a fast patch job. Anchors aweigh.

p, Max Milner; d, Walter Forde; w, Gordon Wellesley, Edward Dryhurst, Brock Williams (from a story by Williams); ph, Basil Emmott, Gus Drisse.

War/Adventure (PR:A MPAA:NR)

FLYING GUILLOTINE, THE**** (1975, Chi.) 110m Shaw Brothers c

Ma Teng (Chen Kuan-tai), Hsuing Kang (Ku Feng), Hsu Shuang-kun (Frankie Wei), Li Yu-ping (Liu Wu-chi), Wan-chu (Ai Ti), Hsieh Tien-fu (Wang Yu), Lo Peng (Lin Wei-tu), Yung Cheng (Chiang Yang).

Teng is a bodyguard for a Chinese emperor. When he is mistakenly accused of a crime, he is forced to flee for his life. The emperor's men track him down but Teng manages to escape. This is a fine example of a Kung Fu film done without the camp qualities that usually permeate such fare. The direction holds tension well, maintaining suspense down to the final moments. The photography is also a cut above most Kung Fu films, and with good performances by the cast, the result is an exciting adventure tale.

d, Ho Meng-hau; w, I. Kuang; ph, Tsao Hui-chi (Shawcolor).

Martial Arts/Adventure (PR:O-C MPAA:R)

FLYING HIGH***** (1931) 78m MGM bw (GB: HAPPY LANDING)

Bert Lahr (Rusty), Charlotte Greenwood (Pansy), Pat O'Brien (Sport), Kathryn Crawford (Eileen), Charles Winninger (Dr. Brown), Hedda Hopper (Mrs. Smith), Guy Kibbee (Mr. Smith), Herbert Braggiotti (Gordon), Gus Arnheim and His Orchestra.

Lahr and Greenwood are a joy in this screwy comedy about a moronic pilot who inadvertently breaks the world record for high-altitude flying. Lahr has especially sharp comic timing in this, his first film role, after playing the part on Broadway. Lahr, of course, went on to play the cowardly lion in THE WIZARD OF OZ. Tunes included were "Happy Landing," and "Dance Til Dawn," which were staged by Busby Berkeley.

d, Charles F. Reisner; w, A.P. Younger, R.E. Hopkins, Reisner; ph, Merritt B. Gerstad; ed, William S. Gray; ch, Busby Berkeley; m/l, Dorothy Fields, James McHugh.

Musical/Comedy (PR:A MPAA:NR)

FLYING HOSTESS**½** (1936) 66m UNIV bw

William Gargan (Hal Cunningham), Judith Barrett (Helen Brooks), William Hall (Guy Edwards), Astrid Allwyn (Phyllis Crawford), Ella Logan (Edna Mulcahy), Andy Devine (Joe Williams), Addison Randall (Earl Spencer), Marla Shelton (Marion Beatty), Michael Loring (Pilot), Mary Alice Rice (Miss Davies), Richard Tucker (Doctor), Dorothea Kent, Maxine Reiner, Diana Gibson, Russell Wade, Kenneth Harlan, Pat Flaherty, Jonathan Hale.

The seemingly delicate Barrett puts a rough edge on her stewardess role when she is forced to land a plane after the pilot has been knocked out. Of course, there's a romance—it's between Barrett and the hostess trainer (Gargan) who's impressed with her daring. A precursor to the onslaught of 1960s' and 1970s' airplane disaster pix, this plug for TWA includes the song, "Bang, the Bell Rang," by Irving Actman and Frank Loesser, sung by Logan.

p, Charles R. Rogers; d, Murray Roth; w, Brown Holmes, Harvey Gates, Harry Clork (from the story "Sky Fever" by George Sayre); ph, James Van Trees; m, Charles Previn.

Romance/Drama (PR:A MPAA:NR)

FLYING IRISHMAN, THE**** (1939) 70m RKO bw

Douglas Corrigan (Doug), Paul Kelly (Butch), Robert Armstrong (Joe Alden), Gene Reynolds (Clyde), Donald McBride (Thompson), Eddie Quillan (Henry), J.M. Kerrigan (Mr. Corrigan), Dorothy Peterson (Mrs. Corrigan), Gene Reynolds (Doug as a Boy), Scotty Beckett (Henry as a Young Boy), Joyce Compton (Sally), Dorothy Appleby (Maybelle), Minor Watson (Personnel Manager), Cora Witherspoon (Mrs. Thompson), Spencer Charters (Smedley), Peggy Ryan (Evelyn Corrigan), Knox Manning (Commentator).

The saga of real-life Douglas "Wrong Way" Corrigan who, in what he said was an attempt to fly cross-country, ended up in Ireland. His Neanderthal navigation brought a flurry of publicity in his favor, but whatever fans he gained were surely lost in this weak portrayal of himself. Corrigan's screen debut was also his finale.

p, Pandro S. Berman; d, Leigh Jason; w, Ernest Pagano, Dalton Trumbo; ph, J. Roy Hunt; ed, Arthur E. Roberts; spec eff, Vernon L. Walker.

Drama   **(PR:A MPAA:NR)**

FLYING LEATHERNECKS***   (1951) 102m Hughes/RKO c

John Wayne (Maj. Dan Kirby), Robert Ryan (Capt. Carl Griffin), Don Taylor (Lt. "Cowboy" Blithe), William Harrigan (Lt. Cmdr. Joe Curan), Janis Carter (Joan Kirby), Jay C. Flippen (Master Sgt. Clancy), Carleton Young (Capt. McAllister), Brett King (Lt. Stark)), Maurice Jara (Lt. Vegay), Steve Flagg (Lt. Jorgensen), Britt Norton (Lt. Tanner), Adam Williams (Lt. Malotke), Lynn Stalmaster (Lt. Castle,), Barry Kelly (General), Sam Edwards (Junior), James Flavin ("Mick," Shore Patrol Commander), Harlan Warde (Admiral's Aide), Harry Lauter (Freddie), John Mallory (Lt. Black), James Dobson (Lt. McCabe), Michael Devery, Douglas Henderson, Ralph Cook, Adam York, Gail Davis, Gordon Gebert, Melville Robert, Elaine Robert.

This overlong but action-filled WW II film offers Wayne in a familiar role, that of a martinet commander of a fighter squadron on Guadalcanal in 1942, a man whose rigid discipline gets the job done but alienates the pilots flying under his orders. Ryan, his easy-going, poetry-reciting second-in-command, thinks Wayne is a fine officer and leader of men but he begins to criticize his uncompromising ways, believing that a freer hand should be taken with the men, that their jobs, as flying specialists who risk their lives more openly and frequently than the average infantryman, demand they receive special consideration. Of course, this is all nonsense to Wayne, who must order up every man he feels fit for duty and able to stare death in the eye. Not that Duke is without compassion; he takes it upon himself to write every family member suffering the loss of one of his pilots and grieves alone in his quarters. Beyond the spectacular dogfights and aerial photography, a blending of Synder's studio footage and newsreel shots cleverly edited by Todd, the story bogs down in spots when Wayne and Ryan get into their seemingly endless debates on how to handle the men. There is a nice respite from this when Wayne visits his wife, Carter, and presents a captured Japanese sabre to his son as a souvenir of a war he hates. It's no lovey-dovey scene, as the manly Wayne can hardly bring himself to tell Carter he loves her until she herself blatantly asks for the statement. FLYING LEATHERNECKS, ably directed by the fiercely independent Ray, is taut and engrossing for the most part, even though it rehashes the stress-of-command theme found in so many other WW II air movies (COMMAND DECISION (1949), FIGHTER SQUADRON (1948), TWELVE O'CLOCK HIGH, (1950), even Wayne's own films, FLYING TIGERS (1942), and, regarding the infantry, SANDS OF IWO JIMA (1949)). Wayne is at his stoic best while Ryan is his usual moody, rambunctious self. Good support comes from Flippen, the seasoned sergeant of the ground crew who manages to scavenge the best food and supplies for his boys. Taylor as a daredevil pilot and Jara as an Indian ace who loses a leg, are standouts. This was the first film under the RKO banner in which producer Hughes took a credit ("Howard Hughes Presents"). The producer also paid Wayne a record $300,000 for his performance, according to one report.

p, Edmund Grainger (for Howard Hughes); d, Nicholas Ray; w, James Edward Grant (based on a story by Kenneth Gamet); ph, William E. Snyder (Technicolor); m, Roy Webb; ed, Sherman Todd; md, C. Bakaleinikoff; art d, Albert S. D'Agostino, James W. Sullivan.

War Drama   **Cas.**   **(PR:C MPAA:NR)**

FLYING MARINE, THE*½   (1929) 60m COL bw

Ben Lyon, Shirley Mason, Jason Robards, Sr.

Only the capable performances by the cast and some nifty airplane sequences keep this tepid tale of brothers romancing the same girl from being a total bore. Mason ditches lover Lyon when his brother (Robards) returns home from the war. When Robards realizes what has happened, he sacrifices his own life to save his brother from a mid-air disaster. Could have been better had more effort been applied to action sequences instead of the dull dramatics.

d, Al Rogell; w, John Natteford.

Drama   **(PR:A MPAA:NR)**

FLYING MATCHMAKER, THE**

                           (1970, Israel) 104m National Showmanship c

Mike Burstein (Kouny-Lemel/Max), Germaine Unikovsky (Libaleh), Rina Ganor (Caroline), Raphel Klatschkin (Reb Kalman, The Matchmaker), Shmuel Rodensky (Pinchas'l), Elisheva Michaeli (Rebeka), Aaron Meskin (Shalmoni), Mordecai Arnon (Beralle), Asher Levy (Loksh), Hanan Goldblatt (Professor), Shlomo Vishinsky (Bullfass), Jetta Luka (Tzipa), Ari Kutai (Dr. Friedberg), Pesach Burstein (Sheile); Voices for English Adaptation: Mike Burstein (Kouny-Lemel/Max), Ken Harvey (The Matchmaker), Bernard Grant (Pinchas'l), Norman Rose (Shalmoni), Lillian Lux (Rebeka), Paulette Rubinstein (Caroline), Lois Brandt (Libaleh).

Comedy starring Klatschkin as a matchmaker with a daughter for whom he can't find a match. Given the for-pay assignment of finding a husband for Ganor, daughter of the wealthy Rodensky, Klatschkin recruits a simpleton from a nearby village. Happily, the dolt could be a twin for Burstein, Ganor's tutor, with whom she is in love—but who has been rejected by her father as too middle-class. The girl pretends she favors Klatschkin's simpleton and thus manages to continue seeing her true love, Burstein. Matters eventually become so confused, as they will in comedies, that Ganor and Burstein are permitted to marry—and Klatschkin's daughter gets the dolt.

p, Mordechai Navon; d, Israel Becker; w, Becker, Alex Maimon (from an 1880 play by Abraham Goldfaden); ph, Romolo Garroni (Totalscope, Cineffects Color); m, Shaul Barzoweski; ed, Nelly Bogor, Nelly Gilad, Edward P. Bartsch.

Musical Comedy   **(PR:A MPAA:G)**

FLYING MISSILE***½   (1950) 91m COL bw

Glenn Ford (Cmdr. Bill Talbot), Viveca Lindfors (Karin Hansen), Henry O'Neill (Adm. Scott), Carl Benton Reid (Dr. Gates), Joe Sawyer ("Fuss" Payne), John Qualen (Lars Hansen), Anthony Ross (Adm. Bradley), Harry Shannon (Vice-Adm. Williams), Ross Ford (Chuck Davis), Zachary A. Charles (Mac), Jerry Paris (Andy Mason), Kenneth Tobey (Pete McEvoy), Paul Harvey (Gen. Benton), Grandon Rhodes (Capt. Whitaker), James Seay (Lt. Jackson), Bill Donnelly (Myers), Richard Quine (Hank Weber), Charles Evans (Chief of Naval Operations).

The idea of using guided missiles on submarines is uppermost in the mind of sub commander Ford. To insure their use, he ignores the naval bureaucracy and proceeds with testing, killing a crew member and injuring himself. Stricken with guilt, he becomes mentally unstable and is temporarily paralyzed. He soon recovers, and—convincing the Navy of his undeterred devotion—is able to continue his tests. Ford gets little support from the other performers or the tired script and, therefore, is left to carry the film on his own.

p, Jerry Bresler; d, Henry Levin; w, Richard English, James Gunn (from a story by Harvey S. Haislip, N. Richard Nash); ph, William Snyder; m, George Duning; ed, Viola Lawrence; md, Mischa Bakaleinikoff; art d, George Brooks.

War/Drama   **(PR:A MPAA:NR)**

FLYING SAUCER, THE***½   (1950) 61m Colonial/FC bw

Mikel Conrad (Mike Trent), Pat Garrison (Vee Langley), Hantz Von Teuffen (Hans), Lester Sharpe (Col. Marikoff), Russell Hicks (Hank Thorn), Frank Darien (Matt Mitchell), Denver Pyle (Turner), Roy Engel (Dr. Carl Lawton), Garry Owen (Bartender in Ernie's), Virginia Hewitt (Nanette), Phillip Morris (Dreamland Bartender), Robert Boon (Barge Captain), Earle Lyon (Alex Muller), Lee Langley.

Early 1950s Commie-phobia links the Russians to space invaders in this historically interesting sci-fi film. Agent Conrad heads to Alaska in search of a UFO which turns out to be a Soviet aircraft. The first film to concern itself with UFO sightings, and to use the term "flying saucer." It is reported that the FBI viewed this film before its release; besides the anti-red propaganda, one hopes that Hoover and Co. appreciated Tannura's fine lensing of the Alaskan landscapes.

p&d, Mikel Conrad; w, Conrad, Howard Irving Young (from a story by Conrad); ph, Philip Tannura; m, Darrell Calker; ed, Robert Crandall.

Science Fiction   **(PR:A MPAA:NR)**

FLYING SAUCER, THE***½   (1964, Ital.) 93m DD bw
                                 (IL DISCO VOLANTE)

Alberto Sordi, Monica Vitti, Silvano Mangano, Eleonora Rossi Drago, Guido Celano, Alberto Fogliani.

Sordi is sort of an Italian Peter Sellers, playing numerous roles in this comedy. They've all got one thing in common: each has seen a Martian flying saucer. Not as zany as it might have been, unfortunately.

p, Dino De Laurentiis; d, Tinto Brass; w, Rudolfo Sonego; ph, Bruno Barcarol.

Comedy   **(PR:A MPAA:NR)**

FLYING SCOT, THE   (SEE: MAILBAG ROBBERY, 1957, Brit.)

FLYING SCOTSMAN, THE**   (1929, Brit.) 61m BIP/WB bw

Moore Marriott (Bob White), Pauline Johnson (Joan White), Raymond Milland (Jim Edwards), Alec Hurley (Crow), Dino Galvani (Headwaiter), Billy Shine (Barman).

Title refers to the train driven by Marriott, a longtime engineer who's made an enemy out of fellow employee Hurley by reporting the latter's drunkenness to higher-ups. Hurley decides to reap his vengeance against the engineer on Marriott's last day before retirement by seeing that the train crashes. The plot fails through the timely interference of Johnson, Marriott's daughter, and Milland, her lover. One of Milland's first feature roles, made prior to his coming to Hollywood, was originally made as a silent, with the soundtrack added a year after initial release.

d, Castleton Knight; w, Victor Kendall, Garnett Weston (based on the story by Joe Grossman); ph, Theodor Sparkuhl.

Drama   **(PR:A MPAA:NR)**

FLYING SERPENT, THE*   (1946) 59m PRC bw

George Zucco (Prof. Forbes), Ralph Lewis (Richard Thorpe), Hope Kramer (Mary Forbes), Eddie Acuff (Jerry Jones), Wheaton Chambers (Lewis Havener), Henry Hall (Billy Hayes), Milton Kibbee (Hastings), Budd Buster (Cordner), Terry Frost (Bennett).

Quetzalcoatl, the ancient Aztec plumed god, is employed by archeological madman Zucco, who wants to protect a hidden treasure he's discovered. When Zucco places a feather on someone's back, the victim is mauled by the crazed bird which wants its feather back. The flying bird/god is on wires, which would probably have been better employed had they been attached to the lifeless Zucco. Five years earlier PRC had done THE DEVIL BAT, which had the same basic plot device.

p, Sigmund Neufeld; d, Sherman Scott [Sam Newfield]; w, John T. Neville; ph, Jack Greenhalgh; ed, Holbrook N. Todd; art d, Edward C. Jewell.

Horror   **(PR:C MPAA:NR)**

FLYING SORCERER, THE*   (1974, Brit.) 52m Anvil/Children's Film
                                          Foundation

Kim Burfield, Debbie Russ, John Bluthal, Tim Barrett, Bob Todd, Erik Chitty.

Transported through time to the Middle Ages, young Burfield returns home with a dragon. The idea has possibilities but as presented is too sweet and simple-minded for its own good.

p, Hugh Stewart; d, Harry Booth; w, Booth, Leo Maguire; ph, Leslie Dear.

Fantasy   **(PR:A MPAA:NR)**

FLYING SQUAD, THE** (1932, Brit.) 80m BL bw

Harold Huth *(Mark McGill)*, Carol Goodner *(Ann Perryman)*, Edward Chapman *(Sedeman)*, Campbell Gullan *(Tiser)*, Harry Wilcoxon *(Inspector Bradley)*, Abraham Sofaer *(Li Joseph)*, Joseph Cunningham *(Simmonds)*.

Returning to London from her Paris art school, Goodner joins up with a gang of drug smugglers in order to avenge her brother's death. She learns that a police inspector offed the lad, even though he had intended to leave the gang. It's not long, however, before she falls in love with the cop. A barely tolerable film which was based on a highly successful stage play.

p, S.W. Smith; d, F.W. Kraemer; w, Bryan Edgar Wallace (from the play by Edgar Wallace).

Crime Drama **(PR:A MPAA:NR)**

FLYING SQUAD, THE* (1940, Brit.) 64m ABF bw

Sebastian Shaw *(Inspector Bradley)*, Phyllis Brooks *(Ann Perryman)*, Jack Hawkins *(Mark McGill)*, Basil Radford *(Sederman)*, Ludwig Stossel *(Li Yoseph)*, Manning Whiley *(Ronnie Perryman)*, Kathleen Harrison *(Mrs. Schifan)*, Cyril Smith *(Tiser)*, Henry Oscar *(Commissioner)*, Kynaston Reeves *(Magistrate)*.

Scotland Yard detective Shaw is helped to capture a drug smuggling czar by Brooks, the sister of a man killed by the crook. She infiltrates the gang and finds out that it is her own employer who murdered her sibling. Routine stuff, just as unimaginatively done here as it was in the 1932 film of the same name.

p, Walter C. Mycroft; d, Herbert Brenon; w, Doreen Montgomery (based on a play by Edgar Wallace); ph, Claude Friese-Greene, W. Harvey.

Crime **(PR:A MPAA:NR)**

FLYING TIGERS*** (1942) 102m REP bw

John Wayne *(Jim Gordon)*, John Carroll *(Woody Jason)*, Anna Lee *(Brooke Elliott)*, Paul Kelly *(Hap Davis)*, Gordon Jones *(Alabama Smith)*, Mae Clarke *(Verna Bales)*, Addison Richards *(Col. Lindsay)*, Edmund MacDonald *(Blackie Bales)*, Bill Shirley *(Dale)*, Tom Neal *(Reardon)*, Malcolm McTaggart *(McCurdy)*, David Bruce *(Lt. Barton)*, Chester Gan *(Mike)*, James Dodd *(McIntosh)*, Gregg Barton *(Tex Norton)*, John James *(Selby)*, Charles Lane *(Airport Official)*, John Seidel *(Barratt)*, Richard Loo *(Doctor)*, Richard Crane *(Airfield Radio Man)*, Willie Fung *(Jim, the Waiter)*.

This was Republic's salute to the all-American Volunteer Group flying for China and Chiang Kai-Shek, under the command of General Claire Chennault, long before Pearl Harbor. These men were both patriotic and mercenary, receiving $500 for every Japanese plane shot down. Wayne is the leader of one squadron of carefree pilots, backed up by Kelly, his tireless second-in-command, a weary veteran whose eyesight is failing. New recruit Carroll arrives with sidekick Jones, and trouble arises when Carroll, a wisecracking nonconformist, disobeys orders and creates dissension among the men. He picks a fight with MacDonald, another new recruit, blaming him for the death of a pilot friend who was killed in a stateside accident during an air show. MacDonald was allowed to fly by Wayne only after his wife, Clarke, begged the squadron commander to employ him. He proves himself heroic by dying nobly in air combat. The incorrigible Carroll, however, continues to make trouble for Wayne, even stealing the attentions of the Duke's girl friend, Lee, a Red Cross worker. In the air, Carroll relentlessly cuts in on the "kill" of other pilots to glean the $500 payoff for knocking down an enemy plane, disregarding orders and jeopardizing his fellow pilots. He misses one hazardous mission Wayne specifically assigns to him because he is off wooing Lee. Carroll's place is taken by Kelly, who has been grounded for poor eyesight. When Kelly dies in flight because of his handicap Carroll is grounded, ordered out of the Flying Tigers by a disgusted Wayne. Carroll begs for one more chance and Wayne reluctantly grants his request. Both men fly a transport plane through dangerous Japanese-infested territory to bomb an important railroad bridge with makeshift TNT bombs, but anti-aircraft batteries hit the plane and Wayne orders Carroll to bail out. Carroll, unknown to Wayne, has been wounded. He pushes Wayne out of the plane and the Duke floats to safety while Carroll gets behind the controls and crash-dives to heroic death into the bridge and a train loaded with enemy troops and ammunition. FLYING TIGERS is wholesale propaganda, but a film that bolstered the American spirit in WW II. All the cliches later presented in combat films dealing with air power are in evidence, particularly the close-ups of Japanese pilots dying horrible deaths, bullets smashing into the canopies of their planes, exploding their faces, blood bursting from their mouths and eyes. This was Wayne's first war film, one that set the pattern for him as a two-fisted combat leader—but one with a soft heart. At one point he displays angry regret about having sent a youth into the air to his death: "Should have stayed in college where he came from, but he begged for a chance and I gave it to him!" At the death of Kelly, his friend, he turns on Carroll and Lee who arrive at the airstrip too late, snarling at them: "I hope you had a good time, because Hap [Kelly] paid the bill!" The film is a direct lift from Howard Hawks' ONLY ANGELS HAVE WINGS (1939) with Kelly taking Thomas Mitchell's role and MacDonald assuming the part of the disgraced pilot played by Richard Barthelmess. Carroll appeared in the 1939 film in a small role and is here promoted to star status. Director Miller provides plenty of action with a sure hand that wastes few scenes; Jones and Fung, a Chinese waiter who refuses to eat the so-called Chinese food Wayne and Lee order from him, offer some much-needed laughs in an otherwise grim story.

p, Edmund Grainger; d, David Miller; w, Kenneth Gamet, Barry Trivers (based on a story by Gamet); ph, Jack Marta; m, Victor Young; ed, Ernest Nims; md, Walter Scharf; art d, Russell Kimball; spec eff, Howard Lydecker.

War Drama **Cas.** **(PR:C MPAA:NR)**

FLYING WILD** (1941) 63m MON bw

Leo Gorcey *(Mugs)*, Bobby Jordan *(Danny Dolan)*, Donald Haines *(Skinny)*, David Gorcey *(Peewee)*, Bobby Stone *(Louie)*, "Sunshine Sammy" Morrison *(Scruno)*, Eugene Francis *(Algernon "Algie" Reynolds)*, Joan Barclay *(Helen Munson)*, David O'Brien *(Tom Larson)*, Herbert Rawlinson *(Mr. Reynolds)*, George Pembroke *(Dr. Richard Nagel)*, Alden "Stephen" Chase *(Jack)*, Dennis Moore *(George)*, Mary Bovard *(Maizie)*, Bob Hill *(Woodward)*, Forrest Taylor *(Forbes)*.

Re-dubbed the Eastside Kids, Dead Enders Gorcey and Jordan wisecrack their way through this pic about a gang of saboteurs out to steal some airplane blueprints. (See BOWERY BOYS series, Index.)

p, Sam Katzman; d, William West; w, Al Martin (from his story); ph, Fred Jackman, Jr.; m, Johnny Lange, Lew Porter; ed, Robert Golden; set d, Fred Preble.

Comedy/Crime **(PR:A MPAA:NR)**

FLYING WITH MUSIC*½ (1942) 71m UA bw

George Givot, Majorie Woodworth, William Marshall, Edward Gargan, Jerry Bergen, Norma Varden.

Minor, forgotten musical stars Givot as a man on the lam who impersonates a tour group leader in Florida. Songs include: "If It's Love," "Rotana," "Pennies for Peppino," "Caribbean Magic," "Song of the Lagoon."

p, Hal Roach; d, George Archainbaud; w, M. Coates Webster, Louis S. Kaye; m, Edward Ward; ed, Richard Currier; m/l, Bob Wright, Chet Forrest.

Musical **(PR:A MPAA:NR)**

FM** (1978) 104m UNIV c (AKA: CITIZEN'S BAND)

Michael Brandon *(Jeff Dugan)*, Eileen Brennan *(Mother)*, Alex Karras *(Doc Holiday)*, Cleavon Little *(Prince)*, Martin Mull *(Eric)*, Cassie Yates *(Laura Coe)*, Norman Lloyd *(Carl Billings)*, Jay Fenichel *(Bobby Douglas)*, James Keach *(Lt. Reach)*, Joe Smith *(Albert Driscoll)*, Tom Tarpey *(Regis Lamar)*, Janet Brandt *(Alice)*, Mary Torrey *(Cathy)*, Roberta Wallach *(Shari Smith)*, Terry Jastrow *(Michael J. Carlyle)*, Cissy Wellman *(Maggie)*, Robert Patten *(Jack Rapp)*, Karen Ciral *(Buxom Blonde)*, Brenda Venus *(Delores Deluxe)*, Tina Ritt *(Alice's Assistant)*, Don Dolan *(Police Captain)*, David Matthau, John Larson, Phillip Epstein, Peter Fox, Bo Kaprall, Keith Jensen, Patricia Marlowe, Tammy Masters, Paul Menzel, Louis Messina, Andrea Claudio, Linda Ronstadt, Jimmy Buffett, Tom Petty, REO Speedwagon, Kevin Cronin, Gary Richrath, Alan Gratzer, Bruce Hall, Neal Doughty.

The going-ons at an FM radio station served primarily as a means for a bombardment of popular rock songs from the time, including some concert footage of Linda Ronstadt and Jimmy Buffet. The story that accompanies the many tunes is a sentimentalized look at the disc jockeys having to face their station taking the plunge away from personalized music into the realm of commercialism. Station master Brandon is so upset by this change that he decides to quit, leaving the rest of the staff to literally hijack the station. But their efforts are for naught, the disillusioned disc jockies receiving little more than a slap on the wrist. Of the various performances comedian Martin Mull, as a space outed D.J., really stole the show, adding an energy with which none of the others, nor the music, is able to compete. Songs included: "FM," "Do It Again," "FM Reprise" (Walter Becker, Donald Fagen), "Livingston Saturday Night" (Jimmy Buffet), "The Key To My Kingdom" (Maxwell Davis, Claude Baum, Joe Josea), "Green Grass And High Tides" (Hugh Thomasson), "Life In The Fast Lane" (Joe Walsh, Don Henley, Glenn Frey), "Bad Man" (J.D. Sputher, Frey), "Poor Poor Pitiful Me" (Warren Zevon), "Love Me Tender" (Elvis Presley, Vera Matson), "Life's Been Good" (Joe Walsh), "Cold As Ice" (Mick Jones, Lew Gramus), "Feels Like The First Time" (Jones), "Slow Ride" (Dave Peverett), "Night Moves" (Bob Seger), "Sentimental Lady" (Bob Welch), "Fly Like An Eagle" (Steve Miller), "Just The Way You Are" (Billy Joel), "Lido Shuffle" (Boz Scaggs), "Hollywood" (Scaggs, Michael Omartin), "Your Smiling Face" (James Taylor), "We Will Rock You" (Brian May, Freddy Mercury), and "More Than A Feeling" (T. Scholz).

p, Rand Holston; d, John A. Alonzo; w, Ezra Sacks; ph, David Myers (Panavision, Technicolor); ed, David Myers; prod d, Lawrence G. Paull; cos, Kent Warner.

Musical/Drama **(PR:C MPAA:PG)**

FOES zero (1977) 90m Coats-Alexander-Coats c

MacDonald Carey *(McCarey)*, Jerry Hardin *(Gen. Mason)*, Jane Wiley *(Diane)*, Alan Blanchard *(Paul)*, Gregory Clemens *(Vic)*, John Coats *(Larry)*.

Terrible sci-fi film starring Carey as a UFO expert who spends the whole film trying to trace a flying saucer that looks like a frisbee. Eventually the "saucer" lands on an island inhabited by Wiley, Blanchard, and Clemens. Director Coats plays the alien's first victim. The film should have ended with his "death."

p, Robert D. E. Alexander, Richard Coats; d&w, John Coats; ph, Michael Sabo; spec eff, John Coats, Scott Farrar, Christopher George, Cinema Research, Film Effects of Hollywood.

Science Fiction **(PR:C MPAA:NR)**

FOG** (1934) 70m COL bw

Donald Cook *(Wentworth Brown)*, Mary Brian *(Mary Fulton)*, Reginald Denny *(Dr. Winstay)*, Robert McWade *(Alonzo Holt)*, Helen Freeman *(Madame Alva)*, Maude Eburne *(Mrs. Jackson)*, Samuel Hinds, G. Pat Collins, Edwin Maxwell, Marjorie Gateson.

A fog-enveloped ocean liner whodunit in which the standard millionaire is murdered and of course the cabins are full of suspects. Another pair of mysterious slayings pops up before the obviously guilty Denny jumps overboard. Most of the plot is mechanically unravelled by an omniscient soothsayer. Unfortunately, the dense fog can't envelop the inane dialog.

d, Albert Rogell; w, Ethel Hill, Dore Schary (from a magazine story by Valentine Williams and Dorothy Rice Sims); ph, Benjamin Kline; ed, Richard Cahoon.

Mystery **(PR:A MPAA:NR)**

FOG 1966 (SEE: STUDY IN TERROR, A, 1966, Brit.)

FOG, THE** (1980) 91m AE c

Adrienne Barbeau *(Stevie Wayne)*, Hal Holbrook *(Fr. Malone)*, Janet Leigh *(Kathy Williams)*, Jamie Lee Curtis *(Elizabeth Solley)*, John Houseman *(Machen)*, Tommy Atkins *(Nick Castle)*, Nancy Loomis *(Sandy Fadel)*, Charles Cyphers *(Dan O'Bannon)*, Ty Mitchell *(Andy Wayne)*, George Buck Flower *(Tommy Wallace)*, John Vick *(Sheriff Simms)*, Jim Jacobus *(Mayor)*, Jim Canning *(Dick Baxter)*, Regina Waldon *(Mrs. Kobritz)*, Darrow Igus *(Mel Sloane)*, Bill Taylor *(Bartender)*, Jim Haynie *(Hank Jones)*, Fred Franklyn *(Ashcroft)*, John Goff *(Al Williams)*, Darwin Joston *(Dr. Phibes)*, Rob Bottin *(Blake)*, Charley Nicklin *(Blake's Voice)*, John Strobel *(Grocery Clerk)*, Lee Sacks, Ric Moreno, Tommy Wallace *(Ghosts)*, Laurie Arent, Lindsey Arent, Shari Jacoby, Christopher Cunday *(Children)*.

A ghost ship occupied by 100-year-old corpses terrorizes a coastal community, which is covered in a heavy fog. Flotsam dialog and an illogical plot tend to negate any chills that the visuals produce. Carpenter calculates the shocks much the same way as in his HALLOWEEN, but with less success. Basically, it is a campfire story which wastes the fine talents of Holbrook and Houseman. Carpenter himself is cast as a church janitor, and has named one of the characters after his one-time collaborator Dan O'Bannon (DARK STAR). The female lead, Barbeau, was his wife in real life. Disappointing.

p, Debra Hill; d, John Carpenter; w, Carpenter, Hill; ph, Dean Cundey (Panavision, Metrocolor); m, Carpenter; ed, Tommy Wallace, Charles Bornstein; prod d, Wallace; art d, Craig Stearns; cos, Bill Whittens, Stephen Loomis; spec eff, Dick Albain, Jr.

Horror Cas. (PR:C-O MPAA:NR)

FOG ISLAND*½ (1945) 70m PRC bw

George Zucco *(Leo Grainger)*, Lionel Atwill *(Alec Ritchfield)*, Jerome Cowan *(Kavanaugh)*, Sharon Douglas *(Gail)*, Veda Ann Borg *(Sylvia)*, John Whitney *(Jeff)*, Jacqueline DeWitt *(Emiline Bronson)*, Ian Keith *(Dr. Lake)*, George Lloyd *(Allerton)*.

A simple tale of a vengeful ex-con, once rich, who invites those suspected of being responsible for his fall to spend a weekend of his foggy island. Why the guilty party accepts the invitation is the film's biggest mystery.

p, Leon Fromkess; d, Terry Morse; w, Pierre Gendron (from a story by Bernadine Angus); ph, Ira Morgan; ed, George McGuire.

Mystery Cas. (PR:A MPAA:NR)

FOG OVER FRISCO*½** (1934) 68m FN/WB bw

Bette Davis *(Arlene Bradford)*, Donald Woods *(Tony Stirling)*, Margaret Lindsay *(Val Bradford)*, Lyle Talbot *(Spencer Carleton)*, Arthur Byron *(Everett Bradford)*, Hugh Herbert *(Izzy Wright)*, Robert Barrat *(Thorne)*, Douglas Dumbrille *(Joshua Maynard)*, Irving Pichel *(Jake Bellow)*, Gordon Westcott *(Joe Bellow)*, Henry O'Neill *(Oren Porter)*, Charles Wilson *(Sgt. O'Hagen)*, Alan Hale *(Chief O'Malley)*, William B. Davidson *(Joe Hague)*, Douglas Cosgrove *(Lt. Davis)*, Harold Minjir *(Archie Van Ness)*, William Demarest *(Spike Smith)*, Harry Seymour *(Bill, the Messenger)*, Dennis O'Keefe *(Van Brugh)*, Ed Peil *(Police Sergeant)*, Robert Walker *(Hood)*, George Chandler *(Taxi Driver)*, Ralph Brooks *(Musician)*, Dick French *(Dick, the Orchestra Leader)*, Selmer Jackson *(Radio Announcer)*, Hal Price *(Bartender)*, Lester Door *(Reporter)*.

German-born director Dieterle, one of Warner Bros.' stalwart helmsmen, herein produced the fastest-paced movie on record by any standard, a technical whirlwind that dazzles and even sometimes befuddles the viewer, overshadowing a rather mundane crime yarn. Lindsay is a society girl who reads in a newspaper report that her stepsister, Davis, has been consorting with underworld figures in an infamous San Francisco nightclub. She upbraids Woods, the reporter who wrote the story, explaining that Davis is merely a thoughtless girl who is not responsible for the company she keeps. Woods takes Lindsay to the nightclub run by Pichel and there they meet Davis, surrounded by underworld types. It is later learned that Davis is not so innocent, that she has been using her fiance Talbot to sell off stolen securities received from Pichel and his gang. Talbot later implores Davis to quit the ring and she promises to do so. She gives Lindsay a sealed envelope that contains evidence that will expose Pichel, telling her to turn this over to police in case she disappears. A short time later, Davis vanishes, kidnaped by Pichel's henchmen when the racketeer decides Davis is too great a risk. Woods and sidekick Herbert get on the trail and find Talbot murdered. They trace Davis to a waterfront hideout and, after a wild gun battle between cooperating police and the hoodlums, the missing Davis is rescued. Pichel's mastermind boss, a member of brokerage house owned by her father, Bryon, is then exposed and the case neatly wrapped up. There's not much to this tale (remade in 1942 as SPY SHIP, a B-programmer), but Dieterle makes the visual most of it with a pace that is astounding, employing every filmic device known to that time—overlapping sound; wipes; iris openings and closings; boom, dolly, and truck shots; and opticals in quick takes—so that the urgency of the story is accelerated and suspense heightened. It's an experimental treat emphasizing movie techniques which enforce Dieterle's concept of filmmaking: "I prefer the direct, forceful method. I believe that a picture's basic idea is more important than the story that is told. A story can be trivial."

p, Robert Lord; d, William Dieterle, Daniel Reed; w, Robert N. Lee, Eugene Solow (based on a story by George Dyer); ph, Tony Gaudio; m, Leo Forbstein; ed, Harold McLernon; art d, Jack Okey; cos, Orry-Kelly.

Crime Drama (PR:A MPAA:NR)

FOLIES BERGERE*** (1935) 83m FOX bw
(GB: THE MAN FROM THE FOLLIES BERGERE)

Maurice Chevalier *(Eugene Charlier/Fernand, the Baron Cassini)*, Merle Oberon *(Baroness Genevieve Cassini)*, Ann Sothern *(Mimi)*, Walter Byron *(Rene)*, Lumsden Hare *(Gustave)*, Robert Grieg *(Henri)*, Eric Blore *(Francois)*, Halliwell Hobbes *(Paulet)*, Philip Dare *(Victor)*, Frank McGlynn, Sr. *(Joseph)*, Ferdinand Munier *(Morizet)*, Ferdinand Gottschalk *(Perishot)*, Barbara Leonard *(Josephine)*, Georges Renavent *(Premier)*, Olin Howland *(Stage Manager)*, Sailor Vincent *(Rubber)*, Robert Graves *(Doorman)*, Paul Kruger *(2nd Doorman)*, Olga Borget, Irene Bentley, Vivian Martin, Jenny Gray, Doris Morton *(Usherettes)*, Joseph E. Bernard *(Butler)*, Albert Pollet *(Male Secretary)*, Perry Ivins *(Airport Official)*, Mario Dominici *(Doctor)*, Paul Toien *(Page Boy)*, Lew Hicks, Leon Baron *(Attendants)*, Nam Dibot *(Ticket Man)*, Harry Holman *(Cafe Waiter)*, Leonard Walker *(Assistant Stage Manager)*, Albert Pollet, Max Barwyn *(Waiters in Box)*, Ed Reinach, Joe Mack, Pop Garson, Bruce Covington, Charles Hagen, Adolph Faylaver, Harry Milton, Conrad Seidermann, Austin Browne *(Bearded Men)*, Marbeth Wright, Lucille Lund, Jeanne Hart, Joan Woodbury, Bernadene Hayes, Marie Wells, Fay Worth, Maryan Dowling *(Girls in Bar)*, Pauline Rosebrook, Shirley Hughes, Dixie McKinley, Libby Marks, Rosa Milano, Zandra Dvorak *(Girl Models)*, Roy Seagus, Eugene Beday, Harry Semek, Hans Schumm, Alex Chevron, Luis Hanore, Rene Mimieux, Dick Allen, Henri Runique *(Bartenders)*, Bob Von Dobeneck, Al Mazzola, Bill O'Brien, Al Constance, Jack Raymond, Boris Fedotoff *(Waiters)*, Audrey Hall, Pokey Champion, Rita Dunn, Claudia Fargo, Myra Jones, Billie Lee, Mary Jane Hodge *(Girls in Shell)*, Helen Mann, Joan Sheldon, Jill Evans, Barbara Roberts, Angela Blue, Nell Rhoades, June Gale, Mae Madison *(Girls in Secretary Number)*, Jenny Gray, Thaya Foster, Ruth Day, Barbara Beall, Gail Goodson, Virginia Dabney *(Girls in Hat Store)*, Wedgwood Nowell, Barlowe Borland, Anders Van Haden, John Ince, Wilson Millar, Yorke Sherwood, Cyril Thornton, Vesey O'Davoren, Robert Cody *(Principals in Montage)*.

This is one of those rare films that was filmed simultaneously in two languages by the same director. Chevalier plays the role in both films, but in the French version Natalie Paley was Baroness Cassini and Mimi was played by Sim Viva. Some of the other French-version actors were Andre Berley, Fernand Ledoux, H.R. Hill, Jules Raucourt, Jacques Louvigny, Andre Cheron, Mario Dominici, and Olga Borget. The plot was a duplicate in both, with Chevalier in two roles. In the first part, he is a wealthy Baron whose fortune is at risk, requiring him to be in two places at once. He's supposed to attend a fancy dress ball as well as a secret meeting about his finances. His partners decide to hire a Folies Bergere performer who is known for his eerie imitations of people, one of whom is the famous Baron. He only has to play the part for the duration of the gala ball and no one tells the Baron's wife, Oberon (they are separated at the time). Chevalier (as the entertainer) is attentive to his "wife" but she rebuffs him. Then he learns that the Baron has been romancing his stage partner, Sothern. The next day, the Baron is not to be found so the performer must again impersonate him. While posing as the Baron he tells Sothern that their affair can no longer go on. At first, Sothern is disappointed, then realizes that she loves the entertainer, not the Baron. Meanwhile, the Baron has engineered a financial deal that garners him a huge amount of francs. Oberon is much more attentive to him than usual, which he likes. What he *doesn't* like is that Sothern now swears her affection to the Baron's look-alike. The Baron finally understands that Oberon is the woman for him but is annoyed by the knowledge that she is back in his arms as the result of the impersonator's efforts and he is forever to wonder how far Oberon went with the charlatan. Worse, he'll never know if *she* knew that it wasn't him for the past two days. This was Oberon's first U.S. film and it did not show her off to great advantage. She used to tell people she was born in Tasmania but that was a fib. Oberon was from India but felt it wouldn't do her career any good if the truth were known. The French version of the film, L'HOMME DES FOLIES BERGERE, was quite a bit spicier and featured topless dancers, something that never could have been shown in the U.S. Two remakes were attempted with the locale changed. One was THAT NIGHT IN RIO (1941) with Don Ameche, Alice Faye, and Carmen Miranda; the other was ON THE RIVIERA (1951), a vehicle for Danny Kaye. Songs in this first version include "Singing a Happy Song," "Rhythm in the Rain," "I Was Lucky," and "Au Revoir l'Amour" by Jack Meskill and Jack Stern (the first two sung by Sothern and Chevalier; the second two by Chevalier alone), "You Took the Words Right Out of My Mouth," by Harold Adamson and Burton Lane, "I Don't Stand a Ghost of a Chance with You," by Victor Young, Ned Washington and Bing Crosby, and "Valentine," by Andre Christien and Albert Willemetz, English lyrics by Herbert Reynolds (M.E. Rourke), all sung by Chevalier.

ex p, Darryl F. Zanuck; assoc p, William Goetz, Raymond Griffith; d, Roy Del Ruth; w, Bess Meredyth, Hal Long (from the play "The Red Cat" by Hans Adler, Rudolph Lothar); ph, Barney McGill, Peverell Marley; md, Alfred Newman; ed, Allen McNeill, Sherman Todd; art d, William Darling; cos, Albert M. Levy, Omar Kiam; ch, Dave Gould.

Musical Comedy (PR:A MPAA:NR)

FOLIES BERGERE½** (1958, Fr.) 100m Sirius c

Eddie Constantine *(Bob Hardie)*, Zizi Jeanmaire *(Claudie)*, Yves Robert *(Jeff)*, Nadia Gray *(Suzy Morgan)*, Jacques Morel *(Director)*, Jacques Castelot *(Philippe Loiselet)*, Pierre Mondy *(Roger)*, Edith Georges *(Rita)*, Serge Perrault *(Max)*.

Tough guy Constantine takes on a musical role as a GI who falls in love with Jeanmaire, a Folies showgirl, after he suspects that she's snatched his wallet. They wed, but their marriage is shaken when a film producer begins eyeing the gal. Constantine is able to shed his Franco-Bogart aura long enough to deliver a fine performance. A successful film in its native France, director Decoin owes much to the U.S. musical tradition.

p, Jacques Roitfeld; d, Henri Decoin; w, Decoin, Jacques Companeez, Georges Tabet, Andre Tabet; ph, Pierre Montazel (Technicolor); m, Phillipe Gerard, Jeff Davis; ed, Claude Durand; set d, Pierre Colombier; ch, Roland Petit, Mary-Jo Weldon.

Musical (PR:C MPAA:NR)

FOLLIES GIRL** (1943) 74m PRC bw

Wendy Barrie *(Anne Merriday)*, Doris Nolan *(Francine La Rue)*, Gordon Oliver *(Pvt. Jerry Hamlin)*, Anne Barrett *(Bunny)*, Arthur Pierson *(Sgt. Bill Perkins)*, J.C. Nugent *(J.B. Hamlin)*, Cora Witherspoon *(Mrs. J.B. Hamlin)*, William Harrigan

(Jimmy Dobson), Jay Brennan (Andre Duval), Lew Hearn (Lew), Cliff Hall (Cliff), Marion McGuire (Trixie), Pat C. Flick (Patsy), Anthony Blair (Somers), Jerry Blanchard (Jerri), Serjei Radamsky (Scarini), G. Swayne Gordon (Doorman), Ray Heatherton and Band, Johnny Long and Band, Bobby Byrne and Band, Ernie Holst and Band, Claire and Arene, Charles Weidman Dancers, Song Spinners, The Heat Waves, Lazare and Castellanos, Fritzi Scheff, Hal Thompson (Specialities).

An army private falls in love with a dress designer while his father decides to put on a ritzy, fashionable burlesque show. There's almost no plot in sight, but the tunes include "Keep The Flag A-Flying" by Mary Schaefer; "No Man In The House" by Nick and Charles Kenny and Sonny Burke; "Someone To Love" by Robert Warren; "I Told A Lie" by Nick Kenny, Kim Gannon, and Ken Lane; "Shall We Gather At The Rhythm?" by Kenny, Burke, and John Murphy; "Fascination," "I Knew Your Father's Son," and "Thoity Poiple Boids" by Fred Wise, Buddy Kaye, and Sidney Lippman.

p&d, William Rowland; w, Marcy Klauber, Charles Robinson (from a story by Klauber and Art Jarrett); ph, George Webber; ed, Samuel Datlowe; md, Ernie Holst.

Musical   **(PR:A   MPAA:NR)**

FOLKS AT THE RED WOLF INN   (SEE: TERROR HOUSE, 1972)

FOLLOW A STAR∗∗   (1959, Brit.) 103m RANK bw

Norman Wisdom (Norman Truscott), June Laverick (Judy), Jerry Desmonde (Vernon Carew), Hattie Jacques (Dymphna Dobson), Richard Wattis (Dr. Chatterway), Eddie Leslie (Harold Franklin), John Le Mesurier (Birkett), Sydney Tafler (Pendlebury), Fenella Fielding (Lady Finchington), Charles Heslop (The General), Joe Melia (Stage Manager), Ron Moody (Violinist).

Wisdom is a tailor with aspirations to fame who gets hired by has-been vocalist Desmonde. The crooner ends up mouthing the tunes while Wisdom does the actual singing in the wings. Jacques, cast as the young performer's wheel-chaired girlfriend, gives him the confidence to take the center stage and become a star in his own right. Songs include "I Love You" and the title cut, both by Wisdom.

p, Hugh Stewart; d, Robert Asher; w, Jack Davies, Henry Blyth, Norman Wisdom; ph, Jack Asher; m, Philip Green; ed, Roger Cherrill; art d, Maurice Carter.

Comedy   **(PR:A   MPAA:NR)**

FOLLOW ME, BOYS!∗∗∗   (1966) 131m BV c

Fred MacMurray (Lemuel Siddons), Vera Miles (Vida Downey), Lillian Gish (Hetty Seibert), Charlie Ruggles (John Everett Hughes), Elliott Reid (Ralph Hastings), Kurt Russell (Whitey), Luana Patten (Nora White), Ken Murray (Melody Murphy), Donald May (Edward White, Jr.), Sean McClory (Edward White, Sr.), Steve Franken (P.O.W. Lieutenant), Parley Baer (Mayor Hi Plommer), William Reynolds (Hoodoo Henderson, as a Man), Craig Hill (Leo, as a Man), Tol Avery (Dr. Ferris), Willis Bouchey (Judge), John Zaremba (Ralph's Lawyer), Madge Blake (Cora Anderson), Carl Reindel (Tank Captain), Hank Brandt (Frankie Martin, as a Man), Richard Bakalyan (Umpire), Tim McIntire (Corporal), Willie Soo Hoo (Quong Lee, as a Man), Tony Regan (Tiger), Robert B. Williams (Artie), Jimmy Murphy (1st P.O.W. Soldier), Adam Williams (P.O.W. Sergeant), Dean Moray (Hoodoo Henderson), Bill Booth (Leo), Keith Taylor (Beefy Smith), Rickey Kelman (Frankie Martin), Gregg Shank (Mickey Doyle), Donnie Carter (Red), Kit Lloyd (Oliver), Ronnie Dapo (Tiger), Dennis Rush (Jimmy), Kevin Burchett (Eggy), David Bailey (Duke), Eddie Sallia (Harry), Bill "Wahoo" Mills (David), Warren Hsieh (Quong Lee), Duane Chase (Joe), Mike Dodge (Phil), Gregor Vigen (Ronnie Larsen), Michael Flatley, Sherwood Ball (Scouts), Colyer Dupont (Scout at Cliff), Dean Bradshaw, Chris Mason, Johnny Bangert (Scouts in War Games).

In a charming role, MacMurray plays an ordinary fellow who packs up his saxophone and relocates to the country, where he plays melodies for the local Boy Scout troop. He soon wins over the town lovely, Miles, who becomes his wife and understands his devotion to the kids. The highlight, however, is the appearance of Lillian Gish as the eccentric and dainty rich lady. She is still able to capture the viewer's attention as well as in her silent days. Disney ladled on the sweetness again, but no real harm is done.

p, Walt Disney; d, Norman Tokar; w, Louis Pelletier (based on the book God and My Country by MacKinley Kantor); ph, Clifford Stine (Technicolor); m, George Bruns; ed, Robert Stafford; art d, Carroll Clark, Marvin Aubrey Davis; set d, Emile Kuri, Frank R. McKelvy; cos, Bill Thomas; spec eff, Eustace Lycett; m/l, title song, Robert B. Sherman, Richard M. Sherman.

Drama   **Cas.**   **(PR:AA   MPAA:NR)**

FOLLOW ME QUIETLY∗∗∗½   (1949) 60m RKO bw

William Lundigan (Grant), Dorothy Patrick (Ann), Jeff Corey (Collins), Nestor Paiva (Benny), Charles D. Brown (Mulvaney), Paul Guilfoyle (Overbeck), Edwin Max (The Judge), Frank Ferguson (McGill), Marlo Dwyer (Waitress), Michael Brandon (Dixon), Douglas Spencer (Phony Judge), Maurice Cass (Bookstore Owner), Wanda Cantlon (Waitress), Howard Mitchell (Don, Bartender), Cy Stevens (Kelly), Robert Emmett Keane (Coroner), Paul Bryar (Sgt. Bryce), Lee Phelps, Art Dupuis (Detectives), Walden Boyle (Intern), Joe Whitehead (Ed), Martin Cichy (Cop), Virginia Farmer (Woman), Nolan Leary (Larson).

A disturbing film noir about a mysterious killer known only as the Judge, who kills anyone he thinks is worthless. Witnesses provide enough evidence for the police to

create a life-size mannequin in the Judge's likeness. The dummy is left sitting on a chair in a shadowy corner of the station where a frustrated detective tells it of his insecurities. The psychotically daring Judge sneaks into the office and assumes the dummy's position in the chair, thus enabling himself to overhear the police strategies. Eventually the cops follow a tip to the killer's hideout, where a chase ensues. Before he falls to his death, the Judge reveals himself to be an ugly, dissatisfied, middle-aged eccentric.

p, Herman Schlom; d, Richard Fleischer; w, Lillie Hayward (from a story by Anthony Mann, Francis Rosenwald); ph, Robert de Grasse; m, Leonid Raab; ed, Elmo Williams; md, Constantin Bakaleinikoff; art d, Albert S. D'Agostino, Walter E. Keller; set d, Darrell Silvera, James Altwies; makeup, Gordon Bau, H.W. Phillips.

Crime   **(PR:C   MPAA:NR)**

FOLLOW THAT CAMEL∗∗   (1967, Brit.) 95m RANK c

Phil Silvers (Sgt. Nocker), Jim Dale (Bertram Oliphant West), Peter Butterworth (Simpson), Charles Hawtrey (Capt. Le Pice), Kenneth Williams (Commandant Burger), Anita Harris (Corktip), Joan Sims (Zigzig), Bernard Bresslaw (Abdul), Angela Douglas (Lady Jane Ponsonby), John Bluthal (Corp. Clotski), Larry Taylor (Riff), William Hurndell (Raff), Gerten Klauber (Algerian Spiv), Peter Gilmore (Bagshaw), Julian Orchard (Doctor), William Mervyn (Ponsonby), Julian Holloway (Ticket Collector), Vincent Ball (Ship's Officer), David Glover (Hotel Manager).

This addition to the "Carry On" series has the craven Dale entering the Foreign Legion to serve directly under the much-decorated fraud, Silvers. Together, their heroism culminates when they successfully protect Douglas and their fort from an attack by Arabs.

p, Peter Rogers; d, Gerald Thomas; w, Talbot Rothwell; ph, Alan Hume (Eastmancolor); m, Eric Rogers; ed, Alfred Roome; cos, Emma Selby-Walker.

Comedy   **(PR:A   MPAA:NR)**

FOLLOW THAT DREAM∗∗½   (1962) 109m UA c

Elvis Presley (Toby Kwimper), Arthur O'Connell (Pop Kwimper), Anne Helm (Holly Jones), Joanna Moore (Alicia Claypoole), Jack Kruschen (Carmine), Jack Oakland (Nick), Roland Winters (Judge), Alan Hewitt (H. Arthur King), Frank de Kova (Jack), Howard McNear (George), Herbert Rudley (Endicott), Gavin and Robin Koon (Eddy and Teddy Bascombe), Robert Carricart (Al), John Duke (Blackie), Harry Holcombe (Governor), Pam Ogles (Adriadne Pennington).

An Elvis vehicle which sends the King to Florida to join forces with his pop and four adorable orphans against a gang of thugs. They spend most of their time defending their squatter's rights to some unclaimed government land, allowing Elvis to show his newfound judo moves. The rest of the time is spent listening to the King croon "Follow That Dream" by Fred Wise and Ben Weisman, "What A Wonderful Life" by Sid Wayne and Jerry Livingston, "I'm Not The Marrying Kind" by Mack David and Sherman Edwards, "Sound Advice" by Bill Giant, Bernie Baum, and Florence Kaye, and "Angel" by Sid Tepper. Only for Elvis fans.

p, David Weisbart; d, Gordon Douglas; w, Charles Lederer (from the novel Pioneer, Go Home by Richard Powell); ph, Leo Tover (Panavision, DeLuxe Color); m, Hans J. Salter; ed, William B. Murphy; art d, Malcolm C. Bert; set d, Gordon Gurnee, Fred McLean; makeup, Dan Striepeke; tech adv, Col. Tom Parker.

Drama/Musical   **(PR:A   MPAA:NR)**

FOLLOW THAT HORSE!∗∗½   (1960, Brit.) 80m Cavalcade/WB bw

David Tomlinson (Dick Lanchester), Cecil Parker (Sir William Crane), Richard Wattis (Hugh Porlock), Mary Peach (Susan Turner), Dora Bryan (Miss Bradstock), Raymond Huntley (Special Branch Chief), Sam Kydd (Farrell), George Pravda (Hammler), John Welsh (Maj. Turner), Peter Copley (Garrod), Cyril Shaps (Dr. Spiegel), Victor Brooks (Blake), Vic Wise (Riley), George A. Cooper (Rudd), Alison Fraser (Harriet), Arthur Lowe (Auctioneer), John Phillips (American Delegate), Guy Deghy (German Delegate), John Crewdson (Pilot), Tony Thawnton (Special Branch Man), John Serret, Edward Dentith, Peter Collingwood, Jonathan Clyde.

Tomlinson gets his hands on some top-secret film after a scientist he is escorting turns out to be a foreign agent. Solely a cinematic contrivance, the top-secret film accidentally ends up in the belly of a race horse. Some humorous situations arise, including Tomlinson's attempt to bid for the horse at an auction. Harmlessly silly.

p, Thomas Clyde; d, Alan Bromly; w, Alfred Shaughnessy, William Douglas Home, Howard Mason (from Mason's novel Photo Finish); ph, Norman Warick; m, Stanley Black; ed, Gerald Turney-Smith; art d, Harry White; makeup, Eric Aylott.

Comedy   **(PR:A   MPAA:NR)**

FOLLOW THAT MAN∗½   (1961, Brit.) 84m Epiney/UA bw

Sydney Chaplin (Eddie Miller), Dawn Addams (Janet Clark), Elspeth March (Astrid Larsen), Joan Heal (Harriet), Peter Bull (Gustav), Jack Melford (Lars Toren), Nicholas Tanner (Olaf), May Hallatt (Nannie), Garry Colleano (Axelrod).

Marginally funny comedy has Chaplin a crook hiding out from the police. He pretends to be the long-lost son of a Swedish widow but her attentions become more alarming than those of the police.

p, Jerry Epstein, Charles Leeds; d&w, Epstein.

Comedy   **(PR:A   MPAA:NR)**

FOLLOW THAT WOMAN** (1945) 70m PAR bw

William Gargan *(Sam Boone)*, Nancy Kelly *(Nancy Boone)*, Ed Gargan *(Butch)*, Regis Toomey *(Barney Manners)*, Don Costello *(Nick)*, Byron Barr *(John Evans)*, Pierre Watkin *(Mr. Henderson)*, Audrey Young *(Marge)*.

Gargan, a detective about to enter the army, is suspected of murder. When he dons his fatigues, his devoted wife, Kelly, continues the search for the guilty party. The private-eye private returns home on a one-week leave and, together with his spouse, solves the mystery.

p, William Pine, William Thomas; d, Lew Landers; w, Winston Miller, Maxwell Shane (from a story by Ben Perry); ph, Fred Jackman, Jr.; m, Alexander Laszlo; ed, Henry Adams; art d, F. Paul Sylos.

Crime (PR:A MPAA:NR)

FOLLOW THE BAND** (1943) 61m UNIV bw (AKA: TROMBONE FROM HEAVEN)

Eddie Quillan *(Marvin Howe)*, Mary Beth Hughes *(Dolly O'Brien)*, Leon Errol *(Big Mike O'Brien)*, Anne Rooney *(Juanita Turnbull)*, Samuel S. Hinds *("Pop" Turnbull)*, Bob Mitchum *(Tate Winters)*, Russell Hicks *(Jeremiah K. Barton)*, Bennie Bartlett *(Cootie)*, Frank Coghlan, Jr. *(Bert)*, Jean Ames *(Lucille Rose)*, Irving Bacon *(Peterson)*, Isabel Randolph *(Mrs. Forbes)*, Frank Faylen *(Brooks)*, Robert Dudley *(Seth Cathcart)*, Paul Dubov *(Alphonse)*, Frank Mitchell *(Charlie)*, Joe Bernard *(Mr. Hawkins)*, Charles Sherlock *(Photographer)*, Leo Carrillo, Skinnay Ennis and the Groove Boys, The King's Men, Alvino Rey, The King Sisters, Ray Eberle, Hilo Hattie, The Bombardiers, Frances Langford.

The flimsy story line is about a farmer (Quillan) visiting New York to accept an award from the National Dairy Association. That alone doesn't make for an exciting flick, so he brings along his trombone. He takes it to a nightspot where a number of musical numbers are heard: "My Melancholy Baby" by George A. Norton and Ernie Burnett; "My Devotion" by Roc Hillman and Johnny Napton; "Ain't Misbehavin' " by Fats Waller, Harry Brooks, and Andy Razaf; "Swingin' The Blues" by Everett Carter and Milton Rosen; "Spellbound" by Carter and Rosen; "Hilo Hattie" by Harold Adamson and Johnny Noble; "The Army Air Corps" by Robert Crawford; "Rosie The Riveter" by Redd Evans and John Jacob Loeb, and "Don't Tread On The Tail Of Me Coat" (composer unknown). All of this doesn't make for excitement either. Sixth-billed Robert Mitchum (as Bob Mitchum) made his first appearance in modern dress, having previously appeared in horse operas only.

p, Paul Malvern; d, Jean Yarbrough; w, Warren Wilson, Dorothy Bennett (from a story by Richard English); ph, Woody Bredell; ed, Milton Carruth; md, Charles Previn; art d, John B. Goodman; ch, Louis Da Pron.

Musical (PR:A MPAA:NR)

FOLLOW THE BOYS*½** (1944) 122m UNIV bw

George Raft *(Tony West)*, Vera Zorina *(Gloria Vance)*, Grace McDonald *(Kitty West)*, Charles Grapewin *(Nick West)*, Charles Butterworth *(Louie Fairweather)*, Ramsay Ames *(Laura)*, Elizabeth Patterson *(Annie)*, Regis Toomey *(Dr. Jim Henderson)*, George Macready *(Walter Bruce)*, Spooks *(Junior)*, Theodore von Eltz *(William Barrett)*, Janet Shaw, Jan Wiley *(Telephone Operators)*, Frank Jenks *(Chick Doyle)*, Molly Lamont *(Secretary)*, Mack Gray *(Lt. Reynolds)*, Addison Richards, Emmett Vogan, Cyril Ring *(Life Staffers)*, Ralph Meredith *(Blind Soldier in MacDonald Number)*, John Estes *(Patient)*, Ralph Gardner *(Patient in Leg Cast in MacDonald Number)*, Doris Lloyd *(Nurse)*, Charles D. Brown *(Col. Starrett)*, Nelson Leigh *(Bull Fiddler)*, Lane Chandler *(Ship's Officer)*, Frank LaRue *(Mailman)*, Tony Marsh *(Officer)*, Stanley Andrews *(Australian Officer)*, Leslie Denison *(Reporter)*, Leyland Hodgson *(Australian Reporter)*, Bill Healy *(Ship's Officer)*, Ralph Dunn *(Loomis)*, Billy Benedict *(Joe, a Soldier)*, Grandon Rhodes *(Guild Member)*, Edwin Stanley *(Film Director)*, Roy Darmour *(Assistant Director)*, Carl Vernell *(Dance Director)*, Wallis Clark *(HVC Committee Man)*, Tony Hughes *(Man)*, Richard Crane *(Marine Officer)*, Frank Wilcox *(Army Doctor)*, Bernard B. Thomas, Jimmy Carpenter, John Whitney, Walter Tetley, Joel Allen, Carlyle Blackwell, Mel Schubert, Stephen Wayne, Charles King *(Soldiers)*, Carey Harrison, William Forrest *(Colonels)*, Steve Brodie *(Australian Pilot)*, Clyde Cook *(Stooge)*, Bobby Barker *(Soldier in Fields' Routine)*, Tom Hanlon *(Announcer)*, Odessa Lauren, Nancy Brinckman *(Telephone Operators)*, Bob Ashley, Lennie Smith *(Jitterbugs)*, Duke York *(MP)*, Don Kramer, Alan Cooke, Luis Torres, Nicholai, John Duane, Ed Browne, Clair Freeman, Bill Meader, Eddie Kover *(Soldiers)*, Daisy *(Fifi)*, Lee Bennett *(Acrobat)*, Baby Marie Osborne *(Nurse)*, George Shorty Chirello *(Welles' Assistant)*, Nicodemus Stewart *(Lt. Reynolds, USAF)*, George Eldredge *(Submarine Officer)*, Linda Brent, Janice Gay, Jane Smith, Marjorie Fectean, Doris Brenn, Rosemary Battle, Lolita Leighter, Mary Rowland, Eleanor Counts *(Magic Maids)*, Bill Wolfe *(Man in Zoot Suit in Fields' Routine)*, Thurston Hall, Jackie Lou Harding, Anthony Warde, Dennis Moore, Martin Ashe, Howard Hickman, George Riley, Jack Wegman, Billy Wayne, Dick Nelson, Jack Whitley, Tom Hanlon, Don McGill, Franklin Parker, Bill Dyer, Michael Kirk, Genevieve Bell. *Stars Appearing as Themselves*: Jeanette MacDonald, Orson Welles' Mercury Wonder Show, Marlene Dietrich, Dinah Shore, Donald O'Connor, Peggy Ryan, W. C. Fields, The Andrews Sisters, Arthur Rubinstein, Carmen Amaya and Her Company, Sophie Tucker, The Delta Rhythm Boys, Leonard Gautier's Dog Act "The Bricklayers," Ted Lewis and His Band, Freddie Slack and His Orchestra, Charlie Spivak and His Orchestra, Louis Jordan and His Orchestra; *In the Hollywood Victory Committee sequence*: Maria Montez, Susanna Foster, Louise Allbritton, Robert Paige, Alan Curtis, Lon Chaney, Jr., Gloria Jean, Andy Devine, Turhan Bey, Evelyn Ankers, Noah Beery, Jr., Samuel S. Hinds, Louise Beavers, Clarence Muse, Gale Sondergaard, Peter Coe, Nigel Bruce, Thomas Gomez, Martha O'Driscoll, Maxie Rosenbloom, Lois Collier, Elyse Knox, Randolph Scott, Philo McCullough, Agustin Castellon Sabicas.

Truly a star-studded array of performers in a plot that's thinner than a hobo's shoe soles. A little more than two hours in length, FOLLOW THE BOYS begins with the demise of vaudeville in New York as the Palace Theatre closes. George Raft, sister Grace McDonald, and dad Charlie Grapewin have just finished their turkey act. They are known as The Three Wests and the manager says, at the end of their performance, "I've seen acts lay an egg, but you guys laid an omelet." Raft tells his family that they would be wise to try California, as there is nothing left for them in The Big Apple. After arriving in The Big Orange, Raft becomes a chorus boy in a film starring Vera Zorina. He criticizes her dancing, gets noticed, and eventually marries her. He becomes a star as well as they appear in a succession of mythical films with titles like "Love In Brazil" and "Moonlight Madness." When the war begins, Raft attempts to enlist but he's turned aside due to a bad knee. He's ashamed of this and doesn't tell Zorina, who takes his non-draftability to mean he's yellow. They soon separate, since he's too proud to tell her the truth. Raft is then asked to get together a troupe of performers for the troops. He agrees to coordinate the shows and asks Zorina to help. She turns him down flat and doesn't tell him that the reason is that she is pregnant. They part once more and he ships out to Australia. Just before the vessel is about to dock, a Japanese torpedo hits it and Raft dies without seeing his new-born son or even knowing of his existence. That, for what it's worth, is the clothesline they hang innumerable excellent musical numbers on. W. C. Fields does his famous pool routine and your sides will ache from laughing. A totally enjoyable bit of cotton candy for the eyes. Wall to wall songs include "Beyond the Blue Horizon" (Richard A. Whiting, W. Franke Harling, Leo Robin) sung by Jeanette MacDonald, who also sings—to a homesick blind soldier—"I'll See You in My Dreams" (Isham Jones, Gus Kahn), Sophie Tucker singing "The Bigger the Army and the Navy" (Jack Yellen) and "Some of These Days" (Shelton Brooks), Dinah Shore singing "I'll Get By" (Roy Turk, Fred E. Ahlert), "I'll Walk Alone" (Jule Styne, Sammy Cahn), and "Mad About Him Blues" (Larry Marks, Dick Charles), and The Andrews Sisters doing a medley of their hits: "Bei Mir Bist Du Schoen," "Beer Barrel Polka," "Apple Blossom Time," and "Shoo, Shoo, Baby." The Delta Rhythm Boys sing "The House I Live In" (Earl Robinson, Lewis Allen), and Arthur Rubenstein plays Chopin's "Liebestraum."

p, Charles K. Feldman, d, Edward Sutherland; w, Lou Breslow, Gertrude Purcell; ph, David Abel; md, Leigh Harline; ed, Fred R. Feitshans, Jr.; art d, John B. Goodman, Harold H. MacArthur; set d, Russell Gausman, Ira S. Webb; cos, Vera West, Howard Greer; spec eff, John P. Fulton; ch, George Hale.

Musical/Comedy (PR:AA MPAA:NR)

FOLLOW THE BOYS*½ (1963) 96m MGM c

Connie Francis *(Bonnie Pulaski)*, Paula Prentiss *(Toni Denham)*, Dany Robin *(Michele)*, Russ Tamblyn *(Lt. "Smitty" Smith)*, *Richard Long (Lt. Peter Langley)*, Ron Randell *(Comdr. Ben Bradville)*, Robert Nichols *(Hulldown)*, Roger Perry *(Radarman F/C Bill Pulaski)*, Janis Paige *(Liz Bradville)*, Paul Maxwell (C.M.A.A.), Eric Pohlmann *(Italian Farmer)*, David Sumner *(Vittorio)*, Sean Kelly *(Duty Officer)*, John McClaren *(Commentator)*, Roger Snowdon *(Italian Barman)*.

Francis is back on the trail of the boys after her success in WHERE THE BOYS ARE. She and her three friends faithfully follow a quartet of sailors who dock in a variety of Riviera ports. Nick-named "seagulls" after the birds which so frequently pester the seafaring lads, the girls warble such tunes as, "Follow The Boys," "Tonight's My Night," "Intrigue," "Waiting For Billy," "Sleepyland" (Benny Davis, Ted Murray, Dramato Palumbo), "Italian Lullabye" (Connie Francis). A mindless and unfunny effort.

p, Lawrence P. Bachmann; d, Richard Thorpe; w, David T. Chantler, David Osborn (based on a story by Bachmann); ph, Ted Scaife (Panavision, Metrocolor); m, Ron Goodwin, Alexander Courage; ed, John Victor Smith; md, Geoff Love; art d, Bill Andrews.

Romantic Comedy (PR:A MPAA:NR)

FOLLOW THE FLEET*½** (1936) 110m RKO bw

Fred Astaire *(Bake Baker)*, Ginger Rogers *(Sherry Martin)*, Randolph Scott *(Bilge Smith)*, Harriet Hilliard *(Connie Martin)*, Astrid Allwyn *(Iris Manning)*, Harry Beresford *(Capt. Ezra Hickey)*, Russell Hicks *(Jim Nolan)*, Brooks Benedict *(Sullivan)*, Ray Mayer *(Dopey)*, Lucille Ball *(Kitty Collins)*, Addison [Jack] Randall *(Lt. Williams)*, Maxine Jennings *(Hostess)*, Jane Hamilton *(Waitress)*, Kay Sutton *(Telephone Operator)*, Doris Lloyd *(Mrs. Courtney)*, Huntley Gordon *(Touring Officer)*, James Pierce *(Bouncer)*, Herbert Rawlinson *(Webber)*, Gertrude Short *(Cashier, Dance Joint)*, George Magrill *(Quartermaster)*, Betty Grable, Joy Hodges, Jeanne Gray *(Trio)*, Thelma Leeds, Lita Chevret *(Girls)*, Tony Martin, Frank Mills, Frank Jenks, Edward Burns, Frank Moran *(Sailors)*, Dorothy Fleisman, Bob Cromer *(Contest Dancers)*.

The first time they hauled this plot around was in a 1925 silent film called SHORE LEAVE, which starred Richard Barthelmess and Dorothy Mackaill. Next, it was a 1930 musical named HIT THE DECK. This time it works as well as can be expected, given the musical talents of Astaire and Rogers, and the inability of Scott and Hilliard to play the comedy co-stars. Fred's an ex-dancer turned gum-chewing, wise-cracking sailor (a far cry from the white tie and tails sophistication usually expected). Ginger, his one-time partner, is now singing in a San Francisco club to make ends meet. Hilliard is Rogers' sister (and although a real blonde, she was forced to don a brunette wig so as not to detract from Rogers). Scott is Astaire's best pal. There's a bit of a plot about obtaining a ship and refurbishing it in order to put on a musical, but that's all frou-frou. The deliciousness of this film is all solidly on the legs of Astaire and Rogers and the subplot could have been lost with no detriment. Irving Berlin, who loved to write for Astaire more than any singer, provides the tunes, which include the magnificent "Let's Face The Music And Dance." This is the only number in which Astaire is garbed in his customary spiffiness. Hilliard and Scott are terribly miscast in their roles. Scott is about as funny as a rain-out at a ball game. Hilliard, though she sings wonderfully, hadn't yet developed the comedy timing that put her 1950s' TV show at the top of the ratings as America watched her marriage to Ozzie Nelson, and her sons, Ricky and David. Lots of dancing and such, but the tale is just an excuse to put Rogers and

Astaire together. By the time they got to this one, the stories were getting to be reworks of earlier films. But the public didn't care, and flocked to this anyhow. One omission is the usual obligatory comic relief, missing here and sorely needed. Still, just to hear Astaire sing Berlin's tunes, and watch him and Rogers trip the light fantastic is enough. The other tunes are "We Saw The Sea," "I'm Putting All My Eggs In One Basket," "But Where Are You?," "I'd Rather Lead A Band," "Let Yourself Go," and "Get Thee Behind Me, Satan." Look for Ball and Grable, both in their early twenties and looking absolutely scrumptious. The Navy technical advisor must have decided he liked show business, because he went on to co-author FLIGHT COMMAND.

p, Pandro S. Berman; d, Mark Sandrich; w, Dwight Taylor, Allan Scott (based on the play "Shore Leave" by Hubert Osborne); ph, David Abel; ed, Henry Berman; md, Max Steiner; art d, Van Nest Polglase; set d, Darrell Silvera; cos, Bernard Newman; spec eff, Vernon Walker; ch, Hermes Pan, Fred Astaire; tech adv, Lt. Cmdr. Harvey Haislip, U.S.N.

Musical/Comedy   **Cas.**   **(PR:AA   MPAA:NR)**

FOLLOW THE LEADER**½   (1930) 76m PAR bw

Ed Wynn (Crickets), Ginger Rogers (Mary Brennan), Stanley Smith (Jimmy Moore), Lou Holtz (Sam Platz), Lida Kane (Ma Brennan), Ethel Merman (Helen King), Bobby Watson (George White), Donald Kirke (R.C. Black), William Halligan (Bob Sterling), Holly Hall (Fritzie Devere), Preston Foster (Two-Gun Terry), James C. Morton (Mickie), Tammany Young (Bull), Jack LaRue (Hood), William Gargan (Chuck), Bill Black, Richard Scott, Jules Epailly, C. Henderson.

Ed Wynn supplies the gags as the screechy-voiced waiter named Crickets who gets mixed up with a gang tagged "The Hudson Dusters." He does his best to find fame for Rogers and succeeds when Merman is kidnaped before the big show. The comedy is silly, but pays off with a few good belly laughs. Paramount cast Merman in her first film role at the last minute, replacing Ruth Etting. Songs highlighted are "Satan's Holiday" (Sammy Fain, Irving Kahal), "Brother, Just Laugh It Off" (E. Y. Harburg, Arthur Schwartz, Ralph Rainger) "Broadway, the Heart of the World" (Lew Brown, Buddy DeSylva, Ray Henderson, from the original play).

d, Norman Taurog; w, Sid Silvers, Gertrude Purcell, Albert Parker (based on the play "Manhattan Mary" by William K. Wells, George White, Buddy DeSylva, Lew Brown, Ray Henderson); ph, Larry Williams; m, Max Manne, Adolph Deutsch; ed, Barney Rogan; art d, William Saulter; cos, Caroline Putnam.

Musical   **(PR:A   MPAA:NR)**

FOLLOW THE LEADER**   (1944) 65m BAN/MON bw
                                  (AKA: EAST OF THE BOWERY)

Leo Gorcey (Muggs McGinnis), Huntz Hall (Glimpy Freedhoff), Dave Durand (Danny), Bud Gorman (James Aloysius "Skinny" Bogerty), Bobby Stone (Speed), Jimmy Strand (Dave), Gabriel Dell (W.W. "Fingers" Belmont), Jack LaRue (Larry), Joan Marsh (Millie McGinnis), Billy Benedict (Spider O'Brien), Mary Gordon (Mrs. McGinnis), Bernard Gorcey (Ginsberg), J. Farrell MacDonald (Clancy), Bryant Washburn (Colonel), "Sunshine Sammy" Morrison (Scruno in Dream), Gene Austin, The Sherrill Sisters.

On Army furlough, Gorcey and Hall find that one of the East Side Kids has been wrongly jailed on a robbery rap and spring into action to catch the real crooks. Standard fare for the boys, which features songs "Now and Then," performed by Austin, and "All I Want to Do Is Play the Drums," performed by The Sherrill Sisters. (See BOWERY BOYS series, Index.)

p, Sam Katzman, Jack Dietz; d, William Beaudine; w, William X. Crowley, Beryl Sachs (based on a story by Ande Lamb); ph, Marcel Le Picard; ed, Carl Pierson; md, Edward Kay; set d, Ernest Hickerson.

Comedy   **(PR:A   MPAA:NR)**

FOLLOW THE SUN**½   (1951) 93m FOX bw

Glenn Ford (Ben Hogan), Anne Baxter (Valerie Hogan), Dennis O'Keefe (Chuck Williams), June Havoc (Norma), Larry Keating (Jay Dexter), Roland Winters (Dr. Graham), Nana Bryant (Sister Beatrice), Sam Snead (Himself), James Demaret (Himself), Dr. Cary Middlecoff (Himself), Harold Blake (Ben Hogan, Age 14), Ann Burr (Valerie, Age 14), Harmon Stevens (Mr. Johnson), Louise Lorimer (Mrs. Clinton), Harry Antrim (Dr. Everett), Jeffrey Sayre (Photographer), Homer Welborne (Announcer), D. Scotty Chisholm (Official), William Janssen (Major), William Forrest (General), Eugene Gericke (Orderly), Gil Herman (Sportswriter), Jewel Rose (Nurse), Jim Pierce (Proprietor), Beverlee White (Gertrude), Emmett Vogan (Temporary Chairman), Grantland Rice (Toastmaster), James Flavin (Henry Gibbs), Myrtle Anderson (Grace), Esther Somers (Mrs. Edwards), Al Demaret (Golf Pro), Lester Dorr (Attendant), John Trebach (Waiter), Warren Stevens (Radio Announcer), William Walker (Golf Club Waiter).

If you like golf, you'll enjoy this story of one of the game's great players. If not, it's a pleasant biography of a man who recovered from an auto accident, then courageously resumed his career. Ford is deeply in love with wife Baxter and is doing quite well on the pro tour until the near-fatal crash. The rest of the film deals with his recovery, culminating in a great tournament victory over Sammy Snead, who plays himself. Author Brennan adapted his own magazine article for the screenplay and showed great sensitivity, and Ford does a fine job in a revealing portrayal of Hogan.

p, Samuel G. Engel; d, Sidney Lanfield; w, Frederick Hazlitt Brennan (based on his article in Reader's Digest); ph, Leo Tover; m, Cyril J. Mockridge; ed, Barbara McLean; md, Lionel Newman; art d, Lyle Wheeler, Richard Irvine.

Biography/Drama   **(PR:A   MPAA:NR)**

FOLLOW THE HUNTER   (SEE: FANGS OF THE WILD, 1954)

FOLLOW THRU**½   (1930) 93m PAR c

Charles Rogers (Jerry Downs), Nancy Carroll (Lora Moore), Zelma O'Neal (Angie Howard), Jack Haley (Jack Martin), Eugene Pallette (J.C. Effingham), Thelma Todd (Ruth Van Horn), Claude King (Mac Moore), Kathryn Givney (Mrs. Bascomb), Margaret Lee (Babs Bascomb), Don Tomkins (Dinty Moore), Albert Gran (Martin Bascomb).

Photographed in vivid two-color Technicolor, this early musical takes place on the golf course. Challenging Todd to 18 holes, Carroll performs as well swinging a club as she does singing a tune. Haley, in his film debut, recreates his Broadway role as a timid millionaire. Songs include: "A Peach Of A Pair" (George Marion, Jr., Richard A. Whiting), "It Must Be You" (Edward Eliscu, Manning Sherwin), "You Wouldn't Fool Me, Would You?," "Button Up Your Overcoat," "I Want to Be Bad" (Lew Brown, Buddy DeSylva, Ray Henderson), "I'm Hard To Please" (Richard Rodgers, Lorenz Hart).

p, Laurence Schwab, Frank Mandel; d&w, Schwab, Lloyd Corrigan (based on the play by Schwab, Buddy DeSylva, Ray Henderson, Lew Brown); ph, Charles B. Boyle, Henry Gerrard (2-color Technicolor); ed, Alyson Shasser; ch, Dave Bennett.

Musical   **(PR:A   MPAA:NR)**

FOLLOW YOUR HEART**   (1936) 82m REP bw

Marion Talley (Marian Forrester), Michael Bartlett (Michael Williams), Nigel Bruce (Henri Forrester), Luis Alberni (Tony), Henrietta Crosman (Madame Bovard), Vivienne Osborne (Gloria), Walter Catlett (Shelton), Eunice Healy (Specialty Dancer), John Eldredge (Harrison Beecher), Clarence Muse (Choir Leader), Ben Blue (Himself), Mickey Rentschler (Tommy Forrester), Si Jenks (Mr. Hawks), Margaret Irving (Louise), Josephine Whittell (Mrs. Plunkett), Hall Johnson Choir.

Opera star Marion Talley, in her only film appearance, is a young vocalist who is unsure about whether she should follow in the footsteps of her operatic mother. Full of music, both popular and classical: the sextet from "Lucia Di Lammermoor," Gaetano Donizetti; the "Page Song" from "Les Huguenots," Giacomo Meyerbeer; "Mignon," Ambroise Thomas; "Magnolias In The Moonlight," "Who Minds About Me?" Walter Bullock, Victor Schertzinger; "Follow Your Heart" (Sidney Mitchell, Schertzinger).

p, Nat Levine; d, Aubrey Scotto; w, Nathanael West, Lester Cole, Samuel Ornitz, Olive Cooper (based on an idea by Dana Burnet); ph, John Mescall, Allyn C. Jones; ed, Ernest Nims, Robert Simpson; md, Dr. Hugo Riesenfeld; ch, Larry Ceballos.

Musical   **(PR:A   MPAA:NR)**

FOLLOW YOUR STAR**½   (1938, Brit.) 80m Belgrave/GFD bw

Arthur Tracy (Arthur Tee), Belle Chrystall (Mary), Mark Daly (Shorty), Horace Hodges (Mr. Wilmot), Nina Boucicault (Mrs. Tee), James Harcourt (Mr. Tee), Dick Tubb (Freddy), Finlay Currie (Maxie).

Tracy gives up his factory job to become a singer and after a series of disappointments he becomes a big star. Sentimental and cliche-ridden, but Tracy's singing wins the day.

p, Harcourt Templeman; d, Sinclair Hill; w, George Pearson, Stafford Dickens (based on a story by Hill, Arthur Tracy); ph, Cyril Bristow.

Musical   **(PR:A   MPAA:NR)**

FOLLY TO BE WISE***   (1953) 91m LFP/FA bw

Alastair Sim (Capt. Paris), Roland Culver (George Prout), Elizabeth Allan (Angela Prout), Martita Hunt (Lady Dodds), Miles Malleson (Dr. Hector McAdam), Colin Gordon (Prof. James Mutch), Edward Chapman (Joseph Byres), Janet Brown (Pvt. Jessie Killigrew), Peter Martyn (Walter), Robin Bailey (Intellectual), Clement McCallin (Colonel), Michael Ripper (Corporal), Leslie Weston (Landlord), Michael Kelly (Staff Sergeant), George Hurst (Bus Conductor), Cyril Chamberlain (Drill Sergeant), George Cole (Private), Jo Powell, Catherine Finn, Enid McCall, Ann Varley (WRACs), Myrette Morven (WRAC Officer), Harold Lang, Martin Boddey.

Above-average comedy that stars the very funny Sim as an army chaplain who tries to organize entertainment for the troops. Tedious at points but worth sifting through.

p, Frank Launder, Sidney Gilliatt; d, Launder; w, Launder, John Dighton (based on the play "It Depends What You Mean" by James Bridie); ph, Jack Hildyard; m, Temple Abady; ed, Thelma Connell; md, Ryalton Kisch; prod d, Arthur Lawson; cos, Anna Duse.

Comedy   **(PR:A   MPAA:NR)**

FOND MEMORIES***   (1982, Can.) 113m National Film Board c

Monique Spaziani (Marie), Julie Vincent (Viviane), R.H. Thomson (Rick), Paul Hebert (Papa), Michel Daigle (Le Gerant), Melanie Daigle (Marie, as a Child), Isabelle Perez (Viviane, as a Child), Georges Delisle (Pharmacist), Mickey Roy (Dancer).

An emotional family struggle begins when a long departed sister returns to her displeased father and younger sister, Spaziani, who uses her father's favoritism against older sis, Vincent. The crafty Spaziani next causes Vincent's boy friend to leave, causing her confused sibling to enter a deep depression. A provoking character study from perceptive Canadian director Mankiewicz.

p, Jean Dansereau, Pierre Lamy; d, Francis Mankiewicz; w, Rejean Ducharme; ph, George Dufaux; m, Jean Cousineau; ed, Andre Corriveau; art d, Normand Sarrazin.

Drama   **(PR:C   MPAA:NR)**

FOOD OF THE GODS, THE zero   (1976) 88m AIP c

Marjoe Gortner (Morgan), Pamela Franklin (Lorna), Ralph Meeker (Bensington), Ida Lupino (Mrs. Skinner), John Cypher (Brian), Belinda Balaski (Rita), Tom Stovall (Tom), John McLiam (Mr. Skinner).

An ambrosia-like substance known as F.O.I.G. (Food Of The Gods) is discovered on a remote island inhabited with giant chickens, wasps, rats, and worms. Preyed upon are island dwellers Lupino and husband McLiam, as well as Gortner, a football player, and his friend Cypher. It's up to Gortner to save the day and do battle with these over-sized foes. Also thrown into the plot is Meeker, a greedy businessman who hopes to market the strange food. Performances are weak all around, and Gordon hits a nadir in his cinematic vision of irregularly sized creatures. Gordon's other films from the late 1950s (THE AMAZING COLOSSAL MAN and ATTACK OF THE PUPPET PEOPLE), although concerned with size, were not much better. Gortner is simply terrible. Actually this is a remake of a film Gordon made some years back titled VILLAGE OF THE GIANTS. Save yourself the trouble, don't even bother looking in the other volume for VILLAGE. It doesn't rate any higher than this pic.

p&d, Bert I. Gordon; w, Gordon (based on part of the novel by H.G. Wells); ph, Reginald Morris (Movielab Color); m, Elliot Kaplan; ed, Corky Ehlers; art d, Graeme Murray; set d, John Stark; spec eff, Tom Fisher, John Thomas, Keith Wardlow, Rick Baker.

Fantasy   Cas.   (PR:O   MPAA:PG)

FOOL AND THE PRINCESS, THE**½   (1948, Brit.) 72m
Merton Park/GFD bw

Bruce Lester (Harry Granville), Lesley Brook (Kate Granville), Adina Mandlova (Moura), Irene Handl (Mrs. Wicker), Murray Matheson (Graham Ballard), MacDonald Parke (Wingfield), Vi Kaley (Mrs. Jenkins), Millicent Russell, Sylvia Harker, Gordon Phillott, Julian Henry, Paul Erikson, Richard Nelson.

Returning home to wife Brook after the war, Lester cannot get Mandlova, a displaced person who claims to be a Russian princess, out of his mind. He leaves Brook to search for her, but when he finds her he realizes she isn't what she claims, and he soon returns home to his wife. Good performances highlight this pleasing romantic comedy.

p, Frank Hoare; d&w, William C. Hammond (based on the novel by Stephen Spender); ph, A.T. Dinsdale.

Comedy/Romance   (PR:A   MPAA:NR)

FOOL KILLER, THE**   (1965) 100m Landau/AA bw
(AKA: VIOLENT JOURNEY)

Anthony Perkins (Milo Bogardus), Edward Albert (George Mellish), Dana Elcar (Mr. Dodd), Henry Hull (Dirty Jim Jelliman), Salome Jens (Mrs. Dodd), Charlotte Jones (Mrs. Ova Fanshawe), Arnold Moss (Rev. Spotts), Sindee Anne Richards (Blessing Angelina), Frances Gaar (Old Crab), Wendell Phillips (Old Man).

After the Civil War, a 12-year-old orphan played by Albert (the son of actors Eddie Albert and Margo, in his film debut) sets out on a journey and meets a crotchety old farmer. The superbly cast Hull tells the youngster the tale of "the fool killer," an axe-murderer who rids the world of its fools. The boy continues his adventures until he comes across Perkins, type-cast as a controlled psychotic, who fascinates and befriends Albert. Together they attend a church revival, but the disturbed anti-religious Perkins leaves. Later the axed body of the preacher is discovered. Naturally, the boy suspects Perkins, who begins to fit the "fool killer" description. After the boy is taken in by a kindly couple, their lives are threatened by enraged Perkins. Albert pleas for their safety, and the finale comes as the killer takes a fatal fall from their roof. Perkins excels again as the cinema's most convincing psycho. Interesting photography makes ample use of close-ups coupled with beautiful panoramics, which punctuate this off-beat portrait of Americana. There is some discrepancy in crediting the editor, and in 1969 Jack Dreyfus, Jr. purchased the rights, re-edited, and rereleased the film.

p, David Friedkin; d, Servando Gonzalez; w, Friedkin, Morton Fine (based on the novel by Helen Eustis); ph, Alex Phillips, Jr.; m, Gustavo Cesar Carreon; ed, Joan Jose Marino, Ralph Rosenblum; prod d, Robert Smith; art d, Rudy Sternad; cos, Dorothy Jeakins; m/l, "The Ballad of the Fool Killer," Mike Phillips, Tillman Franks (sung by David Houston).

Drama   (PR:O   MPAA:NR)

FOOLIN' AROUND**   (1980) 111m COL c

Gary Busey (Wes), Annette O'Toole (Susan), John Calvin (Whitley), Eddie Albert (Daggett), Cloris Leachman (Samantha), Tony Randall (Peddicord), Michael Talbott (Clay), Shirley Kane (Aunt Eunice), W. H. Macy (Bronski), Beth Bosacker (Rickie), Roy Jenson (Blue), Gene Lebell (Paul).

Gary Busey (BUDDY HOLLY STORY, CARNIE) and Annette O'Toole (CAT PEOPLE) try their best with this trite, uneven script. Busey lays on the charm to win over rich girl O'Toole in this throwback to the screwball comedies of the 1930s. It's romantic attempts are constantly undermined by the inadequate supporting cast. Worthwhile only for the lead performances.

p, Arnold Kopelson; d, Richard T. Heffron; w, Mike Kane, David Swift (based on the story by Swift); ph, Philip Lathrop (DeLuxe Color); m, Charles Bernstein; ed, Peter Zinner; prod d, Fernando Carrere; set d, Darrell Silvera; cos, Joe Tompkins; m/l, Bernstein, Jim Seals.

Romantic Comedy   Cas.   (PR:C   MPAA:PG)

FOOLISH HUSBANDS*½   (1948, Fr.) 99m DIF/Siritzky International bw

Fernand Gravet (Gerard Barbier), Micheline Presle (Adelaide Barbier), Marie Dea (Helene Donaldo), Pierre Renoir (Jules Donaldo), Bernard Lancret (Jean-Louis Deshayes), Gilbert Gil (Achille Ballarson).

A talky French comedy about a married couple experimenting with various infidelities, none of which pan out. In the end marriage is better than a series of meaningless affairs. (In French; English subtitles.)

d, Marcel L'Herbier; w, Armand Salacrou (based on his play "Histoire de Rire").

Comedy   (PR:C   MPAA:NR)

FOOLS*   (1970) 93m Translor/Cinerama c

Jason Robards, Jr. (Matthew South), Katharine Ross (Anais Appleton), Scott Hylands (David Appleton), Roy C. Jensen, Mark Bramhall (Men in Park), Marc Hannibal (Dog Owner), Robert C. Ferro, Jr. (Private Detective), Floy Dean, Roy Jelliffe (Couple in Restaurant), Charles B. Dorsett (Dentist), Laura Ash (Patient), Robert Rothwell, Michael Davis (Policemen), Vera Stough (Girl in Movie), James Burr Johnson, Louis Picetti, Jr., Stuart P. Klitsner (FBI Men), Robin Menken, Christopher Pray, Jack Nance (Hippies), Mako (Psychiatrist), Mimi Farina, Rod Arrants.

Robards, a middle-aged ex-horror film star, has had enough of Hollywood—so he moves to San Francisco. There he stumbles on Ross, runaway wife of lawyer Hylands, and the two fall profoundly in love. When the husband sends a detective to pry into their affairs, Ross decides it's time to confront him. She meets Hylands to explain her predicament, but he later shoots her when she tries to ignore him. The cast is misguided and their performances, under Gries' direction, appear unmotivated. Kenny Rogers and the First Edition sing the treacherously "hip" song "Someone Who Cares" (Alex Harvey), and "A Poem I Wrote For Your Hair" (Paul Parrish). Other songs include: "If You Love" (Mimi Farina) sung by Ross, Farina. This film is along the same line as PETULIA and just as bad.

p, Henri Bollinger, Robert H. Yamin; d, Tom Gries; w, Robert Rudelson; ph, Michel Hugo (Eastmancolor); m, Shorty Rogers; ed, Byron Brandt; set d, Louis H. Yates, James T. Mansen.

Drama   (PR:O   MPAA:GP)

FOOLS FOR SCANDAL**   (1938) 81m WB bw

Carole Lombard (Kay Winters), Fernand Gravet (Rene), Ralph Bellamy (Phillip Chester), Allen Jenkins (Dewey Gibson), Isabel Jeans (Lady Paula Malverton), Marie Wilson (Myrtle), Marcia Ralston (Jill), Ottola Nesmith (Agnes), Heather Thatcher (Lady Potter-Porter), Jacques Lory (Papa Joli-Coeur), Tempe Piggott (Bessie), Michellette Burani (Mme. Brioche), Jeni LeGon (Specialty), Albert Petit, Andre Marsaudon (Gendarmes), Three Brown Sisters (Themselves), Elizabeth Dunne, Sarah Edwards (Tourists), Lionel Pape (Photographer), Michael Romanoff, Leon Lasky, Lotus Thompson, Hugh Huntley, Stephani Insull, Tina Smirnova (Party Guests), Rosella Towne (Diana), Elspeth Dudgeon (Cynthia), Lorraine Eddy MacLean (Valerie), Jean Benedict (Evelyn), Norma Varden (Cicely), Ara Gerald (Mrs. Bullit), Leyland Hodgson (Mr. Bullit), John Sutton (Bruce Devon).

A disappointing attempt at comedy in the MY MAN GODFREY genre. Lombard is a famous American film star visiting Paris and sauntering through Montmartre when she meets Gravet, an extremely poor French marquis who is all title and no money. They don't know a thing about each other but have a lovely afternoon, ride in a taxi, and sup together late that night at one of Paris' more soigne boites. She returns to London and Gravet, following her there, gains access to a party she's giving with the theme of Noah's Ark. Pulling his leg, she offers him a job in her household as a servant, and he surprisingly accepts! Gravet proves to be a good butler and cook and now spends his time in keeping Lombard from marrying insurance man Ralph Bellamy. A love affair springs up between them and the conclusion is foregone. Rogers and Hart wrote a number of songs for the movie but most were left on the cutting room floor. The surviving songs are: "There's a Boy In Harlem" and "How Can You Forget?" Bellamy is the only true comedy in the picture. Gravet is boring and even the radiant Lombard leaves much to be desired. In the party scene, you may catch sight of one of Hollywood's greatest characters, the legendary Mike Romanoff, restaurateur to the stars. Romanoff's real name was Harry Gerguson and everyone knew he was a fraud, but he was such a charming boondoggler that nobody in the Hollywood of the 1930s, 1940s, and 1950s cared. After the Rodeo Drive restaurant finally went under, Romanoff attached himself to some of his celebrity buddies and can be seen in later years in a few of Sinatra's pictures, most notably TONY ROME.

p&d, Mervyn LeRoy; w, Herbert and Joseph Fields, Irving Brecher (based on the play "Return Engagement" by Nancy Hamilton, James Shute, Rosemary Casey); ph, Ted Tetzlaff; ed, William Holmes; md, Leo F. Forbstein; art d, Anton Grot; cos, Milo Anderson, Travis Banton; "Le Petite Harlem" sequence directed by Bobby Connolly; m/l, Richard Rodgers, Lorenz Hart.

Comedy   (PR:A   MPAA:NR)

FOOL'S GOLD**   (1946) 63m UA bw

William Boyd (Hopalong Cassidy), Andy Clyde (California Carlson), Rand Brooks (Lucky Jenkins), Robert Emmett Keane (Professor Dixon), Jane Randolph (Jessie Dixon), Stephan Barclay (Bruce Landy), Harry Cording (Duke), Earle Hodgins (Sandler), Bob Bentley (Barton), William "Wee Willie" Davis (Blackie), Forbes Murray (Col. Jed Landy), Glen B. Gallagher (Lieutenant Anderson), Ben Corbett (Sergeant), Fred "Snowflake" Toones (Speed).

Boyd, as Hopalong Cassidy, saves his Army friend's son from a life of crime and breaks up the outlaw gang the boy nearly joined. This second film in a new Hopalong Cassidy series is replete with spectacular outdoor scenery, and the supporting cast is enjoyable to watch. (See HOPALONG CASSIDY Series, Index.)

p, Lewis J. Rachmil; d, George Archainbaud; w, Doris Schroeder (based on characters created by Clarence E. Mulford); ph, Mack Stengler; m, David Chudnow; ed, Fred W. Berger; art d, Harvey T. Gillett.

Western   (PR:A   MPAA:NR)

FOOLS OF DESIRE* (1941) 55m CD bw

Byron Foulger (Wilbur Crane), Constance Bergen (Dorothy), Betty Roadman (Martha), Lynton Brent (Danny).

An unambitious study of the unfaithful husband. When husband Foulger is steadily scorned by his wife, he finds a blonde companion. The sets for this film appear to have been neglected, along with the cast. Foulger's performance is the only item deserving of merit.

d&w, Bernard Ray; md, Modest Altschuler.

Drama (PR:C MPAA:NR)

FOOLS' PARADE*** (1971) 97m COL c
(GB: DYNAMITE MAN FROM GLORY JAIL)

James Stewart (Mattie Appleyard), George Kennedy (Doc Council), Anne Baxter (Cleo), Strother Martin (Lee Cottrill), Kurt Russell (Johnny Jesus), William Windom (Roy K. Sizemore), Mike Kellin (Steve Mystic), Kathy Cannon (Chanty), Morgan Paull (Junior Kilfong), Robert Donner (Willis Hubbard), David Huddleston (Homer Grindstaff), Dort Clark (Enoch Purdy), James Lee Barrett (Sonny Boy), Kitty Jefferson Doepken (Clara), Dwight McConnell (Station Master), Richard Carl (Police Chief), Arthur Cain (Prosecuting Attorney), Paul Merriman (Fireman), Walter Dove (Engineer), Peter Miller (Trusty), George Metro (Train Dispatcher), Suzann Stoehr (Bank Teller), John Edwards (Bank Clerk).

Stewart, along with Martin and Russell, have just been released from prison. Stewart, having worked the mines during his 40-year stint, has saved $25,000, with which the three ex-convicts now plan to open a store. But the money is in check form and can only be cashed in the town of Glory, where Stewart and his friends are not allowed. To complicate matters, the bank president is more than a shade dishonest and he hires Kennedy to eliminate Stewart, which would leave him in possession of the money. Romance enters the picture when the three "good" ex-convicts take refuge in a bordello. Eventually they secure Stewart's money and expose the evil banker. This was Stewart's 75th film, based on Davis Grubb's sentimental but solid novel; it was the many directioned Grubb who also wrote one of the great thrillers, "Night of the Hunter," converted into a masterpiece film noir by actor Charles Laughton in his only directorial bow. Stewart is superb as the tough old ex-con replete with a removable glass eye and so, too, is Baxter, in a scant part as a floozy, who plays it for laughs and gets them with lines like: "We've been puttin' out for soldiers since 1776 but the DAR won't let me in."

p&d, Andrew V. McLaglen; w, James Lee Barrett (based on the novel by Davis Grubb); ph, Harry Stradling, Jr. (Eastmancolor); m, Henry Vars; ed, David Bretherton, Robert Simpson; art d, Alfred Sweeney; set d, Marvin March; cos, Guy C. Verhille; makeup, Frank Westmore, Hank Edds; spec eff, Charles Gaspar.

Western (PR:C MPAA:GP)

FOOLS RUSH IN* (1949, Brit.) 82m
RANK-Pinewood/GFD bw

Sally Ann Howes (Pamela Dickson), Guy Rolfe (Paul Dickson), Nora Swinburne (Angela Dickson), Nigel Buchanan (Joe Trent), Raymond Lovell (Sir Charles Leigh), Thora Hird (Mrs. Coot), Patricia Raine (Millicent), Nora Nicholson (Mrs. Mandrake), Peter Hammond (Tommy), Charles Victor (Mr. Atkins), Esma Cannon (Mrs. Atkins), Guy Verney, Jonathan Field, David Lines, George Mansfield.

A prosaic movie about a girl who backs out of her wedding-day ceremony when her long-missing dad returns. She convinces her mother to remarry the wayward man and finally goes through with her own nuptials. A redundant film which only fools would rush in to see.

p, Aubrey Baring; d, John Paddy Carstairs; w, Geoffrey Kerr (based on a play by Kenneth Horne); ph, Geoffrey Unsworth, Oswald Morris; m, Wilfred Burns; ed, George Clark.

Comedy (PR:A MPAA:NR)

FOOTLIGHT FEVER*½ (1941) 69m RKO bw

Alan Mowbray (Avery), Donald McBride (Crandall), Elisabeth Risdon (Hattie), Lee Bonnell (Carter), Elyse Knox (Eileen), Charles Quigley (Spike), Bradley Page (Harvey), Chester Clute (Holly), Jane Patten (Miss Hughes), Georgia Backus (Imogene).

Mowbray and McBride are hopelessly cast in an old story which, if it were any moldier, would crawl away. The two are trying to raise enough money to put on a show, and are tipped off to a financial source. To get the cash they end up impersonating long-lost pals of a rich woman's childhood sweetheart. A poor follow-up to the livelier CURTAIN CALL. This B-budget flop still managed to lose $40,000.

p, Howard Benedict; d, Irving Reis; w, Ian McLellan Hunter, Bert Granet (based on a story by Granet); ph, Robert de Grasse; ed, Theron Warth.

Comedy (PR:A MPAA:NR)

FOOTLIGHT GLAMOUR** (1943) 68m COL bw

Penny Singleton (Blondie Bumstead), Arthur Lake (Dagwood Bumstead), Larry Simms (Alexander Bumstead), Ann Savage (Vicki Wheeler), Jonathan Hale (J.C. Dithers), Irving Bacon (Mr. Crum), Marjorie Ann Mutchie (Cookie Bumstead), Danny Mummert (Alvin Fuddle), Thurston Hall (Randolph Wheeler), Grace Hayle (Mrs. Cora Dithers), Rafael Storm (Jerry Grant), Arthur Loft (Mr. Clark), James Flavin (Father), Daisy the Dog.

A rich tool manufacturer hires Dagwood (Lake) for the operation of a new plant opening nearby. Blondie throws a wrench into the plans when she casts the manufacturer's daughter in a play against his better wishes. Songs by Ray Evans and Jay Livingston include "What's Under Your Mask, Madame?," "Bamboola." (See BLONDIE series, Index.)

p&d, Frank R. Strayer; w, Karen DeWolfe, Connie Lee (based on the comic strip "Blondie" by Chic Young); ph, Philip Tannura; ed, Richard Fantl; md, M.W. Stoloff; art d, Lionel Banks.

Comedy (PR:A MPAA:NR)

FOOTLIGHT PARADE**** (1933) 102m WB bw

James Cagney (Chester Kent), Joan Blondell (Nan Prescott), Ruby Keeler (Bea Thorn), Dick Powell (Scotty Blair), Guy Kibbee (Silas Gould), Ruth Donnelly (Harriet Bowers Gould), Claire Dodd (Vivian Rich), Hugh Herbert (Charlie Bowers), Frank McHugh (Francis), Arthur Hohl (Al Frazer), Gordon Westcott (Harry Thompson), Renee Whitney (Cynthia Kent), Philip Faversham (Joe Farrington), Juliet Ware (Miss Smythe), Herman Bing (Fralick, the Music Director), Paul Porcasi (George Appolinaris), William Granger (Doorman), Charles C. Wilson (Cop), Barbara Rogers (Gracie), Billy Taft (Specialty Dancer), Marjean Rogers, Pat Wing, Donna La Barr, Marlo Dwyer, Donna Mae Roberts (Chorus Girls), Dave O'Brien (Chorus Boy), George Chandler (Drugstore Attendant), Hobart Cavanaugh (Title Thinker Upper), William V. Mong (Auditor), Lee Moran (Mac, the Dance Director), Billy Barty (Mouse in "Sittin' on a Backyard Fence" Number/Little Boy in "Honeymoon Hotel" Number), Harry Seymour (Joe, the Assistant Director/Desk Clerk in "Honeymoon Hotel" Number), Sam McDaniel (Porter), Fred Kelsey (Hotel Detective), Jimmy Conlin (Uncle), Roger Gray (Sailor-Pal in "Shanghai Lil" Number), John Garfield (Sailor behind Table in "Shanghai Lil" Number), Duke York (Sailor on Table in "Shanghai Lil" Number).

Following the success Warner Brothers had with its blockbusting musicals, 42nd STREET and GOLD DIGGERS OF 1933, the studio launched this lavish production with the dynamic Cagney in the lead. He is a producer of live theatrical entertainment who suddenly finds himself unemployed. His backers, Kibbee and Hohl, think that live theater is finished now that talking films have arrived. Doggedly, Cagney inventively comes up with the idea of doing "prologues," short but stunning musical numbers designed to precede the showing of feature films. Two-thirds of the movie deals with Cagney's behind-the-scenes machinations in putting together these prologues, haggling for backing, exhaustively recruiting and rehearsing armies of singers and dancers, a tough backstage view of Broadway operators, ingenues, and star talent where only the strongest survive. The third part of FOOTLIGHT PARADE provides an astounding array of mass singers and dancers in three Busby Berkeley numbers that have since become movie classics. The first, "Honeymoon Hotel," (Harry Warren, Al Dubin) shows Powell and Keeler arriving at a resort where they are married and then try to get rid of an army of well-wishing relatives so they can enjoy their nuptial night, but, during the hectic routines designed by the inventive Berkeley, the famous Hollywood dwarf, Barty, lingers behind, peeking at the shy couple as they prepare to retire. This number ends on a humorous note with little Barty, not Keeler, winding up in bed with Powell! Next is the mammoth "By A Waterfall" number (Sammy Fain, Irving Kahal), a dazzling 15-minute spectacle featuring more than 100 bathing-suit-clad chorines (more on the leggy-beefy side than would be acceptable by today's standards of feminine pulchritude, the tall and the lean). They splash about in a giant aquacade in kaleidoscopic formations captured by the overhead and long-range shots that were Berkeley's hallmarks. The idea for this number is gotten by Cagney as he is cab-riding along a Manhattan street and sees a group of black children playing in the spray of an open fire hydrant. Yells Cagney, in what a later era would term a racial slur: "That's what the prologue needs! A waterfall splashing on beautiful white bodies!" Powell and Keeler get into this number when they go on a picnic; he falls asleep and she doffs her clothes to reveal a bathing suit, emerging with scores of similarly clad ladies to dive into a giant pool to perform their precision-perfect aquatic routines, which Berkeley photographed above and below the surface. The impressive number ends when Keeler awakens Powell by splashing his face with water. Cagney himself proves his great talent as a hoofer in the final number, "Shanghai Lil" (Warren and Dubin). He is a sailor in search of an Oriental whore who obsesses him. He enters a sprawling, smoke-filled bar peopled by prostitutes, sailors, wharf bums, and cutthroats. He finds her, Keeler (dressed in a white silk outfit, wearing a black wig with huge buns on either side of her head like giant earmuffs), and goes into a wild tap dance on top of tables and bar, with Keeler joining him. (Cagney is the much superior dancer here, making Keeler look as if she is laboring to keep up with him, and her old habit of having to look at her moving feet, as if to check if they are still there, is in evidence. Also, Cagney's voice is more appealing than hers in singing the "Shanghai Lil" tune; it's melodious and on key, where hers is little more than an off-pitch whine.) This number, replete with sailors drill-marching to martial music, reminiscent of the "My Forgotten Man" routine in GOLD DIGGERS OF 1933 ends when a bugle calls, signaling a return-to-ship order. A brawl, however, ensues, and the waterfront dive is destroyed by battling sailors and thugs. (One of the sailors, seen for ten seconds as he peers over a barrel to see if all is clear, is a very young John Garfield, who appeared in the movie as a lark while seeking a film career that would not resume until Broadway success returned him to Hollywood in 1938.) The film, well directed by Bacon, is an enormous skyrocket that explodes into musical and visual fantasy which was seldom equalled. Other songs include "Ah, The Moon Is Here," and "Sitting On A Backyard Fence" (Fain, Kahal). Cagney really carries this film and, for many years, it was his favorite among musicals, although he later believed the film dated with age. He had to argue Jack Warner into giving him the part, pleading that he had song-and-dance talent reaching beyond the tough-guy gangster roles established after PUBLIC ENEMY (1931). The studio agreed after seeing the non-musical Clark Gable appear in an MGM musical, DANCING LADY (1933), the same film offering in a small role a brand new dancing talent, Fred Astaire. Warners Bros. surrounded Cagney with beautiful women in the film, three featured players being Blondell, his protective secretary (Blondell married the film's cinematographer, Barnes, just before the production got under way), Whitney, an ex-wife bleeding his bank account from one end, and Dodd, a gold digger draining it from the other. In addition, hundreds of chorines bobbed in his tap-dancing wake as he instructed them in their routines; two of the chorus girls in the dancing groups are Dorothy Lamour and Ann

Sothern, both then unknown. Berkeley was delighted with Cagney's dancing, later commenting: "He could learn whatever you gave him very quickly. You could count on him to be prepared. And expert mimic that he was, he could pick up the most subtle inflections of movement. It made his work very exciting." Keeler was a different story. Her film career was begun through Al Jolson, whom she later married, and Jack Warner, who gave her a hefty contract. Keeler left Warner Bros. in 1937 at Jolson's suggestion over a contract dispute; Jolson had a bitter argument with Jack Warner which resulted with Keeler leaving the only Hollywood studio that wanted her. This loss caused Keeler to divorce Jolson in 1938 and she remained so embittered about the blackfaced jazz singer that she refused to allow her name to be used when THE JOLSON STORY was made by Columbia in 1949. This was the third time Keeler was paired with Powell, the pair having done 42ND STREET and GOLD DIGGERS OF 1933 together. As for Cagney and Blondell, who had appeared on Broadway together at the onset of their careers in "Penny Arcade," among other stage hits, this p, Darryl F. Zanuck; d, Lloyd Bacon, William Keighley, Busby Berkeley; w, Manuel Seff, James Seymour; ph, George Barnes; ed, George Amy; md, Leo F. Forbstein; art d, Anton Grot; cos, Milo Anderson; ch, Busby Berkeley; m/l, Harry Warren, Al Dubin, Sammy Fain, Irving Kahal; makeup, Perc Westmore.

Musical   **Cas.**   **(PR:A   MPAA:NR)**

FOOTLIGHT SERENADE**½   (1942) 81m FOX bw

John Payne (Bill Smith), Betty Grable (Pat Lambert), Victor Mature (Tommy Lundy), Jane Wyman (Flo LaVerne), James Gleason (Bruce McKay), Phil Silvers (Slap), Cobina Wright, Jr. (Estelle Evans), June Lang (June), Frank Orth (Doorman), Mantan Moreland (Dresser), Irving Bacon (Porter), Charles Tannen (Stage Manager), George Dobbs (Dance Director), Sheila Ryan (Girl), Frank Coghlan, Jr. (Usher), Harry Barris (Composer), Trudy Marshall (Secretary), Don Wilson (Announcer), John Dilson (Clerk), William "Billy" Newell (Writer), Pat McKee (Pug), Wilbur Mack (Boxing Commissioner), George Holmes (Boy), Russ Clark, Frankie Van (Referees), Bud & Jim Mercer (Dance Specialty).

Boxer Mature lands a role in a Broadway play and quickly makes a move on dancer Grable, who is secretly married to another of the actors. Her husband, Payne, is not content to sit back and watch his wife be fawned over. As fate would have it, the play has Payne's character get in a brawl with Mature's. When it comes time to deliver the fake blow, Payne sends the boxer down for a 10-count. The cinematography by Garmes is striking, though the score is feeble. Musical numbers included are, "Are You Kidding?" "I'm Still Crazy About You," "I Hear The Birdies Sing," "Living High," "I'll Be Marching To A Love Song," "Land On Your Feet" (Ralph Rainger, Leo Robin), "I'm Stepping Out With A Memory Tonight" (Herb Magidson, Allie Wrubel).

p, William LeBaron; d, Gregory Ratoff; w, Robert Ellis, Helen Logan, Lynn Starling (based on the story "Dynamite" by Fidel LaBarba, Kenneth Earl); ph, Lee Garmes; ed, Robert Simpson; md, Charles Henderson; art d, Richard Day, Roger Hemen; ch, Hermes Pan.

Musical   **(PR:A   MPAA:NR)**

FOOTLIGHTS AND FOOLS*½   (1929) 70m FN-WB bw-c

Fredric March (Gregory Pyne), Colleen Moore (Betty Murphy/Fifi D'Auray), Raymond Hackett (Jimmy Willet), Virginia Lee Corbin (Claire Floyd), Mickey Bennett (Call Boy), Edward Martindell (Chandler Cunningham), Adrienne D'Ambricourt (Jo), Frederick Howard (Treasurer), Sidney Jarvis (Stage Manager), Cleve Moore (Press Agent), Andy Rice, Jr. (Song Plugger), Ben Hendricks, Jr. (Stage Doorman), Larry Banthim (Bud Burke), Earl Bartlett's Biltmore Trio.

Dim musical starring the barely talented Moore as a sweet and innocent performer sent to Paris by an ambitious Broadway producer to attain a "French" image. He brings her back as the hot and famous musical comedy star "Fifi D'Auray." She soon finds herself pursued by a young hoodlum, Hackett, and a wealthy admirer, March, both of whom have fallen in love with her. She opts for Hackett, but it is only a matter of time before she discovers his true nature after he admits to participating in a robbery of March's firm. In the end Moore is left alone, having lost both men. Some of the dance numbers were filmed in the old two-color Technicolor process that rendered the flesh-tones fairly red. Moore, who had been a reigning silent film star, tried desperately to establish herself in talkies with this one but her thin, unconvincing voice annoyed rather than endeared viewers. The musical numbers included: "If I Can't Have You," "You Can't Believe My Naughty Eyes," "Ophelia Will Fool You," "Pilly Pom Pom Plee" (Alfred Bryan and George W. Meyer).

p, John McCormick; d, William A. Seiter (dance sequences by Max Scheck); w, Katherine Brush, Carey Wilson, Tom Geraghty (based on a story by Brush); ph, Sidney Hickox, Henry Freulich; ch, Max Scheck.

Musical   **(PR:A   MPAA:NR)**

FOOTLOOSE HEIRESS, THE*½   (1937) 61m WB bw

Craig Reynolds (Bruce "Butch" Baeder), Ann Sheridan (Kay Allyn), Anne Nagel (Linda Pierson), William Hopper (Jack Pierson), Hugh O'Connell (John C. Allyn), Teddy Hart (Charlie McCarthy), Hal Neiman (Luke Peaneather), Frank Orth (Justice Abner Cuttler), William Eberhardt (Wilbur Frost), Lois Cheaney (Sarah Cuttler).

Sheridan is a society girl who must wed before midnight on her 18th birthday to win a $5,000 bet. She hooks up with Reynolds, a man below Sheridan's station. Nonetheless, father O'Connell takes a liking to the young man and effortlessly transforms him into a radio copy man. Wholly unbelievable, and a poorly made programmer.

p, Bryan Foy; d, William Clemens; w, Robertson White; ph, Arthur Edeson; ed, Lou Hesse.

Drama   **(PR:A   MPAA:NR)**

FOOTSTEPS IN THE DARK**½   (1941) 96m FN-WB bw

Errol Flynn (Francis Warren), Brenda Marshall (Rita Warren), Ralph Bellamy (Dr. Davis), Alan Hale (Inspector Mason), Lee Patrick (Blondie White), Allen Jenkins (Wilfred), Lucile Watson (Mrs. Archer), William Frawley (Hopkins), Roscoe Karns (Monahan), Grant Mitchell (Carruthers), Maris Wrixon (June Brewster), Noel Madison (Fissue), Jack LaRue (Ace Vernon), Turhan Bey (Ahmed), Frank Faylen (Gus), Garry Owen (Jackson), Sarah Edwards (Mrs. Belgarde), Frank Wilcox (Harrow), Olaf Hytten (Horace), Harry Hayden (Willis), John Dilson (Coroner), Creighton Hale (Harlan), Winifred Harris (Miss Perry), David Newell (June Brewster's Escort), William Hopper (Police Secretary), Sonny Boy Williams (Tommy), Betty Farrington (Mrs. Jenkins).

Flynn, in a delightful, non-historical role, is an amateur criminologist who earns his living as an investment counselor. At night, without wife Marshall knowing, he slips outside and plays sleuth, looking for crimes to solve so he can write some mysteries under his nom-de-plume, F. X. Pettijohn. While prowling about in the fog one night, Flynn encounters a jewel thief who is found dead the next day apparently of acute alcoholism. This appears to be murder to Flynn, who knows the man was a teetotaler, and he spends the rest of the film trying to prove his case. En route he meets a zany stripper (Patrick) while posing as a swaggering Texas cattleman. This further complicates his life when his wife and his mother, Watson, believe he is romantically involved with Patrick; they attend the burlesque house where she is performing to investigate. The police, headed by the obstreperous Hale, also involve Flynn in the death. He finally clears himself and solves the murder by pinpointing oral surgeon Bellamy as the villain. This was not one of Flynn's better films, a fault that can be attributed to a weak script that should have had more humor in it, given the capricious premise.

p, Robert Lord (for Hal B. Wallis); d, Lloyd Bacon, Hugh MacMullen; w, Lester Cole, John Wexley (based on the play "Blondie White" by Ladislaus Fodor, Bernard Merivale, Jeffrey Dell); ph, Ernest Haller; m, Frederick Hollander; ed, Owen Marks; art d, Max Parker; cos, Howard Shoup; spec eff, Rex Wimpy; ch, Robert Vreeland.

Comedy/Mystery   **(PR:A   MPAA:NR)**

FOOTSTEPS IN THE FOG***½ (1955, Brit.) 90m Film Locations/COL c

Stewart Granger (Stephen Lowry), Jean Simmons (Lily Watkins), Bill Travers (David MacDonald), Finlay Currie (Inspector Peters), Ronald Squire (Alfred Travers), Belinda Lee (Elizabeth Travers), William Hartnell (Herbert Moresby), Frederick Leister (Dr. Simpson), Percy Marmont (Magistrate), Margery Rhodes (Mrs. Park), Peter Bull (Brasher), Sheila Manahan (Rose Moresby), Norman Macowan (Grimes), Cameron Hall (Corcoran), Victor Maddern (Jones), Arthur Howard (Vicar), Barry Keegan (Constable Burke), Peter Williams (Constable Farrow).

In London at the beginning of the century, Granger murders his wife but is discovered by maid Simmons, who has always secretly loved him. She blackmails her way into the housekeeper position and Granger decides he has to kill her, too. Pursuing her in the fog he mistakes someone else for her and kills a stranger. Arrested and put on trial, Granger is saved from the gallows by testimony from Simmons, who tightens her grip on him. Granger hits upon a scheme to give himself small doses of poison and have Simmons charged with attempted murder, but he gives himself too much and dies. Simmons is arrested for murder. A well-acted but slow-moving movie, shot in lush Technicolor.

p, M. J. Frankovich, Maxwell Setton; d, Arthur Lubin; w, Dorothy Reid, Leonore Coffee, Arthur Pierson (based on the novel The Interruption by W. W. Jacobs); ph, Christopher Challis (Technicolor); ed, Alan Osbiston; md, Benjamin Frankel; art d, Wilfred Shingleton; cos, Beatrice Dawson, Elizabeth Haffenden.

Drama   **(PR:A   MPAA:NR)**

FOOTSTEPS IN THE NIGHT*½ (1932, Brit.) 59m Associated Talking Pictures/RKO bw (GB: A HONEYMOON ADVENTURE)

Benita Hume (Eve Martin), Harold Huth (Walter Creason), Peter Hannen (Peter Martin), Walter Armitage (Judson), Margery Binner (Josephine), Jack Lambert (Chauffeur), Pollie Emery (Old Woman), Robert English (Mr. Harvey), Frances Ross Campbell (Janet).

A churned-out piece of filler about an evildoer who kidnaps a scientist to nab his secret plans. The inventor's tough wife, however, gives the gang a run for its money.

p, Basil Dean; d, Maurice Elvey; w, Dean, Rupert Downing, John Paddy Carstairs (based on a novel by Cecily Fraser-Smith).

Crime   **(PR:A   MPAA:NR)**

FOOTSTEPS IN THE NIGHT**   (1957) 62m AA bw

Bill Elliott (Lt. Doyle), Don Haggerty (Sgt. Duncan), Eleanore Tanin (Mary Raiken), Douglas Dick (Henry Johnson), Robert Shayne (Fred Horner), James Flavin (Mr. Bradbury), Gregg Palmer (Pat Orvello), Harry Tyler (Dick Harris), Ann Griffith (June Wright), Zena Marshall.

Copper Elliott and Haggerty team up to locate the killer of a gambler, in this stock whodunit. As it turns out, the murderer is a local gas station worker. The producer's studio bungalow office was used as a set for much of the interior action, an interesting money-saving device.

p, Ben Schwalb; d, Jean Yarbrough; w, Albert Band, Elwood Ullman (based on a story by Band); ph, Harry Neumann; m, Marlin Skiles; ed, Neil Brunnenkant; art d, David Milton; cos, Bert Henrikson.

Crime   **(PR:A   MPAA:NR)**

FOR A DOLLAR IN THE TEETH
(SEE: STRANGER IN TOWN, A, 1968, Ital.)

FOR A FEW BULLETS MORE
(SEE: ANY GUN CAN PLAY, 1968, Ital./Span.)

FOR A FEW DOLLARS MORE***½   (1967, Ital./Ger./Span.) 130m
Produzione Europee-Arturo Gonzales-Constantin/UA c
(PER QUALCHE DOLLARO IN PIU)

Clint Eastwood (*The Man With No Name*), Lee Van Cleef (*Col. Douglas Mortimer*), Gian Maria Volonte (*Indio*), Jose Egger (*Old Man Over Railway*), Rosemary Dexter (*Colonel's Sister*), Mara Krup (*Hotel Manager's Wife*), Klaus Kinski (*Hunchback*), Mario Brega, Aldo Sambrell, Luigi Pistilli, Benito Stefanelli (*Indio's Gang*), Roberto Camardiel, Luis F. Rodriguez, Panos Papadopoulos, Diana Rabito, Giovanni Tarallo, Mario Meniconi, Lorenzo Robledo, Tomas Blanco, Werner Abrolat.

The second film in Leone's "Dollar" trilogy (THE GOOD, THE BAD, AND THE UGLY would follow) sees the Italian director in better form and in more control of his style than in A FISTFUL OF DOLLARS. FOR A FEW DOLLARS MORE has better scripting, superior production values, and more interesting characters who complement Eastwood's stoic Man With No Name. Eastwood returns as the mysterious drifter who is locked in a battle with rival bounty hunter Van Cleef to collect the reward for killing psychopathic bandit Volonte. At first the men attempt to capture the crook separately, with little success. The pair forms an uneasy alliance and Van Cleef eventually guns down Volonte in a climactic shootout as Eastwood watches from the sidelines. It turns out Van Cleef is not interested in the money, but revenge. Through a complex series of flashbacks (a structural device that Leone would use in ONCE UPON A TIME IN THE WEST and even more brilliantly in his gangster film ONCE UPON A TIME IN AMERICA) that pops up throughout the film, we see that Van Cleef's sister was raped and murdered by Volonte and it is not until the final moment of the showdown that this all becomes clear. Having had his revenge, Van Cleef rides off, leaving Eastwood with a cart filled with the corpses of Volonte and his men, which undoubtedly will net him another fistful of dollars. By introducing the Van Cleef character, Leone is able to counterpoint Eastwood's cold, amoral gunslinger with a man who has a past and a purpose. A more *human* character, with which the audience can more readily identify, makes Eastwood's character all the more mythical and unearthly. Once again, Ennio Morricone's musical score is a masterwork and he uses specific musical themes for each character. A tune from a musical pocket watch triggers the flashbacks that link Van Cleef and Volonte. In FOR A FEW DOLLARS MORE Leone's thematic concerns are more in focus. His view of the family as a civilizing, motivating force (Van Cleef is more *civilized* than Eastwood because of his family connections whereas Eastwood is never shown to have any), the church's hypocrisy (Van Cleef is first seen reading a Bible, Volonte's blasphemous use of a mission as a hideout, and holy water on his pistols), his sense of humor and the wild, unrelenting landscape where these men suddenly appear and just as suddenly vanish are all more detailed than before. In FOR A FEW DOLLARS MORE we are given the sense that Eastwood has been somewhat affected by Van Cleef, *humanized* a bit. This suspicion would be confirmed in the final part of the trilogy.
p, Alberto Grimaldi; d, Sergio Leone; w, Luciano Vincenzoni, Leone (based on a story by Leone and Fulvio Morsella); ph, Massimo Dallamano (Techniscope, Technicolor); m, Ennio Morricone; ed, Giorgio Ferralonga, Eugenio Alabiso; md, Bruno Nicolai; art d&cos, Carlo Simi.

Western   **Cas.**   **(PR:C   MPAA:NR)**

FOR A FISTFUL OF DOLLARS
(SEE: FISTFUL OF DOLLARS, A, 1964, Ital.)

FOR ATT INTE TALA OM ALLA DESSA KVINNOR
(SEE: ALL THESE WOMEN, 1964, Swed.)

FOR BEAUTY'S SAKE*½   (1941) 62m FOX bw

Ned Sparks (*Jonathan B. Sweet*), Marjorie Weaver (*Dime Pringle*), Ted North (*Bertram Erasmus Dillsome*), Joan Davis (*Dottie Nickerson*), Pierre Watkin (*Middlesex*), Lenita Lane (*Miss Sawter*), Richard Lane (*Mr. Jackman*), Lotus Long (*Ann Kuo*), Glenn Hunter (*Rodney Blynn*), Lois Wilson (*Mrs. Lloyd Kennar*), John Ellis (*Lloyd Kennar*), Tully Marshall (*Julius H. Pringle*), Phyllis Fraser (*Julia*), Olaf Hytten (*Fr. McKinley*), Isabel Jewell (*Amy Devore*), Nigel DeBrulier (*Brother*), Janet Beecher (*Miss Merton*), Helena Phillips Evans (*Mrs. Jellicoe*), Margaret Dumont (*Mrs. Franklin Evans*), Jean Brooks (*Operator*), Cyril Ring (*Hotel Clerk*), Ruth Warren (*Nurse*), Carl Faulkner (*Policeman*), Matt McHugh (*Taxi Driver*), Cliff Clark (*Lt. Dolman*), Ruth Gillette (*Fat Woman*).

A college professor finds himself out of his league when he learns he must run his aunt's beauty parlor to get his inheritance. Put this one under the dryer and forget about it.
p, Lucien Hubbard; d, Shepard Traube; w, Wanda Tuchock, Ethel Hill, Walter Bullock (based on a story by Clarence Buddington Kelland); ph, Charles Clarke; m, Emil Newman; ed, Nick DeMaggio; md, Newman.

Comedy   **(PR:A   MPAA:NR)**

FOR BETTER FOR WORSE***   (1954, Brit.) 84m Associated British-
Pathe-Kenwood/Stratford c
(AKA: COCKTAILS IN THE KITCHEN)

Dirk Bogarde (*Tony Howard*), Susan Stephen (*Anne Purves*), Cecil Parker (*Anne's Father*), Eileen Herlie (*Anne's Mother*), Athene Seyler (*Miss Mainbrace*), Pia Terri (*Mrs. Debenham*), Dennis Price (*Debenham*), James Hayter (*The Plumber*), Thora Hird (*Mrs. Doyle*), George Woodbridge (*Alf*), Charles Victor (*Fred*), Sidney James (*The Foreman*), Peter Jones (*The Dealer*), Robin Bailey (*The Salesman*), Digby Wolfe (*Grocer*), Edwin Styles (*Anne's Boss*), Edmund Hockridge (*The Singer*), Alma Cogan (*Voice*), Mary Law, Leonard Sharp, Dennis Wyndham, Geoffrey Hibbert, Ronnie Stevens, Isobel George, Jackie Lane.

Stephen's not-quite-destitute suitor Bogarde convinces her doubting father (Parker) to let them marry. Bogarde gets a low-paying civil service job, and the giddy newlyweds settle into a small one-room nest. They find themselves at odds with their neighbors, a wide assortment of bill collectors, and even each other. Wedded bliss was never supposed to be like this. Parker comes to the financial rescue with a substantial loan. Deciding Easy Street was only temporarily closed for repairs, the young couple finally decides to tough it out without the loan and lead a more stable married life.
p, Kenneth Harper; d, J. Lee Thompson; w, Thompson, Peter Myers, Alec Grahame (based on the play by Arthur Watkyn); ph, Guy Green (Eastmancolor); m, Wally Stott; ed, Peter Taylor; art d, Michael Stringer; m/l, Sam Coslow.

Romantic Comedy   **Cas.**   **(PR:A   MPAA:NR)**

FOR BETTER FOR WORSE   (SEE: ZANDY'S BRIDE, 1974)

FOR FREEDOM***   (1940, Brit.), 87m Gainsborough/GFD bw

Will Fyffe (*Chief*), Anthony Hulme (*Steve*), E.V.H. Emmett (*Himself*), Guy Middleton (*Pierre*), Albert Lieven (*Fritz*), Hugh McDermott (*Sam*), Billy Russell (*Adolf Hitler*), Capt. Dove, Capt. Pottinger, F.O. Murphy, Arthur Denton, Arthur Goullet, Millicent Wolf, Pat Williams, Jack Raine, Engineer Walker, Engineer Angel, Vice-Admiral J.E.T. Harper (*Narrator*).

Fyffe runs a newsreel company employing his son, Hulme. They determine to make a documentary praising mankind's accomplishments, but when Hitler conquers Czechoslovakia, Fyffe decides to make a film about the Nazis. Hulme quits in protest and travels to Uruguay where he manages to film the scuttling of the German pocket battleship Graf Spee at Montevideo. Actual newsreel footage of the war makes an otherwise routine story interesting. A number of heroes of the battle against the Graf Spee makes appearances as themselves.
p, Edward Black, Castleton Knight; d, Maurice Elvey Knight; w, Miles Malleson, Leslie Arliss (based on a story by Knight); ph, Arthur Crabtree.

Drama   **(PR:A   MPAA:NR)**

FOR HE'S A JOLLY BAD FELLOW
(SEE: THEY ALL DIED LAUGHING, 1964, Brit.)

FOR HEAVEN'S SAKE**½   (1950) 92m FOX bw

Clifton Webb (*Charles*), Joan Bennett (*Lydia*), Robert Cummings (*Jeff Bolton*), Edmund Gwenn (*Arthur*), Joan Blondell (*Daphne*), Gigi Perreau (*Item*), Jack LaRue (*Tony*), Harry Von Zell (*Tex*), Tommy Rettig (*Joe*), Dick Ryan (*Michael*), Charles Lane (*Tax Agent*), Robert Kent (*Joe's Father*), Whit Bissell, Ashmead Scott (*Doctors*), Dorothy Neumann (*Western Union Woman*), Esther Somers (*Dowager*), Jack Daly (*House Detective*), Bob Harlow (*Elevator Boy*), Perc Launders, Richard Thorne (*Doormen*), Albert Pollett, Sid Fields (*Waiters*), Gordon Nelson (*Doorman*), Arno Frey (*Man*), Albert Frey (*Headwaiter*), Jack Daly, Bob Harlow, Richard Thorne, Betty Adams, William O'Leary, Gilbert Fallman, Sue Casey.

Webb is an angel sent on a mission to help a busy theater producer and his wife stop fighting and start having children. He comes down disguised as a wealthy westerner looking to invest some spare change in a play. He plans to meet them socially, never guessing a regular working angel like himself would have such a gift for gambling. He becomes so good dabbling into games of chance that the IRS makes a move to clip his wings. Fellow angel Gwenn finally has to come down from on high and bail the wayward one out.
p, William Perlberg; d&w, George Seaton (based on a play, "May We Come In," by Harry Segal); ph, Lloyd Ahern; m, Alfred Newman; ed, Robert Simpson; art d, Lyle Wheeler, Richard Irvine.

Fantasy/Comedy   **Cas.**   **(PR:A   MPAA:NR)**

FOR LOVE AND MONEY zero   (1967) 75m Crest/J.E.R. c (AKA: FOR
LOVE OF MONEY)

Michelle Angelo, Lionel Nichols, George Caspar, Curly, Norma Mimos, Lee Margill, Janice Kelly, Miki Tani.

Sleazy crime drama involving corporate spies who use women to blackmail executives into spilling company secrets after they have been photographed in compromising situations, which include body painting and LSD.
p&d, Don Davis; w, James Rogers; title song sung by Jose Siemans.

Crime   **(PR:O   MPAA:NR)**

FOR LOVE OF IVY**½   (1968) 101m Palomar/Cinerama c

Sidney Poitier (*Jack Parks*), Abbey Lincoln (*Ivy Moore*), Beau Bridges (*Tim Austin*), Nan Martin (*Doris Austin*), Lauri Peters (*Gena Austin*), Carroll O'Connor (*Frank Austin*), Leon Bibb (*Billy Talbot*), Hugh Hurd (*Jerry*), Lon Satton (*Harry*), Stanley Greene (*Eddie*), Paul Harris, Tony Major, Clark Morgan, Christoper St. John, Bob Carey, Marlene Clark, Laura Greene, Lani Miyazaki, Lisa Moore, Gloria Henry, Yolande Toussaint, Gina Harding, Willis Pinkett, William Matthews, Josip Elic, Cordy Clark, Hope Stansbury, Robert Miller, Nobuko Uenishi, Kyoko Morii, Kedaki Turner, Madge West, Jerome Collamore, Anita Dangler, Peter Dohanos, Jennifer O'Neill, Robert Bannard, Sharon Henesy, Maeve McGuire, John Servetnik, Elliot Wood, Joseph Attles, The Reverend William Glenesk.

Poitier is a trucking executive who runs a gambling operation from inside the trailer of one of his company's trucks. He is coaxed by a pair of white Long Island teenagers to date their maid, who they fear is leaving their household because her life lacks romance. The two hit it off, but the relationship cools when Lincoln learns that Poitier had been blackmailed into dating her in the first place. True love wins out and they finally wed, leaving the family to its own devices back on Long Island.
p, Edgar J. Scherick, Jay Weston; d, Daniel Mann; w, Robert Alan Aurthur (based on a story by Sidney Poitier); ph, Joseph Coffey (Perfect Color); m, Quincy Jones; ed, Patricia Jaffe; prod d, Peter Dohanos; set d, Leif Pederen; m/l title song, Bob Russell, Jones sung by Shirley Horn, "You Put it On Me," Maya Angelou, Jones

(sung by B.B. King), "My Side Of The Sky," Cashmen, Pistilli & West, Jones (sung by Cashmen, Pistilli & West).

Romantic Comedy **Cas.** **(PR:A MPAA:NR)**

FOR LOVE OF MONEY (SEE: FOR LOVE AND MONEY, 1967)

FOR LOVE OF YOU* (1933, Brit.) 61m Windsor/Sterling bw

Arthur Riscoe *(Jack)*, Naunton Wayne *(Jim)*, Franco Foresta *(The Tenor)*, Diana Napier *(The Wife)*, Pearl Osgood *(The Girl)*.

Lame musical sequel to GOING GAY has Riscoe and Wayne as a pair of Englishmen touring the Continent. They stay with an opera star and his wife in Venice, but she starts flirting with Riscoe. Wayne would later gain minor immortality paired with Basil Radford in THE LADY VANISHES, as one of another pair of Englishmen touring the Continent. The two were such a hit as the comic relief in that film that they played more or less the same parts in no less than six other films. Cut from 77 minutes when reissued in 1944.

p, Frank A. Richardson; d, Carmine Gallone; w, Selwyn Jepson; ph, W. Goldberger.

Musical/Comedy **(PR:A MPAA:NR)**

FOR LOVE OR MONEY½** (1934, Brit.) 64m London/Mundus bw (GB: CASH)

Edmund Gwenn *(Edmund Gilbert)*, Wendy Barrie *(Lilian Gilbert)*, Robert Donat *(Paul Martin)*, Morris Harvey *(Meyer)*, Lawrence Grossmith *(Joseph)*, Clifford Heatherley *(Hunt)*, Hugh E. Wright *(Jordan)*, Antony Holles *(Inspector)*.

English businessman Gwenn is preparing his home for a meeting with well-to-do financiers he hopes will provide backing for his scheme to get his ailing business back on its feet. Dodging bill collectors and others of such ilk, he frantically tries to prepare his home, with comic results. The electrician who has arrived to turn out the lights for the long term is not who he wants financiers to see. The electrician becomes very attracted to Gwenn's daughter. Using her as a bargaining chip, he keeps his lights on and finds $100,000 in counterfeit bills left by criminals escaping the law. Gwenn dresses the young man suitably for such a formal occasion and turns him loose flashing the phoney money where the investors can see it. In the end the deal goes through.

p, Alexander Korda; d, Zoltan Korda; w, Arthur Wimperis (based on a story by Anthony Gibbs, Dorothy Greenhill); ph, Robert Martin; ed, Stephen Harrison.

Comedy **(PR:A MPAA:NR)**

FOR LOVE OR MONEY*** (1939) 67m UNIV bw

June Lang *(Susan Bannister)*, Robert Kent *(Ted Frazier)*, Edward Brophy *(Sleeper)*, Richard Lane *(Foster)*, Etienne Girardot *(Poindexter)*, Horace MacMahon *(Dead Eyes)*, Edward Gargan *(Bubbles)*, Cora Witherspoon *(Mrs. Sweringen)*, Raymond Parker, Jerry Marlowe *(Delivery Boys)*, Addison Richards *(Kelly)*, Armand Kaliz *(Nanda)*, Alan Edwards *(Manager)*, Hal K. Dawson *(Cashier)*, Dora Clement *(Miss Upton)*, Eddy Chandler *(John)*, Neely Edwards *(Travel Bureau Clerk)*, Alphonse Martell *(Head Waiter)*, Mary Treen *(Amy the Maid)*, Walter Merrill *(Luke)*, Russ Powell *(Night Watchman)*, Francis Sayles *(Bartender)*, Jack Gardner *(Elevator Boy)*, Charles Regan *(Peter)*, Walter Clinton *(Postman)*, Robin Raymond *(Maid)*.

A zesty picture casting Kent and Brophy as dim-witted bookkeepers to a bookmaker who misplace $50,000 of employer Lane's money. The money shows up on secretary Lang's desk for a very brief time before she spends $44,000 of it in only eight hours. The fun starts when Lane gives the bumbling bookkeepers 36 hours to recover the missing money.

p, Max Golden; d, Albert S. Rogell; w, Charles Grayson, Arthur T. Horman (based on the story by Julian Blaustein, Daniel Taradash, Bernard Feins); ph, Stanley Cortez; ed, Maurice Wright; md, Charles Previn; art d, Jack Otterson.

Comedy **(PR:A MPAA:NR)**

FOR LOVE OR MONEY** (1963) 108m UNIV c

Kirk Douglas *(Deke Gentry)*, Mitzi Gaynor *(Kate Brasher)*, Gig Young *("Sonny" John Dayton Smith)*, Thelma Ritter *(Chloe Brasher)*, Julie Newmar *(Bonnie Brasher)*, William Bendix *(Joe Fogel)*, Leslie Parrish *(Jan Brasher)*, Richard Sargent *(Harvey Wofford)*, Elizabeth MacRae *(Marsha)*, William Windom *(Sam Travis)*, Willard Sage *(Orson Roark)*, Ina Victor *(Nurse)*, Alvy Moore *(George)*, Jose Gonzales Gonzales *(Jaime)*, Don Megowan *(Gregor)*, Billy Halop *(Elevator Operator)*, Joey Faye *(Male Shopper)*, Theodore Marcuse *(Artist)*, Frank Mahony *(Red Beard)*, Alberto Morin *(Maitre D')*, Nydia Westman *(Martha)*, Don Beddoe *(Milo)*, Phil Chambers *(Captain of Crab Boat)*, Karen Norris *(Ava)*, Sean MacGregor *(Seymour)*, John Morley *(Helicopter Pilot)*, Vince Townsend, Jr. *(Guard)*, Charles Thompson *(Uncle Ben)*, Bess Flowers *(Bewildered Woman)*, John Harmon *(Taxi Driver)*, John Indrisano, Ted Fish *(Pugs)*, Claudia Brack, Susan Counter, Evelyn Dutton *(Bridesmaids)*.

The basic flaw with this mediocre comedy is the premise that super-rich hotel millionairess Ritter would have to find a matchmaker for her three daughters, Newmar, Gaynor, and Parrish; three of the most curvaceous women in movies. Ritter, in her private helicopter, flies over her lawyer Douglas' sailboat. He thought he would be rid of his best client on the boat, but Douglas is ordered to manage the three girls' estates and find them suitable husbands who will not spoil the goods beforehand. Gaynor, the most level-headed of the three, winds up with Douglas. Parrish is a beatnik patroness of bizarre modern artists and Newmar is a health-food fanatic. Bendix, who is the security chief of Ritter's hotel chain, is sent to shadow Douglas to make sure he's doing what he claims to be doing. Richard Sargent, a mild-mannered IRS clerk, is recruited for Newmar and William Windom is assigned Parrish. The only truly funny part of the movie is Gig Young, in yet another of his drunken playboy roles. He was the 1960s answer to the 1940s Jack Norton. The film ends with a triple wedding. This movie looks great, has lots of color, superb costumes, and lovely art direction. The only problem is the words Markes and Morris put into the actors' mouths and some very uninventive direction from Michael Gordon, who, when given a great script, can bring brilliance to the screen, as in CYRANO DE BERGERAC, ANOTHER PART OF THE FOREST, or even the lightweight but funny PILLOW TALK. The location shooting was in San Francisco and the remainder was done on the Universal lot. It was originally called THREE ON A MATCH and then THREE WAY MATCH. Bowery Boy Billy Halop is briefly seen as the elevator operator. Burlesque comic Joey Faye is also seen in a bit as a shopper.

p, Robert Arthur; d, Michael Gordon; w, Michael Morris, Larry Markes; ph, Clifford Stine (Eastmancolor); m, Frank De Vol; ed, Alma Macrorie; art d, Alexander Golitzen, Malcolm Brown; set d, Ruby Levitt; md, Joseph Gershenson; cos, Jean Louis; makeup, Bud Westmore, Jack Freeman, Imogene Abbott, Le Vaughn Speer.

Comedy **(PR:A MPAA:NR)**

FOR ME AND MY GAL*½** (1942) 104m MGM bw

Judy Garland *(Jo Hayden)*, George Murphy *(Jimmy K. Metcalf)*, Gene Kelly *(Harry Palmer)*, Marta Eggerth *(Eve Minard)*, Ben Blue *(Sid Simms)*, Richard Quine *(Danny Hayden)*, Keenan Wynn *(Eddie Milton)*, Horace [Stephan] McNally *(Mr. Waring)*, Lucille Norman *(Lily Duncan)*, Betty Welles, Anne Rooney *(Members of Jimmy's Company)*.

This is a delightful trip down memory lane, a nostalgic visit to the innocent vaudeville days before WW I where Garland is trooping the boards with Murphy, Blue, and Norman. Though she loves the hardscrabble life of the backstage, Garland's career is aimed at sending her kid brother Quine to medical school. Smooth talking Kelly appears and tells Garland that she could do much better in his song-and-dance act, that she should leave her partners who are destined to wallow about in the backwaters of show business. Murphy, upon hearing this proposal, is surprisingly generous, urging Garland to better herself. But the new act goes nowhere; Garland and Kelly struggle along for two years while Kelly's promises evaporate day after day. Murphy and Blue, however, hit the big time and Kelly becomes infatuated with top singing star Eggerth (in her American debut). Garland, who now realizes that she's in love with Kelly, sacrifices all, begging Eggerth to help Kelly with an important show biz offer; she does and Kelly is ecstatic, racing to Garland to tell her the news. But, when he finds her in tears, he realizes that she loves him and they plan to marry. WW I interrupts Kelly's big break when he receives a draft notice. To evade service Kelly slams a heavy trunk lid down on his hand and is rejected. Garland's brother Quine is killed in the front lines and when she learns Kelly has purposely maimed himself to avoid serving she rejects him, calling him a coward. To redeem himself, Kelly attempts to enlist but none of the services will have him because of his injured hand. He finally joins a YMCA organization to serve overseas where he distinguishes himself, saving many wounded men. He locates Garland in France where she is singing for troops and they are reunited; they put their act together and head for big time Broadway. The plot and lines of the story are pure hokum but the many great old tunes throughout the film, staged surprisingly by Bobby Connolly (Berkeley, the great choreographer was the overall director but did not stage the dance numbers, his specialty). With this film MGM went all out to raise Garland to superstar status, where her name appeared before the title. For Kelly, it was the big film break of his career; he was spotted on Broadway in "Pal Joey" by producer Arthur Freed and selected to play the part of the heel hoofer, replacing Murphy, who was originally slated for the part. Kelly's debut was aided by Garland who promoted him at every turn and spent a great deal of time teaching Kelly movie techniques. So dislikable was Kelly's role that the preview cards at the premiere overwhelmingly urged that nice guy Murphy get Garland, not Kelly. MGM mogul Louis B. Mayer heard about this and told Murphy when meeting him on a golf course, "You spoiled the picture." Mayer then ordered that a dozen major scenes be reshot where Kelly's part was softened and he was seen in a more heroic and likeable light by movie's end. Murphy later bemoaned his fate in this film in his memoirs, *Say . . . Didn't You Used to Be George Murphy:* " . . . they shot the whole finale again—without me. . . . It wasn't pleasant to discover that my efforts had wound up on the proverbial cutting-room floor." Garland is simply marvelous in a grand visit to a vanished vaudeville era and the public flocked to see her. MGM's coffers bulged with the staggering success of this production, costing slightly more than $800,000 and returning almost $4.8 million at the box office the first time around. Garland and Kelly were here to stay. The highlight of the film, of course, was the great title song (Edgar Leslie, F. Ray Goetz, George W. Meyer), performed by Garland and Kelly. Other songs include: "They Go Wild, Simply Wild Over Me" (Joseph McCarthy, Fred Fisher; danced by Kelly), "The Doll Shop" (Roger Edens), "Oh, Johnny, Oh" (Ed Rose, Abe Olman; danced by Kelly), "Oh You Beautiful Doll" (A. Seymour Brown, Nat D. Ayer; Kelly and Garland duet), "When You Wore A Tulip" (Jack Mahoney, Percy Wenrich; Kelly and Garland), "Don't Leave Me Daddy" (Joe Vergas), "Do I Love You" (Goetz, Henri Christine; sung by Eggerth), "By The Beautiful Sea" (Harold Atteride, Harry Carroll), "After You've Gone" (Henry Creamer, Turner Layton; sung by Garland), "Till We Meet Again" (Ray Egan, Richard A. Whiting; sung by Eggerth), "Tell Me" (Max Kortlander, J. Will Callahan; sung by Eggerth), "We Don't Want The Bacon" (Howard Carr, Harry Russell, Jimmie Havens), "Ballin' the Jack" (Jim Burris, Chris Smith; sung by Garland and Kelly), "Mademoiselle From Armentieres" (authors unknown), "What Are You Going to Do to Help the Boys?" (Gus Kahn, Egbert Van Alstyne), "How Ya Gonna Keep 'Em Down On The Farm" (Sam M. Lewis, Joe Young, Walter Donaldson), "Where Do We Go From Here" (Howard Johnson, Wenrich; sung by Garland), "Goodbye Broadway, Hello France" (C. Francis Riesner, Benny Davis, Billy Baskette), "Smiles" (Callahan, Lee M. Roberts), "It's A Long Way To Tipperary" (Jack Judge, Harry Williams; sung by Garland), "Oh Frenchy" (Sam Ehrlich, Con Conrad), "Pack Up Your Troubles" (George Asuf, Felix Powell; sung by Garland), "When Johnny Comes Marching Home" (Louis Lambert, adapted by Edens; sung by Garland).

p, Arthur Freed; d, Busby Berkeley; w, Richard Sherman, Fred Finklehoffe, Sid Silvers, Jack McGowan, Irving Brecher (based on the story "The Big Time" by Howard Emmett Rogers); ph, William Daniels; ed, Ben Lewis; md, George Stoll; art d, Cedric Gibbons, Gabriel Scognamillo; set d, Edwin B. Willis, Keogh Gleason; cos, Kalloch, Gile Steele; ch, Bobby Connolly, Gene Kelly; makeup, Jack Dawn.

Musical **(PR:A MPAA:NR)**

FOR MEN ONLY*** (1952) 93m N-H/Lippert bw (AKA: THE TALL LIE)

Paul Henreid *(Dr. Stephen Brice)*, Robert Sherman *(Tod Palmer)*, Russell Johnson *(Ky Walker)*, Margaret Field *(Julie)*, Kathleen Hughes *(Tracy)*, Vera Miles *(Kathy)*, James Dobson *(Beanie)*, Douglas Kennedy *(Mayberry)*, Robert Carson *(Hopkins)*, Virginia Mullen *(Mrs. Palmer)*, Steven Clark *(Roy)*, Chris Drake *(Jack)*, Bob Chapman *(Phil)*, O.Z. Whitehead *(Prof. Bixby)*, Arthur Marshall *(Oglethorpe)*, Frank Mathias *(Jerry)*.

Paul Henreid produced, directed, and starred in this study of fraternity hazing. After a dog is killed and a scared pledge is also accidentally done away with, as part of an alleged cover up, a college professor sets out to find out what is going on. A bona-fide attempt to look at a troublesome campus problem.

p&d, Paul Henreid; w, Lou Morheim (from a story by Morheim, Herbert Margolies); ph, Paul Ivano; m, Laving Friedman; ed, Sherman Rose; art d, Frank Durlauf.

Drama (PR:A MPAA:NR)

FOR PETE'S SAKE!* (1966) 90m World-wide c

Billy Graham *(Himself)*, Robert Sampson *(Gas Station Attendant)*, Pippa Scott *(His Wife)*, Johnny Jensen *(Their Son)*, Sam Groom, Al Freeman, Jr., John Milford, Irene Tedrow, Nicholas Surovy, Bob Beach, Pam McMyler, Tim O'Kelly, Danny Bravo, Terry Garr, Cynthia Hull, Connie Sawyer, Len Wayland, Dolores Quinton, Harry Lauter, Tom Peters, Stuart Nisbet, Nicholas Worth, Margaret Muse, Helyn Eby Rock, Ella Edwards.

Tedious religious drama about a lowly gas station attendant (Sampson) who, along with his wife (Scott) and young son (Jensen), is so moved by a Billy Graham revival crusade that they all vow to change their lives and help Jesus stamp out a rowdy teenage motorcycle gang. A really bad movie save for the unintentional laughs.

p, Frank R. Jacobson; d&w, James F. Collier; ph, Richard Batcheller (Eastmancolor); m, Ralph Carmichael; ed, Eugene Pendleton; art d, Theodore Holsopple.

Drama (PR:A MPAA:NR)

FOR PETE'S SAKE** (1977) 90m Rastar/COL c (AKA: JULY PORK BELLIES)

Barbra Streisand *(Henry)*, Michael Sarrazin *(Pete)*, Estelle Parsons *(Helen)*, William Redfield *(Fred)*, Molly Picon *(Mrs. Cherry)*, Louis Zorich *(Nick)*, Vivian Bonnell *(Loretta)*, Richard Ward *(Bernie)*, Heywood Hale Broun *(Judge Hiller)*, Joe Maher *(Mr. Coates)*, Vincent Schiavelli *(Checkout Man)*, Fred Stuthman *(Loan Officer)*, Ed Bakey *(Angelo)*, Peter Mamakos *(Dominic)*, Norman Marshall *(First Worker)*, Joseph Hardy *(Second Cop)*, Wil Albert *(Cop in Drag)*, Jack Hollander *(Loan-shark)*, Gary Pagett *(Assistant Bank Manager)*, Herb Armstrong *(Insurance Man)*, Bella Bruck *(Lady in Supermarket)*, Anne Ramsey *(Telephone Lady)*, Bill McKinney *(Rocky)*, Sid Miller *(Drunk Driver)*, Lew Burke *(Dog Trainer)*, Martin Erlichman *(Man in Theatre)*.

A feeble attempt to do a Hawksian 1930s comedy in the 1970s. The shame of this was that co-authors Shapiro and Richlin both had several light comedies in their resumes (PILLOW TALK, OPERATION PETTICOAT, THAT TOUCH OF MINK, and THE PERFECT FURLOUGH among others). Streisand is a big-mouthed Brooklyn housewife of poor sap Michael Sarrazin, a cabbie who is desperate to go back to school and out of the awful New York City traffic. He is tipped that the U.S.S.R. and the U.S. are about to conclude a deal that will send the price of pork bellies soaring. Streisand and Sarrazin do not have enough money to buy a package of bacon, much less thousands of pork bellies. Streisand goes to Jack Hollander, a loan shark, and borrows $3,000. The Americans and the Soviets cannot come to terms and the loan contract is sold to local madame Picon. Picon tries to get Barbra to hook in the afternoons to pay off the debt. Streisand refuses, gets involved in a couple of other underworld "pranks." (One includes dropping off a time bomb to eliminate some hoodlums, and the other is running rustled cattle into Manhattan.) Eventually, pork bellies go up and Sarrazin is able to buy Streisand out of all of her problems. Although this didn't seem to hurt Streisand (who was coming off the phenomenally successful THE WAY WE WERE), it did nothing for Sarrazin's career, which went from this into such clunkers as CARAVANS, DOUBLE NEGATIVE, and A NIGHT FULL OF RAIN. Streisand had already perfected all of her mannerisms and mugging by this time and used them all. It took several years for her to shed them and learn how to act again (as in YENTL). Her hair was done by her then-lover Jon Peters, who has since become a film producer. The man in the theater was played by Streisand's long-time manager Martin Erlichman as a private joke. Funny it was not. Sidney Miller does a cute drunk driver bit, a reprise of the same character he played many years for Jack Webb's "Dragnet" series. Sports commentator Heywood Hale Broun does a short stint as a judge who wants to bed Streisand. Kovacs produced terrific photography. The picture was originally titled "July Pork Bellies." Even so, changing the title did not help and all concerned with this picture would be wise to omit it from their credits. It grossed less than what Streisand earned for some of her other films.

p, Martin Erlichman, Stanley Shapiro; d, Peter Yates; w, Shapiro, Maurice Richlin; ph, Laszlo Kovacs (Eastmancolor); m, Artie Butler; ed, Frank Keller; art d, Gene Callahan; cos, Frank Thompson.

Comedy Cas. (PR:C MPAA:NR)

FOR SINGLES ONLY zero (1968) 91m UNIV c

John Saxon *(Bret Hendley)*, Mary Ann Mobley *(Anne Carr)*, Lana Wood *(Helen Todd)*, Mark Richman *(Gerald Pryor)*, Ann Elder *(Nydia Walker)*, Chris Noel *(Lily)*, Marty Ingels *(Archibald Baldwin)*, Hortense Petra *(Miss Jenks)*, Milton Berle *(Mr. Parker)*, Charles Robinson *(Jim Allen)*, Duke Hobbie *(Bob Merrick)*, Dick Castle *(Singer)*, Norman Wells *(Clerk In Bursar's Office)*, Norma Foster, Maria Korda, Leslie McRae, Dita Nicole *(Pageant Girls)*, Walter Wanderly Trio with Talya Ferro, Cal Tjader, Nitty Gritty Dirt Band, Lewis and Clarke Expedition, the Sunshine Company.

Swinging "under 30s" get together in this musical romp at an apartment complex that includes one tenant wagering that he can bed Mobley before the week is out, and that leads to the complications that keep this shallow thing going. Before it is over, one tenant moves out, only to be raped by a bunch of waterfront hoods, and she flies back to the complex for safety. Songs: "For Singles Only" (Fred Karger, Milton Berle), "Kee Ka Roo" (Walter Wanderley, Bobby Worth), "Take a Chance With Me" (Wanderley, Talya Ferro), "I'm Not Afraid" (Diane Hilderbrand, Jack Keller), "This Town Ain't the Same Anymore," "Destination Unknown," "Why Need They Pretend?" (Travis Lewis, Bommer Clarke), "Symbol of Love," "Tight Black Gown," "The Loner."

p, Sam Katzman; d, Arthur Dreifuss; w, Dreifuss, Hal Collins; (based on a story by Arthur Hoerl, Albert Derr); ph, John F. Warren (Pathecolor); m, Fred Karger; ed, Ben Lewis; art d, George W. Davis, Leroy Coleman; set d, Henry Grace, Robert De Vestel; spec eff, Edwin J. Fisher; ch, Alex Romero.

Comedy (PR:O MPAA:NR)

FOR THE DEFENSE*½** (1930) 62m PAR bw

William Powell *(William Foster)*, Kay Francis *(Irene Manners)*, Scott Kolk *(Defoe)*, William B. Davidson *(District Attorney Stone)*, John Elliott *(McGann)*, Thomas Jackson *(Daly)*, Harry Walker *(Miller)*, James Finlayson *(Parrott)*, Charles West *(Joe)*, Charles Sullivan *(Charlie)*, Ernest Adams *(Eddie Withers)*, Bertram Marburgh *(Judge Evans)*, Edward Le Saint *(Judge)*, George Hayes *(Ben, the Waiter)*, Billy Bevan *(Drunk)*, Kane Richmond *(Young Man at Speakeasy)*, Sid Saylor *(Evening Sun Reporter)*, Bob Homans *(Lineup Lieutenant)*.

Tightly-edited, well-acted, and fast-moving adaptation of William Fallon's life which took only 15 days to shoot. Fallon, whose life also inspired the film MOUTHPIECE, was the lawyer with the silver tongue in the 1910s and 1920s in New York and Powell plays him with terrific believability. In real life, Fallon was accused of bribing a jury and that is indicated here as well. Great authenticity in all the opening shots of The Tombs and the courts. Once that is established, screenwriter Garrett lets us have a taste of backstage law shenanigans. Powell is mad for Kay Francis and booze, in that order. It's a segmented film in that we are given bits and pieces of the lawyer's life rather than one large case as is so often the story. In the end, Powell is convicted of jury-tampering and sent to Sing Sing where so many of his 'mistakes' now reside. Francis swears to wait the five years until he is released. Silent comics Finlayson and Bevan are seen in bits. Australian Bevan made the transition from silents to talkies with no problem and appeared in a diverse collection of films ranging from PINK PAJAMAS to THE PICTURE OF DORIAN GRAY, LLOYDS OF LONDON, and CLUNY BROWN.

d, John Cromwell; w, Oliver H.P. Garrett (based on a story by Charles Furthman); ph, Charles Lang; ed, George Nichols, Jr.

Courtroom Drama (PR:A-C MPAA:NR)

FOR THE FIRST TIME*** (1959, U.S./Ger./Ital.) 97m Corona/MGM c

Mario Lanza *(Tonio Costa)*, Zsa Zsa Gabor *(Gloria De Vadnuz)*, Johanna von Koczian *(Christa)*, Kurt Kasznar *(Ladislas Tabory)*, Hans Sohnker *(Prof. Bruckner)*, Peter Capell *(Leopold Huebner)*, Renzo Cesana *(Angelo)*, Sandro Giglio *(Alessandro)*.

A touching film about opera singer Lanza's attempts to raise money for the treatment of his deaf girl friend. He goes on a tour of various European capitals playing fund-raising concerts and earning dollars from his magnificent voice. This turned out to be Lanza's final film as he died the same year, at age thirty eight, of a heart attack in a Rome clinic. Songs and operatic pieces include: "Ave Maria" (Giuseppe Verdi), "Oh Mon Amour," "Bavarian Drinking Song," "Vesti La Giubba," from "Pagliacci" (Ruggiero Leoncavallo), "La Donna e Mobile," from "Rigoletto," "Niun Mi Tema," "Grand March" (Verdi), "O Solo Mio" (Eduardo di Capua), "Ich Liebe Dich" (Edvard Grieg), "Come Prima" (M. Panzeri, S. Paola Tacani, Mary Bond), "Capri, Capri," "Pineapple Picker" (George Stoll)."

p, Alexander Gruter; d, Rudolph Mate; w, Andrew Solt; ph, Aldo Tonti (Technirama, Technicolor); ed, Gene Ruggiero; md, George Stoll; art d, Fritz Maurischat.

Musical (PR:A MPAA:NR)

FOR THE LOVE OF BENJI½** (1977) 85m Mulberry Square c

Higgins *(Benji)*, Patsy Garrett *(Mary)*, Cynthia Smith *(Cindy)*, Allen Fiuzat *(Paul)*, Ed Nelson *(Chandler Dietrich)*, Art Vasil *(Stelios)*, Peter Bowles *(Ronald)*, Bridget Armstrong *(Elizabeth)*, Mihalis Lambrinos *(Man in Baggage Room)*.

As far as children's entertainment goes, you can't beat a good dog story for providing the necessary assortment of thrills. FOR THE LOVE OF BENJI fills the bill with one of the most expressive dogs (and actors, for that matter) to come out of Hollywood. The Benji in this film is the two-year-old replacement look-alike for the original Benji. While in Greece, Benji is drugged and kidnaped by Nelson, who stashes an oil secret in the pooch's paw. The main emphasis is on the dog as he wanders through Greece getting in and out of trouble while eluding the crooks. Good for the kids.

p, Ven Vaughn; d&w, Joe Camp (based on a story by Vaughn, Camp); ph, Don Reddy (CFI Color); m, Euel Box; ed, Leon Seith; prod d, Harland Wright; art d, Jack Bennett; spec eff, Bennett; m/l, "Sunshine Smiles," Euel Box, Betty Box, Camp; Benji's trainers, Frank and Juanita Inn.

Juvenile Children Cas. (PR:AAA MPAA:G)

FOR THE LOVE O'LIL* (1930) 67m COL bw

Jack Mulhall *(Wyn Huntley)*, Elliott Nugent *(Sandy Jenkins)*, Sally Starr *(Lil)*, Margaret Livingston *(Eleanor Cartwright)*, Charles Sellon *(Mr. Walker)*, Julia Swayne Gordon *(Mrs. Walker)*, Billy Bevan *(Edward O. Brooks)*, Claire Du Brey *(Mrs. Gardner)*, Joan Standing *(Chambermaid)*.

A boring story of a straight-laced lawyer, who marries a wild, illustrious lady, who learned her tricks from a past love. He wants to live in the quiet house in the country; she insists on life in the fast lane. A loose blonde woman puts the make on the lawyer, and tries to use him as a scapegoat in her divorce proceedings. He is saved by his wife, who bursts in on them in a hotel room before he gets into too much trouble.

p, Harry Cohn; d, James Tinling; w, Dorothy Howell, Bella Cohen, Robert Bruckner (based on a story by Leslie Thrasher); ph, Ted Tetzlaff; ed, Edward Curtiss.

Drama (PR:A MPAA:NR)

FOR THE LOVE OF MARY**½ (1948) 90m UNIV bw

Deanna Durbin (Mary Peppertree), Edmond O'Brien (Lt. Tom Farrington), Don Taylor (David Paxton), Jeffrey Lynn (Phillip Manning), Ray Collins (Harvey Elwood), Hugo Hass (Gustav Heindel), Harry Davenport (Justice Peabody), Griff Barnett (Timothy Peppertree), Katherine Alexander (Miss Harkness), James Todd (Justice Van Sloan), Morris Ankrum (Adm. Walton), Frank Conroy (Samuel Litchfield), Leon Belasco (Igor), Louise Beavers (Bertha), Raymond Greenleaf (Justice Williams), Charles Meredith (Justice Hastings), Adele Rowland (Mrs. Peabody), Mary Adams (Marge), Adrienne Marden (Hilda), Beatrice Roberts (Dorothy), Harry Cheshire (Col. Hedley), Donald Randolph (Assistant Attorney General), William Gould (Sen. Benning).

Light and fun-filled Durbin vehicle in which she plays a White House switchboard operator with deep romantic problems (O'Brien, Lynn, and Taylor are all pursuing her) that can only be sorted out with the help of the president of the U.S. (though he's never shown).

p, Robert Arthur; d, Frederick de Cordova; w, Oscar Brodney; ph, William Daniels; ed, Ted J. Kent; md, Milton Schwarzwald; m/l, "Moonlight Bay," "Let Me Call You Sweetheart," "I'll Take You Home Again, Kathleen," "On the Wings of a Song," "Largo al Factotum," from Gioacchino Antonio Rossini's "The Barber of Seville."

Romantic Comedy (PR:A MPAA:NR)

FOR THE LOVE OF MIKE** (1933, Brit.) 90m BIP/Wardour

Bobby Howes (Bobby Seymour), Constance Shotter (Mike), Arthur Riscoe (Conway Paton), Renee Macready (Stella Rees), Jimmy Godden (Henry Miller), Viola Tree (Emma Miller), Wylie Watson (Rev. James), Hal Gordon (PC), Syd Crossley (Sullivan), Monty Banks, The Carlyle Cousins.

A saucy little story about a man who will do his all for his love. Howes tries to regain the power of attorney now held by heiress Shotter's guardian, who she no longer trusts. He tries a safecracking venture to do so, and is caught red-handed by detective Riscoe. Twist comes at the end when the detective shows Howes how to grab the document, because it turns out they was old school pals.

p, Walter C. Mycroft; d, Monty Banks; w, Clifford Grey, Frank Launder (based on a play by H.F. Maltby); ph, Claude Friese-Greene.

Drama (PR:A MPAA:NR)

FOR THE LOVE OF MIKE** (1960) 87m FOX c
(GB: NONE BUT THE BRAVE

Richard Basehart (Father Phelan), Stuart Erwin (Dr. Mills), Arthur Shields (Father Walsh), Armando Silvestre (Tony Eagle), Elsa Cardenas (Mrs. Eagle), Michael Steckler (Ty Corbin), Rex Allen (Himself), Danny Bravo (Michael).

Orphaned Indian boy Bravo nurses a sickly horse back to health and enters it in a race organized by Allen. The kid's horse crosses the finish line first and he donates the winnings to Basehart and Shields, a pair of monks struggling to keep their financially troubled church from closing. A harmless western soaked in saccharine.

p&d, George Sherman; w, D.D. Beauchamp; ph, Alex Philips (CinemaScope, DeLuxe Color); m, Raul La Vista; ed, Fredrick Y. Smith; art d, Roberto Silva; m/l, Rex Allen.

Children/Western (PR:AAA MPAA:NR)

FOR THE LOVE OF RUSTY** (1947) 68m COL bw

Ted Donaldson (Danny Mitchell), Tom Powers (Hugh Mitchell), Ann Doran (Ethel Mitchell), Aubrey Mather (Dr. Francis Xavier Fay), Sid Tomack (Moe Hatch), George Meader (J. Cecil Rinehardt), Mickey McGuire (Gerald Hobble), Harry Hayden (Hobble), Fred Sears (Doc Levy), Dick Elliott (Bill Worden), Olin Howlin (Frank Foley), Teddy Infuhr (Tommy Worden), Dwayne Hickman (Doc Levy, Jr.), George Nokes (Squeaky), Almira Sessions (Sarah Johnson), Flame (Rusty), Flash the Dog.

Not a lot of plot, just a lot of boy and a lot of dog. The story concerns a boy, Donaldson, who has a series of misunderstandings with his dad, Powers. The two drift apart and are brought back together by a dog, Flash, and a nice old veterinarian, Mather.

p, John Haggott; d, John Sturges; w, Malcolm Stuart Boylan (based on characters created by Al Martin); ph, Vincent Farrar; ed, James Sweeney; md, Mischa Bakaleinikoff; art d, Hans Radon.

Children (PR:AAA MPAA:NR)

FOR THE SERVICE** (1936) 65m UNIV bw

Buck Jones (Buck O'Bryan), Clifford Jones (George Murphy), Edward Keene (Capt. Murphy), Fred Kohler (Bruce Howard), Beth Marion (Benny Carson), Frank McGlynn, Sr. (Jim), Ben Corbett (Ben), Chief Thunderbird (Chief Big Bear), Silver.

Buck Jones stars in, directed, and produced this oater which sees him as the scout of a government outpost in Indian territory who is being pushed out of his job by the commander's son, Clifford Jones, who has been installed as the new scout by his poppa, Keene. Clifford Jones proves to be unsuitable for the job because he has no stomach for the slaughtering of redskins. This, of course, causes Buck Jones to pull up the slack and prove to the kid and his old man that the boy should stick to making eyes at heroine Marion.

p&d, Buck Jones; w, Isadore Bernstein; ph, Allan Thompson, Herbert Kirkpatrick.

Western (PR:A MPAA:NR)

FOR THEM THAT TRESPASS**½ (1949, Brit.) 91m
Associated British Pathe bw (GB: MR. DREW)

Stephen Murray (Christopher Drew), Richard Todd (Herb Logan), Patricia Plunkett (Rosie), Rosalyn Boulter (Frankie), Michael Laurence (Jim Heal), Mary Merrall (Mrs. Drew), Vida Hope (Olive Mockson), Frederick Leister (Vicar Mannersley), Michael Medwin (Len Stevens), John Salew (Public Prosecutor), Robert Harris (Counsel for Defense), Joan Dowling (Gracie), Harry Fowler (Dave), Irene Handl (Mrs. Sams), Helen Cherry (Mary Drew), James Hayter (Jocko), George Curzon (Clark Hall), Valentine Dyall (Sir Archibald), Harcourt Williams (Judge), Kynaston Reeves, George Hayes, Ian Fleming, Edward Lexy, Michael Brennan.

An interesting programmer starring Murray as an upper-class writer who decides he needs some first-hand personal experience to beef up his prose, so he wanders around the more dangerous areas of town to gather some material. Much to his dismay he witnesses a murder, but refuses to help an innocent man, Todd, arrested for the crime, because his presence in such a neighborhood would cause a scandal. Todd is released from prison after serving fifteen years and he hears his "crime" detailed on a radio drama written by Murray which enables him to gather enough evidence to clear his name.

p, Victor Skutezky; d, Cavalcanti; w, J. Lee-Thompson, William Douglas Home (based on the novel by Ernest Raymond); ph, Derek Williams, Val Stewart; m, Philip Green; ed, Margery Saunders.

Drama (PR:A MPAA:NR)

FOR THOSE IN PERIL**½ (1944, Brit.) 67m Ealing bw

David Farrar (Murray), Ralph Michael (Rawlings), Robert Wyndham (Leverett), John Slater (Wilkie), John Batten (Wireless Operator), Robert Griffith (Griffiths), Peter Arne (Junior Officer), James Robertson Justice (Operations Room Officer), Anthony Bushell, William Rodwell, Anthony Bazell, Leslie Clarke.

Unfit for flying duty, Michael half-heartedly joins the air-sea rescue service. On a dangerous mission off the coast of France, his boat encounters German ships, mines, and shore batteries. After picking up a stranded air crew, a German plane strafes the craft and kills Farrar, Michael's commander. Suddenly changed and seeing his importance to the war against fascism, Michael take the helm and guides the boat back to Britain. Exciting, superbly shot wartime drama.

p, S.C. Balcon; d, Charles Crichton; w, Harry Watt, J.O.C. Orton, T.E.B. Clarke (based on a story by Richard Hillary); ph, Douglas Slocombe, Ernest Palmer; ed, Sidney Cole, Erik Cripps; art d, Duncan Sutherland.

War Drama (PR:A MPAA:NR)

FOR THOSE WHO THINK YOUNG** (1964) 96m UA c

James Darren (Gardner "Ding" Pruitt III), Pamela Tiffin (Sandy Palmer), Woody Woodbury (Himself), Paul Lynde (Sid Hoyt), Tina Louise (Topaz McQueen), Nancy Sinatra (Karen Cross), Bob Denver (Kelp), Claudia Martin (Sue Lewis), Robert Middleton (Edgar J. Cronin), Ellen McRae (Dr. Pauline Thayer), Louis Quinn (Gus Kestler), Sammee Tong (Sessue), Addison Richards (Dean Watkins), Mousie Garner (Mousie), Benny Baker (Lou), Anna Lee (Laura Pruitt), George Raft, Roger Smith (Detectives), Amedee Chabot (Beach Girl), Jack LaRue, Allen Jenkins, Robert Armstrong (Cronin's Business Associates), Susan Hart (Sorority Girl), Harry Antrim, Eleanor Audley (Forty-Fifth Anniversary Couple), Anthony Eustrel (Faculty Member), Alberto Morin (Marion the Butler), Sheila Bromley (Mrs. Harkness), Byron Kane (Reporter).

Innocuous beach movie starring popular youth stars of the time Tiffin, Darren, Denver, Sinatra, and Louise as a bunch of aimless adolescents who spend their extra-curricular hours hanging out at the Silver Palms listening to the stiff standup routines of comedian Woodbury. Too bad for them that Darren's uncool granddad Middleton wants to close down the noisy club. Too bad for granddad that the kids learn that he's an ex-bootlegger and they blackmail him into tolerating their activities.

p, Hugh Benson; d, Leslie H. Martinson; w, Dan Beaumont, James O'Hanlon, George O'Hanlon (based on a story by Beaumont); ph, Harold E. Stine (Techniscope, Technicolor); m, Jerry Fielding; ed, Frank P. Keller; md, Fielding; art d, Hal Pereira, Arthur Lonergan; ch, Robert Tucker; m/l, "For Those Who Think Young," "Surf's Up," Jerry Livingston, Mack David (sung by James Darren).

Comedy (PR:A MPAA:NR)

FOR VALOR*** (1937, Brit.) 94m Capitol/GFD bw

Tom Walls (Doubleday/Charlie Chisholm), Ralph Lynn (Maj. Pyke/Willie Pyke), Veronica Rose (Phyllis Chisholm), Joan Marion (Clare Chester), Hubert Harben (Mr. Gallop), Henry Longhurst (Inspector Harding), Gordon James (Fowle), Reginald Tate (Chester), Evan Thomas (Prison Governor), Alan Napier (General), Joyce Barbour (Barmaid), Romilly Lunge (Stafford), Basil Lynn (Solicitor), Walter Lindsay (Butler).

One of Walls and Lynn's better British comedies, FOR VALOR (the inscription on the Victoria Cross) begins during the Boer War and sees foot soldier Walls save the life of his major, Lynn. The grateful Lynn puts Walls in for a Victoria Cross, but his well-intended actions cause Walls' one-way trip back to England to be tried for various crimes he had committed while a civilian. Lynn searches the British prisons for his hero and finally spots him recruiting doughboys for WW I. Lynn offers to raise Walls' boy (who has been a discipline problem) along with his own grandson (who is a goody two-shoes), in the hopes that the good kid will have a decent influence on the bad one. Twenty years later the opposite proves true when Walls' son (also played by Walls) has corrupted Lynn, who ends up in jail, while Walls, Jr. lives comfortably on illegally made monies. Not only that, but young Walls is taking care of old major Lynn, who tells him that his grandson is living happily in the U.S., when in reality he rots in prison.

p, Max Schach; d, Tom Walls; w, Ben Travers; ph, Phillip Tannura.

Comedy (PR:A MPAA:NR)

FOR WHOM THE BELL TOLLS**** (1943) 170m PAR c

Gary Cooper *(Robert Jordan)*, Ingrid Bergman *(Maria)*, Akim Tamiroff *(Pablo)*, Arturo de Cordova *(Agustin)*, Vladimir Sokoloff *(Anselmo)*, Mikhail Rasumny *(Rafael)*, Fortunio Bonanova *(Fernando)*, Eric Feldary *(Andres)*, Victor Varconi *(Primitivo)*, Katina Paxinou *(Pilar)*, Joseph Calleia *(El Sordo)*, Lilo Yarson *(Joaquin)*, Alexander Granach *(Paco)*, Adia Kuznetzoff *(Gustavo)*, Leonid Snegoff *(Ignacio)*, Leo Bulgakov *(Gen. Golz)*, Duncan Renaldo *(Lt. Berrendo)*, George Coulouris *(Andre)*, Frank Puglia *(Capt. Gomez)*, Pedro de Cordoba *(Col. Miranda)*, Michael Visaroff *(Staff Officer)*, Konstantin Shayne *(Karkov)*, Martin Garralaga *(Captain)*, Jean Del Val *(Sniper)*, Jack Mylong *(Col. Duval)*, Feodor Chaliapin *(Kashkin)*, Pedro de Cordoba *(Don Frederico Gonzales)*, Mayo Newhall *(Don Richardo)*, Michael Dalmatoff *(Don Benito Garcia)*, Antonio Vidal *(Don Guillermo)*, Robert Tafur *(Don Faustino Rivero)*, Armand Roland *(Julian)*, Luis Roja *(Drunkard)*, Trini Varela *(Spanish Singer)*, Dick Botiller *(Sergeant)*, Soledad Jiminez *(Don Guillermo's Wife)*, Yakima Canutt *(Young Cavalry Man)*, Tito Renaldo *(1st Sentry)*, Franco Corsaro, Frank Lackteen *(Elias' Men)*, George Sorel *(Bored Sentry)*, John Bleifer *(Peasant Who Flails Gonzalez)*, Harry Cording *(Man Who Flails the Mayor)*, William Edmunds, Alberto Morin, Pedro Regas *(Soldiers)*, Manuel Paris *(Officer of Civil Guards)*, Jose Tortosa, Ernesto Morelli, Manual Lopez *(Civil Guards)*, Maxine Ardell, Yvonne DeCarlo, Marjorie Deanne, Alice Kirby, Marcella Phillips, Lynda Grey, Christopher King, Louise La Planche *(Girls in Cafe)*.

Hemingway's exotic, baroque tale of the Spanish Civil War was brought to the screen with a lavish production and a stellar cast, a film that ages well and, in the light of the groping trends of today's cinema, actually seems to improve as solid drama played against heroic history. Cooper is the American schoolteacher who has volunteered to fight for the Republic against the Fascists, an expert dynamiter. At film's opening he blows up a train and flees across the Spanish countryside with Chaliapin, who is wounded by pursuing soldiers. At Chaliapin's begging request, Cooper shoots him and makes his escape, later appearing in Madrid where he meets with Gen. Golz (Bulgakov), sitting in a nightclub hurriedly cleared by a bombing raid. He is ordered to go into the mountains, organize a small band of guerrillas, and blow up a bridge to prevent the Fascists from counter-attacking when the Republic goes on the offensive. In the mountains Cooper meets Pablo (Tamiroff), the surly, uncooperative leader of the band and a host of colorful, eccentric characters—Pablo's common-law wife, Pilar (Paxinou), Anselmo (Sokoloff), a kindly old man, and other motley types. Also living with the guerrillas is Maria (Bergman) who had been gang-raped and tortured by the Fascists before Tamiroff took her in. She and Cooper are immediately drawn together but Tamiroff resents the intrusion Cooper makes and the respectful attention he is given. He tells Cooper that he is against blowing up the bridge because it will jeopardize his people, and he then takes to drink. Paxinou rallies support for the mission, enlisting all in the band against Tamirff who drunkenly insults everyone and is punched in the mouth by de Cordova. Tamirff smiles through the blood, repeating: "I don't provoke." He later disappears, but returns, apparently repentant and agreeing to lead the retreat after the raid against the bridge. Meanwhile Cooper, Bergman, and Paxinou visit El Sordo's (Calleia's) band and enlist this group in their mission. But a large enemy scouting party discovers Calleia's group and drives them to a mountaintop where they are bombed and destroyed from the air. Cooper learns that the Fascists are aware of the upcoming Republican assault and sends word to Bulgakov to call off the attack. While waiting for a change in orders Cooper and Bergman draw closer together (in the famous sleeping bag scene under the stars). But in the morning Cooper realizes that the Republican attack has begun and he must go ahead with the demolition of the bridge. The band attacks the bridge and other fortifications and Cooper manages to blow up the span just as a column of Fascist tanks approach. Sokoloff and other members of the band are killed and Cooper is mortally wounded when crossing open terrain on horseback. He orders Bergman to be taken out of the mountains by Tamiroff, Paxinou, and others while he stays behind, guarding their retreat with a machinegun. As the pursuing enemy approaches, Cooper opens fire, gunsmoke from the machinegun filling the screen which fades to a huge bell tolling out his death. (The machinegun fire ending is a repeat of Robert Taylor's end in BATAAN, 1943.) Cooper was the perfect Hemingway hero, handpicked by the author (he had played in Hemingway's first novel brought to the screen, A FAREWELL TO ARMS, 1930), taciturn, deliberate, withdrawn, but ready for action. Bergman played the part of the youthful Maria with exuberance and wide-eyed innocence, awkwardly falling in love with her star-crossed hero, her head close-cropped for the part which gave her a startling appearance in the early 1940s when long hair, including her own in films such as CASABLANCA, was mandatory fashion. Bergman, too, had been selected to play her part by Hemingway. The actress had met Hemingway's third wife, newswoman Martha Gellhorn, on board an ocean liner in 1939 and they had become friends; she later met the author in San Francisco and he was as charmed by her as he was by another close actress friend, Marlene Dietrich. Paramount objected to Bergman when Hemingway suggested her for the role, but the author insisted to the point of refusing to sign the deal with the studio so she got the part, and Vera Zorina, who had tested and been assigned the role, was removed. Zorina went to the pains of cutting her hair and spending three weeks of preproduction setups with Cooper in the high Sierra Nevadas where the film was later shot on-location; when she was removed from the film the actress threatened to sue for having to walk about with a near-hairless head without a role to go with it. Paramount settled out of court. Oddly, many of the character actors in the film—Tamiroff, Sokoloff, Rasumny, Kuznetzoff, Snegoff, Bulgakov, Visaroff, Chaliapin—are of Russion extraction and few Spaniards are in evidence. The film was careful not to spell out the enemy as Franco (his name is never mentioned) or the Falangists, and calling the loyalists Republicans. This stance later caused politically minded critics to accuse Paramount of fence-sitting. Retorted Paramount's chief Adolph Zukor: "It's a great picture, without political significance. We are not for or against anybody." Unsubstantiated reports had it that Franco's envoys pressured the studio into a nonpartisan stand. Hemingway received a then whopping $150,000 for the film rights and Cecil B. DeMille originally planned to direct the film but the chore was handed over to Sam Wood, who had been DeMille's assistant as early as 1915; Wood brought in William Cameron Menzies to design the exquisitely mounted production (Menzies had designed Wood's KING'S ROW and GONE WITH THE WIND). Though Wood's pace is a bit slow in a few spots, the story is packed with drama and action, its color photography wonderfully shot, and Young's score is a dynamic and memorable contribution. The film received a bevy of Oscar nominations but only Paxinou won for Best Supporting Actress. Whe re-issued in the 1950s several minutes involving scenes with Shayne and Coulouris were deleted and this truncated version is most often seen. The plotline was unofficially used again for FIGHTER ATTACK, a 1953 B-film programmer from Allied Artists, starring Sterling Hayden and Joy Page.

p&d, Sam Wood; w, Dudley Nichols (based on the novel by Ernest Hemingway); ph, Ray Rennahan (Technicolor); m, Victor Young; ed, Sherman Todd, John Link; prod d, William Cameron Menzies; art d, Hans Dreier, Haldane Douglas; set d, Bert Granger; spec eff, Gordon Jennings; m/l, Victor Young, Ned Washington, Milton Drake, Walter Kent; makeup, Wally Westmore.

Adventure/War (PR:C MPAA:NR)

FOR YOU ALONE*½ (1945, Brit.) 105m BUT bw

Lesley Brook *(Katherine Britton)*, Jimmy Hanley *(Dennis Britton)*, Dinah Sheridan *(Stella White)*, G.H. Mulcaster *(Rev. Peter Britton)*, Robert Griffith *(John Bradshaw)*, Olive Walter *(Lady Markham)*, Manning Whiley *(Max Borrow)*, Irene Handl *(Miss Trotter)*, George Merritt *(Police Constable Blundell)*, Muriel George *(Mrs. Johns)*, Helen Hill, Heddle Nash, Albert Sandler, Hay Petrie, Aubrey Mallalieu, Billy Shine, London Symphony Orchestra.

Soppy musical has Whiley a half-blinded veteran falling in love with Brook, the sister of a war buddy. She, however, loves Griffith, and when Whiley realizes that his love is hopeless, he leaves. Overlong, though later reissue was cut to 98 minutes, then 77 minutes.

p, F.W. Baker; d, Geoffrey Faithfull; w, Montgomery Tully (based on a story by Kathleen Butler); ph, Ernest Palmer.

Musical (PR:A MPAA:NR)

FOR YOU I DIE* (1947) 76m Film Classics bw

Cathy Downs *(Hope Novak)*, Paul Langton *(Johnny Coulter)*, Mischa Auer *(Alec Shaw)*, Roman Bohnen *(Smitty)*, Jane Weeks *(Georgie)*, Marion Kerby *(Maggie Dillon)*, Mannela Callejo *(Louisa)*, Don Harvey *(Gruber)*, Charles Waldron, Jr. *(Jerry)*, Rory Mallinson *(Mac)*.

Hackneyed soap opera starring Langton as an escaped convict who hides out at a secluded tourist camp where he meets and falls in love with the unbearably sweet and noble Downs. Because of his new-found love he reforms from his life of crime and attempts to forget his past.

p, Robert Presnell, Sr., John Reinhardt; d, Reinhardt; w, Presnell; ph, William Clothier; ed, Jason Bernie.

Drama (PR:A MPAA:NR)

FOR YOUR EYES ONLY*** (1981) 127m UA c

Roger Moore *(James Bond)*, Carole Bouquet *(Melina)*, Topol *(Columbo)*, Lynn-Holly Johnson *(Bibi)*, Julian Glover *(Kristatos)*, Cassandra Harris *(Lisl)*, Jill Bennett *(Brink)*, Michael Gothard *(Locque)*, John Wyman *(Kriegler)*, Jack Hedley *(Havelock)*, Lois Maxwell *(Moneypenny)*, Desmond Llewelyn *(Q)*, Geoffrey Keen *(Minister of Defense)*, John Wells *(Denis)*, Janet Brown *(Prime Minister)*, Walter Gotell *(General Gogol)*, James Villiers *(Tanner)*, John Moreno *(Ferrara)*, Charles Dance *(Claus)*, Paul Angelis *(Karageorge)*, Toby Robins *(Iona Havelock)*, Jack Klaff *(Apostis)*, Alkis Kritikos *(Santos)*, Stag Theodore *(Nikos)*, Stefan Kalipha *(Gonzales)*, Graham Crowden *(1st Sea Lord)*, Noel Johnson *(Vice Admiral)*, William Hoyland *(McGregor)*, Paul Brooke *(Bunky)*, Eva Reuber-Staier *(Rublevich)*, Fred Bryant *(Vicar)*, Robbin Young *(Girl in Flower Shop)*, Graham Hawkes *(Mantis Man)*, Max Vesterhalt *(Girl at Casino)*, Lalla Dean *(Girl at Pool)*, Evelyn Drogue, Laoura Hadzivageli, Koko, Chai Lee, Kim Mills, Tula, Vanya, Viva, Lizzie Warville, Alison Worth *(Bond Beauties)*.

After returning to Earth from his MOONRAKER fiasco, Moore resumes his role as James Bond without the excessive technical gadgetry that began to hurt the series. While spending half his time on skis, Moore and the obligatory beauty, Bouquet, set out on a fast-paced chase and counterchase involving a gang of Soviet spies, who also happen to be the killers of Bouquet's father. The success of this picture (perhaps Moore's best in the Bond series), can be attributed to the marvelous direction of John Glen, who had a vault of experience behind him from his days as Bond series second-unit director. The stunts are some of the best in the series, and certainly hold up to previous standards. However, they were not executed without danger. While filming a sequence which has Bond pursued by motorcyclists riding spike-wheeled bikes, a bobsled accident led to the death of one of the stuntmen. A second tragedy followed shortly thereafter when Bernard Lee, the familiar Bond chief known as "M," died before his scenes were shot. Again, the title tune received a ton of air play, pushing Sheena Easton's single to the top of the charts.

p, Albert R. Broccoli; d, John Glen; w, Richard Maibaum, Michael G. Wilson (based on the short stories "For Your Eyes Only" and "Risico" by Ian Fleming); ph, Alan Hume (Panavision, Technicolor); m, Bill Conti; ed, John Grover; prod d, Peter Lamont; art d, John Fenner; set d, Vernon Dixon; cos, Elizabeth Waller; spec eff, Derek Meddings; lyrics, Michael Leeson; m/l "For Your Eyes Only," Conti, Leeson (sung by Sheena Easton); stunts, Rick Sylvester.

Spy/Adventure Cas. (PR:A MPAA:PG)

FORBIDDEN*** (1932) 87m COL bw

Barbara Stanwyck *(Lulu Smith)*, Adophe Menjou *(Bob Grover)*, Ralph Bellamy *(Al Holland)*, Dorothy Peterson *(Helen)*, Thomas Jefferson *(Winkinson)*, Charlotte V. Henry *(Roberta at Age 18)*, Tom Ricketts *(Briggs)*, Halliwell Hobbes *(Florist)*; Myrna Fresholtz *(Roberta as a Baby)*, Helen Parrish *(Roberta at age 8)*; Mary Jo

Ellis (Roberta at Age 12), Bob Parrish, Dick Winslow, Cooke Phelps, Roger Byrne (Office Boys), Helen Stuart (Woman), Carmencita Johnson, Seesel Ann Johnson, Larry Dolan, Lynn Compton (Children in Halloween Scene), Oliver Eckhardt, Claude King, Florence Wix, Robert T. Graves, Gertrude Pedlar, Wilfred Noy, Harry Holman.

Stanwyck is the staid librarian who falls in love with District Attorney Menjou, who conducts an affair with her although he is married to crippled Peterson. Stanwyck has a daughter by him and the child is adopted by Menjou, while Stanwyck gets a job working for muckraking journalist Bellamy, who is continually looking for someone to ruin. Menjou, as the district attorney, works his way up the political ladder to governor. Stanwyck marries Bellamy, but when he learns of her past and threatens to publish it, Stanwyck shoots him. Capra himself described the story as "two hours of soggy, 99.44 percent soap opera." A weepy, implausible melodrama, the only redeeming features here are professional performances by Menjou and Stanwyck and some very good photography by Walker. Stanwyck was the second choice to play the lead in this film. It had been turned down by Helen Hayes after she had been successful in a very similar part in THE SIN OF MADELON CLAUDET.

P, Harry Cohn; d, Frank Capra; w, Jo Swerling (based on a story by Capra); ph, Joseph Walker; ed, Maurice Wright; cos, Edward Stevenson; m/l, "Cupid's Holiday," Irving Bibo, Pete Fylling; makeup, Monte Westmore.

Drama (PR:A-C MPAA:NR)

FORBIDDEN**½ (1949, Brit.) 87m Pennant Pictures/BL bw

Douglass Montgomery (Jim Harding), Hazel Court (Jane Thompson), Patricia Burke (Diana Harding), Garry Marsh (Jerry Burns), Ronald Shiner (Dan Collins), Kenneth Griffith (Johnny), Eliot Makeham (Mr. Thompson), Frederick Leister (Dr. Franklin), Richard Bird (Jennings), Michael Medwin (Cabby), Andrew Cruickshank (Baxter), William Douglas, Dora Stevening, Erik Chitty, Peggy Ann Clifford, Dennis Hawkins, Peter Jones.

Montgomery, a patent medicine seller, falls in love with ice cream girl Court, but his wife (Burke) won't give him a divorce. He increases the shrew's dosage of pills in an attempt to provoke a heart attack, and coming home later he finds her dead. After secretly burying her, he finds the extra pills he had given her. Police track him down after a chase, but they know that Harding died of natural causes. Quite good, if somewhat bleak, drama. One of several films Montgomery, a Hollywood leading man in the 1930s, made over the next decade in England.

p&d, George King; w, Katherine Strueby (based on a story by Val Valentine); ph, Hone Glendinning.

Crime Drama (PR:A-C MPAA:NR)

FORBIDDEN**½ (1953) 84m UNIV bw

Tony Curtis (Eddie), Joanne Dru (Christine), Lyle Bettger (Justin), Marvin Miller (Chalmer), Victor Sen Yung (Allan), Peter J. Mamakos (Sam), Mae Tai Sing (Soo Lee), Howard Chuman (Hon-Fai), Weaver Levy (Tang), Alan Dexter (Barney), David Sharpe (Leon), Harold Fong (Wong), Mamie Van Doren (Singer), Aen Ling Chow, Leemoi Chu (Girl Dealers), Barry Bernard (Black), Harry Lauter (Holly), Reginald Sheffield (Englishman), Alphonse Martell (Guest), Al Ferguson (Harbor Master), Jimmy Gray (Guard), Spencer Chan (Chin).

Curtis is a bright hood who is hired to bring Dru back from the little island of Macao to the States, where she can turn evidence on her mobster husband. Curtis' mission sparks a past romantic flame that existed between the couple, which, by the finale, is burning strong. Curtis turns in a decent performance as the gangster who has both of those stereotypical traits—a hard edge and a gentle interior.

p, Ted Richmond; d, Rudolph Mate; w, William Sackheim, Gil Doud (based on a story by Sackheim); ph, William Daniels; m, Frank Skinner; ed, Edward Curtiss; art d, Bernard Herzbrun, Richard Riedel.

Drama (PR:A MPAA:NR)

FORBIDDEN ALLIANCE
(SEE: BARRETTS OF WIMPOLE STREET, 1934)

FORBIDDEN CARGO** (1954, Brit.) 83m GFD bw

Nigel Patrick (Michael Kenyon), Elizabeth Sellars (Rita Compton), Terence Morgan (Roger Compton), Jack Warner (Alec White), Greta Gynt (Mme. Simonetta), Theodore Bikel (Max), Joyce Grenfell (Lady Flavin Queensway), James Gilbert (Larkins), Eric Pohlmann (Lasovin), Michael Hordern (Director), Martin Boddey (Holt), Hal Osmond (Attendant), Jacques Brunius (Pierre Valance).

Patrick plays a British customs agent who foils a ring of French dope smugglers whose evil contraband has been flooding England. Much attention is devoted to the mechanics of smuggling and its subsequent detection, which gives this thriller an interesting documentary flavor.

p, Sydney Box, Earl St. John; d, Harold French; w, Box; ph, C. Pennington-Richards; m, Lambert Williamson; ed, Anne V. Coates; art d, John Howell.

Crime (PR:A MPAA:NR)

FORBIDDEN COMPANY** (1932) 67m IN/CHES bw

Sally Blane (Janet Blake), John Darrow (Jerry Grant), John St. Polis (David Grant), Myrtle Stedman (Mrs. Grant), Josephine Dunn (Harriet), Dorothy Christy (Louselle), Bryant Washburn (Fletcher), David Durand (Billy), Norma Drew (Diane).

Darrow, falls madly in love with model Blane, who he meets after accidentally running her down with his car. She falls for him, but his parents don't approve. When Darrow's mother, Stedman, gets involved in a car accident, Blane volunteers for the blood transfusion that will save her life, and under this act of charity the romance leaves the forbidden category and joins the company.

d, Richard Thorpe; w, Edward T. Lowe; ph, M.A. Anderson.

Drama (PR:A MPAA:NR)

FORBIDDEN FRUIT*** (1959, Fr.) 97m Gray Film/Films-Around-The-World bw (LE FRUIT DEFENDU)

Fernandel (Dr. Charles Pellegrin), Francoise Arnoul (Martine), Claude Nollier (Armande Pellegrin), Sylvie (Mother Pellegrin), Jacques Castelot (Boquet), Rene Genin (Marchandeau), Fernand Sardou (Fontvielle).

Fernandel plays a doctor married to Nollier who rebels against her and his mother (Sylvie), engaging in an affair with young Arnoul. The rare noncomedic performance by Fernandel is quite good, and the whole film is steadfastly adult and serious. The most effective scenes are those lifted directly out of Simenon's excellent novel. (In French: English subtitles.)

p, A. D'Aguilar; d, Henri Verneuil; w, Jacques Companeez, Jean Manse, Verneuil (based on the novel Act of Passion by Georges Simenon); English Subtitles, R.L. Sokol.

Drama (PR:C MPAA:NR)

FORBIDDEN GAMES**** (1953, Fr.) 90m Silver/Times Film bw (LES JEUX INTERDIT

Brigitte Fossey (Paulette), Georges Poujouly (Michel Dolle), Lucien Hubert (Dolle the Father), Suzanne Courtal (Mme. Dolle), Jacques Marin (Georges Dolle), Laurence Badie (Berthe Dolle), Andre Wasley (Gouard the Father), Amedee (Francis Gouard), Denise Perronne (Jeanne Gouard), Louis Sainteve (Priest), Pierre Merovee (Raymond Dolle).

One of the best films ever about war and its effects, FORBIDDEN GAMES begins slowly and carefully. Refugees fleeing Paris in the face of the Nazi attack jam a road. At a bottleneck on a bridge, German planes swoop down in perfect formation and strafe the confused column. Fossey is seen standing alone on the bridge, her parents and dog dead. When someone takes the dog and throws it over the bridge, Fossey goes after it and meets Poujouly, the 11-year-old son of peasants Hubert and Courtal. The boy takes the girl home with him and his parents take her in. When she sees her parents buried with the other victims in a common grave, she decides that her dog also needs to be buried in a grave with a cross. She and Poujouly steal a cross from the hearse carrying his older brother and when he tries to steal another cross off the altar of the church he is caught by the priest, but released. He and Fossey begin to expand their secret animal cemetery, adding moles, chickens, and even insects, all given elaborate memorial services like the ones said over the dead which they cannot understand. Poujouly steals a number of crosses from the churchyard but the priest names him as the likely thief. Poujouly hides but is found and beaten by his father, who demands to be told where the crosses are. Authorities arrive to take Fossey away; Poujouly promises to reveal the site of the hidden crosses if she is allowed to stay with them. Hubert agrees but when he learns where the crosses are he turns the girl over. Poujouly rushes to the secret cemetery and destroys all the crosses. FORBIDDEN GAMES derives most of its power from Clement's painstakingly methodical direction and the amazing performance of Fossey. The film was originally intended as one episode in an anthology film to be entitled CROSS OF WOOD, CROSS OF IRON, but when he began adapting the Boyer novel for the first episode he realized that it could stand by itself as a feature. The director found Fossey while the 5 year old was vacationing with her aunt, and though he had originally planned to cast an 8 year old in the part whom he thought could understand the subtleties of the character, he was so taken with Fossey's intelligence and look that he gave her the role. Poujouly was found at a summer camp for deprived Parisian kids. The film's final scene, Fossey at the train station crying Poujouly's name and "Mama" over and over as the camera cranes out and loses her in a sea of other displaced persons is one of the most harrowing moments in the cinema. Quite justly, the film was a great critical success, winning every major award in Europe and the Oscar for Best Foreign Language Film. A prolog and epilog were cut from the U.S. prints; the original European running time is 102 minutes. (In French; English subtitles.)

p, Robert Dorfman; d, Rene Clement; w, Clement, Jean Aurenche, Pierre Bost (based on the novel Les Jeux Inconnus by Francois Boyer); ph, Robert Juillard; m, Narciso Yepes; ed, Roger Dwyre; art d, Paul Bertrand; English subtitles, Herman G. Weinberg.

Drama Cas. (PR:C MPAA:NR)

FORBIDDEN HEAVEN* (1936) 68m REP bw

Charles Farrell (Niba), Charlotte Henry (Ann), Beryl Mercer (Agnes), Fred Walton (Pluffy), Phyllis Barry (Sybil), Eric Wilton (Radford), Barry Winton (Allen), Eric Snowden (Speaker).

This plodding political drama has American actor Farrell playing a British worker obsessed with running for Parliament. He rescues a homeless girl, Henry, falls in love, and ends up marrying her. Interesting only in its startling lack of realism because of the many breaks Farrell has in his English accent. A large amount of American slang pockmarks this film though Farrell is playing an Englishman.

p, Trem Carr; d, Reginald Barker; w, Sada Cowan, Jefferson Parker (story by Christine Jope-Slade); ph, Milton Krasner, ed, Jack Ogilvie.

Drama (PR:A MPAA:NR)

FORBIDDEN ISLAND**½ (1959) 66m COL c

Jon Hall (Dave Courtney), Nan Adams (Joanne), John Farrow (Stuart Godfrey), Jonathan Haze (Jack Mautner), Greigh Phillips (Dean Pike), Dave "Howdy" Peters (Fermin Fry), Tookie Evans (Raul Estoril), Martin Denny (Marty), Bob LaVarre (Cal Priest), Bill Anderson (Mike), Abraham Kaluna (Abe).

Underwater programmer featuring Farrow as a psychotic treasure hunter who hires freelance frogmen, headed by Hall, to recover an emerald that went down in a shipwreck. When one diver discovers evidence leading him to believe that Farrow killed someone to get the gem in the first place, Farrow knocks off the diver by damaging his aqualung. This leads to a frogman free-for-all in which everyone is killed. Wickedly offbeat undersea adventure with all of the cast performing superbly. Hall, who had scored well in John Ford's HURRICANE, was pegged as a leading man more than capable of performing his own water stunts; he had been an accomplished swimmer since the age of five and performed his own water acrobatics, including spectacular high dives of more than 130 feet. Other South Seas films where Hall's swimming expertise can be seen include ALOMA OF THE SOUTH SEAS (1941) and ON THE ISLE OF SAMOA (1950).

p,d&w, Charles B. Griffith; ph, Gilbert Warrenton (Columbia Color); m, Alexander Laszlo; ed, Jerome Thoms; m/l "Forbidden Island," Martin Denny; underwater camera, Lamar Boren.

Adventure **(PR:C MPAA:NR)**

FORBIDDEN JOURNEY* (1950, Can.) 95m Selkirk/UA bw

Jan Rubes *(Jan Bartik)*, Susan Douglas *(Mary Sherritt)*, Gerry Rown *(Prof. Bartik)*, Richard Kronold *(Joe)*, Mac Shoub *(Stub)*, Rupert Caplan *(Shipping Agent)*, Blanche Gautier *(Mme. Duval)*, John Colicos *(Student)*, Eleanor Stuart *(Aunt Sherritt)*, Elizabeth Leese *(Dancer)*.

Dull and confusing espionage film starring Rubes as a spy attempting to pass on government secrets to a fellow agent in Montreal. The usual tedium of double-crosses, counter-agents, and paranoia. Panoramic footage of Montreal gives this film what little interest it has, even for fans of the genre.

p,d&w, Dick Jarvis, Cecil Maiden; ph, Roger Racine.

Spy Drama **(PR:A MPAA:NR)**

FORBIDDEN JUNGLE* (1950) 67m EL bw

Don Harvey *(Tom Burton)*, Forrest Taylor *(Trader Kirk)*, Alyce Louis *(Nita)*, Robert Cabal *(Tawa)*, Tamba the Chimp.

Filled with overused stock footage of wild African beasts, this boring entry in the endless series of "jungle boy" films (a subgenre with little redeeming value) follows a great white hunter as he seeks to capture a wild child he believes may be his grandson. The hunter locates the boy, but it is soon obvious that if he were to return to civilization, the boy would die. The hunter nobly decides to let the boy continue his happy life in the wild.

p, Jack Schwarz; d, Robert Tansey; w, Frances Kavanaugh; ph, Clark Ramsey; m, Darrell Calker; ed, Reg Browne.

Adventure **(PR:A MPAA:NR)**

FORBIDDEN LOVE AFFAIR (SEE: FOREVER YOUNG, FOREVER FREE, 1976, South Afr.)

FORBIDDEN MUSIC*** (1936, Brit.) 80m CAP/GFD bw (GB: LAND WITHOUT MUSIC)

Richard Tauber *(Mario Carlini)*, Jimmy Durante *(Jonah J. Whistler)*, Diana Napier *(Princess Regent)*, June Clyde *(Sadie Whistler)*, Derrick de Marney *(Rudolpho Strozzi)*, Esme Percy *(Austrian Ambassador)*, George Hayes *(Capt. Strozzi)*, John Hepworth *(Pedro)*, Edward Rigby *(Maestro)*, George Carney *(Prison Warder)*, Ivan Wilmot *(Chief Bandit)*, Robert Nainby *(Minister for War)*, Joe Monkhouse *(Finance Minister)*, Quinton Mcperson *(Customs Officer)*.

Lighthearted operetta about a small European kingdom where the ruler has outlawed music because he feels it keeps the people from concentrating. Tauber, once one of Europe's most splendid tenor voices, leads a revolt against the decree, which lands him in jail. But the subjects continue rebelling until they win back their beloved music. Performances are adquate, with excellent vocal abilities being exhibited. Direction is well paced, with a balance between the musical numbers and the action of the piquant story. This was one of the films the Austrian-born actor-singer made after emigrating to England because of the Nazi takeover of Germany.

p, Max Schach; d, Walter Forde; w, Rudolph Bernauer, Marian Dix, L. du Garde Peach (based on a story by Fritz Koselka, Armin Robinson); ph, John Boyle; m, Oscar Straus; m/l, Straus.

Musical **(PR:A MPAA:NR)**

FORBIDDEN PARADISE (SEE: HURRICANE, 1979)

FORBIDDEN PLANET**** (1956) 98m MGM c

Walter Pidgeon *(Doctor Morbius)*, Anne Francis *(Altaira)*, Leslie Nielsen *(Comdr. Adams)*, Warren Stevens *(Lt. "Doc" Ostrow)*, Jack Kelly *(Lt. Farman)*, Richard Anderson *(Chief Quinn)*, Earl Holliman *(Cook)*, George Wallace *(Bosun)*, Bob Dix *(Grey)*, Jimmy Thompson *(Youngerford)*, James Drury *(Strong)*, Harry Harvey, Jr. *(Randall)*, Roger McGee *(Lindstrom)*, Peter Miller *(Moran)*, Morgan Jones *(Nichols)*, Richard Grant *(Silvers)*, Robby the Robot.

A superb entry in the science fiction genre, FORBIDDEN PLANET offers an unusually intelligent script, careful and exciting direction by Wilcox, and excellent acting from an entire cast threatened by a strange monster on an exotic planet. It is 2200 A.D. when commander Nielsen lands his United Planets Cruiser C-57D on Altair-4, where the sky is green, the sand pink, and two moons circle above. Moments before landing Nielsen and his 14-man crew have been warned not to land by a Dr. Morbius (Pidgeon), a member of a missing Earth colony sent to the planet 20 years earlier. Undaunted, the spacemen land looking for the missing colony, and are greeted by Robby the Robot, a benign and astounding creation speaking 88 languages and having the ability to perform myriad chores, including the preparation of elaborate meals, the tailoring of exquisite clothes, driving a space vehicle, and, at the behest of mischievous crew member Holliman, producing unlimited quantities of bourbon. The marvelous robot is also harmless, programmed never to use its enormous intellect or physical power against humans. The robot drives Nielsen, Stevens, and Kelly to the futuristic home of Pidgeon where they meet the brilliant scientist and his beautiful daughter, Francis. Pidgeon explains that they are the only survivors of the Earth colony that died many years earlier, its members, including Pidgeon's wife, mysteriously dying at the hands of an invisible, terrible monster that prowls the planet. Francis, who has never seen any man other than her father, is taught how to kiss by Kelly and when she tries it with Nielsen both realize they are attracted to each other. Meanwhile, supplies from the ship vanish and equipment is found mysteriously damaged. Pidgeon later takes the visitors to the underground nerve center of the planet, one created 2000 years earlier by a long-vanished civilization, the Krell. Here he demonstrates a "brain booster" which, if used often enough, will provide infinite knowledge, but it's dangerous to regularly apply this machine, the spacemen later learn. When crew member Anderson, is killed, Pidgeon tells the visitors to depart, that the monster is still present on the planet. Nielsen, however, orders a force field established around his ship and the invisible monster, an enormous fierce animal-like being, is suddenly seen when hit by a crossfire of laser beams. It is truly horrific and almost breaks through the defenses, killing Kelly and others before it relents. Stevens, in order to understand this monstrous creature, applies the "brain booster" and takes a full and fatal charge. Before dying, Stevens manages to tell Nielsen about the nature of the invisible attacker, calling it "the monster of the Id," the force that destroyed the long-ago Krell civilization. The monster then attacks Pidgeon's steel-encased home, punching through armor plate as Pidgeon, Nielsen, and Francis retreat into the Krell nerve center. The monster still pursues them, burning away thick Krell steel, the hardest substance known in the universe. Nielsen finally yells at Pidgeon: "That thing out there—it's you!" He tells the scientist that it's Pidgeon's own subconscious that is bent on destroying them. Pidgeon realizes the truth of Nielsen's statement and screams at the thing melting away the last barrier: "I deny you! I give you up!" The strain of destroying his own subconscious is too much and Pidgeon dies, the Id monster dying with him. Nielsen yanks a doomsday lever that motivates a chain reaction that will explode the Krell furnaces deep inside the planet. He and Francis then board the spaceship which takes off at supersonic speeds, putting them in deep space where they watch Altair-4 explode in an atomic blast that reduces the planet to space dust. FORBIDDEN PLANET was the first science fiction film produced for $1 million—by a major studio. Its writer, Block, had devised the special effects for the standout ROCKET SHIP X-M, 1950. The film is really a futuristic version of Shakespeare's "The Tempest," with Pidgeon in the role of magician Prospero, Francis playing Miranda, the robot-like Spirit Ariel, and the Id being Caliban the witch-child. Block and partner Adler spurned Allied Artists, a top poverty row studio/distributor then grinding out cheap sci-fi movies, and convinced MGM's Dore Schary to produce the film (orignally called FATAL PLANET). The technical achievements of FORBIDDEN PLANET are astounding. The Barrons created an electronic score (reportedly for $25,000) that bubbles, gurgles, rumbles, and screams through scores of circuits. Altair-4's beautiful, eerie atmosphere was achieved through a 10,000-foot cyclorama painting and Gillespie created a 6-foot 11-inch Robby the Robot with a clear plastic head that allows the electronic waves of his brain to be seen in crackling action. Disney animator Meador was hired by Schary to create the Id monster. Lonergan's sets of the spaceship, Pidgeon's home, and the Krell laboratory are massive and stunning. Director Wilcox proved his versatility once more with this superb production, having helmed such diversified films as LASSIE COME HOME (1943) and I PASSED FOR WHITE (1960). Robby the Robot was such a hit that the marvelous machine was employed once again in THE INVISIBLE BOY (1957).

p, Nicholas Nayfack; d, Fred McLeod Wilcox; w, Cyril Hume (based on a story by Irving Block, Allen Adler); ph, George Folsey (CinemaScope, Eastmancolor); m, Louis and Bebe Barron; ed, Ferris Webster; art d, Cedric Gibbons, Arthur Lonergan; set d, Edwin B. Willis, Hugh Hunt; cos, Helen Rose, Walter Plunkett; spec eff, A. Arnold Gillespie, Warren Newcomb, Irving G. Reis, Joshua Meador; makeup, William Tuttle.

Science Fiction **Cas.** **(PR:C MPAA:NR)**

FORBIDDEN RELATIONS** (1983, Hung.) 92m Objektiv Filmstudio-Mafilm/Cinegate c

Lili Monori, Miklos B. Szekely, Mari Torocsik, Jozsef Horvath, Jozsef Toth, Tibor Molnar, Gyorgy Banffy, Laszlo Horvath, Ferenc Palancy, Maria Bajcsay, Klara Leviczki, Judit Balog, Ferenc Nemethy, Laszlo Horesnyi, Juli Nyako, Laszlo Joo, Gyorgy Pogany, Gabor Balassa.

Controversial Hungarian export about an incestuous brother-sister relationship. Monori and Szekely are the sexually intimate siblings, neither attractive nor intelligent, facing a Communist bureaucracy which eventually imprisons them both. Quite explicit sexually, but an interesting film on a subject taboo on both sides of the Iron Curtain.

p, Jozsef Marx; d&w, Zsolt Kezdi-Kovacs; ph, Janos Kende (Eastmancolor); ed, Andrasne Karmento; art d, Tamas Banovich.

Drama **(PR:O MPAA:NR)**

FORBIDDEN STREET, THE (SEE: AFFAIRS OF ADELAIDE, 1949, U.S./Brit.)

FORBIDDEN TERRITORY½** (1938, Brit.) 83m Gaumont bw

Gregory Ratoff *(Alexei Leshki)*, Ronald Squire *(Sir Charles Farringdon)*, Binnie Barnes *(Valerie Petrovna)*, Tamara Desni *(Marie-Louise)*, Barry Mackay *(Michael Farringdon)*, Anthony Bushell *(Rex Farringdon)*, Anton Dolin *(Jack Straw)*, Marguerite Allan *(Fenya)*, Boris Ranevsky *(Runov)*.

A good low-budget thriller that turned out much better than the programmer it was meant to be. A young Englishman in Russia looking for some buried crown jewels stumbles on a secret Russian aircraft site. He lands in jail. Back home, his dad, a nobleman, and brother hear the news and set off to find him. With the help of two Russian women, they do, but not until many minutes of intense excitement pass while they all thwart the Russian secret police. The clever, suspenseful script has much to do with writer Reville being the lifelong wife of pantheon filmmaker Alfred Hitchcock.

p, Richard Wainwright; d, Phil Rosen; w, Dorothy Farnum, Alma Reville (based on the novel by Dennis Wheatley); ph, R. Goldenberg.

Adventure **(PR:A MPAA:NR)**

FORBIDDEN TRAIL** (1936) 65m COL bw

Buck Jones *(Tom Devlin)*, Barbara Weeks *(Mary Middleton)*, Mary Carr *(Mrs. Middleton)*, George Cooper *(Happy)*, Ed Brady *(Snodgrass)*, Frank Rice *(Sheriff)*, Al Smith *(Burke)*, Frank La Rue *(Collins)*, Wong Chung *(Chinese Cook)*, Wallis Clark *(Karger)*, Tom Forman *(Ranch Foreman)*, Gertrude Howard *(Negro Mammy)*, Dick Rush *(Wright)*, Charles Berner *(Johnson)*, Silver the Horse.

Attempt to inject comedy into formula western fails abysmally as Jones is ludicrous as clown-cowboy. When he reverts to his basic strengths, riding and shooting, he regains his stature. He is pitted against bad guy Clark's band of outlaws, who commit virtually every misdeed known to B-westerns. While subduing his foes, Jones falls in love with sagebrush sweetie Weeks. Jones was often attacked by critics for his attempts at comedy, but in the end it was the audiences who counted—and they accepted his antics and the bit of gaiety they injected in the dark days of the Depression.

d, Lambert Hillyer; w, Milton Krims; ph, L. William O'Connell; ed, Gene Milford.

Western **Cas.** **(PR:A MPAA:NR)**

FORBIDDEN TRAILS** (1941) 55m MON bw

Buck Jones *(Buck Roberts)*, Tim McCoy *(Colonel)*, Raymond Hatton *(Sandy)*, Tristram Coffin *(Nelson)*, Charles King *(Fulton)*, Glen Strange *(Howard)*, Lynton Brent *(Bill)*, Jerry Sheldon *(Sam)*, Hal Price *(Bunion)*, Dave O'Brien *(Jim Cramer)*, Christine McIntyre *(Mary)*, Dick Alexander, Silver the Horse.

Two released convicts, who had been sent to the hoosegow by Jones, vow revenge. They trick Jones into a kerosene-doused shack and, only with the heroics of his loyal horse, Silver, does he escape the plot. McCoy and Hatton go undercover to apprehend the outlaws.

p, Scott R. Dunlap; d, Robert North Bradbury; w, Jess Bowers [Adele Buffington] (based on a story by Oliver Drake); ph, Harry Neumann; ed, Carl Pierson.

Western **Cas.** **(PR:A MPAA:NR)**

FORBIDDEN VALLEY*½ (1938) 68m UNIV bw

Noah Beery, Jr. *(Ring)*, Frances Robinson *(Wilda)*, Fred Kohler, Sr. *(Regan)*, Alonzo Price *(Indian Joe)*, Samuel S. Hinds *(Hazzard)*, Stanley Andrews *(Lanning)*, Spencer Charters *(Dr. Scudd)*, Charles Stevens *(Blackjack)*, Soledad Jiminez *(Meetah)*, Ferris Taylor *(Walcott)*, Margaret McWade *(Mrs. Scudd)*, Henry Hunter *(Bagley)*, John Ridgley *(Duke)*, James Foran *(Brandon)*, Sarah Padden *(Mrs. Ragona)*, Glenn Strange *(Corlox)*.

Screenwriter Gittens directed his own material in this film, and it turned out to be popular among matinee-viewing adolescents. Beery plays a boy raised by his father, Hinds, who has been accused of a murder he didn't commit and hides as an escaped convict in the mountains in near isolation. Poor little rich girl Robinson also lives there and Beery falls in love with her. Hinds is killed when he is bumped from his horse and dragged along the rocky terrain. Now on his own, Beery heads for civilization and locates Robinson, who is engaged to be married but loves him nonetheless. He also finds Kohler, who committed the murder blamed on his father, and clears his father's name.

p, Henry McRae, Elmer Tambert; d&w, Wyndham Gittens (based on a novel by Stuart Hardy); ph, Elwood Bredell; ed, Frank Gross.

Western **(PR:AA MPAA:NR)**

FORBIDDEN WORLD* (1982) 86m New World c (AKA: MUTANT)

Jesse Vint *(Mike Colby)*, June Chadwick *(Dr. Barbara Glasser)*, Dawn Dunlap *(Tracy Baxter)*, Linden Chiles *(Dr. Gordon Hauser)*, Fox Harris *(Dr. Cal Tinburgen)*, Raymond Oliver *(Brian Beale)*, Scott Paulin *(Earl Richards)*, Michael Bowen *(Jimmy Swift)*.

A variation of Ridley Scott's amazingly successful sci-fi/horror film ALIEN. Corman and company let loose a blood-sucking, carnivorous monster on the tiny crew of nearly unwatchable performers who populate a scientific research spaceship. If ALIEN seemed gory, FORBIDDEN WORLD makes it look like a Disney film. Eventually, one scientist realizes he is dying from cancer and forces crewman Vint to remove his diseased liver and feed it to the monster so that it will contract the big "C" and die. The film barely avoided an "X" rating from the MPAA after it cut a reportedly vile scene wherein a female crew member is raped by the alien. Trashy, but the suspense scenes are well-directed and the effects are impressive for such a low-budget effort. This one is not for children or adults without iron stomachs.

p, Roger Corman, Mary Ann Fisher; d, Allan Holzman; w, Tim Curnen (based on a story by Jim Wynorski, R.J. Robertson); ph, Tim Suhrstedt (Deluxe Color); m, Susan Justin; ed, Holzman; prod d, Chris Horner, Robert Skotak; art d, Joe Garrity, Wayne Springfield; set d, Chuck Seaton; spec eff, J.C. Buechler, Don Olivera, Mike La Valley.

Horror/Science Fiction **Cas.** **(PR:O MPAA:R)**

FORBIDDEN ZONE*½ (1980) 76m Borack bw

Herve Villechaize *(King Fausto)*, Susan Tyrrell *(Queen)*, Marie-Pascale Elfman *(Frenchy)*, Viva *(Ex-Queen)*.

A bizarre film debut for the equally bizarre rock band Oingo Boingo, directed by the group's founder, Elfman. Filmed in a humorously sly expressionistic style, the film features "Fantasy Island" star Villechaize as the crazed ruler of the Sixth Dimension who, along with his soul-mate Tyrrell, organizes a gross assortment of monsters, varmits, and toadies on whom they perform deviate sexual acts amid Elfman's effective and strange sets. Not everyone's cup of tea, but definitely a must-see for fans of the band.

p&d, Richard Elfman; w, M. Bright, Martin W. Nicholson, Nick Jones; ph, Gregory Sandor; m, Danny Elfman; ed, Nicholson; prod d, Marie-Pascale Elfman; art d, David M. Makler; set d, Ken Corrone.

Musical **Cas.** **(PR:C MPAA:NR)**

FORBIN PROJECT, THE (SEE: COLOSSUS, THE FORBIN PROJECT, 1969)

FORCE BEYOND, THE zero (1978) 94m Film Ventures c

Don Elkins, Peter Byrne.

Some kids out in the Oregon woods see a flying saucer and a scary monster, but of course no one will believe them. The producers of this super low-budget item got just what they paid for—idiocy.

p, Donn Davison; d, William Sachs; w, Davison.

Science Fiction **Cas.** **(PR:C MPAA:NR)**

FORCE: FIVE* (1981) 95m American Cinema c

Joe Lewis *(Jerry Martin)*, Pam Huntington *(Laurie)*, Bong Soo Han *(Rev. Rhee)*, Richard Norton *(Ezekiel)*, Benny "The Jet" Urquidez *(Billy Ortega)*, Sonny Barnes *(Lockjaw)*, Ron Hayden *(Willard)*, Peter MacLean *(Sen. Forrester)*, Mandy Wyss *(Cindy Lester)*, Bob Schott *(Carl)*, Michael Prince *(Stark)*, Matthew Tobin *(Becker)*, Dennis Mancini *(John)*, Patricia Alice Albrecht *(Cathy)*, Edith Fields *(Sarah)*, Mel Novak *(Assassin)*, Tom Vilard *(Disciple)*, Dolores Cantu *(Nina)*, Loren Janes *(Hank)*.

Mercenary Lewis gathers together a band of volunteers to rescue a girl held by a religious cult. The karate-chopping, drop-kicking force saves the gal and deals the death blow to the cult's persuasive leader, Han. As with the rest of this genre, the action is abundant and the intelligence absent.

p, Fred Weintraub; d&w, Robert Clouse (based on screenplay by Emil Farkas, George Goldsmith); ph, Gill Hubbs (CFI Color); m, William Goldstein; prod d, Joel David Lawrence; ed, Bob Bring; art d, Richard Lawrence; stunt coordinator, Pat Johnson.

Adventure **Cas.** **(PR:O MPAA:R)**

FORCE OF ARMS***½ (1951) 100m WB bw (AKA: A GIRL FOR JOE)

William Holden *(Peterson)*, Nancy Olson *(Eleanor)*, Frank Lovejoy *(Maj. Blackford)*, Gene Evans *(McFee)*, Dick Wesson *(Klein)*, Paul Picerni *(Sheridan)*, Katherine Warren *(Maj. Waldron, WAC)*, Ross Ford *(Hooker)*, Ron Hagerthy *(PFC Minto)*, Amelia Kova *(Lea)*, Robert Roark *(Frank)*, Donald Gordon *(Sgt. Weber)*, Slats Taylor *(PFC Yost)*, Ron Hargrave *(Remington)*, Mario Siletti *(Signor Maduvalli)*, Argentina Brunetti *(Signora Maduvalli)*, Anna Dometrio *(Mama Mia)*, Jay Richards *(Guard)*, Henry Kulky *(Sgt. Reiser)*, Andy Mariani, Francesco Cantania *(Barbers)*, Lea Lamedico *(Anna)*, Adriana Page *(Therese)*, Phillip Carey, Bob Ohlen *(M. P.s)*, Joan Winfield *(Nurse)*, John McGuire *(Doctor)*.

A finely directed and sensitively acted WW II romance, FORCE OF ARMS sees Holden, a sergeant, surviving the bloody San Pietro battle in Italy. On R&R, Holden meets WAC officer Olson and the two fall in love after a combative start. When rejoining his unit Holden hesitates during a battle in which his friend and commander Lovejoy and other friends are killed. Upon returning to Olson he proposes and the couple are married. Yet Holden is haunted by the thought that his actions have brought about the deaths of his pals and he atones for his doubts by once more volunteering for front line duty against Olson's wishes. Another battle sees Holden wounded. He is left behind and thought to be dead, but Olson refuses to believe he is gone. Desperately, Olson seeks him out, following the battle lines all the way to Rome and, in a climactic scene, she finds Holden hobbling among repatriated prisoners of war. Director Curtiz does a fine job staging impressive battle scenes which were intercut with actual newsreel footage, and Holden and Olson, who had worked so well in SUNSET BOULEVARD, are believable in a memorable love story. Lovejoy, that stalwart supporting player, is terrific as Holden's concerned friend. The film employs the main story line of Hemingway's A FAREWELL TO ARMS, even though it is based on a Tregaskis novel, the author having penned several superb battle stories that were later filmed, not the least of which was GUADALCANAL DIARY, 1943.

p, Anthony Veiller; d, Michael Curtiz; w, Orin Jannings (based on "Italian Story" by Richard Tregaskis); ph, Ted McCord; m, Max Steiner; ed, Owen Marks; art d, Edward Carrere.

War Drama **(PR:A MPAA:NR)**

FORCE OF EVIL***½ (1948) 78m Enterprise Productions/MGM bw

John Garfield *(Joe Morse)*, Beatrice Pearson *(Doris Lowry)*, Thomas Gomez *(Leo Morse)*, Howland Chamberlin *(Freddy Bauer)*, Roy Roberts *(Ben Tucker)*, Marie Windsor *(Edna Tucker)*, Paul McVey *(Hobe Wheelock)*, Tim Ryan *(Johnson)*, Sid Tomack *(Two & Two Taylor)*, Georgia Backus *(Sylvia Morse)*, Sheldon Leonard *(Ficco)*, Jan Dennis *(Mrs. Bauer)*, Stanley Prager *(Wally)*, Jack Overman *(Juice)*, Raymond Largay *(Bunte)*, Paul Frees *(Elevator Operator)*, Bert Hanlon *(Cigar Man)*, Bob Williams *(Elevator Starter)*, Barbara Woodell *(Receptionist)*, Bill Neff *(Law Clerk)*, Frank Pharr *(Bootblack)*, Joe Warfield *(Collector)*, Beau Bridges *(Frankie Tucker)*, Perry Ivans *(Mr. Middleton)*, Cliff Clark *(Police Lieutenant)*, Larry Blake *(Detective)*, Phil Tully, Paul Newlan, Max Wagner, Chuck Hamilton, Carl Saxe, Capt. Fred Sommers, George Magrill, Ralph Dunn, Jim Davies, Bob Reeves, Bud Wiser, Brick Sullivan, Ray Hyke *(Policemen)*, Jimmy Dundee *(Dineen)*, Mickey McGuire *(Boy)*, Bud Fine *(Butcher)*, Douglas Carter, Sam Ash *(Men)*, Milton Kibbee *(Richards)*, Esther Somers *(Mrs. Lowry)*, Barry Kelley *(Egan)*, Allen Mathews *(Badgley)*, Mervin Williams *(Goodspeed)*, Frank O'Connor *(Bailiff)*, Charles Evans *(Judge)*, Will Lee *(Waiter)*, David McKim *(Cashier)*, William Challee, Joey Ray, David Fresco *(Gunmen)*, John Indrisano *(Henchman)*, Stanley Waxman *(Manager)*, Eileen Coghlin, Barbara Stone, Estelle Etterre, Helen Eby-Rock *(Secretaries)*, Margaret Bert, Jesse Arnold, Betty Corner, Jim Toney, Sherry Hall, Shimen Ruskin *(Sorters)*, Jim Drum, Carl Sklover, John Butler *(Bankers)*, Dick

Gordon, Roger Cole, Jay Eaton, Carl Hanson, Ralph Brooks, Dick Elmore, Bert Davidson *(Attorneys)*, Arthur O'Connell *(Link Hall)*, Murray Alper *(Comptroller)*, Robert Strong *(Court Reporter)*, Joel Fluellen *(Father)*, Mildred Boyd *(Mother)*, Louise Saraydar *(Hatcheck Girl)*, Ray Hirsch *(Newsboy)*, Barbara Combs, John Collum, William H. O'Brien *(Dancers)*, Bob Stebbins *(Norval)*, Ann Duncan *(Norval's Girl Friend)*, Diane Stewart *(Girl)*, Ed Piel, Sr. *(Counterman)*.

Garfield is a slick, self-centered lawyer who not only knows the law but feels he's above it. He practices on Wall Street and has his eyes on millions, working on retainer for racketeer Roberts. The policy czar plans to have the number 776 come up on July 4, knowing that most people will bet it. This will result in most of the little numbers operations going broke paying off; Roberts' big banks will survive and buy up all the little people, making him absolute boss of the New York numbers racket. One of the small-time operators is Gomez, Garfield's kindly brother. Though Roberts orders Garfield not to tell his brother, blood is thicker than set-ups and Garfield asks Gomez to close up his operation on July 4 so he won't go broke. In an act of incredible loyalty to his customers, Gomez refuses to close, telling Garfield he has an obligation to the patrons who have supported him over the years, that they have a right to win now and then. To cure Gomez of his stubborness, Garfield has the police raid his brother's policy operation. Gomez and others, including his attractive young bookkeeper, Pearson, are thrown into jail but are bailed out by Garfield, who is attracted to Pearson. Gomez is furious with his brother and vows that he will quit the racket, but only after July 4, and that he will stay open for business on that scheduled doomsday. He does and he goes bankrupt, but is saved from ruin by Roberts' millions. Absorbed into Roberts' organization, Gomez's people become nervous about the gangsters suddenly in their midst; Chamberlin goes to the police to set up another raid and then, under a death threat, sets up the truculent Gomez for murder when he decides to reveal how Roberts operates. Leonard, another gangster trying to worm his way into Roberts' organization, kills Chamberlin and, beside himself with anxiety, Gomez dies of a heart attack. Garfield thinks Roberts has killed his brother and goes gunning for him, finding him and Leonard together. Through a ruse, Garfield dials the police in Roberts' lavish apartment, hides the tapped phone, then has Leonard admit he killed his brother. Garfield then gets into a shootout with Leonard, who kills Roberts by mistake. Garfield then shoots Leonard and flees, finding his brother's body at the river's edge where the gangsters have dumped it. With him is Pearson. Garfield decides to expose the policy racket and live out a life with Pearson. A dark, brooding film, FORCE OF EVIL offers a powerful performance from Garfield as the cynical, hard-as-nails lawyer (at one point in his on-and-off narrative of this black tale, Garfield states: "I was born dead"). This is a tour-de-force for gifted writer Polonsky, the only film he ever directed before he was blacklisted for being an uncooperative witness before HUAC in 1951, not directing another film for twenty-one years. A *film noir* gem, this is the first production which provides an inside look into the numbers racket, how it works and milks millions from countless hopeful citizens.

p, Bob Roberts; d, Abraham Polonsky, Don Weis; w, Polonsky, Ira Wolfert (based on the novel *Tucker's People* by Wolfert); ph, George Barnes; m, David Raksin; ed, Walter Thompson, Art Seid; md, Rudolph Polk; art d, Richard Day; set d, Edward Boyle; cos, Louise Wilson; makeup, Gus Norin.

Crime Drama Cas. (PR:C MPAA:NR)

FORCE OF IMPULSE* (1961) 84m III Task/Sutton bw

Robert Alda *(Warren Reese)*, J. Carroll Naish *(Antonio Marino)*, Tony Anthony *(Toby Marino)*, Jeff Donnell *(Louise Reese)*, Jody McCrea *(Phil Anderson)*, Brud Talbot *(George)*, Lionel Hampton *(Himself)*, Christina Crawford *(Ann)*, Kathy Barr *(Kathy)*, Teri Hope *(Bunny Reese)*, Paul Daniel *(Uncle Luigi)*.

Monotonous love story about class conflict in high school stars Anthony (who would later appear in several bad spaghetti Westerns) as a dim-witted high school jock in love with wealthy tease Hope. Hope's father, Alda, disapproves of Anthony and forces his daughter into a relationship with upper class McCrea. Defiantly, Hope stays out all night with Anthony (he takes her to nightclubs and the beach) which leads to lots of heavy accusations from Alda until Anthony's father, played by the kindly and wise Naish, calms everybody down and chalks it up to love.

p, Peter Gayle, Tony Anthony; d, Saul Swimmer; w, Francis Swann, Richard Bernstein (based on a story by Swimmer, Anthony); ph, Clifford Poland; m, Joseph Liebman; ed, Gene Milford; md, Lionel Hampton; art d, Leo B. Meyer; m/l, "Strange Feeling," "The Blues I Got Comin' Tomorrow," Joseph Liebman, Mort Goode.

Romance (PR:A MPAA:NR)

FORCE OF ONE, A** (1979) 90m American Cinema c

Jennifer O'Neill *(Detective Mandy Rust)*, Chuck Norris *(Matt Logan)*, Clu Gulager *(Dunne)*, Ron O'Neal *(Rollins)*, James Whitmore, Jr. *(Moskowitz)*, Clint Ritchie *(Melrose)*, Pepe Serna *(Orlando)*, Ray Vitte *(Newton)*, Taylor Lacher *(Bishop)*, Chu Chu Malave *(Pimp)*, Kevin Geer *(Johnson)*, Eugene Butler *(Murphy)*, James Hall *(Moss)*, Charles Cyphers *(Dr. Eppis)*, Bill Wallace *(Jerry Sparks)*, Eric Laneuville *(Charlie Logan)*.

Nam vet Norris is hired to instruct the narcotics squad in the action-packed art of karate. The cops have been rendered ineffective in their fight against a drug boss, suffering a number of losses. When Norris' adopted son is slain because he could identify the boss, Norris goes into action. After the death of Bruce Lee, a gaping hole plagued the genre, but former karate champ Norris helped close that gap. This is the follow-up to GOOD GUYS WEAR BLACK.

p, Alan Belkin; d, Paul Aaron; w, Ernest Tidyman (based on a story by Pat Johnson, Tidyman); ph, Roger Shearman (CFI Color); m, Dick Halligan; ed, Bert Lovitt; art d, Norman Baron.

Martial Arts Cas. (PR:C-O MPAA:PG)

FORCE 10 FROM NAVARONE*½** (1978, Brit.) 118m AIP c

Robert Shaw *(Mallory)*, Harrison Ford *(Barnsby)*, Edward Fox *(Miller)*, Barbara Bach *(Maritza)*, Franco Nero *(Lescovar)*, Carl Weathers *(Weaver)*, Richard Kiel *(Drazac)*, Angus MacInnes *(Reynolds)*, Michael Byrne *(Schroeder)*, Alan Badel *(Petrovich)*, Christopher Malcolm *(Rogers)*, Nick Ellsworth *(Salvone)*, Jonathan Blake *(Oberstein)*, Michael Sheard *(Bauer)*.

Not quite a sequel to THE GUNS OF NAVARONE but close. This time the squad is sent to Yugoslavia to blow up a bridge that is vital to the German war effort. Ford is the American colonel attached to the Force (when he learned about a different Force in STAR WARS, he was much more noticeable) with Weathers as a touchy black soldier who has more than his share of racial hatred come up against him. Fox is the demolitions expert and Bach is a partisan who helps their cause. Huge Richard Kiel is awesome as a Nazi conspirator and his fight with Weathers is a highlight. Nero is a Nazi double agent and Shaw knows it but can't prove it. This occasions a mental exercise with both men knowing that the other knows. There is some tension in that relationship but the major reason to see this is the explosive fireworks and Fox's beautifully understated performance. Filled with action, intrigue and double-crosses, FORCE 10 FROM NAVARONE is worthwhile for war movie fans. It's sort of the European version of THE BRIDGE ON THE RIVER KWAI without all the complex characterizations, and therein lies it's faults. Shaw died before the film was released at the age of 51. He had an interesting reciprocal agreement with actor Donald Pleasence. They were each empowered to commit the other to a project in an emergency. Thus, when Pleasence was paged to star in a "Colombo" episode (he was in England at the time and they needed an answer right away), he told them to send the script to Shaw who was staying at the Beverly Wilshire Hotel. Shaw read it, loved it, called the studio to wonder why they didn't ask *him* to do it, then called Pleasence and told him that it was a brilliant effort. Pleasence flew to the U.S. and began shooting immediately without having read the script. It eventually won a few Emmies.

p, Oliver A. Unger, John R. Sloan, Anthony B. Unger; d, Guy Hamilton; w, Robin Chapman (based on a story by Carl Foreman and the novel by Alistair MacLean); ph, Chris Challis (Panavision, Technicolor); m, Ron Goodwin; ed, Ray Poulton; prod d, Geoffrey Drake; cos, Emma Porteous; spec eff, Rene Albouze; stunts, Eddie Stacey.

War Drama Cas. (PR:A-C MPAA:PG)

FORCED ENTRY* (1975) 82m Century International-Productions Two-Kodiak c (AKA: THE LAST VICTIM)

Ron Max *(Carl)*, Tanya Roberts, Nancy Allen, Brian Freilino.

Slasher film in which Max is a garage mechanic unable to form healthy relationships with women because his mother beat him when he was a child. Rather than go to the self-help section at the paperback stand, he kills the ladies in a typically imaginative variety of methods. When he breaks into Roberts' house and ties her up, he is unable to kill her, instead trying to ask her for a date. She takes advantage of his hesitation and kills him with a butcher knife. Reissued in 1984 with Tanya Roberts top-billed in hopes of cashing in on her name.

p, Jim Sotos, Henry Scarpelli; d, Sotos; w, Scarpelli; ph, A. Kleinman; m, Tommy Vig; spec eff, Bob O'Bradovich, Freddy Sweet.

Horror Cas. (PR:O MPAA:NR)

FORCED LANDING* (1935) 66m REP bw

Esther Ralston *(Ruby)*, Onslow Stevens *(Farraday)*, Sidney Blackmer *(Bernardi)*, Toby Wing *(Amelie)*, Eddie Nugent *(Redfern)*, Barbara Pepper *(Nancy)*, Willard Robertson *(Byrd)*, Bradley Page *(Greer)*, Kane Richmond *(Jimmy)*, Ralf Harolde *(Burns)*, Arthur Aylesworth *(Talcott)*, Julia Griffith *(Fanny)*, Barbara Bedford *(Mrs. Byrd)*, Lionel Belmore *(Warden)*, George Cleveland *(Jolly)*.

A familiar and poorly handled mystery set on a transcontinental flight to New York with a group of kidnapers on board. After spending 15 years in the lock-up, Aylesworth's life is placed in danger by his fellow conspirators, who have been waiting to get their hands on a hidden ransom. The forced landing of the title occurs during a treacherous storm which keeps the cast stranded in a less-than comfortable farmhouse. Not mysterious enough for a movie coscripted by a newspaperman, William Boehnel, who at the time also was a film critic.

p, M.H. Hoffman; d, Melville Brown; w, Scott Darling (based on a story by William Boehnel, M. Helprin); ph, Harry Neumann; ed, Jack Ogilvie.

Mystery (PR:A MPAA:NR)

FORCED LANDING** (1941) 63m PAR bw

Richard Arlen *(Dan Kendall)*, Eva Gabor *(Johanna Van Deuren)*, J. Carroll Naish *(Andros Banshek)*, Nils Asther *(Col. Jan Golas)*, Evelyn Brent *(Doctor's Housekeeper)*, Mikhail Rasumny *(Christmas)*, Victor Varconi *(Hendrick Van Deuren)*, John Miljan *(Gen. Valdane)*, Frank Yaconelli *(Zomar)*, Harold Goodwin *(Petchnikoff)*, Thornton Edwards *(Felig)*, Bobby Dillon *(Nando)*, John Gallaudet *(Maj. Xanders)*, Harry Worth *(Dr. Vidalek)*.

One-time commercial pilot Arlen joins the air corps of a South Seas island, finding himself up against a malevolent politico (Asther) and secretly in love with his girl (Gabor). Asther also happens to be the head of the air corps and, to get rid of the competition, sends Arlen on a suicide run which ends in a dogfight between the two. Arlen makes it back to land in one piece, with Asther experiencing a less enjoyable fate. Better than average (where programmers are concerned), due mostly to the visual sense of director Wiles, a former art director. For Arlen, the long-enduring lead in Hollywood films, the role was not a strange one: he flew for the Royal Canadian Flying Corps before he entered pictures in 1920 and starred in the silent classic WINGS. The film marked the movie debut of the youngest of the Gabor sisters, Eva, a former cabaret singer, who was the first of the glamorous trio to arrive in the U.S. from Budapest.

p, William H. Pine, William C. Thomas; d, Gordon Wiles; w, Maxwell Shane, Edward Churchill; ph, John Alton; ed, Robert Crandall; md, Dimitri Tiomkin; art d, F. Paul Sylos; spec eff, Fred Jackman, Jr.

Aviation Drama/Adventure **Cas.** **(PR:A MPAA:NR)**

FORCED VENGEANCE* (1982) 90m MGM/UA c

Chuck Norris *(Josh Randall)*, Mary Louise Weller *(Claire Bonner)*, David Opatoshu *(Sam Paschal)*, Seiji Sakaguchi *(Cam)*, Frank Michael Liu *(David Paschal)*, Bob Minor *(LeRoy Nicely)*, Lloyd Kino *(Inspector Chen)*, Leigh Hamilton *(Sally Tennant)*, Howard Caine *(Milt Diamond)*, Robert Emhardt *(Carl Gerlich)*, Roger Behrstock *(Ron DiBiasi)*, Jimmy Shaw *(Inspector Keck)*, Camila Griggs *(Joy)*, Michael Cavanaugh *(Stan)*.

Until 1985's CODE OF SILENCE, Norris had karate-chopped his way through several routine kung-fu films like this one. In FORCED VENGEANCE, he once again plays a Vietnam veteran of few words and quick action as he body-slams his way through this mobster movie. Employed by honest businessman Opatoshu, Norris must perform some violent duty on syndicate lord Cavanaugh and his thugs who are trying to pressure Opatoshu into surrendering his livelihood to them. The climax sees a very angry Norris pull his old Vietnam First Airborne uniform out of mothballs and head out after the bad guys. While a few of Norris' earlier efforts showed the promise he would later fulfill with CODE OF SILENCE, FORCED VENGEANCE is a mindless action film.

p, John B. Bennett; d, James Fargo; w, Franklin Thompson; ph, Rexford Metz (Metrocolor); m, William Goldstein; ed, Irving C. Rosenblum; prod d, George B. Chan; set d, Mary Olivia Swanson, Tony Leung.

Martial Arts **Cas.** **(PR:O MPAA:R)**

FORCES' SWEETHEART* (1953, Brit.) 76m New Realm bw

Hy Hazell *(Judy James)*, Harry Secombe *(Harry Llewellyn)*, Michael Bentine *(John Robinson)*, Freddie Frinton *(Aloysius Dimwitty)*, John Ainsworth *(Lt. John Robinson)*, Molly Weir *(The Maid)*, Adrienne Scott *(Audrey)*, Kenneth Henry *(Tommy Tupp)*, Graham Stark *(Simmonds)*, John Fitzgerald *(Producer)*, Michael McCarthy *(Plumber)*, Robert Moore, Russ Allen, The Leslie Roberts Television Girls.

Unfunny comedy has three soldiers using the same name to try to win the affections of singer Hazell. Hopelessly inept, with poor production values to boot, but good singing performances by Hazell, a former musical comedy performer.

p, E.J. Fancey; d, Maclean Rogers; w, Rogers, Michael Bentine; ph, Geoffrey Faithfull.

Comedy **(PR:A MPAA:NR)**

FOREIGN AFFAIR, A*** (1948) 116m PAR bw

Jean Arthur *(Phoebe Frost)*, Marlene Dietrich *(Erika von Schluetow)*, John Lund *(Capt. John Pringle)*, Millard Mitchell *(Col. Rufus J. Plummer)*, Bill Murphy *(Joe)*, Stanley Prager *(Mike)*, Peter von Zerneck *(Hans Otto Birgel)*, Raymond Bond *(Pennecott)*, Boyd Davis *(Griffin)*, Robert Malcolm *(Kraus)*, Charles Meredith *(Yandell)*, Michael Raffeto *(Salvatore)*, James Larmore *(Lt. Hornby)*, Damian O'Flynn *(Lieutenant Colonel)*, Frank Fenton *(Major)*, William Neff *(Lt. Lee Thompson)*, Harland Tucker *(Gen. McAndrew)*, George Carleton *(Gen. Finney)*, Gordon Jones, Freddie Steele *(Military Police)*.

A stinging satirical look at black marketeering in post WW II Berlin, A FOREIGN AFFAIR has simon pure Arthur heading a congressional investigation into the corruptive moral influence Germans are having on occupying GIs. Arthur arrives with a birthday cake for Lund, baked by one of his old girl friends in the U.S. He immediately sells the cake for a mattress which he presents to his German sweetie, Dietrich, an aristocrat turned torch singer in a Berlin bistro, The Lorelei. Arthur pretends to be a German girl and is picked up by some GIs and taken to the notorious club to hear and see Dietrich vamp out some tunes, and she learns that Dietrich is Lund's mistress. She later turns up a photo showing Dietrich with high-ranking Nazis, including Hitler (Bobby Watson). Lund is ordered to continue his affair with Dietrich so he can locate a top Nazi still on the run, Von Zerneck. He can't object since he's altered her records which show her earlier political affiliations so she can stay in Berlin. When confronted with her notorious past, Dietrich delivers a typically biting line: "Politics? Women pick out what's in fashion and change it like a spring hat. Everything is forgiven the eternal female." But she is not forgiven and when Von Zerneck tries to make contact with her, he is shot and she is taken away by no less than five MPs, all of them nervously eyeing her and themselves, uncertain as to whether they can resist her temptations or not. Arthur has been humanized by the experience and, at film's end, discards her spinster-like ways, openly kissing Lund in what appears to be the opening round in a lasting love match. Dietrich, who had dipped in popularity, came back to full box office force in this trampy role which recalled her successes of the 1930s, particularly in THE BLUE ANGEL. At first she declined the role, always worried that her German background would associate her with the Nazis, but clever Wilder showed her a test June Havoc had made for the part and her natrual competitiveness caused her to take on the part. She sings five songs written specifically for her by Hollander: "Iowa Corn Song," "Meadowland," "Ruins of Berlin," "Black Market," and "Illusions." Hollander himself acts as her accompanist in the night-club scenes, a not unfamiliar role for the composer who had performed the same chores in the wedding scene of THE BLUE ANGEL and again in MANPOWER. Her revealing costumes were created by the venerable Edith Head who later commented: "You don't design clothes for Dietrich. You design them *with* her." Dietrich would play an almost identical role in JUDGMENT AT NUREMBERG, 1962. Wilder did some setup shots in bombed out Berlin which gave the impression that the entire film was shot on location, but most of the filming was done at the Paramount studios. This is Wilder at his most acerbic and cynical and the film was originally attacked by critics who considered it a monument to "tastelessness." But the hypnotic performance he draws from sultry Dietrich shows his continuing mastery of the medium.

p, Charles Brackett; d, Billy Wilder; w, Charles Brackett, Billy Wilder, Richard Breen, Robert Harari (based on a story by David Shaw); ph, Charles B. Lang, Jr.; m, Frederick Hollander; ed, Doane Harrison; md, Hollander; art d, Hans Dreier, Walter Tyler; set d, Sam Comer, Ross Dowd; cos, Edith Head; spec eff, Gordon Jennings.

Drama/Romance **(PR:C MPAA:NR)**

FOREIGN AFFAIRES½** (1935, Brit.) 71m Gainsborough/GAU bw

Tom Walls *(Capt. Archibald Gore)*, Ralph Lynn *(Jefferson Darby)*, Robertson Hare *(Mr. Hardy Hornett)*, Norma Varden *(Mrs. Hardy Hornett)*, Marie Lohr *(Mrs. Cope)*, Diana Churchill *(Sophie)*, Cecil Parker *(Lord Wornington)*, Kathleen Kelly *(Milicent)*, Gordon James *(Rope)*, Ivor Barnard *(Count)*.

The British comedy team of the 1930s are together again in this brisk comedy of benign chicanery. Walls, an aging aristocrat with a taste for gambling, borrows from a relative and hits the jackpot at the race track. He goes to Nice and the casinos there and quickly loses all he had just won. He meets Lynn, who also is broke, and the two go to work as touts for a diamond thief disguised as a count, who bilks wealthy visitors to Nice out of their jewels. Walls and Lynn are on their way to the police with this information when they are arrested. At the trial, they, of course, are saved at the last moment to continue their hijinks some place else.

p, Michael Balcon; d, Tom Walls; w, Ben Travers; ph, Roy Kellino.

Comedy **(PR:A MPAA:NR)**

FOREIGN AGENT½** (1942) 62m MON bw

John Shelton *(Jimmy)*, Gale Storm *(Mitzi)*, Ivan Lebedeff *(Okura)*, Hans Schumm *(Werner)*, William Halligan *(Davis)*, George Travell *(Nick)*, Patsy Moran *(Joan)*, Lyle Latell *(Eddie)*, Herbert Rawlinson *(Stevens)*, Kenneth Harlan *(McCall)*, Jack Mulhall *(Editor)*, David Clarke *(Carl Beck)*.

A colorful spy drama set in Hollywood with an enemy gang trying to capture the plans for a searchlight filter, the pet project of a studio technician. A good deal of intrigue, tricky spy techniques, and backlot activity add life to an otherwise typical script. The post-Pearl Harbor fervor is exemplified in nightclub singer Storm's rendition of "It's Taps For The Japs."

p, Martin Mooney, Max King; d, William Beaudine; w, Mooney, John Krafft (based on a story by Mooney); ph, Mack Stengler; ed, Fred Baine; md, Edward Kay; m/l, "Down Deep In My Heart," "It's Taps for the Japs," Beal Mellette, Bill Anderson (sung by Gale Storm).

Spy Drama **(PR:A MPAA:NR)**

FOREIGN CORRESPONDENT***** (1940) 120m UA bw

Joel McCrea *(Johnny Jones/Huntley Haverstock)*, Laraine Day *(Carol Fisher)*, Herbert Marshall *(Stephen Fisher)*, George Sanders *(Scott Ffolliott)*, Albert Basserman *(Van Meer)*, Robert Benchley *(Stebbins)*, Edmund Gwenn *(Rowley)*, Eduardo Ciannelli *(Krug)*, Martin Kosleck *(Tramp)*, Harry Davenport *(Mr. Powers)*, Barbara Pepper *(Doreen)*, Eddy Conrad *(Latvian Diplomat)*, Charles Wagenheim *(Assassin)*, Crauford Kent *(Toastmaster)*, Frances Carson *(Mrs. Sprague)*, Alexander Granach *(Valet)*, Samuel Adams *(Impersonator)*, Dorothy Vaughan *(Jones' Mother)*, Betty Bradley *(Cousin Mary)*, Mary Young *(Auntie Maude)*, Jack Rice *(Donald)*, Jackie McGee, Henry Blair *(Children)*, Rebecca Bohannen *(Sophie)*, Marten Lamont *(Clipper Captain)*, Barry Bernard *(Steward)*, Hilda Plowright *(Miss Pimm)*, Gertrude Hoffman *(Mrs. Benson)*, June Novak *(Miss Benson)*, Roy Gordon *(Mr. Brood)*, Bert White, Thomas Pogue, Jack Voglin, George French *(Passengers)*, William Stelling, John Meredith, George Cathrey *(Flight Officers)*, Leonard Mudie *(Inspector McKenna)*, Holmes Herbert *(Commissioner Ffolliot)*, Frederick Sewall *(Student)*, Emory Parnell *(John Martin, Captain of the Mohican)*, James Finlayson *(Dutch Peasant)*, Hermina Milar *(Little Dutch Girl)*, Loulette Sablon *(Nesta)*, Douglas Gordon *(Taxi Driver)*, Colin Kenny *(Walter)*, Paul Sutton *(Male Nurse)*, Robert C. Fischer *(Manager)*, Jack Dawson *(Schoolmaster)*, Ken Christy, Thomas Mizer *(Plainclothesmen)*, June Heiden *(Two-year-old)*, Terry Kilburn *(Boy)*, Carl Ekberg, Hans Von Morhart *(Dutch Policemen)*, Otto Hoffman *(Telegrapher)*, Charles Halton *(Bradley)*, Joan Brodel [Leslie] *(Jones' Sister)*, Paul Irving *(Dr. Williamson)*, Ferris Taylor *(Jones' Father)*, John T. Murray *(Clark)*, Harry Depp *(Uncle Biren)*, Meeka Aldrich *(Donald's Wife)*, Willy Castello, Bill Gavier *(Dutch Pilots)*, Ian Wolfe *(Stiles the Butler)*, Ernie Stanton, Donald Stuart *(Newsmen)*, Colin Kenny *(Doctor)*, Helena Phillips Evans *(Maid)*, Herbert Evans *(English Doorman)*, Frank Benson *(English Porter)*, Barbara Boudwin *(Barmaid)*, Louis Borrell *(Capt. Lansom)*, Gino Corrado *(Italian Waiter)*, Elspeth Dudgeon, Gwendolyn Logan *(Spinsters)*, Eily Malyon *(English Cashier)*, Bunny Beatty *(Porter)*, John Burton *(English Radio Announcer)*, Raymond Severn *(English Boy)*, Lawrence Osman, Richard Hammond, Joe O'Brien, Billy Bester, Billy Horn, Ronald Brown *(Eton Boys)*, Louise Brien *(Secretary)*, Jack Alfred, George Offerman, Jr. *(Copy Boys)*, E.E. Clive *(Mr. Naismith)*, Alfred Hitchcock *(Man with Newspaper)*, Wheaton Chambers *(Committeeman)*.

One of the truly great espionage films is delivered with taut mastery by the stellar Hitchcock, a film packed with suspense, great atmosphere, and brilliant dialog. Not a scene is wasted from the first moment that American newspaper publisher Davenport reassigns McCrea, a top crime reporter, as foreign correspondent, ordering him to find the most provocative stories swirling about in the cauldron of European politics just prior to WW II. McCrea first goes to London to learn the political ropes from Benchley, a mostly intoxicated newsman who gets him a few introductions to social lions. At one party he meets Marshall who heads a peace organization, along with his attractive daughter, Day. Later McCrea meets Basserman, an important Dutch diplomat who carries about in his memory a secret clause having to do with an Allied agreement to counterattack when a nameless enemy invades his country (the enemy is obviously Germany). In Holland, McCrea works his way through a sea of umbrellas during a downpour to greet Basserman, who is arriving at an important political meeting. A cameraman rushes forward to take Basserman's photo as the politician turns away from McCrea with a look and gesture that says he's never seen the American correspondent before. The camerman takes a photo but the camera is merely a prop behind which is hidden a gun. It goes off, killing the diplomat, while the assassin flees and McCrea tries to pursue him through the dense crowds. Sanders, a British journalist McCrea has befriended in London, along with Day, happen along and McCrea has them drive their car after another auto into which the assassin had leaped. The cars speed beyond the Dutch town and into a countryside dotted with turning windmills. Nothing can be seen of the escape car on a flat road that stretches seemingly to the horizon. McCrea, out of the car, alone approaches a windmill that appears strange. Of the many in sight, it is the only windmill turning against the wind. He slips inside and hears muffled conversations in a foreign language. After eluding secret agents throughout the mill, McCrea finds Basserman in a daze, as if drugged, unable to converse, his babble extolling the beauty of the birds who are perched on the rafters of the mill. Obviously his double has been assassinated. The agents, led by the sinister Ciannelli, enter only seconds after McCrea slips down through a shaft where his trenchcoat is snagged by the cogs of the grinding mill and his arm is almost crushed, but he manages to free himself at the last moment, slipping out the windmill, riding one of the arms to the ground. He then spots a plane landing and races for the road. By the time he hails the police and Sanders the windmill is turning with the wind. Nothing McCrea says or does causes authorities to hunt further for the real Basserman. He insists that a doppleganger has been set up and murdered so the real Basserman could be kidnaped, drugged, and finally made to reveal the secret clause in the Allied agreement. Only Day and Sanders believe McCrea who goes to his hotel to figure out his next move, only to find two suspicious detectives who ask him to accompany them to headquarters. McCrea tells them he'll go along after he takes his bath, then, once in the W.C. he turns on the bath taps and, wearing only his robe, shoes, and socks, goes out the window onto a narrow ledge and works his way along the side of the building. At one point he mistakingly grabs the hotel sign to steady himself and breaks the fluorescent tubing, putting out the lights of the first letter. After almost falling to the street, McCrea manages to get into Day's room. At first she thinks he's boldly attempting to seduce her until he explains that two Dutch cops want to take him in for questioning. He knows they are not policemen but agents who want to shut up his talk of Basserman still being alive. To obtain his clothes, McCrea devises a clever ruse, ordering up a host of hotel servants—the valet, room service, housekeepers—until they are swarming around the befuddled agents in his room, one bellhop retrieving his suit, shirt, tie. In this way he escapes with Day back to London, crossing on a strom-tossed sea by steamer; they leave so hurriedly with agents on their trail that they cannot book staterooms and must huddle on the wave-splashed deck. McCrea, with American bluntness, blurts to Day: "I'm in love with you and I want to marry you." She replies with equal candor: "I'm in love with *you* and I want to marry *you!*" Says McCrea: "That cuts down our love scene quite a bit, doesn't it?" (Hitchcock introduced this chamring bit of dialog right out of the pages of his own life; he had proposed to his wife Alma in 1925 almost the same way and under similar circumstances.) Once in London, Day begs her influential father Marshall to help McCrea, explaining that he is being hunted by secret agents of a foreign country bent on his destruction. Marshall seems to humor her but insists that McCrea be accompanied everywhere by a bodyguard he selects, Gwenn, a cheerful, squat, powerful little fellow. Gwenn takes McCrea on a tour of London but at the first opportunity tries to push McCrea in front of a bus which barely misses the American. "Did you see that?" McCrea asks Gwenn moments later. "Somebody pushed me!" Gwenn smiles and says, "That was me, sir. It was either push or pull . . . you might have been run over." McCrea mumbles his unsure gratitude, actually thanking a man for attempting to murder him. Next, when the two are at the top of Westminster Cathedral Tower, Gwenn engineers McCrea to the edge of the open walkway and, when the other tourists desert the area, rushes forward with a murderous look on his face, his flattened out hands, aimed at McCrea's back, filling the screen. But McCrea survives, later explaining that he stepped aside at the last minute and Gwenn went over the wall and fell to his death. Later, McCrea sees Ciannelli, the top agent who was holding Basserman, visit Marshall at his home in a hush-hush meeting. When McCrea tells Day, implicating her father, she rejects him out of hand, thinking he's gone paranoid. She tells him that she doesn't wish to see him again, that her father is above reproach. McCrea follows Ciannelli and discovers a London hideout where Basserman is being held, injected with truth serum, and interrogated. McCrea takes on the gang of agents and there is a shootout with Sanders leading police to the rescue. Ciannelli is shot and Basserman saved. War is declared and Marshall books passage on the clipper flying from London to America, taking Day with him. Sanders, who is the only one who continues to listen to the generally ignored McCrea, tells the American correspondent that for a long time he's suspected Marshall of not being who the world thought him to be—a cultivated do-gooder trying to maintain peace. Both get on board the transatlantic flight at the last minute and trap Marshall into admitting that he is the leader of the spy ring in London, a confession that's overheard by Day. Just at that moment a German warship, thinking the plane is a British bomber, shoots it down. In a spectacular crash, Marshall unravels his last shred of decency and saves his daughter's life and that of McCrea. An American ship later picks up McCrea, Day, and Sanders and McCrea is allowed to send his dispatch to the U.S., one that exposes Marshall, a report sanctioned by Day. The couple marry and stay on in London where McCrea becomes a famous foreign correspondent. He and Day are broadcasting to America when London undergoes another bombing raid and they stay on in the studio so McCrea can describe the blitz. "Hello, America," McCrea begins, "I've been watching a part of the world being blown to pieces. A part of the world as nice as Vermont, Ohio, Virginia, California, and Illinois lies ripped up and bleeding like a steer in a slaughterhouse. And I've seen things that make the history of the savages read like Pollyanna legend." McCrea is asked to postpone the broadcast, that the bombing is becoming too heavy. He refuses as the lights start to go out and the scene begins to dim. McCrea continues, angry, full of fight: "I can't read the rest of this speech I have because the lights have gone out, so I'll just have to talk off the cuff. All that noise you hear isn't static, it's death coming to London. Yes, they're coming here now. You can hear the bombs falling on the streets and homes. Don't tune me out—hang on—this is a big story, and you're part of it. It's too late now to do anything except stand in the dark and let them come. It feels as if the lights are all out everywhere except in America." The strains of "America" can be heard in the background as McCrea continues urgently: "Keep those lights burning! Cover them with steel! Ring them with guns! Build a canopy of battleships and bombing planes around them. Hello, Amercia! Hang on to your lights! They're the only lights left in the world!" With this stirring plea FOREIGN CORRESPONDENT ends, a rousing, action-filled espionage thriller with a moving propaganda finish. Although it clearly indicts the Nazi regime of Hitler's Third Reich, not once is Germany mentioned. One scene, originally intended as the last, occurs on board the rescue ship where McCrea growls: "The German government will have to answer for this." Sanders states: "Documents will undoubtedly be found, old boy, proving that it is a British trawler disguised as a German battleship, and the whole thing has been organized by the pirate, Churchill, to drag America into the war." These lines were cut but the ending as it stands was clearly intended to alert America and encourage the U.S. to see that the oppressive Nazis would soon be a very real threat. When Nazi propaganda minister Josef Goebbels first saw it, he hailed the Hitchcock film as a masterpiece, calling it "a first class production, a criminological bang-up hit, which no doubt will make a certain impression upon the broad masses of the people in enemy countries. Significantly enough, this film with its absolutely anti-German tendency was allowed to run for months in Sweden. The Swedes and the Swiss are playing with fire. Let us hope they will burn their fingers before the war is over." Goebbels watched FOREIGN CORRESPONDENT innumerable times and it became one of his favorite films, despite the fact that it held him and his evil ilk as everything sinister, inhuman, and destructive. The history of the film was long and complex. Producer Walter Wanger, who had been an aviator during WW I and an embassy attache who worked at the Paris Peace Conference (as well as a member of U.S. intelligence), was fascinated by Vincent Sheean's memoirs, *Personal History* which he purchased for $10,000 in 1936. Sheean had been a European correspondent and his book described a continent in political turmoil but it had no characters, plotline, very few roots upon which to grow a film script. Wanger immediately went after Hitchcock, feeling that the director could give the proper atmospherics to this nebulous European tale. Hitchcock, however, was under contract to David O. Selznick, brought over recently to direct REBECCA, and Wanger had to "rent" the director, paying Selznick $5,000 for 12 weeks of his stellar services while Selznick only paid Hitchcock $2,500 for this schedule, making one hundred percent profit on the deal, an arrangement that rankled Hitchcock for many years to come. (Wanger had originally signed William Dieterle to direct and intended the film to be a vehicle for Charles Boyer and Claudette Colbert.) The script had a long and arduous road to the finish, veteran screenwriter John Howard Lawson initially getting the assignment. Next Wanger hired MARCH OF TIME writers John Meehan and John Lay to work on the script, updating it to keep abreast of fast-moving events in troubled Europe. Originally, the location for the film was to be in Nazi Germany while focusing upon the Spanish Civil War, but when the war in Spain ended in 1939, a new approach had to be taken. Wanger had, to the frustration of all involved in the film, an utter fixation about maintaining absolute timeliness with the production and, as Hitler's armies invaded one European country after another, more and more writers were added then discarded, 14 in all. Charles Bennett and Joan Harrison (the two who actually received the screen credit) worked on the basic script while novelist James Hilton contributed scenes and Ben Hecht was finally brought in to write the stirring ending. Benchley, who played the tipsy London correspondent McCrea was to replace, actually wrote his own scenes; Hitchcock thought it only right that this brilliant humorist and man of belles lettres be responsible for his own screen image. Benchley was told by Hitchcock to be himself, act natural, that the filming would be mere "eavesdropping." Benchley was so at ease during the shooting of his scenes that he appeared to doze at times and finally Hitchcock gave him his only piece of direction, telling him: "Come now, Bob, let's open those *naughty* little eyes!" The script changed so much from day to day that by its finish it had little to do with the original Sheean book, except for the setting in Holland. A second unit crew was sent to Holland but the cameramen lost all of their equipment when their ship was torpedoed and they had to go back for more cameras. The exteriors of the windmills and car chase through the countryside were shot in Holland but the interior of the windmill McCrea enters was a huge set built in the studio at Hitchcock's instructions. The windmill device was the director's own creation. "We'll have the windmill turning against the wind," he was quoted, "and he'll know that's some kind of signal." The treacherous role played by Marshall was also Hitchcock's creation. "I really got that idea about him," he told an interviewer, "from Dr. Buchman of Moral Rearmament—you know—'peace, peace, and everybody love each other,' and all the time he was an agent." With writers coming and going on FOREIGN CORRESPONDENT, coupled to Wanger's constant demands for updating, the cost of the script spiraled upward to $250,000. The overall production would soar to $1.5 million, a staggering amount for those days. (Selznick had spent $1 million on Hitchcock's REBECCA a short time earlier.) Budgeted for $35,000 a day, the film's costs were more the responsibility of the free-spending Wanger than the director who was always precise in his expenses. Hitchcock, as with all his films, would do panel drawings (nothing professional, stick-like characters to show position) for every scene, showing his camera setups. These drawings were turned over to director Golitzen for finished copies and then the director would meet each day with cinematographer Mate and set desinger Menzies to finalize pre-production techniques, so that when it came to the actual shooting, everything was in place, cameramen knew exactly what to do and Hitchcock followed his tightly written script like a locomotive on a straight-as-an-arrow track. The enormous sets Hitchcock ordered for FOREIGN CORRESPONDENT were certainly on the rich side. More than 600 electricians, carpenters, plumbers, and prop men labored on the sets, including the three-tiered interior of the windmill (where 300 linnets were perched on various levels, many of the flighty creatures held in place for shooting by tiny strings); the birds created a mess for cleanup crews but Hitchcock insisted upon using them, an early fascination that would culminate with his production of THE BIRDS. The huge (600 by 125 foot) set recreating Waterloo Station was crowded with more than 500 extras and was used for only a few minutes. The stupendous recreation of a square in Amsterdam was built on a 10-acre set at a cost of $200,000. Because this scene takes place during a rainstorm to show the famous assassination and escape beneath a sea of umbrellas, an elaborate drainage system had to be constructed to handle the overflow of the diverted Colorado River, according to one account. One of the most spectacular scenes in this or any other film was the crashing of the airplane, a ship with four motors, with a 120-foot wingspread and an 84-foot fuselage, smashing into a gigantic studio tank with huge underwater blades churning the contents to create ocean waves while the actors struggled to survive. Just before the crash Hitchcock's cameras record one of the most astounding scenes in the history of movies, one that perplexed experts. It is recorded in one continuous shot over the shoulders of the pilots facing the windshield of the plane as it dives downward toward the ocean. The plane draws closer and closer to the water until, upon impact, the windshield bursts and the cockpit is flooded with water which engulfs pilots and the camera itself. The technique employed here is typical Hitchcock, prosaic yet clever. Using back projection, the director filmed a plane diving toward the water. This strip of film was then shown in rear-view projection, Hitchcock's favorite device, on to a screen that was tissue thin, so that the pilots (and the camera) are actually watching a movie on the other side of the windshield of the cockpit. At the precise moment that the plane appears to crash into the ocean, a pressurized body of water on the other side of the paper thin screen was released, breaking the screen as if it were the windshield to flood the cockpit. Ever the technical perfectionist, Hitchcock, following the crash, insisted upon showing McCrea, Day, Sanders, Marshall, and others survive by clinging to a wing that breaks away from the fuselage of the plane. To do this in the enormous studio tank, technicians had to construct moving branch lines and rails beneath the surface of the water so that the wing would separate from the body of the plane and be swept away. Hitchcock was most pleased with FOREIGN CORRESPONDENT and it remained one of his favorite films. He thought it superior to REBECCA and it was definitely a pure Hitchcock production, even though he did not get his choice of leading players. He wanted Gary Cooper to play the brash American journalist but Cooper turned down the role. At the time, thrillers were considered less important than heavy drama but years later Cooper came to Hitchcock, stating that his decision not to play the part "was a mistake. I should have done it." McCrea, however, is perfect in the role, bringing the kind of fresh-faced apple-pie personality to a film where the lead must be naive and innocent, victimized again by Hitchcockian events he cannot control. Hitchcock's method of casual direction, after laboring over pre-production setups and serious rehearsals, was never more in evidence than in this film. He merely sat back and let the actors step into the shoeprints he himself had designed. Shooting after lunch was always an undemanding period of time for the cast. The director, according to McCrea, had the habit of drinking several glasses of champagne at lunch and he would doze behind the camera. One afternoon McCrea stood talking through his lines and then waited expectedly for Hitchcock to yell "Cut!" The order did not come and finally McCrea himself said, "Cut." Hitchcock awakened in his chair, and, with heavy lids and a slight smile curling about his lips, asked McCrea: "Was it any good?" Replied McCrea: "The best in the picture." Hitchcock nodded and said, "Print it!" Day gives a great performance, full of warmth, and her brunette beauty radiates throughout her scenes, but Hitchcock merely took her for granted and did little to develop her character, early on showing his preference for cool blonde actresses. He did well with British actors Marshall and Sanders and was particularly fond of character actor Basserman who played the kidnapped politician. Basserman migrated from European films to Hollywood in 1938 at the urging of his director friend Ernst Lubitsch, appearing in DR. EHRLICH'S MAGIC BULLET a year before his impressive performance in FOREIGN CORRESPONDENT. In this Hitchcock masterpiece, Basserman, like all of his roles in American films, had no sense of the dialog he was to utter, not knowing a word of English. But he rendered believable lines thanks to his patient wife who taught him every line of dialog phonetically. More than 240,000 feet of film was shot for this 120-minute espionage opus, every foot used containing taut suspense, awesome sets by genius Menzies, striking cinematography by Mate, and, everywhere, the Hitchcock imprint.

p, Walter Wanger; d, Alfred Hitchcock; w, Charles Bennett, Joan Harrison, James Hilton, Robert Benchley; ph, Rudolph Mate; m, Alfred Newman; ed, Otho Lovering, Dorothy Spencer; art d, Alexander Golitzen; set d, William Cameron Menzies; spec eff, Lee Zavitz.

Spy Drama **Cas.** **(PR:A MPAA:NR)**

FOREIGN INTRIGUE½** (1956) 106m UA c

Robert Mitchum *(Bishop)*, Genevieve Page *(Dominique)*, Ingrid Tulean [Thulin] *(Brita)*, Frederick O'Brady *(Spring)*, Gene Deckers *(Sandoz)*, Inga Tidblad *(Mrs. Lindquist)*, John Padovano *(Tony)*, Frederick Schrecker *(Mannheim)*, Lauritz Faulk *(Jones)*, Peter Copley *(Brown)*, Ralph Brown *(Smith)*, George Hubert *(Dr. Thibault)*, Nil Sperber *(Baum)*, Jean Galland *(Danemore)*, Jim Gerald *(Bistro Owner)*, John Stark *(Starky)*, Gilbert Robin *(Dodo)*, Valentine Camax *(Charwoman)*, Robert Le Beal *(Charles)*, Albert Simmons *(Information Desk Clerk)*.

When Galland dies mysteriously, Mitchum, who once worked for him, decides to unravel his mysterious past. He travels to Vienna and learns Galland was a tycoon blackmailer but the proof of his nefarious past is shrouded with the death of an informant and the killer appears to be Page, Galland's widow. O'Brady, a professional agent hired to look into Galland's past, bumps into Mitchum and the two agree to help each other. Mitchum follows leads to Stockholm where he meets Tulean (later Thulin), falling in love with her. Tulean's father had been a traitor during WW II and Galland had been blackmailing him, finally driving him to suicide. Mitchum and Tulean return to Vienna where four agents from the U.S., Sweden, Switzerland, and England reveal more of Galland's past, explaining that Hitler made deals with traitors in every country he invaded (i.e., Quisling in Norway, Laval in France) and, since their countries were never invaded, they were never exposed, yet Galland learned their identities and blackmailed them. Later Page appears, gun in hand, and tries to get Mitchum to blackmail the four traitors but he disarms her and then meets with the shifty O'Brady to pick up the traitors. FOREIGN INTRIGUE is a spinoff of Reynolds' popular TV series by the same name. But this murky, aimlessly plotted espionage saga is less than rewarding, packed with cliches and predictability. Mitchum is the only American actor in the all-European cast and he is decidedly dull, rendering a performance that can be generously called comatose. The production values and on-location shooting in Europe are good. Mitchum's constant wearing of a disheveled raincoat spearheaded a fashion trend in wearing trenchcoats. Page, who appeared in SONG WITHOUT END, is merely a prop, and Tulean, later an Ingmar Bergman actress, is only a prettier one.

p&d, Sheldon Reynolds; w, Reynolds, Harry Jack Bloom, Gene Levitt; ph, Bertil Palmgren (Eastmancolor); m, Paul Durand; ed, Lennart Wallen; art d, Maurice Petri; cos, Pierre Balmain; m/l, "Foreign Intrigue Concerto," Charles Norman; makeup, Joseph Majinsky.

Spy Drama **(PR:C MPAA:NR)**

FOREIGNER, THE*½ (1978) 101m Visions bw

Eric Mitchell *(Max Menace)*, Patti Astor *(Fili Harlow)*, Deborah Harry *(Dee Trick)*, Terens Severine *(Zazu Weather)*, Anya Phillips *(Doll)*, Duncan Hannah *(Shake)*, David Forshtay *(Forbag)*, Klaus Mettig *(The German)*, Ana Marton, Pusante Byzantium *(Rumanians)*, Chirine El Khadem *(The Arab)*.

Frenchman Mitchell is pursued up and down the busy streets of New York City by thugs. Along the way he encounters a couple of bizarre gals—Harry as a new-wave songstress delivering a rendition of Brecht's "Bilbao Song," and Severine as a sadist. Of interest only to those who are attracted to the New York underground scenes, and the big-name rock club CBGB & OM-FUG. A long-forgotten punk band, The Erasers, knocks out a few numbers. Harry would go on to prove that she had some acting ability in the 1980 picture UNION CITY.

p&d, Amos Poe; w, Poe, Eric Mitchell; ph, Chirine El Khadem; m, Ivan Kral; ed, Michael Penland, Poe, Johanna Heer; md, Kral.

Drama **(PR:C MPAA:NR)**

FOREMAN WENT TO FRANCE, THE (SEE: SOMEWHERE IN FRANCE, 1942, Brit.)

FOREPLAY zero (1975) 75m Syn-Frank Enterprises/Cinema National c

Zero Mostel *(President/Don Pasquale)*, Estelle Parsons *(1st Lady/Barmaid)*, Pat Paulsen *(Norman)*, Jerry Orbach *(Lorsey)*, George S. Irving *(Reverend/Muse)*, Michael Clarke-Lawrence *(BBC Announcer)*, Deborah Loomis *(Doll)*, Laurie Heineman *(Trixie)*, Andrew Duncan *(Hurdlemeyer)*, Joe Palmiere *(Alfredo)*, Kevin Sanders *(TV Announcer)*.

Three vignettes, directed and scripted by six people and held together (barely) by a TV interview of Zero Mostel as the ex-President. He explains his downfall by showing CIA file films of White House aides engaging in perverse sexual activities. The first tale has comedian Paulsen enjoying a life-sized doll; the second casts Orbach as a writer who gets sexual help from his mentor; and the final episode (and most embarrassing) has Mostel's daughter being kidnaped by mobster pornographers. As ransom, Mostel must have sex with Parsons on network TV. A waste of time and talent. Directors Malmuth and Avildsen went on to *much* better things, the former directing NIGHTHAWKS (1981) and the later helming ROCKY (1976) and THE KARATE KID (1984).

p, Benni Korzen, David G. Witter; d, Robert J. McCarty, Bruce Malmuth, John G. Avildsen; w, Dan Greenberg, Jack Richardson, David Odell; ph, Jeff Lion Weinstock, Adam Gifford, Ralf Bode; m, Stan Vincent.

Comedy **Cas.** **(PR:O MPAA:R)**

FOREST, THE* (1983) 85m Fury/Wide World of Entertainment c (AKA: TERROR IN THE FOREST)

Dean Russell *(Steve)*, Michael Brody *(John)*, Elaine Warner *(Sharon)*, John Batis *(Charley)*, Ann Wilkinson *(Teddi)*, Jeanette Kelly *(Mother)*, Corky Pigeon *(John, Jr.)*, Becki Burke *(Jennifer)*, Don Jones *(Forest Ranger)*, Tony Gee, Stafford Morgan, Marilyn Anderson.

A typical low-budget horror entry full of the usual nighttime forest frights, including a raving cannibal and the haunting spirits of a dead family. You've seen it done better before.

p&d, Don Jones; w, Evan Jones; ph, Stuart Asbjorsen; m, Richard Hieronymus, Alan Oldfield; art d, Sandra Saunders; makeup, Dana Wolski.

Horror **Cas.** **(PR:O MPAA:R)**

FOREST RANGERS, THE½** (1942) 85m PAR c

Fred MacMurray *(Don Stuart)*, Paulette Goddard *(Celia Huston)*, Susan Hayward *(Tana Mason)*, Lynne Overman *(Jammer Jones)*, Albert Dekker *(Twig Dawson)*, Eugene Pallette *(Mr. Huston)*, Regis Toomey *(Frank Hatfield)*, Rod Cameron *(Jim Lawrence)*, Clem Bevans *(Terry McCabe)*, James Brown *(George Tracy)*, Kenneth Griffith, Keith Richards, William Cabanne, Clint Dorrington, Ronnie Rondell, Bert Stevens, Nick Vehr *(Rangers)*, George Chandler, Tim Ryan, Lee Phelps, Edwin J. Brady *(Keystone Cops)*, Chester Clute *(Judge)*, Pat West *(Bartender)*, Buddy Bowles, Janet Dempsey *(Hansen Kids)*, Sarah Edwards *(Mrs. Hansen)*, Jimmy Conlin *(Mr. Hansen)*, Robert Kent, Jack Mulhall *(Lookouts)*, George Turner *(Boy in Hotel Lobby)*, Bob Kortman, Al Thompson, Myron Geiger, George Bruggeman, Carl Saxe, Harry Templeton, Perc Launders, Ethan Laidlaw, Karl Vess, Arthur Harry Woods, Robert Homans *(Lumbermen)*, Arthur Loft *(John Arnold)*.

MacMurray is a forest ranger who suspects a recent rash of fires in his district is arson. He ventures to a nearby town in search of the criminal and meets Goddard, a beautiful rich girl. They fall in love and marry, but his fellow rangers have trouble accepting this female addition to their domain. Hayward, the daughter of a lumber baron, has always loved MacMurray from afar and is upset by his marriage. Soon the fires get out of hand and the two women in MacMurray's life pull together to help out. Unfortunately, they become trapped behind a wall of flames and MacMurray must hitch a ride on Toomey's small plane in order to parachute into the area. While airborne, he discovers that Toomey (who is flying the plane) is the arsonist and a fight ensues. Toomey sets the plane on fire and parachutes out, leaving the forest ranger knocked out and in a nosedive. Luckily, MacMurray comes to and manages to bail out. He lands near the girls, helps them finish putting out the fire, and learns that the evil Toomey had parachuted himself right into the fire and died. Director Marshall was obsessed with attaining a realistic look for his film, so he sent his cameramen into the flames armed with special heat-resistant film, but the cameras caught fire, causing Marshall to abandon the idea.

p, Robert Sisk; d, George Marshall; w, Harold Shumate (story by Thelma Strabel); ph, Charles Lang; m, Frank Loesser, Joseph J. Lilley; ed, Paul Weatherwax; art d, Hans Dreier, Earl Hedrick.

Action/Adventure **(PR:A MPAA:NR)**

FOREVER AMBER**½ (1947) 140m FOX c

Linda Darnell *(Amber St. Clair)*, Cornel Wilde *(Bruce Carlton)*, Richard Greene *(Lord Almsbury)*, George Sanders *(King Charles II)*, Richard Haydn *(Earl of Radcliffe)*, Jessica Tandy *(Nan Britton)*, Anne Revere *(Mother Red Cap)*, John Russell *(Black Jack Mallard)*, Jane Ball *(Corinne Carlton)*, Robert Coote *(Sir Thomas Dudley)*, Leo G. Carroll *(Matt Goodgroome)*, Natalie Draper *(Countess of Castlemaine)*, Margaret Wycherly *(Mrs. Song)*, Alma Kruger *(Lady Redmond)*, Edmond Breon *(Lord Redmond)*, Alan Napier *(Landale)*, Perry "Bill" Ward *(Little Bruce)*, Richard Bailey *(Bob Starling)*, Houseley Stevenson *(Mr. Starling)*, Bob Adler, Gilchrist Stuart, David Murray, Arthur Elliott *(Cavaliers)*, Skelton Knaggs *(Blueskin)*, Peter Shaw *(Deacon)*, Jimmy Ames *(Galeazzo)*, Vernon Downing *(Fop)*, Lillian Molieri *(Queen Catherine)*, Ian Keith *(Tybalt)*, Frederic Worlock *(Actor)*, Norma Varden *(Mrs. Abbott)*, Edith Evanson *(Sarah)*, Ellen Corby *(Marge)*, James Craven *(Messenger)*, Tempe Pigott *(Midwife)*, Cyril Delevanti *(Cobbler)*, Cecil Weston *(Woman)*, Ottola Nesmith *(Mrs. Chiverton)*, Pati Behrs *(Makeup Artist)*, Eric Noonan *(1st Mate)*, Robert Greig *(Magistrate)*, Glenn Langan *(Rex Morgan)*, Tim Huntley *(Ivers)*, Jimmy Lagano *(Bruce, Age 3)*, Tom Stevenson *(Groom)*, Boyd Irwin *(Lord Rossmore)*, Leonard Carey *(Dead Caller)*, Will Stanton *(Dead-Eye)*, C. C. "Tex" Gilmore *(One-Legged Man)*, David Ralston *(Drunken Pop)*, Victoria Horne *(Quaker)*.

Based on the racy novel by Kathleen Winsor, Darnell stars as a beautiful 17th century English girl born into poverty who sees promiscuity as the only way to wealth and happiness. She bed-hops her way through lovers Wilde, Russell, and Langan, and eventually winds up as the favorite concubine of Sanders, who plays King Charles II. But promiscuity has its price, and Darnell winds up losing the only man she ever really loved, Wilde, who takes their child and moves to America. While the production was surprisingly lavish (the budget was somewhere around $6,500,000), the film suffers from the inability to detail the eroticism of the source material (which was what gave the novel its distinction) due to the censorship problems encountered in the 1940s. The naughty first novel by the much-publicized and photogenic Winsor came out in 1944, the year that also saw the publication of *A Tree Grows in Brooklyn* and Somerset Maugham's *The Razor's Edge*, and became an instant best seller, finishing fourth on the top seller list for the year. The following year it continued its torrid sales record and finished as the year's top seller. In all, three million copies of the book were sold in hardbound and paper cover before it wound down.

p, William Perlberg; d, Otto Preminger; w, Philip Dunne, Ring Lardner, Jr., Jerome Cady (based on the novel by Kathleen Winsor); ph, Leon Shamroy (Technicolor); m, David Raksin; ed, Louis Loeffler; md, Alfred Newman; art d, Lyle Wheeler; set d, Thomas Little, Walter M. Scott; cos, Charles Le Maire, Rene Hubert; spec eff, Fred Sersen; fencing master, Fred Cavens.

Drama **(PR:C-O MPAA:NR)**

FOREVER AND A DAY**** (1943) 104m RKO bw

Anna Neagle *(Miriam [Susan])*, Ray Milland *(Bill Trimble)*, Claude Rains *(Pomfret)*, C. Aubrey Smith *(Adm. Trimble)*, Dame May Whitty *(Mrs. Trimble)*, Gene Lockhart *(Cobblewick)*, Ray Bolger *(Sentry)*, Edmund Gwenn *(Stubbs)*, Lumsden Hare *(Fitts)*, Stuart Robertson *(Lawyer)*, Claud Allister *(Barstow)*, Ben Webster *(Vicar)*, Alan Edmiston *(Tripp)*, Patric Knowles *(Courier)*, Bernie Sell *(Naval Officer)*, Halliwell Hobbes *(Doctor)*, Helena Pickard *(Maid)*, Doris Lloyd, Lionel Belmore *(Bits)*, Louis Bissiner *(Baby)*, Clifford Severn *(Nelson Trimble)*, Charles Coburn *(Sir William)*, Alec Craig *(Butler)*, Ian Hunter *(Dexter)*, Jessie Mathews *(Mildred)*, Charles Laughton *(Bellamy)*, Montagu Love *(Sir John Bunn)*, Reginald Owen *(Mr. Simpson)*, Cedric Hardwicke *(Dabb)*, Noel Madison *(Mr. Dunkinfield)*, Ernest Cossart *(Mr. Blinkinsep)*, Peter Godfrey *(Mr. Pepperdish)*, Buster Keaton *(Dabb's Assistant)*, Wendy Barrie *(Edith)*, Ida Lupino *(Jenny)*, Brian Aherne *(Jim Trimble)*, Edward Everett Horton *(Sir Anthony)*, Isobel Elsom *(Lady Trimble-Pomfret)*, Wendell Hulott *(Augustus)*, Eric Blore *(Selsby)*, June Duprez *(Julia)*, Mickey Martin *(Boy)*, Queenie Leonard *(Housemaid)*, May Beatty *(Cook)*, Merle Oberon *(Marjorie)*, Una O'Connor *(Mrs. Ismay)*, Nigel Bruce *(Maj. Garrow)*, Anita Bolster *(Mrs. Garrow)*, Marta Gale *(Miss Garrow)*, Roland Young *(Mr. Barringer)*, Gladys Cooper *(Mrs. Barringer)*, Robert Cummings *(Ned Trimble)*, Herbert Evans *(Bobby)*, Kay Deslys, Vangie Beilby *(Woman Drunks)*, Richard Haydn *(Mr. Fulcher)*, Emily Fitzroy *(Mrs. Fulcher)*, Odette Myrtil *(Mrs. Dallas)*, Elsa Lanchester *(Mamie)*, Sara Allgood *(Cook in 1917)*, Clyde Cook *(Taxi Driver)*, Dorothy Bell *(WAAC Girl)*, Jean Prescott *(ATS Girl)*, Robert Coote *(Blind Officer)*, Art Mulliner, Ivan Simpson *(Elderly Bachelors)*, Pax Walker, Lola Vanti *(Housemaids in 1917)*, Bill Cartledge *(Telegraph Boy)*, Charles Hall, Percy Snowden *(Men)*, Donald Crisp *(Capt. Martin)*, Ruth Warrick *(Leslie)*, Kent Smith *(Gates Pomfret)*, June Lockhart *(Daughter)*, Lydia Bilbrook *(Mother)*, Billy Bevan *(Cabby)*, Stuart Robertson *(Air Raid Warden)*, Herbert Marshall *(Curate)*, Victor McLaglen *(Spavin)*, Harry Allen *(Cockney Watcher)*, Ethel Griffies *(Wife)*, Gabriel Canzona *(Man with Monkey)*, Joy Harrington *(Bus Conductress)*, Reginald Gardiner *(Man)*, Walter Kingsford *(Man)*, Stuart Hall, Barry Heenan, Barry Norton, Philip Ahlin *(Card Players)*, Daphne Moore *(Nurse)*, Dorothy Bell *(Flower Girl)*, Mary Gordon, Gerald Hamer, Evelyn Beresford, Moyna MacGill, Arthur Treacher, Anna Lee, Cecil Kellaway, Connie Leon, Ernest Grooney, Aubrey Mather, Barbara Everest, Daphne Moore, Doreen Monroe, Charles Irwin, Gerald Oliver Smith.

A salute to England with a cavalcade of stars and directors to make it snap, FOREVER AND A DAY depicts the history of a great manor house in London, built by C. Aubrey Smith, a hell-for-battle admiral of Napoleon's era, and how it passes through the hands of one generation after another. Scores of stars and character actors offer bits and cameos in this stunning film, its only detraction being the brief viewer identification of each player before he or she flits across the screen. Exceptional are Laughton as a comic butler, Hardwicke and Keaton as plumbers, Lanchester as the waitress-maid, Aherne as a coalman, and Lupino the household maid who runs off with him to America. Particularly moving is the WW I sequence when the great mansion has been turned into a rooming house and the love affair that develops between doughboy Cummings and receptionist Oberon during a touching homecoming party for a WW I flying ace who never appears. His parents, Young and Cooper, render superb performances, especially when, at the height of the festivities, they learn that their son has been shot down and killed. A great pageant inside the theme that "there will always be an England," FOREVER AND A DAY comes down to the house's survival (and thereby England's) during the awful WW II blitz of London. RKO used just about everyone in Hollywood's esteemed British acting colony for this one and $500,000 to boot, almost as an act of charity in promoting the British-American cause since the studio saw little return at the box office. The film was nevertheless a memorable event and remains so today, superbly crafted, acted, and directed.

p&d, Rene Clair, Edmund Goulding, Cedric Hardwicke, Frank Lloyd, Victor Saville, Robert Stevenson, Herbert Wilcox; w, Charles Bennett, C.S. Forester, Lawrence Hazard, Michael Hogan, W.P. Lipscomb, Alice Duer Miller, John Van Druten, Alan Campbell, Peter Godfrey, S.M. Herzig, Christopher Isherwood, Gene Lockhart, R.C. Sherriff, Claudine West, Norman Corwin, Jack Hartfield, James Hilton, Emmett Lavery, Frederick Lonsdale, Donald Ogden Stewart, Keith Winters; ph, Robert de Grasse, Lee Garmes, Russell Metty, Nicholas Musuraca; ed, Elmo J. Williams, George Crone; md, Anthony Collins; art d, Albert S. D'Agostino, Lawrence P. Williams, Al Freeman; spec eff, Vernon L. Walker.

Adventure/Romance/History **(PR:A MPAA:NR)**

FOREVER DARLING* (1956) 96m MGM c

Lucille Ball *(Susan Vega)*, Desi Arnaz *(Lorenzo Xavier Vega)*, James Mason *(The Guardian Angel)*, Louis Calhern *(Charles Y. Bewell)*, John Emery *(Dr. Edward R. Winter)*, John Hoyt *(Bill Finlay)*, Natalie Schafer *(Millie Opdyke)*, Mabel Albertson *(Society Reporter)*, Ralph Dumke *(Henry Opdyke)*, Nancy Kulp *(Amy)*, Willis B. Bouchey *(Mr. Clinton)*, Ruth Brady *(Laura)*.

Arnaz and Ball are married sourly due to Arnaz's job as a chemist, which keeps him burning the midnight oil while working on a new insecticide. Ball's guardian angel Mason arrives to help fix things up. He advises Ball to join Arnaz when he takes a trip to test the new insecticide, and Ball does, unfortunately pratfalling her way through a series of misadventures in the woods. A stinker by a once successful comedy team.

p, Desi Arnaz; d, Alexander Hall; w, Helen Deutsch; ph, Harold Lipstein (Eastmancolor); m, Bronislau Kaper; ed, Dann Cahn, Bud Molin; art d, Ralph Berger, Albert Pyke; cos, Elois Jenssen; m/l, "Forever Darling," Sammy Cahn (sung by The Ames Brothers).

Comedy **(PR:A MPAA:NR)**

FOREVER ENGLAND (SEE: BORN FOR GLORY, 1935, Brit.)

FOREVER FEMALE*** (1953) 93m PAR bw

Ginger Rogers *(Beatrice Page)*, William Holden *(Stanley Krown)*, Paul Douglas *(E. Harry Phillips)*, James Gleason *(Eddie Woods)*, Pat Crowley *(Sally Carver)*, Jesse White *(Willie Wolfe)*, Marjorie Rambeau *(Herself)*, George Reeves *(George Courtland)*, King Donovan *(Playwright)*, Vic Perrin *(Scenic Designer)*, Russell Gaige *(Theatrical Producer)*, Marion Ross *(Patty)*, Richard Shannon *(Stage Manager)*, Sally Mansfield, Kathryn Grant, Rand Harper *(Young Hopefuls)*, Henry Dar Boggia *(Felix)*, Victor Romito *(Maitre D')*, Hyacinthe Railla, Alfred Paix *(Waiters)*, Walter Reed *(Leading Man)*, Josephine Whittell *(Katherine)*, Almira Sessions *(Mother)*, Joel Marston *(Photographer)*, Grayce Hampton *(Olga O'Brien)*, David Leonard *(Bill Forrest)*, Maidie Norman *(Emma)*, Vince M. Townsend, Jr. *(Doorman)*, Michael Darrin *(Jack)*, Richard Garland *(Clerk)*, William Leslie *(Bill)*, Dulce Daye *(Drucille King)*.

Fast-paced and funny adaptation of Sir James Barrie's play "Rosalind" brought up to date with several twists added. Smacking slightly of ALL ABOUT EVE, it tells the story of a young supermarket employee, Holden, who writes his first play about a nineteen year-old girl and her forceful mother. Holden truly believes this is modern-day Shakespeare and is adamant about changes (as so many fledgling authors are). He meets Rogers, an aging leading lady, and her ex-husband, Paul Douglas, a stage producer. Douglas agrees to mount the play if Holden alters the age of the lead to twenty nine so Rogers can play it believably (Rogers was actually 42 at the time). Meanwhile, pert Crowley, sort of an Eve to Rogers' Margo, wants the teenage role. Holden bows to pressure, rewrites the play to fit Rogers, and it flops on the road. Holden is terribly charming and both Rogers and Crowley fall in love with him. All that is assuaged when Douglas engineers it so Crowley and Holden get together, thus clearing the way for a reconciliation between him and Rogers. Lots of bright lines, many of them inside jokes for show people, by the Epstein brothers. Rogers overplays somewhat but not enough to cause any winces. Reeves (TV's "Superman") is good as one of Rogers's hangers-on and James

Gleason does his usual excellent job in a supporting role. Marjorie Rambeau plays herself in a Sardi's scene and sparkles. Look for Grant (Mrs. Bing Crosby) as one of the young hopefuls. Her name was still Grandstaff at the time and she goes by very quickly. Jesse White turns in one of his patented good jobs as a New York columnist. The Epsteins wrote many excellent films, not the least of which was CASABLANCA (with Howard Koch). For that alone, you might enjoy their comedy talents in this film. They were always together, so much so that when Jack Warner was walking across his lot and saw one of them, he automatically said "Hi, Boys."

p, Pat Duggan; d, Irving Rapper; w, Julius J. and Philip G. Epstein (suggested by the play "Rosalind" by Sir James M. Barrie); ph, Harry Stradling, Sr.; m, Victor Young; ed, Archie Marshek, Doane Harrison; art d, Hal Pereira, Joseph MacMillan; set d, Sam Comer, Ross Dowd; cos, Edith Head; spec eff, Gordon Jennings; makeup, Wally Westmore.

Comedy **(PR:A MPAA:NR)**

FOREVER MY HEART* (1954, Brit.) 52m BL bw

Douglas Fairbanks, Jr., Muriel Pavlow, Stuart Lindsell, Anouk Aimee, Dermot Palmer, Pierre Lefevre.

Two short stories, of little similarity, are woven together to create a feature whose only redeeming factor seems to be its brevity. The first is a period piece taking place in the jail of the Tower of London, where two prisoners fall in love with each other while being kept in different cells. The male of the pair sacrifices his own life by making sure his female counterpart is able to escape. The second story concerns a prostitute whose guilt over the death of her younger sister has led to hallucinations of the woman's ghost. Despite some capable performers, they were given poor material with which they could do little. The result was extremely dull.

p, Douglas Fairbanks, Jr.; d, Leslie Arliss, Bernard Knowles; w, Selwyn Jepson, Doreen Montgomery, Larry Marcus; ph, Ken Talbot, Eric Cross.

Drama **(PR:C MPAA:NR)**

FOREVER MY LOVE*** (1962) 147m Erma/PAR c

Romy Schneider *(Princess Elisabeth/Sissi)*, Karl Boehm *(Emperor Franz Josef)*, Magda Schneider *(Duchess Ludovika)*, Vilma Degischer *(Archduchess Sophie)*, Gustav Knuth *(Duke Max of Bavaria)*, Joseph Meinrad *(Police Major)*, Uta Franz *(Princess Helene)*, Walther Reyer *(Count Gyula Andrassy)*, Erich Nikowitz *(Archduke Franz-Karl)*, Karl Fochler *(Count Grunne)*, Peter Weck *(Archduke Karl-Ludwig)*, Hilde Wagener *(Princess Helen)*, Senta Wengraf *(Countess Bellegarde)*, Helene Lauterbock *(Countess Esterhazy)*, Klaus Knuth *(Prince Ludwig)*, Egon von Jordan *(Carl)*, Hans Ziegler *(Privy Councillor Dr. Seeburger)*, Albert Rueprecht *(Archduke Ferdinand-Max)*, Sonja Sorell *(Henriette Mendel)*, Peter Neusser *(Count Batthyani)*, Johannes Ferigo *(Count Czaky)*, Ida Gabor *(Margit)*, Chariklia Baxevanos *(Helena)*, Oskar Wegrostek *(Landlord)*, Dolores Hubert *(Governess)*, Herbert Prikopa *(Italian Cook)*, Walter Regelsberger *(Count Windischgraetz)*, Otto Tressler, Ivan Petrovich, Richard Eybner, Josef Egger, Hugo Gottschlich, Franca Parisi Strahl.

Paramount took three Austrian films (SISSI, SISSI-DIE JUNGE KAISERIN, and SISSI-SCHICKSALSJARE EINER KAISERIN), cut them into one lengthy feature, and added a sappy Hal David/Burt Bacharach tune for release in America. The film details the life of Franz Josef (Boehm), the young emperor of Austria, with special attention given to his romance with Schneider, the princess of Bavaria. As the years progress, Schneider becomes a powerful influence in the royal decision-making of Boehm and she eventually convinces him to seek peace with other nations. The film is lavishly produced with great period detail, but in the final analysis a piecemeal effort that would probably have been more interesting if it had been left alone and released as three separate movies. Film was one of many in which Magda Schneider, a popular star of German and Austrian movies in the 1930s, supported her daughter, Romy, and the SISSI version of the movie also was the one that propelled Romy Schneider to stardom. (The Fritz Kreisler operetta "Sissi" had been converted in 1936 by Columbia as THE KING STEPS OUT, directed by Josef von Sternberg.)

p,d&w, Ernest Marischka; ph, Bruno Mondi (Technicolor); m, Anton Profes; ed, Alfred Srp; cos, Gerdago, Leo Bei; ch, Willy Franzl; m/l, "Forever My Love," Hal David, Burt Bacharach (sung by Jane Morgan).

Drama **(PR:A MPAA:NR)**

FOREVER YOUNG, FOREVER FREE** (1976, South Afr.) 87m Film Trust-Milton Okun/UNIV c (AKA: E LOLLIPOP, LOLLIPOP)

Jose Ferrer *(Father Alberto)*, Karen Valentine *(Carol Anne)*, Bess Finney *(Sister Marguerita)*, Muntu Ndebele *(Tsepo)*, Norman Knox *(Jannie)*, Bingo Mbonjeni *(Cash General)*, Simon Sabela *(Rakwaba)*.

A saccharine melodrama starring Knox (who is white) and Ndebele (who is black) as two young boys raised in a South African mission by Ferrer, Finney, and Valentine. Despite the obvious racial tensions in South Africa, the boys become close friends. Tragedy strikes their little world when Knox falls sick and must be flown to New York City for special treatment. Ndebele follows but winds up trapped in Harlem, lost and alone. The boys are reunited for a happy ending. Director Lazarus contrasts the South African scenes with the New York material by portraying the African way of life as simple and pleasant, while Manhattan seems like hell on Earth. Though the message of the film is plain and fairly wholesome, there is a disturbing racial undercurrent prevalent in the early scenes.

p, Andre Pieterse; d&w, Ashley Lazarus (based on a story by Pieterse); ph, Arthur J. Ornitz; m, Lee Holdridge; ed, Lionel Selwyn; art d, Wendy Malan, Phil Rosenberg; cos, John Buckley, Joe Aulisi; m/l, "Forever Young, Forever Free," Rod McKuen, Lee Holdridge (sung by Bernadette Peters).

Juvenile Drama **(PR:AAA MPAA:G)**

FOREVER YOURS** (1937, Brit.) 70m LFP/UA bw (GB: FORGET ME NOT)

Beniamino Gigli *(Enzo Curti)*, Joan Gardner *(Helen)*, Ivan Brandt *(Hugh Anderson)*, Hugh Wakefield *(Curti's Manager)*, Jeanne Stuart *(Irene)*, Allan Jeayes *(London Manager)*, Hay Petrie *(New York Manager)*, Charles Carson *(Arnold)*, Richard Gofe *(Benvenuto)*.

Routine romantic triangle featuring hefty Metropolitan Opera tenor Gigli as a widowed tenor (what else?) who falls into a love affair and then marriage with young British clerical worker Gardner who is on the emotional rebound after a frustrating romance with handsome ship's officer Brandt. Trouble looms on the horizon however, when Gardner and Brandt run into each other while Gigli is on a spectacularly successful world tour. The former lovers are soon mooning over one another again much to the dismay of Gigli who becomes so emotionally distraught that he can't perform. Gardner realizes it is Gigli she truly loves, and she returns to his open arms.

p, Alberto Giacalone, Alexander Korda; d, Zoltan Korda, Stanley Irving; w, Hugh Gray, Arthur Wimperis; ph, Hans Schneeberger; m, Michael [Mischa] Spoliansky; ed, Henry Cornelius; md, Muir Mathieson.

Romance/Musical **(PR:A MPAA:NR)**

FOREVER YOURS** (1945) 83m MON bw

Gale Storm *(Joan Randall)*, Sir C. Aubrey Smith *(Grandfather)*, Johnny Mack Brown *(Tex)*, Frank Craven *(Uncle Charles)*, Conrad Nagel *(Dr. Randall)*, Billy Wilkerson *(1st Soldier)*, Mary Boland *(Aunt Mary)*, Johnny Downs *(Ricky)*, Catherine McLeod *(Martha)*, Selmer Jackson *(Williams)*, Matt Willis *(Alabam)*, Russ Whiteman *(2nd Soldier)*, Leo Diamond and His Harmonaires.

Storm splits her time between horse-riding and singing in a nightclub, the latter a job that brings in extra cash for disabled veterans and handicapped youngsters. She, however, becomes paralyzed, but her father and grandfather, both doctors, can't seem to help. Army surgeon Brown offers his services to the reluctant family, and after much persuading successfully performs an operation. Her recovery is accompanied by the usual film romance between doctor and patient.

p, Jeffrey Bernerd; d, William Nigh; w, Neil Rau, George Sayre; ph, Harry Neumann; ed, Ray Curtiss; m/l, "Close Your Eyes," Al Jaxton, Neil Rau, "You're the Answer," Harry Brown, Robert Watson (sung by Gale Storm).

Drama **(PR:A MPAA:NR)**

FORGED PASSPORT** (1939) 60m REP bw

Paul Kelly *(Dan Frazer)*, June Lang *(Helene)*, Lyle Talbot *(Jack Scott)*, Billy Gilbert *(Nick Mendoza)*, Cliff Nazarro *(Shakespeare)*, Maurice Murphy *(Kansas)*, Christian Rub *(Mr. Nelson)*, John Hamilton *(Harry Rogers)*, Dewey Robinson *(Riley)*, Bruce MacFarlane *(Buck)*, Ivan Miller *(Capt. Ellis)*, Frank Puglia.

Kelly is a U.S. border patrol agent stationed in Tiajuana who loses his job after a friend is gunned down due to his investigation. Kelly then discovers that the bullet was meant for him, sending him on a mission of vengeance. He is nearly blown to pieces when his truck is booby-trapped with a bomb, but succeeds in breaking up the gang. A standard crime pic with comedy relief by smuggler Billy Gilbert, who turned in one of his funniest performances one year later as the governor's messenger in HIS GIRL FRIDAY, a comedy remake of the great THE FRONT PAGE.

p&d, John H. Auer; w, Franklin Coen, Lee Loeb (from an original story by James Webb, Loeb); ph, Jack Marta; m, Cy Feuer; ed, Edward Mann, art d, John Victor Mackay.

Crime **(PR:A MPAA:NR)**

FORGET ME NOT (SEE: FOREVER YOURS, 1937, Brit.)

FORGOTTEN* (1933) 66m Chesterfield bw

Lee Kohlmar *(Papa Strauss)*, June Clyde *(Lena Strauss)*, William Collier, Jr. *(Joseph Meyers)*, Leon [Ames] Waycoff *(Louie Strauss)*, Selmer Jackson *(Hans Strauss)*, Natalie Moorhead *(Myrtle Strauss)*, Natalie Kingston *(May Strauss)*, Otto Lederer *(Uncle Adolph)*, Tom Ricketts *(Old Crony)*, Jean Hersholt, Jr.

A plodding film about a family so adamantly opposed to their "papa's" smelly pipe-smoking that they send the ol' bugger to a retirement home. They think they've cleared the air when he proves them wrong and returns home to confound the family in a business venture. Definitely a forgotten film, and with reason.

p, George R. Batcheller; d, Richard Thorpe; w, Harry Sauber; ph, M.A. Anderson.

Drama **(PR:A MPAA:NR)**

FORGOTTEN COMMANDMENTS zero (1932) 75m PAR bw

Sari Maritza *(Anya Sorin)*, Gene Raymond *(Paul Ossip)*, Marguerite Churchill *(Marya Ossip)*, Irving Pichel *(Prof. Marinoff)*, Harry Beresford *(Priest)*, Edward Van Sloan *(Doctor)*, Kent Taylor *(Gregor)*, Joseph [Sawyer] Sauers *(Ivan Ivanovitch)*, Boris Bullock *(Burly Student)*, Allen Fox *(Second Student)*, Helen Carlyle *(Nurse)*, Frankie Adams *(Registrar)*, John Peter [Carradine], Richmond *(1st Orator)*, William Shawhan *(2nd Orator)*, John Deering *(Room Clerk)*, Harry Cording *(Officer)*, Florence Shreve *(Divorce Clerk)*.

This trite tale centers on an emotionless scientist who kills his mistress after learning that she has taken another lover. The filmmakers decided to add a monk character who relates the story of Moses to a group of children and then has to face the firing squad for "poisoning" children's minds. The story he tells incorporates twenty minutes of footage from C.B. DeMille's 1927 epic, THE TEN COMMANDMENTS, and is intended to further humble the godless Russians. Like oil and water, art and politicizing never mix.

d, Louis Gasnier, William Schorr; w, James Bernard Fagan, Agnes Brand Leahy; ph, Karl Struss.

Drama **(PR:A MPAA:NR)**

FORGOTTEN FACES (1936) 70m PAR bw

Herbert Marshall (Harry Ashton), Gertrude Michael (Cleo Ashton), James Burke (Sgt. Donovan), Robert Cummings (Clinton Faraday), Jane Rhodes (Sally McBride), Robert Gleckler (Mike Davidson), Alonzo Price (Warden Davis), Arthur Hohl (Hi-Jack Eddie), Pierre Watkin (Mr. McBride), Alan Edwards (Steve Deland), Mary Gordon (Mrs. O'Leary), Ann Evers (Maid), Dora Clement (Mrs. McBride), Elizabeth Russell.

After finding his wife in bed with another man, gambler Marshall kills the lover and is jailed. While he may have killed a man he still has a sense of responsibility to his infant daughter, placing her in the home of a wealthy couple. After a number of years his wife, now a stripper, decides to perform an act of blackmail on the foster parents. Marshall hears about the scheme and manages to get himself paroled. He successfully thwarts his ex-wife's plans and saves his daughter's pending marriage without her ever knowing the truth about her parents' past. A shade corny today. Remade as A GENTLEMAN AFTER DARK (1942) with Brian Donlevy in the Marshall part.

p, A.M. Botsford; d, E.A. Dupont; w, Marguerite Roberts, Robert Yost, Brian Marlow (based on a story by Richard Washburn Child); ph, Theodor Sparkuhl.

Drama (PR:A MPAA:NR)

FORGOTTEN GIRLS (1940) 68m REP bw

Louise Platt (Judy Wintale), Donald Woods (Dan Donahue), Wynne Gibson (Frances Wingate), Robert Armstrong (Grover Mullins), Eduardo Ciannelli (Gorno), Jack LaRue (Nolan), Barbara Pepper (Eve), Charles D. Brown (Linton), Sarah Padden (Miss Donaldson), Ann Baldwin (Jackie).

A murder mystery which has little to offer in the genre. Platt is accused of a murder her stepmother, Gibson, committed, but with the help of reporter Woods gets out of prison and proves her innocence. She is nearly the victim of a plot masterminded by her stepmother which would have had her body replaced by that of a corpse. Her cell would then be dynamited, making it impossible for anyone to identify the remains. On her deathbed, however, Gibson confesses, and Woods wins Platt's hand. Plenty to forget in this one, but little to forgive.

p, Robert North; d, Phil Rosen; w, Joseph Moncure March, George Beck, F. Hugh Herbert (based on a story by Frank McDonald); ph, Ernest Miller; ed, Ernest Nims; md, Cy Feuer; art d, John Victor Mackay.

Crime (PR:A MPAA:NR)

FORGOTTEN WOMAN, THE (1939) 68m UNIV bw

Sigrid Gurie (Anne Kennedy), Eve Arden (Carrie Ashburn), William Lundigan (Terence Kennedy), Donald Briggs (District Attorney Burke), Donnie Dunagan (Terry Kennedy, Jr.), Elizabeth Risdon (Margaret Burke), Paul Harvey (Charles Courtenay), Ray Walker (Marty), Virginia Brissac (Mrs. Kimball), Joseph Downing (Johnny Bradshaw), Norman Willis (Stu Mantle), George Walcott (Frank Lockridge), Charles Wilson (Gray), John Hamilton (Dr. May), George Humbert (Proprietor), Selmer Jackson (Man), Alan Edwards (Banker), Grace Hayle (Fat Woman In Beauty Shop), Claire DuBrey (Foxie), Sam McDaniel (Porter), Mariska Aldrich (Homely Woman), Bess Flowers (Beauty Shop Operator), Claire Whitney (Woman Reporter), Louise Lorimer, Pauline Haddon (Women), Betty Roadman, Frances Morris (Matrons), Charles Sherlock, William Thorne, Charles McMurphy (Policemen), Jack Gardner, Ben Lewis (Reporters), William Worthington, Larry Steers (Doctors).

Gurie is wrongly jailed and after four bitter years returns to society. Briggs is the district attorney who jailed her and then clears her name after discovering that the real killers have confessed to the crime. The confession was held over the head of the young district attorney, however, in an attempt to keep him from prosecuting the friends of shifty politician, Harvey. Briggs finally shakes off the nefarious politicians, falls in love with Gurie, and sinks the mighty Harvey. Eve Arden had only been in films for a few years using the name Arden when FORGOTTEN WOMAN was made, but at the time received raves for her comic style, later to be honed into the memorable biting wit and snappy line delivery that would make her famous. Arden appeared in two earlier films in 1929 and 1933 using her real name of Eunice Quedens.

p, Edmund Grainger; d, Harold Young; w, Lionel Houser, Harold Buchman (based on a story by John Kobler); ph, Stanley Cortez; ed, Charles Maynard; md, Charles Previn; art d, Jack Otterson.

Drama (PR:A MPAA:NR)

FORGOTTEN WOMEN (1932) 67m MON bw

Marion Shilling (Patricia Young), Rex Bell (Jimmy Burke), Beryl Mercer (Fern Madden), Virginia Lee Corbin (Sissy Salem), Carmelita Geraghty (Helen Turner), Edna Murphy (Trixie de Forrester), Edward Earle (Sleek Moran), Jack Carlyle (Dugan), Edward Kane (Swineback), G.D. Wood (Walrus).

Newspaper reporter Bell forgets two women in this romance-oriented film. One is a publisher's daughter, Shilling, and the other is stage star Corbin, who, having come to Hollywood, is relegated to extra roles. Bell works hard and becomes city editor due to a couple of big scoops about gangland plots. He romances Corbin, but throws her over for Shilling for most of the film. Corbin takes up with a mob leader as a boy friend. In a car chase with the crooks, Bell has to choose which car he should tail, the one with his former love, or the one with the bad guys. He chooses the one with Corbin, rekindles their love, and forgets Shilling.

d, Richard Thorpe; w, Adele Buffington, Wellyn Totman; ph, Archie Stout.

Drama (PR:A MPAA:NR)

FORGOTTEN WOMEN (1949) 65m MON bw

Elyse Knox (Kate Allison), Edward Norris (Andy Emerson), Robert Shayne (Richard Marshall), Theodora Lynch (Ruth Marshall), Veda Ann Borg (Claire Dunning), Noel Neill (Ellen Reid), Tim Ryan (Harry), Bill Kennedy (Bill Dunning), Warren Douglas (John Allison), Selmer Jackson (Judge Donnell), Paul Frison (Gary), Joel Marston, Sam Balter.

The plot to this one centers on the troubled lives of four women—Knox is nearly divorced, Lynch is a singer whose career is stifled by her hubby, Borg is separated, and Neill doesn't even have a guy, but wants one so she can have problems, too. Neill would go on to play Lois Lane in television's "Superman," where she would continue to have man problems. Real soap opera stuff. Lynch sings "Ave Maria" and "Cielito Lindo."

p, Jeffrey Bernerd; d, William Beaudine; w, W. Scott Darling (based on a story by Bernerd); ph, Marcel LePicard; ed, Roy Livingston, Otho Lovering; md, Edward J. Kay; art d, Dave Milton.

Drama (PR:A MPAA:NR)

FORLORN RIVER (1937) 62m PAR bw

Larry "Buster" Crabbe (Nevada), June Martel (Ina Blaine), John Patterson (Ben Ide), Harvey Stephens (Les Setter), Chester Conklin (Sheriff Grundy), Lew Kelly (Sheriff Jim Warner), Syd Saylor ("Weary" Pierce), William Duncan (Blaine), Raphael Bennett (Bill Hall), Ruth Warren (Millie Moran), Lee Powell (Duke), Oscar G. Hendrian (Sam), Robert Homans (Jeff Winters), Purnell Pratt (David Ward), Larry Lawrence (Ed), Barlowe Borland (Cashier), Tom Ung (Barber), Merrill McCormick (Chet Parker), Vester Pegg (Hank Gordon), Gordon Jones (Lem Watkins), Jay Wilsey, Jr. [Buffalo Bill, Jr.] (Pete Hunter).

Crabbe and his sidekick, Saylor, are hot on the trail of an outlaw gang headed by Stephens. They finally pull him in, making the Nevada town of Zane Grey's novel a more lawful place. Standard oater material. Saylor, perennial sidekick of the heroes in many westerns, floats out of the bleakness now and then with his sturdily working Adam's apple emphasizing his ever-present state of hunger.

p, Harold Hurley; d, Charles Barton; w, Stuart Anthony, Robert Yost (based on the novel by Zane Grey); ph, Harry Hallenberger; m, Boris Morros; ed, John Link.

Western (PR:AA MPAA:NR)

FORMULA, THE (1980) 117m MGM c

George C. Scott (Barney Caine), Marlon Brando (Adam Steiffel), Marthe Keller (Lisa), John Gielgud (Dr. Esau), G.D. Spradlin (Clements), Beatrice Straight (Kay Neeley), Richard Lynch (Kladen/Tedesco), John Van Dreelen (Hans Lehman), Robin Clarke (Maj. Neeley), Ike Eisenmann (Tony), Marshall Thompson (Geologist), Dieter Schidor (Assassin), Werner Kreindl (Schellenberg), Jan Niklas (Gestapo Captain), Wolfgang Preiss (Franz Tauber), Calvin Jung (Sgt. Yosuta), Alan North (Nolan), David Byrd (Obermann), Ferdy Mayne (Siebold), Gerry Murphy (Chauffer), Francisco Prado (Mendosa).

A disappointing screen adaptation of a can't-put-down novel. Since the book and the screenplay were both written by the producer, Steve Shagan, the fault must be laid at his feet although he and director Avildsen have said that the final cut was done by the studio and did not accurately reflect their intentions. Brando appears in just three scenes and was paid one million dollars for each of them. The premise is intriguing: if Germany did not have any access to oil during the war, how did it run its equipment? The film begins as German general Lynch is entrusted with the Nazi secret formula for synthetic fuel. The war is ending and the High Command hopes Lynch can make it to neutral Switzerland, then use the formula to bargain with the Allies for better treatment than what was planned for them at Nuremburg. Lynch is waylaid by U.S. soldier Clarke who spots the secrets for what they are—incredibly valuable. The two decide to join forces. Flash forward to thirty five years hence and Clarke is now dead, murdered as he slept. Clarke became a policeman, then retired, so it is apparent he didn't use the formula to get rich. Scott, a pal of Clarke's, arrives to investigate and learns that Clarke has been dealing with Brando, a billionaire oil tycoon not unlike many of the Texas types we read about. Scott gets nowhere with Brando, then flies to Germany to continue the unraveling of his pal's killing. Once there, he meets Keller, who is a spy, as well as Gielgud, who invented the process. Lynch shows up as well but he is already addle-brained. In the end, Brando and his cohorts win out and keep the synthetic fuel off the market, thereby causing the rest of the world to pay exorbitant prices for oil. Brando was on his way to looking as though he'd sat on an air hose. Perhaps it was his way of saying that the oilmen are fat cats, or maybe it was just that he finally said "the hell with it" after a lifetime of dieting. There is one very long confrontation between Scott and Brando that is worthwhile, if only because two giants are acting in the same room. The only trouble is that their speeches are so pedantic and convoluted that it's not easy to understand what they're saying. The photographer won an Oscar nomination but the rest of the picture is better left forgotten, and that's a shame because the novel was a deserved smash. Shagan was a one-time movie publicity and advertising man who decided to become a novelist and screenwriter. His first picture was the touching SAVE THE TIGER for which he garnered an Academy nomination but lost to Jeremy Larner's THE CANDIDATE.

p, Steve Shagan; d, John G. Avildsen; w, Shagan (based on the novel by Shagan); ph, James Crabe (Metrocolor); m, Bill Conti; ed, Avildsen, David Bretherton; prod d, Herman Blumenthal; art d, Hans-Jurgen Keibach; set d, Lee Poll; cos, Bill Thomas.

Drama **Cas.** (PR:C MPAA:R)

FORSAKEN GARDEN, THE (SEE: OF LOVE AND DESIRE, 1963)

FORSAKING ALL OTHERS (1935) 82m MGM bw

Joan Crawford (Mary Clay), Clark Gable (Jeff Williams), Robert Montgomery (Dill Todd), Charles Butterworth (Shep), Billie Burke (Paula), Frances Drake (Connie), Rosalind Russell (Eleanor), Tom Ricketts (Wiffens), Arthur Treacher (Johnson), Greta Meyer (Bella).

Rollicking slapstick comedy that seems to go against all casting traditions with Crawford in the femme lead. The usual 1930s sophisticated treatment is tossed aside in favor of clowning just this side of Mack Sennett. Crawford and Gable are childhood pals and have stayed on good terms through adolescence and now into their adulthood. Gable comes home from a trip abroad to learn that Crawford is about to marry Montgomery, a cad if there ever was one. Gable adores Crawford and would like to marry her but he keeps mum and hides his affection lest it might cause trouble in her relationship with Montgomery. Just as they are about to be wed, Montgomery leaves her at the church, races off, and marries his ex-girl friend, Drake. Crawford is devastated and turns to Gable for solace. Gable doesn't betray his love for Crawford, preferring instead to play a waiting game until she is ready to hear sweet nothings again. Montgomery realizes he's made an error with Drake and meets Crawford a year later at a party. They go for a bicycle trip and renew their love, planning to wed once more, as soon as he can rid himself of Drake. Gable is hurt and steps back because Crawford's happiness, even without him, is uppermost in his mind. As the wedding nears, Gable's familiarity breeds affection when Crawford realizes that many deeds she'd thought Montgomery had done were in fact done by Gable. Gable bids them goodbye and plans a trip to Spain to forget his heartaches. Crawford now understands that Gable is the man for her. She tells Montgomery that she will not marry him and goes off to find Gable on the ocean liner, just as it is about to leave shore. Montgomery knows in his heart that he doesn't deserve her so he wishes her well and waves goodbye from the pier. Crawford was very funny in her role and those who remember her in all the heavy parts like MILDRED PIERCE or HARRIET CRAIG or Sadie Thompson in RAIN might recall that she came from the musical comedy stage and had a terrific sense of humor about herself. Mankiewicz has always written witty scripts with insights far beyond the plots. This is no exception. His way with words is evident in every scene and there are several big laughs along the predictable way. Bankhead starred in the original play and she was a wonderful farceuse, but it's hard to imagine anyone doing it any better than Crawford.

p, Bernard H. Hyman; d, W.S. Van Dyke; w, Joseph Mankiewicz (based on the play by Edward Barry Roberts and Frank Morgan Cavett); ph, George Folsey, Gregg Toland; m, William Axt; ed, Tom Held; art d, Cedric Gibbons, Edward B. Willis; cos, Adrian; m/l, Gus Kahn, Walter Donaldson.

Comedy **(PR:A MPAA:NR)**

FORT ALGIERS** (1953) 78m UA bw

Yvonne De Carlo *(Yvette)*, Carlos Thompson *(Jeff)*, Raymond Burr *(Amir)*, Leif Erickson *(Kalmani)*, Anthony Caruso *(Chavez)*, John Dehner *(Maj. Colle)*, Robert Boon *(Mueller)*, Henry Corden *(Yessouf)*, Joe Kirk *(Luigi)*, Bill Phipps *(Lt. Gerrier)*, Sandra Gale *(Sandra)*, Charles Evans *(Officer)*.

De Carlo is a French nightclub singer who tries to win over Arab leader Burr to get her hands on secret plans for an attack against the French. She gets into Burr's palace, but her cover is soon blown. Her French Foreign Legionnaire lover, Thompson, comes to her rescue and helps repel the attack on the French. For Canadian-born temptress De Carlo, who wrote the lyrics for the one song she sings in the movie, it was one of four films she made in a very busy year.

p, Joseph N. Ermolieff; d, Lesley Selander; w, Theodore St. John (based on a story by Frederick Stephani); ph, Charles Lawton, Jr.; m, Michel Michelet; ed, Jerome Thoms; md, Raoul Kraushaar; art d, Boris Leven, Robert Peterson; cos, Yvonne Wood; m/l, "I'll Follow You," Michelet, Yvonne De Carlo.

Adventure **(PR:A MPAA:NR)**

FORT APACHE***** (1948) 127m Argosy/RKO bw

Henry Fonda *(Lt.-Col. Owen Thursday)*, John Wayne *(Capt. Kirby York)*, Shirley Temple *(Philadelphia Thursday)*, Ward Bond *(Sgt.-Maj. Michael O'Rourke)*, John Agar *(Lt. Michael "Mickey" O'Rourke)*, George O'Brien *(Capt. Sam Collingwood)*, Irene Rich *(Mrs. Mary O'Rourke)*, Victor McLaglen *(Sgt. Festus Mulcahy)*, Anna Lee *(Mrs. Emily Collingwood)*, Pedro Armendariz *(Sgt. Beaufort)*, Guy Kibbee *(Dr. Wilkens)*, Grant Withers *(Silas Meacham)*, Jack Pennick *(Sgt. Shattuck)*, Dick Foran *(Sgt. Quincannon)*, Miguel Inclan *(Cochise)*, Ray Hyke *(Capt. Gates)*, Mae Marsh *(Mrs. Martha Gates)*, Movita Castenada *(Guadalupe)*, Francis Ford *(Fen, the Stagecoach Guard)*, Hank Worden *(Bald-Headed Southern Recruit)*, Harry Tenbrook *(Courier)*, Frank Ferguson, William Forrest, Archie Twitchell *(Reporters)*, Mary Gordon *(Woman in Stagecoach Station)*, Cliff Clark *(Stage Driver)*, Mickey Simpson *(Non-Commissioned Officer)*, Fred Graham *(Irish Recruit)*, Philip Kieffer *(Man)*.

Superb epic western, FORT APACHE was the first of Ford's U.S. Cavalry trilogy made within two years (the others being SHE WORE A YELLOW RIBBON, 1949, and RIO GRANDE, 1950). The awesome exterior scenes for this film reflect Ford's early training as a painter. Fonda is a martinet commander who had been a famous general during the Civil War. He has been demoted and is bitter at being sent to Fort Apache, Arizona, to fight what he terms "digger Indians," instead of having been assigned to a glory post. For it is glory, fame, and a return to his former rank that he seeks, objectives far beyond his earthbound responsibility to his much-tried men. Fonda arrives at the hardscrabble fort with his daughter Temple and soon his ramrod actions earn him the dislike of his officers and men, but his charming daughter quickly befriends the officers' wives, Rich, Lee, and others, Rich being the mother of a newly arrived lieutenant, Agar (in his film debut), with whom Temple falls in love. Stern Fonda will have none of the relationship since Agar comes from a family of enlisted men, although his father, Bond, is the recipient of the Congressional Medal of Honor, won during the Civil War. West Point-trained Agar further angers Fonda when he takes Temple horseback riding and she accidentally sees two troopers who have been ambushed by the Apaches and burned to death, tied to the wagon wheels of their repair wagon at a site called "Blue Mesa," where the Indians have cut the telegraph wire. Fonda orders Agar and a detail of four men, the most seasoned sergeants on the post it turns out, to retrieve the bodies of the dead troopers. After they depart he follows with two full troops, using the detail as bait to the marauding Indians. As expected, the Indians attack the burial detail which flees, the Indians in pursuit. A wild chase across desert flats culminates with Fonda, Wayne, and the troops intercepting the Indians attacking the burial wagon. When returning to the fort, Fonda forbids his daughter to again see Agar. He next sends Wayne and Spanish-speaking Armendariz across the Rio Grande into Mexico to ask Indian leader Cochise (Inclan) to lead his people back to the reservation and end their warring. Inclan agrees to a truce talk but when Wayne returns to the post he is informed by Fonda that he has tricked Inclan, that Fonda intends to meet him with the entire regiment and force the Indians to return if necessary. Wayne and the rest of the regiment march out with Fonda at their head and make the long journey to the rendezvous point. Here Fonda meets with Inclan; the great Indian chief tells Fonda that neither he nor his people will return to the reservation until Withers, the corrupt Indian agent, is removed from office. His demands are interrupted by a furious Fonda who tells Inclan through interpreter Armendariz that he finds him "without honor," and either he obeys his direct order or his cavalry will charge the Indian camp. Inclan returns to his ranks of Indians and prepares for battle. Fonda orders a charge mounted in fours. "That's suicide, colonel," Wayne rages. Fonda calls Wayne a coward and Wayne challenges him to a duel. Fonda ignores the offer and orders Wayne to stay behind with the wagon train, telling him to take "O'Rourke with you," meaning the elderly sergeant-major, but Wayne takes Agar, the son, while the troops make a wild charge into a box canyon where hundreds of Indians decimate their ranks from mountainside positions. Through his field glasses, Wayne spots Fonda wounded and on foot and rides to his rescue. Fonda ignores the help and takes Wayne's horse so he can rejoin his command. "The command is wiped out, colonel," Wayne tells him. Fonda draws his sabre and tells Wayne that when he ever commands a regiment, "command it!" He then races off to join the remnants of the cavalry which have taken refuge in a small gulley. There the little group makes a futile stand against a horde of Indian cavalry, Inclan at their head. They are killed to the last man, the Apaches roaring toward the wagon train. Wayne tells his men behind the wagons not to fire. He approaches the onrushing Indians unarmed. Inclan rides up to him and plants in the sand next to him the regimental flag he has swooped up in the charge; then the Indians turn back, the huge cloud of dust kicked up by their horses engulfing Wayne, then fading as he watches them go. Wayne later becomes the regimental commander and, for the preservation of the army's good name, allows newspapermen to believe that Fonda's horrific blunder was a magnificent military achievement, one of high myth and glory, before again leading out his men in a long campaign against the Indians. FORT APACHE is rich beyond its wonderful action scenes and outdoor panoramas so dear to Ford's heart. The film expertly depicts the social affairs of a farflung military outpost, the struggle of the females to maintain civilized living conditions, and the routines of the men in day-to-day military duties. Ford's characterization and humor of the Irish cavalrymen, who make up much of the Western troops following the Civil War, is unforgettable; it's a supporting players' field day, with McLaglen, Bond, Foran, Armendariz, and Pennick allowing their caprice to conquer boredom in training raw recruits to march and ride. At one point Fonda finds illegal liquor supplies in Withers' off-post storehouse and orders the sergeants to destroy it. They do so by drinking it down to the last drop and winding up in the guardhouse, later ordered to shovel out the manure pile by a disgusted Bond. The camaraderie of the troopers is overwhelming, comical, and full of wonderful sentiment. Another poignant scene shows Foran, allowed out of the guardhouse for an evening so he can serenade a small social gathering, particularly Temple and Agar; Foran gives a beautiful tenor rendition of "Genevieve." The noncommissioned officers' ball, with its stirring grand march ("Gary Owen") is another highlight among many highlights in a consistently fascinating film. Of course Fonda's role and the doomed course he takes with his heroic regiment is based wholly on the massacre of George Armstrong Custer's 7th Cavalry at the Little Big Horn, but instead of the Sioux, it's the Apaches doing the slaughter. Fonda is superb as the unyielding commander and Wayne, in one of his best roles as an officer concerned for the lives of his men, is the perfect counterpoint to tyrant Fonda. (Ben Johnson, who later became a Ford favorite, was Wayne's stunt double in this film.) Both actors were long-time favorites of Ford; Fonda had made his mark in such earlier Ford masterpieces as THE GRAPES OF WRATH (1940), THE FUGITIVE (1947), and MY DARLING CLEMENTINE (1946), while Wayne had been Ford's darling ever since his electrifying performance in STAGECOACH. Agar, in his first role, got the part because he was married to Temple at the time and the one-time child actress desperately tried to act the adult young lady in a bid for continuing stardom. Both did commendable service but their careers were short-lived as stars thereafter. O'Brien, an old pal of Ford's who had acted in the director's 1924 silent classic, THE IRON HORSE, came out of retirement to play the commander replaced by Fonda. McLaglen, who had won an Oscar in another Ford film, THE INFORMER, thirteen years ealier, heads Ford's stock players Bond, Withers, Pennick, Foran, Armendariz, Lee, and Marsh, the latter having a career trailing back to 1912, with important parts in Griffith's silent masterpieces THE BIRTH OF A NATION (1915) and INTOLERANCE (1916). Paul Fix, who originally had a part in the film, was another Ford fixture and a thick friend of Wayne's. Duke was unsure of some of his lines in the film and asked Fix to coach him from the sidelines. When Ford discovered Fix making hand and face signals he exploded and put Fix through so many rigorous moves that the actor refused to perform and walked off the set. Ford told him never to darken his lighting again. Ford also picked on Temple and was very strict with Agar, making jokes about his inability to ride. Wayne took the youth aside and gave him lessons so he could live up to Ford's expectations, such was the typical consideration of this great star. Ford filmed this picture in Monument Valley (a Navaho Indian tribal park at the Arizona-Utah border, 2,000 square miles of desert and towering sandstone buttes), his favorite on-location area, inaccessible except for summer months because of weather, the same location used for his other two cavalry films, all three stories taken from stories by James Warner Bellah. Ford told Frank Nugent, screenwriter for FORT APACHE, as they outlined the script: "In all westerns, the cavalry rides to the rescue of the beleaguered wagon train or whatever and then it rides off again. I've been thinking about it—what it was like at a cavalry post, remote, people with their own personal problems, and over everything the threat of Indians, of death . . ." As usual, the director labored long, six months in this instance, to prepare script and pre-production set-ups so that he was able to cut his budget from $2.8 million to $2.1 million and shorten the seventy-seven-day shooting schedule to forty-four days. FORT APACHE returned $445,000 in profits to the Argosy/RKO production-distribution team. Though the film ends in defeat, as did Ford's masterful THEY WERE EXPENDABLE (1945), its strong domestic scenes, its colorful coterie of actors, its romantic portrait of an Old West no more, leaves a decided optimistic feeling, something positive and sure as a strong horse beneath the saddle that makes the far horizon reachable.

p, John Ford, Merian C. Cooper; d, Ford (2nd unit, Cliff Lyons); w, Frank S. Nugent (based on the story "Massacre" by James Warner Bellah); ph, Archie J. Stout; m, Richard Hageman; ed, Jack Murray; art d, James Basevi; set d, Joe Kish; cos, Michael Meyers, Ann Peck; spec eff, Dave Koehler; ch, Kenny Williams.

Western **Cas.** **(PR:A MPAA:NR)**

FORT APACHE, THE BRONX½** (1981) 125m FOX c

Paul Newman *(Murphy)*, Edward Asner *(Connolly)*, Ken Wahl *(Corelli)*, Danny Aiello *(Morgan)*, Rachel Ticotin *(Isabella)*, Pam Grier *(Charlotte)*, Kathleen Beller *(Theresa)*, Tito Goya *(Jumper/Detective)*, Miguel Pinero *(Hernando)*, Jaime Tirelli *(Jose)*, Lance William Guecia *(Track Star)*, Ronnie Clanton *(Pimp)*, Clifford David *(Dacey)*, Sully Boyar *(Dugan)*, Michael Higgins *(Hefferman)*, Rik Colitti *(Pantuzzi)*, Irving Metzman *(Applebaum)*, Frank Adu *(Clendennon)*, John Aquino *(Finley)*, Norman Matlock *(Lincoln)*, John Ring *(Donahue)*, Tony DiBenedetto *(Moran)*, Terence Brady, Randy Jurgenson, Marvin Cohen *(Cops at Bar)*, Paul Gleason, Reinaldo Medina *(Detectives)*, Darryl Edwards *(Black Rookie)*, Donald Petrie *(White Rookie)*, Thomas A. Carlin *(Man With Flat Tire)*, Frederick Allen *(Corelli's Brother)*, Dominic Chianese *(Corelli's Father)*, Mike Cichette *(Wild Eyed Man)*, Apu Guecia *(Stabbed Boy)*, Kim Delgado, Reyno, Dadi Pinero, Cleavant Derricks *(Suspects)*, Dolores Hernandez *(Pregnant Girl)*, Santos Morales *(Girl's Father)*, Ruth Last *(Girl's Mother)*, Jose Rabelo *(Girl's Uncle)*, Gilbert Lewis *(Mob Leader)*, Lisa Loomer, Sandi Franklin *(Hookers)*, Eric Mourino, Jessica Costello *(Boy and Girl on Roof)*, Gloria Irizarry *(Drug Dealer)*, Manuel Santiago *(Intern)*, Joaquin LaHabana *(Transvestite)*, Fred Strothers *(Hospital Buyer)*, Sylvia "Kuumba" Williams *(Bartender)*, Patricia Dratel *(Hostage)*, Thomas Fiorello *(Fence)*.

The title of this film comes from an actual police station in the most dilapidated area of that present-day disaster known as The Bronx, a New York borough where arson, murder, thievery, prostitution, assault, gang wars, and gang rapes are as commonplace as sun and rain. Newman is a good cop trying to do his duty inside this hellhole and he is shown in episodic adventures typical in the life of a modern-day galley slave, better known as the cop on the squad beat. Newman talks a mentally unbalanced homosexual queen out of committing suicide, protects a killer prostitute against her murderous pimp, delivers a baby, and disarms a psychopath by making grotesque faces and acting equally crazy. Beyond these unenviable chores, he argues with his superiors for more tolerant procedures with civilians and, when he learns that one of his number (Aiello) has killed a street kid, becomes a pariah on the force by demanding that the murderous cop be exposed, a liberal, rather unbelievable crusade that eventually costs him his shield. Asner is good as the tough cop who takes over the besieged precinct, and Aiello is typically sleazy, but Newman really must carry this rather predictable film wholly on his shoulders and no one actor has ever been big enough for that. The script is sharp and witty but there's no central theme holding it all together.

p, Martin Richards, Tom Fiorello; d, Daniel Petrie; w, Heywood Gould (suggested by the experiences of Thomas Mulhearn, Pete Tessitore); ph, John Alcott (DeLuxe Color); m, Jonathan Tunick; ed, Rita Roland; prod d, Ben Edwards; art d, Christopher Nowak; cos, John Boxer.

Crime Drama **Cas.** **(PR:O MPAA:R)**

FORT BOWIE½** (1958) 80m Bel Air/UA bw

Ben Johnson *(Capt. Thompson)*, Jan Harrison *(Allison Garrett)*, Kent Taylor *(Col. Garrett)*, Jane Davi *(Chenzana)*, Larry Chance *(Victorio)*, J. Ian Douglas *(Maj. Wharton)*, Peter Mamakos *(Sgt. Kukus)*, Jerry Frank *(Lt. Maywood)*, Barbara Parry *(Mrs. Maywood)*, Ed Hinton *(Gentleman)*, Johnny Western *(Sergeant)*.

Johnson's performance is the most exciting element of this familiar cowboy and Indian western. Johnson is in strong opposition to commanding officer Taylor, after the latter massacres a band of Indians who were eager to surrender. Johnson then draws Taylor's wrath when the commander's bored wife falsely accuses him of trying to seduce her. She remains loyal to her husband, however, standing by his side during an Indian attack which results in both their deaths.

p, Aubrey Schenck; d, Howard W. Koch; w, Maurice Tombragel; ph, Carl E. Guthrie; m, Les Baxter; ed, John A. Bushelman; spec eff, Jack Rabin, Louis DeWitt.

Western **(PR:A MPAA:NR)**

FORT COURAGEOUS½** (1965) 72m FOX bw

Fred Beir *(Sgt. Lucas)*, Donald Barry *(Capt. Howard)*, Hanna Landy *(Woman)*, Harry Lauter *(Joe)*, Cheryl MacDonald *(Daughter)*, Walter Reed, Joseph Patridge, Michael Carr, Fred Krone, George Sawaya, Kent Taylor.

An unjustly court-martialed cavalry sergeant, Beir, gallantly takes control of a patrol to Fort Courageous after the commander, Barry, is wounded in an Indian attack. When the men finally reach their destination, they discover that the fort has been wiped out, leaving only one survivor. Forced to stay and face the Indian onslaught, Beir proves himself by organizing his troops to fight off the attacking redskins again and again until, their bravery winning the respect of the Indians, they settle for a draw. Heroism abounds in this briskly told tale of the U.S. Cavalry.

p, Hal Klein; d, Lesley Selander; w, Richard Landau; ph, Gordon Avil; m, Richard LaSalle; ed, John F. Schreyer; md, LaSalle; cos, Patrick Cummings; spec eff, Roger George.

Western **(PR:A MPAA:NR)**

FORT DEFIANCE½** (1951) 81m UA c

Dane Clark *(Johnny Tallon)*, Ben Johnson *(Ben Shelby)*, Peter Graves *(Ned Tallon)*, Tracey Roberts *(Julie)*, George Cleveland *(Uncle Charlie Tallon)*, Dennis Moore *(Lt. Lucas)*, Iron Eyes Cody *(Brave Bear)*, Ralph Sanford *(Stage Coach Driver)*, Craig Woods *(Dave Parker)*, Dick Elliott *(Kincaid)*, Kit Guard *(Barfly)*, Duke York *(Doniger)*, Phil Rawlins *(Jake)*, Jerry Ambler *(Cheyenne)*, Slim Hightower *(Hankey)*, Wesley Hudman *(1st Stranger)*.

Johnson saves this oater about his ride for vengeance against Clark, whose desertion during a battle in the Civil War cost the lives of every man in Johnson's company. Tracking Clark to his desert ranch, Johnson finds the man's younger brother, Graves, who is blind, living with an elderly uncle. While waiting for Clark's arrival, Johnson grows close to Graves and begins to reconsider his mission of revenge. Suddenly the decision is made for him when another vengeance-seeking man arrives and attempts to kill the whole family. Johnson chooses to defend the family and when Clark does return, the former enemies unite to fight off the attack. Another western where Johnson, a former rodeo performer, continues to win his spurs as an actor.

p, Frank Melford; d, John Rawlins; w, Louis Lantz; ph, Stanley Cortez (Cinecolor); m, Paul Sawtell; ed, Tom Pratt; art d, Lucius Croxton.

Western **(PR:A MPAA:NR)**

FORT DOBBS** (1958) 93m WB bw

Clint Walker *(Gar Davis)*, Virginia Mayo *(Celia Gray)*, Brian Keith *(Clett)*, Richard Eyer *(Chad Gray)*, Russ Conway *(Sheriff)*, Michael Dante *(Billings)*.

Clint Walker, star of the short-lived "Cheyenne" television series, made his movie debut in FORT DOBBS, a slow-actioned western. An accused murderer, Walker escapes his lynchers by trading coats with a man he finds dead with an arrow in his back. He comes upon a farm owned by Mayo, and rescues her and her son, Eyer, from raiding Commanches. Walker takes the two to Fort Dobbs, and, on the way, Mayo recognizes Walker's coat as that of her husband's. She mistakes the arrow hole for a bullet hole, and concludes that Walker murdered her mate. Meanwhile, Keith has a sackful of fifteen-shot repeating rifles. Upon arriving at the fort with Mayo and Eyers, Walker masterminds the defense of the stockade from marauding Commanches. With the aid of Keith's rifles, he saves the fort and vindicates his good name to all, including Mayo.

p, Martin Rackin; d, Gordon Douglas; w, Burt Kennedy, George W. George (from the story "Backtrack" by Kennedy, George); ph, William Clothier; m, Max Steiner; ed, Clarence Kolster; art d, Stanley Fleischer; cos, Marjorie Best.

Western **(PR:A MPAA:NR)**

FORT DODGE STAMPEDE** (1951) 60m REP bw

Allan "Rocky" Lane *(Himself)*, Blackjack *(His Stallion)*, Chubby Johnson *(Skeeter)*, Mary Ellen Kay *(Natalie Bryan)*, Roy Barcroft *(Pike Hardin)*, Trevor Bardette *(Sparkler McCann)*, Bruce Edwards *(Jeff Bryan)*, Wesley Hudman *(Butler)*, William Forrest *(Hutchinson)*, Chuck Roberson *(Ragan)*, Rory Mallinson *(Sheriff)*, Jack Ingram *(Cox)*, Kermit Maynard *(Settler)*.

Buried loot from a bank robbery speeds this oater on its way, as two rival groups, Lane's good guys and Barcroft's bad guys, meet in the deserted town of Fort Dodge to find it. Plenty of action and blazing guns accompany Lane as his recruits recover the loot and return it to its rightful owner. Standard story well-handled by Lane and by Johnson and Edwards, his whiskered buddies.

p&d, Harry Keller; w, Richard Wormser; ph, John MacBurnie; ed, Irving M. Schoenberg.

Western **(PR:AA MPAA:NR)**

FORT GRAVEYARD½** (1966, Jap.) 132m Toho bw (CHI TO SUNA)

Toshiro Mifune *(Sgt. Kosugi)*, Tatsuya Nakadai, Yunosuke Ito, Reiko Dan, Makato Sato.

Overlong Japanese war movie starring Mifune as a highly decorated but incorrigible soldier who is sent to the Chinese front as punishment for insubordination. When he arrives, he finds that his brother has been executed for desertion. His rage lands him in a situation where he must choose between a court-martial or a suicide mission. He opts for the mission, which requires him to try to capture a Chinese fort using a crew of released prisoners. Though Mifune succeeds in taking the fort, he cannot hold off the waves of Chinese soldiers and he loses the battle. An interesting Japanese memento of the Sino-Japanese war of 1937-1945.

p, Tomoyuki Tanaka; d, Kihachi Okamoto; w, Okamoto, Kan Saji; ph, Rokuro Nishigaki (Tohoscope); m, Masaru Sato.

War **(PR:C MPAA:NR)**

FORT MASSACRE*** (1958) 80m UA c

Joel McCrea *(Vinson)*, Forrest Tucker *(McGurney)*, Susan Cabot *(Piute Girl)*, John Russell *(Travis)*, Anthony Caruso *(Pawnee)*, Bob Osterloh *(Schwabacker)*, Denver Pyle *(Collins)*, George W. Neise *(Pendleton)*, Rayford Barnes *(Moss)*, Guy Prescott *(Tucker)*, Larry Chance *(Moving Cloud)*, Irving Bacon *(Charlie)*, Claire Carleton *(Adele)*, Francis J. McDonald *(Piute Man)*, Walter Kray *(Chief)*.

McCrea shines as a cavalry sergeant leading his troops through Indian territory after his commanding officer is killed in an ambush. Incredibly, he leads them through restricted Apache territory, telling them it is the shortest route to the fort. The men, however, suspect that McCrea is just looking for an excuse to massacre some Indians because his wife and children were slaughtered by Apaches some years before. As feared, the troops are under constant attack and their numbers dwindle. Sensing that McCrea has gone mad, he is finally killed by one of his own men. While the direction and pace is slow, FORT MASSACRE is well worth sitting through due to McCrea's skillful performance.

p, Walter M. Mirisch; d, Joseph M. Newman; w, Martin N. Goldsmith; ph, Carl Guthrie (CinemaScope, DeLuxe Color); m, Marlin Skiles; ed, Richard Heermance.

Western   **(PR:C MPAA:NR)**

FORT OSAGE*   (1952) 72m MON c

Rod Cameron (*Tom Clay*), Jane Nigh (*Ann Pickett*), Morris Ankrum (*Arthur Pickett*), Douglas Kennedy (*George Keane*), John Ridgely (*Henry Travers*), William Phipps (*Nathan Goodspeed*), I. Stanford Jolley (*Sam Winfield*), Dorothy Adams (*Mrs. Winfield*), Francis McDonald (*Indian Chief*), Myron Healey (*Martin*), Lane Bradford (*Rawlins*), Iron Eyes Cody (*Old Indian*), Barbara Woodell (*Martha Woodling*), Ann Kimbell, Hal Baylor, Russ Conway, Barbara Allen.

Uninspired western starring Cameron as a scout hired to lead a wagon train through Indian territory. Unfortunately, unscrupulous Ankrum and Kennedy have stirred up the redskins by violating a treaty. Cameron confronts the dishonest settlers with his suspicions after dodging one too many arrows. Ankrum's conscience is touched and he decides to reform, but Kennedy kills him. The climax sees Kennedy running for his life from Cameron *and* the Indians. The Indians settle down and allow Cameron to guide the wagon train through their territory unmolested. Stiff-legged script falls down from lack of poise.

p, Walter M. Mirisch; d, Lesley Selander; w, Dan Ullman; ph, Harry Neumann (Cinecolor); m, Marlin Skiles; ed, Richard Heermance; art d, David Milton.

Western   **(PR:A MPAA:NR)**

FORT SAVAGE RAIDERS**½   (1951) 54m COL bw

Charles Starrett (*Steve Drake/The Durango Kid*), Smiley Burnette (*Himself*), John Dehner (*Capt. Michael Craydon*), Trevor Bardette (*Old Cuss*), Peter Thompson (*Lt. James Sutter*), Fred Sears (*Col. Sutter*), John Cason (*Jug*), Frank Griffin (*Rog Beck*), Sam Flint (*Col. Markham*), Dusty Walker.

A surprisingly intense Starrett western which sports a fine performance by Dehner as a crazed army officer who escapes a military prison accompanied by a small band of vicious cons who cut a path of terror through the sagebrush seeking revenge on the army that had imprisoned them. Starrett heads up the posse sent to thwart them and he dons his "Durango Kid" disguise frequently. FORT SAVAGE RAIDERS is also notable as being one of veteran oater director Fred Sears' last performances *before* the cameras.

p, Colbert Clark; d, Ray Nazarro; w, Barry Shipman; ph, Henry Freulich; ed, Paul Borofsky; md, Ross DiMaggio; art d, Charles Clague.

Western   **(PR:A MPAA:NR)**

FORT TI*½   (1953) 73m COL c

George Montgomery (*Capt. Pedediah Horn*), Joan Vohs (*Fortune Mallory*), Irving Bacon (*Sgt. Monday Wash*), James Seay (*Mark Chesney*), Ben Astar (*Francois Leroy*), Phyllis Fowler (*Running Otter*), Howard Petrie (*Maj. Rogers*), Cicely Browne (*Bess Chesney*), Lester Matthews (*Lord Jeffrey Amherst*), George Lee (*Capt. Delecroix*), Louis Merrill (*Raoul de Moreau*).

This was a big year for 3-D movies, and in this one flaming arrows and missiles of all kinds kept coming at the viewers with relentless fury as a group of colonial irregulars, known as Rogers' Rangers, try to oust the French from Fort Ticonderoga, located in the Adirondacks. Montgomery is the hero who, with his ragtag band, dislodges the enemy. Excellent 3-D lensing was spoiled by the paper viewers that always seemed to be falling off during tight spots on the screen. A silly diversion at best.

p, Sam Katzman; d, William Castle; w, Robert E. Kent; ph, Lester H. White, Lothrop B. Worth (Natural Vision 3-D, Technicolor); ed, William A. Lyon.

Western   **(PR:AA MPAA:NR)**

FORT UTAH*   (1967) 84m PAR c

John Ireland (*Tom Horn*), Virginia Mayo (*Linda Lee*), Scott Brady (*Dajin*), John Russell (*Eli Jonas*), Robert Strauss (*Ben Stokes*), James Craig (*Bo Greer*), Richard Arlen (*Sam Tyler*), Jim Davis (*Scarecrow*), Donald Barry (*Harris*), Harry Lauter (*Britches*), Read Morgan (*Cavalry Lieutenant*), Reg Parton (*Rafe*), Eric Cody (*Shirt*)).

Ireland is a tiresome ex-gunfighter who defends a small band of settlers from the machinations of crazed cavalryman Brady and his bloodthirsty band of marauders. Not only have Brady and his killers taken over a cavalry fort, but they also slaughtered a group of Indian women and children, giving Brady the inevitable vengeance-seeking Indians to contend with. The death rattle of the American western film sounds in the distance in this remnant of a once proud genre.

p, A.C. Lyles; d, Lesley Selander; w, Steve Fisher, Andrew Craddock; ph, Lothrop Worth (Techniscope, Technicolor); m, Jimmie Haskell; ed, John F. Schreyer; art d, Hal Pereira, Al Roelofs; set d, Robert R. Benton, John Sturtevant; spec eff, Paul K. Lerpae.

Western   **(PR:A MPAA:NR)**

FORT VENGEANCE**   (1953) 75m AA c

James Craig (*Dick*), Rita Moreno (*Bridget*), Keith Larsen (*Carey*), Reginald Denny (*Maj. Trevett*), Charles Irwin (*Saxon*), Morris Ankrum (*Crowfoot*), Guy Kingsford (*MacRea*), Michael Granger (*Sitting Bull*), Patrick Whyte (*Harrington*), Paul Marion (*Eagle Heart*), Emory Parnell (*Fitzgibbon*).

Craig and Larsen play brothers (one good, one evil) who are forced to flee to Canada after causing an uproar in a high-stakes poker game. Starving, good brother Craig convinces evil brother Larsen that they should join the Royal Canadian Mounted Police, and the Mounties take the strangers due to their detailed knowledge of the Sioux Indians who have been on the warpath and are trying to convince the normally peaceful Black Feet tribe, led by Ankrum, to join them. Larsen steals some furs from a trapper he has murdered and fakes the evidence so that it appears that Ankrum's son, Marion, did the killing. Craig is suspicious and, taking his Mountie code of honor seriously, rides off to bring his

brother to justice. Larsen gets an arrow in the back before Craig finds him. Meanwhile, Marion is about to get his neck snapped by the whites but Craig shows up in the nick of time with his brother head down over a saddle. Story is slower than normal from writer Ullman, who wrote many brisk westerns.

p, Walter Wanger; d, Lesley Selander; w, Dan Ullman; ph, Harry Neumann (Cinecolor); m, Paul Dunlap; ed, Walter Hannemann; art d, David Milton.

Western   **(PR:A MPAA:NR)**

FORT WORTH**   (1951) 80m WB c

Randolph Scott (*Ned Britt*), David Brian (*Blair Lunsford*), Phyllis Thaxter (*Flora Talbot*), Helena Carter (*Amy Brooks*), Dick Jones (*Luther Wick*), Ray Teal (*Gabe Clevenger*), Lawrence Tolan (*Mort*), Paul Picerni (*Castro*), Emerson Treacy (*Ben Garvin*), Bob Steele ("*Shorty*"), Walter Sande (*Waller*), Chubby Johnson (*Sheriff*).

Disappointing Scott oater which features him as a gunslinger in the early days of Texas who hangs up his gun belt and becomes the crusading editor of Fort Worth's finest newspaper. Friend Brian's encouragement backfires on him however, when Scott opposes his plans to buy up all of Fort Worth and turn it into his private cattle shipping center. A vicious band of drifters rides into town to cause trouble and Brian uses them to stop Scott's presses. After doing a slow burn, Scott finally blows the dust off his six guns and stops the baddies in their tracks.

p, Anthony Veiller; d, Edwin L. Marin; w, John Twist (based on the story "Across the Panhandle" by Twist); ph, Sid Hickox (Technicolor); m, David Buttolph; ed, Clarence Kolster; art d, Stanley Fleischer.

Western   **(PR:A MPAA:NR)**

FORT YUMA**   (1955) 78m UA c

Peter Graves (*Lt. Ben Keegan*), Joan Vohs (*Melanie Crowne*), John Hudson (*Sgt. Jonas*), Joan Taylor (*Francesca*), Addison Richards (*Gen. Crook*), William Phillips (*Sgt. Halleck*), James Lilburn (*Cpl. Taylor*), Abel Fernandez (*Mangas*), Lee Roberts, Edmund Penney.

Indians bent on revenge for the slaying of an Apache chief come up with a novel plan: they will dress up as federal soldiers and take the fort by surprise. Trouble is, Graves is with the supply column the Indians attack to get the uniforms, and he escapes the general slaughter to make it back to the fort in time to see the Indian soldiers file into a trap. The redskins are wiped out amidst some gorgeous color scenery.

p, Howard W. Koch; d, Lesley Selander; w, Danny Arnold; ph, Gordon Avil (Technicolor); m, Paul Dunlap; ed, John F. Schreyer.

Western   **(PR:A MPAA:NR)**

FORTRESS, THE**   (1979, Hung.) 92m Hungarofilm (AZ EROD)

Bella Tanai, Sandor Oszter, Jozsef Madaras, Istvan Kovacs, Adam Rajhona, Ferenc Bacs, Gyoergy Tarjan.

A fantasy park offers the public a chance to play organized war games. The bored tourists delight in the sport until they realize that the bullets being fired are real. The state closes the park but recruits its female director to train real-life troops. Written years before the popular American film WESTWORLD, this Hungarian effort separates itself from that film by having heavy doses of political black comedy, a sad commentary on the output from one of the oldest filmmaking countries in Europe.

d, Miklos Szinetar; w, Szinetar, Gyula Hernadi; ph, Miklos Biro.

Drama   **(PR:C MPAA:NR)**

FORTUNATE FOOL, THE*   (1933, Brit.) 73m ABF bw

Hugh Wakefield (*Jim Falconer*), Joan Wyndham (*Helen*), Jack Raine (*Gerald*), Elizabeth Jenns (*Mildred*), Arthur Chesney (*Batty*), Sara Allgood (*Rose*), Bobbie Comber (*Marlowe*), Mary Mayfren (*Mrs. Falconer*), Griffith Humphreys.

Wakefield is an ex-boxer who falls in love with impoverished Wyndham. Jenns, Wakefield's fiancee, has the poor girl framed for a robbery, but wealthy writer Raine intervenes and brings the lovers together while seeing that Jenns gets what's coming to her. Sporadically funny romantic comedy in usual straightforward style of director Walker, who later turned to making religious films. Chesney was the brother of the great character actor Edmund Gwenn, the unforgettable Santa Claus in MIRACLE ON 34TH STREET (1947).

p, Jack Eppel; d, Norman Walker; w, Dion Titheradge (based on a play by Titheradge); ph, Alan Lawson.

Comedy   **(PR:A MPAA:NR)**

FORTUNE, THE****   (1975) 88m COL c

Warren Beatty (*Nicky*), Jack Nicholson (*Oscar*), Stockard Channing (*Freddie*), Florence Stanley (*Landlady*), Richard B. Shull (*Chief Detective*), Tom Newman (*John the Barber*), John Fiedler (*Police Photographer*), Scatman Crothers (*Fisherman*), Dub Taylor (*Rattlesnake Tom*), Ian Wolfe (*Justice of the Peace*), Rose Michtom (*His Wife*), Brian Avery (*Airline Steward*), Nira Barab (*Girl Lover*), Christopher Guest (*Boy Lover*), Jim Antonio (*1st Policeman*), Vic Vallaro (*2nd Policeman*), Joe Tornatore (*Detective*), Kathryn Grody (*Police Secretary*), George Roberts (*Officer*).

An offbeat but hilarious comedy where Beatty and Nicholson are two competing confidence men trying to bilk heiress Channing out of her fortune, one accumulated by Channing's father, a manufacturer of sanitary napkins (which results in more than one tasteless joke). Though she is in love with Beatty, Channing plans to marry slippery Nicholson, then carry on an affair with Beatty who is married and thereby will avoid arrest under the ancient Mann Act (which technically made anyone liable to arrest if they crossed state lines with women other than their wives for decidedly immoral purposes). Nicholson, a failed embezzler, has no intention of playing the cuckolded hubby, but means to have his carnal share of the attractive Channing. When she learns their true intent, Channing tells the boys that she will give her fortune to charity. Alarmed, they conclude that their only course is murder and enact a zany plan where the drugged Channing is placed in a trunk and then set adrift in the ocean. But the trunk does not sink, merely floating away to another beach where Channing frees herself and staggers to shore, wet, confused and picked up by a passing motorist who returns her home. Before she arrives, the guilt-ridden Beatty informs police of the "murder" and this causes no end of trouble for him and Nicholson, especially when Channing arrives very much alive. The entire film is a comedy of slapstick errors that works well through the fine performances of the leads and the superb timing of director Nichols. The director had an entire 1920s block set up on the Columbia lot rather than battle for a period street in Los Angeles replete with TV antennas and modern-day cars. Nicholson first discovered the script and brought it to Nichols who labored long to make it into the subtle little gem that it is. Beatty nervously twitches through his part but is quickly outdone by easygoing Nicholson and the marvelous Channing. A similar type of love triangle, also set in the 1920s, LUCKY LADY, with Gene Hackman, Liza Minnelli, and Burt Reynolds, was made the same year but nowhere approaches the style and wit shown in THE FORTUNE. Songs and musical numbers include "I Must Be Dreaming" (Al Dubin, Pat Flaherty, Al Sherman), "Pretty Trix" (Joe Venuti, Eddie Lang), "My Honey's Lovin' Arms" (Joseph Meyer, Herman Ruby), "Shaking the Blues Away" (Irving Berling), "Cigarette Tango" (John H. Densmore), and "You've Got to See Mama Every Night or You Can't See Mama at All" (Billy Rose, Con Conrad).

p, Mike Nichols, Don Devlin; d, Nichols; w, Adrien Joyce; ph, John A. Alonzo (Technicolor); m, David Shire; ed, Stu Linder; md, Shire; prod d, Richard Sylbert; art d, W. Stewart Campbell; set d, George Gaines.

Comedy **(PR:C MPAA:PG)**

FORTUNE AND MEN'S EYES* (1971, U.S./Can.) 102m Cinemax/MGM c

Wendell Burton *(Smitty)*, Michael Greer *(Queenie)*, Zooey Hall *(Rocky)*, Danny Freedman *(Mona)*, Larry Perkins *(Screwdriver)*, James Barron *(Holyface Peters)*, Lazaro Perez *(Catso)*, Jon Granik *(Sgt. Gritt)*, Tom Harvey *(Warden Gasher)*, Hugh Webster *(Rabbit)*, Kirk McColl *(Guard Gasher)*, Vance Davis *(Sailor)*, Robert Goodier *(Doctor)*, Cathy Wiele *(Cathy)*, Georges Allard *(Fiddler)*, Modesto *(One-Eye)*, Michel Gilbert *(Young Prisoner)*, Robert Saab *(Drummer)*, A. Zeytounian *(Pianist)*.

This was released after THE BOYS IN THE BAND so much of the exploitability of the homosexual subject matter had already been seen, thereby causing this picture to be less well-received than the producers hoped. It takes place in a Canadian prison and our information is that the Canadian government gave assistance to the film. This is hard to believe as the life depicted in the prison is so harsh and terrifying that it reflects poorly on anything north of the border. Burton is arrested for pot possession and sent to an absolute hell-hole where he must either submit to regular sodomization by Hall, who wants to be his protector, or run the risk of being raped regularly by everyone else. He chooses Hall and by the time the picture is over, he's as prison-savvy as all the others and doesn't at all resemble the sweet, naive young man who entered in reel one. Based on a sensational stage play that featured male nudity and brutal scenes, the original stage presentation was a cry for prison reform but that seems to have gone out the window here in favor of all the obvious tawdry elements they thought would turn the stiles. It didn't. Michael Greer is excellent as a screaming queen. He did this once before in THE GAY DECEIVERS and is in danger of being type-cast, no matter how good an actor he can be. Freedman, as an intellectual, is also outstanding but the film's subject matter is so distasteful to most eyes that it failed to find a huge audience. The original director was Jules Schwerin who was replaced by Harvey Hart, and many scenes had to be re-shot. Technical credits are only fair, and composer MacDermot's (HAIR) score is totally wrong for what's on screen. Songs; "It's Free" (Michael Greer), "When Rain Touches Summer" (MacDermot, William Dumareso, sung by Leata Galloway), "Fortune and Men's Eyes" (MacDermot, sung by Ronnie Dyson).

p, Lester Persky, Donald Ginsberg, Lewis M. Allen; d, Harvey Hart; w, John Herbert (based on the play by Herbert); ph, Georges Dufaux (Metrocolor); m, Galt MacDermot; ed, Douglas Robertson; prod d, Earl G. Preston; cos, Marcel Carpenter; ch, Jill Courtney.

Prison Drama **(PR:O MPAA:R)**

FORTUNE COOKIE, THE*** (1966) 125m Mirisch/UA bw (GB: MEET WHIPLASH WILLIE)

Jack Lemmon *(Harry Hinkle)*, Walter Matthau *(Willie Gingrich)*, Ron Rich *(Luther "Boom Boom" Jackson)*, Cliff Osmond *(Mr. Purkey)*, Judi West *(Sandy Hinkle)*, Lurene Tuttle *(Mother Hinkle)*, Harry Holcombe *(O'Brien)*, Les Tremayne *(Thompson)*, Marge Redmond *(Charlotte Gingrich)*, Noam Pitlik *(Max)*, Harry Davis *(Dr. Krugman)*, Ann Shoemaker *(Sister Veronica)*, Maryesther Denver *(Nurse)*, Lauren Gilbert *(Kincaid)*, Ned Glass *(Doc Schindler)*, Sig Roman *(Prof. Winterhalter)*, Archie Moore *(Mr. Jackson)*, Dodie Heath *(Nun)*, Herbie Faye *(Maury)*, Howard McNear *(Mr. Cimoli)*, Bill Christopher *(Intern)*, Bartlett Robinson, Robert P. Lieb, Martin Blaine, Ben Wright *(Specialists)*, Billy Beck *(Locker Room Asst.)*, Judy Pace *(Elvira)*, Helen Kleeb *(Receptionist)*, Lisa Jill *(Ginger)*, John Todd Roberts *(Jeffrey)*, Keith Jackson *(Football Announcer)*, Herb Ellis *(TV Director)*, Don Reed *(Newscaster)*, Louise Vienna *(Girl in Teleblurb)*, Bob Doqui *(Man in Bar)*, Jon Silo *(Tailor)*.

It's a fairly well-known fact that Billy Wilder received his inspiration for this film when he saw a pro football player go on an end-around and wind up falling on a sideline spectator. The Vikings and the Browns are playing in Cleveland (where all of the locations were actually filmed) and CBS cameraman Lemmon is whacked when halfback Rich goes out of bounds. They insist that he go to a hospital for a checkup and he's feeling just fine until his brother-in-law, Matthau (known as "Whiplash Willie" in the insurance business) arrives and convinces Lemmon that a suit against CBS can mean a million bucks. The network is insured, has a ton of money, so who would be hurt, right? Lemmon is a decent sort and totally against the lawyer's pleas but Matthau is insistent and shows Lemmon how to feign the injury. A battery of doctors comes to visit Lemmon, who is immobilized in a wheelchair claiming blindness, dizzy spells, and terrible pain. Lemmon's former wife, a mercenary woman who left him for a failed musician, returns and makes believe she still loves the guy. Rich is deflated by the thought that he was the reason Lemmon is now crippled so he announces that he will now devote his life to being Lemmon's nurse. Meanwhile, Cliff Osmond is a private eye assigned to spying on Lemmon and he is filming all of the man's moves from a house across the road. Osmond can get no proof of a fraud until he confronts Matthau, Rich, and Lemmon and makes some very racist remarks toward the docile halfback. Lemmon, who has grown to care a great deal about Rich, jumps out of his wheelchair and attacks Osmond who had forgotten to put film in his camera. Lemmon repeats the action's for Osmond's camera when he realizes that the only reason his ex-wife, West, has been hanging around was for a chunk of the money. The film ends as Matthau is haranguing Osmond for making racist remarks and promising to sue the man for what he's said. Matthau's performance was a wonder and he took an Oscar as Best Actor. The script and the photography were also nominated. One of the problems was grounding Jack Lemmon who is such a good physical comedian. It's like making Chaplin work in a chair. The comedy slows down several times for Wilder to make some satiric, though not funny, points. It's far too long at 125 minutes and very uneven in the comedy-to-drama ratio, but those funny moments with Matthau at the top of his form are beautiful to behold. All the small roles are well cast, especially Davis, Ruman, Moore, and Christopher, another alumnus of Harvey Lembeck's Comedy Class in Hollywood. Christopher went on to be Father Mulcahy on TV's "M*A*S*H". This was Wilder's second insurance fraud film, the first being the memorable DOUBLE INDEMNITY. He is a treasure who can work in drama (SUNSET BOULEVARD, WITNESS FOR THE PROSECUTION, THE LOST WEEKEND), action (FIVE GRAVES TO CAIRO), or comedy (SOME LIKE IT HOT, ONE TWO THREE, IRMA LA DOUCE).

p&d, Billy Wilder; w, Wilder, I.A.L. Diamond; ph, Joseph LaShelle (Panavision); m, Andre Previn; ed, Daniel Mandell; art d, Robert Luthardt; set d, Edward G. Boyle; cos, Charles Arrico, Paula Giokaris; spec eff, Sass Bedig; m/l, "You'd Be So Nice To Come Home To," Cole Porter (sung by Judi West).

Comedy-Drama **Cas.** **(PR:A-C MPAA:NR)**

FORTUNE IN DIAMONDS (SEE: ADVENTURERS, THE, 1951, Brit.)

FORTUNE IS A WOMAN (SEE: SHE PLAYED WITH FIRE, 1956, Brit.)

FORTUNE LANE** (1947, Brit.) 60m Elstree Independent/GFD bw

Douglas Barr *(Peter Quentin)*, Billy Thatcher *(John)*, Brian Weske *(Tim)*, Angela Glynne *(Margaret Quentin)*, George Carney *(Mr. Quentin)*, Nell Ballantyne *(Mrs. Quentin)*, Antony Holles *(Mr. Carpenter)*.

Young Barr aspires to be an engineer and already is working on an invention. To raise money to finish the gadget, he and a friend (Weske) take jobs as window washers. Weske wants the money to return to Ireland to visit his ailing grandfather, so Barr gives him all the money he has earned. Things work out happily for the boy as he receives praise as a young genius. Pleasant children's film a cut above the usually awful run of the lot.

p&d, John Baxter; w, Geoffrey Orme, Mary Cathcart Borer; ph, Jo Jago, Brendan Stafford.

Children **(PR:AA MPAA:NR)**

FORTUNE TELLER, THE* (1961, Gr.) 90m Finos/Greek Motion Pictures bw (KAPHETZOU; AKA: THE COFFEE FORTUNE TELLER)

Mimi Fotopoulos *(Spyros)*, Georgia Vassiliadou *(Calliopi)*, Smarouli Yiouli *(Kaithi)*, Basil Avlonitis *(Nikitas)*, Pericles Christofarides *(Mr. Giavassis)*.

Primitive Greek comedy stars Vassiliadou as the wizened coffee grounds reader whose predictions complicate lives rather than make them clear, forcing her to set things right again. Lousy subtitles and an almost incoherent story make this film about as deciperable as the Riddle of the Sphinx. (In Greek.)

d&w, Alekos Sakellarios.

Comedy **(PR:A-C MPAA:NR)**

FORTUNES OF CAPTAIN BLOOD*½ (1950) 90m COL bw

Louis Hayward *(Capt. Peter Blood)*, Patricia Medina *(Isabelita Sotomayor)*, George Macready *(Marquis de Riconete)*, Alfonso Bedoya *(Prison Overseer)*, Dona Drake *(Pepita Rosados)*, Lowell Gilmore *(George Fairfax)*, Wilton Graff *(Capt. Alvarado)*, Curt Bois *(King Charles II)*, Lumsden Hare *(Tom Mannering)*, William Bevan *(Billy Bragg)*, Harry Cording *(Will Ward)*, Duke York *(Andrew Hardy)*, Sven Hugo Borg *(Swede)*, Martin Garralaga *(Antonio Viamonte)*, James Fairfax *(Nat Russell)*, Charles Irwin *(Smitty)*, Terry Kilburn *(Kenny Jensen)*, Albert Morin *(Miguel Gonzales)*, Nick Volpe *(Papa Rosados)*, Georges Renavent *(Count)*.

The swashbuckling capitain sails again in yet another rehash of familiar material. This time out, Hayward plays the exiled Irish physician-turned-pirate who sails the seas causing trouble for the Spanish. Macready is commissioned to ferret out the dashing rogue and do him in, but Hayward proves too skillful a pirate (and too popular a character) to be so easily dealt with. Italian-born author Sabatini, who served as an intelligence officer for the British War Office in WW I and wrote high adventure novels for more than forty years, died three months before the release of FORTUNES OF CAPTAIN BLOOD.

p, Harry Joe Brown; d, Gordon Douglas; w, Michael Hogan, Robert Libott, Frank Burt (based on a novel by Rafael Sabatini); ph, George E. Diskant; ed, Gene Havlick; md, Morris Stoloff; art d, George Brooks.

Adventure **(PR:A MPAA:NR)**

FORTY ACRE FEUD*½ (1965) 85m Ormond-Atlanta/Craddock c

Ferlin Husky (Simon Crumb), Minnie Pearl (Ma Culpepper), Bob Corley (Pa Culpepper), Del Reeves (Del Culpepper), Claude Casey (Uncle Foxey Calhoun), Jan Moore (Nancy Calhoun), Sam Tarpley (Postmaster Amos Quint), Ray Price, George Jones, Loretta Lynn, Roy Drusky, Skeeter Davis, Bill Anderson, The Willis Brothers, Hugh X. Lewis, Eddie Hill (Themselves).

Redneck comedy in which an overlooked Tennessee county gets to elect a state representative, which leads to a feud between the Culpeppers and the Calhouns over who should go to the legislature. All is made well when the Smokey Mountain Jamboree arrives to calm the hillbillies down with good ol' country music. Filmed in 16mm in and around Nashville.

p&w, Bill Packham; d, Ron Ormond.

Comedy (PR:A MPAA:NR)

FORTY CARATS**½ (1973) 108m COL c

Liv Ullmann (Ann Stanley), Edward Albert (Peter Latham), Gene Kelly (Billy Boylan), Binnie Barnes (Maud Ericson), Deborah Raffin (Trina Stanley), Billy Green Bush (J. D. Rogers), Nancy Walker (Mrs. Margolin), Don Porter (Mr. Latham), Rosemary Murphy (Mrs. Latham), Natalie Schaefer (Mrs. Adams), Sam Chew, Jr. (Arthur Forbes), Claudia Jennings (Gabriella), Brooke Palance (Polly).

Sometimes amusing adaptation of the French play which Jay Presson Allen turned into a Broadway hit for David Merrick. Liv Ullmann is just turning forty (she was actually thirty seven at the time and looked much younger). She's a successful Manhattan realtor on holiday in Greece where she meets twenty-year-old Albert. They are attracted to each other and spend the night on the beach in each other's arms. Before he wakes, she exits and figures it was just an adventure and she'll never see him again. Back in New York, Albert turns up for a date with Ullmann's daughter, the radiant Raffin in her film debut. Raffin is the result of Ullmann's marriage to Gene Kelly. Ullmann learns that Albert is a whiz-kid businessman from an excellent family and Ullmann's mother, Barnes, encourages him in his efforts to win Ullmann's hand. She attempts to quash her attraction to Albert but everyone else seems to think it's a good idea—her mother, daughter, ex-husband, and even her wise-cracking business associate, Walker. Little by little, she's convinced that the age difference doesn't matter at all if two people love each other and the film ends as she and Albert walk hand in hand on the Greek beach where they spent that first night. Kelly was excellent as a grown-up Noel Airman (MARJORIE MORNINGSTAR) who masquerades as being ten years younger than he is. The producers must have thought the script needed a lift so they had Kelly and Barnes, who had never danced before in movies, do a little turn in a disco. (Barnes was the wife of the producer, Frankovich.) Raffin and Bush have a subplot romance that takes up too much time for what it offers. Ullmann is beautiful but has none of the comedy timing to bring off such a gossamer plot. Too bad, because she does everything else well and can be funny in Swedish. Porter and the immensely talented Rosemary Murphy are perfect as Albert's parents. In the end, it's a cheerful picture but misses the boat in terms of heavy comedy or even meaningful drama.

p, M.J. Frankovich; d, Milton Katselas; w, Leonard Gershe (based on the English adaptation by Jay Presson Allen of the French play by Pierre Barillet and Jean-Pierre Gredy); ph, Charles B. Lang (Metrocolor) m, Michel Legrand; ed, David Blewitt; prod d, Robert Clatworthy; set d, George Hopkins; cos, Jean Louis; m/l, Legrand, Marilyn and Alan Bergman.

Comedy Cas. (PR:A-C MPAA:PG)

FORTY DEUCE** (1982) 89m Island c

Orson Bean (Mr. Roper), Kevin Bacon (Rickey), Mark Keyloun (Blow), Harris Laskaway (Augie), Tommy Citera (Crank), John Anthony (John Noonan), Carol Jean Lewis (Black Woman).

Paul Morrissey directed this less-than-successful adaptation of a seedy off-Broadway play that exposes the dark underbelly of Manhattan's 42nd Street. Bacon (DINER, FOOTLOOSE) plays a male prostitute trying to fund a heroin deal by selling a young runaway boy to middle-aged man Bean. All systems appear to be go until Bacon discovers that the kid has killed himself by overdosing on heroin. Determined to go ahead with this plan, Bacon devises a way to make it appear that the kid's death is Bean's responsibility. From this point, the film is set in Bacon's apartment and Morrissey utilizes the rapidly cliched split-screen technique to generate some excitement in what quickly becomes a stilted and stagy drama. Bacon, however, is excellent as the young hustler. Unfortunately, Bean is downright embarrassing.

p, Jean Jacques Fourgeaud; d, Paul Morrissey; w, Alan Browne (based on a stage play by Browne); ph, Francois Reichenbach, Stefan Stapasik, Steven Fierberg; m, Manu Dibango; ed, Ken Aleuto.

Drama (PR:O MPAA:NR)

48 HOURS*½ (1944, Brit.) 92m EAL/UA bw (GB: WENT THE DAY WELL?)

Leslie Banks (Oliver Wilsford), Elizabeth Allan (Peggy), Frank Lawton (Tom Sturry), Basil Sydney (Ortler), Valerie Taylor (Nora Ashton), Mervyn Johns (Sims), Edward Rigby (Poacher), Marie Lohr (Mrs. Frazer), C.V. France (Vicar), David Farrar (Jung), Muriel George (Mrs. Collins), Thora Hird (Land Girl), Harry Fowler (George Truscott), Patricia Hayes (Daisy), John Slater (German Sergeant), Johnny Schofield (Joe Garbett).

A humdrum tale set in the English countryside during WW II as a group of German paratroopers attempt a takeover of a tiny hamlet. The invaders are aided by the local squire, but meet violent opposition from the villagers. The clue that gives the Germans away is their habit of drawing a line through their 7's. A subject that should make one fill with pride and a sense of country, but only leaves one with heavy eyelids.

p, Michael Balcon; d, Alberto Cavalcanti; w, Angus MacPhail, John Dighton, Diana Morgan (based on a story by Graham Greene); ph, Wilkie Cooper; m, William Walton; md, Ernest Irving; art d, Tom Morahan; spec eff, Roy Kellino.

War Drama (PR:A MPAA:NR)

48 HOURS*** (1982) 96m PAR c

Nick Nolte (Jack Cates), Eddie Murphy (Reggie Hammond), Annette O'Toole (Elaine), Frank McRae (Haden), James Remar (Ganz), David Patrick Kelly (Luther), Sonny Landham (Billy Bear), Brion James (Kehoe), Kerry Sherman (Rosalie), Jonathan Banks (Algren), James Keane (Vanzant), Tara King (Frizzy), Greta Blackburn (Lisa), Margot Rose (Casey), Denise Crosby (Sally), Olivia M. Brown (Candy), Todd Allen (Young Cop), Bill Dearth (Thin Cop), Ned Dowd (Big Cop), Jim Haynie (Old Cop), Jack Thibeau (Detective), Jon St. Elwood (Plainclothesman), Clare Nono (Ruth), Sandy Martin (Policewoman), Matt Landers (Bob), Peter Jason (Cowboy Bartender), Bill Cross, Chris Mulkey (Cops), James Marcelino (Parking Attendant), Bennie Dobbins, Walter Scott, W.T. Zacha (Road Gang Guard), Begona Plaza (Indian Hooker), Loyd Catlett, B. G. Fisher, Reid Cruickshanks (Prison Guards), R. D. Call (Duty Sergeant), Brenda Venus, Gloria E. Gifford (Hookers), John Hauk (Henry), Clint Smith (Leroy), Nick Dimitri, John Dennis Johnston, Rock A. Walker, Dave Moordigian, J. Wesley Huston, Gary Pettinger, Marquerita Wallace, Angela Robinson, Jack Lightsy, Bob Yanez, Luis Contreras, Suzanna M. Regard, Ola Ray, Bjaye Turner, The Busboys.

An extremely popular film at the box office, 48 HRS. has hard-as-granite cop Nolte having Murphy released from prison for 48 hours so he can help track down a pair of maniacal cop killers, Remar and Landham, both former Murphy associates. The pairing of these unlikely partners leads to confrontations and absurd scenes as they race through the underworld, with Murphy under the threat of having his remaining six-month term in prison extended if he doesn't perform well. Nolte, a white cop who would just as soon walk through a brick wall as try the door, mercilessly rides Murphy with physical abuse and racial slurs, even sending the black man into a rowdy country-and-western bar to face down rednecks while getting information. (Murphy later returns the favor by inveigling Nolte into an all-black, all-terrifying nightclub.) The duo finally track down their psychopathic killers and learn to like each other by film's end, although there's not enough reason for it after they've punched each other silly and verbally destroyed the basic roots of each other's character. (The language is excessively and unnecessarily strong in this film which is pock-marked with so many four-letter words that one wonders about the ability of scripters Spottiswoode, Hill, Gross, and Souza to write without using them as quick pit-stops in their race through the West Coast crime world.) Murphy, one of the popular comics of the collegiate "Saturday Night Live" TV show, made his debut in this film and it made a star out of an otherwise fair comedic talent. (He has been playing the same role ever since with less convincing scripts and thinning routines.) Nolte holds his own here, although his weird imitation of Wallace Beery gargling on his own phlegm while delivering his lines is often annoying, as well as hard to understand. Director Hill renders his traditional action-filled pace with excellent lensing from Waite. The score isn't much and about twenty minutes could have been easily cut. No young child should be exposed to the vile (and consistently illiterate) language of this film unless parents are grooming that child for a career in street crime. A press release warned theaters and the theater-going public to stick with the contraction in the title, never spelling is out as "48 Hours", for some inexplicable reason. This was the first feature film to be shot in its entirety on Eastman Kodak's new dim-light-responsive 5293 film, which considerably enhanced the nighttime location scenes. Reportedly, the quartet of writers were delivering pages scene-by-scene to director Hill as shooting proceeded, a slapdash system fraught with peril but one which worked, just as it did with such masterpieces as CASABLANCA (1942).

p, Lawrence Gordon, Joel Silver; d, Walter Hill; w, Roger Spottiswoode, Hill, Larry Gross, Steven E. de Souza; ph, Ric Waite (Movielab Color); m, James Horner; ed, Freeman Davies, Mark Warner, Billy Weber; prod d, John Vallone; set d, Richard C. Goddard; cos, Marilyn Kay Vance.

Comedy/Crime Drama Cas. (PR:O MPAA:R)

48 HOURS TO ACAPULCO** (1968, Ger.) 62m Seven Star/Cinema Service bw (48 STUNDEN BIS ACAPULCO)

Christiane Krueger (Laura), Dieter Geissler (Frank), Monika Zinnenberg (Monika), Rod Carter (Cameron), Alexander Kerst (Laura's Father), Charly Kommer (Gangster), Ted Stauffer (Gangster's Boss).

Fine crime film starring Geissler as a young hustler hired by gangster Krueger to go to Rome and, using money provided by the crook, purchase a portfolio of top secret documents. Accompanying him is the gangster's daughter, Zinnenberg. Geissler, however, goes to Rome, pockets the money, and kills the courier. He then flees to Acapulco and attempts to sell the papers to a more powerful mobster, but is killed when he refuses to sell at a reasonable price. Typical German treatment is given to the material, which means cold detachment from the characters and a slower pace than most Americans are used to.

d, Klaus Lemke; w, Max Zihlmann; ph, Hubs Hagen, Niklas Schilling; m, Roland Kovac.

Crime (PR:C MPAA:NR)

48 HOURS TO LIVE** (1960, Brit./Swed.) 86m Cinema Associates bw (AKA: MAN IN THE MIDDLE)

Anthony Steel (Mike Gibson), Marlies Behrens (Lena), Ingemar Johansson (Himself), Lewis Charles (Marino), Ina Anders (Annika), Birger Malmsten (Paul), Hakan Westergren (Professor Christensen), Rusty Rutledge (Anders), Peter Bourne (Carlson).

This story about international intrigue does not always make sense but retains a fairly high level of suspense. Steel is the correspondent who suddenly finds himself in the middle of a kidnaping plot when a famous nuclear scientist is held for ransom by an international spy ring. The reporter takes it upon himself to see that the scientist is rescued before any harm is done. Inventive direction keeps the film from becoming overly predictable.

p, Eddie Rubin; d&w, Peter Bourne.

Crime (PR:A MPAA:NR)

45 FATHERS** (1937) 71m FOX bw

Jane Withers (Judith Frazier), Thomas Beck (Roger Farragut), Louise Henry (Elizabeth Carter), The Hartmans (Joe McCoy, Flo McCoy), Richard Carle (Bunny Carothers), Nella Walker (Mrs. Carter), Andrew Tombes (Judge), Leon Ames (Vincent), Sammy Cohen (Prof. Ziska), George Givot (Prof. Bellini), Ruth Warren (Sarah), Hattie McDaniel (Beulah), Romaine Callendar (Hastings).

Another routine Withers vehicle. This time the pudgy, impish child star of the 1930s is the darling of her late father's stodgy men's club. The forty-five members of the club agree to adopt the orphan and one is chosen to house her and her obnoxious pet monkey. Of course, Withers sticks her cute nose in the family's business and wins their hearts by singing and dancing.

p, John Stone; d, James Tinling; w, Frances Hyland, Albert Ray (based on a story by Mary Bickel); ph, Harry Jackson; ed, Alex Torffey; md, Samuel Kaylin.

Comedy (PR:AA MPAA:NR)

FORTY GUNS**½ (1957) 76m Globe/FOX bw
(AKA: WOMAN WITH A WHIP)

Barbara Stanwyck (Jessica Drummond), Barry Sullivan (Griff Bonnell), Dean Jagger (Ned Logan), John Ericson (Brockie Drummond), Gene Barry (Wes Bonnell), Robert Dix (Chico Bonnell), Jack "Jidge" Carroll (Barney Cashman), Gerald Milton (Shotgun Spangler), Eve Brent (Louvenia Spangler), Ziva Rodann (Rio), Hank Worden (John Chisum), Neyle Morrow (Wiley), Chuck Roberson (Howard Swain), Chuck Hayward (Charlie Savage), Sandra Wirth (Chico's Girl), Paul Dubov (Judge Macey), Eddie Parks (Sexton).

This picture was trounced by the U.S. critics and beloved by the Europeans when originally released. In the years since, it has become a cult classic and a good example of Fuller's use of the camera, which often serves to make us forget the story. Stanwyck more or less runs Cochise County, Arizona, where she makes her own law by dint of forty cowboys in her employ. The wimpy sheriff is Jagger, in a role played to perfection three years earlier in BAD DAY AT BLACK ROCK. Sullivan, a U.S. Marshal, rides into town on business with his two brothers, Barry and Dix. Their job is to bring law and order to the place and that's a direct clash with Stanwyck and her nutty brother, Ericson (also an alumni of BAD DAY AT BLACK ROCK). Sullivan is an ex-gunslinger now on the right side of the law and he is proud of the fact that he hasn't drawn his gun in a decade. Barry meets and falls in love with local gunsmith Eve Brent. On the day they marry, Ericson kills Barry. Sullivan must get Ericson for that and the young man uses his sister, Stanwyck, as a shield. This doesn't deter Sullivan a bit. He wounds Stanwyck, then kills Ericson. Rather than pay any attention to the prone Stanwyck, he walks past her and orders a doctor, but that's as far as he'll go. The picture concludes with Sullivan leaving town and Stanwyck racing after him. Whether they will eventually unite is left to our imaginations. Much of Fuller's techniques were applauded by Italian and French critics. Sergio Leone was influenced and the series of extreme closeups, weird angle shots, and quick inter-cutting caused the eye to blink more than it should have. There was substance in Fuller's script so why did he attempt to force a phony style onto it? The love scenes between Stanwyck and Sullivan were ungimmicked and therefore the most effective in the movie.

p,d&w, Samuel Fuller; ph, Joseph Biroc (CinemaScope); m, Harry Sukman; ed, Gene Fowler, Jr.; art d, John Mansbridge; set d, Chrester Bavhi, Walter M. Scott; cos, Charles LeMaire, Leah Rhodes; spec eff, Norman Breedlove, L.B. Abbott, Linwood Dunn; m/l, "High Ridin' Woman," Harold Adamson, Sukman, "God Has His Arms Around Me," Adamson, Victor Young (sung by Jack "Jidge" Carroll).

Western (PR:A-C MPAA:NR)

40 GUNS TO APACHE PASS*½ (1967) 95m Admiral/COL c

Audie Murphy (Capt. Coburn), Michael Burns (Doug), Kenneth Tobey (Cpl. Bodine), Laraine Stephens (Ellen), Robert Brubaker (Sgt. Walker), Michael Blodgett (Mike), Michael Keep (Cochise), Kay Stewart (Kate Malone), Kenneth MacDonald (Harry Malone), Byron Morrow (Col. Reed), Willard Willingham (Fuller), Ted Gehring (Barrett), James Beck (Higgins).

Lame Murphy vehicle which sees the heroic cavalry captain single-handedly put down a massive Apache rebellion led by Cochise soon after the Civil War. If that isn't enough, he must first stop an internal rebellion started by shifty corporal Tobey, who convinces the men to sell their rifles to the Indians. Murphy retrieves the guns and defeats Tobey and the redskins. Last western of long-time Roy Rogers director Witney, who went on to broaden out in other genres.

p, Grant Whytock; d, William Witney; w, Willard Willingham, Mary Willingham; ph, Jacques Marquette (Pathe Color); m, Richard LaSalle; ed, Whytock; art d, Paul Sylos; set d, Harry Reif; cos, Joseph Dimmitt; makeup, Ted Coodley.

Western (PR:A MPAA:NR)

FORTY LITTLE MOTHERS**½ (1940) 88m MGM bw

Eddie Cantor (Gilbert J. Thompson), Judith Anderson (Mme. Granville), Rita Johnson (Marian Edwards), Bonita Granville (Doris), Ralph Morgan (Judge Joseph M. Williams), Diana Lewis (Marcia), Nydia Westman (Mlle. Cliche), Margaret Early (Eleanor), Martha O'Driscoll (Janette), Charlotte Munier (Lois), Louise Seidel (Betty), Baby Quintanilla (Chum), Constance Keane [Veronica Lake] (Classmate).

A change of pace for Cantor and director Berkeley (both entrenched in 1930s musicals) who test the waters of high drama in this fairly successful effort. Cantor plays a former college golden boy who, twenty years later, cannot find work. One day he saves a distraught young mother from committing suicide, and he even goes so far as to set her up in a waitressing job. She betrays him however, when

she decides to skip town and leave Cantor with her baby. With the kid in tow, Cantor lands a job as a professor in a girl's school, leaving himself open for the playful abuse of the forty female students in his charge. Their mischievous instincts turn maternal however, when they discover the baby in Cantor's apartment. Knowing he'll be dismissed if the apparently motherless child is discovered by the school's administration, the students aid Cantor in hiding it until the mother is located.

p, Harry Rapf; d, Busby Berkeley; w, Dorothy Yost, Ernest Pagano (based on the play "Monsieur Petiot" by Jean Grulton); ph, Charles Lawton; ed, Ben Lewis; art d, Cedric Gibbons; m/l, "Little Curly Hair In a High Chair," Charles Tobias, Nat Simon.

Drama (PR:A MPAA:NR)

FORTY NAUGHTY GIRLS* (1937) 63m RKO bw

James Gleason (Oscar Piper), ZaSu Pitts (Hildegarde), Marjorie Lord (Joan), George Shelley (Bert), Joan Woodbury (Rita Marlowe), Frank M. Thomas (Jeff), Tom Kennedy (Casey), Alan Edwards (Rickman), Alden Chase (Tommy Washburn), Edward Marr (Christy Bennett), Ada Leonard, Barbara Pepper (Showgirls).

The last of the once-promising Hildegarde Withers/Oscar Piper murder mysteries which had disintegrated into a silly, even stupid, series of inept whodunits. The film opens with the backstage murder of a press agent and then segues into the killing of an actor on stage. Tough cop Gleason shags down the obvious clues and routine suspects, while Pitts sniffs out the real, most unlikely killer.

p, William Sistrom; d, Edward Cline; w, John Gray (based on a story by Stuart Palmer); ph, Russell Metty; ed, John Lockert; md, Roy Webb; art d, Van Nest Polglase.

Mystery (PR:A MPAA:NR)

FORTY-NINE DAYS** (1964, USSR) 80m Mosfilm/Artkino bw (49 DNEY)

Vladimir Buyanovskiy (Sgt. Rakhmatullin), Vitaliy Pivnenko (Pft. Podgornyy), Vladimir Shibankov (Pvt. Fomin), G. Krasheninnikov (Pvt. Boykov), B. Gladkov, A. Zarzhitskaya, E. Knausmyuller, V. Krokhin, N. Rostovikov, V. Filippov, Yu. Levchenko, Ye Loginov, V. Mararov, B. Oya, V. Rogov.

The dramatic story of four Soviet seafarers and their amazing efforts at survival after their barge is wrecked in a storm and they are left adrift in the Pacific off the Siberian coast for forty nine harrowing days. Based on a true incident, which ended happily when the sailors were spotted by U.S. Navy pilots and rescued.

d, Gennadiy Gabay; w, G. Baklanov, Yu. Bondarev, V. Tendryakov; ph, Arkadiy Koltsatyy; m, Aleksey Muravlev; ed, N. Anikeyeva; md, A. Roytman; art d, Boris Nemechek, Arnold Vaysfeld; cos, A. Martinson; spec eff, G. Ayzenberg, F. Krasny; m/l, M. Lvovskiy.

Drama (PR:A MPAA:NR)

FORTY-NINERS, THE* (1932) 59m Freuler Film Associates bw

Tom Tyler, Betty Mack, Al Bridge, Fern Emmett, Gordon Wood, Mildred Rogers, Fred Ritter, Frank Ball, Florence Wells.

Uninteresting depiction of the mass hysteria created when gold was discovered in the California hills. One of the innumerable westerns starring Tyler that have been virtually forgotten, and for good reason.

d, J.P. McCarthy; w, F. McGrew Willis; ph, Edward Kull; ed, Fred Bain.

Western (PR:A MPAA:NR)

FORTYNINERS, THE*½ (1954) 71m AA bw

Wild Bill Elliott (Sam Nelson), Virginia Grey (Stella Walker), Henry Morgan (Alf Billings), John Doucette (Ernie Walker), Lane Bradford (William Norris), Stanford Jolley (Everett), Harry Lauter (Gambler), Earle Hodgins (1st Hotel Clerk), Dean Cromer (Sloane), Ralph Sanford (Bartender).

An almost film noir western (heavy emphasis on voice-over narration) which sees Elliott searching for crooked gambler Morgan who hired the two killers of a federal agent. Posing as a gunman to win the gambler's confidence, Elliott bides his time until he can learn the identity of the murderers. A showdown with the gunmen ends one of "Red Ryder" series veteran Elliott's last oaters.

p, Vincent M. Fennelly; d, Thomas Carr; w, Dan Ullman; ph, Ernest Miller; m, Raoul Kraushaar; ed, Sam Fields.

Western (PR:A MPAA:NR)

FORTY-NINTH MAN, THE** (1953) 73m COL bw

John Ireland (John Williams), Richard Denning (Paul Regan), Suzanne Dalbert (Margo Wayne), Robert C. Foulk (Cmdr. Jackson), Touch Connors (Lt. Magrew), Richard Avonde (Buzz Olin), William R. Klein (Lester), Cicely Browne (Blonde Woman), Tommy Farrell (Reynolds), Joseph Mell (Man), Robert Hunter (Andre), Peter Marshall (Leo Wayne), George Milan (Dave Norton), Genevieve Aumont (Singer), Cris Alcaide (Manning), Michael Colgan (Gray), Jean Del Val (Maurice Ledoux), George Dee (Pierre Neff).

U.S. Security Investigation Division agent Ireland begins to think things odd when his big tip regarding the illegal transportation of atomic devices into the U.S. is explained away by the secretary of the Navy and the SID as part of routine war game exercises. Ireland sets out to prove that his superiors were duped by the bad guys, who are attempting to sneak a big bomb into the country. He tracks down the spies and manages to detonate the deadly device by dumping it out of the saboteur's plane while flying over the nuclear test site in Nevada. Fast-paced and entertaining.

p, Sam Katzman; d, Fred F. Sears; w, Harry Essex (based on a story by Ivan Tors); ph, Lester White; ed, William A. Lyon; art d, Paul Palmentola.

Spy Drama (PR:A MPAA:NR)

FORTY NINTH PARALLEL (SEE: INVADERS, THE, 1941)

FORTY POUNDS OF TROUBLE½** (1962) 106m UNIV c

Tony Curtis *(Steve McCluskey)*, Phil Silvers *(Bernie Friedman)*, Suzanne Pleshette *(Chris Lockwood)*, Claire Wilcox *(Penny Piper)*, Larry Storch *(Floyd)*, Howard Morris *(Julius)*, Stubby Kaye *(Cranston)*, Edward Andrews *(Herman)*, Mary Murphy *(Liz McCluskey)*, Warren Stevens *(Swing)*, Kevin McCarthy *(Blanchard)*, Tom Reese *(Bassett)*, Steve Gravers *(Daytime)*, Karen Steele *(Bambi)*, Gregg Palmer *(Piper)*, Gerald Gordon *(District Attorney)*, Sharon Farrell *(Dolores)*, Charles Horvath *(Stooge)*, Nicky Blair *(Desk Clerk)*, Hallene Hill *(Slot Machine Player)*, Jack LaRue *(Nick the Greek)*, Jim Bannon *(The Westerner)*, Charles Victor *(Madison Avenue Type)*, Ruth Robinson *(Little Old Lady)*, Tito Memminger *(Room Clerk)*, Roman Martinez *(Indian Chief)*, Syl Lamont *(Bellboy)*, Croftt Brook *(Lawyer)*, Paul Comi *(Cavanaugh)*, Ford Rainey *(Judge)*, David Allen *(Singer)*.

Retread of the Damon Runyon standby LITTLE MISS MARKER featuring Curtis as the hard-hearted manager of a swanky Lake Tahoe nightclub owned by Silvers. Enter orphaned tot Wilcox, who latches onto Curtis and forces him to warm to children. Thrown into this sudden change of lifestyle is Pleshette, who enlists Wilcox's aid in convincing Curtis he needs a new wife, even though he's still avoiding the alimony payments from his last holy bonding. The thing climaxes in a slapstick chase through Disneyland that is the film's real showpiece. Director Jewison (IN THE HEAT OF THE NIGHT, ROLLERBALL, F.I.S.T.) was making his big screen debut here after coming over from TV.

p, Stan Margulies; d, Norman Jewison; w, Marion Hargrove (based on the short story "Little Miss Marker" by Damon Runyon); ph, Joseph MacDonald (Panavision, Eastmancolor); m, Mort Lindsay; ed, Marjorie Fowler; art d, Alexander Golitzen, Robert Clatworthy; set d, Ruby Levitt; cos, Rosemary Clatworthy; m/l, "If You" (sung by Suzanne Pleshette), "What's the Scene?" (sung by David Allen), Lindsey, Sydney Shaw.

Comedy **(PR:AAA MPAA:NR)**

42ND STREET***** (1933) 98m WB bw

Warner Baxter *(Julian Marsh)*, Bebe Daniels *(Dorothy Brock)*, George Brent *(Pat Denning)*, Una Merkel *(Lorraine Fleming)*, Ruby Keeler *(Peggy Sawyer)*, Guy Kibbee *(Abner Dillon)*, Dick Powell *(Billy Lawler)*, Ginger Rogers *(Ann Lowell [Anytime Annie])*, George E. Stone *(Andy Lee)*, Robert McWade *(Al Jones)*, Ned Sparks *(Thomas Barry)*, Eddie Nugent *(Terry Neil)*, Allen Jenkins *(Mac Elory)*, Harry Akst *(Jerry)*, Clarence Nordstrom *(Groom, "Shuffle Off to Buffalo")*, Henry B. Walthall *(The Actor)*, Al Dubin, Harry Warren *(Songwriters)*, Toby Wing *("Young and Healthy" Girl)*, Pat Wing *(Chorus Girl)*, Tom Kennedy *(Slim Murphy)*, Wallis Clark *(Dr. Chadwick)*, Jack LaRue *(A Mug)*, Louise Beavers *(Pansy)*, Dave O'Brien *(Chorus Boy)*, Patricia Ellis *(Secretary)*, George Irving *(House Doctor)*, Charles Lane *(An Author)*, Milton Kibbee *(News Spreader)*, Rolfe Sedan *(Stage Aide)*, Harry Seymour *(Aide)*, Gertrude Keeler, Helen Keeler,Geraine Grear [Joan Barclay], Ann Hovey, Renee Whitney, Dorothy Coonan, Barbara Rogers, June Glory, Jayne Shadduck, Adele Lacy, Loretta Andrews, Margaret La Marr, Mary Jane Halsey, Ruth Eddings, Edna Callaghan, Patsy Farnum, Maxine Cantway, Lynn Browning, Donna Mae Roberts, Lorena Layson, Alice Jans, Eve Marcy, Evelyn Joice, Agnes Ray, Grace Tobin *(Chorus Girls)*, Kermit Maynard *(Dancer Who Catches Girl)*, Lyle Talbot *(Geoffrey Waring)*.

Young as this film was in the talkie era, it came along when the public was satiated with musicals, inundated with backstage dramas, flooded with tunes, a genre begun with THE BROADWAY MELODY, produced by MGM in 1929. Yet 42ND STREET turned out to be an all-time blockbuster thanks to the ingenuity of Busby Berkeley, who staged the awesome dance numbers, and a pair of fresh-faced newcomers, Powell and Keeler. Broadway director Baxter wants one more hit so he can retire and recuperate from health problems. The show he undertakes is backed by Kibbee, an old rake after star Daniels. While Daniels rehearses "Pretty Lady," she juggles her off-the-boards time between the nervous Kibbee and her one-time vaudeville partner, Brent, who is now down-and-out. Keeler, a hopeful chorus girl, is given a job in the production by Baxter after Powell, Merkel, and Rogers beg the position for her. She meets Brent and he begins dating her, despite Powell's obvious infatuation with her. Daniels, frustrated at not being able to see Brent, gets drunk at a party held after the Philadelphia tryout, and insults Kibbee, who walks out on the show. It quickly gets worse for Daniels when she learns that Keeler has been seeing her sweet man Brent and, in a tipsy attempt to swing on the chorine, she takes a tumble and breaks her ankle, which immediately puts her out of the show. Kibbee returns to the fold because he is now taken with the curvacious Rogers whom he wants as the new star. Good-hearted chorus girl that she is, Rogers tells Baxter that she can't carry the lead, but that Keeler can. In a marathon rehearsal Baxter trains Keeler for the part, grumbling through the exhausting ordeal: "I'll either have a live leading lady or a dead chorus girl." At the last moment, before she goes on, Daniels hobbles into Keeler's dressing room and wishes her good luck. As she waits in the wings, Baxter comes up to Keeler and delivers what has become an historic filmic line: "You're going out a youngster, but you've *got* to come back a star!" The show is a smash hit and the film ends with the fatigued Baxter sitting on a fire escape next to the theater, listening to the smug first-nighters stream out, overhearing one comment: "All those directors make me sick! Take Marsh [Baxter], he puts his name all over the program. Gets all the credit. Except for kids like Sawyer [Keeler], he wouldn't have a show. Some guys get all the breaks." 42ND STREET is thin on plot and characterization, but what musical isn't? Its charm and fascination are produced by the hectic pace Bacon maintains in his continuous backstage story where all the backdrops hang out and the chorus girls sink exhausted into unglamorous heaps after the routines demanded by the fanatical Baxter, coupled to the ebullient numbers provided by Warren and Dubin. The startling, innovative choreography by Berkeley brings this film to masterpiece level, with absolutely astounding numbers where Berkeley pulled out all the stops, shooting his routines from angles no one ever thought of before. Berkeley's scale of dance numbers rivals traffic jams and stadium crowds, hundreds of dancers moving in unison with hoops, ribbons, and every conceivable kind of prop. Berkeley reportedly screened 5,000 chorus girls for the musical, selecting 300 with the prettiest faces, then taking 200 with the most attractive ankles, then down to 100 with the sexiest knees. More than thirty years later Berkeley told a reporter for the London *Evening Standard* that he had not picked the dancers for 42ND STREET according to only one physical attribute: "I picked the girls for their eyes. Their eyes must talk to me, not flirt with me. I don't need to see girls in bathing costumes to judge them." Berkeley was more than just a choreographer; his limitless talents included incredible set designs. In one production number in this film he had three huge turntables constructed, one higher than the next, and had them spin in opposite directions as girls tap danced on the pyramidal discs. Berkeley, who had made eight films before 42ND STREET, was allowed to go hog-wild by Warner Bros. and the results are spectacular. In the turntable sequence Powell sings to blonde manniquin-type Toby Wing "Young and Healthy." Then, for the wonderful "Shuffle Off To Buffalo" number, where Rogers, Merkel, and other chorines caution a new honeymoon couple, Keeler and Nordstrom, Berkeley has a Pullman car jackknifing open to reveal the inside of the sleeping car. (The lyrics of this number are clever and funny with such lines as "When she knows as much as we know, she'll be on her way to Reno.") The finale is the rousing "42nd Street" number with hordes of dancers doing slice-of-life cameos in song along the Great White Way, culminating in an army of women with slit skirts revealing gartered, nylon-encased legs dancing with meticulous precision until they form a skyscraper with Powell and Keeler peeking from the top. Other Warren-Dubin tunes include the popular "You're Getting To Be A Habit With Me" and "It Must Be June." Berkeley, who had once been a drill instructor, reverted to his old army ways for this production. The ladies of the chorus were put on a rigorous, football-like training program, with strict diets and hard-and-fast rules regulating sleeping hours. Between-meal snacks and desserts were out. During the production schedule, an influenza epidemic ravaged Hollywood, laying waste to the mighty. Berkeley's well-trained chorines survived with nary a sniffle. All in the cast shine, and even though Keeler's slightly nasal singing voice is limited and her dancing is not the best, she is the epitome of the Broadway novitiate while Powell's tenor crooning is full of lark and laughter. Baxter is terrific as the hard-pressed Broadway director. Nepotism was much in evidence here; Keeler was given her lead mostly through the influence of her husband, Al Jolson, Jack Warner's good friend, the man who put the Warner studio on the map with the first talkie, THE JAZZ SINGER (1927). Moreover, Keeler's real-life sisters Helen and Gertrude are in the chorus. The film cost $400,000, which was a mammoth budget for the day, but it returned ten times that amount to Warner Bros. coffers and made Berkeley king of the choreographers.

p, Darryl F. Zanuck; d, Lloyd Bacon; w, James Seymour, Rian James (based on the novel by Bradford Ropes); ph, Sol Polito; ed, Thomas Pratt; md, Leo F. Forbstein; art d, Jack Okey; cos, Orry-Kelly; ch, Busby Berkeley; m/l, Al Dubin, Harry Warren.

Musical **Cas.** **(PR:A MPAA:NR)**

47 SAMURAI (SEE: CHUSHINGURA, 1963, Jap.)

FORTY THIEVES** (1944) 60m UA bw

William Boyd *(Hopalong Cassidy)*, Andy Clyde *(California Carlson)*, Jimmy Rogers *(Himself)*, Douglas Dumbrille *(Tad Hammond)*, Louise Currie *(Katherine Reynolds)*, Kirk Alyn *(Jerry Doyle)*, Herbert Rawlinson *(Buck Peters)*, Robert Frazer *(Judge Reynolds)*, Glenn Strange *(Ike Simmons)*, Jack Rockwell *(Sam Garms)*, Bob Kortman *(Joe Garms)*.

An interesting Hopalong Cassidy entry, the last in the long running series before Boyd bought the rights. Boyd is defeated for sheriff by spineless Alyn who all the crooks in town voted for. After watching the town slide downward, Boyd decides to impeach the sheriff. The leader of the crooks, Dumbrille, hires forty gunslingers to stop him. Incredibly, Boyd takes on all forty and wins. Funnyman Clyde would follow Boyd into his new venture, providing the salty experience and all-around cook- and bottle-washer comic relief the series always enjoyed. (See HOPALONG CASSIDY series, Index.)

p, Harry A. Sherman; d, Lesley Selander; w, Michael Wilson, Bernie Kamins (based on characters created by Clarence E. Mulford); ph, Russell Harlan; m, Mort Glickman; ed, Carol Lewis.

Western **(PR:A MPAA:NR)**

FORTY THOUSAND HORSEMEN½** (1941, Aus.) 100m UNIV bw

Grant Taylor *(Red Gallagher)*, Betty Bryant *(Juliet Rouget)*, "Chips" Rafferty *(Jim)*, Pat Twohill *(Larry)*, Harvey Adams *(Von Hausen)*, Eric Reiman *(Von Schiller)*, Joe Valli *(Scotty)*, Albert C. Winn *(Sheik Abu)*, Kenneth Brampton, John Fleeting, Harry Abdy, Norman Maxwell, Pat Penny, Charles Zoli, Claude Turtin, Theo Lianos, Sgt. Roy Mannix, Edna Emmett, Vera Kandy, Iris Kennedy, Joy Hart.

Early Aussie effort detailing the battles of the famed Australian Light Horse regiment which fought valiantly in Palestine in WW I. Sewn into the action footage is the inevitable romance between Aussie soldier Rafferty and beautiful French girl Bryant on the way to a smashing finish showing a climactic charge by the regiment.

p&d, Charles Chauvel; w, Mrs. Chauvel; ph, George Heath; ed, Bill Shephard; set d, Eric Thompson.

War **(PR:A MPAA:NR)**

FORWARD PASS, THE (1929) 78m FN-WB bw

Douglas Fairbanks, Jr. *(Marty Reid)*, Loretta Young *(Patricia Carlyle)*, Guinn Williams *(Honey Smith)*, Marion Byron *(Mazie)*, Phyllis Crane *(Dot)*, Bert Rome *(Coach Wilson)*, Lane Chandler *(Ass't. Coach Kane)*, Allan Lane *(Ed Kirby)*, Floyd Shackleford *(Trainer)*.

Fair college musical has Fairbanks the star football player who wants to quit the team. His coach persuades campus flirt Young to use her feminine wiles on him, and Fairbanks falls hopelessly in love with her. When she sees the depth of his feelings, she drops the guy she's been seeing and lets Fairbanks know just in time for him to make the title play and win the big game. Young was sixteen years old at the time; Fairbanks was twenty. Songs include: "One Minute Of Heaven," "I Gotta Have You," "Hello Baby," "Huddlin'."

d, Edward Cline; w, Howard Emmett Rogers (based on a story by Harvey Gates); ph, Arthur Todd; ed, Ralph Holt; m/l, Ned Washington, Herb Magidson, Michael Cleary.

Musical (PR:A MPAA:NR)

FOUL PLAY**** (1978) 116m PAR c

Goldie Hawn *(Gloria Mundy)*, Chevy Chase *(Tony Carlson)*, Burgess Meredith *(Hennessey)*, Rachel Roberts *(Gerda)*, Eugene Roche *(Archbishop Thorncrest)*, Dudley Moore *(Stanley Tibbets)*, Marilyn Sokol *(Stella)*, Brian Dennehy *(Fergie)*, Marc Lawrence *(Stiltskin)*, Chuck McCann *(Theater Manager)*, Billy Barty *(J.J. MacKuen)*, Don Calfa *(Scarface)*, Bruce Solomon *(Scott)*, Cooper Huckabee *(Sandy)*, Pat Ast *(Mrs. Venus)*, Frances Bay *(Mrs. Russel)*, William Frankfather *(Albino)*, Ion Teodorescu *(Turk)*, John Hancock *(Coleman)*, Queenie Smith *(Elsie)*, Hope Summers *(Ethel)*, Irene Tedrow *(Mrs. Monk)*, Cyril Magnin *(Pope Pius XIII)*, Chuck Walsh *(Newscaster)*, David Cole *(Theater Usher)*, Bill Gamble *(Dickinson)*, Michael David Lee *(Limo Driver)*, Neno Russo *(Luigi)*, Rollin Moriyama, Mitsu Yashima, M. James Arnett, Jophery Brown, John Hatfield, Joe Bellan, Connie Sawyer, F. Jo Mohrbach, Garry Goodrow, Enrico DiGiuseppe, Glenys Fowles, Kathleen Hegierski, Sandra Walker, Thomas Jamerson, Richard McKee, Jane Shaulis, Craig Baxley, Hal Needham, Glynn Rubin, Shirley the python.

FOUL PLAY is a funny, successful, and very derivative crime-comedy that grossed about $30 million first time around. Colin Higgins wrote and directed it and should have included Hitchcock's name in the credits as the plot totally hinges on a MAN WHO KNEW TOO MUCH twist. Roberts, Roche, Lawrence et al. are a whacky group who want to end the exclusion of religious properties from taxation. To make their point, they intend to murder the Pope who is visiting San Francisco and will be attending a performance of "The Mikado" at the opera house. At the right musical moment, he is to be shot. Hawn, in her best performance to that time, picks up Solomon on the road. He has evidence of the cabal and is dying of a wound. Chase is a detective living on a houseboat in Sausalito and assigned to the Solomon death. He believes Hawn and, after a mess of twists and turns, manages to save the pontiff (played by San Francisco department store magnate Cyril Magnin in a nonspeaking role). Moore is the orchestra leader and a sex freak who frequents massage parlors. It was this job that got him the lead in 10 which instantly catapulted him into stardom. (The role was originally written for Tim Conway, who turned it down.) Chase is at his best, does not overplay, and establishes himself as an excellent light comedian. McCann is superb as the manager of a theater specializing in retrospectives (a little homage on the part of Higgins?). McCann is one of the best second bananas around and can be seen regularly in several commercials (as Oliver Hardy, among others), many of which have won national awards for excellence. A serious as well as comic actor, the breadth of his talent can be seen from his memorable part as the mute in THE HEART IS A LONELY HUNTER to his hysterical portrayal in the title role as THE PROJECTIONIST. Little Billy Barty also deserves praise as a religious bookseller. Charles Fox's music is perfect for the picture; light and bubbly. The theme became a hit for Barry Manilow. Composer Fox worked for producers Miller and Milkis with great success in the past, having written the TV themes for "Happy Days," "Laverne And Shirley" and several other shows including "Love, American Style" and "Wonder Woman."

p, Thomas L. Miller, Edward K. Milkis; d&w, Colin Higgins; ph, David M. Walsh (Panavision, Movielab Color); m, Charles Fox; ed, Pembroke J. Herring; prod d, Alfred Sweeney; set d, Robert R. Benton; m/l, "Ready to Take a Chance Again," Fox, Norman Gimbel (sung by Barry Manilow).

Crime/Comedy Cos. (PR:A-C MPAA:PG)

FOUND ALIVE* (1934) 65m Ideal bw

Barbara Bedford *(The Mother)*, Maurice Murphy *(The Boy)*, Robert Frazer *(The Father)*, Edwin Cross *(Brooke)*, Ernie Adams, Cy Ceeder, Stella Zarco, Audrey Talley, Harry Griffith.

Another standard jungle action melodrama with lots of savage beast stock footage starring Bedford as a woman who loses her son in a divorce settlement. Distraught and confused, she kidnaps the tyke and flees into the jungles of Mexico where she raises the boy, Murphy, with the help of her loyal butler, Brooke. Years later, the kid's father tracks them down and the family is reunited.

d, Charles Hutchinson; w, Adrian Johnson (based on a story by Capt. Jacob Conn); ph, William Thompson; ed, Rose Smith; animal d, Thomas Griffith.

Drama (PR:A MPAA:NR)

FOUNTAIN, THE*½ (1934) 85m RAD bw

Ann Harding *(Julie von Narwitz)*, Brian Aherne *(Lewis Alison)*, Paul Lukas *(Rupert von Narwitz)*, Jean Hersholt *(Baron Von Leyden)*, Ralph Forbes *(Ballater)*, Violet Kemble Cooper *(Baroness Von Leyden)*, Sara Haden *(Sophie)*, Richard Abbott *(Allard Von Leyden)*, Rudolph Amendt *(Goof Von Leyden)*, Barbara Barondess *(Goof's Wife)*, Betty Alden *(Allard's Wife)*, Ian Wolfe *(Van Arkel)*, Douglas Wood *(De Greve)*, Frank Reicher *(Doctor)*, Ferike Boros *(Nurse)*, William Stack *(Commandant)*, Christian Rub *(Kerstholt)*, J. M. Kerrigan *(Shordley)*, Charles McNaughton *(Lampman)*, Desmond Roberts *(Willett)*.

Lukas is a German officer who leaves his loving wife, Harding, at home while he goes off to fight in WW I. She falls in love with dashing young Britisher Aherne in his absence. Lukas returns from the front suffering from the after-effects of poison gas and missing an arm. Guiltily, Harding nurses him but it is only a matter of time before Lukas senses what has transpired while he was gone. Knowing that he is about to die, Lukas lets Harding know that he understands—at least she found someone to replace him. Though well-intended and occasionally moving, the film lumbers slowly along to the fade, dragging disinterest in its wake.

p, Pandro S. Berman; d, John Cromwell; w, Jane Murfin, Samuel Hoffenstein (based on a novel by Charles Morgan); ph, Henry W. Gerrard; m, Max Steiner; ed, William Morgan.

Drama (PR:A MPAA:NR)

FOUNTAIN OF LOVE, THE** (1968, Aust.) 83m Intercontinental/Crown International c (DIE LIEBESQUELLE)

Hans-Jurgen Baumler *(Leif)*, Sieghardt Rupp *(Nils Hansen)*, Eddi Arent *(Alwin Knobbe)*, Ann Smyrner *(Stina)*, Hartmuth Hinrichs *(Carl)*, Christa Linder *(Britta)*, Christiane Rucker *(Grit)*, Marianne Schonauer *(Frau van Weyden)*, Balduin Baas *(Druggist)*, Helga Marlo *(Caroline)*, Walter Buschoff *(Wirt the Innkeeper)*, Ellen Umlauf *(Teacher)*, Werner Abrolat *(John)*, Emely Reuer *(Frieda)*, Herbert Tiede *(Pastor)*, Karin Field *(Victoria)*, Dimiter Panoff *(Lars Pogge)*.

Silly comedy about a small mountain town in Austria whose leaders decide to entice tourists by promoting a legendary "fountain of love" that can be found nearby. The outraged minister of tourism sends one of her agents to investigate but he finds nothing after the town's mayor ordered a three-day moratorium on sex and had the fountain plugged up. The agent wires for the minister to come take a look for herself, but then he is soon dissuaded when he drinks a glass of the aphrodisiatic water. Busloads of tourists arrive to visit the now-opened fountain and the minister claims the waters for the state.

p, Karl Spiehs; d, Ernst Hofbauer; w, Walter Schneider; ph, Franz Lederle (Pathe Color); m, Claudius Alzner; ed, Grete Girinec; art d, Wolf Witzemann; cos, Gerdago.

Comedy (PR:C MPAA:R)

FOUNTAINHEAD, THE½** (1949) 114m WB bw

Gary Cooper *(Howard Roark)*, Patricia Neal *(Dominique)*, Raymond Massey *(Gail Wynand)*, Kent Smith *(Peter Keating)*, Robert Douglas *(Ellsworth Toohey)*, Henry Hull *(Henry Cameron)*, Ray Collins *(Enright)*, Moroni Olsen *(Chairman)*, Jerome Cowan *(Alvah Scarret)*, Paul Harvey, Thurston Hall *(Businessmen)*, Harry Woods *(Superintendent)*, Paul Stanton *(The Dean)*, Bob Alden *(Newsboy)*, Tristram Coffin *(Secretary)*, Roy Gordon *(Vice President)*, Isabel Withers *(Secretary)*, Almira Sessions *(Housekeeper)*, Tito Vuolo, William Haade *(Workers)*, Gail Bonney *(Woman)*, Dorothy Christy *(Society Woman)*, Harlan Warde *(Young Man)*, Jonathan Hale *(Guy Franchon)*, Frank Wilcox *(Gordon Prescott)*, Douglas Kennedy *(Reporter)*, Pierre Watkin, Selmer Jackson *(Officials)*, John Doucette *(Gus Webb)*, John Alvin *(Young Intellectual)*, Geraldine Wall *(Woman)*, Fred Kelsey *(Old Watchman)*, Paul Newlan, George Sherwood *(Policemen)*, Lois Austin *(Woman Guest)*, Josephine Whittell *(Hostess)*, Morris Ankrum *(Prosecutor)*, Griff Barnett *(Judge)*, G. Pat Collins *(Foreman)*, Ann Doran, Ruthelma Stevens *(Secretaries)*, Creighton Hale *(Clerk)*, Philo McCullough *(Bailiff)*.

The 1943 Ayn Rand blockbusting novel came to the screen with the author as the scriptwriter which did not help sort out her obtuse Freudian symbols and her own philosophy of Objectivism. Cooper is the single-minded architect Roark who will not compromise his designs. He meets architecture critic Neal while she surveys a stone quarry when he has taken a job rather than knuckle under to a designing firm. The two fall in love but Cooper suddenly leaves Neal in the proverbial lurch, going to New York to take a commission. She rebounds into the arms of Massey, the arrogant filthy rich publisher of *The Banner*, which later attacks Cooper's radical designs when his star rises. Kent Taylor, a society designer with no scruples, asks Cooper to design a public housing project and he does, on the strict proviso that the buildings never be changed. By the time he completes his design he has befriended one-time enemy Massey while Neal is batting big lids in his direction. Cooper finds that the housing project has been altered drastically and blows up the unfinished buildings with dynamite, which brings him to court on charges. In emotion-packed scenes he defends himself and wins, but before that time Massey, feeling helpless to aid Cooper's cause, has committed suicide. That leaves Cooper to wed Neal and begin building his "mile high" skyscraper in Manhattan. (The final scene shows Neal taking a construction elevator into the unfinished cloud-surrounded tower to Cooper who stands triumphant at the top.) Cooper is wholly miscast as the eloquent architect, surrounded in a sea of words provided by Rand's garrulous script; both Neal and Massey overact with stage mannerisms and the entire production is bloated with symbols (the phallic buildings and equipment employed) and pretentious talk, even though the Roark character is a good profile of maverick architectural genius Frank Lloyd Wright. Carrere and Kuehl provide sumptuous sets and designs, and Steiner's score is brilliant. This was another failed attempt by Warners to make a star out of Neal. Talented director Vidor did what he could with the unmanageable script but it was an upward struggle. Cooper's uneasy rendering of a role that prohibited his usual monosyllabic approach is apparent in every frame. Said Vidor in an interview with *Sight and Sound*: "I didn't think that Cooper was well cast but he was cast before I was. I thought it should have been someone like Bogart, a more arrogant type of man. But after I forgot all that and saw it several years later I accepted Cooper doing it." Good performances come from Smith, the split-the-difference architect, and the venomous columnist portrayed by Douglas. Hull, as the old idealistic architect beaten down by convention and conformity, gives en electrifying performance, but none of it can save a film bent on confusing public and critics alike, which it did, making for a great financial loss.

p, Henry Blanke; d, King Vidor; w, Ayn Rand (based on her novel); ph, Robert Burks; m, Max Steiner; ed, David Weisbart; art d, Edward Carrere; set d, William

Kuehl; cos, Milo Anderson; spec eff, William McGann, Edwin DuPar, H.F. Koenekamp, John Holden; makeup, Perc Westmore, John Wallace.

Drama   Cas.   **(PR:A   MPAA:NR)**

FOUR AGAINST FATE**½   (1952, Brit.) 84m BL bw
(GB: DERBY DAY)

Anna Neagle (*Lady Helen Forbes*), Michael Wilding (*David Scott*), Googie Withers (*Betty Molloy*), John McCallum (*Tommy Dillon*), Peter Graves (*Gerald Berkeley*), Suzanne Cloutier (*Michele Jolivet*), Gordon Harker (*Joe Jenkins*), Gladys Henson (*Gladys*), Ralph Reader (*Bill Hammond*), Alfie Bass (*Spider Wilkes*), Edwin Styles (*Sir George Forbes*), Nigel Stock (*Jim Molloy*), Arthur Hambling (*Col. Tremaine*), Myrette Morven (*Mrs. Tremaine*), Toni Edgar-Bruce (*Mrs. Harbottle-Smith*), Richard Wattis (*Editor*), Raymond Glendenning (*Commentator*), Josephine Fitzgerald, Ewan Roberts, Leslie Weston, H.R. Hignett, Robert Brown, Gerald Anderson, Sam Kydd, Hugh Moxey, Derek Prentice, Michael Ripper, Phillip Ray, Tom Walls, Jr., Cyril Conway, Cecily Walper, John Chandos, Jan Pilbeam, Mary Gillingham, Brian Johnston, Frank Webster.

Episodic horse race film which follows three separate storylines taking place over a few hours at the racetrack. Cloutier, a maid, is escorted to the races by her favorite film star, Graves, whom she has won in a raffle. Wilding and Neagle find solace in each other after both lost loved ones in a plane crash, and Withers and McCallum are a couple who are arrested for murder while at the window collecting their winnings.

p, Herbert Wilcox, Maurice Cowan; d, Wilcox; w, Monckton Hoffe, John Baines, Alan Melville (based on a story by Arthur Austie); ph, Max Greene [Mutz Greenbaum], ed, Bill Lewthwaite.

Drama   **(PR:A   MPAA:NR)**

FOUR BAGS FULL***   (1957, Fr./Ital.) 90m Franco-London-Continentale bw

Jean Gabin (*Grandgil*), Bourvil (*Martin*), Jeanette Batti (*Mariette*), Louis de Funes (*Jambier*), Georgette Anys, Robert Arnoux, Laurence Badie, Myno Burney, Germaine Delbat, Monette Dinay, Jean Dunot, Bernard LaJarrige, Jacques Morin, Hubert De Lapparent, Jean Verner, Hughes Wanner.

Thrill-seeking artist Gabin joins cabbie Bourvil to transport four suitcases of freshly butchered pork across Paris during the WW II occupation. Bourvil gives one of the best performances of his career as the basically honest cabbie driven by circumstances to working in the black market. The structure is very episodic, as the pair avoid German roadblocks, hungry dogs, and collaborationist police. Well worth checking out.

d, Claude Aurant-Lara; w, Jean Aurenche, Pierre Bost (based on a novel by Marcel Ayme); ph, Jacques Natteau; m, Rene Clorec; ed, Madeleine Gug; prod d, Max Douy.

Comedy   **(PR:A   MPAA:NR)**

FOUR BOYS AND A GUN**   (1957) 74m UA bw

Frank Sutton (*Ollie Denker*), Larry Green (*Eddie Richards*), James Franciscus (*Johnny Doyle*), William Hinant (*Stanley Badek*), Otto Hulett (*District Attorney*), Robert Dryden (*Joe Barton*), J. Pat O'Malley (*Fight Manager*), Diana Herbert (*Marie*), Patricia Sloan (*Nita*), Nancy Devlin (*Sophie*), Patricia Bosworth (*Elizabeth*), David Burns (*Television Man*), Anne Seymour (*Mrs. Richards*), Frank Gero (*Slim*), Noel Glass (*Landlord*), Karl Swenson (*Mr. Badek*), Lisa Osten (*Mrs. Badek*), Sid Raymond (*Cab Driver*), George McIver, Frank Campanella.

Four youths become cop killers after losing their nerve in a holdup. They are caught after a brief manhunt and brought before the district attorney who gives them the uncomfortable option of either telling who the triggerman was (which would get the other three lighter sentences) or all four going to the chair. A tragic tale too often retold in real life since then.

p&d, William Berke; w, Philip Yordan, Leo Townsend (based on a novel by Willard Wiener); ph, J. Burgi Contner; m, Albert Glasser; ed, Everett Sutherland, Marie Montagne; md, Glasser; m/l, Stanley Rubin and His Tigertown Five.

Crime Drama   **(PR:C   MPAA:NR)**

FOUR COMPANIONS, THE**   (1938, Ger.) 80m UFA bw (DIE 4 GESELLEN)

Ingrid Bergman (*Marianne*), Sabine Peters (*Kathe*), Ursula Herking (*Franziska*), Carsta Lock (*Lotte*), Hans Sohnker (*Stephan Kohlund*), Leo Slezak, Heinz Weizel, Willi Rose, Erich Ponto, Karl Haubenreiber, Wilhelm P. Kruger, Lotte Braun, Hugo Froelich, Rudolph Klicks, Max Rosenhauer, Ernst G. Schiffner, Hans Jurgen Weidlich.

Early Bergman film sees her as an industrial design student, who, along with three classmates, form a small business upon their graduation. Though pursued by her young and handsome instructor, Sohnker, Bergman rejects his proposal of marriage in favor of her business. When all the girls lose interest (one gets married, one has a child out of wedlock, another decides to devote her energies to serious painting) in the business, leaving Bergman alone, she decides that she, too, will marry and at last agrees to Sohnker's proposal.

d, Carl Froelich; w, Jochen Huth (based on a play by Huth).

Romance/Drama   **(PR:A   MPAA:NR)**

FOUR CORNERED TRIANGLE (SEE: SCREAM OF THE BUTTERFLY, 1965)

4D MAN***   (1959) 85m Fairview/UNIV c (AKA: THE MASTER OF TERROR; GB: THE EVIL FORCE)

Lee Meriwether (*Linda Davis*), Robert Lansing (*Scott Nelson*), James Congdon (*Tony Nelson*), Jasper Deeter (*Mr. Welles*), Guy Raymond (*Fred*), Robert Strauss

(*Roy Parker*), Edgar Stehli (*Dr. Carson*), Dean Newman (*Dr. Schwartz*), Patty Duke (*Marjorie Sullivan*), George Kayara (*Sgt. Todaman*), Elbert Smuiyh (*Capt. Rogers*), Chick James (*B-Girl*).

A surprisingly well executed sci-fi film which sees Lansing as a scientist who has discovered a way for man to walk through solid matter. By hooking a device to his head which scrambles his brain-waves, Lansing is soon able to walk right into banks and steal anything he wants. The only drawback to his new talent is that it tends to age him rapidly. This problem is solved by sapping the life force of other people, which kills them, but makes him stronger. Lansing's fiancee is convinced that her beau has gone off the deep end, so she cons him into shutting off the 4D force and then kills him. In 1985 director Tobe Hooper tread similar ground in the multi-million dollar mess LIFEFORCE.

p, Jack H. Harris, Irvin Shortess Yeaworth, Jr.; d, Yeaworth, Jr.; w, Theodore Simonson, Cy Chermak (based on an original idea by Harris); ph, Theodore J. Pahle (DeLuxe Color); m, Ralph Carmichael; ed, William B. Murphy; md, Carmichael; art d, William Jersey; set d, Don W. Schmitt; spec eff, Barton Sloane.

Science Fiction   **(PR:A   MPAA:NR)**

FOUR DARK HOURS   (SEE: GREEN COCKATOO, THE, 1947, Brit.)

FOUR DAUGHTERS****   (1938) 90m WB bw

Claude Rains (*Adam Lemp*), May Robson (*Aunt Etta*), Priscilla Lane (*Ann Lemp*), Lola Lane (*Thea Lemp*), Rosemary Lane (*Kay Lemp*), Gale Page (*Emma Lemp*), Dick Foran (*Ernest*), Jeffrey Lynn (*Felix Deitz*), Frank McHugh (*Ben Crowley*), John Garfield (*Mickey Borden*), Vera Lewis (*Mrs. Ridgefield*), Tom Dugan (*Jake*), Eddie Acuff (*Sam*), Donald Kerr (*Earl*).

An engrossing, thoroughly enjoyable tale of small-town America and how four girls find romance and marry. When Lynn arrives at Rains' house to board, the music professors' four daughters all fall in love with him. Priscilla Lane becomes engaged to Lynn but later finds out from the cynical Garfield that one of her sisters is devastated by the impending marriage. In a great act of sibling generosity, she gives up Lynn and runs off with the embittered Garfield. It's all for naught when Lynn departs and the sister falls in love with another man. The tough, indolent Garfield realizes that he's breaking Priscilla Lane's heart, and during a snowstorm, drives his car off a cliff so that the girl is finally rid of him. Lane and Lynn are reunited at the end. A grand tearjerker, this is the film that brought Garfield to the screen in his first lead role, one that was tailor-made to his rugged personality. His role called for a shabbily dressed, surly, and wholly disillusioned young old man from the big city where poverty has scarred an otherwise brilliant mind. When he rarely smiles, it is a wry grin and when he laughs it's ironic humor, full of the sardonic. Garfield's rough good looks accompanied well this Depression-built character, one that shouts defiance and defeat at the same time. His remarks to the kindly small-town folks who take him in reflect their innocence and his jaded worldliness. He begins to play one of his own compositions in Rains' home, a piece without a beginning or end, just a fragmentary melody which impresses Priscilla Lane who tells him, "It's beautiful." He gives her a droopy-lidded glance and says through a mouth curled about a smoldering cigarette, "It stinks!" When gentle Robson offers him a cup of tea, Garfield snorts: "You needn't look so noble. Tea is only a little hot water." Garfield later stated that the characterization he developed in this role was drawn from a defiant, cynical pianist with an acerbic wit who had been his friend in New York when he acted in off-Broadway productions, one Oscar Levant. Curtiz does a grand job in hurrying along this marvelous soap opera so well that Warners had him direct two of the film's three sequels. (Gordon Douglas helmed the 1954 remake, YOUNG AT HEART.) Garfield's impact in this film was so overwhelming that he would go on playing the tight-lipped, fatalistic young man from the slums through a slew of Warner Bros. films. Rains is excellent as the tolerant, loving father, and suitors Foran, McHugh, and Lynn are outstanding, as are the Lane sisters and Page. Haller's lensing is as soft and gentle as the story and Steiner's poignant score befits the mood.

p, Hal B. Wallis; d, Michael Curtiz; w, Julius J. Epstein, Lenore Coffee (based on the novel *Sister Act* by Fannie Hurst); ph, Ernest Haller; m, Max Steiner; ed, Ralph Dawson; art d, John Hughes.

Romance   **(PR:A   MPAA:NR)**

FOUR DAYS**   (1951, Brit.) 55m Vandyke/GN bw

Hugh McDermott (*Francis Templar*), Kathleen Byron (*Lucienne Templar*), Peter Reynolds (*Johnny Keylin*), Gordon McLeod (*Mr. Keylin*), H.G. Stoker (*Baxter*), John Harvey (*Hammond Stubbs*), Petra Davies (*Helen*), Francis Roberts.

While McDermott is out of England on business, wife Byron has an affair with sleazy gigolo Reynolds. When McDermott returns and finds out, he jumps off a cliff. He survives but is stricken with amnesia, and his wife nurses him back to health. When Reynolds shows up trying to blackmail the pair, McDermott beats him. Ludicrous melodrama manages to pull off a couple of gripping scenes.

p, Roger Proudlock; d, John Guillermin; w, Lindsay Galloway, J. McLaren Ross (based on a play by Monckton Hoffe); ph, Ray Elton.

Drama   **(PR:A   MPAA:NR)**

FOUR DAYS LEAVE**   (1950, Switz.) 98m Film Classics bw

Cornel Wilde (*Stanley Robin*), Josette Day (*Suzanne*), Simone Signoret (*Yvonne*), John Baragrey (*Jack*), Richard Erdman (*Eddy*), Alan Hale, Jr. (*Joe*), George Petrie (*Sidney*), Leopold Biberti (*Walter Hochull*), Robert Birchler (*Fred*), Christiane Martin (*Madeleine*).

Wilde is a sailor on leave who visits Switzerland and falls in love with Day, the attendant at a watch shop. Before the fadeout he's won a ski contest and put up with the wheezy gags of buddies Hale, Erdman, and Petrie. Competent entertainment.

p, Praesans L. Wechsler; d, Leopold Lindtberg; w, Lindtberg, Curt Siodmak, Ring Lardner, Jr. (based on a story by Richard Schweitzer); ph, Emil Berna; m, Robert Blum.

Comedy   **(PR:A   MPAA:NR)**

FOUR DAYS OF NAPLES, THE** (1963, US/Ital.) 116m Titanus/MGM bw

Regina Bianchi (*Concetta Capuozzo*), Aldo Giuffre (*Pitrella*), Lea Massari (*Maria*), Jean Sorel (*Livornese*), Franco Sportelli (*Prof. Rosati*), Charles Belmont (*Sailor*), Gian Maria Volonte (*Stimolo*), Frank Wolff (*Salvatore*), Luigi De Filippo (*Cicillo*), Pupella Maggio (*Mother of Arturo*), Georges Wilson (*Reformatory Director*), Raffaele Barbato (*Ajello*), Domenico Formato (*Gennaro Capuozzo*), Curt Lowens (*Sakau*), Enzo Turco (*Valente*).

War drama detailing the vicious repression suffered by the Italians after the Nazis occupied the country when the Italian army surrendered to the Allies. The people are forced to watch and cheer the murder of an Italian sailor and soon after all males between the ages of five and fifty are rounded up and sent to slave labor camps. The people of Naples revolt and after a long and bloody uprising the Nazis evacuate the city and the Allies arrive shortly thereafter.

p, Goffredo Lombardo; d, Nanni Loy; w, Pasquale Festa Campanile, Massimo Franciosa, Carlo Benari, Loy (based on a story by Campanile, Franciosa, Loy, Vasco Pratolini); ph, Marcello Gatti; m, Carlo Rustichelli; ed, Ruggero Mastroianni; set d, Gianni Polidori; spec eff, Serse Urbisaglia.

War   **(PR:A   MPAA:NR)**

FOUR DAYS WONDER**½   (1936) 60m UNIV bw

Jeanne Dante (*Judy Widdell*), Kenneth Howell (*Tom Fenton*), Martha Sleeper (*Nancy Fairbrother*), Alan Mowbray (*Archibald Fenton*), Walter Catlett (*Duffy*), Charles Williams (*Kasky*), Margaret Irving (*Aunt Jessica*), Murray Kinnell (*Morris*), Spencer Charters (*Gilroy*), Rollo Lloyd (*The Tramp*).

Based on a story by children's book author A.A. Milne (*Winnie the Pooh*), this charming kiddie opus stars Dante as a thirteen-year-old mystery story enthusiast who becomes embroiled in a real murder case. When she does, she seeks the help of an adult mystery writer to solve the crime before the bumbling police detectives led by Catlett can louse up the case any further.

p, Charles R. Rogers; d, Sidney Salkow; w, Harvey Thews, Michael H. Uris (based on a novel by A.A. Milne); ph, Stanley Cortez.

Juvenile/Mystery   **(PR:AA   MPAA:NR)**

FOUR DESPERATE MEN** (1960, Brit.) 105m EAL-ABF/Continental bw (GB: THE SIEGE OF PINCHGUT)

Aldo Ray (*Matt Kirk*), Heather Sears (*Ann Fulton*), Neil McCallum (*Johnny Kirk*), Victor Maddern (*Bert*), Carlo Justini (*Luke*), Alan Tilvern (*Supt. Hanna*), Barbara Mullen (*Mrs. Fulton*), Gerry Duggan (*Pat Fulton*), Kenneth J. Warren (*Commissioner*), Grant Taylor (*Constable Macey*), Derek Barnes (*Sgt. Drake*), Richard Vernon (*Under Secretary*), Ewan MacDuff (*Naval Captain*), Martin Boddey (*Brigadier*), Max Robertson (*Motorcycle Officer*), John Pusey (*Small Boy*), Fred Abbott (*Constable*), George Woodbridge (*Newspaper Editor*).

An escaped convict (Ray) wants a new trial, for, despite his past criminal record, he knows he had been jailed on false charges. He holes up with his younger brother McCallum and two pals (Maddern and Justini) on a fortress island off Sydney harbor. Ray threatens to blow up the city unless he's given a retrial and the police act accordingly in this no-thrills thriller. The opening holds some good moments of suspense but the direction flags from there on and never recovers. Though the performances are good, this is supposed to be an action-packed suspenser and no amount of good acting can cover its obvious directorial flaws.

p, Eric Williams; d, Harry Watt; w, Inman Hunter, Lee Robinson, Watt, John Cleary (based on a story by Hunter and Robinson); ph, Gordon Dines; m, Kenneth V. Jones.

Action   **(PR:C   MPAA:NR)**

FOUR DEUCES, THE**   (1976) 87m AE c

Jack Palance (*Vic*), Carol Lynley (*Wendy*), Warren Berlinger (*Chico*), Adam Roarke (*Russ*), E.J. Peaker (*Lory*), Gianni Russo, H.B. Haggerty, John Haymer, Cherie Latimer, Martin Kove.

Low-budget exploitation film has Palance a mobster kingpin who falls for Lynley. Fast moving, with some good comic scenes.

p, Yoram Globus; d, William H. Bushnell, Jr.; w, C. Lester Franklin (based on a story by Don Martin); ph, (DeLuxe Color).

Crime   **Cas.**   **(PR:O   MPAA:R)**

FOUR DEVILS**   (1929) 125m FOX bw

First Sequence: Farrell MacDonald (*The Clown*), Anders Randolf (*Cecchi*), Claire McDowell (*Woman*), Jack Parker (*Charles, as a Boy*), Philippe DeLacey (*Adolf, as a Boy*), Dawn O'Day (*Marion, as a Girl*), Anita Fremmault (*Louise, as a Girl*), Wesley Lake (*Old Clown*), Poodle Dog. Second Sequence: Janet Gaynor (*Marion*), Charles Morton (*Charles*), Nancy Drexel (*Louise*), Barry Norton (*Adolf*), Mary Duncan (*The Lady*), Michael Visaroff (*Circus Director*), George Davis (*Mean Clown*), Andre Cheron (*Old Roue*).

F.W. Murnau directed this early soap opera with a circus background, detailing the lives of four children who grow up to take part in the circus. Two of these, Gaynor and Morton, are the lovers who appear as if nothing can keep them apart, that is until Duncan steps into the picture and steals Morton away. Only about one-quarter of FOUR DEVILS had dialog, that which does being extremely hampered by poor recording techniques. The only way this picture is reminiscent of Murnau's earlier works like THE LAST LAUGH is the expressive camera work, the circus

environment being the perfect place to explore camera angles and movement. But as a whole the picture is lacking in impact.

d, F.W. Murnau; w, Carl Mayer, John Hunter Booth (based on the adaptation by Berthold Viertel and Marion Orth of the novel *De Fire Djaevle* by Herman Joachim Bang); ph, Ernest Palmer, L.W. O'Connell; m, S.L. Rothafel; ed, Harold Schuster; m/l, Erno Rapee, Lew Pollack.

Drama   **(PR:A   MPAA:NR)**

FOUR FACES WEST***   (1948) 96m UA bw (AKA: THEY PASSED THIS WAY)

Joel McCrea (*Ross McEwen*), Frances Dee (*Fay Hollister*), Charles Bickford (*Pat Garrett*), Joseph Calleia (*Monte Marquez*), William Conrad (*Sheriff Egan*), Martin Garralaga (*Florencio*), Raymond Largay (*Dr. Eldredge*), John Parrish (*Frenger*), Dan White (*Clint Waters*), Davison Clark (*Burnett*), Houseley Stevenson (*Anderson*), George McDonald (*Winston Boy*), Eva Novak (*Mrs. Winston*), Sam Flint (*Storekeeper*), Forrest Taylor (*Conductor No. 2*).

A refreshingly gentle western starring McCrea as an honest rancher who is forced to rob a bank to save the family homestead, though he leaves the bank an I.O.U. Sheriff Bickford is sent to capture him. On the run, McCrea meets Dee and the pair fall in love, but he is forced to ride off to avoid the ever-vigilant Bickford. As McCrea makes his way across the scorching desert, he discovers a Mexican family suffering from diphtheria. Unable to ignore the pleas of the father, McCrea stays and helps the family, only to be caught by Bickford. Bickford sees that his quarry is no normal bandit, and assures McCrea that he will be let off easy. Though the plot sounds maudlin, McCrea's tough-but-tender performance pulls the whole thing off.

p, Harry Sherman; d, Alfred E. Green; w, Graham Baker, Teddi Sherman (based on the novel *Paso Por Aqui* by Eugene Manlove Rhodes, adaptation by William and Milarde Brent); ph, Russell Harlan; m, Paul Sawtell; ed, Edward Mann; md, Sawtell; art d, Duncan Cramer; set d, Ray Robinson; spec eff, Robert H. Moreland.

Western   **(PR:A   MPAA:NR)**

FOUR FAST GUNS**   (1959) 72m UNIV bw

James Craig (*Sabin*), Martha Vickers (*Mary*), Edgar Buchanan (*Dipper*), Brett Halsey (*Johnny Naco*), Paul Richards (*Hoag*), Blu Wright (*Farmer Brown*), Richard Martin (*Quijano*), John Swift (*Zodie*), Paul Raymond (*Bartender*).

Routine oater starring Craig as a lone rider, fleeing from arrest for a crime he didn't commit. He comes across a secluded western town run ruthlessly by a crippled bartender who avoids being dealt with by the law because nobody wants to harass a cripple. When the townsfolk ask Craig to vacate the varmint, the bartender hires some out-of-town guns to get the stranger before the stranger gets him. The first three guns fail, but the last one happens to be Craig's brother. After hesitation on both sides, the inevitable showdown occurs and Craig shoots down his outlaw brother. This sorry turkey was the first film released from the production studios of the Phoenix Film Studio in Arizona, an ominous augur for the future of the film industry in Arizona.

p&d, William J. Hole, Jr.; w, James Edmiston, Dallas Gaultois; ph, John M. Nickolaus, Jr.; md, Alec Compinsky; ed, Reginald Brown, Harold Wooley, Henry F. Salerno.

Western   **(PR:A   MPAA:NR)**

FOUR FEATHERS, THE*****   (1939, Brit.) 130m Korda-London Film/UA c

John Clements (*Harry Faversham*), Ralph Richardson (*Capt. John Durrance*), C. Aubrey Smith (*Gen. Burroughs*), June Duprez (*Ethne Burroughs*), Allan Jeayes (*Gen. Faversham*), Jack Allen (*Lt. Willoughby*), Donald Gray (*Peter Burroughs*), Frederick Culley (*Dr. Sutton*), Amid Taftazani (*Karaga Pasha*), Henry Oscar (*Dr. Harraz*), John Laurie (*Khalifa*), Robert Rendel (*Colonel*), Hal Walters (*Joe*), Clive Baxter (*Harry as Child*), Archibald Batty (*Adjutant*), Derek Elphinstone (*Lt. Parker*), Norman Pierce (*Sgt. Brown*).

One of the all-time great adventure films, THE FOUR FEATHERS is based on the 1902 tale of cowardice and courage by A.E.W. Mason, many times filmed but never as marvelously as in this masterpiece production. This tale of empire, battle, and redemption begins in the country manor house of Jeayes, a brigadier general who is rough on his young son, Baxter, in an attempt to toughen him up for the service; it is expected that he will follow family tradition and join the army. Smith, a retired general, and father of Duprez, the woman to whom the grown-up Clements becomes engaged, regales one and all with his gruesome tales of the Crimean war, demonstrating the battles by lining up nuts, apples, and a pineapple (the latter representing himself as the commanding general) and then drawing a "thin red line" with wine on the table to represent the British troops. Young Harry Faversham is shown 10 years later as Clements, a sensitive officer who decides he has no obligation to an ancient family tradition by remaining in the service. He resigns his commission just before his regiment leaves for the 1898 Sudan campaign conducted by Lord Kitchener. His friends, Richardson, Gray, and Allen, all officers of Clements' regiment, give him three white feathers, symbolizing cowardice. Duprez, his fiancee who is disgusted by his actions, more or less gives him the fourth feather. Clements finds that she agrees with Richardson and the others and he angrily tears a white feather from her fan and leaves. Clements consults with family doctor Culley, telling him he wants to vindicate himself, that he plans to go to Egypt. Culley gives him the address of a friend, Oscar. Clements, once in Egypt, is helped by Oscar to learn Arabic and disguises himself as a native, having his skin stained. Moreover, to remain speechless, he has the letter "S" branded on his forehead to indicate that he is a Sangali tribesman, the ostracized members of which have had their tongues cut out by their enemies. Later he makes sure that he is captured by Dervishes and used as a laborer, and he witnesses the massacre of his regiment. He wanders the deserted battlefield hours later to find Richardson, wounded and going blind in the searing heat that pounds down on them as he mutely leads the one-time friend to a British outpost. Before departing, Clements places a white feather in Richardson's wallet. Clements finds Allen and Gray captives in a foul-smelling Dervish prison, and helps them escape, blow up the arsenal in Omdurman, and control a vital area of the fortifications until Kitchener's troops sweep into the city triumphant. Both Allen and Gray gratefully take back their feathers. The blind Richardson, recuperating in England, discovers the feather in his wallet and realizes that the speechless native who had helped him in the desert was none other than Clements. Though he is then engaged to Duprez, he gives her up when he hears that Clements has returned to England. Duprez meets Clements again, accepts the return of her feather and melts into his embrace. Clements rejoins his regiment and his last act of bravery is to interrupt Smith who is again dramatically reliving his Crimean battle; Clements sets the record straight by correcting the facts Smith has altered to preserve his own crusty image. THE FOUR FEATHERS is directed by Zoltan Korda with the kind of elan demanded by the action-packed story; this brother of producer Alexander Korda loved and excelled at directing any exotic adventure story. He was also expert in handling huge crowd scenes and it shows in the magnificent battle scenes, particularly the awesome attack of the Fuzzi Wuzzies against the British lines, shown in wide panorama by cameras mounted high on hilltops overlooking the battlefield. Producer Korda spared no expense in this production, using a rich Technicolor process and shooting most of the exteriors in the Sudan. Even the sailing ships pulled by the hordes of natives along the Nile were period vessels constructed at great expense. All of this film, from the smoky, foggy London settings to the desert battles, presents a visual feast that for authenticity and sheer splendor has never been equalled. So rich and moving are the battle scenes that they were used in a host of other films, including ZARAK (1956), MASTER OF THE WORLD (1961), EAST OF SUDAN (1964), and STORM OVER THE NILE (1955), Korda's own less-than-memorable remake of his 1939 film. Korda insisted upon accuracy throughout this production but he also reveled in having the film in color. At one point he entered a ballroom set and was alarmed to find the officers wearing dress blues. "What is this blue uniform?" he asked a military adviser. The British officer replied that it was the correct dress for a private party in the later 1800s. "But this is Technicolor!" roared Korda and the uniforms were changed to red to better show the brilliance of the color. The popular FOUR FEATHERS had been filmed many times, as silents in 1915, 1921, and 1929, the latter being the best of the silent era with Richard Arlen, Fay Wray, William Powell, Clive Brook, and Theodore von Eltz. Three talkies of the story were made in 1939, 1955 (as STORM OVER THE NILE), and 1978, but the 1939 version remains the classic. The Hungarian-born Korda had a bone-deep love of England and its traditions and customs, believing in its concept of a benign empire and most of his great epics reflect his upholding of that British image such as FIRE OVER ENGLAND (1937), DRUMS (1938), THE SCARLET PIMPERNEL (1935). He later refused to produce THE BRIDGE ON THE RIVER KWAI because it reflected badly on British soldiers seemingly willing to aid the Japanese enemy in building a bridge. THE FOUR FEATHERS was his personal salute to the glory of British military traditions. The financial expense was heavy but the box office returns were enormous. However, these profits came six months too late to halt Korda's financially pressed Denham Studios from being taken over by others. Korda made the film knowing he would lose his studio anyway, following in the footsteps of the author to the site of the great tale. Mason related years after writing The Four Feathers how he traveled far and wide to get his background material: "I took a little steamer from Suez down the Red Sea, disembarked at Suakin—there was no Port Sudan in those days and no railway—hired a half a dozen camels with half a dozen Fuzzi Wuzzies, none of whom spoke any English whilst I spoke no Arabic, and pushed off into the eastern Sudan. In due time I arrived at Berber and Khartoum. Omdurman was still much as it had been during the life of Kalifa and the 'house of stone,' his famous prison, still stood. I met Slatin Pasha and a good many of that distinguished group of officers who made the Sudan and its army famous and there was the setting for my story." Korda and his brother simply followed Mason's route to make one of the most memorable films of all time.

p, Alexander Korda; d, Zoltan Korda; w, R.C. Sherriff, Lajos Biro, Arthur Wimperis (based on the novel by A.E.W. Mason); ph, Georges Perinal, Osmond Borradaile, Jack Cardiff (Technicolor); m, Miklos Rozsa; ed, William Hornbeck, Henry Cornelius; md, Muir Mathieson; prod d, Vincent Korda; cos, Godfrey Brennan, Rene Hubert; tech & military adv, Capt. Donald Anderson, Lt. Col. Stirling.

Adventure   Cas.   (PR:A MPAA:NR)

FOUR FLIES ON GREY VELVET**½   (1972, Ital.) 101m PAR c
(QUATRO MOSCHE DI VELLUTO GRIS)

Michael Brandon (Robert), Mimsy Farmer (Nina), Jean Pierre Marielle (Arrosio), Francine Racette (Dalia), Bud Spencer (Godfrey).

Okay Italian mystery which stars Brandon as a rich rock 'n' roll star married to Farmer, who gets embroiled in a murder case. The gimmick in this one is a laser-beam camera able to photograph the last image in the eye of a corpse. As usual, a top-notch score by Ennio Morricone.

p, Salvatore Argento; d&w, Dario Argento (from a story by D. Argento, Luigi Cozzi, Mario Foglietti); m, Ennio Morricone.

Mystery   (PR:C MPAA:R)

FOUR FOR TEXAS*   (1963) 124m WB c

Frank Sinatra (Zack Thomas), Dean Martin (Joe Jarrett), Anita Ekberg (Elya Carlson), Ursula Andress (Maxine Richter), Charles Bronson (Matson), Victor Buono (Harvey Burden), Edric Connor (Prince George), Nick Dennis (Angel), Richard Jaeckel (Mancini), Mike Mazurki (Chad), Wesley Addy (Trowbridge), Marjorie Bennett (Miss Ermaline), Jack Elam (Dobie), Fritz Feld (Maitre D'), Percy Helton (Ansel), Jonathan Hale (Renee), Jack Lambert (Monk), Paul Langton (Beauregard), Jesslyn Fax (Widow), Teddy Buckner and His All Stars, The Three Stooges, Arthur Godfrey, Bob Steele, Virginia Christine, Ellen Corby, Ralph Volkie.

A rather sloppy western-riverboat town saga has Sinatra and Martin as a pair of rival con men who compete for control of the Texas port of Galveston in 1870. The film starts off with brisk action as outlaw Bronson and his desperadoes attack a coach in which Sinatra and Martin are traveling, but they are beaten off by the sharpers. Sinatra is relieved since he is carrying $100,000, but Martin robs him of the money which he takes to Galveston and deposits in a bank run by obese Buono, who had been previously backing Sinatra in his goal to become the city's gambling czar. When Sinatra arrives he is attacked by Bronson but Martin wounds the outlaw who is in Buono's employ. Sinatra then rebuilds an old riverboat and opens it as a lavish casino over which the Sinatra and Martin gangs feud. Buono hopes the two mobs will destroy each other so his own mob, led by Bronson, will take over the riverboat. But this doesn't happen when the mobs of the two con men join forces and defeat Bronson's gang, and all the good-bad-guys live happily ever after with Sinatra and Martin cuddling their two sex queens, Ekberg and Andress. This film is your essential big budget hollow shell with no peas hidden anywhere. Sinatra and Martin merely grin and grunt their way through their sketchy characters, and Ekberg, whose pulchritudinous body fills the screen and engulfs Sinatra's persona, along with slinky Andress take up most of the film from the middle on as two lady sharpers. Bronson is only a snarling prop and Buono does a horrible imitation of Sidney Greenstreet. Director Aldrich has done much better but here his setup shots blatantly focus on the voluptuous Ekberg as she postures her enormous mammaries in any suggestive manner (i.e., leaning over Sinatra's face as she shaves him). Andress attempts to compete with Ekberg in the battle of the busts but loses out by a mile. The story is idiotic, the lensing is erratic, and Riddle's score is a hodge-podge of disconnected melody. Another Sinatra "clan" effort of self-indulgent and wasteful filmmaking but one which did not "con" an already savvy public which stayed away from the box office.

p&d, Robert Aldrich; w, Aldrich, Teddi Sherman; ph, Ernest Laszlo (Technicolor); m, Nelson Riddle; ed, Michael Luciano; art d, William Glasgow; set d, Raphael Bretton; cos, Norma Koch, Joyce Rogers, Charles James; spec eff, Sass Bedig; makeup, Robert Schiffer; stunts, John Indrisano.

Adventure   (PR:C MPAA:NR)

FOUR FOR THE MORGUE*½   (1962) 84m MPA bw

Stacy Harris (Lt. Victor Beaujac), Louis Sirgo (Sgt. John Conroy), Ginny Hostetler (Vivian Miller), Bill White, Clint Bolton, Nicholas Chetta, Leo Bruno, Ed Pyle, Wilson Bourg, Francis Forrest, Val Winter, Pearl Nichols, Jessie Davis, Eugene Sonfield, Roy Longmire, C. Warren Kennedy.

Episodic detective drama starring Harris and Sirgo as New Orleans sleuths who investigate a variety of crimes. Among the cases they solve are: the clearing of the name of a patrolman accused of murdering a thieving young socialite who had stolen a purse; the murder of a bank robber whose body is found in a swamp; the capture of a murderous hitchhiker; and the murder of a cab driver's wife and small dog.

p, Brandon Chase; d, John Sledge; w, Frank Phares; ph, Willis Winford; m, Emil Ascher; ed, Edward Dutriel, Mel Wright.

Crime   (PR:C MPAA:NR)

FOUR FRIENDS***½   (1981) 114m Filmways Pictures c
(GB: GEORGIA'S FRIENDS)

Craig Wasson (Danilo Prozor), Jodi Thelen (Georgia Miles), Jim Metzler (Tom Donaldson), Michael Huddleston (David Levine), Reed Birney (Louie Carnahan), Julia Murray (Adrienne Carnahan), David Graf (Gergley), Zaid Farid (Rudy), Miklos Simon (Mr. Prozor), Elizabeth Lawrence (Mrs. Prozor), Beatrice Fredman (Mrs. Zoldos), James Leo Herlihy (Mr. Carnahan), Lois Smith (Mrs. Carnahan).

A charming, heartfelt, and at times insightful look at a group of four friends who form strong bonds while in high school in the early 1960s and then desperately cling to that love during the turbulent counter-culture movement and social upheavals that marked the end of the decade. Unfortunately, FOUR FRIENDS is so ambitious, and attempts to cover so much ground, that at times the film becomes frustratingly muddled and some of the characters, who looked so promising in the first half hour, tend to get lost in the shuffle. The film's focal point is Wasson, the son of a Yugoslavian immigrant. Simon, the father, has brought his family to East Chicago and becomes a steel worker. Simon has trouble understanding his son, and feels that Wasson's refusal to follow in his footsteps is a condemnation of his own lifestyle. Wasson seeks refuge from this tension in his best friends. Metzler is the good looking jock, Huddleston the overweight momma's boy and, of course, Thelen, the beautiful and vivacious free-spirit who loves them all, but gives the edge to Wasson. Wasson, however, is absolutely terrified of Thelen's open attitudes toward her sexuality and shyly turns down her offer of her virginity. Frustrated, Thelen gives herself to Metzler instead, on the eve of their graduation from high school. At the end of the summer, the gang goes their separate ways. Wasson goes off to college, Metzler to Vietnam, and Thelen, who is carrying Metzler's child, marries Huddleston who inherits his father's mortuary business, though she still loves Wasson. From here the film becomes a series of vignettes that are supposed to dramatize nearly every aspect of life in the late 1960s. Wasson becomes engaged to a young woman from incredibly wealthy parentage, but on the day of their wedding she is shot and killed by her own father, who had been having incestuous relations with her for years. Thelen bumps into Wasson in an increasingly unlikely series of coincidences, and in the end all the friends are reunited for a reaffirmation of their love for each other. Though the film runs out of gas toward the end, it is filmed with an obvious love for the characters and is filled with outstanding performances from Wasson (an underrated actor), Thelen (who saves the film), and Simon (a Chicago-area actor whose final father-son scene is one of the highlights of the movie). Well worth seeing.

p, Arthur Penn, Gene Lasko; d, Penn; w, Steven Tesich; ph, Ghislain Cloquet (Technicolor); m, Elizabeth Swados; ed, Barry Malkin, Marc Laub; prod d, David Chapman; set d, Robert Drumheller; cos, Patricia Norris; ch, Julie Arenal.

Drama **Cas.** **(PR:O MPAA:R)**

FOUR FRIGHTENED PEOPLE*** (1934) 78m DeMille/PAR bw

Claudette Colbert *(Judy Cavendish)*, Herbert Marshall *(Arnold Ainger)*, Mary Boland *(Mrs. Mardick)*, William Gargan *(Stewart Corder)*, Leo Carrillo *(Montague)*, Nella Walker *(Mrs. Ainger)*, Tetsu Komai *(Native Chief)*, Chris Pin Martin *(Native Boatman)*, Joe De La Cruz *(Native)*, Minoru Nisheda, Toru Shimada, E.R. Jinedas, Delmar Costello *(Sakais)*, Ethel Griffies *(Mrs. Ainger's Mother)*.

Moviemaking to DeMille was either epic or, at least, extravagant, and in the case of FOUR FRIGHTENED PEOPLE, one of the director's rare contemporary films, the focus was on the latter. Panic ensues on board a Dutch coastal steamer when passengers learn that bubonic plague has broken out. Four of the passengers escape the doomed ship by stealing a lifeboat and heading for land. They include: Colbert, a prim and proper, thickly bespectacled geography teacher from Chicago; Marshall, a rubber chemist tired of his life and his henpecking wife; Boland, the wife of a British official; and Gargan, a brawling, adventure-seeking newsman a la Richard Harding Davis. Upon reaching shore the foursome meet a half-caste, Carrillo, who prides himself on his drops of Caucasion blood, thinking this racial distinction makes him immune to the jungle terrors, especially vicious native tribes who fear white men. The four are led by Carrillo through wild jungles and face innumerable perils in their attempt to reach the Malayan mainland. Carrillo's fate is particularly horrible at the hands of a bloodlusting tribe of pygmies who don't care whether he's got white blood or not. DeMille indulged himself with this bizarre film and his conduct throughout the production was as bizarre as the story he was telling. After reading the novel by British film critic Robertson, he decided to make the film in the Hawaiian islands. DeMille particularly relished the idea of showing civilized individuals having their sophistication stripped from them in primitive wilds, which left them wandering about in terror from jungle jeopardies, living hand-to-mouth, wearing animal skins, their bodies covered with filth. The director sailed for Honolulu in fall, 1933, to map out the film where he supervised pre-production from his lavish suite in the Royal Hawaiian Hotel. When he received a wire that his leading lady, Colbert, had suffered an appendicitis attack just before she was to set sail to Hawaii, DeMille frantically attempted to replace her, wiring urgent cables to Gloria Swanson and Elissa Landi, offering them Colbert's role. Both stars wired back that they were unable to take on the part due to on-going commitments. DeMille desperately began interviewing hundreds of local white actresses and was on the verge of hiring an unknown when Colbert wired that she would reach Hawaii in a week, recuperating on board the ship taking her there. The director made exhausting tours of many islands and finally selected the biggest, Hawaii, as his central on-location site. As usual, DeMille spent lavishly from Paramount's coffers, ordering 50,000 tons of sawdust spread over the crusty lava beds along the gutted slopes of Mauna Loa, a supposedly extinct volcano. Up those slopes 65 tractors dragged light generators, sound and camera equipment, as well as supplies and tents for the cast members who were soon to undergo the most rigorous work of their careers. DeMille was merciless with his actors, insisting they perform their own stunts. They trekked and staggered and crawled through jungles so dense that they had to be whittled away by knives in spots. They waded through swamps and clomped through lakes of mud while insects covered them and snakes slithered between their legs. When they complained of the hazards DeMille laughed at them. One scene called for the actors to wade ashore in waters that were reportedly full of sharks. The director sneered at the challenge and, before his frightened cast, stripped to the waist and dove into the water from an offshore barge, swimming ashore and then back. Standing triumphant and dripping again on the barge, DeMille snorted, "Now who's afraid of sharks?" Piped Colbert: "I am." Laughed the indefatigable director, "You have nothing to fear. Sharks don't like dark meat, and you have a marvelous tan." Colbert replied, "Yes, but suppose one of those sharks is color blind?" Marshall had a particularly hard time struggling through the swamps because of the wooden leg he pegged around on, the result of losing a limb during WW I, but DeMille ignored this noble actor's plight. Wisecracking Boland, however, made light of the hardships and even Marshall's artificial limb. At one point while they were stumbling through the thick Hawaiian jungle, Boland turned to Marshall struggling behind her and quipped, "Tell me, Bart, do you think the old-fashioned waltz is coming back?" The entire cast and crew suffered incredible hardships, coming down with jungle fever, jaundice, dysentery, intestinal influenza and, because of the thick humidity, headaches so intense that members keeled over from the pain. At night they lay immobile and agony-racked in their skimpy tents with only Colbert's windup Victrola, upon which she played her favorite tunes, to cheer them up. Everywhere spiders the size of saucers scurried over bedding and food, blood-sucking mosquitoes attacked, scorpions, centipedes, and reptiles of every known origin crawled over their bodies and into their clothes. Colbert grew so ill that she had to be lowered from a jungle mountaintop in a rickety cable chair that almost broke, and taken to a hospital to recuperate from the ordeal. The only person totally unaffected by the jungle elements and creatures was the tireless DeMille who considered himself immune to any hazard. When all were prostrate after a 16-hour shooting day, the director would sit in his tent while a single hurricane lamp flickered in front of him and study the next day's location sites on maps and his impossible camera setups. At dawn DeMille would emerge stark naked from his tent, ordering one of his aides to blow a bugle loudly to awaken cast and crew, then he would run madly into the jungle, daring the poisonous reptiles lurking there to bite him to death, and dashing back into the clearing and diving into a bug-infested stream to paddle frantically about for 30 minutes before returning to his tent to get dressed. Though a contemporary story, DeMille still had to get his leading lady naked into a tub or a body of water of some kind. Here, DeMille found the answer to bathing Colbert in the middle of the jungle when he spotted a waterfall. Since the natural falling of the water was not to his liking, DeMille had dozens of laborers place huge boulders at the top to narrow the stream so that the water fell like a bride's veil. Behind this flow of water Colbert took her shower naked, a handy chimpanzee stealing her clothes so that her curvacious body was partly visible as she flitted about looking for some large leafs to cover her form; she and her fellow travelers wind up discarding all their clothes, eaten away by jungle rot, and donning leopard and tiger skins, to make them all the more primitive. FOUR FRIGHTENED PEOPLE, for all of its exotic flavor and bizarre events, failed to attract public interest and the production lost money. Paramount chief Adolph Zukor took DeMille aside and told the flamboyant director, "Better do another historical epic, Cecil, with plenty of sex." DeMille was way ahead of him, already making plans to produce the opulent CLEOPATRA, which would also star his then favorite leading lady, Colbert, and this time her bath would be much more luxurious.

p&d, Cecil B. DeMille; w, Bartlett Cormack, Lenore J. Coffee (based on the novel by E. Arnot Robertson); ph, Karl Struss; m, Karl Hajos, Milton Roder, H. Rohenheld, John Leipold; ed, Anne Bauchens.

Adventure **(PR:C MPAA:NR)**

FOUR GIRLS IN TOWN* (1956) 85m UNIV c

George Nader *(Mike Snowden)*, Julie Adams *(Kathy Conway)*, Marianne Cook *(Ina Schiller)*, Elsa Martinelli *(Maria Antonelli)*, Gia Scala *(Vicki Dauray)*, Sydney Chaplin *(Johnny Pryor)*, Rock Hudson *(Guest)*, Grant Williams *(Spencer Farrington, Jr.)*, John Gavin *(Tom Grant)*, Herbert Anderson *(Ted Larabee)*, Hy Averback *(Bob Trapp)*, Ainslie Pryor *(James Manning)*, Judson Pratt *(William Purdy)*, James Bell *(Walter Conway)*, Mabel Albertson *(Mrs. Conway)*, Dave Barry *(Vince)*, Maurice Marsac *(Henri)*, Helene Stanton *(Rita Holloway)*, Irene Corlett *(Mildred Purdy)*, Eugene Mazzola *(Paul)*, Phil Harvey *(Assistant Director)*, Cynthia Patrick *(Girl)*, Charles Tannen *(Hotel Manager)*, Renata Vanni *(Rosa)*, Robert Boon *(Karl Wagner)*, Jack Mather *(Gaffer)*, Franco Corsaro *(Count)*, John Bryant *(Young Man)*, Helen Andrews *(Wife at Pool)*, Rodney Bell *(Husband at Pool)*, Stephen Ellis *(Reporter)*, Frank Chase *(Larry Arnold)*, Voltaire Perkins *(Business Man)*, Clarence Straight *(Newsreel Man)*, Robert Hoy *(Indian)*, Rex May *(Man Guest)*, Shirley de Burgh, Giselle D'Arc *(French Girls)*, Marie Kassova *(Italian Girl)*, Gisele Verlaine *(German Girl)*, Hubie Kerns *(Casting Man)*, George Calliga *(Frenchman)*, Evelyn Ford, Kitty Muldoon *(American Girls)*, Georg Nardelli.

FOUR GIRLS IN TOWN, tells the story of a talent hunt for a part in a movie vacated by Stanton. It was also an excuse to showcase the talents of some of Universal's contracted talent. The aspiring hopefuls are German girl, Cook, Italian girls, Martinelli and Scala, and American girl, Adams. It turns out that none of them get the part, since Stanton changes her mind and does the film. Don't call us.

p, Aaron Rosenberg; d&w, Jack Sher; ph, Irving Glassberg (CinemaScope, Technicolor); md, Joseph Gershenson; ed, Frederick Y. Smith; art d, Alexander Golitzen, Ted Haworth; cos, Rosemary Odell; spec eff, Clifford Stine; m/l, "Rhapsody For Four Girls," by Alex North.

Drama **(PR:A MPAA:NR)**

FOUR GIRLS IN WHITE** (1939) 72m MGM bw

Florence Rice *(Norma Page)*, Una Merkel *(Gertie Robbins)*, Ann Rutherford *(Patricia Page)*, Mary Howard *(Mary Forbes)*, Alan Marshal *(Dr. Stephen Melford)*, Kent Taylor *(Robert Maitland)*, Buddy Ebsen *(Express)*, Jessie Ralph *(Miss Tobias)*, Sara Haden *(Miss Bennett)*, Phillip Terry *(Dr. Sidney)*, Tom Neal *(Dr. Phillips)*.

Hospital drama about four nurses going through a three-year training course. Nurse Rice decides that nursing is her ticket to a rich husband, and shortly after enrolling, selects brilliant young doctor Marshal as her beau. For a brief change of pace, Rice shifts her affections to rich playboy Taylor, but he's in love with Rutherford. Rice and fellow nurses have their learning put to the test, as they help out with rescue work at a railroad disaster. Rice and Marshal get married at the end. Story was co-scripted by Bucknall, head of the studio's research departments. Ars Gratia Artis.

p, Nat Levine; d, S. Sylvan Simon; w, Dorothy Yost (original by Nathalie Bucknall, Endre Bohem); ph, Leonard Smith; ed, George Boemler; art d, Cedric Gibbons.

Drama **(PR:A MPAA:NR)**

FOUR GUNS TO THE BORDER** (1954) 82m UNIV c

Rory Calhoun *(Ray Cully)*, Colleen Miller *(Lolly Bhumer)*, George Nader *(Bronco)*, Walter Brennan *(Simon Bhumer)*, Nina Foch *(Maggie Flannery)*, John McIntire *(Dutch)*, Charles Drake *(Sheriff Jim Flannery)*, Jay Silverheels *(Yaqui)*, Nestor Paiva *(Greasy)*, Mary Field *(Mrs. Pritchard)*, Robert Hoy *(Smitty)*, Robert Herron *(Evans)*, Reg Parton *(Cashier)*, Donald Kerr *(Town Loafer)*.

An okay action western starring Calhoun, the heavy you hate to love. He is the leader of a group of four cowpokes (McIntire, Nader, and Silverheels are the other three) down on their luck. They successfully rob a bank, and head for the border, but stop to save crusty old Brennan, and sexy Miller from Apaches. Their good deed later leads to the death of McIntire, Nader, and Silverheels, while Calhoun winds up in jail, where he serves his time to pay his debt to society so he may be worthy of Miller. A fairly racy love scene between Calhoun and Miller probably did not come from Louis L'Amour, who wrote the story the film is based on.

p, William Alland; d, Richard Carlson; w, George Van Marter, Franklin Coen (based on story by Louis L'Amour); ph, Russell Metty (Technicolor), ed, Frank Gross.

Western **(PR:A MPAA:NR)**

FOUR HORSEMEN OF THE APOCALYPSE, THE** (1962) 153m Blaustein-Montezuma/MGM c

Glenn Ford *(Julio Desnoyers)*, Ingrid Thulin *(Marquerite Laurier)*, Charles Boyer *(Marcelo Desnoyers)*, Lee J. Cobb *(Julio Madariaga)*, Paul Henreid *(Etienne Laurier)*, Paul Lukas *(Karl Von Hartrott)*, Yvette Mimieux *(Chi-Chi Desnoyers)*, Karl Boehm *(Heinrich Von Hartrott)*, Harriet MacGibbon *(Dona Luisa Desnoyers)*, Kathryn Givney *(Elena Von Hartrott)*, Marcel Hillaire *(Armand Dibier)*, George

Dolenz *(Gen. Von Kleig)*, Stephen Bekassy *(Col. Kleinsdorf)*, Nestor Paiva *(Miguel)*, Albert Remy *(Francois)*, Karlheinz Bohm *(Heinrich Von Hartrott)*, Richard Franchot *(Franz Von Hartrott)*, Brian Avery *(Gustav Von Hartrott)*.

Patriarch Cobb, who has built a vast estate in the Argentine Pampas as a refuge against the ravages of war, holds a family reunion. When he discovers that Boehm, his German-born nephew, and his father, Lukas, have become Nazis, he rages against them, predicting that they will bring down upon the world the Four Horsemen of the Apocalypse—Conquest, Pestilence, War, and Death. Cobb dies in an apoplectic state in the arms of his favorite nephew, playboy Ford and the family drifts back to Europe. Ford and his spineless father, Boyer, enjoy the fruits of wealth while Ford's sister Mimieux joins activists opposing Nazi organizers. Ford meets the idealist Henreid and his wife, Thulin, and when the Nazis march triumphant into Paris, Henreid is imprisoned for partisan activities. Thulin becomes Ford's mistress and Mimieux, now a member of the underground, is captured and killed by the Nazis, despite Ford's pleas to his relatives Lukas and Boehm to spare her. Disgusted with stealing Henreid's wife and his wasteful life, Ford joins the underground while Thulin goes to her husband who has just been released from a concentration camp, deathly ill. Ford agrees to pinpoint Nazi headquarters in Normandy for British bombers and gains access to Boehm's offices; they toast each other and their lost family as the bombs destroy them. This overlong remake of the silent 1921 classic starring Rudolph Valentino in his first role, is ponderous and disjointed with none of the parts fully developed. Thulin is wholly unappealing and her accent was so thick that Angela Lansbury's voice was used to dub her lines. Despite some clever montage scenes by Santillo, there is little artistry here, although Previn's score is soaring and emotion-packed. Austrian actor Boehm, in his U.S. debut, is above average but few of the other cast members register anything but banal lines and bored looks. Most of the blame can be put at director Minnelli's door, although he later claimed that he was rushed through the production by MGM bosses. The studio lost $6 million on this overblown clunker and proved once again that remaking classics is a chancy and very expensive proposition.

d, Vincente Minnelli; w, Robert Ardrey, John Gay (based on the novel by Vicente Blasco Ibanez); ph, Milton Krasner (CinemaScope, Metrocolor); m, Andre Previn; ed, Adrienne Fazan, Ben Lewis; art d, George W. Davis, Urie McCleary, Elliot Scott; set d, Henry Grace, Keogh Gleason; cos, Rene Hubert, Walter Plunkett, Orry-Kelly; spec eff, A. Arnold Gillespie, Lee LeBlanc, Robert R. Hoag; ch, Alex Romero; makeup, Charles Parker.

Adventure/War Drama Cas. (PR:A MPAA:NR)

FOUR HOURS TO KILL** (1935) 71m PAR bw

Richard Barthelmess *(Tony)*, Joe Morrison *(Eddie)*, Gertrude Michael *(Sylvia)*, Helen Mack *(Helen)*, Dorothy Tree *(Mae Danish)*, Roscoe Karns *(Johnson)*, Ray Milland *(Carl)*, Noel Madison *(Anderson)*, Lois Kent *(Little Girl)*, Charles C. Wilson *(Taft)*, Henry Travers *(Mac Mason)*, Paul Harvey *(Capt. Seavers)*, Christian Rub *(Pa Herman)*, Greta Meyer *(Ma)*, Bruce Mitchell *(Healy)*, Olive Tell *(Mrs. Madison)*, John Huettner *(Stanley)*, Alfred Delcambre *(Donald)*, Sam Ash *(Harris)*, Frank Losee, Jr. *(Asst. House Manager)*, Robert Kent *(George Nelson)*, Paul Gerrits *(Phone Repairman)*, Hugh Enfield [Craig Reynolds] *(Frank)*, John Howard *(Asst. Repairman)*, Gertrude Astor *(Little Girl's Mother)*, Lee Kohlmar, Bodil Rosing, Douglas Blackley, John Cox, Jr.

Another in the seemingly endless series of variations on the GRAND HOTEL theme, FOUR HOURS TO KILL follows the lives of a myriad of characters whose paths cross one evening at a fictitious Manhattan theater. The main action follows convicted murderer Barthelmess (he didn't do it, of course) as he plots his escape from copper Wilson so that he can get revenge on the man who set him up to take the fall (he is about to be hanged). Intercut with this are scenes involving the inevitable troubled lovers Morrison and Mack (he's being blackmailed by Tree), and the unfaithful wife and her suave gigolo, Milland. Most of the action takes place in the theater during a performance, and the climax sees Barthelmess freeing himself from Wilson's handcuffs and racing into the playhouse to enact his plot to catch the man who *should* hang for the crimes.

p, Arthur Hornblow, Jr.; d, Mitchell Leisen; w, Norman Krasna (from his play, "Small Miracle"); ph, Theodor Sparkhul; ed, John D. Harrison.

Drama (PR:A MPAA:NR)

FOUR HUNDRED BLOWS, THE***** (1959) 93m SEDIF, Les Films du Carosse/JANUS bw
(LES QUATRES CENTS COUPS)

Jean-Pierre Leaud *(Antoine Doinel)*, Claire Maurier *(Mme. Doinel)*, Albert Remy *(Mon. Doinel)*, Guy Decomble *(Teacher)*, Patrick Auffay *(Rene Bigey)*, Georges Flamant *(Mon. Bigey)*, Yvonne Claudie *(Mme. Bigey)*, Robert Beauvais *(Director of the School)*, Claude Mansard *(Examining Magistrate)*, Jacques Monod *(Commissioner)*, Henri Virlojeux *(Nightwatchman)*, Jeanne Moreau *(Woman with Dog)*, Jean-Claude Brialy *(Man in Street)*, Jacques Demy *(Policeman)*.

THE FOUR HUNDRED BLOWS was François Truffaut's first major work and the start of a cycle that included LOVE AT TWENTY, STOLEN KISSES, BED AND BOARD, and LOVE ON THE RUN, all starring the same actor, Jean-Pierre Leaud in a continuing tale stretching across 20 years that reflected much of Truffaut's own life. In this, Leaud is the overlooked son of Claire Maurier who seems to have time for everything except the child's welfare. Albert Remy is the nominal father but not physically. Despite this, he raises the boy as his own son. Leaud is a terrible student at school and hates his teacher, Decomble, who is referred to by the students as "little sheet." Leaud and his pal, Auffay, take a day off from school and visit an amusement park and, later, Leaud sees his mother hugging her lover on the street. (Truffaut himself appears briefly in the amusement park sequence as one of the adults on the rotor ride.) The next day, Leaud must answer Decomble's questions about the unexplained absence and he is stuck and finally says that he was missing the previous day because his mother died. When Maurier and Remy appear at the school, the lie is discovered and Leaud

runs away and spends the night outside his home. Eventually, Maurier softens and accepts the boy back. The teacher accuses Leaud of plagiarizing Balzac and the boy decides to quit school and leave home. Auffay secretes Leaud in his house for a while, then discovers that life outside the home requires money. He steals a typewriter from his father's office but then is unable to pawn it. He attempts to return it by night and is apprehended by Virlojeux, the watchman. Leaud is taken to police headquarters where Remy tells the chief, Monod, that there is no way he and his wife can handle such an incorrigible boy. The 12-year-old is then tossed into prison with a horde of hardened criminals and hookers. Next, he is sent to an observation center for juvenile delinquents and examined by a psychiatrist. He bares his soul and the family history to the woman. Maurier visits him while he is incarcerated and announces that she still loves him but that Remy has washed his hands. While playing soccer, Leaud escapes from the facility and runs to a beach at Normandy, to the sea, which has always represented freedom to him. In one of the most famous shots in movie history, the confused young man stops at the edge of the Atlantic and turns to the camera, his face reflecting all the confusion of youth and the battering he had received at society's hands and the film ends. THE FOUR HUNDRED BLOWS—in French, idiomatic for raising hell in protest—is a film about injustice, about pain, about all the coincidences in a young boy's life that add up and cause him to be the person he is. And yet, none of it is presented with comment. It's a naturalistic look with virtually no editorializing. The child is average, not good, not bad, just a boy who has been caught up in a maelstrom, not of his own doing. There are no villains or heroes, just the situations that cause the behavior and we wonder how *we* might have acted under the same circumstances. Several scenes are particularly memorable. The camera remains on Leaud's face the entire time he's interrogated by the psychiatrist as he quietly details the horror of his life in an almost off-handed fashion. Decomble takes the boys out on a run through the streets and, one by one, the boys drop off, leaving the teacher talking to himself. THE FOUR HUNDRED BLOWS was originally conceived as a 20-minute film entitled "Antoine Runs Away" which was to appear in a compilation film that included an earlier sketch by Truffaut called "The Mischief Makers." There were to be three other short pictures as well, but all were shelved when Truffaut decided to expand Antoine's 20 minutes. It was shot for peanuts in practical locations on a brief schedule that began November 10, 1958, and concluded January 5, 1959. Truffaut took "Best Director" at Cannes in 1959, the film won "Best Foreign Film" from the New York film critics and the screenplay received an Oscar nomination. In the years since, THE FOUR HUNDRED BLOWS continues to gather accolades and even though Truffaut went on to make many more films in his all-too-brief career, this remained his favorite and the favorite of anyone who ever saw it. Look hard for Jeanne Moreau in a tiny role as the woman with a dog. Leaud stayed with Truffaut through DAY FOR NIGHT, one of the best movies ever made about movies. Phillipe De Broca served as one of the four assistant directors on the film.

p&d, François Truffaut; w, Truffaut, Marcel Moussy (story by Truffaut); ph, Henri Decae; m, Jean Constantin; ed, Marie-Josephe Yoyotte; art d, Bernard Evein; English subtitles, Herman G. Weinberg.

Drama (PR:A-C MPAA:NR)

FOUR IN A JEEP** (1951, Switz.) 100m Praesens Film Zurich bw

Viveca Lindfors *(Franziska Idinger)*, Ralph Meeker *(Sgt. William Long)*, Joseph Yadin *(Sgt. Vassily Voroschenko)*, Michael Medwin *(Sgt. Harry Stuart)*, Dinan *(Sgt. Marcel Pasture)*, Paulette Dubost *(Madame Pasture)*, Hans Putz *(Karl Idinger)*, Eduard Loibner *(Hackl)*, Harry Hess *(Hammond)*, Geraldine Katt *(Steffi)*.

A Swiss-made post-WW II saga detailing the efforts of a multi-national occupation force to keep the peace in Austria. We follow four M.P.'s (Meeker is the American, Medwin, a Brit, Dinan is French, and Yadin a Russian) as their duty to their various countries, and each other, often clouds easy decision-making. Lindfors plays an Austrian girl whose husband, Putz, has escaped from a Russian prison camp. Yadin is afraid he'll be shot if he doesn't turn the fugitive in, despite Meeker's angry attempts to convince him otherwise. The film's action hinges on this one (thin) conflict, and it dawdles to the point of disinterest while getting to the resolution.

p, Lazar Wechsler; d, Leopold Lindtberg; w, Richard Schweizer; ph, Emil Berna; m, Hermann Haller; ed, Robert Blum; sets, Werner Schlieting.

Drama (PR:A MPAA:NR)

FOUR IN THE MORNING** (1965, Brit.) 94m West One Film Producers bw

Ann Lynn *(Girl)*, Brian Phelan *(Boy)*, Judi Dench *(Wife)*, Norman Rodway *(Husband)*, Joe Melia *(Friend)*.

Arty British film that tries to tell a simple tale of two couples whose lives are in trouble due to a lack of emotion and action. The first episode has a young man picking up his girl friend, a dancer, at the nightclub where she works and taking her to the Thames where they play cat-and-mouse with each other's feelings. The second episode has a lonely married woman left to contend with a new-born while her husband is off partying with a male buddy. The two episodes are tied together by a drowning. The filmmakers seem to be making a plea for more emotion in our lives, but their film is curiously lifeless, with camera moves that are too flashy for their own good.

p, John Morris; d&w, Anthony Simmons; ph, Larry Pizer; ed, Fergus McDonnell.

Drama (PR:C MPAA:NR)

FOUR JACKS AND A JILL**½ (1941) 67m RKO bw

Ray Bolger *(Nifty)*, Anne Shirley *(Nine)*, June Havoc *(Opal)*, Desi Arnaz *(Steve)*, Jack Durant *(The Noodle)*, Eddie Foy, Jr. *(Happy)*, Fritz Feld *(Mr. Hoople)*, Henry Daniell *(Bobo)*, Jack Briggs *(Nat)*, William Blees *(Eddie)*, Robert Smith *(Joe)*, Fortunio Bonanova *(Mike)*, Norman Mayes *(Bootblack)*, Mary Gordon *(Landlady)*,

Amarilla Morris *(Girl/Door Gag)*, Leo White *(Perfumer)*, Frank Martinelli *(Ditchdigger)*, Rosemary Coleman *(Salesgirl)*, Jane Woodworth *(Bit)*, Armand "Curley" Wright *(Hot Dog Vendor)*, Florence Lake *(Counter Girl)*, Mantan Moreland *(Attendant)*, Charles Arnt, Ted O'Shea, Grady Sutton *(Drunks)*, Eddie Dunn, Frank Mills *(Cops)*, Raphael Storm *(Headwaiter)*, Eddie Hart *(Taxi Driver)*, Constantine Romanoff, Bob Perry (Gorillas), Nina Waynler *(Katherine)*, Max Luckey *(Otto)*, Roy Crane *(Keva)*, Jack Carr *(Big Guy)*, Jack Gardner *(Usher)*, Joe Bernard *(Jailer)*, Patti Lacey *(Jitterbug Specialty)*.

The third retread of this material (STREET GIRL [1929]; THAT GIRL FROM PARIS [1937]) sees nightclub band members Foy, Jr., Briggs, Bolger, and Blees left in a jam when their female singer, Havoc, quits the gig because her threatening gangster admirer Durant wants her to devote more time to him. Panic sets in and the musicians search the city for a replacement. Bolger discovers Shirley, a down-and-out waif, and drafts her to help the cause. She poses as an important overseas singer and soon cabbie Arnaz gets into the act by masquerading as a Balkan king. The usual set of goofy and contrived complications ensues, leaving this a failed effort. The song titles reflect the level of humor: "I'm In Good Shape for the Shape I'm In"; "You Go Your Way and I'll Go Crazy"; "I Haven't a Thing to Wear"; "Wherever You Are"; "Boogie Woogie Conga" (Mort Greene, Harry Revel).

p, John Twist; d, Jack Hively; w, Twist (story by Monte Brice, suggested by "The Viennese Charmer," by W. Carey Wonderly); ph, Russell Metty; ed, George Hively; spec eff, Vernon L. Walker.

Musical **(PR:A MPAA:NR)**

FOUR JILLS IN A JEEP½** (1944) 89m FOX bw

Kay Francis *(Herself)*, Carole Landis *(Herself)*, Martha Raye *(Herself)*, Mitzi Mayfair *(Herself)*, Jimmy Dorsey and His Band *(Themselves)*, John Harvey *(Ted Warren)*, Phil Silvers *(Eddie)*, Dick Haymes *(Lt. Dick Ryan)*, Alice Faye, Betty Grable, Carmen Miranda *(Guest Stars)*, George Jessel *(Master of Ceremonies)*, Glenn Langan *(Capt. Stewart)*, Lester Matthews *(Capt. Lloyd)*, Miles Mander *(Col. Hartley)*, Frank Wilcox *(Officer)*, Paul Harvey *(General)*, Mary Servoss *(Nurse Captain)*, Dave Willock, Martin Black, B.S. Pully, Mike Kilian, Buddy Yarus, Gordon Wynne *(Soldiers)*, Alex Harford *(Priest)*, Renee Carson *(French Maid)*, Mel Schubert, Kirk Alyn *(Pilots)*, Alex Pollard *(Butler)*, Winifred Harris *(Lady Carlton-Smith)*, Edith Evanson *(Swedish Maid)*, Crauford Kent *(British Officer)*, Frances Morris *(Surgical Nurse)*, James Flavin *(M.P.)*, Bernie Sell, Eddie Acuff *(Sentries)*, Mary Field *(Maid)*, Jimmy Martin *(Aide)*, Lester Dorr *(Soldier)*, Ralph Byrd *(Sergeant)*.

Francis, Landis, Raye and Mayfair went on a USO tour in 1943 and had such an interesting time that the studio decided to make a movie about it. The tour had to have been more interesting than this picture which is the story of Kay Francis wanting to bring some light into the lives of the boys overseas so she constructs a USO unit consisting of herself and the aforementioned trio. The tour takes them into a posh London townhouse, a wet Quonset hut and into the desiccated North African desert. In real life, Landis married an airman she met overseas and that romance is chronicled in the film. It's loaded with guest stars and songs from other Fox movies, some of which include: Grable singing "Cuddle up a Little Closer" (Karl Hoschna and Otto Harbach); Faye with "You'll Never Know" (Mack Gordon and Harry Warren), Miranda with "I'Yi, Yi, Yi, Yi (I Like You Very Much)" (Gordon and Warren), and Raye with "Mr. Paganini" (Sam Coslow). Other songs; "Crazy Me," "You Send Me," "How Blue the Night," "How Many Times Do I Have to Tell You?" (Harold Adamson and Jimmy McHugh), the last three sung by Haymes, making his first screen appearance, "No Love, No Nothing" (Leo Robin and Harry Warren), George M. Cohan's "Over There," and Brig. Genl. Edmund L. Gruber's "When the Caissons Go Rolling Along." Critics didn't like the film very much but it has some merit today as a look at the USO tour groups. There was one song that was cut because it was too explicit for the Hays Office. It was called "Snafu," and the girls kept asking what that word meant. It means "Situation Normal, All Fouled Up," or words to that effect.

p, Irving Starr; d, William A. Seiter; w, Robert Ellis, Helen Logan, Snag Werris (from a story by Froma Sand and Fred Niblo, Jr., suggested by the experiences of Landis, Mayfair, Raye, and Francis); ph, Peverell Marley; md, Emil Newman, Charles Henderson; ed, Ray Curtiss; art d, James Basevi, Albert Hogsett; set d, Thomas Little, Al Orenbach; cos, Yvonne Wood; spec eff, Fred Sersen; ch, Don Loper.

Musical/Comedy **(PR:A MPAA:NR)**

FOUR JUST MEN, THE (SEE: SECRET FOUR, THE, 1939, Brit.)

FOUR KINDS OF LOVE (SEE: BAMBOLE!, 1965, Ital.)

FOUR MASKED MEN** (1934, Brit.) 81m Real Art/UNIV bw

John Stuart *(Trevor Phillips)*, Judy Kelly *(Patricia Brent)*, Miles Mander *(Rodney Fraser)*, Richard Cooper *(Lord Richard Clyne)*, Athole Stewart *(Col. St. John Clive)*, Sebastian Shaw *(Arthur Phillips)*, Victor Stanley *(Potter)*.

Attorney Stuart vows to bring to justice the gang of robbers who shot his brother in a holdup. With the help of a friend he pretends to be a robber himself and infiltrates the gang. Uninspired B movie by the top director of British silents offers nothing new.

p, Julius Hagen; d, George Pearson; w, H. Fowler Mear, Cyril Campion (based on the play "The Masqueraders" by Campion); ph, Sidney Blythe.

Crime **(PR:A MPAA:NR)**

FOUR MEN AND A PRAYER½** (1938) 85m FOX bw

Loretta Young *(Lynn Cherrington)*, Richard Greene *(Geoff Leigh)*, George Sanders *(Wyatt Leigh)*, David Niven *(Christopher Leigh)*, William Henry *(Rodney Leigh)*, C. Aubrey Smith *(Col. Loring Leigh)*, J. Edward Bromberg *(Gen. Torres)*, Alan Hale *(Furnoy)*, John Carradine *(Gen. Adolfo Arturo Sebastian)*, Reginald Denny *(Douglas Loveland)*, Berton Churchill *(Martin Cherrington)*, Claude King *(Gen. Bryce)*, John Sutton *(Capt. Drake)*, Barry Fitzgerald *(Mulcahy)*, Cecil Cunningham *(Piper)*, Frank Baker *(Defense Attorney)*, Frank Dawson *(Mullins)*, Lina Basquette *(Ah-Nee)*, William Stack *(Prosecuting Attorney)*, Harry Hayden *(Cherrington's Secretary)*, Winter Hall *(Judge)*, Will Stanton *(Cockney)*, John Spacey, C. Montague Shaw *(Lawyers)*, Lionel Pape *(Coroner)*, Brandon Hurst *(Jury Foreman)*, Eddie Abdo *(Sheik)*, Frank Lackteen, Noble Johnson *(Natives)*, Chris-Pin Martin *(Soldier)*, Selmer Jackson *(Yacht Captain)*, Barbara Denny, Ruth Clifford *(Telephone Operators)*, Helen Ericson *(Joan)*, George Regas, Francesco Moran *(Egyptian Policemen)*.

Greene, Sanders, Niven and Henry are the sons of cashiered officer C. Aubrey Smith who has been unjustly tossed out of the service and then murdered by criminal businessmen. John Ford directed this sprawling saga that treks from India to South America, London, Egypt and the USA as the young lads seek to uncover the truth about their revered father. What is never explained is how the family of a serviceman became rich enough to allow Niven to be a playboy, Sanders to become a barrister, and Henry to attend Oxford. There are many plots going simultaneously and the brothers use the transatlantic phone to communicate their progress. It turns out the old fella was done in by munitions makers but, by the time we discover that, the mystery has long since been forgotten. What is most unsatisfying is the distinct lack of Ford's usual camaraderie between men. Everyone is so off-handed and dispassionate that we can't get into feeling anything for them. The stiff upper lip was never stiffer. Barry Fitzgerald does a short bit in such an Irish accent that it's hard to discern what he's saying. Loretta Young provides the love interest with Richard Greene but that takes a back seat to the alleged mystery. Good production values.

p, Darryl F. Zanuck; d, John Ford; w, Richard Sherman, Sonya Levien, Walter Ferris (from the novel by David Garth); ph, Ernest Palmer; md, Louis Silvers; ed, Louis Loeffler; art d, Bernard Herzbrun, Rudolph Sternad; set d, Thomas Little; add'l mus, Ernst Toch.

Drama/Mystery **(PR:A MPAA:NR)**

FOUR MOTHERS½** (1941) 85m WB bw

Priscilla Lane *(Ann Lemp Dietz)*, Rosemary Lane *(Kay Lemp Forrest)*, Lola Lane *(Thea Lemp Crowley)*, Gale Page *(Emma Lemp Talbot)*, Claude Rains *(Adam Lemp)*, Jeffrey Lynn *(Felix Dietz)*, Eddie Albert *(Clint Forrest)*, May Robson *(Aunt Etta)*, Frank McHugh *(Ben Crowley)*, Dick Foran *(Ernest Talbot)*, Vera Lewis *(Mrs. Ridgefield)*.

The third—and probably least effective—installment in the Warner Brothers series that traced the loves of four sisters (the first two were FOUR DAUGHTERS and FOUR WIVES). Married life and financial difficulties make up the crux of this melodrama which sees three of the sisters now happy homemakers with babies and hubbies to care for. Trouble looms when poppa Rains brags a bit too much about the success of son-in-law McHugh in the real-estate biz, and the whole town sinks its individual nest-eggs into his Florida land deal. Unfortunately, the land sinks into the proverbial swamp, leaving Rains, McHugh and the townsfolk ruined. Of course the sons-in-law pitch in and make enough dough to pull the old man out of debt so that they can rejuvenate the town. By the climax everybody's happy and the fourth sister even begins to get morning sickness so that she doesn't feel left behind by her sisters.

d, William Keighley; w, Stephen Morehouse Avery (suggested by the novel, *Sister Act*, by Fannie Hurst); ph, Charles Rosher; ed, Ralph Dawson; m/l, "Moonlight And Tears," Jack Scholl, Heinz Roemheld.

Drama **(PR:A MPAA:NR)**

FOUR MUSKETEERS, THE*½** (1975) 108m FOX c
(AKA: THE REVENGE OF MILADY)

Michael York *(D'Artagnan)*, Oliver Reed *(Athos)*, Richard Chamberlain *(Aramis)*, Frank Finlay *(Porthos)*, Raquel Welch *(Mme. Constance Bonaciux)*, Christopher Lee *(Rochefort)*, Faye Dunaway *(Milady)*, Jean-Pierre Cassel *(Louis XIII)*, Geraldine Chaplin *(Queen Anne of Austria)*, Simon Ward *(Duke of Buckingham)*, Charlton Heston *(Cardinal Richelieu)*, Roy Kinnear *(Planchet)*, Nicole Calfan *(Maid Kitty)*.

A sequel to THE THREE MUSKETEERS, both pictures were originally supposed to have been one huge 3-½-hour epic. Then the producers decided to release them as two films—and law suits followed immediately. That aside, this sequel is somewhat better than the original. It's as though director Dick Lester rediscovered the comic style he showed in his earlier work, but didn't get it all together until he was half-way through the picture. This one is laden with slapstick and many tasteless gags and both of them together can't compare to several other versions of the famed Dumas story. The Musketeers, York, Finlay, Chamberlain, and Reed, foiled Dunaway's attempts to discredit Chaplin (the Queen) and now Dunaway plans to wreak revenge upon York and his cohorts, Welch and Ward. York is crazy for Welch (who never looked lovelier or played comedy with a better flair), but Dunaway seduces him and tries to administer a coup de grace. He escapes, but just barely. Dunaway tells Lee to kidnap Welch. She then travels to England where she lets herself be arrested. Once in prison, she convinces the religious fanatic jailer that Ward means to eliminate religion in England. The jailer helps her escape, then assassinates Ward with a dagger. York hears of Ward's death and the fact that his amour, Welch, is being kept in an abbey in Italy. The fortress is guarded by Lee and his men and the Musketeers ride to Welch's rescue. Once at the abbey, a splendid swordfight ensues between York and Lee and Lee is run through. York goes upstairs and finds Welch's body. She has been killed by the nefarious Dunaway. Dunaway is captured later and sentenced to beheading. It doesn't sound like a whole lot of laughs but it is, up until the final reel. Heston reprises his role as Cardinal Richelieu, wears a false nose, and affects a limp. It doesn't help his performance. Lee is excellent as the hateful Rochefort and Jean-Pierre Cassel almost steals the show with his portrayal of a moronic Louis XIII. The Musketeers are not glamorized in these versions and one gets the feeling that Lester and Fraser wanted to hew as close as entertainment permitted to the truth of the way it was in the 1620s. Consequently, many of the characters are portrayed as mercenaries, boors and slobs.

p, Alexander Salkind; d, Richard Lester; w, George MacDonald Fraser (from *The Three Musketeers* by Alexandre Dumas); ph, David Watkins (DeLuxe Color); m, Lalo Schifrin; ed, John Victor Smith; prod d, Brian Eatwell; add'l m, Michel Legrand.

Historical Comedy Drama   Cas.   (PR:A-C MPAA:PG)

FOUR NIGHTS OF A DREAMER*½   (1972, Fr.) 87m Victoria Films-
                                    Albina Films-Del Orso/New Yorker c

Isabelle Weingarten *(Marthe)*, Guillaume Des Forets *(Jacques)*, Maurice Monnoyer *(Lover)*.

Fascinating feature by master director Bresson adapts Dostoyevsky's story "White Night" and puts it in Paris in the modern age. Des Forets is a young artist, living a mostly fantasy life, who meets Weingarten on a bridge one night while she is contemplating suicide. They talk and arrange to meet there the next night. They tell of their lives, he of his painting and his fantasies, she of the man she loves and how he left, promising to meet on this bridge one year later. It was when it became apparent that he wasn't going to show that she thought to kill herself. Des Forets falls in love with the enigmatic woman, walking around Paris with a tape recorder against his heart which just plays him repeating her name. Four nights they meet on the bridge and talk, and on the last night the missing lover does arrive and she goes with him. Des Forets is left with his memories slowly changing into more fantasy. Bresson's spare, totally restrained style is much in evidence here, and he has seldom used it to such effect. An important film by one of the cinema's most important figures.

d&w, Robert Bresson (based on the story "White Nights" by Fyodor Dostoyevsky); ph, Pierre Lhomme (Eastmancolor).

Drama   (PR:O MPAA:NR)

FOUR POSTER, THE*   (1952) 103m COL bw

Rex Harrison *(John)*, Lilli Palmer *(Abby)*.

Charming, sentimental, and unique, THE FOUR POSTER is confined to the masterful acting talents of the husband and wife team of Harrison and Palmer from the moment he carries his bride across the threshold to the time of their deaths. In between they are seen through emotional highlights of their marriage: their children, their son's tragic WW II death, Harrison's flirtations and escapades, his rise and success as a writer, and her faithful support of his dreams. It is nevertheless sometimes stagey and claustrophobic as the master bedroom with its ever-present four poster dominates the scene as the symbol of their marriage. Bridging the episodic scenes are clever animations suggesting the trials and tribulations to come. Harrison and Palmer manage to sidestep boredom and predictability in brilliant performances. Worthwhile and enjoyable.

p, Stanley Kramer; d, Irving Reis; w, Allan Scott (based on the play by Jan de Hartog); ph, Hal Mohr; m, Dmitri Tiomkin; ed, Henry Batista; md, Tiomkin; prod d, Rudolph Sternad; art d, Carl Anderson; set d, William Kiernan, Louis Diage; animation, Paul Julian, Art Babbitt, Lon Keller.

Comedy/Drama   (PR:A MPAA:NR)

FOUR RODE OUT*   (1969, US/Span.) 98m Sagittarius/ADA c

Sue Lyon, Pernell Roberts, Julian Mateos, Leslie Nielsen, Maria Martin, James Daly.

Brutal western about a Mexican outlaw who is being pursued by his girl friend Lyon (who manages to get raped once or twice), his one-time partner Nielsen, and of course, the marshal, Roberts.

p, Pedro Vidal, Richard Landan; d, John Peyser; w, Don Balluck; ph, Rafael Pacheco.

Western   Cas.   (PR:O MPAA:NR)

FOUR SEASONS, THE*   (1981) 107m UNIV c

Alan Alda *(Jack Burroughs)*, Carol Burnett *(Kate Burroughs)*, Len Cariou *(Nick Callan)*, Sandy Dennis *(Anne Callan)*, Rita Moreno *(Claudia Zimmer)*, Jack Weston *(Danny Zimmer)*, Bess Armstrong *(Ginny Newley)*, Elizabeth Alda *(Beth)*, Beatrice Alda *(Lisa)*, Robert Hitt *(Room Clerk)*, Kristi McCarthy *(Waitress)*, David Stackpole *(Doctor)*.

Group friendship is examined in this sometimes too considerate film of six friends—three middle-aged married couples who test their loyalties to each other and their own marriages. Alda and Burnett are the "thoughtful" couple at the center of the sextette which spends a year together, taking vacations through the four seasons. Weston and wife Moreno make up the humorous pairsome while Cariou and Dennis are the star-crossed people whose marriage splits up and Cariou marries a young woman, Armstrong. Much of the first half of the film is spritely and amusing but the effort to become seriously dramatic toward the end, finishing with slapstick as Weston falls through an icy lake, to be rescued by his friends, is a bit hard to take. Alda's debut as a director is nevertheless impressive and Kemper's lensing in the Virgin Islands and New England is often stunning.

p, Martin Bregman; d&w Alan Alda; ph, Victor J. Kemper (Technicolor); m, Antonio Vivaldi; ed, Michael Economou; prod d, Jack Collis; set d, Jerry Wunderlich; cos, Jane Greenwood.

Drama/Comedy   Cas.   (PR:C MPAA:PG)

FOUR SIDED TRIANGLE*½   (1953, Brit.) 74m bw

Barbara Payton *(Lena/Helen)*, Percy Marmont *(Sir Walter)*, James Hayter *(Dr. Harvey)*, Stephen Murray *(Bill)*, John Van Eyssen *(Robin)*, Glyn Dearman *(Bill as a Child)*, Sean Barrett *(Robin as a Child)*, Jennifer Dearman *(Lena as a Child)*, Kynaston Reeves *(Lord Grant)*, John Stuart *(Solicitor)*, Edith Seville.

Pretty silly mad scientist film starring Murray and Van Eyssen as two beaker-brains whose friendship is on the rocks because lovely lady Payton, whom both are attracted to, only has eyes for Van Eyssen. Not wanting to bust up a good friendship over a woman, scientist Murray decides to duplicate his dream girl so that they'll both be happy. After much flashing of lights and other cheap effects (Hammer wouldn't really get cranking in that department until the FRANKEN-STEIN films), Murray comes up with another Payton. Unfortunately he also duplicated her emotions, so Payton No. 2 also only has eyes for Van Eyssen.

p, Alexander Paal, Michael Carreras; d, Terence Fisher; w, Paul Tabori, Fisher (based on a William F. Temple novel); ph, Reginald Wyer; m, Malcolm Arnold; ed, Maurice Bootes.

Science Fiction   (PR:C MPAA:NR)

FOUR SKULLS OF JONATHAN DRAKE, THE*½   (1959) 70m UA
                                                              bw

Eduard Franz *(Jonathan Drake)*, Valerie French *(Alison)*, Henry Daniell *(Dr. Zurich)*, Grant Richards *(Lt. Rowan)*, Paul Cavanagh *(Kenneth Drake)*, Howard Wendell *(Dr. Bradford)*, Paul Wexler *(Zutai)*, Lumsden Hare *(Rogers)*, Frank Gerstle *(Lee Coulter)*.

A staple on the late-night circuit, this low-budget shocker sports black magic as its main menace. Set in the Amazon jungle, the action focuses on an angry tribe of Jivaro Indians whose ancestors had slapped a curse upon the Drake family (white traders) nearly 200 years ago and, of course, are carrying on the tradition into modern times. Descendant of the Drake legacy, Franz, is about to become the next victim of head-shrinking, but he is saved by his daughter, French, and a detective, Richards. Upon further investigation, Franz and Co. discover that the witch doctor's head is actually that of great-granddaddy Drake and it's been sitting on the old fella's shoulders for over 200 years. Fairly atmospheric for those willing to sit up 'til all hours to catch this on the late show.

p, Robert E. Kent; d, Edward L. Cahn; w, Orville H. Hampton; ph, Maury Gertsman; m, Paul Dunlap; ed, Edward Mann.

Horror   (PR:C-O MPAA:NR)

FOUR SONS*½   (1940) 89m FOX bw

Don Ameche *(Chris)*, Eugenie Leontovich *(Frau Bernle)*, Mary Beth Hughes *(Anna)*, Alan Curtis *(Karl)*, George Ernest *(Fritz)*, Robert Lowery *(Joseph)*, Lionel Royce *(Max Sturm)*, Sig Rumann *(Newmann)*, Ludwig Stossel *(Pastor)*, Christian Rub *(Kapek)*, Torben Meyer *(Gustav)*, Egon Brecher *(Richter)*, Eleanor Wesselhoeft *(Frau Richter)*, Michael Visaroff *(Burgomaster)*, Greta Meyer *(Frau Sturm)*, Ernst Hausman *(Schmitt)*, Robert O. Davis *(Hempel)*, Hans Schumm *(Muller)*, Fredrik Vogeding *(Hinckerman)*, William Von Brincken *(Gortner)*, Ragnar Gvale, Robert Conway *(Storm Troopers)*.

An indictment of national socialism, FOUR SONS tells the tale of brothers split in political loyalty with the rise of Nazi Germany. They are Czechs, with Ameche siding with his native country while Curtis becomes a traitorous diehard Nazi and Ernest dies in Poland for the Third Reich, winning an Iron Cross, while the fourth son, Lowery, immigrates to the U.S. to become an artist. Ameche and Curtis give solid performances as the opposing brothers, as does Leontovich in her first American role as the long-suffering mother who joins her one surviving offspring in America after the holocaust swallows up her family. Mayo's lively direction can't bolster the soggy melodrama inherent in the heavy-handed script.

p, Darryl F. Zanuck; d, Archie Mayo; w, John Howard Lawson, Milton Sperling (based on a story by I.A.R. Wylie); ph, Leon Shamroy; ed, Francis D. Lyon; md, David Buttolph; art d, Richard Day, Albert Hogsett.

War Drama   (PR:A MPAA:NR)

FOUR WAYS OUT*   (1954, Ital.) 77m Carroll Pictures bw

Gina Lollobrigida *(Daniela)*, Renato Baldini *(Paolo)*, Corsetta Greco *(Lina)*, Paul Muller *(Guido)*, Enzio Maggio *(Alberto)*, Fausto Tozzi *(Luigi)*, Tamara Lees *(Tamara)*, Emma Baron *(Alberto's Mother)*.

Another in a series of caper films that features fairly sympathetic men who aren't really crooks, but guys who just haven't gotten a fair shake in life and are finally fed up enough to grab what they want. All the standard character motivations are there (one guy's a soccer player whose career was destroyed by an injury; another is a struggling artist; another, a student; and the last one is just plain unemployed with a wife and kids to feed) and when they rip-off the box office of the local soccer stadium, we are moved to rally to their cause. After the heist, the men split up and are picked off by the cops in a variety of melodramatic ways. Not bad, just not fresh. (Italian; dubbed in English.)

p, Eduardo Capolino; d, Pietro Germi.

Crime   (PR:C MPAA:NR)

FOUR WIVES*   (1939) 110m WB bw

Claude Rains *(Adam Lemp)*, Jeffrey Lynn *(Felix Deitz)*, John Garfield *(Mickey Borden)*, Frank McHugh *(Ben Crowley)*, May Robson *(Aunt Etta)*, Gale Page *(Emma Lemp)*, Dick Foran *(Ernest)*, Eddie Albert *(Dr. Clinton Forrest, Jr.)*, Henry O'Neill *(Dr. Clinton Forrest, Sr.)*, Vera Lewis *(Mrs. Ridgefield)*, Priscilla Lane *(Ann Lemp)*, Rosemary Lane *(Kay Lemp)*, Lola Lane *(Thea Lemp)*.

Following on the heels of the surprisingly successful FOUR DAUGHTERS, FOUR WIVES picks right up where the last one left off and sees the daughters of Lemp family patriarch Rains bearing children and finding a new husband for tragically widowed sister Lane. (The suicidal hubbie was played by Garfield in the first film; he reappears in this one as a ghost!) Priscilla Lane, however, discovers that she is expecting to have the late Garfield's baby soon, and this sours her on noble Lynn's proposal of marriage. Meanwhile sister Page is shocked to hear that she can't have children, Lola Lane adopts a kid and then gets pregnant with twins, and Rosemary Lane eventually gets married to Albert. All works out for Priscilla when she gives premature birth to her baby and its life is saved by the still-noble Lynn who volunteers to give the kid a blood transfusion, thus endearing himself to the mama, and they elope. A bit more maudlin than the first pic and Rains is disappointingly absent through much of the film.

p, Hal B. Wallis; d, Michael Curtiz; w, Julius J. and Philip G. Epstein, Maurice Hanline (suggested by the novel, *Sister Act*, by Fannie Hurst); ph, Sol Polito; m, Max Steiner; ed, Ralph Dawson; md, Leo F. Forbstein; art d, John Hughes.

Drama   **(PR:A   MPAA:NR)**

FOUR'S A CROWD**½**   (1938) 91m WB bw

Errol Flynn *(Robert Kensington Lansford)*, Olivia de Havilland *(Lorri Dillingwell)*, Rosalind Russell *(Jean Christy)*, Patric Knowles *(Patterson Buckley)*, Walter Connolly *(John P. Dillingwell)*, Hugh Herbert *(Silas Jenkins)*, Melville Cooper *(Bingham)*, Franklin Pangborn *(Preston)*, Herman Bing *(Barber)*, Margaret Hamilton *(Amy)*, Joseph Crehan *(Pierce, the Butler)*, Joe Cunningham *(Young)*, Dennie Moore *(Buckley's Secretary)*, Gloria Blondell *(Lansford's 1st Secretary)*, Carol Landis *(Lansford's 2nd Secretary)*, Renie Riano *(Mrs. Jenkins)*, Charles Trowbridge *(Dr. Ives)*, Spencer Charters *(Charlie)*.

Change-of-pace role for Flynn who feared type-casting after THE ADVENTURES OF ROBIN HOOD and pressured the studio to cast him in a few screwball comedies, assignments he handled fairly well. This one sees him as an ambitious public relations man who decides to prove his prowess by taking infamous skinflint millionaire Connolly as a client and changing his image. To do this, he begs his old boss Knowles to rehire him as the editor of a newspaper where he can work on Connolly's image in the press. Of course the dashing PR man takes time out to romance Connolly's daughter de Havilland *and* lady reporter Russell. Eventually things get sorted out and Flynn marries Russell, with Knowles taking de Havilland as his bride. The cast does okay, but the script is nothing special. The part played by Flynn is based upon Ivy Ledbetter Lee, a colorful and legendary PR man whose eccentric publicity for the Rockefeller family brought the super rich newspaper headlines. This was one of de Havilland's least favorite roles and she resented Flynn repeatedly calling her a "nitwit" in lines called for by the reckless script.

p, Hal B. Wallis; d, Michael Curtiz; w, Casey Robinson, Sid Herzig (from the novel *All Rights Reserved* by Wallace Sullivan); ph, Ernest Haller; m, Heinz Roemheld, Ray Heindorf; ed, Clarence Kolster; art d, Max Parker; cos, Orry-Kelly.

Comedy/Romance   **(PR:A   MPAA:NR)**

FOURTEEN, THE*****   (1973, Brit.) 105m Anglo-EMI c

Jack Wild *(Reg)*, June Brown *(The Mother)*, John Bailey *(Mr. Sanders)*, Cheryl Hall *(Reena)*, Anna Wing *(Mrs. Booth)*, Diana Beevers *(Miss Field)*, Alun Armstrong *(Tommy)*, Keith Buckley *(Mr. Whitehead)*, Tony Calvin *(Father Morris)*, Liz Edmiston, Christian Kelly, Peter Newby, Frank Gentry, Paul Daly, Richard Heyward, Terry Ives, Christopher Leonard, Sean Hide, Alfons Kaminsky, Wayne Brooks, Mark Hughes, Wayne Dyer.

A British tear-jerker which tells the sad tale of a large family of 14 kids who suddenly become orphans and must face eventual separation. While the children battle against the overzealous social workers who want to ship them into reform schools and foster homes, they are cared for by the oldest brother and his girl friend who serve as surrogate parents. Eventually the brothers and sisters realize that the best, and safest, thing to do is split up, with the family members going their separate ways. Actor David Hemmings directed his second film with THE FOURTEEN and it's a fine, well-balanced movie that manages to tug at the heartstrings without wallowing in the overly-sentimental mawkishness that could have been fallen into.

p, Robert Mintz, Frank Avianca; d, David Hemmings; w, Roland Stark; ph, Ousami Rawl (Panavision, Eastmancolor); m, Kenny Clayton; ed, John Shirley; art d, William McCrow; m/l, title song, Biddu Appiah.

Drama   **(PR:A   MPAA:NR)**

FOURTEEN HOURS***½**   (1951) 92m FOX bw

Paul Douglas *(Dunnigan)*, Richard Basehart *(Robert Cosick)*, Barbara Bel Geddes *(Virginia)*, Debra Paget *(Ruth)*, Agnes Moorehead *(Mrs. Cosick)*, Robert Keith *(Mr. Cosick)*, Howard Da Silva *(Lt. Moksar)*, Jeffrey Hunter *(Danny)*, Martin Gabel *(Dr. Strauss)*, Grace Kelly *(Mrs. Fuller)*, Frank Faylen *(Waiter)*, Jeff Corey *(Sgt. Farley)*, James Millican *(Sgt. Boyle)*, Donald Randolph *(Dr. Benson)*, Willard Waterman *(Mr. Harris)*, Kenneth Harvey *(Police Operator)*, George MacQuarrie *(Evangelist)*, Ann Morrison *(Mrs. Dunnigan)*, Forbes Murray *(Police Commissioner)*, George Putnam *(Radio Announcer)*, Ossie Davis, David Burns, Henry Slate, Harvey Lembeck, Lou Polan *(Cab Drivers)*, Brad Dexter, Shep Menken *(Reporters)*, Joyce Van Patten *(Barbara)*, George Baxter *(Attorney)*, Bernard Burke *(Police Captain)*, Michael Fitzmaurice *(TV Announcer)*, Russell Hicks *(Regan)*.

A superb, tense drama, one that studies the crowd as well as the principals, FOURTEEN HOURS allows the considerable talents of Douglas and Basehart to stun and move viewers. Basehart is the emotionally disturbed young man who climbs out on to the ledge of a New York skyscraper, threatening to jump to his death if anyone approaches him. Traffic cop Douglas is the only human who somehow reaches Basehart, talking to him about poetry and baseball, the joys of life, while shunning all others, including the father Basehart hates (Keith) and the mother who has suffocated him (Moorehead), while girl friend Bel Geddes begs him to live. As the hours drag by and morbid crowds collect, waiting to see Basehart go into a death dive, slices of life all around the skyscraper are shown. A young couple, Paget and Hunter, meet and begin a romance, while commiserating with Basehart perched high above them. Kelly, in a brief but memorable role, witnesses the youth from a neighboring skyscraper where she is preparing to sign divorce papers, and his plight causes her to change her mind, to attempt to make a go of her marriage. A host of characters get into the act, the most effective being Gabel as a police psychiatrist, Da Silva as a police lieutenant, and Faylen as a garrulous waiter. But Douglas, in a beautifully understated performance, dominates the film, while Basehart's intensity of jumbled purpose is often spellbinding. At the last

minute, when Basehart appears to make good his suicide threat, he is saved, snared by a police net and hauled to safety. Hathaway's direction is drum tight as he builds suspense with each scene. (The film is based on the suicide of John Warde who leaped 17 floors to his death on July 26, 1938 from a ledge of the Gotham Hotel, after many people, including traffic cop Charles V. Glasco, tried unsuccessfully for hours to persuade him to save himself.) Film debut for Grace Kelly.

p, Sol C. Siegel; d, Henry Hathaway; w, John Paxton (based on the story "The Man on the Ledge" by Joel Sayre); ph, Joe MacDonald; m, Alfred Newman; ed, Dorothy Spencer; art d, Lyle Wheeler, Leland Fuller.

Drama   **(PR:C   MPAA:NR)**

FOURTH ALARM, THE**½**   (1930) 60m Continental Picture Corp. bw

Nick Stuart *(Dick Turner)*, Ralph Lewis *(Chief Turner)*, Tom Santschi *(Benjamin Griffith)*, Ann Christy *(Helen Griffith)*, Harry Bowen *(Mac)*, Jack Richardson *(Fireman)*.

Stuart's a fireman who catches a pretty little firebug en route to a blaze. After an accident, he becomes a fire inspector along the waterfront. But when he discovers his true love's father illegally manufacturing explosives within city limits he is faced with a moral dilemma. Does he report it or ignore it? Duty, he decides, comes before all else, and the violation is reported. In the end a fire breaks out in the factory, Stuart saves his girl, and her father consents to their marriage. A sweet, if minor, romance with some exciting action at the climax.

p, W. Ray Johnson; d, Phil Whitman; w, Scott Littleton; ph, Herbert Kirkpatrick; ed, Carl Himm.

Action/Romance   **(PR:A   MPAA:NR)**

FOURTH FOR MARRIAGE, A   (SEE: WHAT'S UP FRONT, 1964)

FOURTH HORSEMAN, THE**½**   (1933) 63m UNIV bw

Tom Mix, Margaret Lindsay, Fred Kohler, Raymond Hatton, Edmund Cobb, Buddy Roosevelt, Richard Cramer, Harry Allen, Herman Nolan, Paul Shawhan, Rosita Marstini, Donald Kirke, Duke Lee, C.E. Anderson, Helene Millard, Martha Mattox, Frederick Howard, Grace Cunard, Walter Brennan, Pat Harmon, Hank Mann, Jim Corey, Delmar Watson, Fred Burns, Bud Osborne, Harry Tenbrook, Charles Sullivan, Sandy Sallee, Nip Reynolds, Henry Morris, Clyde Kinney, Jim Kinney, Ed Hendershot, Joe Balch, Augie Gomez, Frank Guskie, "Tony, Jr."

Mix is the noble cowpoke who rides into the life of heroine Lindsay and saves her land from the evil clutches of train robber Kohler who is trying to seize the town through non-payment of delinquent property taxes. The land appears worthless, but Kohler knows of an irrigation plan to bring water which will turn the arid sagebrush community into a thriving metropolis. Kohler and his gang have already decided amongst themselves what major town industries they'll control, so all they have to do is make sure Lindsay doesn't pay off the taxes. Not only does straight-shooter Mix save the day, but he marries Lindsay to boot.

d, Hamilton MacFadden; w, Jack Cunningham (story by Nina Wilcox Putnam); ph, Dan Clark.

Western   **(PR:AA   MPAA:NR)**

FOURTH SQUARE, THE****   (1961, Brit.) 57m Merton Park/AA bw

Conrad Phillips *(Bill Lawrence)*, Natasha Parry *(Sandra Martin)*, Delphi Lawrence *(Nina Stewart)*, Paul Daneman *(Henry Adams)*, Miriam Karlin *(Josetta Alvarez)*, Jacqueline Jones *(Marie Labonne)*, Anthony Newlands *(Tom Alvarez)*, Basil Dignam *(Inspector Forbes)*, Harold Kasket *(Philippe)*.

Another of the string of Edgar Wallace mysteries cranked out by Merton Park Studios in the early 1960s. This one has Phillips as a lawyer proving that the ex-wife of a playboy is a jewel thief and murderer. Usual defects of this low-budget series much in evidence.

p, Jack Greenwood; d, Allan Davis; w, James Eastwood (based on the novel *Four Square Jane* by Edgar Wallace).

Crime   **(PR:A-C   MPAA:NR)**

FOX, THE*****   (1967) 110m Claridge/WB c

Sandy Dennis *(Jill)*, Keir Dullea *(Paul)*, Anne Heywood *(Ellen March)*, Glyn Morris *(Realtor)*.

Director Mark Rydell's first feature film (he had done television previously) sees him at the helm of an uneven adaptation of D.H. Lawrence's novella of lesbian love. Dennis and Heywood star as lovers who have segregated themselves from the world in a lonely farmhouse. Dennis is the dominant female in the relationship and there is a hint that the older, uneasy Heywood harbors a longing for physical contact with a man. These feelings come forth when Dullea enters the scene and sparks the disintegration of the women's relationship. Good performance by Heywood.

p, Raymond Stross; d, Mark Rydell; w, Lewis John Carlino, Howard Koch (based on the novella by D.H. Lawrence); ph, Bill Fraker (DeLuxe Color); m, Lalo Schifrin; ed, Thomas Stanford; art d, Charles Bailey.

Drama   **(PR:O   MPAA:NR)**

FOX AND HIS FRIENDS*****   (1976, Ger.) 123m New Yorker c
      (AKA: FIST-RIGHT OF FREEDOM; FAUSTRECHT DER FREIHEIT, FOX)

Rainer Werner Fassbinder *(Fox)*, Peter Chatel *(Eugen)*, Karl-Heinz Bohm *(Max)*, Harry Baer *(Philip)*, Adrian Hoven *(Father)*, Ulla Jacobsen *(Mother)*, Christiane Maybach *(Hedwig)*, Peter Kern, Hans Zander, Kurt Raab, Irm Herman, Ursula Stratz, Elma Karlowa, Barbara Valentin, Bruce Low, Walter Sedimyn, Evelyn Kunncki, Ingrid Caern, Marquard Bohn, Liselotte Eeer.

Director Fassbinder doubles as the lead in this unusual drama. He is a carnival barker and performer who is also a homosexual. When he wins a fortune in the lottery, he attracts Chatel, the lazy, manipulative scion of a declining aristocratic family. Chatel goes about systematically exploiting Fassbinder as the latter struggles to join the upper classes, typified by Chatel and his parents. One scene has the parents horrified by Fassbinder's table manners but completely accepting the fact that their son is a homosexual milking this working class buffoon for all he's worth. Fassbinder gives an excellent performance as the abused Fox, and the direction is of the usual high standard seen in his works. FOX AND HIS FRIENDS was a moderate success that firmly established Fassbinder's reputation in the U.S. (In German; English subtitles.)

p, Christian Hohoff; d, Rainer Werner Fassbinder; w, Hohoff, Fassbinder; ph, Michael Ballhaus (Eastmancolor); m, Peer Raben; ed, Thea Eymesz; cos, Helga Kempke.

Drama (PR:O MPAA:NR)

FOX AND THE HOUND, THE**** (1981) 83m BV c

The voices of: Mickey Rooney (Tod), Kurt Russell (Copper), Pearl Bailey (Big Mamma), Jack Albertson (Amos Slade), Sandy Duncan (Vixey), Jeanette Nolan (Widow Tweed), Pat Buttram (Chief), John Fiedler (Porcupine), John McIntire (Badger), Dick Bakalyan (Dinky), Paul Winchell (Boomer), Keith Mitchell (Young Tod), Corey Feldman (Young Copper).

Fine Disney outing detailing the lives of a young fox and puppy dog who become close friends one summer. When the dog's owner, a mean hunter, takes him away for the winter, the fox and the hound fully expect to renew their friendship the following spring. When the hunter and the hound return, the fox's former friend has become the man's favorite hunting dog. The dog saves the fox's life once, but warns him to stay away if he doesn't want to be killed. Meanwhile the fox has developed a love interest in another young fox, Vixey. The hunter is determined to catch him and there is a terrifying chase, but the tables turn when the dog is cornered by a large bear. The fox boldly fights off the attacker, saving the dog's life. In turn, the hound stands between his master and the fox, not allowing his friend to be shot. Though they have saved each other's lives, the friends must separate, this time for good. The animation is better-than-average (veteran Disney animators Wolfgang Reitherman and Art Stevens supervised the talents of a new crop of artists that developed during a ten-year program at the studio), but nowhere near the quality of Disney studios in its heyday.

p, Wolfgang Reitherman, Art Stevens; d, Stevens, Ted Berman, Richard Rich; w, Laury Clemmons, Berman, Peter Young, Steve Hulett, David Michener, Burny Mattinson, Earl Kress, Vance Gerry (based on the book by Daniel P. Mannix); m, Buddy Baker; ed, James Melton, Jim Koford; art d, Don Griffith; supervising animators, Randy Cartwright, Cliff Norberg, Frank Thomas, Glen Keane, Ron Clements, Ollie Johnston.

Animated Feature (PR:AAA MPAA:G)

FOX MOVIETONE FOLLIES**½ (1929) 80m FOX bw/c (GB: MOVIETONE FOLLIES OF 1929)

John Breeden (George Shelby), Lola Lane (Lila Beaumont), De Witt Jennings (Jay Darrell), Sharon Lynn (Ann Foster), Arthur Stone (Al Leaton), Stepin Fetchit (Swifty), Warren Hymer (Martin), Archie Gottler (Stage Manager), Arthur Kay (Orchestra Leader), Mario Dominici (Le Maire). Song and Dance Numbers: Sue Carol, Lola Lane, Sharon Lynn, Dixie Lee, Melva Cornell, Paula Langlen, Carolynne Snowden, David Percy, David Rollins, Bobby Burns, Frank Richardson, Henry M. Mollandin, Frank La Mont, Jeanette Dancy.

Slim plot concerns the efforts of a Southern gent to marry the girl of his dreams by buying the major portion of a show in which the girl is performing and firing her. Having followed her all the way from the Deep South to Broadway, he discovers that she would rather devote her time to singing and dancing than to changing diapers and washing dishes. The plot to get her off the stage backfires when the suitor doesn't reckon upon union regulations. Light but enjoyable, with a bit of extra interest being accomplished through the addition of a sequence filmed in Technicolor. Songs include: "The Breakaway," "Walkin With Susie," "Kinkajou," "Varsity Drag," and "Susie."

d, David Butler, Marcel Silver; w, Butler, William K. Wells; ph, Charles Van Enger; ed, Ralph Dietrich; md, Arthur Kay; m/l, Con Conrad, Sidney Mitchell, Archie Gottler.

Musical (PR:A MPAA:NR)

FOX MOVIETONE FOLLIES OF 1930** (1930) 70m FOX bw (AKA: NEW MOVIETONE FOLLIES OF 1930, THE)

El Brendel (Alex Svenson), Marjorie White (Vera Fontaine), Frank Richardson (George Randall), Noel Francis (Gloria De Witt), William Collier, Jr. (Conrad Sterling), Miriam Seegar (Mary Mason), Huntley Gordon (Marvin Kingsley), Yola D'Avril (Maid), Paul Nicholson (Lee Hubert), J.M. Kerrigan.

Following 1929's FOX MOVIETONE FOLLIES, this backstage musical featured Brendel as a butler with a romantic streak who convinces everyone that he's a lumberjack. Along with playboy Collier, Brendel nearly ruins a stage show but disaster is avoided by the finale. In the typical manner the words and music are most important. Songs: "Cheer Up And Smile," "Doin' The Derby" (Con Conrad, Jack Meskill), "You'll Give In" (Joseph McCarthy, James Hanley), "I Wanna Be A Talking Picture Queen" (McCarthy, Hanley, James Brockman), "I Feel A Certain Feeling Coming On," (Cliff Friend, James V. Monaco) "Emily Brown" (Conrad, Meskill).

d, Benjamin Stoloff; w, William K. Wells; ph, L. William O'Connell; m, Con Conrad, Jack Meskill, Joseph McCarthy, James Hanley, James Brockman, Cliff Friend, James V. Monaco; ed, Clyde Carruth; md, Arthur Kay; art d, Stephen Goosson; ch, Danny Dare, Maurice L. Kusell, Max Scheck.

Musical (PR:A MPAA:NR)

FOX WITH NINE TAILS, THE**½ (1969, Jap.) 81m Japan Animated/Daiei c (KYUBI NO KITSUNE TO TOBIMARU)

An animated fable about a beautiful girl who discovers that she is really a nine-tailed fox from the Dark Side whose destiny is to enslave the people of the world to the Devil. Not wanting to give in to do this, she flees to Kyoto, but there she finds that everyone is attracted to her beauty and she begins to fulfill her mission in spite of her better intentions. The people obey her command to destroy the statues of the Buddha and a massive statue of herself is erected in Kyoto. A youth who has known her since childhood destroys the statue and she turns to stone herself.

d, Shinichi Yagi; w, Michio Yoshioka (based on a story by Kido Okamoto); ph, Masayoshi Kishimoto (Fuji Color); m, Shigeru Ikeno; art d, Isamu Kageyama; animation, Taku Sugiyama.

Animated Fantasy (PR:AA MPAA:NR)

FOXES**½ (1980) 106m UA c

Jodie Foster, (Jeanie), Scott Baio (Brad), Sally Kellerman (Mary), Randy Quaid (Jay), Lois Smith (Mrs. Axman), Adam Faith (Bryan), Cherie Currie (Annie), Marilyn Kagan (Madge), Kandice Stroh (Deirdre), Jon Sloan (Loser), Jill Barrie Bogart (Sissie), Wayne Storm (Frank), Mary Margaret Lewis (Gladys), Grant Wilson (Greg), Fredric Lehne (Bobby), E. Lamont Johnson (Detective), Robert Romanus (Scott), Roger Bowen (Counsellor), Mary Ellen O'Neill (Mrs. Steiner), Buddy Foster, Ben Frank, Kay A. Tornberg, Scott Garrett, Laura Dern, Michael Taylor, Gino Baffa, Charles Shull, Tony Termini, Jeff Silverman, Mae Williams, R. Scott Thomson, Ron Lombard, Steve Jones, Jon Benson, Tom Pletts, Ken Novick.

Weakly scripted, but fairly engaging exploration of the lives and problems of four teenage girls, Foster, Currie, Kagan, and Stroh, as they struggle with growing up. Foster (in a fine performance) plays the one girl with a good head on her shoulders who finds herself dealing with the problems of the other three. Currie (the most problematic character in the narrative) is the burnt-out former teenage hooker trying to escape life with her crazed father. Kagan is the overweight, unpopular girl who is trying to free herself of her parent's pampering, and Stroh is a confused, flirtatious, compulsive liar. Though the attempt to explore the problems of modern-day teenagers is admirable, the script is limp in spots, trite in others and ties up all the loose ends with a rather contrived plot device. The other unfortunate drawback is the almost total lack of humor in the film, which tends to make the action all the more depressing.

p. David Puttnam, Gerald Ayres; d, Adrian Lyne; w, Ayres; ph, Leon Bijou (Technicolor); m, Giorgio Moroder; ed, Jim Coblentz; art d, Michael Levesque.

Drama (PR:O MPAA:R)

FOXES OF HARROW, THE***½ (1947) 117m FOX bw

Rex Harrison (Stephen Fox), Maureen O'Hara (Odalie D'Arceneaux), Richard Haydn (Andre LeBlanc), Victor McLaglen (Capt. Mike Farrell), Vanessa Brown (Aurore D'Arceneaux), Patricia Medina (Desiree), Gene Lockhart (The Vicomte), Charles Irwin (Sean Fox), Hugo Haas (Hugo Ludenbach), Roy Roberts (Tom Warren), Dennis Hoey (Master of Harrow), Marcel Journet (St. Ange), Helen Crozier (Zerline), Sam McDaniel (Josh), Libby Taylor (Angelina), Renee Beard (Little Inch), Suzette Harbin (Belle), Perry William Ward (Etienne Fox at Age Six), Clear Nelson, Jr. (Little Inch at Age Three), James Lagano (Etienne at Age Three), Dorothy Adams (Mrs. Fox), Celia Lovsky (Minna Ludenbach), Eugene Borden (French Auctioneer), Bernard DeRoux (Creole Waiter), Frederick Burton (Creole Gentleman), Wee Willie Davis (Sailor), Randy Stuart (Mother of Stephen Fox), Kenneth Washington (Achille), A. C. Bilbrew (Tante Caleen), Henri Letondal (Maspero), Andre Charlot (Dr. Terrebone), Georges Renavent (Priest), Jasper Weldon (Jode), Joseph Crehan (Captain).

This lavish historical drama has Harrison as an Irish rascal and inveterate gambler who uses his considerable skills at the gaming tables of New Orleans to become fabulously rich, beating landowner Haas in a head-to-head card game and winning a vast estate. Harrison is aided by river pirate McLaglen who has picked him up on a sandbar after Harrison was marooned there by a riverboat captain convinced he was a card cheat, an act witnessed by aristocratic southern belle O'Hara. Quickly climbing in society, Harrison is introduced to O'Hara's family and finally wins her heart. They are married but McLaglen's appearance, along with his rowdy pirate crew on their wedding night, alienates the couple and, for three years, they wage a private war, their son being the only bond between them. When crop prices drop drastically and with Harrison away, O'Hara attempts to run their great plantation, Harrow, but she is ineffective. Just as weather threatens to ruin the crops and the field hands shrink from O'Hara who vainly orders them to bring in the harvest, Harrison appears, takes the day, and reunites with the woman he loves. The Yerby bestseller, really an historical soap opera a la Gone with the Wind, is raised above the mediocre by an expensive production and Harrison's magnificent portrayal of the maverick landowner. O'Hara is attractively tempestuous and McLaglen a grinning, scheming brute with a loyal heart. Haydn is excellent as Harrison's new-found New Orleans friend, a fun-loving dandy. Kudos go to Lockhart as O'Hara's generous father and Medina as a sultry lady of the evening. Stahl's direction is imaginative and La Shelle's lensing is moody and excitingly fluid.

p, William A. Bacher; d, John M. Stahl; w, Wanda Tuchock (based on the novel by Frank Yerby); ph, Joseph La Shelle; m, David Buttolph; ed, James B. Clark; md, Alfred Newman; art d, Lyle Wheeler, Maurice Ransford; set d, Thomas Little, Paul S. Fox; spec eff, Fred Sersen.

Historical Drama (PR:A MPAA:NR)

FOXFIRE** (1955) 91m UNIV c

Jane Russell (Amanda), Jeff Chandler (Jonathan Dartland), Dan Duryea (Hugh Slater), Mara Corday (Maria), Robert Simon (Ernest Tyson), Frieda Inescort (Mrs. Lawrence), Barton MacLane (Jim Mablett), Charlotte Wynters (Mrs. Mablett), Eddy Waller (Old Larky), Celia Lovsky (Saba), Arthur Space (Foley), Phil Chambers (Mr.

Riley), Robert Bice (*Walt Whitman*), Vici Raaf (*Cleo*), Grace Lenard (*Rose*), Guy Wilkerson (*Mr. Barton*), Lillian Bronson (*Mrs. Potter*), Mary Carroll (*Mrs. Riley*), Lisabeth Fielding (*Mrs. Foley*), Dabbs Greer (*Bus Driver*), Hal K. Dawson (*Man Tourist*), Chermienne Harker (*Rowena*), Grace Hayle (*Woman Tourist*), Beulah Archuletta (*Indian Woman*), Billy Wilkerson (*Apache Chief*), Chebon Jadi (*Bellhop*), Leon Charles, Jimmy Casino, Charles Soldani, Martin Cichy (*Miners*), Manley Suathojame (*Indian Husband*), R.H. Baldwin (*Hoist Operator*).

A mediocre love story where socialite Russell meets and marries surly Chandler who takes her away from it all, to a broken down Arizona ghost town where he can squeeze out a living as a mining engineer. He is tough to live with, Russell finds out quickly, and their marriage appears headed for the rocks until she has a miscarriage and Chandler stumbles upon a gold mine. Their adversities strengthen their marriage, but Chandler's late-in-coming explanation that he is a half-blooded Apache does little to excuse his brutish, churlish attitude. Duryea gives the most convincing performance as an alcoholic doctor with bottles hidden all over the West. Pevney's direction and Frings' script are unimaginative and downright tame.

p, Aaron Rosenberg; d, Joseph Pevney; w, Ketti Frings (based on a novel by Anya Seton); ph, William Daniels (Technicolor); m, Frank Skinner; ed, Ted J. Kent; md, Joseph Gershenson; art d, Alexander Golitzen, Robert Clatworthy; cos, Bill Thomas; m/l, "Foxfire," Jeff Chandler, Henry Mancini (sung by Chandler).

Drama   **(PR:C MPAA:NR)**

FOXHOLE IN CAIRO   (1960, Brit.) 80m Omnia/BL bw

James Robertson-Justice (*Captain Robertson D.S.O.*), Adrian Hoven (*John Eppler*), Niall MacGinnis (*Radek*), Peter Van Eyck (*Count Almaszy*), Robert Urquhart (*Major Wilson*), Neil McCallum (*Sandy*), Fenella Fielding (*Yvette*), Gloria Mestre (*Amina*), Albert Lieven (*Rommel*), John Westbrook (*Roger*), Lee Montague (*Aberle*), Henry Oscar (*Col. Zeltinger*), Howard Marion Crawford (*British Major*), Anthony Newlands (*S.S. Colonel*), Richard Vernon (*General*), Michael Caine (*Weber*), Storm Durr (*Rommel's Aide*), Nancy Nevinson (*Signorina Signorelli*), John Blythe (*Barman*), Jerome Willis, Lane Meddick.

Overlong, confusing and ultimately dull tale of espionage in Cairo during WW II. Hoven plays a German playboy who becomes Rommel's head spy. Justice is the British counter-intelligence captain who captures Hoven in time to save a Jewish girl who works for the underground and then prevent the Desert Fox from winning The Battle of Algiers.

p, Steven Pallos, Donald Taylor; d, John Moxey; w, Leonard Mosley, Taylor (from the novel *The Cat and the Mice* by Mosley); ph, Desmond Dickinson; m, Wolfram Roehrig, Douglas Gamley, Ken Jones; ed, Oswald Hafenrichter; ch, Patricia Kirschner; makeup, Stuart Freeborn.

Spy Drama   **(PR:A MPAA:NR)**

FOXTROT   (1977, Mex./Swiss) 91m New World c
(AKA: THE OTHER SIDE OF PARADISE)

Peter O'Toole (*Liviu*), Charlotte Rampling (*Julia*), Max Von Sydow (*Larson*), Jorge Luke (*Eusebio*), Helena Rojo (*Alexandra*), Claudio Brook (*Paul*), Max Kerlow (*Captain*), Christa Walter (*Gertrude*), Mario Castillon (*Sailor*), Anne Porterfield (*Marianna*).

A misfire for the brilliant O'Toole who, with his wife, Rampling, and servants, Von Sydow and Luke, retreats to a desert isle to avoid the inconveniences of WW II. Here, he and Rampling languidly explore their past and verbalize over past glories of their civilized generation until the war intrudes upon them and their servants revolt. The whole pretentious mess is an abortive attempt to remake THE RULES OF THE GAME and it fails miserably with a bloodless and wordy script and unrewarding direction and photography. Tunes include "Louise," "Isn't It Romantic," and the title song written by Jay Livingston and Ray Evans.

p, Gerald Green; d, Arturo Ripstein; w, Ripstein, Jose Emilio Pacheco, H.A.L. Craig; ph, Alex Phillips, Jr. (Technicolor); m, Pete Rugolo; ed, Peter Zinner; art d, Lucero Isaac; set d, Jose Rodrigues Granada.

Drama   **(PR:C-O MPAA:R)**

FOXY BROWN   (1974) 91m AIP c

Pam Grier (*Foxy Brown*), Antonio Fargas (*Link*), Peter Brown (*Steve*), Terry Carter (*Michael*), Kathryn Loder (*Katherine*), Harry Holcombe (*Judge*), Sid Haig (*Hays*), Juanita Brown (*Claudia*), Sally Ann Stroud (*Deb*), Bob Minor (*Oscar*), Tony Giorgio (*Eddie*), Fred Lerner (*Bunyan*), Judy Cassmore (*Vicki*).

Very bloody, repulsive black exploitation film featuring Grier as a woman whose drug-dealing brother (Fargas) ratted on her undercover cop boy friend to the mob. Subsequently, the cop is murdered gangland style on Grier's doorstep and she sets out to get revenge on mobsters Loder and Brown. After far too many shootings, fights, rapes, throat-cuttings, and burnings, Grier finally castrates Brown and presents the results of her surgery to Loder in a pickle jar.

p, Buzz Feitshans; d&w, Jack Hill; ph, Brick Marquard (Movielab Color); m, Willie Hutch; ed, Chuck McClelland; art d, Kurt Axtel.

Crime   **(PR:O MPAA:R)**

FOXY LADY½   (1971, Can.) 85m Cinepix c

Alan Gordon (*Hero*), Sylvia Feigel (*Leander*), Robert McHeady (*Mr. Stephens*), Patrick Boxill (*Mr. Seman*), Nicole Morin (*Director*).

Slow-moving romance based on the Hero-Leander myth starring Gordon as a helpful young man and Feigel as the richest girl in the world. The script has the myth's genders reversed, but then it's hard to tell these days. One of director Reitman's (STRIPES, GHOSTBUSTERS) early stabs at comedy.

p&d, Ivan Reitman; w, Matt Seigel, Robert Sandien; ph, Ken Lambert; m, Doug Riley, Reitman; ed, Reitman; set d, Martha Dorlon.

Comedy   **Cas.**   **(PR:A MPAA:NR)**

FRA DIAVOLO   (SEE: DEVIL'S BROTHER, THE, 1933)

FRAGE 7   (SEE: QUESTION 7, 1961, Ger.)

FRAGMENT OF FEAR*   (1971, Brit.) 95m COL c

David Hemmings (*Tom Brett*), Gayle Hunnicutt (*Juliet*), Flora Robson (*Lucy Dawson*), Wilfrid Hyde-White (*Mr. Copsey*), Daniel Massey (*Maj. Ricketts*), Roland Culver (*Mr. Vellacott*), Adolfo Celi (*Bardoni*), Mona Washbourne (*Mrs. Gray*), Mary Wimbush ("*Bunface*"), Bernard Archard (*Priest*), Glyn Edwards (*C.I.D. Superintendent*), Derek Newark (*Sgt. Matthews*), Arthur Lowe (*Mr. Nugent*), Yootha Joyce (*Mrs. Ward-Cadbury*), Patricia Hayes (*Mrs. Baird*), John Rae (*Uncle Stanley*), Angelo Infanti (*Bruno*), Hilda Barry (*Miss Dacey*), Massimo Sarchielli (*Mario*), Philip Stone (*C.I.D. Sergeant*), Edward Kemp (*Kenny*), Kenneth Cranham (*Joe*), Michael Rothwell (*Rocky*), Kurt Christian (*Nino*), Richard Kerr (*Pop Singer*), Jessica Dublin, Louise Cambert (*American Matrons*), Georgina Moon, Petra Markham, Lois Hyett (*Schoolgirls*).

Hemmings is a young, reformed drug-addict turned successful author by writing about the hellish life of a junkie. When his aunt, Robson, is found strangled to death in Pompeii, he decides to investigate, and after a long period of indifference from the authorities (who think he's just a junkie hallucinating), threatening phone calls and paranoiac suspicions, he has a nervous breakdown—and never finds out who the murderers are, or why his aunt was killed. A grim, absorbing, but ultimately frustrating film, sparked with a fine performance from Hemmings.

p, John R. Sloan; d, Richard C. Sarafian; w, Paul Dehn (based on the novel by John Bingham); ph, Oswald Morris; m, Johnny Harris; ed, Malcolm Cooke; art d, Ray Simm; cos, Phyllis Dalton.

Crime/Mystery   **(PR:C-O MPAA:GP)**

FRAGRANCE OF WILD FLOWERS, THE*   (1979, Yugo.) 92m
Centar/New Yorker c

Ljuba Tadic (*Ivan Vasiljevic*), Sonja Divak (*Sonja*), Nemanja Zivic (*Stinky Jeca*), Ratislava Gacic (*Stana*), Aleksandar Bercek (*Film Director*), Cedomir Petrovic (*Inspector*), Gorica Popovic (*Female Reporter*), Olga Spiridonovic (*Desa*), Xica Tomic (*Old Actor*).

Tadic is a popular stage actor who decides to leave fame, fortune, and the crowds that follow by living with a friend and his mistress on an old barge. Avoiding the paparazzi isn't so easy however, as he is followed by a film crew. Crowds arrive and soon are taken by the mistress' singing voice and the tripe that is served at a nearby tavern. As the atmosphere around the barge becomes more Utopian, Tadic grows increasingly disillusioned. A poignant tale of the yearning for a simpler existence (i.e. taking time to smell the flowers) which won the International Critics Award at Cannes.

d, Srdjan Karanovic; w, Rajko Grlic, Karanovic; m, Zoran Simujanovic; art d, Miomir Denic; cos, Danka Pavlovic.

Drama   **(PR:C MPAA:NR)**

FRAIL WOMEN*½   (1932, Brit.) 72m Twickenham/RAD bw

Mary Newcomb (*Lilian Hamilton*), Owen Nares (*Col. Leonard Harvey*), Edmund Gwenn (*Jim Willis*), Jane Welsh (*Sister*), Frederick Peisley (*Peter Farrar*), Athole Stewart (*Father*), Margaret Vines (*Mary Willis*), Frank Pettingell (*McWhirter*), Herbert Lomas (*Solicitor*), Miles Mander (*Registrar*).

Newcomb has an illegitimate daughter during WW I and gives her up to a wealthy old woman. When the woman dies some twenty years later Newcomb, who has been refused a marriage to her true love because of the illegitimacy, weds Nares, the child's father. Nares agrees to the marriage only out of responsibility to his daughter, resulting in Newcomb's suicide. A depressing picture but admirably crafted and performed and directed by the always competent Maurice Elvey.

p, Julius Hagen; d, Maurice Elvey; w, Michael Barringer; ph, Basil Emmott.

Drama   **(PR:C MPAA:NR)**

FRAMED   (1930) 62m RKO bw

Evelyn Brent (*Rose Manning*), Regis Toomey (*Jimmy McArthur*), Ralf Harolde (*Chuck Gaines*), Maurice Black ("*Bing" Murdock*), William Holden (*Inspector McArthur*), Robert Emmett O'Connor (*Sgt. Schulte*), Eddie Kane (*Headwaiter*).

Brent stars as a mobster's daughter out to get revenge on Holden (no relation to the star of SUNSET BOULEVARD or THE WILD BUNCH), the cop who killed her father during a holdup. Five years later, Brent, now the owner of a nightclub, is still bent on vengeance. One night, Brent falls in love with young customer Toomey—who, unbeknownst to her, is Holden's son. When this is discovered she must chose between her love for the son and her hatred for the father. She opts for love and even foils a plot by a murderous bootlegger to kill them both. A well-acted, fast-paced programmer.

p, William Le Baron; d, George Archainbaud; w, Paul Schofield, Wallace Smith; ph, Leo Tover; ed, Jack Kitchin.

Crime   **(PR:A MPAA:NR)**

FRAMED½   (1940) 60m UNIV bw

Frank Albertson (*Henry T. Parker*), Constance Moore (*Phyllis Sanderson*), Jerome Cowan (*Monty de Granville*), Robert Armstrong (*Skippy*), Sidney Blackmer (*Tony Bowman*), Judith Allen (*Gwen Porter*), Herbert Rawlinson (*Walter Billings*), Jack Arnold (*Nick*), Milburn Stone (*Matthew Mattison*), Barbara Pepper (*Goldie Green*), Wade Boteler (*Bartender*), James Flavin (*Cop*), Dick Wessel (*Al*), Anne Gwynne (*Girl*), Lee Phelps (*Police Sergeant*), Eddy Chandler (*Policeman*), Dave Willock (*News Photographer*), Donald Kerr (*Reporter*).

Smart young reporter Albertson is falsely accused of murder and sets out to prove the cops wrong by solving the crime, and gets a front page scoop for his paper as a bonus.

p, Ben Pivar; d, Harold Schuster; w, Roy Chanslor; ph, Jerome Ash; ed, Otto Ludwig; md, H.J. Salter; art d, Jack Otterson.

Crime **(PR:A MPAA:NR)**

FRAMED½** (1947) 82m COL bw (GB: PAULA)

Glenn Ford *(Mike Lambert)*, Janis Carter *(Paula Craig)*, Barry Sullivan *(Stephen Price)*, Edgar Buchanan *(Jeff Cunningham)*, Karen Morley *(Mrs. Price)*, Jim Bannon *(Jack Woodworth)*, Sid Tomack *(Bartender)*, Barbara Wooddell *(Jane Woodworth)*, Paul Burns *(Assay Clark)*, Charles Cane *(Manager, Truck Company)*, Art Smith *(Hotel Clerk)*, Robert Stevens *(Young Man)*, Lillian Wells *(Young Woman)*, Fred Graff *(Bank Clerk)*, Michael Towne *(Boy in Jail)*, Walter Baldwin *(Assistant Manager)*, Eugene Borden *(Julio)*, Martin Garralaga *(Sweeper)*, Kenneth MacDonald, Crane Whitley *(Policemen)*, Alan Bridge *(Judge)*, Snub Pollard *(Dishwasher)*, Jack Baxley *(Bank Guard)*, Stanley Andrews, Gene Stutenroth *(Detectives)*, David Fresco *(Newsboy)*, Mabel Smaney *(Fat Woman)*, Cecil Weston *(Woman in Jail)*, Harry Strang *(Jail Guard)*, Cy Malis *(Crap Shooter)*, Nacho Galindo *(Mexican Shooter)*, William Stubbs *(Houseman)*, Mel Wixson *(Man)*.

Above average crime yarn involves unemployed mining engineer Ford who is making a living as a truck driver and is suddenly seduced by Carter. Her plan is to inveigle Ford into taking an embezzling rap for her look-alike lover, Sullivan a vice president of a bank. Sullivan robs the bank and she kills him for the loot, trying to encourage Ford to run away with her now that she truly loves him. She admits murdering Sullivan but tells Ford that she was drunk when committing the foul deed. He's about to forgive her when he learns that his best friend, Buchanan, is charged with the killing. Ford tricks Carter into confessing to premeditated murder and saves his friend. This is a minor noir entry with some grit provided by Ford and a lot of sex ladled out by Carter. Sullivan, Buchanan, and 1930s leading lady turned character actress Morley produce solid performances. Wallace's direction is rather uninspired despite his action-filled scenes. Opera trained Carter once again (as in NIGHT EDITOR, 1946), demonstrates her bizarre speciality of portraying the sexual excitement that comes to some psychopaths from performing sadistic acts. Here, she conveys intense sexual excitement when Sullivan's car goes over a cliff, showing a noir talent, however repelling, that might have led her to stardom had she not been confined to B pictures for most of the decade she was in the movies.

p, Jules Schermer; d, Richard Wallace; w, Ben Maddow (based on a story by Jack Patrick); ph, Burnett Guffey; m, Marlin Skiles; ed, Richard Fantl; md, M. W. Stoloff; art d, Stephen Gooson; set d, Wilbur Menefee, Sidney Clifford, Fay Babcock; cos, Jean Louis.

Crime Drama **(PR:C MPAA:NR)**

FRAMED** (1975) 106m PAR c

Joe Don Baker *(Ron)*, Conny Van Dyke *(Susan)*, Gabriel Dell *(Vince)*, John Marley *(Sal)*, Brock Peters *(Sam)*, John Larch *(Bundy)*, Warren Kemmerling *(Morello)*, Paul Mantee *(Frank)*, Walter Brooke *(Senator)*, Joshua Bryant *(Andrew)*, Hunter Von Leer *(Dewey)*, Les Lannom *(Gary)*, H.B. Haggerty *(Bickford)*, Hoke Howell *(Decker)*, Lawrence Montaigne *(Deputy Allison)*, Red West *(Mallory)*, Brenton Banks *(Jeremiah)*, Al Hager *(Emmett)*, Ken Lester *(Big Jim)*, Henry O. Arnold *(Lenny)*, Gary Gober *(Kenny)*, Lloyd Tatum *(Deputy Wilson)*, Roy Jenson *(Haskins)*.

Competent, if predictable, violent revenge film from the same people who brought you the WALKING TALL series of vigilante films. Baker stars as a professional gambler who is framed by crooked cops and sent up for a long prison stretch. Upon his release, Baker goes after the crooks with both barrels.

p, Mort and Joel Briskin; d, Phil Karlson; w, Mort Briskin (based on the novel by Art Powers and Mike Misenheimer); ph, Jack A. Marta (Metrocolor); m, Pat Williams; ed, Harry Gerstad; prod d, Stan Jolley; set d, Bert Allen; stunts, Gil Perkins, Carey Loftin.

Crime **(PR:O MPAA:R)**

FRAME-UP THE½** (1937) 59m COL bw

Paul Kelly *(Mark MacArthur)*, Jacqueline Wells [Julie Bishop] *(Betty Lindale)*, George McKay *(Joe Lavery)*, Robert E. O'Connor *(Larry Mann)*, Raphael Bennett *(Franey Forrester)*, Wade Boteler *(Capt. Donovan)*, Edward Earle *(Ellery Richards)*, C. Montague Shaw *(James Weston)*, John Tyrrell *(Soapy Connor)*, Ted Oliver *(Spud Gitale)*, Horace Murphy *(Dr. Phillips)*.

Good little actioner starring Kelly as a race track detective forced to submit to the criminal plans of O'Connor when O'Connor kidnaps the honest cop's gal Wells. With the help of fellow coppers, Kelly outwits the crooks, wins back Wells, and justice is served.

d, D. Ross Lederman; w, Harold Shumate (story by Richard E. Wormser); ph, Benjamin Kline; ed, Otto Meyer.

Crime **(PR:A MPAA:NR)**

FRANCES½** (1982) 140m EMI/Brooksfilm-UNIV c

Jessica Lange *(Frances Farmer)*, Sam Shepard *(Harry York)*, Kim Stanley *(Lillian Farmer)*, Bart Burns *(Ernest Farmer)*, Jonathan Banks *(Hitchhiker)*, Bonnie Bartlett *(Stylist)*, James Brodhead *(Sergeant)*, J. J. Chaback *(Lady in Hotel)*, Jordan Charney *(Harold Clurman)*, Daniel Chodes *(Director)*, Red Colbin *(Judge)*, Donald Craig *(Ralph Edwards)*, Sarah Cunningham *(Alma Styles)*, Lee DeBroux *(Director)*, Jeffrey DeMunn *(Clifford Odets)*, Jack Fitzgerald *(Clapper Man)*, Nancy Foy *(Autograph Girl)*, Anne Haney *(Hairdresser)*, Richard Hawkins *(Bum)*, James Karen *(Judge)*, Darrell Larson *(Spy)*, Patricia Larson *(Mrs. Hillier)*, Albert Lord *(Assistant Director)*, Vincent Lucchesi *(Arresting Sergeant)*, Jack Manning *(Photographer)*, Gerald S. O'Loughlin *(Doctor)*, Woodrow Parfrey *(Dr. Doyle)*, Christopher Pennock *(Dick)*, Rod Pilloud *(Martoni)*, Larry Pines *(Man on Phone)*, John Randolph *(Judge)*, Allan Rich *(Bebe)*, Jack Riley *(Barnes)*, David V. Schroeder *(Lawyer)*, Helen Schustack *(Wardrobe Mistress)*, Sandra Seacat *(Drama Teacher)*, Charles Seaverns *(Realtor)*, Lane Smith *(Dr. Symington)*, Karin Strandjord *(Connie)*, Andrew Winner *(Firechief)*, Vern Taylor *(Executive)*, Biff Yaeger *(Cop)*, Keone Young *(Doctor)*, Alexander Zale *(Man in Screening Room)*.

FRANCES is the relentlessly depressing film biography of the late movie star, Frances Farmer. It's all the more depressing because it's totally true. Farmer, one of the most beautiful actresses of the late 1930s and early 1940s, is shown as the victim of a hateful, driving mother, Kim Stanley, and the foil of a studio system that tolerated no deviations from the norm, as established by the men who ran the movies. Lange is believable in the role. Lange is seen drinking to excess, raped and ravaged in a mental hospital and, in general, handed a bad set of cards by the double-dealers who ran Hollywood at that time. Lange is a rebel, from some early scenes in high school, through the final fade out. Her adherence to individuality is what does her in. The major problem in the film seems to be the fictional punctuation of a lover, Shepard, who always seems to be waiting for Farmer's return to blissful Washington state. And they never really answer the question of whether or not it was alcohol that drove her to erratic behavior. Farmer had a successful career on stage and appeared in such legendary plays as "Golden Boy" (by Clifford Odets) before coming to Hollywood. She retired in 1942, before she was 30, and spent the rest of her life in and out of hospitals until her death at 57 in 1970. As in the fictional ONE FLEW OVER THE CUCKOO'S NEST, Farmer underwent a brain operation and never was the same. The fire went out when the blade went in. Jack Riley, one of the busiest commercial actors around, is seen briefly as Barnes and Jordan Charney, still another graduate of the famed Abraham Lincoln High School in Coney Island, plays Harold Clurman perfectly. John Randolph, veteran stage and screen character man, does a small bit as a judge. He went on to score heavily in 1985's PRIZZI'S HONOR, playing Jack Nicholson's Mafia father. In the hands of others, this could have been a piece of sensationalistic tripe. Credit to Graeme Clifford for holding the lurid aspects as far down as he did. Produced by Mel Brooks' company with the same taste they showed in THE ELEPHANT MAN and with a screenplay by the same authors of that script (Bergren, DeVore), plus Elia's son, Nick Kazan.

p, Jonathan Sanger (co-p, Marie Yates); d, Graeme Clifford; w, Eric Bergren, Christopher DeVore, Nicholas Kazan (perhaps they got some inspiration from Farmer's own autobiography—not credited—*Will There Really Be A Morning?*); ph, Laszlo Kovacs (Technicolor); m, John Barry; ed, John Wright; prod d, Richard Sylbert; art d, Ida Random; set d, Emad Helmey; cos, Patricia Norris.

Biography **Cas.** **(PR:O MPAA:R)**

FRANCHETTE; LES INTRIGUES*½ (1969) 63m Distribpix c

Gary Michaels *(Himself)*, Dan Biller *(The Undercover Agent)*, Kathleen Miller *(Kathy)*, Nick Delgadi *(Rogers)*, Angelo Marcini, Georgio Moffo *(Roger's Torpedoes)*, Barbara Everest, Susan Cooper, Diane Turner.

Distasteful crime drama starring Michaels (who, for reasons known only to himself, plays himself here) as a beach-bum skin diver who meets and falls in love with mysterious British woman, Miller. This idyllic relationship is shattered when he discovers that Miller is the mistress of notorious heroin dealer, Delgadi. The drug kingpin hires the skin diver to dive for him, but the honorable Michaels decides to squeal to the cops. The hood finds out and sends two of his goons to shoot Michaels full of heroin and leave him for the cops in the hopes that his condition will destroy his credibility. Narcotics agent Biller nevertheless enlists Michaels' aid in trapping the criminals. Through all of this Michaels continues to meet Miller in hotel rooms, but they are caught by Delgadi and Miller is tortured and raped. Forced to make another dive for Delgadi (or he will kill Miller), Michaels waits for his chance and kills the mobster's two henchmen, allowing Delgadi to be captured by Biller.

p,d&w, Arlo Shiffen; ph, Gabrial Lister.

Crime **(PR:O MPAA:NR)**

FRANCHISE AFFAIR, THE** (1952, Brit.) 88m ABPC c

Michael Denison *(Robert Blair)*, Dulcie Gray *(Marion Sharpe)*, Anthony Nicholls *(Kevin McDermott)*, Marjorie Fielding *(Mrs. Sharpe)*, Athene Seyler *(Aunt Lin)*, Ann Stephens *(Ketty Kane)*, Hy Hazell *(Mrs. Chadwick)*, John Bailey *(Detective Inspector Grant)*, Avice Landone *(Mrs. Wynn)*, Kenneth More *(Stanley Peters)*, Moultrie Kelsall *(Judge)*, John Warwick *(Carley)*, Maureen Glynne *(Rose Glynn)*, Peter Jones *(Bernard Chadwick)*, Martin Boddey *(Inspector Hallam)*, Olive Sloane, Victor Maddern, Will Ambro, Doris York, Partick Troughton, Hugh Moxey, John Warwick, Earnest Jay, Everley Gregg, Ambrosine Phillpotts, Jean Anderson, Harold Lang, John Forrest, Lawrence Ray.

To have an alibi for her own misdeeds, small-town teenager Stephens falsely accuses local widow Fielding and daughter Gray of kidnapping and abusing her. Country lawyer Denison sorts out the facts and reveals the truth. Tedium triumphs again.

p, Robert Hall; d, Lawrence Huntington; w, Huntington, Hall (based on the novel by Josephine Tey); ph, Gunther Krampff; ed, Clifford Boote.

Crime **(PR:A MPAA:NR)**

FRANCIS*** (1949) 91m UNIV bw

Donald O'Connor *(Peter Stirling)*, Patricia Medina *(Maureen Gelder)*, ZaSu Pitts *(Valerie Humpert)*, Ray Collins *(Col. Hooker)*, John McIntire *(Gen. Stevens)*, Eduard Franz *(Col. Plepper)*, Howland Chamberlin *(Maj. Nadel)*, James Todd *(Col. Saunders)*, Robert Warwick *(Col. Carmichel)*, Frank Faylen *(Sgt. Chillingbacker)*, Anthony [Tony] Curtis *(Capt. Jones)*, Mikel Conrad *(Maj. Garber)*, Loren Tindall *(Maj. Richards)*, Charles Meredith *(Banker Munroe)*, Chill Wills *(Voice of Francis the Talking Mule)*, Judd Holdren *(1st Ambulance Man)*, Al Ferguson *(Capt. Dean)*, Roger Moore *(M.C. Major)*, Harry Harvey, Peter Prouse, Howard Negley *(Correspondents)*, Duke York *(Sgt. Poor)*, Joseph Kim *(Japanese Lieutenant)*, Robert Anderson *(Capt. Grant)*, Jack Shutta *(Sgt. Miller)*, Robert Blunt *(2nd Ambulance Man)*, Tim Graham *(Lt. Bremm)*, Jim Hayward *(Capt. Norman)*, Marvin Kaplan *(1st M.C. Lieutanant)*, Harold Fong *(Japanese Soldier)*, Mickey McCardle *(Capt. Addison)*.

The first in a series of mildly amusing comedies starring O'Connor as a dim-witted G.I. who hooks up with a talking mule named Francis in Burma. With Francis' help, O'Connor performs a series of heroic deeds against the enemy, but the mule will not talk to anyone but O'Connor, and for some reason the soldier insists on telling his superiors that the long-eared beast talks everytime it tries to help him. His C.O. thinks he's nuts, of course, and keeps sending the poor sap to the psycho ward. The truth comes out eventually when a general orders Francis to speak and the obedient mule complies. Hailed as heros, the duo is brought home for post-war duties. These silly comedies made more money than anyone could have expected and director Lubin went on to create another successful talking equine for television in "Mr. Ed."

p, Robert Arthur; d, Arthur Lubin; w, David Stern (based on his novel); ph, Irving Glassberg; m, Frank Skinner; ed, Milton Carruth; art d, Bernard Herzbrun, Richard H. Reidel; set d, Russel A. Gausman, A. Roland Fields, cos, Rosemary Odell.

Comedy **(PR:AA MPAA:NR)**

FRANCIS COVERS THE BIG TOWN** (1953) 86m UNIV bw

Donald O'Connor *(Peter Stirling)*, Yvette Dugay *(Maria Scola)*, Gene Lockhart *(Tom Henderson)*, Nancy Guild *(Alberta Ames)*, Larry Gates *(Dan Austin)*, Silvio Minciotti *(Salvatore Scola)*, Lowell Gilmore *(Garnet)*, William Harrigan *(Chief Hansen)*, Gale Gordon *(Evans)*, Hanley Stafford *(Dr. Goodrich)*, Forrest Lewis *(Judge Stanley)*, Michael Ross *(Parker)*, Louis Mason *(Mason)*, Charles J. Flynn *(Jones)*, Chill Wills *(Voice of Francis the Talking Mule)*.

The fourth in the series of talking-mule movies sees O'Connor trying to become an ace reporter on a New York City newspaper with the help of his braying friend. Francis comes up with several scoops and tips O'Connor so that the fledgling news-hound can impress the city editor. The tables turn, however, and O'Connor is framed on a murder rap and it takes Francis to save him when the big-eared beast-of-burden testifies to his pal's innocence on the witness stand.

p, Leonard Goldstein; d, Arthur Lubin; w, Oscar Brodney (based on "Francis" character created by David Stern); ph, Carl Guthrie; m, Joseph Gershenson; ed, Milton Carruth; art d, Bernard Herzbrun.

Comedy **(PR:AA MPAA:NR)**

FRANCIS GOES TO THE RACES** (1951) 88m UNIV bw

Donald O'Connor *(Peter Stirling)*, Piper Laurie *(Frances Travers)*, Cecil Kellaway *(Col. Travers)*, Jesse White *(Frank Damer)*, Barry Kelley *(Mallory)*, Hayden Rorke *(Rogers)*, Vaughn Taylor *(Harrington)*, Larry Keating *(Head Steward)*, Peter Brocco *(Dr. Marberry)*, Ed Max *(1st Mug)*, Don Beddoe *(Dr. Quimby)*, Jack Wilson *(2nd Mug)*, Bill Walker *(Sam)*, George Webster *(Jockey)*, Chill Wills *(Voice of Francis the Talking Mule)*.

The second talking-mule movie sees O'Connor and friend taking up residence on horsebreeder Kellaway's floundering ranch. While O'Connor falls in love with Kellaway's granddaughter Laurie, and Francis basks in the easy living of the ranch, mobsters grab the horsebreeder's stable as payment of a long-standing debt. To help out, Francis supplies his friends with a list of winners at Santa Anita so that Kellaway and company can raise enough cash to buy one horse to run in a big $100,000 race coming up. O'Connor takes the dough and buys a frustrated mare that doesn't think she can run. Francis comes to the rescue by psychoanalyzing the nag on a couch of straw and inspiring the horse to win, thus enabling Kellaway to get his ranch back.

p, Leonard Goldstein; d, Arthur Lubin; w, Oscar Brodney (based on "Francis" character created by David Stern; story by Robert Arthur); ph, Irving Glassberg; m, Frank Skinner; ed, Milton Carruth.

Comedy **(PR:AA MPAA:NR)**

FRANCIS GOES TO WEST POINT** (1952) 81m UNIV bw

Donald O'Connor *(Peter Stirling)*, Lori Nelson *(Barbara Atwood)*, Alice Kelley *(Cynthia Daniels)*, Palmer Lee [Gregg Palmer] *(William Norton)*, William Reynolds *(Wilbur Van Allen)*, Les Tremayne *(Col. Daniels)*, Otto Hulett *(Chad Chadwick)*, David Janssen *(Cpl. Thomas)*, James Best *(Cpl. Ransom)*, Paul Burke *(Cadet)*, Cliff Clark *(Plant Guard)*, Leonard Nimoy *(Football Player)*, Chill Wills *(Voice of Francis the Talking Mule)*.

The third entry in the talking-mule series sees O'Connor and pal save an atomic plant from sabotage and subsequently being rewarded by being appointed as a freshman at West Point. Francis aids his chum through the usual difficulties with hazing, basic training and grades and even helps Army beat Navy in the big football game.

p, Leonard Goldstein; d, Arthur Lubin; w, Oscar Brodney (based on "Francis" character created by David Stern); ph, Carl Guthrie; ed, Milton Carruth; md, Joseph Gershenson; art d, Bernard Herzbrun, Eric Orbom.

Comedy **(PR:AA MPAA:NR)**

FRANCIS IN THE HAUNTED HOUSE*½ (1956) 80m UNIV bw

Mickey Rooney *(David Prescott)*, Virginia Welles *(Lorna MacLeod)*, James Flavin *(Chief Martin)*, Paul Cavanagh *(Neil Frazer)*, Mary Ellen Kaye *(Lorna Ann)*, David Janssen *(Lt. Hopkins)*, Ralph Dumke *(Mayor Hargrove)*, Richard Gaines *(Dist. Atty. Reynolds)*, Richard Deacon *(Jason)*, Dick Winslow *(Sgt. Arnold)*, Charles Horvath *(Malcolm)*, Timothy Carey *(Hugo)*, Helen Wallace *(Mrs. MacPherson)*, Edward Earle *(Howard Grisby)*, John Maxwell *(Edward Ryan)*, Glen Kramer *(Ephraim Biddle)*, Paul Frees *(Voice of Francis the Talking Mule)*.

Well, it couldn't last forever. After making six of the Francis the talking mule comedies, stars O'Connor and Wills (Francis' voice) and director Lubin had had enough and jumped ship, leaving Rooney to take over the role of the dim-witted pal of the vocal jackass (utilizing the voice talents of Frees). The thin plot here sees Francis rescuing the hapless Rooney who is trapped in a haunted house with a group of crooks trying to steal genuine works of art by replacing them with forgeries. The dumbest—and last—entry in the series.

p, Robert Arthur; d, Charles Lamont; w, Herbert Margolis, William Raynor (based on "Francis" character created by David Stern); ph, George Robinson; ed, Milton Carruth; md, Joseph Gershenson; art d, Alexander Golitzen; cos, Jay Morley, Jr.

Comedy **(PR:AA MPAA:NR)**

FRANCIS IN THE NAVY** (1955) 80m UNIV bw

Donald O'Connor *(Lt. Peter Stirling/Slicker Donovan)*, Martha Hyer *(Betsy Donovan)*, Richard Erdman *(Murph)*, Jim Backus *(Cmdr. Hutch)*, Clint Eastwood *(Jonesy)*, David Janssen *(Lt. Anders)*, Leigh Snowden *(Appleby)*, Martin Milner *(Rick)*, Paul Burke *(Tate)*, Phil Garris *(Stover)*, Myrna Hansen *(Helen)*, Jane Howard *(Standish)*, Virginia O'Brien *(Nurse Kittredge)*, William Forrest *(Admiral)*, Chill Wills *(Voice of Francis the Talking Mule)*.

Overly complicated entry in the talking-mule series sees O'Connor as an Army lieutenant who gets a desperate call from his four-legged friend Francis saying that he's about to be drafted into the Navy. O'Connor comes to his buddie's aid, but is mistaken for a bosun's mate (also played by O'Connor) who looks just like him. The bosun's pals think he's gone nuts and is impersonating an Army lieutenant. Of course the mule straightens everything out. Look for bit-player Clint Eastwood in his second screen appearance (his first was as a lab assistant in REVENGE OF THE CREATURE).

p, Stanley Rubin; d, Arthur Lubin; w, Devery Freeman (based on "Francis" character created by David Stern); ph, Carl Guthrie; ed, Milton Carruth, Ray Snyder; md, Joseph Gershenson; art d, Alexander Golitzen, Bill Newberry; cos, Rosemary Odell.

Comedy **(PR:AA MPAA:NR)**

FRANCIS JOINS THE WACS** (1954) 94m UNIV bw

Donald O'Connor *(Peter Stirling)*, Julie Adams *(Capt. Parker)*, Chill Wills *(Gen. Kaye/Voice of Francis the Talking Mule)*, Mamie Van Doren *(Cpl. Bunky Hilstrom)*, Lynn Bari *(Maj. Louise Simpson)*, ZaSu Pitts *(Lt. Valerie Humpert)*, Joan Shawlee *(Sgt. Kipp)*, Allison Hayes *(Lt. Dickson)*, Mara Corday *(Kate)*, Karen Kadler *(Marge)*, Elsie Holmes *(Bessie)*, Olan Soule *(Capt. Creavy)*, Anthony Radecki *(Aide)*, Richard Deems *(Jeep Driver)*, Sam Woody *(Blue Soldier)*.

The fifth entry in the talking-mule series sees ex-G.I. O'Connor working as bank teller and finding himself drafted back into the service due to a clerical error, only this time he is to serve in the WACS. Francis comes along to make sure he stays out of trouble with the lovely ladies whom O'Connor is to assist in a camouflage mission. Wills, the voice of Francis, also plays the commanding general.

p, Ted Richmond; d, Arthur Lubin; w, Devery Freeman (based on "Francis" character created by David Stern; story by Herbert Baker); ph, Irving Glassberg; ed, Ted J. Kent, Russell Schoengarth; art d, Alexander Golitzen.

Comedy **(PR:AA MPAA:NR)**

FRANCIS OF ASSISI** (1961) 105m FOX c

Bradford Dillman *(Francis Bernardone)*, Dolores Hart *(Clare Scefi)*, Stuart Whitman *(Paolo)*, Pedro Armendariz *(Sultan)*, Cecil Kellaway *(Cardinal Hugolino)*, Eduard Franz *(Pietro Bernardino)*, Athene Seyler *(Aunt Buona)*, Finlay Currie *(Pope Innocent III)*, Mervyn Johns *(Brother Juniper)*, Russell Napier *(Brother Elias)*, John Welsh *(Canon Cattanei)*, Harold Goldblatt *(Bernard)*, Edith Sharpe *(Donna Pica Bernardone)*, Jack Lambert *(Scefi)*, Oliver Johnston *(Father Livoni)*, Malcolm Keen *(Bishop Guido)*, Evi Marandi *(Saracen Girl)*, Manuela Ballard *(Lucia)*, Jole Mauro *(Elfrida)*, Uti Hof *(Regina)*, Nicholas Hannen *(Beggar)*, Paul Muller, John Karlssen, Jack Savage, David Maunsell, Cyrus Elias, Curt Lowens, Renzo Cesana, Walter Maslow *(Friars)*, Feodor Chaliapin *(Cardinal Savelli)*.

Opulently lensed on location in Italy and Spain, this movie proves once again that even the most interesting religious stories can become dull if placed in the wrong hands. Dillman is the hedonistic son of an Assisi textile man. He becomes aware that there must be more to life than wine, women and song, and joins the army of Pope Innocent III (Currie) to fight for Sicily's liberation. Whitman is a poor nobleman and Dillman's best amici. While in the thick of the fray, Dillman responds to an inner voice telling him to return home. For this, he is marked as a coward and a deserter and tossed into the slammer. Upon his release, he hears the voice once more. This time, it tells him to rebuild the ruins of a church in Assisi. He gathers a bunch of locals and establishes a new religious order and together, they reconstruct the house of worship. Whitman falls in love with Hart, a wealthy young woman. She turns from Whitman and answers Dillman's religious call, forsaking worldly goods to become a nun. (Two years after this film, she did that in real life and is now known as Mother Dolores.) Whitman is enraged and rides off to join the Crusades. The Franciscan order grows rapidly and Dillman is then requested to journey to the Holy Land to help the Crusaders fight the sultan's army. He walks through fire to prove his faith and that mightily impresses the Sultan, Armendariz. Dillman is appalled by the Crusaders plundering and turns from their leader, Whitman. Upon returning to Assisi, he discovers that some of his flock have ignored their vows of poverty. He leaves and takes up residence in a cave and becomes progressively blinder until he is about to die and is visited by Hart and Whitman, who say their farewells. Much of St. Francis' work with animals is not seen here and if it had been, that is what might have made it work. He was the 13th-century version of Dr. Doolittle but you wouldn't know it for all the extraneous material in this film. A very lavish, but essentially tedious movie. Irish actor Harold Goldblatt is seen briefly as Bernard. A small bit is done by Renzo Cesana, who used to be a television sensation as "The Continental" in the early years of the tube. This was one of director Curtiz's dullest pictures.

p, Plato A. Skouras; d, Michael Curtiz; w, Eugene Vale, James Forsyth, Jack Thomas (based on the novel *The Joyful Beggar* by Louis De Wohl); ph, Piero Portalupi (CinemaScope, DeLuxe Color); m, Mario Nascimbene; ed, Louis Loeffler; art d, Edward Carrere; set d, Walter M. Scott, Fernandino Ruffo; cos, Vittorio Nine Novarese; spec eff, Joseph Natanson; tech adv, Vincenzo Labella.

Biography **(PR:A MPAA:NR)**

FRANCOISE (SEE: ANATOMY OF A MARRIAGE, MY DAYS WITH JEAN-MARC, 1964, Fr.)

FRANKENSTEIN**** (1931) 71m UNIV bw

Colin Clive *(Frankenstein)*, Mae Clarke *(Elizabeth)*, John Boles *(Victor)*, Boris Karloff *(The Monster)*, Edward Van Sloan *(Dr. Waldman)*, Dwight Frye *(Fritz, the Dwarf)*, Frederick Kerr *(The Baron)*, Lionel Belmore *(The Burgomaster)*, Michael Mark *(Ludwig, Peasant Father)*, Marilyn Harris *(Maria the Child)*, Arletta Duncan, Pauline Moore *(Bridesmaids)*, Francis Ford *(Villager)*.

"If you have a weak heart and cannot stand intense excitement or even shock, we are advising you NOT to see this production," warned Universal in its advertisements for this granddaddy of horror films. "If, on the contrary, you like an unusual thrill you will find it in FRANKENSTEIN." What viewers found was more than one "unusual thrill" as they followed slightly mad scientist Clive crawling about a fog-bound, eerie graveyard with his hunchbacked dwarf assistant, Frye, in search of dead bodies to steal, the freshly deceased with which he can piece together his obsessive creation. Many male corpses have been stitched together by doctor Clive to form a single breathless cadaver stretched out at the top of an abandoned watchtower which he has converted into a laboratory. All is about finished except that Clive lacks a brain for his giant. He dispatches Frye to the medical department of a nearby university. Here the dim-witted hunchback scans several jars in which brains have been kept alive for study. He selects one and begins to leave when a chime goes off, frightening him, causing him to drop the jar. Quickly he grabs another, oblivious to the ominous label on the second jar: "Criminal Brain." Clive later inserts the brain into his lifeless experiment, then waits for the appropriate electrical storm before turning on the strange machines he has constructed, devices that conduct the trapped lightning bolts and course them through the Monster's body. In attendance during this bizarre experiment is Clive's one-time tutor, Van Sloan, his horrified fiancee Clarke, and best friend Boles. All vainly plead with Clive to cease and desist but he is now berserk with anxiety and flits about the laboratory, electrically infusing life into his strange creature, raising it on a movable platform to the top of the tower so that the shafts of lightning strike it directly, then lowering the immense table as the transformers, dynamos, and electrodes crackle to a halt. At first there is no sign of life, but then one of the hands twitches. Clive is hysterical with scientific triumph, shouting: "It's moving, it's alive! It's alive!" He has created an artificial man from the flesh and blood of the dead, a creature so awful to behold that it is kept out of sight. Clive summons the Monster into his laboratory and it lurches forward on leaden limbs, its huge skull jerkily turning toward its master, a flat-topped, lizard-eyed, heavily scarred hulk with grotesque electrodes protruding from its neck and steel clamps pressed down into a clammy forehead affixing the top of its head. It is everything repugnant and detestable, a truly sinister thing oozing ignorant evils. The Monster becomes troublesome and Clive keeps him chained in a dungeon where Frye taunts the creature with a torch which he thrusts into his face. Incensed, the Monster breaks his chains and kills Frye, then breaks out of his cell before Van Sloan, who intends to dissect the creature, can prevent further murders. He crushes Van Sloan, then wanders aimlessly into the countryside. Later, the Monster comes upon an innocent little girl, Harris, who does not fear him. He joins her in a game, tossing flower petals into a lake. When there are no more petals, the murderous creature becomes enraged and throws the girl into the water, where she drowns. He stumbles away from the scene, a flicker of remorse shown in a small gesture as he wrings his hands, perhaps dimly comprehending the awful act he has committed. Then Mark, the dead child's father, finds the body and brings it into the town, to the very door of the burgomaster, Belmore, who promises revenge for the murder. Meanwhile, Clive has abandoned his creature altogether, thinking Van Sloan has destroyed it, and makes plans to marry Clarke, who is preening before a mirror in the Frankenstein mansion, admiring her bridal gown. At this moment, the Monster, seeking its creator, crashes into the room, plodding toward a horrified Clarke. He is driven off by servants and by Clive, answering Clarke's screams of terror. The villagers, with Clive leading them, then grab torches and begin to hunt the Monster through the night. The creature grabs Clive and drags his creator into an old windmill which is quickly surrounded by shouting villagers. At the top ledge of the windmill Clive and his Monster battle and the scientist is finally lifted up by his creation and hurled downward, his fall broken by one of the arms of the moving windmill. The villagers set fire to the creaking wooden structure and it burns to the ground, the Monster ostensibly dying in the flames. Clive later recovers and marries Clarke. FRANKENSTEIN was released only ten months after Universal's classic horror film DRACULA, starring Bela Lugosi. So successful was the Lugosi film that he was originally cast as the Monster in FRANKENSTEIN, with Robert Florey contracted to direct. But Lugosi's test footage, including Lugosi's sympathetic view of the monster as also depicted in the Webling play (and in the original novel by Mary Shelley), was rejected in favor of a more sinister and devastating monster and a director who would project a baroque view, one where a nightmare pageant would be staged, was selected, this being the theatrically bent Whale. Whale urged Universal to cast Karloff in the role of the monster, a part that would forever typecast this accomplished actor in horror films, although he would only play the monster twice more, in THE BRIDE OF FRANKENSTEIN, 1935, and in SON OF FRANKENSTEIN, 1939. Karloff had had a long but uneventful film career up to this time, having first appeared as an extra as early as 1916 in a Universal silent entitled THE DUMB GIRL OF PORTICI; he had made 80 films before FRANKENSTEIN and was so in demand as a character player by the time he was cast as the Monster that in the year 1931 alone he had appeared in eighteen films. Whale's selection of this stellar actor occurred accidentally. Karloff happened to be eating in the studio commissary where Whale spotted him and called him over to his table, telling him: "Your face has startling possibilities . . . I'd like you to test for the Monster in FRANKENSTEIN." Karloff was delighted and immediately huddled with the studio's greatest makeup artist, Jack Pierce, who would go on to oversee the creation of every monster Universal put on the screen from 1931 to his retirement in 1947. Karloff wanted to appear just right and he spent countless hours with Pierce perfecting his appearance until making a test that stunned Whale and got him the part. Pierce explained how he designed the Monster's hideous image in a 1939 interview with the New York *Times*: "There are six ways a surgeon can cut the skull and I figured Dr. Frankenstein, who was not a practicing surgeon, would take the easier. That is, he would cut the top of the skull off straight across like a pot lid, hinge it, pop the brain in, and clamp it tight. That's the reason I decided to make the Monster's head square and flat like a box and dig that scar across his forehead and have two metal clamps hold it together. The two metal studs that stick out the sides of his neck are inlets for electricity—plugs. Don't forget the Monster is an electrical gadget and that lightning is his life force . . . The lizard eyes were made of rubber, as was his false head. I made his arms look longer by shortening the sleeves of his coat. His legs were stiffened by steel struts and two pairs of pants. His large feet were the boots asphalt-spreaders wear. His face was coated with blue-green grease paint, which photographs [in black and white] gray." Pierce's coloring briefly affected other technicians on the production and it was decided to tint the prints of this film a sickly green but it made all the actors look bilious, so these prints were discarded and the black-and-whites were officially released. Director Whale later took some credit for Karloff's frightening makeup, having studied art before entering WW I, and later becoming a magazine cartoonist. Said Whale: "Karloff's face has always fascinated me, and I made drawings of his head, added sharp, bony ridges where I imagined the skull might have joined. His physique was weaker than I could wish but that queer, enetrating personality of his, I felt, was more important than his shape, which could easily be altered." Karloff himself helped in the creation of the nightmare figure, later commenting: "The Monster was inarticulate, and I had to make him understood. When the audience first sees him he is only five hours old. My first problem was not to let his eyes be too intelligent, which is why I decided to use the false eye-lids that half-veil the eyes." Physically, Karloff was put through agony. His body was elevated to a height of seven feet six inches by huge boots with thirty pound weights at the bottom of each so he was forced to clomp ponderously about, and, coupled to the steel struts affixed to his legs, gave him that weird lurching effect. Heavy padding bulked up his drab clothing and his hands were thickly coated with plaster. Added to this was the weighty artificial skull, many layers of greasepaint, strips of cotton, and mounds of gum arabic. To merely attempt to walk in this incredible ensemble Karloff had to struggle to the point of exhaustion (he lost 20 pounds during the six-week shooting) and, when the script compelled him to carry Clive on his back in the windmill scenes, he severely strained his back and would later be hospitalized and require a spinal fusion. To make matters worse, producer Laemmle, Jr., youthful son of the studio owner whose inspirations DRACULA and FRANKENSTEIN were, decided that Karloff's incredible appearance must be kept secret until the film's release. Once he was made up he was not allowed to leave the set, see visitors, or even smoke since he might flick an ash onto the highly flammable parts of his makeup. When he was allowed to go to his dressing room and into other soundstages while still made up, an assistant director placed a black hood over his head and gloves on his hands. His meals were served in private and Uncle Carl Laemmle gave strict orders that Karloff was never ever to be seen by his office staff, commenting: "Some of our nice little secretaries are pregnant and they might be frightened if they saw him." The makeup and costume took Karloff and Pierce five hours to put on each day and two hours to remove. (As a souvenier of his ordeal Karloff later took home the box-top headpiece and the asphalter's shoes.) When Uncle Carl Laemmle saw the rushes of FRANKENSTEIN he recoiled in horror, telling his son: "This is scary stuff and we must warn moviegoers." He ordered a prolog written and delivered by Van Sloan (later deleted, as was the murdering of the child, thought by the elder Laemmle to be too brutal to tolerate). Van Sloan appears on the screen to tell audiences: "How do you do. Mr. Carl Laemmle feels it would be a little unkind to present this picture without just a word of friendly warning. We are about to unfold the story of Frankenstein, a man of science, who sought to create a man after his own image without reckoning upon God. It is one of the strangest tales ever told. It deals with the two great mysteries of creation, life and death. I think it will thrill you. It may even shock you. It might even horrify you. So if any of you do not care to subject your nerves to such a strain, now's your chance to . . . Well, we've warned you!" Van Sloan was the perfect choice for Laemmle's warning since he had delivered the creepy epilog for DRACULA. Uncle Carl threw out a line delivered by Clive, one the studio mogul felt would upset the clergy. Clive, ecstatic at bringing life to his misshapen creation, initially cried out: "Now I know what it feels like to be God!" The film premiered on December 6, 1931 in Santa Barbara, California, but Universal thought so little of Karloff that he was not invited; Clive and Clarke were on hand to take the plaudits of the public. When the Monster appeared on screen the image produced a wave of fear greater than any Grand Guignol of the past. People, especially women and children, went screaming up the aisles. The theater manager got a call at 3 a.m. the following morning from an irate male patron who shouted over the phone (according to the ever alert Universal publicity department): "I saw FRANKENSTEIN at your place last night and can't sleep—I have no intention that you should either!" Karloff, who had only seen some of the rushes, took his wife and one of her friends to see the film in San Francisco. After he appeared on screen, Mrs. Karloff's friend became hysterical, shaking Dorothy Karloff (a librarian) and screaming as she shielded her eyes with one hand: "Dot, how can you live with that *creature?*" Although Whale and Laemmle agreed with the censors to cut the scene where the Monster kills the little girl to see if she will float, Karloff objected. He felt that this was his one scene whereby he could display the Monster's one spark of humanity by wringing his hands and emitting cries of agony. This scene played in England, but the British censor board cut the scenes where the Monster threatens bride-to-be Clarke and kills Van Sloan. For all of his inability to act beyond the restrictions of his horrific makeup, mail to Karloff flooded the studio, where he became the superstar of monster movies. The public flocked to the film which was made for less than $250,000 and returned $12 million the first time around, making almost as much in 1938 when it was rereleased on a double bill with DRACULA, these two films playing to record crowds throughout the U.S. (In one instance during the 1938 rerelease, a crowd of 4,000 people broke into a theater where prints were late in arriving, creating a near-riot until frantic technicians got the film rolling.) Karloff was ever mindful through his long career of his debt to the strange, lumbering creature, once saying: "God bless the old boy—without him I would have been nowhere." Clive's twitchy performance is almost a duplicate of his role in JOURNEY'S END, which is why Whale picked him. Clarke had already appeared in a Whale film, WATERLOO BRIDGE, and he liked her frail appearance, the perfect screaming fright victim. Boles was a singer who had appeared in THE KING OF JAZZ and was seeking to change his roles to the dramatic, succeeding in typecasting himself as a handsome supporting player in a spate of horror films. The role of the fragile fiancee almost went to Bette Davis instead of Clarke, but Whale rejected Davis after viewing her in a costume test as being "too aggressive." FRANKENSTEIN'S success, of course, owes much to Whale's conception of the man-made monster and his masterful and expeditious direction, along with Florey's vivid script, albeit the film takes much from the story lines of THE GOLEM, 1922 and THE CABINET OF DR. CALIGARI, 1919. The skimpy musical score in this 1931 monster epic enhances rather than detracts from the suspense and terror of the film. This netherworld film had been produced many times both before and after Universal's 1931 landmark effort, first in 1910 as FRANKENSTEIN with Charles Ogle by the Edison Company (no prints are presently known to exist), in 1915 as LIFE WITHOUT SOUL, and an Italian effort in 1920 known as MASTER OF FRANKENSTEIN. Sequels: THE BRIDE OF FRANKENSTEIN, 1935; SON OF FRANKENSTEIN, 1939; GHOST OF FRANKENSTEIN, 1941; FRANKENSTEIN MEETS THE WOLF MAN, 1943; HOUSE OF FRANKENSTEIN, 1945; HOUSE OF DRACULA, 1945; ABBOTT AND COSTELLO MEET FRANKENSTEIN, 1948. British productions about the monster were ground out by Hammer Studios for fifteen years, along with a spate of cheapie Hollywood productions where the Monster was played for laughs. The Monster was so often confused by the public with his creator's name "Frankenstein" has come to signify the Monster himself. (See FRANKENSTEIN series, Index.)

p, Carl Laemmle, Jr.; d, James Whale; w, Garrett Fort, Francis Edwards Faragoh, John L. Balderston, Robert Florey (based on the novel by Mary Shelley and the play by Peggy Webling); ph, Arthur Edeson; m, David Brockman; ed, Maurice Pivar, Clarence Kolster; art d, Charles D. Hall; set d, Herman Rosse; spec eff, John P. Fulton; makeup, Jack P. Pierce.

Horror   Cas.   (PR:C-O   MPAA:NR)

FRANKENSTEIN AND THE MONSTER FROM HELL**
(1974, Brit.) 93m Hammer/PAR c

Peter Cushing (Baron Frankenstein), Shane Briant (Simon Helder), Madeline Smith (Sarah), Dave Prowse (Monster), John Stratton (Asylum Director), Charles Lloyd-Pack (Prof. Durendel), Bernard Lee (Tarmud), Patrick Troughton (The Body Snatcher), Sydney Bromley (Muller), Janet Hargreaves (Chatter), Philip Voss (Ernst).

The sixth, last, and worst of the Hammer Frankenstein series sees Briant as a young doctor performing experiments with human bodies (a la Dr. Frankenstein). When he is discovered, he is thrown into an asylum by the authorities. As it turns out, the asylum is run by—none other than Dr. Frankenstein himself, Cushing. Together they continue their work, this time to transfer the brain of a brilliant mathematician into the head of an ugly, hairy brute of a man played by the future Darth Vader in STAR WARS, Prowse. Everything goes fine until the monster develops a craving for human flesh. Really lame, but released on a double bill with the vastly superior CAPTAIN KRONOS: VAMPIRE HUNTER.

p, Roy Skeggs; d, Terence Fisher; w, John Elder [Anthony Hinds]; ph, Brian Probyn (Studio Film Lab Processing); m, James Bernard; ed, James Needs; art d, Scott Macgregor.

Horror   (PR:O   MPAA:R)

FRANKENSTEIN CONQUERS THE WORLD zero   (1964, Jap./US)
87m Toho/AIP c (FUHARANKENSHUTAIN TAI BARAGON; AKA: FRANKENSTEIN VERSUS THE GIANT DEVILFISH; FRANKENSTEIN AND THE GIANT LIZARD)

Nick Adams (Dr. James Bowen), Tadao Takashima (Scientist), Kumi Mizuno (Woman Doctor), Yoshio Tsuchiya, Takashi Shimura, Kenchiro Kawaji, Seuko Togami.

Pitiful attempt by the Japanese monster-movie industry to adapt the Frankenstein monster to their milieu. The results are barely laughable. The plot involves the transfer of the Frankenstein monster's heart from Nazi Germany to Japan during WW II, where it is caught in the atomic blast that destroyed Hiroshima, and subsequently eaten by an unwitting Japanese youngster (got that?). Suddenly the little cannibalistic tyke finds himself growing into a giant who sports a large forehead (yeah, it kinda looks like Frankenstein's) and ugly, nasty teeth. Dressing himself like a cave man, the "monster" goes to live on Mount Fuji where he fights off another giant Japanese monster, Baragon (it looks a little like Godzilla). This creature was originally supposed to be a giant octopus, but for some reason, the molluscan scenes were shelved (though this battle can be seen in some production stills that pop up occasionally). American actor Adams actually acted his scenes during the production (as opposed to the usual Japanese practice, where the American actor is hired after the fact and his scenes inserted later for U.S. release, as was done with Raymond Burr in GODZILLA) and he plays the usual lame scientist who's around to help rebuild Hiroshima. Really awful, even for a Japanese monster movie.

p, Tomoyuki Tanaka; d, Inoshiro Honda; w, Kaoru Mabuchi (from a synopsis by Jerry Sohl, based on a story by Reuben Bercovitch); ph, Hajime Koizumi (Tohoscope, Eastmancolor); m, Akira Ifukube; ed, Ryohei Fujii; art d, Takeo Kita.

Science Fiction/Horror   (PR:C   MPAA:NR)

FRANKENSTEIN CREATED WOMAN***   (1965, Brit.) 92m Seven
Arts-Hammer/FOX c

Peter Cushing (Baron Frankenstein), Susan Denberg (Christina), Thorley Walters (Dr. Hertz), Robert Morris (Hans), Peter Blythe (Anton), Barry Warren (Karl), Derek Fowlds (Johann), Alan MacNaughtan (Kleve), Peter Madden (Police Chief), Stuart Middleton (Hans As a Boy), Duncan Lamont (Prisoner), Colin Jeavons (Priest), Ivan Beavis (New Landlord), John Maxim (Police Sergeant), Philip Ray (Mayor), Kevin Flood (Jailer), Bartlett Mullins (Bystander), Alec Mango (Spokesman).

The fourth and one of the best of Hammer's Frankenstein series sees mad doctor Cushing once again experimenting with human bodies. This time he transplants the soul of an executed young man into the disfigured body of his female lover, Denberg (a former Playboy centerfold), who had committed suicide after her beau was killed. Cushing then performs plastic surgery and turns the ugly girl into a blonde beauty, but the revenge impulse of her male soul takes over and she seeks out those who brought about her/his unjust execution, and then seduces and kills them. An interesting variation of the Frankenstein theme presented with fine production values. This is the sequel to EVIL OF FRANKENSTEIN. Then along came FRANKENSTEIN MUST BE DESTROYED.

p, Anthony Nelson Keys; d, Terence Fisher; w, John Elder [Anthony Hinds]; ph, Arthur Grant (DeLuxe Color); m, James Bernard; ed, James Needs, Spencer Reeve; prod d, Bernard Robinson; md, Philip Martell; art d, Don Mingaye; cos, Rosemary Burrows, Larry Stewart; spec eff, Les Bowie; makeup, George Partleton.

Horror   (PR:O   MPAA:NR)

FRANKENSTEIN-ITALIAN STYLE zero   (1977, Ital.) 97m Euro
International c (FRANKENSTEIN ALL'ITALIANA)

Aldo Maccione (The Monster), Gianrico Tedeschi (Prof. Frankenstein), Ninetto Davoli (Igor), Jenny Tamburi (Janet), Anna Mazzananio (Maud), Lorenza Guerrieri (Alice).

Crude Italian sexploitation film wherein Frankenstein's monster interrupts his creator's wedding ceremony, dies, is revived, and then performs stud services for the good doctor's assistant, wife, and servant before the doc transplants the monster's large sex organs onto himself—a rip-off of a similar scene in Mel Brooks' YOUNG FRANKENSTEIN (1974). Wretched.

p, Filiberto Bandino; d, Armando Crispino; w, Massimo Franciosa, Maria Luisa Montagnana; ph, Giuseppe Aquari; m, Stelvio Cipriani; prod d, Mario Molli; ed, Angela Cipriani.

Comedy/Horror   (PR:O   MPAA:NR)

FRANKENSTEIN MEETS THE SPACE MONSTER zero (1965) 75m
AA bw (AKA: MARS INVADES PUERTO RICO, FRANKENSTEIN MEETS
THE SPACEMEN)

James Karen (Dr. Adam Steele), Nancy Marshall (Karen Grant), Robert Reilly (Col. Frank Saunders/Frankenstein), Marilyn Hanold (Princess Marcuzan), Lou Cutell (Nadir), David Kernan (Gen. Bowers).

One of the all-time worst sci-fi movies ever made. It has nothing to do with Mary Shelley's Frankenstein. Rather, the Frankenstein of the title refers to a NASA android named Frank (Reilly), who crash-lands his space ship near the evil but beautiful alien Princess Hanold's ship, which has arrived in Puerto Rico to capture Earth women to take back to her home planet in order to repopulate. With the aid of her bald dwarf Cutell and her pet space monster, Hanold sends her minions out to capture some girls wildly dancing to rock 'n' roll music at a pool party. Unfortunately, one of the aliens stumbles across Reilly extricating himself from his smashed capsule, and blasts him in the face with his ray-gun. Now, with only half a face (a few transistors are clearly visible on the side of his horribly scarred skull) the NASA android goes haywire, wreaking havoc. Luckily, he is found and rewired by Karen and Marshall and then sent off to do battle with the invaders. After a long, silly fight with the pet monster (he almost pulls his mask off), Reilly rescues the kidnaped Earth girls, and destroys the alien craft in a blaze of NASA stock footage. Really bad, full of silly rock 'n' roll songs, inane dialog and laughable "special effects."

p, Robert McCarthy; d, Robert Gaffney; w, George Garrett (based on a story by Garrett, John Rodenbeck, R. H. W. Dillard); ph, Saul Midwall; ed, Laverne Keating.

Horror/Science Fiction   (PR:C   MPAA:NR)

FRANKENSTEIN MEETS THE WOLF MAN*** (1943) 72m UNIV bw

Lon Chaney, Jr. (The Wolf Man/Lawrence Talbot), Ilona Massey (Baroness Elsa Frankenstein), Patric Knowles (Dr. Mannering), Lionel Atwill (Mayor), Bela Lugosi (Monster), Maria Ouspenskaya (Maleva), Dennis Hoey (Inspector Owen), Don Barclay (Franzec), Rex Evans (Vazec), Dwight Frye (Rudi), Harry Stubbs (Gune), Martha Vickers (Little Girl), Doris Lloyd (Hospital Nurse), Adia Kuynetzoff, Beatrice Roberts (Villager), Jeff Corey, Torben Meyer.

This was the fifth Frankenstein film in the Universal series. Chaney searches out Dr. Frankenstein to cure his lycanthropy. The good doctor is dead and Chaney meets and battles the doctor's monster. The townspeople, not wanting to see the monster back in their village, blow up the dam and wash the Wolf Man and Frankenstein's monster away. Lugosi was sick for most of the shooting and stuntman Eddie Parker doubled for him through most of the filming. The first close-up is of Parker. The film is really a sequel to THE WOLF MAN (1941) and originally Chaney was to play both the Wolf Man and Frankenstein's monster in this film. This became too complicated and Lugosi was then called in.

p, George Waggner; d, Roy William Neill; w, Curt Siodmak; ph, George Robinson; ed, Edward Curtiss; art d, John Goodman; makeup, Jack Pierce, Ellis Burman; spec eff, John P. Fulton; stunts, Eddie Parker.

Horror   (PR:C   MPAA:NR)

FRANKENSTEIN MUST BE DESTROYED!*** (1969, Brit.) 97m
Hammer/WB c

Peter Cushing (Baron Frankenstein), Veronica Carlson (Anna Spengler), Freddie Jones (Prof. Richter), Simon Ward (Dr. Karl Holst), Thorley Walters (Inspector Frisch), Maxine Audley (Ella Brandt), George Pravda (Dr. Brandt), Geoffrey Bayldon (Police Doctor), Collette O'Neal (Madwoman), Harold Goodwin (Burglar), Frank Middlemass, Norman Shelley, Michael Gover, George Belbin (Guests), Peter Copley (Principal), Jim Collier (Dr. Heidecke), Alan Surtees, Windsor Davies (Police Sergeants).

The fifth in the Hammer Frankenstein series sees the good doctor, Cushing, interested in brain transplants. Anxious to work with an expert in the field, Pravda, he travels to his town only to find that his colleague has gone mad and been put in an asylum. By blackmailing young doctor Ward and his girl Carlson (they had been selling drugs stolen from the hospital where Ward works), Cushing gets them to help him kidnap Pravda from the asylum. In their escape, Cushing inadvertently causes the death of Pravda. Undaunted, Cushing drags the body to the basement of Carlson's rooming house where he performs a brain transplant, taking Pravda's brain out of his body and putting it into the head of an unfortunate asylum employee whom he had murdered (Jones). The operation is a success, but Jones' skull is horribly scarred. Suddenly a water main that runs through the boarding-house property bursts, uncovering the buried shell of Pravda. Cushing and Carlson barely manage to move the corpse before the authorities arrive to inspect the pipe. Jones, meanwhile has wandered off to visit his (Pravda's) wife. When confronted with this ugly man who knows intimate details about her life with her husband, Audley becomes terrified and flees. Saddened by this turn of events, Jones realizes that brain transplants are a horrible wrong to perform on the part of the patients and he seeks out Cushing to destroy him and his unholy work. Eventually creator and creation face each other and die together in a fiery climax. A well-done Hammer horror film, with a thoughtful screenplay that finally injects some compassion and intelligence into the monster. One of director Fisher's best.

p, Anthony Nelson Keys; d, Terence Fisher; w, Bert Batt (based on a story by Keys, Batt); ph, Arthur Grant (Technicolor); m, James Bernard; ed, James Needs, Gordon Hales; md, Philip Martell; art d, Bernard Robinson; cos, Rosemary Burrows; makeup, Eddie Knight.

Horror (PR:C-O MPAA:NR)

FRANKENSTEIN 1970** (1958) 83m AA bw

Boris Karloff (Baron Victor von Frankenstein), Tom Duggan (Mike Shaw), Jana Lund (Carolyn Hayes), Donald Barry (Douglas Row), Charlotte Austin (Judy Stevens), Irwin Berke (Inspector Raab), Rudolph Anders (Wilhelm Gottfried), John Dennis (Morgan Haley), Norbert Schiller (Shuter), Mike Lane (Hans).

In this Frankenstein horror outing Karloff finally gets to play the creator instead of the created. As the grandson of the late Baron Frankenstein who was horribly scarred by the Nazis during the war, Karloff plans to recreate his grandpa's experiments, but he needs cash to purchase an atomic reactor to bring his creature to life. To do this he allows a television crew to rent his historic castle to shoot a TV show. With the money, and spare parts to work with, Karloff succeeds in bringing his monster (it stands about seven feet tall and is wrapped up like a mummy) to life, but the creature attacks him and during the struggle atomic steam is released, killing them both. The members of the TV crew that have survived unravel the monster's bandages and are shocked to discover that its face is that of Karloff, before the Nazis scarred him. Karloff hams it up and the whole thing is pretty silly (including the title, which means nothing) but FRANKENSTEIN 1970 is an odd combination of classic and nuclear horror.

p, Aubrey Shenck; d, Howard W. Koch; w, Richard Landau, George Worthing Yates (based on a story by Shenck, Charles A. Moses); ph, Carl E. Guthrie; (CinemaScope) m, Paul Dunlap; ed, John A. Bushelman; art d, Jack Collins; set d, Paul Dunlap; makeup, Gordon Bau.

Horror (PR:C MPAA:NR)

FRANKENSTEIN, THE VAMPIRE AND CO.* (1961, Mex.) 80m
Cinematografia Calderon (FRANKENSTEIN, EL VAMPIRO Y COMPANIA)

Manuel Loco Valdes, Jose Jasso, Joaquin Garcia Vargas Borolas, Quintin Bulnes, Antonio Bravo, Jorge Mondragon, Martha Elena Cervantes, Nora Veryan, Roberto G. Rivera.

Mexican rip-off of ABBOTT AND COSTELLO MEET FRANKENSTEIN (1948) starring the less-than-hilarious comedy team of Loco Valdes and Jasso who deliver the bodies of a vampire (Bulnes) and Frankenstein's monster to a mysterious castle, where the vampire plans to have doctor Veryan transplant the virtually unused brain of Valdes into the head of the monster (sound familiar?). Soon the werewolf arrives and we have a complete photocopy of the plot of the Abbott and Costello film. This doesn't even come close to touching Bud and Lou's version.

p, Guillermo Calderon; d, Benito Alazraki; w, Alfredo Salazar; ph, Enrique Wallace.

Comedy/Horror (PR:C MPAA:NR)

FRANKENSTEIN VS. THE GIANT DEVILFISH
(SEE: FRANKENSTEIN CONQUERS THE WORLD, 1966, Jap.)

FRANKENSTEIN'S BLOODY TERROR* (1968, Span.) 83m
Maxper/Independent International c
(LA MARCA DEL HOMBRE LOBO)

Paul Naschy (Count Waldemar Daninsky), Diana Zura (Countess), Michael Manza (Rudolph), Julian Ugarte (Mikelhov), Rossanna Yanni (Wandessa).

For some reason Spanish horror star Naschy has a rabid (pardon the joke) cult of fans in this country, but his films sure don't betray the reason for such loyalty. In this, the most favored Naschy effort, our hero is a werewolf who goes to an occult specialist seeking a cure for his lycanthropy. Unfortunately the experts turn out to

be vampires. Originally shown in Spain in 3-D, 70-mm "Chil-o-rama" and Eastmancolor (as are most of Naschy's films); only flat prints survive in this country.

d, Enrique L. Equiluz [Henry L. Egan]; w, Jacinto Molina [Paul Naschy]; ph, Emilio Foriscot (70-mm "Chil-O-Rama/Eastmancolor 3-D); m, Angel Arteaga; ed, Francisco Janmandreu; art d, Jose Luis R. Ferrer.

Horror (PR:C MPAA:PG)

FRANKENSTEIN'S DAUGHTER zero (1958) 85m Astor bw (AKA: SHE MONSTER OF THE NIGHT)

John Ashley (Johnny Bruder), Sandra Knight (Trudy Morton), Donald Murphy (Oliver Frank), Sally Todd (Suzie), Harold Lloyd, Jr. (Don), Felix Locher (Carter Morton), Wolfe Barzell (Elsu), John Zaremba, Robert Dix, Harry Wilson, Voltaire Perkins, Charlotte Portney, Bill Coontz, George Barrows, Page Cavanaugh Trio.

Murphy stars as a mad scientist living in the suburbs who is not really Oliver Frank, as he tells everyone, but Oliver Frankenstein, a descendant of the old doctor himself. He creates a monster from the corpse of a teenage girl, who terrorizes the city until she and her maker meet their maker. It's hard to fathom Mary Shelley's original appearing so poorly, but FRANKENSTEIN'S DAUGHTER succeeds in being that.

p, Marc Frederic; d, Dick Cunha; w, M.E. Barrie; ph, Meredith Nicholson; m, Nicholas Carras; ed, Everett Dodd; spec eff, Ira Anderson; makeup, Harry Thomas.

Horror Cas. (PR:C-O MPAA:NR)

FRANKIE AND JOHNNY* (1936) 66m REP bw

Helen Morgan (Frankie), Chester Morris (Johnny), Florence Reed (Lou), Walter Kingsford (Timothy), William Harrigan (Curley), John Larkin (Andy), Cora Witherspoon ("Lumpy"), Lilyan Tashman [not billed] (Nellie Bly).

A mess from beginning to end. This was one of the first pictures to be based on a song. Since then, there have been several others such as ODE TO BILLY JOE (1976), TAKE THIS JOB AND SHOVE IT (1981), and more. Chester Morris is dull as Johnny, a country bumpkin who wanders into a St. Louis sporting house (read: brothel) where Helen Morgan is Frankie, the in-house vocalist. They marry; he begins cheating on her with Lilyan Tashman (Bly), who died before the picture was released, two years after it was made (lots of hassles with the Hays Office over the depiction of the bordello). Dying was taken as a personal affront by the studio bosses of the 1930s; as was usually the case with deceased cast or crew members, Tashman was unbilled in the screen credits on the picture's release. Morgan is about to shoot Morris for his transgressions when the deed is done for her by an angry gambler. With a screenplay by Moss Hart, more wit would have been expected, but he was busy that year working with Kaufman on what was to be "You Can't Take It With You" for Broadway. Dumb dialog, badly directed, jerkily edited; even the songs don't work. Morgan thrushes "Give Me A Heart To Sing To," "Get Rhythm In Your Feet," "If You Want My Heart," and, of course, "Frankie and Johnny."

p, William Saal; d, Chester Erskin, John H. Auer; w, Moss Hart, Lou Goldberg (based on a story by Jack Kirkland); ph, Joseph Ruttenberg; md, Victor Young; m/l, Young, Ned Washington, J. Russell Robinson, William Livingstone.

Drama Cas. (PR:A-C MPAA:NR)

FRANKIE AND JOHNNY** (1966) 87m UA c

Elvis Presley (Johnny), Donna Douglas (Frankie), Harry Morgan (Cully), Sue Anne Langdon (Mitzi), Nancy Kovack (Nellie Bly), Audrey Christie (Peg), Robert Strauss (Blackie), Anthony Eisley (Braden), Jerome Cowan (Wilbur), Wilda Taylor, Larri Thomas, Dee Jay Mattis, Judy Chapman (Earl Barton Dancers).

Another mediocre Presley vehicle, this one based on the famous title song. Presley is Johnny, a gambler/singer on a Mississippi riverboat and Douglas (of TV's "Beverly Hillbillies" fame) is Frankie, his girl. Presley has a string of bad luck with his gambling until he meets red-haired Kovack, who brings him good fortune. The jealous Douglas inadvertently shoots Presley, but he lives and sings. Directed by Freddy (BONZO GOES TO COLLEGE, (1952), "The Tonight Show") de Cordova. Songs include: "When The Saints Go Marching In," "Look Out Broadway," Fred Wise, Randy Starr; "Shout It Out," Bill Giant, Bernie Baum, Florence Kaye; "Frankie And Johnny," new words and arrangement by Fred Karger, Alex Gottlieb, Ben Weisman; "Chesay," Weisman, Syd Wayne, Karger; "Come Along," David Hess; "Petunia," "The Gardner's Daughter," "Beginner's Luck," Sid Tepper, Roy C. Bennett; "What Every Woman Lives For," Doc Pomus, Mort Shuman; "Everybody Come Aboard," Giant, Baum, Kaye; "Hard Luck," Weisman, Wayne; "Please Don't Stop Loving Me," Joy Byers.

p, Edward Small; d, Frederick de Cordova; w, Alex Gottlieb (based on a story by Nat Perrin); ph, Jacques Marquette (Technicolor); m&md, Fred Karger; ed, Grant Whytock; art d, Walter Simonds; set d, Morris Hoffman; ch, Earl Barton; makeup, Dan Greenway.

Musical (PR:A MPAA:NR)

FRANK'S GREATEST ADVENTURE (SEE: FEARLESS FRANK, 1967)

FRANTIC*** (1961, Fr.) 90m Nouvelles Editions de Films/Times Film Corp.
bw (ASCENSEUR POUR L'ECHAFAUD)

Jeanne Moreau (Florence Carala), Maurice Ronet (Julien Tavernier), Georges Poujouly (Louis), Yori Bertin (Veronique), Jean Wall (Simon Carala), Ivan Petrovich (Horst Bencker), Lino Ventura (Inspector Cherier), Elga Andersen (Madame Bencker), Felix Marten (Subervie), Bandeira, Hubert Deschamps, Sylvianne Aisenstein.

Famed documentarist/feature filmmaker Louis Malle—MURMUR OF THE HEART (1971), PRETTY BABY (1978), ATLANTIC CITY (1980)—in his first feature film tells the parallel story of two disparate criminal enterprises, interestingly joined by circumstance and coincidence. Moreau and Ronet, lovers, plot the murder of her husband—his employer—Wall. Having secretly affixed a rope outside Wall's office window (one story above his own office), Ronet very publicly lets it be known that he is sequestering himself in his own office for a brief period one afternoon. He climbs the rope to Wall's chambers, shoots him dead, and then returns to his own office. Following his customary habit pattern, he leaves his office—making certain he is observed doing so—at his usual hour. Once in the street, he glances upward, to see the rope—mute but deadly evidence of his involvement—dangling between the two offices. He re-enters the building to retrieve the indicting hemp, with which he may have fashioned a noose for himself, but a cost-conscious management has decreed that the building's electric power be shut off after working hours; he finds himself trapped in an elevator between two floors. During Ronet's entrapment, delinquent teenagers Poujouly and Bertin steal his car and go for a ride, discovering his gun and camera in the glove compartment. The youngsters befriend an older adventurous German couple, Petrovich and Anderson, then try to steal their luxury car, killing the pair with Ronet's pistol when they are caught in the act. In the morning, with the return of electric power, Ronet is freed from his suspended prison, only to be arrested for the murder of the German couple. The enamored Moreau turns detective on his behalf, tracing the teens to a motel. Police inspector Ventura has tracked them there also. Ronet's camera has been recovered by him, and with it, photographs establishing the teens' guilt—and Ronet's innocence—in the murder of the German couple, pictured with the youngsters in a happier moment. However, negatives exposed previously prove to compromise Moreau and Ronet in the death of Wall, as well.

p, Jean Thuillier; d, Louis Malle; w, Roger Nemier, Malle (based on the play *Ascenseur Pour L'Echafaud* by Noel Calef); ph, Henri Decae; m, Miles Davis; ed, Leonide Azar; art d, Rino Mondellini, Jean Mandaroux; makeup, Boris de Fast.

Crime **Cas.** **(PR:C MPAA:NR)**

FRASIER, THE SENSUOUS LION** (1973) 97m Shuster-Sandler/LCS c

Michael Callan *(Marvin Feldman)*, Katherine Justice *(Allison Stewart)*, Victor Jory *(Frasier's Voice)*, Frank de Kova *(The Man)*, Malachi Throne *(Bill Windsor)*, Marc Lawrence *(Chiarelli)*, Peter Lorre, Jr. *(Boscov)*, Patrick O'Moore *(Worcester)*, Arthur Space *(Dredge)*, Lori Saunders *(Minerva Dolly)*, Joe E. Ross *(Kuback)*, Fritzi Burr *(Marvin's Mother)*, A. E. Gould-Porter *(Motel Manager)*, Ralph James *(Newspaper Reporter)*, Jerry Kobrin *(Newspaper Editor)*, John Qualen *(Old Man On Porch)*, Florence Lake *(Old Woman On Porch)*, Maryesther Denver *(Nurse)*, Allison McKay *(Wife In Kitchen)*, Charles Woolf *(Man In Kitchen)*, John J. Fox *(Heavyset Man)*, Paul (Mousie) Garner *(Man In Bar)*, Frank Biro *(Host At Cocktail Party)*, Shurze, Neil *(Frasier the Lion)*.

Callan plays a young zoologist who goes to the California Lion Country Safari preserve to study Frasier, an incredibly potent and amorous lion who has fathered 37 cubs with seven different lionesses. To his surprise, the lion talks (using Jory's voice) and confides his secrets to his new-found friend. Billionaire de Kova wants to slaughter Frasier for his glands, hoping to attain the feline's incredible potency (a step up from the old monkey-gland scenario). Soon there are run-ins with criminals, chases through the animal kingdom, and the usual nonsense that accompanies these talking animal movies. This one's okay if you like this sort of thing.

p, Allan Sandler; d, Pat Shields; w, Jerry Kobrin (based on a story by Sandy Dore); ph, David L. Butler (DeLuxe Color); m, Robert Emenegger; ed, Michael Brown.

Comedy **(PR:AA MPAA:PG)**

FRATERNITY ROW*½** (1977) 101m PAR c (AKA: OH BROTHERHOOD)

Peter Fox *(Rodger Carter)*, Gregory Harrison *(Zac Sterling)*, Scott Newman *(Chunk Cherry)*, Nancy Morgan *(Jennifer Harris)*, Wendy Phillips *(Betty Ann Martin)*, Robert Emhardt *(Brother Bob Abernathy)*, Robert Matthews *(Lloyd Pope)*, Bernard R. Kantor *(The Professor)*, Cliff Robertson *(Narrator)*, Scott Brown *(Russell)*, Garrett Gibbs *(Greg)*, Dan Millington *(Scott)*, Michael J. McAlister *(Arthur)*, Jim Negele *(Doug)*, Dean Rallis, Jr. *(Ted)*, Steve Shortridge *(Mel)*, Dean Smith *(Andy)*, Scott Stuckman *(Randy)*, Thomas Thomas *(Warren)*, Scott Tolstad *(Bruce)*, Robert Matthews *(Lloyd Pope)*, Colleen Casey *(Nora)*, Katie Finnegan *(Nancy)*, Eden Ginn *(Sharon)*, Nancy Glogow *(Georgianna)*, Nancy Haden *(Phyllis)*, Tracy Hayward *(Lorna)*, Darrlynn Kaun *(Louise)*, Marilyn Miller *(Lois)*, Carlene Olson *(Cissy)*, Angela Aber *(Ruth)*, Cher Chelton *(Lucy)*, Marlena Crews *(Jeanette)*, Douglas Davidson *(Collin)*, Glenn Deigan *(Hollis)*, Dwayne L. Foster *(John)*, Mark Leffler *(Mark)*, Barbara Ellen Lyle *(Mavis)*, Penelope Meier *(Alice)*, Ed Shaw *(Larry)*, David S. Starr *(David)*, Jeffrey Tolstad *(Jim Jenson)*, Mary Ann Thompson *(KDA Housemother)*, Robert Oram *(Ambulance Doctor)*, Peter Schleger *(Ambulance Attendant)*, F. Brent Keast *(Voice of Disc Jockey)*, Gene Weed *(Voice of Newscaster)*.

Hard-nosed, realistic view of college fraternity life circa 1954. Harrison plays a young pledge trying to get accepted into a fraternity run by understanding frat pledge master Fox and sadistic frat brother Newman. Morgan plays Harrison's girl friend who thinks the whole frat system is elitist and corrupt, and begs him to abandon his desire to join before it is too late. Uncompromising in its brutal examination of the hazing and prejudice practiced in the fraternity system, the film is filled with excellent performances from a cast of newcomers (especially Newman, the son of Paul Newman, who died tragically of a drug overdose soon after this film's release). Produced and scripted by USC graduate student Allison, he employed a student cast and crew with advice from Hollywood professionals. Made on a low budget, with the help of several foundation grants, the picture won three awards. Original songs include "If You Can Dream," "The Pattern Is Broken," Don McLean; "Oh Brotherhood," "The Dreamsinger," "Pinning Call Out Song," "We're Looking Towards a New Life," "Hey Gamma Nu," "The Fellowship Greeting Song," John Phillips Hutton, Matthew Row; "The Birdland Dance," Hutton; "The Song of the Pledges," Michael Corner.

p, Charles Gary Allison; d, Thomas J. Tobin; w, Allison; ph, Peter Gibbons (CFI color); m, Don McLean, Michael Corner, John Phillips Hutton, Mathew Row; ed, Eugene A. Fournier; art d, James Sbardellati; set d, Greg Mellott; cos, Beverly Ihnen; makeup Gary Burlingame.

Drama **(PR:O MPAA:PG)**

FRAULEIN½** (1958) 95m FOX c

Dana Wynter *(Erika Angermann)*, Mel Ferrer *(Foster MacLain)*, Dolores Michaels *(Lori)*, Maggie Hayes *(Lt. Berdie Dubbin)*, Theodore Bikel *(Dmitri)*, Luis Van Rooten *(Fritz Graubach)*, Helmut Dantine *(Hugo)*, Herbert Berghof *(Karl)*, James Edwards *(Corp. S. Hanks)*, Ivan Triesault *(Professor Angermann)*, Blandine Ebinger *(Berta Graubach)*, Jack Kruschen *(Grischa)*.

Wartime romance starring Wynter as an innocent German girl who aids an escaped American soldier, Ferrer, when he flees a prisoner-of-war camp. After the war they meet again in Berlin. Wynter, harassed by the Russians, mistakenly registers as a prostitute. Ferrer falls in love with the girl, but she is determined to find her wounded German fiance, Dantine, who is hospitalized somewhere. Ferrer helps the girl find Dantine, and when it becomes apparent that the ex-Nazi no longer cares for her, she turns to the American. When she attempts to leave Germany with Ferrer, her dreams are nearly shattered when the health department balks because her records state she's a prostitute. Luckily, a kindly American corporal changes the records and allows her and Ferrer their happiness. Shot on location in Germany.

p, Walter Reisch; d, Henry Koster; w, Leo Townsend (based on the novel by James McGovern); ph, Leo Tover (CinemaScope, DeLuxe Color); m, Daniele Amfitheatrof; ed, Marjorie Fowler; art d, Lyle R. Wheeler, Leland Fuller; cos, Mary Wills; spec eff, L. B. Abbott.

War/Romance **(PR:C MPAA:NR)**

FRAULEIN DOKTOR½** (1969, Ital./Yugo.) 102m Cinematografica-Avala/PAR c (GOSPODJICA DOKTOR—SPIJUNKA BEZ IMENA)

Suzy Kendall *(Fraulein Doctor)*, Kenneth More *(Col. Foreman)*, Capucine *(Dr. Saforet)*, James Booth *(Meyer)*, Alexander Knox *(Gen. Peronne)*, Nigel Green *(Mathesius)*, Roberto Bisacco *(Hans Schell)*, Malcolm Ingram *(Cartwright)*, Giancarlo Giannini *(Lt. Hans Ruppert)*, Mario Novelli *(Sgt. Otto Latemar)*, Kenneth Poitevin *(Lt. Ernest Wiechert)*, Bernard de Vries *(Lt. Wilhelm von Oberdorff)*, Ralph Nossek *(Lean Agent)*, Michael Elphick *(Tom)*, Olivera Vuco *(Marchioness de Haro)*, Adreina Paul *(Dona Elena de Rivas)*, Silvia Monti *(Margarita)*, Virginia Bell *(Dona Julia)*, Colin Tapley *(Gen. Metzler)*, Gerard Herter *(Capt. Munster)*, Walter Williams *(Gen. von Hindenburg)*, John Atkinson *(Maj. Rops)*, Neale Stainton *(Sergeant)*, John Webb *(1st Agent)*, Joan Geary *(Landlady)*, Aca Stojkovic *(Chemist)*, Mavid Popovic *(Chaplain)*, Dusan Bulajic *(Col. Delveaux)*, Miki Micovic *(Blondel)*, James Mishler *(Gen. von Ludendorff)*, Janez Vrhovec *(Belgian Colonel)*, Bata Paskaljevic, Zoran Longinovic *(Wounded English Soldiers)*, Dusan Djuric *(Aide to Ludendorff)*, Maggie McGrath *(Mrs. MacPherson)*, Gyorgy Nagyajtay *(Chilean Ambassador)*, Andreas Voutsinas.

In a muddled espionage story, Kendall plays a shifty German master spy during WW I, a mystery woman who brought about devastation to the Allies far beyond the boudoir exploits of the more infamous Mata Hari. She is seen with two German agents landing from a sub at Scapa Flow in the Scottish Orkney Islands where the British fleet lies at anchor. Her job is to kill the redoubtable British military leader, Field Marshall Lord Kitchener. Though her confederates are captured, Kendall manages to escape back to the submarine with information detailing the movements of the warship taking Kitchener to Russia on a hush-hush mission. The sub lays a pattern of mines in the path of the H.M.S. *Hampshire* and the ship is blown up, taking Kitchener and 700 more victims to a watery death. Kendall celebrates by taking morphine injections. Her unsavory past is examined by British intelligence officer More who sends Booth to Germany to kill the lethal woman. Meanwhile, Kendall forms an association with lesbian French scientist Capucine, creator of a poison gas against which gas masks are ineffective. She murders Capucine, steals the formula, and turns it over to the Germans who use it with devastating results. Booth tracks down Kendall and makes plans to kill her, an act sanctioned by the Germans as they have no more use for their drug-addicted spy, but Booth falls in love with Kendall and the Germans merely stage Kendall's death; she later turns up in Spain impersonating a noblewoman arranging a Red Cross train to aid Allied wounded but as a cover for German spies to steal attack plans. She is discovered by More who is killed by Booth over his love for the beautiful but deadly spy. Booth is killed by Germans and Kendall laughs like a maniac, then breaks into hysterical sobbing, realizing the slaughter she has brought about. The Germans unleash the poison gas along the Allied front and thousands of men are shown dying horribly from the effects, their skin peeling away, their faces eroding. Kendall vanishes and is never heard from again. The production values of this film are superior and the battle scenes are outright spectacular, but the script is confusing and the direction so disjointed as to be distracting. The viewer seldom realizes that the point of view has abruptly changed from one character to the other and before identification is established, the focus shifts jerkily to another incident, another cast of characters. Although the producers claimed that the Kendall character was based upon someone called "Anna Maria Lesser," the real "Fraulein Doktor" was Elsbeth "Tiger Eyes" Schragmuller (1887-1940), a German Ph.D who operated a school for spies in Antwerp during WW I, a clever, inventive creature who adopted academic approaches to espionage, believing that intensive training was the true making of an agent. Schragmuller instituted the system of "sacrificing" her own agents so that those moles buried deeper would survive. This intellectual spymaster, who seldom left her offices (which were almost bombed a few times by Allied agents), was basically a plain looking, dark-haired, and unspectacular woman whom the Allies, in their frustration to halt her methodical information-gathering, altered into the romantic image of a blonde, blue-eyed vixen whose carnal exploits exceeded Mata Hari and whose ruthless ambitions encompassed any and all manner of heinous war crimes. Schragmuller's only distinctive physical attribute were huge animal-like eyes which earned her the nickname of "Tiger Eyes." She remained unknown during WW I and her identity was not learned until shortly before her death in 1940 when she was still teaching history at Munich University, one of those ubiquitous humans who survives all retribution, living out an obscure life which this and other films would later transform into the incredible, the mysterious, the unbelievable.

p, Dino De Laurentiis; d, Alberto Lattuada; w, Duilio Coletti, Stanley Mann, Harry A.L. Craigh, Vittoriano Petrilli, Lattuada (based on a story by Petrilli); ph, Luigi Kuveiller (Technicolor); m, Ennio Morricone; ed, Nino Baragli; md, Bruno Nicolai; prod d, Mario Chiari; set d, Enzo Eusepi; cos, Maria De Matteis, Enzo Bulgarelli; spec eff, Dusan Piros; makeup, Otello Fava, Marija Kordic.

Spy Drama **(PR:C-O MPAA:M)**

FREAKS**** (1932) 64m MGM bw (AKA: NATURE'S MISTAKES, FORBIDDEN LOVE, THE MONSTER SHOW)

Wallace Ford *(Phroso)*, Leila Hyams *(Venus)*, Olga Baclanova *(Cleopatra)*, Rosco Ates *(Roscoe)*, Henry Victor *(Hercules)*, Harry Earles *(Hans)*, Daisy Earles *(Frieda)*, Rose Dione *(Mme. Tetrallini)*, Daisy, Violet Hilton *(Siamese Twins)*, Edward Brophy, Matt McHugh *(Rollo Brothers)*, Olga Roderick *(Bearded Lady)*, Johnny Eck *(Boy with Half a Torso)*, Randian *(Hindu Living Torso)*, Schlitzie, Elvira, Jennie Lee Snow *(White Pin Heads)*, Pete Robinson *(Living Skeleton)*, Koo Coo *(Bird Girl)*, Josephine-Joseph *(Half Woman-Half Man)*, Martha Morris *(Armless Wonder)*, Frances O'Connor *(Turtle Girl)*, Angelo Rossito *(Midget)*, Zip, Pip, Elizabeth Green *(Specialties)*, Albert Conti *(Landowner)*, Michael Visaroff *(Jean the Caretaker)*, Ernie Adams *(Sideshow Patron)*, Louise Beavers *(Maid)*.

This bizarre cult classic, directed by that master of the macabre, Browning, came about after MGM's Irving Thalberg took one look at the staggering receipts gleaned by Universal through their horror classics. Demanded Thalberg of Browning, "Give me something that will out-horror FRANKENSTEIN." He did, but this production is so offbeat, so strange, that it took decades for it to find an audience. Baclanova, a physically normal trapeze artist, has a dark and avaricious heart. Although she is involved with Victor, the strong man, she encourages flirtatious moves by Harry Earles, one of the midgets in Dione's traveling circus, who forsakes Daisy Earles (his real-life midget sister) for the "big woman." Harry Earles does not believe he is really a man unless he is normal size. Baclanova and Victor laugh at the little man for his blatant adoration of the sexy trapeze star but then Daisy Earles reveals that Harry Earles is rich, that he has inherited a fortune. The cruel Baclanova conspires with Victor to obtain the money; she will marry the midget, then they will posion the little fellow and take his money. Daisy tells pretty seal trainer Hyams and Ford, chief clown, that Baclanova is no good and means to harm her Harry. But Harry Earles is too infatuated with sexy Baclanova to think clearly, even when she makes fun of him, calling him "my little green-eyed monster," and "dirty, slimy freak." She cozies up to Harry Earles and they are married. Later, the circus freaks gather around the wedding table. Their tricks and dances upon the table, their awkward movements and odd manners, repel Baclanova who shrinks back in disgust as they begin to chant, "We accept you, one of us." Baclanova then insults them all, telling them she will never be one of them, a grotesque freak, while her boy friend Victor howls with laughter. She turns and kisses Victor repeatedly while he fondles her, all in front of Harry Earles, her midget husband, who is now thoroughly humiliated and disgraced. Baclanova and Victor begin to systematically poison Harry but the freaks rally round Earles once they begin to suspect he is being murdered. Then, Victor sneaks into Hyams' wagon; he had lived with her until being kicked out, the seal trainer realizing that he was no good. Victor tries to rape Hyams but Ford arrives and the two battle. Victor actually gets the best of Ford, pounding him senseless and sending him into screaming pain by pinning him to a hot stove. In the struggle, the wagon overturns and, just as Victor is about to kill Ford, a knife strikes him. Howling in pain, he takes to the forest, the scores of hideous circus freaks hopping, slithering, crawling toward him, one, Randian, the Hindu living torso, an armless, legless creature, snakes after him in a raging rainstorm like a wild reptile squiggling through the mud, a huge, gleaming knife between his teeth. It is implied that, before killing the vicious Victor, the freaks intend to castrate the rapist. Baclanova cowers in her wagon as the freaks seek her out, pulling guns and knives as they approach her. Savagely they carve up her face and body, turning her into a freak more grotesque than any in their number, a legless chicken woman with webbed hands and a face that would stop Big Ben, and this is the very last scene the viewer is shown, the evil Baclanova on display at the carnival, paying for her evil ways. Browning drew upon his childhood experiences when making FREAKS; he had run away and joined a circus in the 1890s, befriending sideshow freaks and observing how the public reacted to them with mixed feelings of morbid curiousity, revulsion, and genuine empathy. The real-life freaks Browning collected for this superb film of the grotesque are much more appealing than most of the normal sized people in the production, exhibiting the kind of loyalty and group protection seldom found in the normal world. When Thalberg and his boss Louis B. Mayer took one look at FREAKS they shrank back in horror, as did the public, even though Browning took only 36 days to film the story at a cost of $316,000. So revolted and disgusted were critics and viewers that the film lost $164,000 by the time—a matter of weeks—it was withdrawn by MGM after loud outcries from pressuring social groups. The film was banned in England for more than 30 years and never shown on TV, although it now enjoys popular showings in revival houses. The assortment of oddities collected included Olga Roderick, the bearded lady; Johnny Eck, a boy with only half a torso; bird girl Koo Coo; Josephine-Joseph, the half-man, half-woman; Randian, the armless, legless living torso; human skeleton Pete Robinson; midgets; pinheads; dwarfs; and the incredible Daisy and Violet Hilton, Siamese twins (who would later be exploited in the cheapie CHAINED FOR LIFE, 1950). FREAKS is not a study in deformity, however, but an old-fashioned morality play where the defenseless and hopeless triumph over evil. MGM vainly tried to get into the horror film genre in a big way with FREAKS, advertising with such lines as, "Can a full-grown woman truly love a midget? Here's the strangest romance in the world—the love story of a giant, a siren, and a midget!" When critics blasted the film as "loathsome," and "nauseating," MGM added a preface to it, almost as a disclaimer (since discarded) which stated that "history and religion, folklore and legend abound in tales of misshapen misfits who have altered the world's course. Goliath, Caliban, Frankenstein, Cloucester, Tom Thumb, and Kaiser Wilhelm, are just a few." It didn't help but MGM kept trying to sneak the film back into public favor by rereleasing it under different titles. Calling it NATURE'S MISTAKES some years later, the studio tried to tantalize viewers with such obnoxious promotional lines as "Do Siamese twins make love? What sex is the half-man, half-woman?"

p&d, Tod Browning; w, Willis Goldbeck, Leon Gordon, Edgar Allan Woolf, Al Boasberg (based on the short story "Spurs" by Ted Robbins); ph, Merritt B. Gerstad; ed, Basil Wrangell.

Horror **(PR:O MPAA:NR)**

FREAKS!, 1966 (SEE: SHE FREAK, 1966)

FREAKY FRIDAY*½** (1976) 95m Disney/BV c

Barbara Harris *(Ellen Andrews)*, Jodie Foster *(Annabel Andrews)*, John Astin *(Bill Andrews)*, Patsy Kelly *(Mrs. Schmauss)*, Vicki Schreck *(Virginia)*, Dick Van Patten *(Harold Jennings)*, Sorrell Booke *(Mr. Dilk)*, Alan Oppenheimer *(Mr. Joffert)*, Kaye Ballard *(Coach Betsy)*, Ruth Buzzi *(Opposing Coach)*, Marc McClure *(Boris Harris)*, Marie Windsor *(Mrs. Murphy)*, Sparky Marcus *(Ben Andrews)*, Ceil Cabot *(Miss McGuirk)*, Brooke Mills *(Mrs. Gibbons)*, Karen Smith *(Mary Kay Gilbert)*, Marvin Kaplan *(Carpet Cleaner)*, Al Molinaro *(Drapery Man)*, Iris Adrian *(Bus Passenger)*, Barbara Walden *(Mrs. Benson)*, Shelly Juttner *(Hilary Miller)*, Charlene Tilton *(Bambi)*, Lori Rutherford *(Jo-Jo)*, Jack Shelton *(Lloyd)*, Laurie Main *(Mills)*, Don Carter *(Delivery Boy)*, Fuddle Bagley *(Bus Driver)*, Fritz Feld *(Jackman)*, Dermott Downs *(Harvey Manager)*, Jimmy Van Patten *(Cashier)*.

Offbeat live-action Disney film starring Harris and Foster as bickering mother and daughter who wish they could change places for one whole day. Magically, their wish is granted and what follows sees Harris acting immature, running about the neighborhood playing pranks, and Foster wearing make-up and acting like an adult. Interjected into the material are the nearly unavoidable Freudian themes that arise from the situation, especially in scenes where Harris is chasing after her daughter's teenage boy friend and Foster's jealousy when she meets her father's gorgeous secretary—highly unusual for a Disney film. Nevertheless, the film plows through these elements by bouncing more sight gags at the viewer to gloss over the darker aspects of the story. In the end, once they have returned to normal, Foster has gained some maturity, and Harris some insight into her daughter.

p, Ron Miller; d, Gary Nelson; w, Mary Rodgers (based on her book); ph, Charles F. Wheeler (Technicolor); m, Johnny Mandel; ed, Cotton Warburton; art d, John B. Mansbridge, Jack Senter; set d, Robert Benton; cos, Chuck Keehne, Evelyn Kennedy; makeup, Robert J. Schiffer; spec eff, Eustace Lycett, Danny Lee, Art Cruickshank; m/l, Al Kasha, Joel Hirschhorn.

Comedy **Cas.** **(PR:AA MPAA:G)**

FRECKLES** (1935) 69m RKO bw

Tom Brown *(Freckles)*, Virginia Weidler *(Laurie Lou)*, Carol Stone *(Mary Arden)*, Lumsden Hare *(James McLean)*, James Bush *(Ralph Barton)*, Dorothy Peterson *(Mrs. Duncan)*, Addison Richards *(Jack Carter)*, Richard Alexander *(Butch)*, George Lloyd, Louis Natheaux, Wade Boteler.

Third version of the Gene Stratton-Porter novel (the others were filmed in 1917 and 1928) sees Brown as the turn-of-the-century young orphan who wanders into a lumber camp and lands a job as a watchman. There he meets schoolteacher Stone who turns her romantic attentions from the disagreeable paymaster to the adolescent orphan. Enter cutesy youngster Weidler, whom Brown saves from the clutches of evil bandits to gain the respect of the town. Usual sentimental homespun drama.

p, Pandro S. Berman; d, Edward Killy, William Hamilton; w, Dorothy Yost (based on the novel by Gene Stratton-Porter); ph, Robert de Grasse; ed, Desmond Marquette.

Drama **(PR:A MPAA:NR)**

FRECKLES** (1960) 84m FOX c

Martin West *(Freckles)*, Carol Christensen *(Chris)*, Jack Lambert *(Duncan)*, Steven Peck *(Jack Barbeau)*, Roy Barcroft *(McLean)*, Lorna Thayer *(Miss Cooper)*, Ken Curtis *(Wessner)*, John Eldridge *(Mr. Cooper)*.

Yet another adaptation of the Gene Stratton-Porter novel detailing the adventures of young, one-handed orphan West as he ventures into the Big Bear Lake territory of California looking for work. He finds a job as a guard at a logging company and it is his job to protect the timber against bandits. There he meets and falls in love with the daughter, Christensen, of his boss, lumber-baron Barcroft, and proves himself worthy by capturing a gang of thieves that's after the timber.

p, Harry Spalding; d, Andrew V. McLaglen; w, Spalding (based on the novel by Gene Stratton-Porter); ph, Floyd Crosby (CinemaScope, DeLuxe Color); m, Henry Vars; ed, Harry Gerstad; m/l, By Dunham (sung by Jack Lambert).

Drama **(PR:A MPAA:NR)**

FRECKLES COMES HOME** (1942) 63m MON bw

Johnny Downs *(Freckles)*, Gale Storm *(Jane)*, Mantan Moreland *(Jeff)*, Bradley Page *(Quigley)*, Betty Blythe *(Mrs. Potter)*, Marvin Stephens *(Danny)*, Walter Sande *(Leach)*, Max Hoffman, Jr. *(Hymie)*, Lawrence Criner *(Roxbury)*, John Ince *(Potter)*, Irving Mitchell *(Winslow)*, Gene O'Donnell *(Monk)*, Irving Bacon *(Constable)*.

Another chapter in the homespun Stratton-Porter saga starring Downs, a clever college boy who comes home from school determined to make his home town a shaker-and-mover in the country. Before he can do that, though, he must rid the burg of a group of fancy gangsters who have come to rob the bank owned by

Storm's daddy. Storm's first big role after she was discovered through a radio talent search.

p, Lindsley Parsons; d, Jean Yarbrough; w, Edmond Kelso (based on a story by Gene Stratton-Porter); ph, Max Stengler; ed, Jack Ogilvie.

Drama (PR:A MPAA:NR)

FREDDIE STEPS OUT✶✶ (1946) 75m MON bw

Freddie Stewart, June Preisser, Ann Rooney, Warren Mills, Noel Neill, Jackie Moran, Frankie Darro, Milt Kibbee, Belle Mitchell, Edythe Elliott, Murray Davis, Claire James, Douglas Fowley, Charlie Barnet, Emmett Vogan, Terry Lee Carlson, Neta Geddes, Chuy Reyes.

Stewart handles two roles in this average musical comedy—an amiable schoolboy and a popular swing vocalist. When the singer drops out of sight, Stewart's mischievous friends report that their fellow classmate is actually the star. Confusion abounds, especially when the singer's wife shows up. Songs include: "Patience and Fortitude" (Billy Moore, Jr., Blackie Warren), "Let's Drop The Subject" (Hal Collins, Joe Sanns), "Don't Blame Me" (Dorothy Fields, Jimmy McHugh).

p, Sam Katzman; d, Arthur Dreifuss; w, Hal Collins; ph, Ira Morgan; ed, Ace Herman; md, Lee Zahler; art d, Paul Palmentola; ch, Jack Boyle.

Musical/Comedy (PR:A MPAA:NR)

FREDDY UNTER FREMDEN STERNEN✶½ (1962, Ger.) 97m Melodie/Casino c

Freddy Quinn (Himself), Christian Machalet (Stephan), Vera Tschechowa, Gustav Knuth, Dieter Eppler, Ursula Krieg, Benno Sterzenbach, Hannelore Elsner, Marlies Behrens, Helga Sommerfeld, Dagmar Biener, Cammila Spira.

A German musical comedy starring singer Quinn, who travels to Canada, where he plans to build a home away from it all. Soon he discovers that there is copper on his land, and a spiteful neighbor spins a plot to grab the treasure for himself. Luckily, through the force of his charm and talent, Quinn is able to defeat his rival, much to the delight of the community.

d, Wolfgang Schleif; w, Gustav Kampendonk, Aldo von Pinelli; ph, Heinz Pehlke (Eastmancolor); m, Lothar Olias; ed, Hermann Ludwig; art d, Gabriel Pellon, Peter Rohrig; cos, Eva Maria Schroder; makeup, Friedrich Havenstein, Eva Schreckling.

Comedy/Musical (PR:A MPAA:NR)

FREE AND EASY✶✶✶½ (1930) 73m MGM bw (AKA: EASY GO)

Buster Keaton (Elmer Butts), Anita Page (Elvira), Trixie Friganza (Ma), Robert Montgomery (Larry), Fred Niblo (Director), Edgar Dearing (Officer), Gwen Lee, John Miljan, Lionel Barrymore (Themselves), William Haines (Guest), William Collier Sr. (Master Of Ceremonies), Dorothy Sebastian, Karl Dane (Cave Scene—Themselves), David Burton (Director), Cecil B. DeMille, Jackie Coogan, Joe Farnham, Arthur Lange (Themselves).

Keaton's first sound film sees him as the inept manager of beauty contest winner Page who takes her (with her mother, Friganza) to Hollywood to become a star. After gatecrashing his way into the MGM studio it is he who is "discovered" and ends up in front of the cameras. Luckily, Page falls in love with Montgomery, so her trip to California wasn't a total washout. Not an outstanding Keaton vehicle by any means, but it provides a fascinating view into the MGM studio system as it existed in 1930. Great cameo appearances by Coogan, Barrymore and DeMille.

d, Edward Sedgwick; w, Richard Schayer, Al Boasberg, Paul Dickey; ph, Leonard Smith; ed, William Levanway, George Todd; art d, Cedric Gibbons; cos, David Cox; ch, Sammy Lee; m/l, Fred E. Ahlert, William Kernell, Roy Turk.

Comedy (PR:A MPAA:NR)

FREE AND EASY✶ (1941) 56m MGM bw

Robert Cummings (Max Clemington), Ruth Hussey (Martha Gray), Judith Anderson (Lady Joan Culver), C. Aubrey Smith (The Duke), Nigel Bruce (Florian Clemington), Reginald Owen (Sir George Kelvin), Tom Conway (Capt. Ferris), Forrester Harvey (Briggs/Landlord), Charles Coleman (Powers), Theresa Maxwell Conover (Lady Ridgeway), Frederic Worlock (Manager).

Dull look at British society (made once before as BUT THE FLESH IS WEAK, 1932) sees Bruce and Cummings as father and son who try everything to catch a pair of high-society wives. Cummings first finds himself a rich but boring prospect in Anderson, but then he dumps her for his true love, Hussey. Bruce gets lucky also and both guys marry great girls. Trite and uninvolving. This was famed musical-comedy director Sidney's debut as a feature film director (he'd been an Academy Award-winning short subjects director for the studio for some time). Nepotism sometimes pays off; Sidney was the son of an MGM executive.

p, Milton Bren (uncredited); d, George Sidney; w, Marvin Borowsky (based on the play "The Truth Game" by Ivor Novello); ph, Charles Lawton, George Folsey; ed, Frank E. Hull.

Comedy/Romance (PR:A MPAA:NR)

FREE, BLONDE AND 21✶✶ (1940) 67m FOX bw

Lynn Bari (Carol), Mary Beth Hughes (Jerry), Joan Davis (Nellie), Henry Wilcoxon (Dr. Mayberry), Robert Lowery (Dr. Stephen Craig), Alan Baxter (Mickey), Katharine Aldridge (Adelaide), Helen Ericson (Amy), Chick Chandler (Gus), Joan Valerie (Vicki), Elyse Knox (Marjorie), Dorothy Dearing (Linda), Herbert Rawlinson (Mr. Crane), Kay Linaker (Mrs. Crane), Thomas Jackson (Insp. Saunders), Richard Lane (Lt. Luke), Dorothy Moore (Susan), Gwen Kenyon (New Girl), Frank Coghlan Jr. (Bell Boy), Mickey Simpson (Cop), Jerry Fletcher (Hotel Clerk), Edward Cooper (Butler).

Soap opera tale of a woman's hotel in New York and the love lives of the various residents. Among the ladies is gold-digger Hughes who gets herself in hot water

when she becomes too involved with a gangster, and Bari as a dedicated artist who winds up marrying a millionaire.

p, Sol M. Wurtzel; d, Ricardo Cortez; w, Frances Hyland; ph, George Barnes; ed, Norman Colbert; md, Samuel Kaylin.

Drama (PR:A MPAA:NR)

FREE FOR ALL✶✶½ (1949) 83m UNIV bw

Robert Cummings (Christopher Parker), Ann Blyth (Alva Abbott), Percy Kilbride (Mr. Abbott), Ray Collins (Mr. Blair), Donald Woods (Roger Abernathy), Mikhail Rasumny (Dr. Torgelson), Percy Helton (Mr. Hershey), Harry Antrim (Mr. Whiting), Wallis Clark (Mr. Van Alstyne), Frank Ferguson (Hap Ross), Dooley Wilson (Aristotle), Russell Simpson (Farmer), Lester Matthews (Mr. Aberson), Murray Alper (McGuinness), Bill Walker (Herbert), Kenneth Tobey (Pilot), Harris Brown (Colonel), Willard Waterman (Commander).

Amusing enough comedy about Ohio inventor Cummings who travels to Washington, D.C. to get a patent on his latest creation—making gasoline from plain water. Once he arrives he finds himself entangled in the usual bureaucratic red-tape until kindly government employee Kilbride offers Cummings a place to stay. There, Cummings is exposed to a strange house with more bizarre contraptions than he's ever seen. But love springs eternal and he falls for Kilbride's daughter Blyth.

p, Robert Buckner; d, Charles T. Barton; w, Buckner (based on a story by Herbert Clyde Lewis); ph, George Robinson; m, Frank Skinner; ed, Ralph Dawson; art d, Bernard Herzbrun, Nathan Juran.

Comedy (PR:A MPAA:NR)

FREE GRASS✶ (1969) 83m Hollywood Star Pictures c (AKA: SCREAM FREE)

Richard Beymer (Dean), Russ Tamblyn (Link), Lana Wood (Karen), Elisabeth Thompson (Margo), Warren Finnerty (Barney), Casey Kasem (Phil), Joel Dee McCrea [Jody McCrea] (Agent No. 1), Lindsay Crosby (Agent No. 2), Dave Hull (Lieutenant).

Pretty odd film starring Beymer (still trying to live down his WEST SIDE STORY image) and Wood (Natalie's sister) as lovers who need cash. They fall in with low-life gang leader Tamblyn, who talks them into smuggling marijuana on motorcycles from Mexico to Los Angeles. When Beymer balks at the killing of two narcotics agents and backs out of the deal, Tamblyn and his cronies put LSD in his drink, try to set him on fire and kidnap Wood. Eventually Beymer snaps out of it, rescues Wood and warns the hippies to stay away from the "free grass." Classic trash seemingly inspired by WEST SIDE STORY, or at least the actors' images from it.

p, John Lawrence; d, Bill Brame; w, Lawrence, James Gordon White, Gerald Wilson, Paul Stevenson; ph, Austin McKinney (Eastmancolor); m, Sidewalk Productions.

Crime (PR:O MPAA:R)

FREE LOVE✶½ (1930) 70m UNIV bw

Conrad Nagel (Stephen Ferrier), Genevieve Tobin (Hope Ferrier), Monroe Owsley (Rush Begelow), Bertha Mann (Helena), Ilka Chase (Pauline), George Irving (Judge Sturgis), Reginald Pasch (Dr. Wolheim), Slim Summerville (Gas Inspector), ZaSu Pitts (Ada The Maid), Sidney Bracey (Butler), Bert Roach.

Nagel and Tobin are a married couple who just can't seem to get along. Tobin tries a counsellor who only empties her pockets, then she finally decides to move out with her children. Nagel convinces her to come back, but it takes a punch in the face to bring the little woman around to seeing things his way. It's all pretty ineffective, except of course for matinee idol Nagel's punching a woman around.

d, Hobart Henley; w, Edwin Knopf, Winifred Dunn (based on the play "Half Gods" by Sidney Howard); ph, Hal Mohr; ed, Maurice Pivar, Ted Kent.

Comedy (PR:C MPAA:NR)

FREE SOUL, A✶✶✶½ (1931) 91m MGM bw

Norma Shearer (Jan Ashe), Leslie Howard (Dwight Winthrop), Lionel Barrymore (Stephen Ashe), Clark Gable (Ace Wilfong), James Gleason (Eddie), Lucy Beaumont (Grandma Ashe), Claire Whitney (Aunt Helen), Frank Sheridan (Prosecuting Attorney), E. Alyn Warren (Bottomley, Ace's Chinese Boy), George Irving (Defense Atty. Johnson), Edward Brophy (Slouch), William Stacy (Dick), James Conlin (Reporter), Sam McDaniel (Valet), Lee Phelps (Court Clerk), Roscoe Ates (Men's Room Patron Who is Shot At), Larry Steers (Casino Proprietor), Frances Ford (Skidrow Drunk), Henry Hall (Detective), Bess Flowers (Birthday Party Guest).

In this film the prim and proper MGM queen Shearer, wife of production chief Irving Thalberg, discarded her ladylike image to project a free-and-easy, carnal craving socialite who has been "liberated" from the restrictions of her upperclass upbringing, a sensational turn about that had Shearer's legions of fans agog. A FREE SOUL opens in San Francisco with brilliant but alcoholic attorney Barrymore successfully defending no-good gangster Gable against a murder charge, then showing up with his disreputable client at the mansion of his mother, Beaumont, to celebrate her birthday. Here his flapper-like daughter is immediately drawn to the animalistic Gable, dumping her social prince, Howard, a polo playing aristocratic type. She defends Gable from her snobbish family and leaves with him in his flashy roadster, going to his gambling den where she spends a night with him, then becomes his mistress. Barrymore, on the drunken skids, visits Gable's speakeasy and, while trying to avoid arrest by raiding police, hides in Gable's secret apartment where he meets his daughter, Shearer, approaching him in a revealing, slinky nightgown. Barrymore, full of disgust, confronts Gable, stating, "The only time I hate democracy is when one of you mongrels forgets his place!" He takes Shearer home and the two make a pact; she will stop seeing gangster Gable if he will stop drinking. Father and daughter take a trip to

Yosemite where, for three months, they relax and get to know each other. Then Barrymore disappears into a bottle and Shearer returns home, only to be ostracized by her family. Again she takes up with Gable who reverts to his thug nature, attacking her in her apartment, shoving her around (shoving Norma Shearer?). Howard arrives and later shoots Gable down like a dog. Accused of murder, Howard refuses to defend himself to protect Shearer's on-and-off good name. Shearer desperately seeks her famous criminal lawyer father and, at the last minute, finds him stewed to the gills in a seedy flophouse. Barrymore is cleaned up, pumped full of hot coffee, and then he races into the courtroom to deliver one of the most dramatic defense speeches in the history of film, his summation ending with an admission of his own parental failure, "There is only one breast that you can pin the responsibility for this murder on..." At that moment Barrymore drops dead. Howard is found not guilty and Shearer departs for New York City, announcing she will begin life anew. Howard tells her that he will follow her, and they will find happiness together. Out of character as Shearer's role was, her husband Thalberg felt the part of the vampy socialite would turn around his wife's sweet and delicate image, although she had won an Oscar for her gentle role in THE DIVORCEE only a year earlier. It was a wise choice. Shearer's screen image loomed even larger and her ability to handle a variety of roles seemed to broaden, so that for the next eight years her persona dominated MGM films. Howard, that fine British actor, was mostly wasted in this film, used as a love interest prop. It was Barrymore who electrified audiences with his superb portrayal of the alcoholic lawyer. Studio mogul Louis B. Mayer had to beg Barrymore to take the part; the actor had decided that he would direct and never again step in front of a camera. The role, however, was too meaty to resist chewing upon and Barrymore's incredible histrionics won him an Oscar for Best Actor. So overjoyed with the results was Mayer that he offered Barrymore a lucrative lifetime contract with his studio, one which the actor immediately accepted. Gable was another matter. He had scored heavily in THE EASIEST WAY in 1930 and MGM signed him to a two-year contract at $350-a-week. Following the premiere of THE EASIEST WAY Thalberg personally queried viewers about what they thought of newcomer Gable. He then, according to Samuel Marx in *Mayer and Thalberg*, gathered MGM executives in the theater's parking lot, stating: "We've got ourselves a new star!" Head of MGM's B-production unit Harry Rapf snorted, "He's more a heavy than a hero." Thalberg nodded: "That means strong matinee business. Women love heavies; they'll come out afternoons to see him." From this film on, the women (and men) of America did. Early in the film Gable is appealing, even charming, but he turns cruel and brutish at the end, manhandling Hollywood's ultrachic queen to the delight of goose-pimpled female viewers whose eyes popped when Gable shoved Shearer into a chair, snarling: "Sit down and take it and like it! You're an idiot—a spoiled, silly brat that needs a hairbrush now and then!" Shearer was later to say: "It was Clark who made villains popular." Gable owed much to Barrymore who actually got him the role of the gangster in A FREE SOUL, persuading Thalberg to give him the part. The veteran actor had always been a supporter of Gable's; the two had acted together as early as 1926 when appearing in the play, "The Copperhead." Barrymore eventually arranged for and directed Gable's screen test, dressing the future king of the lot as a scantily clad Indian warrior, walking him through the lot to the sound stage while Gable begged him to return so he could put on a coat. Said Gable later: "Guys were whistling at me, and the girls coming out of the commissary were yoo-hooing. I was never so embarrassed in my life." When Gable complained to Barrymore, the crusty old thespian croaked: "The hell with all of them. Haven't they ever seen feathers before?" The role of Ace Wilfong was the largest Gable had ever handled and he worried about delivering his lines. He was quoted in Bob Thomas' *Thalberg: Life and Legend*: "I don't know what I'll do if Brown stops me in the middle of a speech. I've got a photographic memory, and I think of everything in one piece—that's my stock company training. If I'm stopped I'll have to go back to the beginning again." Director Brown didn't interfere with Gable's speeches and A FREE SOUL went on to become a smash hit, earning a $244,000 profit beyond its $529,000 price tag the first time around. MGM tore up Gable's contract and gave him another, at $1,150 a week. The publicity department had written only 750 words about Gable in the many years he had been on the lot; now it ground out 1,000 words a day about the new king of Hollywood. Within a year he would be starring with Greta Garbo in SUSAN LENOX—HER FALL AND RISE, and he would appear with Shearer in two more big budget films, STRANGE INTERLUDE (1932), and IDIOT'S DELIGHT (1939). A FREE SOUL was remade in a 1953 lackluster production entitled THE GIRL WHO HAD EVERYTHING, with Elizabeth Taylor, William Powell, Fernando Lamas and Gig Young. Powell assumed the Barrymore role, a part created by author Adela Rogers St. John with intimate knowledge; she had pieced together the profile of the brilliant but alcoholic lawyer from the exploits of her own father, criminal lawyer Earl Rogers, whose West Coast courtroom antics, gimmicks, and stunts in winning cases were legendary, as were his Homeric drinking escapades. Her book was adapted by Willard Mack for Broadway, the play running only 100 performances in 1928.

d, Clarence Brown; w, John Meehan (based on the novel by Adela Rogers St. John and the play by Willard Mack); ph, William Daniels; m, William Axt; ed, Hugh Wynn; art d, Cedric Gibbons; cos, Adrian.

Drama **(PR:C MPAA:NR)**

FREE SPIRIT (SEE: BELSTONE FOX, 1973, Brit.)

FREE, WHITE AND 21* (1963) 102m Falcon International/AIP bw

Frederick O'Neal *(Ernie Jones)*, Annalena Lund *(Greta Mae Hansen)*, George Edgely *(Judge)*, George Russell *(Defense Attorney Tyler)*, John Hicks *(Prosecuting Attorney Atkins)*, Hugh Crenshaw *(Assistant Prosecuting Attorney)*, Miles Middough, James Altgens, Bill McGee, Jonathan Ledford, Ted Mitchell, Jack Dunlop *(Witnesses)*.

O'Neal plays a black motel owner accused of raping a beautiful white woman, Lund, who came to Texas from Sweden to support the civil rights cause by becoming a Freedom Rider. Eventually the whole case is presented to a jury and the verdict goes in favor of the defendant. Supposedly an insightful look at race relations at the time, now it's just stilted and archaic.

p&d, Larry Buchanan; w, Buchanan, Hal Dwain, Cliff Pope; ph, Ralph K. Johnson; ed, Buchanan; art d, Dennis Adams; m/l, Joe Johnson and his Orchestra.

Drama **(PR:C MPAA:NR)**

FREEBIE AND THE BEAN½** (1974) 112m WB c

Alan Arkin *(Bean)*, James Caan *(Freebie)*, Loretta Swit *(Meyers' Wife)*, Jack Kruschen *(Red Meyers)*, Mike Kellin *(Lt. Rosen)*, Linda Marsh *(Freebie's Girl)*, Paul Koslo *(Whitey)*, John Garwood *(Chauffeur)*, Alex Rocco *(District Attorney)*, Valerie Harper *(Bean's Wife)*, Christopher Morley *(Transvestite)*.

Fairly obnoxious cop comedy/action picture starring Arkin and Caan as two relentless cops who practically destroy San Francisco to capture big-shot gangster Kruschen. The humor is tasteless and racist, but the action scenes are fantastically choreographed and executed. A minor masterpiece for fans of mindless car-chase movies.

p&d, Richard Rush; w, Robert Kaufman (based on a story by Floyd Mutrux); ph, Laszlo Kovacs (Panavision, Technicolor); m, Dominic Frontiere; ed, Frederic Steinkamp, Michael McLean; art d, Hilyard Brown; set d, Ruby Levitt.

Crime/Comedy **Cas.** **(PR:O MPAA:R)**

FREEDOM FOR US (SEE: A NOUS LA LIBERTE, 1931, Fr.)

FREEDOM OF THE SEAS** (1934, Brit.) 74m BIP/Wardour bw

Clifford Mollison *(Smith)*, Wendy Barrie *(Phyllis Harcourt)*, Zelma O'Neal *(Jennie)*, H.F. Maltby *(Harcourt)*, Tyrell Davis *(Cavendish)*, James Carew *(Bottom)*, Cecil Ramage *(Berkstrom)*, Henry Wenman *(Wallace)*, Frederick Peisley *(Jackson)*, Frank Atkinson *(O'Hara)*, Charles Paton *(Gamp)*.

A quiet clerk, Mollison, surprises his fellow employees when he enlists for service in the British navy during WW I and saves a passenger ship from becoming the victim of a spy plot. He adds his coup de grace by sinking a German U-boat. A witty little story which was director Varnel's first.

p, Walter C. Mycroft; d, Marcel Varnel; w, Roger Burford (based on a play by Walter C. Hackett); ph, Otto Kanturek; ed, Sidney Cole; art d, Cedric Dawe.

Comedy **(PR:A MPAA:NR)**

FREEDOM RADIO (SEE: VOICE IN THE NIGHT, A, 1941, Brit.)

FREEDOM TO DIE** (1962, Brit.) 61m Bayford/BUT bw

Paul Maxwell *(Craig Owen)*, Felicity Young *(Linda)*, Bruce Seton *(Felix)*, Kay Callard *(Coral)*, T.P. McKenna *(Mike)*, Laurie Leigh *(Julie)*, Charlie Byrne *(Happy Joe)*.

A routine crime meller which has a fugitive hunting down the daughter of a fellow burglar in order to get her to unlock a safe deposit box.

p, Charles A. Leeds; d, Francis Searle; w, Arthur La Bern.

Crime **(PR:A MPAA:NR)**

FREEWHEELIN'*½ (1976) 80m Turtle Releasing Organization c

Stacy Peralta, Camille Darrin, Russ Howell, Ken Means, Tom Sims, Mike Weed, Paul Constantineau, Bobby Pierce, Stevie Monahan, Desiree Von Essen, Guy Grundy, Waldo Autrey.

Paper-thin plot has Peralta as a skate board enthusiast who lives only to be able to roll down the street on this weird item that consists of a board about a foot and a half long resting on four small wheels. This desire outweighs anything else a normal youth might devote himself to, such as romance or the pursuit of an education.

p&d, Scott Dittrich; w, George Van Noy; ph, Pat Darrin; m, Stephen Freud; ed, Van Noy.

Drama **(PR:A MPAA:G)**

FREIGHTERS OF DESTINY** (1932) 60m RKO bw

Tom Keene, Barbara Kent, Frank Rice, Mitchell Harris, Fred Burns, Tom Bay, Slim Whitaker, Billy Franey, William Welsh, Frederick Burton.

This oater has Keene play the son of a wagon train leader transporting a group of settlers to populate the Old West. The film's title alludes to these famed wagons which brought civilization to the frontier. A greedy banker with designs on taking over the franchise dispatches his band of outlaws to steal from and attack the trailblazers every inch of the way.

d, Fred Allen; w, Adele Buffington; ph, Ted McCord; md, Arthur Lange; art d, Carroll Clark.

Western **(PR:A MPAA:NR)**

FRENCH CANCAN**** (1956, Fr.) 93m Franco-London Films-Jolly/United Motion Picture Organization c (AKA: ONLY THE FRENCH CAN)

Jean Gabin *(Danglard)*, Maria Felix *(La Belle Abesse)*, Francoise Arnoul *(Nini)*, Jean-Roger Caussimon *(Baron Walter)*, Gianni Esposito *(Prince Alexandre)*, Philippe Clay *(Casimir)*, Michel Piccoli *(Valorgueil)*, Jean Paredes *(Coudrier)*, Lydia Johnson *(Guibole)*, Max Dalban *(Manager Of The Reine Blanche)*, Jacques Jouanneau *(Bidon)*, Jean-Marc Tennberg *(Savate)*, Hubert Deschamps *(Isidore The Waiter)*, Franco Pastorino *(Paulo The Baker)*, Valentine Tessier *(Mme. Olympe, Nini's Mother)*, Albert Remy *(Barjolin)*, Annik Morice *(Therese)*, Dora Doll *(Le Genisse)*, Anna Amendola *(Esther Georges/The Voice Of Cora Vaucaire)*, Leo Campion *(The Commandant)*, Mme. Paquerette *(Mimi Prunelle)*, Sylvine Delannoy *(Titine)*, Anne-Marie Mersen *(Paquita)*, Michelle Nadal *(Bigoudi)*, Gaston Gabaroche *(Oscar The Pianist)*, Jaque Catelain *(The Minister)*, Pierre Moncorbier *(The Bailiff)*, Jean Mortier *(The Hotel Manager)*, Numes Fils *(The Neighbor)*, Robert Auboyneau *(The Elevator Attendant)*, Laurence Bataille *(La Pygmee)*, Pierre Olaf *(Pierrot The Heckler)*, Jacques Ciron *(1st Dandy)*, Claude Arnay *(2nd Dandy)*,

France Roche *(Beatrix)*, Michele Philippe *(Eleonore)*, R.J. Chauffard *(Police Inspector)*, Gaston Modot *(Danglard's Servant)*, Jacques Hilling *(The Surgeon)*, Patachou *(Yvette Guilbert)*, Andre Claveau *(Paul Delmet)*, Jean Raymond *(Paulus)*, Edith Piaf *(Eugenie Buffet)*, Jedlinska *(La Gigolette)*, Jean Sylvere *(The Groom)*, Palmyre Levasseur *(The Laundry Woman)*, Andre Philip, Bruno Balp, Jacques Marin, H.R. Herce, Rene Pascal, Martine Alexis, Corinne Jansen, Maya Jusanova, the voice of Mario Luillard.

After a 15-year hiatus from filmmaking in France, Renoir returned with a high-spirited celebration called FRENCH CANCAN, which brought to life the dawning days of the Moulin Rouge complete with high-kicking, frilly, lacy chorus gals. Gabin turns in one of his most memorable performances as an aging theater impresario who is known for his ability to take common girls and transform them into dancehall sensations, as well as successfully seducing them. Before long, however, he becomes captivated with a different girl and the idea of turning her into a star, while ignoring his previous love. Arnoul becomes the next in his long line of targets when he spots her working as a laundry girl in Montmarte of the 1880s. Caussimon agrees to give Gabin enough money to open a new theater and the impresario decides to make Arnoul the star of his new "Moulin Rouge." With the help of former dance star Johnson, Arnoul and her fellow dancers begin a gruelling episode of stretching, kicking, and CanCan-ing. Gabin's mistress, the spicy Felix, demands that she be part of the show and makes it quite obvious that she is insanely jealous of Arnoul. When opening night arrives it appears that Arnoul will not dance because of her fear that she is losing Gabin and a young man who wants to marry her. The adage that "the show must go on" is fully enforced in a finale which has Arnoul and her fellow dancers exploding into a flurry of vibrant color and swirling skirts. A deceptively simple picture, FRENCH CANCAN does a superb, breathtaking job of transcending time and letting us relive the era which previously lived only in the posters and paintings of Toulouse-Lautrec and Jean's father Auguste Renoir. Renoir, whose films have consistently served as a training grounds for a number of prominent directors (Jacques Becker on LA CHIENNE, 1981; Yves Allegret and Luchino Visconti on the short A DAY IN THE COUNTRY, 1936; Robert Aldrich on THE SOUTHERNER, 1945), also gave a start to "New Wave" director Jacques Rivette on this picture by letting him serve as a directorial trainee.

p, Louis Wipf; d&w, Jean Renoir (based on an idea by Andre-Paul Antoine); ph, Michel Kelber (Technicolor); m, Georges Van Parys; ed, Boris Lewin; art d, Max Douy; cos, Rosine Delamare; ch, G. Grandjean; makeup, Yvonne Fortuna.

Musical (PR:A MPAA:NR)

FRENCH CONNECTION, THE***** (1971) 104m FOX c

Gene Hackman *(Jimmy "Popeye" Doyle)*, Fernando Rey *(Alain Charnier)*, Roy Scheider *(Buddy Russo)*, Tony Lo Bianco *(Sal Boca)*, Marcel Bozzuffi *(Pierre Nicoli)*, Frederic De Pasquale *(Devereaux)*, Bill Hickman *(Mulderig)*, Ann Rebbot *(Marie Charnier)*, Harold Gary *(Weinstock)*, Arlene Farber *(Angie Boca)*, Eddie Egan *(Walter Simonson)*, Andre Ernotte *(La Valle)*, Sonny Grosso *(Klein)*, Pat McDermott *(Chemist)*, Alan Weeks *(Drug Pusher)*, The Three Degrees *(Themselves)*, Ben Marino *(Lou Boca)*, Al Fann *(Undercover Agent)*, Maureen Mooney *(Bicycle Girl)*, Robert Weil *(Auctioneer)*.

A brilliant, tough, street crime film has Hackman as the indefatigable Popeye Doyle, who passionately hates any and all drug pushers. Professional hit man Bozzuffi kills a French detective in Marseilles, France, while, in Brooklyn, N.Y., Hackman and his partner Scheider roust a drug dealer in a vacant lot. Later that night Hackman and Scheider spot a group of drug-connected people celebrating and tail Lo Bianco and his wife. This leads to a massive surveillance of a large U.S. drug ring where Hackman and Scheider are ordered to work with federal agents Hickman and Grosso; Hackman and Hickman have a long-standing feud which begins to boil to the surface. Meanwhile, Rey, the mastermind of the French drug traffic, "The French Connection," plants 120 pounds of heroin in the Lincoln Continental car of TV actor De Pasquale, who unwittingly escorts the shipment to New York. Rey contacts Lo Bianco in Manhattan to arrange for the sale of the herion but is spotted by Hackman who has staked out Lo Bianco, trailing the pair to a hotel. Hackman follows Rey, who is aware that he is being tailed, and the wiley Frenchman outwits Hackman, escaping on a subway train, smugly waving good-bye to Hackman as the cop is left standing on the platform, gritting and cursing out his frustration. Later Bozzuffi positions himself as a sniper and squeezes off a shot at Hackman, killing a female passerby. Hackman pursues the killer to the top of a building, then to the street where Bozzuffi escapes momentarily via elevated train. In a rage, the obsessed cop commandeers a civilian car and races wildly through the streets, attempting to overtake the elevated train. Hackman knocks over garbage cans and newsstands, narrowly missing pedestrians and careening around the steel structure of the elevated while caroming off cars. Bozzuffi threatens to shoot the motorman running the train, killing a transit cop who comes to the rescue; the motorman collapses in terror and the train goes out of control, hurtling down the tracks at breakneck speed, Hackman driving relentlessly through traffic beneath the speeding train which suddenly crashes. Bozzuffi leaps from it and Hackman, the commandeered car wrecked, is in hot pursuit, finally shooting the killer several times in the back when he refuses to halt. The TV actor's car has been located by then and is taken to a police garage where it is carefully taken apart and inspected but no drugs are found. Hackman insists that "the car is dirty," and technicians finally remove the rocker arms where the heroin is found. The car is put back together and returned with apologies by the police to the actor, who is told that it has been stolen and recovered. The car is then trailed as it is driven by Rey's henchmen to deserted buildings at Ward's Island where Lo Bianco and his group meet to make the pickup and payoff. Hackman, Scheider, and local and federal cops close in and, when ordering the gangsters inside the buildings to surrender, are suddenly fired upon. A full scale gun battle ensues with Hackman pursuing nemesis Rey. He kills Hickman by mistake. Lo Bianco and others are rounded up (later given light sentences), but Rey escapes and is never caught. For

their unorthodox behavior, Hackman and Scheider are transferred to another department. Young director Friedkin produced a spine-twisting, suspenseful, and utterly absorbing film which incorporated thrills with street humor, routine police work with highly dramatic scenes. His chase scene is, without exception, including the car chase in BULLITT (1968), the most incredible, hair-raising sequence in this or any other film, shot from within Hackman's car, cameras mounted in the back seat, and on the front fenders, recording straight and fish-eye shots of harrowing image. To be sure, the police are portrayed as being almost as brutal as the criminals, with Hackman shown to be a near maniac who will stop at nothing to corral drugsters. Friedkin later stated to *Newsday* that he had Hackman fire a random shot off camera "to show how his obsession with catching the French connection had made him a psychotic. He was so trigger-happy by then he was ready to shoot at anything once he rounded the corner. He was shooting at ghosts." Hackman deservedly won an Oscar for his portrayal, as did the film, Friedkin, Tidyman for the script, and Greenberg for editing. Hackman's performance is totally riveting, revealing the harsh, jolting, and gutter brutality that is the policeman's lot in combatting illegal drug traffic, the dirtiest business in the world. His role is based upon the career of a spectacular New York City cop, Eddie Egan, who, with his partner Sonny Grosso (portrayed by Scheider, both appearing in THE FRENCH CONNECTION), smashed a dope operation and confiscated a whopping 120 pounds of heroin worth $32 million. After Egan appeared as a technical adviser and took a small part in the film, and, with only seven hours before his retirement papers were to be signed, he was summarily dismissed from the NYPD at age 42. Robin Moore, the author of the novel upon which this spectacular film is based, later stated in *New York* magazine that Egan was dismissed because the "image" he projected was not sanctioned by the department, that "the police department, like the military or any other institution, prefers to make its own heroes for its own purposes and not have men become legends on their own initiative, in their own way." Egan, according to Friedkin, "didn't feel we did him an injustice. He loved the picture." The intrepid policeman later went on to become a top technical adviser for Hollywood crime productions, often appearing in such films as PRIME CUT (1972) with Lee Marvin and Hackman. Filmed on location in New York City, THE FRENCH CONNECTION became an overnight box office smash, earning more than $27,500,000 in its first run. (The language is raw, wholly unsuited to youngsters.)

p, Philip D'Antoni; d, William Friedkin; w, Ernest Tidyman (based on the book by Robin Moore); ph, Owen Roizman (DeLuxe Color); m, Don Ellis; ed, Jerry Greenberg; md, Ellis; art d, Ben Kazaskow; set d, Ed Garzero; cos, Joseph Fretwell; spec eff, Sass Bedig; makeup, Irving Buchman; stunts, Bill Hickman.

Crime Drama Cas. (PR:O MPAA:R)

FRENCH CONNECTION II***½ (1975) 119m FOX c

Gene Hackman *(Popeye Doyle)*, Fernando Rey *(Charnier)*, Bernard Fresson *(Barthelemy)*, Jean-Pierre Castaldi *(Raoul Diron)*, Charles Millot *(Miletto)*, Cathleen Nesbitt *(Old Lady)*, Pierre Collet *(Old Pro)*, Alexandre Fabre *(Young Tail)*, Philippe Leotard *(Jacques)*, Jacques Dynam *(Inspector Genevoix)*, Raoul Delfosse *(Dutch Captain)*, Patrick Floersheim *(Manfredi)*.

This is a virtuoso performance for Hackman in a top-drawer followup to the marvelous original that appeared four years earlier, one where the hard-nosed cop is sent to Marseilles, France, to unearth the shifty Rey, the man who got away in THE FRENCH CONNECTION. Hackman is treated with disdain by top French cop Fresson, who resents his intrusive, loud-mouth, bad-mannered ways. Hackman is decidedly out of place in a setting he does not understand, laboring with a language that proves more difficult each day. He does not know that he is being used as bait by Fresson to lure Rey into the open. Further complicating matters, Hackman eludes his French police bodyguards in an effort to find Rey on his own and succeeds in getting kidnaped by the drug czar's henchmen, taken to a sleazy hotel, and, at Rey's orders, injected with heroin so that he soon becomes so addicted he will tell everything he knows about the drug ring. Rey, whom Hackman calls "Frog One," is surprised to learn that Hackman knows next to nothing about his international drug smuggling operation and decides to let the displaced cop live, contemptously dumping him in front of police headquarters. Hackman, with Fresson's help, is kept incommunicado and undergoes a horrific withdrawal from heroin, quitting "cold turkey." When recovering Hackman follows his memory back to the hotel where he had been kept prisoner and finally locates the building. He calls Fresson, then sets fire to the place, rooting out Rey's henchmen whom he and arriving police shoot and capture. Police and Hackman later fight it out with Rey's main gang at the Marseilles docks where Fresson and Hackman are almost drowned in a drydock. Again, Rey appears to make his escape but, at the last moment, Hackman races to the end of a dock to see the culprit fleeing in a small motorboat. He calls his name, Rey turns, and Hackman shoots him to death. This is a stunning sequel and is tightly directed by Frankenheimer, a master of suspense (THE MANCHURIAN CANDIDATE, 1962, SEVEN DAYS IN MAY, 1964, SECONDS, 1966, BLACK SUNDAY, 1976). Hackman's performance is astounding and believable, the sequences dealing with his withdrawal from heroin presenting a frightening and realistic look at the effects of hard drugs. Shot on location in Marseilles, FRENCH CONNECTION II grossed $5,600,000 in its initial run. All the production people are outstanding, in particular Renoir's breathtaking cinematography, Frazee's special effects, and Needham's stuntwork.

p, Robert L. Rosen; d, John Frankenheimer; w, Alexander Jacobs, Robert Dillon, Lauri Dillon (based on a story by Robert and Lauri Dillon); ph, Claude Renoir (DeLuxe Color); m, Don Ellis; ed, Tom Rolf; prod d, Jacques Saulnier; art d, Gerard Viard, Georges Glon; cos, Jacques Fonterary; spec eff, Logan Frazee; makeup, Monique and Alex Archambault; stunts, Hal Needham.

Crime Drama Cas. (PR:O MPAA:R)

FRENCH CONSPIRACY, THE*½

(1973, Fr.) 125m Two Worlds Films/Cine Globe c (L'ATTENTAT)

Jean-Louis Trintignant (Darien), Michel Piccoli (Kassar), Gian Maria Volonte (Sadiel), Jean Seberg (Edith), Francois Perier (Rouannet), Philippe Noiret (Garcin), Michel Bouquet (Lempereur), Bruno Cremer (Vigneau), Daniel Ivernel (Acconeti), Roy Scheider (Howard).

A fictionalized version of a scandal which occurred in France in 1965 when Moroccan leftist leader Ben Barka was kidnaped, compromising the French government. The film, however, receives a dismal treatment that lacks any sense of drama. A fine score by Morricone and Semprun's writing (he also penned Z by Costa-Gavras and STAVISKY by Alain Resnais, both centering on political conspiracy) should help, but do not.

p, Yvon Guedel; d, Yves Boisset; w, Ben Barzman, Basilio Franchina, Jorge Semprun; ph, Ricardo Aronovich; m, Ennio Morricone; cos, Pierre Nourry.

Drama   **(PR:A   MPAA:PG)**

FRENCH DRESSING**

(1964, Brit.) 86m WB bw

James Booth (Jim), Roy Kinnear (Henry), Marisa Mell (Francoise Fayol), Alita Naughton (Judy), Bryan Pringle (The Mayor), Robert Robinson (Himself), Norman Pitt (Westebourne Mayor), Henry McCarthy (Bridgemouth Mayor), Sandor Eles (Vladek).

Shaky first effort from director Russell sees him presiding over a light-hearted comedy concerning a dying British resort. Ambitious deck chair attendant Booth and his American girl friend Naughton convince the town fathers to stage a film festival in the village. To attract crowds they enlist the aid of sexy French newcomer Mell (patterned after Bridgette Bardot) to host the festivities. Of course there are the usual set of disasters when the event attracts more patrons than the townfolk can handle. Amusing but forgettable.

p, Kenneth Harper; d, Ken Russell; w, Peter Myers, Ronald Cass, Peter Brett (based on a story by Myers, Cass; additional dialog, Johnny Speight); ph, Ken Higgins; m, Georges Delerue; ed, Jack Slade.

Comedy   **(PR:A   MPAA:NR)**

FRENCH GAME, THE**

(1963, Fr.) 86m Atlantic Pictures bw (FR: LE COEUR BATTANT)

Francoise Brion (Dominique), Jean-Louis Trintignant (Francois), Raymond Gerome (Pierre Mallet), Penelope Portrait.

Somewhat dull romance featuring Trintignant as a young painter who meets and falls in love with young and beautiful Brion while vacationing on the French Riviera. Brion however, is there to meet her lover, an older, married Chilean diplomat, but he never shows up, leaving the pair to explore the pleasures of the Riviera together. Despite their new closeness, Trintignant is unable to distract Brion from her obsession with the Chilean and their love is never fulfilled.

d&w, Jacques Doniol-Valcroze; ph, Christian Matras; m, Michel Legrand; ed, Nadine Marquand.

Romance   **(PR:C   MPAA:NR)**

FRENCH KEY, THE**

(1946) 67m REP bw

Albert Dekker (Johnny Fletcher), Mike Mazurki (Sam Cragg), Evelyn Ankers (Janet Morgan), John Eldredge (John Holterman), Frank Fenton (Horatio Vedder), Selmer Jackson (Walter Winslow), Byron Foulger (Peabody), Joe DeRita (Fox), Marjorie Manners (Betty Winslow), David Gorcey (Eddie Miller), Michael Brandon (Murdock), Sammy Stein (Percy), Alan Ward (Madigan), Walter Soderling (George Polson), Emmett Vogan (Desk Clerk).

Murder mystery starring Dekker and musclebound sidekick Mazurki who find themselves locked out of their hotel room because they haven't paid the rent. The clever duo use the fire escape, and find a dead man in their room clutching a gold coin. To avoid being blamed for the murder the pair set out to track down the real killer and they encounter a trail of nightclubs, coin dealers and more corpses. The mystery becomes so convoluted that there is never any clear resolution.

p&d, Walter Colmes; w, Frank Gruber; ph, Jockey Feindel; m, Alexander Laszlo; ed, Robert Jahns.

Mystery   **(PR:A   MPAA:NR)**

FRENCH LEAVE*

(1931, Brit.) 60m A&D/Talking Picture Epics bw

Madeleine Carroll (Mlle. Juliette/Dorothy Glenister), Sydney Howard (Cpl. Sykes), Arthur Chesney (Gen. Root), Haddon Mason (Capt. Harry Glenister), Henry Kendall (Lt. George Graham), George de Warfaz (Jules Marnier), May Agate (Mme. Denaux), George Owen (Pte. Jenks).

Lame comedy set during WWI, about a young British woman who is so desperate to be near her soldier husband that she poses as a local girl in the French town where he is stationed to be near him. This leads to complications which see her being suspected of spying for the Germans. Long and tedious at 60 minutes, the original British cut ran 100 minutes.

p, Henry Defries, Sam Harrison; d, Jack Raymond; w, Reginald Berkeley, W.P. Lipscomb (based on the play by Berkeley); ph, Bernard Knowles.

War/Comedy   **(PR:A   MPAA:NR)**

FRENCH LEAVE**

(1937, Brit.) 86m Welwyn/Pathe bw

Betty Lynne (Dorothy Glennister), Edmond Breon (Col. Root), John Longden (Lt. Glennister), John Wickham (Lt. Graham), Arthur Hambling (Cpl. Sykes), Frederick Burtwell (Nobby), Michael Morel (Jules Marnier), Margaret Yarde (Mme. Dernaux), Oliver Wakefield, The Roosters.

Lynne and her army lieutenant husband Longden figure out a way to stay together during WW I in France. Lynne pretends to be just a friend of Longden's, avoiding the suspicion of his fellow soldiers, and Breon, a colonel who's fallen in love with her. The truth comes out when she is accused of being an enemy agent, but

Longden clears her name and by doing so implicates himself. Everything works out fine by the finale as the loving couple take a leave in Paris.

p, Warwick Ward; d, Norman Lee; w, Vernon Clancey (based on a play by Reginald Berkeley); ph, Bryan Langley.

Comedy   **(PR:A   MPAA:NR)**

FRENCH LEAVE**

(1948) 65m MON bw

Jackie Cooper (Skitch), Jackie Coogan (Pappy), Ralph Sanford (Muldoon), Curt Bois (Marcel), Renee Godfrey (Mimi), William Dambrosi (Pierre), Claire DuBrey (Mom LaFarge), John Bleifer (Pop LaFarge), Larry Blake (Shultz), Robin Raymond, George Lloyd, Frank Scannell, Pedro Regas, Jimmy Cross, Dick Winslow, Alphonse Martell, Billy Snyder, Manuel Paris, Vivian Mason, Robert Coogan, Charles LaTorre.

Former child stars Coogan and Cooper team up as merchant seamen who are more interested in the ladies on shore than performing their shipboard duties. They conspire with French food smugglers who loot ships of chow and sell it on the black market. A modest comedy programmer.

p, Sid Luft; d, Frank McDonald; w, Jameson Brewer, Jack Rubin; ph, William Sickner; ed, Ace Herman; md, Edward Kay; art d, Dave Milton.

Comedy   **(PR:A   MPAA:NR)**

FRENCH LIEUTENANT'S WOMAN, THE*

(1981) 127m UA c

Meryl Streep (Sarah/Anna), Jeremy Irons (Charles/Mike), Hilton McRae (Sam), Emily Morgan (Mary), Charlotte Mitchell (Mrs. Tranter), Lynsey Baxter (Ernestina), Jean Faulds (Cook), Peter Vaughan (Mr. Freeman), Colin Jeavons (Vicar), Liz Smith (Mrs. Fairley), Patience Collier (Mrs. Poulteney), John Barrett (Dairyman), Leo McKern (Dr. Grogan), Arabella Weir (Girl on Undercliff), Ben Forster (Boy on Undercliff), Catherine Willmer (Dr. Grogan's Housekeeper), Anthony Langdon (Asylum Keeper), Edward Duke (Nathaniel), Richard Griffiths (Sir Tom), Graham Fletcher-Cook (Delivery Boy), Richard Hope (3rd Assistant), Michael Elwyn (Montague), Toni Palmer (Mrs. Endicott), Cecily Hobbs (Betty Anne), Doreen Mantle (Lady on Train), David Warner (Murphy), Alun Armstrong (Grimes), Gerard Falconetti (Davide), Penelope Wilton (Sonia), Joanna Joseph (Lizzie), Judith Alderson (Red Haired Prostitute), Cora Kinnaird (2nd Prostitute), Orlando Fraser (Tom Elliott), Fredricka Morton (Girl), Alice Maschler (2nd Girl), Vicky Ireland, Claire Travers-Deacon, Harriet Walter, Janet Rawson, Mia Soteriou, Mary McLeod, Peter Fraser, Rayner Newmark.

This film was a mistake from start to finish, a self-indulgent effort to translate the Fowles novel to the screen when everyone knew that the epic romance novel was impossible to translate, everyone but the public and viewers who paid top dollar to learn the same thing. Streep is the social pariah in mysterious mourning who has been dishonored after a disastrous affair with a French officer in 1867 England, and Irons is the Victorian young man of principle who finds her and falls hopelessly in love with her. The story is told on two levels, from the historical point of view, as in the novel, and from a contemporary focus of the same lovers as the actors of the film, falling in love on the set during the production. The intercutting between the two perspectives is disorienting, fragmentary, and utterly confusing, creating a sloppy, senseless production. Streep, an on-and-off actress who is vastly overrated as a multi-talented person able to cope with any role, overacts embarrassingly, affecting a flighty style that could only be called early Miriam Hopkins; she swallows lines, turns her back to the camera, and displays a general disregard for both roles she attempts to enact. Irons is a wooden prop who delivers his lines with all the energy of an unpainted mannequin. Pinter's screenplay is as much an inside joke as is the direction and overall production, one where the public didn't laugh or cry. A terrible waste of time and money.

p, Leon Clore; d, Karel Reisz; w, Harold Pinter (based on the novel by John Fowles); ph, Freddie Francis (Technicolor); m, Carl Davis; ed, John Bloom; prod d, Assheton Gorton; art d, Norman Dorme, Terry Pritchard, Allan Cameron; cos, Tom Rand.

Romance   **Cas.**   **(PR:O   MPAA:NR)**

FRENCH LINE, THE**

(1954) 102m RKO c

Jane Russell (Mary Carson), Gilbert Roland (Pierre), Arthur Hunnicutt ("Waco" Mosby), Mary McCarty (Annie Farrell), Joyce MacKenzie (Myrtle Brown), Paula Corday (Celeste), Scott Elliott (Bill Harris), Craig Stevens (Phil Barton), Laura Elliot (Katherine Hodges), Steven Geray (Francois), John Wengraf (1st Mate), Michael St. Angel (George Hodges), Barbara Darrow (Donna Adams), Barbara Dobbins (Kitty Lee), Jean Moorhead, Mary Rodman, Charmienne Harker, Dolores Michaels, Suzanne Alexander, Eileen Coghlan, Rosemary Colligan, Millie Doff, Jane Easton, Helene Hayden, Ellye Marshall, Jarma Lewis, Marilyn [Kim] Novak, Pat Sheehan, Maureen Stephenson, Shirley Tegge, Beverly Thompson, Doreen Woodbury, Devvy Davenport, Barbara Lohrman, Dolly Summers, Phyllis St. Pierre, Shirley Buchanan (Models), Ray Bennett (Foreman), Al Cavens, Jo Gilbert, Frank Marlowe, Nick Stuart, Charles Smith, Allen Ray, Jeffrey Sayre, Ralph Volkie, Carlos Albert, Robert Dayo, Donald Moray, Joseph Rubino, Renald Dupont (Reporters), Bess Flowers (Saleslady), Theresa Harris (Clara), Peggy Leon, Leoda Richards (Customers), Ramona Magrill (Seamstress), John Mooney, George Wallace, Lane Bradford (Cowboys), Edward Short (Willie), Edward Coch, Wayne Taylor (French Bellhops), Pierre Chandler, Frederick Stevens, Arthur Dulac (French Stewards), Jack Chefe (Wine Steward), William Forrest (Sam Baker), Louis Mercier (Steward), Buck Young (Photographer), Sue Casey, Mary Ellen Gleason, Mary Langan, Bobette Bentley, Gloria Watson, Dede Moore, Helen Chapman, Gloria Pall, Dawn Oney, Joi Lansing, Joyce Johnson, Lonnie Pierce (Showgirls), Mary Jane Carey (American Nurse), Toni Carroll (Toni), Sandy Drescher (Girl), Wanda Ottoni (French Nurse), Shirley Patterson (Elsie), Lucien Plauzoles (Boy), Lomax Study (French Waiter), Billy Daniel (Andre), Jack Boyle, Joel Friend (Actordancers), Suzanne Ames, Babs Cox (Maids), Anne Ford, Virginia Bates, Katherine Cassidy (Paris Models), Lizz Slifer (French Woman), Stanley Farrar (French Man), Marina Cisternas (Customer at Paris Salon), Dan Bernaducci, Fritz Feld (French Cabbies), Marie Rabasse (Flower Woman), Bert Le Baron (Doorman).

A cheap spinoff of GENTLEMEN PREFER BLONDES, this is strictly a Russell vehicle where she is a Texas heiress who desperately wants to be loved, not for her millions but for her own voluptuous self. In Texas she discards stuffy, acquisitive Stevens and takes off on a transcontinental sea trip, pretending to be a model for McCarty's troupe, while hiring the statuesque MacKenzie to impersonate her, even though the double is newly married and her anxious bridegroom is along for the ride and must hide out incognito, salivating for his wife. Also along for the trip is playboy Roland whose job it is (being hired by Hunnicutt, Russell's avuncular cowboy protector) to safeguard the heiress. He believes MacKenzie is the real heiress, or so we are led to believe, and he puts the make on Russell as he might any attractive but penniless female. But the truth is Roland knows all along that Russell is miss moneybucks and his machinations lead her to reject him, particularly when she comes to believe he's truly interested in MacKenzie, which he is not. By the time the troupe reaches Europe and puts on a successful fashion show, Russell and Roland are at fighting odds but all ends well when he confesses that he knew she was the lady with the pursestrings and he loves her in spite of her filthy rich background. It's not much of a story but Howard Hughes, by offering up the Amazonian Russell in 3-D and squeezing her sizzling figure into the skimpiest of costumes, was able to hype this predictable potboiler into heavy profits. Most of the story, dialog, and songs are merely a buildup to a white-hot number Russell sings at the finale, "Lookin' for Trouble" (Andre Josef Myrow, Ralph Blaine, Robert Wells), where she wears only high heels, gloves, and what was loosely termed a bikini, a one-piece affair, opened at below and above the waist, low cut to show off Russell's considerable mammary allure. She had a diamond buried in her naval and the whole thing is really an old burlesque approach as she discards an ankle-length ermine cape and goes into a quaking, shaking, bumping, grinding, hip-shooting number that immediately got Hughes criticism from social groups, pulpits, and reviewers howling at the bad taste. The film did not get the production code seal of approval, which created even greater box office receipts. Russell later commented in her autobiography: "I did the whole number very tongue in cheek, and I saw nothing wrong with it." Hughes played Russell's attributes for all they were worth, blatantly advertising the film with such suggestive lines as "J.R. in 3-D. It'll knock *both* your eyes out!" When the Catholic Legion of Decency condemned the film, theaters overflowed with customers, despite the fact that Archbishop Ritter of St. Louis stated that "since no Catholic can with a clear conscience attend such an immoral movie, we feel it is our solemn duty to forbid our Catholic people under penalty of mortal sin to attend this presentation." This was, of course, all carefully planned by the calculating Hughes, who released the film in St. Louis after learning that 65 percent of the city's 857,000 people were Catholic. Kim Novak, using her given name of Marilyn, appears briefly as a model. Songs include: "Comment Allez-Vous?" "Well, I'll Be Switched," "Any Gal From Texas," "What Is This That I Feel?" "With A Kiss," "By Madame Fuelle," "Wait Till You See Paris," "Poor Andre," and (cut) "The French Line" (Myrow, Blane, Wells).

p, Edmund Grainger; d, Lloyd Bacon; w, Mary Loos, Richard Sale (based on a story by Matty Kemp and Isabel Dawn); ph, Harry J. Wild (3-D, Technicolor); m, Walter Scharf; ed, Robert Ford; md, C. Bakaleinikoff; art d, Albert S. D'Agostino, Carroll Clark; cos, Michael Woulfe, Howard Greer; ch, Billy Daniel.

Musical/Comedy Cas. (PR:C MPAA:NR)

FRENCH MISTRESS½** (1960, Brit.) 98m BL bw

Cecil Parker *(Headmaster)*, James Robertson Justice *(Robert Martin)*, Ian Bannen *(Colin Crane)*, Agnes Laurent *(Madeleine Lafarge)*, Raymond Huntley *(Rev. Edwin Peake)*, Irene Handl *(Staff Sgt. Hodges)*, Edith Sharpe *(Matron)*, Kenneth Griffith *(Mr. Meade)*, Robert Bruce *(Mr. Ramsay)*, Thorley Walters *(Col. Edmonds)*, Henry Longhurst *(Second Governor)*, Brian Oulton *(Third Governor)*, Scot Finch *(Edmonds)*, Richard Palmer *(Milsom)*, Peter Greenspan *(Wigram)*, Jeremy Bulloch *(Baines)*, Athene Seyler *(Beatrice Peake)*, Cardew Robinson *(Ambulance Attendant)*, Paul Sheridan *(Monsieur Fraguier)*.

British comedy set in a stuffy boys' school that goes up for grabs when the sexy, young, and French Laurent arrives as the learning institution's new French tutor. The boys stage a literal revolt on the administration when it is announced that she is being dismissed because she is attracting too much attention. Typical jokes regarding the adolescent boys reactions to their enticing new teacher wear thin quickly.

p, John Boulting; d, Roy Boulting; w, Roy Boulting, Jeffrey Bell (based on a play by Robert Monro); ph, Max Greene; m, John Addison; ed, John Jympson.

Comedy (PR:A MPAA:NR)

FRENCH POSTCARDS** (1979) 95m Geria/PAR c

Miles Chapin *(Joel)*, Blanche Baker *(Laura)*, David Marshall Grant *(Alex)*, Valerie Quennessen *(Toni)*, Debra Winger *(Melanie)*, Mandy Patinkin *(Sayyid)*, Marie-France Pisier *(Mme. Tessier)*, Jean Rochefort *(Mon. Tessier)*, Lynn Carlin *(Mrs. Weber)*, George Coe *(Mr. Weber)*, Christophe Bourseiller *(Pascal)*, Francois Lalande *(Mon. Levert)*, Anemone *(Christine)*, Veronique Janot *(Malsy)*, Marie-Anne Chazelk *(Cecile)*, Laurence Ligneres *(Mme. Levert)*, Andre Penvern *(Jean-Louis)*, Patrick Fierry *(Jean-Claude)*, Ronald Neunreuther *(Bus Driver)*, Gloria Katz *(Chief Snail)*, Jean Champagne, Guy Bouchet *(Staffers)*, Jean-Jose Richer *(Medieval Knight)*, Jean-Pierre Kohut-Svelko *(Photographer)*, Susan Bredhoff *(Iranian Maid)*.

The naive escapades of a group of American students studying in France for a year is given a charming, somewhat corny treatment by the authors of AMERICAN GRAFFITI—Huyck (who also directed) and Katz. Pisier is a teacher who offers her culture to the students, while at the same time expressing an interest in the U.S. As the film progresses, she has an affair with one of her students, Chapin, though it soon ends when he leaves for Spain. Meantime, the students visit famous sights (as many of the Michelin Guide's 212 major sights as they can) and destroy the language in their attempts to sound Parisian. Winger appears in an early role and DIVA director Jean-Jacques Beineix acts as assistant director. Imagine a weakly directed version of AMERICAN GRAFFITI set in France.

p, Gloria Katz; d, Willard Huyck; w, Huyck, Katz; ph, Bruno Nuytten; m, Lee Holdridge; ed, Carol Littleton; art d, Jean-Pierre Kohut-Svelko; cos, Catherine Leterrier, Joan Mocine.

Drama/Comedy Cas. (PR:A-C MPAA:PG)

FRENCH QUARTER½** (1978) 101m Crown International c

Bruce Davison *(Kid Ross/Inspector Sordik)*, Virginia Mayo *(Countess Piazza/Ida)*, Lindsay Bloom *(Big Butt/Policewoman)*, Lance Legault *(Tom/Burt)*, Ann Michelle *(Coke-Eyed Laura/Policewoman)*, Alisha Fontaine *(Trudy/Christine)*, Vernel Bagneris *(Jelly Roll/Policeman)*, Rebecca Allen *(Bricktop/Girl in Square)*, Laura Mish Owens *(Ice Box Jose/Girl in Square)*, Anna Filamento *(Mme. Papaloos/Mme. Beaudine)*, William Simms *(Aaron Harris/Pimp)*, Stocker Fontelieu *(Dr. Miles/Old Man)*, Stanley Reyes *(Bellocq/Drunk)*, Ronald Bolden *(Satchelmouth/Shoeshine Boy)*, Sylvia "Kuumba" Williams *(Wisterie/Cleaning Woman)*, Dino Head *(Lady Lil/Stripper)*, Don Hood *(Detective/Policeman)*, Barry Sullivan.

Interesting obscurity has Fontaine the reincarnation of a New Orleans prostitute from the turn of the century. Dual story line has each performer both in modern times and in the past. Hardly noticed when originally released, the film is worth seeing if it ever resurfaces.

p&d, Dennis Kane; w, Barney Cohen, Kane; ph, Jerry Kalogeratos (Movielab Color); m, Dick Hyman; ed, Ed Fricke, George Norris; cos, Ellen Mirojnick; ch, Donnis Hunnicutt.

Drama Cas. (PR:O MPAA:R)

FRENCH, THEY ARE A FUNNY RACE, THE** (1956, Fr.) 105m GAU-Continental bw (LES CARNETS DU MAJOR THOMPSON; AKA: FRENCH ARE A FUNNY RACE; NOTEBOOKS OF MAJOR THOMPSON; DIARY OF MAJOR THOMPSON)

Jack Buchanan *(Major Thompson)*, Martine Carol *(Martine)*, Noel-Noel *(Taupin)*, Totti Truman Taylor *(Nurse)*, Andre Luguet *(Editor)*, Genevieve Brunet *(Secretary)*, Catherine Boyl *(Wife)*.

Based on essays allegedly written by an English major about his adjustment to the carefree French life. Buchanan is the retired officer who lives in Paris with his air-headed, but beautiful, French wife; the two appearing to have nothing better to do than argue over how to raise their child. Except for a few sequences which draw a great deal of humor by contrasting French and English lifestyles, this is a far cry from such brilliant works like THE MIRACLE OF MORGAN CREEK or SULLIVAN'S TRAVELS, both minor masterpieces filled with Sturges' cunning wit.

p, Paul Wagner; d&w, Preston Sturges (based on the book *The Notebooks Of Major Thompson* by Pierre Daninos); ph, Maurice Barry, Christian Matras; ed, Raymond Lanny.

Comedy (PR:A MPAA:NR)

FRENCH TOUCH, THE½** (1954, Fr.) 84m Times Film bw (COIFFURE POUR DAMES)

Fernandel *(Marius-Mario)*, Renee Devillers *(Aline)*, Arlette Poirier *(Edmonde)*, George Chamarat *(M. Brochand)*, Blanchette Brunoy *(Mme. Brochand)*, Jane Sourza *(Denise)*, Jose Noguero *(Admirer of Mme. Brochand)*.

Farcical French comedy about a sheep-shearer, Fernandel, who decides to become a hairdresser and soon finds himself the rage of the Parisian ladies. Lots of not-as-bad-as-it-looks bedroom comedy which sees Fernandel constantly trying to explain things to his wife. An average goofy comedy.

d, Jean Boyer; w, Serge Veber, Boyer (based on a play by P. Armont, M. Gerbidon); ph, Ch. Suin; m, Paul Misraki.

Comedy (PR:A MPAA:NR)

FRENCH WAY, THE** (1952, Fr.) 73m L. Barry Bernard bw

Josephine Baker *(Zazu)*, Micheline Presle *(Claire)*, Georges Marchal *(Bernard)*, Almos *(M. Honore)*, Jean Tissier *(Pierre)*, Lucien Baroux *(Leon/The Tramp)*, Gabrielle Dorziat *(Mme. Ancelot)*, Saturnin Fabre *(M. Dalban)*, Marguerite Perry *(Mlle. Esperajou)*.

Strange little French farce concerning a young romantic couple who are forbidden to marry because of their parents who are constantly feuding. Enter French nightclub sensation Baker (a bit past her prime) who lives in the apartment house owned by the boy's father and who sees that the young lovers' plans to marry are carried through. Baker of course takes time to sing and dance her way through: "To Live Alone Under One Roof" and "No Nina." Baker begins to do her trademark dance routine, but the scene was cut.

p&d, Jacques De Baroncelli; m, Wal-Berg; ed, Reine Dorian; m/l, Vincent Scotto.

Drama (PR:A MPAA:NR)

FRENCH WAY, THE** (1975, Fr.) 105m Peppercorn-Wormser c (LE MOUTON ENRAGE; AKA: LOVE AT THE TOP)

Jean-Louis Trintignant *(Nicholas)*, Romy Schneider *(Roberta)*, Jean-Pierre Cassel *(Fabre)*, Jane Birkin *(Marie-Paule)*, Florinda Bolkan *(Flora)*, Georges Wilson *(Lourceuil)*, Henri Garcin *(Berthoud)*.

Mousy bank clerk Trintignant becomes an almost overnight success when placed under the plotting of hard-up novelist Cassel. Before long he's impressing all of Paris with his power over women and his ability to attain great wealth. Highly stylized film lacks much thematic content and virtually wastes the talented cast. (In French; English subtitles.)

p, Leo Fuchs; d, Michel Deville; w, Christopher Frank (based on the novel by Roger Blondel); ph, Claude Lecomte (Movielab Color); m, Saint-Saens.

Drama (PR:O MPAA:R)

FRENCH WITHOUT TEARS** (1939, Brit.) 86m PAR bw

Ray Milland *(Alan Howard)*, Ellen Drew *(Diana Lake)*, Janine Darcy *(Jacqueline Maingot)*, Roland Culver *(Cmdr. Rogers)*, David Tree *(Chris Neilan)*, Jim Gerald *(Maingot)*, Guy Middleton *(Brian Curtis)*, Kenneth Morgan *(Kenneth Lake)*, Margaret Yarde *(Marianne)*, Toni Gable *(Chi-Chi)*.

Uninspired schoolboy comedy set in France has a group of Englishmen studying French under the guidance of a stuffy tutor. Enter the sexy and flirtatious Drew, the sister of one of the students, who proceeds to seduce every one of her brother's classmates except Milland who'll have nothing to do with her—until they marry. Editing supervised by Lean.

p, Mario Zampi; d, Anthony Asquith; w, Terence Rattigan, Ian Dalrymple, Anatole de Grunwald (based on the play by Rattigan); ph, Bernard Knowles, Jack Hildyard; m, Nicholas Brodsky; ed, Davis Lean; art d, Paul Sheriff.

Comedy (PR:A MPAA:NR)

FRENCHIE** (1950) 80m UNIV c

Joel McCrea (*Tom Banning*), Shelley Winters (*Frenchie Fontaine*), Paul Kelly (*Pete Lambert*), Elsa Lanchester (*Countess*), Marie Windsor (*Diane*), John Russell (*Lance Cole*), John Emery (*Clyde Gorman*), Regis Toomey (*Carter*), Paul E. Burns (*Rednose*), Frank Ferguson (*Jim Dobbs*), Vincent Renno (*Tony*), Larry Dobkin (*Bartender*), Lucille Barkley (*Dealer*).

For some reason Universal decided to rework the Marlene Dietrich, Jimmy Stewart oater classic DESTRY RIDES AGAIN (1939) and they came up with this lame imitation starring Winters in the Dietrich role and McCrea filling in for Stewart. The result is a flat western that sees Winters as a New Orleans gambling house madame returning to her home town of Bottleneck to avenge the murder of her father. McCrea is the town sheriff she falls for—without abandoning her plot for vengeance. She eventually uncovers that respected banker Emery and Kelly, are the real killers. There is even a knock down drag out between Winters and Windsor (the banker's wife) that is ripped-off from the fight in DESTRY RIDES AGAIN between Dietrich and Una Merkel. Winters is just plain sloppy in her role.

p, Michel Kraike; d, Louis King; w, Oscar Brodney; ph, Maury Gertsman (Technicolor); m, Hans Salter; ed, Ted J. Kent.

Western (PR:A MPAA:NR)

FRENCHMAN'S CREEK*** (1944) 112m PAR c

Joan Fontaine (*Lady Dona St. Columb*), Arturo de Cordova (*The Frenchman*), Basil Rathbone (*Lord Rockingham*), Nigel Bruce (*Lord Godolphin*), Cecil Kellaway (*William*), Ralph Forbes (*Harry St. Columb*), Harold Ramond (*Edmund*), Billy Daniels (*Pierre Blanc*), Moyna MacGill (*Lady Godolphin*), Patricia Barker (*Henrietta*), David James (*James*), Mary Field (*Prue*), David Clyde (*Coachman*), Charles Coleman (*Footman*), Paul Oman (*Luc*), Arthur Gould Porter (*Thomas Kustick*), Evan Thomas (*Robert Penrose*), Leslie Denison (*John Nankervia*), Denis Green (*Philip Rashleigh*), George Kirby (*Dr. Williams*), David Thursby (*Ostler*), Lauri Betty (*Alice*), Ronnie Rondell, George Barton, Victor Romito, Bob Clark, Allen Pinson, Patrick Desmond, Jimmy Dime, Harvey Easton, Henry Escalanate, Art Foster, Vincent Gironda, Jacques Karre, John Latito, Rube Schaffer, Sammy Stein, Armand Tanny, Fred Kohler, Jr., John Roy, Neal Clisby, Noble Blake (*Pirate Crew*), Constance Worth, Phyllis Barry (*Women in Gambling House*), Edward Cooper (*Croupier*), Bob Stevenson, Alfred George Ferguson (*Jail Guards*), Frank Hagney (*Cornishman*), Keith Hitchcock (*Watchman*), Leyland Hodgson, Kenneth Hunter, Boyd Irwin, Gordon Richards (*Guests*).

This lavish romance epic set in the 17th century has gentle British noblewoman Fontaine fleeing her spineless husband, Forbes, and his lecherous, dangerous friend, Rathbone, who lusts after her. She finds French pirate de Cordova's ship anchored in a creek near her country estate, and falls in love with the swashbuckler. In a fit of caprice, Fontaine accompanies de Cordova in a raid against the estate of pompous landowner Bruce. When she hears that her husband and Rathbone are en route to capture the dashing adventurer, Fontaine sends her favorite servant, Kellaway, to warn him. She then entertains the pursuers at dinner, only to be interrupted by de Cordova who captures the palatial estate. He locks up Forbes and Rathbone, then pleads with Fontaine to run away with him. She tells him she must remain for the sake of her young children and he leaves. Rathbone, who later tells Fontaine he has overheard her conversation with the pirate, first tries to blackmail the lady. When she sneers at his threat he attempts to rape her but Fontaine flees up a staircase, Rathbone in hot pursuit. Fontaine pulls down a heavy suit of armor which kills her tormentor. Next she hears that de Cordova has been taken prisoner. She helps him escape but refuses to sail with him, nobly pledging her life to her children. The production is stunning in lush color, superb art direction by Dreier and Fegte and astounding sets by Comer, who won an Oscar. Most memorable is Young's unforgettable score, at the center of which is Claude Debussy's "Clair de Lune." It's a wonderful tearjerker and Rathbone excels as the menace.

p, B.G. DeSylva; d, Mitchell Leisen; w, Talbot Jennings (based on the novel by Daphne du Maurier); ph, George Barnes; process ph, Farciot Edouart (Technicolor); m, Victor Young; ed, Alma Macrorie; art d, Hans Dreier, Ernst Fegte; set d, Sam Comer; cos, Raoul Pene Du Bois; spec eff, Gordon Jennings.

Historical Romance (PR:A MPAA:NR)

FRENZY**½ (1946, Brit.) 75m Four Continents bw (GB: LATIN QUARTER)

Derrick de Marney (*Charles Garrie*), Frederick Valk (*Dr. Krasner*), Joan Greenwood (*Christine*), Joan Seton (*Lucille*), Beresford Egan (*Minetti*), Lily Kann (*Maria*), Valentine Dyall (*Prefect of Police*), Martin Miller (*Morgue Keeper*), Espinoza (*Ballet Master*), Margaret Clarke (*Ballet Mistress*), Sybilla Binder (*Medium*), Anthony Hawtrey (*Specialist*), Gerhardt Kempinski (*Police Sergeant*), Bruce Winston (*Friend*), Rachel Brodrar, Cleo Nordi, Billy Holland.

Creepy thriller starring de Marney as a Paris sculptor who has an affair with the wife of another sculptor who is slowly going mad. When the madman discovers the infidelity, he snaps completely, kills his wife and plasters her up in a statue. He is eventually arrested for another murder, that of his mistress, but de Marney becomes involved in the occult trying to find out what happened to his lover. Good suspenseful moments somewhat weakened by long, slow passages and an overly complicated flashback structure.

p, Louis Jackson, Derrick de Marney; d&w, Vernon Sewell (based on the play "L'Angoise," by Pierre Mills and C. Vylars); ph, Gunther Kramph, Gerald D. Moss.

Suspense (PR:A MPAA:NR)

FRENZY***½ (1972, Brit.) 116m UNIV c

Jon Finch (*Richard Blaney*), Barry Foster (*Robert Rusk*), Barbara Leigh-Hunt (*Brenda Blaney*), Anna Massey (*Babs Milligan*), Alec McCowen (*Chief Inspector Oxford*), Vivien Merchant (*Mrs. Oxford*), Billie Whitelaw (*Hetty Porter*), Clive Swift (*Johnny Porter*), Bernard Cribbins (*Felix Forsythe*), Michael Bates (*Sgt. Spearman*), Jean Marsh (*Monica Bailing*).

Hitchcock's first film he'd done in England in almost two decades, was not a smash at the box office (under $10 million, according to our figures), but it was a smashing return to his earlier style after the dull TORN CURTAIN and TOPAZ. With a funny, literate script adaptation by Shaffer (author of SLEUTH and twin brother of Peter Shaffer, author of AMADEUS, ROYAL HUNT OF THE SUN and many more), Hitchcock takes us over some familiar territory but never with more fun and cinematic energy. This is not a mystery, we know the real killer early on. Hitchcock preferred suspense to mystery and liked letting the audience in on matters, then defied you to not be on the edge of your seat. Finch is accused of several murders; his ex-wife, Leigh-Hunt, who is a professional matchmaker, and his girlfriend, Massey. Someone has been strangling women with neckties and Finch is the obvious suspect. The real killer, however, is Foster, one of the best villains since Robert Walker in STRANGERS ON A TRAIN. Foster is a vegetable monger who is Finch's pal. His charming demeanor hides a psychopathic rapist mentality that is only seen when he is committing his crimes. Hitchcock's touches abound and the humor gets screamingly funny when the inspector, McCowen, clues in his wife, Merchant, at dinner. Merchant is one of those women who likes to make gourmet meals for her tired husband and each successive dinner scene gets more hysterical as he attempts to eat the slop she's serving. Nothing would please him more than bangers and mash or shepherd's pie but she insists on testing her new and disgusting concoctions on him. There's more sex and violence in this than usual and Hitchcock is more explicit in both than ever before. Still, he is nowhere near what his copier (Brian De Palma) attempts and everything is understated. Foster is sensational as the killer and Finch is almost as good. Many of the faces were new to Americans and that helped in the credibility of the story. Cribbins has been a working British comic actor for years and scored well in the National Theatre's version of "Guys and Dolls" in 1984, where he played Nathan Detroit without dropping an "h." Marsh (from TV's "Upstairs, Downstairs") does a neat job as the prudish assistant to Leigh-Hunt. The humor begins at the top as a politician states that the Thames has been absolutely cleared of pollution. At that precise moment, a dead woman's body floats to the surface. Despite the tongue-in-cheek overview, there are several real moments of terror and the final effect is one of having been well entertained by a movie, which is exactly what Hitchcock always wanted to do.

p&d, Alfred Hitchcock; w, Anthony Shaffer (from the novel *Goodbye Picadilly, Farewell Leicester Square* by Arthur LaBern); ph, Gil Taylor (Technicolor); m, Ron Goodwin; ed, John Jympson; prod d, Syd Cain; art d, Bob Laing; set d, Simon Wakefield.

Crime Drama Cas. (PR:C-O MPAA:R)

FRESH FROM PARIS*½ (1955) 72m Mercury-International/AA c (AKA: PARIS FOLLIES OF 1956)

Forrest Tucker (*Dan Bradley*), Margaret Whiting (*Margaret Walton*), Dick Wesson (*Chuck Russell*), Martha Hyer (*Ruth Harmon*), Barbara Whiting (*Barbara Walton*), Lloyd Corrigan (*Alfred Gaylord*), Wally Cassell (*Harry*), Fluff Charlton (*Taffy*), James Ferris (*Jim*), William Henry (*Wendell*), The Sportsmen, Frank Parker.

A gardener, Corrigan, posing as a millionaire, offers to finance a show put on by Tucker, but Tucker discovers he's a fraud. The quickly made film (five days) contains all the stereotyped characters who are involved in musical productions including a dizzy singer, Margaret Whiting, and a girl who is just in awe of the whole goings-on. The original title dated the film too much for all save memorabilia lovers, so when the film was re-released its ripeness was concealed with this new title. Songs include "Can This Be Love?," "I Love A Circus," "Have You Ever Been In Paris?," "I'm All Aglow Again," "I'm In A Mood Tonight" (Pony Sherrell, Phil Moody); "The Hum Song" (Sid Kuller).

p, Bernard Tabakin; d, Leslie Goodwins; w, Milton Lazarus; ph, Edwin Du Par (DeLuxe Color); ed, Gene Fowler, Jr.; md, Frank DeVol; cos, Don Loper, Lucille Sothern; ch, Donn Arden.

Musical (PR:A MPAA:NR)

FRESHMAN, THE (SEE: BACHELOR OF HEARTS, 1958, Brit.)

FRESHMAN LOVE**½** (1936) 65m WB bw (GB: RHYTHM ON THE RIVER)

Frank McHugh *(Coach Hammond)*, Patricia Ellis *(Joan Simpkins)*, Warren Hull *(Bob Wilson)*, Joe Cawthorn *(Wilson, Sr.)*, George E. Stone *(E. Prendergast Biddle)*, Mary Treen *(Squirmy)*, Henry O'Neill *(Pres. Simpkins)*, Alma Lloyd *(Sandra)*, Anita Kerry *(Princess Oggi)*, Johnny Arthur *(Fields)*, Walter Johnson *(Tony Foster)*, Joseph Sawyer *(Coach Kendall)*, Florence Fair *(Mrs. Norton)*, Spec O'Donnell *(Eddie)*.

Silly campus comedy concerning rowing-team coach McHugh's efforts to keep his job by pushing his team to its limits. His efforts are constantly frustrated by gorgeous gal Ellis who keeps luring the husky oarsmen away from practice. McHugh manages to turn the tables by sending enticing letters to rowers from other schools encouraging them to enroll in his college by enclosing in the letters a sexy photo of Ellis. A win is ultimately attained after bandleader Stone is recruited as coxswain and introduces a jazz beat to the striving oarsmen. Songs include "The Collegiana," "That's What I Mean," "Freshman Love," and "Romance After Dark." Harmless fun with a few good jazz tunes to liven things up.

p, Bryan Foy; d, William McGann; w, Earl Felton, George Bricker (based on a story by George Ade); ph, Sid Hickox; m, M.K. Jerome; ed, James Gibbons; md, Leo F. Forbstein; art d, Esdras Hartley; cos, Orry-Kelly; m/l, Jerome, Jack Scholl, Joan Jasmyn.

Comedy **(PR:A MPAA:NR)**

FRESHMAN YEAR**** (1938) 65m UNIV bw

Dixie Dunbar *(Dotty)*, William Lundigan *(Bob)*, Constance Moore *(Marian)*, Ernest Truex *(Professor)*, Stanley Hughes [Mark Daniels] *(Jay)*, Frank Melton *(Dave)*, Tommy Wonder *(Tommy)*, Fay McKenzie, Marjorie Montgomery, Marjorie Deane, Kay Stewart, Alan Ladd *(Students)*, Don Defore *(Upperclassman)*, Alden [Stephen] Chase, Raymond Parker, Three Diamond Brothers, Three Murtagh Sisters, The Lucky Seven Choir.

Somewhat amusing campus comedy featuring Lundigan as an enterprising underclassman who hits upon the idea of selling "flunk" insurance to students for 50 cents a policy. If a student flunks his or her test, the insurance pays a ten-dollar settlement. The scheme sells like wildfire, but disaster strikes when professor Truex fails nearly the whole class, causing Lundigan to teeter on the brink of bankruptcy until he makes a bundle promoting the annual college show. Look for perennial costar Don Defore in a small role, as well as Alan Ladd in one of his many bit parts during the time he roomed with other struggling young actors Rory Calhoun and Sunset Carson. Universal announced its intention to make three other college caper films using the same top-billed cast members. It never happened. Fun little programmer punctuated by several songs including,"Chasin' You Around" by Frank Loesser, Irving Actman; "Ain't That Marvellous," "Swing That Cheer," by Joe McCarthy, Harry Barris.

p, George Bilson; d, Frank McDonald; w, Charles Grayson (based on a story by Thomas Ahearn, F. Maury Grossman); ph, Elwood Bredell; ed, Ed Curtis; md, Charles Previn; art d, Jack Otterson.

Comedy **(PR:A MPAA:NR)**

FREUD**½** (1962) 140m UNIV bw (AKA: THE SECRET PASSION)

Montgomery Clift *(Sigmund Freud)*, Susannah York, *(Cecily Koertner)*, Larry Parks *(Dr. Joseph Breuer)*, Susan Kohner *(Martha Freud)*, Eric Portman *(Dr. Theodore Meynert)*, Eileen Herlie *(Frau Ida Koertner)*, Fernand Ledoux *(Professor Charcot)*, David McCallum *(Carl von Schlosser)*, Rosalie Crutchley *(Frau Freud)*, David Kossoff *(Jacob Freud)*, Joseph Furst *(Jacob Koertner)*, Allan Cuthbertson *(Wilkie)*, Moira Redmond *(Nora Wimmer)*, Maria Perschy *(Magda)*, Elisabeth Neumann-Viertel *(Frau Bernays)*, Ursula Lyn *(Mitzi Freud)*, Alexander Mango *(Babinsky)*, Leonard Sachs *(Brouhardier)*, Victor Beaumont *(Dr. Gruber)*, Manfred Andrea *(Student Doctor)*, Anita Gutwell, Charles Regnier, P. V. Polnitz, Herr Rabb, Friedrich V. Lederbur, J. Swarbrick, M. V. Eden, M. Haufler, A. Vanderhyde, F. Moyne, M. Herbst, Voigt, Vogel, E. Roth, Ol Abdou, J. Holzleitner, U. Emmer, S. Brecht, Y. Maralon, A. V. Loeben, Dr. Ohrenstein, E. Lenkers, Cutty, A. P. Wolff, B. Taubenberger, M. Schanauer, Stefan Schnabel, Mrs. Marks, M. Freeman, G. Woodfine.

Overlong, tedious and far too complex, FREUD attempts to synthesize so much into 140 minutes that it misses the couch on many levels. Clift was miscast as the eminent Jewish doctor from Vienna. Not in a trillion years could that Yankee face be realistic as Sigmund. Instead of showing several patients, the authors composited York as a woman who had every neurosis known to humanity; she's fixated on her father (an Electra complex), hysterical, *and* sexually repressed. It begins as the 30-year-old Freud takes a leave of absence from his work at Vienna's General Hospital where he has been regularly arguing with his superior, Portman. Freud wants to delve deeper into the reasons for hysteria; he travels to Paris where he studies with Ledoux and learns that hypnosis can be used to artificially induce the condition. He marries Kohner, then goes to work for Parks, who also believes in hypnotherapy. Together, they treat York, who is also suffering from insomnia and temporary loss of full sight. Their other case is McCallum, a youth who attacked his father because of his repressed incestuous love for his mother. Clift's published works offend the medical establishment but he is dogged in his belief that he is doing the right thing. Soon, he foregoes hypnosis in favor of what was to become known as "free association." As his work with York continues, Clift begins writing his theories, and eventually presents them to total derision on the part of the listeners. History proves him to be right. This was Larry Parks' first job in many years since being hunted down by the McCarthy types in the 1950s. He was so ingrained in the public eye as Al Jolson that some laughter was heard in the theaters (not unlike George Reeves when he attempted to play roles other than Superman). Occasionally, a one-on-one scene between an analyst and a patient can be electrifying (as in THE FOUR HUNDRED BLOWS, 1959, when Leaud speaks to an unseen listener) but in this film, the star is the psychiatrist—not the patient—and the result is dull. Clift was suffering from a thyroid problem while making the picture, as well as cataracts, and his inability to remember lines, especially medical terms, slowed the production down. McCallum came to the USA shortly afterwards and became well known as the Russian in TV's "The Man From UNCLE." A one-man play about Freud was done several years later (authored by Lynn Roth) and covered the same ground even more effectively because there were no other detracting characters and the essence of Freud was allowed to emerge. This was filmed entirely in England and all the sets are perfect. Too bad the rest of it wasn't.

p, Wolfgang Reinhardt; d, John Huston; w, Charles Kaufman, Reinhardt (based on a story by Kaufman and a script by Jean-Paul Sartre); ph, Douglas Slocombe; m, Jerry Goldsmith; ed, Ralph Kemplen; md, Joseph Gershenson (electronic music by Henk Badings); art d, Stephen B. Grimes; cos, Doris Langley Moore; makeup, Robert Schiffer, Raimund Stangl.

Biography **(PR:A-C MPAA:NR)**

FRIC FRAC**½** (1939, FR.) 95m Distributeurs Francais bw

Fernandel *(Marcel)*, Michel Simon *(Jo)*, Arletty *(Loulou)*, Helene Robert *(Renee)*, Andrex *(Marcandieu)*, Marcel Vallee *(Mons. Blin)*.

Average comedy concerning young rustic jeweler's assistant Fernandel, who dumps his boss' daughter when he becomes infatuated with Arletty who, unbeknownst to him, is the moll of a jewel thief serving time in prison. Through Arletty, he becomes friendly with Simon, which soon leads to his unwitting involvement in the burglary of his employer's store. Eventually he realizes the error of his ways, dumps the crooks, and falls back into the arms of the boss' daughter. Routine material helped by an outstanding cast of French stars. The attempt of the subtitler to capture the spirit of the underworld argot is a tragicomedy in itself. Direction of the film was erroneously credited to producer Lehmann, who was fond of claiming the Hosannas actually earned by the then-poor, overworked Autant-Lara in the period before his success with DEVIL IN THE FLESH (1949). (In French; English subtitles.)

p, Maurice Lehmann; d, Claude Autant-Lara; w, Michel Duran (based on the play by Edouard Bourdet); ph, Armand Thirard; m, Casimir Oberfeld; ed, Elizabeth Harris; prod d, Rene Renoux.

Comedy **(PR:A MPAA:NR)**

FRIDAY FOSTER**** (1975) 89m AIP c

Pam Grier *(Friday Foster)*, Yaphet Kotto *(Colt Hawkins)*, Godfrey Cambridge *(Ford Malotte)*, Thalmus Rasulala *(Blake Tarr)*, Eartha Kitt *(Madame Rena)*, Jim Backus *(Enos Griffith)*, Scatman Crothers *(Rev. Noble Franklin)*, Ted Lange *(Fancy Dexter)*, Tierre Turner *(Cleve)*, Paul Benjamin *(Sen. David Lee Hart)*.

Average Grier vehicle sees the durable exploitation star as a newspaper photographer who stumbles across a plot to assassinate black politicians. The trail leads through a maze of underworld and political types that ends up at the desk of the big-shot mobster Jim Backus (Mr. Magoo?!). Of course, there's the necessary sex and violence, and when the smoke clears, Grier comes out on top. Good cast of black talents that should have been making better movies.

p&d, Arthur Marks; w, Orville Hampton (from a story by Marks based on the comic strip "Friday Foster"); ph, Harry May (Movielab Color); m, Luchi De Jesus; ed, Stanley Frazen; m/l, Bodie Chandler; stunts, Richard Geary.

Crime **(PR:O MPAA:R)**

FRIDAY THE 13TH***** (1934, Brit.) 70m Gainsborough/GAU bw

"On The Bus": Sonnie Hale *(Alf)*, Cryil Smith *(Fred)*, Muriel Aked *(Miss Twigg)*, Richard Hulton *(Johnny)*, Harold Warrender, John Clifford. "Jackson the Shipping Clerk": Eliot Makeham *(Jackson)*, Ursula Jeans *(Eileen Jackson)*, D.A. Clarke-Smith *(Max)*, Gibb McLaughlin *(Florist)*."Blake the Gentleman of Fortune": Emlyn Williams *(Blake)*, Frank Lawton *(Frank Parsons)*, Belle Chrystal *(Mary)*, O. B. Clarence *(Clerk)*, Wally Patch. "Joe of the Caledonian Market": Max Miller *(Joe)*, Alfred Drayton *(Detective)*, Hartley Power *(American)*, Percy Parsons. "Wakefield the City Man": Edmund Gween *(Wakefield)*, Mary Jerrold *(Flora Wakefield)*, Gordon Harker *(Hamilton Briggs)*. "Mr. Lightfoot in the Park": Robertson Hare *(Mr. Lightfoot)*, Martita Hunt *(Agnes Lightfoot)*, Leonora Corbett *(Dolly)*, Clive Morton. "Millie the Non-Stop Variety Girl": Jessie Matthews *(Milly)*, Ralph Richardson *(Schoolmaster)*, Donald Calthrop *(Hugh Nichols)*, Ivor McLaren *(Dance Instructor)*.

Nothing at all like the 1980 teeny-bopper gore film with the same title, or its sequels, this plot was a terrific idea which predated and anticipated a spate of later disaster pictures such as THE CROWDED SKY (1960) and THE HIGH AND THE MIGHTY (1954), bringing together a disparate group of passengers united only by transitory tragedy. Big Ben features prominently as we see the clock face registering a minute before midnight on the title date. A lightning bolt causes a London omnibus, filled with unrelated, unacquainted passengers, to crash into a shop. Events of the prior twenty-four hours in the lives of six of them are detailed in separate sequences; suspensefully, we know not which of them have survived the crash, until the final moments. Matthews, the chorine who quarreled with her sweetheart, was traveling to an assignation with a bounder. The disaster saves her from seduction and effects a reunion, in the meatiest of the several stories. Witty dialog and good performances by a cast of excellent actors combine with fine continuity to make this trend-setter well worth watching.

p, Michael Balcon; d, Victor Saville; w, G.H. Moresby-White, Sidney Gilliat, Emlyn Williams; ph, Charles Van Enger.

Drama **(PR:A MPAA:NR)**

FRIDAY THE 13TH zero   (1980) 95m PAR c

Betsy Palmer (*Mrs. Voorhees*), Adrienne King (*Alice*), Harry Crosby (*Bill*), Laurie Bartram (*Brenda*), Mark Nelson (*Ned*), Jeannine Taylor (*Marcie*), Robbi Morgan (*Annie*), Kevin Bacon (*Jack*), Ari Lehman (*Jason*), Peter Brouwer (*Steve*), Rex Everhart (*Truck Driver*), Ronn Carroll (*Sgt. Tierney*), Ron Millkie (*Dorf*), Walt Gorney (*Crazy Ralph*), Willie Adams (*Barry*), Debra S. Hayes (*Claudette*), Dorothy Kobs (*Trudy*), Sally Anne Golden (*Sandy*), Mary Rocco (*Operator*), Ken L. Parker (*Doctor*).

Rancid, bloody excuse for a horror film sees seven young camp counselors finally opening up Camp Crystal Lake for business after it had been boarded up for years following a nasty murder that had never been solved. Of course, the killer is still on the loose, and proceeds to eliminate the counselors one by one in a series of tedious, repetitive, ghastly murders that leaves only one teenager left. No intelligence, no characterization, no socially redeeming value whatsoever, FRIDAY THE 13TH embodies everything that was wrong with the latest cycle of horror films—totally mindless bloodletting. This trash spawned several equally vile sequels and imitations (the only exception is the somewhat interesting THE BURNING). The one good thing is the inventive and well done special makeup effects by Tom Savini, whose talents have been used better elsewhere (especially in the horror films of George Romero). A wretched film. Stay away.

p&d, Sean S. Cunningham; w, Victor Miller; ph, Barry Abrams (Panavision); m, Harry Manfredini; ed, Bill Freda; art d, Virginia Field; spec eff & stunts, Tom Savini.

Horror   **Cas.**   **(PR:O   MPAA:R)**

FRIDAY THE 13TH PART II zero   (1981) 87m PAR c

Amy Steel (*Ginny*), John Furey (*Paul*), Adrienne King (*Alice*), Kirsten Baker (*Terry*), Stu Charno (*Ted*), Warrington Gillette (*Jason*), Walt Gorney (*Crazy Ralph*), Marta Kober (*Sandra*), Tom McBride (*Mark*), Bill Randolph (*Jeff*), Lauren-Marie Taylor (*Vickie*), Russell Todd (*Scott*), Betsy Palmer (*Mrs. Voorhees*), Cliff Cudney (*Max*), Jack Marks (*Cop*), Steve Daskawisz (*Jason's Stunt Double*), Jerry Wallace (*Prowler*), David Brand, China Chen, Carolyn Loudon, Jaime Perry, Tom Shea, Jill Voight (*Counselors*).

Somehow, this one's even worse than the first. Called a sequel, it's basically the same movie except this time a different cast of teen-agers gets killed in the usual, very graphic, manner (the excess gore was trimmed to avoid an "X" rating by the MPAA). Once again, it made a ton of money. True fans of horror movies should boycott this trash because it's excessive, mindless gore like this that threatens to destroy the whole genre.

p, Steve Miner, Dennis Murphy; d, Miner; w, Ron Kurz (based on characters created by Victor Miller); ph, Peter Stein (DeLuxe Color); m, Harry Manfredini; ed, Susan E. Cunningham; prod d, Virginia Field; cos, Ellen Lutter; spec eff, Steve Kirshoff; stunts, Cliff Cudney.

Horror   **Cas.**   **(PR:O   MPAA:R)**

FRIDAY THE 13TH PART III*   (1982) 95m PAR c

Dana Kimmel (*Chris Higgins*), Richard Brooker (*Jason*), Catherine Parks (*Vera*), Paul Kratka (*Rick*), Jeffrey Rogers (*Andy*), Larry Zerner (*Shelly*), Tracie Savage (*Debbie*), Rachel Howard (*Chili*), David Katims (*Chuck*), Nick Savage (*Ali*), Gloria Charles (*Fox*), Kevin O'Brien (*Loco*), Annie Gaybis (*Cashier*), Cheri Maugans (*Edna*), Steve Miner (*Newscaster*), Gianni Standaart (*Newswoman*), Steve Susskind (*Harold*), Perla Walter (*Mrs. Sanchez*), David Wiley (*Abel*), Terry Ballard, Terence McCorry, Charlie Messenger (*State Troopers*), Steve Daskawisz.

Once again, the same movie filled with different corpses, but at least this sequel boasts some decent 3-D work (probably the best 3-D effects in the new wave of 3-D movies). It contains the same stupid, gross plot as the others, but the gore is a bit de-emphasized with the special-effects crew concentrating on the nicely done 3-D depth work for a change. It's still trash, and this one also made an immoral amount of money. As of this writing there have been a mind-numbing five FRIDAY THE 13TH films with no sign of a letup (though our hopes were raised by FRIDAY THE 13TH PART 4—THE FINAL CHAPTER. They lied.).

p, Frank Mancuso, Jr., Tony Bishop; d, Steve Miner; w, Martin Kitrosser, Carol Watson (based on characters created by Victor Miller, Ron Kurz); ph, Gerald Feil (Panavision, Movielab Color, in 3-D); m, Harry Manfredini; ed, George Hively; art d, Robb Wilson King.

Horror   **Cas.**   **(PR:O   MPAA:R)**

FRIDAY THE 13TH . . . THE ORPHAN*   (1979) 80m Gilman-
Westergaard/World Northal c
(AKA: KILLER ORPHAN)

Peggy Feury (*Aunt Martha*), Joanna Miles (*David's Mother*), Donn Whyte (*David's Father*), Stanley Church (*Dr. Thompson*), Eleanor Stewart (*Mary*), Afolabi Ajayi (*Akin*), Jane House (*Jean Ford*), David Foreman (*Percy Ford*), Mark Owens (*David*).

Stupid horror movie about a ten-year-old boy who is told by his aunt that he is to be put in a boarding school. For some reason the boy imagines he is to be put in an orphanage, and fantasizes what his confinement would be like in such a place. Of course, he gets his revenge in a bloody manner. This film was actually released before Sean S. Cunningham's rancid FRIDAY THE 13TH.

d&w, John Ballard; ph, Beda F. Patka; m, Ted Macero; art d, Sidney Ann MacKenzie; m/l, Janis Ian.

Horror   **(PR:O   MPAA:R)**

FRIEDA***   (1947, Brit.) 97m RANK/UNIV bw

David Farrar (*Robert Dawson*), Glynis Johns (*Judy Dawson*), Mai Zetterling (*Frieda Dawson*), Flora Robson (*Nell Dawson*), Albert Lieven (*Richard Mannsfeld*), Barbara Everest (*Mrs. Dawson*), Gladys Henson (*Edith*), Ray Jackson (*Tony Dawson*),

Patrick Holt (*Alan Dawson*), Milton Rosmer (*Tom Merrick*), Barry Letts (*Jim Merrick*), Gilbert Davis (*Lawrence*), Renee Gadd (*Mrs. Freeman*), Douglas Jefferies (*Hobson*), Barry Jones (*Holliday*), Eliot Makeham (*Bailey*), Norman Pierce (*Crawley*), John Ruddock (*Granger*), D.A. Clarke-Smith (*Herriot*), Garry Marsh (*Beckwith*), Aubrey Mallalieu (*Irvine*), John Molecey (*Latham*), Stanley Escane (*Post-boy*), Gerhard Hinze [Gerard Heinz] (*Polish Priest*), Arthur Howard (*First Official*).

Restrained drama starring Zetterling as the German wife of an RAF officer who is brought home to his small home town in England at the closing days of WW II. She is rejected by her husband's family, and the townsfolk, whose attitudes toward Germans are understandably bitter and distrustful. To make things worse, her still actively Hitlerite brother arrives to stir up more trouble, fueling more harsh feelings and suspicion between her and the locals. Eventually, she wins the British over and rejects her brother. Surprisingly progressive in its understanding of the postwar prejudice so soon after the conflict.

p, Michael Relph; d, Basil Dearden; w, Ronald Millar, Angus MacPhail (based on the play by Millar); ph, Gordon Dines; m, John Greewood; ed Leslie Norman; md, Ernest Irving; art d, Jim Morahan; cos, Bianca Mosca; spec eff, Cliff Richardson makeup, Ernest Taylor.

Drama   **(PR:A   MPAA:NR)**

FRIEND OF THE FAMILY**   (1965, Fr./Ital.) 95m Belstar/International
Classics bw (AKA: PATATE)

Jean Marais (*Noel Carradine*), Danielle Darrieux (*Edith Rollo*), Anne Vernon (*Veronique Carradine*), Sylvie Vartan (*Alexa Rollo*), Pierre Dux (*Leon "Patsy" Rollo*), Jane Marken (*Berthe*), Noel Roquevert (*Monsieur Michalon*), Hubert Deschamps (*Adrien*), Jacques Jouanneau (*Marcel*), Henri Virlojeux (*Professor Richard*), Mike Marshall (*Jean Francois*), Laurence Badie (*Jeannette*), Daniel Ceccaldi (*Michel*), Francois Charet (*Bernard*), Jules Dassin.

A French farce starring Dux as a toy inventor who goes to his boyhood friend Marais, now a wealthy industrialist, to convince him to invest in his new invention. The meeting goes badly when old childhood sore spots resurface (Marais persists in calling Dux by his childhood nickname "Patsy," which the latter loathes) but Dux's wife Darrieux manages to calm things down. Soon after, Darrieux finds some love letters owned by their teen-age daughter Vartan, and Dux immediately suspects Marais as the unnamed lover. Seeing an opportunity to get what he wants from Marais by blackmailing him with the letters, Dux eventually abandons his plan when his daughter finds a new boy friend. Finally, their differences cleared, the two men go into business together. Look for director/actor Jules [Julius] Dassin, an expatriate due to the McCarthy-era witch hunts, in a bit part. At the time of the film's U.S. release, one reviewer wrote, "It appears to be a comedy," which may serve as an appropriate warning. (In French; English subtitles).

p, Andre Hakim; d&w, Robert Thomas (based on the play *Patate* by Marcel Achard); ph, Robert Lefebvre (CinemaScope); m, Raymond Le Senechal; ed, Henri Taverna; md, Jacques Metehen; set d, Max Douy; m/l, Hubert Rostaing, Jean Drejac.

Comedy   **(PR:A   MPAA:NR)**

FRIEND WILL COME TONIGHT, A***   (1948, Fr.) A.C.G.C. 92m
Films/Lopert bw
(UN AMI VIENDRA CE SOIR)

Michel Simon (*Michel Lemaret*), Madeleine Sologne (*Helen Asselin*), Louis Salou (*Commissioner Martin/Commander Gerard*), Saturnin Fabre (*Phillippe Prunier*), Paul Bernard (*Dr. Tiller*), Marcel Andre (*Dr. Lestrade*), Jacques Clancy (*Jacques Leroy*), Daniel Gelin (*Pierre Ribault*), Claude Lehmann (*Dr. Pigaut*), Lily Mounet (*The Baroness*), Yvette Andreyor (*Beatrice*), Cecilia Paroldi (*Claire*).

Taut spy thriller set in the French Alpine region near Switzerland in the fall of 1944. The Nazis invade an insane asylum in search of the leader of the underground movement, whom they are convinced is hiding out among the patients. Simon plays a slightly crazed inmate who babbles world philosophy while fending off the brutal interrogations of the Nazis. Though Salou is actually the brains behind the underground, Simon allows himself to be thought the ringleader and sacrifices his life so that Salou can escape and carry on the fight. (In French; English subtitles).

p, Constantin Geftman; d, Raymond Bernard; w, Jacques Companeez, Bernard; ph, Robert Lefebvre; m, Arthur Honegger.

Spy/Drama   **(PR:A   MPAA:NR)**

FRIENDLIEST GIRLS IN THE WORLD, THE
(SEE: COME FLY WITH ME, 1963)

FRIENDLY ENEMIES*½   (1942) 95m UA bw

Charles Winninger (*Karl Pfeiffer*), Charlie Ruggles (*Henry Block*), James Craig (*William Pfeiffer*), Nancy Kelly (*June Block*), Otto Kruger (*Anton Miller*), Ilka Gruning (*Mrs. Pfeiffer*), Greta Meyer (*Gretchen*), Addison Richards (*Inspector McCarty*), Charles Lane (*Braun*), John Piffle (*Schnitzler*), Ruth Holly (*Nora*).

Winninger plays an old German (who now lives in the U.S.) sympathetic to the Nazi cause and Ruggles plays his friend, also German, whose sympathies lie with the good ol' red, white and blue. The performers basically spend their time trapped on one set and argue their respective positions constantly. Winninger finally relents after he is duped into funding German sabotage operations that included the sinking of a transport that carried his own son. Badly done wartime propaganda based on a play written in 1918 and updated to apply to WW II. A remake, this was originally filmed in 1925, starring the famed comedy vaudevillians (Joe) Weber and (Lew) Fields.

p, Edward Small; d, Allan Dwan; w, Adelaide Heilbron (from the stage play by Samuel Shipman, Aaron Hoffman); ph, Edward Cronjager; m, Lucien Moraweck;

ed, Grant Whytock, William Claxton; md, Lud Gluskin; art d, John Du Casse Schulze.

Drama (PR:A MPAA:NR)

FRIENDLY KILLER, THE** (1970, Jap.) 90m Nikkatsu c
(NOBORIRYU TEKKAHADA)

Hiroko Ogi (Katsumi), Akira Kobayashi (Masa), Toru Abe (Yasukawa), Tatsuya Fuji, Kokan Katsura, Yoko Yamamoto, Tomoo Koike, Shoki Fukae, Eiji Goo, Hideki Takahashi, Kiyoko Tange, Setsuko Minami, Tomoko Aki, Hatsue Tonooka, Toru Yuri, Shunji Sayama.

Ogi plays the daughter of a murdered gangster who picks up where he left off and takes control of her father's mob. A gang war between Ogi and rival gang boss Abe breaks out, and the woman gang leader suddenly finds herself being aided by a mysterious stranger, Kobayashi. When she attempts to call a truce and settle differences, she is double-crossed and forced to kill a rival gang member. In jail, Ogi wages a war to improve prison conditions and is eventually released. Upon Ogi's return to her territory, she learns that Abe has take much of her power; she demands a confrontation. The climax sees an attack on her headquarters in which Abe is finally killed and the loyal Kobayashi mortally wounded. In his dying words, Kobayashi confesses to Ogi that it was he who was hired by Abe to murder her father.

d&w, Teruo Ishii; ph, Sei Kitaizumi (Nikkatsu Scope, Fuji Color); m, Masao Yagi; art d, Takeo Kimura.

Crime (PR:C-O MPAA:NR)

FRIENDLY NEIGHBORS** (1940) 67m REP bw

Leon Weaver (Abner), Frank Weaver (Cicero), June Weaver (Elviry), Lois Ranson (Nancy), Spencer Charters (Bumblebee Hibbs), Cliff Edwards ("Notes"), John Hartley (Breeze Kid), Loretta Weaver (Violey), Al Shean (Doc), Thurston Hall (The Governor), Margaret Seddon (Martha Williams), Clarence H. Wilson (Silas Barton), J. Farrell MacDonald (Sheriff Potts), Al St. John (Smokey).

Average hillbilly hokum starring the Weavers as a backwoods family forced to leave their land because of drought and seek their fortunes elsewhere. Along the way they hook up with various hobos and wanderers until they come to rest in a small town which is dying because of periodic floods that hit the burg occasionally. The Weavers decide to save the town, and with the help of their newfound friends they successfully petition the governor to allow a levee to be constructed to stem the rising waters and make the town a nice place to settle. The sixth of the eleven "Weaver Brothers and Elviry" series which Republic produced between 1938 and 1943. The popular "Grand Ole Opry" radio performers—billed for the airwaves as "The Arkansas Travelers"—were well known to rural America, and their modestly budgeted pictures returned a good profit. (See WEAVER BROTHERS AND ELVIRY series, Index.)

p, Armand Schaefer; d, Nick Grinde; w, Dorell and Stuart McGowan; ph, Ernest Miller; ed, Charles Craft; md, Cy Feuer.

Drama (PR:A MPAA:NR)

FRIENDLY PERSUASION***½ (1956) 137m AA c

Gary Cooper (Jess Birdwell), Dorothy McGuire (Eliza Birdwell), Marjorie Main (Widow Hudspeth), Anthony Perkins (Josh Birdwell), Richard Eyer (Little Jess), Phyllis Love (Mattie Birdwell), Robert Middleton (Sam Jordan), Mark Richman (Gard Jordan), Walter Catlett (Professor Quigley), Richard Hale (Elder Purdy), Joel Fluellen (Enoch), Theodore Newton (Army Major), John Smith (Caleb), Mary Carr (Emma, Quaker Woman), Edna Skinner, Marjorie Durant, Frances Farwell (Widow Hudspeth's Daughters), Samantha (The Goose), Russell Simpson, Charles Halton, Everett Glass (Elders), Richard Garland (Bushwhacker), James Dobson (Rebel Soldier), John Compton (Rebel Lieutenant), James Seay (Rebel Captain), Diane Jergens (Young Girl-Elizabeth), Ralph Sanford (Business Man), Jean Inness (Mrs. Purdy), Nelson Leigh (Minister), Helen Kleeb (Old Lady), William Schallert (Young Husband), John Craven (Shell Game Man), Frank Jenks (Lemonade Vendor), Jack McClure (Soldier), Charles Courtney (Reb Courier), Tom Irish (Young Rebel), Mary Jackson (Country Woman), Joe Turkel, James Anderson (Poor Losers), Harry Hines (Barker), Henry Rowland (O'Hara), Ivan Rasputin (Billy Goat), Donald Kerr (Manager), Steve Warren (Haskell), Earle Hodgins (Shooting Gallery Operator), John Pickard (Ex-Sergeant), Norman Leavitt (Clem), Dan Kennedy (Buster).

Long and sometimes preachy, FRIENDLY PERSUASION remembers better than it actually was. The making of the film was easy enough and the fireworks began when the screenwriter, Michael Wilson, did not get his screen credit as Allied Artists exercised their right to "deny credit to a writer revealed to be a member of the Communist Party or one who refused to answer charges of Communist affiliation." Wilson had invoked the Fifth Amendment of the Constitution when called as a witness in 1951 by the House Committee on Un-American Activities (HUAC). Based on the book by Jessamyn West, Wilson's script tells the story of a peaceful family of Quakers in Indiana whose sanctity is disturbed by the coming Civil War in 1862. Cooper is the patriarch, married to a beautiful Dorothy McGuire. Their son, Perkins, listens to a young Union officer make a plea for young men to take up the Blue cudgel. Although morally opposed to war, Perkins wonders if he's hiding behind his religion to mask a cowardly streak. When the news comes in that the southern band known as Morgan's Raiders is nearing their town, Perkins joins the local militia and prepares to fight. McGuire is totally against this but Cooper understands that their son feels he must stand up and be counted. There is a battle and Perkins is hurt. Cooper goes into the war zone to save his son and finds his pal, Middleton, who has been ambushed. Middleton dies and Cooper goes after the killer. He nabs him but cannot bring himself to kill the man, so he allows him to escape. At the end, Cooper locates Perkins and brings the wounded boy home. Perkins has convinced himself and everyone else that he's a brave man and the picture fades out. There's humor galore, especially in a scene with Marjorie Main

and her three lonesome daughters, Skinner, Farwell, and Durant. There are many tearful moments and several incisive looks into the lives of the "Friends." Oscar nominations were made for the picture, the script, Perkins, Best Sound, and Best Song. McGuire took Best Actress of the year as voted by the National Board of Review. Twenty minutes excised from the film would have made it a classic. As it is, FRIENDLY PERSUASION still must rank as one of Wyler's best comedy-dramas, even with the bloated length. Mark Richman (now known as Peter Mark Richman) is seen in one of his earliest films as Gard Jordan. Richman has since established himself as one of Hollywood's best character men and has a secondary, and very successful, career as a painter. Tiomkin and Paul Francis Webster wrote a few songs for the film, one of which became a hit as sung by Pat Boone, "Friendly Persuasion, (Thee I Love)," the others were "Mocking Bird In A Willow Tree," "Coax Me A Little," "Indiana Holiday," and "Marry Me, Marry Me."

p&d, William Wyler; w, Michael Wilson (uncredited) (from the novel The Friendly Persuasion by Jessamyn West); ph, Ellsworth Fredericks (CinemaScope, DeLuxe Color); m, Dmitri Tiomkin; ed, Robert Swink, Edward A. Biery, Jr., Robert A. Belcher; art d, Edward S. Haworth; set d, Joe Kish; cos, Dorothy Jeakins, Bert Henrikson; makeup, Emile La Vigne; m/l, Tiomkin, Paul Francis Webster; tech adv, Jessamyn West.

Drama Cas. (PR:A MPAA:NR)

FRIENDS* (1971, Brit.) 101m PAR c

Sean Bury (Paul Harrison), Anicee Alvina (Michelle LaTour), Pascale Roberts (Annie), Sady Rebbot (Pierre), Ronald Lewis (Harrison), Toby Robins (Mrs. Gardner), Joan Hinkson (Lady in Bookshop).

Terrible teenage drama starring Bury and Alvina as two unloved French kids who run off together and set up housekeeping on a deserted beach. They have a baby and, shortly thereafter, their apologetic parents show up and take them away. Devoid of any insight into the teenage mind, the film seems to revel in its unnecessarily explicit nudity which gave it an "R" rating, thereby eliminating its targetted audience. Filmmaker Gilbert (THE ADVENTURERS; YOU ONLY LIVE TWICE), who was a child star himself, gave the lead to French actress Alvina after she perfected her English especially to qualify for the part. Includes songs by Elton John. Yes! They even made a sequel: PAUL AND MICHELLE-1974.

p&d, Lewis Gilbert; w, Jack Russell, Vernon Harris (based on a story by Gilbert); ph, Andreas Winding (Technicolor); m, Elton John, Paul Buckmaster; ed, Anne V. Coates; art d, Marc Frederix; cos, Jeanine Herrly; m/l, John, Bernie Taupin; makeup, Maguy Vernadet.

Drama (PR:O MPAA:R)

FRIENDS AND HUSBANDS*** (1983, Ger.) 106m Bioskop Film-Les Films du Losange-Westdeutscher Rundfunk/Miracle c

Hanna Schygulla, Angela Winkler, Peter Striebeck, Christine Fersen, Franz Buchriesser, Jochen Striebeck, Therese Affolter, Werner Eichhorn, Karl Striebeck, Peter Aust, Helga Ballhaus, Selda Bondy, Carla Egerer, Alexander Volz, Irene Clarin, Felix von Manteuffel, Axel Milberg, Doris Schade.

One of the common themes in the work of Trotta has been the concentration of strong relationships between women, expressing bonds which the men of the films are usually unable to understand or break, and often feel alienated from. Such is the thrust of FRIENDS AND HUSBANDS, a look into the evolving friendship between Schygulla and Winkler as they discover greater and greater need for each other's companionship. Concentration is placed on character development and so the movie's pace is sometimes extremely slow, but for those with patience, infinitely rewarding.

p, Eberhard Junkersdorf; d&w, Margarethe von Trotta; ph, Michael Ballhaus; m, Nicholas Economou; ed, Dagmar Hirtz; art d, Jurgen Henze, Werner Mink.

Drama (PR:C MPAA:NR)

FRIENDS AND LOVERS*½ (1931) 66m RKO bw

Adolphe Menjou (Capt. Roberts), Lily Damita (Alva Sangrito), Erich von Stroheim (Victor Sangrito), Laurence Olivier (Lt. Nichols), Hugh Herbert (McNellis), Frederick Kerr (Gen. Armstrong), Blanche Friderici (Lady Alice), Yvonne D'Arcy (French Maid), Dorothy Wolbert (English Barmaid), Kay Deslys (Waitress).

When you consider all the heavyweight talents involved in this picture, one wonders how they could think that they were making something of value. Von Stroheim uses his wife, Damita, to blackmail unsuspecting men in India. She makes the mistake of actually falling in love with Menjou, a captain assigned to the area. While working on the frontier, Menjou meets Olivier, an early victim of Damita's charms. The two men argue, then realize what has happened and unite. They've been rivals before but understand the importance of their friendship. Back in England, they quarrel once more. Von Stroheim is killed and Olivier convinces Menjou to leave with the woman he loves, Damita. The film tries to cram two hour's worth of story into one hour and in this case, less is not more. It's so badly conceived and poorly edited that the plots have a tendency to blend into each other. It doesn't seem that a scene runs more than two minutes before another one cuts in. Only worth looking at to see a very young Olivier and the always pleasing and believable von Stroheim. Director Schertzinger also worked on the score with Steiner. Originally a concert violinist, Schertzinger was born in Belgium and his first movie credit was writing the music for Thomas Ince's silent CIVILIZATION.

p, William LeBaron; d, Victor Schertzinger; w, Jane Murfin (based on the novel The Sphinx Has Spoken by Maurice de Kobra); ph, Roy Hunt; m, Max Steiner, Schertzinger. (Note, in some reviews, the screenplay is wrongly credited to Wallace Smith.)

Drama (PR:A MPAA:NR)

FRIENDS AND LOVERS (SEE: VIXENS, THE, 1969)

FRIENDS AND NEIGHBORS** (1963, Brit.) 79m Valiant/Schoenfeld bw

Arthur Askey *(Albert Grimshaw)*, Megs Jenkins *(Lily Grimshaw)*, Peter Illing *(Nikita)*, Tilda Thamar *(Olga)*, Reginald Beckwith *(Wilf Holmes)*, June Whitfield *(Doris Holmes)*, Danny Ross *(Sebastian Green)*, Catherine Feller *(Susan Grimshaw)*, Jess Conrad *(Buddy Fisher)*, George Wheeler *(George Cooper)*, Linda Castle *(Gloria Stockwell)*, Max Robertson *(Himself)*, Ken Parry, Steven Scott, Richard Walter, Donald Bisset, Anatole Smirnoff, Laurence Herder, Arthur Howard, Paul Bogdan, Alan Scott.

Askey, a British bus conductor, wins the grand prize in a lottery which turns out to be a visit from two Russian social workers. Panicking, Askey's wife Jenkins turns the visit into a vodka party which is much enjoyed by the Russians who, after they leave, encourage all their comrades to drop in on the Askey household when visiting England.

p, Bertram Ostrer; d, Gordon Parry; w, Val Valentine, Talbor Rothwell (based on the stage play "Friends and Neighbours" by Austin Steele); ph, Arthur Grant; m, Philip Green; ed, Bill Lenny; art d, Ivan King; set d, John Cox, Richard Marden.

Comedy **(PR:A MPAA:NR)**

FRIENDS FOR LIFE** (1964, Ital.) 100m Cines bw (AMICI PER LA PELLE)

Geronimo Meynier *(Mario)*, Andrea Scire *(Franco)*, Luigi Tosi, Paolo Ferrari, Dina Perbellini, Marcella Rovena, Carlo Tamberlani, Vera Carmi, Bianca Maria Bettinali.

Mushy melodrama has Meynier and Scire become boyhood buddies when Meynier helps Scire recover from the hurt of losing a motorscooter race that he bragged about winning. Their friendship strengthens and Meynier convinces Scire's widowered father, who is planning to take his son on a Middle East business trip, that the lad should best remain with Meynier's family. On the day the father is to depart, the two pals quarrel over Scire's antics during a school sporting event and Scire decides to leave with his father. Filled with sorrow, Meynier dashes to the airport to patch things up, but, alas, he arrives too late. (Another last scene was shot in which Meynier met Scire at the airport and had the two consolidating a lifelong pact of friendship.)

p, Carlo Civallero; d, Franco Rossi; w, Rossi, Leo Benvenuti, Piero De Bernardi, Ugo Guerra, Giandomenico Giagni (based on a story by Rossi, Ottavio Alessi, Benvenuti, De Bernardi, Guerra); ph, Gabor Pogany; m, Nino Rota; ed, Otello Colangeli; art d, Franco Lolli.

Comedy/Drama **(PR:A MPAA:NR)**

FRIENDS OF EDDIE COYLE, THE***½ (1973) 102m PAR c

Robert Mitchum *(Eddie Coyle)*, Peter Boyle *(Dillon)*, Richard Jordan *(Dave Foley)*, Steven Keats *(Jackie Brown)*, Alex Rocco *(Scalise)*, Joe Santos *(Artie Van)*, Mitchell Ryan *(Waters)*, Helena Carroll *(Sheila Coyle)*, Peter MacLean *(Partridge)*, Kevin O'Morrison *(Manager of 2nd Bank)*, Carolyn Pickman *(Nancy)*, Marvin Lichterman *(Vernon)*, James Tolkan *(The Man's Contact Man)*, Matthew Cowles *(Pete)*, Margaret Ladd *(Andrea)*, Jane House *(Wanda)*, Michael McCleery *(The Kid)*, Alan Koss *(Phil)*, Dennis McMullen *(Webber)*, Judith Ogden Cabot *(Mrs. Partridge)*, Jan Egleson *(Pale Kid)*, Jack Kehoe *(The Beard)*, Robert Anthony *(Moran)*, Gus Johnson *(Ames)*, Ted Maynard *(Sauter)*, Sheldon Feldner *(Ferris)*.

Mitchum is Coyle and he is a three-time loser. One more offense and he goes into prison for life, no parole, no hope. Police learn of an impending Boston bank robbery and go to Mitchum, telling him that they know he earns a living for his destitute family by running illegal goods across state lines. They will put him away unless he informs on the robbery gang. He reluctantly agrees to help and, after selling the gang some guns, contacts detectives but his information is insufficient, he is told. He must go on being a permanent informer and is ordered to help capture gang boss Rocco. Before he can move, however, Rocco is arrested and the underworld friends of Mitchum point the finger at him, ordering him murdered. Boyle, the man who receives the murder assignment is actually the informant but he carries out his mission anyway, taking Mitchum to a hockey game then driving into the country where he shoots Mitchum and leaves his body in a car. This is a tough look at the world of petty crooks and the sleazy side of the underworld. Mitchum is surprisingly effective at the down-and-out cheap thief, as if worn out through the decades from earlier *film noir* escapades in THE RACKET and OUT OF THE PAST. Boyle is terrific as the thug with synthetic friendship, willing to sell out his own mother for survival in a system he knows will destroy him anyway. Mitchum had his usual downbeat perspective of this film, attributing any good aspects of his role to the haircut he ordered for the part. Yates' direction is grimly taut and Monash's script pulls no punches, but for some the tale may prove too gruesome, too gory and even grotesque to take.

p, Paul Monash; d, Peter Yates; w, Monash (based on the novel by George V. Higgens); ph, Victor J. Kemper (Panavision, Technicolor); m, Dave Grusin; ed, Patricia Lewis Jaffe; prod d, Gene Callahan; art d, Callahan; set d, Don Galvin; cos, Eric Seelig; makeup, Irving Budham.

Crime Drama **(PR:O MPAA:R)**

FRIENDS OF MR. SWEENEY*** (1934) 68m WB bw

Charles Ruggles *(Asaph)*, Ann Dvorak *(Beulah)*, Eugene Pallette *(Rixey)*, Dorothy Burgess *(Millie)*, Dorothy Tree *(Olga)*, Robert Barrat *(Alex)*, Berton Churchill *(Brumbaugh)*, Harry Tyler *(Mike)*, Harry Beresford *(Claude)*, William Davidson *(Prime)*.

Ruggles is the milquetoast editorial writer for a conservative periodical and, along with his fellow employees, is forever being bullied by the editor, a sanctimonious prig. Upset with his lot as the groveling flunky, Ruggles strives to add a little pizzazz to his life. The final straw occurs when a soda jerk belittles him with insults. Ruggles seeks out his old pal Pallette and the two embark on a wild escapade of gambling, drinking, and confrontation with the underworld. An everything-but-the-kitchen-sink comedy in which Ruggles' unrestrained performance carries the day.

p, Sam Bischoff; d, Edward Ludwig; w, Warren Duff, Sidney Sutherland (based on the novel by Elmer Davis); ph, Ira Morgan; ed, Thomas Pratt; art d, Robert Haas.

Comedy **(PR:A MPAA:NR)**

FRIGHT (SEE: SPELL OF THE HYPNOTIST, 1956)

FRIGHT**½ (1971, Brit.) 87m BL/AA c (AKA: NIGHT LEGS)

Susan George *(Amanda)*, Honor Blackman *(Helen)*, Ian Bannen *(Brian)*, John Gregson *(Dr. Cordell)*, George Cole *(Jim)*, Dennis Waterman *(Chris)*, Tara Collinson *(Tara)*, Maurice Kaufman *(Police Inspector)*, Michael Brennan *(Police Sergeant)*, Roger Lloyd Pack *(Constable)*.

George stars as a babysitter hired by Blackman to watch her son. Soon George finds herself being terrorized by Blackman's crazed husband Bannen who has just escaped from a mental hospital and is searching for his wife and three-year-old son. After murdering the sitter's boy friend, Bannen gains access to the house and cuts off all communication. Trying to play for time, George allows the killer to make love to her and eventually the police arrive and surround the house. Bannen grabs the sitter and his son and holds the police back by pressing a large shard of broken glass to their throats. He is finally captured. Violent and distasteful, but a well-directed thriller.

p, Harry Fine, Michael Style; d, Peter Collinson; w, Tudor Gates; ph, Ian Wilson (Humphries, Eastmancolor); m, Harry Robinson; ed, Raymond Poulton; prod d, Disley Jones; art d, Scott Wodehouse; makeup, George Blackler; m/l, "Ladybird," Robinson, Bob Barrett (sung by Nanette).

Suspense **(PR:O MPAA:NR)**

FRIGHTENED BRIDE, THE** (1952, Brit.) 95m GN bw (GB: TALL HEADLINES)

Andre Morell *(George Rackham)*, Flora Robson *(Mary Rackham)*, Michael Denison *(Philip Rackham)*, Jane Hylton *(Frankie Rackham)*, Mervyn Johns *(Uncle Ted)*, Dennis Price *(Maurice Fletcher)*, Hugh Dempster *(Police Inspector)*, Michael Ward *(Dentist)*, Mai Zetterling *(Doris Richardson)*, Olive Sloane *(Mrs. Baker)*, Peter Burton *(Graham Moore)*, Barbara Blair *(Nancy Richardson)*, Celia Lipton *(Sandra)*, Don Phillips *(Lonie)*, Joan Hickson *(Waitress)*, Naunton Wayne *(Police Inspector)*, Sydney James *(Mr. Spencer)*.

An unbelievable story hurts decent performances by some well-known British actors and actresses. Taken from the Audrey Erskine Lindop novel, it tells the woes of a middle class family after their eldest boy is executed for murder. The family leaves town in shame, changes its name, and the father will not let the son's name be spoken anymore. The mother looks for help through the spirits while the daughter remains stoic. The family must fight its feelings when it appears their other son will follow his older brother when his wife is found dead. The family struggles with the guilt feelings but they are lifted at the climax when the police tell them that the death was an accident.

p, Raymond Stross; d, Terence Young; w, Audrey Erskine, Lindop and Dudley Leslie; ph, Pennington Richards; m, Hans May; ed, Vera Campbell.

Drama **(PR:A MPAA:NR)**

FRIGHTENED CITY, THE*** (1961, Brit.) 97m Zodiac-Anglo Amalgamated/AA bw

Herbert Lom *(Waldo Zhernikov)*, John Gregson *(Det. Insp. Sayers)*, Sean Connery *(Paddy Damion)*, Alfred Marks *(Harry Foulcher)*, Yvonne Romain *(Anya)*, Olive McFarland *(Sadie)*, Kenneth Griffith *(Wally)*, David Davies *(Alf Peters)*, Frederick Piper *(Sgt. Ogle)*, Robert Cawdron *(Nero)*, Tom Bowman *(Tanky Thomas)*, Patrick Jordan *(Frankie Farmer)*, George Pastell *(Sanchetti)*, Patrick Holt *(Supt. Carter)*, Bruce Seton *(Asst. Commissioner)*, Robert Percival *(Wingrove)*, Joan Haythorne *(Miss Rush)*, Arnold Diamond *(Moffat)*, Jack Stewart *(Tyson)*, Douglas Robinson *(Salty Brewer)*, Marianne Stone *(Barmaid)*, Neal Arden *(Head Waiter)*, Norrie Paramor *(Pianist)*, Malcolm Clare *(Choreographer)*, J.G. Devlin *(Informer)*, John Witty *(TV Announcer)*.

Tough British gangster movie starring Lom as an ambitious hood who hits upon the idea of organizing all of the six main rackets' gangs into one big conglomerate that would control London. The plan works for awhile, but then Lom begins to make even bigger, more dangerous deals. One of the gangsters, Marks, breaks off from the organization and forms his own gang. This sparks a bloody war between the factions which leads to Lom sending Connery (in an early role) to bump off Marks. Connery does so, but then panics and turns against the mob by "squealing" in court. Well done, fast paced gangster film filled with good performances.

p, John Lemont, Leigh Vance; d, Lemont; w, Vance (based on a story by Vance and Lemont); ph, Desmond Dickinson; m, Norrie Paramor; ed, Bernard Gribble; art d, Maurice Carter; cos, Laura Nightingale; m/l, "Marvelous Lie," "I Laughed At Love," Paramor, Bunny Lewis.

Crime **(PR:A MPAA:NR)**

FRIGHTENED LADY, THE (SEE: CRIMINAL AT LARGE, 1932, Brit.)

FRIGHTENED LADY (SEE: CASE OF THE FRIGHTENED LADY, THE, 1941, Brit.)

FRIGHTENED MAN, THE** (1952, Brit.) 69m Tempean/Eros bw

Dermot Walsh *(Julius Roselli)*, Barbara Murray *(Amanda)*, Charles Victor *(Mr. Roselli)*, John Blythe *(Maxie)*, Michael Ward *(Cornelius)*, Thora Hird *(Vera)*, John Horsley *(Harry)*, Annette Simmonds *(Marcella)*, Martin Benson.

The dreams of junk dealer Victor to have his son make something of himself diminish when the son is thrown out of Oxford because of poor grades. The boy hooks up with a gang of jewel thieves, for which his father is secretly the fence, and Victor tries to keep him from participating in a dangerous foray. The son does so anyway and is killed. Decent crime drama written and directed by John Gilling, known for his efficient low-budget adventures and thrillers.

p, Robert Baker, Monty Berman; d&w, John Gilling; ph, Berman.

Crime **(PR:A MPAA:NR)**

FRIGHTMARE** (1974, Brit.) 86m Ellman c

Rupert Davies *(Edmund)*, Sheila Keith *(Dorothy)*, Deborah Fairfax *(Jackie)*, Paul Greenwood *(Graham)*, Kim Butcher *(Debbie)*, Fiona Curzon *(Merle)*, Jon Yule *(Robin)*, Tricia Mortimer *(Lilian)*, Pamela Farbrother *(Delia)*, Edward Kalinski *(Alec)*, Victor Winding *(Detective Inspector)*, Anthony Hennessy *(Sergeant)*, Noel Johnson *(Judge)*, Michael Sharvell-Martin *(Barman)*, Tommy Wright *(Nightclub Manager)*, Andrew Sachs *(Barry)*, Nicholas John *(Pete)*, Jack Dagmar *(Old Man)*, Leo Genn *(Dr. Lytell)*, Gerald Flood *(Matthew)*.

A stylishly directed grisly film about a married couple Davies and Keith who live on a farm and have a bizarre gustatory taste—they're cannibals.

p&d, Peter Walker; w, David McGillivray (based on a story by Walker); ph, Peter Jessop (Eastmancolor); m, Stanley Myers; ed, Robert Dearburg; art d, Chris Burke.

Horror **(PR:O MPAA:R)**

FRIGHTMARE* (1983) 86m Atlantic TV/Saturn International c (AKA: THE HORROR STAR)

Ferdinand [Ferdy] Mayne *(Conrad)*, Luca Bercovici *(Saint)*, Nita Talbot *(Mrs. Rohmer)*, Leon Askin *(Wolfgang)*, Jennifer Starrett *(Meg)*, Barbara Pilavin *(Etta)*, Carlene Olson *(Eve)*, Scott Thomson *(Bobo)*, Donna McDaniel *(Donna)*, Jeffrey Combs *(Stu)*, Peter Kastner *(Director)*, Chuck Mitchell *(Detective)*, Jesse Ehrlich *(Professor)*.

Dead horror film star is brought back to life after devotees steal his body from its resting place. It's not these ghoulish types who perform the magic, but the dead man's wife, angered that the sacred tomb has been tampered with. The regenerated body then goes on a mass killing spree on the persons responsible for disturbing his rest. Worthless in both conception and performance.

p, Patrick and Tallie Wright; d&w, Norman Thaddeus Vane; ph, Joel King; m, Jerry Moseley; ed, Robert Jackson; art d, Anne Welch; spec eff, Knott, Ltd., Chuck Stewart.

Horror **Cas.** **(PR:O MPAA:R)**

FRIGID WIFE (SEE: MODERN MARRIAGE, A, 1950)

FRISCO JENNY½** (1933) 70m WB/FN bw

Ruth Chatterton *(Frisco Jenny)*, Donald Cook *(Dan Reynolds)*, James Murray *(Dan McAllister)*, Louis Calhern *(Steve Dutton)*, Hallam Cooley *(Willie Gleason)*, Pat O'Malley *(O'Hoolihan)*, Robert Warwick *(Kelly)*, Harold Huber *(Weaver)*, Helen Jerome Eddy *(Amah)*, Frank McGlynn Sr. *(Good Book Charlie)*, J. Carroll Naish *(Harris)*, Robert Emmet O'Connor *(Jim Sandoval)*, Sam Godfrey, Franklin Parker.

Trite melodrama set in the Barbary Coast circa 1906-1933 features Chatterton as the orphaned daughter of a kindly saloonkeeper (her parents were killed in the San Francisco earthquake) who rises to become the madame of a popular bordello. Along the way she bears an illegitimate son whom she gives away to rich parents. As the years go by Chatterton becomes one of the driving forces in the San Francisco underworld, but to her dismay her son grows up to become a crusading district attorney committed to wiping out all crime. Chatterton's lieutenant Calhern decides the only way to stop this law-and-order binge is to eliminate the district attorney, but Chatterton kills him before he can carry out his assassination. Ironically, the district attorney sends Chatterton to the gallows for the murder, and she goes to her fate without ever revealing her identity to her son. Unbelievable storyline helped by good production and direction.

p, Raymond Griffith; d, William A. Wellman; w, Wilson Mizner, Robert Lord (based on a story by Gerald Beaumont, Lillie Hayward, John Francis Larkin); ph, Sid Hickox; ed, James Morley; art d, Robert Haas.

Drama **(PR:A MPAA:NR)**

FRISCO KID*** (1935) 80m WB/FN bw

James Cagney *(Bat Morgan)*, Margaret Lindsay *(Jean Barrat)*, Ricardo Cortez *(Paul Morra)*, Lily Damita *(Bella Morra)*, Donald Woods *(Charles Ford)*, Barton MacLane *(Spider Burke)*, George E. Stone *(Solly)*, Addison Richards *(William T. Coleman)*, Joseph King *(James Daley)*, Robert McWade *(Judge Crawford)*, Joseph Crehan *(McClanahan)*, Robert Strange *(Graber)*, Joseph Sawyer *(Slugs Crippen)*, Fred Kohler *(Shanghai Duck)*, Edward McWade *(Tupper)*, Claudia Coleman *(Jumping Whale)*, John Wray *(The Weasel)*, Ivar McFadden *(1st Lookout)*, Lee Phelps *(2nd Lookout)*, William Wagner *(Evangelist)*, Don Barclay *(Drunk)*, Jack Curtis *(Captain)*, Walter Long *(Miner)*, James Farley *(Man)*, Milton Kibbee *(Shop Man)*, Harry Seymour *(Salesman)*, Claire Sinclair *(Madame)*, Alan Davis *(Young Drunk)*, Karl Hackett *(Dealer)*, Wilfred Lucas *(1st Policeman)*, John T. "Jack" Dillon *(2nd Policeman)*, Edward Mortimer *(1st Man)*, William Holmes *(2nd Man)*, Don Downen *(Usher)*, Mrs. Wilfred North *(Mrs. Crawford)*, Charles Middleton *(Speaker)*, Joe Smith Marba *(Man)*, Landers Stevens *(Doctor)*, Frank Sheridan *(Mulligan)*, J.C. Morton, Harry Tenbrook *(Men)*, Lew Harvey *(Dealer)*, Eddie Sturgis *(Rat Face)*, William Desmond *(Captain/Vigilante)*, Jessie Perry *(Maid)*, Edward Keane, Edward LeSaint *(Contractors)*, Robert Dudley, Dick Rush *(Vigilante Leaders)*, John Elliott *(Doctor)*, Helene Chadwick, Bill Dale, Dick Kerr, Alice Lake, Vera Stedman, Jane Tallent.

A rousing, no-holds-barred actioner set in 19th century San Francisco, FRISCO KID almost duplicates the story of BARBARY COAST, written by Ben Hecht and Charles MacArthur. Yet it's singularly fascinating because of the irrepressible performance of Cagney, the one and only. He is a penniless seaman who plans to pan the gold streams of California but is waylaid by notorious shanghaier Kohler and almost dragged aboard a ship. Cagney battles for his freedom and life and kills the much-hated Kohler which makes him a local hero along the Barbary Coast. He gambles his way to riches and fame, opening a saloon and gambling den and then happily leads many a San Francisco citizen to perdition. Involved in a killing not of his own doing, Cagney is about to be lynched but is saved by the nice girl, Lindsay, who begs for his life, persuading a grizzled jury that he is just a rough-raised lad who fell into bad company. Cagney gives a performance that has a bit more ham in it than was his usual delivery, perhaps feeling uncomfortable in his fancy gambler's waistcoat and cutaway with a tight wing collar to choke off the usual banter. This would be Cagney's last film with Lindsay. Lily Damita, who replaced Estelle Taylor in a fire-eating saloon gal role, married Errol Flynn shortly after this film and her career soon went into eclipse. Fans of the silent era will note the many bit parts taken by a host of personalities from that fading era, including director Dick Kerr, Helene Chadwick, Bill Dale, Alice Lake, Jane Tallent, and Vera Stedman. Many of these no longer wanted talents were included in the cast at Cagney's request; it was typical of this great star to find work for fellow players no longer on top, a custom he practiced throughout his long and wonderful career.

p, Samuel Bischoff; d, Lloyd Bacon; w, Warren Duff, Seton I. Miller; ph, Sol Polito; ed, Owen Marks; md, Leo F. Forbstein; art d, John Hughes; cos, Orry-Kelly.

Adventure **(PR:A MPAA:NR)**

FRISCO KID, THE** (1979) 122m WB c (AKA: NO KNIFE)

Gene Wilder *(Avram Belinsky)*, Harrison Ford *(Tommy)*, Ramon Bieri *(Mr. Jones)*, Val Bisoglio *(Chief Gray Cloud)*, George Ralph DiCenzo *(Darryl Diggs)*, Leo Fuchs *(Chief Rabbi)*, Penny Peyser *(Rosalie)*, William Smith *(Matt Diggs)*, Jack Somack *(Samuel Bender)*, Beege Barkett *(Sarah Mindl)*, Shay Duffin *(O'Leary)*, Walter Janowitz, Joe Kapo, Clyde Kusatsu, Cliff Pello, Allan Rich, Rolfe Sedan.

A weak and unfunny ripoff of BLAZING SADDLES, this Wilder opus depicts a Polish rabbi who is making his way through the Old Wild West to get to a leaderless congregation in San Francisco. He is victimized by sharpers, almost killed by outlaws, and nearly misses being sizzled on a stake by irate Indians, saved repeatedly by Ford, a grim-faced gunman who inexplicably adopts this wandering Jew. Wilder is occasionally funny but the racial jokes fall flat and Aldrich's direction is heavy-handed, as forced as his 1963 effort to make a comedy out of a period production titled FOUR FOR TEXAS. The action scenes are downright sadistic, brutality for its own sake, and the set pieces presented are disjointed, making for a confusing story. Wilder is simply not humorous which says much against a trite and often distasteful script by Elias and Shaw, for Wilder is indeed a great clown who should have had more with which to work. Then again, the comedian was on top when this film was made and elected to do it, which confirms the belief that most actors, irrespective of deep and abiding talent, have no sense of role selectivity. The only pluses here are Marsh's superior production design and Hauser's inventive cinematography. These are simply not enough to make anyone accept this mudpie.

p, Mace Neufeld; d, Robert Aldrich; w, Michael Elias, Frank Shaw; ph, Robert B. Hauser; m, Frank DeVol; ed, Maury Winetrobe, Irving Rosenblum, Jack Horger; prod d, Terence Marsh; set d, Marvin March.

Comedy **Cas.** **(PR:C MPAA:PG)**

FRISCO LILL*½ (1942) 60m UNIV bw

Irene Hervey *(Lillian Grayson)*, Kent Taylor *(Peter Brewster)*, Minor Watson *(Jeff Gray)*, Jerome Cowan *(Vince)*, Samuel S. Hinds *(James Brewster)*, Milburn Stone *(Mike)*, Matty Fain *(Garrity)*, Claire Whitney *(Nell Brewster)*, Emmett Lynn *(Devers)*, Dave Willock *(Student)*.

Hervey joins a gambling casino as a dealer in an effort to clear her father, Watson, of a murder charge. Attorney Taylor provides the love interest. Poor little programmer.

p, Paul Malvern; d, Erle C. Kenton; w, George Bricker, Michael Jacoby (based on a story by Arthur V. Jones, Dorcas Cochran); ph, Charles Van Enger; ed, Otto Ludwig.

Drama **(PR:A MPAA:NR)**

FRISCO SAL** (1945) 94m UNIV bw

Susanna Foster *(Sally)*, Turhan Bey *(Dude)*, Alan Curtis *(Ric)*, Andy Devine *(Bunny)*, Thomas Gomez *(Dan)*, Collette Lyons *(Mickey)*, Samuel S. Hinds *(Doc)*, Fuzzy Knight *(Hallelujah)*, Billy Green *(Billy)*, Ernie Adams *(McKinney)*, George Lloyd *(Judge)*, Bert Fiske *(Eddie)*.

New England gal Foster travels to the Barbary Coast and goes undercover by getting a job singing in Bey's saloon to unearth her brother's murderer. Bey clashes with crime boss Curtis over control of coastal operations. Foster falls for Bey but is put off when Bey is implicated in her brother's disappearance. All turns out well when it is revealed that Foster's brother isn't dead after all. Universal originally slated this film as a technicolor western with Foster, Robert Paige and Ella Raines but decided to cut back on cost, changing the story setting to the Barbary Coast to avail itself of existing sets, going to black and white and dumping Paige and Raines. Songs include: "Beloved" (George Waggner, Edward Ward), "Good Little Bad Little Lady" (Jack Brooks).

p&d, George Waggner; w, Curt Siodmak, Gerald Geraghty; ph, Charles Van Enger; ed, Edward Curtiss; md, Edward Ward; art d, John B. Goodman, Robert Clatworthy; ch, Lester Horton.

Mystery **(PR:A MPAA:NR)**

FRISCO TORNADO*½ (1950) 60m REP bw

Allan "Rocky" Lane *(Himself)*, Eddy Waller *(Nugget Clark)*, Martha Hyer *(Jean)*, Stephen Chase *(Jim Crall)*, Ross Ford *(Paul Weston)*, Mauritz Hugo *(Brod)*, Lane Bradford *(Mike)*, Hal Price *(Thompson)*, Rex Lease *(Mac)*, George Chesebro *(Gun Guard)*, Edmund Cobb *(Stage Driver)*, Bud Geary and Black Jack the horse.

Lane is a U.S. marshal out to break up a ring of conniving insurance salesmen who are providing protection coverage against a gang of outlaws that are ravaging a small cattletown. As it turns out, the outlaws work for the salesmen. True to "B" western tradition, good guy Lane saves the day. Lane later gained fame as the voice of TV's talking horse, Mr. Ed.

p, Gordon Kay; d, R.G. Springsteen; w, M. Coates Webster; ph, John MacBurnie; m, Stanley Wilson; ed, Robert M. Leeds; art d, Frank Arrigo.

Western   **(PR:A   MPAA:NR)**

FRISCO WATERFRONT**   (1935) 66m REP bw

Ben Lyon (Glenn Burton), Helen Twelvetrees (Alice), Rod LaRocque (Dan Elliott), Russell Hopton (Eddie), James Burke (Corrigan), Henry Kolker (District Attorney), Purnell Pratt (Dr. Stevens), Barbara Pepper (The Stranger), Lee Shumway (Foreman), Norman Houston (Johnson).

Contrived tale about a successful politician, Lyon, who is a candidate for governor of California. As he is about to cast his vote (the polling place is in a tent), a truck careens off the road and crashes into the voting booth, critically injuring the candidate and his opponent. In a flashback we see Lyon's rise to power from unemployed WW I veteran to a powerful waterfront dock worker, finally becoming a lawyer and politician. Twelvetrees plays his long-suffering wife, who leaves him during his rise to power. The tearful Twelvetrees, sudser queen of the early 1930s, was at the zenith of her career with this film. After 1935, her popularity plummeted; she appeared in only three more pictures during the decade.

p, Trem Carr; d, Arthur Lubin; w, Norman Houston; ph, Harry Neumann; ed, Carl Pierson.

Drama   **(PR:A   MPAA:NR)**

**FRISKY*½   (1955, Ital.) 98m Titanus/DCA bw
(PANE AMORE E GELOSIA; AKA: BREAD, LOVE, AND JEALOUSY)

Gina Lollobrigida (Frisky), Vittorio De Sica (Marshal Antonio Carotenuto), Marisa Merlini (Midwife Annarella), Roberto Risso (Carabiniere Stelluti), Virgilio Riento (Priest Don Emidio), Tina Pica (Housekeeper Caramel).

A dreadful sequel to BREAD, LOVE, AND DREAMS, using the same setting and the same list of characters but without expanding on the farcical nature of the original, and, in fact, failing to capture the same flavor. Middle-aged DeSica gets himself into hot water with Merlini when she thinks he is fooling around with Lollobrigida. He is not, of course, but the efforts to prove his innocence just are not amusing. A thoroughly disappointing effort.

p, Nino Misiano; d, Luigi Comencini; w, Marcello Girosi (based on the story by Comencini and E.M. Margadonna); ph, Carlo Montuori; m, (Alessandro Cicognini).

Comedy   **(PR:A   MPAA:NR)**

FROG, THE   (1937, Brit.) 75m FOX bw

Gordon Harker (Sergeant Elk), Jack Hawkins (Capt. Gordon), Esme Percy (Philo Johnson), Felix Aylmer (John Bennett), Vivian Gaye (Stella Bennett), Richard Ainley (Ray Bennett), Noah Beery (Joshua Broad), Gordon McLeod (Chief Commissioner), Carol Goodner (Lola Bassano), Cyril Smith (P.C. Balder), Julien Mitchell (John Maitland), Harold Franklyn (Hagen).

Scotland Yard attempts to smash a mysterious ring of murderers, blackmailers, and thieves in this film version of a stage play based on Edgar Wallace's novel The Fellowship Of The Frog.

p, Herbert Wilcox; d, Jack Raymond; w, Ian Hay, Gerald Elliott (based on the play by Hay from the novel The Fellowship Of The Frog by Edgar Wallace); ph, F. A. Young; ed, Fred Wilson, Merrill White.

Crime   **(PR:A   MPAA:NR)**

FROGMEN, THE*   (1951) 96m FOX bw

Richard Widmark (Lt. Comdr. John Lawrence), Dana Andrews (Flannigan), Gary Merrill (Lt. Comdr. Pete Vincent), Jeffrey Hunter (Creighton), Warren Stevens (Hodges), Robert Wagner (Lt. j.g. Franklin), Harvey Lembeck (Carnarsie), Robert Rockwell (Lt. Doyle), Henry Slate (Sleepy), Robert Adler (Chief Ryan), Bob Patten (Lt. Klinger), Harry Flowers (Kinselia), William Bishop (Ferriso), Fay Roope (Adm. Dakers), William M. Neil (Comdr. Miles), James Gregory (Chief Petty Officer Lane), Russell Hardie (Capt. Radford), Parley Baer (Dr. Ullman), Peter Leeds (Pharmacist's Mate), Richard Allan, Frank Donahue, Jack Warden (Crew Members), Norman McKay (Capt. Phillips), Sydney Smith (Gen. Coleson), Ray Hyke (Repair Man), George Yoshinaga (Swimmer), Harry Hamada (Gunner), Rush Williams (Soldier).

Swift WW II action drama explodes with Widmark as a tough and unloved commander of Navy frogmen. Widmark takes over a UDT (Underwater Demolition Team) after its former, kindly commander has been killed. He is tough and uncompromising, giving curt orders and showing no compassion, a cold attitude which earns him the resentment and dislike of his men, particularly Andrews, the ranking noncom. Almost all of the men request transfers but then Widmark, assisted by Andrews, defuses an unexploded bomb lodged beneath the hospital ward of a ship, saving all on board. Further instilling confidence and respect from his men, Widmark leads his team on to a beach defended by Japanese and, while the shore emplacements strafe the water's edge, manages to blow up the water obstacles so the Marines can land. Widmark is still a man with the bark on, as he proves when lambasting Hunter for planting a sign welcoming the Marines to a beach cleared for them by the UDT. A terrific finale sees the UDT heroes wearing oxygen tanks and swimming underwater into a Japanese submarine pen, cutting the undersea nets, and planting explosives that later destroy the enemy vessels, then fighting their way to freedom past Japanese frogmen who have spotted the gurgling bubbles from the UDT's underwater equipment. Widmark gives one of his best performances and Andrews is solid as his friendly adversary. Merrill, as a captain of one of the boats landing the frogmen, is also effective, as are Hunter, Wagner, and group clown Lembeck.

p, Samuel G. Engel; d, Lloyd Bacon; w, John Tucker Battle (based on a story by Oscar Millard); ph, Norbert Brodine; m, Cyril J. Mockridge; ed, William Reynolds; md, Lionel Newman; art d, Lyle Wheeler, Albert Hogsett.

War Drama   **(PR:A   MPAA:NR)**

FROGS**½   (1972) 90m AIP c

Ray Milland (Jason Crockett), Sam Elliott (Pickett Smith), Joan Van Ark (Karen Crockett), Adam Roarke (Clint Crockett), Judy Pace (Bella Berenson), Lynn Borden (Jenny Crockett), Mae Mercer (Maybelle), David Gilliam (Michael), Nicholas Cortland (Kenneth), George Skaff (Stuart), Lance Taylor, Sr. (Charles), Holly Irving (Iris), Dale Willingham (Tina), Hal Hodges (Jay), Carolyn Fitzsimmons (Lady In Car), Robert Sanders (Young Boy In Car).

A revenge-of-nature film along the lines of Hitchcock's THE BIRDS sees thousands of frogs, snakes, turtles, and lizards attack Deep South plantation owner Milland (in a wheelchair) and his family on his birthday, which happens to be on the Fourth of July. Silly, but surprisingly effective.

p, George Edwards, Peter Thomas; d, George McCowan; w, Robert Hutchison, Robert Blees (based on a story by Hutchison); ph, Mario Tosi (Movielab Color); m, Les Baxter; ed, Fred R. Feitshans, Jr.; md, Baxter, Al Simms; cos, Phyllis Garr; makeup, Tom Burman; spec eff, Joe Sidore.

Horror   Cas.   (PR:C   MPAA:PG)

**FROM A ROMAN BALCONY*½   (1961, Fr./Ital.) 84m Transcontinental-
Euro International/CD bw (LA GIORNATA BALORDA; CA S'EST PASSE A
ROME; AKA: A CRAZY DAY; LOVE IS A DAY'S WORK; PICKUP IN
ROME)

Jean Sorel (David), Lea Massari (Freya), Jeanne Valerie (Marina), Rik Battaglia (Carpiti), Valeria Ciangottini (Ivana), Isabelle Corey (Sabina), Paolo Stoppa (Moglie), Marcella Valeri (Sora Tosca), Luigi Giacosi (Romani), Enrico Glori, Elvy Lissiak, Irene D'Aloisi.

Tedious "art" film rife with overly obvious political symbolism and allegory which was co-written by Pier Paolo Pasolini, whose own films aren't much better. The story concerns a day in the life of an obnoxiously simple tenement-dwelling young man, Sorel, who spends much of the movie looking for a job so that he can marry his sweetheart, Ciangottini. He goes to the office of a shady lawyer for work, but the lawyer ignores him. Depressed, Sorel spots a former lover, Valerie, who is now a prostitute; he makes love to her. Bored, he accompanies her to her next trick. The customer turns out to be the lawyer, and Sorel blackmails him into providing a job. Soon Sorel finds himself driving an olive oil truck, but this job ends when he is seduced by the wife of the company's owner. While in the throes of passion, his truck rolls down a hill and explodes. Once again out of work, Sorel decides to steal a ring from a corpse's finger (which he had seen laid out in an apartment earlier in the film) and use the money to marry his girl friend, legitimize their child, and start a new life. Interesting particularly as a travelog; the film shows both the seamy and seductive sides of postwar Rome: the towering tenements cloaked by clotheslines, billowing washwork covering the concrete; the barren business buildings; the swanky surroundings of the sybaritic rich.

p, Paul Graetz; d, Mauro Bolognini; w, Alberto Moravia, Pier Paolo Pasolini, Marco Visconti (inspired by "Roman Tales" and "New Roman Tales", by Moravia); ph, Aldo Scavarda; m, Piero Piccioni; ed, Borys Lewin, Nino Baragli; md, Piccioni; art d, Carlo Egidi; subtitles, Herman G. Weinberg.

Drama   **(PR:C   MPAA:NR)**

FROM BEYOND THE GRAVE** (1974, Brit.) 98m Amicus/WB c (AKA:
THE CREATURES FROM BEYOND THE GRAVE; CREATURES)

Peter Cushing (Proprietor); The Gate Crasher: David Warner (Edward Charlton), Wendy Allnutt (Pamela), Rosalind Ayres (Prostitute), Marcel Steiner ("Face"); An Act of Kindness: Donald Pleasence (Underwood), Ian Bannen (Christopher Lowe), Diana Dors (Mabel Lowe), Angela Pleasence (Emily Underwood); The Elemental: Margaret Leighton (Mme. Orloff), Ian Carmichael (Reggie Warren), Nyree Dawn Porter (Susan Warren); The Door: Ian Ogilvy (William Seaton), Lesley-Anne Down (Rosemary Seaton), Jack Watson (Sir Michael Sinclair); Tommy Godfrey, Ben Howard, John O'Farrell.

A pretty horror anthology which tells four separate tales of terror interconnected by Cushing, who plays the owner of a creepy antique shop. Good cast, but spoiled by poor directing which telegraphs the outcomes. Illustrating W. C. Fields' famous maxim YOU CAN'T CHEAT AN HONEST MAN (1939), grim fates await those who attempt to fleece Cushing. The best performance is that of Leighton, in what may be her last film (she died shortly after completing the part). This was one of a series of well-done horror films from the producing team of Subotsky and Rosenberg; others included DR. TERROR'S HOUSE OF HORRORS (1965) and VAULT OF HORROR (1973). Warner Bros. deferred release of this film in the U.S., apparently feeling that it was not up to the standard set by others in the series.

p, Max J. Rosenberg, Milton Subotsky; d, Kevin Connor; w, Raymond Christodoulou, Robin Clarke (based on stories from The Unbidden by R. Chetwynd-Hayes); m, Douglas Gamley; ph, Alan Hume (Technicolor); ed, John Ireland; md, Gamley; art d, Maurice Carter; set d, Simon Wakefield; cos, John Hilling; makeup, Neville Smallwood; spec eff, Alan Bryce.

Horror   **(PR:C   MPAA:PG)**

**FROM HEADQUARTERS*   (1929) 71m WB bw

Monte Blue (Happy Smith), Guinn Williams (Sgt. Wilmer), Gladys Brockwell (Mary Dyer), Lionel Belmore (Senor Corroles), Henry B. Walthall (Buffalo Bill Ryan), Eddie Gribbon (Pvt. Murphy), Ethlyne Claire (Innocencia), Pat Hartigan (Spike Connelly), John Kelly (O'Farrell), Otto Lederer (Bugs McGuire), Joseph Giraud (Major), William Irving (Fritz), Pat Somerset (Hendricks).

Listless effort to show the valor of the Marines has Blue as the tough captain in search of tourists who get lost in the jungles of Central America. Williams as the tough Marine sergeant saves this one from being a complete washout.

d, Howard Bretherton; w, Harvey Gates, Francis Powers (based on the story "Marines Are Coming" by Samuel Hartridge); ph, William Rees; ed, Harold McLernon.

Adventure (PR:A MPAA:NR)

FROM HEADQUARTERS** (1933) 62m WB bw

George Brent (*Lt. J. Stevens*), Margaret Lindsay (*Lou Ann Winton*), Eugene Pallette (*Sgt. Boggs*), Hugh Herbert (*Manny*), Dorothy Burgess (*Dolly White*), Theodore Newton (*Jack Winton*), Hobart Cavanaugh (*Muggs Manton*), Robert Barrat (*Anderzian*), Henry O'Neill (*Inspector Donnelly*), Edward Ellis (*Dr. Van de Water*), Ken Murray (*Mac*), Kenneth Thomson (*Gordon Bates*), Robert E. Homans (*Sgt./ Orderly*), Frank Darien (*Manly*).

A detailed early look at the inner workings of a (then) modern police department. The emphasis is on fingerprint detection, hair samples, chemical labs, booking procedures, and radio rooms. The plot that's threaded through all this concerns detective Brent as he pursues a murderer who has killed a blackmailer. Burgess' stereotype of a cocaine addict in an era when the drug was low in price, and used primarily by those who were low in class, is interesting in view of what was later to become Hollywood's hippest high-ticket habit.

p, Sam Bischoff; d, William Dieterle; w, Robert N. Lee, Peter Milne, Arthur Greville Collins (based on a story by Lee); ph, William Reese; ed, William Clemens; art d, Anton Grot.

Crime (PR:A MPAA:NR)

FROM HELL IT CAME** (1957) 71m AA bw

Tod Andrews (*Dr. William Arnold*), Tina Carver (*Dr. Terry Mason*), Linda Watkins (*Mrs. Kilgore*), John McNamara (*Prof. Clark*), Gregg Palmer (*Kimo*), Robert Swan (*Witch Doctor Tano*), Baynes Barron (*Chief Maranka*), Suzanne Ridgway (*Korey*), Mark Sheeler (*Eddie*), Lee Rhodes (*Norgu*), Grace Matthews (*Orchid*), Tani Marsh (*Naomi*), Chester Hayes (*Maku*), Lenmana Guerin (*Dori*).

Silly horror film set on a faraway south-sea island sees native prince Palmer sentenced to death by witch doctor Swan for fraternizing with white scientists Andrews and Carver, who are investigating the radiation residue left over from an atomic bomb blast. Swan stabs Palmer in the chest and buries him upright in a coffin, but not before the prince vows vengeance. Soon after, he keeps his promise by coming back to life as a walking tree stump (with a stern look on its face) that grows out of the grave. The tree monster then lumbers (pun intended) around getting his revenge on those who murdered him until he eventually wanders into some quicksand and disappears. Really goofy.

p, Jack Milner; d, Dan Milner; w, Richard Bernstein (story by Bernstein, J. Milner); ph, Brydon Baker; m, Darrell Calker; ed, Jack Milner; art d, Rudi Feld; spec eff, James H. Donnelly; monster creation, Paul Blaisdell.

Horror (PR:C MPAA: NR)

FROM HELL TO HEAVEN**½ (1933) 67m PAR bw

Carole Lombard (*Colly Tanner*), Jack Oakie (*Charlie Bayne*), Adrienne Ames (*Joan Burt*), David Manners (*Wesley Burt*), Sidney Blackmer (*Cuff Billings*), Verna Hillie (*Sonny Lockwood*), James C. Eagles (*Tommy Tucker*), Shirley Grey (*Winnie Lloyd*), Bradley Page (*Jack Ruby*), Walter Walker (*Pop Lockwood*), Berton Churchill (*Toledo Jones*), Donald Kerr (*Steve Wells*), Nydia Westman (*Sue Wells*), Cecil Cunningham (*Mrs. Chadman*), Thomas Jackson (*Lynch*), Allen Wood (*Pepper Murphy*), Rita LaRoy (*Elsie*), Clarence Muse (*Sam*), Dell Henderson.

Here is a racetrack tale that would finish a poor second had it not been for the ebullient talents of Lombard. She is a blonde handicapper who appears at a hotel peopled by gamblers, horse owners and enthusiasts, and a bevy of racetrack touts. The many stories shown before the deadline of the big race highly imitate those of GRAND HOTEL. One couple desperately bets on a favorite nag so that the husband can win back $5,000 he has embezzled from his firm. Two crooks are betting money taken from a murder victim. A jockey stakes everything on his own ability, and a vegetable stand owner puts up a life's savings to make a final killing. Lombard is no exception to this mania. Her horse, Sir Rapid, is bound to win, she is convinced, but she needs $10,000 to bet on him. Her only money contact is an old beau, Blackmer, a man she jilted to wed a rich merchant. Now divorced, she is so desperate that she accepts Blackmer's cynical and lustful agreement to advance her the money against herself. If she loses, she is to submit to his carnal desires—at least that's the implication. It's winner take all and Lombard loses, her horse running third. True to her word she delivers herself up to Blackmer but he proves himself a man of honor by insisting that she owes him nothing. His nobility impresses Lombard no end and it is obvious to her that he truly loves her in spite of her callous behavior in the past. They plan to pick winners together thereafter. This was not one of Lombard's better efforts but she was limited by the multi-roles offered others, stories that attempted variety rather than a single theme. Oakie plays sort of a Lewis Stone role, commenting on the riffraff that rattles through the gambler's hotel, almost mimicking Stone's final ironic comment at the end of GRAND HOTEL when stating: "People come and go but nothing ever happens." Ames is alluring as Oakie's sultry companion while jut-jawed Blackmer is smooth as silk in his role of the cuckolded lover.

d, Erle Kenton; w, Percy Heath, Sidney Buchman (based on a story by Lawrence Hazard); ph, Henry Sharp; m/l, Sam Coslow, Arthur Johnston, Leo Robin, Ralph Rainger.

Sports Drama (PR:C MPAA:NR)

FROM HELL TO TEXAS***½ (1958) 100m FOX c (GB: MANHUNT)

Don Murray (*Tod Lohman*), Diane Varsi (*Juanita Bradley*), Chill Wills (*Amos Bradley*), Dennis Hopper (*Tom Boyd*), R.G. Armstrong (*Hunter Boyd*), Jay C.

Flippen (*Jake Leffertfinger*), Margo (*Mrs. Bradley*), John Larch (*Hal Carmody*), Ken Scott (*Otis Boyd*), Rodolfo Acosta (*Bayliss*), Salvador Baguez (*Cardito*), Harry Carey, Jr. (*Trueblood*), Jerry Oddo (*Morgan*), Jose Torvay (*Miguel*), Malcolm Atterbury (*Hotel Clerk*).

Handsome western starring Murray as a kindly cowboy who suddenly finds himself the object of a massive manhunt through the badlands of New Mexico after he accidentally kills one of powerful rancher Armstrong's three sons. Armstrong vows vengeance and sets off with an army of gunslingers (including his two remaining sons) to capture and kill Murray. Barely keeping one step ahead of the posse, Murray finds himself under even greater pressure when another of Armstrong's sons is trampled to death in a cattle stampede and after he kills several members of the posse in self defense. Murray receives some help from kind-hearted rancher Wills and his daughter Varsi, but Armstrong catches up with him and there is a dramatic showdown in the moonlight that comes to an end without bloodshed when Murray throws down his gun to save the life of Armstrong's last surviving son, Hopper. The rancher concedes and calls off the hunt. Well directed with an outstanding cast and beautiful cinematography.

p, Robert Buckner; d, Henry Hathaway; w, Buckner, Wendell Mayes (based on the book *The Hell Bent Kid* by Charles O. Locke); ph, Wilfrid M. Cline (CinemaScope, DeLuxe Color); m, Daniele Amfitheatrof; ed Johnny Ehrin; art d, Lyle R. Wheeler, Walter M. Simonds.

Western (PR:C MPAA:NR)

FROM HELL TO VICTORY** (1979, Fr./Ital./Span.) 100m New Film-Princess Films-Jose Frade c

George Peppard (*Bret*), George Hamilton (*Maurice*), Horst Buchholz (*Jurgen*), Capucine (*Nicole*), Sam Wanamaker (*Ray*), Jean Pierre Cassel (*Bick*), Annie Duperey (*Fabienne*), Ray Lovelock, Angel Aranda, Antonio Mayans.

Close friends of different nationalities (American, German, French, English) find themselves torn apart when WW II erupts. Before they go their separate ways, they vow to meet each year at the same cafe. During the war most find themselves fighting the Nazis for the Allies, but the German reluctantly must fight on the opposing side. During the war some of the friends lose their lives, but most survive to meet together on the day Paris is liberated. A big-budget war picture punctuated with some fairly exciting battle scenes, the film was never released theatrically in the U.S.

d, Hank Milestone; w, Umberto Lenzi, Jose Luis Martinez Molls, Gianfranco Clerici; ph, Jose Luis Alcaine (Eastmancolor); m, Riz Ortolani; ed, Vincenzo Tomasi; set d, Giuseppe Bassan, Rafael Ferry.

War   **Cas.** (PR:C MPAA:NR)

FROM HERE TO ETERNITY***** (1953) 118m COL bw

Burt Lancaster (*Sgt. Milton Warden*), Deborah Kerr (*Karen Holmes*), Montgomery Clift (*Robert E. Lee Prewitt*), Frank Sinatra (*Angelo Maggio*), Donna Reed (*Alma Lorene*), Ernest Borgnine (*Sgt. "Fatso" Judson*), Philip Ober (*Capt. Dana Holmes*), Jack Warden (*Cpl. Buckley*), Mickey Shaughnessy (*Sgt. Leva*), Harry Bellaver (*Mazzioli*), George Reeves (*Sgt. Maylon Stark*), John Dennis (*Sgt. Ike Galovitch*), Tim Ryan (*Sgt. Pete Karelsen*), Barbara Morrison (*Mrs. Kipfer*), Kristine Miller (*Georgette*), Jean Willes (*Annette*), Merle Travis (*Sal Anderson*), Arthur Keegan (*Treadwell*), Claude Akins (*Sgt. Baldy Thom*), Robert Karnes (*Sgt. Turp Thornhill*), Robert Wilke (*Sgt. Henderson*), Douglas Henderson (*Cpl. Champ Wilson*), Don Dubbins (*Friday Clark*), John Cason (*Cpl. Paluso*), John Bryant (*Capt. Ross*), Joan Shawlee (*Sandra*), Angela Stevens (*Jean*), Mary Carver (*Nancy*), Vicki Bakken (*Suzanne*), Margaret Barstow (*Roxanne*), Delia Salvi (*Billie*), Willis Bouchey (*Lieutenant Colonel*), Al Sargent (*Nair*), Weaver Levy (*Bartender*), Tyler McVey (*Maj. Stern*), William Lundmark (*Bill*), Robert Healy (*Soldier*), Brick Sullivan (*Military Guard*), Moana Gleason (*Rose, Waitress*), Freeman Lusk (*Col. Wood*), Robert Pike (*Maj. Bonds*), Carleton Young (*Col. Ayres*), Fay Roope (*Gen. Slater*), Louise Saraydar, Joe Roach, Patrick Miller, Norman Wayne, Joe Sargent, Mack Chandler, Edward Laguna, John D. Veitch, John Davis, Carey Leverette, Alan Pinson, Guy Way, James Jones, Manny Klein and His Trumpet.

The massive James Jones novel, thought to be impossible to convert to the screen, is brought forth in a powerful, unforgettable portrait of pre-WW II enlisted men, their women, and the grim destiny that overtook them all. All the principals are enormous in their telling characterizations—Lancaster, Clift, Kerr, Sinatra, Reed, even the utterly reprehensible character Ernest Borgnine. The film opens with Clift arriving at Schofield Barracks, the army base at Pearl Harbor, transferring because he refused to continue being a company boxer at his previous post. His new commander, Ober, a brutal, insecure officer, promises Clift that if he boxes on the company team he will be given the post of bugler, a job he very much wants. But Clift refuses, haunted by ugly experiences in the ring, particularly one bout where he blinded his best friend and he has vowed never again to put on the gloves. For Clift's obstinacy, Ober orders Lancaster, his top sergeant, to give Clift every dirty detail in the company. Lancaster, a by-the-book almost perfect soldier, empathizes with Clift, respecting and befriending him, but is angered when, after trying to convince Clift to compromise, he is stone-walled. Lancaster is also involved with Ober's blonde sluttish wife, Kerr, and he secretly meets with her, developing a torrid affair. They meet in cars, on piers, on the beach to make love; nagging Lancaster are the rumors that Kerr has had many affairs on many Army posts and when he raises questions about this to Kerr she explodes. Ober himself is cheating on his wife and treats her as an unwanted concubine. Clift bears up under the harsh treatment Ober administers, his suffering eased by a newly established relationship with Reed, a hostess he has met at the New Congress Club, a dance hall frequented by enlisted men. She has a shady past but he accepts her, asking that she see only him during her off-hours. Meanwhile, Clift's only other friend, Sinatra, a wise-cracking, tough enlisted man, commits several small offenses and draws repeated company punishment. He and Clift meet with their friends in a smoky saloon one night and Sinatra shows his friends some family photos. Borgnine, the beer-bellied, sadistic sergeant of the dreaded stockade, saunters by, picks up a photo of Sinatra's sister, and makes an obscene remark about her. Sinatra goes berserk and slams a stool down on the back of Borgnine's head. The giant sergeant turns, amazed; "You hit me," he says. "Yeah," snarls Sinatra, "and I'm about to do it again!" Borgnine spits out a racial slur. "Only my friends call me wop," Sinatra shouts back. The two face each other in what is obviously an uneven match. When Borgnine pulls a switchblade and announces that he intends to carve up Sinatra, Lancaster, who has been sitting with some other sergeants, jumps up and tells both men to stop. Sinatra obeys but Borgnine sneers and makes a move toward Sinatra. Lancaster breaks a bottle and juts the jagged edge toward the huge Borgnine, telling him that he will take on the stockade sergeant if he doesn't quit. Borgnine will not face Lancaster and puts the knife away, but, before leaving, warns Sinatra that someday he will wind up in the stockade where he will be waiting. Clift continues to pull dirty details; saddled with kitchen police he jokes with Lancaster about it, telling him he might find a pearl in the dishwater. He is less jocular with Reed, explaining that his real dream has always been to play taps at Arlington National Cemetery, and he has demonstrated his wonderful ability to play the bugle during the barroom scene; he forever carries his own bugle mouthpiece to remind him of his ambition. Yet he is unmovable in his resolve to resist Ober's pressures to fight, later explaining his philosophy, and that of most of the old Army regulars, by stating that "a man's gotta go his own way or he's nothin'," and "a man's gotta do what a man's gotta do." He backs this up by telling the noncoms of his company: "I can take anything you can dish out." The pressure increases but Clift remains loyal to the only home he has ever had, the service, telling Reed that he's been in the Army since age 17 and that "I'm a 30-year man. I'm in for the whole ride." One night he gets drunk with Lancaster and the two declare their friendship while sitting in the middle of the road. Lancaster is of the same mold as Clift. "Prewitt stays right here till the bitter end," Clift says of himself to Lancaster. Just then Sinatra, who has gone AWOL and been thrown in the stockade, staggers down the road and collapses into Clift's arms. He is battered and bleeding, explaining how he has escaped the stockade after not being able to take Borgnine's beatings anymore. Sinatra explains in a halting, gasping voice that every time Borgnine beat him he spat in his face but that the beatings became so bad that he had to escape, smuggling himself aboard a garbage truck and then falling off the truck and being injured internally. He dies in Clift's arms and Clift vows revenge. Later Clift finds Borgnine coming out of a downtown Pearl Harbor bar and inveigles him into an alley where he confronts him with Sinatra's death. The sneering, vicious stockade brute pulls his knife but Clift is prepared, yanking out a switchblade of his own. Both men rush each other, Borgnine severely wounding Clift, but Clift manages to mortally wound Borgnine who dies in the alley. Clift staggers off to take refuge in Reed's house, recuperating until he can rejoin his outfit. Lancaster carries Clift on the rollcall even though he is AWOL. By this time, Ober has been relieved of his command. Earlier, Dennis, the heavyweight of the company boxing team, has tried to embarrass Clift and then picked a fight with him in the parade ground, beating him mercilessly until Clift fights back, jarring the heavyweight and pounding him senseless while Ober watches without attempting to interfere. Staff officers see the fight and Ober's do-nothing attitude which later causes him to be relieved. Lancaster, meanwhile, has broken off with Kerr, preferring, like his friend Clift, to give his whole allegiance to the Army. Then, early Sunday morning, December 7, while Lancaster and other soldiers are entering the mess hall for breakfast, a roar of engines is heard; Lancaster steps outside to see a lone soldier running across the parade ground, screaming unintelligibly, a lone fighter plane following him, strafing the barracks and field, killing the running soldier. Lancaster races into the mess hall and organizes his noncoms, ordering all enlisted men to put on their helmets and get beneath their bunks. The bombs start falling, shaking the barracks, while distant explosions signal the sinking of the U.S. battleships helplessly anchored in the harbor. Lancaster breaks into the armory and issues automatic weapons to his sergeants and they clamber to the roofs of Schofield Barracks to return fire at the Zeros streaming overhead, strafing and bombing. Lancaster, holding a heavy machinegun, knocks down a Japanese fighter to the cheers of his men. Clift, that evening, though still bleeding from his knifefight wound, insists upon returning to his company now that war has broken out. Reed tries to stop him but he gives his last loyalty to the service that has been so rigid with him. In attempting to reach his company, running past nervous sentinels on guard against Japanese invasion forces, Clift is shot to death when not halting to be identified. Lancaster finds him dead and tells an officer that Clift "was always a hardhead but the best damned soldier I ever knew." With WW II begun, civilians depart Pearl Harbor by boat, among them Reed and Kerr who meet on a liner, both looking back at the receding Pearl Harbor where they leave behind lost loves. Reed lies to Kerr, telling her that Clift was a fighter pilot who was killed while taking off to meet the Japanese fighters. They toss their leis into the water at film's end. FROM HERE TO ETERNITY was thought difficult to produce as a film since the novel was so heavily laced with foul language. It is not much more than a male soap opera in literary form but Zinnemann's masterful direction and Taradash's tough, emotion-packed script, coupled to the outstanding portrayals by all the cast members, produced a flawless film. But it was an uphill battle for Zinnemann all the way. Most of the war was with Columbia's dictator, Harry Cohn, who had purchased the novel for $82,000 and was determined to retain its seamy story, raw language, and violence, rejecting one adaptation after another. The Army was not happy with Jones' fierce indictment of its system and refused use of Schofield Barracks unless some major concessions were made. One chief point involved the role of Ober. In the novel he gets away with everything, even being promoted to major, but in the film he is cashiered for his cruelty and malfeasance. The feature roles were also difficult to cast over Cohn's whimsical supervision; he thought to use one of two Columbia contract players, John Derek or Aldo Ray. Both, said Zinnemann, would be wrong for the Prewitt role. He wanted Clift and Cohn refused, saying that the actor was too temperamental. "Thank you," said the quiet-voiced Zinnemann, "but if I can't have Clift it's no deal." "I'm president of this company," roared King Cohn. "You can't give me ultimatums!" Replied Zinnemann: "I'm not giving you ultimatums. I want to make a good picture, and I don't see how I can make this picture without Monty Clift." Cohn relented and Clift was hired for $150,000. He was delighted with the tight, realistic script hammered out by Taradash, and immediately went into training for the role, one where he stayed drunk through most of the production. In the drunk scene with Lancaster, Clift actually was intoxicated. His drinking was so serious that he missed scenes and muffed lines. It was Sinatra who befriended Clift and helped him through his hard times, talking him into drinking enough coffee and sobering for difficult scenes, even though they went on benders together. His performance was nevertheless stunning, perhaps the finest of his career, one, he was positive, would win him an Oscar. It was ironic, many felt unfair, that Clift was denied the award, although this was his third nomination. Awards did go to Columbia for Best Picture, Zinnemann for Best Direction, Taradash for Best Screenplay, and to Sinatra and Reed for best supporting roles, among eight Oscars in all. Clift was at his pinnacle with this film but he suddenly lost his grasp on his life and career following the critical and popular smash FROM HERE TO ETERNITY became, grossing $19 million in its first run. Clift took to the bottle thereafter, refusing one good script after another—none were "exceptional," in his estimation, including ON THE WATERFRONT (1954) and EAST OF EDEN (1955). Oddly, FROM HERE TO ETERNITY provided just the opposite fate for the volatile and colorful Sinatra. His career as a singer was fading since his vocal cords had hemorrhaged and his film career was limited to some tuneful Gene Kelly musicals where he was not required to act. Sinatra's wooing of his then present wife Ava Gardner had created notoriety which caused Hollywood to shun him. He was deeply in debt, owing the government more than $100,000 in back taxes. When his own agency, MCA, dropped him, Sinatra personally sent note after note to Cohn, begging for the Maggio role. Cohn ignored him. Then Gardner pleaded with Cohn and both she and Sinatra flew from Nairobi, Africa, where she was working with Clark Gable in the production of MOGAMBO, to make a personal appeal. Much has been said and written about how Sinatra eventually did get the part and there were even stories that mob men pressured Cohn into deciding in Sinatra's favor. Another story had it that Sinatra offered to *pay Cohn* if he would give him the role, or, according to Norman Zierold writing in *The Moguls*, Sinatra told Cohn: "If you give me the part of Maggio in FROM HERE TO ETERNITY, I'll do it for nothing." Cohn reportedly told the singer he would think it over but said when Sinatra left his office: "They'll laugh at that skinny little runt." Moreover, Zinnemann had already decided that Eli Wallach was to play Maggio and he had been cast, but Wallach bowed out, opting to appear in the Broadway production of "Camino Real" under Elia Kazan's direction. Sinatra was then given a test and impressed both Cohn and Zinnemann. Cohn hired Sinatra at rock-bottom prices, paying him a mere $8,000. Sinatra's performance was nothing less than electrifying and he suddenly turned his entire career around, becoming a much sought-after actor. He was in awe of Clift, whom he considered an actor's actor, and Clift admired Sinatra because he could sing and he, Clift, couldn't carry a note. (It was Manny Klein who dubbed the wonderful blues Clift plays on the bugle, including the "Reenlistment Blues".) Lancaster was obtained through producer Hal B. Wallis, getting $120,000, and Edmond O'Brien, originally slated for the role of the top sergeant, was dropped. Even Kerr was a remote possibility for the fine role she finally rendered. The part of the slatternly, lonely officer's wife was initially given to the unpredictable Joan Crawford but when she was told what plain attire she would have to wear she exploded; no designer originals, no Crawford. Kerr, a rather distant actress, was thought to be perfect for the trysting wife, all the more sensuous by virtue of her cool posture which quickly thawed in the memorable beach scene where she and Lancaster press hot bodies as the surf washed over them. Even Reed was not the first choice for her part, Julie Harris being selected by Zinnemann. Cohn objected, calling Harris a "child frightener," and insisted that Reed play the role of the prostitute, changed to a hostess for the film, her middle-class image being more proper for the role, he believed. Cohn also had to one-up MGM with Reed; she had been a contract player for eight years there before joining Columbia and Cohn intended to make a star out of someone Louis B. Mayer had overlooked. Cohn personally oversaw the entire production, flying to Hawaii to visit the on-location shootings and sets. When he learned that Sinatra was giving Zinnemann a hard time on a particular scene, he rushed to the set and upbraided the entire cast. Though he was worried that Sinatra's name might suggest the film was a musical, he reluctantly agreed to have Sinatra's name included with the other four stars above the title. The mogul spent lavishly, allowing a $2 million budget, but he demanded that it be brought in promptly and Zinnemann wrapped up the production in 41 days. Cohn was elated with the success of the film, made in standard black and white when the industry was turning to 3-D, widescreen, and rampant color, proving that the old Hollywood formula could still generate profits. The production would eventually soar beyond $80 million in receipts. Clift was utterly depressed at not winning an Academy Award for Best Actor; he considered this his superlative effort. Zinnemann gave him a consolation prize he kept all his life, a miniature gold trumpet mounted like an Oscar.

p, Buddy Adler; d, Fred Zinnemann; w, Daniel Taradash (based on the novel by James Jones); ph, Burnett Guffey; m, George Duning; ed, William Lyon; md, Morris Stoloff; art d, Gary Odell; set d, Frank Tuttle; cos, Jean Louis; makeup, Clay Campbell; song, "Re-enlistment Blues," m/l, James Jones, Fred Karger, Robert Wells; boxing adv, Mushy Callahan; tech adv, Brig. Gen. Kendall J. Fielder.

Drama **(PR:C-O MPAA:NR)**

FROM NASHVILLE WITH MUSIC* (1969) 87m Bradford/Craddock c

Marilyn Maxwell *(Mabel)*, Leo G. Carroll *(Arnold)*, Jose Gonzalez Gonzalez *(Film Director)*, Marty Robbins, Merle Haggard, Buck Owens, Charley Pride, Tammy Wynette, Wynn Stewart, Bill Anderson, George Jones, Carl Smith, Don Gibson, Jo Ann Steele, The Jordanaires, Bonnie Owens, Big Jim Bradford, John C. Bradford, The Strangers, The Jones Boys, The Buckaroos, Cousin Jody, Susan Raye, Eddie Fukano, Buddy Alan.

The music is the only thing to see (or hear) in this daft picture about a New York couple, Carroll and Maxwell, who take a trip to Nashville. They meet country singer Robbins when their car stalls, and he gives them a pair of tickets to the Grand Ole Opry. Thinking that they are off to the opera they go, but are shocked to find casually dressed good-ol-boys and knee-slapping country fiddlin'. Aghast, Maxwell returns to New York, while Carroll dances to the mountain boogie. The feudin' couple reconcile by the finale, after an almost endless parade of southern music stars go by. Songs: "Jody Special," "Play Off" (Cousin Jody), "Hey Joe" (Boudleaux Bryant), "Deep Water" (Fred Rose), "White Lightning" (J.P. Richardson), "Stand By Your Man" (Billy Sherrill, Tammy Wynette), "Walk Through This World With Me" (Sandra Seamons, Kay Savage), "Your Good Girl's Gonna Go Bad" (Sherrill, Glenn Sutton), "Wild Weekend," "A Happy State of Mind" (Bill Anderson), "I've Got a Tiger By the Tail" (Buck Owens, Harlan Howard), "Act Naturally" (Johnny Russell, Vonie Morrison), "It's Such a Pretty World Today" (Dale Noe), "Branded Man," "Hungry Eyes" (Merle Haggard), "Today I Start Loving You Again" (Bonnie Owens, Haggard), "Lead Me On" (Leon Copeland), "Kaw Liga" (Fred Rose, Hank Williams), "Cotton Fields" (arr, The Jordanaires), "Walking In The Sunshine" (Roger Miller), "Granada" (Agustin Lara), "I'll Be a Legend In My Time" (Don Gibson), "Hello Daily News" (Jim Easterby), "Singin' the Blues" (Melvin Endsley), "Crystal Chandelier" (Ted Harris), "The Shoe Goes On the Other Foot Tonight" (Buddy Mize), "Spoke In the Wheel" (Clay Boland, Bix Reichner), "The Green Green Grass of Home" (Claude Putnam, Jr.).

p&d, Eddie Crandall, Robert Patrick; ph,m&ed, Will Zens.

Musical   **(PR:AAA   MPAA:G)**

FROM NOON TO THREE**½**   (1976) 98m UA c

Charles Bronson (Graham Dorsey), Jill Ireland (Amanda Starbuck), Douglas V. Fowley (Buck Bowers), Stan Haze (Ape), Damon Douglas (Boy), Hector Morales (Mexican), Bert Williams (Sheriff), William Lanteau (Rev. Cabot), Betty Cole, Davis Roberts (Amanda's Servants), Fred Franklyn (Postmaster), Sonny Jones (Dr. Finger), Hoke Howell (Deke), Howard Brunner (Foster), Donald "Red" Barry (Outlaw Leader), Elmer Bernstein, Alan Bergman (Songwriters).

Interesting, but unsuccessful, Bronson vehicle which has an excellent script dealing with the making of western myths. Bronson plays a drifter outlaw who, after a brief liaison with Ireland, is transformed into an outlaw legend by her soon after his death. She builds a giant commercial empire based on her fictional stories about the now-infamous "Graham Dorsey," and his name is forever emblazoned on the history of the Old West. When Bronson turns up very much alive, no one, not even Ireland, recognizes him or will believe his protestations that he is Dorsey. He ends up in an insane asylum where the doctors just nod and smile at his delusions of having been a great gunfighter. It is admirable that Bronson chose to break type and play a likable, almost goofy character, but the film is miscast and misdirected, sapping the material of its true power.

p, M.J. Frankovich, William Self; d&w, Frank D. Gilroy; ph, Lucien Ballard (Panavision, DeLuxe Color); m, Elmer Bernstein; ed, Maury Winetrobe; prod d, Robert Clatworthy; art d, Dick Lawrence; set d, George Robert Nelson; cos, Moss Mabry; spec eff, Augie Lohman; m/l, "Hello and Goodbye," Bernstein, Alan and Marilyn Bergman.

Western/Comedy   **(PR:C   MPAA:PG)**

FROM RUSSIA WITH LOVE**   (1963, Brit.) 110m UA c

Sean Connery (James Bond), Daniela Bianchi (Tatiana Romanova), Pedro Armendariz (Kerim Bey), Lotte Lenya (Rosa Klebb), Robert Shaw (Red Grant), Bernard Lee ("M"), Eunice Gayson (Sylvia), Walter Gotell (Morzeny), Francis de Wolff (Vavra), George Pastell (Train Conductor), Nadja Regin (Kerim's Girl), Lois Maxwell (Miss Moneypenny), Alizia Gur (Vida), Martine Beswick (Zora), Vladek Sheybal (Kronsteen), Leila (Belly Dancer), Hasan Ceylan (Foreign Agent), Fred Haggerty (Krilencu), Neville Jason (Chauffeur), Peter Bayliss (Benz), Nushet Atear (Tempo), Peter Madden (McAdams), Peter Brayham (Rhoda), Desmond Llewelyn (Boothroyd), Jan Williams (Masseuse).

The second and possibly the best of the Bond movies sees Connery as 007 sent to mysterious Istanbul to grab a top-secret Russian decoding machine. There he falls for Russian agent Bianchi, who is an unwitting pawn of Spectre. Also on Bond's tail are female assassin Lenya (who carries a poisonous switchblade in her shoe) and crazed blonde killer Shaw (the deadliest and most human Bond villain yet). The highlight is a terrific battle to the death between Shaw and Connery on the Orient Express. Well-written and well-acted, with little evidence of the gadgets that would plague the series from this point on.

p, Harry Saltzman, Albert R. Broccoli; d, Terence Young; w, Richard Maibaum, Johanna Harwood (based on the novel by Ian Fleming); ph, Ted Moore (Technicolor); m, John Barry; ed, Peter Hunt; art d, Syd Cain; set d, Freda Pearson; cos, Jocelyn Rickards; spec eff, John Stears; m/l, "From Russia With Love," Lionel Bart (sung by Matt Monro), "James Bond Theme," Monty Norman.

Spy Drama   **Cas.**   **(PR:A   MPAA:NR)**

FROM THE EARTH TO THE MOON½**
                                                                       (1958) 100m WB c

Joseph Cotton (Victor Barbicane), George Sanders (Stuyvesant Nicholl), Debra Paget (Virginia Nicholl), Don Dubbins (Ben Sharpe), Patric Knowles (Josef Cartier), Carl Esmond (J.V. [Jules Verne]), Henry Daniell (Morgana), Melville Cooper (Bancroft), Ludwig Stossel (Aldo Von Metz), Morris Ankrum (U.S. Grant).

Boring Jules Verne adaptation sees mad scientist Cotton inventing a source of infinite energy called "Power X" after the close of the Civil War. He soon designs a missile to send beings into outer space and back that would use his fuel for power. He, along with rival scientist Sanders, crewman Dubbins and Sanders' stowaway daughter, Paget, blast off to the moon. After countless dull adventures the climax sees Paget and Dubbins, now lovers, returning to Earth and leaving the cranky scientists on the moon.

p, Benedict Bogeaus; d, Byron Haskin; w, Robert Blees, James Leicester (based on the novel by Jules Verne); ph, Edwin B. DuPar (Giantscope, Technicolor); m, Louis Forbes; ed, Leicester; art d, Hal Wilson Cox; cos, Georgette.

Science Fiction   **Cas.**   **(PR:A   MPAA:NR)**

FROM THE LIFE OF THE MARIONETTES**½**
                                                               (1980, Ger.) 104m ITC c/bw

Robert Atzorn (Peter Egerman), Christine Buchegger (Katarina), Martin Benrath (Mogens Jensen), Rita Russek (Ka), Lola Muethel (Cordelia Egerman), Walter Schmidinger (Tim), Heinz Bennent (Arthur Brenner), Ruth Olafs (Nurse), Karl Heinz Pelser (Interrogator), Gaby Dohm (Secretary), Toni Berger (Doorman).

Just after the rumours had been spread that Ingmar Bergman was to retire from the realm of feature film production to devote himself to his first love, the theater, he made yet another in-depth inquiry into the forces acting upon individual motivation. Somewhat of a follow-up to SCENES FROM A MARRIAGE, FROM THE LIFE OF THE MARIONETTES concentrates on the emotional and sexual repression resulting from Atzorn's relationship to his wife, the psychological antithesis of which can account for his bizarre sexual murder of a young prostitute. Bergman uses a mixture of black and white and color to relate the events which center around this murder, only the actual murder portrayed in color and appearing at the beginning of the film. The rest, in black and white to lend an air of documentation concentrates on the details that surround his alienating marriage, as well as a brief look at the police inquiry into the murder of the prostitute. The major theme that Bergman seems to be getting at is that the philosophical traditions instigated by materialistic determinism has made man's emotional life a vast void. Thus the title, FROM THE LIFE OF THE MARIONETTES, signifies that Atzorn is just another puppet in the scheme of things, unable to properly respond to sensual and emotional arousal that varies from the routine structure. Many of these complex thoughts are delivered through speeches and the characters' attempts to explain their lives, despite which Nykvist is still able to perform quite a bit of provocative camera work.

p, Lord Grade, Martin Starger; d&w, Ingmar Bergman; ph, Sven Nykvist; m, Rols Wilhelm; ed, Petra Voelffen; prod d, Rolf Zechetbauer; art d, Herbert Strabel; cos, Charlotte Fleming.

Drama   **Cas.**   **(PR:O   MPAA:NR)**

**FROM THE MIXED-UP FILES OF MRS. BASIL E.
FRANKWEILER****½**   (1973) 105m Cinema 5 c
                                                             (AKA: THE HIDEAWAYS)

Ingrid Bergman (Mrs. Frankweiler), Sally Prager (Claudia), Johnny Doran (Jamie), George Rose (Saxonburg), Richard Mulligan (Mr. Kincaid), Georgann Johnson (Mrs. Kincaid), Madeline Kahn (Schoolteacher), Donald Symington (Museum Director), Linda Selman (Museum Secretary), Brucie Conover (Kevin), Mike Hammett (Brucie), Peter Turgeon (Counterman), Robert Packer (2nd Guard).

Pleasant film starring Prager and Doran as brother and sister bored with their dull suburban home who take off to New York City for a week on a lark. They wind up spending most of their trip hiding out in the Metropolitan Museum of Art undetected until Prager becomes obsessed with finding out whether a white statue she is fond of is an authentic Michelangelo. She traces the donor of the piece to a spacious mansion in New Jersey owned by the friendly Bergman. Prager and Bergman form a close friendship in which they exchange secrets about each other and discuss their love for the arts. This was Bergman's first film appearance in three years, and, fifty eight years old at the time, played a woman in her middle seventies.

p, Charles G. Mortimer Jr.; d, Fielder Cook; w, Blanche Hanalis (based on the novel by E.L. Konigsburg); ph, Victor J. Kemper; m, Donald Devor; ed, Eric Albertson; art d, Philip Rosenberg; set d, Ed Stewart.

Drama/Children   **Cas.**   **(PR:AA   MPAA:G)**

FROM THE TERRACE**   (1960) 144m FOX c

Paul Newman (Alfred Eaton), Joanne Woodward (Mary St. John), Myrna Loy (Martha Eaton), Ina Balin (Natalie), Leon Ames (Samuel Eaton), Elizabeth Allen (Sage Rimmington), Barbara Eden (Clemmie), George Grizzard (Lex Porter), Patrick O'Neal (Dr. Jim Roper), Felix Aylmer (MacHardie), Raymond Greenleaf (Fritz Thornton), Malcolm Atterbury (George Fry), Raymond Bailey (Mr. St. John), Ted de Corsia (Mr. Benziger), Howard Caine (Duffy), Mae Marsh (Governess), Kathryn Givney (Mrs. St. John), Dorothy Adams (Mrs. Benziger), Lauren Gilbert (Frolick), Blossom Rock (Nellie), Cecil Elliott (Josephine), Rory Harrity (Steve Rimmington), Ottola Nesmith (Lady Sevringham), Clive L. Halliday (Lord Sevringham), Gordon B. Clarke (Weinkoop), Ralph Dunn (Jones), Felippa Rock (Jean Duffy), Jimmy Martin (Sandy), William Quinn (Von Elm), Stuart Randall (Kelly), John Harding (Newton Orchid), Sally Winn (Mrs. Pearson), Elektra Rozanska (Mrs. Ripley).

It's never been easy to adapt John O'Hara's sprawling novels to the screen and this is no exception. They attempted to boil more than one thousand pages into a picture that runs nearly two and a half hours. Then they thought they'd hedge their bets by casting hearthrob Newman and wife Woodward, thus insuring box office receipts. Boy, were they wrong. Newman is a Navy flier who comes home after the war to rest at the mansion of his wealthy family in O'Hara's fictional Pennsylvania town. His old father, Ames, and his drunken, cheating mother, Loy, get on his nerves quickly, so he moves to New York and starts a business with his pal, Grizzard. Visiting the posh Long Island south shore resort of Southhampton, he meets and woos Woodward, who is rich and veddy veddy social. They marry and seem to have it all together. Now, Newman rescues wealthy Aylmer's grandson, Martin, and is given a job with the old man's successful Wall street investment company. Business is all that matters to Newman and he begins to ignore Woodward, who becomes increasingly needy. Desperate for affection, she renews an affair with O'Neal, a psychiatrist with enough neuroses to populate Park Avenue. Newman and Woodward quarrel and he goes to Pennsylvania on some delicate business negotiations. Once there, he falls hard for Balin, the daughter of a local businessman, De Corsia. They have a steamy affair and she eventually comes to New York City where they tryst in a Manhattan hotel room. One of Newman's co-workers, Caine, discovers the affair and threatens to blow the whistle unless Newman helps him with what is obviously a fraudulent investment scheme. Aylmer is a prude and would not tolerate Newman's behavior. Newman must make a decision and he opts to bare his soul to the company's directors, bid Woodward goodbye, and take off for a simpler life with Balin, thereby salvaging whatever integrity he has remaining. The novel was sexually explicit (as is so much of O'Hara's work) and that was lost in the screenplay due to the tight hand of the censor in 1960. Director Robson had a big hit with PEYTON PLACE just prior and thought he could do the same thing with this material. It was not to be and the fault must be laid at Robson and Lehman's feet. Lehman is one of the best screenwriters around (SOUND OF MUSIC, NORTH BY NORTHWEST, WEST SIDE STORY, THE SWEET SMELL OF SUCCESS) but he may have been too respectful of O'Hara in his attempt to cram most of the original material into the screenplay. When Paul Newman is on his game, he's marvelous, as in HUD, HARPER, AND HOMBRE (to name three pictures that begin with "H" his lucky letter). But when he's bad, as in THE SECRET WAR OF HARRY FRIGG, WHAT A WAY TO GO! and THE LIFE AND TIMES OF JUDGE ROY BEAN, he is dreadful. This picture ranks with the latter. One of the few saving graces was the work of Myrna Loy as Newman's mother. She did the best of anyone with a sharply etched portrayal of a tortured alcoholic married to an iceberg and having to seek warmth in the arms of other men. Character actress Blossom Rock was Jeanette MacDonald's sister who labored in the bit part vineyards for decades.

p&d, Mark Robson; w, Ernest Lehman (based on the novel by John O'Hara); ph, Leo Tover (CinemaScope, DeLuxe Color); m, Elmer Bernstein; ed, Dorothy Spencer; art d, Lyle Wheeler, Howard Richman, Maurice Ransford; set d, Walter M. Scott, Paul S. Fox; cos, Travilla; spec eff, James B. Gordon, L.B. Abbott.

Drama   Cas.   (PR:C MPAA:NR)

FROM THIS DAY FORWARD**½   (1946) 95m RKO bw

Mark Stevens (Bill Cummings), Joan Fontaine (Susan), Rosemary DeCamp (Martha), Henry Morgan (Hank), Wally Brown (Jake), Arline Judge (Margie), Renny McEvoy (Charlie), Bobby Driscoll (Timmy), Queenie Smith (Mrs. Beesley), Doreen McCann (Barbara), Erskine Sanford (Higgler), Mary Treen (Alice), Ellen Corby (Mother), George Magrill (Man), Jack Gargan (Milkman), Tom Noonan (Attendant), Moroni Olsen (Tim Bagley), Ralph Dunn (Bailiff), Ida Moore (Hairdresser), Nan Leslie (Girl), Charles Wagenheim (Hoffman), Milton Kibbee (Factory Foreman).

Stevens is a returned war hero who settles down with his new wife, Fontaine, in New York's tenement district. Their story is told in flashback (a convenient method to cover an unsure script) revealing the beginnings of their romance, the draft, and his hassles with government employment centers. Their undying love, however, conquers all, including the Great Depression—and the critics' pen.

p, William L. Pereira; d, John Berry; w, Garson Kanin, Edith R. Sommer, Hugo Butler, Charles Schnee (based on the novel All Brides Are Beautiful by Thomas Bell); ph, George Barnes; m, Leigh Harline; ed, Frank Doyle; md, C. Bakaleinikoff; art d, Albert S. D'Agostino, Alfred H. Herman; set d, Darrell Silvera; spec eff, Vernon L. Walker; m/l, "From This Day Forward," Mort Greene, Harline.

Drama   (PR:A MPAA:NR)

FROM TOP TO BOTTOM**½   (1933, Fr.) 80m Tobis-Klangfilm/Films Sonores Tobis bw (DU HAUT EN BAS)

Jean Gabin (Charles Boulla), Jeannine Crispin (Marie de Ferstel), Michel Simon (Maximilian Podeletz), Mauricet (Binder), Wladimir Sokoloff (Berger), Leon Morton (Concierge), Milly Mathis (Poldi), Margo Lion (Mme. Binder), Catherine Hessling (Girl In Love), Peter Lorre (Beggar), Pauline Carton (Seamstress).

A disappointing comedy of manners from the great German director, G.W. Pabst, which concentrates mostly on Viennese community life while telling the tale of an uneducated soccer player, Gabin, who meets and is tutored by an unemployed teacher, Crispin. Failing with this picture, his second made in France after he left Germany when the Nazis took over, Pabst set out for America, but made only one film, A MODERN HERO (staring Richard Barthelmess) before returning, disillusioned, to France. FROM TOP TO BOTTOM also marked the last time Pabst worked with the noted German expressionist art director Metzner. (Metzner made a major contribution to German silents by directing the landmark short, DER UEBERFALL.) Also notable is this film's cinematographer, Schuefftan, who created a "glass shot" technique where real backgrounds are blended with mirror images, one that later became known as the "Schuefftan Effect." There has been some confusion as to whether Lorre or Paul Lukas appeared in the role of the beggar in FROM TOP TO BOTTOM, some saying that Lorre only dubbed his voice. It is obvious from studying frames of this film, even though the tramp is shown in some distance, that, indeed, Lorre appears in the role.

p, Georges Root; d, G.W. Pabst; w, Anna Gneynner (based on a play by Ladislaus Bus Fekete); ph, Eugen Schuefftan; m, Marcel Lattes; ed, Jean Oser; art d, Erno Metzner; m/l, "Chaque Semaine a Sept Jours," Herbert Rappoport.

Comedy   (PR:A MPAA:NR)

FRONT, THE*½   (1976) 94m COL c

Woody Allen (Howard Prince), Zero Mostel (Hecky Brown), Herschel Bernardi (Phil Sussman), Michael Murphy (Alfred Miller), Andrea Marcovicci (Florence Barrett), Remak Ramsey (Hennessey), Marvin Lichterman (Myer Prince), Lloyd Gough (Delaney), David Margulies (Phelps), Joshua Shelley (Sam), Norman Rose (Howard's Attorney), Danny Aiello (Danny La Gattuta), Scott McKay (Hampton), Julie Garfield (Margo), Charles Kimbrough (Committee Counselor), M. Josef Sommer (Committee Chairman), Georgann Johnson, David Clarke, I.W. Klein, John Bentley, Murray Moston, McIntyre Dixon, Rudolph Wilrich, Burt Britton, Albert M. Ottenheimer, William Bogert, Joey Faye, Marilyn Sokol, John J. Slater, Renee

Paris, Gino Gennaro, Joan Porter, Andrew Bernstein, Jacob Bernstein, Matthew Tobin, Marilyn Persky, Sam McMurray, Joe Ramrog, Michael Miller, Lucy Lee Flippin, Jack Davidson, Donald Symington, Patrick McNamara.

Uninspired comedy, THE FRONT has Allen as a cashier who "fronts" for blacklisted artists during the witchhunting McCarthy era, including many in the production who were really blacklisted—Ritt, Bernstein, and Mostel. Disjointed, with a story line so thin it could pass for linguine, the film flits from one conspiratorial meeting to the next, one allegation to the next, without resolve and few laughs. It's not a funny subject and Allen's attempt to sneak a message behind the belly humor fails miserably. Mostel is good in the serious role of a comic ruined by political hate-mongers. He is asked to spy on Allen so he can squeeze out a living and refuses, committing suicide rather than betraying a friend. (The Mostel role is patterned after Philip Loeb, according to one report. Loeb was the on-air partner of Gertrude Berg, starring in the TV show, "The Goldbergs." The left-leaning Loeb was fired from his job and, when he could no longer pay to have his mentally ill son kept in a private hospital, causing the youth to be put in a state institution, he committed suicide.) Everybody is uncomfortable in this messy production which was undoubtedly the product of a bull session where a retribution against the Red Hunters was decided upon, but it came 20 years too late. The 1950s newsreel footage interspersed with the dramatic scenes does not help but merely appears to be a forced device to establish the era—shots of President Harry Truman, Sen. Joe McCarthy, battle scenes of the Korean war, etc—and the "ironic" music overlapping, that of Frank Sinatra singing "Young At Heart," is a ripoff of Vera Lynn's vocal at the end of DR. STRANGELOVE. Allen is in love with newsreel footage, as this and many of his other productions (ZELIG 1983) show, as a method, no doubt, to authenticate his filmic statements. The device merely appears contrived in that the newsreel clips are jammed between dramatic scenes, often as not having no relevancy. Nothing works here.

p&d, Martin Ritt; w, Walter Bernstein; ph, Michael Chapman (Panavision, Technicolor); m, Dave Grusin; ed, Sidney Levin; art d, Charles Bailey; set d, Robert Drumheller; cos, Ruth Morley.

Drama/Comedy   Cas.   (PR:C MPAA:PG)

FRONT LINE KIDS**   (1942, Brit.) 80m Signet/BUT bw

Leslie Fuller (Nobby Clarkson), Marion Gerth (Elsa la Rue), Anthony Holles (Hotelier), Gerald Rex (Bert Wragg), John Singer (Ginger Smith), George Pughe (Pinski), Ralph Michael (Paul), Eric Clavering (Carl), O.B. Clarence, David Keir, Norman Pierce, Vi Kaley, Douglas Stewart, Ben Williams, Vincent Holman, Norah Gordon, Gerald Moore, John Tacchi, David Anthony, Michael John, Brian Fitzpatrick, Derek Prendergast, Kay Lewis.

A bunch of street kids are given jobs at a hotel run by a man hoping to use his pretty female companion to take advantage of jewel thieves. The kids use the wisdom they've gained from the streets to thwart the plotting of the manager as well as of the thieves. Evenly paced in both direction and screenplay to create a pleasant little effort.

p, Hugh Perceval; d, Maclean Rogers; w, Kathleen Butler, H.F. Maltby (based on a story by John Byrd); ph, Stephen Dade.

Comedy   (PR:AA MPAA:NR)

FRONT PAGE, THE*****   (1931) 101m Caddo/Hughes/UA bw

Adolphe Menjou (Walter Burns), Pat O'Brien (Hildy Johnson), Mary Brian (Peggy), Edward Everett Horton (Bensinger), Walter Catlett (Murphy), George E. Stone (Earl Williams), Mae Clarke (Molly), Slim Summerville (Pincus), Matt Moore (Kruger), Frank McHugh (McCue), Clarence H. Wilson (Sheriff Hartman), Fred Howard (Schwartz), Phil Tead (Wilson), Eugene Strong (Endicott), Spencer Charters (Woodenshoe), Maurice Black (Diamond Louie), Effie Ellsler (Mrs. Grant), Dorothea Wolbert (Jenny), James Gordon (The Mayor), Dick Alexander (Jacobi).

A virile, dizzy-paced drama which has become the classic film on newspapers and newsmen, THE FRONT PAGE portrayed a glorious headline era, one that will be thankfully remembered because of this Milestone classic. O'Brien, in his film debut, is the fast-talking Hildy Johnson, the sensation hunting star of the Chicago press. His shifty, wholly untrustworthy editor, Menjou, is trying to prevent his star reporter from quitting the business and moving from Chicago to a New York advertising job, following his impending marriage to goodie-goodie Brian. Most of the action takes place in the press room of Chicago's Criminal Courts Building. (This building is still standing as a detective center, behind which, in the days of Hecht and MacArthur, the condemned were hanged in a courtyard with bleachers holding press and public alike, spectators of these macabre executions vying for tickets doled out by the local, corrupt sheriff.) Brian hates Menjou, O'Brien's job, and the sleazy tabloid world which has made him famous, and she pressures O'Brien to finish his last day's work so they can flee to New York on the Twentieth Century, the fastest luxury train available, with her mother, Ellsler, in tow. In his last visit to the press room to say goodbye to his newspaper cronies, O'Brien gets caught up in the escape of an anarchist, Stone, who is scheduled for execution that night. (Typical of the raucous death-house humor is a request by one of the reporters of the sheriff, asking him if he will move up the hanging so he can meet his 5 p.m. deadline.) O'Brien finds Stone hiding in the rolltop desk used by Tribune reporter Horton and tries to shield him so that his paper can get the exclusive on the story. Much of the action involves Menjou and O'Brien trying to keep Stone in the desk and move it out of the press room before the other reporters discover the anarchist's presence. O'Brien also has to contend with Clarke, Stone's prostitute friend who jumps from a window to prove her love for the condemned man (she survives), and his fiancee and her mother. In the end, the conniving reporter and editor are exposed and threatened by the sheriff and mayor with arrest for harboring a fugitive. But Menjou, ever the resourceful newsman, has enough on the politicians to send them into their own jail. When O'Brien discovers that Stone escaped by using the sheriff's own gun, one the sheriff lent to Stone to reenact a killing for the prison psychiatrist, the newsmen are off the hook. Nothing can now stop O'Brien from leaving for New York with Brian. As a parting gift, and to show his deep fondness for O'Brien, Menjou gives him his gold watch, one inscribed: "To the chief from the boys." O'Brien departs but Menjou has no intention of losing his star reporter. He calls police and tells them to stop the train at the next stop, stating at film's comic end: "The son-of-a-bitch stole my watch!" (Part of this statement was obliterated by the noise of a typewriter carriage.) THE FRONT PAGE is an excellent production with superior performances from film novice O'Brien and a wonderful rascally part rendered by the sophisticated but ever wily Menjou. (O'Brien's role is patterned after co-author Charles MacArthur and his wild and unpredictable editor Menjou is based upon Walter Howey of the Chicago *Tribune*, a man who would stop at nothing for a news story, even to the point of creating it himself.) Hughes, who used the name of his own firm, the Caddo Rock Drill Bit Company, as the production company, let Milestone have has creative way with the film which shows in its no-holds-barred action and dialog of wit and wacky humor, presented with a pace that whirls the story past the viewer like an "extra" shooting off the press. Hughes did make two decisions on the film, vetoing the director's first two choices for the remarkable Hildy Johnson role. Milestone first selected James Cagney to play the brash newsman, but Hughes said no, calling the great actor "a little runt." Then Milestone proposed Clark Gable and Hughes rejected the future King of Hollywood, saying that Gable's "ears make him look like a taxi-cab with both doors open!" O'Brien, who had been acting in New York and had appeared in the stage version of "The Front Page," was contacted by a Hughes agent and signed at $750 a week on a five-year contract. When O'Brien showed up at the studio he shocked MIlestone by telling him he had never played Hildy Johnson on Broadway, that he had played the editor's part and only in a road show in Cleveland. He kept the part anyway. The editor's role was first given to the great character actor Louis Wolheim, but he died of a stroke three weeks into production and a rush for a replacement ensued with Arthur Byron and Richard Bennett (father of actresses Joan and Constance) suggested and discarded. (No one ever thought of using Osgood Perkins, father of Tony, who had played the role on Broadway.) Milestone performed a coup by signing the urbane, polished Menjou as the scheming editor Walter Burns. The decision first surprised everyone but Menjou adjusted to the low-down role with relish. When he first appeared on the set, he found O'Brien shooting dice with character actors McHugh and Catlett. Barging in and kneeling down to join the action, he said: "Hi, suckers. Save the introductions for later. I await my turn at the dice." The debonair lothario of films discarded his sleek pose and knelt on knifeblade creases in his pants, rolling the dice until dawn when he stood up, dusted himself off, and said with aplomb: "Bring on some real plungers!" All of the character actors shine in the reporter roles, from the cynical Catlett and McHugh to the fussy, sanitary-obsessed Horton, the reporter who believes himself to be a poet. Horton is hired by Menjou from the *Tribune* for his own rag just to get him out of the press room and, while going to Menjou's paper to be given his poetry column, is fired by Menjou via a phone conversation with Menjou's city editor who is told to "kick him down the stairs!" The dialog from the play was kept almost intact, with all the wild newspaper argot, glib quips, and slurs delivered rapid-fire by the actors as in the play. Remade as HIS GIRL FRIDAY, 1940.

p, Howard Hughes; d, Lewis Milestone; w, Bartlett Cormack and (uncredited) Ben Hecht, Charles Lederer (based on the play by Ben Hecht and Charles MacArthur); ph, Glen McWilliams, Hal Mohr, (uncredited) Tony Gaudio; ed, W. Duncan Mansfield; art d, Richard Day.

Drama/Comedy **Cas.** **(PR:A MPAA:NR)**

FRONT PAGE, THE*** (1974) 105m UNIV c

Jack Lemmon *(Hildy Johnson)*, Walter Matthau *(Walter Burns)*, Carol Burnett *(Mollie Malloy)*, Susan Sarandon *(Peggy Grant)*, Vincent Gardenia *(Sheriff)*, David Wayne *(Bensinger)*, Allen Garfield *(Kruger)*, Austin Pendleton *(Earl Williams)*, Charles Durning *(Murphy)*, Herbert Edelman *(Schwartz)*, Martin Gabel *(Dr. Eggelhofer)*, Harold Gould *(The Mayor)*, Cliff Osmond *(Jacobi)*, Dick O'Neill *(McHugh)*, Jon Korkes *(Rudy Keppler)*, Lou Frizzell *(Endicott)*, Paul Benedict *(Plunkett)*, Doro Merande *(Jennie)*, Noam Pitlik *(Wilson)*, Joshua Shelley *(Cab Driver)*, Allen Jenkins *(Telegrapher)*, John Furlong *(Duffy)*, Biff Elliot *(Police Dispatcher)*, Barbara Davis *(Myrtle)*, Leonard Breman *(Butch)*.

This slick remake of the ebullient original falls short of the film it could have been, despite the presence of master filmmaker Wilder. Lemmon, as the cock-sure reporter, and Matthau as his calculating editor, are both standouts but the rest of the cast try too hard to fill the giant footsteps of those who earlier occupied the roles. Lemmon is bound for New York with Sarandon to begin a new life but Matthau uses the escape of anarchist Pendleton to hold him on the job, ignoring the pleas of prostitute Burnett who is in love with the condemned man. The hide-and-seek game the newsmen play with authorities in covering up the wanted man's whereabouts is forced and only Gabel, as the balmy psychiatrist, gives a hillarious performance. Durning is too vicious for the newsman role he plays, as is Garfield; Hecht and MacArthur had drawn their characters as jocular, not sadistic, personalities but this posturing is no doubt Wilder's doing, the work of an absolute cynic, gifted as he was, where the mean-streaked German flaw, the "fatal flaw" Goethe once cited, overpowered the script and even the superb performances of the leads. Despite the obvious charismatic interaction between Lemmon and Matthau, the film is oddly stilted. Pendleton overacts with a mindless, flaky attitude while Burnett is simply awful in reprising the Mary Brian role. She projects only one emotion—a gratingly annoying hysteria, as if trying to screech around a sword reluctantly swallowed before stepping onto the set. Wilder was much more effective with Lemmon and Matthau in THE FORTUNE COOKIE (1966) and their teaming in THE ODD COUPLE (1968) was even more humorous. This one just doesn't have the big story at press time. Wilder also mistakenly attempted to "modernize" the story, though it retains its 1929 setting, by introducing more vulgarity than the original Hecht, MacArthur script depicted.

p, Paul Monash; d, Billy Wilder; w, Wilder, I.A.L. Diamond (based on the play by Ben Hecht, Charles MacArthur), ph, Jordan S. Cronenweth (Panavision, Technicolor); m, Billy May; ed, Ralph E. Winters; art d, Henry Bumstead; set d, James W. Payne; cos, Burton Miller; m/l, "Button Up Your Overcoat," B. G. DeSylva, Lew Brown, Ray Henderson (sung by Susan Sarandon), "That Old Gang of Mine" (sung by Jack Lemmon and male chorus).

Drama/Comedy **(PR:C-O MPAA:PG)**

FRONT PAGE STORY½** (1954, Brit.) 99m 1954 BL bw

Jack Hawkins *(John Grant)*, Elizabeth Allan *(Susan Grant)*, Eva Bartok *(Mrs. Thorpe)*, Derek Farr *(Teale)*, Michael Goodliffe *(Kennedy)*, Martin Miller *(Dr. Brukmann)*, Patricia Marmont *(Julie)*, Joseph Tomelty *(Dan)*, Jenny Jones *(Jenny)*, Stephen Vercoe *(Craig)*, Helen Haye *(Susan's Mother)*, Michael Howard *(Barrow)*, Guy Middleton *(Gentle)*, Henry Mollison *(Lester)*, Gordon Bell *(Jackson)*, Tristram Rawson *(Judge)*, John Stewart *(Prosecution)*, Bruce Beeby *(Defense)*, Ronald Adam *(Editor)*, Walter Fitzgerald *(Black)*.

Hawkins is a newsman who is too devoted to his paper to take a much-needed vacation with his wife (Allan). Instead, he stays in the office and handles a number of interesting stories. The routine newsroom soap opera technique is neatly followed here, allowing for a substantial amount of drama. The hot items of the day—four kids evicted from their home, a woman charged with mercy killing, and a drunken ex-reporter on the hunt for an atomic scientist—culminate with the story of a plane crash. Hawkins' wife, Allan, is listed as one of the passengers, but it turns out that she did not take the plane. A lucid look behind the headlines at the people who make and write the news.

p, Jay Lewis; d, Gordon Parry; w, Lewis, Jack Howells, William Fairchild, Guy Morgan (based on the novel *Final Night* by Robert Gaines); ph, Gilbert Taylor; m, Michael Carr; ed, Bill Lewthwaite; md, Jackie Brown.

Drama **(PR:A MPAA:NR)**

FRONT PAGE WOMAN½** (1935) 81m WB bw

Bette Davis *(Ellen Garfield)*, George Brent *(Curt Devlin)*, Roscoe Karns *(Toots)*, Winifred Shaw *(Inez Cordova)*, Joseph Crehan *(Spike Kiley)*, Joseph King *(Hartnett)*, J. Farrell Macdonald *(Hallohan)*, Addison Richards *(District Attorney)*, Dorothy Dare, June Martel *(Show Girls)*, Selmer Jackson *(Joe Davis)*, Gordon Westcott *(Maitland Colter)*, J. Carroll Naish *(Mr. Roberts)*, Walter Walker *(Judge Rickard)*, DeWitt C. Jennings *(Lieutenant)*, Huntley Gordon *(Marvin Q. Stone)*, Adrian Rosley *(Tailor)*, Georges Renevant *(Chinard)*, Miki Morita *(Fuji)*, Adrian Morris, Eddie Shubert *(Guards)*, George Guhl, James Burtis *(Motor Cops)*, Frank Glendon, Edward Keane, Jack Norton, Charles E. Delaney, Harry Seymour *(Reporters)*, Mary Treen *(Nurse)*, Mary Foy *(Landlady)*, Dick Winslow *(Copy Boy)*, Leo White, Ben F. Hendricks *(Taxi Drivers)*, James Farley *(Bailiff)*, Wade Boteler *(Cop)*, Charles Moore *(Black Boy)*, Lester Dorr, Jerry Mandy *(Waiters)*, Torben Meyer *(Janitor)*, Grace Hayle, Mike Monk.

As far-fetched a newspaper yarn as ever concocted, FRONT PAGE WOMAN is not quite funny enough to rank as a full-fledged comedy but it has enough moments in it to please undiscerning audiences. George Brent is the Ben Hecht of his newspaper. Bette Davis writes the agony column for a rival rag. They are in love but Brent is a chauvinist who thinks a woman's place is not in the editorial office. Davis wants to marry Brent but she won't do it until she can show Brent that women have printer's ink running just as thickly in their veins. While covering a greater alarm fire, Davis sees two men leave the burning edifice and race away in a taxi. She follows them as well as she can but eventually loses the trail. Later, she's at a local hospital and she recognizes a man who is there, mortally wounded from stab wounds (Gordon). She writes the story and scoops the other papers, tying in the dead man with the fire. Brent ho-hums her story, says she was just lucky and that a real newshound would have been able to hunt down the murderer. Davis goes out to attempt that. Meanwhile, Brent gets some circumstantial evidence together and Westcott is arrested for Gordon's death. In his investigations, Brent interviews Shaw, who promptly vanishes after the conversation. A trial begins and Brent, with the aid of Karns, the staff photographer, eavesdrops on the jury's deliberations by cutting a hole in the wall. Now, to have some fun with Davis, Brent tosses some "not guilty" ballots into the jury's ballot box and Davis falls for that. She phones in what she thinks is a scoop and her paper runs the headline that Westcott was found innocent. However, the jury finds him guilty and Brent gets that scoop. Davis is fired for her miscue, goes to the jail, and talks to Wescott. After a brief meeting, she is determined that he's been railroaded, Brent is also in jail for contempt-of-court. Davis finds Shaw and learns she is the real killer. She secures a written confession and gets it to her former editor, Crehan. The man is so impressed with her work that he gives her the old job back. Brent is released and reluctantly agrees that there are some women who actually do make "good newspapermen." You don't believe it for one second, but the picture is so good-natured and some of the lines are so witty that you are willing to forgive story holes so large that the entire rolling stock of AMTRAK could ride through.

p, Sam Bischoff; d, Michael Curtiz; w, Roy Chanslor, Lillie Hayward, Laird Doyle (based on the story "Women Are Bum Newspapermen" by Richard Macauley); ph, Tony Gaudio; m, Heinz Roemheld; ed, Terry Morse; md, Leo F. Forbstein; art d, John Hughes.

Comedy/Drama **(PR:A MPAA:NR)**

FRONTIER AGENT*½ (1948) 56m MON bw

Johnny Mack Brown *("Nevada" Jack McKensie)*, Raymond Hatton *(Sandy Hopkins)*, Reno Blair, Kenneth MacDonald, Dennis Moore, Riley Hill, Frank LaRue, Ted Adams, Virginia Carroll, William Ruhl, Kansas Moehring, Bill Hale, Lane Bradford, Bob Woodward, Boyd Stockman.

Brown is cast as a government agent who dons chaps and a ten-gallon hat in order to catch the bad guys. He does so with his usual flair and the assistance of fellow lawman and comic sidekick "Oldtimer" Hatton.

p, Barney Sarecky; d, Lambert Hillyer; w, J. Benton Cheney; ph, Harry Neumann; ed, Fred Maguire; md, Edward Kay.

Western **(PR:A MPAA:NR)**

FRONTIER BADMEN**½ (1943) 77m UNIV bw

Robert Paige (Steve), Anne Gwynne (Chris), Noah Beery, Jr. (Jim), Diana Barrymore (Claire), Leo Carrillo (Chinito), Andy Devine (Slim), Thomas Gomez (Ballard), Frank Lackteen (Cherokee), William Farnum (Courtwright), Lon Chaney, Jr. (Chango), Tex Ritter (Kimball), Robert Homans (Sheriff), Tom Fadden (Thompson), Arthur Loft (Lindsay), Norman Willis (Randall), Jack Rockwell (Mack), Stanley Price (Blackie), George Eldredge (Cattle Buyer), Earle Hodgins (Desk Clerk), Eddy Waller (Auctioneer), Charles Wagenheim (Melvin), Fern Emmett (Milliner), Kermit Maynard (Townsman), Beverly Mitchell (Waitress).

A good B oater with a decent supporting cast sees Paige and his sidekick Beery as cattlemen who drive their herd down the Chisholm Trail to Abilene, Kansas, only to discover that evil Gomez has a stranglehold on the local cattle market, which is enforced by Chaney. Paige and Beery decide to short-circuit Gomez's operation by starting up their own independent exchange. The usual fistfights and showdowns occur and in the end Paige and Beery end up on top.

p&d, Ford Beebe, co-d, William McGann; w, Gerald Geraghty, Morgan B. Cox; ph, William Sickner; ed, Fred Feitshans; md, H.J. Salter; art d, John B. Goodman, Ralph DeLacy; set d, Russell Gausman, Leigh Smith.

Western (PR:A MPAA:NR)

FRONTIER CRUSADER*½ (1940) 62m PRC bw

Tim McCoy (Trigger Tim Rand), Dorothy Short (Jenny Mason), Lou Fulton (Lanky Lent), Karl Hackett (Barney Bronson), Ted Adams (Jack Trask), John Merton (Hippo Potts), Forrest Taylor (John Stoner), Hal Price (Sheriff Dolan), Kenne Duncan (Mesa Kid), George Chesebro, Frank Ellis, Reed Howes, Lane Bradford.

McCoy battles bad guys Merton and Hackett, who steal a payroll in attempting to prevent an honest mining company from developing a rich vein of gold. Some more clatter of hoofbeats and cracking of heads and pistols from Producers Releasing Corp. in Gower Gulch.

p, Sigmund Neufeld; d, Peter Stewart [Sam Newfield]; w, William Lively (based on a story by Arthur Durlam); ph, Jack Greenhalgh; ed, Holbrook N. Todd.

Western (PR:A MPAA:NR)

FRONTIER DAYS** (1934) 61m Spectrum bw

Bill Cody, Ada Ince, Wheeler Oakman, Franklyn Farnum, William Desmond, Bill Cody, Jr., Lafe McKee, Vic Potel, Chico the Horse.

Cody is an undercover agent for the Fargo Express who is assigned to capture the head of a stagecoach robbery gang. Along the way he meets Ince and her father, Farnum. When the gang cheats Farnum out of his ranch and then kills him, Cody charges forward and finally brings the leader of the gang, crooked banker Oakman, to justice.

p, Al Alt [Ray Kirkwood]; d, Bob Hill; w, James Shawkey (based on a story by Norman Springer); ph, Brydon Baker; ed, S. Roy Luby.

Western (PR:A MPAA:NR)

FRONTIER FEUD** (1945) 54m MON bw

Johnny Mack Brown (Nevada), Raymond Hatton (Sandy), Dennis Moore (Joe), Christine McIntyre (Blanche), Jack Ingram (Don Graham), Edwin Parker (Murphy), Frank La Rue (Chalmers), Steve Clark (Bill Corey), Jack Rockwell (Sheriff Clancy), Mary MacLaren (Sarah Moran), Edmund Cobb (Moran), Lloyd Ingraham (Si Peters) Charles King, Stanley Price.

Every kid's hero Brown and his comic sidekick Hatton are federal marshals investigating a series of murders tied to a ranchers' feud. Though good rancher Moore is a likely suspect, he is cleared when the marshals catch the real culprits.

p, Charles J. Bigelow; d, Lambert Hillyer; w, Jess Bowers [Adele Buffington] (based on a story by Charles N. Hecklemann); ph, Harry Neumann; ed, Dan Milner.

Western (PR:A MPAA:NR)

FRONTIER FUGITIVES* (1945) 58m PRC bw

Tex Ritter, Dave O'Brien, Guy Wilkerson, Lorraine Miller, I. Stanford Jolley, Jack Ingram, Frank Ellis, Jack Hendricks, Charles King, Karl Hackett, Budd Buster.

Ritter and his fellow Rangers investigate the murder of a trapper supposedly killed by Indians. They then discover that his killers were really whites in disguise trying to locate some furs the trapper had hidden. (See TEXAS RANGERS series, Index.)

p, Arthur Alexander; d, Harry Fraser; w, Elmer Clifton; ph, Robert Cline; ed, Holbrook N. Todd; md, Lee Zahler.

Western (PR:A MPAA:NR)

FRONTIER FURY** (1943) 55m COL bw

Charles Starrett (Steve Langdon), Arthur Hunnicutt (Arkansas Tuttle), Roma Aldrich (Stella Larkin), Clancy Cooper (Dan Bentley), I. Stanford Jolley (Nick Dawson), Edmund Cobb (Tracy Meade), Bruce Bennett (Clem Hawkins), Ted Mapes (Jim Wallace), Bill Wilkerson (Chief Eagle Feather), Stanley Brown (Gray Bear), Joel Friedkin (Doc Hewes), Jimmy Davis and His Singing Buckaroos, Frank LaRue, Lew Meehan, Chief Yowlachie, Johnny Bond.

Starrett plays an honest Indian agent who loses his job when he is robbed of the government monies allotted to the tribe. Not wanting to see his redskin charges starve through a rough winter, he sets out to capture the thieves by tracing some rare coins that were among the cash. After a couple of rough run-ins with the bandits, his Indian friends ride to the rescue and recover the money. Another in a long stream of westerns (going back before Wally Wales/Hal Taliaferro in the middle 1920s) by Burbridge, that most unusual of movie scenarists, a woman writer of western movies.

p, Jack Fier; d, William Berke; w, Betty Burbridge; ph, Benjamin Kline; ed, Jerome Thoms; art d, Lionel Banks.

Western (PR:A MPAA:NR)

FRONTIER GAL*** (1945) 84m UNIV c
(GB: THE BRIDE WASN'T WILLING)

Yvonne De Carlo (Lorena Dumont), Rod Cameron (Johnny Hart), Andy Devine (Big Ben), Fuzzy Knight (Fuzzy), Sheldon Leonard (Blackie), Andrew Tombes (Judge Prescott), Beverly Sue Simmons (Mary Ann Hart), Clara Blandick (Abigail), Frank Lackteen (Cherokee), Claire Carleton (Gracie), Eddie Dunn, Harold Goodwin (Bailiffs), Jack Overman (Buffalo), Jan Wiley (Sheila Winthrop), Rex Lease, George Eldredge, Jack Ingram, Joseph Haworth (Henchmen), Lloyd Ingraham, Joseph E. Bernard, Douglas Carter, Lou Wood, Paul Bratti (Dealers), Edward M. Howard (Henchman at Bar), Jean Trent, Joan Fulton [Shawlee], Kerry Vaughn, Karen Randle (Hostesses), Eddie Lee (Wing Lee, Candy-Shop Proprietor), Jack O'Shea, Billy Engle (Barflies), Cliff Lyons (Brawler in Candy Shop/Double for Blackie), Jack Rutherford (Bit at Table), Eddie Borden (Man at Table), William Desmond, Kit Guard (Extras in Saloon).

Fun comedy western sees De Carlo as a saloon owner who falls for dashing bandit Cameron while he is on the run from a posse. She quickly pushes him into a shotgun wedding when she finds that his intentions are not strictly honorable, and then turns him over to the law. He escapes and shows up at the saloon for a one-night honeymoon before he disappears into the badlands. Six years later he resurfaces to discover he is the father of scene-stealing moppet Simmons, whose purpose on Earth, it seems, is to reunite her parents. Cute little oater that established De Carlo as a star.

p, Michael Fessier, Ernest Pagano; d, Charles Lamont; w, Fessier, Pagano; ph, George Robinson, Charles P. Boyle (Technicolor); m, Frank Skinner; ed, Ray Snyder; md, Skinner; art d, John S. Goodman, Richard H. Riedel; set d, Russell A. Gausman, Oliver Emert; spec eff, John P. Fulton; m/l, "Set 'Em Up, Joe," "What Is Love," (sung by Yvonne De Carlo), "Johnny's Comin' Home" (sung by Fuzzy Knight), Jack Brooks, Edgar Fairchild.

Western (PR:A MPAA:NR)

FRONTIER GAMBLER* (1956) 70m ARC bw

John Bromfield, Coleen Gray, Jim Davis, Kent Taylor, Margia Dean, Veda Ann Borg, Tracey Roberts, Stanley Andrews, Roy Engel, Nadene Ashdown, Frank Sully, Pierce Lyden, Ewing Brown, Rick Vallin, John Merton, Helen Jay.

When the most powerful woman in a small western town disappears, the lover she jilted is naturally blamed. A typical low-budget affair cranked out of the oater mill.

p, Sigmund Neufeld; d, Sam Newfield; w, Orville Hampton.

Western (PR:A MPAA:NR)

FRONTIER GUN** (1958) 70m Regal/FOX bw

John Agar (Jim Crayle), Joyce Meadows (Peg Barton), Barton MacLane (Simon Crayle), Robert Strauss (Yubo), Lyn Thomas (Kate Durand), Morris Ankrum (Andrew Barton), James Griffith (Cash Skelton), Leslie Bradley (Rev. Jacob Hall), Doodles Weaver (Eph Loveman), Mike Ragan (Tanner), Sammy Ogg (Virgil Barton), George Brand (Judge Ard Becker), Tom Daly (Cowhand), Claire DuBrey (Bess Loveman), Daniel White (Sam Kilgore), Dan Simmons (Harry Corman), Sydney Mason (Doc Studdeford), Boyd Stockman (Marshall Swain).

After bad man Strauss terrorizes his small town, Agar volunteers to become town marshal and eliminate the beast. The odds are against him because he is slow in the draw due to a wrist injury, but when Strauss kills his father, the new marshal puts a bullet in the outlaw's head. Good cinematography by Walter Strenge, but audiences found that it was becoming increasingly hard for spiritless Agar to carry a film.

p, Richard E. Lyons; d, Paul Landres; w, Stephen Kandel; ph, Walter Strenge (Regalscope); m, Paul Dunlap; ed, Robert Fritch.

Western (PR:A MPAA:NR)

FRONTIER HELLCAT** (1966, Fr./Ital./Ger./Yugo.) 98m Rialto-Atlantis-S.N.C.-Jadran/COL c (UNTER GEIRN; PARMI LES VAUTOURS; MEDJU JASTREBOVIMA; AKA: AMONG VULTURES)

Stewart Granger (Old Surehand), Pierre Brice (Winnetou), Elke Sommer (Annie), Gotz George (Martin Baumann), Walter Barnes (Baumann), Sieghardt Rupp (Preston), Miha Baloh (Weller), Renato Baldini (Leader), Mario Girotti (Baker), Louis Velle (Gordon), Paddy Fox (Old Wabble), Voja Miric (Steward), Stole Arandjelovic (Milton), Djordje Nenedovic (Miller), Georg Mitic (Wakadeh), Gordana Cosic (Wakadeh's Sister), Dusan Bulajic (Bloomfield), Dunja Rajter (Betsy), Milan Srdoc.

Granger, a self-appointed lawman, gets himself in a bind with a band of outlaws known as the Vultures, who disguise themselves as Indians to terrorize local prospectors. Sommer is kidnaped by the gang while carrying some diamonds, but she is rescued by her true love, George, who in turn gets captured. This time it's Granger's chance to prove his bravery. After performing some daring feats he saves George's skin. Together with Granger's blood brother, Brice, the pair defeat the bad guys. A multi-national production supposedly set in Arizona. Released in Germany in 1964 at 102m.

p, Preben Philipsen; d, Alfred Vohrer; w, Eberhard Keindorff, Johanna Sibelius (based on the novel by Karl May); ph, Karl Loeb (CinemaScope, Eastmancolor); m, Martin Boettcher; ed, Hermann Haller; art d, Vladimir Tadej; cos, Irms Pauli.

Western (PR:A MPAA:NR)

FRONTIER INVESTIGATOR** (1949) 60m REP bw

Allan "Rocky" Lane (Himself), Eddy Waller (Nugget Clark), Roy Barcroft (Flint Fleming), Gail Davis (Janet Adams), Robert Emmett Keane (Erskine Doubleday), Clayton Moore (Scott Garnett), Francis Ford (Ed Garnett), Claire Whitney (Molly

Bright), Harry Lauter *(Kenny)*, Tom London *(Jed)*, George H. Lloyd *(Milton Leffingwell)*, Marshall Reed *(Outlaw)*.

Lane sets out to avenge the death of his younger brother who was shot by a man using a rifle with a telescopic sight (unusual for B westerns). The trail leads him to a frontier town where he takes a job as a stagecoach driver to have more time to hunt the killer. He soon finds himself embroiled in a shooting war between rival stagecoach companies and he captures his man. Fast-paced and well-shot by veteran cameraman Ernest Miller.

p, Gordon Kay; d, Fred C. Brannon; w, Bob Williams; ph, Ernest Miller; m, Stanley Wilson; ed, Arthur Roberts; art d, Frank Hotaling.

Western   **Cas.**   **(PR:A MPAA:NR)**

FRONTIER JUSTICE*½   (1936) 56m FD bw

Hoot Gibson *(Brent)*, Jane Barnes *(Ethel)*, Richard Cramer *(Ware)*, Roger Williams *(Wilton)*, John Elliott *(Ben)*, Franklyn Farnum *(Lessin)*, Lloyd Ingraham *(Dr. Crane)*, Joseph Girard *(Halston)*, Snowflake *(Snowflake)*, George Yeoman *(Sheriff)*, Lafe McKee.

Gibson is his usual silly self as the son of cattle owner who was framed by evil sheepherders who have managed to have the old man committed to an insane asylum. The conflict is over water rights and Gibson puts down his exploding cigars long enough to straighten things out. Cowboy Gibson felt that his comedy was growing stale and retired from the screen soon after FRONTIER JUSTICE, not to return to it for seven years.

p, Walter Futter; d, Robert McGowan; w, W. Scott Darling (based on a novel by Col. George B. Rodney); ph, Art Reed.

Western   **Cas.**   **(PR:A MPAA:NR)**

FRONTIER LAW*½   (1943) 55m UNIV bw

Russell Hayden *(Jim Warren)*, Jennifer Holt *(Lois Rogers)*, Dennis Moore *(Dusty)*, Fuzzy Knight *(Ramblin' Rufe Randall)*, Jack Ingram *(Hawkins)*, Hal Taliaferro *(Rogers)*, George Eldredge *(Slinger)*, I. Stanford Jolley *(Weasel)*, Frank LaRue *(Vernon)*, James Farley *(Bates)*, Art Fowler *(Dirk)*, Mike Vallon *(Ferrell)*, Earle Hodgins *(Coroner)*, Roy Butler *(Sheriff)*, Tex Cooper, Johnny Bond and his Red River Valley Boys.

Hayden leads a group of cowboys against an outlaw gang in order to clean up the town and clear the name of a friend wrongly accused of murder.

p, Oliver Drake; d&w, Elmer Clifton.

Western   **(PR:A MPAA:NR)**

FRONTIER MARSHAL**½   (1934) 66m FOX bw

George O'Brien *(Michael Wyatt)*, Irene Bentley *(Mary Reid)*, George E. Stone *(Abe Ruskin)*, Alan Edwards *(Doc Warren)*, Ruth Gillette *(Queenie LaVerne)*, Berton Churchill *(Hiram Melton)*, Frank Conroy *(Oscar Reid)*, Ward Bond *(Ben Murchison)*, Edward LeSaint *(Judge Walters)*, Russell Simpson *(Editor Pickett)*, Jerry Foster *(Jerome)*.

A novel that laid the basis for the Wyatt Earp legend, *Wyatt Earp, Frontier Marshal*, here is used a second time around (the first was for a silent film), with Earp's name changed to "Michael Wyatt" to forestall any suits the novelization of Earp's life might have opened up. O'Brien rides into town as a mysterious stranger, to bring law and order to a chaotic community ruled by a corrupt mayor. Routine formula stuff but engaging nevertheless.

p, Sol Lesser; d, Lew Seiler; w, William Conselman, Stuart Anthony (based on the novel *Wyatt Earp, Frontier Marshal* by Stuart N. Lake); ph, Robert Planck.

Western   **(PR:A MPAA:NR)**

FRONTIER MARSHAL***   (1939) 71m FOX bw

Randolph Scott *(Wyatt Earp)*, Nancy Kelly *(Sarah Allen)*, Cesar Romero *(Doc Halliday)*, Binnie Barnes *(Jerry)*, John Carradine *(Ben Carter)*, Edward Norris *(Dan Blackmore)*, Eddie Foy, Jr. *(Eddie Foy)*, Ward Bond *(Town Marshal)*, Lon Chaney, Jr. *(Pringle)*, Chris-Pin Martin *(Pete)*, Joe Sawyer *(Curly Bill)*, Harry Hayden *(Mayor Henderson)*, Ventura Ybarra *(Pablo)*, Charles Stevens *(Indian Charlie)*, Tom Tyler *(Buck Newton)*, Del Henderson *(Proprietor of Bella Union Cafe)*, Si Jenks *(Prospector)*, Gloria Roy *(Dance Hall Girl)*, Margaret Brayton *(Mother)*, Pat O'Malley *(Customer)*, Harry Woods, Dick Alexander *(Curly Bill's Men)*, John Bleifer, Hank Mann, Edward Le Saint, Heinie Conklin, George Melford *(Men)*, Fern Emmett *(Hotel Maid)*, Kathryn Sheldon *(Mrs. Garvey)*, Ferris Taylor *(Doctor)*, John Butler *(Harassed Man)*, Arthur Aylesworth, Eddie Dunn *(Card Players)*, Philo McCullough, Ethan Laidlaw *(Toughs)*.

Scott is the redoubtable western lawman Earp who enters Tombstone only to find it a wild and lethal hellhole. He goes to work with a vengeance, first subduing a drunken half breed, Stevens, who is shooting up the town, by merely clouting him over the head with his gun butt. He befriends Romero, playing the deadly Doc Holliday, and the two of them compete for Kelly while Barnes, Romero's sometimes dancehall girl friend, vies for the gunfighter's attentions. Romero has a bad heart (the real Doc had TB) and he is gunned down by Sawyer and his gang, which causes Scott to meet the bad guys in the famous battle at the O.K. Corral, emerging victorious and winning Kelly. This action-jammed film, based on a lot of fiction created by Earp biographer Lake, is expertly helmed by Dwan, a stellar silent film director. This same Earp life story had been filmed in 1934 with George O'Brien in the Earp role. John Ford's masterpiece, MY DARLING CLEMENTINE (1947), was wholly drawn from this 1939 film. Although the facts are sometimes fractured in this version, it is nevertheless enjoyable, with Scott and Romero giving top-notch performances and Eddie Foy, Jr. impersonating his father, who really was kidnapped by the Curly Bill Brocious gang and compelled to perform his act at their pleasure (Alan Mowbray reprised this role in MY DARLING CLEMENTINE with excellent results). Fox mogul, Darryl Zanuck, insisted the actual name of Wyatt Earp be used in this production, which caused the studio to pay $5,000 to an Earp relative for the use of the name, and yet the relative still sued Fox after

the film was released, saying that the Scott-Kelly romance was fictitious and a distortion of the truth.

p, Sol M. Wurtzel; d, Allan Dwan; w, Sam Hellman (based on the novel *Wyatt Earp, Frontier Marshal* by Stuart N. Lake); ph, Charles G. Clarke; ed, Robert Bischoff; md, Samuel Kaylin; art d, Richard Day, Lewis Creber; set d, Thomas Little; cos, Herschel.

Western   **(PR:A MPAA:NR)**

FRONTIER MARSHAL IN PRAIRIE PALS
(SEE: PRAIRIE PALS, 1942)

FRONTIER OUTLAWS**   (1944) 58m PRC bw

Buster Crabbe *(Billy Carson)*, Al "Fuzzy" St. John *(Fuzzy Jones)*, Frances Gladwin *(Pat)*, Marin Sais *(Ma Clark)*, Charles King *(Barlow)*, Jack Ingram *(Taylor)*, Kermit Maynard *(Wallace)*, Edward Cassidy *(Sheriff)*, Emmett Lynn *(Judge)*, Budd Buster *(Clerk)*.

Crabbe plays a clever cowboy who poses as a Mexican interested in buying stolen cattle to trap a gang of outlaws led by King. When the gang attempts to sell the cattle the trap is closed and the knavery is stopped. Bewhiskered sidekick St. John provides some nice comedy, as does Lynn playing the judge.

p, Sigmund Neufeld; d, Sam Newfield; w, Joe O'Donnell; ph, Robert Cline; ed, Holbrook N. Todd.

Western   **(PR:A MPAA:NR)**

FRONTIER OUTPOST***½   (1950) 55m COL bw

Charles Starrett *(Steve Lawton, The Durango Kid)*, Smiley Burnette *(Smiley Burnette)*, Lois Hall *(Alice Tanner)*, Steve Darrell *(Forsythe)*, Fred Sears *(Copeland)*, Bob Wilke *(Krag Benson)*, Paul Campbell *(Capt. Tanner)*, Jock O'Mahoney *(Lt. Peck)*, Bud Osborne *(Stage Driver)*, Charles "Chuck" Roberson *(Gopher)*, Pierre Watkin *(Col. Warick)*, Dick Wessel *(Sgt. Murphy)*, Hank Penny, Slim Duncan *(Musicians)*.

Starrett stars as a U.S. marshal who, along with partner Burnette, is assigned to capture crooks who have been intercepting gold shipments due to be delivered to a fort. To their surprise, they find the fort abandoned and report their discovery to headquarters. Before he knows it, Starrett is thrown into jail because of false information that cites him as the mastermind behind the gold heists. He breaks out of prison, dons a mask, and sets out as the "Durango Kid" to solve the robberies. A better than average Starrett oater. (See DURANGO KID series, Index).

p, Colbert Clark; d, Ray Nazarro; w, Barry Shipman; ph, Fayte Browne; ed, Paul Borofsky; art d, Charles Clague.

Western   **(PR:A MPAA:NR)**

FRONTIER PHANTOM, THE** (1952) 56m Western Adventure/REA bw

Al "Lash" LaRue, Al "Fuzzy" St. John, Archie Twitchell, Clarke Stevens, Virginia Herrick, Bud Osborne, Cliff Taylor, Kenne Duncan, George Chesebro, Sandy Sanders, Buck Garrett, Jack O'Shea, Frank Ellis, Roy Butler, Larry Barton.

LaRue and St. John are a pair of U.S. marshals in pursuit of a gang of counterfeiters. LaRue goes undercover, calling himself "The Frontier Phantom," but instead of capturing the outlaws they themselves are captured. They have a tough time convincing the sheriff that they're on the side of the law, though eventually they are released and bring the counterfeiters in.

p&d, Ron Ormond; w, Maurice Tombragel, June Carr.

Western   **(PR:A MPAA:NR)**

FRONTIER PONY EXPRESS**   (1939) 58m REP bw

Roy Rogers *(Roy Rogers)*, Mary Hart [Lynne Roberts] *(Ann)*, Raymond Hatton *(Horseshoe)*, Edward Keane *(Lassiter)*, Noble Johnson *(Cantrell)*, Monte Blue *(Cherokee)*, Donald Dillaway *(Brett)*, William Royle *(Garrett)*, Ethel Wales *(Mrs. Murphy)*, George Letz [Montgomery], Charles King, Bud Osborne, Fred Burns, Jack Kirk, Bob McKenzie, Ernie Adams, Hank Bell, Jack O'Shea, Trigger, the Horse.

Rogers plays a pony express rider operating between California and the frontier territory. He becomes involved in a plot by Confederate spy Dillaway and southern politician Keane to get California to enter the Civil War on the rebel side. Keane, however, is playing both sides (Confederate and Union) against each other so he can walk in and claim the territory as his own. Luckily Rogers and his golden palomino Trigger are on hand to put an end to his plot in another virile Rogers actioner directed by the studio's top director, Joseph Kane. As usual in Rogers' films, little nuggets of history are offered along the way, in this case the influence of the pony express on the Civil War. Hart was another of the many talented and lovely women Rogers performed with before the studio's discovery of Dale Evans, his long-time costar and later his wife. George Montgomery, here still calling himself by his real name, Letz, changed the name the next year when he began taking over leading roles.

p&d, Joseph Kane; w, Norman Hall; ph, William Nobles; ed, Gene Milford; md, Cy Feuer.

Western   **Cas.**   **(PR: MPAA:NR)**

FRONTIER REVENGE** (1948) 57m Western Adventure/Screen Guild bw

Al "Lash" LaRue *(Himself)*, Al St. John *(Fuzzy Q. Jones)*, Jim Bannon *(Brant)*, Peggy Stewart *(Joan De Lysa)*, Ray Bennett *(Deuce Rago)*, Sarah Padden *(Widow Owens)*, Jimmie Martin *(Pete)*, Jack Hendricks *(Red)*, Lee Morgan *(Jake)*, Sandy Sanders *(Bart)*, Billy Dix *(Bartender)*, Cliff Taylor *(Bartender)*, Steve Raines *(Bart)*, Bud Osborne *(Dawson Brothers)*, George Chesebro *(Col. Winston)*, Kermit Maynard *(Outlaw)*, Jack Evans *(Saloon Extra)*.

LaRue and St. John pose as the Dawson Brothers, a pair of stagecoach robbers, in order to put an end to an outlaw racket headed by Bennett. Bennett, unaware that he is being tricked, plans a mine robbery with LaRue and St. John in the hope that he can get his hands on the Dawson Brothers' loot. With the help of Stewart, a saloon singer working for the government, LaRue and St. John bring the whip down on Bennett and his men, putting them behind bars.

p, Ron Ormond; d&w, Ray Taylor; ph, James S. Brown, Jr.; m, Walter Greene; ed, Hugh Winn.

Western (PR:A MPAA:NR)

FRONTIER SCOUT*

(1939) 60m FA/GN bw

George Houston (Wild Bill Hickok), Al St. John (Whiney), Beth Marion (Mary), Dave O'Brien (Steve Hickok), Guy [Alden] Chase (Bennett), Charles Whitaker (King), Kenne Duncan (Davis), Carl Matthews (Crandall), Kit Guard (Slim), Rob Woodward (Shorty), Jack Smith (Grant), Roger Williams (Jessup), Budd Buster (Mr. Jones), Walter Byron (Adams), Mantan Moreland, Minerva Urecal.

Former opera singer Houston plays Wild Bill Hickok whom Gen. Grant sends off to force Lee to surrender. After singlehandedly ending the Civil War in the first reel, the film tones down a bit and concentrates on Houston's efforts to corral cattle rustler, Chase. Very uneven direction by Newfield. Film was a sudden change of pace for Houston, who had been playing in musicals and dramas since his entry in the movies in 1935. The role led the next year to "The Lone Rider" series which he starred in before his death of a heart attack in 1944.

p, Franklyn Warner, Maurice Conn; d, Sam Newfield; w, Frances Guihan; ph, Jack Greenhalgh; ed, Dick Wray.

Western (PR:A MPAA:NR)

FRONTIER TOWN*

(1938) 58m GN bw

Tex Ritter (Tex), Ann Evers (Gail), Snub Pollard (Peewee), Charles King (Denby), Horace Murphy (Stubby), Karl Hackett (Regan), Lynton Brent (Grayson), Don Marion (Hawthorne), Ed Cassidy (Welsh), Forrest Taylor (Lane), Jack C. Smith, Babe Lawrence, Hank Worden, John Elliott, Jimmy LeFieur's Saddle Pals, White Flash the Horse.

The awful song "Yip, Yow, I'm an Eagle" is about par for the course in this poor horse opera with Country Music Hall of Famer Ritter. Ritter is saddled with a pair of dimwits, Murphy and Pollard, as they hit all the rodeos, allowing the singing cowboy to show off his skill with a rope. He wins all the prizes so the rodeo sponsors cook up a murder frameup to get rid of him. Other songs: "Old Cayusey," "Streets of Laredo," "Brass Wagon."

p, Edward Finney; d, Ray Taylor; w, Lindsay Parsons; ph, Gus Peterson; ed, Frederick Bain.

Western (PR:A MPAA:NR)

FRONTIER UPRISING*½

(1961) 68m Zenith/UA bw

James [Jim] Davis (Jim Stockton), Nancy Hadley (Consuela), Ken Mayer (Beaver), Nestor Paiva (Montalvo), Don O'Kelly (Kilpatrick), Stuart Randall (Ben Wright), David Renard (Lopez), John Marshall (Gen. Torena), Eugene Iglesias (Lt. Ruiz), Herman Rudin (Chief Taztay), Addison Richards (Cmdr. Kimball), Renata Vanni, Tudor Owen, Jan Arvan, Norman Pabst, Allan Ray, Dina Caesar, Barbara Mansell, Sid Kane.

Davis stars as a tough frontier scout battling hordes of Mexicans and Indians while trying to gain control of California for the U.S. Stunning cinematography by Maury Gertsman of the dry desert country helps the weak narrative move along.

p, Robert E. Kent; d, Edward L. Cahn; w, Owen Harris (based on a short story "Kit Carson" by George Bruce); ph, Maury Gertsman; m, Paul Sawtell, Bert Shefter; ed, Kenneth Crane; art d, Serge Krizman; set d, James Roach.

Western (PR:A MPAA:NR)

FRONTIER VENGEANCE*

(1939) 57m REP bw

Don "Red" Barry (Jim Sanders), Betty Moran (Ruth Hunter), George Offerman, Jr. (Clay Blackburn), Ivan Miller (Frank Blackburn), Obed "Dad" Pickard (Rocky), Cindy Walker (Dancer), Kenneth MacDonald (Slash), Griff Barnett (Joel Hunter), Yakima Canutt (Zack), Jack Lawrence (Moyer), Matty Roubert (Pinto), Fred "Snowflake" Toones (Snowflake).

Poor oater sees Barry falsely accused of the murder of his best friend. Interspersed with this dilemma is the battle between two rival stagecoach lines and Barry's romance with one of the drivers, Moran. The stagecoach race at the finale, winner getting the contract, has been seen before and will be seen many more times, with, here, nothing added of any importance.

p, George Sherman; d, Nate Watt; w, Bennett Cohen, Barry Shipman (based on a story by Cohen); ph, Reggie Lanning; ed, Edward Mann; md, Cy Feuer.

Western **Cas.** (PR:A MPAA:NR)

FRONTIERS OF '49*½

(1939) 54m COL bw

Bill Elliott (John Freeman), Luana de Alcaniz (Dolores de Cervantes), Charles King (Howard Brunon), Hal Taliaferro [Wally Wales] (Kit), Charles Whittaker (Brad), Octavio Girard (Don Miguel), Carlos Villarias (Padre), Joe de la Cruz (Romero), Jack Walters (Pete), Al Ferguson (Red), Kit Guard, Bud Osborne, Jack Ingram, Lee Shumway, Ed Cassidy, Frank Ellis.

Elliott stars as a cavalry officer sent down to the Spanish territory to stop evil land thief King—head of a gang practicing legal robbery of the property—from snatching any more real estate. Elliott's second western for Columbia. The dust raised by the cavalry settles down to bury this one without much loss.

p, Larry Darmour; d, Joseph Levering; w, Nate Gatzert; ph, James S. Brown; m, Lee Zahler; ed, Dwight Caldwell.

Western (PR:A MPAA:NR)

FRONTIERSMAN, THE**

(1938) 71m PAR bw

William Boyd (Hopalong Cassidy), George "Gabby" Hayes (Windy), Russell Hayden (Lucky), Evelyn Venable (June Lake), William Duncan (Buck Peters), Clara Kimball Young (Amanda Peters), Charles A. "Tony" Hughes (Mayor Judson Thorpe), Dickie Jones (Artie Peters), Roy Barcroft (Sutton), Emily Fitzroy (Miss Snook), John Beach (Quirt), Robert Mitchell's St. Brendan Boys Choir (School Kids), Blackjack Ward (Rustler), George Morrell (Townsman), Jim Corey (Bar 20 Cowboy), Jesse Cavan (Townsman).

Boyd helps schoolteacher Venable run a little red schoolhouse on the range populated by members of the St. Brendan Boys Choir, who sing at the drop of a Stetson. It's pretty dull going until the Bar 20 boys jump in the saddle and take off in a fierce chase after rustler Barcroft and his gang, corralling them in a gun battle. Unusual domesticized western that doesn't pump the triggers until the last fifteen minutes. (See HOPALONG CASSIDY series, Index).

p, Harry Sherman; d, Lesley Selander; w, Norman Houston, Harrison Jacobs (based on the character created by Clarence E. Mulford); ph, Russell Harlan; ed, Sherman Rose; art d, Lewis J. Rachmil.

Western (PR:A MPAA:NR)

FRONTIERSMAN, THE, 1968

(SEE: BUCKSKIN, 1968)

FROU-FROU**

(1955, Fr.) 115m Gamma/Film Cine-Italgamma c

Dany Robin (Frou-Frou), Philippe Lemaire (Artus), Gino Cervi (Vladimir), Jean Wall (Sabatier), Louis de Funes (Major), Mischa Auer (Archduke), Marie Sabouret (Grand Duchess).

Pre-WW I drama concerning young cigarette girl Robin who is discovered by four rich middle-aged men who decide to take her in and make her a lady. She soon becomes a singer and, between falling in love with a gigolo who betrays her and finally marrying one of the rich men, she finds time to croon a few tunes. (In French.)

d, Augusto Genina; w, A.E. Carr, Cecil Saint-Laurent; ph, Henri Alekan (CinemaScope, Eastmancolor); m, Louiguy; ed, Leonide Azar.

Drama (PR:A MPAA:NR)

FROZEN ALIVE*

(1966, Brit./Ger.) 80m Alfa-Creole/Magna bw (DER FALL X701)

Mark Stevens (Frank), Marianne Koch (Helen), Delphi Lawrence (Joan), Joachim Hansen (Tony), Walter Rilla (Sir Keith), Wolfgang Lukschy (Inspector Prentow), Albert Bessler (Martin), Sigurd Lohde (Dr. Merkheimer), Wolfgang Gunther (Sgt. Grun), Helmut Weiss (Chairman), John Longden (Prof. Hubbard).

A coldly directed picture which fails on just about all levels. The story is about Stevens and his experiments with freezing living creatures. He persuades his girl friend into running the tests with himself as a guinea pig. During the experiment, while he is immobilized, his ex-wife is killed. Naturally, he is suspected, but his rock-solid alibi gets him off the hook. The attempt at suspense has the emotionally shaken girl friend struggling to carry on with the testing and revive her chilly lover when the cops arrive to question Stevens. Produced in Germany in 1964, though not released in England until 1967, at a slim 63 minutes.

p, Artur Brauner, Ronald Rietti; d, Bernard Knowles; w, Evelyn Frazer; ph, Robert Ziller; ed, Steven Collins; art d, Jurgen Kiebach; cos, Vera Mugge; makeup, Heinz Stamm.

Science Fiction/Crime (PR:A MPAA:NR)

FROZEN DEAD, THE*½

(1967, Brit.) 96m Gold Star/WB bw/c

Dana Andrews (Dr. Norberg), Anna Palk (Jean Norberg), Philip Gilbert (Dr. Roberts), Kathleen Breck (Elsa Tenney), Karel Stepanek (Gen. Lubeck), Basil Henson (Capt. Tirpitz), Alan Tilvern (Essen), Ann Tirard (Mrs. Schmidt), Edward Fox (Prisoner No. 3), Oliver MacGreevy (Joseph), Tom Chatto (Inspector Witt), John Moore (Stationmaster), Charles Wade (Porter).

Ridiculous and unintentionally funny horror drama starring Andrews as a mad scientist determined to bring dozens of frozen Nazis back to life after he has kept them in a meat locker (in uniform) since the end of WW II. He succeeds in making the Germans ambulatory, but he can't get their brains to work. To remedy this, his colleague snips the head off a female friend of Andrew's niece which they put in a box and hook up to a complicated apparatus in the hopes that her telepathic powers will aid them in their experiments. As it turns out the girl/head will have none of it and she uses her telepathy to mobilize some dismembered arms hanging on the lab wall, which strangle the Nazi scientists to death. Too strange to thaw out initial disinterest. This film was shot in Eastmancolor but was released only in black and white in the U.S.

p,d&w, Herbert J. Leder; ph, Davis Boulton; m, Don Banks; ed, Tom Simpson; md, Philip Martell; art d, Scott MacGregor.

Horror (PR:C MPAA:NR)

FROZEN GHOST, THE**

(1945) 61m UNIV bw

Lon Chaney, Jr. (Alex Gregor), Evelyn Ankers (Maura Daniel), Milburn Stone (George Keene), Douglas Dumbrille (Inspector Brant), Martin Kosleck (Rudi Poldan), Elena Verdugo (Nina Coudreau), Arthur Hohl (Skeptic), Tala Birell (Valerie Monet).

Chaney, Jr., is a hypnotist who has the misfortune of having an onstage volunteer die. His business agent gets him a job at a wax museum. An aide at the museum, jealous of Chaney's way with women, sets out, with the help of the business agent, to drive the hypnotist insane. Creepy in parts but ineffectively directed, with some poor supporting roles.

p, William Cowan; d, Harold Young; w, Bernard Schubert, Luci Ward (based on a story by Harrison Carter and Harry Sucher, from the radio program "Inner Sanctum"); ph, Paul Ivano; md, H.J. Salter; art d, John B. Goodman, Abraham Grossman; cos, Vera West.

Horror/Suspense   **(PR:C MPAA:NR)**

FROZEN JUSTICE**   (1929) 73m FOX bw

Lenore Ulric (Talu), Robert Frazer (Lanala), Louis Wolheim (Duke), Ullrich Haupt (Capt. James), Laska Winter (Douglamana), Tom Patricola (Dancer), Alice Lake (Little Casino), Gertrude Astor (Moosehide Kate), Adele Windsor (Boston School Ma'am), Warren Hymer (Bartender), Neyneen Farrell (Yukon Lucy), El Brendel (Swede), Lou Morrison (Proprietor), Charles Judels (French Sailor), Joe Rochay (Jewish Character), Meyers Sisters (Harmony Duo), Landers Stevens (Mate Moore), Arthur Stone (French Pete), Jim Spencer (Medicine Man), Jack Ackroyd (English Eddie), Gertrude Chorre (Talu's Mother).

A weeper using the frozen tundra of the Arctic landscapes as a background, has Ulric the half-Eskimo woman who leaves the tribe with whom she has dwelled to seek out the fun and excitement offered by a visiting sea captain. As always the new encounters of the Eskimo girl are hardly what she expected, being forced to support the shiftless captain through her singing abilities, which aren't all that much. Her attempts to return to her husband and the other Eskimos fail when she and the captain fall into an icy chasm. Story is a pretty good one, though it is treated a bit too melodramatically and some of the depictions of Eskimo culture are totally ridiculous. This was the first talking role for Ulric, in a film career that was less than exceptional. Veteran character actor Landers Stevens, here playing a tough salt, was the father of pantheon film director George Stevens.

d, Allan Dwan; w, Sonya Levien (based on a story by Emjor Mikkelsen); ph, Harold Rosson; ed, Harold Schuster.

Adventure/Drama   **(PR:A MPAA:NR)**

FROZEN LIMITS, THE***   (1939, Brit.) 84m Gainsborough/GFD bw

Bud Flanagan & Chesney Allen (Bud & Ches), Jimmy Nervo & Teddy Knox (Cecil & Teddy), Charlie Naughton & Jimmy Gold (Charlie & Jimmy), Moore Marriott (Tom Tiddler), Eileen Bell (Jill), Anthony Hulme (Tex O'Brien), Bernard Lee (Bill McGrew), Eric Clavering (Foxy).

Three English music hall comedy duos teamed to form the Crazy Gang, which made five films between 1937 and 1959, of which this is probably the best. The sextet read in a forty-year-old paper their fish and chips are wrapped in that gold has been found in Alaska. They chuck their carnival jobs and head north, where they find Marriott, an old coot of a prospector who knows he has a mine around somewhere, but just can't think where. Fast-paced comedy well worth checking out, co-authored by Val Guest, an outstanding comedy writer.

p, Edward Black; d, Marcel Varnel; w, Marriott Edgar, Val Guest, J.O.C. Orton; ph, Arthur Crabtree.

Comedy   **(PR:A MPAA:NR)**

FROZEN RIVER*   (1929) 61m WB bw

"Rin-Tin-Tin," Davey Lee, Nina Quartero, Josef Swickard, Raymond McKee.

Rin-Tin-Tin got first billing in this lacklustre feature, and rightfully so as he proves to have much more acting ability than any of the humans in the cast. The canine is up to his usual heroics, saving a damsel-in-distress from the grip of money hungry thieves. Dialogue is at an extreme minimum, and is marred by poor recording techniques. Most of the sound track consists of the dog barking, making as much sense as the spoken lines.

d, Harmon Weight; w, Anthony Coldeway (based on the story by John Fowler); m, Louis Silver.

Adventure   **(PR:A MPAA:NR)**

FRUIT IS RIPE, THE**   (1961, Fr./Ital.) 90m Contact-P.I.P.-Transmonde/Janus bw (LES FILLES SEMENT LE VENT)

Scilla Gabel (Kissa), Francoise Saint-Laurent (Josine), Eva Damien (Margo), Philippe Leroy (Armand), Saro Urzi (Buonacasa), Michel Lemoine (Berto), Vittorio Prada, Sandrine, Jacques Fabbri, Philippe Mory, Francoise Dannel, Helene Tossy, Gisele Gallois, Elsa Kine, Janine Vila, Rene Tereusa, Roger Crouzet.

Three girls—a tease, a tough, and a romantic—are employed as fruit pickers during the summer months. The blistering hot sun, however, turns them and their male coworkers into passionate lovers. They all pair off, but a sour finale leads to the accidental death of one of the guys. In between there is a strike by the workers, which succeeds. Love's turmoil cooks up a tempestuous film.

p, Rene Thevenet; d&w, Louis Soulanes; ph, Paul Coteret; m, Michel Magne; ed, Alice Green.

Drama   **(PR:C MPAA:NR)**

FRUSTRATIONS* (1967, Fr./Ital.) 89m Radius-Pamec/Audubon bw (LA TRIATE DES BLANCHES; LA TRATTA DELLE BIANCHE; AKA: HOT FRUSTRATIONS)

Reine Rohan (Marisa), Magali Noel (Louisa), Paul Guers (Jean), Jean-Marc Tennberg (Mario), Evelyne Boursotti (Edith), Jean-Louise Tristan (Bob).

Rohan runs away with playboy Guers, her head filled with thoughts of marriage. When she learns that he heads a white slave racket, she is naturally upset. She is even more surprised when she finds herself working as a prostitute on board a yacht. After an aborted escape attempt, she is captured and sent to a place called "The Hole," a concentration camp of sorts. Her playboy-pimp realizes he really loves her and gets her released, and she escapes from him. The police are on the pimp's trail as he chases her and after a crash he dies. Rohan exposes the operation to the police, and they smash it. Realistic but repugnant portrayal of the sexual nether world.

p&d, Georges Combret; w, Combret, Pierre Mandru; ph, Pierre Lebon; m, Rene Sylviano; art d, J.-Paul Coutan-Laboureur.

Crime/Drama   **(PR:O MPAA:NR)**

FU MANCHU AND THE KISS OF DEATH (SEE: KISS & KILL, 1969, U.S./Brit./Span./Ger.)

FUEGO   (SEE: PYRO, 1964, U.S./Span.)

FUGITIVE, THE**   (1933) 56m MON bw

Rex Bell, Cecilia Parker, George "Gabby" Hayes, Robert Kortman, Tom London, Gordon DeMain, Phil Dunham, Theodore Lorch, Dick Dickinson, Earl Dwire, George Nash.

Bell gets arrested and thrown into jail but escapes with a notorious mail robber. It turns out that Bell is a U.S. Secret Service agent trying to infiltrate a mail-robbing gang. Well directed, some good acting but basically routine. Typical of the serious western roles lovable old Gabby Hayes played before he developed into the favorite comic sidekick in the history of the genre. Actress Cecilia Parker would go on to become better known as Mickey Rooney's older sister in MGM's ANDY HARDY series.

p, Paul Malvern, Trem Carr; d&w, Harry O. Jones [Harry Fraser]; ph, Archie Stout.

Western   **(PR:A MPAA:NR)**

FUGITIVE, THE**½ (1940, Brit.) 76m G&S/UNIV bw (GB: ON THE NIGHT OF THE FIRE)

Ralph Richardson (Will Kobling), Diana Wynyard (Kit Kobling), Romney Brent (Jimsey Jones), Mary Clare (Lizzy Crane), Henry Oscar (Pilleger), Dave Crowley (Jim Smith), Gertrude Musgrove (Dora Smith), Frederick Leister (Inspector Carr), Ivan Brandt (Wilson), Sara Allgood (Charwoman), Glynis Johns (Mary Carr), Maire O'Neill, Mai Bacon, Phyllis Morris, Teddy Smith, Joe Mott, Joe Cunningham, Harry Terry, Irene Handl.

Richardson stars in this insightful thriller as a barber who steals a small amount of cash to appease his wife's spending habits. She pays off a bill to Oscar, a drape maker, and the stolen bills are traced back to Oscar. He blackmails the couple, but Richardson retaliates by killing him. His wife takes the car and leaves town for a safer place, while Richardson stays behind. He is eventually surrounded and killed by police after learning his wife was involved in a fatal collision. Twenty minutes cut from British release.

p, Josef Somlo; d, Brian Desmond Hurst; w, Hurst, Terence Young, Patrick Kirwan (based on the novel On The Night Of The Fire by Frederick Laurence Green); ph, Gunther Krampf.

Crime Drama   **(PR:A MPAA:NR)**

FUGITIVE, THE*****   (1947) 104m RKO bw

Henry Fonda (The Fugitive), Dolores Del Rio (Mexican Woman), Pedro Armendariz (Police Lieutenant), Ward Bond (El Gringo), Leo Carrillo (Chief of Police), J. Carroll Naish (Police Spy), Robert Armstrong (Police Sergeant), John Qualen (Doctor), Fortunio Bonanova (Governor's Cousin), Chris-Pin Martin (Organ Player), Miguel Inclan (Hostage), Fernando Fernandez (Singer), Jose I. Torvay (Mexican), Melchor Ferrer.

A powerful passion play in a modern, mythical south-of-the-border country, THE FUGITIVE is moviemaking at its technical best and it offers a performance from Fonda that this sensitive actor seldom matched. He is a saintly priest who is hunted in a country that has outlawed the clergy, a revolutionary government led by savage fanatics such as Armendariz, who intend to purge with blood all traces of the Catholic religion. Fonda hides in a small village, abandoning his collar and passing for a peasant. He performs secret religious rites and is revered by all, including Del Rio, the ravishingly beautiful mistress to Armendariz. She has had an illegitimate child with the military police lieutenant and begs Fonda to baptize the infant, which he does. Then an American criminal on the run, Bond, who has been wounded, is comforted by Fonda and both Del Rio and Bond help him escape to another country where there is no religious persecution. Naish comes to him in his new sanctuary and tells him that Bond is dying and begs him to return to the hostile land so that he can receive the last rites. Fonda, ever loyal to his holy orders, returns only to find Bond upbraiding him for being so stupid as to fall into a police trap, that he has not asked for absolution. Naish, the half-breed police spy, is guilt-ridden as Fonda is arrested, and he begs the priest for forgiveness. Fonda forgives the betrayal and is jailed. Even Armendariz is full of apprehension and guilt for having to execute the man who risked his life to baptize his child. Fonda is nevertheless martyred while the villagers pray for him. But even as he is being led to his death, another priest is being smuggled into the village to administer spiritual needs to the people. Among all of Ford's films, he considered this to be his true masterpiece and it is a visual feast for the eyes, its magnificent black and white and contrasting scenes photographed by the superb cinematographer Figueroa. Shot in six weeks around Taxco, Choiula, and Cuernavaca, Mexico, THE FUGITIVE presents Fonda as an almost other world saint whose only existence is to serve his religion and its followers. That perennial Ford scriptwriter Nichols, who could perform any literary miracle Ford desired, cleaned up the priest character from the Greene novel where he was originally a "whiskey priest," who has lost almost all vestiges of his own moral code, sinking so low as to live with a fallen woman. Ford never tired of telling Fonda over the years that his role in THE FUGITIVE was the best performance of his career, an evaluation the actor debated with himself for years, but never with the great John Ford. Fonda is absolutely riveting and compelling, his only consistent doubt in a stupendous portrayal is that he cannot sacrifice himself enough for those who believe in him. THE FUGITIVE is really a companion film to Ford's marvelous THE INFORMER, a tale of personal betrayal, challenged morality, and physical sacrifice, and, as both films exemplify, a noble image of a peasant people that focuses upon purity and beauty. Here

Fonda is the true Ford hero, quiet, contemplative, nonviolent, capable of superhuman sacrifice. This was the first joint production of RKO and Argosy Pictures, a company headed by Ford and Cooper, and it proved a financial failure. Interior shots were made at Churubusco Studios in Mexico City. This film was remade for TV starring Laurence Olivier under the British title of the novel, THE POWER AND THE GLORY.

p, John Ford, Merian C. Cooper; d, Ford; w, Dudley Nichols (based on the novel *The Labyrinthine Ways* or *The Power and the Glory* by Graham Greene); ph, Gabriel Figueroa; m, Richard Hageman; ed, Jack Murray; md, Hageman; art d, Alfred Ybarra; set d, Manuel Parra; spec eff, Fred Sersen.

Drama **(PR:C MPAA:NR)**

FUGITIVE AT LARGE** (1939) 66m COL bw

Jack Holt *(Storm/Farrow)*, Patricia Ellis *(Patricia)*, Stanley Fields *(Manning)*, Arthur Hohl *(Curtis)*, Weldon Heyburn *(Corrick)*, Guinn "Big Boy" Williams *(Conway)*, Don Douglas *(Stevens)*, Leon Ames *(Carter)*, Cy Kendall *(Captain)*, Leon Beaumont, Ben Welden, Jonathan Hale.

Holt plays a dual role of a robber who sets up his civil engineer look-alike as a patsy for his crime. The engineer is arrested and the robber continues his spree. But goodness prevails and the robber, his wife, and their gang are arrested. Another of the "escape-for-the-moment" action films Holt made during the Depression years, which made him at the time one of the top draws in the B program category.

p, Larry Darmour; d, Lewis D. Collins; w, Eric Taylor, Harvey Gates (based on a story by Taylor); ph, James S. Brown, Jr.; ed, Dwight Caldwell; m/l, Hall Johnson.

Drama **(PR:A MPAA:NR)**

FUGITIVE FROM A PRISON CAMP* (1940) 58m COL bw

Jack Holt *(Sheriff Lawson)*, Marian Marsh *(Ann Baldwin)*, Robert Barrat *(Chester Russell)*, Phillip Terry *(Bill Harding)*, Dennis Moore *(Slugger Martin)*, Jack LaRue *(Red Nelson)*, George Offerman, Jr. *(Ted Baldwin)*, Frankie Burke *(Sobby Taylor)*, Donald Haines *(Burly Bascomb)*, Alan Baldwin *(Jerome Davis)*, Frank LaRue *(Robert O'Brien)*, Ernest Morrison *(Chuckles)*.

Nice guy sheriff Holt believes in prisoner rehabilitation. These guys aren't so bad, right? A lot of first-time offenders in a prison resembling a summer camp more than a detention camp work hard to redeem themselves on a road construction project. There's some dirty deals and a pallid love interest but the lame story, the hackneyed script, and all-around bad acting indicate the slow death of the long-running Holt series for Columbia.

p, Larry Darmour; d, Lewis D. Collins; w, Albert DeMond, Stanley Roberts; ph, James S. Brown, Jr.; ed, Dwight Caldwell.

Prison Drama **(PR:A MPAA:NR)**

FUGITIVE FROM JUSTICE, A*** (1940) 54m WB bw

Roger Pryor *(Dan Miller)*, Lucille Fairbanks *(Janet Leslie)*, Eddie Foy, Jr. *(Ziggy)*, Shiela Bromley *(Ruby Patterson)*, Morgan Conway *(Julie Alexander)*, Donald Douglas *(Lee Leslie)*, John Gallaudet *(Mark Rogers)*, Lottie Williams *(Mrs. Leslie)*, Joe Devlin *(Hinky-Dink)*, Steven Darrell *(Zorrila)*, John Harmon *(Gorwin)*, Robert E. O'Connor *(Murphy)*, Thomas Jackson *(Corkery)*, Eddy Chandler *(Gray)*, Ed Keane *(Partridge)*, Willis Claire *(Binke)*, Gus Glasmire *(Calhoun)*, Bernice Pilot *(Della)*, George Lloyd *(Bartender)*, Michael Conroy *(Office Boy)*.

Tight little gangster flick with Pryor as an insurance investigator trying to keep million-dollar policyholder Douglas away from gangsters and cops. Foy has some humorous moments as Pryor's assistant. Though Fairbanks, the niece of Douglas Fairbanks, Sr., has a top billing, she has relatively little to do. Short, but well done.

p, Bryan Foy; d, Terry Morse; w, Alex Gottlieb (based on the story "Million Dollar Fugitive" by Leonard Neubauer); ph, Arthur L. Todd; ed, Thomas Pratt.

Crime **(PR:A MPAA:NR)**

FUGITIVE FROM SONORA½** (1943) 57m REP bw

Don "Red" Barry *(Keeno Phillips/Dave Winters)*, Wally Vernon *(Jackpot Murphy)*, Lynn Merrick *(Dixie Martin)*, Harry Cording *(Iron Joe Martin)*, Ethan Laidlaw *(Hack Roberts)*, Pierce Lyden *(Slade)*, Gary Bruce *(Tom Lawrence)*, Kenne Duncan *(Cole)*, Tommy Coats *(Ed)*, Frank McCarroll *(Harris)*.

Barry plays a dual role of paroled outlaw and his twin brother, a parson bringing "salvation" to the lawless old West. The parson helps the niece of a gang leader who's trying to force parolees to join him or go back to prison. Barry's parolee is caught up in the gang but recants and dies to save his brother's life. Some good performances make this an above-average western. It was another double role for Barry, the thing he liked to do best because it gave him a chance to play heavies, bad guy roles where he thought the real acting was.

p, Eddy White; d, Howard Bretherton; w, Norman S. Hall; ph, William Bradford; m, Mort Glickman; ed, Richárd van Enger; art d, Russell Kimball.

Western **(PR:A MPAA:NR)**

FUGITIVE IN THE SKY** (1937) 60m WB bw

Jean Muir *(Rita Moore)*, Warren Hull *(Terry Brewer)*, Gordon Oliver *(Bob White)*, Carlyle Moore, Jr. *(Johnny Martin)*, Howard Phillips *(Killer Madson)*, Winifred Shaw *(Autumn Day)*, Mary Treen *(Agatha Ormsby)*, John Litel *(Mike Phelan)*, Gordon Elliott *(Ramon Duval)*, Gordon Hart *(Charles Holmberg)*, Nedda Harrigan *(Mrs. Tristo)*, John Kelly *(Kid Gouch)*, Joe Cunningham *(Spike)*, Don Barclay *(Ronald DeWitt)*, Charles Foy *(Steve Fanning)*, Spencer Charters *(Henry Staeger)*, Lillian Harmer *(Martha Staeger)*, Tom Jackson *(Dave Brandon)*.

Aboard an airplane originating from Los Angeles, reporters, government agents, and gangsters tussle, forcing the plane down in the middle of a dust storm. Complicated and farfetched plot twists along with mediocre to middling performances. Anything can happen aboard this plane and does.

d, Nick Grinde; w, George Bricker; ph, Ted McCord, Fred Jackman; ed, Frank Dewar.

Drama **(PR:A MPAA:NR)**

FUGITIVE KIND, THE** (1960) 119m UA bw

Marlon Brando *(Val Xavier)*, Anna Magnani *(Lady Torrance)*, Joanne Woodward *(Carol Cutrere)*, Maureen Stapleton *(Vee Talbott)*, Victor Jory *(Jabe Torrance)*, R.G. Armstrong *(Sheriff Talbott)*, Emory Richardson *(Uncle Pleasant)*, Spivy *(Ruby Lightfoot)*, Sally Gracie *(Dolly Hamma)*, Lucille Benson *(Beulah Binnings)*, John Baragrey *(David Cutrere)*, Ben Yaffee *(Dog Hamma)*, Joe Brown, Jr. *(Pee Wee Binnings)*, Virgilia Chew *(Nurse Porter)*, Frank Borgman *(Gas Station Attendant)*, Janice Mars *(Attendant's Wife)*, Debbie Lynch *(Lonely Girl)*.

Even fair Tennessee Williams is better than no Tennessee Williams and this is just about that; fair. He wrote the original play "Orpheus Descending" for Brando and Magnani to do on Broadway, but she was busy making movies and he didn't like the role. The play closed quickly and Brando was right to refuse the stage part. He might have done the same thing here with no loss to his career. Brando is a snakeskin jacketed guitarist-singer who leaves New Orleans after a judge admonishes him. On the road, his car breaks down and he makes his way to the local police station at Two Rivers, Mississippi, where the sheriff's wife, Stapleton, offers him food and a night's rest in one of the prison cells. Next day, she points him in the direction of the local general store owned by Jory, who is dying of cancer (not unlike Big Daddy in CAT ON A HOT TIN ROOF), and his Italian wife, Magnani. They need a clerk and Brando might be able to have the job. Magnani hires the young man. Woodward is the local nymphomaniac who attempts to bed Brando in the local cemetery. Brando stays away from her, which causes a scene. Jory gets home from the hospital, sees some electricity between Brando and Magnani, and is determined to stay alive, rather than allow her to take Brando in as the man of the house. Magnani makes it clear to Jory that she's always hated him, and everyone else in the town. (She'd had a stillborn child by a prominent townsman who then deserted her. Further, the liquor store she ran with her father was burned to the ground by Klansmen-types because he sold alcohol to the local blacks.) Later, Brando steals some money from the store, uses it to bet in a local gambling game, wins, and then comes back to the store to replace the stolen money. He now has enough of a stake to get out of town. Magnani is up waiting for him, calls him a crook, they argue and she eventually admits that she must have him there, if only for her sanity. He agrees to stay on and, over Jory's objections, Magnani decides to open a candy store. While she's off buying gear and candy, Brando is accused of messing with Stapleton by the same ones who burned Magnani's liquor store. He's ordered to leave town by sundown or they'll do him harm. Jory's mean-spirited nurse, Chew, thinks that Magnani is pregnant by Brando, and that that's why he's leaving. Brando asks Magnani to join him later and go off together to a new life. Jory is in his bedroom, lights a bunch of newspapers and tosses them downstairs into the candy store, which has been built onto the house. Brando tries to stop the fire by using his prized snakeskin jacket. Magnani is shot by Jory and Brando is trapped in the flames, unable to get out because the townspeople are outside and ready to kill him once he flees the fire. Later, Woodward finds the jacket among the smoking debris and says: "Wild things leave skins behind, so that the fugitive kind can always follow their kind." Somewhat based on the legend of Orpheus descending into hell to rescue Eurydice, the picture was mired in a morass of verbiage that only must have meant something to Williams. It was made in Milton, New York, which resembled the tacky town Williams imagined. Interiors were done in the Bronx. Although the acting was, as you might reckon, first-rate, the picture imploded under the weight of all the personal significance Williams attached to this particular story. It was originally produced in 1940 as "Battle Of Angels" and Williams kept working on it until he thought it was right. It never was.

p, Martin Jurow, Richard A. Shepherd (and Brando's company, Pennebaker); d, Sidney Lumet; w, Meade Roberts, Tennessee Williams (based on Williams' play "Orpheus Descending"); ph, Boris Kaufman; m, Kenyon Hopkins; ed, Carl Lerner; art d, Richard Sylbert; cos, Frank Thompson.

Drama **(PR:C MPAA:NR)**

FUGITIVE LADY½** (1934) 66m COL bw

Neil Hamilton *(Donald Brooks)*, Florence Rice *(Ann Duncan)*, Donald Cook *(Jack Howard)*, Clara Blandick *(Aunt Margaret)*, Nella Walker *(Mrs. Brooks)*, William Demarest *(Steve Rogers)*, Wade Boteler *(Rudy Davis)*, Ernest Wood *(Joe Nelson)*, Rita Le Roy *(Sylvia Brooks)*, Rita Gould *(Mrs. Clifford)*, Matt McHugh *(Bert Higgins)*, Harvey Clark *(Mr. Creswell)*, Maidel Turner *(Mrs. Young)*, Harry Holman *(Mr. Young)*, James Curtis *(Motorcycle Officer)*, Jessie Pringle *(Mrs. Carfax)*, Warner Richmond *(Saunders)*, Howard Hickman *(Doctor)*, Betty Alden *(Nurse)*, Maude Truax *(Mrs. Adams)*, Gladys Gale *(Miss Smith)*, Edward Le Saint *(Judge)*, Billie Seward *(Miss Hyland)*, Phillips Smalley *(Mr. Wolsey)*, Margaret Morgan *(Mrs. Wolsey)*, Sam Flint *(Conductor)*, Bill Dooley *(Simmons)*, Pat O'Malley *(Renham)*, Lucille Ball, Virginia Pine, Bess Flowers *(Beauty Operators)*, Isabelle La Mal *(Mrs. Brown)*, A. R. Haysel *(Hallahan)*, Beulah Hutton *(Edna)*, Wilson Benge *(Butler)*, Buddy Roosevelt *(Fight Double)*, Adalyn Hall *(Mrs. Goddard)*, Wedgwood Nowell *(Court Clerk)*, James Adamson *(Black Man)*, Cy Schindell, Mike Lally, Bert Starkey, Allen Caran *(Men)*, Irene Colman, James Blakely *(Bridal Couple)*, Evelyn Mackert *(Stand-in for Florence Rice)*.

A beautiful girl elopes with a jewel thief. She doesn't know about his occupation though, so when he takes it on the lam she takes the fall. She is pronounced guilty but is involved in a train wreck on her way to prison. Her identity is mixed up with the fiancee of a rich, handsome young man. Naturally they fall in love, but who should appear but the fiancee as well as the jewel thief, the fiancee's brother, and the police. It all works out in the end with the girl being cleared of all charges and marrying her new love. Rice is fine as the plucky heroine and a strong supporting cast makes this a good, if minor, adventure.

d, Al Rogell; w, Herbert Asbury, Fred Niblo; ph, Al Seigler; ed, John Rawlins.

Drama **(PR:C MPAA:NR)**

FUGITIVE LADY**½ (1951) 78m REP bw

Janis Paige (Barbara Clementi), Binnie Barnes (Esther Clementi), Massimo Serato (Gene), Eduardo Ciannelli (Ralph Clementi), Tony Centa (Jeff), Alba Arnova (Francine), Dino Galvani (Guissepe), Rosina Galli (Teresa), John Fostini (Beppo), Luciana Danieli (Maria), Michael Tor (Bob), Alex Serberoli (Chauffeur), Joop Van Hulsen (Druggist), Guilio Marchetti (Giovanni).

When Ciannelli falls to his death from a cliff, insurance agent Canta becomes suspicious. Was it suicide or murder? The two suspects include Paige, Ciannelli's gold-digging adulteress wife, and Barnes, Ciannelli's stepsister, who secretly loved him herself and was bitter over the marriage. Through flashbacks the true nature of the crime is discovered. After a drinking bout, Paige has sent inebriated Ciannelli out for more booze. Unbeknownst to him, she has changed the road signs to insure his death. In the end she suffers a similar fate, driving off the same cliff while running from the police. Some nice costumes and great Italian scenery, but the story is hampered by its slow exposition.

p, M.J. Frankovich; d, Sidney Salkow, w, John O'Dea (based on the novel by Doris Miles Disney); ph, Tonino Delli Colli; ed, Nino Baragli; md, Willy Ferrero; m/l,"My Guy" Alberto Barberis and Suzanne MacPherson (sung by Paige).

Drama/Mystery (PR:O MNAA:NR)

FUGITIVE LOVERS** (1934) 74m MGM bw

Robert Montgomery (Paul Porter), Madge Evans (Letty Morris), Ted Healy (Hector Withington, Jr.), Nat Pendleton (Legs Coffee), C. Henry Gordon (Daly), Ruth Selwyn (Babe Callahan), Moe Howard, Larry Fine, Jerry Howard (The Three Julians), Mary Emmons (News Vendor), Earl of Chichester (Extra), George Gorman (Bus Driver), "Dad" Mills (Blind Man), Akim Tamiroff (Bus Passenger).

While traveling via a transcontinental bus, a chorus girl is pursued by a fugitive from justice who is in love with her. Trite dialog and contrived situations destroy any chance at plausibility. Film's most distinctive feature is the appearance of the Three Stooges (billed as the Three Julians) as the goofy sidekicks of drunk Healy.

d, Richard Boleslawski; w, Albert Hackett, Frances Goodrich, George B. Seitz (based on a story by Ferdinand Reyher and Frank Wead); ph, Ted Teztlaff; ed, William S. Gray.

Comedy (PR:A MPAA:NR)

FUGITIVE ROAD** (1934) 69m INV/CHES bw

Erich von Stroheim (Hauptmann Oswald Von Traunsee), Wera Engels (Sonia Vallanoff), Leslie Fenton (Riker), George Humbert (Vinocchio), Harry Holman (Burgomaster), Hank Mann, Ferdinand Schumann-Heinck, Michael Visaroff, Bangie Beilly, Hans Ferberg.

Von Stroheim is a hardened border guard with a marshmallow center. He detains Humbert, an Italian trying to get to Austria. Later he detains Russian immigrant Engels for his own lusty purposes but has a change of heart and fixes her up with a fugitive gunman from Brooklyn. Eventually all detainees are allowed to go to America. Von Stroheim played his usual character well, but overall this is a minor film.

d, Frank Strayer; w, Charles S. Belden and Robert Ellis; ph, M.A. Anderson, Ted McCord.

Drama (PR:A MPAA:NR)

FUGITIVE SHERIFF, THE** (1936) 61m COL bw

Ken Maynard (Ken Marshall), Beth Marion (Jane Roberts), Walter Miller (Flamer), Hal Price (Louder Lucas), John Elliott (Judge Roberts), Arthur Millett (John), Virginia True Boardman (Mrs. Ball), Frank Ball (Prospector), Edmond Cobb (Wally), Lafe McKee, Art Mix, William Gould, Bob Burns, Horace Murphy, Vernon Dent, Tex Palmer, Bud Osborne, Slim Whitaker, Al Taylor, Frank Ellis, Horace B. Carpenter, Oscar Gahan, Glenn Strange, Fred Burns, Lew Meehan, Blackjack Ward, Tex Cooper, Roy Bucko, Buck Bucko, Art Dillard, Jack King, Bud Jamison, Bud McClure, Tarzan the Horse.

Maynard is elected sheriff over a candidate backed by outlaws. He is subsequently framed for a crime but wins out in the end. Along the way he meets and falls for Marion, engages in gun play, and harmonizes with his cowboy friends. Average western with some fancy riding stunts as usual by Maynard and his horse Tarzan.

p, Larry Darmour; d, Spencer G. Bennett; w, Nate Gatzert; ph, James S. Brown, Jr.; ed, Dwight Caldwell.

Western (PR:A MPAA:NR)

FUGITIVE VALLEY*½ (1941) 61m MON bw

Ray Corrigan (Crash), John King (Dusty), Max Terhune (Alibi), Julie Duncan (Ann), Glenn Strange (Gray), Bob Kortman (Langdon), Ed Brady (Doctor), Tom London (Warren), Reed Howes (Brandon), Carl Matthews (Slick), Edward Peil, Sr. (Jailer), Doye O'Dell (Jim).

Unlikely and confusing western from Monogram's "Range Buster" series. Corrigan and King are stage robbers turned deputy marshals. The story involves their following some outlaws, stolen money, and ranchers. King sings three songs. Terhune has some fun bits with magic and ventriloquism, which he did as a vaudevillian before he entered the movies. Songs, "My Little Prairie Annie," "Chisholm Trail," "Riding Along."

p, George W. Weeks; d, S. Roy Luby, John Vlamos, R. Finkel; w, Oliver Drake; ph, Robert Cline; m, Frank Sanucci; ed, Roy Claire.

Western (PR:A MPAA:NR)

FUGITIVES FOR A NIGHT** (1938) 63m RKO bw

Frank Albertson (Matt Ryan), Eleanor Lynn (Ann Wray), Allan Lane (Nelson), Bradley Page (Poole), Adrianne Ames (Eileen Baker), Jonathan Hale (Captain), Russell Hicks (Tenwright), Paul Guilfoyle (Monks).

Aspiring actor Albertson is hired to be a stooge for big film star Page. When big shot Hicks is murdered in a night club, Albertson is thought to be the killer. Innocent of the charges, he goes into hiding with his studio publicist girl friend Lynn. Then he is exonerated when Page is arrested for the murder. Some interesting behind-the-scenes glimpses at a film studio but pretty much routine. Script gives no hint of what Trumbo was to become.

p, Lou Lusty; d, Leslie Goodwins; w, Dalton Trumbo (based on a story by Richard Wormser); ph, Frank Redmond; ed, Desmond Marquette.

Mystery/Drama (PR:C MPAA:NR)

FULL CIRCLE zero (1935, Brit.) 55m WB bw

Rene Ray (Margery Boyd), Garry Marsh (Max Reeves), Graham Pocket (Mark Boyd), Betty Shale (Mrs. Boyd), Margaret Yarde (Agatha), Patricia Hilliard (Jeanne Westover), Bruce Belfrage (Clyde Warren), John Wood (Tony Warren), Elizabeth Jenns (Leonora Allway).

A salesman steals a will to appease a blackmailer, but when he learns that the beneficiary is deserving of the cash he steals it back again. The plot can barely travel in a straight line without problems, much less going "full circle."

p, Irving Asher; d, George King; w, Michael Barringer.

Crime (PR:A MPAA:NR)

FULL CIRCLE**½ (1977, Brit./Can.) 98m Fester c
(AKA: THE HAUNTING OF JULIA)

Mia Farrow (Julia), Keir Dullea (Magnus), Tom Conti (Mark), Jill Bennett (Lily), Robin Gammell (Swift), Cathleen Nesbitt (Mrs. Rudge), Anna Wing (Mrs. Flood), Pauline Jameson (Mrs. Branscombe), Peter Sallis (Mr. Branscombe), Sophie Ward (Kate), Samantha Gates (Olivia).

In a gruesome opening, Farrow is a mother trying to save her choking daughter by performing a tracheotomy with a kitchen knife. It is to no avail and her daughter dies. After getting over her shock Farrow leaves her husband and moves into an old, creaky Victorian house, where spooky things happen. Her husband is found in the basement with his throat slit. Her boy friend is electrocuted in the bathtub. The ending is mysterious: did Farrow commit the murders or the ghostly child who had been murdered near the house thirty years previously? Farrow herself ends up with her throat cut. Some creepy moments, but Farrow did this all much better in ROSEMARY'S BABY. Still, there are enough scares in this and some nice atmospheric touches that make it worthwhile.

p, Peter Fetterman, Alfred Pariser; d, Richard Longcraine; w, Dave Humphries; ph, Peter Hannan (Eastmancolor); m, Colin Towns; ed, Ron Wisman; art d, Brian Morris; cos, Shuna Harwood.

Horror (PR:O MPAA:NR)

FULL CONFESSION*** (1939) 72m RKO bw

Victor McLaglen (McGinnis), Sally Eilers, (Molly), Joseph Calleia (Father Loma), Barry Fitzgerald (Michael O'Keefe), Elisabeth Risdon (Norah O'Keefe), Adele Pearce (Laura Mahoney), Malcolm McTaggart (Frank O'Keefe), John Bliefer (Weaver), William Haade (Moore), George Humbert (Mercantonio).

A brutal murder takes place and Fitzgerald is convicted and sentenced to die. Problem is, he's innocent. McLaglen is the real killer and confesses to his priest, Calleia. Calleia tries to get him to give up, but McLaglen refuses. In a climactic ending Calleia is attacked by McLaglen. A crisis of conscience ensues and McLaglen gives a lifesaving blood transfusion to the priest. He admits to the crime, saving Fitzgerald from the chair. An interesting film, though some critics complained that it was nothing more than an inferior version of the 1935 John Ford film THE INFORMER.

p, Robert Sisk; d, John Farrow; w, Jerry Cady (based on a story by Leo Birinski); ph, J. Roy Hunt; ed, Harry Marker.

Drama (PR:C MPAA:NR)

FULL MOON HIGH* (1982) 93m Larco/Filmways c

Adam Arkin (Tony Walker), Elizabeth Hartman (Miss Montgomery), Ed McMahon (Mr. Walker), Kenneth Mars, Roz Kelly, Joanne Nail, Pat Morita, Alan Arkin, Louis Nye, John Blythe Barrymore, Demond Wilson.

A horror comedy which casts Adam Arkin as a werewolf who, after visiting Transylvania, returns to the high school of the title. Full of silly jokes and pokes at modern life and the possibility of having a werewolf on your block. Arkin finally pairs off with a feminine werewolf (a wolfwoman?) in the hopes of starting a family. Director Cohen has had better luck with IT'S ALIVE, IT LIVES AGAIN, and Q. Ed McMahon appears as Adam Arkin's father, even though his real life father, Alan Arkin, is also cast.

p,d&w, Larry Cohen; ph, Daniel Pearl; m, Gary W. Friedman; art d, Robert Burns; makeup, Steve Neill.

Horror/Comedy (PR:A-C MPAA:NR)

FULL OF LIFE*** (1956) 91m COL bw

Judy Holliday (Emily Rocco), Richard Conte (Nick Rocco), Salvatore Baccaloni (Papa Rocco), Esther Minciotti (Mama Rocco), Joe DeSantis (Father Gondolfo), Silvio Minciotti (Joe Muto), Penny Santon (Carla), Arthur Lovejoy (Mr. Jameson), Eleanor Audley (Mrs. Jameson), Trudy Marshall (Nora Gregory), Walter Conrad (John Gregory), Sam Gilman (Dr. Atchison).

Charming domestic comedy/drama about a girl without any religious convictions who has married into a very Catholic Italian family. The picture begins as Holliday is in her last month of pregnancy by husband Conte, a writer with no money. Based on a novel by Italian John Fante, there's probably a lot of truth in the story as it appears to be a thinly disguised fiction of reality. Holliday falls through the floor of her termite-ridden kitchen and Conte's father, Metropolitan Opera basso Baccaloni, is a carpenter who will fix the floor. That done, he proceeds to build them a huge and totally unnecessary fireplace, complaining all the while about the fact that Conte and Holliday seem to be on a path of planned parenthood, rather than having one of those enormous Italian families. Although officially married, they haven't had a Catholic wedding and so the enormous Holliday (who seems to be about to give birth to the entire film) is taken in a maternity wedding gown to the church to do things properly. After the service, she's rushed to the hospital to deliver. That's the plot, but the fun is in the extremely believable characters and dialog by Fante. Good taste is in evidence everywhere and what could have been a dumb slapstick farce is handled very well. Esther Minciotti, who played virtually the same mama role in MARTY, is superb and Baccaloni is a revelation. All-around good fun.

p, Fred Kohlmar; d, Richard Quine; w, John Fante (based on the novel by Fante); ph, Charles Lawton, Jr.; m, George Duning; ed, Charles Nelson; md, Morris W. Stoloff; art d, William Flannery; set d, William Kiernan, Louis Diage.

Comedy/Drama   (PR:A   MPAA:NR)

FULL SPEED AHEAD*   (1936, Brit.) 71m PAR bw

Paul Neville (Capt. Murton), Moira Lynd (Jean Hunter), Richard Norris (Tim Brent), George Mozart (Chief Smith), Geoffrey Clark (Dunn), Victor Hagen (Smith), George Turner (Oily Short), Arthur Seaton (Irving Hunter), Julien Vedey (Mendoza), Syd Crossley (Moggridge), Arthur Brander, Dorothy Dewhurst.

Neville, a chauffeur to a shipping tycoon, and Lynd, the tycoon's daughter, stow away on one of the company's ships. The captain, however, plans to sink the ship in an insurance scam until Neville and Lund uncover the scheme.

p&d, Lawrence Huntington; w, Gerald Elliott (based on a story by Huntington, Elliott); ph, Stanley Grant.

Crime Drama   (PR:A   MPAA:NR)

FULL SPEED AHEAD**   (1939, Brit.) 60m Education & General
                                                      Services/GFD bw

Michael Osler (John Elwood), Frederick Peisley (Michael Elwood), Dinah Sheridan (Joan Barrymore), Morland Graham (Gordon Tweedie), H.G. Stoker (Sir Robert Barrymore), Betty Shale (Mrs. Elwood).

A better example of British naval technology than of filmmaking, FULL SPEED AHEAD trudges through a weak script about a pair of brothers—one who climbs the ladder of command, the other who becomes a ship designer whose new craft is instrumental in rescuing his brother's fiancee in a sea disaster.

p&d, John Hunt; w, "Bartimeus"; ph, W. Winterton.

Drama   (PR:A   MPAA:NR)

FULL TREATMENT, THE   (SEE: STOP ME BEFORE I KILL!, 1961)

FULLER BRUSH GIRL, THE***   (1950) 87m COL bw (GB: THE
                                                      AFFAIRS OF SALLY)

Lucille Ball (Sally Elliot), Eddie Albert (Humphrey Briggs), Carl Benton Reid (Christy), Gale Robbins (Ruby Rawlings), Jeff Donnell (Jane Bixby), John Litel (Watkins), Fred Graham (Rocky Mitchell), Lee Patrick (Claire Simpson), Arthur Space (Inspector Rodgers), Sid Tomack (Bangs), Billy Vincent (Punchy), Lorin Raker (Deval), Lelah Tyler (Mrs. North), Sarah Edwards (Mrs. East), Lois Austin (Mrs. West), Isabel Randolph (Mrs. South), Isabel Withers (Mrs. Finley), Donna Boswell (Sue/Lou), Gregory Marshall (Alvin/Albert), Gail Bonney (Baby Sitter), Joel Robinson, Shirley Whitney (Dancers), Sumner Getchell (Magazine Salesman), Red Skelton (Fuller Brush Man), Jay Barney (Fingerprint Man), John Doucette, Charles Hamilton, Cy Malis, Joseph Palma (Cops), Jack Little, James L. Kelly (Comics), Myron Healey (Employee), Bud Osborne (Old Sailor), Barbara Pepper, Paul Bryar (Couple), Jean Willes (Mary), Frank Wilcox (Roberts), Syd Saylor (Wardrobe Man), Paul E. Burns (Stage Doorman), Val Avery (Burlesque Patron), George Lloyd (Sea Captain on Dock), Cliff Clark (Ship's Captain), Joseph Creman (Captain of Police Boat).

Ball is a door-to-door salesgirl linked to a murder. She has to escape from the cops, taking along boy friend Eddie Albert. Lots of slapstick, chases, and some great comic bits that are Ball's specialty. Albert is fine as her not-too-bright beau. Red Skelton makes a brief appearance as an in-joke reference to his own film THE FULLER BRUSH MAN.

d, Lloyd Bacon; w, Frank Tashlin; ph, Charles Lawton, Jr.; m, Heinz Roemheld; ed, William Lyon; md, Morris W. Stoloff; art d, Robert Peterson.

Comedy   (PR:AAA   MPAA:NR)

FULLER BRUSH MAN**½**   (1948) 92m COL bw
                                                      (GB: THAT MAN MR. JONES)

Red Skelton (Red Jones), Janet Blair (Ann Elliot), Don McGuire (Keenan Wallick), Hillary Brooke (Mrs. Trist), Adele Jergens (Miss Sharmley), Ross Ford (Freddie Trist), Trudy Marshall (Sara), Nicholas Joy (Commissioner Trist), Donald Curtis (Gregory Crackston), Arthur Space (Lt. Quint), Selmer Jackson (Henry Seward), Roger Moore (Detective Foster), Stanley Andrews (Detective Ferguson), Bud Wolfe (Jiggers), David Sharpe (Skitch), Chick Collins (Blackie), Billy Jones (Herman), Jimmy Lloyd (Chauffeur), Jimmy Logan (Butler), Jimmy Hunt (Junior).

Red Skelton is at his best in the slapstick tale of a Fuller Brush salesman mixed up in a murder mystery. With Blair, Skelton tries a little sleuthing to clear himself of the crime. They follow the clues to a war surplus factory where the final scene is thoroughly madcap, ranking with the early Mack Sennett silents. Coscripted by Frank Tashlin (THE GIRL CAN'T HELP IT, WILL SUCCESS SPOIL ROCK HUNTER?), one of Hollywood's most gifted comic directors.

p, Edward Small; d, S. Sylvan Simon; w, Frank Tashlin, Devery Freeman (based on a story by Roy Huggins); ph, Lester White; m, Heinz Roemheld; ed, Al Clark; art d, Stephen Gooson, Carl Anderson.

Comedy/Crime   Cas.   (PR:AAA   MPAA:NR)

FUN AND FANCY FREE**   (1947) 73m RKO c

Edgar Bergen with Mortimer Snerd and Charlie McCarthy, Luana Patten, and the voices of: Dinah Shore (Narrator), Anita Gordon (The Singing Harp), Cliff Edwards (Jiminy Cricket), Billy Gilbert (The Giant), Clarence Nash (Donald Duck), The King's Men, The Dinning Sisters, The Starlighters.

A weak Disney film, actually two shorts strung together using Jiminy Crickett as the unifying thread. The first episode, narrated by Dinah Shore, tells the story of Bongo, a circus bear who escapes to the wilderness. He meets a girl bear and her bear boy friend, as well as an early version of Chip and Dale. Eventually, the sappy Bongo becomes brave and wins over the girl. Stretched out to one reel, the story (a Sinclair Lewis adaptation) could have been leisurely told in five minutes. The second and more ambitious short combines live action—Edgar Bergen (and his dummies Charlie McCarthy and Mortimer Snerd) and Luana Patten—with animated standards—Mickey Mouse, Donald Duck and Goofy. The result, however, is an uninspired version of "Jack and the Beanstalk." One of the highlights is Billy Gilbert, as the voice of Willie the Giant, performing his familiar sneezing-fit bit. Tunes include: "My Favorite Dream" (William Walsh, Roy Noble), "Too Good To Be True," "Say It With A Slap" (Buddy Kaye, Eliot Daniel), "Lazy Countryside" (Bobby Worth), "Fun and Fancy Free" (Bennie Benjamin, George Weiss), "Fee Fi Fo Fum" (Paul J. Smith, Arthur Quenzer), "I'm A Happy-Go-Lucky Fellow" (Leigh Harline, Ned Washington), "Beanero" (Oliver Wallace), "My, What A Happy Day" (Walsh, Noble).

p, Walt Disney; d, Jack Kinney, W.O. Roberts, Hamilton Luske; live-action d, William Morgan; w, Homer Brightman, Harry Reeves, Ted Sears, Lance Nolley, Eldon Dedini, Tom Oreb (BONGO segment from a story by Sinclair Lewis); live-action ph, Charles P. Boyle (Technicolor); m, Paul J. Smith, Oliver Wallace, Eliot Daniel; ed, Jack Bachom; directing animators, Ward Kimball, Les Clark, John Lounsbery, Fred Moore, Wolfgang Reitherman; character animators, Hugh Fraser, Phil Duncan, Judge Whitaker, Arthur Babbitt, John Sibley, Marc Davis, Harvey Toombs, Hal King, Ken O'Brien, Jack Campbell; backgrounds, Ed Starr, Claude Coats, Art Riley, Brice Mack, Ray Huffine, Ralph Hulett.

Animated Feature   Cas.   (PR:AAA   MPAA:NR)

FUN AT ST. FANNY'S***   (1956, Brit.) 80m BL/Grand Alliance c

Fred Emney (Dr. Septimus Jankers), Cardew Robinson (Cardew the Cad), Vera Day (Maisie), Johnny Brandon (Fanshawe), Davy Kaye (Ferdy), Freddie Mills (Harry the Scar), Gerald Campion (Fatty Gilbert), Miriam Karlin (Mildred), Claude Hulbert (Winkle), Kynaston Reeves (McTavish), Gabrielle Brune (Matron), Stanley Unwin (The Guide), Dino Galvani (Pumpernickel), Peter Butterworth (The Potter), Paul Daneman (Fudge), Roger Avon (Horsetrough), Ronald Corbett (Chumleigh), Aud Johansen (Praline), Tom Gill (Constable), Marianne Stone, Francis Langford's Singing Scholars.

Emney is headmaster of a British boarding school that stands to inherit the fortune of a twenty-five-year-old student (Robinson), if only they can get the "lad" expelled. A plan is conceived to plant a stolen painting on Robinson, but this is averted by a private detective hired by school trustees. Robinson finally graduates at the film's end. Robinson gives a fun performance as the would-be scholar. Good supporting cast.

p, David Dent; d, Maurice Elvey; w, Antony Verney, Fred Emney (based on a story by Peter Noble and Denis Waldock); ph, Eric Cross; m, Edwin Astley; ed, Robert Hill.

Comedy   (PR:AA   MPAA:NR)

FUN IN ACAPULCO**   (1963) 100m PAR c

Elvis Presley (Mike Windgren), Ursula Andress (Margarita Dauphine), Elsa Cardenas (Dolores Gomez), Paul Lukas (Maximillian), Larry Domasin (Raoul Almeido), Alejandro Rey (Moreno), Robert Carricart (Jose), Teri Hope (Janie Harkins), Charles Evans (Mr. Harkins), Alberto Morin (Hotel Manager), Francisco Ortega (Desk Clerk), Robert De Anda (Bellboy), Linda Rivera (Telegraph Clerk), Darlene Tomkins (1st Girl), Linda Rand (2nd Girl), Eddie Cano, Carlos Mejia, Leon Cardenas, Fred Aguirre (Musicians), Tom Hernandez (Photographer), Adele Palacios (Secretary).

Presley is a trapeze artist crippled by a sudden fear of heights. He is hired as a lifeguard/singer at an Acapulco hotel where he meets Andress, hotel social director, and falls in love. Problem is that high diver Rey also has his eye on her. At the film's climax Presley conquers his fear of heights in a cliff dive and wins the lady's affections. With ten nonmemorable numbers, FUN IN ACAPULCO is just a travelog cashing in on Presley's slowly diminishing box office appeal. Songs: (All sung by Presley) "Fun In Acapulco" (Sid Wayne, Ben Weisman), "Vino, Dinero y Amor," "Mexico," "The Bullfighter was a Lady" (Sid Tepper, Roy C. Bennett), "El Toro" (Bill Giant, Bernie Baum, Florence Kaye), "Marguerita" (Don Robertson), "(There's) No Room to Rhumba (In a Sports Car)" (Fred Wise, Dick Manning), "I Think I'm Gonna Like It Here" (Hal Blair, Don Robertson), "Bossa Nova Baby" (Jerry Leiber, Mike Stoller), "You Can't Say No in Acapulco" (Dee Fuller, Lee Morris, Sid Feller), "Guadalajara" (Pepe Guizar).

p, Hal Wallis; d, Richard Thorpe; w, Allan Weiss; ph, Daniel L. Fapp (Technicolor); m, Joseph J. Lilley; ed, Stanley E. Johnson; art d, Hal Pereira, Walter Tyler; set d, Sam Comer, Robert R. Benton; cos, Edith Head; spec eff, Paul K. Lerpae; ch, Charles O'Curran.

Musical   Cas.   (PR:A   MPAA:NR)

FUN LOVING   (SEE: QUACKSER FORTUNE HAS A COUSIN IN THE
                                              BRONX, 1970, Ire.)

FUN ON A WEEKEND***   (1979) 93m UA bw

Eddie Bracken (P. P. Porterhouse III), Priscilla Lane (Nancy Crane), Tom Conway (Van), Allen Jenkins (Joe Morgan), Arthur Treacher (B. O. Moffatt), Clarence Kolb (Quigley Quackenbush), Alma Kruger (Mrs. Van Orsdale), Russell Hicks (John

Biddle), Fritz Feld (Sergei Stronganoff), Richard Hageman (Mr. Cowperwaithe), Lester Allen (Stooge at Lunch Counter), Bill Kennedy (Bill Davis).

Bracken is a quiet man with big dreams. He teams with grandiose schemer deluxe Lane and the two attempt a get-rich-quick scam. They shed their clothing for some swim suits and socialize at a beach frequented by the affluent. No one knows the two of them are poor when they're in swim gear, right? Bracken has some wonderful moments getting out of implausible situations and the direction is nicely paced. A good cast of clowns and comic actors rounds out the cast.

p,d&w, Andrew Stone; ph, Paul Ivano; m, Lucien Caillet, ed, Paul Weatherwax; art d, Rudi Feld.

Comedy (PR:AA MPAA:NR)

FUN WITH DICK AND JANE** (1977) 95m COL c

George Segal (Dick Harper), Jane Fonda (Jane Harper), Ed McMahon (Charlie Blanchard), Dick Gautier (Dr. Will), Allan Miller (Loan Company Manager), Hank Garcia (Raoul Esteban), John Dehner, Mary Jackson (Jane's Parents), Walter Brooke (Mr. Weeks), Sean Frye (Billy-Harper), James Jeter (Immigration Officer), Maxine Stuart (Blanchard's Secretary), Fred Willard (Bob), Thalmus Rasulala (Mr. Johnson), Ji-Tu Cumbuka (Guard), Selma Archerd (Beverly Hills Matron), John Brandon (Pete Winston), Burke Byrnes (Roger), William Callaway (Record Store Clerk), Jean Carson (Paula), Richard Crystal (Motel Manager), Thayer David (Deacon), Cora Lee Day (Cleaning Lady), Jon Christian Erickson (Trans-Sexual), Art Evans (Man at Bar), Richard Foronjy (Landscape Man), Louis Guss (Phone Company Customer), Harry Holcombe (Pharmacist), Darrow Igus, DeWayne Jessie (Robbers), J. Rob Jordon (Cop), Richard Karron (Pool Builder), Richard Keith (Senator), Robert Lussier (Unemployment Clerk), Edward Marshall (Phone Company Clerk), Isaac Ruiz, Jimmy Martinez, Santos Morales (Raoul's Friends), Mickey Morton (Tippy), Tom Peters (Restaurant Owner), William Pierson (Nesbitt), Anne Ramsey (Employment Applicant), Joan Spiga (Carmen), Debi Storm (Baby Sitter), Gloria Strook (Mildred Blanchard), Fred Willard (Bob).

After Segal loses his job with the aerospace industry he and wife Fonda turn to armed robbery to make ends meet. Not as funny or socially relevant as it could be, but a nice chemistry between Fonda and Segal. McMahon does a great job as Segal's alcoholic boss.

p, Peter Bart, Max Palevsky; d, Ted Kotcheff; w, David Giler, Jerry Belson, Mordecai Richler (based on a story by Gerald Gaiser); ph, Fred Koenekamp (Metrocolor); m, Ernest Gold, Lamont Dozier, Gene Page; ed, Danford B. Greene; prod, D James G. Hulsey; set d, Jack Stevens; cos, Donfeld, Lambert E. Marks, Margo Baxley; m/l, "Ahead of the Game," The Movies (sung by The Movies); stunts, Paul Baxley.

Comedy Cas. (PR:C-O MPAA:PG)

FUNDOSHI ISHA (SEE: LIFE OF A COUNTRY DOCTOR, 1961, Jap.)

FUNERAL FOR AN ASSASSIN*½ (1977) 90m Epoh-Four Star c

Vic Morrow, Peter Von Dissel, Gaby Getz, Gillian Garlick, Siegfried Mayhardt, Stewart Parker.

A hitman lives life on the edge, avoiding numerous close calls, as he receives the most important assignment of his career. Standard television-styled police work.

p, Walter Brough, Ivan Hall; d, Hall; w, Brough.

Crime Cas. (PR:A MPAA:PG)

FUNERAL HOME* (1982, Can.) 93m MPM-Wescom/CFDC c (AKA: 2 CRIES IN THE NIGHT)

Lesleh Donaldson (Heather), Kay Hawtrey (Maude), Barry Morse (Davis), Dean Garbett (Rick), Stephen Miller (Billy), Harvey Atkin (Harry), Alf Humphries (Joe), Peggy Mahon (Florie), Doris Petrik (Ruby), Les Rubie (Sam), Bob Warners (Fred).

Hawtrey, a peculiar old woman who lives in a small motel which formerly housed a funeral home, is visited one summer by her teenage granddaughter Donaldson. The young girl is soon haunted by frightening voices in the cellar, which turn out to be those of her dead grandfather. It seems grandma has been pretending to be grandpa while storing his decaying corpse in the house. If this doesn't sound familiar then you've never seen PSYCHO.

p&d, William Fruet; w, Ida Nelson; ph, Mark Irwin; m, Jerry Fielding; ed, Ralph Brunjes; prod d, Roy Forge Smith, Susan Longmire; spec eff, Dennis Pike; makeup, Shonagh Jabour.

Horror Cas. (PR:O MPAA:R)

FUNERAL IN BERLIN***½ (1966, Brit.) 102m PAR c

Michael Caine (Harry Palmer), Paul Hubschmid (Johnny Vulkan), Oscar Homolka (Col. Stok), Eva Renzi (Samantha Steel), Guy Doleman (Ross), Rachel Gurney (Mrs. Ross), Hugh Burden (Hallam), Thomas Holtzmann (Reinhart), Gunter Meisner (Kreutzmann), Heinz Schubert (Aaron Levine), Wolfgang Volz (Werner), Klaus Jepsen (Otto Rukel), Herbert Fux (Artur), Rainer Brandt (Benjamin), Ira Hagen (Monika), Marthe Keller (Brigit), Uschi Heyer (Bar Girl).

Caine repeats his role from THE IPCRESS FILE as he heads to Berlin to investigate the "death" of Homolka, whose funeral is being faked to get him through the Berlin Wall. An excellent look at espionage and the spy business with an interesting view of postwar Berlin. A fine cast in a strong film. Sequel: BILLION DOLLAR BRAIN.

p, Harry Saltzman, Charles Kasher; d, Guy Hamilton; w, Evan Jones (based on the novel by Len Deighton); ph, Otto Heller (Panavision, Technicolor); m, Conrad Elfers; ed, John Bloom; prod d, Ken Adam; md, Harry Rabinowitz; art d, Peter Murton; set d, Michael White, Vernon Dixon.

Spy Drama (PR:C MPAA:NR)

FUNHOUSE, THE** (1981) 96m UNIV c

Elizabeth Berridge (Amy), Cooper Huckabee (Buzz), Miles Chapin (Richie), Largo Woodruff (Liz), Sylvia Miles (Mme. Zena), Kevin Conway (The Barker), William Finley (Marco The Magnificent), Wayne Doba (The Monster), Shawn Carson (Joey Harper), Jeanne Austin (Mrs. Harper), Jack McDermott (Harper), David Carson (Geek), Sonia Zomina (Bag Lady), Ralph Marino (Truck Driver), Herb Robins (Carnival Manager), Mona Agar (Stripper), William Finley (Marco), Susie Malnik (Carmella), Sid Raymond (M.C.), Larry Ross (Heckler), Frank Grimes (Voyeur), Frank Schuller (Poker Player), Peter Conrad (Midget), Mildred Hughes (Tall Lady), Glen Lawrence, Mike Montalvo (Spectators), Shawn McAllister, Sandy Mielke (Garbage Collectors).

A group of teenagers high on pot stay all night in a carnival funhouse and witness the murder of a carnival stripper by a mutant son of the funhouse operator. When the monster's father realizes that the teenagers have witnessed the crime, he sends his son after them. Directed by the man who did TEXAS CHAINSAW MASSACRE, this film has a number of scary sequences, but isn't coherent enough to stand above the glut of teenage horror films done at this time. The film runs totally out of gas and original situations during the last fifteen minutes.

p, Derek Powers, Steven Bernhardt; d, Tobe Hooper; w, Larry Block; ph, Andrew Laszlo (Panavision, Technicolor); m, John Beal; ed, Jack Hofstra; prod. d, Morton Rabinowitz; art d, Jose Duarte; set d, Tom Coll.

Horror Cas. (PR:O MPAA:R)

FUNNY FACE***½ (1957) 103m PAR c

Audrey Hepburn (Jo Stockton), Fred Astaire (Dick Avery), Kay Thompson (Maggie Prescott), Michel Auclair (Prof. Emile Flostre), Robert Flemyng (Paul Duval), Dovima (Marion), Suzy Parker, Sunny Harnett, Don Powell, Carole Eastman (Specialty Dancers), Sue England (Laura), Ruta Lee (Lettie), Alex Gerry (Dovitch), Iphigenie Castiglioni (Armande), Jean Del Val (Hairdresser), Albert D'Arno (Beautician), Nina Borget (Assistant Hairdresser), Marilyn White, Dorothy Colbert (Receptionists), Louise Glenn, Heather Hopper, Cecile Rogers (Junior Editors), Nancy Kilgas (Melissa), Emilie Stevens (Assistant Dance Director), Paul Smith (Steve), Diane Du Bois (Mimi), Karen Scott (Gigi), Gabriel Curtiz (Man Next to Hand Stand), Peter Camlin (Man Buyer), Elizabeth Slifer (Mme. La Farge), Donald Lawton (Airport Clerk), Karine Nordman (French Girl), Genevieve Aumont (French Actress), Nesdon Booth (Southern Man), George Dee, Marcel de la Brosse, Albert Godderis (Seedy Men), Jerry Lucas (Bruiser), Jack Chefe (Frenchman), Jan Bradley (Crying Girl), Jerry Chiat (Man on Head), Elsa Peterson (Woman Buyer), Fern Barry (Southern Wife).

Not a great musical plot, FUNNY FACE does provide us with a host of George and Ira Gershwin songs and that alone is worth the price of admission. In the 1920s, the Gershwins did a musical called "Funny Face" but it hasn't a thing to do with this story, which was based on an unproduced musical called "Wedding Day." A satire of fashion, beatniks, existentialists, FUNNY FACE is a May-December romance between Astaire, a Madison Avenue fashion photographer based on real-life Richard Avedon (who was the visual consultant on the movie) and Greenwich Village bookseller Hepburn. Astaire finds the sweet, young thing and plays Henry Higgins to her Eliza, then takes her to Paris where, with the help of Kay Thompson, a magazine editor, they transform the waif into the top Vogue-type model in the world. Okay, that's the story, now you can forget it. It's just a hatrack on which to hang some of Gershwin's best tunes and some wonderful dancing choreographed by Astaire and Eugene Loring. Songs included: "Let's Kiss and Make Up," "He Loves and She Loves" (danced by Astaire), "Funny Face" (Astaire, Hepburn), "How Long Has This Been Going On?" (Hepburn), "Clap Yo' Hands" (Astaire, Thompson), "S'Wonderful" (Astaire, Hepburn, all by George, Ira Gershwin), "Bonjour Paris" (Astaire, Thompson, Hepburn), "On How To Be Lovely" (Thompson, Hepburn; Roger Edens, Leonard Gershe), "Marche Funebre" (Edens). Many of the songs were later used in the Tommy Tune/Twiggy Broadway show "My One And Only." Not many laughs but beautifully photographed and executed.

p, Roger Edens; d, Stanley Donen; w, Leonard Gershe (based on "Wedding Day," an unproduced musical libretto by Gershe); ph, Ray June (VistaVision, Technicolor); m, George Gershwin, Ira Gershwin, Roger Edens, Gershe; ed, Frank Bracht; md, Adolph Deutsch; art d, George W. Davis, Hal Pereira; set d, Sam Comer, Ray Moyer; cos, Edith Head, Hubert de Givenchy; spec eff, John P. Fulton; ch, Astaire, Eugene Loring; makeup, Wally Westmore.

Musical/Comedy Cas. (PR:AA MPAA:NR)

FUNNY FARM, THE** (1982, Can.) 96m New World-MUT c

Miles Chapin (Mark), Tracy Bregman (Amy), Jack Carter (Philly), Eileen Brennan (Gail), Peter Aykroyd (Stephen), Mike MacDonald (Bruce), Howie Mandel (Larry), Jack Blum (Peter), Marjorie Gross, Lou Dinos.

An attempt to do justice to stand-up comedians, with Chapin traveling to California from the Midwest to perform his routine. Brennan turns in a staunch performance as the owner of a comedy club.

p, Claude Heroux; d&w, Ron Clark; ph, Rene Verzier; m, Pierre Brousseau; ed, Marcus Manton; art d, Carol Spier.

Comedy/Drama Cas. (PR:C MPAA:NR)

FUNNY GIRL**** (1968) 151m Rastar/COL c

Barbra Streisand (Fanny Brice), Omar Sharif (Nick Arnstein), Kay Medford (Rose Brice), Anne Francis (Georgia James), Walter Pidgeon (Florenz Ziegfeld), Lee Allen (Eddie Ryan), Mae Questel (Mrs. Strakosh), Gerald Mohr (Branca), Frank Faylen (Keeney), Mittie Lawrence (Emma), Gertrude Flynn (Mrs. O'Malley), Penny Santon (Mrs. Meeker), John Harmon (Company Manager), Thordis Brandt, Bettina Brenna, Virginia Ann Ford, Alena Johnston, Karen Lee, Mary Jane Mangler, Inga Neilsen, Sharon Vaughn (Ziegfeld Girls).

There was hardly a more auspicious film debut for any actor or actress than this one for Barbra Streisand. She shared the Oscar as Best Actress with Katharine Hepburn (LION IN WINTER), the first time that had happened since 1931-32, when Fredric March (DR. JEKYLL AND MR. HYDE) and Wallace Beery (THE CHAMP) did the same thing. Streisand played the part on Broadway and had it perfected by the time Wyler brought it to the screen. It's the early 1900s and young Fanny Brice, an ugly duckling with a nonstoppable ambition to be a star, is determined to get out of her lower East Side life. Streisand is a wonder as Brice and milks every last laugh out of the situation. She loses a job in a chorus line and then tries to perform in a roller skating number. She slips, slides, gets loads of laughs and evokes gales of laughter from the crowd. Sharif (as Nicky Arnstein, a notorious gambler) sees her and helps her get the eye of Ziegfeld (Pidgeon) who hires her for his new Follies presentation. She walks on stage dressed as a pregnant bride (totally out of place in Pidgeon's mind and he is furious) and wows the crowd. Pidgeon is miffed at her chutzpah but mollified by the audience response and allows her to stay in the show and choose her own songs. Sharif appears again, takes her to a party at her mother's beer hall (Medford in an Oscar-nominated role), then leaves for horse racing in Kentucky. They meet again when she is touring in Maryland with the show. Love happens quickly and Sharif loses a fortune on a horse, then plans to go steamship cruising across the Atlantic where he can meet and bilk passengers out of their money. Streisand is on her way to Chicago and receives roses from Sharif. She calls Pidgeon, resigns, gets a train to NYC then leaps aboard a tugboat to catch Sharif's ocean liner. (That scene ends the first half of the road-show version and Wyler uses a helicopter to fly into an incredible close-up of Streisand's face for the song.) In act two, Streisand and Sharif move into a Long Island mansion, then she gives birth to a daughter (who, by the way, is married in real life to producer Ray Stark). Later, while rehearsing a new show, Streisand is shocked when Sharif loses all their money and they have to sell the house. Sharif is dwarfed by his wife's celebrity and begins gambling heavily. He owes lots of money and gets involved in a phony bond deal that causes him to be sent to jail. He returns after a year in prison and bids her goodbye in her dressing room and the picture concludes. They augmented the Broadway score with several tunes from Brice's life, including her signature "My Man" (Maurice Yvain, A. Willemetz, Jacques Charles, Channing Pollock) as well as "Second Hand Rose" (Grant Clarke, James Hanley) and "I'd Rather Be Blue" (Fred Fisher, Billy Rose). This was Wyler's first musical and he did it well, securing an Oscar nomination. Other nominations went to the picture, Stradling, Scharf, and the title song. Other songs: "People," "Don't Rain On My Parade," "I'm the Greatest Star," "Sadie, Sadie," "His Love Makes Me Beautiful," "You Are Woman, I Am Man," "If a Girl Isn't Pretty," "The Swan," "Roller Skate Rag," "Funny Girl," (Jule Styne, Bob Merrill). Sharif was offbeat casting but acquitted himself well. Good supporting work from all concerned and superb technical credits. Sequel: FUNNY LADY.

P, Ray Stark; d, William Wyler; w, Isobel Lennart (based on the musical by Jule Styne, Bob Merrill, Lennart); ph, Harry Stradling (Panavision, Technicolor); ed, Maury Winetrobe, William Sands; prod d, Gene Callahan; md, Walter Scharf; art d, Robert Luthardt; set d, William Kiernan; cos, Irene Sharaff; ch, Herbert Ross.

Musical/Comedy Cas. (PR:A MPAA:NR)

FUNNY LADY*½** (1975) 136m Rastar/COL c

Barbra Streisand *(Fanny Brice)*, James Caan *(Billy Rose)*, Omar Sharif *(Nick Arnstein)*, Roddy McDowall *(Bobby)*, Ben Vereen *(Bert Robbins)*, Carole Wells *(Norma Butler)*, Larry Gates *(Bernard Baruch)*, Heidi O'Rourke *(Eleanor Holm)*, Samantha Huffaker *(Fran)*, Matt Emery *(Buck Bolton)*, Joshua Shelley *(Painter)*, Corey Fischer *(Conductor)*, Garrett Lewis *(Production Singer)*, Don Torres *(Man at Wedding)*, Raymond Guth *(Buffalo Handler)*, Gene Troobnick *(Ned)*, Royce Wallace *(Adele)*, Cliff Norton, Paul Bryar.

Sequels are seldom as good as the originals but this one comes close. Streisand reprises her role as Fanny Brice and the picture begins in 1930. She's gotten Sharif (briefly reprising as Nick Arnstein, the gambler who was her first husband) out of her guts and now meets tiny Billy Rose, Caan, an entrepreneur-showman-songwriter and the shorthand champion of the U.S. It was with that shorthand talent that he became secretary to Bernard Baruch and got a lot of inside dope on the stock market, something that made Rose rich. Streisand and Rose marry but his running around and their separate careers keep them apart until the eventual breakup. A lot of fiction was added to the truth for this film and it suffered for that. It cost slightly under $9 million to make and tripled that in rentals but was essentially unsatisfying as a story. However, there was enough music in the movie to satisfy anyone and there were songs culled from several sources to fill out the Kander and Ebb score. Ross moved up from choreographer to helm this and he does a good job, considering the thin script he has to work with and the minor musical talents of Caan. FUNNY LADY garnered Oscar nominations for Howe, Matz, and best song "How Lucky Can You Get?" by Kander and Ebb. It didn't win anything in the Academy Award sweepstakes. Other Songs: "Great Day," "More Than You Know" (Vincent Youmans, Edward Eliscu, Billy Rose), "Blind Date," "So Long, Honey Lamb," "Isn't This Better?" "Let's Hear It for Me," "I Like Him/I Like Her" (John Kander, Fred Ebb), "It's Only A Paper Moon" (Harold Arlen, E.Y. Harburg, Rose), "I Found A Million Dollar Baby In a Five and Ten Cent Store" (Harry Warren, Mort Dixon, Rose), "Beautiful Face, Have a Heart" (James V. Monaco, Fred Fisher, Rose), "If You Want the Rainbow, You Must Have the Rain" (Oscar Levant, Dixon, Rose), "I Caught a Code In My Dose" (Arthur Fields, Fred Hall, Rose), "Am I Blue?" (Harry Akst, Grant Clarke, Rose), "Clap Hands, Here Comes Charley" (Joseph Meyer, Ballard MacDonald, Rose), "Me and My Shadow" (Al Jolson, Dave Dreyer, Rose), "If I Love Again" (Jack Murray, Ben Oakland). (Sequel to FUNNY GIRL.)

p, Ray Stark; d, Herbert Ross; w, Arnold Schulman, Jay Presson Allen (based on a story by Schulman); ph, James Wong Howe (Panavision, Technicolor); ed, Marion Rothman; prod d, George Jenkins; md, Peter Matz; set d, Audrey Blasdel; cos, Ray Aghayan, Bob Mackie, Shirley Strahm; spec eff, Albert Whitlock; ch, Betty Walberg. (Note: Various sources note that the picture is done in Metrocolor, Eastmancolor, or Technicolor.)

Musical/Comedy (PR:A MPAA:PG)

FUNNY MONEY zero (1983, Brit.) 97m Norfolk International/Cannon c

Gregg Henry, Elizabeth Daily, Gareth Hunt, Derren Nesbitt, Annie Ross, Joe Praml, Rose Alba, Stephen Yardley, Nigel Lambert, Bill McAllister, Lyndam Gregory, Al Matthews, Carol Cleveland, Mildred Shay, Charles Keating, Robert Henderson, Alan Campbell, Rai Bartonious, Fred S. Ronnow, Johnny Wade, Ronald Chenery, Richard Borthwick, Amanda Kemp, Melanie Hughes, Tony Allef, Marianne Stone, Dave Cooper, Kara Nobel, Roy Evan, Derek Deadman, Maggie Flint, Bill Gavin.

A sleazy little social satire which targets life in Britain and the characters' addiction to credit card buying. It's not especially pointed for a satire, or funny for a comedy despite a fairly accomplished cast.

p, Selwyn Roberts; d&w, James Kenelm Clarke; ph, John Wyatt; m, Ed Welch; ed, Bill Lennie; prod d, Harry Pottle.

Drama/Satire (PR:O MPAA:NR)

FUNNY PARISHIONER, THE (SEE: THANK HEAVEN FOR SMALL FAVORS, 1965, Fr.)

FUNNY THING HAPPENED ON THE WAY TO THE FORUM, A*** (1966) 99m UA c

Zero Mostel *(Pseudolus)*, Phil Silvers *(Lycus)*, Jack Gilford *(Hysterium)*, Buster Keaton *(Erronius)*, Michael Crawford *(Hero)*, Michael Hordern *(Senex)*, Annette Andre *(Philia)*, Patricia Jessel *(Domina)*, Leon Greene *(Miles Gloriosus)*, Inga Neilsen *(Gymnasia)*, Myrna White *(Vibrata)*, Pamela Brown *(Priestess)*, Jennifer & Susan Baker *(Geminae)*, Beatrix Lehmann *(Domina's Mother)*, Alfie Bass *(Gatekeeper)*, Roy Kinnear *(Instructor)*, Lucienne Bridou *(Panacea)*, Helen Funai *(Tintinabula)*, Janet Webb *(Fertilla)*, Frank Elliot, Bill Kerr, Jack May, Frank Thornton.

Mostel is a Roman slave desperately trying to win his freedom. Gilford is his unwitting accomplice. Plot complications involve Silvers as a brothel owner, Andre and Crawford as the young lovers, and Keaton, in what was to be his final U.S. film (he made one more in Canada before he died, the year FORUM was released) searching for his lost children. Lester's direction is a hit-and-miss effort with some really great moments of farce. The production numbers bog down the story but overall performances make this one worth watching. It is a great cast and Gilford is a gem. Taken from the Broadway show. Oscar winner for Best Adapted Score in 1966. Songs: "Everybody Ought to Have a Maid (Sweeping Out, Sleeping In)" (sung by Mostel, Silvers, Gilford, Hordern), "Comedy Tonight" (Mostel), "Lovely" (Mostel, Crawford, Andre, Gilford), "Bring Me My Bride" (Greene), "The Dirge" (Greene).

p, Melvin Frank; d, Richard Lester; w, Melvin Frank, Michael Pertwee (based on the musical comedy book by Burt Shevelove, Larry Gelbart); ph, Nicolas Roeg (DeLuxe Color); ed, John Victor Smith; prod d, Tony Walton; cos, Walton; spec eff, Cliff Richardson; ch, Ethel and George Martin; m/l, Stephen Sondheim.

Comedy Cas. (PR:C MPAA:NR)

FUNNYMAN½** (1967) 102m Korty/New Yorker c/bw

Peter Bonerz *(Perry)*, Sandra Archer *(Sue)*, Carol Androsky *(Sybil, Costumer)*, Larry Hankin *(Roger)*, Barbara Hiken *(Molly, Cook)*, Gerald Hiken *(Mahlon, Director)*, Nancy Fish *(Jan)*, Budd Steinhilber *(Vogel)*, Ethel Sokolow *(Vera, Agent)*, Marshall Efron *(Sid, Photographer)*, George Ede *(Advertising Executive)*, Jane House *(Girl in Bikini)*, Herb Beckman *(Watson, Ad Man)*, Manuela Ruecker *(Heidi)*, Rodger Bowen *(Lester, Social Scientist)*, Mel Stewart *(Phil)*, Dick Stahl *(Zach, Comic Salesman)*, Stephen D. Newman *(Sculptor)*, Alan Myerson *(Seymour, Electronics Man)*, Jerry Mander *(Arnie, Publicist)*, Lucille Bliss *(Girl of 1000 Voices)*, Ellsworth Milburn *(Piano Player)*, Anne Bownen *(Social Scientist's Wife)*, Arthur Okamura *(Painter)*.

Finding increasing monotony in his routines along with an unfulfilling sex life, a San Francisco comic takes a hiatus. Along the way he has a humorous encounter with a Japanese family and a model, Archer, who becomes his first meaningful relationship. The characters are extremely likable and Bonerz's monologs are very funny. There's some incisive social commentary and provocative musings on the serious business of being funny. However, Bonerz's vacation is anticlimatic and quickly rambles off into a series of disconnected events. The film is poorly photographed, though there are some interesting uses of animation.

p, Hugh McGraw, Stephen Schmidt; d, John Korty; w, Korty, Peter Bonerz; ph, Korty; m, Peter Schickele; ed, David Schickele; animation, Korty.

Comedy/Drama (PR:C MPAA:NR)

FUOCO FATUO (SEE: FIRE WITHIN, THE, 1964, Fr./Ital.)

FUR COLLAR, THE* (1962, Brit.) 71m Albatross/RFD bw

John Bentley *(Mike Andrews)*, Martin Benson *(Inspector Legrain)*, Philip Friend *(Eddie Morgan)*, Nadja Regin *(Marie Lejeune)*, Balbina *(Jacqueline Legrain)*, Hector Ross *(Roger Harding)*, Gordon Sterne *(Duclos)*, Guy Middleton *(Resident)*, Brian Nissen *(Carl Jorgensen)*.

Bentley is a reporter in Paris who collars a fugitive involved in an espionage operation. By pretending to be dead, Bentley fools the crook and foils his plans.

p,d&w, Lawrence Huntington.

Crime (PR:A MPAA:NR)

FURESSHUMAN WAKADISHO (SEE: YOUNG GUY GRADUATES, 1969, Jap.)

FURIA*** (1947, Ital.) 90m Franchini-AGIC/Film Classics bw

Isa Pola *(Clara)*, Rossano Brazzi *(Antonio)*, Gino Cervi *(Oreste)*, Adriana Bennetti *(Marietta)*, Umberto Spadaro *(Rocco)*, Camillo Pilotto *(Priest)*, Bella Starace Sainati *(Priest's Sister)*.

One of the many films to come out of the postwar Italian Neo-Realism movement. Pola is a bored housewife cheating on her horse breeder husband with Brazzi, an employee of her husband. The husband's daughter by a former marriage ends up marrying Brazzi, but this doesn't stop the affair. In the end, Pola is strangled by a crude stablehand who has lusted after her throughout the film. Daring for its time with a sensuality not found in American films. (In Italian, English subtitles.)

d&w, Geofredo Alessandrini; ed, Herman G. Weinberg; English subtitles by Weinberg.

Drama **(PR:O MPAA:NR)**

FURIES, THE*½ (1930) 69m FN/WB bw

Lois Wilson *(Fifi Sands)*, H. B. Warner *(Oliver Bedlow)*, Theodore Von Eltz *(Owen McDonald)*, Natalie Moorhead *(Caroline Leigh)*, Jane Winton *(Gwendolyn Andrews)*, Tyler Brooke *(Smith)*, Alan Birmingham *(Dr. Cummings)*, Purnell Pratt *(District Attorney)*, Byron Sage *(Alan Sands)*, Ben Hendricks, Jr. *(Bedlow's Butler)*, Carl Stockdale *(Bennett)*.

Who murdered Wilson's husband? The answer is somewhere in the continual stream of entrances and exits this unexciting adaptation of a stage play brings forth. The only entertainment is provided by the district attorney's investigation that produces a lot of laughs when it is discovered that the lawyer for Mrs. Wilson has coached the servants to fib, and her son discovers the ruse.

d, Alan Crosland; w, Forrest Halsey (based on the play by Zoe Akins), ph, Robert Kurrle.

Mystery **(PR:A MPAA:NR)**

FURIES, THE*** (1950) 109m PAR bw

Barbara Stanwyck *(Vance Jeffords)*, Wendell Corey *(Rip Darrow)*, Walter Huston *(T.C. Jeffords)*, Judith Anderson *(Florence Burnett)*, Gilbert Roland *(Juan Herrera)*, Thomas Gomez *(El Tigre)*, Beulah Bondi *(Mrs. Anaheim)*, Albert Dekker *(Reynolds)*, John Bromfield *(Clay Jeffords)*, Wallace Ford *(Scotty Hyslip)*, Blanche Yurka *(Herrera's Mother)*, Louis Jean Heydt *(Bailey)*, Frank Ferguson *(Dr. Grieve)*, Lou Steele *(Aguirre Herrera)*, Movita Casteneda *(Chiquita)*, Myrna Dell *(Dallas Hart)*, Jane Novak *(Woman)*, Arthur Hunnicutt, James Davies, Douglas Grange *(Cowhands)*, Baron Lichter *(Waiter)*, Pepe Hern *(Felix Herrera)*, Rosemary Pettit *(Carol Ann)*, Craig Kelly *(Young Anaheim)*, Charles Evans *(Old Anaheim)*, Joe Dominguez *(Wagon Driver)*, Artie Del Rey *(Wagon Driver's Son)*, Eddy C. Waller *(Old Man)*, Georgia Clancy *(Wedding Guest)*, Nolan Leary *(Drunk Guest)*, Sam Finn *(Dealer)*, Richard Kipling *(Bit Man)*.

Huston is a rancher about to marry socialite Anderson. His daughter Stanwyck tries to talk him out of it, but to no avail. Stanwyck attacks her stepmother and when Huston hangs an old ranchhand she vows revenge on her father. She and her lover, Corey, force Huston into bankruptcy and he is shot for hanging the ranchhand. A moody, dark western with overtones of Greek tragedy. A particularly vicious performance by Stanwyck, and the last film for Huston, who died of a heart attack two months before the film was released.

p, Hal B. Wallis; d, Anthony Mann; w, Charles Schnee (based on the novel by Niven Busch); ph, Victor Milner; m, Franz Waxman; ed, Archie Marshek; art d, Hans Dreier, Henry Bumstead; set d, Sam Comer, Bertran Granger; cos, Edith Head; spec eff, Gordon Jennings; m/l, "T.C. Round-up Time," Jay Livingston, Ray Evans.

Western **(PR:C MPAA:NR)**

FURIN KAZAN (SEE: UNDER THE BANNER OF SAMURAI, 1969, Jap.)

FURTHER ADVENTURES OF THE WILDERNESS FAMILY—PART TWO½** (1978) 105m PI c (AKA; WILDERNESS FAMILY, PART 2)

Robert Logan *(Skip Robinson)*, Susan D. Shaw *(Pat Robinson)*, Heather Rattray *(Jenny Robinson)*, Ham Larsen *(Tony Robinson)*, George "Buck" Flower *(Boomer)*, Brian Cutler *(Doctor)*, Kurt Grayson *(Pilot)*.

Sequel to the highly successful ADVENTURES OF THE WILDERNESS FAMILY. A simple story line follows the Robinson family as they encounter various woodland creatures (ranging from cute to vicious), assorted natural disasters, and Shaw's bout with pneumonia. Good performances and plenty of outdoor footage to satisfy any nature lover. Sequel: MOUNTAIN FAMILY ROBINSON.

p, Arthur Dubs; d, Frank Zuniga; w, Dubs; ph, John Hora; m, Douglas Lackey; m/l, Gene Kauer, Dennis Brockman (songs performed by Barry Williams).

Nature **(PR:AAA MPAA:G)**

FURTHER UP THE CREEK!*** (1958, Brit.) 91m COL bw

David Tomlinson *(Lt. Fairweather)*, Frankie Howerd *(Bos'n)*, Shirley Eaton *(Jane)*, Thora Hird *(Mrs. Galloway)*, Lionel Jeffreys *(Barker)*, Lionel Murton *(Perkins)*, Sam Kydd *(Bates)*, John Warren *(Cooky)*, David Lodge *(Scouse)*, Ian Whittaker *(Lofty)*, Amy D'Alby *(Edie)*, Esma Cannon *(Maudie)*, Tom Gill *(Phillipe)*, Jack Le White, Max Day *(Kentoni Brothers)*, Mary Wilson *(1st Model)*, Katherine Byrne *(2nd Model)*, Eric Pohlmann *(President)*, Michael Goodliffe *(Lt. Commander)*, Wolfe Morris *(Algeroccan Major)*, John Singer *(Dispatch Rider)*, Larry Noble *(Postman)*, Ballard Berkeley *(Whacker Payne)*, Judith Furse *(Chief Wren)*, Michael Ripper *(Ticket Collector)*, Joe Gibbon *(Taxi Driver)*, Victor Brooks *(Policeman)*, Cavan Malone *(Signalman)*, Desmond Llewellyn *(Chief Yeoman)*, Basil Dignam *(Flagship Commander)*, John Stuart *(Admiral)*, Jean Conrad *(Signals)*, Patrick Holt *(First Lieutenant)*, George Herbert *(Algeroccan Officer)*, Charles Lloyd Pack *(El Diabolo)*, Walter Hudd *(British Consul)*, John Hall *(Sea Scout)*.

A follow-up to the highly successful UP THE CREEK, and less rather than more, as most follow-ups are. Tomlinson repeats his role as the naive naval officer who is commander of "The Aristotle." The ship has been sold to the country of Algerocco and it's his job to deliver it. After leaving port he discovers the bos'n has sold tickets to nine passengers for a luxury cruise. Howerd has replaced Peter Sellers, UP THE CREEK's original bos'n, and changes the character to fit his own comic style.

p, Henry Halsted; d, Val Guest; w, Guest, John Warren, Len Heath; ph, Len Harris (Megascope); m, Stanley Black; ed, Bil Lenny.

Comedy **(PR:AA MPAA:NR)**

FURY***** (1936) 90m MGM bw

Spencer Tracy *(Joe Wheeler)*, Sylvia Sydney *(Katherine Grant)*, Walter Abel *(District Attorney)*, Edward Ellis *(Sheriff)*, Walter Brennan *(Buggs Meyers)*, Bruce Cabot *(Bubbles Dawson)*, George Walcott *(Tom)*, Frank Albertson *(Charlie)*, Arthur Stone *(Durkin)*, Morgan Wallace *(Fred Garrett)*, George Chandler *(Milt)*, Roger Gray *(Stranger)*, Edwin Maxwell *(Vickery)*, Howard C. Hickman *(Governor)*, Jonathan Hale *(Defense Attorney)*, Leila Bennett *(Edna Hooper)*, Esther Dale *(Mrs. Whipple)*, Helen Flint *(Franchette)*, Edward Le Saint *(Doctor)*, Everett Sullivan *(New Deputy)*, Murdock MacQuarrie *(Dawson's Friend)*, Ben Hall *(Goofy)*, Janet Young, Jane Corcoran, Mira McKinney, Mary Foy, Edna Mae Harris *(Women)*, Edwin J. Brady, James Quinn, Al Herman, Frank Mills *(Dawson's Friends)*, George Offerman, Jr. *(Defendant)*, Frank Sully *(Dynamiter)*, Dutch Hendrian *(Miner)*, Albert Taylor *(Old Man)*, Ray Brown *(Farmer)*, Guy Usher *(Assistant Defense Attorney)*, Nora Cecil *(Albert's Mother)*, Frederick Burton *(Judge Hopkins)*, Tom Mahoney *(Bailiff)*, Tommy Tomlinson *(Reporter)*, Sherry Hall *(Court Clerk)*, Carlos Martin *(Donelli)*, Jack Daley *(Factory Foreman)*, Duke York *(Taxi Driver)*, Charles Coleman *(Innkeeper)*, Will Stanton *(Drunk)*, Esther Muir *(Girl in Nightclub)*, Bert Roach *(Waiter)*, Raymond Hatton *(Hector)*, Victor Potel *(Jorgeson)*, Clara Blandick *(Judge's Wife)*, Erville Aderson *(Plumber)*, Herbert Ashley *(Oscar)*, Harry Hayden *(Lookup Keepr)*, Si Jenks *(Hillbilly)*, Christian Rub *(Ahem)*, Carl Stockdale *(Hardware Man)*, Elsa Newell *(Hot Dog Stand Owner)*, Alexander Cross, Robert E. Homans *(Guards)*, Arthur Hoydt *(Grouch)*, Ward Bond *(Objector)*, Franklin Parker, Wally Maher, Huey White *(Men)*, Gertrude Sutton *(Mrs. Tuttle)*, Minerva Urecal *(Fanny)*, Daniel Haynes *(Taxi Driver)*, Sam Hayes *(Announcer)*, Harvey Clark *(Pippen)*, Clarence Kolb *(Burgermeister)*.

German director Lang presents a trenchant indictment against the rule of the mob in this penetrating study of injustice and inhumanity, with Tracy providing an outstanding performance as the wronged man. En route to see his fiancee, Sidney, Tracy is arrested as a suspected kidnaper and jailed pending trial. The evidence against him is strictly circumstantial; he possesses a bill from a ransom payment. A mob forms around the jail but Ellis, the sheriff, manages to disband them, ordering them home. Ellis gets nervous and calls the governor, Hickman, begging him to put the national guard on alert in the event a lynch mob is formed, telling him he has not enough guards to withstand a full-scale assault on his small jail. Hickman tells him he will consider the action. Cabot and other mob leaders are drinking in a local bar when they learn about the bills found on Tracy, and the lynch legion is quickly formed, scores of vengeance-seeking citizens marching toward the jail carrying all manner of weapons and ropes. Ellis musters his guards and puts another urgent call through to Hickman, but the governor believes that it would be politically unwise to send out the national guard against his constituents and ignores the plea. The mob vents its wrath on the jail, hurling a shower of bricks through the windows and storming the line of guards outside. The jailers are overpowered but the mob cannot break into the jail. In frenzied frustration the mob sets the building on fire, also dynamiting it, and Tracy and other prisoners are trapped in a hellish inferno. Tracy has watched the mob do its dirty work from his cell window. Sydney, in the crowd, witnesses his agonized helplessness. The flames consume the building, ostensibly killing all inside. Yet Tracy survives and goes into hiding. Meanwhile, Abel, the local district attorney, reveals that the real kidnaper has been found and has confessed, that Tracy was innocent all along and that he has been a murder victim by the mob. Tracy, hidden by his brothers Walcott and Albertson, refuses to surface when Abel indicts more than 20 members of the mob for murder. He wants revenge and insists these lynch-law advocates be tried for his own murder. No one, however, including Ellis and other officials, will testify against Cabot and other mob members who smugly feel they will be freed. Sydney, who believes Tracy dead, testifies that she saw him at the window of his cell just before the jail was dynamited by mob members, offsetting the defense's contention that since Tracy's body was never found he was not killed. Abel then produces Tracy's charred engagement ring to prove he perished, albeit Tracy has purposely left this evidence of his own demise behind. When it appears that the defendants will get off, Tracy orders his brothers to obtain a newsreel taken at the site of the riot, showing the lynch mob members and the burning of the jail. The film is turned over to Abel and shown in court, horrifying spectators and many of those standing trial; one of the defendants, a woman, screams in guilt-ridden agony and confesses, leading many others to do the same. They are found guilty, but Tracy, his heart softened by appeals from Sydney, appears in court at the last minute and the would-be murderers are dismissed. This was Lang's favorite American film and rightfully so, for it demonstrates his directorial genius in wasting not a frame of film, telling his story with sharp cross-cutting between victim and tormentors, while unraveling the mindless and murderous passion of a mob out of control through the actions of its members. It is still a wonder that MGM, the "family oriented" studio, managed to release such a socially conscious "message" film. Lang had been hired in Paris in 1934 by David O. Selznick, then working for MGM, and he happily left Europe where the Nazi regime was fast taking over. The monocle-wearing Lang arrived in Hollywood in 1935 to find the community treating him with disdain; it was thought that he was another eccentric German director in the unpredictable mold of Erich von Stroheim. He was put to work writing scripts, a modern version of *Dr. Jekyll and Mr. Hyde*, adapted from a story by James Warner Bellah, "The Man Behind You." MGM never saw this script but Lang did show Selznick a screenplay alternately entitled PASSPORT TO HELL or JOURNEY TO HELL. The producer first told him he liked the script, then later said it was no good at all. Moreover, Lang made the mistake of snubbing studio mogul Louis B. Mayer and, with his year's contract about to run out, the great director was told that he was being released. He desperately offered up a project he had been working on with writer Norman Krasna, called "Mob Rule." Mankiewicz, a one-time contract writer at Paramount, was given the project, both Mayer and his production chief Eddie Mannix hoping the production would be a flop so they could be rid of the aloof Lang. The front office pecked away at Lang; he was called in by Mannnix once and accused of altering the approved dialog in the script, now called FURY. Lang quashed the objection by informing Mannix that his English was not good enough for him to change any of the script's dialog. (Lang had nevertheless spent months traveling through the U.S., talking to taxicab drivers, truck drivers, waitresses, gas station attendants, to learn English and the customs of America; he actually refused to speak German during the Nazi hold upon his homeland.) Used to absolute control at the UFA studio in Germany, Lang had no idea that union rules demanded that rest and food breaks were called for in his unrelenting schedule and he was soon in hot water. Even Tracy sided with the hordes of extras in the film, feeling they were being abused. Lang inserted some scenes showing how blacks were victimized by mobs of whites, but Mayer personally had these scenes cut, stating that his studio was not in business to produce social commentary. The studio, at Mayer's connivance, went so far as to bury the film on a double bill, released in a small West Coast theater, so it would go unnoticed and result in a box office failure MGM could use to send Lang packing. But W.R. Wilkerson, who published the influential *Hollywood Reporter*, and who was a Lang fan, heard about the film and called the studio to ask why it was being released in a remote theater. He was reportedly told by a studio executive: "Oh, don't go . . . it's a lousy picture." He went anyway and found the film to be the masterpiece it is. His enthusiasm and that of other critics, forced MGM to give the film a major publicity campaign and release it in first-run houses on the East Coast. The film, along with MGM's release of SAN FRANCISCO a month later, made a top star out of Tracy. Lang touches are present in FURY everywhere, particularly close-ups of newspaper headlines, wanted posters, elements of grim reality to document the tale he unfolds. MGM was astounded by the success of the film which Lang saw at the New York premiere, accompanied by Marlene Dietrich. Even though he had succeeded, Lang's tremendous accomplishment, his vivid and horrifying portrait of mob violence, was thought by the studio to be a fluke and Lang soon left MGM when the studio refused to make any more such films. The director moved on to United Artists to make YOU ONLY LIVE ONCE (1937) with Henry Fonda and Sylvia Sydney and would not return to MGM until 1955 to direct MOONFLEET. The story for FURY comes wholly from the lynching of two kidnapers, Thomas Harold Thurmond and John Maurice Holmes, who had abducted and murdered Brooke Hart, son of a department store owner in San Jose, California. They were dragged out of the San Jose jail on the night of Novemeber 9, 1933, by an enraged mob bent on lynch law, thousands of citizens attacking the jail and dragging the two men out and stringing them up in a local park, their actions recorded by news photographers and newsreel cameramen. After lynching the kidnapers, scores of citizens drove their cars to the spot and turned on auto lights to play upon the bodies swaying from tree limbs. State police had to fight the mob to cut down the bodies and remove them. Even in death the kidnapers were not immune to the mob's wrath, scores of women, children and men spitting and striking the corpses as they were taken away. California Gov. James "Sunny Jim" Rolfe, who had been repeatedly asked by San Jose Sheriff William Emig to send state militia to prevent the lynching, refused to lift a finger to stem the tide of the mob. Upon hearing about the lynchings, this less than distinguished state official remarked that the mob had "the best lesson ever given the country. I would pardon those fellows if they were charged. I would like to parole all kidnapers in San Quentin and Folsom to the fine patriotic citizens of San Jose." No one was charged in the lynchings.

p, Joseph L. Mankiewicz; d, Fritz Lang; w, Bartlett Cormack, Lang (based on the story "Mob Rule" by Norman Krasna); ph, Joseph Ruttenberg; m, Franz Waxman; ed, Frank Sullivan; art d, Cedric Gibbons, William A. Horning, Edwin B. Willis; set d, Willis; cos, Dolly Tree.

Crime Drama **(PR:C MPAA:NR)**

FURY, THE*½ (1978) 117m FOX c

Kirk Douglas *(Peter Sandza)*, John Cassavetes *(Childress)*, Carrie Snodgress *(Hester)*, Amy Irving *(Gillian Bellaver)*, Andrew Stevens *(Robin Sandza)*, Fiona Lewis *(Dr. Susan Charles)*, Charles Durning *(Dr. Jim McKeever)*, Carol Rossen *(Dr. Ellen Lindstrom)*, Joyce Easton *(Katharine Bellaver)*, William Finley *(Raymond Dunwoodie)*, Jane Lambert *(Vivian Knuckells)*, Sam Laws *(Blackfish)*, Melody Thomas *(LaRue)*, Hilary Thomas *(Cheryl)*, Patrick Billingsley *(Lander)*, Jack Callahan *(DeMasi)*, Dennis Franz *(Bob)*, Michael O'Dwyer *(Marty)*, Felix Shuman *(Dr. Ives)*, J. Patrick McNamara *(Robertson)*, Bernie Kuby *(Nuckles)*, Rutanya Alda *(Kristen)*, Frank Yablans *(Goon on Radio)*.

Not to be confused with FURY, a superb Spencer Tracy film, this is another one of De Palma's muddles, although it may be the best picture he's done. If you've been reading the MPG, you must know by this time how we feel about DePalma's work. If he isn't taking ideas from Hitchcock (BODY DOUBLE, DRESSED TO KILL), then he's taking from himself (CARRIE) as he details yet another telekinesis story. Andrew Stevens (real-life son of actress Stella Stevens) is on vacation with his father, Douglas, at a resort on the Mediterranean. Douglas is a U.S. secret agent and his cohort, Cassavetes, is the chief of a shadowy U.S. agency investigating psychic phenomena. Terrorists attack the resort and it looks as though Douglas has been killed. Cassavetes takes Stevens out during the gunplay. Now we learn that Cassavetes doesn't work for the U.S., he's in it for his own profit and he knows that Stevens has the ability he wants to duplicate. The "terrorists" were not that at all, rather they were murderers hired by Cassavetes to erase Douglas so the villain could get the lad all to himself. Douglas is not dead, however, and he returns to the States where he hires a psychic, Finley, to help find Stevens. Meanwhile, Amy Irving is also telekinetic and currently being studied at the Paragon Institute (which we later find out is a cover for Cassavetes). Finley informs Douglas that Irving is sending out "vibrations" and might know where the lost Stevens is. At Cassavetes's secret country place, he is altering Stevens' mind and hopes to use the young man for evil purposes and auction him off to the highest bidder. It is presumed that one of the Arab bloc countries will pay through the turban for him. The powers are taking over Stevens and he is rapidly becoming psychotic. Douglas gets Irving out of the Institute and, together, they will attempt to find Stevens at Cassavetes' hideout. Stevens is far gone now, a real nut-case, and he is in love with his doctor, Lewis. When he thinks she is cheating on him, he uses his powers to kill her. Douglas and Irving arrive (she has pictured the place in her mind) and see Stevens die from a fall off the top of the mansion. Douglas responds by committing suicide. Now that Stevens is gone, Cassavetes attempts to get Irving into the same situations but she responds by concentrating and blowing Cassavetes up into a million shards of flesh and gristle and bone. The best part of the movie was the makeup by Tuttle and the special makeup effects by Rick Baker. This was probably better than the other De Palma tripe because someone else wrote the screenplay. His long suit is fancy camerawork and lots of blood and guts. His short suit is everything else. Producer Yablans couldn't resist taking a part in this film, babbling in a bit part on radio.

p, Frank Yablans; d, Brian De Palma; w, John Farris (based on his novel); ph, Richard H. Kline (DeLuxe Color); m, John Williams; ed, Paul Hirsch; prod d, Billy Malley; set d, Audrey Blasdel-Goddard; cos, Theoni V. Aldredge; spec eff, A.D. Flowers; makeup, William Tuttle; spec makeup eff, Rick Baker.

Horror **Cas.** **(PR:O MPAA:R)**

FURY AND THE WOMAN** (1937) 65m Rialto bw

William Gargan *(Bruce Corrigan)*, Molly Lamont *(June McCrae)*, James McGrath *(Kinky)*, Reginald Hincks *(Engineer)*, J.P. McGowan *(Anderson)*, Libby Taylor *(Sarah)*, Harry Hastings *(Ling)*, Ernie Impett *(Bart)*, Arthur Kerr *(Lester)*, Bob Rideout *(Red)*, David Clyde *(McCrae)*.

Gargan, a new arrival in a logging camp, is actually the owner's son. Though he keeps his identity a secret, he soon discovers a plot by some workers dealing with a rival logging company. The camp is run, incredulously, by his father's beautiful partner, Lamont. He falls in love with her but not before having to work his way through some misunderstandings and plenty of rugged action. Some nice logging footage helps the film. Unbelievable but entertaining.

p, Kenneth J. Bishop; d, Lewis D. Collins; w, Philip Conway; ph, Henry Forbes; ed, William Austin.

Adventure/Romance **(PR:A MPAA:NR)**

FURY AT FURNACE CREEK*** (1948) 88m FOX bw

Victor Mature *(Cash)*, Coleen Gray *(Molly Baxter)*, Glenn Langan *(Rufe)*, Reginald Gardiner *(Capt. Walsh)*, Albert Dekker *(Leverett)*, Fred Clark *(Bird)*, Charles Kemper *(Peaceful Jones)*, Robert Warwick *(Gen. Blackwell)*, George Cleveland *(Judge)*, Roy Roberts *(Al Shanks)*, Willard Robertson *(Gen. Leads)*, Griff Barnett *(Appleby)*, Frank Orth *(Evans)*, J. Farrell MacDonald *(Pops)*, Charles Stevens *(Artego)*, Jay Silverheels *(Little Dog)*, Robert Adler *(Leverett Henchman)*, Harry Carter *(Clerk)*, Mauritz Hugo, Howard Negley *(Defense Counsels)*, Harlan Briggs *(Prosecutor)*, Si Jenks *(Jury Foreman)*, Guy Wilkerson, Edmund Cobb *(Court Clerks)*, Kermit Maynard *(Scout)*, Paul Newlan *(Bartender)*, Ted Mapes *(Man)*, George Chesebro, Al Hill, Jerry Miley *(Card Players)*, Minerva Urecal *(Mrs. Crum)*, Ray Teal *(Sergant)*, Alan Bridge *(Lawyer)*, Oscar O'Shea *(Jailer)*, Robert Williams *(Stranger)*, James Flavin *(Judge Advocate)*.

Well done action-packed western has Mature and Langan as the sons of Warwick, the commanding officer of an outpost who is cashiered after being charged with conspiring with renegade Indians. The brothers go about clearing their father's name but using divergent methods. Mature, a rugged adventurer, takes the abrupt approach, while Langan, an officer in the army, conducts a methodical search. Both alienate each other in their desperate search for the truth but reconcile by the finish when they discover that silver tycoon Dekker has framed their father so he can buy up mineral rich Indian lands for a pittance. Mature is terrific as the maverick son and Dekker is solid as the culprit. Gardiner is also good as the spineless army officer in Dekker's grip who sets up Warwick's frame. Gray, who loves both brothers, is fetching. Although a B feature, everything about this production is above average, from the tight direction by Humberstone to Jackson's photography and Raskin's memorable score.

p, Fred Kohlmar; d, H. Bruce Humberstone; w, Charles G. Booth, Winston Miller (based on a story by David Garth); ph, Harry Jackson; m, David Raskin; ed, Robert Simpson; md, Alfred Newman; art d, Lyle Wheeler, Albert Hogsett; set d, Thomas Little; cos, Rene Hubert; spec eff, Fred Sersen; makeup, Ben Nye, George Lane.

Western **(PR:A MPAA:NR)**

FURY AT GUNSIGHT PASS**½ (1956) 68m COL bw

David Brian *(Whitey Turner)*, Neville Brand *(Dirk Hogan)*, Richard Long *(Roy Hanford)*, Lina Davis *(Kathy Phillips)*, Katharine Warren *(Mrs. Boggs)*, Percy Helton *(Boggs)*, Morris Ankrum *(Doc Phillips)*, Addison Richards *(Charles Hanford)*, Joe Forte *(Andrew Ferguson)*, Wally Vernon *(Okay, Okay)*, Paul E. Burns *(Squint)*, Frank Fenton *(Sheriff Meeker)*, James Anderson *(O'Neil)*, George Keymas *(Daley)*, Robert Anderson *(Sam Morris)*, Fred Coby *(Spencer)*, John Lehmann *(Forrest)*, Guy Teague *(Hammond)*.

Brian is an outlaw who tries to pull one over on his boss. He holds up a bank before the designated time but the cash is stolen by the town undertaker, whose wife steals the money when he's accidentally killed. Meanwhile, the robbers are holding the town hostage until the money is found, threatening to kill a citizen an hour. Eventually, the money is returned and the wrongdoers are punished. Though a little too short to achieve everything it sets out to accomplish, FURY AT GUN-SIGHT PASS is well directed with some strong scenes. The script is sharply written, though a little complex.

p, Wallace MacDonald; d, Fred F. Sears; w, David Lang; ph, Fred Jackman, Jr.; m, Mischa Bakaleinikoff; ed, Saul Goodkind; art d, George Brooks.

Western   **(PR:O   MPAA:NR)**

FURY AT SHOWDOWN*** (1957) 75m UA bw

John Derek (*Brock Mitchell*), John Smith (*Miley Sutton*), Carolyn Craig (*Ginny Clay*), Nick Adams (*Tracy Mitchell*), Gage Clarke (*Chad Deasey*), Robert E. Griffin (*Sheriff Clay*), Malcolm Atterbury (*Norris*), Rusty Lane (*Riley*), Sydney Smith (*Van Steeden*), Frances Morris (*Mrs. Williams*), Tyler McDuff (*Tom Williams*), Robert Adler (*Alabam*), Norman Leavitt (*Swamper*), Ken Christy (*Mr. Phelps*), Tom McKee (*Sheriff of Buckhorn*).

Derek is an ex-gunslinger trying to overcome his past reputation with the help of his exuberant younger brother Adams. An evil attorney, played by Clarke, is seeking revenge on Derek for the killing of Clarke's brother years earlier. An attempt is made to swindle land from Derek, then a hired gun kills Adams. Derek kills the hired gun and has Clarke arrested for his crimes. The end finds Derek with girl friend Craig, who has spent the film wrestling with her conscience about her love for Derek. Moody and atmospheric, FURY AT SHOWDOWN is a remarkable achievement considering that it was shot in only five days. The existential feel, though a little heavy-handed, works well within the setting.

p, John Beck; d, Gerd Oswald; w, Jason James (based on a novel by Lucas Todd); ph, Joseph LaShelle; m, Henry Sukman; ed, Robert Golden; art d, Leslie Thomas.

Western   **(PR:O   MPAA:NR)**

FURY AT SMUGGLERS BAY** (1963, Brit.) 92m Mijo/EM bw

John Fraser (*Chris Trevenyan*), Peter Cushing (*Squire Trevenyan*), Bernard Lee (*Black John*), June Thorburn (*Jenny Trevenyan*), Michele Mercier (*Louise Lejeune*), William Franklyn ("*The Captain*"), George Coulouris (*Francois Lejeune*), Liz Fraser (*Betty*), Miles Malleson (*Duke of Avon*), Katherine Kath (*Maman*), Jouma (*Jouma*), Tom Duggan ("*Red Friars*"), Humphrey Heathcote (*Roger Treherne*), Christopher Carlos (*The Tiger*), Maitland Moss (*Tom*).

Fraser, the son of local magistrate Cushing, discovers a gang of pirates ruthlessly led by Lee. Cushing, however, makes no attempt to disarm the outlaws, instead blaming a series of smuggling incidents on some local fisherman. Fraser enlists some help and learns that dad fears Lee will blackmail him. A battle ensues and both Cushing and Lee are killed. Fraser, of course with a romantic interest, becomes the new magistrate.

p,d&w, John Gilling; ph, Harry Waxman (PanaScope); m, Harold Geller; ed, John Victor Smith; art d, Duncan Sutherland; cos, Phyllis Dalton.

Adventure/Drama   **(PR:A   MPAA:NR)**

FURY BELOW*½ (1938) 58m J. E. Baum bw

Russell Gleason (*Jim Cole III*), Maxine Doyle (*Mary Norsen*), Leroy Mason (*Fred Johnson*), Sheila Terry (*Claire Johnson*), Matthew Betz (*Dorsky*), Rex Lease (*Joe Norsen*), John Merton (*Emil*), Ruth Frazer (*Molly*), Phil Dunham (*Cole, Sr.*), Elliott Sullivan (*Miner*).

A comedy in a coal mine. Gleason is a young mine operator, Merton is a mad mine driller, and Lease is the foreman. Conflict comes in the form of Betz, doing one of his patented heavies. The film is poorly written and is disjointed. Gleason does manage to have a few funny lines but the film is forgettable.

p, G.R. Mercader; d, Harry Fraser; w, Phil Dunham (based on a story by Mercader); ph, Paul Ivano; ed, Arthur Brooks.

Comedy   **(PR:A   MPAA:NR)**

FURY IN PARADISE* (1955, U.S./Mex.) 77m Filmmakers c

Peter Thompson, Rea Iturbi, Edwards Noriega, Felipe Nolan, Jose Espinosa, Fran Schiller, Carlos Rivas, Claud Brooks.

Thompson, while vacationing in Mexico, gets entangled in a revolutionary plot and the lives of a powerful hacienda owner. He readily falls for the owner's daughter—one of the staple acts in oaterville. Filmed in Mexico, which may not be paradise, but at least it's in color.

p, Alfonso Sanchez-Tello; d&w, George Bruce; ph, (Eastmancolor).

Western   **(PR:A   MPAA:NR)**

FURY OF HERCULES, THE*½ (1961, Ital.) 95m Medallion c
(LA FURIA DI ERCOLE; AKA: FURY OF SAMSON)

Brad Harris, Brigitte Corey, Mara Berni, Carlo Tamberlani, Serge Gainsbourg, Elke Arendt, Alan Steele.

Another of the innumerable muscleman films made in Italy during the early 1960s, all spectacles of physical exaggeration in terms of both beauty and muscles. Not deviating too heavily from the standard plot, Harris is the bronze-bodied hero instrumental in freeing a group of people forced to live under the thumb of an evil ruler.

d, Gianfranco Parolini; w, P. Parolini, Giorgio C. Simonelli, C. Madison; ph, Francesco Izzarelli; ed, Mario Sansoni; spec eff, R. Morelli, F. Cardinali.

Adventure   **(PR:A   MPAA:NR)**

FURY OF THE CONGO**½ (1951) 69m COL bw

Johnny Weissmuller (*Jungle Jim*), Sherry Moreland (*Leta*), William Henry (*Ronald Cameron*), Lyle Talbot (*Grant*), Joel Friedkin (*Prof. Dunham*), George Eldredge (*Barnes*), Rusty Wescoatt (*Magruder*), Paul Marion (*Raadi*), Blanca Vischer (*Mahara*), Pierce Lyden (*Allen*), John Hart (*Guard*).

Deep in the Congo jungles dwells the Okongo, a giant spider that produces a potent narcotic after ingesting certain jungle plants. A group of evildoers want the

drug. They kidnap a tribe of white jungle natives who worship the Okongo, then force them to round up the special plant. Also being held captive is a professor who is being searched for by Weissmuller, who does battle with assorted beasts and natural disasters before confronting the smugglers and restoring peace to the Congo once more. Standard jungle genre. (See JUNGLE JIM series, Index.)

p, Sam Katzman; d, William Berke; w, Carroll Young (based on the comic strip "Jungle Jim" by A. Raymond); ph, Ira H. Morgan; ed, Richard Fantl; md, Mischa Bakaleinikoff; art d, Paul Palmentola.

Adventure   **(PR:AA   MPAA:NR)**

FURY OF THE JUNGLE* (1934) 55m COL bw

Donald Cook (*Allen*), Peggy Shannon (*Joan*), Alan Dinehart (*Taggart*), Harold Huber (*Frenchy*), Dudley Digges (*Parrish*), Toshia Mori (*Chita*), Clarence Muse, Fredrik Vogeding, Charlie Stevens.

White men from various countries, along with a South American native girl, live in a small village when along comes the first white woman they've seen in a long time. She has brought along her sick brother, who quickly succumbs to disease, leaving the sister to contend with the male population. The native girl becomes jealous as the men all vie for the unfortunate woman's attentions. This film was cheaply made with painfully phony accents by the actors. The same stock shot of a jaguar is used twice. The blatant racism is unforgivable.

d, Roy William Neill; w, Ethel Hill, Dore Schary (based on a story by Horace McCoy); ph, John Stumar; ed, Ray Curtiss.

Drama   **(PR:O   MPAA:NR)**

FURY OF THE PAGANS*½ (1963, Ital.) 86m Arion/COL bw-c (LA FURIA DEI BARBARI)

Edmund Purdom (*Toryok*), Rossana Podesta (*Lianora*), Livio Lorenzon (*Kovo*), Carla Calo, Daniele Vargas, Andrea Fantasia, Vittorio Feri, Ljubica Jovic, Amedeo Novelli, Niksa Stefanian, Giulio Massimi, Simonetta Simeoni, Raffaella Pelloni, Luciano Marin.

A long-running rivalry between Purdom and Lorenzon set in northern Italy during the sixth century. After Lorenzon does some killing and raping of Purdom's women, the victimized leader is enraged. After a few years, Lorenzon returns to the village with gal Podesta. Purdom single-handedly kills him and takes Podesta.

d, Guido Malatesta; w, Gino Mangini, Umberto Scarpelli (based on a story by Mangini); ph, Vincenzo Seratrice (Dyaliscope, Eastmancolor); m, Gian Stellari, Guido Robuschi; ed, Roberto Giandalia; art d, Pier Vittorio Marchi, Alfonso Russo.

Action/Drama   **(PR:C   MPAA:NR)**

FURY OF THE VIKINGS (SEE: ERIK THE CONQUEROR, 1961, Ital.)

FUSS OVER FEATHERS*** (1954, Brit.) 84m Group 3/BL c
(GB: CONFLICT OF WINGS)

John Gregson (*Bill Morris*), Muriel Pavlow (*Sally*), Kieron Moore (*Squadron Leader Parsons*), Niall MacGinnis (*Harry Tilney*), Harry Fowler (*Buster*), Guy Middleton (*Adjutant*), Sheila Sweet (*Fanny Bates*), Campbell Singer (*F/S Campbell*), Barbara Hicks (*Mrs. Thompson*), Brian Moorehead (*3rd Pilot*), Harold Siddons (*Range Officer*), Howard Connell (*Flight Officer, Control*), Charles Lloyd Pack (*Bookie*), Bartlett Mullins (*Soapy*), Russell Napier (*Wing Cmdr. Rogers*), Frederick Piper (*Joe Bates*), Edwin Richfield (*Smother Brooks*), Dorothea Rundle (*Mrs. Trotter*), George Woodbridge, William Mervyn, David Spenser, Peter Swanwick, Gwenda Wilson, Margaret Withers, Hugh Moxey, Beryl Cooke, Brian Harding, Humphrey Lestocq, Guy Verney, Tony Doonan.

Legend-ridden villagers fight to save a bird sanctuary scheduled as a target area for the air force. Local folk prove the land was planned by Henry VIII as a public preserve, but they are overruled by a high court, so they take matters into their own hands. The Norfolk fields are colorful stretches of country suitably captured for romantic action through Grant's lens. Direction and screenplay follow suit.

p, Herbert Mason; d, John Eldridge; w, Don Sharp, John Pudney (based on a novel by Sharp); ph, Arthur Grant (aerial), Martin Curtis (Eastmancolor); m, Philip Green; ed, Lito Carruthers.

Drama   **(PR:AAA   MPAA:NR)**

FUTARI NO MUSUCKO (SEE: DIFFERENT SONS, 1962, Jap.)

FUTUREWORLD*** (1976) 107m AIP c

Peter Fonda (*Chuck Browning*), Blythe Danner (*Tracy Ballard*), Arthur Hill (*Duffy*), Yul Brynner (*Gunslinger*), John Ryan (*Schneider*), Stuart Margolin (*Harry*), Jim Antonio (*Ron*), Allen Ludden (*Game Show M.C.*), Nancy Bell (*Erica*), Angela Greene (*Mrs. Reed*), Robert Cornthwaite (*Mr. Reed*), Darrell Larson (*Eric*), John Fujioka (*Mr. Takaguchi*), Dana Lee (*His Aide*), Burt Conroy (*Gen. Karnovski*), Dorothy Konrad (*Mrs. Karnovski*), Alex Rodine (*KGB Man*), Joanna Hall (*Maiden Fair*).

In this sequel to 1973's WESTWORLD, it is three years later and investigative reporters Fonda and Danner are looking over the revamped futuristic theme park Delos. They meet Hill, the director of Futureworld, and stumble onto his plot to replace all world leaders with look-alike robots. Brynner has a small cameo, reprising his role from the first film. In the end it is discovered that Hill is also a robot. Though not as clever or original as its predecessor, FUTUREWORLD is effective. Some location shooting at NASA facilities is used particularly well. Both Fonda and Danner give strong performances.

p, Paul Lazarus III, James T. Aubrey, Jr.; d, Richard T. Heffron; w, Mayo Simon, George Schenck; ph, Howard Schwartz, Gene Polito (Metrocolor); m, Fred Karlin; ed, James Mitchell; art d, Trevor Williams; set d, Dennis Peeples, Marvin March; cos, Ann McCarthy; spec eff, Brent Sellstrom, Gene Griggs.

Science Fiction/Thriller   **Cas.**   **(PR:C   MPAA:PG)**

FUZZ*** (1972) 92m Filmways/UA c

Burt Reynolds (*Detective Steve Carella*), Jack Weston (*Detective Meyer Meyer*), Tom Skerritt (*Detective Bert Kling*), Raquel Welch (*Detective Eileen McHenry*), Yul Brynner (*Deaf Man*), James McEachin (*Detective Arthur Brown*), Steve Ihnat (*Detective Andy Parker*), Stewart Moss (*Detective Hal Willis*), Dan Frazer (*Lt. Byrnes*), Bert Remsen (*Sgt. Murchison*), H. Benny Markowitz (*Patrolman Levine*), James Victor (*Patrolman Gomez*), Roy Applegate (*Patrolman Cramer*), Tom Lawrence (*Patrolman Crosby*), Norman Burton (*Police Commissioner Nelson*), Vince Howard (*Patrolman Marshall*), Jake Lexa (*Patrolman Miscolo*), Britt Leach, Brian Doyle Murray, Harold Oblong (*Detectives*), J.S. Johnson (*Telephone Technician*), Harry Eldon Miller (*Police Garage Attendant*), David Dreyer (*Mayor's Uniformed Guard*), William Martel (*Mayor's Bodyguard*), Peter Bonerz (*Buck*), Cal Bellini (*Ahmad*), Don Gordon (*LaBresca*), Charles Tyner (*Pete*), Gary Morgan (*Jimmy*), Charlie Martin Smith (*Baby*), Tamara (*Rochelle*), George Reynolds (*Tiny*), Albert Popwell (*Lewis*), Ron Tannas (*Dominick*), Barry Hamilton (*Young Prisoner*), Roy Morton (*Rapist*), Felipe Turich (*Puerto Rican Prisoner*), Gino Conforti, Gerald Hiken (*Painters*), Robert Jaffe (*Alan*), Neile Adams (*Teddy*), Martine Bartlett (*Sadie*), Peter Brocco (*Man with Garbage*), Mia Bendixsen (*Little Girl*), Christopher Wheeler (*Little Boy*), David Fresco (*Vicenzo*), Vincent Van Lynn (*Mayor Jefferson*), Jack Perkins (*Parks Commissioner*), Bunny Summers (*Mrs. Cooper*), Russ Grieve (*Deputy Mayor*), Cay Forester (*Mrs. Scanlon*), Athena Lorde (*Mrs. Jefferson*), Patti Tee Byrne (*Abigail*), Cynthia Lane (*Louise*), Dominic Chianese (*Panhandler*), Richard Stahl (*Vagrant*), Charles Picerni (*Chauffeur*), Larry Barton (*Bald Man*).

An episodic police comedy in the same vein as M*A*S*H and THE HOSPITAL. Reynolds is a Boston cop searching for bomber Brynner who has been killing local politicians. In between are various episodes and characters, including Welch as a policewoman undercover in a sleeping bag with Skerritt, and Morgan and Smith as two punks who get cheap thrills turning winos into bonfires. Fast-paced film that makes good points though the humor may be offensive to some. Don't miss Reynolds in the nun's habit.

p, Jack Farren; d, Richard A. Colla; w, Evan Hunter (based on the novel by Ed [Evan Hunter] McBain); ph, Jacques Marquette (Panavision, DeLuxe Color); m, Dave Grusin; ed, Robert Kimble; art d, Hilyard Brown; set d, Philip Abramson; cos, Dorothy Jeakins; m/l, "I'll Be Seeing You" (sung by Dinah Shore).

Comedy **Cas.** **(PR:O MPAA:PG)**

FUZZY PINK NIGHTGOWN, THE (1957) 87m UA bw

Jane Russell (*Laurel Stevens*), Keenan Wynn (*Dandy*), Ralph Meeker (*Mike Valla*), Fred Clark (*Sgt. McBride*), Una Merkel (*Bertha*), Adolphe Menjou (*Arthur Martin*), Renay Venuta (*Daisy Parker*), Robert H. Harris (*Barney Baylies*), Bob Kelley (*TV Announcer*), Dick Haynes (*Disk Jockey*), John Truax (*Flack*), Milton Frome (*Lt. Dempsey*).

A muddled and limp story shows Russell as a sexy film star who is kidnaped just as her new film, "The Kidnaped Bride" is about to be released. She plays along with abductors Meeker and Wynn, thinking it all a studio stunt to promote the film, but they are for real. After spending some time with Russell, however, both fall for her, particularly Meeker, and they want to call off the kidnaping. But by now Russell wants them to go through with the actual abduction, fearing that her fans will feel that it was only a cheap publicity stunt after all and it will ruin her film at the box office. The film is stilted, and, beyond the skimpy wardrobe designed to show off Russell's magnanimous mammaries and Amazonian figure, the whole thing appears forced and unfunny. Much of the failure for this film was later assumed by Russell who insisted on a black-and-white film with the accent on romance, while director Taurog wanted a color film which caricatured the entire story. He lost. Moreover, Dean Martin was scheduled for the Meeker role but Russell could not get him hired. She later claimed that because of this she was never allowed on Martin's TV show. Russell's filmmaking decisions since leaving Howard Hughes' protective umbrella had not been on the money. She turned down the lead role in LOVE ME OR LEAVE ME (1955) opposite James Cagney and the part went to Doris Day, the film becoming a smash hit. Russell declined the role while believing she would get the lead part in I'LL CRY TOMORROW (1956) which went to Susan Hayward. THE FUZZY PINK NIGHTGOWN is mere puff, a quickie put together after Hollywood starlet Marie "The Body" McDonald was allegedly kidnaped in January, 1957, and was found on a desert path outside of Indo, California, clad only in her pajamas. She claimed she had been abducted by two men but the whole thing appeared to be nothing more than a publicity gimmick designed to bolster a collapsing career. The producer of this mediocre, slapstick-loaded production was Russell's husband, one-time football star Waterfield.

p, Robert Waterfield; d, Norman Taurog; w, Richard Alan Simmons (based on the novel by Sylvia Tate); ph, Joseph LaShelle; m, Billy May; ed, Archie Marshek; art d, Serge Krizman; cos, Billy Travilla.

Comedy/Romance **(PR:A MPAA:NR)**

FUZZY SETTLES DOWN* (1944) 60m PRC bw

Buster Crabbe (*Billy Carson*), Al St. John (*Fuzzy*), Patti McCarthy, Charles King, John Merton, Frank McCarroll, Hal Price, John Elliott, Edward Cassidy, Robert Hill, Ted Mapes, Texas Palmer.

St. John actually doesn't settle down but he does make an attempt. He buys himself a newpaper office but before long is accused of stealing some of the paper's funds. They were stolen by someone else, however, and Crabbe is the one who locates and kills the real culprit. St. John, his name cleared of any wrongdoing, leaves the city and tries to "settle down" in the country. (See BILLY CARSON series.)

p, Sigmund Neufeld; d, Sam Newfield; w, Louise Rousseau; ph, Jack Greenhalgh; ed, Holbrook N. Todd.

Western **Cas.** **(PR:A MPAA:NR)**

G

G.I. BLUES** (1960) 115m PAR c

Elvis Presley *(Tulsa McCauley)*, James Douglas *(Rick)*, Robert Ivers *(Cookey)*, Juliet Prowse *(Lili)*, Leticia Roman *(Tina)*, Sigrid Maier *(Marla)*, Arch Johnson *(Sgt. McGraw)*, The Jordanaires.

Presley's first movie after returning from military service. G.I. Elvis sets up a combo with two other soldiers and plays at a large army show in Germany. Prowse plays an icy cabaret singer, and Elvis bets $300 that he'll spend the night with her. Elvis wins, falls in love with the singer, and makes marriage plans in the end. Songs include "Shopping Around" (Sid Tepper, Roy C. Bennett, Schroeder); "Tonight Is So Right For Love," "What's She Really Like?" (Sid Wayne, Silver); "Frankfurt Special," "Didya Ever," "Big Boots," (Wayne, Edwards); "Pocketful of Rainbows" (Wise, Weisman); "Doin' The Best I Can" (Thomas, Schumann); "Blue Suede Shoes" (Carl Perkins); title song (Tepper, Bennett); "Wooden Heart" (Wise, Weisman).

p, Hal Wallis; d, Norman Taurog; w, Edmund Beloin, Henry Garson; ph, Loyal Griggs (Technicolor); ed, Warren Low; md, Joseph J. Lilley; art d, Hal Pereira, Walter Tyler; ch, Charles O'Curran.

Musical **Cas.** **(PR:A MPAA:NR)**

G.I. HONEYMOON** (1945) 63m MONO bw

Gale Storm *(Ann)*, Peter Cookson *(Bob)*, Arline Judge *(Flo)*, Frank Jenks *(Blubber)*, Jerome Cowan *(Ace)*, Virginia Brissac *(Lavinia)*, Ralph Lewis *(Lt. Randall)*, Earl Hodgins *(Jonas)*, Ruth Lee *(Mrs. Barton)*, Andrew Tombes *(Rev. Horace)*, Jonathan Hale *(Col. Smith)*, Lois Austin *(Mrs. Smith)*, John Valentine *(Maj. Brown)*, Claire Whitney *(Mrs. Brown)*, Frank Stevens *(Capt. Stein)*, Jack Overman *(Sgt. Harrigan)*.

A comedy about a WW II army couple prevented from consummating their marriage. Cookson is assigned to night-sentry duty just as his wife, Storm, slips into her negligee, for example. Or, when they do get a chance for bedroom romance, he's too tired from a 37-mile hike. Then, a gambler with a grudge against the bride frames Cookson's company, leading to his being jailed. Storm's aunt saves the day—or bridal night—through her WW I friendship with Cookson's colonel.

p, Lindsley Parsons; d, Phil Karlstein; w, Richard Weil, Jr. (based on a play by A.J. Rubien, Robert Chapin and Marion Page Johnson); ph, Harry Neumann; ed, William Austin.

Comedy **(PR:A MPAA:NR)**

G.I. JANE** (1951) 62m Lippert bw

Jean Porter *(Jan)*, Tom Neal *(Tim)*, Iris Adrian *(Lt. Adrian)*, Jimmy Dodd *(Tennessee)*, Jean Mahoney *(Hilda)*, Jimmy Lloyd *(Lt. Bradford)*, Mara Lynn *(Pilsnick)*, Michael Whalen *(Major)*, Robert Watson *(Colonel)*, Phil Arnold *(Mousey)*, Jimmy Cross *(Winkie)*, Alan Ray *(Chuck)*, Richard Monahan *(Tired P.F.C.)*, Jean Coleman, Amie Bates, Jeri Strong, Olive Krushat *(WAC Quartet)*, Jack Reitzen *(Corporal)*, Mark Lowell *(Private)*, Loren Welch *(Recruiting Sergeant)*, Garnet Marks *(Captain)*, Jimmie Parnell *(Sergeant)*, Diana Mumby *(WAC)*, Monty Pittman *(Lieutenant)*, Vic Massey *(MP Driver)*.

T.V. producer Neal faints when he gets his army induction notice. He dreams that he has been stationed at a desert radar post and orders a company of WACs to join his men. WAC officer Adrian tries to keep the two camps from fraternizing, but her efforts are fruitless. Neal falls in love with Porter and wakes up to start a romance with Porter in reality. Songs include "Gee, I Love My GI Jane," "I Love Girls" (Jimmy Dodd); "Baby I Can't Wait" (Dian Manners, Johnny Clark); "What's To Be Is Gonna Be," (Teepee Mitchell, Johnny Anz).

p, Murray Lerner; d, Reginald Le Borg; w, Jan Jeffries (based on a story by Lerner); ph, Jack Greenhalgh; m, Walter Greene; ed, William Austin.

Musical **(PR:A MPAA:NR)**

G.I. WAR BRIDES*½ (1946) 69m REP bw

Anna Lee *(Linda Powell)*, James Ellison *(Steve Giles)*, Harry Davenport *(Grandpa Giles)*, William Henry *(Capt. Roger Kirby)*, Stephanie Bachelor *(Elizabeth Wunderlich)*, Doris Lloyd *(Beatrice Moraski)*, Robert Armstrong *(Dawson)*, Joseph Sawyer *(Sgt. Frank Moraski)*, Mary McLeod *(Kathleen Fitzpatrick)*, Carol Savage *(Joyce Giles)*, Pat Walker *(Margaret Lee)*, Helen Gerald *(Ruth Giles)*, Pat O'Moore *(Harold R. Williams)*, Maxine Jennings *(Sgt. Polly Williams)*, Russell Hicks *(Inspector Ramsaye)*, Francis Pierlot *(Mr. Wunderlich)*, Pierre Watkin *(Editor)*, Eugene Lay *(Donnie)*, Lois Austin *(Miss Nolan)*, Virginia Carroll *(Helen Mayo)*.

Lee trades places with one of many English war brides heading to the States to get through immigration. A reporter discovers her masquerade, and when she finds her pretended U.S. husband wants nothing to do with her, the journalist saves her from deportation.

p, Armand Schaefer; d, George Blair; w, John K. Butler; ph, Alfred Keller; m, Morton Scott; ed, Tony Martinelli.

Comedy **(PR:A MPAA:NR)**

G-MAN'S WIFE (SEE: PUBLIC ENEMY'S WIFE, 1936)

G-MEN**** (1935) 85m WB bw

James Cagney *(James "Brick" Davis)*, Ann Dvorak *(Jean Morgan)*, Margaret Lindsay *(Kay McCord)*, Robert Armstrong *(Jeff McCord)*, Barton MacLane *(Brad Collins)*, Lloyd Nolan *(Hugh Farrell)*, William Harrigan *(McKay)*, Edward Pawley *(Danny Leggett)*, Russell Hopton *(Gerard)*, Noel Madison *(Durfee)*, Regis Toomey *(Eddie Buchanan)*, Addison Richards *(Bruce J. Gregory)*, Harold Huber *(Venke)*, Raymond Hatton *(The Man)*, Monte Blue *(Analyst)*, Mary Treen *(Secretary)*, Adrian Morris *(Accomplice)*, Edwin Maxwell *(Joseph Kratz)*, Emmett Vogan *(Bill the Ballistics Expert)*, James Flavin *(Agent)*, Stanley Blystone, Pat Flaherty *(Cops)*, James T. Mack *(Agent)*, Jonathan Hale *(Congressman)*, Ed Keane *(Bank Cashier)*, Charles Sherlock *(Short Man)*, Wheeler Oakman *(Henchman at Lodge)*, Eddie Dunn *(Police Broadcaster)*, Gordon "Bill" Elliott *(Intern)*, Perry Ivins *(Doctor at Store)*, Frank Marlowe *(Hood Shot at Lodge)*, Gertrude Short *(Collins' Moll)*, Marie Astaire *(Gerard's Moll)*, Florence Dudley *(Durfee's Moll)*, Al Hill *(Hood)*, Huey White *(Gangster)*, Glen Cavender *(Headwaiter)*, John Impolito *(Tony)*, Bruce Mitchell *(Sergeant)*, Monte Vandegrift *(Deputy Sheriff)*, Frank Shannon *(Chief)*, Frank Bull *(Announcer)*, Martha Merrill *(Nurse)*, Gene Morgan *(Lounger)*, Joseph De Stefani *(J.E. Glattner, the Florist)*, George Daly, Ward Bond *(Machine Gunners)*, Tom Wilson *(Prison Guard)*, Henry Hall *(Police Driver)*, Lee Phelps *(McCord's Aide)*, Marc Lawrence *(Hood at Lodge)*, Brooks Benedict *(Man)*.

This is a turnabout film for Cagney, one where he changed his film image, from ruthless gangster to fearless FBI man. Harrigan is a bigshot gangster who generously puts Cagney through law school. When Toomey, Cagney's pal, becomes an FBI man and is gunned down without a chance, not legally able to bear arms Cagney joins the FBI to seek revenge. He is considered a good recruit in that his knowledge of gangster methods is extensive. But Armstrong, his FBI superior, dislikes Cagney because of his braggadoccio ways and makes life rough for him during his rigorous training; Armstrong really becomes incensed when Cagney makes a play for his sister, Lindsay, who is attracted to the brash young FBI recruit. Cagney gets word that Harrigan wants to see him and he travels to New York to visit with the crime kingpin, also seeing his old girl friend, Dvorak, who sings in Harrigan's nightclub. Cagney tells him that he is committed to the Bureau and that he will stop at nothing to put any crook in jail. Harrigan tells his law-abiding protege to go right ahead. It won't matter to him, Harrigan explains, since he's quitting the rackets and opening a small resort in northern Wisconsin. Before leaving New York, Cagney runs into Harrigan's associates, MacLane and company, telling them they are on warning. He also rejects Dvorak and she immediately takes up with MacLane. Cagney returns to Bureau headquarters and is confronted by Armstrong and others; he has been followed, they tell him, and spotted with Harrigan. Cagney explains that he owed it to Harrigan to tell him that his loyalty was to the Bureau. Cagney is kept on but Armstrong is suspicious that Cagney's one-time ties to the underworld might undermine FBI operations. Cagney disproves that by capturing Public Enemy Number One, Pawley, who is taken by train to Leavenworth, but, in Kansas City, MacLane, Bond, and other gangsters meet the lawmen escorting the gangsters and shoot them down, escaping with Pawley. (This is a direct reenactment of the infamous "Kansas City Massacre" in 1933 where outlaws Verne Miller, Solly Weisman, and Maurice and Homer Denning shot down five lawmen in an attempt to free gangster Frank Nash, killing Nash in the wholesale slaughter.) The massacre inflicted by the gangsters points out the helplessness of FBI agents not legally entitled to bear arms and Richards, playing the role of the FBI Director (a benign profile of J. Edgar Hoover), convinces Congress to pass a law which will arm his agents. Word comes that Pawley, MacLane, Bond, and others are hiding out in Harrigan's Wisconsin resort and the FBI agents, including Cagney and Armstrong, fly to the remote area and storm the lodge. A terrific gun battle ensues in which Harrigan, who has been held prisoner by the gangsters while playing their reluctant host, is killed. MacLane escapes with other gangsters. (This gun battle is based upon the abortive FBI raid against the Little Bohemia Lodge in Wisconsin in 1934, in a vain attempt to capture the Dillinger gang, one in which the reckless FBI agent, Melvin Purvis, led his men in a frontal attack against the lodge and where three CCC workers were accidentally shot, one killed, by murderous FBI gunfire as they emerged from the lodge restaurant and got into their car, mistaken for the gangsters who escaped through back windows of the lodge.) MacLane, as an act of vengeance against Cagney, kidnaps Lindsay, holding her for ransom. Dvorak, who still loves the feisty agent, calls Cagney and tells him where Lindsay is being held. MacLane finds Dvorak making the call in a drugstore phone booth, snarls "at it again, huh," and shoots her to death. Cagney alerts agents and goes to an underworld garage where he shoots it out with MacLane and frees Lindsay, winning the gratitude of Armstrong. G-MEN (the first time the term was used in a film) was made for a then whopping $450,000, with Cagney receiving $4,500 a week, and took six weeks to shoot. Keighley's direction is frantic with so much action as to astound any viewer trying to keep up with the nonstop movement. The gangsters, drawn loosely from the spectacular crime careers of John Dillinger, Baby Face Nelson and others, spray their machinegun bullets through almost every frame, their souped-up escape cars careening around corners in breathtaking chases. Keighley was a devil-may-care director and in his films anything went, including the use of real machinegun bullets. This was the second time Cagney had been faced with being actually shot at (by an expert gunman stationed off camera); he had almost been hit by a spray of machinegun bullets in PUBLIC ENEMY. In one scene Cagney had to hide behind a pile of logs which were sprayed with real machinegun bullets. He was nervous about the scene and told Keighley so. "I promise you, Jim," the director soothed, "the guy firing that gun will not do anything that will injure you." The bullets came close but the actor went unscratched. When director Michael Curtiz was directing Cagney in ANGELS WITH DIRTY FACES three years later another scene called for the actor to stand next to a window while an expert machinegunner shot at him. By then he was definitely gun-shy and refused to do the scene, insisting above Curtiz's admonitions, that the scene would require two takes, one with the bullets hitting without his presence, the other with him in the scene without the bullets, both takes to be intercut into one later. Said Cagney afterward: "I got out of the scene, and Burke, the professional machinegunner, fired the shots. One of the bullets hit the steel edge of the window, was deflected, and went right through the wall where my head had been. That convinced me, need I say it, that flirting with real bullets was ridiculous." With G-MEN, Cagney's popularity as a tough guy fighting on the right side of the law soared and he became one of the "Ten Top Moneymakers" in Hollywood; all of his films within a year's period had earned more than $1 million. G-MEN's director, Keighley, was not one of Cagney's favorite helmsmen; he thought he was affectatious, preferring to speak French to his cast and crew than English, he and his wife recently having learned the language in nonstop lessons. Lindsay also bothered the down-to-earth Cagney. In getting her first role in CAVALCADE, 1932, Lindsay, who came from Dubuque, Iowa, had fibbed to producers, saying she was British, that accent being sought as the best understood in the early sound era. She continued to affect a slightly British accent with broad "As" even in G-MEN, which annoyed Cagney. "They needed women who looked like her," he said in his autobiography, "pretty, that's all." G-MEN was a pet project of Hoover's who loaned several real agents to appear in the film, ostensibly to lend credibility to the production but really to make sure that the Bureau's story was told the way Hoover wanted it told. It was nevertheless exciting and absorbing fare, enhanced by the presence of the dynamic Cagney. So durable was this film that Warner Bros. re-released G-MEN many times for box office bonanzas. In the 1949 go-around, the studio added a prolog to the film with David Brian as the Chief and Douglas Kennedy as an agent. Brian is teaching a class of recruits and introduces the film to them by saying: "You are about to see the granddaddy of them all!"

p, Lou Edelman; d, William Keighley; w, Seton I. Miller (based on the novel *Public Enemy No. 1* by Gregory Rogers); ph, Sol Polito; ed, Jack Killifer; md, Leo F. Forbstein; art d, John J. Hughes; cos, Orry-Kelly; ch, Bobby Connolly; tech adv, Frank Gompert; m/l, "You Bother Me An Awful Lot" Sammy Fain, Irving Kahal (sung by Dvorak).

Crime Drama **(PR:A MPAA:NR)**

GABLE AND LOMBARD* (1976) 131m UNIV c

James Brolin *(Clark Gable)*, Jill Clayburgh *(Carole Lombard)*, Allen Garfield [Goorwitz] *(Louis B. Mayer)*, Red Buttons *(Ivan Cooper)*, Melanie Mayron *(Dixie)*, Carol McGinnis *(Noreen)*, S. John Launer *(Judge)*, William Bryant *(Colonel)*, Joanne Linville *(Ria Gable)*, Noah Keen *(A. Broderick)*, Alice Backes *(Hedda Hopper)*, Morgan Brittany *(Vivien Leigh)*, Robert Karnes *(Gable's Director)*, Ross Elliott *(Lombard's Director)*, Andy Albin *(Forest Ranger)*.

A cardboard re-telling of the Clark Gable and Carol Lombard romance and marriage. They meet at a Hollywood party and fall in love. He's married and Garfield is worried about a newspaper scandal, but they marry and have a short but happy time together. Clayburgh as Lombard is adequate, but Brolin has none of the charisma that made Gable a premier screen idol. The major problem is the superficial script.

p, Harry Korshak; d, Sidney J. Furie; w, Barry Sandler; ph, Jordan S. Cronenweth (Technicolor); m, Michel Legrand; ed, Argyle Nelson.

Drama **(PR:O MPAA:R)**

GABLES MYSTERY, THE*½ (1931, Brit.) 70m BIP/Powers bw (GB: THE MAN AT SIX)

Anne Grey *(Sybil Vane)*, Lester Matthews *(Campbell Edwards)*, Gerald Rawlinson *(Frank Pine)*, John Turnbull *(Inspector Dawford)*, Kenneth Kove *(Joshua Atkinson)*, Charles Farrell *(George Wollmer)*, Arthur Stratton *(Sgt. Hogan)*, Herbert Ross *(Sir Joseph Pine)*, Minnie Rayner *(Mrs. Cummerpatch)*.

What seemed like a good idea—having a woman play a detective—may have looked like a mild stroke of genius to its creators, but without a well-constructed plot it's not very captivating. Grey is the woman who devotes herself to sleuthing to track down a slippery jewel thief and his gang. This leads her to a country estate at which the kingpin has taken over the identity of the owner to pursue his goals. A mild hair-raiser at best.

p, Warwick Ward; d, Harry Hughes; w, Hughes, Victor Kendall (based on the play "The Man At Six" by Jack Celestin, Jack de Leon); ph, H.E. Palmer; ed, A.R. Gobbett.

Crime **(PR:A MPAA:NR)**

GABLES MYSTERY, THE* (1938, Brit.) 66m Welwyn/MGM bw

Francis L. Sullivan *(Power)*, Antoinette Cellier *(Helen Vane)*, Leslie Perrins *(Inspector Lloyd)*, Derek Gorst *(Frank Rider)*, Jerry Verno *(Potts)*, Aubrey Mallalieu *(Sir James Rider)*, Sidney King *(Mortimer)*, Laura Wright *(Mrs. Mullins)*, Ben Williams, Charles Howard, J. Neil More, Vernon Harris, Richard Littledale.

This film, originally made in 1931 under the title THE MAN AT SIX, was such an atrocious film it's hard to understand what motivated the remake. Yarn centers around the efforts of a lady detective, Cellier, to track down a notorious jewel thief. Absolutely nothing has been done to improve the original.

p, Warwick Ward; d, Harry Hughes; w, Victor Kendall, Hughes (based on the play "The Man At Six" by Jack Celestin, Jack de Leon); ph, H.E. Palmer; ed, A.R. Gobbett.

Crime **(PR:A MPAA:NR)**

GABRIEL OVER THE WHITE HOUSE*** (1933) 87m COS/MGM bw

Walter Huston *(Hon. Judson Hammond)*, Arthur Byron *(Jasper Brooks)*, Karen Morley *(Pendota Molloy)*, Franchot Tone *(Hartley Beekman)*, Dickie Moore *(Jimmy Vetter)*, C. Henry Gordon *(Nick Diamond)*, David Landau *(John Bronson)*, Samuel Hinds *(Dr. Eastman)*, William Pawley *(Borell)*, Jean Parker *(Alice Bronson)*, Claire Dubrey *(Nurse)*.

This bizarre but wholly fascinating film shows the American presidency as a postion of incredible power wielded by either a lunatic or an inspired genius, take your pick. That marvelous character actor Huston carries the whole load here on broad, capable shoulders. He is a newly elected president, a completely venal partisan politician with too quick a smile for his constituents and a sneer for the Constitution. A pleasure-seeking man of easy ways, Huston calls everyone by a nickname and insists upon being addressed as "Mayor," a position he once held, in mock humility. He is irresponsible, driving his car at breakneck speeds so he can outdistance his motorcycle escort, and his first Cabinet appointments are whimsical, at best, as Huston indifferently nods at the first names suggested by his corrupt secretary of state, Byron. Obviously, this party hack has no intention of honoring the highest office of the land. (At this stage of Huston's profile, his character and administration sharply mirror the corrupt Harding administration.) Then he is seriously injured in an auto accident. While recuperating, Huston sees a heavenly vision, or so it is is later reported, shown by the fluttering of a curtain on his window. It is a visit from the Archangel Garbriel, his devoted secretary Tone later states, who has brought him a message from On High. Huston is suddenly and frighteningly a changed man with a crusade to launch. He is now all law and order, decent, concerned, and conscientious. First, he fires his calculating and thoroughly crooked secretary of state. Then he goes after the bevy of boondogglers he has named to his Cabinet, getting rid of the lot of them. Crisis rears its roaring head when a million unemployed men begin marching on Washington. Huston races to Baltimore to meet them but their leader, Landau, is shot and killed at orders from powerful gangster Gordon for arcane reasons. Huston invites Gordon to visit him in the White House and here puts the crime czar on warning, that Huston will stop at nothing to place him and his minions behind bars or, if they resist the forces of law, have him and others shot to death. Gordon declares war and directs his goons to attack the White House with machineguns. Tone, following the President's orders, attacks first, leading a small army in armored cars to Gordon's headquarters. The gangsters let loose a murderous fusillade which is ineffective. The armored cars open fire and destroy the building, with the gangsters being backed up against a wall and executed en masse. With quick reforms, Huston beats back unemployment, but Byron and other enemies force Congress to adopt impeachment proceedings, many stating that Huston is simply insane. But Huston storms into the House of Representatives and demands martial law, insisting he be made a virtual dictator, albeit benevolent. He is given absolute power. On board the presidential yacht, Huston gathers the world's great leaders and lambasts them, telling them that while the U.S. has been scrapping ancient war vessels, according to old treaties, foreign powers have scrapped only their blueprints, not their navies. Moreover, Huston goes on the radio regularly to communicate his ideas with an American public that endorses his methods and beliefs. While using a quill once employed by President Abraham Lincoln (to sign the Emancipation Proclamation), Huston signs a far-reaching disarmament proclamation, after predicting that a future war would see airplanes "bomb cities, kill populations." As the strains of "The Battle Hymn of the Republic" are heard in the background, Huston slumps forward and dies a martyr's finish. This film, as oddball as it may seem today, was superbly directed by LaCava, whose forte was really comedy, as his W.C. Fields films testified, yet he excels here, perhaps because the ludicrousness of the story is carried through with a straight face by Huston. He is so believable that his powerhouse performance made GABRIEL OVER THE WHITE HOUSE one of the six top hits in spring, 1933. Of course, much of the story first indicts the Republican administrations that had occupied the White House, chiefly Warren G. Harding's, then takes on the personality of Roosevelt's up-coming administration. This was not a fluke. Cosmopolitan, the producing company, was owned by newspaper czar William Randolph Hearst, and he had urged producer Wanger to put this story onto film. Wanger got the project approved by Irving Thalberg, MGM's boy wonder, but Wanger worried about the reaction of top studio boss Louis B. Mayer, a diehard Republican. "What do I do about Mayer?" Wanger asked Thalberg. The production chief replied: "Don't pay any attention to him." The film was shot in just 18 days for a cost of $180,000 and was premiered in a Glendale, California theater. Mayer and his cronies went to see it. The MGM mogul was amazed that the film even existed and was seeing it for the first time. After viewing the film, Mayer marched out of the theater in a rage, yelling to Eddie Mannix, his top executive: "Put that picture in its can. Take it back to the studio and lock it up!" Mayer saw the film as a promotion for Franklin D. Roosevelt, a man about to occupy the White House and one he hated (although he later became a supporter), and a slur on his one-time friends, Presidents Harding and Herbert Hoover. He little realized that Hearst had changed his allegiances and was all for FDR, at least in the mold of Huston's dictatorial president who would rule America with an iron hand but with the best interests of the people. The whole device of Huston speaking to the nation via radio was prophetic in that FDR would become a familiar voice over the airwaves with his "Fireside Chats." Huston's setting up a million jobs through public works programs foreshadowed FDR's CCC and WPA projects. But Mayer could not really shelve the film. He distributed Hearst's Cosmopolitan Pictures and he could not afford to make an enemy of the newspaper czar who might turn his influential columnists, particularly Louella Parsons, loose upon MGM productions. The studio had also invested heavily in the film. Mayer ordered several cuts and retakes (which cost an additional $30,000) and then released GABRIEL OVER THE WHITE HOUSE. The liberal press attacked it relentlessly but it was a great hit in rural areas, especially in the South, where despotic leaders like Huey Long reigned. An oddity today, Huston's dynamic and compelling performance still packs a wallop.

p, Walter Wanger; d, Gregory LaCava; w, Carey Wilson, Bertram Bloch (based on the novel *Rinehard* by T.F. Tweed); ph, Bert Glennon; m, Dr. William Axt; ed, Basil Wrangell.

Drama **(PR:C MPAA:NR)**

GABY** (1956) 96m MGM c

Leslie Caron *(Gaby)*, John Kerr *(Gregory Y. Wendell)*, Cedric Hardwicke *(Mr. Carrington)*, Taina Elg *(Elsa)*, Margalo Gillmore *(Mrs. Carrington)*, Scott Marlowe *(Jan)*, Ian Wolfe *(Registrar)*, Joe Di Reda *(Allen)*, Joseph Corey *(Pete)*, James Best *(Jim)*, Lisa Montell *(Claire)*, Ruta Lee *(Denise)*, Marda Onyx *(Olga)*, Gloria Wood *(Singer)*.

In this remake of WATERLOO BRIDGE, Caron is an English ballerina and Kerr an American paratrooper on leave before the WW II D-Day invasion. They fall in love, but their love can't be consummated because he must leave to join the invasion. Caron learns that he was killed in action and, upset that she wasn't able to give herself to him, comforts other young soldiers in the bedroom. When Kerr shows up alive, Caron refuses to marry him because she can't come clean to the altar, but Kerr's love is so strong he forgives her.

p, Edwin H. Knopf; d, Curtis Bernhardt; w, Albert Hackett, Frances Goodrich, Charles Lederer (based on a screenplay by S.N. Behrman, Paul H. Rameau, George Froeschel and the play "Waterloo Bridge" by Robert E. Sherwood); ph, Robert Planck (CinemaScope, Eastmancolor); m, Conrad Salinger; ed, John McSweeney, Jr.; md, Charles Wolcott; art d, Cedric Gibbons, Daniel B. Cathcart; ch, Michel Panaieff; m/l, "Where or When," Richard Rodgers, Lorenz Hart.

Drama   **(PR:A   MPAA:NR)**

GAIETY GEORGE   (SEE: SHOWTIME, 1946, Brit.)

GAIETY GIRLS, THE**   (1938, Brit.) 72m London-Denham/UA bw (GB: PARADISE FOR TWO)

Jack Hulbert (*Rene Martin*), Patricia Ellis (*Jeannette*), Arthur Riscoe (*Jacques Thibaud*), Googie Withers (*Miki*), Sydney Fairbrother (*Miss Clare*), Wylie Watson (*Clarence*), David Tree (*Marcel*), Cecil Bevan (*Renaud*), Antony Holles (*Brand*), Roland Culver (*Paul Duval*), H.F. Maltby (*Director*), Finlay Currie (*Creditor*).

A musical with chorus girl Ellis meeting millionaire Hulbert. Hulbert is masquerading as a reporter and Ellis persuades him to pose as her millionaire husband.

p, Gunther Stapenhorst; d, Thornton Freeland; w, Arthur Macrae, Robert Stevenson; ph, Gunther Krampf; m, Michale [Mischa] Spoliansky; ed, E. B. Jarvis; md, Muir Mathieson; cos, Rene Hubert; ch, Philip Buchel, Jack Donohue; m/l, Spoliansky, William Kernell.

Musical/Comedy   **(PR:A   MPAA:NR)**

GAL WHO TOOK THE WEST, THE**   (1949) 84m UNIV c

Yvonne De Carlo (*Lillian Marlowe*), Charles Coburn (*Gen. Michael O'Hara*), Scott Brady (*Lee O'Hara*), John Russell (*Grant O'Hara*), Myrna Dell (*Nancy*), James Millican (*Hawley*), Clem Bevans (*Hawley as Old Timer*), Bob Stevanson (*Ted*), Houseley Stevenson (*Ted as Old Timer*), Robin Short (*Bartender*), Russell Simpson (*Bartender as Old Timer*), John Litel (*Col. Logan*), James Todd (*Douglas Andrews*), Edward Earle (*Mr. Nolan*), Jack Ingram, Francis McDonald, Glenn Strange, William Tannen, Steve Darrell, Pierce Lyden, Ross Elliott, John James, Richard Farmer, Martin Cichy (*Men*), Audrey Young (*Sue*), Ann Pearce, June Fulton, Patricia Hall (*Dance Hall Girls*), Howard Negley (*Potkins*), Charles Cane (*Grant's Man*), William Haade (*Lee's Man*), Louise Lorimer (*Mrs. Logan*), Forrest Taylor (*Servant*), Charles Jordan (*Customer*), George Stern (*Barber*), Paul Brinegar (*Salesman*), William Donnelly (*Cavalry Captain*), Steve Crandall, Jon Riffel (*Young Men*), House Peters, Jr. (*Trooper*), Russ Whiteman (*Corp. Trooper*), Fraser McWinn (*Sentry*), Peggie Leon, Ella Ethridge, Verna Korman, William Bailey, Roger Moore, David Alison, Forbes Murray, Mildred Sellers, Louise Bates, Philip Ahlm, Helen Dickson (*Guests*), Harlan Hoagland (*Bartender*), Chalky Williams, Paul Palmer (*Men in Saloon*), Patrick Griffin, Gary Teague.

A satirical western has three old men telling their versions of the story of the legendary O'Hara family and the two cousins (Russell and Brady) feuding over singer DeCarlo. Someone forgot to put the satire and humor in this comedy. Excellent cinematography from William Daniels.

p, Robert Arthur; d, Frederick de Cordova; w, William Bowers, Oscar Brodney; ph, William Daniels (Technicolor); m, Frank Skinner; ed, Milton Carruth; art d, Bernard Herzbrun, Robert Boyle.

Comedy   **(PR:A   MPAA:NR)**

GAILY, GAILY***   (1969) 117m Mirisch-Cartier/UA c (GB: CHICAGO, CHICAGO)

Beau Bridges (*Ben Harvey*), Melina Mercouri (*Queen Lil*), Brian Keith (*Francis X. Sullivan*), George Kennedy (*Axel P. Johanson*), Hume Cronyn ("*Honest" Tim Grogan*), Margot Kidder (*Adeline*), Wilfrid Hyde-White (*The Governor*), Melodie Johnson (*Lilah*), Joan Huntington (*Kitty*), John Randolph (*Father Harvey*), Claudie Bryar (*Mother Harvey*), Eric Shea (*Virgil Harvey*), Merie Earle (*Grandma Harvey*), James Christy (*Frankie*), Charles Tyner (*Dr. Lazarus*), Harry Holcombe (*The Stranger*), Roy Poole (*Dunne*), Clark Gordon (*Wally Hill*), Peter Brocco (*Swami*), Maggie Oleson (*Mrs. Krump*), Nikita Knatz (*Chauffeur*), Roy Barcroft, J.S. Johnson, Tom Peters, Harvey Jason, Les Podwell, Martin Friedberg, Nora Marlowe, Don Keefer.

A sentimental look backward to Chicago of 1910, based on Ben Hecht's colorful journalistic memories, this film begins with directorial care and style, then slowly erodes into mindless slapstick for a predictable Hollywood ending. Bridges, playing the young Ben Hecht, is shown at the Galena, Illinois, Fourth of July celebration, where he is enamored of lucious Johnson, mistress to Chicago political bigwig Kennedy, who passes her off as his niece. Bridges later embarks for Chicago to seek his fame and fortune, a naive rube who gets his pocket picked and is soon so hungry that he steals a little girl's ice cream cone and flees into heavy traffic where he is almost run over by the touring car in which wealthy madam Mercouri is riding. She takes Bridges in (not unlike the way Shirley MacLaine was to instantly "adopt" Peter Sellers in BEING THERE), putting him up at her lavish bordello where Bridges later meets and entertains Mercouri's girls by telling them the stories he intends to write. (Hecht himself unwittingly took a room in a brothel when first arriving in Chicago.) Mercouri asks her capricious ne'er-do-well newsman lover Keith to take the boy under his wing and she arranges to get him a job on the sensation-seeking Chicago *Journal* where he is put to work as a "picture-chaser," stealing photos of persons involved in crimes and scandals. Classic lines are delivered by the paper's editor to Bridges before the novice newsman is sent out to obtain a photo of an alleged "sex maniac." The alarmed Bridges begins to leave the busy city room but the editor stops him, shouting: "Do you know what a sex maniac does?" "N-n-n-no," stammers Bridges. Booms the editor: "He *sells* newspapers!" After a few wild adventures, Bridges learns quickly the wiles of the street, and Keith, the hard-drinking Irish newsman, completes his education by

taking Bridges on a tour of Chicago's great saloons, getting him tipsy and explaining how there are good crooks like Cronyn who want to share the spoils and thieves like Kennedy who want it all. Bridges catches sight of Cronyn later at a party held by Mercouri where Cronyn buries his face in a cake resembling the city treasury and Holcombe, playing poet Carl Sandburg, recites his "Chicago" poem. Kidder, who is one of Mercouri's girls and who has slept with and is in love with Bridges, takes Cronyn to her bedroom where she avoids a sexual liaison and absconds with the politician's "Big Mitt Ledger," a hand-written notebook in which Cronyn has recorded every bribe and kickback taken by every important politician in Illinois. When Bridges discovers he has been living in a whorehouse and that all about him are corrupt, he goes berserk, stealing the ledger from Kidder, who immediately gives up prostitution and joins the Salvation Army. Everyone goes after Bridges and the ledger. Kennedy tries to wheedle it out of him; his sexy mistress Johnson attempts to seduce Bridges to get it. Cronyn and his forces, even Keith, try to obtain it, chasing Bridges about the city until, trapped on an upraised bridge, the youth falls into the river and is presumed drowned. He is saved by a quack who injects adrenaline into him, the same crackpot who had earlier tried to revive, at Keith's insistence, a hanged murderer (a stunt Ben Hecht and Charles MacArthur actually performed in the glory days of Chicago journalism). Bridges witnesses his own funeral, then shocks one and all by appearing. Another scramble for the ledger ends with Mercouri given the dangerous document for safekeeping. Bridges winds up with Kidder and the film ends on a happy if not nitwit note. This was a lavish production with director Jewison capturing great historic landmarks and period scenes in and around Chicago. Keith is a humorous and lovable standout as the alcoholic, reckless reporter. Mercouri is exotic and mysterious, but most of the cast do poor caricatures of their roles. Kidder is unconvincing, Kennedy all huff-and-puff, and Johnson's protruding bosom acts for her. Cronyn excels as the sleazy politician, his overacting actually enhancing his part, while Hyde-White is memorable as the venal governor. The whole thing falls apart in the middle when Jewison abandoned a tight and historically alluring story for a Keystone Kops conclusion where all the earlier shown style and wit are dumped for scant belly laughs. There are some charming but lightweight tunes scattered throughout the aimless script, including "Gaily, Gaily," "Xmas Eve on Skid Row," "The Tango I Saved for You," (Henry Mancini); "Sentimental Dream," "Tomorrow is My Friend," (sung by Jimmie Rodgers); "There's Enough to Go Around" (Alan and Marilyn Bergman, Mancini, sung by Mercouri).

p&d, Norman Jewison; w, Abram S. Ginnes (based on the book *Gaily, Gaily* by Ben Hecht); ph, Richard Kline (DeLuxe Color); m, Henry Mancini; ed, Ralph Winters; prod d, Robert Boyle; art d, George Chan; set d, Edward G. Boyle, Carl Biddiscombe; cos, Ray Aghayan; spec eff, Sass Bedig; m/l, Mancini, Alan and Marilyn Bergman; makeup, Del Armstrong.

Comedy   **(PR:C-O   MPAA:M)**

GAL YOUNG UN**½   (1979) 105m Nunez Films c

Dana Preu (*Matt*), David Peck (*Trax*), J. Smith (*Elly*), Gene Densmore (*Storekeeper*), Jennie Stringfellow (*Edna*), Tim McCormack (*Blaine*), Casey Donovan (*Jeb*), Mike Garlington (*Eddy*), Marshal New (*Edgar*), Bruce Cornwell (*Phil*), John Pieters, Gil Lazier, Tina Moore, Marc Glick, Kerry McKenney, Sarah Drylie, Randy Ser, Bernie Cook, Fred Wood, Sissy Wood, Lewis Ivey, J.D. Henry, Billie Henry, Susan Holzer, Brian Lietz, Gus Holzer, Ross Sturlin, Pat Garner.

A virtual one-man project for Victor Nunez, a young American independent filmmaker, who did everything except compose the music and act. Set in the backwoods of Florida, GAL YOUNG UN is an insightful and sensitive depiction of a woman who has retired from the world to work on her property and seek contentment through her ability to be by herself and take pleasure in her surroundings. An upsetting force in the form of a shiftless young man pops into her life, romances the woman many years his senior, and asks her to marry him. Though the woman has a decidedly positive effect upon the young man, it is not long before he begins to use her to help set up a moonshining business (story takes place during Prohibition). Though the woman is taken advantage of, she deals with the proceedings in a patient and understanding manner that always allows her to stay on top of the situation. A moving and subtle film that manages to retain its power without lapsing into sentiment. Taken from a story by Marjorie Kinnan Rawlings.

p,d,w,&ph, Victor Nunez; m, Azalea Blossom String Band; ed, Nunez; cos, Allen Eggleston, Susan Holzer.

Drama   **(PR:C   MPAA:NR)**

GALAXINA*   (1980) 95m Marimar/Crown International c

Stephen Macht (*Thor*), Dorothy R. Stratten (*Galaxina*), James David Hinton (*Buzz*), Avery Schreiber (*Capt. Butt*), Ronald Knight (*Ordric*), Lionel Smith (*Maurice*), Tad Horino (*Sam Wo*), Herb Kaplowitz (*Rock Eater/Kitty/Ugly Alien Woman*), Nancy McCauley (*Elexia*), Fred D. Scott (*Commander*), George E. Mather (*Horn Man*).

This uninspired SF spoof was the last film of "Playboy" Playmate and starlet Dorothy Stratten. The day the film premiered in Kansas City she was murdered by her estranged husband. Stratten is a robot navigator on a space police cruiser. Macht falls in love with her and tries to transform her into a real woman as they journey to the planet Altar 1. Take-off of STAR WARS.

p, Marilyn J. Tenser; d&w, William Sachs; ph, Dean Cundy (Panavision); ed, Larry Bock; prod d, Tom Turlley.

Comedy   **Cas.**   **(PR:O   MPAA:NR)**

GALAXY EXPRESS**½   (1982, Jap.) 91m Toei/New World c (AKA: GALAXY EXPRESS 999)

Voices: Corey Burton, Fay McKay, Anthony Pope, Booker Bradshaw, Barry Seegar, B.J. Ward, William Woodson.

Daring both visually and thematically, this feature-length cartoon follows the journey of a young boy in space to gain vengeance against the machine man responsible for the death of his mother. The boy encounters a woman resembling his mother, who aids him in his quest. They arrive at a cold and dead planet that derives its energy from the hearts of people whose bodies have become machines. The journey of the youth is highly symbolic and could be related to his overcoming the bonds which keep him tied to his mother. In this sense the film closely resembles a mythic dream.

p, Chiaki Imada; d, Taro Rin; w, Shiro Ishimori, Paul Grogan (based on a TV series by Leiji Matsumoto); m, Nozumi Aoki; ed, Robert Kizer, Masaaki Hanai, Skip Schoolnik; anim. d, Kazuo Komatsubara.

Animated Fantasy   Cas.   (PR:A   MPAA:PG)

GALAXY OF TERROR(1981) 80m New World c (AKA: MINDWARP; AN INFINITY OF TERROR; PLANET OF HORRORS)

Edward Albert (Cabren), Erin Moran (Alluma), Ray Walston (Kore), Bernard Behrens (Ilvar), Zalman King (Baelon), Robert Englund (Ranger), Taaffe O'Connell (Damelia), Sid Haig (Quuhod), Grace Zabriskie (Capt. Trantor), Jack Blessing (Cos), Mary Ellen O'Neill (Mitre).

Rip-off of ALIEN, this Corman production has plenty of gore and a mindless storyline. A group of astronauts are sent to rescue a stranded spaceship. A female astronaut is raped by a giant worm, another female, Moran, blows up, and Haig cuts off his own arm. Excellent special effects. Second unit director Jim Cameron went on to write and direct the superior SF film THE TERMINATOR (1984).

p, Roger Corman, Marc Siegler; d, B.D. Clark; w, Siegler, Clark; ph, Jacques Haitkin (uncredited color); m, Barry Schrader; ed, Robert J. Kizer, Larry Boch, Barry Zetlin; spec eff, Tom Campbell.

Science Fiction   Cas.   (PR:O   MPAA:R)

GALIA   (1966, Fr./Ital.) 105m Speva-Cine Alliance-Variety/Zenith bw (AKA: I AND MY LOVERS; I AND MY LOVE)

Mireille Darc (Galia), Venantino Venantini (Greg), Francoise Prevost (Nicole), Jacques Riberolles (Wespyr), Francois Chaumette (Matik), Edward Meeks, Philippe Castelli.

A bizarre melodrama which has Darc rescue Prevost from a suicidal leap into the Seine. Prevost tells Darc that she tried to kill herself because her husband was cruel to her. Darc decides to get back at the husband, Venantini, by leaving the suicide note Prevost had previously written in place. While spying on him to gauge his reaction, she meets him and before long falls in love with him. He tells her that Prevost won't agree to a divorce and that he knows his wife is still alive. When Prevost learns of the affair she kills her husband, explaining to Darc that she did it to protect her. So much for credibility, but it does have an interesting cast—Darc went on to play the lead in Jean-Luc Godard's classic WEEKEND, and Prevost had appeared previously in Jacques Rivette's PARIS BELONGS TO US. The Johann Sebastian Bach theme is sung by The Swingle Sisters.

p, Michel Safra, Serge Silberman; d, Georges Lautner; w, Lautner, Vahe Katcha (based on a story by Katcha); ph, Maurice Fellous; m, Michel Magne; ed, Michele David; art d, Jean d'Eaubonne.

Drama   (PR:C   MPAA:NR)

GALILEO½   (1968, Ital./Bul.) 108m Fenice Cinematografica-Rizzoli-Kinozenter c

Cyril Cusack (Galileo), Lou Castel (Friar), Gigi Ballista (Trial Judge), Paolo Graziosi (Bernini), Irene Kokonova (Galileo's Mistress), Piero Vida (Pope Urban VIII), Gheorghi Kolaiancey (Giordano Bruno).

This first Italian-Bulgarian co-production centers around Galileo's fight for his scientific findings against the Vatican's dogma. This one telescopes its finale with too much talk.

p, Leonardo Pescarolo; d, Liliana Caviani; w, Caviani, Tullio Pinelli, Fabrizio Onofri; ph, Alfio Contini (Eastmancolor); m, Ennio Morricone; ed, Nino Baragli; art d, Ezio Frigerio.

Drama   (PR:A   MPAA:NR)

GALILEO*   (1975, Brit.) 145m American Film Theatre c

Topol (Galileo Galilei), Edward Fox (Cardinal Inquisitor), Colin Blakely (Priuli), Georgia Brown (Ballad Singer's Wife), Clive Revill (Ballad Singer), Margaret Leighton (Court Lady), John Gielgud (Old Cardinal), Michael Gough (Sagredo), Michael [Michel] Lonsdale (Cardinal Barberini/Pope), Richard O'Callaghan (Fulganzio), Tim Woodward (Ludovico), Judy Parfitt (Angelica Sarti), John McEnery (Federzoni), Patrick Magee (Cardinal Bellarmin), Mary Larkin (Virginia), Ian Travers (Andrea as a Boy), Tom Conti (Andrea as a Man).

From Landau's American Film Theatre series this adaptation of the Brecht play is brought in high-class fashion to the screen. Topol plays Galileo fighting to have his findings on the planetary system accepted by the 17th-century Catholic church.

p, Ely Landau; d, Joseph Losey; w, Barbara Bray, Losey (based on Charles Laughton's adaptation of the play by Bertolt Brecht); ph, Michael Reed; m, Hans Eisler, Richard Hartley; ed, Reginald Beck.

GALLANT BESS**   (1946) 99m MGM c

Marshall Thompson (Tex), George Tobias (Lug), Clem Bevans (Smitty), Donald Curtis (Lt. Bridgeman), Murray Alper (Johnny), Wally Cassell (Mike), Jim Davis (Harry), Chill Wills (C.P.O.), John Burford ("Shorty"), Johnny Bond (Oakie), Gallant Bess the Horse.

Thompson joins the Seabees when WW II breaks out. He leaves behind the prize horse he had raised from a colt. The young man finds another horse—Bess—on a Pacific island and adopts the mare. It brings his unit luck and when Thompson is sent state-side he brings the horse with him. Whoa, Bess.

p, Harry Rapf; d, Andrew Marton; w, Jeanne Bartlett (based on an incident as told by Lt. Marvin Park); ph, John W. Boyle (Cinecolor); m, Rudolph G. Kopp; ed, Harry Komer; art d, Cedric Gibbons.

Drama   (PR:A   MPAA:NR)

GALLANT BLADE, THE**   (1948) 81m COL c

Larry Parks (Lt. David Picard), Marguerite Chapman (Nanon de Lartigues), Victor Jory (Marshal Mordore), George Macready (Gen. Cadeau), Edith King (Mme. Chauvignac), Michael Duane (Paul Brissac), Onslow Stevens (Gen. de la Garance), Peter Brocco (Sgt. Jacques), Tim Huntley (Maj. Lanier), Ross Ford (Henri), Paul Campbell (Georges), Fred Sears (Lawrence), Nedrick Young (Sgt. Martine), Wilton Graff (Duc d' Orleans).

A swashbuckler set in 17th-century France and loosely based on fact. The ruling factions and a group of generals and soldiers struggle for power. Jory kidnaps Macready hoping to break the rebels. Parks' sword frees the general at the last second. Good action, lame script.

p, Irving Starr; d, Henry Levin; w, Walter Ferris, Morton Grant (based on a story by Ted Thomas and Edward Dein); ph, Burnett Guffey, Charles Lawton (Cinecolor); m, M.W. Stoloff, George Duning; ed, Viola Lawrence; art d, Stephen Goosen, Sturges Carne.

Action/Adventure   (PR:A   MPAA:NR)

GALLANT DEFENDER½   (1935) 60m COL bw

Charles Starrett (Johnny Flagg), Joan Perry (Barbara McGrall), Harry Woods (Munro), Edward J. Le Saint (Campbell), Jack Clifford (Sheriff), Al Bridge (Salty Smith), George Billings (Jimmy), George Chesebro (Swale), Edmund Cobb, Frank Ellis, Jack Rockwell, Tom London, Stanley Blystone, Lew Meehan, Merrill McCormack, Glenn Strange, Al Ferguson, Slim Whitaker, Bud Osborne; Roy Rogers, Bob Nolan, Tim Spencer, Hugh and Carl Farr (The Sons of the Pioneers).

This was the first of the series of Starrett westerns for Columbia. Starrett is wrongly accused of murder and goes about proving his innocence while homesteaders fight off the cattlemen. Starrett made 132 westerns for Columbia, ending with THE KID FROM BROKEN GUN in 1952.

p, Harry Decker; d, David Selman; w, Ford Beebe (based on a story by Peter B. Kyne); ph, Benjamin Kline.

Western   (PR:A   MPAA:NR)

GALLANT FOOL, THE½   (1933) 60m MON bw

Bob Steele, Artletta Duncan, George Hayes, John Elliott, Theodore Lorch, Perry Murdock, George Nash, Pascale Perry.

One in a series of seven features whirlwind fighter Steele was to appear with George Hayes (before he became "Gabby") for Monogram pictures; the often-used oater theme here concerns a man wrongly accused of murder trying to keep himself out of the grip of the law, while figuring a way to clear his name.

p, Trem Carr; d, Robert N. Bradbury; w, Bradbury, Harry O. Jones [Harry Fraser].

Western   (PR:A   MPAA:NR)

GALLANT HOURS, THE*   (1960) 115m UA bw

James Cagney (Fleet Adm. William F. Halsey, Jr.), Dennis Weaver (Lt. Cmdr. Andy Lowe), Ward Costello (Capt. Harry Black), Richard Jaeckel (Lt. Cmdr. Roy Webb), Les Tremayne (Capt. Frank Enright), Robert Burton (Maj. Gen. Roy Geiger), Raymond Bailey (Maj. Gen. Archie Vandegrift), Carl Benton Reid (Adm. Ghormley), Walter Sande (Capt. Horace Keys), Karl Swenson (Capt. Bill Bailey), Vaughn Taylor (Cmdr. Mike Pulaski), Harry Landers (Capt. Joe Foss), Richard Carlyle (Fr. Gehring), Leon Lontoc (Manuel), James T. Goto (Adm. Isoroku Yamamoto), James Yagi (Rear Adm. Jiro Kobe), John McKee (Lt. Harrison Ludlum), John Zaremba (Maj. Gen. Harmon), Carleton Young (Col. Evans Carlson), William Schallert (Capt. Tom Lanphier), Nelson Leigh (Adm. Callaghan), Sydney Smith (Adm. Scott), Herbert Lytton (Adm. Murray), Selmer Jackson (Adm. Chester Nimitz), Tyler McVey (Adm. Ernest J. King), Maggie Magennis (Red Cross Girl), Robert Montgomery, Jr., James Cagney, Jr. (Marines), Robert Montgomery, Art Gilmore (Narrators).

James Cagney was the perfect choice to play Admiral Halsey. He more than resembled the man, he became him in this very truthful documentary-style story about the five weeks between October 18 through December 1, 1942. Halsey had a personal grudge against the Japanese Admiral Yamamoto. Although they admired each other for their military expertise, Cagney uses his superior strategy to outwit Goto in the battle of Guadalcanal (so wonderfully depicted by Tregaskis in his book Guadalcanal Diary). Although the story of a great victory, there is almost no battle action on screen and director Montgomery focuses in on the human side of the war. There are so many ordeals that a commander must endure and Montgomery takes the time to show the inner workings of a great leader. Cagney is subtle in his portrayal, perhaps one of his best. No doubt he felt that it was important to accurately depict the man. It gets a bit slow for what was thought to be a "war" movie but it is that leisurely pace that makes it all the more believable. There was a bit too much narration and the personal side of Halsey's life is overlooked, but that's a quibble. "Bull" Halsey came on the set of the film and was asked by Cagney if he liked the way a particular scene was going. Halsey's reply was "You would know that better than I would. You're the pros." Halsey was also a pro and couldn't have had a better person to portray him than Cagney. Les Tremayne (Enright) and Karl Swenson (Bailey) were both veteran radio actors who came to film late. Tremayne was a regular on various night-time dramas and Swenson was the star of the very popular "Lorenzo Jones" radio soap.

p&d, Robert Montgomery; w, Frank D. Gilroy, Beirne Lay, Jr.; ph, Joe MacDonald; m, Roger Wagner; ed, Frederick Y. Smith; art d, Wiard Ihman; set d,

Frank McKelvey; cos, Jack Martell; tech adv (U.S.), Captain Idris B. Monahan; tech adv (Japan), James T. Goto.

Biography/War **(PR:A MPAA:NR)**

GALLANT JOURNEY*½ (1946) 86m COL bw

Glenn Ford *(John Montgomery)*, Janet Blair *(Regina Cleary)*, Charlie Ruggles *(Jim Montgomery)*, Henry Travers *(Thomas Logan)*, Jimmy Lloyd *(Dan Mahoney)*, Charles Kemper *(Father Ball)*, Arthur Shields *(Father Kenton)*, Willard Robertson *(Zachary Montgomery)*, Selena Royle *(Mrs. Montgomery)*, Robert DeHaven *(Jim Montgomery as a Boy)*, Loren Tindall *(Jim Logan)*, Byron Morgan *(John Logan)*, Eula Morgan *(Mrs. Logan)*, Michael Towne *(Raymond Walker)*, Paul Marion *(Tony Dondaro)*, Henry Rowland *(Cornelius Rheinlander)*, Robert Hoover *(Dick Ball as a Boy)*, Paul E. Burns *("Peacock" Fox)*, Chis-Pin Martin *(Pedro Lopez)*, Fernando Alvarado *(Juan Morales)*, Bobby Cooper *(Tom)*, Rudy Wissler *(Hep)*, Tommy Cook *(Cutty)*, Buddy Swan *(Sharkey)*, Conrad Binyon *(Snort)*.

A film biography of lesser known late 19th-century aviation pioneer John J. Montgomery, whose experiments with gliders brought him notoriety, but no money. He invents a gold separator, but the money he makes from that goes to fight patent infringement lawsuits. He begins a relationship with a Jesuit, Blair, who helps him through his hard times. Then he contracts vertigo, preventing him from flying, and dies. Wellman's lack-luster direction keeps the film from being a compelling drama.

p&d, William A. Wellman; w, Wellman, Byron Morgan; ph, Burnett Guffey, George B. Meehan, Jr., Elmer Dyer; m, Marlin Skiles; ed, Al Clark; md, M.W. Stoloff; art d, Stephen Goosson, Carl Anderson.

Drama **(PR:A MPAA:NR)**

GALLANT LADY** (1934) 81m Twentieth Century/UA bw

Ann Harding *(Sally)*, Clive Brook *(Dan)*, Otto Kruger *(Phillip Lawrence)*, Tullio Carminati *(Cynario)*, Dickie Moore *(Deedy)*, Janet Beecher *(Maria)*, Betty Lawford *(Cynthia)*, Charles Coleman, Adrienne D'Ambricourt.

Harding is a mother whose fatherless child is taken from her. She accidentally finds her son in Paris and ends up marrying his adopted father. Couldn't have worked out better if it had been planned that way. Remade in 1938 as ALWAYS GOODBYE.

p, Darryl F. Zanuck; d, Gregory La Cava; w, Sam Mintz (based on an original story by Gilbert Emery, Douglas Doty); ph, Peverell Marley; ed, Richard Day.

Drama **(PR:A MPAA:NR)**

GALLANT LADY*½ (1942) 70m Motion Picture Associates/PRC bw

Sidney Blackmer, Rose Hobart, Claire Rochelle, Lynn Starr, Vince Barnett, Jack Baxley, Crane Whitley, John Ince, Frank Brownley, Richard Clarke, Spec O'Donnell, Inez Call, Pat McKee, Ruby Dandridge, Henry Hastings.

After being convicted for participating in mercy killings, a woman doctor is sent to prison. She escapes and hides out in the home of a country medic who protects her from the law. Eventually she attains freedom. A bottom-of-the-barrel drama.

p, Lester Cutler; d, William Beaudine; w, Arthur St. Claire (based on a story by Octavus Roy Cohen); ed, Fred Bain; md, Lee Zahler.

Drama **(PR:A MPAA:NR)**

GALLANT LEGION, THE** (1948) 88m REP bw

William Elliott *(Gary Conway)*, Adrian Booth *(Connie Faulkner)*, Joseph Schildkraut *(Clarke Faulkner)*, Bruce Cabot *(Beau Laroux)*, Andy Devine *(Windy Hornblower)*, Jack Holt *(Captain Banner)*, Grant Withers *(Wesley Hardin)*, Adele Mara *(Catalina)*, James Brown *(Tom Bauner)*, Hal Landon *(Chuck Conway)*, Tex Terry *(Sgt. Clint Mason)*, Lester Sharpe *(Matt Kirby)*, Hal Taliaferro *(Billy Smith)*, Russell Hicks *(Sen. Beale)*, Herbert Rawlinson *(Maj. Grant)*, Marshall Reed *(Bowling)*, Steve Drake *(Dispatch Rider)*, Harry Woods *(Lang)*, Roy Barcroft, Bud Osborne, Hank Bell, Jack Ingram, George Chesebro, Rex Lease, Noble Johnson, Emmett Vogan, John Hamilton, Trevor Bardette, Gene Stutenroth, Ferris Taylor, Iron Eyes Cody, Kermit Maynard, Jack Kirk, Merrill McCormack, Augie Gomez, Cactus Mack, Fred Kohler, Glenn Strange, Joseph Crehan, Peter Perkins.

Texas ranger Elliott, with the help of journalist Booth stop Schildkraut from breaking up the Texas Rangers. Schildkraut had hoped to split Texas into two sections after disbanding the protectors, preventing the territory from becoming a single state. Adele Mara sings three songs: "A Gambler's Life," "Lady from Monterey," and "A Kiss or Two."

p&d, Joseph Kane; w, Gerald Adams (based on a story by John K. Butler, Gerald Gerraghty); ph, Jack Marta; ed, Richard L. Van Enger; md, Morton Scott.

Western **(PR:A MPAA:NR)**

GALLANT ONE, THE** (1964, U.S./Peru) 65m Gillman c

Henry Heller *(Arturo)*, Gil Goluskin *(Uncle Felipe)*, Laya Raki, Ricardo Bonnemaison, Jorge Montoro, Toby Fox, Fernando Samillan, Jim Parker, Harold E. Wyman, Kenny Miller, Hank Nichols.

Ten-year old Heller's father is imprisoned for stealing and the boy moves in with his uncaring uncle. The boy plans to sell his pet burro for his father's defense, but the animal is sold by the uncle for food and liquor. Heller persists in his quest to prove his father innocent and finally does, upon which the village priest presents him with another burro.

p, Aaron Stell, Ron Randell; d&w, Stell; ph, J. Carlos Carbajal; m, Eduard Ingris; ed, Milton Citron.

Drama **(PR:A MPAA:NR)**

GALLANT SONS** (1940) 71m MGM bw

Jackie Cooper *(Byron "By" Newbold)*, Bonita Granville *(Kate Pendleton)*, Gene Reynolds *(Johnny Davis)*, Gail Patrick *(Clare Pendleton)*, Ian Hunter *("Natural" Davis)*, June Preisser *(Dolly Matson)*, Leo Gorcey *("Doc" Reardon)*, William Tracy *("Beefy" Monrose)*, Tommy Kelly *(Harwood "Woody" Hollister)*, Edward Ashley *(Al Posna)*, El Brendel *(Olaf Larsen)*, Minor Watson *(Barton Newbold)*, Ferike Boros *(Madame Wachek)*, Charlotte Wynters *(Estelle)*, Donald Douglas *(Hackberry)*, George Lessey *(Judge)*.

Jackie Cooper leads a band of youngsters on the trail of a murderer. Reynolds' father has taken the rap for the murder so other people won't have their names smeared in the trial. The group of kids, however, outsmarts the police and unmasks the real murderer at a high school play. Patrick went on to become the producer of the "Perry Mason" TV series.

p, Frederick Stephani; d, George B. Seitz; w, William R. Lipman, Marion Parsonnet; ph, Sidney Wagner; ed, Ben Lewis.

Mystery **(PR:A MPAA:NR)**

GALLERY OF HORRORS

(SEE: DR. TERROR'S GALLERY OF HORRORS, 1967)

GALLIPOLI****** (1981, Aus.) 110m PAR c

Mark Lee *(Archy)*, Bill Kerr *(Jack)*, Mel Gibson *(Frank Dunne)*, Ron Graham *(Wallace Hamilton)*, Harold Hopkins *(Les McCann)*, Charles Yunupingu *(Zac)*, Heath Harris *(Stockman)*, Gerda Nicolson *(Rose Hamilton)*, Robert Grubb *(Billy)*, Tim McKenzie *(Barney)*, David Argue *(Snowy)*, Reg Evans, Jack Giddy *(Officials)*, Dane Peterson *(Announcer)*, Paul Linkson *(Recruiting Officer)*, Jenny Lovell *(Waitress)*, Steve Dodd *(Billy Snakeskin)*, Harold Baigent *(Stumpy)*, Robyn Galwey *(Mary)*, Don Quin *(Lionel)*, Phyllis Burford *(Laura)*, Marjorie Irving *(Gran)*, John Murphy *(Dan Dunne)*, Bill Hunter *(Major Barton)*, Peter Ford *(Lt. Gray)*, Diane Chamberlain *(Anne Barton)*, Ian Govett *(Army Doctor)*, Geoff Parry *(Sgt. Sayers)*, Clive Bennington, Giles Holland-Martin *(English Officers)*, Moshe Kedem *(Egyptian Shopkeeper)*, John Morris *(Col. Robinson)*, Don Barker *(N.C.O. at Ball)*, Kiwi White *(Soldier on Beach)*, Paul Sonkkila *(Sniper)*, Peter Lawless *(Observer)*, Saltbush Baldock *(Sentry)*, Les Dayman *(Artillery Officer)*, Stan Green *(Sgt. Major)*, Max Wearing *(Col. White)*, Graham Dow *(Gen. Gardner)*, Peter R. House *(Radio Officer)*.

GALLIPOLI is a medium-sized film of epic proportions. If it had been given the big budgets allocated to HEAVEN'S GATE or some of the other nuclear disasters turned out in recent years, this would have been one of the most spectacular movies ever made. Australian director Weir (THE LAST WAVE, PICNIC AT HANGING ROCK) has added another gem to his string of pearls with GALLIPOLI. Lee and Gibson are two runners living in the Australian Outback during WW I. Both want to join the army but Lee is too young. He fakes his way into the service and Gibson joins him. We then see the futility of the British campaign to rid the Dardanelles of the Turkish menace and fight their way to Istanbul. The British chiefs of staff must have known that their efforts would be difficult but they sent a force of 35,000 ANZACS (Australians and New Zealanders) into the fray on the off-chance that this small army might be able to make it happen. The remainder of the film details the fate of the men and the inevitable tragic climax which was caused by inept commanders and a poor choice of messengers. This losing campaign would be rationalized, as all losing campaigns are, and today Gallipoli for Aussies and New Zealanders stands for something akin to the Alamo for Texans. Lee and Gibson are superb in their depictions of two star-crossed young men ground by the cruel jaws of war. Weir went on to helm THE YEAR OF LIVING DANGEROUSLY and WITNESS. The effective use of music in GALLIPOLI utilized an excellent score by May as well as some futuristic sounds by Jean Michel Jarre and the haunting "Adagio in G Minor" by Albioni to enhance the splendid production. This film and BREAKER MORANT are typical of some of the fine work coming over from Down Under.

p, Robert Stigwood, Patricia Lovell; d, Peter Weir; w, David Williamson (story by Weir); ph, Russell Boyd (Panavision, Eastmancolor); m, Brian May; ed, William Anderson; prod d, Wendy Weir; art d, Herbert Pinter.

Historical Drama **Cas.** **(PR:A-C MPAA:PG)**

GALLOPING DYNAMITE*½ (1937) 57m Ambassador bw

Kermit Maynard *(Jim)*, Ariane Allen *(Jane)*, John Merton *(Reed)*, David Sharpe *(Wilkes)*, Stanley Blystone *(Jenkins)*, Earl Dwire *(Pop)*, Francis Walker, Tracy Layne, Robert Burns, Allen Greer, John Ward, Budd Buster.

Maynard, a Texas Ranger, hunts down the murderer of his brother. The Ranger discovers that gold was behind the killing and quickly rounds up the criminals.

p, Maurice Conn; d, Harry Fraser; w, Sherman Lowe, Charles Condon (based on the "Mystery of Dead Man's Isle" by James Oliver Curwood); ph, Jack Greenhalgh; m, Connie Lee; ed, Martin G. Cohn.

Western **Cas.** **(PR:A MPAA:NR)**

GALLOPING MAJOR, THE** (1951, Brit.) 82m IFD bw

Basil Radford *(Maj. Arthur Hill)*, Jimmy Hanley *(Bill Collins)*, Janette Scott *(Susan Hill)*, A.E. Matthews *(Sir Robert Medleigh)*, Rene Ray *(Pam Riley)*, Hugh Griffith *(Harold Temple)*, Joyce Grenfell *(Maggie)*, Charles Victor *(Sam Fisher)*, Sidney Tafler *(Mr. Leon)*, Julien Mitchell *(Sgt. Adair)*, Charles Lamb *(Ernie Smart)*, Charles Hawtrey *(Lew Rimmel)*, Kenneth Evans *(Bert)*, Alfie Bass *(Newsboy)*, Sidney James *(Bookmaker)*, Gilbert Davis, Tom Walls, Jr., James Lomas, Ellen Pollock, Raymond Rollett, Arthur Denton, Sam Kydd, Michael Ward, Leslie Phillips, Clifford Cobbe, Dick Courtenay, Mary Matthews, Jacqueline Maude, Billy Russell, Duncan Lamont, Donovan Winter, Arthur Lovegrove, Derek Ensor, Roy Carr, Thora Hird, Ernie Metcalfe, Joe Day, Pat Ray, Joe Clarke, Dan Malvern, Ben Williams, Charlie Smirke, Raymond Glendenning, Bruce Belfrage, Marion Harris, Jr., Mr. Hawkins.

Radford plays a retired army major now running a pet store. He rounds up 300 investors to buy a race horse but buys the wrong horse. Never fear—the horse redeems him by winning the Grand National.

p, Monja Danischewsky; d, Henry Cornelius; w, Danischewsky, Cornelius (based on a story by Basil Radford); ph, Stanley Pavey; m, Georges Auric; ed, Geoffrey Foot.

Comedy (PR:A MPAA:NR)

GALLOPING ROMEO*½ (1933) 59m MONO bw

Bob Steele, Doris Hill, George Hayes, Frank Ball, Ernie Adams, Lafe McKee, Ed Brady, George Nash, Earl Dwire.

Steele couldn't quite pull off the light comedy he was asked to do in this film. Clips from previous Steele films were used to pad the movie, one of the earliest uses of this lengthening device.

p, Trem Carr; d, Robert N. Bradbury; w, Harry O. Jones [Harry Fraser] (based on a story by Bradbury); ph, Archie Stout.

Western (PR:A MPAA:NR)

GALLOPING THRU**½ (1932) 58M MONO bw

Tom Tyler, Betty Mack, Al Bridge, Si Jenks, Stanley Blystone, G.D. Woods [Gordon DeMain], John Elliott, Artie Ortego.

Tyler's best western for Monogram. He is out to revenge the murder of his father and Bridge is the man who feels his wrath. Scenes are dramatically well staged, including that in which Blystone, Tyler's best friend, steps aside so that Tyler may have Mack.

p, Trem Carr; d, Lloyd Nosler; w, Wellyn Totman; ph, Archie Stout.

Western (PR:A MPAA:NR)

GALS, INCORPORATED*½ (1943) 60m UNIV bw

Leon Errol (Cornelius Rensington III), Harriet Hilliard (Gwen), Grace McDonald (Molly), David Bacon (Bill), Betty Kean (Bets Moran), Maureen Cannon (Bubbles), Lillian Cornell (Vicki), Minna Phillips (Jennifer), Marion Daniels (Virginia), Margery Daye (Acrobatic Dancer); Glen Gray and His Casa Loma Orchestra, The Pied Pipers.

Millionaire Errol bankrolls a nightclub for a group of gold-digging women until his daughter arrives to cut off the money. Then her brother shows up and falls in love with one of the girls. Songs include "Here's Your Kiss," "Hep, Hep, Hooray," and "All The Time It's You" (Milton Rosen, Everett Carter).

p, Will Cowan; d, Leslie Goodwins; w, Edward Dein (based on a story by Dave Gould and Charles Marion); ph, Jerome Ash; m, Charles Previn; ed, Arthur Hilton.

Comedy (PR:A MPAA:NR)

GAMBIT*** (1966) 107m UNIV c

Shirley MacLaine (Nicole), Michael Caine (Harry), Herbert Lom (Shahbandar), Roger C. Carmel (Ram), Arnold Moss (Abdul), John Abbott (Emile), Richard Angarola (Col. Salim), Maurice Marsac (Hotel Clerk), Paul Bradley (Man in Cafe).

A 27-minute dream sequence at the start of this film shows how a heist can be accomplished, but. . . . MacLaine is a red-headed Eurasian woman toiling in a Hong Kong nightspot when Caine approaches her with a proposition. He and pal, Abbott, want to use her talents to help them steal a priceless Chinese work of art from Arab multimillionaire Lom. The face on the statuette is similar to that of the Arab's departed wife. By a scriptwriter's coincidence, those features also happen to be the same as on MacLaine's face. Caine and MacLaine pretend to be British nobility when they travel to the city where Lom reigns supreme. It goes without saying that Lom is immediately attracted to MacLaine, but Lom is no ninny and suspects the real reason for the visit, so he substitutes a fake statue for the real one. By another coincidence, Caine finds the real statuette and takes it. He then disappears, leaving MacLaine in a heckuva lurch. She is told that unless Caine returns the artwork, he will be found and jailed. Caine tells MacLaine that Abbott is so good at duplicating art treasures that no one will ever suspect that one was put in place of the other. Lom gets a wire from Caine saying that the real statuette is still in his possession. Now Caine plans to sell a duplicate made by Abbott some time before. The crime was, in fact, not a theft at all. Caine is attempting to sell the copy to some other art collector. Caine wants MacLaine to stay with him but she refuses. To prove his love for her, Caine ostensibly makes one last copy and destroys it to show he is through with criminal activities. As Caine and MacLaine depart, Caine winks at Abbott. After they've left, Abbott opens a closet in which repose three more duplicates of the statuette. This was Caine's first Hollywood film and he impressed everyone with his combination of tight-lipped doggedness and underplayed sense of humor. This was also producer Fuchs' first picture and marked an auspicious beginning for the one-time movie studio still photographer. GAMBIT was a slightly-veiled copy of TOPKAPI and RIFIFI, down to the elaborate planning sequence in both films. The major difference is that this picture had some very funny dialog. A delight to the eye and ear.

p, Leo L. Fuchs; d, Ronald Neame; w, Alvin Sargent, Jack Davies (based on the novel by Sidney Carroll); ph, Clifford Stine (Techniscope, Technicolor); m, Maurice Jarre; ed, Alma Macrorie; art d, Alexander Golitzen, George C. Webb; set d, John Austin, John McCarthy; cos, Jean Louis; makeup, Bud Westmore; hairstyles, Sidney Guilaroff.

Crime Comedy (PR:A-C MPAA:NR)

GAMBLER, THE*½ (1958, Fr.) 105m GAU c (LE JOUEUR)

Gerard Philipe (Alexei), Liselotte Pulver (Pauline), Nadine Alari (Blanche), Bernard Blier (Zagoriensky), Jean Danet (Des Grieux), Francoise Rosay (Grandmother), Carette (Muzjik).

Screen adaptation of Dostoyevsky done in an obvious, overblown style that wallows in melodramatics. The story details the sordid life of an aging general who lives high-on-the-hog in 19th-century France while waiting for his elderly, rich aunt to die so he can claim her fortune. In the meantime, he cons a dim-witted French adventurer into providing his living expenses by offering his beautiful daughter as

the Frenchman's mistress. Enter Philipe, the daughter's young tutor, who is in love with her and is determined to take her away from all this. Unfortunately for all concerned, the aunt lives long enough to be struck with gambling fever herself and she loses her fortune at the tables, causing the general's proud daughter to commit suicide. A superior version of this story is THE GREAT SINNER, starring Gregory Peck.

p, Franco London; d, Claude Autant-Lara; w, Jean Aurenche, Pierre Bost, Francois Boyer (based on the novel by Feodor Dostoyevsky); ph, Jacques Natteau (Eastmancolor); ed, Madeleine Gug.

Drama (PR:C MPAA:NR)

GAMBLER, THE*** (1974) 109m PAR c

James Caan (Axel), Paul Sorvino (Hips), Lauren Hutton (Billie), Morris Carnovsky (A.R. Lowenthal), Jacqueline Brookes (Naomi), Burt Young (Carmine), Carmine Caridi (Jimmy), Vic Tayback (One), Steven Keats (Howie), London Lee (Monkey), M. Emmet Walsh (Las Vegas Gambler), James Woods (Bank Officer), Carl W. Crudup (Spencer), Allan Rich (Bernie), Stuart Margolin (Cowboy), Ric Mancini (Sal), Joel Wolfe (Moe), Raymond Serra (Benny), William Andrews (Basketball Coach), Joseph Attles (Singer in the Park), Antonio Fargas (Pimp), Ernest Butler (Vernon), Sully Boyar (Uncle Hy), Gregory Rozakis (Joe), Starletta De Paur (Monique), Lucille Patton (Ricky's Wife), Ed Kovens (Ricky), Baron Wilson (Basketball Janitor), Richard Foronjy (Donny), Frank Sivero (Donny's Driver), Frank Scioscia (Man in Park with Donny), Philip Sterling (Sidney), Beatrice Winde (Receptionist), Patricia Fay (Teller), Leon Pinkney (Street Basketball Boy), Alisha Fontaine (Howie's Girl), Presley Caton (Monkey's Girl), Mitch Stein, Jonathan Koshner (College Announcers), Charles Polk (Bartender), Dick Schaap (TV Announcer), Chick Hearn (Radio Announcer).

Uneven but interesting drama documenting the anger, frustration, and self-destruction of a gambler. Caan is good as a college professor so deeply in debt to his bookies that he must borrow money from his mother, Brookes, in order to keep Sorvino from killing him. Caan runs off to Las Vegas with girl friend Hutton and wins a bundle at the tables, but his desire to lose is so strong that he squanders it all on dumb sports bets. (One of the flaws of the film is that writer Toback says that all gamblers want to lose, an oversimplified analysis of a complex problem.) We now see that we are in the presence of what George C. Scott called Paul Newman in THE HUSTLER (1961), a "loser." Caan comes very close to being killed but gets out of it when he convinces a student of his to shave points in a basketball game that is getting heavy play from the bettors. Suddenly, the picture takes a left turn and Caan inexplicably winds up in a tough black area where he picks up a hooker and then gets beaten up by the woman's pimp. This sequence has almost nothing to do with the picture save to show us that he is on a downward spiral that can only end in tragedy. Good acting from all concerned and an excellent job by Carnovsky, as Caan's rich grandfather who refuses to lend Caan any money. Burt Young, a pal of Caan's in real life, is excellent as a quietly brutal collector for a loan shark. James Woods is seen in a small role and several sports announcers play themselves, including Lakers' broadcaster Chick Hearn and Dick Schaap. London Lee, the Catskill comic, proves that he should stay there and forget about acting. It could have been great if they hadn't larded on all the pretentiousness and stuck with the story.

p, Robert Chartoff, Irwin Winkler; d, Karel Reisz; w, James Toback; ph, Victor J. Kemper (Eastmancolor); m, Jerry Fielding (based on Gustav Mahler's Symphony Number One); ed, Roger Spottiswoode; prod d, Philip Rosenberg; set d, Edward Stewart; cos, Albert Wolsky.

Drama **Cas.** (PR:O MPAA:R)

GAMBLER AND THE LADY, THE*½ (1952, Brit.) 74m Hammer/ Exclusive bw

Dane Clark (Jim Forster), Kathleen Byron (Pat), Naomi Chance (Lady Susan Willens), Anthony Forwood (Peter Willens), Meredith Edwards (Dave), Eric Pohlmann (Arturo Colonna), Julian Somers (Licasi), Anthony Ireland (Farning), Enzo Cottichia (Angelo Colonna), Thomas Gallagher (Sam), Max Bacon (Maxie), Jane Griffiths (Janey Greer), Percy Marmont (Lord Hortland), Eric Boon (Boxer), Mona Washbourne, Richard Shaw, George Pastell, Martin Benson, Felix Osmond, Robert Adair, Mark Singleton, Peter Hutton, Andre Mikhelson, Paul Sheridan, Robert Brown, David Keir, Irissa Cooper, Laurie Taylor, The Valencia Trio.

Unimaginative gangster yarn in which Clark plays a hotshot gambler whose winnings and ownership of several casinos are not enough to keep him content. His yen to become part of the upper crust in society takes the form of an affair with Chance, a member of England's aristocracy, something that doesn't set too well with the nightclub singer he has left behind. She in turn takes the final stab at doing him in, after the efforts of greedy gangsters prove unfruitful. Though an intriguing crime drama exists somewhere beneath this depiction, the way it was brought to the screen in both script and direction does little to take advantage of its possibilities.

p, Anthony Hinds; d, Pat Jenkins, Sam Newfield; w, Newfield; ph, Walter Harvey.

Crime (PR:A MPAA:NR)

GAMBLER FROM NATCHEZ, THE**½ (1954) 88m FOX c

Dale Robertson (Vance Colby), Debra Paget (Melanie Barbee), Thomas Gomez (Capt. Barbee), Lisa Daniels (Yvette Rivage), Kevin McCarthy (Andre Rivage), Douglas Dick (Claude St. Germaine), John Wengraf (Cadiz), Donald Randolph (Pierre Bonet), Henri Letondal (Renard), Jay Novello (Garonne), Woody Strode (Josh), Peter Mamakos (Etienne), Ivan Triesault (Raoul).

A colorful, but standard, western which takes place in the early 1800s. Robertson is the son of a gambler who was killed by three of his associates. He travels the region in an attempt to track down the murderers. Expect nothing more than average shoot-'em-up action.

p, Leonard Goldstein; d, Henry Levin; w, Gerald Drayson Adams, Irving Wallace (based on a story by Adams); ph, Lloyd Ahern (Technicolor); m, Lionel Newman; ed, William Murphy.

Western   **(PR:A   MPAA:NR)**

GAMBLER WORE A GUN, THE*½   (1961) 67m Zenith/UA bw

Jim Davis (Case Silverthorn), Mark Allen (Dex Harwood), Addison Richards (Doc Devlin), Merry Anders (Sharon Donovan), Don Dorrell (Jud Donovan), Bob Anderson (Tray Larkin), Keith Richards (Het Larkin), John Craig (Rebe Larkin), Charles Cane (Kelly Barnum), Joe McGuinn (Hastings), Morgan Shaan (Thompson), Eden Hartford (Woman), Brad Trumbull (Deputy), Jack Kenny (Bartender), Boyd Stockman (Dave), Boyd "Red" Morgan (Luke).

Davis purchases a ranch via mail order, but when he heads west to claim it he learns that the owner had been lynched before the deed was registered. He discovers that his property is being used by a local cattle rustler. With the help of the dead owner's kids he brings the marshal down on the outlaws, but not before he himself is falsely accused of murder. A remake of THE LONE GUN.

p, Robert E. Kent; d, Edward L. Cahn; w, Owen Harris (based on a story by L. L. Foreman); ph, Floyd Crosby; ed, Kenneth Crane; art d, Serge Krizman.

Western   **(PR:A   MPAA:NR)**

GAMBLERS, THE**   (1929) 60m Warner Bros. Vitaphone bw

H.B. Warner (James Darwin), Lois Wilson (Catherine Darwin), Jason Robards, Sr. (Carvel Emerson), George Fawcett (Emerson, Sr.), Johnny Arthur (George Cowper), Frank Campeau (Raymond), Pauline Garon (Isabel Emerson), Charles Sellon (Tooker).

Two Wall Streeters appropriate their firm's money and gamble it on the stock market. Shades of 1929 in 1929. Director Curtiz's first sound film, a weak one.

d, Michael Curtiz; w, J. Grubb Alexander (based on a play by Charles Klein); ph, William Reese; ed, Thomas Pratt.

Comedy/Drama   **(PR:A   MPAA:NR)**

GAMBLERS, THE 1948   (SEE: JUDGE, THE, 1948)

GAMBLERS, THE**   (1969) 93m U-M Film Distributors c

Suzy Kendall (Candace), Don Gordon (Rooney), Pierre Olaf (Cozzier), Kenneth Griffith (Broadfoot), Stuart Margolin (Goldy), Richard Woo (Koboyashi), Massimo Serato (Del Isolla), Faith Domergue (Signora Del Isolla), Relja Basic (Yakov), Tony Chinn (Nono).

Gordon is a successful gambler, and a very crooked card player. Serato poses as a wealthy man to trap Gordon, which he does—but Gordon doesn't mind: he gets Kendall.

p, William A. Berns; d&w, Ron Winston (based on a play by Nikolai Gogol); ph, Tomislav Pinter (Eastmancolor); m, John Morris; ed, Richard Bracken; art d, Veljko Despotovic.

Drama   **(PR:A   MPAA:NR)**

GAMBLER'S CHOICE**   (1944) 66m PAR bw

Chester Morris (Ross Hadley), Nancy Kelly (Vi Parker), Russell Hayden (Mike McGlennon), Sheldon Leonard (Chappie Wilson), Lee Patrick (Fay Lawrence), Lloyd Corrigan (Ulysses S. Rogers), Tommy Dugan (Benny), Lyle Talbot (Yellow Gloves Weldon), Charles Arnt (McGrady), Maxine Lewis (Bonnie D'Arcy), Billy Nelson (Danny May).

Hayden, a boyhood friend of gambler Morris is a 1910 NYC police lieutenant raiding gambling joints. A fellow officer is killed in a raid and Hayden is transferred to the Bronx, where he meets Kelly, a nightclub singer. Hayden and Morris both fall in love with Kelly. Morris saves his friend from a frame-up and is killed in a gunfight. No problem. Another take-off of MANHATTAN MELODRAMA.

p, William Pine, William Thomas; d, Frank McDonald; w, Maxwell Shane, Irving Reis (based on a story by Howard Emmett Rogers and James Edward Grant); ph, Fred Jackman; ed, Howard Smith; md, Mort Glickman; art d, F. Paul Sylos.

Drama   **(PR:A   MPAA:NR)**

GAMBLIN' MAN   (SEE: BORN TO KILL, 1974)

GAMBLING*½   (1934) 82m FOX bw

George M. Cohan (Al Draper), Wynne Gibson (Maizie Fuller), Dorothy Burgess (Dorothy Kane), Theodore Newton (Ray Braddock), Walter Gilbert (Inspector Freelock), Percy Ames, Cora Witherspoon, Harold Healy, David Morris, E. J. De Varney, Robert Strange, John T. Doyle, Joseph Allen, Fred Miller, Hunter Gardner.

Cohan is a gambler hunting down the killer of his ward. Too much talk, too little action.

p, Harold B. Franklin; d, Rowland V. Lee; w, Garrett Graham (based on a play by George M. Cohan); ph, Jack Mackenzie.

Murder/Mystery   **(PR:A   MPAA:NR)**

GAMBLING DAUGHTERS*½   (1941) 65m PRC bw

Cecilia Parker (Diana Cameron), Roger Pryor (Chance Landon), Robert Baldwin (Jimmy Parker), Gale Storm (Lillian), Sig Arno (Prof. Bedoin), Janet Shaw (Katherine), Charles Miller (Walter Cameron), Eddie Foster (Nick), Alfred Hall (Dean), Judy Kilgore (Gloria), Gertrude Messinger (Jane), Marvelle Andre (Dorothy), Roberta Smith (Mary).

Parker and Storm are two young, rich women who get involved with gambling types. There's a murder, a comic insurance inspector, Baldwin, and a story that goes nowhere.

p, T.H. Richmond; d, Max Nosseck; w, Joel Kay, Arnold Phillips (based on a story by Sidney Sheldon and Ben Roberts); ph, Mack Stengler.

Mystery   **(PR:A   MPAA:NR)**

GAMBLING HOUSE**½   (1950) 80m RKO bw

Victor Mature (Marc Fury), Terry Moore (Lynn Warren), William Bendix (Joe Farrow), Zachary A. Charles (Willie), Basil Ruysdael (Judge Ravinek), Donald Randolph (Lloyd Crane), Damian O'Flynn (Ralph Douglas), Cleo Moore (Sally), Ann Doran (Della), Eleanor Audley (Mrs. Livingston), Gloria Winters (B. J. Warren), Don Haggerty (Sharky), William E. Green (Doctor), Jack Kruschen (Burly Italian), Eddy Fields (Fat Man Pickpocket), Victor Paul, Joseph Rogato, Guy Zanette (Italian Immigrants), Kirk Alyn (FBI Man), Jack Stoney (Detective), Sherry Hall (Robbins), Vera Stokes (Stationwagon Driver), Leonidas Ossetynski (Mr. Sobieski), Loda Halama (Mrs. Sobieski), Homer Dickinson (Doorman), Forrest Burns (Milkman), Carl Davis (Big), Chester Jones (Elevator Attendant), Bert Moorhouse (Burke), Art Dupuis (Porter), Stanley Price (Gorman).

Mature is a foreign-born gambler who becomes the fall guy for a murder committed by crime boss Bendix. Mature beats the murder charge, but Bendix informs the judge that Mature doesn't have naturalization papers. When he is helped by social worker Moore, Mature realizes the importance of American citizenship, and a sympathetic judge allows him to stay in the country. Only in America.

p, Warren Duff; d, Ted Tetzlaff; w, Marvin Borofsky, Allen Rivkin (based on a story by Erwin Gelsey); ph, Harry J. Wild; ed, Roland Gross; md, C. Bakaleinikoff; art d, Albert S. D'Agostino, Alfred Herman.

Drama   **(PR:A   MPAA:NR)**

GAMBLING LADY**½   (1934) 66m FN/WB bw

Barbara Stanwyck (Lady Lee), Joel McCrea (Garry Madison), Pat O'Brien (Charlie Lang), C. Aubrey Smith (Peter Madison), Claire Dodd (Sheila Aiken), Phillip Reed (Steve), Philip Faversham (Don), Robert Barrat (Mike Lee), Arthur Vinton (Fallin), Ferdinand Gottschalk (Cornelius), Robert Elliott (Graves), Arthur Treacher (Pryor), Margaret Morris (Operator), Willie Fung (Ching), Stanley Mack (Secretary), Renee Whitney (Baby Doll), Rev. Neal Dodd (Minister), Brooks Benedict (Lou), Leonard Carey (Butler), Frank Thornton (Manservant), Edward Kane (Duke), Jay Eaton (Clerk), Charles C. Wilson, James Burke (Detectives), James Donlan (Lawyer), Wade Boteler (Cop), Ernie Alexander (Bell Boy), Milton Kibbee (1st Reporter), Maurice Brierre (Croupier), Albert Conti (French Lawyer), Laura Treadwell (Guest), Willard Robertson (District Attorney), Edward Le Saint (Sheila's Attorney), Louis Natheaux (Dope), Edward Keane (Duke), Bob Montgomery (Crooked Gambler), Eddie Shubert, Ralph Brooks (Reporters).

Stanwyck is the daughter of a gambler who killed himself when he couldn't pay his debts. She becomes a gambler herself and meets and falls in love with gambler McCrea. Stanwyck is married to another man and when a friend of hers is killed, the blame points to her husband. She saves him from being jailed, divorces him and goes off with McCrea. This was the first of several films in which Stanwyck and McCrea would co-star.

d, Archie Mayo; w, Ralph Block, Doris Malloy (based on a story by Malloy); ph, George Barnes; ed, Harold McLernon; art d, Anton Grot; cos, Orry-Kelly.

Drama   **(PR:A   MPAA:NR)**

GAMBLING ON THE HIGH SEAS**   (1940) 56m WB bw

Wayne Morris (Jim Carter), Jane Wyman (Laurie Ogden), Gilbert Roland (Greg Morella), John Litel (U.S. District Attorney), Roger Pryor (Max Gates), Frank Wilcox (Stone), Robert Strange (Larry Brill), John Gallaudet (Steve Sterling), Frank Ferguson (District Attorney), Harry Shannon (Chief of Police), George Reeves (Reporter), George Meader (Secretary to District Attorney), William Pawley (Frank), Murray Alper (Louie).

Morris is a reporter out to dig up evidence on Roland, a gangster-owner of a gambling ship and a murderer. On board he meets and falls in love with Wyman and gets the dirt on the gambler. She helps him do both.

d, George Amy; w, Robert E. Kent (based on a story by Martin Mooney); ph, L. William O'Connell; ed, Frederick Richards.

Drama   **(PR:A   MPAA:NR)**

GAMBLING SAMURAI, THE***   (1966, Jap.) 101m Toho c
                                                (KUNISADA CHUJI)

Toshiro Mifune (Chuji), Michiyo Aratama, Kumi Mizuno, Daisuke Kato, Yosuke Natsuki, Kankuro Nakamura.

Japanese Samurai great Mifune, returning to his village after a two-year absence, finds it oppressed by a thoughtless government. His sister is assaulted by an official and commits suicide; then her fiance is killed. Instead of going on a rampage, however, Mifune bides his time, devoting his energies to undermining the government by stealing rice from a warehouse and distributing it to the suffering farmers. After three years, he finally gets his revenge. Then he leaves the village, promising someday to return. The character of Chuji is also portrayed in Sadeo Yamanaka's CHUJI KUNISADA, and Daisuke Ito's silent A DIARY OF CHUJI'S TRAVELS. This film was originally released in Japan in 1960.

d, Senkichi Taniguchi; w, Kaneto Shindo; ph, Rokuro Nishigaki (Tohoscope, Agfa Color).

Action/Drama   **Cas.**   **(PR:C   MPAA:NR)**

GAMBLING SEX*½   (1932) 60m Monarch bw

Ruth Hall, Grant Withers, Maston Williams, John St. Polis, Jean Porter, Jimmy Eagles, Murdock McQuarrie.

Hall is a rich society woman who gets the gambling bug. She loses all her money but Withers, the poor but honest hero, takes her away from the mess she created.

Though set in Florida, California mountains can be seen in the background of some shots.

d, Henry Knight; w, F. McGrew Willis; ph, Fred Bain; ed, Homer Ackerman.

Drama (PR:A MPAA:NR)

GAMBLING SHIP**½ (1933) 72m PAR bw

Cary Grant (*Ace Corbin*), Benita Hume (*Eleanor La Velle*), Roscoe Karns (*Blooey*), Glenda Farrell (*Jeanne Sands*), Jack La Rue (*Pete Manning*), Arthur Vinton (*Joe Burke*), Charles Williams (*Baby Face*), Edwin Maxwell (*District Attorney*), Harry Shutan (*1st Gunman*), Frank Moran (*2nd Gunman*), Spencer Charles (*1st Detective*), Otho Wright (*2nd Detective*), Evelyn Silvie (*Indian Woman*), Kate Campbell (*Woman Detective*), Edward Gargan (*1st Deputy*), Jack Grey (*2nd Deputy*), William Welsh (*Conductor*), Sid Saylor (*The Sailor*), Hooper Atchley (*Doctor*), Larry Alexander (*Telephone Operator*), Louis Natheaux (*Croupier*), Gum Chung (*Cook*).

A mediocre melodrama with added interest because of Grant's charming presence, GAMBLING SHIP has Grant as a big-time gambler, on board a transcontinental train, pretending to be a successful businessman. He meets Hume (later Ronald Colman's real-life wife), who appears to be a wealthy socialite but she isn't. Hume is really a mistress to Vinton, owner of a failing gambling ship. She convinces Grant to buy the boat after he learns that a gambling rival, vicious La Rue, owns another boat servicing the same high rollers. Grant's only desire is to ruin La Rue's business and even an old score. La Rue will have none of it, and he and his goons board Grant's ship, set it on fire, and kill Vinton. By then Grant and Hume know what each other really is, but it doesn't matter since they're in love. They're also lucky. A storm comes up, washes all the gangsters overboard, and sinks the ship, but not before Grant and Hume are safely on land, in each other's arms, and betting on the future together. A rather limp script is held together with some lively action and Grant's winning ways. La Rue adds to the flavor as a truly rotten-to-the-core villain, a specialty that would become most pronounced in THE STORY OF TEMPLE DRAKE.

d, Louis Gasnier, Max Marcin; w, Marcin, Seton I. Miller, Claude Binyon (based on stories by Peter Ruric); ph, Charles Lang.

Drama (PR:A MPAA:NR)

GAMBLING SHIP*½ (1939) 62m UNIV bw

Robert Wilcox (*Larry Mitchell*), Helen Mack (*Mollie Riley*), Ed Brophy (*Innocent*), Joseph Sawyer (*Tony Garzoni*), Irving Pichel (*Professor*), Selmer Jackson (*Steve Riley*), Sam McDaniel (*Speedy*), Dorothy Vaughn (*Matron*), Al Hill (*Fingers*), John Harmon (*Cramer*), Rudolph Chavers (*Snowflake*), Tim Davis (*Nick*).

A crooked gambling tycoon, Pichel, kills an honest competitor when he won't sell his gambling ship. The dead man's daughter, Mack, takes over her father's business and Wilcox is the investigator out to nab Pichel.

p, Irving Starr; d, Aubrey H. Scotto; w, Alex Gottlieb (based on a story by G. Carleton Brown and Emanuel Manheim); ph, George Meehan; ed, Ed Curtis; md, Charles Previn; art d, Jack Otterson.

Drama (PR:A MPAA:NR)

GAMBLING TERROR, THE** (1937) 53m REP bw

Johnny Mack Brown (*Jeff*), Iris Meredith (*Betty*), Charlie King (*Brett*), Ted Adams (*Sheriff*), Earl Dwire (*Bradley*), Dick Curtis (*Dirk*), Horace Murphy (*Missouri*), Bobby Nelson (*Jerry*), Frank Ellis (*Blackie*), Frank Ball (*Garet*), Sherry Tansey, Steve Clark, George Morrell, Art Dillard, Tex Palmer, Jack Montgomery.

Nonchalant cowboy Brown goes after mobster Dwire who wants protection money from the ranchers. Brown puts a quick stop to *that* plan.

p, A.W. Hackel; d, Sam Newfield; w, George H. Plympton, Fred Myton; ph, Bert Longenecker; ed, S. Roy Luby.

Western Cas. (PR:A MPAA:NR)

GAME FOR SIX LOVERS, A** (1962, Fr.) 86m Falcon bw
(L'EAU A LA BOUCHE; AKA: GAMES FOR SIX LOVERS)

Bernadette Lafont (*Prudence*), Francoise Brion (*Milena*), Alexandra Stewart (*Fifine*), Michel Galabru (*Cesar*), Jacques Riberolles (*Robert*), Gerard Barray (*Miguel*), Paul Guers (*Jean-Paul*), Florence Loinod (*Florence*).

Brion and two cousins whom she's never met are named as beneficiaries in their grandmother's will. Then Brion mistakes one of her cousin's friends for her cousin, a seductive maid (Lafont) seduces the butler, and Brion's female cousin (Stewart) falls for the lawyer (Barray). Finally, Guers, the real cousin of Brion arrives, and all ends well. Lafont is no stranger to fans of Claude Chabrol, appearing in LE BEAU SERGE and LES BONNES FEMMES. Producer Braunberger also had his hand in on Truffaut's SHOOT THE PIANO PLAYER and Godard's MY LIFE TO LIVE.

p, Pierre Braunberger; d&w, Jacques Doniol-Valcroze; m, Serge Gainsbourg; ph, Roger Fellous; ed, C. Negri, Nadine Marquand.

Comedy/Drama (PR:A MPAA:NR)

GAME FOR THREE LOSERS** (1965, Brit.) 55m Merton Park/AE bw

Michael Gough (*Robert Hilary*), Mark Eden (*Oliver Marchant*), Toby Robins (*Frances Challinor*), Rachel Gurney (*Adele*), Allan Cuthbertson (*Garsden*), Al Mulock (*Nick*), Roger Hammond (*Peter Fletcher*), Lockwood West (*Justice Tree*), Mark Dignam (*Attorney General*), Catherine Wilmer (*Miss Stewart*), Catherine Anne Pichon (*Miss Fawcett*), Leslie Sarony (*Harley*).

When a successful politician gets involved in some underhand activities, everything he had struggled to obtain looks as if it's about to go up in smoke. Fairly intriguing political-crime thriller, hampered only by the inability of the scripter to bring any new material into the aged proceedings.

p, Jack Greenwood; d, Gerry O'Hara; w, Roger Marshall (based on a novel by Edgar Lustgarten).

Crime/Drama (PR:A MPAA:NR)

GAME FOR VULTURES, A* (1980, Brit.) 90m
Pyramid/New Line Cinema c

Richard Harris, Richard Roundtree, Joan Collins, Ray Milland, Sven-Bertil Taube, Denholm Elliott, Ken Gampu, Tony Osoba, Neil Hallett, Alibe Parsons, Elaine Proctor, Mark Singleton, Jana Cilliers, John Parsonson.

In the racially-torn country of Rhodesia, a man fighting sanctions becomes an angry black revolutionary. Rather than take an intelligent approach towards this emotional topic, this story goes for easy stereotypes and a plethora of violence. The results are pretentious, bloody and, at times, unintentionally funny.

p, Hazel Adair; d, James Fargo; w, Phillip Baird (based on the novel by Michael Hartmann).

Drama (PR:O MPAA:R)

GAME IS OVER, THE*** (1967, Fr.) 98m Marceau-Cocinor/Royal c
(LA CUREE)

Jane Fonda (*Renee Saccard*), Peter McEnery (*Maxime Saccard*), Michel Piccoli (*Alexandre Saccard*), Tina Marquand (*Anne Sernet*), Jacque Monod (*Mon. Sernet*), Simone Valerie (*Mme. Sernet*), Ham Chao Luong (*Mr. Chou*), Howard Vernon (*Lawyer*), Douglas Read (*Maitre d'Hotel*), Germaine Montero (*Guest*).

Fonda is cast as the wealthy young wife of Piccoli, bored with her husband. When his stepson, who is the same age as Fonda, pays a visit, she is much taken by him, which leads to her request for a divorce. Piccoli agrees and Fonda goes to Switzerland to annul the marriage. While she is away, Piccoli pressures his spineless stepson into getting engaged to the daughter of a banker. Fonda returns and is near suicide when she attends her lover's engagement party. The finale has Fonda, dripping wet from a death leap into a pool, sitting alone in acceptance of a now empty life. As usual in a Vadim film there is a vast amount of nudity, though Fonda, who once sued *Playboy* for printing nude photos, commented that this film did more for her career as a serious actress than any other film she had made.

p&d, Roger Vadim; w, Vadim, Jean Cau, Bernard Frechtman (based on the novel *La Curee* by Emile Zola); ph, Claude Renoir (Panavision, Technicolor); m, Jean-Pierre Bourtayre, Jean Bouchety; ed, Victoria Mercanton; art d, Jean Andre.

Drama/Romance (PR:O MPAA:NR)

GAME OF CHANCE, A* (1932, Brit.) 65m EPC bw

John F. Argyle (*Dick Weston*), Margaret Delane (*Ruth*), Jack Marriott (*Jack Andrews*), Eileen Lloyd (*Mrs. Weston*), Thomas Moss (*Bookie*).

Inconsequential early British talker centering around the illegalities that take place behind bet placing in the sporting scene. The bookie responsible for the chicanery gets his comeuppance when a trainer gets wind of one naive soul being an easy game for the crook.

d, Charles Barnett; w, John F. Argyle.

Crime/Drama (PR:A MPAA:NR)

GAME OF DANGER (SEE: BANG! YOU'RE DEAD, 1954, Brit.)

GAME OF DEATH, A**½ (1945) 72m RKO bw

John Loder (*Rainsford*), Audrey Long (*Ellen*), Edgar Barrier (*Kreiger*), Russell Wade (*Robert*), Russell Hicks (*Whitney*), Jason Robards (*Captain*), Gene Stutenroth (*Pleshke*), Noble Johnson (*Carib*), Robert Clarke (*Helmsman*).

A remake of THE MOST DANGEROUS GAME done in 1932 by RKO. Barrier is the maniacal hunter of humans, in this case Loder, Long, and Wade, on his island. Loder tricks the madman and saves Long but not before Wade is killed. Johnson repeats his role from the 1932 original, and Fay Wray's 1932 screams are also used.

p, Herman Schlom; d, Robert Wise; w, Norman Houston (based on a story by Richard Connell); ph, J. Roy Hunt; m, Paul Sawtell; ed, J.R. Whittredge; md, C. Bakaleinikoff; art d, Albert S. D'Agostino, Lucius Croxton.

Suspense (PR:A MPAA:NR)

GAME OF DEATH, THE* (1979) 102m COL c
(AKA: GOODBYE BRUCE LEE: HIS LAST GAME OF DEATH)

Bruce Lee (*Billy Lo*), Gig Young (*Jim Marshall*), Dean Jagger (*Dr. Land*), Hugh O'Brian (*Steiner*), Colleen Camp (*Ann Morris*), Robert Wall (*Carl Miller*), Mel Novak (*Stick*), Kareem Abdul-Jabbar (*Hakim*), Chuck Norris (*Fighter*), Danny Inosanto (*Pasqual*), Billy McGill (*John*), Hung Kim Po (*Lo Chen*), Roy Chaio (*Henry Lo*).

To cash in on footage from a film Lee did not finish before his death, producer Chow puts in a double and uses out-takes for this kung fu mess. Most of the time we see the double only from the back, with close-ups of Lee's face or eyes cut in. Same old plot: Lee (and his double) break up a crime syndicate. The original Lee footage includes a fight with Kareem Abdul-Jabbar. There are also out-takes of Chuck Norris from Lee's RETURN OF THE DRAGON.

p, Raymond Chow; d, Robert Clouse; w, Jan Spears; ph, Godfrey A. Godar (Panavision); m, John Barry; ed, Alan Pattillo.

Martial Arts Cas. (PR:O MPAA:R)

GAME OF LOVE, THE** (1954, Fr.) 108m Franco-London/Times Film bw
(LE BLE EN HERBE)

Nicole Berger (*Vinca*), Pierre-Michel Beck (*Phil*), Edwige Feuillere (*Madame Dalleray*), Charles Deschamps (*Vinca's Father*), Helene Tossy (*Vinca's Mother*), Renee Devillers (*Phil's Mother*), Julienne Paroli (*Vinca's Grandmother*), Louis De Funes (*Movie Projectionist*), Simone Duhart (*Pianist*), Robert Berri (*Policeman*).

Feuillere is cast as the older woman who seduces the teenage Beck. Director Autant-Lara felt that he had a subject that would get at the hearts of all those who had experienced young love, and he did hit upon a marketable success—as well as winning the Grand Prix du Cinema—but his impression of amorous youth has no sense of passion. He merely provided a scandalous entertainment. As such, the film was the target of religious organizations and was banned in both Nice and Chicago, where it was declared to be "immoral and obscene"—which only further hiked the sales receipts. Autant-Lara had previously spent some time in court after accusing Roger Leenhardt of plagiarizing his script—a case which Autant-Lara lost. Aurenche and Bost again (as with DIARY OF A COUNTRY PRIEST) took the liberty of altering Colette's novel by adding a lesbian character, which was removed only weeks before the shooting began, obviously by someone with greater intelligence.

d, Claude Autant-Lara; w, Autant-Lara, Jean Aurenche, Pierre Bost (based on the novel *The Ripening Seed* by Colette); ph, Robert Le Febvre; m, Rene Cloeree; ed, Madeleine Gug.

Drama **(PR:C MPAA:NR)**

GAME OF TRUTH, THE** (1961, Fr.) 80m Cocinor bw (LE JEU DE LA VERITE)

Robert Hossein *(Inspector)*, Francoise Prevost *(Guylaine)*, Paul Meurisse *(Borquere)*, Jean Servais *(Verlat)*, Nadia Gray *(Solange)*, Thien-Huong *(Girl)*, Perrette Pradler *(Florence)*, Jeanne Valerie *(Francine)*, Georges Riviere *(Bernard)*, Jean-Louis Trintignant *(Guy)*, Jacques Dacqmine *(Industrialist)*, Marc Cassot *(Husband)*.

A writer throws a party and a man arrives with an envelope. In the envelope is a large amount of money, and while the man puts everyone through a game of answering questions, he's killed. The guests call the police and another man arrives, who turns out to be the killer, there to blackmail the man who hired him—who turns out to be . . . .

d, Robert Hossein; w, Jean Serge, Robert Chazal, Louis Martin, and Steve Passeur; ph, Christian Matras; ed, Gilbert Natol.

Murder/Mystery **(PR:C MPAA:NR)**

GAME THAT KILLS, THE*½ (1937) 55m COL bw

Charles Quigley *(Alec Ferguson)*, Rita Hayworth *(Betty Holland)*, John Gallaudet *(Sam Erskine)*, J. Farrell MacDonald *(Joe Holland)*, Arthur Loft *(Rudy Maxwell)*, John Tyrell *(Eddie)*, Paul Fix *(Dick Adams)*, Max Hoffman, Jr. *(Bill Drake)*, Dick Wessel *(Leapfrog Soule)*, Maurice Black *(Jeff)*, Clyde Dilson *(Steve Moran)*, Harry Strang *(Walter)*, Dick Curtis *(Whitey)*, Lee Prather *(Bronson)*, Jack Dougherty, Edmund Cobb *(Cops)*, Ralph Dunn *(Detective)*, Ethan Laidlaw, Eddie Fetherston *(Cab Drivers)*, George Chesebro *(Waiter)*, Bud Weiser, Lloyd Ford *(Motor Cops)*, Sammy McKim *(Jack)*.

Hayworth's first major screen role was in this forgettable film. Quigley joins a professional hockey team to find out who killed his brother, who was murdered in a faked rink accident. Hayworth plays the daughter of the team's trainer. Offscreen, as part of her glamorization, she was having her hairline raised by electrolysis.

d, D. Ross Lederman; w, Grace Neville, Fred Niblo, Jr. (based on a story by J. Benton Cheney); ph, Benjamin Kline; m, Morris Stoloff; ed, James Sweeney.

Drama **(PR:A MPAA:NR)**

GAMEKEEPER, THE½** (1980, Brit.) 84m ATV Network c

Phil Askham *(George Purse)*, Rita May *(Mary)*, Andrew Grubb *(John)*, Peter Steels *(Ian)*, Michael Hinchcliffe *(Bob)*, Philip Firth *(Frank)*, Lee Hickin *(Jack)*, Jackie Shinn *(Lord)*, Paul Brian *(Butcher)*, Ted Beyer *(Alf)*, Chick Barratt *(Henry)*, Willoughby Gray *(Duke)*, Mark Elwes *(Lord Dronfield)*.

A sensitive, realistic, documentary-type film from the director of KES (1972). Askham is a one-time millworker who, with his small family, has elected to lead the natural life. He takes the position of gamekeeper on a large country estate owned by absentee landlord Elwes. The latter makes occasional grouse-hunting forays with his titled friends, but generally chooses to spend his time elsewhere. Askham takes his responsibilities seriously; he lectures would-be poachers and trespassing children sternly, raises pheasants, and repairs fences. However, other fences in the rural community are not so readily mended; many villagers are resentful of the archaic feudal system, one which Askham defends. Gradually, the unthinking humiliations of a system of near-servitude, however infrequent, begin to befoul his nest. Budding antagonism builds until, finally, he espouses the view of his neighbors: the landed gentry must go, and they won't go without being pushed.

d, Kenneth Loach; w, Loach, Barry Hines (based on a novel by Hines); ph, Chris Menges and Charles Stewart; ed, Roger James; art d, Martin Johnson, Graham Tew; cos, Maxine Henry.

Drama **(PR:A MPAA:NR)**

GAMERA THE INVINCIBLE zero (1966, Jap.) 86m Daiei/World Entertainment bw (DAIKAIJU GAMERA; AKA: GAMERA; GAMMERA; GAMMERA THE INVINCIBLE)

Albert Dekker *(Secretary of Defense)*, Brian Donlevy *(Gen. Terry Arnold)*, Diane Findlay *(Sgt. Susan Embers)*, John Baragrey *(Capt. Lovell)*, Dick O'Neill *(Gen. O'Neill)*, Eiji Funakoshi *(Dr. Hidaka)*, Harumi Kiritachi *(Kyoke)*, Junichiro Yamashita *(Aoyagi)*, Yoshiro Uchida *(Toshio)*, Michiko Sugata *(Nobuyo)*, Yoshiro Kitahara *(Sakurai)*, Jun Hamamura *(Dr. Murase)*, Mort Marshall *(Jules Manning)*, Alan Oppenheimer *(Dr. Contrare)*, Stephen Zacharias *(Senator Billings)*, Bob Carraway *(Lt. Simpson)*, Gene Bua *(Lt. Clark)*, John McCurry *(Airman First Class Hopkins)*, Walter Arnold *(American Ambassador)*, Louis Zorich *(Russian Ambassador)*, Robin Craven *(English Ambassador)*, George Hirose *(Japanese Ambassador)*.

First in the long-running series about Gamera, who ranks right up there with Godzilla and Mothra in the Japanese monster hall of fame. Gamera is a gigantic, fire-spitting turtle created in the aftermath of an atomic bomb explosion. He flies by pulling his tail and spinning (sort of like an outboard motor), and goes around destroying city after city. An international assemblage of governmental and military heads collaborate and conceive of Plan Z to thwart this rampaging creature. The turtle is caught in a rocket and fired off to Mars. Perhaps they should have smuggled the sequel scripts aboard.

p, Yonejiro Saito; d, Noriyaki Yuasa; w, Fumi Takahashi, Saito, Richard Kraft; ph, Nobuo Munekawa, Julian Townsend (Totalscope); ed, Ross-Gaffney, Tatsuji Nakashizu; art d, Hank Aldrich; spec eff, Yonesaburo Tsukiji; m/l, title song, Wes Farrell (sung by The Moons).

Monster/Science Fiction **(PR:A MPAA:NR)**

GAMERA VERSUS BARUGON*½ (1966, Jap./U.S.) 101m Daiei c (GAMERA TAI BARUGON; AKA: GAMBARA VERSUS BARUGON, THE WAR OF THE MONSTERS)

Kojiro Hongo, Kyoko Enami, Akira Natsuki, Koji Fujiyama, Yuzo Hayakawa, Ichiro Sugai.

The rocket that sent everyone's favorite spinning turtle, Gamera, into space in GAMERA, THE INVINCIBLE has been hit by a meteor (a likely story), sending the nasty critter tumbling back to earth. An added option has been installed this time—a jet-propulsion exhaust system which allows him to zip about even faster than before. He's pitted against the horn-spiked 130-foot lizard Barugon, whose field of energy (a deadly rainbow which melts whatever it touches) draws Gamera near. Tokyo and Osaka are smashed into smithereens in the process. Gamera tosses the lizard into Lake Biwa to rid the East of his awful presence, turning the lake blue (the color of his blood). Yuasa, whose fine special effects are the highlight, was rewarded with the opportunity to direct the remainder of the GAMERA series. Good Saturday morning hangover material.

p, Hidemasa Nagata; d, Shigeo Tanaka; w, Fumi Takahashi; ph, Michio Takahashi; spec eff, Noriyaki Yuasa.

Monster/Science Fiction **(PR:A MPAA:NR)**

GAMERA VERSUS GAOS*½ (1967, Jap.) 87m Daiei c (GAMERA TAI GAOS; AKA: GAMERA VERSUS GYAOS, THE RETURN OF THE GIANT MONSTERS, BOYICHI AND THE SUPERMONSTER)

Kojiro Hongo, Kichijiro Ueda, Naoyuki Abe, Reiko Kasahara, Taro Marui, Yukitaro Hotaru, Yoshio Kitahara.

Gamera's third outing has him completing the transformation from a nasty turtle which snapped at kids to a friendly old thing, much to the pleasure of Daiei Studios, competing with Godzilla for a share of the market. Gaos is the protaganist this time around—a scaly flying fox of sorts who shoots fire-extinguishing smoke from its chest. He's not too fond of the moppets either, which means Gamera is pretty busy saving the little buggers. Gamera's no dummy though as he out foxes Gaos by getting him to fly too close to the sun. An Icarus complex?

p, Hidemasa Nagata; d, Noriyaki Yuasa; w, Fumi Takahashi; ph, Akira Uehara; spec eff, Kazafumi Fujii, Yuzo Kaneko.

Monster/Science Fiction **(PR:A MPAA:NR)**

GAMERA VERSUS GUIRON*½ (1969, Jap.) 88m Daiei c (GAMERA TAI GUIRON: AKA: ATTACK OF THE MONSTERS)

Nobuhiro Kashima, Christopher Murphy, Miyuki Akiyama, Yuko Hamada, Eiji Funakoshi, Kon Omura.

Gamera's nemesis is now Guiron, a spear-headed monster who lives on the other side of the sun (luckily for the busy construction workers of Tokyo and Osaka). Gamera tucks in his head and arms and does his spinning-turtle routine to make the trip. Once there, he saves a couple of kiddies (Yeah, Gamera!) from two gorgeous but evil native women who eat brains. Sure it's getting routine, but what do you want from a giant superturtle—art?

p, Hidemasa Nagata; d, Noriyaki Yuasa; w, Fumi Takahashi; ph, Akira Kitazaki; spec eff, Kazafumi Fujii.

Monster/Science Fiction **(PR:A MPAA:NR)**

GAMERA VERSUS MONSTER X*½ 1970, Jap.) 83m Daiei/AIP-TV c (GAMERA TAI DAIMAJU JAIGA; AKA: GAMERA VERSUS JIGER, MONSTERS INVADE EXPO '70)

Tsutomo Takakuwa, Kelly Varis, Katherine Murphy, Kon Omura, Junko Yashiro.

Big turtle Gamera is pushed into a really bizarre and demented episode this time around (for those of you who are counting, this was Gamera's sixth film). When the organizers of Expo '70 dig up an old sacred statue, they accidentally (as if anyone would do this on purpose) set free big lizard Jiger. In the midst of a battle between the two creatures, Jiger whacks Gamera in the chest with its tail, implanting some eggs in the wound. Baby Jiger soon hatches and viciously begins to suck Gamera's blood, slowly but surely emptying out our heroic turtle. A couple of kids save Gamera by piloting a submarine through the turtle's veins (not unlike FANTASTIC VOYAGE), and destroying the bloodsucker. Expo '70 went on without a single problem. Weird . . . sometimes people in film *can* be very weird.

p, Hidemasa Nagata; d, Noriyaki Yuasa; w, Fumi Takahashi; ph, Akira Kitazaki.

Monster/Science Fiction **(PR:A MPAA:NR)**

GAMERA VERSUS VIRAS*½ (1968, Jap) 75m Daiei c (GAMERA TAI VIRAS; AKA: GAMERA VERSUS OUTER SPACE MONSTER VIRAS, DESTROY ALL PLANETS)

Kojiro Hongo, Toru Takatsuka, Carl Crane, Michiko Yaegaki, Mari Atsumi, Junko Yashiro, Peter Williams.

Number four for ol' Gamera is a lot more tame than the films which were to follow (see GAMERA VERSUS JIGER). Gamera is taken over by an alien force which causes him to be a nasty turtle again, capturing two boys who were innocently playing around in a submarine. They work to free Gamera from the alien grip, and after he recovers, Gamera battles the octopus-ish Viras. More in the line of child entertainment than the others in the series.

p, Hidemasa Nagata; d, Noriyaki Yuasa; w, Fumi Takahashi; ph, Akira Kitazaki; spec eff, Kazafumi Fujii, Yuso Kaneko.

Monster/Science-Fiction (PR:A MPAA:NR)

GAMERA VERSUS ZIGRA*½ (1971, Jap.) 87m Daiei c (GAMERA TAI SHINKAI KAIJU JIGARA; AKA: GAMERA VERSUS THE DEEP SEA MONSTER ZIGRA)

Reiko Kasahara, Mikiko Tsubouchi, Koji Fujiyama, Isamu Saeki, Yasushi Sakagami, Arlene Zoellner, Gloria Zoellner.

Gamera meets one heck of a challenge in this, his 7th film, as he battles the people of Zigran. Led by a powerful female alien who can cause earthquakes, the Zigrans have come to Earth to take over our friendly planet before we ruin it with our careless pollution. When Gamera objects, he is promptly extinguished. He sinks to the bottom of the sea—dead, but not without hope. Japan's loving kids act in everyone's interest and revive the big turtle by sending a powerful electric current through his shell. He wakes up, kills the Zigrans and flies off into the sunset (sort of). In one sense this picture is worse than the others—no longer are the monsters all powerful, they have merely been reduced to playing-pieces for more powerful humans. But, in a positive sense, these monster pictures have taken up a social context by which they address the issue of our own self-induced destruction and not that of a killer monster. Director Yuasa, by this time, had become the second most prolific director of monster films trailing Inoshiro Honda who had directed the Godzilla films for Toho Studios.

p, Yoshihiko Manabe; d, Noriyaki Yuasa; w, Fumi Takahashi; ph, Akira Uehara; spec eff, Kozufumi Fujii.

Monster/Science Fiction (PR:A MPAA:NR)

GAMES½** (1967) 100m UNIV c

Simone Signoret *(Lisa)*, James Caan *(Paul)*, Katharine Ross *(Jennifer)*, Don Stroud *(Norman)*, Kent Smith *(Harry)*, Estelle Winwood *(Miss Beattie)*, Marjorie Bennett *(Nora)*, Ian Wolfe *(Dr. Edwards)*, Antony Eustrel *(Winthrop)*, Eloise Hardt *(Celia)*, George Furth *(Terry)*, Carmen Phillips *(Holly)*, Peter Brocco *(Count)*, Florence Marly *(Baroness)*, Carl Buttenberger *(Arthur)*, Pitt Herbert *(Pharmacist)*, Stuart Nisbet *(Detective)*, Kendrick Huxham *(Bookseller)*, Richard Guizon *(Masseur)*, William O'Connell, Ena Hartman, Joanne Medley, Jeff Scott, Eddra Gale, Rachel Rosenthal, Luana Anders, Robert Aiken, Max Lewin.

Caan and Ross are a pair of hedonistic Manhattan socialites with a penchant for fun and games. Signoret is an immigrant who has been reduced to selling cosmetics door-to-door. She is welcomed into their art-laden residence and asked to join in their playtime. As an amateur medium, Signoret is called upon to help conceive some pleasures for the bored duo. One of the ploys is Ross's seduction of Stroud, a slack-jawed post-pubescent delivery boy. Then Caan comes in, feigns surprise, and shoots the boy dead. Stroud is dipped in plaster and set up in the apartment as an art object. Caan and Signoret go off on a "business trip" and Ross, a nervous neurotic, is left alone with the sculpture. Suddenly, the "dead" Stroud reappears and begins to terrorize Ross. She responds by shooting him again, this time for real. Caan returns, sees what has happened and tells Ross that the first "murder" was nothing more than another game. Now she's done it and must pay the price. Ross falls apart and Caan has her sent to a mental hospital. Once she has been disposed of, we realize that Caan and Signoret are in cahoots. They sell the expensive art and plan to go away together. In the last sequence, Signoret and Caan toast the success of their plan. But Caan's drink is poisoned and he falls dead at Signoret's feet. So the last game, set, and match goes to Signoret. Harrington is one of the best directors at this kind of film but GAMES misses in many ways. The atmosphere is all there but much of the needed suspense is not. Some good second lead work by Smith as the family lawyer and Winwood as the dotty neighbor. In an homage to other films of this genre, Harrington casts Florence Marly (QUEEN OF BLOOD) and Luana Anders (NIGHT TIDE) as well as using a clip from Universal's own DRACULA (starring Bela Lugosi). Caan was, as usual, posturing in his part and was as shallow as a soap dish.

p, George Edwards; d, Curtis Harrington; w, Gene Kearney (based on a story by Harrington, Edwards) ph, William A. Fraker (Techniscope, Technicolor); m, Samuel Matlovsky; ed, Douglas Stewart; md, Joseph Gershenson; art d, Alexander Golitzen, William D. De Cinces; set d, John McCarthy; makeup, Bud Westmore.

Crime/Drama (PR:O MPAA:NR)

GAMES, THE** (1970) 95m FOX c

Michael Crawford *(Harry Hayes)*, Stanley Baker *(Bill Oliver)*, Ryan O'Neal *(Scott Reynolds)*, Charles Aznavour *(Pavel Vendek)*, Jeremy Kemp *(Jim Harcourt)*, Elaine Taylor *(Christine)*, Athol Compton *(Sunny Pintubi)*, Fritz Wepper *(Kovanda)*, Kent Smith *(Kaverley)*, Sam Elliott *(Richie Robinson)*, Reg Lye *(Gilmour)*, Mona Washbourne *(Mrs. Hayes)*, Don Newsome *(Cal Wood)*, Emmy Werner *(Vera Vendek)*, Harvey Hall *(Stuart Simmonds)*, June Jago *(Mae Harcourt)*, Karel Stepanek *(Kubitsek)*, Gwendolyn Watts *(Barmaid)*, John Alkin *(John)*, Dale Ishimoto *(Dr. Tselsura)*, Alexander Werner *(Juri Vendek)*, Rafer Johnson, Rod Pickering, Adrian Metcalfe *(Commentators)*, Bob Cunningham *(Fred Gardner)*, Colin Jeavons *(Earnest Man)*, Paddy Webster *(Jocelyn)*, Tina Carter *(Miss Gibb)*, Stephanie Beacham *(Angela Simmonds)*, Basil Dignam *(Weston)*, Hugh McDermott, Warren Stanhope, Leigh Taylor-Young.

Human sacrifice story of four marathoners from different countries and their obstacles in getting ready for the Rome Olympics. British milkman Crawford is trained by the hard-driving Baker, a former track star. Yale runner O'Neal prepares for the race heedless of his delicate heart condition. Aznavour is a 41-year-old Czech athlete, whose government orders him to compete for the glory of his country. Compton is an Australian aborigine who must strive against the sting of second-class citizenship in his own country. He ignores the pressures of black militants to use the race as a forum for protest and goes on to win the gold medal.

p, Lester Linsk; d, Michael Winner; w, Eric Segal (based on a novel by Hugh Atkinson); ph, Robert Paynter (Panavision, DeLuxe Color); m, Francis Lai; ed, Bernard Gribble; art d, Albert Witherick, Fred Carter, Roy Stannard.

Drama (PR:A MPAA:G)

GAMES FOR SIX LOVERS (SEE: GAME FOR SIX LOVERS, A, 1962, Fr.)

GAMES MEN PLAY, THE*½ (1968, Arg.) 92m Tinayre-Borras S.R.L./Brenner-Day and Day bw (LA CIGARRA NO ES UN BICHO; AKA: THE HOTEL, THE CICADA IS NOT AN INSECT)

Maria Antinea *(The Wife)*, Amelia Bence *(The Prostitute)*, Elsa Daniel *(The Bride)*, Martha Legrand *(Secretary)*, Malvina Pastorino *(Teacher)*, Jose Cibrian *(Industrialist)*, Narcisco Ibanez Menta *(Ventriloquist)*, Angel Magana *(Journalist)*, Luis Sandrini *(Taxi Driver)*, Enrique Serrano *(Musician)*, Teresa Blasco *(Maid)*, Guillermo Bredeston *(Bridegroom)*, Diana Ingro *(Model)*, Miryan de Urquijo *(Lady)*, Leda Zanda *(Nurse)*, Guillermo Battaglia *(Doctor)*, Hector Calcano *(Police Commissioner)*, Homero Carpena *(Manager)*, Ludio de Val *(Sergeant)*, Hector Mendez *(Police Inspector)*.

There are some interesting ideas in this story of six couples who get trapped in a hotel when one of the guests is diagnosed as having bubonic fever. Anything of value in this picture, however, is owed to Albert Camus who exhausted the subject in his brilliant novel *The Plague*. The quarantine changes the lives of almost everyone involved—a married couple rekindles their love, two young lovers decide to wed, two people having an affair realize their relationship has no spark without the threat of being caught. The only one who emerges unchanged when the quarantine clears is a prostitute who re-enters the hotel with a customer. Originally released in Argentina in 1963, though a Spanish language version was shown in the United States in 1964. Additional nude footage was included for the English-language version.

p, Eduardo Borras; d, Daniel Tinayre; w, Borras; ph, Alberto Etchebehere; m, Lucio Milena; ed, Jorge Garate; art d, Gori Munoz.

Drama (PR:O MPAA:NR)

GAMES THAT LOVERS PLAY*½ (1971, Brit.) Border Film c

Joanna Lumley *(Fanny Hill)*, Penny Brahms *(Constance Chatterley)*, Richard Wattis *(Mr. Lothran)*, Jeremy Lloyd *(Jonathan Willoughby)*, Diana Hart *(Mrs. Hill)*, Nan Munro *(Lady Evelyn)*, John Gatrell *(Bishop)*, Charles Cullum *(Charles)*, Leigh Anthony *(Keeper)*, George Belbin *(Maj. Thumper)*, June Palmer *(Girl)*, Graham Armitage *(Young Photographer)*, New Temperance Seven.

Two madames, Hart and Munro, wager over whose best girl is the better trick. Set in the Roaring Twenties, this ribald farce has Hart's girl taking a drag queen to bed while Munro's girl plies her trade on a rotund bishop. Round one is declared a draw. To decide matters, the madames randomly use the phone book and pick the number of wine seller Wattis. Neither girl alone can arouse him, but when they jump in bed with him together it's seduction galore. The bet ends in a draw.

p, O. Negus-Fancey, Judith Smith; d&w, Malcolm Leigh; ph, Ken Higgins (Eastmancolor); m, Davis Lindup; ed, Peter Austin Hunt; art d, Bill Hutchins.

Comedy (PR:O MPAA:NR)

GAMLET (SEE: HAMLET, 1964, U.S.S.R.)

GAMMA PEOPLE, THE** (1956) 78m Warwick/COL bw

Paul Douglas *(Mike Wilson)*, Eva Bartok *(Paula Wendt)*, Leslie Phillips *(Howard Meade)*, Walter Rilla *(Boronski)*, Philip Leaver *(Koerner)*, Martin Miller *(Lochner)*, Michael Caridia *(Hugo)*, Pauline Drewett *(Hedda)*, Jackie Lane *(Anna)*, Olaf Pooley *(Bikstein)*, Rosalie Crutchley *(Frau Bikstein)*, Paul Hardtmuth *(Hans)*, Cyril Chamberlain *(Graf)*, Leonard Sachs *(Telegraph Clerk)*, St. John Stuart *(Goon)*.

Newsman Douglas and his photographer, Phillips, are on a European train heading for Salzburg. They end up, though, in a communist country called Gudavia. There they find a mad scientist shooting the kids with gamma rays. This turns a few into geniuses, but most into idiots, called goons. Douglas and Phillips put a swift stop to things with the help of Bartok. A small science fiction film with an intriguing plot.

p, John Gossage; d, John Gilling; w, Gilling and Gossage (based on a story by Louis Pollock); ph, Ted Moore; m, George Melachrino; ed, Jack Slade, Alan Osbiston; art d, John Box.

Science Fiction (PR:A MPAA:NR)

GAMMERA THE INVINCIBLE (SEE: GAMERA THE INVINCIBLE, 1966, Jap.)

GANDHI***** (1982) 188m International Film Investors-Goldcrest Films International-Indo-British Films-National Film Development/COL c

Ben Kingsley *(Mahatma Gandhi)*, Candice Bergen *(Margaret Bourke-White)*, Edward Fox *(Gen. Dyer)*, John Gielgud *(Lord Irwin)*, Trevor Howard *(Judge Broomfield)*, John Mills *(The Viceroy)*, Martin Sheen *(Walker)*, Rohini Hattangady *(Kasturba Gandhi)*, Ian Charleson *(Charlie Andrews)*, Athol Fugard *(Gen. Smuts)*, Gunter Maria Halmer *(Herman Kallenbach)*, Saeed Jaffrey *(Sardar Patel)*, Geraldine James *(Mirabehn)*, Alyque Padamsee *(Mohammed Ali Jinnah)*, Amrish Puri *(Khan)*, Roshan Seth *(Pandit Nehru)*, Ian Bannen *(Sr. Police Officer)*, Michael Bryant *(Principal Secretary)*, John Clements *(Advocate General)*, Richard Griffiths *(Collins)*, Nigel Hawthorne *(Kinnoch)*, Bernard Hepton *(G.O.C.)*, Michael Hordern *(Sir George Hodge)*, Peter Harlowe *(Lord Mountbatten)*, Jane Myerson *(Lady Mountbatten)*, Shreeram Lagoo *(Prof. Gokhale)*, Om Puri *(Nahari)*, Virendra Razdan *(Maulana Azad)*, Richard Vernon *(Sir Edward Gait)*, Harsh Nayyar *(Nathuram Godse)*, Prabhakar Patankar *(Prakash)*, Vijay Kahsyap *(Apte)*, Nigam Prakash *(Karkare)*, Supriya Pathak *(Manu)*, Nina Gupta *(Abha)*, Shane Rimmer *(Commentator)*, Anang Desai *(J. B. Kripalani)*, Alok Nath *(Tyeb Mohammed)*, Dean Gaspar *(Singh)*, David Gant *(Daniels)*, Daniel Day Lewis *(Colin)*, Avis Bunnage *(His*

Mother), Sunila Pradhan (Mrs. Motilal Nehru), Manohar Pitale (Shukla), Ernest Clark (Lord Hunter), Pankaj Mohan (Mahadev Desai), Bernard Horsfall (Gen. Edgar), Daleep Tahil (Zia), Terrence Hardiman (Ramsey MacDonald), John Vine (A. D. C. to Gen. Dyer).

Sir Richard Attenborough ("Dickie" to his pals) spent nearly 20 years attempting to convince studios that the life story of Gandhi was crying to be made. It had already been touched upon in the adaptation of Indian expert Stanley Wolpert's book in NINE HOURS TO RAMA (1963) and, amazingly, that was a dull picture. Writing a synopsis of this film would be like doing a precis of the Encyclopedia Brittanica. It *could* be done but much would be lost in the compressing. Gandhi is a movie nearly as long as the great man's life was. Ben Kingsley's Academy Award-winning performance as Gandhi is a marvel on many levels. It was his first film and he was seen to age over half a century as he metamorphosed from a young attorney in South Africa to the leader of a sub-continent. The picture opens with the youthful lawyer being tossed off a train by a man who is not fit to mend his loincloth. And the only reason for the treatment is that Kingsley's skin is a few tones darker than those around him. From there, matters take a turn for the worse as Kingsley is beaten, jailed, and exiled. He develops his theory of "passive resistance" and uses that as his steppingstone to power among his people. It's as naturalistic as a film can get without actually watching the entire life of a human being in home movies. That is not to say that the sheer cinematic energy is the same as something taken by an 8-millimeter camera. But we are so caught up with the vast saga that we often forget these are actors and they are being told what to do by a director. The style and grace of Gandhi is almost as gentle and placid as the man was (in the intimate scenes when Indians were not being mowed down by British soldiers). Yet, even the battle sequences have a sanity about them, a kind of rightness which is stamped with great authenticity and can only be the result of Attenborough's talent, his maturity, and his unwillingness to compromise. It may well be impossible to compartmentalize the long life of a great human being (or even a terrible human being) in just over three hours, but Attenborough and author Briley have magnificently collaborated to offer us what can only be described as a balanced view of Gandhi's life, from trauma to triumph to his eventual death by assassination. Each scene is almost a story in itself and the pace is never rushed to get out of the scene as fast as possible. Instead, the subtlety builds and it is almost as though Gandhi's life is a huge drawing, with each incident helping to fill in the colors until we are regaled by the sight of a mural. Kingsley is spellbinding every time we see him, so the length of the picture does not have any boredom factor. The use of matte paintings mixed with the sprawling vistas blend to give us panoramic size as counterpoint to the small moments. Every supporting actor is well cast with the exception of Bergen as famed photographer Bourke-White. She seems to do not much more than snap pictures and try to look interested in what Kingsley is talking about. What she is doing in this movie is anybody's guess. Seth, as Nehru, is excellent, as are Fox, Howard, Mills, and Sheen. The well-known South African author, Athol Fugard (Master Harold And The Boys among others) is believable as Smuts. Gandhi takes us on a roller coaster of emotions; we get angry when the Indians are slaughtered, we are shocked when he asks his wife to swab the latrine, we smile when he achieves power and we are crushed when he is murdered. Making a true story is never easy and when most people have some sort of idea of what happened, the problem becomes "how to show it and still keep the audience intrigued." From the opening credits, we are drawn into the vortex of Gandhi's life and the highest accolade we can offer as our feeling on the movie is that, after seeing this picture, we wish we could have met the man. Academy Awards for Best Picture, Best Actor, Best Direction, Best Writing, Best Cinematography, Best Costume Design, Best Art Direction, Best Set Design, Best Editing.

p&d, Richard Attenborough; w, John Briley; ph, Billy Williams, Ronnie Taylor (Panavision, Technicolor); m, Ravi Shankar, George Fenton; ed, John Bloom; prod d, Stuart Craig; art d, Bob Laing, Ram Yedekar, Norman Dorme; set d, Michael Seirton; cos, John Mollo, Bhanu Athaiya; spec eff, David Hathaway.

Biography   **Cas.**   **(PR:A MPAA:PG)**

GANG, THE**   (1938, Brit.) 69m Syndicate/GFD bw
(GB: THE GANG SHOW)

Ralph Reader (Skipper), Gina Malo (Marie), Stuart Robertson (Raydon), Richard Ainley (Whipple), Leonard Snelling (Len), Syd Palmer (Syd), Roy Emerton (Proprietor), Percy Walsh (McCullough), Sandy Williamson, Don Dalvin.

Reader plays a Boy Scout leader who likes to think of himself as a theatrical genius. But his plans to run a show starring nothing but scouts reveals to the high-minded man that creating a successful show is not a piece of cake. Luckily for Reader, the good-natured Malo takes an interest in seeing the boys get on stage and helps in obtaining the necessary funding.

p, Herbert Wilcox; d, Alfred Goulding; w, Marjorie Gaffney (based on a story by Ralph Reader); ph, Ernest Palmer; m/l, Reader.

Musical   **(PR:A MPAA:NR)**

GANG BULLETS*   (1938) 62m MON bw

Anne Nagel (Patricia), Robert Kent (Carter), Charles Trowbridge (Wayne), Morgan Wallace (Anderson), J. Farrell MacDonald (Reardon), John T. Murray (Meade), Arthur Loft (Wallace), John Merton (Red), Donald Kerr (Armstrong), Carleton Young (Newell), Isabell LaMalle (Mrs. Jones), Benny Bartlett (Billy).

Racketeer Wallace is thrown out of one town, relocates to another, and resorts to his crooked ways. District attorney Trowbridge and his assistant, Kent, finally outfox the clever hood and put him in jail.

p, E.B. Derr; d, Lambert Hillyer; w, John T. Neville; ph, Arthur Martinelli; ed, Russ Schoengarth.

Crime   **(PR:A MPAA:NR)**

GANG BUSTER, THE**½   (1931) 65m PAR bw

Jack Oakie (Charlie "Cyclone" Case), Jean Arthur (Sylvia Martine), William "Stage" Boyd (Sudden Mike Slade), Wynne Gibson (Zella), William Morris (Andrew Martine), Francis McDonald (Pete Caltek), Albert Conti (Carlo), Tom Kennedy (Gopher Brant), Harry Stubbs (Faulkner), Ernie Adams (Sammy), Constantin Romanoff (Otto), Pat Harmon (McGinty), Joseph Girard (Lieutenant), Eddie Dunn (Taxi Driver), Arthur Hoyt (Phone Caller).

Comedian Oakie is a small-town stooge who, through his own bumbling, puts a number of gangsters behind bars. He gets himself caught in the crossfire of two warring gangs, and when a mob boss orders him to abduct a young woman, Oakie comes into his office and tells him that it's against the law and he'll get arrested. A well-written comedy using the then very popular gangster genre with hilarious results.

d, A. Edward Sutherland; w, Percy Heath, Joseph L. Mankiewicz; ph, Harry Fischbeck; ed, Jane Loring.

Comedy   **(PR:A MPAA:NR)**

GANG BUSTERS*   (1955) 75m Visual Drama Inc.-Terry Turner/Film Division of General Teleradio bw

Myron Healey (John Omar Pinson), Don C. Harvey (Detective Walsh), Sam Edwards (Long), Frank Gerstle (Detective Fuller), Frank Richards (Bennett), Kate MacKenna (Aunt Jenny), Rusty Wescoatt (Mike), William Justine (Louie), Allan Ray (Slick Harry), William Fawcett (Truck Driver), Ed Colbrook (Pool Hall Operator), Charles Victor (Officer Rondeau), Bob Carson (Doctor), Joyce Jameson (Girl in Car), Mike Ragan (Police Officer), Ed Hinton (1st Guard), Robert Bice (2nd Guard).

Adapted from the successful radio drama, GANG BUSTERS contains nothing fresh or insightful. The film centers around Healey, Public Enemy No. 4, and his repeated prison escapes. Shot in documentary style in Oregon, the film's story line drags because of uninspired and cliche sequences.

p, William J. Faris and William H. Clothier; d, Bill Karn; w, Phillips H. Lord (revisions by Karn); ph, Clothier; m, Richard Aurandt; ed, Faris.

Crime   **(PR:A MPAA:NR)**

GANG SHOW, THE   (SEE: GANG, THE, 1938, Brit.)

GANG THAT COULDN'T SHOOT STRAIGHT, THE*   (1971) 98m MGM c

Jerry Orbach (Kid Sally Palumbo), Leigh Taylor-Young (Angela Palumbo), Jo Van Fleet (Big Momma), Lionel Stander (Baccala), Robert DeNiro (Mario), Irving Selbst (Big Jelly), Herve Villechaize (Beppo), Joe Santos (Ezmo), Carmine Caridi (Tony the Indian), Frank Campanella (Water Buffalo), Harry Basch (DeLauria), Sander Vanocour (TV Commentator), Phil Bruns (Gallagher), Philip Sterling (District Attorney Goodman), Roy Shuman (Mayor), Alice Hirson (Mayor's Wife), Jack Kehoe (Scuderi), Despo (Mourner), Sam J. Coppola (Julie), James J. Sloyan (Joey), Paul Benedict (Shots O'Toole), Burt Young (Willie Quarequio), Jackie Vernon (Herman), Louis Criscuolo (Junior), George Loros (Jerry), Harry Davis (Dominic Laviano), Ted Beniades, Fat Thomas Rand, Michael V. Gazzo (Black Suits), Robert Gerringer (Commissioner O'Grady), Walter Flanagan (The Super), Dan Morgan (Muldoon), Dorothi Fox (Meter Maid), Johnny Addie (Race Announcer), Robert Weil (Circus Supply Manager), Leopold Badia (Old Waiter), Fran Stevens (Baccala's Wife), Florence Tarlow (Police Matron), Alisha Fontaine, Lorrie Davis (Jelly's Girls), Rita Karin (Mrs. Goldfarb), Tom Lacy (Religious Salesman), William H. Boesen (Jury Foreman), Gary Melkonian (Greek Racer), Sully Boyar (Bald Bartender), Gustave Johnson (Detective Jenkins), George Stefans (Greek Captain), Frank Jourdano (TV Reporter), Elsa Raven (Mrs. Water Buffalo), Gloria Le Roy (Ida the Waitress).

What a waste of money, time, and talent. Based on newspaper columnist Jimmy Breslin's hilarious novel, producers Chartoff and Winkler and screenwriter Salt let this thing get so far out of hand that Goldstone's pedestrian direction couldn't save it. Salt, who wrote the screenplay for MIDNIGHT COWBOY and should have known better, has fallen flat with this script about a bunch of incompetent hoodlums who try to kill a Mafia chief but fail time after time. It's one flat sight gag after another as Orbach leads his clods against Stander. The only reason to watch this at all is to see young Robert DeNiro as a crooked immigrant. Villechaize got his big American break in the movie and proves to be just as bad in this as he went on to be on TV. How so many good people could have been gathered together to make such a turkey is a wonderment. Good music from Dave Grusin and fine lensing from Roizman couldn't save this from sinking to the bottom of the East River. A total caricature with virtually no characterizations.

p, Robert Chartoff, Irwin Winkler; d, James Goldstone; w, Waldo Salt (based on the novel by Jimmy Breslin); ph, Owen Roizman (Metrocolor); m, Dave Grusin; ed, Edward A. Biery; art d, Robert Gundlach; set d, George Diditta; cos, Joseph Garibaldi Aulisi; makeup, Robert Laden.

Comedy   **(PR:A-C MPAA:PG)**

GANG WAR*½   (1928) 70m FBO bw

Prolog: Lorin Raker, Jack McKee, Mabel Albertson, David Hartman; Story: Olive Borden (Flowers), Jack Pickford (Clyde Baxter), Eddie Gribbon (Blackjack), Walter Long (Mike Luege), Frank Chew (Wong).

The film starts out with a synchronized sound prolog, with two reporters going out to get a scoop on the doings of the city's underworld. They meet a cafe singer, who tells them Pickford's story, flashing back into the silent body of the film. Pickford is a musician in love with taxi dancer Borden, but gangster Gribbon has eyes for her too. The gangster ends up marrying the girl, killing a half-dozen rival gangsters, and gets killed himself saving Pickford. He dies before consummating the marriage, sustaining Borden's purity for true love Pickford.

d, Bert Glennon; w, Fred Myton, Edgar Allan Wolff (based on a story by James Ashmore Creelman); ph, Virgil Miller; ed, Archie Marshek.

Crime (PR:A MPAA:NR)

GANG WAR* (1940) 60m Sack bw

Ralph Cooper (Killer Meade), Gladys Snyder (Mazie), Reggie Fenderson (Danny), Lawrence Criner (Lou Baron), Monte Hawley (Bill), Jesse C. Brooks (Lt. Holmes), Johnny Thomas (Phil), Maceo Sheffield (Bull Brown), Charles Hawkins (Pip), Robert Johnson (Waxy), Henry Roberts (Slim), Harold Garrison (Slicum).

An all-black gangster film which suffers from a low budget. Two gangs fight it out for control of the jukeboxes in Harlem. The lack of funds to acquire a professional writer and director puts this film under.

p, Harry M. Popkin; d, Leo C. Popkin; w, Lou Sherman (based on a story by Walter Cooper); ph, Marcel Picard; m, Lew Porter; ed, Michael Luciano; m/l, "Remember the Night," Porter and Johnny Lange.

Crime (PR:C MPAA:NR)

GANG WAR*** (1958) 75m FOX bw

Charles Bronson (Alan Avery), Kent Taylor (Bryce Barker), Jennifer Holden (Marie), John Doucette (Maxie Matthews), Gloria Henry (Edie Avery), Gloria Grey (Marsha Brown), Barney Phillips (Sam Johnson), Ralph Manza (Axe Duncan), George Eldredge (Sgt. Ernie Tucker), Billy Snyder (Mr. Tomkins), Jack Reynolds (Joe Reno), Dan Simmons (Bob Cross), Larry Gelbmann (Little Abner), Jack Littlefield (Johnny), Ed Wright (Henchman No. 1), Shirle Haven (Nicki), Arthur D. Gilmore (Capt. Finch), Don Giovanni (Mike Scipio), Jack Finch (Police Sergeant), Stephen Masino (Hood No. 1), Stacey Marshall (Millie), Lynn Guild (Diane Barker), Lennie Geer (Slick Connors), Helen Jay (Street Girl), Marion Sherman (Agnes), Whit Bissell (Mark).

Bronson is an unassuming Los Angeles high-school teacher who witnesses a gangland slaying and reluctantly agrees to testify against the hit men. The gang retaliates and Bronson's pregnant wife, Henry, is killed during an attack on his house. The incensed Bronson seeks revenge and goes after the gang leader, Doucette, who has gotten embroiled with the national syndicate. After breaking into Doucette's mansion and seeing him go crazy, Bronson lets the police and the court system take care of the rest. This film paved the way for the development of the Bronson character stereotype, that of a quiet, peaceful man driven to violence (DEATH WISH).

p, Harold E. Knox; d, Gene Fowler, Jr.; w, Louis Vittes (based on the novel The Hoods Take Over by Ovid Demaris), ph, John M. Nickolaus, Jr. (RegalScope); m, Paul Dunlap; ed, Frank Baldridge; md, Dunlap; art d, John Mansbridge; set d, Walter M. Scott, Bertram Granger; makeup, Jack Obringer.

Crime Drama (PR:C-O MPAA:NR)

GANG WAR*½ (1962, Brit.) 65m Danziger/UA bw

Sean Kelly (Inspector Bob Craig), Eira Heath (Maria Alexis), David Davies (Jim Alexis), Sean Sullivan (Al Hodges), John Gabriel (Doc Tobin), Mark Singleton (Tony Danton), Colin Tapley (Paul Alexis), Leon Cortez (Grimes).

Unexciting attempt to create a gangland thriller, set in London instead of New York or Chicago, though a Chicago figure is introduced, perhaps as a means to heighten believability. The Chicago crook and a Londoner team up to try to get a piece of the jukebox racket. This being London in the early 1960s it was probably a very profitable business. Remake of the 1940 programmer.

p, Brian Langslow; d, Frank Marshall; w, Mark Grantham.

Crime (PR:A MPAA:NR)

GANGA (SEE: RIVER, THE, 1961, India)

GANG'S ALL HERE, THE
(SEE: AMAZING MR. FORREST, THE, 1943, Brit.)

GANG'S ALL HERE*½ (1941) 63m MON bw

Frankie Darro (Frankie), Marcia Mae Jones (Patsy), Jackie Moran (Chick), Mantan Moreland (Jeff), Keye Luke (George), Robert Homans (Pop), Irving Mitchell (Saunders), Ed Cassidy (Norton), Pat Gleason (Marty), Jack Kenney (Dink), Lawrence Criner (Ham Shanks), Paul Bryar (Bob), Jack Ingraham (Matt).

Darro joins up with a trucking firm that is being put out of business by a rival's sabotaging. The competitor is ramming the rigs off the road and hijacking the contents. Darro and Moreland are captured by the crooks, escape, are recaptured, then put an end to the whole mess. Interesting mostly for the presence of CHARLIE CHAN regulars Luke and Moreland, the irrepressible black sidekick.

p, Lindsley Parsons; d, Jean Yarbrough; w, Edmond Kelso; ph, Mack Stengler; ed, Jack Ogilvie.

Drama (PR:A MPAA:NR)

GANG'S ALL HERE, THE*** (1943) 103m FOX c
(GB: THE GIRLS HE LEFT BEHIND)

Alice Faye (Eadie Allen), Carmen Miranda (Dorita), Phil Baker (Himself), Benny Goodman and his Orchestra (Themselves), Eugene Pallette (Mr. Mason, Sr.), Charlotte Greenwood (Mrs. Peyton Potter), Edward Everett Horton (Peyton Potter), Tony DeMarco (Himself), James Ellison (Andy Mason), Sheila Ryan (Vivian), Dave Willock (Sgt. Casey), June Haver (Maybelle), Miriam Lavelle (Specialty Dancer), Charles Saggau (Jitterbug Dancer), Deidre Gale (Jitterbug Dancer), George Dobbs (Benson), Leon Belasco (Waiter), Frank Faylen (Marine), Russell Hoyt (Sailor), Virginia Sale (Secretary), Leyland Hodgson (Butler), Lee Bennett (Bit Man), Jeanne Crain (Girl by the Pool), Lillian Yarbo (Maid), Frank Darien (Doorman), Al Murphy (Stage Manager), Hallene Hill (Old Lady), Gabriel Canzona (Organ Grinder), Fred Walburn (Newsboy), Virginia Wilson (Dancing Partner).

Aside from the papier-mache thin plot, this film has a lot going for it. It was Faye's last big musical and no expense was spared by the studio. It was also Berkeley's first color picture and he took great advantage of his new film freedom. The plot, such as it was, concerns Faye as a chorus girl at a Big Apple nightclub where the star is Miranda (who had her largest role and was just wonderful). Baker is also appearing at the club and is a pal of young Ellison, an Army sergeant who stops by the club to say hello and see his father, Pallette, having some fun with their nervous Nellie neighbor, Horton. Ellison falls hard for Faye and trails her to a local canteen where she puts in some time between shows. Back at the club later that night, Faye brings Ellison backstage and lets him watch the show from the wings. Still later, the couple take a ride on the Staten Island ferry where she sings one of her new numbers for him. Next day, Ellison takes off for his duty in the Pacific. They start writing letters to each other. As the months fall off the calendar, Faye becomes the star of the show and sings her songs to a photo of Ellison. Ellison becomes a war hero and returns to a party that Pallette has arranged for him in Horton's garden. Any monies received will be given to the war-bond efforts. At the party, Baker meets Greenwood, Horton's wife, an old pal from her days in Paris when she was still young and wild. Miranda uncovers the fact that Ryan is unofficially affianced to Ellison, despite the fact that he and Faye are apparently speaking for each other. There's a large show in the garden with Goodman and others. The plot complications develop with a few misplaced words, and some further coincidences but, in the end, Faye and Ellison, as you might imagine, get together. The major reasons to see this are for the Warren tunes, the Berkeley inventiveness and a few of the performances. Look hard for young Jeanne Crain in a one-line bit and June Haver as a hat-check girl in her debut. Miranda's version of "The Lady In The Tutti Frutti Hat" established her as a major star. During much of the production time, Faye was pregnant with her second child. She made a cameo singing appearance in only one other film, FOUR JILLS IN A JEEP in 1944, and then switched her style to essay a straight dramatic role in FALLEN ANGEL (1946). After that, she retired from films altogether for 16 years. Her lackluster performance in this film stemmed as much from Berkeley's deficient dialog direction as from her morning sickness. Widely viewed as the high point of choreography in Berkeley's career, this lavish, costly spectacle was nearly seven months in shooting. The Freudian overtones in some of the production numbers—notably the one in which 60 chorines pranced about with giant phallic bananas—sufficed to get the film banned in Brazil, the nominal homeland of many of the film's characters.

p, William LeBaron; d, Busby Berkeley; w, Walter Bullock (from a story by Nancy Winter, George Root, Jr., and Tom Bridges); ph, Edward Cronjager (Technicolor); md, Alfred Newman, Charles Henderson; ed, Ray Curtiss; art d, James Basevi, Joseph C. Wright; set d, Thomas Little; cos, Yvonne Wood; spec eff, Fred Sersen; ch, Berkeley; m/l, "No Love, No Nothin'," "A Journey to a Star," "The Lady in the Tutti-Frutti Hat," "The Polka-Dot Polka," "You Discover You're in New York," "Paducah," "Minnie's in the Money," Leo Robin, Harry Warren; "Brazil," Ary Barroso, S.K. Russell; "Soft Winds," Benny Goodman; "Polka Dot Ballet," David Raksin.

Musical (PR:A MPAA:NR)

GANGS INCORPORATED (SEE: PAPER BULLETS, 1941)

GANGS OF CHICAGO** (1940) 66m REP bw

Lloyd Nolan (Matty Burns), Barton MacLane (Ramsey), Lola Lane (June), Ray Middleton (Bill Whitaker), Astrid Allwyn (Virginia), Horace MacMahon (Cry-Baby), Howard Hickman (Judge), Leona Roberts (Mrs. Whitaker), Charles Halton (Bromo), Addison Richards (Blake), John Harmon (Rabbit), Dwight Frye (Pinky), Alan Ladd.

As a teenager, Nolan witnessed his thief father gunned down by cops. He goes to college, and becomes a criminal lawyer, aiding the bad guys. He gets hooked up with gangster boss MacLane, and helps build an underworld empire. Nolan's partner is Middleton, hired by the FBI to spy on him. When Middleton is shot, Nolan saves his life, and informs on his mob client. Ladd's part is so small that if you blink you'll miss him.

p, Robert North; d, Arthur Lubin; w, Karl Brown; ph, Elwood Bredell; ed, Murray Seldeen, Lester Orlebeck; md, Cy Feuer; art d, John Victor Mackay.

Crime (PR:A MPAA:NR)

GANGS OF NEW YORK**½ (1938) 67m REP bw

Charles Bickford ("Rocky" Thorp/John Franklin), Ann Dvorak (Connie), Alan Baxter (Dancer), Wynne Gibson (Orchid), Harold Huber (Panatella), Willard Robertson (Sullivan), Maxie Rosenbloom (Tombstone), Charles Trowbridge (Attorney Lucas), John Wray (Maddock), Jonathan Hale (Warden), Fred Kohler (Kruger), Howard Phillips (Al Benson), Robert Gleckler (Nolan), Elliot Sullivan (Hopkins), Maurice Cass (Phillips).

Bickford plays a dual role as a top gangster, and a police officer. The gang leader is in jail, but still runs his crime operations through a short-wave radio hidden in his cell. When Bickford, the gangster, is put in solitary, away from his radio, Bickford, the cop, takes the mobster's place within the gang. The cop has all the gangsters keep records to become more business-like, and so he can collect enough evidence to put them all behind bars. When the gang leader escapes from jail, the intended peaceful round-up turns into a shoot-out.

p, Armand Schaefer; d, James Cruze; w, Wellyn Totman, Sam Fuller, Jack Townley, Charles Francis Royal (based on an original story by Sam Fuller, suggested by Herbert Asbury's book, Gangs of New York); ph, Ernest Miller; m, Alberto Columbo; ed, William Morgan; art d, John Victor Mackay.

Crime (PR:A MPAA:NR)

GANGS OF SONORA** (1941) 56m REP bw

Robert Livingston (Stony Brooke), Bob Steele (Tucson Smith), Rufe Davis (Lullaby Joslin), June Johnson (June Conners), Ward "Bud" McTaggart (David Conners), Helen MacKellar (Kansas Kate Conners), Robert Frazer (Sam Tredwell), William Farnum (Ward Beecham), Budd Buster (Jed Pickins), Hal Price (Sheriff), Wally West, Bud Osborne, Bud Geary, Jack Kirk, Al Taylor, Griff Barnett, Curley Dresden, Jack Lawrence.

Another in Republic's THREE MESQUITEERS series, with Livingston, Steele, and Davis going after a crooked town boss, Frazer, in the territory of Wyoming. Wyoming is trying to become a state, and Frazer is doing everything in his power to prevent it. His gang kills the crusading newspaper editor and his assistant. The Mesquiteers arrive to clean up as an elderly woman, MacKellar, takes over the newspaper. (See THREE MESQUITEERS series, Index.)

p, Louis Gray; d, John English; w, Albert DeMond, Doris Schroeder (based on characters created by William Colt MacDonald); ph, Bud Thackery; m, Cy Feuer; ed, Ray Snyder.

Western   Cas.   (PR:A   MPAA:NR)

GANGS OF THE WATERFRONT*½ (1945) 55m REP bw

Robert Armstrong (Dutch Malone/Peter Winkly), Stephanie Bachelor (Jane Rodgers), Martin Kosleck (Anjo Ferranti), Marian Martin (Rita), William Forrest (District Attorney Brady), Wilton Graff (Commissioner Hogan), Eddie Hall (Miler), Jack O'Shea (Ortega), Davison Clark (Dr. Martin), Dick Elliott (Chief Davis).

Armstrong is a taxidermist wanting revenge for his brother's gang-related murder. When the mobster boss is hospitalized in an auto accident, district attorney Forrest has lookalike Armstrong take his place. Through Armstrong, the gang is broken and its members put in jail.

p&d, George Blair; w, Albert Beich (based on a story by Sam Fuller); ph, Marcel Le Picard; m, Richard Cherwin; ed, Fred Allen.

Crime   (PR:A   MPAA:NR)

GANGSTER, THE*** (1947) 84m AA bw

Barry Sullivan (Shubunka), Belita (Nancy Starr), Joan Lorring (Dorothy), Akim Tamiroff (Nick Jammey), Henry Morgan (Shorty), John Ireland (Karty), Fifi D'Orsay (Mrs. Ostroleng), Virginia Christine (Mrs. Karty), Sheldon Leonard (Cornell), Leif Erickson (Beaumont), Charles McGraw (Dugas), John Kellogg (Sterling), Elisha Cook, Jr. (Oval), Ted Hecht (Swain), Jeff Corey, Peter Whitney, Clancy Cooper (Brothers-in-law), Murray Alper (Eddie), Shelley Winters (Hazel), Edwin Maxwell (Politician), Rex Downing (Boy with Note), Ruth Allen (Girl Singer), Billy Gray (Little Boy), Norma Jean Nilsson (Little Girl), Dewey Robinson (Pool Player), Larry Steers (Headwaiter), Pat Emery (Miss Callister), Maxine Semon (Hotel Maid), Marie Blake (House Mistress), Anita Turner (Essie), Phyllis Ayres (Wife on Street), Dolores Castle (Cigarette Girl), Sidney Melton (Stage Manager), Delese Daudet, Jean Harrison (Dancers), Tommy Reilly (Piano Player), Don Haggerty (Stranger), Griff Barnett (Dorothy's Father), Ralph Freto, Gene Collins (Boys), Michael Vallon (Man on Boardwalk), Jane Weeks (Girl in Corridor), Parker Gee (Man in Corridor), Greta Grandstedt, Marguerita Padula, Jean Calhoun, Helen Alexander, Zona Eaton, Irene Brooks (Women), Mike Lally, Sammy Shack, Jay Eaton, Lennie Bremen, Alec Pope, Mike Gaddis, Andy Andrews, Phil Arnold (Men), Bill Kennedy, Mike Conrad, Jack Reynolds, Larry Thompson (Thugs).

Crime boss Sullivan, a thief since childhood, then an apprentice hoodlum, finally a top man in the underworld but wholly a product of a mean environment, begins to doubt himself. He ignores mob business, doting on his gun moll Belita, whom he comes to believe is two-timing him. Tamiroff warns Sullivan that his men are losing ground to a rival gangster, Leonard, but Sullivan cannot be bothered. He goes to an ice cream parlor, a hangout of his youth, and there finds Lorring, who attacks him for his crooked life. Sullivan begins to inspect his background, his purposes, and he now not only doubts but fear creeps into his heart and overtakes his judgment. He cannot act as he ponders his fate while a local gambler, Ireland, begs him for money. One by one, Sullivan's henchmen shrink from his ranks until he is alone, waiting for death as Leonard's thugs close in. He flees to the streets and is shot down. THE GANGSTER is an offbeat entry in the film noir genre, one that places the accent on the psychological. Though at times muddled, the script strives to maintain a deeper approach than such overt films as PUBLIC ENEMY or AL CAPONE. In its day this film was considered a somewhat artistic triumph and some sources claim that Fuchs is not the true scriptwriter here, but that the aesthetic Dalton Trumbo really wrote the screenplay. Sullivan, Tamiroff, Ireland, and others are a bit too theatrical under Wiles' moody direction and a certain staginess is ever present. Yet it is an often absorbing curiosity which profiles the kind of intelligence and perception no American gangster ever demonstrated in reality.

p, Maurice, Frank King; d, Gordon Wiles; w, Daniel Fuchs (based on his novel Low Company); ph, Paul Ivano; m, Louis Gruenberg; ed, Walter Thompson; md, Irvin Talbot; art d, F. Paul Sylos; set d, Sidney Moore; cos, Norma; spec eff, Roy W. Seawright; m/l, "Paradise," Gordon Clifford, Nacio Herb Brown; makeup, Ern Westmore.

Crime Drama   (PR:C   MPAA:NR)

GANGSTER STORY**½ (1959) 70m Releasing Corporation of Independent Producers-States Rights bw

Walter Matthau (Jack Martin), Carol Grace (Carol), Bruce McFarlan (Earl Dawson), Garrett Wallberg (Adolph), Raiken Ben Ari (Hood)

The only feature film versatile Matthau ever directed. He also held starring status as an independent gangster struggling to make a mark for himself in the territory of local boss McFarlan. Understandably angered by this new crime figure, McFarlan initially makes several useless attempts to trap Matthau. The two forces eventually combine to create what would be the beginning of their demise. An unusual role for Matthau in that his abilities seem not to be limited to his customary growling type of comedy. Overall, a good effort.

p, Jonathan Daniels; d, Walter Matthau; w, Paul Purcell (based on a story by Richard Grey and V.J. Rhems); m/l, "The Itch For Scratch," Leonard Barr, Ronald Bloomberg (sung by Ted Stanford).

Crime   (PR:A   MPAA:NR)

GANGSTER VIP, THE* (1968, Jap.) 94m Nikkatsu/Toho c (DAIKANBU)

Tetsuya Watari (Goro Fujikawa), Chieko Matsubara (Yukiko Hashimoto), Mitsuo Hamada (Takeo Tsujikawa), Tamio Kawaji (Isamu Tsujikawa), Kyosuke Machida (Katsuhiko Sugiyama), Kayo Matsuo (Yumeko).

A tale of organized crime which tries to impress with a message about the evils of gang warfare. Watari grows up in the slums of Japan, the son of a prostitute. His petty thievery soon leads to bigger things as he hooks up with a powerful mob. He decides to go straight and pay more attention to his family. He attends the funeral of a slain friend, taking a pistol as a precaution. The police raid the gathering and send Watari to prison for carrying a concealed weapon.

d, Toshio Masuda; w, Kaneo Ikegami, Reiji Kubota (based on a story by Goro Fujita); ph, Kurataro Takamura (Fuji Color, Nikkatsu Scope); m, Naozumi Yamamoto; art d, Takeo Kimura.

Crime Drama   (PR:C   MPAA:NR)

GANGSTER'S BOY*½ (1938) 80m MON bw

Jackie Cooper (Larry Kelly), Lucy Gilman (Julie Davis), Robert Warwick (Tim "Knuckles" Kelly), Louise Lorimer (Molly Kelly), Tommy Wonder (Bill Davis), Selmer Jackson (Judge Roger Davis), Bobby Stone (Salvatore), Betty Blythe (Mrs. Davis), Bradley Metcalfe (Arthur), Huntley Gordon (Principal Benson), William Gould (District Attorney Edward Jameson), Jack Kennedy (Sergeant), Herbert Evans (Stevens the Butler), Buddy Pepper (Boy), Hooper Atchley (Sammy Trip the Gangster), Byron Foulger (District Attorney's Secretary), Joe Devlin (Jim, a Cop), Edward Piel (Editor), Jack Gardner (Photographer), Harry Harvey (Reporter).

Cooper is a hard-working high-school kid who strives to be accepted by society and to rid himself of the taint associated with his ex-convict father, Warwick. Later he takes the rap for a crime committed by a well-respected friend. No longer an MGM child star, the 17-year-old Cooper made a number of such "special" films for low-budget Monogram. The film has some music, with dancing and acting by choreographer Wonder, and with Cooper playing the drums.

p, William T. Lackey; d, William Nigh; w, Robert D. Andrews (based on a story by Andrews, Karl Brown); ph, Harry Neumann; ed, Russell Schoengarth; md, Abe Meyer; ch, Tommy Wonder; m/l, Edward Kay, Beckley Reichne, Clay Boland.

Drama   (PR:A   MPAA:NR)

GANGSTER'S BRIDE, THE (SEE: SECRET VALLEY, 1937)

GANGSTER'S ENEMY NO. 1 (SEE: TRAIL OF TERROR, 1935)

GANGSTERS OF THE FRONTIER*½ (1944) 56m PRC bw

Dave O'Brien, Tex Ritter, Guy Wilkerson, Patti McCarty, Harry Harvey, Betty Miles, I. Stanford Jolley, Marshall Reed, Charles King, Jr., Clarke Stevens.

A deviation from the normal oater theme has the people of Red Rock enslaved and forced to work the local mines by two brothers who have just escaped from jail. It doesn't take long before O'Brien, Ritter, and company are able to rescue the town from this tyrannical grip. Through a clever ruse, the big bad brothers are made to inadvertently lay siege to themselves, and they shoot and kill each other. (See TEXAS RANGER series, Index.)

p, Arthur Alexander; d&w, Elmer Clifton; ph, Robert Cline; ed, Charles Hinkel, Jr.; md, Lee Zahler.

Western   Cas.   (PR:A   MPAA:NR)

GANGSTER'S REVENGE (SEE: GET OUTTA TOWN, 1964)

GANGWAY*½ (1937, Brit.) GAU 90m bw

Jessie Matthews (Pat Wayne), Barry Mackay (Inspector Bob Deering), Olive Blakeney (Nedda Beaumont), Liane Ordeyne (Greta Brand), Patrick Ludlow (Carl Freemason), Nat Pendleton ("Smiles" Hogan), Noel Madison (Mike Otterman), Alastair Sim (Taggett), Doris Rogers (Mrs. Van Tuyl), Laurence Anderson (Tracy), Blake Dorn (Benny the Gent), Graham Moffatt (Joe), Peter Gawthorne (Assistant Commissioner), Henry Hallatt (Smithers), Warren Jenkins (Foreign Dancer), Edmon Ryan (Red Mike), Danny Green (Shorty).

Matthews is a London newspaper reporter aboard a New York-bound ocean liner angling for an interview with alleged Hollywood actress, Blakeney, who is actually a jewel thief. Scotland Yard inspector Mackay is also on board, searching for the thief, and he suspects Matthews. So does gangster Pendleton, another passenger on the ship, who kidnaps Matthews to work for his boss when they dock in New York. Mackay finally realizes who the criminal is and rescues Matthews. The film is a musical but most of it is devoted to tracking down the thief amidst a hail of gunfire. This was the third of Gaumont-British's vehicles for Matthews, "The Dancing Divinity," the English equivalent of America's popular Eleanor Powell. Like the others, this was directed by her husband, Hale, himself a popular British song-and-dance man. Critics of the time contended that this picture wasted Matthews' terpsichorean talents in favor of the hackneyed gangster theme.

p, Michael Balcon; d, Sonnie Hale; w, Lesser Samuels, Hale (based on an original story by Dwight Taylor); ph, Glen MacWilliams; ed, Al Barnes; m/l, Sam Lerner, Al Goodhart, and Al Hoffman; ch, Buddy Bradley.

Musical/Crime   (PR:A   MPAA:NR)

GANGWAY FOR TOMORROW**½   (1943) 69m RKO bw

Margo (Lizette), John Carradine (Wellington), Robert Ryan (Joe), Amelita Ward (Mary), William Terry (Bob Nolan), Harry Davenport (Fred Taylor), James Bell (Burke), Charles Arnt (Jim Benson), Wally Brown (Sam), Alan Carney (Swallow), Erford Gage (Dan Barton), Richard Ryen (Colonel Mueller), Warren Hymer (Pete), Michael St. Angel (Mechanic), Don Dillaway (Mechanic), Sam McDaniel (Hank), John Wald (Radio Announcer), Bruce Edwards (Rogan), Carole Gallagher (Peanuts), Wheaton Chambers (Priest), Hope Landin (Emma), Earle Hodgins (Constable), Anne Kundee (Sara Henry), Al Kundee (Sam Kowalski), Al Ferguson (Ed Gilroy), Angelos Desfis (Worker), Richard Martin (Jules), Ida Shoemaker (Grandma), Harro Meller (Officer), Dave Thursby (Fogarty), Edythe Elliott (Mary's Mother), Noelle DeLorme (French Girl In Truck), Chester Carlisle, Brandon Beach (Judges), Robert Bice (Stooge), Frederick Brunn (General Sergeant), Hooper Atchley (Desk Clerk), John Sheehan (Producer Bell).

Five people work in a defense plant during WW II pooling a ride together in Arnt's car. Arnt thinks he knows each one of them, but finds his assumptions are way off. Using flashbacks and narrations, the stories of Margo, Ryan, Ward, Bell, and Carradine are revealed. Margo was a French underground fighter who escaped to America, and works in the plant to help her countrymen. Ryan, a race car driver, has racetrack injuries which kept him from joining the Air Force, Ward is a "Miss America" who becomes disillusioned about her world. Bell is a prison warden who had to execute his own brother, and hobo Carradine decided to do something worthwhile for a change. Though war-time propaganda, the attempt at interweaving the separate stories is entertaining. For you compound flashback collectors, this is another gem, with flashbacks within flashbacks.

p&d, John H. Auer; w, Arch Oboler (based on an original story by Aldar Laszlo and Oboler); ph, Nicholas Musuraca; m, Roy Webb; ed, George Crone; md, Constantin Bakaleinikoff; art d, Albert D'Agostino, Al Herman; spec eff, Vernon L. Walker.

Drama   (PR:A   MPAA:NR)

GANJA AND HESS*   (1973) 110m Kelly-Jordan c
(AKA: DOUBLE POSSESSION; BLOOD COUPLE).

Duane Jones (Dr. Hess Green), Marlene Clark (Ganja), Bill Gunn (George), Sam Waymon (Rev. Williams), Leonard Jackson (Archie), Candece Tarpley (Girl in Bar), Richard Harrow (Dinner Guest), John Hoffmeister (Jack), Betty Barney (Singer), Mabel King (Queen of Myrthia), Betsy Thurman (Poetess), Enrico Fales (Green's Son), Tommy Lane (Pimp), Tara Fields (Woman With Baby).

Not without serious flaws, this black vampire picture does have some interesting pluses. Set in the present, Jones is cast as a vampire who longs for his native Africa. The thin plot is confusingly told (it was rereleased in a re-edited version) and has Jones marrying Clark, a veteran of Russ Meyer's films. Jones' claim to fame is being the only person to survive THE NIGHT OF THE LIVING DEAD, and he proves that his performance in that film wasn't a fluke. One version of this film has some eerily atmospheric African music, while others have typically early 70s soul music.

p, Chris Schultz; d&w, Bill Gunn; ph, James E. Hinton; m, Sam Waymon; ed, Victor Kanefsky; prod d, Tom John; cos, Scott Barrie.

Horror   (PR:O   MPAA:R)

GAOL BREAK**½   (1936, Brit.) 64m FN/WB bw

Ralph Ince (Jim Oakley), Pat Fitzpatrick (Mickie Oakley), Basil Gill (Dr. Walter Merian), Raymond Lovell (Duke), Lorna Hubbard (Daisy Oakley), Roy Findlay (Louie), Elliot Mason (Euphie), Desmond Roberts (Paul Kendall), Vincent Holman, Beryl Mills, Billy Shine, Jim Regan.

Ince is a convict who gets wind of the fact that his wife is hanging out with a gang of thugs, one of whom wants to sell Ince's son to a wealthy family who lost their own child. He breaks out of prison to thwart the plan, tracks the boy to the yacht of the rich family, but then realizes that the life the family plans for the boy would be best for him after all. Ince heads back for prison. An intriguing story of self-sacrifice, with thrills to boot.

p, Irving Asher; d, Ralph Ince; w, Michael Barringer; ph, Basil Emmott.

Crime/Drama   (PR:A   MPAA:NR)

GAOLBREAK*½   (1962, Brit.) 61m BUT bw

Peter Reynolds (Eddie Wallis), Avice Landone (Mrs. Wallis), David Kernan (Len Rogerson), Carol White (Carol Marshall), David Gregory (Ron Wallis), John Blythe (Slim), Robert Desmond (Page), Geoffrey Hibbert (Dr. Cambus).

A hard-working news agent discovers that he has two sons devoting themselves to crime. After one is put in jail, the other needs assistance in a job and manages to break the other out. Not exactly the most comforting family.

p, Francis Searle, Ronald Liles; d, Searle; w, A.R. Rawlinson.

Crime   (PR:A   MPAA:NR)

GAP, THE   (SEE: JOE, 1970)

GAPPA THE TRIFIBIAN MONSTER*½   (1967, Jap.) 90m Nikkatsu c
(DAIKYOJU GAPPA; AKA: MONSTER FROM A PREHISTORIC PLANET)

Tamio Kawaji, Yoko Yamamoto, Yuji Okada, Koji Wada, Tatsuya Fuji.

Wonderful, as Japanese monster movies go. This is the only time Japan's Nikkatsu Studios entered into the monster movie genre (the Kaiju Eiga, as they call it). It is more of a farce than anything else, with no intention of being taken seriously. After a baby Gappa monster is kidnaped and put into a sideshow, its parents try to recover it. They stomp up and down on Tokyo, hitting all the tourist spots, and eventually get their little Gappa back. Excellent special effects and a witty script make this a must for monster mavens.

p, Hideo Koi; d, Haruyasu Noguchi; w, Iwao Yamazaki, Ryuzo Nakanishi; ph, Muneo Keda; spec eff, Akira Watanabe.

Science-Fiction/Satire   (PR:A   MPAA:NR)

GARAKUTA   (SEE: RABBLE, THE, 1965)

GARBAGE MAN, THE**   (1963) 86m Cinema Distributors of America bw/c
(AKA: THE GARBAGE MAN COMETH)

Toney Naylor (Garbage Man), Venita Beautrice (Dream Girl), Joseph Lincoln, "Miss" Baby Bailey.

Garbageman Taylor lives a content existence running a small trash cart which is pulled by a talking horse. The horse has a habit of knocking the mechanized system of sanitation that surrounds them. Taylor later meets a lusty lady who helps him to overcome the pressures of modernization.

p, Robert Steuer; d&w, Eric Sayers.

Comedy   (PR:C   MPAA:NR)

GARDEN MURDER CASE, THE*½   (1936) 61m MGM bw

Edmund Lowe (Philo Vance), Virginia Bruce (Zalia Graem), Gene Lockhart (Lowe Hammle), Benita Hume (Nurse Beeton), Nat Pendleton (Sgt. Heath), H.B. Warner (Maj. Ralston), Kent Smith (Woode Swift), Grant Mitchell (Markham), Frieda Inescort (Mrs. Ralston), Douglas Walton (Floyd Garden), Henry B. Walthall (Dr. Garden), Jessie Ralph (Mrs. Hammle), Charles Trowbridge (Inspector Colby), Etienne Girardot (Doremus), William Austin (Sneed), Rosalind Ivan (Japson).

Lowe was the fifth actor to play Van Dine's detective, and this time he's hunting down a murderer who uses hypnosis as his weapon. A person is killed on a racetrack, the murderer's wife falls from a bus, and Lowe discovers that Warner is the one putting them under a deadly spell. (See PHILO VANCE series, Index.)

p, Lucien Hubbard, Ned Marin; d, Edwin L. Marin; w, Bertram Milhauser (based on a story by S.S. Van Dine); ph, Charles Clarke; ed, Ben Lewis.

Murder Mystery   (PR:A   MPAA:NR)

GARDEN OF ALLAH, THE****   (1936) 85m SELZ/UA c

Marlene Dietrich (Domini Enfilden), Charles Boyer (Boris Androvsky), Basil Rathbone (Count Anteoni), C. Aubrey Smith (Father Roubier), Tilly Losch (Irena), Joseph Schildkraut (Batouch), John Carradine (Sand Diviner), Alan Marshall (De Trevignac), Lucille Watson (Mother Superior), Henry Brandon (Hadj), Helen Jerome Eddy (A Nun), Charles Waldron (The Abbe), John Bryan (Brother Gregory), Nigel De Brulier (The Lector), Pedro De Cordoba (Gardener), Ferdinand Gottschalk (Hotel Clerk), Adrian Rosely (Mustapha), "Corky" (Bous-Bous), Robert Frazer (Smain), David Scott (Larby), Andrew McKenna (Mueddin), Bonita Granville, Marcia Mae Jones, Betty Jane Graham, Ann Gillis (Children in Convent), Marian Sayers, Betty Van Auken, Edna Harris, Frances Turnham (Oasis Girls), Leonid Kinskey (Voluble Arab), Louis Aldez (Blind Singer), Barry Downing (Little Boris), Jane Kerr (Ouled Nails Madam), Russell Powell (Ouled Nails Proprietor), Eric Alden (Anteoni's Lieutenant), Michael Mark (Coachman), Harlan Briggs (American Tourist), Irene Franklin (Wife), Louis Mercier, Marcel De La Brosse, Robert Stevenson (De Trevignac's Patrol).

Dietrich is all nobility here, nursing her long-sick father until his death. Her spiritual adviser Watson suggests she seek rest and peace in the Algerian desert. En route to the desert town of Beni-Mora, Dietrich meets the moody, almost hostile Boyer who has broken his vows and left a Trappist monastery near Tunis. This sorrowful, introspective man attracts Dietrich. Later a flamboyant guide, Schildkraut, takes Dietrich to a dancing den where sultry Losch does a fiery dance (she almost repeats it step by step a decade later in DUEL IN THE SUN). She stops to attack Brandon, Schildkraut's brother, trying to stab him, is jealous of another woman who has caught Brandon's eye. A riot breaks out and Dietrich is almost trampled, pulled from the nightclub by Boyer, who had been watching the dancers. From that moment on, they are drawn together, forming a strong emotional bond that deepens into love. Rathbone, a nobleman attracted to Dietrich, spends a short time with her in a bazaar where a sand diviner, Carradine, scratches out a future for her, predicting travel, intense joy, then he stops abruptly. Ominously, he refuses to continue telling Dietrich's future. Not long after Smith marries Dietrich and Boyer and they go off into the desert on their honeymoon. In the desert a French army patrol encounters the honeymooners and its officer, Marshal, recognizes Boyer as the runaway monk. Dietrich then learns her husband's terrible secret, the reason why he has been so distant from her. They agree that the only right thing to do is for Boyer to return to his monastery so he can atone for his great sin. Dietrich accompanies her husband to the doors of the monastery and then leaves him for the last time. This thick melodrama is saved from over-ripening by stirring performances from Boyer and Dietrich and Boleslawski's sensitive direction of a lavish production. The color is gorgeous and Steiner's score is as rich as the plot and characterizations. Rathbone is good as Dietrich's loyal friend, but appears all too briefly. Dietrich insisted upon approving of the three-color Technicolor process in this film, insisting that the shots be made "in soft light," which allowed her to wear her specially selected designer white gowns without having them glare. Greene and Rosson won Oscars for their marvelous color cinematography, while Steiner was nominated. The 1904 Hichens' novel was dramatized in 1911 and first filmed by Selig in 1917 with Helen Ware and Thomas Santschi. Another silent was made by MGM in 1927, starring Alice Terry and Ivan Petrovich. Shot on location in the desert surrounding Yuma, Arizona, the film was not one of Dietrich's favorites; she hated parts of the dialog, particularly having to talk about God in the middle of her love scenes with Boyer. Said Dietrich later: "Imagine having to say, as I did, 'Nobody but God and I know what is in my heart.' The conceit of it! I tell you I very nearly died!"

p, David O. Selznick; d, Richard Boleslawski; w, W.P. Lipscomb, Lynn Riggs (based on the novel by Robert Hichens); ph, W. Howard Greene (Technicolor); m,

Max Steiner; ed, Hal. C. Kern, Anson Stevenson; art d, Sturges Carne, Lyle Wheeler, Edward Boyle; spec eff, Earl A. Wolcott.

Romance **(PR:C MPAA:NR)**

GARDEN OF EDEN*½ (1954) 70m Excelsior Pictures c

Mickey Knox *(John Patterson)*, Jamie O'Hara *(Susan Lattimore)*, Karen Sue Trent *(Jean Lattimore)*, John Gude *(Roy)*, R.G. Armstrong *(Jay Lattimore)*, Jane Rose, Paula Morris, Stephen Gray, Arch W. Johnson, Norval E. Packwood, Jane Sterling, John Royal.

Obscure exploitation film that details the struggle of a nudist camp to gain respect from the community. O'Hara stars as the daughter-in-law of stodgy tycoon Armstrong. She feels compelled to begin a new way of life after the untimely death of her husband. Quite by accident, she stumbles upon a nudist camp, and decides that fun-in-the-sun is just what the doctor ordered. Outraged by her actions, Armstrong arrives at the camp to drag her back, but he too is soon converted over to nudism (yes, that's R.G. Armstrong, the burly guy who's always beating people up in Sam Peckinpah's movies). Really strange and silly, a must-see for fans of irregular cinema.

p, Walter Bibo; d, Max Nosseck; w, Nat Tanchuck, Nosseck; ph, Boris Kaufman (Tri-Art Color); m, Robert McBride; ed, Paul Falkenberg.

Drama **(PR:O MPAA:NR)**

GARDEN OF EVIL½** (1954) 100m FOX c

Gary Cooper *(Hooker)*, Susan Hayward *(Leah Fuller)*, Richard Widmark *(Fiske)*, Hugh Marlowe *(John Fuller)*, Cameron Mitchell *(Luke Daly)*, Rita Moreno *(Singer)*, Victor Manuel Mendoza *(Vicente Madariaga)*, Fernando Wagner *(Captain)*, Arturo Soto Bangel *(Priest)*, Manuel Donde *(Waiter)*, Antonio Bribiesca *(Bartender)*, Salvado Terroba *(Victim)*.

Adventurers Cooper, Widmark, and Mitchell are headed for the California gold mines when their ship is dismantled and they are stranded in a Mexican village. Hayward hears about the soldiers of fortune and approaches them with a proposition: Her husband is trapped in a gold mine cave-in and she will pay them handsomely if they will lead her through wild Indian territory and help rescue him. The thought of gold makes them all willing and they push on into the wild interior of a mountainous province. Their guide, Mendoza, Hayward notices, is marking the trail as he leads them into the primeval region. She obliterates the markers and must later contend with Mitchell's animal advances until Cooper stops the lust-driven gold-seeker. The group arrives at a remote area the Indians call "The Garden of Evil," where they find Hayward's husband, Marlowe, who has a broken leg and shows no gratitude toward the wife who has risked her life to rescue him. They all have gold but they also have a horde of murderous Indians surrounding them. Hayward, fed up with her husband and life in general, offers to build a bonfire and pretend they are still in camp, offering to stay behind while the men save themselves. Cooper argues with her but can only win by knocking out the headstrong woman and carrying her away. Next Marlowe sacrifices himself to the following Indians by riding back into their midst. The others find him studded with arrows, nailed upside down to a cross. The Indians kill the interlopers one by one, first Mitchell, then Mendoza. High in a narrow mountain pass Cooper, Hayward, and Widmark halt to see the Indians still in pursuit. The men draw lots to see who stays behind to hold off the savages and who takes Hayward to safety. Widmark loses and stays behind to put up a fight. Before Cooper and Hayward leave, he looks at the burning red sun setting and says: "There it goes. Every day it goes and somebody goes with it. Today, it's me." Cooper takes Hayward to safety, then returns to help Widmark but he is mortally wounded, piles of dead Indians strewn about him. Cooper catches up with Hayward and they ride to safety together, Cooper ruefully commenting: "If the world were made of gold men would die for a handful of dirt." The plot here is routine but the acting is above average with a handsome production and dazzling on-location shots in Mexico. Hayward overacts to the point where her nerves seem to about burst from her skin, a condition she later claimed was the result of her then tempestuous marriage with actor Jess Barker; in fact she planned to divorce Barker once the film was made. Moreover, Mitchell was emotionally involved with the actress, even after she used her sons as an excuse to return to the U.S. for Christmas while the rest of the cast and crew were stuck in Mexico. The actress later went to a jammed Mexican cafe in Cuernavaca with the cast to celebrate New Year's Eve. After a few brandies she leaned over to Mitchell, knowing his attraction to her, and ran her long fingernails deeply along his cheek, drawing blood and leaving wounds that caused director Hathaway to delay further shooting until the scabs vanished. Mitchell was scarred for life. Hathaway had a difficult time with Hayward who delayed productions and often walked off the set when annoyed with his brusque ways. The film went over budget and beyond schedule, although Cooper remained mute about the temperament his co-star displayed; Hayward was then one of the top box office actresses. He had not appeared with her since BEAU GESTE (1939), in which Hayward played a small but significant part as his childhood sweetheart. This was Cooper's 81st film and he did his heroic best with a weak script and Hathaway's on-and-off direction. Hayward was a real heroine off camera. During the shooting around the volcano Paricutin, she noticed a small boy slip off a ledge. He was about to fall from a lethal height when she jumped from her horse (she was an excellent horsewoman) and raced to grab him, saving his life. Oddly enough, the actress had herself been saved from falling to her death from a mountain-top years earlier when she was in another production, I'D CLIMB THE HIGHEST MOUNTAIN (1951).

p, Charles Brackett; d, Henry Hathaway; w, Frank Fenton (based on a story by Fred Freiberger and William Tunberg); ph, Milton Krasner, Jorge Stahl, Jr. (CinemaScope, Technicolor); m, Bernard Herrmann; ed, James B. Clark; art d, Lyle Wheeler, Edward Fitzgerald; set d, Pablo Galvan; cos, Travilla; spec eff, Ray Kellogg; m/l, "La Negra Noche," Emilio D. Uranga, "Aqui," Ken Darby, Lionel Newman; makeup, Ben Nye.

Adventure **(PR:C MPAA:NR)**

GARDEN OF THE FINZI-CONTINIS, THE****** (1976, Ital./Ger.) 103m TITANUS c (IL GIARDINO DEL FINZI-CONTINI)

Dominique Sanda *(Micol)*, Lino Capolicchio *(Giorgio)*, Helmut Berger *(Alberto)*, Fabio Testi *(Malnate)*, Romolo Valli *(Giorgio's Father)*, Raffaele Curi *(Ernesto)*, Camillo Angelini-Rota *(Micol's Father)*, Katina Viglietti *(Micol's Mother)*, Inna Alexeiff *(Micol's Grandmother)*, Barbara Pilavin, Gianpaolo Duregon, Katina Morisani, Cinzia Bruno, Marcella Gentile, Camillo Cesarei, Ettore Geri, Franco Nebbia, Alessandro D' Alatie.

De Sica is at his apex with this brilliant film. There are Best Film lists made every year. GONE WITH THE WIND and CITIZEN KANE, and CASABLANCA, are usually found on the all-time docket and one obscure De Sica picture may also be seen, THE BICYCLE THIEF. That was a rough neo-realistic black-and-white film. This is anything but and it's almost too colorful and cool for the subject matter. Just as THE BICYCLE THIEF, was simple and straightforward in its semi-documentary way, THE GARDEN OF THE FINZI-CONTINIS uses that same no-comment type of direction and just asks you to be caught up with the protagonists without taking a stance. Set in Ferrara, Italy, during WW II, this story of love and culture unfurls effortlessly, albeit a trifle lethargically. The Finzi-Continis are a wealthy Jewish-Italian family who cannot believe that the war will ever invade their hallowed garden walls. Rather than flee, they stay on in the false hope that they will not be betrayed. As they sit, posteriors barely touching their exquisite furniture, they realize that Fascism is not going to go away and that they must take a position and join the fight against it. Sanda is the austere daughter of the F-C family and she has a relationship with Capolicchio, son of another Jewish family, not nearly as wealthy and more politically involved. Their love began when they were in school as children and it was always assumed that they would marry. Enter Testi, a militant Communist who is as anti-Fascist as the Jews of Ferrara. Sanda and Testi have a physical attraction and she passes on her engagement to take up with Testi. He goes off to war in the Italian army and is killed. The Jews of Ferrara are gathered up and taken to the death camps where De Sica spares us the horror and subtly indicates their deaths by the singing of the traditional Jewish "Kaddish" (the prayer for the dead). This is one of those rare films where flashbacks not only work, but are absolutely necessary. It's told in a time layer so we see what's happening now, what happened then, and what happened even before that. De Sica's handling of the unknowns in the cast is peerless. The camerawork is perfect and the sentiments are honest. De Sica's son did the music. Before dying at the age of 72, De Sica had appeared in more than 150 films as an actor as well as having directed some of the finest movies ever to come out of Italy. There is not one wasted word in the screenplay, but the slowness in the first half is what takes this out of the classic category. Sanda was radiant in her role and a huge career was forecast. It still hasn't become reality. During the Fascist regime, Jews *were* systematically rounded up and slaughtered in Italy. De Sica has been quoted as saying, "We were *all* guilty." This film was his personal attempt at expiation. Author Bassani, who collaborated on the screenplay, repudiated the film. De Sica said, "Always the author is against me."

p, Arthur Cohn, Gianni Hecht Lucari; d, Vittorio De Sica; w, Cesare Zavattini, Vittorio Bonicelli, Ugo Pirro, Giorgio Bassani (disavowed) (based on the novel by Bassani); ph, Ennio Guarnieri (Eastmancolor); m, Manuel De Sica; ed, Adriana Novelli; md, Carlo Savina; art d, Giancarlo Bartolini Salimbeni; set d, Franco D'Andria; cos, Antonio Randaccio; makeup, Giulio Natalucci.

War-Drama **Cas.** **(PR:C MPAA:R)**

GARDEN OF THE DEAD zero (1972) Clover/Entertainment Pyramid c

John Dennis, Duncan McCloud, Marland Proctor, Eric Stern.

A stupid NIGHT OF THE LIVING DEAD rip-off (what other kinds of horror rip-offs are there?) which has some dead prisoners returning from the grave to kill their prison guards. Not even capital punishment can stop these convicts.

p, Daniel Cady; d, John Hayes; w, John Jones.

Horror **(PR:O MPAA:PG)**

GARDEN OF THE MOON** (1938) 94m WB bw

Pat O'Brien *(John Quinn)*, Margaret Lindsay *(Toni Blake)*, John Payne *(Don Vincente)*, Johnnie Davis *(Slappy Harris)*, Melville Cooper *(Maurice)*, Isabel Jeans *(Mrs. Lornay)*, Mabel Todd *(Mary Stanton)*, Penny Singleton *(Miss Calder)*, Dick Purcell *(Rick Fulton)*, Curt Bois *(Maharajah of Sind)*, Granville Bates *(Angus McGillicuddy)*, Edward McWade *(Duncan McGillicuddy)*, Larry Williams *(Trent)*, Jimmie Fidler *(Himself)*, Ray Mayer, Jerry Colonna, Joe Venuti and his Swing Cats *(Musicians)*.

This small musical was director Berkeley's last film for Warner Bros. O'Brien is the owner of the "Garden of the Moon" night club and Payne is his bandleader. They're fighting for press agent Lindsay's hand. Dick Powell was originally slated for the bandleader and Bette Davis for the Lindsay role (she preferred suspension). Songs include "The Girl Friend of the Whirling Dervish," "Love Is Where You Find It" (not the well-known number from THE KISSING BANDIT), "The Lady On the Two Cent Stamp," "Confidentially," and the title song.

p, Louis Edelman; d, Busby Berkeley; w, Jerry Wald, Richard Macaulay (based on a story by H. Bedford-Jones, Barton Browne); ph, Tony Gaudio; ed, George Amy; md, Leo F. Forbstein; m/l, Harry Warren, Al Dubin, Johnny Mercer.

Musical **(PR:A MPAA:NR)**

GARDENER, THE (SEE: SEEDS OF EVIL, 1974)

GARMENT JUNGLE, THE*** (1957) 88m COL bw

Lee J. Cobb *(Walter Mitchell)*, Kerwin Mathews *(Alan Mitchell)*, Gia Scala *(Theresa Renata)*, Richard Boone *(Artie Ravidge)*, Valerie French *(Lee Hackett)*, Robert Loggia *(Tulio Renata)*, Joseph Wiseman *(Kovan)*, Harold J. Stone *(Tony)*, Adam Williams *(The Ox)*, Wesley Addy *(Mr. Paul)*, Willis Bouchey *(Dave Bronson)*, Robert Ellenstein *(Fred Kenner)*, Celia Lovsky *(Tulio's Mother)*, Jon Shepodd *(Alredi)*,

Judson Taylor *(Latzo)*, Dick Crockett *(Miller)*, Suzanne Alexander *(Joanne)*, Ellie Kent *(Stephanie)*, Gloria Pall *(Fitting Model)*, Millicent Deming, Shirley Buchanan *(Announcers)*, Ann Carroll, Laurie Mitchell, Kathy Marlowe, Peggy O'Connor, Bonnie Bolding, Marilyn Hanold, June Tolley *(Models)*, Madeline Darrow, Jan Darlyn, June Kirby *(Models On Line)*, Jean Lewis *(Receptionist)*, Joan Granville *(Girl Operator)*, Irene Seidner *(Old Lady Operator)*, Betsy Jones Moreland *(Secretary)*, Dale Van Sickel *(Helper)*, Irene King *(Model)*, Hal Taggart, Paul Knight, Paul Weber, Donald Kirke, Paul Power *(Salesmen)*, Archie Savage *(Elevator Operator)*, Dorothe Kellogg, Lillian Culver, Kenneth Gibson *(Buyers)*, Sidney Melton *(Male Operator)*, Bob Hopkins *(Bartender)*, Betty Koch *(High Fashion Model)*, Frank Marlowe *(Onlooker)*, Diane DeLaire *(Head Seamstress)*, George Robotham *(Truck Driver)*.

Mathews, a Korean war veteran, finds that his father, a garment company owner, has become involved with a union-busting syndicate. He tries to get his father, Cobb, to change his mind about unions, but Cobb won't listen to him. Mathews goes to union leader Loggia and hears what he has to say about unionization. When Cobb tells syndicate boss Boone what the union leader has told his son, Loggia is brutally killed. Horrified by this, Cobb tries to break from Boone and is killed himself. Mathews, with the help of French, digs up records of pay-offs to Boone. As French goes to the district attorney Mathews, in revenge, beats up the mob boss before the police cart him away. Director Aldrich was replaced by Vincent Sherman five days before the end of schedule, and shooting then continued for 16 days. Aldrich said he had never seen the film, and doesn't know how much of his footage was re-shot.

p, Harry Kleiner; d, Vincent Sherman (Uncredited: Robert Aldrich); w, Kleiner (based on a series of articles, *Gangsters In The Dress Business*, by Lester Velie); ph, Joseph Biroc; m, Leith Stevens; ed, William Lyon; art d, Robert A. Peterson; set d, William Kiernan, Frank A. Tuttle; cos, Jean Louis; makeup, Clay Campbell.

Crime   **(PR:A   MPAA:NR)**

GARNET BRACELET, THE***   (1966, USSR) 90m Mosfilm/Artkino c
                                              (GRANATOVYY BRASLET)

Ariadna Shengelaya *(Vera Nikolayevna)*, Igor Ozerov *(Zheltkov)*, O. Basilashvili *(Vasily Lvovitch)*, Vladislav Strzhelchik *(Nikolay Nikolayevich)*, N. Malyavina *(Anna Nikolayevna)*, Yuriy Averin *(Von Friesse)*, Olga Zhizneva *(Mme. Zarzhitskaya)*, Leonid Gallis *(Anosov)*, Zh. Terteryan *(Zhenni Reyter)*, G. Gai *(A. I. Kuprin)*, Stanislav Neygauz *(Pianist)*, David Ashkinazi *(Violinist)*, Pavel Massalskiy, T. Loginova, V. Rautbart, S. Karnovich-Valua, N. Latinskiy, P. Shpringfeld, Z. Chekulayeva, V. Kulik, O. Lapiado, S. Afansyev, A. Barushnoy.

The ideas of obsessive love and the class system are interwoven when Ozerov, a poor clerk, falls in love with Shengelaya, a gorgeous princess. He constantly follows her, wherever she goes, and writes her letters which express his undying desire for her. She understands that his feelings are genuine, but realizes that she is a princess and he is a commoner. He decides to send her an expensive golden bracelet with garnet inlays. It is the only thing he possesses of worth, an heirloom from his mother. When the princess receives it she is touched, but those around her are amused. When he hears that he has been mocked by them, he commits suicide. The princess goes against the acceptable norm and pays her condolences. A depressing film which occasionally touches on the humanism of Jean Renoir. Directed by Abram Room, who has been working in the Soviet film industry since the mid 1920s.

d, Abram Room; w, Room, A. Granberg (based on the story by Aleksandr Kuprin); ph, Leonid Kraynenkov (Widescreen, MagiColor); m, Ludwig von Beethoven; art d, O. Alikin, A. Freydin, I. Shreter.

Drama   **(PR:A   MPAA:NR)**

GARRISON FOLLIES**   (1940, Brit.) 64m Signet/But bw

Barry Lupino *(Alf Shufflebotham)*, Nancy O'Neil *(Sally Richards)*, H.F. Maltby *(Maj. Hall-Vett)*, John Kevan *(Dick Munro)*, Hugh Dempster *(Adjutant)*, Gabrielle Brune *(Lady Cynthia Clayton)*, Neville Brook *(Commanding Officer)*, Dennis Val Norton *(Plummer)*, Jack Vyvyian, David Tomlinson, Rita Grant, Martyn Box, Harry Herbert, Sylvia Kellaway and Leslie, Ann Lenner, Joan Davis' Eight Rose Petals, Dorothy Lloyd, Percival Mackey's Band.

To keep Britons' minds off WW II, Signet came out with this supposedly uproarious comedy about a plumber who doubles on the cornet (Lupino) and a retired major (Maltby). Their plans to organize a show for the troops goes haywire, but by the finale everything is running smoothly.

p, Hugh Perceval, Ernest Gartside; d, Maclean Rogers; w, Rogers, Kathleen Butler, H.F. Maltby; ph, Geoffrey Faithfull.

Comedy   **(PR:A   MPAA:NR)**

GARU, THE MAD MONK   (SEE: GURU, THE MAD MONK, 1970)

GAS zero   (1981, Can.) 94m Filmplan International/PAR c

Donald Sutherland *(Nick the Noz)*, Susan Anspach *(Jane Beardsley)*, Howie Mandel *(Matt Lloyd)*, Sterling Hayden *(Duke Stuyvesant)*, Sandee Currie *(Sarah Marshall)*, Peter Aykroyd *(Ed Marshall)*, Keith Knight *(Ira)*, Helen Shaver *(Rhonda)*, Alf Humphries *(Lou Picard)*, Philip Akin *(Lincoln Jones)*, Michael Hogan *(Guido Vespucci)*, Paul Kelman *(Nino Vespucci)*, Dustin Waln *(Earl Stuyvesant)*, Vlasta Vrana *(Baron Stuyvesant)*, Harvey Chao *(Lee Kwan)*, Brian Nasimok *(Fawsi Ibn Fawsi)*, Vincent Marino *(Uncle Leo)*, Videt Bussy *(Mrs. Botts)*, Carl Marotte *(Bobby)*, Bob Parson *(Ordway)*, Richard Donat *(Fred)*, Domenico Fiore, Dino Tosques *(Hoods)*, Art Grosser *(Lester)*, Dieto Kretzchmar *(Juggler)*, Gershon Resnick *(Yassir)*, Walter Massey *(Maj. Bright)*, Jeff Diamond *(Bandit)*, Mac Bradden *(Announcer)*, Terry Haig *(Reporter)*, Ralph Pettofrezzo, Joe Sanza, Joost Davidson, Tony Angelo, Tony Nardi, George Wilson, Barry Edward Blake, Kirsten Bishopric, Rollie Nincheri, Steve Michaels, Michael Mololey, Armand Monroe, Carolyn Maxwell, Caroline Plamondon, Charles Biddles, Jr., Malcolm Nelthorpe,

Walker Boone, Sam Montesano, Norris Dominigue, Lawrence Steinberg, Pierre Lemieux, Linda Lonn, Robert Blais.

A moronic film that is totally unwatchable. The story, if you can call it that, is about a small American town going through a fuel shortage, and the situations the characters get themselves into. Anspach, Hayden, and Aykroyd sleepwalk through their performances. Sutherland is a jive-talking disc jockey directing folks to gas stations, and his talent is wasted. Gas should have been given to the script, along with a match. Another tax-shelter bonanza for investors wishing to take advantage of the host country's liberal laws, obviously intended to keep its film-industry technicians and bit-part players off the public welfare roles.

p, Claude Heroux; d, Les Rose; w, Richard Wolf (based on a story by Wolf, Susan Scranton); ph, Rene Verzier (Bellevue Pathe color); m, Paul Zaza; ed, Patrick Dodd; prod d, Carol Spier; cos, Gaudeline Soriol.

Comedy   **Cas.**   **(PR:O   MPAA:R)**

GAS HOUSE KIDS*½   (1946) 71m PRC bw

Robert Lowery, Teala Loring, Billy Halop, Carl "Alfalfa" Switzer, Rex Downing, Paul Bryar, David Reed, Rocco Lanza, Ralph Dunn, Nanette Vallon, Charles Wilson, Hope Landin.

The first in a series of three films in which PRC tried to copy the success of The Dead End Kids by developing their own stories about a gang of ornery youths from New York City's lower East Side. The common goal of the gang in this feature is to aid a crippled veteran in trying to make something out of his life by opening up a chicken ranch. A contrived solution comes in the form of a reward for a criminal, whom the youths combine their forces to pursue, thus getting the veteran back onto his feet. (See GAS HOUSE KIDS series, Index.)

p, Sigmund Neufeld; d, Sam Newfield; w, Raymond Schrock, George Bricker, Elsie Bricker (based on a story by George and Elsie Bricker); ph, Jack Greenhalgh; m, Leo Erdody; ed, Holbrook N. Todd; md, Erdody; art d, Frank Sylos.

Comedy/Drama   **(PR:A   MPAA:NR)**

GAS HOUSE KIDS GO WEST*   (1947) 62m Ben Stoloff/PRC bw

Emory Parnell *(Sgt. Casey)*, Chili Williams *(Nan Crowley)*, Vince Barnett *(Steve)*, William Wright *(Jim Kingsley)*, Lela Bliss *(Mrs. Crowley)*, Ronn Marvin *(Pulaski)*, Ray Dolciame *(Corky)*, Carl "Alfalfa" Switzer *(Alfalfa)*, Bennie Bartlett *(Orvie)*, Rudy Wissler *(Scat)*, Tommy Bond *(Chimp)*.

One from the GAS HOUSE KIDS series, and a dismal entry at that. The gang goes on vacation at a ranch with their policeman friend, Parnell. They discover the foreman is using the ranch to hide stolen cars, and the kids put a quick end to it. (See GAS HOUSE KIDS series, Index.)

p, Sam Baerwitz; d, William Beaudine; w, Robert E. Kent, Robert A. McGowan, Eugene Conrad (based on a story by Baerwitz); ph, William Sickner; m, Alvin Levin, Hans Sommer; ed, Harry Reynolds.

Adventure   **(PR:A   MPAA:NR)**

GAS HOUSE KIDS IN HOLLYWOOD*   (1947) 62m PRC-EL bw

Carl "Alfalfa" Switzer, Rudy Wissler, Benny Bartlett, Tommy Bond, James Burke, Jan Bryant, Michael Whalen, Douglas Fowley, Frank Orth, Lyle Latell, Milton Parsons.

Not only is this the last film of the short-lived series, but it is also the last film to be produced under PRC guardianship. As was typical for this company, which concentrated on very low-budget pictures aimed for the lower half of double bills, GAS HOUSE KIDS IN HOLLYWOOD offers very little to get excited about. The gang journeys out to the land of movie idols for a bit of star-gazing and, instead, finds itself in the middle of an adventure concerning robbery and murder. (See GAS HOUSE KIDS series, Index.)

p, Sam Baerwitz; d, Edward Cahn; w, Robert E. Kent; ph, James Brown; m, Albert Glasser; ed, Al DeGaetano, W. Donn Hayes; art d, F. Paul Sylos.

Crime/Comedy   **(PR:A   MPAA:NR)**

GASBAGS**½   (1940, Brit.) 77m Gainsborough/GFD bw

Bud Flanagan *(Bud)*, Chesney Allen *(Ches)*, Jimmy Nervo *(Cecil)*, Teddy Knox *(Knoxy)*, Charlie Naughton *(Charlie)*, Jimmy Gold *(Goldy)*, Moore Marriott *(Jerry Jenkins)*, Wally Patch *(Sergeant-Major)*, Peter Gawthorne *(Commanding Officer)*, Frederick Valk *(Sturmfuehrer)*, Eric Clavering *(Scharffuehrer)*, Anthony Eustrel *(Gestapo Officer)*, Carl Jaffe *(Gestapo Chief)*, Manning Whiley *(Colonel)*, Torin Thatcher *(SS Man)*, Irene Handl *(Wife)*, George Merritt.

An exhilarating comedy starring the popular British comedy troupe The Crazy Gang in another zany adventure. This time out they balloon into enemy territory and befriend an old eccentric prisoner Marriott who has plans for a tunnel-boring tank drawn on his back. With Marriott disguised as Hitler, they manage to get the tank and pilot it home to the Queen's country. It definitely lives up to its crazy title.

p, Edward Black; d, Marcel Varnel; w, Val Guest, Marriot Edgar (based on a story by Val Valentine, Ralph Smart); ph, Arthur Crabtree.

Comedy/War   **(PR:A   MPAA:NR)**

GASLIGHT****   (1940) 88m BNP/Anglo Amer. Film Corp bw
                                              (AKA: ANGEL STREET)

Anton Walbrook *(Paul Mallen)*, Diana Wynyard *(Bella Mallen)*, Frank Pettingell *(Rough)*, Cathleen Cordell *(Nancy)*, Robert Newton *(Vincent Ullswater)*, Jimmy Hanley *(Cobb)*, Minnie Rayner *(Elizabeth)*, Mary Hinton *(Lady Winterbourne)*, Marie Wright *(Alice Barlow)*, Jack Barty *(Chairman)*, Angus Morrison *(Pianist)*, Aubrey Dexter *(House Agent)*, The Darmora Ballet.

This British psychological thriller, repeated with equal success in the U.S. four years later, is a forgotten masterpiece, due to the machinations of MGM's Louis B. Mayer. In one of her finest roles, Wynyard is a wealthy patrician lady who marries the urbane but calculating Walbrook. They move into an 1880 mansion, Wynyard's ancestral London home where Cordell is the ever-present brazen maid. Through clever and subtle measures, Walbrook slowly drives Wynyard to the brink of insanity, convincing her that she is losing her memory by misplacing jewelry, forgetting names, and having no touch with reality. Through the weeks she also notices the gaslight in her rooms flicker downward nightly, coming to believe that this, too, is part of her hallucinations. Pettingell, a kindly and perceptive Scotland Yard detective, meets Wynyard socially and begins paying attention to her and Walbrook, too much attention for the strange master of the house. The detective actually is investigating the mysterious Walbrook, following him on his nightly walks and losing him in the vicinity of his own house. He later discovers Walbrook rummaging madly about the attic of his house, frantically trying to find the hidden jewels of Wynyard's deceased grand actress aunt; the real reason why Walbrook had married Wynyard is to find the fabulous jewels he knew through careful research her grandmother had owned but which never surfaced. While in the attic he had turned up the gas jets to enlighten his search, thus creating the drain on the gas outlets in Wynyard's rooms. Pettingell not only convinces Wynyard that she is sane but that her husband has murdered her aunt. He is exposed by Wynyard who takes a devastating psychological revenge. Walbrook is magnificent as the arch villain, his extravagant middle-European acting style bordering on the flamboyant. He is loaded with dark charm to shroud his evil purposes. Pettingell is solidly effective as the detective who has been on his trail almost from the beginning. This film barely survived the ruthless scheming of MGM's Louis B. Mayer. Columbia purchased the rights of the film in 1941, intending an American remake with Irene Dunne in the lead. Then MGM bought the property for a Hedy Lamarr vehicle and Mayer, when the Ingrid Bergman-Charles Boyer production was set in 1944, ordered his minions to track down all the prints of the original GASLIGHT and destroy them so it would never compete with his lavish production. Prints, however, survived, and GASLIGHT was shown under that title and, in a 1952 U.S. art house release, under the title of ANGEL STREET, the title of the play of the same story used for a 1941 Broadway production starring Vincent Price and Judith Evans. (The British production was based upon a London stage hit produced in 1938 as GASLIGHT.) This film is one of the most stylish British efforts to be made before WW II, one of director Dickinson's most polished works, each scene carefully setup as the tension is mounted brilliantly frame by frame. Cameraman Knowles achieves a consistently eerie mood throughout by brilliant angles and lighting.

p, John Corfield; d, Thorold Dickinson; w, A.R. Rawlinson, Bridget Boland (based on the play by Patrick Hamilton); ph, Bernard Knowles; m, Richard Addinsell; ed, Sydney Cole.

Mystery **(PR:C MPAA:NR)**

GASLIGHT***** (1944) 114m MGM bw
(GB: THE MURDER IN THORNTON SQUARE)

Charles Boyer *(Gregory Anton)*, Ingrid Bergman *(Paula Alquist)*, Joseph Cotten *(Brian Cameron)*, Dame May Whitty *(Miss Thwaites)*, Angela Lansbury *(Nancy Oliver)*, Barbara Everest *(Elizabeth Tompkins)*, Eustace Wyatt *(Budge)*, Emil Rameau *(Mario Gardi)*, Edmund Breon *(Gen. Huddleston)*, Halliwell Hobes *(Mr. Mufflin)*, Tom Stevenson *(Williams)*, Heather Thatcher *(Lady Dalroy)*, Lawrence Grossmith *(Lord Dalroy)*, Jakob Gimpel *(Pianist)*, Terry Moore *(Paula, Age 14)*, Harry Adams *(Policeman)*, Charles McNaugton *(Wilkins)*, Bobby Hale *(Lamplighter)*, Alix Terry *(Girl of Ten)*, Eric Wilton *(Valet)*, Simon Oliver *(Boy in Museum)*, Alec Craig *(Turnkey)*, Leonard Carey *(Guide)*, Pat Malone *(Policeman)*, George Nokes *(Boy)*, Lillian Bronson *(Lady)*, Joy Harrington *(Miss Pritchard)*, Arthur Blake *(Butler)*, Ronald Bennett *(Footman)*, Phyllis Yuse *(Young Girl)*.

Bergman is stupendous in her Academy Award winning role of the wealthy socialite who marries the witty, charming Boyer, who is equally spellbinding as he transforms into an insidious monster in his attempt to drive his ravishing wife stark raving mad. Beautiful but naive Bergman encounters the urbane Boyer and, after a short courtship, they wed and leave for a two-week honeymoon in Italy where Bergman has studied opera, her Aunt Alice having been a famous opera star who was later mysteriously murdered, Bergman, as a child, finding her body. Returning to London, the couple move into Bergman's ancestral home, once owned by her celebrated Aunt Alice Alquist, at 10 Thornton Square. Among the servants are Everest, who has cooked for the family for years, and Lansbury, a flirtatious maid who cozies up to Boyer the minute he takes residence. Boyer orders the top of the mansion sealed off, explaining to Bergman that it is for her own good since that is where her aunt was murdered; he intends to shield her from ugly memories. Then Bergman begins to misplace things with Boyer finding them. Worse, he confronts her with deliberately stealing items, including his own possessions, and hiding them. He demonstrates this by uncovering items in secret places where she has obviously put them. Boyer increasingly reminds Bergman that her memory lapses are beginning to disturb their social life; she forgets invitations and planned events. He also reveals to others that his poor wife's mother died in an insane asylum. At one social occasion Boyer rebukes Bergman for her erratic behavior and this is observed by Cotten, a Scotland Yard detective. He takes a close interest in the couple and begins to make inquiries, particularly into the long ago unsolved murder of Alice Alquist. Local gossip Whitty provides background information on the couples' habits and Cotten's suspicions of Boyer increase. Cotten tries to see Bergman alone but is foiled several times by her ever-watchful husband. Finally, Cotten manages to meet Bergman alone in her rooms just as she is on the verge of a nervous breakdown. She explains that she notices the gaslight in her rooms flicker and diminish but no one else notices this and she believes it is another hallucination. As they talk the gaslight dims and Cotten confirms it as fact. Cotten then finds items ostensibly lost by Bergman locked in her husband's desk, along with a letter Boyer had written 20 years earlier, apparently to Bergman's murdered aunt. Cotten follows Boyer on one of his evening strolls and discovers that he has simply gone around the block, through an alleyway and reentered his own house to climb into the attic, turning up the gasjets above Bergman's rooms and causing the light below to diminish, inadvertantly providing another measure to drive his lovely wife mad. In the attic, where Alice Alquist's belongings are stored, Boyer has been systematically searching for the opera star's fabulous jewelry which was never located after her death. At the moment he is exposed by Cotten, he has found the priceless gems, sewn onto the front of an ancient evening gown, hidden among the costume jewelry. Cotten prevents Boyer from murdering Bergman and ties him up in the attic until more police are summoned, leaving Bergman alone with her tormentor. He begs her to get a knife and untie him. She picks one up, puts it down, and pretends to have "misplaced" it, torturing him as he has tortured her. Boyer becomes desperate, pleading with her to help him escape, for it is now known that he had killed her aunt decades earlier. Bergman finally screams at him: "I hate you! Without a shred of pity, without a shred of regret, I watch you go with glory in my heart!" He is led away by policemen as Bergman is supported by Cotten from the scene; it is obvious that they will face the future together. Cukor's direction is amazingly tense for a helmsman used to soft stories tailored to genteel ladies. He builds the tale carefully and draws magnificent performances from Bergman, Boyer, and Cotten. Bergman, who had just finished making FOR WHOM THE BELL TOLLS, was first alarmed at seeing herself in the rushes, thinking she did not appear to be the frail and faltering victim. "I look so *healthy,*" she told Cukor who told her that such an appearance would all the more convince audiences that she was indeed on the verge of a breakdown. Both Bergman and Cotten had to be borrowed from Selznick for the production and David O. Selznick initially refused to allow Bergman to appear unless she was listed in the credits first, before Boyer. The actress confronted the producer, saying she didn't care if her name followed Boyer's, just as long as she got the juicy part. She had to put on an act, crying great tears before Selznick would relent. Cukor suggested that she learn about nervous breakdowns by going to a mental institution and studying the patients. She did, concentrating upon one slightly deranged female, and it was this patient's habits and physical quirks Bergman used to authenticate her own character in GASLIGHT. The actress, adept with almost any role, had one bugbear, that of having to do a love scene as an opening shot with her leading man. She asked Cukor not to begin with a clinch in GASLIGHT, but, as recalled later in her memoirs, *My Story:* "Our opening shot, out of sequence as always, was when I arrived at a railway station in Italy. I leapt out of the carriage and raced across to where Charles [Boyer] was standing in the middle of the platform waiting to catch me in his arms, passionately embrace me, and kiss me." This was her introduction to Boyer, made all the more ridiculous in that she was several inches taller than he and during the railway scene and others where they stood together, Boyer had to perch upon a wooden box so he would appear taller. (The great French romantic actor would have to assume the same elevated stance years later when he again acted with Bergman in ARCH OF TRIUMPH.) Boyer had been married for 10 years to retired British actress Pat Patterson and the couple had been unsuccessful in having children. During the GASLIGHT production Boyer's wife delivered a boy, Michael. The cast gave him a party and Boyer was so overjoyed with the birth of his son that he visibly wept into his champagne glass. (Either by accident or intentionally, Michael Boyer killed himself while in his 20s; Boyer took his own life in 1978, three days after his wife died of a brain tumor.) The most astounding element of the film was the debut of Lansbury, who was nominated for an Oscar for Best Supporting Player, astounding in that she never had a bit of acting experience, although her mother was British character actress Moyna MacGill. When she heard that MGM was casting for the film she tried out for the cheap, flirtatious part of Nancy the maid and, despite objections from the studio's publicity department which thought her without sex appeal, Lansbury got the part and chewed it to pieces. Up to that time, Lansbury had been wrapping packages in Bullock's Wilshire Department Store. She celebrated her eighteenth birthday on the set. She was later to state: "I happened to see GASLIGHT not long ago on television. I was amazed. I thought, My God, how did I have all that assurance." Oddly, Jack Benny later did a burlesque of the movie which he called "Autolight" for his TV show, in which the comedian vexes Barbara Stanwyck. MGM brought an infringement suit, despite the fact that the Benny bit was strictly a parody. The suit was later dropped after going through the courts and the skit was shown. Boyer's performance is a study in obsession, one that won him an Oscar nomination (he lost Best Actor to Bing Crosby in GOING MY WAY). The closeup scene where Boyer describes the jewels in the Tower of London with a passion that engulfs his entire wide-eyed being is a marvel.

p, Arthur Hornblow, Jr., d, George Cukor; w, John Van Druten, Walter Reisch, John L. Balderston (based on the play "Angel Street" by Patrick Hamilton); ph, Joseph Ruttenberg; m, Bronislau Kaper; ed, Ralph E. Winters; art d, Cedric Gibbons, William Ferrari; set d, Edwin B. Willis, Paul Huldschinsky; spec eff, Warren Newcombe.

Mystery **Cas.** **(PR:C MPAA:NR)**

GASOLINE ALLEY½** (1951) 76m COL bw

Scotty Beckett *(Corky)*, Jimmy Lydon *(Skeezix)*, Susan Morrow *(Hope)*, Don Beddoe *(Walt Wallet)*, Patti Brady *(Judy)*, Madelon Mitchel *(Phyllis)*, Dick Wessel *(Pudge)*, Gus Schilling *(Joe Allen)*, Kay Christopher *(Nina)*, Byron Foulger *(Charles D. Haven)*, Virginia Toland *(Carol Rice)*, Jimmy Lloyd *(Harry Dorsey)*, William Forrest *(Hacker)*, Ralph Peters *(Reddick)*, Charles Halton *(Pettit)*, Charles Williams *(Mortie)*, Christine McIntyre *(Myrtle)*.

The first of an announced intended series based on the popular comic strip—then 30 years of age—of the same name. The story line, taken directly from the daily newspaper, concentrates on the younger Wallets, chubby Corky (Beckett) and Hope (Morrow). They wed, then attempt to attain self-sufficiency by opening a diner. Beset by all the customary troubles of undercapitalization, they are assisted by family and friends, with comic relief supplied by Wessel and Schilling as their new employees.

p, Milton Feldman; d&w, Edward Bernds (based on Frank O. King's comic strip); ph, Lester White; ed, Aaron Stell; md, Mischa Bakaleinikoff; art d, Victor Green.

Comedy **(PR:AA MPAA:NR)**

GAS-S-S-S!*** (1970) 79m AIP c
(AKA: GAS-S-S-S, OR IT BECAME NECESSARY TO DESTROY THE WORLD IN ORDER TO SAVE IT)

Robert Corff (Coel), Elaine Giftos (Cilla), Pat Patterson (Demeter), George Armitage (Billy the Kid), Alex Wilson (Jason), Alan Braunstein (Dr. Drake), Ben Vereen (Carlos), Cindy Williams (Marissa), Bud Cort (Hooper), Talia Coppola [Shire] (Coralie), Country Joe [McDonald] and The Fish (F.M. Radio), Lou Procopio (Marshall McLuhan), Jackie Farley (Ginny), Phil Borneo (Quant), David Osterhout (Texas Ranger), Bruce Karcher (Edgar Allan Poe), Mike Castle (Hippie), Jim Etheridge, Gary Treadwell (Renegade Cowboys), Peter Fain (Policeman), Stephen Graham (Thief), Bob Easton (Fanatic Religious Leader), Juretta Taylor, Johnny & The Tornados, The Gourmet's Delight.

Director Corman's legendary ability to take advantage of every small circumstance to make low-budget films that appear to have cost real money is stretched to the limit in this Fellini-like retrospection. The apocalypse arrives in the form of a nerve-gas leak from a plant in Alaska that has the effect of speeding up human metabolism to the extent that all people over 25 are goners. Conservative kids take over Texas, turning the territory into a police state, in one of many anomalous occurrences. Young Corff and Giftos, faced with this phenomenon of the betrayal of youth by youth, gather four friends and depart for a commune of the like-minded, located in an old pueblo in New Mexico. Along the way, they encounter Hells Angels turned guardians of tradition, a squad of ravaging football players determined to rape, burn, and loot, and a further threat from the upwardly mobile, led by Marshall McLuhan. Dusky in-gags abound as the group meets other one-time youth heroes in a landscape reminiscent of James Branch Cabell's Jurgen. Critics of the time thought the picture passe, just another youth-culture-oriented film. AIP apparently shared this view; the studio chopped up the original version, excising the dialog between the very Jewish God and Christ, which resulted in Corman's departure to form his own New World Pictures. This, Corman's next-to-last directorial effort, was one of his few money-losers. Many of his young players went on to considerable success in cinema. An excessive film, but one well worth seeing. Songs include "I'm Looking For a World," "Please Don't Bury My Soul," "Maybe It Really Wasn't Love," "Don't Chase Me Around," "Got To Get Movin'," "This Is the Beginning," "The Pueblo Pool," "Bubble Gum Girl," Barry Melton; "Cry a Little," "Gas Man," "Juke Box Serenade," Greg Dewey, Mark Kapner, Doug Metzner, Melton; "First Time, Last Time," "Today Is Where," Toni Brown; "Castles," Brown, Terry Garthwaite; "World That We All Dreamed Of," Joe McDonald.

p&d, Roger Corman; w, George Armitage; ph, Ron Dexter; m, Country Joe and The Fish, Barry Melton; ed, George Van Noy; art d, David Nichols; set d, Stephen Graham.

Drama   (PR:O MPAA:GP)

GASU NINGEN DAIICHIGO (SEE: HUMAN VAPOR, THE, 1964, Jap.)

GATE OF FLESH* (1964, Jap.) 90m Nikkatsu c (NIKUTAI NO MON)

Yumiko Nogawa, Kayo Matsuo, Misako Tominaga, Joe Shishido, Satoko Kasai, Tomiko Ishi.

A Japanese pimp treats his prostitutes in a brutal manner when the girls team up with a gang of organized criminals after WW II comes to a close.

d, Seijun Suzuki; w, Goro Tanada; ph, Shigeyoshi Mine (Nikkatsu Scope, Eastmancolor).

Drama   (PR:O MPAA:NR)

GATE OF HELL**** (1954, Jap.) 89m Daiei c (JIGOKUMEN)

Machiko Kyo (Lady Kesa), Kazuo Hasegawa (Moritoh), Isao Yamagata (Wataru), Koreya Senda (Kiyomori), Yataro Kurokawa (Shigemori), Kikue Mohri (Sawa), Kotaro Bando (Rokuroh), Jun Tazaki (Kogenta), Tatsuya Ishiguro (Yachuta), Kenjiro Uemura (Masanaka), Gen Shimizu (Saburosuke).

A dazzlingly beautiful and poetically simple Japanese tale set in the 12th century. Matinee idol Hasegawa is cast as a feudal warlord who desires the beautiful Kyo, though she is already married. Hasegawa sneaks into their bedroom at night and drives his sword into the bed in an attempt to kill his rival. However, he kills Kyo, who has sacrificed herself for her husband. Filled with shame, sorrow, and remorse Hasegawa begs for the husband to kill him, but he refuses. Hasegawa leaves everything behind and decides to live the life of a monk. The hauntingly simple story is enriched by its hypnotically colorful photography which has been hailed by some as "the most beautiful color photography ever to grace the screen." (The Japanese Film, Richie and Anderson). It went on to receive international praise by winning two Academy Awards (foreign film; costume design, color) and the Grand Prize at Cannes. Oddly it was barely recognized by the Japanese critics, none of whom even placed it on their top 10 lists. The gently sexy Kyo also appears in the classics RASHOMON and UGETSU. (In Japanese; English subtitles.)

p, Masaichi Nagata; d&w, Teinosuke Kinugasa (based on a play by Kan Kikuchi); m, Yasushi Akutagawa; ph, Kohei Sugiyama (Eastmancolor); cos, Sanzo Wada.

Drama   Cas.   (PR:C-O MPAA:NR)

GATES OF HELL, THE zero (1983, U.S./Ital.) 93m Motion Picture Marketing/Robert Warner c (PAURA NELLA CITTA DEI MORTI VIVENTI; AKA: CITY OF THE LIVING DEAD; THE FEAR; TWILIGHT OF THE DEAD; FEAR IN THE CITY OF THE LIVING DEAD)

Venantino Venantini, Carlo de Mejo, Daniela Doria, Robert Sampson.

It's stretching the definitions of a movie to place this monstrosity under such a heading; rather, it's more an excuse to indulge in some sadistic gore. The slight story line has the dead coming back to life—on All Saint's Day, of course—in the city that was once known as Salem, Massachusetts. An electric drill through a person's head and a maggot-filled hand are just two of the pleasantries this film has to offer.

d, Lucio Fulci; w, Fulci, D. Sacchetti; ph, S. Salvati; m, Fabio Frizzi; art d, M.A. Geleng, O. Taito; spec eff, Gino de Rossi; makeup, Rufini, Restopino.

Horror   Cas.   (PR:O MPAA:NR)

GATES OF PARIS*** (1958, Fr./Ital.) 95m FS-Rizzoli/Lopert bw (PORTE DES LILAS)

Pierre Brasseur (Juju), George Brassens (L'Artiste), Henri Vidal (Pierre Barbier), Dany Carrel (Maria), Raymond Bussieres (Alphonse), Amedee (Paulo), Alain Bouvette (Paulo's Pal), Bugette (Police Sergeant), Gerard Buhr, Jacques Marin, Annette Poivre, Teddy Bilis, Alice Tissot, Gabrielle Fontan, Albert Michel, Paul Faivre, Georges Bever, Charles Bouillaud, Sylvain, Philippe Houy, Joel Montheilet, Jeon Rieuben, Michel Lucas, Christian Denhez.

Brasseur, a drunk, and his good friend Brassens, a troubadour, meet gangster Vidal and offer him refuge in Brassens' house. Brasseur takes the time to care for Vidal, benefiting from his newfound friendship. Vidal warms up to Carrel, a girl Brasseur has eyes for, and cons her into stealing some money from her cafe owner father. Brasseur prevents Vidal from carrying out his plan and, when the gangster tries to escape, shoots him. A grim look at friendship which is not without its charm, but certainly lacks the comedy that Clair feels he has included. GATES OF PARIS was awarded the Grand Prix of the Cinema Francais.

p, Andre Daven; d, Rene Clair; w, Clair, Jean Aurel (based on the novel La Grande Ceinture by Rene Fallet); ph, Robert Le Febvre; m, George Brassens; ed, Louisette Hautecoeur, Arlette Lalande; md, Marc Lanjean; art d, Leon Barsacq.

Drama   (PR:C MPAA:NR)

GATES OF THE NIGHT*** (1950, Fr.) 87m Pathe-London/Films International of America bw (LES PORTES DE LA NUIT)

Nathalie Nattier (Malou), Yves Montand (Diego), Pierre Brasseur (Georges), Saturnin Fabre (Monsieur Senechal), Raymond Bussieres (Raymond Lecuyer), Serge Reggiani (Guy), Jean Carette (Mons. Quinquina), Jean Vilar (Le Clochard), Sylvia Bataille (Claire Lecuyer), Mady Berry (Madame Quinquina), Christian Simon (Cri-Cri), Dany Robin (Etiennete).

A surrealistic drama set in Paris after the liberation from the Nazis. Montand is a resistance hero who meets a harmonica-playing vagabond. This mysterious man, who represents destiny, leads Montand to Nattier, a woman he had fallen in love with and had been searching for. Her husband is a war profiteer and her brother a Nazi collaborator who commits suicide. A mixture of reality and mythology that didn't attract an audience at the box office. This was Carne's final collaboration with Prevert. A large-budget film, with nominal exteriors constructed within studio walls by the talented Trauner, it lacked the panache of earlier wartime efforts by the team, made under conditions of great privation. Jean Gabin and Marlene Dietrich were originally selected as the leading players, but refused the assignments—with apparent good reason—at the last minute. The film was screened in the U. S. four years after its Paris premiere. (In French; English subtitles.)

p&d, Marcel Carne; w, Jacques Prevert (based on his ballet Le Rendez-Vous); ph, Philippe Agostini; m, Joseph Kosma; ed, Jean Feyte; prod d, Alexandre Trauner.

Drama   (PR:C-O MPAA:NR)

GATES TO PARADISE** (1968, Brit./Ger.) 75m Jointex c

Lionel Stander (Monk), Ferdy Mayne (Count Ludovic), John Fordyce (Jacob), Matthieu Carriere (Alexis), Pauline Challoner (Blanche), Jenny Agutter (Maud).

Director Wajda, who lost his cavalry-officer father and who himself experienced the Polish resistance during WW II, was obsessed by the apparent futility of acts of heroism in wartime situations. This picture, based on the Children's Crusade of the 13th century, expresses that view in the extreme, stressing the hidden motives which often lie behind acts of presumed courage. The Children's Crusade was an early peace march, one in which thousands of youngsters, armed only with their moral convictions, attempted to halt the long-lasting carnage of the battles between Moslems and Christians for possession of the holy land. Some 50,000 of the child marchers were lost, many of them sold into slavery in Egypt and in Marseilles, France. Stander is the sympathetic monk accompanying the youthful marchers. During the journey, he hears the confessions of several of the latter, discovering that their motivations have more to do with their physical attraction to the march's charismatic leaders, Carriere and Fordyce, than to pacifistic inclination. Further investigation discloses that the "vision" which impelled one of the young leaders to begin the crusade was dictated to him by the decadent count, Mayne, who has a lecherous desire for both young leaders. Observing that the entire massive undertaking was conceived in passions more of the flesh than of the spirit, Stander attempts to halt the march to Jerusalem, but he is trampled underfoot by the juggernaut of pacifism. Stander was an unlikely choice for the part of the monk; he had played comics and heavies for the most part. This was one of a number of films he undertook as an exile from the McCarthy-era witch-hunts.

p, Sam Waynberg; d, Andrzej Wajda; w, Jerzy Andrzejewski, Donald Kravanth (based on a novel by Andrzejewski); ph, Wieczyslaw Jahoda (CinemaScope Technicolor); m, Ward Swingle.

Drama   (PR:C MPAA:NR)

GATEWAY*** (1938) 73m FOX bw

Don Ameche (Dick), Arleen Whelan (Catherine), Gregory Ratoff (Prince Michael), Binnie Barnes (Mrs. Simms), Gilbert Roland (Tony), Raymond Walburn (Mr. McNutt), John Carradine (Leader of Refugees), Maurice Moscovich (Grandpa Hlawek), Harry Carey (Commissioner Nelson), Marjorie Gateson (Mrs. McNutt), Lyle Talbot (Henry), Fritz Leiber (Dr. Weinlander), Warren Hymer (Guard-Waiter), Eddy Conrad (Davonsky), E.E. Clive (Room Steward), Charles Coleman (Purser), Gerald Oliver Smith (Englishman), Albert Conti (Count), Russell Hicks (Ernest).

Most of the action in this film takes place on an ocean liner filled with immigrants bound for New York. Ameche is a journalist returning from the Spanish Civil War. He meets Whelan, an Irish girl en route to meet her fiance. She is sexually attacked by Walburn and he's injured in her struggle to escape. He presses charges and she is detained at Ellis Island. Her fiance, Talbot, refuses to marry her and Ameche goes to her aid, almost causing a riot in the process.

p, Darryl F. Zanuck; d, Alfred G. Werker; w, Lamar Trotti (based on a story by Walter Reisch); ph, Edward Cronjager; ed, James B. Morley; md, Arthur Lange; art d, Bernard Herzbrun, Albert Hogsett.

Drama   **(PR:A MPAA:NR)**

GATEWAY TO GLORY*   (1970, Jap.) 122m Daiei c
                                          (AA, KAIGUN)

Kichiemon Nakamura (Ichiro Hirata), Shogo Shimada (Adm. Yamamoto), Ryunosuke Minegishi, Masayuki Mori, Sachiko Murase, Eiko Azusa, Ken Utsui, Kojiro Hongo, Jun Fujimaki.

Nakamura is a lad enrolled in the Etajima Naval Academy who'd rather study than deal with militarism. He sympathizes, however, with his comrades who go off to fight in the Sino-Japanese War. His mother dies, and after graduating at the top of the class, he returns home to visit her grave. He becomes a pilot assigned to escort a bomber, and is shot down by the Allies while escorting Japan's best-known military man, Admiral Yamamoto.

d, Mitsuo Murayama; w, Ryuzo Kikushima, Yoshihiro Ishimatsu; ph, Akira Uehara (Daiei Scope, Eastmancolor); m, Seitaro Omori; art d, Koichi Takahashi.

War Drama   **(PR:C MPAA:NR)**

GATHERING OF EAGLES, A**   (1963) 115m UNIV c

Rock Hudson (Col. Jim Caldwell), Rod Taylor (Hollis Farr), Leif Erickson (Gen. Hewitt), Mary Peach (Victoria Caldwell), Barry Sullivan (Col. Fowler), Kevin McCarthy (Gen. Kirby), Henry Silva (Col. Garcia), Leora Dana (Mrs. Fowler), Robert Lansing (Sgt. Banning), Richard Anderson (Col. Josten), Richard LePore (Sgt. Kemler), Robert Bray (Lt. Col. Gales), Jim Bannon (Col. Morse), Nelson Leigh (Gen. Aymes), Russ Bender (Col. Torrance), John McKee (Maj. Tarvis), Ben Wright (Leighton), Dorothy Abbott (Mrs. Josten), John Holland (Beresford), John Pickard (Controller), Ed Prentiss (Duty Controller), Ray Montgomery (Capt. Linc), R. Wayland Williams (Capt. Hutchens), Ted Stanhope (Prentiss), Marjorie Stapp (Ann Morse), Steve Mitchell (Master Sergeant), Frances Mercer (Grey Lady), Mary Benoit (Nurse).

An undistinguished Air Force film with Hudson as a SAC commander in post-war time. He's a hard-driving leader wanting perfection from his men, and not giving enough time to his British bride, Peach. A conflict builds inside him that is a well-worn air-defense film subject. The best thing about this tired production is "The SAC Song," written by witty satirical songsmith Tom Lehrer.

p, Sy Bartlett; d, Delbert Mann; w, Robert Pirosh (based on a story by Bartlett); ph, Russell Harlan (Eastmancolor); m, Jerry Goldsmith; ed, Russell F. Schoengarth; art d, Alexander Golitzen, Henry Bumstead; set d, Robert Priestly; cos, Irene, Seth Banks, Norman Mayreis, Olive Koenitz; makeup, Bud Westmore, Mark Reedall.

Drama   **(PR:A MPAA:NR)**

GATLING GUN, THE*½   (1972) 93m Western/Ellman International c

Guy Stockwell (Lt. Malcolm), Woody Strode (Runner), Barbara Luna (Leona), Robert Fuller (Sneed), Patrick Wayne (Jim Beland), Pat Buttram (Tin Pot), John Carradine (Rev. Harper), Phil Harris (Boland), Judy Jordan (Martha Boland), Carlos Rivas (Two-Knife).

A tired and ragged cavalry tale which goes through the standard Indian attacks on the troops. This time, though, the cavalry has a Gatling gun and needless to say arrows prove to be no match for it. There's a bit too much use of slow-motion—a blatant rip-off of Peckinpah's patented technique.

p, Oscar Nichols; d, Robert Gordon; w, Joseph Van Winkle, Mark Hanna; ph, Jacques Marquette (Techniscope, Technicolor); ed, Edward Mann.

Western   **(PR:C MPAA:PG)**

GATOR**   (1976) 115m UA c

Burt Reynolds (Gator McKlusky), Jack Weston (Irving Greenfield), Lauren Hutton (Aggie Maybank), Jerry Reed (Bama McCall), Alice Ghostley (Emmeline Cavanaugh), Dub Taylor (Mayor Caffrey), Mike Douglas (Governor), Burton Gilliam (Smiley), William Engesser (Bones), John Steadman (Ned McKlusky), Lori Futch (Suzie McKlusky), Stephanie Burchfield (Teenage Addict), Bob Yeager (Man In Hospital), Dudley Remus (Pogie), Alex Hawkins (Police Chief).

This was Reynolds' first directorial effort and he continues the adventures of his character from the movie WHITE LIGHTNING (1973). Reynolds is forced by federal agents to help nab a corrupt political boss and school friend, Reed. The agents get his cooperation by threatening to throw his father into jail for moonshining. Reynolds is followed by incompetent federal agent Weston and TV reporter Hutton, who becomes Burt's love interest. An entertaining piece of "good ol' boy" fluff with plenty of car and boat chases. Reynolds continued to star in this type of film (SMOKEY AND THE BANDIT (1980), HOOPER (1978), CANNONBALL RUN (1981)) becoming a parody of the character he portrayed. The film is notable for good performances from inexperienced cinema actors, notably country-and-western composer/singer Reed (in his second feature film) and TV interviewer Mike Douglas (in his feature-picture debut).

p, Jules Levy, Arthur Gardner; d, Burt Reynolds; w, William Norton; ph, William A. Fraker (DeLuxe Color); m, Charles Bernstein; ed, Harold F. Kress; art d, Kirk Axtell; spec eff, Cliff Wenger.

Action   **Cas.**   **(PR:C MPAA:PG)**

GATOR BAIT*   (1974) 93m Sebastion International c

Clyde Ventura, Bill Thurman, Don Baldwin, Janet Baldwin, Ben Sebastion, Tracy Sebastion, Claudia Jennings, Sam Gilman, Doug Dirkson,

A vile independent feature for lower class markets and minds. A group of locals are all chasing a beautiful girl of the swamp (named "Desiree," no less), but she'll have nothing to do with them. Instead, the sexy woman gives the burly males a few surprises, some of which are appallingly violent. Between that and the giggle-giggle attitude towards sex, there's no shame in missing this one.

p,d&w, Ferd and Beverly Sebastion.

Drama   **Cas.**   **(PR:O MPAA:R)**

GAUCHO SERENADE**   (1940) 66m REP bw

Gene Autry (Gene), Smiley Burnette (Frog), June Storey (Joyce), Duncan Renaldo (Gaucho), Mary Lee (Patsy), Clifford Severn, Jr. (Ronnie), Lester Matthews (Alfred Willoughby), Smith Ballew (Buck Benson), Joseph Crehan (Martin), William Ruhl (Carter), Wade Boteler (Rancher), Ted Adams (Jenkins), Wendell Niles, Fred Burns, Julian Rivero, George Lloyd, Edward Cassidy, Joe Dominguez, Olaf Hytten, Fred Toones, Gene Morgan, Jack Kirk, Harry Strang, Hank Worden, Kernan Cripps, Jim Corey, Tom London, Walter Miller, Frankie Marvin, Buck Bucko, The Velascos, Jose Eslava's Orchestra, Champion, the horse.

A very boring western with nothing happening until the last 15 minutes of the film. A group of big businessmen want to kidnap the son of a former partner, so the latter won't squeal. Autry makes sure this doesn't happen. There's more singing than horse riding. Songs include, "The Singing Hills," "Give Out With A Song," "Wooing Of Kitty MacFuty," "A Song At Sunset," and the title song. (See GENE AUTRY series, Index.)

p, William Berke; d, Frank McDonald; w, Betty Burbridge, Bradford Ropes; ph, Reggie Lanning; ed, Tony Martinelli; m/l, Connie Lee, Gene Autry, John Marvin, John Redmond, James Cavanaugh, Nat Simon, Mack Davis, Dick Sanford, Sammy Mysels, Smiley Burnette.

Western   **(PR:A MPAA:NR)**

GAUCHOS OF EL DORADO*½   (1941) 56m REP bw

Bob Steele (Tucson Smith), Tom Tyler (Stony Brodie), Rufe Davis (Lullaby Joslin), Lois Collier (Ellen), Duncan Renaldo (Gaucho), Rosina Galli (Isabella), Norman Willis (Bart), William Ruhl (Tyndal), Tony Roux (Miguel), Raphael Bennett (Monk), Yakima Canutt (Snakes).

A young man robs a bank, getting away with $5,000 and a bullet in him. The Mesquiteers find him dying and the trio promises to take the money to his mother for the mortgage. Mistaken identities and other problems befall the cowboys before everything gets squared away. One of 51 of the THREE MESQUITEERS series (see Index), begun by RKO and later picked up by Republic. Steele had been in the first picture of the series, but played a secondary role. In Republic's 23 of the series, from 1940 through 1943, Steele was top-billed as Tucson Smith. Director Orlebeck directed ten of the films; he had previously worked as a film editor. (See THREE MESQUITEERS series, Index.)

d, Les Orlebeck; w, Albert DeMond (based on a story by Earle Snell and characters created by William Colt MacDonald); ph, Reggie Lanning; ed, Charles Craft; m/l, "Bird and the Wolf," Jule Styne and Sol Meyer.

Western   **(PR:A MPAA:NR)**

GAUNT STRANGER, THE (SEE: PHANTOM STRIKES, THE, 1938, Brit.)

GAUNTLET, THE**   (1977) 110m Malpaso/WB c

Clint Eastwood (Ben Shockley), Sondra Locke (Gus Mally), Pat Hingle (Josephson), William Prince (Blakelock), Bill McKinney (Constable), Michael Cavanaugh (Feyderspiel), Carole Cook (Waitress), Mara Corday (Jail Matron), Douglas McGrath (Bookie), Jeff Morris (Desk Sergeant), Samantha Doane, Roy Jenson, Dan Vadis (Bikers).

Eastwood does a reprise of his "Dirty Harry" character here, only this time he's working for the Phoenix, Arizona, police department. His superior, Prince, orders him to Las Vegas to extradite a prisoner, Locke, who is to testify in a trial. Eastwood, an alcoholic cop with little hope for promotion, let alone a pension, goes to Las Vegas and picks up Locke who tells him that they will never get back to Phoenix, that both will be killed before she gets into court to testify against high-ranking police officials in Eastwood's department. He scoffs at her but when a bevy of cops unleash a fusillade against the bungalow where they are staying temporarily, he quickly comes to believe she has a point. They flee by taking a cop hostage and having him drive his squad car toward Phoenix. On a dark road, the couple get out of the squad car which is then blasted to bits by an army of cops, killing the driver. Hiding out in a desert cave, Eastwood and Locke grow friendly toward each other in a hostile sort of way and the cop interrupts a motorcycle gang the next morning as they stop to get their bearings and smoke some pot. Eastwood commandeers a cycle and sends the gang packing. He and Locke again proceed to their destination as a machinegun firing helicopter tries to strafe them. Next Eastwood takes over a bus and has it plated with armor, and he and Locke climb aboard, intending to drive into Phoenix and confront Prince, the head of the police department who has set them up and is the person Locke will testify against. Prince, who is told by Eastwood that he is coming, sets up an incredible police gauntlet, hundreds of cops who riddle the bus as it roars into the city. But Eastwood and Locke survive to drive the battered vehicle onto the steps of Prince's grandiose office building. Prince races through the scores of cops surrounding the couple and orders them killed but the cops refuse, and, when he tries to kill them, Locke shoots him to death. The couple then go off to face the music together. THE GAUNTLET is thoroughly unbelievable hokum which any 10-year-old will dismiss as nonsense. Eastwood sleepwalks through his role and Locke is simply repulsive as the feisty hooker, a nonactress with a grating voice, obnoxious manners, and the personality of a gila monster. The production is expensively mounted and returned $17 million plus from the pockets of diehard Eastwood fans. The violence is bloody, nonstop, and as pointless as the script.

p, Robert Daley; d, Clint Eastwood; w, Michael Butler, Dennis Shryack; ph, Rexford Metz (Panavision, DeLuxe Color); m, Jerry Fielding; ed, Ferris Webster, Joel Cox; art d, Allen E. Smith; set d, Ira Bates; cos, Glenn Wright; spec eff, Chuck Gaspar; stunts, Wayne Van Horn, makeup, Don Schoenfeld.

Crime Drama   **Cas.**   **(PR:O MPAA:R)**

GAVILAN**   (1968) 85m International/Craddock c
                                             (AKA: BALLAD OF GAVILAN)

Christopher George, George De Vries.

When a young man's family is abused by a nefarious type, the veangeful son tracks down and kills the outlaw. A typical 1940s western plot that got held over for 20 years.

p,d&w, William J. Jugo; m, Pete Seeger.

Western   **(PR:C   MPAA:NR)**

GAWAIN AND THE GREEN KNIGHT**½   (1973, Brit.) 93m
               UA-Sancrest c (AKA: SIR GAWAIN AND THE GREEN KNIGHT)

Murray Head (Gawain), Nigel Green (Green Knight), Ciaran Madden (Linet), Robert Hardy (Sir Bertilan), Davil Leland (Humphrey), Anthony Sharp (King), Ronald Lacey (Oswald), Murray Melvin (Seneschal), Willoughby Goddard (Knight), Richard Hurndall (Bearded Man), Tony Steedman (Fortinbras), George Merritt (Old Knight), Peter Copley (Pilgrim), Pauline Letts (Lady of Lyonesse), Geoffrey Bayldon (Wiseman), Jerold Wells (Sergeant), Jack Woolgar (Porter), Michael Crand (The Giant).

The familiar legend of the Round Table is brought to the screen in a low-budget, but surprisingly effective, effort. Green Knight Green comes to court and asks any of the knights to take his best chop, on the condition that he then be allowed to return the favor. Head takes up the challenge and with one swing of his broadsword lops the challenger's head off. Green calmly picks up the severed head and places it atop his shoulders, then tells Head to come to his castle to receive his side of the bargain. After a terrific start the picture lags as Head waits and worries for the appointed time he's to have his head chopped off. Not often seen, but worth checking out.

p, Carlo Ponti; d, Stephen Weeks; w, Philip Breen, Weeks (based on a medieval poem); ph, Ian Wilson (Panavision, Technicolor); m, Ron Goodwin; art d, Anthony Woollard.

Fantasy   **(PR:C-O MPAA:NR)**

GAY ADVENTURE, THE*   (1936, Brit.) 73m Grosvenor/Pathe bw

Yvonne Arnaud (Julie), Barry Jones (Darnton), Nora Swinburne (Fay D'Allary), Betty Worth (Baby), Sybil Grove (Miss Darnton), Finlay Currie (Porter), Guy Middleton (Aram), Robert Holmes (D'Allary), Antony Holles (Charles), Kenneth Warrington (Mickey Blane), Ralph Truman (Buck), Percy Parsons (Pete), Andrea Malandrinos (Hotel Manager).

A complicated mess of a comedy that bites off more than it can chew. A duo of American crooks (Currie, Middleton) convince a timid English gentleman (Jones) that he's a descendant of D'Artagnan, the fourth Musketeer, with resulting fantasies and derring-do. The story is too involved to put coherently on the screen.

p, Harcourt Templeman; d, Sinclair Hill; w, D.B. Wyndham-Lewis (based on the play by Walter Hackett); ph, Cyril Bristow.

Comedy   **(PR:A   MPAA:NR)**

GAY ADVENTURE, THE*   (1953, Brit.) 82m UA bw
                 (GB: GOLDEN ARROW; AKA: THREE MEN AND A GIRL)

Burgess Meredith (Dick), Jean-Pierre Aumont (Andre Marchand), Paula Valenska (Suzy/Sonia/Hedy), Kathleen Harrison (Isobel), Richard Murdoch (David Felton), Julian Dalbie [d'Albie] (Waterhouse), Jose de Almeyda (Jones), Kenneth Cove (Clergyman), Henry Pascal (Photographer), Karel Stepanek (Schroeder), Glyn Lawson (Max), Edward Lexy (The Colonel), Derek Blomfield (First Officer), D'Arcy Conyers (Second Officer), Eva Savage (Mimi), Milo Sperber (Black Marketeer), Richard Warner (Captain), Ivan Sampson (Commanding Officer), Hilda Bayley (Mrs. Felton), Ernest Jay (Mr. Felton), Natasha Parry (Betty Felton), Sandra Dorne (Night Club Girl), James Crabbe (John Felton), Colin Gordon (Connelly), Hugh Morton (Perdrelli), Richard Molinas (Schloss), Philip Slessor (BBC Man), Gordon Tanner (Bixby), Patrick Barr (Hedy's Husband).

No, not a film about an emergence from a closet. An interesting trio of fantasies, all provoked by a glimpse of the same blonde Venus, Valenska, a wooden actress with an unintelligible accent whom apparently smitten producer De Grunwald seemed to be grooming for Marlene Dietrich-style stardom. For some reason, this picture, completed in 1949, was held back from release for nearly four years, even in its native Britain. Harrison, who appears in only one of the three episodes, became a star in the interim, which was doubtless the reason for her high billing among the cast members. The British title, GOLDEN ARROW, refers to the train traveling from Paris on which the dream girl is first spotted by French bus driver Aumont; no doubt the U. S. title was chosen to allay the suspicion that the opus might be of the cowboys-and-Indians genre. Aumont visualizes Valenska as a sexy photographer's model with whom he has an amorous adventure on the French Riviera. Meredith, the American army officer, spots Valenska on the channel boat. He sees her as a singer in a sleazy cabaret in occupied Berlin, from which he rescues her. Murdoch, the proper Britisher, spying her on the boat train to London, views her as a prima-donna movie star who enlists his assistance in avoiding the pesky paparazzi of the press, taking refuge in his stodgy middle-class home. Each of the three fantasies is shattered as the dreamy trio see Valenska disentrain to the waiting arms of a husband and three children.

p, Anatole De Grunwald; d, Gordon Parry; w, Paul Darcy, Sid Colin, De Grunwald; ph, Guy Drisse; m, Mischa Spoliansky; ed, Gerald Turney-Smith; art d, Tom Goswell.

Comedy   **(PR:A   MPAA:NR)**

GAY AMIGO, THE**   (1949) 60m UA bw

Duncan Renaldo (Cisco), Leo Carrillo (Pancho), Armida (Rosita), Joe Sawyer (Sgt. McNulty), Walter Baldwin (Stoneham), Fred Kohler, Jr. (Brack), Kenneth MacDonald (Capt. Lewis), George Denormand (Corporal), Clayton Moore (Lieutenant), Fred Crane (Duke), Helen Servis (Old Maid), Beverly Jons (Girl), Bud Osborne (Driver), Sam Flint (Paulsen).

The second of producer Krasne's five in the Cisco Kid series for United Artists (there were 23 in all). Renaldo is O. Henry's character, and he and Carrillo are mistaken for the leaders of a band of desperados. As the cavalry chases after them, the duo hunt down the real bandits. (See CISCO KID series, Index.)

p, Philip N. Krasne; d, Wallace Fox; w, Doris Schroeder (based on the characters created by O. Henry); ph, Ernest Miller; m, Albert Glasser; ed, Martin Cohn.

Western   **(PR:A   MPAA:NR)**

GAY BLADES**   (1946) 67m REP bw

Allan Lane (Andy Buell), Jean Rogers (Nancy Davis), Edward Ashley (Ted Brinker), Frank Albertson (Frankie Dowell), Anne Gillis (Helen Dowell), Robert Armstrong (McManus), Paul Harvey (J.M. Snively), Ray Walker (Bill Calhoun), Jonathan Hale (Whittlesey), Russell Hicks (Buxton), Emmett Vogan (Doctor), Edward Gargan (Bartender), Nedrick Young (Gary Lester).

Rogers is a talent scout searching for a hunk to star in a movie titled "The Behemoth." She goes to New York and finds hockey player Lane. He's reluctant and Rogers ends up dropping her Hollywood job to be a hockey player's wife. The handsome Lane, a former Notre Dame football star, had worked for the major studios before sliding over to Republic. The year following this "inside Hollywood" opus, he became Allan "Rocky" Lane, specializing in B-westerns for the studio (51 in all).

p&d, George Blair; w, Albert Reich (based on a story by Marcel Klauber from a magazine story by Jack Goodman and Albert Rice); ph, William Bradford; m, Dale Butts; ed, Tony Martinelli; md, Morton Scott; art d, Gano Chittenden; spec eff, Howard and Theodore Lydecker.

Comedy   **(PR:A   MPAA:NR)**

GAY BRIDE, THE**   (1934) 82m MGM bw

Carole Lombard (Mary), Chester Morris (Office Boy), ZaSu Pitts (Mirabelle), Leo Carrillo (Mickey), Nat Pendleton (Shoots Magiz), Sam Hardy (Dingle), Walter Walker (MacPherson), Joe Twerp (Lafcadio), Louis Nathoaux (Honk), Edward Le Saint (Justice of Peace), Frank Darien (Minister), Fred Malatesta (French Officer), William Von Brincken (German Official), Herbert Evans (British Official), Bobby Watson (Auto Salesman), Norman Ainsley (Waiter), Fred "Snowflake" Toones (Bootblack), Garry Owen, Ray Mayer, Fuzzy Knight (Cameramen), Clay Drew (Stage Doorman), Wedgwood Nowell (Stage Manager), Jack Baxley (Bum), Wilbur Mack (Banker), Lew Harvey (Gangster), Willie Fung (Chinaman), Mary Carr (Mrs. Bartlett), Gordon DeMain (Sergeant), Boothe Howard, Francis McDonald (Crooks).

Unfortunately, the word "gay" has taken on a very different meaning since this picture was titled. In 1934, it meant "happy" or "carefree" but this movie was neither. A feeble attempt at a gangland satire, it tells the tale of gold-digger Lombard who vamps Pendleton, the mobster who is backing the show in which Lombard is appearing. She doesn't really like him, the way he dresses, or his Hell's Kitchen manner of speech, but she marries him anyhow for his money and in the full knowledge that the business he is in may leave her in widow's weeds at any moment. They go off on a European honeymoon where she talks him into buying an expensive painting. Once that's done, she sells the painting at a $20,000 profit and replaces it with a cheap imitation, knowing that he will never know the difference. Then she buys a car, makes a deal with the auto salesman, and gets the man to send a bill for twice the amount to her unsuspecting husband. Pendleton is shot to death by her next conquest, Hardy, who in turn is bumped off by Carrillo, leaving her penniless with several creditors having laid claims on her property. Lombard winds up marrying the office boy, Morris. The screenplay was by the Spewacks, two of the best writers on Broadway and in the movies. It was a misfire from the start and audiences stayed away in droves. Even on Bingo nights.

p, John Considine, Jr.; d, Jack Conway; w, Sam and Bella Spewack (based on the story "Repeal" by Charles Francis Coe); ph, Ray June; m, Jack Virgil; ed, Frank Sullivan; art d, Cedric Gibbons; cos, Dolly Tree.

Crime Comedy/Drama   **(PR:A-C   MPAA:NR)**

GAY BUCKAROO, THE*½   (1932) 66m Allied bw

Hoot Gibson (Clint Hale), Merna Kennedy (Mildred Field), Roy D'Arcy (Dave Dumont), Edward Peil (Hi Low Jack), Charles King ("Faro" Parker), Lafe McKee ("Sporty Bill" Field), Sidney de Grey ("Uncle Abner"), The Hoot Gibson Cowboys.

Gibson is a rancher trying to win the hand of Kennedy. So is gambler and bad guy D'Arcy, and he gives Gibson a very hard time.

p, M.H. Hoffman, Jr.; d, Phil Rosen; w, Philip Graham White (based on a story by Lee R. Brown); ph, Harry Neumann; ed, Mildred Johnston.

Western   **(PR:A   MPAA:NR)**

GAY CABALLERO, THE**   (1932) 60m FOX bw

George O'Brien (Ted Radcliffe), Victor McLaglen (Don Bob Harkness), Conchita Montenegro (Adela Morales), Linda Watkins (Ann Grey), C. Henry Gordon (Don Paco Morales), Weldon Heyburn (Jito), Willard Robertson (Maj. Blount), Martin Garralaga (Manuel), Juan Torena (Juan Rodrigues).

O'Brien is an Easterner, a football star who comes West to undertake the supervision of his legacy, a cattle ranch, which has supported him in collegiate abundance for some years. He discovers that Hispanic cattle king Gordon has greatly diminished his fortune through nefarious efforts to build an empire. Gordon has been partly thwarted in his evil doings by a mysterious outlaw, El Coyote, who is, in reality, friendly old Don Bob (McLaglen). O'Brien and McLaglen get together to combat the acquisitive hidalgo and his hideous henchman, the gigantic Heyburn. O'Brien's budding romance with the lovely Montenegro is complicated by the fact that she is the daughter of his nemesis, Gordon. After a succession of shootouts and a terrific battle in a cantina in which O'Brien bests the huge Heyburn with some college wrestling throws as McLaglen looks on, all works out well.

p, Edmund Grainger; d, Alfred Werker; w, Philip Klein, Barry Connors (based on the novel *Gay Bandit* by Tom Gill); ph, George Schneiderman; ed, Al De Gaetano.

Western (PR:A MPAA:NR)

GAY CABALLERO, THE✶✶ (1940) 58m FOX bw

Cesar Romero (*Cisco Kid*), Sheila Ryan (*Susan Wetherby*), Robert Sterling (*Billy Brewster*), Chris-Pin Martin (*Gordito*), Janet Beecher (*Kate Brewster*), Edmund MacDonald (*Joe Turner*), Jacqueline Dalya (*Carmelita*), Montague Shaw (*George Wetherby*), Hooper Atchley (*Sheriff McBride*).

The best of Fox's Cisco Kid series. Romero and his sidekick Martin arrive in town and find that he's assumed dead. It also seems that before his death, Romero tried to cheat Ryan out of her land. Romero reveals that female crook Beecher used his name to perpetrate the deed and puts an end to her scam. (See CISCO KID series, Index.)

p, Walter Morosco, Ralph Dietrich; d, Otto Brower; w, Albert Duffy, John Larkin (based on a story by Walter Bullock, Duffy, and characters created by O. Henry); ph, Edward Cronjager; ed, Harry Reynolds; md, Emil Newman.

Western (PR:A MPAA:NR)

GAY CITY, THE (SEE: LAS VEGAS NIGHTS, 1941)

GAY DECEIVERS, THE✶½ (1969) Fanfare 97m bw

Kevin Coughlin (*Danny Devlin*), Brooke Bundy (*Karen*), Larry Casey (*Elliot Crane*), Jo Ann Harris (*Leslie Devlin*), Michael Greer (*Malcolm*), Sebastian Brook (*Craig*), Jack Starrett (*Col. Dixon*), Richard Webb (*Mr. Devlin*), Eloise Hardt (*Mrs. Devlin*), Jeanne Baird (*Mrs. Conway*), Marishka (*Carolyn*), Mike Kopscha (*Psychiatrist*), Joe Tornatori (*Sgt. Kravits*), Robert Reese (*Real Estate Agent*), Christopher Riordan (*Duane*), Doug Hume (*Corporal*), Dave Osterhout (*Stern*), Marilyn Wirt (*Sybil*), Ron Gans (*Freddie*), Rachel Romen (*Dorothy*), Tom Grubbs (*Paul*), Louise Williams (*Bunny*), Randee Lynne (*Sheryl*), Meridith Williams (*Phil*), Harry Sodoni (*Georgette*), Lenore Stevens (*Laverne*), Trigg Kelly (*Jackie*), Tony Epper (*Vince*).

Coughlin and Casey avoid the draft by pretending they're gay. The army lets them go, but recruiting officer Starrett isn't too sure about their story. He stakes out Casey's apartment and when the pair realizes they're being watched, they really have to act gay. They move into a gay apartment and by the time Starrett gives up, Coughlin loses his fiancee. In the end, suspicious Starrett proves less than straight. A decent idea that never was developed to its potential.

p, Joe Solomon; d, Bruce Kessler; w, Jerome Wish (based on a story by Abe Polsky and Gil Lasky); ph, Dick Glouner; m, Stu Phillips; ed, Renn Reynolds, Reg Browne; art d, Archie Bacon; set d, Ray Boltz; cos, Norman Saling; makeup, Brian Perrow.

Comedy (PR:O MPAA:R)

GAY DECEPTION, THE✶✶½ (1935) 75m FOX bw

Francis Lederer (*Sandro*), Frances Dee (*Mirabel*), Benita Hume (*Miss Channing*), Alan Mowbray (*Lord Clewe*), Akim Tamiroff (*Spellek*), Lennox Pawle (*Consul-General*), Adele St. Maur (*Lucille*), Ferdinand Gottschalk (*Mr. Squires*), Richard Carle (*Mr. Spitzer*), Lenita Lane (*Peg DeForrest*), Barbara Fritchie (*Joan Dennison*), Paul Hurst (*Bell Captain*), Robert Greig (*Adolph*), Luis Alberni (*Ernest*), Lionel Stander (*Gettel*).

Dee is a small-town girl who wins a $5,000 lottery and goes to New York City to live like a queen. She meets Lederer, a bellboy who turns out to be a real-life prince, and Dee gets her wish to be a queen. This light but artful effort was one of director Wyler's rare comedies. For those interested in semantic coincidence and linguistic development, Wyler's other major directorial effort that same year was titled THE GOOD FAIRY.

p, Jesse L. Lasky; d, William Wyler; w, Stephen Avery, Don Hartman, Arthur Richman; ph, Joseph Valentine.

Comedy (PR:A MPAA:NR)

GAY DESPERADO, THE✶✶✶½ (1936) 86m Pickford-Lasky/UA bw

Nino Martini (*Chivo*), Ida Lupino (*Jane*), Leo Carrillo (*Pablo Braganza*), Harold Huber (*Campo*), James Blakeley (*Bill*), Stanley Fields (*Butch*), Mischa Auer (*Diego*), Adrian Rosley (*Radio Station Manager*), Paul Hurst (*American Detective*), Alan Garcia (*Police Captain*), Frank Puglia (*Lopez*), Michael Visaroff (*Theatre Manager*), Chris-Pin Martin (*Pancho*), Harry Semels (*Manuel*), George Du Count (*Salvador*), Alphonso Pedroza (*Coloso*), Trovadores Chinacos (*Guitar Trio*), Len Brixton (*Nick*), M. Alvarez Maciste (*Guitar Soloist*).

Carrillo is a music-loving Mexican bandit who patterns himself after American screen gangsters. He kidnaps opera star Nino Martini, playing a singing caballero, and heiress Lupino. Martini gets plenty of time to sing, but bad guy Carrillo and his partner Huber steal the show with their comical performances. A really terrific musical comedy for its time. Unfortunately, this second of the films produced by the new Pickford-Lasky team was also the last by the team. Songs include "The World Is Mine Tonight," Holt Marvell [Eric Maschwitz], George Posford; "Cielito Lindo," Neil Wilson, Carlo Fernandez, Sebastian Yradier; "Estralita," Frank LaForge, Manuel Ponce; "Adios Mi Terra," Miguel Sandoval; "Lamento Gitano,"

Walter Samuels, Leonard Whitcup; "Mamacita Mia," Anon.; "Celeste Aida," Giuseppe Verdi.

p, Mary Pickford, Jesse L. Lasky; d, Rouben Mamoulian; w, Wallace Smith (based on a story by Leo Birinski); ph, Lucien Andriot; ed, Margaret Clancey; md, Alfred Newman; art d, Richard Day.

Musical/Comedy (PR:A MPAA:NR)

GAY DIPLOMAT, THE✶ (1931) 66m RKO bw

Ivan Lebedeff (*Capt. Orloff*), Genevieve Tobin (*Diana Dorchy*), Betty Compson (*Baroness Corri*), Ilka Chase (*Blinis*), Purnell Pratt (*Col. Gorin*), Rita LaRoy (*Natalie*), Colin Campbell (*Gamble*), Edward Martindel (*Ambassador*), Arthur Edmund Carew (*The Suave Man*).

Suavely continental supporting actor Lebedeff in his first starring role as a handsome captain in the Russian army during WW I (Russia was on our side, remember) dispatched to Bucharest to trap an important spy—a veritable Mata Hari. In a confusing plot, the charming captain encounters a number of beautiful, sophisticated ladies, any one of whom could be his quarry. Ultimately, the choice narrows to Tobin and Compson, for either of whom a man might well forsake his allegiance to his country. The counterspy captain captures both, Compson for her devilish deeds and Tobin for his heart's delight. This film marked another debut, that of Pandro S. Berman in his first producing job (the task was known as "supervising" at the time; production was customarily credited to the studio entity itself). Berman, who went on to become RKO's stock-company supervisor/producer, had been studio mogul William LeBaron's assistant; he was assigned to this film when supervisor Henry Hobart walked off the job.

d, Richard Boleslavsky; w, Doris Anderson (based on a story by Benn W. Levy); ph, Leo Tover.

Spy/Drama (PR:A MPAA:NR)

GAY DIVORCEE, THE✶✶✶✶ (1934) 107m RKO bw
(GB: GAY DIVORCE, THE)

Fred Astaire (*Guy Holden*), Ginger Rogers (*Mimi Glossop*), Alice Brady (*Hortense Ditherwell*), Edward Everett Horton (*Egbert Fitzgerald*), Erik Rhodes (*Rodolfo Tonetti*), Eric Blore (*Waiter*), Lillian Miles (*Hotel Guest*), Charles Coleman (*Valet*), William Austin (*Cyril Glossop*), Betty Grable (*Hotel Guest*), Paul Porcasi (*Nightclub Proprietor*), E.E. Clive (*Customs Inspector*), George Davis, Alphonse Martell (*French Waiters*), Charles Hall (*Call Boy at Dock*), Art Jarrett.

After a brief dance together in FLYING DOWN TO RIO (1933), this marked the first of many Astaire/Rogers co-starring vehicles. Nominated for three Academy Awards (best picture, best musical/adaptation), it won the first Best Song Oscar for "The Continental" (Con Conrad, Herb Magidson), which was a 22-minute production number, broken up by dialog because director Sandrich didn't like songs that had little to do with the plot. Only one tune was salvaged from Cole Porter's original Broadway score: "Night and Day." The play was called *The Gay Divorce*, but the Hays Office decreed that divorces are anything but "happy," although the divorcee just might be, so they added the extra "E" and everyone was satisfied. Once again, as in so many of these 1930s movies, the plot only served as a reason to make music and dance. Only ten minutes of actual dancing were seen, but they were sheer poetry and made Astaire and Rogers the most memorable team in pictures. Rogers wants to get a divorce from her husband but in those days it wasn't as easy as it is today. Thus, a correspondent has to be named in order to prove infidelity, even where there was none. Lawyer Horton and Rogers' aunt, Brady, hire a professional to serve as the necessary correspondent. Astaire is an American dancer in England and meets Rogers in a seaside resort (called Brightbourne, for some reason, but actually Brighton). He runs after her for several songs but she thinks he is the hated correspondent. There are several cases of mistaken identity, sub-plots, etc., and in the end, they realize that he is not who she thinks he is. They fall in love and are presumed to dance on together forever. Rhodes is the real correspondent and plays it well. The producers weren't certain that Astaire and Rogers could handle the movie on their own so they "insured" success with several of the best second bananas around; Horton, Blore and a number of others. Betty Grable does one number with Horton and establishes herself as a force to contend with. The settings were superb, the dances, choreographed by Dave Gould, were excellent. The following year, Gould went to MGM and staged the dances for FOLIES BERGERE, for which he won an Oscar. Astaire and assistant Hermes Pan did the choreography for his dances. Max Steiner's orchestrations were a marvel to listen to then and still are today. Lots of laughs in the script and high-energy performances by all. One of the best examples of Depression-era musicals. Lou Brock, who customarily produced musicals for RKO, scoffed at this formula plot, stating "I can blow a better script than that out of my nose." He was overruled by new production chief Pandro S. Berman, who went to London, saw Astaire in the stage version, and purchased the rights for an incredibly low $20,000. Other songs include "Don't Let It Bother You," "Let's K-nock K-nees," Harry Revel, Mack Gordon; "A Needle In a Haystack," "The Continental," Con Conrad, Herb Magidson.

p, Pandro S. Berman; d, Mark Sandrich; w, George Marion, Jr., Dorothy Yost, Edward Kaufman (based on the musical play "The Gay Divorce" by Dwight Taylor and Cole Porter; musical adaptation by Kenneth Webb, Samuel Hoffenstein); ph, David Abel; ed, William Hamilton; md, Max Steiner; art d, Van Nest Polglase, Carroll Clark; cos, Walter Plunkett; spec eff, Vernon Walker; ch, Dave Gould; Astaire's ch, Astaire, Hermes Pan (uncredited).

Musical/Comedy Cas. (PR:AA MPAA:NR)

GAY DOG, THE✶½ (1954, Brit.) 87m Coronet/Eros bw

Wilfred Pickles (*Jim Gay*), Petula Clark (*Sally Gray*), Megs Jenkins (*Maggie Gay*), John Blythe (*Peter Nightingale*), Margaret Barton (*Peggy Gowland*), Russell Enoch (*Leslie Gowland*), Cyril Raymond (*Vicar*), Harold Goodwin (*Bert Gay*), Jon Pertwee, Peter Butterworth, Douglas Ives, Nuna Davey.

As a man who loves his greyhound more than anything in the world, Pickles devotes himself totally to grooming it for the track. But when he goes out of town and discovers a competitor with a better chance of winning, he bets against his own dog and his friends lose money betting on his. Comic situations abound, but fall far short in the execution, which is surprising coming from eminently competent director Elvey.

p, Ernest Gartside; d, Maurice Elvey; w, Peter Rogers (based on the play by Joseph Colton); ph, James Wilson.

Comedy   (PR:A   MPAA:NR)

GAY FALCON, THE**½**   (1941) 67m RKO bw

George Sanders (*Falcon*), Wendy Barrie (*Helen Reed*), Allen Jenkins (*Goldy*), Anne Hunter (*Elinor*), Gladys Cooper (*Maxine*), Edward S. Brophy (*Bates*), Arthur Shields (*Waldeck*), Damian O'Flynn (*Weber*), Turhan Bey (*Retana*), Eddie Dunn (*Grimes*), Lucille Gleason (*Mrs. Gardiner*), Willie Fung (*Jerry*), Hans Conried (*Herman*), Jimmy Conlin (*Bartender*), Walter Soderling (*Morgue Attendant*), Robert Smith (*Cop at Morgue*), Bobby Barber (*Waiter*), Paul Norby (*Cigar Clerk*), Mickey Phillips (*Newsboy*), Frank O'Connor (*Cop*), Lew Kelly (*Jailer*), Polly Bailey (*Landlady*), James Baline (*Cop in Hallway*), Joey Ray (*Orchestra Leader*), Lee Bonnell, Virginia Vale.

Sanders, an amateur detective and a ladies' man, goes after a gang of jewel thieves. They're in cahoots with some down-on-their-luck socialites trying to defraud insurance companies. The Falcon gets the pretty leading lady, breaks up the scam, and brings the gang to justice. An entertainingly fast-paced film that started a series of FALCON films. Leslie Charteris sued RKO, claiming the FALCON was a rip-off of THE SAINT. (See THE FALCON series, Index.)

p, Howard Benedict; d, Irving Reis; w, Lynn Root, Frank Fenton (based on characters created by Michael Arlen); ph, Nicholas Musuraca; m, Paul Sawtell; ed, George Crone; art d, Van Nest Polglase.

Mystery   (PR:A   MPAA:NR)

GAY IMPOSTERS, THE   (SEE: GOLD DIGGERS IN PARIS, 1938)

GAY INTRUDERS, THE*****   (1946, Brit.) 100m
BN/Anglo American bw (MEDAL FOR THE GENERAL)

Godfrey Tearle (*Gen. Victor Church*), Jeanne de Casalis (*Lady Frome*), Morland Graham (*Bates*), John Laurie (*McNab*), Mabel Constanduros (*Mrs. Bates*), Patric Curwen (*Dr. Sargeant*), Michael Lambert (*Lord Ottershaw*), Irene Handl (*Mrs. Farnsworth*), Maureen Glynne ("*Snarrer*"), Gerald Moore (*Harry*), Brian Weske (*Limpy*), Petula Clark (*Irma*), David Trickett (*Bobby*), Pat Geary (*Violet*), Thorley Walters (*Andrew*), Alec Faversham (*Hank*), Rosalyn Boulter (*Billeting Officer*), H. F. Maltby (*Mayor*), Janette Scott.

Released in Britain in 1944, the film is a tour-de-force for Tearle, as a once-jingoistic general—holder of the Victoria Cross—whose WW II services are refused by what he considers an ungrateful government. Resolved to take no interest in the conflict, he retires to his gracious country manor, avoiding newspapers and the wireless and contemplating suicide. His bitter reflections are rudely interrupted when a sextet of cockney tykes is forced upon him, billeted—by circumstance of the war he has tried to ignore—in his home. He and his large domestic staff find the language of the urchins unintelligible and their conduct unbearable, especially that of guttersnipe Moore, the little devil who makes off with his medals. In the end, the unregenerate general is brought back to a reconciliation with the world he thought to leave through an understanding with the kids. With their assistance, he saves a downed and wounded RAF pilot, winning yet another medal in the process.

p, Louis H. Jackson; d, Maurice Elvey; w, Elizabeth Baron (based on the novel by James Ronald); ph, James Wilson, Arthur Grant; ed, Grace Garland.

Drama   (PR:A   MPAA:NR)

GAY INTRUDERS, THE*½**   (1948) 68m FOX bw

John Emery (*John Newberry*), Tamara Geva (*Maria Ivar*), Leif Erickson (*Dr. Harold Matson*), Roy Roberts (*Charles McNulty*), Virginia Gregg (*Dr. Susan Nash*), Si Wills (*Arthur*), Sara Berner (*Ethel*), Harry Lauter (*Male Secretary*), Marilyn Williams (*Female Secretary*).

Two successful theater stars, Emery and Geva, have marital problems offstage. They go to psychiatrists Erickson and Gregg to straighten things out. In the end, the married doctors become the bickering ones as the acting pair reconcile.

p, Frank N. Seltzer; d, Ray McCarey; w, Francis Swann (based on a story by Swann, McCarey); ph, Mack Stengler; m, Ralph Stanley; ed, Bert Jordan; md, David Chudnow; art d, Jerome Pycha, Jr.

Comedy   (PR:A   MPAA:NR)

GAY LADY, THE, 1935   (SEE: LADY TUBBS, 1935)

GAY LADY, THE** (1949, Brit.) 96m TC/GFD c (GB: TROTTIE TRUE)

Jean Kent (*Trottie True*), James Donald (*Lord Digby Landon*), Hugh Sinclair (*Maurice Beckenham*), Lana Morris (*Bouncie Barrington*), Andrew Crawford (*Sid Skinner*), Bill Owen (*Joe Jugg*), Harcourt Williams (*Duke of Wellwater*), Michael Medwin (*Marquis Monty*), Hattie Jacques (*Daisy Delaware*), Joan Young (*Mrs. True*), Heather Thatcher (*Angela Platt-Brown*), Mary Hinton (*Duchess*), Harold Scott (*Mr. True*), Dilys Laye (*Trottie as a Child*), Daphne Anderson (*Bertha*), Carol Lesley (*Clare*), Irene Browne (*Duchess of Wellwater*), Francis de Wolff, Gladys Young, Anthony Halfpenny, Patricia Deane, Shirley Mitchell, David Lines, Campbell Cotts, Elspet Gray, Mary Jones, Ian Carmichael, Christopher Lee, Anthony Steel, Roger Moore, Sam Kydd.

Light-hearted romantic comedy set during the last decade of the nineteenth century centers on the affairs of the heart of Kent as her career advances from small theater bits in London to starring in the best houses. Along the way she

dumps balloonist Crawford, her first admirer and love, for more prominent suitors, eventually marrying a lord. When she becomes nostalgic for the simpler times of her life, Kent goes on a romp with the balloon man, an affair that makes her realize the life she has chosen for herself is really the one she is most content with. Horror film star Christopher Lee and James Bond hero Roger Moore are seen in small roles early in their careers.

p, Hugh Stewart; d, Brian Desmond Hurst; w, C. Denis Freeman (from the play by Caryl Brahms and S.J. Simon); ph, Harry Waxman (Technicolor); m, Benjamin Frankel; ed, Ralph Kemplen; md, Muir Mathieson; art d, Ralph Brinton; set d, Colleen Browning; m/l, Carroll Gibbons.

Drama/Comedy   (PR:A   MPAA:NR)

GAY LOVE**½**   (1936, Brit.) 77m BL/Marcy bw

Florence Desmond (*Gloria Fellowes*), Sophie Tucker (*Herself*), Sydney Fairbrother (*Dukie*), Enid Stamp-Taylor (*Marie Hopkins*), Ivor McLaren (*Lord Tony Eaton*), Garry Marsh (*Freddie Milton*), Leslie Perrins (*Gerald Sparkes*), Ben Welden (*Ben*), Finlay Currie (*Highams*).

The greatest boons to this musical comedy are the talents of impressionist Desmond and irrepressible overweight torcher Tucker, at their very best in a time before the title phrase was expropriated and gained another meaning. The simple story deals with a music-hall actress who, unbeknownst to her fellow-trouper sister, becomes smitten with the sister's titled fiance. Swallowing her amorous secret, she resolves to deal with her dilemma by dropping out. All is made well when the sister rediscovers an old flame, with whom she elopes, leaving the coast clear for the mellifluous martyr. Desmond's impressions of Greta Garbo and Mae West are the high points of this happy hoopla. Released in Britain in 1934.

p, Herbert Smith; d, Leslie Hiscott; w, Charles Bennett, Billie Bristow, John Paddy Carstairs (based on the play by Audrey and Waveney Carton); ph, Alex Bryce, Harry Rose.

Musical/Comedy   (PR:A   MPAA:NR)

GAY NINETIES   (SEE: FLORO DORA GIRL, THE, 1930)

GAY OLD DOG*½**   (1936, Brit.) 62m EM/RKO bw

Edward Rigby (*Tom Bliss*), Moore Marriott (*George Bliss*), Ruby Miller (*Mrs. Vernon*), Marguerite Allan (*Judith*), Annie Esmond (*Mrs. Gambit*), Joan Wyndham (*Betty*), Patrick Barr (*Phillip*), Johnny Singer (*Andrew V. Oakes*), Billy Holland (*Capt. Black*), Vi Kaley, Norman Pierce, Ben Williams.

Dull depiction of the trials and tribulations of two brothers in a small English village. Trouble starts when a husbandless woman with a new-born baby takes refuge in their home. Complications arise when one of the brothers becomes involved with a woman whose only intent is to make off with as much of his cash as possible—which is exactly what she does. Luckily for the man, his brother is around to help him out of the jam. Absent of any life.

p, George King, Randall Faye; d, King; w, Faye (based on the story by Enid Fabia).

Dramatic Comedy   (PR:A   MPAA:NR)

GAY PURR-EE**½**   (1962) 85m UPA/WB c

Voices of: Judy Garland (*Mewsette*), Robert Goulet (*Jaune-Tom*), Red Buttons (*Robespierre*), Hermione Gingold (*Mme. Rubens-Chatte*), Paul Frees (*Meowrice*), Morey Amsterdam, Mel Blanc, Julie Bennett, Joan Gardiner.

The feeble attempt at a pun in the title of this full-length cartoon should give you some sort of indication of the writing level. In the hands of the geniuses at Disney, this might have amounted to something because they backed their visual prowess with strong scripts. This, however, is several cuts below Disney in most departments. Produced by the man who gave us "Mr. Magoo," it is the story of Garland (Mewsette), a country cat who longs for the excitement of Paris. She flees the farm to seek fame and Friskies in the big town. Her presumed lover, Goulet (Jaune-Tom), follows her there with his amusing sidekick, Buttons (Robespierre) to keep an eye on her and make sure she doesn't fall in with bad company. Once in Paris, Garland is catnaped by Frees (Meowrice) who takes her off to Gingold's (Rubens-Chatte) beauty school. They intend to marry her off to some fat cat in Pittsburgh. (Why they chose Pittsburgh is a puzzlement. Perhaps they thought it the funniest-sounding town in the U.S. It may have looked great on paper, but it wasn't funny on film.) Meanwhile, Goulet and Buttons are sent to Alaska by Frees, but they turn the tables and come back rich, paws laden with gold. They get Garland and take her off to live happily ever after and raise lots of kittens. Songs by E.Y. "Yip" Harburg and Harold Arlen include: "Mewsette," "Roses Red-Violets Blue," "Take My Hand, Paree," "The Money Cat," "Little Drops of Rain," "Bubbles," "Paris Is A Lonely Town," "The Horses Won't Talk." And none of them compare to any of the tunes this same pair did for THE WIZARD OF OZ (1939). The artwork was good with the Provence exteriors drawn in a Van Gogh style. One particularly memorable sequence featured the impressionist works of almost a dozen famous artists. The kind of movie that will appeal to a precocious but not too demanding French nine year old. You'll recognize Frees' voice if you've ever been to Southern California, as he is the unofficial voice of Disneyland and can be heard at several park attractions.

p, Henry G. Saperstein; d, Abe Levitow; w, Dorothy and Chuck Jones, Ralph Wright; ph, Roy Hutchcroft, Jack Stevens, Dan Miller, Duane Keegan (Technicolor); ed, Ted Baker, Sam Horta, Earl Bennett; prod d, Edward Levitt, Richard Ung, "Corny" Cole, Ray Aragon, Robert Singer, Ernest Nordli; color stylists, Don Peters, Gloria Wood, Robert Inman, Phil Norman, Richard Kelsey; animators, Fred Madison, Art David, Ken Harris, Ben Washam, Phil Duncan, Hal Ambro, Ray Patterson, Grant Simmons, Irv Spence, Don Lusk, Volus Jones, Harvey Toombs, Hank Smith.

Animated Feature   (PR:AAA   MPAA:NR)

GAY RANCHERO, THE**½ (1948) 72m REP c

Roy Rogers (Himself), Tito Guizar (Nicci Lopez), Jane Frazee (Betty Richards), Andy Devine (Cookie Bullfincher), Estelita Rodriguez (Consuelo Belmonte), George Meeker (Vance Brados), LeRoy Mason (Mike Ritter), Dennis Moore (Tex), Keith Richards (Slim), Betty Gagnon (Reception Clerk), Robert Rose (Breezy), Ken Terrell (Roberts), Bob Nolan and the Sons of the Pioneers, "Trigger."

The clash of the old and new West is the central theme of this Roy Rogers western. Rogers is a horse-riding sheriff after gangsters trying to gain control of an airport by sabotaging the planes. Roy's six-shooters put an end to their doings, but not until after a nasty beating by the gangsters. Songs include Tito Guizar singing "Granada," "You Belong To My Heart," Frazee and Rogers dueting "Wait'll I Get My Sunshine In The Moonlight," and Estelita singing the title song. This was one of eight Rogers pictures—five of them co-starring Frazee—made during a brief hiatus in which Dale Evans was replaced as Rogers' leading lady by other actresses. Studio bosses apparently felt that the public could not be expected to believe that a hero would pursue his own wife so ardently, and the Rogers-Evans nuptials had occurred the previous New Years' Eve. (See ROY ROGERS series, Index.)

p, Edward J. White; d, William Witney; w, Sloan Nibley; ph, Jack Marta (Trucolor); ed, Tony Martinelli; md, Morton Scott; art d, Frank Hotaling; m/l, Abe Tuvim, Francia Luban, J.J. Espinosa, Harry Glick, Jimmy Lambert, Dave Olsen, Augstin Lara, Ray Gilbert.

Western   Cas.   (PR:A MPAA:NR)

GAY SENORITA, THE** (1945) 69m COL bw

Jinx Falkenburg, Jim Bannon, Steve Cochran, Corinna Mura, Isabelita, Thurston Hall, Isabel Withers, Marguerita Sylva, Lusite Triana, Lola Mentes, Tommy Cook, Nina Bara, Leander de Cordova, Antonio Triama.

Enterprising young Bannon is given a heavy dosage of love from Falkenburg squelching his plan to drive the inhabitants of the Mexican portion of a California town out to make room for business developments. Breezy bit of entertainment.

p, Jay Gorney; d, Arthur Dreifuss; w, Edward Eliscu (based on a story by J. Robert Bren); ph, Burnett Guffey; ed, Al Clark; art d, Jerome Pycha; ch, Antonio Triana; m/l "Buenos Noches," Don George, Serge Walters.

Musical/Drama   (PR:A MPAA:NR)

GAY SISTERS, THE*½ (1942) 108m FN-WB bw

Barbara Stanwyck (Fiona Gaylord), George Brent (Charles Barclay), Geraldine Fitzgerald (Evelyn Gaylord), Donald Crisp (Ralph Pedloch), Gig Young [Byron Barr] (Gig Young), Nancy Coleman (Susanna Gaylord), Gene Lockhart (Herschell Gibbon), Larry Simms (Austin), Donald Woods (Penn Sutherland Gaylord), Grant Mitchell (Gilbert Wheeler), William T. Orr (Dick Tone), Anne Revere (Ida Orner), Helene Thimig (Saskia), George Lessey (Judge Barrows), Charles D. Waldron (Mr. Van Rennseler), Frank Reicher (Dr. Bigelow), David Clyde (Benson), Mary Thomas (Fiona at Age Eight), Edward McNamara (Policeman), Dorothea Wolbert (Woman), Virgil Cain (Mr. Keith), Carol Joyce Combes (Evelyn as a Child), Charlene Salerno (Susanna as a Child), Harry C. Bradley (Clerk), Ray Montgomery (Joe), Joseph Crehan (City Editor), Joan Winfield (Receptionist), George Meeker (Clerk), Charles Drake (First Clerk), Bill Edwards (Second Clerk), Vera Lewis (First Woman), Flo Promis (Second Woman), Jack Mower (Court Attendant), Murray Alper (Elevator Operator), Hobart Bosworth (Clergyman), Creighton Hale (Simmons), Claire Du Brey (Matron), Inez Palange, Walter Brooke, Hank Mann, Garry Owen, Sarah Edwards, Erville Alderson, Fern Emmett, Mary Field, Frank Darien, George Haywood.

THE GAY SISTERS was anything but that. A long, boring, and gray, rather than gay, story. Stanwyck, Coleman, and Fitzgerald are left motherless when their mom goes down on the Lusitania. Their father is also killed in France, and they must now oversee their huge Fifth Avenue mansion on their own. Stanwyck married Brent in order to get an inheritance from her aunt, and Brent, a real-estate developer, now wants to get his hands on the family's mansion in order to raze it and build a huge complex. (Note: There is a real parallel here as the Vanderbilts of Fifth Avenue were prevailed upon by the Rockefellers to sell their property to make way for Radio City and Rockefeller Center.) Stanwyck and Brent were married years before and she's kept that a secret. She begins a personal campaign against Brent and vows to "never sell the land." Big buildings soon surround the house. Brent wants revenge for her having walked out on him and neglecting to tell him that he fathered a son during their marriage. Several court scenes take up the middle of the film and the whole thing leaves a sour taste in the mouth. Fitzgerald conveniently marries a duke and Coleman winds up with Gig Young, whose character name is the same as his real one. Young, born Byron Barr (he also used the pseudonym Bryant Fleming), took his name from the role he played. He died by his own hand in 1978 after, police theorized, he murdered his wife of three weeks in their New York apartment. His last film, released after his suicide, was THE GAME OF DEATH (1979), an ironic note. Stephen Longstreet, who wrote the novel Coffee's screenplay was based upon, is also a superb graphic artist who specializes in works of famous faces.

p, Henry Blanke; d, Irving Rapper; w, Lenore Coffee (based on novel by Stephen Longstreet); ph, Sol Polito; m, Max Steiner; ed, Warren Low; md, Leo F. Forbstein; art d, Robert Haas; cos, Edith Head; makeup, Perc Westmore.

Drama   (PR:A-C MPAA:NR)

GAY VAGABOND, THE*½ (1941) 66m REP bw

Roscoe Karns (Arthur Dixon/Jerry Dixon), Ruth Donnelly (Kate Dixon), Ernest Truex (A.J. Wilbur), Margaret Hamilton (Agatha Badger), Abner Biberman (Ratmar), Bernadene Hayes (Spring Rutherford), Lynn Merrick (Betty Dixon), Rod Bacon (Franklin Atwater), Gloria Franklin (Sonya), Carol Adams (Lucille), Byron Foulger (Vogel), Paul Newlan (Lobang).

Karns plays a dual role of small-town twin brothers. One is the meek, reclusive type and the other is a skirt-chasing adventurer returning from China. The two get

mixed up, causing a few laughs. A near-reprise of the roles played by Karns and Donnelly in Republic's HIGGINS FAMILY series, roles they had inherited from their originators, James and Lucille Gleason. (See HIGGINS FAMILY series, Index.)

p, Robert North; d, William Morgan; w, Ewart Adamson, Taylor Caven; ph, Bud Thackery; m, Cy Feuer; ed, Howard O'Neill; art d, John Victor Mackay.

Comedy   (PR:A MPAA:NR)

GAZEBO, THE*** (1959) 102m Avon/MGM bw

Glenn Ford (Elliott Nash), Debbie Reynolds (Nell Nash), Carl Reiner (Harlow Edison), John McGiver (Sam Thorpe), Mabel Albertson (Mrs. Chandler), Doro Merande (Matilda), Bert Freed (Lt. Joe Jenkins), Martin Landau (The Duke), Robert Ellenstein (Ben), Richard Wessell (Louis the Louse), Herman (The Pigeon).

Ford is a television writer married to Broadway star Reynolds in this amusing black comedy. A blackmailer shows up with pictures of an unclothed Reynolds, posed during her leaner days (financially, not physically). Ford decides that murder is the only way to take care of the situation. He hides the body where his new gazebo is to be placed. But it turns out that the blackmailer is found dead somewhere else, and Ford doesn't know who is buried in the back yard. Reynolds sings "Something Called Love," Walter Kent, Walton Farrar.

p, Lawrence Weingarten; d, George Marshall; w, George Wells (based on a play by Alec Coppel from a story by Myra and Alec Coppel); ph, Paul C. Vogel; m, Jeff Alexander; ed, Adrienne Fazan; art d, George W. Davis, Paul Groesse; cos, Helen Rose.

Comedy   (PR:A MPAA:NR)

GEEK MAGGOT BINGO zero (1983) 73m Weirdo Films c
(AKA: THE FREAK FROM SUCKWEASEL MOUNTAIN)

Robert Andrews (Dr. Frankenberry), Brenda Bergman (Buffy), Richard Hell (The Rawhide Kid), Donna Death (Scumbalina), Zacherle (Host), Bruno Zeus (Geeko), Gumby Sangler (Flavian), Jim Giacama (Dean Quagmire), Robert Martin (Street Hawker), Bob Elkin (Victim), Tyler Smith (Formaldehyde Man).

A nothing little zit of a 16mm movie which attempts to make fun of horror pictures, but instead makes fun of technical Renaissance man Nick Zedd. Andrews plays Dr. Frankenberry, a mad scientist who devotes his existence to chemosynthetic regeneration—bringing dead tissue back to life. The film tries too hard to be camp, constantly reminding us how funny it should be. In a rather dumb role as The Rawhide Kid is Richard Hell, the punk-rock leader of the Voidoids, who also appeared in SMITHEREENS (1982), a role in which he displayed even less talent. Is this what happens when parents give their kids extra cash?

p,d&w, Nick Zedd (based on a story by Robert Kirkpatrick, Zedd); ph,ed&prod d, Zedd; set d, Zedd, Donna Death; spec eff, Tyler Smith, Ed French.

Horror/Satire   (PR:O MPAA:NR)

GEHEIMINISSE IN GOLDEN NYLONS
(SEE: DEAD RUN, 1969, Fr./Ital./Ger.)

GEISHA, A*** (1978, Jap.) 87m Daiei/New Yorker Films bw
(GIONBAYASHI; AKA: GION MUSIC)

Michiyo Kogure (Miyoharu), Ayako Wakao (Eiko), Seizaburo Kawazy (Kusada), Chieko Naniwa (Okimi), Eitaro Shindo (Sawamoto), Mikio Koshiba (Kanzaki), Ichiro Sugai (Saeki), Haruo Tanaka (Ogawa).

Originally made in 1953, A GEISHA did not make its way to the U.S. until 1978, and, like the majority of Mizoguchi's work, has remained virtually unknown to American filmgoers. A thoughtful and subtle look at the changes going on in Japanese social attitudes, the film examines the friendship between two geishas, upholders of that ancient Japanese art that lost a lot of dignity as a result of WW II. Kogure plays the passive elderly geisha who has agreed to train the young Wakao in the secrets of her art, but when the younger woman's romantic vision of her role proves a far cry from reality, she opts out. Much of the focus is placed on the developing relationship between the two women, as their combined recognition of what the geisha has degenerated into becomes a force that binds them together. The younger Wakao has the choice of changing her direction, while Korgure is forced to remain with the only thing she knows.

d, Kenji Mizoguchi; w, Yoshikata Yoda (based on a story by Matsutaro Kawaguchi); ph, Kazuo Miyagawa; m, Ichiro Saito; ed, Mitsuzo Miyata; art d, Kazumi Koike.

Drama   (PR:A MPAA:NR)

GEISHA BOY, THE*** (1958) 95m PAR c

Jerry Lewis (Gilbert Wooley), Marie McDonald (Lois Livingston), Sessue Hayakawa (Mr. Sikita), Barton MacLane (Maj. Ridgley), Suzanne Pleshette (Put. Betty Pearson), Nobu McCarthy (Kimi Sikita), Robert Hirano (Mitsuo Watanabe), Ryuzo Demura (Ichiyama), Harry Hare (Himself), The Los Angeles Dodgers.

Lewis found the most success when Tashlin was directing, and THE GEISHA BOY is a perfect example. A zany comedy with Lewis as an unsuccessful magician who takes a job with a USO tour show in the Orient. He gets into situations with McDonald, the troupe's headliner, and with MacLane, an officer who can't wait for his own funeral because he loves "Taps." In Japan, Lewis falls in love with a Japanese widow, McCarthy, and her son adopts him. Plenty of sight gags, parodies, and physical comedy that work well, thanks to Lewis' timing and Tashlin's writing and strong direction.

p, Jerry Lewis; d&w, Frank Tashlin (based on a story by Rudy Makoul); ph, Haskell Boggs (VistaVision, Technicolor); m, Walter Scharf; ed, Alma Macrorie; art d, Tambi Larsen, Hal Pereira; set d, Sam Comer, Robert Benton; cos, Edith Head.

Comedy   (PR:A MPAA:NR)

GEISHA GIRL*½ (1952) 67m REA bw

Martha Hyer *(Peggy Burns)*, William Andrews *(Rocky Wilson)*, Archer MacDonald *(Archie)*, Kekao Yokoo *(Zoro)*, Teddy Nakamura *(Nakamura)*, Henry Okawa *(Police Inspector)*, Tatsuo Saito *(Professor)*, Michiyo Naoki *(Michiko)*, Ikio Suwamura *(Fumi)*, Ralph Nagara *(Betto)*, Shinzo Takada *(Tanaka)*, Pearl Hamada *(Stripteaser)*.

Andrews and MacDonald are soldiers on their way home from Korea, stopping in Japan enroute. They meet stewardess Hyer and break up a Japanese ring that has developed explosive pills to use for sabotage. Hyer turns out to be a detective who has been tracking the gang for months. A low-budget trip via the screen through Tokyo.

p&d, George Breakston, C. Ray Stahl; w, Stahl; ph, Ichiro Hoshijima; m, Albert Glasser; ed, Irving Schoenberg.

Drama **(PR:A MPAA:NR)**

GELIEBTE BESTIE (SEE: HIPPODROME, 1961, Ger.)

GELIGNITE GANG (SEE: DYNAMITERS, THE, 1956, Brit.)

GEN TO FUDO-MYOH (SEE: YOUTH AND HIS AMULET, THE, 1963, Jap.)

GENDARME OF ST. TROPEZ, THE* (1966, Fr./Ital.) 93m S.N.C.-Franca/Magna c (LE GENDARME DE SAINT-TROPEZ; UNA RAGAZZA A SAINT TROPEZ)

Louis de Funes *(Ludovic Cruchot)*, Genevieve Grad *(Nicole Cruchot)*, Michel Galabru *(Gerber)*, Jean Lefebvre *(Fougasse)*, Christian Marin *(Merlot)*, Daniel Cauchy *(Richard)*, Jean-Paul Bertrand *(Eddie)*, Franck Vilcour *(Jean-Luc)*, Maria Pacome, Pierre Barouh, Claude Pieplu, Jacques Famery, Madeleine Delavaivre, Martine de Breteuil, France Rumilly, Patrice Laffont, Fernand Sardou, Gabriele Tinti, Giuseppe Porelli, Michelle Wargnier, Norma Dugo.

A lame French-Italian coproduction about a new police sergeant who pays a visit to the French resort town of St. Tropez with his lovely daughter, Grad. He takes his new-found power too seriously and tries to round up a number of beach nudists. Grad, meanwhile, has made up a story that her father is a millionaire yachtsman. She gets mixed up with criminals who lift a priceless Rembrandt from a local museum. The spunky gendarme saves the day, the painting, and his daughter.

p, Rene Pigneres, Gerard Beytout; d, Jean Girault; w, Richard Balducci, Jacques Vilfrid, Girault (based on the story by Balducci); ph, Marc Fossard (Dyaliscope, Eastmancolor); m, Raymond Lefevre; ed, Jean-Michel Gautier, Jean Feyte; art d, Sidney Bettex.

Comedy **(PR:O MPAA:NR)**

GENE AUTRY AND THE MOUNTIES½** (1951) 70m COL bw

Gene Autry *(Gene Autry)*, Pat Buttram *(Scat Russell)*, Elena Verdugo *(Marie Duval)*, Carleton Young *(Pierre LaBlond)*, Richard Emory *(Terry Dillon)*, Herbert Rawlinson *(Inspector Wingate)*, Trevor Bardette *(Raoul Duval)*, Francis McDonald *(Batiste)*, Jim Frasher *(Jack Duval)*, Gregg Barton *(Sgt. Stuart)*, House Peters, Jr. *(Hogan)*, Jody Gilbert *(Squaw)*, Nolan Leary *(Dr. Sawyer)*, Boyd Stockman, Bruce Carruthers, Robert Hilton, Teddy Infuhr, Billy Gray, John R. McKee, Roy Butler, Steven Elliott, Chris Allen, Champion, Jr. the Horse.

Another fun to watch Autry film with Gene and Buttram Montana marshals on the trail of a bank-robbing gang. The marshals enlist the help of the Mounties when the bad guys cross the U.S.-Canada border. The gang leader is killed in a fire that almost destroys a whole town. One of the better films in the Autry series as the hero continues to sing and philosophize his way aross the ever-varying landscapes. Verdugo went on to be a busy TV performer, her most prominent role being that of a nurse on "Marcus Welby," starring Robert Young. Billy Gray also went on to TV fame on "Father Know Best," starring—you guessed it—Robert Young. (See GENE AUTRY series, Index.)

p, Armand Schaefer; d, John English; w, Norman S. Hall; ph, William Bradford; m, Mischa Bakaleinikoff; ed, James Sweeney; art d, Charles Clague; m/l, "Blue Canadian Rockies" (Cindy Walker); "Anetora" (Doris Anderson, Gene Andrea, sung by Autry); "Love's Ritorneall" (sung by Verdugo).

Western **(PR:A MPAA:NR)**

GENE KRUPA STORY, THE½** (1959) 102m COL bw (GB: DRUM CRAZY)

Sal Mineo *(Gene Krupa)*, Susan Kohner *(Ethel Maguire)*, James Darren *(Eddie Sirota)*, Susan Oliver *(Dorissa Dinell)*, Yvonne Craig *(Gloria Corregio)*, Lawrence Dobkin *(Speaker Willis)*, Celia Lovsky *(Mother)*, Red Nichols *(Himself)*, Bobby Troup *(Tommy Dorsey)*, Anita O'Day *(Herself)*, Ruby Lane *(Blues Singer)*, Gavin McLeod *(Ted Krupa)*, John Bleifer *(Father)*, Shelley Manne *(Davey Tough)*, Buddy Lester *(Himself)*.

Sal Mineo was far too young and the direction far too pedestrian to make this anything but an ordinary filmography of an extraordinary musician. Krupa was a heavy drinker and a well-known pot smoker so there was plenty of room for fireworks in his exciting life. It is true-to-life, but the reading of newspaper accounts are more interesting than the film. Krupa's father wanted him to be a priest, but he chose music instead. He loses Kohner, his childhood sweetheart, then gets involved with a "bad" girl, Oliver. The best parts of the movie are the songs and the performances by the stars who play themselves; O'Day, Nichols, and Buddy Lester. In a small role as Mineo's dad is Gavin McLeod, of "Love Boat" fame. Yvonne Craig, who went on to become TV's "Bat Girl" registers strongly as a youthful nymphet. Although Mineo is seen at the skins, it is Krupa recording the drum work that puts a driving beat behind the picture's score. Musical numbers: "I Love My Baby" (Bud Green, Harry Warren; sung by Lane); "Memories of You" (Eubie Blake, Andy Razaf; sung by O'Day); "Royal Garden Blues" (Spencer Williams, Clarence Williams, played by Krupa Orchestra); "Cherokee" (Ray Noble; Krupa Orchestra); "Indiana" (Ballard MacDonald, James Hanley; Krupa Orchestra, Nichols); "Way Down Yonder In New Orleans" (Henry Creamer, J. Turner Layton; Krupa Orchestra); "Let There Be Love" (Ian Grant, Lionel Rand; Darren); "Song of India" (Rimsky-Korsakov); "Drum Crazy," "Spiritual Jazz."

p, Philip A. Waxman; d, Don Weis; w, Orin Jannings; ph, Charles Lawton, Jr.; m, Leith Stevens; ed, Maurice Wright, Edwin Bryant; art d, Robert Peterson.

Biography **(PR:A-C MPAA:NR)**

GENERAL CRACK** (1929) 97m WB bw/c

John Barrymore *(Prince Christian/Gen. Crack/Duke of Kurland)*, Lowell Sherman *(Leopold II)*, Marian Nixon *(Archduchess)*, Armida *(Fidelia)*, Hobart Bosworth *(Count Hensdorff)*, Jacqueline Logan *(Countess Carola)*, Otto Matieson *(Col. Gabor)*, Andrea de Segurola *(Col. Pons)*, Douglas Gerrard *(Capt. Sweeney)*, William von Brincken *(Capt. Schimdt)*, Theodore Lodi *(Capt. Banning)*, Nick Thompson *(Gypsy Chieftain)*, Julanne Johnston *(Court Lady)*, Gus Schacht *(Pietro)*, Curt Rehfeld *(Lt. Dennis)*, Mme. Daumery *(Mme. Frump)*.

This was the Great Profile's first all-talking picture and a good example of how they misused matinee idols in those days. He was still slim enough to look good in costumes and they decked him out well in doublet and hose. Barrymore plays a military mercenary who will hire himself and his cadre of cutthroats out to the highest bidder. In this case, he's employed by the Austrian Emperor, Sherman, and must secure the crown of the Holy Roman Empire. Along the way, Barrymore, who is married to a gypsy (Armida), marches off to war and leaves his wife behind in Vienna. Sherman goes after the woman while Barrymore is off fighting, infuriating Barrymore. In what seems like just a few minutes, Barrymore and some of his men win the war and get back in time for him to dethrone Sherman. Not a terrific movie and notable only for the use of Technicolor in a coronation scene. Expensive but basically shallow vehicle for the handsome heartthrob.

d, Alan Crosland; w, J. Grubb Alexander (based on an adaptation by Walter Anthony of a dramatization by Thomas Broadhurst of a story by George Preddy); ph, Tony Gaudio; ed, Harold McLernon.

Historical Drama **(PR:A-C MPAA:NR)**

GENERAL DIED AT DAWN, THE*½** (1936) 97m PAR bw

Gary Cooper *(O'Hara)*, Madeleine Carroll *(Judy Perrie)*, Akim Tamiroff *(Gen. Yang)*, Dudley Digges *(Mr. Wu)*, Porter Hall *(Peter Perrie)*, William Frawley *(Brighton)*, J. M. Kerrigan *(Leach)*, Philip Ahn *(Oxford)*, Lee Tung Foo *(Mr. Chen)*, Leonid Kinskey *(Stewart)*, Val Duran *(Wong)*, Walter Wong, Willie Fung *(Bartenders)*, Hans Fuerberg *(Yang's Military Advisor)*, Sarah Edwards, Paul Harvey *(American Couple)*, Spencer Chan *(Killer)*, Harold Tong, Charles Leong, Thomas Chan, Harry Yip, Swan Yee, Kam Tong *(House Boys)*, Frank Young *(Clerk)*, Carol DeCastro *(Clerk)*, Barnett Parker *(Englishman)*, Hans Von Morhart *(Mandarin)*, Dudley Lee, Walter Lem, Thomas Lee, George Wong Wah *(Waiters on Train)*, Tom Ung *(Steward on Train)*, Taft Jung, Sam Laborador, Richard Young, Jung Kai, Harry Leong, Chan Suey, Paul Tom, Loo Loy, Quon Gong, Wong Fong, Leo Abbey, Bob Jowe *(Guards)*, George Chan *(Porter)*, Clifford Odets, John O'Hara, Sidney Skolsky, Lewis Milestone *(Reporters)*.

An exotic adventure story sees Cooper as an American soldier of fortune in the Northern provinces of China during the days when many warlords terrorized China, controlling districts as fiefdoms and draining them of money, land, and goods. The worst of these is Tamiroff, a cunning, savage bandit chief who, with his 12 top aides, intends to take over the entire country, each of the aides slated to rule one of China's 12 provinces. Cooper despises Tamiroff and his plug-uglies and works against them, agreeing to smuggle gold to Shanghai where he will buy ammunition and arms to supply a peasant uprising against Tamiroff and company. In Pengwa, Cooper waits to fly to Shanghai after meeting revolt leader Diggs. Ahn, chief henchman of Tamiroff, tries to assassinate Cooper, but Cooper survives. The assassin then hires destitute and cowardly American Hall, who is to engineer Cooper on board a train en route to Shanghai. When he fails, Hall inveigles his beautiful daughter, Carroll, into luring the adventurer onto the train. Here Cooper romances Carroll, meets a bunch of wise-cracking newsmen, and, after Tamiroff's troops stop the train, is abducted. The gold he is carrying is turned over to avaricious Hall to take to Shanghai, but Hall intends to keep it for himself. Cooper, who manages to escape Tamiroff's guards, goes to Shanghai and, while recouping the gold, kills Hall in self-defense, an act Carroll cannot forgive, even though she is in love with Cooper. Both are again captured by Tamiroff's men and taken on board his huge junk in the harbor. Also on board is drunken gunrunner Frawley, from whom Cooper was to purchase arms for the rebels. Frawley becomes so obstreperous, stabbing Tamiroff, that he is shot to death. Then the fatally wounded Tamiroff orders both Cooper and Carroll executed, but Cooper devises a clever scheme whereby he and his lady love are set free and Tamiroff, to test the loyalty of his followers, orders his henchmen to commit mass suicide. They do, dying out of blind loyalty to him just as he himself dies. It's a thick melodrama but loaded with action and bizarre scenes, mostly proving how Occidental logic outdoes Oriental inscrutability. All of Milestone's directorial devices, the dolly and pan shots, the boom shots to encompass large masses of people, are incorporated in this absorbing but considerably dated film. The script is tight, witty, and ingenious, the first screenplay of budding playwright Odets. The playwright rounded up some of his literary pals who partied with Milestone and three of them, Odets, Hollywood gossip columnist Sidney Skolsky, and novelist John O'Hara, along with Milestone, appear in one scene—paid the $5-a-day extra fee—as foreign correspondents traveling on the train which carries Cooper and Carroll into Tamiroff's jeopardy. O'Hara, at the time, was trying to break into films as a screenwriter and was delighted to appear in the film. He has one line, delivered to Cooper in the rumbling dining car, saying: "Oh, hello, O'Hara." Cooper, whose name was O'Hara in the movie, muffed his response line so many times that Milestone took him aside and asked him why he was so bothered. Replied Cooper: "That's wrong. He can't call *me* O'Hara. *His* name's O'Hara." Director Milestone would then patiently explain that "we've been shooting this picture for 43 days, and all that time you've been O'Hara, remember?" It was a while before Cooper got it right. THE GENERAL DIED AT DAWN is similar in story and production values to SHANGHAI EXPRESS, but Carroll is less of a trampy vamp than Marlene Dietrich. (Carroll replaced Merle Oberon who had commitments elsewhere.) The British actress had an up-and-down career through programmers and major films during the 1930's, until appearing in THE PRISONER OF ZENDA (1937), Hitchcock's SECRET AGENT (1936) and, most notably, THE 39 STEPS (1935), the latter offering Carroll a role as mysterious as that in THE GENERAL DIED AT DAWN. These were the films that established her fame as the most beautiful blonde in 1930s movies. Where Cooper is the perfect resolute hero, Tamiroff is the best possible villain, vainglorious, crude, rapacious, wise in his search for power. Hall gives his usual good rendition of a weak-willed and unscrupulous person, while Frawley is absolutely and engrossingly reckless, insulting, and violent, one of the greatest early portraits of the "ugly American" on record. Milner's artfully lit camera work brought an Oscar nomination, as did Janssen's score and Tamiroff's part, the latter for the first Academy Award for a supporting role. Others in the running in this newly created category were Mischa Auer for MY MAN GODFREY, Stuart Erwin for PIGSKIN PARADE, Basil Rathbone for ROMEO AND JULIET and Walter Brennan who took the Oscar for COME AND GET IT; Brennan would take another Academy Award for Supporting Actor two years later for KENTUCKY and then win an unprecedented third Oscar in the same category in 1940 for his crusty role as Judge Roy Bean in THE WESTERNER.

p, William Le Baron; d, Lewis Milestone; w, Clifford Odets (based on a novel by Charles G. Booth); ph, Victor Milner; m, Werner Janssen; ed, Eda Warren; md, Boris Morros; art d, Hans Dreier, Ernst Fegto; cos, Travis Banton; spec eff, Gordon Jennings, Arthur Smith.

Adventure   **(PR:C   MPAA:NR)**

GENERAL JOHN REGAN**   (1933, Brit.) 74m
                                                       British & Dominions/UA bw

Henry Edwards (Dr. O'Grady), Chrissie White (Moya Kent), Ben Welden (Billing), Pegeen Mair (Mary Ellen), David Horne (Maj. Kent), W.G. Fay (Golligher), Fred O'Donovan (Doyle), Denis O'Neil (Kerrigan), Eugene Leahy (Sgt. Colgan), George Callaghan (Moriarty), Mary O'Farrell (Mrs. Gregg).

A friendly, wholesome comedy featuring Edwards as a wily Irishman who pulls out the stops, while inventing a character that might make headlines. His goal: to create a celebrity to foist on a visiting American newspaper publisher, bringing notoriety to his small town, Ballymoy. Edwards, the darling of England in the days of the silents, married his co-star Chrissie White in the 1920s, and she appears here in her last film role.

p, Herbert Wilcox; d, Henry Edwards; w, Lenox Robinson (based on the play by George A. Birmingham); ph, Cyril Bristow, G. F. Stegmann.

Comedy   **(PR:A MPAA:NR)**

GENERAL MASSACRE**   (1973, U.S./Bel.) 90m Burr Jerger c

Burr Jerger (Gen. Massacre), Christine Gish (Daughter), Tiffany Tate (Wife), Tsai (Corporal), Al Grundy (Lieutenant), Guy Williams (General, as a Young Man).

This one-man show for producer-writer-director-actor Jerger focuses on an army general (played by Jerger) who carries the ethics of war to an almost absurd extreme. Jerger seems to take his position much too seriously, using the morals developed in the military to approach civilian life. Plot centers around his stay in Belgium while waiting for his trial on the killing of innocent civilians in Viet Nam. Flashbacks show Jerger catching his wife in an affair and then killing her. He does the same thing to his daughter when he finds her with his orderly, who then murders Jerger in retaliation. Though Viet Nam is the setting for much of the film, GENERAL MASSACRE is not another criticism of that war, but of the sadistic personality that thrives on violence and war. The thrust is psychological, but unfortunately Jerger is never able to express the complexities beneath the surface of his character.

p&d, Burr Jerger; w, Jerger, Herman Wuyts; ph&ed, Wuyts (Gevacolor).

War/Drama   **(PR:O MPAA:NR)**

GENERAL SPANKY**½   (1937) 73m MGM bw

Spanky McFarland (Spanky), Phillips Holmes (Marshall Valient), Ralph Morgan (Yankee General), Irving Pichel (Simmons), Rosina Lawrence (Louella), Billie Thomas (Buckwheat), Carl Switzer (Alfalfa), Hobart Bosworth (Col. Blanchard), Robert Middlemass (Overseer), James Burtis (Boat Captain), Louise Beavers (Cornelia), William Best (Henry).

After his plantation-owner boss, the elegant Holmes, goes off to fight in the Civil War, "Our Gang's" Spanky rounds up his pals and takes up the Confederate cause. Together with Alfalfa (Switzer), and Buckwheat (Thomas), they outwit some bumbling Yankee soldiers and save Holmes from the firing squad, thanks to kindly Yankee general Morgan. Switzer sings a rousing rendition of "Just Before the Battle, Mother." GENERAL SPANKY was an attempt to have the "gang" joke, make faces, and slam-bang their way through a full-length feature film after hundreds of one and two-reelers since the series was born in 1921. The reception, however, was so lukewarm that no other feature film of the "gang" was ever made.

p, Hal Roach; d, Fred Newmeyer, Gordon Douglas; w, Richard Flournoy, Hal Yates, John Guedel; ph, Art Lloyd, Walter Lundin; m, Marvin Hatley; ed, Ray Snyder.

Comedy   **(PR:AA MPAA:NR)**

GENERAL SUVOROV***   (1941, USSR) 90m Mosfilm/Artkino bw
                                                                  (SUVOROV)

N.P. Cherkasov-Sergeyev (Gen. Suvorov), A. Yachnitsky (Paul I), M. Astangov (Arakcheyev), S. Kiligin (Bagration), V. Aksenov (Meshcherski), A. Khanov (Platonich), G. Kovrov (Prokhor), A. Antonov (Tiurin).

Soviet director V.I. Pudovkin (MOTHER) expertly cast Nikolai Cherkasov-Sergeyev, a minor actor in his mid-sixties, in the title role. The emphasis of the saga is placed on Suvorov's victories over Napoleon, and his antagonistic relations with Czar Paul I. The film led up to a risky crossing of the Alps which the elderly actor met with enthusiasm. Jay Leyda wrote in his Kino of Sergeyev's acceptance of danger " . . . as he rides along the precipice (he) shows his soldiers a great snow-covered peak ahead, and shouts back to them—'Well, brothers, there's a hill for us to jump over!' " (In Russian; English subtitles.)

d, V.I. Pudovkin, Mikhail Doller; w, G. Grebner, H. Ravich; ph, A. Golovnya, T. Lobova; m, Yuri Shaporin; set d, V. Yegorov, K. Yefimov.

Biography/Drama   **(PR:A   MPAA:NR)**

GENERALE DELLA ROVERE***½ (1960, Ital./Fr.) 160m Zebra-GAU/
                                                  Continental bw (IL GENERALE DELLA-ROVERE)

Vittorio De Sica (Bardone/Grimaldi), Hans Messemer (Col. Mueller), Vittorio Caprioli (Banchelli), Giuseppe Rossetti (Fabrizio/Pietro Valeri), Sandra Milo (Olga), Giovanna Ralli (Valeria), Anne Vernon (Mrs. Fassio), Baronessa Barzani (Contessa della Rovere), Kurt Polter (German Officer), Kurt Selge (Schrantz), Mary Greco (The Madam), Lucia Modugno (The Prostitute), Linda Veras (German Attendant).

De Sica is an Italian black marketeer during WW II. The Nazis force him to go undercover in Milan's San Vittore jail, posing as an Italian general to find out who the resistance leaders are. In prison, he slowly identifies spiritually with the role he is playing and soon the men look up to him for comfort and guidance. This essentially dooms him, for he decides not to betray the rebel leaders and is summarily executed by the Germans in a powerful climax to a powerful film by the director of OPEN CITY. (In Italian; English subtitles.)

p, Morris Ergas; d, Roberto Rossellini; w, Sergio Amidei, Diego Fabri, Indro Montanelli (based on a novel by Montanelli); ph, Carlo Carlini; m, Renzo Rossellini, Jr.; art d, Piero Zuffi.

Drama   **(PR:C   MPAA:NR)**

GENERALS OF TOMORROW   (SEE: TOUCHDOWN ARMY, 1938)

GENERALS WITHOUT BUTTONS**½   (1938, Fr.) 80m Forester-
                                                             Parant/Mayer-Burnstyn bw

Jean Murat (Jean Delcourt), Claude May (Aline Sorbier), Saturnin Fabre (Simon), Serge Grave (Lebrac), Marcel Mouloudji (La Crique), Jacques Tavoli (Aztec), Rognoni (Father of Lebrac), Bouzauquet (Gaspard), Caliman (Father of Gibus), Vera Phares (Marie Tintin), Clairette Founier (Tavie), Ginette Marbeauf (A Kid).

Adults in two rival towns whose families have been feuding for centuries resume the brawling, leaving a bitter impression on the town's children. The senselessness of their quarreling raises questions in their minds about peace in the future. It is amusing to see the youngsters' viewpoints, who appear more intelligent than their parents. The novel the picture was based on won the prestigious Goncourt Prize for literature in France. (In French; English subtitles.)

d, Jacques Daroy; w, Jacques Maury (based on the novel La Guerre Des Boutons by Louis Pergaud); m, Wal-Berg.

Satire   **(PR:A   MPAA:NR)**

GENERATION*½   (1969) 104m AE c (GB: A TIME FOR GIVING)

David Janssen (Jim Bolton), Kim Darby (Doris Bolton Owen), Peter Duel (Walter Owen), Carl Reiner (Stan Herman), Andrew Prine (Winn Garand), James Coco (Mr. Blatto), Sam Waterston (Desmond), David Lewis (Arlington), Don Beddoe (Gilbert), Jack Somack (Airline Policeman), Lincoln Kilpatrick (Hey Hey).

Geared toward young adults, this artificially sweetened and supposedly humorous look at a couple's home pregnancy is pointless and self-important. Janssen is nowhere near as defined in his character as Henry Fonda, who played the role on stage. He is cast as the father of an anti-establishment lass who has decided to have her baby delivered in a Greenwich Village loft. Necessity, however, forces her and her husband to call in a doctor, humorously played by Carl Reiner. On par with any one of many average made-for-TV movies.

p, Frederick Brisson; d, George Schaefer; w, William Goodhart (based on the play by Goodhart); ph, Lionel Linden (Technicolor); m, Dave Grusin; ed, James Heckert; prod d, Robert E. Smith; set d, Hoyle Barrett; cos, Noel Taylor; m/l, "Generation," Dino Fekaris, Nick Zesses, Bea Verdi (sung by Rare Earth).

Comedy   **(PR:C   MPAA:M)**

GENEVIEVE***½   (1953, Brit.) 86m Sirius/UNIV c

John Gregson (Alan McKim), Dinah Sheridan (Wendy McKim), Kenneth More (Ambrose Claverhouse), Kay Kendall (Rosalind Peters), Geoffrey Keen (1st Speed Cop), Harold Siddons (2nd Speed Cop), Reginald Beckwith (J.C. Callahan), Arthur Wontner (Elderly Gentleman), Joyce Grenfell (Hotel Proprietress), Leslie Mitchell (Himself), Michael Medwin (Husband), Michael Balfour (Conductor), Edie Martin (Guest).

A wonderful British comedy about two couples, classic car enthusiasts, who participate in the annual London-to-Brighton rally. The title comes from the 1904 roadster owned by Gregson and Sheridan who, on the return trip, challenge their friends, More and Kendall, to a friendly race. Their playfulness becomes increasingly intense as they speed to the Westminster Bridge finish line. A joy to watch. Picked as the Best British Film of the year.

p&d, Henry Cornelius; w, William Rose; ph, Christopher Challis (Technicolor); m, Larry Adler; ed, Clive Donner; ch, Eric Rogers; harmonica theme played by Adler.

Comedy   Cas.   (PR:A MPAA:NR)

GENGHIS KHAN**½   (U.S./Brit./Ger./Yugo.) (1965) 124m COL c
                                        (DSCHINGIS KHAN: DZINGIS-KAN)

Stephen Boyd (*Jamuga*), Omar Sharif (*Temulin-Genghis Khan*), James Mason (*Kam Ling*), Eli Wallach (*Shah of Khwarezm*), Francoise Dorleac (*Bortei*), Telly Savalas (*Shan*), Robert Morley (*Emperor of China*), Michael Hordern (*Green*), Yvonne Mitchell (*Katke*), Woody Strode (*Sengal*), Kenneth Cope (*Subodai*), Roger Croucher (*Kassar*), Don Borisenko (*Jebai*), Patrick Holt (*Kuchluk*), Suzanne Hsaio (*Chin Yu*), George Savalas (*Toktoa*), Carlo Cura (*Genghis, as a Child*), Gustavo Rojo (*Altan*), Dusan Vujisic (*Ho Mun Tim*), Jovan Tesic (*Fut Su*), Andreja Marcic (*Chagedei*), Thomas Margulies (*Jochi*), Yamata Pauli, Linda Loncar (*Indian Girls*), Branislav Radovic, Zvonko Jovcic (*Slave Dealers*), Dominique Don, Edwina Carroll, Carmen Dene, Nora Forster, Jatta Falke, Hannalore Maeusel, Yvonne Shima, May Spils, Sally Douglas, Chieko Huber, Elke Kroger, Ursel Mumoth, Lucille Soong, Ester Anderson (*Concubines*).

The saga of famed Mongolian leader Genghis Khan, played convincingly by Omar Sharif. After being raised by the evil leader Jamuga, he escapes and forms his own tribe in the mountains. He returns to steal away and marry Jamuga's girl, taking off for China. It is there that he gains the respect of Mason, the leader of the Chinese, by fending off the attacking Jamuga warriors. Though many players were miscast, the film does have some moments which, however epic in nature, are still handled on a personal level. Location shots filmed in Yugoslavia also help.
p, Irving Allen; d, Henry Levin; w, Clarke Reynolds, Beverley Cross (based on a story by Berkely Mather); ph, Geoffrey Unsworth (Panavision, Technicolor); m, Dusan Radic; ed, Geoffrey Foot; art d, Maurice Carter; set d, Toni Sarzi-Braga; cos, Cynthia Tingey; spec eff, Bill, David Warrington; makeup, Neville Smallwood.

Adventure/Drama   (PR:C MPAA:NR)

GENIE, THE**   (1953, Brit.) 75m BL bw

Bill Travers, Scott McKay, Patricia Cutts, Tom Duggan, Sean Barrett, Bernadette O'Farrell, Douglas Fairbanks, Jr., Yvonne Furneaux, Martin Miller.

Three stories with little in common were combined to create this single feature. The first takes place in a prisoner-of-war camp where two men fight for a seat on an escape plane. The next story centers around the disillusionment of a son when he discovers that his dead mother was not the madonna he had always romanticized her to be—a fantasy which made the attempts of the father to pursue romance almost impossible. The final story concerns a love affair between a genie and a human, with the supernatural character sacrificing his own desires in order that another man, the grandfather of the girl he loves, can remain free.
p, Douglas Fairbanks, Jr.; d, Lance Comfort, Lawrence Huntington; w, Noel Charles, Peter Gordon Scott, Doreen Montgomery; ph, Eric Cross, Brendan J. Stafford.

Drama   (PR:A MPAA:NR)

GENIUS, THE**½   (1976, Ital./Fr./Ger.) 126m
                                        Rafran-AMLF-Rialto/Titanus c
                                        (UN GENIO, DUE COMPARI, UN POLLO)

Terence Hill (*Joe Thanks*), Miou-Miou (*Lucy*), Robert Charlebois (*Locomotive Bill*), Patrick McGoohan (*Maj. Cabot*), Klaus Kinski (*Doc Foster*).

Director Damiani trespasses into Sergio Leone's territory in this spaghetti western about Hill's fight for Indian liberation, which plays more to a point of buffoonery than would be expected. A multinational effort which includes a magnetic, off-beat performance by Kinski as an outlaw, and marked by the inimitable Morricone score.
p, Fulvio Morsella, Claudio Mancini; d, Damiano Damiani; w, Damiani, Morsella, Ernesto Gastaldi; ph, Giuseppe Ruzzolini (Technicolor); m, Ennio Morricone; ed, Nino Baragli; art d, Francesco Bronzi, Carlo Simi.

Western/Farce   (PR:C MPAA:NR)

GENIUS AT WORK*½   (1946) 61m RKO bw

Wally Brown (*Jerry*), Alan Carney (*Mike*), Anne Jeffreys (*Ellen*), Lionel Atwill (*Marsh*), Bela Lugosi (*Stone*), Marc Cramer (*Rick*), Ralph Dunn (*Gilley*), Robert Clarke, Philip Warren, Harry Harvey.

The Abbott and Costello-esque pairing of Brown and Carney has them cast as radio detectives on the hunt for murderous criminologist Atwill, known as "The Cobra." This was smoothie villain Atwill's final film before his sudden death, and marked the end of the Brown-Carney duo. Lugosi fulfilled his three-picture deal with RKO by taking this mindless role of Stone, the Cobra's right-hand man. Modestly funny at times but mostly not. A remake of the 1937 SUPER SLEUTH.
p, Herman Schlom; d, Leslie Goodwins; w, Robert E. Kent, Monte Brice; ph, Robert de Grasse, Vernon L. Walker; m, Constantin Bakaleinikoff; ed, Marvin Coil; art d, Albert S. D'Agostino, Ralph Berger.

Crime/Comedy   (PR:A MPAA:NR)

GENTLE ANNIE**   (1944) 80m MGM bw

James Craig (*Lloyd Richland*), Donna Reed (*Mary Lingen*), Marjorie Main (*Annie Goss*), Henry Morgan (*Cottonwood Goss*), Paul Langton (*Violet Goss*), Barton MacLane (*Sheriff Tatum*), John Philliber (*Barrow*), Morris Ankrum (*Gansby*), Arthur Space (*Barker*), Frank Darien (*Jake*), Noah Beery, Sr. (*Hansen*), Norman Willis (*Cowboy*), Lee Phelps, Ray Teal (*Expressmen*), Lee Shumway (*Fireman*), Art Miles, Jim Farley (*Conductors*), John Merton (*Engineer*), Charlie Williams (*Candy Butcher*), Jake Clifford, Wade Crosby (*Brakeman*).

A U.S. marshal takes a liking to a couple of bank-robbing brothers and their equally lawbreaking mother Annie, played endearingly by Marjorie Main. He

takes a chance by putting them up in his Oklahoma ranch house while they get together enough funds to return home to Missouri. Originally W.S. Van Dyck was assigned the directorial role but he was taken sick and unfortunately replaced by the lifeless Marton.
p, Robert Sisk; d, Andrew Marton; w, Lawrence Hazard (based on the novel by MacKinlay Kantor); ph, Charles Salerno, Jr.; m, David Snell; ed, Chester W. Schaeffer; art d, Cedric Gibbons, Leonid Vasian.

Western   (PR:A MPAA:NR)

GENTLE ART OF MURDER   (SEE: CRIME DOES NOT PAY, 1962, Fr.)

GENTLE CREATURE, A****   (1971, Fr.) 88m
                                        Parc-Marianne/New Yorker c (UN FEMME DOUCE)

Dominique Sanda (*She*), Guy Frangin (*He*), Jane Lobre (*Anna*).

A hauntingly simple film about a young wife who commits suicide, leaving no explanation for her obsessively dominant husband. The opening is sparse; a bedroom door opens and the maid enters, followed by a shot of a swaying rocker and a tipping table, then a shot of a scarf gently falling to the ground. We next see Sanda's frail, lifeless body on the ground, a crowd quickly gathering around. Her husband, Frangin, must then find the reason she took her life, wrestling with the weight of his guilt. A pawnbroker, Frangin retells of his meeting with Sanda, a free-spirit who visits his shop. They marry, but Sanda must adapt her life style to his, being subjected to his accusations and jealousies. She toys with murdering him, pointing a gun at his head but lacking the ability to pull the trigger. She falls ill and Frangin realizes his love for her. He takes a positive outlook on the marriage and plans for a future together, only to have her shut the door on his hopes. Bresson's first film in color and only his ninth in 26 years, A GENTLE CREATURE (it opened in Paris in 1969 as UN FEMME DOUCE) marked the film debut of former model Sanda, who would the same year be seen in Bertolucci's THE CONFORMIST. (In French; English subtitles.)
p, Mag Bodard; d&w, Robert Bresson (based on the novella *A Gentle Creature* by Fyodor Dostoyevsky); ph, Ghislain Cloquet (Eastmancolor); m, Jean Wiener; ed, Raymond Lamy; art d, Pierre Charbonnier; makeup, Alex Marcus.

Drama   (PR:C MPAA:NR)

GENTLE GANGSTER, A**   (1943) 57m REP bw

Barton MacLane (*Mike Hallit*), Molly Lamont (*Ann Hallit*), Dick Wessel (*Steve Parker*), Joyce Compton (*Kitty Parker*), Jack LaRue (*Hugo*), Cy Kendall (*Al Malone*), Rosella Towne (*Helen Barton*), Ray Teal (*Joe Barton*), Crane Whitley (*Rev. Hamilton*), Elliott Sullivan (*Lefty*), Anthony Warde (*Charles*).

Gangster MacLane and pals lose their adventurous instinct and settle down with their girl friends. Twenty years later, menacing LaRue, a mug from the past, disrupts their peaceful family lives, only to be driven out of town by the now respectable folks. An antihero look at the romanticized era of the speakeasy and the mob.
p, A.W. Hackel; d, Phil Rosen; w, Jefferson Parker, Al Martin; ph, Harry Neumann; m, Lee Zahler; ed, Martin G. Cohn.

Crime   (PR:A MPAA:NR)

GENTLE GIANT***   (1967) 93m PAR c

Dennis Weaver (*Tom Wedloe*), Vera Miles (*Ellen Wedloe*), Clint Howard (*Mark Wedloe*), Ralph Meeker (*Fog Hanson*), Huntz Hall (*Dink*), Charles Martin (*Mike*), Rance Howard (*Tater*), Frank Schuller (*Charlie*), Robertson White (*Swenson*), Ric O'Feldman (*Mate*), James Riddle (*Skipper*), Jerry Newby (*1st Townsman*), Frank Logan (*2nd Townsman*), Alfred Metz (*1st Fisherman*), Levirne DeBord (*2nd Fisherman*), Ben the Bear.

The "Gentle Giant" of the film is a big, friendly bear, who 7-year-old Clint Howard and his parents, Weaver and Miles, befriend and come to own, much to the horror of their neighbors. Eventually, Clint Howard leads Ben back to the wilds and frees him, and his dad, a wildlife officer, comes across him in the Everglades. Heroic actions of Ben the Bear and Clint Howard bring the story to a predictable conclusion.
p, Ivan Tors; d, James Neilson; w, Edward J. Lakso, Andy White (based on the novel *Gentle Ben* by Walt Morey); ph, Howard Winner (Eastmancolor); m, Samuel Matlovsky; ed, Warren Adams, Peter Colbert; md, Matlovsky; art d, Bruce Bushman; set d, Don Ivey; spec eff, Jack Johnson; zoological cons, Ralph Helfer.

Drama   Cas.   (PR:AAA MPAA:NR)

GENTLE GUNMAN, THE***   (1952, Brit.) 84m EAL/GFD bw

John Mills (*Terence Sullivan*), Dirk Bogarde (*Matt Sullivan*), Robert Beatty (*Shinto*), Elizabeth Sellars (*Maureen Fagan*), Barbara Mullen (*Molly Fagan*), Eddie Byrne (*Flynn*), Joseph Tomelty (*Dr. Brannigan*), Gilbert Harding (*Henry Truethorne*), James Kenney (*Johnny Fagan*), Liam Redmond (*Connolly*), Jack McGowran (*Patsy McGuire*), Michael Golden (*Murphy*), Michael Dunne (*Brennan*), Patricia Stewart (*Girl at Docks*), Harry Brogan (*Barney*), Seamus Cavanagh (*Publican*), Terence Alexander (*Ship's Officer*), Jean St. Clair (*Rosie O'Flaherty*), Patrick Doonan (*Sentry*), John Orchard, Tony Quinn, Doris Yorke, E.J. Kennedy.

Mills and Bogarde deliver first-rate performances in this subtle pro-British look at IRA terrorists. With action shifting between London and Belfast, revolutionary Mills decides that the violent nationalistic spirit of his fellow rebels is not the right way. He gives up the fight and tries to convince brother Bogarde to do the same, but is accused of being a traitor. In a moment of propaganda, and perhaps wishful thinking on the part of the directors, both brothers renounce their loyalty to the IRA.
p&d, Michael Relph, Basil Dearden; w, Roger Macdougall (based on a play by Macdougall); ph, Gordon Dines; m, John Greenwood; ed, Peter Tanner; art d, Jim Morahan.

Drama   (PR:C MPAA:NR)

GENTLE JULIA***

(1936) 63m FOX bw

Jane Withers (Florence Atwater), Tom Brown (Noble Dill), Marsha Hunt (Julia Atwater), Jackie Searl (Herbert Atwater), Francis Ford (Mr. Tubbs), George Meeker (Mr. Crum), Maurice Murphy (Newland Sanders), Harry Holman (Grandpa Atwater), Myra Marsh (Mrs. Atwater), Jackie Hughes (Henry Rooter), Hattie McDaniel (Kitty Silvers), Eddie Buzard (Wallie Torbin).

Interestingly, the main character in this down-home tale isn't Hunt, who plays the title role of Julia, but her little sister, Withers. After sweet-talking Meeker struts into town, Withers notices big sister's infatuation with him. She does all that she can to make sure her fickle sister doesn't make the wrong decision and leave behind Brown, the shy boy who is her real love. A pleasant and satisfying romance.

p, Sol M. Wurtzel; d, John Blystone; w, Lamar Trotti (based on a novel by Booth Tarkington); ph, Ernest Palmer; ed, Fred Allen; md, Samuel Kaylin.

Romance   (PR:A MPAA:NR)

GENTLE PEOPLE AND THE QUIET LAND, THE*½

(1972) 115m BJW/Commerical c (AKA: THE GENTLE PEOPLE)

Patsy McBride (Tess Ziegler), Reed Apaghian (Claude Souders), Robert Counsel (Jacob Ziegler), Jeff Warren (Terry McAllister), Harold Ayer (Mr. Souders), Charles Knapp (Bishop), Martha Hully (Mrs. Ziegler), Philip Kurtz, Jr. (Little Eli), Pat Boyer (Mrs. Souders).

A surface glance at the Pennsylvania Amish community, which follows the indecisive McBride as she leaves the sect for a religious fanatic hippie. She becomes pregnant and purposely falls from a horse, hoping for a miscarriage. The ploy is a success and she decides to return to the Amish where she finds the peace she had been searching for. An oversimplified, preachy, and unintentionally funny view of the Amish people, who are not especially fond of such attention.

p,d&w, Richard H. Bartlett (based on the writings and photographs of James Warner); ph, (Warnercolor).

Drama   (PR:A MPAA:G)

GENTLE RAIN, THE*½

(1966, Braz.) 110m Comet/AA c

Christopher George (Bill Patterson), Lynda Day (Judy Reynolds), Fay Spain (Nancy Masters), Maria Helena Dias (Gloria), Lon Clark (Harry Masters), Barbara Williams (Girl Friend), Robert Assumpaco (Hotel Manager), Herbert Moss (Jimmy), Lorena (Jewelry Girl), Nadyr Fernandes (Nightclub Girl), Bert Caudle, Jr. (Party Guest).

A frigid seventeen-year-old girl from New York City, Day, runs away to Rio where she falls in love with architect George, who has become mute since an accident in which his girl friend was killed. She tries to convince him to see a psychiatrist but he refuses, thinking she wants him to return with her to her socialite crowd. The psychotic pair never quite get their act together and the wimpering Day, after giving George an ultimatum, takes off. Day and George do have a convincing screen presence and try their best with this elementary script. Day later becomes Lynda Day-George.

p, Bert Caudle, Jr., Bert Balaban; d, Balaban; w, Robert Cream; ph, Mario Di Leo (Eastmancolor); m, Luiz Bonfa; ed, Fima Noveck; art d, Carmellio Cruz.

Drama   (PR:O MPAA:NR)

GENTLE SEX, THE**½

(1943, Brit.) 92m TC-Concanen/GFD bw

Joan Gates (Gwen), Jean Gillie (Good Time Dot), Joan Greenwood (Betty), Joyce Howard (Ann Lawrence), Rosamund John (Maggie Fraser), Lilli Palmer (Erna), Barbara Waring (Joan), John Justin (David Sheridan), Frederick Leister (Col. Lawrence), Mary Jerrold (Mrs. Sheridan), Everley Gregg (Mrs. Simpson), Elliott Mason (Mrs. Fraser), John Laurie (Corporal), Meriel Forbes (Commander), Harry Welchman (Captain), Rosalyn Boulter (Sally), Noreen Craven (Convoy Sergeant), Anthony Bazell (Ted), Ronald Shiner (Racegoer), Jimmy Hanley (Soldier), Miles Malleson (Guard), Peter Cotes (Taffy), Roland Pertwee, Nichola Stuart, Frank Atkinson, Maud Dunham, Amy Dalby, Grace Arnold, Claude Bailey, Richard George, Clifford Buckton, Frederick Peisley, James Sadler, Leslie Howard (Narrator).

WW II propaganda film about seven girls who join Britain's women's army, ATS. Their day-in and day-out routine is tossed onto the screen along with a string of heroic acts by all concerned. Some lucid and funny moments in a capable and intelligent production for its time.

p, Derrick de Marney, Leslie Howard; d, Howard, Maurice Elvey; w, Moie Charles, Aimee Stuart, Roland Pertwee, Phyllis Rose (based on a story by Charles); ph, Robert Krasker, Ray Sturges.

War   (PR:A MPAA:NR)

GENTLE TERROR, THE*½

(1962, Brit.) 67m Danziger/UA bw

Terence Alexander (David), Angela Douglas (Nancy), Jill Hyem (Daphne), Laidman Browne (Byrne), Malcolm Webster (Ian), Patrick McAlinney (Sam), Victor Spinetti (Joe), Jack Melford (Inspector Miles).

Lame comedy in which the most unlikely person is accused of having a hand in an embezzlement scheme. The only way for him to clear his name is to pin down the actual crook, which he does in haphazard fashion.

p, Brian Taylor; d, Frank Marshall; w, M.M. McCormack.

Comedy   (PR:A MPAA:NR)

GENTLE TOUCH, THE**

(1956, Brit.) 91m EAL/Rank c (GB: THE FEMININE TOUCH)

George Baker (Dr. Jim Alcott), Belinda Lee (Susan Richards), Delphi Lawrence (Pat Martin), Adrienne Corri (Maureen O'Brien), Henryetta Edwards (Ann Bowland), Barbara Archer (Liz Jenkins), Diana Wyngard (The Matron), Joan Haythorne (Home Sister), Beatrice Varley (Sister Snow), Joan Carol (Theater Sister), Mandy (Jessie), Constance Fraser (Assistant Matron), Christopher Rhodes (Dr. Ted Russell), Joss Ambler (Bateman), Newton Blick (Lofty), Dorothy Alisen (The Suicide),

Dandy Nichols (Skivvy), Richard Leech (Casualty Doctor), Vivienne Drummond, Mark Daly, Olwen Brookes, Barbara Leake, Iris Russell, Enda Landor, Sylvia Bidmead, Yvonne Faithful, Shirley Lawrence, Sally Pearce, Rosamund Waring, Tarna Gwynne, Madge Brindley, Margaret Halstan, Helene Burls, Molly Hamley Clifford, John Orchard, John Warren.

Sentimental treatment of the encounters of five young women as they train to become nurses. Though each has her own personal conflict with which she must contend, major emphasis is placed on the relationship between Lee and Baker, who plan to share their life together in the backwoods of Canada by film's end. Efficient technical handling helps to gloss over the script's triteness.

p, Michael Balcon; d, Pat Jackson; w, Ian McCormick (based on the novel A Lamp Is Heavy by Sheila Mackay Russell); ph, Paul Beeson (Technicolor); m, Clifton Parker; ed, Peter Bezencenet; md, Dock Mathieson; art d, Edward Carrick; cos, Anthony Mendleson.

Drama   (PR:A MPAA:NR)

GENTLE TRAP, THE*

(1960, Brit.) 59m BUT bw

Spencer Teakle (Johnny Ryan), Felicity Young (Jean), Dorinda Stevens (Mary), Martin Benson (Ricky Barnes), Dawn Brooks (Sylvia), Alan Edwards (Al Jenkins), Hugh Latimer (Vic Carter).

Another distasteful British effort to make a crime film reminiscent of those in the 1930s from Hollywood centers around the efforts of a crook to escape both the law and head of the gang, who is the victim of the thief's double-dealing. For a while, at least, he's able to find some camouflage with the assistance of a girl.

p, Jack Parsons; d, Charles Saunders; w, Brock Williams, Alan Osborne (from the story by Guido Coen).

Crime   (PR:A MPAA:NR)

GENTLEMAN AFTER DARK, A**

(1942) 74m UA bw

Brian Donlevy (Harry Melton), Miriam Hopkins (Flo Melton), Preston Foster (Tom Gaynor), Harold Huber (Stubby), Philip Reed (Eddie), Gloria Holden (Miss Clark), Douglass Dumbrille (Enzo Calibra), Sharon Douglas (Diana), Bill Henry (Paul Rutherford), Ralph Morgan (Morrison), Jack Mulhall (Desk Clerk), William Haade (Relief Cop), William Ruhl (Detective), Edgar Dearing (Joe), David Clarke (Bellboy).

Donlevy breaks out of prison to kill his blackmailing wife and protect the honor of his daughter, so that she can marry without knowing the knavery of her parents. The bad scripting and direction doesn't hurt Donlevy, who comes across strongly in spite of a production that seems intent on shooting him down. A remake of FORGOTTEN FACES of 1936.

p, Edward Small; d, Edwin L. Martin; w, Patterson McNutt, George Bruce (based on a story by Richard Washburn Child); ph, Milton Krasner; ed, Arthur Roberts; m, Dimitri Tiomkin; art d, John DuCasse Schulze; spec eff, Howard Anderson.

Crime   (PR:A MPAA:NR)

GENTLEMAN AT HEART, A***

(1942) 67m FOX bw

Cesar Romero (Tony Miller), Carole Landis (Helen Mason), Milton Berle (Lucky Cullen), J. Carroll Naish (Gigi), Richard Derr (Stewart Haines), Rose Hobart (Claire Barrington), Jerome Cowan (Finchley), Elisha Cook, Jr. (Genius), Francis Pierlot (Appleby), Chick Chandler (Louie), Steve Geray, Matt McHugh, Kane Richmond, Syd Saylor, Charles Lane, William Halligan.

To wipe his horse-racing debts clean, Berle hands over his art gallery to bookie Romero. After meeting gallery manager Landis, Romero begins to take a greater interest in the art world. Soon they hook up with Naish, an egotistical painter of forgeries, who brings it all to a humorous head when they start auctioning off the copies he's done. Elisha Cook, Jr. also appears, supplying some laughs as a wisecracking, starving artist.

p, Walter Morosco; d, Ray McCarey; w, Lee Loeb, Harold Buchman (based on the story "Masterpiece" by Paul Hervey Fox); ph, Charles Clarke; ed, J. Watson Webb; md, Emil Newman.

Comedy   (PR:A MPAA:NR)

GENTLEMAN CHAUFFEUR

(SEE: WHAT A MAN, 1930)

GENTLEMAN FROM ARIZONA, THE**

(1940) 72m MON c

Ruth Reece (Juanita), J. Farrell MacDonald (Coburn), John King (Pokey), John Barclay (Georgie), Craig Reynolds (Van Wyck), Nora Lane (Martha), Doc Pardee (Doc), Ross Santee (Ross), Adrianna Galvez (Adrianna), John Morris (Peewee), Sherry Hall (Gimp), and The Golden Westerners.

Reece plays Cupid-on-the-ranch, matchmaking for the locals, who include a mindless millionaire, his heiress, and a horse trainer. Plot culminates at the track, where the millionaire's semi-wild stallion is stirring up a cloud of dust as a surprise entry in the important race.

p, Charles E. Goetz; d, Earl Haley; w, Haley, Jack O'Donnell; ph, John Boyle, Edward Cohen (Cinecolor); m, C. Bakaleinikoff; ed, Ed Curtiss.

Western   (PR:A MPAA:NR)

GENTLEMAN FROM CALIFORNIA, THE

(SEE: CALIFORNIAN, THE, 1937)

GENTLEMAN FROM DIXIE**

(1941) 61m MON bw

Jack LaRue (Thad Terrill), Marian Marsh (Margaret), Clarence Muse (Jupe), Mary Ruth (Betty Jean), Robert Kellard (Lance), John Holland (Brawley), Herbert Rawlinson (Warden), Joe Hernandez (Announcer), I Stanford Jolley (Kirkland), Lillian Randolph (Aunt Eppie), Phyllis Barry (Secretary), John Elliott, Clarence Muse Singers.

LaRue is released from prison and, having turned the proverbial new leaf mends his brother's family life and gets revenge on the man who sent him up the river. All too familiar, although it is one of the rare movies in which LaRue plays a sympathetic role instead of the mean gangster.

p, Edward Finney; d, Al Herman; w, Fred Myton; ph, Marcel Le Picard; ed, Fred Bain.

Drama   **(PR:A   MPAA:NR)**

GENTLEMAN FROM LOUISIANA***   (1936) 67m REP bw

Edward Quillan (Tod Mason), Charles "Chic" Sale (Deacon Devlin), Charlotte Henry (Linda Costigan), Marjorie Gateson (Fay Costigan), John Miljan (Baltimore), Pierre Watkin (Roger Leland), Charles Wilson (Diamond Jim Brady), Ruth Gillette (Lillian Russell), Holmes Herbert (Chief Steward), Matt McHugh (Steve Brodie), John Kelly (John L. Sullivan), Arthur Wanzer (Moran), Snub Pollard (Hadley), Kenneth Lawton, Lowden Adams, Gertrude Hoffman, Harrison Greene.

Better-than-average tale of an innovative kid jockey who gets railroaded by some crooks only to emerge victorious on the track and regain his respect. A period piece with fidelity to costuming at the turn of the century.

p, Nat Levine; d, Irving Pichel; w, Gordon Rigby, Joseph Fields (based on a story by Jerry Chodorov, Bert Granet); ph, Ernest Miller, Jack Marta; ed, Charles Craft.

Crime   **(PR:A   MPAA:NR)**

GENTLEMAN FROM NOWHERE, THE**½   (1948) 65m COL bw

Warner Baxter (Earl Donovan), Fay Baker (Catherine Ashton), Luis Van Rooten (Barton), Charles Lane (Fenmore), Wilton Graff (Larry Hendricks), Grandon Rhodes (Edward Dixon), Noel Madison (Vincent Sawyer), Victoria Horne (Miss Kearns), Don Haggerty (Bill Cook), William Forrest (Henry Thompson), Pierre Watkin (Hoffman), Robert Emmet Keane (Marshal).

"Scare" director William Castle is at the reins of this hard-to-swallow tale of a presumed dead boxer who resurfaces after a lengthy disappearance following a chemical plant robbery. A detective spots him and together they try to wipe clean his past slate, so he can live again. Standard film for its time, but nowhere today.

p, Rudolph C. Flothow; d, William Castle; w, Edward Anhalt; ph, Vincent Farrar; ed, Henry Batista.

Crime   **(PR:A   MPAA:NR)**

GENTLEMAN FROM TEXAS*   (1946) 55m MON bw

Johnny Mack Brown, Raymond Hatton, Claudia Drake, Reno Blair [Browne], Christine McIntyre, Curt Barrett and the Trailsmen, Tris Coffin, Marshall Reed, Terry Frost, Jack Rockwell, Steve Clark, Pierce Lyden, Wally West, Artie Ortego, Bill Wolfe, Ted Adams, Lynton Brent, Frank LaRue, Tom Carter, Jack Rockwell.

Brown is up to his usual antics of swooning and riding, though devoting the majority of his time to the pursuit of pretty women. Hardly a gripping romance.

p, Scott R. Dunlap; w, Lambert Hillyer; w, J. Benton Cheney; ph, Harry Neumann; ed, Fred Maguire; md, Edward Kay; art d, Vin Taylor.

Western   **(PR:A   MPAA:NR)**

GENTLEMAN JIM****   (1942) 104m WB-FN bw

Erroll Flynn (James J. Corbett), Alexis Smith (Victoria Ware), Jack Carson (Walter Lowrie), Alan Hale (Pat Corbett), John Loder (Clinton DeWitt), William Frawley (Billy Delaney), Minor Watson (Buck Ware), Ward Bond (John L. Sullivan), Madeleine LeBeau (Anna Held), Rhys Williams (Harry Watson), Arthur Shields (Father Burke), Dorothy Vaughn (Ma Corbett), James Flavin (George Corbett), Pat Flaherty (Harry Corbett), Wallis Clark (Judge Geary), Marilyn Phillips (Mary Corbett), Art Foster (Jack Burke), Edwin Stanley (President McInnes), Henry O'Hara (Colis Huntington), Harry Crocker (Charles Crocker), Frank Mayo (Gov. Stanford), Carl Harbaugh (Smith), Fred Kelsey (Sutro), Sammy Stein (Joe Choynski), Charles Wilson (Gurney), Jean Del Val (Renaud), William B. Davidson (Donovan), Mike Mazurki (Jake Kilrain), Frank Hagney (Mug), Wee Willie Davis (Flannagan), Wade Crosby (Manager), Lon McCallister (Page Boy), Georgia Caine (Mrs. Geary), Wade Boteler (Policeman), Mary Gordon (Irish Woman), Emmet Vogan (Stage Manager), Monte Blue, William Hopper, Milton Kibbee, Hooper Atchley (Men), Lester Dorr (Reporter), Lee Phelps, Pat O'Malley (Detectives).

Flynn's role here, like that of his splendid portrayals in THE ADVENTURES OF ROBIN HOOD (1938) and THEY DIED WITH THEIR BOOTS ON (1941) (where he played George Armstrong Custer), fits him like a glove, in this case, two of them which he uses to become heavyweight champion of the world. Flynn and his role model, James J. Corbett, were almost identical in their colorful temperaments, capricious moods, and utterly daring natures. As a brash San Francisco bank clerk, Flynn attends a waterfront prizefight, then illegal in 1887, which is raided by police. The quick-witted young man spots Watson and Clark, two of his bank's bigwigs, about to be arrested and he spirits them out of the arena. In gratitude, they sponsor his membership at the exclusive Olympic Club and here, using his method of "scientific" boxing techniques, he manages to show Williams, the boxing instructor, a thing or two. His braggadocio ways causes him to be set up with a professional fighter for the club's private match viewing, an event that the beautiful Smith looks forward to; Flynn has made advances to this patrician lady and she wants him to get his comeuppance. It's the other way around as Flynn makes short work of the professional but he later embarrasses himself with conservative members by getting drunk with his loudmouth sidekick Carson. The two wake up in a flea-bitten Salt Lake City hotel, hung over and with blank memories. They have no idea what they're doing there and, worse, they don't have a penny to their names. Fight manager Frawley barges into the room and tells Flynn that he's got to get ready for the professional fight he's agreed to wage that night. Flynn doesn't remember signing a contract to enter the ring but since he's broke he decides to earn his train fare back to San Francisco by boxing. Thus his ring career begins while his Irish family lives for each of his boxing triumphs, although Flynn's father, Hale, and his brawny, brawling brothers, Flavin and Flaherty, are fanatical followers of John L. Sullivan, the heavyweight champion of the world (played by Bond). In one scene Hale returns home to his small San

Francisco home where the family also operates a livery stable; he is happily tipsy, announcing that he has just met the Great John L, showing his hand and saying: "That's the hand that shook the hand of John L. Sullivan . . . I'll never wash it again." The family is shown prospering as Flynn wins fight after fight, moving into a large home and opening a popular saloon (only two of Corbett's five brothers are shown, and Harry Corbett actually did open a successful sporting cafe in San Francisco; another brother, George, became a successful baseball pitcher). Flynn is not without detractors, some of whom learn that there is one man he has never been able to defeat since childhood, Stein, playing Joe Choynski. A huge crowd assembles to see the pair battle on a San Francisco barge, including Smith, still looking to see the man she loves (and won't admit to loving) humbled, accompanied by Loder, who loves her but respects Flynn. It's a battle royal with Hale, Frawley, Carson, and even Shields, as the family priest, in Flynn's corner, each offering his own peculiar coaching on how to beat the brute Stein. Flynn wins but it's a tough bout, and now he's ready to take on the great champion, Bond. The fight is set in New Orleans and the town is invaded by Flynn's Irish clan who go about battling through the rooms of their elegant hotel. Here, Flynn more or less proposes to Smith but she puts him off. The fight with Bond ensues, a titanic struggle of 21 rounds which is fought under the new glove-wearing Marquis of Queensberry rules (one of the main features of these new regulations demanded that an opponent go to a neutral corner when knocking down his adversary, a rule that confused Sullivan, who was used to knocking down a man with bare knuckles and standing over him to knock him down again as he rose to fight, each knockdown becoming a round which explained apparently marathon fights going 70 or 80 rounds). Flynn boxes where Bond slugs and the young challenger demonstrates his "dancing" footwork, including a side-stepping defensive technique that made him all-elusive to the ponderous, toe-to-toe type fighters such as Sullivan. Bond lurches and lumbers about while Flynn slowly chops him to pieces and finally wins the fight. Bond, in a wonderfully touching scene, delivers his championship belt to Flynn in the winner's hotel suite, interrupting a victory celebration. Flynn's gracious, kind words to the defeated champion show the watching Smith his true humility and decency and she later agrees to marry him. The rollicking, humorous, and action-jammed film ends when Flavin and Flaherty get into another donnybrook, and Carson, running toward the camera, shouts a line which is heard throughout this splendid film: "The Corbetts are at it again!" This is one of Walsh's best efforts and he never allows his cameras to rest for a moment as he records the pell-mell tale. Warner Bros. pulled out all the stops for GENTLEMAN JIM, using their largest facilities on the lot for the crowd scenes. The Choynski fight was set up on the enormous SEA HAWK's ship stage and huge tank to represent San Francisco Bay in the background with a ship from THE SEA WOLF, made a year earlier, riding at anchor next to the barge holding the boxing ring. The enormous set of the New Orleans fight, shot in the studio's largest sound stage, 22, was first masked by art director Smith who had a large backdrop painted with more than 500 dummy spectators watching the fight in the shadows. When the Screen Extras Guild heard about this, a strong protest brought down the backdrop and 500 real extras occupied the rear areas of the arena to cheer Flynn on to victory. The actor was physically ideal for his role as Corbett who, in his heyday, was a slim 178 pounds, stood 6 foot 1 inch and cut a dashing, handsome figure who went on to a successful stage and silent screen career after his boxing days. Flynn, however, found the role one of his most demanding. He had recently been turned down for WW II duty by the Army and Navy because of what military medicos termed an "athlete's heart." Flynn could only work for a minute at a time during the boxing sequences which prove amazingly realistic. In the Sullivan-Corbett match Ed "Strangler" Lewis doubled for Bond and one-time fight champion Freddie Steele doubled for Flynn. Former welterweight champ Mushy Callahan trained the actor for six weeks in the Warners' gymnasium, teaching the naturally right-handed Flynn to effectively use Corbett's famous left jab. "Luckily," Callahan later remembered for one Flynn biographer, "he had excellent footwork, he was dodgey, he could duck faster than anybody I saw. And by the time I was through with him, he'd jab, jab, jab, with his left like a veteran." At the time of the film's release, the actor had just been cleared in a notorious rape charge case and lines from GENTLEMAN JIM Flynn delivered to Smith caused double-entendre audience reactions. When Smith tells him that "I'm no lady," Flynn roughhouses her, kisses her, and replies: "I'm no gentleman." This caused snickers to ripple through audiences. The film nevertheless is great fun and remains one of Flynn's best efforts as well as being one of his favorite productions.

p, Robert Buckner; d, Raoul Walsh; w, Vincent Lawrence, Horace McCoy, (based on the autobiography The Roar of the Crowd by James J. Corbett); ph, Sid Hickox; m, Heinz Roemheld; ed, Jack Killifer; art d, Ted Smith; cos, Milo Anderson; makeup, Perc Westmore.

Sports Drama   **Cas.**   **(PR:A   MPAA:NR)**

GENTLEMAN JOE PALOOKA   (SEE: JOE PALOOKA, CHAMP, 1946)

GENTLEMAN MISBEHAVES, THE*   (1946) 70m COL bw

Robert Stanton, Osa Massen, Hillary Brooke, Frank Sully, Dusty Anderson, Shemp Howard, Sheldon Leonard, Jimmy Lloyd, Chester Clute.

A decent cast, which included Shemp Howard of THE THREE STOOGES, was totally wasted in this failing attempt to combine a bit of underworld intrigue with backstage Broadway happenings. The producer of a show destined to be a hit is hard-up for the dough to see the thing through. After his attempt to obtain the needed cash through marriage falls through, he turns to a gambler for aid.

p, Alexis Thurn-Taxis; d, George Sherman; w, Robert Wyler, Richard Weill (based on the story by Wyler, John B. Clymer); ph, Philip Tannura; ed, Gene Havlick; md, Marion Silva, Jr.; art d, Jerome Pycha, Jr.

Musical/Comedy   **(PR:A   MPAA:NR)**

GENTLEMAN OF VENTURE

(SEE: IT HAPPENED TO ONE MAN, 1941, Brit.)

GENTLEMAN OF PARIS, A*½ (1931) 78m GAU bw

Arthur Wontner *(Judge Le Fevre)*, Vanda Greville *(Paulette Gerrard)*, Hugh Williams *(Gaston Gerrard)*, Phyllis Konstam *(Madeleine)*, Sybil Thorndike *(Lola Duval)*, Arthur Goullet *(Bagot)*, George Merritt *(M. Duval)*, Frederick Lloyd *(Advocate-General)*, George de Warfaz *(Valet)*, Florence Wood *(Concierge)*, Peter Lawford *(Child)*, Frederick Burtwell, Joan Pereira, Hector Abbas, Flora Robson, Ellen Pollock, Millicent Wolff.

A French judge, always on a lark with the women, witnesses a murder while dining with his latest. When another woman from his past is charged with the killing, he conceals what he knows and coincidentally gets the case at trial. The jury convicts, conscience strikes, and the judge reveals what he knows, ruining his career. Powerful stuff in 1931 perhaps, but judicial meanness has rarely been punished since.

p, Michael Balcon; d, Sinclair Hill; w, Sewell Collins, Sidney Gilliat (based on the novel *His Honor the Judge* by Niranjan Pal); ph, Mutz Greenbaum.

Crime **(PR:A MPAA:NR)**

GENTLEMAN'S AGREEMENT* (1935, Brit.) 71m B&D/PAR bw

Frederick Peisley *(Guy Carfax)*, Vivien Leigh *(Phil Stanley)*, Antony Holles *(Bill Bentley)*, David Horne *(Sir Charles Lysle)*, Vera Bogetti *(Dora Deleamere)*, Victor Stanley *(Williams)*, Ronald Shiner *(Jim Ferrin)*, Kate Saxon *(Mrs. Ferrin)*.

Only of interest to catch a glimpse of Vivien Leigh in her first starring role. Unfortunately, very little of her talent was revealed in this age-old tale in which two men switch social positions. A poor man suddenly becomes rich, while the rich one has a chance to sit back and enjoy life's simpler pleasures, which is where Leigh comes in. Nothing very original was added to help the development of the plot or for laughter's sake.

p, Anthony Havelock-Allan; d, George Pearson; w, Basil Mason (based on the story "The Wager" by Jennifer Howard).

Comedy **(PR:A MPAA:NR)**

GENTLEMAN'S AGREEMENT**** (1947) 118m FOX bw

Gregory Peck *(Phil Green)*, Dorothy McGuire *(Kathy)*, John Garfield *(Dave)*, Celeste Holm *(Anne)*, Anne Revere *(Mrs. Green)*, June Havoc *(Miss Wales)*, Albert Dekker *(John Minify)*, Jane Wyatt *(Jane)*, Dean Stockwell *(Tommy)*, Nicholas Joy *(Dr. Craigie)*, Sam Jaffe *(Prof. Lieberman)*, Harold Vermilyea *(Jordan)*, Ransom M. Sherman *(Bill Payson)*, Roy Roberts *(Mr. Calkins)*, Kathleen Lockhart *(Mrs. Minify)*, Curt Conway *(Bert McAnny)*, John Newland *(Bill)*, Robert Warwick *(Weisman)*, Louise Lorimer *(Miss Miller)*, Howard Negley *(Tingler)*, Victor Killan *(Olsen)*, Frank Wilcox *(Harry)*, Marilyn Monk *(Receptionist)*, Wilton Graff *(Maitre D')*, Morgan Farley *(Clerk)*, Mauritz Hugo *(Columnist)*, Olive Deering, Jane Green, Virginia Gregg *(Women)*, Jesse White *(Elevator Starter)*.

This was Hollywood's first major attack on anti-Semitism, a subtle, timely and, for its day, widely controversial production. Peck, in one of his most convincing portrayals, is a magazine writer who decides to research and write a series of important articles dealing with anti-Semitism. At first he fails to achieve an in-depth perception of the problem which he solves by pretending to be Jewish and bringing down upon himself contempt and hostility from bigots. One of the film's most telling moments is where Peck tries to explain this race-religious hatred to his young son, Stockwell, who is later abused at school because his schoolmates think him Jewish, a fact that causes Peck no end of anxiety, along with what his new identity will do to his weak-hearted mother, Revere. Supporting him through one crisis after another is McGuire, but even fellow magazine workers such as Havoc, who is a Jew using a non-Jewish identity, is herself anti-Semitic. War hero Garfield, in an almost cameo role, demonstrates the hatred some have for him because he is Jewish in a powerful restaurant scene. (The Jewish actor later stated that he felt this role was "important . . . I didn't have to act this one, I felt it.") In another painful but effective scene, Peck tries to check into a swanky hotel that secretly restricts Jewish patrons. His encounter with hotel manager Roy Roberts is a study in unforgettable bigotry and prejudice practiced on a terrifyingly subtle level. The strain of Peck's impersonation almost wrecks his life and relationship with McGuire, but he manages to produce his dynamic series. This film, extremely relevant today, shocked and taught audiences of 1947, and it was a truly heroic endeavor personally sponsored by producer Zanuck (who, ironically, was one of the few Hollywood studio bosses who was not Jewish; in fact his 20th Century-Fox organization was known, in filmdom's argot, as "the goyem studio"). Later that year RKO brought forth CROSSFIRE, also dealing with anti-Semitism, but as a violent crime film that dealt with prejudice on the level of the uneducated and brutal. From start to end, Zanuck personally supervised this production, persuading playwright Hart to travel to Hollywood, which he disliked, to write the script and asking stellar director Kazan to helm the project. Hart and Zanuck developed a deep friendship during the production as the playwright tightened Hobson's original novel, the author being present through most of the production as an advisor. Said Hart's widow, Kitty Carlisle (quoted in Zanuck's biography, *Don't Say Yes Until I Finish Talking* by Mel Gussow): "He [Hart] felt Darryl had great courage to do the picture. There was great pressure from some not to do it. Moss did it as a labor of love." Kazan, who was never friendly with mogul Zanuck, later stated that, though he and the producer argued over individual scenes, Zanuck became a friendlier person while involved in the production. Said Kazan: "His actions made him seem like a warm person. Lots of rich Jews in Hollywood didn't want GENTLEMAN'S AGREEMENT. Don't stir it up!" Zanuck scrutinized every scene nightly and asked Kazan to reshoot a particular sequence. "When?" Kazan asked. "Tomorrow," ordered Zanuck. The producer later wrote to Hart, saying: "I would rather get it good now than have to chop it up and try to trim after the picture is finished." Zanuck would glean for his studio a Best Picture Oscar (his first since HOW GREEN WAS MY VALLEY), and Academy Awards went to Kazan for directing and Holm for Best Supporting Actress. Zanuck was proud of his production and its cast but he quickly resorted to his tough boss role when Holm later insisted upon a salary increase called for in her contract. Zanuck broke the contract and fired the actress. Holm later told gossip columnist Sheila Graham: "Then he called the head of every other studio and said he had fired me because I was too difficult to work with." Garfield also received an Oscar nomination that year, but for BODY AND SOUL as best actor. He had initially debated taking a supporting part in GENTLEMAN'S AGREEMENT, although he received star billing with Peck and McGuire. He asked David Niven's advice and the British actor told him "when in doubt, be in a hit." In the end, Garfield registered a powerful though brief performance. "The picture says something I believe, and it needs to be said," Garfield concluded when taking the role of the Jewish-American Army lieutenant. Shot mostly on location in New York, GENTLEMAN'S AGREEMENT remains a classic crusading film which exposed an ugly scar on the human character and brought revelation and enlightenment to appreciative audiences worldwide.

p, Darryl F. Zanuck; d, Elia Kazan; w, Moss Hart (based on the novel by Laura Z. Hobson); ph, Arthur Miller; m, Alfred Newman; ed, Harmon Jones; art d, Lyle Wheeler, Mark Lee Kirk.

Drama **Cas.** **(PR:A MPAA:NR)**

GENTLEMAN'S FATE½** (1931) 90m MGM bw

John Gilbert *(Jack Thomas)*, Louis Wolheim *(Frank)*, Leila Hyams *(Marjorie)*, Anita Page *(Ruth)*, Marie Prevost *(Mabel)*, John Miljan *(Florio)*, George Cooper *(Mike)*, Ferike Boros *(Angela)*, Ralph Ince *(Dante)*, Frank Reicher *(Francesco)*, Paul Porcasi *(Mario)*, Tenen Holtz *(Tony)*.

After turning out LITTLE CAESAR, director LeRoy delivered this lightweight peek at underworld bootlegging. While the film has some fine moments, it is a sloppy assembly-line piece. Faults in LeRoy's work were not surprising considering that he turned out more than 20 films in the period 1930-33. This one was hailed as a comeback picture for legendary screen idol Gilbert, whose slide began with the advent of talkies, but audiences failed to buy it.

d, Mervyn LeRoy; w, Leonard Praskins (based on a story by Ursula Parrott); ph, Merritt B. Gerstad; ed, William S. Gray.

Crime **(PR:C MPAA:NR)**

GENTLEMAN'S GENTLEMAN, A*½ (1939, Brit.) 70m FN-WB bw

Eric Blore *(Heppelwhite)*, Marie Lohr *(Mrs. Handside-Lane)*, Peter Coke *(Tony)*, Patricia Hilliard *(Judy)*, David Hutcheson *(Bassy)*, David Burns *(Alfred)*, Ian Maclean *(Fox)*, Wallace Evennett *(Magnus Pomeroy)*, C. Denier Warren *(Dr. Bottom)*.

A failed attempt at creating a whimsical farce in which Blore plays a valet to an aging man of wealth. After this man passes out during a party, Blore comes up with a blackmail scheme evolving around an attempted poisoning. None of it makes much sense, nor is it much fun.

p, Jerome Jackson; d, Roy William Neill; w, Austin Melford, Elizabeth Meehan (based on the play by Philip Macdonald); ph, Basil Emmott.

Comedy **(PR:A MPAA:NR)**

GENTLEMEN ARE BORN** (1934) 75m FN-WB bw

Franchot Tone *(Bob Bailey)*, Jean Muir *(Trudy Talbot)*, Margaret Lindsay *(Joan Harper)*, Ann Dvorak *(Susan Merrill)*, Ross Alexander *(Tom Martin)*, Nick [Dick] Foran *(Smudge Casey)*, Charles Starrett *(Stephen Hornblow)*, Russell Hicks *(Editor)*, Robert Light *(Fred Harper)*, Arthur Aylesworth *(Mr. Gillespie)*, Henry O'Neill *(Mr. Harper)*, Addison Richards *(Martinson)*, Marjorie Gateson *(Mrs. Harper)*, Bradley Page *(Al)*.

A stark look at four young men who graduate college during the Depression, and their struggles to make ends meet for themselves and their families. A film untimely for its time, since it was a bad luck theme in a bad luck era, and now long past its time, except for an interesting look at an early Tone picture. Also a regular role for Starrett before he became a western film hero.

d, Alfred E. Green; w, Robert Lee Johnson, Eugene Solow (based on a story by Johnson); ph, James Van Trees; ed, Bert Levy; art d, Robert Haas.

Drama **(PR:A MPAA:NR)**

GENTLEMEN OF THE NAVY (SEE: ANNAPOLIS FAREWELL, 1935)

GENTLEMEN MARRY BRUNETTES½** (1955) 97m UA c

Jane Russell *(Bonnie/Mimi Jones)*, Jeanne Crain *(Connie/Mitzi Jones)*, Alan Young *(Charlie Biddle/Mrs. Biddle/Mr. Biddle, Sr.)*, Scott Brady *(David Action)*, Rudy Vallee *(Himself)*, Guy Middleton *(Earl of Wickenware)*, Eric Pohlmann *(Mons. Ballard)*, Ferdy Mayne *(Mons. Dufond)*, Leonard Sachs *(Mons. Dufy)*, Guido Lorraine *(Mons. Marcel)*, Derck Sydney *(Stage Manager, Monte Carlo)*, Boyd Caheen *(Pilot)*, Robert Favart *(Hotel Manager)*, Duncan Elliot *(Couturier)*, Gini Young, Carmen Nesbitt *(Two Blondes)*, Maurice Lane *(Western Union Messenger, Paris)*, Penny Dane *(Wardrobe Woman)*, Michael Balfour *(Stage Doorman, New York)*, Edward Tracy *(Chauffeur)*.

Sexy Russell and pert Crain are Broadway sister/showgirls who become fed up with stagedoor Johnnies pestering them and they move to Paris to appear in musical productions. They are emulating the careers of their mother and aunt who were the rage in the 1920s and these American flappers are seen in flashback, both played by Russell and Crain. Brady, their agent, creates publicity for the girls, along with his rather bumbling aide, Young, who is stagestruck and, unknown to anyone, a multi-millionaire. Vallee, playing his crooning self, and Middleton, a wealthy earl, had both wooed the 1920s girls and pick up with their modern counterparts, although the girls' hearts eventually go to Brady and Young. The story is tired, but the song and dance numbers are lively, with Russell and Crain showing a lot of leg and cleavage. Aside from the shimmy-and-shake routines which seem to be offered more as men's smoker entertainment than as a standard musical, the production is just above average. Enhancing the film are the exotic

Paris and Riveria settings and stunning costumes by Travilla and Christian Dior. Brady's vocals are dubbed by Robert Farnom and Anita Ellis dubs Crain's vocals. Songs include: "Gentlemen Marry Brunettes" (Herbert Spencer, Earle Hagen), "You're Driving Me Crazy" (Walter Donaldson), "Have You Met Miss Jones?" "My Funny Valentine" (Richard Rodgers, Lorenz Hart), "Miss Annabelle Lee" (Sidney Clare, Lew Pollack), "I Wanna Be Loved By You" (Bert Kalmar, Harry Ruby), "Ain't Misbehavin'" (Andy Razaf, Fats Waller). This is the follow-up to 1953's GENTLEMEN PREFER BLONDES.

p, Richard Sale, Robert Waterfield; d, Sale; w, Sale, Mary Loos (based on the story "But Gentlemen Marry Brunettes" by Anita Loos); ph, Desmond Dickinson (CinemaScope, Technicolor); m, Robert Farnon; ed, G. Turney Smith; md, Farnon; cos, Travilla, Christian Dior; ch, Jack Cole.

Musical/Comedy   **(PR:A MPAA:NR)**

GENTLEMEN OF THE PRESS**½   (1929) 75m PAR bw

Walter Huston (*Wickland Snell*), Katherine [Kay] Francis (*Myra May*), Charles Ruggles (*Charlie Haven*), Betty Lawford (*Dorothy Snell*), Norman Foster (*Ted Hanley*), Duncan Penwarden (*Mr. Higgenbottom*), Lawrence Leslie (*Red*), Harry Lee (*Copy Desk Editor*), Brian Donlevy (*Bit*).

Huston is a hard-bitten newspaperman in this weak adaptation of newspaperman Ward Morehouse's play. It never quite works as we see Huston miss all of the events a man wants to be at due to the pressure of his business. His daughter is born and he is off on assignment; she gets married and he is somewhere else, and he doesn't even make it to her side when she dies in childbirth. Unremittingly depressing, this movie is enough to talk anyone out of being in the news business. The final scene has Huston at his desk as a Yale graduate interviews him about what it's like to be in the newspaper game. Huston tells the youngster to get out of it before it poisons him. The only comedy is provided by Ruggles as a sot reporter. He has all the funny lines and does well with them. It's authentic in many ways but the authors have striven to add even more drama to what is already a dramatic vocation and it smacks of overkill. Look for Donlevy in one of his first movie roles.

d, Millard Webb; w, John Meehan, Bartlett Cormack (based on the play by Ward Morehouse); ph, George Folsey; ed, Morton Blumenstock.

Newspaper Drama   **(PR:A MPAA:NR)**

GENTLEMEN PREFER BLONDES***   (1953) 91m FOX c

Jane Russell (*Dorothy*), Marilyn Monroe (*Lorelei*), Charles Coburn (*Sir Francis Beekman*), Elliott Reid (*Malone*), Tommy Noonan (*Gus Esmond*), George Winslow (*Henry Spofford III*), Marcel Dalio (*Magistrate*), Taylor Holmes (*Gus Esmond, Sr.*), Norma Varden (*Lady Beekman*), Howard Wendell (*Watson*), Steven Geray (*Hotel Manager*), Henri Letondal (*Grotier*), Leo Mostovoy (*Phillipe*), Alex Frazer (*Pritchard*), Harry Carey, Jr. (*Winslow*), George Davis (*Cab Driver*), Alphonse Martell (*Headwaiter*), Jimmie and Freddie Moultrie (*Boy Dancers*), Jean de Briac, George Dee, Peter Camlin (*Gendarmes*), Jean Del Val (*Ship's Capt*), Ray Montgomery (*Peters*), Alvy Moore (*Anderson*), Robert Nichols (*Evans*), Charles Tannen (*Ed*), Jimmy Young (*Stevens*), Charles De Ravenne (*Purser*), John Close (*Coach*), William Cabanne (*Sims*), Philip Sylvestre (*Steward*), Jack Chefe (*Proprietor*), Alfred Paix (*Pierre*), Max Willenz (*Court Clerk*), Rolfe Sedan (*Waiter*), Robert Foulk, Ralph Peters (*Passport Officials*), Harry Seymour (*Captain of Waiters*).

A flashy, campy song and dance film with the ever-alluring Monroe doing her wiggling bit to entice *any* millionaire into walking down the aisle. MM is the famous blonde Lorelei and Russell her supposed down-to-earth friend and co-entertainer. The showgirls leave for Paris after Monroe gets word from wealthy Noonan that they will marry when she arrives. Armed with a letter of credit from Noonan, the girls board the luxury liner *Ile de France*. Also on board is Reid, a private eye paid to observe sexy MM by Holmes, Noonan's father, who believes the bounteous blonde beauty is only after his son's money. Russell tumbles for Reid but Monroe, believing Russell can do better, scans the passenger list to see if any wealthy available males are sailing with them. She discovers the name of Henry Spofford III, and thinks this aristocratic name is certainly borne by an eligible bachelor. Upon closer investigation she learns that this candidate is a precocious little boy, Winslow, he of the famous "fog-horn voice." The child responds to the attractive MM with humorous adult-like statements, telling her: "You have a great deal of animal magnetism." Coburn, a flirtatious but doddering diamond merchant—the mere mention of such gems sends MM into a swooning paroxysm of ecstasy—dallies innocently with the blonde bombshell. When he demonstrates how a goat is embraced by a python, with MM as the goat and himself as the snake, the lurking Reid takes a photo. Russell discovers her boyfriend's true identity and she and Monroe get the photo by dosing him with drugs. In retaliation, Reid collects more ostensibly damaging evidence which is really innocent frolicking but it's enough for Holmes to use to convince Noonan to reject poor MM. Worse, the diamond tiara Coburn has given Monroe for capturing the photo of his goat-python routine turns out to be his wife's and she insists it be returned. Once in Paris the girls get jobs in a nightclub where Monroe wiggles through her famous song, "Diamonds Are a Girl's Best Friend" (Jule Styne, Leo Robin). Then the girls are told that Coburn's wife has had a warrant for Monroe's arrest taken out, charging her with theft of the tiara. While Monroe tries to get Noonan to help her out of the mess, Russell slips on a blonde wig, allows herself to be arrested and, once in court, tries to prove she is Monroe by going into a wild hip-grinding routine in tawdry imitation of Monroe. Reid shows up just as Russell is about to be taken to a cell and proves that Coburn has stolen his own tiara. All charges are dropped and Noonan winds up with Monroe and Reid with Russell. The story is thin but the music and dance numbers are fat with bustling entertainment. Monroe and Russell fairly burst from their revealing costumes with Russell far surpassing Monroe in pulchritude; she is a Juno of limb, breast, and hip, all of which is quaked and wriggled with abandon in the final number. Russell, who received top billing, also renders a poor acting job and an almost permanent sneer as she caustically spits out her lines. Her part did call for practicality, to balance Monroe's whimsy, but not sustained sarcasm. This, Monroe is the showstopper, coy, cute, sensuous in a sort of innocent manner. This,

her 19th film, was one of her most popular hits and the film moves along with Hawks' typical brisk pace and gusto, capitalizing on the garish, the gauche, the blatant vulgarity of blood red colors, jiggling flesh, and brainless femininity. Never one to ignore a good idea, Hawks obviously remembered how Erich von Stroheim in the silent classic THE MERRY WIDOW (1925) had Roy D'Arcy lustfully ogle Mae Murray's necklace which lights up like an electric sign. In one scene, he has MM view Coburn's head as a huge, glimmering diamond. The studio eyed the film much the same way as the production poured more than $5 million into Fox's coffers. Other songs include: "Ain't There Anyone Here For Love" (Hoagy Carmichael, Harold Adamson, sung by Russell while surrounded by musclemen in a gymnasium), "Bye Bye Baby," "A (Two) Little Girl(s) From Little Rock" (Styne, Robin, both sung by Monroe and Russell), "When Love Goes Wrong" (Carmichael, Adamson). Remade from the 1928 silent. The sequel for this film was 1955's GENTLEMEN MARRY BRUNETTES.

p, Sol C. Siegel; d, Howard Hawks; w, Charles Lederer (based on the play by Anita Loos, Joseph Fields); ph, Harry J. Wild (Technicolor); ed, Hugh S. Fowler; md, Lionel Newman; art d, Lyle Wheeler, Joseph C. Wright; set d, Claude Carpenter; cos, Travilla; spec eff, Ray Kellog; ch, Jack Cole.

Musical   **Cas.**   **(PR:A MPAA:NR)**

GENTLEMEN WITH GUNS*½   (1946) 53m PRC bw

Buster Crabbe (*Billy*), Al St. John (*Fuzzy*), Patricia Knox (*Matilda*), Steve Darrell (*McAllister*), George Chesebro (*Slade*), Karl Hackett (*Justice of the Peace*), Budd Buster (*Sheriff*), Frank Ellis (*Cassidy*), George Morrell.

Buster Crabbe is in the lead as gunslinger Billy Carson in this addition to the Carson series. Together with pal St. John, they outwit the heavies who are trying to get the water rights to Fuzzy's ranch. Slapstick comedy and gunfire bore after a few minutes, and from there on it is strictly late Gower Glutch material with all "excess fat" trimmed from the budget by the master of the art, producer Neufeld. (See BILLY CARSON series, Index.)

p, Sigmund Neufeld; d, Sam Newfield; w, Fred Myton; ph, Jack Greenhalgh; ed, Holbrook N. Todd; md, Lee Zahler.

Western   **(PR:A MPAA:NR)**

GEORDIE   (SEE: WEE GEORDIE, 1955, Brit.)

GEORG**½   (1964) 55m Ariadne/Film-Makers bw

Stanton Kaye (*Georg*), Lynn Averill (*Wife*), Mark Cheka.

An interesting though self-indulgent idea which incorporates the use of the movie camera into the movie. Stanton Kaye plays Georg, a cameraman in Germany during WW II. While filming a battle, his camera continued to run, even though it was unattended. What he captured on film was the image of people dying all around him. He returns home, telling people of the destruction he saw, showing the film and slides. Understandably, they do not care to hear of it. Emigrating to the U.S., he settles in Illinois, marries, and soon his wife dies in childbirth, leaving him on his own. The finale has him taunting soldiers at a missile base. He is shot, his camera sitting on a tripod still running. There are some nice moments where Kaye delivers his pleas directly to the audience, via his camera, and acts as narrator. A personal and ambitious "diary" which unfortunately is long forgotten.

p,d&w, Stanton Kaye; ph, Detlev Wiede; ed, Kaye.

Drama   **(PR:C MPAA:NR)**

GEORGE**   (1973, U.S./Switz.) 86m Thompson-Telepool-Intertel/CAP c

Marshall Thompson (*Jim Paulsen*), Jack Mullaney (*Walter Clark*), Inge Schoner (*Erika Walters*), Linda Caroll (*Regina*), Ursula Von Wiese (*Frau Gerber*), Hermann Frick (*Herr Werner*), Erwin Parker (*Air Freight Man*), Raimund Bucher (*Boat Owner*), Frank Schacher (*Control Tower Operator*), Elisabeth Vonallmen (*Ursula*), Edgar Reiser (*Monk*), Brigitte Graubner (*1st Girl Tourist*), Dagmar Balmer (*2nd Girl Tourist*), Wallace Bennett (*American Tourist*), Jeffery Barter (*Bellboy*).

Thompson plays an airplane pilot whose peaceful existence in Switzerland is suddenly interrupted when he inherits a 250-pound dog from his sister, who is embarking on her fourth marriage. The constant battle between Thompson's attempts to have some peace with the presence of the large and obnoxious dog doesn't find a resolution until the dog saves his new master's life during an avalanche. Light in both attitude and presentation.

p, Marshall Thompson; d&w, Wallace C. Bennett (based on a story by Thompson); ph, Peter Rohe (Eastmancolor); m, Herman Thieme; ed, Margut Von Oven; md, Thieme; art d, Barbara Long; cos, Valerie Genco; dog trainers, Jeffery Barter, Bill Hayes.

Comedy   **Cas.**   **(PR:A MPAA:G)**

GEORGE AND MARGARET***   (1940, Brit.) 70m WB bw

Marie Lohr (*Alice*), Judy Kelly (*Frankie*), Noel Howlett (*Malcolm*), Oliver Wakefield (*Roger*), John Boxer (*Claude*), Ann Casson (*Gladys*), Arthur Macrae (*Dudley*), Margaret Yarde (*Cook*), Irene Handl (*Beer*), Gus McNaughton (*Wolverton*).

A suburban family's life is thrown into turmoil when Lohr announces that old friends George and Margaret are stopping by for a visit. Add to that three riotous brothers, one of whom unveils plans to wed the maid, and a kitchen strike organized by the cook. After all is finally under control and ready to go, George and Margaret fail to show up. Unlike most sitcoms, it is full of laughs.

p, A.M. Salomon; d, George King; w, Rodney Ackland, Brock Williams (based on the play by Gerald Savory); ph, Basil Emmott.

Comedy   **(PR:A MPAA:NR)**

GEORGE AND MILDRED*   (1980, Brit.) 93m Chips-ITC c

Yootha Joyce, Brian Murphy, Stratford Johns, Norman Eshley, Sheila Fearn, Kenneth Cope.

A weak spinoff of a popular British television situation comedy, this film has the male half of the title pair suspected of being a professional assassin. Star Joyce died shortly before this film was released.

d, Peter Frazer Jones; w, Dick Sharples.

Comedy **(PR:A-C MPAA:NR)**

GEORGE IN CIVVY STREET*½ (1946, Brit.) 79m COL bw

George Formby *(George Harper)*, Rosalyn Boulter *(Mary Colton)*, Ronald Shiner *(Fingers)*, Ian Fleming *(Uncle Shad)*, Wally Patch *(Sprout)*, Philippa Hiatt *(Lavender)*, Enid Cruickshank *(Miss Gummidge)*, Mike Johnson *(Toby)*, Frank Drew *(Jed)*, Moore Raymond, Robert Ginns, Daphne Elphinstone, Rita Varien, John Coyle, Roddy Hughes, Lyn Evans, Johnny Claes and His Claepigeons.

The final screen appearance for the popular British comedian Formby was a lifeless farce in which he played the owner of a tavern in love with a waitress from a rival pub. The battle that ensues as a result of Formby's attempts to win this girl from her manager makes up the bulk of this tasteless romp.

p, Marcel Varnel, Ben Henry; d, Varnel; w, Peter Fraser, Ted Kavanagh, Max Kester, Gale Pedrick (based on the story by Howard Irving Young); ph, Phil Grindrod.

Comedy **(PR:A MPAA:NR)**

GEORGE RAFT STORY, THE½** (1961) 105m AA bw (GB: SPIN OF A COIN)

Ray Danton *(George Raft)*, Jayne Mansfield *(Lisa Lang)*, Julie London *(Sheila Patton)*, Barrie Chase *(June)*, Frank Gorshin *(Moxie Cusack)*, Barbara Nichols *(Texas Guinan)*, Brad Dexter *(Benny Siegel)*, Robert Strauss *(Frenchie)*, Herschel Bernardi *(Sam)*, Margo Moore *(Ruth Harris)*, Neville Brand *(Al Capone)*, Joe De Santis *(Frankie Donatella)*, Argentina Brunetti *(Mrs. Raft)*, John Bleifer *(Mr. Raft)*, Pepper Davis, Tony Reese *(M.C. Team)*, Jack Lambert *(Jerry Fitzpatrick)*, Cecile Rogers *(Charleston Dancer)*, Tol Avery *(Mizner)*, Robert H. Harris *(Harvey)*, Jack Albertson *(Milton)*, Murvyn Vye *(Johnny)*.

There are not too many people who have had their life story filmed while they were still alive, but George Raft's story was worth telling. Raft's life reads like a series of show business-crime cliches but Wilbur's screenplay was true to the reality so we have to accept it. Ray Danton, who bears no resemblance to Raft, wisely foregoes any attempt at duplication and seeks to create his own interpretation of the well-known actor. Danton is seen as a dancer who began his career in New York's Hell's Kitchen neighborhood and starts out by hoofing in a gangster-owned nightspot where he becomes friendly with all of the lowlifes and highbrows who frequent the place. (It may be apocryphal, but there are those who feel that it was Raft's character that was the basis for the movie star in COTTON CLUB.) When a lecherous crime boss lusts after a comely cigarette girl, Danton comes to her aid and is rewarded by being bounced out of a job. He goes to Hollywood and gets his big chance in Howard Hawks' SCARFACE where he establishes his coin-flipping, tough-talking persona. (Despite Muni's brilliant performance, Raft's work was not overlooked and he was soon getting role after role.) Danton begins hanging out with the California mob and straddles the worlds between Hollywood and Hoodlumwood. His career begins to wane and he gets involved with a casino operation in Havana, then has that rug pulled out from under when Fidel Castro wrests power from Fulgencio Batista in 1959. His story ends as he gets the part in SOME LIKE IT HOT where he parodized himself. Five different women are seen as part of his life; London, Mansfield, Chase, Nichols, and Moore, and each is little more than a brief interlude. Several gangsters are seen: Brand is Capone, Dexter is Bugsy Siegel, plus a series of unidentified bent-nose types. Danton's career continued until he decided that he liked being behind the cameras. He has since gone on to become a successful TV director for "Cagney and Lacey," "Quincy," and several others. What most people don't know about Danton is that he has a beautiful singing voice and appeared on Broadway in the stage version of THE RAINMAKER as well as other musicals. Married at one time to actress Julie Adams, he also spent many years in Europe with French star Pascale Petit, by whom he has a daughter.

p, Ben Schwalb; d, Joseph M. Newman; w, Crane Wilbur; ph, Carl Guthrie; m, Jeff Alexander; ed, George White; art d, David Milton; set d, Joseph Kish; cos, Roger J. Weinberg, Norah Sharpe; spec eff, Milt Olsen; ch, Alex Romero.

Biography **(PR:A MPAA:NR)**

GEORGE TAKES THE AIR* (SEE: IT'S IN THE AIR, 1940, Brit.)

GEORGE WASHINGTON CARVER** (1940) 69m Bryant bw

Dr. George Washington Carver *(Himself)*, Booker T. Washington III *(Grandfather)*, Ralph Edwards *(Carver as a Boy)*, Milton Sprague *(Carver as a Man)*, Tim Campbell *(Friend of Carver)*, Raye Gilbert *(Girl)*, Tuskegee Institute Choir.

A straightforward biography of Carver, the innovative black scientist who is played by Carver himself. We see him in his orphaned childhood developing his probing instincts, and as an adult discovering countless uses for the peanut. After making that tasty treat into a profitable industry, Carver went on to head the Tuskegee Institute Agricultural Department. Rarely enthralling, the amateur acting is stilted, and the photography just passable, but it is of educational and historical value.

p, Allen McDowell, Ira Greene; d, Ben Parker; w, Robert Shurr; ph, Ernest St. George; narrator, John Martin.

Drama/Biography **(PR:A MPAA:NR)**

GEORGE WASHINGTON SLEPT HERE**** (1942) 93m WB bw

Jack Benny *(Bill Fuller)*, Ann Sheridan *(Connie Fuller)*, Charles Coburn *(Uncle Stanley)*, Percy Kilbride *(Mr. Kinsher)*, Hattie McDaniel *(Hester)*, William Tracy *(Steve Eldridge)*, Joyce Reynolds *(Madge)*, Lee Patrick *(Rena Leslie)*, Charles Dingle *(Mr. Prescott)*, John Emery *(Clayton Evans)*, Douglas Croft *(Raymond)*, Harvey Stephens *(Jeff Douglas)*, Franklin Pangborn *(Mr. Gibney)*, Chester Clute *(Man)*, Isabel Withers *(Woman)*, Hank Mann, Cliff Saum *(Moving Men)*, Sol Gorss, Glenn Cavender *(Well Diggers)*, Dudley Dickerson *(Porter)*, Jack Mower *(Passenger)*, Gertrude Carr *(Wife)*.

The deadpan, penny-pinching Benny was never funnier than in this filmed version of the Kaufman and Hart Broadway comedy. He is happily living with wife Sheridan in a cozy Manhattan apartment, a successful businessman with not much more on his mind than what maid McDaniel is making for dinner. Sheridan, however, has a reckless passion for anything antique or rustic. She is forever bringing home wholly useless artifacts, until she finally decides that she and Benny must move into one, a broken-down colonial shack which she buys without his knowledge. While shaving in his bathroom, a little baldheaded stranger barges in and asks him if the water is hot. Benny tells him yes, then explodes, chasing the interloper out and following after him, razor in hand, to find Sheridan who tells him that she's just rented their apartment to another couple, that she's purchased her dream house in the country. Benny and Sheridan drive to their country estate only to find that Dingle, their neighbor who owns the road leading to their house, has set up a toll stop to milk the new suckers. Benny refuses to pay and drives his car across open land, nearly wrecking the auto. He reaches a house on the brink of total collapse. One disaster follows another, including rotten timbers breaking away so that Benny falls through a floor. Later, while searching for a fresh water supply with laconic, stoic Kilbride, the inept caretaker, Benny falls into a well. Walls are missing, plumbing practically nonexistent. For weeks, then months, Benny and Sheridan slave to shape up the ancient dwelling, but the toll exacted, particularly by Kilbride, who insists upon dumping tons of gravel on the grounds and endlessly pumping for fresh water, all but depletes Benny's once considerable bank account. Dingle, the ever hateful neighbor, intends to buy up the Connecticut farm but is momentarily thwarted when Coburn, Benny's rich uncle, appears to come to the rescue. Coburn, however, is proved a phony millionaire. Moreover, Croft, Benny's obnoxious nephew, creates havoc with Dingle who is about to take over. The hard-pressed couple, just before being evicted, unearth a letter written by George Washington, a priceless document which will provide the money for Benny and Sheridan to retain their home. With the country house looking beautiful, the fresh water pumping into the sink, and a beautiful summer day blossoming, Benny surveys his splendid home with Kilbride walking at his side. The caretaker looks to the sky and drones: "Here they come." Benny looks up to see a black swarm darkening the sun. "Here who comes?" Shrugs Kilbride: "The seven-year locusts," he says matter-of-factly, and the massive swarm swoops down out of the sky, zeroing in on only one spot, Benny's house, and Benny specifically, who begins a St. Vitus dance as he and Kilbride are stripped by the locusts to their underwear. The Kaufman and Hart comedy was altered to some degree for the film version. Here Benny is the victim of his wife's love of the past where the play had the wife the victim and the locale is changed from Bucks County, Pennsylvania, to Connecticut. Though it's heavy on the slapstick, the comedy is punctured with belly laughs as Benny undergoes one outrage after another. One of the many priceless scenes shows Benny, Sheridan, Coburn, and Kilbride trying to cheer themselves by guzzling strong cider before being thrown out. Kilbride, who scores heavily with offbeat humor, renders a side-splitting reaction when he breaks his stoic silence to loudly and unexpectedly sing "I'll Never Smile Again." If you're a Benny fan (and who in his right humor isn't?) you'll be in heaven with this film and the man who hilariously descended from there for THE HORN BLOWS AT MIDNIGHT (1945), another laugh riot.

p, Jerry Wald; d, William Keighley; w, Everett Freeman (based on the play by George S. Kaufman and Moss Hart); ph, Ernest Haller; ed, Ralph Dawson; art d, Max Parker.

Comedy **(PR:A MPAA:NR)**

GEORGE WHITE'S 1935 SCANDALS** (1935) 83m FOX bw

Alice Faye *(Honey Walters)*, James Dunn *(Eddie Taylor)*, Ned Sparks *(Elmer White)*, Lyda Roberti *(Manya)*, Cliff Edwards *(Dude Holloway)*, Arline Judge *(Midgie Malone)*, Eleanor Powell *(Marilyn Collins)*, Emma Dunn *(Aunt Jane)*, Benny Rubin *(Louis)*, Charles Richman *(Harriman)*, Roger Imhof *(Officer Riley)*, Donald Kerr *(Grady)*, Walter Johnson *(Daniels)*, Fred Santley *(M.C.)*, Jack Mulhall *(Ticket Seller)*, Sam McDaniel *(Porter)*, George White *(Himself)*, Lois Eckhart *(Mme. DuBarry)*, Fuzzy Knight *(Sam Fagel)*, Jed Prouty *(Al Lee)*, Lynn Bari, Anne Nagel *(Chorus Girls)*, Tamara Shayne *(Russian Girl)*, Thomas Jackson, Iris Shunn, Harry Dunkinson, Esther Brodelet, Marbeth Wright, Aloha Wray, Edna Mae Jones, Madelyn Earle, Florine Dickson, Kay Hughes, Mildred Morris.

Hot off the heat of the previous year's GEORGE WHITE'S SCANDALS, they rushed another one before the cameras and it suffered the fate that most sequels suffer—it wasn't as good as the first one. This time, White and Roberti take a holiday in Florida to rest up after having a smashing success with a review in New York and, on their way down to the Sunshine State, they stop in Georgia where they see a show advertised as "White's Scandals." Wondering what *that's* all about, they soon learn it's a silly melange put together by Sparks, whose name is also White. Faye is the star of the show and impresses White so much that he offers her a job in his next New York production. Her aunt, Emma Dunn, finagles a job for James Dunn in the show as well. Next thing he knows, White has hired a coterie and must take Sparks and Judge along with him as well. They all go back to New York and the new show is a smash. Everything's just jake until Powell comes along and vamps Dunn away from Faye. Dunn and Powell are seen hitting the high spots around the city and soon enough Faye decides that she's not going to sit and wait for Dunn so she begins to do the same. Both of their work suffers and they are fired and exit in different directions. Aunt Jane (Dunn), comes to New York and learns what's happened. She and White begin looking for the two missing kids and find them through the aid of Rubin, a booking agent. They return to the show, meet again, and decide that they want to spend the rest of their lives together. It's mostly notable for Powell's short but effective debut. She was a revelation in tap dancing and Fox missed the boat by not signing her to a contract. She went to

MGM and became an enormous star for the next decade. Due to the Depression, costs were kept down on the picture and it didn't have nearly the production values of the first SCANDALS. A pleasant trifle but hardly as good as many other films of the era, it had the problem of Mr. White's attempting to be all things to all people by producing, directing, choreographing and co-starring himself in the picture. His ego got in the way of his taste. Musical numbers: "Oh, I Didn't Know" (sung by Alice Faye), "According to the Moonlight" (Jack Yellen, Herb Magidson, Joseph Meyer), "I Was Born Too Late" (Yellen, Meyer), "You Belong To Me" (Yellen, Cliff Friend, sung by Faye), "It's An Old Southern Custom" (Yellen, Meyer, sung by Faye), "I Got Shoes, You Got Shoesies," "Hunkadola" (Yellen, Friend, Meyer), "It's Time to Say Goodnight" (Friend, Meyer).

p&d, George White; w, Jack Yellin, Patterson McNutt (based on an idea by White); ph, George Schneiderman; m, Louis De Francesco; art d, Gordon Wiles; cos, Charles Le Maire.

Musical/Comedy   **(PR:A MPAA:NR)**

GEORGE WHITE'S SCANDALS**½   (1934) 83m FOX bw

Rudy Vallee (Jimmy Martin), Jimmy Durante (Happy McGillicuddy), Alice Faye (Kitty Donnelly), Adrienne Ames (Barbara Loraine), Gregory Ratoff (Nicholas Mitwoch), Cliff Edwards (Stew Hart), Dixie Dunbar (Patsy Dey), Gertrude Michael (Miss Lee), Richard Carle (Minister), Warren Hymer (Pete Pandos), George White (Himself), Thomas Jackson (Al Burke), Armand Kaliz (Count Dekker), Roger Grey (Sailor Brown), William Bailey (Harold Bestry), George Irving (John R. Loraine), Ed Le Saint (Judge O'Neill), Edna May Jones (Eleanor Sawyer), Irving Bacon (Hick), Dewey Robinson (Garbage King), Creighton Hale (Theater Treasurer), Alma Mott, Lee Lawrence, Ethlyn Howard (Sally, Irene and Mary), Dick Alexander (Iceman), Frances Raymond (Landlady), Howard Hickman (Doctor).

Alice Faye became a star in this movie that was not nearly as good as it should have been. George White had many successes on the stage in New York and went to Hollywood in hopes of doing the same. He wrote the story, co-directed, and even took a large part in the goings-on: too many hats. There was much too much plot for what is basically a song and danceathon. Gertrude Michael is a reporter who wants to get some material for a feature article. She secures White's okay to go backstage and watch one of his stage musicals in action. Faye is one of the show's stars and in love with Vallee, the headliner, but he has been entranced by Ames, a society deb. In Faye's dressing room, the two women quarrel and Faye whacks Ames across the face. Vallee sees this and rushes to Ames' side, thus disappointing Faye who plans to leave the show. Meanwhile, Durante is in love with Faye and, after a fight with Dunbar, also plans to quit the proceedings. Ratoff is a nutsy salesman who is pestering producer White to buy one of his many items which range from life insurance to a bulletproof vest. They do a radio show and Ames is there and exposed as being a "groupie" and little more. White convinces Vallee and Faye to sign what he says are new contracts for the show but what they are really signing is a marriage license. Vallee and Faye are married and White is thrilled, now knowing that he'll have a successful and long run of his show. Lillian Harvey was supposed to co-star with Vallee but created a stir with the producers and wanted her part made larger. The producers responded by firing her and hiring Faye, Vallee's band vocalist, for the lead. Until then, she was supposed to have a small part and do one song. They were so impressed by her work that they combined the two parts in a rewrite and Faye became a star. Durante does a blackface number and it's just silly. There is no amount of dark makeup that's going to make The Schnozz look any different. Some terrif dance numbers (George Hale) that borrowed their originality from Busby Berkeley. No great songs but fun anyhow. The tunes include: "Nasty Man," "So Nice," "Hold My Hand," "My Dog Loves Your Dog," "Sweet and Simple," "Six Women," "Following in Mother's Footsteps," "Every Day Is Father's Day With Baby," (Ray Henderson, Jack Yellen, Irving Caesar), "Picking Cotton" (Buddy De Sylva, Lew Brown, Henderson), "The Man On the Flying Trapeze" (revised by Walter O'Keefe).

p, George White; d, White, Thornton Freeland, Harry Lachman; w, Jack Yellen (based on a story by White); ph, Lee Garmes, George Schneiderman; ed, Paul Weatherwax; md, Louis De Francesco; cos, Charles LeMaire.

Musical   **(PR:AA MPAA:NR)**

GEORGE WHITE'S SCANDALS**   (1945) 95m RKO bw

Joan Davis (Joan Mason), Jack Haley (Jack Williams), Philip Terry (Tom McGrath), Martha Holliday (Jill Martin), Ethel Smith (Swing Organist), Margaret Hamilton (Clarabell), Glenn Tryon (George White), Bettejane [Jane] Greer (Billie Randall), Audrey Young (Maxine Manner), Rose Murphy (Hilda), Fritz Feld (Montescu), Beverly Wills (Joan as a Child), Rufe Davis (Impersonations), Wesley Brent, Grace Young, Lorraine Clark, Diana Mumby, Linda Claire, Susanne Rosser, Marilyn Buford, Marie McCardle, Vivian Mason, Vivian McCoy, June Frazer, Virginia Belmont, Rusty Farrell, Nan Leslie, Chili Williams, Virginia Cruzon, Annelle Hayes, Joy Barlow, Barbara Thorson, Ruth Hall, Ethelreda Leopold, Alice Eyland, Linda Ennis, Lucy Cochrane, Zas Varka (Showgirls), Betty Farrington (Buxom Woman), Tom Noonan (Joe), Larry Wheat (Pop), Carmel Myers (Leslie), Holmes Herbert (Lord Asbury), Dorothy Christy (Lady Asbury), Sid Melton (Songwriter), Florence Lake (Mother), Minerva Urecal (Teacher), Crane Whitley (Father), Effie Laird, Hope Landin (Scrubwomen), Neely Edwards (Lord Quimby), Gene Krupa and His Band, Frank Mitchell, Lyle Latell (Ladder Gag), Shelby Bacon, Edwin Davis, Edwin Johnson, John Stanley, Allen Cooke, Eric Freeman, Vonn Hamilton, Walter Stone (Dancers), Ed O'Neil (John the Baptist), Harry Monty, Buster Brodie (Box Gag), Rosalie Ray (Chorus Dame), Edmund Glover (Production Man), Nino Tempo (Drummer), Sammy Blum (Cafe Proprietor), Harold Minjir (Hotel Clerk).

On the lines of Florenz Ziegfeld's "Follies" and Earl Carroll's "Vanities," George White delivers another SCANDALS with about as much scandal as there is story. Davis and Haley are lovebirds, as are Terry and Holliday. The latter is a dancer who runs off before the show begins, sending panic through boy friend-stage manager Terry. Gene Krupa is spotlighted in some of the musical numbers, which

include "Bolero in the Jungle," "E.H.S.," "Leave Us Leap" (Krupa), "I Want to be a Drummer In the Band" (Jack Yellen, Sammy Fain, performed by Krupa), "How did you Get Out of My Dreams?" (Yellen, Fain), "I Wake Up In the Morning," "Who Killed Vaudeville?" (Yellen, Fain, sung by Davis and Haley), "Scandals" (from the 1931 original, sung by Beverly Sills, written by Lew Brown, Ray Henderson), "Liza," "Os Pintinhos No Perreiro," "Wishing" (played on the organ by Ethel Smith, the latter written by Buddy De Sylva); "Life Is Just a Bowl of Cherries" (Brown, Henderson), "Bouquet and Lace" (Leigh Harline).

p, Jack J. Gross, Nat Holt, George White; d, Felix E. Feist; w, Hugh Wedlock, Howard Snyder, Parke Levy, Howard Green (based on a story by Wedlock, Snyder); ph, Robert de Grasse; ed, Joseph Noriega; md, Constantin Bakaleinikoff; art d, Albert S. D'Agostino, Ralph Berger; spec eff, Vernon L. Walker; ch, Ernest Matray.

Musical   **Cas.**   **(PR:A MPAA:NR)**

GEORGIA, GEORGIA*   (1972) 91m Cinerama c

Diana Sands (Georgia Martin), Dirk Benedict (Michael Winters), Minnie Gentry (Alberta Anderson), Roger Furman (Herbert Thompson), Terry Whitmore (Bobo), Diana Kjaer, Lars Eric Berenett, Stig Engstrom, Artie Sheppard, James Thomas Finlay, Jr., Andrew Bates, Jr., Randolph Henry, Tina Hedstrom, Beatrice Wendin.

Sands, a black entertainer performing in Sweden, meets and falls for Benedict, a white photographer from America. Her traveling companion, Gentry, hates whites and decides to take matters into her own vindictive hands. Uneven scripting, confused morality, bad acting, and all done in a location that couldn't have meant less to the unfolding of the tale.

p, Jack Jordan; d, Stig Bjorkman; w, Maya Angelou; ph, Andreas Bellis; m, Sven Olaf Waldorf; ed, Sten-Goran Camitz; ch, Herman Howell; m/l, "I Can Call Down Rain," Angelou (sung by Diana Sands).

Drama   **(PR:O MPAA:R)**

GEORGY GIRL****   (1966, Brit.) 100m Everglades/COL bw

James Mason (James Leamington), Alan Bates (Jos), Lynn Redgrave (Georgy), Charlotte Rampling (Meredith), Bill Owen (Ted), Clare Kelly (Doris), Rachel Kempson (Ellen), Denise Coffey (Peg), Dorothy Alison (Health Visitor), Peggy Thorpe-Bates (Hospital Sister), Dandy Nichols (Hospital Nurse), Terence Soall (Salesman), Jolyan Booth (Registry Office Clerk).

Redgrave is Georgy, a chubby virgin in her early twenties who is suffering from a self-esteem neurosis. Her parents are servants employed by Mason, a well-to-do married man who never sired any children. Through the years, Mason has treated Redgrave like a daughter but as she grows older, his affection undergoes a subtle alteration and he eventually asks her to become his mistress. Redgrave lives with Rampling, a sensual young violinist who has more affairs than the local catering hall. Rampling is patronizing toward her roommate whom she regards as not much more than a live-in maid. Rampling announces that she is preggers by her new lover, Bates. Redgrave and Bates meet and fall in love, which causes Rampling to say she is going to give up the child for adoption. Redgrave will not hear of this and becomes the baby's surrogate mother. By picture's end, Redgrave is impaled on the horns of a dilemma; should she marry Bates, should she keep the baby, or should she marry Mason and keep the baby? Mason's wife has conveniently died, and she opts for him after he says he will adopt the child and they can raise it together. Mason is wonderful as the older man, harried by a nagging, often sickly wife. Redgrave shot to stardom in this role, and rightly so. She showed her range as she grew from a self-conscious and uncertain waif to a woman with responsibilities. It's an honest turn of events in that Mason's character is so un-cliched (he is not the Humbert Humbert who loves young girls just because they are young. He loves Redgrave because she is Redgrave) that we hope from the start that he will get the happiness long denied him. A charming movie that aided the careers of all concerned, GEORGY GIRL was also helped by the title song, which became a hit on two continents. The music was by Tom Springfield and the lyrics by that excellent farceur, Jim Dale. Mason, Redgrave, and cinematographer Higgins were nominated for Oscars. "Georgy Girl" is sung by The Seekers and "I'm Gonna Leave Her" is done by the Mirage. Kempson is the mother of Redgrave.

p, Otto Plaschkes, Robert A. Goldston; d, Silvio Narizzano; w, Margaret Forster, Peter Nichols (based on the novel by Forster); ph, Ken Higgins; m, Alexander Faris; ed, John Bloom; art d, Tony Woollard; cos, Mary Quant; addt'l m, Brian Hunter; ch, Marjory Sigley; m/l, Tom Springfield, Jim Dale.

Comedy/Drama   **(PR:A-C MPAA:NR)**

GERALDINE**   (1929) 80m Pathe bw

Marian Nixon (Geraldine), Eddie Quillan (Eddie Able), Albert Gran (Mr. Wygate), Gaston Glass (Bell Cameron).

Sweet little rich girl Nixon fails to impress the guy she's fallen for. Her wealthy dad pays for charm school lessons and she ends up in love with her instructor. One of those "how they did it then can still impress us now" things: a memorable bit of work for those days.

p, Paul Bern; d, Melville Brown; w, Carey Wilson, George Dromgold, Peggy Prior (based on a story by Booth Tarkington); ph, David Abel; ed, Barbara Hunter.

Romance   **(PR:A MPAA:NR)**

GERALDINE**   (1953) 90m REP bw

John Carroll (Grant Sanborn), Mala Powers (Janey Edwards), Jim Backus (Jason Ambrose), Stan Freberg (Billy Weber), Kristine Miller (Ellen Blake), Leon Belasco (Dubois), Ludwig Stossel (Berger), Earl Lee (Palmer), Alan Reed (Frederick Sterling), Nana Bryant (Dean Blake), Carolyn Jones (Kitty).

Freberg is a recording star who tries to record a musical find of folk music instructor Carroll's. The tune is in public domain so a battle begins. At the finale, Carroll's name is on the platter. Tunes include: "Wintertime Of Love" (Edward

Heyman, Victor Young), "Geraldine" (Sidney Clare, Young), "Flaming Lips" (Stan Freberg), "Rat Now" (Fuzzy Knight), "Black is the Color," "Along the Colorado Trail," "The Foggy Dew" (traditionals, lyrics by Irwin Coster).

p, Sidney Picker; d, R.G. Springsteen; w, Peter Milne, Frank Gill, Jr. (based on a story by Milne, Doris Gilbert); ph, John L. Russell, Jr.; m, R. Dale Butts; ed, Tony Martinelli; art d, Frank Hotaling.

Musical **(PR:A MPAA:NR)**

GERMAN SISTERS, THE** (1982, Ger.) 107m Bioskop/Miracle c (DIE BLEIERNE ZEIT)

Jutta Lampe, Barbara Sukowa, Rudiger Vogler, Doris Schade, Verenice Rudolph, Luc Bondy, Franz Rudnick, Julia Biedermann, Ina Robinski, Patrick Estrada-Pox, Samir Jawad, Barbara Paepcke, Rebecca Paepcke, Margit Czenki, Carola Hembus, Anna Steinmann, Wulfhild Sydow, Ingeborg Weber, Satan Deutscher, Karin Bremer, Rolf Schult, Anton Rattinger, Lydia Billiet, Hannelore Minkus, Wilbert Steinmann, Felix Moeller, Christoph Parge, Michael Sellmann.

The German director and wife of fellow director Wolker Schlondorff (THE TIN DRUM), von Trotta has combined two of her strongest elements in this picture—feminism and politics. The sisters—one a terrorist for the Baader-Meinhof terrorist gang and the other a reporter—move slowly through the film, allowing for the maximum of character study. Sukowa is a standout, turning in an equally strong performance in the same year with Fassbinder's LOLA.

p, Eberhard Junkersdorf; d&w, Margarethe von Trotta; ph, Franz Rath (Fujicolor); m, Nicolas Economou; ed, Dagmar Hirtz; art d, Georg von Kieseritzky, Barbara Kloth.

Drama **(PR:C-O MPAA:NR)**

GERMANY IN AUTUMN** (1978, Ger.) 123m Projekt-Filmverlag der Autoren-Hallelujah-Kairos Film c (DEUTSCHLAND IM HERBST)

Hannelore Hoger, Katja Rupe, Hans Peter Cloos, Angela Winkler, Franzisca Walser, Vadim Glowna, Helmut Griem, Dieter Laser, Enno Patalas, Mario Adorf, Horst Mahler, Wolf Biermann, Manfred Rommel, Wolfgang Baechler, Heinz Bennent, Joachim Bissmeyer, Joey Buschmann, Caroline Chaniolleau, Otto Friebel, Hildegard Friese, Michael Gahr, Horatius Heberle, Petra Kiener, Lisi Mangold, Eva Meier, Franz Priegel, Werner Possardt, Leon Rainer, Walter Schmiedinger, Gerhard Schneider, Corinna Spies, Eric Vilgertshofer, Manfred Zapatka, and the Collective "Rote Ruebe."

Referred to, at least thematically, as the birth of the New German Cinema, GERMANY IN AUTUMN is a collection of short pieces both fictive and documentary by nine directors, including Alexander Kluge, Volker Schlondorff, and R.F. Fassbinder. It is a response to the political terrorism in West Germany in August 1977, as well as the German government's reaction to that terrorism. While it's held together by Kluge's voice-over, it is still disjointed, which comes as no surprise considering the number of people involved. Of the eight episodes the most memorable is Fassbinder's—the longest and most personally intense segment. Discussing the Baader-Meinhof terrorist deaths and the kidnaping and murder of a public official, Fassbinder's episode has been compared to Godard's in LOIN DU VIETNAM. The episode is visually stark—a naked and slobbish Fassbinder sits in his apartment discussing the month's events with his homosexual lover and his mother. Fassbinder's personality boldly dominates the picture in the same way that he headed the New German Cinema. Also provocative is Heinrich Boell's episode which pokes fun at German television for its refusal to air a production of Sophocles' "Antignone." While GERMANY IN AUTUMN is a compelling and historically significant addition to German cinema, it is a difficult picture for those unfamiliar with that country's political situation. Originally released at 134m. (In German.)

p, Theo Hinz, Eberhard Junkersdorf; d, Alf Brustellin, Alexander Kluge, Maximiliane Mainka, Edgar Reitz, Katja Rupe, Hans Peter Cloos, Volker Schloendorff, Rainer Werner Fassbinder, Bernhard Sinkel, Beate Mainka-Jellinghaus, Peter Schubert; w, Heinrich Boell, Peter Steinbach (in addition to the directors); ph, Juergen Juerges, Bodo Kessler, Dietrich Lohmann, Michael Ballhaus, Colin Mounier, Joerg Schmidt-Reitwein; ed, Juliane Lorenz, Heide Genee, Mulle Goetz-Dickopp, Tanja Schmidbauer, Christine Warnick; set d, Henning von Gierke, Winfried Henning, Toni Luedi.

Drama **(PR:O MPAA:NR)**

GERMANY, YEAR ZERO*** (1949, Ger.) 75m Tevere-Sadfilm/Superfilm bw (GERMANIA, ANNO ZERO)

Edmund Moeschke *(Edmund)*, Franz Kruger *(His Father)*, Barbara Hintz *(Eva)*, Werner Pittschau *((Karlheinz)*, Erich Guhne *(The Professor)*, Alexandra Manys, Baby Reckvell, Ingetraut Hintze, Hans Sange, Hedi Blankner, Count Treiberg, Karl Kauger.

Shortly after WW II, Roberto Rossellini took his cameras to the war-torn city of Berlin: a place filled with starving people, rampant crime, and a generation confused by the role their fathers had played in one of history's greatest tragedies. Using the techniques that worked so successfully in ROMA, OPEN CITY, and PAISAN, Rossellini took people off the streets of Berlin to play the roles in the film. Among them was Moeschke, superb as a young boy who kills his sickly father, and then, unable to live with such a deed, kills himself. GERMANY, YEAR ZERO, poignantly captured the impoverished state of Berlin. Some incredible images were recorded which will serve as a reminder to later generations of the events that took place in this once glorious city. Though this could safely be called Rossellini's last Neo-Realist film, he stretched the definition (which has always been open to discussion) by taking to the studios in Rome when the cold climate of Germany became too much for him to contend with. (In German; English subtitles.)

p&d, Roberto Rossellini; w, Rossellini, Carlo Lizzani, Max Kolpet (based on a story by Rossellini); ph, Robert Juillard; m, Renzo Rossellini; ed, Eraldo Da Roma, Findeisen; set d, Roberto Filippone; English subtitles, Charles Clement.

Drama **(PR:A MPAA:NR)**

GERMINAL** (1963, Fr.) 110m Marceau-Cocinor, Metzger & Woog, Laetitia/Cocinor bw

Jean Sorel *(Etienne)*, Berthe Grandval *(Catherine)*, Claude Brasseur *(Chavel)*, Bernard Blier *(Director)*, Lea Padovani *(Mother)*, Simone Valere *(Clotilde)*, Philippe Lemaire *(Engineer)*, Claude Cerval *(Grocer)*.

Director Allegret succeeds in sifting out anything of value in Emile Zola's novel and leaving it in the cutting room floor. A group of coal miners strike at the urgings of fellow worker Sorel. Their gamble fails, but they plant the seed in the townsfolks' minds for later action. Allegret, as with the other directors of the "Quality of Tradition," provides nothing more than the numbing illusion of intellect by trying to transfer the literary aspects of classic novels to the screen. Read the book instead.

d, Yves Allegret; w, Charles Spaak (based on the novel by Emile Zola); ph, Jean Bourgoin (Dyaliscope); ed, Henri Rust.

Drama **(PR:A MPAA:NR)**

GERONIMO*** (1939) 89m PAR bw

Preston Foster *(Capt. Starrett)*, Ellen Drew *(Alice Hamilton)*, Andy Devine *(Sneezer)*, William Henry *(Lt. Steele)*, Ralph Morgan *(Gen. Steele)*, Gene Lockhart *(Gillespie)*, Marjorie Gateson *(Mrs. Steele)*, Kitty Kelly *(Daisy Devine)*, Monte Blue *(Interpreter)*, Addison Richards *(Frederick Allison)*, Pierre Watkin *(Col. White)*, Joseph Crehan *(President U.S. Grant)*, Chief Thundercloud *(Geronimo)*, Joe Domingues *(Pedro)*, William Haade *(Cherrycow)*, Ivan Miller *(Hamilton Fish)*, Frank M. Thomas *(Politician)*, Syd Saylor *(Sergeant)*, Richard Denning *(Lt. Larned)*, Steve Gaylord Pendleton *(Pvt. Young)*, Pat West *(Soldier)*, Francis Ford, Billy Edmunds, Russell Simpson *(Scouts)*, Cecil Kellogg *(Soldier Kells)*, Harry Templeton *(Soldier Burns)*, Archie Twitchell *(General's Orderly)*, Stanley Andrews *(Presidential Advisor)*.

One of the best action-packed westerns of the 1930s, GERONIMO did not spare the Indian leader upon whose awful exploits this film is based. Played with a cross-eyed vengeance by Chief Thundercloud, Geronimo is profiled as living only to draw the blood of any white person, preferring to slaughter helpless women and children. Henry arrives at a remote cavalry post where his father, Morgan, is the commander. Morgan, a ramrod general and petty tyrant who lives by the book, hardly acknowledges Henry's existence, warning him that he will show no favoritism. Morgan goes out of his way to snub and hurt his sensitive son, who later goes AWOL and is followed by Foster, a seasoned officer who has taken the young lieutenant under his wing. Though Henry discloses the whereabouts of the troops commanded by his father and the route they are taking to confront the Apaches, Foster takes the blame and he is tortured rather than betray his regiment. Chief Thundercloud and his Apaches ambush Morgan's troops and all but annihilate them. Foster, Henry, and Devine join the beleaguered troops who are surrounded on an island and dwindling fast. At the last minute, as the Apaches group to form a charge that will sweep over the survivors, a relief column dashes to the rescue. Foster is killed by Geronimo while saving the lives of others and the fierce Indian leader is captured by Henry, who redeems himself. In a stirring final scene, President Grant (Crehan) awards the Congressional Medal of Honor to Foster posthumously while his saddle mates look on proudly. The GERONIMO script is wholly lifted from the successful Gary Cooper opus, LIVES OF A BENGAL LANCER, 1935 and is less than inspired. It ignores fact for Hollywood fiction, savaging the savages and endorsing the racial adage that "the only good Indian is a dead Indian." Foster is solid and convincing as the hearty and experienced cavalry officer and Devine provides his usual roly-poly laughs. Morgan and Henry overact woefully, particularly in scenes where they test their father-son relationship. Chief Thundercloud has only one expression—murderous. Footage from THE PLAINSMAN, THE TEXAS RANGERS (both 1936) and WELLS FARGO (1937) is employed freely to enhance action scenes, especially rear projection sequences from THE PLAINSMAN for the scenes depicting the troops under siege on the island.

d&w, Paul H. Sloane; ph, Henry Sharp; m, Gerald Carbonara, John Leopold; ed, John Link; art d, Hans Dreier, Earl Hendrick; spec eff, Farciot Edouart.

Western **(PR:C MPAA:NR)**

GERONIMO½** (1962) 101m UA c

Chuck Connors *(Geronimo)*, Kamala Devi *(Teela)*, Ross Martin *(Mangus)*, Pat Conway *(Maynard)*, Adam West *(Delahay)*, Enid Jaynes *(Huera)*, Larry Dobkin *(Gen. Crook)*, Denver Pyle *(Sen. Conrad)*, Armando Silvestre *(Natchez)*, John Anderson *(Burns)*, Amanda Ames *(Mrs. Burns)*, Mario Navarro *(Giantah)*, Eduardo Noriega *(Col. Morales)*, Nancy Rodman *(Mrs. Marsh)*, Joe Higgins *(Kincaide)*, Robert Hughes *(Corporal)*, James Burk *(Cavalryman)*, Bill Hughes *(Indian Scout)*, Bravado *(The Horse)*.

Connors is convincing as the title character who goes on the warpath against the U.S., after fleeing to Mexico over a broken treaty. One of a handful of films which is in favor of the Indian nation. Unfortunately, these redskins come across as too gentle to be believed, and curiously speak in unfaltering English. Magnificent photography from South of the border is a big plus, but that cannot forgive the upbeat ending, which implies that the Indians got a square deal. They did not, and never have.

p&d, Arnold Laven; w, Pat Fielder (based on a story by Fielder, Laven); ph, Alex Phillips (Panavision, Technicolor); m, Hugo Friedhofer; ed, Marsh Hendry; md, Herschel Burke Gilbert; art d, Robert Silva; set d, Carlos Granjean; spec eff, Leon Ortega.

Western **(PR:C MPAA:NR)**

GERT AND DAISY CLEAN UP** (1942, Brit.) 85m BUT bw

Elsie Waters *(Gert)*, Doris Waters *(Daisy)*, Iris Vandeleur *(Ma Butler)*, Elizabeth Hunt *(Hettie)*, Joss Ambler *(Mr. Perry)*, Ralph Michael *(Jack Gregory)*, Tonie Edgar Bruce *(Mrs. Wilberforce)*, Douglas Stewart *(Mayor)*, Harry Herbert *(Old Cheerful)*, Angela Glynne *(Girl)*, Uriel Porter *(Snow White)*.

An energetic comedy which paired Elsie and Doris Waters as cockney cafe workers who get themselves fired after consistently turning the place upside down with their antics. They manage to win respect, however, by preventing local grocer Ambler from carrying out his black market activities.

p, F.W. Baker; d, Maclean Rogers; w, Kathleen Butler, H.F. Maltby; ph, Stephen Dade.

Comedy **(PR:A MPAA:NR)**

GERT AND DAISY'S WEEKEND** (1941, Brit.) 79m BUT bw

Elsie Waters *(Gert)*, Doris Waters *(Daisy)*, Iris Vandeleur *(Ma Butler)*, John Slater *(Jack Densham)*, Elizabeth Hunt *(Maisie Butler)*, Wally Patch *(Charlie Peters)*, Annie Esmond *(Lady Plumtree)*, Aubrey Mallalieu *(Barnes)*, Gerald Rex *(George the Terror)*.

A rambunctious comedy which teamed the Waters sisters and placed them in charge of some rowdy child evacuees. Their mischievous escapades turn to crime fighting when they uncover the plot of a pair of jewel thieves. The youngsters are blamed when Esmond's gems disappear, but the kids easily clear their names.

p, F.W. Baker; d, Maclean Rogers; w, Rogers, Kathleen Butler, H.F. Maltby; ph, Stephen Dade.

Comedy **(PR:A MPAA:NR)**

GERTRUD½** (1966, Den.) 115m Palladium/Pathe Contemporary bw

Nina Pens Rode *(Gertrud Kanning)*, Bendt Rothe *(Gustav Kanning)*, Ebbe Rode *(Gabriel Lidman)*, Baard Owe *(Erland Jannson)*, Axel Strobye *(Axel Nygren)*, Anna Malberg *(Kanning's Mother)*, Eduoard Mielche *(The Rector Magnificus)*, Vera Gebuhr *(Kanning's Maid)*, Karl Gustav Ahlefeldt, Lars Knutzon, William Knoblauch, Valso Holm, Ole Sarvig.

Unhappily married to a successful lawyer, Rode leaves, accusing him of being too devoted to his career. She has an affair with a young musician, but her hopes of romance are dashed when she learns that he has been bragging about the affair. She then admits to her friend Strobye that she is depressed because she falls in love only with men who cannot pay full attention to her. She goes to Paris alone, but is reunited 30 years later with Strobye. The finale has her reading him a poem ("Look at me, am I beautiful? No, but I have loved") about love which she wrote when she was 16. Dreyer's fans had to wait 10 years for this picture and were disappointed. What is most disturbing is its talkiness, prompting one critic to call it a "two-hour study of sofas and pianos." The film capped off the career of the 75 year old Dreyer.

p, Jorgen Nielsen; d&w, Carl Theodore Dreyer (based on a play by Hjalmar Soderberg); ph, Henning Bendtsen, Arne Abrahamsen; m, Jorgen Jersild; ed, Edith Schlussel; art d, Kai Rasch; m/l, Grethe Risbjerg Thomsens, Robert Schumann, Heinrich Heine.

Drama **(PR:A MPAA:NR)**

GERVAISE*** (1956, Fr.) 120m Delahaie-Silver-CICC/Corona bw

Maria Schell *(Gervaise)*, Francois Perier *(Henri Coupeau)*, Suzy Delair *(Virginie)*, Armand Mestral *(Lantier)*, Jacques Harden *(Goujet)*, Mathilde Casadesus *(Mme. Boche)*, Jacques Hilling *(Mon. Boche)*, Andre Wasley *(Pere Colombe)*, Hubert de LaParrent *(Mon. Lorilleaux)*, Jany Holt *(Mme. Lorilleaux)*, Lucien Hubert *(M. Poisson)*, Chantal Gozzi *(Nana)*, Florelle *(Maman Coupeau)*, Pierre Duverger *(M. Gaudron)*, Jacqueline Morane *(Mme. Gaudron)*, Peignot *(M. Madinier)*, Rachel Devirys *(Mme. Fauconnier)*, Max Elbeze *(Zidore)*, Micheline Luccioni *(Clemence)*, Helene Tossy *(Mme. Bijard)*, Christian Denhez *(Etienne at 8)*, Christian Ferez *(Etienne at 13)*, Patrice Catineau *(Claude)*, Marcelle Tery, Denise Perronne, Simone Duhart, Amedee, Aram Stephan, Rachel Devirys, Jean Reiet, Roger Dalphin, Yvonne Claudie, Leurville, Jean Gautrat, Christian Denhez, Christian Ferez, Patrice Catineaud, Michele Caillaud, Gilbert Sanjakian, Yvette Cuvelier.

Based on a relatively obscure Zola novel about the evils of alcoholism, the emphasis has been switched to show the life of Schell as a poverty-stricken woman with more problems in two hours than the average soap opera gives you in a year. She's only eighteen years old and already has two children by her lover, Mestral, who leaves her. The time is the 1850s and the location is the poorest section of Montmartre in Paris. After Mestral departs, Schell goes to a local bathhouse and learns that he has fled with Delair, the sister of a neighbor. She has a fight with Delair and, although Schell is physically handicapped, she beats the woman to smithereens. Some time later, Schell marries a kind and gentle man, Perier, who is a roof repairer. They have a daughter and life seems to have a glimmer of hope in it at last. Schell is saving money so she can open her own laundry, then Perier has an accident and is incapacitated for many months. Schell uses up all her money taking care of her husband and he loses his desire to work. Harden, a blacksmith friend, offers Schell the money to open her laundry. It is not too hard to see that he is madly in love with her. She opens the shop and again runs into Delair. She pretends that all is forgiven but she is merely gulling the woman so she can exact revenge for what happened so many years before. At the same time, Perier has now recovered enough to begin drinking and stealing money from the laundry. Schell decides to celebrate her birthday by catering a huge dinner in her store. Delair, who is married to someone else now, is in cahoots with Mestral. She is going to get even with Schell. She tells everyone at the house that Mestral is in the neighborhood. Perier goes across the street, gets Mestral, and brings him back, knowing full well that he was his wife's lover and the father of the children. Once Schell sees Mestral, she realizes that she is still under his influence and she doesn't know how to handle that. What complicates matters is that her husband now invites Mestral to stay with them as a guest in their extra bedroom. Rather than deal with Mestral, she becomes the lover of Harden. Later, Harden is sent to prison for his political involvement in a strike. When he gets out of his short jail stay, he is stunned to see Mestral at the house. There is a brief flashback sequence (which didn't have to be there) that shows Mestral forcing his attentions on Schell when they get home one night and find Perier passed out. The young daughter, Gozzi, sees this happen and is understandably scarred. Harden is disgusted by Schell, takes her son with him into apprenticeship, and exits Paris. Perier is now a terrible drunk, given to attacks of delirium tremens. Schell learns that Mestral is still seeing Delair and she is hurt. Her business begins to disintegrate. When Delair offers to buy the store, Schell refuses. Perier, by now a hulk of a man who lives only to drink, destroys the store. He is taken away to a hospital. Schell is unbearably depressed and takes up drinking. Delair gets hold of the laundry, turns it into a candy store, and lives there happily with her current husband, Hubert, and her lover of so many years, Mestral. Schell sits in a tavern and reaches out for her daughter, who cannot bear to see her mother in that condition and leaves, racing away in the streets, searching for some happiness that she will never have. Zola wrote a twenty volume set of books and this one, *L'Assommoir*, was the seventh of that series. Rene Clement, who made a career out of directing comedies, does a superb job with his actors and the settings. It is such a downer, though. There are so few people one can care about that it is not easy to get involved with the story. And yet GERVAISE won several awards, Best Actress, Schell, Best Film at Venice Film Festival, the Oscar nomination for Best Foreign Film, The British Film Academy's award as Best Film as well as the New York Film Critics Awards for Best Foreign Film. (In French; English subtitles.)

p, Annie Dorfmann; d, Rene Clement; w, Jean Aurenche, Pierre Bost (based on the novel *L'Assommoir* by Emile Zola); ph, Rene Julliard; m, Georges Auric; ed, Henri Rust; English subtitles, Mai Harris.

Drama **(PR:C-O MPAA:NR)**

GESTAPO (SEE: NIGHT TRAIN, 1940, Brit.)

GET BACK** (1973, Can.) 90m Clearwater c

Michael Parks *(Toby)*, Bonnie Bedelia *(Ellie)*, Chuck Shamata *(Chino)*, Henry Beckman *(Will)*, Hugh Webster *(Coker)*.

Two old-time surfing pals reunite after a long absence and plan a holdup, at a local mill, but love gets in their way. One partner falls for the other's girl, putting an end to their plan—and their lives. Few bright spots brighten the tragic scenario, where sadness and fate seem to prevail.

d, Donald Shebib; w, Claude Harz; ph, Richard Leiterman (Eastmancolor); m, Matthew McCauley; ed, Shebib, Tony Lower.

Crime **(PR:C MPAA:NR)**

GET CARTER*** (1971, Brit.) 111m MGM c

Michael Caine *(Jack Carter)*, Ian Hendry *(Eric Paice)*, Britt Ekland *(Anna Fletcher)*, John Osborne *(Cyril Kinnear)*, Tony Beckley *(Peter)*, George Sewell *(Con McCarty)*, Geraldine Moffat *(Glenda)*, Dorothy White *(Margaret)*, Rosemarie Dunham *(Edna the Landlady)*, Petra Markham *(Doreen Carter)*, Alun Armstrong *(Keith Lacey)*, Bryan Mosley *(Cliff Brumby)*, Glynn Edwards *(Albert Swift)*, Bernard Hepton *(Thorpe)*, Terence Rigby *(Gerald Fletcher)*, John Bindon *(Sid Fletcher)*, Godfrey Quigley *(Eddie Appleyard)*, Kevin Brennan *(Harry)*, Maxwell Dees *(Vicar)*, Liz McKenzie *(Mrs. Brumby)*, John Hussey, Ben Aris *(Architects)*, Kitty Attwood *(Old Woman)*, Denea Wilde *(Pub Singer)*, Geraldine Sherman *(Girl in Cafe)*, Yvonne Michaels, Joy Merlyn *(Women in Post Office)*, Alan Hockey *(Scrap Dealer)*.

An impressive theatrical film debut from director Hodges who had thrilled British television viewers with a series of well-crafted dramas for the BBC. Set in the North of England, Caine plays a small-time hood from London who arrives in Newcastle to arrange his brother's funeral. While preparing for the burial, Caine becomes obsessed with learning who murdered his sibling and why. Seeking out his brother's friends and acquaintances, Caine tries to question them, but finds a wall of stony silence. Operating on a hunch, he follows penny ante hood Hendry to local crime lord Osborne's home and is surprised to find himself more than welcome. Before he leaves, Caine is warned to return to London before he causes any trouble. Caine ignores the warning, and soon attempts are made on his life. After a narrow escape, he is rescued by Osborne's girl friend, Moffatt, and she takes him to her place. The pair make love, and afterwards, while Moffatt is out of the room, Caine discovers a porno film starring Moffatt, his brother's ex-mistress, White, an old boy friend, Edwards, and Markham, his brother's daughter. Surmising that Markham must have been drugged, Caine brutally interrogates Moffatt, who reveals that Osborne and his associates produced the film as a lever against Caine's brother. When Mosley, a slot-machine operator anxious to rid himself of Osborne, got hold of the film, he screened it for Caine's brother in the hopes that the enraged father would kill the mob boss. Mosley's plan went awry, however, when Caine's brother went to the police instead. Osborne, fearing the worst, ordered Hendry to kill Caine's brother. Finally, having learned the truth, Caine kills Moffatt, Edwards, Mosley, and White. Knowing he can't get near Osborne because of Hendry, Caine tells the police the details of the crime boss' activities. Before Osborne is arrested, he arranges for Caine's death. The next morning, Caine traps Hendry on a lonely beach and kills him, but before he has a chance to relish his revenge, the London gangster is blown away by one of Osborne's assassins. Grim, violent, and stylishly directed, GET CARTER is an interesting film that brings some freshness to the crime film, especially the British variety which had been stuck in a rut for some time. Director Hodges immediately establishes his debt to the works of Raymond Chandler and Dashiell Hammett by showing Caine reading Chandler's *Farewell My Lovely* on the train to Newcastle. While Caine would like to think of himself as one of Chandler's or Hammett's lonely avengers, he is really nothing more than a vicious brute with a warped sense of honor. Caine is an archaic character trapped between the past and the present. This theme is beautifully illustrated by the milieu in which the film is set. In the film, Newcastle is a city in transition. The urban slum, *film noir* buildings are in the process of being displaced by cold, efficient high-rise structures that symbolize the increasing business-like mentality of a crime world that has no place for violent mavericks like Caine. GET CARTER was remade in 1972 with an all black cast under the title HIT MAN.

p, Michael Klinger; d&w, Mike Hodges (based on the novel *Jack's Return Home* by Ted Lewis); ph, Wolfgang Suschitzky (Metrocolor); m, Roy Budd; ed, John Trumper; md, Budd; prod d, Assheton Gorton; art d, Robert King; cos, Vangie Harrison; spec eff, Jack Wallis; m/l, Jack Fishman; makeup, George Partleton.

Crime (PR:O MPAA:R)

GET CHARLIE TULLY** (1976, Brit.) 97m Quintain/TBS c

Dick Emery (*Charlie Tully*), Derren Nesbitt (*Sid Sabbath*), Ronald Fraser (*Reggie Campbell Peek*), Pat Coombs (*Libby Niven*), William Franklyn (*Arnold Van Cleef*), Cheryl Kennedy (*Jo Mason*), Norman Bird (*Warder Burke*), Roland Curran (*Vivian*), Liza Goddard (*Liza Missenden Green*), Ambrosine Phillpotts (*Lady Missenden Green*), Brian Oulton (*Funeral Director*), Steve Plytas (*Vittorio Ferruchi*), Neil Wilson (*Attendant Price*), Henry Gilbert (*Don Luigi*), Antony Stamboulieh (*Dino*), Guido Adorni (*Carlo*), Stefan Gryff (*Capo Mafiosa*), Louis Mansi (*Mancini*), Frank Coda (*Mafioso*), Shiela Keith (*Lady Magistrate*), Tucker Maguire (*American Woman*), Phil Brown (*American Man*), Joan Ingram (*Woman in Art Gallery*), Julia Grosthwaite (*Patsy*), Anna Gilcrist (*Jane*), Margaret Courtenay (*W.P.O.*), Dinnie Powell (*Arthur*), Larry Taylor (*Hood*).

Emery is the title character who, along with sidekick Nesbitt, tries to put this gross picture across. They are on the chase for four women who have the location of some missing bonds tattooed on their bottoms. The Mafia gets involved in the scheme, pursuing Emery through London to Rome, where the amiable con man ends up trying to sell the Sistine Chapel to some naive Americans.

p, E.M. Smedley Aston; d, Cliff Owen; w, John Warren, John Singer; ph, Ernest Steward (Eastmancolor); m, Christopher Gunning; ed, Bill Blunden; md, Marcus Dods; art d, Geoffrey Tozer; cos, Verena Coleman.

Comedy (PR:C MPAA:PG)

GET CRACKING**½ (1943, Brit.) 96m COL British bw

George Formby (*George Singleton*), Edward Rigby (*Sam Elliott*), Frank Pettingell (*Alf Pemberton*), Ronald Shiner (*Everett Manley*), Dinah Sheridan (*Mary Pemberton*), Wally Patch (*Sgt. Joe Preston*), Mike Johnson (*Josh*), Irene Handl (*Maggie Turner*), Vera Frances (*Irene*), Jack Vyvyan, Harry Fowler.

Formby, a crazy mechanic, becomes the village hero when he defeats the town's neighboring rival in a Home Guard exercise. The other villagers get their hands on a valuable army weapon but Formby recaptures it by turning a truck into a tank, easily defeating the opponent. Far-fetched but full of laughs.

p, Ben Henry; d, Marcel Varnel; w, L. DuGarde Peach; ph, Stephen Dade.

Comedy (PR:A MPAA:NR)

GET CRAZY**½ (1983) 92m EMB c

Malcolm McDowell (*Reggie*), Allen [Garfield] Goorwitz (*Max*), Daniel Stern (*Neil*), Gail Edwards (*Willy*), Miles Chapin (*Sammy*), Ed Begley, Jr. (*Colin*), Stacey Nelkin (*Susie*), Bill Henderson (*King Blues*), Lou Reed (*Auden*), Howard Kaylan (*Capt. Cloud*), Lori Eastside, Lee Ving, John Densmore, Anna Bjorn, Robert Picardo, Bobby Sherman, Fabian Forte, Franklyn Ajaye, Denise Galik, Tim Jones, Dan Frischman, Mary Woronov, Barry Diamond, Paul Bartel, Jackie Joseph, Dick Miller, Charlie Stavola, Charity James, Sam Laws.

Living up to its title, GET CRAZY is an uproarious, anarchistic celebration of rock 'n' roll which takes place during a New Year's Eve concert at a Fillmore East-type venue in New York City. Begley, Jr. and his henchmen Sherman and Forte (or does anyone still call him Fabian?) are the bad guys—three of the prettiest, clean cut bad guys ever seen—with plans of destroying the concert hall and ruining the show. Stern and Goorwitz do their best to keep the music coming and stop the villainous Begley. The good guys win out, but not without the help of the musicians. McDowell is wonderfully bizarre as a Mick Jagger character whose body goes through a strange metamorphosis by the finale. Real life rockers Lee Ving (from the L.A. punk band Fear) and John Densmore (ex-drummer of The Doors) also make cameos. The one who steals the show, however, is Lou Reed, sitting in the back of a taxi trying to get to the show before midnight while playing his guitar. He finally gets there but after everyone's left—nevertheless he still performs a final tune.

p, Hunt Lowry; d, Allan Arkush; w, Danny Opatoshu, Henry Rosenblum, David Taylor; ph, Thomas Del Ruth (Metrocolor); m, Michael Boddicker; ed, Mark Goldblatt, Kent Beyda, Michael Jablow; art d, Elayne Cedar.

Comedy/Musical Cas. (PR:O MPAA:R)

GET GOING*** (1943) 57m UNIV bw

Robert Paige (*Bob Carlton*), Grace McDonald (*Judy King*), Vera Vague (*Matilda Jones*), Walter Catlett (*Horace Doblem*), Lois Collier (*Doris*), Maureen Cannon (*Bonnie*), Milburn Stone (*Mr. Tuttle*), Jennifer Holt (*Vilma Walters*), Nana Bryant (*Mrs. Daugherty*), Frank Faylen (*Hank*), Wally Vernon (*Bit*), Lillian Cornell (*Nightclub Singer*), Claire Whitney.

A delightful comedy in which McDonald gets a job in WW II Washington and, housing and shortages of males being what they were then, pretends to be a spy to catch the attention of Paige. Curious, he shadows her, and soon they fall in love. McDonald does a little snooping of her own and leads Paige to the doorstep of the actual spy headquarters.

p, Will Cowan; d, Jean Yarbrough; w, Warren Wilson; ph, George Robinson; ed, Ray Snyder; md, H.J. Salter; art d, John Goodman; m/l, "Got Love," "Hold That

Line," Everett Carter, Milton Rosen (sung by Cannon), "Siboney" (sung by Cornell).

Comedy (PR:A MPAA:NR)

GET HEP TO LOVE**½ (1942) 79m UNIV bw (GB: IT COMES UP LOVE)

Gloria Jean (*Doris Stanley*), Donald O'Connor (*Jimmy Arnold*), Jane Frazee (*Ann Winters*), Robert Paige (*Stephen Winters*), Peggy Ryan (*Betty Blake*), Edith Barrett (*Miss Roberts*), Cora Sue Collins (*Elaine Sterling*), Nana Bryant (*Aunt Addie*), Irving Bacon (*Mr. Hardwicke*), John Abbott (*Prof. Radowsky*), Millard Mitchell (*McCarthy*), Tim Ryan (*Detective*), Douglas Scott (*Ronald Stacey*), Oliver Prickett (*Man*), Dorothy Babb, Jean McNab, Jane McNab, Delores Mitchell (*The Jivin' Jills*), Joe "Corky" Geil, Tommy Rall, Ronald Stanton (*The Jivin' Jacks*), Mary Field (*Woman Judge*), Harry Hayden (*Judge Ramsey*), Billy Benedict (*Soda Jerk*), Norma Drury (*1st Woman*), Virginia Brissac (*Mrs. Bruce*), Sidney Miller (*Boy Waiter*), Wade Boteler (*Stacey*), Ruth Lee (*Woman*), Dot Chester (*2nd Woman*), Chester Clute (*Mr. Tolly*).

Fourteen-year-old Gloria Jean is cast as a child prodigy who runs away from the concert hall and an overbearing aunt. She turns up at the doorstep of a childless couple who adopt her and send her to school. Ryan is a private eye hired by the aunt to locate Jean. Sharing the headlining spot is O'Connor, who is Jean's school chum. Musical numbers include: "Sempre Libre" (Giuseppe Verdi), "Villanelle" (Eva Dell Acqua, Ralph Freed), "Drink To Me Only With Thine Eyes" (music anonymous, lyrics by Ben Jonson), "Siboney" (Dolly Morse, Ernesto Lecuona; all sung by Gloria Jean), "Let's Hitch a Horsie to the Automobile" (Al Hoffman, Mann Curtis, Jerry Livingston; sung by Peggy Ryan), "Those Endearing Young Charms" (Thomas Moore, Matthew Locke), "Heaven For Two" (Don Raye, Gene DePaul).

p, Bernard W. Burton; d, Charles Lamont; w, Jay Dratler (based on a story by M.M. Musselman); ph, L.W. O'Connell; md, Charles Previn.

Musical (PR:A MPAA:NR)

GET MEAN*½ (1976, Ital.) 84m Cee Note c

Tony Anthony, Lloyd Battista.

One of the strangest and most obscure spaghetti westerns ever to come out of Italy as director Baldi and producer-star Anthony pull out all the stops. "Stranger" Anthony battles all manner of villains, including vikings who turn up in a small western ghost town, and a mad family that appears to have been taken out of a Shakespearian epic in their Elizabethan splendor, complete with a castle, in the middle of the desert. The climax sees Anthony fighting medieval knights, and their swords and arrows with his vast array of weapons, which includes machine guns, dynamite, and his trusty six-shooter. The whole mess is connected by a mysterious silver sphere that turns up in every scene as if it were a supernatural observer to the crazy proceedings. Anthony was responsible for a long series of "Stranger" spaghetti westerns in the 1970s and he also started a 3-D revival with his COMIN' AT YA! (1981) which was directed by Baldi and was even worse than GET MEAN.

p, Tony Anthony; d, Ferdinando Baldi; w, Lloyd Battista, Wolfe Lowenthal; ph, (Techniscope, Technicolor).

Western (PR:C MPAA:PG)

GET OFF MY FOOT* (1935, Brit.) 82m WB/FN bw

Max Miller (*Herbert Cronk*), Jane Carr (*Helen Rawlingcourt*), Dorothy "Chili" Bouchier (*Marie*), Norma Varden (*Mrs. Rawlingcourt*), Morland Graham (*Maj. Rawlingcourt*), Anthony Hankey (*Algy*), Reginald Purdell (*Joe*), Vera Bogetti (*Matilda*), Wally Patch (*Tramp*), John Devereaux.

Miller skips town after believing he drowned a man and ends up working as a butler for a major. The major hopes to marry his daughter off to Miller when he learns that he's inherited a fortune, but instead Miller weds the maid. One of Beaudine's British films, GET OFF MY FOOT has a promising title and that's all.

p, Irving Asher; d, William Beaudine; w, Frank Launder, Robert Edmunds (based on a play "Money By Wire" by Edward Paulton); ph, Basil Emmott.

Comedy (PR:A MPAA:NR)

GET ON WITH IT** (1963, Brit.) 86m Governor bw (GB: DENTIST ON THE JOB)

Bob Monkhouse (*David Cookson*), Kenneth Connor (*Sam Field*), Ronnie Stevens (*Brian Dexter*), Shirley Eaton (*Jill Venner*), Eric Barker (*Col. J.J. Proc/The Dean*), Richard Wattis (*Macreedy*), Reginald Beckwith (*Duff*), Charles Hawtrey Roper (*Pharmacist*), Graham Stark (*Man*), Charlotte Mitchell (*Mrs. Burke*), Jeremy Hawk (*Prof. Lovitt*), David Horne (*Adm. Southbound*), Ian Whittaker (*Fuller*), Patrick Holt (*Newsreader*), Michael Miles (*Himself*), Keith Fordyce (*Himself*), David Glover (*Bull*), Richard Caldicot (*Prison Governor*), Cyril Chamberlain (*TV Director*), Mercy Haystead (*Miss Figg*), Sheena Marshe (*Lolita Roughage*), Valli Newby (*Cheeky Brunette*).

Silliness abounds as usual in this addition to the "Carry On" series. This time a couple of whacky dentists invent a new wonder toothpaste tagged "Dreem . . . with a built-in beam!" and the rest of the story is of their antics in promoting it. Tail end of a once witty series from England. (See CARRY ON series, Index.)

p, Bertram M. Ostrer; d, C.M. Pennington-Richards; w, Hazel Adair, Hugh Woodhouse, Bob Monkhouse; ph, Stephen Dade; m, Ken Jones; ed, Bill Lenny; art d, Tony Masters.

Comedy (PR:A MPAA:NR)

GET OUT OF TOWN (SEE: GET OUTTA TOWN, 1962)

GET OUT YOUR HANDKERCHIEFS**½   (1978, Fr.) 108m Les Films Ariane-C.A.P.A.C.-Belga-SODEP/New Line c

Gerard Depardieu (Raoul), Patrick Dewaere (Stephane), Carol Laure (Solange), Riton (Christian Beloeil), Michel Serreaul (Neighbor), Eleonore Hirt (Mrs. Beloeil), Sylvie Joly (Passerby), Jean Rougerie (Mr. Beloeil).

An entertaining comedy which tried to be naughty and was well rewarded for its efforts. Depardieu is the husband of Laure, a sexually unresponsive woman. He hits on the idea of getting her a lover, and chooses Dewaere. But Dewaere has no more luck than Depardieu, so they put their heads together and decide that perhaps a baby will do the trick, but again they are defeated. It takes a 13-year-old boy from summer camp to solve their problem when Laure finds satisfaction with him and he makes her pregnant. An Oscar winner for Best Foreign Film and Georges Delerue's score also won a French Cesar. (In French; English subtitles.)

p, Paul Claudon; d&w, Bertrand Blier; ph, Jean Penzer (Eastmancolor); m, Georges Delerue; ed, Claudine Merlin; art d, Eric Moulard.

Comedy   Cas.   (PR:O MPAA:NR)

GET OUTTA TOWN*½ (1960) 63m MCP bw (AKA: GET OUT OF TOWN; THE DAY KELLY CAME HOME; GANGSTER'S REVENGE)

Doug Wilson (Kelly Olson), Jeanne Baird (Jill), Marilyn O'Connor (Claire), Tony Lewis (Rico), Frank Harding (Sgt. Wills), Steve Bradley (Officer Kemper), Beppi De Vries (Kelly's Mother), Tommy Holden (Squirrel), Lee Kross (Tony), Frank McCully (Bartender), Edith Clair (Waitress), Sam Chiodo, Fred Chiodo, Robert Biggers John O'Hara.

Ex-con Wilson returns home to find his brother murdered. Because of his criminal history he is suspected, but clues lead to the syndicate. Wilson is cleared but he gets out of town anyway, taking his girl friend, Baird, with him. That's about it and maybe the screenwriter should have got outta town before he laid this egg.

p, Charles Davis, Douglas Wilson; d, Davis; w, Bob Wehling; ph, Larry Raimond; m, Bill Holman; ed, Richard Llewellyn, Davis.

Crime   (PR:C MPAA:NR)

GET THAT GIRL* (1932) 67m Talmadge bw

Richard Talmadge, Shirley Grey, Carl Stockdale, Fred Malatesta, Jimmy Guilfoyle, Lloyd Ingram, Geneva Mitchell, Victor Stanford, Billy Jones.

Munich-born Talmadge produced and starred in this hodge-podge of western action which is all put in order by the swinging fists of the producer-star, whose heavy German accent soon put the skids to any more acting in oaters such as this.

d, George Crone (based on a story by Charles R. Condon).

Western   (PR:C MPAA:NR)

GET THAT GIRL, 1936   (SEE: CARYL OF THE MOUNTAINS, 1936)

GET THAT MAN*½ (1935) 67m Empire Films bw

Wallace Ford, Finis Barton, E. Alyn Warren, Leon Ames, Lillian Miles, Laura Treadwell, William Humphries, Johnstone White.

A case of mistaken identity makes life a bit too exciting for a lowly taxi driver. His resemblance to the supposedly dead heir to a vast fortune spices up the doldrums of riding around the city behind a steering wheel.

p, Lester Scott, Jr.; d, Spencer Gordon Bennett; w, Betty Burbridge (based on a story by Robert Bridgewood); ph, James S. Brown, Jr.

Mystery/Drama   (PR:A MPAA:NR)

GET TO KNOW YOUR RABBIT** (1972) 91m WB c

Tom Smothers (Donald Beeman), John Astin (Mr. Turnbull), Suzanne Zenor (Paula), Samantha Jones (Susan), Allen [Goorwitz] Garfield (Vic), Katharine Ross (Girl), Orson Welles (Mr. Delasandro), Hope Summers (Mrs. Beeman), Charles Lane (Mr. Beeman), Robert Ball (Mr. Weber), Larry D. Mann (Mr. Seager), King Moody (TV Reporter), Jack Collins (Mr. Reese), George Ives (Mr. Morris), M. Emmet Walsh (Mr. Wendel), Helen Page Camp (Mrs. Wendel), Pearl Shear (Flo), Timothy Carey (Cop), Jessica Myerson (Mrs. Reese), Anne Randall (Stewardess), Bob Einstein (Police Officer), Judy Marcione (Miss Parsons).

Brian DePalma directed this heavy satire starring Tom Smothers as a businessman fed up with the establishment. He enrolls in Orson Welles' school of magic and soon is performing his newly learned tricks while tap dancing. His free-spirited life soon takes on a familiar tone when his business manager tries to exploit him, again subjecting him to the money-oriented mentality he tried to leave behind. This project, shelved for two years, shows DePalma at his most intelligent and moralistic which, commendable as those traits are, tended to overshadow the charm which might have made this film work.

p, Steve Bernhardt, Paul Gaer; d, Brian DePalma; w, Jordon Crittenden; ph, John Alonzo (Technicolor); m, Jack Elliott, Allyn Ferguson; ed, Frank Urioste, Peter Colbert; art d, William Malley; set d, Jim Payne; magic stunts advisor, Harry Blackstone, Jr.

Satire   (PR:O MPAA:R)

GET YOUR MAN* (1934, Brit.) 67m B&D/PAR bw

Dorothy Boyd (Nancy McAlpine), Sebastian Shaw (Robert Halbeam), Clifford Heatherley (Parker Halbeam), Hugh E. Wright (Rev. John Vivien), Kay Walsh (Mary Vivien), Helen Ferrers (Agatha McAlpine), Rex Harrison (Tom Jakes), Charles Barrett.

Rivals in the toothpaste business join forces and assure success by marrying off their children to each other. Shaw and Walsh, however, have different plans and, much to the business owners' chagrin, become romantically tied to others. A standard British programmer which has hit the screens in countless other forms, most of them funnier.

p&d, George King; w, George Dewhurst (based on the play "Tu M'Espouseras" by Louis Verneuil).

Comedy   (PR:A MPAA:NR)

GET YOURSELF A COLLEGE GIRL* (1964) 87m Four Leaf MGM c (AKA: GO-GO SET)

Mary Ann Mobley (Terry), Joan O'Brien (Marge), Nancy Sinatra (Lynne), Chris Noel (Sue), Chad Everett (Gary), Willard Waterman (Senator Hubert Morrison), Fabrizio Mioni (Armand), James Milhollin (Gordon), Paul Todd (Ray), Donnie Brooks (Donnie), Hortense Petra (Donna), Dorothy Neumann (Dean), Marti Barris (Secretary), Mario Costello (Bellboy), The Dave Clark Five, The Animals, The Jimmy Smith Trio, Stan Getz, Astrud Gilberto, The Standells, Roberta Linn, Freddie Bell and the Bell Boys.

Good-looking Mobley nearly flunks out of college when it is discovered that she is a writer of pop songs on the side. Waterman is cast as a senator seeking the youth vote, who saves her from getting ousted, in a story that is so trite that the swinging set of that day even thought it was bad. Songs: "Get Yourself a College Girl" (Fred Karger, Sidney Miller), "The Swinging Set" (Karger, Donnie Brooks, Miller), "The Girl from Ipanema" (Stan Getz version).

p, Sam Katzman; d, Sidney Miller; w, Robert E. Kent; ph, Fred H. Jackman (Panavision, Metrocolor); m, Fred Karger; ed, Ben Lewis; art d, Addison Hehr, George W. Davis; set d, Henry Grace, Jack Mills; spec eff, J.E. Christensen; ch, Hal Belfer.

Musical Comedy   (PR:A MPAA:NR)

GET-AWAY, THE** (1941) 88m MGM bw

Robert Sterling (Jeff Crane), Charles Winninger (Dr. Josiah Glass), Donna Reed (Maria Theresa O'Reilly), Henry O'Neill (Warden Alcott), Dan Dailey, Jr. (Sonny Black), Don Douglas (Jiff Duff), Ernest Whitman ("Moose"), Grant Withers (Parker), Chester Gan (Sam), Charles Wagenheim (Hutch), Guy Kingsford (George), Matty Fain (Bryan).

Sterling is a G-man who goes undercover as an inmate sharing a cell with the deadly Dailey. Sterling, as part of a government plan, organizes a prison break so the FBI can capture the rest of Dailey's powerful gang. As Mr. Hoover would have it, the gang is bullet-ridden by the sharp-shooting agents in a predictable but exciting finale. The film marked the first screen appearance of Reed, the farm-fed beauty who developed into a leading lady for almost two decades and who won an Oscar for her role as the prostitute Alma in FROM HERE TO ETERNITY in 1953.

p, J. Walter Ruben; d, Edward Buzzell; w, Wells Root, W.R. Burnett (based on a story by Ruben, Root); ph, Sidney Wagner; m, Daniele Amfitheatrof; ed, James E. Newcom; art d, Cedric Gibbons.

Crime   (PR:C MPAA:NR)

GETAWAY, THE***½ (1972) 122m Solar-First Artists/NG c

Steve McQueen (Doc McCoy), Ali McGraw (Carol McCoy), Ben Johnson (Jack Benyon), Sally Struthers (Fran Clinton), Al Lettieri (Rudy Butler), Slim Pickens (Cowboy), Richard Bright (Thief), Jack Dodson (Harold Clinton), Dub Taylor (Laughlin), Bo Hopkins (Frank Jackson), Roy Jensen (Cully), John Bryson (Accountant), Bill Hart (Swain), Tom Runyon (Hayhoe), Whitney Jones (Soldier), Raymond King, Ivan Thomas (Boys on Train), Brenda W. King, C.W. White (Boys' Mothers), W. Dee Kutach (Parole Board Chairman), Brick Lowry (Parole Board Commissioner), Martin Colley (McCoy's Lawyer), O.S. Savage (Field Captain), Bruce Bissonette (Sporting Goods Salesman), Tom Bush (Cowboy's Helper), Dick Crockett (Bank Guard), A.L. Camp (Hardware Store Owner), Bob Veal (TV Shop Proprietor), Jim Kannon (Cannon), Maggie Gonzalez (Carhop), Doug Dudley (Max), Stacy Newton (Stacy), Tom Bush (Cowboy's Helper).

In one of his most hard-bitten roles, taciturn McQueen is released on a parole arranged for by his wife McGraw. She has had to sleep with political big-shot Johnson, who pulled the strings for the parole; he wants McQueen to lead a group of professional thieves on a bank raid. McQueen organizes the small band, including McGraw as a getaway driver and cocky Lettieri and Hopkins as gun-happy goons. Through an elaborate plan, McQueen and cohorts successfully rob the southwestern bank of $500,000 but Hopkins spoils the caper by panicking and killing a guard. The thieves rendezvous and McQueen learns that Lettieri has murdered Hopkins. The gunman tells him: "He didn't make it . . . neither did you," and draws a gun to shoot McQueen. But McQueen has anticipated the suspected traitor's move and is quicker, firing several shots into Lettieri's chest, the blast driving him into a pit. To be sure, McQueen fires another round into Lettieri's prone body, the bullet striking the gunman's shoulder. McQueen and McGraw drive off, heading for Johnson's ranch. McQueen now realizes that Johnson has set him up, that Lettieri was ordered to kill him and he even suspects his wife of being in league with the boss. In a confrontation with Johnson, McQueen's suspicions are confirmed. He also learns that Johnson slept with McGraw and, in a rage, is about to kill Johnson when McGraw shoots him. McQueen flees with the money and McGraw. Later he accuses her of being Johnson's mistress, slapping her about for her infidelity, even though she explains that she did it to get him released from prison. "You sent me to him," she whines. Driving frantically, the couple head for El Paso and the Mexican border with Johnson's army of gunmen on their trail. Lettieri is also after them. He had worn a bulletproof vest and only McQueen's last bullet injured him. Lettieri has abducted a veterinarian, Dodson, and his sluttish wife, Struthers, forcing them to drive to El Paso after McQueen and the money. McQueen and McGraw have a series of adventures en route to El Paso, one of which sees petty thief Bright steal McGraw's bag carrying the stolen money. This McQueen recovers by boarding the same train Bright takes and slugging the thief unconscious, getting off at the next stop to rejoin his wife and buy a car, then driving to a cheap El Paso hotel run by Taylor where they hide out, scheming a way to cross into Mexico. Johnson's henchmen and Lettieri catch up with them and a fierce shootout takes place where

McQueen kills Lettieri for real and mows down the Johnson goons. He and McGraw then stop Pickens, who is driving a pickup truck, and order him to take them up to the border. They offer him a fortune for his beat-up truck and he laughingly sells it to them, promising to tell no one. McQueen and McGraw then safely drive into Mexico and opulent freedom at film's end. This violent film, typical of Peckinpah's slam-bang action movies, relentlessly depicts ruthless robbery, killing, and murder, not to mention adultery, kidnaping, bribery, extortion, and general mayhem. The vivid direction and lightning pace, however, make the film completely fascinating as the culprits attempt to destroy the culprits and the viewer finds himself actually rooting for McQueen and McGraw, thieves that they might be, hoping they will get away. The film breaks all code precedents in that antiheroes and out-and-out criminals, McQueen and McGraw are allowed to totally escape punishment for their crimes. (The bank robbery is offhandedly excused in that insurance will cover the loss but nothing is said about the killing of the bank guard, other than this was the work of an out-of-control thief.) Lettieri gives a wonderful study in evil and Struthers, who allows him to flop her ample breasts about like blobs of Jello, is about as repugnant a female as ever bounced across a screen, encouraging the gunman to murder her husband, obsessed with his guns and menacing manner. No one in this film is honorable or attractive, a fact symbolized in one cynical Peckinpah scene where, to escape detection, McQueen and McGraw hide in a garbage truck and are dumped, along with their stolen loot, in a vast waste area. Human waste walking is what the film is all about and, as such, is a lesson in amorality, which may or may not have been the director's intention. McGraw is just a waste of time, having no acting ability at all and projecting the attitude of a spoiled rich girl whose Neiman-Marcus charge card has been taken away. Her open-mouth appearance and wide-eyed stares pass for her acting talent which is zero. This film, which was originally intended to be a Paramount production, is Peckinpah's biggest hit, though certainly not his best film, grossing more than $18 million. Peter Bogdanovich was initially slated to direct the film and Jack Palance was tentatively scheduled to play the vicious Lettieri role. National General took over the distributing responsibilities in cooperation with the newly formed First Artists Production Company which had been organized by Paul Newman, Sidney Poitier, Barbra Streisand, and McQueen, this being McQueen's first production selected by him. The story, originally set in the 1940s, was made contemporary. The actor dominated every aspect of the film, reediting the work himself and discarding an entire score done by Jerry Fielding and bringing in Jones to compose another score, one as cacophonous as the bullet-banging noise permeating the film. The violence here is nonstop and inexcusable under most circumstances, but as a study in bloodletting, it's hard to match. Certainly this film is not for youngsters.

p, David Foster, Mitchell Brower; d, Sam Peckinpah; w, Walter Hill (based on the novel by Jim Thompson); ph, Lucien Ballard (Todd-AO 35, Technicolor); m, Quincy Jones; ed, Robert Wolfe; art d, Ted Haworth, Angelo Graham; set d, George R. Nelson; cos, Ray Summers; spec eff, Bud Hulburd; stunts, Carey Loftin; makeup, Al Fleming, Jack Petty.

Crime Drama **Cas.** **(PR:O MPAA:PG)**

GETTING AWAY WITH MURDER (SEE: END OF THE GAME, 1976, Ger./Ital.)

GETTING EVEN* (1981) 55m Quantum c

Matthew Faison *(Leonard)*, Kate Zentall *(Karen)*.

A financially pressured artist and her accountant friend concoct a plan to rob a bank, after they hit upon hard times. Attempts at humor fall far short of the target as the bumbling pair nervously go through with the heist. A short independent film which, though it fits the Hollywood mold, thankfully never found wide distribution.

p, Emil Safier, Zepporah Safier; d&w, Mark Feldberg; ph, Ernest Holzman (CFI Color); m, Richard Greene; ed, Duane Hartzell; cos, Susan Lilly.

Comedy **(PR:C MPAA:NR)**

GETTING GERTIE'S GARTER*** (1945) 72m UA bw

Dennis O'Keefe *(Ken)*, Marie McDonald *(Gertie)*, Barry Sullivan *(Ted)*, Binnie Barnes *(Barbara)*, Sheila Ryan *(Patty)*, J. Carroll Naish *(Charles, the Butler)*, Jerome Cowan *(Billy)*, Vera Marshe *(Anna, the Maid)*, Donald T. Beddoe *(Clancy)*, Frank Fenton *(Winters)*, Richard Le Grand *(Dr. Clark)*.

A broad farce which was a successful Broadway comedy has O'Keefe as a retiring scientist whose past comes back to haunt him. He had once given luscious McDonald a bejeweled garter before marrying pretty Ryan. Now his best friend Sullivan is about to marry McDonald, who tells O'Keefe she intends to keep the sexy keepsake in case his marriage fails and he returns to her arms. To prevent embarrassment with his wife and friend, O'Keefe goes to wild extremes to obtain the elusive garter which encircles McDonald's leg. It's one belly laugh after another and director Dwan does not spare the slapstick. The overall production is above average. Worth more than a peek. Take-off of UP IN MABEL'S ROOM, 1944.

p, Edward Small; d, Allan Dwan; w, Dwan, Karen DeWolfe (based on a play by Wilson Collison, Avery Hopwood); ph, Charles Lawton, Jr; ed, Walter Hanneman, Truman K. Wood; md, Louis Forbes; art d, Joseph Sternad.

Comedy **(PR:A MPAA:NR)**

GETTING OF WISDOM, THE*** (1977, Aus.) 100m Southern Cross/Roadshow c

Susannah Fowle *(Laura)*, Barry Humphries *(Rev. Strachey)*, John Waters *(Rev. Shepherd)*, Sheila Helpmann *(Mrs. Gurley)*, Patricia Kennedy *(Miss Chapman)*, Julia Blake *(Isabella Shepherd)*, Dorothy Bradley *(Miss Hicks)*, Kay Eklund *(Mrs. Rambotham)*, Max Fairchild *(Mr. O'Donnell)*, Jan Friedl *(Miss Snodgrass)*, Diana Greentree *(Maisie Shepherd)*, Maggie Kirkpatrick *(Sarah)*, Monica Maughan *(Miss Day)*, Candy Raymond *(Miss Zielinski)*, Terence Donovan *(Tom Macnamara)*, Kerry Armstrong, Celia de Brugh, Kim Deacon, Alix Longman, Jo-Anne Moore, Amanda Ring, Hilary Ryan, Janet Shaw, Karen Sutton, Sigrid Thornton *(Girls)*.

Fowle is a 13-year-old enrolled in a girls' boarding school. In episodic fashion, we see her go through an initiation process, as well as adjust to her schoolmates and instructors. A refreshing directorial job from Beresford, who also delivered DON'S PARTY and TENDER MERCIES.

p, Phillip Adams; d, Bruce Beresford; w, Eleanor Witcombe, Moya Iceton (based on the novel by Henry Handel Richardson); ph, Don McAlpine (Panavision, Eastmancolor); ed, William Anderson; prod d, John Stoddart; art d, Richard Kent; cos, Anna Senior.

Drama **Cas.** **(PR:C MPAA:NR)**

GETTING OVER* (1981) 108m Maverick/Continental c

John R. Daniels *(Mike Barnett)*, Gwen Brisco *(Gwen)*, Mary Hopkins *(Mary)*, Bernice Givens *(Bernice)*, Sheila Dean *(Sheila)*, Renee Gentry *(Renee)*, Sandra Sully *(Sandy)*, Paulette Gibson *(Paulette)*, Donniece Jackson *(Penny)*, George Pelster *(Lou Lesser)*, John F. Goff *(Arnold Stanfield Stone)*, Sheldon Lee *(Sol Comfort)*, Andrew "Buzz" Cooper *(Deff Jeff Marvelous)*, Dap Sugar Willie *(Willie)*, Floyd "Wildcat" Chatman *(Noble)*, Arthur Adams *(Baron Sporty)*, Don Edmonds *(Millstine)*, Aurelia Sweeney *(Zulu)*, Mabel King *(Mabel Queen)*, Bryan O'Dell *(Claude)*, David Hubbard *(Clyde)*, Michael Hiat *(Waldo Perfect)*, Peggy Foster *(Cleo)*.

Essentially a production to feature a rock group called The Love Machine, this film was shown in tandem with love performances by that group for the short time it was in release. It's a silly, exaggerated ride through the business known as "show." Every stereotype in recent memory has been placed into the screenplay. Goff is the standard unscrupulous record producer. He hires promoter Daniels to help satisfy the government employment standards (black employees' ratio to white). Right there is the first hole in this hole-laden story. Of all the businesses that the government has on file, show business is the least likely to have any problems acceding to quotas. The lowly promoter, Daniels, finds and develops The Love Machine, an all-girl musical group. Next, he attempts to lure Cooper away from a record company run by broken-nose types (read Cosa Nostra) by offering a multi-million dollar contract which, of course, he could not possibly fulfill. There's a huge music awards show and Cooper, supposedly a major star, finds it impossible for him to perform unless he gets the cues from his gangster managers. Next thing you know, Cooper is kidnaped and The Love Machine walks away with the show. There are more plot contrivances in this 108 minutes than you would find in a lifetime of reading Dickens. A must miss, except for the very undiscerning. The best part of the film is the music; the acting, script, and direction all serve to make up the worst parts. It was produced by the star, which says something. He also wrote the story and the original idea and it may be presumed that he also found the money.

p, John R. Daniels, Cassius V. Weathersby, Jr.; d&w, Bernie Rollins (based on a story by Rollins and Daniels from an original idea by Daniels); ph&ed, Stephen B. Kim (CFI Color); m, Johnny Rodgers; art d, Hayward Perkins, Laurence Lochard; set d, Boris Caper.

Musical Drama **(PR:A-C MPAA:PG)**

GETTING STRAIGHT*½** (1970) 126m COL c

Elliott Gould *(Harry Bailey)*, Candice Bergen *(Jan)*, Jeff Corey *(Dr. Willhunt)*, Max Julien *(Ellis)*, Robert F. Lyons *(Nick)*, Cecil Kellaway *(Dr. Kasper)*, Jon Lormer *(Vandenburg)*, Leonard Stone *(Lysander)*, William Bramley *(Wade Linden)*, Jeannie Berlin *(Judy Kramer)*, John Rubinstein *(Herbert)*, Billie Bird *(Landlady)*, Richard Anders *(Dr. Greengrass)*, Brenda Sykes *(Luan)*, Gregory Sierra *(Garcia)*, Jenny Sullivan *(Sheila)*, Hilarie Thompson *(Cynthia)*, Harrison Ford *(Jake)*, Irene Tedrow *(Mrs. Stebbins)*, Elizabeth Lane *(Alice Linden)*, Joanna Serpe *(Roommate)*, Harry Holcombe *(Dean Chesney)*, Scott Perry *(Airline Representative)*, Richard Eymann, Warren Merrill.

Richard Rush just doesn't make enough movies. He seems to get around to them once every six or seven years (THE STUNT MAN, 1980, etc.) and that's not enough for us. It is Rush's stylish direction that almost saves Kaufman's screenplay from being the overdone and often sloppy work it must have been on paper. Gould is a returning Vietnam soldier who goes back to college at a fictional university to secure a teaching degree. While studying, he gets caught up with the lives of his fellow students, many of whom are 10 years younger than he is and light-years more naive, and is caught up in the tumultuous uprisings that characterize the waning years of the 1960s decade. Bergen is Gould's girl friend and never looked more attractive. Shot at a small community college near Eugene, Oregon, it is a most bucolic setting for the anger displayed. Gould is forced by Corey, the department head, to teach remedial English, a job he hates. Corey doesn't like Gould's smart-aleck attitude and is going to make life difficult for him. Gould looks at teaching as a calling and Corey sees it as a job and therein is the crux of their differences. Julien is a black militant who tries to enlist Gould in the cause, but he refuses for the time being, as he is trying to get straight. Lyons is a former pal of Gould who tries to sabotage Gould's career by stealing his exams and then reporting it to Corey. Meanwhile, Gould is seeing Bergen as well as several other women on campus and cutting a swath through the flower of Oregonian womanhood. Once the riots begin, Gould is asked to be a liaison between the students and the school by school president Lormer. He is then called before a panel of professors and has an argument with one of them over the man's interpretation of THE GREAT GATSBY, which he feels was motivated by homosexuality. Gould responds by denouncing them all, dancing on the table, and winds up kissing the boorish and pedantic questioner on the mouth. And with that, he races out to accompany Bergen and Julien as they demonstrate. Gould is wonderful playing himself (and nobody does Gould better than Gould) and this is one of several films made at that time which showed off his quirky personality to perfection. The few sexual scenes are done with taste and when it gets funny, it's very funny. It's also very dated by today's standards, a not uncommon problem when a picture is so specifically geared to be *au courant*. Still, as a youth picture, it towers above much of the tripe being made in the 1980s. Jeannie Berlin (Elaine May's daughter who went on to star in Neil Simon's THE HEARTBREAK KID, 1972) and Jenny Sullivan (Barry Sullivan's daughter) are good in their small roles. The assistant director, Howard Koch, Jr., went on to become a film producer and eventually ran Rastar for Ray Stark. Songs include "Getting Straight," Ronald Stein, Dan Payton, Marty Kaniger, Caroline Arnell; "Feelings," "Shades of Gray," Barry Mann, Cynthia Weil; "Ain't No Way," Dan Payton, Marty Kaniger; "Moon Rock and Talk," Ronald Stein (sung by P. K. Limited); "I'll Build a Bridge," Jack Keller, Ernie Sheldon (sung by The New Establishment).

p&d, Richard Rush; w, Bob Kaufman (based on the novel by Ken Kolb); ph, Laszlo Kovacs (Eastmancolor); m, Ronald Stein; ed, Maury Winetrobe; art d, Sydney Z. Litwack; set d, Edward Parker; cos, Gene Ashman; spec eff, Ira Anderson; stunts, Chuck Bail; makeup, Leo Lotito, Ben Lane.

Comedy/Drama   **Cas.**   **(PR:C-O MPAA:R)**

GETTING TOGETHER zero   (1976) 110m Total Impact c

Malcolm Groome (David), Kathleen Seward (Shiela), Rhonda Hansome (Reb), Tony Collado (Carlos), Charles Douglass (Randy), Helga Kopperl (Vivian).

A narcissistic view of some young So Ho artists, who have no one to blame for their cinematic failure but themselves. Groome is a copywriter who gives it all up for a free and easy existence. When conservative girl friend Seward walks out, weirdo Hansome takes her place. She ties him up and fills him in on her perverse fantasies which include her homosexual brother. An embarrassment for everybody, and a joy to none.

p, Joey Asaro, David Sector; d&w, Sector; ph, Marty Knopf; m, Tony Camillo; ed, Jane Brodsky Altschuler; prod d, Theodore S. Hammer; art d, Gerald Holbrook; cos, Neil Cooper.

Drama   **(PR:O MPAA:NR)**

GHARBAR   (SEE: HOUSEHOLDER, THE, 1963, U.S./Ind.)

GHASTLY ONES, THE zero   (1968) 81m JER c

Veronica Radbrook, Hal Belsoe, Eileen Hayes, Don Williams, Maggie Rogers, Carol Vogel, Richard Ramos, Anne Linden, Fib LaBlanque, Haal Borske, Neil Flanders, Hal Sherwood.

A hopeless case in terms of the horror genre which must have been churned out on a negative budget. Three couples must stay in a haunted mansion in order to receive their dead father's estate. The three men are killed off—one is hanged, another disemboweled, and a third is jabbed in the throat with a pitchfork. Of the three girls, only two make it to the final credits, with one having her head served on a dinner plate. The killer turns out to be an old woman who claims to be the illegitimate half sister of the dead man. She is prepared to kill the remaining gals, but is stopped by her hunchback friend. She sets the hunchback on fire; he smacks her with a cleaver. They both die, as does this picture, which alas, was resurrected 10 years later and remade as LEGACY OF BLOOD.

p, Jerome Frederick; d, Andy Milligan; w, Milligan, Hal Sherwood; ph, Milligan, D. Mills; ed, Gerald Jackson.

Horror   **Cas.**   **(PR:O MPAA:NR)**

GHIDRAH, THE THREE-HEADED MONSTER**½ (1965, Jap.) 85m
Toho/Continental c
(GHIDORAH SANDAI KAIJU CHIKYU SAIDAI NO KESSAN; AKA: GHIDORA, THE THREE-HEADED MONSTER; GHIDRAH; THE GREATEST BATTLE ON EARTH: THE BIGGEST RIGHT ON EARTH: MONSTER OF MONSTERS)

Yosuke Natsuki (Shindo), Yuriko Hoshi (Naoko), Hiroshi Koizumi (Prof. Murai), Takashi Shimura (Dr. Tsukamoto), Emi Ito, Yumi Ito ("The Peanuts," Little Sisters), Akiko Wakabayashi (Princess Salno), Hisaya Ito (Malness), Akihiko Hirata (Okita), Kenji Sahara (Kanamaki), Eiji Okada.

The three heads of Japanese monster Ghidrah may be better than Mothra's one, but not if fellow monsters Godzilla and Rodan are called in to give a hand. The big brawl takes place on Mount Fuji, which has come to be a familiar stomping grounds for these destructive critters. The people of Tokyo are just as surprised as ever when their city gets trampled under foot by the fire-breathers. The three-against-one match comes to a head when the quick-thinking Mothra spins a silky web which ensnares Ghidrah. Honda's direction, as usual, is up to camp standards, as well as the miniatures. The most notable aspect of this genre, however, is the dubbing "technique" which a blind man could have done better. Interestingly cast is Takashi Shimura from Kurosawa's IKURU, and Eiji Okada from Alain Resnais' HIROSHIMA MON AMOUR.

p, Tomoyuki Tanaka; d, Inoshiro Honda; w, Shinichi Sekizawa; ph, Hajime Koizumi (Tohoscope, Eastmancolor); m, Ikira Ifukube; ed, Ryohei Fujii; art d, Takeo Kita; spec eff, Eiji Tsuburaya.

Monster/Science Fiction   **Cas.**   **(PR:A MPAA:NR)**

GHETTO FREAKS   (SEE: SIGN OF AQUARIUS, 1970)

GHOST, THE zero   (1965, Ital.) 96m Panda/Magna c
(LO SPETTRO)

Barbara Steele (Margaret), Peter Baldwin (Dr. Charles Livingstone), Leonard Elliott (Dr. Hichcock), Harriet White (Catherine), Raoul H. Newman [Umberto Raho] (Canon), Reginald Price Anderson (Notary Fisher), Carlo Kechler (Police Superintendent), Carol Bennet.

Steele is driven mad when the ghost of the husband she murdered appears and tells her where he has hidden his precious jewels. She looks for them but they are not there. It turns out that her husband is still alive and plotting with the housekeeper to drive her crazy, a method employed with much more grace in

Clouzot's DIABOLIQUE. Steele is the only reason to watch this. A sequel to the tolerable HORRIBLE DR. HICHCOCK.

p, Louis Mann [Luigi Carpentieri], Ermanno Donati; d, Robert Hampton [Riccardo Freda]; w, Hampton, Robert Davidson (based on a story by Davidson); ph, Donald Green [Raffaele Masciocchi] (Technicolor); m, Frank Wallace [Franco Mannino]; ed, Donna Christie [Ornella Micheli]; art d, Samuel Fields [Mario Chiari].

Horror   **(PR:O MPAA:NR)**

GHOST AND MR. CHICKEN, THE***   (1966) 89m UNIV c

Don Knotts (Luther Heggs), Joan Staley (Alma), Liam Redmond (Kelsey), Dick Sargent (Beckett), Skip Homeier (Ollie), Reta Shaw (Mrs. Maxwell), Lurene Tuttle (Mrs. Miller), Philip Ober (Simmons), Harry Hickox (Police Chief Fuller), Charles Lane (Whitlow), Jesslyn Fax (Mrs. Hutchinson), Nydia Westman (Mrs. Cobb), George Chandler (Judge), Robert Cornthwaite (Springer), James Begg (Herkie), Sandra Gould (Loretta Pine), James Millhollin (Mr. Maxwell), Cliff Norton (Bailiff), Ellen Corby (Miss Tremaine), Jim Boles (Billy Ray), Hope Summers (Suzanna Blush), Hal Smith (Calver Weems), Eddie Quillan (Elevator Operator), J. Edward McKinley (Mayor).

Don Knotts is surprisingly funny as a bug-eyed typesetter for a newspaper who yearns to become a reporter. While tracking down a murder for a story, he has to spend the night in a haunted house. Combining Knotts, who seems to be afraid of his own shadow, with a ghoul-filled mansion leaves endless opportunities for laughs. Staley, who is cast as the reporter's gal, was the 1958 Playboy centerfold.

p, Edward J. Montagne; d, Alan Rafkin; w, James Fritzell, Everett Greenbaum; ph, William Margulies (Technicope, Technicolor); m, Vic Mizzy; ed, Sam E. Waxman; art d, Alexander Golitzen, George Webb; set d, John McCarthy, Oliver Emert; cos, Rosemary Odell.

Comedy/Mystery   **(PR:A MPAA:NR)**

GHOST AND MRS. MUIR, THE****   (1942) 104m FOX bw

Gene Tierney (Lucy), Rex Harrison (The Ghost of Capt. Daniel Gregg), George Sanders (Miles Fairley), Edna Best (Martha), Vanessa Brown (Anna), Anna Lee (Mrs. Fairley), Robert Coote (Coombe), Natalie Wood (Anna as a Child), Isobel Elsom (Angelica), Victoria Horne (Eva), Whitford Kane (Sproule), Brad Slaven (Enquiries), William Stelling (Bill), Helen Freeman (Author), David Thursby (Sproggins), Heather Wilde (Maid), Stuart Holmes (Man on Train), Housely Stevenson.

There's really nothing scary about this wonderful fantasy/romance where the beautiful widow Tierney buys a remote seacoast house which was once occupied by a dashing merchant captain. Shortly after Tierney moves in with her little daughter Wood she encounters some strange doings but is not alarmed even though Coote and other neighbors have already warned the headstrong woman that the cottage is haunted. Tierney is more curious than apprehensive and after a few pranks practiced by the cantankerous ghost, Harrison, she demands he show himself. He does, in all his handsome, bearded glory, not only befriending Tierney and her daughter but falling in love with the lovely lady. Tierney eventually faces financial problems and Harrison comes to the rescue by dictating his 19th century sea adventures which Tierney puts into novel form and for which a publisher pays handsomely to put the salty tales between covers. Through her publisher, Tierney meets writer Sanders who courts her with genteel manners, but she finds that he's a cad, a dallying married man who takes his wife, Lee, for granted. The true lover is Harrison but he realizes the impossibility of the situation and, while Tierney sleeps, whispers in her ear, telling her that their ethereal relationship has been but a dream and that's the only way she will remember it. This fragile story would have immediately collapsed into unbelievability had it not been for the fine performances of Harrison and Tierney, whose wonderful interaction was materially brought forth by director Mankiewicz. The production is deeply enhanced by Lang's contrasting photography which earned him an Oscar nomination. Herrmann's score is both whimsical and full of other-world lyricism. In this, his second American film, Harrison is superb as the sharp-tongued affectionate ghost and Tierney shines as his earthbound object of love. Remade in 1955 as STRANGER IN THE NIGHT and a 1968-70 TV series.

p, Fred Kohlmar; d, Joseph L. Mankiewicz; w, Philip Dunne (based on the novel by R.A. Dick); ph, Charles Lang; m, Bernard Herrmann; ed, Dorothy Spencer; art d, Richard Day, George Davis; set d, Thomas Little, Stuart Reiss, cos, Oleg Cassini; spec eff, Fred Sersen.

Fantasy   **(PR:A MPAA:NR)**

GHOST AND THE GUEST***   (1943) 59m PRC bw

James Dunn (Webster Frye), Florence Rice (Jackie Frye), Mabel Todd (Mabel), Sam McDaniel (Harmony Jones), Robert Dudley (Ben Bowron), Eddy Chandler (Herbie), Jim Toney (Police Chief), Robert Bice (Smoothie Lewis), Renee Carson (Josie), Tony Ward (Killer Blake), Anthony Caruso (Ted), Eddie Foster (Harold).

Dunn and Rice are newlyweds who take their vacation in a quiet country home, which turns out to be occupied by gangsters in search of some hidden diamonds. Secret passages and hidden panels make for some zany hocus-pocus, in this picture scripted by old-time comedian Morey Amsterdam.

p, Arthur Alexander, Alfred Stern; d, William Nigh; w, Morey Amsterdam (based on the story by Milt Gross); ph, Robert Cline; ed, Charles Henkel, Jr.; md, Lee Zahler; art d, James Altweid.

Comedy   **(PR:A MPAA:NR)**

GHOST BREAKERS, THE***½   (1940) 83m PAR bw

Bob Hope (Larry Lawrence), Paulette Goddard (Mary Carter), Richard Carlson (Geoff Montgomery), Paul Lukas (Parada), Willie Best (Alex), Pedro De Cordoba (Havez), Virginia Brissac (Mother Zombie), Noble Johnson (The Zombie), Anthony Quinn (Ramon/Francisco Maderos), Tom Dugan (Raspy Kelly), Paul Fix (Frenchy Duval), Lloyd Corrigan (Martin), Emmett Vogan (Announcer), Grace Hayle (Screaming Woman), Herbert Elliott (Lt. Murray), James Blaine (Police Sergeant),

Jack Hatfield *(Elevator Boy)*, David Durand *(Bellhop)*, James Flavin *(Hotel Porter)*, Leonard Sues *(Newsboy)*, Jack Edwards *(Ship Bellboy)*, Max Wagner *(Ship Porter)*, Paul Newlan *(Baggage Man)*, Francisco Maran *(Headwaiter)*, Jack Norton *(Drunk)*, Blanca Vischer *(Dolores)*, Douglas Kennedy, Robert Ryan *(Internes)*, Kay Stewart *(Telephone Girl)*.

Looking for a follow-up to their successful Hope/Goddard 1939 comedy thriller THE CAT AND THE CANARY, Paramount dusted off an old haunted house film called THE GHOST BREAKERS that had been made twice in the silent days, once in 1914 with H.B. Warner, and again in 1922 with Wallace Reid. The result was a stylish, frequently funny little scare show that was even better than THE CAT AND THE CANARY. Hope plays a radio commentator known for his crime exposes (obviously inspired by Walter Winchell) who inadvertently becomes involved with a murder when he arrives at a hotel for a talk with gangster Fix. Before he enters Fix's room, Hope witnesses one of the mobster's goons, Quinn, attempt to murder Lukas, a lawyer. In a panic, Hope produces a pistol and kills Quinn. Hysterical, Hope dashes into the next open room and jumps into a steamer trunk owned by Goddard. Soon the trunk is placed aboard a ship bound for Cuba, with Hope still inside. When Hope finally emerges from the trunk he learns that Goddard has inherited a mansion in Cuba and Lukas is the lawyer for the estate. A romance soon develops between Goddard and Hope, and they both become worried when repeated warnings that her house is haunted greet them in Havana. While visiting the city, Goddard is given an ominous warning by the twin brother of the man Hope killed (also played by Quinn), who demands to know the identity of his brother's murderer. Meanwhile Hope has been nosing around the mansion and finds some strange goings-on. Organ music, ghosts, and a room full of caskets are investigated by Hope, Goddard, and valet Best. Lawyer Lukas turns up murdered, but he manages to mutter something about hidden treasure before he dies. During their rummaging, the trio uncover a secret passageway that leads to a hidden silver mine. In the mine are Quinn and gangster Carlson. Carlson brandishes a gun and things look grim, but Best accidentally hits the switch for a trap door and eliminates the gangster. As it turns out, Quinn and his twin brother were only trying to protect the mine from intruders! Naturally, all winds up well in the end. Though really a comedy, THE GHOST BREAKERS has its fair share of effective and spooky horror scenes, directed with an atmospheric flavor by Marshall. The balance between laughs and chills is expertly handled, making the film a pleasure to watch. In 1953 the film was remade as SCARED STIFF with Dean Martin and Jerry Lewis. THE GHOST BREAKERS was listed, along with the Bowery Boys film GHOST CHASERS, as the principal sources of inspiration for the phenomenally successful 1984 film GHOSTBUSTERS.

p, Arthur Hornblow, Jr.; d, George Marshall; w, Walter De Leon (based on the play by Paul Dickey, Charles Goddard); ph, Charles Lang; m, Ernst Toch; ed, Ellsworth Hoagland; art d, Hans Dreier, Robert Usher; set d, Mel Epstein; spec eff, Farciot Edouart.

GHOST CAMERA, THE½** (1933, Brit.) 68m REA/RAD bw

Henry Kendall *(John Grey)*, Ida Lupino *(Mary Elton)*, John Mills *(Ernest Elton)*, S. Victor Stanley *(Albert Sims)*, George Merritt *(Inspector)*, Felix Aylmer *(Coroner)*.

A photograph is taken of a murder, but the camera is tossed out a window to destroy the evidence. Luckily for the innocent man accused of the killings, the camera lands in a passing auto, preventing any damage to the film. Lupino, 15 years old at the time, would make one more film in England before going to Hollywood as a Paramount player.

p, Julius Hagen, d, Bernard Vorhaus; w, H. Fowler Mear (based on a story by J. Jefferson Farjeon.

Mystery/Crime **(PR:A MPAA:NR)**

GHOST CATCHERS*** (1944) 67m UNIV bw

Ole Olsen *(Ole)*, Chic Johnson *(Chic)*, Gloria Jean *(Melinda)*, Martha O'Driscoll *(Susanna)*, Leo Carrillo *(Jerry)*, Andy Devine *(Bear)*, Lon Chaney *(Horsehead)*, Kirby Grant *(Clay)*, Walter Catlett *(Colonel)*, Ella Mae Morse *(Virginia)*, Henry Armetta *(Signatelli)*, Morton Downey, Tor Johnson, Mel Torme *(Drummers)*, Walter Kingsford, Tom Dugan, Edgar Dearing, Wee Willie Davis, Ralph Peters, Frank Mitchell, Bess Flowers, Jack Norton, Edward Earle.

An exceptionally wild comedy from the team of Olsen and Johnson who are pitted against ghosts this time. They are the owners of a nightclub who aid their new neighbor and his family when their house is discovered to be haunted. Lon Chaney, Jr. plays a bear, while Andy Devine is cast as a horse. This strange film is full of such oddities, another being a cameo by singer Mel Torme playing the drums. Tunes include: "Blue Candlelight" (Paul Francis Webster, Harry Revel); "These Foolish Things" (Harry Link, Holt Marvell, Jack Strachey); "I'm Old Enough to Dream" (Everett Carter, Edward Ward); "Three Cheers For The Customer," (Webster, Revel); "Swanee River," "Quoth The Raven."

p, Edmund L. Hartmann; d, Edward F. Cline; w, Hartmann (based on the story "High Spirits" by Milt Gross, Cline); ph, Charles Van Enger; ed, Arthur Hilton; md, Edward Ward; art d, John B. Goodman, Richard H. Riedel.

Musical/Comedy **(PR:A MPAA:NR)**

GHOST CHASERS** (1951) 67m MON bw

Leo Gorcey *(Slip Mahoney)*, Huntz Hall *(Sach)*, William Benedict *(Whitey)*, David Gorcey *(Chuck)*, Buddy Gorman *(Butch)*, Bernard Gorcey *(Louie Dumbrowsky)*, Jan Kayne *(Cynthia)*, Philip Van Zandt *(Dr. Granville)*, Robert Coogan *(Jack Eagen)*, Lela Bliss *(Margo The Medium)*, Hal Gerard *(Dr. Siegfried)*, Marshall Bradford *(Prof. Krantz)*, Argentina Brunetti *(Mrs. Parelli)*, Doris Kemper *(Mrs. Mahoney)*, Belle Mitchell *(Mme. Zola)*, Michael Ross *(Gus)*, Lloyd Corrigan *(Edgar)*, Donald Lawton *(Leonard)*, Paul Bryar *(First Reporter)*, Pat Gleason *(Second Reporter)*, Bob Peoples *(Photographer)*.

After one of the Bowery Boys' neighbors is cheated, the gang sets out to break up a seance scheme. In the midst of his investigation, Hall bumps into a real ghost, which only he can see, who is also out to crack the same ring. Another frail entry in the four dozen Bowery Boys series. A clever touch is the ghost, who takes the boys' side and bedazzles with ghostly acts in their favor. (See BOWERY BOYS series, Index).

p, Jan Grippo; d, William Beaudine; w, Charles R. Marion, Bert Lawrence; ph, Marcel Le Picard; ed, William Austin; art d, Dave Milton.

Comedy/Crime **(PR:A MPAA:NR)**

GHOST CITY* (1932) 60m MON bw

Bill Boyd, Andy Shuford, Helen Foster, Walter Miller, Kate Campbell, Charles King, Walter Shumway, Jack Carlyle.

Boyd contends with the masked gang responsible for the ghostly appearance of a once-thriving town in this below-par oater. For one who once was a rotten horseman, Boyd shows he is learning fast in GHOST CITY.

d&w, Harry Fraser; ph, Archie Stout.

Western **(PR:A MPAA:NR)**

GHOST COMES HOME, THE½** (1940) 78m MGM bw

Frank Morgan *(Vern Adams)*, Billie Burke *(Cora Adams)*, Ann Rutherford *(Billie Adams)*, John Shelton *(Lanny Shea)*, Reginald Owen *(Hemingway)*, Donald Meek *(Mortimer Hopkins, Sr.)*, Nat Pendleton *(Roscoe)*, Frank Albertson *(Ernest)*, Harold Huber *(Tony)*, Hobart Cavanaugh *(Ambrose Bundy)*.

Morgan returns home after a two-month absence to find his family living a life of luxury. Since he was presumed dead, wife Burke was able to collect his insurance benefits, only to have to return the cash due to Morgan's reappearance. A fair comedy which is saved from the cellar by a wonderfully likable cast.

p, Albert E. Levoy; d, William Thiele; w, Charles Maibaum, Harry Ruskin (based on a play "The Courageous Seaman" by George Kaiser); ph, Leonard Smith; m, David Snell; ed, William Terhune; art d, Cedric Gibbons.

Drama **(PR:A MPAA:NR)**

GHOST CREEPS, THE (SEE: BOYS OF THE CITY, 1940)

GHOST DIVER** (1957) 76m FOX bw

James Craig *(Roger Bristol)*, Audrey Totter *(Anne Stevens)*, Pira Louis *(Pelu Rico)*, Nico Minardos *(Manco Capao)*, Lowell Brown *(Bob Bristol)*, Rodolfo Hoyos, Jr. *(Rico)*, George Trevino *(Bartender)*, Elena Da Vinci *(Marguerita)*, Paul Stader *(Stunt, Actor)*, Diane Webber, Robert Lorenz *(Stunt Doubles)*, Richard Geary, Tom Garland, Michael Dugan *(Stunts)*.

Craig is the star of a TV adventure show who is determined to uncover a hidden South American treasure, and tells his viewers so. Also taking part in the underwater search is Minardos, a local diver who is even more obsessed with the treasure. An earthquake shakes everything up, and both men surface empty-handed.

p, Richard Einfeld; d&w, Einfeld, Merrill G. White; ph, Jack M. Nickolaus, Jr. (RegalScope); m, Paul Sawtell, Bert Shefter; ed, White.

Adventure **(PR:A MPAA:NR)**

GHOST GOES WEST, THE**** (1936) 85m LFP/UA bw

Robert Donat *(Murdoch/Donald Glourie)*, Jean Parker *(Peggy Martin)*, Eugene Pallette *(Joe Martin)*, Elsa Lanchester *(Lady Shepperton)*, Ralph Bunker *(Ed Bigelow)*, Patricia Hilliard *(Shepherdess)*, Everley Gregg *(Gladys Martin)*, Morton Selten *(Gavin Glourie)*, Chili Bouchier *(Cleopatra)*, Mark Daly *(Groom)*, Herbert Lomas *(Fergus)*, Elliot Mason *(Mrs. NcNiff)*, Jack Lambert, Colin Leslie, Richard Mackie, J. Neil More, Neil Lester *(Sons of MacLaggan)*, Hay Petrie *(The MacLaggan)*, Quintin McPherson *(MacKaye)*, Arthur Seaton, David Keir *(Creditors)*.

This was the first English-speaking film for French master director Clair and it proved a winner. The story begins in Scotland where Donat, an 18th century clan leader, is insulted by another clan chief but dies before he can remedy the stain upon his stiff honor. His modern-day descendant, also Donat, winds up trying to maintain the sprawling family castle and is slowly going broke, creditors waiting for him behind every door. Salvation arrives in the form of loud, acquisitive Pallette with his pretty daughter Parker, who immediately falls for Donat. It's two worlds meshing uncomfortably; Donat is refined, dignified, and brimming with ancient culture, where Parker is outgoing, down-to-earth, and utterly candid. While Donat shows her his cavernous castle she remarks: "You don't know what it means to us to see something that's not new." Her mother, Gregg, is simply suffering from a vacuous mentality; during dinner Gregg states: "Ever since I had my nervous breakdown, I've been psychic." This dinner in the grand ballroom is prepared and served by Donat's creditors, who have been chasing him about his castle's halls for money until Pallette's family appeared to buy the place and are now so eager to recoup their losses that they act out the parts of servants. Pallette does buy the castle and has it transported by pieces to the U.S., rebuilding stone by stone on his vast Florida estate. Parker and Donat—he goes along with the castle as caretaker—are emotionally involved and eyeing the altar but matters become complicated when it is discovered that the castle which has been haunted in Scotland by Donat's ancestor, also played by Donat, has come along with the pieces and goes on haunting everyone in sight. More mirth is added when Parker confuses the spooky ancestor with the flesh and blood man she loves. In the end the ghost is able to remove the stigma of insult to his honor and find eternal rest while his living descendant winds up with Parker and a bright American future. Clair's light comedic touch is everywhere in the film which is loaded with the kind of screwball comedy so popular in the 1930s, personified by Pallette's brassy ways, and Gregg's scatterbrained ideas. Stereotyped elements of American materialism are stressed but U.S. audiences took it all good-naturedly and made the film a hit. Clair and his overpowering producer, Korda, however, did not always see eye to eye. Korda had signed Clair to a three-year contract in 1935 and convinced the director to leave France after his latest satire on dictators, LE DERNIER

MILLIARDAIRE (1934) was poorly received. THE GHOST GOES WEST was a wide departure for Clair and he was constantly interrupted in the shooting of the film by Korda, who thought that barging onto a set or into a sound stage to make changes was his inalienable right. He arbitrarily changed lines in the Clair-Sherwood script and even threw out scenes dealing with the transporting of the castle from Scotland to Florida, stating that the shipboard sequences were too long and not funny enough. At one point Clair even debated removing his name from the film but enough of his touch remained to have him reconsider. The film, as released in England, ran 90 minutes with 5 minutes chopped out of it by Korda for American release. A sepia tint was applied to all original prints.

p, Alexander Korda; d, Rene Clair; w, Robert E. Sherwood, Clair, Geoffrey Kerr (based on the story "Sir Tristram Goes West" by Eric Keown) ph, Hal Rosson; m, Misha Spoliansky; ed, Harold Earle-Fishbacher, Henry Cornelius; prod d, Vincent Korda; md, Muir Mathieson; cos, Rene Hubert, John Armstrong; spec eff, Ned Mann.

Fantasy/Comedy   **(PR:A   MPAA:NR)**

GHOST GOES WILD, THE** (1947) 66m REP bw

James Ellison, Anne Gwynne, Ruth Donnelly, Stephanie Bachelor, Grant Withers, Lloyd Corrigan, Emil Rameau, Jonathan Hale, Charles Halton, Edward Everett Horton, Edward Gargan, Gene Garrick, Michael Hughes, William Austin.

Artist Ellison takes to masquerading as a spiritualist, using the ruse as a means of escaping a court date. But he gets more than he bargained for when a real ghost pops into the picture. Luckily for Ellison, this spirit is friendly and helps to get him out of the jam he's gotten himself into. A light-hearted mystery, strictly for those seeking entertainment.

p, Armand Schaefer; d, George Blair; w, Randall Faye; ph, John Alton; m, Joseph Dubin; ed, Fred Allen; md, Morton Scott; art d, Hilyard Brown.

Mystery/Comedy   **(PR:A   MPAA:NR)**

GHOST GUNS** (1944) 60m MON bw

Johnny Mack Brown, Raymond Hatton, Evelyn Finley, Sarah Padden, Riley Hill, Ernie Adams, Jack Ingram, Tom Quinn, Frank LaRue, John Merton, Bob Cason, Marshall Reed, Steve Clark, George Morrell.

There's something mysterious happening out on the range. Muscular and hardy hero Brown spends the film's 60 minutes checking out what's behind it all.

p, Charles J. Bigelow; d, Lambert Hillyer; w, Frank H. Young (based on a story by Bennett Cohen); ph, Marcel Le Picard; ed, Pierre Janet; md, Edward Kay; set d, Vin Taylor.

Western   **(PR:A   MPAA:NR)**

GHOST IN THE INVISIBLE BIKINI*½ (1966) 82m AIP c

Tommy Kirk (Chuck Phillips), Deborah Walley (Lili Morton), Aron Kincaid (Bobby), Quinn O'Hara (Sinistra), Jesse White (J. Sinister Hulk), Harvey Lembeck (Eric Von Zipper), Nancy Sinatra (Vicki), Claudia Martin (Lulu), Francis X. Bushman (Malcolm), Benny Rubin (Chicken Feather), Bobbi Shaw (Princess Yolanda), George Barrows (Monstro), Basil Rathbone (Reginald Ripper), Patsy Kelly (Myrtle Forbush), Boris Karloff (The Corpse), Susan Hart (The Ghost), Luree Holmes (Shirl), Alberta Nelson (Alberta), Andy Romano (J.D.), Piccola Pupa (Piccola), Myrna Ross, Bob Harvey, John Macchia, Alan Fife (Rat Pack), Ed Garner, Mary Hughes, Patti Chandler, Frank Alesia, Salli Sachse, Sue Hamilton, Jerry Brutsche (Girls and Boys), The Bobby Fuller Four, Elena Andreas, Herb Andreas (The Statues).

Karloff is wasted in this big-budget beach picture as a recently deceased corpse who, with the help of gal ghost Hart, tries to get into heaven. The catch is that he must perform one good deed within twenty-four hours. Rathbone is the sinister lawyer and executor of the estate who plans to kill the benefactors. Karloff sees his chance and with Hart's help foils Rathbone's plan and gets through the pearly gates. AIP decided to retire the beach genre after this picture, their seventh, failed miserably at the box office. The Bobby Fuller Four provides the rock'n'roll.

p, James H. Nicholson, Samuel Z. Arkoff; d, Don Weis; w, Louis M. Heyward, Elwood Ullman (based on a story by Heyward); ph, Stanley Cortez (Panavision, Pathe color); m, Les Baxter; ed, Fred Feitshans, Eve Newman; art d, Daniel Haller; set d, Clarence Steensen; cos, Richard Bruno; spec eff, Roger George; ch, Jack Baker; l, "Geronimo" "Swing-A-Ma-Thing," "Don't Try to Fight It, Baby," "Stand Up and Fight," "Make the Music Pretty," Guy Hemric, Jerry Styner; "Geronimo" sung by Nancy Sinatra.

Comedy   **(PR:C   MPAA:NR)**

GHOST OF DRAGSTRIP HOLLOW zero (1959) 65m AIP bw

Jody Fair (Lois), Martin Braddock (Stan), Russ Bender (Tom), Leon Tyler (Bonzo), Elaine Dupont (Rhodo), Henry McCann (Dave), Sanita Pelkey (Amelia), Dorothy Neuman (Anatasia), Kirby Smith (Wesley), Jean Tatum (Alice), Jack Ging (Tony), Nancy Anderson (Nita), Beverly Scott (Hazel), Bill St. John (Ed), Judy Howard (Sandra), Tom Ivo (Allen), Paul Blaisdell (Monster), George Dockstader (Motor Cop), Marvin Almars (Leon), Rosemary Johnston (Lois's Double), Marilyn Moe (Nita's Double).

Hot rods, monsters, and rock 'n 'roll—an instant giveaway to the mentality of this teen-oriented picture. The hint of a plot has a gang of greasers holing up in a haunted mansion after getting evicted from their garage. This deformed script could have only been helped by a complete rewrite. There are a few unromantic romances, a brawl with a rival gang, and the appearance of a gym-shoed "She Creature."

p, Lou Rusoff; d, William Hole, Jr.; w, Rusoff; ph, Gil Warrenton; m, Ronald Stein; ed, Frank Keller, Ted Sampson; art d, Dan Haller; m/l, "Charge Geronimo!" "Ghost Train," Nick Venet, "Tongue Tied," Jimmy Maddin, "He's My Guy," Charlotte Brasser, "I Promise You," Bruce Johnston, Judy Harriet.

Comedy/Horror   **(PR:C   MPAA:NR)**

GHOST OF FRANKENSTEIN, THE*** (1942) 65m UNIV bw

Lon Chaney, Jr. (Monster), Sir Cedric Hardwicke (Frankenstein), Ralph Bellamy (Erik), Lionel Atwill (Dr. Bohmer), Bela Lugosi (Ygor), Evelyn Ankers (Elsa), Janet Ann Gallow (Cloestine), Barton Yarborough (Dr. Kettering), Doris Lloyd (Martha), Leyland Hodgson (Chief Constable), Olaf Hytten (Russman), Holmes Herbert (Magistrate), Dwight Frye (Village Man), Michael Mark (Mayor's Assistant), Harry Cording (Villager), Otto Hoffman, Lawrence Grant, Brandon Hurst, Julius Tannen, Dick Alexander, Ernie Stanton, George Eldredge, Teddy Infuhr, Lionel Belmore.

Lon Chaney, Jr. takes over Karloff's role as the famous squarehead in this dully scripted third sequel. Again details change from film to film. After being tossed into the blazing sulphur pit at the end of SON OF FRANKENSTEIN, the monster appears here unscarred. He is also now able to speak, a gift he possessed in the first sequel, BRIDE OF FRANKENSTEIN, but lost again in the second. Lugosi, as Ygor, dutifully brings the monster to the country castle of Hardwicke, the second son of Dr. Frankenstein. The doctor decides Chaney needs a brain transplant and pulls out Lugosi's, who doesn't seem to be using it anyway. The monster becomes more intelligent, but also malevolent. He goes on a rampage through the nearby town and kidnaps a small girl. He is captured, chained, and brought to trial. While it doesn't stand up to its predecessors, it can boast an enjoyable cast. It also has the honor of being perhaps the last of the classic horror film era, giving way to the days of sci-fi and psychological horror. The destruction footage of the laboratory in the climax of the film was later used in the finale of HOUSE OF DRACULA (1945). After this came FRANKENSTEIN MEETS THE WOLFMAN. (See FRANKEN-STEIN series, Index.)

p, George Waggner; d, Erle C. Kenton; w, Scott Darling (based on a story by Eric Taylor); ph, Milton Krasner, Woody Bredell; ed, Ted Kent; md, Charles Previn; art d, Jack Otterson; spec eff, John P. Fulton.

Horror   **(PR:C   MPAA:NR)**

GHOST OF HIDDEN VALLEY*½ (1946) 50m PRC bw

Buster Crabbe (Billy Carson), Al St. John (Fuzzy Jones), Jean Carlin (Kaye), John Meredith (Henry), Charles King (Dawson), Jimmy Aubrey (Tweedle), Karl Hackett (Jed), John L. "Bob" Cason (Sweeney), Silver Harr (Stage Guard), Zon Murray (Arnold), George Morrell, Bert Dillard, Cecil Trenton.

Stale oater which has Englishman Meredith go West to run his father's ranch. He finds himself having to battle cattle rustlers who are traveling across his land. With the aid of Crabbe and St. John they run the bandits off his property. Crabbe was to make one more film for low-budget Producers Releasing Corp. after six years on the lot and 40 features. (See BILLY CARSON series, Index.)

p, Sigmund Neufeld; d, Sam Newfield; w, Ellen Coyle; ph, Art Reed; ed, Holbrook N. Todd; md, Lee Zahler.

Western   **(PR:A   MPAA:NR)**

GHOST OF JOHN HOLLING (SEE: MYSTERY LINER, 1934)

GHOST OF ST. MICHAEL'S, THE**½ (1941, Brit.) 82m EAL/ABF bw

Will Hay (William Lamb), Claude Hulbert (Hilary Teasdale), Charles Hawtrey (Percy Thorne), Raymond Huntley (Mr. Humphries), Felix Aylmer (Dr. Winter), Elliott Mason (Mrs. Wigmore), John Laurie (Jamie), Hay Petrie (Procurator Fiscal), Roddy Hughes (Amberley), Manning Whiley (Stock), Derek Blomfield (Sunshine), Brefni O'Rorke (Sgt. MacFarlane).

Hays is a half-witted schoolteacher at a London boys' school from where the boys are evacuated to a damp and dreary Scottish castle during WW II. Legend has it that when someone is near death in the castle, bagpipes play. The pipes blow and Aylmer dies; they play again and Huntley dies. The pipes let out another bellow, but before a third victim is claimed Hays discovers that Mason, a collaborator with the Germans, is responsible for the deaths. An enjoyable comedy with a few thrills tossed in.

d, Marcel Varnel; w, Angus Macphail, John Dighton; ph, Derek Williams.

Comedy   **(PR:A   MPAA:NR)**

GHOST OF THE CHINA SEA** (1958) 73m COL bw

David Brian (Martin French), Lynn Bernay (Justine Woolf), Jonathan Haze (Larry Peters), Harry Chang (Hito Matsumo), Gene Bergman (Sabatio Trinidad), Kam Fong Chun (Pvt. Hakashima), Mel Prestige (Gaetano Gato), Jaime Del Rosario (Himself), Dan Taba (Capt. Zaikaku), Bud Pente (Col. McCutcheon).

Brian is the tough, embittered captain of a ship tagged the "U.S.S. Frankenstein" which is trying to escape a Japanese invasion during WW II. The problem, however, is a lack of food and supplies, most importantly, gasoline. To get what they think is a Dutch cruiser to save them, they jump ship and set it afire, hoping they'll be noticed. They are, but the ship is Japanese, which is torpedoed by a British vessel before the men can be taken captive. A typical actioner which was one of veteran director Sears' final pictures.

p, Charles B. Griffith; d, Fred F. Sears; w, Griffith; ph, Gilbert Warrenton; m, Alexander Laszlo; ed, Charles Nelson; md, Laszlo.

Action/War Drama   **(PR:A   MPAA:NR)**

GHOST OF ZORRO** (1959) 69m REP bw

Clayton Moore (Ken Mason/Zorro), Pamela Blake (Rita White), Roy Barcroft (Hank Kilgore), George J. Lewis (Moccasin), I. Stanford Jolley (Paul Hobson), Steve Clark (Jonathan R. White), Marshall Reed (Fowler), Jack O'Shea (Freight Agent), Steve Darrell (Ben Simpson), John Crawford (Mulvaney), Eugene Roth (Crane), Dale Van Sickel (Hodge), Tom Steele (Brace), Alex Montoya (Yellow Hawk), Frank O'Connor (Doctor), Holly Bane (Larkin), Bob Reeves (Andy).

Moore dons a mask and battles a gang of outlaws who are trying to prevent the extension of a telegraph line. Moore's performance, with and without his mask, is solid, but the film is a re-edited version of a 12-chapter serial from 1949, resulting in a confusing and choppy feature.

d, Fred C. Brannon; w, Royal Cole, William Lively, Sol Shor; ph, John MacBurnie; m, Stanley Wilson; ed, Cliff Bell, Harold Minter, DeWitt McCann; art d, Fred A. Ritter; set d, John McCarthy, Jr., James Redd; makeup, Bob Mark; spec eff, Howard Lydecker, Theodore Lydecker.

Western   **(PR:A   MPAA:NR)**

GHOST PATROL**   (1936) 58m Puritan bw

Tim McCoy (Tim Caverly), Claudia Dell (Natalie Brent), Walter Miller (Dawson), Wheeler Oakman (Kincaid), Jim Burtis (Henry), Dick Curtis (Charlie), Lloyd Ingraham (Brent), Jack Casey (Mac), Slim Whitaker (Frank), Artie Ortego (Ramon), Art Dillard (Shorty), Fargo Bussey (Bill).

Miller and Oakman are a sinister cowboy duo who kidnap the inventor of a ray gun. They put the weapon to use by pulling mail planes out of the sky, but their mischief stops when G-man McCoy and his pals hear of their doings. Essentially, this film is a western disguised by gangsters and sci-fi traits. The six-guns are replaced with death rays and horses with aircraft. Interesting only in retrospect.

p, Sigmund Neufeld, Leslie Simmonds; d, Sam Newfield; w, Wyndham Gittens (based on a story by Joseph O'Donnell); ph, John Greenhalgh; ed, Jack English.

Western/Science-Fiction   Cas.   (PR:A   MPAA:NR)

GHOST RIDER, THE*   (1935) 56m Argosy/Superior bw

Rex Lease, Ann Carol, Lloyd Ingraham, Bill Patton, Bobby Nelson, William Desmond, Franklyn Farnum, Lafe McKee, Art Mix, Blackie Whiteford, Roger Williams, Ed Coxen, Denver Dixon [Victor Adamson], Blackjack Ward, Eddie Parker, John Alexander.

Rex Lease is a deputy who gets some help in his quest to clean up the West from the forays of a ghostly gunfighter. An interesting idea which doesn't nearly reach its potential.

p, Louis Weiss; d, Jack Levine [Jack Jevne]; w, John West [Jack Jevne].

Western   (PR:A   MPAA:NR)

GHOST SHIP, THE***½   (1943) 69m RKO bw

Richard Dix (Captain), Russell Wade (Tom), Edith Barrett (Ellen), Ben Bard (Bowns), Edmund Glover (Sparks), Skelton Knaggs (Finn), Tom Burton (Benson), Steve Winston (Ausman), Robert Bice (Raphael), Lawrence Tierney (Louie), Dewey Robinson (Boats), Charles Lung (Jim), George de Normand (John), Paul Marion (Peter), Sir Lancelot (Billy), Boyd Davis (Roberts), Harry Clay (McCall), Russell Owen, John Burford, Eddie Borden, Mike Lally, Charles Regan (Crew Members), Nolan Leary (Stenographer), Herbert Vigran (Chief Engineer), Shirley O'Hara (Silhouette Girl), Alex Craig (Blind Beggar), Bob Stevenson, Charles Norton (German Sailors), Norman Mayes (Carriage Driver).

A heavily atmospheric study of Dix, the psychotic captain of a ship, and the effects of his terrorization of third-mate Wade. The tormented Wade tries to inform the rest of the crew of Dix's sadistic behavior, but is ignored. The captain continues on his monstrous path until he is knocked out by fellow crew member Knaggs. This film was for many years out of distribution because of a lawsuit brought by Samuel Golding and Norbert Faulkner, who felt producer Lewton had stolen their like-titled play. The court agreed and pulled the film from theatrical release. It can now be heralded as an excellent example of Lewton's ability to create a dark and sinister mood through subtlety. Director Mark Robson (THE HARDER THEY FALL, THE BRIDGES AT TOKO-RI) is able to stylishly bring the script to life. Songs "Blow the Man Down" (sung by the Blind Beggar and Billy Radd), "Home Dearie Home," "Come to San Sebastian," "I'm Billy Radd from La Trinidad" (all sung by Radd).

p, Val Lewton; d, Mark Robson; w, Donald Henderson Clarke; ph, Nicholas Musuraca; m, Roy Webb; ed, John Lockert; md, Constantin Bakaleinikoff; art d, Albert S. D'Agostino, Walter E. Keller; set d, Darrell Silvera, Claude Carpenter; cos, Edward Stevenson; spec eff, Vernon L. Walker.

Drama/Horror   (PR:C   MPAA:NR)

GHOST SHIP**   (1953, Brit.) 69m ABTCON/Lippert bw

Dermot Walsh (Guy), Hazel Court (Margaret), Hugh Burden (Dr. Fawcett), John Robinson (Mansel), Joss Ambler (Yard Manager), Joan Carol (Mrs. Martineau), Hugh Latimer (Peter), Mignon O'Doherty (Mrs. Manley), Laidman Browne (Coroner), Meadows White (Yard Surveyor), Pat McGrath (Bert), Josh Ackland (Ron), John King-Kelly (Sid), Colin Douglas, Patricia Owens, Melissa Stribling, Jack Stewart, Anthony Marlowe, Geoffrey Dunn, Ian Carmichael, Anthony Hayes, Barry Phelps, Robert Moore, Ewen Solon, Jock Finlay, Madoline Thomas, Graham Stuart, Gordon Bell.

Barely staying afloat, this average tale is about a young couple who purchase a yacht they are told is haunted. The unbelievers ignore the warnings and strange things begin to happen. They call in an expert on the supernatural and discover that the former owner killed and stored on board two bodies. The ship is exorcised and the couple sail off, content with the bargain-priced boat.

p&d, Vernon Sewell; w, Sewell, Philip Thornton; ph, Stanley Grant; m, Eric Spear; ed, Francis Bieber; art d, George Haslam.

Drama   Cas.   (PR:A   MPAA:NR)

GHOST STORIES   (SEE: KWAIDAN, 1965, Jap.)

GHOST STORY**   (1974, Brit.) 89m Stephen Weeks c

Murray Melvin, Larry Dann, Vivian Mackerall, Marianne Faithfull, Anthony Bate, Leigh Lawson, Barbara Shelley.

Old friends gathered at a country house get involved with the ghosts that haunt the place. This occasionally effective scare piece suffers from bad acting and lax direction.

p&d, Stephen Weeks; w, Weeks, Rosemary Sutcliff; ph, Peter Hurst (Fujicolor); m, Ron Geesin.

Horror   (PR:C   MPAA:NR)

GHOST STORY***½   (1981) 110m UNIV c

Fred Astaire (Ricky Hawthorne), Melvyn Douglas (John Jaffrey), Douglas Fairbanks, Jr. (Edward Wanderley), John Houseman (Sears James), Craig Wasson (Don/David), Alice Krige (Alma/Eva), Jacqueline Brookes (Milly), Patricia Neal (Stella), Miguel Fernandes (Gregory Bate), Lance Helcomb (Fenny Bate), Mark Chamberlin (Young Hawthorne), Tom Choate (Young Jaffrey), Kurt Johnson (Young Wanderley), Ken Olin (Young James), Brad Sullivan (Sheriff), Guy Boyd, Robert Burr, Helena Carroll, Robin Curtis, Breon Gorman, Cagle D. Green, Kyra Carleton, James Greene, Ruth Hunt, Virginia P. Bingham, Deborah Offner, Russell R. Bletzer, Alfred Curven, Michael O'Neil, William E. Conway, Terrance Mario Carnes, Hugh Hires, Raymond J. Quinn, Barbara von Zastrow, Edward F. Dillon, Alvin W. Fretz.

Four elderly men—Astaire, Douglas, Fairbanks, Jr., and Houseman—meet regularly in New England to tell each other ghost stories. One year strange occurrences upset the stream of things. It's then revealed that 50 years earlier these men had accidently killed a lovely young tease. To cover their tracks they had put her in a car and driven it into a lake, only to see her frantically but unsuccessfully try to escape. Krige (CHARIOTS OF FIRE) turns in an eerie performance as the vengeful ghost. The film suffers from a number of holes in the script (it was penned by CARRIE screenwriter Lawrence Cohen), but that seems quite standard for a ghost story. Excellent mood and atmosphere of the New England winter setting and four enjoyable performances from the leads are satisfying. It unfortunately resorts to some stupid special effects at the finale, forgetting that the power of any ghost story lies in the imaginary and not the actual.

p, Burt Weissbourd; d, John Irvin; w, Lawrence D. Cohen (based on the novel by Peter Straub); ph, Jack Cardiff (Technicolor); m, Philippe Sarde; ed, Tom Rolf; art d, Norman Newberry; makeup, Dick Smith.

Horror   Cas.   (PR:O   MPAA:R)

GHOST TALKS, THE**   (1929) 61m FOX bw

Helen Twelvetrees (Miriam Holt), Charles Eaton (Franklyn Green), Carmel Myers (Marie Haley), Earle Foxe (Heimie Heimrath), Henry Sedley (Joe Talles), Joe Brown (Peter Accardi), Clifford Dempsey (John Keegan), Stepin Fetchit (Christopher C. Lee), Baby Mack (Isobel Lee), Arnold Lucy (Julius Bowser), Bess Flowers (Sylvia), Dorothy McGowan (Miss Eva), Mickey Bennett (Bellboy).

By mistake, a daffy detective graduates at the top of his private-eye class, which pits him against a barrage of crooks and spooks. An early talkie which is hampered by a gross overusage of the microphone. A good piece of ammunition if one wants to make a case for the "purity" of silent cinema.

d, Lew Seiler; w, Frederick Brennan, Harlan Thompson (based on the play "Badges" by Max Marcin, Edward Hammond); ph, George Meehan.

Crime/Comedy   (PR:A   MPAA:NR)

GHOST THAT WALKS ALONE, THE*   (1944) 63m COL bw

Arthur Lake, Janis Carter, Lynne Roberts, Frank Sully, Warren Ashe, Arthur Space, Barbara Brown, Matt Wills, Ida Moore, Jack Lee, Paul Hurst, Robert Williams, John Tyrrell.

A dull comedy in which a man who does the sound effects for a radio station finds his imagination working overtime when his honeymoon is interrupted by the appearance of a dead body in his hotel room. The film manages a chuckle here and there, but not enough to keep one from falling asleep.

p, Jack Fier; d, Lew Landers; w, Clarence Upson Young (based on the story by Richard Shattuck); ph, L.W. O'Connell; ed, Jerome Thoms; md, M.W. Stoloff; art d, Lionel Banks, Paul Murphy.

Mystery/Comedy   (PR:A   MPAA:NR)

GHOST TOWN*½   (1937) 65m COMM bw

Harry Carey (Cheyenne Harry), Ruth Findlay (Jane), Jane Novak (Rose), David H. Sharpe (Bud Ellis), Lee Shumway (Mr. Morrell), Edward Cassidy (Sheriff), Roger Williams (Ed Gannon), Phil Dunham (Abe Rankin), Earl Dwire (McCall), Chuck Morrison (Blackie Hawks), Sonny the "Marvel Horse."

Carey crosses the path of an old friend who plans on buying an abandoned mining town. The friend is killed and, as always, good guy Carey is blamed and is tossed into the lockup. Follow this with his escape and proven innocence and the result is the standard, unimaginative oater. The poor pacing doesn't help.

p, William Berke; d, Harry Fraser; w, Weston Edwards (based on a story by Monroe Talbot); ph, Robert Cline; m, Lee Zahler; ed, Arthur Brooks.

Western   (PR:A   MPAA:NR)

GHOST TOWN**   (1956) 77m Bel-Air/UA bw

Kent Taylor (Anse Conroy), John Smith (Duff Dailey), Marian Carr (Barbara Leighton), John Doucette (Doc Clawson), William [Bill] Phillips (Kerry McCabe), Serena Sande (Maureen), Joel Ashley (Sgt. Dockery), Gilman H. Rankin (Simon Peter Wheedle), Ed Hashim (Dull Knife), Gary Murray (Alex).

A diverse group of whites takes refuge in a deserted town when local Cheyenne Indians get into the firewater. Under pressure of the attack, their ammunition exhausted, the beseiged travelers reveal their true characters to one another. Good-guy Taylor proves to be a purveyor of illegal arms to the murdering heathen; Carr, affianced to brave Eastern newspaperman Smith, demonstrates her avarice in electing to go for her recently discovered gold strike rather than for his person. Salvation arrives in the nick of time and justice triumphs. The revelations of the ordeal result in the union of Smith and the truly noble halfbreed, Sande.

p, Howard W. Koch; d, Allen Miner; w, Jameson Brewer; ph, Joseph F. Biroc; m, Paul Dunlap; ed, Mike Pozen; cos, Wesley V. Jefferies.

Western (PR:A MPAA:NR)

GHOST TOWN GOLD** (1937) 57m REP bw

Robert Livingston (Stony Brooke), Ray Corrigan (Tucson Smith), Max Terhune (Lullaby Joslin), Kay Hughes (Sabina), LeRoy Mason (Barrington), Burr Carruth (Thornton), Bob Kortman (Monk), Milburn Moranti (Jake), Frank Hagney (Kamatski), Don Roberts (Manager), F. Herrick Herrick (Catlett), Robert C. Thomas (Champ), Yakima Canutt (Buck), Horace Murphy, Earle Hodgins, Edward Piel, Sr., Harry Harvey, Hank Worden, Bud Osborne, Bob Burns, Wally West, I. Stanford Jolley.

The THREE MESQUITEERS series (see Index) continues as the Dumas-esque trio of Livingston, Corrigan, and Terhune race to return some stolen cash before the bank it was stolen from is foreclosed. Terhune, a vaudeville ventriloquist for more than 20 years, uses his skills here for a few laughs.

p, Nat Levine, William Berke; d, Joseph Kane; w, John Rathmell, Oliver Drake (based on a story by Bernard McConville, and characters created by William Colt MacDonald); ph, Jack Marta; m, Harry Grey; ed, Lester Orlebeck.

Western Cas. (PR:A MPAA:NR)

GHOST TOWN LAW*** (1942) 62m MON bw

Buck Jones (Buck Roberts), Tim McCoy (Tim), Raymond Hatton (Sandy), Virginia Carpenter (Josie Hall), Murdock McQuarrie (Judge Crail), Charles King (Gus), Howard Masters (Tom Cook), Ben Corbett (Red Larkin), Tom London, Silver the Horse.

An off-beat combination of western and mystery which spends most of the opening sequence in darkness with hooded figures on horseback. As part of the Rough Rider series, Buck and the boys battle a gang who methodically kill anyone who nears their hideout. The trio gets tough after two marshalls are killed and, as expected, overpower the black hats. (See ROUGH RIDER series, Index.)

p, Scott R. Dunlap; d, Howard Bretherton; w, Jess Bowers (Adele Buffington); ph, Harry Neumann; m, Edward Kay; ed, Carl Pierson.

Western/Mystery (PR:C MPAA:NR)

GHOST TOWN RENEGADES** (1947) 57m PRC bw

Al "Lash" La Rue (Cheyenne), Al "Fuzzy" St. John (Fuzzy), Jennifer Holt (Diane), Jack Ingram (Sharpe), Terry Frost (Flint), Steve Clark (Trent), Lee Roberts (Johnson), Lane Bradford (Wace), Henry Hall (Jennings), William Fawcett (Watson), Mason Wynn, Dee Cooper.

A familiar plot which offers nothing more than is expected. LaRue and St. John are a pair of government agents trailing Ingram, who is trying to gain control of an abandoned mining town. The property is rich in unmined gold but the feds never give him a chance to take advantage of it.

p, Jerry Thomas; d, Ray Taylor; w, Patricia Harper; ph, Ernest Miller; m, Walter Greene; ed, Joe Gluck.

Western (PR:A MPAA:NR)

GHOST TOWN RIDERS*½ (1938) 54m UNIV bw

Bob Baker, Fay Shannon, George Cleveland, Hank Worden, Forrest Taylor, Glenn Strange, Jack Kirk, Martin Turner, Reed Howes, Murdock McQuarrie, Merrill McCormack, George Morrell, Frank Ellis, Oscar Gahan, Tex Phelps.

The West is terrorized by an outlaw gang that holes up in an abandoned town littered with tumbleweeds. Baker foils their plan to scam Eastern lass Shannon out of her gold mine, paving the way for a romance between the pair.

p, Trem Carr; d, George Waggner; w, Joseph West.

Western (PR:A MPAA:NR)

GHOST TRAIN, THE** (1933, Brit.) 70m Gainsborough/GAU bw

Jack Hulbert (Teddy Deakin), Cicely Courtneidge (Miss Bourne), Ann Todd (Peggy Murdock), Cyril Raymond (Richard Winthrop), Allan Jeayes (Dr. Sterling), Donald Calthrop (Saul Hodgkin), Angela Baddeley (Julia Price), Henry Caine (Herbert Price), Tracy Holmes (Charles Bryant), Carol Coombe (Elsie Bryant).

Stranded in a desolate train station, a group of people are spooked by the thundering sounds of what they believe to be a "ghost train." These folks aren't too bright, however, and the train turns out to be very real. A shallow detective learns that the tracks are used by the Russians to transport Commie propaganda in England. Of course the wicked Reds are outwitted in the finale. The same story was done on the stage and as a silent.

p, Michael Balcon; d, Walter Forde; w, Angus Macphail, Lajos Biro, Sidney Gilliat (based on the play by Arnold Ridley); ph, Lesie Rowson.

Comedy (PR:A MPAA:NR)

GHOST TRAIN, THE** (1941, Brit.) 85m Gainsborough/GFD bw

Arthur Askey (Tommy Gander), Richard Murdoch (Teddy Deakin), Kathleen Harrison (Miss Bourne), Morland Graham (Dr. Sterling), Linden Travers (Julie Price), Peter Murray Hill (Richard Winthrop), Carole Lynn (Jackie Winthrop), Herbert Lomas (Saul Hodgkin), Raymond Huntley (John Price), Betty Jardine (Edna), Stuart Latham (Herbert), D.J. Williams (Ben Isaacs).

A group of folks forced to stay overnight at a train station are frightened by stories of a "ghost train" which the stationmaster tells. The answer to the mysterious train is far from supernatural, as the bumbling Askey discovers that it is being engineered by a gang of gunrunners. Good for a few laughs and a couple of chilling surprises.

p, Edward Black; d, Walter Forde; w, Marriott Edgar, Val Guest, J.O.C. Orton, Sidney Gilliat (based on a play by Arnold Ridley); ph, John J. Cox.

Comedy (PR:A MPAA:NR)

GHOST VALLEY**½ (1932) 54m RKO bw

Tom Keene, Merna Kennedy, Mitchell Harris, Billy Franey, Harry Bowen, Kate Campbell, Ted Adams, Buck Moulton, Harry Semels, Al Taylor, Slim Whitaker.

Keene and Kennedy inherit some property in an abandoned gold town which is rich in unmined ore. Harris, the administrator, learns of the potential wealth and tries to scare Kennedy off the land. Keene shows up and, not divulging his identity, is hired to assist Harris. Before long Keene has completely foiled Harris' scheme.

d, Fred Allen; w, Adele Buffington (based on a story by Buffington); ph, Ted McCord; ed, William Clemens; art d, Carroll Clarke.

Western (PR:A MPAA:NR)

GHOST VALLEY RAIDERS** (1940) 57m REP bw

Donald Barry (Tim Brandon), Lona Andre (Linda), LeRoy Mason (Frank Ewing), Tom London (Sheriff), Jack Ingram (Kennelly), Horace Murphy (Ringleader), Ralph Peters (Deputy Sheriff), Curley Dresden (Rawhide), Yakima Canutt (Marty Owens), John Beach, Bud Osborne, Al Taylor, Jack Montgomery, Fred Burns.

Barry is hired to put the stop to a gang terrorizing stagecoach riders. He goes undercover and, dressed like a bandit, cracks the thieving ring. Standard shoot-'em-up entertainment. A good chance to see the legendary stunt performer Canutt in a regular role.

p&d, George Sherman; w, Bennett Cohen (based on a story by Connie Lee); ph, Ernest Miller; ed, Lester Orlebeck; md, Cy Feuer.

Western (PR:A MPAA:NR)

GHOST WALKS, THE***½ (1935) 69m IN bw

John Miljan (Prescott Ames), June Collyer (Gloria Shaw), Richard Carle (Wood), Spencer Charters (The Professor), Johnny Arthur (Erskine), Henry Kolker (Dr. Kent), Donald Kirke (Terry), Eve Southern (Beatrice), Douglass Gerrard (Carroway), Wilson Benge (Jarvis), Jack Shutta (Head Guard), Harry Strang (Guard).

A determined playwright who has just penned a mystery invites a stage producer to his home. With the aid of some professional actors, the whodunit is played out, but without the knowledge of the producer, who thinks there has been an actual murder. When people really do begin disappearing, the playwright gets spooked. It turns out that an escaped lunatic has been doing the body snatching and preparing them for unscheduled operations. A well-written script and sharp performances support the unique premise, with tricky lighting effects proving startling in the old house setting.

p, Maury M. Cohen; d, Frank Strayer; w, Charles S. Belden; ph, M.A. Anderson; ed, Roland Reed; md, Abe Meyer; art d, Edward Jewell.

Mystery (PR:A MPAA:NR)

GHOSTS, ITALIAN STYLE** (1969, Ital./Fr.) 92m Ponti/MGM bw-c
(QUESTI FANTASMI; AKA: THREE GHOSTS)

Sophia Loren (Maria), Vittorio Gassman (Pasquale), Mario Adorf (Alfredo), Margaret Lee (Sayonara), Aldo Giuffre (Raffaele), Francesco Tensi (Prof. Santanna), Marcello Mastroianni (Guest-Ghost), Francis De Wolff, Augusta Merola, Piera Degli Esposti, Giovanni Tarollo, Nietta Zocchi, Valentino Macchi.

It's 1967 in Naples, Italy. Loren, an angry and succulent woman, is annoyed at the deal life has given her. She's poor, she has a bad marriage, and absolutely no money. Married to Gassman, they decide there is nothing left for them to live for and they attempt a double suicide but fail even at that. She decides to take up with Adorf, a man who has wanted her ever since she was a teenager. He ran an orphane and used the children to make bogus religious icons and such and Loren had been raised there under his lustful eye. What she doesn't know is that Adorf has been the reason why her husband has been unable to keep a job as Adorf has been in the background, making certain that the man would stay at any given employment. Adorf, still trying to get close to Loren, lets Loren and Gassman stay at a haunted palace where they will be the caretakers. Adorf allows them to move in and doesn't tell them that he is in the room above theirs. Loren doesn't know the palace is haunted and that Adorf is allowing them to live so he can dispel the rumors of the ghosts. Gassman sees Adorf late one night and thinks he is a ghost. He also finds a packet of money that Adorf has dropped and believes the ghost is trying to help the couple. Now Gassman rents a room to a dizzy hooker, Lee. Loren is outraged and mistakenly believes that Gassman is pimping for Lee so she leaves and doesn't allow anyone to know where she's gone. Gassman is arrested by police for his wife's 'murder' and tossed in jail. Adorf lights a perpetual candle in Loren's memory in the basement underneath the mansion. After a while, Gassman is released as there was no evidence to prove he'd killed his wife. Seven months have passed when Gassman finds Loren back at home, hiding. Gassman and Loren are back in love and determined to make a new life when Adorf sees Loren and thinks she is a ghost. He falls to his knees and wants to make up for all of the transgressions he's ever been guilty of. Loren says it would be well if Adorf gives all of the terrible money he's earned over the years to some charity and donate it in her memory. Further, Loren suggests that Adorf marry Lee. Adorf gives Gassman a ton of money and the couple leave, before he realizes he's been duped. They travel to Scotland to work as domestics for a crazed nobleman in a really haunted castle. This picture must have read better than it played. Even with Mastroianni in a cameo and the always delightful Gassman as the male lead, it didn't make it either at the box office or in the critics' eyes. Based on a play by De Filippo in 1946, it didn't translate well to the screen. Although only slightly longer than an hour and a half, it felt like forever.

p, Carlo Ponti; d, Renato Castellani; w, Castellani, Adriano Baracco, Leo Benvenuti, Piero De Bernardi, Ernest Pintoff (based on the play "Questi Fantasmi" by Eduardo De Fillipo); ph, Tonino Delli Colli (Technicolor); m, Luis

Enriquez Bacalov; ed, Jolande Benvenuti; art d, Pierro Poletto; cos, Piero Tosi (for Loren), Enrico Sabbatini.

Comedy   **(PR:C   MPAA:G)**

GHOSTS IN THE NIGHT   (SEE: GHOSTS ON THE LOOSE, 1943)

GHOSTS OF BERKELEY SQUARE**½(1947, Brit.) 85m Pathe/BN bw

Robert Morley (Gen. Burlap), Felix Aylmer (Col. Kelsoe), Yvonne Arnaud (Millie), Robert Beaumont (King's Equerry), Madge Brindley (Matron), Strelsa Brown (Rajah's Amazon Attendant), Harry Fine (1914 Colonel), Ronald Frankau (Tex), James Hayter (Capt. Dodds), Claude Hulbert (Merryweather), Martita Hunt (Lady Mary), Mary Jerrold (Lettie), Gerard Kempinski (Croupier), Edward Lexy (Briga-dier), Marie Lohr (Lottie), John Longden (Mortimer Digby), Aubrey Mallalieu (Butler), Anthony Marlowe (Speaking Red Indian), Mary Martlew (Maybella), A. E. Matthews (Gen. Bristow), Esme Percy (Vizier), J. H. Roberts (Doctor), Pamela Roberts (Decoy Girl), Abraham Sofaer (Disraeli), Ernest Thesiger (Investigator), Tom Walls, Jr. (Provost Marshal), Martin Miller (Professor), Wilfrid Hyde-White (Staff Captain), Wally Patch (Foreman).

Morely and Aylmer, upset with the war's progress, devise a plan to rectify things and get killed while implementing their scheme. Furious, Queen Anne has them appear before a court in the afterlife and they are sentenced to haunt a mansion. Through the aid of trick photography, the "ghosts" can assume human forms at will. Entertaining fluff.

p, Louis H. Jackson; d, Vernon Sewell; w, James Seymour (based on the novel No Nightingales by Caryl Brahms, S. J. Simon); ph, Ernest Palmer, Moray Grant; m, Hans May; ed, Joseph Sterling; prod d, Fred A. Swan; art d, Wilfred Arnold; cos, Beresford Egan.

Comedy   **Cas.**   **(PR:A   MPAA:NR)**

GHOSTS ON THE LOOSE**
(1943) 64m MON bw
(GB: GHOSTS IN THE NIGHT;
AKA: THE EAST SIDE KIDS MEET BELA LUGOSI)

Leo Gorcey (Muggs McGinnis), Huntz Hall (Glimpy Williams), Bobby Jordan (Danny), "Sunshine Sammy" Morrison (Scruno), Billy Benedict (Skinny, Benny), Stanley Clements (Stash), Bobby Stone (Rocky, Dave), Bill Bates ("Sleepy" Dave), Bela Lugosi (Emil), Rick Vallin (John "Jack" Gibson), Ava Gardner (Betty Williams Gibson), Minerva Urecal (Hilda), Wheeler Oakman (Tony), Frank Moran (Monk), Peter Seal (Bruno), Jack Mulhall (Lt. Brady), Kay Marvis Gorcey (Bridesmaid), Robert F. Hill (Minister), Tom Herbert.

Lugosi plays a Nazi spy hiding out in an ostensibly abandoned New York mansion. When the Bowery Boys stumble on his abode, he tries to scare them away by making the place appear haunted. Unfortunately, there was not enough focus on Lugosi as the film centered on the usual high jinks buffoonery of Gorcey, Hall, and company, whose antics make them a sort of poor man's Three Stooges. The subplot had Gardner playing Hall's soon-to-be-wed sister, which coincided with her real life walk down the aisle with Mickey Rooney, and some exhibitors were sharp and aggressive enough to bill her as "Mrs. Mickey Rooney" on their marquees. (See BOWERY BOYS series, Index.)

p, Sam Katzman, Jack Dietz; d, William Beaudine; w, Kenneth Higgins; ph, Max Stengler; ed, Carl Pierson; md, Edward Kay; art d, David Milton.

Comedy   **Cas.**   **(PR:A   MPAA:NR)**

GHOUL, THE***   (1934, Brit.) 73m GAU bw

Boris Karloff (Prof. Morlant), Cedric Hardwicke (Broughton), Ernest Thesiger (Laing), Dorothy Hyson (Betty Harlow), Anthony Bushell (Ralph Morlant), Kathleen Harrison (Kaney), Harold Huth (Aga Ben Dragore), D.A. Clarke-Smith (Mahmoud), Ralph Richardson (Nigel Hartley), Jack Raine (Chauffeur).

Interesting but minor Karloff vehicle (he appears only in the beginning of the film and at the end), the first he starred in produced in his native England which he had left in 1909. Karloff plays an eccentric English Egyptologist obsessed with the powers of the ancient Egyptian gods. On his death bed he commands his servant, Thesiger, to bind the sacred jewel known as "The Eternal Light" to his hand. He warns Thesiger that if the jewel is stolen, he will return from the grave seeking revenge. After Karloff's death, a greedy lawyer, a bogus priest, and an Egyptian student arrive at the estate and search for the jewel. When it is wrenched out of his hand, the dead Karloff indeed comes back to life, strangles the guilty party, and returns to his tomb with the jewel. Made and released on the heels of Karloff's hit THE MUMMY (some of the story elements in THE GHOUL were obviously inspired by the earlier film), THE GHOUL relies totally on the horror king's presence for any spooky power it may have. By killing him off at the beginning and bringing him back, the film suffers from the long, dull stretch in the middle that has no dynamic power of its own. No prints of THE GHOUL existed until recently (a print was discovered in New York City in 1969) and the film is hardly ever shown. It was the first English attempt at a horror film, and to help it along Gaumont imported a top-flight makeup artist to do Karloff's visage. Made as a comedy in 1962 under the title NO PLACE LIKE HOMICIDE!

p, Michael Balcon; d, T. Hayes Hunter; w, Roland Pertwee, John Hastings Turner, Rupert Downing, L. DuGarde Peach (based on the novel and play by Dr. Frank King, Leonard J. Hines); ph, Gunther Krampf; ed, Ian Dalrymple; makeup, Heinrich Heitfeld.

Horror   **(PR:C   MPAA:NR)**

GHOUL, THE**½   (1975, Brit.) 88m RANK c

Peter Cushing (Dr. Lawrence), John Hurt (Tom), Alexandra Bastedo (Angela), Gwen Watford (Ayah), Veronica Carlson (Daphne), Stewart Bevan (Billy), Ian McCulloch (Geoffrey), Don Henderson (The Ghoul).

Cushing is a defrocked clergyman who tries to hide his son's cannibalism. Set in the 1920s English countryside during a major auto race, the film sees a series of

drivers disappear one by one (apparently the son has a taste for *fast* food). In the end, Cushing shoots the son to death. Hurt gives a stellar performance as the gardener, who is an unequivocable lunatic in his own right. While underplaying gore, the film fails to intrigue due to its cold and calculating approach.

p, Kevin Francis; d, Freddie Francis; w, John Elder; ph, John Wilcox (Eastmancolor); m, Harry Robinson; ed, Henry Richardson; md, Philip Martell; art d, Jack Shampar.

Horror   **Cas.**   **(PR:O   MPAA:NR)**

GHOUL IN SCHOOL, THE   (SEE: WEREWOLF IN A GIRLS' DORMITORY, 1963, Ital.)

GIANT****   (1956) 201m WB c

Elizabeth Taylor (Leslie Benedict), Rock Hudson (Bick Benedict), James Dean (Jett Rink), Carroll Baker (Luz Benedict II), Jane Withers (Vashti Snythe), Chill Wills (Uncle Bawley), Mercedes McCambridge (Luz Benedict), Sal Mineo (Angel Obregon III), Dennis Hopper (Jordan Benedict III), Judith Evelyn (Mrs. Horace Lynnton), Paul Fix (Dr. Horace Lynnton), Rod Taylor (Sir David Karfrey), Earl Holliman (Bob Dace), Robert Nichols (Pinky Snythe), Alexander Scourby (Old Polo), Fran Bennett (Judy Benedict), Charles Watts (Whiteside), Elsa Cardenas (Juana), Carolyn Craig (Lacey Lynnton), Monte Hale (Bale Clinch), Mary Ann Edwards (Adarene Clinch), Sheb Wooley (Gabe Target), Victor Millan (Angel Obregon I), Mickey Simpson (Sarge), Pilar del Rey (Mrs. Obregon), Maurice Jara (Dr. Guerra), Noreen Nash (Lorna Lane), Napoleon Whiting (Swazey), Tina Menard (Lupe), Ray Whitley (Watts), Felipe Turich (Gomez), Francisco Villalobos (Mexican Priest), Ana Maria Majalca (Petra), Guy Teague (Harper), Nativadid Vacio (Eusebio), Max Terhune (Dr. Walker), Ray Bennett (Dr. Borneholm), Barbara Barrie (Mary Lou Decker), George Dunne (Verne Decker), Slim Talbot (Clay Hodgins), Tex Driscoll (Clay Hodgins, Sr.), Juney Ellis (Essie Lou Hodgins), Charles Meredith (Minister), Rush Williams (Waiter), Bill Hale (Bartender), Tom Monroe, Mark Hamilton (Guards), John Wiley (Assistant Manager), Ina Poindexter (Young Woman), Carl Moore (Toastmaster), Ella Ethridge (General's Wife), Paul Kruger (General), Eddie Baker (Governor), Ethel Greenwood (Governor's Wife), Fernando Alvarado, Tony Morella (Busboys), Julian Rivero (Old Man), Maxine Gates (Mrs. Sarge), Richard and David Bishop (Jordan as an Infant), Steven Kay (Jordan at Age 4), Mary Ann and Georgann Cashen (Judy as an Infant), Christine Werner (Luz as an Infant), Judy and Jill Lent (Luz at Age 2), John Garcia (Angel as an Infant), David Jiminez (Angel at Age 5), Colleen and Marlene Crane (Judy II as an Infant), Wanda Lee Thompson (Judy II at Age 2), Perfideo Aguilar and Margaret Trujillo (Jordy IV at an Infant), Ramon Ramirez (Jordy IV at Age 2).

Everything about GIANT is like its title, immense, towering, vast, and so too are the talents brought to it, from that of the master director Stevens to leads Taylor, Hudson, and Dean. In the case of the former two, they expanded their native abilities to the demanding roles and exceeded themselves. In Dean's case, it was a matter of a naturally great talent expanding in a part that gave him more freedom from the typecast role of young rebel. Headstrong, spoiled, and rich Taylor leaves her green Virginia countryside and land-wealthy family after falling in love with and marrying tall, dark Hudson, who takes her home to his endless Texas ranch, Reata, where she becomes mistress of the house and his cattle empire but soon learns that when Hudson and fellow cattle barons talk business she is expected to leave the room. Taylor must also contend with Hudson's resentful older sister, McCambridge, who dislikes her intrusion into the family. The two women are constantly in head-to-head conflict which ends when the obstinate McCambridge insists upon riding a wild horse which kills her. Her loathing of Hudson and Taylor lingers bitterly in the form of her will in which she bequeaths a small part of Reata to Dean, a surly, ambitious ranch hand who hates Hudson, mostly for marrying Taylor; Dean loves Taylor from afar with an obsessive passion. Dean is a thorn in Hudson's side and the wound runs even deeper, straight down, when Dean strikes oil, a wildcat well that gushes up a multi-million dollar fortune. Dean begins buying up other property, sinking more wells, and his oil empire, over the years, rivals Hudson's cattle kingdom. Hudson is a man of the old school and, despite the pleas of friends and business associates, refuses to sully his vast ranges by puncturing the land with ugly oil wells. Most of his neighbors go into the oil business with a vengeance and are either bought up by Dean or become his satellites. A new generation by then has grown up in the Old West tradition of Hudson's Reata. Mineo, the son of one of Hudson's myriad Mexican wranglers, goes off to WW II and is killed. Hudson's son, Hopper, becomes a doctor and refuses to take on his father's mantle, insisting upon doctoring the Mexican community, and, to the shock of the family, marrying Cardenas, an attractive Mexican woman. One of Hudson's daughters, Bennett, marries ranch hand Holliman who becomes Hudson's candidate to take over his empire when he dies (no Texan ever retires). Baker, the other daughter, really infuriates Hudson by becoming the queen of "Jet Rink Day" and becomes personally involved with Dean, who is an aging cowboy, still pathetically alone despite his immense riches. A huge banquet is scheduled to honor Dean and Hudson's clan reluctantly attends. When Cardenas is turned away from a beauty salon owned by Dean because she is Mexican, Hopper explodes and confronts Dean just as he enters the banquet hall to receive a standing ovation. Hopper attempts to strike the wealthy Dean but Dean's goons grab and hold him as Dean beats Hopper senseless. Hudson jumps from his seat and waits for Dean at the end of the entrance aisle, fists at the ready. The two step into a wine room where Dean, so drunk he cannot defend himself, sinks against a wall. Hudson, in disgust, walks away, but not before crashing down rack after rack of expensive wine. Later that night Dean slouches drunkenly at the speaker's table, the great hall long emptied, mumbling into the microphone the speech he never delivered to his guests. Baker, led to the scene by Wills, Hudson's long-time friend, witnesses Dean's emotional collapse and hears him raving about Taylor, her mother, the one woman he loved and never possessed. Baker's shock of recognition is that Dean attempted to possess her mother by making her his mistress. She leaves Dean alone to wallow in his oil-glutted fate. En route to Reata, Hudson drives his family homeward, forsaking his private plane. He stops in a diner owned by mammoth Simpson who refuses to serve a Mexican family. Hudson intervenes, asking Simpson to serve the Mexicans and a fight ensues, a battle royal where the huge proprietor is rocked by one powerhouse punch after another but manages to administer winning blows that send Hudson sprawling. The fight is significant; Hudson loses, but he wins the hearts of his family that had suspected him of hidden aristocratic prejudices. It is a courageous act that makes Hudson more than big; it makes him great. GIANT was big for everyone connected with it, returning a whopping $12 million in receipts the first time around. Stevens helmed with care the enormously popular Edna Ferber tale, carefully building the complex story scene by scene, establishing his characters with sensitivity. Stevens, as he had with A PLACE IN THE SUN and SHANE, took great pains with detail, as shown with the day-to-day workings of the fabled Reata ranch and, conversely, the bonehard labor of Dean's oil drilling. Always an extravagant director, he spared no expense in his many "takes" so that each scene was to his liking. Old Texas is convincingly and meticulously shown transforming to the new under his superb guidance. He deservedly won an Oscar for Best Director, overwhelming other epic helmsmen, King Vidor for WAR AND PEACE; Walter Lang for THE KING AND I and Michael Anderson for AROUND THE WORLD IN 80 DAYS, along with William Wyler for FRIENDLY PERSUASION. Taylor, who had appeared in Stevens' emotion-packed A PLACE IN THE SUN, found the director more demanding in GIANT, annoying her with his penchant for excruciatingly detailed setups and retakes but this may have resulted in Stevens' original desire to have Grace Kelly play the lead role and his impatience with the 23-year-old Taylor, who did not have the ranging abilities of the Oscar-winning Kelly. Hudson was moved about perfectly by Stevens as the personification of Old Texas, big, brawling, and with as much pride as the horizonless land he owned. It remained Hudson's favorite film performance until the day he died, one that won him an Oscar nomination. The film received 10 Academy Award nominations but only Stevens took one home, perhaps justifiably so in that this film was more his film than any other, the total expression of one man. Dean also received an Oscar nomination for his truculent role but he was dead by then, having been killed in an auto accident only days after the film was completed. Ginsberg, who had headed Paramount studios from 1940 to 1950 (under the watchful eye of Chairman of the Board Adolph Zukor) oddly coproduced GIANT with Stevens and then dropped out of films altogether, involving himself in commercial and industrial financing. Tiomkin's score is powerful but a bit too sprawling, like the film, on occasions. Mellor's lensing is superb, along with the editing. The Warner Color used, however, which bears a shot of overall rust-brown hue, distracts with flesh tones too dark which makes the actor's makeup obvious, especially in Taylor's closeups. Yet this color works well with the outdoors scenes. It's nevertheless a broadly appealing film that has the classic look and feel of true Americana, one that is heartfelt, sincere, and brave, wonderfully capsulized in Stevens' extreme closeups of two infants, one Anglo, one Mexican, looking wide-eyed to the future, with the "eyes of Texas," and, for that matter, all of America.

p, George Stevens, Henry Ginsberg; d, Stevens; w, Fred Guiol, Ivan Moffat (based on the novel by Edna Ferber); ph, William C. Mellor (Warner Color); m, Dmitri Tiomkin; ed, William Hornbeck, Fred Bohanan, Phil Anderson; prod d, Boris Leven, Ralph Hurst; md, Tiomkin; cos, Marjorie Best, Moss Mabry; m/l, Tiomkin, Paul Francis Webster.

Drama/Historical Epic   Cas.   (PR:A   MPAA:NR)

GIANT BEHEMOTH, THE   (SEE: BEHEMOTH, THE SEA MONSTER, 1959, Brit.)

GIANT CLAW, THE*   (1957) 76m Clover/COL bw

Jeff Morrow, Mara Corday, Morris Ankrum, Louis D. Merrill, Edgar Barrier, Robert Shayne, Morgan Jones, Clark Howat, Ruell Shayne.

An infinitely preposterous-looking giant bird from outer space terrorizes our Earth and lays an egg on Quebec. Flown by visible wires, the winged horror is able to avoid detection by the use of a radar-resistant shield. But the critter can't pull one over on scientists Morrow, Corday, and Ankrum (an old pro after EARTH VS. THE FLYING SAUCER and KRONOS), who send the bird to the bottom of the sea. One of the more comic moments is when the bird attacks a train, picks it up in its beak, and flies off with it—a cute analogy to a worm. Corday does a fine job standing around and looking sexy, especially since she was Playboy's Miss October in 1958. The "special" effects are laughable.

p, Sam Katzman; d, Fred F. Sears; w, Samuel Newman, Paul Gangelin; ph, Benjamin H. Kline; ed, Samuel A. Goodkind, Tony DiMarco; md, Mischa Bakaleinikoff; art d, Paul Palmentola.

Science-Fiction   (PR:A   MPAA:NR)

GIANT FROM THE UNKNOWN zero (1958) 76m Screencraft/Astor bw

Edward Kemmer (Wayne Brooks), Sally Fraser (Janet Cleveland), Buddy Baer (Vargas, the Giant), Morris Ankrum (Prof. Cleveland), Bob Steele (Sheriff Parker), Joline Brand (Ann Brown).

A preposterous story in which Baer plays a giant conquistador who is brought back to life after being struck by lightning. The grande senor employs his new-found sprightliness to go on a murder rampage in a remote and hapless California village. Producer Jacobs went on to do THE PLANET OF THE APES series.

p, Arthur F. Jacobs; d, Richard E. Cunha; w, Frank Hart Taussig, Ralph Brooke; ph, Cunha; m, Albert Glasser; spec eff, Harold Banks.

Horror   (PR:C   MPAA:NR)

GIANT GILA MONSTER, THE½** (1959) 74m Hollywood/McLendon Radio bw

Don Sullivan (Chace Winstead), Lisa Simone (Lisa), Shug Fisher (Mr. Harris), Jerry Cortwright (Bob), Beverly Thurman (Gay), Don Flourney (Gordy), Clarke Browne (Chucky), Pat Simmons (Sherry), Pat Reeves (Rick), Anne Sonka (Whila), Fred Graham (Sheriff), Bob Thompson (Wheeler), Cecil Hunt (Compton), Ken Knox

(Steamroller Smith), Yolanda Salas (Liz Humphries), Howard Ware (Eb Humphries), Stormey Meadows (Agatha Humphries), Desmond Dhooge (Hitchhiker).

A rear-projected monster just doesn't put the audiences in a deep state of fear, especially when it's a lizard. It does, however, induce occasional uncontrolled laughter. Sullivan and his merry band of hip teenagers battle the giant gila that has been threatening northern Texas, and even disturbing a local record hop. Directed by veteran cameraman Kellogg, whose only other claim to fame is as co-director with John Wayne of THE GREEN BERETS.

p, Ken Curtis; d, Ray Kellogg; w, Kellogg, Jay Sims (based on a story by Kellogg); ph, Wilfred Cline; m, Jack Marshall; ed, Aaron Stell; spec eff, Ralph Hammeras, Wee Risser.

Science Fiction   (PR:A   MPAA:NR)

GIANT LEECHES, THE   (SEE: ATTACK OF THE GIANT LEECHES, 1959)

GIANT OF MARATHON, THE**   (1960, Ital.) 90m Titanus-Galatea/MGM c

Steve Reeves (Philippides), Mylene Demongeot (Andromeda), Daniela Rocca (Karis), Ivo Garrani (Creuso), Philippe Hersent (Callimaco), Sergio Fantoni (Teocrito), Alberto Lupo (Milziade), Daniele Varga (Dario, King of Persians), Miranda Campa (Un'Ancella), Gianni Loti (Teucro).

Though the character is patterned after an ancient Greek marathon runner, Reeves is cast as a pretty-boy hunk who muscles the Persian armed forces out of Athens. Don't count on any 26-mile foot races here. Olympian Reeves uses a horse to go from Athens to Sparta in order to recruit more musclemen from the latter to defend the former against Varga's Persians. The Athenians have been betrayed by traitorous Fantoni who, with the help of the ravishing Rocca, has sold them out. Rocca's romantic regard for Reeves makes her change hats again, and as she informs him of the plot, Fantoni kills her. Too late, though: Reeves has learned that the Persians—here's a switch—are going to attack the Greeks from the rear. With a small but brave band of bodybuilders, he routs the wretches and sinks their fleet just as the Spartans gallop in to clean up. Reeves wins the divine Demongeot and Athens is saved. A gory, overwrought spectacle which barely seems like it was directed by the usually subtle Jacques Tourneur. He is out of place, and thankfully returned to the U.S. after this picture. Some striking underwater photography (thanks to those Totalscope lenses) puts some zest into the otherwise standard naval battles.

p, Bruno Vailati; d, Jacques Tourneur; w, Ennio De Concini, Augusto Frassinetti, Vailati (based on an idea by Alberto Barsanti, Raffaello Pacini); ph, Mario Bava (Dyaliscope, Totalscope, Eastmancolor); m, Roberto Nicolosi; ed, Mario Serandrei; art d, Marcello de Prato; set d, Massimo Tavazzi; cos, Marisa Crimi, Pier Luigi Pizzi.

War/Adventure   (PR:O   MPAA:NR)

GIANT OF METROPOLIS, THE½** (1963, Ital.) 92m Centro/Seven Arts c (IL GIGANTE DI METROPOLIS; AKA: GIANT OF METROPOLIS)

Gordon Mitchell (Obro), Roldano Lupi (Yotar), Bella Cortez (Mesede), Liana Orfei (Queen Texen), Furio Meniconi (Egor), Marietto (Elmos), Omero Gargano.

An Italian muscleman movie, one of those in vogue in the early 1960s thanks to HERCULES (1959) star Steve Reeves. In this one it's Mitchell who goes around without a shirt. He travels to an above-sea-level Atlantis where he is confronted by the immortal Cortez and his magnetic death ray. Cortez is bent on ruling sadistically, but is stopped by Mitchell. The battle is destructive enough to send Atlantis gurgling under the ocean waters. Some interesting sets and bizarre torture rituals put this film a cut above the rest. Released in Italy in 1961.

p, Emimmo Salvi; d, Umberto Scarpelli; w, Salvi, Sabatino Ciuffino, Oreste Palella, Ambrogio Molteni, Gino Stafford; ph, Mario Sensi; m, Armando Trovajoli; ed, Leo Scuccuglia, Adriana Bellanti; art d, Giorgio Giovannini.

Fantasy   (PR:A   MPAA:NR)

GIANT SPIDER INVASION, THE zero   (1975) 76m Transcentury/Group I c

Barbara Hale (Jenny), Leslie Parrish (Ev), Robert Easton (Kester), Steve Brodie (Dr. Vance), Alan Hale (Sheriff), Dianne Lee Hart (Terri), Bill Williams (Dutch), Christianne Schmidtmer (Helga), Kevin Brodie.

Why this film was made in 1975 is a minor mystery. This throwback to early science-fiction pictures such as TARANTULA (1955) is moronic, plain and simple. It has no basis to be set in the mid-1970s, whereas the mutation-radiation films of the 1950s were responding to a very real notion of the time. The title is self-explanatory, except that the spider eggs are mistaken for diamonds by Wisconsin farmer, Easton. Come on now, no one in the midwest is that dumb.

p, Richard L. Huff, Bill Rebane; d, Rebane; w, Huff, Robert Easton; ph, Jack Willoughby; spec eff, Richard Albain, Robert Millay.

Science-Fiction   (PR:A   MPAA:PG)

GIANTS A' FIRE   (SEE: ROYAL MOUNTED PATROL, 1941)

GIBRALTAR   (SEE: IT HAPPENED IN GIBRALTAR, 1948, Fr.)

GIBRALTAR ADVENTURE   (SEE: CLUE OF THE MISSING APE, THE, 1953)

GIDEON OF SCOTLAND YARD***   (1959, Brit.) 91m COL bw-c (GB: GIDEON'S DAY)

Jack Hawkins (Inspector George Gideon), Dianne Foster (Joanna Delafield), Anna Lee (Kate Gideon), Anna Massey (Sally Gideon), Andrew Ray (P.C. Simon Farnaby-Green), Cyril Cusack (Herbert "Birdy" Sparrow), James Hayter (Mason),

Ronald Howard *(Paul Delafield)*, Howard Marion-Crawford *(The Chief)*, Laurence Naismith *(Arthur Sayer)*, Derek Bond *(Det. Sgt. Eric Kirby)*, Griselda Harvey *(Mrs. Kirby)*, Frank Lawton *(Det. Sgt. Liggott)*, John Loder *(Ponsford, "The Dupe")*, Marjorie Rhodes *(Mrs. Saparelli)*, Hermione Bell *(Dolly Saparelli)*, Michael Trubshawe *(Sgt. Golightly)*, Jack Watling *(Rev. Julian Small)*, Henry Longhurst *(Rev. Mr. Courtney)*, Michael Shepley *(Sir Rupert Bellamy)*, Nigel Fitzgerald *(Inspector Cameron)*, Robert Raglan *(Dawson)*, Maureen Potter *(Ethel Sparrow)*, Doreen Madden *(Miss Courtney)*, Miles Malleson *(Judge at Old Bailey)*, Donal Donnelly *(Feeney)*, Billie Whitelaw *(Christine)*, Malcolm Ranson *(Ronnie Gideon)*, Mavis Ranson *(Jane Gideon)*, Francis Crowdy *(Fitzhubert)*, David Aylmer *(Manners)*, Brian Smith *(White-Douglas)*, Barry Keegan *(Riley, Chauffeur)*, Charles Maunsell *(Walker)*, Stuart Saunders *(Chancery Lane Policeman)*, Dervis Ward *(Simmo)*, Joan Ingram *(Lady Bellamy)*, John Warwick *(Inspector Gillick)*, John Le Mesurier *(Prosecuting Attorney)*, Peter Godsell *(Jimmy)*, Robert Bruce *(Defending Attorney)*, Alan Rolfe *(C.I.D. Man at Hospital)*, Derek Prentice *(1st Employee)*, Alastair Hunter *(2nd Employee)*, Helen Goss *(Woman Employer)*, Susan Richmond *(Aunt May)*, Raymond Rollett *(Uncle Dick)*, Lucy Griffiths *(Cashier)*, Mary Donevan *(Usherette)*, O'Donovan Shiell, Hart Allison, Michael O'Duffy *(Policemen)*, Diana Chesney *(Barmaid)*, David Storm *(Court Clerk)*, Gordon Harris *(C.I.D. Man)*.

A late film in the long career of John Ford that isn't at all bad; it's just not one of his masterpieces. Shot in Britain, GIDEON OF SCOTLAND YARD stars Hawkins as an overworked Scotland Yard inspector. The action takes place during one of his typically complicated, harrowing days. When word is on the street that one of his sergeants has been on the take. Hawkins confronts the officer and receives an uneasy denial. Soon after, the cop is killed in a hit-and-run car wreck. Hawkins is distracted from this event by a maniacal killer who commits murder in Manchester and then heads to London to pull a safe robbery where he kills again. To add to his headaches, Hawkins finds himself the victim of a hold-up *and* he receives a bullet wound from another thief. If that isn't enough for one day, Hawkins even earns the loving wrath of his family when he forgets to bring home some salmon *and* by being late for his daughter's first concert. Ford and screenwriter Clarke cram the film with many vignettes and sub-plots, all of which are dramatized with the great director's usual skill at characterization and humor. Hawkins performs with the right amount of determination (the cop in him) and likeable, human foibles that make his Gideon worth following for a day. Unfortunately, the film was looked upon as minor stuff when it was released in the U.S., and the distributor cut the film down to a running time of 54 minutes and stuck it on the lower half of a double bill. If that wasn't enough insult, the beautiful Technicolor prints that were released to theaters in Europe were transferred to cheaper black & white prints for American distribution. Luckily, American television prints have been restored to their original state and the bastardized prints have all but disappeared. Not one of Ford's labors of love, but mediocre Ford is better than the best of most other filmmakers then or now.

p, John Ford, Michael Killanin; d, Ford; w, T.E.B. Clarke (based on the novel *Gideon's Day* by J.J. Marric [John Creasey]); ph, Frederick A. Young (Technicolor; released in black & white); m, Douglas Gamley; ed, Raymond Poulton; md, Muir Mathieson; art d, Ken Adam.

Crime (PR:A MPAA:NR)

GIDEON'S DAY (SEE: GIDEON OF SCOTLAND YARD, 1958, Brit.)

GIDGET*** (1959) 95m COL c

Sandra Dee *(Francie)*, James Darren *(Moondoggie)*, Cliff Robertson *(Kahoona)*, Arthur O'Connell *(Russell Lawrence)*, The Four Preps *(Themselves)*, Mary LaRoche *(Dorothy Lawrence)*, Joby Baker *(Stinky)*, Tom Laughlin *(Lover Boy)*, Sue George *(B.L.)*, Robert Ellis *(Hot Shot)*, Jo Morrow *(Mary Lou)*, Yvonne Craig *(Nan)*, Doug McClure *(Waikiki)*, Burt Metcalfe *(Lord Byron)*, Richard Newton, Ed Hinton *(Cops)*, Patti Kane *(Patty)*.

The All-American ideal is wholesomely embodied in happy-go-lucky Dee, who became the model of countless teenagers in the late 1950s. Dee plays Gidget (a nickname meaning "girl midget"), a sad-faced youngster who doesn't quite measure up to the chesty, bikinied girls on the beach. Her mom's reassurances come true when the two grooviest surfers in town, Darren and Robertson, start paying Dee some attention. She falls in love with Darren, who gives up his surfboard at the summer's end and returns to college. The first and best of the series, it is saved primarily by a fine cast; Sandra Dee had just appeared in Douglas Sirk's IMITATION OF LIFE, and Robertson, who turned in a commendable performance as Kahoona, was later praised for his role in CHARLY. Also "hanging-ten" was Tom Laughlin, who much later made BILLY JACK. Tunes include "The Next Best Thing To Love" (Stanley Styne, Fred Karger). (See GIDGET series, Index.)

p, Lewis J. Rachmil; d, Paul Wendkos; w, Gabrielle Upton (based on the novel by Frederick Kohner); ph, Burnett Guffey (CinemaScope, Eastmancolor); m, Morris Stoloff; ed, William A. Lyon; md, Stoloff; art d, Ross Bellah.

Comedy Cas. (PR:A MPAA:NR)

GIDGET GOES HAWAIIAN** (1961) 101m COL c

James Darren *(Jeff Mather)*, Michael Callan *(Eddie Horner)*, Deborah Walley *(Gidget)*, Carl Reiner *(Russ Lawrence)*, Peggy Cass *(Mitzie Stewart)*, Eddy Foy, Jr. *(Monty Stewart)*, Jeff Donnell *(Dorothy Lawrence)*, Vicki Trickett *(Abby Stewart)*, Joby Baker *(Judge Hamilton)*, Don Edmonds *(Larry Neal)*, Bart Patton *(Wally Hodges)*, Jan Conaway *(Barbara Jo)*, Robin Lory *(Dee Dee)*, Arnold Merritt *(Clay Anderson)*, Vivian Marshall *(Lucy)*, Johnny Gilbert *(Johnny Spring)*, Terry Huntingdon *(Stewardess)*, Jerardo de Cordovier *(Waiter)*, Guy Lee *(Bellboy)*, Yankee Chang *(Mr. Matsu)*.

The great appeal of Dee, the original Gidget, is lost in this innocuous sequel. Taking her place is Deborah Walley, who does a fair job as Darren's displeased girl friend. She takes off to Hawaii with her parents, and has some fun in the sun with a group of well-tanned beach bums. Darren complicates things when he surprises Walley with a visit. Fred Karger and Stanley Styne provided a pair of tunes: "Gidget Goes Hawaiian" and "Wild About That Girl." (See GIDGET series, Index.)

p, Jerry Bresler; d, Paul Wendkos; w, Ruth Brooks Flippen (based on Frederick Kohner's characters); ph, Robert J. Bronner (Eastmancolor); m, George Duning; ed, William A. Lyon; art d, Walter Holscher; set d, Darrell Silvera; ch, Roland DuPree; makeup, Ben Lane.

Comedy Cas. (PR:A MPAA:NR)

GIDGET GOES TO ROME*½ (1963) 103m COL c

Cindy Carol *(Gidget)*, James Darren *(Jeff)*, Jessie Royce Landis *(Aunt Albertina)*, Cesare Danova *(Paolo Cellini)*, Danielle de Metz *(Daniela Serrini)*, Joby Baker *(Judge)*, Trudi Ames *(Libby)*, Noreen Corcoran *(Lucy)*, Peter Brooks *(Clay)*, Lisa Gastoni *(Anna Cellini)*, Claudio Gora *(Alberto)*, Don Porter *(Russ Lawrence)*, Jeff Donnell *(Dorothy Lawrence)*, Joe Kamel *(Pinchman)*, Antonio Segurini, Leonardo Botta *(Italian Boys)*, Umberto Raho *(Mario)*, Audrey Fairfax *(Contessa)*, Vadim Wolkowsky *(Prince Bianchi)*, Edra Gale *(Fat Woman)*, Irina Vasailchikoff *(Lean Woman)*, Milly Monti *(Henrietta)*, Charles Borromel *(Whitefaced Poet)*, David Munsell, Jan Coomer *(Listeners)*, Leon Auerbach *(East Indian Yoga)*, Norma Nedici *(Normal Woman)*, Matilda Calnan *(Old Woman)*, John Stacy *(Drunk Butler)*, Carmen Scarpita, Melina Vukotic *(Caviar Women)*, Eva Marandi *(Receiptionist)*, Mimo Billi *(Fontana Doorman)*, Veronica Wells *(Major Domo Dresser)*, Sylvia Llore, May Sariola, Adria Ramaccia, Tina Lepri *(Models)*, Jim Dolen *(Nelson)*.

It seems that the further Gidget wanders away from the West coast, the worse the films become. This one has Darren returning to the role for the third time and trying out his charms on yet another Gidget—Cindy Carol. The pair is now "steadies" on vacation in Rome. Both allow their love to wander, which leads to minor affairs. Needless to say, they are reunited at the finale. Songs include "Gegetta," "Big Italian Moon," George David Weiss, Al Kasha (sung by James Darren). This turned out to be the worst (save for the made-for-TV versions) and thankfully the last of the teeny-bopper series. Arrividerci, Gidget. (See GIDGET series, Index.)

p, Jerry Bresler; d, Paul Wendkos; w, Ruth Brooks Flippen, Katherine Eunson, Dale Eunson (based on Frederick Kohner's characters); ph, Enzo Barboni, Robert J. Bronner (Eastmancolor); m, Johnny Williams; ed, William A. Lyon; art d, Antonio Sarzi-Braga, Robert Peterson; set d, Ferdinando Ruffo; cos, Pat Barto, Sorelle Fontana; makeup, Mel Berns; m/l, George David Weiss, Al Kasha.

Comedy (PR:A MPAA:NR)

GIFT (SEE: VENOM, 1968, Swed.)

GIFT, THE** (1983, Fr./Ital.) 105m Goldwyn c

Pierre Mondy *(Gregoire)*, Claudia Cardinale *(Antonella)*, Clio Goldsmith *(Barbara)*, Jacques Francois *(Loriol)*, Cecile Magnet *(Charlotte)*, Renzo Montagnani *(Emir Faycal)*, Remi Laurent *(Laurent)*, Leila Frechet *(Sandrine)*, Henri Guybet *(Andre)*, Yolande Gilot *(Jennifer)*, Diulio Del Prete *(Umberto)*.

A tame sex comedy which centers on the attempts of a group of office workers who combine their cash and resources to get a retiring co-worker a prostitute as a special gift. As usual, the French idea of a sex comedy is neither sexy nor funny and succeeds only in appeasing U.S. audiences who see French films only to be in vogue.

p, Gilbert de Goldschmidt; d&w, Michel Lang (based on the play "Bankers Also Have Souls" by Valme and Terzolli); ph, Daniel Gaudry; m, Michel LeGrand; set d, Jean-Claude Gallouin; cos, Tanine Autre.

Comedy Cas. (PR:O MPAA:R)

GIFT HORSE, THE (SEE: GLORY AT SEA, 1952, Brit.)

GIFT OF GAB½** (1934) 70m UNIV bw

Edmund Lowe *(Philip Gabney)*, Gloria Stuart *(Barbara Kelton)*, Ruth Etting *(Ruth)*, Phil Baker *(Doctor)*, Ethel Waters *(Ethel)*, Alice White *(Margot)*, Victor Moore *(Col. Trivers)*, Hugh O'Connell *(Patsy)*, Helen Vinson *(Nurse)*, Gene Austin *(Crooner)*, Thomas Hanlon *(Announcer)*, Henry Armetta *(Janitor)*, Andy Devine *(McDougal)*, Wini Shaw *(Singer)*, Marion Byron *(Telephone Girl)*, Sterling Holloway *(Sound Effects Man)*, Edwin Maxwell *(Norton)*, Leighton Noble *(Orchestra Leader)*, Maurice Block *(Auction Room Owner)*, Tammany Young *(Mug)*, James Flavin *(Alumni President)*, Billy Barty *(Baby)*, Richard Elliott *(Father)*, Florence Enright *(Mother)*, Warner Richmond *(Cop)*, Sid Walker, Skins Miller, Jack Harling *(The Three Stooges [not the famous trio])*, Sidney Skolsky, Dennis O'Keefe, Dave O'Brien, Boris Karloff, Bela Lugosi, Alexander Woollcott, Paul Lukas, Chester Morris, Roger Pryor, The Downey Sisters, Douglass Montgomery, Candy and Coco, Douglas Fowley, Binnie Barnes, June Knight, The Beale Street Boys, Rian James, Graham McNamee, Gus Arnheim and his Orchestra *(Themselves)*.

Physical proof that lots of talented folks and musical numbers do not an entertaining film make. Lowe gets fired from his radio-announcer job after an erroneous interview, and turns to the bottle. His girl Stuart sets him straight and gets him a scoop. His enthusiasm returns and he sets out to find a downed airplane that's been missing. His search proves effective and, as a publicity stunt, he broadcasts his report as he is parachuting to the plane. Karloff and Lugosi seem to be tossed in just to fulfill a contract. Whatever the reasons, they are the highlight of this pic. Karloff is cast as the top-hatted Phantom, and Lugosi as an Apache dancer donning a checkered cap! Well, maybe sometimes contracts should be broken. Tunes include: "Talking To Myself," "I Ain't Gonna Sin No More," "Gift Of Gab," Herb Magidson, Con Conrad; "Somebody Looks Good," George Whiting, Albert von Tilzer; "Don't Let This Waltz Mean Goodbye," "Walkin' On Air," Jack Meskill, von Tilzer; "What A Wonderful Day," Harry Tobias, Al Sherman; "Tomorrow—Who Cares?" Murray Mencher, Charles Tobias; "Blue Sky Avenue." For the curious Moe, Larry, and Curly fans, The Three Stooges listed in the credits are a bogus act who were competing against the real trio.

p, Carl Laemmle, Jr.; d, Karl Freund; w, Rian James, Lou Breslow (based on the story by Jerry Wald, Philip G. Epstein); ph, George Robinson, Harold Wenstrom; ed, Raymond Curtis; md, Edward Ward.

Musical **(PR:A MPAA:NR)**

GIFT OF LOVE, THE** (1958) 105m FOX c

Lauren Bacall *(Julie Beck)*, Robert Stack *(Bill Beck)*, Evelyn Rudie *(Hitty)*, Lorne Greene *(Grant Allan)*, Anne Seymour *(McMasters)*, Edward Platt *(Dr. Miller)*, Joseph Kearns *(Mr. Rynicker)*.

An equally sappy remake of SENTIMENTAL JOURNEY (1946) (as if one version of this story wasn't enough). Bacall is the seriously ill wife of Stack, who fears her husband's impending loneliness. She adopts a young girl and gives this "gift of love" to him just before she dies. He soon finds the tot to be more of a nuisance than a blessing, and returns her to the orphanage (for a full refund?). His sixth-sense one day takes hold of him and he rushes to an oceanside cliff. At the last moment he spots the child and comes to her rescue. And the disgustingly sweet pair live happily ever after. Bacall doesn't know how lucky she was to have died.

p, Charles Brackett; d, Jean Negulesco; w, Luther Davis (based on a story by Nelia Gardner White); ph, Milton Krasner (CinemaScope, DeLuxe Color); m, Cyril J. Mockridge; ed, Hugh S. Fowler; md, Lionel Newman; art d, Lyle R. Wheeler, Mark Lee Kirk; cos, Charles LeMaire; m/l, "The Gift of Love," Sammy Fain, Paul Francis Webster (sung by Vic Damone).

Drama **(PR:A MPAA:NR)**

GIGANTES PLANETARIOS** (1965, Mex.) 80m Estudios America/Corsa bw (AKA: GIGANTES INTERPLANETARIOS)

Guillermo Murray *(Daniel)*, Adriana Roel *(Sylvia)*, Rogelio Guerra *(The Boxer)*, Jose Angel Espinosa Ferrusquilla *(The Manager)*, Jose Galvez *(The Protector)*, Jacqueline Fellay, Evita Munoz, Irma Lozano, Nathanael Leon Frankenstein, Carlos Nieto.

A science-fiction kid's story about a group of Earthlings who travel to the distant planet of Eternal Night, where they liberate the underground-dwelling inhabitants from the grip of a mad ruler bent on destroying the Earth.

p, Emilio Gomez Muriel; d, Alfredo B. Crevenna; w, Alfredo Ruanova.

Science-Fiction/ Children's Adventure **(PR:A MPAA:NR)**

GIGANTIS*½ (1959, Jap./U.S.) 78m Toho/WB bw (GOJIRO NO GYAKUSHYU; AKA: THE RETURN OF GODZILLA; THE FIRE MONSTER; THE VOLCANO MONSTER; GODZILLA RAIDS AGAIN; GODZILLA'S COUNTERATTACK; COUNTERATTACK OF THE MONSTER)

Hiroshi Koizumi *(Tsukioka)*, Setsuko Wakayama *(Hedemi)*, Minoru Chiaki *(Kobayashi)*.

This time it's Osaka that gets trampled under foot by the A-bomb-awakened Godzilla. His wrath sends the entire population running frantically, screaming out-of-synch pleas for help. Originally released in Japan in 1955, this first sequel to GODZILLA, KING OF THE MONSTERS was "Americanized" in 1959 by Warner Bros. Two major differences distinguishing this from the orignial are a remodeling of the monster's body, and the loss of director Honda, who thankfully returned in the following RODAN. The American title resulted from the fact that Warner Bros. neglected to secure the rights to the name "Godzilla."

p, Tomoyuki Tanaka, Paul Schreibman (U.S.); d, Motoyoshi Oda, Hugo Grimaldi (U.S.); w, Takeo Murata, Sugeaki Hidaka; ph, Seichi Endo; m, Rex Lipton (U.S.); ed, Grimaldi (U.S.); art d, Takeo Kita; spec eff, Eiji Tsuburaya, Akira Watanabe, Hiroshi Mukoyama, Masao Shirota.

Science-Fiction **(PR:A MPAA:NR)**

GIGI***** (1958) 116m MGM c

Leslie Caron *(Gigi)*, Maurice Chevalier *(Honore Lachaille)*, Louis Jourdan *(Gaston Lachaille)*, Hermione Gingold *(Mme. Alvarez)*, Eva Gabor *(Liane D'Exelmans)*, Jacques Bergerac *(Sandomir)*, Isabel Jeans *(Aunt Alicia)*, John Abbott *(Manuel)*, Monique Van Vooren *(Showgirl)*, Lydia Stevens *(Simone)*, Edwin Jerome *(Charles the Butler)*, Dorothy Neumann *(Designer)*, Marilyn Sims *(Redhead)*, Richard Bean *(Harlequin)*, Pat Sheahan *(Blonde)*, Leroy Winebrenner *(Lifeguard)*, Marya Ploss *(Model)*, Jack Trevan *(Coachman)*.

One might have to search the thesaurus for new words to describe the wonderment of GIGI. There were those who carped that it was a reworking of "My Fair Lady" by the authors of that milestone, but GIGI can stand on her own two lovely legs, thank you. This is actually the fifth time around for the story which began as a Colette novel (which she must have lifted from Shaw's PYGMALION, which he took from an old legend that had already been written as a straight play by W.S. Gilbert of Gilbert and Sullivan fame in the 1800s). The novel was adapted as a French film in 1950 starring Daniele Delorme and then done as a straight stage play in 1951 starring Audrey Hepburn on Broadway. Odd that they overlooked Hepburn for the screen musical, then used her in MY FAIR LADY after overlooking Julie Andrews. Lavish, glossy, and eminently tuneful, GIGI tells the story of Caron, an illegitimate waif in the late 1800s Paris who lives with her aunt, Jeans, and her grandmother, Gingold. Their plan is to transform this waif into a courtesan so she can become the mistress to Jourdan, the wealthy heir to a fortune gleaned from the sugar industry. Jourdan, at first, is willing to accept Caron as his mistress, then realizes that he truly loves her and that the only way he can keep her from becoming his mistress is to make her his wife. This throws Gingold for a loop; never before has anyone ever wanted to actually marry one of the family. Their tradition, for so many years, has been to be kept women and Gingold had, in fact, once been the lover of Jourdan's father, Chevalier. Gingold doesn't quite know how to handle this fresh situation and finally agrees to allow her granddaughter to marry the young man. Caron had played the role in the Paris stage play and does well here with her singing voice being dubed by Betty Wand. Produced in Paris, it is a delight to watch from the first frame. All of the usual Parisian landmarks are seen, the Tuileries, the Bois de Boulogne, the Palais de Glace, etc., and they add much to the backdrop. Chevalier steals every single scene he's in, save one, in which he sings the memorable "I Remember It Well" with Gingold. Lerner and Loewe were perfect for the job of adapting the Collette play for a musical. While treading the same path as they did with MY FAIR LADY, they were able to write a perfect screenplay and score and not let you feel they were stealing from themselves. The score ranks as one of the best ever written specifically for the screen and every song feels organic to the story. Cecil Beaton, who also did the design for MY FAIR LADY, does a smashing job with all of his sets and costumes and manages to recreate the Paris of the Gay Nineties with such aplomb that you could dial out the sound on this film and just revel in the sights. Director Minnelli reaches his greatest pinnacle with his firm, yet tender, handling of a subject that might have been distasteful in a lesser director's hands. Gigi took nine Oscars and one special Oscar for Chevalier's "contributions to the world of entertainment for more than half a century." The awards were given for Best Film, Best Direction (Minnelli), Cinematography (Ruttenberg), screenplay (Lerner), scoring (Previn), song ("Gigi" by Lerner and Loewe), editing (Fazan), costumes (Beaton), art direction (Horning and Ames). As perfect a film musical as you can ever expect to see. Some of the songs have gone on to become classics. They include; "Gigi," "Ah Yes, I Remember It Well," "Thank Heaven For Little Girls," "The Night They Invented Champagne," "She's Not Thinking Of Me (Waltz at Maxim's)," "It's A Bore," "Gossip," "I'm Glad I'm Not Young Anymore," "The Parisians," "Gaston's Soliloquy," "Say A Prayer For Me Tonight," and the ice skating sequence "A Toujours."

p, Arthur Freed; d, Vincente Minnelli, w, Alan Jay Lerner (based on the play "Gigi" dramatized by Anita Loos from the novel by Colette); ph, Joseph Ruttenberg, Ray June (CinemaScope, Metrocolor); m, Frederick Loewe; ed, Adrienne Fazan; prod d, Cecil Beaton; md, Andre Previn; art d, William Horning, Preston Ames; set d, Henry Grace; cos, Beaton; makeup, William Tuttle, Charles Parker.

Musical **Cas.** **(PR:A MPAA:NR)**

GIGOLETTE*½ (1935) 70m SEL/RKO bw (GB: NIGHT CLUB)

Adrienne Ames *(Kay Parrish)*, Ralph Bellamy *(Terry Gallagher)*, Donald Cook *(Gregg Emerson)*, Robert Armstrong *(Chuck Ahearn)*, Harold Waldridge *(Ginsy)*, Robert T. Haines *(Kingsley Emerson)*, Grace Hampton *(Mrs. Emerson)*, Milton Douglas Orchestra.

Ames is the society swell, a dame rendered destitute by the Depression, who is forced to the demeaning expedient of seeking employment. She finds it in gangster Bellamy's bistro, the Club Hee-Haw. Her friendly patron soon upgrades her status from Hee-Haw hostess to "gigolette"—gigolo gender-equivalent—in his swanky new Casino de Monaco. Her love interest, Cook, finds her promotion degrading, and the budding romance is threatened. Additional assaults on amour arrive as booze barons battle about business in this already dated prohibition-formula picture. Able actors are squandered in this anachronism, with Bellamy (the ultimate FDR impersonator) seeming very much out of character.

p, Burt Kelly; d, Charles Lamont; w, Gordon Kahn; ph, Joseph Ruttenberg; m, Charles Williams, Marcy Klauber; ed, William Thompson.

Drama **(PR:AC MPAA:NR)**

GIGOLETTES OF PARIS* (1933) 64m Equitable bw

Madge Bellamy, Gilbert Roland, Natalie Moorhead, Theodore von Eltz, Molly O'Day, Henry Kolker, Paul Porcasi, Albert Conti, P. Schumann-Heink.

Cheaply made and poorly produced, this picture aspires to be a sizzling love story, supposedly set in the back streets of Paris. Bellamy is the shop girl who has her heart broken by the shiftless von Eltz, but manages to get back on her feet again to start an affair with Roland. Von Eltz is a real lady's man (he could, in fact, be called a gigolo), but he is willing to reform upon discovering the wonders of true love. A decent cast is given no material with which to show their abilities, with inexcusable film techniques a further hindrance to the slack story.

d&w, Alphonse Martel; ph, Henry Cronjager, Herman Schopp; m, Darby St. John; ed, Tom Parsons, Otis Garrett.

Drama **(PR:A MPAA:NR)**

GIGOT*½** (1962) 104m Seven Arts/FOX c

Jackie Gleason *(Gigot)*, Katherine Kath *(Colette)*, Gabrielle Dorziat *(Mme. Brigitte)*, Jean Lefebvre *(Gaston)*, Jacques Marin *(Jean)*, Albert Remy *(Alphonse)*, Yvonne Constant *(Lucille Duval)*, Germaine Delbat *(Mme. Greuze)*, Albert Dinan *(Bistro Proprietor)*, Diane Gardner *(Nicole)*, Camille Guerini *(Priest)*, Rene Harvard *(Albert)*, Louis Falavigna *(Mon. Duval)*, Jean Michaud *(Gendarme)*, Richard Francoeur *(Baker)*, Paula Dehelly *(Baker's Wife)*, Jacques Ary *(Blade)*, Franck Villard *(Pierre)*.

Filmed entirely in Paris with obvious love and affection, GIGOT was an enormous flop at the box office. Gleason, in an attempt to bring Chaplinesque pantomime back to the screen, wrote the story and the music and starred in the film. He and director Kelly were so disappointed by Fox's handling of the movie that they felt it was their most unhappy experience in the picture business. Gleason based the character on his TV "poor soul" portrayal and attempted to lengthen it into a full film. It works, but no one wanted to shell out money to see a character they'd seen so often for nothing on the small screen. Kelly and Gleason also carped about the fact that the studio edited the film after they handed it in. We'll never know what it might have been but what it was was still pretty good, even if you're not a Gleason enthusiast. The major problem is that we never get a full story. Rather, we get a study. Gleason is a big, mute oaf who works as a maintenance man at a small pension in Paris. Loved by the children and the various dogs in the neighborhood, he is the butt of all the jokes by his needling employer, Dorziat, a mean miser.

Gleason's hobby appears to be going to funerals, where he can feel as though he belongs to some sort of group, depressing though it may be. He meets Kath, a street hooker, and her daughter, Gardiner, and invites them to stay with him in his seedy basement apartment. Gleason and Gardiner have a special relationship and when Kath says she wants to leave because she cannot afford to stay there, Gleason steals some francs from the bakery in order to keep her there. Kath goes out one night with her lover and returns to the basement to find that her daughter and Gleason have disappeared. She believes that Gleason has kidnaped the child and alerts everyone in the area. It's not true. Gleason and Gardiner are actually in a sub-basement below the regular subterranean room, where he is amusing her. The ceiling of the room falls and the child is hurt. Gleason takes her through back alleys to his priest, who immediately calls for a doctor. He goes back to the boarding house and is spotted by an angry crowd who believe he is a child abuser, or perhaps a murderer. They chase after him and he falls into the Seine. When all they see of him is his floating hat, they assume he is dead. Gardiner appears and tells them what has happened and now the neighborhood is filled with guilt so they throw him a huge funeral, the kind of sendoff Gleason would have loved to attend. Up in a tree, like a latter day Tom Sawyer, Gleason watches his own final rites and is delighted. Soon enough, he is spotted by one of the tearful attendees and the chase begins again as the picture concludes. GIGOT is beautifully photographed but could have been pruned by ten minutes for greater effectiveness. Gleason proves again that he is one of the best mimes since silent films. He has never had the career in movies that he wanted. After a series of small parts in pictures (NAVY BLUES, ALL THROUGH THE NIGHT, ORCHESTRA WIVES, SPRING-TIME IN THE ROCKIES), he went to TV and became a giant, then distinguished himself in THE HUSTLER and REQUIEM FOR A HEAVYWEIGHT. But the rest of his pictures, such trifles as MR. BILLION, HOW DO I LOVE THEE, and the atrocious SMOKEY AND THE BANDIT (twice), are better forgotten.

p, Kenneth Hyman; d, Gene Kelly; w, John Patrick (based on a story by Jackie Gleason); ph, Jean Bourgin (DeLuxe Color); m, Gleason; ed, Roger Dwyre; md, Michel Magne; art d, Auguste Capelier.

Comedy/Drama **(PR:A MPAA:NR)**

GILBERT AND SULLIVAN (SEE: GREAT GILBERT AND SULLIVAN, THE, 1953, Brit.)

GILDA**** (1946) 110m COL bw

Rita Hayworth *(Gilda)*, Glenn Ford *(Johnny Farrell)*, George Macready *(Ballin Mundson)*, Joseph Calleia *(Obregon)*, Steven Geray *(Uncle Pio)*, Joseph Sawyer *(Casey)*, Gerald Mohr *(Capt. Delgado)*, Robert Scott *(Gabe Evans)*, Ludwig Donath *(German)*, Don Douglas *(Thomas Langford)*, Lionel Royce *(2nd German)*, Saul Z. Martel *(Little Man)*, George J. Lewis *(Huerta)*, Rosa Rey *(Maria)*, Ruth Roman *(Girl)*, Ted Hecht *(Socialite)*, Argentina Brunetti *(Woman)*, Jerry DeCastro *(Doorman)*, Robert Stevens *(Man at Masquerade)*, Fernanda Eliscu *(Bendolin's Wife)*, Frank Leyva *(Argentine)*, Forbes Murray, Sam Flint, Bob Board *(Americans)*, Jean DeBriac, Oscar Lorraine *(Frenchmen)*, George Humbert *(Italian)*, Eduardo Ciannelli *(Bendolin)*, Russ Vincent *(Escort)*, Herbert Evans *(Englishman)*, Robert Tafur *(Clerk)*, Rodolfo Hoyos *(Peasant Man)*, Robert Kellard, Ernest Hilliard, Frank Leigh, Jean Del Val, Paul Regas, Phil Van Zandt *(Men)*, Erno Verebes, Eugene Borden *(Dealers)*, Alphonse Martell, Leon Lenoir *(Croupiers)*, Soretta Raye *(Harpy)*, J.W. Noon, Nobel G. Evey *(Bunco Dealers)*, George Sorel, Jack Chefe, Albert Pollet, Lou Palfy *(Assistant Croupiers)*, Sam Appel *(Black Jack Dealer)*, Jack Del Rio *(Cashier)*, Julio Abadia *(Newsman/Waiter)*, Cosmo Sardo, Paul Bradley, Nina Bara, Ruth Roman, John Tyrrell *(Bits)*, Ted Hecht *(Social Citizen)*, Leander De Cordova *(Servant)*, Fred Godoy *(Bartender)*, Lew Harvey, John Merton *(Policemen)*, Herman Marks, Carli Elinor, Joseph Palma, Alfred Paix, Herman Marks, Ralph Navarro *(Waiters)*, Ramon Munox *(Judge)*, Argentina Brunetti *(Woman)*, Sam Ash *(Gambler)*.

Superlative trash as it is, GILDA is also a landmark film in that it made Rita Hayworth a superstar and one of Hollywood's most durable sex queens, as well as providing Ford with one of his most intriguing roles, just after his return from WW II duties with the Marines. Ford changes a bad gambling streak by using loaded dice, while playing a bunch of toughs on the Buenos Aires waterfront. Cleaning out his adversaries, he is later attacked by one of the plug-ugly players who tries to steal his winnings. From the shadows steps Macready, drawing a sword from his walking cane and running through the attacker. He not only saves Ford's life but, after telling him that he had been observing the young man's crafty dice rolling, hires him to work in his posh casino as a dealer. Ford, advised by shrewd Geray, a washroom attendant who knows the ins and outs of the club, rises rapidly until he is the manager and Macready's friend and confidant. Macready, who takes mysterious trips, vanishes and returns with luscious Hayworth, a voluptuous temptress, who has become his wife. Though he pretends to meet her for the first time, Ford knows this vixen well; they once had a torrid affair but she left him. Macready is no fool, however, and knows the two are eyeballing each other with carnal thoughts. As a devilish ploy, Macready assigns Ford the job of watching his wife so she won't get into trouble. Resenting Ford's protective role and her husband's distrustful nature, Hayworth gets high and then puts on a sexy spectacle, doing an impromptu striptease to the tune "Put the Blame on Mame," which turns Macready's male patrons into drooling mashers who have to be restrained from crushing the lovely long-haired lady as she leaves the dance floor. Hayworth has done the unpardonable; shamed both her husband and former lover in public but she cannot get Ford to discard his honor by having an affair with her. Macready, meanwhile, has been the business agent for a rich organization that is Nazi-dominated, and he murders a man on behalf of the vile cartel. When arriving home to pack his bags he finds Ford struggling with Hayworth, who is drunk and threatening to run away. Macready assumes they are resuming their old affair and departs, fleeing in a plane that crashes into the ocean. Ford is oddly loyal to Macready in death, defending his name to detractors. Hayworth could care less, vowing her love for Ford. They marry but Ford has no love for his sensuous wife, a woman he feels must be punished for betraying his friend Macready. She runs away to sing in another club but Ford finds her and brings her back to the Buenos Aires casino where Macready himself returns. He had not been killed in the plane crash after all, but had parachuted to safety at the last minute. He confronts wife and friend, intending to murder both of them for their disloyalty. But when drawing his deadly sword from its cane scabbard, Geray, the washroom attendant loyal to Ford, shoots him to death. Calleia, the local cop who has been trying to establish Macready's Nazi connections throughout the film, shows up and lets Geray off. Ford and Hayworth are now free to start their fiery romance all over again. GILDA's script is *almost* as complicated and confusing as THE BIG SLEEP, made that same year, one where Columbia released 53 features to lead all studios which, combined, produced 300 theatrical films, big, small, and indifferent. Some real blockbusters appeared that year, including THE BEST YEARS OF OUR LIVES and THE JOLSON STORY, but none were as provocative as GILDA where Hayworth jiggles in and out of one strapless evening gown after another, her long neck and elongated torso, her long, hefty legs twisting and turning snakelike to heart-thumping music. Critics remained indifferent to the film but returning GIs flocked with their wives and sweethearts to see Columbia's sex goddess who accented her role with such lines as: "If I'd have been a ranch they would have called me the Bar *Nothing*!" That Hayworth was a reigning pinup star with servicemen before GILDA, was undisputed. Painted upon the test A-bomb dropped on Bikini Atoll was her likeness and the name "Rita." Though Hayworth reprises a few bars of "Put the Blame on Mame," her songs are sung by Anita Ellis ("Put the Blame on Mame" and "Amado Mio" by Doris Fisher and Allan Roberts). Columbia mogul Harry Cohn, considered Hayworth his private property and reportedly went so far as to plant hidden microphones in her dressing room to listen in on conversations she might be having with co-star Ford, thinking they might develop an affair. Hayworth and Ford quickly found the microphones and taunted the eavesdropping boss with risque conversation. Both had appeared six years earlier in THE LADY IN QUESTION and they enjoyed vexing Cohn, who finally began calling down from his office to the studio after the day's shooting had ended to find the two stars present. "What the hell are you doing down there?" queried Cohn. "Just having a drink," Ford replied. "Why don't you go home?" demanded Cohn, "I can't keep the studio open all hours of the night. It costs money! Now get the hell out and don't forget to shut off the lights when you leave!" Yet Cohn spared no expense in the production and choreography designer Cole lavished Hayworth with sex-oriented dances which he patterned after a professional stripper he had known, both numbers brought into the production long after director Vidor began shooting, which indicates the haphazard fashion by which this film was shaped. It was Hayworth's film from the beginning; Vidor began shooting the story before Ford was actually signed and joined the production. The original story was written exclusively for Hayworth by producer Van Upp, named to oversee the production by Cohn himself. She was later blamed by Hayworth for establishing a sex goddess no woman could ever hope to be in reality. When she had problems with Aly Khan, Hayworth told Van Upp: "It's all your fault . . . you wrote GILDA. And every man I've known has fallen in love with Gilda and wakened with me." Vidor brought about a minor miracle in directing GILDA, exacting sterling performances, even from the hammy Geray, a man known for overacting. But in the character actor's case it was success through browbeating. Vidor upbraided Geray constantly during the shooting, often taking him aside and shouting at him in his native Hungarian tongue. The volatile director later tried to escape his Columbia contract by suing the studio, which brought mogul Cohn's vicious personality to the limelight. Cohn's sharp, foul tongue was exposed during court testimony, along with his mistreatment of any talent under contract to his studio. One incident cited occurred after GILDA's completion when Cohn invited Vidor and his wife to dinner. They arrived a few minutes late at the studio, which caused Cohn to explode, telling his secretary to "give him [Vidor] a drink, then throw him out!" Cohn was ordered to apologize for calling Vidor names but never did and in the end, two years later, after Vidor directed Hayworth and Ford in another film, THE LOVES OF CARMEN, he bought up his Columbia contract for $75,000 and departed Columbia, thinking himself lucky to get out alive.

p, Virginia Van Upp; d, Charles Vidor; w, Marion Parsonnet (based on Jo Eisinger's adaptation of E.A. Ellington's original story), ph, Rudy Mate, Marlin Skiles; ed, Charles Nelson; md Morris Stoloff; art d, Stephen Goosson, Van Nest Polglase; set d, Robert Priestly; cos, Jean Louis; ch, Jack Cole; makeup, Clay Campbell.

Drama **Cas.** **(PR:C MPAA:NR)**

GILDED CAGE, THE** (1954, Brit.) 77m Tempean/Eros bw

Alex Nicol *(Steve Anderson)*, Veronica Hurst *(Marcia Farrell)*, Clifford Evans *(Ken Aimes)*, Ursula Howells *(Brenda Lucas)*, Elwyn Brook-Jones *(Bruno)*, John Stuart *(Harding)*, Michael Alexander *(Harry Anderson)*, Trevor Reid *(Inspector Brace)*, Roman O'Casey, Patrick Jordan.

Two brothers get enmeshed in a plot to steal a valuable painting and smuggle it out of England. Nicol, a security officer from the States, works to clear the name of his brother who was wrongly accused of being behind the operation. The brothers succeed in polishing off the crooks and returning the artwork back to the wall.

p, Robert S. Baker, Monty Berman; d, John Gilling; w, Brock Williams (based on a story by Paul Erickson); ph, Berman.

Crime **(PR:A MPAA:NR)**

GILDED LILY, THE*½** (1935) 85m PAR bw

Claudette Colbert *(Lillian David)*, Fred MacMurray *(Peter Dawes)*, Ray Milland *(Charles Gray/Granville)*, C. Aubrey Smith *(Lloyd Granville)*, Eddie Craven *(Eddie)*, Luis Alberni *(Nate)*, Donald Meek *(Hankerson)*, Michelette Burani *(Lily's Maid)*, Claude King *(Boat Captain)*, Charles Irwin *(Oscar)*, Ferdinand Munier *(Otto Bushe)*, Rita Carlyle *(Proprietor's Wife)*, Forrester Harvey *(English Inn Proprietor)*, Edward Gargan *(Guard)*, Leonid Kinskey *(Vocal Teacher)*, Jimmy Aubrey *(Purser)*, Charles Wilson *(Pete's Editor)*, Walter Shumway *(Assistant Editor)*, Rollo Lloyd *(City

Editor), Reginald Barlow (Managing Editor), Esther Muir (Divorcee), Grace Bradley (Daisy), Pat Somerset (Man in London Club), Eddie Dunn (Reporter), Tom Dugan (Bum), Warren Hymer (Taxi Driver), Rudy Cameron, Jack Egan, Jack Norton (Photographers), Hayden Stevenson, Perry Ivans, Cherry Campbell, Samuel E. Hines (Cameramen at New York Apartment), Mel Ruick (English Band Leader), Stanley Mann (Steward with Telegram), Ambrose Barker, David Thursby (British Reporters), William Begg, Dick French, Ronald Rondell, Rebecca Wassem, Adele Corliss, Gale Ronn (Patrons at Nate's Cafe), Albert Pollet, Cyril Ring (Headwaiters).

A charming and often overlooked comedy, this was the first of a septet of pairings for MacMurray and Colbert. She was already a major star (the year before she Oscared for IT HAPPENED ONE NIGHT) and he was two years younger, a newcomer at 27. Chemistry was instant and they had such a good time working with each other that it was to become one of the best duos in that era. MacMurray is a New York shipping news reporter and Colbert a stenographer who meet on the subway and love spending their afternoons discussing such world-shaking topics as the merits of peanuts versus popcorn for serious snacking at the movies. MacMurray is mad for her but she has just a tinge of the golddigger in her personality and has her chapeau set for Milland, a rich and titled Englishman, son of Smith. It looks as though she'll get her wish and marry Milland, but they have an argument and she refuses his proposal of marriage. MacMurray is delighted and writes a newspaper story about her and she becomes famous as "The No Girl" (the girl who said "No" to what every girl might want; a wedding to a wealthy and handsome young man). Due to her notoriety, she is booked in a nightclub as a singer (they used to do that in those days; anyone who had any sort of celebrity, even a murderess who had been acquitted, or someone like golfer Babe Zaharias, got booked in either the vaudeville or the nightclub circuit). She makes her debut and it is a shambles. Dressed to kill, she forgets the words to the song, gets nervous, and ad-libs some charming lines that convinces the crowd she is a lovely person and not just the media freak she appears to be. She is united with Milland in England and tries to live life the way he wants it lived but she soon comes to the conclusion that she would be lots happier with MacMurray, a man cut from the same cloth. Sharp dialog from Claude Binyon, in his first solo screenplay effort, and smooth helming from Wesley Ruggles, director brother of Charles Ruggles. Prior to movies, MacMurray had been a vocalist and saxaphone player. He also costarred on Broadway in "Roberta" where he imitated Rudy Vallee. Odd that he seldom used that good singing voice in films, preferred instead to settle into a light comedy niche after some fine dramatic work in such films as DOUBLE INDEMNITY and THE CAINE MUTINY. He is married to actress June Haver. Two years after this film, he and Colbert did it on the air for "Lux Radio Theatre" the show hosted for so many years by Cecil B. DeMille. A good example of the 1930s screwball comedy.

p, Albert Lewis; d, Wesley Ruggles; w, Claude Binyon (based on a story by Melville Baker, Jack Kirkland); ph, Victor Milner; m, Arthur Johnston; ed, Otho Lovering; cos, Travis Banton; m/l, Sam Coslow, Arthur Johnston "Something About Romance."

Comedy   (PR:AA MPAA:NR)

GILDERSLEEVE ON BROADWAY**½   (1943) 65m RKO bw

Harold Peary (Gildersleeve), Billie Burke (Mrs. Chandler), Claire Carleton (Francine Gray), Richard LeGrand (Peavey), Freddie Mercer (Leroy), Hobart Cavanaugh (Homer), Margaret Landry (Margie), Leonid Kinskey (Window Washer), Ann Doran (Matilda), Lillian Randolph (Birdie), Michael Road (Jimmy).

Peary postpones his impending nuptials with Doran to attend a pharmacist's convention in the big city, and we all know what happens then, don't we? Wealthy widow Burke covets his manly frame, and tart Carleton believes him to be well-fixed. The romantic ribaldry is not aided by a cupid figure, a maniacal archer, who attempts to pierce his sought-after substance for real. A misunderstanding results in his pursuit by police; he escapes by doing a Harold Lloyd-style window-ledge walk. This errant nonsense was well attended due to the popularity of the concurrent radio show. (See GREAT GILDERSLEEVE series, Index.)

p, Herman Schlom; d, Gordon Douglas; w, Robert E. Kent; ph, Jack Mackenzie; ed, Les Millbrook; md, C. Bakaleinikoff; art d, Albert S. D'Agostino, William Stevens.

Comedy   (PR:A MPAA:NR)

GILDERSLEEVE'S BAD DAY**   (1943) 62m RKO bw

Harold Peary (Gildersleeve), Jane Darwell (Aunt Emma), Nancy Gates (Margie), Charles Arnt (Judge Hooker), Freddie Mercer (Leroy), Russell Wade (Jimmy), Lillian Randolph (Birdie), Frank Jenks (Al), Douglas Fowley (Louie), Alan Carney (Toad), Grant Withers (Henry Potter), Richard LeGrand (Peavey), Dink Trout (Otis), Harold Landon (George Peabody), Charles Cane (Police Chief), Ken Christy (Bailiff), Joey Ray (Tom), Joan Barclay (Julie Potter), James Clemons, Jr. (Boy), W. J. O'Brien, Morgan Brown, Ralph Robertson, Broderick O'Farrell, Lou Davis, Herbert Berman, Richard Bartell, Eddie Borden, Larry Wheat (Jurors), Warren Jackson (Joe, the Cop), Earle Hodgins (Mason, the Cop), Fern Emmett (Mrs. Marvin), Lee Phelps (Ryan), Danny Jackson (Messenger Boy), Fred Trowbridge (Defense Attorney), Arthur Loft (Lucas), Jack Rice (Hotel Clerk), Edgar Sherrod (Minister), Ann Summers, Patti Brill, Betty Wells, Margie Stewart, Barbara Hale.

It may have been a bad day for Gildersleeve, but it was an even worse one for the audience. Peary returns for the second time to the role which one can laugh at but not with, this time mixing with some crooks. The dimwit becomes a jury foreman who refuses to believe that the obviously guilty gangster has done wrong—the only one in the court still unconvinced. He redeems himself when, captured by

gangsters and forced to drive their getaway car, he rams it into a tree to bring them to justice. This series was a spinoff of a popular radio show of the time. (See GREAT GILDERSLEEVE series, Index.)

p, Herman Schlom; d, Gordon Douglas; w, Jack Townley; ph, Jack Mackenzie; ed, Les Millbrook; md, C. Bakaleinikoff; art d, Albert S. D'Agostino, Carroll Clark.

Comedy   (PR:A MPAA:NR)

GILDERSLEEVE'S GHOST**   (1944) 63m RKO bw

Harold Peary (Gildersleeve/Randolph/Jonathan), Marion Martin (Terry Vance), Richard LeGrand (Peavey), Amelita Ward (Marie), Freddie Mercer (Leroy), Margie Stewart (Margie), Marie Blake (Harriet Morgan), Emory Parnell (Haley), Frank Reicher (John Wells), Joseph Vitale (Henry Lennox), Lillian Randolph (Birdie), Nicodemus Stewart (Chauncey), Charles Gemora (Gorilla).

Another exercise in zany comedy from the dynamic duo of Schlom and Douglas. The producer-director team again try their hand at Gildersleevian humor. Writer Kent brings in the poltergeists and makes Peary a police-commissioner nominee. The ghosts do their best to get the bumbling idiot into office. (See GREAT GILDERSLEEVE series, Index.)

p, Herman Schlom; d, Gordon Douglas; w, Robert E. Kent; ph, Jack Mackenzie; ed, Les Millbrook; md, C. Bakaleinikoff; art d, Albert D'Agostino, Carroll Clark; spec eff, Vernon L. Walker.

Comedy   (PR:A MPAA:NR)

GINA**½   (1961, Fr./Mex.) 92m Dismage-Producciones Tepeyac/Omat-
                                    Sutton-Pathe America c
    (LA MORT EN CE JARDIN; LA MUERTE EN ESTA JARDIN; AKA: EVIL
                                                    EDEN)

Simone Signoret (Gina), Georges Marchal (Chark), Michel Piccoli (Fr. Lizzardi), Michele Girardon (Maria), Charles Vanel (Castin), Tito Junco (Chenko), Luis Aceves Castaneda (Alberto), Jorge Martinez de Hoyos (Capt. Ferrero), Alberto Pedret (Lieutenant), Stefani, Marc Lambert (Workers), Raul Ramirez (Alvaro), Alicia del Lago, Francisco Reiguera.

The film opens in a South American diamond-mining village with the miners taking arms against an oppressive military regime. Marchal, a soldier of fortune, goes to bed with prostitute Signoret, who robs him and has him arrested for being a revolutionary. Marchal escapes and blows up an ammunition dump. He encounters Signoret again and they, along with some of the villagers, struggle through a hazardous jungle without supplies or sustenance. At last they come upon a plane loaded with food and jewels. Vanel, one of the rebel villagers, goes berserk and kills Signoret and is in turn shot by Marchal. Marchal then takes deaf-mute villager Girardon with him on a raft down a river to freedom. This film is one of Bunuel's lesser works, and it suffers from the tight demands of his French co-producers, a problem that lasted from 1955-1961. Some truly Bunuelian ideas come through, such as the cache of jewels discovered on the plane, but it is mostly an overguarded effort. Released in France in 1956 at 104 minutes and in Mexico in 1960 at 145 minutes.

p, David Mage, Oscar Dancigers; d, Luis Bunuel; w, Bunuel, Luis Alcoriza, Raymond Queneau, Gabriel Arout; ph, Jorge Stahl, Jr. (Eastmancolor); m, Paul Misraki; ed, Marguerite Renoir, Alberto Valenzuela, Denise Chardein; art d, Edward Fitzgerald.

Adventure/Drama   (PR:C MPAA:NR)

GINGER**   (1935) 80m FOX bw

Jane Withers (Ginger), O.P. Heggie (Rexford Whittington), Jackie Searl (Hamilton Parker), Katharine Alexander (Mrs. Parker), Walter King (Daniel Parker), Tommy Bupp, Richard Powell, Brendon Fowler, Walter Johnson, Leonard Carey.

Kid actor Jane Withers is an orphan who goes through the same situations made popular by the infinitely superior Shirley Temple.

p, Sol M. Wurtzel; d, Lewis Seiler; w, Arthur Kober; ph, Bert Glennon; md, Samuel Kaylin.

Drama   (PR:A MPAA:NR)

GINGER**   (1947) 74m MON bw

Frank Albertson, Barbara Reed, Johnny Calkins, Janet Burton, Gene Collins, Lee "Lasses" White, Dick Elliott, Oliver Blake, Edythe Elliott, Wally Walker.

Ginger is the dog at the center of this canine tearjerker. She steals the hearts of all who come in contact with her and makes a grab for those of the audience as well.

p, Lindsley Parsons; d&w, Oliver Drake (based on a story by Donald C. McKean); ph, James Brown; ed, Ace Herman; md, Edward J. Kay.

Drama   (PR:A MPAA:NR)

GINGER IN THE MORNING**   (1973) 92m National Film c

Monte Markham, Susan Oliver, Slim Pickens, Mark Miller, Sissy Spacek.

A tender romance about a quiet salesman in need of company who picks up a hitchhiker with whom he falls in love. Spacek appears in an early role (her first was PRIME CUT), then in the same year in BADLANDS.

d, Gordon Wiles.

Romance   **Cas.**   (PR:A MPAA:NR)

GION MATSURI   (SEE: DAY THE SUN ROSE, THE, 1969, Jap.)

GIORDANO BRUNO***
(1973, Ital.) 115m Ponti-Champion Cinematografica/Euro c

Gian Maria Volonte (Giordano Bruno), Charlotte Rampling (Fosca), Hans Christian Blech (Sartori), Mathieu Carriere (Orsini), Mark Burns (Bellarmino), Renato Scarpa (Fra Tragagliolo).

A spectacular look at 16th-century Italian philosopher and defrocked monk Bruno who was accused of trying to destroy church doctrines. Director Montaldo succeeds in developing the character as a complex and provocative figure. Beautifully photographed by Storaro and with the recognizable musical stamp of Morricone.

p, Leo Pescarolo; d, Giuliano Montaldo; w, Montaldo, Lucio De Caro, Pergiovanni Anchisi; ph, Vittorio Storaro (Technicolor); m, Ennio Morricone; ed, Antonio Siciliano; art d, Sergio Canevari.

Drama (PR:O MPAA:NR)

GIORNI DI FUOCO
(SEE: LAST OF THE RENEGADES, 1966, Fr./Ital./Ger./Yugo.)

GIPSY BLOOD
(SEE: CARMEN, 1931, Brit.)

GIRARA*½
(1967, Jap.) 89m Shochiku c
(GUIRARA; GUILALA; UCHU DAIKAIJU GUILALA; AKA: THE X FROM OUTER SPACE)

Eiji Okada, Toshiya Wazaki, Peggy Neal, Itoko Harada, Shinichi Yanagisawa, Franz Gruber, Keisuke Sonoi, Mike Daning, Torahiko Hamada.

Outer space monster Girara grows to a phenomenal size when it hitches a ride on board a spaceship. It absorbs the energy of the weapons meant to destroy it and gets even larger. It's reduced to a manageable size, however, and sent back into orbit.

p, Akihiko Shimada; d, Kazui Nihonmatsu, w, Nihonmatsu, Hidemi Motomochi, Moriyoshi Ishida; ph, Shizuo Hirase; spec eff, Hiroshi Ikeda.

Science Fiction (PR:G MPAA:NR)

GIRDLE OF GOLD*½
(1952, Brit.) 66m Screenplays-London/Eros bw

Esmond Knight (William Evans), Maudie Edwards (Mrs. Griffiths), Meredith Edwards (Mr. Griffiths), Petra Davies (Mary Rees), Glyn Houston (Dai Thomas), Tonie MacMillan (Mrs. Macie), Kenneth Evans (Sgt. Mortimer).

Edwards stars as a Welsh undertaker who sews his cash in his wife's girdle for safekeeping, never thinking she'll give the girdle away. She does and Edwards begins a desperate search for his fortune. Besides losing all his money, he nearly loses his wife to Knight, but by the finale both his finances and romance are secure.

p, Audrey Hirst, D'Arcy Conyers; d, Montgomery Tully; w, Jack Dawe; ph, Jack Asher.

Comedy (PR:A MPAA:NR)

GIRL, A GUY AND A GOB, A***
(1941) 90m RKO bw
(GB: THE NAVY STEPS OUT)

George Murphy (Coffee Cup), Lucille Ball (Dot Duncan), Edmond O'Brien (Stephen Herrick), Henry Travers (Abel Martin), Franklin Pangborn (Pet Shop Owner), George Cleveland (Pokey), Kathleen Howard (Jawme), Marguerite Chapman (Cecilia Grange), Lloyd Corrigan (Pigeon), Mady Correll (Cora), Frank McGlynn (Pankington), Doodles Weaver (Eddie), Frank Sully (Salty), Nella Walker (Mrs. Grange), Richard Lane (Recruiting Officer), Irving Bacon (Mr. Merney), Rube Demarest (Ivory), Charles Smith (Messenger), Nora Cecil (Charwoman), Bob McKenzie (Porter), George Lloyd, George Chandler, Vic Potel (Bits), Vince Barnett (Pedestrian), Jimmy, Bush, Jack Lescoulie (Sailors), Joe Bernard (Tattoo Artist), Fern Emmett (Middle-Aged Woman), Wade Boteler (Uniformed Attendant), Charles Irwin (Dance Hall Emcee), Carol Hughes (Dance Hall Girl), Warren Ashe (Opera Ticket Taker), Jimmy Cleary (Program Boy), Ralph Brooks, Cy Ring, Tommy Quinn (Hustlers), Alex Pollard (Butler), Mary Field (Woman on Street), Snub Pollard (Attendant), Geraldine Fissette (Native Dancer), Leon Belasco (Taxi Driver), Hal K. Dawson (Photographer), Dewey Robinson (Bouncer), Andrew Tombes (Bus Conductor).

Genius comedian Lloyd acted as producer in this wonderfully funny, though entirely familiar, love triangle. O'Brien is a shy rich boy who is enamored of Ball. She, however, has plans with the obnoxious Murphy. When Ball is dumped by her beau, she ends up in the arms of O'Brien. Lloyd is successful at transferring his slapstick techniques to director Wallace and the enjoyable cast.

p, Harold Lloyd; d, Richard Wallace; w, Frank Ryan, Bert Granet (based on a story by Grover Jones); ph, Russell Metty; ed, George Crone; spec eff, Vernon L. Walker.

Comedy **Cas.** (PR:A MPAA:NR)

GIRL AGAINST NAPOLEON, A
(SEE: DEVIL MADE A WOMAN, THE, 1959, Span.)

GIRL AND THE BUGLER, THE***
(1967, USSR) 76m Mosfilm/Artkino bw (ZVONYAT, OTKROYTE DVER)

Lena Proklova (Tanya), Rolan Bykov (The Bugler), Victor Belokurov (Petya), Lena Zolotuhina (Girl Friend), Sergey Nikonenko, Olya Semyonova, Vitya Kosykh, Vitya Sysoyev, A. Aleynikova, L. Veytsler, V. Vladimirova, A. Denisova, Oleg Yefremov, A. Maksimova, E. Nekrasova, Lyudmila Ovchinnikova, Iya Savvina, Misha Metyolkin, Mark Bernes.

A heart-warming children's tale about a young girl's infatuation with a scouting leader. Her infatuation fades when she spots her "love" with "another woman." The title comes from a show put on by a bugler who charms and captivates all the kids. Winner of Venice's Children's Film Festival.

d, Alexander Mitta; w, Alexander Volodin; ph, A. Panasyuk; m, V. Basner; art d, P. Kiselyov.

Children (PR:AA MPAA:NR)

GIRL AND THE GAMBLER, THE**
(1939) 62m RKO bw

Leo Carrillo (El Rayo), Tim Holt (Johnny Powell), Steffi Duna (Dolores), Donald MacBride (Mike), Chris-Pin Martin (Pasqual), Edward Raquello (Rodolfo), Paul Fix (Charlie), Julian Rivero (Pedro), Frank Puglia (Gomez), Esther Muir (Madge), Paul Sutton (Manuelo), Charles Stevens (Andres), Frank Lackteen (Tomaso), Henry Rocquemore.

Replaying his Mexican Robin Hood role seen in GIRL OF THE RIO, Carrillo bets his fellow gang members that he can woo dancer Duna back to their hideout. When he finds her in love with the impressionable Holt, he brings them back by force until he relents near the Mexican border and releases the captured couple.

p, Cliff Reid; d, Lew Landers; w, Joseph A. Fields, Clarence Upson Young (based on the play "The Dove" by Willard Mack); ph, Russell Metty; ed, Desmond Marquette; m/l, "La Gunga Timbalero," "Mi Ultimo Adios," Aaron Gonzales.

Western (PR:A MPAA:NR)

GIRL AND THE GENERAL, THE**
(1967, Fr./Ital.) 105m Champion-Concordia/MGM c

Rod Steiger (The General), Virna Lisi (Ada), Umberto Orsini (Private Tarasconi), Toni Gaggia (The Lieutenant), Marco Mariani (The Corporal), Jacques Herlin (The Veterinary), Valentino Macchi (Soldier).

Steiger is a one-armed general in the Italian Army who is captured by the incompetent Orsini. After just a short time Steiger escapes, and with Lisi locks Orsini in a railroad car. The pair stay in an abandoned farmhouse where Steiger nurses a gimpy leg. Ragged and hungry, Lisi shows some soldiers a little skin in return for some food. Eventually they meet up with Orsini again, who has come to like Steiger and Lisi. A minefield, however, takes the lives of the general's companions. Fed up with the war and the pain it brings, Steiger turns himself in to the Austrian authorities. Also released at 113 minutes.

p, Carlo Ponti; d, Pasquale Festa Campanile; w, Luigi Malerba, Campanile (based on the story by Massimo Franciosa, Campanile); ph, Ennio Guarnieri (Technicolor); m, Ennio Morricone; ed, Iolanda Benvenuti; art d, Luciano Spandoni; set d, Dario Micheli; cos, Maria De Matteis; makeup, Nilo Jacoponi.

War Drama (PR:C MPAA:NR)

GIRL AND THE LEGEND, THE*½
(1966, Ger.) 90m N.D.F./Comet c
(ROBINSON SOLL NICHT STERBEN)

Romy Schneider (Maud), Horst Buchholz (Tom), Erich Ponto (Daniel Defoe), Magda Schneider (Mother), Mathias Wieman (King), Gustav Knuth (Gangster Chief), Rudolf Vogel (Valet), Gunther Luders (Drinkwater), Roland Kaiser, Wolfgang Condrus, Urs Hess (Children), Gert Frobe, Siegfried Lowitz, Mario Adorf, Elisabeth Flickenschildt, Joseph Offenbach, Ernst Fritz Furbringer, Willy Leyrer, Heinrich Gretler, Karl Heinz Peters, Rudolf Rhomberg.

A band of kids, both rich and poor, come to the aid and comfort of 17th-century author (The Adventures of Robinson Crusoe) Daniel Defoe. Romy Schneider, herself, should feel a little like Crusoe, having been marooned by the script. Released in West Germany in 1957 at 98 minutes.

p, Georg Richter; d, Josef von Baky; w, Emil Burri, Johannes Mario Simmel; ph, Gunther Anders, Gunter Senftleben (Agfacolor); m, Georg Haentzschel; ed, Claus von Boro; art d, Hein Heckroth; set d, Heckroth, A. Windau, Walter J. Blokesch; cos, Charlotte Flemming; makeup, Raimund Stangl, Anita Greil.

Drama (PR:A MPAA:NR)

GIRL AND THE PALIO, THE
(SEE: LOVE SPECIALIST, THE, 1958, Ital.)

GIRL CAN'T HELP IT, THE**
(1956) 99m FOX c

Tom Ewell (Tom Miller), Jayne Mansfield (Jerri Jordan), Edmond O'Brien (Murdock), Henry Jones (Mousie), Julie London (Herself), John Emery (Wheeler), Juanita Moore (Hilda), Barry Gordon (Barry), Ray Anthony, Little Richard, Fats Domino, Gene Vincent and His Blue Caps, The Platters, The Treniers, Eddie Fontaine, Abbey Lincoln, The Chuckles, Johnny Olenn, Nino Tempo, Eddie Cochran.

A weak spoof designed to take advantage of the new rock 'n' roll craze and the buxom talents of Mansfield—at best an inept actress with an annoyingly high voice—this film has three or four guffaws and a script designed for the mindless. In her first starring role Mansfield is a gangster's moll with no talent (typecasting) who is sent to agent Ewell by mobster O'Brien to be turned into a star. Ewell creates a rock 'n' roll act for Mansfield, who wiggles and quakes from her top-heavy top to her bouncing bottom, imitating, as usual, Marilyn Monroe, or Mamie Van Doren, or Sheree North. Mansfield becomes a star, falls in love with Ewell, and dumps thug O'Brien in her climb to rock 'n' roll fame. Of course, the entire film is just a flimsy excuse to parade a host of the new music genre talent. Fox allowed a heavy budget for this sexpot film, with $35,000 given to Mansfield's 18 wardrobe changes. Seventeen tunes puncture a script already full of holes. Mansfield's mammaries were blatantly advertised by Fox. In one promotional slogan, the copy ran: "She mesmerizes every mother's son—if she smiles then beefsteak becomes well done," drawing from the Little Richard title song. Director Tashlin projected a humorous macho philosophy about this film and, when asked to evaluate his leading lady quipped: "There's nothing more hysterical to me than big-breasted women—like leaning Towers of Pisa." Songs include: "Blue Monday" (sung by Fats Domino), "Twenty Flight Rock" Eddie Cochran, "Be Bop a Lula" (Gene Vincent and the Bluecaps), "She's Got It" (Little Richard), "Cry Me A River" (Julie London) and are among the few understandable standards sung).

p&d, Frank Tashlin; w, Tashlin, Herbert Baker; ph, Leon Shamroy (CinemaScope, De Luxe Color); ed, James B. Clark; md, Lionel Newman; art d,

Lyle R. Wheeler, Leland Fuller; cos, Charles LeMaire; m/l, Bobby Troup (new songs).

Musical   **(PR:C MPAA:NR)**

GIRL CAN'T STOP, THE*½   (1966, Fr./Gr.) 87m Les Films Marceau-Cocinor-Sport Films-Fanayotopoulos/U.S. Films bw
(LES CHIENS DANS LA NUIT)

Maria Xenia (Tassoula), George Riviere, Claude Cerval, Jean Sobieski, Jenny Astruc, Georges Lycan, Jacques Ardennes.

After becoming the mistress of an embezzler, Xenia discovers that her husband and the embezzler killed an old banker to collect his inheritance. Having been raped by one of her husband's henchmen, she seeks guidance from a priest, who advises her to go to the police. She is cleared of any wrongdoing and happily retires to a remote Greek island.

p&d, Willy Rozier; w, Xavier Vallier, Rozier (based on the novel *Ho Chatze Manouel: Mythistorema* by Thrasos Kastanakes); ph, Michel Rocca; m, Jean Yatove.

Crime Drama   **(PR:C MPAA:NR)**

GIRL CRAZY**½   (1932) 75m RKO bw

Bert Wheeler (Jimmy Deegan), Robert Woolsey (Slick Foster), Eddie Quillan (Danny Churchill), Dorothy Lee (Patsy), Mitzi Green (Tessie Deegan), Kitty Kelly (Kate Foster), Arline Judge (Molly Gray), Stanley Fields (Lank Sanders), Lita Chevret (Mary), Chris-Pin Martin (Pete), Brooks Benedict, Monte Collins.

Wheeler and Woolsey are a pair of city boys who take a taxi to Custerville, Arizona, and get mixed up in a variety of adventures. Wheeler, in a fixed vote, becomes the sheriff and finds himself up against Fields who has this problem with doing in sheriffs. Adding to the madcap antics is Quillan's decision to turn his dad's ranch into a local hot spot, complete with dancing girls and gambling. Based on a Gershwin musical, it was later remade with Mickey Rooney and Judy Garland, and again as WHEN THE BOYS MEET THE GIRLS (1967). The wonderful tunes include,"Could You Use Me?," "But Not For Me," "Embraceable You," "Sam and Delilah," "I Got Rhythm," "Bidin' My Time," "You've Got What Gets Me," by the Gershwins.

p, William LeBaron; d, William A. Seiter; w, Tim Whelan, Herman J. Mankiewicz, Edward Welch, Walter DeLeon (based on the Broadway musical comedy, and the book by John McGowan, Guy Bolton); ph, Roy Hunt; m, George Gershwin, Ira Gershwin; ed, Artie Roberts; art d, Max Ree.

Musical/Comedy   **(PR:A MPAA:NR)**

GIRL CRAZY****   (1943) 97m MGM bw
(AKA: WHEN THE GIRLS MEET THE BOYS)

Mickey Rooney (Danny Churchill, Jr.), Judy Garland (Ginger Gray), Gil Stratton (Bud Livermore), Robert E. Strickland (Henry Lathrop), Rags Ragland (Rags), June Allyson (Specialty), Nancy Walker (Polly Williams), Guy Kibbee (Dean Phineas Armour), Tommy Dorsey and His Band (Themselves), Frances Rafferty (Marjorie Tait), Howard Freeman (Gov. Tait), Henry O'Neill (Mr. Churchill, Sr.), Sidney Miller (Ed), Eve Whitney (Brunette), Carol Gallagher, Kay Williams (Blondes), Jess Lee Brooks (Buckets), Roger Moore (Cameraman), Charles Coleman (Maitre d'Hotel), Harry Depp (Nervous Man), Richard Kipling (Dignified Man), Henry Roquemore (Fat Man), Alphonse Martel (Waiter), Frances MacInerney, Sally Cairns (Checkroom Girls), Barbara Bedford (Churchill's Secretary), Victor Potel (Stationmaster), Joseph Geil, Jr., Ken Stewart (Students), William Beaudine, Jr. (Tom), Irving Bacon (Reception Clerk), George Offerman, Jr. (Messenger), Mary Elliott (Southern Girl), Katharine Booth (Girl), Georgia Carroll, Aileen Haley, Noreen Nash, Natalie Draper, Hazel Brooks, Eve Whitney, Mary Jane French, Inez Cooper, Linda Deane (Showgirls), Don Taylor, Jimmy Butler, Peter Lawford, John Estes, Bob Lowell (Governor's Secretary), William Bishop, James Warren, Fred Beckner, Jr. (Radio Men), Blanche Rose, Helen Dickson, Melissa Ten Eyck, Vangie Beilby, Julia Griffith, Lillian West, Sandra Morgan, Peggy Leon, Bess Flowers (Committee Women), Harry C. Bradley (Governor's Crony), Bill Hazlett (Indian Chief), Rose Higgins (Indian Squaw), Spec O'Donnell (Fiddle Player).

A fast-moving and funny film, GIRL CRAZY was the eighth pairing of Garland and Rooney and surely one of their best. Based on a play by Guy Bolton and Jack McGowan (with music by the Gershwins), it was first made by RKO as a Wheeler and Woolsey comedy. This time, MGM turned out a delightful picture that was unfortunately remade in 1965 as WHERE THE BOYS MEET THE GIRLS with Connie Francis and Harve Presnell, which is like trying to remake CITIZEN KANE with Dom De Luise in the Welles role. On the stage, Ginger Rogers did the Garland part and Merman played the role Nancy Walker did in the film. Rooney is the rich son of newspaper publisher O'Neill. He is sent to an all-boy's mining school where wake-up time is six a.m., which is the usual hour when he goes to sleep. Stuck out in the desert, Rooney finds it hard to exercise his girl-crazy attitude as the only woman of any consequence nearby is the granddaughter of the dean (Kibbee) who is, of course, Garland. Rooney hates being at the school and lets everyone know it but he is in love with Garland by this time and determined to make a go of it. Now we learn that the school is to be shuttered because they can't get enough students. Rooney gets the others behind him and proposes that they stage a rodeo and see if they can raise enough money to save the school. He gets a two-month stay from governor Freeman. Rooney meets Freeman's daughter, Rafferty, at a party, and tells her and all the other sweet young debs at the party that they are about to name a rodeo queen and that each of them just might be that winner. The girls show up for the rodeo, which is a huge hit. The vote for the queen is split evenly between Garland and Rafferty. Rooney announces that Rafferty is the winner and Garland takes it like a pro, never knowing that it was a tie. Rooney's motivations were for the national publicity it could achieve. He's right. Applications pour in for the school but most of them are from women and the school is turned into a co-ed

institution. Rooney and Garland can now continue their love affair and the school is saved. This was originally to be directed by Busby Berkeley but he and MGM musical maven Edens didn't get along and Garland didn't like him due to some friction on FOR ME AND MY GAL the year before. Still, they did bring him in to stage the spectacular "I Got Rhythm" number and left the rest of the musical work to Charles Walters who did a splendid job. Other songs were: "Sam and Delilah," "Embraceable You," "I Got Rhythm," "Fascinating Rhythm," "Treat Me Rough," "Bronco Busters," "Bidin' My Time," "But Not for Me," "Do," "When It's Cactus Time in Arizona," "Boy, What Love Has Done to Me," "Barbary Coast," all by George and Ira Gershwin, and "Happy Birthday, Ginger," by Roger Edens. Rooney played his own piano in a tune with the Tommy Dorsey band and acquitted himself well. He was also a sensational drummer as seen in various other films. This was June Allyson's third picture of 1943 (the others were BEST FOOT FORWARD and THOUSANDS CHEER) and "the blonde with the brunette voice" more than held her own with Rooney in the "Treat Me Rough" number. Rags Ragland has a small, funny bit as the school handyman, and Gil Stratton, who went on to become a Los Angeles sportscaster for many years, is seen in one of his early roles as Bud Livermore. Stratton will be best recalled for his work in THE WILD ONE. Taurog directed well but we can't help but think about what this might have been if Berkeley and Garland could have mended their fences before the picture began. Look for Peter Lawford and Don Taylor as a couple of boys.

p, Arthur Freed; d, Norman Taurog; w, Fred Finklehoffe, uncredited contributions on the screenplay by Dorothy Kingsley, Sid Silvers, and William Ludwig (based on the play by George and Ira Gershwin, Guy Bolton, Jack McGowan); ph, William Daniels, Robert Planck; ed, Albert Akst; md, George Stoll; art d, Cedric Gibbons; set d, Edwin B. Willis, Mac Alper; cos, Irene Sharaff, Irene; ch, Charles Walters, Busby Berkeley.

Musical/Comedy   **(PR:AAA MPAA:NR)**

GIRL CRAZY, 1965   (SEE: WHEN THE BOYS MEET THE GIRLS, 1965)

GIRL DOWNSTAIRS, THE**½   (1938) 73m MGM bw

Franciska Gaal (Katerina Linz), Franchot Tone (Paul Wagner), Walter Connolly (Mr. Brown), Reginald Gardiner (Willie), Rita Johnson (Rosalind Brown), Reginald Owen (Charlie), Franklin Pangborn (Adolf Pumpfel), Robert Coote (Karl), Barnett Parker (The Butler), Priscilla Lawson (Freda), James B. Carson (Rudolph), Charles Judels (Fritz), Billy Gilbert (Garage Proprietor).

A Cinderella story starring Hungarian Gaal as a maid who wins the affections of a rich man courting the lovely daughter of her millionaire boss. A pleasing little romance which, though implausible, is well-acted and expertly directed. Gilbert stands out in a bit comic routine.

p, Harry Rapf; d, Norman Taurog; w, Harold Goldman, Felix Jackson, Karl Noti (based on the short story by Sandor Hunyady); ph, Clyde De Vinna; m, Bob Wright, Chet Forrest; ed, Elmo Vernon.

Romance   **(PR:A MPAA:NR)**

GIRL FEVER*   (1961) 72m Y.P. Artists-Leo/General Screen-Leo c

Count Gregory, George Camarinos III, Choo-Choo Collins, Danielle Clary, Geraldine, Dick Richards, Edna Thayer.

Count Gregory makes a global excursion to find himself a new star for his Broadway stage show. He searches Egypt, Italy, Spain, Japan, and Paris for the right person. He winds up being taken prisoner by a harem, then has an encounter with a group of apaches who are holding a meeting in a Parisian cafe. He has a brilliant revelation that the most talented performers are right there in the Big Apple, and decides to continue his hunt at home. Bad.

p, Sherman Price; d, Price, Yevsie Petrushansky.

Musical/Comedy   **(PR:A MPAA:NR)**

GIRL FOR JOE, A   (SEE: FORCE OF ARMS, 1951)

GIRL FRIEND, THE**½   (1935) 67m COL bw

Ann Sothern (Linda), Jack Haley (Henry), Roger Pryor (George), Thurston Hall (Harmon), Victor Kilian (Sunshine), Ray Walker (Doc), Margaret Seddon (Grandma), Inez Courtney (Hilda), Geneva Mitchell, Lee Kohlmar, Victor Potel, John T. Murray.

Haley is a pretentious but amiable rustic who has written a serious drama about the life of Napoleon, an epic work unlikely to attain a staging. Sothern is his charming sister and Seddon his grandmother. An actor and a pair of balladmongers decide to save themselves from impending starvation by impersonating a high-powered Broadway producer and his two assistants and pretending interest in Haley's opus. Lodging for the summer at the family farmhouse, they sing for their supper by mock-rehearsing the Napoleonic nonsense in the adjacent barn. When Grandma Seddon sinks her life savings into a brief run in the local town's theater, the rascals relent and revise the rube's writings, turning the maudlin melodrama into a musical. A *real* Broadway producer views the result and purchases the package for a happy ending, with actor-impersonator Pryor and budding stage star Sothern a romantic duo.

p, Samuel Briskin; d, Edward Buzzell; w, Gertrude Purcell, Benny Rubin (based on a story by Gene Towne, Graham Baker); ph, Joseph Walker; ed, John Rawlins; ch, Seymour Felix; m/l, Arthur Johnston, Gus Kahn.

Musical   **(PR:A MPAA:NR)**

GIRL FRIENDS, THE   (SEE: LE AMICHE, 1962, Fr.)

GIRL FROM ALASKA**   (1942) 75m REP bw

Ray Middleton (Steve Bentley), Jean Parker (Mary "Pete" McCoy), Jerome Cowan (Ravenhill), Robert H. Barrat (Frayne), Ray Mala (Charley), Francis McDonald (Pelly), Raymond Hatton (Shorty), Milton Parsons (Sanderson), Nestor Paiva (Geroux).

Middleton, the surly hero of this gold-rush drama, celebrates his impending nuggetless withdrawal from the icy territory, sans strike and disillusioned. The debaucherie of the departure ceremony leads to the apparent death of a local lawman; Middleton is forced to flee to avoid prosecution. He falls in with another felon, Cowan, a well-fixed Englishman who wants to get further fixed, and plans to get that way by robbing and murdering an elderly prospector whose panning has paid off. Parker, the prospector's progeny, is menaced by the villain after her father's demise, but she and Middleton escape across the ice floes of a thawing frozen river. Middleton, his spirits revived by his regard for Parker, discovers that he was not responsible for the lawman's death and all ends well.

p, Armand Schaefer; d, Nick Grinde; w, Edward T. Lowe, Robert Ormond Case (based on *The Golden Portage* by Case); ph, Jack Marta, Bud Thackerey; ed, Ernest Nims; md, Cy Feuer; art d, Russell Kimball.

Western **(PR:A MPAA:NR)**

GIRL FROM AVENUE A** (1940) 73m FOX bw

Jane Withers *(Jane)*, Kent Taylor *(MacMillan)*, Katharine Aldridge *(Lucy)*, Elyse Knox *(Angela)*, Laura Hope Crews *(Mrs. Forrester)*, Jessie Ralph *(Mrs. Van Dyne)*, Harry Shannon *(Timson)*, Vaughan Glaser *(Bishop)*, Rand Brooks *(Steve)*, Ann Shoemaker *(Mrs. Maddox)*, George Humbert *(Gallupi)*.

Set in horse-and-buggy times, this Withers comedy/drama is a reprise of George Bernard Shaw's play "Pygmalion." Withers plays a street urchin who uses her wits to stay alive on the city streets. Taylor saves her from a scrape with a man she tries to beat for a fancy meal. Taylor, a wealthy part-time playwright, takes her home to use for reference for street slang in a play he plans to write. His entire family is opposed to her living with them, but Taylor keeps her around, watching her like a zoo specimen. She ends up winning over the whole family as she becomes transformed into a perfect lady.

p, Sol M. Wurtzel; d, Otto Brower; w, Frances Hyland (based on the play, "The Brat", by Maude Fulton); ph, George Barnes, Lucien Andriot; ed, Louis Loeffler; md, Emil Newman; art d, Richard Day, Chester Fore.

Comedy **(PR:A MPAA:NR)**

GIRL FROM CALGARY** (1932) 64m CHAD/MON bw-c

Fifi D'Orsay, Paul Kelly, Astrid Allwyn, Robt. Warwick, Edward Featherstone, Ed Maxwell.

Bad, spotty color is a feature of the opening scenes of this mediocre effort, with stock footage of a genuine rodeo parade and introduction intercut with shots of heroine D'Orsay riding a rope-manipulated phony bucking bronco. The remainder of the picture is in black-and-white. The delightful D'Orsay is spotted astride her barrel-bronco by theatrical flack Kelly, who decides he will Svengali her to stardom. An Atlantic City beauty contest falls to her favor, and then a stage production. She resists the big-city importunities of the lustful, devilish angel of the show—Warwick—who, by way of warning, has his heavies beat rival Kelly to a bloody pulp. Hurrying hospitalward, she comforts Kelly; at the film's close, marriage to her mentor seems imminent.

d, Phil Whitman, Leon D'Usseau; w, D'Usseau, Sig Schlager; ph, Harry Neuman; m, Albert Hay Malotte.

Drama **(PR:A MPAA:NR)**

GIRL FROM CHINA, THE (SEE: SHANGHAI LADY, 1930)

GIRL FROM GOD'S COUNTRY** (1940) 75m REP bw

Chester Morris *(Jim Holden)*, Jane Wyatt *(Anne Webster)*, Charles Bickford *(Bill Bogler)*, Mala *(Joe)*, Kate Lawson *(Koda)*, John Bleifer *(Ninimook)*, Mamo Clark *(Mrs. Bearfat Tillicoot)*, Ferike Boros *(Mrs. Broken Thumb)*, Don Zelaya *(Tom Broken Thumb)*, Clem Bevans *(Ben)*, Ed Gargan *(Poker Player)*, Spencer Charters *(Dealer)*, Thomas Jackson *(Poker Player)*, Vic Potel *(Barber)*, Si Jenks *(Trapper)*, Gene Morgan *(Man at the Dock)*, Ace *(Blitzen the Dog)*.

A stern, self-exiled, selfless doctor, Morris, wanted for prosecution for the drug-murder of his terminally ill father back home, ministers to the medical needs of the ill, indigent Inuit in the far reaches of the frozen North. Newly arrived nurse Wyatt finds the circumstances of her unwanted exile to the same outpost revolting, her happy but hapless lice-ridden charges disgusting. Enter dogged detective Bickford on the track of mercy killer Morris. After many a chase, Morris ministers to the snow-blinded sleuth, who sybaritically saves the samaritan from certain incarceration by way of reward, forgetting that he found the felon. Wyatt quells her queasiness and opts to stay in the snowy surroundings with her heroic healer. Notable among the natives in this Northerner is Mala, the half-Jewish Eskimo who plays the lead Inuit.

p, Armand Schaefer; d, Sidney Salkow; w, Elizabeth Meehan, Robert Lee Johnson, Malcolm Stuart Boylan (based on a story by Ray Millholland); ph, Jack Marta; ed, William Morgan; md, Cy Feuer; art d, John Victor Mackay.

Drama **(PR:A MPAA:NR)**

GIRL FROM HAVANA, THE**** (1929) 65m FOX bw

Lola Lane *(Joan Anders)*, Paul Page *(Allan Grant)*, Kenneth Thomson *(William Dane)*, Natalie Moorhead *(Lona Martin)*, Warren Hymer *(Spike Howard)*, Joseph Girard *(Dougherty)*, Adele Windsor *(Babe Hanson)*, Marcia Chapman *(Sally Green)*, Dorothy Brown *(Toots Nolan)*, Juan Sedillo *(Detective)*, Raymond Lopez *(Joe Barker)*.

An excellent, suspenseful early talkie with decent dialog and few give-aways, this picture features one of the all-time great theft sequences. A clerk in a jewelry store, Page, bravely defends the patrons by leaping to attack a frothy-mouthed "mad" dog that has wandered into the posh establishment. Wrestling the presumably rabid pooch to a standstill, the heroic pearl peddler finds himself roundly upbraided by the store's manager when it is discovered that a number of valuable trinkets have vanished. The occupants of the establishment are searched, but to no avail; the gems have jetted. Next, we find the intrepid ex-clerk aboard an ocean liner bound for Cuba, with his one-time jewelry patrons Thomson and Moorhead, principals in the gem-theft ring. The pooch reappears; the missing bracelets had been stuffed by Page into a pouch worn by the "rabid" mutt. But, Lo! Female detective Lane has boarded also, hot on the trail of the trio and their henchmen. En route, a ship's concert offers opportunities for the singing, dancing Lane—one of three successful cinematic sisters, the others being Priscilla and Rosemary—to warble "Time Will Tell," at which point the purloining Page promptly falls in love with her. But wait! Page has only pretended perfidy in order to get the goods on one member of the mob, who murdered his father. After a brisk battle, the clever crooks are caught, their venture come to naught, lovers Lane and Page unite, and everthing seems right.

d, Benjamin Stoloff; w, John Stone, Edwin H. Burke.

Crime **(PR:A MPAA:NR)**

GIRL FROM HAVANA** (1940) 69m REP bw

Dennis O'Keefe *(Woody Davis)*, Claire Carlton *(Havana)*, Victor Jory *(Tex Moore)*, Steffi Duna *(Chita)*, Gordon Jones *(Tubby Waters)*, Bradley Page *(Cort)*, Addison Richards *(Harrigan)*, Abner Biberman *(Capt. Lazear)*, William Edmunds *(Ricco)*, Trevor Bardette *(Drenov)*, Jay Novello *(Mancel)*, Frank Lackteen *(Peon)*.

O'Keefe and Jory star as two buddies who venture into the oil drilling business seeking fame and fortune. Regrettably, forces beyond their control conspire to thwart their entrepreneurial efforts. Rebel uprisings in the area threaten to destroy the oil site, while the charming attentions of femme fatale Carlton threaten to destroy their friendship. Eventually the pair trace the political trouble to an unscrupulous gunrunner who'll sell weapons to anybody. MGM released the same basic story at the same time in BOOM TOWN (1940), starring Clark Gable and Spencer Tracy as the feuding friends. Guess which of the two entries became a classic?

p, Robert North; d, Lew Landers; w, Karl Brown, Malcolm Stuart Boyland; ph, Ernest Miller; ed, William Morgan; md, Cy Feuer; m/l, Jule Styne, George R. Brown, Sol Meyer.

Drama **(PR:A MPAA:NR)**

GIRL FROM HONG KONG** (1966, Ger.) 95m Nero-Neue Deutsche/Comet c (BIS ZUM ENDE ALLER TAGE)

Akiko *(Anna Suh)*, Helmut Griem *(Glen Dierks)*, Carl Lange *(Hamburg Innkeeper)*, Ursula Lillig *(Glen's Former Girl Friend)*, Hanns Lothar, Peter Carsten, Carla Hagen, Eva Pflug, Klaus Kindler.

Griem is a German sailor who falls in love with a Chinese girl who has a spotted past. The girl, Akiko, returns with Griem to his home, but doesn't receive a very warm welcome. Akiko flees, Griem follows, hope exists.

p, Seymour Nebenzahl, Wolf Schwarz; d, Franz Peter Wirth; w, Kurt Heuser, Oliver Hassencamp (based on the novel *Brackwasser* by Heinrich Hauser); ph, Klaus von Rautenfeld; m, Michel Michelet; ed, Lilian Seng; art d, Hans Berthel, Johannes Ott; cos, Hartinut Bake; makeup, Herbert Griesner, Gertrud Heinz-Werner.

Romance **(PR:A MPAA:NR)**

GIRL FROM IRELAND (SEE: KATHLEEN MAVOURNEEN, 1934)

GIRL FROM JONES BEACH, THE½** (1949) 77m WB bw

Ronald Reagan *(Bob Randolph/Robert Venerik)*, Virginia Mayo *(Ruth Wilson)*, Eddie Bracken *(Chuck Donovan)*, Dona Drake *(Connie Martin)*, Henry Travers *(Judge Bullfinch)*, Lois Wilson *(Mrs. Wilson)*, Florence Bates *(Miss Shoemaker)*, Jerome Cowan *(Mr. Graves)*, Helen Westcott *(Miss Brooks)*, Paul Harvey *(Jim Townsend)*, Lloyd Corrigan *(Mr. Evergood)*, Myrna Dell *(Lorraine Scott)*, William Forrest *(Mr. Moody)*, Gary Gray *(Woody Wilson)*, Mary Stuart *(Hazel)*, Lennie Bremen *(News Vendor)*, Buddy Roosevelt *(Conductor)*, Chester Clute *(Collection Agent)*, Dick Bartell *(Man at Phone Booth)*, Billy Wayne *(Mac the Bartender)*, Jeff Richards, Dale Robertson *(Lifeguards)*, Guy Wilkerson *(Janitor)*, Angi O. Poulos *(Foreigner in Hallway)*, Antonio Filauri *(Italian)*, Gregory Golubeff *(Italian)*, Peter Camlin *(Frenchman)*, Robert O'Neil *(Irishman)*, Nancy Valentine *(Margot)*, Lola Albright *(Vickie)*, William Yetter *(Mr. Schwarzholz)*, Glen Gallagher, Dolores Castle *(Samba Team)*, Creighton Hale *(Waiter)*, Jack Gargan, Tony Merrill, Henry Iblings, Cary Harrison, Broderick O'Farrell, Ray Bailey, Kay Mansfield, Grayce Hampton *(Guests)*, Joan Vohs, Carol Brewster, Betty Underwood, Alice Wallace, Joi Lansing, Lorraine Crawford, Vonne Lester, Karen Gaylord *(Models)*.

Reagan proves himself an amiable farceur in this lightweight piece of froth about a famous illustrator (no doubt patterned after popular artists Petty and Vargas) who needs to find the perfect woman. He's been drawing women for quite some time and a TV company offers to put him and his model on the air. But he doesn't have one model—they are a composite of several models he's used. When he sees his dream girl (Mayo) in the flesh at Jones Beach, promoter Bracken (who mugged so much that it's ugly to watch) makes her an offer but she declines. She works as a schoolteacher and is more involved with people's minds than their eyes. Reagan poses as a Czech immigrant and registers in her American history class to get closer to her and does some thick-accented dialog that is very funny (especially funny when you know where he went from there). Mayo soon recognizes him for who he is but continues her relationship with him as the mutual attraction grows. A local paper prints a copy of her in her bathing suit and the school board goes up in arms. They fire her and she takes them to court (not unlike what really happened several decades later when a teacher and a police officer were both fired for appearing in a national men's magazine). Travers is the judge and finds for her. She and Reagan decide to get married and he will now use his abilities for something better than the cheesecake for which he is famous. A cute film that did well at the box office, perhaps better than it should have. Mayo is lovely and plays well off Reagan. In one particular scene Bracken was so involved watching the women that he allegedly tripped Reagan by mistake, causing the future chief exec to fall and break a small bone in his back. The script by I.A.L. Diamond (working without Billy Wilder for a change) was filled with bright remarks and almost managed to overcome the ham acting of Bracken.

p, Alex Gottlieb; d, Peter Godfrey; w, I.A.L. Diamond (based on a story by Allen Boretz); ph, Carl Guthrie; m, David Buttolph; ed, Rudi Fehr; art d, Stanley Fleischer; set d, William Kuehl; cos, Leah Rhodes; spec eff, William McGann, Edward DuPar; m/l, Harry Warren, Al Dubin, Sol Marcus, Eddie Seiler; makeup, Gordon Bau.

Comedy   **(PR:AA MPAA:NR)**

GIRL FROM LORRAINE, A*   (1982, Fr./Switz.) 107m
Phenix-Gaumont-Fr.-SSR/New Yorker c (LA PROVINCIALE)

Nathalie Baye (Christine), Bruno Ganz (Remy), Angela Winkler (Claire), Patrick Chesnais (Pascal), Pierre Vernier, Dominique Paturel, Roland Monod, Jean Obe, Henri Poirier, Robert Rimbaud, Jean Davy, Jacques Lalande.

One of Europe's most delightful actresses, Nathalie Baye, is cast in an elementary tale about a girl from the country who looks for a new life in Paris. Though it is no more than the standard country-girl-finds-disillusionment-in-the-city story, it is made thoroughly engaging by Baye (DAY FOR NIGHT, 1973, THE GREEN ROOM, 1978) and Ganz (THE AMERICAN FRIEND, 1977). The City of Light never looked darker as Baye finds lust rather than love in the arms of Swiss executive Ganz who, after briefly bedding Baye, bolts to Japan to bolster his business. She befriends equally disenchanted actress Winkler who, weary of the couches of the casting directors, converts to courtesan. Seeing herself starting to become as brittle as her city surroundings, Baye ultimately returns to her parental province to find peace.

p, Yves Peyrot, Raymond Pousaz; d, Claude Goretta; w, Goretta, Jacques Kirsner, Rosina Rochette; ph, Philippe Rousselot, Dominique Bringuier; m, Arie Dzierlatka; ed, Joele Van Effenterre, Xavier Castano; art d, Jacques Bufnoir.

Drama   **(PR:O MPAA:NR)**

GIRL FROM MANDALAY*   (1936) 68m REP bw

Conrad Nagel (John Foster), Kay Linaker (Jeanie), Donald Cook (Kenneth Grainger), Esther Ralston (Mary Trevor), Harry Stubbs (Trevor), Reginald Barlow (Dr. Collins), George Regas (Headman), David Clyde (Malone), Jack Santos (Bongai), Joe Bautista (Oswald), John Bouer (Mannering), Daisy Belmore (Mrs. Collins), Harry Allen (Captain).

Nagel stars as a lonely Britisher in Mandalay who seeks emotional refuge in a marriage with local nightclub entertainer Linaker after his fiancee in England gets fed up and marries another. Unfortunately, Linaker gets little respect from Nagel's British buddies until she helps out during a tiger attack and fever epidemic. Hopelessly contrived.

p, Nat Levine, Victor Zobel; d, Howard Bretherton; w, Wellyn Totman, Endre Bohem (based on the novel Tiger Valley by Reginald Campbell); ph, Ernest Miller, Jack Marta.

Drama   **(PR:A MPAA:NR)**

GIRL FROM MANHATTAN**   (1948) 80m UA bw

Dorothy Lamour (Carol Maynard), George Montgomery (Reverend Tom Walker), Charles Laughton (The Bishop), Ernest Truex (Homer Purdy), Hugh Herbert (Aaron Goss), Constance Collier (Mrs. Brooke), William Frawley (Mr. Bernouti), Sara Allgood (Mrs. Beeler), Frank Orth (Oscar Newsome), Howard Freeman (Sam Griffin), Raymond Largay (Wilbur J. Birch), George Chandler (Monty), Selmer Jackson (Dr. Moseby), Adelaide De Walt Reynolds (Old Woman), Maurice Cass (Mr. Merkel), Eddy Waller (Jim Allison), Everett Glass (Committee Man), Marie Blake (Committee Woman).

Minister Montgomery—a former star football player—finds himself being manipulated by a rotten realtor who connives a scheme to buy out boardinghouse owner Truex, build a new church on his property, raze the old church, and then sell the property to a hotel chain that plans to build in the area. Lamour, a successful New York model and niece of Truex comes home to find out what's going on. To stay in business, Truex needs enough dough to finish off his mortgage, so noble and saintly minister Montgomery takes the money out of his personal savings to help Truex, while sacrificing a new church.

p, Benedict Bogeaus; d, Alfred E. Green; w, Howard Estabrook; ph, Ernest Laszlo; m, Heinz Roemheld; ed, James E. Smith; md, David Chudnow; art d, Jerome Pycha.

Drama   **(PR:A MPAA:NR)**

GIRL FROM MAXIM'S, THE* (1936, Brit.) 53m LFP/J.H. Hoffberg bw

Frances Day ("La Mome"), Lady Tree (Mme. Petypon), Leslie Henson (Dr. Petypon), George Grossmith (Le General), Desmond Jeans (Etienne), Evan Thomas (Corignon), Sterling Holloway (Mongincourt), Gertrude Musgrove (Clementine), Eric Portman.

Dull British comedy set in Paris in 1904 and starring Day as a lovely singer and frequent visitor of Maxim's who becomes embroiled in the personal life of a henpecked doctor. Through a series of increasingly hard-to-take circumstances, the doctor finds himself forced to pass off the sexy singer as his wife, which leads to many routine mistaken-identity situations. For some reason this film took five years to reach American shores, and by that time producer/director Korda had gone on to bigger and better things. At the time he made this low-level farce—simultaneously filmed in French—he was just beginning the English phase of his career, working with low budgets and poor technical help (Korda had previously produced and directed in Hungary and the U.S.).

p, Alexander Korda, Ludovico Toeplitz; d, Korda; w, Harry Graham, Arthur Wimperis (based on Georges Feydeau's play "La Dame Chez Maxim"); ph,

Georges Perinal; m, Kurt Shroeder; ed, Harold Young, R. Bettinson; set d, Vincent Korda; cos, Jean Oberle.

Comedy   **(PR:A MPAA:NR)**

GIRL FROM MEXICO, 1930   (SEE: MEXICALI ROSE, 1930)

GIRL FROM MEXICO, THE½**   (1939) 71m RKO bw

Lupe Velez (Carmelita), Donald Woods (Dennis), Leon Errol (Uncle Matt), Linda Hayes (Elizabeth), Donald MacBride (Renner), Edward Raquello (Romano), Elizabeth Risdon (Aunt Della), Ward Bond (Mexican Pete).

Velez made a comeback with GIRL FROM MEXICO which stars her as a sexy South-of-the-border entertainer who is discovered by ad agency worker Woods when he drafts her to perform for his company on a new radio program. Of course he gets more than he bargained for in the wild Velez, who proceeds to take Manhattan and Woods by storm. The film was surprisingly successful at the box office and spawned a series of films starring Velez as the "Mexican Spitfire," with the facially mobile Errol as her constant foil. Songs include "Negra Consentida" (Joaquin Pardave) "Chiapanecas" (Romero, Garuse, De Torre). (See MEXICAN SPITFIRE series, Index.)

p, Robert Sisk; d, Leslie Goodwins; w, Lionel Houser, Joseph A. Fields (based on a story by Houser); ph, Jack MacKenzie; ed, Desmond Marquette; md, Roy Webb; art d, Van Nest Polglase.

Comedy   **(PR:A MPAA:NR)**

GIRL FROM MISSOURI, THE*   (1934) 75m MGM bw
(GB: ONE HUNDRED PERCENT PURE)

Jean Harlow (Eadie), Lionel Barrymore (T.B. Paige), Franchot Tone (Tom Paige), Lewis Stone (Frank Cousins), Patsy Kelly (Kitty Lennihan), Alan Mowbray (Lord Douglas), Clara Blandick (Miss Newberry), Russell Hopton (Bert), Hale Hamilton (Charles Turner), Henry Kolker (Sen. Titcombe), Nat Pendleton (Lifeguard), Marion Lord (Wardrobe Mistress), Carol Tevis (Baby Talker), Desmond Roberts (Butler), Bert Roach (Willie), Norman Ainsley (2nd Butler), Howard Hickman (Senator), James Burke, Lee Phelps (Policemen), Alice Lake (Manicurist), Lane Chandler (Doorman), Richard Tucker (Office Manager), Gladys Hulette (Secretary), Charles C. Wilson (Lieutenant), Charles Williams, Fuzzy Knight (Cameramen), Dennis O'Keefe (Dance Extra), Larry Steers (Extra in Stateroom), William "Stage" Boyd (Eadie's Stepfather).

Harlow is the daughter of an innkeeper in a small resort town and she's annoyed at the fact that her stepfather wants her to "entertain" the clientele, somewhat beyond the usual ways. She is best friends with Patsy Kelly and the two decide to run off to New York and find a better life there. She gets a job as a chorine but nurtures the hope that she will eventually be able to marry the millionaire of her dreams. Despite lots of double entendres, Harlow remains very virginal and will not give up her chastity until Mr. Right drives up in his Bentley and marries her. She gets a job performing at a stag party along with several other chorus types, a party hosted by Stone who is quite blue because he is flatter than the Texas Panhandle. Stone wants Barrymore, a very wealthy man, to advance him some money until he gets back on his feet. Barrymore, in one of his patented miserly roles, foregoes the pleasure of lending Stone any money, which causes the man to take his own life but not before he gives Harlow his golden cuff links because he is taken with her breezy personality. The cops enter and think that Harlow may have stolen the prized possessions from the dead man, but Barrymore confirms they were a present from the late ne'er-do-well. Harlow thinks providence may have sent Barrymore her way as the man she will marry. He's rich, a widower, and apparently lonely. Harlow follows him to Florida where he lives aboard a yacht. Once there, she meets Barrymore's son, Tone, and falls in love with him. Tone likes her enough to propose that she become his mistress, which throws Harlow into hysteria. She wants to be a wife, not the "other woman." Through her tears, she acquiesces to his request. Now Tone realizes that Harlow is truly a virtuous girl and is willing to toss that aside because she really loves him. Once that gets through his thick skull, he proposes marriage and she eagerly accepts. Barrymore, remembering how and where he met the platinum blonde, wants that romance put aside right away. No son of his is going to marry a cheap, tawdry chorus girl. In an attempt to prove to Tone that Harlow is just a gold digger, Barrymore has her framed by hiring a man to go to her hotel room. Tone is despondent at what appears to be duplicity on his intended's account and refuses to believe that she is innocent of any charges. Hamilton, who is richer than Barrymore, pays Harlow's bail and gets her out of the false imprisonment so she agrees to become his mistress. But first, she is going to wreak some vengeance on Barrymore. He is about to leave for Europe to attend a conference and is busy talking to a cadre of cameramen when she arrives, dressed only in a revealing slip, runs up to the old codger, gives him a squeeze, and exits as fast as she entered. Tone by now has realized that she was innocent and wants to apologize. When Barrymore tells Tone what Harlow did, Tone represses a smile and knows she did it out of revenge. He accuses his father of framing Harlow and Barrymore admits it. Next, the two men go out looking for Harlow. They locate her at Hamilton's sumptuous apartment, still a virgin but slightly tipsy with celebration drinks. Tone and Harlow marry quickly, which also gets Barrymore off the hook when he explains to curious newshawks that Harlow is, in fact, his daughter-in-law and was only being cute as she showed her affection for the old coot. Fade out with Tone and Harlow looking forward to a long and happy life together. Lots of funny lines, lots of raucous action, and the scene where Harlow arrives at the yacht in Florida is a riot. The picture was released in England as ONE HUNDRED PERCENT PURE and had two titles before the final one. Originally called, "Eadie Was A Lady," they then tried "Born To Be Kissed," and settled on THE GIRL FROM MISSOURI. Sharp dialog from John Emerson and Anita Loos, who was also responsible for GENTLEMEN PREFER BLONDES as well as at least fifty other screenplays.

p, Bernard H. Hyman; d, Jack Conway; w, Anita Loos, John Emerson; ph, Ray June; m, Dr. William Axt; ed, Tom Held.

Comedy   (PR:A-C MPAA:NR)

GIRL FROM MONTEREY, THE**   (1943) 69m PRC bw

Armida (Lita), Edgar Kennedy (Doc Hogan), Veda Ann Borg (Flossie), Jack LaRue (Johnson), Terry Frost (Jerry O'Leary), Anthony Caruso (Baby), Charles Williams (Harry), Bryant Washburn (Commissioner), Guy Zanett (Perrone), Wheeler Oakman (Announcer).

A stock romance/boxing film starring Armida as the manager/sister of pugilist Caruso who seeks to convince her brother not to fight boxer Frost, because she's in love with him. To make matters worse, Frost's crooked manager hires a bombshell, Borg, to seduce Caruso and keep him out of shape so that the fight will be a cake walk. Luckily all the dishonest dealings are revealed to the boxing commission at the last minute and nobody gets hurt. Songs include "Jive, Brother, Jive," "Last Night's All Over," and "The Girl From Monterey" (Louis Herscher).

p, Jack Schwarz; d, Wallace Fox; w, Arthur Hoerl (based on an original story by George Green, Robert Gordon); ph, Marcel Le Picard; ed, Robert Crandall; md, Mahlon Merrick; art d, Frank Sylos.

Drama   (PR:A MPAA:NR)

GIRL FROM PARIS, THE   (SEE: THAT GIRL FROM PARIS, 1937)

GIRL FROM PETROVKA, THE*½   (1974) 103m UNIV c

Goldie Hawn (Oktyabrina), Hal Holbrook (Joe), Anthony Hopkins (Kostya), Gregoire Aslan (Minister), Anton Dolin (Ignatievitch, Balletmaster), Bruno Wintzell (Alexander), Zoran Andric (Leonid), Hanna Hertelendy (Judge), Maria Sokolov (Old Crone), Zitto Kazann (Passport Black Marketeer), Inger Jensen (Helga Van Dam), Raymond O'Keefe (Minister's Driver), Richard Marner (Kremlin Press Official), Michael Janisch (Police Chief Valinikov), Harry Towb (American Reporter), Ted Grossman (Jogging Companion), Elisa Georgiadis (Minister's Wife), Heinz Marecek (Cafe Waiter), Anatol Winogradoff (Shipyard Caretaker).

Hawn struggles mightily with this dim material provided by screenwriters Bryant and Scott, but she just can't seem to shake the basic inanity of the concept. She plays a Russian girl who falls in love with American reporter Holbrook with typical and unimaginative complications to follow. While purporting to be a social comedy, the film is never very funny, and the ending (which sees Hawn sent to prison because her papers weren't in order) ruins any good feelings that may have slipped through.

p, Richard D. Zanuck, David Brown; d, Robert Ellis Miller; w, Chris Bryant, Allan Scott (based on the novel by George Feifer); ph, Vilmos Zsigmond (Panavision/Technicolor); m, Henry Mancini; ed, John F. Burnett; art d, George C. Webb; set d, Hal G. Gausman, Joe Chevalier; cos, Deidre Clancy; m/l, Roy Budd, Jack Fishman.

Comedy/Drama   (PR:A MPAA:PG)

GIRL FROM POLTAVA**½   (1937) 86m Avramenko/Kinotrade bw
                                                              (AKA: NATALKA POLTAVKA)

Thalia Sabanieeva (Natalka), Dimitri Creona (Petro), Olena Dibrova (Terpylykha), Michael Shvetz (Vyborny), Mathew Vodiany (Vozny), Theodore Swystun (Mykola), Vladimir Zelitsky (Palamar), Lydia Berezovska (Mariyka), Mykola Novak (Landlord), Michael Skorobohach (Office Clerk), Fedir Braznick (Peasant), Maria Lavryk (His Wife), Peter Kushabsky (Terpylo), Andrew Stanislavsky (Lirnyk).

An American-made adaptation of the Russian operetta "Natalka Poltavka" performed entirely in Russian and directed by M.J. Gann and low-budget master Edgar G. Ulmer. Produced and released at about the same time a Russian-made version of the material was released in New York City, GIRL FROM POLTAVA is the more accessible version as it is balanced with a lively mix of music, drama, and humor shot in a manner that does not betray its stage origins. (In Russian; English subtitles.)

d, M.J. Gann, E.G. Ulmer; w, Vasile Avramenko, Gann; m, C.N. Shvedoff.

Musical   (PR:A MPAA:NR)

GIRL FROM RIO, THE**   (1939) 63m MON bw

Movita (Marquita), Warren Hull (Steven), Alan Baldwin (Carlos), Kay Linaker (Vicki), Clay Clement (Mitchell), Adele Pearce (Annette), Soledad Jiminez (Lola), Richard Tucker (Montgomery), Dennis Moore (Collins), Byron Foulger (Wilson).

A mystery/musical that unfortunately moves at a turtle's pace. And this turtle doesn't win the race. Heavily dependent on Movita's singing talents, it has her in New York to bail her brother out of trouble. Her brother is being framed; Movita enlists the aid of her American boy friend, Hull, who is a newspaperman. She starts singing at a nightclub where the owner is under suspicion of starting some fires at his previous clubs. Movita's scheme is discovered and club owner Clement traps her in his office. She gets to his gun before him and fires some shots. The tracer bullets start a fire and that's been Clement's method. Hull and others arrive like the cavalry; the mystery is solved and Movita can once again sing a happy tune, including "The Burro Song," "Romance In Rio," and "Daddy Mine."

p, E.B. Derr; d, Lambert Hillyer; w, Milton Raison, John T. Neville; ph, Paul Ivano; ed, Russell Schoengarth; m/l, Johnny Lange, Lew Porter, Harry Tobias, Emile de Recat.

Mystery   (PR:A MPAA:NR)

GIRL FROM SAN LORENZO, THE**   (1950) 59m UA bw

Duncan Renaldo (Cisco), Leo Carrillo (Pancho), Jane Adams (Nora), Bill Lester (Jerry), Byron Foulger (Cal), Don Harvey (Kansas), Lee Phelps (Sheriff), Edmund Cobb (Wooly), Leonard Penn (McCarger), David Sharpe (Blackie), Wes Hudman (Rusty).

An average CISCO KID series (see Index) film starring Renaldo as Cisco and Carrillo as sidekick Pancho. The baddies are robbing the stagecoaches and placing the blame on the redoubtable Renaldo and his constant companion. Following the customary chases and gunplay—and with a little romance between Adams and Lester, fostered by the dashing duo—Renaldo rounds up the wretches and brings them to justice. (See CISCO KID series, Index.)

p, Philip N. Krasne; d, Derwin Abrahams; w, Ford Beebe (based on characters created by O. Henry); ph, Kenneth Peach; m, Albert Glasser; ed, Marty Cohn; art d, Fred Preble.

Western   (PR:A MPAA:NR)

GIRL FROM SCOTLAND YARD, THE**   (1937) 61m PAR bw

Karen Morley (Viola Beech), Robert Baldwin (Derrick Holt), Katherine Alexander (Lady Lavering), Eduardo Cianelli (Franz Borg), Milli Monti (Herself), Lloyd Crane (Bertie), Bud Flanagan [Dennis O'Keefe] (John), Phil Steelman, Alphonse Martel, Don Brodie, Odette Myrtil, Lynn Anders, Major Farrell.

Things have been blowing up and Scotland Yard has assigned Morley to track the perpetrators down in this thriller that is so poor it evokes more laughs than anything. With help from American newspaperman Baldwin, she tracks down the culprit during a long, drawn-out airplane chase. Cianelli is the evil man with the death ray that can blow up anything he wants to destroy. Not believable.

p, Emanuel Cohen; d, Robert Vignola; w, Doris Anderson, Dore Schary (based on a story by Coningsby Dawson); ph, Robert Pittack; ed, George McGuire.

Crime   (PR:A MPAA:NR)

GIRL FROM STARSHIP VENUS, THE zero   (1975, Brit.) 90m
                                                                 Intercontinental c

Monika Ringwald, Andrew Grant, Mark Jones, Tanya Ferova.

A trashy sex fantasy about a creature from another galaxy that transforms itself into a voluptuous woman in order to fully understand human ways and emotions. Cinema will be a better place once the girl goes back to Starship Venus.

p, Morton Lewis; d&w, Derek Ford.

Science Fiction   (PR:O MPAA:R)

GIRL FROM TENTH AVENUE, THE**½   (1935) 70m FN-WB bw
                                                              (GB: MEN ON HER MIND)

Bette Davis (Miriam Brady), Ian Hunter (Geoffrey Sherwood), Colin Clive (John Marland), Alison Skipworth (Mrs. Martin), John Eldredge (Hugh Brown), Phillip Reed (Tony Hewlett), Katharine Alexander (Valentine French Marland), Helen Jerome Eddy (Miss Mansfield, the Secretary), Adrian Rosley (Marcel), Andre Cheron (Max), Edward McWade (Art Clerk), Brooks Benedict (Diner), Gordon "Bill" Elliott (Clerk at Club), Jack Norton (Man), Bess Flowers (Woman Guest), Mary Treen (Secretary), Heinie Conklin.

Made the year after Davis scored her first major starring success in her triumphal role in OF HUMAN BONDAGE (1934), this film was something of a letdown. Hunter, a society attorney of questionable character, has been dumped by his fiancee, Alexander, who marries another man, Clive. By way of recompense for the desertion, Hunter gets blind drunk. Davis, who is not of his social caste, rescues Hunter from serious embarrassment and joins him in his unhappy carousal. Upon awakening, they discover they have gotten married. Davis suggests an annulment, but Hunter convinces her to wait and see whether things will work out. With her assistance and support, he renews his career, which begins to flourish. Meanwhile, Alexander realizes that her marriage to Clive was a mistake; she wants to get back together with Hunter. Good hearted Davis agrees to step aside for the society scions and get a divorce, but then she meets Alexander and realizes what the lady truly is: no lady at all. She tells her as much in the middle of a flossy restaurant, disquieting Hunter, who moves out on her. Couched in his club, he meets fellow clubman Clive, who convinces him that his coarsely bred cutie should continue as his consort.

p, Henry Blanke; d, Alfred E. Green; w, Charles Kenyon (based on the play "Outcast" by Hubert Henry Davies); ph, James Van Trees; ed, Owen Marks; md, Leo F. Forbstein; art d, John Hughes; cos, Orry-Kelly.

Drama   (PR:A MPAA:NR)

GIRL FROM THE MARSH CROFT, THE**   (1935, Ger.) 82m UFA bw
                                                              (DAS MADCHEN VON MOORHOF)

Hansi Knoteck (Helga Christmann), Ellen Frank (Gertrud Gerhart), Kurt Fischer-Fehling (Karsten Dittmar), Friedrich Kayssler (Mr. Dittmar), Eduard von Winterstein (Mr. Gerhart), Jeanette Bethge (Mrs. Dittmar), Lina Carstens (Mrs. Christmann), Franz Stein (Mr. Christmann), Erwin Klietsch (Peter Nolde), Theodor Loos (Judge), Fritz Hoopts, Erich Dunskus, Hans Meyer-Hanno, Maria Seidler, Anita Duvel, Ilse Petri, Klaus Pohl, Dorothea Thies, Betty Sedlmayr, Hilde Sessak.

A young farmer is engaged to a young socialite, but is in love with the girl from the marsh. After he gets involved in a brawl in a local bar, the engagement is called off by the debutante's parents, freeing him to wed his true love. Originally filmed as a silent in 1919—a Swedish production. Remade in 1958 under the same title.

p, Peter Paul Brauer; d, Detlef Sierck [Douglas Sirk]; w, Lothar M. Mayring (based on the novel by Selma Lagerlof); ph, Willi Winterstein; m, Hans-Otto Borgmann; ed, Fritz Stapenhorst; set d, C.L. Kirmse.

Drama   (PR:A MPAA:NR)

GIRL FROM TRIESTE, THE*   (1983, Ital.) 103m Faso/Golden Era c

Ben Gazzara, Ornella Muti, Mimsy Farmer, Andrea Ferreol, Jean-Claude Brialy, William Berger, Consuelo Ferrara, Romano Puppo, Diego Pesaola.

Gazzara again teams up with Muti after their initial pairing in TALES OF ORDINARY MADNESS (1983) in this considerably less interesting picture, this time saving her from a suicide attempt. Gazzara, an on-and-off actor (ANATOMY OF A

MURDER, 1959, SAINT JACK, 1979), in this picture simply resorts to mediocrity.

p, Achille Manzotti; d, Pasquale Festa Campanile; w, Ottavio Jemma (based on the novel by Campanile); ph, Alfio Contini (Technicolor); m, Riz Ortolani; ed, Amedeo Salfa; prod d, Ezio Altieri.

Drama   (PR:C MPAA:NR)

GIRL FROM VALLADOLID*½   (1958, Span.) 95m
Cinematograficas/UNIV c (MUCHACHITA DE VALLADOLID)

Alberto Closas (Patricio), Analia Gade (Mercedes), Lina Rosales (Alexandra Aymat), Alfredo Mayo (Canciller), Lopez Vazquez (Secretary), Vicky Lagos (Erika).

Gade plays the ignorant, provincial young bride of diplomat Closas who proves she's smarter than she looks by wooing a rich oil deal for her husband by using her folksy charm. Based on a stage play and it shows.

d, Luis Amadori; w, Luis Marquina, Amadori (from the play by Calvo Sotelo); ph, Jose Aguayo (Eastmancolor); m, Cristobal Halffter; art d, Enrique Alarcon.

Comedy   (PR:A MPAA:NR)

GIRL FROM WOOLWORTH'S, THE*½   (1929) 60m FN-WB bw

Alice White (Pat King), Charles Delaney (Bill Harrigan), Wheeler Oakman (Lawrence Mayfield), Rita Flynn (Tillie Hart), Ben Hall.

An early all-talking musical about a singing salesgirl, White, in the music department of the title store. She sings her way into show business, but drops stardom for a marriage to Delaney. Some unmemorable tunes from this film are, "Crying for Love" and "What I Know About Love."

p, Ray Rockett; d, William Beaudine; w, Richard Weil, Edward Luddy (based on Adele Commandini's story); ph, Jackson Rose; m/l, Al Bryan, George Meyer.

Musical   (PR:A MPAA:NR)

GIRL GAME*   (1968, Braz./Fr./Ital.) 90m Victoria-France Cinema-
Consorcio/Cinema Distributors of America c (AKA: COPACABANA PALACE, THE SAGA OF THE FLYING HOSTESSES)

Sylva Koscina (Ines), Walter Chiari (Ugo), Mylene Demongeot (Zina von Raunacher), Paolo Ferrari (De Fonseca), Gloria Paul (Michele), Claude Rich (Buby von Raunacher), Raymond Bussieres, Francis De Wolff, Ruggero Baldi, Franco Fabrizi.

Call it what you will, but by any name this glorification of the jet-setter's lifestyle during Rio's Carnival is strictly worthwhile only for the scenery. Released at both 90 and 125 minutes.

p, Franco Cancellieri, Abilio Pereira de Almeida; d, Steno; w, Sergio Amidei, Luciano Vincenzoni; ph, Massimo Dallamano (Dyaliscope/Technicolor); m, Gianni Ferrio.

Drama   (PR:C MPAA:NR)

GIRL GETTERS, THE**½   (1966, Brit.) 93m Bryanston/AIP bw
(GB: THE SYSTEM)

Oliver Reed (Tinker), Jane Merrow (Nicola), Barbara Ferris (Suzy), Julia Foster (Lorna), Harry Andrews (Larsey), Ann Lynn (Ella), Guy Doleman (Philip), Andrew Ray (Willy), John Porter Davison (Grib), Clive Colin Bowler (Sneakers), David Hemmings (David), Iain Gregory (Sammy), John Alderton (Nidge), Jeremy Burnham (Ivor), Mark Burns (Michael), Derek Nimmo (James), Pauline Munro (Sylvie), Derek Newark (Alfred), Stephanie Beaumont (Marianne), Talitha Pol (Helga), Dora Reisser (Ingrid), Susan Burnet (Jasmin), Victor Winding (Stan Atty), Jennifer Tafler (Sonia), Ross Parker (Fred), Gwendolyn Watts.

Reed delivers a fine performance as a young seaside photographer who takes pictures of the local girls as a ploy to find romance. When he takes Merrow's photo he gets more than he bargained for from the independent London fashion model. The finale has Reed, though struck with love, realizing that she has gotten the better of him. Photographed by Nicolas Roeg and featuring David Hemmings in an early role.

p, Kenneth Shipman; d, Michael Winner; w, Peter Draper; ph, Nicolas Roeg; m, Stanley Black; ed, Fred Burnley; art d, Geoffrey Tozer; cos, Bridget Sellers; makeup, Gerry Fletcher; m/l, "The System," Bobby Richards, Mike Pratt.

Drama/Romance   (PR:C MPAA:NR)

GIRL GRABBERS, THE zero   (1968) 89m August/RAF c

Paul Cox (Paul Desmond), Jackie Richards (Lynn), Ludmilla Tchor (Tania), John Spence (Nick), Sebastian Dangerfield [Stefan Peters] (Louie), June Francis (Ruth), Alaistair Burr (Frank), Louise Violet, Linda Boyce (Go-Go Dancers).

A contemporary drama reflecting the popular concern with violence and crime in the big city. Cox is out for revenge against the hoodlums who raped his girl friend during an intended burglary of her Greenwich Village apartment. He tracks down a prostitute friend of one of the thugs, Spence, and discovers the latter's whereabouts by posing as a friend. Captured by the drug-dealing, thieving rapists, Spence and Dangerfield, Cox is sentenced to death by them, along with rape victim Tchor and prostitute Richards, whom they believe to have betrayed them. The intended murder victims, including the unwitting Richards, are taken for a gangland-style ride. Richards, getting wind of the fact that Spence and Dangerfield plan to dispose of her as well as the other two, attacks them. Spence fires, killing Richards and, inadvertently, Dangerfield. Cox manages to get control of the car and runs Spence down. Actor Dangerfield appears to have taken his nom de cinema from J. P. Donleavy's novel The Ginger Man.

p&d, Simon Nuchtern.

Drama   (PR:O MPAA:NR)

GIRL HABIT*½   (1931) 77m PAR bw

Charlie Ruggles (Charlie Floyd), Tamara Geva (Sonya Maloney), Sue Conroy (Lucy Ledyard), Margaret Dumont (Blanche Ledyard), Allen Jenkins (Tony Maloney), Donald Meek (Jonesy), Douglas Gilmore (Huntley Palmer), Jerome Daley (Warden Henery), Betty Garde (Hattie Henery), Ed Gargan (Detective), Murray Alper (Hood), Jean Ackerman, Paulette Goddard, Erica Newman, Norma Taylor (Lingerie Salesgirls).

Ruggles is a rich bachelor who likes to play around and finds himself being pursued by the mobster husband of one of his conquests in this nice little farce that gets some pleasant chuckles. He finally does land in prison, but right next to the guy who was chasing him. Once out, he resumes his unabashed flirting, much to the chagrin of his fiancee. Instead of the girl batting the eyelashes, this time it's the guy.

d, Edward Cline; w, Owen Davis, Gertrude Purcell (based on a play by A. E. Thomas, Clayton Hamilton); ph, Larry Williams; ed, Barney Rogan.

Comedy   (PR:A MPAA:NR)

GIRL HAPPY**   (1965) 96m MGM c

Elvis Presley (Rusty Wells), Shelley Fabares (Valerie), Harold J. Stone (Big Frank), Gary Crosby (Andy), Joby Baker (Wilbur), Nita Talbot (Sunny Daze), Mary Ann Mobley (Deena), Fabrizio Mioni (Romano), Jackie Coogan (Sgt. Benson), Jimmy Hawkins (Doc), Peter Brooks (Brentwood Von Durgenfeld), John Fiedler (Mr. Penchill), Chris Noel (Betsy), Lyn Edgington (Laurie), Gale Gilmore (Nancy), Pamela Curran (Bobbie), Rusty Allen (Linda).

Presley, leader of a four-piece rock 'n' roll group, has the incredible good fortune to land a job in a Fort Lauderdale nightclub during Easter week, when vacationing collegians take over the town. Sent there by the club's owner, Chicago mobster Stone, Presley is commissioned to keep an eye on Stone's errant daughter Fabares—who is mad about him—during his spare time. Lothario Mioni's attempts to romance the wild wanton involve all in numerous scrapes, which the kindly cop, Coogan, attempts to ameliorate. All ends well as Presley subdues Fabares by offering her what she really wants. Songs include "Girl Happy" (Doc Pomus, Norman Mead); "Cross My Heart and Hope to Die" (Ben Weisman, Sid Wayne); "Do Not Disturb," "Spring Fever," "Wolf Call" (Bill Giant, Bernie Baum, Florence Kaye); "Do the Clam" (Weisman, Wayne, Dolores Fuller); "Fort Lauderdale Chamber of Commerce," "Puppet On a String" (Sid Tepper, Roy C. Bennett); "I've Got to Find My Baby," "The Meanest Girl in Town" (Joy Byers); "Startin' Tonight" (Lenore Rosenblatt, Victor Millrose).

p, Joe Pasternak; d, Boris Sagal; w, Harvey Bullock, R. S. Allen; ph, Philip H. Lathrop (Panavision, Metrocolor); m, George Stoll; ed, Rita Roland; art d, George D. Davis, Addison Hehr; set d, Henry Grace, Hugh Hunt; cos, Lambert Marks, Elva Martien; ch, David Winters; makeup, William Tuttle, Ron Berkeley.

Musical   (PR:A MPAA:NR)

GIRL HE LEFT BEHIND, THE**½   (1956) 101m WB bw

Tab Hunter (Andy Sheaffer), Natalie Wood (Susan Daniels), Jessie Royce Landis (Madeline Sheaffer), Jim Backus (Sgt. Hanna), Henry Jones (Hanson), Murray Hamilton (Sgt. Clyde), Alan King (Maguire), James Garner (Preston), David Janssen (Capt. Genaro), Vinton Hayworth (Arthur Sheaffer), Wilfrid Knapp (Congressman Hardison), Les Johnson (Lt. Taylor), Raymond Bailey (General), Florenz Ames (Mr. Hillaby), Fredd Wayne (Sgt. Sheridan), Ernestine Wade (Lorna).

This occasionally cumbersome comedy has Hunter a wealthy, spoiled draftee in the peacetime Army, longing only to get out and away, back to his sweetheart Wood. During basic training, his purposeful ineptitude—which leads to most of the few laughs, usually at the expense of his training sergeant, Hamilton—results in the Army offering him a discharge from the service, albeit a dishonorable one. Desperate to depart the confines of the encampment, he accepts the proffered paper, but before his exit occurs he finds himself in the midst of a war-games exercise. In the confusion of the games, he saves the lives of four of his fellow soldiers. Redeemed by this adventure, he elects to serve out his time, the manhood ritual having had its inexorable effect. The English do this sort of thing much better. Takeoff of SEE HERE PRIVATE HARGROVE.

p, Frank P. Rosenberg; d, David Butler; w, Guy Trosper (based on a novel by Marion Hargrove); ph, Ted McCord; m, Roy Webb; ed, Irene Morra; art d, Stanley Fleisher; cos, Moss Mabry.

Comedy   (PR:A MPAA:NR)

GIRL HUNTERS, THE**½   (1963, Brit.) 103m Fellane/Colorama bw

Mickey Spillane (Mike Hammer), Shirley Eaton (Laura Knapp), Lloyd Nolan (Art Rickerby), Hy Gardner (Himself), Scott Peters (Pat Chambers), Guy Kingsley Poynter (Dr. Larry Snyder), James Dyrenforth (Bayliss Henry), Charles Farrell (Joe Grissi), Kim Tracy (the Nurse), Benny Lee (Nat Drutman), Murray Kash (Richie Cole), Bill Nagy (Georgie), Clive Endersby (Duck-Duck), Richard Montez (Skinny Guy), Larry Cross (Red Markham), Tony Arpino (Cab Driver), Hal Galili (Bouncer), Nelly Hanham (Landlady), Bob Gallico (Dr. Leo Daniels), Michael Brennan, Howard Greene, Grant Holden (Police), Francis Napier (Detective), Larry Taylor (The Dragon).

Frontier-style justice prevails over law and order once again as judge-and-jury private detective Mike Hammer—here played by his creator, Spillane—is forcibly pulled from seven years of alcoholic abandon by his one-time friend, the police captain, Peters. The latter wants the streetwise Spillane's assistance in interrogating the dying Kash, who will speak to none save he. The resentful Spillane, whose spiritous self-flagellation results from despondency over the apparent death of his sexy secretary Velda years before, gains the desired data but refuses to transmit it to the authorities until persuaded by federal agent Nolan. Kash, it appears, was a fellow agent, murdered by the same weapon that killed a prestigious U.S. senator, an assassination laid to the red hands of communist spies. With the help of a syndicated columnist, Gardner, Spillane tracks the communist syndicate led by

Taylor. The trail leads to the senator's wonderful widow, the estimable Eaton, whom he romances. Starting to suspect that the vagrant Velda may yet be viable, Spillane renews the chase with vigor, locating the leader of the spy ring, Taylor, and nailing his hands to the floor to ensure his capture by his more conventional pursuers. He then confronts Eaton about her suspected complicity with the spies, after first spiking her shotgun, which explodes and kills her as the guilty girl attempts to shoot him. As in the rest of Spillane's literary *corpus,* any lady who dallies with the detective pays a heavy penalty. Fast and farcical, with girls and gore, a film favored by those who can stomach the Jehovan judgments therein expressed.

p, Robert Fellows, Charles Reynolds; d, Roy Rowland; w, Mickey Spillane, Rowland, Fellows (based on Spillane's novel); ph, Ken Talbot (Panavision); m, Phil Green; ed, Sidney Stone; art d, Tony Inglis; cos, Rene Coke, Dan Millstein; ch, Douglas Robinson; makeup, Sydney Turner.

Mystery (PR:C-O MPAA:NR)

GIRL I ABANDONED, THE*½ (1970, Jap.) 116m Nikkatsu c
(WATASHI GA SUTETA ONNA)

Choichiro Kawarazaki *(Tsutomu Yoshioka),* Toshie Kobayashi *(Mitsu),* Ruriko Asaoka *(Mariko),* Chikako Natsumi *(Shimako),* Haruko Kato, Shoichi Ozawa, Takeshi Kato, Teruko Kishi, Hideaki Ezumi, Toru Emori, Hisataka Yamane, Ryutaro Tatsumi, Kunie Origa, Hideharu Otaki, Fumie Kitahara, Tadao Nakamaru, Minako Sakaguchi, Hiroshi Shimada, Sumie Sasaki, Toshio Hayano, Asao Sano, Junko Kuroda, Shigeru Tsuyuguchi, Shusaku Endo.

Upwardly mobile office worker Kawarazaki's marriage to a relative of the chief executive of his employing firm is disrupted when he renews his acquaintance with one-time lover Kobayashi—now fallen upon hard times after an abortion of his prospective progeny—whom he deemed an unsuitable wife. A mutual woman friend, Natsumi, tells him of his former sweetheart's troubles; following his self-serving wedding, his compassionate nature compels him to see her again. Their passion is rekindled, but its fulfillment is photographed by an ally of the sinister go-between, Natsumi. Attempting to save her beloved's career, the once-abandoned Kobayashi tries to recover the blackmail photographs, but dies in an accidental fall from a window. An interesting contemporary oriental account of the dilemma expressed in Theodore Dreiser's *An American Tragedy.*

d, Kirio Urayama; w, Hisashi Yamanouchi (based on a story by Shusaku Endo); ph, Shohei Ando; m, Toshiro Mayuzumi; art d, Yoshinaga Yokoo.

Drama (PR:C-O MPAA:NR)

GIRL I MADE, THE (SEE: MADE ON BROADWAY, 1933)

GIRL IN A MILLION, A** (1946, Brit.) 90m Broca/Oxford bw

Hugh Williams *(Tony),* Joan Greenwood *(Gay Sultzman),* Basil Redford *(Prendergast),* Naunton Wayne *(Fotheringham),* Wylie Watson *(Peabody),* Hartley Power *(Col. Sultzman),* Yvonne Owen *(Molly),* Garry Marsh *(General),* Edward Lexy *(Policeman),* James Knight *(Pavilion Manager),* Julian D'Albie *(Dr. Peters),* Eileen Joyce *(Pianist),* Charles Rolfe *(Attendant),* Gwen Clark [Jane Hylton] *(Nurse),* Millicent Wolf *(Sister),* Aubrey Mallalieu *(Judge),* Michael Hordern, John Salew, John Olson.

A celebration of silence in which the delights of distaff dumbness are made evident. Inventor Williams, endlessly beset by a shrewish, nagging, vocal spouse, sheds her through the agency of the divorce court, to the congratulatory plaudits of the judge, Mallalieu. Seeking surcease from sirens, he seizes the solace of a sojourn in a scientific cell administered by the War Office. In this quiet community of creative craftsmen there are no women until the untimely arrival of American colonel Power and his daughter—Greenwood, in her first starring role—who, traumatized by a torpedo attack on the trip to Blighty, has lost her powers of speech. Charmed by this contrast, the misogynistic mister makes her his missus. Following a further shock, his mute mate regains the use of her vocal cords and proves to be as verbose as his previous spouse. They fight: she flees, pregnant with his child. The vacant vixen volunteers to return to him, but his situation strengthens when the clever coquette feigns muteness for his gratification. All ends happily (and quietly).

p, Sydney Box; d, Francis Searle; w, Muriel and Sydney Box; ph, Reginald H. Wyer, Bert Mason, Bernie Lewis.

Comedy (PR:A MPAA:NR)

GIRL IN BLACK STOCKINGS** (1957) 75m UA bw

Lex Barker *(David Hewson),* Anne Bancroft *(Beth Dixon),* Mamie Van Doren *(Harriet Ames),* Ron Randell *(Edmund Parry),* Marie Windsor *(Julia Parry),* John Dehner *(Sheriff Holmes),* John Holland *(Norman Grant),* Diana Vandervlis *(Louise Miles),* Richard Cutting *(Dr. Younger),* Larry Chance *(Indian Joe),* Gene O'Donnell *(Joseph Felton),* Gerald Frank *(Frankie Pierce),* Karl MacDonald *(Fred, a Deputy Sheriff),* Norman Leavitt *(Amos),* David Dwight *(Justice of the Peace Fred Walters),* Mark Bennett *(Brackett),* Stuart Whitman *(Prentiss),* Mickey Whiting *(Hib, a Deputy Sheriff).*

A non-western set in the West which anticipated the plot of Alfred Hitchcock's classic PSYCHO (1960) by three years. Requiring a rest from his legalistic rigors, a young lawyer—Barker—seeks respite in a Utah lodge. He soon becomes friendly with lodge employee Bancroft, despite the distractions of the voluptuous Van Doren, a fellow guest, and Windsor, sister of the crippled proprietor, Randell. A mass of mutilation murders of missing maidens occurs, and all are suspect to sheriff Dehner. Barrister Barker brings culprit Bancroft, his beloved, to bay; she, psychotic, has taken pains to see that she is the only attractive female remaining in the picture.

p, Aubrey Schenk; d, Howard W. Koch; w, Richard Landon (based on the story *Wanton Murder* by Peter Godfrey); ph, William Margulies; m, Les Baxter; ed, John F. Schreyer; prod d, Jack T. Collins.

Mystery/Suspense (PR:C MPAA:NR)

GIRL IN DANGER** (1934) 57m COL bw

Ralph Bellamy *(Trent),* Shirley Grey *(Gloria Gale),* J. Carroll Naish *(Russo),* Charles Sabin *(Dan Terrence),* Arthur Hohl *(Beckett),* Ward Bond, Ed Le Saint, Vincent Sherman, Francis McDonald, Edward Keane, Eddy Chandler, Pat O'Malley.

A second-rate entry in the popular INSPECTOR TRENT series (see Index). Zany, thrill-seeking society girl Grey brings a little excitement into her life by assisting a gem thief and concealing a valuable emerald in her elegant apartment. Inspector Trent—Bellamy—rigs his customary clever ruses in an attempt not only to recover the stolen stone, but also to bring a gang to justice. Members of the gang are attempting to recover the jewel themselves, and to wreak vengeance on the bold brigand who double-crossed them by seizing the stone himself.

d, D. Ross Lederman; w, Harold Shumate; ph, Benjamin Cline; ed, Otto Meyer.

Crime (PR:A MPAA:NR)

GIRL IN DISTRESS**½ (1941, Brit.) 101m Tansa/GFD bw
(GB: JEANNIE)

Barbara Mullen *(Jeannie McLean),* Wilfrid Lawson *(James McLean),* Gus MacNaughton *(Angus Whitelaw),* Phyllis Stanley *(Mrs. Whitelaw),* Michael Redgrave *(Stanley Smith),* Percy Walsh *(French Customs Man),* Albert Lieven *(Count Erich Von Wittgenstein),* Kay Hammond *(Margaret),* Edward Chapman *(Mr. Jansen),* Hilda Bailey *(Mrs. Jansen),* Marjorie Fielding *(Mrs. Murdoch),* Phillip Godfrey *(Restaurant Carman),* Googie Withers *(Laundry Girl),* Frank Cellier, Anne Shelton, Joan Kemp-Welch, Rachel Kempson, Percy Walsh, Meinhart Maur, Esme Percy, Joss Ambler, Katie Johnson, Lynn Evans, Ian Fleming, James Knight.

A Cinderella story of sorts, GIRL IN DISTRESS tells of a delightful Scottish girl, Mullen, who inherits a few hundred pounds and decides to spend it all on a terrific vacation in Vienna. She meets washing-machine salesman Redgrave and then Austrian gigolo Lieven, who poses as a count. Lieven mistakes Mullen for a rich girl, but when he finds out the truth, he instantly drops her, leaving Redgrave to pick her up on the rebound.

p, Marcel Hellman; d, Harold French; w, Anatole de Grunwald, Roland Pertwee, Aimee Stuart (based on a play by Stuart); ph, Bernard and Arthur Knowles; m, Mischa Spoliansky; ed, Edward B. Jarvis; md, Percy McKay.

Romance/Drama (PR:A MPAA:NR)

GIRL IN EVERY PORT, A**½ (1952) 86m RKO bw

Groucho Marx *(Benny Linn),* Marie Wilson *(Jane Sweet),* William Bendix *(Tim Dunnevan),* Don DeFore *(Bert Sedgwick),* Gene Lockhart *(Garvey),* Dee Hartford *(Millicent),* Hanley Stafford *(Navy Lieutenant),* Teddy Hart *("High Life"),* Percy Helton *(Drive-In Manager),* George E. Stone *(Skeezer),* Rodney Wooten *(The Pearl).*

Groucho Marx began working as a single—without his brothers—in COPACABANA (1947). In this one, he worked as a double with new teammate William Bendix, who had just signed a lucrative new contract with RKO. Marx and the less-than-cerebral Bendix are troublemaking tars, multiply hashmarked misfits in the Navy. Boob Bendix gets a small bequest, which he spends on a racehorse which proves to have multiple maladies. Shipmate Marx attempts to bail out his buddy by returning the horse to stable-owner DeFore and redeeming the dollars it cost. Curvaceous carhop Wilson, he discovers, owns the sound and speedy twin of the ailing equine. Sagacious salt Marx decides to switch the two nags after entering the crippled colt in a race, ensuring a win and making a mass of money at the mutuel window. A horsenaping ensues, with the quick and the near-dead both stabled aboard a Navy vessel. At the track, the fleet and the footsore finish neck-and-neck; the terrible tars inadvertently capture some saboteurs; DeFore captures well-endowed Wilson; the mettlesome shipmates are bemedalled.

p, Irwin Allen, Irving Cummings, Jr.; d&w, Chester Erskine (based on the story *They Sell Sailors Elephants* by Frederick Hazlett Brennan); ph, Nicholas Musuraca; m, Roy Webb; ed, Ralph Dawson; art d, Albert S. D'Agostino, Walter Keller.

Comedy Cas. (PR:A MPAA:NR)

GIRL IN 419**½ (1933) 63m PAR bw

James Dunn *(Dr. Dan French),* Gloria Stuart *(Mary Dolan),* David Manners *(Dr. Nichols),* William Harrigan *(Peter Lawton),* Shirley Grey *(Nurse Blaine),* Johnny Hines *(Slug),* Jack LaRue *(Sammy),* Vince Barnett *(Otto),* Kitty Kelly *(Telephone Girl),* Clarence Wilson *(Mr. Horton),* Gertrude Short *(Lucy),* Effie Ellsler *(Mrs. Young),* Edward Gargan *(Lt. Riley),* James Burke, Hal Price.

A big-city general hospital story, the institution filled with disenchanted burnouts hardened to horror, seemingly uncaring, playing pranks and toying with tragedy. Talented surgeon Dunn, alternately womanizing and pontificating, accompanies an ambulance on a call to a hotel where a big-time gambler has been shot to death during a card game (an occurrence resembling the slaying of "Mr. Big," Arnold Rothstein, in 1928). In the hotel suite, he notices lipstick on a cigarette butt: *cherchez la femme.* He doesn't need to *cherchez* for very long, however; the sorely beaten Stuart shows up in the hospital, the victim of a vicious attack. By heroic means, Dunn saves her life, then falls in love with her. During her recuperation, mobster Harrigan visits, bearing a bouquet for a policeman who has killed two members of a rival mob. Spotting Stuart, he later sends LaRue, his henchman, to reverse her recovery. Stuart's demise is delayed when young intern Manners interferes, only to be wounded for his pains. Clever villain Harrigan has himself admitted to the hospital with plans to pursue the persecution of the pretty Stuart. Manners, the intern, injects him with poison and then claims that he was dead on arrival, and our heroine's peril is past. Too many subplots make this flim difficult to follow.

p, B. P. Schulberg; d, George Somnes, Alexander Hall; w, Allen Rivkin, P. J. Wolfson, Manuel Seff (based on a story by George Furthman); ph, Karl Struss.

Crime   (PR:A MPAA:NR)

GIRL IN GOLD BOOTS*   (1968) 108m Geneni c

Jody Daniels (Critter Jones), Leslie McRae (Michele Casey), Tom Pace (Buz Nichols), Bara Byrnes (Joanie Nichols), Mark Herron (Leo McCabe), William Bagdad (Marty), Victor Izay (Mr. Casey), Harry Lovejoy (Harry Blatz), James Victor (Joey), Rod Wilmoth (Officer), Chris Howard (Chris), Mike Garrison (Gas Station Attendant), Michael Derrick (Car Attendant), Sheila Roberts (Store Clerk), Duke Graham, Jerry Ambler (Motorcyclists), Anne McAnn (Waitress), Genji (Cocktail Waitress), Rafael Campos.

Portraying the youth culture of the 1960s without letup, this musical has sex, drugs, death, draft-dodging, motorcycles, and rock 'n' roll among its period appurtenances. Amiable draft evader Daniels joins delinquent biker Pace and his new-found friend McRae, an aspiring starlet, on their trip to Hollywood. Pace introduces his friend to his go-go girl sibling, Byrnes, and her boss, club manager Herron. The latter, piqued with his star prancer because of her drug habit, plans to replace her with the gilt-shod McRae. The eavesdropping Jones, now janitoring, discovers that Pace, Herron, and Bagdad have committed a murder during a drug theft. Faced with exposure exceeding even that of the female leads, the evil drug disseminators threaten the lives of Daniels and McRae, but are outfought and apprehended. Daniels manfully elects to serve his country after all. Songs include the title song, "Do You Want To Laugh or Cry?" "For You," "Hello, Michelle," "One Good Time, One Place," Chris Howard; "Lonesome Man," George Eddy; "You Gotta Come Down," Jody Daniels, Bobby Batson; "Everything I Touch Turns to Gold," Denise Norwood; "Cowboy Santa," Nick Busillo; "Wheels of Love," "Sin," "Minnie Shimmy," Jay Colonna, Jerry Wallace; "Jimmy's Girl," Laurence Gray; "Strange Things," Jay Schlessinger.

p&d, Ted V. Mikels; w, Leighton L. Peatman, Art Names, John T. Wilson; ph, Robert Maxwell (Eastmancolor); m, Nicholas Carras; ed, Leo Shreve; cos, Nora Maxwell; makeup, Gene Mikels; singers, Chris Howard, Jody Daniels, Larry Cartell, Joe Valino, The Third World; harmonica, Danny Walton.

Crime/Musical   (PR:O MPAA:NR)

GIRL IN HIS POCKET   (SEE: NUDE IN HIS POCKET, 1962, Fr.)

GIRL IN LOVER'S LANE, THE zero   (1960) 78m Filmgroup bw

Brett Halsey (Bix), Joyce Meadows (Carrie), Lowell Brown (Danny), Jack Elam (Jesse), Selette Cole (Peggy), Cal Anders, Emile Meyer.

Itinerant Halsey gets romantically involved with a small-town girl, Meadows. When she's murdered, he becomes the prime suspect. Halsey is saved from the wrath of the irate townsfolk when the runaway boy he befriended, Brown, extracts a confession from village idiot Elam. Interesting primarily for the latter's performance, a change from his customary western/gangster sharply sinister villain roles.

p, Robert Roark; d, Charles R. Rondeau; w, Jo Heims.

Drama/Crime   (PR:A MPAA:NR)

GIRL IN OVERALLS, THE   (SEE: SWINGSHIFT MAISIE, 1943)

GIRL IN PAWN   (SEE: LITTLE MISS MARKER, 1934)

GIRL IN POSSESSION**   (1934, Brit.) 65m FN-WB bw

Laura La Plante (Eve Chandler), Henry Kendall (Sir Mortimer), Claude Hulbert (Cedric), Monty Banks (Caruso), Bernard Nedell (de Courville), Millicent Wolf (Julie Garner), Ernest Sefton (Wagstaffe), Charles Paton (Saunders), Charlotte Perry.

An interesting early British talking-picture comedy. Expatriate American La Plante, inveigled into thinking she has received a valuable legacy—a stately English manor with abundant grounds—arrives in Britain to find the estate in virtual escrow. The real owner, the titled Kendall, hasn't a son. Parlaying her pulchritude, La Plante helps the hapless Kendall to sell his stately suzerainty. La Plante, Universal's top non-talking star during the 1920s, is widely believed to have played no more starring parts subsequent to 1931. Perfidious Albion! She slipped across the water to do this one last ingenue role, her first and only in Britain, but the film was never released to theaters in her native land.

p, Irving Asher; d&w, Monty Banks.

Comedy   (PR:A MPAA:NR)

GIRL IN ROOM 17, THE   (SEE: VICE SQUAD, 1953)

GIRL IN ROOM 13*   (1961, U.S./Braz.) 79m Layton-Sinofilmes/Astor c

Brian Donlevy (Steve Marshall), Andrea Bayard (Kitty Herman), Elizabeth Howard (Elizabeth), Victor Merinow (Victor Marlow), John Herbert (Police Captain), Pedro Paulo Hatheyer, Carmen Marineo, Ari Ferreira, Nelson Oliver.

An aging Donlevy is wasted in this Brazilian quickie as a private eye from the States who is tracking a murderer. While hunting her down he stumbles upon a counterfeiting operation. He sets a trap to catch the gang, and after a double-cross, emerges victorious. Not an elegant way for Donlevy to wind down his career.

p, Marc Frederic; d, Richard Cunha; w, H.E. Barrie, Cunha; ph, Konstantin Tkaczenko (Eastmancolor); m, Gabriel Migliori; ed, Lucio Braun; art d, Pierino Massenzi; cos, Alice Piavetti; makeup, Flavio Torres.

Crime   (PR:A MPAA:NR)

GIRL IN THE BIKINI, THE*½   (1958, Fr.) 76m Atlantis bw (MANINA, LA FILLE SANS VOILE; GB: THE LIGHTHOUSE KEEPER'S DAUGHTER)

Brigitte Bardot (Manina), Jean-Francois Calve (Gerard), Howard Vernon (Eric), Espanita Cortez (Franchucha), Raymond Cordy (Francis), Robert Arnoux.

Made when BB was just 18 years old in 1952 and released in the States six years later after she had created a stir with her screen presence all over the world. Bardot plays the daughter of a lighthouse keeper on a coast where two men are searching for treasure. One is a fairly young man who takes an interest in the girl and she in him; the relationship saves his life when his partner betrays him. On its release, Bardot's father was extremely upset at the scanty dress his daughter wore and he demanded several scenes be cut.

p&d, Willy Rozier; w, Xavier Vallier, Rozier; ph, Michael Rocca; m, Jean Yatove; ed, Suzanne Baron.

Drama   (PR:C MPAA:NR)

GIRL IN THE CASE**   (1944) 65m COL bw

Edmund Lowe (William Warner), Janis Carter (Myra Warner), Robert Williams (Malloy), Richard Hale (John Heyser), Stanley Clements (Tuffy), Carole Mathews (Sylvia Manners), Robert Scott (Tommy Rockwood), Dick Elliott (Smith), Gene Stutenroth (Roberts).

An unsuccessful attempt at selling Lowe and Carter to the movie going public as the next Powell and Loy in an effort to capitalize on the popularity of the THIN MAN series. Lowe, a lawyer who just happens to be an expert lock-picker, finds himself hired by Scott to pick the lock of an old chest. Incredibly, Lowe suddenly becomes embroiled in an espionage scheme involving enemy agents and mysterious motivations. Quick and inoffensive, it has a few redeeming comedic moments.

p, Sam White; d, William Berke; w, Joseph Hoffman, Dorcas Cochran (based on a story by Charles F. Royal); ph, L.W. O'Connell; ed, Paul Borofsky; md, M.W. Stoloff; art d, Lionel Banks, Paul Murphy.

Mystery/Comedy   (PR:A MPAA:NR)

GIRL IN THE CROWD, THE*½   (1934, Brit.) 52m FN-WB bw

Barry Clifton (David), Googie Withers (Sally), Patricia Hilliard (Marian), Harold French (Bob), Clarence Blakiston (Peabody), Margaret Gunn (Joyce), Richard Littledale (Bill Manner), Phyllis Morris (Mrs. Lewis), Patric Knowles (Tom Burrows), Eve Lister (Ruby), Betty Lynne (Phyllis), John Wood (Harry), Elizabeth Vaughan, Marjorie Corbett, Brenda Lawless, Barbara Waring, Melita Bell.

A ridiculous idea for a film has Clifton as a man desperate to find a girl, leading him to seek the advice of a happily married man. Clifton does exactly what this friend recommends—that is, just take a girl out of the crowd. But this chance pick just happens to be his friend's wife. It isn't long before this skirt-chaser finds himself sitting in jail in proceedings that makes absolutely no sense, but at least provide a couple of laughs.

p, Irving Asher; d, Michael Powell.

Comedy   (PR:A MPAA:NR)

GIRL IN THE FLAT, THE*   (1934, Brit.) 65m B&D-PAR bw

Stewart Rome (Sir John Waterton), Belle Chrystal (Mavis Tremayne), Vera Boggetti (Girda Long), Jane Millican (Kitty Fellows), John Turnbull (Inspector Grice), Noel Shannon (Maj. Crull).

Naive country girl goes to the big city and gets herself in a jam when invited to a party by one of her girl friends. This friend turns out to be no friend at all, but a killer and blackmailer willing to take advantage of her country pal. Brought to the screen in a pretty decrepit manner.

p&d, Redd Davis; w, Violet Powell (based on a story by Evelyn Winch); ph, Percy Strong.

Crime   (PR:A MPAA:NR)

GIRL IN THE GLASS CAGE, THE*½   (1929) 72m FN-WB bw

Loretta Young (Gladys Cosgrove), Carroll Nye (Terry Pomfret), Matthew Betz ("Doc" Striker), Lucien Littlefield (Sheik Smith), Ralph Lewis (John Cosgrove), George E. Stone (Carlos), Julia Swayne Gordon (Mrs. Pomfret), Majel Cleman (Isabelle Van Court), Charles Sellon (Dan Jackson, The Prosecutor), Robert Haine (Pomfret's Attorney).

Movie theater cashier Young really has some problems. A gangster has fallen for her, and a nefarious uncle has stolen her money. Only in Hollywood, as they say. The story is far-fetched nonsense, dragged on for a tedious 72 minutes.

p, Ned Marin; d, Ralph Dawson; w, James Gruen (based on the story by George Kibbe Turner); ed, Terry Morse; art d, John H. Hughes.

Drama   (PR:A MPAA:NR)

GIRL IN THE HEADLINES, THE (SEE: MODEL MURDER CASE, THE, 1963, Brit.)

GIRL IN THE INVISIBLE BIKINI, THE   (SEE: GHOST IN THE INVISIBLE BIKINI, THE, 1966)

GIRL IN THE KREMLIN, THE zero   (1957) 81m UNIV bw

Lex Barker (Steve Anderson), Zsa Zsa Gabor (Lili Grisenko/Greta Grisenko), Jeffrey Stone (Mischa Rimilkin), Maurice Manson (Molda [Stalin]), William Schallert (Jacob Stalin), Natalie Daryll (Dasha), Aram Katcher (Laurenti Beria), Norbert Schiller (Ivan Brubof), Michael Fox (Igor Smetka), Elena Da Vinci (Olga Smetka), Phillipa Fallon (Nina), Charles Horvath (Deshilow), Kurt Katch (Commissar), Vanda Dupre (Girl at Cafe), Alfred Linder (Tata Brun), Gabor Curtiz (Dr. Petrov), Della Maltzahn (Dancer), Wanda Ottoni (Girl in Sidewalk Cafe), Richard Richonne (Vedishky), Carl Sklover (Rashti), Peter Besbas (Wine Shop Owner), Franz Roehn (Old Man), Albert Szabo (Truck Driver), Henry Rowland (Policeman), Dale Van Sickel (Cabby).

A ferociously awful picture which presents the idea that Stalin (who had been dead since 1953) was actually alive and living with Zsa Zsa Gabor in Greece (?!). Former O.S.S. man Barker is approached by Gabor's twin (Gabor in a dual role) in an attempt to help her find her missing sister. It seems that the missing Gabor disappeared the same day Stalin supposedly died. To avoid detection, Stalin had his face surgically altered (an improvement, no doubt), but that doesn't stop Barker who not only locates the former dictator, but also runs him off a winding, mountain road. One scene which serves as a nice little shocker has the lovely Daryll getting her flowing locks shaved off by the Reds—this new Stalin has a fetish for bald women.

p, Albert Zugsmith; d, Russell Birdwell; w, Gene L. Coon, Robert Hill (based on a story by Harry Ruskin, DeWitt Bodeen); ph, Carl Guthrie; m, Joseph Gershenson; ed, Sherman Todd; art d, Alexander Golitzen, Eric Orbom; cos, Bill Thomas.

Mystery   (PR:A MPAA:NR)

GIRL IN THE LEATHER SUIT   (SEE: HELLS BELLES, 1969)

GIRL IN THE NEWS, THE*½   (1941, Brit.) 77m FOX/MGM bw

Margaret Lockwood (Anne Graham), Barry K. Barnes (Stephen Farringdon), Emlyn Williams (Tracy), Roger Livesey (Bill Mather), Margaretta Scott (Judith Bentley), Wyndham Goldie (Edward Bentley), Basil Radford (Dr. Treadgrove), Irene Handl (Miss Blaker), Mervyn Johns (James Fetherwood), Betty Jardine (Elsie), Kathleen Harrison (Cook), Felix Aylmer (Prosecuting Counsel).

Scripted by Sidney Gilliat (THE LADY VANISHES) and directed by Carol Reed, this murder mystery is filled with twisting plot points and a few stabs at humor. Contributing to the moviedom adage, "the butler did it," this picture has butler Williams poisoning his employer and then putting the blame on Lockwood, a nurse who had previously been acquitted of a similar charge. The courtroom scene, which is nearly obligatory for British crime pictures, is played out with painstaking suspense, ultimately proving Williams' guilt. The movie was reissued in 1948.

p, Edward Black; d, Carol Reed; w, Sidney Gilliat (based on the novel by Roy Vickers); ph, Otto Kanturek; m, Louis Levy; ed, R.E. Dearing.

Crime   (PR:A MPAA:NR)

GIRL IN THE NIGHT, THE**   (1931, Brit.) 65m Wardour bw

Henry Edwards (Billie), Dorothy Boyd (Cecile), Sam Livesey (Ephraim Tucker), Reginald Bach (Schmidt), Eric Maturin (Fenton), Diana Wilson (Mrs. Fenton), Charles Paton (Prof. Winthrop), Harvey Braban (Inspector).

Edwards and Boyd meet on a stormy evening and take shelter in what they believe to be an abandoned house. That alone wouldn't make for a very compelling film, so the filmmakers have occupied the house with an assortment of crooks and smugglers. It turns out that Boyd has been wrongly accused of auto theft, but by the finale her name has been cleared.

p&d, Henry Edwards; w, Edwin Greenwood (based on a story by Edwards).

Crime   (PR:A MPAA:NR)

GIRL IN THE PAINTING, THE***   (1948, Brit.) 90m
                                        Gainsborough/UNIV bw (GB: PORTRAIT FROM LIFE)

Mai Zetterling (Hildegarde), Robert Beatty (Campbell Reid), Guy Rolfe (Maj. Lawrence), Herbert Lom (Hendlemann), Patrick Holt (Ferguson), Arnold Marle (Prof. Menzel), Sybilla Binder (Eitel), Thora Hird (Mrs. Skinner), Gerard Heinz (Heine), Yvonne Owen (Helen), Ernest Thesiger (Bloomfield), John Blythe (Johnnie), Philo Hauser (Hans), George Thorpe, Cyril Chamberlain, Betty Lynne, Nellie Arno, Richard Molinas, Donald Sinden, Hugo Schuster, Eric Messiter, Dorothea Glade, Michael Hordern, Peter Murray, Gordon Bell, Sam Kydd, Eric Pohlmann, Anthony Steel.

An interesting British drama about an army officer who is obsessed by a portrait in a gallery of a young woman. He ventures off to Germany to find the girl, and, discovering that she is an amnesiac victim, tries to help her regain her memory. Fisher went on to direct horror films for Hammer such as THE CURSE OF FRANKENSTEIN and THE HORROR OF DRACULA.

p, Anthony Darnborough; d, Terence Fisher; w, Muriel Box, Sidney Box, Frank Harvey, Jr. (based on a story by David Evans); ph, Jack Asher; ed, V. Sagovsky; md, Muir Mathieson; art d, George Provis.

Drama   (PR:A MPAA:NR)

GIRL IN THE PICTURE, THE**   (1956, Brit.) 63m Cresswell/Eros bw

Donald Houston (John Deering), Patrick Holt (Inspector Bliss), Maurice Kaufmann (Rod Molloy), Junia Crawford (Pat Dryden), Paddy Joyce (Jack Bates), John Miller (Duncan), Tom Chatto (George Keefe), Colin Cleminson, Lloyd Lamble.

An oft-told crime tale about a reporter who is searching for the identity of a killer, supposedly known only by a girl in a photo. With the snapshot as his only lead, the reporter (Houston) finally locates the girl. In keeping with formula, he falls in love with her and saves her from the murderous criminal. Enjoyable but familiar.

p, Edward Lloyd; d, Don Chaffey; w, Paul Rogers; ph, Ian Struthers.

Crime   (PR:A MPAA:NR)

GIRL IN THE RED VELVET SWING, THE*½   (1955) 109m FOX c

Ray Milland (Stanford White), Joan Collins (Evelyn Nesbit Thaw), Farley Granger (Harry K. Thaw), Luther Adler (Delphin Delmas), Cornelia Otis Skinner (Mrs. Thaw), Glenda Farrell (Mrs. Nesbit), Frances Fuller (Mrs. White), Philip Reed (Robert Collier), Gale Robbins (Gwen Arden), James Lorimer (McCaleb), John Hoyt (William Travers Jerome), Harvey Stephens (Dr. Hollingshead), Emile Meyer (Greenbacher), Richard Travis (Charles Dana Gibson), Harry Seymour (Arthur), Ainslie Pryor (Sport Donnally), Kay Hammond (Nellie), Betty Caulfield (Alice), Carolee Kelly (Margaret), Jack Raine (Mr. Finley), Hellen Van Tuyl (Mrs. Jennings), Robert Simon (Stage Manager), Paul Glass (Assistant Stage Manager), Paul Power (Van Ness), Fred Essler (Leopold Boerner), Ivan Triesault (Maitre D'), Raymond Bailey (Judge Fitzgerald), Charles Tannen (Court Clerk), Edmund Cobb (Judy Foreman), James Conaty (Rev. McEwen), Marjorie Hellen, Diane DuBois, Suzanne Alexander, Peggy Connelly, Rosemary Ace, Jean McCallen, Leslie Parrish (Flora

Dora Girls), Oliver Cross (Head Steward), Max Wagner, Steve Darrell, Henry Kulky (Wardens), Edith Evanson (Josie), William Forrest (Simpson), Stuart Holmes (Old Man at Restaurant), Major Sam Harris (Old Man at Show).

This film is a recreation of the sensational 1906 murder of Stanford White, famous architect, by Harry K. Thaw, infamous crackpot, on the Winter Garden roof in front of hundreds of theatergoers. Milland (as White) is shown as a dirty old man, lusting after Collins, who plays showgirl Evelyn Nesbit and wife of Thaw (Granger). The film's viewpoint is that of the defense Thaw mounted with his mother's millions after the killing, one that incredibly saw this ruthless killer escape the death penalty. Milland casts a covetous eye upon pretty Collins at the beginning of her showgirl career, taking her to his posh Manhattan lair where she swings high on a red velvet swing, pushed by the lacivious architect. After she marries Granger, she witnesses her deranged husband become so incensed at the memory of Thaw that he works his insanity into lethal action after seeing White during a musical. Little of the real facts are presented in this obvious vehicle for Collins as the trampy Nesbit. Milland does a caricature of the victim, one far from the true character of White, while Granger mutters and mumbles like a cretin dressed in a tuxedo. The flavor of the turn-of-the-century is well-captured in the sets by Wheeler and the lensing by Krasner is sharp, but Fleischer's direction is slow-paced and almost crawls at times.

p, Charles Brackett; d, Richard Fleischer; w, Walter Reisch, Charles Brackett; ph, Milton Krasner (CinemaScope, DeLuxe Color); m, Leigh Harline, Edward B. Powell; ed, William Mace; md, Lionel Newman; art d, Lyle R. Wheeler, Maurice Ransford; cos, Charles LeMaire; ch, David Robel.

Crime Drama   (PR:C MPAA:NR)

GIRL IN THE SHOW, THE*½   (1929) 74m MGM bw

Bessie Love, Raymond Hackett, Nanci Price, Eddie Nugent, Jed Prouty, Ford Sterling, Mary Doran, Lucy Beaumont, Richard Carlyle, Alice Moe, Frank Nelson, Jack McDonald, Ethel Wales, John F. Morrissey.

A harmless little tale about a touring company of "Uncle Tom's Cabin," who find themselves in trouble when their manager leaves. Love decides to settle down with fellow actor Prouty, who offers to marry her and take care of her little sister. Hackett, the lead thespian, arranges some performances for the inactive troupe and breaks up the Love-Prouty marriage. Love and Hackett fall for each other and, after some confusion on who will play the lead femme role on stage, Love becomes the star of the show. The first feature for Edgar Selwyn, whose name served as the "wyn" part of Goldwyn Pictures when the firm was founded in 1916.

d&w, Edgar Selwyn (based on the play "Eva the Fifth" by John Kenyon Nicholson, John Golden); ph, Arthur Reed; ed, Harry Reynolds, Truman K. Wood.

Drama   (PR:A MPAA:NR)

GIRL IN THE STREET**   (1938, Brit.) 75m GAU bw
                                        (GB: LONDON MELODY)

Anna Neagle (Jacqueline), Tullio Carminati (Marius Andreani), Robert Douglas (Nigel Taplow), Horace Hodges (Father Donnelly), Grizelda Hervey, Miki Hood (Friends of Marius), Davina Craig, Joan Kemp-Welch (Maids), Leonard Snelling (Organ Grinder's Son), Arthur Chesney (Marius' Butler), Henry Wolston (Snodgrass).

Cockney street singer Neagle is taken under the wing of Carminati, a member of the diplomatic corps. She joins a touted review and then gets engaged to an undersecretary. Unfortunately her fiance is about to be dismissed. Of course, benefactor Carminati saves the day in this average musical. It's passable entertainment.

p&d, Herbert Wilcox; w, Florence Tranter, Monckton Hoffe (based on a story by Ray Lewis); ph, F.A. Young.

Musical   (PR:A MPAA:NR)

GIRL IN THE TAXI*   (1937, Brit.) 70m ABF bw

Lawrence Grossmith (Baron des Aubrais), Helen Haye (Delphine), Jean Gillie (Jacqueline), Mackenzie Ward (Hubert), Ben Field (Dominique), Lawrence Hanray (Charencey), Joan Kemp-Welch (Suzanne Dupont), Albert Whelan (Alexis), Henri Garat (Rene Boislurette), John Deverell (Emile Pomarel), Frances Day (Suzanne Pommarel).

This British-made musical takes place in Paris, where a respected father and husband loves to carouse at night in the city's hot spots. His son follows in his footsteps and dates a wild widow, whom the father also is chasing. The young man-about-town the father has rejected as a son-in-law discovers the two roustabouts and blackmails dad into letting him have the daughter's hand. Lighthearted and naughty, but oh, so old-fashioned.

p, Kurt Bernhardt, Eugene Tuscherer; d, Andre Berthomieu; w, Fritz Gottfurcht, Val Valentine, Austin Melford (based on an operetta by Georg Okonkowsky) ph, Roy Clark; m, Jean Gilbert; m/l Arthur Wimperis, Frank Eyton.

Musical   (PR:A MPAA:NR)

GIRL IN THE WOODS**   (1958) 71m AB-PT/REP bw

Forrest Tucker (Steve Cory), Maggie Hayes (Belle Cory), Barton MacLane (Big Jim), Diana Francis (Sonda), Murvyn Vye (Whitlock), Paul Langton (Luke Plummer), Joyce Compton (Aunt Martha), Kim Charney (Jerry Plummer), Mickey Finn (Samson), Bartlett Robinson (Dr. Wyndham), Harry Raybould (Marty), George Lynn (Operator), Joey Ray (Bartender).

Tucker is a lumberjack who packs his axe and wife, Hayes, and heads for a new place to make a living. He ends up in the middle of a feud between lumberjacks Langton and Vye, taking the rap for a robbery. The whole town turns against him but he courageously sticks around and proves his innocence.

p, Harry L. Mandell; d, Tom Gries; w, Oliver Crawford, Marcel Klauber (based on Crawford's novel *Blood On The Branches*); ph, Jack Marta; m, Albert Glasser; ed, Doug Stewart; md, Glasser; art d, Walter Keller.

Drama   **(PR:A   MPAA:NR)**

GIRL IN 313**   (1940) 54m FOX bw

Florence Rice *(Joan Matthews)*, Kent Taylor *(Gregg Dunn)*, Lionel Atwill *(Russell Woodruff)*, Katharine Aldridge *(Sarah Sorrell)*, Mary Treen *(Jenny)*, Jack Carson *(Pat O'Farrell)*, Elyse Knox *(Judith Wilson)*, Joan Valerie *(Francine Edwards)*, Dorothy Dearing *(Emmy Lou Bentley)*, Dorothy Moore *(Happy)*, Jacqueline Wells *(Lorna)*, Charles C. Wilson *(Brady)*, William Davidson *(Grayson)*.

An average crime thriller has Rice as a police agent going undercover to discover the ringleader of a gang of jewel thieves. She falls in love with one of the hoods, Taylor, before she discovers that the crooks are working together with a double-dealing insurance firm. Before their love can blossom, Taylor is killed in a battle with police. One of a handful of films skillfully directed by Latin-lover actor Ricardo Cortez, who was known for his "bedroom eyes."

p, Sol M. Wurtzel; d, Ricardo Cortez; w, Barry Trivers, Clay Adams (based on a story by Hilda Stone); ph, Edward Cronjager; m, Emil Newman; ed, Louis Loeffler; art d, Richard Day, Lewis Creber.

Crime   **(PR:A   MPAA:NR)**

GIRL IN TROUBLE*   (1963) 82m Vanguard bw

Tammy Clark *(Judy Collins)*, Ray Menard *(John Watson)*, Neomie Salatich *(Mona Dwick)*, Larry Johnson *("Mr. Smith")*, Martin Smith *(Harry Calhoun)*, Bettina Johnson *(Loni)*, Charles Murphy *(Hotel Clerk)*, Jay Houck *(Intern)*, L. Foster Rouse *(Ambulance Attendant)*, C.F. Counce *("The Mark")*, Marie Cavanaugh *(Bella)*.

Wanting to enjoy life before she gets married, Clark takes to the road. She gets a ride from a stranger who attacks her, and she smashes his head on a rock after a struggle. She ends up on Bourbon Street where she becomes a hooker, and soon gets used to her lavish surroundings. Her fiance comes looking for her and takes her away from the evils of street life. The finale has her receiving word that the stranger she thought she had killed was only knocked out. A movie in trouble.

p&d, Lee Beale [Brandon Chase]; w, Anthony Naylor; ph, Leo J. Hebert; ed, Edmond Lacoste; md, George Simson; cos, Arthur Sherrick.

Drama   **(PR:C   MPAA:NR)**

GIRL IN WHITE, THE****   (1952) 92m MGM bw
(AKA: SO BRIGHT THE FLAME)

June Allyson *(Dr. Emily Barringer)*, Arthur Kennedy *(Dr. Ben Barringer)*, Gary Merrill *(Dr. Seth Pawling)*, Mildred Dunnock *(Dr. Marie Yeomans)*, Jesse White *(Alec)*, Marilyn Erskine *(Nurse Jane Doe)*, Guy Anderson *(Dr. Barclay)*, Gar Moore *(Dr. Graham)*, Don Keefer *(Dr. Williams)*, Ann Tyrrell *(Nurse Bigley)*, James Arness *(Matt)*, Curtis Cooksey *(Commissioner Hawley)*, Carol Brannon *(Nurse Wells)*, Ann Morrison *(Nurse Schiff)*, Jo Gilbert *(Nurse Bleeker)*, Erwin Kaiser *(Dr. Schneider)*, Kathryn Card *(Mrs. Lindsay)*, Jonathon Cott *(Dr. Ellerton)*, Joan Valerie *(Nurse Hanson)*, Coleman Francis *(Orderly)*, A. Cameron Grant *(Elevator Boy)*, David Fresco *(Patient)*.

An excellent period biography of Emily Dunning Barringer and her struggles to become a doctor in the male-dominated medical profession in 1902. Related in a semi-documentary style, the story traces her through medical school to New York's Bellevue Hospital. A large portion of the film concentrates on the medical practices at the turn of the century, which certainly promotes realism in the picture but does little to enhance its entertainment value.

p, Armand Deutsch; d, John Sturges; w, Irmgard Von Cube, Allen Vincent, Philip Stevenson (based on the book *Bowery to Bellevue*, by Emily Dunning Barringer); ph, Paul C. Vogel; m, David Raksin; ed, Ferris Webster; art d, Cedric Gibbons, Leonid Vasian.

Biography/Drama   **(PR:A   MPAA:NR)**

GIRL IS MINE, THE**   (1950, Brit.) 51m Touchstone/BL bw

Patrick Macnee *(Hugh Hurcombe)*, Pamela Deeming *(Betty Marriott)*, Lionel Murton *(James Rutt)*, Arthur Melton *(Pringle)*, Richard Pearson *(Sergeant)*, Ben Williams *(Policeman)*, Len Sharp *(Watchman)*, Elwyn Stock, Simon de Wardener, Patricia Dickson, Valerie Agnew.

MacNee and Deeming are a pair of boat owners who encounter some difficulties with a malicious dock owner. An American, Murton, helps them out of their bind and falls in love with Deeming.

p, Freda Stock; d&w, Marjorie Deans (based on a story by Ralph Stock); ph, Ben Hart.

Drama   **(PR:A   MPAA:NR)**

GIRL LOVES BOY**   (1937) 73m GN bw

Eric Linden *(Robert Conrad)*, Cecilia Parker *(Dorothy McCarthy)*, Roger Imhof *(Charles Conrad)*, Dorothy Peterson *(Mrs. McCarthy)*, Pedro de Cordoba *(Signor Montefiori)*, Bernadene Hayes *(Sally Lacy)*, Otto Hoffman *(Gus Wilkey)*, Patsy O'Connor *(Penny McCarthy)*, Rollo Lloyd *(Dr. Williams)*, Buster Phelps *(Ned McCarthy)*, John T. Murray *(Venable)*, Spencer Charters *(Rufus Boggs)*, Sherwood Bailey *(Tim McCarthy)*, Edwin Mordant *(Parson Meeker)*, Jameson Thomas *(Lawyer Mack)*.

A lightweight romance which is as banal as the title. Parker hopes to win the affections of dapper youngster Linden, whose head is swirling for a gold-digging dame instead. He gets his just desserts, however, when he learns that his new wife never got divorced from her first husband. A technically weak picture, with a screenplay that isn't much better.

p, Bennie F. Zeidman; d, Duncan Mansfield; w, Mansfield, Carroll Graham (based on a story by Karl Brown, Hinton Smith); ph, Edward Snyder; ed, Edward Schroeder.

Drama   **(PR:A   MPAA:NR)**

GIRL MADNESS   (SEE: BEAST OF YUCCA FLATS, THE, 1961)

GIRL MERCHANTS   (SEE: SELLERS OF GIRLS, 1967, Fr.)

GIRL MISSING*   (1933) 69m WB bw

Ben Lyon *(Henry Gibson)*, Glenda Farrell *(Kay Curtis)*, Mary Brian *(June Dale)*, Peggy Shannon *(Daisy)*, Lyle Talbot *(Raymond Fox)*, Guy Kibbee *(Kenneth Van Dusen)*, Harold Huber *(Jim Hendricks)*, Ferdinand Gottschalk *(Alvin Bradford)*, Helen Ware *(Mrs. Bradford)*, George Pat Collins, Edward Ellis, Louise Beavers, Mike Marita, Fred Kelsey.

A slow-moving mystery cranked out of the Warner Bros. programmer mill, which centers on a plot by a showgirl and her boy friend to hoodwink a millionaire into marriage. As the title suggests, the girl disappears on her wedding night and the groom offers a hefty reward. A gold-digging pair of chorus girls start following the clues that lead to the girl, the reward, and an eventual marriage to the millionaire.

d, Robert Florey; w, Ben Markson, Carl Erickson, Don Mullaly; ph, Arthur Todd; ed, Ralph Dawson.

Mystery   **(PR:A   MPAA:NR)**

GIRL MOST LIKELY, THE**½   (1957) 98m RKO/UNIV c

Jane Powell *(Dodie)*, Cliff Robertson *(Pete)*, Keith Andes *(Neil)*, Kaye Ballard *(Marge)*, Tommy Noonan *(Buzz)*, Una Merkel *(Mom)*, Kelly Brown *(Sam)*, Judy Nugent *(Pauline)*, Frank Cady *(Pop)*, Nacho Galindo, Chris Essay, Valentin de Vargas, Joseph Kearns, Julia Montoya, Paul Garay, Gloria De Ward, Gail Ganley, Harvey Hohneckey, Bob Banas, Joyce Blunt, Tex Brodus, Buddy Bryant, Maurice Kelly, Tommy Ladd, Todd Miller, Dean Myles, Howard Parker, Donna Poyet, Paul Rees, Bruce Stowell, Lida Thomas.

A musical remake of the Ginger Rogers starrer TOM, DICK AND HARRY that fails to live up to the original, even with some nice tunes. Powell is simultaneously engaged to Noonan, Robertson, and Andes and can't decide who is the man for her. Andes is a wealthy playboy, Noonan is a real estate man, and Robertson is a mechanic specializing in diesel engines. It was a fairly dumb story in 1941 when they made the first version but it was saved by a sharp screenplay and some superb performances. The script for this one falls down in the humor department and Robertson is a total lox when it comes to playing comedy. Several contrived situations including Powell's fleeing from Andes just prior to her marriage. She winds up with Robertson at the conclusion, poor but happy. Gower Champion staged the musical numbers and saves the day with his creativity. Although the original screenplay of TOM, DICK AND HARRY was by Paul Jarrico, he was given no credit on the screen which occasioned a brouhaha between the studio and the Writers Guild. He surely deserved the credit but this remake would have done nothing for his career. Musical numbers: "The Girl Most Likely" (Bob Russell, Nelson Riddle); "All the Colors of the Rainbow," "I Don't Know What I Want," "Balboa," "We Gotta Keep Up With the Joneses," "Crazy Horse" (Hugh Martin, Ralph Blane).

p, Stanley Rubin; d, Mitchell Leisen; w, Devery Freeman (based on an uncredited story and screenplay by Paul Jarrico); ph, Robert Planck (Technicolor); md, Nelson Riddle; ed, Harry Marker, Dean Harrison; art d, Albert S. D'Agostino, George W. Davis; cos, Renie; ch, Gower Champion.

Musical Comedy   **Cas.**   **(PR:AA   MPAA:NR)**

GIRL MUST LIVE, A***   (1941, Brit.) 89m Gainsborough/FOX bw

Margaret Lockwood *(Leslie James)*, Renee Houston *(Gloria Lind)*, Lilli Palmer *(Clytie Devine)*, George Robey *(Horace Blount)*, Hugh Sinclair *(Earl of Pangborough)*, Naunton Wayne *(Hugo Smythe)*, Moore Marriott *(Bretherton Hythe/Lord Grandonald)*, Mary Clare *(Mrs. Wallis)*, David Burns *(Joe Gold)*, Kathleen Harrison *(Penelope)*, Drusilla Wills *(Miss Polkinghorne)*, Wilson Coleman *(Mr. Joliffe)*, Helen Haye *(Aunt Primrose)*, Frederick Burtwell *(Hodder)*, Martita Hunt *(Mme. Dupont)*, Muriel Aked, Joan White, Merle Tottenham, Kathleen Boutall, Michael Hordern.

A runaway schoolgirl, Lockwood, is the contrast to the vampishness of Palmer and Houston, both of whom are Lockwood's fellow chorus gals. When the femmes fatales plot to blackmail Sinclair, Lockwood does her own bit of deceiving and saves the earl's day. Tightly directed by Carol Reed, who followed this picture (released in Britain in 1939) with his excellent tale of coal miners, THE STARS LOOK DOWN.

p, Edward Black; d, Carol Reed; w, Frank Launder (based on a story by Emery Bonett); ph, Jack Cox; m/l, "Who's Your Love," "I'm a Savage," Eddie Pola, Manning Sherwin.

Drama   **(PR:A   MPAA:NR)**

GIRL NAMED TAMIKO, A**½   (1962) 110m PAR c

Laurence Harvey *(Ivan Kalin)*, France Nuyen *(Tamiko)*, Martha Hyer *(Fay Wilson)*, Gary Merrill *(Max Wilson)*, Michael Wilding *(Nigel Costairs)*, Miyoshi Umeki *(Eiko)*, Steve Brodie *(James Hatten)*, Lee Patrick *(Mary Hatten)*, John Mamo *(Minya)*, Bob Okazaki *(Kimitaka)*, Richard Loo *(Otani)*, Philip Ahn *(Akiba)*, Davis Lewis, Ray Teal.

Set in Tokyo, John Sturges' A GIRL NAMED TAMIKO seems to be a natural extension of his Japanese sympathies which date to the murdered war hero in BAD DAY AT BLACK ROCK and the debt paid to Akira Kurosawa in THE MAGNIFICENT SEVEN. Here, however, Sturges is away from the western ground on which he made his finest pictures. After photographer Harvey's parents are killed by the Japanese he tries to get a visa to the States. His only chance is to become friendly with U.S. embassy employee Hyer, with whom he has an affair. Before he is able to leave he falls in love with Nuyen, a Japanese girl from a traditional family. Against her parents' wishes, Nuyen plans to wed Harvey, but he is still under the control of Hyer, his only ticket out. He gets the visa and leaves his Japanese lover, but before boarding the plane, runs back to her.

p, Hal Wallis, Joseph H. Hazen; d, John Sturges; w, Edward Anhalt (based on the novel by Ronald Kirkbride); ph, Charles Lang, Jr. (Panavision, Technicolor); m, Elmer Bernstein; ed, Warren Low; art d, Walter Tyler, Hal Pereira; set d, Sam Comer, Arthur Krams; cos, Edith Head.

Drama (PR:A MPAA:NR)

GIRL NEXT DOOR, THE**½ (1953) 92m FOX c

Dan Dailey (*Bill Carter*), June Haver (*Jeannie*), Dennis Day (*Reed Appleton*), Billy Gray (*Joe Carter*), Cara Williams (*Rosie*), Natalie Schafer (*Evelyn*), Clinton Sundberg (*Samuels*), Hayden Rorke (*Fields*), Mary Jane Saunders (*Kitty*), Donna Lee Hickey (*Mitzi*), Lyn Wilde (*Peggy*), Mona Knox (*Smitty*), June Wurster (*Maggie*), Beverly Thompson (*Susie*), Gregg Sherwood (*Franny*), Michael Ross (*O'Toole*), Herbert Vigran (*Sergeant*), Charles Wagenheim (*Junkman*), Don Kohler (*Customs Official*), Robert Carraher (*Policeman*).

An innocuous musical comedy which casts Haver as a Broadway star tired of city life. Her manager, intent on keeping her in the limelight, sets her up in a snazzy home. Her next door neighbor is cartoonist Dailey and his son, Gray. Much to the dismay of the child, the two adults get involved, but his understanding girl friend explains that people come in pairs just like the animals on Noah's Ark. Includes a pleasant cartoon sequence and the tunes: "If I Love You A Mountain," "I'd Rather Have A Pal Than A Gal—Anytime," and "Nowhere Gal" (Mack Gordon, Josef Myrow). This prim and proper picture was Haver's last before entering a convent, where she remained several months before leaving it for marriage to actor Fred MacMurray.

p, Robert Bassler; d, Richard Sale; w, Isobel Lennart (based on a story by L. Bush-Fekete, Mary Helen Fay); ph, Leon Shamroy (Technicolor); m, Cyril J. Mockridge; ed, Robert Simpson; md, Lionel Newman; ch, Richard Barstow.

Musical Comedy (PR:A MPAA:NR)

GIRL OF MY DREAMS
(SEE: SWEETHEART OF SIGMA CHI, THE, 1933)

GIRL O' MY DREAMS** (1935) 63m MON bw

Mary Carlisle (*Gwen*), Sterling Holloway (*Spec Early*), Eddie Nugent (*Larry Haynes*), Arthur Lake (*Bobby Barnes*), Creighton [Lon] Chaney (*Don Cooper*), Gigi Parrish (*Mary*), Tommy Dugan (*Joe Smiley*), Jeanie Roberts (*Kittens*), Lee Shumway (*Coach*).

A fluffy tale that deals with a group of college kids and their lives and loves on the campus. Holloway is the school newspaper editor, Nugent the most popular boy with the women, and Chaney the big track star who barely notices the distaff side until he wins the senior class election. A track meet is the center for the action in the film, instead of the over-used football game. Perennial "sweet coed" of the 1930s, Carlisle, here again does her thing. She then was 23 years old.

p, William T. Lackey; d, Raymond McCarey; w, George Waggner; ph, Ira Morgan; m, Waggner, Edward Ward; ed, Jack Ogilvie.

Comedy (PR:A MPAA:NR)

GIRL OF THE GOLDEN WEST**½ (1930) 78m FN-WB bw

Ann Harding (*Minnie*), James Rennie (*Dick Johnson*), Harry Bannister (*Jack Rance*), Ben Hendricks, Jr. (*Handsome Charlie*), J. Farrell MacDonald (*Sonora Slim*), George Cooper (*Trinidad Joe*), Johnny Walker (*Nick*), Richard Carlyle (*Jim Larkins*), Arthur Stone (*Joe Castro*), Arthur Housman (*Sidney Dick*), Norman McNeil (*Happy Holiday*), Fred Warren (*Jack Wallace*), Joe Girard (*Ashby*), Newton House (*Pony Express Rider*), Princess Noola (*Wowkle*), Chief Yowlachie (*Billy Jackrabbit*).

The first sound version of the 1904 Belasco standby (it had already been made famous on the stage, in opera (Puccini), and was filmed in the silent era) which stars Harding as a young girl who falls into a romance with dashing crook Rennie. Soon sheriff Bannister comes after the outlaw and it looks as though the lovers will be serving some time in jail, but Harding strikes a deal with the lawman that will win them their freedom if she can beat him at poker. She does, and they ride off into the sunset. Harding, who gives the film its spunk, was only cast because she was married to Bannister and he had her participation as Minnie written into his contract.

d, John Francis Dillon; w, Waldemar Young (based on a play by David Belasco); ph, Sol Polito.

Western (PR:A MPAA:NR)

GIRL OF THE GOLDEN WEST, THE**½ (1938) 120m MGM bw

Jeanette MacDonald (*Mary Robbins*), Nelson Eddy (*Ramerez/Lt. Johnson*), Walter Pidgeon (*Jack Rance*), Leo Carrillo (*Mosquito*), Buddy Ebsen (*Alabama*), Leonard Penn (*Pedro*), Priscilla Lawson (*Nina Martinez*), Bob Murphy (*Sonora Slim*), Olin Howland (*Trinidad Joe*), Cliff Edwards (*Minstrel Joe*), Billy Bevan (*Nick*), Brandon Tynan (*The Professor*), H.B. Warner (*Father Sienna*), Monty Woolley (*Governor*), Charley Grapewin (*Uncle Davy*), Noah Beery, Sr. (*General*), Billy Cody, Jr. (*Gringo*), Jeanne Ellis (*The Girl Mary*), Ynez Seabury (*Wowkle*), Victor Potel (*Stage Driver*), Nick Thomason (*Billy Jack Rabbit*), Tom Mahoney (*Handsome Charlie*), Phillip Armenta (*Long Face*), Chief Big Tree (*Indian Chief*), Russell Simpson (*Pioneer*), Armand "Curley" Wright, Pedro Regas (*Renegades*), Gene Coogan (*Manuel*), Sergei Arabeloff (*Jose*), Alberto Morin (*Juan*), Joe Dominguez (*Felipe*), Frank McGlynn (*Pete, a Gambler*), Cy Kendall (*Hank, a Gambler*), E. Alyn Warren, Francis Ford (*Miners*), Hank Bell (*Deputy*), Walter Bonn (*Lt. Johnson*), Richard Tucker (*Colonel*), Virginia Howell (*Governor's Wife*).

This was the fifth time around for this story. Originally a play by David Belasco (he also produced) in 1905, it was made three times before as films and also done as an opera. In this version, MacDonald and Eddy (at the top of their popularity, having just done ROSE MARIE) couldn't save the slow-moving direction and ho-hum screenplay with their talents. She is the girl who owns a rough and tumble saloon in a mining town out west and he's sort of a Zorro character but on the wrong side of the law. They fall in love an she saves him when she plays cards with Pidgeon, the sheriff of the town, with Eddy as the stakes. Pidgeon is also in love with MacDonald, so it's a bit of a triangle, but her heart belongs to Eddy (as it did in so many films) and there's no doubt whom she'll wind up with at the finis. Shot in sepia tone, it's a curiosity piece that will have TV viewers fiddling with their dials if it's broadcast in the original hues. The best number is the elaborate Rasch staging of "Mariachi," the only piece of excitement in an otherwise dreary movie. No laughs to speak of other than Ebsen's turn on "The West Ain't Wild Anymore." TV viewers under the age of 40 won't remember but Ebsen was one of the best song and dance men around for many years before he went straight in various television series. He was supposed to play The Tin Man in THE WIZARD OF OZ but his skin rebelled against the silver make-up and Jack Haley, Sr., got the part. Coincidentally, Ray Bolger, the Scarecrow in THE WIZARD OF OZ, did some singing and dancing in this picture, but his scenes were deleted by the studio, fearful that the film was already too long. In a small role as the governor, the irrepressible Monty Woolley manages to make the most out of the least. Other musical numbers (music by Sigmund Romberg and lyrics by Gus Kahn unless otherwise noted): "Sun-up to Sundown" (Jeanne Ellis, Chorus); "Camptown Races," "Shadows on the Moon" (Ellis); "Soldiers of Fortune" (Beery, Cody, Jr.); "Soldiers of Fortune" reprise (Cody, Eddy, Male Chorus); "Shadows on the Moon" reprise (Eddy, MacDonald); "The Wind in the Trees" (Eddy); "Liebestraum" (MacDonald, music by Franz Liszt, English lyrics by Kahn); "Ave Maria" (MacDonald, Boys' Choir, music by Johann Sebastian Bach and Charles Gounod); "Senorita" (Eddy, Chorus), "Who Are We to Say" (Eddy); "Who Are We to Say" reprise (MacDonald).

p, William Anthony McGuire; d, Robert Z. Leonard; w, Isabel Dawn, Boyce DeGaw (based on the play by David Belasco); ph, Oliver T. Marsh (Sepiatone); m, Herbert Stothart; ed, W. Donn Hayes; art d, Cedric Gibbons; cos, Adrian; spec eff, Slavko Vorkapich; ch, Albertina Rasch.

Musical (PR:AA MPAA:NR)

GIRL OF THE LIMBERLOST** (1934) 86m MON bw

Louise Dresser (*Katherine Comstock*), Ralph Morgan (*Wesley Sinton*), Marian Marsh (*Elnora Comstock*), H.B. Walthall (*Dr. Amon*), Gigi Parrish (*Edith Carr*), Helen Jerome Eddy (*Margaret Sinton*), Betty Blythe (*Mrs. Parker*), Barbara Bedford (*Elvira Carney*), Robert Ellis (*Frank Comstock*), Tommy Bupp (*Billy*).

Overwrought soap opera with some surprisingly grim moments starring Dresser, the uncaring mother of swamp child Marsh, who has despised the child since the womb because it was Dresser's pregnancy that led to the death of her husband. Dresser's husband fell into quicksand while sloshing through the bayou with his wife one day, and due to her rotund child-bearing state she had to stand helplessly by and watch him die. After Marsh's birth, Dresser ignores the child and refuses to send her to school. Sympathetic neighbors come to Marsh's aid and Dresser has a change of heart when she discovers that her "loving" husband had carried on with other women.

d, Christy Cabanne; w, Adele Comandini (based on the novel *A Girl Of the Limberlost* by Gene Stratton Porter); ph, Ira Morgan; ed, Carl Pierson.

Drama (PR:A MPAA:NR)

GIRL OF THE LIMBERLOST, THE** (1945) 60m COL bw

Ruth Nelson (*Kate Comstock*), Dorinda Clifton (*Elnora Comstock*), Loren Tindall (*Pete Reed*), Gloria Holden (*Miss Nelson*), Ernest Cossart (*Roger Henley*), Vanessa Brown (*Helen Brownlee*), James Bell (*Wesley Sinton*), Joyce Arling (*Margaret Sinton*), Charles Arnt (*Hodges*), Warren Mills (*Chester Hopple*), Gloria Patrice (*Amy Thurston*), Lillian Bronson (*Miss Blodgett*), Peggy Converse (*Jessie Reed*), Jimmy Clark (*Bob Stewart*), Carol Morris (*Carrie*).

The second melodramatic film adaptation of Gene Stratton Porter's novel of irrational hatred, this time starring Nelson as the vengeful mother who mentally and physically tortures her hated daughter Clifton because she blames the child for the death of her husband. The narrative plays along the same lines as the earlier version, and it is only the performance of Clifton (who attempts to steer clear of histrionics) that separates this from its predecessor.

p, Alexis Thurn-Taxis; d, Melchor G. Ferrer; w, Erna Lazarus (based on the novel *A Girl Of the Limberlost* by Gene Stratton Porter); ph, Burnett Guffey; m, Ernest Gold; ed, Al Clark; md, M. R. Bakaleinikoff.

Drama (PR:A MPAA:NR)

GIRL OF THE MOORS, THE** (1961, Ger.) 87m Real/Casino c
(DAS MADCHEN VOM MOORHOF)

Maria Emo, Claus Holm, Wolfgang Lukschy, Werner Hinz, Horst Frank, Eva-Ingeborg Scholz, Alice Treff, Hans Nielsen, Hilde Korber, Joseph Offenbach, Berta Drews, Josef Dahmen.

Another version of Swedish romantic writer Selma Lagerlof's novel which was previously filmed in 1917 and 1947 in Sweden, 1935 in Germany (THE GIRL FROM THE MARSH CROFT), and in Finland in 1940. This time Emo, a maid, is impregnated by her scoundrel boss and tries to commit suicide, but she is saved. When her boss later is killed, she is free to marry the man she loves.

p, Gyula Trebitsch; d, Gustav Ucicky; w, Adolf Schutz (based on Selma Lagerlof's novel *The Girl From The Marsh Croft*); ph, Albert Benitz (Agfacolor); m, Siegfried Franz.

Drama (PR:C-O MPAA:NR)

GIRL OF THE MOUNTAINS** (1958, Gr.) 90m
Finos/Greek Motion Pictures bw (GOLFO)

Antigoni Valakou (Golfo), Nikos Kazis (Tassos), Kyvell Theochari (Stavroula), Byron Pallis (Kitso), Yorgos Glynos (Old Thanassoula), Mimi Fotopoulos (Yanos), Dora Stratou Dance Ensemble.

Kazis is a handsome young shepherd trapped between a rich, vengeful widow (Theochari), who seeks to dominate him, and the meek and beautiful Valakou, whom he wants to marry. Theochari manages to woo the youngster away from his girl, but when he snaps to his senses and returns to Valakou, it is too late because she had taken poison. Grief-stricken, Kazis kills himself, leaving Theochari truly alone. Gorgeous scenery and a likable performance from Valakou make this one tolerable. (In Greek; English subtitles.)

d&w, Orestis Laskos (based on a story by Spyros Peresiadi); m, Takis Morekis.

Drama   (PR:C-O MPAA:NR)

GIRL OF THE NIGHT** (1960) 93m Vanguard/WB bw

Anne Francis (Bobbie), Lloyd Nolan (Dr. Mitchell), Kay Medford (Rowena), John Kerr (Larry), Arthur Storch (Jason Franklin, Jr.), James Broderick (Dan Bolton), Lauren Gilbert (Mr. Shelton), Eileen Fulton (Lisa), Julius Monk (Swagger).

The hackneyed saga of an unwilling streetwalker, Francis, who relates all she knows about her seamy life to her attentive psychiatrist, Nolan, as she tries to straighten out her life. Flashbacks tell the dreary tale and they are over-used and badly structured. Nolan, true to his psychiatric oath, helps her regain her self-esteem and embark on a new life of her own. Francis does a nice job with the drawn-out script that for its time did deal frankly with the sordid aspects of the street trade.

p, Max J. Rosenberg; d, Joseph Cates; w, Ted Berkman, Raphael Blau (based on the book The Call Girl by Dr. Harold Greenwald); ph, Joseph Brun; m, Sol Kaplan; ed, Aram A. Avakian; art d, Charles Bailey; cos, Theonie V. Aldredge.

Drama   (PR:C-O MPAA:NR)

GIRL OF THE OZARKS**½ (1936) 68m PAR bw

Virginia Weidler (Edie Moseley), Leif Erikson (Tom Bolton), Elizabeth Russell (Gail Rogers), Henrietta Crosman (Granny Moseley), Janet Young (Maw Moseley), Russell Simpson (Bascomb Rogers), Nora Cecil (Miss Trent), Lois Kent (Claire Rogers), Louis Mason (Lem), Arthur Aylesworth (Buck Wilder), Harry Bates (Jonas Toler), Nelson McDowell (Seth Tanner), Ben Hall (Clerk), Jane Keckley (Mrs. Wilder).

A tiny hillbilly town is the home for generous newspaper editor Erikson. When he lays eyes on the orphaned Weidler, he immediately makes room for her in his household. He soon realizes that three's company and takes on Russell as a wife. The picture ends with his family portrait being completed. A triumph in miscasting in general, except for brat Weidler, nine years old at the time, who covers up what she can with comedy, singing, and bouncing around in mischief.

p, A.M. Botsford; d, William Shea; w, Stuart Anthony, Michael Simmons (based on a story by Maurice Babb, John Bright, Robert Trasker); ph, George Clemons; art d, Hans Dreier, John Goodman.

Comedy/Drama   (PR:A MPAA:NR)

GIRL OF THE PORT* (1930) 65m RKO bw

Sally O'Neil, Reginald Sharland, Mitchell Lewis, Duke Kahanamoku, Donald MacKenzie, Renee Macready, Arthur Clayton, Gerald Barry, Barrie O'Daniels, John Webb Dillon, William Burt, Crauford Kent, Hugh Grumplin.

A strangely entertaining adventure picture set in the Fiji Islands which has New York show-girl O'Neil meeting up with a cannibal who, instead of making her his dinner, gives her a job as a barmaid. She falls in love with a visiting Englishman who came to the island to overcome his fear of fire. With an island full of fire-worshippers he figured this would be the best way to beat his phobia. O'Neil survives the cannibals' appetite and falls in love with the Brit, who for a grande finale walks over 20 feet of coals into her arms. A mind-bender for sure for those in the mood.

d, Bert Glennon; w, Beulah Marie Dix, Frank Reicher (based on the story "The Firewalker" by John Russell); ph, Leon Tover.

Adventure   (PR:A MPAA:NR)

GIRL OF THE RIO** (1932) 70m RKO bw (GB: THE DOVE)

Dolores Del Rio (Dolores), Leo Carrillo (Don Jose Tostado), Norman Foster (Johnny Powell), Lucille Gleason (Matron), Ralph Ince (O'Grady), Edna Murphy (Madge), Stanley Fields (Mike), Frank Campeau (Bill), Roberta Gale (Mabelle).

Dancehall gal Del Rio stars in this version of the hit Broadway play "The Dove," and she spends her time trying to give caballero Carrillo the brushoff. She has a vendetta against him because he sent her lover, Foster, to a foreign jail. A remake of a 1928 silent, and remade again as THE GIRL AND THE GAMBLER in 1939.

d, Herbert Brenon; w, Elizabeth Meehan (based on the play "The Dove" by Willard Mack from a story by Gerald Beaumont); ph, Leo Tover; ed, Artie Roberts; m/l, "Querida," Victor Schertzinger.

Drama   (PR:A MPAA:NR)

GIRL OF THE YEAR (SEE: PRETTY GIRL, THE, 1950)

GIRL ON A CHAIN GANG* (1966) 96m Jerry Gross Productions bw

William Watson, Julie Ange, R.K. Charles.

The title of this one pretty much gives it away—Ange is a girl on the run from the police who gets caught and does time on an all-male chain gang. Pitifully improbable.

p,d&w, Jerry Gross (based on a story by Don Olsen).

Drama   (PR:O MPAA:NR)

GIRL ON A MOTORCYCLE, THE** (1968, Fr./Brit.) 91m Mid-Atlantic-Ares/Claridge c (LA MOTOCYCLETTE; AKA, NAKED UNDER LEATHER)

Alain Delon (Daniel), Marianne Faithfull (Rebecca), Roger Mutton (Raymond), Marius Goring (Rebecca's Father), Catherine Jourdan (Catherine), Jean Leduc (Jean), Jacques Marin (Pump Attendant), Andre Maranne (French Superintendent), Bari Johnson, Arnold Diamond (French Customs Officers), John G. Heller (German Customs Officer), Marika Rivera (German Waitress), Richard Blake, Christopher Williams, Colin West, Kit Williams (Students).

One-time Rolling Stones groupie Faithfull is clad in black leather as a bored housewife who hops on a motorcycle in Alsace and takes off for Heidelberg to meet her lover, Delon. During a long erotic ride through the countryside she recalls various meetings with Delon—some romantic, others sexual. As she nears Delon's house, the bike seeming increasingly more powerful, she is killed in a crash that sends her flying into the windshield of an oncoming car. A perversely morbid and erotic tale which is blessed with Faithfull's aura, but damned by Cardiff's pretensions. Originally released with an "X" rating but toned down to get its "R," and shot in bilingual versions.

p, William Sassoon; d, Jack Cardiff; w, Ronald Duncan, Gillian Freeman (based on the novel La Motocyclette by Andre Pieyre de Mandiargues); ph, Cardiff (Technicolor); m, Les Reed; ed, Peter Musgrave; art d, Russell Hagg, Jean d'Eaubonne; cos, Lanvin; stunts, David Watson.

Drama/Romance   (PR:O MPAA:R)

GIRL ON APPROVAL*½ (1962, Brit.) 75m Eyeline/Bry bw

Rachel Roberts (Anne Howland), James Maxwell (John Howland), Annette Whitley (Sheila), Ellen McIntosh (Mary Gardner), John Dare (Stephen Howland), Pauline Letts (Mrs. Cox), Michael Clarke (William Howland).

The relationship between a teenage girl and her imprisoned mother is strained when the girl is forced to live with foster parents. Frend, who directed for 25 years, began his career as an editor for Hitchcock, cutting WALTZES FROM VIENNA (1933), SECRET AGENT (1936), SABOTAGE (1937), and YOUNG AND INNOCENT (1937).

p, Anthony Perry, Harold Orton; d, Charles Frend; w, Kathleen White, Kenneth Cavander (based on a story by White).

Drama   (PR:A MPAA:NR)

GIRL ON THE BARGE, THE*½ (1929) 80m UNIV bw

Jean Hersholt, Sally O'Neill, Malcom McGregor, Morris McIntosh, Nancy Kelly, George Offerman, Jr., Henry West.

Bible-toting barge captain Hersholt maintains his hold over daughter O'Neill by not teaching her to read. When she makes the acquaintance of tugboat worker, McGregor, she is taught the things her father tried to keep from her. Hersholt, of course, goes into a rage, beating his daughter and nearly killing McGregor. Hersholt has a change of heart, however, when McGregor's tugboat rescues Hersholt's barge which is helplessly adrift. The romance comes to an obligatory end with O'Neill and McGregor marrying and having a child.

d, Edward Sloman; w, Rupert Hughes, Charles Henry Smith; ph, Jackson Rose.

Drama/Romance   (PR:A MPAA:NR)

GIRL ON THE BOAT, THE** (1962, Brit.) 91m Knightsbridge bw

Norman Wisdom (Sam), Millicent Martin (Billie Bennett), Richard Briers (Eustace Hignett), Sheila Hancock (Jane), Bernard Cribbins (Peters), Athene Seyler (Mrs. Hignett), Philip Locke (Bream Mortimer), Noel Willman (Webster), Ronald Fraser (Colonel), Reginald Beckwith (Barman), Timothy Bateson (Purser), Dick Bentley (American), Peter Bull (Blacksmith).

Wisdom delivers his patented brand of comedy and throws his lecturer aunt's cottage up for grabs in 1920s England. A typically mediocre treatment of a P.G. Wodehouse story which relies solely on Wisdom's slapstick performance.

p, John Bryan; d, Henry Kaplan; w, Reuben Ship (based on a novel by P.G. Wodehouse).

Comedy   (PR:A MPAA:NR)

GIRL ON THE BRIDGE, THE zero (1951) 76m FOX bw

Hugo Haas (David), Beverly Michaels (Clara), Robert Dane (Mario), Tony Jochim (Mr. Cooper), Johnny Close (Harry), Darr Smith (Councilman), Judy Clark, Maria Bibikoff, Al Hill, Richard Pinner, Rose Marie Valenzuea, Joe Duval, Alan Ray, William Kahn, Jimmy Moss.

Hugo Haas, one of the cinema's consistently poor directors, continues to bat one thousand with this useless piece of drivel. Haas stars as a kind-hearted old watchmaker who hires Michaels and soon works up the courage to ask her to marry him. She agrees, but before long her ex-lover's cousin is trying blackmail. Haas kills him and the lover is tried for the crime. The guilty Haas, no longer able to bear the weight of his suffering, kills himself. Michaels is simply bad (though who wouldn't be under Haas' direction?), and it is incomprehensible that she could make a dog heel, much less drive a man to suicide. Bad, very bad.

p&d, Hugo Haas; w, Haas, Arnold Phillips; ph, Paul Ivano; m, Harold Byrns; ed, Merrill White, Albert Shaff; art d, Rudi Feld.

Drama   (PR:A MPAA:NR)

GIRL ON THE CANAL, THE** (1947, Brit.) 63m EAL bw (GB: PAINTED BOATS)

Jenny Laird (Mary Smith), Robert Griffith (Ted Stoner), Bill Blewett (Pa Smith), May Hallatt (Ma Smith), Madoline Thomas (Mrs. Stoner), Harry Fowler (Alf Stoner), Grace Arnold (His Sister), Megs Jenkins (Barmaid), James McKechnie (Narrator), John Owers.

The lives of two families living on canal barges in England are the subject of this well-made film. Blewett dies after an illness and Griffith goes off to fight the

Germans, his marriage to Laird postponed, although she, unknown to him, is pregnant. Crichton, a former editor, would later direct some of the best of Ealing comedies, including THE TITFIELD THUNDERBOLT and THE LAVENDER HILL MOB.

p, Henry Cornelius; d, Charles Crichton; w, Stephen Black, Louis MacNeice, Michael McCarthy (based on a story by Black); ph, Douglas Slocombe; m, John Greenwood; ed, Leslie Allen; art d, Jim Morahan.

Drama   (PR:A MPAA:NR)

GIRL ON THE FRONT PAGE, THE**   (1936) 75m UNIV bw

Edmund Lowe (Hank Gilman), Gloria Stuart (Joan Langford), Reginald Owen (Biddle), David Oliver (Flash), Spring Byington (Mrs. Langford), Gilbert Emery (Thorne), Robert Gleckler (Bill), Clifford Jones (Edward), Maxine Reiner (Annette).

A mediocre story about a society woman, Stuart, who takes over her father's newspaper, much to the consternation of the editor, Lowe. He decides not to resign, however, and instead attempts to thwart a plot by Stuart's butler to blackmail her. Stuart undertakes some reporting work unknown to Lowe, and when he discovers that, he falls for her, and she for him. Standard stuff that would scarcely make a headline today.

p, Charles R. Rogers; d, Harry Beaumont; w, Austin Parker, Alice D.G. Miller, Albert R. Perkins (based on a story by Roy and Marjorie Chanslor); ph, Milton Krasner; m, Herman Heller; ed, Philip Cahn.

Comedy   (PR:A MPAA:NR)

GIRL ON THE PIER, THE*   (1953, Brit.) 65m Major/Apex bw

Veronica Hurst (Rita Hammond), Ron Randell (Nick Lane), Charles Victor (Inspector Chubb), Marjorie Rhodes (Mrs. Chubb), Campbell Singer (Joe Hammond), Eileen Moore (Cathy Chubb), Brian Roper (Ronnie Hall), Anthony Valentine (Charlie Chubb), Thorp Devereaux, Diana Wilding, Raymond James, Steve Conway.

Singer, a waxworks curator on England's Brighton Pier, kills his former partner-in-crime, Randell, when he catches him with his wife, Hurst. Singer, while being pursued by the police, accidentally runs off the pier and dies a watery death.

p, Lance Comfort, John Temple-Smith; d, Comfort; w, Guy Morgan; ph, Bill McLeod.

Crime   (PR:A MPAA:NR)

GIRL ON THE RUN*   (1961) 64m Rose Tree/Astor bw

Richard Coogan (Bill Martin), Rosemary Pettit (Janet), Frank Albertson (Hank), Harry Bannister (Clay Reeves), Edith King (Carnival Girl), Charles Bollender (Dwarf), George Marsh (Managing Editor), Renee De Milo, Joseph Sullivan, Mike O'Dowd, John Krollers, Scott Hale.

Newsman Coogan investigates the murder of his managing editor, which he is accused of committing, by snooping around a carnival for clues. With the help of his secretary, he uncovers a partnership between his dead boss and a shady politician. Little to it, like yesterday's newspaper.

p, Robert Presnell, Sr.; d, Joseph Lee, Arthur J. Beckhard; w, Cedric Worth, Beckhard.

Crime/Mystery   (PR:A MPAA:NR)

GIRL ON THE SPOT**   (1946) 75m UNIV bw

Lois Collier (Kathy Lorenz), Jess Barker (Rick), George Dolenz (Leon), Fuzzy Knight (Bim), Ludwig Stossell (Popsy Lorenz), Richard Lane (Weepy McGurk), Donald MacBride (Gleason), Edward S. Brophy (Fingers), Billy Newell (Lightfoot), Ralph Sanford (Thomas), Delos Jewkes (Pirate King), Russell Horton (Frederick), Carole Hughes (Cuddles), Joseph Crehan (Editor), Sarah Edwards (Mrs. Richards), John Hamilton (Commissioner), Marie Harmon (Girl), John Shay (Mathews), Dulce Daye (Woman), Bert Roach (Man), Boyd Irwin (Confidence Man), Selmer Jackson (Ridgeway), James Carlisle (Colt), Cy Ring (Hobart), Ernie Adams (Pickpocket), Jack Cheatham (Cop), Nolan Leary, Carey Harrison (Men), John Mertin, Howard Mitchell, Roger Cole, Jimmy Lucas, Dick Dickinson, Frank Hagney (Mugs), Gene Stutenroth (Gambler), Alec Craig (Murgatroid), Forrest Taylor (Inky), Dick French (Bill), George Lynn (Bracken), Bob Homans (Clancy), Ray Walker (Dawson).

Collier gets herself in a colossal jam when she arrives for an audition at a nightclub just as the owner is getting polished off by some unfriendly gangsters—Lane, Newell, and Brophy. Barker, a photographer, helps her out of her spot and in the process falls in love with her. Collier does manage to make it to the stage in a performance of "The Pirates Of Penzance," after which the killers are jailed.

d, William Beaudine; w, Dorcas Cochran, Jerry Warner (based on a story by George Blake, Jack Hartfield); ph, M. Gertzman; ed, Saul Goodkind; art d, Abe Grossman; ch, Louis Da Pron; m/l, "Poor Wandering One," "A Policeman's Lot," W.S. Gilbert, Sir Arthur Sullivan.

Crime/Musical   (PR:A MPAA:NR)

GIRL OVERBOARD*½   (1929) 65m UNIV bw

Mary Philbin, Fred Mackaye, Edmund Breese, Otis Harlan, Francis McDonald.

Parolee Mackaye gets out of prison under the limits of a certain "Rule No. 3" which states that he cannot romance or marry. However, when he rescues wide-eyed beauty Philbin after she falls into the water, he cannot help but break the unfair rule. The parole office, luckily, has a heart and grants Mackaye and his bride-to-be special permission to marry. Barely a talkie, GIRL OVERBOARD, contains only about four minutes of dialog and one song ("Port of Dreams"), but that was enough to help sink Philbin, who, after three more attempts to break through to talkies, retired from the movies.

d, Wesley Ruggles; w, John B. Clymer.

Drama   (PR:A MPAA:NR)

GIRL OVERBOARD*   (1937) 64m UNIV bw

Gloria Stuart (Mary Chesbrooke), Walter Pidgeon (Paul Stacey), Billy Burrud (Bobby Stacey), Hobart Cavanaugh (Joe Gray), Gerald Oliver Smith (Harvey), Sidney Blackmer (Alex LeMaire), Jack Smart (Charlie Jenkins), David Oliver ("Dutch"), Charlotte Wynters (Molly Shane), Russell Hicks (Sam Le Maire), Robert Emmett O'Connor (Sgt. Hatton), Edward McNamara (Capt. Murphy).

Stuart enlists district attorney Pidgeon's aid in clearing her name in the murder of her former employer. She, Pidgeon, and the real killer are all traveling on board an ocean liner which sinks, drowning the guilty one. An uneventful programmer which sinks faster than the ship.

p, Robert Presnell; d, Sidney Salkow; w, Tristram Tupper (based on the story "Person-To-Person Call" by Sarah Elizabeth Rodger); ph, Ira Morgan; ed, Philip Cahn; md, Charles Previn.

Drama   (PR:A MPAA:NR)

GIRL RUSH**   (1944) 65m RKO bw

Wally Brown (Jerry Miles), Alan Carney (Mike Strager), Frances Langford (Flo Daniels), Vera Vague (Suzie Banks), Robert Mitchum (Jimmy Smith), Paul Hurst (Muley), Patti Brill (Claire), Sarah Padden (Emma), Cy Kendall (Bartlan), John Merton (Scully), Diana King (Martha), Michael Vallon (Prospector), Paul Newlan (Miner), Sherry Hall (Monk), Kernan Cripps (Bartender), Wheaton Chambers (Dealer), Ernie Adams (Dave), Lee Phelps (Mac), Byron Foulger (Oscar), Chili Williams (Girl), Rita Corday, Elaine Riley, Rosemary LaPlanche, Duan Kennedy, Virginia Belmont (Members of Troupe), Bud Osborne, Ken Terrell, Bert LeBaron, Dale Van Sickel.

A musical comedy featuring an inferior comedy team, Brown and Carney, playing a couple of vaudevillians stranded in California during the 1849 gold rush. They decide to do some prospecting on their own, and stumble into the womanless town of Red Creek, where they are promised sacks of gold dust if they find some women. The pair do, by bringing a revue into town, and strike gold with the idea. Songs included: "Annabella's Bustle," "Rainbow Valley," "If Mother Could Only See Us Now," "Walking Arm in Arm With Jim" (Harry Harris, Lew Pollack). Sleepy-eyed screen newcomer Mitchum won critical raves for his "likable" personality, beginning his long relationship with RKO.

p, John Auer; d, Gordon Douglas; w, Robert E. Kent (based on a story by Laszlo Vadnay, Aladar Laszlo); ph, Nicholas Musuraca; m, Gene Rose; ed, Duncan Mansfield; md, Constantin Bakaleinikoff; art d, Albert S. D'Agostino, Walter Keller; spec eff, Vernon L. Walker.

Musical Comedy/Western   (PR:A MPAA:NR)

GIRL RUSH, THE**½   (1955) 84m PAR c

Rosalind Russell (Kim Halliday), Fernando Lamas (Victor Monte), Eddie Albert (Elliot Atterbury), Gloria De Haven (Taffy Tremaine), Marion Lorne (Aunt Clara), James Gleason (Ether Ferguson), Robert Fortier (Pete Tremaine), Matt Mattox, Don Crichton, George Chakiris (Specialty Dancers), Douglas Fowley (Charlie), Jesse White (Pit Boss), Larry Gates (Hap Halliday), George Chandler, Lester Dorr, Shelley Fabares, Dorothy Gordon, Frances Lansing, Marjorie Bennett, Karolee Kelly, Hal Dawson, Hickey Kamm, Orlando Sicilia, Sherlock Feldman, Alexander Rhein, Vincent Padula, Arthur Gould Porter, Sid Tomack, Eddie Ryder, Lyle Latell, Freeman Lusk, George Pembroke, Frank Mills, Len Hendry, Darlene Fields, Marcoreta Hellman, Mike Mahoney, Kathy Johnson, Richard Kipling, Ralph Montgomery, Deborah Sydes, Lorna Simans.

A lightweight and often frivolous farce that served as a pale followup to Russell's WONDERFUL TOWN hit. Russell and her aunt, Lorne, come to Las Vegas to get into the hotel game with Gleason, a former partner of Russell's late father. She's under the mistaken impression that she owns 50 percent of the Flamingo Hotel, but it turns out that her hotel is a decrepit old place where nobody goes. Gleason had lost a bundle at the tables and the hotel is in hock. Lamas owns the Flamingo and he and Russell have a romance that winds up with them gazing into each other's eyes at the finale. Other than "An Occasional Man," the score wasn't anything to write home about. Other tunes included: "Take A Chance," "We're Alone," "The Girl Rush," "Champagne," "Birmingham," "Out Of Doors," "Choose Your Partner," "My Hillbilly Heart," (Hugh Martin, Ralph Blane). At a brief 84 minutes, considering all the music and the story, it still feels overlong and could have done with some judicious snipping. The movie looked more like a travelog for Las Vegas and is rampant with plugs for the various hotels. One of the speciality dancers was George Chakiris who went on to stardom in WEST SIDE STORY, then almost disappeared. De Haven and Albert figure in a small subplot that goes nowhere. The producer was Russell's long-time spouse, Fred Brisson.

p, Frederick Brisson; d, Robert Pirosh; w, Pirosh, Jerome "Jerry" Davis (based on a story by Phoebe and Henry Ephron); ph, William Daniels (VistaVision, Technicolor); m, M.S.I. Spencer-Hagen; ed, William Hornbeck; art d, Hal Pereira, Malcolm Bert; cos, Edith Head; ch, Robert Alton.

Musical/Comedy   (PR:A MPAA:NR)

GIRL SAID NO, THE*   (1930) 90m MGM bw

William Haines (Tom Ward), Leila Hyams (Mary Howe), Polly Moran (Polly), Marie Dressler (Hetty Brown), Francis X. Bushman (McAndrews), Clara Blandick (Mrs. Ward), William Janney (Jimmy Ward), Junior Coghlan (Eddie Ward), Phyllis Crane (Alma Ward), William V. Mong.

A tasteless comedy romance in which breezy Haines, as a young lady killer, tries to capture the heart of Hyams who has turned him down for Bushman. Haines plots dozens of extreme measures to win her over, and finally goes so far as to drag her from the altar, bound and gagged, leading to a merciful close to a sappy movie for which co-screenwriter Charles MacArthur, co-author of THE FRONT PAGE, should have felt mortified.

d, Sam Wood; w, Sarah Y. Mason, Charles MacArthur (based on a story by A.P. Younger); ph, Ira Morgan; ed, Frank Sullivan, Truman K. Wood, George Boemler; m/l, Martin Broones, Fred Fisher.

Comedy (PR:A MPAA:NR)

GIRL SAID NO, THE*½ (1937) 72m GN bw

Robert Armstrong (*Jimmie Allen*), Irene Hervey (*Pearl*), Paula Stone (*Mabel*), Edward J. Brophy (*Pie*), Vivian Hart (*Beatrice*), William Danforth (*Howard Hathaway*), Holmes Herbert (*Charles Dillon*), Gwill Andre (*Flo*), Vera Ross, Harry Tyler, Richard Tucker, Mildred Rogers, Frank Moulan, Josef Swickard, Arthur Kay, Horace Murphy, Bert Roach, Allan Rogers, Max Davidson, Caritz Crawford.

Hervey is a dance hall girl who has a penchant for spending other people's money. Armstrong is a bookie whom she soaks for a wallet-full one romantic evening. His plan of revenge is to make her into a show business name, represent her, and retrieve the money she got from him. Excerpts from Gilbert and Sullivan's "The Mikado," "Patience," "Pirates of Penzance," and "Ruddigore" make up a large portion of the film's second half.

p&d Andrew L. Stone; w, Betty Laidlaw, Robert Lively (based on a story by Stone); ph, Ira Morgan, ed, Thomas Neff; md, Arthur Kay; art d, Lewis J. Rachmil.

Musical (PR:A MPAA:NR)

GIRL SMUGGLERS* (1967) 63m Sack Amusement bw

Lucky Kargo.

Kargo prevents his sister from being sold into a prostitution ring organized by Puerto Rican gangsters. The young girls are snagged out of school, shipped to Puerto Rico, and then prepared for a life on New York's streets.

p&d, Barry Mahon.

Crime (PR:O MPAA:NR)

GIRL STROKE BOY**½ (1971, Brit.) 86m London Screen c

Joan Greenwood (*Lettice*), Michael Hordern (*George*), Clive Francis (*Laurie*), Straker (*Jo*), Patricia Routledge, Peter Bull, Rudolph Walker, Elizabeth Welch.

A generation gap tale with middle-class parents, Hordern and Greenwood, shocked that their son suddenly has an interest in the opposite sex. One day he brings home Straker, an androgynous West Indian girl, which makes the parents raise questions about their son's sexuality. A few lively scenes, but the majority of the picture is a prisoner of the loose-living, gross-talking era.

p, Ned Sherrin; d, Bob Kellett; w, Caryl Brahms, Sherrin (based on the play "Girl Friend," by David Percival); ph, Ian Wilson (Eastmancolor/Humphries); m, John Scott; ed, Brian Smedly Aston.

Drama (PR:C MPAA:NR)

GIRL SWAPPERS, THE (SEE: TWO AND TWO MAKE SIX, 1962, Brit.)

GIRL, THE BODY, AND THE PILL, THE zero (1967) 80m

Creative/Dominant-Box Office Spectaculars c (AKA: THE PILL)

Pamela Rhea (*Marcia Barrington*), Bill Rogers (*Wesley Nichols*), Valedia Hill (*Irene Hunt*), Nancy Lee Noble (*Randy Hunt*), Otto Schlesinger (*Mr. Price*), Roy Collodi (*Pike Grover*), George Brown (*Brad Martin*), Eleanor Vaill (*Grace Nichols*), James Nelson (*Ray Stanton*), Kay Ross (*Alice Nichols*), Todd Harris (*Charlie*), Sue Puccinelli (*Nancy Foster*), Pat Tenerelli (*Freddy*), Ray Sager, (*Tony*), The Fly-By-Nytes (*Themselves*).

King of gore, Herschell Gordon Lewis (2000 MANIACS, GORE GORE GIRLS), turns out a bloodless soap opera this time around. Wild teen sex runs rampant until Hill pays dearly when she becomes pregnant. Since she was on the pill she's understandably suspicious and learns that someone replaced them with saccharine tablets. All ends well after both an abortion and forgiveness are granted.

p&d, Herschell Gordon Lewis; w, Louise Downe; ph, Roy Collodi; ed, Richard Brinkman; md, Larry Wellington; art d, Dean Alexander; set d, Robert Enrietto; m/l, "The Pill," Sheldon Seymour.

Drama (PR:O MPAA:R)

GIRL THIEF, THE* (1938) 64m ABF bw (GB: LOVE AT SECOND SIGHT)

Marian Marsh (*Juliet*), Anthony Bushell (*Bill*), Claude Hulbert (*Allan*), Ralph Ince (*Mackintosh*), Joan Gardner (*Evelyn*), Stanley Holloway (*PC*), Neil Kenyon (*Uncle Angus*), Vivian Reynolds (*Butler*).

A confusing romantic comedy has the daughter of a match king, Marsh, feigning love for the inventor of an everlasting match, Hulbert. However, Marsh discovers that she really loves Hulbert's friend, Bushell, while Hulbert decides to go back to a former girl friend. Marsh and Bushell end up at the altar in what presumably is another everlasting match.

p, Julius Haimann; d, Paul Merzbach; w, Frank Miller, Jack Dies Davies (based on a story by Harold Simpson); ph, Jack Cox, Philip Grindrod; ed, John Neill Brown; m/l, Mischa Spolianski, Clifford Grey.

Comedy (PR:AA MPAA:NR)

GIRL TROUBLE**½ (1942) 81m FOX bw

Don Ameche (*Don Pedro Sullivan*), Joan Bennett (*June Delaney*), Billie Burke (*Mrs. Rowland*), Frank Craven (*Ambrose Murdock Flint*), Alan Dinehart (*Charles Barrett*), Helene Reynolds (*Helen*), Fortunio Bonanova (*Cordoba*), Ted North (*George*), Doris Merrick (*Susan*), Dale Evans (*Ruth*), Roseanna Murray (*Pauline*), Janis Carter (*Virginia*), Vivian Blaine (*Barbara*), Trudy Marshall (*Miss Kennedy*), Robert Greig (*Fields*), Joe Crehan (*Kuhn*), Arthur Loft (*Burgess*), Mantan Moreland (*Edwards*), John Kelly (*Mug*), Matt McHugh (*Driver*), George Lessey (*Morgan*), Ed Stanley (*Lehman*), Edith Evanson (*Hulda*), Lee Bennett (*Tom*), Bruce Warren (*Jerry*),

Frank Coghlan, Jr. (*Elevator Boy*), Frances Cain, Gayne Kinsey (*Dance Team*), Forbes Murray (*Mr. Lawson*), Lois Landon (*Mrs. Lawson*), Arno Frey (*Anton*), Jeff Corey (*Mr. Mooney*), Ruth Cherrington (*Large Woman*), Henry Roquemore (*Man*), Eddie Acuff (*Taxi Driver*), Jack Stoney (*Mac*), Doodles Weaver (*Ticket Taker*), Marjorie "Babe" Kane (*Cashier*), Mary Currier (*Secretary*).

A WW II screwball comedy about Ameche, the son on a Venezuelan rubber planter, who travels to New York to negotiate a loan to expand his father's company. Bennett is a rich American girl whose assets have been frozen in England for the duration of the war, rendering her penniless. She rents her apartment to Ameche, and stays on as his maid. After some typically goofy situations in the apartment, the two fall in love, split, and then reunite after Bennett helps Ameche get his loan.

p, Robert Bassler; d, Harold Schuster; w, Ladislas Fodor, Robert Riley Crutcher (based on a story by Fodor, Vicki Baum, Guy Trosper); ph, Edward Cronjager; m, Alfred Newman; ed, Robert Fritsch; art d, Richard Day, Boris Leven.

Comedy (PR:A MPAA:NR)

GIRL WAS YOUNG, THE (SEE: YOUNG AND INNOCENT, 1937, Brit.)

GIRL WHO CAME BACK, THE*½ (1935) 65m CHES/FD bw

Sidney Blackmer (*Rhodes*), Shirley Grey (*Gilda*), Noel Madison (*Brewster*), Mathew Betz (*Smoky*), Torben Myer (*Zarabella*), May Beatty (*Aunty*), Frank LaRue (*Burke*), Robert Adair (*Mathews*), Ida Darling (*Mrs. Rhodes*), Edward Martindel (*Madison*), John Dilson (*Wadsworth*), Lou Davis (*Sims*), Don Brodie (*Jason*).

A far below par crime film, THE GIRL WHO CAME BACK has Grey as a gangster's moll who goes straight when she moves to California. Although she is through with the rackets, Grey pulls off a jewel heist for a mob, but double-crosses the gangsters, for no apparent reason.

p, George R. Batcheller; d, Chas. Lamont; w, Ewart Adamson; ph, M.A. Andersen; ed, Roland Reed.

Crime (PR:A MPAA:NR)

GIRL WHO COULDN'T QUITE, THE** (1949, Brit.) 85m Monarch bw

Bill Owen (*Tim*), Elizabeth Henson (*Ruth*), Iris Hoey (*Janet*), Betty Stockfeld (*Pamela*), Stuart Lindsell (*John Pelham*), Vernon Kelso (*Paul Evans*), Rose Howlett (*Rosa*), Fred Groves (*Tony*).

Owen is a hobo who befriends Henson and makes her happy for the first time since her treacherous childhood. She succumbs to amnesia, however, and forgets who Owen is. The hobo succeeds in bringing her memory back, but she ungratefully leaves him out of her life. A calculated tearjerker which bears too much sorrow for any one audience to handle.

p, John Argyle; d, Norman Lee; w, Lee, Marjorie Deans (based on a play by Leo Marks); ph, Geoffrey Faithfull.

Drama (PR:A MPAA:NR)

GIRL WHO COULDN'T SAY NO, THE** (1969, Ital.) 83m Italnoleggio-Prima-Fulco/FOX c (IL SUO MODO DI FARE; AKA: TENDERLY)

Virna Lisi (*Yolanda*), George Segal (*Franco*), Lila Kedrova (*Yolanda's Mother*), Akim Tamiroff (*Uncle Egidio*), Paola Pitagora (*Widow*), Luciano Mondolfo (*Professor*), Mario Brega (*Cripple*), Vera Nandi (*Luisa Belli*), Richard Bill (*Salesman*), Ciccio Barbi (*Passenger on Train*), Gianni Di Benedetto, Nora Ricci, Adriano Amidei Migliano, Germano Longo, Ugo Adinolfi, Mirella Pamphili, Felicity Mason, Jeffrey Copplestone.

An amusing comedy which has Segal playing a dim-witted doctor who falls in love with Lisi, a childhood sweetheart and now a wild hippie. He is promoted in spite of her unconventional ideas around the hospital, and soon ends up owning the place. He finally tires of her habit of hopping into other men's beds and decides to devote himself to medicine.

p, Luciano Perugia; d, Franco Brusati; w, Brusati, Ennio de Concini; ph, Ennio Guarnieri; m, Riz Ortolani; ed, Franco Arcalli; art d, Pier Luigi Pizzi; cos, Pizzi.

Romantic Comedy (PR:A MPAA:GP)

GIRL WHO DARED, THE*½ (1944) 54m REP bw

Lorna Gray, Peter Cookson, Grant Withers, Veda Ann Borg, John Hamilton, Willie Best, Vivien Oakland, Roy Barcroft, Kirk Alyn.

What starts as an innocent good time for a group voyaging to an island off the coast of Georgia, soon turns into a murder mystery when one of their members turns up dead. Barely enough suspense to sustain the short duration of the film.

p, Rudolph E. Abel; d, Howard Bretherton; w, John K. Butler (based on the story "Blood On Her Shoe" by Medora Field); ph, Bud Thackery; ed, Arthur Roberts; md, Morton Scott; art d, Gano Chittenden.

Mystery (PR:A MPAA:NR)

GIRL WHO FORGOT, THE* (1939, Brit.) 79m BUT bw

Elizabeth Allan (*Leonora Barradine*), Ralph Michael (*Tony Stevenage*), Enid Stamp-Taylor (*Caroline Tonbridge*), Basil Radford (*Mr. Barradine*), Jeanne de Casalis (*Mrs. Barradine*), Murial Aked (*Mrs. Badger*), David Keir (*Drawbridge*).

Allan is the girl who forgets and what she forgot is her mother. She nearly becomes the victim of the scheming Aked, who makes a move to take over the girl's trust fund. She is befriended, however, by Michael. He leaves his socialite fiancee behind and ends up walking the aisle with Allan. An easily forgettable melodrama with a dose of comedy.

p, Daniel Birt, Louise Birt; d, Adrian Brunel; w, Louise Birt (based on the play "The Young Person In Pink" by Gertrude Jennings).

Drama/Comedy (PR:A MPAA:NR)

GIRL WHO HAD EVERYTHING, THE½** (1953) 69m MGM bw

Elizabeth Taylor *(Jean Latimer)*, Fernando Lamas *(Victor Y. Ramondi)*, William Powell *(Steve Latimer)*, Gig Young *(Vance Court)*, James Whitmore *(Charles "Chico" Menlow)*, Robert Burton *(John Ashmond)*, William Walker *(Julian)*, Harry Bartell *(Joe)*, Elmer Peterson *(Himself)*, Dan Riss *(Counsel)*, Paul Harvey *(Sen. Drummond)*, Dean Miller *(Radio Announcer)*, Wilson Wood *(Newsman)*, Doug Carter *(Bellboy)*, Emory Parnell *(Auctioneer)*, Earle Hodgins *(Spotter)*, Frank Dae *(Old Man Kinkaid)*, Roy Butler *(Trainer)*, John McKee *(Male Secretary)*, Bobby Johnson *(Attendant)*, Anthony Warde, Philip Van Zandt *(Colleagues)*, Jonathan Cott, John Maxwell, Stu Wilson *(Newspaper Men)*, James Horne, Perry Sheehan, Dee Turnell, Sally Musick *(Guests in Town House)*, George Brand, A. Cameron Grant, George Sherwood, Pat O'Malley *(Senate Board Members)*, Jack Sterling *(Cab Driver)*.

Based on the 1931 film, A FREE SOUL, which starred Norma Shearer, Clark Gable, and Lionel Barrymore (in the roles played by Taylor, Lamas, and Powell in this version). The story stars Taylor as the spoiled daughter of Powell, a prominent criminal lawyer. Taylor falls in love with Lamas, a ringleader of a gambling syndicate and one of Powell's clients. Despite the opposition of Powell and her ex-boy friend, Young, she is determined to marry Lamas. On the eve of her wedding, Taylor discovers that Lamas is about to be brought before a crime investigation committee. Lamas assaults Powell in front of Taylor, making her come to her senses just before Lamas is bumped off by his fellow mobsters, allowing Taylor to go into the open arms of Young. Taylor was pregnant with her first child during the shooting of THE GIRL WHO HAD EVERYTHING and the shooting schedule was skillfully reorganized so that her more revealing scenes could be filmed before her pregnancy became too obvious. This was also Powell's last film for MGM, the studio where he had done most of his best work.

p, Armand Deutsch; d, Richard Thorpe; w, Art Cohn (based on the novel *A Free Soul* by Adela Rogers St. John); ph, Paul Vogel; m, Andre Previn; ed, Ben Lewis; art d, Cedric Gibbons, Randall Duell; cos, Helen Rose.

Drama **(PR:A MPAA:NR)**

GIRL WHO KNEW TOO MUCH, THE* (1969) 95m United-Westco/COM c

Adam West *(Johnny Cain)*, Nancy Kwan *(Revel)*, Robert Alda *(Allardice)*, Nehemiah Persoff *(Lt. Crawford)*, Patricia Smith *(Tricia)*, David Brian *(Had Dixon)*, Buddy Greco *(Lucky)*, Weaver Levy *(Wong See)*, John Napier *(Danny Deshea)*, Mark Roberts *(Stephen)*, Steven Peck *(Tony Grinaldi)*, Diane Van Valin *(Stripper)*, Chick Chandler *(Hunley)*, Lisa Todd *(Sugar Sweet)*.

Television's "Batman" star West socked his way into action as an ex-CIA agent turned nightclub owner who finds himself battling a massive Communist conspiracy against the free world. Ensnared by his former bosses, the CIA, and a major Mafia family into helping repel the Reds, West fights off dozens of Oriental (presumably Chinese) Commies and reveals that the kingpin mobster's wife is in reality a Communist agent and only married the gangster to further her insidious plans. Confusing, pointless, and stupid, the only entertainment value here is the unintentionally funny performance of West, who, outside of his *intentionally* funny "Batman" role, always comes off tight-lipped and dull.

p, Earle Lyon; d, Francis D. Lyon; w, Charles A. Wallace; ph, Alan Stensvold (Eastmancolor); m, Joe Green; ed, Terry O. Morse; art d, Paul Sylos.

Spy Drama **(PR:O MPAA:R)**

GIRL WITH A PISTOL, THE½** (1968, Ital.) 100m Documento/PAR c (LA RAGAZZA CON LA PISTOLA)

Monica Vitti *(Assunta Borello)*, Stanley Baker *(Dr. Osborne)*, Carlo Giuffre *(Vincenzo Maccaluso)*, Corin Redgrave *(Frank)*, Anthony Booth *(John)*, Aldo Puglisi *(1st Mafioso)*, Tiberio Murgia *(2nd Mafioso)*, Deborah Stanford *(Mrs. Sullivan)*, Dominic Allen *(Mr. Sullivan)*, Catherine Feller *(Rosina)*, Helen Downing *(Ada)*, Janet Brandes *(Nurse)*, Natasha Harwood *(Mrs. Osbourne)*, Stefano Satta Flores *(Waiter)*.

An amusing Italian comedy starring Vitti as a naive young Sicilian girl who is snatched and dragged up to a mountain retreat by Giuffre, where he can compromise her reputation and instantly win her hand in marriage to avoid further embarrassment. Little does he know what he got himself into, however, because Vitti suddenly becomes a nymphomanic who drives the exhausted Sicilian boy away. Vitti returns to her village without a husband and sets out to find the louse and bring him back. Her search leads her to England where her provincial Sicilian ways stick out like a sore thumb. Soon some culture rubs off on Vitti and she begins to assimilate more British manners until she ensnares local doctor Baker. Eventually she runs into Giuffre and gets her revenge by slapping him in the face and running off to marry Baker.

p, Gianni Hecht Lucari; d, Mario Monicelli; w, Rodolfo Sonego, Luigi Magni (English adaptation, Ronald Harwood); ph, Carlo Di Palma (Technicolor); m, Peppino Dev-Luca; ed, Ruggero Mastroianni; art d, Renzo Marignano.

Comedy **(PR:A MPAA:NR)**

GIRL WITH A SUITCASE*½** (1961, Fr./Ital.) 111m Titanus-S.G.C./Ellis bw (LA RAGAZZA CON LA VALIGIA; LA FILLE A LA VALISE; AKA: PLEASURE GIRL)

Claudia Cardinale *(Aida Zepponi)*, Jacques Perrin *(Lorenzo Fainardi)*, Corrado Pani *(Marcello Fainardi)*, Luciana Angelillo *(Aunt Marta)*, Gian Maria Volonte [Carlo Hintermann] *(Piero)*, Riccardo Garrone *(Romolo)*, Renato Baldini *(Francia)*, Romolo Valli *(Father Introna)*, Ciccio Barbi *(Crosia)*, Nadia Bianchi *(Nuccia)*, Edda Soligo *(Teacher)*, Elsa Albani *(Lucia)*.

After being dropped by Perrin's older brother, Cardinale gains the sympathy and friendship of Perrin himself. He soon falls in love with the older Cardinale, buying her clothes which he cannot afford and giving her his allowance. She, however, meets a musician, and, knowing that things will never work between her and the sixteen-year-old Perrin, leaves with him. His heart says to follow and he does, but he is beaten up by the musician. Concerned for his safety, she insists that Perrin return home to his family. He complies, but gives her an envelope full of money before he leaves. Cardinale is exceptionally gorgeous in her role, and, like the rest of the cast, gives a likable and sensitive performance.

p, Maurizio Lodi Fe; d, Valerio Zurlini; w, Leo Benvenuti, Piero De Bernardi, Enrico Medioli, Giuseppe Patroni-Griffi, Giuseppe Bennati, Zurlini (based on a story by Zurlini); ph, Tino Santoni; m, Mario Nascimbene; ed, Mario Serandrei; art d, Flavio Mogherini.

Drama **(PR:A MPAA:NR)**

GIRL WITH GREEN EYES*½** (1964, Brit.) 91m Woodfall/Lopert bw

Peter Finch *(Eugene Gaillard)*, Rita Tushingham *(Kate Brady)*, Lynn Redgrave *(Baba Brenan)*, Marie Kean *(Josie Hannigan)*, Arthur O'Sullivan *(Mr. Brady)*, Julian Glover *(Malachi Sullivan)*, T.P. McKenna *(Priest)*, Lislott Goettinger *(Joanna)*, Patrick Laffan *(Bertie Counihan)*, Eileen Crowe *(Mrs. Byrne)*, Kay Craig *(Aunt)*, Joe Lynch *(Andy Devlin)*, Yolande Turner *(Mary)*, Harry Brogan *(Jack Holland)*, Michael Hennessey *(Davey)*, Joe O'Donnell *(Patrick Devlin)*, Michael O'Brian *(Lodger)*, Dave Kelly *(Ticket Collector)*, Oliver MacGreevy *(Duggan)*.

Edna O'Brien successfully adapted her own novel into what used to be called "a woman's picture" before people's sensibilities were raised. Filmed in and around Dublin, GIRL WITH GREEN EYES tells the story of young Rita Tushingham who leaves her father's barren farm in County Clare to come to Dublin where she gets a job in a grocery and shares a flat with Redgrave, an old pal from Catholic school. She meets Finch, a divorced writer many years older than she, and they become friends after she runs after him, then moves into his home. Despite their propinquity and the underlying attraction, she remains chaste due to a combination of her youth, her shyness, and her religious upbringing. When her father, O'Sullivan, learns that she is living with a man, he gets her to return home as that is no situation for a decent, God-fearing Catholic girl to be in. Her priest, McKenna, rebukes her for that lax behavior and she leaves home again and goes to Finch's home. She is tailed by O'Sullivan and a horde of his besotted buddies. They break into Finch's house and only leave when Finch points his aged shotgun at them. Tushingham finally relents and sleeps with Finch. It's not the best relationship because there are so many years between them and they have little in common beyond their passion. She feels quite inadequate around Finch and his older cronies and eventually becomes somewhat of a shrew, attempting to keep him all for herself and not allow him the pleasure of his buddies' company. They battle over this and she leaves, taking up residence again with Redgrave, a lively lass with a lust for life. Tushingham thinks that Finch will come after her but when he doesn't, she resigns herself to the fact that it was fun while it lasted, but now it's time to move ahead and get on with her life. It was originally titled "Once Upon A Summer" and featured several of the best Irish actors around. All the roles were well played and the dialog smacked of Irish reality, though at rare times a trifle stilted for the American ear. Lots to recommend this film, including good first-time direction by Desmond Davis, long-time cinematographer for executive producer Richardson as well as debut photography by Manny Wynn. Turner, Finch's real-life wife, does an excellent cameo as a bitch. It was Redgrave's second film for Richardson, the first having been TOM JONES. Lovingly made, it's a fine introduction to the Ireland of lyrical romance, rather than the strife-torn area we see so often.

p, Oscar Lewenstein; d, Desmond Davis; w, Edna O'Brien (based on her novel *The Lonely Girl*); ph, Manny Wynn; m, John Addison; ed, Anthony Gibbs, Brian Smedley-Aston; md, Addison; art d, Ted Marshall; makeup, Bob Lawrence.

Drama **(PR:A-C MPAA:NR)**

GIRL WITH IDEAS, A*** (1937) 70m UNIV bw

Wendy Barrie *(Mary Morton)*, Walter Pidgeon *(Micky McGuire)*, Kent Taylor *(Frank Barnes)*, Dorothea Kent *(Isabelle Foster)*, George Barbier *(John F. Morton)*, Ted Osborn *(Pete Dailey)*, Henry Hunter *(William Duncan)*, Samuel S. Hinds *(Rodding Carter)*, George Humbert *(Toni)*, Horace MacMahon *(Al)*, Ed Gargan *(Eddie)*, Norman Willis *(Hanlon)*, Theodore Osborn *(Bailey)*, George Cleveland *(Malladay)*, Michael Fitzmaurice *(Reggie)*, Robert Dalton *(Greg)*, Frances Robinson *(Maggie)*, Drew Demarest *(Hill)*, Robert Spencer *(Charlie)*, Fay Helm *(Genevieve)*, Jimmy Lucas *(Tom)*, William Lundigan *(Herman)*, Billy Bletcher *(McKenzie)*, Pat Flaherty *(Motorcycle Cop)*, Sam Hayes *(Wallie Waldron)*, Edward McWade *(Judge)*, Harry Allen *(Janitor)*, Sherry Hall *(Jury Foreman)*, Thomas Braidon *(Butler)*, Fern Emmett, Sidney Bracy *(Secretaries)*, Otto Fries *(Policeman)*, Monte Vandergrift *(Truck Driver)*, James Farley *(Private Policeman)*, Bobby Watson *(Vendor)*, Anthony Warde *(Gangster)*, Mary Jane Shauer *(Adele)*, Art Yeoman, Jack Gardner *(Reporters)*, Matty Roubert *(Messenger Boy)*, Jack Daley *(Traffic Officer)*, Bob McClung *(Newsboy)*, Charles Sullivan *(Waiter)*, Heinie Conklin *(Street Sweeper)*, George Ovey *(Bookkeeper)*, Rebecca Wassem *(Girl)*, Allen Fox *(Uniformed Messenger)*, Kathleen Nelson *(Stenographer)*.

Barrie is a rich girl who buys the newspaper that once libeled her. Through her society contacts she prints a better paper than its former owner, Pidgeon, did. Pidgeon, who had hoped to repurchase the paper after Barrie wrecked it, is so disturbed by the events that he fakes the kidnaping of Barrie's father, Barbier, and gives the story to a rival paper. Barbier is delighted with his kidnaping, as it is the first vacation he has had in years. A lot of fun and a fine cast make this highly viewable.

p, Edmund Grainger; d, S. Sylvan Simon; w, Bruce Manning, Robert T. Shannon (based on the story "Mightier Than The Sword" by William Rankin); ph, Milton Krasner; ed, Philip Cahn; md, Charles Previn; art d, Jack Otterson.

Comedy   **(PR:A MPAA:NR)**

GIRL WITH THE GOLDEN EYES, THE*½   (1962, Fr.) 90m
Madeleine/Kingsley-Union bw (LA FILLE AUX YEUX D'OR)

Marie Laforet (Girl), Paul Guers (Henri Marsay), Francoise Prevost (Eleanore San-Real), Jacques Verlier (Paul de Manneville), Francoise Dorleac (Katia), Alice Sapritch (Madame Alberte), Carla Marlier (Sonia), Frederic de Pasquale (Willy), Guy Martin (Chabert), Philippe Moreau.

Guers falls in love with golden-eyed Laforet, but is unable to learn anything about her, not even her name. He turns to Prevost, a business associate, for help, but soon discovers that the girls are lovers. He enlists the aid of a powerful group of men known as "The Thirteen," who locate the girl. Before Guers is able to get to her, the jealous Prevost stabs her to death. Another French look at filles engaged in hedonism.

p, Gilbert de Goldschmidt; d, Jean-Gabriel Albicocco; w, Pierre Pelegri, Albicocco, Philippe Dumarcay (based on The Story of the Thirteen by Honore de Balzac); ph, Quinto Albicocco; m, Narciso Yepes, Arcangelo Corelli; ed, Georges Klotz; art d, Jacques d'Ovidio, Frederic de Pasquale.

Drama   **(PR:C MPAA:NR)**

GIRL WITH THE RED HAIR, THE**   (1983, Neth.) 116m
Movies Filmproductions-VNU-Trio-VaraTv-Querido-Meteor/UA c

Renee Soutendijk (Hannie), Peter Tuinman (Hugo), Loes Luca (An), Johan Leysen (Frans), Robert Delhez (Floor), Ada Bouwman (Tinka), Lineke Rijxman (Judith), Maria De Booy (Mother), Henk Rigters (Father), Adrian Brine (German Officer), Chris Lomme (Mrs. DeRuyter), Lou Landre (Otto), Jan Retel (Professor), Elsje Scherjon (Carlien), Hennie Van Den Akker (Van Den Heuvel).

The true story of a female resistance fighter from Holland during WW II, which is interesting when it sticks to the story but gets hopelessly muddled when it tries to moralize on the philosophical line between worthwhile violence and terrorism. A lot of feminist symbolism also mars a story that needed to be told straight. Lensing by Theo Van De Sande deserves a special nod.

p, Chris Brouwer, Haig Balian; d, Ben Verbong; w, Verbong, Peter de Vos (based on the novel by Theun De Vries); ph, Theo Van De Sande (Fujicolor); m, Nicolai Piovani; ed, Ton De Graff; art d, Dorus Van Der Linden; cos, Jan Tax.

War Drama   **(PR:A MPAA:PG)**

GIRL WITH THREE CAMELS, THE**   (1968, Czech.) 98m
Barrandov/Continental bw (DIVKA S TREMI VELBLOUDY)

Slavka Budinova (Bobina's Mother), Zuzana Ondrouchova (Bobina), Radovan Kukavsky (Alfred), Jan Langsadl (Josef Pepik), Vladimir Pospisil (Mother's 1st Lover).

A teenage girl is made pregnant by a man on the night before he is to go to Algeria to work in construction. The only word she thereafter receives from him is written on the back of a postcard with three camels on it. Her mother, who also was illegitimate, gives her money for an abortion, which the girl uses instead to check into a hospital and have the child. After an amusing and unsuccessful attempt to pierce the bureaucracy and list the father's name on the birth records, she throws the postcard in front of a portrait of her grandmother, who also was illegitimate. A lot of laughs in this one for those with a mordant sense of humor.

d, Vaclav Krska; w, Miloslav Stehlik, Krska (based on a story by Stehlik); ph, Rudolf Stahl; m, Jiri Sust.

Comedy/Drama   **(PR:A MPAA:NR)**

GIRL WITHOUT A ROOM**   (1933) 72m PAR bw

Charles Farrell (Tom Duncan), Charles Ruggles (Vergil Crock), Marguerite Churchill (Kay Loring), Gregory Ratoff (General), Walter Woolf (Arthur Copeland), Grace Bradley (Nada), Leonid Snegoff (Trotsky), Mischa Auer (Walksky), Leonid Kinskey (Gallopsky), Alex Melesh (Sitsky), August Tollaire (Pierre), Adrien Rosley (Henri), Perry Ivans (De Bergerac), William P. Colvin (Art Judge), Sam Ash (Street Singer).

A silly little art school comedy starring Farrell as a Tennessee boy who wins a scholarship to study painting in Paris. Encouraged, he is surprised when he learns that his style of painting has fallen out of favor in France and is considered garbage. He switches to the more bizarre, modern style and soon becomes the rage, winning a big award. Nobody knows, however, that the masterwork is hanging upside down. A lot of singing, dancing, cabaret numbers, and assorted nutty characters give this contrived story a certain untoward charm.

p, Charles R. Rogers; d, Ralph Murphy; w, Frank Butler, Claude Binyon (based on the novel by Jack Lait); ph, Leo Tover; ch, Larry Ceballos; m/l, "You Alone," "Roof-Top Serenade," "The Whistle Has to Blow," Val Burton, Will Jason.

Comedy   **(PR:A MPAA:NR)**

GIRLFRIENDS***½   (1978) 86m Cyclops/WB c

Melanie Mayron (Susan Weinblatt), Anita Skinner (Anne Munroe), Eli Wallach (Rabbi Gold), Christopher Guest (Eric), Bob Balaban (Martin), Gina Rogak (Julie), Amy Wright (Ceil), Viveca Lindfors (Beatrice), Mike Kellin (Abe), Jean de Baer (Terry), Ken McMillan (Cabbie), Russell Horton (Photo Editor), Tania Berezin (Rabbi's Wife), Kathryn Walker (Carpel's Receptionist), Roderick Cook (Carpel), Kristoffer Tabori (Charlie).

A refreshing little film that marked the directorial debut of Weill, GIRLFRIENDS strips away the pretentiousness often seen in small movies and offers us a real look

at real people. Weill spent many years as a documentarian; she uses her experience and her ear and eye for realism to present us with an episodic story that mixes comedy and poignancy for excellent results. Mayron is a chubby Jewish photographer whose roommate, Skinner, is leaving to get married. Mayron must now go it alone and contemplate her life, new insecurities, and her cellulite. She is so good in the role that we are hard-pressed to find a false note; she seems closer to "being" than acting. Not unlike SHEILA LEVINE IS DEAD AND LIVING IN NEW YORK (1975), it is a character study of a certain type of urban Jewish woman that never hits a false note. Bob Balaban is Mayron's boy friend. He is depicted as likable and believable, an honest human being with honest problems. Mayron flirts with Wallach, a rabbi, and almost has a fling with him but she winds up as the house photographer doing weddings and bar mitzvahs. It's unsentimental, emotional, and made with great affection. GIRLFRIENDS began as an American Film Institute project with a small grant. As the picture was being made, various investors chimed in and contributed. One hopes they made their money back. A New York story that may not have made much sense west of New Jersey, GIRLFRIENDS is not mired in the seventies; the problems of these people will be as real in twenty years as they were when the movie was made.

p, Claudia Weill, Jan Saunders; d, Weill; w, Vicki Polon (based on a story by Polon and Weill); ph, Fred Murphy (DuArt Color); m, Michael Small; ed, Suzanna Pettit; art d, Patrizia von Brandenstein.

Comedy/Drama   **Cas.**   **(PR:A-C MPAA:PG)**

GIRLS, THE**   (1972, Swed.) 100m Lindgren-Sandrews bw (FLICKORNA)

Bibi Andersson, Harriet Andersson, Gunnel Lindblom, Gunnar Bjornstrand, Erland Josephson, Stig Engstrom, Ake Lindstrom, Frank Sundstrom.

A touring theatrical company performing Aristophanes' "Lysistrata" serves as the backdrop for this feminist drama exploring the roles and directions of the three female leads. Bibi Andersson must deal with a husband who has a pair of mistresses; Harriet Andersson has a lover who will not marry her; and Lindblom is married to a man who takes care of her children dutifully. All three, however, find themselves looking for a way to cope with their dilemmas and anxieties. If you like strong feminist statements, heavy symbolism, and a reliance on flashbacks then this one's for you. Released in Sweden in 1969. (In Swedish; English subtitles.)

p, Goran Lindgren; d, Mai Zetterling; w, Zetterling, David Hughes; ph, Rune Ericson; m, Michael Hurd; ed, Wicl Kjellin.

Drama   **(PR:O MPAA:NR)**

GIRLS ABOUT TOWN***½   (1931) 80m PAR bw

Kay Francis (Wanda Howard), Joel McCrea (Jim Baker), Lilyan Tashman (Marie Bailey), Eugene Pallette (Benjamin Thomas), Allan Dinehart (Jerry Chase), Lucile Webster Gleason (Mrs. Benjamin Thomas), Anderson Lawler (Alex Howard), George Barbier (Webster), Robert McWade (Simms), Judith Wood (Winnie), Lucille Brown, Louise Beavers, Adrienne Ames, Hazel Howard, Claire Dodd, Patricia Caron.

A screwball comedy starring Francis and Tashman as roommates who live in a swank apartment and wear fancy clothes and who are funded by sappy businessmen vamped by the pair. Problems arise for Francis when she falls in love with handsome and rich hick McCrea. They have a turbulent romance that leads to a marriage proposal, but the frustrated gold digger finally confesses that she's married and her husband left her long ago. Luckily, after an investigation, it is discovered that she'd been divorced all along and just didn't know it. Though the plotting gets convoluted and a bit much at times, Cukor's direction concentrates on snappy dialog and clever comedy sequences. Author Akins had written a very similar plot in the Broadway hit play filmed by United Artists, THE GREEKS HAD A WORD FOR IT. This time, Paramount beat the rival studio into the theaters.

d, George Cukor; w, Raymond Griffith, Brian Marlow (based on a story by Zoe Akins); ph, Ernest Haller.

Comedy/Drama   **(PR:O MPAA:NR)**

GIRLS AT SEA**   (1958, Brit.) 80m ABF/Seven Arts c

Guy Rolfe (Captain), Ronald Shiner (Marine Ogg), Alan White (Commander), Michael Hordern (Adm. Hewitt), Anne Kimbell (Mary), Nadine Tallier (Antoinette), Fabia Drake (Lady Hewitt), Mary Steele (Jill), Richard Coleman (Capt. Randall), Lionel Jeffries (Tourist), Teddy Johnson (Singer), Daniel Massey (Flag Lieutenant), David Lodge (Cpl. Duckett), Warren Mitchell, Michael Ripper, Mercy Haystead, Brian Wilde, Harold Goodwin, David Aylmer, Richard Briers, Marie Devereux, Shane Cordell, Josephine Lisle.

An amusing comedy which details the sticky situation that arises when three good-looking women, Kimbell, Steele, and Tallier, are left behind during a shipboard party on the HMS Scotia, a battleship. Before lean and handsome captain Rolfe can arrange for the girls to be brought back to shore, the ship is called out on maneuvers off the coast of Italy. Having no choice but to take the women along, Rolfe spends much of the film hiding their presence from the admiral.

p, Vaughn N. Dean, Gilbert Gunn; d, Gunn; w, T.J. Morrison, Gunn, Walter C. Mycroft (based on the play "The Middle Watch" by Stephen King-Hall, Ian Hay); ph, Erwin Hillier (Technicolor); m, Laurie Johnson; ed, E.B. Jarvis; art d, Peter Glazier.

Comedy   **(PR:A MPAA:NR)**

GIRLS CAN PLAY**   (1937) 59m COL bw (AKA: FIELDER'S FIELD)

Jacqueline Wells (Ann Casey), Charles Quigley (Jimmy Jones), Rita Hayworth (Sue Collins), John Gallaudet (Foy Harris), George McKay (Sluggy), Gene Morgan (Pete), Patricia Farr (Peanuts), Guinn "Big Boy" Williams (Lt. Flannigan), Joseph Crehan (Brophy), John Tyrrell (Danny Mashio), Richard Terry (Cisto), James Flavin (Bill O'Malley), Beatrice Curtis, Ruth Hilliard (Infielders), Lee Prather

(Coroner), Harry Tyler (Dugan), Beatrice Blinn (Mae), George Lloyd (Blater), Michael Breen (Man), Fern Emmett (Anna), Richard Kipling (Mr. Raymond), Bruce Sidney (Doctor), Lucille Lund (Jane Harmon), Evelyn Selbie (Fortune Teller), Lee Shumway (Capt. Curtis), Ann Doran (Secretary).

GIRLS CAN PLAY is a bizarre crime drama dealing with a girls' baseball team, a murder, gangsters, and newspaper reporters. Ex-convict Gallaudet, who sells cheap liquor with bogus labels, runs a drugstore and sponsors a girls' baseball team. The action shifts between the crime plot and the baseball diamond where the beautiful girls practice. Gallaudet's ex-con pal shows up and Gallaudet kills him to keep him quiet. Later the girl catcher is poisoned on the playing field. On the trail of the murderer is dim-witted police officer Williams and an equally lamebrained cub reporter, Quigley. Gallaudet sells the drugstore and the illegal liquor, and tries to get away with the money before the slow law can catch up with him. Rita Hayworth makes one of her early screen appearances as Gallaudet's moll.

p, Ralph Cohn; d&w, Lambert Hillyer (based on a story by Albert DeMond); ph, Lucien Ballard; m, Morris Stoloff; ed, Byron Robinson; art d, Stephen Goosson; cos, Kalloch.

Crime   **(PR:A   MPAA:NR)**

GIRLS DEMAND EXCITEMENT*   (1931) 64m FOX bw

Virginia Cherrill (Joan Madison), John Wayne (Peter Brooks), Marguerite Churchill (Miriam), Helen Jerome Eddy (Gazella Perkins), Marion Byron (Margery), Martha Sleeper (Harriet Mundy), William Janney (Freddie), Eddie Nugent (Tommy), Winter Hall (The Dean), Addie McPhail (Sue Street), Ralph Welles, George Irving, Terrance Ray, Ray Cooke, Jerry Mandy, Emerson Treacy.

An inane film set on a co-ed college campus in which tension explodes between the boys and the girls, leading to the guys trying to clear the girls from the institution. Wayne, not yet a major star, played the leader of the boys, while Cherrill, who starred opposite Charlie Chaplin in CITY LIGHTS, is the leader of the girls.

d, Seymour Felix; w, Harlan Thompson; ph, Charles Clarke; ed, Jack Murray.

Comedy   **(PR:A   MPAA:NR)**

GIRLS DISAPPEAR   (SEE: ROAD TO SHAME, THE, 1962)

GIRLS' DORMITORY***   (1936) 65m Darryl F. Zanuck/FOX bw

Herbert Marshall (Dr. Stephen Dominik), Ruth Chatterton (Prof. Anna Mathe), Simone Simon (Marie Claudel), Constance Collier (Prof. Augusta Wimmer), J. Edward Bromberg (Dr. Spindler), Dixie Dunbar (Luisa), John Qualen (Toni), Shirley Deane (Fritzi), Tyrone Power, Jr. (Count Vallais), Frank Reicher (Dr. Hoffenreich), George Hassell (Dr. Wilfinger), Lynne Berkeley (Dora), June Storey (Greta), Christian Rub (Forester), Rita Gould (Prof. Emma Kern), Lillian West (Prof. Josephine Penz), Symona Boniface (Prof. Clotilde Federa), Lynn Bari, Lillian Porter (Students).

Gene Markey's sharp, romantic script introduced Simone Simon to American audiences after several successful films in France. It also served to bolster young Tyrone Power (when he was still using "junior" in his name; his father had been a famous matinee idol and star of early silent films) and spring him to stardom. Actually, the father was Frederick Tyrone Power and he dropped the first name. Nowadays, there's yet another Tyrone Power and he uses the "junior" whereas he should really be Tyrone Power III. He is seen briefly in COCOON. But enough background, what about the picture? Simon is a student at an Alpine finishing school with a reputation as being a no-nonsense institution. Marshall is the headmaster and Simon falls tete over sabots for him, even though he's almost twenty years her senior. She attends the spring fete and asks him to dance with her but he declines and she is embarrassed. A bit later, Marshall and his comely assistant, Chatterton, discover a love letter that was anonymously written to him and they seek to learn who wrote it. Once Simon is discovered as having been the author of the steamy missive, she laughs it off and says it was merely a letter to a sweetheart who existed only in her mind. Although having written it, she didn't intend to ever let it get to Marshall and she tells this to Chatterton, without knowing that Chatterton is also in love with Marshall. Because of the school's strict rules, a convening of a faculty committee censures Simon for the note and when they contact her mother, Simon races off to a sheer precipice known as Lover's Leap where lovers have been known to leap. Marshall finds Simon there, contemplating a jump into oblivion, and he realizes that what he thought was avuncular affection has now metamorphosed into love. Later, he tells Chatterton that he and Simon intend to get married. This stuns Chatterton, who responds by quitting her job. Now Simon understands that Chatterton has yearned for Marshall for many years. Simon decides that the only decent thing to do is pretend that her love for Marshall is of the puppy variety and she stays away from him until the day she is to graduate. Power, a handsome young count, arrives and takes her away at the graduation dance. Marshall is heartsick and runs after Simon, only to be informed that she doesn't want to see him and that Power's appearance was well-conceived to show Marshall that it was all over between them. Marshall goes back to Chatterton and asks her to stay on. She says she'll do that and it is presumed they will eventually get together once Marshall rids himself of the passion for Simon, not an easy thing. Marshall was a bit awkward in the role that James Mason did in LOLITA, that of an older man with a teenage love. Simon was breathtaking and demonstrated a wide range of acting ability. Power was in the film only as a counterpoint but his screen persona registered so strongly that Darryl F. Zanuck gave him larger roles in the next few months and he was soon one of Fox's leading actors. All he said in GIRLS' DORMITORY was, "Can I have this dance?" and the preview cards overwhelmingly mentioned him above everyone else in the picture. Such is the power of stardom.

p, Raymond Griffith; d, Irving Cummings; w, Gene Markey (based on the play by Ladislaus Fodor); ph, Merritt Gerstad; m, Charles Maxwell, Arthur Lange; ed,

Jack Murray; md, Lange; art d, Hans Peters; set d, Thomas Little; cos, Gwen Wakeling.

Drama   **(PR:A   MPAA:NR)**

GIRLS FROM THUNDER STRIP, THE zero   (1966) 82m
                                          Borealis/American General c

Jody McCrea, Maray Ayres, Mick Mehas, Casey Kasem, Lindsay Crosby.

A mid-1960s drive-in picture which offered the usual doses of leather-clad bikers, beer-drinking rednecks, and sexy women. The girls of the title manage to get in the middle of a moonshine battle which leaves a number of people dead. A bottom-of-the-barrel addition to the biker genre. Another young lead played by McCrea, son of the handsome star of the 1940s Joel McCrea, and Frances Dee.

p, David L. Hewitt, Michael Mehas; d, Hewitt; w, Pat Boyette.

Action/Drama   **(PR:O   MPAA:NR)**

GIRLS! GIRLS! GIRLS!**½   (1962) 101m PAR c

Elvis Presley (Ross Carpenter), Stella Stevens (Robin Gantner), Jeremy Slate (Wesley Johnson), Laurel Goodwin (Laurel Dodge), Benson Fong (Kin Yung), Robert Strauss (Sam), Guy Lee (Chen Yung), Frank Puglia (Alexander Stavros), Lili Valenty (Mama Stavros), Beulah Quo (Mme. Yung), Barbara Beale (Leona), Betty Beall (Linda), Nestor Paiva (Arthur Morgan), Ann McCrea (Mrs. Morgan), Ginny Tiu (Mai Ling), Elizabeth Tiu (Tai Ling), Alexander Tiu, The Jordanaires.

GIRLS! GIRLS! GIRLS! was Presley's fourth movie of 1962, as he churned out musical after musical. This time he is a poor tuna boat fisherman in Hawaii, who also works as a nightclub singer to make enough dough to get his old man's sailboat out of hock. A singer, Stevens, and rich girl pretending to be poor, Goodwin, both want Presley's love, but he gives it to Goodwin. She buys his father's boat for him, and hurts his pride. Nevertheless, Elvis saves Goodwin from the Sleazy attentions of tuna boat owner Slate, and marries her. He ends up making her sell his father's boat, and they build their own. Musical numbers: "The Nearness of You" (Ned Washington, Hoagy Carmichael, sung by Stella Stevens), "Never Let Me Go" (Jay Livingston, Ray Evans, sung by Stevens), "Girls, Girls, Girls" (Jerry Leiber, Mike Stoller), "Return to Sender," "We're Coming In Loaded" (Otis Blackwell, Winfield Scott), "A Boy Like Me, A Girl Like You," "Song of the Shrimp," "Earth Boy," "The Walls Have Ears" (Sid Tepper, Roy C. Bennett), "Thanks to the Rolling Sea," "Because of You," "Where Do We Come From?" (Ruth Batchelor, Bob Roberts), "We'll Be Together, Mama" (Charles O'Curran, Dudley Brooks), "I Don't Wanna Be Tied" (Bill Giant, Bernie Baum, Florence Kaye), "I Don't Want To" (Janice Torre, Fred Spielman).

p, Hal B. Wallis; d, Norman Taurog; w, Edward Anhalt, Allan Weiss (based on a story by Weiss); ph, Loyal Griggs (Panavision, Technicolor); m, Joe Lilley; ed, Stanley I. Johnson; art d, Hal Pereira, Walter Tyler; set d, Sam Comer, Frank R. McKelvy; cos, Edith Head; ch, Charles O'Curran; makeup, Gary Morris.

Musical   Cas.   (PR:A   MPAA:NR)

GIRLS HE LEFT BEHIND, THE (SEE: GANG'S ALL HERE, THE, 1943)

GIRLS IN ACTION   (SEE: OPERATION DAMES, 1959)

GIRLS IN ARMS   (SEE: OPERATION BULLSHINE, 1963)

GIRLS IN CHAINS*½   (1943) 72m PRC bw

Arline Judge (Helen), Roger Clark (Frank Donovan), Robin Raymond (Rita), Barbara Pepper (Ruth), Dorothy Burgess (Mrs. Peters), Clancy Cooper (Marcus), Allan Byron, (Johnny Moon), Patricia Knox (Jean), Sidney Melton (Pinkhead), Russell Gaige (Dalvers), Emmet Lynn (Lionel Cleeter), Richard Clarke (Tom Havershield), Betty Blythe (Mrs. Grey), Peggy Stewart (Jerry), Beverly Boyd (George), Bob Hill (Dr. Orchard), Henry Hall (Judge Coolidge), Mrs. Gardener Crane (Mrs. McCarthy), Crane Whitley (Rev. Greene), Francis Ford (Jury Foreman).

A strange murder mystery that has the murderer revealed at the beginning of the film. The title refers to girls in a reformatory behind barbed wire. Clark plays a detective who helps Arline, the sister-in-law of a crook, Byron, get him behind bars. Judge is fired from her teaching job because her sister is married to Byron. Suddenly unemployed, she takes a job teaching the dangerous girls in the reformatory and there gets enough evidence on Byron, due to his illegal dealings with the corrupt superintendent of the institution, to convict him.

p, Peter Van Duinen; d, Edgar R. Ulmer; w, Albert Reich (based on a story by Ulmer); ph, Ira Morgan; m, Leo Erdody; ed, Charles Henkel, Jr.

Crime   **(PR:A   MPAA:NR)**

GIRLS IN PRISON*½   (1956) 86m Golden Slate/AIP bw

Richard Denning (Rev. Fulton), Joan Taylor (Anne Carson), Adele Jergens (Jenny), Helen Gilbert (Melanee), Lance Fuller (Paul Anderson), Jane Darwell (Matron Jamieson), Raymond Hatton (Pop Cadson), Phyllis Coates (Dorothy), Diana Darrin (Meg), Mae Marsh (Grandma), Laurie Mitchell (Phyllis), Diane Richards (Night Club Singer), Luana Walters (Female Guard), Riza Royce (Female Guard).

Taylor is sent to jail for a bank holdup she did not commit, and Denning is the prison chaplain who believes she was wronged. Other women prisoners, though, are sure she knows where a stolen $38,000 is buried and they plan to break out with Taylor in tow to lead them to the cache. An earthquake helps them in their break and the showdown comes when they run into Fuller, who was in on the original robbery and also is hunting the stolen money.

p, Alex Gordon; d, Edward L. Cahn; w, Lou Rusoff; ph, Frederick E. West; m, Ronald Stein; ed, Ronald Sinclair; m/l, "Tom's Beat," Stein, sung by Diane Richards.

Crime   **(PR:C   MPAA:NR)**

GIRLS IN THE NIGHT*½   (1953) 83m UNIV bw

Joyce Holden (*Georgia*), Glenda Farrell (*Alice Haynes*), Harvey Lembeck (*Chuck Haynes*), Patricia Hardy (*Hannah Haynes*), Glen Roberts (*Joe Spurgeon*), Don Gordon (*Irv Kelleher*), Jaclynne Greene (*Vera*), Anthony Ross (*Charlie Haynes*), Susan Odin (*Hilda Haynes*), Billy Wayne (*Bit*).

Boring account of juvenile delinquents that follows a poor family's struggles in trying to escape its surroundings by moving to a better neighborhood. The son rips off a blind man, who is not actually blind. Lembeck, the son, finds out that the "blind" man has been killed by the area bad guys. While the family struggles on with its own battles, Lembeck sets out to find the real killer and redeem himself.

p, Albert J. Cohen; d, Jack Arnold; w, Ray Buffum; ph, Carl Guthrie; m, Joseph Gershenson; ed, Paul Weatherwax; art d, Alexander Golitzen, Robert Boyle; ch, Hal Belfer.

Crime   (PR:C MPAA:NR)

GIRLS IN THE STREET*½   (1937, Brit.) 75m GFD bw
                                       (GB: LONDON MELODY)

Anna Neagle (*Jacqueline*), Tullio Carminati (*Marius Andreani*), Robert Douglas (*Nigel Taplow*), Horace Hodges (*Father Donnelly*), Grizelda Hervey (*Friend*), Miki Hood (*Marius*), Davina Craig (*Maid*), Joan Kemp-Welch (*Maid*), Leonard Snelling (*Organ Grinder's Son*), Arthur Chesney (*Marius' Butler*), Henry Wolston (*Snodgrass*).

Neagle, a street singer and dancer, gets into a heated argument with the chauffeur of Carminati, and ends up romancing the dashing ambassador. Trouble arises when Carminati is accused of spilling governmental secrets. It seems he took Neagle's former fiance, Douglas, into his confidence, and Douglas blabbed the information out of spite. Carminati resigns, but Neagle stays with him anyway. Pleasant fluff, nicely made all around.

p&d, Herbert Wilcox; w, Florence Tranter, Monckton Hoffe (based on a story by Ray Lewis); ph, F.A. Young; ed, Fred Wilson.

Musical   (PR:A MPAA:NR)

GIRLS IN UNIFORM, (1932)   (SEE: MAEDCHEN IN UNIFORM, 1932, Ger.)

GIRLS IN UNIFORM, 1965   (SEE: MAEDCHEN IN UNIFORM, 1965)

GIRLS NEVER TELL   (SEE: HER FIRST ROMANCE, 1951)

GIRLS OF PLEASURE ISLAND, THE**½   (1953) 95m PAR c

Don Taylor (*Lt. Gilmartin*), Leo Genn (*Roger Halyard*), Elsa Lanchester (*Thelma*), Philip Ober (*Col. Reade*), Joan Elan (*Violet Halyard*), Audrey Dalton (*Hester Halyard*), Dorothy Bromiley (*Gloria Halyard*), Peter Baldwin (*Pvt. Henry Smith*), Gene Barry (*Capt. Beaton*), A.E. Gould-Porter (*Rev. Bates*), Barry Bernard (*Wilkinson*), Richard Shannon, Leon Lontok, Michael Ross, Johnny Downs.

Bromiley, Dalton, and Elan live on a secluded South Pacific Island with their dad, Genn, when fifteen hundred U.S. Marines land in the closing days of WW II to build an airstrip. Genn doesn't like it because his daughters have never before met eligible men and they quickly become involved with the handsome young guys from the States. Dad loses his little war, of course, to red-blooded youth. A natural for plenty of comedy, nicely handled by all concerned.

p, Paul Jones; d, F. Hugh Herbert, Alvin Ganzer; w, Herbert (based on the novel *Pleasure Island* by William Maier); ph, Daniel Fapp, W. Howard Greene (Technicolor); m, Lyn Murray; ed, Ellsworth Hoagland; art d, Hal Pereira, Roland Anderson.

War Comedy   (PR:A MPAA:NR)

GIRLS OF SPIDER ISLAND (SEE: IT'S HOT IN PARADISE, 1962, Ger.)

GIRLS OF THE BIG HOUSE**   (1945) 68m REP bw

Lynne Roberts (*Jeanne Crail*), Virginia Christine (*Bernice*), Marian Martin (*Dixie*), Adele Mara (*Harriet*), Richard Powers (*Barton Sturgis*), Geraldine Wall (*Head Matron*), Tala Birell (*Alma Vlasek*), Norma Varden (*Mrs. Thelma Holt*), Stephen Barclay (*Smiley*), Mary Newton (*Dr. Gale Warren*), Erskin Sanford (*Prof. O'Neill*), Sarah Edwards (*Dormitory Matron*), Ida Moore (*Mother Fielding*), William Forrest (*District Attorney*), Verna Felton (*Agnes*).

Small-town woman Roberts is framed by a man she meets in a big-city night club and finds herself behind bars. The old timers don't take kindly to the newcomer, forcing two camps in the prison to spring up, which culminates in a murder. Roberts finally is freed by the efforts of her home town lawyer and an interesting women's prison film comes to a close. Two songs sung by the inmates in the prison's recreation room lift that segment of the picture into the extraordinary.

p, Rudolph E. Abel; d, George Archainbaud; w, Houston Branch; ph, John Alton; m, Joseph Dubin; ed, Arthur Roberts; md, Morton Scott; art d, Gano Chittenden; spec eff, Howard and Theodore Lydecker; m/l, "There's A Man In My Life," Jack Elliott, "Alma Mater," Sanford Green, June Carroll.

Drama   (PR:A MPAA:NR)

GIRLS OF LATIN QUARTER*   (1960, Brit.) 69m Border/New Realm c

Bernard Hunter (*Clive Smedley*), Jill Ireland (*Jill*), Sheldon Lawrence (*Mac*), Danny Green (*Hodgson*), Joe Baker (*Finch*), Mimi Pearce, Cherry Wainer, Sonya Cordeaux, Cuddly Dudley.

An empty musical about a mousy heir who must take over a farm before he can get the fortune willed to him. He does, and Ireland, with her dancing talent (she once danced with the Monte Carlo Ballet), helps him get what he is after.

p, O'Negus Fancey; d, Alfred Travers; w, Dick Vosburgh, Brad Ashton (based on a story by Travers, Bernard Hunter).

Musical   (PR:A MPAA:NR)

GIRLS OF THE ROAD*½   (1940) 61m COL bw

Ann Dvorak (*Kay Warren*), Helen Mack (*Mickey*), Lola Lane (*Elly*), Ann Doran (*Jerry*), Marjorie Cooley (*Irene*), Mary Field (*Mae*), Mary Booth (*Edna*), Madelon Grayson (*Annie*), Grace Lenard (*Stella*), Evelyn Young (*Sadie*), Bruce Bennett (*Officer Sullavan*), Eddie Laughton (*Footsy*), Don Beddoe (*Sheriff*), Howard Hickman (*Gov. Warren*).

A bizarre story about female hoboes during the Depression. Dvorak, the daughter of the governor, goes among them to learn the real story of their plight, and hitchhikes and cooks her meals over the campfire with the unluckies, and Beddoe, as the sheriff, doesn't make life for the drifters any easier.

d, Nick Grinde; w, Robert D. Andrews; ph, George Meehan; ed, Charles Nelson.

Drama   (PR:C MPAA:NR)

GIRLS ON PROBATION*   (1938) 63m WB bw

Jane Bryan (*Connie Heath*), Ronald Reagan (*Neil Dillon*), Sheila Bromley (*Hilda Engstrom*), Anthony Averill (*Tony Rand*), Henry O'Neill (*Judge*), Elisabeth Risdon (*Kate Heath*), Sig Rumann (*Roger Heath*), Dorothy Peterson (*Jane Lennox*), Susan Hayward (*Gloria Adams*), Larry Williams (*Terry Mason*), James Nolan (*Dave Warren*), Esther Dale (*Mrs. Engstrom*), Arthur Hoyt (*Mr. Engstrom*), Lenita Lane (*Marge*), Peggy Shannon (*Ruth*), Janet Shaw (*Inmate*), Kate Lawson (*Matron*), Brenda Fowler (*Head Matron*), Joseph Crehan (*Todd*), James Spottswood (*Public Defender*), Pierre Watkin (*Prosecuting Attorney*), Maud Lambert, Kate Lawson (*Matrons*), Jan Holm (*Girl Clerk*), Fern Barry, Sally Sage, Marian Alden, Paulette Evans, Clara Horton (*Prisoners*), Glen Cavender (*Cop*), Reid Kilpatrick (*Police Broadcaster*), Nat Carr (*Pawnbroker*).

Time is truly a relative commodity. Watch a great movie and two hours goes by in a flash. Watch a boring film and sixty three minutes feels like eternity. Such is the case with GIRLS ON PROBATION, an ordinary prison drama with little to recommend it other than Hayward's first decent role and the appearance of Reagan in the part of an attorney. Bryan is a sweet, naive kid who happens to be at a party where Hayward accuses her of stealing the gown she's wearing. Bryan is arrested for the theft and then we learn that Bromley, a pal of Bryan's, works at the shop where the gown was in for cleaning and had "lent" her the dress. Hayward withdraws the robbery accusation but the insurance company for the cleaning shop decides to go ahead and prosecute. Bryan is tried for grand larceny. Reagan believes her story and gets her off with a suspended sentence. But Bryan's father, Rumann, is livid and throws her out of his home. Bryan moves to another town and meets Bromley again. This time, Bromley is in cahoots with her boy friend, Averill, and they are in the midst of robbing a bank when the two girls re-encounter each other. Bryan is pushed into the car during the robbers' getaway and when the long arm of the law catches up with them, she is convicted as an accomplice and gets off with three years probation. She goes home, meets Reagan again, who is, by now, the assistant district attorney, and she takes a job in his office as his secretary. They also fall in love and all seems well until Bromley reappears and wants to blackmail Bryan. Unless she comes across with some money, Bromley will inform Reagan about Bryan's conviction. Bryan responds by telling the cops about the whereabouts of Averill, who has just escaped from jail. There's a huge gun battle and Averill is shot to death after having accidentally shot Bromley. With both of them dead, Bryan's secret is safe and she and Reagan can get married and raise a brood of little Clarence Darrows. From the above description, it seems like a lot of story in just over an hour but they managed to make it dull as dirt. Done better with Sylvia Sidney in YOU AND ME and only worth watching on TV if the alternative is test patterns or color bars.

p, Bryan Foy; d, William McGann, Harry Seymour; w, Crane Wilbur; ph, Arthur Todd; ed, Frederick Richards; art d, Hugh Reticker; cos, Howard Shoup.

Crime Drama   (PR:A MPAA:NR)

GIRLS ON THE BEACH**   (1965) 80m PAR c (AKA: SUMMER OF '64)

Martin West (*Duke*), Noreen Corcoran (*Selma*), Peter Brooks (*Stu*), Brian Wilson, Michael Love, Alan Jardin, Carl Wilson, Dennis Wilson (*Beach Boys*), Jerry Allison, Jerry Naylor, Sonny Curtis (*Crickets*), Arnold Lessing (*Frank*), Linda Marshall (*Cynthia*), Steven Rogers (*Brian*), Ann Capri (*Arlene*), Aron Kincaid (*Wayne*), Sheila Bromley (*Mrs. Winters*), Mary Mitchel (*Emily*), Gale Gerber (*Georgia*), Linda Saunders (*Patricia*), Mary Kate Denny (*Jenny*), Nan Morris (*1st Sorority Sister*), Lana Wood (*Bonnie*), Pat Deming, Michele Corcoran, Larry Merrill (*Dancers*), Dennis Jones (*Guy 1*), Bill Sampson (*Guy 2*), Carol Jean Lewis (*Dancer*), Joan Conrath (*2nd Sorority Sister*), Rick Newton (*Parking Lot Attendant*), Lesley Gore (*Herself*), Nancy Spry (*Betty*), Ron Kennedy (*M.C.*), Bruno Ve Sota (*Pops*), Lynn Cartwright (*Waitress*), Richard Miller (*1st Waiter*), Leo Gordon (*2nd Waiter*), Helen Kay Stephens (*Contestant and Dancer*).

The Alpha Beta sorority is trying to raise $10,000 during Easter vacation in sunny California to pay off the mortgage on their sorority house. They plan a benefit musical performance and are fooled into thinking the Beatles will make an appearance. They do not, of course, so the girls work up a convincing imitation and come out on top with the money. Songs include: "Leave Me Alone," "It's Gotta Be You," "I Don't Want to Be a Loser" (sung by Lesley Gore), "Lonely Sea, La Bamba" (performed by the Crickets), "Girls On the Beach," "Little Honda" (sung by the Beach Boys).

p, Harvey Jacobson; d, William Witney; w, David Malcolm; ph, Arch R. Dalzell (Pathe Color); m, Cary Usher; ed, Morton Tubor.

Musical   (PR:A MPAA:NR)

GIRLS ON THE LOOSE**½   (1958) 77m Jewel Enterprises/UNIV bw

Mara Corday (*Vera Parkinson*), Lita Milan (*Marie Williams*), Barbara Bostock (*Helen*), Mark Richman (*Lt. Bill Hanley*), Joyce Barker (*Joyce Johanneson*), Abby Dalton (*Agnes Clark*), Jon Lormer (*Doctor*), Ronald Green (*Danny*), Fred Kruger (*Mr. Grant*), Paul Lambert (*Joe*), Monica Henreid (*Cigarette Girl*).

The title implies a sex farce but this is a deadly story about five women who band together to steal a $200,000 payroll. Led by Corday, the gang members hide the loot in the woods and soon conscience rises to the fore. Dalton is about to squeal but is murdered. Internal squabbling tears the gang apart. All meet violent ends as they try to stop one another from going to the cops. Two awkward songs mar the forward movement of this interesting psychological drama and melodrama appears now and then. But popular actor Henreid's direction is fine when he lets the story unfold naturally. Monica Henreid, the Cigarette Girl, is his daughter.

p, Harry Rybnick, Richard Kay; d, Paul Henreid; w, Alan Friedman, Dorothy Raison, Allen Rivkin (story by Friedman, Raison, Julian Harmon; ph, Philip Lathrop; ed, Edward Curtiss; m/l, "How Do You Learn to Love?" "I Was a Little Too Lonely," Jay Livingston, Ray Evans, Dixie Philpott, Ray Whitaker, Dolores Hampton.

Crime   **(PR:O   MPAA:NR)**

GIRLS PLEASE!*½   (1934, Brit.) 73m British and Dominions/UA bw

Sydney Howard (*Trampleasure*), Jane Baxter (*Renee van Hoffenheim*), Meriel Forbes (*Ann Arundel*), Edward Underdown (*Jim Arundel*), Peter Gawthorne (*Van Hoffenhiem*), Lena Halliday (*Miss Prout*), Cecily Oates (*Miss Kinter*), Sybil Arundale (*Matron*), Moore Marriott (*Oldest Inhabitant*), Neva Carr-Glyn, Edna Earle.

Howard stars in this sub-par comedy as a gym teacher who comes between the romance of Baxter and Underdown, a pair of college students. The situation gets crazier and crazier until Howard is forced to disguise himself as the school's headmistress.

p, Herbert Wilcox; d, Jack Raymond; w, R.P. Weston, Bert Lee, Jack Marks (based on a story by Michael Hankinson, Basil Mason).

Comedy   **(PR:A   MPAA:NR)**

GIRLS' SCHOOL*½   (1938) 71m COL bw

Anne Shirley (*Natalie Freeman*), Nan Grey (*Linda Simpson*), Ralph Bellamy (*Michael Hendragin*), Dorothy Moore (*Betty Fleet*), Gloria Holden (*Miss Laurel*), Marjorie Main (*Miss Armstrong*), Margaret Tallichet (*Gwennie*), Peggy Moran (*Myra*), Kenneth Howell (*Edgar*), Cecil Cunningham (*Miss Brewster*), Pierre Watkin (*Mr. Simpson*), Doris Kenyon (*Mrs. Simpson*), Heather Thatcher (*Miss Bracket*), Virgina Howell (*Miss MacBeth*), Joanne Tree (*Sudie*), Martha O'Driscoll, Sherrie Overton.

A winning light comedy about some rich girls in a boarding school for proper young ladies. The delightful plot twist finds one of the prim young women planning to elope with a youthful dolt, but her scheme sinks under a load of irony when the school's most popular teacher runs off with the boy instead and gets married. Lots of ancillary fun in keeping the thin story moving.

p, Samuel Marx; d, John Brahm; w, Tess Slesinger, Richard Sherman (based on a play by Slesinger); ph, Franz Planer; m, Gregory Stone; ed, Otto Mayer; md, Morris Stoloff; art d, Stephen Goosson.

Comedy   **(PR:A   MPAA:NR)**

GIRLS' SCHOOL*   (1950) 61m COL bw

Joyce Reynolds (*Peggy Donovan*), Ross Ford (*Barry Sheppard*), Laura Elliot (*Lucille Farnsworth*), Julia Dean (*Emily Matthews*), Thurston Hall (*Col. Selby Matthews*), Leslie Banning (*Martha Frawley*), Joyce Otis (*Connie Watkins*), Louise Beavers (*Hatti*), Sam McDaniel (*Willie Jackson*), Wilton Graff (*Dave Vickers*), Grant Calhoun (*Carter Ingraham*), Mary Ellen Kay (*Elspeth*), Boyd Davis (*Ephraim Baines*), Harry Cheshire (*Calhoun Robie*), Joan Vohs (*Jane Ellen*), Diantha Pattison (*Louise*), Toni Newman (*Henrietta*).

Reynolds' father dies and leaves her $30,000 of his gambling winnings. She flees to a girls' finishing girl when she thinks her dad's partner is after the money. A tradeoff of sorts is made when the money later is returned to the victim who lost it and Reynolds finds love with Ford, a gas station owner. Scarcely fuel enough in this one to bring it home safely.

p, Wallace MacDonald; d, Lew Landers; w, Brenda Weisberg (based on a story by Jack Henley); ph, Henry Freulich; ed, Edwin Bryant; md, Mischa Bakaleinikoff.

Drama   **(PR:A   MPAA:NR)**

GIRLS' TOWN**   (1942) 66m PRC bw

Edith Fellows (*Sue*), June Storey (*Myra*), Kenneth Howell (*Kenny*), Alice White (*Nicky*), Anna Q. Nilsson (*Mother*), Warren Hymer (*Joe*), Vince Barnett (*Dimitri*), Paul Dubov (*Fontaine*), Peggy Ryan (*Penny*), Dolores Diane (*Sally*), Helen McCloud (*Mayor*), Bernice Kay (*Ethyl*), Charlie Williams (*Coffer*).

Nilsson is an ex-actress who runs a boarding house for other aspiring starlets. Storey is the beauty queen, who will walk over anyone to get into films, including her loving sister (Fellows) and the woman who gave her a place to stay. Fellows is the younger sister just along for the ride who has to put up with her prima donna sister and all of her actions. Another of the many films made in wartime Hollywood whose sole point seemed to be to utilize the talents of women in the absence of actors who had gone off to war.

p, Lou Brock, Jack Schwarz; d, Victor Halperin; w, Gene Kerr, Victor McLeod; ph, Arthur Reed; m, Lee Zahler; ed, Martin G. Cohn.

Drama   **(PR:A   MPAA:NR)**

GIRLS' TOWN*   (1959) 92m MGM bw (AKA: THE INNOCENT AND THE DAMNED)

Mamie Van Doren (*Silver Morgan*), Mel Torme (*Fred Alger*), Paul Anka (*Jimmy Parlow*), Ray Anthony (*Dick Culdane*), Maggie Hayes (*Mother Veronica*), Cathy Crosby (*Singer*), Gigi Perreau (*Serafina Garcia*), Elinor Donahue (*Mary Lee Morgan*), Gloria Talbott (*Vida*), Sheilah Graham (*Sister Grace*), Jim Mitchum (*Charley Boy*), Dick Contino (*Stan Joyce*), Harold Lloyd, Jr. (*Chip Gardner*), Charles

Chaplin, Jr. (*Joe Cates*), The Platters (*Themselves*), Peggy Moffitt (*Flo*), Jody Fair (*Gloria Barker*), Peter Leeds (*Michael Clyde*), Nan Peterson (*Carhop*), Grabowski (*Skin*), Karen Von Unge, Susanne Sydney, Nancy Root, Wendy Wilde, Bobi Byrnes, Gloria Rhoads, Phyllis Douglas.

Another bad-girls-doing-carnal-things exploitation film from Albert Zugsmith. Van Doren is sent to a correctional institution run by nuns, for her part in the accidental death of a young man. There she falls under the influence of the nuns and drops her tough exterior and all works out in the end. A host of popular stars of the time helped sell this one at the box office, but its tawdriness lingers to embarrass them all. With one song, "Wish It Were Me" (Buck Ram).

p, Albert Zugsmith; d, Charles Haas; w, Robert Smith (based on a story by Robert Hardy Andrews); ph, John L. Russell; m, Van Alexander; ed, Leon Barsha; md, Alexander; art d, Hans Peters, Jack T. Collis.

Drama   **(PR:C   MPAA:NR)**

GIRLS UNDER TWENTY-ONE*½   (1940) 64m COL bw

Bruce Cabot (*Smiley Ryan*), Rochelle Hudson (*Frances White*), Paul Kelly (*Johnny Cane*), Tina Thayer (*Jennie White*), Roberta Smith (*Sloppy Krupnik*), Lois Verner (*Fatso Cheruzzi*), Beryl Vaughan (*Marge Dolan*), Joanne Tree (*Gertie Dolan*), Debbie Ellis (*Tessa Mangione*), William Edmunds (*Tony Mangione*), John Dilson (*Albert Carter*), John Tyrell (*Rusty*).

Six girls with a tough streak running through them try to emulate Thayer's sister, Hudson, who has married a gangster and lives high on the hog until she is railroaded to prison through her association with the hood. When she is free again she gets involved with old flame Kelly, who reforms her. Then she tries to reform the other girls but it is not until one of them is killed during a pilfering expedition in a department store that the others see the light and become decent persons again. Story stands tall and stays that way until the thrilling finish.

p, Ralph Cohn; d, Max Nosseck; w, Jay Dratler, Fanya Foss; ph, Barney McGill; m, M.W. Stoloff; ed, Charles Nelson.

Crime   **(PR:A   MPAA:NR)**

GIRLS WILLS BE BOYS*½   (1934, Brit.) 70m Associated British/ Alliance bw

Dolly Haas (*Pat Caverley*), Cyril Maude (*Duke of Bridgwater*), Esmond Knight (*Geoffrey Dawson*), Irene Vanbrugh (*Princess of Ehrenstein*), Edward Chapman (*Grey*), Ronald Ward (*Bernard*), Charles Paton (*Sanders*), H.F. Maltby, Alfred Wellesley.

Maude is the crusty duke who secludes himself on an all-male estate after his son runs off with a foreign dancer. He receives a letter and a picture of a young man named Pat (Haas). Pat is actually Patricia and the predictable situations and laughs occur. The duke's secretary wouldn't dare bring a woman to his boss but Haas shows up at the estate anyway and poses as the duke's grandson. Thinking he/she's too skinny, grandpa puts Haas on a strict exercise program under the tutelage of the steward of the estate. Only after rescuing her in a swimming crisis (she went in nude) does the steward find out the secret. Of course, they fall in love. Grandpa is none too happy, but eventually laughs it off. Another fun-producer for the British public by French-born director Marcel Varnel.

p, Walter C. Mycroft; d, Marcel Varnel; w, Kurt Siodmak, Clifford Grey, Roger Burford (based on the play "The Last Lord" by Siodmak); ph, Claude Friese-Greene, Ronald Neame; ed, A.S. Bates.

Comedy   **(PR:A   MPAA:NR)**

GIRLY   (SEE: MUMSY, NANNY, SONNY AND GIRLY, 1970, Brit.)

GIRO CITY*   (1982, Brit.) 102m Silvarealm-channel 4-Redifuusion/Cinegate c (AKA: AND NOTHING BUT THE TRUTH)

Glenda Jackson (*Sophie*), Jon Finch (*O'Mally*), Kenneth Colley (*Martin*), James Donnelly (*James*), Emrys James (*Williams*), Karen Archer (*Brigitte*), Simon Jones (*Henderson*), Huw Ceredig (*Elwyn Davies*), Alun Lewis (*Photographer*), Dermot Crowley (*Flynne*), Bruce Alexander, Robert Austin, Frank Baker, Gerwyn Baker, Valerie Baker, Colette Baker, David Beames, James Benson, Bob Blythe, Norman Caro, Simon Coady, Philip Compton, Peter Halliday, Jennifer Hill, William Ingrams, John Kearney, Sophie Kind, Michael Lees, Sharon Morgan, Marion McLoughlin, Roger Nott, Robert Pugh, David Quilter, Celestine Randall, Madhav Sharma, Tallulah Turney, Arthur Whybrow, Matthew Long, Elisabeth Lynne.

Corruption and the attitudes fostered by television come under close scrutiny in this British thriller. A farm family in South Wales takes on the town government which is given kickbacks by a huge corporation to stay on the land. Jackson and Finch, a filmmaker and a reporter, go after the story and encounter obstacles thrown out by their own executives and corporate bigwigs bent on hiding the story. The drama comes as Jackson and Finch go on to take a look at the Irish Republican Army, another hot topic no one wants them to touch. Jackson and Finch are superb and give the audience something to think about on how opinions are formed.

p, Sophi Balhetchet, David Payne; d&w, Karl Francis; ph, Curtis Clark; m, Alun Francis; ed, Neil Thomson; art d, Jamie Leonard.

Drama   **(PR:C   MPAA:NR)**

GIT!**½   (1965) 92m World-Cine/EM c

Jack Chaplain (*Deke*), Heather North (*Elaine*), Leslie Bradley (*Finney*), Richard Webb (*Andrew Garrett*), Hannah Landy (*Mrs. Finney*), Emory Parnell (*T.C. Knox*), Joseph Hamilton (*Jed*), Richard Valentine (*District Attorney*), Jeff Burton (*Police Sergeant*), Sherry Moreland (*Dr. Allen*), Shug Fisher (*Sam Lewis*), Seldom Seen Sioux (*Rock, a Dog*).

Seventeen-year-old Chaplain saves a dog from being killed, and with the help of North trains it to become a hunting dog. Passable for kid viewers, and eminently viewable in the sequences devoted to training the dog.

p&d, Ellis Kadison; w, Homer McCoy (based on the story by McCoy, Kadison); ph, Gordon Avil (Technicolor); m, Phillip Lambro; ed, Donald Tait; md, Lambro; set d, Kenneth Tolman; m/l, "Git!" Leon Thomas, "No Drums, No Trumpets!" Phillip Landro, Ellis Kadison, "Where I Belong," Llyn Paul, C.C. Jones.

Children's Drama   **(PR:AAA MPAA:NR)**

GIT ALONG, LITTLE DOGIES*   (1937) 60m REP bw

Gene Autry (*Himself*), Smiley Burnette (*Frog*), Maple City Four (*Themselves*), Judith Allen (*Doris*), Weldon Heyburn (*Wilkins*), William Farnum (*Maxwell*), Willy Fung (*Sing Low*), Carleton Young (*Man*), Will and Gladys Ahearn (*Themselves*), The Cabin Kids (*Themselves*), G. Raymond Nye, Frankie Marvin, George Morrell, Horace B. Carpenter, Rose Plummer, Earle Dwire, Lynton Brent, Jack Kirk, Al Taylor, Frank Ellis, Jack C. Smith, Murdock McQuarrie, Oscar Gahan, Monte Montague, Sam McDaniel, Eddie Parker, Bob Burns, Champion the Horse.

The sparse plot of this Autry outing deals with a war between cattle ranchers and oilmen. Autry leads the ranchers, who are trying to prevent well-drilling because it will poison the creek their herds drink from. He changes his mind, however, when he learns that the well will bring a railroad to the town. Heyburn, the oil driller, is stalling bringing in the well until his partner, the town banker, runs out of funds, thus giving Heyburn control of the well. Autry thwarts the plan and wins the love of the banker's daughter, Allen. A lot of warbling, but little action makes this one turn up lame. (See GENE AUTRY series, Index.)

p, Armand Schaefer; d, Joseph Kane; w, Dorrell McGowan, Stuart McGowan; ph, Gus Peterson; ed, Tony Martinelli; m/l, Sam H. Stept, Sidney Mitchell, Fleming Allen, Smiley Burnette, the McGowans.

Western/Musical   **Cas.**   **(PR:A MPAA:NR)**

GIU LA TESTA   (SEE: DUCK, YOU SUCKER!, 1972, Ital.)

GIULIETTA DEGLI SPIRITI (SEE: JULIET OF THE SPIRITS, 1975, Ital.)

GIULIO CEASRE IL CONQUISTATORE DELLE GALLIE
       (SEE: CAESAR THE CONQUEROR, 1963, Ital.)

GIUSEPPE VENDUTO DAI FRATELLI   (SEE: STORY OF JOSEPH AND HIS BRETHREN, THE, 1962, Ital.)

GIVE A DOG A BONE*   (1967, Brit.) 77m Westminster/MRA c

Ronnie Stevens (*Ringo*), Robert Davies (*Mickey Merry*), Ivor Danvers (*Mr. Space*), Richard Warner (*Rat King*), Bryan Coleman (*Lord Swill*), Len Maley (*Pa Merry*), Patricia O'Callaghan (*Ma Merry*).

Unimpressive final effort for Cass, not one of Britain's more prominent film artists, is an inane conception taking the form of a boy and his dog story. With the help of his dog, a boy battles a vicious rat that has dreams of taking over the world from the human species.

p,d&w, Henry Cass (based on the play by Peter Howard).

Fantasy   **(PR:A MPAA:NR)**

GIVE A GIRL A BREAK**½   (1953) 81m MGM c

Marge Champion (*Madelyn Corlane*), Gower Champion (*Ted Sturgis*), Debbie Reynolds (*Suzy Doolittle*), Helen Wood (*Joanna Moss*), Bob Fosse (*Bob Dowdy*), Kurt Kasznar (*Leo Belney*), Richard Anderson (*Burton Bradshaw*), William Ching (*Anson Pritchett*), Laurene Tuttle (*Mrs. Doolittle*), Larry Keating (*Felix Jordan*), Donna Martell (*Janet Hallson*).

This harmless little musical has three would-be stage stars, Marge Champion, Reynolds, and Wood, who compete for a part in a big Broadway musical, directed by Gower Champion, when the star, Martell, walks out. To complicate matters, all three girls have the support of a different production staff member. Lots of singing and dancing results, and in the end it is Reynolds who wins out. Director Donen demonstrates his usual flair, with strong support from Fosse and Gower Champion. Musical numbers: "Give a Girl a Break," "In Our United State," "It Happens Every Time," "Nothing is Impossible," "Applause, Applause" (Ira Gershwin, Burton Lane), "Challenge Dance" (Andre Previn, Saul Chaplin).

p, Jack Cummings; d, Stanley Donen; w, Albert Hackett, Frances Goodrich (based on a story by Vera Caspary); ph, William Mellor (Technicolor); ed, Adrienne Fazan; md, Andre Previn, Saul Chaplin; art d, Cedric Gibbons, Paul Groesse; ch, Stanley Donen, Gower Champion.

Musical   **(PR:A MPAA:NR)**

GIVE AND TAKE*½   (1929) 81m UNIV bw

Jean Hersholt, George Sidney, George Lewis, Sharon Lynn, Charles Miller, Sam Hardy.

Frustratingly stagey comedy-drama which takes skilled actors Hersholt and Sidney and turns them into statues who must remain still for fear of lousing up the all-important sound recording. Hersholt plays the owner of a fruit cannery who is attacked by employees threatening a strike that would ruin his business. Things begin to look up when kindly mogul Hardy comes to the rescue and offers to save the business by putting in a large order. Unfortunately, Handy turns out to be an escaped looney-tune, which throws everyone into a panic. Luckily it all turns out well when Hardy proves he's sane and rich. While the basic material is funny the stiffness of the presentation saps vitality from the situations.

d, William Beaudine; w, Harvey Thew, Albert DeMond (based on a play by Aaron Hoffman); m, Joseph Cherniavsky.

Drama   **(PR:A MPAA:NR)**

GIVE AND TAKE   (SEE: SINGING IN THE CORN, 1946)

GIVE 'EM HELL, HARRY!***½ (1975) 102m THEATRE TELEVISION c

James Whitmore (*Harry S. Truman*).

This is the filmed version of Whitmore's one-man show that he has toured around the country for many seasons. Truman was a president who grew to meet the challenge of the most important position in the world. Looking back as his presidency through the mire of Nixon, the failure of Johnson, the incompetence of Ford and Carter, and the imperious terms for Reagan, he is brought to life brilliantly by Whitmore (who did the same as Teddy Roosevelt and Will Rogers) under the guiding hand of director Binder, a TV veteran. Shot at a Seattle theater, Gallu's script crackles with wit and two performances which were shot are craftily edited into one piece of film by Binder. By the time the evening is over, you'll feel that you spent it with a real, live Harry Truman and that's the best compliment to give this movie. Whitmore is flawless as he jumps, glides, and bounces his way through Truman's life in a spirited and rollicking display of acting techniques that young thespians would be wise to study.

p, Al Ham, Joseph E. Bluth; d&e, Steve Binder; w, Samuel Gallu; ph, Ken Palius (Technicolor); set d, James Hamilton.

Comedy/Drama   **Cas.**   **(PR:A MPAA:G)**

GIVE HER A RING*   (1936, Brit.) 65m BIP bw

Clifford Mollison (*Paul Hendrick*), Wendy Barrie (*Karen Swenson*), Zelma O'Neal (*Trude Olsen*), Erik Rhodes (*Otto Brune*), Bertha Belmore (*Miss Hoffman*), Olive Blakeney (*Mrs. Brune*), Diamond Brothers (*Repair Men*), Nadine March (*Karen's Friend*), Jimmy Godden (*Uncle Rifkin*), Syd Crossley (*Gustav*), Richard Hearne (*Drunk*), Stewart Granger (*Diner*), Maurice Winnick's Ciro's Club Band (*Themselves*).

A poor British attempt at an American-1930s-style musical, GIVE HER A RING tells the story of some telephone switchboard operators who tend to get involved in the love lives of the people who call them for help. Barrie plays one of the operators who falls in love with her boss, Mollison. Songs are easily forgotten, and that's not good in a musical.

p, Walter C. Mycroft; d, Arthur Woods; w, Clifford Grey, Ernst Wolff, Marjorie Deans, Wolfgang Wilhelm (based on the play "Fraulein Falsch Verbunden," by H. Rosenfeld); ph, Claude Friese-Greene, Ronald Reame; m, Harry Acres; ed, E.B. Jarvis; art d, W. Macdonald Sutherland;; m/l Grey, Hans May.

Musical   **(PR:A MPAA:NR)**

GIVE HER THE MOON*** (1970, Fr./Ital.) 92m Artistes Associes-P.E.A./ UA c (LES CAPRICES DE MARIE)

Philippe Noiret (*Gabriel*), Bert Convy (*Broderick MacPower*), Dorothy Marchini (*Dorothy Golden*), Valentina Cortese (*Madeleine de Lepine*), Fernand Gravey (*Capt. Ragot*), Marthe Keller (*Marie Panneton*), Jean-Pierre Marielle (*Leopold Panneton*), Didi Perego (*Aurore Panneton*), Henri Cremieux (*Postman*), Francoise Perier (*Jean-Jules de Lepine*).

An original and strangely funny film about a millionaire (Convy) who decides to go to the small French town of Angevine to marry the winner of a beauty contest (Noiret). Though she has a beau, Noiret agrees to see Convy, who tries to charm her by moving her entire village to his New York home. The trick is set up on Bedloe's Island and becomes a hit with the tourist trade. He learns his lesson, however, and sends the French back to France, and Noiret back to her true love. Wonderfully funny director de Broca (THAT MAN FROM RIO) has assembled an interesting and perfect cast with Noiret (ZAZIE), Cortese (DAY FOR NIGHT) and TV game show veteran Convy, who oddly enough fits the bill here. A fine score from Georges Delerue.

p, Christian Ferry; d, Philippe de Broca; w, de Broca, Daniel Boulanger; ph, Jean Penzer (De Luxe Color); m, Georges Delerue; ed, Henri Lanoe; set d, Theo Meurisse; cos, Baba; makeup, Jackie Reynal.

Comedy   **(PR:A MPAA:G)**

GIVE ME A SAILOR**½   (1938) 71m PAR bw

Martha Raye (*Letty Larkin*), Bob Hope (*Jim Brewster*), Betty Grable (*Nancy Larkin*), Jack Whiting (*Walter Brewster*), J.C. Nugent (*Mr. Larkin*), Clarence Kolb (*Capt. Tallant*), Nana Bryant (*Mrs. Brewster*), Emerson Treacy (*Meryl*), Bonnie Jean Churchill (*Ethel May Brewster*), Kathleen Lockhart (*Mrs. Hawks*), Ralph Sanford (*Ice Man*), Edward Earle (*1st Businessman*), Eddie Kane (*2nd Businessman*).

Nice musical farce concerns a love triangle involving two pairs of siblings, Hope and Whiting, who are fellow officers in the Navy, and Raye and Grable, who live on shore. The four meet while the brothers are on leave. Whiting falls for Grable, but Raye is smitten with Whiting, while Hope wants Raye and Whiting to get together so he will be able to worm his way into Grable's good graces. Hope coaches Raye on how to get Whiting interested in her, but nothing seems to work until a photograph of Raye accidentally turns up in a best legs contest. Raye garners a lot of attention from the picture, and is finally able to turn Whiting's head. Their relationship almost leads to a wedding, but the couples get confused at the last second, resulting in a Raye and Hope and a Grable and Whiting walk down the aisle. Songs include: "What Goes Here in My Heart?" "A Little Kiss at Twilight," "Give Me a Sailor," "The US And You," "It Don't Make Sense" (Ralph Rainger, Leo Robin).

p, Jeff Lazarus; d, Elliott Nugent; w, Doris Anderson, Frank Butler (based on a play by Anne Nichols); ph, Victor Milner; ed, William Shea; md, Boris Morros; art d, Hans Dreier, Earl Hedrick; ch, LeRoy Prinz.

Musical/Comedy   **(PR:A MPAA:NR)**

GIVE ME MY CHANCE**   (1958, Fr.) 95m Sirius (DONNEZ-MOI MA CHANCE)

Michele Mercier (*Nicole*), Nadine Tallier (*Kiki*), Danick Patisson (*Brigitte*), Ivan Desny (*Gilbert*), Francois Guerin (*Georges*), George Chamaret (*Father*).

Mercier is a young girl who wins a contest that brings her from her country home to a Paris film studio. She fails her screen test but keeps on rehearsing in hopes of another try. But an unscrupulous studio employee uses the girl and she decides to kill herself. At the last minute her finance comes to her rescue, bringing a spanking new movie contract. The story is all formula as are the production values. Mercier shows some talent in the lead, though, like her character, she could use a few more acting lessons.

p, Jacques Roitfeld; d, Leonide Moguy; w, Andre and Georges Tabet, Moguy; ph, Maurice Barry; ed, Henri Taverna.

Drama **(PR:C MPAA:NR)**

GIVE ME THE STARS** (1944, Brit.) 90m BN/Anglo-American bw

Leni Lynn *(Toni Martin)*, Will Fyffe *(Hector McTavish)*, Jackie Hunter *(Lyle Mitchell)*, Olga Lindo *(Lady Lester)*, Emrys Jones *(Jack Ross)*, Margaret Vyner *(Patricia Worth)*, Antony Holles *(Achille Lebrun)*, Grace Arnold *(Mrs. Gossage)*, Patric Curwen *(Sir John Worth)*, Joss Ambler *(George Burns)*, Hilda Bayley *(Mrs. Ross)*, Angela Glynne *(Janie)*, Robert Griffith, Johnnie Schofield, Janet Morrison, Hal Gordon, David Trickett, George Merritt, David Keir, Alan Johnstone, Stanley Paskin, Harry Herbert, Sidney Arnold, George Spence, Larry Jay, Ben Williams, Vi Kaley, Desmond Roberts, Kenneth Mosely, Peter Lowry, Jack Williams, George Pughe, Jack May, Trixie Scales, Philip Hillman, Brookes Turner, Keith Shepherd.

Sappy treatment of a story in which Lynn gets her chance to hit the big time at the expense of her down-and-out uncle who is unable to make his music hall performances. The girl goes all the way from the U.S. to England to find her uncle in a state of drunkenness, and tries to reform him. Alas, he is injured in an accident and she takes over, winning wide acclaim.

p, Fred Zelnik; d, Maclean Rogers; w, Rogers, Austin Melford (based on the story by A. Hilarius and Rudolf Bernauer); ph, James Wilson.

Musical/Drama **(PR:A MPAA:NR)**

GIVE ME YOUR HEART*½ (1936) 77m Cosmopolitan/WB bw (GB: SWEET ALOES; AKA: I GIVE MY HEART)

Kay Francis *(Belinda Warren)*, George Brent *(Jim Baker)*, Roland Young *(Tubbs Barrow)*, Patric Knowles *(Robert Melford)*, Henry Stephenson *(Edward, Lord Farrington)*, Frieda Inescort *(Rosamond Melford)*, Helen Flint *(Dr. Florence Cudahy)*, Zeffie Tilbury *(Miss Esther Warren)*, Elspeth Dudgeon *(Alice Dodd)*, Halliwell Hobbes *(Oliver Warren)*, Russ Powell *(Cab Driver)*, Edgar Norton *(Servant)*, Dick French, Ethel Sykes *(Guests)*, Bruce Warren *(Young Man)*, Elsa Peterson *(Young Woman)*, Louise Bates *(Hostess)*, Ed Mortimer *(Host)*, Carlyle Moore, Jr. *(Elevator Man)*, Phyllis Godfrey *(Maid)*, Eric Wilton *(Johnson the Butler)*, Demetrius Emanuel *(Waiter)*, Mitchell Ingraham *(Bartender)*, Alphonse Martel *(Dining Room Captain)*, Toekie Trigg *(Baby Edward)*, Helena Grant *(Nurse)*, Wayne and Teske *(Dance Team)*.

A well-made weepie that stars Francis as the woman torn by the decisions she must live with. Francis is a well-bred American woman who has fallen on hard times and is living with her stingy aunt, Tilbury. She enters into an affair with the son of an English lord, Knowles, who is married to invalid Inescort. Francis has a child by Knowles and decides to give it up so it may be raised by Knowles and Inescort, who is unable to have children. Francis flees to America and marries lawyer Brent and tells him nothing of her past, but still longs for her missing child. Young, a writer friend of Francis, effects a reunion and eventually all works out for the best.

d, Archie Mayo; w, Casey Robinson (based on the play, "Sweet Aloes," by Jay Mallory [Joyce Carey]); ph, Sid Hickox; ed, James Gibbons; md, Leo F. Forbstein; art d, Max Parker, C.M. Novi; cos, Orry-Kelly.

Drama **(PR:A MPAA:NR)**

GIVE MY REGARDS TO BROADWAY*** (1948) 89m FOX c

Dan Dailey *(Bert)*, Charles Winninger *(Albert)*, Nancy Guild *(Helen)*, Charlie Ruggles *(Toby)*, Fay Bainter *(Fay)*, Barbara Lawrence *(June)*, Jane Nigh *(May)*, Charles Russell), Arthur Waldron, Jr.), Sig Ruman *(Dinkel)*, Howard Freeman *(Mr. Waldron)*, Herbert Anderson *(Frank Doty)*, Pat Flaherty *(Wallace)*, Harry Seymour *(Emcee)*, Paul Harvey *(Mr. Boyd)*, Lela Bliss *(Mrs. Boyd)*, Georgia Caine *(Mrs. Waldron)*, Matt McHugh *(Fan)*.

Nostalgic old-time vaudevillian Winninger, though retired from the stage and working in a factory, pines for the lost days when he and his wife Bainter were out on the boards knocking audiences dead. Though he and Bainter played such places as the Palace, they could never manage to become headliners, and it is to this end that Winninger raises his children as performers in the hope that vaudeville will return. Filled with a love for the stage and fanciful notions of show-biz fame, the kids actively participate in their father's fantasy. After 20 years of waiting, the family is finally given a chance to prove its mettle on stage. The act is a hit and the family is offered a 16-week booking, but the kids regrettably must turn down the contract because they have their own lives to live. In a powerful scene, son Dailey finally convinces his father that vaudeville is dead and the children should be allowed to live their own lives, not his fantasy. Winninger is brought to his senses and decides to stop trying to resurrect his past, content to simply cherish his memories. Badly received by critics who were tired of backstage musicals, GIVE MY REGARDS TO BROADWAY is a fine, small song-and-dance show that provides some fascinating footage of the mechanics involved in vaudeville and glimpses at several interesting old-time acts. The characterizations in the film are well drawn and solid, with standout performances by Winninger and Dailey as father and son. Songs include: "Give My Regards to Broadway" (George M. Cohan); "When Frances Dances With Me" (Benny Ryan, Sol Violinsky); "Let a Smile Be Your Umbrella" (Sammy Fain, Irving Kahal, Francis Wheeler); "Whispering" (John Schonberger, Richard Coburn, Vincent Rose); "Where Did You Get That Hat?" (J. W. Kelly); "Linger Awhile" (Harry Owens, Rose).

p, Walter Morosco; d, Lloyd Bacon; w, Samuel Hoffenstein, Elizabeth Reinhardt (based on a story by John Klempner); ph, Harry Jackson (Technicolor); ed, William Reynolds; md, Lionel Newman; art d, Lyle Wheeler, J. Russell Spencer; ch, Seymour Felix.

Musical **(PR:A MPAA:NR)**

GIVE OUT, SISTERS** (1942) 65m UNIV bw

The Andrews Sisters *(Themselves)*, Dan Dailey, Jr. *(Bob Edwards)*, Grace McDonald *(Gracie Waverly)*, Charles Butterworth *(Prof. Woof)*, Walter Catlett *(Gribble)*, Richard Davies *(Kendall)*, Donald O'Connor *(Don)*, Peggy Ryan *(Peggy)*, Edith Barrett *(Agatha Waverly)*, Fay Helm *(Susan Waverly)*, Marie Blake *(Blandina Waverly)*, Emmett Vogan *(Batterman the Costumer)*, Leonard Carey *(Jamison the Butler)*, Jivin' Jacks and Jills *(Themselves)*, Irving Bacon *(Dr. Howard)*, Leon Belasco *(Waiter)*, Robert Emmett Keane *(Peabody the Lawyer)*, Lorin Raker *(Dr. Bradshaw)*, Jason Robards, Sr. *(Drunk)*, Duke York *(Louie)*, Alphonse Martel *(Headwaiter)*, Emmett Smith *(Porter)*, Fred "Snowflake" Toones *(Valet)*, William Frawley *(Harrison)*.

Silly, witless musical that would have been better off as a short subject rather than attempting to make it into a full-length feature. The Andrews Sisters are starring at a nightclub and, in a totally unbelievable turn of events, some local dance students are asked to join in their latest show. One of them is Grace McDonald, a wealthy young heiress whose three spinster aunts refuse to allow her to be in show business (Barrett, Helm, Blake). Butterworth is the school proprietor and in bad financial trouble due to the shenanigans of his ex-partner, Catlett, so he can use the booking. Meanwhile, there's a love story brewing with McDonald and Dan Dailey (when he was still using the "junior" in his name) who is the nightclub's bandleader. Club owner Frawley needs to get permission from the old aunts because McDonald is underage, and when he goes to their home they are impersonated by the Andrews Sisters who dress up in biddy clothes. They give their assent and McDonald is allowed to work. Now the three real aunts find out about it and race to the club, fully expecting to raise a ruckus. Once there, they are entranced by the show and especially by McDonald and they join the cast for the finale on the stage as everyone sings "The Pennsylvania Polka" (Lester Lee, Zeke Manners). With a musical cast that includes Donald O'Connor, Peggy Ryan, Dan Dailey, and a number of other veterans, one would have hoped for more from this yawner but it was not to be. Songs from several sources include: "The New Generation" (Walter Donaldson), "Who Do You Think You're Fooling?" (Ray Stillwell, Ray Gold), "Jiggers, the Beat" (Al Lerner, Sid Robin), "You're Just A Flower From An Old Bouquet," and the aforementioned polka from Pennsylvania. Blake was Jeanette MacDonald's sister and had a running role as the telephone operator in the DR. KILDARE series of MGM films.

p, Bernard W. Burton; d, Edward F. Cline; w, Paul Gerard Smith, Warren Wilson (based on a story by Lee Sands, Fred Rath); ph, George Robinson; ed, Paul Landres; md, Charles Previn; art d, Jack Otterson; ch, John Mattison; m/l, Al Lerner, Sid Robin, Ray Stilwell, Ray Gold, Lester Lee, Zeke Manners, Walter Donaldson, Gwynee & Lucien Denni.

Musical/Comedy **(PR:A MPAA:NR)**

GIVE US THE MOON** (1944, Brit.) 95m GFD bw

Margaret Lockwood *(Nina)*, Vic Oliver *(Sascha)*, Peter Graves *(Peter Pyke)*, Roland Culver *(Ferdinand)*, Max Bacon *(Jacobus)*, Frank Cellier *(Pyke)*, Jean Simmons *(Heidi)*, Eliot Makeham *(Dumka)*, Iris Lang *(Tania)*, George Relph *(Otto)*, Gibb McLaughlin *(Marcel)*, Irene Handl *(Miss Haddock)*, Henry Hewitt *(Announcer)*, Alan Keith *(Raphael)*, Jonathan Field, John Salew, Rosamund Greenwood, Arty Ash, Frank Atkinson, George Hirste, Dorothy Bramhall, Jean Capra, Monte de Lyle, Gertrude Kaye, Pat(ricia) Owens, Harry Fowler, Charles Paton, Joy Millan, Lysbeth Sydney, Owen Fellows, Arthur Denton.

Lockwood is the head of a group of citizens who, three years after WW II is over, form a society in Soho that refuses to work. Graves comes across this group during his post-war wanderings and decides to run a hotel in the area. Despite the fact that the group has disavowed the work-ethic, the members slowly get involved in helping Graves run the business and chaos soon sweeps the area. Lovely Jean Simmons, then 14, was picked from among a group of dance students for the role of Heidi, Lockwood's sister.

p, Edward Black; d, Val Guest; w, Guest, Caryl Brahms, S.J. Simon, Howard Irving Young (based on the novel *The Elephant Is White* by Brahms, Simon); ph, Phil Grindrod.

Comedy **(PR:A MPAA:NR)**

GIVE US THIS DAY (SEE: SALT TO THE DEVIL, 1949, Brit.)

GIVE US THIS NIGHT** (1936) 73m PAR bw

Jan Kiepura *(Antonio)*, Gladys Swarthout *(Maria)*, Philip Merivale *(Marcello Bonelli)*, Benny Baker *(Tomasso)*, Michelette Burani *(Francesca)*, William Collier, Sr. *(Priest)*, Sidney Toler *(Carabiniere)*, John Miltern *(Vincenti)*, Alan Mowbray *(Forcellini)*, Mattie Edwards *(Elena)*, Chloe Douglas *(Lucrezia)*.

Singing fisherman Kiepura replaces over-the-hill tenor Mowbray as just the man to sing to Swarthout, leading diva for operatic impresario Merivale. It all turns out to be merely an opportunity to bill Swarthout and the Polish immigrant and plot falls to pieces before it's over. Action takes place in Sorrento and Naples and quickly becomes stilted as the pair raise their voices, mostly Kiepura's, throughout. Songs: "Sweet Melody of Night," "I Mean To Say I Love You," "My Love and I," "Music In the Night," "Give Us This Night," "Was There Ever A Voice" (Erich Wolfgang Korngold, Oscar Hammerstein II). After singlehandedly sinking the show, Kiepura never made another film in the U.S.

p, William LeBaron; d, Alexander Hall; w, Edwin Justus Mayer, Lynn Starling (based on a story by Jacques Bachrach); ph, Victor Milner, Gordon Jennings; ed, Elseworth Hoagland; art d, Hans Drier, Roland Anderson.

Musical **(PR:A MPAA:NR)**

GIVE US WINGS** (1940) 60m UNIV bw

Billy Halop (Tom), Huntz Hall (Pig), Gabriel Dell (String), Bernard Punsley (Ape), Bobby Jordan (Rap), Wallace Ford (York), Anne Gwynne (Julie), Victor Jory (Carter), Shemp Howard (Whitey), Milburn Stone (Tex), Harris Berger (Bud), Billy Benedict (Link), James Flavin (White), Addison Richards (Capt. Stern), Etta McDaniel (Mammy), Paul White (Servant), Milton Kibbee (Gas Station Attendant), Ben Lewis (Foreman).

Universal lumped together the "Dead End Kids" and the "Little Tough Guys" to come up with this routine comedy effort which sees the boys attempting to become pilots in the Army Air Corps by taking aeronautical mechanics classes in a study program. Unfortunately, they don't make it into the service, but crooked cropduster fleet operator Jory enthusiastically signs them up to fly his ancient deathtraps. Luckily, Ford refuses to allow them in the air without more training and he is proved correct when Jory overrides him and lets Jordan take a cropduster out, only to crash it. (See BOWERY BOYS series, Index.)

p, Ken Goldsmith; d, Charles Lamont; w, Arthur T. Horman, Robert Lee Johnson (based on a story "Crop Dusters" by Eliot Gibbons); ph, John Boyle; ed, Frank Gross; md, Charles Previn; art d, Jack Otterson; cos, Vera West.

Adventure   (PR:A   MPAA:NR)

GIVEN WORD, THE**½ (1964, Braz.) 98m Oswaldo Massaini
Productions/Lionex bw (O PAGADOR DE PROMESSAS)

Leonardo Vilar (Ze), Gloria Menezes (Rosa), Dionisio Azevedo (Father Olavo), Norma Bengell (Marli), Geraldo d'el Rey (Bonitao/"Handsome"), Roberto Ferreira (Dede), Othon Bastos (Reporter), Gilberto Marques (Galego), Carlos Torres (Monsignor), Antonio L. Sampaio (Coca), Milton Gaucho (Policeman), Joao Desordi (Detective), Irenio Simoes (Editor), Enoch Torres (Inspector), Maria Conceicao (Auntie), Veveldo Diniz (Church Clerk), Walter da Silveira, Napoleao Lopes Filho (Bishops), Copoeira Dancers of Cangiquinha.

Effective depiction of the creation of a martyr from a lowly peasant. Vilar plays the peasant who only intends to place a large wooden cross on a church's altar after traveling to a nearby village when his donkey is saved from death, but soon finds himself the seed of great commotion when the church refuses to accept his cross. (In Portuguese; English subtitles.)

p, Oswaldo Massaini; d&w, Anselmo Duarte (based on the story by Alfredo Dias Gomes); ph, Chick Fowle; m, Gabriel Migliori; ed, Carlos Coimbra; art d, Jose Teixeira de Araujo; spec eff, Josef Reindl; English subtitiles; Reine Dorian.

Drama   (PR:A   MPAA:NR)

GLAD RAG DOLL, THE** (1929) 70m WB bw

Dolores Costello (Annabel Lea), Ralph Graves (John Fairchild), Audrey Ferris (Bertha Fairchild), Albert Grant (Nathan Fairchild), Maude Turner Gordon (Aunt Fairchild), Thomas Ricketts (Admiral), Claude Gillingwater (Sam Underlane), Arthur T. Rankin (Jimmy Fairchild), Dale Fuller (Miss Peabody), Douglas Gerrard (Butler), Andre Beranger (Barry, an Actor), Lee Moran (Press Agent), Tom Kennedy (Manager Foley), Louise Beavers (Hannah), Stanley Taylor (Chauffeur).

One of director Curtiz' early talkies for Warner Bros. He directed well over a hundred films for this studio, including CASABLANCA (1943) and most of the Errol Flynn classics. This film has a shocker opening, with Costello's rejected suitor putting a pistol to his head and pulling the trigger. The initial scene is a Pirandello-like twist; it proves to be a stage play, with Costello the lovely heroine. After the performance, the lovesick Rankin visits Costello, bearing blossoms, and persuades her to visit his ancestral Philadelphia mansion. She meets his family: the stern and disapproving Graves, dirty old man Grant, snobbish but lascivious and kleptomaniacal Gordon, and the rest. Unfairly accorded the soubriquet of gold digger, she accepts money from attorney Gillingwater for the return of the wimpy Rankin's compromising missives, only to turn the full sum over to the foolish Rankin to keep him out of serious trouble. Ultimately, the sagacious showgirl's true colors are revealed to grave Graves, who woos and wins her. This title has little bearing on the story line; it was apparently selected solely to take advantage of the popularity of a then-current song hit, used thematically throughout the movie, "Glad Rag Doll" (Milt Ager, Dan Dougherty, Jack Yellin). The talented Beavers, as Costello's maid, belts out the blues classic "Some of These Days."

d, Michael Curtiz; w, Graham Baker (based on a story by Harvey Gates); ph, Byron Haskin.

Comedy   (PR:O   MPAA:NR)

GLAD TIDINGS*½ (1953, Brit.) Insignia/Eros bw

Barbara Kelly (Kay Stuart), Raymond Huntley (Tom Forester), Ronald Howard (Cpl. Nicholas Brayne), Jean Lodge (Celia Forester), Terence Alexander (Spud Cusack), Diana Calderwood (Josephine Forester), Laurence Payne (Clive Askham), Arthur Howard (Mr. Roddington), Brian Smith (Derek Forester), Harry Green (Golfer), Roger Maxwell, Yvette Wyatt, Doris Yorke.

Despite having to go against the wishes of his children, Huntley comes to the conclusion that it is time to resign from his army career and take a new wife. The bride-to-be is finally able to get onto the good side of Huntley's offspring by arranging marriages for the desperate daughters, which, combined with her other abilities, makes her another member of the family. Plodding domestic trifle.

p, Victor Hanbury; d&w, Wolf Rilla (based on the play by R. F. Delderfield); ph, Eric Cross.

Comedy/Drama   (PR:A   MPAA:NR)

GLADIATOR, THE***½ (1938) 70m COL bw

Joe E. Brown (Hugo Kipp), Man Mountain Dean (Himself), June Travis (Iris Bennett), Dickie Moore (Bobby), Lucien Littlefield (Prof. Danner), Robert Kent (Tom Dixon), Ethel Wales (Mrs. Danner), Donald Douglas (Coach Robbins), Lee Phelps (Coach Stetson), Eddie Kane (Speed Burns), Wright Kramer (Dr. DeRay).

Great comedy in which unassuming Brown accidentally drinks a new serum developed by Littlefield. He quickly becomes a campus hero—a star football player—thanks to the super stregthening powers of the serum. Trouble arises when the serum wears off and Brown faces a wrestling champion. Travis is Brown's steadfast girl friend and wrestling performer Man Mountain Dean (think about it!) is the wrestler Brown faces. Some wonderful moments for Brown including some great physical stuff on the football field and wrestling mat, along with a neat impersonation bit. The film is full of gags, nicely held together by the cast and director Sedgwick. The story line is based on the first of famed author Philip Wylie's novels. Wylie, best known for his works of social criticism such as Generation of Vipers, which vituperated good old Mom, was a talented science-fiction writer, who provided the story for George Pal's Oscar-winning WHEN WORLDS COLLIDE (1951).

p, David L. Loew; d, Edward Sedgwick; w, Charlie Melson, Arthur Sheckman, James Mulhauser, Earle Snell, George Marion, Jr. (based on the novel by Philip Wylie); ph, George Schneiderman; ed, Robert Crandall; md, Victor Young; art d, Albert D'Agostino; m/l, Walter G. Samuels, Charles Newman.

Comedy   (PR:AAA   MPAA:NR)

GLADIATOR OF ROME* (1963, Ital.) 105m C.I.R.A.C./Medallion c
(IL GLADIATORE DI ROMA)

Gordon Scott (Marcus), Wandisa Guida (Nisa), Roberto Risso (Valerio), Ombretta Colli (Aglae), Alberto Farnese (Vezio Rufo), Gianni Solaro (Macrino), Eleonora Vargas (Prisca), Andrea Aureli (Settimio), Charles Barman (Annio), Miranda Campa (Porzia), Mirko Ellis (Frasto), Pietro De Vico (Pompilio), Piero Lulli (Astarte), Nando Tamberlani (Valerio's Father).

Guida is a princess who is kept as a slave girl for 14 years. When her parents are sentenced to die she is thrown into jail with them and her friend Scott. He becomes a big strong gladiator. Because Guida is the last surviving heir to the throne, she is ordered to be executed. Muscleman Scott saves the day when he bends the iron bars to her prison cell and frees the girl.

p, Giorgio Agliani; d, Mario Costa; w, Gian Paolo Callegari, Giuseppe Mariani; ph, Pierludovico Pavoni (Euroscope, Eastmancolor); m, Carlo Franci; ed, Antonietta Zita; art d, Piero Poletto; cos, Giorgio Desideri.

Action/Drama   (PR:C   MPAA:NR)

GLADIATORERNA (SEE: GLADIATORS, THE, 1971, Swed.)

GLADIATORS, THE*½ (1970, Swed.) 90m Sandrews/New Line Cinema c
(GLADIATORERNA; AKA: THE PEACE GAME)

Arthur Pentelow (British General), Frederick Danner (British Staff Officer), Hans Bendrik (Capt. Davidsson), Daniel Harle (French Officer), Hans Berger (West Germany Officer), Rosario Gianetti (American Officer), Tim Yum (Chinese Staff Officer), Kenneth Lo (Chinese Colonel), Bjorn Franzen (Swedish Colonel), Christer Gynge (Assistant Controller), Jurgen Schling (East German Officer), Stefan Dillan (Russian Officer), Ugo Chiari (Italian Officer), Chandrakant Desai (Indian Officer), George Harris (Nigerian Officer), Jeremy Child (B1), Erich Stering (B2), Jean-Pierre Delamour (B3), Richard Friday (B4), Roy Scammel (B5), J.Z. Kennedy (B6), Eberhard Fehmers (B7), Terry Whitmore (B8), Nguyen (B9), To Van Minh (B10), Pik-Sen Lim (C2), Michael Cheuk, Taras Lee, Eng Chee Gan, Heng Ko Lei, Henry Chan, Louis Cheng, Sik-Yng Waung, Bill Fay (Members of Chinese Team), Keith Bradfield (Narrator). (In Swedish; English dialog and subtitles.)

Peter Watkins, whose brilliant THE WAR GAME (1965) is still banned by the BBC, falls flat this time as he ventures into sub-B movie territory. Set in the near future, countries engage in televised gladiatorial bouts known as The Peace Games. Sponsored by a spaghetti company, they are intended to subdue man's aggressive tendencies. During the 256th game (China vs. the West) a radical French student intervenes and inadvertently causes the computer to assassinate a British soldier and the Chinese prisoner he loves. A disappointing failure.

p, Goran Lindgren; d, Peter Watkins; w, Watkins, Nicholas Gosling; ph, Peter Suschitzky (Eastmancolor); m, Gustav Mahler; ed, Lars Hagstrom; art d, William Brodie; cos, Chris Collins; spec eff, Stig Lindberg.

Science-fiction   Cas.   (PR:C-O   MPAA:NR)

GLADIATORS 7*½ (1964, Span./Ital.) 92m Cieto Fontini-Italo
Zingarelli/MGM c (I SETTE GLADIATORI; LOS SIETE ESPARTANOS)

Richard Harrison (Darius), Loredana Nusciak (Aglaia), Livio Lorenzon (Panurgus), Gerard Tichy (Hiarba), Edoardo Toniolo (Milon), Joseph Marco (Xeno), Barta Barry (Flaccus), Tony Zamperla (Vargas), Francis Badeschi (Licia), Enrique Avila (Livius), Antonio Molino (Macrobius), Antonio Rubio (Mados), Emila Wolkowics (Ismere).

The hapless city of Sparta is under the evil rule of the Roman Empire. Good-guy gladiator Harrison and six skirted cohorts decide a little revolt might be in order and take on the tyrants. There's a good deal of swordplay, hand-to-hand combat, along with some blood and guts and a bit of cheesecake sex. Guess who wins in the end? The bad acting isn't helped by the poor-quality dubbing, but there are some fairly well directed action sequences. This is typical of the gladiator films of the early sixties—quick and cheap. The lucky number of the title—inspired, doubtless, by the success of SEVEN SAMURAI (1954) and THE MAGNIFICENT SEVEN (1960)—didn't help.

p, Cleto Fontini, Italo Zingarelli; d, Pedro Lazaga; w, Sandro Continenza, Bruno Corbucci, Alberto De Martino, Rafael Garcia Serrano, Giovanni Grimaldi, Zingarelli; ph, Adalberto Albertini, Eloy Mella (CinemaScope, Eastmancolor); m, Marcello Giombini; ed, Otello Colangeli; art d, Piero Poletto, Antonio Simont; cos, Mario Giorsi.

Action/Drama   (PR:O   MPAA:NR)

GLAMOUR*½   (1931, Brit.) 70m British International bw

Seymour Hicks *(Henry Garthorne)*, Ellaline Terriss *(Lady Belton)*, Margot Grahame *(Lady Betty Enfield)*, Basil Gill *(Lord Westborough)*, A. Bromley Davenport *(Lord Belton)*, Beverley Nichols *(Hon. Richard Wells)*, Betty Hicks *(Lady Armadale)*, Clifford Heatherley *(Edward Crumbles)*, Naomi Jacob *(Rosalind Crumbles)*, David Hawthorne *(Charlie Drummond)*, Philip Hewland *(Millett)*, Arthur Stratton *(Fireman)*, Charles Paton *(Clockwinder)*, Margery Binner *(Reede)*, Eric Marshall *(Singer)*, Irene Potter, Molly Edmunds, David Miller.

A tour de force for Hicks who co-directed, scripted, and starred in the film, but without the payoff he must have been hoping for. Hicks is a charming old gent, a famous actor who has no problem finding women. But then trouble brews up in the form of Grahame, his latest romance who it turns out is engaged to marry Nichols, Hicks' son. When her father finds out he confronts Hicks who devises a wild scheme that frees her from his affections, leaving her to believe his son is no relation in the process. The script is not what it should be considering the material. Dialog is stiff and the acting is fairly poor (Nichols was a news reporter apparently doing the film for a lark). Though there are some good, if dumb, gags the film is a disappointment.

p, Seymour Hicks; d, Hicks, Harry Hughes; w, Hicks; ph, Jack Cox.

Comedy/Romance   **(PR:A   MPAA:NR)**

GLAMOUR*½   (1934) 75m UNIV bw

Paul Lukas *(Victor Bankl)*, Constance Cummings *(Linda Fayne)*, Phillip Reed *(Lorenzo Valenti)*, Joseph Cawthorn *(Ibsen)*, Doris Lloyd *(Nana)*, David Dickinson *(Stevie)*, Peggy Campbell *(Amy)*, Olaf Hytten *(Dobbs)*, Alice Lake *(Secretary)*, Lita Chevret *(Grassie)*, Lyman Williams *(Forsyth)*, Phil Teed *(Jimmy)*, Luis Alberni *(Mons. Paul)*, Yola d'Avril *(Renee)*, Grace Hale *(Miss Lang)*, Wilson Benge *(Pritchard)*, Louise Beavers *(Millie)*, Jessie McAllister.

Trite story about a dancer (well played by Cummings despite the material) who jilts her husband, Lukas, for her dance partner, Reed. Husband No. 2 fools around on her and she ends up, a little worse for wear and tear, with husband No. 1. The film was adapted from a short story by Edna Ferber that took place in one day. The script padded out the story, but it proved to be too much (15 minutes were cut between the Hollywood and New York premieres) and the film quickly becomes a dud. Songs include "Heaven On Earth."

d, William Wyler; w, Doris Anderson, Gladys Unger (based on a short story by Edna Ferber); ph, George Robinson; ed, Ted Kent; m/l, Walter Donaldson, David Klatzkin, Howard Jackson, Harry Akst.

Drama   **(PR:C   MPAA:NR)**

GLAMOUR BOY, 1940   (SEE: MILLIONAIRE PLAYBOY, 1940)

GLAMOUR BOY*½**   (1941) 79m Colbert Clark/PAR bw

Jackie Cooper *(Tiny Barlow)*, Susanna Foster *(Joan Winslow)*, Walter Abel *(A.J. Colder)*, Darryl Hickman *(Billy Doran)*, Ann Gillis *(Brenda Lee)*, William Demarest *(Papa Doran)*, William Wright *(Hank Landon)*, Katherine Booth *(Helen Trent)*, Jackie Searle *(Georgie Clemons)*, Norma Varden *(Mrs. Lee)*, John Gallaudet *(Mickey Fadden)*, Edith Meiser *(Jenny Sullivan)*, Olive Blakeney *(Miss Trent)*, Josephine Whittell *(Helga Harris)*, Jack Chapin *(Man)*.

Hollywood looks backward in this film with a neat gimmick: 18-year-old Cooper plays an ex-child star, now working as a soda jerk. When he overhears producer Abel wondering how to use new child star Hickman, Cooper suggests a remake of the real Cooper's famous film SKIPPY (1931). The producer agrees and hires Cooper as Hickman's coach. On the lot he meets Foster and they fall in love, but problems arise and Cooper leaves town. En route he finds Hickman in the back seat of his car, and in classic child-actor style the boy talks Cooper into getting back together with Foster. An interesting and enjoyable film that is well acted. Watching Cooper watch SKIPPY is a slightly surreal experience. Watch for Searle as a heavy, having grown up from being SKIPPY's tattle-tale. Songs include "The Magic of Magnolias," "Love Is Such an Old-Fashioned Thing," Victor Schertzinger, Frank Loesser; "Sempre Libera," from the opera *La Traviata*, F. M. Piave, Giuseppe Verdi.

p, Sol C. Siegel; d, Ralph Murphy; w, Bradford Ropes, Val Burton, F. Hugh Herbert; ph, Dan Fapp; ed, William Shea; art d, Hans Dreier, Haldane Douglas.

Comedy/Drama   **(PR:AA   MPAA:NR)**

GLAMOUR FOR SALE**   (1940) 60m COL bw

Anita Louise *(Ann Powell)*, Roger Pryor *(Daly)*, Frances Robinson *(Betty)*, June MacCloy *(Peggy)*, Don Beddoe *(Regan)*, Paul Fix *(Manell)*, Arthur Loft *(Braddock)*, Veda Ann Borg *(Lucille)*, Myra Marsh, Evalyn Young, Madelon Grayson, Ann Doran, Ruth Fallow, Lynn Browning, Dorothy Fay, Jeanne Hart, Bonnie Bennett.

Daring for 1940, though mild stuff today. Film deals with a police investigation of escort services. The film goes out of its way to sanitize the business, showing "nice girls" with services that are strictly business and harpies with the sleazier services (i.e., the ones that use blackmail and extortion but no prostitution!) Louise is the nice girl accidentally caught up in the schemes of bad girl MacCloy. Pryor is a cop who helps Louise, stopping MacCloy and clearing the good girls' names. The film reflects the Hollywood standards of the time: good is good, bad is bad, and there are no shades of gray in between.

d, D. Ross Lederman; w, John Bright; ph, Franz Planer; m, Ben Oakland; ed, Viola Lawrence; art d, Lionel Banks; m/l Oakland, Milton Drake, Herb Magidson.

Drama   **(PR:A   MPAA:NR)**

GLAMOUR GIRL**   (1938, Brit.) 68m WB bw

Gene Gerrard *(Dean Webster)*, Lesley Brook *(Connie Stevens)*, Ross Landon *(Taylor Brooks)*, Betty Lynne *(Vicki)*, Leslie Weston *(Murphy)*, Robert Randel *(J. J. Andex)*, Dennis Arundell *(Sir Raymond Bell)*, James Carew *(Collins)*, Jimmy Godden *(Arnold)*.

What might have been a decent farce loses impact through the stale handling of undeveloped material. Gerrard is a photographer who decides to throw over his successful career to try his hand at painting, for which he doesn't have the talent. Luckily, he has maintained the admiration of his former secretary, who does not remain a secretary for long but becomes his bride. Lacks verve.

p, William Collier; d, Arthur Woods; w, John Meehan, Jr. Tom Phipps; ph, Basil Emmott.

Comedy   **(PR:A   MPAA:NR)**

GLAMOUR GIRL*½**   (1947) 68m COL bw

Gene Krupa *(Himself)*, Virginia Grey *(Lorraine Royle)*, Michael Duane *(Johnny Evans)*, Susan Reed *(Jennia Higgins)*, Jimmy Lloyd *(Buddy Butterfield)*, Jack Leonard *(Ray Royle)*, Pierre Watkin *(T.J. Hopkins)*, Eugene Borden *(Luigi Tamarini)*, Netta Packer *(Aunt Hattie Higgins)*, Noel Neill *(Gertrude)*, Jeann Bell *(Rosa)*, Carolyn Grey *(Vocalist)*.

A familiar "small town girl takes on the big city" film with thoroughly complete results. This time the girl is zither-playing Reed, who gets discovered in a small Tennessee town. She is taken by talent scout Grey to the city and then quickly abandoned. Undaunted, Grey forms her own company with Duane and quickly makes Reed an overnight sensation. Typical formula stuff, its real excuse for being is to show off the talents of Krupa and his band. Songs include "Gene's Boogie," Segar Ellis, George Williams; "Anywhere," Jule Styne, Sammy Cahn; "Without Imagination," Allan Roberts, Doris Fisher.

p, Sam Katzman; d, Arthur Dreifuss; w, M. Coates Webster, Lee Gold (based on a story by Gold); ph, Ira H. Morgan; ed, Charles Nelson; md, Mischa Bakaleinikoff; art d, Paul Palmentola.

Drama/Musical   **(PR:A   MPAA:NR)**

GLAMOROUS NIGHT*½**   (1937, Brit.) 65m ABF/REP bw

Mary Ellis *(Melitza Hjos)*, Otto Kruger *(King Stefan)*, Victor Jory *(Baron Lyadeff)*, Barry Mackay *(Anthony Allan)*, Trefor Jones *(Lorenti)*, Maire O'Neill *(Phoebe)*, Antony Holles *(Maestro)*, Charles Carson *(Otto)*, Felix Aylmer *(Diplomat)*, Finlay Currie *(Angus Mackintosh)*, Jeanne Carpenter.

Big, ambitious film adapted from a play by Novello, this is the story of a king (Kruger) who becomes infatuated with gypsy girl Ellis and thinks about abdicating. Jory is an evil prime minister who tries to use this to his advantage. The film is overdone, with crowd scenes that just don't work, and flat photography. Still, it's an interesting subject for a British film considering that shortly before release England's own King Edward VIII had abdicated for "the woman I love," Wallis Warfield Simpson. At the time author/actor/songsmith Novello actually wrote the play, it was redolent of another royal romance entirely, that of King Carol II of Romania and his young mistress Magda Lupescu. The Jewish Lupescu had a great influence on her lover; she was instrumental later in assisting many Jews to flee from the persecutions of the Nazi-influenced Iron Guard. The famed pair were the subject of a popular limerick, "A lady named Magda Lupescu/For her monarchy came to the rescue/She said, 'It's a grand thing/ To be under a king/Is democracy better, I esk you?'"

p, Walter C. Mycroft; d, Brian Desmond Hurst; w, Dudley Leslie, Hugh Brooke, William Freshman (based on the play by Ivor Novello); ph, Fritz Arno Wagner; m/l, Novello, Christopher Hassall.

Drama   **(PR:C   MPAA:NR)**

GLASS ALIBI, THE**   (1946) 68m REP bw

Paul Kelly *(Max Anderson)*, Douglas Fowley *(Joe Eykner)*, Anne Gwynne *(Belle Marlin)*, Maris Wrixon *(Linda Vale)*, Jack Conrad *(Benny Brandini)*, Selmer Jackson *(Dr. Lawson)*, Cyril Thornton *(Riggs)*, Cy Kendall *(Red Hogan)*, Walter Soderling *(Coroner)*, Vic Potel *(Gas Attendant)*, George Chandler *(Bartender)*, Phyllis Adair *(Nurse)*, Ted Stanhope *(Drug Clerk)*, Dick Scott *(Frank)*, Eula Guy *(Connie)*, Forrest Taylor *(Charlie)*.

Fowley is a reporter who marries Wrixon, a wealthy Santa Monica socialite. He knows she's got a heart ailment and with girl friend Gwynne he plots her murder. He lays out the plans and shoots Wrixon, not knowing she is already dead of heart failure. He is caught and convicted, with tough homicide detective Kelly holding back the true nature of Wrixon's death which would have cleared Fowley. Routine material is held together with some strong direction and an equally strong cast. The script has just enough plot twists to keep it interesting. A nice little thriller.

p&d, W. Lee Wilder; w, Mindret Lord; ph, Henry Sharp; ed, John F. Link; md, Alexander Laszlo.

Crime   **(PR:A   MPAA:NR)**

GLASS BOTTOM BOAT, THE**   (1966) 110m Arwin-Reame/MGM c

Doris Day *(Jennifer Nelson)*, Rod Taylor *(Bruce Templeton)*, Arthur Godfrey *(Axel Nordstrom)*, John McGiver *(Ralph Goodwin)*, Paul Lynde *(Homer Cripps)*, Edward Andrews *(Gen. Wallace Bleecker)*, Eric Fleming *(Edgar Hill)*, Dom De Luise *(Julius Pritter)*, Dick Martin *(Zack Molloy)*, Elisabeth Fraser *(Nina Bailey)*, George Tobias *(Mr. Fenimore)*, Alice Pearce *(Mrs. Fenimore)*, Ellen Corby *(Anna Miller)*, Dee J. Thompson *(Donna)*, Robert Vaughn *(Napoleon Solo)*.

Day is a public relations worker at a space laboratory in this wacky comedy, who gets caught up (accidentally of course) in the world of spy secrets and espionage. Taylor's her boss, a whiz technician who falls for Day and contrives to have her write a biography of him so she'll always be close to him. Between calling up her dog Vladimir on the phone (the ring cues him to exercise) and burning all paper as instructed, Day quickly becomes suspected as a Soviet spy. Wonderful supporting cast includes De Luise as an inept spy and Lynde as a security agent who is suspicious of Day. Watch for a brief cameo by Robert Vaughn, playing Napoleon Solo from "the Man From U.N.C.L.E." television series. Day also sings "Que Sera, Sera," Jay Livingston, Ray Evans, which quickly became her theme song. Other songs: "The Glass Bottom Boat," Joe Lubin, "Soft As the Starlight," Lubin, Jerome Howard. Snappy direction from Tashlin.

p, Martin Melcher, Everett Freeman; d, Frank Tashlin; w, Freeman; ph, Leon Shamroy (Panavision, Metrocolor); m, Frank De Vol; ed, John McSweeney; art d, George W. Davis, Edward Carfagno; set d, Henry Grace, Hugh Hunt; cos, Ray Aghayan; spec eff, J. McMillan Johnson, Carroll L. Shepphird; makeup, William Tuttle, Harry Maret.

Comedy **(PR:A MPAA:NR)**

GLASS CAGE, THE (SEE: GLASS TOMB, THE , 1955)

GLASS CAGE, THE** (1964) 84m Futuramic bw
(AKA: DEN OF DOOM; DON'T TOUCH MY SISTER; BED OF FIRE)

Arline Sax *(The Girl/Her Older Sister)*, John Hoyt *(Det. Jeff Bradley)*, Elisha Cook, Jr. *(Her Father)*, Robert Kelljan *(Police Detective)*, King Moody *(Beatnik)*.

Sax is a young woman who is arrested for shooting a prowler, but let off the hook thanks to amorous detective Kelljan. After her older sister disappears (also played by Sax) and her father (Cook) becomes even more intense, Sax runs away to a zoo. She falls into a bear pit and is rescued before becoming a grizzly's lunch. An interesting and semi-experimental mystery which has been cut to 78 minutes for television, deleting a nude rape scene.

p, John Hoyt, Paul Lewis; d, Antonio Santean; w, Hoyt, Santean; ph, Jean-Philippe Carson.

Mystery/Drama **(PR:O MPAA:NR)**

GLASS HOUSES½** (1972) 103m Magellan/COL c

Bernard Barrow *(Victor)*, Deirdre Lenihan *(Kim)*, Jennifer O'Neill *(Jean)*, Ann Summers *(Wife)*, Phillip Pine *(Ted)*, Lloyd Kino *(Katayama)*, Clarke Gordon *(The Novelist)*, Gar Campbell, Lorna Thayer, Maury Hill, Mary Carver, Joan Kaye, Tom Toner, Logan Ramsey, Holly Irving, Al Checco, Janice Barr, Alma Beltran, Tom J. Halligan, William Cort, Albert Popwell, Robert Karnes, Eve McVeagh, James Wellman, Laurie Hagen, Karen Lind, David Morick, Anita Raffi, Elizabeth Ross, John Wyler, Chris Carmody, Pat Walter, George Berkley, Jack Grinnage, Jack Mattis, Davis Roberts, Rhoda Anderson, Ruth Stanley.

A post-BOB & CAROL & TED & ALICE adultery story. Here the characters include an author of sex books, an affluent but frustrated middle-aged couple, and young women exploring different relationships for the first time. There are hints at incest, handled in a tense but highly sensitive manner. They all meet at a California retreat near the film's end. Well-done characterizations that satirize but never caricature. Direction captures the mood of southern California. Made in 1970, the film was not released until 1972, probably to capitalize on the stardom O'Neill had achieved the year before in THE SUMMER OF '42.

p, George Folsey, Jr.; d, Alexander Singer; w, A. Singer, Judith Singer; ph, George Folsey, Sr. (Eastmancolor); m, David Raskin; ed, Folsey, Jr.

Drama **(PR:O MPAA:NR)**

GLASS KEY, THE*** (1935) 80m PAR bw

George Raft *(Ed Beaumont)*, Claire Dodd *(Janet Henry)*, Edward Arnold *(Paul Madvig)*, Rosaline Keith *(Opal Madvig)*, Ray Milland *(Taylor Henry)*, Robert Gleckler *(Shad O'Rory)*, Guinn "Big Boy" Williams *(Jeff)*, Tammany Young *(Clarkie)*, Harry Tyler *(Henry Sloss)*, Charles C. Wilson *(Farr)*, Emma Dunn *(Mom)*, Matt McHugh *(Puggy)*, Patrick Moriarity *(Mulrooney)*, Mack Gray *(Duke)*, Frank Marlowe *(Walter Ivans)*, Herbert Evans *(Senator's Butler)*, George H. Reed *(Black Serving Man)*, Percy Morris *(Bartender)*, Irving Bacon *(Waiter)*, Ann Sheridan *(Nurse)*, Henry Roquemore *(Rinkle)*, Frank O'Connor *(McLaughlin)*, Michael Mark *(Swartz)*, Del Cambre *(Reporter)*, Veda Buckland *(Landlady)*, George Ernest *(Boy)*, Charles Richman *(Sen. Henry)*.

The hard-nosed Hammett novel about political corruption saw a top-notch production in its first film outing. Raft is a close-mouthed henchman of political bigshot Arnold, who always does the boss' bidding right up to the brink of death. Arnold makes a deal with crooked senator Richman which Raft thinks will end in disaster. Kingmaker Arnold agrees to help Richman get reelected. Inexplicably, Arnold gets religion, abandons his corrupt ways, and uses his contacts to close down a notorious gambling casino run by Gleckler. Crime boss Gleckler is not happy with this move and, in retaliation, murders Richman's playboy son, Milland, who has been going with Arnold's daughter, Keith, then frames Arnold for the slaying. Raft goes to the rescue, taking on Gleckler's goons to find the real killer. For his pains he is beaten to a pulp by Williams in one of the most brutal scenes in film history, a sado-masochistic ritual that incredibly got by the 1935 censors. Raft finally manages to get enough evidence to free Arnold and pin the murder on Gleckler, deftly engineering another homicide charge pinned to the bad guy's chest. Raft is the perfect tough guy who says little but gets the job done, while Arnold is wonderful as the soft-hearted political mover and shaker, the kind of part he played to perfection, especially when he was required to have no heart at all as in the case of Capra's MEET JOHN DOE (1941) and MR. SMITH GOES TO WASHINGTON (1939). This was a money-maker for author Hammett who was paid a then substantial $25,000 for the rights to film his novel. Remade in 1942 with Alan Ladd, Brian Donlevy, and Veronica Lake.

p, E. Lloyd Sheldon; d, Frank Tuttle; w, Kathryn Scola, Kubec Glasmon, Harry Ruskin (based on the novel by Dashiell Hammett); ph, Henry Sharp; ed, Hugh Bennett.

Crime Drama **(PR:C MPAA:NR)**

GLASS KEY, THE***½** (1942) 85m PAR bw

Brian Donlevy *(Paul Madvig)*, Veronica Lake *(Janet Henry)*, Alan Ladd *(Ed Beaumont)*, Bonita Granville *(Opal Madvig)*, Richard Denning *(Taylor Henry)*, Joseph Calleia *(Nick Varna)*, William Bendix *(Jeff)*, Frances Gifford *(Nurse)*, Donald MacBride *(Farr)*, Margaret Hayes *(Eloise Matthews)*, Moroni Olsen *(Ralph Henry)*, Eddie Marr *(Rusty)*, Arthur Loft *(Clyde Matthews)*, George Meader *(Claude Tuttle)*, Pat O'Malley, Ed Peil, Sr., James Millican *(Politicians)*, Edmund Cobb, Frank Bruno, Jack Luden, Jack Gardner, Joe McGuinn, Frank Hagney *(Reporters)*, John W. DeNoria *(Groggins)*, Jack Mulhall *(Lynch)*, Joseph King *(Fisher)*, Al Hill *(Bum)*, Freddie Walburn *(Kid)*, Conrad Binyon *(Stubby)*, Vernon Dent *(Bartender)*, Stanley Price, Kenneth Chryst *(Men in Barroom)*, Dane Clark *(Henry Sloss)*, Norma Varden *(Dowager)*, Frank Elliott *(1st Butler in Henry Home)*, George Cowl *(2nd Butler in Henry Home)*, Broderick O'Farrell, Arthur Hull, Tom O'Grady, Jack Fowler *(Guests at Henry Dinner)*, Tom Fadden *(Waiter)*, William Wagner *(Butler)*, Charles Sullivan *(Taxi Driver)*, Francis Sayles *(Seedy-looking Man)*, George Turner *(Doctor)*, Tom Dugan *(Jeep)*, William Benedict *(Sturdy)*, Lillian Randolph *(Entertainer at Basement Club)*.

The remake of the Hammett tale of political corruption and murder is better by a hair than the original which was good to begin with, this production having a bigger budget and a stronger cast. Donlevy is a political boss who backs Senator Olsen, a reform candidate for governor. Ladd, who is Donlevy's loyal aide, tells him he's making a mistake but will support him. First Donlevy closes up Calleia's notorious gambling casino and this satisfies his new girl friend, Lake, who is Olsen's daughter, she being the reason why Donlevy has gone straight. Calleia pays Donlevy a visit and tells him that because he pays for protection, he intends to run wide open. Donlevy calls his police contact and, in front of the scowling Calleia, tells the cop to close the club again if it reopens, to "slam it down so hard it'll splash!" He then asks Calleia if he gets the point. The surly gangster walks out of Donlevy's office, but his hulking henchman, Bendix, spits contemptuously on the floor before turning away. Donlevy hits him in the back with a shoe so hard he sends Bendix flying through the doorway. Bendix turns in a rage, arms outstretched like an ape man, and starts back, but Ladd slams the door in his face. Meanwhile, Denning, the no-good playboy son of Olsen, is taking Donlevy's young sister, Granville, to nightclubs and Ladd keeps pulling her out of trouble. This causes Donlevy to make threats against Denning, who is later found murdered. Ladd finds the body and tells Donlevy, who is brushing his teeth at the time and who takes the news as if Ladd were informing him that the milkman forgot a delivery. When Ladd asks Donlevy if he understood what he just told him, Donlevy rinses his mouth and says: "What do you want me to do about it—bust out crying?" Later, at Denning's funeral, Bendix not-so-jokingly suggests that he and Calleia "knock off Madvig [Donlevy] right here—that way they won't have to take him far to bury him!" Calleia tells Olsen at the cemetery that the local press is already hinting that Donlevy killed his son to stop him from seeing Granville. Since Donlevy's aide Ladd has found the body, it is assumed that Donlevy is the killer. Ladd asks his pal Donlevy to dump Lake and her blueblood associations and make peace with Calleia, but Donlevy refuses. The two begin a fight in the back room of their favorite bar and part on unfriendly terms, Ladd planning to leave for New York. Ladd then goes to Calleia, pretending to work for the gambling czar, but he is really trying to get information about how Calleia plans to frame his friend Donlevy. Calleia shows Ladd an affidavit signed by a henchman, Clark, which claims that he saw Donlevy kill Denning. Ladd rips up the affidavit and Calleia sics his German Shepherd on Ladd, then his vicious goon Bendix. Ladd wakes up in a sleazy room where Bendix beats him again and again. When Marr cautions psychopath Bendix to go easy, Bendix grins maniacally and states: "You can't croak him—he's tough!" Calleia arrives and Ladd is revived to be asked to set up Donlevy but he refuses and Calleia orders Bendix to beat Ladd senseless, which he does, despite the protests of Loft, a local newspaper editor Calleia is using to frame Donlevy with stories implicating him with Denning's murder. While Bendix and Marr are preparing a meal, Ladd sets fire to the room where he is kept prisoner. Bendix and Marr busy themselves with putting out the fire and Ladd smashes a third story window, rolls down a roof, and drops through a skylight, crashing on to a kitchen table where a family is eating. He is taken to a hospital. Donlevy visits him and just before he passes out Ladd tells him how Calleia is setting up a phony witness against him. Donlevy departs to attend to the fake witness, then turns and says to a doctor: "If that guy dies, I'll turn this place into a warehouse!" Ladd recovers and Lake tells him that she has fallen for him but he brushes this off. Donlevy arrives at his hospital bedside and shows Ladd an engagement ring with a diamond as big as the Ritz on Lake's finger. "How do you like that," beams Donlevy. "Fifteen Gs!" After Donlevy leaves, Lake asks Ladd why he took such an awful beating for Donlevy. "Because he's my friend and he's square." Later, after nurse Gifford finds out where Loft's country estate is located, at Ladd's request, Ladd dresses and goes there to find Donlevy's sister, Loft and his wife Hayes, and Calleia and goons Bendix and Marr. Ladd explains to Granville that Calleia intends to force Loft to print an open accusation of murder against her brother. Trampy Hayes, when learning that her husband is broke and doing Calleia's bidding for money, plays up to Ladd. Loft, witnessing his wife blatantly kissing Ladd, goes to his room and blows out his brains. Ladd hurries to his room and finds a hastily written will appointing Calleia as his executor; he destroys this paper so that Donlevy can appoint his own executor and control the newspaper, which is about to print Calleia's lies about Donlevy, all stemming from an anonymous letter writer whom Ladd accurately guesses is Lake. She has been convinced all along that Donlevy murdered her brother and has played along with him to get information on the killing. Ladd turns the tables on Lake, however, by having her arrested for killing her brother Denning, knowing that Olsen will come forward to save his daughter. The Senator comes forth, confessing that he killed his son accidentally in an argument. Donlevy was present at the time and, for Lake's sake, helped Olsen to cover up the killing. When Donlevy discovers that Lake and Ladd "got it bad for each other," he magnanimously bows out. He shakes Ladd's hand and says, "I suppose you think I'm nuts." Then he takes back the expensive engagement ring from Lake, pulling it from her finger and walking out, saying: "But if you think you're getting married with my rock, *you're nuts!*" Ladd earlier makes a little trip to a basement bar where he finds lunatic Bendix and easily convinces him that Calleia is setting him up for the killing of phony witness Clark, that Calleia will allow him to go to the electric chair. Calleia shows up and Bendix drunkenly attacks him, strangling him to death as Ladd watches,

Calleia's gun in his hand. After strangling Calleia, Bendix snorts: "I'm just a big, good-natured slob everybody thinks they can push around." Ladd calls the waiter of the dive into the back room and tells him to call the police and get a doctor in case Calleia is still alive. Bendix laughs madly and adds: "Or an undertaker in case he isn't." Ladd has had his vengeance without having to lift a finger; Calleia is dead and his vicious henchman Bendix will go to the chair for the murder. This is a tough crime yarn that pulls no punches, too raw for viewing by youngsters, but a faithful adaptation of the Hammet novel and an improvement over the 1935 original film with taut direction from film noir specialist Heisler and excellent low-key photography by Sparkuhl. Latimer's script works hard to capture the Hammet dialog and scenes and mostly succeeds, pumping underworld lines out of Bendix's mouth such as "gimme the roscoe [gun]" and "we got to give him the works [kill him]." This film was put into production before Ladd's electric performance in THIS GUN FOR HIRE was seen by the public, a film Paramount quickly mounted to support its new tough leading man. Patricia Morrison was selected to play the female lead but was replaced because she was too tall for Ladd and Lake, his partner in THIS GUN FOR HIRE, was given the role of the rich daughter. Donlevy is superb as the nonchalant political boss from the wrong side of the tracks, a role tailored after his wonderful performance in THE GREAT MCGINTY. Ladd is as strong and stoic as the character Hammett envisioned and Lake is solid as the manipulative daughter. Bendix steals almost every scene he's in, being both frightening and an object of pity, a cretinous killer whose only joy in life is sadistically administering a beating. While Bendix was beating up Ladd, the rugged six-footer slipped and struck Ladd square on the jaw, knocking him out. Director Heisler, never one to let a convincing scene go unrecorded, ordered the shot printed and it appears in the film. Bendix, however, became so distraught at actually cold-cocking Ladd that he burst into tears, blubbering: "God, what have I done?" Ladd, who was taciturn and tough, a loner in real life, came around to find bruiser Bendix bawling over him. He was so touched that he befriended the character actor immediately. Ladd was a reclusive type without a lot of friends, living quietly with his wife apart from the social Hollywood community. When shooting to stardom and making a great deal of money, Ladd lavished gifts on those friends he did have, the Bendixes included. When the actor heard that Bendix and his wife and child were living in a cramped rented bungalow, he located a spacious house the couple thought ideal to buy. Ladd also requested Bendix for many of his future films, helping him every way he could, all because a punch actually landed on his jaw. Famed director Akira Kurosawa has said that this film inspired him to do YOJIMBO, 1961.

p, Fred Kohlmar; d, Stuart Heisler; w, Jonathan Latimer (based on the novel by Dashiell Hammett); ph, Theodore Sparkuhl; m, Victor Young; ed, Archie Marshek; art d, Hans Dreier, Haldane Douglas.

Crime Drama **(PR:O MPAA:NR)**

GLASS MENAGERIE, THE*** (1950) 106m WB bw

Jane Wyman *(Laura Wingfield)*, Kirk Douglas *(Jim O'Connor)*, Gertrude Lawrence *(Amanda Wingfield)*, Arthur Kennedy *(Tom Wingfield)*, Ralph Sanford *(Mendoza)*, Ann Tyrrell *(Clerk)*, John Compton *(Young Man)*, Gertrude Graner *(Woman Instructor)*, Sara Edwards *(Mrs. Miller)*, Louise Lorrimer *(Miss Porter)*, Cris Alcaide *(Eddie)*, Perdita Chandler *(A Girl)*, Sean McClory *(Richard)*, James Horn, Marshall Romer *(Callers)*.

The lyrically superb Williams play, one of the most popular in American theater revivals, saw a film adaptation by Warner Bros. that was sensitive and well-constructed but somewhat misdirected. The prosaic story involves a proud but dominating mother, Lawrence, her crippled, day-dreaming daughter, Wyman, and her disillusioned son, Kennedy. The three live in a run-down apartment in St. Louis' tenement district. Lawrence's husband is long gone, a runaway "telephone man who fell in love with long distance." She is forever telling her grown children that when she was a southern belle there was no end to the "gentlemen callers" knocking on her door, anxious suitors all. Her son, Kennedy, who writes poetry, is also a romantic but it is his hard reality to provide the financial support for the family by slaving in a warehouse. Lawrence incessantly nags her children to improve their lot, Kennedy to get a better job and Wyman to see young men and select a husband. Wyman, however, retreats to her room to clean and fondle her glass figurine collection, her "glass menagerie," using this as an escape from her crippled foot and natural inability to seek male companionship. Concluding that Wyman will never make a move on her own, Lawrence goads Kennedy into bringing home a fellow warehouse worker, Douglas, a "gentleman caller" Lawrence comes to believe will sweep her daughter off her feet and into a wedding ceremony. Douglas is actually doing Kennedy a favor but he is gentle and kind toward the shy Wyman, drawing her out. This he has little trouble doing in that she remembers Douglas from high school where she had a secret crush on him. Douglas takes her to a dance hall and patiently encourages her to dance with him, which she does. Later, he tenderly kisses her but realizes that he has gone too far, quickly explaining that he is engaged. Yet Wyman is not devastated. Douglas has shown Wyman that even though she has a crippled foot she can still enjoy life, that if she reaches out, someone will be there for her. Lawrence later blames Kennedy for bringing home a man almost married and falsely building up Wyman's hopes, the very thing she herself had been doing all along. Disgusted, Kennedy leaves home, taking a job as a merchant seaman but promising to send money home every month. At film's end Wyman is seen sitting on the apartment fire escape with her mother, waiting for another "gentleman caller," believing that some day he will come. This bittersweet, delicate story is handled with care by director Rapper, but the accent is placed more on laughs than pensive study, which somewhat shreds the play's original intent. Burks' fluid camera, however, avoids a stagey look to the production. Lawrence overacts a bit but Kennedy and Wyman are both convincing and sympathetic as the young adults trapped by poverty. Douglas, who was then just impacting in films, is terrific as the kind-hearted, understanding "gentleman caller." Wyman's part is similar to her Oscar-winning performance in JOHNNY BELINDA (1948), only here she has a deformed foot instead of being mute. At first it was thought to have her wear a leg brace but this proved too cumbersome, so a special shoe was made to give her the appearance of having a deformed foot. At 36 Wyman was too old for her part, which called for a young woman, but makeup artist Westmore gave Wyman a youthful appearance by removing all makeup. She was given a hairpiece to wear, but it made her head look too big. Westmore convinced Wyman to let him thin out her hair and cut it to what was later described as a "short, fluffy bob she has worn ever since." This allowed the wig to fit well over her cut down real hair and gave her a natural, younger look. She, Douglas, and Kennedy were standouts in this almost reverential production. The producer of THE GLASS MENAGERIE, Wald, later stated that "Jane [Wyman] isn't fresh anymore. She's mellowed . . . In the old days, she'd read a script and 10 minutes later be in the picture; a script was a script and to hell with it. Now she reads a script, studies the character for weeks and months, discusses it thoroughly, and has a deep and perfect understanding of the part before she goes before the cameras." Of course the role Kennedy so wryly played was autobiographical, based on Williams himself, and the Wyman character, withdrawing into a tiny fantasy world of glass figurines, is much like Blanche in A STREETCAR NAMED DESIRE, who withdraws into the past, and even the mother, a one-time attractive southern belle who relishes the genteel traditional of a long-dead Old South and the "gentlemen callers" of her youth, also parallels the neurotic Blanche. Douglas, too, is similar to the "gentleman caller" of STREETCAR, who calls upon Blanche with old manners but lecherous ideas, so superbly played in that film by Karl Malden. Lawrence, though not top billed, has the largest part as the ambitious mother, a role first thought to be assigned to Tallulah Bankhead (the part was magnificently played on Broadway by Laurette Taylor).

p, Jerry Wald, Charles K. Feldman; d, Irving Rapper; w, Tennessee Williams, Peter Berneis (based on the play by Williams); ph, Robert Burks; m, Max Steiner; ed, David Weisbart; art d, Robert Haas; makeup, Perc Westmore.

Drama **(PR:A MPAA:NR)**

GLASS MOUNTAIN, THE** (1950, Brit) 97m Victoria/Renown bw

Michael Denison *(Richard Wilder)*, Dulcie Gray *(Ann Wilder)*, Valentine Cortese *(Alida)*, Tito Gobbi *(Tito)*, Sebastian Shaw *(Bruce McLeod)*, Antonio Centa *(Gino)*, Sidney King *(Charles)*, Elena Rizzieri *(Singer)*, Arnold Marle, Ferdinand Terschack, Venice Opera House Orchestra and Chorus.

The famed fairly tale transcribed by the Brothers Grimm from ancient peasant legends has it that a legendary mountain of glass cannot be climbed. The protagonist of the tale discovers that for each step he takes up the mountain, he slides back *two* steps. To win his princess' love, he must climb the mountain so, cleverly, he turns about and climbs it *backwards*, gaining double elevation with each downward step. Perhaps the producers should have reversed the direction of this rather cumbersome film, which soars to the heights only in its music and scenery. The plot deals with British wartime airman Denison who, shot down in Italy's Dolomite mountains, is rescued by pretty partisan Cortese. Returning home to wife Gray, he attempts to compose an opera based on an ancient Dolomite peasant legend, which obsesses him. Inspiration does not come readily in his domestic milieu; haunted by memories of the curvaceous, courageous Cortese, he returns to the scene of his wartime solace, where he completes his operatic opus. The successful premiere performance of the piece proves purgative of his passion; when Gray is injured in her own air crash, he returns to her long-suffering arms. Cortese's performance is outstanding; Denison and Gray, husband and wife in reality, handle their familiar relationship well, but the real stars of the picture are the music, with operatic baritone Gobbi, and the beautiful mountain scenery.

p, John Sutro, Fred Zelnik, Joseph Janni; d, Henry Cass; w, Cass, Janni, John Hunter, Emery Bonnet, John Cousins; ph, William McLeod, Arthur Grant; m, Vivian Lambelet, Nino Rota, Elizabeth Anthony; ed, Lister Laurance; art d, Terence Verity.

Drama **(PR:A MPAA:NR)**

GLASS OF WATER, A*½ (1962, Ger.) 84m Deutsche Film Hansa/Casino c/bw (DAS GLAS WASSER)

Gustaf Grundgens *(Henry St. John, Viscount Bolingbroke)*, Liselotte Pulver *(Queen Anne)*, Hilde Krahl *(Lady Churchill, Duchess of Marlborough)*, Sabine Sinjen *(Abigail)*, Horst Janson *(Arthur Marsham)*, Rudolf Forster *(Marquis de Torcy)*, Joachim Rake *(Lord Avondale)*, Hans Leibelt *(Butler)*, Herbert Weissbach *(Beichvater, Father Confessor)*, Bobby Todd.

Released in Germany in 1960, based on a French play, and set in England in the early part of the 18th century, this cumbersome comedy misses the mark. When Krahl, as Duchess of Marlborough, attempts to subvert the signing of a treaty that would have ended hostilities with Spain, clever Bolingbroke—Grundgens—dispatches young cadet Janson to the bedchamber of Queen Anne—Pulver—to get her to sign the document. Apprehended by Krahl, Janson is ordered to compensate for his effrontery by wedding one of the queen's handmaidens, Sinjen, who happens to be the lady he favors. The film fails to catch the mood and mystique of the place and period.

p, Georg Richter; d, Helmut Kautner; w, Kautner (based on Eugene Scribe's play *Le verre d'eau, ou les effets et les causes*); ph, Gunther Anders; m, Bernard Eichhorn, Roland Sonder-Mahnken; ed, Klaus Dudenhofer; art d, Herbert Kirchhoff, Albrecht Becker; cos, Werner Boehm.

Drama **(PR:A MPAA:NR)**

GLASS SLIPPER, THE** (1955) 93m MGM c

Leslie Caron *(Ella)*, Michael Wilding *(Prince Charles)*, Keenan Wynn *(Kovin)*, Estelle Winwood *(Mrs. Toquet)*, Elsa Lanchester *(Widow Sonder)*, Barry Jones *(Duke)*, Amanda Blake *(Birdena)*, Lisa Daniels *(Serafina)*, Lurene Tuttle *(Cousin Loulou)*, Lillane Montevecchi *(Tehara)*, Walter Pidgeon *(Narrator)*, Ballet de Paris.

A re-telling of the Cinderalla story with a few new twists added. Caron is the lead and is far less attractive than the two evil stepsisters but is transformed into a beauty by the film's end. Winwood is the fairy godmother who really doesn't work any magic. She's more of an eccentric old woman who lives in the forest and "inspires" Caron. The best thing THE GLASS SLIPPER has going for it is three well-staged ballets (though Wilding is inept when he tries his hand at it). Theme song, "Take My Love," Helen Deutsch, Bronislau Kaper.

p, Edwin H. Knopf; d, Charles Walters; w, Helen Deutsch; ph, Arthur E. Arling (Eastmancolor); m, Bronislau Kaper; ed, Ferris Webster; art d, Cedric Gibbons, Daniel B. Cathcart; cos, Helen Rose, Walter Plunkett; ch, Roland Petit.

Romance   **(PR:A MPAA:NR)**

GLASS SPHINX, THE*   (1968, Egypt/Ital./Span.) 91m
Italian International-P.I.C.A.S.A.—Copro/AIP c LA ESFINGE
DE CRISTAL; LA SFINGE D'ORO; UNA SFINGE TUTTA D'ORO)

Robert Taylor (Prof. Karl Nichols), Anita Ekberg (Paulette), Gianna Serra (Jenny), Jack Stuart (Ray), Angel Del Pozo (Alex), Jose Truchado (Theo), Remo De Angelis (Mirko), Emad Hamdy (Fouad), Ahmed Kamis (Chief Shoukry), Lidia Biondi.

Taylor is a famed archeologist digging in Egypt to find the legendary Glass Sphinx, which contains an immortalizing elixir. His secretary, Ekberg, is involved with a gang that not only wants the potion, but wants Taylor dead as well. She finds, however, that she cannot go on with the plot after she falls in love with him. The outlaws are not easily stopped and finally get the elixir, which turns out to be the best thing since baked bread. Taylor does his best to get Ekberg back; she has fled with the gang, but his hopes are shot down at the same time Ekberg is. This depressing decline for Taylor was released only a year before his death.

p, Fulvio Lucisano; d, Luigi Scattini, Kamel El Sheik; w, Rafael Sanchez Campoy, Jaime Camas Gil, Jose Antonio Cascales, Adalberto Albertini (Eng. dialog, Louis M. Hayward, Adriano Bolzoni; based on a story by Bolzoni, Albertini), ph, Felix Miron Martinez (Techniscope, Eastmancolor); m, Roberto Pregadio, Les Baxter (Eng. version); art d, Luis Arguello.

Adventure   **(PR:A MPAA:NR)**

GLASS TOMB, THE*   (1955, Brit.) 59m Hammer/Lippert bw
(THE GLASS CAGE)

John Ireland (Pel), Honor Blackman (Jenny), Geoffrey Keen (Stanton), Eric Pohlmann (Sapolio), Sidney James (Tony Lewis), Liam Redmond (Lindley), Sydney Tafler (Rorke), Valerie Vernon (Bella), Arnold Marle (Pop Manoni), Stan Little (Mickelwitz), Tonia Bern, Anthony Richmond, Norah Gordon, Arthur Howard.

The "Starving Man" at a carnival, Pohlmann, is found dead in the cage where he was to perform his next feat. It is discovered that he had seen the murder of a blackmailer and the killer turned on him to keep him quiet. Carnival vignettes keep this one lively.

p, Anthony Hinds; d, Montgomery Tully; w, Richard Landau (based on the novel The Outsiders by A. E. Martin); ph, Walter Harvey; m, Leonard Salzedo.

Crime   **(PR:A MPAA:NR)**

GLASS TOWER, THE**   (1959, Ger.) 104m Bavaria Filmkunst/Ellis Films
bw (DER GLASERNE TURM)

Lilli Palmer (Katja Fleming), O. E. Hasse (Robert Fleming), Peter Van Eyck (John Lawrence), Brigitte Horney (Dr. Bruning), Hans Messemer (Dr. Krell), Ludwig Linkmann (Blume), Gerd Brudern (Staatsanwalt), Hintz Fabricus (Gerichts-Prasident), Else Ehser (Mrs. Wiedecke), Werner Stock (Wendland), Ewald Wenck (Policeman), Gaby Fehling (Sister Margarethe).

Palmer's desire to return to the stage is forbidden by husband Hasse, mainly because this rich industrialist is too insecure to allow his wife to run around with free-wheeling theater people, especially playwright Van Eyck. When Palmer's passions are not met, Hasse winds up losing his wife completely. Despite a highly emotional performance by Palmer and a fittingly stiff one from Hasse, the material remains despairingly uninteresting.

d, Harold Braun; w, Wolfgang Koeppen (based on the novel by Odo Krohmann and Koeppen); m, Werner Eisbrenner.

Drama   **(PR:A MPAA:NR)**

GLASS WALL, THE½**   (1953) 78m Shane-Tors/COL bw

Vittorio Gassman (Peter), Gloria Grahame (Maggie), Ann Robinson (Nancy), Douglas Spencer (Inspector Bailey), Robin Raymond (Tanya), Jerry Paris (Tom), Elizabeth Slifer (Mrs. Hinckley), Richard Reeves (Eddie), Joseph Turkel (Freddie), Else Neft (Mr. Zakolya), Michael Fox (Toomey), Ned Booth (Monroe), Kathleen Freeman (Fat Woman), Juney Ellis (Girl Friend), Jack Teagarden, Shorty Rogers and His Band.

Gassman is a European who has jumped ship in a desperate attempt to immigrate to America. He flees to New York City where he is helped by a social outcast (Grahame) and Paris as a jazzman who knows about Gassman's underground activities for the Allies during World War II. An interesting premise for an American film considering that the Cold War was underway at the time. Documentary-style photography and atmospheric lighting work very nicely. A brief appearance by Teagarden and Rogers and his band, along with a hard jazzy score, give the story an even more kinetic feel.

p, Ivan Tors; d, Maxwell Shane; w, Tors, Shane; ph, Joseph F. Biroc; m, Leith Stevens; ed, Stanley Frazen; art d, Serge Krizman.

Drama   **(PR:A MPAA:NR)**

GLASS WEB, THE½**   (1953) 81m UNIV bw (3-D)

Edward G. Robinson (Henry Hayes), John Forsythe (Don Newell), Marcia Henderson (Louise Newell), Kathleen Hughes (Paula Ranier), Richard Denning (Dave Markson), Hugh Sanders (Lt. Stevens), Jean Willes (Sonia), Harry O. Tyler (Jake), Clark Howat (Bob Warren), Paul Dubov (Other Man), John Hiestand (Announcer), Bob Nelson (Plainclothesman), Dick Stewart (Everett), Jeri Lou James (Barbara

Newell), Duncan Richardson (Jimmy Newell), Jack Kelly (First Engineer), Alice Kelly (Waitress), Lance Fuller (Ad Lib), Brett Halsey (Lew), Kathleen Freeman (Mrs. O'Halloran), Eve McVeagh (Viv), Beverly Garland (Sally), Jack Lomas (Cliffie), Helen Wallace (Mrs. Doyle), Howard Wright (Weaver), Herbert C. Lytton (Gilbert), James Stone (Mr. Weatherby), John Verros (Fred Abbott), Benny Rubin (Tramp Comic), Eddie Parker (Tourist), Tom Greenway (District Attorney), Donald Kerr (Paper Man).

A minor crime melodrama made interesting by the use of 3-D. Hughes is an aggressive young actress who appears on a regular "Crime Of The Week" TV show. She had once had an affair with scriptwriter Forsythe and is now using that dalliance as blackmail to keep her on his show and to keep her purse lined with extra cash. He is about to pay her the last of the money and gets to her flat to find her murdered. Much as he would have wanted to do the job himself, he is innocent. Hughes was also blackmailing Robinson, the research director for the show. Since the crime remains unsolved, they decide to use it as the basis for one of the TV show's episodes. Robinson, who provides the data for the scripts, keeps feeding information to writer Forsythe. The evidence keeps pointing to Forsythe as the killer until Robinson gives himself away as the real criminal when he includes some facts that only the killer would know. When Forsythe realizes that, he confronts Robinson, and is about to be killed. However, this takes place in an empty studio and someone has conveniently left the cameras in operation. The police see what's happening and arrive to save Forsythe so he can go on to great stardom in TV's "Dynasty" 30 years later. The best part of the film was the authentic TV studio setting and Robinson's performance. The movie features several early appearances by actors who became famous on TV; Jack Kelly, Beverly Garland, Lance Fuller, Brett Halsey and Richard Denning all had their own starring or co-starring roles in series. This was one of Jack Arnold's four 3-D projects and not a very good one from the man who also directed THE INCREDIBLE SHRINKING MAN (1957), THE MOUSE THAT ROARED (1959), THE CREATURE FROM THE BLACK LAGOON (1954) as well as scores of TV comedies.

p, Albert J. Cohen; d, Jack Arnold; w, Robert Blees, Leonard Lee (based on the novel by Max Simon Ehrlich); ph, Maury Gertsman (3-D); m, Joseph Gershenson; ed, Ted J. Kent; art d, Bernard Herzbrun, Eric Orbom.

Mystery   **(PR:A MPAA:NR)**

GLEN OR GLENDA zero   (1953) 65m Screen Classics/PAR bw
(AKA: I LED TWO LIVES; I CHANGED MY SEX;
HE OR SHE; THE TRANSVESTITE)

Bela Lugosi (The Spirit), Lyle Talbot (Police Inspector Warren), Daniel Davis [Edward D. Wood, Jr.] (Glen/Glenda), Dolores Fuller (Barbara), "Tommy" Haynes (Alan/Ann), Timothy Farrell (Dr. Alton), Charles Crofts, Conrad Brooks, Henry Bederski, George Weiss.

Consistently voted as one of the worst movies of all time (if not the reigning champ) GLEN OR GLENDA, in its own unique way, is something of a classic. Davis (who was actually director Wood) is a regular guy who gets his kicks by dressing up in women's clothing and having a night on the town as "Glenda." Of course his fiance Fuller (Wood's real-life wife) is not too pleased with the situation. Haynes is Alan/Ann, an ex-Marine who undergoes a sex-change operation. Lugosi appears at intervals in the film to offer commentary on the proceedings. Surrounded by skeletons, shrunken heads and voodoo paraphernalia, Lugosi offers ominous warnings such as, "Beware of the green dragon that sits at your doorstep. . . .he eats little boys." Though everything about the film was decidedly on the cheap side, it does offer some insights into the then prevailing attitudes towards transvestites and sex changes. This was Wood's first directorial effort, and he went on to make several other camp classics, including ROBOT MONSTER (1953) and the infamous PLAN NINE FROM OUTER SPACE (1959). Famous sex-change personality Christine Jorgenson was approached to do this film but refused. A final footnote: Wood claims to have fought in WW II with silk panties beneath his khakis.

p, George G. Weiss; d&w, Edward D. Wood, Jr.; ph, William C. Thompson; ed, Bud Schelling.

Drama   **(PR:O MPAA:PG)**

GLENN MILLER STORY, THE**   (1953) 115m UNIV c

James Stewart (Glenn Miller), June Allyson (Helen Burger Miller), Charles Drake (Don Haynes), George Tobias (Si Schribman), Henry [Harry] Morgan (Chummy MacGregor), Marion Ross (Polly Haynes), Irving Bacon (Mr. Miller), Kathleen Lockhart (Mrs. Miller), Barton MacLane (Gen. Arnold), Sig Ruman (Mr. Krantz), Phil Garris (Joe Becker), James Bell (Mr. Burger), Katherine Warren (Mrs. Burger), Frances Langford, Louis Armstrong, Gene Krupa, Ben Pollack, Archie Savage Dancers, The Modernaires with Paula Kelly (Themselves), Dayton Lummis (Col. Spaulding), Deborah Sydes (Jonnie Dee), Anthony Sydes (Herbert), Ruth Hampton (Girl Singer), Damien O'Flynn (Col. Baker), Carleton Young (Adjutant General), William Challee (Sergeant), Steve Pendleton (Lt. Col. Baessell), Harry Harvey, Sr. (Doctor), Leo Mostovoy (Schillinger), Dick Ryan (Garage Man), Hal K. Dawson (Used Car Salesman), Lisa Gaye (Bobby-Soxer), Nino Tempo (Wilbur Schwartz), Babe Russin (Himself), Carl Vernell (Music Cutter), Bonnie Eddy (Irene), Robert A. Davis (Boy), The Mello Men, The Rolling Robinsons (Specialties), Roland Jones (Waiter), Kevin Cochran (Boy), Cicily Carter (Bobby-Soxer).

Unlike so many film bios, this one is an honest, intelligent depiction of one of America's greatest musical influences and doesn't merely string together a series of hit tunes in between gratuitous scenes. Well-told, well-acted and well-directed, all that's missing is Tex Beneke, who was the "boy singer" for Miller for years and even went on to lead the band after Miller's death. The omission of Beneke as part of the Miller coterie is a major mistake as Tex even appeared as himself with Miller in such pictures as ORCHESTRA WIVES (1942) and SUN VALLEY SERENADE (1941). In this, Stewart is Miller, a bright young man with a love for the trombone and a desire to create music. He encounters Allyson at the University of Colorado and she is struck by his shyness and sincerity; they are soon in love. After graduation, he goes to work for Ben Pollack (playing himself) and then in the pit of a Broadway show. On his wedding night, Allyson is shocked to find him at a hot jazz session in Harlem with Krupa, Satchmo, and several more. After studying for a while, he becomes best friends with George Tobias, who operates a Boston dance palace. Soon enough, he forms his own group and becomes a hot property. The war breaks out and he joins the Army, spending most of his time entertaining the troops that Bob Hope overlooked. His life is cut tragically short when he's flying over the English Channel in December, 1944, heading for Paris where he's going to do a concert and his plane mysteriously disappears. The famous Miller sound is discovered when he's working at Tobias dance hall and his trumpet player splits his lip, thereby causing the clarinet to play the lead on "Moonlight Serenade," (Mitchell Parish, Miller). It was an accident that was most fortuitous and from that moment on, you could always tell a Miller record. Stewart learned how to handle the trombone, but the actual playing was dubbed, variously credited to Murray MacEachern and to Joe Yukl. Many great tunes punctuate the excellent dialog. They include: "In The Mood," Andy Razaf, Joe Garland; "Tuxedo Junction," Buddy Feyne, Erskine Hawkins, William Johnson, William Dash; "Little Brown Jug," J. E. Winner; "Adios," Eddie Woods, Enric Madraguera; "String of Pearls," Eddie De Lange, Jerry Grey; "Pennsylvania 6-5000," Gray, Carl Sigman; "Stairway to the Stars," Mitchell Parish, Matt Malneck, Frank Signorelli; "American Patrol," E. H. Meacham; "I Know Why," "Chattanooga Choo Choo," Mack Gordon, Harry Warren; "Bidin' My Time," George and Ira Gershwin; "I Dreamed I Dwelt In Marble Halls," Alfred Bunne, Michael Balfe; "St. Louis Blues March," Ray McKinley, Perry Burgett, Jerry Gray, Glenn Miller (based on W. C. Handy's "St. Louis Blues.")

p, Aaron Rosenberg; d, Anthony Mann; w, Valentine Davies, Oscar Brodney; ph, William Daniels (Technicolor); m, Joseph Gershenson (adaptation, Henry Mancini); ed, Russell Schoengarth; ch, Kenny Williams; tech adv, Chummy MacGregor.

Musical/Biography   **(PR:AAA   MPAA:NR)**

GLENROWAN AFFAIR, THE*½   (1951, Aus.) 70m Australian
                                                     Action/British Empire Films bw

Bob Chitty (Ned Kelly), Ben Crowe (Dan Kelly), Larry Crowhurst (Joe Byrne), Bill Crowe (Steve Hart), Rupe Kathner (Aaron Sherritt), Alma King (Kate Kelly), John Fernside (Father Gibney), Frank Ransome (Sergeant Steele), Charles Tasman (Commissioner Nicholson), George Webb (Supt. Hare), Edward Smith (Mr. Standish), Alan Bardsley (Old Man), Arthur Hemsley (Barfly).

One of many films, songs, and stories about the Ned Kelly gang, outlaws of the outback, as famous down under as the Jesse James legend in the U.S. (and closely paralleling it in many ways). THE GLENROWAN AFFAIR, in which the police-hating Kelly mob lured a trainload of cops to that town after removing a section of track, thinking to cause a derailment, is as well known in the bush country as the James boys' THE GREAT NORTHFIELD, MINNESOTA RAID (1972). Unfortunately, this poorly made representation of that auspicious event doesn't begin to come up to its American counterpart. Largely interesting as a slice of Australian history for the cobber lovers among us. The inventive Ned Kelly (Chitty) is captured by being shot in the legs after police bullets fail to penetrate his armor plate, made—in a strange inversion of the Biblical injunction—from plowshares. Kelly was tried and hanged in Melbourne in 1880.

d&w, Rupe Kathner; ph, Harry Malcolm.

Crime/Biography   **(PR:C   MPAA:NR)**

GLIMPSE OF PARADISE, A*½   (1934, Brit.) 56m WB-FN bw

George Carney (Jim Bogsworth), Eve Lister (Marion Fielding), Robert Cochran (Norman Ware), Wally Patch (Harry), Winifred Oughton (Mrs. Latter), Roddy Hughes (Walter Fielding), Katie Johnson (Mrs. Fielding), Margaret Yarde (Mrs. Kidd), D. J. Williams (Bert Kidd), Fred Groves (Joshua Ware), Reg Marcus, Sydney Monckton, Claude Horton, Fletcher Lightfoot, Eve Llewellyn, Phyllis Baker, Quinton McPherson.

Self-sacrificing father Carney has a chance to prove his worth by keeping his daughter out of the grips of a vicious blackmailer. He does this good deed without ever letting her on to his true identity, his having been in prison and without contact from the kid since she was an infant.

p, Irving Asher; d, Ralph Ince; w, Michael Barringer (based on a story by Sam Mintz); ph, Basil Emmott.

Crime/Drama   **(PR:A   MPAA:NR)**

GLITTERBALL, THE*   (1977, Brit) 56m Mark Forstater/Children's Film
                                                              Foundation c

Ben Buckton, Keith Jayne, Ron Pember, Marjorie Yates, Barry Jackson, Andrew Jackson.

A compelling children's film which pre-dates Steven Spielberg's E.T. by five years. Essentially the story is the same; a little alien (Glitterball) is abandoned on Earth and Buckton and Jayne are the kids who help it get home. The finale has the alien mother ship come to the rescue. It has some commendable special effects and is short enough to keep the little ones' attention.

p, Mark Forstater; d, Harley Cockliss; w, Howard Thompson; ph, Alan Hall; spec eff, Brian Johnson, Charles Page.

Children's Film/Fantasy/
Science-Fiction   **(PR:AAA   MPAA:NR)**

GLOBAL AFFAIR, A   (1964) 84m Seven Arts MGM bw

Bob Hope (Frank Larrimore), Lilo Pulver (Sonya), Michelle Mercier (Lisette), Elga Andersen (Yvette), Yvonne DeCarlo (Dolores), Miiko Taka (Fumiko), Robert Sterling (Randy), Nehemiah Persoff (Sigura), John McGiver (Snifter), Jacques Bergerac (Louis Duval), Mickey Shaughnessy (Policeman), Barbara Bouchet (Girl), Billy Halop (Cabby), Adlai Stevenson (Passerby), Reta Shaw (Nurse Argyle), Henry Kulky (Charlie), Francis de Sales (U. S. Delegate), Rodolfo Hayes, Jr. (Spanish Delegate), Lester Mathews (U. K. Delegate), Boothe Coleman (Delegate), William

Newell (Waiter), Tanya Lemani (Panja), Georgia Hayes (Jean), Edmon Ryan (Gavin), Baby Monroe (First Citizen of the World), Rafer Johnson (Nigerian Representative), Hugh Downs (TV Commentator), Martin Blaine, Inez Pedroza, Francoise Ruggieri, Voltaire Perkins.

Hope is a United Nations department head who finds an abandoned baby in the internationally owned building. Since no one knows who the baby is or where he's from, Hope is wooed by a variety of international beauties in a strange kind of contest to see which country will get the kid. Hope finally decides to keep the baby and delivers a speech to the General Assembly about international brotherhood. There are some good laughs for Hope and a nice supporting cast, but the plot is pretty standard and predictable. Hope's final speech is unbelievably pretentious. Look for Adlai Stevenson's walk-on and sports legend Rafer Johnson's brief bit. Songs include "So Wide the World" (sung by Vic Dana) "Fais Do Do," "A Global Affair," Dorcas Cochran, Dominic Frontiere.

p, Hall Bartlett; d, Jack Arnold; w, Arthur Marx, Bob Fisher, Charles Lederer (based on a story by Eugene Vale); ph, Joseph Ruttenberg; m, Dominic Frontiere; ed, Bud Molin; art d, George W. Davis, Preston Ames; set d, Henry Grace, Charles Thompson; cos, Bill Thomas; makeup, William Tuttle, Layne Britton.

Comedy   **(PR:A   MPAA:NR)**

GLORIA*½**   (1980) 123m COL c

Gena Rowlands (Gloria Swenson), Juan Adames (Philip Dawn), Buck Henry (Jack Dawn), Julie Carmen (Jeri Dawn), Lupe Guarnica (Margarita Vargas), Jessica Castillo (Joan Dawn), Tony Knesich (1st Man/Gangster), Ralph Dolman (Kid 1/Back of the Bus), Israel Castro (Kid 2/Back of the Bus), Carlos Castro (Kid 3/Back of the Bus), Philomena Spagnolo (Old Lady), Tom Noonan (2nd Man/Gangster), Gregory Gleghorne (Kid in Elevator), Kyle-Scott Jackson (1st Policeman), Gary Klarr (2nd Policeman), Roman Rodriguez (Escape Cab Driver), George Yudzevich (Heavyset Man), Ronnie Maccone (3rd Man/Gangster), Asa Quawee (Cab Driver No. 2).

A gutsy, spellbinding performance by Rowlands makes GLORIA a must for crime film fans, although the story requires sustaining a surrealistic point of view. A woman in her forties, Rowlands lives alone with her cats and her savings, a comfortable nestegg built up from turning tricks with high-placed mobsters over the decades. She borrows a cup of coffee from her neighbors, Henry and his Puerto Rican wife, and quickly learns that they are marked for death by the Mafia, Henry having been the bookkeeper for the mob and having kept a diary of all illegal actions which the mob has discovered. Rowlands is asked by the family to take the children, an 8-year-old boy, Adames, and an older girl. The girl insists upon staying with her family but the boy goes to Rowlands' apartment. Minutes later the Mafia goons slaughter the family. Rowlands shields the boy, then flees with him, and the much sought after diary. The chase is on, with the goons hunting all over Manhattan for Rowlands and the boy. Guns explode, cars and cabs careen and squeal around corners and race up and down streets until Rowlands can stand it no more. She pulls a gun and blasts a packed car of pursuing gangsters, killing the driver and causing the car to crash, then shooting the rest of the occupants and escaping with the child. But it's a one-sided war. Rowlands knows this and goes to a Mafia don with whom she has had an affair, begging for the life of the child and offering to turn over the diary. The answer is a firm and cold-blooded no. It's a matter of Mafia honor that the entire family be killed, including the boy, who might grow up to kill Mafia people. The boy must die. Rowlands manages to escape the Mafia don's lair and again flee with the boy. By film's end we are led to believe that both will live, albeit in anonymity. Rowlands gives the finest portrayal of her career, that of the nervous, apprehensive woman who finds somewhere in her insides the courage to defy an evil system and fight it to a bloody standstill. Adames is both precocious and fascinating, a child with boyish temperament who uncannily becomes adult in pressure situations. Director Cassavetes (Rowlands' husband) proves his probing expertise with incisive scenes while maintaining a chillingly brisk pace; he is marvelously supported by cinematographer Schuler whose fluid cameras record the terrible unfolding action and penetrating closeups of the hunted pair. This is, nevertheless, a traumatizing study of extreme violence and, as such, is not for youngsters.

p,d&w, John Cassavetes; ph, Fred Schuler; m, Bill Conti; ed, Jack McSweeney; prod d, Rene D'Auriac, Fred Schuler; cos, Peggy Farrell.

Crime Drama   **Cas.**   **(PR:O   MPAA:R)**

GLORIFYING THE AMERICAN GIRL½**   (1930) 96m PAR bw/c

Mary Eaton (Gloria Hughes), Edward Crandall (Buddy), Olive Shen (Barbara), Dan Healey (Miller), Kaye Renard (Mooney), Sarah Edwards (Mrs. Hughes), Eddie Cantor, Rudy Vallee and His Orchestra, Mr. and Mrs. Florenz Ziegfeld, Mayor and Mrs. James Walker, Ring Lardner, Noah Beery, Texas Guinan, Johnny Weissmuller, Irving Berlin, Adolph Zukor, Charles Dillingham, Norman Brokenshire (Narrator), Helen Morgan.

Eaton's a chorus girl with an internal struggle: does she want the love of Crandall or the love of teeming millions as she performs in the Ziegfeld Follies? The thin plot line is really just an excuse for the production numbers, songs, and sketches contained in this film. Some great songs, Cantor's marvelous tailor bit, and a host of celebrity "first nighters" dutifully noted by the offscreen narrator. This is the only film Ziegfeld ever produced and it had been his hope for it to be the first all-singing, all-talking film. But due to production delays, including sound problems and Ziegfeld's financial notoriety, the dream was not to be. The film suffers from being shot at Paramount's Astoria, Long Island Studio, for superior sound equipment was already being used in California. Songs include "What Wouldn't I Do For That Man," E. Y. Harburg, Jay Gorney; "Blue Skies," Irving Berlin; "I'm Just a Vagabond Lover," Leon Zimmerman, Rudy Vallee; "Baby Face," Harry Akst, Benny Davis; "At Sundown," "Beautiful Changes," "Sam the Old Accordion Man," "There Must Be Someone Waiting For Me," Walter Donaldson.

d, Millard Webb; w, Webb, J. P. McEvoy; ph, George Folsey (Part 2—Technicolor); ch, Frank Tours (musical numbers), Ted Shawn (ballet ensembles).

Musical   **Cas.**   **(PR:A MPAA:NR)**

GLORIOUS SACRIFICE   (SEE: GLORY TRAIL, THE, 1937)

GLORY**½   (1955) 99m David Butler/RKO c

Margaret O'Brien (Clarabel Tilbee), Walter Brennan (Ned Otis), Charlotte Greenwood (Miz Tilbee), John Lupton (Chad Chadburn), Byron Palmer (Hoppy Hollis), Lisa Davis (Candy Trent), Gus Schilling (Joe Page), Theron Jackson (Alexander), Hugh Sanders (Sobbing Sam Cooney), Walter Baldwin (Doc Brock), Harry Tyler (Beed Wickwire), Leonid Kinskey (Vasily), Paul Burns (Squeaky Bob), Madge Blade (Aunt Martha).

Pretty standard fare involving grown-up O'Brien as a racehorse owner in the blue grass of Kentucky. She and her grandmother can't raise the money to buy horse feed but somehow with Brennan's help can get the funds to put their filly in the Kentucky Derby. Guess who wins the big race? The story is padded with a romantic interest for O'Brien. Does Lupton love her or snooty society woman Davis? All is resolved when the horse wins the big one, and Lupton wins O'Brien. She even gets a chance to sing during the film, though the voice is that of Norma Zimmer. Overlong and predictable stuff, although the Kentucky scenery and some footage of horses looks pretty good.

p&d, David Butler; w, Peter Milne (based on a story by Gene Markey); ph, Wilfrid M. Cline (Superscope, Technicolor); m, Frank Perkins; ed, Irene Morra; art d, Albert D'Agostino; cos, Michael Woulfe; m/l, "Glory," "Gettin' Nowhere Road," "Kentucky (Means Paradise)," M. K. Jerome, Ted Koehler.

Family Drama   **(PR:AAA MPAA:NR)**

GLORY ALLEY**   (1952) 79m MGM bw

Ralph Meeker (Socks Barbarrosa), Leslie Caron (Angela), Kurt Kasznar (The Judge), Gilbert Roland (Peppi Donnato), John McIntire (Gabe Jordan), Louis Armstrong (Shadow Johnson), Jack Teagarden (Himself), Dan Seymour (Sal Nichols "The Pig"), Larry Gates (Dr. Robert Ardley), Pat Goldin (Jabber), John Indrisano (Spider), Mickey Little (Domingo), Dick Simmons (Dan), Pat Valentino (Terry Walker), David McMahon (Frank the Policeman), George Garver (Newsboy Addams).

A weak psychological drama has Meeker as a promising boxer from the Latin Quarter of New Orleans who panics on the eve of his attempt to take the middleweight crown, thus disgracing himself and all his friends, who reside in a side street known as Glory Alley. His close friend, Kasznar, who is the blind father of Meeker's dancer girl friend, Caron, brands Meeker a coward when he shows up to offer a half-hearted explanation to cronies in the gym owned by Roland. Kasznar's rage is such that it puts a damper on the Meeker-Caron romance and the prizefighter leaves New Orleans, joining the army and fighting in Korea. Meeker returns a great hero, holder of the Congressional Medal of Honor. He hangs around Glory Alley, wallowing in hero worship, while Caron goes on supporting her blind father by doing snaky, sexy burlesque dances in a local bistro (with "Satchmo" Armstrong accompanying her in a particular steamy version of "St. Louis Blues" where Caron does a sizzling, leggy, hip-grinding dance). She's true-blue to Meeker but most still feel that when it comes to the ring he's still a coward. Meeker backs Kasznar in a business that fails, then half-heartedly begins training for the championship fight all over again. He admits to Caron that he took it on the run earlier because, of all things, he was terrified that the fight crowd would see an ugly scar on his head! Caron and others persuade him to overlook this distracting disfigurement and Meeker goes into the ring and wins the crown, becoming the hero of Glory Alley and the idol of his hootchy-cootch dancer. The story is muddled and disjointed and the direction by Walsh, normally a top-flight helmsman, is inexplicably weak. Caron's dancing stands out as does Armstrong's wonderful artistry on the horn when playing the title song and a hot number entitled "That's What the Man Said."

p, Nicholas Nayfack; d, Raoul Walsh; w, Art Cohn; ph, William Daniels; ed, Gene Ruggiero; md, Georgie Stoll; art d, Cedric Gibbons, Malcolm Brown; ch, Charles O'Curran.

Drama   **(PR:C MPAA:NR)**

GLORY AT SEA**½   (1952, Brit.) 100m Molton-BL/IF bw
     (GB: THE GIFT HORSE)

Trevor Howard (L/C Hugh Fraser), Richard Attenborough (Dripper Daniels), Sonny Tufts (Yank Flanagan), James Donald (Lt. Richard Jennings), Joan Rice (June Mallory), Bernard Lee (Stripey Wood), Dora Bryan (Glad), Hugh Williams (Capt), Robin Bailey (Lt. Michael Grant), Meredith Edwards (Jones), John Forrest (Appleby), Patric Doonan (PO Martin), Sidney James (Ned Hardy), James Kenny (John Fraser), James Carney (Bone), Russell Enoch (Adams), Anthony Oliver, Harold Siddons, Harry Towb, George Street, Glyn Houston, John Gabriel, Michael Ashlin, Peter Hobbes, John Warren, Hugh Hastings, Tony Quinn, David Oake, Gwenda Wilson, Peter Bathurst, Lyn Evans, Robert Moore, John Wynn, Harold Ayer, Alan Rolfe, Michael Mulcaster, John Brooking, Tim Turner, Cyril Conway, Ann Wheatley, Charles Lloyd Pack, John Clevedon, Olaf Pooley.

Howard plays the demanding and unpopular commanding officer of a broken down battleship. His attitude toward his men and theirs toward him begin to turnabout after a conflict with the Germans proves the ancient battleship is still able to perform. A well-paced effort.

p, George Pitcher; d, Compton Bennett; w, William Fairchild, William Rose, Hugh Hastings (based on a story by Ivan Goff and Ben Roberts); ph, Harry Waxman.

War   **Cas.**   **(PR:A MPAA:NR)**

GLORY BOY*½   (1971) 93m Waxman/Cinerama c
     (AKA: MY OLD MAN'S PLACE; THE OLD MAN'S PLACE)

Arthur Kennedy (Walter Pell), Mitchell Ryan (Sgt. Martin Flood), William Devane (Jimmy Pilgrim), Michael Moriarty (Trubee Pell), Topo Swope (Helen), Lloyd Gough (Dr. Paul), Ford Rainey (Sheriff Coleman), Peter Donat (Car Salesman), Sandra Vacey (Darlene Pilgrim), Paula Kauffman (Bubbles), Eve Marchand (Streetwalker).

Rapes, scrapes, and shootings on the old homestead as Viet Nam vet Moriarty and his buddy, lower-East-side kid Devane, visit dad Kennedy on their return from a conflict in which Moriarty—to his shame—has been forced to kill a Vietnamese woman. Meeting happy psychopathic-killer-sergeant Ryan, encountered while roughing up a San Francisco transvestite, Moriarty decides to invite him to come and meet dear old dad, jingoistic Kennedy, who espouses the homilies of machodom and delights in his memories of WW II. The intended therapy of confrontation with a younger mirror-image carried to an illogical extreme fails to take, at least at the outset; dad retains his misguided ideals despite his humiliations by the sadistic sergeant. Devane attempts to hunt down his cuckolding wife and, unsuccessful, returns to the farm with Swope—daughter of actress Dorothy McGuire in real life—a Canadian peace-worker hitchhiker, whom the rabid Ryan attempts to rape. Diverted from his violence by a gunshot wound at the hands of the dim-witted Devane, the convalescing Ryan evinces a born-again humility and swears to mend his meretricious ways. Moriarty and Swope fall in love; Kennedy hopes they will remain on the old homestead, reprising his own history. The recovered Ryan, re-enlisting, celebrates his departure by raping Swope and firing a shotgun at the others. The mortally wounded Kennedy kills Ryan and then makes his peace with son Moriarty. Originally intended to be a starring vehicle for actor Robert Blake, the film features strong performances from an excellent cast of relative unknowns. Devane went on to become one of the kings of TV soap operas before landing other solid movie parts. Moriarty developed into a fine character actor. This was one of many films to exploit the Viet Nam war theme, and not one of the most successful. Barring the sex and violence, GLORY BOY is slow in pace and low in production values.

p, Philip A. Waxman; d, Edwin Sherin; w, Stanford Whitmore (based on the novel The Old Man's Place by John Sanford); ph, Richard C. Glouner (Technicolor); m, Charles Gross; ed, Ferris Webster; art d, Robin Wagner; cos, Thomas Walsh; spec eff, Aubrey P. Pollard; m/l, "Glory Boy," Gross, Norma Green (sung by Gary Lemel); makeup, Joseph Di Bella.

Drama   **(PR:O MPAA:R)**

GLORY BRIGADE, THE***   (1953) 82m FOX bw

Victor Mature (Lt. Sam Prior), Alexander Scourby (Lt. Niklas), Lee Marvin (Corp. Bowman), Richard Egan (Sgt. Johnson), Nick Dennis (Corp. Marakis), Roy Roberts (Sgt. Chuck Anderson), Alvy Moore (Pvt. Stone), Russell Evans (Pvt. Taylor), Henry Kulky (Sgt. Smitowsky), Gregg Martell (Pvt. Ryan), Lamont Johnson (Capt. Adams), Carleton Young (Capt. Davis), Frank Gerstle (Maj. Sauer), Stuart Nedd (Lt. Jorgenson), George Michaelides (Pvt. Nemos), John Verros (Capt. Charos), Alberto Morin (Sgt. Lykos), Archer MacDonald (Sgt. Kress), Peter Mamakos (Col. Kallicles), Father Patrinakos (Chaplain), John Haretakis, Costas Morfis, David Gabbai, Nico Minardos (Greek Soldiers), George Saris (Medic), Jonathan Hale (Col. Peterson).

Mature stars as a U.S. Army lieutenant of Greek descent who volunteers to command a joint American/Greek regiment into Communist territory during the Korean conflict. The purpose of the mission is to gather intelligence information regarding the enemy troop strength and tactics. Tension flairs between the Americans and the Greeks after the first skirmish with the enemy when it appears that the Greeks avoided combat since their bayonets are free of blood stains. The crisis mounts when Mature begins to lose most of his American men while the Greeks emerge virtually unscathed. Eventually Mature learns that the Greek soldiers traditionally cleanse their bayonets of blood, and he and the Americans realize that they have been wrong about their comrades all along. Pulling together for the first time, the soldiers are finally able to cut their losses and accomplish their mission, while gaining new respect for each other. Better than average war film helped immensely by a strong cast (it was one of Lee Marvin's earliest roles), fast pace, and crisp photography by cinematographer Ballard.

p, William Bloom; d, Robert D. Webb, w, Franklin Coen; ph, Lucien Ballard; ed, Marlo Mora; art d, Lyle Wheeler, Lewis Creber; ch, Matt Mattox.

War   **(PR:C MPAA:NR)**

GLORY GUYS, THE**   (1965) 111m UA c

Tom Tryon (Demas Harrod), Harve Presnell (Sol Rogers), Senta Berger (Lou Woodward), James Caan (Dugan), Andrew Duggan (Gen. McCabe), Slim Pickens (Gregory), Peter Breck (Hodges), Jeanne Cooper (Mrs. McCabe), Laurel Goodwin (Beth), Adam Williams (Crain), Erik Holland (Gentry), Robert McQueeney (Marcus), Wayne Rogers (Moyan), William Meigs (Treadway), Alice Backes (Mrs. Poole), Walter Scott (Lt. Cook), Michael Forest (Marshall Cushman), George Ross (Hanavan), Dal McKennon (Gunsmith), Stephen Chase (Gen. Hoffman), Henry Beckman (Salesman), Michael Anderson, Jr. (Martin Hale).

Duggan is a general who has political ambitions and will stop at nothing—including sacrificing his troops—to gain his intended end. Pretty routine stuff that screenwriter Peckinpah also dealt with that year in his directorial effort MAJOR DUNDEE. The large supporting cast is terrific. Caan is good as a stubborn recruit, and veteran character actor Pickens provides his usual comic relief. Though the direction is uninspired, the film is greatly enhanced by the photography of veteran cameraman Howe. The battle sequences are excellent and there's a nice use of slow zooms.

p, Arnold Laven, Arthur Gardner, Jules Levy; d, Laven; w, Sam Peckinpah (based on the novel The Dice of God by Hoffman Birney); ph, James Wong Howe (Panavision, DeLuxe Color); m, Riz Ortolani; ed, Melvin Shapiro, Ernst R. Rolf;

prod d, Edward S. Haworth; art d, Roberto Silva; set d, Ray Moyer; cos, Frank C. Beetson, Jr.; makeup, Donald W. Roberson.

Western **(PR:C MPAA:NR)**

GLORY OF FAITH, THE**½ (1938, Fr.) 70m Film de Koster/French Film Exchange bw

Gabriel Farguette *(Jean Renaut)*, Jacqueline Francell *(Marie-Therese)*, Alice Tissot *(Madame Renaut)*, Raymond Galle *(Louis Rateur)*, Jean Dax *(Monsieur Renaut)*, Germaine Sablon *(Rose)*.

A modernization of the story of Saint Theresa in which Francell is a seamstress with an overwhelming and passionate faith. The Francell character is introduced followed by a recounting of the life of St. Theresa. Parallels between their two lives encompass the rest of the film. There is a nice blend of humor and drama within the film and the script is nicely paced. In its original American showing, some theaters chose to book it with a newsreel on the beatification of Mother Cabrini. (In French; English subtitles.)

d, Georges Pallu; m, Jane Bos.

Drama **(PR:A MPAA:NR)**

GLORY STOMPERS, THE zero (1967) 84m Norman T. Herman/AIP c

Dennis Hopper *(Chino)*, Jody McCrea *(Darryl)*, Chris Noel *(Chris)*, Jock Mahoney *(Smiley)*, Jim Reader *(Paul)*, Saundra Gale *(Jo Ann)*, Robert Tessier *(Magoo)*, Astrid Warner *(Doreen)*, Gary Wood *(Pony)*, Lindsay Crosby *(Monk)*, Casey Kasem *(Mouth)*, Al Quick, Paul Prokop, Tony Acone, Ed Cook.

Pre-EASY RIDER (1969) Hopper is a motorcycle gang leader who kidnaps rival gang leader McCrea and gal pal Noel. He gets beaten and left for dead; she nearly gets sold into the Mexican white slave market. Of course McCrea recovers and rounds up his buddies for a little old-fashioned biker-picture revenge. Pretty routine biker stuff with some fine camera work. Don't miss an appearance by dee jay Kasem. Try to stay awake during the much-ballyhooed "love-in."

p, John Lawrence; d, Anthony M. Lanza; w, Lawrence, James Gordon White; ph, Mario Tossi (Colorscope, Pathe Color); m, Sidewalk Productions, Inc., Mike Curb; ed, Len Miller.

Drama **(PR:O MPAA:NR)**

GLORY TRAIL, THE*½ (1937) 64m Crescent bw (AKA: GLORIOUS SACRIFICE)

Tom Keene *(John Morgan)*, Joan Barclay *(Lucy Strong)*, E. H. Calvert *(Col. Strong)*, Frank Melton *(Gilchrist)*, William Royle *(Capt. Fetterman)*, Walter Long *(Riley)*, Allen Greer *(Indian Joe)*, William Crowell *(Wainwright)*, Harve Foster *(Hampton)*, Ann Hovey *(Julie Morgan)*, John Lester Johnson *(Toby)*, Etta McDaniel *(Mandy)*, James Bush *(David Kirby)*.

While building railroad lines, a group of workers and soldiers have to fight off constant trouble from the Indians. Keene plays a scout, with Barclay and Royle as the love interest. The direction and camera work are typical of B-Western standards, but the acting is lackluster.

p, E. B. Derr; d, Lynn Shores; w, John T. Neville; ph, Arthur Martinelli; ed, Don Barrett; md, Abe Meyer; art d, Paul F. Sylos.

Western **(PR:A MPAA:NR)**

GLOVE, THE*½ (1980) 90m Tommy J./Pro International c (AKA: BLOOD MAD)

John Saxon *(Sam Kellough)*, Roosevelt Grier *(Victor Hale)*, Joanna Cassidy *(Sheila Michaels)*, Joan Blondell *(Mrs. Fitzgerald)*, Jack Carter *(Walter Stratton)*, Keenan Wynn *(Bill Schwartz)*, Aldo Ray *(Prison Guard)*, Michael Pataki *(Harry Iverson)*, Misty Bruce *(Lisa)*, Howard Honig *(Lt. Kruger)*.

Saxon is an ex-ballplayer, ex-policeman who now makes a living as a bounty hunter. A $20,000 reward is offered for the capture of Grier after he attacks a prison guard with a "riot glove," a metal-loaded number that gives Grier a ROLLERBALL-chic look. But Grier's a psychotic with a conscience: when not attacking assorted victims he plays guitar for ghetto children. There is, of course, the inevitable showdown that resorts to mob action for excitement. Pretty bad all around, with a pseudo-*film noir* narration by Saxon. Blondell, in a cameo, is completely wasted and Cassidy is little more than decoration. Uninspired and violent, though Grier gives a hint that with better material he could really be something.

p, Julian Roffman; d, Ross Hagen; w, Roffman, Hubert Smith; ph, Gary Graver (Metrocolor); m, Robert O. Ragland; ed, Bob Fitzgerald; action and fight d, Roffman.

Crime/Action **Cas.** **(PR:O MPAA:R)**

GLOWING AUTUMN** (1981, Jap.) 137m Toho-Mitsukoshi/Toho c (MOERU AKI)

Kyako Maya, Shin Saburi, Kinya Kitaoji, Mayumi Ogawa.

Masaki Kobayashi is a superb director when it comes to visual images. He is rivaled in Japan only by Kurosawa for his technical expertise and his ability to provide memorable imagery. However, visuals only do not a motion picture make. This is the major fault with GLOWING AUTUMN. Kobayashi creates a sumptuous world of images but, in the end, loses the audience to a silly plot twist that confuses and angers as well. A young woman is living with an older businessman who has brought out the animal passion in her. She vacations in Kyoto and meets a handsome young photographer who is a breath of fresh air after she has spent so much time with her older, brooding lover. She wants to develop a relationship with the youth but can't shake the hold her benefactor has on her. Until now, the movie is wonderful to watch and the love triangle is interesting. Then the film falls apart when the older lover dies and the woman is willed a round-trip ticket to Iran. She is partial to Persian rugs, and now can go to the source and buy what she likes. The photographer then shows up with some hare-brained scheme to make Persian rugs in Japan and sell them as real, for very low prices. And that's about that. Like many Japanese films, this one takes a long time getting where it's going, which is often nowhere. A misfire, but exquisitely shot.

p, Sanezumi Fujimoto; d, Masaki Kobayashi; w, Shun Inagaki; ph, Kozo Okazaki; m, Toru Takemitis; ed, Keiichi Uraoka.

Drama **(PR:A-C MPAA:NR)**

GNOME-MOBILE, THE**** (1967) 84m BV c

Walter Brennan *(D.J. Mulrooney/Knobby)*, Tom Lowell *(Jasper)*, Matthew Garber *(Rodney Winthrop)*, Ed Wynn *(Rufus)*, Karen Dotrice *(Elizabeth Winthrop)*, Richard Deacon *(Ralph Yarby)*, Sean McClory *(Horatio Quaxton)*, Jerome Cowan *(Dr. Conrad Ramsey)*, Charles Lane *(Dr. Scroggins)*, Norman Grabowski *(Male Nurse #1)*, Gil Lamb *(Gas Station Attendant)*, Maudie Prickett *(Katie Barrett)*, Cami Sebring *(Violet)*, Ellen Corby *(Etta Pettibone)*, Frank Cady *(Charlie Pettibone)*, Hal Baylor *(Male Nurse #2)*, Karl Held *(Paul)*, Charles Smith *(Airport Attendant)*, Byron Foulger *(Hotel Clerk)*, Susan Flannery *(Airline Stewardess)*, Ernestine Barrier *(Nell)*, Dee Carroll *(Second Secretary)*, William Fawcett *(Chauffeur)*, Robert S. Carson *(Twin Oaks Attendant)*, Jack Davis *(Manson)*, John Cliff *(Night Watchman)*, Mickey Martin *(Bellboy)*, Alvy Moore *(Gas Station Mechanic)*, Dale Van Sickel *(Uniformed Guard)*, Parley Baer *(Voice of Owl)*, Jimmy Murphy *(Voice of Raccoon)*, Jesslyn Fax, Dee Carroll *(Voices of Bluejays)*, Pamela Gail *(Snapdragon)*, Susan Henning, Judy Van Wormer, Dyane Robins, Toni O'Connor, Kathy Foley, Barbara Halpern, Joyce Menges, Bunny Henning, Mimi Zerbini, Kathee Francis, Pat Ann Reid, Cindy Taylor, Susan Gates, Marianna Case, Jacquelyn Mary Ray, Shawn Scott, Sandra Gimpel, Virginia Aldridge *(Gnome Maidens)*, Amedee Chabot, Carla Borelli, Jeanne Shipman, Nancy Gould, Karin Blake, Carol O'Kane, Pamela Howard, Carol Merrill, Jackie Andre, Brenda Power, Dorothy Duffy *(Married Gnomes)*.

Brennan enacts what was said to be his first dual role in this terrific children's movie based on a novel by social reformer Upton Sinclair, author of the famed *The Jungle*. Brennan is an elderly timber tycoon, an arch conservative. He takes his grandchildren, Garber and Dotrice (from MARY POPPINS, 1964, as was Wynn in this, the last picture he made before his death) for a ride among the redwoods in his prized 1930 Rolls Royce. When the trio stops to picnic, Dotrice ambles off and runs into Lowell, a youthful, tiny gnome, and his 943-year-old ailing grandfather (also Brennan, who plays the role as a stereotypical leprechaun, brogue and all). The two explain their situation: isolated from the rest of their ilk, Lowell seems fated to be the last of his line, a situation which has his grandfather depressed to the point of illness. Enlisting the aid of Garber and Brennan the lumber baron, Dotrice offers to assist the ill-fated duo to find others of their kind. The quintet takes to the trail in the limousine, now dubbed "The Gnome-Mobile." Staying the night in a motel—the petite pair concealed in a picnic basket for protection from prying eyes—gnome Brennan discovers that tycoon Brennan is the financier foe of the forest. He raises a ruckus which results in his discovery by freak-show operator McClory, who promptly gnabs the gnomes, intending to put them on display. Irate tycoon Brennan, on discovering their disappearance, contacts his company's vice-president, Deacon, alerting him to marshal the security forces of the firm and institute a search. Deacon promptly has his gnome-knowing boss consigned to the funny farm. His grandchildren free him, resulting in one of the best Disney car chases of all time as the trio flee in THE GNOME-MOBILE, rescuing Lowell in the process. Gnome Brennan, who had escaped by his own devices, is found by the four in a sylvan glade chatting with the king of the gnomes. Fortuitously, this personage is attended by dozens of diminutive damsels, all eager to land Lowell as lord and master. A footrace is arranged to decide the bride; the winner is shy Violet, the personal preference of the groom. The lumber lord allots a lot of land to the little folk as a nuptial gift, and all enter the limousine for a parting joyride to the strains of "The Gnome-Mobile Song."

p, Walt Disney, James Algar; d, Robert Stevenson; w, Ellis Kadison (based on the novel *The Gnomobile; a Gnice Gnew Gnarrative With Gnonsense, But Gnothing Gnaughty* by Upton Sinclair); ph, Edward Coleman (Technicolor); m, Buddy Baker; ed, Norman R. Palmer; art d, Carroll Clark, William H. Tuntke; set d, Emile Kuri, Hal Gausman; cos, Bill Thomas, Chuck Keehne, Neva Rames; spec eff, Eustace Lycett, Robert A. Mattey; makeup, Pat McNally.

Fantasy **Cas.** **(PR:AAA PR:NR)**

GOBEN NO TSUBAKI (SEE: SCARLET CAMELLIA, THE, 1965, Jap.)

GO-BETWEEN, THE**** (1971, Brit.) 118m MGM-EMI/COL c

Julie Christie *(Marian Maudsley)*, Alan Bates *(Ted Burgess)*, Dominic Guard *(Leo Colston)*, Margaret Leighton *(Mrs. Maudsley)*, Michael Redgrave *(The Older Leo)*, Michael Gough *(Mr. Maudsley)*, Edward Fox *(Hugh Trimingham)*, Richard Gibson *(Marcus Maudsley)*, Simon Hume-Kendall *(Denys)*, Amaryllis Garnett *(Kate)*, Roger Lloyd Pack *(Charles)*.

Harold Pinter wrote the screenplay adaptation of L.P. Hartley's novel and it's a stylish look back into an old man's memories. Redgrave reviews the crossroads of his life in painstaking and sometimes dizzying detail under Losey's deft direction. Julie Christie is engaged to Edward Fox, a member of the British aristocracy, but she is in love with Bates, a lowly farmer. Guard is Redgrave as a young man and he is hired as the go-between to deliver messages from Christie to Bates and vice versa. It is this assignment which gives the youth his first taste of love. In doing his job, Guard also falls for Christie—and what red-blooded boy wouldn't? We later learn that Redgrave never married and we are given to believe it was this feeling for Christie that kept him a bachelor for seven decades. Set in Norfolk in the 1900s, the film flashes forward and backward (a trick Pinter loves) with several twists and such attention to fine shadings that you cannot watch this movie without giving it your utmost attention. The cover for the affair is blown when Christie's mother, Leighton, forces young Guard to take her to where Christie and Bates are trysting. Several shocking incidents, including Bates shooting himself, keep this film constantly surprising. The ending, where an aged Christie asks the aged Redgrave to once more act as a go-between, is a smashing climax to a superb film. Pinter and Losey had previously collaborated on THE SERVANT and ACCIDENT, both of which were huge critical successes but failed to make much money. This won several awards, sweeping the 1971 Cannes Film Festival. Leighton was nominated for an Oscar. Witty, poignant and just a tad slow, THE GO-BETWEEN is gorgeously photographed by Gerry Fisher and it is only the languid pace Losey chooses that keeps this from being perfect.

p, John Heyman, Norman Priggen; d, Joseph Losey; w, Harold Pinter (based on the novel by L.P. Hartley); ph, Gerry Fisher (Technicolor); m, Michel Legrand; ed, Reginald Beck; art d, Carmen Dillon; cos, John Furniss.

Drama **Cas.** **(PR:A-C MPAA:PG)**

GO-GETTER, THE** (1937) 90m COS/WB bw

George Brent *(Bill Austin)*, Anita Louise *(Marguerite Ricks)*, Charles Winninger *(Cappy Ricks)*, John Eldridge *(Lloyd Skinner)*, Henry O'Neill *(Cdr. Tisdale)*, Joseph Crehan *(Karl Stone)*, Willard Robertson *(Matt Peasley)*, Herbert Rawlinson *(Lester Brent)*, Ed Gargan *(Policeman)*, Harry Beresford *(Barker)*, Eddie Acuff *(Bob)*, Mary Treen *(Bride)*, Craig Reynolds, Carlyle Moore, Jr. *(Macon Survivors)*, Gordon Oliver *(Mr. Luce)*, James Robbins *(Information Clerk)*, Helen Lowell *(Mr. Luce's Mother)*, Helen Valkis *(Skinner's Secretary)*, Minerva Urecal *(Cappy Ricks' Secretary)*, Edward Price *(Radio Operator)*, Max Hoffman, Jr. *(Navigating Officer)*, Lane Chandler *(Radio Officer)*, Myrtle Stedman *(Nurse)*, George Chandler *(Card Printer)*, Ann Doran *(Maizie, the Maid)*, Charles Coleman *(Butler)*, Ward Bond, Ben Hendricks, Alan Bridge, Pat Flaherty *(Loggers)*, Sam McDaniel *(Black Man)*, Etta McDaniel *(Black Woman)*, Harrison Greene, Harry Depp *(Men)*, Mathilde Comont *(Marie)*, Harry Fox.

A re-make of a 1923 silent feature, THE GO-GETTER is the story of Brent, a man who loses his leg in a navy dirigible crash (in the original, the hero lost his leg in the war). He gets a job with a lumber company and promptly falls in love with the boss's daughter (Louise). But general manager Eldridge also has designs on her and sends Brent off on "the blue vase test." This is a company test where an employee must find a vaguely described blue vase and bring it back to headquarters via railway. Of course Brent succeeds, winning his true love's heart and becoming the new G.M. as well. The film starts off with an interesting premise but quickly becomes just another unbelievably simplistic romance. It was director Berkeley's first non-musical effort and he clearly was not cut out for such fare. Hokey plots that work for musicals just don't make it as straight drama.

p, Hal B. Wallis; d, Busby Berkeley; w, Delmer Daves (based on a story by Peter B. Kyne); ph, Arthur Edeson; ed, William Holmes; md, Leo F. Forbstein; art d, Hugh Relicker; cos. Orry-Kelly; m/l, "It Shall Be Done," Jack Scholl, M.K. Jerome.

Drama **(PR:A MPAA:NR)**

GO CHASE YOURSELF*** (1938) 70m RKO bw

Joe Penner *(Wilbur Meely)*, Lucille Ball *(Carol Meely)*, June Travis *(Judith Daniels)*, Richard Lane *(Nails)*, Fritz Feld *(Count Pierre de Louis-Louis)*, Tom Kennedy *(Ice-Box)*, Granville Bates *(Halliday)*, Bradley Page *(Frank)*, George Irving *(Daniels)*, Arthur Stone *(Warden)*, Jack Carson *(Warren Miles)*, Frank M. Thomas *(Police Chief)*, Jack Green *(Officer)*, George Shelley *(Detective)*, Ted Oliver *(Detective Clark)*, Margaret Armstrong *(Mrs. Daniels)*, Phillip Morris *(Cop)*, John Ince *(John Weatherby)*, Lynton Brent *(Photographer)*, Clayton Moore, Alan Bruce, William Corson *(Reporters)*, Napoleon Whiting *(Porter)*, Donald Kerr *(Gas Station Attendant)*, Edith Craig *(Mother)*, Bobs Watson *(Junior)*, Diana Gibson, Rita Oehmen *(Diners)*, Billy Dooley *(Linesman)*, Edward Hern *(Raffle Seller)*, Chester Clute *(Excited Man)*.

Penner ("Wanna buy a duck?"), a popular radio comedian of the day, had difficulty finding the right film to suit his talents until GO CHASE YOURSELF. Here, he's an unassuming bank clerk who, after a series of events, ends up in a trailer being towed by some gangsters. His wife (Ball) and the cops think he's stolen the bank's loot, and the chase is on. In the end, Penner saves the day and clears his name. While nothing memorable, GO CHASE YOURSELF is a thoroughly enjoyable farce, and Penner is terrific. The direction never lags behind the frenzied pace of the film. Ball is fine as the hardboiled wife. Perhaps this hardness reflected her off-screen character: she eventually ended up owning RKO.

p, Robert Sisk; d, Edward F. Cline; w, Paul Yawitz, Bert Granet (based on a story by Walter O'Keefe); ph, Jack MacKenzie; ed, Desmond Marquette; md, Roy Webb; art d, Van Nest Polglase, Feild M. Gray; cos, Renie; spec eff, Vernon L. Walker; m/l "I'm From the City," Hal Raynor, Burton Lane, Joe Penner.

Comedy **(PR:A MPAA:NR)**

GO FOR BROKE*** (1951) 92m MGM bw

Van Johnson *(Lt. Michael Grayson)*, Lane Nakano *(Sam)*, George Miki *(Chick)*, Akira Fukunaga *(Frank)*, Ken K. Okamoto *(Kaz)*, Henry Oyasato *(O'Hara)*, Harry Hamada *(Masami)*, Henry Nakamura *(Tommy)*, Warner Anderson *(Col. Charles W. Pence)*, Don Haggerty *(Sgt. Wilson I. Culley)*, Gianna Canale *(Rosina)*, Dan Riss *(Capt. Solari)*.

At the height of WW II inexperienced Army lieutenant Johnson undergoes an enlightenment of attitude when his first command assignment sees him in charge of the 442nd Regimental Combat Team which consists entirely of Japanese Americans. Johnson is wary of his troops at first and subjects them to intensive training. By the time the group is sent off to fight in Italy, Johnson's attitude changes toward them—for the better. What's more, their attitude toward him also begins to improve. As the troops push the huns out of Italy, Johnson grows close to his men and realizes that they are just as American as he is. Eventually the regiment fights its way into France where their fighting skills are put to the test when they must take a hill in a heavily wooded area. The men of the 442nd prove their mettle when they accomplish their mission. They are even honored by President Truman and General Mark W. Clark for their bravery. Johnson is fine as the narrow-minded lieutenant who finally sees the light, and the casting of actual Oriental actors as the men of the 442nd was a brave and commendable decision so soon after the war, especially considering the paranoid political climate of the time. The liberal message of the film (that people of different ethnic backgrounds are just as honorable, intelligent, brave, and moral as the white majority) was typical of the work produced by Dore Schary for MGM. However, these humanistic themes had fallen out of vogue by 1951 and soon Schary was trying to defend himself from the likes of Senator Joseph McCarthy. Writer/director Pirosh's screenplay was nominated for an Academy Award.

p, Dore Schary; d&w, Robert Pirosh; ph, Paul C. Vogel; m, Alberto Colombo; ed, James E. Newcom; art d, Cedric Gibbons, Eddie Imazu.

War **(PR:A MPAA:NR)**

GO-GO SET (SEE: GET YOURSELF A COLLEGE GIRL, 1964)

GO INTO YOUR DANCE**½ (1935) 92m FN-WB bw
(GB: CASINO DE PAREE; CASINO DE PARIS)

Al Jolson *(Al Howard)*, Ruby Keeler *(Dorothy Wayne)*, Glenda Farrell *(Sadie Howard)*, Helen Morgan *(Luana Bell)*, Barton MacLane *(The Duke)*, Sharon Lynne *(Blonde)*, Patsy Kelly *(Irma)*, Benny Rubin *(Himself)*, Phil Regan *(Eddie Rio)*, Gordon Westcott *(Fred)*, William Davidson *(McGee)*, Joyce Compton *(Show Girl)*, Akim Tamiroff *(Mexican)*, Joseph Crehan *(Jackson)*, Joseph Cawthorn, Harry Warren, Al Dubin.

Backstage musical comedy with overtones of mobdom features Jolson and real-life wife Keeler in a contrived story that's the usual thin stuff, counterpointed by some terrific numbers by Harry Warren and Al Dubin in one of their earlier jobs for Warners. Jolson is a famous performer whose drinking has caused him to be banned from the musical stage by the producers and other actors who have had to work with him. He needs to make a comeback and, with the aid of a dancer, Keeler, he opens a nightclub, teams up with her, and climbs back into the good graces of everyone who matters. In the course of events, he gets mixed up with mobster MacLane, there's a bit of gunplay, and it finishes with Jolson back at the pinnacle of success. The comedy-drama style of the picture hurts it in that the first half is played for yuks (when he's nipping at the flask) and the second half is drowned in bathos. Comedy relief is by Patsy Kelly, and what little she has to do is done well. Farrell plays Jolson's adoring sister and Helen Morgan is seen briefly in one of her last screen appearances as a nightery thrush. Even hoofers Warren and Dubin get a moment on screen in one of the rare times when the creators have a chance to be acknowledged by the public. Warner Brothers had specialized in crime pictures (LITTLE CAESAR, 1930, etc.) and backstage musicals (42ND STREET, 1933, etc.) and in this one, they attempted to combine the two. It didn't quite work, sort of like attempting to eat two of your favorite foods together that don't meld. The dancing was only fair and could have used someone like Busby Berkeley to make it snap to attention. Still, it's a pleasant enough diversion and gives us the opportunity to see Jolson at the top of his talent, doing a blackface number. Songs include: "Mammy," "She's A Latin from Manhattan," "About A Quarter To Nine," "A Good Old Fashioned Cocktail With A Good Old Fashioned Girl," "Go Into Your Dance," "Little Things You Used To Do," "Casino De Paree" (Harry Warren, Al Dubin).

p, Sam Bischoff; d, Archie Mayo; w, Earl Baldwin (based on a story by Bradford Ropes); ph, Tony Gaudio, Sol Polito; ed, Harold McLernon; ch, Bobby Connoly.

Musical/Comedy **(PR:A MPAA:NR)**

GO, JOHNNY, GO!**½ (1959) 75m HR bw

Alan Freed *(Himself)*, Jimmy Clanton *(Johnny)*, Sandy Stewart *(Julie Arnold)*, Chuck Berry *(Himself)*, Herb Vigran *(Bill Barnett)*, Frank Wilcox *(Mr. Arnold)*, Barbara Woodell *(Mrs. Arnold)*, Milton Frome *(Mr. Martin)*, Joe Cranston *(Band Leader)*, Inga Boling *(Secretary)*, Eddie Cochran, The Flamingos, The Cadillacs, Jackie Wilson, Jo Ann Cambell, Harvey, Ritchie Valens.

Clanton plays a young orphan taken in by the manic deejay Freed and transformed into rock sensation "Johnny Melody." The hip dialog of the 1950s rock scene plays as great camp today, but there are some terrific performances by some great names here. It's the only film appearance by Valens, who died in a plane crash with Buddy Holly shortly before the film's release. Wilson and Berry also give good performances. Freed himself was the subject of a film biography, AMERICAN HOT WAX, in 1978.

p, Alan Freed; d, Paul Landres; w, Gary Alexander; ph, Ed Fitzgerald; m, Leon Klatzkin; ed, Walter Hannemann; art d, McClure Capps.

Musical **Cas.** **(PR:A MPAA:NR)**

GO KART GO** (1964, Brit.) 55m Fanfare/CFF bw

Dennis Waterman *(Jimpy)*, Jimmy Capehorn *(Squarehead)*, Frazer Hines *(Harry)*, Pauline Challenor *(Patchy)*, Melenie Garland *(Squirt)*, Robert Ferguson *(Stiggy)*, John Moulder Brown *(Spuggy)*, Graham Stark, Campbell Singer *(Policemen)*, Wilfrid Brambell *(Junkman)*, Cardew Robinson *(Postman)*, Gladys Henson *(Housewife)*, Alan White and Harry Locke *(Fathers)*.

Tale of a classic childhood event centers around the efforts of a group of kids to band together and build a go-cart to enter in a race. Of course the moppets manage to pull out in front to win on the big day.

p, George H. Brown; d, Jan Darnley-Smith; w, Michael Barnes (based on the story by Frank Wells).

Children **(PR:AAA MPAA:NR)**

GO, MAN, GO!*** (1954) 82m UA bw

Dane Clark *(Abe Saperstein)*, Pat Breslin *(Sylvia Saperstein)*, Sidney Poitier *(Inman Jackson)*, Edmon Ryan *(Zack Leader)*, Bram Nossen *(James Willoughby)*, Anatol Winogradoff *(Papa Saperstein)*, Celia Boodkin *(Mama Saperstein)*, Carol Sinclair

(Fay Saperstein), Ellsworth Wright *(Sam)*, Slim Gaillard *(Slim)*, Frieda Altman *(Ticket Seller)*, Mort Marshall *(Master of Ceremonies)*, Jean Shore *(Secretary)*, Jule Benedic *(1st Bathing Beauty)*, Jerry Hauer *(2nd Bathing Beauty)*, Marty Glickman, Bill Stern *(Announcers)*, Lew Hearn *(Appraiser)*, Ruby Dee *(Irma Jackson)*, Harlem Globetrotters *(Themselves)*.

An interesting film about the beginnings of the comedy basketball team the Harlem Globetrotters that says as much about racism in the 1930s as it did about Hollywood in the 1950s. Clark is the Jewish coach who finds a group of blacks playing basketball on a street corner. Determined to see that they get the attention they deserve, Clark organizes the team and takes them off barnstorming until at last they achieve recognition and fame. Poitier is Clark's eventual associate and the friendship between the two and their wives is genuine. This film never blatantly states the inherent racism within the story, but it certainly is there—and is by no means subtle. The players on the white team the Globetrotters play at the film's end are portrayed as White Knights. Defeat would mean the end of any hope for the Globetrotters. It is a clear case of black versus white and to the victor will go the spoils. This film is far more important as a social statement than it appears to be. This was the second movie featuring the dusky dunkers; their first was THE HARLEM GLOBETROTTERS (1951), directed by Phil Brown. In 1981, they were exploited in a real dog, the third comeback of the abortive TV comedy series, THE HARLEM GLOBETROTTERS ON GILLIGAN'S ISLAND. GO, MAN, GO! was famed cinematographer James Wong Howe's first directorial effort; he did a creditable job.

p, Anton M. Leader; d, James Wong Howe; w, Arnold Becker; ph, Phil Steiner; m, Alex North; ed, Faith Elliott; md, North; m/l, Sy Oliver, Mike Shore.

Drama **(PR:A MPAA:NR)**

GO NAKED IN THE WORLD** (1961) 103m Arcola/MGM c

Gina Lollobrigida *(Giulietta Cameron)*, Anthony Franciosa *(Nick Stratton)*, Ernest Borgnine *(Pete Stratton)*, Luana Patten *(Yvonne Stratton)*, Will Kuluva *(Argus Diavolos)*, Philip Ober *(Josh Kebner)*, John Kellogg *(Cobby)*, Nancy R. Pollock *(Mary Stratton)*, Tracey Roberts *(Diana)*, Yale Wexler *(Charles Stacy)*, Rodney Bell *(Parkson)*, John Gallaudet *(Rupert)*, Chet Stratton *(Jack)*, Maggie Pierce *(Girl)*, Bill Smith *(Boy)*, Jacqueline Smith *(Teenager)*.

One of several La Traviata-based films released in the late 1950s-early 1960s that dealt with ladies of the evening, most of which were the old story of the "hooker with a heart of gold." This time it's Lollobrigida who's the call girl. Franciosa is the son of wealthy manufacturer Borgnine. The rebellious son is head over heels for Lollobrigida and doesn't know a thing about her past. Pity, because his father certainly does. After learning the truth, Franciosa goes into a rage, but finally forgives his lady love. Too late, though. She can't handle the emotional pressure and ends it all by leaping off a hotel balcony into the sea. The camerawork is good—intimate and personal. And, as always, Lollobrigida is a pleasure to look at.

p, Aaron Rosenberg; d&w, Ranald MacDougall (based on the book by Tom T. Charles); ph, Milton Krasner (CinemaScope, Metrocolor); m, Adolph Deutsch; ed, John McSweeney, Jr.; art d, George W. Davis, Edward Carfagno; set d, Henry Grace, Dick Pefferle; cos, Helen Rose; spec eff, Robert R. Hoag; makeup, William Tuttle.

Drama **(PR:O MPAA:NR)**

GO TELL THE SPARTANS*½** (1978) 114m Spartan/AE c

Burt Lancaster *(Maj. Asa Barker)*, Craig Wasson *(Cpl. Stephen Courcey)*, Jonathan Goldsmith *(Sgt. Oleonowski)*, Marc Singer *(Capt. Al Olivetti)*, Joe Unger *(Lt. Raymond Hamilton)*, Dennis Howard *(Cpl. Abraham Lincoln)*, David Clennon *(Lt. Finley Wattsberg)*, Evan Kim *(Cowboy)*, John Megna *(Cpl. Ackley)*, Hilly Hicks *(Signalman Toffer)*, Dolph Sweet *(Gen. Harnitz)*, Clyde Kasatsu *(Col. Minh)*, James Hong *(Cpl. Oldman)*, Denice Kumagai *(Butterfly)*, Tad Horino *(One-Eyed Charlie)*, Phong Diep *(Minh's Interpreter)*, Ralph Brannen *(Minh's Aide-de-Camp)*, Mark Carlton *(Capt. Schlitz)*.

Lost in the shuffle between THE DEER HUNTER and APOCALYPSE NOW, this neat little war movie told of the U.S. presence in Vietnam in 1964, with "advisor" Lancaster commanding a small group of combat advisors. Ordered to send a platoon of Vietnamese militia (old men with shotguns, commanded by communist-hating mercenary Kim) and a squad of American advisors under green lieutenant Unger to garrison an old French stronghold, Lancaster, a veteran of three wars, argues that the site is of no value and that the only effect of putting troops there will be to entice the Viet Cong to mass for an attack. He is overruled on the grounds that the French abandoned the spot and lost the war, "and we don't want to make the same mistake the French did." Lancaster is proved right, though, and before long the Vietcong have besieged the isolated outpost. A helicopter arrives to evacuate the men, but it is only big enough for the Americans. Wasson, a draftee who volunteered to serve in Vietnam, refuses to leave the old militiamen at the mercy of the Vietcong, so he stays behind as the helicopter lifts off, and when the dust clears he sees Lancaster standing there. They make plans to lead the evacuation, but an attack kills most of the men and Lancaster. Wasson awakens wounded the next morning and begins limping home. The film features a typically fine performance by Lancaster, who spends most of the film trying to understand why a draftee like Wasson would volunteer for combat duty. When Wasson explains that he wanted to know what a war was like, Lancaster exclaims "I should have known it—you're a tourist!" Even at this point in the war, it is obvious that we don't belong there; the U.S. Army command is seen as greedy and stupid, while the South Vietnamese are seen as thoroughly corrupt (Lancaster has to bribe the local warlord to give the battle some air support). The title derives from the inscription above the French cemetery, quoting the doomed Spartans at Thermopylae: "Stranger, go tell the Spartans how we lie, loyal to their laws, here we die." An excellent war movie, one that puts the Vietnam war in a historical context and points up the futility of the whole thing.

p, Allan F. Boddoh, Mitchell Cannold; d, Ted Post; w, Wendell Mayes (based on the novel *Incident at Muc Wa* by Daniel Ford); ph, Harry Stradling, Jr.; m, Dick Halligan; ed, Millie Moore; art d, Jack Senter; cos, Ron Dawson.

War **Cas.** **(PR:O MPAA:R)**

GO TO BLAZES½** (1962, Brit.) 84m ABF/Warner-Pathe c

Dave King *(Bernard)*, Robert Morley *(Arson Eddie)*, Daniel Massey *(Harry)*, Dennis Price *(Withers)*, Coral Browne *(Colette)*, Norman Rossington *(Alfie)*, Maggie Smith *(Chantal)*, Miles Malleson *(Salesman)*, Finlay Currie *(Judge)*, James Hayter *(Smoker)*, Wilfrid Lawson *(Scrap Dealer)*, John Welsh *(Fire Officer)*, David Lodge *(Sergeant)*, John Le Mesurier *(Fisherman)*, Kynaston Reeves *(Clubman)*.

After a series of inept crimes a trio of crooks buys an old fire engine in hopes of using it as a ruse for clean getaways. Alas, they have to put out a real fire instead. Finally they hire a scandal-ridden ex-fire chief, Price, and arsonist Morley, who help them stage a fire in the boutique next to a bank. Some good comic stuff involving the crooks' ineptitude and bad luck, as well as marvelously funny "fire training" scenes, but sequences are stretched out and lose the humor. The cast is terrific, with Morley and Price leading the way. The female roles, however, are not fleshed out and are a real waste of talent.

p, Kenneth Harper; d, Michael Truman; w, Patrick Campbell, Vivienne Knight (based on a story by Peter Myers, Ronald Cass); ph, Erwin Hillier (CinemaScope, Technicolor); m, John Addison; ed, Richard Best.

Comedy **(PR:A MPAA:NR)**

GO WEST½** (1940) 79m MGM bw

Groucho Marx *(S. Quentin Quale)*, Chico Marx *(Joe Panello)*, Harpo Marx *(Rusty Panello)*, John Carroll *(Terry Turner)*, Diana Lewis *(Eve Wilson)*, Walter Woolf King *(Beecher)*, Robert Barrat *(Red Baxter)*, June MacCloy *(Lulubelle)*, George Lessey *(Railroad President)*, Mitchell Lewis *(Halfbreed)*, Tully Marshall *(Dan Wilson)*, Clem Bevans *(Official)*, Joe Yule *(Bartender)*, Arthur Houseman *(Drunk)*.

It starts off promising and quickly goes downhill. The opening of GO WEST finds slick-talking Groucho being outwitted by Chico and Harpo in a very funny sequence, but much of the rest of the film simply doesn't live up to its promise. The plot has something to do with a land deed, but it's really an excuse for the Marxes to clown around. At the studio's insistence, a thoroughly boring romantic sub-plot was grafted onto the story. Chico gets a piano solo and Harpo turns an Indian loom into his namesake instrument. Groucho sings, looking completely bored with the whole process. The brothers, best work was clearly behind them by 1940, though they continued making films. Studio indifference and poor writing that clearly misunderstood the Marx brand of humor is evident. An interesting sidenote: Groucho's character was named after a crude inside Hollywood joke about the young girls at an actor's disposal: San Quentin Quail. This film was originally to have been scored by Harry Ruby and Bert Kalamar, who scripted the more successful DUCK SOUP (1933) and HORSE FEATHERS (1932), and it seems a shame that it wasn't. Songs include "Ridin' the Range," Gus Kahn, Roger Edens; "As If I Didn't Know," "You Can't Argue With Love," Kahn, Bronislau Kaper; "Land of the Sky Blue Water," Charles Wakefield Cadman; "Beautiful Dreamer," "Oh Susanna," Stephen Foster.

p, Jack Cummings; d, Edward Buzzell; w, Irving Brecher; ph, Leonard Smith; ed, Blanche Sewell; md, Georgie Stoll; art d, Cedric Gibbons, Stan Rogers; set d, Edwin B. Willis.

Comedy **Cas.** **(PR:A MPAA:NR)**

GO WEST, YOUNG LADY** (1941) 71m COL bw

Glenn Ford *(Tex Miller)*, Penny Singleton *(Belinda Pendergast)*, Ann Miller *(Lola)*, Charlie Ruggles *(Jim Pendergast)*, Allen Jenkins *(Hank)*, Jed Prouty *(Judge Harmon)*, Onslow Stevens *(Tom Hannegan)*, Bob Wills *(Bob)*, Edith Meiser *(Mrs. Hinkle)*, Bill Hazlet *(Chief Big Thunder)*, Waffles *(Himself)*, The Foursome, Bob Wills and His Texas Playboys.

A brave attempt, though not successful, to combine slapstick comedy, cowboy film aesthetics, and musical numbers into one package. It's the old story of a marshal (Ford) sent to clean up a small town terrorized by an outlaw. Singleton and Miller are the two ladies vying for (and fighting over) Ford's attentions. The real problem with GO WEST, YOUNG LADY is that it's never really sure what sort of film it wants to be. Consequently, it goes everywhere at once, and the results are not what was intended. Wills was a major country-and-western artist at the time and put together his biggest band ever for this film. Songs include "Ida Red," Bob Wills and His Texas Playboys, "Doggie, Take Your Time," "Gentlemen Don't Prefer a Lady," "I Wish That I Could Be a Singing Cowboy," "Rise To Arms (The Pots and Pans Parade)," "Somewhere Along the Trail," "Go West, Young Lady," Sammy Kahn, Saul Chaplin.

p, Robert Sparks; d, Frank R. Strayer; w, Richard Flournoy, Karen DeWolf (based on a story by DeWolf); ph, Henry Freulich; ed, Gene Havlick; md, M. W. Stoloff; art d, Lionel Banks; cos, Walter Plunkett; ch, Louis DaPron.

Comedy/Musical/Western **(PR:A MPAA:NR)**

GO WEST, YOUNG MAN** (1936) 80m Major Pictures/PAR bw

Mae West *(Mavis Arden)*, Warren William *(Morgan)*, Randolph Scott *(Bud Norton)*, Alice Brady *(Mrs. Struthers)*, Elizabeth Patterson *(Aunt Kate)*, Lyle Talbot *(Francis X. Harrigan)*, Isabel Jewell *(Gladys)*, Margaret Perry *(Joyce)*, Etienne Giradot *(Prof. Rigby)*, Maynard Holmes *(Clyde)*, John Indrisano *(Chauffeur)*, Alice Ardell *(Maid)*, Nicodemus Stewart *(Nicodemus)*, Charles Irwin *(Master of Ceremonies)*, Walter Walker *(Andy Kelton)*, Jack LaRue *(Rico)*, G.P. Huntley, Jr. *(Embassy Officer)*, Robert Baikoff *(Officer)*, Xavier Cugat and his Orchestra *(Themselves)*, Dick Elliott *(Reporter)*, Si Jenks *(Bumpkin)*, Eddie Dunn.

By the time this one was made, the blue-nosed censors and several conservative groups had been up in arms about West's suggestiveness in many other movies and much of her humor was snipped from the script, even before it got to the sound stage. West is a movie star whose latest picture is previewing in a small town. In the movie within the movie, "Drifting Lady," Jack LaRue and Xavier Cugat are among the actors seen. She's allowed to be somewhat more sensual and satirical here in that it's supposed to be a depiction of one of her films, rather than what is happening "live" in the movie. Once that's over, the picture gets bogged down. West is introduced to the movie theater audience watching the preview and creates a sensation with the small-town crowd. She meets Scott, all muscles and little else, and likes the cut of his jib, so she stays on in the little burg to see if she can have a little fun with the rawboned young man. Scott's girl friend, Perry, is furious over West's advances and threatens to tell all to the 1930s version of the "National Enquirer," with the goading of a snobbish professor, Giradot. To get the heat off, William (West's press agent) promises Giradot a part in West's next movie, and the ham in him succumbs. Talbot is the local governor and an old pal of West's and when he hears some dialog about a kidnaping, he assumes that West is to be the victim. Meanwhile, West is still trying to nail Scott and would like to take him back to Hollywood. About ten other bogus plot turns complicate matters, and the whole thing winds up a morass. West adapted a play by Lawrence Riley for her own use and failed to keep a through-line story, thus confusing audiences. It wasn't a large hit. Scott is his customary wooden self, and the wrong man to play opposite West. Missing from the screenplay are West's usual barbs and satirical darts, no doubt the result of the script's bowdlerizing at the hands of those at the top. She gets to sing "I Was Saying To The Moon," "Go West, Young Man," and "On A Typical Tropical Night," as well as "When You Stepped Into My Life." A generally unsatisfying film for Mae West fans, still it has enough laughs to make the 80 minutes pass painlessly. Directed by Hathaway, an odd choice for this type of material.

p, Emanuel R. Cohen; d, Henry Hathaway; w, Mae West (based on the play "Personal Appearance" by Lawrence Riley); ph, Karl Struss; m, George Stoll; ed, Ray Curtiss; m/l, Arthur Johnston, Johnny Burke.

Comedy   (PR:C MPAA:NR)

GOBS AND GALS✶✶   (1952) 86m REP bw
                                           (GB: CRUISING CASANOVAS)

George Bernard (*Sparks Johnson*), Bert Bernard (*Salty Conners*), Robert Hutton (*Lt. Steve Smith*), Cathy Downs (*Betty Lou*), Gordon Jones (*Mike Donovan*), Florence Marly (*Sonya DuBois*), Leon Belasco (*Peter*), Emory Parnell (*Senator Prentice*), Leonid Kinskey (*Ivan*), Tommy Rettig (*Bertram*), Minerva Urecal (*Mrs. Pursell*), Donald MacBride (*Cdr. Gerrens*), Henry Kulky (*Boris*).

Two bored sailors on a South Seas island bide their time by sending romantic letters to various feminine pen pals, enclosing a picture of their chief officer with every letter. Eventually, the officer's fiancee finds out and thinks she's being two-timed. Meanwhile, one of the pen pals is secretly a Soviet spy, all too eager to get to an American officer. Though a funny premise, the film is not nearly as daring as it could be. The Bernards as the two sailors are not the comic actors necessary for their roles and resort to mugging and pratfalls. At the film's end, they have neatly cleared up the romantic troubles and captured some Soviet spies to boot. But at that point, the film has gone on long enough and the humor is all spent. Some good editing helps the pace, but not by much.

p, Sidney Picker; d, R. G. Springsteen; w, Arthur T. Horman; ph, John MacBurnie; m, Stanley Wilson; ed, Arthur Roberts; art d, Al Ybarra.

Comedy   (PR:A MPAA:NR)

GOD FORGIVES—I DON'T!✶½   (1969, Ital./Span.) 101m
                                Crono Cinematografica-P.E.F.S.A. Films/AIP
                                (TU PERDONAS . . . YO NO; DIO PERDONA . . . IO NO)

Terence Hill (*Cat*), Frank Wolff (*Bill San Antonio*), Bud Spencer (*Earp Hargitay*), Gina Rovere (*Rose*), Jose Manuel Martin (*Bud*), Tito Garcia, Paco Sanz, Giovanna Lenzi, Jose Canalejas, Bruno Arie, Remo Capitani, Juan Olaguible, Rufino Ingles, Roberto Alessandri, Luis Bar Boo, Arturo Fuento, Giancarlo Bastianoni.

Wolff is a train robber who kills everyone aboard his latest hijacking venture. He rides off and buries the money, but Hill hears about this and is determined to find the loot. The two face each other in a gun fight after a crooked game of cards. But it's not only the card game that's crooked, for Hill is given a gun loaded with blanks and is tricked into believing he has killed his adversary. Spencer is an insurance agent who teams up with Hill to find the cash. They do and hide it in a new spot, but they are ambushed and tortured by Wolff and his henchmen. Spencer escapes, but Hill is taken by a guard to the hidden cache. Hill kills his guard and sends word to Wolff demanding a showdown. They meet and are surprised by Spencer, who is then shot by Wolff. But Hill shoots his adversary and sets off a dynamite charge near the stolen money. Wolff crawls to the dynamite in a desperate effort to extinguish the fuse, but it explodes, killing him. As it turns out, Hill and Spencer have really hidden the money elsewhere and ride off to retrieve it. Not much of anything that is particularly new or fresh can be found in this spaghetti Western.

p, Enzo D'Ambrosio; d, Giuseppe Colizzi; w, Colizzi, Gumersindo Mollo; ph, Alfio Contini; m, Angel Oliver Pina; ed, Sergio Montanari; art d, Gastone Carsetti, Luis Vazquez; cos, Marilu Cortenty; spec eff, Cataldo Galliano, Alfredo Segoviano.

Western   (PR:O MPAA:M)

GOD GAME, THE   (SEE: MAGUS, THE, 1968, Brit.)

GOD GAVE HIM A DOG   (SEE: BISCUIT EATER, THE, 1940)

GOD IS MY CO-PILOT✶✶✶½   (1945) 90m WB bw

Dennis Morgan (*Col. Robert L. Scott*), Dane Clark (*Johnny Petach*), Raymond Massey (*Maj. Gen. Chennault*), Alan Hale (*"Big Mike" Harrigan*), Andrea King (*Catherine Scott*), John Ridgely (*Tex Hill*), Stanley Ridges (*Col. Meriam Cooper*), Craig Stevens (*Ed Rector*), Warren Douglas (*Bob Neale*), Stephen Richards (*Sgt. Baldridge*), Charles Smith (*Pvt. Motley*), Minor Watson (*Col. Caleb V. Haynes*),

Richard Loo (*Tokyo Joe*), Murray Alper (*Sgt. Aaltonen*), Bernie Sell (*Gil Bright*), Joel Allen (*Lt. Doug Sharp*), John Miles (*Lt. "Alabama" Wilson*), Paul Brooke (*Lt. Jack Horner*), Clarence Muse (*"Prank"*), William Forrest (*Dr. Reynolds*), Frank Tang (*Chinese Captain*), Philip Ahn (*Japanese Announcer*), Dan Dowling (*Frank Schiel*), Paul Fung (*Gen. Kitcheburo*), Frances Chan (*Specialty Dancer*), Sanders Clark (*British Officer Prisoner*), Phyllis Adair (*American Girl Prisoner*), Dale Van Sickle, Tom Steele, Art Foster (*American Pilots*), Buddy Burroughs (*Scott as a Boy*), George Cleveland (*Catherine's Father*), Gigi Perreau (*Robin Lee*), Don McGuire, William Challee (*A.V.G. Groundmen*), Joel Friedkin (*Newspaper Editor*), James Flavin (*Major*).

A stirring but sometimes sanctimonious war drama shows Morgan portraying a WW II flying ace who battles the Japanese over China while piloting for Gen. Claire Chennault's "Flying Tigers." It's really a tale of one boy's love of flight, beginning with Morgan's childhood when he first jumps off the barn roof with an umbrella, expecting to float earthward instead of crashing on his backside, which he does. In various sequences Morgan is depicted practicing with model planes, then going through West Point, on to flying the mail through stormy weather, then instructing other pilots and finally accepting a hazardous mission to China just after Pearl Harbor is bombed. He winds up flying with Chennault's all-volunteer group and learns that no pilot flies alone, that there is also a spiritual hand on the stick. Morgan is particularly upset after he strafes a Japanese military column, killing scores. He seeks solace from missionary Hale who gives him a prayer for pilots. Morgan's faith is tested when he is shot down and has to survive in enemy territory, finally being rescued in a wounded state and returned to Allied lines by the Chinese. The florid performances and occasionally mawkish attempts at injecting a religious philosophy are overcome by a solid story and startling camerawork by Hickox. Aerial photography is superlative and Florey's overall direction sings. Of value is the straightforward manner in which the life of the 34-year-old Macon, Georgia, ace is told. Scott was involved in the bombing of Hong Kong and was shot down, severely wounded, but evaded capture and returned to train myriad pilots on survival methods and aviation techniques. Massey is authoritative as Chennault, and solid performances are put forth by Clark, Ridgeley, Hale, Stevens, Douglas, Ridges, and those two good old Japanese enemies, Loo (a Hawaiian by birth) and Ahn (Chinese).

p, Robert Buckner; d, Robert Florey; w, Peter Milne, Abem Finkel (based on the book by Col. Robert L. Scott); ph, Sid Hickox; m, Franz Waxman; ed, Folmer Blanksted; md, Leo F. Forbstein; art d, John Hughes; spec eff, Roy Davidson, Edwin DuPar, Robert Burks; tech adv, Col. Robert Lee Scott, Jr.

War Drama   (PR:A MPAA:NR)

GOD IS MY PARTNER✶½   (1957) 82m FOX bw

Walter Brennan (*Dr. Charles Grayson*), John Hoyt (*Gordon Palmer*), Marion Ross (*Francis Denning*), Jesse White (*Louis*), Nelson Leigh (*Rev. Goodwin*), Charles Lane (*Judge Warner*), Ellen Corby (*Mrs. Dalton*), Paul Cavanaugh (*Dr. Brady*), Nancy Kulp (*Maxine Spelvana*), John Harmon (*Ben Renson*), Charles Gray.

Overly simplistic story about retired surgeon Brennan who decides to give $50,000 to religious causes. His family files suit, saying he's incompetent and can't handle his money. Niece Ross defends her uncle, who claims that without the Lord he never would have been able to become such a great surgeon. Of course the jury believes him and he is allowed to donate money as he sees fit. The script is hackneyed and one-sided; the direction tired and tedious. Producer Hersh was known for his strong religious feelings, which probably explains the preachiness of the film.

p, Sam Hersh; d, William F. Claxton; w, Charles Francis Royal; ph, Walter Strenge (Regalscope); m, Paul Dunlap; ed, Robert Fritch; md, Dunlap; art d, Ernest Fegte.

Drama   (PR:A MPAA:NR)

GOD IS MY WITNESS✶✶✶   (1931) 77m Astor bw

Bob McKenzie (*William Hastings*), John Aldredge (*Leo Turer*), George Grossmith (*God*), Alice White (*Betty James*), Flora Sheffield (*Louise Bleeker*), Barry Norton (*Officer Jurgens*), Clyde Cook (*Berman*), Joan Marsh (*Hat-Check Girl*).

A very amusing early talkie that was, surprisingly, never remade. Based on a short story by Runyon that appeared as a newspaper feature, it tells of Long Island tough guys, McKenzie and Aldredge, who have been having a run of bad luck and, instead of making the traditional deal with the devil in order to change their lives, they make a deal with Grossmith, who must have been one of the earliest people to play God in a movie. They meet God when he is running the Times Square newspaper stand where they get their racing forms. The two promise to always tell the truth and to only do things that will benefit other people, with no thought for their own welfare. This includes having to marry their long-time girl friends, White and Sheffield, with whom they have been keeping company since before Prohibition. (This must have been a precursor to Runyon's story of Nathan Detroit and Adelaide who were engaged for 14 years.) Their lives have been complicated by the presence of local beat cop Norton whose main object in life seems to be nabbing the two men and sending them to Sing Sing. Everyone in the Broadway community is pleasantly surprised and somewhat shocked by the turnabout of these two suburban hoodlums (even though none of Runyon's heroes ever did anything beyond some illegal gambling or rum-running or the occasional protection racket) as they suddenly assume an almost-angelic attitude in their relationships with others. They help Cook, a down-at-the-heels coffee shop operator, by working behind his counter while he tends to his ailing wife. They save the life of chorine-hat check girl Marsh when she decides that she no longer wants to be the moll of a noted Mafia-type don. Meanwhile, they help little old ladies across the street, give money to charity, and become paragons of virtue. As their attitudes change, so do their lives. Suddenly, they are included in the guest list of a charity ball at the Waldorf and begin to meet all the right people. Their backgrounds arise when they think they can steal the furs at the ball, but they stop short when they realize that God is their witness. In the end, Marsh marries an Astor-type, and she is so grateful to the two men that she sets them up in their own dry-cleaning business. When they return to the newsstand to thank God, they discover that the old man wasn't God at all, just a misguided old geezer with a mental problem. Grossmith has died and left the two men his newsstand, as well as his fortune. In his will, he states that if he could change the lives of anyone, they would be the beneficiary of his lifetime of work. And it turns out that the old fella owned eight buildings on Broadway. It sounds corny, but the lines are witty and not at all dated. Further, the scene where these plaid-jacketed thugs attempt to cook and serve food at a lunch counter is a comedy classic of timing as the dishes pile up and the orders fall behind. With the Marx Brothers in the leads, this would have been a smash. A couple of undistinguished tunes dot the action: "With All My Heart" and "Heaven Sends It's Love." This was Grossmith's only film in the U.S. He had been Gilbert and Sullivan's "patter man" for many years and was renowned for his ability to clearly enunciate the tricky lyrics that Gilbert penned.

p&d, Berthold Viertel; w, John Weaver (based on the story "Two Gentlemen of Corona" by Damon Runyon); ph, George Barnes; m, W. Franke Harling; ed, Gene Ruggiero; art d, Leland Burke; set d, Miles W. Henderson; m/l, Harling, Mathew Hyman.

Crime/Comedy/Fantasy **(PR:A MPAA:NR)**

GOD TOLD ME TO*** (1976) 89m Larco/New World c (AKA: DEMON)

Tony LoBianco *(Peter Nicholas)*, Deborah Raffin *(Casey Forster)*, Sandy Dennis *(Martha Nicholas)*, Sylvia Sidney *(Elizabeth Mullin)*, Sam Levene *(Everett Lukas)*, Robert Drivas *(David Morten)*, Mike Kellin *(Deputy Commissioner)*, Richard Lynch *(Bernard Phillips)*, Sammy Williams *(Harold Gorman)*, Jo Flores Chase *(Mrs. Gorman)*, William Roerick *(Richard)*, Lester Rawlins *(Board Chairman)*, Harry Bellaver *(Cookie)*, George Patterson *(Zero)*, Walter Steele *(Junkie)*, John Heffernan *(Bramwell)*, Alan Cauldwell *(Bramwell as a Youth)*, Robert Nichols *(Fletcher)*, Andy Kaufman *(Police Assassin)*, Al Fann, James Dixon, Bobby Ramsen, Peter Hock, Alex Stevens, Harry Madsen, Randy Jurgensen *(Detective Squad)*, Sherry Steiner *(Bernard's Mother as a Young Woman)*, James Dukas *(Doorman)*, Mason Adams *(Obstetrician)*, William Bressant *(Police Officer)*, Armand Dahan *(Fruit Vendor)*, Vida Taylor *(Miss Mullin as a Girl)*, Adrian James *(Prostitute)*, Leila Martin *(Nurse Jackson)*, Michael Pendry *(Attendant)*, Dan Resin, Alexander Clark, Marvin Silbisher *(Wall Street Executives)*, Harry Eno *(Medical Examiner)*.

LoBianco is a Catholic police officer investigating a series of sniper murders. His trail leads him to a weird religious cult that has its origins in alien beings. Lynch is the man behind the killings, half-human and half-alien. His mother, played by Sidney, had been raped by an alien creature, giving birth to an anti-Christ. Some excellent sequences as well at its haunting themes of repression, sexual guilt, and ultimate faith make this a cut above most films of this ilk. Don't miss an appearance by dadaist comedian Kaufman as an off-the-wall cop. Originally released as GOD TOLD ME TO, the title was changed to DEMON as most television stations refused to advertise the film with the former title.

p,d&w, Larry Cohen; ph, Paul Glickman; m, Frank Cordell; ed, Arthur Mandelberg, William J. Waters, Christopher Lebenzon, Mike Corey; cos, Ralston; spec eff, Steve Neill; m/l, "Sweet Momma Sweet Love," Robert O. Ragland, Janelle Webb (sung by George Centre Griffin).

Crime Drama **(PR:O MPAA:R)**

GODDESS, THE½** (1958) 104m COL bw

Kim Stanley *(Emily Ann Faulkner)*, Betty Lou Holland *(Mother)*, Joan Copeland *(Aunt)*, Gerald Hiken *(Uncle)*, Burt Brinckerhoff *(Boy)*, Steve Hill *(John Tower)*, Gerald Petrarca *(Minister)*, Linda Soma *(Bridesmaid)*, Curt Conway *(Writer)*, Joan Linville *(Joanna)*, Joyce Van Patten *(Hillary)*, Lloyd Bridges *(Dutch Seymour)*, Bert Freed *(Lester Brackman)*, Donald McKee *(R.M. Lucas)*, Louise Beavers *(Cook)*, Elizabeth Wilson *(Secretary)*, Roy Shuman and John Lawrence *(G.I.s)*, Chris Flanagan, Patty Duke, Mike O'Dowd, Sid Raymond, Margaret Brayton, Werner Klemperer, Fred Herrick, Gail Haworth.

A probing inquiry into the making of a film star fails by its inability to present anything beyond the expected. That is, all the typical situations one would expect a woman working to be a star to encounter are presented without deviations from the pattern. This is mainly the fault of screenwriter Chayevsky—the first time he had ever ventured to the West Coast to put his pen to work. Luckily a subtle and workmanlike job was delivered from Cromwell at the helm. Stanley plays the woman who rose from squalor in a Southern slum to become one of the hottest idols of the screen, a journey she makes not so much on talent as on her looks. Ultimately she cannot remain in the spotlight for long; her demise shows her as a woman dependent upon other forms of stimulation, mainly drugs and alcohol, to keep going. Those people closest to her are also affected by the changes she must go through, her mother eventually turning to religion. What could have been a powerful portrayal of the darker side of a glamourized lifestyle remains but a naive and ordinary expose that makes an actor's life look empty and shallow. It has been said that this film profiles the careers of either Ava Gardner or, especially, Marilyn Monroe, yet Chayevsky has always insisited that he was really drawing from the goddess Success as profiled by American philosopher William James.

p, Milton Perlman; d, John Cromwell; w, Paddy Chayevsky; ph, Arthur J. Ornitz; m, Virgil Thompson; ed, Carl Lerner; art d, Edward Haworth; set d, Richard Meyerhoff, Tom Oliphant; cos, Frank L. Thompson; makeup, Robert Jiras.

Drama **(PR:C-O MPAA:NR)**

GODDESS, THE*** (1962, India) 95m Satyajit Ray/Harrison Pictures bw (DEVI)

Chhabi Biswas *(Kalikinkar)*, Soumitra Chatterjee *(Umaprasad)*, Sharmila Tagore *(Doyamoyee)*, Purnendu Mukherjee *(Taraprasad)*, Karuna Bannerjee *(Harasundari)*, Arpen Choudhury *(Khoka)*, Anil Chatterjee *(Bhudev)*, Mohamed Ibn Israel *(Sick Boy's Father)*, Kali Sarkar *(Prof. Jarkar)*, Khagesh Chakravarty *(Doctor)*, Nagendra Nath *(Priest)*.

Biswas, a wealthy, religious man, dreams that his 17-year-old daughter-in-law Tagore is a reincarnated Hindu goddess. He has her placed on an altar outside his home and all the town agrees with Biswas' dream when a child is seemingly cured by her. Tagore starts to wonder herself, and begins doubting the meaning of her true nature. When her husband S. Chatterjee returns from school, he demands that his wife stop this nonsense. But Tagore fears divine retribution if she does this, and refuses. There are two different endings for the film. Originally, Tagore dies by a river when her husband returns; a later version has her going insane after being unable to heal a sick nephew. In either case, the hand of India's best-known director is well seen. Ray shows compassion, and insight into these people, telling the story in a subdued but fascinating manner.

p,d&w, Satyajit Ray (based on the works of Prabhatkumar Mukherjee, Rabindranath Tagore); ph, Subrata Mitra; m, Ali Akbar Khan; ed, Dulal Dutta; art d, Bansi Chandragupta.

Drama **(PR:C MPAA:NR)**

GODDESS OF LOVE, THE** (1960, Ital./Fr.) 68m FOX c

Belinda Lee *(Helen)*, Jacques Sernas *(Laertes)*, Massimo Girotti *(Praxiteles)*, Maria Frau, Luigi Tosi, Claudio Gora, Elli Parvo, Camillo Pilooto, Enzo Fiermonte.

Girotti is a sculptor in 4th century Greece. Using Lee as a model, he creates a replica of Aphrodite, though he completely ignores the beauty of his model. Sernas is a Macedonian soldier who falls in love with Lee. The jealous sculptor turns Sernas over to Greek soldiers and is rejected by Lee for his actions. She runs off and becomes a prostitute, then begins to think of suicide. But Sernas, now a great hero, returns and the two are once more united. This is little more than soap opera with a historical setting. The story and acting are trite in this film dubbed for the American market.

p, Gian Paolo Bigazzi; d, Victor von Tourjansky; w, Damiano Damiani; ph, (CinemaScope, Deluxe Color); m, Michel Michelet.

Historical Romance **(PR:O MPAA:NR)**

GODFATHER, THE***** (1972) 175m PAR c

Marlon Brando *(Don Vito Corleone)*, Al Pacino *(Michael Corleone)*, James Caan *(Sonny Corleone)*, Richard Castellano *(Clemenza)*, Robert Duvall *(Tom Hagen)*, Sterling Hayden *(McCluskey)*, John Marley *(Jack Woltz)*, Richard Conte *(Barzini)*, Diane Keaton *(Kay Adams)*, Al Lettieri *(Sollozzo)*, Abe Vigoda *(Tessio)*, Talia Shire *(Connie Rizzi)*, Gianni Russo *(Carlo Rizzi)*, John Cazale *(Fredo Corleone)*, Rudy Bond *(Cuneo)*, Al Martino *(Johnny Fontane)*, Morgana King *(Mama Corleone)*, Lenny Montana *(Luca Brasi)*, John Martino *(Paulie Gatto)*, Salvatore Corsitto *(Bonasera)*, Richard Bright *(Neri)*, Alex Rocco *(Moe Greene)*, Tony Giorgio *(Bruno Tattaglia)*, Vito Scotti *(Nazorine)*, Tere Livrano *(Theresa Hagen)*, Victor Rendina *(Phillip Tattaglia)*, Jeannie Linero *(Lucy Mancini)*, Julie Gregg *(Sandra Corleone)*, Ardell Sheridan *(Mrs. Clemenza)*, Simonetta Stefanelli *(Apollonia)*, Angelo Infanti *(Fabrizio)*, Corrado Gaipa *(Don Tommasino)*, Franco Citti *(Calo)*, Saro Urzi *(Vitelli)*.

The ultimate in modern gangster fare, this moody, murky, murderous film is a cult classic of film noir, an almost mythical production that chronicles the rise, fall, and rise of a single Mafia family in New York. Brando, his cheeks stuffed with gum and his throat jammed with colloquialisms, is the rasping, thoughtful, shrewd, and lethal Godfather whose crime empire is held together by the muscle of his son, Caan, and an army of Italian street soldiers, not the least of whom is the stoic giant, Montana (Luca Brasi). The film opens with gaiety, an outdoor Italian wedding at Brando's fortress-like estate where Brando's daughter, Shire, is about to marry Russo, a bookie in the Godfather's fiefdom. Cirsitto, an undertaker, is seen begging Brando in his private office for "justice," revenge really, against a gang of thugs who have raped his daughter. Brando reminds him that he has never shown him any recognition nor respect but his anguished pleas move the crime czar and he promises that "these men will be dealt with," but that he, Brando, may some day call up Cirsitto to return "the favor," whatever it might be. On the grounds is Brando's second son, Pacino, who has just returned from WW II, a much-decorated Marine captain. College educated, sensitive, and perceptive, he is unlike almost all present, except for college girl Keaton, his non-Italian girl friend. Pacino points out gangster luminaries to Keaton like a small boy might designate heroes in a baseball park. Then Martino shows up, the singing idol of countless bobbysoxers, to croon a love song for the wedding couple which sends young girls in the crowd into ecstatic squeals. Martino, whose role is reportedly based upon Frank Sinatra, as in Puzo's book, meets with Brando, sobbingly telling him that a movie mogul in Hollywood is withholding an important role in an upcoming blockbuster film from him, one that will give vitality to his sagging career. Brando slaps him, telling him to behave like a man, then promises he will do what he can. The favor is done later by Duvall, who acts as Brando's consigliari (lawyer); he takes a trip to Hollywood to request in the name of Brando that Hollywood mogul Marley give Martino the movie role he is seeking. Marley dines with Duvall, showing him every courtesy, then explodes over dessert, saying that the singer ruined one of his finest actresses and that he will, under no circumstances, give the part to him. Sprinkled throughout the studio boss' tirade are such words as "guinzo, wop, and dago," none of which endear the film czar to Duvall or the man he reports to, Brando. The mob has other ways to persuade Marley to its way of thinking. He awakens in his silk sheeted bed with blood all over him. Throwing back the sheets, he finds the head of his prized racehorse next to him. His screams are heard at dawn echoing over his vast Hollywood estate and, naturally, Martino gets the part. "We made him an offer he can't refuse," Duvall later reports to the family in New York. Real problems for Brando and company arise with the appearance of Lettieri, a maverick gangster who has the backing of a rival Mafia family headed by Rendina and his son Giorgio. Lettieri, in a meeting with Brando, Caan, and others, tells the family that he intends to establish wide-scale narcotics sales in NYC but he requires the permission of Brando and his heavy political protection. Brando, an old school Mafia don, is disgusted by the thought of narcotics and says so, saying that he is content with his gambling, prostitution, protection, and other rackets, and sends Lettieri packing. This decision on

Brando's part leads to an assassination attempt on Brando's life. He is gunned down in the street while his weak-willed son Cazale stands by helplessly. Brando is rushed to a hospital while Lettieri kidnaps Duvall, telling him that he must persuade Caan, heir apparent to the Corleone family, that he must cooperate with him and the rival Mafia clan and go into the narcotics trade. Duvall is released but Lettieri's plans go awry when he learns that Brando still lives. Meanwhile, the hulking Montana, Brando's chief executioner, meets with Giorgio and is strangled to death by Giorgio's goons and Lettieri. Pacino, going to visit his father in the hospital, discovers that the family's gunmen supposed to be on guard have vanished. He improvises an appearance of guards to ward off a second assassination attempt against Brando. Hayden, a crooked police captain in Lettieri's employ, arrives at the hospital entrance to confront Pacino, ordering him from the premises so Lettieri's goons can kill Brando unmolested. But Pacino stands up to the brutish cop who smashes him in the face while two cops pinion his arms, despite a police aide pointing out that Pacino is a war hero. Just then Duvall shows up with an army of private detectives and upbraids Hayden, telling him that unless he allows the detectives to take their guard positions he will be brought into court where he will have to provide a "rule to show cause" for his unorthodox and illegal actions. Hayden departs in a rage but Brando's life is saved. A war council sees Pacino stepping into the family business against his father's wishes. Pacino proposes that he meet with Lettieri and Hayden, his bodyguard, ostensibly to establish a truce, but to kill both of them. Before setting up this killing, the family receives a package containing the bullet-proof vest which Montana had worn when going to see the Tattaglias. "What's this?" Caan says. Clemenza (Castellano) snorts: "It's a Sicilian message—means Luca Brasi sleeps with the fishes." Pacino meets with Lettieri and Hayden in a small, remote Italian restaurant. He carries on a lengthy conversation in Italian with Lettieri while Hayden stuffs his face, then excuses himself and goes to the washroom where a gun has been hidden behind the toilet fixture. Taking this back to the table with him, he suddenly shoots and kills both Lettieri and Hayden, then calmly walks out of the restaurant where his own men pick him up and drive off. Pacino must go into hiding; Brando, recovered and returned home, sends him off to Sicily where he marries Stefanelli and is constantly guarded by those in league with Brando. Meanwhile, in the U.S. a full scale war breaks out between the Brando and Rendina families. After months of slaughter another don, Conte, calls a truce meeting. Brando confronts Rendina and, after Conte chastises Brando for not sharing his political connections and police protection, a reconciliation is made with Brando reluctantly agreeing to allow narcotics operations. Afterward, he states that Conte is the man who backed Lettieri from the beginning. By this time Brando has lost his son Caan, who has been ambushed at a toll stop by several carloads of gangsters who machinegun his corpse over and over again (in the most violent scene of this most violent movie). Pacino himself is almost killed when his car in Sicily has a bomb planted in it which kills his young wife. Pacino return to the U.S. to again take up with Keaton and assume the leadership of his family since Brando is in ill health. Brando gives his advice to his son, the sum total of which is "trust no one," and shortly thereafter dies while playing with a little grandson. Pacino organizes his family into an even more powerful force, expanding his interest to Las Vegas where his brother Cazale has been working with Moe Greene (Rocco). When Pacino visits Las Vegas and tells Rocco that he is in charge, Rocco insults him, telling him that *he* built Las Vegas and he takes orders from no one, that he will never sell out his interest nor lose control of his desert gambling empire. Pacino, however, is no explosive, unpredictable Caan. In fact, he is unlike any Mafia don of the past. He is a cultured, educated, and iceberg cool person who relies upon careful strategy to defeat his enemies. He prepares well to deal with them all. Married now to Keaton, he attends a baptism as a godfather; the camera cuts from this scene to show Pacino's men killing Conte, Rendina, Rocco, and others, a terrible cross-country slaughter while Pacino's church vows are heard in hypocritical voice-over. Even Tessio (Vigoda), one of his father's closest and longest allies, is murdered since he tried to set up Pacino for execution. Also murdered is Russo, Pacino's brother-in-law, for it was Russo who set up the killing of Caan. After Pacino goes through the baptism services for Russo's and Shire's child, he orders Russo murdered. He is strangled inside of a car. At film's end Keaton sees one Mafioso after another enter her husband's office to kiss his hand and swear allegiance. The door closes slowly on this chilling scene where Pacino has now become the boss of bosses, the most powerful crime leader in America. THE GODFATHER is three hours of stunning and shocking film, realistically and grimly portraying the insidious crime cartel that grew to omnipotent power in the U.S., holding nothing back. All of the leads are stupendous in their unforgettable roles, even the supporting players. It is really Pacino's film, although Brando's intermittent appearances were so convincingly played that it won this extraordinary actor his second Oscar. (The film also took Academy Awards for Best Picture and Best Screenplay.) Pacino himself is marvelous as the college-trained son whose blood is thicker than a crime-free profession. Caan is perfect as the hedonistic, volatile son whose bloody ways end in his own bloodshed. Duvall, the quick-witted lawyer and adopted son, provides a slick, almost reassuring performance as one of the saner persons in a gun-happy underworld. Keaton, the naive but loving wife gives a good counterbalance to the evil goings-on, but, expectedly, she is the big loser. Hayden as the corrupt cop is a standout, as is the sleazy Lettieri. All the thugs are amazingly believable, Castellano, Vigoda, Rocco (doing Bugsy Siegel), and others providing the murder and mayhem with chilling precision. Coppola's direction is absolutely brilliant in piecing together a movie of many scenes, divergent and far-flung, yet cohesive scenes that meld a dark, brooding saga that was to earn more than $150 million, one of the all-time box office blockbusters. Not only is the direction and acting flawless in this somber masterpiece but the technical credits are outstanding, particularly the obsessively gripping cinematography by Willis, and Rota's haunting score. Unlike the hallmark gangster films of the past, PUBLIC ENEMY (1931), LITTLE CAESAR (1930) and WHITE HEAT (1949), this film relies on no proven formula but tells its story in visual vignettes strung together by Brando's almost mythic presence, the image that holds the movie together as it does his Mafia family. Of course, the Puzo novel is structured on the same principle and incorporates many a gangster myth and reality. Who is the real godfather upon which this crime epic is based? Carlo Gambino probably, with a little Willie Moretti and a little Lucky Luciano thrown in. It really doesn't matter except that the film unrealistically elevates the 1940s Mafia to a position of power it was not to attain until the 1970s. Its callous philosophy of killing anyone opposing it as "just business" is, of course, the rationale for the Mafia's continued existence. The real Mafia leaders of the U.S. enjoyed the glamour, the prestige, and the everlasting film image accorded to it. In fact, at the Chicago premier, a host of Mafia-syndicate figures showed up in a seemingly endless line of limousines to view the film and applaud its primitive contentions. No longer was the message from the screen that crime did not pay; it was now clear that it paid very well indeed. Brando himself echoed this somewhat perverse viewpoint when talking to *Newsweek* later, stating: "In a way the Mafia is the best example of capitalists we have. Don Corleone is just an ordinary business magnate who is trying to do the best he can for the group he represents and for his family." Brando took only $100,000 and a percentage of the film as payment which reportedly yielded $16 million. (His part was not assigned to him initially; first producers thought about approaching Edward G. Robinson or even Laurence Olivier, although producer Ruddy and director Coppola wanted Brando all along). Coppola had heard that Brando was difficult to deal with but was surprised with the ease of his performance and his good cooperation during the 35 days the star allowed for the filming of his role (between April 12 and May 28, 1971). Endowed with a $6 million budget, Coppola shot most of the film on location in Hollywood, Las Vegas, and New York, using exteriors in the Bronx, Brooklyn, Manhattan, and in Richmond, New York. The scene where Brando is almost assassinated was shot on dilapidated Mott Street but here Coppola had to set the period by taking down all the TV antennas. Antique cars and costumes of the post WW II era were dredged up from everywhere. Also shown are such NYC instutitions as Bellevue Hospital and the New York Eye and Ear Clinic. In addition, Pacino and a second-unit spent two weeks in a small village in Sicily. Brando's raspy voiced role (later to be mimicked by a host of impersonators) was difficult in one respect for Coppola in that the actor was 47 at the time, much too young for the aging Mafia don. The problem was solved by makeup expert Dick Smith who had accomplished makeup wonders in THE EXORCIST (1973) and LITTLE BIG MAN (1970), where he aged Dustin Hoffman to a century. Smith added wrinkles to Brando's skin by applying liquid latex, especially around the eyes and nose. A leathery appearance was also achieved the same way, along with loose flesh, and bags beneath the eyes, and olive skin tones to give him that Mediterranean appearance. A special denture was inserted along his lower jawline which jutted the actor's jaw, gave him a completely different bite, and caused more sag in his cheeks. His cheeks were then stuffed with a gummy substance to affect heavy jowls and it was this device that altered the actor's appearance drastically, giving rise to wild speculations that Brando spent hours stuffing his cheeks with cotton, nose tissue, newspapers. Author Puzo, who later claimed that he had Brando in mind when developing the Vito Corleone character, sold the film rights to his book for $35,000 while the book was still in galley form and long before it became a bestseller. Paramount gave him the added incentive of paying him $100,000 for writing the screenplay and a reported small percentage of the profits. The studio allowed for only $2 million in the film's original budget and executives wanted a strictly contemporary view shown. Paramount then hired Coppola to direct, although his previous films—FINIAN'S RAINBOW (1968), YOU'RE A BIG BOY NOW (1966), and THE RAIN PEOPLE (1969)—were flops. Producer Ruddy was even less established as essentially a television producer. Yet the pair managed to convince Paramount to increase its budget and go bigger with THE GODFATHER, even though its recent Mafia profile, THE BROTHERHOOD (1968) with Kirk Douglas, had been a dismal failure. The words "Mafia" and "Cosa Nosta" caused turmoil among the upstanding Italian communities in the U.S. Even before the film was completed, the Italian-American Civil Rights League raised $600,000 at an enormous rally in Madison Square Garden, this money to be used to halt the production. Part of that movement was Frank Sinatra upon whom the Johnny Fontane character is reportedly based. (Puzo later supported this idea in *The Godfather and Other Confessions*, stating how he met Sinatra in a Hollywood restaurant and how "Sinatra started to shout abuse . . . I felt depressed, because I thought Sinatra hated the book and believed that I had attacked him personally in the character of Johnny Fontane.") Others felt the same way. Vic Damone accepted the Fontanne role but then walked out on the film, not from the reported outside pressure, but, according to his own statement, because it "was not in the best image of Italian-Americans." Italian-American author Puzo staunchly disagreed. In fact, in an article for the New York *Times*, Puzo had written: "Do Italians and American-Italians control organized crime in America? The answer must be a reluctant but firm yes." Ten days before THE GODFATHER went into production, Ruddy met with leaders of the Italian-American Civil Rights League and agreed to delete from the screenplay all mention of the words "Mafia" and "Cosa Notra." Prior to this meeting Paramount had reportedly received a deluge of mail which threatened union walkouts during the production and even massive countrywide boycotts of the film. Ruddy later announced the results of his meeting, implying that the concern was really about the quality of the film to be produced. He is quoted as saying: "We had to get the word out to the Italian-American community in a very bona fide way that we had no intention of doing a schlock exploitation gangster film." That THE GODFATHER certainly was not. A mind-scaring chronicle of violence and blood-letting it is, one where the most powerful medium on earth all but excused the Mafia's existence on the grounds that, like Everest, "it's there," and it must therefore be profiled in dramatic exploration. A cure for cancer will certainly be discovered long before the public recognizes the reasons for its deep attraction to this film and its equally absorbing sequel. The GODFATHER films touch upon something perpetually dark in the human character, a fearfully widening black hole into which humanity vanishes and reason itself cannot exist.

p, Albert S. Ruddy; d, Francis Ford Coppola; w, Mario Puzo, Coppola (based on the novel by Puzo); ph, Gordon Willis (Technicolor); m, Nino Rota; ed, William Reynolds, Peter Zinner, Marc Laub, Murray Solomon; prod d, Dean Tavoularis; md, Carlo Savina; art d, Warren Clymer; set d, Philip Smith; cos, Anna Hill Johnstone; spec eff, A.D. Flowers, Joe Lombardi, Sass Bedig; stunts, Paul Baxley; makeup, Dick Smith, Phillip Rhodes.

Crime Drama Cas. (PR:O MPAA:R)

GODFATHER, THE, PART II***** (1974) 200m PAR c

Al Pacino *(Michael)*, Robert Duvall *(Tom Hagen)*, Diane Keaton *(Kay)*, Robert DeNiro *(Vito Corleone)*, Talia Shire *(Connie)*, John Cazale *(Fredo)*, Lee Strasberg *(Hyman Roth)*, Michael V. Gazzo *(Frank Pentangeli)*, Richard Bright *(Al Neri)*, Gaston Moschin *(Fanutti)*, Frank Sivero *(Genco)*, Morgana King *(Mama)*, Marianna Hill *(Deanna)*, Troy Donahue *(Merle Johnson)*, Joe Spinell *(Willie Cicci)*, Abe Vigoda *(Tessio)*, Fay Spain *(Mrs. Marcia Roth)*, Maria Carta *(Vito's Mother)*, G.D. Spradlin *(Sen. Geary)*, Oreste Baldini *(Vito Andolini as a boy)*, Tom Rosqui *(Rocco Lampone)*, B. Kirby, Jr. *(Young Clemenza)*, Francesca deSapio *(Young Mama Corleone)*, Leopoldo Trieste *(Signor Roberto)*, Dominic Chianese *(Johnny Ola)*, Amerigo Tot *(Michael's Bodyguard)*, John Aprea *(Young Tessio)*, Gianni Russo *(Carlo)*, Guiseppe Sillato *(Don Francesco)*, Mario Cotone *(Don Tommasino)*, James Gounaris *(Anthony Corleone)*, Harry Dean Stanton *(FBI No. 1)*, David Baker *(FBI No. 2)*, Ezio Flagello *(Impresario)*, Peter Donat *(Questadt)*, Roger Corman *(Sen. No. 2)*, James Caan *(Sonny)*, Tere Livrano *(Theresa Hagen)*, Carmine Caridi *(Carmine Rosato)*, Danny Aiello *(Tony Rosato)*, Carmine Foresta, Nick Discenza *(Bartender)*, Father Joseph Medeglia *(Father Carmelo)*, William Bowers *(State Committee Chairman)*, Joe Della Sorte, Carmen Argenziano, Joe Lo Grippo *(Michael's Buttonmen)*, Ezio Flagello *(Impresario)*, Livio Giorgi *(Tenor)*, Kathy Beller *(Girl in "Senza Mamma")*, Saveria Mazzola *(Signora Colombo)*, Tito Alba *(Cuban President)*, Johnny Naranjo *(Translator)*, Elda Maida *(Pentangeli's Brother)*, Ignazio Pappalardi *(Mosca)*, Andrea Maugeri *(Strollo)*, Peter La Corte *(Abandando)*, Vincent Coppola *(Vendor)*, Tom Dahlgren *(Corngold)*, Paul B. Brown *(Sen. Ream)*, Phil Feldman *(Sen. No. 1)*, Yvonne Coll *(Yolanda)*, J.D. Nichols *(Attendant at Brothel)*, Edward Van Sickle *(Ellis Island Doctor)*, Gabria Belloni *(Ellis Island Nurse)*, Richard Watson *(Customs Official)*, Venancia Grangerard *(Cuban Nurse)*, Erica Yohn *(Governess)*, Theresa Tirelli *(Midwife)*, James Caan *(Sonny Corleone)*.

In this sequel to the awesome original Pacino now reigns supreme as Mafia don of Brando's crime empire which Pacino rules from his vast Lake Tahoe, Nevada, estate. At a lavish party Pacino entertains Spradlin, a slick, self-serving, and smug senator from Nevada who tells him that he is opposed to the Mafia's gambling operations in his state and that he intends to wipe out the organization. Spradlin later wakes up in a sleazy whorehouse next to a prostitute he appears to have murdered in a drunken orgy but it is obvious that he has been set up. Pacino ostensibly comes to his rescue by covering up the killing and Spradlin is thus in his control thereafter. An assassination attempt is made on Pacino and his family, machinegunners spraying his posh home in Lake Tahoe in the middle of the night, but the family and the don survive. Later Pacino meets with Strasberg in Havana, where the pair open a swank hotel-casino, but Pacino is guarded against the wily and untrustworthy Strasberg, believing it was he who was behind the assassination attempt. When Pacino discovers that his brother, Cazale, worked with Strasberg to set up the abortive Lake Tahoe raid he marks him for death, ostracizing him. Cazale has been resentful for having to take a back seat in family operations and being treated like a lackey and has formed a secret liaison with Strasberg to take over the entire Corleone cartel. Keaton, who is carrying Pacino's child, miscarries and Pacino's problems are compounded when he is called to testify before a Senate Investigative Committee probing organized crime operations. One of the old Mafia lieutenants, Gazzo, has offered to tell all he knows, but his testimony is cut short when Pacino has his brother brought from Sicily to sit in the courtroom with the obvious implication that if Gazzo talks his brother will be murdered. Gazzo later commits suicide after talking to Duvall who visits him in his solitary confinement quarters, convincing him that he must uphold Mafia traditions. Keaton then tells Pacino that she purposely aborted his child so it would not grow up to become the corrupt creature he is; Pacino slaps her and orders her never to darken his door again, giving instructions that she is never again to see their two small children. In cold and calculating wrath Pacino orders the deaths of his enemies. Following Castro's takeover of Cuba, the gangsters flee Havana with Batista and Strasberg becomes a world traveler. Pacino's goons kill him as he arrives at an airport. Another Pacino hit man takes Cazale out fishing on Lake Tahoe and executes Pacino's brother for his involvement with Strasberg. Throughout the contemporary story, the rise of Pacino's father in an immigrant era is shown in flashback, with De Niro playing the elder Corleone. De Niro establishes himself with his cronies in New York's Little Italy through bribery, compromise, extortion, and "doing favors" for local businessmen who, in turn, do him the favor of paying protection. De Niro, who fled Sicily as a child after his family was slaughtered in a vendetta by a local don, returns to his native land a wealthy man years later, to plunge a stiletto into the chest of the don. THE GODFATHER, PART II proved to be unusual in that it is actually better than the original with dynamic and gripping performances by Pacino and De Niro as the younger and older dons. The flashback sequences are superbly portrayed in period, achieved cinemagraphically by Willis who applied a tint to the turn-of-the-century scenes, giving that faded era a softer, richer look than the sharp image of the contemporary story. De Niro's amazing essaying of Vito Corleone, done in Italian with subtitles to achieve more authenticity, won a deserved Oscar. Academy Awards were also gleaned for Best Picture, Direction, Screenplay, Art Direction, and Musical Score. Strasberg, in a role that profiles crime syndicate treasurer Meyer Lansky, provided a cold-blooded look at the blood-and-money philosophy of Pacino's brutal world, gloating with lip-smacking relish over the success of the crime cartel's operations with the line "we're bigger than U.S. Steel." Coppola had a free hand with this sequel and his deft directorial touches are everywhere, particularly in his fine feel for the historical sequences with the fascinating De Niro, an epic portrayal of crime in the new land, which was later emulated to the hilt in Sergio Leone's visually stunning but poorly scripted ONCE UPON A TIME IN AMERICA (1984). THE GODFATHER, PART II took in more than $30 million at the box office, against its original budget of about $12 million. More millions were added in 1977 when a media event occured; at that time TV aired both GODFATHER and GODFATHER, PART II, including out-takes.

p, Francis Ford Coppola, Gary Frederickson, Fred Roos; d, Coppola; w, Coppola, Mario Puzo, (based on characters from the novel by Puzo); ph, Gordon Willis (Technicolor); m, Nino Rota, Carmine Coppola; ed, Peter Zinner, Barry Malkin, Richard Marks; prod d, Dean Tavoularis; md, Carmine Coppola; art d, Angelo Graham; set d, George R. Nelson; cos, Theodora Van Runkle; spec eff, J.D. Flowers, Joe Lombardi.

Crime Drama Cas. (PR:O MPAA:R)

GODLESS GIRL, THE** (1929) 90m C. B. De Mille/Pathe bw

Lina Basquette *(Judith Craig)*, Marie Prevost *(Mame)*, George Duryea *(Bob Hathaway)*, Noah Beery *(Head Guard)*, Eddie Quillan *("Goat")*, Mary Jane Irving *(Victim)*, Clarence Burton, Dick Alexander *(Guards)*, Kate Price, Hedwig Reicher *(Matrons)*, Julia Faye, Viola Louie, Emily Barrye *(Inmates)*, Jimmy Aldine, Vivian Bay, Elaine Bennett, Wade Boteler, Betty Boyd, Julia Brown, Archie Burke, Colin Chase, Cameron Coffey, Cecilia De Mille, Jacqueline Dyris, George Ellis, Anielka Elter, James Farley, Larry Fisher, Evelyn Francisco, May Giraci, Grace Gordon, Milton Holmes, William Humphrey, George Irving, Peaches Jackson, Dolores Johnson, Jane Keckley, Nora Kildare, Richard Lapan, Ida McKenzie, Don Marion, Edith May, Mary Mayberry, Collette Merton, Buddy Messinger, Pat Moore, Jack Murphy, Pat Palmer, Janice Peters, Hortense Petra, Gertrude Quality, Rae Randall, Billie Van Avery, Dorothy Wax.

The evangelistic plot of THE GODLESS GIRL has to do with the invidious secret high-school organization, the Atheist Society, led by Basquette, which is assaulted by the religious group led by Duryea, flinging fruits and vegetables (director De Mille was reportedly hit in the face by a melon during the shooting). The melee ends up in a fist-fight, during which a 15-year old girl is accidentally catapulted to her death from a third-story landing. The two opposed leaders and Quillan, convicted of complicity, are sent to a reformatory, where assorted brutalities are visited on them. There they meet Prevost, a hardened female inmate, with whom Quillan initiates a through-the-wire-fence comic romance. Rebelling against the sadism of brutal head guard Beery and that of matrons Price and Reicher, Duryea escapes in a grocery wagon with Basquette inside. On the outside, in the pastoral countryside, each discovers virtue in the other. Recaptured, they undergo more indignities, but Basquette finds God (her hands pressed against Duryea's through the mesh of the screen that separates the genders bear cross-shaped singe marks upon her conversion). Suddenly, a fire breaks out in the reformatory (the dictatorial De Mille, always a stickler for realism, actually had Leisen's wonderful set torched; several young actresses almost lost their lives when the fire raged out of control). Risking death in the inferno, Duryea and Basquette heroically rescue Beery, their tormentor, who has been overcome by smoke. In return, they are granted their freedom, Basquette returning to society with a new faith. An interesting, though seriously flawed, picture which scored a number of firsts in the odyssey of autocratic director De Mille who here, as in previous pictures, employed a four-piece orchestra to play a personal overture whenever he appeared on a set ready to direct a scene. Released with its last two scenes having been reshot with dialog, this part-talkie was De Mille's first sound film (while the great director was busy preparing his first *all*-talkie at MGM, the dialog scenes were actually directed by German actor Fritz Feld, in his directorial debut). It was the first and last film De Mille directed in the new consortium finances forced him to enter into with Pathe, then owned by Joseph P. Kennedy, father of President John Kennedy (De Mille had objected to the merger, saying: "Pathe . . . a name which stands for cheap pictures . . . "). It was his first film to be shot entirely with one camera, barring a few preliminary shots made by special technical director George Ellis at the State Training School for Girls at Gainesville, Texas. The camera set-up was a marvel to behold, comprising a monorail overhead tram with a platform holding four men—including the director—which could be raised, lowered, tracked, and dollied over an entire set, floating virtually anywhere and everywhere (a technique rediscovered by French director Max Ophuls at a much later time). It was the first film in which the director enjoyed the fruits of nepotism; he cast his only natural child, 17-year-old Cecilia, in a small part. It was also the first film in which the director melded such an atrocious amalgam of themes: religious fundamentalism mixed with sex (his forte for years), prison reform, slapstick comedy, adventure, and high-school expose. Scripted by De Mille's long-time collaborator (both on the screen and off) MacPherson, the picture was De Mille's answer to a growing number of people who had begun to question his religiosity and his personal morals. His recently released KING OF KINGS had been thought by some fundamentalists to dwell a little too long on the relationship between Jesus Christ and Mary Magdalene; in the wake of his studio's financial upheavals, his business ethics were being questioned; his romances with women other than his long-suffering wife Constance were well known in Hollywood circles. As was the case with many other monarchs throughout history, De Mille diverted attention from his personal shortcomings by starting a war. His enemy: the atheists. When he announced his plans for the picture, he received an immediate reward in the form of an angry telegram from the American Association for the Advancement of Atheism, which his publicists quickly forwarded to all the wire services. De Mille and his experienced crew took great pains with the picture, interviewing reformatory inmates and officials, having young female staff members go behind bars disguised as convicted criminals to observe conditions, collecting hundreds of pamphlets and books dealing with atheism, and going over floor plans and diagrams of dozens of reformatories. Casting was no less slapdash; the studio had announced that the entire cast would comprise "persons of high-school age." Instead, the stars were seasoned troupers. Basquette was a one-time Follies girl, a recent widow, who had worked in several silents. Duryea had played opposite her on Broadway in the hit "Abie's Irish Rose." Prevost had been a Mack Sennett bathing beauty in 1917, and was addicted to drugs. Quillan had worked in Sennett comedies. The first title selected for the new feature was, simply, ATHEIST. The second, continuing the director's string of biblical allegories, was THE FIERY FURNACE. The course of the filming was marked by romance and jealousy. De Mille had found a part for his new mistress, Faye, whose presence—according to one De Mille biographer—was always galling to his long-time associate, writer MacPherson. Cinematographer Marley was smitten with star Basquette, and the two married shortly after the picture was canned. De Mille had objected strongly to sound being added to the film, despite the recent success of THE JAZZ SINGER. After its release, he recanted, stating, "Oh God, what I will be able to do with sound!" and so he did.

p&d, Cecil B. De Mille; w, Jeanie MacPherson; ph, Peverell Marley, J. F. Westerberg, Franklin McBride; ed, Anne Bauchens; art d, Mitchell Leisen.

Drama   **(PR:C MPAA:NR)**

GOD'S COUNTRY*½   (1946) 64m Action Pictures/Screen Guild bw

Robert Lowery, Helen Gilbert, William Farnum, Buster Keaton, Si Jenks, Stanley Andrews, Al Ferguson, Ace the Dog.

The Wild West becomes the victim of some more of Keaton's madcap antics. This film marked the absolute nadir in the great comedian's career, before the beginning of his resurrection in France the following year.

p, William B. David; d, Robert Tansey; w, Frances Kavanaugh (based on the story by James Oliver Curwood).

Western/Comedy   **(PR:A MPAA:NR)**

GOD'S COUNTRY AND THE MAN*½   (1931) 59m SYN bw
(AKA: GOD'S COUNTRY; ROSE OF THE RIO GRANDE)

Tom Tyler, Betty Mack, George Hayes, Ted Adams, Julian Rivero, Al Bridge, John Elliott, Gordon DeMain, Artie Ortego.

Tyler, a two-fisted cowboy and then some, goes undercover, posing as a bad guy to capture outlaw Bridge. While undercover he falls for Mack but she won't have anything to do with an outlaw. Seems she's a government agent under wraps as well. Of course they fall in love at the end, but not before Tyler takes on six men in a fist fight and 10 men in a shootout. Hokey stuff with typical production values for the genre. This was the last film made by Syndicate before the change to Monogram.

p&d, J.P. McCarthy; w, Wellyn Totman; ph, Archie Stout.

Western   **(PR:A MPAA:NR)**

GOD'S COUNTRY AND THE MAN**   (1937) 56m MON bw

Tom Keene (Jim), Betty Compson (Roxy), Charlotte Henry (Betty), Charles King, Jr. (Gentry), Billy Bletcher (Sandy), Ed Parker (Bill), Rob McKenzie (Storekeeper), Merrill McCormick (Henchman).

Typical cowboy plot about a gunman whose murder spree is nipped by law-abiding Keene. The difference in this oater is in the performances of two strong women, Compson and Henry, a dance hall girl who strikes it rich, and the love interest, respectively. Too bad, they don't get much of a chance to develop their characters in between all the heavy two-fisted action.

p&d, R. N. Bradbury; w, Robert Emmett; ph, Bert Longenecker.

Western   **(PR:A MPAA:NR)**

GOD'S COUNTRY AND THE WOMAN**   (1937) 83m WB c

George Brent (Steve Russett), Beverly Roberts (Jo Barton), Barton MacLane (Bullhead), Robert Barrat (Jefferson Russett), Alan Hale (Bjorn Skalka), Joseph King (Red Munro), El Brendel (Ole Oleson), Joseph Crehan (Jordan), Addison Richards (Gaskett), Roscoe Ates (Gander Hopkins), Billy Bevan (Plug Hat), Bert Roach (Kewpie), Vic Potel (Turpentine), Mary Treen (Miss Flint), Herbert Rawlinson (Doyle), Harry Hayden (Barnes), Pat Moriarity (Tim O'Toole), Max Wagner (Gus), Susan Fleming (Grace Moran), Eily Malyon (Mrs. Higginbottom), Shirley Lloyd (Secretary), Andre Cheron (Mon. Gagnon), Georgette Rhodes (French Teletype Operator), Robert Bell (French Messenger), Joan Woodbury (Frenchwoman), Minerva Urecal (Maisie), Hal Craig (Motorcycle Cop), Saul Gorss (Logger), Mathilde Comont (Mary), Bob Stevenson (Lars), George Chandler (Flunky).

Brent's just arrived from Paris to brother Barrat's logging camp. His brother is in fierce competition with a rival logging camp—which just happens to be run by the beautiful Roberts. Brent forgets all about blood being thicker than water and crosses the river to work for the competition. Hackneyed and unbelievable nonsense with a lot of overacting, but the Technicolor scenery is gorgeous to look at and beautiful shots of the forest abound. Beware though—at times Brent's hair appears to be purple.

p, Hal B. Wallis; d, William Keighley; w, Norman Reilly Raine, Peter Milne, Charles Belden (based on the novel by James Oliver Curwood); ph, Tony Gaudio (Technicolor); ed, Jack Killifer.

Drama   **PR:A MPAA:NR)**

GOD'S GIFT TO WOMEN**   (1931) 72m WB bw

Frank Fay (Jacques Duryea), Laura La Plante (Diane), Joan Blondell (Fifi), Charles Winninger (Mr. Churchill), Arthur Edmund Carewe (Mr. Dumont), Alan Mowbray (Auguste), Louise Brooks (Florine), Tyrell Davis (Basil), Billy House (Cesare), Yola d'Avril (Dagmar), Margaret Livingston (Tania), Ethlyn Claire (Yvonne), Nena Quartaro (Suzanne), Hazel Howell (Camille), The "G" Sisters (Marie, Mabelle).

Poor Fay. He's got loads of trouble, namely women just can't keep their hands off him. Of course he's more than happy to honor their requests until he meets millionairess La Plante. The amorous Frenchman falls for the beautiful American but she'll have nothing to do with him. She and her father pay off a doctor to tell Fay that one more kiss will mean death. Alas, La Plante means more to him than life itself and in the film's best sequence he kisses her despite the risk. Though it's a

funny premise, the film just doesn't work. There are too many supporting characters, and gaps in the story suggest that some juicier sections were edited out by nervous producers. Still Fay is fun and director Curtiz gives him a free reign.

d, Michael Curtiz; w, Joseph Jackson, Raymond Griffith (based on the play "The Devil Was Sick" by Jane Hinton); ph, Robert Kurrie; ed, James Gibbons.

Comedy   **(PR:A MPAA:NR)**

GOD'S GUN*½   (1977) 93m Irwin Yablans Co. c

Lee Van Cleef, Jack Palance, Richard Boone, Cody Palance, Robert Lipton, Sybil Danning, Leif Garrett.

Though thought to be dead, a preacher who is handy with a gun makes things tough for those who tried to do him in. Good cast wasted in an exploitive effort.

p, Menachem Golan, Yoram Globus; d, Frank Kramer [Gianfranco Parolini].

Western   **Cas.**   **(PR:O MPAA:R)**

GOD'S LITTLE ACRE***   (1958) 112m UA bw

Robert Ryan (Ty Ty Walden), Aldo Ray (Bill Thompson), Tina Louise (Griselda), Buddy Hackett (Pluto), Jack Lord (Buck Walden), Fay Spain (Darlin' Jill), Vic Morrow (Shaw Walden), Helen Wescott (Rosamund), Lance Fuller (Jim Leslie), Rex Ingram (Uncle Felix), Michael Landon (Dave Dawson).

Ryan, in a wonderful performance, is a Georgia farmer who believes there is buried treasure somewhere on his farm. With the help of sons Lord and Morrow, he tries to find the treasure. Only one spot is not touched: an acre of land with a cross on it, specifically set for tithing (hence the title of the film). However the blessed little acre is constantly being changed around in the never-ending search. A sub-plot involving Ryan's son-in-law, Ray, concerns the younger man's efforts to re-start the local cotton mill. Unfortunately he does in a fruitless effort. This is a splendid balance of the comic and the tragic. A fine supporting cast includes a surprisingly good performance from Buddy Hackett.

p, Sidney Harmon; d, Anthony Mann; w, Philip Yordan (based on the novel by Erskine Caldwell); ph, Ernest Haller; m, Elmer Bernstein; ed, Richard C. Meyer; cos, Sophia Stutz.

Drama   **Cas.**   **(PR:O MPAA:NR)**

GODSEND, THE*   (1980, Can.) 90m Cannon c

Cyd Hayman (Kate Marlowe), Malcolm Stoddard (Alan Marlowe), Angela Pleasence (Stranger), Patrick Barr (Dr. Collins), Wilhelimina Green, Lee Gregory, Joanne Boorman.

Hayman and Stoddard have a new arrival in the house, and the kid is a little demon. Seems it's real mom (Pleasance) dropped by the house, had a baby, and left before dawn. So being the nice movie couple they are, Hayman and Stoddard decide to adopt it. The baby is an albino but is by no means pure as snow. Somehow she's responsible for the death of the couple's four natural children, Hayman's miscarriage, and Stoddard's mumps, which render him sterile. Of course all this happens off-screen. Another THE OMEN, but tame.

p&d, Gabrielle Beaumont; w, Olaf Pooley (based on the novel by Bernard Taylor); ph, Norman Warwick; m, Roger Webb; ed, Michael Ellis; art d, Tony Curtis.

Horror   **Cas.**   **(PR:O MPAA:R)**

GODSON, THE***   (1972, Ital./Fr.) 103m C.I.C.C.-Fida
                                                   Cinematografica/Artists International c (LE SAMOURAI)

Alain Delon (Jef Costello), Nathalie Delon (Jan Lagrange), Francois Perier (The Inspector), Cathy Rosier (Valerie), Jacques Leroy (The Gunman), Jean-Pierre Posier (Olivier Rey), Catherine Jourdan (Hatcheck Girl), Michel Boisrond (Wiener), Robert Favart (Barman), Andre Salgues (Garage Man), Roger Fradet, Carlo Nell, Robert Rondo, Andre Thorent (Policemen), Georges Casati (Damolini), Jack Leonard (Garcia), Jacques Deschamps (Police Clerk).

Assassin Delon lives a life of precision and timing, and must always remain aloof from contact with other human beings, exemplified by his barren room with only a caged bird for company. He undertakes the job of killing a nightclub owner, which places him under total survelliance by the Paris police. At the same time he discovers that the man he is working for has marked him for death. Delon tries to hunt down this kingpin, and ends up being killed by the police who are tailing his every move. This bad American version has a dubbing track, which is a mistake when subtitles could have handled it much better.

p, Eugene Lepicier; d&w, Jean-Pierre Melville (based on the novel The Ronin by Joan McLeod); ph, Henri Decae, Jean Charvein; m, Francois De Roubaix; ed, Monique Bonnot, Yolande Maurette.

Crime   **(PR:C-O MPAA:PG)**

GODSPELL**   (1973) 103m COL c

Victor Garber (Jesus), David Haskell (John/Judas), Jerry Sroka (Jerry), Lynne Thigpen (Lynne), Katie Hanley (Katie), Robin Lamont (Robin), Gilmer McCormick (Gilmer), Joanne Jonas (Joanne), Merrell Jackson (Merrell), Jeffrey Mylett (Jeffrey).

Another film in the tradition of JESUS CHRIST, SUPERSTAR, GODSPELL gives us the Gospel according to St. Matthew but it looks more like it's according to Bozo. Originally a project by a group of Carnegie Mellon University students, it had a run at New York's La Mama theater as a straight play, then Schwartz added a score and it is probably still running in some small theater somewhere, even as you read this. It's overly simple and tells the story of Jesus as a New York flower child living and dying in the Big Apple. When it's good, it's filled with energy, fun, and zip. When it's bad, which is more often, it's insulting to anyone who has read the Bible. With Manhattan's landmarks as the background (Central Park, the Brooklyn Bridge, Grant's Tomb, Times Square, Lincoln Center, and more), Garber is Jesus, a sexless creature in a sweatshirt and overalls. The entire production denigrates the awe and wonder of the Good Book because of the silly way in which they handle matters, as opposed to the brilliance of the conception of Connelly's GREEN PATURES. The best number is by Garber and Haskell ("All For The Best") as they softshoe their ways across New York and wind up at the Bulova Watch sign. Many of the elements would have been better left on the off-off Broadway stage. The worst part of the direction is the mugging that Greene allowed. Just when you're beginning to like these people, he goes in for a close-up and the actors twist their faces into Jerry Lewis masks. It's as though Emmett Kelly and Marty Feldman were doing the New Testament. Schwartz's score is rousing but often repetitious and the picture looks more like a rock 'n' roll travelog of New York than anything else. Were it not for the fact that we know where the story came from, this might have stood on it's own as an interesting curiosity piece. Anyone who lived through the Hippie 1960s will enjoy it more than someone who hasn't. Good dancing but a generally disappointing film version of a small cast play that rocked the audiences with its fervor. In this case, opening it up for the camera did it a disservice. Produced by Angela Lansbury's brother, Edgar. Songs include "Day By Day," "By My Side," "Alas For You," "On The Willows," "O,Bless The Lord My Soul," "Prepare Ye The Way Of The Lord," "Turn Back O Man," "Beautiful City," "Save The People," All Good Gifts," "Light Of The World," and the aforementioned "All For The Best."

p, Edgar Lansbury; d, David Greene; w, Greene, John-Michael Tebelak (based on the musical book by Tebelak with score by Stephen Schwartz); ph, Richard G. Heimann (TVC Color); m, Stephen Schwartz; ed, Alan Heim; prod d, Brian Eatwell; art d, Ben Kasazkow; cos, Sherrie Sucher; ch, Sam Bayes; m/l, Schwartz, Jay Hamburger, Peggy Gordon.

Musical (PR:C MPAA:G)

GODY MOLODYYE (SEE: TRAIN GOES TO KIEV, THE, 1961, U.S.S.R)

GODZILLA (SEE: GODZILLA, KING OF THE MONSTERS, 1956, Jap.)

GODZILLA, KING OF THE MONSTERS**½ (1956, Jap.) 80m Toho Productions bw (GOJIRA)

Raymond Burr (*Steve Martin*), Takashi Shimura (*Dr. Yamane*), Momoko Kochi (*Emiko*), Akira Takarado (*Ogata*), Akihiko Hirata (*Dr. Serizawa*), Sachio Sakai (*Hagiwara*), Fuyuki Murakami (*Dr. Tabata*), Ren Yamamoto (*Sieji*), Toyoaki Suzuki (*Shinkichi*), Tadashi Okabe (*Dr. Tabata's Assistant*), Toranosuke Ogwawa (*President of Company*), Frank Iwanaga (*Security Officer*).

There is a temptation to call this a camp classic, for in many ways it is. But the version Americans saw in 1956 was much different from the original version in Japan. Dubbed into English, the American version cleverly intercuts footage of Burr giving the appearance that he is interacting with his Japenese companions. It is the morning after a terrible explosion and Burr is in the hospital. From his bed he recounts the story of the film in flashback. Awakened from a deep, undersea sleep by atomic testing, the prehistoric monster Godzilla goes ashore, destroying much of Tokyo. Bullets and bombs cannot stop it. Finally a scientist devises a system of removing oxygen from the sea, thus killing the monster. But he cannot live with the tought of his destruction and commits suicide. The American version ends with Burr realizing that the scientist died for humanity. In Japan, GODZILLA is looked upon with reverence, much in the same way Americans view KING KONG. In 1979, a 25th anniversary showing was an overwhelming success. In 1982, the original Japanese cut, GOJIRA, had its American debut sans dubbing and Burr.

p, Tomoyuki Tanaka; d, Ishiro Honda, Terry Morse; w, Takeo Murata, Honda (based on a story by Shigeru Kayama); m, Akira Ifukube; ed, Morse; spec eff, Eiji Tsuburaya, Akira Watanabe, Hiroshi Mukoyama, Kuichiro Kishida.

Monster/Horror Cas. (PR:C MPAA:NR)

GODZILLA TAI MOTHRA (SEE: GODZILLA VS. THE THING, 1964, Jap.)

GODZILLA VS. MEGALON*½ (1976, Jap.) 74m Toho/Cinema Shares c (GOJIRA TAI MEGARO)

Katsuhiko Sasaki, Hiroyuki Kawase, Ytaka Hayashi, Kotaro Tomita.

Godzilla engages in a slug fest with a giant cockroach, unleashed by the evil Seatopians to conquer the world. The world isn't too keen on the idea and sends a robot to fetch Godzilla, who has apparently become a good guy in his old age. There are a couple of other creatures both good (the Jet Jaguar, a flying cyborg that can change its size to be more compatible with enemies) and bad (the Gaigan, another flying metal creature, with a buzzsaw for a stomach). Good fun from the "So Bad It's Good" school. The advertising campaign tried to capitalize on the Dino DeLaurentiis KING KONG ads by showing Godzilla and the Megalon duking it out over the World Trade Center. In the film their final battle takes place in a far sparser set, a desert.

p, Tomoyuki Tanaka; d, Jun Fukuda; w, Fukuda, Shinichi Sekizawa; ph, Yuzuru Aizawa

Monster/Horror (PR:C MPAA:G)

GODZILLA VERSUS THE COSMIC MONSTER*½ (1974, Jap.) 80m Toho/Cinema Shares c (GOJIRA TAI MEKA-GOJIRA; AKA: GODZILLA VERSUS THE BIONIC MONSTER)

Masaki Daimon, Kazuya Aoyama, Akihiko Hirata, Hiroshi Koizumi, Masao Imafuku, Beru-Bera Lin, Mori Kishida, Kenji Sahara, Barbara Lynn.

Godzilla turns 20 years old with this film and gets a metal clone as a gift. Faced with this new menace, he turns to King Seeser, an Okinawan monster god. Together they fight off the new menace. Don't miss Anzilla, returning for his third monster appearance with Godzilla. Though some attempts at humor, Sergio Leone parodies, and real-life feuds between the Japanese and the Okinawans are hinted at, nothing is ever given much more than a standard Grade-Z treatment. The title was changed after the creators of the television shows "The Six Million

Dollar Man" and "The Bionic Woman" sued over this film's attempt to cash in on their popularity.

p, Tomoyuki Tanaka; d, Jun Fukuda; w, Hiroyasu Yamamura, Fukuda; ph, Yuzuru Aizawa (Tohoscope); spec eff, Shokei Nakano.

Monster/Horror (PR:C MPAA:G)

GODZILLA VERSUS THE SEA MONSTER*½ (1966, Jap.) 87m Toho/Continental c (NANKAI NO KAI KETTO; AKA: EBIRAH, TERROR OF THE DEEP; BIG DUEL IN THE NORTH)

Akira Takarada, Toru Watanabe, Hideo Sunazuka, Kumi Mizuno, Jun Tazaki, the Alilena twins.

No one in the movies seems to have a better record for making friends out of enemies than Godzilla. Here he's joined by former rival Mothra (in the creature's fourth movie) to fight off a new menace—Ebirah, a monster lobster. This new foe has a different sort of power base than most of Godzilla's opponents. He's financed by Red Bamboo, a totalitarian group that wants to take over the world. But Mothra runs an airlift, saving a group of people from an island about to explode. The real action is when Godzilla takes on the Ebirah, who can regenerate a new one whenever a tentacle is torn off. As usual, our hero wins in another of his poorly made though fun outings.

p, Tomoyuki Tanaka; d, Jun Fukuda; w, Shinichi Sekizawa; ph, Kazuo Yamada; spec eff, Eiji Tsuburaya.

Monster/Horror Cas. (PR:C MPAA:NR)

GODZILLA VERSUS THE SMOG MONSTER zero (1972, Jap.) 85m Toho/AIP (GOJIRA TAI HEDORA; AKA: GODZILLA VS. HEDORA)

Akira Yamauchi (*Dr. Yano*), Hiroyuki Kawase (*Ken*), Toshie Kimura (*Mrs. Yano*), Toshio Shibaki (*Yukio*), Keiko Mari (*Miki*).

In the early 1970s, radiation was no longer the big fear of people everywhere. Pollution was now the No. 1 bad guy and who better to combat it than the old monster-fighter himself, Godzilla? Yamauchi discovers some growing mass in a polluted lake. He thinks its a giant tadpole but before he knows what's happening the mass turns into a 400-foot glob of sewage with big red eyes. It brushes up against him, leaving some acid burns on his face. His son, Kawese, dubs the creature "Hedora," which is Japanese for "pollution." The boy has a dream that Godzilla will come and save the day and informs his father of this vision. Meanwhile, Hedora is attacking Japanese discos where the teenie-boppers dance the night away to anti-pollution songs. When he goes off in search of other things to destroy the kids continue their fun on the slopes of Mt. Fuji. Who should come to spoil the party but the evil Hedora! Things don't look good for our group until from out of nowhere Godzilla arrives. He engages in battle with the muddy monster, helped by Yamauchi, who has invented a device that dehydrates sea monsters. Hedora is reduced to dust but a smaller version of him appears from the ruins. Godzilla stomps this lump into a pancake and heads off into the hills, as Kawase shouts "Godzilla. Thanks a lot." The English dubbing is awful and so is the film.

p, Tomoyuki Tanaka; d, Yoshimitsu Banno; w, Banno, Kaoru Mabuchi; ph, Yoichi Manoda (Colorscope); m, Riichiro Manabe; ed, Yoshitami Kuroiwa; art d, Taiko Inoue; spec eff, Shokei Nakano.

Monster/Horror (PR:C MPAA:G)

GODZILLA VS. THE THING*½ (1964, Jap.) 90m AIP/Toho c (MOSURA TAI GOIRA; GOJIRA TAI MOSURA: AKA: GODZILLA VS. MOTHRA: GODZILLA VS. THE GIANT MOTH: MOTHRA VS. GODZILLA: GODZILLA FIGHTS THE GIANT MOTH)

Akira Takarada (*News Reporter*), Yuriko Hoshi (*Girl Photographer*), Hiroshi Koisumi (*Scientist*), Yu Fujiki (*2nd Reporter*), Eimi Ito, Yumi Ito (*Twin Girls*), Yoshifumi Jajima (*Kumayama*), Kenji Sahara (*Banzo Torahata*), Jun Tazaki (*Newspaper Editor*), Ikio Sawamura (*Priest*), Kenzo Tadake (*Mayor*), Susumu Fujita (*Public Relations Officer*), Yutaka Sada (*Old Man*), Yoshio Kosugi (*Old Man In the Village*), Yutaka Nakayama, Hiroshi Iwamoto, Joji Uno (*Fishermen*), Yasuhisa Tsutsumi (*Longshoreman*), Ren Yamamoto (*Sailor*), Haruo Nakajima (*Godzilla*).

Mothra, the giant moth, is back for his second feature after surviving his encounter with King Kong. Of course this time he's got Godzilla to tangle with. Mothra is living the quiet life of an island deity when Godzilla returns (for his fourth picture) to wreak the havoc he has made into cult. Mothra finally gives in to the pleadings of the Peanut Sisters and tries to stop the fire breathing nemesis. It is to no avail. As luck would have it, Mothra's giant egg, which is being held in a carnival as an exhibit, hatches and the two junior Mothras avenge their elder's name. Good camp with the added element of cute little monsters.

p, Tomoyuki Tanaka; d, Inoshiro Honda; w, Shinichi Sekizawa; ph, Hajime Koizumi (Tojoscope, Eastmancolor); m, Akira Ifukube; spec eff, Eiji Tsuburaya, Sadamasa Arikawa, Akira Watanabe, Motoyoshi Tomioka, Kuichiro Kishida.

Monster/Horror Cas. (PR:C MPAA:NR)

GODZILLA'S REVENGE* (1969) 92m Toho/UPA c (ORU KAIJU DAISHINGEKI)

Kenji Sahara, Tomonori Yazaki, Machiko Naka, Sachio Sakao, Chotaro Togin, Yoshibumi Tajima.

A young boy is bothered by bullies and runs off. He falls asleep and dreams about an isle of monsters where he meets Godzilla and son. The pair teach the young lad a thing or two about fighting, via recycled scenes from SON OF GODZILLA and GODZILLA VERSUS THE SEA MONSTER. Some of the creatures from DESTROY ALL MONSTERS also make an appearance. Extremely bad, though the kids may enjoy it, this is also the last GODZILLA film directed by the creature's originator, Honda. Considering the quality of the first film, it was sad to see what a joke the creature had become over the years.

p, Tomoyuki Tanaka; d, Inoshiro Honda; w, Shinichi Sekizawa; ph, Mototaka Tomioka (Tojoscope); spec eff, Eiji Tsuburaya.

Monster/Horror   (PR:C   MPAA:NR)

GOFORTH   (SEE: BOOM! 1968)

GOG**   (1954) 82m UA c

Richard Egan (David Sheppard), Constance Dowling (Joanna Merritt), Herbert Marshall (Dr. Van Ness), John Wengraf (Dr. Zeltman), Philip Van Zandt (Dr. Elzevir), Valerie Vernon (Mme. Elzevir), Steve Roberts (Maj. Howard), Byron Kane (Dr. Carter), David Alpert (Peter Burden), Michael Fox (Dr. Hubertus), William Schallert (Engle), Marian Richman (Helen), Jeanne Dean (Marna), Tom Daly (Senator), Alex Jackson (Vince), Patti Taylor, Beverly Jocher (Girl Acrobats), Aline Towne (Dr. Kirby), Al Bayer (Pilot), Andy Andrews, Julian Ludwig (Security Guards).

Cheap 3-D thrills as only 1950s science fiction films developed. Egan is investigating some problems at a secret underground laboratory. Work on the world's first space station is being sabotaged and it is up to him to find out who is responsible. He discovers that Novac, the nuclear powered robot brains of the plant, has been toyed with by enemy agents. There are some aerospace battles, robot destruction, exciting action beyond belief, and, in general, good clean fun. It's a bit talky for its own good and the direction tends to slow things down for explanations, but overall it's a good way to spend a Saturday afternoon.

p, Ivan Tors; d, Herbert L. Strock; w, Tom Taggart, Richard G. Taylor (based on a story by Ivan Tors); ph, Lothrop B. Worth (Color Corp. of America); m, Harry Sukman; ed, Strock; spec eff, Harry Redmond, Jr.

Science Fiction   (PR:A   MPAA:NR)

GOHA**½   (1958, Tunisia) 85m UGC c

Omar Cheriff, Zina Bouzaiane, Laurro Gazzalo, Gabriel Jabbour, Daniel Emilfark.

A story-teller spins the tale of a young man, thought stupid by his family and neighbors. But this is the lad's cover, for his mind is alive with imagination. The film takes a dramatic turn when he becomes involved with the wife of a town wise man. The sudden switch from folksy humor to a dramatic tale of adultery is well handled by the director, making this an interesting and offbeat little feature. This was the debut for Baratier as an avant garde director, in an adaptation of a Tunisian folk tale.

d, Jacques Baratier; w, Georges Schehade; ph, Jean Bourgoin (Agfacolor); ed, Trmand Becque.

Drama   (PR:O   MPAA:NR)

GOIN' COCONUTS**½   (1978) 93m Osmond c

Donny Osmond (Donny), Marie Osmond (Marie), Herbert Edelman (Sid), Kenneth Mars (Kruse), Chrystin Sinclaire (Tricia), Ted Cassidy (Mickey), Marc Lawrence (Webster), Khigh Dhieg (Wong), Harold Sakat (Ito), Charles Walke (Jake), Danny Well (Al), Jack Collin (Charlie), Tommy Fujiwara (Alecki).

While on a trip in Hawaii, Marie becomes the proud owner of a necklace, not knowing that it is wanted by a group of bad guys, led by Mars. Sinclaire is a mystery lady who also wants the necklace. This is little more than an extended sketch from the Osmonds' popular television variety show of the time. Their "acting" here differs little from the show: lots of singing, toothy smiles, and cutesy insults. Lots of Hawaiian scenery as well for when things slow down, which is often.

p, John Cutts; d, Howard Morris; w, Raymond Harvey; ph, Frank Phillips (DeLuxe Color); ed, Frank Bracht.

Family Comedy/Adventure   (PR:AAA   MPAA:PG)

GOIN' DOWN THE ROAD**½   (1970, Can.) 96m Evenden/Chevron c

Doug McGrath (Peter), Paul Bradley (Joey), Jayne Eastwood (Betty), Cayle Chernin (Celina), Nicole Morin (Nicole), Pierre La Roche (Plant Foreman), Sheila White (Girl in Record Shop), Ted Sugar, Don Steinhouse, Ron Martin (Workers at Plant), Denise Bishop (Clerk in Grocery), Max Jones, Jack Zimmerman, Mary Black, Ivor Jackson, Ralph Struh, Stan Ross, Stuart Marwick.

An excellent example of how a small budget film easily can outdo a multi-million dollar extravaganza. Made for only $78,000, this story is about two small-town workers looking for something better in life. McGrath and Bradley head from their little Nova Scotia home to the big time of Toronto. There they find work in a soda pop factory and find life even more dismal. Though constantly fighting, they depend on each other's friendship. One marries a girl he has made pregnant and then loses his job. McGrath and Bradley once more run off from their troubles at the film's end, looking for their dreams elsewhere. The acting by the leads is exceptional. Bradley is fine as a simple man, happy with beer and television. McGrath is the more tortured of the two. He wants, and yet knows he'll never attain, the finer things in life. Eastwood is excellent as the hapless waitress who becomes pregnant. Her role is small but she gives a gem of a performance. The dialog is earthy but not coarse. Direction is self-conscious but overall does a nice job of giving the film its humanity. The only real technical problem is an inherent graininess caused by enlarging the film from 16mm to 35mm. The film was partially financed by the Canadian Film Development Corp., as well as Phoenix Films.

p&d, Donald Shebib; w, William Fruet (based on a story by Shebib and Fruet); ph, Richard Leiterman (Eastmancolor); m, Bruce Cockburn; ed, Shebib.

Drama   (PR:O   MPAA:R)

GOIN' HOME**½   (1976) 97m Prentiss Productions c

Todd Christiansen (Todd), Bernard Triche (Bernard), Kevin Oliver (Kevin), Melvin Ruffin (Ruffin), Robert Dale Poole (Dusty), Marion Forbes (Evil), Delia Bradford (Delia).

Sentimental film about a boy (Christiansen) who flees his home state of Florida when his dog is accused of biting a child. The two head off on a travelog tour towards California. Along the way they meet assorted stereotypes, including a wise old hobo, a New Orleans shoeshiner (the inevitable "hip black person"), an abused tugboat cabin boy, and Forbes as "Evil." There's plenty of slow motion, sunset against the hills, and lush, heart-tugging music. A "family picture" with a clear audience in mind.

p,d&w, Chris Prentiss; ph, Prentiss, Christopher Sloan Nibley III (DeLuxe Color); m, Lee Holdridge; ed, Prentiss.

Family Adventure   (PR:AAA   MPAA:G)

GOIN' SOUTH**   (1978) 105m PAR c

Jack Nicholson (Henry Moon), Mary Steenburgen (Julia Tate), Christopher Lloyd (Towfield), John Belushi (Hector), Veronica Cartwright (Hermine), Richard Bradford (Sheriff Kyle), Jeff Morris (Big Abe), Danny DeVito (Hog), Tracey Walter (Coogan), Gerald H. Reynolds (Polty), Luana Anders (Mrs. Anderson), George W. Smith (Mr. Anderson), Lucy Lee Flippin (Mrs. Haber), Ed Begley, Jr. (Mr. Haber), Maureen Byrnes (Mrs. Warren), B.J. Merholz (Mr. Warren), Britt Leach (Parson Weems), Georgia Schmidt (Florence), Nancy Coan Kaclik (Mrs. Standard), R.L. Armstrong (Farmer Standard), Barbara Ann Walters, Anne Ramsey, Marsha Ferri, Lin Shaye, Don McGovern, Dennis Fimple, Anne T. Marshall, Anita Terrian, Roger L. Wilson, Carlton Risdon, May R. Boss, Loren Janes.

Horse thief Nicholson, who had unsuccessfully tried to become a member of the Younger gang, beats it across the Mexican border but an unscrupulous posse ignores the international border laws and crosses the river to capture him. Nicholson brings about his own bad end in that he has jeered and sneered at the exhausted pursuers. He is taken back to town and sentenced to death. Members of his old horse thieving gang visit him in his last hours, his old flame, Cartwright, telling him sorrowfully: "You was the best I ever had, except for that circus fella." Desperate, Nicholson discovers in the 11th hour an old law that permits his release if a woman of the town agrees to marry him. He stands on the gallows like a slave on the block, begging any and all females in the crowd to select him as a husband. The rope goes around his neck, the executioner fondles the trap lever, but, at the last moment, an ancient woman (Schmidt) croaks out her willingness to marry Nicholson. She, however, is overcome with anxiety at the hurried wedding ceremony and drops dead. The horse thief is dragged back to the gallows and once more undergoes the ordeal. Then a high-pitched voice, that of Steenburgen, is heard asking to marry the condemned man. He is released and weds, on the proviso that he work her small ranch for her. Actually, she wants him to dig with her in an old gold mine to scratch out a dying yellow vein. This he does, rushing with her into fatigue to glean the meager riches before a railroad forecloses on the land and/or his old gang gets wind of the mine and takes what gold they have clawed from the rocks. The couple take time out to warily investigate each other's personalities and Nicholson, who can't wait anymore, conducts an awkward husbandly rape of his headstrong wife. His triumph over her iron-willed aggressive nature apparently appeals to her since she later asks that he tie her up again and reenact the sexual attack. (She's weird to begin with, hanging her dining room chairs on wall hooks.) In the end, the gang arrives, pursued by another posse, and a long drawn-out shootout ensues while Nicholson and Steenburgen head south with their sacks of gold, moving like frantic gypsies toward the border and happiness. Though the premise of GOIN' SOUTH is clever, the story is unbelievable and, under Nicholson's first grip as a director, unwieldy and directionless with the tale presented in disjointed, poorly set sequences that will confuse the viewer. Nicholson the actor is mildly amusing, as are some of his riotous gang members, DeVito and Belushi (the latter appearing only briefly, irrespective of his high billing). But the whole thing bogs down in amateurish mugging and slapstick midway in the film. Steenburgen is a terrible mistake in her film debut, a leading lady with no sex appeal, no presence, no charisma, no nothing. The one thing Steenburgen does have is one of the most annoyingly shrill, grating, and inexcusable voices ever to go on to a sound track. Ridiculous is the only way to describe the reason why this young widow would ever pick such a dirty, foul-smelling, creepy little bum like Nicholson to save from the hangman's rope to work her land when she could have any law-abiding single man in town. But then there would not have been a story without her inexplicable selection and there is little story after that. Poor direction and Nicholson's casting of himself as a character actor on the level of Smiley Burnette when a leading man was desperately needed add up to a boring waste of time.

p, Harry Gittes, Harold Schneider; d, Jack Nicholson; w, John Herman Shanner, Al Ramrus, Charles Shyer, Alan Mandel (based on a story by John Herman Shanner, Al Ramrus); ph, Nestor Almendros (Panavision, Metrocolor); m, Van Dyke Parks, Perry Botkin, Jr.; ed, Richard Chew, John Fitzgerald; prod d, Roby Carr Rafelson; cos, William Ware Theiss.

Western   **Cas.**   (PR:O   MPAA:PG)

GOIN' TO TOWN**   (1935) 74m PAR bw

Mae West (Cleo Borden), Paul Cavanagh (Edward Carrington), Gilbert Emery (Winslow), Marjorie Gateson (Mrs. Grace Brittony), Tito Coral (Taho), Ivan Lebedeff (Ivan Valadov), Fred Kohler, Sr. (Buck Gonzales), Monroe Owsley (Fletcher Colton), Grant Withers (Young Fellow), Luis Alberni (Signor Vitola), Lucio Villegas (Senor Ricardo Lopez), Mona Rico (Dolores Lopez), Wade Boteler (Foreman of Ranch), Paul Harvey (Donovan), Joe Frye (Laughing Eagle), Adrienne D'Ambricourt (Annette), Tom London, Syd Saylor, Irving Bacon, Bert Roach, James Pierce (Buck's Gang), Francis Ford (Sheriff), Dewey Robinson (Bartender), Julian Rivero (Bet Taker), Stanley Andrews (Engineer), Rafael Storm (Senor Alvarez), Vladimir Bykoff (Lt. Mendoza), Andres De Segurola (President Racing Association), Pearl Eaton (Girl), Jack Pennick (Dancing Cowboy), Robert Dudley (Deputy), Albert Conti (Head Steward), Frank Mundin (Mrs. Brittony's Jockey), Harold Entwhistle (Colton's Butler), Stanley Price (Attendant), Frank McGlynn (Judge), Leonid Kinskey (Interior Decorator), Virginia Hammond (Miss Plunkett),

Laura Treadwell, Nell Craig *(Society Women)*, Morgan Wallace *(J. Henry Brash)*, Cyril Ring *(Stage Manager)*, Tom Ricketts *(Indian Seller)*, Tom Monk *(English Butler)*, Paulette Paquet, Mirra Rayo *(French Maids)*, Henry Roquemore *(Match King)*, Ted Oliver, Charles McMurphy *(Policemen)*, Franco Cersaro *(Italian Officer)*, Bert Morehouse, Sheldon Jett, J.P. McGowan, Sam Stein, James Pierce, Max Lucke, O.M. Steiger, Myra Royl, Tom Monk, James Cowles, Lew Kelly, George Guhl, Eugene Berden, Frank Corsara, Germaine DeNeel.

Not one of Mae West's best, GOIN' TO TOWN tried to pack too much in 74 minutes. West wrote the screenplay so you know there are plenty of smart and sassy wisecracks, but it covers so much ground that we barely have enough time to get interested in something. This time around, West is a cattle baroness who inherits an oil field from a guy who has won her in a dice game (Kohler). Next thing you know, she's the wealthiest woman in the state. Kohler has been shot but gave her the deed to the oil before he turned up his toes. She has her property surveyed by British engineer Cavanagh and falls for him. (There's a scene where she actually ropes him with a lariat after he ignores her advances.) She tries to win him over but he resists. He is then sent to Buenos Aires on business and she follows him there (does this woman have no shame?). She finds a copy of a posh magazine and sees a photo of Gateson, a real lady, and she realizes that the only way she can charm the stiff-upper-lip of Cavanagh is to become a lady. With the help of an employee, Emery, she does a Pygmalion on herself and is soon the doyenne of Buenos Aires. She is going to run her horse in a huge race against the horse owned by Gateson. Gateson, who will stop at nothing, has her lover, Lebedeff, attempt to drug West's horse the night before the race. To insure her winning, West has her trainer, Coral, stand at the finish line to fire a gun when her horse nears the wire. The only way the animal responds is when hearing sharp noises (not unlike "Jeepers Creepers" in GOLD DIGGERS OF '33, who would only calm down when he heard Louis Armstrong sing). Lebedeff sees the horse win, then changes his allegiance from Gateson to West, but she sees right through him for the gigolo he is. She says, "We're intellectual opposites. I'm intellectual and you're opposite." He protests by saying that he's a nobleman and "the backbone of my family." West responds and says, "Then your family had better see a chiropractor." West wants Cavanagh but he still won't tumble so she arranges a marriage, in name only, to Gateson's nephew, Owsley, who was just about to take his own life due to financial losses at the gaming tables. They get married and move to Southhampton where she is now in residence as a pillar of society. She invites Gateson and some of her snobbish friends over but it's a bust. Now Gateson hires a private eye to find out if West is a woman of low morals. She also hires Lebedeff and ships him in from Argentina so he can be found in West's bed. There's a big gala, and Cavanagh, who is now an earl, arrives and declares his love, finally, to West and asks that she marry him. Meanwhile, Owsley goes to get her money from the bedroom safe as he is still in heavy hock. He catches Lebedeff in the bedroom, there's a fight, and Owsley is killed with the gun he had in his hand. Lebedeff races off and goes into hiding. Downstairs, there is a huge opera being performed with West singing one of the leads for the assemblage. At the interval, she goes up to her bedroom and finds her dead husband as well as a monogrammed case left behind by the killer. The private detective attempts to blame West for the murder but Lebedeff is apprehended by Coral and admits his guilt as well as implicates Gateson and her plot to discredit West. With no husband to stand in the way, West marries Cavanagh and goes off to Jolly Olde England as the wife of the Earl of Stratton. Now that's enough for two movies but in between all the action there's time for such songs as "Now I'm A Lady," "He's A Bad Bad Man But He's Good Enough For Me," "Love Is Love In Any Woman's Heart," as well as the aria from Saint-Saens' opera "Samson And Delilah," known as "My Heart At Thy Still Voice." Phew. Some good one-liners from West and a few sharp moments from others in the cast but it's a misfire, mostly, because it doesn't quite know if it wants to be funny or not. For example, she plays the opera totally straight and that was a perfect spot for humor against the mayhem that was taking place upstairs between her husband and the hired lover. Not everything West did was perfection and this one was the proof of that pudding.

p, William LeBaron; d, Alexander Hall; w, Mae West (based on a story by Marion Morgan, George B. Dowell); ph, Karl Struss; m, Sammy Fain; ed, LeRoy Stone; art d, Hans Dreier, Robert Usher; cos, Travis Banton; m/l, Fain, Irving Kahal.

Musical Comedy **(PR:C MPAA:NR)**

GOIN' TO TOWN½** (1944) 68m RKO bw

Chester Lauck *(Lum)*, Norris Goff *(Abner)*, Barbara Hale *(Patty)*, Florence Lake *(Abigail)*, Dick Elliott *(Squire)*, Grady Sutton *(Cedric)*, Herbert Rawlinson *(Wentworth)*, Dick Baldwin *(Jimmy Benton)*, Ernie Adams *(Zeke)*, Jack Rice *(Clarke)*, Sam Flint *(Dr. Crane)*, Andrew Tombes *(Parker)*, George Chandler *(Jameson)*, Ruth Lee *(Mrs. Wentworth)*, Danny Duncan *(Grandpappy Spears)*, Marietta Canty *(Camellia)*, Nils T. Granlund *(N.T.G.)*

Lauck and Goff take their popular "Lum and Abner" characters off the radio and onto the big screen in this short feature. Fooled by a city slicker, they talk their neighbors into mortgaging their property and investing in a supposed pool of oil beneath the Jot-Em-Down Store. Of course, no oil is found but all is well in the end when the pair unload their property on the city slicker. A pleasant comedy with direction and script adequate for the material and even some showgirls for an added production number.

p, Jack William Votion; d, Leslie Goodwins; w, Charles E. Roberts, Charles H. Marion; ph, Robert Pittack; ed, Hanson T. Fritch; md, Lud Gluskin; art d, Alfred C. Ybarra; ch, Paul Oscard.

Comedy **(PR:A MPAA:NR)**

GOING APE!*½ (1981) 87m PAR c

Tony Danza *(Foster)*, Jessica Walter *(Fiona)*, Stacey Nelkin *(Cynthia)*, Danny De Vito *(Lazlo)*, Art Metrano *(Joey)*, Frank Sivero *(Bad Habit)*, Rick Hurst *(Brandon)*, Howard Mann *(Jules Cohen)*, Joseph Maher *(Gridley)*, Leon Askin *(Zabrowski)*, Jacquelyn Hyde *(Zelda)*, Ted White, Bob Terhune, Jay Durkus *(Goons)*, Angus Duncan *(Farley)*, Ellen Gerstein, Poppy Lagos, Marji Marvin, Donna Ponterotto, D.J. Sullivan *(Sisters)*, Hamilton Mitchell *(Marcin)*, Ruth Gillette *(Marianne)*, Henry Charles *(Ringmaster)*, Gene LeBell *(Faraday)*, Merie Earle *(Binocular Lady)*, Luke Andreas *(Carter)*.

A lot of monkey business involving Danza, some orangutans, and $5 million. Seems Danza's father has died and the will stipulates that Tony can have the money if he can take care of his father's beloved pets for five years. If any of them should come down with as much as a sniffle the money will go to the local zoo. Nelkin is Danza's girl who grows fond of the hairy beasts and Walter is her money-mad mother, scheming ways to get her daughter married off. Kronsberg made his directorial debut with this number after beginning a successful career in the orangutan film business with Clint Eastwood, writing EVERY WHICH WAY BUT LOOSE and ANY WHICH WAY YOU CAN. The same apes were used in all three films under the guidance of Bobby Berosini. GOIN APE! is about as creative as its title. There's little humor and no room for the actors to show their stuff.

p, Robert L. Rosen; d&w, Jeremy Joe Kronsberg; ph, Frank V. Phillips (Movielab Color); m, Elmer Bernstein; ed, John W. Wheeler; art d, Robert Kinoshita; set d, Richard Goddard; orangutan stunts ch, Bobby Berosini.

Comedy **Cas.** **(PR:A MPAA:PG)**

GOING BERSERK zero (1983) 85m UNIV c

John Candy *(John Bourgignon)*, Joe Flaherty *(Chick Leff)*, Eugene Levy *(Sal di Pasquale)*, Alley Mills *(Nancy Reese)*, Pat Hingle *(Ed Reese)*, Ann Bronston *(Patti)*, Eve Brent Ashe *(Mrs. Reese)*, Elizabeth Kerr *(Grandmother Ashe)*, Dixie Carter *(Angela)*, Paul Dooley *(Dr. Ted)*, Richard Libertini *(Sun Yi)*, Ronald E. House *(Bruno)*, Kurtwood Smith *(Clarence)*, Ernie Hudson *(Muhammed)*, Gloria Gifford *(Francine)*, Frantz Turner *(Wallace)*, Murphy Dunne *(Public Defender)*, Dan Burrows *(Minister)*, Julius Harris *(Judge)*, Bill Saluga *(Skipper, Kung Fu Leader)*, Kathy Bendett *(News Reporter)*, Brenda Currin *(Sal's Secretary)*, Hope Haves *(Princess)*, Natasha Ryan *(Kitten)*, Mark Bringelson *(Mom, Jr.)*, John Paragon *(Rooster)*, Mimi Seton *(Pink Punker)*, Mike Moroff *(Biker Leader)*, Tino Insana *(Outside Biker)*, Lynn Hallowell *(Misty)*, Larry Poindexter *(Claudell)*, Marianne Muellerlemle *(Waitress)*, Ken Letner *(Bailiff)*, Mark Yerkes *(Stunt Double)*, Rosalind Chato *(Kung Fu Girl)*, Jeff Imada, George Cheung, James Lew, Eric Lee, Danny Wong *(Kung Fu Fighters)*, Karen Lee Hopkins *(Aerobics Leader)*, Sioux Marcelli, Margie Deneke, Jennifer Perito, Ade Small, Patricia Ann Douglas, Ercelle Johnson, Kathleen White, Elaine Bolton, Sarah M. Miles, Judy Pierce, Sara Jane Gould, Helene Phillips, Lainie Manning, Denise McKenna, Leeyan Granger *(Aerobics Dancers)*, Peter Wilcox, Aaron King *(Elvis Presley Lookalikes)*, Sharon Peters *(Dolly Parton Lookalike)*, Archie Lang *(Man With Bag)*, Don Sherman *(Prisoner #1)*, Robert Bakanic *(Cameraman)*, Jeff Vida *(Usher)*, Elinor Donahue *(Margaret Anderson)*.

A stupendously unfunny and crude comedy which stars Candy as a limousine driver who falls in love with the daughter of a congressman. Opposing the congressman is a bizarre religious leader/aerobics studio owner who wants his sect to live in freedom from the law. Candy is captured and brainwashed into killing the congressman at the sight of a playing card (the five of diamonds). The spell doesn't quite work, however, and Candy turns into a lascivious goon concerned only with his anatomy. The assassination attempt, which is to take place during Candy's wedding, is foiled when he realizes that he was brainwashed. A pathetic attempt at filmmaking which should not be seen by children—not because of sex or violence, but because of its gutter humor.

p, Claude Heroux; d, David Steinberg; w, Steinberg, Dana Olsen; ph, Bobby Byrne (Panavision, Technicolor); m, Tom Scott; ed, Donn Cambern; prod d, Peter Lansdown Smith; m/l, "Mom Is Dead," Scott, Lee Ving; "Going Berserk," Scott, Rob Preston.

Comedy **Cas.** **(PR:O MPAA:R)**

GOING GAY (SEE: KISS ME GOODBYE, 1933, Brit.)

GOING HIGHBROW** (1935) 68m WB bw

Guy Kibbee *(Matt Upshore)*, ZaSu Pitts *(Caro Upshore)*, Edward Everett Horton *(Augie)*, Ross Alexander *(Harley Marsh)*, June Martel *(Sandy)*, Gordon Westcott *(Samuel Long)*, Judy Canova *(Annie)*, Nella Walker *(Mrs. March)*, Jack Norton *(Sinclair)*, Arthur Treacher *(Waiter)*, Milton Kibbee *(Acme Press Man)*, Frank Dufrane *(Officer)*, Walter Clyde *(Captain)*, Christine Gess *(French Actress)*, Sherry Hall *(United Newsman)*, Joseph E. Bernard, Jack H. Richardson *(Stewards)*, Olaf Hytten *(Butler)*, Irving Back *(Clerk)*, William Jeffrey *(Proprietor)*, Maude Turner Gordon *(Mrs. Vandergrift)*.

Kibbee and Pitts are a *nouveau riche* pair determined to break into society. They consult eccentric Horton on possible methods. He suggests throwing a lavish party for their daughter. There's just one slight problem: they have no daughter. This is resolved soon enough when Martel is whisked away from a lunch counter and into "daughterdom." It's all pretty routine material, with barely competent direction by Florey. Poor camera angles and pacing.

d, Robert Florey; w, Edward Kaufman, Sy Bartlett (based on the play "Social Pirates" by Ralph Spence); ph, William Rees; ed, Harold McLernon; md, Leo F. Forbstein; art d, Esdras Hartley; cos, Orry-Kelly; m/l, Louis Alter, John Scholl.

Comedy **(PR:A MPAA:NR)**

GOING HOLLYWOOD*** (1933) 80m COS/MGM bw

Bing Crosby *(Bill Williams)*, Marion Davies *(Sylvia Bruce)*, Fifi D'Orsay *(Lili Yvonne)*, Stuart Erwin *(Ernest P. Baker)*, Patsy Kelly *(Jill)*, Bobby Watson *(Jack Thompson)*, Ned Sparks *(Bert)*, Lennie Hayton, The Three Radio Rogues.

Lighthearted and unpretentious, this musical comedy is delightfully enacted by Crosby in his first MGM film and Davies in one of her best performances. Davies is an attractive French teacher in an exclusive girls' school; she meets Crosby, an aspiring crooner, and falls in love. But he's got the movie bug and is heading for

Hollywood and stardom. Once in Hollywood, Crosby becomes an overnight sensation and is set to star with sultry D'Orsay in a big musical production. Davies leaves her school and runs after Crosby, finding him in the clutches of D'Orsay, who has been leading him astray. When Davies finds Crosby drunk in a speakeasy dive with D'Orsay she gives the vixen a savage upbraiding and saves the crooner from Old Demon Rum. Moreover, the talented Davies replaces D'Orsay in the movie and becomes the star of the film, winding up with Crosby, fame, and fortune to boot. Director Walsh handled the production with great skill and a brisk pace that was to become his trademark. Crosby, in collegiate sweaters, spectator shoes, and white golf pants, is the essence of the casual crooner. He sings one of his biggest early-day hits, "Temptation" (Nacio Herb Brown, Arthur Freed). This production was lavishly sponsored by Cosmopolitan Productions, the filmmaking arm of newspaper czar William Randolph Hearst, who allowed his leading lady and mistress Davies all the luxuries of an empress during production. The snail-like pace of the production was astounding for that period, six months in which the actors more or less performed in their off-hours. Crosby was later to state in his autobiography *Call Me Lucky*: "It was the most leisurely motion picture I ever had anything to do with." Davies never arrived at the MGM lot until after 10 a.m. and spent two hours in her lavish dressing rooms—really a bungalow outfitted with office, kitchen, and dining room—preparing sumptuous high cuisine lunches for herself and leading players. Walsh, having nothing to do, whiled away the morning hours by playing golf. The long lunches involved conversation having little to do with the film they were making but Walsh, on occasion, would try to work in discussions about a few scenes and these would be worked into the schedule, time permitting. No one worked beyond 5 p.m. because of Hearst's refusal to pay heavy overtime costs. The film, when finally released, was an enormous success and made Crosby one of the 10 top box office kings. The crooner never forgot GOING HOLLYWOOD, remembering this film as "an example of the way the big movie queens of a bygone era—stars like Barbara LaMarr and Clara Bow and Pola Negri—sailed into action. In its day it spelled glamour. I got in on the twilight of this colorful era. It was quite an experience." Crosby's salary zoomed skyward with this production. He had been under contract to Paramount and, when Hearst specifically asked that MGM make a deal with Paramount for Crosby, the singer used this to negotiate another Paramount contract that called for $200,000 for three films to be made in 1934-35. He was also allowed to keep $50,000 in payment from MGM for his role in GOING HOLLYWOOD, plus, according to one report, a $5,000-a-week stipend. Within six months of the release of this musical Crosby was earning $500,000 a year, a staggering amount in the Depression-torn era when whole families were surviving, or attempting to survive, on a few thousand dollars a year. The literate and amusing script was penned by Stewart, a witty Hollywood scribe of the Robert Benchley school, and the supporting cast for GOING HOLLYWOOD is solid with Sparks as the cynical film director, Erwin as the bumbling producer, Hayton as the versatile pianist and conductor, and slapstick galore from Kelly in her film debut after smashing successes on Broadway. Songs include: "We'll Make Hay While the Sun Shines," "Going Hollywood," "Our Big Love Scene," "After Sundown," "Cinderella's Fella," "Beautiful Girl" (Freed, Brown), "Just an Echo In the Valley" (Reginald Connelly, Jimmy Campbell, Harry Woods).

p&d, Walter Walsh; w, Donald Ogden Stewart (based on a story by Frances Marion); ph, George Folsey; ed, Frank Sullivan; md, Lennie Hayton.

Musical **(PR:A MPAA:NR)**

GOING HOME** (1971) 97m MGM c

Robert Mitchum *(Harry K. Graham)*, Brenda Vaccaro *(Jenny)*, Jan-Michael Vincent *(Jimmy Graham)*, Jason Bernard *(Jimmy at 6)*, Sally Kirkland *(Ann Graham)*, Joe Attles *(Bible Man)*, Lou Gilbert *(Mr. Katz)*, Josh Mostel *(Bonelli)*, Carol Gustafson *(Ella)*, Barbara Brownell *(Betsy)*, David Wilson, Glenn Walken, Clay Watkins, Bruce Kornbluth *(Sailors)*, Thomas Spratley *(Guard)*, Louis Criscuolo *(Angry Man)*, Richard Goode *(Pleasant Man)*, Vicki Sue Robinson *(Hippie Girl)*, Lawrence E. Bender *(Pass Clerk)*, Tim Wallace, Jules Sicilia *(Bowling Alley Drunks)*, George Mathews *(Malloy)*, Mary Louise Wilson *(Real Estate Lady)*, Ann Thomas *(Lady in Nursery)*, George DiCenzo *(Sergeant)*, Hope Clarke *(Mother at Prison)*, William K. Leech *(Portman)*, Lynn Terry, Ben Terry *(Night Club Entertainers)*, Shari Marcell *(Waitress)*, Hank Luba, Edward Steinfeld, Jack C. Harper, Ginny Heller *(Friends at the Beach)*, Paula Stewart *(Girl at Trailer Park)*, William R. Tebbs *(Mechanic)*, Carol Wilkerson *(Girl at Prison)*, Winkie Miller *(Girl at Party)*, Robert Rinier *(Bowler)*.

Herbert Leonard, who successfully produced many TV shows like "Route 66," makes his directorial debut with this and is defeated by Mitchum's sleep-walking. It's an off-beat story about Mitchum, a man who murdered his wife, coming out of jail 13 years later and attempting to establish a relationship with his son, Vincent, who saw him dispatch the woman in a gruesome fashion. Vincent is not only 13 years older, he hates his father 13 times as much. Mitchum settles in a seaside town and Vincent goes looking for him. Mitchum is now an empty hulk of a man and living with Vaccaro, who acts as the go-between for the two men. Vaccaro is good as the woman and Vincent is believable as the confused and angry young man. It was interesting to see Mitchum break out of his tough-guy mold but he may have stretched for something beyond his talents with this one. A bunch of songs are interspersed so it almost becomes a musical tragedy. Songs include: "Way Back Home In West Virginia," "The Lala Song," "You Never Know How Much" (Bill Walker), "Time After Time" (Sammy Cahn, Jule Styne), "Blue Moon" (Richard Rodgers, Lorenz Hart), "Tell Me About Love" (Danny Vic, sung by Red Lane), "Silver Bird" (Lane), "Rope Around the Wind," "Singaree Singaroh" (Lane, Harry Henley, sung by Lane)

p&d, Herbert B. Leonard; w, Lawrence B. Marcus; ph, Fred Jackman (Metrocolor); m, Bill Walker; ed, Sig Neufeld, Jr.; art d, Peter Wooley; set d, Audrey Blaisdel; cos, Guy Verhille; spec eff, Ira Anderson.

Drama **(PR:O MPAA:GP)**

GOING IN STYLE**** (1979) 97m WB c

George Burns *(Joe)*, Art Carney *(Al)*, Lee Strasberg *(Willie)*, Charles Hallahan *(Pete)*, Pamela Payton-Wright *(Kathy)*, Siobhan Keegan *(Colleen)*, Brian Neville *(Kevin)*, Constantine Hartofolis *(Boy in Park)*, Mary Testa *(Teller)*, Jean Shevlin *(Mrs. Fein)*, James Manis *(Hot Dog Vendor)*, Margot Stevenson *(Store Cashier)*, Tito Goya *(Gypsy Cab Driver)*, William Pabst *(Bank Guard)*, Christopher Wynkoop *(Bank Manager)*, Joseph Sullivan *(Moon)*, Bob Maroff *(Cab Driver)*, Vivian Edwards *(Bellhop)*, Barbara Ann Miller *(Waitress)*, Catherine Billich, Betty Bunch *(Cashiers)*, Anthony D. Call, William Larson, Reathal Bean, Alan Brooks *(FBI Agents)*.

An hilarious comedy where three elderly gents, Burns, Carney, and Strasberg, tired of the indifference society shows them, along with the pervasive feeling of uselessness that shrouds their lives, decide to robs a bank. It's really Burns who conceives of the idea, more as a way of relieving boredom than increasing the thickness of his wallet. Also, the idea is appealing to Strasberg and Carey as a method by which they, the senior citizens, can strike back at a system that has abandoned them as human beings. Wearing funny masks and wielding guns, the threesome robs a Manhattan bank of a small fortune, but Strasberg dies of a heart attack some days later while the three sit on their favorite park bench watching small children play. Burns and Carney then fly to Las Vegas, and, using their ill-gotten loot, take the casinos to the cleaners, flying back to New York with a great fortune in cash. Carney then dies in his sleep and Burns turns the money over to Carney's likable nephew, Hallahan, to use to open a business. He is noncommital when FBI and police finally close in on him and he is sent to prison for his caprice, meeting with Hallahan in the visitor's room to tells him to keep the money and jokingly tells him before disappearing once again behind bars that no prison can hold him. Burns is absolutely fascinating in his portrayal of a crafty, wise, and wholly adaptable old man outwitting the fast-moving young world about him. There are some sublimely serious parts to give the whole thing roots, such as a moving scene where Burns looks through a box of old photos which actually show Burns in his youth as a vaudeville trooper and some shots with his real life wife Gracie Allen. He begins to weep as he looks back on days no more, images that drag at his heart. This nostalgic interlude is brought to an abrupt halt when Burns suddenly stands up, swearing, as he realizes that he has wet his trousers—age again, intruding upon his reveries. Director Brest does a great job with a sensitive subject, drawing fine performances from everyone. Carney is a standout as the jovial, ready-for-anything sidekick who has the time of his life rolling points in Las Vegas and really dies happy, flattered to glowing pride that a pretty young thing in gambler's paradise propositioned *him*. A consistently funny and warm movie.

p, Tony Bill, Fred T. Gallo; d&w, Martin Brest (based on a story by Edward Cannon); ph, Billy Williams (Technicolor); m, Michael Small; ed, Robert Swink, C. Timothy O'Meara; prod d, Stephen Hendrickson; art d, Gary Weist; cos, Anna Hill Johnstone.

Comedy **Cas.** **(PR:C MPAA:PG)**

GOING MY WAY***** (1944) 130m PAR bw

Bing Crosby *(Father Chuck O'Malley)*, Rise Stevens *(Genevieve Linden)*, Barry Fitzgerald *(Father Fitzgibbon)*, Frank McHugh *(Father Timothy O'Dowd)*, Gene Lockhart *(Ted Haines, Sr.)*, William Frawley *(Max Dolan)*, James Brown *(Ted Haines, Jr.)*, Jean Heather *(Carol James)*, Porter Hall *(Mr. Belknap)*, Fortunio Bonanova *(Tomasso Bozzani)*, Eily Malyon *(Mrs. Carmody)*, George Nokes *(Pee Wee)*, Tom Dillon *(Officer McCarthy)*, Stanley Clements *(Tony Scaponi)*, Carl "Alfalfa" Switzer *(Herman Langerhanke)*, Hugh Maguire *(Pitch Pipe)*, Sybyl Lewis *(Maid at Metropolitan Opera House)*, George McKay *(Mr. Van Heusen)*, Jack Norton *(Mr. Lilley)*, Anita Bolster *(Mrs. Quimp)*, Jimmie Dundee *(Fireman)*, Adeline Reynolds *(Mother Fitzgibbon)*, Gibson Gowland *(Churchgoer)*, Julie Gibson *(Taxi Driver)*, Bill Henry *(Intern)*, Robert Tafur *(Don Jose)*, Martin Garralaga *(Zuniga)*, Robert Mitchell Boy Choir.

A warm and moving film, GOING MY WAY was a sleeper that turned into an enormous box office hit. Crosby is an easy-going, trouble-shooting priest who arrives at St. Dominic's Church, a Catholic institution that has seen better days, as has its curate, elderly Fitzgerald. The old priest, set in his ways, has helmed the parish for 45 years and recently the Church has gotten heavily in debt with overdue mortgages. Even the parishioners are disillusioned. The local kids are on the verge of turning into street toughs. Clements and Switzer (of Our Gang fame) are caught by Fitzgerald crossing through the church yard, lugging a turkey they have just stolen from a poultry truck. Nervously they turn it over to Fitzgerald as a gift. Crosby, of course, knows what they've been up to, but Fitzgerald is blissfully oblivious to their nefarious activities. That night, while eating a succulent turkey dinner, Crosby voices his suspicions of the boys. "Nonsense," Fitzgerald says. "I'll have you know that the very food before us was donated to the parish by two of the boys that you say have been accused of stealing. I gave them both my blessing." Crosby responds: "And they gave you the bird." Crosby manages to round up the youths and turn them into a fine choir. He writes a song, "The Day After Forever" (Johnny Burke, Jimmy Van Heusen, sung by Crosby and Heather), but music publisher Frawley shakes his head and labels it too "schmaltzy." He later hears another ditty by the priest, "Swingin' On A Star," (Burke, Van Heusen, sung by Crosby and choir) and snatches it up. It's a big hit and its proceeds help to pay off the church debts. Holder of the mortgage Lockhart proves tough to deal with but Crosby gets around him with his Irish charm, even managing to help out Brown, Lockhart's son, and Heather, so they can get married. All appears right with the world until McHugh, a fellow priest from another parish, runs in with the news that the church is on fire. Gutted, the stark remains indicate the finish for Fitzgerald's parish, yet Crosby approaches opera diva Stevens, an old flame who is surprised to see he is a priest. She agrees to help restore the church and takes Crosby's choir on tour, raising the needed funds to rebuild the church. Meanwhile, Crosby and Fitzgerald have grown fond of each other and, in one scene where Fitzgerald is ill in bed, Crosby sings him a grand old song from the Old Sod, "Too-ra-loo-ra-loo-a" (J.R. Shannon), accompanied by a music box. Moreover, at the end of the film, just before packing his bag and leaving the parish intact, Crosby manages to bring Fitzgerald's 90-year-old mother from Ireland for an emotional reunion with her son. McCarey's direction here is simply masterful as he brings the story just short of being maudlin, mawkish, and soaked with sentimentality. It all works like magic, especially the unbeatable chemistry between Crosby and Fitzgerald. It was box office dynamite, with $6 million returned to Paramount coffers. The film also enjoyed a grand sweep of Oscars, with Academy Awards going to the studio for Best Picture (Paramount had not gotten this award since WINGS, 16 years earlier), for Best Director, Best Screenplay, Best Song ("Swingin' On A Star") and to Crosby and Fitzgerald for Best Actor and Best Supporting Actor (Fitzgerald was actually nominated for Best Actor and Best Supporting Actor, the last to receive nominations in two categories, the Academy eliminating this procedure after 1945). Paramount had second thoughts about casting Crosby as a priest but McCarey, whose project this was, convinced studio executives that he would be perfect as the unflappable cleric. Crosby was forever grateful that McCarey would "take me by the hand and lead me through the picture." This film and its equally wonderful sequel, THE BELLS OF ST. MARY'S, found immense popularity with the Catholic Church and Pope Pius XII who later gave a private audience to Crosby to thank him for his portrayal. Other songs include: "Going My Way" (Burke and Van Heusen; sung by Crosby and Stevens), "Silent Night" (Franz Gruber, Joseph Mohr; sung by Crosby, Robert Mitchell Boy Choir), "Habanera" (from Bizet's "Carmen," sung by Stevens), "Ave Maria" (Schubert, sung by Stevens, Robert Mitchell Boy Choir).

p&d, Leo McCarey; w, Frank Butler, Frank Cavett (based on a story by McCarey); ph, Lionel Lindon; ed, Leroy Stone; md, Robert Emmett Dolan; art d, Hans Dreier, William Flannery, set d, Gene Merritt, John Cope; spec eff, Gordon Jennings; cos, Edith Head.

Drama/Musical   **Cas.**   **(PR:AAA MPAA:NR)**

GOING PLACES**   (1939) 84m COS/WB bw

Dick Powell (*Peter Mason*), Anita Louise (*Ellen Parker*), Allen Jenkins (*Droopy*), Ronald Reagan (*Jack Withering*), Walter Catlett (*Franklin Dexter*), Harold Huber (*Maxie*), Larry Williams (*Frank*), Thurston Hall (*Col. Withering*), Minna Gombell (*Cora Withering*), Joyce Compton (*Joan*), Robert Warrick (*Frome*), Louis Armstrong (*Cabe, the Black Hostler*), Maxine Sullivan (*Specialty*), John Ridgely (*Desk Clerk*), Joe Cunningham (*Night Clerk*), Eddie Anderson (*Black Groom*), George Reed (*Sam*), Ferdinand Munier (*Mr. Beckman*), Sidney Bracey (*Cooper*), Janet Shaw, Rosella Towne (*Young Ladies*), Ward Bond, Eddy Chandler (*Cops*), Frank Mayo (*Flagman*), Jesse Graves (*Butler*), Charlotte Treadway (*Woman Guest*), John Harron (*Guest*).

This was the fourth time around for this story and Powell's third bomb in a row, the other two being HARD TO GET and COWBOY FROM BROOYLYN. Based on "The Hottentot", a play by Victor Mapes and William Collier, it was first made as a silent HOTTNETOT, starring Douglas MacLean, then again as a talkie with Edward Everett Horton and Patsy Ruth Miller. Later, it was the basis for a Joe E. Brown comedy called POLO JOE. Powell is a sporting goods salesman who needs to get some business so he poses as a famous jockey and gets in with the horsey set. He falls in love with wealthy Louise and then has to ride her uncle's steed, "Jeepers Creepers" in the big race. Do we have to tell you if he wins or loses? Louis Armstrong plays the horse's groom and gets to sing the big song based on the horse's name. Ronald Reagan is the devil-may-care son of the rich horse owner, Hall, and Louise is the lovely niece. The horse is very jumpy and can only be calmed when Armstrong sings to him so the race takes place with Powell aboard in the silks and Armstrong riding alongside with a bunch of musicians as they sing to the animal. Unlikely, you say? Well of course. And that was about the most logical element of the movie. Reagan does well in a small part but it's Armstrong who steals what little there is to steal. Once again, the best thing in the film was the music by Harry Warren. The tunes include "Jeepers Creepers," "Say It With A Kiss," "Oh, What A Horse Was Charley," and "Mutiny In The Nursery." Good musical cameos by the Dandridge Sisters and Maxine Sullivan.

p, Hal B. Wallis; d, Ray Enright; w, Jerry Wald, Sig Herzig, Maurice Leo (based on the play "The Hottentot" by Victor Mapes, William Collier); ph, Arthur L. Todd; md, Leo F. Forbstein; ed, Clarence Kolster; art d, Hugh Reticker; m/l, Harry Warren, Johnny Mercer.

Musical Comedy   **(PR:A MPAA:NR)**

GOING PLACES**½   (1974, Fr.) 117m C.A.P.-U.P.E.-SN/Cinema 5 c (LES VALSEUSES)

Gerard Depardieu (*Jean-Claude*), Patrick Dewaere (*Pierrot*), Miou-Miou (*Marie-Ange*), Jeanne Moreau (*Jeanne*), Jacques Chailieux (*Jacques*), Michel Peurilon (*Surgeon*), Brigitte Fossey (*Young Mother*), Isabelle Huppert (*Jacqueline*), Christiane Muller (*Jacqueline's Mother*), Christian Alers (*Jacqueline's Father*), Dominique Davray (*Ursula*), Jacques Rispal (*Beautician*), Marco Perrin (*Warden*), Gerard Boucaron (*Garage Owner*), Michel Pilorge (*Market Manager*).

One of those films designed to display the empty ideals and general despondence of the French youth of the 1970s is technically efficient but never seems to do anything but gloss over the issues it's trying to address. Depardieu and Dewaere are two buddies who spend their time galivanting across France, showing little respect for the people they come across. The idea of robbing or raping some innocent victim mars their consciences as much as a cat is bothered pouncing on an unsuspecting mouse. These two guys are little more than animals, and like the cat they conceal their ruthless exteriors long enough to be incredibly cute. A brief stint by Jeanne Moreau as an ex-con trying to get back on the right track is the one sparkling moment of the film; unfortunately her brilliant presence is much too short, and then it's back to putting up with the antics of Depardieu and Dewaere.

p, Paul Claudon; d, Bertrand Blier; w, Blier, Philippe Dumarcay (based on the novel by Blier); ph, Bruno Nuyten; m, Stephane Grappelli; ed, Kenout Peltier.

Drama   **Cas.**   **(PR:O MPAA:R)**

GOING STEADY**   (1958) 82m COL bw

Molly Bee (*Julie Ann*), Alan Reed, Jr. (*Calvin Potter*), Bill Goodwin (*Gordon Turner*), Irene Hervey (*Grace Turner*), Ken Miller (*Woody Simmons*), Susan Easter (*Olive Nelson*), Linda Watkins (*Aunt Lola*), Byron Foulger (*Mr. Potter*), Hugh Sanders (*Mr. Ahern*), Florence Ravenel (*Mrs. Potter*), Ralph Moody (*Justice of the Peace*), Carlyle Mitchell (*Arthur Priestley*).

Bee and Reed are two high school sweethearts who run off and get married one weekend after she fools her parents into thinking she's going to an out-of-town basketball game. They move in with her parents and soon discover they are to become parents as well. Bee and Reed are fine as the young couple, with Goodwin and Hervey appropriately bewildered as Bee's parents.

p, Sam Katzman; d, Fred F. Sears; w, Budd Grossman (based on a story by Grossman, Sumner A. Long); ph, Benjamin H. Kline; md, Mischa Bakaleinikoff; ed, Charles Nelson; art d, Paul Palmentola.

Comedy   **Cas.**   **(PR:A MPAA:NR)**

GOING STRAIGHT*   (1933, Brit.) 51m WB bw

Moira Lynd (*Peggy Edwards*), Helen Ferrers (*Lady Peckham*), Tracy Holmes, Joan Marion, Hal Walters, Huntley Wright, Eric Stanley, George Merritt, Gilbert Davis.

Poorly handled in all respects, this picture attempts to make a farce out of the goings-on in a wealthy home which takes on two ex-convicts as employees. Boring and routine.

p, Irving Asher; d, John Rawlings.

Comedy   **(PR:A MPAA:NR)**

GOING TO TOWN   (SEE: MA AND PA KETTLE GO TO TOWN, 1949)

GOING WILD**   (1931) 68m FN-WB bw

Joe E. Brown (*Rollo Smith*), Lawrence Gray (*Jack Lane*), Laura Lee (*Peggy Freeman*), Walter Pidgeon ("*Ace" Benton*), Ona Munson (*Ruth Howard*), Frank McHugh ("*Rickey" Freeman*), May Boley (*May Bunch*), Harvey Clark (*Herndon Reamer*), Anders Randolf (*Edward Howard*), Sam Cantor (*Sammy Cantor*), Arthur Hoyt (*Robert Story*), Johnny Arthur (*Simpkins*), Fred Kelsey (*Conductor*), Larry Banthin.

Brown is a down-on-his-luck newspaperman who is mistaken for a famous aviator. Since it is a pair of pretty girls who think he is someone else, Brown plays along. Before he knows it he's caught up in a web of lies and finds himself being chased by an Amazon dead-set on killing him. The plot has some confusing twists, though Brown is funny as always. Poor backdrop on closeups destroys the illusion of Brown doing wild stunt flying. The rest of the cast never really gets a chance to shine. Standard comedy fare of the period.

d, William A. Seiter; w, Humphrey Pearson, Henry McCarthy (based on a story by Pearson); ph, Sol Polito; ed, Peter Fritch.

Comedy   **(PR:A MPAA:NR)**

GOJIRA TAI MOSURA   (SEE: GODZILLA VS. THE THING, 1964, Jap.)

GOJUMAN-NIN NO ISAN   (SEE: LEGACY OF THE 500,000, THE, 1964, Jap.)

GOKE, BODYSNATCHER FROM HELL* (1968, Jap.) 84m Shochiku c (KYUKETSUKI GOKEMIDORO; AKA: GOKE THE VAMPIRE)

Hideo Ko, Teruo Yoshida, Tomomi Sato, Eizo Kitamura, Masay Takahashi, Cathy Horlan, Kazuo Kato, Yuko Kusunoki.

An airliner, with Yoshida as captain and Sato as stewardess, passes through a mysterious cloud mass and crash-lands in a desert. Everyone seems to be okay except for one passenger, Ko who has been turned into a vampire by the cloud. Before long everyone is turning into a vampire, but Yoshida and Sato manage to escape. When they finally find safety, they discover a mysterious outer space source that is turning all of Earth's population into vampires. Coupled with bad acting and sloppy direction, this resembles INVASION OF THE BODY SNATCHERS, though not nearly as well done.

p, Takashi Inomata; d, Hajime Sato; w, Susumu Takaku, Kyuzo Kobayashi; ph, Shizuo Hirase; m, Shunsuke Kikuchi; art d, Tadataka Yoshida.

Science Fiction/Horror   **(PR:O MPAA:NR)**

GOLD**   (1932) 58m Majestic bw

Jack Hoxie, Alice Day, Hooper Atchley, Jack Clifford, Bob Kortman, Tom London, Lafe McKee, Mathew Betz, Harry Todd, Archie Ricks, Jack Kirk, Jack Byron.

Hoxie is an ex-rancher turned gold miner. He splits his claim with an old-timer but the latter is killed by outlaws who take his money. Hoxie, the prime suspect, loses his social standing and also his girl, the victim's daughter. But Hoxie fools the villains and wins his girl's heart in the end. An average horse opera that overcomes its stereotypes with some good acting. Even Hoxie's horse Dynamite gets in on the action, stealing the final scene.

p, Larry Darmour; d, Otto Brower; w, Scott Darling (based on a story by Jack Natteford); ph, Art Reed, Charles Marshall; ed, S. Roy Luby.

Western   **(PR:A MPAA:NR)**

GOLD**   (1934, Ger.) 120m UFA bw

Hans Albers, Brigitte Helm, Friedrich Kayssler, Lien Deyers, Michael Bohnen, Eberhard Leithoff, Rudolf Platte.

Kayssler is a modern day alchemist, who, along with his assistant, Albers, creates an atomic reactor capable of changing lead to gold. They are made a handsome offer by Bohnen for their discovery but decide gold-making is beneath their talents and the machine is destroyed. The photography gives a nice atmospheric look to GOLD and the acting is quite strong. Helm is especially good as the assistant who is also the lover. A French version, entitled L'OR, was shot simultaneously by Serge de Poligny, with some of the actors taking different roles. Helm, however, played the same character in both versions. After WW II, a nervous U.S. government had the film screened by nuclear experts, fearful that GOLD was proof that the Germans had the know-how to build an atomic reactor.

p, Alfred Zeisler; d, Karl Hartl; w, Rolf E. Banloo; ph, Guenther Rittau, Otto Baecker, Werner Bohne.

Drama **(PR:C MPAA:NR)**

GOLD** (1974, Brit.) 118m AA c

Roger Moore *(Rod Slater)*, Susannah York *(Terry Steyner)*, Ray Milland *(Hurry Hirschfeld)*, Bradford Dillman *(Manfred Steyner)*, John Gielgud *(Farrell)*, Simon Sabela *(Big King)*, Tony Beckley *(Stephen Marais)*, Bernard Horsfall *(Kowalski)*, Marc Smith *(Tex Kiernan)*, John Hussey *(Plummer)*, Norman Coombes *(Frank Lemmer)*, George Jackson *(Doctor)*, Michael McGovern *(Jackson)*, Andre Maranne *(French Man)*, John Bay *(American)*, Paul Hansard *(Swiss)*, Paul Mafela *(Jimmy)*, Ralph Norvel *(Girl in Bar)*, Garth Tuckett, Albert Raphael, Lloyd Lilford, Alan Craig, John Kingley *(Miners)*, Karl Duering, Nadim Sawalha, Gideon Kolb, John Bay *(Syndicate Members)*

Unscrupulous South African mine owners plot to flood their holdings, thus raising gold prices around the world. Moore is a mine foreman who is unwittingly used by the owners, as is York, the wife of a mine operator. This is a grimly realistic film with a suspenseful climax. The flooding of the mine looks brutally honest. Bernstein's dramatic music score works well, adding emotion and tension to the flooding sequences. Shot on location in South Africa.

p, Michael Klinger; d, Peter Hunt; w, Wilber Smith, Stanley Price (based on the novel *Goldmine* by Smith); ph, Ousama Rawi (Panavision, Technicolor); m, Elmer Bernstein; ed, John Glen; prod d, Alec Vetchinsky, Syd Cain; art d, Robert Laing; m/l, Don Black (songs sung by Jimmy Helms, Maureen McGovern, Trevor Chance).

Drama **(PR:O MPAA:PG)**

GOLD DIGGERS IN PARIS**½ (1938) 100m WB bw (GB: GAY IMPOSTORS)

Rudy Vallee *(Terry Moore)*, Rosemary Lane *(Kay Morrow)*, Hugh Herbert *(Maurice Giraud)*, Allen Jenkins *(Duke Dennis)*, Gloria Dickson *(Mona)*, Melville Cooper *(Pierre LeBrec)*, Mabel Todd *(Leticia)*, Fritz Feld *(Luis Leoni)*, Ed Brophy *(Mike Coogan)*, Curt Bois *(Padrinsky)*, Victor Kilian, George Renevant *(Gendarmes)*, Armand Kaliz *(Stage Manager)*, Maurice Cass *(Vail)*, Eddie Anderson *(Doorman)*, The Schnickelfritz Band.

Last and weakest of the GOLD DIGGER films, the Parisian setting was an attempt to both breathe some life into the series and make a bonafide movie star out of Vallee. The results are passable. This time around the Gold Diggers visit France and there's some confusion between a club named "Ballet" and the American Ballet. That's really just an excuse for some good old-fashioned Busby Berkeley production numbers. Though the studio budgeted this film well below the others, Berkeley did his usual fine job. The direction is fine, considering the thin plot Enright had to work with. Songs: "The Latin Quarter," "I Wanna Go Back to Bali," "Put That Down in Writing," "A Stranger in Paree" (Al Dubin, Harry Warren), "Day Dreaming All Night Long," "Waltz of the Flowers," "My Adventure" (Johnny Mercer, Warren).

p, Sam Bischoff; d, Ray Enright; w, Earl Baldwin, Warren Duff (based on a story by Jerry Wald, Richard Macaulay, Maurice Leo, Jerry Horwin, James Seymour); ph, Sol Polito, George Barnes; md, Leo F. Forbstein; art d, Robert Haas; ed, George Amy.

Musical **(PR:A MPAA:NR)**

GOLD DIGGERS OF BROADWAY**½ (1929) 105m WB c

Nancy Welford *(Jerry)*, Conway Tearle *(Stephen Lee)*, Winnie Lightner *(Mable)*, Ann Pennington *(Ann Collins)*, Lilyan Tashman *(Eleanor)*, William Bakewell *(Wally)*, Nick Lucas *(Nick)*, Helen Foster *(Violet)*, Albert Gran *(Blake)*, Gertrude Short *(Topsy)*, Neely Edwards *(Stage Manager)*, Julie Swayne Gordon *(Cissy Gray)*, Lee Moran *(Dance Director)*, Armand Kaliz *(Barney Barnett)*.

First of the talkie GOLD DIGGERS (a silent version of the original stage play was made in 1923) tells the now-familiar story of three chorus girls meeting men in the big city and trying to get juicy parts in a big show. Welford, Pennington, and Lightner are the gold diggers, with Lightner stealing the picture. She's a delight to watch, with a wonderful voice to boot. Some great production numbers that are big and brassy. Tap dancing was used effectivly to play around with the new sound medium. Lucas's number, "Tip Toe Through the Tulips," became a big hit for pop singer Tiny Tim in 1968. Other songs: "Painting the Clouds with Sunshine" (sung by Lucas). "In a Kitchenette," "Go to Bed," "And They Still Fall in Love," "What Will I do Without You?" "Mechanical Man," "Song of the Gold Diggers" (Al Dubin, Joe Burke).

d, Roy Del Ruth; w, Robert Lord (based on the play by Avery Hopwood); ph, (Technicolor); ch, Larry Ceballos.

Musical **(PR:A MPAA:NR)**

GOLD DIGGERS OF 1933**** (1933) 94m WB bw

Warren William *(J. Lawrence Bradford)*, Joan Blondell *(Carol King)*, Aline MacMahon *(Trixie Lorraine)*, Ruby Keeler *(Polly Parker)*, Dick Powell *(Brad Roberts/Robert Treat Bradford)*, Guy Kibbee *(Faneuil H. Peabody)*, Ned Sparks *(Barney Hopkins)*, Ginger Rogers *(Fay Fortune)*, Clarence Nordstrom *(Gordon)*, Robert Agnew *(Dance Director)*, Sterling Holloway *(Messenger Boy)*, Tammany Young *(Gigolo Eddie)*, Ferdinand Gottschalk *(Clubman)*, Lynn Browning *(Gold Digger Girl)*, Charles C. Wilson *(Deputy)*, Billy Barty *("Pettin' in the Park" Baby)*, Fred "Snowflake" Toones, Theresa Harris *(Black Couple)*, Joan Barclay *(Chorus Girl)*, Wallace MacDonald *(Stage Manager)*, Charles Lane, Wilbur Mack, Grace Hayle *(Society Reporters)*, Hobart Cavanaugh *(Dog Salesman)*, Bill Elliott *(Dance Extra)*, Dennis O'Keefe *(Extra During Intermission)*, Busby Berkeley *(Call Boy)*, Fred Kelsey *(Detective Jones)*, Frank Mills *(1st Forgotten Man)*, Etta Moten *("Forgotten Man" Singer)*, Billy West *(Medal of Honor Winner)*, Eddie Foster *(Zipky's Kentucky Hill Billies—2nd Man)*, Loretta Andrews, Adrien Brier, Lynn Browning, Monica Bannister, Maxine Cantway, Bonnie Bannon, Margaret Carthew, Kitty Cunningham, Gloria Faythe, Muriel Gordon, June Glory, Ebba Hally, Amo Ingraham, Lorena Layson, Alice Jans, Jayne Shadduck, Bee Stevens, Anita Thompson, Pat Wing, Renee Whitney, Ann Hovey, Dorothy Coonan *(Gold Diggers)*.

After Warner Bros. released 42ND STREET to a huge response, they quickly put this one into script and onto the stages as they knew they had something in musicals. It was based on a 1929 play by Avery Hopwood called "Gold Diggers Of Broadway" and was to spawn several more in the same genre. Blondell, MacMahon, and Keeler are a trio of unemployed showgirls who are thrilled when producer Sparks tells them he is about to start a new show. Then they learn he hasn't got a penny. Meanwhile, Powell is a songwriter who lives across the way from the girls and is mad for Keeler (Powell and Keeler were to repeat this love story may times in years to come). When he hears about the new show, "Forgotten Melody," and the fact that Sparks' wallet is full of empty, he offers to lend them the needed lucre, the sum of $15,000. The girls think he is either putting them on or daft, but when he arrives at Sparks' office with a check, the show goes into immediate rehearsal. Soon enough, Powell has a part in the show, singing some of his own tunes. Blondell and MacMahon think something is fishy. Where did Powell get that kind of money? Is he a crook? Keeler, ever the soul of naivete, believes in Powell and knows, deep in her heart of hearts, that he's a legit guy. Now we learn where he came by the moolah. Seems that Powell is a very rich young man indeed and his brother, William, arrives in New York with old-line Boston lawyer Kibbee to put a stop to Powell's attempts at a show business career. That kind of thing just isn't done by the Beacon Hill families from which Powell has sprung. It is a definite blot on their escutcheon and William is jut-jawed about ending the whole matter. By this time, Powell is ready to marry Keeler and William thinks the girl is only in it for the money, so he goes to the trio's apartment in an attempt to buy Keeler out of the relationship. Once he gets to their residence, nothing goes the way it should. Keeler is out, so Blondell masquerades as her roommate and she and MacMahon go to lunch with William and Kibbee. William is captivated by Blondell. That night, they go to dinner and William gets schnockered. Blondell returns him to her apartment where he has to sleep it off. Later, MacMahon comes home and decides to play a prank on William. They take his clothes off and put him into Blondell's bed. Next morning, William awakens to find himself in this compromising position. He writes a check to Blondell (whom he still thinks is Keeler) for ten grand, then rushes out. Blondell finds the check and frames it. Now William learns that Keeler and Powell have gotten married and Blondell is someone else. He is crazy about her and wants to continue the relationship and he really isn't a bad sort so Blondell says she'll go on seeing him, but only after he agrees to shake hands and give his blessing to his brother and his new sister-in-law. William agrees and everyone is happy. At the end, MacMahon has her heart set on Kibbee, a lifelong bachelor, and the odds are they'll get together sometime after the fadeout. That's the story; a pretty good one at that. In the following GOLD DIGGERS, there were never that many things going on. Hopwood's play served the music well. And what music it was. Harry Warren and Al Dubin, fresh from their 42ND STREET success (it was later made into a Broadway play that ran many seasons and although Warren wrote more hits than almost everyone, with the exceptions of Cole Porter, Richard Rodgers, and, perhaps, Irving Berlin, no one knew him then and fewer people know him now) wrote this score which included, "We're In The Money," "Pettin' In The Park," "The Shadow Waltz," "My Forgotten Man," "I've Got To Sing A Torch Song." Berkeley did some startling work on this film. In the opening number, Ginger Rogers leads the chorus in an extravagant "We're In The Money" as the girls, all dressed in gold coin costumes, dance among a series of giant coins. This was, no doubt, a slap in the face at the Depression, when no one was in the money, except those people who made these kind of movies. In "Pettin' In The Park," the ubiquitous chorines are all dressed in armor and attacked by a chorus of boy dancers armed with can openers. In "Shadow Waltz," Berkeley wired the dancers with electric violins and neon lights, then had them dance on a huge curved staircase. The most powerful number was sung by Etta Moten, "My Forgotten Man," a tribute to the men who fought in "The Great War" (WW I) and who were now unemployed and attempting to find something to do to beat the Depression (the absolute opposite of the opening). More than 150 extras were in the scene which almost rivaled "Brother, Can You Spare A Dime" for sheer pathos. After Moten did her piece, Blondell takes up the tune and finishes it (with singing dubbed by opera star Marian Anderson) as the picture fades to black. Rogers was billed eighth but opened the movie and there were those who felt that she received such a plum because she and director LeRoy were a romantic item at that time. It may have been the case but Rogers went on to prove that she didn't need anyone to help her be a star, except Fred Astaire. And after a while, she didn't even need him. In the "Pettin' In The Park" sequence, look hard after the dancers race offstage to change out of their wet clothes caused by a downpour. They step behind shades, are back-lit and there is no mistaking the fact that they are totally nude. A young Billy Barty, the very small actor who has been making movies for 50 years and was so funny as the bible salesman in FOUL PLAY, has a tiny role as a backstage employee. Barty never let the fact that he was a dwarf stand in his way and he is one of the most beloved actors in movies. The picture is loaded with inside jokes. Famed agent Louis Schurr's name is seen on screen as Ned Sparks' secretary and several other gags were put in there just for pals. If you have but one 1930s Warner Bros. musical to see, make it his one. Dennis O'Keefe does a small bit as an extra and Berkeley himself takes a role as the Call Boy. Remade in 1951 as PAINTING THE CLOUDS WITH SUNSHINE.

p, Robert Lord; d, Mervyn LeRoy; w, Erwin Gelsey, James Seymour, David Boehm, Ben Markson; (based on the play "Gold Diggers Of Broadway" by Avery

Hopwood); ph, Sol Polito; md, Leo F. Forbstein; ed, George Amy; art d, Anton Grot; cos, Orry-Kelly; ch, Busby Berkeley; m/l, Harry Warren, Al Dubin.

Musical Comedy Cas. **(PR:A MPAA:NR)**

GOLD DIGGERS OF 1935*** (1935) 95m WB-FN bw

Dick Powell (Dick Curtis), Gloria Stuart (Amy Prentiss), Adolphe Menjou (Nicoleff), Glenda Farrell (Betty Hawes), Grant Mitchell (Louis Lamson), Dorothy Dare (Arline Davis), Alice Brady (Mrs. Mathilda Prentiss), Frank McHugh (Humboldt Prentiss), Hugh Herbert (T. Mosely Thorpe), Winifred Shaw (Winny), Joe Cawthorn (Schulz), Ramon & Rosita (Dancers), Matty King (Tap Dancer).

A minor plot but handled in a major fashion by Berkeley's brilliant direction and choreography. The scene is a summer resort in an unnamed New England town and the story concerns a number of romantic pairings. The highlight is a production number done for a charity show at the hotel and features the remarkable "Lullaby Of Broadway" sequence that shows the last day in the life of a "Broadway Baby" before she falls out of a window to her death. It begins with a white dot on the screen (Winnie Shaw's face) and gets larger and larger until it's full screen. The dance number follows and the scene ends with Shaw putting a cigarette in her mouth and the silhouette of her face becoming the skyline of Manhattan, then receding into the same small speck. In between, there are more than one hundred dancers, seen from evey possible angle and doing some of the most precise dancing ever put on celluloid. There is also a baby grand piano ballet (seen in a sort of fashion in the 1984 Olympics opening number) with 56 pianos and 56 of the most beautiful women Berkeley could find. Berkeley himself was a rakehell, married several times, and there was always gossip about his having his ways with many of the women in his films. (So much for the myth about choreographers being poofs.) The inn's employees live on the tips left by the guests (hence the title) and the characters include Powell, as a desk clerk studying to be a doctor (no longer the songwriter as he was in the prior films); Menjou, as the cheating and often angry owner of the hotel; Gloria Stuart, as the attractive ingenue and Frank McHugh, as the ne'er-do-well comedy relief, a man who has had three wives and has a current crush on Dare. The key to all the fun is the Harry Warren-Al Dubin score which features the aforementioned "Lullaby Of Broadway" (a reprise from their score for FORTY SECOND STREET) as well as "I'm Going Shopping With You" and "The Words Are In My Heart." It is around these and other tunes that Berkeley has devised what was to some the apex of his choreographic career. One of the visual highlights was the sequence that was shot backwards and showed the 56 pianos moving about with seemingly no one to move them. The secret was that 56 men were hidden under the pianos and pushed them on casters. Reviewers were mixed on their opinion of this film. Some disliked it and some hated it.

d, Busby Berkeley; w, Manuel Seff, Peter Milne (based on a story by Milne, Robert Lord); ph, George Barnes; ed, George Amy; art d, Anton Grot.

Musical Comedy **(PR:A MPAA:NR)**

GOLD DIGGERS OF 1937*** (1936) 101m FN-WB bw

Dick Powell (Rosmer Peek), Joan Blondell (Norma Parry), Glenda Farrell (Genevieve Larkin), Victor Moore (J.J. Hobart), Lee Dixon (Boop Oglethorpe), Osgood Perkins (Mory Wethered), Charles D. Brown (John Huge), Rosalind Marquis (Sally), Irene Ware (Irene), William Davidson (Andy Callahan), Joseph Crehan (Chairman at Insurance Convention), Susan Fleming (Lucille Bailey), Charles Halton (Dr. Warshoff), Olin Howland (Dr. McDuffy), Paul Irving (Dr. Henry), Harry Bradley (Dr. Bell), Fred "Snowflake" Toones (Snowflake), Pat West (Drunken Salesman), Iris Adrian (Verna), Cliff Saum (Conductor), Jane Wyman, Irene Coleman, Shirley Lloyd, Betty Mauk, Naomi Judge, Betty Mcivor, Sheila Bromley, Lois Lindsay, Marjorie Weaver, Lucille Keeling, Virginia Dabney, Jane Marshall (Girls), Wedgwood Nowell (Penfield), Tom Ricketts (Reginald), Bobby Jarvis (Stage Manager), Myrtle Stedman, Jacqueline Saunders (Nurses), Gordon Hart (White).

This time around, Dick Powell is an insurance agent coerced by Perkins and Brown to sell a $1 million policy to Moore, who then discovers that the old man could kick the bucket at any given moment. Moore is a Broadway producer kept alive by Powell and Blondell, a showgirl and part-time secretary. Produced by Hal B. Wallis (who did so many fabulous films for Warner Bros.), it was based on a Broadway play that was co-written by Richard Maibaum (who authored many of the James Bond films 30 years later). The original play was called "Sweet Mystery Of Life" and provided more than the usual story fodder for the musical numbers. Berkeley stepped back from his directing chores and only did the musical staging. He was not enraptured by the original score by E.Y. Harburg and Harold Arlen so he called upon Warner contract writers Harry Warren and Al Dubin to supplement the songs. There was nothing to compare with the "Lullaby Of Broadway" number but it was a fairly good score that included "With Plenty Of Money And You" (The Gold Digger's Song), "All's Fair In Love And War," "Speaking Of The Weather," "Hush Ma Mouth," "The Life Insurance Song," and "Let's Put Our Heads Together." The final number had 70 young lovelies doing interminable marching drills led by Blondell. Moore was delightful as the 1930s version of David Merrick, and Glenda Farrell scored well in a small role. Big and glossy, it was a great success at the theaters.

p, Hal B. Wallis; d, Lloyd Bacon; w, Warren Duff (based on the play "Sweet Mystery Of Life" by Richard Maibaum, Michael Wallace, George Haight); ph, Arthur Edeson; md, Leo F. Forbstein; ed, Thomas Richards; ch, Busby Berkeley.

Musical Comedy **(PR:A MPAA:NR)**

GOLD DUST GERTIE*½ (1931) 66m WB bw
(GB: WHY CHANGE YOUR HUSBAND?)

Winnie Lightner (Gertie), Chic Johnson (Harlan), Ole Olsen (Guthrie), Dorothy Christie (Mabel), Claude Gillingwater (Arnold), Arthur Hoyt (Dr. Tate), George Byron (Capt. Osgood), Vivian Oakland (Lucille), Charles Judels (Pestalozzi), Virginia Sale (Secretary).

The vaudeville and Broadway comedy team of Olsen and Johnson are a pair of bathing suit salesmen who have more than a common occupation: they are both ex-husbands of Lightner. She's set on getting as much alimony as she can from the two, so they team up and try to escape her clutches. It's a thin plot line that wastes three fine comic talents. Lightner starts out fine but the situations and poor dialog defeat her every attempt at comedy. The direction is as uninspired as the script and a boat chase scene is stolen from the movie TOP SPEED filmed the year before. This was the first and only time Olsen wore a mustache for the movies.

d, Lloyd Bacon; w, W.K. Wells, Ray Enright, Arthur Caesar (based on the play "The Life of the Party" by Len D. Hollister); ph, James Van Trees.

Comedy **(PR:A MPAA:NR)**

GOLD EXPRESS, THE* (1955, Brit.) 58m GAU/Rank bw

Vernon Gray (Bob Wright), Ann Walford (Mary Wright), May Hallatt (Agatha Merton), Ivy St. Helier (Emma Merton), Patrick Boxill (Mr. Rover), John Serrett (Luke Dubois), Delphi Lawrence (Pearl).

Their honeymoon interrupted because of a robbery attempt on the train on which they are traveling, reporters Gray and Walford put their skills to use to uncover the culprit behind the thieving. A feeble attempt to add some humor to the script has two eccentric old ladies, who also happen to write crime novelettes, come to the assistance of the reporters. Not worth the trip.

p, Frank Wells; d, Guy Fergusson; w, Jackson Budd; ph, Frank North.

Crime/Comedy **(PR:A MPAA:NR)**

GOLD FEVER** (1952) 63m MON bw

John Calvert (John Bonar), Ralph Morgan (Nugget Jack), Ann Cornell (Rusty), Gene Roth (Bill Johnson), Tom Kennedy (Big Tom), Judd Holdren (Jud Jerson), Danny Rense (Ward Henry), Bobby Graham (Cougar), George Murrell (Recorder), King the Horse.

Typical Monogram fare with Morgan as an old prospector who teams up with Bonar in a search for gold. Roth is the villain who tries to seize their claim, and Cornell is long-lost daughter-love interest. There's the usual amount of fights and chases, well-directed by Goodwins.

p, John Calvert; d, Leslie Goodwins; w, Edgar C. Anderson, Jr., Cliff Lancaster (based on a story by Calvert); ph, Maj. Clark Ramsey, Glenn Gano; m, Johnny Richards; ed, John F. Link.

Western **(PR:A MPAA:NR)**

GOLD FOR THE CAESARS*½ (1964) 85m Adelphia Campagnia/MGM c

Jeffrey Hunter (Lacer), Mylene Demongeot (Penelope), Ron Randell (Rufus), Massimo Girotti (Maximus), Giulio Bosetti (Scipio), Ettore Manni (Luna), Georges Lycan (Malendi), Furio Meniconi (Dax), Jacques Stany.

Handsome Hunter is a Roman slave with a talent for architecture and an eye for the ladies. Problems arise when he falls for Demongeot, the slave girl of Roman bigwig Girotti. Hunter is sent off to find gold in a nearby valley, but that's just an excuse for some standard fighting with the enemy. The whole thing is predictable, though competently directed and fun to watch.

p, Joseph Fryd; d, Andre De Toth; w, Arnold Perl, Sabatino Ciuffini (based on the novel by Florence A. Seward); ph, Raffaele Masciocchi (Panavision, Technicolor); m, Franco Mannino; ed, Franco Fraticelli; art d, Ottavio Scotti; set d, Arrigo Breschi; cos, Mario Giorsi; spec eff, Erasmo Bacciucchi.

Historical Drama **(PR:C MPAA:NR)**

GOLD GUITAR, THE*½ (1966) 84m Airlon/Craddock c

Del Reeves, Roy Drusky, Hugh X. Lewis, Margie Bowes, Skeeter Davis, Arnold Dorfman, George Ellis, Don Barber, John Fox, Mary Nell Santacroce, Bill Anderson, Eddie Hill, Bill Carlisle, Charlie Louvin.

There's something about that Nashville sound. Elvis had it, Johnny Cash has it, and now some gangsters from the Big Apple want it as well. They head off to the South to discover the secret to the sound but apparently get their directions wrong at the service station. Though the story is about the Nashville sound, this was filmed entirely in Atlanta, something more than a stone's throw from that town in Tennessee. Songs include: "A Dollar Ain't A Dollar Anymore" (Tom Glazer), "I Can't See Me Without You" (Sandra Rhodes), "It's A Mean Ol' World" (Hugh X. Lewis), "Anywhere U.S.A." (Del Reeves, Ellen Reeves), "Alone With You" (Roy Drusky, Lester Vanadore), "One Bum Town" (Hank Mills), "7-11" (Margie Bowes), "The Gold Guitar" (Harry Middlebrooks).

p, Bill Packham; d, J. Hunter Todd; w, Packham; ph, Jack Steeley; m, Harry Middlebrooks.

Comedy **(PR:A MPAA:NR)**

GOLD IS WHERE YOU FIND IT*** (1938) 91m FN/WB c

George Brent (Jared Whitney), Olivia De Havilland (Serena Ferris), Claude Rains (Col. Ferris), Margaret Lindsay (Rosanne Ferris), John Litel (Ralph Ferris), Tim Holt (Lanceford Ferris), Barton MacLane (Slag Minton), Henry O'Neill (Judge), Marcia Ralston (Molly Featherstone), George F. Hayes (Enoch Howitt), Sidney Toler (Harrison McCoy), Robert McWade (Crouch), Clarence Kolb (Sen. Walsh), Russell Simpson (McKenzie), Harry Davenport (Dr. Parsons), Willie Best (Helper), Moroni Olsen (Sen. Hearst), Granville Bates (Nixon), Charles Halton (Turner), Erville Alderson (Cryder), Cy Kendall (Kingan), Robert Homans (Grogan), Eddy Chandler (Deputy), Richard Botiller (Ramon), Cliff Saum (Medicine Man), Arthur Aylesworth, Raymond Brown, Guy Wilderson, Jack Rutherford, Frank Pharr (Ranchers), Walter Rogers (Gen. Grant), Edmund Cobb, James Farley (Miners), Milton Kibbee, Sarah Edwards, Sue Moore (Guests), Alan Davis (Clerk), Wilfred Lucas, Thomas Mills, John Harron (Men at Stock Exchange), Daisy Lee (Chinese Maid), Eric Wilton (Butler).

Thirty years after the California gold rush, mining is largely run by companies. Brent is an engineer sent to supervise an operation in Perris, Californa. After saving Lance from a barroom brawl, he falls for Lance's sister, De Havilland. But to no avail; she's a farmer's daughter and farmers hate the miners. A war breaks out between the two forces and Lance is killed. Before he dies he is able to blow up a dam that sets off a landslide. The film ends with Brent becoming a farmer and marrying De Havilland. The simplistic plot line was used many times over in such diverse westerns as OKLAHOMA and HEAVEN'S GATE, but here the thinness of the plot is overcome by strong production values. The Technicolor photography is lush and beautifully captures the on-location scenery. Based on a true story.

p, Hal B. Wallis; d, Michael Curtiz; w, Warren Duff, Robert Buckner (based on a story by Clements Ripley); ph, Sol Polito (Technicolor); m, Max Steiner; ed, Clarence Kolster; md, Leo F. Forbstein; spec eff, Byron Haskin.

Western **(PR:A MPAA:NR)**

GOLD MINE IN THE SKY∗∗ (1938) 60m REP bw

Gene Autry (Gene), Smiley Burnette (Frog), Carol Hughes (Cody Langam), Craig Reynolds (Larry Cummings), Cupid Ainsworth (Jane Crocker), Le Roy Mason (Sykes), Frankie Marvin (Joe), Robert Homans ("Lucky" Langham), Eddie Cherokose (Kuzak), Ben Corbett (Spud Grogan), Milburn Morante (Mugsy Malone), Jim Corey (Chet), George Guhl (Cy Wheeler), Stafford Sisters (Themselves), Fred Toones (Snowflake), George Letz (Montgomery), Charles King, Lew Kelly, Joe Whitehead, Matty Roubert, Anita Bolster, Earl Dwire, Maude Prickett, Al Taylor, Art Dillard, J.L. Frank's "Golden West Cowboys," Stafford Sisters, Champion the Horse.

Autry's a singing ranch foreman who becomes executor of the owner's will. It's his job to see that the late owner's daughter, Hughes, doesn't marry unless Autry has final approval of her intended. No surprises as to who she ends up with! Still, there's some competition from a city slicker but he's no match for Autry. Enjoyable though standard fare. (See GENE AUTRY series, Index.)

d, Joseph Kane; w, Jack Natteford, Betty Burbridge; ph, William Nobles; m, Alberto Colombo; ed, Lester Orlebeck; m/l, "Gold Mine in the Sky," "Dude Ranch Cowboys," "As Long As I Have My Horse," "That's How Donkeys Were Born," "I'm a Tumbleweed Tenor," Autry, Johnny Marvin, Fred Rose, Charles and Nick Kenny.

Western **Cas.** **(PR:A MPAA:NR)**

GOLD OF NAPLES∗∗ (1957, Ital.) 74m Ponti-De Laurentiis-Gala/DCA bw (L'ORO DI NAPOLI)

"The Racketeer": Toto (The Husband), Lianella Carrell (His Wife), Pasquale Cennamo (The Racketeer); "Pizza on Credit": Sophia Loren (The Wife), Giacomo Furia (The Husband), Alberto Farnese (The Lover), Paolo Stoppa (The Widower); "The Gambler": Vittorio De Sica (The Count), Mario Passante (His Valet), Irene Montalto (The Countess), Piero Bilancioni (The Boy), Enrico Borgstrom (His Father, the Porter); "Theresa": Silvana Mangano (Theresa), Erno Crisa (The Husband), Ubaldo Maestri (The Intermediary).

A series of vignettes, a style dear to the heart of Italian filmmakers, make up this disjointed, sometimes incomprehensible, production. In "The Racketeer" pantomimist Toto outwits and undoes a bullying friend who has intruded into his home as a permanent guest. "Pizza on Credit" shows the heftily endowed Loren as a cheating wife who loses her wedding ring while trysting with Farnese, which causes husband Furia to become suspicious plus a frantic search for the ring (returned by the lover at the last moment). De Sica, the director, plays the lead role in "The Gambler," an inveterate gamester who has squandered away every dime his family ever had, but who continues to believe he is a grand sharper. De Sica, in the best of the vignettes, has a marvelous scene with the young son of the doorman where he resides, Bilancioni, who wearily wins every hand, cleaning out the old man once again. Mangano is an alluring prostitute in "Theresa" who marries a mentally unbalanced young man and has to apply her own brand of psychology to straighten out their relationship. Though the acting is generally above average here, particularly by De Sica and Mangano, GOLD OF NAPLES is not 14 karat, mostly because of the erratic story lines and little or no logical transition between vignettes. This film marked one of Sophia Loren's earliest appearances and she mugs and hams for the camera with amateur flamboyance, displaying as much of her voluptuous body and busty build as then permissible by censors. She has one scene where she hip-sways herself along a Neopolitan street while smugly enjoying the many sets of male eyes coveting her ample endowments. This was done in an artificial rain shower to allow her skimpy clothes to cling to her shapely body, a sexy ploy later used in BOY ON A DOLPHIN when she was depicted as a deep-sea diver. (Loren reportedly got bronchial pneumonia after doing this wet scene.) This segment, with Loren as the pizza-maker's sluttish spouse, is very close to the French movie, THE BAKER'S WIFE (1940). Two episodes of the six-episode film were cut before the U.S. release. (In Italian; English subtitles.)

p, Dino De Laurentiis, Carlo Ponti; d, Vittorio De Sica; w, Cesare Zavattini, De Sica, Giuseppe Marotta (based on the novel by Marotta); ph, Otello Martelli; m, Alessandro Cicognini; ed, Evaldo da Roma; English titles, Herman G. Weinberg.

Drama/Comedy **(PR:C-O MPAA:NR)**

GOLD OF THE SEVEN SAINTS∗∗ (1961) 89m WB bw

Clint Walker (Jim Rainbolt), Roger Moore (Shaun Garrett), Leticia Roman (Tita), Robert Middleton (Gondora), Chill Wills (Doc Gates), Gene Evans (McCracken), Roberto Contreras (Armanderez), Jack C. Williams (Ames), Art Stewart (Ricca).

Moore is an Irish cowboy who, with partner Walker, has to transport a cache of gold through the desert and mountains. Of course they're chased by marauders who want the gold. In the end the gold is lost in the rapids. A harkening back to the tidy adventure TREASURE OF THE SIERRE MADRE, this film was cheaply

made and poorly written. Walker isn't given much to do and the direction is undistinguished. Black and white stock adds nothing to the film's mood.

p, Leonard Freeman; d, Gordon Douglas; w, Leigh Brackett, Freeman (based on the novel Desert Guns by Steve Frazee); ph, Joseph Biroc (Warnerscope); m, Howard Jackson; ed, Folmar Blangsted; art d, Stanley Fleischer; set d, Fay C. Babcock.

Western **(PR:A MPAA:NR)**

GOLD RACKET, THE∗ (1937) 66m GN bw

Conrad Nagel (Alan O'Connor), Eleanor Hunt (Bobbie Reynolds), Fuzzy Knight (Scotty), Frank Milan (Steve), Charles Delaney (Joe), Karl Hackett (Lefty), Warner Richmond (Doc), Albert J. Smith (Fraser), W. L. Thorne (McKenzie), Paul Weigel (Assayer), Fred Malatesta (Ricardo), Edward Le Saint (Dixon).

Nagel and Hunt are federal agents on the trail of smugglers. She goes undercover in a Mexican nightclub, which gives the film a handy excuse to stick in a few songs. She vamps the head smuggler, who is a nightclub regular, and snares him into a trap. A simple-minded story with acting and production value to match.

p, George A. Hirliman; d, Louis J. Gasnier; w, David S. Levy (based on a story by Howard Higgin); ph, Mack Stengler; ed, Robert Jahns.

Crime **(PR:A MPAA:NR)**

GOLD RAIDERS, THE∗ (1952) 56m UA bw

George O'Brien (George), Moe Howard, Shemp Howard, Larry Fine (The Three Stooges), Sheilah Ryan (Laura), Clem Bevans (Doc), Monte Blue (Sawyer), Lyle Talbot (Taggert), John Merton (Clete), Al Baffert (Utah), Hugh Hooker (Sandy), Bill Ward (Red), Fuzzy Knight (Sheriff), Dick Crockett (Blake), Roy Canada (Slim).

A forgotten Three Stooges film, and rightly so. The three team with O'Brien, an insurance agent and former sheriff, to stop outlaws from hijacking gold shipments. The usual Stooges mayhem, way past its prime, keeps delaying O'Brien and it is all really substandard stuff.

p, Bernard Glasser; d, Edward Bernds; w, Elwood Ullman, William Lively; ph, Paul Ivano; m, Alexandre Starr; ed, Fred Allen.

Comedy **Cas.** **(PR:A MPAA:NR)**

GOLD RUSH MAISIE∗∗ (1940) 84m MGM bw

Ann Sothern (Maisie Ravier), Lee Bowman (Bill Anders), Virginia Weidler (Jubie Davis), John F. Hamilton (Bert Davis), Mary Nash (Sarah Davis), Slim Summerville (Fred Gubbine), Scotty Beckett (Harold Davis), Irving Bacon (Harry), Louis Mason (Elmo Beecher), Victor Kilian, Jr. (Ned Sullivan), Wallace Reid, Jr. (Matt Sullivan), Clem Bevans (Graybeard), John Sheehan (Drunk), Charles Judels (Greek), Virginia Sale (Harry's Wife), Eldy Waller (Ben Hartley), Kathryn Sheldon (Mrs. Sullivan).

Third film in the MAISIE series finds Sothern trying to make it as a singer in gold rush territory, only to find a depressed and hungry farm folk. She forgets all about the dreamed-of riches and helps the farmers instead. The film starts off as a comedy but quickly turns to drama when it shows the plight of the farmers. Such a mood switch in this sort of film was an unexpected and daring twist. The MAISIE films were one of several cheap and profitable series MGM put out at the time. (See MAISIE series, Index).

p, J. Walter Ruben; d, Edwin L. Marin; w, Betty Reinhardt, Mary C. McCall, Jr. (based on a story by Wilson Collison); ph, Charles Lawton; ed, Frederick Y. Smith.

Comedy **(PR:A MPAA:NR)**

GOLDBERGS, THE∗∗∗½ (1950) 83m PAR bw (AKA: MOLLY)

Gertrude Berg (Molly Goldberg), Philip Loeb (Jake Goldberg), Eli Mintz (Uncle David), Eduard Franz (Alexander), Larry Robinson (Sammy), Arlene McQuade (Rosalie), Betty Walker (Mrs. Kramer), Sara Krohner (Tante Elka), David Opatoshu (Mr. Dutton), Barbara Rush (Debby), Peter Hanson (Ted), Edit Angold (Mrs. Schiller), Helen Brown (Mrs. Morris), Josephine Whittell (Mrs. Van Nest), Shari Robinson (Nomi), Erno Verebes (Mr. Mondel).

A spinoff of a popular CBS radio and television series, "The Goldbergs," with the same cast. Here an old flame of Berg's shows up for a visit, bringing along his young fiancee. She's quite a bit younger than him and promptly falls for a young music teacher closer to her age. Scorned, the older man promptly backs out of a business deal with Loeb. Berg settles all by arranging a meeting between a neighbor widow and her old flame, and the film ends with everyone at peace. Berg had tight control over the film, co-writing the screenplay. Molly Goldberg was Berg and she wasn't about to let her famous character be destroyed in a bad film.

p, Mel Epstein; d, Walter Hart; w, Gertrude Berg, N. Richard Nash; ph, John F. Seitz; m, Van Cleave; ed, Elisworth Hoagland; art d, Hal Pereira, Henry Bumstead.

Comedy **(PR:A MPAA:NR)**

GOLDEN AGE, THE (SEE: L'AGE D'OR, 1930, Fr.)

GOLDEN APPLES OF THE SUN zero (1971, Can.) 85m Sine Qua Non/Gendon c

Percy Harkness (Richard), Elizabeth Suzuki (Janet), Leon Morenzie (Jarvis), Derek Lamb (Troubadour).

A cross between a sex film and Ingmar Bergman, there's an unexplained, random killing and a lot of soft focused love-making in the woods in this film. No one seems to know what's going on but there is some gorgeous photography. MacDermot did the music for the musical "Hair."

p, Robert Lawrence; d, Barrie Angus McLean; w, McLean, Kristin Weingartner; ph, Roger Moride (Eastmancolor); m, Galt MacDermot; ed&prod d, McLean, Weingartner.

Drama **(PR:O MPAA:NR)**

GOLDEN ARROW, THE**½** (1936) 60m FN-WB bw

Bette Davis *(Daisy Appleby)*, George Brent *(Johnny Jones)*, Carol Hughes *(Hortensa Burke-Meyers)*, Eugene Pallette *(Mr. Meyers)*, Dick Foran *(Tommy Blake)*, Catharine Doucet *(Mrs. Pommesby)*, Craig Reynolds *(Jorgenson)*, Hobart Cavanaugh *(De Wolfe)*, Henry O'Neill *(Mr. Appleby)*, Ivan Lebedeff *(Count Giggi Guilliano)*, G.P. Huntley, Jr. *(Aubrey Rutherford)*, Rafael Storm *(Prince Peter)*, E. E Clive *(Walker)*, Eddie Acuff *(Davis)*, Earle A. Foxe *(Parker)*, Carlyle Moore, Jr. *(Mr. Rogers)*, Naomi Judge *(Mrs. Clarke)*, Colleen Coleman *(Miss Jones)*, Shirley Lloyd *(Miss French)*, Larry Kent *(Mr. Smith)*, George Andre Beranger *(Florist)*, Billy Arnold *(Officer)*, Ed Hart *(Steward)*, Rudolf Amendt [Anders] *(Max)*, Josie Rubic *(Renaldo)*, Bess Flowers *(Miss Hackett)*, Eddie Shubert *(Swing Operator)*, Mary Treen *(Secretary)*, Bill Elliott, Don Brodie, Eddie Fetherston, Frank Faylen *(Reporters)*, Richard Powell *(Motor Cop)*, Alma Lloyd *(Telephone Girl)*, John T. Murray *(City Editor)*, Elsa Peterson *(Woman)*, George Sorrell *(Marcel)*, Edward Keane *(Bixby)*, Vesey O'Davoren *(Butler)*, Viola Lowry *(Woman)*, Major Nichols *(Man)*.

Lightweight comedy with Davis as a cafeteria worker who is hired by a cosmetics company to pose as an heiress for publicity. A rumor starts that the "heiress" is about to marry Lebedeff, a famous, if poverty-stricken, count. This irks Hughes, who really wants to marry Lebedeff, and she engages a private detective to find out Davis' real background. Meanwhile, reporter Brent, in an interview with Davis, is told she wants no business with fortune-hunters. He proposes a marriage of convenience; she'll be free to make the social scene without worry of men, and he'll be wealthy enough to write a novel. She agrees and a marriage takes place. But soon Brent tires of being excess baggage and runs off to Hughes in revenge. Hughes tells him the truth about Davis, and, realizing where his true love lies, he returns to her. This was a light film, competently directed and well acted, but nothing special. Being forced to make THE GOLDEN ARROW after the successes of THE PETRIFIED FOREST and OF HUMAN BONDAGE embittered Davis with the studio. She felt the lighter material was below her talents and she began a long fight for better quality scripts.

p, Samuel Bischoff; d, Alfred E. Green; w, Charles Kenyon (based on the play by Michael Arlen); ph, Arthur Edeson; m, W. Franke Harling, Heinz Roemheld; ed, Thomas Pratt; md, Leo F. Forbstein; cos, Orry-Kelly.

Comedy **(PR:A MPAA:NR)**

GOLDEN ARROW, THE, 1949 (SEE: GAY ADVENTURE, THE, 1949, BRIT.)

GOLDEN ARROW, THE*½** (1964, Ital.) 91m MGM c (LA FRECCIA D'ORO)

Tab Hunter *(Hassan)*, Rossana Podesta *(Jamila)*, Umberto Melnati *(Thin Genie)*, Giustino Durano *(Absent-Minded Genie)*, Mario Feliciani *(Baktiar)*, Jose Jaspe *(Sabrath)*, Giampaolo Rosmino *(Mokbar)*, Renato Baldini *(Prince of Bassora)*, Rosario Borelli *(Prince of Aleppo)*, Ceco Zamurovich *(Prince of Samarkand)*, Calisto *(Prince of Bassora's General)*, Dominique Boschero *(Queen of Rocky Valley)*, Abdel Moneim Ibrihim *(Capt. Hamit)*, Claudio Scachilli *(Bandit)*, Omar Zoulfikar *(Magician of Rocky Valley)*, Franco Scandurra, Gloria Milland, Renato Montalbano.

Saturday matinee fare featuring Hunter as a bandit who discovers he is an heir to a sultan. He has to fetch the Golden Arrow to prove himself and he meets assorted genies, princes, and magicians en route. The editing is choppy and the post-dubbing barely passable. Hunter looks like he's having a hard time with the language barrier. The special effects are not bad, especially some flaming monsters.

p, Goffredo Lombardo; d, Antonio Margheriti; w, Bruno Vailati, Augusto Frassinetti, Filippo Sanjust, Giorgio Prosperi, Giorgio Alorio; ph, Mario Capriotti (Technirama, Technicolor); m, Mario Nascimbene; ed, Giorgio Serandrei; art d, Flavio Mogherini; set d, Massimo Tavazzi; cos, Giorgio Desideri; spec eff, Fernando Mazza, Technicolor Italiana.

Fantasy/Adventure **(PR:A MPAA:NR)**

GOLDEN BLADE, THE**½** (1953) 80m UNIV c

Rock Hudson *(Harun)*, Piper Laurie *(Princess Khairuzan)*, Gene Evans *(Hadi)*, Kathleen Hughes *(Bakhamra)*, George Macready *(Jafar)*, Steven Geray *(Barcus)*, Edgar Barrier *(Caliph)*, Alice Kelley, Anita Ekberg, Erika Norden, Valerie Jackson, Renate Huy *(Handmaidens)*, Vic Romito *(Sherkan)*, Jack Bason *(Chamberlain)*, Harry Wilson *(Old Soldier)*, Olga Lunick *(Tavern Dancer)*, Dorinda Clifton *(Dancer)*, Dennis Weaver *(Rabble Rouser)*, Guy Williams *(Town Crier)*, Dayton Lummis *(Munkar)*, Bill Radovich *(Eunuch)*, Harry Mendoza *(Chinese Magician)*, Harry Lang *(Magician)*, Fred Graham *(Sergeant)*, Zachary Yaconelli *(Waiter)*, George "Shorty" Chirello *(Artist)*, Martin Cichy *(Adjustment)*.

A good-versus-evil story with Hudson the noble one. He has to rescue Laurie from the clutches of Macready who is the meanest vizer around. Though it's only a one-hero job, Hudson employs use of "the magic sword of Damascus." It looks good both in front and behind the lens but that's no surprise. By 1953 Universal was turning out similar mystical Eastern fare on a regular basis, with each component perfected by the time THE GOLDEN BLADE was filmed.

p, Richard Wilson, Leonard Goldstein; d, Nathan Juran; w, John Rich; ph, Maury Gertsman (Technicolor); m, Joseph Gershenson; ed, Ted J. Kent; art d, Bernard Herzbrun, Eric Orbom; ch, Eugene Loring.

Fantasy/Adventure **(PR:A MPAA:NR)**

GOLDEN BOX, THE**** (1970) 79m Hollywood Cinema c

Marsha Jordan *(Diane)*, Ann Myers *(Donna)*, Jim Gentry *(Slade Rivers)*, Mark Edwards *(Gene Lackey)*, Steve Vincent *(The Boss)*, Bernard Bossick *(Numero Uno)*, Forman Shain *(Kirby)*, Gene Massey *(Bellboy)*, Barbara O'Bryant *(Girl Friend in Washington)*, Mike Perry *(Charlie, the Bartender)*, Frank Mills *(Brother)*, Barbara Mills *(Sister)*.

A nightclub pianist is killed and his piano book stolen. The book contains secret codes telling where a treasure is hidden. Two ex-mistresses of the murdered man follow the hired killers, hop-scotching across the U.S. in hopes of retrieving the book and cracking the code. Their adventures include a nude gin rummy game, seduction of a bellboy, and finally cracking the code book. Average fare that's hardly memorable.

p&d, Don Davis.

Crime/Thriller **(PR:O MPAA:R)**

GOLDEN BOY****** (1939) 99m COL bw

Barbara Stanwyck *(Lorna Moon)*, Adolphe Menjou *(Tom Moody)*, William Holden *(Joe Bonaparte)*, Lee J. Cobb *(Mr. Bonaparte)*, Joseph Calleia *(Eddie Fuseli)*, Sam Levene *(Siggie)*, Edward S. Brophy *(Roxy Lewis)*, Beatrice Blinn *(Anna)*, William H. Strauss *(Mr. Carp)*, Don Beddoe *(Borneo)*, Frank Jenks *(Boxer)*, Charles Halton *(Newspaperman)*, John Wray *(Manager-Barker)*, James "Cannonball" Green *(Chocolate Drop)*, Thomas Garland *(Fighter)*, Charles Lane *(Drake)*, Harry Tyler *(Mickey)*, Stanley Andrews *(Driscoll)*, Robert Sterling *(Elevator Boy)*, Clinton Rosemond *(Father)*, Alex Melesh *(Stranger)*, Minerva Urecal *(Costumer)*, Eddie Fetherston *(Wilson)*, Lee Phelps *(Announcer)*, Larry McGrath *(Referee)*, Sam Hayes *(Broadcaster)*, Alfred Grant *(Daniel)*, Bob Ryan, Charles Sullivan *(Referees)*, John Harmon, George Lloyd *(Gamblers)*, Mickey Golden, Gordon Armitage, Joe Gray *(Fighters)*, Bruce Mitchell *(Guard)*, Earl Askam *(Cop)*, Irving Cohen *(Ex-Pug)*, Onest Conley, Sid Saylor, Dora Clement, Landers Stevens, Anne Kay, Al Lang, Don Brodie, Charles Sherlock, Pat McKee, Charles Randolph.

Not a faithful film adaptation of the powerful Odets play but one that nevertheless is an excellent production that keeps the spirit of the play intact, GOLDEN BOY marked the first major appearance of Holden, one that established him as a star. Holden is a gifted violinist who takes up boxing to earn enough money to advance his musical education. He is also a talented prizefighter but his savvy manager, Menjou, sees that he is holding back on his punches and asks Stanwyck to cozy up to his promising protege and discover why he won't let loose on the jaws of his opponents. Of course, it's because Holden wishes to preserve his hands for his violin and it's Stanwyck's rotten job to convince Holden to give up his musical ambitions. Then Stanwyck meets Holden's father, Cobb, who has sacrificed his entire life so his son can pursue his musical career, a dream shared by the principled Holden. Holden falls in love with Stanwyck but is quickly disillusioned with her when he finds that she has feigned her affection for him to get him back in the ring. She taunts him to the point where he must prove himself and returns to the fighting, killing an opponent and breaking a hand. He is finished as a prizefighter and a violinist and Stanwyck is devastated, realizing that she loves him. She goes to Holden, begs forgiveness, and convinces the youth that there is much in life to live for. Though certain characters have been shaved from the original play and the protagonist lives instead of dies for a happy ending, director Mamoulian does a wonderful job retaining the essential story and basic character, building beautifully upon both through his careful scenes, as sensitively handled as the gentle nature of the Holden character. Menjou is terrific as the wily, self-serving manager, and Cobb overwhelms as the self-sacrificing immigrant father. But it is really Stanwyck's picture and she dominates every scene she's in without her usual excessive histrionics. Here she is subtle and subdued as the fresh-faced manipulator, an attractive female Iago who undergoes a stunning transition to an understanding, compassionate human being. Holden is the epitome of the innocent young idealist whose personal visions are trampled by an unfeeling world, one whose basically fine instincts manage to survive. His role was one of the most coveted in film history. John Garfield established the part on Broadway, but he was not in the running. A ton of actors were tested for the role, including Elia Kazan, later a fine director, Robert Taylor, Robert Cummings, Tyrone Power, Henry Fonda, and Richard Carlson. In fact, Carlson was announced as the lead but Stanwyck changed all that. Her own role was much in debate. At first Jean Arthur was to play the scheming lady, then Ann Sheridan (both Frances Farmer and Nancy Carroll had played the role on stage). Mamoulian leaned in favor of Stanwyck and Stanwyck insisted that a young Paramount contract player, 21-year-old Holden, be tested. Mamoulian saw the test which Holden did with Joan Perry, the future wife of Harry Cohn, head of Columbia. He wanted the young man right away, which caused Cohn to scream: "The kid's a nobody!" Mamoulian persisted and Cohn called Holden to his office. After admitting that he wasn't even sure he could act and definitely could not box nor play a violin, Holden stood mute before the acid-tongued mogul. "Then what the hell are you doing here?" Holden replied simply: "I'm here because you sent for me." Cohn put him in the picture after picking up Holden's contract from Paramount dirt cheap. In fact, he was paying the youthful actor so little Holden could not afford to meet his rent and threatened to quit the production unless Cohn advanced enough money to him to make ends meet, which the mogul reluctantly did. From the first day's shooting Stanwyck calmed the nervous novice, telling him to rely upon her for any advice, any help she could give him. By then Stanwyck was a big star, having appeared in films for a decade. She bolstered him at every opportunity and spent hours working with him on his lines, his presence, and how to achieve real feeling for his character. Holden would always look back upon this film with fondness, and with great affection for Stanwyck, although he hated the curly locks tinged with blonde highlights the makeup department put on top of his head. At the 1978 Academy Awards Holden and Stanwyck were presenters and at that time Holden publicly declared his great debt to the movie queen. She repaid the compliment in 1982 when Holden was dead. Stanwyck accepted an Oscar for her long and lustrous career, then stated: "A few years ago, I stood on this stage with William Holden as a presenter. I loved him very much and I miss him. He always wished I would get an Oscar. And so tonight, my Golden Boy, you got your wish." GOLDEN BOY was neither a critical nor popular success. The critics at the time resented the alterations in the play and it was noted that Odets had refused to write the screenplay. Yet the film holds up today surprisingly well and the performances, Holden's included, are outstanding. Of special note are Mamoulian's prizefight scenes which are both realistic and brutal, with the director masterfully presenting a biting portrait of that corrupt world of gangsters, promoters and blood-lusting spectators.

p, William Perlberg; d, Rouben Mamoulian; w, Lewis Meltzer, Daniel Taradash, Sara Y. Mason, Victor Heerman (based on the play by Clifford Odets); ph, Nicholas Musuraca, Karl Freund; m, Victor Young; ed, Otto Meyer; md, Morris W. Stoloff; art d, Lionel Banks; cos, Kalloch.

Drama   **Cas.**   **(PR:A MPAA:NR)**

GOLDEN BULLET   (SEE: IMPASSE, 1969)

GOLDEN CAGE, THE**   (1933, Brit.) 62m Sound City/MGM bw

Anne Grey (Venetia Doxford), Anthony Kimmins (Paul Mortimer), Frank Cellier, Julian Sande (Jane Morris), Mackenzie Ward (Claude Barrington), Cecil Parker, Andrea Malandrinos.

Decent romantic story focusing on the affairs of Grey, who marries into wealth despite being in love with another, poorer man. As the jilted lover, Kimmins has his new affair with Sande interrupted by Grey, who wants to continue where they had left off. Then, fearing that she will not be able to live the life style to which she has become accustomed, Grey backs out and returns to her money man.

p, Norman Loudon; d, Ivar Campbell; w, D.B. Wyndham-Lewis, Pamela Frankau (based on the play by Lady Trowbridge).

Drama   **(PR:A MPAA:NR)**

GOLDEN CALF, THE**   (1930) 69m FOX bw

Jack Mulhall (Philip Homer), Sue Carol (Maybelle Cobb), El Brendel (Knute Olson), Marjorie White (Alice), Richard Keene (Tommie), Paul Page (Edwards), Walter Catlett (Master of Ceremonies), Ilka Chase (Comedienne).

A secretary, played by Carol, leads a simple, rather humdrum life. But her good friend White decides it is time for a Pygmalion-style job on the girl, complete with mud packs and silk dresses. The result is ravishing beauty, and the inevitable romance by Carol's employer who, of course, does not recognize his secretary. There are lots of songs, dances, and spirit in this energetic musical. Though the idea is nothing original, the production is pretty good, breathing life into seemingly routine stuff. Songs include: "A Picture No Artist Can Paint" (sung by Brendel), "You Gotta Be Modernistic" (sung by White, Keene), "I'm Telling the World About You," "Maybe Someday" (sung by Carol), and "Can I Help It" (sung by White, Keene).

p, Ned Marin; d, Millard Webb; w, Harold Atteridge (based on a story by Aaron Davis); ph, Lucien Andriot; ch, Earl Lindsay; m/l, Cliff Friend, Jimmie Monaco).

Musical/Comedy   **(PR:AA MPAA:NR)**

GOLDEN COACH, THE**½   (1953, Fr./Ital.) 105m Hoche-Dalphinus/Corona c (LE CARROSSE D'OR)

Anna Magnani (Camilla), Odoardo Spadaro (Don Antonio), Nada Fiorelli (Isabella), Dante (Harlequin), Duncan Lamont (Viceroy), George Higgins (Martinez), Ralph Truman (Duke), Gisella Mathews (Marquise), Raf De La Terre (Chief Justice), Elena Altieri (Duchess), Paul Campbell (Felipe), Riccardo Rioli (Bullfighter), William Tubbs (Innkeeper), Jean Debucourt (Bishop).

In this beautifully photographed film Lamont plays a 16th Century South American businessman. Bored with his work and his mistress, he turns his attentions to Magnani, a lusty actress from a touring Commedia Dell Arte troupe. But two other locals, a toreador and a nobleman, also fall for Magnani's charms. A local war looms as the three vie for her attentions. Lamont gives her his golden coach and Magnani defuses tension by giving it away to a church to be used as a hearse. The intriguing story is slowed down by scenes of the Commedia troupe intercut within the plot. Even so, the film is quite good with strong direction from Renoir and beautiful uses of color.

p, Francesco Alliata; d, Jean Renoir; w, Renoir, Renzo Avanzo, Jack Kirkland, Giulio Macchi (based on the play by Prosper Merimee); ph, Claude Renoir (Technicolor); m, Antonio Vivaldi; ed, David Hawkins.

Drama   **(PR:A-C MPAA:NR)**

GOLDEN DAWN**   (1930) 81m WB c

Walter Woolf (Tom Allen), Vivienne Segal (Dawn), Noah Beery (Shep Keyes), Alice Gentle (Mooda), Lupino Lane (Pigeon), Lee Moran (Blink), Marion Byron (Johanna), Nigel De Brulier (Hasmali), Otto Matieson (Capt. Eric), Dick Henderson (Duke), Sojin (Piper), Nina Quartaro (Maid-in-Waiting), Julanne Johnston (Sister Hedwig), Nick De Ruiz (Napoli), Edward Martindel (Col. Judson).

Based on a minor 1927 Broadway musical, GOLDEN DAWN is a simplistic story about jungle natives versus white men during WW I. Dismissed as a minor film in its day, GOLDEN DAWN ranks as a masterpiece of camp. There are a number of plot inconsistencies and some hokey musical numbers. Beery plays in blackface, reflecting the racist attitudes of the studios at that time. This film features a crude Technicolor process which is really a two-strip color technique, giving actors a heavy jaundiced look. Don't miss the tender song "My Bwana" (Oscar Hammerstein II, Emmerich Kalman). Other songs: "Whip Song," "Dawn," "We Too" (Hammerstein, Kalman), "My Heart's Love Call," "Africa Smiles No More," "Mooda's Song," "In a Jungle Bungalow" (Grant Clarke, Harry Akst).

d, Ray Enright; w, Walter Anthony (based on a play by Otto Harbach, Oscar Hammerstein II); ph, Dev Jennings (Technicolor); md, Larry Ceballos; ch, Eduardo Cansino.

Musical   **(PR:A MPAA:NR)**

GOLDEN DEMON**½   (1956, Jap.) 95m Daiei/Edward Harrison c (KONJIKI YASHA)

Jun Negami (Kan-ichi), Fujiko Yamamoto (Miya), Kenji Sugawara (Arao), Mitsuko Mito (Akagashi), Kazuko Fushimi (Aiko), Eiji Funakoshi (Tomiyama), Shizue Natsukawa (Mrs. Minowa), Kumeko Urabe (Tose), Kinzo Shin (Mrs. Shigisawa), Shiko Saito (Wanibuchi), Teppei Endo (Mr. Minowa), Jun Miyazaki (Kamata), Yuki Hayakawa (Kazahaya), Yoshio Takee (Yusa), Sachiko Meguro (Mrs. Yusa).

Tragic tale of two star-crossed lovers forced into separation when a wealthy man asks the girl's parents for their daughter's hand. Although she doesn't want to, Yamamoto marries the man, leading a loveless existence in isolation. Meanwhile Negami has thrown himself headfirst into his career as a usurious moneylender, the only thing on his mind being vengeance against the woman who jilted him. Metaphoric ending has Negami's house going up in flames, helping the young man to see clearly again. Tends to pour on the sentiment in heavy doses, but the acting, photography, and direction are all superbly handled, making this a powerful and moving love story. (In Japanese; English subtitles.)

p, Masaichi Nagata; d&w, Koji Shima (based on the adaptation by Matsutaru Kawaguchi of the novel by Koyo Ozaki); ph, Michio Takahashi (Eastmancolor); m, Ichiro Saito.

Drama   **(PR:C-O MPAA:NR)**

GOLDEN DISK   (SEE: INBETWEEN AGE, THE, 1958, BRIT.)

GOLDEN EARRINGS**½   (1947) 95m PAR bw

Ray Milland (Col. Ralph Denistoun), Marlene Dietrich (Lydia), Murvyn Vye (Zoltan), Bruce Lester (Byrd), Dennis Hoey (Hoff), Quentin Reynolds (Himself), Reinhold Schunzel (Prof. Krosigk), Ivan Triesault (Maj. Reimann), Hermine Sterler (Greta Krosigk), Eric Feldary (Zweig), Gisela Werbiseck (Dowager), Larry Simms (Page Boy), Hans Von Morhart (S.S. Trooper), Mme. Louise Colombet (Flower Woman), Robert Val, Pepito Perez, Gordon Arnold (Gypsy Boys), Martha Bamattre (Wise Old Woman), Antonia Morales (Gypsy Dancer), Jack Wilson (Hitler Youth Leader), Fred Nurney, Otto Reichow (Agents), Haldor de Becker (Telegraph Boy), Gordon Richards, Vernon Downing (Club Members), Leslie Denison (Miggs), Tony Ellis (Dispatch Rider), Gwen Davies (Stewardess), Robert Cory (Doorman), Henry Rowland (Peiffer), William Yetter, Sr., Henry Guttman (Peasants), William Yetter, Jr., James W. Horne, Leo Schlesinger (Soldiers), Ellen Baer (Girl), Carmen Beretta (Tourist), Frank Johnson (Waiter), Maynard Holmes (Private), Fred Giermann (Sergeant), Roberta Jonay (Peasant Girl), Harry Anderson (German Farmer), Caryl Lincoln (Farmer's Wife), Bob Stephenson, Henry Vroom (S.S. Guards), George Sorel, Hans Schumm (Policemen), John Dehner (S.S. Man), Howard Mitchell (Naval Officer), Arno Frey (Major), John Good (S.S. Lieutenant), Walter Rode, Jack Worth (Nazi Party Officials), Peter Seal (Chief of Police), John Peters (Lieutenant Colonel), Margaret Farrell (Woman), John Gilbreath (Soldier), Al Winters (Elite Guard Colonel), Greta Ullmann, Catherine Savitsky (German Wives).

This absurd clunker is so bad that it became a camp classic overnight, even in an era when camp was unknown. Dietrich is at her most outlandish as a fierce gypsy whose sanitary habits would repel a mongoose, and the cultured Milland is bewildered by it all, when not sneering his disgust at dirty Dietrich and a script that is best termed mentally incompetent. This impossible tale begins just after WW II when Milland, a British major general, receives a box at his London hotel; it contains a pair of simple golden earrings. He is soon en route to Paris by plane, with foreign correspondent Reynolds at his side, to get his strange story, and strange it is, especially when it comes to explaining Milland's pierced ears. Milland tells Reynolds how six years earlier, before England was involved in WW II, he and Lester, as British intelligence officers, were held prisoner by Nazis who questioned them about their knowledge of a new poison gas formula developed by Schunzel. A flashback shows Milland and Lester overpowering their guards and, dressed as German officers, each going his own way in seach of Schunzel and his all-important formula. They agree to meet in Stuttgart but Milland gets sidetracked in the Black Forest. He buries his stolen uniform and then hears a woman singing. Upon investigating, Milland finds a lone gypsy woman, Dietrich, stirring a fish stew. She explains that she lives apart from her band for unexplained reasons. Dietrich displays an amazing knowledge of the back roads snaking through the dense Black Forest and Milland accepts her offer to travel with her. She disguises him as a gypsy, staining his skin as dark as her own, piercing his ears and affixing golden earrings, and outfitting him in gypsy clothes. They finally overtake the band to which Dietrich belongs. The bulky, towering, and cretinous leader, Vye, immediately picks a fight with Milland because he is wearing Vye's jacket. Dietrich encourages Milland to fight to prove he is worthy of her affection. He does, but merely to protect himself. He wins not only the battle but Vye's respect and Dietrich's undying love since she is convinced he fought for her. Milland is now a full-fledged gypsy who is also an expert palm reader, thanks to Dietrich, who has taught him the technique. The band comes to an area outside of Stuttgart where Milland meets with Lester, as planned. As a troop of Nazi youth marches past, Milland reads Lester's palm and believes he sees a death sign. Lester, dressed in Tyrolean garb, is off to find Schunzel. Dietrich calms Milland's fears, telling him that no one can alter destiny. Lester, indeed, is killed. Milland later unearths the professor who, as his palm is being read, refuses to believe the dark hued Milland is a British spy. Gestapo agents then arrive and denounce Schunzel as a traitor. With nothing to lose, he passes on his secret formula written on a five-mark note to Milland as payment for having his fate prophesied. Dietrich then spirits Milland to the Rhine where he takes a boat to freedom, but not before promising to return to Dietrich after the war. In a flash forward, Milland is shown entering the Black Forest and finding Dietrich waiting for him. He climbs into her wagon and they roll off into the dense woodlands to live the gypsy life together. This film, competently directed by Leisen, was to Milland a sophomoric story he could definitely live without. He was top box office at the time, age 43, having won an Oscar for Best Actor a year earlier for his magnificent performance in THE LOST WEEKEND. He considered this production a come-down and made no bones about it. Dietrich had not appeared in a film in three years, her last being KISMET where she had performed a very sexy dance in skimpy attire which maintained her sex goddess image. Since that time she had been entertaining American troops close to the battle lines in Europe and making anti-Nazi broadcasts in England; being German-born she had much to prove or disprove. This was also the first film she made at Paramount in 10 years and, after the makeup department finished with her, there would have been no way of anyone knowing that she was one of the world's great glamour queens. She donned a black wig plastered down with what appeared to be bear grease. Her skin was stained so dark she seemed ready for a minstrel show instead of a part enacting a Hungarian gypsy. Her clothes were bulky, torn rags, and her hands and face were constantly smudged with dirt. There was nothing appealing about this repulsive image, not even the husky voice that floated up from the pounds of makeup to hum in Hungarian a few bars of the title song (which Vye sang in English with a painful bass). The approach was supposed to be something called "neo-realism" but it was really a massacre of believability. The production was not helped either when the Catholic Legion of Decency "condemned" the film since Dietrich and Milland were decidedly shown to be living together without the benefit of matrimony. (This, of course, did nothing but stimulate box office receipts.) It was all so tame and sloppy with only a few peeks at Dietrich's famous gams. For Milland, urbane and polished, the film was an ordeal and, unlike most males on earth, he had no interest in acting opposite Dietrich. He balked at having to play love scenes with "the old bag," (Dietrich was then 45) and threatened to walk out on his contract. The two battled constantly during the production which caused no end of problems for the rest of the cast and the harried crew. Dietrich considered Milland a boor and from the first moment she showed her contempt for the sophisticated actor, and she displayed it brutally. Quoted later, Leisen remembered the confrontation with shock: "When we were shooting the scene where he first meets her as she's stirring stew, Marlene stuck a fishhead into her mouth, sucked the eye out, and then pulled out the rest of the head. Then, after I yelled cut, she stuck her finger down her throat to make herself throw up. The whole performance made Ray violently ill."

p, Harry Tugend; d, Mitchell Leisen; w, Abraham Polonsky, Frank Butler, Helen Deutsch (based on the novel by Yolanda Foldes); ph, Daniel L. Fapp; m, Victor Young; ed, Alma Macrorie; art d, Hans Dreier, John Meehan; set d, Sam Comer, Grace Gregory; cos, Kay Dodson; spec eff, Gordon Jennings; ch, Billy Daniels; m/l, "Golden Earrings" by Young, Jay Livingston, Ray Evans; makeup, Wally Westmore.

Drama   **(PR:C   MPAA:NR)**

GOLDEN EYE, THE   (SEE: MYSTERY OF THE GOLDEN EYE, 1948)

GOLDEN FLEECING, THE**   (1940) 68m MGM bw
Lew Ayres (Henry Twinkle), Rifa Johnson (Mary Blake), Lloyd Nolan (Gus Fender), Virginia Grey (Lila Hanley), Nat Pendleton ("Fatso" Werner), Leon Errol (Uncle Waldo), George Lessey (Buckley Sloan), Richard Carle (Pattington), Ralph Byrd (Larry Kelly), Marc Lawrence ("Happy" Dugan), Thurston Hall (Charles Engel), James Burke (Sibley), Spencer Charters (Justice of Peace), William Demarest (Swallow).

Ayres is an insurance salesman who sells a big policy to a gangster. The gangster leaves town so Ayres has to find him before he is killed, or it could be financial disaster for the company and unemployment for Ayres. There's some nonsense about a worthless stock paying off, and reward money. Of course, the gangster is found and Ayres wins the heart of the boss' secretary. The lame script is not helped by the ineffectual direction or Ayres' constant mugging.

p, Edgar Selwyn; d, Leslie Fenton; w, S.J. and Laura Perelman, Marion Parsonnet (based on a story by Lynn Root, Frank Fenton, John Fante); ph, Leonard Smith; ed, Conrad A. Nervig.

Comedy   **(PR:A   MPAA:NR)**

GOLDEN GATE GIRL**   (1941) 110m Golden Gate bw
Tso Yee Man (The Girl), Wong Hok Sing (The Boy), Moon Quan (The Father), Liu Nom (Salesman), Luk Won Fee (The Cook).

In San Francisco's Chinatown, the daughter of a stern shopkeeper disobeys her parents and goes to the Chinese opera. With the help of her father's salesman, Nom, she sneaks into a club and meets the opera's star. They fall in love and marry, much to the wrath of Quan. He stops speaking to her and fires the salesman. The singer has to return to China while the girl has a baby, but she dies in childbirth. The baby grows up to look like her mother (Man in a dual role) and eventually reconciles with her grandfather. The first all-Chinese language picture shot in Chinatown, its director was also a noted female film director in her native country. (In Chinese.)

d, Esther Eng; w, Moon Quan; ph, J. Sunn; ed, Quan.

Drama   **(PR:C   MPAA:NR)**

GOLDEN GIRL***   (1951) 107m FOX c
Mitzi Gaynor (Lotta Crabtree), Dale Robertson (Tom Richmond), Dennis Day (Mart), James Barton (Mr. Crabtree), Una Merkel (Mrs. Crabtree), Raymond Walburn (Cornelius), Gene Sheldon (Sam Jordan), Carmen D'Antonio (Lola Montez), Michael Ross (Bouncer), Harry Carter (Union Officer), Lovyss Bradley (Mrs. Probe), Emory Parnell (McGuire), Luther Crockett (Man in Box), Harris Brown (Stagehand), Kermit Maynard (Manager), Robert Nash (Stage Manager), Jessie Arnold (Wardrobe Woman).

Gaynor is terrific as a showgirl who finds fame during the Civil War, going from town to town. Robertson is a Confederate spy who is in love with her and follows her trail. Overall, enjoyable entertainment. Day is fun to watch as her timid admirer-inspirer. Direction is good, with musical numbers particularly well-handled. Produced by comedian toastmaster Jessel. Songs: "Dixie" (Daniel Decatur Emmett, sung by Mitzie Gaynor), "Carry Me Back to Old Virginny," "Oh, Dem Golden Slippers" (James A. Bland), "California Moon" (Jessel, Sam Lerner, Joe

Cooper), "Sunday Morning" (Eliot Daniel, Ken Darby), "Kiss Me Quick and Go My Honey" (Daniel), "Never" (Daniel, Lionel Newman), "When Johnny Comes Marching Home" (Patrick S. Gilmore), "Believe Me If All Those Endearing Young Charms" (Thomas Moore, Matthew Locke), "La Donna E. Mobile" (from "Rigoletto" by Giuseppe Verdi).

p, George Jessel; d, Lloyd Bacon; w, Walter Bullock, Charles O'Neal, Gladys Lehman (based on a story by Albert and Arthur Lewis, Edward Thompson); ph, Charles G. Clarke (Technicolor); ed, Louis Loeffler; md, Lionel Newman; ch, Seymour Felix.

Musical   **(PR:AA   MPAA:NR)**

GOLDEN GLOVES, 1939   (SEE: EX-CHAMP, 1939)

GOLDEN GLOVES**   (1940) 66m PAR bw
Richard Denning (Bill Crane), Jean Cagney (Mary Parker), J. Carrol Naish (Joe Taggerty), Robert Paige (Wally Matson), William Frawley (Emory Balzar), Edward S. Brophy (Potsy Brill), Robert Ryan (Pete Wells), George Ernest (Joey Parker), David Durand (Gumdrop Wilbur), James Seay (Jimmy), Sidney Miller (Sammy Sachs), Alec Craig (MacDonald), Pierre Watkin, John Gallaudet, Leona Roberts, Lorraine Krueger, Thomas E. Jackson, Frank Coghlan, Jr., Johnnie Morris.

Nice guy Paige is a sports writer who sets up a boxing league to compete with bad guy Naish's group. Naish bribes a professional fighter to enter Paige's group and teach them a lesson. He loses to charming fighter Denning, who wins a girl in addition to the fight. In an attempt to cash in on popular boys' boxing competitions, this film was released with a short, GOLDEN GLOVES. The acting is passable. Cagney is Jimmy's little sister.

d, Edward Dmytryk; w, Maxwell Shane, Lewis R. Foster (based on a story by Shane); ph, Henry Sharp; ed, Doanne Harrison; md, Sigmund Krumgold; art d, Hans Dreier, William Flannery.

Drama   **(PR:A   MPAA:NR)**

GOLDEN GLOVES STORY, THE**   (1950) 76m EL bw
James Dunn (Joe Riley), Dewey Martin (Nick Martel), Gregg Sherwood (Iris Anthony), Devin O'Morrison (Bob Gilmore), Kay Westfall (Patti Riley), Arch Ward (Himself), Johnny Behr (Himself), Dickie Conon (Jerry Burke), Fern Persons (Mrs. Burke), John "Red" Kullers (Bernie Dooling), Tony Zale (Himself), Issy Kline (Himself), Jack Brickhouse (Ring Side Announcer), Dick Mastro (Announcer in Ring), Michael McGuire (Capt. Mahoney), Art van Harvey (Father McGuire).

Nasty amateur boxer Martin and gentleman boxer O'Morrison are both vying for a championship and a referee's daughter. Martin has some rough going attaining these items but reforms and wins all around in the end. Real boxing footage livens it up a bit. Watch for cameos by professional boxers Behr, Zale, and Kline, and footage on the late Arch Ward, founder of the famed boys' boxing classic.

p, Carl Krueger; d, Felix Feist; w, Joe Ansen, Feist (based on a story by D.D. Beauchamp, William F. Sellers); ph, John L. Russell, Jr.; m, Arthur Lange; ed, William F. Claxton; md, Emil Newman.

Drama   **(PR:A   MPAA:NR)**

GOLDEN GOOSE, THE**½   (1966, E. Ger.) 72m
                   DEFA/Murray-Trans-International c (DIE GOLDENE GANS)
An unspectacular animated version of the Grimms' fairy tale about a goose that lays golden eggs and the sorrow and joy that this brings to a peasant. (English version.)

p, K. Gordon Murray (based on the fairy tale by Jakob Grimm, Wilhelm Grimm); ph, (Eastmancolor).

Children   **(PR:AA   MPAA:NR)**

GOLDEN HARVEST**½   (1933) 72m PAR bw
Richard Arlen (Walt Martin), Chester Morris (Chris Martin), Genevieve Tobin (Cynthia Flint), Roscoe Ates (Loopey Lou), Julie Haydon (Ellen), Burton Churchill (Eben Martin), Elizabeth Patterson (Lydia), Charles Sellon (Jason), Frederick Burton (Judge Goodhue), Lawrence Gray (Hugh), Richard Carle (Doctor), Henry Kolker (Henry Flint).

Morris, a farm boy with big dreams, heads off to Chicago and in no time is a big dealer on the Board of Trade. There are several love interests (six!) among the principals and some nice footage of the Kansas wheat fields. But reality catches up and makes GOLDEN HARVEST a boring slice of life.

p, Charles R. Rogers; d, Ralph Murphy; w, Casey Robinson (based on a story by Nina Wilcox Putnam); ph, Milton Krasner.

Drama   **(PR:A   MPAA:NR)**

GOLDEN HAWK, THE**½   (1952) 83m COL c
Rhonda Fleming (Rouge), Sterling Hayden (Kit Gerardo), Helena Carter (Bianca del Valdiva), John Sutton (Luis del Toro), Paul Cavanagh (Jeremy Smithers), Michael Ansara (Bernardo Diaz), Raymond Hatton (Barnaby Stoll), Alex Montoya (Homado), Poppy A. del Vando (Dona Elena), Albert Pollet (Gov. Ducasse), David Bond (Prosecutor), Donna Martell (Emilie Savonez), Mary Munday (Maria).

Typical swashbuckling sea story finds lady pirate Fleming held by evil governor Sutton. Hayden comes to her rescue and finds out a few things about his past in the process. For her part, the sensuous Fleming is really a rich lady trying to recover a stolen fortune via pirating. Good fun if taken lightly. Some nice action sequences manage to overcome stiff directing.

p, Sam Katzman; d, Sidney Salkow; w, Robert E. Kent (based on the novel by Frank Yerby); ph, William V. Skall; ed, Edwin Bryant; md, Mischa Bakaleinikoff; art d, Paul Palmentola; set d, Sidney Clifford.

Adventure   **(PR:A   MPAA:NR)**

GOLDEN HEAD, THE** 　　　　　(1965, Hung., U.S.) 115m
　　　　　　　　　　　　　　Cinerama-Hungarofilms c

George Sanders (Basil Palmer), Buddy Hackett (Lionel Pack), Jess Conrad (Michael Stevenson), Lorraine Power (Milly Stevenson), Robert Coote (Braithwaite), Denis Gilmore (Harold Stevenson), Cecilia Esztergalyos (Anne), Douglas Wilmer (Inspector Stevenson), The Hungarian Folk Dancers, Hungarian Opera Ballet.

Sanders, along with cohort Hackett, plans to steal the priceless Golden Head of Saint Lazslo. But the children of a British detective on holiday in Budapest discover the plan and report it to daddy. This leads to a climactic chase via speedboat on the Blue Danube. The plot is too simplistic to be believed and the film's pacing is far too slow. Lots of travelog style footage is tacked on but has nothing to do with the film other than serve as filler. Hackett's endless mugging is annoying.

p, Alexander Paal; d, Richard Thorpe; w, Stanley Goulder, Ivan Boldizsar (based on the novel by Roger Pilkington); ph, Istvan Hildebrand (Technirama-Technicolor); m, Peter Fenyes; ed, Frank Clarks; m/l, Mitch Murray.

Comedy/Crime　　　　　　　　　　　　　**(PR:A　MPAA:NR)**

GOLDEN HEIST, THE　　　　　　(SEE: INSIDE OUT, 1975, Brit.)

GOLDEN HELMET　　　　　　　(SEE: CASQUE D'OR, 1952)

GOLDEN HOOFS*½ 　　　　　　　(1941) 68m FOX bw

Jane Withers (Jane Drake), Charles "Buddy" Rogers (Dean MacArdle), Katharine Aldridge (Cornelia Hunt), George Irving (Dr. Timothy Drake), Buddy Pepper (Morthy Witherspoon), Cliff Clark (Booth), Phillip Hurlick (Mose), Sheila Ryan (Gwen), Howard Rickman (Calvin Harmon).

Withers trains horses on her grandfather's farm. The old man has to sell the farm though, and millionaire Rogers buys it to get rid of Withers' trotters and build a training area for flat racehorses. She gets a crush on him and, in a surprise for the genre, her horse loses a big race but she wins his heart. Grandfather Irving's pet project, a community hospital, gets some of the winning money, too. Good family fare, with some nice footage of the horses. This was Rogers' first film after a long break from the movies and he is fine in the role.

p, Walter Morosco, Ralph Dietrich; d, Lynn Shores; w, Ben Grauman Kohn (based on a story by Roy Chanslor, Thomas Lanigan); ph, Lucien Andriot; ed, James R. Clark; md, Cyril J. Mockridge.

Family Drama　　　　　　　　　　**(PR:AAA　MPAA:NR)**

GOLDEN HORDE, THE*½ 　　　　(1951) 75m UNIV c
　　　　　　　(AKA: GOLDEN HORDE OF GENGHIS KHAN)

Ann Blyth (Princess Shalimar), David Farrar (Sir Guy), George Macready (Shaman), Henry Brandon (Juchi), Howard Petrie (Tucluk), Richard Egan (Gill), Marvin Miller (Genghis Khan), Donald Randolph (Torga), Peggie Castle (Lailee), Poodles Hanneford (Friar John), Leon Belasco (Nazza), Lucille Barkley (Azalah), Karen Varga (Nina), Robert Hunter (Herat).

Blyth is the princess of a city threatened by Mongol Miller. Farrar and his band of English Crusaders offer their help, but Blyth prefers to do it on her own. She concocts a plan that pits Brandon, Miller's son, against a rival and thus saves the city with her cunning. Lots of soldiers and swords, along with catapults, horses, and other implements of destruction (circa 1220) are used in the process. The action is fast, furious, and there is good use of color in the battle scenes.

p, Howard Christie, Robert Arthur; d, George Sherman; w, Gerald Drayson Adams (based on a story by Harold Lamb); ph, Russell Metty (Technicolor); m, Hans J. Salter; ed, Frank Gross; art d, Bernard Herzbrun, Alexander Golitzen.

Historical Drama/Action　　　　　　**(PR:A　MPAA:NR)**

GOLDEN IDOL, THE** 　　　　　　(1954) 71m AA bw

Johnny Sheffield (Bomba), Anne Kimbell (Karen Marsh), Lane Bradford (Joe Hawkins), Paul Guilfoyle (Ali Ben Mamoud), Leonard Mudie (Barnes), Smoki Whitfield (Eli), Roy Glenn (Gomo), Rick Vallin (Abdullah), James Adamson (Ezekial), William Tannen (Reed), Don Harvey (Graves).

One of 11 films in the BOMBA series, THE GOLDEN IDOL again cast former-TARZAN Boy Sheffield in the role of the juvenile jungle hero. This time he helps a Watusi tribe get their golden idol back from a villainous Arab chieftain. As good as can be expected and better than most of the non-Weissmuller TARZANs. (See BOMBA THE JUNGLE BOY series, Index.)

p,d&w, Ford Beebe (based on the characters created by Roy Rockwood); ph, Harry Neumann; ed, John Fuller; art d, David Milton.

Adventure　　　　　　　　　　　**(PR:AA　MPAA:NR)**

GOLDEN IVORY　　　　　　　(SEE: WHITE HUNTRESS, 1954)

GOLDEN LADY, THE* 　　　　　　(1979, Brit.) 96m
　　　　　　Jean Ubaud-Keith Cavele/Target International c

Christina World (Julia Hemmingway), Suzanne Danielle (Dahlia), June Chadwick (Lucy), Anika Pavel (Carol), Stephan Chase (Max Rowlands), Edward De Souza (Yorgo Praxis), David Wing (Dietmar Schuster), Patrick Newell (Charlie Whitlock), Richard Oldfield (Wayne Bentley).

Lady supersleuth World and her gang of female helpers are the major forces in keeping an Arab country from falling into the grasp of the KGB. At first, World (as the lady James Bond) and company work toward helping the KGB reach its goal, but start undoing what they have done once they realize the Soviet intentions. Situations are all terribly predictable, with the premise of the film relying much too heavily on sex.

p, Paul Cowan; d, Jose Larraz; w, Joshua Sinclair; ph, David Griffiths; m, Georges Garvarentz; ed, David Campling; art d, Norris Spencer; cos, Sandy Moss.

Spy Drama　　　　**Cas.**　　　　**(PR:O　MPAA:NR)**

GOLDEN LINK, THE** 　　　　　　(1954, Brit.) 83m Parkside/Archway bw

Andre Morrell (Supt. Blake), Thea Gregory (Joan Blake), Patrick Holt (Terry Maguire), Jack Watling (Bill Howard), Arnold Bell (Detective Inspector Harris), Olive Sloane (Mrs. Pullman), Bruce Beeby (Sgt. Baker), Alexander Gauge (Arnold Debenham), Dorinda Stevens (Norma Sheridan), Elsie Wagstaff (Mrs. West), Edward Lexy (Maj. Grey), Maria Landt (Maria), Charlie Drake (Joe), Ellen Pollack (Mme. Sonia).

A well-crafted crime mystery which stars Morrell as a police superintendent investigating the death of a neighbor who fell four floors to her death outside their apartment building. Morrell learns that his own daughter was in love with the dead woman's husband and tried to get him to divorce her. The real killer turns out to be not the husband or lover as expected, but a helpful neighbor.

p, Guido Coen; d, Charles Sanders; w, Allan Mackinnon; ph, Harry Waxman; m, Eric Spear; ed, Jack Slade.

Crime　　　　　　　　　　　　　**(PR:A　MPAA:NR)**

**GOLDEN MADONNA, THE **½ 　　　(1949, Brit.) 88m MON bw

Phyllis Calvert (Patricia Chandler), Michael Rennie (Mike Christie), Tullio Carminati (Signor Higone), David Greene (Johnny Lester), Aldo Silvani (Don Vincenzo), Franco Coop (Esposito), Pippe "Palsa" Benucci (Pippo), Francesca Bondi (Maria), Claudio Ermeli (Antonio).

The Golden Madonna is a painting Italian villagers would pray to during dry spells. Hidden from the Nazis during WW II, it is now tucked away in a villa inherited by Calvert. Not knowing the importance of the painting, she sells it to a junk dealer. Once its relevance is known she sets out with Rennie to retrieve it, but it has ended up in the hands of some swindlers who pretend to give it back but they actually have sold it to black-market dealer Carminati. After undergoing a religious conversion, they steal it back and all is well. Calvert is as lively and fun as Rennie is grim. There is good use of the Italian countryside but that and Calvert's performance just aren't enough to save any sort of interest. Re-released in 1953 by Warner Bros.

p, John Stafford; d, Ladislas Vajda; w, Askos Tolnay; ph, Anchise Brizzi, Otello Martelli; ed, Carmen Beliaoff.

Drama　　　　　　　　　　　　　**(PR:A　MPAA:NR)**

GOLDEN MARIE　　　　　　　(SEE: CASQUE D'OR, 1952)

GOLDEN MASK, THE*½ 　　　　　(1954, Brit.) 88m Mayflower/UA c
　　　　　　　　　　　　　　　(GB: SOUTH OF ALGIERS)

Van Heflin (Nicholas Chapman), Wanda Hendrix (Anne Burnet), Eric Portman (Dr. Burnet), Charles Goldner (Petris), Jacques Francois (Jacques Farnod), Jacques Brunius (Kress), Aubrey Mather (Prof. Sir Arthur Young), Alec Finter (Workman), Noelle Middleton (Stewardess), Rene Leplat (Dr. Farnod), Simone Silva (Zara), Pierre Chaminade (Concierge), Marne Maitland (Thank You), George Pastell (Hassan), Marie France (Yasmin), Arnold Diamond (Spahi Officer), Messaoud (Abdel), Michael Mellinger (Spahi N.C.O.), Alec Mango (Mahmoud), Maxwell Setton (Donkey Buyer), Aubrey Baring (1st Camel Rider).

Portman and daughter Hendrix, along with Van Heflin and Hendrix's fiance, Francois, are on a search for the lost tomb of Marcus Manilius. There they hope to find the golden mask of Moloch, which is worth a fortune. They run into the standard bandits but are saved by the equally standard military. Hendrix and Van Heflin fall for each other and Francois relinquishes his intended. Competent direction helps this flow smoothly and the acting is fine for the material. Scenes of the desert and ancient ruins are marvelously shot.

p, Maxwell Setton, Aubrey Baring; d, Jack Lee; w, Robert Westerby; ph, Oswald Morris (Technicolor); m, Robert Gill; ed, V. Sagovsky.

Drama　　　　　　　　　　　　　**(PR:A　MPAA:NR)**

GOLDEN MISTRESS, THE** 　　　　(1954) 82m UA c

John Agar (Bill Buchanan), Rosemarie Bowe (Ann Dexter), Abner Biberman (Carl Dexter), Andre Narcisse (Iznard), Jacques Molant (Ti Flute), Kiki (Christofe), Pierre Blain (The Houngan), Shibley Talamas (DuPuis), Andre Contant, Napoleon Bernard (Domballa Soloists), Andre Germain (Untamed Spearman), The National Folklore Theatre Of Haiti.

Agar is talked into using his boat to locate a voodoo treasure by Bowe, daughter of the greedy Biberman. Biberman gets struck down by a voodoo curse and never makes it to the treasure. Agar and Bowe do, however, but are nearly killed by enraged natives for their trouble. They escape to begin an existence of romantic bliss together. The Technicolor photography, authentic extras, and picturesque Haiti locale make up for the predictable plotline.

p, Richard Kay, Harry Rybnick; d, Joel Judge; w, Judge, Lew Hewitt (based on a story by Hewitt); ph, William C. Thompson (Technicolor); m, Raoul Kraushaar; ed, Howard Smith; art d, James R. Connell.

Adventure　　　　　　　　　　　**(PR:A　MPAA:NR)**

GOLDEN MOUNTAINS*½ 　　　　(1958, Den.) 89m AS Nordisk c
　　　　　　　　　　　　　　(GULD OG GRONNE SKOVE)

Axel Bang, Verner Tholsgaard, Mogens Viggo Petersen, Cay Christiansen, Karl Stegger.

Two small Danish islands are engaged in a long-running feud. Three boys on one island love three girls on the other, but the parents of each loving couple refuse to allow marriage. But when Americans find oil on one of the islands, all disputes and feuds are settled and the couples all marry. A felicitous little story, nicely handled, with an excellent use of color.

p, Vinod S. Pathak; d, Gabriel Axel; w, Johannes Allen; ph, Joergen Skov (Eastmancolor); m, Svend Erik Tarp; ed, Carsten Dahl; set d, Kai Rasch.

Comedy　　　　　　　　　　　　　**(PR:A　MPAA:NR)**

GOLDEN NEEDLES*½ (1974) 93m Sequoia/AIP c
(AKA: CHASE FOR THE GOLDEN NEEDLES)

Joe Don Baker (Dan), Elizabeth Ashley (Felicity), Jim Kelly (Jeff), Burgess Meredith (Winters), Ann Sothern (Finzie), Roy Chiao (Lin Toa), Frances Fong (Su Lin), Tony Lee (Kwan), Alice Fong (Lotus), Clarence Barnes (Claude), Pat Johnson (Winter's Man), Edgar Justice (Bobby).

Sordid but fun Kung Fu-type story with an unusual twist. A legendary 30-inch-tall statue has seven gold needles inserted. Put these seven needles in the exact same position in an adult male and he will become a sexual dynamo: put them in otherwise and it's the big sleep. Naturally, everyone is after the little darling including Baker, Ashley, and Meredith (who deserved better roles than this). The direction holds to a nice pace with the story and sharp editing keeps things moving. Shot on location in Hong Kong.

p, Fred Weintraub, Paul Heller; d, Robert Clouse; w, S. Lee Upgostin, Sylvia Schneble; ph, Gilbert Hubbs (Movielab Color); m, Lalo Schifrin; ed, Michael Kahn.

Drama/Action (PR:O MPAA:PG)

GOLDEN NYMPHS, THE (SEE: HONEYMOON OF HORROR, 1964)

GOLDEN PLAGUE, THE*½ (1963, Ger.) 95m Occident/Bakros bw
(DIE GOLDENE PEST)

Ivan Desny (Sergeant Hartwig), Karl Boehm (Karl Hellmer), Gertrud Kuckelmann (Franziska Hellmer), Wilfried Seyferth (Wenzeslaw Lolowrat), Elise Aulinger (Johanna), Heinz Hilpert (Tonder), Ilse Furstenberg (Mrs. Foesterling).

Desny is a U.S. soldier who returns to his German girl friend at the end of WW II but finds himself at odds with her brother, an amusement park owner involved in the black market. Released in Germany in 1954.

d, John Brahm; w, Dieter Werner.

Drama (PR:A MPAA:NR)

GOLDEN RABBIT, THE* (1962, Brit.) 64m Argo/RANK bw

Timothy Bateson (Henry Tucker), Maureen Beck (Sally), Willoughby Goddard (Clitheroe), Dick Bentley (Insp. Jackson), John Sharp (Peebles), Kenneth Fortescue (Detective Wilson), Raymond Rollett (Manager), Humphrey Lestocq, Ronald Adam.

When a bank clerk with amateur alchemist standing develops a way to manufacture gold he becomes the target of a scheme by some greedy businessmen. His girl friend is kidnaped to pressure the clerk into giving up his formula, but by the finale the sweethearts are safe and a gold rush is avoided.

p, Jack Lamont, Barry Delmaine; d, David MacDonald; w, Dick Sharples, Gerald Kelsey.

Comedy (PR:A MPAA:NR)

GOLDEN RENDEZVOUS* (1977) 103m
Film Trust-Milton Okun/Golden Rendezvous c

Richard Harris (John Carter), Ann Turkel (Susan Janssen), David Janssen (Charles Conway), Burgess Meredith (Van Heurden), John Vernon (Luis Carreras), Gordon Jackson (Dr. Marston), Keith Baxter (Preston), Dorothy Malone (Elizabeth Taubman), John Carradine (Fairweather).

A muddled mess of a picture with Vernon as a mercenary hijacking a ship. He's got an atomic device and he'll blow up the cruiser (a floating casino that holds every stock movie type available) unless he gets money from the U.S. Treasury. Poor character motivations, gaping plot holes, and television movie aesthetics make this a film well worth missing.

p, Andre Pieters; d, Ashley Lazarus; w, John Gay, Stanley Price (based on the novel by Alistair MacLean), ph, Ken Higgins; ed, Ralph Kemplen.

Drama Cas. (PR:O MPAA:NR)

GOLDEN SALAMANDER*** (1950, Brit.) 87m GFD bw

Trevor Howard (David Redfern), Anouk (Anna), Herbert Lom (Ranki), Miles Malleson (Douvet), Walter Rilla (Serafis), Jacques Sernas (Max), Wilfred Hyde-White (Agno), Peter Copley (Aribi), Eugene Deckers (Police Chief), Henry Edwards (Jeffries), Marcel Poncin (Dommic), Percy Walsh (Guillard), Sybilla Binder (Mme. Labree), Kathleen Boutall (Mme. Guillard), Valentine Dyall (Ben Ahrim).

Howard is an archeologist combing Tunisia for lost treasures. He accidentally confronts some gun runners and soon discovers the entire district is run by one man. With the help of Anouk, he saves the day. Though the acting is fine and the on-location photography top notch, the direction is a bit slow.

p, Alexander Galperson; d, Ronald Neame; w, Neame, Victor Canning, Lesley Storm (based on a novel by Canning); ph, Dudley Lovell, Freddie Francis; m, William Alwyn; ed, Jack Harris; md, Muir Mathieson.

Drama (PR:A MPAA:NR)

GOLDEN SEAL, THE** (1983) 94m Samuel Goldwyn Co.—New Realm c

Steve Railsback (Jim Lee), Penelope Milford (Tania Lee), Michael Beck (Crawford), Torquil Campbell (Eric), Sandra Seacat (Gladys), Seth Sakai (Semeyon), Richard Narita (Alexei), Peter Anderson (Tom), Terrence Kelly (Mongo), Tom Heaton (Stutterer).

A family living on an isolated island in British Columbia is visited by a rare golden seal, which comes there every seven years to bear young. She and Campbell (age 10) make fast friends and the lad helps save her from bounty hunters. This is a fine family drama. Photography is lush but the pace of direction is too slow. The friendship between the boy and the seal seems genuine.

p, Samuel Goldwyn, Jr.; d, Frank Zuniga; w, John Groves (based on the novel A River Ran Out of Eden by James Vance Marshall); ph, Eric Saarinen (Metrocolor); m, Dana Kaproff; ed, Robert Q. Lovett; prod d, Douglas Higgins.

Family Adventure Cas. (PR:AAA MPAA:PG)

GOLDEN STALLION, THE**½ (1949) 67m REP bw

Roy Rogers (Himself), Dale Evans (Stormy Billings), Estelita Rodriguez (Pepita Valdez), Pat Brady (Sparrow Biffle), Greg McClure (Jeff Middleton), Frank Fenton (Sheriff), Greg McClure (Ben), Dale Van Sickel (Ed Hart), Clarence Straight (Spud), Jack Sparks (Guard), Chester Conklin (Old Man), Foy Willing and the Riders of the Purple Sage, Trigger the Horse.

Rogers' horse Trigger is in love and what's a cowboy to do? Diamond smugglers hide their booty in the horseshoe of a beautiful palomino. Rogers captures the herd she's in and Trigger falls for her. When Trigger sees her being maltreated, he kills the party responsible. Great guy that he is, Rogers takes the blame but then Trigger, Jr. saves the day by exposing the smugglers. Amusing entry in the Roy Rogers series with sensitive direction that makes it all believable. (See ROY ROGERS series, Index.)

p, Edward J. White; d, William Whitney; w, Sloan Nibley; ph, Jack Marta; m, Nathan Scott; ed, Tony Martinelli; art d, Frank Hotaling; m/l, Sid Robin, Foy Willing, Nathan Gluck, Ann Parentean, Eddie Cherkose, Sol Meyer, Jule Styne.

Western Cas. (PR:A MPAA:NR)

GOLDEN TRAIL, THE 1937 (SEE: RIDERS OF THE WHISTLING SKULL, THE, 1937)

GOLDEN TRAIL, THE** (1940) 53m MON bw

Tex Ritter (Tex), Slim Andrews (Slim), Ina Guest (Chita), Patsy Moran (Patsy), Gene Alsace (Rat), Stanley Price (Prader), Warner Richmond (Chris), Eddie Dean (Injun), Forrest Taylor (Rawls).

Typical cowboy yarn in which Ritter and Andrews face a gang of claim jumpers intent on killing unsuspecting prospectors who have struck it rich. The bad guys are in cahoots with a county clerk who forges signatures and documents for a piece of the action. Ritter overcomes all to defeat the forces of evil and bring peace to the land once more. Standard stuff, with songs including a new arrangement of the old favorite "Clementine." Other songs: "Gold Is Where You Find It" (Ritter, Frank Harford), "Donohue's Done It Again" (Jack Frost), "They're Hanging Pappy Early In the Morning" (Johnny Lange, Lew Porter).

p, Edward Finney; d, Al Herman; w, Roland Lynch, Robert Emmett, Roger Merton; ph, Marcel LePicard; ed, Robert Golden; m/l, Ritter, Frank Harford, Jack Frost, Johnny Lange, Lew Porter.

Western (PR:A MPAA:NR)

GOLDEN VOYAGE OF SINBAD, THE***½ (1974, Brit.) 105m COL c

John Phillip Law (Sinbad), Caroline Munro (Margiana), Tom Baker (Koura), Douglas Wilmer (Vizier), Martin Shaw (Rachid), Gregoire Aslan (Hakim), Kurt Christian (Haroun), Takis Emmanuel (Achmed), John D. Garfield (Abdul), Aldo Sambrell (Omar).

Good fun with a minimum of plot and a maximum of wonderful Harryhausen special effects. Law is the famed sailor in search of a mythical gold tablet that will bring untold riches. En route he does battle with one-eyed centaurs, a winged griffin, and a host of other creatures. It's not up to the quality of THE SEVENTH VOYAGE OF SINBAD but it's enormous fun to watch. Direction is adequate as is the acting, both of which take a back seat to the special effects.

p, Charles H. Schneer, Ray Harryhausen; d, Gordon Hessler; w, Brian Clemens; ph, Ted Moore (Dynarama); m, Miklos Rozsa; ed, Roy Watts; prod d, John Stoll; art d, Fernando Gonzales; set d, Julian Mateos; spec eff, Harryhausen.

Fantasy/Adventure Cas. (PR:AAA MPAA:G)

GOLDEN WEST, THE** (1932) 74m FOX bw

George O'Brien, Janet Chandler, Marion Burns, Onslow Stevens, Julia Swayne Gordon, Emmett Corrigan, Edmund Breese, Sam West, Arthur Pierson, Bert Hanlon, Hattie McDaniels, Charles Stevens, Stanley Blystone, George Rigas, Dorothy Ward, Sam Adams, Ed Dillon, Chief Big Tree, John War Eagle.

How the West was won a la Zane Grey. This is an early programmer telling of a theme that would later be expanded in numerous epic-sized films and television movies.

d, David Howard; w, Gordon Rigby (based on a story by Zane Grey); ph, George Schneiderman; ed, Ralph Dietrich.

Western (PR:A MPAA:NR)

GOLDENGIRL zero (1979) 104m AE c

Susan Anton (Goldengirl), James Coburn (Dryden), Curt Jurgens (Serafin), Leslie Caron (Dr. Lee), Robert Culp (Esselton), James A. Watson, Jr. (Winters), Harry Guardino (Valenti), Ward Costello (Cobb), Michael Lerner (Sternberg), John Newcombe (Armitage), Julianna Field (Ingrid), Sheila DeWindt (Debbie), Andrea Brown (Teammate), Anette Tannader (Krull), Nicholas Coster (Dr. Dalton).

Anton's dad is proud of his daughter, a great runner heading for the Olympics. What she doesn't realize is that daddy Jurgens was an old buddy of Hitler and has been using some left-over experiments to raise a superhuman daughter. There's some nonsense about corporate sponsorship and lots of shots with Anton in tight garb. Produced in association with NBC, which planned to run it as a two-night television picture the next year when the real Olympics were to occur. Script and direction are laughable and, as for Anton, she should have stayed with her cigar ads.

p, Danny O'Donovan; d, Joseph Sargent; w, John Kohn (based on the novel by Peter Lear); ph, Stevan Larner (Eastmancolor); m, Bill Conti; ed, George Nicholson; art d, Syd Litwack; set d, Gerald Adams.

Drama Cas. (PR:O MPAA:PG)

GOLDFINGER**** (1964, Brit.) 112m UA c

Sean Connery *(James Bond)*, Gert Frobe *(Goldfinger)*, Honor Blackman *(Pussy Galore)*, Shirley Eaton *(Jill Masterson)*, Tania Mallett *(Tilly Masterson)*, Harold Sakata *(Oddjob)*, Bernard Lee *("M")*, Martin Banson *(Solo)*, Cec Linder *(Felix Leiter)*, Lois Maxwell *(Moneypenny)*, Nadja Regin *(Bonita)*, Desmond Llewelyn *("Q")*, Bill Nagy *(Midnight)*, Alf Joint *(Capungo)*, Varley Thomas *(Old Lady)*, Raymond Young *(Sierra)*, Richard Vernon *(Smithers)*, Denis Cowles *(Brunskill)*, Michael Mellinger *(Kisch)*, Bert Kwouk *(Mr. Ling)*, Hal Galili *(Strap)*, Lenny Rabin *(Henchman)*.

Easily the best of the gadget-oriented James Bond extravaganzas, this third film in the Bond series probably has the most endurance. This time out Connery is pitted against one of his most memorable villians, a heavy-set, filthy rich, power hungry maniac who calls himself Goldfinger, played with obvious zest by Frobe. Having secured all the private stocks of gold throughout the world, Frobe plans to invade, plant, and detonate a small atomic device (procured from the Red Chinese) inside Fort Knox in order to contaminate its huge gold supply with deadly radiation, thus rendering it worthless. If his plan succeeds, Frobe would possess the vast majority of saleable gold in the world, and become the richest, most powerful man on Earth. With the help of his bizarre oriental assistant Oddjob (Sakata), who kills his victims with a razor-edged bowler hat, and martial arts expert Pussy Galore (played by Blackman, who abandoned her spot on the highly successful TV series "The Avengers" for this role) who is also a pilot, Frobe puts his plan into action. Connery uncovers the plan after meeting Frobe at a Miami Beach hotel where the villain cheats at poker, using an elaborate system he has devised with his secretary, Eaton. Eaton watches the other players' cards from across the table by using a telescope, and then informs Frobe of the hands through a transmitter in the big man's hearing aid. Eaton falls in love with Connery, and when their tryst is discovered, Frobe has his secretary's body covered with a gold paint which clogs her pores and suffocates her (it is perhaps the most enduring image in any Bond film). Frobe then leaves for Europe and Bond follows, learning that the evildoer's smuggled gold is transported in his solid-gold Rolls Royce. Connery is captured by Blackman and then shipped back to the U.S. and winds up in Frobe's headquarters in Kentucky. There it is revealed that Frobe plans to subdue the soldiers guarding Fort Knox with a nerve gas that will be sprayed over the gold vault by Blackman's planes. Still held captive, Connery is handcuffed to the atomic bomb and left to die. Meanwhile, Blackman, who has finally fallen for Connery (she was a challenge for Bond due to the subtle lesbian undertones suggested by the script), flies off to Washington to inform the authorities of Frobe's scheme. With only seconds to detonation, Connery is saved and has a showdown with Sakata, who loses the fight when his flying derby is used against him. Frobe escapes, however, but foolishly tries to get revenge on Connery, who is being flown to a meeting with the President, by disguising himself as an American general. The big man corners the secret agent in the airplane but when their fight breaks a window, Frobe is sucked out of the plane. GOLDFINGER contains more crowd-pleasing moments than any other Bond film. The golden girl, Oddjob's flying hat, the deadly lazer beam that almost cuts Connery in half, the amazing Astin-Martin with its dozens of gadgets and, of course, Shirley Bassey's terrific rendition of the theme song (which became a big hit) immediately became an integral part of the James Bond lore. The production is stunning and lavish with special kudos to production designer Ken Adam and art director Peter Murton, whose impressive Fort Knox set was a testament to imagination and execution (the designers were not allowed a peek at the real Fort Knox). Another unique aspect of the GOLDFINGER phenomenon was the (at the time) unparalleled marketing strategy which saw scads of toys, games, model cars, dolls, soundtrack albums, and standard publicity stunts (armed, bikini-clad female guards escorting prints of the film to the premiere) which peppered stores and newspapers for months. In the end it is a tribute to first-time Bond series director Hamilton (who had assisted Carol Reed and John Huston on previous projects) that he was able to keep all the gadgets, wild characters, and strange locations in check long enough to produce a balanced, entertaining film that does not rely totally on the flash and effects that would weaken the subsequent entries in the series.

p, Harry Saltzman, Albert R. Broccoli; d, Guy Hamilton; w, Richard Maibaum, Paul Dehn (based on the novel by Ian Fleming); ph, Ted Moore (Technicolor); m, John Barry; ed, Peter Hunt; prod d, Ken Adam; art d, Peter Murter; set d, Freda Pearson; m/l, Title song, Leslie Bricusse, Anthony Newley, Barry; spec eff, John Stears; makeup, Paul Rabiger.

Spy/Adventure **Cas.** **(PR:C-O MPAA:NR)**

GOLDIE* (1931 58m FOX bw

Spencer Tracy *(Bill)*, Warren Hymer *(Spike)*, Jean Harlow *(Goldie)*, Lina Basquette *(Constantina)*, Maria Alba *(Dolores)*, Eleanor Hunt *(Russian Girl)*, Leila Karnelly *(Wife)*, Ivan Linow *(Husband)*, Jesse DeVorska *(Gonzales)*, Eddie Kane *(Barker)*, George Raft *(Man at Carnival)*.

There is almost nothing to recommend this film other than the fact that it gives us the chance to see Harlow and Tracy when they were very young, and George Raft in a tiny bit. Hymer is a sailor who finds a little black book filled with women's names and addresses. After dating each girl, he finds that they all have something in common, a tattoo. Hymer is angered that some guy had the nerve to tattoo these women as a mark of his conquest. He plans to give the guy "what for" if he ever meets him. Tracy steps into the scene. He is another sailor and a rival for the affections of a woman. But the two men become fast pals and learn that they have a great deal in common. They travel to Calais where Hymer falls hard for Harlow, who works at the local carnival as a high diver. Tracy tells Hymer that all she is interested in is Hymer's money and that causes a rift between the two men. Harlow attempts to get Tracy on her side but he is not swayed. It is only when Hymer sees that Harlow wears Tracy's tattoo on her body that he realizes that Tracy knows the woman well, very well, and was only trying to help his pal. Hymer walks out on Harlow and the film ends with the two men still friends.

d, Benjamin Stoloff; w, Gene Towne, Paul Perez; ph, Ernest Palmer; ed, Alex Troffey.

Drama **(PR:A MPAA:NR)**

GOLDIE GETS ALONG** (1933) 65m RKO bw

Lili Damita *(Goldie LaFarge)*, Charles Morton *(Bil Tobin)*, Sam Hardy *(Sam Muldoon)*, Nat Pendleton *(Cassidy)*, Lita Chevret *(Marie Gardner)*, Arthur Hoyt *(Mayor Simms)*, Henry Fink *(Flynn)*, Bradley Page *(Hawthorne)*, Lee Moran *(Kaplan)*.

Damita, tired of small-town life, leaves New Jersey and boy friend Morton for fame and fortune in Hollywood. Along the way she gets mixed up in a shady beauty contest run by Hardy. Escaping this, she arrives in movieland only to discover that her former beau is now a star. She is soon as big a star as he. But he's sick of the movie business and they decide to head back to New Jersey and the simple life. Though clearly one of the many fairy tales Hollywood was churning out at the time, there is a nice glimpse of life on a film studio in GOLDIE GETS ALONG. Other than that this is standard Hollywood fluff.

p, J.G. Bachmann; d, Malcolm St. Clair; w, Hawthorne Hurst; ph, Merritt Gersted.

Comedy **(PR:A MPAA:NR)**

GOLDSTEIN½** (1964) 85m Montrose bw

Lou Gilbert *(Old Man)*, Ellen Madison *(Sally)*, Thomas Erhart *(Sculptor)*, Benito Carruthers *(Jay)*, Charles Fischer *(Mr. Nice)*, Severn Darden *(Doctor)*, Anthony Holland *(Aid)*, Nelson Algren *(Himself)*.

An unusual independent film shot in Chicago and based loosely on the tale of the prophet Elijah. Gilbert, seemingly a bum, emerges from the waters of Lake Michigan and meets a variety of characters until, like Elijah, he mysteriously disappears when the film ends. The plot, like Gilbert, meanders. We meet a woman undergoing an abortion, a begger with a violin, and a struggling artist. Their stories are all loosely strung together by their encounters with Gilbert. Algren appears in a nice cameo as he listens to a sculptor's tale of artistic dilemma. GOLDSTEIN is a funny, black comedy, well directed by Manaster and Kaufman. The gruesome abortion scene is sensitively handled and the camera work is terrific throughout. Chicago is equally a star in this film, with well chosen locations beautifully photographed. GOLDSTEIN is not an easy film, but is definitely an intriguing one.

p, Zev Braun; d&w, Philip Kaufman, Benjamin Manaster; ph, Jean-Phillippe Carson; m, Meyer Kupferman; ed Adolfas Mekas.

Fantasy/Satire **(PR:O MPAA:NR)**

GOLDTOWN GHOST RIDERS** (1953) 57m COL bw

Gene Autry *(Himself)*, Smiley Burnette *(Himself)*, Gail Davis *(Cathy Wheeler)*, Kirk Riley *(Ed Wheeler)*, Carleton Young *(Jim Granby)*, Neyle Morrow *(Teeno)*, Denver Pyle *(Bernie Malloy)*, Steve Conte *(Blackwell)*, John Doucette *(Bailey)*, Champion the Horse.

Strangely plotted Autry oater has the singing cowboy playing a circuit court judge presiding over a murder trial where the accused claims he has already served time for the killing. Years before, the murderer, thinking he had killed his swindler-partner, was tried and sent to jail. Unbeknownst to him, his victim lived and assumed a new identity. When the killer was released from prison and discovered he had served time for a murder he didn't actually commit, he tracked the ex-partner down and did the job right. (See GENE AUTRY series, Index.)

p, Armand Schaefer; d, George Archainbaud; w, Gerald Geraghty; ph, William Bradford; ed, James Sweeney; md, Mischa Bakaleinikoff; art d, George Brooks.

Western **(PR:A MPAA:NR)**

GOLDWYN FOLLIES, THE** (1938) 115m Goldwyn/UA c

Adolphe Menjou *(Oliver Merlin)*, The Ritz Brothers *(Themselves)*, Vera Zorina *(Olga Samara)*, Kenny Baker *(Danny Beecher)*, Andrea Leeds *(Hazel Dawes)*, Helen Jepson *(Leona Jerome)*, Phil Baker *(Michael Day)*, Ella Logan *(Glory Wood)*, Bobby Clark *(A. Basil Crane, Jr.)*, Jerome Cowan *(Lawrence)*, Nydia Westman *(Ada)*, Charles Kullmann *(Alfredo)*, Frank Shields *(Assistant Director)*, Edgar Bergen and Charlie McCarthy *(Themselves)*, the American Ballet of the Metropolitan Opera, Joseph Crehan *(Theater Manager)*, Roland Drew *(Igor)*, Frank Mills *(Prop Man)*, Walter Sande *(Westinghouse)*, Alan Ladd *(Auditioning Singer)*, Vivian Coe [Austin], Marjorie Deane, Betty Douglas, Ann Graham, Jane Hamilton, Lynne Berkeley, Judith Ford, Evelyn Terry, Gloria Youngblood (The "Gorgeous" Goldwyn Girls).

Ten writers attempted to solve this mish-mash with the final script done by Oscar-winner Ben Hecht in what was reputed to be two weeks. The other writers included Dorothy Parker and Anita Loos and none of it helped a whit. Goldwyn wanted to be the Ziegfeld of movies and was determined to make some huge movies of the same stripe as the great Flo had done for Broadway. This was to be the first of many but it was such a disaster that he wisely took his losses, licked his wounds, and went on to make some other, very wonderful movies. Critics were united in their scathing comments on this picture but it wasn't nearly as bad as they felt. Any picture that introduces Charlie McCarthy and Edgar Bergen can't be all bad and this wasn't. Menjou is a film producer with a long string of flops. He meets Leeds who tells him why his pictures have been laughed at by the audiences and the critics (this may have been Hecht being prophetic at his typewriter). He hires Leeds to be his "voice of the people" but keeps her away from the Hollywood crowd he feels will spoil her. Instead he smuggles her in and out of the studio, buys her a small house, hires a chaperone, and spends his evenings reading scripts to her so she can make some sage comments about what "the people" will like. One of the films she works on is Menjou's version of "Romeo and Juliet" and she feels that it will *never* work because they both die at the end. So she insists he change the ending in order for the two star-crossed lovers to live happily ever after. Menjou has a larger problem. He must get several actors together in a film not unlike THE GOLDWYN FOLLIES. He interviews The Ritz Brothers, Bergen and dummy, Vera Zorina (ballerina wife of George Balanchine), and just about everyone else in Hollywood who isn't working, then comes up with a yarn that will use all their dubious talents. Phil Baker is a talentless accordion player who flees Zorina, an equally ungifted Russian actress. In the middle of this there is a large water ballet, featuring Zorina, a few arias from "La Traviata" and several songs from George Gershwin, who died while they were making this and whose songs were completed by Vernon Duke. Menjou needs to find a young fellow to play the boy juvenile and Leeds locates Baker, the short order cook at a local burger stand. Baker gets the role and she is thrilled. Now Menjou realizes he is in love with Leeds and threatens to fire Baker if she doesn't leave him. In the last reel, Baker tells Menjou that he is willing to give up his big break in order to marry Leeds. Menjou likes the lad's spunk, changes his mind, and gives the youth a five-year contract. Picture ends with everyone sitting around the piano singing "Love Walked In." Sure, it's dumb and yes, it's about as real as a trip to Mars by streetcar, but there is some fun in the sheer silliness. Duke had some help from Gershwin's best pal, Oscar Levant, in finishing the music left behind by Gershwin's untimely demise. Several other songs by other writers served to give the magic absolutely no sense of style whatsoever. H.C. Potter did some uncredited direction as well, to no avail. The musical program consisted of "Romeo And Juliet" (ballet), "Water Nymph" (ballet), "Here, Pussy, Pussy" (Ray Golden, Sid Kuller), "Serenade To A Fish" (performed by the Ritz Brothers), and Kenny Baker singing "Love Walked In" and "Love Is Here To Stay" (George, Ira Gershwin), "Spring Again" (Vernon Duke, Ira Gershwin). Charles Kullman and Helen Jepson sang arias from Giuseppe Verdi's "La Traviata," Ella Logan presented "I was Doing Alright" by the Gershwins, Jepson returned with "La Serenata" (Alfred Silvestri, Enrico Toselli), and "I Love To Rhyme" (the Gershwins, featuring Phil Baker, Edgar Bergen and Charlie McCarthy).

p, Samuel Goldwyn; d, George Marshall; w, Ben Hecht, Sam Perrin, Arthur Phillips; ph, Gregg Toland (Technicolor); ed, Sherman Todd; md, Arthur Newman; art d, Richard Day, cos, Omar Kiam; ch, George Balanchine.

Musical Comedy (PR:A MPAA:NR)

GOLEM, THE*   (1937, Czech./Fr.) 91m AB/Metropolis bw

Harry Baur (Emperor Rudolf), Roger Karl (Chancellor Lang), Ferdinand Hart (Golem), Charles Dorat (Rabbi Jacob), Almos (Toussaint), Roger Duchesne (Trignac), Gaston Jacquet (Chief Of Police), Germaine Aussey (Countess Strada), Jenny Holt (Rachel), Tanja Doll (Mme. Benoit).

The third version (the first talkie) of the legendary tale of the Golem was shot with a French cast in Prague where the myth is said to have been born. Rudolf II, played by Baur, has become a vicious and oppressive dictator who practices the black arts and treats the ghetto Jews poorly. He lives in constant fear of the Golem, a giant formed from clay to protect Jews. Rabbi Jacob (Dorat) finds the Golem (Hart) and enscribes God's name on its forehead bringing the statue to life. The creature breaks free from the prison where he was enchained and goes on a vengeful rampage that sees all of Baur's armies fall before it. In the end, the Golem has destroyed most of Prague, including Baur's palace. Having completed his work, Dorat removes the name from the Golem's forehead and the statue shatters. Effectively directed with some fairly amazing special effects, though the narrative drags somewhat in spots. (In French; English subtitles.)

p, Jozef Stern; d, Julien Duvivier; w, Duvivier, Andre-Paul Antoine (based on play by Jan Werich and Jiri Voskovec); ph, Jan Stallich, Vaclav Vich; m, Kumok; ed, Martin J. Lewis; set d, Andrejev, Kopecky.

Horror (PR:C MPAA:NR)

GOLEM   (1980, Pol.) 92m Zespoly Filmowe/Perspekty c (AKA: THE GOLEM)

Marek Walczewski (Pernat), Krystyna Janda (Rozyna), Joanna Zolkowska (Miriam), Krzysztof Majchrzak (Student), Mariusz Dmochowski (Holtrum), Wieslaw Drzewica (Miriam's Father), Henryk Bak, Wojciech Pszoniak, Jan Nowicki, Ryszard Pietruski, Andrzej Seweryn, Marian Opania, Boguslaw Sobczuk.

A futuristic view of the Golem legend brought to the screen by Polish experimental filmmaker Szulkin. This time the tale is of a Golem in reverse. The future sees the total control of humanity by technology and computers. The "human" beings have been created by mad doctors who have fused communication technology and flesh into one, enabling them to control the populace's very movements. One of the products of this union of man and machine, Walczewski, fails and becomes an alienated outsider, more human than machine, that must be destroyed. Walczewski wanders through the urban rubble, one step ahead of the doctors, trying to find a way out of the technological madness of his existence. Interesting but overlong film was done in sepia tints. (In Polish.)

d, Piotr Szulkin; w, Szulkin, Tadeusz Sobolewski; (based on the legend and the novel by Gustav Meyrink); ph, Zygmunt Samosiuk; set d, Zbigniew Warpechowski, Janusz Wlasow.

Science Fiction (PR:C MPAA:NR)

GOLFO   (SEE: GIRL OF THE MOUNTAINS, 1958)

GOLGOTHA½   (1937, Fr.) 97m Film Union bw

Harry Baur (Herod), Robert Le Vigan (Jesus), Jean Gabin (Pontius Pilate), Charles Granval (Calaphas), Andre Bacque (Annas), Hubert Preiler (Peter), Lucas Gridoux (Judas), Edwige Feuillere (Claudia), Juliette Verneuil (Mary), Vana Yami (Mary Magdaleine), Van Daele (Gerron).

The first sound film to be made about the life of Christ, this English version covered only the final week of his life. Le Vigan is cast as Christ and, in an interesting choice, Jean Gabin plays Pontius Pilate. While an exceptional and lavish film, it is too large and crafted to have much emotional effect. (In French.)

p, A. d'Aguiar; d, Julien Duvivier; w, Forrest Izard, I.E. Lopert; ph, G.J. Kruger; m, Jacques Ibert.

Historical Drama (PR:A MPAA:NR)

GOLIATH AGAINST THE GIANTS*   (1963, Ital./Span.) 95m Cineproduzioni Associate-Procusa/Medallion c (GOLIATH CONTRO I GIGANTI, GOLIAT CONTRA LOS GIGANTES; AKA: GOLIATH AND THE GIANTS)

Brad Harris (Goliath), Gloria Milland (Elea), Fernando Rey (Bokan), Barbara Carroll (Daina), Jose Rubio, Lina Rosales, Carmen de Lirio, Angel Aranda, Mimmo Palmara, Fernando Sancho, Ray Martino, Ignazio Dolce, Luigi Marturano, Nello Pazzafini, Manuel Arbo, Rufino Ingles, Gianfranco Gasparri, Francisco Bernar, Angel Ortiz, Luis Marco.

Harris plays the Beirathian king, who, while away from home fighting a war, learns that Rey has taken over his throne. Angrily, he sails back home to claim his rightful place, encountering storms and sea monsters en route. He also rescues the beautiful Milland, who was sent by Rey to kill Harris. But the two fall in love and Milland is imprisoned as a traitor when she returns home. When Harris finally arrives in Beirath, after defeating Amazons and killing Rey, he rescues his true love. Strictly for the kiddies with its overly simplistic characters and presentation.

p, Cesare Seccia, Manuel Perez; d, Guido Malatesta; w, Seccia, Gianfranco Parolini, Giovanni Simonelli, Arpad De Riso, Sergio Sollima (based on a story by Seccia); ph, Alejandro Ulloa (Super TotalScope, Eastmancolor); m, Carlo Innocenzi; ed, Mario Sansoni, Edmondo Lozzi; art d, Ramiro Gomez, Carlo Santonocito.

Fantasy/Adventure (PR:A MPAA:NR)

GOLIATH AND THE BARBARIANS**   (1960, Ital.) 85m Standard/AIP c (IL TERROR DEI BARBERI)

Steve Reeves (Emiliano), Chelo Alonso (Londo), Bruce Cabot (Alboyna), Giulia Rubini (Sabina), Livio Lorenzon (Igor), Luciano Marin (Svevo), Arturo Dominici (Delfo), Furio Meniconi (Marco), Fabrizio Capucci (Bruno), Andrea Checci (Agnese), Gino Scotti (Count Daniele).

Another Reeves muscleman epic, this one set in Italy of 568 A.D. with Cabot as the leader of an army of vicious barbarians who come out of the Alps seeking to conquer the sleepy town of Verona. Unfortunately for the barbarians, Verona is also the hometown of the mighty Reeves, who single-handedly makes short order of the invaders by beating the daylights out of them.

p, Emimmo Salvi; d, Carlo Campogalliani; w, Campogalliani, Gino Mangini, Nino Stresa, Giuseppe Taffarel (based on a story by Salvi, Mangini); (TotalScope, Eastmancolor); m, Les Baxter; cos, Giovanna Matili.

Adventure Cas. (PR:A MPAA:NR)

GOLIATH AND THE DRAGON½   (1961, Ital./Fr.) 90m AIP c (LA VENDETTA DE ERCOLE)

Mark Forest (Goliath), Broderick Crawford (King Eurystheus), Eleonora Ruffo (Dejanara), Phillipe Hersent (Illus), Sandro Maretti (Ismene), Federica Ranchi (Thea), Gaby Andre (Alcinoe).

Laughable adventure-action picture that desperately tries to emulate the success of the Steve Reeves epics (a dubious proposition at best). This one pits the muscular Forest against the many insidious beasts and devices of the evil King Eurystheus, played with relish by Crawford. Bad special effects include a three-headed dragon dog, a giant killer-bat, and a hysterical looking dragon. A must-see for fans of ludicrous films.

p, Archille Piazzi, Gianni Fuchs; d, Vittorio Cottafavi; w, Marco Piccolo, Archibald Zounds, Jr.; ph, Mario Montuori (Colorscope); m, Les Baxter; ed, Maurizio Lucidi; cos. Peruzzi.

Adventure (PR:A MPAA:NR)

GOLIATH AND THE SINS OF BABYLON**   (1964, Ital.) 80m Leone Film/AIP c (MACISTE, L'EROE PIU GRANDE DEL MONDO)

Mark Forest (Goliath), Eleanora Bianchi (Regia/Chelima), Jose Greci (Xandros), Giuliano Gemma (Alceo), John Chevron (Evandro), Erno Crisa (Pergaso), Piero Lulli (Meneos), Arnaldo Fabrizio (Morakeb), Mimmo Palmara, Livio Lorenzon, Jacques Herlin, Paul Muller.

After Crisa, an ancient ruler, conquers the neighboring city of Nefer, he demands twenty-four virgins as a tribute. Forest, playing the hero, frees one of the women and joins up with Greci and Chevron to rescue the others. Bianchi, playing the mystery woman who Greci is in love with, convinces him to enter a chariot race in which the first prize is Greci's daughter. During it, Greci is wounded by Crisa's henchmen and is replaced by Forest who wins the race but is then accused of treason. As they attempt to arrest him, he escapes and leads a revolt that overthrows Crisa. At last Greci marries Bianchi, who is really the princess of the land and the two reign over Nefer while Forest returns to his country life and the film ends. It's a confusing story with too many characters and plot twists. But action is plentiful and fun to watch. In this dubbed English version Forest is called Goliath, though his character's name is "Maciste" in the Italian original.

p, Elio Scardamaglia; d, Michele Lupo; w, Roberto Gianviti, Francesco Scardamaglia, Lionello De Felice; ph, Mario Sbrenna (Techniscope, Technicol); m, Francesco De Masi; ed, Alberto Gallitti; art d, Pier Vittorio Marchi; makeup, Amato Garbini.

Historical Adventure (PR:A MPAA:NR)

GOLIATH AND THE VAMPIRES* (1964, Ital.) 91m Ambrosiana Cinematografica/AIP c (MACISTE CONTRO IL VAMPIRO; AKA: THE VAMPIRES)

Gordon Scott *(Goliath)*, Gianna Maria Canale *(Astra)*, Jacques Sernas *(Buono)*, Leonora Ruffo *(Julia)*, Annabella Incontrera *(Magda)*, Van Aikens, Rocco Vitolozzi, Mario Feliciani.

Scott plays another muscular hero whose sworn duty is to protect the weak and innocent from the likes of a superhuman vampire whose bite turns men into robots. Scott rescues a group of slave women from the evil fiend who then assumes the muscle man's identity. The stunning climax sees Scott in a bruising battle with himself! Who will win?

p, Paolo Moffa; d, Giacomo Gentilomo, Sergio Corbucci; w, Corbucci, Duccio Tessari; ph, Alvaro Mancori (TotalScope, Technicolor); m, Angelo Francesco Lavagnino; ed, Eraldo Da Roma; art d, Gianni Polidori.

Adventure/Horror (PR:C MPAA:NR)

GOLIATHON zero (1979, Hong Kong) 83m World Northal c (AKA: THE MIGHTY PEKING MAN)

Li Hsiu-hsien *(Chen Cheng-feng)*, Evelyne Kraft *(Ah Wei)*, Hsaiao Yao *(Huang Tsui-hua)*, Ku Feng *(Lu Tiern)*, Lin Wei-ty *(Chen Shi-yu)*, Usu Shao-shing *(Ah Lung)*, Chen Ping *(Lucy)*, Wu Wang-sheng *(Ah Pi)*.

Kraft, the star of LADY DRACULA, is a gorgeous jungle woman who befriends a giant ape. She falls in love with an Oriental explorer who takes her back to Hong Kong along with her simian buddy. The latter is exhibited in an arena but he won't stand for it and a clairvoyant is not needed to figure out what happens next. Every giant ape movie cliche is firmly intact in this KING KONG ripoff. The bad special effects and ridiculous dialog often bring this film to a new low in filmmaking.

p, Runme Shaw; d, Homer Gaugh; w, Li Chen; spec eff, Andrew Rayan.

Thriller/Adventure (PR:C MPAA:PG)

GONE ARE THE DAYS*** (1963) 100m Hammer bw (AKA: THE MAN FROM C.O.T.T.O.N., PURLIE VICTORIOUS)

Ruby Dee *(Lutiebelle)*, Ossie Davis *(Purlie Victorious)*, Sorrell Booke *(Capt. Cotchipee)*, Godfrey Cambridge *(Gitlow)*, Hilda Haynes *(Missy)*, Alan Alda *(Charlie Cotchipee)*, Beah Richards *(Idella)*, Charles Welch *(Sheriff)*, Ralph Roberts *(Deputy)*.

Davis, a self-ordained minister, returns to Cotchipee, Georgia, his native community, with his wife Dee. He has a plan to obtain a barn on the plantation owned by tyrant Booke. He intends to purchase the building and turn it into an integrated church, passing off Dee as a dead cousin who is entitled to $500 being held by cruel master Booke. The plan fails but Alda, Booke's liberal-thinking son, helps Davis accomplish his mission. The barn is converted and the first church meeting is a somber one, a burial ceremony for Booke who has died of a stroke at being outwitted by Davis. Based on the play "Purlie Victorious," there is a lot of sermonizing about civil rights, bigotry, and intolerance but posited in a farcical manner where the viewer might be in doubt as to whether to laugh or cry. Dee and Davis are fine but a bit too hortatory in spots. Alda is good as the educated white southerner with progressive views, and Booke is a round-bellied caricature of an antebellum, bullwhip toting Simon Legree. Hilarious is Cambridge as the boss black of the plantation who feigns absolute slavish devotion to Booke while mocking him at every instant, especially when singing "Old Black Joe." The direction by Webster is sharp and smart but the dialog gets a bit wordy, smacking of stage roots. This film would mark the film debut of Alda.

p&d, Nicholas Webster; w, Ossie Davis (based on his play "Purlie Victorious"); ph, Boris Kaufman; m, Henry Cowen, Milton Okun; ed, Ralph Rosenblum; prod d, Kim Swados; cos, Tauhma Seid; makeup, Herman Buchman.

Comedy/Drama (PR:A MPAA:NR)

GONE IN 60 SECONDS** (1974) 105m H.B. Halicki International c

H.B. Halicki, Marion Busia, Jerry Daugirda, James McIntyre, George Cole, Ronald Halicki, Markos Kotsikos, Parnelli Jones, Gary Bettenhausen, Jonathan E. Fricke, Hal McClain, J.C. Agajanian, Sr., J.C. Agajanian, Jr., Christopher J.C. Agajanian, Billy Englehart, Mayor Sak Yamamoto of Carson, California.

Assistance of local police and fire department officials in a half dozen communities in Southern California was needed to make this drawn-out film, purported to be an expose on car theft rings. The movie is saved, however, by a spectacular 40-minute police chase scene in which 93 cars are destroyed, 48 of them police vehicles.

p,d&w, H.B. Halicki; ph, John Vacek (Eastmancolor); m, Ronald Halicki, Philip Kachaturian; ed, Warner E. Leighton.

Crime Cas. (PR:C MPAA:PG)

GONE TO EARTH (SEE: WILD HEART, THE, 1950, Brit.)

GONE TO THE DOGS*½ (1939, Aus.) 82m Cinesound/British Empire Films bw

George Wallace, Lois Green, John Dobbie, John Fleeting, Alec Kellaway.

The title of this early Australian picture would perhaps be the best description of this non-stop barrage of old gags via the hand of comedian Wallace. Basically a vehicle to display Wallace's form of outdated humor; one can't help but let out a chuckle or two as he goes from one weird situation to another.

d, Ken G. Hall; w, George Wallace, Frank Harvey, Frank Coffey; ph, George Heath.

Comedy (PR:A MPAA:NR)

GONE WITH THE WIND***** (1939) 220m SELZ/MGM c

The Cast (in order of appearance): AT TARA—Fred Crane *(Brent Tarleton)*, George Reeves *(Stuart Tarleton)*, Vivien Leigh *(Scarlett O'Hara)*, Hattie McDaniel *(Mammy)*, Everett Brown *(Big Sam)*, Zack Williams *(Elijah)*, Thomas Mitchell *(Gerald O'Hara)*, Oscar Polk *(Pork)*, Barbara O'Neil *(Ellen O'Hara)*, Victor Jory *(Jonas Wilkerson)*, Evelyn Keyes *(Suellen O'Hara)*, Ann Rutherford *(Careen O'Hara)*, Butterfly McQueen *(Prissy)*, Tom Seidel *(Guest)*; AT TWELVE OAKS—Howard Hickman *(John Wilkes)*, Alicia Rhett *(India Wilkes)*, Leslie Howard *(Ashley Wilkes)*, Olivia de Havilland *(Melanie Hamilton)*, Rand Brooks *(Charles Hamilton)*, Carroll Nye *(Frank Kennedy)*, Marcella Martin *(Cathleen Calvert)*, Clark Gable *(Rhett Butler)*, James Bush *(Gentleman)*, Marjorie Reynolds *(Gossip)*, Ralph Brooks *(Gentleman)*, Philip Trent *(Gentleman, later bearded Confederate on steps at Tara)*; AT THE BAZAAR IN ATLANTA—Laura Hope Crews *(Aunt Pittypat Hamilton)*, Harry Davenport *(Dr. Meade)*, Leona Roberts *(Mrs. Caroline Meade)*, Jane Darwell *(Dolly Merriwether)*, Albert Morin *(Rene Picard)*, Mary Anderson *(Maybelle Merriwether)*, Terry Shero *(Fanny Elsing)*, William McClain *(Old Levi)*; OUTSIDE THE EXAMINER OFFICE—Eddie "Rochester" Anderson *(Uncle Peter)*, Jackie Moran *(Phil Meade)*, Tommy Kelly *(Boy)*; AT THE HOSPITAL—Cliff Edwards *(Reminiscent Soldier)*, Ona Munson *(Bell Watling)*, Ed Chandler *(Sergeant)*, George Hackathorne *(Wounded Soldier)*, Roscoe Ates *(Convalescent Soldier)*, John Arledge *(Dying Soldier)*, Eric Linden *(An Amputation Case)*, Guy Wilkerson *(Wounded Card Player)*; DURING THE EVACUATION—Tom Tyler *(Commanding Officer)*, Frank Faylen *(Soldier Aiding Dr. Meade)*, Junior Coghlan *(Exhausted Boy)*; DURING THE SEIGE—William Bakewell *(Mounted Officer)*, Lee Phelps *(Bartender)*; GEORGIA AFTER SHERMAN—Paul Hurst *(Yankee Deserter)*, Ernest Whitman *(Carpetbagger's Friend)*, William Stelling *(Returning Veteran)*, Louis Jean Heydt *(Hungry Soldier)*, Isabel Jewell *(Emmy Slattery)*, William Stack *(Minister)*; DURING RECONSTRUCTION—Robert Elliott *(Yankee Major)*, George Meeker, Wallis Clark *(His Poker-Playing Captains)*, Irving Bacon *(Corporal)*, Adrian Morris *(Carpetbagger Orator)*, J.M. Kerrigan *(Johnny Gallagher)*, Olin Howland *(Yankee Businessman)*, Yakima Canutt *(Renegade)*, Blue Washington *(His Companion)*, Ward Bond *(Yankee Captain Tom)*, Cammie King *(Bonnie Blue Butler)*, Mickey Kuhn *(Beau Wilkes)*, Lillian Kemble Cooper *(Bonnie's Nurse)*, Si Jenks *(Yankee on Street)*, Harry Strang *(Tom's Aide)*, Emerson Treacy, Trevor Bardette, Lester Dorr, John Wray.

A masterful movie milestone, GONE WITH THE WIND is the best-remembered and most publicized film in Hollywood's colorful history, the greatest single product the system ever offered up to generations of viewers. It is as powerful and moving today as it was when first released on December 15, 1939. Margaret Mitchell's super bestselling 1,037-page novel was brought to the screen in the most lavish treatment accorded a literary property up to that time by Selznick, who was determined to make this the pinnacle achievement of his career. He did. The film opens in magnificent color, portraying the verdant grounds of Tara, the great plantation owned by one-time Irish immigrant Mitchell. On the veranda of the great mansion sits Leigh, Mitchell's beautiful, headstrong teenage daughter, Scarlett O'Hara, the oldest of three girls, who is toying with two southern gentlemen, Crane and Reeves, twins and slavish suitors who beg her to consider selecting one of them to take her to the upcoming barbecue at another grand plantation, Twelve Oaks. She coquettishly plays the twins off one another, not really interested in either, but questioning them about the man she obsessively loves, Howard (Ashley Wilkes), the gentle, aesthetic eldest son of Hickman, owner of Twelve Oaks. Suddenly, Leigh spots a horse galloping across the meadow, its white-haired rider wildly racing the animal. She jumps up and, gathering her white hoop skirts about her, runs down the road to meet Mitchell. He rides up to her, dismounts, and she begins complaining about staying at Tara. Mitchell's Irish temperament rears as he firmly tells her that Tara is her priceless inheritance, that "land is the only thing worth living for, worth dying for—it's the only thing that lasts." But Leigh has only visions of Howard before her. Later, to entice his aristocratic eye, Leigh dons her best dress to attend the barbecue at his plantation, with the help of her protective Mammy, McDaniel, who laces her into a corset so tightly she can hardly breathe. At Twelve Oaks Leigh is the center of attention, by far the most beautiful southern belle in attendance, with scores of young beaus hovering about her like anxious bees about a hive. But she can only think of Howard and corners him alone in the library. There she tells him how deeply she loves him but is rudely jolted when he tells her that he is engaged to her cousin, de Havilland, the selfless Melanie Hamilton, and that he loves her. He admits he does love her in a brotherly way: "You've always had my heart—you cut your teeth on it." Leigh explodes at the rejection and slaps Howard's face; he leaves her alone in the library and she grabs an expensive vase and hurls it against the fireplace mantel. From a couch where he has been dozing rises Gable, the dashing Rhett Butler, adventurer and handsome ladies' man. He admonishes Leigh for her temperamental outburst and she lashes back that he is "no gentleman." He retorts: "And you are no lady." Their confrontation is a fiery one, but it is clear that Gable is drawn to the beautiful Leigh, who vows that she will somehow win Howard's heart away from de Havilland. Later, when all the females take a nap in the sultry afternoon, Leigh stands outside the library to overhear a heated debate between the men attending the party. The young southerners boast that if war breaks out between the North and South, the South will surely defeat the Yankees within months. The lone holdout of this proud contention is Gable, who stands defiantly in their midst and tells them that the war will be a prolonged struggle and that the North stands to win in the long run, that it is equipped with heavy industry to produce unlimited war supplies and a vast population from which to draw enormous armies. A galloping horseman arrives at Twelve Oaks a short time later to announce that Georgia has joined the Confederacy and that the Civil War has commenced. The southern men are uproariously joyful, anxiously looking forward to winning glory "on the field of honor." Howard, who watches the celebrating southerners with de Havilland at his side, is reserved about it all, secretly sharing Gable's viewpoint. Leigh, in a spiteful mood, has meanwhile busied herself with enticing Brooks (de Havilland's brother) away from his fiancee Rhett (India Wilkes, Ashley's sister) and the ebullient young man proposes marriage. Leigh accepts almost absent-mindedly. Ashley and the others leave to join their regiment and, following a quick marriage to Brooks, Leigh soon finds herself a young widow, Brooks having died of pneumonia following an attack of measles in training camp. To brighten her spirits, Leigh tells her family that she must leave Tara and go to Atlanta to visit Crews, her Aunt Pittypat. Mammy McDaniel correctly guesses Leigh's intentions, telling her that she really intends to stay with de Havilland so that she, Leigh, will be present when Howard returns on leave, and "you jus' waitin' there like a spider!" But, as usual, Leigh has her way and goes to Atlanta, attending a charity bazaar designed to raise money for the South's war effort. Wearing widow's weeds, Leigh again meets Gable, who bluntly tells her that she is longing to shed her mourning garb and enjoy life. When a collection is taken for wounded Confederates, the self-sacrificing de Havilland leads the women to donate their gold wedding rings so the metal can be melted down and used to purchase supplies. Leigh happily dumps Brooks' ring into the collection basket. Then Davenport conducts an auction whereby gentlemen must bid money to dance with the lady of their choice. Gable shocks the crowd by bidding a fortune to dance with Leigh. Davenport informs Gable that "she is in mourning," and cannot accept Gable's offer. With a sprightly move, Leigh leaves her booth and shouts, "Oh, yes I will!" While dancing, Gable tells Leigh that he is captivated by her and he knows she is attracted to him, that they are both made of the same stubborn, adventuresome cloth and that some day she will admit that she loves him. "That's something you'll never hear," she tells him. The war drags on and finally Howard returns home on leave, weary, disillusioned; his only desire is to spend the few days he has been granted with his gracious wife de Havilland. Yet Leigh intrudes upon them everywhere, trying to get Howard alone. Just before Howard returns to the front, Leigh has a moment alone with him, telling him that her whole heart belongs to him, that she still loves him and will always love him. He tells her he belongs to de Havilland but loves her in his own way. She begs that he tell her that he loves her so she can "live on it for the rest of my life." He does and goes back to the war which the South is now losing and losing badly. De Havilland is pregnant with Howard's child and soon the news comes that the Yankees under Sherman are advancing upon Atlanta. The population panics and Crews flees to the country, leaving Leigh and a simple-minded black servant, McQueen, to tend to the bedridden de Havilland. Leigh has promised Howard that she will take care of de Havilland and she does but begins to worry when the attending doctor, Davenport, tells her that he will be busy tending to the thousands of wounded soldiers pouring into Atlanta. She is assured by McQueen that she knows what to do when de Havilland gives birth. De Havilland goes into painful labor and Leigh races off to the railroad yards where the wounded are being treated to fetch Davenport. There, she is appalled at the awesome sight of thousands of horribly wounded Confederate soldiers strewn over the yards and she must pick her way through this prostrate horde, hands clutching her skirt hem, hundreds of voices begging for aid, water, food. She finds Davenport, his doctor's smock coated with blood, as he frantically attempts to administer to the endless wounded. Leigh begs him to return with her to deliver de Havilland's child. He stares at her with sleepless eyes and says he cannot go, that "men are dying here," but that she can handle it, that the birth will be a simple thing. Leigh returns home and summons McQueen, telling her to prepare for the birth. McQueen then whines hysterically that she "don't know nothin' about birthin' babies." In a rage, Leigh slaps McQueen, then catches hold of herself and goes to de Havilland's room where she delivers the child. De Havilland, barely conscious, tells Leigh how grateful she is, then passes out. Leigh steps outside of her aunt's home during the sultry evening to notice the streets deserted. Then a lone Confederate officer comes riding fast down the dirt street. She stops him and asks if the Yankees are coming. He tells her that they have already entered parts of the city and that there is only one road open for evacuation, urging her to flee. Frantic, Leigh sends McQueen to a bordello run by Munson, knowing Gable will be there. McQueen begs Gable to bring a horse and wagon for Leigh, de Havilland, and the baby so they can escape the Yankees. Some time later Gable shows up with a broken-down nag and a battered wagon into which he loads the women and child and then proceeds out of the city. The Confederates have torched the city, adopting a "scorched earth" policy, intending to leave nothing but cinders for the occupying Union troops, and Gable drives the wagon past towering fires as the granaries and warehouses blaze all about them. The horse becomes so terrified that Gable must cover its eyes and lead the animal through the inferno to safety. Once beyond the fire the wagon is attacked by thugs and looters but Gable manages to beat off the dregs of the city and join the last bedraggled column of exhausted Confederate troops, the rear guard leaving Atlanta which burns behind them, turning the whole sky amber. Leigh rides beside Gable as McQueen comforts de Havilland and the baby in the back of the wagon. The feisty southern belle calls the southern soldiers fools for having started a war they could not win and tells Gable that he should be proud that he never joined the army, that he was smart to stay a blockade runner for mercenary reasons. Gable stares glumly at the creeping column of shadow figures in tattered gray uniforms, boys passing out from wounds and fatigue while seasoned veterans step forward to lift them onto their shoulders. Says Gable: "I'm not so proud . . . Take a good look, my dear, an historic moment—you can tell your grandchildren how you watched the Old South disappear." Once at a safe point, Gable leaves Leigh, telling her that he's going to join the Confederates because he's "a sucker for lost causes once they're really lost." He embraces her, telling her that he loves her and that they belong together someday because they are both alike, "bad lots, the both of us, selfish," but realistic. He kisses her and she lambastes him as he goes off. Driving through desolated areas where battles have scorched the land, Leigh manages to bring de Havilland, her baby, and McQueen back to Tara which, unlike Twelve Oaks, still stands, although the lands have been ravaged. She finds her father driven half insane, her mother O'Neil dead from typhoid, her sisters ill and only McDaniel, Polk, and McQueen to help out. There is no food and little prospect of it. She is starving and, exhausted, goes to the fields where she digs up a root vegetable and tries to eat it, then vomits. She stands on a little hill in a rage and swears that she will "lie, cheat, steal, or kill, but I'll never be hungry again! As God is my witness!" Leigh goes about the hard business of trying to revive Tara by putting everybody to work, even making her spoiled younger sisters, Keyes and Rutherford, work by picking cotton in the fields. A Union scavenger shows up (Hurst) and, after taking her mother's jewelry, demands Leigh give him what she's hiding behind her skirt. As he approaches her menacingly, Leigh pulls forth the pistol Gable had given her before leaving her on the road to Tara. She aims it at Hurst and sends a bullet crashing into his head, killing him. De Havilland arrives, having pulled herself out of her sickbed, dragging her brother's sword. The two women drag the body to a field and bury it, saying nothing to no one. The weeks drag on and then one day Mitchell bursts through the front door to shout: "It's over, it's all over! Lee's surrendered!" De Havilland is delighted, saying "Ashley will be coming home now." Leigh is overjoyed at the prospect that the man she also loves will be returning. The tattered Confederate soldiers straggle past Tara, Leigh and de Havilland feeding and cleaning them. Then a lone soldier is seen approaching and de Havilland, her hand going to her throat in a deep emotional shock of recognition, sees it's Howard. She races down the road and into his arms. Leigh is about to run to him also but McDaniel holds her back, reminding her that "he's her husband, ain't he?" Later, carpetbagging Yankees levy $300 in taxes against Tara, a payment Leigh can't make. In desperation, she goes to Howard who is splitting rails in the field. He has no help to give her, only a bittersweet look backward to the soft summers of the antebellum years. "The South is dead, dead," she tells Howard, "the Yankees and the carpetbaggers have got it." She proposes that he go to Mexico with her, that she is "sick and tired" of everything. Howard refuses, saying that he must stay with de Havilland and the baby. "There's nothing to keep us here," she insists. "Nothing," Howard replies, "except honor." Crying, Leigh insists that he tell her he loves her. Howard says he does but he will take his wife and child and leave. "Then there's nothing left for me." Howard takes some earth and presses it into her hand. "Yes, there is," he tells her, "Tara." She agrees and goes back to preserving the one thing she loves more than anything else, the plantation. Jory, the sleazy one-time overseer of Tara, shows up with his wife, Jewell, and offers to buy the plantation so she can pay the taxes. Leigh throws a handful of dirt into Jory's face, saying: "That's all you'll ever get of Tara!" Jory and Jewell drive away yelling threats. Mitchell, aroused from his manic state, mounts his horse and gives pursuit, but is thrown and killed. Plagued with demands for taxes, Leigh shrewdly concludes that Gable will have the money. She has no clothes but improvises a beautiful gown by having McDaniel use the living room drapes of green velvet to shape the dress. She then leaves for Atlanta to see Gable, who is a prisoner of the Yankees. He is treated generously by Union officers with whom he plays losing poker. He is allowed to see Leigh, who sweeps into the makeshift prison, a stable. "Thank heavens, you're not in rags," Gable tells her. "I'm sick of seeing women in rags." She plays on his emotions, and he is about to promise her anything until he discovers her hands covered with callouses. Snarls Gable: "You've been working like a field hand. What do you really *want*?" She tells him she needs $300. He replies: "You're not worth $300; you'll never be anything but misery to any man." He tells her he can't put his hands on his money which is in an English bank. "So you see, my dear, you've abased yourself for nothing." In a rage, Leigh sweeps out of the jail, vowing never to speak to Gable again. In the carpetbagger-clogged streets she finds Nye, now a successful merchant, who is engaged to her sister, Keyes. Leigh quickly vamps the gullible Nye and steals him from Keyes by telling him that her sister is planning to marry another. Leigh and Nye are married a short time later and she obtains the tax money. Howard later tells her that he's planning to go to New York to work, but Leigh insists that he stay and help build a lumber empire in Atlanta. When he resists, she feigns a crying fit and de Havilland upbraids Howard, telling him that they owe Leigh everything, that their child would not have been born had it not been for Leigh. Howard gives in, saying "I can't fight you both." To build their mill, Leigh resorts to any means, including the use of convict labor. She ruthlessly does business with the carpetbaggers and arouses the dislike of the southern community. Gable meets her later and asks: "Do you never shrink from marrying men you don't love?" She ignores him and rides off to inspect her mill, driving her carriage alone through shanty town where several men waylay her, trying to take her carriage. Brown, who had been the foreman at Tara, comes to the rescue, smashing the attackers and driving Leigh to safety. That night Nye, Howard, Davenport, and others attend a "political" meeting, which is a vigilante gathering leading to a raid on shanty town and the carpetbaggers. Leigh, de Havilland, and other women anxiously await the return of their men at Howard's home. Gable shows up to ask where the men have gone, saying he's been told by some Yankee friends that they will be raiding the vigilante meeting. De Havilland tells Gable the location of the meeting site and he rushes off to warn them. Union troopers under Bond's command then arrive and surround the house after finding Howard not at home. Under guard, de Havilland begins reading *David Copperfield* to the nervous women. Her words are interrupted by raucous singing from outside and Gable shows up with Howard and Davenport, all appearing drunk. They stumble past Bond and his soldiers but Bond insists that Howard led a raid on shanty town and he intends to arrest him. Gable tells him that he and the other gentlemen have been celebrating at Munson's bordello, which embarrasses all the wives present and nonpluses Bond who apologizes and leaves. Howard, it is discovered, has been superficially wounded, and Leigh's concern for him is witnessed bitterly by Gable who asks her if she has any concern about her own husband. When she offhandedly asks where Nye is, Gable tells her that he was killed in the raid. Once again in mourning, Leigh takes to drinking alone in her rooms. Gable calls on her. Leigh, crying and hiccupping, demands to know what he wants. He wants her, he says. "I can't go through all my life waiting to catch you between husbands." He proposes and she calls him a fool, telling him that she will always love another. He bullies her into accepting his proposal of marriage. They sail to New Orleans on their honeymoon where they dine in exquisite restaurants and spend a fortune on fine clothes, but Leigh is restless, awakening with nightmares about Tara's destruction. Gable takes her back to Tara and, to please her, spends a fortune to restore the plantation, as well as buying a magnificent mansion in Atlanta. Leigh and Gable have a child but

Leigh is disturbed that motherhood will destroy her beauty (especially after trying to get into an old dress when McDaniel tells her "you ain't never again gonna be no eighteen-and-a-half inches" at the waist). She refuses to sleep with husband Gable, fearing to have more children. This alienates Gable who seeks solace with Munson. Leigh pays a surprise visit to her lumber mill where she meets Howard, whom she still loves. He is lost in the nostalgia for yesterday, speaking of "its golden warm security." She replies: "Don't look back, don't look back. It drags at your heart until there's nothing you can do but look back." She kisses him just as Roberts and Rhett enter to witness their embrace. Hearing about the tryst, Gable angrily orders Leigh to attend Howard's birthday party, forcing her to dress in a lurid gown and telling her to wear plenty of rouge so she will look the part of the vamp he believes her to be. She attends alone and is welcomed only by the ever-gracious de Havilland. Returning home, she finds Gable drunk and he pours her a drink. Then he tells her that he's sick of her persistent love for Howard, places his hands on either side of her head, and tells her that he intends to remove Howard from her mind by "squashing your head like a walnut!" Leigh brushes him away, then begins to leave. Gable sweeps her up and forcibly takes her to their bedroom. The next morning Leigh is happy after her night with Gable, but he is contrite and resentful over having to force himself upon her. They argue and Gable tells Leigh he's taking their daughter, King, to London. Once in England, however, the child has nightmares and asks to go home. Upon returning to Atlanta, Gable and Leigh have another explosive encounter and Leigh accidentally falls down the stairway, aborting the child she is carrying. Leigh survives but the strain between the pair is painful and, as before, both reach out for each other but at the wrong times. Then King is killed while riding her pony, which crushes both of them. Gable takes the child's body into the nursery and will not give it up until de Havilland persuades Gable to open his rooms so the child can be buried. Before leaving the mansion de Havilland collapses and later dies in childbirth, but not before Leigh promises that she will take care of Howard and her son. With the death of de Havilland, Leigh realizes that she does not love Howard, but it's been Gable all along. She rushes home and tells him she loves him. It's too late. Gable's long-suffering love for her is gone, he says and he leaves her. At the doorway of their resplendant mansion she stops him, saying: "But if you go what'll I do?" Gable replies: "Frankly, my dear, I don't give a damn!" Then he vanishes into a mist. Leigh is beside herself, consoling herself with thoughts about Tara, then saying: "Tara, home, I'll go home . . . there must be some way to bring him back . . . After all, tomorrow is another day." This splendid production ends on Leigh's optimistic note, a last line that would remain the most memorable in the history of American film. In fact, this line was originally author Mitchell's first title for her colorful novel, one that her publisher, Macmillan, rejected, saying it had published too many books with the word "tomorrow" in them. Everything about GONE WITH THE WIND is superlative, from the direction, mostly by Fleming but with contributary scenes from George Cukor, through the leading roles where Gable, Leigh, Howard, and de Havilland brilliantly shine and interplay in a marvelously balanced chemistry. All the supporting players, from Mitchell to McDaniel, the younger sisters Keyes and Rutherford, to the evil cameos by Jory and Hurst, are simply outstanding. The technical values remain unchallenged; Haller's cinematography is softly historic in keeping with the image of the Old South and Steiner's lyrical, poignant score emotionally fits every scene, sensitively caressing the images before the viewer; for this work alone Steiner joined the ranks of the best film composers on record. The man mostly responsible for "the greatest film ever made," according to one survey, was producer genius Selznick who tirelessly drove himself and all concerned with the production, striving ceaselessly for perfection and coming as close to it as humanly possible. Oddly enough, Selznick declined to buy the book rights to GONE WITH THE WIND after his representative Kay Brown read it when it was first published in 1936 and sent him the book and then a wire reading: "I beg, urge, coax, and plead with you to read this at once. I know that after you read the book you will drop everything and buy it." But Selznick hesitated. Paramount had produced a Civil War film, SO RED THE ROSE, at gigantic cost a year earlier and it had failed miserably at the box office, even under the able direction of King Vidor. He also didn't like the price tag Mitchell's agents were demanding, $50,000, then an enormous fee, the highest ever asked for book rights. Selznick's initial reaction to the novel was even more perplexing, shared by other studios and Hollywood powerhouses. The Motion Picture Producers Association had agreed not to bid on the novel so the price would not be driven up, and set an expensive precedent. Jack Warner at Warner Bros. nixed purchasing the book. Director Mervyn LeRoy said no, believing that Civil War dramas simply weren't box office. RKO's Pandro Berman said it was impossible because only Katharine Hepburn could play Scarlett O'Hara and she was "box office poison." Actress Constance Bennett thought about buying the rights early on for $25,000 but backed off, saying the price was too high. Louis B. Mayer of MGM played with buying the novel but his brilliant head of production, Irving Thalberg, who normally had excellent instincts in selecting box office blockbusters, rejected the idea, telling Mayer: "Forget it, Louis. No Civil War picture ever made a nickel." Selznick's mind was made up for him by John Hay "Jock" Whitney, Selznick International's chairman of the board. Whitney had read the novel and wired Selznick that if the producer didn't buy it for their firm, he would. Later Selznick would state: "This was all the encouragement I needed." Selznick found that he would have to struggle madly to bring the classic tale to the screen, fighting with the cast to appear in it. The millions who read the book universally envisioned Gable as Rhett Butler, although Errol Flynn, Gary Cooper, and Ronald Colman were seriously considered for the part. When asked her choice, author Mitchell jocularly said she thought Groucho Marx should play the hero, then seriously added (quoted from Margaret Mitchell's *Gone With the Wind Letters, 1936-1949*): "Clark Gable . . . has never been the choice for Rhett down here . . . In looks and in conduct Basil Rathbone has been the first choice in this section." It was later stated that Mitchell actually wrote the book with Gable in mind but that would have been impossible, since she began the novel in 1926, as Gable himself was to point out (quoted by one of his biographers, Lynn Tornabene in *Long Live the King*): "When the book was being written I was a four-dollar-a-day laborer in Oklahoma and not in anybody's mind for anything, much less the hero in a Civil War novel." Gable's friends, and particularly his future wife, Carole Lombard, nagged him to read the book. He later stated: "My reaction to Rhett was immediate and enthusiastic. 'What a part for Ronald Colman,' I said. I cannot say I did not want to play Rhett. I did. But he was too popular. Miss Mitchell had etched him into the minds of millions, each of whom knew exactly how Rhett would look and act. It would be impossible to satisfy them all." Selznick offered the role to Gable as the actor knew he would but he turned it down flat, telling the producer: "I don't want the part for money, marbles, or chalk," adding that he was tied up by his MGM contract anyway. But everywhere the king of Hollywood went he was hailed as GONE WITH THE WIND's future leading man. His friend Spencer Tracy knew Gable was avoiding the role and loved to tease him about it; every time Tracy passed Gable on the MGM lot he would shout out: "Hi ya, Rhett!" Nevertheless Selznick got what he wanted and he wanted Gable. He made a deal with MGM whereby that studio would put up half of the estimated $2.5 million in production expenses in return for distributing the film, getting half of the profits, and part of this momentous deal was that Selznick got Gable as a loan-out actor. Gable's MGM contract stipulated that the studio could sell his services to another studio with the star receiving a portion of the other studio's payment to MGM; in this case $100,000 went to the actor, which ameliorated his apprehensions considerably. But Gable went reluctantly and, though he performed his role superbly, was truculent throughout the production, refusing to take coaching lessons in how to affect a southern accent. When Leigh complained that their kissing scenes repelled her because of the strong odor produced by his dentures, Gable merely laughed and refused to do anything about it. It was Gable who really brought about the firing of George Cukor as director of the film. Early on Gable felt that Cukor, who was known as a "woman's director," was paying too much attention to Leigh, de Havilland, and other females in the cast, minimizing the male roles and the general thrust of the film. He got this message to Selznick, who, after viewing many new scenes, fired Cukor and hired Gable's friend, Fleming, an action director who had helmed RED DUST (1932), TEST PILOT (1938), and THE WIZARD OF OZ (1939). (Actually Gable was given a list of directors by Selznick to choose from before the producer dumped Cukor and these included Jack Conway, King Vidor, Robert Z. Leonard, and Fleming.) When Fleming read the script and viewed the footage Cukor had already shot, he announced that "I'm going to make this picture a melodrama." Leigh and de Havilland were deeply upset about the change, going to Selznick, carping and weeping before him in a three-hour marathon plea which availed them nothing, since Selznick kept his back turned to them constantly, refusing to talk. But the ladies never gave up on their man Cukor; even after he had been fired they each met secretly with him at his home and in remote restaurants where he coached them for up-coming scenes. Neither actress was aware the other was seeing Cukor. De Havilland felt guilty seeking this guidance in such a furtive way and told the director that it was probably unfair to Leigh. Cukor laughed and told her that Leigh was seeing him on the sly, too. It was never publicly stated but the shrewd Selznick may have been behind these clandestine directing sessions to soothe the ruffled feathers of his stars. Cukor would later state that many important scenes he had supervised remained intact in the released version of the movie: "I believe all the stuff I shot is still in the picture. As I remember, it included the opening scene on the steps of Tara, the bazaar, and the scene where Vivien Leigh came downstairs and slapped Butterfly McQueen." Howard was almost as reluctant to play Ashley Wilkes as Gable was hesitant to enact the Rhett Butler role. Selznick always had Howard in mind for the sensitive Ashley, but the British actor responded in 1938 to Selznick's offer with the remark: "I haven't the slightest intention of playing another weak, watery character such as Ashley Wilkes. I've played enough ineffectual characters already." Howard, one of the finest actors on screen during the 1930s, said that he was too old for the part (he was then 45) and his face was careworn with discernible wrinkles. Lamely, Selznick ordered a test of Melvyn Douglas (in which Lana Turner appeared as Scarlett) but the producer rejected him as being "too beefy" after seeing the test. Several others were suggested for the important role—Ray Milland, Richard Carlson, Jeffrey Lynn, Shepperd Strudwick, John Howard, Robert Young—but Selznick kept coming back to Howard. Selznick knew the actor longed to produce and direct films, and learned that Howard had just started his own production company and had purchased several literary works such as *They Shoot Horses, Don't They?* (a project so hampered by censorship that it would be three decades before it was turned into an absorbing but offbeat film). To get Howard to agree to play Ashley, Selznick offered him the position of associate producer for INTERMEZZO which Selznick was then about to put into production with Howard in the leading role opposite Ingrid Bergman. This post satisfied Howard's behind-the-cameras ambitions for the time being. Moreover, Howard was given a hefty contract for both films with handsome six figure payments. He is quoted as writing to his daughter (in *Scarlet, Rhett, and A Cast of Thousands* by Roland Flamini): "Money is the mission here and who am I to refuse it?" The part of Melanie Hamilton, the saintly lady dear to all hearts, was never in doubt with Selznick. He wanted de Havilland for that part all along as he stated in a letter dated November 18, 1938, to Selznick International vice president Daniel T. O'Shea (quoted from *Memo from David O. Selznick*, edited by Rudy Behlmer): "I would give anything if we had Olivia de Havilland under contract to us so that we could cast her as Melanie." The idea of having de Havilland for the part was credited to Joan Fontaine by de Havilland herself, who later stated that this notion began when Fontaine read for the part of Scarlett before Cukor. "When he asked her to read for the part of Melanie instead," commented de Havilland, "she declined and said, 'If it's a Melanie you are looking for, why don't you try my sister?' And he did." But de Havilland was under contract to shifty Jack Warner and the only way he would release her on loan-out to Selznick would be if Selznick took an entire Warner Bros. package deal. Warner proposed that Selznick use Warner Bros. stars Errol Flynn as Rhett and Bette Davis as Scarlett, and *then* he could have de Havilland. This plan was quashed almost immediately by Davis herself. Not that she didn't want the Scarlett O'Hara part; she coveted the role as much as any actress in America (which was every one of them who could walk and talk and was under age 90), but she hated Flynn to the marrow and refused to act with him under any circumstances, a posture rigidly assumed after her disastrous encounter with him in THE SISTERS (1938). De Havilland, who wanted the role of Melanie badly, enlisted the help of Jack Warner's wife, a friend, and Mrs. Warner convinced her mogul husband to loan out de Havilland to Selznick. Before this Warner decision was painfully extracted, Selznick had been fielding about wildly for any promising actress to fill the void, considering Geraldine Fitzgerald, Elizabeth Allen, Frances Dee (who also tested for Scarlett), Anne Shirley, Priscilla Lane, Andrea Leeds, and contract Paramount player Marsha Hunt. In fact, at one point, Selznick had decided on Hunt after viewing her second screen test for the Melanie role, embracing her and bombastically stating: "I've found my Melanie." He told her to keep his decision secret until he called her in a few days. One day later Marsha Hunt picked up a trade paper and read that de Havilland had been signed for the part. Maureen O'Sullivan was also disappointed since MGM mogul Louis B. Mayer had lobbied for her as Melanie. All of these machinations paled before the incredible nation-wide hunt Selznick conducted for two years in his search for the perfect woman to play the most coveted movie role in films, that of Scarlett O'Hara, someone with the varied capabilities of enacting the selfish, dynamic, stupid, brave, and often pathetic southern belle. The hunt was real but it also served to keep the nation breathlessly awaiting the discovery, a public relations stunt unequalled in film history, conducted by Selznick's flamboyant publicity and advertising director Russell Birdwell. He would spend about $100,000 in two years, sending 110 talent agents throughout the nation to hunt through campuses, drama schools, little theater groups, nightclubs, even burlesque houses. More than 2,000 females were seen in tests, interviews, and stills by Selznick who doggedly ploughed through phalanxes of female hopefuls. During the first year of hunting, thousands of letters from readers of the novel poured into Selznick, suggesting every actress who ever appeared before the cameras, including Marie Dressler and ZaSu Pitts! Norma Shearer, considered seriously by Selznick, however, was undone by her enormous fan mail which decidedly went *against* this regal MGM queen of sophisticated roles appearing as "a scheming little bitch," and Shearer bowed out to please her supporters. At least, that was the public story. It was the author herself, Mitchell, who wrote to Selznick, telling the producer that Shearer "has too much dignity and not enough fire for the part," and these remarks sealed Shearer's fate. Joan Crawford was next suggested and rejected as being "too hard looking." Early on there was a strong public surge for southern-born Miriam Hopkins who had scored heavily in BECKY SHARP, but her tests were unpromising. The same applied to Frances Dee, Loretta Young, Jean Harlow, Margaret Sullavan, Ann Sheridan, Carole Lombard, Claudette Colbert, Jean Arthur, Joan Bennett, and Irene Dunne. Director Cukor suggested Katharine Hepburn, but Selznick said no, she was not sexy enough. Then Cukor wired Selznick that "we've got our Scarlett," before bringing Tallulah Bankhead from San Francisco to Los Angeles for a much-publicized screen test. Selznick had received a telegram from the governor of Alabama urging him to star Bankhead, a native of that state and a true southern belle. But Bankhead's screen test went poorly; she was too theatrical and too demanding, insulting almost everyone in the studio before leaving the set to await approval. What she got was a scathing rejection from a woman who hated her and whose tongue dripped as much acid as her own, William Randolph Hearst's syndicated and all-powerful gossip-monger, Louella Parsons, who had written in her column: "Tallulah Bankhead breezed into town last night to make a test for Scarlett O'Hara in GONE WITH THE WIND. Her friend, George Cukor, is going to direct. Jock Whitney, another friend, is backing it, so I'm afraid she'll get the part. If she does, I personally, will go home and weep, because she is NOT Scarlett O'Hara in any language and if David Selznick gives her the part he will have to answer to every man, woman, and child in America." And that was too much correspondence for Selznick to handle, tireless though he was. Bankhead was sent packing, and the hunt went on and on. Other studios emptied their lots of starlets at Selznick's request, ordering young contract players to test for the role. Even tall, redheaded Lucille Ball was told to try out by her RKO superior. "Are you kidding?" she asked, but went anyway, got lost and soaked in a downpour while looking for the Selznick studio, and belted down a shot of brandy before going into Selznick's office. He wasn't there, so she dried off before the burning fireplace; he entered while she was still kneeling before the flames. He handed her a sheet with a few lines on it and Ball read it off quickly. Selznick thanked her and told her they'd let her know. Ball was out of the office before she realized that she had read for the role of Scarlett O'Hara on her knees! Ironically, she would occupy Selznick's very office years later as the head of her own studio, Desilu, after buying up the Selznick lot with the enormous profits from her long-running TV show, "I Love Lucy." Other starlets followed, including Mary Anderson (given the role of Maybelle Merriweather), Alicia Rhett (awarded the part of India Wilkes), Lana Turner and Edythe Marrener, later known as Susan Hayward. Hayward, then a New York model, had been spotted by Cukor in the pages of *The Saturday Evening Post* and he reportedly sent for her to test for the coveted role. She did test for the part but, Cukor said years later, debunking a Hollywood legend, she read a few of Scarlett's lines so he and Selznick could find a spot for her in the studio's ranks of novice actresses, never seriously considering her for the most important film lead in Hollywood. Hayward later echoed those feelings (quoted from *Portrait of a Survivor, Susan Hayward* by Beverly Linet): "I looked like a snub-nosed teenager. What did I know about southern belles?" Selznick told her to return to New York and get some acting experience in summer stock. "I like oranges," she replied tartly, "I'm staying." In fact, she cashed in her return ticket provided by Selznick and used the money to find a room before making the studio rounds. She had no chance of becoming Scarlett O'Hara but she was definitely in Hollywood to stay. Candidates came from all quarters and strata, including Atlanta socialite Catherine Campbell, who read for the part unsuccessfully. She was successful, however, in marrying William Randolph Hearst, Jr., heir to the giant newspaper empire, and became the mother of the hapless Patty Hearst, who later robbed banks on behalf of a crackpot revolutionary movement. All of a sudden a new name began to appear in the gossip columns as *the* frontrunner for the Scarlett O'Hara role, a fiery, attractive, sexy actress Selznick had put under a five-year contract and had already been given a role in Selznick's THE YOUNG IN HEART (1938). This was Paulette Goddard who was scheduled to star in DRAMATIC SCHOOL (1938) and THE WOMEN (1939). Selznick had been impressed with her test and announced to the world that she would "probably" get the part. But the flood of mail that met this announcement made Selznick jittery. Thousands of protests were made by those condemning the actress' association with the great Charlie Chaplin, who had recently been chastised by the press for his reported anti-American postures. Worse, it was generally understood that Goddard was "living in sin" with Chaplin, though she staunchly insisted that she had married the comedian secretly on board ship during a 1936 around-the-world cruise. Selznick, through his press hound Birdwell, put the problem directly to Goddard. She would get the part but only on one condition, a condition that later became legendary. She would have to produce a marriage license or other substantial proof that, indeed, verified her claim that she was legally married to Chaplin. Birdwell told her: "If you're announced in the part and there's a press conference they will certainly ask you when and where you were married." The hot-tempered Goddard yelled: "It's none of their goddamn business!" Then she stormed out of the office and out of the picture. The search went on, getting ridiculous. Would-be Scarletts chased Cukor around New York when he briefly visited there on a talent hunt, one young girl following him by train all the way to Washington, D.C., opening every door of the Pullman cars of the train on which he was reportedly riding to find him. She had to be physically ejected at the next stop. On another occasion, a large box stamped with big letters OPEN AT ONCE was delivered to Selznick's office. When it was pried open, a young girl dashed out, reciting Scarlett's lines from the book, racing into Selznick's inner office, and disrobing at the same time. Later, Selznick opened the door of his home on Christmas Eve, 1937, to see a huge object shaped like a book and decorated like the book jacket of *Gone With the Wind*. The cover swung open and a pretty girl wearing a mid-19th Century dress stepped out to tell the producer: "Merry Christmas, Mr. Selznick. I am your Scarlett O'Hara!" Perhaps the wildest rumor in late 1938 was that the search was a put-up job, that Selznick knew all along who would be starring in his epic film—it was Margaret Mitchell herself whom he had been secretly coaching in Atlanta for almost two years to prepare her for the role! Selznick's time schedule demanded that he begin shooting GONE WITH THE WIND and he took the plunge on the night of December 10, 1938, and he had no Scarlett O'Hara. The first scenes were magnificent, recording the burning of Atlanta where Selznick ordered more than 30 acres of the old Pathe backlot of tinderbox sets, mostly useless to Selznick International, put to the torch. As scores of firemen from three communities stood by, the flames shot upward to turn the sky over Culver City crimson. As the sky burned bright, all of Hollywood knew that Selznick had begun his Civil War epic. Black clouds rolled eastward through Beverly Hills where many a mogul saw the smoke drift through lawn parties and waft over pools. The inferno was incredible, leaping hundreds of feet skyward, firemen shooting out drifting blazes with their hoses when firebrands threatened to ignite Selznick buildings to be left intact. Every Technicolor camera in Hollywood, all seven of them, had been brought to the site of the fire to record the fiery scene from several angles. Many an old set burned that night, including the village and towering gates that had been used for the original KING KONG (1933). To capture this incredible holocaust on film cameraman Haller used up two of his precious Technicolor cameras to film the same scene in synchronization, supported by angled mirrors, the first attempt at a wide-screen process; although these shots were not employed in the general release of GWTW, they were salvaged and incorporated into a release 32 years later. Culver City Fire Chief Ernest Grey stood by nervously watching the leaping, crackling flames. He had expressed his fears to Selznick directly, telling the mogul that he had had nightmares about the fire ever since he had been informed about it, that he had seen in his fitful sleep the fire leap out of control and rage through the entire studio, then eat its way through the heart of his community, gutting all of Culver City and beyond. Every available man and truck on his force was present, stationed at specific positions by Lee Zavitz, Hollywood's top "fire and powder man," a technician, Selznick reminded Chief Grey, who was the best in the business. But to calm Grey's fears, Selznick added another 200 Selznick technical employees to stand by as a reserve firefighting force. Grey's nervousness was shared by the brilliant William Cameron Menzies who was in overall charge of production design for the film. It was he who had convinced Selznick not to show the burning of Atlanta in miniature models to save money, as producer Eddie Mannix suggested, but to give the world an authentic looking inferno, one that would convince audiences all over the world that Atlanta was really burning. Zavitz had made sure that there would be plenty of time to film the sequence. He had installed throughout the set area two elaborate sprinkler systems, one containing rock gas and distillate, the other water and extinguishing solution. By alternating each system, Zavitz managed to turn the fire on and off eight times, prolonging the blaze for hours as three different buckboards were pulled by three different horses carrying Rhett, Scarlett, Prissy, Melanie, and baby, three separate groups of actors, these doubles all seen at a distance, through various stages of the fire. All the while, supervising this spectacular scene, Selznick stood on a high tower overlooking the blaze, shouting orders most of his technicians could no longer hear. Upon the platform were studio dignitaries and friends invited to view the colossal scene. Arriving just as the last blaze simmered over the embers of the charred sets was Selznick's brother Myron, a flamboyant hard-drinking talent agent, the most powerful and successful in Hollywood. He had brought along two of his clients, British actor Laurence Olivier and his wife to be, Vivien Leigh. Leigh, who had appeared in significant British films such as FIRE OVER ENGLAND (1937) and A YANK AT OXFORD (1938), stepped forward as Myron Selznick, then drunk after partying, boomed to his brother: "Here, genius, I want you to meet Scarlett O'Hara!" To David Selznick at that moment, a vision of arresting and electric beauty stood before him, her exquisite face lit by the glow of the dying fires about them. He peered into her mesmerizing gray-green eyes, noted her long auburn hair falling out of a halo hat, and her lithe figure beneath a mink coat. As the 25-year-old Leigh stepped forward, Selznick smiled and nodded. He would later state in a magazine article: "I took one look and knew that she was right . . . At least, right as far as appearance went. At least right as far as my conception of how Scarlett O'Hara looked . . . I'll never recover from that first look." Neither did audiences around the world who would agree with Selznick for years to come. Ironically, Selznick had forgotten that only short weeks before he had approved of Leigh's screen test for the role but then she had been only another applicant in an endless list of possibles. Leigh did do her test for the role and both Cukor and Selznick were ecstatic about her. When she attended a Christmas Day party in 1938 at Cukor's place the director took her aside and unofficially told her, "Well, I guess we're stuck with you." The official announcement that Leigh would be Scarlett O'Hara was the culmination of the greatest publicity campaign Hollywood would ever know. More than 150,000 feet of black and white film and 13,000 feet of Technicolor film was used in the testing of hundreds of applicants while America ignored two years of earth-shaking events and clung to daily reports about who the lucky lady might be. Typical of the isolationist attitude of the U.S. during that time, the nation was utterly absorbed by this media-manipulated fantasy that became part of the country's social fabric, an indelible memory where one generation after another would hear the rustling of Mammy's red petticoat and Scarlett's green velvet dress. Leigh was put under contract and paid $30,000 for her role, with Selznick having to make a side deal with British film mogul Alexander Korda who had her under contract. Korda inexplicably told Leigh that the part was not right for her, but he benefitted greatly from that role after Selznick made Leigh a world-wide star. She was, of course, magnificent as the high-spirited Scarlett, shining particularly in those scenes directed by Cukor and working hard to please his action-director replacement Fleming. She and Gable were emotional opposites and their naturally competitive natures added greatly to their scenes. Gable had too easy an air about him for Leigh's liking and he had a habit of taking many coffee breaks and rest periods. The all-business Leigh would then yell at him: "What are you f------ about for?" According to Anne Edwards, author of *Vivien Leigh: A Biography*: "Gable admired his leading lady's vocabulary, as did Fleming, but otherwise he was a bit put off by her intellect and her dedication to work. She regarded Gable as lazy, not too bright, and an unresponsive performer (though she was always laudatory about his kindness and good manners to her)." She was also bothered by the obvious fact that the focus shifted to Gable when Cukor left the production and Fleming took over. Gable and Fleming were drinking pals and they, along with Ward Bond, would take breaks to run out to their motorcycles parked in the studio lot and race around the countryside before returning to do love scenes. Fleming, who had just finished directing THE WIZARD OF OZ, released the same year as GWTW, another proof of his towering genius, was a moody, rough-and-tumble helmsman who had little patience with temperamental female stars. Oddly, he had condemned the notion of directing the film when Selznick approached him, telling him that Cukor's perspective was too limiting and that he wanted Fleming to take over the production. "Don't be a damn fool, David," he reportedly told Selznick. "This picture is going to be one of the biggest white elephants of all time." Yet Fleming put his heart and soul into the film once he took the reins. He drove the cast and technicians and himself to exhaustion and is responsible for most of the spectacular scenes in the movie, particularly the awesome depot scene where thousands of Confederates are shown wounded and dying in the sun. Menzies and Fleming had designed this scene to encompass a long, overhead shot that would literally show thousands of extras as wounded soldiers lying about the tracks of the Atlanta depot. This was not a day in which helicopters were available and the highest boom equipment in Hollywood reached only 25 feet; the shot, as Menzies designed it, would require a crane that could reach 90 feet above the scene and Fleming was in a quandary as to how to get the camera to that height, especially the heavy Technicolor equipment of that day. Then an enormous crane was located some miles away, one that could be elevated to 125 feet, and this was quickly rented from a construction firm and brought to the Selznick lot where it was packed with camera equipment, Fleming, assistants and then sent precariously skyward. The great pull-back crane shot began with a closeup of Leigh entering the awful, bloody yard and, as she made her way across the expanse of tracks laden with countless wounded men, the camera retreated to show more and more and more of the battered army to suggest a whole nation crippled and lost, the apex of the shot including the torn but proud Confederate banner defiantly waving over the whole terrible scene while the heart-wrenching strains of "Swanee River" are heard as a plaintive lament, a dirge for the Old South. The scene itself was packed with thousands of extras, some alive, some stuffed. In a test shot, Menzies noticed that the top of the frame for the pull-back scene was barren of bodies. "We've got to put in more men, more men!" he chanted to his assistants. A frantic call went out to the Screen Actors Guild to send over every extra in Hollywood (that guild then representing extras), and a flood of men poured onto the lot, but still it wasn't enough; the Guild could only muster about 950 extras for the scene, and many of these were foreign-born Filipinos, Chinese, Japanese, men kept far in the distance so their Oriental features would not be discerned. Still Menzies and Fleming screamed for more men but there were no more to be had, so about 1,500 stuffed dummies were placed strategically through the decimated ranks of the wounded troopers with the live soldiers pulling strings attached to the arms and legs of the dummies to give them animation. The Screen Actors Guild later sued Selznick, demanding salaries for these dummies, but Selznick proved that the Guild could not provide the needed men in the short time originally allowed for the casting call and the suit was later dropped. Next to Selznick, who supervised each and every frame of GWTW, Fleming and the brilliant William Cameron Menzies were mostly responsible for the extraordinary product that became the world's most famous movie. Menzies, a one-time illustrator of children's books, provided detailed sketches of each character in the film, including costumes and sets, detailing their exits and entrances, with marginal notes next to each box containing a sketch suggesting how the scene should be lit and the specific camera set-up and angle, more than 2,500 sketches in all. The long hours and incredible demands on Fleming took a great toll as he relentlessly met every challenge the indefatigable Selznick made, along with his own improvements and drawing a performance from Gable that was unforgettable. Fleming began to sink into dark moods and would often explode over trivial problems. He talked to assistants about committing suicide by driving his car off a cliff in Malibu (two of the cast did later commit suicide, George Reeves, one of the Tarleton brothers and later Superman in the TV series; Ona Munson, enacting bordello madam Belle Watling, would die by her own hand in 1955). Leigh proved difficult with Fleming, seeming to resist his exhortations to "ham it up, will you?" He finally exploded directly in the actress' face, yelling: "Miss Leigh, you can take this royal script and shove it up your royal British ass!" Some days later the director was rushed to a hospital in an unconscious state, suffering from a complete nervous breakdown. Selznick, desperate, brought in journeyman director Sam Wood to finish some scenes and then stay on as Fleming's assistant when a much subdued Fleming returned to the production, the fire having gone out of his personality forever. He did manage to direct a great scene with Gable after that, one where Rhett was required to weep over Scarlett's miscarriage. Gable resisted the idea, saying that people would laugh at seeing Clark Gable cry. The night before the scene was to be shot Gable could not sleep, was seized with stomach cramps, and had to be nursed by wife Lombard. He arrived on the set jittery and red-eyed and then rendered a weeping scene that he himself could not believe when he later looked at the rushes, saying to Fleming: "Did I do that? What the hell happened?" Gable was so elated about that scene that he celebrated in the next scene (shot out of sequence) where Leigh/Scarlett has her first baby and Rhett toasts the occasion with the marvelous McDaniel (chosen for Mammy over Louise Beavers and Hattie Noel). They are supposed to be drinking sherry which was in reality tea but Gable had his special bottle of whiskey brought from his dressing room and he secretly substituted it for the tea. He poured a stiff drink for himself and McDaniel as the cameras rolled and when Mammy gulped down the fiery liquid her eyes popped and her great girth shook but she maintained her composure without registering surprise and even took another belt, the camera catching a smile on that wonderful face, and this is the print used in the film, sanctioned by the amused Fleming. The director, noted for his action films, surprisingly did not provide any real battle scenes, even though most think they remember scenes of clashing armies. The devastation of the war is graphically shown in crowds of wounded and dead on stilled battlefields but actual combat is only seen in some clever montages showing silhouettes of marching men over which explosions occur, these later being attributed to substitute director Wood. This and many another scene found its way into a film that was written piecemeal and, like CASABLANCA (1942), finalized on paper only a few days before the cameras recorded the image for posterity. From the beginning, the script for GWTW was treated with reverence by Selznick, who considered Mitchell's novel sacrosanct; actually he was frightened of altering any characters or scenes and incurring the wrath of the millions of moviegoers who had read the book. Selznick and Cukor actually wrote the first draft of the film, but when Fleming appeared in the production he looked over the manuscript and then announced to Selznick: "David, our f---- script is no f---- good!" A host of writers, good and great, labored over the enormous work, 1,037 pages in print, and these included Jo Swerling, John Van Druten, Michael Foster, Winston Miller, John Balderston, Charles MacArthur, Edwin Justus Mayer, Oliver H.P. Garrett. Even the great novelist F. Scott Fitzgerald was put to work on the script early on. Selznick had always admired Fitzgerald and the novelist had stayed in contact with the producer over the years, sending him autographed copies of each of his novels as they appeared. Fitzgerald had been writing in Hollywood to make ends meet since his popularity as a novelist had dropped off. He had been working at MGM on MADAME CURIE (not released until 1943) when the studio took him off that script and loaned him out to Selznick for some "polishing" of the GWTW script. In a letter to his daughter Scottie, Fitzgerald wrote (collected in *The Letters of F. Scott Fitzgerald* by Andrew Turnbull): "Day of rest! After a wild all-night working on *Gone With the Wind* and more to come tomorrow. I read it—I mean really read it—it is a good novel—not very original, in fact leaning heavily on *The Old Wives' Tale, Vanity Fair*, and all that has been written on the Civil War. There are no new characters, new techniques, new observations—none of the elements that make literature—especially no new examination into human emotions. But on the other hand it is interesting, surprisingly honest, consistent, and workmanlike throughout, and I felt no contempt for it but only a certain pity for those who considered it the supreme achievement of the human mind." To his editor, Max Perkins at Scribner's, Fitzgerald later wrote: "You know in that GONE WITH THE WIND job I was absolutely forbidden to use any words except those of Margaret Mitchell, that is, when new phrases had to be invented one had to thumb through as if it were Scripture and check out phrases of hers which would cover the situation!" Fitzgerald worked for about two weeks at $1,250 a week, polishing and straightening out scenes, but mostly he blue-penciled bad lines written by predecessors. In one scene Leigh wraps a sash around Howard, who says: "It looks like gold." Fitzgerald crossed that line out, astutely pointing out to Selznick that it was superfluous since "this is Technicolor." In another scene Howard tells Leigh about the destitute and starving Confederate armies, saying his men have "no arms . . . no food." Fitzgerald wrote in the margin on the manuscript a note to Selznick reading: "It's news that the South fought without arms?" He added poetic phrases to describe the terrible condition of the troops, putting into Howard's mouth the telling line: "When our shoes wear out—well, some of the men are barefoot now and the snow is deep in Virginia." He crossed out hundreds of lines written by other Hollywood contributors, labeling these over and over again on the manuscript, "trite, stagey," then went back to Mitchell's own dialog, considering it "infinitely more moving" than those lines hacked out earlier. In still another change, dialog flooded the scene where the jealous, possessive Leigh watches Howard and de Havilland go upstairs to the bedroom. Fitzgerald cut out all the dialog, merely retaining the longing look Leigh gives the couple as they retreat from her. "It seems to me stronger in silence," Fitzgerald told Selznick. It was. Fitzgerald was told by the producer: "Look, don't let Scarlett romp all over Rhett

Butler. George [Cukor, the woman's director favoring Leigh] will throw everything to her. You and I have got to watch out for Clark." But Cukor, even though he was an old friend of Fitzgerald's, was the author's undoing. In one all night session with the script where Donald Ogden Stewart was briefly brought in to help Fitzgerald, Cukor grabbed a manuscript page and read, just as Selznick entered the office: " 'Aunt Pitty bustles quaintly across the room' . . . How can I photograph that? How do you 'bustle quaintly across the room?' It may be funny when you read about it, but it won't look like anything at all." Fitzgerald, in a state of exhaustion and a bit disgusted at Cukor stood up, later telling girl friend Sheilah Graham (quoted in her book *The Real F. Scott Fitzgerald)*: "I gave him a demonstration with my rear end swinging from side to side, but it only made him laugh more." Three hours later the laughter stopped when Selznick fired Stewart on the spot. The next morning Fitzgerald received a telegram from Selznick which told him that he, too, had been fired from the script. The producer respected Fitzgerald too much to hurtfully fire him to his face. After working on WINTER CARNIVAL (1939) for Walter Wanger and getting drunk on the job and being fired, Fitzgerald's Hollywood career came to a sad end the year after GWTW was released; he died while reading a Princeton alumni magazine and eating a Hershey bar in Sheilah Graham's company. Other writers like Jo Swerling were used on the script and even the highest paid screenwriter of all time, Ben Hecht, was brought in at a flat fee of $15,000 to do some final polishing. Hecht, who had not read the book, worked for a solid week rewriting scenes from the by then basically Sidney Howard draft (Howard was killed while driving a tractor and his Academy Award was made posthumously). Hecht later outlined in *Child of the Century* the work schedule Selznick maintained on GWTW, one he was expected to duplicate: "Four Selznick secretaries who had not yet been to sleep that night staggered in with typewriters, paper, and a gross of pencils. Twenty-four hour work shifts were quite common under David's baton. David himself sometimes failed to go to bed for several nights in a row. He preferred to wait till he collapsed on his office couch. Medication was often necessary to revive him." Selznick kept Hecht and Fleming working this schedule for a week, with only four hours sleep allowed each night. Fleming had a blood vessel in one eye burst before he collapsed, and Selznick refused to allow anyone to have lunch, stating that food would slow the writing process. He supplied a curious menu to keep the threesome going, salted peanuts and bananas. Said Hecht: "On the fifth day Selznick toppled into a torpor while chewing a banana. The wear and tear on me was less, for I had been able to lie on the couch and half doze while the two darted about acting. Thus, on the seventh day, I had completed, unscathed, the first nine reels of the Civil War epic." Despite the army of writers who worked on GWTW, only Sidney Howard received credit for the screenplay. Upon completion, after 140 days, Leigh working 125 days, Gable, 71, the film was premiered on December 15, 1939 at the Grand Theater in Atlanta. Mitchell, Selznick, Leigh, Gable, and de Havilland were in attendance. Every one of the theater's 2,051 seats was sold out at $10 each. The crowds were enormous, over one million persons clogging Atlanta's streets to see the stars, and this would be the reaction throughout the world as millions flocked to see the film, made for $4,250,000, including advertising and promotion. (Had the film been made in 1959, estimates state, it would have cost $40 million to produce.) The film opened in London when England was already at war and continued throughout WW II, right through the blitz, running continuously until the war was over six years later. Although Leslie Howard was killed in 1943 when Nazi planes shot down the commercial plane in which he was flying, Selznick and the rest of the leading players never tired of talking about the film in interviews and neither did the rest of the world. GWTW found its way into popular songs like "The Lady Is a Tramp" by Richard Rodgers and Lorenz Hart, one verse stating that she won't play Scarlett in GONE WITH THE WIND. In a Bugs Bunny cartoon, the irascible rabbit dons a disguise and calls himself Crimson O'Hare-Oil. References to the film appeared in other films even before it was completed, such as THE AWFUL TRUTH (1937), KING OF GAMBLERS (1937), and HOLLYWOOD HOTEL (1938). Bob Hope, in LOUISIANA PURCHASE (1941), conducts a filibuster by reading what appears to be GWTW. Even Al Capp got into the act and also into some trouble. In one "Li'l Abner" strip the cartoonist parodied the film with names like Wreck Butler, Melancholy Hamilton, and Ashcan Wilkes. Author Mitchell, who usually ignored such awkward attempts to spoof her work, was this time angered enough to go to court and have Capp cease and desist. GWTW was everyone's favorite movie, or, at least, through the decades had been in a virtual tie with CASABLANCA, and over the years, until the 1970s and 1980s inflation dollars exploded box office receipts for THE GODFATHER (1972), STAR WARS (1977), and ROCKY (1976) out of sight, it was the all-time box office champ. More than $32 million flowed into MGM-Selznick coffers for GWTW by 1943. World receipts totaled $50 million by 1959 and this spiraled upward to $70 million by 1967 when it was released by MGM with the print expanded from 35mm to 70mm for widescreen viewing and stereophonic sound added. By 1983 the film had gleaned in U.S. rentals alone $76.7 million. On November 6-7, 1976, NBC aired the film on TV after paying $5 million for the one-shot privilege, receiving a 47.6 Neilsen rating, the highest ever recorded, which meant that 130 million persons watched GWTW on those two nights. Two years later CBS leased the classic film for 20 years, paying MGM a staggering $35 million to air the film 20 times. In 1978 producers Richard Zanuck and David Brown announced that they would create a film entitled: TARA: THE CONTINUATION OF GONE WITH THE WIND but after much huffing and puffing, the project died stillborn. Musical and dramatic versions of the book were produced in Japan for live theater and TV release and one of these condensed versions, in English, opened at London's Drury Lane Theater in 1972. The musical version that reached the U.S., called "Scarlett," saw a West Coast production in 1973 but it never opened on Broadway, nor did its LP albums achieve any kind of popularity as did the original Max Steiner score. The 40th anniversary celebration of GWTW's Hollywood premiere was held on December 28, 1979, in the Los Angeles County Museum of Art and some of the younger cast members appeared, including Rand Brooks, Evelyn Keyes (who had written a best-selling book about her life, cleverly entitled *Scarlett O'Hara's Younger Sister)*, and Ann Rutherford. Alone of the principal players still alive was Olivia de Havilland, who commented then: "Every time I see it, I find something fresh, some shade of meaning that I hadn't noticed before . . . How fortunate that so many gifted people found artistic immortality in GONE WITH THE WIND." Rutherford, who played Scarlett's youngest sister, was grateful to have had her small role in the film, commenting in The New York *Times* on December 31, 1979, "If nothing else, it assured me of an epitaph. It was a passport to the world. It was something for the ages. There is something quite timeless about the appeal of GONE WITH THE WIND." Even down to the smallest bit part, those who had appeared in GWTW for a few seconds would cling to that memory more than to other films where their roles were meatier. And there were legions of actors who never made it into the film but later talked endlessly about their also-ran possibilities. Lillian Gish and Cornelia Otis Skinner lost out to Barbara O'Neil for the role of Mrs. O'Hara. Billie Burke was rejected for the role of Aunt Pittypat, filled by the flighty Laura Hope Crews. Lionel Barrymore was inched out of the cantankerous character of Dr. Meade by Harry Davenport and even Tallulah Bankhead missed out *twice*, rejected as Scarlett, then, as if adding insult to injury, was offered the role of the slattern Belle Watling in a round-about way by Selznick. He asked a representative to approach the temperamental actress to see if she might be interested in the lesser role, adding, "and for God's sake, don't mention my name in connection with it." When Tallaluh was told that she wasn't wanted as Scarlett but could play a whore in GWTW her verbal rejection of the role was similar to the volcanic explosion of Krakatoa and largely unprintable. Cammie King, who played the tragic little Bonnie Blue Butler, only got that role because her older sister, originally selected for the part, outgrew the role because the film was so long in production and Cammie was the right age and size. Even the minor role of Careen O'Hara, Scarlett's youngest sister, hung in the balance. Selznick tried to get Judy Garland for the role which eventually went to Rutherford. Only Butterfly McQueen, as the vacuous Prissy, was undisputed in her role and, oddly enough, this was the one and only character author Mitchell later stated was based on a real person. There was never any question as to what would happen when the Academy met to honor its own in February 1940. GWTW swept the Oscars in almost all major categories, the lone exception being that of Gable, whose performance in GONE WITH THE WIND was one of his finest, an historic appearance that, most thought later, should have won for Best Actor, but he lost out to Robert Donat for GOODBYE, MR. CHIPS. In the other categories it was a rout, with nine major Oscars and two special Oscars going to those connected with what members of the American Film Institute later voted as "The Greatest Film Ever Made." These included: Best Picture; Victor Fleming, Best Director; Vivien Leigh for Best Actress; Hattie McDaniel, Best Supporting Actress (beating out de Havilland for her performance in GWTW, and notable in that McDaniel was the first black to win an Oscar); Sidney Howard, Best Screenplay (awarded posthumously, Howard having died in August, 1939); Ernest Haller, Ray Rennahan, Best Color Cinematography; Lyle Wheeler, Best Art Direction; Hal C. Kern and James Newcom, Best Film Editing; William Cameron Menzies, Special Oscar for outstanding achievement in the use of color for the enhancement of dramatic mood; Don Musgrave and Selznick International Pictures, Inc., for pioneering in the use of coordinated equipment; David O. Selznick, an Oscar for the Irving G. Thalberg Memorial Award. That night, and the legend of the film begun long before, belonged to one man, designated in a congratulatory quip by master of ceremonies Bob Hope: "Isn't it wonderful—this benefit for David O. Selznick!"

p, David O. Selznick; d, Victor Fleming (uncredited, George Cukor, Sam Wood, William Cameron Menzies, Sidney Franklin); w, Sidney Howard (uncredited, Jo Swerling, Charles MacArthur, Ben Hecht, John Lee Mahin, John Van Druten, Oliver H.P. Garrett, Winston Miller, John Balderston, Michael Foster, Edwin Justus Mayer, F. Scott Fitzgerald, Selznick) (based on the novel by Margaret Mitchell); ph, Ernest Haller, Lee Garmes (Technicolor); m, Max Steiner; ed, Hal C. Kern, James E. Newcom; md, Louis Forbes; prod d, Menzies; art d, Lyle Wheeler, Hobe Erwin; set d, Edward G. Boyle; cos, Walter Plunkett; spec eff, Jack Cosgrove, Lee Zavitz; ch, Frank Floyd, Eddie Prinz.

Drama/Historical Epic Cas. (PR:A MPAA:NR)

GONG SHOW MOVIE, THE zero (1980) 89m UNIV c

Chuck Barris *(Himself)*, Robin Altman *(Red)*, Mabel King *(Mabel)*, Lillie Shelton *(Mama)*, Jaye P. Morgan *(Herself)*, James B. Douglas *(Buddy Didio)*, Rip Taylor *(Maitre D')*, Brian O'Mullin, Jack Bernardi, Satisfaction, William Tregoe, Harvey Alpert, Herman Alpert, Harvey Lembeck, Ed Marinaro, Murrary Langston, Melvin Presar, Steve Garvey, Jamie Farr, Pat Cranshaw, Cathleen Cordell, Jim Winburn, Bella Bruck, Starr Hester, David Sheiner, Pat McCormick, Patty Andrews, Gary Mule Deer, Rosy Grier, Norman Blankenship, Darvy Traylor, Ronald Carr.

Idiotic movie version of an obnoxious television program, which exploited the "talents" of those whose unfortunate ambition it was to be in show business. The movie version is even worse because in it show host Chuck Barris makes a ridiculous attempt at serious drama by portraying himself as a sensitive TV host who is being driven to madness by all the craziness his show has unleashed. The result of this movie has the same, basic, inhuman appeal of a freak show. Sleazy.

p, Budd Granoff; d, Chuck Barris; w, Barris, Robert Downey; ph, Richard C. Glouner (CFI color); m, Milton De Lugg; ed, James Mitchell; art d, Robert K. Konoshita.

Comedy (PR:C MPAA:R)

GONKS GO BEAT*½ (1965, Brit.) 92m Titan/Anglo-Amalgamated c

Kenneth Connor *(Wilco Roger)*, Frank Thornton *(Mr. A&R)*, Barbara Brown *(Helen)*, Iain Gregory *(Steve)*, Terry Scott *(PM)*, Pamela Donald *(Tutor)*, Reginald Beckwith *(Professor)*, Jerry Desmonde *(Great Galaxian)*, The Long & The Short, The Nashville Teens, Lulu & The Lovers, The Troles, Ray Lewis & The Trekkers, The Vacqueros, The Graham Bond Organization, Elaine & Derek, Alan David.

Connor, a player in many of the CARRY ON pictures, stars in this rock 'n' roll comedy about an alien who comes to Britain to spread peace, love, and understanding. Only fans of obscure mod bands will enjoy this teen exploitation item.

p, Peter Newbrook, Robert Hartford-Davis; d, Hartford-Davis; w, Jimmy Watson.

Musical (PR:A MPAA:NR)

GOOD BAD GIRL, THE** (1931) 67m COL bw

Mae Clarke (Marcia), James Hall (Bob Henderson), Marie Prevost (Trixie), Robert Ellis (Tyler), Nance O'Neil (Mrs. Henderson), Edmund Breese (Mr. Henderson), James Donlan (Donovan), Paul Porcasi (Pagano), Paul Fix (Roach), Wheeler Oakman (Moreland), George Berliner (Spike).

Melodramatic gangster tale opens with Clarke telling her mobster boy friend Ellis that she's dumping him for true love. The other man is rich-boy Hall, who marries Clarke, knowing nothing of her sordid past. After the wedding and a baby, former lover Ellis busts out of prison and comes seeking revenge for her assumed betrayal of him. Her in-laws are outraged at her past life and pressure her into giving up the baby and never darkening the proverbial doorway again. Hall goes off to Paris to get a divorce and Clarke ends up making her living in a nightclub. Soon Ellis shows up to kill her, but before he gets the chance he is gunned down by a detective. Hall returns from Paris, having had a change of heart and takes Clarke and the baby back.

d, Roy William Neill; w, Jo Swerling (based on a story by Winifred Van Duzer); ph, Teddy Telzlaff; ed, Edward Curtiss.

Crime/Romance (PR:C MPAA:NR)

GOOD BEGINNING, THE* (1953, Brit.) 65m ABF-Pathe bw

John Fraser (Johnny Lipson), Eileen Moore (Kit Lipson), Peter Reynolds (Brian Watson), Lana Morris (Evie Watson), Humphrey Lestocq (Thorogood), Hugh Pryse (Braithwaite), Anne Stephens (Polly), Peter Jones (Furrier), Robert Raglan (Shelley), David Kossoff (Dealer), Victor Maddern, Roland Curram, Virginia Clay, Oliver Johnston, Lou Jacobi, Ronnie Harries, Barbara Cavan, Rosemary Whitfield, Eddie Vitch, Alma Cookson.

Fraser, to keep up with the Joneses (actually the Watsons—Reynolds and Morris) buys his wife, Moore, a fur coat but soon realizes he can't keep up the payments. He digs himself deeper and deeper in the credit hole until he is finally forced to sell the jacket. Although the evils of credit spending and the desperateness of debt are powerful subjects, THE GOOD BEGINNING fails to live up to its subject's potential.

p, Robert Hall; d, Gilbert Gunn; w, Hall, Gunn, Janet Green (based on a story by Green); ph, Lionel Banes.

Drama (PR:A MPAA:NR)

GOOD COMPANIONS** (1933, Brit.) 110m GAU/FOX bw

Jessie Matthews (Susie Dean), Edmund Gwenn (Jess Oakroyd), John Geilgud (Inigo Jolifant), Mary Glynne (Miss Trant), Percy Parsons (Morton Mitcham), A.W. Baskcomb (Jimmy Nunn), Dennis Hoey (Joe Brundit), Viola Compton (Mrs. Brundit), Richard Dolman (Jerry Jerningham), Margery Binner (Elsie), D.A. Clarke-Smith (Ridvers), Florence Gregson (Mrs. Oakroyd), Frank Pettingell (Sam Oglethorpe), Alex Fraser (Dr. MacFarlane), Finlay Currie (Monte Mortimer), Max Miller (Milbrau), Ivor Barnard (Eric Tipstead), Olive Sloane (Effie), Muriel Aked (Vicar's Wife), J. Fisher White (Vicar), Jack Hawkins (Albert), Cyril Smith (Leonard Oakroyd), Lawrence Hanray (Mr. Tarvin), Annie Esmond (Mrs. Tarvin), Ben Field (Mr. Droke), George Zucco (Fauntley), Arnold Riches (Hilary), Wally Patch (Driver), Barbara Gott (Big Annie), Margaret Yarde (Mrs. Mounder), Hugh E. Wright (Librarian), Pollie Emery (Miss Thong), Harold Meade, Mignon O'Doherty, Daphne Scorer, Henry Crocker, Gilbert Davis, John Clifford, George Manship, J.B. Spendlove, Tom Shale, Fred Piper, Jane Cornell, John Burch, Jimmy Bishop, Henry Adnes, Violet Lane, Robert Victor, Mai Bacon, Mike Johnson, Henry Ainley (Narrator).

Forgettable British musical comedy of the "Hey gang—let's put on a show!" variety. Plot sees a floundering concert party saved from financial ruin due to the combined efforts of a lonely spinster who invests some cash in the operation out of a sense of adventure, a schoolteacher who writes jazz tunes on the side, and a vastly talented chorus girl who rises to become the star of the show. Songs include, "Lucky For Me," "Three Wishes," and "I'll be Happy" (George Posford, Douglas Furber).

p, T.A. Welsh, George Pearson; d, Victor Saville; w, W.P. Lipscomp, Angus Macphail, Ian Dalrymple (based on the story and play by J.B. Priestley); ph, Bernard Knowles; m, George Posford.

Comedy/Musical (PR:A MPAA:NR)

GOOD COMPANIONS, THE**½ (1957, Brit.) 105m ABF/AB-Pathe c

Eric Portman (Jess Oakroyd), Celia Johnson (Miss Trant), Hugh Griffith (Morton Mitcham), Janette Scott (Susie Dean), John Fraser (Inigo Jolifant), Bobby Howes (Jimmy Nunn), Rachel Roberts (Elsie and Effie Longstaff), John Salew (Mr. Joe), Mona Washbourne (Mrs. Joe), Paddy Stone (Jerry Jerningham), Irving Davis (Partner), Shirley Ann Field, Margaret Simons, Kim Parker (The Three Graces), Beryl Kaye (Principal Dancer), Thora Hird (Mrs. Oakroyd), Beatrice Varley (Mrs. Jimmy Nunn), Alec McCowen (Albert), Jimmy Caroll (Leonard), Jeremy Burnham (Felton), Anna Turner (Daisy), Fabia Drake (Mrs. Tarvin), Brian Oulton (Fauntley), Lloyd Pearson (Mr. Tarvin), Ralph Truman (Memsford), Joyce Grenfell (Lady Parlitt), John Le Mesurier (Monte Mortimer), Agnes Bernelle (Ethel Georgia), Lloyd Lamble (Pitsnar), Nicholas Bruce (Chauffeur), Leslie Carol (Film Star), Larry Cross (TV Commentator), Campbell Cotts (The Critic), Shane Cordell (Critic's Secretary), Tom Gill (Critic's Friend), Marianne Stone, Max Butterfield (Honeymoon Couple), Marjorie Rhodes (Mrs. Mounder), Richard Leech (Ridvers), Barbara Archer (Barmaid), George Rose (Theater Owner), Ian Wilson (Mr. Droke), Melvyn Hayes

(Telegraph Boy), Claude Bonser (Pit Man), Owlen Brookes (Woman On Tram), Anthony Newley (Mulbrau), Richard Thorp (David), George Woodbridge (Ripe Gentleman).

Remake of the 1933 musical comedy about the efforts of a group of friends who try to save a dying concert party from financial ruin. Johnson plays the rich spinster willing to invest the money, Fraser the talented composer/schoolteacher, and Scott the singer who rises to become a big star. Not much improvement on the original.

p, Hamilton G. Inglis; d, J. Lee-Thompson; w, T.J. Morrison, J.L. Hodgson, John Whiting (based on a novel by J.B. Priestley); ph, Gilbert Taylor (CinemaScope, Technicolor); m, C. Alberto Rossi, Paddy Roberts, Geoffrey Parsons; m/l, Roberts, Parsons.

Musical (PR:A MPAA:NR)

GOOD DAME* (1934) 72m PAR bw

Sylvia Sydney (Lillie Taylor), Fredric March (Mace Townsley), Jack LaRue (Blush Brown), Noel Francis (Puff Warner), Russell Hopton ("Spats" Edwards), Bradley Page (Regan), Guy Usher (Fallon), Kathleen Burke (Zandra), Joseph J. Franz (Scanion), Miami Alverez (Cora), Walter Brennan (Elmer Spicer), John Marston (Judge Goddard), James Crane (Mr. Hill), William Farnum (Judge Flynn), Patricia Farley (Emily), Florence Dudley (Stella), Jill Bennett (Rose), Erin LaBissoniere (Mac), Ernest S. Adams (Night Clerk), Kenneth McDonald (Assistant to Hill), Cecil Weston (Mrs. Hill), James Burke (Cop), Jack Baxley (Barker For Dame Show), Edward Gargan (Man In Hotel Room).

Surprisingly bad March/Sidney vehicle which sees the duo as platonic friends working for a traveling carnival, he the overly tough card shark and she a member of the girlie show. The film opens as the pair are tossed off the carny train for different reasons. They decide to make a go of it together and check into a hotel with adjoining rooms. Sidney constantly frustrates March's attempts at romance and he eventually grows to respect her "good girl" stance and she his likable tough-guy image. They try to scrape up a living, but both are eventually arrested, March for robbery and Sidney on an old charge of a past indiscretion. March's chivalry surfaces when he makes an eloquent appeal to the judge on Sidney's behalf, and the judge is so moved that instead of sentencing them both, he marries them. March is terribly miscast as the overblown, fast-talking thug who punches half the characters in the face, and Sidney's talents are wasted sustaining the role of the overly sweet, patient gal who deep down loves her man.

d, Marion Gering; w, William K. Lipman, Vincent Lawrence, Frank Partos, Sam Hellman (based on a story by Lipman); ph, Leon Shamroy; ed, Jane Loring.

Drama (PR:A MPAA:NR)

GOOD DAY FOR A HANGING**½ (1958) 85m COL c

Fred MacMurray (Ben Cutler), Maggie Hayes (Ruth Granger), Robert Vaughn (The Kid), Joan Blackman (Laurie Cutler), James Drury (Paul Ridgely), Wendell Holmes (Tallant Joslin), Edmon Ryan (William Selby), Stacy Harris (Coley), Kathryn Card (Molly Cain), Emile Meyer (Marshall Hiram Cain), Bing Russell (George Fletcher), Russell Thorson (Landers), Denver Pyle (Moore), Phil Chambers (Avery), Howard McNear (Olson), Rusty Swope (Midge), Harry Lauter (Matt Fletcher), Greg Barton (Frank), Michael Garth (Pike), Ed Hinton, Paul Donovan (Citizens), William "Tiny" Baskin (Man), Tom London, William Fawcett (Farmers), Bob Bice (Griswald).

Vaughn is captured by a posse under the lead of MacMurray who wants to send "the Kid" to the gallows. Surprisingly the townsfolk sympathize with the good-looking, charismatic youngster and do what they can to prevent his execution, accusing MacMurray of being cold-blooded. No one, not even his daughter, believes MacMurray's evidence in this offbeat western which, unfortunately, is too slow-paced to hold much attention. MacMurray, as he so consistently does, delivers a moving portrayal as the frustrated marshal.

p, Charles H. Schneer; d, Nathan Juran; w, Daniel B. Ullman, Maurice Zimm (based on a story by John Reese); ph, Henry Freulich (Eastmancolor); ed, Jerome Thoms; art d, Robert Peterson.

Western (PR:A MPAA:NR)

GOOD DAY FOR FIGHTING (SEE: CUSTER OF THE WEST, 1967)

GOOD DIE YOUNG, THE**½ (1954, Brit.) 98m Remus/IF bw

Laurence Harvey (Miles "Rave" Ravenscourt), Gloria Grahame (Denise), Richard Basehart (Joe), Joan Collins (Mary), John Ireland (Eddie), Rene Ray (Angela), Stanley Baker (Mike), Margaret Leighton (Eve Ravenscourt), Robert Morley (Sir Francis Ravenscourt), Freda Jackson (Mrs. Freeman), James Kenney (David), Susan Shaw (Doris), Lee Patterson (Tod Maslin), Sandra Dorne (Girl), Leslie Dwyer (Stookey), Walter Hudd (Dr. Reed), Patricia McCarron (Carole), Thomas Gallagher (Burns), George Rose (Bunny), Alf Hinds (Milton), MacDonald Parke (Carruthers), Patsy Hagate, Marianne Stone, Sheila McCormack, Zena Barry, Hugh Moxey, Harold Siddons, John McRae, Alexander Davion, Stella Hamilton, Philip Ray, Joan Heal, Joe Bloom, Patricia Owens, Edward Judd.

A gripping crime tale of four characters thrown together who end up in a tensely violent situation when a planned heist goes afoul. Harvey, an aristocratic bum, organizes Basehart, a penniless war vet, Baker, a former boxer, and Ireland, a U.S. Army deserter, for a bank robbery. When problems occur, Harvey guns down both Ireland and Baker with the intention of dealing Basehart the same fate. Basehart, however, sends a fatal bullet into Harvey underneath a sign that carries the message "No Way Out." An atmospheric thriller which provides 98 minutes of entertainment.

p, Jack Clayton; d, Lewis Gilbert; w, Gilbert, Vernon Harris (based on a novel by Richard Macauley); ph, Jack Asher; ed, Ralph Kemplen; md, Georges Auric; art d, Bernard Robinson; cos, Rahvis.

Crime (PR:C MPAA:NR)

GOOD DISSONANCE LIKE A MAN, A*½** (1977) 60m bw

John Bottoms *(Charles E. Ives)*, Richard Ramos *(George E. Ives)*, Sandra Kingsbury *(Harmony Ives)*, Louis Zorich *(George W. Chadwick)*, Louis Turenne *(Franz Milke)*, Joshua Hamilton *(Young Charles)*, Bob McIlwain *(Horatio Parker)*.

The life of American avant-garde composer Charles E. Ives is re-created in a vivid film. Based on Ives' actual notebooks, the story traces him from early childhood, to Yale days, to the eventual composition of his works. The heavy influence of Ives' father, himself an experimental musician, is portrayed as well. Interspersed with the drama are reminiscences of Ives' friends and family, which give the film a better feeling of honesty. Characterizations are well drawn by the ensemble, under strong direction. A fine example of independent filmmaking at its best.

p&d, Theodore W. Timreck (based on Charles Ives' memos, and reminiscences and taped interviews with relatives and friends); ph, Peter Stein.

Drama **(PR:C MPAA:NR)**

GOOD EARTH, THE***** (1937) 138m MGM bw/sepia

Paul Muni *(Wang Lung)*, Luise Rainer *(O-Lan)*, Walter Connolly *(Uncle)*, Tilly Losch *(Lotus)*, Charley Grapewin *(Old Father)*, Jessie Ralph *(Cuckoo)*, Soo Yong *(Aunt)*, Keye Luke *(Elder Son)*, Roland Lui *(Younger Son)*, Chingwah Lee *(Ching)*, Harold Huber *(Cousin)*, Olaf Hytten *(Roland Liu, Grain Merchant)*, William Law *(Gateman)*, Mary Wong *(Little Bride)*, Lotus Lui *(The Voice of Lotus)*, Soo Young *(Old Mistress Aunt)*, Charles Middleton *(Banker)*, Suzanna Kim *(Little Fool)*, Caroline Chew *(Dancer)*, Chester Gan *(Singer in Teahouse)*, Miki Morita *(House Guest of Wang)*, Philip Ahn *(Captain)*, Sammee Tong *(Chinaman)*, Richard Loo *(Farmer/Rabble Rouser/Peach Seller)*.

"Who wants to see a picture about Chinese farmers?" asked MGM chief Louis B. Mayer of his production head Irving Thalberg, who proposed what was to become a classic man-and-wife saga and their struggle to exist and thrive off the mean land of China. Muni, in a powerful role—another marvelous rendering of offbeat characterization—is a simple rice farmer who weds Rainer, a kitchen slave; this is a marriage of convenience where Muni does not set eyes on his bride until the last minute. Through incredible labor, Muni and Rainer make their little farm into a success until Muni can buy many more rice fields, prospering. They produce three children and all seems promising until severe draught turns the land into an unyielding crust. When famine sets in, the family begins to starve, forcing Rainer to feed her children cooked earth. Connolly, Muni's uncle, begs the farmer to sell off his land but Muni is adamant. They will all starve first, and they almost do before Muni moves his family to the southern provinces, temporarily abandoning his land. Starvation and poverty are rife here, too, and the family continues to suffer as he vainly looks for work. Suddenly the city streets are filled with revolutionaries and swarms of people are swept along with the rioting tide, including Rainer who has been out scavenging for food. She is carried with the throngs right into a royal palace that is being looted and then stomped unconscious. She awakens to find a bag of jewels dropped by one of the looters. Troops move in to stop the wholesale sacking. Rainer, hiding the priceless gems, is herded into a large group awaiting execution for looting, but manages to escape. Injured, she makes her way back to Muni and her children to give him the jewels. The family travels back north to reclaim its land and Muni purchases a marvelous mansion, becoming the wealthiest landowner in the province. Riches corrupt the simple farmer, who begins to indulge in minor vices; he meets sensuous Losch, a tea dancer, who seduces him and becomes his mistress. Muni goes on ignoring his long-suffering wife Rainer and then learns that his youngest son Lui has also been seeing Losch and mercilessly beats him. Calamity occurs when the farming area is invaded by swarms of locusts that begin to eat up the vital crops. Muni's oldest son Luke, who has been studying agriculture, shows Muni and the others how to combat the destructive insects and the locusts are beaten off. Tranquility is restored and one of Muni's sons is married. Rainer, who has been ill for some time, dies just after the ceremonies and it is only at this point that Muni comes to realize that it was she who had kept the family together and was responsible for his success. He stands weeping next to a peach tree Rainer planted on the night of their wedding and cries out her name, saying: "O-Lan, you are the earth!" This superlative production was three years in the making and was Thalberg's last production, one he personally oversaw. He had never taken a film credit and died before THE GOOD EARTH was completed; in memory of this young, driving force, who was responsible for a string of majestic films (GRAND HOTEL, 1932, DINNER AT EIGHT, 1933, MUTINY ON THE BOUNTY, 1935, ROMEO AND JULIET, 1936), Mayer had the following credit inserted into the credits of THE GOOD EARTH: "To the memory of Irving Grant Thalberg we dedicate this picture, his last great achievement." Rainer is positively captivating as the self-sacrificing wife and deservedly won an Oscar for best actress, beating out Greta Garbo in CAMILLE, and accomplishing the seemingly impossible in winning back-to-back Oscars, having won for Best Actress the previous year for THE GREAT ZIEGFIELD. (Only Katharine Hepburn was to equal this feat and, going one better, winning her first Oscar for Best Actress in 1933 for MORNING GLORY then back-to-back Oscars in 1967 and 1968 for her performances in GUESS WHO'S COMING TO DINNER and THE LION IN WINTER.) To prepare themselves for their Oriental roles, Muni and Rainer went to the Chinese settlements in San Francisco to study customs, postures, accents, and social conduct. MGM spent a fortune on this film for those days, $2,816,000, its most expensive film since 1925's BEN HUR. The film paid off big, returning more than $3,500,000 for its initial release, due mostly to its two brilliant stars whom MGM hyped as being Oscar winners, Muni also having gleaned an Oscar the year earlier for his electrifying protrait in THE STORY OF LOUIS PASTEUR. His role is flawlessly rendered as the strong, stoic farmer who learns too late the magnificent qualities of his loving wife. (Muni later complained that he was miscast and rejected his own performance.) The Pearl Buck novel, which won her the Pulitzer Prize, marched through the bestseller lists for almost two years following its 1931 publication. The story was dramatized and brought to Broadway by the Theater Guild in 1933 and starred Claude Rains and Nazimova. Thalberg saw the play and decided to make it into an epic. He immediately sent George Hill, a talented but alcoholic director, to China to get background footage and gather important props. His wife, Francis Marion, went along to do research since she was originally slated to write the screenplay. Hill and Marion returned with more than two million feet of background footage, some of which was used in the released film. This second unit also brought back eighteen tons of properties, dismantled farmhouses with thatched roofs, water buffalo and countless antiquated farming implements; the only Western prop used in the film was an alarm clock. MGM converted more than 500 acres of land in the San Fernando Valley to a Chinese province and crowded it with 1,500 extras during the mob scenes. A great deal of money was spent on having agricultural specialists plant Chinese crops of leek, bamboo, and cabbage, along with developing a special irrigation system for the stretching rice paddies. Director Hill was then preparing his opening shots but took to the bottle and, in fact, was so drunk during a story conference at the studio that he almost collapsed. Embarrassed before Thalberg, his wife and others, Hill managed to return home where he put a bullet through his head. Victor Fleming was brought in to direct and Marion, too grief-stricken to write the script, was replaced by Jennings, Schlesinger, and West. Fleming cast some sixty orientals in speaking roles, but the leads were played by occidentals, including Muni, Rainer, Connolly, Grapewin, and Ralph. When one critic personally pointed out to Thalberg that no oriental actor received a leading role, the producer smiled and said: "I'm in the business of creating illusions." Fleming grew ill and had to be hospitalized; the same situation occured with Fleming when he was at work on GONE WITH THE WIND three years later. Thalberg, with costs mounting, brought in Sidney Franklin to replace Fleming. Franklin was cautioned at the outset by Thalberg that he must strive for a major achievement in THE GOOD EARTH, quoting the film philosophy expressed by playwright-screenwriter Laurence Stallings (and later adopted by director Howard Hawks, this appearing in Samuel Marx's *Mayer and Thalberg*): "Every film of major importance must have one great sequence from the standpoint of the camera, in acting and story, in light and shadow, in sound and fury." There were *several* great sequences in THE GOOD EARTH, not the least of which were the terrifying mob scenes when the palace is ransacked. These were really directed by General Ting-Hsiu Tu, who had been loaned to MGM by the Chinese Nationalists of the Nanking government to preserve accuracy of Chinese settings and history. The most astounding scene in this film, or many another, was the invasion of the locusts. Hundreds of extras, Muni, Rainer and family in the lead, took to the jeopardized fields to combat the pests which blackened the sky, frantically digging fire lanes, disorienting the insects by banging gongs, then beating them with shovels, their feet, their hands. Every known photographic gimmick up to that time was employed in the locust invasion scene. The Chinese location footage was used as a backdrop; closeups of the locusts on a miniature soundstage were intercut, along with inserting special effects paintings on the film to produce a startling montage of the menace. Among the horde of extras used in this scene was a very young James Stewart. While cameras rolled, he was suddenly yanked from the rows of extras as awkwardly standing out; he was simply too tall for the oriental crowd scene at 6'4" and was fired. Among the supporting players, German dancer Losch cut a sinuous, sensuous figure as the tearoom dancer captivating Muni's gaze. A discovery of Max Reinhardt, Losch would perform almost lascivious dances in THE GARDEN OF ALLAH (1936), DUEL IN THE SUN (1946), and THE GOOD EARTH; in this film one spectator describes her as "a dream person," snaking into the scene, her fingers bedecked with jewels, her head adorned with a gem-encrusted tiara, her lithe body wrapped in white brocade. Losch lived a mysterious Hollywood life and vanished completely from the movie scene after marrying a nobleman. Of all the cast members none equalled the meteoric rise and instant collapse as a star as did Rainer. Another discovery of Reinhardt's, Rainer was brought from Europe in 1934 by MGM and electrified the world by her startling performance as Anna Held in THE GREAT ZIEGFELD (1936), her second film, which won for her the first of her two Oscars. A nonconformist, Rainer walked about Hollywood in slacks, her face barren of makeup, her hair in disarray at the height of 1930s glamor when such conduct was thought by studio moguls to be eccentric if not sinful. The 5'3" dark-haired beauty further infuriated studio bosses by telling all who cared to listen that she was a stage actress and that she disliked the movies. She was echoing the anti-Hollywood sentiments of her then boy friend—later her husband—playwright Clifford Odets and so contemptuous of films was Rainer that she told Academy officials that she refused to attend the ceremonies on March 10, 1938 at the Biltmore Bowl unless they assured her she would win a statuette. When told they could not make such a promise, Rainer stayed home. MGM chief Mayer exploded when hearing that Rainer was ignoring the ceremonies and, on that night, he sent several studio representatives to her home where they found the actress in her pajamas, her hair in curlers. She was ordered to hurriedly dress in an evening gown and was whisked to the banquet where, two hours later, she was given an Oscar which she accepted as her uncombed hair fell in front of her lovely face. Rainer continued to be a thorn in the ample side of Louis B. Mayer and he made sure that her films thereafter were, at best, mediocre, except for THE GREAT WALTZ in 1938. A year later, after marrying Odets, the actress told the mogul that she intended to return to Europe, explaining that "my sources have dried up." Snorted Mayer: "Why do you need sources? You've got a director, haven't you?" Rainer had never made big money in Hollywood; MGM had paid her a mere pittance for her work in THE GOOD EARTH, $250 a week, the lowest scale for any nameless contract player. Not that she hadn't had opportunities to increase her salary; Rainer, however, was disinclined to accept the method of negotiation offered by Mayer. The mogul once said to her: "Why won't you sit on my lap when we're discussing your contract the way the other girls do?" The final meeting between fiery actress and totemic studio chief was explosive. Rainer told Mayer to throw her contract into the garbage can. "We made you and we're going to kill your career!" roared Mayer. Said Rainer softly: "God made me." The actress' incredible performance in THE GOOD EARTH, however, one where she never laughed, seldom spoke, and expressed everything in wide-eyed silence, pierced the heart of Pearl Buck's phlegmatic heroine and remains an artful classic. It was first thought to have the film's musical score composed by the distinguished Arnold Schoenberg. Thalberg sent a representative to discuss the proposition with the composer. "Think of it!" extolled the MGM official to Schoenberg. "A terrific storm is going on. The wheatfield is swaying in the wind and suddenly the earth begins to tremble! In the midst of an earthquake, O-Lan gives birth to a baby! What an opportunity for music!" Schoenberg shrugged and replied: "With all that going on, why do you need music?" When the composer finally met with Thalberg he demanded $50,000 for a musical score. Thalberg was happy to pay it. Then Schoenberg demanded "an absolute guarantee that not a single note of my score will be altered." That Thalberg would never approve. Schoenberg was sent back to his scriptorium sans contract and Herbert Stothart took over the score assignment.

p, Irving G. Thalberg, Albert Lewin; d, Sidney Franklin; w, Talbot Jennings, Tess Schlesinger, Claudine West [Frances Marion uncredited] (based on the novel by Pearl S. Buck); ph, Karl Freund, montages, Slavko Vorkapich; m, Herbert Stothart; ed, Basil Wrangel; art d, Cedric Gibbons, Harry Oliver, Arnold Gillespie; set d, Edwin B. Willis; cos, Dolly Tree.

Drama **Cas.** **(PR:A MPAA:NR)**

GOOD FAIRY, THE*½** (1935) 98m UNIV bw

Margaret Sullavan *(Luisa "Lu" Ginglebusher)*, Herbert Marshall *(Dr. Max Sporum)*, Frank Morgan *(Konrad)*, Reginald Owen *(Detlaff)*, Alan Hale *(Schlapkohl)*, Beulah Bondi *(Dr. Schultz)*, Cesar Romero *(Joe)*, Al Bridges *(Doorman)*, George Davis *(Chauffeur)*, Hugh O'Connell *(Gas Collector)*, June Clayworth *(Actress)*, Eric Blore.

Charming romantic comedy starring Sullavan as a young woman just released from an asylum, whose innocence attracts the amorous advances of millionaire Morgan. To escape she tells him she's married, and when she is forced to produce a husband, she grabs the first name in the phone book. The unwitting victim is a lawyer, Marshall, who suddenly finds Morgan offering him a contract that will make him rich (Morgan hopes to impress Sullavan with his generosity and then woo her away from her "husband"). Meanwhile Marshall and Sullavan inevitably fall in love. When the truth comes out, Morgan softens and allows them to marry, yet continues as their benefactor. Morgan steals the show as the millionaire and the rest of the cast performs with vigor. Remade in 1947 with Deanna Durbin as I'LL BE YOURS.

p, Henry Hennigson; d, William Wyler; w, Preston Sturges (based on the play by Ferenc Molnar); ph, Norbert Bodine, ed, Daniel Mandell.

Comedy **(PR:A MPAA:NR)**

GOOD FELLOWS, THE** (1943) 69m PAR bw

Cecil Kellaway *(Jim Hilton)*, Mabel Paige *(Miss Kent)*, Helen Walker *(Ethel Hilton)*, James Brown *(Tom Drayton)*, Diana Hale *(Spratt)*, Kathleen Lockhart *(Mary Hilton)*, Douglas Wood *(John Drayton)*, Norma Varden *(Mrs. Drayton)*, Olin Howlin *(Reynolds)*, Tom Fadden *(Harvey)*, William B. Davidson *(Blake)*, Rod Cameron, Wade Boteler, Chester Clute, Irving Bacon, Norman Ainsley, Henry Edgar Dearing, Maurice Cass, Edward Earle, Robert Winkler, Kerman Cripps, Oscar Smith.

Dim comedy starring Kellaway as the head of a small town fraternal lodge who alienates his family emotionally and financially due to his devotion to the men's club. Trite conclusion sees Kellaway miraculously hitting the jackpot and solving all his problems.

p, Walter MacEwen; d, Jo Graham; w, Hugh Wedlock, Jr., Howard Snyder (based on the play by George S. Kaufman, Herman Mankiewicz); ph, Theodor Sparkuhl; ed, Arthur Schmidt, art d, Hans Dreier, Haldane Douglas.

Comedy **(PR:A MPAA:NR)**

GOOD GIRLS GO TO PARIS½** (1939) 75m COL bw

Melvyn Douglas *(Ronald Brooke)*, Joan Blondell *(Jenny Swanson)*, Walter Connolly *(Olaf Brand)*, Alan Curtis *(Tom Brand)*, Joan Perry *(Sylvia Brand)*, Isabel Jeans *(Caroline Brand)*, Stanley Brown *(Ted Dayton)*, Alexander D'Arcy *(Paul Kingston)*, Henry Hunter *(Dennis)*, Clarence Kolb *(Dayton, Sr.)*, Howard Hickman *(Jeffers)*, Barlowe Borland *(Chambers)*, Helen Jermone Eddy *(Tearoom Hostess)*, Donald Dillaway, Forbes Murray, Johnny Tyrrell, James Craig *(Men)*, Dave Willock, Richard Fiske, Robert Sterling, Dick Winslow, Jack Chapin, Robert Cherry, Tommy Seidel *(Students)*, Dorothy Comingore, Beatrice Blinn *(Girls)*, Ann Doran, Adrian Booth *(Bridesmaids)*, Don Beddoe *(Burton)*, Wright Kramer *(Prof. Guthrie)*, George Guhl *(Constable)*, Sam McDaniel *(Porter)*, George Douglas *(Baxter)*, Leon Belasco *(Violinist)*, George Lloyd *(Schultz)*, William Newell *(Waiter)*, Dora Clement, Jean Acker, Lillian Teneycke *(Women)*, Harry Bailey *(Wedding Guest)*, Jane K. Loofbourrow, Catherine Courtney *(Old Maids)*, Dorothy Fowler *(Maid)*, Ray Turner *(Red Cap)*, Leigh DeLacey *(Cook)*, Bill Irving *(Chef)*, Eleanor Counts, Beatrice Curtis *(Waitresses)*, Mary Field *(Ada)*, John Maurice Sullivan *(Minister)*, Jack Daley *(Train Conductor)*, Walter Sande, Walter Merrill *(Ticket Agents)*.

Amiable and frothy farce produced by Perlberg before he joined with Director George Seaton to become a major force in films. Douglas is a British professor in the U.S. on an exchange program. Blondell is a waitress at the campus restaurant. Douglas is engaged to someone else but through a series of totally implausible events, he and Blondell wind up in each others arms. To examine the plot line would be to destroy the whole fun of the movie, almost like having to explain why a joke about Rene Descartes is funny to someone who doesn't know who Descartes is. There's a little bit of what appears to be blackmail, some silly breach of promise business, a satire of cafe society in New York and several small subplots, none of which can stand any sort of logical scrutiny but all of which add to the overall enjoyment. Look for Dorothy Comingore (CITIZEN KANE) in a small bit part. Also, a very young James Craig, the comedic Dave Willock and Robert Sterling can be seen in tiny spots. It's the kind of movie that's just right at two in the morning when you can't sleep. Not that this will put you under, just that it's a pleasant way to spend some late night insomniac hours.

p, William Perlberg; d, Alexander Hall; w, Gladys Lehman, Ken Englund (based on a story by Lenore Coffee, William Joyce Cowen); ph, Henry Freulich; m, Morris W. Stoloff; ed, Al Clark; art d, Lionel Banks; cos, Kalloch.

Comedy **(PR:A MPAA:NR)**

GOOD GUYS AND THE BAD GUYS, THE*½ (1969) 90m WB c

Robert Mitchum *(Flagg)*, George Kennedy *(McKay)*, David Carradine *(Waco)*, Tina Louise *(Carmel)*, Douglas V. Fowley *(Grundy)*, Lois Nettleton *(Mary)*, Martin Balsam *(Mayor Wilker)*, John Davis Chandler *(Deuce)*, John Carradine *(Ticker)*, Marie Windsor *(Polly)*, Dick Peabody *(Boyle)*, Kathleen Freeman *(Mrs. Stone)*, Jimmy Murphy *(Buckshot)*, Garrett Lewis *(Hawkins)*, Nick Dennis *(Engineer)*, David Cargo *(Newspaperman)*, Buddy Hackett *(Townsman)*.

If you saw RIDE THE HIGH COUNTRY then you'll recognize the derivative source for Cohen and Shryack's flabby screenplay. Kennedy is back in town and Mitchum, the local marshal, doesn't like that one bit. He's run up against Kennedy before and the guy is bad news so he warns the mayor, Balsam, that the little town of Progress is in for some big trouble. Balsam is up for re-election and doesn't want to rile the populace, so he retires Mitchum and replaces him with Peabody, a bumbling deputy. Mitchum, now no longer carrying the lawman's "tin," begins his own investigation of Kennedy's intentions. Kennedy is running with a new gang, but when that cut-throat cadre want to kill Mitchum (they are planning a huge robbery and fear that Mitchum will thwart them), Kennedy puts his foot down. He has a grudging admiration for his old nemesis and would hate to see Mitchum die with (or without) his boots on. Kennedy and Mitchum join forces to defeat the gang, headed by David Carradine. Fowley is sweet as an old hermit who brings Kennedy and Mitchum back to town after the two have beaten each other to a pulp. He is rewarded by being killed by the gang. Nettleton is Mitchum's pal, a boarding house owner with a heart of gold-plate. In the end, Balsam offers Mitchum his former job but that's declined as the old gunfighter realizes it's time to change careers. John Carradine is briefly seen as an aged conductor aboard the train that is the target for the gang. Shot on location in New Mexico, director Kennedy did his best to overcome the flat jokes and the trite situation, but he was defeated by the script.

p, Ronald M. Cohen, Dennis Shryack; d, Burt Kennedy; w, Cohen, Shryack; ph, Harry Stradling, Jr. (Panavision, Technicolor); m, William Lava; ed, Howard Deane, Otho Lovering; prod d & art d, Stan Jolley; set d, Ralph S. Hurst; cos, Yvonne Wood, Robert Richards, Dominic Di Bona, Lyle Field, Patricia Norris, Audrey Newell; m/l, "The Ballad Of Marshal Flagg," Lava, Ned Washington (sung by Glen Yarbrough); makeup, Perc Westmore.

Western/Comedy/Drama **(PR:A-C MPAA:M)**

GOOD GUYS WEAR BLACK½** (1978) 96m Mar Vista c

Chuck Norris *(John T. Booker)*, Anne Archer *(Margaret)*, Lloyd Haynes *(Murray)*, James Franciscus *(Conrad Morgan)*, Dana Andrews *(Government Man)*, Jim Backus *(Doorman)*.

Decent Norris action picture sees the martial arts master as a Viet Nam vet-turned-schoolteacher whose military past is brought up by a woman investigating his unit's last mission. It was a CIA operation that saw most of the men left behind in the jungles waiting for a rescue chopper that never arrived. The investigator suggests that perhaps the soldiers were never meant to survive and that he and his men may have been set up by the government. Norris becomes obsessed with finding out what really happened and soon discovers the remaining members of his unit are being systematically killed. He is aided by a small group of investigators (Archer, Haynes, and Andrews), who join forces to help him solve the mystery. Eventually the bloody trail leads to corrupt politician, Franciscus, who Norris discovers sold him and his men out. Unbelievable action scene sees Norris kick through the front windshield of a speeding car and come out without a scratch. Followed by the sequel A FORCE OF ONE (1979).

p, Allan F. Bodoh; d, Ted Post; w, Bruce Cohn, Mark Medoff (based on a story by Joseph Fraley); m, Craig Safan.

Action/Mystery **Cas.** **(PR:O MPAA:PG)**

GOOD HUMOR MAN, THE*** (1950) 79m COL bw

Jack Carson *(Biff Jones)*, Lola Albright *(Margie Bellew)*, George Reeves *(Stuart Nagel)*, Jean Wallace *(Bonnie Conroy)*, Peter Miles *(Johnny Bellew)*, Frank Ferguson *(Inspector Quint)*, David Sharpe *(Slick)*, Chick Collins *(Fats)*, Eddie Parker *(John)*, Pat Flaherty *(Officer Rhodes)*, Richard Egan *(Officer Daley)*, Arthur Space *(Steven)*, Jack Overman *(Stoker)*, Victoria Horne *(Bride)*.

A surprisingly successful resurrection of Mack Sennett-style slapstick written by cartoonist/gagwriter/director Tashlin and directed by the ever-steady hand of Bacon. Rubber-faced comic Carson stars as a hapless ice-cream-truck driver who must suffer the slings and arrows of outrageous sight gags. While out on his route, Carson is seduced into participating in a payroll robbery by sexy vamp Wallace. After the job, Carson finds himself running both from the crooks (led by TV's George "Superman" Reeves) who want to bump him off and from the cops who want him in the hoosegow. This, of course, opens the floodgates for an abundance of well-staged slapstick gags which manage to capture the Keystone Kops flair. Accompanied by his girl friend Albright, Carson hides out in a schoolhouse. Just as things look grim for the hapless confection salesman, he and his sweetie are rescued by the "Captain Marvel Club," a group of kids who happen to be some of Carson's regular customers. Genuinely funny, THE GOOD HUMOR MAN is a joy for fans of Tashlin, who got his start in movies in 1930 as a cartoonist. From there, Tashlin wrote gags for Hal Roach, became a story editor for Walt Disney, and even assisted Harpo Marx with gags for A NIGHT IN CASABLANCA. Tashlin's experience with cartoons and goofy comedy marked the fresh, quirky, innovative style that would surface in his own films as a director. He produced two campy 1950s comedies, THE GIRL CAN'T HELP IT (1956) and WILL SUCCESS SPOIL ROCK HUNTER (1957). In 1985, a film similar to Tashlin's unique brand of comedy brightened America's movie screens in PEE WEE'S BIG ADVENTURE directed by Tim Burton, another former animator/cartoonist turned live-action filmmaker who was obviously inspired by the work of Tashlin.

p, S. Sylvan Simon; d, Lloyd Bacon; w, Frank Tashlin (based on the story "Appointment with Fear" by Roy Huggins); ph, Lester White; m, Heinz Roemheld; ed, Jerome Thoms; md, Morris Stoloff; art d, Walter Holscher.

Comedy **(PR:A MPAA:NR)**

GOOD INTENTIONS** (1930) 70m FOX bw

Edmund Lowe *(David Creason)*, Marguerite Churchill *(Helen Rankin)*, Regis Toomey *(Richard Holt)*, Earle Foxe *(Flash Norton)*, Eddie Gribbon *(Liberty Red)*, Robert McWade *(Cyrus Holt)*, Georgia Caine *(Miss Huntington)*, Owen Davis, Jr. *(Bud Finney)*, Pat Somerset *(Babe Gray)*, J. Caroll Naish *(Charlie Hatrick)*, Henry Kolker *(Butler)*, Hale Hamilton *(Franklin Graham)*.

Lowe stars as the suave leader of a gang of high-class mobsters who use their social standing to gain access to the safes of unsuspecting rich folks. Lowe moves throughout the upper-crust circles with ease, and even begins a romance with the bank president's daughter, Churchill. Eventually the truth comes out, ruining the gang's phony prestige, as well as Lowe's romance with Churchill. Slow-moving.

d, William K. Howard; w, George Manker Watters, Howard (based on a story by Howard); ph, George Schneiderman; ed, Jack Murray; m/l "Slave to Love," Cliff Friend, Jimmie Monaco.

Crime **(PR:A MPAA:NR)**

GOOD LUCK, MISS WYCKOFF zero (1979) 105m Bel Air-Gradison c (AKA: THE SIN)

Anne Heywood *(Evelyn Wyckoff)*, Donald Pleasence *(Dr. Steiner)*, Robert Vaughn *(Dr. Neal)*, Carolyn Jones *(Beth)*, Dorothy Malone *(Mildred)*, Ronee Blakely *(Betsy)*, Dana Elcar *(Havermeyer)*, Doris Roberts *(Rene)*, John Lafayette *(Rafe)*, Earl Holliman *(Ed Eckles)*, Jocelyn Brando *(Lisa Hemmings)*.

Heywood stars as a 35-year-old schoolteacher (a bit unconvincing; she was 47 at the time) whose first sexual experience is a rape by a black janitor. Doctors Pleasence and Vaughn try to help her through the trauma, but the result is nothing more than a clinician's viewpoint, lacking any sort of emotional basis. The only worthwhile part of the film is Jocelyn Brando's reference to brother Marlon's role in A STREETCAR NAMED DESIRE (1951). A normally fine cast is utterly wasted in this pile of steaming racist garbage which is only further marred by Chomsky's grotesque television style. Not surprisingly, the film never found a distributor, was peddled by the producers, and ended up being known as THE SIN in order to reach a less discriminating market.

p, Raymond Stross; d, Marvin J. Chomsky; w, Polly Platt (based on the novel by William Inge); ph, Alex Phillips, Jr. (Metrocolor); m, Ernest Gold; ed, Rita Roland; art d, Jim Bissell; set d, Roy Stennard; cos, Tom Rasmussen.

Drama **(PR:O MPAA:R)**

GOOD LUCK, MR. YATES** (1943) 89m COL bw

Claire Trevor *(Ruth Jones)*, Edgar Buchanan *(Jonesey Jones)*, Jess Barker *(Oliver Yates)*, Tom Neal *(Charlie Edmonds)*, Albert Basserman *(Dr. Carl Hesser)*, Tommy Cook *(Johnny Zaloris)*, Scotty Beckett *(Jimmy Dixon)*, Frank Sully *(Joe Briggs)*, Douglas Leavitt *(Monty King)*, Henry Armetta *(Mike Zaloris)*, Rosina Galli *(Katy Zaloris)*, Billy Roy *(Plunkett)*, Conrad Binyon *(Bob Coles)*, Bobby Larson *(Ross)*, Rudy Wissler *(Wilson)*, The Bob Mitchell Boy Choir, The Sheriff's Boys Band.

Silly war-time drama starring Barker as a teacher at a military school who has lost the respect of his students because he is not in uniform. Crushed, Barker convinces the draft board to release him from his "essential" status and he enlists, only to discover he is unacceptable due to a punctured eardrum. Rather than face his students with this latest humiliation, he takes a job at a shipyard and leads the kids to believe he is in the army by answering letters from them addressed to boot camp but forwarded to him by a soldier buddy. Soon suspicions arise that he is a deserter at best and a Nazi spy at worst. This puts a strain on the new romance he has developed with fellow welder Trevor, but all turns out fine in the end when Buchanan emerges the hero of a shipyard fire. This story's credibility is stretched to the limit.

p, David J. Chatkin; d, Ray Enright; w, Lou Breslow, Adele Commandini (based on a story by Hal Smith, Sam Rudd); ph, Philip Tannura; ed, Richard Fantl; art d, Lionel Banks.

Drama **(PR:A MPAA:NR)**

GOOD MORNING . . . AND GOODBYE zero (1967) 78m Eve c

Alaina Capri *(Angel)*, Stuart Lancaster *(Burt)*, Pat Wright *(Stone)*, Haji *(Witch)*, Karen Ciral *(Lana)*, Don Johnson *(Ray)*, Tom Howland *(Herb)*, Megan Timothy *(Lottie)*, Toby Adler *(Betty)*, Sylvia Tedemar *(Dancer)*, Carol Peters *(Nude)*.

More Russ Meyer mammary lensing stars Capri as a sexually frustrated wife who seeks satisfaction anywhere she can find it. Construction worker Wright is her favorite lover, but she also finds time to spend with Timothy, the wife of Wright's assistant, and teen surfer Johnson, who is the boy friend of her stepdaughter, Ciral. A witch, played by Haji, comes to Capri's impotent husband, Lancaster, and turns him on—and finally into—a real man.

p&d, Russ Meyer; w, John E. Moran (based on a story by Meyer); ph, Meyer; m, Igo Kantor; ed, Meyer, Richard Brummer.

Drama **Cas.** **(PR:O MPAA:NR)**

GOOD MORNING, BOYS (SEE: WHERE THERE'S A WILL, 1937, Brit.)

GOOD MORNING, DOCTOR (SEE: YOU BELONG TO ME, 1941)

GOOD MORNING, JUDGE**½ (1943) 66m UNIV bw

Dennis O'Keefe *(David Barton)*, Louise Allbritton *(Elizabeth Christine Smith)*, Mary Beth Hughes *(Mira Bryon)*, J. Carroll Naish *(Andre)*, Louise Beavers *(Cleo)*, Samuel S. Hinds *(J. P. Gordon)*, Frank Faylen *(Ben Pollard)*, Ralph Peters *(Harry Pollard)*, Oscar O'Shea *(Magistrate)*, Marie Blake *(Nicky Clark)*, Don Barclay *(Biscuit Face)*, Murray Alper *(Charlie Martin)*, Eddie Acuff *(Cab Driver)*, Ruth Lee *(Paula)*, Lee Phelps *(Court Clerk)*, Phil Warren *(Orchestra Leader)*, Ruth Warren *(Katie Bevins)*, Billy Newell *(Bartender)*, Edward Earle *(Ducky Evans)*, Harry Strang *(Bailiff)*, Jack Rice *(Hotel Clerk)*, Eddie Coke *(Reporter)*, Margaret Marquis *(Girl)*, Rebel Randell *(Sunbather)*, Albert Ray *(Tommy Bevins)*, Pierce Lyden *(Policeman)*, Hal Craig *(Bailiff)*, Billy Bletcher *(Voice of Radio Announcer)*, Charles Sherlock *(Waiter)*, Chief Red Robe *(Indian Dancer)*, Harry S. Smith [Jay Silverheels], Ralph Lonewolf, Byron Topetchy *(Indians)*, Linda Ann Bieber *(Little Bevins' Girl)*, William Edritt *(Headwaiter)*, Virginia Engels *(Sunbather)*, Cyril Ring *(Elizabeth's Escort)*.

Well done B comedy starring O'Keefe as a music publisher who finds himself being sued for plagiarism by his former singer-girl friend Hughes. One night he meets the lovely Allbritton and while dining together, realizes she is the lady lawyer who is going to be prosecuting him in the morning. Seeing this as an opportunity to win his case, he slips a knockout drop into her drink, hoping she'll be too far gone to state her case in court the next day. After a round of goofy scenes in and out of court and several more doses of knockout drinks, Allbritton and O'Keefe realize their love for each other and clinch for the fadeout.

p, Paul Malvern; d, Jean Yarbrough; w, Maurice Geraghty, Warren Wilson (based on a story by Geraghty, Winston Miller); ph, John W. Boyle; ed, Edward Curtiss; md, Charles Previn; art d, John B. Goodman, Robert Boyle; m/l, "Spellbound," "Sort Of A Kinda," Milton Rosen, Everett Carter (sung by Hughes).

Comedy **(PR:A MPAA:NR)**

GOOD MORNING, MISS DOVE*** (1955) 107m FOX c

Jennifer Jones *(Miss Dove)*, Robert Stack *(Tom Baker)*, Kipp Hamilton *(Jincey Baker)*, Robert Douglas *(Mr. Porter)*, Peggy Knudsen *(Billie Jean)*, Marshall Thompson *(Mr. Pendleton)*, Chuck Connors *(Bill Holloway)*, Biff Elliott *(Alex Burnham)*, Jerry Paris *(Maurice)*, Mary Wickes *(Miss Ellwood)*, Ted Marc *(David Burnham)*, Dick Stewart *(Dr. Temple)*, Vivian Marshall *(Mrs. Meggs)*, Richard Deacon *(Mr. Spivey)*, Bill Walker *(Henry)*, Than Wyenn *(Mr. Levine)*, Leslie Bradley *(Alonso Dove)*, Robert Lynn, Sr. *(Dr. Hurley)*, Edward Firestone *(Fred Makepeace)*, Cheryl Callaway *(Annabel)*, Mark Engel *(Markie)*, Tim Cagney *(Bobsie)*, Linda Bennett *(Peggy)*, Kenneth Osmond *(Tommy Baker at Age 9)*, Paul Engel *(Alex Burnham at Age 9)*, Tiger Fafara *(Fred Makepeace as a Child)*, Martha Wentworth *(Grandma Holloway)*, Virginia Christine *(Mrs. Rigsbee)*, Junius Matthews *(Mr. Pruitt)*, Reba Tassell *(Polly Burnham)*, Gary Diamond *(Harrison)*, Myna Cunard *(Mrs. Aldredge)*, A. Cameron Grant *(Mr. Prouty)*, Janet Brandt *(Mrs. Levine)*, Linda Brace *(Jacqueline Wood)*, Ann Tyrell *(Mrs. Makepeace)*, Nan Dolan *(Mrs. Wood)*, Betty Caulfield *(Mother)*, Elmore Vincent *(Mailman)*, Vincent Perry *(Principal)*, Steve Darrell *(Police Captain)*, Milas Clark, Leonard Ingoldsby, Cary Savage, Tim Haldeman, Michael Gainey *(Boys)*, Ernest Dotson *(Boy at Fountain)*, Mary Carroll, Sarah Selby *(Teachers)*, Jo Gilbert *(Young Matron)*, Pamela Beaird, Carol Sydes, Lydia Reed *(Girls)*, Jean Innes *(Night Nurse)*, Maude Prickett, Catherine Howard *(Nurses)*, John Hiestand *(Prison Guard)*, Edward Mundy *(Hearse Driver)*, Tim Johnson *(Freshman)*, Jean Andren *(Secretary to Mr. Dove)*, Jane Crowley, Eleanore Vogel *(Women)*, Mae Marsh *(Woman in Bank)*, Virginia Carroll *(Ann)*, Elizabeth Flournoy *(Mildred)*, George Dunn *(Janitor)*, Herb Virgran *(Police Surgeon)*, Charles Webster, Richard Cutting *(Husbands)*, Sam McDaniel *(Man)*, William Hughes.

Jennifer Jones is a prim and proper spinster teacher who is at the end of a long and useful life as the schoolteacher in a small New England town. She is on what *might* be her deathbed, awaiting news of whether or not an operation can save her life. The picture is one long flashback of the way she has influenced all the people in the village. One of her students, Stack, is now a brilliant young doctor who can save her life with a new procedure. When she falls ill, the town takes it upon itself to see what can be done for this one-of-a-kind person who has changed all their lives. Chuck Connors is a tough guy who could have gone either way but chose to be a police officer due to Miss Dove. Jerry Paris is a playwright who was gently pushed into his career by his loving teacher, et al. (Paris would go on to become an enormously successful TV director who helmed such hits as "Happy Days" and "Laverne And Shirley.") GOOD MORNING, MISS DOVE is more a character study than a story and it was a best-selling book before being made into a film. Not a huge hit, it was nevertheless the stepping stone for a few actors and proved that Jones had a wider range than was previously thought. A warm, loving picture with a lot of humanity, it did not garner the results MGM had hoped for. But how many movies do?

p, Samuel G. Engel; d, Henry Koster; w, Eleanore Griffin (based on the novel by Frances Gray Patton); ph, Leon Shamroy (CinemaScope, DeLuxe Color); m, Leigh Harline; ed, William Reynolds; md, Lionel Newman; art d, Lyle R. Wheeler, Mark-Lee Kirk; set d, Walter M. Scott, Paul S. Fox; cos, Mary Wills; spec eff, Ray Kellogg; makup, Ben Nye.

Drama **(PR:A MPAA:NR)**

GOOD NEIGHBOR SAM***½ (1964) 130m COL c

Jack Lemmon *(Sam Bissel)*, Edward G. Robinson *(Simon Nurdlinger)*, Romy Schneider *(Janet Lagerlof)*, Dorothy Provine *(Minerva Bissel)*, Michael Connors *(Howard Ebbets)*, Anne Seymour *(Irene Krump)*, Charles Lane *(Jack Bailey)*, Louis Nye *(Reinhold Shiffner)*, Edward Andrews *(Burke)*, Robert Q. Lewis *(Earl)*, Joyce Jameson *(Prostitute)*, Peter Hobbs *(Phil Reisner)*, Tris Coffin *(Sonny Blatchford)*, Neil Hamilton *(Larry Boling)*, Riza Royce *(Miss Halverson)*, William Forrest *(Millard Mellner)*, The Hi-Lo's *(Themselves)*, Linda Watkins *(Edna)*, Bernie Kopell *(Taragon)*, Patrick Waltz *(Wyeth)*, William Bryant *(Hausner)*, Vickie Cos *(Jenna)*, Kym Karath *(Ardis)*, Quinn O'Hara *(Marsha)*, Hal Taggart *(McVale)*, Jan Brooks *(Gloria)*, Peter Camlin *(French Waiter)*, Tom Anthony *(Assistant Director)*, Bess Flowers *(Mrs. Burke)*, Dave Ketchum *(Hertz Commercial Man)*, Gil Lamb *(Drunk)*, Harry Ray *(Milkman)*, Joe Palma *(Postman)*, David Swift *(TV Director)*, Zanouba *(Belly Dancer)*, Barbara Bouchet *(Receptionist)*.

Happily married advertising executive Lemmon is thrilled by the news that he has been entrusted with the firm's most valuable account, that of Nurdlinger's Dairy Company owned and run by old man Nurdlinger (Robinson). Robinson is impressed by the clean-cut young Lemmon; in fact, the milk magnate is obsessed with wholesomeness and decency. When Lemmon arrives home he is surprised to find his wife, Provine, entertaining her former college roommate Schneider, a vivacious and sexy lady about to inherit millions of dollars from her grandfather's estate. Unfortunately, there is a snafu with the inheritance. A stipulation in her grandfather's will states that she must be married and living with her husband in order to collect, and the fact of the matter is that Schneider's husband, Connors, has just walked out on her. Desperate because two of her cousins are out to catch her apart from her husband—and have hired private detective Nye to shadow her (they stand to inherit the fortune if she is not eligible)—Schneider has rented the house next door and begs Lemmon to pretend he's her husband until she gets the money. If he agrees to do this, she'll pay him $1 million. Lemmon agrees, but the deception soon gets out of hand because Nye's constant surveillance has him trapped in bed with Schneider every night. To make things worse, Schneider's husband Connors returns home and is forced to live with Lemmon's wife Provine so as not to louse up the plan. This leads to further complications when Robinson comes to believe that Schneider is actually Lemmon's wife and decides that since they make such a nice, wholesome couple, he will plaster their faces across every billboard in town to promote his milk products. The billboard campaign is put into action without Lemmon's knowledge and Schneider is thrown into hysterics because her cousins might see it. That night Lemmon and Schneider don painters gear and comb the city defacing every billboard they can find with their images in an effort to salvage the charade. The plan works and the next day sees Schneider with Connors, Lemmon with Provine, and everyone millions of dollars richer. A consistently funny screwball comedy despite its somewhat excessive length, GOOD NEIGHBOR SAM reaches back to the classic comedies of Lubitsch, Hawks, and Sturges for its inspiration and succeeds admirably. Lemmon is great as the basically decent, wholesome family man that Robinson's milk tycoon thinks he is, bringing his usual manic energy to the role. Robinson is solid as always in his humorous supporting role, but it is Schneider, in her first Hollywood film, who steals the show. Her spunky, sexy, extremely funny portrayal demonstrates her versatility as an actress and is an interesting counterpoint to such serious ventures as her role in Orson Welles' adaptation of Franz Kafka's THE TRIAL (1962).

p&d, David Swift; w, James Fritzell, Everett Greenbaum, Swift (based on the novel by Jack Finney); ph, Burnett Guffey (Eastmacolor); m, Frank DeVol; ed, Charles Nelson; prod d, Dale Hennesy; set d, Ray Moyer; cos, Micheline, Jacqueline; ch, Miriam Nelson; makeup, Ben Lane.

Comedy **Cas.** **(PR:A-C MPAA:NR)**

GOOD NEWS** (1930) 78m MGM bw

Mary Lawlor *(Connie)*, Stanley Smith *(Tom)*, Bessie Love *(Babe)*, Cliff Edwards *(Kearney)*, Gus Shy *(Bobbie)*, Lola Lane *(Patricia)*, Thomas Jackson *(Coach)*, Delmer Daves *(Beef)*, Billy Taft *(Freshman)*, Frank McGlynn *(Prof. Kenyon)*, Dorothy McNulty *(Flo)*, Helen Virgil, Vera Marsh, Abe Lyman and His Band.

Based on a 1927 musical which starred former California senator George Murphy in the lead, GOOD NEWS was the essential cliche college musical and even in 1930 was already old hat. A football star, Smith, is in danger of losing his eligibility to play in the big game if he doesn't improve his grades. He is placed in the hands of shy, plain Lawlor who helps him get better marks and, at the same time, blossoms from an ugly duckling into a raving beauty. Truly a rah-rah musical, the best dancing comes at the feet of Dorothy McNulty (who later became Penny Singleton, of BLONDIE fame and later the president of AGVA). Director Delmer Daves began as an actor and appears in a small bit part as Beef. The most famous tune is "Varsity Drag" (Buddy De Sylva, Ray Henderson, Lew Brown) in the release print. "He's A Lady's Man," "Good News," "Tait Song," "Students Are We," "Just Imagine" (De Sylva, Henderson, Brown), "If You're Not Kissing Me," and "Football" (Arthur Freed, Nacio Herb Brown), "I Feel Pessimistic" (J. Russell Robinson, George Waggner), "I'd Like To Make You Happy" (Reggie Montgomery), "My Blue Heaven" (Donaldson). The picture was remade in 1947, by which time it had become a nostalgia piece and actually was better than the original.

d, Nick Grinde, Edgar J. MacGregor; w, Frances Marion, Joe Franham (based on the stage play by Lawrence Schwab, Lew Brown, Frank Mandel, Ray Henderson, Buddy De Sylva); ph, Percy Hilburn; ed, William Levanway.

Musical/Comedy **(PR:A MPAA:NR)**

GOOD NEWS**** (1947) 92m MGM c

June Allyson *(Connie Lane)*, Peter Lawford *(Tommy Marlowe)*, Patricia Marshall *(Pat McClellan)*, Joan McCracken *(Babe Doolittle)*, Ray McDonald *(Bobby Turner)*, Mel Torme *(Danny)*, Robert Strickland *(Peter Van Dyne, III)*, Donald MacBride *(Coach Johnson)*, Tom Dugan *(Pooch)*, Clinton Sundberg *(Prof. Burton Kennyone)*, Loren Tindall *(Beef)*, Connie Gilchrist *(Cora, the Cook)*, Morris Ankrum *(Dean Griswold)*, Georgia Lee *(Flo)*, Jane Green *(Mrs. Drexel)*, Richard Tripper, Bill Harbach.

Lavish remake of the 1930 film version of the Broadway musical features Peter Lawford as the football hero with June Allyson as the young student who is working her way through Tait College as a librarian. Marshall is the college sexpot and she has her heart set on Lawford, but he succumbs to the purity of Allyson and all winds up well. Same plot as original version; hero can't make his grades so he must be tutored by bright female. She does the job and Lawford is able to play in the big game. The color, new songs, and sensational choreography all contributed to making this a big hit for MGM in 1947. Almost every song was a winner and director Walters, up to then a choreographer, made an impressive debut in this film. Superb supporting work by Mel Torme (who was still known as "The Velvet Fog" at that time) and Joan McCracken who had come from a successful stage career in "Bloomer Girl" and "Billion Dollar Baby." New songs that were added to the score included "Pass That Peace Pipe" (Hugh Martin, Ralph Blane, Roger Edens) and "The French Lesson" (Betty Comden, Adolph Green, Edens). Add that to the others from the 1930 version and you can see this was a vast improvement.

p, Arthur Freed; d, Charles Walters; w, Betty Comden, Adolph Green (based on the musical comedy by Lawrence Schwab, Frank Mandel, Buddy De Sylva, Lew Brown, Ray Henderson); ph, Charles Schoenbaum (Technicolor); ed, Albert Akst; md, Lennie Hayton; art d, Cedric Gibbons, Edward Carfagno; set d, Edwin B. Willis, Paul G. Chamberlain; cos, Helen Rose, Valles; makeup, Jack Dawn.

Musical/Comedy **(PR:AA MPAA:NR)**

GOOD OLD DAYS, THE** (1939, Brit.) 79m WB-FN bw

Max Miller *(Alexander the Greatest)*, Hal Walters *(Titch)*, H. F. Maltby *(Randolph Macaulay)*, Martita Hunt *(Sara Macaulay)*, Kathleen Gibson *(Polly)*, Anthony Shaw *(Lovelace)*, Allan Jeayes *(Shadwell)*, Roy Emerton *(Grimes)*, Phyllis Monkman *(Mrs. Bennett)*, Sam Wilkinson *(Croker)*.

British comedy situated in London circa 1840, involves a group of actors trying to make a living in a society that still continues to think of them as nothing more than talented beggars. Their efforts to entertain are rewarded by a stiff fine and imprisonment, but all works out well when they rescue a nobleman's son from a band of gypsies who have kidnaped the boy. The boy's father is so grateful, he bails the actors out of their predicament.

p, Jerome Jackson; d, Roy William Neill; w, Austin Melford, John Dighton (based on the story by Ralph Smart); ph, Basil Emmott.

Comedy **(PR:A MPAA:NR)**

GOOD OLD SOAK, THE** (1937) 67m MGM bw

Wallace Beery *(Clem Hawley)*, Una Merkel *(Nellie)*, Eric Linden *(Clemmie Hawley)*, Judith Barrett *(Ina)*, Betty Furness *(Lucy)*, Ted Healy *(Al Simmons)*, Janet Beecher *(Matilda Hawley)*, George Sidney *(Kennedy)*, Robert McWade *(Webster)*, James Bush *(Tom)*, Margaret Hamilton *(Minnie)*.

Beery stars as a likable small-town drunkard who bails out young Linden when the boy juggles the company books for the benefit of showgirl Barrett. All turns out well after Beery pressures snide banker McWade into coming up with the money he swindled out of Linden through a shady stock market deal.

p, Harry Rapf; d, J. Walter Ruben; w, A. E. Thomas (based on the play "The Old Soak" by Don Marquis); ph, Clyde DeVinna; m, Edward Ward; ed, Frank Sullivan; ch, Val Raset; m/l Walter Donaldson, Bob Wright, Chet Forest.

Drama **(PR:A MPAA:NR)**

GOOD SAM½** (1948) 112m Rainbow Productions/RKO bw

Gary Cooper *(Sam Clayton)*, Ann Sheridan *(Lu Clayton)*, Ray Collins *(Rev. Daniels)*, Edmund Lowe *(H.C. Borden)*, Joan Lorring *(Shirley Mae)*, Clinton Sundberg *(Nelson)*, Minerva Urecal *(Mrs. Nelson)*, Louise Beavers *(Chloe)*, Dick Ross *(Claude)*, Lora Lee Michel *(Lulu)*, Bobby Dolan, Jr. *(Butch)*, Matt Moore *(Mr. Butler)*, Netta Packer *(Mrs. Butler)*, Ruth Roman *(Ruthie)*, Carol Stevens *(Mrs. Adams)*, Todd Karns *(Joe Adams)*, Irving Bacon *(Tramp)*, William Frawley *(Tom)*, Harry Hayden *(Banker)*, Irmgard Dawson, Jane Allan *(Girls)*, *Tom Dugan (Santa Claus)*, Sarah Edwards *(Mrs. Gilmore)*, Ruth Sanderson *(Sam's Secretary)*, Marta Mitrovich *(Mysterious Woman)*, Mimi Doyle *(Red Cross Nurse)*, Franklin Parker *(Photographer)*, Ida Moore *(Old Lady)*, Florence Auer *(Woman on Bus)*, Dick Wessel *(Bus Driver)*, Sedal Bennett *(Woman Chasing Bus)*, Cliff Clarke *(Probation Officer)*, Jack Gargan, Bess Flowers *(Parents)*, Almira Sessions *(Landlady)*, Garry Owens *(Taxi Driver)*, Stanley McKay *(Young Minister)*, Bert Roach *(Whispering Usher)*, Bob Tidwell *(Telegraph Boy)*, Ann Lawrence *(Salvation Army Girl)*, Joe Hinds, Francis Stevens *(Salvation Army Workers)*, Joseph Crehan *(Casey)*, William Haade *(Taxi Driver)*, Bert Moorehouse *(Man)*, Dick Elliott, Bert Roach *(Politicians)*, Louis Mason *(Mr. Duffield)*, Effie Laird *(Mrs. Duffield)*.

This is not one of Cooper's better performances in a twisted comedy where the normally brilliant McCarey presented an awkward story in a manner as bumbling and inept as its likable but uninspired hero. Cooper is the manager of a department store who just can't say no to a host of spongers and hangers-on. He lends his car to a neighbor who wrecks it and then further vexes his wife Sheridan by inviting the car repairman to dinner. Cooper next lends his life's savings, which Sheridan had been planning to use for a new house, to an impoverished young couple to begin a business. He also tolerantly feeds and houses Sheridan's loafing brother Ross who refuses to look for a job. Then he gets tangled with Lorring, an abrasive salesgirl working for him, and prevents her suicide. Cooper eventually faces bankruptcy and ruin; he goes on a colosssal binge to forget his troubles and wakes up vice president of the firm and with repayment from his friends. Cooper provides only a sheepish, befuddled look throughout this slapdash production and serves as a straight man to one-liners from undistinguished character actors. Only Sheridan comes through with a stellar performance. This was really Frank Capra's meat but when McCarey chewed on it, nothing remained but a barebones comedy with a few funny highlights and a lot of missed opportunities.

p&d, Leo McCarey; w, Ken Englund (based on a story by McCarey, John Klorer); ph, George Barnes; m, Robert Emmet Dolan; ed, James McKay; art d, John B. Goodman; spec eff, Russell A. Cully.

Comedy **Cas.** **(PR:A MPAA:NR)**

GOOD SOLDIER SCHWEIK, THE*** (1963, Ger.) 98m CCC-Filmkunst-Weinfilm/Lionex Films bw (DER BRAVE SOLDAT SCHWEJK)

Heinz Ruhmann *(Schweik)*, Ernst Stankowski *(Lt. Lucas)*, Ursula Borsodi *(Kathi)*, Senta Berger *(Gretl)*, Erika von Thellmann *(Baroness)*, Franz Muxeneder *(Woditschka)*, Hugo Gottschlich *(Sgt. Flanderka)*, Edith Elmay, Fritz Imhoff, Franz Boheim, Karl Fochler, Hans Thimig, Erika Frey, Michael Jansich, Egon von Jordan, Lazlo Szemere, Fritz Muliar, Alma Seidler, Otto Schmole, Jane Tilden.

Ruhmann portrays a mild-mannered dog salesman who is drafted into the German army during WW I. Despite his frantic attempts to show patriotism and respect for his superiors, he manages to get himself caught up in several mishaps, including being captured by his own comrades and narrowly escaping execution by firing squad. Filled with Rabelaisian humor, and taken from a masterpiece of Czechoslovakian literature. (In German; English subtitles.)

p, Karl Ehrlich; d, Axel Von Ambesser; w, Hans Jacoby (based on a novel by Jaroslaw Hasek); ph, Richard Angst; m, Bernhard Eichhorn; ed, Angelika Appel, Hermann Haller; art d, Werner Schlichting, Isabella Schlichting; cos, Dr. Leo Blei.

Satire   (PR:C MPAA:NR)

GOOD SPORT**½   (1931) 67m FOX bw

Linda Watkins (*Marilyn Parker*), John Boles (*Boyce Cameron*), Greta Nissen (*Peggy Burns*), Minna Gombell (*Virginia*), Hedda Hopper (*Mrs. Atherton*), Allan Dinehart (*Rex Parker*), Claire Maynard (*Queenie*), Ethel Kenyon (*Loretta*), Louise Beavers (*September*), Sally Blane (*Marge*), Betty Francisco (*Laura*), Joyce Compton (*Fay*), Eleanor Hunt, Chrystine Maple, Nadine Dore, Genevieve Mitchell.

This witty romantic drama takes a light view of prostitution, indicating that love, the type that makes one lose all self control, is not all that it's cracked up to be. This look into the realm of high-class ladies-of-the-night has a thin plot of a young married woman (Watkins) who discovers that her honorable husband has been carrying on some affairs on the side. In an attempt to try to get to the bottom of this, Watkins winds up getting herself into a mess by having an extramarital affair of her own. Though the subject is a little risque, it is kept low key, approached in a manner to emphasize the humor.

d, Kenneth MacKenna; w, William Hurlbut; ph, Charles Clarke; ed, Alex Troffey.

Drama/Comedy   (PR:A MPAA:NR)

GOOD, THE BAD, AND THE UGLY, THE****   (1967, Ital./Span.) 161m Produzioni Europee/UA c (IL BUONO, IL BRUTTO, IL CATTIVO)

Clint Eastwood (*Joe*), Eli Wallach (*Tuco*), Lee Van Cleef (*Setenza*), Aldo Giuffre, Chelo Alonso, Mario Brega, Luigi Pistilli, Rada Rassimov, Enzo Petito, Claudio Scarchilli, Livio Lorenzon, Antonio Casale, Sandro Scarchilli, Benito Stefanelli, Angelo Novi, Silvana Bacci, Antonio Casas, Aldo Sambrell.

Leone's epic, and the last of the Eastwood "Dollars" trilogy, is a stunning, panoramic view of the West during the Civil War. THE GOOD, THE BAD, AND THE UGLY is a deceptively simple story detailing the efforts of three drifters, Eastwood (the Good), Eli Wallach (the Ugly), and Van Cleef (the Bad), to find a fortune hidden in the unmarked grave of a man named Bill Carson. Eastwood once again plays the silent but supremely self-confident "Man-with-no-name" (he's called "Blondie" by Wallach) who meets renegade Mexican bandit Wallach, a lecherous, cruel, obnoxious crook who has a large price on his head. Eastwood and Wallach decide to make a few bucks by having the silent stranger "capture" the bandit and turn him in for the reward money. When the townsfolk send the horse out from under Wallach (whose head is in a noose of course) Eastwood takes careful aim from a distance and shoots the rope, allowing the bandit to escape. Later, when they reunite, they split the money. This system works for awhile, but Wallach balks at his share, and states that he should get more because it is his neck in the rope. Eastwood sees his point and calmly states, "but I'm the guy that does the cutting." Eventually Wallach gets fed up and the partnership ends when he drags Eastwood through the desert, hoping to kill him. There they happen across an abandoned carriage. Inside is Bill Carson (the man whom the totally evil bounty hunter played by Van Cleef has been trying to find); Carson's last words tell where the gold is buried. Unfortunately, Wallach only hears half of the secret and Eastwood the other half, so the men are stuck with each other until they can locate the gold. When the pair is captured by the Union Army (they had been posing as Confederates to get through some enemy territory) they are brutally tortured by Van Cleef, who has become an Army sergeant in the hopes that it will lead him closer to the gold. The men refuse to talk, and the three form an uneasy alliance. Eventually this leads to a three-way showdown in a giant cemetery which sees Van Cleef killed by Eastwood and Wallach surprised to find he wasn't really a participant (Eastwood had previously removed the bullets from his gun). Eastwood then puts a noose around Wallach's neck, strings it to a tree, and leaves him precariously perched atop a tombstone with half the gold at his feet and rides off. After a mighty struggle, Wallach finally slips, but Eastwood shoots the rope in half, saving the bandit's life (the trick gives Eastwood enough time to make good his getaway from the treacherous bandit). Leone's narrative structure is incredibly complex, with the characters' paths intersecting and sometimes intertwining (at various points in the story two of the characters appear to team up against the other, but *all* of them want the treasure for themselves) and, as their personal brutality increases (to themselves and others), the Civil War begins to enter their lives and dwarf their petty crimes. The war is a minor disturbance at first, which slowly intrudes into their territory and eventually sees Eastwood and Wallach involved in a massive battle for an unimportant bridge where hundreds of soldiers go to their pointless doom. The scale of violence shocks these two violent men; Eastwood (whose character begins to show a humanity only hinted at in the previous two films) states that he has never "seen so many men wasted so badly." It is Leone's most violent film (which is necessary when contrasting the level of brutality men can perform on each other) but also one of his most compassionate. One of the most memorable scenes shows the Union troops organizing an orchestra of Confederate prisoner/musicians to play an idyllic, beautiful tune (this is one of Morricone's finest musical scores) to cover the noise of Van Cleef's torture of his prisoners. The effect is haunting and conjures up memories of similar behavior by the Nazis in the WW II death camps. Another touching moment occurs when Eastwood comes across a dying young soldier and the bounty hunter covers the shivering man with his duster and helps him smoke his final cigarette. Unlike the previous two films of the trilogy, this was a big-budget effort; Leone expended more than $1 million on it, more than the first two put together. Nearly one-fourth of that sum went to Eastwood, suddenly one of the high-ticket actors of the world.

Though not Leone's masterpiece (which would come with ONCE UPON A TIME IN THE WEST, 1969, where he synthesizes elements of scale, narrative, casting, and style), THE GOOD, THE BAD, AND THE UGLY is a massive, many faceted film that continues to hold up, viewing after viewing.

p, Alberto Grimaldi; d, Sergio Leone; w, Luciano Vincenzoni, Leone (based on a story by Age-Scarpelli, Vincenzoni, Leone); ph, Tonino Delli Colli (Techniscope, Technicolor); m, Ennio Moricone; ed, Nino Baragli, Eugenio Alabiso; md, Bruno Nicolai; art d, Carlo Simi; cos, Simi; spec eff, Eros Bacciucchi.

Western   **Cas.**   (PR:O MPAA:NR)

GOOD TIME GIRL***½   (1950, Brit.) 81m Rank/FC bw

Jean Kent (*Gwen Rawlings*), Dennis Price (*Red*), Herbert Lom (*Max*), Bonar Colleano (*American*), Peter Glenville (*Jimmy the Waiter*), Flora Robson (*Chairman of Juvenile Court*), George Carney (*Mr. Rawlings*), Beatrice Varley (*Mrs. Rawlings*), Hugh McDermott (*2nd American*), Griffith Jones (*Danny Martin*), Amy Venesa (*Mrs. Chalk*), Elwyn Brook-Jones (*Mr. Pettinger*), Orlando Martins (*Kelly*), Renee Gadd (*Probation Officer*), Jill Balcon (*Roberta*), Joan Young (*Mrs. Bond*), Margaret Barton (*Agnes*), Jack Raine (*Detective Sgt. Girton*), Nora Swinburne (*Reform School Matron*), Diana Dors (*Lyla Lawrence*), George Merritt (*Police Sergeant*), Michael Hordern (*Seddon*), Garry Marsh (*Mr. Hawkins*), Harry Ross (*Fruity Lee*), Dorothy Vernon (*Mrs. Chudd*), Vera Francis (*Edie*), June Byford (*Joan Rawlings*), John Blythe (*Art Moody*), Edward Lexy (*Mr. Morgan*), Phyl French (*Sonia*), Danny Green (*Smiling Billy*), Noel Howlett (*Clerk*), Mollie Palmer (*A Girl*), Zena Marshall (*Red's Wife*), Ilena Sylva (*Ida*), Betty Nelson (*Connie*), Rosalind Atkinson (*Doctor*), Iris Vandeleur (*Lodger*), Jane Hylton (*Maid*), Lionel Grose (*Doorman*).

Grim drama starring Kent as a slum girl who runs away from home and gets mixed up with gangsters. Driving home drunk one night she runs over and kills a policeman. She then joins up with two American G.I. deserters and the trio goes off on a spree of robbery and crime, culminating in the murder of a young cabbie who incredibly turns out to be Kent's former beau. Based on a real murder committed in 1945.

p, Sydney Box; d, David MacDonald; w, Muriel Box, Sydney Box, Ted Willis (based on the novel *Night Darkens the Streets* by Arthur la Bern); ph, Stephen Dade; m, Lambert Williamson; ed, Vladimir Sagovsky; art d, Maurice Carter; makeup, W. T. Partleton.

Crime/Thriller   (PR:O MPAA:NR)

GOOD TIMES*½   (1967) 92m Motion Picture International/COL c

Sonny and Cher (*Themselves*), George Sanders (*Mordicus*), Norman Alden (*Warren*), Larry Duran (*Smith*), Kelly Thordsen (*Tough Hombre*), Lennie Weinrib (*Garth*), Peter Robbins (*Brandon*), Edy Williams, China Lee, Diane Haggerty (*Mordicus' Girls*), James Flavin (*Lieutenant*), Phil Arnold (*Solly*), Hank Worden (*Kid*), Morris Buchanan (*Proprietor*), Charles Smith (*Telegrapher*), John Cliff (*Gangster*), Herk Reardon, Bruce Tegner (*Wrestlers*), Richard Collier (*Peddler*), Howard Wright (*Old Timer*), Joe Devlin (*Bartender*), Mike Kopach (*Deputy*).

Pop musical starring 1960s singing sensations Sonny and Cher as themselves. Plot sees movie producer Sanders offering the duo a chance to star in pictures. The film then becomes a series of fantasy scenes by Sonny as he imagines himself and Cher in a variety of film genres (western, gangster, Tarzan) with Sanders as the villain in each. Sonny snaps back to reality and decides he no longer trusts Sanders and turns down his offer. Songs include: "I Got You Babe," "It's The Little Things," "Good Times," "Trust Me," "Don't Talk To Strangers," "I'm Gonna Love You," and "Just A Name." Trivial, but imaginative, this was the first feature film directed by William Freidkin (THE FRENCH CONNECTION, THE EXORCIST).

p, Lindsley Parsons; d, William Friedkin; w, Tony Barrett (based on a story by Nicholas Hyams); ph, Robert Wyckoff (DeLuxe Color); m, Sonny Bono; ed, Melvin Shapiro; cos, Leah Rhodes; spec eff, Bob Peterson; ch, Andre Tayir; makeup, Ed Butterworth.

Musical   (PR:A MPAA:NR)

GOODBYE AGAIN**½   (1933) 64m WB bw

Warren William (*Kenneth Bixby*), Joan Blondell (*Anne*), Genevieve Tobin (*Julie*), Helen Chandler (*Elizabeth*), Ruth Donnelly (*Maid*), Wallace Ford (*Arthur Westlake*), Hugh Herbert (*Harvey Wilson*), Hobart Cavanaugh (*Clayton*), Jay Ward (*Theodore*), Ferdinand Gottschalk (*Hotel Manager*), Ray Cook (*Bellboy*).

Sharp romantic comedy stars William as a famous author and playboy who attempts to rekindle a romance with former flame Tobin, much to the dismay of her husband, Herbert. Blondell plays William's secretary who is in love with him from afar and jealously disapproves of his actions regarding Tobin.

d, Michael Curtiz; w, Ben Markson (based on a play by George Haight, Alan Scott); ph, George Barnes; ed, Thomas Pratt.

Romance   (PR:A MPAA:NR)

GOODBYE AGAIN***   (1961) 120m Argus/UA bw

Ingrid Bergman (*Paula Tessier*), Yves Montand (*Roger Demarest*), Anthony Perkins (*Philip Van Der Besh*), Jessie Royce Landis (*Mrs. Van Der Besh*), Jackie Lane (*Maisie I*), Pierre Dux (*Maitre Fleury*), Jean Clarke (*Maisie II*), Uta Taeger (*Gaby*), Andre Randall (*Mons. Steiner*), David Horne (*British Lawyer*), Lee Patrick (*Mme. Fleury*), A. Duperoux (*Madeline Fleury*), Raymond Gerome (*Jimmy*), Jean Hebey (*Mons. Cherel*), Michel Garland (*Young Man in Club*), Paul Uny (*Waiter*), Colin Mann (*Assistant Lawyer*), Diahann Carroll (*Singer*), Peter Bull (*The Client*), Michele Mercier (*Maisie III*).

Bergman stars as a beautiful Parisian interior decorator, approaching middle-age, whose lover, Montand, has a penchant for younger women and leaves her in pursuit of them frequently. Fearing loneliness and sensing that Montand will never marry her, she finds herself irresistibly attracted to Perkins, the son of one of her wealthy clients, American socialite Landis. This sparks jealous spats between Montand and Bergman and, upon returning from a business trip, he is outraged to find that Perkins has moved in with her. Montand seeks solace in the company of a string of other women, but he cannot forget Bergman, while she begins to realize that she does not really love Perkins and has just been using him to feel loved and needed. Montand finally proposes to Bergman and she accepts, but soon after they are married, the cycle starts again and Bergman realizes that Montand is continuing his affairs. Powerful performances by the three principal stars turned this depressing script into a fine examination of middle-aged romance.

p&d, Anatole Litvak; w, Samuel Taylor (based on the novel *Aimez-Vous Brahms* by Francoise Sagan); ph, Armand Thirard; m, Georges Auric; ed, Albert Bates; art d, Alexandre Trauner; cos, Christian Dior; m/l, Dory Langdon; makeup, John O'Gorman, Georges Bouban.

Romance (PR:C MPAA:NR)

GOODBYE BROADWAY** (1938) 69m UNIV bw

Alice Brady *(Molly Malloy)*, Charles Winninger *(Pat Malloy)*, Tom Brown *(Chuck Bradford)*, Dorothea Kent *(Jeanne Carlyle)*, Frank Jenks *(Harry Clark)*, Jed Prouty *(J.A. Higgins)*, Willie Best *("Jughead")*, Donald Meek *(Oglethorpe)*, Henry Roquemore *(Henry Swanzey)*, Del Henderson *(Cromwell)*, Jack Daley *(Lancaster)*, Rollo Lloyd *(Merriweather)*, Charles Sullivan *(Freddie)*, Steve Strelich *(Elmer)*, Virginia Howell *(Mrs. Pettengale)*, Tommy Riggs and "Betty Lou."

Winninger and Brady star as husband and wife vaudeville troopers who get conned into plunking down $4,000 for a seedy hotel in New England. After the standard set of gags and twists, the clever couple manage to turn around and sell the hotel back to the dishonest real estate man for $10,000, a fortune in those days. Good cast of character performers make this one breezy entertainment.

p, Edmund Grainger; d, Ray McCarey; w, Roy Chanslor, A. Dorlan Otvos (based on the play "The Shannons of Broadway," by James Gleason); ph, George Robinson; ed, Maurice Wright.

Drama/Comedy (PR:A MPAA:NR)

GOODBYE BRUCE LEE: HIS LAST GAME OF DEATH

(SEE: GAME OF DEATH, 1976)

GOODBYE CHARLIE½** (1964) 117m FOX c

Tony Curtis *(George Tracy)*, Debbie Reynolds *(Charlie Sorel/The Woman)*, Pat Boone *(Bruce Minton)*, Joanna Barnes *(Janie)*, Ellen McRae [Burstyn] *(Franny)*, Laura Devon *(Rusty)*, Martin Gabel *(Morton Craft)*, Roger Carmel *(Inspector)*, Harry Madden *(Charlie Sorel, the Male)*, Myrna Hansen *(Starlet)*, Michael Romanoff *(Patron)*, Michael Jackson *(Himself)*, Antony Eustrel *(Butler)*, Donna Michelle *(Guest on Yacht)*, Walter Matthau *(Sir Leopold Sartori)*, Jerry Dunphy *(TV Newscaster)*, Carmen Nisbet, Sydney Guilaroff *(Patrons at Beauty Salon)*, Jack Richardson *(Party Guest)*, Rudy Hansen, Edward Wermel *(Germans in Bistro)*, Natalie Martinelli *(Italian Girl)*.

Novel comedy plot involves a suave Hollywood writer and ladies' man who is murdered by angry Hungarian film producer Matthau when he catches the writer in bed with his wife. The playboy returns to life in the form of the beautiful and sexy Reynolds who moves in with his/her old friend Curtis, who has returned from Paris to deliver the eulogy and settle his buddy's estate. He is a bit confused by this woman who, despite her female charm, acts like the male friend he knew so well. Reynolds uses his/her new-found freedom to cash in on affairs he/she has had with other Hollywood wives, and uses the opportunity to get his/her revenge on Matthau. Funny but far-fetched entertainment from director Minnelli, who doesn't need to rely on strange plot devices to make a good movie.

p, David Weisbart; d, Vincente Minnelli; w, Harry Kurnitz (based on a play by George Axelrod); ph, Milton Krasner (CinemaScope, DeLuxe Color); m, Andre Previn; ed, John W. Holmes; art d, Jack Martin Smith, Richard Day; set d, Walter M. Scott, Keogh Gleason; cos, Helen Rose; m/l, "Goodbye Charlie" and "Seven At Once", Previn, Dory Langdon (sung by Jerry Wallace); spec eff, L.B. Abbott, Emil Kosa, Jr.

Comedy (PR:C MPAA:NR)

GOODBYE COLUMBUS* (1969) 105m Willow Tree/PAR c

Richard Benjamin *(Neil Klugman)*, Ali MacGraw *(Brenda Patimkin)*, Jack Klugman *(Mr. Patimkin)*, Nan Martin *(Mrs. Patimkin)*, Michael Meyers *(Ron Patimkin)*, Lori Shelle *(Julie Patimkin)*, Royce Wallace *(Carlotta)*, Sylvie Straus *(Aunt Gladys)*, Kay Cummings *(Doris)*, Michael Nurie *(Don Farber)*, Betty Greyson *(Aunt Molly)*, Monroe Arnold *(Uncle Leo)*, Elaine Swain *(Sarah Ehrlich)*, Richard Wexler *(Busboy)*, Rubin Schafer *(Uncle Max)*, Jaclyn Smith *(Model)*, Bill Derringer *(John McKee)*, Mari Gorman *(Simp)*, Gail Ommerle *(Harriet)*, Jan Peerce *(Wedding Guest)*, Max Peerce, Anthony McGowan, Chris Schenkel, David Benedict, Ray Baumel, Delos Smith.

A tepid insipid comedy-romance, GOODBYE, COLUMBUS profiles two unorthodox Jewish families and their in-love offspring. Benjamin is an impoverished librarian and MacGraw is a spoiled Jewish princess (both in their film debuts). He spends a few weeks at her home while MacGraw's well-to-do-father, Klugman, exhorts Benjamin to make something of himself. Benjamin sneaks into MacGraw's room to make love to her but is later dismayed to learn that she won't take birth control pills because they make her ill. They later rendezvous in a sleazy hotel where MacGraw explains how the diaphragm he insisted she get was found by her mother and she is now labelled a fallen girl. Benjamin packs his bag and leaves her forever. There's not much to this film and there wasn't much to the Roth novella, little to which any broad-based Amercian audience could relate. Benjamin's performance is so lackadaisical that he bores by his mere presence. A terrible actor in every respect, Benjamin's subsequent performances never improved. Vying with him in thespian ineptitude is MacGraw, foisting herself upon filmgoers with a grating voice and annoying mannerisms. She simply cannot act convincingly on any level and it is a wonder that her career ever went beyond this trifle. Klugman is the only professional who gives a good performance here as the money-clutching businessman. Peerce's direction is slipshod, almost indifferent, one where he provides a patchy and confusing story—a home movie, really—that wouldn't be acceptable on a Saturday night by its players. Songs include "Goodbye, Columbus," "So Kind to You," "It's Got to Be Real" (composed and sung by The Association). Look for Jaclyn Smith in a cameo role as a model.

p, Stanley R. Jaffe; d, Larry Peerce; w, Arnold Schulman (based on the novella by Philip Roth); ph, Gerald Hirschfeld (Technicolor); m, Charles Fox; ed, Ralph Rosenblum; art d, Manny Gerard; cos, Gene Coffin; makeup, Andy Cianella.

Comedy Cas. (PR:O MPAA:R)

GOODBYE EMMANUELLE zero (1980, Fr.) 95m Trinacra-Parafrance/Miramax c

Sylvia Kristel *(Emmanuelle)*, Umberto Orsini *(Husband)*, Alexandra Stewart *(Dorothee)*, Jean-Pierre Bouvier *(Lover)*, Olga Georges Picot *(Woman)*.

Kristel stars in this second sequel to the X-rated EMMANUELLE, but appears more tame than usual, accounting for the picture's R-rating. She is married to an ultra-understanding husband who doesn't want to know about her affairs. She takes up with a film director and all of a sudden hubby goes a bit jealous in the head. Kristel says goodbye and heads for Paris with her lover. So much for dramatic construction. GOODBYE EMMANUELLE, though directed by the competent Leterrier, appeals solely to the erotica market, but even they won't be satisfied with this one's reserved approach.

p, Yves Rousset-Rouard; d, Francois Leterrier; w, Leterrier, Monique Lange (based on the characters created by Emmanuelle Astier); ph, Jean Badal (Eastmancolor); m, Serge Gainsbourg; ed, Marie-Josephe Yoyette.

Drama Cas. (PR:O MPAA:R)

GOODBYE FRANKLIN HIGH½** (1978) 94m Cal-Am c

Lane Caudell, Ann Dusenberry, Darby Hinton, Julie Adams, William Windom.

High-school student Caudell approaches his graduation day with a number of career choices and must choose between his girl friend, his baseball aspirations, and that old standby—a college education. A well-acted, though minor, film about growing up in the 1970s.

p&d, Mike MacFarland; w, Stu Krieger; m/l, Lane Caudell.

Drama/Comedy (PR:A MPAA:PG)

GOODBYE GEMINI* (1970, Brit.) 89m Cinerama c

Judy Geeson *(Jacki)*, Martin Potter *(Julian)*, Michael Redgrave *(James Harrington-Smith)*, Alexis Kanner *(Clive Landseer)*, Mike Pratt *(Rod Barstowe)*, Marion Diamond *(Denise Pryce-Fletcher)*, Freddie Jones *(David Curry)*, Peter Jeffrey *(Detective Inspector Kingsley)*, Terry Scully *(Nigel Garfield)*, Daphne Heard *(Mrs. McLaren)*, Laurence Hardy *(Minister)*, Joseph Furst *(Georgiu)*, Brian Wilde *(Taxi Driver)*, Ricky Renee *(Myra)*, Barry Scott *(Audrey)*, Hilda Barry *(Stallholder)*, Jack Connell *(Barman)*.

Disturbing psychological drama starring Potter and Geeson as 20-year-old incestuous twins living in London's Chelsea area. When another man gets too friendly with his sister, Potter gets him drunk and takes him to a homosexual orgy, where he blackmails him into leaving his sister alone. Afterwards, he convinces Geeson to help him kill this intruder into their lives. Then Potter goes completely mad and kills his sister and himself. Pretty wretched.

p, Joseph Shaftel, Peter Snell; d, Alan Gibson; w, Edmund Ward (based on the novel *Ask Agamemnon*, by Jenni Hall); ph, Geoffrey Unsworth (Eastmancolor); m, Christopher Gunning; ed, Ernest Holser; prod d, Wilfred Shingleton; md, Marcus Dods; art d, Fred Carter; cos, Sandy Moss; m/l, "Tell The World We're Not In," Dennis King, Don Black (sung by The Peddlers), "Nothing's Good And Nothing's Free," "Forget About The Day," Christopher Gunning, Peter Lee Stirling (sung by Stirling), title song by Rick Jones, J. Alexander Ryan (sung by Jackie Lee); makeup, Harry Frampton.

Crime/Drama (PR:O MPAA:R)

GOODBYE GIRL, THE**** (1977) 110m MGM/WB c

Richard Dreyfuss *(Elliott Garfield)*, Marsha Mason *(Paula McFadden)*, Quinn Cummings *(Lucy McFadden)*, Paul Benedict *(Mark Morgenweiss)*, Barbara Rhodes *(Donna Douglas)*, Theresa Merritt *(Mrs. Crosby)*, Michael Shawn *(Ronnie)*, Patricia Pearcy *(Rhonda Fontana)*, Gene Castle *(Assistant Choreographer)*, Daniel Levans *(Dance Instructor)*, Nichol Williamson *(Oliver Frye)*, Marilyn Sokol *(Linda)*, Anita Dangler *(Mrs. Morganweiss)*, Victoria Boothby *(Mrs. Bodine)*, Robert Costanzo *(Liquor Store Salesman)*, Poncho Gonzales, Jose Machado, Hubert Kelly *(Muggers)*, Dana Laurita *(Cynthia)*, Dave Cass *(Drunk)*, Esther Sutherland *(Strip Club Manager)*, Loyita Chapel, Caprice Clarke *(Strip Club Dancers)*, Clarence Felder *(Critic)*, Kensuke Haga, Ryohei Kanokogi *(Japanese Salesmen)*, Ruby Holbrook *(Woman in Audience)*, Kristina Hurrell *(Gretchen)*, David Matthau, Milt Oberman *(Furniture Movers)*, Eddie Villery *(Painter)*, Joseph Carberry, Eric Uhler, Ray Barry, Munson Hicks, Robert Kerman, Jeanne Lange, Robert Lesser, Fred McCarran, Nicholas Mele, Maureen Moore, Joseph Regalbuto, Peter Vogt, Wendy Cutler, Susan Elliott, Andy Goldberg, Paul Willson.

Of all the Simon productions, and these seem myriad in the last decade from a prolific author in search of laughs, THE GOODBYE GIRL perfectly blends humor, sentiment, and romance on a level so pleasant it's almost suspicious. Mason is a divorced ex-Broadway hoofer in her thirties living with her precocious daughter in an apartment suddenly subleased by aspiring actor Dreyfuss, who arrives to take possession in the middle of the night. This is shocking news to Mason who thus learns that her departed lover, also an actor, has not only made her homeless, along with her daughter, Cummings, but has jilted her without notification. Dreyfuss makes it easy on Mason by offering to share the apartment, provided she pays half the rent. She agrees out of desperation and the two strike up an uneasy truce but they battle through the days. Dreyfuss finally gets a lead role in "Richard III," the off-Broadway production directed by a crackpot revisionist, Benedict, who insists that Dreyfuss play the classic role as a swishy gay. He fights this but yields when told he will lose the part. Mason attends opening night which is a disaster; no one likes the play except the wacky Benedict and his weird mother. Dreyfuss and the bizarre production get a universal panning from the critics and the distraught actor is consoled by Mason who has fallen in love with him, going back on her vow never to love again, particularly an actor. He, too, falls for Mason and the two meet romantically on the rooftop of their apartment house, Dreyfuss dressed in a white dinner jacket, having prepared a meal under the stars for her. Mason limbers up and gets a chorus girl job after sweating for the position to help Dreyfuss make ends meet. He then gets a small comedy role and is discovered by Williamson and offered an eight-week movie role out of town. Dreyfuss promises Mason and her daughter that he will return for them as he leaves but, as it begins to rain, the girl every man always says goodbye to grows depressed, feeling that she has been abandoned once more. The phone rings; it's Dreyfuss, calling from a corner booth, asking her and Cummings to go with him. She is overjoyed, now knowing he truly loves her, telling him that it isn't necessary, that she'll be waiting. This is a superb lighthearted comedy deftly directed by Ross who helmed such hits as PLAY IT AGAIN, SAM (1972) and THE TURNING POINT (1977) and produced by Stark, who had backed box office bonanzas such as LOLITA (1962) and FUNNY GIRL (1967). Mason is wonderfully warm and sensitive in her precarious role while her charisma is matched in a flawless performance by Dreyfuss who won an Oscar for Best Actor. Cummings is a charming little girl whose premature sophistication provides some good humor. Benedict steals his scenes as the introspective, nutty theater director whose oddball notions are not far from the unreality of today's off-Broadway mentors. The film was a box office blockbuster, gleaning almost $42 million in its first outing. Next to THE SUNSHINE BOYS, this may be Simon's best script.

p, Ray Stark; d, Herbert Ross; w, Neil Simon; ph, David M. Walsh (Metrocolor); m, David Grusin; ed, John F. Burnett; prod d, Albert Brenner; set d, Jerry Wunderlich; cos, Ann Roth; spec eff, Albert Griswold; m/l, David Gates.

Comedy **Cas.** **(PR:C MPAA:PG)**

GOODBYE LOVE*½ (1934) 65m Jefferson/RKO bw

Charlie Ruggles, Verree Teasdale, Sidney Blackmer, Mayo Methot, Phyllis Barry, Ray Walker, John Kelly, Grace Hale, Luis Alberni.

Dull tale of the trials and tribulations of alimony-payers stars Blackmer as a rich man in "alimony jail" just to spite his ex-wife. Ruggles, his valet, is also sent to jail because he can't afford to make his alimony payments. When Ruggles does get hold of enough cash to pay up, he takes the money and runs off to Atlantic City where he pretends to be an English lord and big-game hunter. During the pretense, he falls for gold digger Teasdale, but she has other plans and marries Blackmer. When he learns of the girl's mercenary intentions, Blackmer frames Teasdale, as well as his first wife. Blackmer finally gets off the alimony hook and goes on to marry his secretary instead.

p, Joseph I. Schnitzer, Samuel Zierler; d, H. Bruce Humberstone; w, Hampton Del Ruth, George Rosener, John Howard Lawson; ph, Charles Schoenbaum.

Comedy/Romance **(PR:A MPAA:NR)**

GOODBYE MR. CHIPS**** (1939, Brit.) 114m MGM bw

Robert Donat *(Charles Chipping)*, Greer Garson *(Katherine Ellis)*, Terry Kilburn *(John/Peter Colley)*, John Mills *(Peter Colley as a young man)*, Paul Henreid *(Max Staefel)*, Judith Furse *(Flora)*, Lyn Harding *(Dr. Wetherby)*, Milton Rosmer *(Charteris)*, Frederick Leister *(Marsham)*, Louise Hampton *(Mrs. Wickett)*, Austin Trevor *(Ralston)*, David Tree *(Jackson)*, Edmund Breon *(Col. Morgan)*, Jill Furse *(Helen Colley)*, Guy Middleton *(McCulloch)*, Nigel Stock *(John Forrester)*, Scott Sunderland *(Sir John Colley)*, Ronald Ward, Patrick Ludlow, Simon Lack, Caven Watson, Cyril Raymond, John Longden.

Donat is nothing less than smashing as the shy and retiring British schoolteacher who guides several generations of young boys to manhood in this superlative Saville production. Boys are shown entering tradition-bound Brookfield School at the beginning of a new term, their names called off a roster and then a flashback to 1870 to show Donat as Mr. Chipping, "Chips" for short, arriving at the same school as a withdrawn novice instructor whose bowler hat is soon knocked off by boys at play. His class runs amuck and causes a commotion that brings headmaster Harding on the run to chastise new teacher Donat. The experience deeply affects him, and, to insulate himself against similar embarrassments, Donat becomes a strict disciplinarian, so aloof and hard with the boys that he becomes the most unpopular teacher in the school, especially after he keeps a failing star athlete from playing in an important match. Promotions elude Donat because of his unyielding attitudes and he is largely forgotten in the backwaters of the school. At forty he takes his first vacation and travels to Austria on a hiking tour. Here he meets and falls in love with Garson. They marry and she brings forth his natural compassion and consideration for his students. Soon his humanity brings him to high esteem among pupils and faculty alike. Garson then tragically dies in childbirth, along with their baby, but the courage and kindness she has exemplified remains with Donat who lingers long into the next century to be revered as the school's most memorable institution. Even in his eighties, when retired, he lives close to the school, tutoring and nurturing his boys. On his deathbed he hears a doctor and teacher conferring, saying that it's a shame he never had any children of his own. Murmurs Donat at the end: "You're wrong. I have—thousands of them, thousands of them, and all my boys." So moving was Donat's performance that he beat out the most popular American candidate for the Best Actor Oscar, Clark Gable for his role of Rhett Butler in GONE WITH THE WIND. Garson also shines brightly in this, the first film to introduce her to American audiences, essaying a role not dissimilar to her marvelous part as MRS. MINIVER (1942). The script is bright and the directing crisp but it is Donat's bravura role that totally captivates, one that almost went to Charles Laughton who was first considered for the part. The story enacted here was written in novella form (about 20,000 words) by James Hilton, or rather gushed out in four days to meet a magazine deadline in 1934. The author was later to state: "I don't think I have ever written so quickly, easily, and with so much certitude that I needn't think twice about a word, a sentence, or a movement in the narrative." The story would have gone unnoticed had not American literary critic Alexander Woollcott raved about it on his syndicated radio show, one overheard by MGM executive Irving Thalberg who immediately bought it for his studio but never lived to see it filmed. (Hilton's father had been a headmaster but the author denied basing the story on him.) The MGM division in England produced this film, constructing the most lavish and expensive sets created for a movie in that country up to that time. Following this film, Garson, who never felt she had a chance for the part and had her bags packed after a Hollywood screen test she believed was a failure, became the personal protege of Louis B. Mayer, who felt she embodied the very essence of decency and good-living. He would go on to star her in PRIDE AND PREJUDICE (1940), BLOSSOMS IN THE DUST (1941), and RANDOM HARVEST (1942). Donat was another matter. He was a huge star by the time he made this film, having scored in such fine films as THE PRIVATE LIFE OF HENRY VIII (1933), THE COUNT OF MONTE CRISTO (1934), THE 39 STEPS (1935), THE GHOST GOES WEST (1936), and THE CITADEL (1938). Since his contract called for script approval, he was able to turn down many MGM scripts, often as not B-grade material, which Mayer attempted to foist upon him, and some major productions such as DR. JEKYLL AND MR. HYDE (1940), the lead for which went to Spencer Tracy, and STAND BY FOR ACTION (1943) which later starred Robert Taylor. He did star in two MGM films of his own selection, ADVENTURES OF TARTU (1943) and PERFECT STRANGERS (1945, also known as VACATION FROM MARRIAGE), both being unimportant productions. Donat, never healthy throughout his life, died prematurely of a severe asthma condition in 1958, at age 53. (He made only 19 films in his lifetime.) A musical remake of this brilliant film starred Peter O'Toole but, aside from the charming performance of its lead, it was lackluster from beginning to end.

p, Victor Saville; d, Sam Wood; w, W.C. Sheriff, Claudine West, Eric Maschwitz, Sidney Franklin (based on the novella by James Hilton); ph, Frederick A. Young; m, Richard Addinsell; ed, Charles Frend; md, Louis Levy; art d, Alfred Junge; cos, Julie Harris.

Drama **(PR:AAA MPAA:NR)**

GOODBYE MR. CHIPS½** (1969, U.S./Brit.) 151m APJAC/MGM c

Peter O'Toole *(Arthur Chipping)*, Petula Clark *(Katherine Bridges)*, Michael Redgrave *(Headmaster)*, George Baker *(Lord Sutterwick)*, Sian Phillips *(Ursula Mossbank)*, Michael Bryant *(Max Staefel)*, Jack Hedley *(William Baxter)*, Alison Leggatt *(Headmaster's Wife)*, Clinton Greyn *(Bill Calbury)*, Barbara Couper *(Mrs. Paunceforth)*, Michael Culver *(Johnny Longbridge)*, Elspet Gray *(Lady Sutterwick)*, Clive Morton *(Gen. Paunceforth)*, Ronnie Stevens *(Algie)*, John Gugolka *(Sutterwick, Jr.)*, Michael Ridgeway *(David)*, Tom Owen *(Farley)*, Mario Maranzana *(Pompeii Guide)*, Sheila Steafel *(Tilly)*, Jeremy Lloyd *(Johnson)*, Elspeth March *(Mrs. Summersthwaite)*, Craig Marriott *(New Boy)*, Jack May *(Price)*, Leo Britt *(Elder Master)*, Boyston Tickner *(Policeman)*, Patricia Hayes *(Miss Honeybun)*, The Boys of Sherborne School.

A misfired musical remake of the classic 1939 Robert Donat-Greer Garson film stars O'Toole in fine form as Chips and pop-singer Clark less-than successful as his bride. O'Toole, a shy and unassuming schoolmaster in England circa 1924, grows frustrated with a student body that he seems unable to communicate with. While on holiday, he is taken to a music hall by a former student and it is there he meets Clark, an uneducated singer. Later, while vacationing at Pompeii, O'Toole again meets Clark and the couple fall in love and marry. The union is surprisingly successful, with O'Toole educating Clark and she teaching him how to come out of his shell. When school begins again, Baker, an important benefactor, learns of O'Toole's marriage to the dance hall girl and tries to have him fired. Luckily, Clark knows the man's former mistress and, when confronted by her, Baker backs down. As the years go by O'Toole and Clark are happy and content, though he never seems able to land the headmaster's position at the school. When WW II erupts, Clark volunteers to entertain the troops and while away she is killed in a bomb explosion. Tragically, O'Toole is finally named headmaster just before Clark's death but he is unable to relay the news to her. Eventually, O'Toole retires and gives a memorable, impassioned farewell address to the students and faculty before he leaves. GOODBYE MR. CHIPS was given a lavish production by the studio with most of the film shot on location at Sherborne School in Dorset, England, and also in Pompeii. The musical numbers are passable but far from memorable, save for O'Toole's atrocious attempt at singing in the "Where Did My Childhood Go?" number. Overall, rookie director Ross stumbles over the material, neither destroying nor enhancing the talents of O'Toole, Clark and company. (He would improve vastly with such hits as THE GOODBYE GIRL, 1977.) Aside from the obvious addition of music to the basic story, other things were changed as well. The time frame of the film is shifted from WW I to WW II and Mrs. Chips undergoes a metamorphosis from educated society lady to poor, down-to-earth, dance hall girl. The changes are of negligible importance because irrespective of what the producers decided to do, they took on a losing proposition by trying to top Robert Donat's masterful performance in the original version of GOODBYE MR. CHIPS with O'Toole and a fistful of songs. Leslie Bricusse penned the tunes which include: "Fill The World with Love" (sung by boy's chorus), "Where Did My Childhood Go?" (O'Toole), "London Is London" (Clark and chorus), "And the Sky Smiled" (Clark), "Apollo" (Clark), "When I Am Older" (boy's chorus), "Walk Through the World" (chorus), "What Shall I Do with Today?" (Clark), "What a Lot of Flowers" (O'Toole), "Schooldays" (Clark and chorus), "When I Was Younger" (O'Toole), "You And I" (Clark).

p, Arthur P. Jacobs; d, Herbert Ross; w, Terence Rattigan (based on the novelette by James Hilton); ph, Oswald Morris (Panavision, Metrocolor); m, John Williams; ed, Ralph Kemplen; prod d, Ken Adams; art d, Maurice Fowler; cos, Julie Harris; ch, Nora Kaye.

Musical **(PR:A MPAA:G)**

GOODBYE, MOSCOW**   (1968, Jap.) 97m Toho c
(SARABA MOSUKUWA GURENTAI)

Yuzo Kayama (The Promoter), Toshiko Morita, Shigeru Koyama, Toshio Kurosawa.

Cynical film features Kayama as a jazz musician turned promoter. Although he is highly successful, Kayama is bored with his life so he travels to Moscow, putting off his decision to quit the business. There he befriends a young dissident trumpet player. The boy is encouraged by Kayama, much to the anger of both the Japanese embassy and the boy's youth leader brother. After the boy is arrested for fighting, Kayama finds himself alone and bitter once again. Filmed on location in Japan and Moscow.

p, Masumi Fujimoto; d, Hiromichi Horikawa; w, Takeshi Tamura; ph, Yasumichi Fukuzawa (Eastmancolor); m, Toshiro Mayuzumi, Massao Yagi; art d, Shinobu Muraki.

Drama   **(PR:O   MPAA:NR)**

GOODBYE, MY FANCY**   (1951) 106m WB bw

Joan Crawford (Agatha Reed), Robert Young (Dr. James Merrill), Frank Lovejoy (Matt Cole), Eve Arden (Woody), Janice Rule (Virginia Merrill), Lurene Tuttle (Ellen Griswold), Howard St. John (Claude Griswold), Viola Roache (Miss Shackleford), Ellen Corby (Miss Birdeshaw), Morgan Farley (Dr. Pitt), Virginia Gibson (Mary Nell Dodge), John Qualen (Prof. Dingley), Ann Robin (Clarissa Carter), Mary Carver (Jon Wintner), Creighton Hale (Butler), Frank Hyer (Man), John Alvin (Jack White), John Hedloe (Telephone Man), Phil Tead (Reporter), Larry Williams, Fredrick Howard, Lucius Cook (Congressman).

To bridge the gap between comedy and drama, GOODBYE MY FANCY accomplishes neither. Based on a play by Fay Kanin, it is the story of Crawford, an aggressive and assertive congresswoman, who returns to her alma mater to receive a degree. The irony is that she had been expelled from the school two decades previously, and she agrees to take the award if only to rub their noses in her success. Her one-time lover, Young, is now president of the school and she is looking forward to seeing him again. Her expulsion had been as the result of an all-night escapade with Young when he was a fledgling professor and she was a student. She left the school in tears and has not seen him since. It should go without saying that sparks fly the moment they see each other once more. But there's a problem: Lovejoy is a journalist-photographer who has been trailing Crawford for quite some time, gathering material for a story. He is crazy in love with her and a triangle begins to form. Lovejoy wants to marry Crawford and does what he can to break up the budding re-romance between her and Young. Meanwhile, in a sub-plot, Farley is a professor at the school who feels that the college is mired in old-fashioned methods. He wishes to bring it up to date, instead of allowing it to continue using outdated teaching systems. St. John and Tuttle, trustees of the school, are rock-ribbed conservatives and totally against any alterations in the curriculum. Crawford joins Farley in his crusade. Several complications arise and Crawford sees that Young is wishy-washy and that she would be much happier with Lovejoy. She bids farewell to Young as the picture ends. It was not a hit on Broadway and failed at the movie box office as well. There are not enough laughs in the Goff/Roberts screenplay to make us feel lighthearted and there is far too much preachiness to take it seriously. Mostly worth watching for Lovejoy's performance.

p, Henry Blanke; d, Vincent Sherman; w, Ivan Goff, Ben Roberts (based on the play by Fay Kanin); ph, Ted McCord; m, Ray Heindorf; ed, Rudi Fehr; art d, Stanley Fleischer; cos, Sheila O'Brien.

Romance/Drama   **(PR:A   MPAA:NR)**

GOODBYE, MY LADY***   (1956) 94m Batjac/WB bw

Walter Brennan (Uncle Jesse), Phil Harris (Cash), Brandon de Wilde (Skeeter), Sidney Poitier (Gates), William Hopper (Grover), Louise Beavers (Bonnie Drew).

Rites-of-passage childhood drama starring de Wilde as a 14-year-old orphan who lives in the Mississippi swamps with his elderly uncle, Brennan. One day de Wilde finds a stray dog and adopts it. After becoming attached to the animal, the boy finds out that the dog actually has another owner and there is a large reward posted for its return. Torn between his love for the dog and his conscience which tells him to return her, he makes the first mature decision of his life and brings the dog back to its rightful owners. An appealing family film with some tender moments.

d, William A. Wellman; w, Sid Fleischman (based on a novel by James Street); ph, William H. Clothier; m, Laurindo Almeida, George Field; ed, Fred MacDowell; art d, Donald A. Peters; cos, Carl Walker; m/l, "When Your Boy Becomes A Man," Don Powell, Moris Erby.

Drama   **(PR:AA   MPAA:NR)**

GOODBYE, NORMA JEAN zero (1976) 95m Austamerican/Filmways c

Misty Rowe (Norma Jean Baker), Terrence Locke (Ralph Johnson), Patch Mackenzie (Ruth Latimer), Preston Hanson (Hal James), Marty Zagon (Irving Olbach), Andre Philippe (Sam Dunn), Ivey Bethune, Steve Brown, Adele Claire, Frank Curcio, Jean Sarah Frost, Stuart Lancaster, Lilyan McBride, Burr Middleton, Paula Mitchell, Garth Pillsbury.

Rancid movie-bio of Marilyn Monroe's early years when she was just a movie fan by the name of Norma Jean Baker, played by Rowe. The film opens in 1941 and sees a young Rowe raped by a highway patrolman as payment for a speeding ticket. This incident, presumably, is meant to illustrate Rowe's dissatisfaction with sex that would ironically plague her the rest of her life. After she wins a beauty contest, it is a series of sleazy sexual encounters from there to Hollywood and fame. Sensationalistic and slimy with no real insight into Monroe's character.

p&d, Larry Buchanan; w, Lyn Hubert, Buchanan; ph, Bob Sherry; m, Joe Beck, m/l, "Norma Jean Wants To Be A Movie Star," Johnny Cunningham (sung by Cunningham).

Biography   **Cas.**   **(PR:O   MPAA:R)**

GOODBYE PORK PIE**½ (1981, New Zealand) 105m New Zealand Film
Commission/Brent Walker c

Tony Barry, Kelly Johnson, Claire Oberman, Shirley Gruar, Jackie Lowitt, Don Selwyn, Shirley Dunn, Paki Cherrington, Christine Lloyd, Maggie Maxwell, John Ferdinand, Clyde Scott, Steven Tozer, Phil Gordon, Bruno Lawrence, Adele Chapman, Ian Watkin, Frances Edmond, Marshall Napier, Bill Juliff, John Bach, Liz Simpson, Alan Wilke, Paul Watson, Timothy Lee, Michael Woolf, Andrew Dungan, Frank Prythetch, Linus Murphy, Matthew Nieuwlands, Danny O'Connel, Paul Paino, David Pottinger, Keith Richardson, Roy Sanders, Gene Saunders, Doug Aston, Charles Barlow, Len Bernard, Mike Booth, Morris Bruce, Bill Carson, Norman Fairley, Norman Fletcher, Ged Sharp, Peter Sledmere, Kevin Simpson, The Wizard, Brain Ward, John Galvin, Dee Kelly, Max Kennard, Melissa Lawrence, Chris Lines, Jim Woodfine.

A road movie set in New Zealand (is there enough road there to accommodate a road movie?) about three fun-loving youngsters pursued by police. The plot, as in many road movies from THEY LIVE BY NIGHT (1948) to KINGS OF THE ROAD (1976) to THE ROAD WARRIOR (1982), is kept to a minimum, concentrating instead on the characters, the surroundings, and the desire to live free and drive fast.

p, Nigel Hutchinson, Geoff Murphy; d, Murphy; w, Murphy, Ian Mune; ph, Alaun Bollinger (Eastmancolor); m, John Charles; ed, Mike Horton; art d, Kal Hawkins, Robin Outterside.

Drama/Adventure   **Cas.**   **(PR:C   MPAA:NR)**

GOODBYE TO THE HILL   (SEE: PADDY, 1970, Ireland)

GOODNIGHT, LADIES AND GENTLEMEN**½   (1977, Ital.) 119m
Maggio Cooperativa/Titanus c
(SIGNORE E SIGNORI, BUONANOTTE)

Senta Berger, Adolfo Celi, Vittorio Gassman, Nino Manfredi, Marcello Mastroianni, Ugo Tognazzi, Paolo Villaggio.

A fragmentary movie with several different segments written and directed by a variety of Italian talents. All of the stories are witty looks at Italian political and social life. One of the standout segments, "The Bomb," directed by Monicelli, is a political satire which sees a silly bomb scare at a police station snowball into an actual terrorist plot wherein the commissioner is blown to bits. Other segments include a look at Christmas in Naples through the eyes of a child who sees all the public officials who participate in the ceremonies as pompous and eccentric, and a satire on the CIA. The whole thing is cemented through the use of an Italian Broadcasting Corp. news show that introduces each segment and is anchored by Mastroianni. Most of the material is fine, but a few of the segments would have benefitted from cutting.

p, Franco Committeri; d&w, Age/Scarpelli, Leo Benvenuti, Luigi Comencini, Piero De Bernardi, Nanni Loy, Ruggero Maccari, Luigi Magni, Mario Monicelli, Ugo Pirro, Ettore Scola; ph, Claudio Ragona (Eastmancolor); m, Lucio Dalla, Antonello Venditti, Giuseppe Mazzuca, Nicola Samale; ed, Amedeo Salfa; art d, Lucia Mirisola, Lorenzo Baraldi, Luciano Spadoni.

Satire   **(PR:C-O   MPAA:NR)**

GOODNIGHT SWEETHEART*½   (1944) 67m REP bw

Robert Livingston (Johnny Newsome), Ruth Terry (Caryl Martin), Henry Hull (Jeff Parker), Grant Withers (Matt Colby), Thurston Hall (Judge James Rutherford), Lloyd Corrigan (Police Chief Davis), Maude Eburne (Johnny's Landlady), Olin Howlin (Slim Taylor), Lucien Littlefield (Collins), Ellen Lowe (Caryl's Landlady), Chester Conklin (Bottle Man), Emmett Lynn (Pete), Billy Benedict (Bellboy).

Uninspired programmer featuring ex-cowboy star Livingston as the cocky, big-city reporter who moves to a small town to take over a newspaper he half owns. Of course he brings his tough, antagonistic reporting style with him and stirs up plenty of trouble for the opposition's mayoral candidate until the politician's pretty niece, Terry, teaches the brash reporter a lesson.

d, Joseph Santley; w, Isabel Dawn, Jack Townley (based on a story by Frank Fenton, Joseph Hoffman); ph, Bud Thackery; m, Morton Scott; ed, Ralph Dixon; md, Morton Scott; art d, Fred A. Ritter.

Drama   **(PR:A   MPAA:NR)**

GOODNIGHT VIENNA   (SEE: MAGIC NIGHT, 1933, Brit.)

GOOSE AND THE GANDER, THE**   (1935) 65m WB bw

Kay Francis (Georgiana), George Brent (Bob McNear), Genevieve Tobin (Betty Summers), John Eldredge (Lawrence), Claire Dodd (Connie Thurston), Helen Lowell (Aunt Julia), Ralph Forbes (Ralph Summers), William Austin (Arthur Summers), Spencer Charters (Winklesteinberger), Eddie Shubert (Sweeney), John Sheenan (Murphy), Charles Coleman (Jones), Wade Boteler, Davison Clark, Nick Copeland, Cliff Saum, Glen Cavender (Detectives), Al Woods (Bellboy), Milton Kibbee (Garageman), Jack Richardson (Baggage Man), David Newell (Hotel Clerk), Eddy Chandler (Policeman), Guy Usher (Sergeant), Edward McWade (Justice of Peace), Helen Woods (Violet), Bill Elliot (Teddy), Jan Buckingham (Mrs. Burns), Carlyle Blackwell, Jr. (Barkley), Olive Jones (Miss Brent).

Overly complicated bedroom farce starring Francis, who is divorced from Forbes, and who shockingly overhears his second wife, Tobin, make plans to spend an adulterous weekend with Brent while her husband is away on business. Wanting Forbes to catch the pair in the act, Francis fixes things so that Brent and Tobin cannot make it to their destination and they have to stay in her house. Francis then arranges for Forbes to come over and witness his wife's infidelity, but things go haywire when a pair of jewel thieves, Dodd and Eldredge, become stranded at Francis' house as well. The situation gets worse when Francis realizes she cannot go through with the plot because she has fallen in love with Brent. Happily, the jewels are recovered by Tobin, and Forbes makes his way to the house just in time to witness the wedding of Brent and Francis.

p, James Seymour; d, Alfred E. Green; w, Charles Kenyon; ph, Sid Hickox; ed, Howard Leonard; md, Leo F. Forbstein; art d, Robert M. Haas; cos, Orry-Kelly.

Comedy **(PR:A MPAA:NR)**

GOOSE GIRL, THE½ (1967, Ger.) 78m
Fritz Genschow-Film/Childhood Productions c
(DIE GANSEMAGD)

Rita-Maria Nowotny, Fritz Genschow, Renee Stobrawa, Renate Fischer, Theodor Vogeler, Gunter Hertel, Alexander Welbat, Wolfgang Draeger, Peter Hack.

Based on a Grimm Brothers' story, this is the tale of an enchanted princess on her way to marry a prince. During her travels she loses her magical powers and is forced to change identities with her evil maid-servant. After their arrival, the phony princess puts the true one to work as a goose tender. She then decapitates a magical talking horse so he will not give away the secret. But the horse head is mounted and the king overhears the goose-tending princess talking with it. The king discovers the true story and the rightfully betrothed marries the prince. The decapitation ruins this one for children.

p,d&w, Fritz Genschow (based on "Die Gansemagd" by Jakob and Wilhelm Grimm); ph, Gerhard Huttula (Agfacolor); m, Richard Stauch; ed, Erika Petrik; art d, Siegfried Kiok; cos, Grete Gorlich.

Fairy Tale **(PR:C-O MPAA:NR)**

GOOSE STEP (SEE: BEASTS OF BERLIN, 1939)

GOOSE STEPS OUT, THE** (1942, Brit.) 79m EAL/UA bw

Will Hay (William Potts/Muller), Frank Pettingell (Prof. Hoffman), Julien Mitchell (Gen. Von Glotz), Charles Hawtrey (Max), Peter Croft (Hans), Anne Firth (Lena), Leslie Harcourt (Vagel), Jeremy Hawk (ADC), Raymond Lovell (Schmidt), Aubrey Mallalieu (Rector), Barry Morse (Kurt), Lawrence O'Madden (Col. Truscott), Peter Ustinov (Krauss).

A harmless wartime comedy which casts Hay in a dual role—that of a British spy and a Nazi spy to whom he bears a remarkable resemblance. He manages to infiltrate a German university, pose as the Nazi, confuse the students (telling them that the "V for Victory" symbol is used instead of the traditional Nazi salute), and steals a top-secret bomb. A funny programmer which served solely as an alternative to watching the news reports on the real war.

p, S.C. Balcon; d, Will Hay, Basil Dearden; w, Angus Macphail, John Dighton (based on a story by Bernard Miles, Reginald Groves); ph, Ernest Palmer.

Comedy **(PR:A MPAA:NR)**

GORATH*½ (1964, Jap.) 83m Toho/COL c
(YOSEI GORASU)

Ryo Ikebe, Akihiko Hirata, Jun Tazaki, Yumi Shirakawa, Takashi Shimura, Kumi Mizuno.

Slow Japanese sci-fi effort set in the future detailing the terror caused by a giant runaway planet known as "Gorath," that is hurtling its way on a collision course with Earth. Clever scientists band together and move Earth into a different orbit with large rockets, removing it from Gorath's path. Too bad this is where the American release prints end. In the Japanese prints, the film continues and we see the earthquakes and destruction caused by the change in the Earth's orbit which releases a giant walrus from underneath the South Pole. Directed by veteran GODZILLA helmsman, Honda.

d, Inoshiro Honda; w, Takeshi Kimuri; ph, Hajime Koizumil (Tohoscope, Eastmancolor); m, Kan Ishil; spec eff, Eiji Tsuburaya.

Science Fiction **Cas.** **(PR:C MPAA:NR)**

GORBALS STORY, THE*½ (1950, Brit.) 74m
New World/Eros bw

Howard Connell (Willie Mutrie), Betty Henderson (Peggie Anderson), Russell Hunter (Johnnie Martin), Marjorie Thomson (Jean Mutrie), Roddy McMillan (Hector), Isobel Campbell (Nora Reilly), Jack Stewart (Peter Reilly), Archie Duncan (Bull), Sybil Thomson, Eveline Garrett, Lothar Lewinsohn.

A well-meaning attempt at showing how the sleazy Glasgow tenement atmosphere can lead to violence. Connell is cast as a decent, soft-spoken chap who comes desperately close to committing murder. Instead, he leaves the slums and devotes his life to art. All the fine intentions in the world can't keep this from appearing second-rate.

p, Ernest Gartside; d&w, David MacKane (based on a play by Robert McLeish); ph, Stanley Clinton.

Drama **(PR:C MPAA:NR)**

GORDEYEV FAMILY, THE**½ (1961, U.S.S.R.) 96m Gorky Film
Studio/Artkino bw (FOMA GORDEYEV)

Sergey Lukyanov (Ignat Gordeyev), Georgiy Yepifantsev (Foma Gordeyev), Pavel Tarasov (Yakov Mayakin), Alla Labetskaya (Lyuba), Marina Strizhenova (Sasha), Mariya Milkova (Sofiya Pavlovna Medynskaya), I. Sretenskiy (Yezhov), G. Sergeyev (Smolin), A. Glushchenko (Krasnoshchyokov), I. Gurov (Ukhtishchev), B. Sitko (Knyazev), Boris Andreyev (Zvantsev), Sasha Balitskiy (Foma as a Child), Lyusya Nikiforova, Ira Nikiforova (Lyuba as a Child), Vladik Lebedev (Smolin as a Child), Sasha Kukareko (Yezhov as a Child), A. Timontayev, A. Zhukov, A. Karpov, A. Solovyov, A. Geleva, A. Baranov, S. Troitskiy, Konstantin

Nemolyayev, L. Sokolova, A. Tsinman, N. Butuzov, A. Garichev, L. Dobkevich, Ye. Pavlova, I. Nechanov.

This film is set in St. Petersburg at the turn of the century where Lukyanov, a wealthy grain merchant, wants his son, Yepifantsev, to follow in his footsteps. After a night of drunken abandon, Lukyanov dies, and his business partner, played by Tarasov, tries to teach the grain trade to Yepifantsev. But the boy is enraged by the hypocrisy of the business world and shows little interest in acquiring wealth. Although he can easily marry Tarasov's daughter and settle into a comfortable life, he instead flits from one affair to another, becoming further disillusioned with life. When the merchants decide they can no longer tolerate his antics, they have him thrown into an insane asylum. Eventually released, Yepifantsev lives out his days as a pauper at a flophouse established with his father's money. An interesting plot of a Soviet film, taken from the socialist writings of the great pre-revolutionary thinker Maxim Gorky.

d, Mark Donskoy; w, Boris Byalik, Donskoy (based on the novel Foma Gordeyev by Maxim Gorky); ph, Margarita Pilikhina; m, Lev Shvarts; ed, A. Klebanova; md, A. Zhyuraytis; art d, Pyotr Pashkevich; set d, B. Duksht; cos, E. Rappoport; spec eff, S. Ivanov; makeup, A. Smirnov.

Drama **(PR:O MPAA:NR)**

GORDON IL PIRATA NERO (SEE: RAGE OF THE BUCCANEERS, 1962, Ital.)

GORDON'S WAR* (1973) 89m FOX c

Paul Winfield (Gordon), Carl Lee (Bee), David Downing (Otis), Tony King (Roy), Gilbert Lewis (Spanish Harry), Carl Gordon (Luther the Pimp), Nathan C. Heard (Big Pink), Grace Jones (Mary), Jackie Page (Bedroom Girl), Charles Bergansky (Caucasian), Adam Wade (Hustler), Hansford Rowe (Dog Salesman), Warren Taurien (Goose), Ralph Wilcox (Black Hit Man), David Connell (Hotel Proprietor), Richelle LeNoir (Gordon's Wife), Michael Galloway (Gray-Haired Executive).

An uninspired and ultra-violent film that has returning Vietnam vet Winfield becoming enraged after his wife overdoses on drugs. He forms a vigilante group and goes after fellow blacks who are pushing dope in Harlem, creating an all-out street war. The blood flows freely and as senselessly as in any martial arts movie and is not helped by a motorcycle chase finish. The script is abysmal, the acting barely professional, and Davis' direction is almost invisible. Just another black exploitation mess which puts on social consciousness airs which any 10-year-old will see through.

p, Robert L. Schaffel; d, Ossie Davis; w, Howard Friedlander, Ed Spielman; ph, Victor J. Kemper (Panavision, DeLuxe Color); m, Horace Ott; ed, Eric Albertson; art d, Perry Watkins; set d, Robert Drumheller; cos, Anna Hill Johnstone; m/l, Andy Badale, Al Elias.

Crime Drama **(PR:O MPAA:R)**

GORGEOUS HUSSY, THE**½ (1936) 103m MGM bw

Joan Crawford (Peggy O'Neal Eaton), Robert Taylor (Bow Timberlake), Lionel Barrymore (Andrew Jackson), Melvyn Douglas (John Randolph), James Stewart ("Rowdy" Roderick Dow), Franchot Tone (John Eaton), Louis Calhern (Sunderland), Alison Skipworth (Mrs. Beall), Beulah Bondi (Rachel Jackson), Melville Cooper (Cuthbert), Edith Atwater (Lady Vaughn), Sidney Toler (Daniel Webster), Gene Lockhart (Maj. O'Neal), Phoebe Foster (Emily Donaldson), Clara Blandick (Louisa Abbott), Frank Conroy (John C. Calhoun), Nydia Westman (Maybelle), Louise Beavers (Aunt Sukey), Charles Trowbridge (Martin Van Buren), Willard Robertson (Secretary Ingham), Greta Meyer (Mrs. Oxenrider), Fred "Snowflake" Toone (Horatius), William Orlamond (Herr Oxenrider), Tom Herbert (Slave Dealer), Lee Phelps (Bartender), Rubye de Remer (Mrs. Bellamy), Betty Blythe (Mrs. Wainwright), George Reed (Braxton), Bert Roach (Maj. Domo), Else Janssen (Dutch Minister's Wife), Oscar Apfel (Tompkins), Richard Powell (Doorman), Lee Harvey, Sid Saylor, Wade Boteler, Hooper Atchley (Agitators), Zeffie Tilbury (Mrs. Daniel Beall), Harry Holman (Auctioneer), Morgan Wallace (Slave Buyer), Ward Bond (Officer), Samuel S. Hinds (Commander), Sam McDaniel (Butler), Harry Strang (Navigator).

Joan Crawford could do a lot of things in her day but she was quite miscast in the role of THE GORGEOUS HUSSY, though there's no questioning the fact that she was gorgeous and that there was no less a hussier. Surrounded by several leading men (Stewart, Tone, Barrymore, Douglas, and Taylor), Crawford is the daughter of an innkeeper in 1830s Washington, D.C. She looks terrific in her first costume role and struts and preens as well as Irene Dunne could have. Barrymore is President Jackson and currently staving off the liberal types who are eager to secede from the union. Washington society members turn up their noses at Jackson because his wife, Bondi, had been a backwoods girl before he met her. She'd moved in with Barrymore before the divorce from her first husband was granted and thus had been living in what might have been deemed "sin" for quite a while. Barrymore and Bondi stay at the inn where he befriends Crawford, a forward-thinking woman who advocates female suffrage. Since the inn is so close to Washington, Crawford is friendly with most of the politicians, as is her father, Lockhart. All of the notables of the time surround her and attempt to win her hand. She's in love with Melvin Douglas but he keeps her at arms's length. She is hurt by the rejection and marries Taylor, a young Navy lieutenant, on the rebound. But he is killed soon after in war-related action and she begins a romantic alliance with Tone, who later becomes a cabinet member. Crawford and Tone are happy with each other and her star rises in polite society but the snobby women oppose her. Meanwhile, their husbands, as most men in Washington, find her pert, attractive, bright, and worthwhile. Crawford and Barrymore continue their friendship and she becomes the unofficial White House "niece," a person to whom Barrymore can unload his worries and fear no betrayal. The closer she gets to Barrymore, the more she is hated by those who can not get near the man. They start a campaign against her and sully her name, saying she is disloyal to the country. Barrymore investigates the allegations and determines that the guilty parties are the members of his cabinet. Then he dismisses them all for their roles in the cabal against Crawford. Rather than cause any further problems, Crawford exits Washington and the nation carries on. This was a lot of story in 103 minutes, and it has lots of facets of a little-known woman in U.S. history. But that is no guarantee that anyone will be interested in her life. A disappointment at the box office and no amount of advertising could save it. Ward Bond is seen in one of his earliest roles as an unnamed officer, and Sidney Toler, who was later to make his mark as the Asian Charlie Chan, is Daniel Webster. There has yet to be a great movie success based on American history. And we wonder if it isn't because we are taught so much of it at school that we hate the thought of paying for it at the box office.

p, Joseph Mankiewicz; d, Clarence Brown; w, Ainsworth Morgan, Stephen Morehouse Avery (based on the book by Samuel Hopkins Adams); ph, George Folsey; m, Herbert Stothart; ed, Blanche Sewell; art d, Cedric Gibbons; cos, Adrian; ch Val Raset.

Historical Drama   **(PR:AA MPAA:NR)**

GORGO**½   (1961, Brit.) 79m MGM c

Bill Travers (Joe), William Sylvester (Sam), Vincent Winter (Sean), Christopher Rhodes (McCartin), Joseph O'Conor (Prof. Hendricks), Bruce Seton (Prof. Flaherty), Martin Benson (Dorkin), Maurice Kauffman (Radio Reporter), Basil Dignam (Admiral), Barry Keegan (Mate), Thomas Duggan (Naval Officer), Howard Lang (Colonel), Dervis Ward (Bosun), Connie Tilton, David Wilding, Michael Dillon, Peter Brace, Peter Perkins (Stunt Artists).

Giant monster tale set in England details the discovery and subsequent exploitation of a 65-foot prehistoric dinosaur called Gorgo, caught off the coast of Ireland. The critter is brought back to London and shown off by unscrupulous exhibitors in a circus, until Gorgo's 250-foot mom arrives and destroys half the city to rescue her baby and bring him home. Director Lourie rips off sequences from his earlier film, BEAST FROM TWENTY-THOUSAND FATHOMS, which was better and boasted fantastic stop-motion animation effects from Ray Harryhausen.

p, Wilfred Eades; d, Eugene Lourie; w, John Loring, Daniel Hyatt; ph, F.A. Young (Technicolor); m, Angelo Lavagnino; ed, Eric Boyd-Perkins; art d, Elliott Scott; spec eff, Tom Howard.

Science Fiction   **Cas.**   **(PR:C MPAA:NR)**

GORGON, THE**½   (1964, Brit.) 83m Hammer/COL c

Peter Cushing (Namaroff), Christopher Lee (Meister), Richard Pasco (Paul), Barbara Shelly (Carla), Michael Goodliffe (Heitz), Patrick Troughton (Kanof), Jack Watson (Eatoff), Jeremy Longhurst (Bruno), Toni Gilpin (Sascha), Redmond Phillips (Hans), Joseph O'Conor (Coroner), Alister Williamson (Cass), Michael Peake (Policeman), Sally Nesbitt (Nurse), Prudence Hyman (Chatelaine).

Slow but atmospheric Hammer film, set in Germany of 1910, stars Lee as a professor who arrives in a small hamlet to investigate the rash of mysterious murders that have literally turned a portion of the male populace into stone. The trail leads to eccentric brain surgeon Cushing, who is protecting his lovely assistant, Shelly. It is she who is possessed with a strange affliction that transforms her into a modern day Medusa at night, replete with snakes in her hair. After Cushing has also been turned to stone, Lee cuts off Shelly-Medusa's head and ends the terror.

p, Anthony Nelson Keys; d, Terence Fisher; w, John Gilling (based on a story by J. Liewellyn Devine); ph, Michael Reed (Technicolor); m, James Bernard; ed, James Needs; prod d, Bernard Robinson; art d, Don Mingaye; spec eff, Syd Pearson; makeup, Roy Ashton.

Horror   **Cas.**   **(PR:C-O MPAA:NR)**

GORILLA, THE*½   (1931) 58m WB bw

Lila Lee (Alice Denby), Joe Frisco (Garrity), Joe Gribbon (Mulligan), Walter Pidgeon (Arthur Marsden), Purnell Pratt (The Stranger), Edwin Maxwell (Cyrus Stevens), Roscoe Karns (Simmons), Landers Stevens (The Inspector), William Philbrick (Servant).

Slapstick mystery stars Frisco as a bumbling detective hired to flush a wild gorilla out of a spooky mansion. Nonsensical sequences include a spot in which the detective dresses up like a gorilla himself. Filmed as a silent in 1927.

d, Bryan Foy; w, Ralph Spence, Herman Ruby, W. Harrison Orkow (based on a play by Spence); ph, Sid Hickox; ed, George Amy.

Comedy/Mystery   **(PR:A MPAA:NR)**

GORILLA, THE**   (1939) 65m FOX bw

Jimmy Ritz (Garrity), Harry Ritz (Harrigan), Al Ritz (Mulligan), Anita Louise (Norma Denby), Patsy Kelly (Kitty), Lionel Atwill (Walter Stevens), Bela Lugosi (Peters), Joseph Calleia (Stanger), Edward Norris (Jack Marsden), Wally Vernon (Seaman), Paul Harvey (Conway), Art Miles (The Gorilla).

The third film version of the comedy-mystery stage play by Ralph Spence is used as a vehicle for the Ritz Brothers. The boys play three bumbling detectives hired by wealthy Atwill to capture a killer known only as "The Gorilla" (he dresses like one), who has threatened his life. The three goofs stake out the mansion, which is filled with trap doors and secret passages, and await the arrival of the killer. Unfortunately, a real gorilla escapes from the local circus and shows up at the mansion, adding to the confusion and comedy. The Ritz Brothers do their usual mugging and grimacing, and Lugosi is totally wasted as a menacing butler (the role was originally cast for Peter Lorre). It was not a happy set as the Ritz Brothers tried to back out of the film after the screenplay had been adapted to fit their bits into it. Fox suspended the comedians and filed a lawsuit against them for $150,000 and the boys trotted quickly back to the set. Their compliance came a bit too late, for after the shooting Fox dropped the comics from its payroll. (See RITZ BROTHERS series, Index.)

p, Darryl F. Zanuck, Harry Joe Brown; d, Allan Dwan; w, Rian James, Sid Silvers (based on the play by Ralph Spence); ph, Edward Cronjager; ed, Allen McNeil; md, David Buttolph; art d, Richard Day, Lewis Creber; makeup, Perc Westmore.

Comedy/Mystery   **Cas.**   **(PR:A MPAA:NR)**

GORILLA, 1944   (SEE: NABONGA, 1944)

GORILLA**   (1964, Swed.) 90m Terrafilm-Alf Jorgensen/Herts-Lion International c

Georges Galley (Game Warden), Gio Petre (Journalist).

A gorilla goes on the rampage in the Belgian Congo and the local witch doctor decides the only way to stop the terror is to sacrifice a new-born infant. A local game warden, along with a journalist who is researching the natives, work together to stop the enraged animal and fall in love along the way. After they accomplish their task, she must return home, but the couple promise they will meet again one day. An early work for cinematographer Nykvist, who later worked with Ingmar Bergman and other important directors. It was filmed on location in the Belgian Congo and released in Sweden eight years before the American release.

p, Lorens Marmstedt; d, Lars Henrik Ottoson, Sven Nykvist; w, Ottoson; ph, Nykvist (AgaScope, Eastmancolor).

Adventure   **Cas.**   **(PR:C MPAA:NR)**

GORILLA AT LARGE**½   (1954) 84m Panoramic/FOX c

Cameron Mitchell (Joey Matthews), Anne Bancroft (Laverne Miller), Lee J. Cobb (Detective Sgt. Garrison), Raymond Burr (Cyrus Miller), Charlotte Austin (Audrey Baxter), Peter Whitney (Kovacs), Lee Marvin (Shaughnessy), Warren Stevens (Mack), John G. Kellogg (Morse), Charles Tannen (Owens).

This often hilarious 3-D thriller stars Bancroft as a trapeze artist at an amusement park, where the top attraction is a ferocious gorilla. After several murders take place, the main suspect is Mitchell, a law student working at the park as a costumed gorilla. Also suspect is Bancroft's husband, park owner Burr. Another murder then takes place, and this time it's the gorilla who is suspect. As it turns out, the actual criminal behind all the murders is Bancroft—dressed in an ape outfit. The suspenseful climax sees the real gorilla carry her to the top of a roller coaster before he is shot down. The excellent cast somehow pulls it off, cheap gorilla suits and all.

p, Robert L. Jacks; d, Harmon Jones; w, Leonard Praskins, Barney Slater; ph, Lloyd Ahern (Technicolor); md, Lionel Newman.

Thriller   **(PR:C MPAA:NR)**

GORILLA GREETS YOU, THE**½   (1958, Fr.) 105m Pathe (LE GORILLE VOUS SALUE BIEN)

Lino Ventura (Gorille), Bella Darvi (Moll), Charles Vanel (Colonel), Rene Lefevre (Inspector), Pierre Dux (Lawson), Robert Manuel (Kanas).

"The Gorilla" is a code name for a top French secret agent, who divides his time between the criminal underground and espionage. Investigating some stolen missile plans, Ventura finds himself among counterfeiters, dope dealers, and assorted spies. This is an effective little thriller. Ventura handles the lead role well, making the standard cliches fresh.

p, Raoul Ploquin; d, Bernard Borderie; w, Antoine Dominique, Jacques Robert, Borderie (based on the novel by Dominique); ph, Louis Page (Franscope); ed, Pierre Gaudin.

Spy Drama   **(PR:C MPAA:NR)**

GORILLA MAN**   (1942) 64m WB bw

John Loder (Capt. Craig Killian), Marian Hall (Patricia Devon), Ruth Ford (Janet Devon), Richard Fraser (Walter Sibley), Paul Cavanagh (Dr. Wolf), Lumsden Hare (General Devon), John Abbott (Dr. Ferris), Mary Field (Nurse Kruger), Rex Williams (Eric), Joan Winfield (Mrs. Tanner), Charles Irwin (Inspector Cady), Peggy Carson (Oliver), Walter Tetley (Sammy), Art Foster (Constable), Creighton Hale (Ryan), Frank Mayo (Fletcher).

Implausible spy tale starring Loder as a shell-shocked British commando who is proclaimed clinically insane by ruthless Nazi spies, posing as doctors. Portrayed by Cavanagh and Abbott, the spies are trying to prevent Loder from spilling out secret information he gathered about the enemy. To convince the hospital staff of Loder's insanity, they even go so far as to murder several women and pin the blame on him. Loder finally snaps out of his dazed condition just in time to foil their evil scheme.

d, D. Ross Lederman; w, Anthony Coldeway; ph, James Van Trees; ed, James Gibbon; art d, Stanley Fleischer.

Espionage   **(PR:A MPAA:NR)**

GORILLA SHIP, THE*   (1932) 60m Mayfair bw

Ralph Ince (Capt. Larsen), Vera Reynolds (Mrs. Wells), Reed Howes (Dave Burton), Wheeler Oakman (Mr. Wells), James Bradbury, Jr. (Dumb Sailor), George Chesebro (1st Mate), Ben Hall (Cabin Boy).

Lame action tale set on a yacht owned by insanely jealous Oakman, who suspects that his best friend, Howes, is flirting with his wife, Reynolds.

p, Ralph M. Like; d, Frank Strayer; w, George Wagner; ph, Jules Cronjager; ed, Byron Robinson.

Drama   **(PR:A MPAA:NR)**

GORKY PARK***   (1983) 103m Orion/Rank c

William Hurt (Arkady Renko), Lee Marvin (Jack Osborne), Brian Dennehy (William Kirwill), Ian Bannen (Iamskoy), Joanna Pacula (Irina), Michael Elphick (Pasha), Richard Griffiths (Anton), Rikki Fulton (Pribluda), Alexander Knox (General), Alexei Sayle (Golodkin), Ian McDiarmid (Prof. Andreev), Niall O'Brien (KGB Agent

Rurik), Henry Woolf *(Levin)*, Tusse Silberg *(Natasha)*, Patrick Field *(Fet)*, Jukka Hirvikangas *(James Kirwill)*, Marjatta Nissinen *(Valerya Davidova)*, Hekki Leppanen *(Kostia Borodin)*, Lauri Torhonen *(Director)*, Elsa Salamaa *(Babuska)*, Anatoly Davydov *(KGB Agent Nicky)*, Lasse Lindberg, Jussi Parvianen *(Shadowers)*, Black Pearls *(Russian Tea Band)*, Bad Sign *(Rock and Roll Band)*.

Intriguing spy thriller in which three bodies found in Moscow's Gorky Park have been stripped of their faces and fingertips, making identification nearly impossible. Hurt, in a highly polished performance, plays the Moscow police inspector assigned to the case. His trail leads to Marvin, an American fur trader, who has all of Moscow at his disposal. Pacula is a young dissident, a friend of one of the victims, who gets caught up between Hurt and Marvin. Though a little confusing at times, this is an interesting mystery, giving a harshly realistic picture of the average man's life behind the Iron Curtain. Filmed in Helsinki, as the Soviets refused permission to film in Moscow.

p, Gene Kirkwood, Howard W. Koch, Jr.; d, Michael Apted; w, Dennis Potter (based on the novel by Martin Cruz Smith); ph, Ralf D. Bode (Technicolor); m, James Horner; ed, Dennis Virkler; prod d, Paul Sylbert; cos, Richard Bruno.

Mystery/Thriller   **Cas.**   **(PR:O MPAA:R)**

GORP zero   (1980) 90m AIP/Filmways c

Michael Lembeck *(Kavell)*, Dennis Quaid *(Mad Grossman)*, Philip Casnoff *(Bergman)*, Frank Drescher *(Evie)*, David Huddleston *(Walrus Wallman)*, Robert Trebor *(Rabbi Blowitz)*, Lou Wagner *(Federman)*, Richard Beauchamp *(Ramirez)*, Julius Harris *(Fred The Chef)*, Lisa Shure *(Vicki)*, Debi Richter *(Barbara)*, Rosanna Arquette *(Judy)*, Dale Robinette *(Irvington)*, Mark Deming *(Lobster Newburg)*.

"Summer-camp" comedy in the MEATBALLS vein that is tasteless and unfunny. All of the humor is based on dim jokes involving drugs, sex, or racism, none of which is even remotely inspired or humorous—just obnoxious. A failure.

p, Jeffrey Konvitz, Louis S. Arkoff; d, Joseph Ruben; w, Konvitz (based on a story by Konvitz, Martin Zweiback); ph, Michael Hugo (Movielab Color); ed, Bill Butler.

Comedy   **(PR:O MPAA:R)**

GOSPEL ACCORDING TO ST. MATTHEW, THE*** (1966, Fr., Ital.) 136m Arco-C.C.F. Lux/CD bw (IL VANGELO SECONDO MATTEO; L'EVANGILE SELON SAINT-MATTHIEU

Enrique Irazoqui *(Jesus Christ)*, Margherita Caruso *(Mary, as a Girl)*, Susanna Pasolini *(Mary, as a Woman)*, Marcello Morante *(Joseph)*, Mario Socrate *(John the Baptist)*, Settimo Di Porto *(Peter)*, Otello Sestili *(Judas)*, Ferruccio Nuzzo *(Matthew)*, Giacomo Morante *(John)*, Alfonso Gatto *(Andrew)*, Enzo Siciliano *(Simon)*, Giorgio Agamben *(Philip)*, Guido Cerretani *(Bartholomew)*, Luigi Barbini *(James, Son of Alpheus)*, Marcello Galdini *(James, Son of Zebedee)*, Elio Spaziani *(Thaddeus)*, Rosario Migale *(Thomas)*, Rodolfo Wilcock *(Caiaphas)*, Alessandro Tasca *(Pontius Pilate)*, Amerigo Bevilacqua *(Herod the Great)*, Francesco Leonetti *(Herod Antipas)*, Franca Cupane *(Herodias)*, Paola Tedesco *(Salome)*, Rossana Di Rocco *(Angel)*, Eliseo Boschi *(Joseph of Arimathea)*, Natalia Ginzburg *(Mary of Bethany)*, Renato Terra *(A Pharisee)*, Enrico Maria Salerno *(Voice of Jesus)*.

Pasolini's epic film, telling the life story of Jesus in a semi-documentary filmmaking style. His use of non-actors, including his mother as Mary, works well. Pasolini, a Marxist, dedicated this film to Pope John XXIII. The director strongly objected to the word "saint" being added to the English title but his wishes were ignored. Bacolov was nominated for an academy award for his arrangements of the Bach, Mozart, Webern, and Prokofiev music used in the film. An interesting approach to the Biblical genre, far and away better than most in the category. The classic American spiritual "Sometimes I Feel Like a Motherless Child" is sung by Odetta.

p, Alfredo Bini; d&w, Pier Paolo Pasolini (based on The Gospel According to St. Matthew); ph, Tonino Delli Colli; m, Luis Enriquez Bacalov, Johann Sebastian Bach, Wolfgang Amadeus Mozart, Sergei Prokofiev, Anton Webern; ed, Nino Baragli; md, Bacalov; art d, Luigi Scaccianoce; cos, Danilo Donati; spec eff, Ettore Catallucci; makeup, Marcello Ceccarelli.

Biblical Drama   **Cas.**   **(PR:A MPAA:NR)**

GOSPEL ROAD, THE**   (1973) 93m FOX c

Robert Elfstrom *(Christ)*, June Carter Cash *(Mary Magdalene)*, Larry Lee *(John The Baptist)*, Paul Smith *(Peter)*, Alan Dater *(Nicodemus)*, Robert Elfstrom Jr. *(Christ Child)*, Gelles LaBlanc *(John)*, Terrance Winston Mannock *(Matthew)*, Thomas Leventhal *(Judas)*, John Paul Kay *(James The Elder)*, Sean Armstrong *(Thomas)*, Lyle Nicholson *(Andrew)*, Steven Chernoff *(Philip)*, Stuart Clark *(Nathaniel)*, Ulf Pollack *(Thaddeus)*, Jonathan Sanders *(Simon)*.

Folksy, Southern semi-documentary about the life and times of Jesus Christ, narrated in Jerusalem by Johnny Cash, who points out historical landmarks. The film then cuts to dramatized incidents in Christ's life (the Messiah is played by the director, Elfstrom, in a questionable bit of egotism) which are punctuated with country-and-western songs by the likes of John Denver and Kris Kristofferson. Well intentioned, but more than a little odd. June Carter Cash does a wonderful rendition of Denver's "Follow Me."

p, June and Johnny Cash; d, Robert Elfstrom; w, Johnny Cash, Larry Murray; ph, Elfstrom, Tom McDonough (Eastmancolor); ed, John Craddock; m, Larry Butler; m/l, John Denver, Larry Gatlin, Kris Kristofferson, Joe South, Harold and Don Reid, Christopher Wren, Johnny Cash.

Religious   **(PR:A MPAA:NR)**

GOT IT MADE**   (1974, Brit.) 86m c

Lalla Ward, Michael Latimer, Katya Wyeth, Fabia Drake, Douglas Lambert.

Ward stars as a young British socialite who questions her impending marriage to an equally well-off lad. Her change of heart comes when she meets a promiscuous lass and a free-spirited American traveler who clue her in on the real world. A slow-moving class-struggle picture which is saved only by Ward's vibrant personality.

p&d, James Kenelm Clarke; w, Clarke, Michael Robson; m, Clarke; ed, Paul Davies; set d, Roger King.

Drama   **(PR:C-O MPAA:NR)**

GOT WHAT SHE WANTED*   (1930) 87m TIF bw

Betty Compson *(Mahyna)*, Lee Tracy *(Eddie)*, Allan Hale *(Dave)*, Gaston Glass *(Boris)*, Dorothy Christy *(Olga)*, Fred Kelsey *(Dugan)*.

Lackluster programmer starring Compson as a bored foreign wife who goes after smart-aleck hoofer Tracy as a solution to her romantic problems. Unfortunately, Tracy is an irresponsible vagabond who leaves the girl in the lurch, and she happily returns to her husband. Pretty dim, and shot almost entirely in close-up.

d, James Cruze; w, George Rosener; ph, C.F. Schoenbaum.

Drama   **(PR:A MPAA:NR)**

GOUPI MAINS ROUGES (SEE: IT HAPPENED AT THE INN, 1943, Fr.)

GOVERNMENT GIRL**   (1943) 94m RKO bw

Olivia de Havilland *(Smokey)*, Sonny Tufts *(Browne)*, Anne Shirley *(May)*, Jess Barker *(Dana)*, James Dunn *(Sergeant Joe)*, Paul Stewart *(Branch)*, Agnes Moorehead *(Mrs. Wright)*, Harry Davenport *(Senator MacVickers)*, Una O'Connor *(Mrs. Harris)*, Sig Ruman *(Ambassador)*, Jane Darwell *(Miss Trask)*, George Givot *(Count Bodinsky)*, Paul Stanton *(Mr. Harvester)*, Art Smith *(Marqueenie)*, Joan Valerie *(Miss MacVickers)*, Harry Shannon *(Mr. Gibson)*, Ray Walker *(Tom Holliday)*, Emory Parnell *(The Chief)*, Larry Steers, Russell Huestes, James Carlisle, Bert Moorhouse, Fred Norton *(Businessmen)*, Warren Hymer, Harry Tenbrook *(MPs)*, Karl Miller *(Janitor)*, Charles Meakin *(Businessman)*, Bruce Edwards, Lawrence Tierney *(FBI Men)*, Ian Wolfe *(Hotel Clerk)*, Babe Green, Fred Fox, Frank McClue, James Kirkwood, Wally Dean, Louis Payne, Donald Hall, Harry Bailey *(Senators)*, J. O. Fowler *(Man)*, Demetrius Alexis, Larry Williams, Chester Carlisle, Harry Denny, Tom Costello, Ronnie Rondell *(Businessmen)*, Norman Mayes *(Janitor)*, Clive Morgan *(Officer)*, Harold Miller *(Naval Officer)*, Major Sam Harris *(American General)*, Rita Corday, Barbara Hale, Patti Brill, Margaret Landry, Mary Halsey, Barbara Coleman, Marion Murray *(Bits)*, Ralph Dunn, Al Hill, David Newell, George Ford, Alex Melesh *(FBI Men)*, Ralph Linn, Josh Milton, Tom Burton, Harry Clay, Steve Winston *(Reporters)*, June Booth *(Secretary)*, Ivan Simpson *(Judge Leonard)*, Charles Halton *(Clerk)*, Ian Wolfe *(Hotel Clerk)*, David Hughes *(Guest)*, J. Louis Johnson *(Mr. Wright's Father)*, Chef Milani *(Hotel Waiter)*, Frank Norman *(Tough Sergeant)*, John Hamilton, Edward Keane, George Melford *(Irate Men)*, Joe Bernard *(Workman)*, George Riley *(Cop)*.

Famed screenwriter Dudley Nichols (STAGECOACH, 1939, THE INFORMER, 1935, BRINGING UP BABY, 1938) tried his hand at producing, directing, and writing and came up with a dud. Tufts is a successful Detroit auto executive brought to Washington, D.C. to help speed up the wartime bomber output. De Havilland plays the loyal secretary who guides him through the mounds of entangling red tape that Tufts constantly finds himself caught in. Fed up with the bureaucracy, Tufts goes on the rampage and cuts through channels, short-circuiting the system. He soon finds himself hauled before a Senate investigating committee, but he is acquitted thanks to an eloquent appeal on his behalf by de Havilland, who browbeats the senators into submission with her "after all, there's a war on!" declarations. Interlaced with this lame narrative is a preponderance of sub-plots which yank the film in a dozen different, unfocused directions. De Havilland gives one of her weakest performances (she didn't want to do the film in the first place) and Tufts is . . . well, Tufts. Nichols would try his hand at directing twice more (SISTER KENNY, 1946, a modest success, and MOURNING BECOMES ELECTRA, 1947, a failure) before giving up for awhile and returning to writing.

p,d&w, Dudley Nichols (adapted by Budd Schulberg from a story by Adela Rogers St. John); ph, Frank Redman; m, Leigh Harline; ed, Roland Gross; md, C. Bakaleinikoff; art d, Albert S. D'Agostino; set d, Darrell Silvera, Al Fields.

Comedy   **(PR:A MPAA:NR)**

GOYOKIN** (1969, Jap.) 124m Fuji Telecasting-Tokyo Eiga/Toho International c

Tatsuya Nakadai *(Magobei Wakizaka)*, Tetsuro Tamba *(Rokugo Tatewaki)*, Kinnosuke Nakamura *(Samon Fujimaki)*, Isao Natsuyagi *(Kunai)*, Yoko Tsukasa *(Shino)*, Kunie Tanaka *(Hyosuke)*, Ruriko Asaoka *(Oriha)*.

Tamba steals some gold to pay off an oppressive government tax, then brutally murders a group of fishermen who were witness to the theft. Both acts are violations of ancient samurai codes and Tamba's brother-in-law Nakadai denounces the actions. Tamba expels Nakadai from the family but Nakadai joins up with a shogunite to seek revenge. They watch as Tamba misplaces some shore lights in order to wreck a ship, and the two former family members engage in a swordfight. Tamba is the loser and Nakadai's honor remains intact. Typical samurai stuff in a piratical setting.

d, Hideo Gosha; w, Gosha, Kei Tasaka; ph, Kozo Okazaki (Panavision, Eastmancolor); m, Masaru Sato; art d, Motoji Kojima.

Samurai/Pirate   **(PR:O MPAA:NR)**

GRACIE ALLEN MURDER CASE** (1939) 74m PAR bw

Warren William (Philo Vance), Ellen Drew (Ann Wilson), Kent Taylor (Bill Brown), Jed Prouty (Uncle Ambrose), Jerome Cowan (Daniel Mirche), Donald MacBride (District Attorney Markham), H. B. Warner (Richard Lawrence), William Demarest (Sgt. Heath), Judith Barrett (Dixie Del Marr), Horace MacMahon (Gus, the Waiter), Al Shaw, Sam Lee (Thugs), Richard Denning (Fred), Irving Bacon (Clerk), Gracie Allen (Herself).

Silly but fun Philo Vance mystery pitting the famed detective against the befuddling verbal patter of Gracie Allen. Allen and friend Taylor are near the scene of the murder of an escaped convict and Taylor is accused of the killing. Enter William, who must patiently sift through Allen's ramblings until he can sort out the facts and catch the real killer. (See PHILO VANCE series, Index.)

p, George Arthur; d, Alfred E. Greene; w, Nat Perrin (based on a novel by S.S. Van Dine); ph, Charles Lang; ed, Paul Weatherwax; art d, Hans Dreier, Earl Hedrick; m/l, Matty Malneck, Fred Loesser.

Comedy/Mystery   (PR:A   MPAA:NR)

GRADUATE, THE***** 1967 105m Lawrence Turman/EM c

Anne Bancroft (Mrs. Robinson), Dustin Hoffman (Ben Braddock), Katharine Ross (Elaine Robinson), William Daniels (Mr. Braddock), Murray Hamilton (Mr. Robinson), Elizabeth Wilson (Mrs. Braddock), Brian Avery (Carl Smith), Walter Brooke (Mr. Maguire), Norman Fell (Mr. McCleery), Elisabeth Fraser (Lady #2), Alice Ghostley (Mrs. Singleman), Buck Henry (Room Clerk), Marion Lorne (Miss DeWitt), Harry Holcombe (Minister), Lainie Miller (Nightclub Stripper), Eddra Gale (Woman on Bus), Richard Dreyfuss (Berkeley Student), Jonathan Hole (Mr. DeWitt).

One of the most subtle comedies ever put on film, THE GRADUATE was a tour de force for newcomer Hoffman and made him and Ross, his young lover, overnight sensations. Hoffman is the graduate, a pensive and somewhat shy youth of wealthy Southern California suburbia. Upon completion of his college studies, Hoffman is pressured by family and friends to "get going" with his life, encouraged too much at every turn to find a job, marry, and become a doppelganger of his parents. Bancroft, doing a sultry imitation of Lauren Bacall, vamps Hoffman who cannot believe the older, married woman—she and Hamilton are his parents' best friends—is actually attempting to seduce him. He relents under her persistence and their clandestine affair is strictly sex, although Hoffman tries, with youthful innocence, to establish a more platonic affair. Through Bancroft, Hoffman falls in love with her daughter Ross, and is put in the exhausting position of maintaining relationships with mother and daughter. He finally decides that Ross will be his wife, although Bancroft is wholly opposed to the marriage. When Ross goes off to a San Francisco college, Hoffman drives up the coast to convince her to marry him, an attempt foiled by Hamilton's awkward confrontation with Hoffman. Ross then decides she will marry another and, at the last minute, Hoffman rushes to the church, banging on the glass of an enclosed area to get the bride's attention. Just before saying "I do," Ross hitches up her bridal gown, throws back her veil, and rushes outside to clasp hands with Hoffman; the two flee, with irate family and friends in pursuit, to catch a bus to nowhere in particular. This comedy is wonderfully sculptured by director Nichols who presents a half-dozen hilarious scenes—Hoffman escaping from a patio party and the badgering advice of adults by submerging himself in the family pool in scuba gear; the vamping of Hoffman by an intoxicated Bancroft who suddenly changes from middleaged housewife to Theda Bara, hiking her skirts lasciviously and purring promises of smoldering sex which almost puts Hoffman into a comatose state; the final frantic wedding scene where Hoffman appears to rescue Ross from marrying a man she does not love. Nichols was to declare: "I think Benjamin and Elaine will end up exactly like their parents; that's what I was trying to say in that last scene." Yet the well-to-do younger audiences of the day interpreted this sequence of blatant heroics as a wonderful act of defiance by two young persons whose destinies were being manipulated by their parents. The film was an enormous hit, gleaning $40 million from grateful viewers. Overnight, Nichols, who had scored heavily with his WHO'S AFRAID OF VIRGINIA WOOLF? (1966), became the most important director in Hollywood by virtue of THE GRADUATE. He was sought after as a director who was both commercial and artistic, although much of the credit for the innovative and fluid graphics in the film must go to cameraman Surtees, who was allowed a free hand to widely experiment. Surtees took distant shots and brought them down into a microscopic view such as showing Hoffman driving across the Golden Gate Bridge and then narrowing a wide, beautiful vista down to him in his car, then a fly-away shot to the heavens. On another occasion Surtees shot Hoffman running to prevent the wedding with a telescopic shot; though he is racing to the church he never appears to get anywhere, almost as if he is running in place. All in all, THE GRADUATE is a phenomenal film with a flawless cast and production people providing one of the most memorable movies of the 1960s, a decade where film achievement was at an all-time low. Songs include "Scarborough Fair," "The Big, Bright Green Pleasure Machine," "Sounds of Silence," "Mrs. Robinson," "April Come She Will" (sung by Simon and Garfunkel).

p, Lawrence Turman; d, Mike Nichols; w, Calder Willingham, Buck Henry (based on the novel by Charles Webb); ph, Robert Surtees (Panavision, Technicolor); m, Dave Grusin; ed, Sam O'Steen; prod d, Richard Sylbert; set d, George R. Nelson; cos, Patricia Zipprodt; m/l, Paul Simon; makeup, Harry Maret.

Comedy   Cas.   (PR:A   MPAA:NR)

GRADUATION DAY* (1981) 85m IFI/Scope III c

Christopher George (Coach), Patch MacKenzie (Anne), E. Danny Murphy (Kevin), E.J. Peaker (Blondie), Michael Pataki (Principal).

Another bloody attempt at horror during the HALLOWEEN-inspired resurgence of the genre. This one sees the members of a high-school track team being killed off one by one in a variety of fiendish and gross ways. The main suspects include track coach George and school principal Pataki. Dull, dull, dull.

p, David Baughn, Herb Freed; d, Freed; w, Anne Marisse, Freed; ph, Daniel Yarussi; ed, Martin Jay Sadoff; spec eff, Jill Rockow.

Horror   Cas.   (PR:O   MPAA:R)

GRAFT** (1931) 72m UNIV bw

Regis Toomey (Dusty Hotchkiss), Sue Carol (Constance Hall), Dorothy Revier (Pearl Vaughan), Boris Karloff (Joe Terry), William Davidson (M.H. Thomas), Richard Tucker (Carter Harrison), Willard Robertson (Scudder), Harold Goodwin (Speed Hansen), George Irving (M.T. Hall), Carmelita Geraghty (Secretary).

Toomey is an overeager cub reporter determined to bring in a hot story. He is sent to interview a building contractor played by Davidson, and overhears an argument between the man and Revier, Davidson's former mistress. She is about to inform the district attorney about Davidson's illegal dealings, thereby ruining any chance for his political future. Davidson has the D.A. killed and Revier kidnaped. Toomey implicates Carol in his story but when she is proven innocent his editor fires him. Determined to get to the bottom of things, Toomey follows the trail to a yacht where Revier is being held captive. He fights off Karloff, the real murderer, and frees Revier. Getting his story to the paper on time, he not only wins back his job but Carol's love as well. Unrealistic and silly stuff, though the pace keeps things somewhat on edge. While working on this film, Karloff was seen by James Whale one day at the studio commissary. He offered the relatively unknown actor a screen test for FRANKENSTEIN and the rest is film history.

d, Christy Cabanne; w, Barry Barringer; ph, Jerome Ash; ed, Maurice Pivar.

Newspaper Drama/Thriller   (PR:C   MPAA:NR)

GRANATOVYY BRASLET (1966, U.S.S.R.)
(SEE: GARNET BRACELET, THE)

GRAN VARIETA*** (1955, Ital.) 103m EX/CD c

Maria Fiore (Mariantonia), Alberto Sordi (Premoli), Lauretta Masiro (Beautiful Girl), Carlo Croccolo (Battaglia), Vittorio De Sica (Luciano), Lea Padovani (Anna), Delia Scala (Mizzy), Renato Rascel (The Comic).

A five-part look at Italian vaudeville from the turn of the century to the present. "A Star Is Born" stars Fiore as a sprightly singer/comedienne on her way to the top. The second segment features Sordi as a quick-change artist trying to romance Masiro. The third story, "Military Affair," stars Croccolo as a nightclub performer who does a military parody and winds up being drafted and killed in the real army. "The Fading Actor" stars De Sica as a once-popular and famous actor whose celebrity is now fading. "The Censor," the final and most interesting episode, details the difficulties producers and writers had dealing with the Fascist censors. (Italian; English subtitles.)

p, Carlo Infescelli; d, Domenico Paolella; w, Dino Falconi, Oreste Biancoli, Vinicio Marinucci, Michele Gualdieri, Paolella; ph, Carlo Carlini (Ferraniacolor); m, M. Rustichelli; ed, Raniero Mangione.

Drama   (PR:A   MPAA:NR)

GRAND CANARY*½ (1934) 78m FOX bw

Warner Baxter (Dr. Harvey Leith), H. B. Warner (Dr. Ismay), Madge Evans (Lady Mary Fielding), Juliette Compton (Elissa Baynham), Zita Johann (Suzan Tranter), Barry Norton (Robert Tranter), Gerald Rogers (Steward), Roger Imhof (Jimmy Corcoran), Marjorie Rambeau (Daisy Hemingway), Gilbert Emery (Capt. Renton), John Rogers (Trout), Desmond Roberts (Purser), Carrie Daumery (Marquesa).

Labored adaptation of A.J. Cronin's novel about a shipload of passengers on their way to the Canary Islands. Baxter stars as the washed-up, alcoholic doctor who takes a cruise to escape a scandal back in Blighty. He spends most of the film staring at his stateroom walls and flashing back to past successes. A young female missionary, Johann, is in love with him from afar, but he's too interested in married woman Evans. Johann's brother, Norton, a religious zealot, finds himself involved in an affair with an older, bitter and cynical woman, but not much is done with this potentially interesting story line. Baxter finally is given a chance to redeem himself when it appears that the island is infested with yellow fever. He sobers up enough to save the victims stricken with the dread disease. To wind up everything on a happy note, Evans gets a convenient divorce from her husband and she and Baxter make a go of it.

p, Jesse Lasky; d, Irving Cummings; w, Ernest Pascal (based on the novel by A.J. Cronin); ph, Bert Glennon.

Drama   (PR:A   MPAA:NR)

GRAND CANYON** (1949) 64m Lippert/Screen Guild bw

Richard Arlen (Mike Adams), Mary Beth Hughes (Terry Lee), Reed Hadley (Mitch Bennett), James Millican (Tex Hartford), Olin Howlin (Windy), Grady Sutton (Halfnote), Joyce Compton (Mabel), Charlie Williams (Bert), Margia Dean (Script Girl), Anna May Slaughter (Little Girl), Stanley Price (Makeup Man), Holly Bane (Rocky), Frank Hagney (First Thug), Kid Chissel (Second Thug), Zon Murray (Morgan).

Misfired parody of the western genre shot on location in the Grand Canyon. Story details the efforts of an oater movie crew to shoot a sagebrush epic in the Canyon. The star of the movie, Millican, breaks his leg and is replaced by local mule-caretaker Arlen. Most of the comedy arises from the efforts of "director" Hadley and "leading lady" Hughes to guide the rookie hayseed along in the art of movie thesping. Okay comedy, but could have been much funnier.

p, Carl K. Hittleman; d, Paul Landres; w, Jack Harvey, Milton Luban (based on a story by Hittleman); ph, Ernest W. Miller; m, Albert Glasser; ed, Landres; md, Glasser; art d, F. Paul Sylos.

Comedy/Western   (PR:A   MPAA:NR)

GRAND CANYON TRAIL**½ (1948) 67m REP c

Roy Rogers (Himself), Jane Frazee (Carol Martin), Andy Devine (Cookie Bullfincher), Robert Livingston (Bill Regan), Roy Barcroft (Dave Williams), Charles Coleman (J. Malcolm Vanderpool), Emmett Lynn (Ed Carruthers), Ken Terrell (Mike Delsing), James Finlayson (Sheriff), Tommy Coats (Bannister), Foy Williams & Riders Of The Purple Sage, Trigger the Horse.

Typical Rogers oater sees our hero as the down-and-out owner of a dried-up silver mine. Livingston, a one-time Three Mesquiteers star, plays the shifty mining engineer who tries to swindle Rogers out of his mine because he suspects there's much more silver to be found, if you know where to look. This is the first appearance of Riders of the Purple Sage, who replaced the Sons of the Pioneers. The film was made during Dale Evans' post-marital hiatus from the series, as decreed by Republic president Herbert Yates, who thought no one would believe Rogers' pursuit of his own wife. (See ROY ROGERS series, Index.)

p, Edward J. White; d, William Witney; w, Gerald Geraghty; ph, Reggie Lanning (Trucolor); ed, Tony Martinelli; md, Morton Scott; art d, Frank Hotaling; m/l, Jack Elliot, Foy Willing.

Western **Cas.** **(PR:A MPAA:NR)**

GRAND CENTRAL MURDER*** (1942) 72m MGM bw

Van Heflin ("Rocky" Custer), Patricia Dane (Mida King), Cecilia Parker (Constance Furness), Virginia Grey (Sue Custer), Samuel S. Hinds (Roger Furness), Sam Levene (Inspector Gunther), Connie Gilchrist (Pearl Delroy), Mark Daniels (David V. Henderson), Horace McNally ("Turk"), Tom Conway (Frankie Ciro), Betty Wells ("Baby" Delroy), George Lynn (Paul Rinehart), Roman Bohnen (Ramon), Millard Mitchell (Arthur Doolin).

This exciting and often thrilling mystery was raised from its B-production level by a solid cast and a fascinating portrayal by the moody Heflin, who plays a private eye investigating the killing of a beautiful actress, Dane. Although she is found dead early on, in a train car parked inside the enormous bowels of Grand Central Station, Dane is seen throughout in a series of clever flashbacks which occur when police inspector Levene—in a role he had essayed many times—questions a variety of colorful suspects, including Heflin himself. The sets are unpretentious but the story is well written and Simon's direction wastes no frames in unraveling the puzzle and revealing the killer.

p, B. F. Zeidman; d, S. Sylvan Simon; w, Peter Rurie (based on the novel by Sue MacVeigh); ph, George Folsey; m, David Snell; ed, Conrad A. Nervig; art d, Cedric Gibbons.

Mystery **(PR:A MPAA:NR)**

GRAND DUKE AND MR. PIMM (SEE: LOVE IS A BALL, 1963)

GRAND ESCAPADE, THE** (1946, Brit.) 70m Elstree Independent/BL bw

James Harcourt (Old Traveller), Patrick Curwen (Author), Peter Bull (Jennings), Edgar Driver (Night Watchman), Ernest Sefton (Simon Archer), Ben Williams (Jack Barrow), Howard Douglas (Mark Han), Ivor Barnard (Fisherman), Charles Rolfe (First Farmhand), Arthur Denton (Second Farmhand), Pat Kay (Pianist), Sydney Shaw (Harmonica Player), Bobbie and Nornie Dwyer (Dancers), Peter Artemus (Tom), Philip Artemus (Dick), Jackie Artemus (Harry).

Three young boys travel through London down to the southern coast of England in the company of an old junk dealer whose intent is to help get the goods on the crook he feels is responsible for the death of his smuggler son. Routine children's film with pretty scenery but little else.

p&d, John Baxter; w, Geoffrey Orme, Barbara K. Emary; ph, Jo Jago; m, Kennedy Russell; ed, Vi Burdon; art d, Dennis Wreford; m/l, Pat Kay.

Children **(PR:A MPAA:NR)**

GRAND EXIT** (1935) 68m COL bw

Edmund Lowe (Tom Fletcher), Ann Sothern (Adrienne Martin), Onslow Stevens (John Grayson), Robert Middlemass (Fire Chief Mulligan), Wyrley Birch (Warden), Selmer Jackson (District Attorney Cope), Guy Usher (Police Chief Roberts), Miki Morita (Noah), Arthur Rankin (Dave), Russell Hicks (Drake), Edward Van Sloan (Klorer).

Lowe plays an insurance investigator hot on the trail of an arsonist who is setting fire to big buildings all over the city. Good supporting cast includes Stevens, Van Sloan, and Sothern as the love interest. Good, tough dialog and well-paced by director Kenton.

d, Erle Kenton; w, Bruce Manning, Lionel Houser (based on a story by Gene Towne, Graham Baker); ph, Henry Freulich; ed, Gene Milford.

Crime **(PR:A MPAA:NR)**

GRAND FINALE* (1936, Brit.) 71m B&D/PAR British bw

Mary Glynne (Lina Parsons), Guy Newall (Hugo Trench), Eric Cowley (Sir Thomas Portland), Glen Alyn (Pat Mainwaring), Douglas Rhodes (Peter Trench), Philip Holles (Collins), Dorothy Dewhurst (Miss Pittaway), Kim Peacock (Editor), Afrique (Himself).

Romantic farce that just isn't funny centers around the romantic quest of a journalist for a model engaged to a man being chased by his ex-wife. After an ungracious amount of figuring out who's able to go with whom, everything ends happily for all involved. Pure tedium.

p, Anthony Havelock-Allan; d, Ivar Campbell; w, Vera Allinson (based on a story by Paul Hervey Fox).

Comedy **(PR:A MPAA:NR)**

GRAND HOTEL***** (1932) 115m MGM bw

Greta Garbo (Grusinskaya), John Barrymore (Baron Felix von Gaigern), Joan Crawford (Flaemmchen), Wallace Beery (General Director Preysing), Lionel Barrymore (Otto Kringelein), Jean Hersholt (Senf), Robert McWade (Meierheim), Purnell B. Pratt (Zinnowitz), Ferdinand Gottschalk (Pimenov), Rafaella Ottiano (Suzette), Morgan Wallace (Chauffeur), Tully Marshall (Gerstenkorn), Murray Kinnell (Schweimann), Edwin Maxwell (Dr. Waitz), Mary Carlisle (Honeymooner), John Davidson (Hotel Manager), Sam McDaniel (Bartender), Rolfe Sedan, Herbert Evans (Clerks), Lee Phelps (Extra in Lobby), Lewis Stone (Dr. Otternschlag), Frank Conroy (Rohna), Bodil Rosing.

This was the MGM blockbuster, a pet project of Irving Thalberg, that established for the first time the multistar movie. Even today the film crackles with wit, temperament, and vitality, all stemming from the cream of the studio's then-finest talent. Much of the credit for the success of this film is due to director Goulding who managed a minor miracle in preventing the raging egos of his great stars from destroying the film and each other. He was not called "the lion tamer" for nothing. The film opens as wealthy guests enter and leave the Grand Hotel, the finest hostelry in Berlin. Stone, a war-scarred WW I veteran and physician, approaches the front desk to ask porter Hersholt if he has received any mail. As usual, he has not. Complains Stone: "Grand Hotel . . . nothing ever happens." But it is happening, the fiery romances, the violent confrontations, the schemes, deceits, and tempestuous relationships, right behind the doors of the guest rooms. Five guests are profiled, their stories intercutting each other. Garbo, an internationally famous ballerina, arrives at the hotel with her retinue; she will be performing an important ballet in Berlin. John Barrymore, an impoverished baron, also comes to the hotel, but with a sinister purpose; his dire finances have caused him to become a "second-story" thief and he intends to steal Garbo's much-publicized jewels. Also ensconced in a hotel suite is a clerk, Lionel Barrymore, who is dying but intends to use up his life's savings by enjoying his last days in comfort and luxury. Just the opposite of the meek-mannered clerk is Beery, a bombastic, crude and larcenous industrialist who has arrived in Berlin to put over a big business deal. He immediately calls up for a stenographer to take down his last-minute business notes and Crawford arrives to perform his clerical chores. Beery notices her earthy beauty and immediately begins to make moves on her. (In one scene where she affixes her stocking to a garter, displaying attractive legs, Beery's lustful eyes pop lewdly.) Garbo realizes that her heyday is over as a dancer and she is frightened over the prospect of going to the theater to perform, begging assurance from backers that the house will be full. They lie to her, saying a packed audience will be waiting for her. As she leaves for the theater, John Barrymore watches her go, making sure that her room will be empty. Before undertaking his nefarious mission, Barrymore spots sexy Crawford and asks her to go to a dance with him the following night. Later, while taking dictation from Beery, Crawford is propositioned by the industrialist and is attracted to his money and power but is repelled by his brutal manner, especially when he later makes fun of harmless Lionel Barrymore in the hotel bar. Lionel Barrymore, however, is not completely helpless; he gets into a card game with some sharpers and wins a vast amount of money. Fortune goes the other way for Beery, whose crooked methods result in his being exposed on the business deal, which collapses. He is now facing bankruptcy and ruination. Meanwhile, John Barrymore has managed to get into Garbo's suite and is rummaging through her jewelry, fondling her pearls, when the ballerina unexpectedly returns. He hides behind some drapes to see her enter and prepare to go to bed. She is utterly devastated; the theater had only been half full and her performance was a disaster. She studies a bottle containing poison, thinking to end her life. Just then Barrymore makes his presence known, startling Garbo, who asks: "Who are you?" Barrymore answers: "Someone who loves you," and goes on to state that he has long been her secret admirer. Garbo gives a reply which later became umbilically tied to her persona: "I want to be alone." But Barrymore refuses to leave. Overwhelmed by her incredible beauty he returns her pearls, admitting that he is a thief, and then soulfully begs for her attention. "I'd like to take you in my arms," he tells her. "I've never seen anything in my life as beautiful as you are . . . . Let me stay for just a little while." Her life is suddenly turned around by Barrymore's charm and eloquence and she allows him to stay with her. Later, Barrymore, even more desperate for money since he has told Garbo he will meet her in Vienna and make a life with her—enters Beery's suite, but the industrialist catches him red-handed going through his things and picks up a phone, using the heavy stand to club Barrymore to death. Crawford, terrified after witnessing the killing, races off to get Lionel Barrymore; the lowly clerk arrives and stands up to bully-boy Beery, calling the police. Through the lobby of the Grand Hotel pass these guests once more, John Barrymore as a body on its way to the morgue. Garbo, later—hurried along excitedly by her maid, Ottiano, who lies to her, saying John Barrymore will be on the train to Vienna with them—rushes out gushing farewells, happy for the first time in years, tragically looking forward to a mythical rendezvous. Lionel Barrymore and Crawford next appear, the clerk given hope by Crawford, who has agreed to go to Paris with him and begin a new life together. But the passing parade fails to impress the dour Stone who stands at the front desk and drones: "Grand Hotel. Always the same. People come, people go. Nothing ever happens." GRAND HOTEL had long been in the mind of Thalberg before he put it into production, having read the 1930 best-selling novel (Menschen im Hotel as originally published in German) by Vicki Baum, and seen the Broadway play based on the novel which played for 444 nights. (The play starred Eugenie Leontovitch in the Garbo role (Garbo received $68,000 for her film role), Henry Hull in the John Barrymore part (Barrymore received $55,750), Hortense Alden in Crawford's role (Crawford got $60,000), Sig Rumann in Beery's part (Beery received $55,000) and Sam Jaffe as the clerk essayed by Lionel Barrymore in the film (Lionel Barrymore got $25,000); only Ottiano, as the maid, was picked up from the original play production for the MGM film.) The studio production chief thought this the perfect vehicle to pack with MGM stars and he bought the rights to the books for $13,500, but the stars he chose did not approach the project with his enthusiasm. The great Greta Garbo, whose reputation in the movies was legendary, approached the acting assignment with considerable concern. Was she too old to play a graceful ballerina (even though the part called for an aging lady)? How would she appear opposite such sterling stars as the Barrymores and Beery? (And she was vexed at the onset when hearing that Louis B. Mayer's hatred for her one-time lover and leading man John Gilbert had caused Gilbert to be scratched from the role of the nobleman thief to be replaced by John Barrymore). The studio also had difficulty in billing their greatest star, since her contract stated that her name always came first in the credits. Executives proposed to her that she simply be signified above the rest of the cast as "Garbo," and she agreed to this verbally, but MGM could not get her to sign an agreement to that effect because Greta Garbo did not sign papers. Garbo was also temperamental and Thalberg purposely sought out Goulding who had a reputation for carefully handling difficult actresses. Mayer stepped in to caution Thalberg that the freelance director had been dumped by Paramount after running up a heavy budget of more than $600,000 for NIGHT ANGEL and that he did not take orders easily. Thalberg still hired Goulding, paying him $52,000 for his services. Goulding proved his worth, cleverly avoiding confrontations between the stars, notably Garbo and the very ambitious Crawford. (The two never appear together on screen and were shown in only one group photo together on the GRAND HOTEL set, although the photo is clearly doctored, with Garbo wearing outdoor apparel and looking off into space while the rest of cast stand under hot overhead lights sans coats and stare back into the camera; in other words a cut-out of Garbo was inserted with the rest of the cast, but even common sense would tell any discerning observer that "The Great Sphinx" of movies would never tolerate such a democratic lineup shot.) But the world saw only rosy relationships between all the sterling cast members during the 49 days of shooting, thanks to MGM's publicity department. According to the releases, when Garbo swept on to the set John Barrymore swooped forward, took her hand, kissed it, and exclaimed: "My wife and I think you are the most beautiful woman in the world!" Garbo, after playing her first love scene with the Great Profile, kissed him passionately with the camera turned off, and oozed: "You have no idea what it means to me to play opposite so perfect an artist!" Such compliments were liberally strewn about the set, Crawford reportedly telling newsmen: "Every single day, Mr. Lionel Barrymore would say something nice to me. He'd say: 'How are you, baby? I never saw you look so beautiful.' He'd tell me that I had acted better than any other day that week. I know he didn't mean it, but it was nice to hear." It was reported that gruff and tough Beery gave Garbo the keys to his Yosemite mountain retreat so she could "really be alone" and rest on weekends. And to Beery, the polished John Barrymore allegedly said: "Not that I'm falling in love with you or anything, but I'd like to make a statement. You're the best actor on this set!" Most of these reports were pure publicity hokum, fairy tales for the fan magazines. The leading players were not only less than cordial to each other, all vying for their own scenes, but most of them didn't want to make the picture. Beery saw the original play and afterwards remarked about the character Preysing, the role he would later enact: "He doesn't murder women, but he's lower than anybody *I've* every played." When he was eventually assigned this role, Beery exploded. He went on a two-day strike, refusing to go before the cameras, running about the studio to beg one producer after another to get him released from the role of the ogre. When he did report for work, he was truculent and hard to budge into scenes, later commenting: "I hate the lousy part I'm playing in GRAND HOTEL. I told them I didn't want to do it. I shot my mouth off to everyone in power on the lot and it didn't do a hell of a bit of good!" But once Beery did jump into the role he made the most of it, displaying a sneering, greedy, and brutish villain who would linger long in the viewer's memory. Beery employed his favorite trick to steal scenes, particularly with Crawford. He would alter or ad-lib his lines slightly so that Crawford would have to concentrate so hard on his cue lines that it would limit her ability to act. Director Goulding put his foot down at Crawford's insistence and Beery reluctantly played it straight. Crawford was no slouch at stealing scenes herself, and in this film, her worst fear (as was that of Garbo) was that the "other female lead" would outact her and get the raves. She also had to fend off the Barrymore brothers, classic scene stealers. Once she came on the set and said sharply to the Barrymores: "All right, boys, but don't forget that the American public would rather have one look at my back than watch both of your faces for an hour." Crawford got on everyone's nerves when she ordered her personal secretary to bring a phonograph to her dressing room where she would play somber songs (sung by Marlene Dietrich, Garbo's rival) very loudly so that all could hear, ostensibly to put her in the right mood for her upcoming scenes. This particularly vexed Beery, who got even the next week. He had several drinking companions dress up in gold-braided uniforms. At his signal, just when Crawford was coming on the set, he raised his hand and the bozos marched forward loudly banging on bass drums while one shrilly played "Marching Through Georgia" on a piccolo. "Joan wouldn't speak to me, except professionally, for a week," he later guffawed. Goulding managed to prevent the fiery temperaments of his stars from destroying each other by having them play many scenes separately, addressing an invisible person, and then cutting to another separate take of that person, brought on to the set to act alone, then cross-cutting the scenes, to give the illusion that both actors were in the same scene at the same time. All of it worked marvelously and Garbo outshone her fellow thespians, even though she appears somewhat gawky with her long legs and notoriously large feet in her ballerina costume. She and John Barrymore overact in their love scenes as was the style of the silent era that spawned their fame and Lionel Barrymore whines his way along in a cringing, often unsympathetic part, albeit his is the role that demands empathy. Yet these wonderful characters sparked their vignettes like live wires hopping freely about the set. Made at a cost of $695,341.20, GRAND HOTEL took in $2,594,000 in its first year of release and remains a classic of its kind. MGM shrewdly marketed this film by withholding its general release for many months after its premiere at Sid Grauman's Chinese Theater in Hollywood on April 16, 1932, allowing a tremendous word-of-mouth campaign to heighten expectation from viewers and critics alike. And the critics cheered, along with the Academy, which voted the film an Oscar for Best

Picture. The enormous success of GRAND HOTEL set the stage for many all-star films to come. MGM used this casting formula to great success with such films as DINNER AT EIGHT (1933) and ROMEO AND JULIET (1936) and this concept would later be employed by a spate of poorly made opuses decades later—AIRPORT, EARTHQUAKE, THE TOWERING INFERNO. In 1945 GRAND HOTEL was remade as the frothy WEEKEND AT THE WALDORF with Ginger Rogers, Lana Turner, Walter Pidgeon, Van Johnson and Edward Arnold in the lead roles. In 1959 a West German production, using the original title MENSCHEN IM HOTEL, starred Michele Morgan, O. W. Fischer, Sonja Ziemann, Heinz Ruhmann, and Gert Frobe. The story got another reworking as a musical entitled AT THE GRAND, with songs by Robert Wright and George Forrest, which opened in Los Angeles with Paul Muni, Neile Adams, Cesare Danova, Joan Diener, David Opatoshu, and Vladimir Sokoloff in the lead roles. It flopped miserably and never saw a Broadway opening. MGM announced in 1976 that it would remake the original again but the production never got past the drawing board. As a tribute to this film, the studio opened its multimillion-dollar casino operation in Las Vegas in the 1970s when it abandoned its film production arm, calling its new resplendent hostelry "The MGM Grand Hotel."

d, Edmund Goulding; w, William A. Drake (based on the play *Menschen im Hotel* by Vicki Baum and the American version by Drake); ph, William Daniels; ed, Blanche Sewell; art d, Cedric Gibbons; cos, Adrian.

Drama   Cas.   (PR:A MPAA:NR)

GRAND ILLUSION***   (1938, Fr.) 95m RAC/World Pictures bw

Jean Gabin (*Marechal*), Pierre Fresnay (*Capt. de Boeldieu*), Erich von Stroheim (*Von Rauffenstein*), Dalio (*Rosenthal*), Dita Parlo (*Peasant Woman*), Carette (*An Actor*), Gaston Modot (*A Surveyor*), Georges Peclet (*A Soldier*), Edouard Daste (*A Teacher*), Sylvain Itkine (*Demolder*), Jacques Becker (*The English Officer*), Werner Florian (*Arthur Krantz*).

A Renoir classic study of men in prison—gentlemen officers in this case—coddled by another gentleman officer, GRAND ILLUSION is a fascinating portrait of military customs, courtesies, and attitudes that evaporated with the coming of WW II. The film opens during WW I, showing Gabin and Fresnay on a reconnaissance flight. They are shot down in flames by German ace von Stroheim but survive the crash. Von Stroheim lands and then cavalierly invites them to have lunch with him before ground troops arrive to cart the French officers off to a POW camp. Both men are sent to Hallbach and placed in barracks where French officer Dalio, a Jew, befriends them, along with several British officers who have also been taken prisoner. The newcomers join the others in working on an escape tunnel beneath the barracks and later they witness a musical performed by the British officers, many of whom don wigs in performing the female roles. The German officers of the camp have been invited to the performance but they are offended when Gabin, who has just been given important news through the grapevine, announces a great French victory on the Western Front. The French and British prisoners band together to patriotically sing "La Marseillaise" (in as stirring a scene as CASABLANCA provided when utilizing the French national anthem four years later). For this brazen offense, Gabin is sent to solitary confinement, and is released as the tunnel is finished. A mass escape is then planned but foiled when the Germans suddenly order all the prisoners to move to another camp. Incoming British officers do not learn of the escape tunnel since Gabin cannot tell them about it, unable to speak English, and since none of the British prisoners understand French, a frustrating scene full of grim irony. Fresnay and Gabin are sent to another prison, a bastion-like keep commanded by von Stroheim, now retired from the skies, having injured himself so badly that he must wear a neck brace at all times. He warmly welcomes the Frenchmen, pointing out that this prison, Wintersborn, is escape-proof and designed to hold those prisoners who have repeatedly attempted to escape. Von Stroheim treats his prisoners with great deference, having them to dinner and extending what meager courtesies he can, talking with Fresnay about how this war will bring to an end the gentlemen class of officers from the "Old World," dispensing with the honor and dignity of their rank and bloodlines. When some Russian prisoners create a disturbance over a shipment of books instead of food, Fresnay concocts a plan by which Gabin and Dalio can escape. He climbs a battlement and, perched high, begins playing a flute which brings German guards. They are about to shoot him down but von Stroheim arrives to stop them, pleading with the French officer to come down. While this is going on, Gabin and Dalio lower themselves by rope over the high walls and flee. Fresnay continues playing and finally von Stroheim sends a bullet into him out of frustration, intending to wound him. But the shot proves fatal and Fresnay later dies. Von Stroheim, truly grief-stricken, has the Frenchman taken to his own room and stays at Fresnay's deathbed, comforting him. Fresnay is fatalistic in his last moments, saying that it is all for the best, a "good solution" to having to maintain a futile prison life. Gabin and Dalio trek 200 miles to freedom; exhausted and starving, they are taken in by German widow Parlo. Gabin falls in love with Parlo and promises to return for her after the war. He and Dalio then cross into Switzerland. GRAND ILLUSION is directed with patience and care by Renoir who allowed von Stroheim great latitude with his role (it was von Stroheim who suggested he play both the pilot and the warden when first offered just the flying ace role; he was allowed by Renoir to rewrite these roles, blending them). This film was banned in Germany by Nazi Propaganda Minister Josef Goebbels who labeled it "Cinematographic Enemy Number 1" and he compelled his Italian counterpart to have the film banned in that country, although the 1937 Venice Film Festival gave the film a "Best Artistic Ensemble" award. It was thought that all European prints of the film were destroyed by the Nazis, but American troops uncovered a negative in Munich in 1945, one strangely preserved by the Germans themselves. Gabin, Fresnay, Dalio, and von Stroheim all give impressive performances in this beautifully directed and written film. Authenticity was achieved by Renoir's insistence that the various characters speak in their own tongues (with subtitles) and his deep focus photography and always moving cameras make for stunning visuals. The film is loaded with fine scenes but none so memorable as that of von Stroheim clipping his lone geranium, a single image of hope, following Fresnay's death. Forgotten in the U.S. at the time of his death in 1957, von Stroheim was awarded the Legion of Honor by the French.

d, Jean Renoir; w, Renoir, Charles Spaak; ph, Christian Matras; m, Joseph Kosma; ed, Marguerite Renoir; m/l, Vincent Telly, Albert Valsien.

War Drama   **Cas.**   **(PR:A   MPAA:NR)**

GRAND JURY*½   (1936) 60m RKO bw

Fred Stone (Commodore Taylor), Louise Latimer (Edith Taylor), Owen Davis, Jr. (Steve), Moroni Olsen (Bodyguard), Frank M. Thomas (Taylor), Guinn Williams (Britt), Harry Beresford (Evans), Russell Hicks (Hanify), Harry Jans (Sullivan), Robert Emmet Keane (Walters), Robert Middlemass (Chief), Margaret Armstrong (Martha), Charles Wilson (Editor), Edward Gargan, Billy Gilbert.

Stone plays an elderly, public-minded man outraged at the holes in the judicial system that allow murderers to walk off scot-free. Together with reporter Davis, Jr. and granddaughter Latimer, the old coot rounds up a group of gangsters secretly led by one of the city's most respected citizens.

p, Lee Marcus; d, Albert S. Rogell; w, Joseph A. Fields, Philip G. Epstein (based on a story by James Grant, Thomas Lennon); ph, Vernon Walker; ed, Jack Hively.

Crime   **(PR:A   MPAA:NR)**

GRAND JURY SECRETS*½   (1939) 68m PAR bw

John Howard (John Keefe), Gail Patrick (Agnes Carren), William Frawley (Bright Eyes), Harvey Stephens (Michael Keefe), Jane Darwell (Mrs. Keefe), Porter Hall (Anthony Pelton), John Hartley (Robson), Morgan Conway (Thomas Reedy), Elisha Cook, Jr. (Robert Austin/Norman Hazlitt), Kitty Kelly, Jack Norton, Richard Denning, Frank M. Thomas, Edward Marr.

Howard plays the clever, crusading reporter/brother of district attorney Stephens, who is constantly at odds with his sibling over his news-gathering methods, which tend to interfere with the wheels of justice. Among Howard's amazing systems is the use of a series of short-wave transmitters planted around the city enabling him to get scoops fast. This network of news helps him out when he is kidnaped by a big-time hood who's sick of his nosing around. A small army of ham-radio enthusiasts comes to his rescue.

p, Sam Engel; d, James Hogan; w, Irving Reis, Robert Yost (based on a story by Reis, Maxwell Shane); ph, Harry Fischbeck; ed, Hugh Bennett; art d, Hans Dreier, Franz Bachelin.

Crime   **(PR:A   MPAA:NR)**

GRAND MANEUVER, THE****   (1956, Fr.) 104m FS-Rizzoli/United
                                 Motion Picture c (LES GRANDES MANOEUVRES)

Michele Morgan (Marie Louise Riviere), Gerard Philipe (Lt. Armand de la Verne), Brigitte Bardot (Lucie), Yves Robert (Felix), Jean Desailly (Victor Duverger), Pierre Dux (Colonel), Jacques Francois (Rudolph), Lise Delamare (Jeanne), Jacqueline Maillan (Juliette), Magalie Noel (Therese), Simone Valere (Gisele), Catherine Anouilh (Alice), Jacques Fabbri (Armand's Batman), Raymond Cordy (Photographer), Olivier Hussenote (Prefect).

In a pre-WW I garrison town, Philipe makes a bet that he can seduce a lovely and sophisticated town lady before he goes off to maneuvers in the summer. He wins the bet but in the process falls under the spell of love. Director Rene Clair has commented on the idea of love in the film: "In order to avoid any ambiguity, let us say right now that love is the only concern of THE GRAND MANEUVER and that a love adventure is the entire subject." Historian Georges Sadoul has written that "this is Rene Clair's only truly romantic film and one that contains more genuine emotion than any of his others." The atmospheric elegance and pastoral colors (Clair's first picture in color) beautifully typify what is termed "poetic realism." After a premier screening in Moscow, Clair found himself in a conversation with a member of the audience, who regretted that the subject of the film was so "lacking in seriousness." "Lacking in seriousness?," Clair replied. "It deals only with love," the Russian added. To which Clair retorted, "For us, love is a very serious matter."

p&d, Rene Clair; w, Clair, Jerome Geronimi, Jean Marsan (based on a story by Courteline); ph, Robert Le Febvre, Robert Juillard (Eastmancolor); m, Georges van Parys; ed, Louisette Hautecoeur; art d, Leon Barsacq; cos, Rosine Delamare.

Drama/Romance   **(PR:C   MPAA:NR)**

GRAND NATIONAL NIGHT   (SEE: WICKED WIFE, THE, 1953, Brit.)

GRAND OLD GIRL*   (1935) 70m RKO bw

Fred MacMurray (Sandy), Alan Hale (Click Dade), May Robson (Laura Bayles), Hale Hamilton (Mr. Killaine), Mary Carlisle (Gerry Killaine), Etienne Girardot (Mellis), William Burress (Butts), Edward Van Sloan (Holland), Fred Kohler, Jr. (Bill Belden), Onest Conley (Neptune), Ben Alexander (Tom Miller), George Offerman, Jr. (Walter), Theodor von Eltz (The New Principal), Gavin Gordon (The President).

Absolutely ridiculous slice of sentimentality concerning veteran schoolteacher Robson, who is drummed out of the educational system after 38 years for getting involved in local politics by making trouble for a powerful gambler, who has been corrupting students from the back of the drugstore. After many desperate appeals, she is finally forced to go to the top; she hauls in the President of the United States (one of her former students, of course) to wax eloquent on the wholesome, patriotic duties of teaching the nation's young. Really corny.

p, Cliff Reid; d, John S. Robertson; w, Milton Krims, John Twist, Arthur T. Horman (based on a story by Wanda Tuchock); ph, Lucien Andriot; ed, George Crone.

Drama   **(PR:A   MPAA:NR)**

GRAND OLE OPRY**   (1940) 68m REP bw

Leon Weaver (Abner), Frank Weaver (Cicero), June Weaver (Elviry), Lois Ranson (Susie Ann Weaver), Allan Lane (Fred Barnes), Henry Kolker (William C. Scully), John Hartley ("Hunch" Clifton), Loretta Weaver (Violey), Purnell Pratt (Attorney General), Claire Carleton (Ginger), Ferris Taylor (Lt. Governor), Uncle Dave Macon and Dorris, Roy Acuff and Smoky Mountain Boys with Rachel, George Dewey Hay.

Another backwoods Weaver family drama. This time the hillbillies manage to outwit a group of corrupt city politicians and install Leon Weaver as the governor of the state. Entertaining blue-grass tunes provided by Roy Acuff's Smoky Mountain Boys, George Dewey Hay, and Uncle Dave Macon and Dorris. Typical country corn. (See WEAVER BROTHERS AND ELVIRY series, Index.)

p, Armand Schaefer; d, Frank McDonald; w, Dorrell and Stuart McGowan; ph, Jack Marta; ed, Ray Snyder; md, Cy Feuer.

Comedy/Musical   **(PR:A   MPAA:NR)**

GRAND PARADE, THE*½   (1930) 81m Pathe bw

Helen Twelvetrees (Molly), Fred Scott (Kelly), Richard Carle (Rand), Marie Astaire (Polly), Russell Powell (Calamity), Bud Jameson (Sullivan), Jimmy Adams (Jones), Lillian Leighton (Madam Stitch), Spec O'Donnell (Call Boy), Sam Blum (Sam), Tom Malone (Daugherty), Jimmy Aubrey (The Drunk).

Tired come-back tale set in 1910 and starring Twelvetrees as the loyal girl who picks up has-been minstrel singer Scott, gets him off the bottle and away from the evil influence of blonde bombshell Astaire, whom she blames for the entertainer's decline. Songs include: "Molly"; "Sweetheart"; "Grand Parade"; "Alone In The Rain"; and "It's All In Me."

p, Edmund Goulding; d, Fred Newmeyer, Frank Reicher; w, Goulding; ph, David Abel; ch, Richard Boleslavsky; m/l, Goulding, Dan Dougherty.

Musical/Drama   **(PR:A   MPAA:NR)**

GRAND PRIX**   (1934, Brit.) 70m Clowes and Stock/COL bw

John Stuart (Jack Holford), Gillian Sande (Jean McIntyre), Milton Rosmer, Peter Gawthorne (John McIntyre), Wilson Coleman, Lawrence Andrews.

Romance centering around the auto racing track stars Stuart as a driver in love with Sande, but unable to pursue his desires at all because the car he invented killed her father during a test run. Stuart's winning of a big race proves the worth of his car and redeems him in the eyes of Sande. A bit sappy in points but maintains interest through the interweaving of the romantic theme with the race car setting.

p, L.S. Stock, St. John L. Clowes; d&w, Clowes.

Drama   **(PR:A   MPAA:NR)**

GRAND PRIX*½   (1966) 179m Douglas & Lewis/MGM c

James Garner (Pete Aron), Eva Marie Saint (Louise Frederickson), Yves Montand (Jean-Pierre Sarti), Toshiro Mifune (Izo Yamura), Brian Bedford (Scott Stoddard), Jessica Walter (Pat), Antonio Sabato (Nino Barlini), Francoise Hardy (Lisa), Adolfo Celi (Agostini Manetta), Claude Dauphin (Hugo Simon), Enzo Fiermonte (Guido), Genevieve Page (Monique Delvaux Sarti), Jack Watson (Jeff Jordan), Donald O'Brien (Wallace Bennett), Jean Michaud (Children's Father), Albert Remy (Surgeon), Rachel Kempson (Mrs. Stoddard), Ralph Michael (Mr. Stoddard), Alan Fordney, Anthony Marsh, Tommy Franklin (Sportscasters), Phil Hill (Tim Randolph), Graham Hill (Bob Turner), Bernard Cahier (Journalist), Chris Amon, Lorenzo Bandini, Jean Pierre Beltoise, Bob Bondurant, Joakim Bonnier, Jack Brabham, Ken Costello, Juan Manuel Fangio, Nino Farina, Paul Frere, Dan Gurney, Dennis Hulme, Tony Lanfranchi, Guy Ligier, Michael Parkes, Andre Pillette, Teddy Pillette, Peter Revson, Jochen Rindt, Jim Russell, Ludovico Scarfiotti, Jo Schlesser, Skip Scott, Joe Siffert, Mike Spence (Themselves), Bruce McLaren (Douglas McClendon), Richie Ginther (John Hogarth), Evans Evans (Mrs. Tim Randolph), John Bryson (Photographer David), Arthur Howard (Claude), Alain Gerard (American Boy), Tiziano Feroldi (Doctor at Monza), Gilberto Mazzi (Rafael), Raymond Baxter (BBC Interviewer), Eugenio Dragoni (Ferrari Official), Maasaki Asukai (Japanese Interpreter), Albert Remy (Doctor at Monte Carlo).

The personal lives and loves of professional auto racers are randomly mingled with lots of racing footage. Various affairs, accidents, blackmail, and crashes are the loosely connected and poorly told plot's content, and it all gets pretty tedious after awhile. The use of split-screen images is fine but overdone, and quickly becomes run-of-the-mill, and not nearly as exciting as it pretends to be. Filmed on location at several important European competitions.

p, Edward Lewis; d, John Frankenheimer; w, Robert Alan Aurthur, Bill Hanley; ph, Lionel Lindon (Cinerama-SuperPanavision, Metrocolor); m, Maurice Jarre; ed, Fredric Steinkamp; prod d, Richard Sylbert; md, Jarre; cos, Sydney Guilaroff; spec eff, Milt Rice; makeup, Guilaroff, Giuliano Laurenti, Alfio Meniconi; racing advisor, Phil Hill, Joakim Bonnier, Richie Ginther; technical consultant, Carroll Shelby.

Racing/Drama   **Cas.**   **(PR:O   MPAA:NR)**

GRAND SLAM**½   (1933) 65m WB bw

Paul Lukas (Peter Stanislavsky), Loretta Young (Marcia Stanislavsky), Frank McHugh (Philip), Glenda Farrell (Blondie), Helen Vinson (Lola Starr), Walter Byron (Barney), Ferdinand Gottschalk (Van Dorn), Joseph Cawthorne (Alex), Paul Porcasi (Nick), Mary Doran (Dot), Lucien Prival (Gregory), Tom Dugan (Artie), Maurice Black (Paul), Lee Moran (Harry), Ruthelma Stevens (Muriel), Emma Dunn (Sob Sister), Reginald Barlow (Theodore), Harry C. Bradley, Charles Levison, Roscoe Karns, De Witt Jennings, George Cooper, John Sheehan.

Unusual light comedy concerning the national craze for bridge tournaments. Lukas plays the Russian waiter (who would rather be pursuing a career as a serious author) who stumbles into a bridge match with the undisputed king of bridge,

Gottschalk. Soon Lukas and his wife (who plays on his team) become the "Bridge Sweethearts Of America" and promote their playing method as a way to solve marital problems. Unfortunately the couple split temporarily due to an argument while playing, leaving Lukas to battle Gottschalk alone. It soon begins to appear that Lucas will lose, until his wife returns and together they expose Gottschalk as a fraud whose last con was pretending he was an Indian at a traveling medicine show. Fine comic performance from Lukas holds the silly material together.

p, Hal Wallis; d, William Dieterle; w, David Boehm, Ernest Gelsey (based on the novel by B. Russell Herts); ph, Sid Hickox; ed, Jack Killifer; cos, Orry-Kelly.

Comedy **(PR:A MPAA:NR)**

GRAND SLAM*** (1968, Ital., Span., Ger.) 101m
Jolly/Coral/Constantin/PAR c (AD OGNI COSTO; DIAMANTES A GO-GO; AKA: TOP JOB)

Edward G. Robinson *(Prof. James Anders)*, Janet Leigh *(Mary Ann)*, Adolfo Celi *(Mark Milford)*, Klaus Kinski *(Erich Weiss)*, Georges Rigaud *(Gregg)*, Robert Hoffman *(Jean Paul Audry)*, Riccardo Cucciolla *(Agostino)*, Jussara *(Setuaka)*, Miguel Del Castillo *(Manager)*, Luciana Angiolillo, Valentino Macchi.

Shot in Spain, London, New York, Rome, and Rio de Janeiro, this exciting suspense picture had several titles. In Italy, it was known as AD OGNI COSTO. In Germany it was TOP JOB, and in Spain it was DIAMANTES A GO-GO. All four versions were of different lengths and it's not surprising, as the film was one of those co-production deals that involves companies from various countries and stars from various countries that will guarantee an audience in each venue. Robinson is a teacher in Rio. Twice each year, he's looked out of his classroom window and seen a huge cache of gems delivered to a diamond company across the way. After three decades of toiling in the groves of academé, he goes to New York and asks Celi, an old pal, to help him rob the jewels. Celi assembles a cadre of crooks, Kinski, Rigaud, Cucciolla, and Hoffman, to aid in the theft. So, with a safecracker, an electronics wizard, a professional gigolo (to seduce the manager's secretary) and a leader, they return to Rio to do the deed. It's the day before Carnival in Brazil and the gang learns that a new security system, known as the Grand Slam 70, has been installed in the strong-room. They regroup and make a new plan but Leigh, the secretary, smells something unkosher and calls in the police. The gang begin bickering and the plan is altered. Cut to Rome where Leigh meets Robinson and she is about to hand over the gems (it was a double cross all the way) when a young purse snatcher goes by on a Vespa, takes Leigh's handbag, and disappears down the street. Good acting and direction and more than a little nod of appreciation to several movies which have used similar plots like TOPKAPI, RIFIFI, and Kubrick's THE KILLING which also had a twist ending, just when you thought they were going to get away with the caper. Somebody must have been having a private joke when they named former Nazi Kinski Erich Weiss (a Jewish name), which is the real name of Houdini. A good movie that deserved a better fate than it got at the box office.

p, Harry Colombo, George Papi; d, Giuliano Montaldo; w, Mino Roli, Marcello Fondato, Antonio de la Loma, Augusto Caminito, Marcello Coscia (based on a story by Paolo Bianchini, Roli, Caminito); ph, Antonio Macasoli (Techniscope, Technicolor); m, Ennio Morricone; ed, Nino Baragli; md, Bruno Nicolai; art d, Alberto Boccianti, Juan Alberto Soler.

Crime **(PR:A-C MPAA:NR)**

GRAND SUBSTITUTION, THE½** (1965, Hong Kong) 116m
Shaw Brothers/Frank Lee International c

Li Li-hua *(Chuang Chi)*, Ivy Ling Po *(Chao Wu)*, Yen Chun *(Cheng Ying)*, Li Ting *(Po Fung)*, Chen Yen-yen *(Madam Cheng)*, Ching Miao *(Chao Tun)*, Li Yeng *(Chao Su)*, Yang Tse-ching *(Kung Sun)*, Chen You-hsin *(Chin Kung)*, Li Ying *(Tu An-chia)*, Chao Ming *(Han Chieh)*, Tung Di *(Gen. Wei Chiang)*, Tien Feng *(Chui Ying)*, Liang Ruey *(Chin Ling Kung)*, Chen Ying Chieh *(Wei Chung)*, Hsia Yi-chiu *(Chuen Lan)*.

A Chinese opera on film. After the emperor hands over many affairs of state to a crooked and ruthless prime minister (Ying), trouble brews. After an uprising, Di is sent for, though Ying would rather have seen the riots go through. He persuades the emperor to purge Po and his family, which numbers over three hundred. Li-hua, the emperor's sister and Po's daughter-in-law, is the only one spared from death. Li-hua gives birth to a son. The boy's life is in danger, but a friend, Chun, substitutes his baby, who is ultimately killed. The real heir is taken into Ying's home and raised as his own. Fifteen years go by and he is informed of his past history. He kills Ying and avenges his family's honor.

p, Run Run Shaw; d, Yen Chun; w, Chen E-hsin; ph, Yu Tsang-shan (Shawscope, Eastmancolor); m, Sian Hua; ed, Chiang Hsing-lung; art d, Chen Chin-shen, Chen Chi-jui; m/l, Hua and E-hsin.

Chinese Opera **(PR:C MPAA:NR)**

GRAND THEFT AUTO½** (1977) 89m New World c

Ron Howard *(Sam Freeman)*, Nancy Morgan *(Paula Powers)*, Marion Ross *(Vivian Hedgeworth)*, Pete Isacksen *(Sparky)*, Barry Cahill *(Bigby Powers)*, Hoke Howell *(Preacher)*, Lew Brown *(Jack Klepper)*, Elizabeth Rogers *(Priscilla Powers)*, Rance Howard *(Ned Slinker)*, Don Steele *(Curley Q. Brown)*, Paul Linke *(Collins Hedgeworth)*, Leo Rossi *(Sal)*, Robby Weaver *(Harold Hingleman)*, Clint Howard *(Ace)*, Jim Ritz *(Officer Tad)*, Bill Conklin *(Engle Hingleman)*, Ken Lerner *(Benny)*, Jack Perkins *(Shadley)*, Rev. Bobs Watson *(Minister)*, Gary K. Marshall *(Underworld Boss)*, Karen Kaysing *(Bride)*, Paul Bartel *(Groom)*, Rick Seaman *(Max Hingleman)*, Tom Waters *(Lester)*, Ancel Cook *(Dink)*, Vic Rivers *(Muskovitz)*, Cal Naylor *(Car Salesman)*, Jim Costigan *(Hiram)*, Reed Chenault *(Rex)*, Phyliss Citas *(Lupe)*, Leo Michelson *(Farmer)*, Jim Begg *(Businessman)*, Jimi Fox *(Engineer)*, Gisella Blake *(Accordionist)*, Larry Cruickshank *(Elder Spokesman)*, Gene Hartline *(Gas Station Attendant)*, George Wagner *(Camera Operator)*, Bill Denochelle, Eddie Mulder *(Derby Drivers)*, Wayne Goodwin *(Mysterious Man)*, Lars Fredriksen *(Stony)*, Glen Towery *(Tony)*, Todd McCarthy *(Reporter)*.

Howard's directorial debut (he would soon go on to direct NIGHT SHIFT and SPLASH) starring himself as he and heiress Morgan borrow her daddy's big Rolls Royce and drive from L.A. to Las Vegas to elope. Daddy Cahill bands together a small army of drivers (including Mafia hit-men waiting in Vegas) and takes off after the couple in a 90-minute car chase that eventually sees the Rolls destroyed and the couple wed. The usual Corman cast of regulars includes a cameo appearance by director Paul Bartel (DEATHRACE 2000, 1975, EATING RAOUL, 1982), second unit direction provided by Allan Arkush (ROCK 'N' ROLL HIGH SCHOOL, 1979, GET CRAZY, 1983) and the film was edited by Joe Dante who would go on to direct THE HOWLING (1981) and GREMLINS (1984).

p, Jack [Jon] Davidson; d, Ron Howard; w, Rance Howard, Ron Howard; ph, Gary Graver (Metrocolor); m, Peter Ivers; ed, Joseph Dante; art d, Keith Michaels; set d, Charles Nixon; spec eff, Roger George; cos, Jane Rhum, Linda Pearl; stunts, Victor Rivers; makeup, Leigh Mitchell.

Comedy/Action **Cas.** **(PR:C MPAA:PG)**

GRANDAD RUDD½** (1935, Aus.) 93m
Cinesound/British Empire Films bw

Bert Bailey, Fred McDonald, Elaine Hamill, Lilias Adeson, John D'Arcy, John Cameron, George Lloyd.

This Australian feature is a sequel to ON OUR SELECTION, the first major talkie for that country. In this outing, popular comic Bailey finds himself on a ranch, engaging in a series of zany misadventures. The episodic structure is well handled, with the comedy backed by strong direction. American audiences might find the Australian accents difficult, if not impossible, to decipher.

p, Bert Bailey; d, Ken G. Hall; w, Victor Roberts, George Parker (based on a play by Bailey and Steele Rudd); ph, Frank Hurley.

Comedy **(PR:A MPAA:NR)**

GRANDPA GOES TO TOWN** (1940) 66m REP bw

James Gleason *(Joe Higgins)*, Lucile Gleason *(Lil Higgins)*, Russell Gleason *(Sidney Higgins)*, Harry Davenport *(Grandpa)*, Lois Ranson *(Betty Higgins)*, Maxie Rosenbloom *(Al)*, Tommy Ryan *(Tommy Higgins)*, Ledda Godoy *(Ledda)*, Noah Beery *(Sam)*, Douglas Meins *(Bill)*, Garry Owen *(Muggsy)*, Ray Turner *(Homer)*, Lee "Lasses" White *(Ike)*, Walter Miller *(Director)*, Emmett Lynn *(Jasper)*, Joe Caits *(Woodrow)*, Arturo Godoy *(Himself)*.

Another, somewhat bizarre, Higgins family drama that mainly concerns itself with Grandpa Higgins (Davenport) and his discovery of gold in a ghost town where ma had invested most of their life savings after being hoodwinked by a shady real estate dealer. The discovery of the mother lode of course makes the little hotel in the middle of nowhere a booming success. Things get strange when unnecessary scenes starring recent (in 1940) boxing whiz Arturo Godoy (he had gone 15 rounds with Joe Louis) dancing a rhumba with his wife and then participating in a lame heavyweight bout. Walter Miller, one of the best known romantic leads of the silents, died before this film's release. He played the director of a film within the film. Songs include "Sunshine For Sale." (See HIGGINS FAMILY series, Index.)

p&d, Gus Meins; w, Jack Townley; ph, Reggie Lanning; ed, Murray Seldeen; md, Cy Feuer; art d, John Victor Mackay; m/l, Walter Samuels.

Comedy **(PR:A MPAA:NR)**

GRANNY GET YOUR GUN* (1940) 55m FN-WB bw

May Robson *(Minerva Hatton)*, Harry Davenport *(Nate)*, Margot Stevenson *(Julie Westcott)*, Hardie Albright *(Phil Westcott)*, Clem Bevans *(Smokey)*, Clay Clement *(Riff Daggett)*, William Davidson *(Fitzgerald)*, Arthur Aylesworth *(Sheriff Quinn)*, Granville Bates *(Tom Redding)*, Ann Todd *(Charlotte)*, Vera Lewis *(Carrie)*, Max Hoffman, Jr. *(Frayne)*, Archie Twitchell *(Joe)*, Walter Wilson *(Judge)*, Nat Carr *(Wadsworth)*.

Unbelievable yarn starring Robson as a gun-toting granny of Gold City, Nevada, who doesn't take any guff from anybody. When her granddaughter, Stevenson, is accused of the murder of her soon-to-be-ex-husband, Robson grabs her guns and sets out to find the real killer.

p, Bryan Foy; d, George Amy; w, Kenneth Gamet (based on the novel *The Case of the Dangerous Dowager* by Erle Stanley Gardner); ph, L. William O'Connell; ed, Jack Killifer.

Crime **(PR:A MPAA:NR)**

GRAPES OF WRATH**** (1940) 129m FOX bw

Henry Fonda *(Tom Joad)*, Jane Darwell *(Ma Joad)*, John Carradine *(Casey)*, Charley Grapewin *(Grandpa Joad)*, Dorris Bowdon *(Rosaham)*, Russell Simpson *(Pa Joad)*, O.Z. Whitehead *(Al)*, John Qualen *(Muley)*, Eddie Quillan *(Connie)*, Zeffie Tilbury *(Grandma Joad)*, Frank Sully *(Noah)*, Frank Darien *(Uncle John)*, Darryl Hickman *(Winfield)*, Shirley Mills *(Ruth Joad)*, Grant Mitchell *(Guardian)*, Ward Bond *(Policeman)*, Frank Faylen *(Tim)*, Joe Sawyer *(Accountant)*, Harry Tyler *(Bert)*, Charles B. Middleton *(Conductor)*, John Arledge *(Davis)*, Hollis Jewell *(Muley's Son)*, Paul Guilfoyle *(Floyd)*, Charles D. Brown *(Wilkie)*, Roger Imhof *(Thomas)*, William Pawley *(Bill)*, Arthur Aysleworth *(Father)*, Charles Tannen *(Joe)*, Selmer Jackson *(Inspector)*, Eddie C. Waller *(Proprietor)*, David Hughes *(Frank)*, Cliff Clark *(Townsman)*, Adrian Morris *(Agent)*, Robert Homans *(Spencer)*, Irving Bacon *(Conductor)*, Kitty McHugh *(Mae)*, Georgia Simmons *(Woman)*, James Flavin *(Guard)*, George O'Hara *(Clerk)*, Thornton Edwards *(Motor Cop)*, Jack Pennick *(Committeeman)*, Walter McGrail *(Gang Leader)*, Harry Cording, Paul Sutton, Pat Flaherty, Tom Tyler, Ralph Dunn *(Deputies)*, George Breakstone *(Boy)*, Ted Oliver *(State Policeman)*, Ben Hall *(Gas Station Attendant)*, Gloria Roy *(Waitress)*, Norman Willis *(Joe)*, Erville Anderson *(Storekeeper)*, Harry Strang *(Fred the Truck Driver)*, Rex Lease *(Cop)*, Ienz Palange *(Woman in Camp)*, Louis Mason *(Man in Camp)*, Harry Tenbrook *(Deputy/Troublemaker)*, Frank O'Connor *(Deputy)*, Herbert Heywood *(Gas Station Man)*, Walter Miller *(New Mexico Border Guard)*, Gaylor [Steve] Pendleton, Robert Shaw *(Gas Station Attendants)*, Lee

Shumway *(1st Deputy)*, Dick Rich *(2nd Deputy)*, Trevor Bardette *(Jule)*, William Haade *(Deputy Driver)*, Peggy Ryan, Wally Albright, Shirley Coates, Mae Marsh, Francis Ford.

One of John Ford's greatest films, a certain masterpiece that captured forever on film a tragic element of American society in a time when the very fabric of that society was almost irreparably torn. Here is the painful and poignant odyssey of the Joad family, tenant farmers from Oklahoma, whose saga came to symbolize the plight of the "Okies." Fonda is the eldest Joad son who appears on a desolate stretch of land slashed by a stark road; he has just served a four-year prison term for manslaughter and is returning to his family farm, hitchhiking. After getting a short ride from a suspicious trucker, Fonda hoofs it to a clearing where he meets slightly mad Carradine, a one-time preacher who "has lost the call." Carradine no longer administers to the spiritual needs of the backward Oklahoma tenant farmers. Together, the two walk to the farm worked by Fonda's parents but they only find Qualen, who has lost more of his mental balance than Carradine. He is hiding in the old Joad house and tells how sheriff's deputies in the employ of the banks and farming combines have been searching for him ever since he knocked one unconscious. He relates with fearful detail how he and his family were driven off their own sharecropping farm by tractors that crushed his ramshackle house, how he had cried out against the invaders that he and his people were born on the land and some of them died on it. But it made no difference; he was driven off all the same. Now, he tells Fonda, it's the turn of the Joad family and many others. Fonda and Carradine travel to the farm of Fonda's uncle, Darien, where all the Joads have gathered to prepare for their trek Westward into the unknown. There is a joyous reunion between Fonda and his mother, Darwell, playing the eternal Ma Joad. In the morning the entire family, a dozen people, pile into a broken down truck, loaded to the axels with all of the family's belongings, and set out for California where jobs can be had, according to a handbill Pa Joad (Simpson) has received. Before leaving, Darwell, alone in the clapboard farmhouse, holds up a pair of ancient earrings, putting them to her ears in the dim light and remembering her youth. She clutches a few meager belongings, and then emerges to say, "I'm ready." The rattling heap jumps forward, creaking and groaning under its weight, its tired radiator soon steaming. To the younger Joad children, Hickman and Mills, the trip is a grand adventure, but it's torture to Grandpa and Grandma Joad, Grapewin and Tilbury, and soon Grapewin dies. Fearful of being detained with only $150 to sustain them, the Joads bury Grapewin alongside the road. Carradine says a few words over him, then, to make sure anyone finding the body is assured that the old man was not the victim of foul play, Fonda leaves a note in a bottle at graveside. It reads: "This here is William James Joad, died of a stroke, old, old man. His folks buried him because they got no money to pay for funerals. Nobody kilt him. Just a stroke and he died." En route, the family stops at a campsite and hears not of the rewards of the "Promised Land," but the horrors of the migrant farm communities, how thousands of Okies have flocked to California for those 800 jobs offered in handbills and how they are paid dirt cheap wages, barely enough on which to survive. In the mass exodus from the Dust Bowl, created by the winds that dried up the lands, the Joads continue along Route 66. Their numbers decrease again when Tilbury dies in Darwell's arms; Ma does not tell the family, afraid that agricultural inspectors will turn them back if she makes it known that Grandma is dead. The family crosses the forbidding desert in the middle of the night and enters California where Darwell tells Fonda of the death, saying: "I guess she'll get to rest her head in California after all." They move from one miserable campsite after another, treated by club-toting goons as cattle, cheated out of their wages by unscrupulous landowners who drive them to their picking chores like slaves. They are used as scabs to break strikes without knowing their purpose. Everywhere the migrants are starving. In one camp, the sight of starving children so disturbs the family that Darwell orders them to eat their meal in their tent, then charitably gives the remains of her pot of stew to children, telling them to get flat sticks to eat from. Fonda has no idea of politics, asking "What's these Reds anyway?" as the family moves along. At one camp deputy sheriffs seek out a labor organizer, Guilfoyle, who runs when they order him to surrender. A deputy shoots at him, killing a woman and then Fonda knocks the deputy senseless to prevent him from getting off another shot. Carradine takes the blame for hitting the man and is taken smilingly away. Fonda later finds Carradine (a sort of Christ figure; even his initials are "J.C.") later in a hidden camp outside one of the large farms. He convinces Fonda that the workers must stand up to the landowners to get a fair wage. Just then deputies raid the encampment and one crushes Carradine's head with a club. Fonda takes the club and kills the murderer but is scarred on his left cheek before fleeing. The family must now run with Fonda being sought and they find a safe haven in a government sponsored camp with clean living conditions. Nearby farmers give them work for good wages. For the first time since their arduous journey began the Joads encounter decency and the prospects of survival. When the camp dwellers hold a dance local thugs attempt to break it up but are foiled by the workers who have been tipped off by a local farmer. More seriously, investigators appear at the camp looking for a young man who bears a scar on the left cheek. Fonda is warned and must now leave his family. Fonda goes to Darwell, waking her, taking her outside to tell her he's leaving in the middle of the night so he won't cause the family more trouble. He tells her that Carradine has opened his eyes that "he was like a lantern. He helped me to see things, too." He intends to organize the workers "for a better way of life." Darwell asks where he will be and Fonda replies: "Well, maybe it's like Casey says. Fella ain't got a soul of his own. Just a little piece of a big soul. One big soul that belongs to everybody . . . I'll be around in the dark—I'll be everywhere. Wherever you can look—wherever there's a fight, so hungry people can eat, I'll be there. Wherever there's a cop beating up a guy, I'll be there. I'll be there in the way guys yell when they're mad. I'll be there in the way kids laugh when they're hungry, and they know supper's ready, and when people are eatin' the stuff they raised, and livin' in the houses they built, I'll be there, too." Fonda kisses his mother, even though, she admits "we ain't the kissin' kind," then leaves, much the way he had appeared, unexpectedly and with hope. The family is later shown on the road again. As Darwell and Simpson ride along, Ma becomes introspective. She is the real rock upon which the family has built its trust and she looks to the future with gritty determination, saying to Pa: "Rich fellers come up. They die. Their kids ain't no good and they die out. But we keep a-comin'. We're the people that live. Can't wipe us out. Can't lick us. We'll go on forever, 'cause we're the people!" With these stirring words THE GRAPES OF WRATH comes to an end, one of the most powerful documents ever put to film. Ford's visual interpretation of the Steinbeck classic is so gripping and telling that this incredible film whirlwinds past the viewer, piling up so many memorable scenes that emotions are jarred from one sequence to the next. The director's shots are framed so that everywhere are the endless, almost barren landscapes, overcast skies, bleak exteriors offering little hope, all to accentuate the plight of the displaced Okies. To accomplish his vision Ford employed Gregg Toland, greatest cinematographer of his day and pioneer in deep-focus photography. Here the camera is everywhere, dominating every scene, showing a microscopic tale of a fragment of society, the broken part, from the very beginning when Fonda is seen as a tiny figure walking down a seemingly endless road. The roads and countryside dominate, as do barbed wire and broken-down shacks and the rattletrap trucks in which the migrants move and live, for these are their only true homes, always on the verge of collapse. There is a pervasive feeling of constant doom until the Joads find the government camp and its guardian, Mitchell, who not too coincidentally bears a resemblance to then President Franklin D. Roosevelt, a benevolent figure representing good and security. Though Ford does not shrink from indicting the banks and the landgrabbing companies who took advantage of the cropless farmers, driving them without conscience from their land and crushing their spirits, he also turned one of the bleakest tales ever penned into one of optimism by portraying an American family, displaced but not emotionally or spiritually uprooted, one that still had faith in the future and in America, and therein lies the film's greatness. The performances rendered by the cast are nothing less than superb, drawn carefully by Ford in understated portrayals. Producer Zanuck took great pains to preserve the Steinbeck classic, for which he paid a then staggering $100,000, inserting in the author's contract the promise that the film would "fairly and reasonably retain the main action and social intent of said literary property." Zanuck did insert the "we're the people" speech made by Darwell but with Steinbeck's approval. Zanuck had no trouble in getting Fonda to play a role he knew the actor wanted more than anything. He lured him into a lengthy contract by letting it be known that he was thinking of Tyrone Power or Don Ameche for the part of Tom Joad, which he was not. Fonda's sensitive performance is undoubtedly the greatest of his career, a role that established him as one of the world's top actors. He later credited Ford with this effort, stating how Ford, for the most part, made only one take, never bothering to rehearse his actors. The fabulous farewell scene between Darwell and Fonda was shot only once. The actor recalled in *Fonda, My Life* (as told to Howard Teichmann): "We'd never done it [the scene] out loud, but Ford called for action, the cameras rolled, and he had it in a single take. After we finished the scene, Pappy didn't say a word. He just stood up and walked away. He got what he wanted." Ford did send a second unit to the Oklahama Dust Bowl for some background shooting but for the most part the entire film was shot in California, right in the migrant camps around Pomona. Enhancing the theme and posture of the film were the down home tunes "Red River Valley" and "Home on the Range" which were occasionally inserted to add musical poignancy to certain scenes. Johnson's superlative script tightened the 619-page novel, cleaning up the rough language, but retaining the basic characters and story intent. The result, with Ford's mastery in control, is that the film presents a powerful message without sermonizing. Literary critic Edmund Wilson early on labeled the novel so "cinematic" that Ford could "pour" it onto the screen when ready. Zanuck, who made this film his personal project, involved himself with every aspect of the production. He edited Johnson's script brilliantly so that he later won accolades from this fine screenwriter: "Every script I wrote was improved by his editing." The studio chief inserted little bits of business and technical touches into the film. In the scene where Carradine and other "radicals" are camped near a riverbed, Zanuck had the sound of crickets put on the soundtrack so that viewers would know the group was located in a swampy area. The instrument most often used in the sparse Newman score is the accordian, selected by Zanuck as being the most American and correct for the story. Ford had no objections to Zanuck's involvement but lauded the producer, especially for the tacked-on Ma Joad speech at the end, stating: "The way Zanuck changed it, it came out on an upbeat." Zanuck, not Ford, edited the film after seven weeks of shooting, then released it to universal raves from critics and public alike. It took considerable courage to make THE GRAPES OF WRATH in 1939 when the industry at large warned against producing such a strong social document on film which bordered on indicting the capitalistic system and served almost as a cry for socialism. The Academy Awards the following year honored Ford by giving him an Oscar for Best Director of this film and to Darwell for her magnificent performance as Ma Joad (her part almost went to Beulah Bondi), but the man everyone expected to win, Henry Fonda, lost to his close friend James Stewart for Best Actor (THE PHILADELPHIA STORY). This surprised Stewart, who, before attending the ceremonies, stated that Fonda should win, that he himself had voted for Fonda. Yet, it was later reasoned that the Academy, forever playing catch-up, had voted Stewart the award for his role a year earlier in MR. SMITH GOES TO WASHINGTON. Viewing THE GRAPES OF WRATH today one realizes just how flawless and wonderful it is, with characters and drama as powerful as when it was first released, its evocative scenes as sharply etched as the real life still photography of Dorothea Lange, Arthur Rothstein and Ben Shahn who recorded the actual devastation of the Dust Bowl in Depression torn 1933-34. This film certainly ranks as one of the 10 best films of all time.

p, Darryl F. Zanuck; d, John Ford; w, Nunnally Johnson (based on the novel by John Steinbeck); ph, Gregg Toland; m, Alfred Newman; ed, Robert Simpson; art d, Richard Day, Mark-Lee Kirk; set d, Thomas Little; theme song "Red River Valley."

Drama **Cas.** **(PR:A MPAA:NR)**

GRASS EATER, THE* (1961) 63m Leder-Norton bw

Paul Leder (*Pete Boswell*), Rue McClanahan (*Loraina*), Leon Schrier (*Harvey*), Patricia Manning (*Mary*), Helen Goodman (*Melba*), Richard Villard (*Bartender*), Ted Roter (*Waiter*), Bernard Dukore (*Bookstore Owner*), Bill Guhl (*Man on Street*).

Dull, self-consciously "arty" film adaptation of the equally boring and pretentious stage play by William Norton (who co-produced). The story, such as it is, circles around a vagabond-ish Leder (who co-produced), who wins his girl's affections by demonstrating to her the corruption inherent in the normal marriage structure; he picks a married couple, seduces the wife, and reduces the husband to a bowl of jello. Tripe.

p, Paul Leder, William Norton; d, John Patrick Hayes; w, Hayes (based on the play by Norton); ph, John Morrill; m, Jaime Mendoza-Nava; ed, Thomas Conrad; set d, Ray Creevey.

Drama (PR:C MPAA:NR)

GRASS IS GREENER, THE** (1960) 105m Grandon/UNIV c

Cary Grant (*Victor Rhyall*), Deborah Kerr (*Hilary Rhyall*), Robert Mitchum (*Charles Delacro*), Jean Simmons (*Hattie Durant*), Moray Watson (*Trevor Sellers*).

Some stage plays are best seen in the proscenium light and lose all of their intimacy when expanded to meet the needs of the screen. Such was the case for THE GRASS IS GREENER. Originally seen on the London stage where it was a fair hit, THE GRASS IS GREENER is filled with ten-pound words, overly verbose and often stultifying in its prose. The long-winded story concerns a British earl, Grant, and his earlette, Kerr, who have opened their palatial manse to the—cringe—public, so they can afford to keep it up, pay the gardeners, and continue living in the style in which their forebears lived. (This really does happen in Jolly Olde and so the premise is sound.) Mitchum, a cliched Texas oilman, enters the house and, showing no couth whatsoever, walks into Kerr's boudoir, a sacrosanct area of the house, without being announced or invited. Bells ring when these two see each other. The remainder of the movie concerns Grant's attempts at retrieving Kerr and rekindling the love they once knew. A series of contrived plot twists include enlisting an old girl friend, Simmons, to parade around the house in garish clothing and pretend that she is mad for him; this being a dumb attempt to elicit jealousy on Kerr's part. Lots of jingoistic dialog rapping the USA while lauding the U.K. also helps to mar the film. Kerr and Grant are united at the end; Mitchum and Simmons have now discovered each other and, it is presumed, they will live happily ever after while roping doggies or capping gushers. Mitchum is leaden as the oil man. Not that he doesn't look the part, it's just that he plays light comedy the way Dom De Luise plays believable drama. In other words, not at all. Mitchum is as comfortable with a witty quip as Queen Elizabeth might be with a damp mop. The only person who seems at home in the morass of verbiage is Grant, who could read the Korean dictionary and make it sound charming. Donen takes us for a few romps in the green countryside only to ease the claustrophobia and gratuitous meandering outdoors only serves to make us realize how hidebound the story is. The saving grace is Noel Coward's music and his song "The Stately Homes Of England." Seeing the film today and hearing that song makes us recall Quentin Crisp's comment (he's the gay raconteur who writes and performs so well and was portrayed by John Hurt in a magnificent PBS special "The Naked Civil Servant") where he referred to himself as one of the "Stately Homos Of England." Shallow and trite, it's almost, but not quite, rescued by Grant's performance. Other songs include "Mad Dogs and Englishmen" and "I'll Follow My Secret Heart."

p&d, Stanley Donen; w, Hugh and Margaret Williams (based on their play); ph, Christopher Challis (Technirama, Technicolor); m, Noel Coward; ed, James Clark; md, Muir Mathieson; art d, Paul Sheriff; set d, Vernon Dixon; cos, Hardy Amies, Christian Dior; m/l, Coward; makeup, John O'Gorman, Eric Allwright.

Comedy Cas. (PR:A MPAA:NR)

GRASS IS SINGING, THE** (1982, Brit./Swed.) 110m Chibote-Swedish Film Institute/Mainline c

Karen Black, John Thaw, John Kani, John Moulder-Brown, Patrick Mynhardt, Bjorn Gedda.

Filmed depiction of a novel by Doris Lessing does a good job in capturing the anguish a woman goes through in trying to adapt to the climate of Africa, both social and environmental, after marrying a landowner who is himself too sickly to live there. Any power the film does have is mainly a result of Black as the newlywed; everything else just seems a background to allow her to go through her histrionics.

p, Mark Forstater; d&w, Michael Raeburn (based on the novel by Doris Lessing); ph, Bille August; m, Lasse Dahlberg, Bjorn Isfalt, Temba Tana; ed, Thomas Schalm.

Drama (PR:A MPAA:NR)

GRASSHOPPER, THE*** (1970) 96m NGP c

Jacqueline Bisset (*Christine*), Jim Brown (*Tommy Marcott*), Joseph Cotten (*Richard Morgan*), Corbett Monica (*Danny*), Ramon Bieri (*Roosevelt Dekker*), Christopher Stone (*Jay Rigney*), Roger Garrett (*Buck*), Stanley Adams (*Buddy Miller*), Dick Richards (*Lou Bellman*), Tim O'Kelly (*Eddie Molina*), Stefanianna Christopherson (*Libby*), Ed Flanders (*Jack Bishop*), Wendy Farrington (*Connie*), Sandi Gaviola (*Kyo*), Eris Sandy (*Vicky*), John David Wilder (*Timmy*), Jay Laskay (*Manny*), Jim Smith (*Larry*), Therese Baldwin (*Gigi*), Chris Wong (*Billy*), Kathalyn Turner (*Ann Marie*), William H. Bassett (*Aaron*), Marc Hannibal (*Walters*), David Duclon (*Miller's Son*), Jessica Myerson (*Saleswoman*).

This might well be named "A Star Is Aborted." A sincere and sordid story with far more verisimilitude than the customary rags-to-riches or knife-in-the-back hackneyed Hollywood tale. Bissett, bored by British Columbia, elects to travel to Los Angeles to join her old home-town sweetheart O'Kelly. Diverted when her car breaks down, she joins Monica—a club comic—and goes to the bright lights of Las Vegas. Fascinated by the city that never sleeps, she yet continues her travels,

joining O'Kelly and settling in to a life of domesticity, working as a bank teller. Haunted by the glamor she has seen, the restless 19 year old hops to the greener grass of Vegas, where her physical attributes land her a job as a showgirl. Settling in with new friends, she meets Brown—as in real life, a one-time football great—who has been hired as a handshaker by a hotel. She marries the black, disgruntled Brown and, to advance his career beyond the confines of meeting and greeting, joins mob-connected Bieri in his hotel room, only to be brutally beaten when she rejects his sexual advances. Husband Brown retaliates with a vicious attack on Bieri; he and his bride then, wisely, leave town. Again longing for excitement, Bisset decides to leave her husband. Before she can do so, he is murdered. Bisset returns to Las Vegas, but the pervasive influence of Bieri prevents her from finding legitimate employment. She turns high-ticket call-girl, then becomes the mistress of millionaire Cotten. Ultimately, she chooses to leave the comfort of Cotten for what she views as independence. Grasshopper turned ant, she peddles her pulchritude with the assistance of panderer Stone, a rock musician, to raise enough money to purchase a ranch. Stone absconds with Bisset's body-earned bankroll. Burned out and bitter at 22, Bissell gets blasted and persuades a similarly stoned skywriter to deliver her message to the world: the single word F____; ephemeral, transitory, drifting on the wind. A well done film, with a fine performance by Bisset.

p, Jerry Belson, Garry Marshall; d, Jerry Paris; w, Belson, Marshall (based on the novel *The Passing Of Evil* by Mark McShane); ph, Sam Leavitt (Technicolor); m, Billy Goldenberg; ed, Aaron Stell; art d, Tambi Larsen; set d, Donald J. Sullivan; spec eff, Thol O. Simonson; makeup, Gustaf M. Norin; cos, Donfeld.

Drama (PR:O MPAA:R)

GRAVE OF THE VAMPIRE zero (1972) 95m Entertainment Pyramid c (AKA: SEED OF TERROR)

William Smith, Michael Pataki, Lynn Peters, Diane Holden, Jay Adler, Kitty Vallacher, Jay Scott, Lieux Dressler.

Vile and disgusting film features Pataki as a vampire who rapes a woman in an open grave, thus fathering her child. The baby drinks her blood out of a bottle, but she finally kicks off from anemia. Smith plays the grown-up version of the vampire lad, reluctant to do what his heritage commands. He decides to kill his old man, finding him teaching occultism at a university. Problems arise when a neighbor falls in love with Smith and wants to join him in the world of the undead. Shocking, grisly, and disgusting. Vampire daddy Pataki went on to similar garbage, playing in DRACULA'S DOG a few years later. Smith had just finished doing "Hawaii Five-O" for television, and this apparently was the best offer he had.

p, Daniel Cady; d, John Patrick Hayes; w, Hayes, David Chase (based on the novel *The Still Life* by Chase); ph, Paul Hipp; ed, Ron Johnson; art d, Earl Marshall; makeup, Tino Zacchia.

Horror Cas. (PR:O MPAA:PG)

GRAVE ROBBERS FROM OUTER SPACE (SEE: PLAN 9 FROM OUTER SPACE, 1959)

GRAVEYARD OF HORROR zero (1971, Span.) 86m International c (EL DESCUARTIZADOR DE BINBROOK; AKA: NECROPHAGUS)

Bill Curran, Francisco Brana, Beatriz Lacy, Victor Israel, Catherine Ellison, Yocasta Grey, J.R. Clark, Marisa Shiero.

When an experiment goes astray, a scientist is transformed into a combination animal-vegetable-mineral whom his brother has to bury underground and keep supplied with a fresh corpse daily. Positively wretched, but good for a laugh in some quarters.

p, Tony Recorder; d&w, Miguel Madrid; ph, Alfonso Nieva; m, Alfonso Santisteben; ed, Maria Luisa Soriano; art d, Barbara Hyde; spec eff, Antonio Molina.

Horror (PR:O MPAA:NR)

GRAVESIDE STORY, THE (SEE: COMEDY OF TERRORS, THE, 1963)

GRAVY TRAIN, THE*** (1974) 94m Tomorrow Entertainment/COL c (AKA: THE DION BROTHERS)

Stacy Keach (*Calvin*), Frederic Forrest (*Rut*), Margot Kidder (*Margie*), Barry Primus (*Tony*), Richard Romanus (*Carlo*), Denny Miller (*Rex*), Clay Tanner (*Bather*), Robert Phillips (*Gino*), Mary L. Honaker (*Mother*), Jack Starrett (*Rancher*), Lorna Thayer (*TV Interviewer*), Francesca Bellini (*Receptionist*).

Decent crime drama featuring outstanding performances by Keach and Forrest as hayseed West Virginia brothers who leave their coal-mining community and go off on their own to strike it rich. Soon they end up with gang leader Primus, and together with the klutzy Miller, they pull a big armored-car robbery. Primus does a double-cross and skips town with the loot, leaving Keach, Forrest, and Miller to the cops. In the ensuing shootout, Miller is killed and the brothers take off after Primus, seeking revenge. Climax sees a massive gun battle between the parties in a rotten building that is in the midst of being torn down. Well-directed by Starrett, with a good script filled with plenty of black humor by DAYS OF HEAVEN (1978) director Terrence Malick who used a pseudonym because he didn't direct.

p, Jonathan T. Taplin; d, Jack Starrett; w, Bill Kerby, David Whitney [Terrence Malick]; ph, Jerry Hirschfeld (CFI color); m, Fred Karlin; ed, John Horger; prod d, Stan Jolley; set d, Bill Calvert; spec eff, Cliff Wenger; m/l, Fred and Marsha Karlin.

Crime (PR:O MPAA:R)

GRAY LADY DOWN* (1978) 111m Mirisch/UNIV c

Charlton Heston (*Capt. Paul Blanchard*), David Carradine (*Capt. Gates*), Stacy Keach (*Capt. Bennett*), Ned Beatty (*Mickey*), Stephen McHattie (*Murphy*), Ronny Cox (*Cmdr. Samuelson*), Dorian Harewood (*Fowler*), Rosemary Forsyth (*Vickie*), Hilly Hicks (*Page*), Charles Cioffi (*Adm. Barnes*), William Jordan (*Waters*), Jack

Rader *(Harkness)*, Anthony Ponzini *(Caruso)*, Michael O'Keefe *(Harris)*, Charlie Robinson *(McAllister)*, Christopher Reeve *(Phillips)*, Melendy Britt *(Liz)*, David Wilson *(Hanson)*, Robert Symonds *(Secretary of the Navy)*, Lawrason Driscoll *(Bloome)*.

A rare, dull disaster film. Rare for the fact that Irwin Allen had absolutely nothing to do with it, GRAY LADY DOWN manages to take an interesting subject and make it celluloid Valium. There isn't one turn or twist that we haven't seen several times before, and it's as suspenseful as a Donald Duck cartoon, but not nearly as entertaining. Heston is his usual stoical self as the captain of a nuclear submarine that is crippled and sits at the bottom of the ocean, teetering on a shaky precipice. If it goes over the side, it will sink even deeper, the hull will crack from the water pressure, and all hands will be lost. It's only about an hour out of Hartford; Keach is put in charge of the rescue operation. Aboard the ship, Harewood—the ship's second officer—goes berserk from the pressure (or was it from Heston's bad acting?). They are in radio contact with Keach as Carradine, a retired naval man, and Beatty go into the depths in Carradine's experimental bathyscape, the Snark. Do we have to tell you if they live or die? Based on a novel that had to be better than this film, GRAY LADY DOWN lost money at the box office, and rightly so. It is, to coin a phrase, sub-standard. If you watch this movie thinking it's a comedy, you may laugh a great deal.

p, Walter Mirisch; d, David Greene; w, Howard Sackler, James Whittaker (adapted by Frank P. Rosenberg, based on the novel *Event 1000* by David Lavallee); ph, Steven Larner (Panavision, Technicolor); m, Jerry Fielding; ed, Robert Swink; prod d, William Tuntke; set d, John Dwyer; spec eff, Curtis Dickson.

Disaster/Drama **Cas.** **(PR:C MPAA:PG)**

GRAYEAGLE** (1977) 104m AIP c

Ben Johnson *(John Colter)*, Iron Eyes Cody *(Standing Bear)*, Lana Wood *(Beth Colter)*, Jack Elam *(Trapper Willis)*, Paul Fix *(Running Wolf)*, Alex Cord *(Grayeagle)*, Jacob Daniels *(Scar)*, Jimmy Clem *(Abe Stoud)*, Cindy Butler *(Ida Colter)*, Charles B. Pierce *(Bugler)*, Blackie Wetzell *(Medicine Man)*.

Even Johnson can't save this low-budget rehash of John Ford's western classic THE SEARCHERS (1956), this time told from the point of view of the Indians. Johnson plays a tough frontier trapper who launches a lengthy search for his daughter, who was kidnaped by a young Cheyenne brave. As the girl is dragged back to the deathbed of Chief Running Wolf—Fix—through a variety of beautiful western locales, we gradually learn that the Cheyenne chief is her real father. Inane attempt at making the Indians sympathetic through the character of Johnson family friend Cody—who is really a sort of "Uncle Tom" of the redskins—fails because of Pierce's racist view of Indians in general. The cutting of 40 minutes for varied markets further hurts the Indian perspectives.

p,d&w, Charles B. Pierce; ph&ed, Jim Roberson (Movielab Color); m, Jaime Mendoza-Nava; art d, John Ball.

Western **(PR:C MPAA:PG)**

GRAZIE ZIA (SEE: THANK YOU, AUNT, 1967, Ital.)

GREASE*½** (1978) 110m PAR c

John Travolta *(Danny)*, Olivia Newton-John *(Sandy)*, Stockard Channing *(Rizzo)*, Jeff Conaway *(Kenickie)*, Didi Conn *(Frenchy)*, Jamie Donnelly *(Jan)*, Dinah Manoff *(Marty)*, Barry Pearl *(Doody)*, Michael Tucci *(Sonny)*, Kelly Ward *(Putzie)*, Susan Buckner *(Patty Simcox)*, Eddie Deezen *(Eugene)*, Lorenzo Lamas *(Tom Chisum)*, Dennis C. Stewart *(Leo)*, Annette Charles *(Cha Cha)*, Dick Patterson *(Mr. Rudie)*, Fannie Flagg *(Nurse Wilkin)*, Darrell Zwerling *(Mr. Lynch)*, Ellen Travolta *(Waitress)*, Eve Arden *(Principal McGee)*, Frankie Avalon *(Teen Angel)*, Joan Blondell *(Vi)*, Edd Byrnes *(Vince Fontaine)*, Sid Caesar *(Coach Calhoun)*, Alice Ghostley *(Mrs. Murdock)*, Dody Goodman *(Blanche)*, Sha-Na-Na *(Johnny Casino and the Gamblers)*.

If you're looking for good, clean, high-spirited fun, then GREASE is the word for you. Steve Krantz, who now spends most of his time producing the works of his wife, Judith Krantz, originally had the rights to this film and intended to do it as a cartoon (He'd once been partnered with Ralph Bakshi). When he could find no one to agree with his concept (a wise choice on the part of the studios) he let the project go and it was picked up by Allan Carr, who made a deal with Robert Stigwood, and the die was cast. The Broadway play is probably still running somewhere, and the movie is a fine rendition of the play, and reaped huge rewards at the box office, perhaps the highest grosses accorded to any film musical. It takes place in the 1950s, which have become a serious haven for nostalgics. Travolta and Newton-John make auspicious impressions as two kids who attend Rydell High. If this movie were made in the 1960s it would have starred Frankie Avalon and Sandra Dee in the roles. If not them, substitute Fabian and Annette Funicello. (Avalon does make an appearance in the picture, just to titillate the older crowd.) The story is a chaotic look at young love; the plot turns are not really important. There are the usual misunderstandings, the satire of the teachers, a car race between rivals and several production numbers. Travolta is one of those cool dudes who feels he has to stay above the travails of his contemporaries. Newton-John loves him dearly and wants their summer romance to continue once they go to school together. Everyone in the picture was at least five to ten years out of High School when they made it, but disbelief was suspended in favor of the enjoyment. Lots of attention was paid to the details, and it shows in every frame. The clothes, the manner of speech, the hair styles, the musical arrangements were all on the nose. There are several extended "cameos" by various stars; Eve Arden reprises her "Our Miss Brooks" role, but this time she is a principal. Sid Caesar is a fine coach, and even ageless Joan Blondell comes on for a fast, funny bit. A lot of people made their first appearances in GREASE. It was Kleiser's premier directing effort (for the screen). He had already done a good job directing Travolta in a TV show called "The Boy In The Glass Bubble" in which Travolta played the true story of a young man with a rare disease who could not leave the bubble he lived in or he would die. Travolta fell in love with the woman who played his mother, Diana Hyland, and they stayed together until her early death of cancer while she was still in her thirties). Stockard Channing had already appeared in THE FORTUNE, where she was dwarfed by her co-stars. In GREASE, she was able to step out and make a large dent. Didi Conn, who starred in the mawkish YOU LIGHT UP MY LIFE, proves that she is a one-note actress with a whiny voice. (She married screen composer David Shire, former husband of Talia Shire, sister of Francis Ford Coppola, but what the heck, you knew that, didn't you?) Edd "Kookie" Byrnes, who was a heartbreaker in the 1950s, makes a small appearance. He is good, and should be getting more work. Travolta was never better, and his film career went straight downhill from here as he starred in a host of garbage pictures that made very little money. Composer Charles Fox ("Happy Days", many TV shows, as well as FOUL PLAY and a host of movies) was supposed to do the score for the film, but he and producer Carr didn't see eye to eye, so Louis St. Louis was brought in and his barely credited contribution was excellent. Newton-John is adorable in her virginal way, and just about all the secondary parts are well-cast. It is a first-rate depiction of a fifth-rate genre (BEACH PARTY, BEACH BLANKET BINGO, DON'T KNOCK THE ROCK, etc.) and you just can't hate anything *this* energetic and happy. Songs include "Grease," "Summer Nights," "Hopelessly Devoted To You," "You're The One That I Want," "Sandy," "Beauty School Dropout," "Look At Me, I'm Sandra Dee," "Greased Lightnin," "It's Raining On Prom Night," "Alone at a Drive-In Movie," "Blue Moon," "Rock 'n' Roll Is Here to Stay," "Those Magic Changes," "Hound Dog," "Born to Hand-Jive," "Tears On My Pillow," "Mooning," "Freddy My Love," "Rock 'n' Roll Party Queen," "There Are Worse Things I Could Do," "We Go Together," "Love is a Many Splendored Thing."

p, Robert Stigwood, Allan Carr; d, Randal Kleiser; w, Bronte Woodard (adapted by Carr from the musical by Jim Jacobs, Warren Casey); ph, Bill Butler (Panavision, Metrocolor); ed, John F. Burnett; prod d, Phillip Jefferies; md, Bill Oakes; set d, James Berkey, ch, Patricia Birch, cos, Albert Wolsky; m/l, Jacobs, Casey, Barry Gibb, John Farrar, Scott J. Simon, Louis St. Louis, others.

Musical/Comedy **Cas.** **(PR:A MPAA:PG)**

GREASE 2½** (1982) 114m PAR c

Maxwell Caulfield *(Michael Carrington)*, Michelle Pfeiffer *(Stephanie Zinone)*, Pamela Segall *(Dolores Rebchuck)*, Didi Conn *(Frenchy)*, Eve Arden *(Ms. McGee)*, Sid Caesar *(Coach Calhoun)*, Dody Goodman *(Blanche)*, Tab Hunter *(Mr. Stuart)*, Dick Patterson *(Mr. Spears)*, Connie Stevens *(Miss Mason)*, Adrian Zmed *(Johnny Nogerilli)*, Christopher McDonald *("Goose" McKenzie)*, Peter Frechette *(Lou Di Mucci)*, Leif Green *(Davey Jaworski)*, Lorna Luft *(Paulette Rebchuck)*, Maureen Teefy *(Sharon Cooper)*, Alison Price *(Rhonda Ritter)*, Eddie Deezen, Matt Lattanzi, Liz Sagal, Dennis C. Stewart.

Several repeaters from the first GREASE, but not the important ones. Maxwell Caulfield has been tapped to replace Travolta, and it's too bad, because Caulfield can't lift Travolta's comb. Pfeiffer fares somewhat better as the ingenue, but the whole movie looks as though it was slapped together to take advantage of the incredible success of its predecessor, and, no doubt, it was. GREASE did over $100 million dollars at the wickets, much to the chagrin of many of the reviewers, who felt it had nothing to offer a sophisticated audience. They were right, of course, in that it had little to recommend it to the crowd that reads *Vogue* or *Forbes*, but what it *did* have was sheer fun and silliness. In GREASE 2, much of that has been removed. Lame jokes and stilted direction by Pat Birch, who did the choreography on the first film. They must have thought that qualified her to direct this one. They were wrong. The time is tranquil 1961. Ike is gone; JFK is everyone's favorite president. Matter of fact, it was quite a dull era for America, and that is accurately depicted by the dull screenplay. Caulfield is the new boy at Rydell, an English lad who would like to fit in. He falls for Pfeiffer, a member of the Pink Ladies club, the members of which are not allowed to date anyone not a biker with the T-Birds gang. Caulfield saves Pfeiffer from some meanies, but never allows himself to be seen, so he's sort of *Captain Marvel* or *The Green Hornet* or *The Lone Ranger* on a motorcycle. The last thirty minutes are there because they obviously ran out of story. It's a talent show at a luau in the old Mickey Rooney "Hey, I've got a barn, let's put on a show," attitude. Didi Conn comes back to annoy one's eardrums with a voice that sounds like a cat scratching his claws on a blackboard. Lorna Luft (daughter of Judy Garland) has a small role as one of the Pink Ladies. Pamela Segall, third-billed, is the daughter of well-known TV writer-producer Don Segall, but nepotism had nothing to do with it, and he was just as surprised as anyone when he read that she'd gotten the part. Arden, Caesar, and Goodman are holdovers. In a tiny role is the man who later married Newton-John, star of the first GREASE. His name is Matt Lattanzi and, as far as anyone can gather, this was the highlight of his dim acting career. Tab Hunter and Connie Stevens are the nostalgia roles (as was Frankie Avalon in the first) and are lost. A waste of time for everyone concerned, and yet it did make enough money to make the producers think about another sequel. Thank heaven they let it go at this.

p, Robert Stigwood, Allan Carr; d&ch, Patricia Birch; w, Ken Finkleman; ph, Frank Stanley (Panavision, Metrocolor); m, Louis St. Louis; ed, John F. Burnett; prod d, Gene Callahan; set d, Lee Poll; cos, Robert De Mora.

Musical/Comedy **Cas.** **(PR:C-O MPAA:PG)**

GREASED LIGHTNING*** (1977) 96m Third World Cinema/WB c

Richard Pryor *(Wendell Scott)*, Beau Bridges *(Hutch)*, Pam Grier *(Mary Jones)*, Cleavon Little *(Peewee)*, Vincent Gardenia *(Sheriff Cotton)*, Richie Havens *(Woodrow)*, Julian Bond *(Russell)*, Earl Hindman *(Beau Welles)*, Minnie Gentry *(Mrs. Scott)*, Lucy Saroyan *(Hutch's Wife)*, Noble Willingham *(Billy Joe Byrnes)*, Bruce Atkins, Steve Fifield *(Deputies)*, Bill Cobbs, Georgia Allen *(Mary's Parents)*, Maynard Jackson *(Minister)*, Danny Nelson *(Wayne Carter)*, Cara Dunn *(Restaurant Owner)*, Alvin Huff *(Moonshiner)*, Willie McWhorter *(Wendell Jr.)*, Frederick Dennis Greene *(Slack)*, Bill Connell *(Speedway Announcer)*.

Good comedy-biography of the first black NASCAR stock-car racer Wendell Scott (played by Pryor, once again proving he can act), spanning a twenty-five year period from the end of WW II to 1971. The story begins during the closing days of the war and we see Pryor striving to overcome the prejudice and close-mindedness in the racing business with a sense of purpose and humor. Climax sees Pryor in 1971 finally participating in a championship race. Real-life Georgia politicians Bond and Jackson have small bits. Songs are "Maybe Tomorrow," Fred Karlin, Bradford Craig (sung by Roberta Flack); "All Come True," Karlin, Norman Gimbel (sung by Richie Havens).

p, Hannah Weinstein; d, Michael Schultz; w, Kenneth Vose, Lawrence DuKore, Melvin Van Peebles, Leon Capetanos; ph, George Bouillet (Movielab Color); m, Fred Karlin; ed, Bob Wyman, Christopher Holmes, Randy Roberts; art d, Jack Senter; set d, James I. Berkey; cos, Celia Bryant, Henry Salley; spec eff, Candy Flanagan, Tom Ward.

Drama/Comedy   **Cas.**   **(PR:C MPAA:PG)**

GREASER'S PALACE**½   (1972) 91m Greaser's Palace Ltd. c

Albert Henderson (Seaweedhead Greaser), Michael Sullivan (Lamy Greaser), Luana Anders (Cholera Greaser), James Antonio (Vernon), George Morgan (Coo Coo), Ron Nealy (Card Man), Larry Moyer (Captain Good), John Paul Hudson (Smiley), Jackson Haynes (Rope Man), Lawrence Wolf (French Padre), Alex Hitchcock (Nun), Pablo Ferro (Indian), Toni Basil (Indian Girl), Stan Gottlieb (Spitunia), Herve Villechaize (Mr. Spitunia), Don Smolen (Gip), Joe Madden (Man With Painting), Donald Calfa (Morris), Woody Chambliss (Father), Ron Nealy (Ghost), Allan Arbus (Zoot Suit), Elsie Downey (The Woman), Rex King (Turquoise Skies).

Offbeat (what did one expect from the director of PUTNEY SWOPE, 1969) telling of Christ's passion tale set in the old west. Arbus plays the Messiah, a dude from the East, who parachutes into a crazy little sagebrush town on his way to the promised land to become a singer. There he runs into trouble in the form of nasty town boss Henderson. Arbus brings the baddie's son Sullivan back to life after the old man has killed him because he suspects he's a "homo." Eventually crazy woman Downey crucifies Arbus to purge her soul of evil. Very strange, but well done and creative.

p, Cyma Rubin; d&w, Robert Downey; ph, Peter Powell (Eastmancolor); m, Jack Nitzsche; ed, Bud Smith; set d, David Forman; cos, Sharon Sachs; makeup, Pat Dobie.

Drama   **Cas.**   **(PR:C MPAA:NR)**

GREAT ADVENTURE, THE*** (1955, Swed.) 80m Sandrew-Baumanfilm bw (DET STORA ÄVENTYRET)

Anders Norborg (Anders), Kjell Sucksdorff (Kjell), Arne Sucksdorff (Father), Norman Shelley (Narrator).

A highly impressive film mainly because of Sucksdorff's ability to capture a unique vision of the wilderness and the forces which separate the wild from more structured systems. A thin plot revolves around two farmboys who capture and attempt to tame a wild otter, a goal that fails when the young animal has a yearning to join his kind in the forest.

p,d,w,ph&ed, Arne Sucksdorff; md, Lars Erik Larsson.

Adventure   **(PR:AAA MPAA:NR)**

GREAT ADVENTURE, THE*½   (1976, Span./Ital.) 87m Pacific International c

Jack Palance, Joan Collins, Fred Romer [Fernando Romero], Elisabetta Virgili, Manuel de Blas, Remo de Angelis.

Lame adaptation of a Jack London story has Romer roaming the Alaskan wilderness with his faithful hound and running up against Palance as a corrupt town boss and Collins as a vampish dancehall girl.

p, Elliot Greisinger, Joseph Allegro; d, Paul Elliotts [Gianfranco Baldanello].

Adventure   **Cas.**   **(PR:A MPAA:G)**

GREAT ALLIGATOR* (1980, Ital.) (IL FIUME DEL GRANDE CAIMANO)

Mel Ferrer, Barbara Bach, Richard Johnson.

Cheapie in all respects makes the supposition that a thrill or two may be got by having a giant alligator loose in the vicinity of an African resort run by Ferrer. Bach is among the guests who have to put up with the possibility of having a leg chomped off.

p, Lawrence Martin; d&w, Sergio Martino.

Horror   **Cas.**   **(PR:O MPAA:NR)**

GREAT AMERICAN BROADCAST, THE*** (1941) 90m FOX bw

Alice Faye (Vicki Adams), Jack Oakie (Chuck Hadley), John Payne (Rix Martin), Cesar Romero (Bruce Chadwick), Four Ink Spots (Specialty), James Newill (Singer), Nicholas Brothers, Wiere Brothers (Specialty), Mary Beth Hughes (Secretary), Eula Morgan (Mme. Rinaldi), William Pawley (Foreman), Lucien Littlefield (Justice of the Peace), Edward Conrad (Conductor), Gary Breckner, Mike Frankovich, John Hiestand (Announcers), Eddie Acuff (Jimmy), Mildred Gover (Jennie), Syd Saylor (Brakeman), Eddie Kane (Headwaiter), William Halligan (Mr. Porter), Frank Orth (Counterman), Herbert Heywood (Doorman), Charles Tannen (Usher), Dorothy Dearing (Bruce's Girl Friend), Snowflake, Sam McDaniel (Porters), John Sinclair (Lineman), Arno Frey (Waiter).

Oakie and Payne play a pair of enterprising WW I vets determined to strike it rich in the business world. Financed by another buddy, Romero, the duo bomb out in nearly every venture they enter into until someone suggests giving the fledgling medium of radio a try. With the enthusiastic help of Oakie's girl friend Faye, they begin to build their radio empire. Looking to broadcast an event of major significance in order to snare an audience, the team decides to do a play-by-play of the upcoming Willard-Dempsey fight of 1919. The broadcast is an unqualified success, with Faye and Payne falling in love during the excitement. Payne and Oakie

have a parting of the ways shortly thereafter. Soon the couple are married and running a small radio station, but stiff competition from the giant corporations is forcing them out. Unable to secure a loan to expand and modernize his business, Payne feels defeated. To save the station, Faye goes to Romero for help and he agrees to finance the loan. Payne learns of the deal and leaves Faye in anger. Lonely and unable to run the station by herself, Faye goes to New York to work for Romero and Oakie, who now own and operate the biggest radio station in the city. As the years go by Faye becomes a radio singing sensation and considers going to Reno for a quickie divorce from Payne, who has yet to resurface. Oakie, finally admitting to himself that Faye never loved him, encourages her to remain married and vows to help her find her husband. To do this, Oakie devises the first nationwide radio broadcast, an idea originally thought up by Payne, and plans to take credit for the scheme in all the papers, knowing that the news will enrage Payne enough to force a confrontation. The big day comes and the broadcast goes on the air featuring dozens of top-name performers including Jack Benny, Kate Smith, Rudy Vallee, Eddie Cantor, and of course, Faye. Oakie's plan works. Payne arrives at the station and is reunited with Faye. A solid variety musical, THE GREAT AMERICAN BROADCAST is a fast-paced, often funny, and at times a fascinating look at the early days of radio. Though the production at times is a bit slipshod (none of Faye's gowns are circa 1920; the chorus' costumes are the same worn in ALEXANDER'S RAGTIME BAND, 1939), the film moves at such a rapid and entertaining rate that only the persnickety would be bothered. Faye is vivacious and charming as ever in her fifth and final appearance in a radio-inspired musical extravaganza. Songs include: "I've Got a Bone to Pick With You," "It's All In a Lifetime," "I Take to You," "Long Ago Last Night," "Where You Are," "The Great American Broadcast" (Mack Gordon, Harry Warren), "Albany Bound" (Buddy De Sylva, Bud Green, Ray Henderson), "Give My Regards to Broadway" (George M. Cohan), "If I Didn't Care" (Jack Lawrence).

p, Darryl F. Zanuck; d, Archie Mayo; w, Don Ettlinger, Edwin Blum, Robert Ellis, Helen Logan; ph, Leon Shamroy, Perverell Marley; ed, Robert Simpson; md, Alfred Newman; art d, Richard Day, Albert Hogsett; set d, Thomas Little; cos, Travis Banton.

Musical   **(PR:A MPAA:NR)**

GREAT AMERICAN BUGS BUNNY-ROAD RUNNER CHASE*** (1979) 97m WB c (AKA: THE BUGS BUNNY-ROAD RUNNER MOVIE)

Mel Blanc (Voice Characterizations).

An outstanding compilation of some of Chuck Jones' finest Bugs Bunny cartoons released on the irrepressible rabbit's 40th birthday. Some twenty minutes of new animated footage showing Bugs in his Beverly Hills home looking back over the years at his past triumphs provide the structure for this nostalgic look at Daffy Duck, Elmer Fudd, and Porky Pig from the years 1939-1962. Also making a brief appearance is a montage of scenes with Road Runner and Wile E. Coyote culled from 16 different cartoons. Good fun.

p&d, Chuck Jones; w, Mike Maltese, Jones; m, Carl Stalling, Milt Franklyn, Dean Elliott; ed, Treg Brown, Horta Editorial; prod d, Maurice Noble, Ray Aragon; graphics, Don Foster.

Cartoon   **(PR:AAA MPAA:G)**

GREAT AMERICAN PASTIME, THE**½   (1956) 89m MGM bw

Tom Ewell (Bruce Hallerton), Anne Francis (Betty Hallerton), Ann Miller (Mrs. Doris Patterson), Dean Jones (Buck Rivers), Rudy Lee (Dennis Hallerton), Judson Pratt (Ed Ryder), Raymond Bailey (George Carruthers), Wilfrid Knapp (Mr. Dawson), Bob Jellison (Mr. O'Keefe), Raymond Winston (Herbie Patterson), Tod Ferrell (Man Mountain O'Keefe), Paul Engle (Foster Carruthers), Ann Morriss (Mrs. George Carruthers), Gene O'Donnell (Samuel J. Garway), Smidgeon the Dog, Nathaniel Benchley.

A comedic look at suburban little-league baseball, and its effects on both youngsters and adults, that pre-dates THE BAD NEWS BEARS by nearly 20 years. Ewell plays a young attorney who agrees to manage a baseball team in order to get closer to his son. Soon the father-son activity turns into a nightmare, as all the kids' parents pressure Ewell to give their children the top spots on the team. When sexy young widow Miller comes on to Ewell to make sure her child is allowed to pitch, the coach's jealous wife Francis, who hates baseball, learns how to keep score so she can keep an eye on her husband. Ewell steals the show as the somewhat bumbling coach who tries hard to keep everybody happy.

p, Henry Berman; d, Herman Hoffman; w, Nathaniel Benchley; ph, Arthur E. Arling; m, Jeff Alexander; ed, Gene Ruggiero; art d, William A. Horning, Randall Duell; set d, Edwin B. Willis, Edward G. Boyle; spec eff, A. Arnold Gillespie; makeup, William Tuttle.

Comedy   **(PR:A MPAA:NR)**

GREAT ARMORED CAR SWINDLE, THE** (1964) 58m Falcon bw

Peter Reynolds (Eric Winlatter), Dermot Walsh (Robert Wade), Joanna Dunham (Cherry Winlatter), Lisa Gastoni (Eva), Brian Cobby (Peter de Savory), Jack Allen (Ernest Winlatter), Geoffrey Denton (Debt Collector), Arnold Diamond (Telling), Richard Golding (Mintos), John G. Heller (Mel), Mercia Mansfield (Ernest's Secretary), Peter Walker (Alex), Eric Corrie (Wilson), Desmond Cullon-Jones (Evans), Charles Russell (Cappel), Joe Wadham (Boxer), Gertan Klauber (Lofty), John Lawrence (Security Officer).

Routine espionage thriller starring Reynolds as a confused English businessman who becomes a less-than-willing pawn in an international scheme involving the shipment of currency to a Middle Eastern government under the communist gun. The whole plan to substitute counterfeit notes goes down the tubes as Reynolds' nosy wife Dunham spoils the works when she goes poking around in search of her husband.

p, Peter Lambert; d, Lance Comfort; w, Lambert (based on the novel *The Breaking Point* by Laurence Meynell); ph, Basil Emmott; m, Albert Elms; ed, Peter Pitt; art d, John Earl.

Spy Drama (PR:A MPAA:NR)

GREAT AWAKENING, THE (SEE: NEW WINE, 1941)

GREAT BALLOON ADVENTURE, THE (SEE: OLLY, OLLY OXEN FREE, 1978)

GREAT BANK HOAX, THE**½ (1977) 93m Jacoby c (AKA: THE GREAT GEORGIA BANK HOAX; SHENANIGANS)

Burgess Meredith (*Jack*), Richard Basehart (*Emanuel*), Ned Beatty (*Julius*), Charlene Dallas (*Cathy*), Paul Sand (*Richard*), Michael Murphy (*Manigma*), Constance Forslund (*Patricia*), Arthur Godfrey (*Bryer*).

An off-beat comedy that attempts to expose the greed in a small town community. Sand plays a bank teller who embezzles $100,000 just to show it is possible. Bank president Meredith thinks up a scheme to steal $200,000 from the bank and thus cover up the teller's embezzlement. Sands then gives the money back after insurance had already covered the stolen money. The whole town eventually gets in the act, including the local minister, in attempts to right the confusion. A witty caper in spots, laced with barbs of ridicule at the town's self-righteousness.

d&w, Joseph Jacoby; ph, Walter Lassally (Movielab Color); m, Arthur B. Rubenstein; ed, Ralph Rosenbaum; prod d, Gary Weist; cos, Dian Finn Chapman.

Comedy Cas. (PR:C MPAA:NR)

GREAT BANK ROBBERY, THE** (1969) 97m WB c

Zero Mostel (*Reverend Pious Blue*), Kim Novak (*Lyda Kabanov*), Clint Walker (*Ben Quick*), Claude Akins (*Slade*), Akim Tamiroff (*Papa Pedro*), Larry Storch (*Juan*), John Anderson (*Kincaid*), Sam Jaffe (*Brother Lilac*), Mako (*Secret Service Agent Eliot Fong*), Elisha Cook, Jr. (*Jeb*), Ruth Warrick (*Mrs. Applebee*), John Fielder (*Brother Dismas*), John Larch (*Sheriff*), Peter Whitney (*Brother Jordan*), Norman Alden (*The Great Gregory*), Guy Wilkerson, Burt Mustin (*Glaziers*), Royden Clark (*Commandant*), Janet Clark (*Lady*), Jerry Brown (*Driver*), Grady Sutton (*Reverend Sims*), William Zuckert (*Ranger Commander*), Bob Steele, Ben Aliza, Mickey Simpson (*Guards*), Byron Keith (*Deputy*), Kenny Endoso, Roy Ogata, George Sasaki, Yoneo Iguchi, Hiroshi Hissamuni (*Chinese Laundrymen*), Chuck O'Brien, Philo McCullough, Fred Krone, Dick Hudkins, Emile Avery, Everett Creach, Bob Mitchell Boy Choir.

Dim western comedy starring Mostel as an evangelist/con-man and Novak as his assistant who try to rob the most impregnable bank in the west (Jesse James reportedly keeps his money there), which is located in the town of Friendly circa 1880. Unfortunately other robbers have their eye on the bank, including Mexican bandit Tamiroff and his dim-witted son Storch, guilt-ridden gunslinger Akins and his sidekick Cook Jr., and incognito Texas Ranger Walker, who is posing as a laundryman with six Chinese/American federal agents who want to catch suspected crooked mayor Anderson. Of course all the characters' paths collide and much slapstick comedy is made of the ensuing madness. Two songs by Sammy Cahn and James Van Heusen, "The Rainbow Rider" and "Heaven Helps Him Who Helps Himself" don't help.

p, Malcolm Stuart; d, Hy Averback; w, William Peter Blatty (based on the novel by Frank O'Rourke); ph, Fred J. Koenekamp (Panavision, Technicolor); m, Nelson Riddle; ed, Gene Milford; prod d, Jack Poplin; set d, William L. Kuehl; m/l, Sammy Cahn, James Van Heusen; cos, Moss Mabry; ch, Miriam Nelson; sp eff, Ralph Webb; makeup, Al Greenway.

Western/Comedy (PR:A MPAA:NR)

GREAT BARRIER, THE (SEE: SILENT BARRIERS, 1937, Brit.)

GREAT BIG THING, A* (1968, U.S./Can.) 80m Argofilm c

Reni Santoni (*Vinny Shea*), Louise Latraverse (*Michelle*), Paul Sand (*Morrie*), Marcy Plotnick (*Laurie*), Gerard Parkes (*Appie*), Francois Yves Carpentier (*Holly*), Roberta Maxwell (*Eve*), Leon Pownall (*Ray*), Heath Lamberts (*Bill*).

Tedious youth film starring Santoni as a 23-year-old Canadian loser wandering aimlessly through life with no apparent purpose. We watch Santoni as he borrows money, shoplifts, and talks to friends about his urge to write a novel, but he never seems to really do anything but exist. Santoni tries hard to pull something out of the material, but it's a losing battle.

p, Martin Rosen; d, Eric Till; w, Terence Heffernan; ph, Jean Claude Labrecque (Eastmancolor); m, Robert Prince; ed, Ralph Rosenblum.

Drama (PR:C MPAA:NR)

GREAT BIG WORLD AND LITTLE CHILDREN, THE*** (1962, Pol.) 102m Start Unit bw (WIELKA WIELKSZA NAJWIELKSZA)

Kinja Sienko, Woychiech Purzynski, B. Bilewski, Zbigniew Josefowicz, J. Klosinski, Z. Kucowna, Z. Malowski, E.B. Mickus, B. Pawlik.

Three short stories presented in one film, this is probably the first all-Polish science fiction film. The first two stories deal with children and how objects come alive to help them. The third features Sienko and Purzynski as two children who are taken by a magical silver sphere to the planet Vega. There they see what the world would look like after an atomic war. Sets and costumes are excellent, helping create the right feeling in these sensitive film stories. The production was supervised by Wanda Jakubowska, who directed the autobiographical Auschwitz drama OSTATNI ETAP in 1948.

p, Wanda Jakubowska; d, Anna Sokolowska; w, Sokolowska, Jerzy Broszkiewicz; ph, Kazimierz Vavrzyniak, Jacik Korcelli.

Science Fiction (PR:A MPAA:NR)

GREAT BRAIN, THE** (1978) 82m Osmond c

Jimmy Osmond, Pat Delaney, Fran Ryan, Cliff Osmond, Arthur Roberts, Lynn Benesch, Len Birman, James Jarnigan, John Fredric Hart.

The singing family "The Osmonds" took a shot at becoming involved in filmmaking with this childish tale that is on much the same level as their music. Jimmy Osmond (not known as part of the singing group) is the star, playing a young squirt who manages his way about through his abilities of deception. Good clean family fun that tries its hardest to keep from offending anything.

p, Richard Bickerton; d, Sidney Levin; w, Alan Cassidy (based on the book by John D. Fitzgerald); m/l, Donny Osmond.

Comedy (PR:AA MPAA:NR)

GREAT BRAIN MACHINE, THE (SEE: BRAIN MACHINE, THE, 1956, Brit.)

GREAT BRITISH TRAIN ROBBERY, THE*** (1967, Ger.) 104m Norddeutscher Rundfunk-Real Film-Stella Film/Peppercorn-Wormser bw (DIE GENTLEMEN BITTEN ZUR KASSE; AKA: DER POSTZUG-UBERFALL)

Horst Tappert (*Michael Donegan*), Hans Cossy (*Patrick Kinsey*), Karl Heinz Hess (*Geoffrey Black*), Gunter Neutze (*Archibald Arrow*), Hans Reiser (*Thomas Webster*), Rolf Nagel (*Gerald Williams*), Harry Engel (*George Slowfoot*), Wolfran Schaerf (*Andrew Elton*), Gunther Tabor (*Ronald Cameron*), Franz Mosthav (*Walter Lloyd*), Wolfried Lier (*Alfred Frost*), Kurt Conradi (*Arthur Finnegan*), Horst Beck (*Twinky*), Paul Edwin Roth (*Peter Masterson*), Kai Fischer (*Inge Masterson*), Grit Bottcher (*Jennifer Donegan*), Hannelore Schroth (*Eileen Black*), Sylvia Lydi (*Suzy Fast*), Siegfried Lowitz (*Dennis MacLeod*), Lothar Grutzner (*Sgt. Robbins*), Dirk Dautzenberg (*Sgt. Davies*), Albert Hoerrmann (*Montague*), Isa Miranda (*Mona*).

Exciting German true-story caper film about the detailed planning and execution of a daring robbery of the British mails by a clever group of criminals. Though the robbery goes well, some of the members of the gang make fatal mistakes that enable police to capture them. The film does not end with their capture, however, because the criminal syndicate devises a plan to break them out of prison. Taut, well directed, and beautifully photographed in crisp black and white. Location scenes filmed in England.

p, Egon Monk; d, John Olden, Claus Peter Witt; w, Henry Kolarz, Robert Muller (based on the book *The Robbers' Tale: The Real Story of the Great Train Robbery* by Peta Fordham); ph, Gerald Gibbs, Frank A. Banuscher; m, Heinz Funk; ed, Monika Tadsen-Erfurth, Oswald Hafenrichter, Gisela Quicker; art d, Mathias Matthies.

Crime (PR:A MPAA:NR)

GREAT CARUSO, THE***½ (1951) 109m MGM c

Mario Lanza (*Enrico Caruso*), Ann Blyth (*Dorothy Benjamin*), Dorothy Kirsten (*Louise Heggar*), Jarmila Novotna (*Maria Selka*), Richard Hageman (*Carlo Santi*), Carl Benton Reid (*Park Benjamin*), Eduard Franz (*Giulio Gatti-Casazza*), Ludwig Donath (*Alfredo Brazzi*), Alan Napier (*Jean de Reszke*), Paul Javor (*Antonio Scotti*), Carl Milletaire (*Gino*), Shepard Menken (*Fucito*), Vincent Renno (*Tullio*), Nestor Paiva (*Egisto Barretto*), Peter Edward Price (*Caruso as a Boy*), Mario Siletti (*Papa Caruso*), Angela Clarke (*Mama Caruso*), Ian Wolfe (*Hutchins*), Yvette Duguay (*Musetta*), Argentina Brunetti (*Mrs. Barretto*), Edit Angold (*Hilda*), Peter Brocco (*Father Bronzetti*), David Bond (*Father Angelico*), Matt Moore (*Max*), Anthony Mazola (*Fucito at Age Eight*), Mae Clarke (*Woman*), Blanche Thebom, Teresa Celli, Nicola Moscona, Giuseppe Valdengo, Lucine Armara, Marina Koshetz, Robert E. Bright, Gilbert Russell (*Opera Singers*), Mario DeLaval (*Ottello Carmini*), Sherry Jackson (*Musetta as a Child*), Maurice Samuels (*Papa Gino*).

Despite the egotistical rampages of star Mario Lanza on the set, THE GREAT CARUSO was completed, released, and became a huge hit for MGM. Lanza, of course, plays Caruso in this very fanciful film version of the great tenor's life. The movie opens in Naples, 1873, when Caruso is born. The little boy demonstrates his amazing vocal talents at an early age when he attracts the attention of the congregation at his church while singing in the choir. As he gets older (now played by Lanza), the struggling singer tries to scratch out a living by crooning in cabarets and on street corners for whatever money is tossed his way. Luck finally smiles on Lanza when two opera singers discover the young tenor and place him in the opera's chorus. From there, Lanza's star rises swiftly and he is soon touring Europe while being hailed the world's greatest tenor. Eventually, America calls and Lanza makes the trip accompanied by a boatload of friends and associates who have aided him in his career. Before his debut in New York, Lanza inadvertently insults the opera's major benefactor, Reid, and the tension spoils his first appearance. Irrespective of Reid's feelings, Lanza become a sensation and even manages to woo Reid's daughter, Blyth. Soon Lanza and Blyth marry, have a child, and bask in the glory of the singer's spectacular career. Storm clouds arrive, however, when Lanza comes down with a painful throat ailment at the age of 47. Refusing to give his voice a rest, Lanza continues singing and during a performance of Floyow's "Martha" he collapses and dies. While THE GREAT CARUSO plays fast and loose with the facts (the screenplay was based on wife Dorothy Caruso's biography of her husband and she later regretted selling the rights to MGM), the appeal of the film lies in Lanza's stunning performance as Caruso and, of course, the incredible 27 musical numbers that play practically nonstop during the 109 minute running time. This was Lanza's third and best film, and the singer's ego was as big as his waistline; during shooting he often declared, "I am Caruso!" On the set Lanza proved himself to be an absolute terror by making ridiculous demands, refusing to bathe, relieving himself without bothering to find a toilet, and other vulgarities that caused tension and loathing on the set. When Lanza would return to work after the weekend, the costumers were shocked to find that two days of binge eating had swelled the singer-actor into a new size, forcing them to make last minute changes in his wardrobe. Luckily for MGM and the public, the studio decided to adopt a grin-and-bear it attitude and finish the picture. In the film Lanza is superb. His voice, according to a few critics, was equal to, if not better than,

Caruso himself. Lanza, of course, *knew* he was better than Caruso and took great pains to remind everyone of that. Tragically, Lanza's outbursts grew worse, making him less and less desirable to work with. He would complete only one other film for MGM, BECAUSE YOUR MINE (1952), and walk out during the production of THE STUDENT PRINCE (1954), which forced the studio to replace him with Edmund Purdom, who lip-synched the songs the volatile tenor had already recorded. After three more films for other studios, Lanza died in Rome at the age of 38. Songs include the hit, "The Loveliest Night of the Year" (sung by Blyth, adapted by Irving Aaronson and Paul Francis Webster from "Over the Waves" by Juventino Rosas), "Vesti la Giubba" (from the opera "I Pagliacci" by Ruggero Leoncavallo), "M'Appari" (from the opera "Martha" by Friedrich von Flotow), "The Last Rose of Summer" (Thomas Moore, Richard Alfred Milliken), "Celeste Aida," "Numi, Pieta," "La Fatal Pietra" (from the opera "Aida" by Guiseppe Verdi), the Sextet from the opera "Lucia di Lammermoor" by Gaetano Donizetti, "La Donne a Mobile" (from the opera "Rigoletto" by Verdi), "Che Gelida Manina!" (from the opera "La Boheme" Giacomo Puccini), "E Lucevan Le Steele" (from the opera "Tosca" Puccini), "Sweethearts" (Victor Herbert, Robert B. Smith), "Because" (Teschemacher, Guy d'Hardelot), "Ave-Maria" (Johan Sebastian Bach, Charles Francis Gounod), "Mattinata."

p, Joe Pasternak; d, Richard Thorpe; w, Sonia Levien, William Ludwig (based on the story by Dorothy Caruso); ph, Joseph Ruttenberg; m, Johnny Green; ed, Gene Ruggiero; art d, Cedric Gibbons, Gabriel Scognamillo; cos, Gile Steele, Helen Rose.

Musical/Biography **Cas.** **(PR:A MPAA:NR)**

GREAT CATHERINE* (1968, Brit.) 98m Keep Films/WB c

Peter O'Toole *(Capt. Charles Edstaston)*, Zero Mostel *(Prince Patiomkin)*, Jeanne Moreau *(Catherine The Great)*, Jack Hawkins *(Sir George Gorse)*, Akim Tamiroff *(Sergeant)*, Marie Lohr *(Lady Gorse)*, Marie Kean *(Princess Dashkoff)*, Kenneth Griffith *(Naryshkin)*, Angela Scoular *(Claire)*, Kate O'Mara *(Varinka)*, Lea Seidl *(Grand Duchess)*, Claire Gordon *(Elizabeth Vokonska)*, Oliver MacGreevy *(General Pskov)*, James Mellor *(Col. Pugachov)*, Declan Mulholland *(Count Tokhtamysh)*, Janet Kelly *(Anna Schuvalova)*, Henry Woolf *(Egrebyomka)*, Catherine Lancaster *(Sophia)*, Alfred Ravel, Gordon Rollings *(Glaziers)*, Sean Barrett *(Andrei Strelkin)*, Alf Joint *(Russian General)*, Reuben Martin, Yuri Borienko, Rupert Evans, Milton Reid *(Henchmen)*, Dinny Powell, Tom Clegg *(Mongols)*, Gerald Lawson, Norma Foster, Scobie *(A Dog)*.

George Bernard Shaw wrote this as a one-act play that opened in November of 1913. They waited 55 years to make it into a film and would have been well-advised to wait another 55 years. What a mish-mash! In the inept hands of director Flemyng, this is a flat-footed farce that was a waste of Warner Bros. money and the audience's time. O'Toole is a dim-witted captain of the Light Dragoons. He and Hawkins, the British ambassador, want to have an audience with Moreau, queen of all the Russians. Mostel is the prince, protector of the Winter Palace at St. Petersburg; the place looks like Tobacco Road, Soviet-style. Animals run along the marble floors while Mostel is happily besotted. Mostel thinks that the queen needs a boy friend so he contrives to get O'Toole into the royal bed. Moreau thinks that's a fine idea, but O'Toole races away with his girl friend, Scoular, who is Hawkins' daughter. The queen is not amused and orders O'Toole arrested by her cossacks, who take him back to the palace. She wants to know all about his adventures in the United States where he was present at various Revolutionary War skirmishes. She's built a huge model of a battle in her bathroom and they play soldier until she wades into her tub to sink a British frigate. He's enraged by this, escapes once more, and is captured again and returned to the palace to attend a great ball. Once there, he dances with a troupe of Russian terpsichoreans, then is taken to a secret hideaway where Moreau intends to have her way with him. Before his virtue is compromised, Scoular arrives and takes him away, but not before he preaches about the benefits of English life. It fails on several levels. Shaw never thought this was one of his best works but producers, clamoring to find works in the public domain by famous authors, often pounce on trifles and attempt to inflate them into full-blown films. The fact that Shaw wrote this probably helped secure the financing. Mostel, unless held in check, always overacts and this is a prime example of a stage actor, accustomed to having to play "big" for the people in the last row, overdoing things for the close-up camera. Lots of money was lavished on the production and it sank in Catherine's bathtub, right where it should have.

p, Jules Buck; d, Gordon Flemyng; w, Hugh Leonard (from the play "Great Catherine Whom Glory Still Adores" by George Bernard Shaw); ph, Oswald Morris; m, Dmitri Tiomkin; ed, Anne V. Coates; prod d, John Bryan; art d, Bill Hutchinson; set d, Pamela Cornell; cos, Margaret Furse; ch, Paddy Stone; makeup, Bill Lodge.

Historical Comedy **(PR:AA MPAA:G)**

GREAT CHICAGO CONSPIRACY CIRCUS, THE**
(SEE: CHICAGO '70, 1970)

GREAT CITIZEN, THE*½ (1939, USSR) 114m Lenfilm/Amkino bw

N. Bogoliubov *(Shakhov)*, I. Bersenov *(Kartashov)*, O. Zhakov *(Borovsky)*, Boris Chirkov *(Maxim)*, G. Semionov *(Kolesnikov)*, A. Zrajevsky *(Dubok)*, E. Altus *(Katz)*, P. Kirillov *(Briantzev)*, B. Poslavsky *(Sizov)*, V. Kiselev *(Gladkikh)*, N. Raiskaya-Dore *(Shakhov's Mother)*, N. Rashevskaya *(Olga)*, Z. Fedorova *(Nadya)*, E. Nemchenko *(Bronov)*, C. Riabinkin *(Kriuchkov)*, A. Polibin *(Soloviev)*.

Josef Stalin's own version of the famed Moscow "show trials" of 1937, in which hundreds of dissidents—presumed followers of Leon Trotsky—were liquidated or transported to Siberian prison camps for long terms. Historically interesting, if only for its revelations of the party-disciplined defendants sealing their own warrants of doom by publicly confessing their revisionism. Overlong, overacted, and excessively polemical, but a fascinating view of the party line of the time. Fedorova—unusual for this type of Soviet film—is a knockout. (In Russian; English subtitles.)

d, Friederich Ermler; w, Ermler, M. Bleiman, M. Bolshintsov; m, Dmitri Shoshtakovich.

Historical Drama **(PR:A MPAA:NR)**

GREAT COMMANDMENT, THE*½ (1941) 78m FOX bw

John Beal *(Joel)*, Maurice Moscovich *(Lamech)*, Albert Dekker *(Longinus)*, Marjorie Cooley *(Tamar)*, Warren McCullum *(Zadok)*, Lloyd Corrigan *(Jemuel)*, Ian Wolfe *(Tax Collector)*, Olaf Hytten *(Nathan)*, Anthony Marlowe *(Singer)*, Lester Scharff *(First Zealot)*, Albert Spehr *(Second Zealot)*, Marc Loebell *(Judas)*, Harold Minjir *(Andrew)*, Earl Gunn *(Wounded Man)*, George Rosener *(Merchant)*, John Merton *(Under Officer)*, Perry Evans *(First Elder)*, Stanley Price *(Second Elder)*, D'Arcy Corrigan *(Blind Man)*, Max Davidson *(Old Man)*.

Christian drama, set in 30 A.D. in Judea, starring Beal as the son of a scholar who attempts to start a rebellion against the oppressive Roman Empire. He is aided by his brother, Dekker, who is married to the girl Beal truly loves, Cooley. This problem is solved when Dekker is killed by a Roman soldier, freeing Cooley and Beal to go off together after the young rebel—suddenly influenced by the teachings of Christ—gives up his revolution. Pretty dull.

p, John T. Coyle; d, Irving Pichel; w, Dana Burnet; ph, Charles P. Boyle; m, Hans Salter, Walter Jurman; ed, Ralph Dixon; art d, Edward Jewell.

Drama **(PR:A MPAA:NR)**

GREAT DAN PATCH, THE½** (1949) 92m W.R. Frank/UA bw

Dennis O'Keefe *(David Palmer)*, Gail Russell *(Cissy Lathrop)*, Ruth Warrick *(Ruth Treadwell)*, Charlotte Greenwood *(Aunt Neddy)*, Henry Hull *(Dan Palmer)*, John Hoyt *(Ben Lathrop)*, Arthur Hunnicutt *(Chet)*, Clarence Muse *(Voodoo)*, Harry Lauter *(Bud Ransome)*.

Race-track movie biography of famed trotter Dan Patch, a horse that was so fast he ran out of opponents and had to race against his own records toward the end of his career. O'Keefe plays a middle-class chemist with a penchant for horseflesh which he acquired on the farm where he was raised. The usual tear-jerking episodes ensue, including a barn fire. Race-track philosopher Muse sings two forgettable tunes: "Mixed Team" and "Can't Git You Then, Can't Git You Now". Toned a rather pleasing sepia.

p&w, John Taintor Foote; d, Joe Newman; ph, Gilbert Warrenton; ed, Fred W. Berger; md, David Chudnow; art d, Jerome Pycha, Jr.; m/l, Foote, Alex Laszlo, Martin Broones.

Sports Drama **(PR:AA MPAA:NR)**

GREAT DAWN, THE** (1947, Ital.) 90m Scalera/Superfilm bw

Pierino Gamba *(Himself)*, Rossano Brazzi *(Renzo Gamba)*, Renee Faure *(Anna Gamba)*, Giovanni Grasso *(Oreste Bellotti)*, Michele Riccardini *(Don Terenzio)*, Yvonne Samson *(Daisy)*, Fausto Guerzoni *(Fausto)*, Loris Gizzi *(Cooky)*, Guglielmo Sinay *(Salesman)*.

Overblown, nearly operatic Italian melodrama starring Gamba, an extremely talented musical youngster, here seen to be constantly at odds with his rich grandfather, Grasso, about his pursuing a career in music. Meanwhile the kid's dad, Brazzi, a less-than-successful composer, has taken a job as a clown in Paris to raise some cash to send to mom, Faure, so she can regain custody of Gamba. Gamba, however, devises his own path to stardom, and with the help of local priest Riccardini, he organizes a full-scale orchestra to play an open-air concert featuring his conducting. In the end, mom and dad are reunited, and grandpa gives in. (Italian, English subtitles).

d, G.M. Scotese; m, Ludwig van Beethoven, Franz Schubert, Giacchino Rossini; English titles, A.V. Macaluso.

Drama **(PR:A MPAA:NR)**

GREAT DAY*½ (1945, Brit.) 82m RKO bw

Eric Portman *(Capt. Ellis)*, Flora Robson *(Mrs. Ellis)*, Sheila Sim *(Margaret Ellis)*, Isabel Jeans *(Lady Mott)*, Walter Fitzgerald *(John Tyndale)*, Philip Friend *(Geoffrey Winthrop)*, Marjorie Rhodes *(Mrs. Mumford)*, Margaret Withers *(Miss Tyndale)*, Maire O'Neill *(Mrs. Walsh)*, Beatrice Varley *(Miss Tracy)*, Joan Maude, Ivor Barnard, John Laurie, Patricia Hayes, Irene Handl, Kathleen Harrison, Leslie Dwyer, Jacqueline Clarke, Norman Pierce, Pauline Tennant, John McLaren, Valentine Dunn, O. B. Clarence, Jean Shepherd, David Ward, Roy Malcolm.

British soap opera concerning the lives of a small-town women's guild as its members prepare for a visit by American first lady Eleanor Roosevelt. The main story line is devoted to Robson and Sim, the wife and daughter of bitter and alcoholic WW I veteran Portman, who makes their life a hell. His raving antics nearly drive Sim into a foolish marriage with her employer just for the sake of stability, but the wise girl changes her mind at the last minute, opting for young military man Friend.

p, Victor Hanbury; d, Lance Comfort; w, Wolfgang Wilhelm, John Davenport (based on the play by Lesley Storm); ph, Erwin Hillier; m, William Alwyn; ed, Sidney J. Stone; art d, William C. Andrews.

Drama **(PR:A MPAA:NR)**

GREAT DAY, THE, 1977 (SEE: SPECIAL DAY, A, 1977)

GREAT DAY IN THE MORNING½** (1956) 91m RKO c

Virginia Mayo *(Ann Merry Alaine)*, Robert Stack *(Owen Pentecost)*, Ruth Roman *(Boston Grant)*, Alex Nicol *(Stephen Kirby)*, Raymond Burr *(Jumbo Means)*, Leo Gordon *(Zeff Masterson)*, Regis Toomey *(Father Murphy)*, Carlton Young *(Col. Gibson)*, Donald McDonald *(Gary Lawford)*, Peter Whitney *(Phil the Cannibal)*, Dan White *(Rogers)*.

Unusually sluggish film from director Tourneur set in the Colorado Territory in 1861 at the start of the Civil War. Rebel sympathizer Stack is pitted against Northern secret agent Nicol in a race to grab as much Colorado gold as possible to finance the war. Stack soon finds himself torn between a true belief for the cause and the amorous advances of saloon entertainer Roman and East-coast couturier Mayo. Atmospheric, but strangely uninvolving.

p, Edmund Grainger; d, Jacques Tourneur; w, Lesser Samuels (based on the novel by Robert Hardy Andrews); ph, William Snyder (SuperScope, Technicolor); m, Leith Stevens; ed, Harry Marker; md, Constantin Bakaleinikoff; art d, Albert D'Agostino, Jack Okey; cos, Gwenn Wakeling.

Western **(PR:A MPAA:NR)**

GREAT DEFENDER, THE* (1934, Brit.) 72m British International/Wardour bw

Matheson Lang *(Sir Douglas Rolls)*, Margaret Bannerman *(Laura Locke)*, Arthur Margetson *(Leslie Locke)*, Richard Bird *(Eric Hammond)*, Jeanne Stuart *(Phyllis Ware)*, J. Fisher White *(Judge)*, Sam Livesey *(Sir Henry Lingard)*, Lawrence Hanray *(Parker)*, O.B. Clarence *(Mr. Hammond)*, Mary Jerrold *(Mrs. Hammond)*, Frank Atkinson *(Pope)*, Kathleen Harrison *(Maid)*, Jimmy Godden *(Inspector Holmes)*, Hal Gordon, [C.] Denier Warren, Gladys Hamer, Robert Horton, Alec Fraser.

Courtroom drama that sees ailing super-barrister Lang prove that Bannerman's husband Margetson did not stab his mistress, Stuart, to death. The killer is, in fact, homicidal maniac Bird, who is obsessed with The Bible. Lang wins his case, but the trauma of the trial proves too great for him; he dies, in a performance well reprised by Charles Laughton in the strangely similar WITNESS FOR THE PROSECUTION (1957), based on a play by Agatha Christie.

p, Walter C. Mycroft; d, Thomas Bentley; w, Marjorie Deans, Paul Perez (based on a story by John Hastings Turner); ph, John J. Cox.

Crime **(PR:A MPAA:NR)**

GREAT DIAMOND ROBBERY** (1953) 69m MGM bw

Red Skelton *(Ambrose C. Park)*, Cara Williams *(Maggie Drumman)*, James Whitmore *(Remlick)*, Kurt Kasznar *(Tony)*, Dorothy Stickney *(Emily Drumman)*, George Mathews *(Duke Fargoh)*, Reginald Owen *(Bainbridge Gibbons)*, Harry Bellaver *(Herb)*, Connie Gilchrist *(Blonde)*, Steven Geray *(Van Goosen)*, Sig Arno *(Mr. Sahutsky)*.

Skelton's last film for MGM came up a dud. The comedian plays a young diamond cutter who was abandoned on a park bench as a baby and subsequently taken to an orphanage. While out celebrating the anniversary of his bundle being found on the bench, Skelton drinks too much and ends up in the slammer next to dishonest lawyer Whitmore, who, upon hearing the diamond cutter's sad tale, "discovers" a phony family for him. His "uncles" happen to be two hoods, Kasznar and Bellaver, who use Skelton's jewel knowledge to help them steal a diamond worth two million, but the plot goes haywire when his bogus "mother" and "sister" soften and spill the beans. In the end, Skelton is cleared, and he marries his "sister."

p, Edwin H. Knopf; d, Robert Z. Leonard; w, Laslo Vadnay, Martin Rackin (based on a story by Vadnay); ph, Joseph Ruttenberg; ed, George White; md, Rudolph G. Kopp; art d, Cedric Gibbons, Edward Carfagno.

Comedy/Crime **(PR:A MPAA:NR)**

GREAT DICTATOR, THE**** (1940) 127m UA bw

Charles Chaplin *(Hynkel, Dictator of Tomania, a Jewish Barber)*, Paulette Goddard *(Hannah)*, Jack Oakie *(Napaloni, Dictator of Bacteria)*, Reginald Gardiner *(Schultz)*, Henry Daniell *(Garbitsch)*, Billy Gilbert *(Herring)*, Maurice Moscovich *(Mr. Jaeckel)*, Emma Dunn *(Mrs. Jaeckel)*, Grace Hayle *(Madame Napaloni)*, Carter de Haven *(Bacterian Ambassador)*, Bernard Gorcey *(Mr. Mann)*, Paul Weigel *(Mr. Agar)*, Chester Conklin, Hank Mann, Esther Michelson, Florence Wright, Eddie Gribbon, Robert O. Davis, Eddie Dunn, Nita Pike, Peter Lynn.

THE GREAT DICTATOR is almost, but not quite, a classic comedy. What went on behind the cameras may have been more interesting than the film itself, which was an early flogging of Hitler, long before much of the rest of the world woke up to the monster that existed in Germany. Chaplin had begun the film's script three years before and was told by the sales executives at United Artists that he should abandon the project as Germany was a large market and there was a great deal of sympathy for the mad Austrian, and even some from several of America's leading lights; most notably Joseph Kennedy and Charles Lindbergh. Undaunted, Chaplin continued his preparation for the film, and, by the time it came out, audiences were clamoring for it. Hitler was so annoyed at the depiction that he had Chaplin on his murder list for when the Third Reich attacked the USA. Other than some gibberish in MODERN TIMES, this was the first time audiences heard the Little Tramp speak and there was some disappointment. Chaplin had waited until 13 years after sound to make his first full talkie; it was a revelation. This was his only picture since MODERN TIMES in 1936. It had been eagerly awaited, and were it not for a long (six-minute) sermon at the end of the picture, the impact would have been far more definitive. The film is filled with satire as Chaplin takes pot shots at Hitler (Hynkel), Mussolini (Napaloni), Goebbels (Garbitsch) and Goering (Herring). Chaplin plays an unnamed Jewish barber in a "Tomanian" ghetto who is just recovering from what appears to be amnesia and wakes up to find himself living under the thumb of a madman (also played by Chaplin). He is beaten up by some of the brownshirts and escapes, then is mistaken for Hynkel in Austria (recently "liberated" by Hynkel). As Hynkel, Chaplin speaks in a combination of German double-talk, gibberish, and what used to be known as "Dutch" dialect on the old vaudeville stage. The most telling comedy scene is Hynkel playing with a gigantic balloon of the world and using it in a ballet sequence. The next best scene is a meeting between the two dictators (Oakie was absolutely magnificent as the jut-jawed leader of "Bacteria") where the two men are seated next to each other in chairs that can be raised and, like the King in THE KING AND I, neither will allow the other's head to be above his, so they keep raising the barber-type chairs to gain higher altitude. Goddard (Mrs. Chaplin at the time, or so it seemed) is a downtrodden Jewish laundress who is in love with the barber and escapes with him to Austria. Watching the film today, we realize that Chaplin must have had information about Hitler that the government did not or would not release to the public. This film made everyone feel that Chaplin must have been born of the Jewish faith, a fact he never denied. But the truth is that he was the son of a born-again Christian woman who went mad and sent him and half-brother Sidney to a home for foundlings. Chaplin's father was an Irish drunk with a music-hall act that never did gain him any fame. Charles Chaplin, Senior, died before he was 40. When Chaplin was questioned on his motives for making the movie, one of the reporters asked if he did it because he was Jewish. "Does one have to be Jewish to hate the Nazis?" was his reply, "But you *are* Jewish, aren't you?" persisted the reporter. Chaplin mused about that a moment, then said: "Actually, I'm not sure, but as many of the world's great geniuses have had some Jewish blood in their veins, I'd like to think so." The confusion probably came from the fact that Charlie's brother Sidney was the son of a Jewish bookmaker from South Africa and was adopted by Charles Chaplin, Senior, when the latter married Charlie's mother, Hannah. In THE GREAT DICTATOR, Chaplin surrounded himself with some of the best actors he could muster. Particularly good were Billy Gilbert as Herring and Henry Daniell as Garbitsch. Daniell had usually been known for his dramatic roles, but he was exquisite as the skinny propaganda minister. The music was by Meredith Willson, long before he was lionized for his work on THE MUSIC MAN. Nominated for best picture, best actor and writer, as well as best supporting actor and best music, it won none of those awards. By this time, Chaplin was hip to the effectiveness of music in films; he used an air by Brahms as counterpoint while he shaved a patron in the barber shop. It's a highlight sequence in a film filled with several brilliant touches. In the years to come, Chaplin's life was marred by controversy. He jettisoned Miss Goddard, then married Oona, the teenage daughter of Eugene O'Neill, with whom he had several children. In the 1950s, while on a trip to Europe, he received word that he would not be allowed back in the US unless he testified before a committee investigating Communist infiltration in the movie business. If anything, Chaplin was a supreme capitalist, but he never did attain US citizenship and refused to testify, preferring instead to be exiled to Vevey, Switzerland, where he spent the rest of his days. He was then knighted by the Queen, and returned to the US to receive a special Oscar. He said those two moments were the highlights of his incredible life. THE GREAT DICTATOR was the last film in which he wore the Little Tramp mustache and one wonders if Hitler ever realized how silly he looked to a world that had grown up watching Chaplin.

p,d&w, Charles Chaplin; ph, Roland Totheroh, Karl Struss; m, Meredith Willson; ed, Willard Nico; md, Willson; art d, J. Russell Spencer.

Comedy **Cas.** **(PR:AAA MPAA:NR)**

GREAT DIVIDE, THE*½ (1930) 72m FN/WB bw

Dorothy Mackaill *(Ruth Jordan)*, Ian Keith *(Stephen Ghent)*, Lucien Littlefield *(Texas Tommy)*, Ben Hendricks, Jr. *(Dutch Romero)*, Myrna Loy *(Manuella)*, Frank Tang *(Wong)*, Creighton Hale *(Edgar Blossom)*, George Fawcett *(MacGregor)*, Jean Laverty *(Verna)*, Claude Gillingwater *(Winthrop Amesbury)*, Roy Stewart *(Joe Morgan)*, James Ford *(Ruth's Friend)*, Jean Lorraine *(Polly)*, Gordon Elliott *(Ruth's Friend)*, Marjorie Kane.

A remake of a 1925 silent film adaptation of writer Moody's popular play, which melded the dancing-daughter jazz-baby genre of the 1920s with the stock western mythos. Keith, a fine stage actor, plays a well-to-do businessman who, garbed as a *bandido* after a Mexican fiesta, abducts Mackaill—British, but a one-time Ziegfeld girl—in order to sway her from her sluttish, profligate Roaring-Twenties life style. She is unaware that her captor is her late father's former business partner, the man who has been financially supporting that self-same life style. Keith carts Mackaill to his isolated mountain cabin near the Mexican border, where she runs into a number of western stereotype characters including comic villain Hendricks Jr.—in a role well-played by Wallace Beery in the 1925 silent version—and fiery Mexican servant girl Loy. Loy, speaking in the standard ethnic accent which served her so well in her customary Gypsy/Arab/Hispanic parts of the time, cavils at Keith's concupiscient captive; she begs to bed the brave buccaneer herself in a series of exotic Mexican dances. Keith, intent on imparting moral verities on wayward wanton Mackaill, spurns the lascivious Latin. Mackaill's hatred of her late father's puritanical partner gradually changes to desire; Loy leaves; the abduction turns amorous. Oddly, First National released this picture in both sound and titled silent versions—despite the fact that sound films had been ascendant for more than a year—apparently hoping to catch bookings in unconverted rural theaters. Songs include "The End of the Lonesome Trail" and "Si, Si, Senor."

p, Robert North; d, Reginald Barker; w, Fred Myton, Raul Perez (based on the play "West of the Great Divide" by William Vaughn Moody); ph, Lee Garmes, Alvin Knechtel; ed, Ray Curtiz; m/l, Herman Ruby, Ray Perkins.

Western **(PR:A MPAA:NR)**

GREAT DREAM, THE (SEE: EMBRACERS, THE, 1966)

GREAT ESCAPE, THE**** (1963) 169m UA c

Steve McQueen *("Cooler King" Hilts)*, James Garner *("The Scrounger" Hendley)*, Richard Attenborough *("Big X" Bartlett)*, James Donald *(Senior Officer Ramsey)*, Charles Bronson *(Danny Velinski)*, Donald Pleasence *("The Forger" Blythe)*, James Coburn *("The Manufacturer" Sedgwick)*, David McCallum *(Ashley-Pitt)*, Gordon Jackson *(MacDonald)*, John Leyton *(Willie)*, Angus Lennie *("The Mole" Ives)*, Nigel Stock *(Cavendish)*, Jud Taylor *(Goff)*, William Russell *(Sorren)*, Robert Desmond *("The Tailor" Griffith)*, Tom Adams *(Nimmo)*, Lawrence Montaigne *(Haynes)*, Hannes Messemer *(Von Luger)*, Robert Graf *(Werner)*, Harry Riebauer *(Strachwitz)*, Hans Reiser *(Kuhn)*, Robert Freitag *(Posen)*, Heinz Weiss *(Kramer)*, Til Kiwe *(Frick)*, Ulrich Beiger *(Preissen)*, George Mikell *(Dietrich)*, Karl Otto Alberty *(Steinach)*.

A classic escape picture, this film portrays hundreds of the most hardened Allied prisoners all thrown together into a special German prison camp which is considered escape-proof. Here are those prisoners who have made so many escape attempts that they are considered by the Nazis to be incorrigibles. These include Attenborough, known as Big X, the British master escape planner, Bronson, a Polish officer who is in charge of the tunnel digging, Pleasence, responsible for forging passports and papers, and Americans Garner, in charge of assembling needed supplies, and McQueen, who has his own ideas of escape. Attenborough plans to dig three tunnels and allow for the escape of not just a few prisoners, but hundreds, which will cause havoc in Germany and keep thousands of their troops searching for the Allied officers, drawing them away from front line duties. Garner, the clever scrounger who amasses everything needed for the mass exodus, from butter to cameras, discovers that Pleasence is going blind but persuades Attenborough to allow him to escape with the rest, that he will responsible for the older man. The tunnels are painstakingly dug, the earth from the excavations scattered about the prison compound and even in the attics of the barracks. The tunnel walls are shored up by slats taken from bunks and tunnel entries are cleverly made under stoves and washroom drains. During a 4th of July celebration staged by the Americans, the Germans find one tunnel but the main escape route remains intact and, during an air raid, scores flee to freedom. Bronson, who has supervised the digging of this tunnel, is overcome by a claustrophobic attack but manages to come to his senses at the last minute and escapes. The Germans round up 50 of the prisoners, including in-charge officers Attenborough and Jackson, executing them out of hand. Others like McCallum are shot while fleeing. Some do make it to safety, including Bronson and Coburn, the latter getting to France and then, with the help of the French underground, to Spain. Garner and Pleasence steal a German training plane but it runs out of gas and they crash-land. Pleasence is killed by a German patrol and Garner recaptured. McQueen is one of the last still at large. He steals a motorcycle and leads the pursuing Germans in a spectacular cross-country chase, finally trying to sail the cycle over a huge barbed wire barrier and failing. He tumbles into the wire and is recaptured, returned to the camp, and thrown into solitary confinement where he has spent most of his time scheming up new escape attempts. At the end McQueen is heard to thump his baseball against the wall of his cell, a sign that he is again at work dreaming up a new over-the-wall adventure. Based on a book detailing a real-life mass escape of Allied troops in 1942, this film is beautifully directed and well-written, enacted superbly by the entire cast, even Messemer, the aristocratic German commandant. Not since THE MAGNIFICENT SEVEN had director-producer Sturges been in better form and, even though the film is long, it's done with such a hearty pace that the viewer will not feel it drag. There is a great deal of humor in the film, provided through the dry wits and actions of Garner and McQueen for the most part. This was McQueen's first real standout role, one where he played a James Dean type character who is somewhat alienated but not too much of a maverick to desert the common cause. Bernstein's score is exhilarating and memorable and perfectly blends with the nonstop tension. THE GREAT ESCAPE was a box office smash and went down well with the critics, joining the ranks of such masterful similar-themed productions as THE BRIDGE ON THE RIVER KWAI (1957), GRAND ILLUSION (1937), and STALAG 17 (1953).

p&d, John Sturges; w, James Clavell, W.R. Burnett (based on the book by Paul Brickhill); ph, Daniel L. Fapp (DeLuxe Color); m, Elmer Bernstein; ed, Ferris Webster; art d, Fernando Carrere; cos, Bert Henrikson; makeup, Emile Lavigne.

War Prison Drama Cas. (PR:A MPAA:NR)

GREAT EXPECTATIONS**½ (1934) 97m UNIV bw

Henry Hull *(Magwitch)*, Phillips Holmes *(Pip)*, Jane Wyatt *(Estella)*, Florence Reed *(Miss Havisham)*, Alan Hale *(Joe Gargery)*, Rafaela Ottiano *(Mrs. Joe)*, Walter Armitage *(Herbert Pocket)*, Jackie Searl *(Young Herbert)*, Eily Malyon *(Sarah Pocket)*, Virginia Hammond *(Molly)*, Ann Howard *(Young Estella)*, George Breakston *(Young Pip)*, Forrester Harvey *(Uncle Pumblechook)*, Harry Cording *(Orlick)*, Douglas Wood *(Compeyson)*, Philip Dakin *(Drummle)*, Francis Sullivan *(Jaggers)*.

Uninspired Hollywood version of the Charles Dickens classic starring Holmes as Pip, the young orphan boy who rises to prominence with the help of his life-long, mysterious benefactor. A weak adaptation filled with disappointing performances from a cast capable of better. Hobson shone much brighter as Estella in the vastly superior 1946 version directed by David Lean. At the time of initial release, the picture suffered from critical comparison with the nearly simultaneous release of THE OLD CURIOSITY SHOP, the first of a series of British productions of the works of Dickens.

d, Stuart Walker; w, Gladys Unger (based on the novel by Charles Dickens); ph, George Robinson; art d, Albert D'Agostino; ed, Edward Curtiss.

Drama (PR:AA MPAA:NR)

GREAT EXPECTATIONS***** (1946, Brit.) 118m Cineguild/UNIV bw

John Mills *(Pip Pirrip)*, Valerie Hobson *(Estella/Her Mother)*, Bernard Miles *(Joe Gargery)*, Francis L. Sullivan *(Jaggers)*, Martita Hunt *(Miss Havisham)*, Finlay Currie *(Abel Magwitch)*, Anthony Wager *(Pip as Child)*, Jean Simmons *(Estella as Child)*, Alec Guinness *(Herbert Pocket)*, Ivor Barnard *(Wemmick)*, Freda Jackson *(Mrs. Gargery)*, Torin Thatcher *(Bentley Drummle)*, Eileen Erskine *(Biddy)*, Hay Petrie *(Uncle Pumblechook)*, George Hayes *(Compeyson)*, O.B. Clarence *(Aged Parent)*, Richard George *(Sergeant)*, Everley Gregg *(Sarah Pocket)*, John Burch *(Mr. Wopsle)*, Grace Denbigh-Russell *(Mrs. Wopsle)*, John Forrest *(Pale Young Gentleman)*, Anne Holland *(A Relation)*, Frank Atkinson *(Mike)*, Gordon Begg *(Night Porter)*, Edie Martin *(Mrs. Whimple)*, Walford Hyden *(Dancing Master)*, Roy Arthur *(Galley Steersman)*.

A banquet for the ears, a feast for the ears, a table laden with goods from Dickens and realized brilliantly by director David Lean from a script by himself, Ronald Neame, Anthony Havelock-Allan, Cecil McGivern, and Kay Walsh. Dickens may be one of the most difficult authors to adapt to manageable length due to all of his magnificent sidebar characters and numerous subplots. The proof of that is the nine hours of NICHOLAS NICKLEBY that was done for the stage, then shown on public television. This was the third of four versions of GREAT EXPECTATIONS. The first was a silent starring Jack Pickford and Mary Huff. Universal did a remake in 1934 with Jane Wyatt, Phillips Holmes, and Francis Sullivan (who also appeared in this version in the same role as Jaggers) and the final was made for US TV in 1975 and released elsewhere as a feature. It starred Michael York, Sarah Miles, and James Mason (see review) and, even though a color film, paled by comparison. Young Wager is an orphan being raised by Jackson, his married sister in lowly straits. He is called to the large mansion on the hill and asked to be a playmate to Jean Simmons, the ward of slightly mad Martita Hunt, an eccentric who lives in a rotting house, surrounded by memories. Simmons takes great pleasure insulting and teasing the young boy, who is hopelessly in love with her. Dissolve and Wager is replaced by Mills, who is working as an assistant/apprentice to his brother-in-law, Miles, a blacksmith. Mills is visited by the rotund Sullivan, a London solicitor, who tells him that he is now a rich young man, the result of having been left a great sum of money by someone who prefers to remain anonymous. The stipulation of the legacy is that Mills must quit the country life and make his way to London, where he is now to be a young man of "great expectations." He believes that the money must have come from the wacky Hunt. He goes to London and shares a flat with Guinness, a charming rakehell. (This was Guinness' belated introduction to films at the age of 32, after having had many distinguished roles in West End productions). He meets Hobson (replacing Simmons, who was never more radiant in her small role) and their relationship begins once more. (Hobson was, at the time, married to the film's executive producer, Havelock-Allan, but she did a good job despite that). Mills becomes accustomed to the life of a wealthy young man; his bucolic attitudes soon become almost distastefully high-nosed. Then he meets Currie and learns that this rough old man is the benefactor. (The picture had begun in a graveyard where young Wager met a convict, brought him some victuals, and handed him a file so the man could escape prison.) But Mills, as an adult, barely remembered his good deed and can't believe that this tough coot has bestowed such riches upon him. Currie is being chased by an old enemy after having come back from a voyage overseas where he made a fortune. Thinking his only daughter dead, Currie had mentally taken Mills on as his "son" and, having no one else to leave his fortune to, gave it to Mills. There is a steamer leaving London, but the ship's dock is being watched by the authorities who still want to get Currie for his long-ago crime. Mills and Guinness get a boat and row out into the Thames where they hope to stop the already-departed steamer and put Currie aboard. Things don't work out, and the paddle-wheeler knocks everyone into the water in the most action-packed scene in the film. Currie is mortally wounded and dies in prison with Mills by his side, but not before we learn that Hobson is his daughter! Mills returns to Hunt's mansion to tell Hobson what he has learned. Hunt, who had been deserted on her wedding day, keeps the room where the wedding dinner was to have taken place exactly as it was many years ago. Further, she wears the same clothes she wore on that fateful day. There is an accident, and the old woman dies when a coal from the fireplace sets her clothes on fire. Mills then discovers that Hobson is living the same sort of hermit-like life as Hunt had and, with his proposal of marriage (sort-of), he manages to convince her that there's more to be seen out there than what's inside the decaying house. This is a very dense picture. Every scene is crammed with exposition and information, although it feels more like revelation. Oscars were awarded the production design and art direction, and the film was also nominated for best picture, as well as for best script and best direction. Dickens fans will probably say that it was too simply done, but to correctly make GREAT EXPECTATIONS, with all the accompanying situations and people, would be to have attempted a six-hour film and in 1946, that would have been impossible. The black-and-white lensing by Guy Green enhanced the mood of the movie; color (in the later version) didn't help one bit. The color was in the story and in the memorable Dickensian characterizations. Charles Dickens had rightly been called "one of the greatest story tellers in history" and this is a good example of his narrative powers. Technically, Guinness had appeared 12 years before in a very small role in EVENSONG but he, and we, prefer to think of this as his debut. Co-author Neame went on to become a successful director on his own, with credits such as TUNES OF GLORY, THE MAN WHO NEVER WAS, THE PRIME OF MISS JEAN BRODIE, THE POSEIDON ADVENTURE, THE ODESSA FILE, and many others. Since this film, there have been several attempts to bring Dickens to the stage and screen, the most notable being OLIVER TWIST, OLIVER, and PICKWICK. Dickens was a commercial author and often was paid by the word. Many critics took him to task for doing such things as describing a table and taking a page to do it. Never mind that. As a commercial author, he knew what a good yarn was, and how to delight his readers. GREAT EXPECTATIONS is, arguably, his best work and ranks with Lean's OLIVER TWIST as the best cinematic adaptation of his writing. It has action, adventure, fabulous characters, and a marvelous sense of actually "being there." If you hear that it's playing anywhere (in an uncut version) within one hundred miles, race to see it.

p, Ronald Neame; d, David Lean; w, Lean, Neame, Anthony Havelock-Allan, Cecil McGivern, Kay Walsh (from the novel by Charles Dickens); ph, Guy Green; m, Walter Goehr; ed, Jack Harris; prod d, John Bryan; art d, Wilfrid Shingleton; cos, Sophia Harris.

Drama Cas. (PR:AAA MPAA:NR)

GREAT EXPECTATIONS*** (1975, Brit.) 124m Transcontinental c

Michael York *(Pip)*, Sarah Miles *(Estella)*, Margaret Leighton *(Miss Havisham)*, James Mason *(Magwitch)*, Robert Morley *(Pumblechook)*, Anthony Quayle *(Jaggers)*, Heather Sears *(Biddy)*, Joss Ackland *(Joe Gargery)*, Andrew Ray *(Herbert Pocket)*, James Faulkner *(Drummle)*, Rachel Roberts *(Mrs. Gargery)*, Simon Gipps-Kent *(Pip, as a Boy)*, Maria Charles *(Sarah Pocket)*, Elaine Garreau *(Cousin Camilla)*, Richard Beaumont *(Pocket, as a Boy)*, Eric Chitty *(Old Man)*.

Even adeqate Dickens is better than no Dickens at all and this version of the great story teller's saga is somewhat more than adequate. Gipps-Kent is young Pip, an orphan living with Roberts and Ackland, his sister and brother-in-law. His uncle, Morley, tells him that he has been selected by Leighton, a wealthy old recluse, to come to her mansion and play there with her ward. The lad's life is not as dull as one might think, living in the country, as he has already been involved in one unique incident whereby he aided an escaped convict, Mason, in his flight from authority. At the manor house, the lad meets Miles, a snobbish young miss who does not hide the fact that she feels the young man is common as muck. Miles taunts and tweaks the boy and lets him know, in no uncertain terms, that he can never worm his way into her affections until such time as he becomes a gentleman, a goal he sets up for himself right then and there. Quayle appears as a London barrister and informs the lad that an anonymous source wishes to help him become a young man of "great expectations." He is to be given a generous stipend each year. York is now the older Pip; he goes to live with Ray in London. Ray is a devil-may-care lad with an eye for the lasses. Once in London, York again meets Miles, but she is just as persnickety with him as before. York thinks that the source of the money is Leighton (he hardly knows anyone else nearly that rich), a crazed woman who lives with the nightmare of the day she was to be married and was abandoned at the altar. This caused her to cease functioning in the outside world and enclose herself within her mansion's decaying walls. Enter Mason again. After his escape years ago, he went Down Under, made a fortune, and, thinking his only daughter dead, bestowed the benefits of his labors on York, mentally adopting the young orphan. Mason is still a fugitive from justice in England and has risked his freedom in order to come back to London to meet the older Pip, York. York thinks he might like to go back to Australia with Mason and then send for Miles. Now York learns that Miles is to marry Faulkner, a cad if there ever was one. York feels it's Leighton's fault for making Miles into a cynical woman, old beyond her years. York then learns that Miles is, in fact, Mason's daughter and he tells him that just before the old man dies attempting to flee his pursuers in an exciting sequence. York travels to India and returns as a very rich man. He is determined to aid those who have helped him. He meets Miles and learns that Faulkner has treated her horribly, but has since died. Miles and York are reunited and will share the rest of their lives together. Yellen's screenplay for this version was not nearly as rich as the earlier, 1946, picture, and Hardy's direction falters. Hardy came from a successful stage career (as did Yellen) and their inability to understand the difference between stage and screen is what does this in. Good music from Maurice Jarre, and nice work from all the technical departments, but the heart of the matter was left somewhere on the cutting room floor. And so were all the songs. Originally made as a musical, they edited all of the tunes out and we'll never know if it worked in that form.

p, Robert Fryer; d, Joseph Hardy; w, Sherman Yellen (based on the novel by Charles Dickens); ph, Freddie Young (Panavision, Eastmancolor) m, Maurice Jarre; ed, Bill Butler; art d, Alan Tomkins; m/l, (out of the final print) Norman Sachs, Mel Mondel.

Drama   **(PR:AAA MPAA:NR)**

GREAT FEED, THE   (SEE: LA GRANDE BOUFFE, 1973, Fr./Ital.)

GREAT FLAMARION, THE***   (1945) 78m REP bw
Erich von Stroheim (Flamarion), Mary Beth Hughes (Connie Wallace), Dan Duryea (Al Wallace), Stephen Barclay (Eddie), Lester Allen (Tony), Esther Howard (Cleo), Michael Mark (Night Watchman), Joseph Granby (Detective), John R. Hamilton (Coroner), Fred Velasco, Carmen Lopez (Mexican Dancers), Tony Ferrell (Mexican Singer).

Von Stroheim is at his dark best in this melodrama about a performer who makes his living as a vaudeville marksman. He is a woman-hater, the result of a failed love affair some 15 years before. His aide is Hughes, who is married to Duryea, who also works for von Stroheim. After the succulent Hughes begins to make eyes at von Stroheim, Duryea is killed "accidentally" and—and then Hughes leaves von Stroheim for a bicycle rider. The Great Flamarion has been flim-flammed by a femme once again.

p, William Wilder; d, Anthony Mann; w, Anne Wighton, Heinz Herald, Richard Weil (from the story "Big Shot" by Vicki Baum); ph, James Spencer Brown; m, Alexander Laszlo; ed, John F. Link; md, David Chudnow; art d, F. Paul Sylos.

Drama   **(PR:A-C MPAA:NR)**

GREAT FLIRTATION, THE*½   (1934) 71m PAR bw
Elissa Landi (Zita Marishka), Adolphe Menjou (Karpath), David Manners (Larry Kenyon), Lynne Overman (Joe Lang), Raymond Walburn (Henry Morgan), Adrian Rosley (Mikos), Paul Porcasi (Herr Direktor), George Baxter (Arpad), Judith Vosselli (Queen), Akim Tamiroff (Paul Wengler), Vernon Steele (Bigelow).

Backstage melodrama starring Menjou as an egotistical actor whose career is on the downslide, and Landi as his long-suffering actress wife whom he's oppressed since their marriage. After moving from Budapest to New York, the couple fall on hard times until they are both cast in a play written by dashing young playwright Manners. Menjou is a hit on stage, but he walks when he discovers his wife's infatuation with Manners. This doesn't bother Manners, who simply cranks out another play and stars Landi in the lead. The play is a smash—but the loyal Landi sacrifices her career to save her marriage.

p, Charles R. Rogers; d, Ralph Murphy; w, Humphrey Pearson (based on a story by Gregory Ratoff); ph, Milton Krasner.

Drama   **(PR:A MPAA:NR)**

GREAT GABBO, THE***   (1929) 71m Sono-Art World Wide bw
Erich von Stroheim (Great Gabbo), Betty Compson (Mary), Don Douglas (Frank), Marjorie King (Babe), Otto Gabbo (A dummy), Helen Kane.

This bizarre, often unintentionally funny and very campy film has von Stroheim as a half crazy ventriloquist who is losing his personality to his own dummy, Otto, while punishing his pretty assistant, Compson, for imagined wrongs. Von Stroheim (in the first talkie in which he appeared) becomes so jealous of his helper Compson that he drives her from his side, the dummy actually insulting her and heaping so much abuse on her head that she quits the act, even though she loves von Stroheim. The ventriloquist loses his identity to the dummy altogether and goes

berserk at the end, smashing the dearest thing to his heart, Otto, the wooden extension of his personality. Poorly produced with a grainy texture and erratic sound, talkies then being in the experimental stage, THE GREAT GABBO is fascinating merely for von Stroheim's presence. He does the best he can with an improbable story which is awkwardly directed by Cruze, a one-time famous silent screen helmsman who failed to make the transition to talkies. Compson's presence adds little and is explained by the fact that she was the director's wife at the time. It's crude and disjointed but there are priceless scenes such as von Stroheim singing with his dummy on stage. Some absurd attempts at dance numbers are made, including one maniacal routine entitled "The Web of Love," showing scantily clad chorines trapped and writhing in a massive cobweb controlled by an actor dressed in a loose-fitting wild spider costume. To those still responding to the magic name of von Stroheim, a name that really meant importance during the silent era, the film was a let-down, only offering another "crazy artist" story. Von Stroheim did the film because he was desperate for money and later hated the role, coming to believe it symbolized his own crackup and failure. He tried to buy the rights to the film years later, presumably to destroy all the prints, but found that someone else had purchased the property, a real-life ventriloquist named Edgar Bergen. Songs include: "The New Step," "I'm Laughing Ickey," "I'm in Love With You," "The Ga-Ga Bird," "The Web of Love," "Every Now and Then" (Paul Titsworth, Donald McNamee, Lynn Cowan and King Zany).

p&d, James Cruze; w, Hugh Herbert (based on the Ben Hecht story, "The Rival Dummy"); ph, Ira Morgan; ch, Maurice Kusell.

Drama/Musical   **Cas.**   **(PR:C MPAA:NR)**

GREAT GAMBINI, THE**   (1937) 70m PAR bw
Akim Tamiroff (Gambini), John Trent (Grant Naylor), Marian Marsh (Ann Randall), Genevieve Tobin (Mrs. Randall), Reginald Denny (Mr. Randall), William Demarest (Kirby), Edward Brophy (Buckie), Lya Lys (Luba), Allen Birmingham (Lamb), Roland Drew (Stephen Danby), Ralph Peters (Bartender).

Tamiroff plays a not-so-clever murderer who happens to be a night-club clairvoyant. To throw the cops off his trail, Tamiroff pretends to help solve the murders by predicting future deaths, but in the end he only traps himself. A decent "B" thriller.

p, B. P. Schulberg; d, Charles Vidor; w, Frederick Jackson, Frank Partos, Howard Irving Young (based on a story by Jackson); ph, Leon Shamroy; ed, Robert Bischoff; md, Boris Morros; art d, Albert D'Agostino.

Crime   **(PR:A MPAA:NR)**

GREAT GAME, THE*   (1930) 75m GAU bw
John Batten (Dicky Brown), Renee Clama (Peggy Jackson), Jack Cock (Jim Blake), Randle Ayrton (Henderson), Neil Kenyon (Jackson), Kenneth Kove (Bultitude), A.G. Poulton (Banks), Billy Blyth (Billy), Lew Lake (Tubby), Wally Patch (Joe Miller), Rex Harrison (George).

To Americans, fairly uninteresting British sport film which details the trials and tribulations of a mismanaged soccer team. Ayrton, the chairman, seeks to purchase star players by offering enticing salaries, while the team's manager, Kenyon, wishes to build a loyal and lasting ball-club by nurturing the young talent at hand. Eventually Kenyon has his way and the team goes on to victory in the closing minutes.

p, L'Estrange Fawcett; d, Jack Raymond; w, W.P. Lipscomb, Ralph Gilbert Bettinson, (from a story by William Hunter, John Lees); ph, Basil Emmott.

Sports Drama   **(PR:A MPAA:NR)**

GREAT GAME, THE**   (1953, Brit.) 80m Advance/Adelphi bw
James Hayter (Joe Lawson), Thora Hird (Miss Rawlings), Diana Dors (Lulu Smith), Sheila Shand Gibbs (Mavis Pink), John Laurie (Wells), Glyn Houston (Ned Rutter), Geoffrey Toone (Jack Bannerman), Jack Lambert (Mr. Blake), Meredith Edwards (Skid Evans), Alexander Gauge (Ben Woodhall), Frank Pettingell (Sir Julius), Glenn Melvyn (Heckler), Tommy Lawton, Brentford Football Club, Charles Leno, Sydney Vivian, Roddy Hughes.

Uneven depiction of a man who forfeits all for the sake of the football team he runs; this includes his honesty when he uses underhanded methods to obtain a much-needed player, something that causes him to lose his position when discovered. The business he had always had to fall back upon is still there, but is left in a bad way. Decent portrayal of a man driven by greed who eventually meets his downfall through this selfishness.

p, David Dent; d, Maurice Elvey; w, Wolfgang Wilhelm (based on the play "Shooting Star" by Basil Thomas); ph, Phil Grindrod.

Drama   **(PR:A MPAA:NR)**

GREAT GARRICK, THE***   (1937) 82m WB bw
Brian Aherne (David Garrick), Olivia De Havilland (Germaine De Le Corbe), Edward Everett Horton (Tubby), Melville Cooper (M. Picard), Luis Alberni (Basset), Lionel Atwill (Beaumarchais), Marie Wilson (Nicolle), Lana Turner (Auber), Linda Perry (Molee), Craig Reynolds (Janin), Dorothy Tree (Madame Moreau), Chester Clute (Moreau), Etienne Girardot (Jean Cabot), Albert Dekker (LeBrun), Milton Owen (Capt. Thierre), Trevor Bardette (Noverre, the Blacksmith), E.E. Clive (Vendor), Harry Davenport (Innkeeper of Turk's Head), Paul Everton (Innkeeper of Adam and Eve), Jack Norton (Drunken Gentleman), Leyland Hodgson (Man in Box), Fritz Leiber (Horatio), Fritz Leiber, Jr. (Fortinbras), Corbet Morris (Osric), Olaf Hytten (Ambassador), Constance Tellissier (Woman in Box), Connie Leon (Woman in Audience), Elspeth Dudgeon (Old Witch), Ben Welden (Blacksmith).

A very amusing picture that could have been a comedy classic if more attention had been given to the script. Aherne is the great David Garrick, a successful and renowned British actor of the 18th century and is finishing a stint at the Drury Lane Theater in London when he tells the crowd that he is about to work at Paris' Comedie Francaise as a guest artist. Some of the crowd don't appreciate the fact that he will be going off to the City Of Light and he makes a facetious remark that he might be able to teach the French actors a thing or two. When the people at the Comedie Francaise hear about that comment, they decide to play a prank on him. The idea is to embarrass Garrick and their plot would make a terrific French stage farce. They take over an inn on the Calais-Paris road and stage an entire play for Aherne's benefit. Everyone from the innkeeper to the servants are part of the comedy troupe. Even the guests are actors. Arguments occur, duels are fought, murder takes place, all for the sake of the British actor. Eventually, he sees through their sham and decides to play along with it. It's then that De Havilland arrives at the inn, a legitimate guest. Aherne believes she is one of the conspirators. In the end, Aherne informs the others that he knew the truth from somewhere near the middle of their plot. Now he looks for De Havilland, whom he has fallen in love with, and discovers that she was not one of the actors at all. She has run off to Paris. Aherne will play "Don Juan" at the Comedie Francaise but is so heartsick at the loss of De Havilland (whom he made blush by telling her that she was an inferior actress and should leave the stage forever) that he feels he cannot go on stage and play the role. But then he looks up at a box and sees De Havilland and he goes on to play the greatest "Don Juan" of his career. It's an apocryphal story (but who is around to dispute it?) but charming nevertheless. Aherne and De Havilland were an item during the making of the film but they eventually broke up and he became her brother-in-law two years later when he married her sister Joan Fontaine. Lots of good work from all the second bananas, especially Horton and Cooper. Lana Turner and Marie Wilson supply what little sex appeal can be sensed under those heavy dresses.

p, Mervyn LeRoy; d, James Whale; w, Ernest Vadja (based on his play, "Ladies And Gentlemen"); ph, Ernest Haller; m, Adolph Deutsch; ed, Warren Low; md, Leo F. Forbstein; art d, Anton Grot; cos, Milo Anderson.

Comedy (PR:A MPAA:NR)

GREAT GATSBY, THE**** (1949) 92m PAR bw

Alan Ladd (Jay Gatsby), Betty Field (Daisy Buchanan), Macdonald Carey (Nick Carraway), Ruth Hussey (Jordan Baker), Barry Sullivan (Tom Buchanan), Howard Da Silva (Wilson), Shelley Winters (Myrtle Wilson), Henry Hull (Dan Cody), Carole Mathews (Ella Cody), Ed Begley (Myron Lupus), Elisha Cook, Jr. (Klipspringer), Nicholas Joy (The Guest), Walter Greaza (Kinsella), Tito Vuolo (Mavromichaelis), Diane Nance (Pamela), Ray Walker (Real Estate Man), Jack Lambert (Reba), Jack Gargan (Golf Pro), Lynne Romer, Jeanne Romer (Twins).

A tailor-made role for Ladd, THE GREAT GATSBY in its first talking version is far superior to its silent predecessor and botched remake in 1974. Most of this is due to Ladd in one of the greatest performances of his career. Ladd, as the mysterious Gatsby, is seen driving to West Egg, an exclusive New York suburb, with Cook, a henchman, and Begley, an associate in the rackets. It's the 1920s and Ladd is a handsome, incredibly wealthy gangster and bootlegger. He selects a mansion and moves in, inspecting the enormous building, walking through the cavernous rooms. As he does, Cook sits down at a piano and plays "Just a Cottage Small by a Waterfall." As he and Begley stand on the patio and look across the bay, Ladd tells the older man about a woman he has known in Louisville, Kentucky, years ago, Daisy Faye, now known as Daisy Buchanan (Field). The mansion opposite across the bay is Field's home. Into Ladd's resplendent mansion pour scores of revelers, all enjoying the sumptuous parties he throws, replete with oceans of bootleg booze, jazz-playing bands, and Charleston-hopping flappers and sheiks. Carey, who is Field's cousin and lives in a small cottage next to Ladd's estate, attends one of the parties and Ladd, who has kept himself distant from his guests, suddenly appears to eagerly introduce himself. Ladd spews forth obvious lies about his background, then abruptly asks Carey: "Now that you have met me, what do you think of me?" Beyond Ladd's fabrications are the facts of his real life, then seen in flashback (never shown in the 1974 remake). As impoverished Jimmy Gatts, Ladd befriends Hull, a wealthy old playboy who invites him to sail around the world with him on his yacht and during the voyage Mathews, Hull's sensuous wife, leads Ladd on. All of it amuses Hull who later tells Ladd that his wife will never leave him for Ladd since he has money and the youth is broke, adding ruefully: "Money is the only thing that counts." Armed with this shallow philosophy, Ladd goes after riches in the most direct manner, later becoming one of New York's most successful bootleggers. Carey, whose interest in Ladd's background is now deep, pumps Hussey, Field's close friend, and she admits that she and Field knew Ladd in Kentucky during WW I when he was in the army. Though Field and Ladd were deeply in love, Hussey relates, Ladd was shipped overseas to fight and, tired of waiting for him, Field married wealthy socialite Sullivan. But the marriage has proven rocky, especially after Sullivan has taken up with a cheap married floozey, Winters, who busies herself by cuckolding husband Da Silva, a dim-witted garage mechanic. Ladd is so eager to see Field again that he buys Hussey a yellow roadster identical to his own and one she admires, so she will set up a clandestine rendezvous with Field at Carey's cottage. Here the two meet again over tea in a highly charged scene and their love for each other is rekindled. Field tells Ladd she will tell Sullivan that she is leaving him for Ladd. But it's an empty promise; she can't bring herself to desert certain old line luxury for Ladd's bootleg wealth, even though Ladd repeatedly urges her to tell Sullivan. "She won't do it," Carey cautions Ladd, "not Daisy." The following day, Ladd resolves to take Field away with him. He arrives at the Sullivan estate and the entire group—Ladd, Field, Sullivan, Hussey, and Carey—go into Manhattan where Ladd finally confronts Sullivan, telling him: "Look here, old sport, Daisy doesn't love you. She has loved me since 11 years ago." Sullivan explodes, confronts and confuses Field, then screams at Ladd that he is a gangster. The trip back to Long Island proves disastrous. Driving Ladd's yellow roadster, Field accidentally runs over Winters as she passes Da Silva's garage; the mindless mistress raced into the road, thinking her lover Sullivan was in the car and stepped right into the front of the car. Beside herself, Field refuses to stop and Ladd nobly states that he will tell authorities he was driving. Field goes home to Sullivan, cowardly melting into his protective riches; both of them are selfish and self-centered to the core. Sullivan

smirks at the thought of Ladd taking the responsibility for killing his unwanted mistress, then tells Field: "Let him take the blame! He has it coming! We'll all say it was him if we have to—it was his car." Carey protests and Sullivan snarls: "Since when were you a friend of Gatsby's?" "Since one minute ago," replies Carey. Field agrees to let Ladd take the fall and when Carey goes outside he finds Ladd, who has heard his one-time lover's words; the betrayal has devastated him. Carey visits Ladd at his mansion to see servants departing and Ladd sitting at poolside, waiting for a phone call. Ladd tells Carey he is abandoning the pretense of being a gentleman; he is closing the house and moving on. "But you are a gentleman," Carey tells him, "the only one I know." Nothing seems to matter to Ladd anymore, except that he intends to keep his promise to the spoiled Field. He will take the blame for Winters' death since "Daisy can't help being Daisy." He stands up and walks toward the pool. A shot rings out and Ladd staggers forward, falling into the water. He lamely swims a few strokes, then dies, his body floating face downward. Standing at poolside dumbly holding a smoking revolver is Da Silva, the cuckolded garageman, who has taken mistaken vengeance on Ladd for the death of his cheating wife. It is the end of the Great Gatsby. Carey later attends Ladd's funeral, placing flowers on the grave. The only other person in attendance is Hussey, who agrees to accompany Carey back to his Midwest home. Ladd's performance in THE GREAT GATSBY is a perfect match to the tragic hero drawn by author F. Scott Fitzgerald—embodying youthful disillusionment, quiet gentility, fatal nobility. He is tough but vulnerable to the nostalgic love that obsessively drives him to his own doom. He is admirable, but a man to be pitied as much as to be remembered. No one has ever come closer to capturing Gatsby's melancholy, mythical persona than Alan Ladd. Curiously, the traumatic scene where Da Silva shoots Ladd at poolside was witnessed by Alana Ladd, the actor's 5-year-old daughter who was watching on the set with her mother. It took two hours to prepare the blood blister on Ladd's back so that, upon being shot by Da Silva's blank-firing revolver, the actor fell into the pool and the blister would explode to spread apparent blood in the crystal clear water. But, after the fall, the sound of a child crying was heard, that of Alana Ladd, who believed her father had actually been killed. It took hours for her very much alive father to convince her that "it's just pretend, just a movie." The child was taken home to ponder the mysteries of movie-making while the scene was reshot. Da Silva, who had appeared in four movies with Ladd, and who would appear as Wolfsheim 25 years later in the 1974 remake (a character from the original novel who is represented by Begley in the Ladd film) would later state: "It was so curious, doing GATSBY again—with Redford this time. But as much as I admired Redford as an actor, I felt he could never play a man from the opposite side of the tracks. And Ladd could and did. In retrospect, I think his Gatsby was very underrated, unfortunately." Again, Ladd was troubled with the height of other male actors who towered above him, except for Da Silva. To put him on equal footing with Carey and Sullivan, the studio built a special carpeted ramp for interior scenes, one that sloped downward to the sound stage floor so that Ladd could stand above the taller actors and appear the same height. This proved embarrassing to the actor. Beverly Linet, in Ladd, A Hollywood Tragedy, has makeup man Hal Lierley remembering Ladd telling him: "No more, no more . . . from now on I'm going to demand approval of the other male actors I work with." Supporting cast members do well with their satellite roles but Field appears a bit too old for Daisy. Carey is convincing as the empathetic Nick Carraway, ostensible narrator of Gatsby's tragic tale, and Sullivan is properly despicable as the sneering and worthless man of wealth. Winters does her tawdry little bit well with the small part of Myrtle, the frustrated and mindless cheat. Winters later recalled in her memoirs, Shelley: Also Known as Shirley, that she learned how to smoke so she could properly portray "bad girl" Myrtle, but admitted to Clark Gable and Errol Flynn at a party that, even though she had a role in the upcoming film, she had never read a word of F. Scott Fitzgerald. Gable and Flynn immediately launched into a colorful discussion of their drinking escapades with Fitzgerald in Malibu bars when the author lived in Hollywood and was writing scripts. Then Flynn told Winters that "he had all of Fitzgerald's first editions, and he would lend me The Great Gatsby, as I really ought to be familiar with all of his work before I did that film. He added wistfully, 'I wonder why no one ever offers me films like that.' " Da Silva again is solid as is Hussey, and the overall production provides top values. The script is taut and more faithful to the novel than any other, before or after. Seitz's excellent photography sharply details the 1920s period, a better representation of that wild and lawless era, oddly enough, than the original silent production made in 1926 by Paramount, starring Warner Baxter and Lois Wilson. Fitzgerald had been dead for nine years by the time this film was made and most of his books were out of print, the renaissance of his writings to begin about a year after the release of this version, so there was sketchy public identification with the story, but Ladd's name drew considerable response and the film made money, though it did not do the box office it deserved. Prior to the release of the poorly made 1974 talkie remake of THE GREAT GATSBY, Paramount removed all prints of the 1949 version from public circulation and banned its use on TV, a great disservice to a significant film.

p, Richard Maibaum; d, Elliott Nugent; w, Cyril Hume, Maibaum (based on the novel by F. Scott Fitzgerald and the play by Owen Davis); ph, John F. Seitz; m, Robert Emmett Dolan; ed, Ellsworth Hoagland; art d, Hans Dreier, Roland Anderson; cos, Edith Head; makeup, Perc Westmore.

Drama (PR:A MPAA:NR)

GREAT GATSBY, THE* (1974) 144m PAR c

Robert Redford (Jay Gatsby), Mia Farrow (Daisy Buchanan), Bruce Dern (Tom Buchanan), Karen Black (Myrtle Wilson), Scott Wilson (George Wilson), Sam Waterston (Nick Carraway), Lois Chiles (Jordan Baker), Howard Da Silva (Meyer Wolfsheim), Roberts Blossom (Mr. Gatz), Edward Herrmann (Klipspringer), Elliot Sullivan (Wilson's Friend), Arthur Hughes (Dog Vendor), Kathryn Leigh Scott (Catherine), Beth Porter (Mrs. McKee), Paul Tamarin (Mr. McKee), John Devlin (Gatsby's Bodyguard), Patsy Kensit (Pamela Buchanan), Marjorie Wildes (Pamela's Nurse), Jerry Mayer (Reporter), Bob Sherman, Norman Chauncer (Detectives at Pool), Regina Baff (Miss Baedeker), Janet Arters, Louise Arters (Twins), Oliver

Clark *(Fat Man)*, Vincent Schiavelli *(Thin Man)*, Sammy Smith *(Comic)*, Tom Ewell *(Mourner)*.

The color is rich, the photography superb, and the atmospherics of the roaring twenties are realistically and stunningly in evidence in this film version of F. Scott Fitzgerald's masterpiece novel, but that's it. The script is weak, short-cutted to play up scenes the author intended to be understated, particularly those interminable soft-focus love sequences between Farrow and Redford, the direction is haphazard at best, and the acting is positively abysmal by all parties concerned, except that rendered by Da Silva, a wonderful old pro who appeared in the 1949—and best—version of this classic tale. Redford essays Gatsby, the charade-playing gangster who loves married Mia from afar, throwing fabulous parties to get her attention, meeting her secretly in Waterston's cottage, renewing his love for her and she for him, each having loved the other in the bittersweet past of WW I and she having married into wealth, he wedding violence. Dern is the smug-ugly wealthy husband and Chiles the purring cousin who arranges the assignation between Farrow and Redford. Black plays the sluttish, violence-prone Myrtle, cheating wife of garageman Wilson (same name as the character) who is seeing Dern on the side. There's a bit of drama—only a bit—when the Long Island aristocrats meet in a sweaty Plaza hotel suite to drink and confront each other—Redford demanding Farrow leave filthy rich Dern, she undecided, Dern in a rage, and Redford ultimately out in the cold and dead in his swimming pool, the murder victim of Wilson who believes Redford has run over Black on the road when it was precious, precocious, and utterly revolting Mia. The film is really a disgrace to Fitzgerald's wonderful novel, one that may have satisfied the roaring egos of the actors but does nothing but emphasize the fact that the 1949 version starring Alan Ladd was the best. Director Clayton was all wrong for this film, a British helmsman whose sole thrust was to cover the story with a heavy blanket of hot jazz, bootleg gin, and wild parties where ladies in evening gowns and men in tuxedos jump willy-nilly into pools. Clayton obviously misunderstood the story or ignored it purposely, portraying its fringe images as the main attractions. The Coppola script is a hodge-podge of Fitzgeraldania that eliminates important elements of the tale; Coppola completely fails to develop Gatsby's character. Here, Redford, looking Ivy League and prep school, is anything but a tough gangster with high social aspirations. He appears from nowhere and goes to nowhere. His performance is as mechanical, wooden, and uninspiring as Farrow's is stupid, shallow, and simpy. Dern is merely a stumbling, scowling malcontent and Waterston mangles the sensitive role of the narrator with a smirky, mindless grin and a delivery that has all the enthusiasm of a dead mongoose. Black is frenetic in her lust for rich man Dern, so much so that she appears instantly certifiable; in one idiotic scene she slashes her arm while jamming it through a window to get Dern's attention and then has an orgasmic response to the sight of the blood and the mere thought of her lover. From her absolute manic postures one can only assume that director Clayton suggested she play the mad scene from *Macbeth* and let it go at that. Wilson as the cuckolded garage owner is a walking cadaver with unblinking eyes whose zenith of emotion is an annoying monotoned voice (heavily laced with a hillbilly accent). Chiles does not even attempt to act, but merely lounges around in silk ensembles looking sexy and batting her eyes in the direction of any male present. They're awful, all of them, dreadful and, yes, repulsive in the form of characters with original substance who have been twisted into grotesque caricatures. Clayton, Coppola, and producer Merrick simply raped Fitzgerald's work (for which his daughter Scottie Smith was paid a whopping $350,000), then foisted off the brutal attack on the public as a consenting act. The attitudes of all the principals here were fantastically presumptuous. Redford jumped at the part of Gatsby when Paramount offered it, later stating: "I wanted Gatsby badly," and then pompously added, "he is not fleshed out in the book." The question is: How would Redford know? If "fleshing out" (a term used only by hacks who insist upon bettering classics with their own trite images and stereotyped words to inflate already bloated egos) means that Gatsby had to be portrayed as a glossy model out of *Gentleman's Quarterly* with slicked down hair, robot gestures, replacing lines with squints and genuine sensitivity with arthritic fist-clenching, then Redford "fleshed" him out indeed, in his own glinting way, one that had nothing to do with Jay Gatsby, F. Scott Fitzgerald, or the great story that could have been put onto celluloid. Clayton and clique merely filmed a reputation and called it their own. There was trouble right from the beginning when Paramount initially hired precious Truman Capote to write the script; a more unlikely and unsympathetic scribe could not be found. Capote's screenplay was rejected quickly when he turned it in, and one report had it that he had portrayed Nick (Waterston's role) as a swishy homosexual and Jordan Baker (the role enacted by Chiles) had been transformed into a snaky lesbian. Indignant, Capote sued the studio but dropped his case after a settlement of $110,000 was made to him. Paramount then hired Coppola who spent all of three weeks adapting the great novel for the screen. Coppola later stated that "Clayton should get co-author credit," since the director reportedly worked on the script. Its idiotic posture and framing shows it. Credit, credit, credit is what the inane production was all about, everybody bowing inside the great gray ghost of Fitzgerald. Clayton, Redford, Coppola, Farrow—all of them—should get the credit they deserve for this expensive insult, which cost the studio more than $13 million to produce. Each one of these individuals should wear for the rest of their lives a placard about their necks which states: "I helped to destroy a literary classic!" It might have been worse. Worse? Steve McQueen was proposed for the Gatsby role and Ali McGraw as Daisy. Katharine Ross, Candice Bergen, and Faye Dunaway (the latter the only real actress in the whole bunch of them) were also suggested for the role. Then Mia Farrow sent a cute wire from London to production chief Bob Evans (then at outs with soon-to-be-divorced wife McGraw) which read: "Dear Bob, may I be your Daisy?" After her test studio executives felt she was the perfect Daisy. So much for the taste of front office arbiters. The perfection vanished with box office receipts that barely inched over the break-even point. The irony, one might imagine, would not be lost on a dead, boyish gangster grinning in eternal oblivion at such perverse extravagance, such outlandish disregard for a not-so-hard-earned buck.

p, David Merrick; d, Jack Clayton; w, Francis Ford Coppola (based on the novel by F. Scott Fitzgerald); ph, Douglas Slocombe (Panavision, Eastmancolor); m, Nelson Riddle; ed, Tom Priestly; prod d, John Box; art d, Eugene Rudolf, Robert Laing; cos, Theoni V. Aldredge; ch, Tony Stevens.

Drama   **Cas.**   **(PR:A   MPAA:PG)**

GREAT GAY ROAD, THE∗∗½   (1931, Brit.) 88m STOLL/But bw

Stewart Rome *(Hilary Kite)*, Frank Stanmore *(Crook Perkins)*, Kate Cutler *(Aunt Jessie)*, Arthur Hardy *(Sir Crispin)*, Pat Paterson *(Nancy)*, Billy Milton *(Rodney)*, Hugh E. Wright *(Backus)*, Frederick Lloyd *(Col. Trigg)*, Ethel Warwick *(Lizzie)*, Wally Patch *(Joe)*, Charles Paton, Bruce Winston, Petra Charpentier, Alf Cordery, Aubrey Fitzgerald, The Kirkby Sisters.

Cute tale about a tramp who is really a man of some means, but who gave up his patrimony in order to pursue the carefree life of a bum. Getting a yen to visit his old home and family, Rome, as the tramp, returns home and quickly finds himself falling in love with his cousin. The chance of them having a romance is aborted through the woman's promise to marry another. Not wishing to upset the status quo, Rome takes to the road again, doing the honorable thing by leaving the woman to the original claimer.

p&d, Sinclair Hill; w, Leslie Howard Gordon (based on the novel by Tom Gallon); ph, Desmond Dickinson.

Drama   **(PR:A   MPAA:NR)**

GREAT GEORGIA BANK HOAX   (SEE: GREAT BANK HOAX, 1977, Brit.)

GREAT GILBERT AND SULLIVAN, THE∗∗½   (1953, Brit.) 105m
London Film Productions/UA c
(GB: THE STORY OF GILBERT AND SULLIVAN)

Robert Morley *(W.S. Gilbert)*, Maurice Evans *(Arthur Sullivan)*, Eileen Herlie *(Helen Lenoir)*, Martyn Green *(George Grossmith)*, Peter Finch *(Richard D'Oyley Carte)*, Dinah Sheridan *(Grace Marston)*, Isabel Dean *(Mrs. Gilbert)*, Wilfrid Hyde-White *(Mr. Marston)*, Muriel Aked *(Queen Victoria)*, Michael Ripper *(Louis)*, Bernadette O'Farrell *(Jessie Bond)*, Ann Hanslip *(Bride)*, Eric Berry *(Rutland Barrington)*, Yvonne Marsh *(Second Bride)*, Lloyd Lamble *(Joseph Bennett)*, Ian Wallace *(Captain)*, Owen Brannigan *(Principal Bass Baritone)*, Richard Warner *(Cellier)*, Perlita Neilson *(Lettie)*, Charlotte Mitchell *(Charlotte)*, Kenneth Downey *(Counsel for the Plaintiff in "Trial by Jury")*, Sylvia Clarke *(Gianetta in "The Gondoliers" and Peep-Bo in "The Mikado")*, Stella Riley *(Millicent)*, Leonard Sachs *(Smythe)*, Philip Ray *(Theater Manager)*, John Rae *(Ferguson)*, George Cross *(Stage Manager)*, George Woodbridge *(Reporter)*, Robert Brookes Turner *(Doorman)*, Anthony Green *(Office Boy)*, Gron Davies *(The Ancestral Ghost in "Ruddigore")*, Arthur Howard *(Usher in "Trial by Jury")*, John Banks *(Strephon in "Iolanthe")*, John Hughes *(Train Bearer in "Iolanthe")*, Thomas Round *(Defender in "Trial by Jury" and Nanki-Poo in "The Mikado")*, Harold Williams *(Judge in "Trial by Jury")*, Muriel Brunskill *(Principal Contralto)*, Harold Lang, Jennifer Vyvyan, Joan Gillingham, Gordon Clinton, John Cameron, Marjorie Thomas, Webster Booth *(Singers)*.

An accurate portrayal of the famed Victorian comic operetta writing duo. Morley is the caustic writer/lyricist and Evans is the composer. Finch is the man who brings them together. The highly enjoyable music is sung by members of the famed D'Oyly Carte company, including Green, one of the premier Gilbert and Sullivan tenors. It's great fun, though not quite as engaging as one might hope.

p, Frank Launder, Sidney Gilliat; d, Gilliat; w, Gilliat, Leslie Bailey, Vincent Korda (based on *The Gilbert and Sullivan Book* by Bailey); ph, Christopher Challis (Technicolor); m, Arthur Sullivan; ed, Gerald Turney-Smith; prod d, Hein Heckroth; md, Sir Malcolm Sargent; m/l, W.S. Gilbert, Sullivan.

Musical/Biography   **(PR:AAA   MPAA:NR)**

GREAT GILDERSLEEVE, THE∗∗   (1942) 61m RKO bw

Harold Peary *(Gildersleeve)*, Jane Darwell *(Aunt Emma)*, Nancy Gates *(Margie)*, Charles Arnt *(Judge Hooker)*, Freddie Mercer *(LeRoy)*, Thurston Hall *(Governor Stafford)*, Lillian Randolph *(Birdie)*, Mary Field *(Amelia Hooker)*, George Carleton *(Mr. Powers)*.

Rotund comedian Peary, bringing his popular radio character "The Great Gildersleeve" to the screen, is up to his neck in problems, as usual. Chief problem is the local judge's sister (Field), who wants to marry him. His adopted niece and nephew (Gates and Mercer), do everything in their power to keep her a spinster. It was better on radio. (See GREAT GILDERSLEEVE series, Index.)

p, Herman Schlom; d, Gordon Douglas; w, Jack Townley, Julien Josephson; ph, Frank Redman; ed, John Lockert; md, C. Bakaleinikoff; art d, Albert S. D'Agostino, Walter E. Keller.

Comedy   **Cas.**   **(PR:A   MPAA:NR)**

GREAT GOD GOLD∗∗   (1935) 65m MON bw

Sidney Blackmer *(John Hart)*, Martha Sleeper *(Marcia Harper)*, Regis Toomey *(Phil Stuart)*, Gloria Shea *(Gert)*, Edwin Maxwell *(Nitto)*, Ralf Harolde *(Frank Nitto)*, Maria Alba *(Eleana Nitto)*, John T. Murray *(Simon)*.

Topical at the time of its release, GREAT GOD GOLD deals in specific with the receivership frauds that flourished after the '29 market crash, in general with money lust. Blackmer stars as an honest financier who gets caught up in a criminal scheme. The scheme is thwarted through the efforts of Sleeper and Toomey, and Blackmer is left a broke and broken man.

p, Trem Carr; d, Arthur Lubin; w, Norman Houston, Jefferson Parker (from a story by Albert J. Meserow, Elynore Dalkhart); ph, Milton Krasner; ed, Jack Ogilvie.

Drama   **(PR:A   MPAA:NR)**

GREAT GUNDOWN, THE*½   (1977) 95m Sun Productions c

Robert Padilla (*Mario Ochoa, "The Savage"*), Malila St. Duval (*Teresa*), Richard Rust (*Joe Riles*), Steven Oliver (*Arden*), David Eastman (*Edgely*), Stanley Adams (*Buck*), Rockne Tarkington (*Sutton*), Michael Christian (*Darwood*), Michael Green (*Preacher Gage*), Owen Orr (*Happy Hogan*).

An independently produced western which has Padilla, as "The Savage," leading a group of motley mercenaries (a la THE WILD BUNCH) on a search for the villainous Rust. Director Hunt can be credited for attempting a western in the midst of the STAR WARS craze, but his over-indebtedness to Sam Peckinpah's violence conveys a disturbing lack of originality. You might as well watch the real thing.

p, Paul Nobert; d, Paul Hunt; w, Steve Fisher (based on a story by Robert Padilla); ph, Ronald V. Garcia (Technicolor); m, Alan Caddy, Ronald Fallon; ed, Tony de Zarraga.

Western   Cas.   (PR:O MPAA:PG)

GREAT GUNFIGHTER, THE   (SEE: GUNFIGHT AT COMMANCHE CREEK, 1963)

GREAT GUNS**½   (1941) 73m FOX bw

Stan Laurel (*Stan*), Oliver Hardy (*Oliver*), Sheila Ryan (*Ginger Hammond*), Dick Nelson (*Dan Forrester*), Edmund MacDonald (*Hippo*), Charles Trowbridge (*Col. Ridley*), Ludwig Stossel (*Dr. Schickel*), Kane Richmond (*Capt. Baker*), Mae Marsh (*Aunt Martha*), Ethel Griffies (*Aunt Agatha*), Paul Harvey (*Gen. Essick*), Charles Arnt (*Doctor*), Pierre Watkin (*Col. Wayburn*), Russell Hicks (*Gen. Burns*), Irving Bacon (*Postman*), Alan Ladd (*Soldier*).

Stan and Ollie are the chauffeur and gardener for Nelson, a silver-spoon-in-the-mouth son of a millionaire. He's drafted into the service and Stan and Ollie (who with his weight couldn't possibly have been drafted) join the Army to be near him. Nelson would much prefer to make it on his own but they are like mother hens. MacDonald is their sergeant at the cavalry camp in Texas and he goes through several Edgar Kennedy tantrums of frustration in his attempts to train them. Nelson falls for a postal worker, Ryan, and Stan and Ollie conclude their careers by helping win a maneuvers campaign by some of the weirdest planning ever seen. Not one of their funniest but enough to keep you smiling. Look for Alan Ladd in a small part as a soldier in a photography store. (See LAUREL & HARDY series, Index.)

p, Sol M. Wurtzel; d, Monty Banks; w, Lou Breslow, ph, Glen MacWilliams; ed, Al DeGaetano; md, Emil Newman; art d, Richard Day, Albert Hogsett; set d, Thomas Little; cos, Herschel.

Comedy   (PR:AAA MPAA:NR)

GREAT GUY**½   (1936) 75m GN bw (GB: PLUCK OF THE IRISH)

James Cagney (*Johnny Cave*), Mae Clarke (*Janet Henry*), James Burke (*Pat Haley*), Edward Brophy (*Pete Reilly*), Henry Kolker (*Conning*), Bernadene Hayes (*Hazel Scott*), Edward J. McNamara (*Capt. Pat Hanlon*), Robert Gleckler (*Cavanaugh*), Joe Sawyer (*Joe Burton*), Ed Gargan (*Al*), Matty Fain (*Tim*), Mary Gordon (*Mrs. Ogilvie*), Wallis Clark (*Joel Green*), Douglas Wood (*The Mayor*), Jeffrey Sayre (*Clerk*), Eddy Chandler (*Meat Clerk*), Henry Roquemore (*Store Manager*), Murdock MacQuarrie (*Client*), Kate Price (*Woman at Accident*), Frank O'Connor (*Detective*), Arthur Hoyt (*Furniture Salesman*), Jack Pennick (*Truck Driver*), Lynton Brent (*Reporter*), John Dilson (*City Editor*), Bud Geary, Dennis O'Keefe (*Guests*), Robert Lowery (*Parker*), Bobby Barber (*Grocery Clerk*), Gertrude Green (*Nurse*), Ethelreda Leopold (*Burton's Girl Friend*), Bruce Mitchell (*Cop at Accident*), James Ford, Frank Mills, Ben Hendricks, Jr. (*Party Guests*), Kernan Cripps (*Deputy*), Bill O'Brien (*2nd Meat Clerk*), Lester Dorr (*Chauffeur*), Harry Tenbrook (*Receiving Clerk*), Lee Shumway (*Mike the Cop*), Gertrude Astor, Vera Steadman, Mildred Harris, Bert Kalmar, Jr., Walter D. Clarke, Jr.

A disappointing entry from an otherwise sterling list of films, GREAT GUY offers a low-pressure performance from Cagney, who is an ex-boxer given the public post of chief deputy of the Bureau of Weights and Measures. His honesty soon results in trouble. When Cagney discovers that racketeers are cheating the public in the food market, such as weighing down chickens with lead slugs and inserting false bottoms in strawberry baskets, he goes after the chiselers. Racketeers try to bribe him and, when that fails, they beat him up. Meanwhile, his sweetheart, Clarke, tries to get him to stop risking his neck. Unknown to Clarke, her boss (Kolker) is one of the big shots behind the racket. With help from politician Brophy, Cagney's one-time ring opponent, and tough cop Burke, Cagney finally gets enough evidence to send Kolker, Gleckler, and other miscreants to jail, emerging victorious and with Clarke on his arm. Cagney appeared in this Grand National film at a time when he was feuding with his home studio, Warner Bros., and GN took full advantage of the situation, cashing in on his fame but providing a cheap production with little value and a poor script. The supporting cast is good and Grand National felt that bringing Cagney and Clarke back together again for the first time since THE PUBLIC ENEMY, the team would provide the same kind of box office dynamite. But the film fizzled. Cagney received $100,000 from Grand National and would make one more film with this independent firm, SOMETHING TO SING ABOUT, a movie nobody crowed about. By then his battle with Warners ended and he was back in the fold, making bigger and better films for WB. The theme of crooked weights and measures was one Cagney would later resurrect for another independent production years later, A LION IS IN THE STREETS, but this film would be much more successful than THE GREAT GUY.

p, Douglas MacLean; d, John G. Blystone; w, Henry McCarty, Horace McCoy, Henry Johnson, Henry Ruskin (based on the "Johnny Cave Stories" by James Edward Grant); ph, Jack McKenzie; ed, Russell Schoengarth; md, Merlin Skiles; art d, Ben Carre; cos, Dorothy Beal.

Crime Drama   Cas.   (PR:A MPAA:NR)

GREAT HOPE, THE**½   (1954, Ital.) 91m EX/Minerva c LA GRANDE SPERANZA)

Renato Baldini (*Captain*), Lois Maxwell (*Lily*), Folco Lulli (*First Mate*), Carlo Bellini (*Officer*), Aldo Bufi Landi (*Lieutenant*), Earl Cameron (*Johnny*), Edward Flemming (*Carter*), Henri Vidon (*Steiner*), Carlo Delle Piane (*Ciccio*), Jose Jaspe (*Fernandez*), Tom Middleton (*Jackie*).

An Italian submarine cruising the Atlantic shortly before the end of World War II picks up some survivors of a British ship wreck. Along with the crew is nurse Maxwell who becomes romantically involved with the submarine captain. Based on a true story, this film gives a nice pacifist message that, happily, does not come across as trite or heavy-handed. The ensemble acting within the claustrophobic mise-en-scene is underplayed and never hammy, and the episodic story is held together well by the direction.

d, Duilio Coletti; w, Coletti, Marc Antonio Bragadin (from a story by Bragadin); ph, Leonida Barboni (Ferraniacolor); m, Nino Rota; ed, Giuliana Attenni.

War/Romance   (PR:C MPAA:NR)

GREAT HOSPITAL MYSTERY, THE**   (1937) 58m FOX bw

Sally Blane (*Ann Smith*), Thomas Beck (*Dr. David McKerry*), Jane Darwell (*Miss Keats*), Sig Rumann (*Dr. Triggert*), Joan Davis (*Flossie Duff*), Wade Boteler (*Detective Lt. Mattoon*), William Demarest (*Mr. Beatty*), George Walcott (*Allen Tracy*), Howard Philips (*Tom Kirby*), Ruth Peterson (*Desk Nurse*), Carl Faulkner, Frank C. Fanning (*Policmen*), Margaret Brayton (*Chart Room Nurse*), Lona Andrew (*Miss White*), Tom Mahoney (*Bank Guard*).

Darwell and Blane are hospital workers who get mixed up in gangster activities when they learn that Blane's brother is being chased by a bunch of hoods. They make a few switches among the hospital beds and fix it so it appears that Blane's brother is a recently deceased patient. Thanks to the brave, gangster-fighting comic Demarest, the hoods are apprehended.

p, John Stone; d, James Tinling; w, Bess Meredyth, William Conselman, Jerry Cady (based on a story by Mignon Eberhard); ph, Harry Jackson; ed, Nick DeMaggio; md, Samuel Kaylin.

Crime/Mystery   (PR:A MPAA:NR)

GREAT HOTEL MURDER**   (1935) 70m FOX bw

Edmund Lowe (*Roger Blackwood*), Victor McLaglen (*Andy McCabe*), Rosemary Ames (*Elinor Blake*), Mary Carlisle (*Olive Temple*), Henry O'Neill (*Mr. Harvey*), C. Henry Gordon (*Dr. Temple*), William Janney (*Harry Prentice*), Charles C. Wilson (*Anthony Wilson*), John Wray ("*Feets*" *Moore*), John Qualen, Herman Bing, Madge Bellamy, Robert Gleckler, Clarence H. Wilson.

A routine murder mystery which casts Lowe as a writer of such stories. While staying in a plush hotel, he helps house detective McLaglen uncover clues to a recent murder, much to the latter's dismay. The dead man was found in one of the hotel's rooms, but it was not the one he registered for. According to one of the suspects, he had asked to change rooms, leading the private eye to suspect the guest he had switched with. McLaglen, however, follows the wrong set of clues and must rely on the assistance of Lowe, who solves the mystery.

p, John Stone; d, Eugene Forde; w, Arthur Kober (based on a story from Vincent Starrett's *Recipe For Murder*); ph, Ernest Palmer; m, Samuel Kaylin.

Mystery   (PR:A MPAA:NR)

GREAT IMPERSONATION, THE**   (1935) 64m UNIV bw

Edmund Lowe (*Baron Leopold Von Ragenstein/Sir Everard Dominey*), Valerie Hobson (*Lady Eleanor Dominey*), Wera Engels (*Princess Stephanie*), Henry Mollison (*Eddie Pelham*), Murray Kinnell (*Seaman*), Leonard Mudie (*Mangam*), Lumsden Hare (*Duke Henry*), Spring Byington (*Duchess Caroline*), Brandon Hurst (*Middleton*), Claude King (*Sir Gerald Hume*), Esther Dale (*Mrs. Unthank*), Charles Waldron (*Sir Ivan Brun*), Ivan F. Simpson (*Dr. Harrison*), Frank Reicher (*Dr. Schmidt*), Nan Grey (*Middleton's Daughter, the Maid*), Willy Castello (*Duval*), Priscilla Lawson (*Maid*), Pat O'Hara (*Chauffeur*), Virginia Hammond (*Lady Hume*), Thomas R. Mills (*Bartender*), Tom Ricketts, Frank Terry, Robert Bolder (*Villagers*), Lowden Adams (*Waiter*), Violet Seaton (*Nurse*), Dwight Frye (*Roger Unthank*), David Dunbar, Frank Benson (*English Farmers*), John Powers (*English Police*), Leonid Snegoff (*Wolff*), Harry Worth (*Hugo*), Adolph Milar (*German*), Larry Steers (*Army Officer*), Harry Allen (*Parkins*), Douglas Wood (*Nobleman*).

Lowe plays a German spy posing as a nobleman who tries to take over an English castle. Lowe works for an organization of unconscionable weapons dealers, whose sole concern is money. Remade in 1942 with Ralph Bellamy.

p, Edmund Grainger; d, Alan Crosland; w, Frank Wead, Eve Greene (based on the novel by E. Phillips Oppenheim); ph, Milton Krasner, John P. Fulton; ed, Phil Cahn.

Spy Drama   (PR:A MPAA:NR)

GREAT IMPERSONATION, THE***   (1942) 70m UNIV bw

Ralph Bellamy (*Sir Edward Dominey/Baron von Ragenstein*), Evelyn Ankers (*Muriel*), Aubrey Mather (*Sir Ronald*), Edward Norris (*Bardinet*), Kaaren Verne (*Baroness Stephanie*), Henry Daniell (*Seaman*), Ludwig Stossel (*Dr. Schmidt*), Mary Forbes (*Lady Leslie*), Rex Evans (*Sir Tristram*), Charles Coleman (*Mangan*), Robert O. Davis (*Hofmann*), Charles Irwin (*Yardly*), Fred Vogeding (*Stengel*), Victor Zimmerman (*Nazi Soldier*), Marcelle Corday (*Frenchwoman*), Olaf Hytten (*Tobacconist*), Fred Giermann (*Stamin*), Henry Guttman (*Hans*), Val Stanton (*English Porter*), Hans von Morhart (*Muller*), Audrey Long (*Anna*), Eric Wilton, Hans Herbert (*Clerks*), Charles Flynn (*Nazi Soldier*), Yvette Dugay, Sylvia Arslan (*French Children*), Napoleon Simpson (*Tall Black*).

An improvement over the 1935 original with Edmund Lowe, this remake of THE GREAT IMPERSONATION takes place during WW II instead of WW I. Bellamy plays a dual role as an Englishman and his German doppelganger. At the war's outbreak Bellamy kills his German look-alike and returns to England, posing as a master spy for the Nazis, funneling false secret plans to German agents there. The enemy spies are rounded up while Bellamy returns to Germany. He is almost exposed before persuading Rudolph Hess to make his notorious plane trip to Scotland to ostensibly rendezvous with British Nazis, only to be captured and thrown into the Tower of London. Bellamy is convincing and empathetic in a wild, provocative film that tip-toes through real incidents in an attempt to lend credibility to an incredible tale.

p, Paul Malvern; d, John Rawlins; w, W. Scott Darling (based on the novel by E. Phillips Oppenheim); ph, George Robinson; ed, Russell Schoengarth; md, H.J. Salter; art d, Jack Otterson.

Spy Drama **(PR:A MPAA:NR)**

GREAT IMPOSTOR, THE½** (1960) 112m UNIV bw

Tony Curtis *(Ferdinand Waldo Demara, Jr.)*, Karl Malden *(Fr. Devlin)*, Edmond O'Brien *(Capt. Glover)*, Arthur O'Connell *(Warden Chandler)*, Gary Merrill *(Pa Demara)*, Joan Blackman *(Catherine Lacey)*, Raymond Massey *(Abbott Donner)*, Robert Middleton *(Brown)*, Jeanette Nolan *(Ma Demara)*, Sue Anne Langdon *(Eulalie)*, Larry Gates *(Cardinal)*, Mike Kellin *(Thompson)*, Frank Gorshin *(Barney)*, Cindi Wood *(WAC Lieutenant)*, Robert Crawford, Jr. *(Demara, Jr. as a Boy)*, Richard Sargent *(Hotchkiss)*, Ward Ramsey *(Executive Officer Howard)*, Doodles Weaver *(Farmer)*, Philip Ahn *(Hun Kin)*, Harry Carey, Jr. *(Dr. Joseph Mornay)*, Jerry Paris *(Defense Lieutenant)*, Herbert Rudley *(Senior Officer)*.

A biography of Ferdinand Waldo Demara, Jr., a real-life impostor, the film begins with Curtis masquerading as a Harvard professor to join the Marines, and proceeds through a series of false identities including that of a Trappist monk, a jail warden, and a surgeon in the Royal Canadian Navy. Played for comedy, the film never quite works, perhaps because Curtis can't handle the title role. The best scenes in this disjointed production occur when Curtis takes on the role of a prison reform administrator and not only quells a potentially bloody riot but brings a new understanding between warden and inmates.

p, Robert Arthur; d, Robert Mulligan; w, Liam O'Brien (based on the book by Robert Crichton); ph, Robert Burks; m, Henry Mancini; ed, Frederic Knudtson; art d, Alexander Golitzen; set d, Julia Heron; makeup, Bud Westmore.

Biography/Comedy **(PR:A MPAA:NR)**

GREAT JASPER, THE½** (1933) 83m RKO bw

Richard Dix *(Jasper Horn)*, Wera Engels *(Norma McGowd)*, Edna May Oliver *(Madame Talma)*, Florence Eldredge *(Jenny Horn)*, Walter Walker *(Mr. McGowd)*, David Durand *(Andrew Horn as a Boy)*, Bruce Line *(Roger McGowd as a Boy)*, James Bush *(Andrew Horn)*, Bruce Cabot *(Roger McGowd)*, Betty Furness *(Sylvia)*, Dorothy Gray *(Sylvia as a Girl)*, Robert Emmett O'Connor.

Dix is an Irish Don Juan who gets into a lot of trouble because of his amorous tendencies. A motorman at the turn of the century, he is loyal to his wife, only in that he doesn't run away with any of the many women he makes love to. We see him changing jobs and women, until finally he retires in Atlantic City as a somewhat moralistic reader of women's fortunes, and dies after doing some good.

p, Kenneth Macgowan; d, J. Walter Ruben; w, Samuel Ornitz, H.W. Hanemann (based on the novel by Fulton Oursler); ph, Leo Tover.

Comedy/Drama **(PR:A MPAA:NR)**

GREAT JESSE JAMES RAID, THE*½ (1953) 73m Lippert c

Willard Parker *(Jesse James)*, Barbara Payton *(Kate)*, Tom Neal *(Arch Clements)*, Wallace Ford *(Elias Hobbs)*, James Anderson *(Jorrette)*, Jim Bannon *(Bob Ford)*, Richard Cutting *(Sam Wells)*, Barbara Woodell *(Zee)*, Mary Treen *(Mrs. Angus)*, Earl Hodgins *(Soapy Smith)*, Tom Walker *(Jesse James as a Youth)*, Joann Arnold *(Brunette)*, Helene Hayden *(Redhead)*, Steve Pendleton *(Todd)*, Bob Griffin *(Morgan)*, Robin Morse *(Anderson)*, Ed Russell *(Sheriff)*, Rory Mallinson *(Cavalry Officer)*, Marin Sais.

Bannon (Bob Ford) sets up a $300,000 mine theft with Parker (Jesse James) as a partner. Even though Parker has been living in retirement, he can't resist a good heist, and quickly gathers the best men for the job. It turns out, however, that Bannon has set Parker up, and the gang discovers his deception. In the finale, neither of the men get their hands on the gold and they ride off in separate directions. A let-down oater with little to do with the facts.

p, Robert L. Lippert, Jr.; d, Reginald Le Borg; w, Richard Landau; ph, Gilbert Warrenton (Anscolor); m, Bert Shefter; ed, Carl Pierson; m/l, "That's The Man For Me," Shefter, Lou Herscher.

Western **(PR:A MPAA:NR)**

GREAT JEWEL ROBBER, THE*** (1950) 91m WB bw

David Brian *(Dennis)*, Marjorie Reynolds *(Martha)*, Jacqueline de Wit *(Mrs. Vinson)*, Alice Talton *(Brenda)*, John Archer *(Sampter)*, Perdita Chandler *(Peggy)*, Robert B. Williams *(Capt. Ryan)*, Warren Douglas *(Altman)*, John Morgan *(Rogers)*, Bigelow Sayre *(Benson)*, Mayor Stanley Church of New Rochelle *(Himself)*.

Brian plays the likable real-life Gerard Dennis who, during a two-year period, stole over $1,000,000 in jewels and furs from the homes of wealthy families. The story follows his criminal escapades from Canada, through Buffalo, and across the continent to the West Coast. An intriguing and exciting picture that illustrates, once again, that while criminals can be glamorous, crime "does not pay," since Dennis, during production of his life story on film, was in Sing Sing, doing 18 years to life.

p, Bryan Foy; d, Peter Godfrey; w, Borden Chase (based on the story, "Life of Gerard Graham Dennis" by Chase, G.G. Dennis); ph, Sid Hickox; m, William Lava; ed, Frank Magee; art d, Stanley Fleischer.

Crime **(PR:A MPAA:NR)**

GREAT JOHN L, THE*** (1945) 96m Crosby/UA bw (GB: A MAN CALLED SULLIVAN)

Greg McClure *(John L. Sullivan)*, Linda Darnell *(Anne Livinstone)*, Barbara Britton *(Kathy Harkness)*, Lee Sullivan *(Mickey)*, Otto Kruger *(Richard Martin)*, Wallace Ford *(McManus)*, George Mathews *(John Flood)*, Robert Barrat *(Billy Muldoon)*, J.M. Kerrigan *(Father O'Malley)*, Simon Semenoff *(Mons. Claire)*, Joel Friedkin *(Michael Sullivan)*, Harry Crocker *(Arthur Brisbane)*, Hope Landin *(Maura Sullivan)*, Rory Calhoun *(James J. Corbett)*, Fritz Feld *(Claire's Manager)*, Dick Curtis *(Waldo)*, Tom Jackson *(McCullough)*, Edwin Maxwell *(Exhibition Ring Announcer)*, Nolan Leary *(Restaurant Waiter)*, Dewey Robinson *(Diner)*, George Eldredge *(Crony)*, Milton Parsons *(Health Restaurant Waiter)*, George Brasno *(Tom Thumb)*, Ernie S. Adams *(Waiter)*, George Lloyd *(Boss)*, Tom Fadden *(Clerk)*, Rex Lease *(Corbett's Manager)*.

A zesty film, THE GREAT JOHN L was the first independent production from crooner Bing Crosby and it proved to be a winner. McClure is the brash, brusque, and bold John L. Sullivan, the Boston Strong Boy, as he was called in his youthful heyday, who is shown entering the ring to make name and fame. As one victory follows another, McClure's head swells, as do his pockets. After he becomes heavyweight champion of the world—in a day when fighters squared off in the ring bare knuckles, mind—McClure loses control, takes to drinking and carousing and abandons his training discipline. When contender Calhoun, as the dapper James J. Corbett, meets McClure in the ring, the champ is a flabby figure headed for the bin of the has-beens. He loses his girl, his title, his championship belt, and, most importantly, his self-respect. Drinking his way through life, bullying his own reputation to impress other drunks, McClure finally sinks to the gutter. In a powerful scene, he orders a drink at a bar with his last bit of change, then looks in the mirror opposite to see a disgusting, scowling, mean-streaked bum. McClure hurls the glass of booze into the mirror, smashing it, then loudly announces: "I'll never take another drink as long as I live!" He becomes a crusading exponent of clean living, a reformer, grand example of the good life, ending the film on a decidedly upbeat note. This film is top drawer on every level, with fine production values and excellent period sets, costumes, and atmospherics. Tuttle peoples the film with strong supporting players and a humorous Irish flavor. McClure, a virtual unknown in his first film and first starring role, is a standout, ideally playing the great slugger. Oddly, McClure was never again to make a film as good as this one. Born Dale Easton, one-time day laborer and stevedore, he was discovered by Crosby while playing in a little theater group in Los Angeles. There are many moving moments in this film, one of them being hilarious, showing McClure nonplussed while attempting to punch a French fighter in a Paris match. The fighter, Semenoff, is a *la savotte* expert who uses his feet to kick his opponent, a style of fighting never seen on film before this picture.

p, Frank R. Mastroly, James Edward Grant; d, Frank Tuttle; w, Grant; ph, James Van Trees ed, Theodore Bellinger; md, Victor Young; m/l, Johnny Burke, James Van Heusen; stunts, John Indrisano.

Sports Drama **(PR:A MPAA:NR)**

GREAT LIE, THE*** (1941) 102m WB bw

Bette Davis *(Maggie Patterson)*, George Brent *(Pete Van Allen)*, Mary Astor *(Sandra Kovak)*, Lucile Watson *(Aunt Ada)*, Hattie McDaniel *(Violet)*, Grant Mitchell *(Joshua Mason)*, Jerome Cowan *(Jock Thompson)*, Sam McDaniel *(Jefferson)*, Thurston Hall *(Worthington James)*, Russell Hicks *(Col. Harrison)*, Olin Howland *(Ed)*, J. Farrell MacDonald *(Dr. Ferguson)*, Doris Lloyd *(Bertha)*, Alphonse Martell *(Waiter)*, Georgia Caine *(Mrs. Pine)*, Charlotte Wynters *(Mrs. Anderson)*, Cyril Ring *(Harry Anderson)*, Georges Renavent *(Maitre d'Hotel)*, Napoleon Simpson *(Parker)*, Charles Trowbridge *(Sen. Greenfield)*, Virginia Brissac *(Sadie)*, George Kirby *(Minister)*, Addison Richards *(Mr. Talbot)*, Richard Clayton *(Page Boy)*, George Reed *(Butler)*.

Grand soap opera at its best, here Davis is a wealthy socialite in love with Brent, a reckless playboy flyer. Astor, a concert pianist, is also in love with Brent who marries her on the spur of the moment but later they find out the wedding may be invalid. Brent offers to go down the aisle again with Astor but is secretly relieved when she puts him off, saying she must play a concert first. Next Brent goes to Davis' Maryland plantation where he proposes to her—he's definitely got marriage on his mind—but Davis, who had broken off her engagement with him before because of his irresponsible ways, tells him no, or, at least, she will hold judgment until his recent marriage to Astor is thrown out as illegal. Before any of this can happen Brent goes off on a government-sponsored flight to South America and is lost, apparently dead of a crash in the jungle. On a trip to New York Davis meets Astor who tells her that she is pregnant with Brent's child and the ever-magnanimous Davis takes Astor to her Arizona ranch. There the boy is born and Davis passes the child off as her own to save Astor's career. Then, while Astor is off on an Australian tour, Brent shows up very much alive, having survived his jungle exploit. Davis hides the truth about the baby from Brent but, when Astor returns from her tour, she insists that Davis tell all. Brent does not go into shock, only upbraids Davis for withholding the truth, then tells her he still loves her and wants her to be his bride. He, too, is generous, saying that Astor can have the child but he intends to stay with Davis. Confronted with this, Astor opts for a clean break, giving up Brent to Davis, and the baby, stating that he should stay with his real "mother." It's all improbable hogwash but women loved this film (and still do) and director Goulding pulled off a minor miracle by putting forth a splendid production without sinking completely into the saccharine. A very soupy but effective score was produced by Steiner; the great Warner Bros. composer preferred to score Davis films. Astor, who played the piano, and actually performed part of the difficult Tchaikovsky Piano Concerto, got her part and subsequently an Oscar for Supporting Actress, through Davis. "I insisted she play Sandra," Davis later said. "Plus Astor was in her own right a skilled pianist." The overweight Astor frantically went on a diet for the film but still appeared fat before the camera, so designer Orry-Kelly suggested she cut her long hair severely. When Davis heard about it, she almost challenged Astor to do it, asking: "Would you really *dare*?"

Astor had hair stylists clip her locks near to the skull in a close-cropped manner. The look was shockingly similar (for that day and age) to that of a man's haircut. The hair slashing, however, gave Astor a slimmer appearance and, once the film was released, her hairstyle soon became the rage in America. Davis, after beginning the film, sat down with Astor and told her that she thought the film was "going to stink . . . It's too incredible for words . . . All I do is mewl to George about 'That woman you married when you were drunk,' and to 'please come back to me,' and all that crap." She had the writers enlarge Astor's part so she could play off her and the beefed up role was certainly the reason why Astor won her Oscar. The two were beautifully combative and many came to believe that Astor and Davis actually feuded off screen the way Davis and Miriam Hopkins had years earlier. But they enjoyed each other's company and actually reworked many of the scenes together. Astor later stated in her autobiography, A Life on Film:, how they reshaped "the relationship between the two women—the savage bargaining . . . A couple of cats who had to shield their claws for expediency." Director Goulding was often amazed at their invention. He was a man of simple guidance. Goulding outlined Astor's role for the actress with this prosaic caption: "A piano, brandy, and men. In that order." When the women worked over one scene and came on to the set, Goulding said: "Well, ladies—if you're ready—would you kindly inform me as to what we're going to do?" Davis, of course, had the top lines and delivered an unforgettable and ruthless statement to Astor after the child is born: "That child is mine. Your part was finished the minute you gave that baby to me. From that day on, I had only one purpose in my life, to make that baby mine and forget you ever existed." And she did.

p, Hal B. Wallis; d, Edmund Goulding; w, Lenore Coffee (based on the novel January Heights by Polan Blanks); ph, Tony Gaudio; m, Max Steiner; ed, Ralph Dawson; md, Leo F. Forbstein; art d, Carl Jules Weyl; cos, Orry-Kelly; spec eff, Byron Haskin, Robert Burks.

Drama   **(PR:A   MPAA:NR)**

GREAT LOCOMOTIVE CHASE, THE***   (1956) 87m BV c
                                            (AKA: ANDREWS' RAIDERS)
Fess Parker (James J. Andrews), Jeffrey Hunter (William A. Fuller), Jeff York (William Campbell), John Lupton (William Pittenger), Eddie Firestone (Robert Buffum), Kenneth Tobey (Anthony Murphy), Don Megowan (Marion A. Ross), Claude Jarman Jr. (Jacob Parrott), Harry Carey Jr. (William Bensinger), Lennie Geer (J.A. Wilson), George Robotham (William Knight), Stan Jones (Wilson Brown), Marc Hamilton (John Wollam), John Wiley (John M. Scott), Slim Pickens (Pete Bracken), Morgan Woodward (Alex), W.S. Bearden (A Switchman), Harvey Hester (Jess McIntyre), Douglas Bleckley (Henry Haney).

A Civil War picture from Disney in which battles take a back seat to almost nonstop action. Parker is a Union soldier who, with a small band of men, tries to get into Confederate territory and destroy railway supply lines. He and his men board a locomotive and wait for the appropriate time to take it over. They are pursued by Hunter, a determined conductor who takes off after them via a handcar and then procures a locomotive for himself. Soon a full-steam chase is in progress, with enough twists and turns to keep everyone interested. The finale has Parker brought to trial and awaiting execution, but (small consolation) he has gained the respect of his pursuers. Photographed in CinemaScope, THE GREAT LOCOMOTIVE CHASE, takes advantage of its wide screen in the same way Edwin S. Porter did in his silent short THE GREAT TRAIN ROBBERY. The breath-taking massiveness of the thundering locomotive rips through the theater as it passes from one side of the frame to the other—an effect not possible during a television viewing. Walt Disney, himself a train fanatic, supervised production on weekends when not too busy with the construction of his California amusement park, Disneyland.

p, Lawrence Edward Watkin; d, Francis D. Lyon; w, Watkin; ph, Charles Boyle (CinemaScope, Technicolor); m, Paul J. Smith; ed, Ellsworth Hoagland; art d, Carroll Clark; set d, Emile Kuri, Pat Delaney; cos, Chuck Keehne, Joseph Dimmitt; makeup, David Newell, Louis Haszillo; m/l, Watkin, Paul Smith, Stan Jones.

Adventure   Cas.   (PR:AA   MPAA:NR)

GREAT LOVER, THE**½   (1931) 72m MGM bw
Adolphe Menjou (Jean Paurel), Irene Dunne (Diana Page), Ernest Torrence (Potter), Neil Hamilton (Carlo), Olga Baclanova (Savarova), Cliff Edwards (Finny), Hale Hamilton (Stapleton), Roscoe Ates (Rosco), Herman Bing (Losseck), Else Janssen (Mme. Neumann Baumbach).

Menjou is an aging opera star who courts budding young singer Dunne, devoting much of his attentions to her, but also to an array of others. She is attracted to his talent though she refuses to put up with his philandering. When a past love of hers suddenly emerges, she leaves Menjou, preferring honesty to artistry. A very young Dunne turns in a fine performance.

d, Harry Beaumont; w, Gene Markey, Edgar Allan Woolf (based on an original stage play by Leo Dietrichstein, Frederick Hatton, Fanny Hatton); ph, Merritt B. Gerstad; ed, Helen Warne.

Drama/Musical   (PR:A   MPAA:NR)

GREAT LOVER, THE**½   (1949) 80m PAR bw
Bob Hope (Freddie Hunter), Rhonda Fleming (Duchess Alexandria), Roland Young (C.J. Dabney), Roland Culver (Grand Duke Maximillian), Richard Lyon (Stanley), Gary Gray (Tommy), Jerry Hunter (Herbie), Jackie Jackson (Joe), Karl Wright Esser (Steve), Orley Lindgren (Bill), Curtis Loys Jackson, Jr. (Humphrey), George Reeves (Williams), Jim Backus (Higgins), Sig Arno (Attendant).

While chaperoning a group of teenage boys on a return trip from Europe to the States, Hope gets mixed up with a sharpie gambler and a duchess who believes him to be a wealthy American. The duchess' father gets his pockets emptied in a card game with the cheat, and when Hope intervenes he is pursued from bow to stern. Following the standard plot of these pictures, Hope gets the girl and

emerges heroic. The card sharp is also a murderer but it doesn't really matter. Songs: "A Thousand Violins" and "Lucky Us" (Jay Livingston, Ray Evans).

p, Edmund Beloin; d, Alexander Hall; w, Beloin, Melville Shavelson, Jack Rose; ph, Charles B. Lang, Jr.; m, Joseph J. Lilley; ed, Ellsworth Hoagland; md, Lilley; art d, Hans Dreier, Earl Hedrick.

Comedy   (PR:A   MPAA:NR)

GREAT MACARTHY, THE**½   (1975, Aus.) 93m Stony Creek/
                                            Seven Keys c
John Jarratt (MacArthy), Judy Morris (Miss Russell), Kate Fitzpatrick (Andrea), Sandra MacGregor (Vera), Barry Humphries (Colonel Ball-Miller), John Frawley (Webster), Colin Croft (Tranter), Chris Haywood (Warburton), Colin Drake (Ackerman), Ron Fraser (Twentyman), Max Gillies (Stan), Dennis Miller (Macguinness), Jim Bowles (Les), Bruce Spence (Bill Dean), Peter Cummins (Rerk), Cul Cullen (MacArthy Senior).

Highly popular Australian tale told on stage, television, and in print, traces the exploits of a great soccer player from the outback who signs up with a big league team in Melbourne. He has a series of bedroom romps, some corporate ventures, a failed marriage, and his sports career is eventually brought down by behind-the-scenes manipulation.

p&d, David Baker; w, John Romeril (based on the novel A Salute to the Great McCarthy by Barry Oakley); ph, Bruce McNaughton; m, Bruce Smeaton; ed, John Scott.

Sports Drama   (PR:C-O   MPAA:NR)

GREAT MAN, THE***   (1957) 92m UNIV bw
Jose Ferrer (Joe Harris), Dean Jagger (Philip Carleton), Keenan Wynn (Sid Moore), Julie London (Carol Larson), Joanne Gilbert (Ginny), Ed Wynn (Paul Beasley), Jim Backus (Nick Cellantano), Russ Morgan (Eddie Brand), Edward C. Platt (Dr. O'Connor), Robert Foulk (Mike Jackson), Lyle Talbot (Harry Connors), Vinton Hayworth (Charley Carruthers), Henry Backus (Mrs. Rieber), Janie Alexander (Mary Browne), Vicki Dugan (Receptionist), Robert Schwartz (Mailboy), Mallene Hill (Old Woman).

A compelling though often heavy-handed drama, THE GREAT MAN is told in interviews Ferrer conducts concerning the life and times of a prominent radio personality who has recently died in a car accident. Ferrer is an investigative reporter who is assigned by his network to work up an in-depth profile on the deceased to present in an hour-long nationwide program, a tribute to the departed "great man." Accompanied by pretty assistant Gilbert, Ferrer interviews Ed Wynn, an overly pious New England station owner who gave the "great man" his first break; his mistress, London; his one-time manager, Keenan Wynn; and network president Jagger. What emerges is a portrait of a callous, manipulative, and thoroughly rotten apple. When Ferrer confronts Jagger with the truth about his subject, he is told that the tribute will still take place and that no critical remarks about the deceased will be tolerated. Ferrer himself goes on the air, but throws away the lying script and reveals the truth about the dead man, knowing it will mean the end of his career. This was the first indictment of network manipulation of public opinion and it was almost as revealing and shocking as A FACE IN THE CROWD which followed the next year. Ferrer, who also directed and wrote the script, does a stunning job and is ably supported by London as the sultry and discarded mistress. Ed Wynn and son Keenan are also impressive in the roles as background characters.

p, Aaron Rosenberg; d, Jose Ferrer; w, Al Morgan, Ferrer (based on a novel by Morgan); ph, Harold Lipstein; m, Herman Stein; ed, Sherman Todd, Al Joseph; art d, Richard H. Riedel, Eric Orbom, Alexander Golitzen; cos, Bill Thomas; m/l, "The Meaning of the Blues," Bobby Troup, Leah Worth (sung by Julie London).

Drama   (PR:A   MPAA:NR)

GREAT MAN VOTES, THE***   (1939) 70m RKO bw
John Barrymore (Vance), Peter Holden (Donald), Virginia Weidler (Joan), Katherine Alexander (Miss Billow), Donald MacBride (Iron Hat McCarthy), Bennie Bartlett (Davy McCarthy), Brandon Tynan (Chester Ainslee), Elisabeth Risdon (Phoebe Ainslee), Granville Bates (The Mayor), Luis Alberni (Manos), J.M. Kerrigan (Hot Shot Gillings), William Demarest (Charles Dale), Roy Gordon (Mr. Byrne).

Barrymore's real-life declining health cast him into this role perfectly as an alcoholic college professor continually depressed since the death of his wife. To support his two precocious children, he teaches and becomes a night watchman. The children plan to have their father earn back his self-respect and do it by creating a situation in which their father's lone vote will decide who the town's next mayor will be. So once again the father becomes an important man, not only to himself, but also to his children.

p, Cliff Reid; d, Garson Kanin; w, John Twist (based on a story by Gordon Malherbe Hillman); ph, Russell Metty; ed, Jack Hively; art d, Van Nest Polglase.

Drama   (PR:A   MPAA:NR)

GREAT MANHUNT, THE, 1949   (SEE: DOOLINS OF OKLAHOMA,
                                            THE, 1949)

GREAT MANHUNT, THE***½   (1951, Brit.) 104m LFP/COL bw
                                            (GB: STATE SECRET)
Douglas Fairbanks, Jr. (Dr. John Marlowe), Glynis Johns (Lisa), Jack Hawkins (Colonel Galcon), Herbert Lom (Karl Theodor), Walter Rilla (General Niva), Karel Stepanek (Dr. Revo), Carl Jaffe (Janovik Prada), Gerard Heinz (Bendel), Hans Moser (Sigrist), Gerik Schjelderup (Bartorek), Guido Lorraine (Lt. Prachi), Anton Diffring (Policeman), Peter Illing (Macco), Olga Lowe (Baba), Therese Van Kye (Theresa), Leonard Sachs (Dr. Poldoi), Robert Ayres (Buckman), Martin Boddey, Russell Waters, Howard Douglas, Arthur Howard (Clubmen), Leslie Linder (Andre), Leo Bieber (Man at Phone), Nelly Arno (Shop Assistant), Paul Demel

(Barber), Arthur Reynolds *(Compere)*, Richard Molinas *(Red Nose)*, Eric Pohlmann *(Cable-Car Conductor)*, Louis Wiechert *(Christian)*, Henrik Jacobson *(Mountain Soldier)*.

A highly exciting and gripping tale of political intrigue centering around the sojourn of a doctor, Fairbanks, invited to the mythical country of Vosnia under false pretenses. Once there he finds that he is required to peform a complicated operation on the tyrannical head of state, who has but a short time left in this world. When Fairbanks becomes aware of the political climate of Vosnia he realizes an escape is his only chance, which he undertakes with Johns, the part-British lass he encounters along the way. Also joining in the escape attempt is two-bit gangster Lom, but even his abilities are not enough to see the threesome to safety. Captured, Fairbanks is only allowed to go free when a rapid change in government takes place. A mythical language was created to fulfill the requirements of Vosnia, whose exact location is only hinted at, but seems to be located somewhere behind the Iron Curtain.

p, Frank Launder, Sidney Gilliat; d&w, Gilliat (based on the novel *Appointment With Fear* by Roy Huggins); ph, Robert Krasker, John Wilcox; m, William Alwyn; ed, Thelma Myers; md, Muir Mathieson; art d, Wilfred Shingleton.

Adventure/Spy Drama (PR:A MPAA:NR)

GREAT MAN'S LADY, THE½** (1942) 90m PAR bw

Barbara Stanwyck *(Hannah Sempler)*, Joel McCrea *(Ethan Hoyt)*, Brian Donlevy *(Steely Edwards)*, Katharine Stevens *(Girl Biographer)*, Thurston Hall *(Mr. Sempler)*, Lloyd Corrigan *(Mr. Cadwallader)*, Etta McDaniel *(Delilah)*, Frank M. Thomas *(Senator Knobs)*, Lillian Yarbo *(Mandy)*, Helen Lynd *(Bettina)*, Mary Treen *(Persis)*, Lucien Littlefield *(City Editor)*, John Hamilton *(Senator Grant)*, Fred "Snowflake" Toones *(Fogey)*, Damian O'Flynn *(Burns)*, Charles Lane *(Pierce)*, Anna Q. Nilsson *(Paula Wales)*, Milton Parsons *(Froman)*, Fern Emmett *(Secretary to City Editor)*, Irving Bacon *(Parson)*, Monte Blue *(Man at Hoyt City)*, Bob Perry *(Miner)*, George Chandler *(Forbes)*, George P. Huntley *(Quentin)*, George Irving *(Dr. Adams)*, David Clyde *(Bartender)*, Eleanor Stewart *(Daughter)*, Ottola Nesmith *(Mrs. Frisbee)*, Pat O'Malley *(Murphy the Policeman)*, Hank Bell, Larry Lawson, Lee Phelps, Theodore Von Eltz, Lee Moore, Buck Mack, Charles Williams.

Protracted melodrama told mostly in flashback. Film opens at the unveiling of a statue honoring a U.S. senator who amassed great power and apparently did wonderful deeds during the settling of the West. Stanwyck is interviewed by reporters who want to confirm the rumor that she was the late senator's secret wife. After first denying the story, she confides in one writer and spills it all. As it turns out, Stanwyck was the substance behind the senator's (McCrea's) reputation. Anything good that was accomplished resulted from her efforts, not McCrea's, who was really a spineless money grubber.

p&d, William A. Wellman; w, W.L. River, Adela Rogers St. John, Seena Owen (based on the story "The Human Side" by Vina Delmar); ph, William C. Mellor; m, Victor Young; ed, Thomas Scott; art d, Hans Dreier, Earl Hedrick; cos, Edith Head; spec eff, Gordon Jennings; makeup, Robert Ewing.

Western (PR:A MPAA:NR)

GREAT McGINTY, THE**** (1940) 81m PAR bw (GB: DOWN WENT McGINTY)

Brian Donlevy *(Dan McGinty)*, Muriel Angelus *(Catherine McGinty)*, Akim Tamiroff *(The Boss)*, Allyn Joslyn *(George)*, William Demarest *(The Politician)*, Louis Jean Heydt *(Thompson)*, Harry Rosenthal *(Louis, the Bodyguard)*, Arthur Hoyt *(Mayor Tillinghast)*, Libby Taylor *(Bessie, the Colored Maid)*, Thurston Hall *(Mr. Maxwell)*, Steffi Duna *(The Girl)*, Esther Howard *(Madame La Jolla)*, Frank C. Moran *(The Boss' Chauffeur)*, Jimmy Conlin *(The Look Out)*, Dewey Robinson *(Benny Feigman)*, Richard Carle *(Dr. Jarvis)*, Donnie Kerr *(Catherine's Boy, 4)*, Mary Thomas *(Catherine's Girl, 6)*, Drew Roddy *(Catherine's Boy, 9)*, Sheila Sheldon *(Catherine's Girl, 11)*. Jean Phillps *(Manicurist)*, Lee Shumway *(Cop)*, Pat West *(Pappia)*, Byron Foulger *(Secretary)*, Charles Moore *(McGinty's Valet)*, Emory Parnell *(Policeman)*, Vic Potel *(Cook)*, Harry Hayden *(Watcher)*, Robert Warwick *(Opposition Speaker)*.

An hilarious spoof of American politics, this film marked the directorial debut of the mercurial and brilliant Preston Sturges, one of the best writer-directors of the 1940s, who specialized in screwball comedies and undoubtedly was responsible for reviving slapstick in movies. The film opens in a smoky banana republic bar. Heydt, a one-time chief cashier of a major bank who has embezzled funds and then fled to this steamy exile is so dejected with his plight that he attempts to commit suicide in the men's room but he is stopped by the bartender, Donlevy. Back at the bar, Donlevy smirks at Heydt's complaint that a man of his distinction should not have to lead such a life. "Cashier of a bank" snorts Donlevy. He leans forward conspiratorially and says: "I used to be the governor of a state." His story then unravels in flashback, showing Donlevy as a seedy hobo looking to make a dishonest dollar. He gets the perfect opportunity during an election in a large city (probably Chicago because such street names as "Van Buren" and "Clark" are used, or maybe St. Louis since the corrupt mayor to be re-elected by the venal political machine is named Tillinghast which is close to Pendergast, who bossed Missouri). Ward heeler Demarest hires Donlevy to vote for persons who "are sick in bed, or croaked, but that don't mean that the mayor should be cheated out of their support." Dimwitted Donlevy is to be paid $2 for his phony vote but he decides to run up the tally, so he votes 37 times as a repeater, returning with chits given to him by crooked poll workers to redeem them for a total of $74. Demarest is flabbergasted, saying he does not have that kind of money to pay him off, then takes Donlevy down to the party hall where political boss Tamiroff orders Donlevy paid off. Donlevy and Tamiroff have words and Donlevy gets slapped by the swarthy sachem for his comments. He slaps Tamiroff back and the boss' thugs close in. Tamiroff waves them off, telling them: "He don't know no better." Tamiroff lectures the truculent tramp but Donlevy snarls: "Get your fingers out of my face!" The boldness of the man startles Tamiroff, who breaks into hysterical laughter, saying: "He thinks he's me!" Tamiroff is so delighted by the feisty Donlevy that he appoints him a collector of funds in his protection racket. From bars to bordellos, Donlevy is shown making his rounds and, before using his brawn, he exercises the peculiar philosophy of his brain in persuading clients to pay up, telling one: "You want to be at the mercy of every slug who wears a uniform? You need someone to protect you from human greed." He collects handsomely, even when he has to use his muscle. Tamiroff is pleased with the results but realizes that his protege Donlevy is still a diamond in the rough, especially noting the loud suit he wears. Says the boss to Donlevy: "The reason you're alive and walking around in that horse blanket isn't because I like you. . . . This is the land of opportunity. Everybody lives by chiseling everybody else." He makes Donlevy an alderman, although their fierce battles continue. In one scene, a short discussion leads to a wild fist fight right in the back of the boss' limousine while Tamiroff's aides in the front seat, now used to this weird friendship, ignore the battle and go right on with their small talk. Donlevy's big break comes when Tamiroff puts him up for mayor, but on the proviso that he marry because voters prefer a married man. "Marriage," waxes Tamiroff, "has always been the most beautiful setup between the sexes." This marriage of political convenience takes place between Donlevy and his secretary, Angelus, who truly loves him and thinks of him as basically good and decent. After he becomes mayor, Angelus urges her errant husband to reform and aid the impoverished and indigent. "They want to be left alone," he squawks, "they like to be dirty," but he puts through aid measures to help the poor anyway. Tamiroff next pushes his political creation into the state's highest office, that of governor. By this time Donlevy has thoroughly reformed and has two small children from Angelus' former marriage of whom he has grown fond; Angelus guides him through a commendable beginning, telling him: "You're going to be the finest governor the state ever had." But Donlevy never gets to fullfill that prediction. A scandal erupts over a bridge he constructed through a graft-laced deal while mayor and Donlevy is arrested. He has already caused Tamiroff to be sent to prison for attempted assassination after he refused to play ball with the crook and Tamiroff took a shot at him. Now, ironically, he winds up in a cell right next to that of Tamiroff. Both men break out of prison, aided by their old crony, Demarest, and make good their escape. Donlevy stops long enough to call Angelus and tell her to go on with her life without him, and to tell her how to get at his safe deposit boxes where he has stashed his money so she and the children will have some security. In a flash forward we now see Donlevy concluding his tale to Heydt in the bar. Suddenly the owner of the club appears and accuses Donlevy of loafing; it is Tamiroff and both of them go at each other like old times with Demarest, now a grumpy waiter cleaning tables, complaining about the racket they are making. Donlevy, in his first starring role, gives a marvelous performance as a dim-witted plug-ugly who is transformed into a decent crusader for good and provides side-splitting laughs throughout in tandem with the flamboyant Tamiroff, whose rendering of the boss is masterful. He is wily, slippery, devious, deceitful, and utterly corrupt—the perfect political boss—and, in his savage way, crudely humorous. Demarest, one of the most durable and effective character actors, is colorful and full of street savvy and wit, once remarking: "If you didn't have graft, you'd have a lower class of people in politics!" This terrific satire was the brainchild of screenwriter Sturges, who had labored long in the script departments of Hollywood studios. After completing the outline for this story, he took it to Paramount's chief of production, William Le Baron. When the story was approved, Sturges asked to direct the film but Le Baron said no; Sturges had no experience. The writer then said he would sell the story to Paramount for $10 if he was allowed to direct. This was an offer no cost-conscious studio executive could refuse and Sturges was given the green light. His film captured raves from critics and the public loved the raucous humor and slap-happy characterizations. THE GREAT McGINTY launched Sturges as a major writer-director and he went on to produce a wonderful string of comedies, including CHRISTMAS IN JULY (1940), SULLIVAN'S TRAVELS (1941), THE LADY EVE (1941), THE MIRACLE OF MORGAN'S CREEK (1943), and HAIL THE CONQUERING HERO (1944). During the 1940s Sturges was Hollywood's wonder man, writing and directing one smash hit after another; he was Frank Capra with a banana peel who never lost touch with the common man. By the 1950s he was broke, his talent ostensibly flown, and no one would give him a job in the movies. The slim, mustachioed, and dynamic Sturges was still dreaming of a comeback when he died in his room in the Algonquin Hotel in New York in 1959.

p, Paul Jones; d&w, Preston Sturges; ph, William Mellor; m, Frederick Hollander; ed, Hugh Bennett; art d, Hans Dreier, Earl Hedrick; set d, A. E. Freudeman; cos, Edith Head; makeup, Wally Westmore.

Comedy (PR:A MPAA:NR)

GREAT MCGONAGALL, THE* (1975, Brit.) 95m Darltan/Scotia American c

Spike Milligan *(William McGonagall)*, Peter Sellers *(Queen Victoria)*, Julia Foster *(Mrs. McGonagall)*, John Bluthal, Valentine Dyall, Clifton Jones, Julian Chagrin, Victor Spinetti, Charlie Atom.

Hitting a low in British humor, this tale of an unemployed Scot (Milligan) trying to become Britain's poet laureate starts slowly, then stops. Milligan and Sellers have together done some side-splitting in the past, but here their luck runs out, though Sellers adds a bright spot with his portrayal of a sexually preoccupied Queen Victoria.

p, David Grant; d, Joseph McGrath; w, McGrath, Spike Milligan; ph, John Mackey (Eastmancolor); m, John Shakespeare, Derek Warne; prod d, George Djurkovic.

Comedy (PR:O MPAA:NR)

GREAT, MEADOW, THE*½ (1931) 80m MGM bw

John Mack Brown *(Berk Jarvis)*, Eleanor Boardman *(Diony Hall)*, Lucille La Verne *(Elvira Jarvis)*, Anita Louise *(Betty Hall)*, Gavin Gordon *(Evan Muir)*, Guinn Williams *(Reuben Hall)*, Russell Simpson *(Thomas Hall)*, Sarah Padden *(Mistress Hall)*, Helen Jerome Eddy *(Sally Tolliver)*.

Ambitious but utterly abysmal account of the hardships endured by an intrepid band of pioneers journeying from Virginia to Kentucky in 1775. Battling Indians, clearing forests, and foraging for food are minor annoyances in comparison to watching this monstrosity, which reportedly took a year to film. Leading lady Boardman retired the year of its release—not soon enough.

d, Charles Brabin; w, Edith Ellis, Brabin (based on the novel by Elizabeth Maddox Roberts); ph, William Daniels, Clyde De Vinna; ed, George Hively, Anne Bauchens.

Historical Drama **(PR:A MPAA:NR)**

GREAT MIKE, THE½** (1944) 72m PRC bw

Stuart Erwin *(Spencer)*, Robert "Buzzy" Henry *(Jimmy)*, Pierre Watkin *(Whitley)*, Gwen Kenyon *(Erin)*, Carl "Alfalfa" Switzer *(Speck)*, Edythe Elliott *(Mrs. Dolan)*, Marian Martin *(Kitty)*, Bob Meredith *(Sandy)*, Lane Chandler *(Hildur)*, Ed Cassidy *(Pronnett)*, William Halligan *(Doc Scott)*, Leon Tyler *(Junior)*, Charlie King *(Doc Slagle)*, Eddie Rocco *(Bill Slagle)*, Mike, Corky, Mickey *(Themselves)*.

Touching and improbable story about a boy, his dog, and a horse. The lad, Henry, believes that a horse carting a milk wagon has the makings of a champion racer and persuades a sportsman to let it run against his prized thoroughbred. The milk wagon puller wins and an illegal betting ring is broken up. The dog dies while heroically saving the horse from injury.

p, Leon Fromkess; d, Wallace W. Fox; w, Raymond L. Schrock (based on an original story by Martin Mooney); ph, Jockey A. Feindel; m, Lee Zahler; ed, Hugh Winn; art d, Paul Palmentola.

Children's Drama **(PR:A MPAA:NR)**

GREAT MISSOURI RAID, THE½** (1950) 84m PAR c

Wendell Corey *(Frank James)*, MacDonald Carey *(Jessie James)*, Ward Bond *(Major Trowbridge)*, Ellen Drew *(Bee Moore)*, Bruce Bennett *(Cole Younger)*, Bill Williams *(Jim Younger)*, Anne Revere *(Mrs. Samuels)*, Edgar Buchanan *(Dr. Samuels)*, Lois Chartrand *(Mary Bauer)*, Louis Jean Heydt *(Charles Ford)*, Barry Kelley *(Mr. Bauer)*, James Millican *(Sgt. Trowbridge)*, Paul Lees *(Bob Younger)*, Guy Wilkerson *(Clell Miller)*, Ethan Laidlaw *(Jim Cummings)*, Tom Tyler *(Allen Parmer)*, Steve Pendleton *(Arch Clements)*, Bob Bray *(Charlie Pitts)*, Paul Fix *(Sgt. Brill)*, James Griffith *(Jack Ladd)*, Bob Osterloh *(August)*, Alan Wells *(Dick Liddil)*, Whit Bissell *(Bob Ford)*.

Well done rendition of the James brothers' oft-recounted battles with the law. Corey stars as Frank and Carey stars as Jessie. After the Civil War, they murder a Union soldier who was questioning their parents about Frank's connection with William Quantrell, the notorious Kansas raider. Bond, the soldier's brother, vows revenge and dedicates his life to tracking them down. The boys hook up with the Younger brothers and go off on a spree of bank and train robberies and gunfights with the law. Like most James films, the movie ends with the Ford brothers, Heydt and Bissell, shooting Jessie in the back.

p, Nat Holt; d, Gordon Douglas; w, Frank Gruber; ph, Ray Rennahan (Technicolor); m, Paul Sawtell; ed, Philip Martin; art d, John Goodman.

Western **(PR:A MPAA:NR)**

GREAT MR. HANDEL, THE*½ (1942, Brit.) 89m Independent Producers-GHW/Midfilm c

Wilfrid Lawson *(Mr. Handel)*, Elizabeth Allan *(Mrs. Cibber)*, Malcolm Keen *(Lord Chesterfield)*, Michael Shepley *(Sir Charles Marsham)*, Max Kirby *(Frederick, Prince of Wales)*, Hay Petrie *(Phineas)*, Morris Harvey *(Heidegger)*, A.E. Matthews *(Charles Jennens)*, Frederick Cooper *(Pooley)*, Andrew Leigh *(Captain Coram)*, Trefor Jones *(Singer)*, Gladys Ripley *(Singing Voice of Mrs. Cibber)*, Robert Atkins, H.F. Maltby, Michael Hunt, Alan Wren, Ivan Samson, Charles Groves, Alfred Sangster, D.J. Williams, Amy Dalby, Alfred Harris, Dorothy Vernon, Charles Doe, Frank Atkinson, Len Sharr, Judith Nelmes, Victor MacClure, Jean Stanley.

The story of the 18th-century composer Handel, and his struggles with royalty and the church. Lawson plays the German composer who adopts England as his homeland. He has an altercation with a bishop of the church of England as he is to rehearse a choir to sing for the king's coronation, telling the bishop that he is a better Englishman than the bishop because he picked his nationality rather than being born to it. He also has a falling out with the Prince of Wales, Kirby, but atones by writing "The Messiah." The great composer's music makes up a large portion of the film score.

p, James B. Sloan; d, Norman Walker; w, L. Du Garde Peach, Gerald Elliott, Victor MacClure (based on a radio play by Peach); ph, Claude Friese-Greene, Jack Cardiff (Technicolor); ed, Sam Simmons; md, Ernest Irving.

Biography **(PR:A MPAA:NR)**

GREAT MR. NOBODY, THE½** (1941) 71m WB bw

Eddie Albert *(Dreamy)*, Joan Leslie *(Mary)*, Alan Hale *(Skipper)*, William Lundigan *(Amesworth)*, John Litel *(Wade)*, Charles Trowbridge *(Dillon)*, Paul Hurst *(O'Connor)*, Dickie Moore *(Limpy)*, John Ridgely *(Williams)*, Douglas Kennedy *(McGraw)*, George Campeau *(Hanes)*, William Benedict *(Jig)*, Helen MacKellar *(Mrs. Barnes)*, Joyce Tucker *(Janet)*, Mary Field *(Miss Frane)*.

Albert plays a bumbling newspaper classified ad salesman who is always getting into trouble with his employers. He hands out preprinted copy of job ads to his unemployed buddies and his creative promotional ideas are stolen from him and credited to others. He daydreams about marrying Leslie—a coworker—buying a boat, and sailing the seven seas with her and his roommate, Hale. He gets into all kinds of trouble and, of course, finally manages to straighten himself out.

p, William Jacobs; d, Ben Stoloff; w, Ben Markson, Kenneth Gamet (based on a story "The Stuff of Heroes" by Harold Titus); ph, Arthur Todd; m, Adolph Deutsch; ed, Rudi Fehr.

Comedy **(PR:A MPAA:NR)**

GREAT MOMENT, THE*** (1944) 83m PAR bw

Joel McCrea *(W. T. G. Morton)*, Betty Field *(Elizabeth Morton)*, Harry Carey *(Prof. Warren)*, William Demarest *(Eben Frost)*, Louis Jean Heydt *(Dr. Horace Wells)*, Julian Tannen *(Dr. Jackson)*, Edwin Maxwell *(V.P. Medical Society)*, Porter Hall *(President Pierce)*, Franklin Pangborn *(Dr. Heywood)*, Grady Sutton *(Homer Quinby)*, Donivee Lee *(Betty Morton)*, Harry Hayden *(Judge Shipman)*, Torben Meyer *(Dr. Dahlmeyer)*, Vic Potel *(Dental Patient)*, Thurston Hall *(Senator Borland)*, J. Farrell MacDonald *(The Priest)*, Robert Dudley *(Cashier-Charles)*, Robert Frandsen *(Mr. Abbott)*, Sylvia Field *(Young Mother)*, Reginald Sheffield *(Young Father)*, Robert Greig *(Morton's Butler)*, Sheila Sheldon *(Servant Girl)*, Harry Rosenthal *(Mr. Chamberlain)*, Frank Moran *(Porter)*.

McCrea plays the Boston dentist who discovered an agent to take most of the pain out of extracting teeth—and other surgical operations—anesthesia (the name given it by Dr. Oliver Wendell Holmes). The film follows McCrea from young student forced to turn to dentistry because of the expense of medical school to his experiments with ether. His not always understanding wife, Field, and his human guinea pig, Demarest, support him through all his trials and eventually he, first, becomes wealthy from his discovery, then donates it to mankind. Director Sturges, better known for his comedies, handles the drama and story well.

p,d&w, Preston Sturges (from the biography by Rene Fulop-Miller); ph, Victor Milnor; m, Victor Young; ed, Stuart Gilmore; art d, Hans Dreier, Ernst Fegte.

Biography **(PR:A MPAA:NR)**

GREAT MUPPET CAPER, THE*** (1981) 95m UNIV c

Jim Henson *(Kermit, Rowlf, Dr. Teeth, Waldorf, Swedish Chef)*, Frank Oz *(Miss Piggy, Fozzie Bear, Animal, Sam the Eagle)*, Dave Goelz *(The Great Gonzo, Beauregard, Zoot, Dr. Bunsen, Honeydew)*, Jerry Nelson *(Floyd, Pops, Lew Zealand)*, Richard Hunt *(Scooter, Statler, Sweetums, Janice, Beaker)*, Charles Grodin *(Nicky Holiday)*, Diana Rigg *(Lady Holiday)*, John Cleese, Robert Morley, Peter Ustinov, Jack Warden *(Guest Stars)*, Steve Whitmore *(Rizzo the Rat, Lips)*, Carroll Spinney *(Oscar the Grouch)*, Erica Creer *(Marla)*, Kate Howard *(Carla)*, Della Finch *(Darla)*, Michael Robbins *(Guard)*, Joan Sanderson *(Dorcas)*, Peter Hughes *(Maitre D')*, Peggy Aitchison *(Prison Guard)*, Tommy Godfrey *(Bus Conductor)*, Katia Borg, Valli Kemp, Michele Ivan-Zadeh, Chai Lee *(Models)*, Louise Gold, Kathryn Muller, Boy Payne, Brian Muehl, Mike Quinn, Robert Barnett, Hugh Spight, Brian Henson, Suzanne Church, Ian Hanham, David Ludwig, Christine Nelson, Rodney Lovick, Mary Mazstead, Patti Dalton, Cynthia Ashley, Lynn Latham, Susan Backlinie, Cynthia Leake, Sherrill Cannon, Kahren Lohren, Christine Cullen, Tricia McFarlin, Susie Guest, Denise McKenna, Wendy Holker, Melina Lee Phelps, Linda Horn, Denise Potter, Lee Keenan, Ann Rynne, Darine Klega, Roberta Ward, Peter Falk.

The Muppet menagerie cavorts in the middle of London in this, their second, film. Kermit, Fozzie Bear, and Gonzo are reporters investigating a jewel robbery of fashion queen Rigg. Rigg's brother, Grodin, sets up Miss Piggy for the blame for the theft, but the other muppets save the day by exposing Grodin as the real criminal. There are not as many guest-star cameo appearances as in the Muppets' first movie, but the ones that are here do a good job, and Miss Piggy's Busby Berkley-type dance and the Esther Williams-type water ballet are fun to watch.

p, David Lazer, Frank Oz; d, Jim Henson; w, Tom Patchett, Jay Tarses, Jerry Juhl, Jack Rose; ph, Oswald Morris (Technicolor); prod d, Harry Lange; ed, Ralph Kemplen; art d, Charles Bishop, Terry Ackland-Snow, Leigh Malone; m/l, Joe Raposo; cos, Julie Harris; ch, Anita Mann; Muppet cos, Calista Hendrickson, Mary Strieff, Joanne Green, Carol Spier, Danielle Obinger.

Comedy/Musical **Cas.** **(PR:AAA MPAA:G)**

GREAT NORTHFIELD, MINNESOTA RAID, THE**** (1972) 91m UNIV bw

Cliff Robertson *(Cole Younger)*, Robert Duvall *(Jesse James)*, Luke Askew *(Jim Younger)*, R.G. Armstrong *(Clell Miller)*, Dana Elcar *(Allen)*, Donald Moffat *(Manning)*, John Pearce *(Frank James)*, Matt Clark *(Bob Younger)*, Wayne Sutherlin *(Charley Pitts)*, Robert H. Harris *(Wilcox)*, Jack Manning *(Heywood)*, Elisha Cook, Jr. *(Bunker)*, Royal Dano *(Gustavson)*, Mary Robin Redd *(Kate)*, Bill Callaway *(Calliopist)*, Arthur Peterson *(Jefferson Jones)*, Craig Curtis *(Chadwell)*, Barry Brown *(Henry Wheeler)*, Nellie Burt *(Doll Woman)*, Liam Dunn *(Drummer)*, Madeleine Taylor Holmes *(Old Granny Woman)*, Herbert Nelson *(Chief Detective)*, Jack Manning *(Landlord)*, Erik Holland *(Sheriff)*, Anne Barton *(Clell's Wife)*, Marjorie Durant *(Maybelle)*, Inger Stratton *(Singing Whore)*, Velda J. Hansen *(Nude Girl)*, William Challee *(Old Timer)*, Robert Gravage *(Farmer)*.

An offbeat, ragged but totally absorbing western, this film profiles the James-Younger gang in realistic terms, showing them for the murderous and desperate men they truly were. The Missouri legislature prepares to vote on granting amnesty to outlaws Jesse James (Duvall) and Cole Younger (Robertson), members arguing that these men and their followers were driven into crime by powerful behind-the-scenes interests (railroads) that appropriated their lands. Robertson is willing to accept the amnesty and return to farming, but Duvall argues with him, telling him that the railroads will go on stealing their land anyway, that the persecution will never stop. He is right. Railroad magnates bribe the state's Speaker of the House to rule the amnesty motion out of order and Duvall makes plans to rob the big bank in Northfield, Minnesota, after reading a newspaper account about its financial standing as "the biggest bank west of the Mississippi." Robertson, portrayed as the real leader of the notorious outlaw band, withholds judgment and, through a Pinkerton ruse, is later shot in a bordello. He manages to escape to a cave where a hillbilly woman, Holmes, known as Old Granny Woman, mends him with secret herbal medication. He then hears that Duvall and the gang have departed for Northfield and rides ahead of them, getting to the town first. It's a Swedish community of hard-working farmers and shopkeepers and Robertson befriends the local banker, conning him out of a sack of gold and then publicly announcing that he intends to put his wealth into the bank's vault because the

James gang and other notorious outlaws make it too risky to carry money about, thus beefing up the deposits which he later intends to rob. The outlaw spends his time chatting with townspeople, visiting a local brothel, and admiring a calliope that sits outside the bank. When Duvall and men arrive, Robertson outlines the robbery for them but everything goes wrong. Dano, the town idiot, interferes with one of the gang members on watch outside the bank and is shot, falling upon the calliope which shrieks out a warning to the town. The hardy citizens arm themselves and, when the outlaws emerge from the bank, they are met with lethal gunfire. Several members are shot down but the James and Younger brothers manage to ride out of town, all terribly wounded except Duvall and Pearce. They take refuge with an old woman, Burt, who cares for the wounded men. Duvall had earlier "loaned" Burt money to pay off her mortgage but he later murders her and dresses in her clothes to escape, his brother Frank (Pearce) riding at his side as "her husband" back to Missouri. By then Robertson and his brothers, Askew and Clark, have gone in another direction and have been shot to pieces and captured by a massive posse. They are paraded back through the streets of Northfield in a rolling cage and Robertson, shot 11 times, stands up in a half-conscious state to accept the cheers of the citizens who applaud his grit. Although director-writer Kaufman claimed to have researched the real tale of the James-Younger gang while studying history at the University of Chicago, many of his facts are inaccurate and some scenes are outright fabrications (there is no evidence to support the scene where James killed the old lady who helped the gang and then escaped in drag), although the psychotic nature of Jesse James as portrayed in the film is well-founded, and Duvall gives a masterful interpretation of this mysterious and mythical outlaw. Robertson is superb as Cole Younger, a cunning, intelligent, and even sensitive person, while the supporting players are all believable and the well-mounted production drips of authenticity. The robbery (which occurred on September 7, 1876) is particularly well-staged and the awkward, crude, and unsophisticated dialog fits in nicely with how the times and people really were. This is not a western in any traditional sense but a violent, murky drama of the Middle West when it was still a frontier, as rough and unsure as its terrain and the polyglot immigrants who peopled it. This is one of the best profiles of the James-Younger gang, although THE LONG RIDERS more aptly captures the gang's character.

p, Jennings Lang; d, Philip Kaufman; w, Kaufman, ph, Bruce Surtees (Technicolor); m, Dave Grusin; ed, Douglas Stewart; art d, Alexander Golitzen, George Webb; set d, Hal Gausman; cos, Helen Colvig.

Western **(PR:O MPAA:PG)**

GREAT O'MALLEY, THE*** (1937) 71m WB bw

Pat O'Brien *(James Aloysius O'Malley)*, Humphrey Bogart *(John Phillips)*, Frieda Inescort *(Mrs. Phillips)*, Henry O'Neill *(Attorney for Defense)*, Hobart Cavanaugh *(Pinky Holden)*, Mary Gordon *(Mrs. O'Malley)*, Frank Sheridan *(Father Patrick)*, Delmar Watson *(Tubby)*, Sybill Jason *(Barbara Phillips)*, Ann Sheridan *(Judy Nolan)*, Donald Crisp *(Capt. Cromwell)*, Craig Reynolds *(Motorist)*, Gordon Hart *(Doctor)*, Mabel Colcord *(Mrs. Flaherty)*, Lillian Harmer *(Miss Taylor)*, Frank Reicher *(Dr. Larson)*, Jack Mower, Arthur Millet *(Detectives)*, Max Wagner *(Bus Driver)*, Charles Wilson *(Cop)*, Bob Perry *(Man Getting Shine)*.

O'Brien is a tough, uncompromising cop in this fast-paced vehicle where he gives out a ticket to one and all for the slightest infraction. So rule-book crazy is O'Brien that he is friendless on the force and in the streets; even his kind old mother, Gordon, is reserved about her intractable son. When reporter Cavanaugh lampoons O'Brien's strict code of law enforcement, his chief, Crisp, becomes incensed at having the police department ridiculed in the press. He demotes the cop, assigning him to the lowly position of crossing guard at an intersection. One of O'Brien's first victims is Bogart, who is unemployed and is driving to a job appointment in his rattletrap car. O'Brien stops him and gives him a ticket for a broken muffler and noisy exhaust. Moreover, O'Brien delays Bogart so long that he loses the job. Bogart returns home, thoroughly disillusioned, to his wife, Inescort, and crippled daughter, Jason, and becomes desperate for money with which to feed and house his family. He takes his medals won during WW I to a pawn shop and there gets into a squabble with the owner (a scene enacted many times in 1930s films, including I AM A FUGITIVE FROM A CHAIN GANG where WW I hero Paul Muni attempts to pawn his *Croix de Guerre)*. During the fight, Bogart knocks out the pawnbroker and, in a moment of weakness, takes all the money from the till. A short time later O'Brien arrests Bogart—unware of the robbery—for not having fixed his muffler. When the press learns of the kind of arrest O'Brien has made and how the police later discover Bogart's more serious crime, the newspapers have a field day chiding the cops. Next, Bogart's little lame daughter is run over at O'Brien's crossing and the cop, with the help of her school teacher, Sheridan, carries the injured girl home. Here O'Brien learns that she is the daughter of the man he has persecuted over a trivial infraction and that he was the cause of Bogart's wild moment of law-breaking. O'Brien becomes a changed man. He begs a great surgeon to operate on Jason and the girl is completely restored. O'Brien then testifies on behalf of Bogart and gets him released. He does more, going to the company where Bogart applied for a job and persuading the management to hire him. None of this is made known to Bogart who, when released, becomes half crazy at what O'Brien has done to him. He gets a gun and slightly wounds the cop but O'Brien prevents his arrest, claiming that the gun went off accidentally. When back on duty, O'Brien has a new outlook on life and becomes a tolerant though just policeman. His transformation brings love from Sheridan and friendship from Bogart. All is right with the world. THE GREAT O'MALLEY is performed charmingly and convincingly by O'Brien, and his supporting players, Bogart and Sheridan are, as always, top drawer. Dieterle's direction is speedy and Haller's lensing is sharp and fluid, although the script becomes occasionally syrupy. Bogart disliked this film, a comedown, he felt, from his stellar role as Duke Mantee in THE PETRIFIED FOREST. Actually, Jack Warner had not wanted Bogart as a contract player and was forced to take him on by Leslie Howard, the star Warner *had* to have for THE PETRIFIED FOREST. From that time on, Warner tried to get Bogart to break his contract by putting him in parts he knew he would despise, such as the role he played in THE GREAT O'MALLEY. Bogart, however, hung on until better roles came his way. Said the actor of this film: "It was terrible, but it was one of those things we did at that goddamed sweatshop *[Warner Bros]*. Pat was very good. Pat was never bad."

p, Harry Joe Brown; d, William Dieterle; w, Milton Krims, Tom Reed (based on the story "The Making of O'Malley" by Gerald Beaumont); ph, Ernest Haller; ed, Warren Low; m, Heinz Roemheld; art d, Hugh Reticker; cos, Milo Anderson; spec eff, James Gibbons, Fred Jackman, Jr., H.F. Koenekamp.

Drama **(PR:A MPAA:NR)**

GREAT PLANE ROBBERY, THE** (1940) 55m COL bw (AKA: KEEP HIM ALIVE)

Jack Holt *(Mike Henderson)*, Stanley Fields *(Frankie Toller)*, Vicki Lester *(Helen Carver)*, Noel Madison *(Joe Colson)*, Granville Owen *(Jim Day)*, Theodore Von Eltz *(Rod Brothers)*, Hobart Cavanaugh *(Homer Pringle)*, Milburn Stone *(Krebber)*, Paul Fix *(Eddie Lindo)*, Harry Cording *(Nick Harmon)*, John Hamilton *(Dr. Jamison)*, Doris Lloyd *(Mrs. Jamison)*, Lane Chandler *(Bill Whitcomb)*.

This B picture has insurance investigator Holt on board the same plane as recently released racketeer Madison. A $500,000 policy on Madison is shortly to expire and his old gang hijacks the plane. The heroic Holt subdues the bad guys and makes sure the plane doesn't crash and that Madison lives.

p, Larry Darmour; d, Lewis D. Collins; w, Albert DeMond (based on a story by Harold Greene); ph, James S. Browne, Jr.; m, Les Zahler; ed, Dwight Caldwell.

Crime **(PR:A MPAA:NR)**

GREAT PLANE ROBBERY*½ (1950) 61m UA bw

Tom Conway *(Ned Johnson)*, Margaret Hamilton *(Mrs. Judd)*, Steve Brodie *(Murray)*, Lynne Roberts *(Mary)*, David Bruce *(Carter)*, Marcel Journet *(Sebastian)*, Gilbert Frye *(Bill Arthur)*, Ralph Dunn *(Police Inspector Bruce)*, Lucille Barkley *(Miss Bennett)*, Paul Campbell *(George Harris)*, Beverly Jons *(Jane)*.

Cornball wisecracks add nothing to this lackluster drama. Plot centers around a murder and one accidental killing. Conway is the pilot of the plane where all this takes place, and Brodie is cast as the villain. With the unrealistic characters and terrible dialog given them, maybe the creators of this mess are the real villains.

p, Sam Baerwitz; d, Edward L. Cahn; w, Richard G. Hubler, Baerwitz (based on a story by Russell Rouse, Clarence Greene); ph, Jackson J. Rose; m, Edward J. Kay; ed, Norman A. Cerf; art d, F. Paul Saylos.

Drama **(PR:A MPAA:NR)**

GREAT PONY RAID, THE*½** (1968, Brit.) 58m AB-Pathe/CFF bw

Edward Underdown *(Snowy)*, Michael Brennan *(Butch)*, Christian Comber *(Tom)*, Tina Paget Brown *(Joan)*, Andrew Purcell *(Jim)*, Shelley Crowhurst *(Angela)*, Tim Killinback *(Joe)*, Patrick Barr *(Col. Gore)*.

When the English countryside of Dartmoor is invaded by a gang of rustlers who satisfy themselves with stealing ponies, it is up to a group of kids anxious for the safety of the ponies to organize a means of stopping the thieves.

p, Lionel Hoare; d, Frederic Goode; w, Wallace Bosco, Geoffrey Hayes (based on a story by Bosco).

Children's Adventure **(PR:AA MPAA:NR)**

GREAT POWER, THE zero (1929) 83m MGM bw

Hirshel Mayall *(John Power)*, Minna Gombell *(John Wray)*, Alan Birmingham *(Bruce Power)*, Nelan Jaap *(Frank Forrest)*, G. Davison Clark *(Judge Ben Forrest)*, John Anthony *(Sen. Dick Wray)*, Helen Shipman *(Peggy Wray)*, Jack Leslie *(Graves)*, Walter Walker *(Sen. Charles Davis)*, Conway Wingfield *(Rev. Dr. Elliott)*, Alfred Swenson *(District Attorney Crane)*, Walter F. Scott *(Jordan)*, Eleanor Martin *(Maid)*.

This disaster is based on a Broadway play which also flopped. The entire stage production was moved to Waterbury, Connecticut for filming, where it had to be shot twice because of an amateurish first effort. A new director, Rock, and a professional film crew were called in to finish this early talkie. Mayall is a multi-millionaire facing Judgment Day, and he can't find any witnesses for his defense. He is uniformly described as being cold, cruel, and miserly.

p, Franklin Warner; d, Joe Rock; w, Myron Fagan (based on his play); ed, Fagan.

Drama **(PR:A MPAA:NR)**

GREAT PROFILE, THE*** (1940) 79m FOX bw

John Barrymore *(Evans Garrick)*, Mary Beth Hughes *(Sylvia)*, Gregory Ratoff *(Boris Mefoofsky)*, John Payne *(Richard Lansing)*, Anne Baxter *(Mary Maxwell)*, Lionel Atwill *(Dr. Bruce)*, Edward Brophy *(Sylvester)*, Willie Fung *(Confucius)*, Joan Valerie *(Understudy)*, Charles Lane *(Director)*, Marc Lawrence *(Tony)*, Cecil Cunningham *(Miss Perkins)*, Hal K. Dawson *(Ticket Seller)*, William Pawley *(Electrician)*, Eddie Dunn *(Furniture Man)*, James Flavin *(Detective)*, Dorothy Dearing *(Debutante)*.

Art imitates life as Barrymore spoofs himself while playing a character who is a thinly-veiled version of the way he was living at the time. He's a drunken ham who gets thrown off a film and goes astray on a three-day drunk. Now he finds a lousy play and secures some backers for it, takes it to Chicago and opens it. Act One is a bust and Barrymore decides that he can ad-lib a better Act Two than what was written. So he juices up during the intermission and the second act is a riot. Ratoff plays Barrymore's long-suffering manager and Hughes his equally long-suffering wife. Ratoff is in the hole to gangster Brophy in a sub-plot that's quickly over. The smaller parts are all well cast, especially Atwill, Lane and Lawrence. But the major interest in the movie has to be Barrymore as himself and knowing full well that *we* knew that he was near the end of a career. He chews up the scenery with abandon, but that's exactly what we expect him to do so there is no surprise. It's almost a step past satire into burlesque, but Lang's direction keeps it in tow for the cheery ending. Payne is the backer and Baxter is the authoress; these roles could have been played by anyone for all the impact they had. Brophy and Ratoff are funny, although it's sad to see Barrymore, who was probably the greatest Hamlet the United States had ever seen, making such sport of himself. But he probably enjoyed doing it, at least that was the impression that one received from seeing this extraordinary film. Marc Lawrence plays his usual heavy, a role he's been doing for almost 50 years . . . and nobody does it better.

p, Darryl F. Zanuck; d, Walter Lang; w, Milton Sperling, Hilary Lynn; ph, Ernest Palmer; ed, Francis D. Lynon; md, Cyril Mockridge; art d, Richard Day, Joseph C. Wright.

Comedy   **Cas.**   **(PR:A MPAA:NR)**

GREAT RACE, THE*** (1965) 157m WB c

Tony Curtis (*The Great Leslie*), Jack Lemmon (*Prof. Fate*), Natalie Wood (*Maggie DuBois*), Peter Falk (*Max*), Keenan Wynn (*Hezekiah*), Arthur O'Connell (*Henry Goodbody*), Vivian Vance (*Hester Goodbody*), Dorothy Provine (*Lily Olay*), Larry Storch (*Texas Jack*), Ross Martin (*Baron Rolfe Von Stuppe*), George Macready (*Gen. Kuhster*), Marvin Kaplan (*Frisbee*), Hal Smith (*Mayor of Boracho*), Denver Pyle (*Sheriff*), William Bryant (*Baron's Guard*), Ken Wales (*Baron's Guard*), J. Edward McKinley (*Chairman*), Art Stewart (*Man*), Maria Schroeder (*Women in Tobelsk*), Patricia King, Joyce Nizzari (*Women in Western Scene*), Greg Benedict, Chuck Hayward (*Soldiers*), Francis McDonald (*Russian*), Dick Alexander (*Extra*), Robert S. Carson (*Vice Chairman*), Paul Smith, actor 1 (*First Employee*) Frank Kreig (*Starter*), Charles Fredericks (*M.C.*), Clegg Hoyt (*Man*), Charles Steel (*Freight Agent*), Joe Palma (*Conductor*), Paul Bryar (*Policeman*), Chester Hayes (*Man in Bear Suit*), John Truax (*Prison Guard*), Johnny Silver, Hal Riddle (*Bakers*).

A silly, happy, zany, cross-continental romp, THE GREAT RACE would have cost more than $50 million if made today. Both panned and praised when it was released, THE GREAT RACE zooms ahead full throttle for all of its 157 minutes. Tony Curtis is "The Great Leslie" and Lemmon is the arch villain, "Professor Fate." They battle each other the instant the green flag is dropped. Falk is Lemmon's cackling Igor-like sidekick, Max, and together they scheme to best Curtis in a 22,000-mile road race from New York City to the Eiffel Tower in Paris. The year is 1908 and the period cars are a delight to the eye. Wood is the femme fatale who also hopes to win the race. It begins and they're off. Well, at least *some* are off. Wood's car breaks down almost instantly and she reluctantly rides along with Curtis and his ace mechanic, Wynn. Lemmon's car is sort of an evolutionary precursor to the MAD MAX vehicle. The Hannibal 8 is equipped with a cannon, smoke screen sprayer, and sundry other gadgets especially intended to wipe out Curtis, a gleaming-toothed, jut-jawed hero in the old mold. Curtis is always dressed in glowing white and when the most elaborate pie fight in filmdom takes place, he comes out spotless. Right from the start it's a two-car race, as Lemmon knocks off all the other autos. The mishaps that follow include a Western brawl and just about every sight gag devised by anyone who made a silent movie. That's the problem with this film: we get the feeling that we've seen it all before, in black and white, and with a lot more taste and artistry. The two cars meet in Alaska enroute to Siberia. As they ride side-by-side on ice floes, Lemmon and Falk kidnap Wood and whisk her off to the mythical country of Carpania where Lemmon, in a spoof of THE PRISONER OF ZENDA, plays an effete king. Watching Lemmon camp it up and the villainous Falk is almost worth the price of admission. In another satire of film (the Errol Flynn and Basil Rathbone swashbuckling clashes), Curtis sword fights with Ross Martin, the nefarious Baron Von Stuppe (the same name used by Mel Brooks for Madeline Kahn's character in BLAZING SADDLES). Curtis foils Martin's plans to incite revolution. The pie fight ensues and some have hailed this as the transcendent masterpiece of slapstick on film. Wood rejoins Curtis and from there it's a race to the finish. Once defeated, Lemmon demands a rematch via a return to New York, and they're off again. Several attempts at "big" comedies followed this, but none approached this success. THE GREAT RACE runs far too long however, and its direction is far too indulgent. Many of the jokes don't pay off, but it's still funny enough to merit your attention. The technical credits are wonderful and the costumes and sets seem authentic. Mancini's fun score adds pace and flow. Don't expect the controlled lunacy of Laurel and Hardy. This spectacle is almost totally uncontrolled and therein lies much of its charm.

p, Martin Jurow; d, Blake Edwards; w, Arthur Ross (based on a story by Ross and Edwards); ph, Russell Harlan (Panavision, Technicolor); m, Henry Mancini; ed, Ralph E. Winters; prod d, Fernando Carrerre; set d, George James Hopkins; cos, Edith Head; ch, Hermes Pan; m/l, Mancini, Johnny Mercer ("The Sweetheart Tree" sung by Wood).

Comedy   **Cas.**   **(PR:A-C MPAA:NR)**

GREAT RADIO MYSTERY, THE   (SEE: TAKE THE STAND, 1934)

GREAT RUPERT, THE*** (1950) 86m Eagle Lion bw

Jimmy Durante (*Mr. Amendola*), Terry Moore (*Rosalinda*), Tom Drake (*Peter Dingle*), Frank Orth (*Mr. Dingle*), Sarah Haden (*Mrs. Dingle*), Queenie Smith (*Mrs. Amendola*), Chick Chandler (*Phil Davis*), Jimmy Conlin (*Joe Mahoney*), Hugh Sanders (*Mulligan*), Donald T. Beddoe (*Mr. Haggerty*), Cindy Candido (*Molineri*), Clancy Cooper (*Policeman*), Harold Goodwin (*FBI Man*), Frank Cady (*Tax Investigator*).

Entertaining fluff stars Durante and a squirrel (which is actually a puppet) in renowned animator Pal's directorial debut in feature film. Durante heads a hard luck family of acrobats who suddenly find gobs of money stashed throughout their house. The squirrel has been stealthily taking money from a miserly neighbor. The family's bubble bursts when a suspicious FBI agent starts snooping around to find out the source of their riches. Just as Durante is about to be hauled off to jail as a racketeer, a fire exposes the mystery of the money. Moore and Drake provide the romance, while Durante wonderfully mugs his way through the film.

p, George Pal; d, Irving Pichel; w, Laslo Vadnay (based on a story by Ted Allen); ph, Lionel Lindon; m, Fred Spielman, Buddy Kaye; ed, Duke Goldstone.

Comedy   **(PR:AA MPAA:NR)**

GREAT ST. LOUIS BANK ROBBERY, THE*½ (1959) 85m UA bw

Steve McQueen (*George Fowler*), David Clarke (*Gino*), Crahan Denton (*John Egan*), Molly McCarthy (*Ann*), James Dukas (*Willie*), The St. Louis Police Department.

This attempt to create a realistic depiction of the scheming and actual undertaking of a bank heist is a failure in that the long- drawn-out expose of four men going through routine tasks gets to be a bit boring, and can only leave the viewer fidgeting about in his seat. McQueen is the driver of the getaway car for the heist that ends in tragedy as the police come around to greet the four men before they can make a clean escape. Though some headway is gained by showing fears and acts of irrationality (McCarthy, sister to one robber and McQueen's supposed girl friend, is needlessly shot for objecting to the plan) the young men are driven to, but much more action is needed for the entire hour and half.

p&d, Charles Guggenheim; d, Guggenheim, John Stix; w, Richard Heffron; ph, Victor Duncan; m, Bernardo Segall; ed, Warren Adams; md, Hershy Kay; m/l, Segall, Peter Ude, Jim Symington (sung by Symington).

Crime   **(PR:C-O MPAA:NR)**

GREAT ST. TRINIAN'S TRAIN ROBBERY, THE**½ (1966, Brit.) 94m Braywild BL c

Frankie Howard (*Alphonse Askett*), Reg Varney (*Gilbert*), Desmond Walter Ellis (*Leonard Edwards*), Cyril Chamberlain (*Maxie*), Arthur Mullard (*Big Jim*), Stratford Johns (*The Voice*), Raymond Huntley (*The Minister*), Richard Wattis (*Bassett*), Peter Gilmore (*Butters*), Eric Barker (*Culpepper Brown*), George Benson (*Gore-Blackwood*), Michael Ripper (*Liftman*), Godfrey Winn (*Truelove*), Dora Bryan (*Amber Spottiswood*), Barbara Couper (*Mabel Radnage*), Margaret Nolan (*Susie Naphill*), Elspeth Duxbury (*Veronica Bledlow*), Maggie McGrath (*Magsa O'Riley*), Carole Ann Ford (*Albertine*), Jean St. Clair (*Drunken Dolly*), George Cole (*Flash Harry*), Portland Mason (*Georgina*), Maureen Crombie (*Marcia Askett*), Colin Gordon (*Noakes*), Leon Thau (*Pakistani Porter*), Meredith Edwards (*Chairman*), Norman Mitchell (*William*), Larry Martin (*Chips*), Lisa Lee (*Miss Brenner*), Edwina Coven (*Dr. Judd*), Jeremy Clyde (*Monty*), Aubrey Morris (*Hutch*), William Kendall (*Mr. Parker*), Terry Scott.

Madcap yarn dealing with the farcical exploits of the trouble-making girls of St. Trinian. The plot involves a group of train robbers who hide $7 million in a deserted country mansion, and upon returning years later find the mansion has been converted into the St. Trinian School. They try to recover the loot, but are booted out by the hockey stick toting girls. Their problems really multiply when they make a second attempt to retrieve the money on parent's day, climaxing in a slapstick train chase between the robbers and the girls.

p&d, Frank Launder, Sidney Gilliat; w, Launder, Ivor Herbert (based on Ronald Searle's cartoon characters); ph, Kenneth Hodges (Eastmancolor); m, Malcolm Arnold; ed, Geoffrey Foot; art d, Albert Witherick.

Comedy   **Cas.**   **(PR:AA MPAA:NR)**

GREAT SANTINI, THE**** (1979) 115m ORION/WB c

Robert Duvall (*Bull Meechum*), Blythe Danner (*Lillian Meechum*), Michael O'Keefe (*Ben Meechum*), Lisa Jane Persky (*Mary Anne Meechum*), Julie Anne Haddock (*Karen Meechum*), Brian Andrews (*Matthew Meechum*), Stan Shaw (*Toomer Smalls*), Theresa Merritt (*Arrabelle Smalls*), David Keith (*Red Pettus*), Paul Mantee (*Col. Hedgepath*).

A touching drama with standout performances by everyone concerned, and yet THE GREAT SANTINI fared poorly at the box office. The problem may have been the name, which came from a novel by Pat Conroy (author of CONRACK) and may have been a fine title for a novel, but as a film it led people to believe they were going to see something different. Duvall is a harsh military man who raises his children as though they were soldiers in his cadre. His methods go far beyond the usual martinet's, and he abuses almost everyone who comes into contact with his sharp tongue. The major difficulty in the man's life is that he is a soldier with no war to fight. His main target is his son, O'Keefe, star of the local basketball team. One of the highlights of the film is a one-on-one basketball game between father and son whereby Duvall uses every sort of underhanded move to beat the boy. As a military man, Duvall never spends more than 18 months in any given location, hardly enough time for the kids to make any permanent friends, so they must rely upon each other and their relationship with their parents. Tension begins almost immediately, as we see the cruel treatment handed out by Duvall to his recruits. As the "warrior without a war," Duvall is superb, and this performance was probably better than the one that landed him the Oscar in TENDER MERCIES. Danner does her usual good work as Duvall's long-suffering wife, forever making excuses for the man she loves. O'Keefe scores as the young man who has the misfortune to be born the son of the wrong kind of father, a man who is only happy when dominating everyone around him. Persky, who is rapidly becoming a force on the stage (she appeared in the American version of "Steaming," the British play that featured female nudity) is totally believable as the eldest daughter. The picture becomes bogged down in an unnecessary subplot with O'Keefe's best friend, Shaw, a black man being teased and pestered by bigot Keith. The ending is a disappointment in dramaturgy, but probably very true to life. To reveal what happens to Duvall would be to do a disservice to anyone interested in seeing this film. Veteran character actor Mantee is seen in a small but telling role, the kind he does so well. Filmed in Beaufort, South Carolina, the surroundings are as authentic as corn pone. Academy nominations went to both Duvall and O'Keefe.

p, Charles A. Pratt; d&w, Lewis John Carlino (based on the novel by Pat Conroy); ph, Ralph Woolsey; m, Elmer Bernstein; ed, Houseley Stevenson; prod d, Jack Poplin; set d, Jeff Haley, Don Sullivan.

Drama **Cas.** **(PRC: MPAA:PG)**

GREAT SCHNOZZLE, THE (SEE: PALOOKA, 1934)

GREAT SCOUT AND CATHOUSE THURSDAY, THE* (1976) 102m AIP c (AKA: WILDCAT)

Lee Marvin *(Sam Longwood)*, Oliver Reed *(Joe Knox)*, Robert Culp *(Jack Colby)*, Elizabeth Ashley *(Nancy Sue)*, Strother Martin *(Billy)*, Sylvia Miles *(Mike)*, Kay Lenz *(Thursday)*, Howard Platt *(Vishniac)*, Joe Zacha *(Trainer)*, Phaedra *(Friday)*, Leticia Robles *(Saturday)*, Luz Maria Pena *(Holidays)*, Erika Carlson *(Monday)*, C.C. Charity *(Tuesday)*, Ann Verdugo *(Wednesday)*.

Plenty of dull jokes and childish slapstick doom this supposed comedy from the start. Two former partners in crime, Marvin and Reed, get together to plot revenge on Culp, a third partner who cheated them out of some money they had stolen. Only problem, Culp has used the money to join high society, and getting to him will be tougher than they thought. Lenz plays a prostitute who has a May-December romantic fling with Marvin. Fling this one right out the window.

p, Jules Buck, David Korda; d, Don Taylor; w, Richard Shapiro; ph, Alex Phillips, Jr. (Technicolor); m, John Cameron; ed, Sheldon Kahn; prod d, Jack Martin Smith; set d, Enrique Esteves; cos, Rene Conley; stunts, Jerry Gatlin.

Western Comedy **Cas.** **(PR:O MPAA:PG)**

GREAT SINNER, THE*½** (1949) 110m MGM bw

Gregory Peck *(Feodor Dostoyevsky)*, Ava Gardner *(Pauline Ostrovski)*, Melvyn Douglas *(Armand Le Glasse)*, Walter Huston *(Gen. Osrtrovski)*, Ethel Barrymore *(Granny)*, Frank Morgan *(Aristide Pitard)*, Agnes Moorehead *(Emma Getzel)*, Ludwig Stossel *(Hotel Manager)*, Ludwig Donath *(Doctor)*, Erno Verebes *(Hotel Valet)*, Curt Bois *(Jeweler)*, Martin Garralaga *(Maharajah)*, Antonio Filauri *(Senor Pinto)*, Frederick Ledebur *(Le Glasse's Secretary)*, Vincent Renno *(Casino Inspector)*, William H. Hawes *(Nervous Englishman)*, Andre Charlot *(Distinguished Man)*, Sam Scar *(Turk)*, Elsa Heims *(Woman with Cigar)*, Joan Miller *(Cold Sexy Woman)*, John Piffle *(Fat Man)*, Emil Rameau *(Fearful Old Man)*, Elspeth Dudgeon *(Fearful Old Woman)*, James Anderson *(Nervous Young Man)*, Charles Wagenheim *(Man with Ring)*, Gisella Werbisek *(Greedy Woman)*, Hannelore Axmann *(Staring Woman)*, Lorraine Crawford *(Pretty Blonde)*, Ann Sturgis *(Pretty Brunette)*, Leonid Kinskey *(Band Leader)*, Ilka Gruning *(Duenna)*, Fred Nurney *(Porter)*, David McMahon *(Station Master)*, Bob Stevenson, Daniel DeJohghe, Michael Macey, Joe Ploski, Victor Denny *(Hotel Valets)*, Sue Casey *(Pretty Girl)*, Frank Elliott *(Englishman)*, Lisa Golm *(Elderly Lady)*, Jean Del Val, Sayre Deering, Perry Ivins, John Arnold *(Croupiers)*, Bert Hanlon *(Porter)*, Jeraldine Jordan *(Maid)*, George Paris *(Soldier)*, Tom Ingersoll, Wheaton Chambers *(Priests)*, Peter Scott *(Cabaret Waiter)*, Erica Strong *(Girl in Flower Shop)*, Martha Bamattre *(Woman Fountain Attendant)*, Everett Glass *(Pince-nez Man)*, Frank Jacquet *(Doorman)*, Neal Dowd *(Young Man)*, Eloise Hardt *(Young Girl)*, Dick Simmons *(Voice)*, Irene Seidner *(Woman Vendor)*, Fred Lorenz *(Conductor)*, Hans Hopf *(Hurdy-Gurdy Man)*, Marianne Budrow *(Little Girl)*, Lotte Stein *(Buxom Woman)*, Ken Tobey *(Cabby)*, Walter Rode, June Booth *(Couple in Room)*, Max Willenz *(Policeman)*, Manfred Furst *(Mr. Huber)*, Betty Jane Howarth *(Girl at Baccarat Table)*, John Cortay *(Inspector)*.

An often gripping film, based on Dostoyevsky's classic 1866 story, "The Gambler" (though uncredited by the producers of this film), Peck is an honorable writer who falls in love with Gardner, but learns that her father, Huston, an inveterate gambler, is horribly in debt to casino owner Douglas and that he and she are almost chattel to the smooth gambling czar. Peck thinks to rescue the pair and redeem their IOU's by beating Douglas at this own gaming tables. At first, it appears as though he will be able to accomplish the impossible. He wins and wins, his beginner's luck triumphing with every turn of the cards, roll of the dice, spin of the wheel. Magnanimously, Peck begins to repay Huston's debt to Douglas who takes it all with smiling smugness; he knows the outcome. Then Peck's luck turns bad and his long losing streak plummets his personal fortunes so that he uses up his money, his future royalties, even the gems Gardner has long held back from her own father's use. There are stunning scenes that haunt such as the grand entrance into the casino by noblewoman Barrymore, Ava's grandmother, who is accompanied by a retinue of servants carrying a large silver box containing the family's heirlooms. She intends to redeem the family fortune herself but is devastated when she gambles herself into bankruptcy. The upbeat ending is contrived by Hollywood in that Peck is shown dashing off a literary masterpiece which saves all from ruination. (Undoubtedly writers Fodor and Isherwood had in mind *Crime and Punishment* which appeared in the same year Dostoyevsky wrote "The Gambler.") Peck is powerful as the obsessed gambler, and Gardner was never more ravishing. Huston is a wonderful bewhiskered rapscallion and Douglas, as the slick casino operator, is a man you love to hate. The art and set people excelled here, recreating sumptuous sets of the high fashion gambling rooms, hotels, and salons of 19th century Wiesbaden. Of course Peck's role is not only based on the Dostoyevsky character in the short story, one Aleksei Ivanovich, but on the author himself, who lost his entire fortune not once but several times at the gambling tables in Leipzig. Gardner's role is based on the author's mistress, Polina Suslov, who deserted him when the money ran out. Peck, then still an aspiring actor, though well established with such films as YELLOW SKY (1948), DUEL IN THE SUN (1946), THE PARADINE CASE (1948), THE YEARLING (1946) and GENTLEMAN'S AGREEMENT (1947), sought out Huston's advice during the production. The older man, one of the greatest character actors ever, would not, however, impart any real information about acting. He disliked it, he said, and talked about sports instead. When Peck persisted, Huston's advice came down to one line: "Give 'em a good show and always travel first class."

p, Gottfried Reinhardt; d, Robert Siodmak; w, Ladislas Fodor, Christopher Isherwood (based on a story by Fodor, Rene Fulop-Miller, and, uncredited Feodor Dostoyevsky's "The Gambler"); ph, George Folsey; m, Bronislau Kaper; ed, Harold F. Kress; md, Andre Previn; art d, Cedric Gibbons, Hans Peters; set d, Edwin B. Willis, Henry W. Grace; cos, Irene Valles; spec eff, Warren Newcombe; makeup, Jack Dawn.

Drama **(PR:A MPAA:NR)**

GREAT SIOUX MASSACRE, THE½** (1965) 92m F.&F./COL c (AKA: CUSTER MASSACRE; THE MASSACRE AT THE ROSEBUD)

Joseph Cotten *(Maj. Reno)*, Darren McGavin *(Capt. Benton)*, Philip Carey *(Col. Custer)*, Julie Sommars *(Caroline Reno)*, Nancy Kovack *(Libbie Custer)*, John Matthews *(Dakota)*, Michael Pate *(Sitting Bull)*, Don Haggerty *(Sen. Blaine)*, Frank Ferguson *(Gen. Terry)*, Stacy Harris *(Mr. Turner)*, Iron Eyes Cody *(Crazy Horse)*, House Peters, Jr. *(Reporter)*, John Napier *(Tom Custer)*, William Tannen *(Miner)*, Blair Davies *(Presiding Officer)*, Louise Serpa *(Mrs. Turner)*.

Another look at what happened to Custer and his troopers at the Battle of Little Big Horn. This time the story is told through the eyes of two of Custer's officers, played by Cotten and McGavin. Custer, as portrayed by Carey, is an outspoken believer in fair treatment for the Indians and goes so far as to accuse powerful Washington politicians of corruption in their dealings with them. For this Carey is ousted from his post and forced into retirement. At this point, he is approached by Haggerty, a senator who convinces the former colonel to forget his high ideals and join him in a plan to make Carey the next president. Ambition takes over and Carey decides to upstage Gen. Terry, played by Ferguson, at Little Big Horn. But in his rush to do battle, Carey ultimately meets his death. Ironically, a military board later dismisses the entire matter as innocent.

p, Leon Fromkess; d, Sidney Salkow; w, Fred C. Dobbs (based on a story by Salkow, Marvin Gluck); ph, Irving Lippman (Pathe Color); m, Emil Newman, Edward B. Powell; ed, William Austin; art d, Frank P. Sylos.

Western **(PR:A MPAA:NR)**

GREAT SIOUX UPRISING, THE** (1953) 79m UNIV c

Jeff Chandler *(Jonathan Westgate)*, Faith Domergue *(Joan Britton)*, Lyle Bettger *(Stephen Cook)*, Stacy Harris *(Uriah)*, Peter Whitney *(Ahab Jones)*, Walter Sande *(Joe Baird)*, Stephen Chase *(Maj. McKay)*, John War Eagle *(Red Cloud)*, Glenn Strange *(Stand Watie)*, Charles Arnt *(Gist)*, Julia Montoya *(Heyoka)*, Dewey Drapeau *(Teo-Ka-Ha)*, Boyd "Red" Morgan *(Ray)*, Lane Bradford *(Lee)*, Jack Ingram *(Sam)*, Clem Fuller *(Jake)*, Ray Bennett *(Sgt. Manners)*.

Dull western sees Chandler as a surgeon-turned-horse-doctor due to a hand injury, who moves West to lead the quiet life. Yet things are anything but peaceful in the small town of Laramie Junction, which is also the headquarters of crooked horse dealer Bettger. Though he appears to be a fair playing rancher, Bettger actually makes a living rustling horses from the Sioux Indians and selling them to the army. The smaller ranchers hate him because of his underhanded buying tactics with them, and to complicate matters, the Sioux are soon on his warpath, as well. Along comes Chandler, who calms the Indian chief by promising to find the rustler, and helps organize the ranchers so they can sell their horses directly to the army, rather than using Bettger as their middleman. But Bettger frames the doctor and tries to throw the ranchers and Indians against him, which nearly causes the army troops to attack the Sioux. Chandler acts quickly to clear himself, thus preventing a war and bringing Bettger to justice.

p, Albert J. Cohen; d, Lloyd Bacon; w, Melvin Levy, J. Robert Bren, Gladys Atwater (based on a story by Bren, Atwater); ph, Maury Gertsman (Technicolor); ed, Edward Curtiss; art d, Alexander Golitzen, Alfred Sweeney.

Western **(PR:A MPAA:NR)**

GREAT SMOKEY ROADBLOCK, THE½** (1978) 100m Mar Vista-Ingo Preminger/Dimension c (AKA: THE LAST OF THE COWBOYS)

Henry Fonda *(Elegant John)*, Eileen Brennan *(Penelope)*, Robert Englund *(Beebo)*, John Byner *(Disc Jockey)*, Austin Pendelton *(Guido)*, Susan Sarandon *(Ginny)*, Melanie Mayron *(Lulu)*, Marya Small *(Alice)*, Leigh French *(Glinda)*, Dana House *(Celeste)*, Gary Sandy, Johnnie Collins III, Valerie Curtin, Bibi Osterwald.

Fonda is an aging trucker, ready to make one last cross-country run before packing it in. After he is hospitalized with a minor illness, his beloved 18-wheel rig is repossessed and he breaks out to steal it back. He then heads out to see his old flame, Brennan, who now runs a brothel and is having some problems with the law. They decide that Fonda's last run should include taking her and the girls across the country, so everyone piles in and they head off, with the police in hot pursuit. The girls use their talents along the way to make gas money and the entire effort receives media attention from both television, as well as a wild disc jockey, played by Byner. The climactic finish sees Fonda ram his truck through a three car-deep police blockade. He dies in Brennan's arms with a look of profound achievement. Though completed in 1976, this was not released for two years. The original title was THE LAST OF THE COWBOYS, and Fonda, not knowing that truckers were popularly referred to as "cowboys," at first said he wouldn't take the part because he didn't want to ride a horse at his age. This film has a good sense of fun to it and Fonda seemed to be having the time of his life, giving a good performance despite the fact he was wearing both a pacemaker and hearing aid during filming.

p, Allan F. Bodoh; d&w, John Leone; ph, Ed Brown, Sr.; m, Craig Safan.

Action/Drama **Cas.** **(PR:C MPAA:PG)**

GREAT SPY CHASE, THE½** (1966, Fr.) 84m S.N.E. Gaumont/A.I.P. bw (LES BARBOUZES)

Lino Ventura *(Lagneau)*, Bernard Blair *(Cafarelli)*, Francis Blanche *(Vassilieff)*, Mireille Darc *(Amaranthe)*, Charles Millot *(Muller)*, Andre Weber *(Rossini)*, Jess Hahn *(O'Brien)*, Jacques Balutin *(Le Douanier)*, Robert Dalban *(Le Camionneur)*, Michele Marceau *(Rosalinde)*, Noel Roquevert.

Silly farce involving the exploits of four secret agents—French, Russian, Swiss, and German—and their efforts to ply some secrets from the widow of a scientist. Of course things are just a little out of the ordinary, seeing how her husband died in a brothel and she is a retired stripper. The CIA and some Chinese Communists are also along for the fun. Eventually the Frenchman uses his native skills to seduce the poor woman, only to end up in trouble with his wife. Some good satire and farcical elements here.

p&d, Georges Lautner; w, Michel Audiard, Albert Simonin; ph, Maurice Fellous; m, Michel Magne; art d, Jacques D'Ovidio.

Spy Comedy   **(PR:C   MPAA:NR)**

GREAT SPY MISSION, THE   (SEE: OPERATION CROSSBOW, 1965)

GREATEST BATTLE ON EARTH, THE   (SEE: GHIDRAH, THE THREE-HEADED MONSTER, 1965, Jap.)

GREAT STAGECOACH ROBBERY**   (1945) 56m REP bw

Bill Elliott, Bobby Blake, Alice Fleming, Francis McDonald, Don Costello, Sylvia Arslan, Bud Geary, Leon Tyler, Freddie Chapman, Henry Wills, Hank Bell, Bob Wilke, John James, Tom London, Dickie Dillon, Bobby Dillon, Raymond ZeBrack, Patsy May, Chris Wren, Horace Carpenter, Grace Cunard, Frederick Howard.

A twist to the usual oater theme throws in an element of humanity when Elliott takes it upon himself to set an example for a young man lost in idealized romanticism about his outlaw father. Ample opportunity remains for Elliott to display his fancy form of gun handling, enough at least to convince the youth that a life of crime is not necessarily the most heralded. (See RED RYDER Series, Index).

p, Louis Gray; d, Lesley Selander; w, Randall Faye; ph, Bud Thackery; ed, Charles Craft; md, Richard Cherwin; art d, Fred A. Ritter.

Western   **(PR:A   MPAA:NR)**

GREAT STUFF*   (1933, Brit.) 50m BL/FOX bw

Henry Kendall (Archie Brown), Betty Astell (Vera Montgomery), Alfred Wellesley (Vernon Montgomery), Barbara Gott (Claudette Montgomery), Hal Walters (Spud), Ernest Sefton (Captain), Gladys Hamer (Cook), Ernest Childerstone.

Inane farce based on the attempts of a millionaire couple to keep their daughter Astell from marrying a man, Kendall, they fear may have reasons other than love for taking the girl to the altar. However, all their worries prove to be unwarranted. First, though, the parents must make fools out of themselves by pretending to rob their own house. One of the innumerable British comedies from the 1930s which never withstood the test of time.

p, Herbert Smith; d, Leslie Hiscott; w, Michael Barringer (based on a story by Brandon Fleming).

Comedy   **(PR:A   MPAA:NR)**

GREAT SWINDLE, THE*½   (1941) 58m COL bw

Jack Holt (Jack Regan), Jonathan Hale (Swann), Henry Kolker (Stewart Cordell), Marjorie Reynolds (Margaret Swann), Don Douglas (Bill Farrow), Boyd Irwin (Thomas Marshall), Sidney Blackmer (Dave Lennox), Douglas Fowley (Rocky Andrews), Tom Kennedy (Capper Smith).

A trite tale of crusading insurance investigator Holt, who is called in to uncover the source of a warehouse arson. Holt manages to get some incriminating photographs, only to have them stolen from his apartment before they can be used for evidence. He goes on to accuse everyone but the right person of the crime and even gets himself fired from his job before finally tracking down the culprit. Plot is slow and confusing at times.

p, Larry Darmour; d, Lewis D. Collins; w, Albert DeMond (story by Eric Taylor); ph, James S. Brown, Jr.; ed, Dwight Caldwell.

Mystery   **(PR:A   MPAA:NR)**

GREAT TEXAS DYNAMITE CHASE, THE**½   (1976) 90m Yasny Talking Pictures II/New World Pictures c (AKA: DYNAMITE WOMEN)

Claudia Jennings (Candy Morgan), Jocelyn Jones (Ellie Jo Turner), Johnny Crawford (Slim), Chris Pennock (Jake), Tara Strohmeier (Pam Morgan), Miles Watkins (Boyfriend), Bart Braverman (Freddie), Nancy Bleier (Carol), Buddy Kling (Mr. Sherman), Tom Rosqui (Jason Morgan), Eric Boles (Johnny), Stefan Gierasch (Robert Simon), Don Elson (Mr. Smith).

This low budget sexploitation film stars Jennings and Jones as a couple of female bank robbers who prefer dynamite instead of guns. It starts with Jennings blasting her way out of prison, and then blowing up a bank where Jones has just been fired from her job. The two join forces and go on a bank-robbing spree. When Jones gets caught shoplifting, the two hole up in the store and take Crawford as a hostage. He and Jones become lovers and the women use him as a hostage in all the banks they knock off. After some narrow escapes, including one where Crawford gets shot, they get trapped in a barn by police. But in a rousing climax, they blow up their car and ride away on horses in the confusion. Jennings was the 1970 Playboy Playmate of the year and made a few B films (GATOR BAIT and DEATHSPORT) before dying in a 1979 car crash in California.

p, David Irving; d, Michael Pressman; w, David Kirkpatrick, Mark Rosin; ph, Jamie Anderson (Metrocolor); m, Craig Safan; ed, Millie Moore; prod d, Russell Smith.

Crime   **Cas.**   **(PR:O   MPAA:R)**

GREAT TRAIN ROBBERY, THE*½   (1941) 62m REP bw

Bob Steele (Tom Logan), Claire Carleton (Kay Stevens), Milburn Stone (Duke Logan), Helen MacKellar (Mrs. Logan), Si Jenks (Whiskers), Monte Blue (The Super), Hal Taliaferro (Pierce), George Guhl (Jones), Jay Novello (Santos), Yakima

Canutt (Klefner), Dick Wessel (Gorman), Lew Kelly (Dad Halliday), Guy Usher (Barnsdale).

Steele is a railroad detective sent to guard a shipment of gold. Looking to steal the gold is Steele's crooked brother Stone, and of course the old triangle—two brothers in love with the same girl, Carleton—complicates matters.

p&d, Joseph Kane; w, Olive Cooper, Garnett Weston, Robert T. Shannon; ph, Reggie Lanning; m, Cy Feuer; ed, Lester Orlebeck.

Crime/Drama   **(PR:A   MPAA:NR)**

GREAT TRAIN ROBBERY, THE***   (1979, Brit.) 110m UA c (GB: THE FIRST GREAT TRAIN ROBBERY)

Sean Connery (Edward Pierce), Donald Sutherland (Agar), Lesley-Anne Down (Miriam), Alan Webb (Edgar Trent), Malcolm Terris (Henry Fowler), Robert Lang (Inspector Sharp), Wayne Sleep (Clean Willy), Michael Elphick (Burges), Pamela Salem (Emily Trent), Gabrielle Lloyd (Elizabeth Trent), James Cossins (Inspector Harranby), Peter Benson (Station Dispatcher), Janine Duvitski (Maggie), Clive Swift (Mr. Chubb), John Bett (McPherson), Agnes Bernelle, Frank McDonald, Brian De Salvo, Joe Cahill, Michael Muldoon, Derry Power, George Downing, Susan Hallinan, John Dunne, Cecil Nash, Donald Churchill, Andre Morell, Brian Glover, Oliver Smith, Jenny Till, John Altman, Paul Kember, Geoff Ferris, Craig Stokes, Noel Johnson, Donald Hewlett, Peter Butterworth, Patrick Barr, Hubert Rees.

Connery is a British thief who, in 1855, pulls off the first moving train robbery. Based on real events, the movie has Connery enlisting the help of master safecracker Sutherland and Sleep to pull off the crime. Down, Connery's mistress, sets up his escape after being caught by police. An involving thriller that stumbles occasionally on over-long dialog exchanges. Connery did his own stunt work when on top of the train cars. This is one of writer-director Crichton's best productions.

p, John Foreman; d&w, Michael Crichton (based on his novel); ph, Geoffrey Unsworth; m, Jerry Goldsmith; ed, David Bretherton; prod d, Maurice Carter; art d, Bert Davey; cos, Anthony Mendleson.

Crime   **Cas.**   **(PR:A   MPAA:PG)**

GREAT VAN ROBBERY, THE**½   (1963, Brit.) 73m Danziger/UA bw

Denis Shaw (Caesar Smith), Kay Callard (Ellen), Tony Quinn (Mercer), Philip Saville (Carter), Tony Doonan (Wally), Geoffrey Hibbert (Venner), Vera Fusek (Mara), Carl Duering (Delgano), Peter Elliott, Bob Simmons, Gordon Sterne, Guido Lorraine, Hal Osmond, June Rodney, Brian Weske, Carl Conway, Michael Bell, Jacques Cey, Julian Orchard, John Mackin, Robert Raglan, Paul Stassino, Peter Allenby.

A private bank account in Rio de Janeiro has some bank notes deposited in it which are ultimately traced to a robbery from a Royal Mint van. Scotland Yard contacts Interpol and Shaw is soon on the trail. His investigation leads him to Saville's coffee storehouse where a warehouse worker is found murdered, and the rest of the missing money is located. Shaw and Saville fight it out and Saville's girl friend, Callard, tries to run down the agent with her car. But the auto hits a pile of coffee beans, sending the car into a skid that kills her lover instead. The cinematography is by future director Roeg.

p, Edward J. Danziger, Harry Lee Danziger; d, Max Varnel; w, Brian Clemens, Eldon Howard; ph, Nicolas Roeg; m, Leon Young, Edwin Astley, Albert Elms; ed, Maurice Rootes; art d, Eric Blakemore.

Crime   **(PR:O   MPAA:NR)**

GREAT VICTOR HERBERT, THE***   (1939) 96m PAR bw

Allan Jones (John Ramsey), Mary Martin (Louise Hall), Walter Connolly (Victor Herbert), Lee Bowman (Dr. Richard Moore), Susanna Foster (Peggy), Judith Barrett (Marie Clark), Jerome Cowan (Barney Harris), John Garrick (Warner Bryant), Pierre Watkin (Albert Martin), Richard Tucker (Michael Brown), Hal K. Dawson (George Faller), Emmett Vogan (Forbes), Mary Currier (Mrs. Victor Herbert), James Finlayson (Lamp Lighter).

Biographical account of the great turn-of-the-century composer of musicals and operettas, Victor Herbert, takes a back seat to the plot revolving around the marriage of tenor Jones and soprano Martin. Not much insight given into the life of Herbert, played by Connolly, with most of the story line spent on the tangled affairs of the actors who staged his works. Connolly is the peace-maker between Jones and Martin when they have domestic clashes due to the opposite direction of their careers. Martin made her movie debut in this film. A total of 28 Herbert songs are heard during the course of the film, including "Someday" (lyrics by William LeBaron); "Al Fresco," "Thine Alone," "Punchinello," "Kiss Me Again," "All For You," "Neapolitan Love Song" (lyrics by Henry Blossom); "Absinthe Frappe," "Rose Of The World," "March Of The Toys" (lyrics by Glen Macdonough); "There Once Was An Owl," "To The Land Of Romance," "Sweethearts" (lyrics by Henry B. Smith); "Ah, Sweet Mystery Of Life," "I'm Falling In Love With Someone" (lyrics by Rida Johnson Young).

p&d, Andrew L. Stone; w, Russel Crouse, Robert Lively (based on a story by Lively, Stone); ph, Victor Milner; ed, James Smith; md, Phil Boutelje; art d, Hans Dreier, Ernst Fegte; ch, LeRoy Prinz.

Biography/Musical   **(PR:AAA   MPAA:NR)**

GREAT WALDO PEPPER, THE***   (1975) 107m UNIV c

Robert Redford (Waldo Pepper), Bo Svenson (Axel Olsson), Bo Brundin (Ernst Kessler), Susan Sarandon (Mary Beth), Geoffrey Lewis (Newt), Edward Herrmann (Ezra Stiles), Philip Bruns (Dillhoefer), Roderick Cook (Werfel), Kelly Jean Peters (Patsy), Margot Kidder (Maude), Scott Newman (Duke), James S. Appleby (Ace), Patrick W. Henderson, Jr. (Scooter), James Harrell (Farmer), Elma Aicklen (Farmer's Wife), Deborah Knapp (Farmer's Daughter), John A. Zee (Director Western Set), John Reilly (Western Star), Jack Manning (Director Spanish Set), Joe

Billings *(Policeman)*, Robert W. Winn *(Theater Manager)*, Lawrence Casey *(German Star)*, Greg Martin *(Assistant Director)*.

A handsomely mounted aviation adventure, this film deals with that colorful era of the early 1920s when barnstorming—performing aerial feats before rural crowds—was so popular. Among the flyers of the day is Redford who had been a WW I flyer without much distinction but who claims to have met German ace Brundin in combat. His friend and competitor in the skies and on the ground over the love of women they meet is Svenson. When he arrives in a small town, Redford discovers that Svenson's air show is already being touted and Redford undoes his competitor by loosening the wheels on Svenson's plane so that he must crash-land. Svenson gets even by exposing Redford's fabrication of meeting Brundin in the skies over France during WW I. The antics of both men lead to several mishaps and crashes, one where Redford winds up in a cast and recuperates in the home of Kidder, with whom he falls in love. When recovered, Redford teams up with Svenson to perform more daredevil sky feats, convincing Sarandon to wing-walk as the "It Girl of the Skies." Her fame is short-lived; she falls to her death while trying to walk from one wing to the wing of another plane while in flight. For this and other crazy stunts, government air official Lewis grounds both Redford and Svenson. Redford travels to the West Coast, however, and, using an assumed name, becomes a stunt pilot in an epic movie about WW I which is loosely based upon Brundin's own fabulous war record. Brundin himself, the German ace Redford never really met in combat, is an advisor on the film. The two become friendly and Redford finds that the German is as displaced and disillusioned with life as himself. Ignoring commands from the film's director, the two men take up planes and actually perform incredible stunts, outdoing each other. Then, as if enacting a wordless agreement, they battle each other in the sky without live ammunition, flying close to each other and using their planes as weapons to tear at each other's ships. Brundin is finally bested and Redford flies off into oblivion, finally tasting the victory that had eluded him during the Great War. The story, told better in such films as THE TARNISHED ANGELS, takes much from an obscure Erich von Stroheim vehicle, THE LOST SQUADRON (1932) which dealt with WW I pilots performing impossible barnstorming and movie stunts. Redford is fine as the boy-man of the air who cannot find a place in a society that has no more need of heroes. The stunts themselves are spectacular and worth the whole film. Even Redford performed some incredible feats, wing-walking at 3,000 feet, which the studio ballyhooed later, but an act that gave Universal studio executives the jitters at the time. ("I felt incredible freedom," Redford was later quoted, "but then I thought—what am I doing here?") Brundin is outstanding as the misplaced German ace but the rest of the cast, particularly Kidder and Lewis, walk about and sound like zombies with little tape recordings in their throats which bleat out their lines. Kidder, a terrible actress in any movie (she always appears as if she is annoyed at having to be in any movie), has no presence whatsoever, only a voice so gratingly vexing that she is thankfully not missed once Redford leaves her side. The production values here are good and Hill's direction is up to the story but becomes a bit draggy in spots where he is consumed by the notion to infuse logic in an illogical tale. The whole thing is more like a comic book with feeble attempts to impart deeper images and thoughts, but it's still pretty good entertainment.

p&d, George Roy Hill; w, William Goldman (based on a story by Hill); ph, Robert Surtees (Technicolor); m, Henry Mancini; ed, Peter Berkos, William Reynolds; art d, Henry Bumstead; set d, James Payne; cos, Edith Head; stunts, Tallmantz Aviation: James S. Appleby, Wayne Berg, Howard Curtis, Mike Dewey, John Kazian, Thomas Mooney, Frank Pine, Frank Price, Audrey Saunders, Art Scholl, Frank Tallman, Ralph Wiggins; makeup, Gary Liddiard.

Adventure **Cas.** **(PR:C MPAA:PG)**

GREAT WALL, THE½** (1965, Jap.) 104m Daiei/Magna c (SHIN NO SHIKOTEI)

Shintaro Katsu *(Emperor Shih Huang Ti)*, Fujiko Yamamoto *(Princess Chu)*, Ken Utsui *(Crown Prince Tan)*, Hiroshi Kawaguchi *(Hsi Liang)*, Ayako Wakao *(Chiang-nu)*, Kojiro Hongo *(Li Hei)*, Raizo Ichikawa *(Ching Ko)*, Ganjiro Nakamura *(Hsu Fu)*, Eijiro Tono *(Li Tang)*, Isuzu Yamada *(Dowager Empress)*, Ken Mitsuda *(Mencius)*, Junko Kano, Kazuo Hasegawa, Machiko Kyo.

A Chinese historical epic, taking place in 230 B.C., features Katsu as a conquering tyrant who attempts to unite all of China's warring tribes. He marries Yamamoto, though she tries to murder him as he was responsible for her father's death. Inaugurating vast changes for the country, his life is soon threatened once again as Ichikawa is hired by enemies to assassinate the new ruler. The plot fails, but enemies from the north attack, killing Yamamoto. This moves Katsu to build the great Chinese wall to protect his country. He becomes mad in his obsession with the project, taking his wrath out on Kawaguchi, a young scholar. When an earthquake stops the wall's erection, Katsu has Kawaguchi sacrificed to the gods and orders the dead man's fiancee, Wakao, to be executed. But Hongo, the son of Katsu's favorite guard, saves them, while Katsu, having incurred the wrath of the people, is finally assassinated.

p, Masaichi Nagata; d, Shigeo Tanaka; w, Fuji Yahiro; ph, Michio Takahashi (Technirama, Technicolor); m, Akira Ifukube; ed, Tatsuji Nakashizu.

Historical Drama **(PR:O MPAA:NR)**

GREAT WALL OF CHINA, THE zero (1970, Brit.) 93m bw

Wayne Mockett *(K)*, Dennis Dynsley *(Max Brod)*, Peter Stanton *(Richard)*, Frank Hatherley *(Norman)*, Peter Neumann *(Max)*.

A confusing and overly pretentious film done in a documentary style, with the actors partly portraying themselves. The film is divided into six chapters, each one titled from a Franz Kafka novel or story. The vignettes touch on Maoism, the Chinese cultural revolution, student protests, bureaucracy, and pacifism. Hard to say what this film is really about.

p, Mark Forstater; d&w, Joel Tuber; ph, Barry Salt; ed, John Newsome, Forstater, Tuber.

Drama **(PR:C-O MPAA:NR)**

GREAT WALTZ, THE*** (1938) 107m MGM bw

Luise Rainer *(Poldi Vogelhuber)*, Fernand Gravet *(Johann Strauss)*, Miliza Korjus *(Carla Donner)*, Hugh Herbert *(Hofbauer)*, Lionel Atwill *(Count Hohenfried)*, Curt Bois *(Kienzl)*, Leonid Kinskey *(Dudelman)*, Al Shean *(Cellist)*, Minna Gombell *(Mrs. Hofbauer)*, George Houston *(Schiller)*, Bert Roach *(Vogelhuber)*, Greta Meyer *(Mrs. Vogelhuber)*, Herman Bing *(Dommayer)*, Alma Kruger *(Mrs. Strauss)*, Henry Hull *(Franz Joseph)*, Sig Rumann *(Wertheimer)*, Christian Rub *(Coachman)*.

The first of two films dealing with the life of Johann Strauss (the second was done in 1972), this was a sacher torte of pleasure for anyone who loves his music as much as did MGM mogul Louis Mayer. Gravet (whose real name is Gravey, but the studio bosses thought that would be laughed at by English-speaking audiences) does a good job as Strauss. Korjus, who was sort of the European version of Mae West, has a brilliant voice, but reigning MGM musical star Jeanette MacDonald made it clear that there wasn't room on the Culver City lot for two sopranos so Korjus faded into obscurity soon afterward. Our story sees Gravet quit his job in a Viennese banking house to follow his star. He gets a job leading a local orchestra and batoning his own works. Soon after, he marries Rainer, the local baker's daughter, but in a brief time is carrying on with Korjus, an opera singer. Rainer keeps mum for a while, then decides to fight for her man and storms the theater after the opening of Gravet's first full opera. It all works out in the end, but the fun is in the telling and in the glorious Strauss music. Solid comedy from Herbert as Strauss' publisher, as well as stalwart work from Hull in the role of Emperor Franz Joseph. No Oscars for this film, an overlooked gem.

p, Bernard Hyman; d, Julien Duvivier (Josef von Sternberg, uncredited); w, Samuel Hoffenstein, Walter Reisch (based on a story by Gottfried Reinhardt); ph, Joseph Ruttenberg; m, Johann Strauss (adapted by Dmitri Tiompkin); ed, Tom Held; md, Arthur Gutman; art d, Cedric Gibbons; ch, Albertina Rasch; m/l, "Tales Of Vienna Woods," "There'll Come A Time," "One Day When We Were Young" (sung by Korjus), "Voices Of Spring," "Du Und Du," "The Bat," "I'm In Love With Vienna," "Revolutionary March," "There'll Come A Time," Strauss, Oscar Hammerstein II.

Musical/Biography **(PR:AA MPAA:NR)**

GREAT WALTZ, THE** (1972) 135m MGM c

Horst Buchholz *(Johann Strauss, Jr.)*, Mary Costa *(Jetty Treffz)*, Rossano Brazzi *(Baron Tedesco)*, Nigel Patrick *(Johann Strauss, Sr.)*, Yvonne Mitchell *(Anna Strauss)*, James Faulkner *(Josef Strauss)*, Vicki Woolf *(Lili Weyl)*, Susan Robinson *(Emilie Trampusch)*, George Howe *(Karl Frederick Hirsch)*, Lauri Lupino Lane *(Donmayer)*, Michael Tellering *(Karl Haslinger)*, Willard Parker *(Karl Treffz)*, Ingrid Wayland *(Theresa Strauss)*, Lorna Nathan *(Olga)*, Hermione Farthingale *(Louise)*, Franz Aigner *(Josef Weyl)*, Elizabeth Muthsam *(Caroline Strauss)*, Marty Allen *(Johann Herbeck)*, Dominique Weber *(Jacques Offenbach)*, Guido Wieland *(Max Steiner)*, Paola Loew *(Princess Pauline Metternich)*, Prince Johannes Schonburg-Hartenstein *(Emperor Franz-Josef)*, Helmut Janatsch *(Havemeyer)*.

Basically the same story as the original, this overblown color version still has the same wonderful music but that is where the similarity ends. None of the players in this remake compare with the first ones, and even though it is in color and Panavision, it seems older and stodgier than the 1938 original. Andrew Stone, who is so good when it comes to suspense films (THE LAST VOYAGE, etc.), sinks deep in a morass of rich Viennese cream on this one. The dialog is stilted and the performances mannered. Worth watching only for the listening.

p,d&w, Andrew L. Stone; ph, Dave Boulton (Panavision, Metrocolor); m, Johann Strauss, Jr., Johann Strauss, Sr., Josef Strauss, Jacques Offenbach; ed, Ernest Walker; art d, William Albert Havenmeyer; cos, David Walker, Emmi Minnich, Josef Wanke; ch, Onna White; m/l, "The Blue Danube Waltz," "Tritsch-Tratsch Polka," "Louder And Faster," "Pitter Patter Polka," "Love Is Music," "Say Yes," "Crystal And Gold," "Six Drinks," "Nightfall," "Warm," "Who Are You," "The Radetzky March," "With You Gone," Strauss, George Forrest, Robert Craig Wright (narration sung by Kenneth McKellar).

Musical/Biography **(PR:AA MPAA:G)**

GREAT WAR, THE** (1961, Fr., Ital.) 118m DD-Gray/Lopert bw (LA GRANDE GUERRE; LA GRANDE GUERRA)

Vittorio Gassman *(Giovanni Busacca)*, Alberto Sordi *(Oreste Jacovacci)*, Silvana Mangano *(Constantina)*, Folco Lulli *(Bordin)*, Bernard Blier *(Capitano Castelli)*, Romolo Valli *(Tenente Gallina)*, Vittorio Sanipoli *(Maggiore Venturi)*, Nicola Arigliano *(Giardino)*, Mario Valdemarin *(Aspirante Loquenzi)*, Tiberio Mitri *(Mandrich)*, Livio Lorenzon *(Sergente Battiferri)*, Tiberio Murgia *(Nicotra)*, Carlo D'Angelo *(Capitano Ferri)*, Marcello Giorda *(Il Generale)*, Guido Celano *(Italian Major)*, Luigi Fainelli *(Giacomazzi)*, Gerard Herter *(German Captain)*, Achille Compagnoni *(Military Chaplain)*, Geronimo Meynier *(Messenger)*, Elsa Vazzoler *(Bordin's Wife)*, Ferruccio Amendola *(Deconcini)*.

In this war comedy that takes place in Italy during WW II, Gassman must enlist in the army in exchange for a pardon of criminal charges against him. He meets Sordi at the enlistment center and tries unsuccessfully to bribe the man into giving him a deferment. The two later meet on a transport train and combine their wits to escape duties. After a prostitute steals Gassman's wallet, he spends the next day in a bloody battle on the front. When he and Sordi are sent to town for more supplies, Gassman confronts the prostitute once more. He gets his wallet back but falls in love in the process. The two soldiers don't want to go back to the terrible battle and spend the night in town. But when they awake in the morning they find their company has been wiped out and the town now regards them as heroes. When the two regain a sense of loyalty and decide to go back to the war, they are sent on a special mission to deliver a message, but are captured by Austrians.

After refusing to give up any information to the enemy Gassman and Sordi are both killed. Their commanding officer, not surprised by their long absence, assumes they have once more pulled off a scam. The comical beginning that leads to a tragic end is similar to WHAT PRICE GLORY?, though the earlier film was much better and far more even-handed than this one.

p, Dino De Laurentiis; d, Mario Monicelli; w, Luciano Vincenzoni, Mario Monicelli, Age and Scarpelli (based on a story by Vincenzoni); ph, Giuseppe Rotunno, Roberto Gerardi (Cinema Scope); m, Nino Rota; ed, Adriana Novelli; md, Franco Ferrara; art d, Mario Garbuglia.

War/Comedy (PR:O MPAA:NR)

GREAT WHITE, THE* (1982, Ital.) 88m Film Ventures c

James Franciscus, Vic Morrow, Joshua Sinclair, Timothy Brent, Chuck Kaufman, Thomas Moore, Joyce Lee.

An out-and-out ripoff of JAWS. While most shark films inspired by the 1975 film changed the plot around, this comes off as a near clone. Universal Studios, producers of the original film, sued this filmmaker and got a preliminary injunction, which stopped any further showings of this bad, though often unintentionally funny, film.

p, Maurizio Amati, Ugo Tucci; d, Enzo G. Castellari; w, Marc Princi; ph, A. Spagnoli, Mattei, Moglia; m, Morton Stevens; spec eff, G. Ferrari, G. Pozzi, A. Corridori.

Adventure (PR:O MPAA:PG)

GREAT WHITE HOPE, THE*½** (1970) 102m FOX c

James Earl Jones (Jack Jefferson), Jane Alexander (Eleanor), Lou Gilbert (Goldie), Joel Fluellen (Tick), Chester Morris (Pop Weaver), Robert Webber (Dixon), Marlene Warfield (Clara), R.G. Armstrong (Cap'n Dan), Hal Holbrook (Cameron), Beah Richards (Mama Tiny), Moses Gunn (Scipio), Lloyd Gough (Smitty), George Ebeling (Fred), Larry Pennell (Frank Brady), Roy E. Glenn, Sr. (Pastor), Bill Walker (Deacon), Marcel Dalio (French Promoter), Rodolfo Acosta (El Jefe), Virginia Capers (Sister Pearl), Rockne Tarkington (Rudy), Oscar Beregi (Ragosy), Manuel Padilla, Jr. (Paco), Karl Otto Alberty (Hans), Jim Beattie (The Kid), Scatman Crothers (Barker), Basil Dignam (English Official).

Based on Howard Sackler's thinly veiled depiction of Jack Johnson's life, this big period drama is a character study of a man and woman of different races who try to maintain some happiness while living in a racially tense atmosphere. In the story, Jones beats Pennell in the fight at Reno and becomes the first black heavyweight champion of the world. He incurs the wrath of his live-in, Warfield, and his pal, Gunn, when he takes up with a white divorcee, Alexander. They cross a state line and he is arrested for having broken the Mann Act in a kangaroo court situation where they are going to teach that "uppity nigger" a lesson. The judge sentences him to three years at Joliet but he escapes by dressing as a member of the prison baseball club. Once out, he flees north of the border to Canada, then on to England with Alexander, where he applies for a license to box, but is refused. He goes to France and pounds his opponents, then travels to Germany where no one will accept a bout. With no money to speak of, he appears in a Hungarian version of "Uncle Tom's Cabin" as Tom. A federal agent, played by Webber, agrees to reduce the prison charge against Jones if Jones will agree to throw a fight in Cuba, but Jones refuses. He and Alexander travel south of the border now and are barely making a living in Mexico. She begs him to take the Havana fight but he is adamant so she drowns herself. Jones finally accepts the bout, and after a terrible beating, regains his pride and tries to win but it is too late. The heavyweight champion's belt is returned to the white majority. Shot in Spain, Arizona, and on the "Hello Dolly" set at Fox Studios, THE GREAT WHITE HOPE was a triumph in many ways. It showed the climate of the time without the usual preaching that director Ritt sometimes likes to show, and the love story between Jones and Alexander was touchingly portrayed. Some overacting on Jones' part, but he was bringing his stage presence (he'd also starred in the Broadway version) and Ritt neglected to take him down for the big screen. All of the people portrayed were real and the names were changed so author Sackler could take some liberties, but anyone who knows ring history will recognize the other boxers.

p, Lawrence Turman; d, Martin Ritt; w, Howard Sackler (based on his play); ph, Burnett Guffey (Panavision, DeLuxe Color); m, Lionel Newman; ed, William Reynolds; prod d, John De Cuir; art d, Jack Martin Smith; set d, Walter M. Scott, Raphael Bretton; cos, Irene Sharaff; ch, Donald McKayle; m/l, "Let Me Hold You In My Arms Tonight," Jesse Fuller; makeup, Ed Butterworth, Paul Stanhope.

Biography **Cas.** (PR:C-O MPAA:GP)

GREAT YEARNING, THE** (1930, Ger.) 110m Cicero-Deutsch Universal bw (DIE GROSSE SEHNSUCHT)

Camilla Horn, Theodor Loos, Harry Frank, Berthe Ostyn, Irma Godau, Anna Muller-Lincke, Ferdinand Bonn, Walter Steinbeck.

This early German talkie is a biography of Camilla Horn, a popular German actress of her time. Horn plays herself as she goes from an unknown to become a big star. A fairly unimaginative film, THE GREAT YEARNING is also a valuable one, due to its fascinating view of the German studio system in the late 1920s.

d, Stefan Szekely; w, Hans H. Zerlett; ph, Mutz Greenbaum; m/l, Friedrich Hollaender, Rudolf Eisner, Karl Bruell.

Biography (PR:A MPAA:NR)

GREAT ZIEGFELD, THE*** (1936) 170m MGM bw

William Powell (Florenz Ziegfeld), Luise Rainer (Anna Held), Myrna Loy (Billie Burke), Frank Morgan (Billings), Reginald Owen (Sampston), Nat Pendleton (Sandow), Virginia Bruce (Audrey Lane), Ernest Cossart (Sidney), Robert Greig (Joe), Raymond Walburn (Sage), Fannie Brice (Herself), Jean Chatburn (Mary Lou), Ann Pennington (Herself), Ray Bolger (Himself), Harriett Hoctor (Herself), Charles Trowbridge (Julian Mitchell), Gilda Gray (Herself), A.A. Trimble (Will

Rogers), Joan Holland (Patricia Ziegfeld), Buddy Doyle (Eddie Cantor), Charles Judels (Pierre), Leon Errol (Himself), Marcelle Corday (Marie), Esther Muir (Prima Donna), Herman Bing (Customer), Paul Irving (Erlanger), William Demarest (Gene Buck), Alfred P. James (Stage Door Man), Miss Morocco (Little Egypt), Suzanne Kaaren (Miss Blair), Sarah Edwards (Wardrobe Woman), James P. Burtis (Bill), Mickey Daniel (Telegraph Boy), William Griffith (Husband), Grace Hayle (Wife), Richard Tucker, Clay Clement, Lawrence Wheat, Selmer Jackson (Customers), Alice Keating (Alice), Rosina Lawrence (Marilyn Miller), Jack Baxley (Detective), Charles Coleman (Carriage Starter), Eric Wilton (Desk Clerk), Mary Howard (Miss Carlisle), Bert Hanlon (Jim), Evelyn Dockson (Fat Woman), Franklyn Ardell (Allen), John Larkin (Sam), David Burns (Clarence), Phil Tead (Press Agent), Susan Fleming (Girl with Sage), Adrienne d'Ambricourt (Wife of French Ambassador), Charles Fallon (French Ambassador), Boothe Howard (Willie Zimmerman), Edwin Maxwell (Charles Froman), Ruth Gillette (Lillian Russell), John Hyams (Dave Stamper), Wallis Clark (Broker), Ray Brown (Inspector Doyle), Pat Nixon (Extra).

Opulent, lavish, melodious, and true to the subject, THE GREAT ZIEGFELD was, for its time, the best musical biography ever done. Powell didn't look like Ziegfeld, nor did Rainer look like Held nor Loy like Burke, but it made no difference as the magic of their acting convinced us they were who they portrayed. For the rest of time, we'll always think of Powell as the great Flo. Filled with cameos of stars playing themselves (Brice, Bolger, Pennington), as well as many famous performers in other roles, this movie also served to introduce a young actress whose husband was to hold an important position in American history. You'll have to look hard, but there's former first lady Pat Nixon as an extra. It cost almost $2 million, a king's ransom in those days, and every penny is up there on the screen. Screenwriter McGuire worked for Ziegfeld and knew him intimately, so we can be sure that much of the story is accurate, save for some inventions that had to be included, such as Flo dying in a New York hotel next to his theater. The truth was that he died in Los Angeles, but that's a piffle compared to the great things about this film. Powell is seen as a sideshow barker shouting the talents of Sandow (Pendleton), The Strong Man. He makes a fortune at the World's Great Columbian Exposition in Chicago, then blows it on a trip to Monte Carlo. But his voyage does bear fruit as he meets and signs Rainer to a contract. She'd been approached by his rival, Morgan, but she became attracted to the brash young impresario, decided to put her career, and later her life, into his hands. Their marriage is turbulent and marked by her jealous nature, as well as his total lack of regard for money. She catches him innocently kissing a chorus girl, and that leads to their divorce. His career continues rocketing and he meets a lovely young actress, Loy, whom he takes as the second Mrs. Ziegfeld. She is adoring and manages to curtail his extravagances. They become parents to a baby daughter but his career goes straight down until he is broke. Loy hocks her jewels to finance a new show and Ziegfeld is a hit again. When the stock market crashes, he is heavily invested and loses everything. Sick and depressed, he dies a broken man. It's a no-holds-barred study of the larger-than-life showman that would have stood on its own as an excellent biography even without the many songs and production numbers that punctuate the production. Oddly, Powell's Oscar nomination that year was not for his work as Ziegfeld, but for a totally different kind of portrayal, that of MY MAN GODFREY. He lost to Paul Muni's LOUIS PASTEUR, then came back to play a ghostly Ziegfeld 10 years later, when MGM made ZIEGFELD FOLLIES. The screenwriter and the director were also nominated and lost, but it did win as Best Picture, and Rainer took the first of two consecutive Oscars. A year later, she won for THE GOOD EARTH. Dennis Morgan is seen as the boy singer (with his voice looped by Allan Jones) but his name, at that time, was Stanley Morner. Huge sets, dazzling dance numbers, and many songs from a passel of writers. Tunes include: "A Pretty Girl Is Like A Melody," "You Gotta Pull Strings," "You," "She's A Ziegfeld Follies Girl," "You Never Looked So Beautiful," "A Circus Must Be Different In A Ziegfeld Show," "Rhapsody In Blue," "On With The Motley," "One Fine Day (Une Bel Di)," "Humoresque Number 7 in G Flat," "My Man," "Yiddle On Your Fiddle," "Won't You Come And Play With Me?" "If You Knew Susie," "Parade Of The Glorified Girls," "Queen Of The Jungle," "Look For The Silver Lining," "March of The Musketeers," "Ol' Man River," "Makin' Whoopee," "Rio Rita," "Tulip Time," "Someone Loves You After All," "It's Delightful to be Married," and more. Everything about this Stromberg production was first-rate and stands as a shining example of how to make a musical biography. Ziegfeld was a temperamental, complex man and he is shown, warts and all, in this outstanding film.

p, Hunt Stromberg; d, Robert Z. Leonard; w, William Anthony McGuire; ph, Ray June, Oliver T. Marsh, Karl Freund, Merritt B. Gerstad, George Folsey; ed, William S. Gray; md, Arthur Lange; art d, Cedric Gibbons; cos, Adrian; ch, Seymour Felix; m/l, Walter Donaldson, Harold Adamson, Irving Berlin, George Gershwin, Con Conrad, Herb Magidson, Jerome Kern, Rudolph Friml, Gus Kahn, Dave Stamper, Buddy De Sylva, Channing Pollock, Maurice Yvain, Anna Held, Vincent Scotto, Henri Christine, Joseph Meyer, Anton Dvorak, Puccini, Johann Strauss, Leoncavallo, Tierney and McCarthy.

Musical/Biography (PR:AAA MPAA:NR)

GREATEST, THE zero (1977, U.S./Brit.) 101m M.V./COL c

Muhammad Ali (Himself), Ernest Borgnine (Angelo Dundee), Lloyd Haynes (Herbert Muhammad), John Marley (Dr. Pacheco), Robert Duvall (Bill McDonald), David Huddleston (Cruikshank), Ben Johnson (Hollis), James Earl Jones (Malcolm X), Dina Merrill (Velvet Green), Roger E. Mosley (Sonny Liston), Paul Winfield (Lawyer), Annazette Chase (Belinda Ali), Mira Waters (Ruby Sanderson), Phillip MacAllister (Young Cassius Clay, Jr.), Arthur Adams (Cassius Clay, Sr.), Dorothy Meyer (Odessa Clay), Lucille Benson (Mrs. Fairlie), Theodore R. Wilson (Gardener), Skip Homeier (Major), Sally Gries, Elizabeth Marshall (Sponsor's Wife), Malachi Throne (Payton Jory), Richard Gullage (Commission Doctor), Richard Venture (Colonel), Stack Pierce (Johnson), Ben Medina (Ronnie), Paul Mantee (Carrara), George Garro (Mr. Curtis), David Clennon (Captain), Ernie Wheelwright (Bossman Jones), George Cooper (Lawyer), James Gammon ("Mr. Harry"), Toni Crabtree

(Hooker), Don Dunphy *(Commentator)*, Fernand A. Larrieu, Jr. *(Grocer)*, Nai Bonet *(Suzie Gomez)*, Alberto Martin *(Doctor)*, Ray Holland *(Reporter)*, Drew "Bundini" Brown, Rahaman Ali, Howard Bingham, W. Youngblood Muhammad, Lloyd Wells, Pat Patterson, Gene Kilroy, Harold Conrad *(Themselves)*.

He might have been "the Greatest" in the boxing ring, but on the screen he's more like "the stiffest" as he portrays himself in the story of his life up to the George Foreman fight. Turtle-paced story shows his beginnings as a fighter under trainer Dundee, portrayed by Borgnine. We see Ali win back his heavyweight title after refusing to be inducted into the Army, and his conversion to Islam under the tutelage of Malcolm X. Added in to please the boxing fan is actual footage of Ali's fights during his rise to the top. The movie climaxes with his Foreman clash in a somewhat puzzling documentary style. This was the last film for director Gries (known for such films as WILL PENNY, BREAKHEART PASS) before his sudden death in 1976.

p, John Marshall; d, Tom Gries; w, Ring Lardner, Jr. (based on the book *The Greatest: My Own Story*, by Muhammad Ali, Richard Durham, Herbert Muhammad); ph, Harry Stradling, Jr. (Metrocolor); m, Michael Masser; ed, Byron Brandt; prod d, Bob Smith; set d, Solomon Brewer; cos, Eric Seelig, Sandra Stewart; spec eff, Candy Flanagin; m/l, "The Greatest Of All," Masser, Linda Creed (sung by George Benson), "I Always Knew I Had It In Me," Masser, Jerry Goffin (sung by Benson); makeup, William Tuttle, Tom Tuttle.

Biography/Sports Drama Cas. (PR:C-O MPAA:G)

GREATEST BATTLE ON EARTH, THE (SEE: GHIDRAH, THE THREE-HEADED MONSTER, 1965, Jap.)

GREATEST LOVE, THE*** (1954, Ital.) 118m Ponti-DD/Lux bw (AKA: EUROPE '51)

Ingrid Bergman *(Irene)*, Alexander Knox *(George)*, Ettore Giannini *(Andrea)*, Giulietta Masina *(Passerotto)*, Sandro Franchina *(Michele)*, Teresa Pellati *(Ines)*, William Tubbs *(Family Doctor)*, Alfred Browne *(Hospital Priest)*.

Shaken by the suicide of her son, society woman Bergman sets out to understand the crumbling world around her. A Communist friend sends her out to the people, where she sees poverty and works alongside the poor in some kind of contrition. But when she helps a young criminal escape the police, her husband has her committed to an asylum, where she suffers in silence. Depressing and overlong, but Bergman's performance was her best in years. (In English.)

p&d, Roberto Rosselini; w, Rosselini, Sandro de Leo, Mario Pannunzio, Ivo Perilli, Brunello Rondi, Fabbri (based on a story by Rosselini); ph, Aldo Tonti; m, Renzo Rosselini; ed, Jolanda Benvenuti; set d, Virgillio Marchi.

Drama (PR:C MPAA:NR)

GREATEST SHOW ON EARTH, THE**** (1952) 153m PAR c

Betty Hutton *(Holly)*, Cornel Wilde *(Sebastian)*, Charlton Heston *(Brad)*, Dorothy Lamour *(Phyllis)*, Gloria Grahame *(Angel)*, James Stewart *(Buttons, a Clown)*, Henry Wilcoxon *(Detective)*, Lyle Bettger *(Klaus)*, Lawrence Tierney *(Henderson)*, John Kellogg *(Harry)*, John Ridgely *(Jack Steelman, Assistant Manager)*, Frank Wilcox *(Circus Doctor)*, Bob Carson *(Ringmaster)*, Lillian Albertson *(Button's Mother)*, Julia Faye *(Birdie)*, Emmett Kelly, Cucciola, Antoinette Concello, John Ringling North *(Themselves)*, Gloria Drew *(Ann)*, Anthony Marsh *(Tony)*, Bruce Cameron *(Bruce)*, Noel Neill *(Noel)*, Charmienne Harker *(Charmienne)*, Dorothy Crider *(Dorothy)*, Patricia Michon *(Patricia)*, Vicki Bakken *(Vicki)*, Gay McEldowney *(Gay)*, Hugh Prosser *(Hugh)*, Rus Conklin *(Rus)*, John Crawford *(Jack)*, Claude Dunkin *(Claude)*, Keith Richards *(Keith)*, Rosemary Dvorak *(Rosemary)*, Lorna Jordan *(Lorna)*, Mona Knox *(Mona)*, Gertrude Messinger *(Gertrude)*, John Parrish *(Jack Lawson)*, William Hall *(Bill)*, Brad Johnson *(Reporter)*, William J. Riley, Robert W. Rushing *(Policemen)*, Adele Cook Johnson *(Mabel)*, Lane Chandler *(Dave)*, Howard Negley *(Truck Boss)*, Erik Nelson *(Boy)*, Beverly Washburn *(Girl)*, Syd Saylor, Lester Dorr *(Circus Barkers)*, Milton Kibbee *(Townsman)*, Fred Kohler, Jr. *(Fireman)*, Greta Grandstedt, Mary Field, Kathleen Freeman *(Women)*, Ross Bagdasarian *(Man)*, Edmond O'Brien *(Midway Barker)*, Dale Van Sickel *(Man in Train Wreck)*, William Boyd *(Himself)*, Bing Crosby, Bob Hope, Mona Feeman *(People in Grandstands)*, Tuffy Genders *(Tuffy)*, Ethan Laidlaw *(Hank)*, Stanley Andrews *(Man)*, Lydia Clarke *(Circus Girl)*, John Merton *(Chuck)*, Bradford Hatton *(Osborne)*, Herbert Lytton *(Foreman)*, Norman Field *(Truesdale)*, Everett Glass *(Board Member)*, Lee Aaker *(Boy)*, Nancy Gates, Ken Christy, Clarence Nash, Bess Flowers *(Spectators)*, Lou Jacobs, Felix Adler, Liberty Horses, The Flying Concellos, Paul Jung, The Maxellos *(Circus Acts)*, Dolores Hall, Robert St. Angelo, Davidson Clark, Dorothy Adams, Ottola Nesmith, David Newell, Josephine Whitell.

It's big, it's garish, it's loud, most of all, it's wonderful, DeMille's superlative salute to the circus world. Here all the glamour and the flashy hoopla fits perfectly with the director whose middle name was epic. Heston, whose acting career would be forever linked to film epics, was selected by showman DeMille to play the boss of the sprawling, almost unwieldy circus. In love with Heston is the big top's star aerialist, Hutton, but she is crushed when the boss hires a French star, Wilde, who takes away Hutton's spotlight, although Heston honestly insists that he has made this decision for the good of the circus. And Wilde, upon arrival, quickly proves he is master of the air, performing tricks that amaze even the amazing Hutton who first resents the strutting Frenchman, then develops a fascination that hovers around love. Other stories interplay with this one, Heston's constant struggle to maintain and motivate the circus, Bettger, the elephant trainer, who is spurned by showgirl Grahame whom he loves desperately and who mistreats him at every turn. Further, Lamour is a glamourous aerialist and Stewart a mysterious clown who never removes his makeup. The competition between Hutton and Wilde becomes fierce as she tries to battle her way back to the center arena. Wilde attempts an impossible feat without using a net to prove his superiority and almost falls to his death, horribly damaging one arm. Hutton becomes even more infatuated with Wilde who bears up nobly with his injuries, going off to see a special surgeon when some nerves begin jumping in his otherwise paralyzed hand. Meanwhile, Bettger, hating Grahame for also throwing herself at Wilde, wrecks the circus train en route to another performance, killing himself accidentally and causing a major disaster. Performers are thrown about, wild animals let loose in the countryside, and Heston is injured when pinned under wreckage, so badly hurt that he requires immediate medical attention. Hutton begs Stewart to do something, knowing he is a master surgeon in disguise. Following the circus is detective Wilcoxen who is searching for a doctor who has been charged with the mercy killing of his wife and he watches as Stewart, still wearing his clown's makeup, performs a major operation on Heston in a makeshift surgery, saving his life and revealing his identity in the process. Stewart is led away to face the euthanasia charges and the circus struggles to reassemble its tattered remnants. In torn costumes and covered with bruises and bandages, the Big Top still goes up and the performers give "the greatest show on earth" to the audience. In the end, the fully restored Wilde winds up with Grahame, and Hutton, realizing that she is still in love with Heston, finishes in a happy clinch with the boss. This film was a superb DeMille production, carefully and expensively constructed, filmed with love in every frame and its 153 minutes are loaded with charm and excitement. The entire cast, particularly Heston, do outstanding jobs. Hutton overacts a bit (as usual) but Wilde is perfect as the egotistical aerialist, Stewart touching as the tragic clown, and Graham a sexy, manipulative circus lady. Some amusing tidbit shots are thrown in by DeMille where he peopled the circus audience with Paramount celebrities. In one scene two agog spectators peering upward anxiously at the aerial artist while nervously munching peanuts are Bob Hope and Bing Crosby. Since the early 1920s DeMille had planned on producing a spectacular circus film but his biblical epics got in the way. Finally, in 1949, when Paramount paid Ringling Brothers $250,000 for the right to use the circus name, equipment and talent, DeMille began elaborate preparations. The director wanted to make a journal of circus activities so he spent several months touring with the Ringling Brothers and Barnum & Bailey Circus, traveling in John Ringling North's personal railway car, attended by a valet, chef, butler, and maid, and enjoying the car's lavish three bedrooms, kitchen, baths, and sumptuous dining room. Sketch artist John Jensen made hundreds of sketches at DeMille's direction as the mighty helmsman investigated every bit of circus life on the road, in preparation for this production. The film would follow the circus as it left its winter camp in Sarasota, Florida and through several towns, depicting the roustabouts who sweated to haul up the mammoth canvas big tops to the pole tops at dawn, the performers in their daily routines, the social life or the lack of it in all hard-working ranks. It was a gritty experience for the great showman and he put the colorful lifestyles right into his enormous film, his most successful to date. At first, DeMille thought to cast either Kirk Douglas or Burt Lancaster in the boss role but he selected Heston, after seeing him in an offbeat film version of JULIUS CAESAR. Many female stars were considered for the aerialist role that later went to Hutton. DeMille said no to Hedy Lamarr, Marlene Dietrich, and Paulette Goddard. He had grown disgusted with Goddard in UNCONQUERED when she displayed fright at some of his battle scenes; DeMille could not abide a coward and he upbraided any of his stars who would not face the fury of his action sequences. When Victor Mature proved fearful of hand-to-hand combat in SAMSON AND DELILAH, DeMille chastised him before the entire cast and crew. Wilde, who was playing the aerialist, learned that he suffered from acrophobia, a fear of heights, and DeMille sneered his contempt for the actor throughout the film. Once, when spotting Wilde putting on clogs, he reportedly shouted to the actor: "Better not put those on, Mr. Wilde. Remember—you're afraid of heights!" Hutton, on the other hand, proved to be utterly fearless and actually performed many of her own stunts. (As did Lamour who really twisted about on a rope 40 feet above the audience, hanging from a metal ring by her teeth.) Hutton actually lobbied for her role, sending a $1,000 floral wreath to DeMille when she heard he was casting. The wreath showed her as a miniature trapeze artist swinging at the top of the wreath. The bravura act caused DeMille to send Hutton a wire in which he stated: "Definitely favor your directing as well as playing in the picture." Actually, actress Grahame had the most hazardous role as the assistant of elephant trainer Bettger. At one point, while her anxious husband, director Nicholas Ray, watched bug-eyed, Grahame lay back on the sawdust while a huge elephant put its leaden foot to her face; one wrong move and her head would have been crushed. She later hung from the mouth of the elephant by one leg as the ponderous pachyderm lumbered about the show ring. The railroad wreck was done in miniature but so well was it constructed that it appeared quite real. DeMille was extremely inventive, mounting his cameras on pulleys and having them slide up and down the support poles of the main tent. He also raised and lowered himself on huge booms and created tracking shots by affixing a blimp to one camera the size of a desk. This was the last film DeMille made in three-strip Technicolor and the result was lavish photography under the inspired supervision of Barnes, Marley, and Kelly. The film is authentic and awesome and earned an Oscar as Best Picture. DeMille got the first Oscar of his life, an Irving Thalberg Academy Award for the role of producer. Oddly, all of the on-location shooting went on without mishap. Not until making studio shots back at Paramount did DeMille have trouble. When filming the aftermath of the train wreck, scores of monkeys were released to scamper before the roaming lions, tigers, leopards. The larger, tame animals were rounded up after the usual roars but the monkeys were so terrified that they fled the sound stage and raced wildly through the studio back lot, most of them fleeing into the Hollywood cemetery, many never to be located again. (There is a strange little history of such events throughout decades of filmmaking; in the mid-1920s a film company making a movie on Catalina Island off the California coast imported some buffalo and wild boar and, when production was complete, left the animals on the isle. They have since populated in great numbers and inhabit the area beyond the hills surrounding the tiny town of Avalon.) Songs include: "Be a Jumping Jack," "The Greatest Show on Earth" (Ned Washington, Victor Young), "Popcorn and Lemonade," "Sing a Happy Song," "A Picnic in the Park" (John Murray Anderson, Henry Sullivan), "Lovely Luawana Lady" (E. Ray Goetz, John Ringling North).

p&d, Cecil B. DeMille; w, Fredric M. Frank, Barre Lyndon, Theodore St. John (based on a story by Frank, St. John, Frank Cavett); ph, George Barnes, J. Peverell Marley, Wallace Kelly (Technicolor); m, Victor Young; ed, Anne Bauchens; art d, Hal Pereira, Walter Tyler; set d, Sam Comer, Ray Moyer; cos, Miles White, Edith Head, Dorothy Jeakins; spec eff, Gordon Jennings, Paul Lerpae, Devereaux Jennings; ch, Richard Barstow; makeup, Wally Westmore.

Adventure/Circus Epic **Cas.** **(PR:AAA MPAA:NR)**

GREATEST STORY EVER TOLD, THE*½** (1965) 141m George Stevens/UA c

Max Von Sydow *(Jesus)*, Dorothy McGuire *(Mary)*, Robert Loggia *(Joseph)*, Claude Rains *(Herod The Great)*, Jose Ferrer *(Herod Antipas)*, Marian Seldes *(Herodias)*, John Abbott *(Aben)*, Rodolfo Acosta *(Captain of Lancers)*, Philip Coolidge *(Chuza)*, Michael Ansara *(Herod's Commander)*, Dal Jenkins *(Philip)*, Joe Perry *(Archelaus)*, Charlton Heston *(John the Baptist)*, Donald Pleasence *(The Dark Hermit)*, David McCallum *(Judas Iscariot)*, Roddy McDowall *(Matthew)*, Michael Anderson, Jr. *(James the Younger)*, David Sheiner *(James the Elder)*, Gary Raymond *(Peter)*, Robert Blake *(Simon the Zealot)*, Burt Brinckerhoff *(Andrew)*, John Considine *(John)*, Jamie Farr *(Thaddaeus)*, David Hedison *(Philip)*, Peter Mann *(Nathaniel)*, Tom Reese *(Thomas)*, Telly Savalas *(Pontius Pilate)*, Angela Lansbury *(Claudia)*, Johnny Seven *(Pilate's Aide)*, Paul Stewart *(Questor)*, Harold J. Stone *(Gen. Varus)*, Cyril Delavanti *(Melchior)*, Mark Leonard *(Balthazar)*, Frank Silvera *(Caspar)*, Joanna Dunham *(Mary Magdalene)*, Janet Margolin *(Mary of Bethany)*, Ina Balin *(Martha of Bethany)*, Michael Tolan *(Lazarus)*, Carroll Baker *(Veronica)*, Pat Boone *(Man at Tomb)*, Sal Mineo *(Uriah)*, Van Heflin *(Bar Armand)*, Ed Wynn *(Old Aram)*, Shelley Winters *(Woman of No Name)*, Chet Stratton *(Theophilius)*, Ron Whelan *(Annas)*, John Lupton *(Speaker of Capernaum)*, Russell Johnson *(Scribe)*, Abraham Sofaer *(Joseph of Arimathaea)*, Martin Landau *(Caiaphas)*, Nehemiah Persoff *(Shemiah)*, Joseph Schildkraut *(Nicodemus)*, Victor Buono *(Sorak)*, Robert Busch *(Emissary)*, John Crawford *(Alexander)*, John Wayne *(Roman Captain)*, Sidney Poitier *(Simon of Cyrene)*, Richard Conte *(Barabbas)*, Frank De Kova *(Tormentor)*, Joseph Sirola *(Dumah)*, John Pickard *(Peter's 2nd Accuser)*, Celia Lovsky *(Woman Behind Railings)*, Mickey Simpson *(Rabble Rouser)*, Richard Bakalyan *(Good Thief on Cross)*, Marc Cavell *(Bad Thief on Cross)*, Renata Vanni *(Weeping Woman)*.

THE GREATEST STORY EVER TOLD was unmercifully ripped to shreds by the critics, a fate it did not deserve. It cost more than $20 million and included a cast of some of filmdom's biggest (though not necessarily best) stars. But it appeared that the movie mavens were lying in wait for it to come out, and nothing short of the actual "Second Coming" would have satisfied them. The story goes over familiar turf for anyone who has ever spent any time in a hotel room with nothing else to read but the Bible put there by the Gideons. (Sky Masterson in GUYS AND DOLLS prides himself on his knowledge of The Good Book because he's spent more lonely nights in more hotel rooms than almost anyone). Familiar scenes include Christ's birth, the decree by Herod to slaughter all male children in Jerusalem, the flight into Egypt, John the Baptist immersing Jesus, the gathering of the Apostles, John's death, Lazarus' resurrection, the money-lenders being chased from the temple, the Passover dinner that was to be Jesus' last supper, his crucifixion, and the ultimate resurrection. At almost four hours originally, and with a staggering price tag, this movie never did make its money back. Von Sydow is as convincing as he can be under Stevens' slogging direction. United Artists fully expected it to sweep the Oscars and hoped that would take it out of its financial doldrums, but all it garnered was three nominations, as that was the year of THE SOUND OF MUSIC, DOCTOR ZHIVAGO, CAT BALLOU, DARLING, SHIP OF FOOLS, THUNDERBALL, and THE GREAT RACE, some heavy competition. With so many well-known faces in the picture as insurance, it worked against the believability of the film as people just sat there and pointed to their favorites in tiny parts and lost the thread of the narrative. There is a story, perhaps apocryphal, about John Wayne's appearance as the Roman centurion. His one line in the picture was: "Truly, this man was the Son of God." After attempting it a couple of times, Stevens gently said: "Duke, what we need in this line is something more. Look up at the man and give us some. . . some awe." Wayne nodded, Stevens signaled the cameras to begin rolling, and Wayne said: "Awww, truly this man was the Son of God." Shot on location in Utah and Arizona when they discovered that those places looked like what they thought Palestine must have looked like at that time, it was a monumental shoot with thousands of extras, countless crew members and many arguments due to Stevens' penchant for re-takes. The overtime pay was larger than the regular salaries of many of the people involved. At one point, shooting went into cold weather and snow marred the landscape of what was supposed to be a desert, and several snowplows had to be brought in, along with wheelbarrows, shovels, and butane flame throwers, to clear away the white stuff. Eventually, they had to move back to Hollywood and construct a huge replica of Jerusalem, thereby sending the price even higher. With all the recutting, the movie eventually came down to just over two hours, but even that didn't bring the customers in. Until HEAVEN'S GATE, this had been the biggest bomb ever. Fox had originally paid $100,000 for Oursler's novel and he and Denker had been using the Bible to make a fine living since 1947, when they began a radio show that depicted the stories in sort of a soap opera fashion. For the next 10 years, with more than 500 episodes, they let us in on Christ's life. That 10 years was substantially more time than Jesus himself preached. The novel was issued in 1949, sold more than 3 million and Fox, who had great success with THE ROBE, thought they could do the same with this. Phillip Dunne, who had written the scripts for THE ROBE, DAVID AND BATHSHEBA, as well as DEMETRIUS AND THE GLADIATORS, was approached to write the adaptation for this, but declined and Stevens was brought in, at a fee of $1 million, to handle the producing and directing assignment. If all goes well, and barring any unforeseen events like another attempt at making the story, enough people should see this picture on TV that it may make the money back by the year 2000.

p&d, George Stevens; w, Stevens, James Lee Barrett (based on The Bible, other ancient writings, the book *The Greatest Story Ever Told* by Fulton Oursler, and radio scripts by Henry Denker); ph, William C. Mellor, Loyal Griggs (Ultra Panavision 70, Cinerama, Technicolor); m, Alfred Newman; ed, Harold F. Kress, Argyle Nelson, Jr., Frank O'Neill; art d, Richard Day, William Creber, Hall; set d, David Hall; spec eff, J. McMillan Johnson, Clarence Slifer, A. Arnold Gillespie, Robert R. Hoag; cos, Vittorio Nino Novarese, Marjorie Best.

Biblical Epic **Cas.** **(PR:AAA MPAA:NR)**

GREED IN THE SUN½** (1965, Fr./Ital.) 122m GAU-Trianon-Ultra/MGM bw (CENT MILLE DOLLARS AU SOLEIL; CENTOMILA DOLLARI AL SOLE)

Jean-Paul Belmondo (Rocco), Lino Ventura (Herve), Reginald Kernan (Hans Steiner), Andrea Parisy (Pepa), Gert Frobe *(Castigliano)*, Bernard Blier *(Mitch-Mitch)*, Doudou Babet *(Khenouche)*, Pierre Mirat *(Halibi)*.

Kernan portrays a naive truck driver assigned to haul a load from Morocco to Nigeria. Unknown to him, the shipment contains guns and ammunition to be used in a border war. But another driver, Belmondo, discovers the secret of the cargo and, along with girl friend Parisy, hijacks the truck. Frobe, the manager of the trucking firm, offers Kernan and Ventura a reward if they can recover the shipment. After a breakneck chase through deserts and winding mountain roads, they catch up with the stolen vehicle. Belmondo's truck breaks down and he forces Ventura and Kernan to carry the load in their truck. He and Parisy ride off, leaving the two would-be heroes behind. After arriving at the final destination, Belmondo leaves the truck with Parisy and heads off for the nearest brothel. Ventura appears and the two begin to duke it out—only to have the battle end when Belmondo suddenly bursts out laughing, realizing Parisy has run off with the truck. Fast-paced and furious, and great for action fans.

p, Alain Poire; d, Henri Verneuil; w, Michel Audiard (based on the novel by Claude Veillor); ph, Marcel Grignon (CinemaScope); m, Georges Delerue; ed, Claude Durand; art d, Robert Clavel; set d, Pierre Charron.

Crime/Action **(PR:O MPAA:NR)**

GREED OF WILLIAM HART, THE½** (1948, Brit.) 78m BUS/Ambassador bw (AKA: HORROR MANIACS)

Tod Slaughter *(William Hart)*, Henry Oscar *(Mr. Moore)*, Jenny Lynn *(Helen Moore)*, Winifred Melville *(Meg Hart)*, Patrick Addison *(Hugh Alston)*, Arnold Bell *(Doctor Cox)*, Aubrey Woods *(Jamie Wilson)*, Mary Love *(Mary Patterson)*, Ann Trego *(Janet Brown)*, Edward Malin *(David Patterson)*, Hubert Woodward *(Swanson)*, Denis Wyndham *(Sgt. Fisher)*.

Intriguing crime thriller centers on the escapades of grave-robbers Slaughter and Oscar as the providers of cadavers for local Edinburgh medical students. When the supply becomes low, with the demand still great, the two decide to create their own dead bodies, a maneuver that proves profitable when they only stick to lowly types, such as bums, prostitutes, and drunkards. But when they murder a likable retarded man known to everybody, things get a bit tense. Not the worst retelling of the Burke and Hare legend. Something a fan of demented killers can get his teeth into.

p, Gilbert Church; d, Oswald Mitchell; w, John Gilling; ph, D.P. Cooper, S.D. Onions.

Crime/Biography **(PR:C-O MPAA:NR)**

GREEK STREET (SEE: LATIN LOVE, 1930, Brit.)

GREEK TYCOON, THE* (1978) 106m Abkco/UNIV c

Anthony Quinn *(Theo Tomasis)*, Jacqueline Bisset *(Liz Cassidy)*, Raf Vallone *(Spyros Tomasis)*, Edward Albert *(Nico Tomasis)*, James Franciscus *(James Cassidy)*, Camilla Sparv *(Simi Tomasis)*, Marilu Tolo *(Sophia Matalas)*, Charles Durning *(Michael Russell)*, Luciana Paluzzi *(Paola Scotti)*, Robin Clarke *(John Cassidy)*, Kathryn Leigh Scott *(Nancy Cassidy)*, Roland Culver *(Robert Keith)*, Tony Jay *(Doctor)*, John Bennett *(Servant)*, Kathryn Schofield *(Helena)*, Joan Benham *(Lady Allison)*, Linda Thorson *(Angela)*, Guy Deghy *(Tahlib)*, Jill Melford *(Magda)*, Lucy Gutteridge *(Mia)*, Nasis Kedrakas, John Denison, Carolle Rousseau, Danos Lygizos, Cassandra Harris, Patricia Kendall-John, Sandor Eles, Beulah Hughes, Vicki Michelle, Carol Royle, Mimi Denissi, Athene Fielding, Bonnie George, Charles Maggiore, Jeff Pomerantz, Richard Fasciano, John Bolt, Henderson Forsythe, Michael Prince, Gordon Oas-Heim, William Stelling, John Hoffmeister, Carinthia West, Dimitri Nikolaidis, Dimos Starenios, John Ioannou, David Masterman.

If you can't guess who the characters are in this, then you must have been living on Mars for the last few decades. A thin copy of the truth, THE GREEK TYCOON gives us Quinn (though born in Mexico, he's made a living for years playing Hellenics) in a lavish soap opera as an Onassis type, who falls in love with Jackie Kennedy clone Bisset. Made in 1978, it had a fair run at the theaters, but seems more at home next to the 1980s TV shows like "Dynasty" and "Dallas" in its style and content. In the story Bisset is wed to Franciscus, a U.S. senator, and Quinn begins to slyly court her, despite the fact that she is apparently happily married. Franciscus is busy talking to the British prime minister while Bisset goes aboard his yacht where Quinn sows the seeds for his later reaping. Quinn is married to Sparv, but taunts her by sleeping around. His son, played by Edward Albert, is the gyro of his eye, and his brother is Vallone, whom he taunts mercilessly. In the course of events, Albert dies in an accident (it really did happen to Onassis' son), Franciscus becomes President of the U.S. and is later assassinated, and Bisset, now a widow, takes up with Quinn. The only honest scenes in this tripe are when Quinn reprises his ZORBA THE GREEK role. In one scene he dances with some Greek peasants in a poor restaurant and later he commiserates about his son's death in a dance with some fishermen. If scenery, greenery, and seeing all the comforts that megabucks can bring are what you like, you may enjoy THE GREEK TYCOON. If honesty, drama, and real feelings are what turns you on, read a book. Superb lensing by Tony Richmond and a pretty good score by Myers. Quinn is an immense talent with some legendary roles to his credit (LUST FOR LIFE, VIVA ZAPATA), but he has to get off this kick of playing Greeks and get on with playing other characters so we can, once again, enjoy his work. Enough is enough.

p, Allen Klein, Ely Landau; d, J. Lee Thompson; w, Mort Fine (based on a story by Fine, Nico Mastorakis, Win Wells); ph, Tony Richmond (Technovision, Technicolor); m, Stanley Myers; ed, Alan Strachan; prod d, Michael Stringer; art d, Tony Readin, Gene Gurlitz, Mel Bourne; set d, Vernon Dixon.

Drama **Cas.** **(PR:C MPAA:R)**

GREEKS HAD A WORD FOR THEM*** (1932) 77m Goldwyn/UA bw (AKA: THREE BROADWAY GIRLS)

Madge Evans *(Polaire)*, Joan Blondell *(Schatze)*, Ina Claire *(Jean)*, David Manners *(Dey Emery)*, Lowell Sherman *(Boris Feldman)*, Phillips Smalley *(Justin Emery)*, Sidney Bracey *(The Waiter)*, Betty Grable *(Showgirl)*.

The tale of three golddigging gals, Evans, Blondell, and Claire, who go out on the hunt for rich husbands. The trio are well cast and provide many laughs as they battle each other for the affections of the males in the picture. Offscreen, the affections of another male, photographer Barnes, were also won over when he and star Blondell fell in love on the set and later married. Remade a few times, including HOW TO MARRY A MILLIONAIRE.

p, Samuel Goldwyn; d, Lowell Sherman; w, Sidney Howard (based on the stage play of the same name by Zoe Akins); ph, George Barnes; ed, Stuart Heisler; art d, Richard Day; cos, Chanel.

Comedy **(PR:A MPAA:NR)**

GREEN BERETS, THE *** (1968) 141m Batjac/WB c

John Wayne *(Col. Mike Kirby)*, David Janssen *(George Beckworth)*, Jim Hutton *(Sgt. Petersen)*, Aldo Ray *(Sgt. Muldoon)*, Raymond St. Jacques *(Doc McGee)*, Bruce Cabot *(Col. Morgan)*, Jack Soo *(Col. Cai)*, George Takei *(Capt. Nim)*, Patrick Wayne *(Lt. Jamison)*, Luke Askew *(Sgt. Provo)*, Irene Tsu *(Lin)*, Edward Faulkner *(Capt. MacDaniels)*, Jason Evers *(Capt. Coleman)*, Mike Henry *(Sgt. Kowalski)*, Craig Jue *(Hamchunk)*, Chuck Roberson *(Sgt. Griffin)*, Eddy Donno *(Sgt. Watson)*, Rudy Robins *(Sgt. Parks)*, Richard "Cactus" Pryor *(Collier)*, Bach Yen *(Vietnamese Singer)*, Frank Koomen *(Lt. Sachs)*, William Olds *(Gen. Phan Son Ti)*, Yodying Apibal *(ARVN Soldier)*, Chuck Bail *(Sgt. Lark)*, Vincent Cadiente *(Viet Cong Soldier)*, William Shannon *(Sgt. White)*.

Though propagandistic and mostly oblivious to the kind of war it was depicting, this guts-and-glory Vietnam war film is packed with excitement and impressive battle scenes. Wayne, who co-directed with Kellogg, commands a regiment that holds back swarms of Viet Cong troops on top of a hill, a position that is eventually overrun but then retaken when U.S. planes strafe the area with automated machine guns that devastate the enemy. Wayne next leads a mission to kidnap a Viet Cong general and this proves to be both suspenseful and triumphant. Throughout Wayne tries to educate cynical newsman Janssen as to the worth of fighting the Communists and is eventually successful after Janssen witnesses torture and merciless slaughter inflicted by the enemy. Hutton, who adopts an orphan Vietnamese boy, is killed during the abduction assignment but Janssen takes the boy under his wing at the end. Wayne is good in his usual heroic role, replaying a part he made traditional during WW II films. The supporting cast is as strong as the realistic and awesome battle scenes (these being directed by Kellogg). Critics unfairly lambasted this film for political reasons when it was released at the height of the Vietnam controversy rather than evaluating its production values. The message was a simple one which even unsophisticated audiences could determine without the aid of political activists passing for film reviewers. The film was Wayne's patriotic expression of "what those lads are going through" during the war and, as such, it well depicted the horrors of that losing struggle. One reviewer, attempting to stop popular support for the film, was so stupid as to call it "dull." That it is not and the public streamed to see it, dumping $11 million at the box office. Wayne was unperturbed by the critical blasts, stating: "I think those terrible reviews help us a great deal. I've been in this business for forty years and any statements I've made in movies have been pretty truthful, I think. When people read those reviews I'm sure they couldn't believe them . . . THE GREEN BERETS simply says that a lot of our brave boys are fighting and dying for us out there. The ridiculously one-sided criticism of the picture only made people more conscious of it and they are proving that the reviews were not very effective." The critics reviewed the war, not the film, and lost the battle.

p, Michael Wayne; d, John Wayne, Ray Kellogg; w, James Lee Barrett (based on the novel by Robin Moore); ph, Winton C. Hoch (Panavision, Technicolor); m, Miklos Rozsa; ed, Otho Lovering; prod d, Walter M. Simonds; set d, Ray Moyer; cos, Jerry Alpert; spec eff, Sass Bedig; makeup, Dave Grayson.

War Drama **Cas.** **(PR:C MPAA:NR)**

GREEN BUDDHA, THE* (1954, Brit.) 62m REP bw (AKA: THE GREEN CARNATION; THE MAN WITH THE GREEN CARNATION)

Wayne Morris *(Gary Holden)*, Mary Germaine *(Vivien Blake)*, Walter Rilla *(Frank Olsen)*, Mary Merrall *(Mrs. Rydon-Smith)*, Arnold Marle *(Vittorio Miranda)*, Lloyd Lamble *(Inspector Flynn)*, Kenneth Griffith *(Nobby)*, Leslie Linder *(Harry Marsh)*, George Woodbridge *(Farmer)*, Percy Herbert *(Casey O'Rourke)*, Marcia Ashton, Victor Platt, Wolf Frees, Frank Atkinson, Bartlett Mullins, Dan Lester.

Yankee charter pilot Morris inadvertently finds himself in the midst of thieves who have purloined a costly antique jade figure from an exhibit. He tracks the thieves to Battersea—they have resorted to a resort in their flight—where he rescues the fair Germaine from their unsavory clutches, and the Buddha boosters gain only jaded justice. An unusual effort for Republic, this film was shot in England using local talent for the most part, rather than the company's own familiar Hollywood studio, locations, and personnel. With the near-demise of the B-picture, the troubled Republic was, at the time, attempting to make the transition to material of a higher grade. This wasn't it.

p, William N. Boyle; d, John Lemont; w, Paul Erickson; ph, Basil Emmett; m, Lambert Williamson; ed, John Seabourne; md, Williamson; art d, John Stoll.

Crime **(PR:A MPAA:NR)**

GREEN CARNATION (SEE: TRIALS OF OSCAR WILDE, THE, 1960)

GREEN COCKATOO, THE* (1947, Brit.) 63m Devonshire Films bw (AKA: FOUR DARK HOURS; RACE GANG)

John Mills *(Jim Connor)*, Rene Ray *(Eileen)*, Robert Newton *(Dave Connor)*, Charles Oliver *(Terrell)*, Bruce Seton *(Madison)*, Julian Vedey *(Steve)*, Allan Jeayes *(Inspector)*, Frank Atkinson *(Butler)*.

This poor imitation of an early American gangster film is about song and dance man Mills, who, with the help of Ray, uncovers the murderers of his brother, played by Newton.

p, William K. Howard, Robert T. Kane; d, William Cameron Menzies, Howard (uncredited); w, Edward O. Berkman, Arthur Wimperis (based on a story by Graham Greene); ph, Mutz Greenbaum; m, Miklos Rozea.

Crime **(PR:A MPAA:NR)**

GREEN DOLPHIN STREET*** (1947) 140m MGM bw

Lana Turner *(Marianne Patourel)*, Van Heflin *(Timothy Haslam)*, Donna Reed *(Marguerite Patourel)*, Richard Hart *(William Ozanne)*, Frank Morgan *(Dr. Edmund Ozanne)*, Edmund Gwenn *(Octavius Patourel)*, Dame May Whitty *(Mother Superior)*, Reginald Owen *(Capt. O'Hara)*, Gladys Cooper *(Sophie Patourel)*, Moyna MacGill *(Mrs. Metivier)*, Linda Christian *(Hin-Moa)*, Bernie Gozier *(Jacky-Pato)*, Pat Aherne *(Kapua-Manga)*, Al Kikume *(Native)*, Edith Leslie *(Sister Angelique)*, Gigi Perreau *(Veronica at Age 4)*, Douglas Walton *(Sir Charles Maloney)*, Leslie Dennison *(Capt. Hartley)*, Lumsden Hare *(Anderson)*, William Fawcett *(Nat)*, Wyndham Standing *(Government General)*, Lucille Curtis *(Mrs. Samuel Kelly)*, Carol Nugent *(Veronica at Age 7)*, James Leong *(Chinese Longshoreman)*, Guy Kingsford *(Young Fisherman)*, Ramsey Ames *(Corinne)*, Tetsu Komai *(Chinaman)*, Patricia Emery *(Niece)*.

MGM instituted a new way of buying rights with their Book Award in 1947. They paid $200,000 for the novel by Elizabeth Goudge, then bought four more but only filmed one, RAINTREE COUNTY. GREEN DOLPHIN STREET took Oscars for visual effects (Arnold Gillespie, Warren Newcombe) and sound effects (Douglas Shearer, Michael Steinore), which was a disappointment for the studio as they had sunk more than $4 million into the production, a huge amount at the time. The film's most spectacular scene, the wrecking of a specially-built ship, was deleted from the final cut of the movie. It would have added to the overall impression of this larger-than-life story. Our story takes place in 1840. Turner and Reed are the two daughters of a wealthy man in the Channel Islands, the cherubic Gwenn. Richard Hart arrives on the island and both women fall in love with him but he prefers Reed, the gentler of the two, over the aggressive Turner (a brunette in this film). Turner wants to keep Reed from Hart so she arranges for him to join the Navy, one of his lifelong ambitions. He goes off to China in the service of England but inadvertently misses his ship and is frightened that he will be branded a deserter. Now a fugitive, he meets old pal Heflin, another fugitive, and the two travel to New Zealand to operate a lumber business in the wilds. One night, under the influence of alcohol, Hart writes a letter to his beloved and mistakenly writes the name of Marianne (Turner), asking her to join him in New Zealand and become his wife. She believes the letter was meant for her, not sister Marguerite (Reed), and takes a long and difficult sea voyage to New Zealand, steps off the ship at the port in Wellington where Hart must now take her in as his wife, rather than admit his mistake. A further complication arises when we learn that Heflin, a native of the town where Turner and Reed were born, has been in love with Turner ever since he was a small boy. Turner can sense that all is not well in the marriage; it's nothing concrete, just a feeling. She is a sensational administrator and the company begins making money until their entire investment is ruined by an earthquake and tidal wave. The next few plot turns come hard on the heels of each other. Turner gives birth, a Maori revolt takes place, and Heflin helps Turner and Hart escape to a nearby island where they again become wealthy. Turner goes home to St. Pierre Island and finally learns that Hart had made a mistake and really meant to marry Reed. She offers him the chance to get out of the marriage and wed Reed. But Hart now realizes that he truly and deeply loves Turner with much more of a mature love than he ever had for Reed so many years ago when they and the world were much younger. Hart understands that only a woman who loved him that much would make that kind of gesture. He declares his love for Turner in no uncertain terms. In the meantime, Reed now has encountered her destiny in religion. In the film's final sequence, Reed is about to be ordained as a nun. Technically, this was a first-rate picture and audiences made it MGM's biggest picture of 1947. Young Richard Hart was being groomed as a star but suddenly died of a heart attack at age 35. Costumes and all art direction were top notch. The love story at the core of the film was rooted in a false note (Hart getting drunk and substituting Turner's name for Reed's) but if you can swallow that, you'll have a good time watching GREEN DOLPHIN STREET. Nice work from all the secondary actors with special kudos to an exquisite Linda Christian.

p, Carey Wilson; d, Victor Saville; w, Samson Raphaelson (based on the novel by Elizabeth Goudge); ph, George Folsey; m, Bronislau Kaper; ed, George White; art d, Cedric Gibbons, Malcolm Brown; set d, Edwin B. Willis; spec eff, Warren Newcombe, A. Arnold Gillespie; cos, Walter Plunkett, Valles; makeup, Jack Dawn.

Adventure/Drama **(PR:A-C MPAA:NR)**

GREEN EYES*½ (1934) 68m Chesterfield bw

Shirley Grey *(Jean Kester)*, Charles Starrett *(Bill Tracy)*, Claude Gillingwater *(Stephen Kester)*, John Wray *(Inspector Crofton)*, William Bakewell *(Cliff)*, Dorothy

Revier (Mrs. Pritchard), Ben Hendricks, Jr. (Regan), Alden Chase (Pritchard), Arthur Clayton (Hall), Aggie Herring (Dora), Edward Keane (Raynor), Edward Le Saint (Banker), Robert Frazer (Broker), John Elliott (Chemist), Lloyd Whitlock (Howe), Elmer Ballard (Lenox the Butler), Frank Hagney (Policeman).

A far below-par detective film that has Starrett as a writer of detective stories who also does some real sleuthing. The usual murder, which is followed by the usual questioning of everyone involved, until the usual culprit is found, makes up the filling of this usual murder mystery.

p, George R. Batcheller; d, Richard Thorpe; w, Melville Shyer (based on the novel The Murder of Stephen Kester by H. Ashbrook); ph, M.A. Anderson; md, Abe Meyer; art d, Edward Jewell.

Mystery   **(PR:A   MPAA:NR)**

GREEN FIELDS**   (1937) 103m Collective Film Producers/New Star bw
(GRUNER FELDER)

Michael Goldstein (Levy-Yitzchok), Helen Beverley (Tzineh), Isidore Cashier (David-Noich), Anna Appel (Rochel), Leo Noimi (Gittel), Dena Drute (Stera), Max Vodnoy (Aikuneh), Saul Levine (Hersh-Ber), Herschel Bernardi (Avrum-Yankon), Aron Ben-Ami.

Aimed primarily at the Jewish population of America, this slowly paced but otherwise charming picture follows the adventures of a young student of the Talmud when he leaves the shelter of the synagogue in order to find out what people are really like in the world. Taking up residence at a small farm, he quickly finds himself the center of a battle between two families, both wanting the young student as a tutor and suitor to their daughters. But the youth is really unable to take any control of his fate, becoming prey to the whimsy of the farmers. A minor work by Edgar G. Ulmer, who directed in conjunction with stage director Jacob Ben-Ami. A first feature film for former Yiddish theater actor Bernardi, the only one of the cast to go on to greater things, including many character roles in Hollywood films, and legitimate Broadway stardom. Much of the action is extremely subdued, depending upon dialogue to move the action showing that the material is much more suited for the stage. (In Yiddish; English subtitles).

d, Edgar G. Ulmer, Jacob Ben-Ami; w, Peretz Hirschbein (based on his play); ph, William Miller, Burgi Contner; m, Vladimir Heifetz; ed, Jack Kemp.

Comedy   **(PR:A   MPAA:NR)**

GREEN FINGERS**   (1947) 87m BN/Anglo-American bw

Robert Beatty (Thomas Stone), Carol Raye (Jeannie Mansell), Nova Pilbeam (Alexandra Baxter), Felix Aylmer (Daniel Booth), Moore Marriott (Pickles), Brefni O'Rourke (Coroner), Charles Victor (Joe Mansell), Harry Welchman (Dr. Baxter), Edward Rigby (Albert Goodman), Ellis Irving (Jones), Olive Walters (Mrs. Mansell), Wally Patch (Dawson), Daisy Burrell (Receptionist), Felicity Deveraux (Pamela), Doreen Lawrence (Angela), Frederick Morant (Dr. Miles), Howard Douglas (Johnson), Gerald Moore (Pete), Leslie Weston (Sam), George Pelling (Squiffy), Patric Curwen (Managing Director), Carol Lawton (Secretary), Arsene Kirilloff (Booth's Receptionist), John England (Chauffeur), Paul Blake (George), Richard Barclay (Wilson), Doris Bloom (Nurse), Brookes Turner (Second Coroner's Officer), Charles Paton (Hudson), Roddy Hughes (Mr. Green), Percy Coyte (Night Watchman), Mr. Gratham (Coroner), Robert Moore (First Coroner's Officer), Nora Gordon (Mrs. Green), Ernie Priest (Policeman).

Beatty is a fisherman who decides to become a doctor. Before finishing with medical school, he treats Raye, the daughter of his landlady, thought to be incurable by the reigning medical profession. The case receives great attention, not only because she is cured, but because Beatty was not a licensed doctor at the time. Despite having no degree and being shunned by the experts, he goes into osteopathy, marries Raye, and embarks on a very successful life. Along the way, he has an affair with Pilbeam. After deciding to break off the affair, Beatty dumps her and she commits suicide. During the autopsy, it is discovered that Beatty misdiagnosed her illness and his treatment led to her death. Shattered, he takes off for the seas again. But his wife's disease recurs and she begs of him to use his "Green Fingers" once more. She is soon cured, and they live happily ever after.

p, Louis H. Jackson; d, John Harlow; w, Jack Whittingham (based on the novel, The Persistent Warrior by Edith Arundel); ph, Ernest Palmer; m, Hans May; ed, Joseph Sterling; art d, Wilfred Arnold; makeup, Harry Hayward.

Medical Drama   **(PR:A   MPAA:NR)**

GREEN FIRE**   (1955) 100m MGM c

Stewart Granger (Rian X. Mitchell), Grace Kelly (Catherine Knowland), Paul Douglas (Vic Leonard), John Ericson (Donald Knowland), Murvyn Vye (El Moro), Jose Torvay (Manuel), Robert Tafur (Father Ripero), Joe Dominguez (Jose), Nacho Galindo (Officer Perez), Charlita (Dolores), Natividad Vacio (Hernandez), Rico Alaniz (Antonio), Paul Marion (Roberto), Bobby Dominguez (Juan), Charles Stevens, Joe Herrera (Bandits), Martin Garralaga (Gonzales), Alberto Morin (Carlos), Rudolfo Hoyos, Jr. (Pedro, the Bartender), Lillian Molieri (Mexican Girl), Marie Delgado, Juli Loffredo, Frances Dominguez, Tina Menard (Women).

Granger is an emerald miner in Colombia, South America, where he meets coffee plantation owner Kelly, and the usual complications and eventual romance fall suit. Despite some good natural-disaster footage, including landslides, storms, and flooding, the dialog here is deadly dull. The characters are cliched as are most of the sequences between the two leads.

p, Armand Deutsch; d, Andrew Marton; w, Ivan Goff, Ben Roberts; ph, Paul Vogel (CinemaScope, Eastmancolor); m, Mikols Rozsa; ed, Harold F. Kress; art d, Cedric Gibbons, Malcolm Browne; set d, Edwin B. Willis, Ralph Hurst; cos, Helen Rose; spec eff, A. Arnold Gillespie, Warren Newcombe; m/l, Rozsa, Jack Brooks; makeup, William Tuttle.

Drama/Romance   **(PR:C   MPAA:NR)**

GREEN FOR DANGER**   (1946, Brit.) 91m Individual Picture/GFD bw

Sally Gray (Nurse Linley), Trevor Howard (Dr. Barney Barnes), Rosamund John (Esther Sanson), Alistair Sim (Inspector Cockrill), Leo Genn (Mr. Eden), Judy Campbell (Marion Bates), Megs Jenkins (Nurse Woods), Moore Marriott (Joe Higgins), Henry Edwards (Mr. Purdy), Ronald Adam (Dr. White), George Woodbridge (Sgt. Hendricks), Wendy Thompson (Sister Carter), Frank Ling (Rescue Worker), Elizabeth Sydney, John Rae, Hattie Jacques.

An unorthodox detective, Sim, is on a strange double murder case that takes place within a British emergency hospital during WW II. A postman is slightly wounded by a buzz bomb and brought to the hospital where he dies under anesthesia. When Campbell discovers that the postman was in fact murdered, she's stabbed to death. Sim has great fun asking all sorts of questions that irk the suspects. Each one of the six, who was present in the operating room during the time of the murder, has a motive, but Campbell's death and a murder attempt on Gray narrows the field to four. Sim finally stages a fake operation which the suspects believe to be the real thing and which enables the sly detective to unmask to real culprit.

p, Frank Launder, Sidney Gilliat; d, Gilliat; w, Gilliat, Claude Guerney (based on a novel by Christianna Brand); ph, Wilkie Cooper; m, William Alwyn; ed, Thelma Myers; prod d, Peter Proud; md, Muir Mathieson.

Mystery/Comedy   **Cas.**   **(PR:A   MPAA:NR)**

GREEN GLOVE, THE**   (1952) 88m Benagoss/UA bw

Glenn Ford (Michael Blake), Geraldine Brooks (Chris Kenneth), Sir Cedric Hardwicke (Father Goron), George Macready (Count Paul Rona), Gaby Andre (Gaby Saunders), Jany Holt (Countess), Roger Treville (Inspector Faubert), Georges Tabet (Jacques Piotet), Meg Lemonnier (Madame Piotet), Paul Bonifas (Inspector), Juliette Greco (Singer), Jean Bretonniers (Singer).

This routine cops and robbers chase film is set in and around Monte Carlo. The title refers to a priceless medieval relic that had belonged to a small rural French church. It's stolen during WW II by jewel thief and German collaborator, Macready. American paratrooper Ford is dropped behind enemy lines and enlisted by the church to return the glove. He gets it away from Macready, but loses it when his shelter is bombed. Ford returns to France after the war, hoping to find the glove and make his fortune, but Macready, now the head of an international crime ring, has been waiting for Ford to lead him to the relic. Ford finds the glove after a series of mountain chases and returns it to the church.

p, Georges Maurer; d, Rudolph Mate; w, Charles Bennett; ph, Claude Renoir; m, Joseph Kosma; ed, Lola Barache; art d, Alexander Trauner.

Crime   **(PR:A   MPAA:NR)**

GREEN GODDESS, THE**½   (1930) 80m WB bw

George Arliss (The Rajah), H.B. Warner (Maj. Crespin), Alice Joyce (Lucilla Crespin), Ralph Forbes (Doctor Traherne), David Tearle (High Temple Priest), Reginald Sheffield (Lt. Cardew), Nigel de Brulier (Hermit Priest), Betty Boyd (Ayah), Ivan Simpson (Hawkins).

This film revolves around a group of Britishers who survive a plane crash in the Himalayas only to find themselves prisoners of a tyrannical, English-hating Rajah, played by Arliss. This film, which is marred by poor sound recording, is a remake of a 1923 silent version which also starred Arliss. It was remade again in 1943 as ADVENTURE IN IRAQ.

d, Alfred E. Green; w, Julian Josephson (based on the play of the same name by William Archer); ph, James Van Trees; ed, James Gribbon.

Adventure   **(PR:A   MPAA:NR)**

GREEN GRASS OF WYOMING**½   (1948) 89m FOX c

Peggy Cummins (Carey Greenway), Charles Coburn (Beaver), Robert Arthur (Ken), Lloyd Nolan (Rob McLaughlin), Burl Ives (Gus), Geraldine Wall (Neil McLaughlin), Robert Adler (Joe), Will Wright (Jake), Herbert Heywood (Storekeeper Johnson), Richard Garrick, Charles Hart (Old Timers), Charles Tannen (Veterinarian).

Based on a novel by Mary O'Hara, who also wrote the "Flicka" and "Thunderhead" series of horse stories, GREEN GRASS OF WYOMING has a good blend of human and animal relationships. On the human side is Cummins, the niece of ranch owner, Coburn, who falls in love with Arthur, the son of another ranch owner, Nolan. On the horse side, the romance involves a black mare owned by Arthur and a wild stallion, Thunderhead. The stallion lures the mare away, but Arthur brings both of them back to the ranch. The story then moves to the racetrack where the climax shows Coburn's horse beating out Nolan's mare which is about to give birth to the offspring of Thunderhead. Cummins and Arthur get together for a happy ending also.

p, Robert Bassler; d, Louis King; w, Martin Berkeley (based on the novel by Mary O'Hara); ph, Charles Clarke (Technicolor); m, Cyril Mockridge; ed, Nick DeMaggio; md, Lionel Newman.

Drama   **(PR:AA   MPAA:NR)**

GREEN GROW THE RUSHES**½   (1951, Brit.) 77m ACT/BL bw
(AKA: BRANDY ASHORE)

Roger Livesey (Capt. Biddle), Honor Blackman (Meg), Richard Burton (Hammond), Frederick Leister (Col. Gill), John Salew (Finch), Colin Gordon (Fisherwick), Geoffrey Keen (Prudhoe), Cyril Smith (Hewitt), Eliot Makeham (Urquhart), Vida Hope (Polly), Russell Waters (Bainbridge), Archie Duncan (Pettigrew), Jack McNaughton, Bryan Forbes, Arnold Ridley, Gilbert Davis, Harcourt Williams, John Stamp, Harold Goodwin, Henrik Jacobsen, Betty Shale.

A lightweight comedy about a group of brandy smugglers along England's southern shore who function under the protection of an ancient charter. When the authorities catch on, however, they try to find enough evidence to haul the perpetrators in. Eventually, a shipload of brandy reaches the port, but the townspeople drink it up before the authorities discover it. An entertaining picture produced by a group of film technicians who had nothing but troubles when it came to distributing the film, which suffered by comparison with similar—but earlier—Ealing comedies.

p, John Gossage; d, Derek Twist; w, Howard Clewes, Twist (based on a novel by Clewes); ph, Harry Waxman; m, Lambert Williamson; ed, Hazel Wilkinson.

Comedy **(PR:A MPAA:NR)**

GREEN HELL ** (1940) 87m UNIV bw

Douglas Fairbanks, Jr. *(Keith Brandon)*, Joan Bennett *(Stephanie Richardson)*, George Sanders *(Forrester)*, Vincent Price *(David Richardson)*, Alan Hale *(Dr. Emil "Nils" Loren)*, Gene Garrick *(Graham)*, George Bancroft *(Jim "Tex" Morgan)*, John Howard *(Hal Scott)*, Francis McDonald *(Gracco)*, Ray Mala *(Mala)*, Peter Bronte *(Santos)*, Kay Linaker *(Woman)*, Lupita Tovar, Yola d'Avril, Nena Quartaro, Anita Camargo *(Native Girls)*, Eumenio Blanco *(Well-Dressed Native)*, Tony Paton *(Bartender)*, Wilson Benge *(Butler)*, Iron Eyes Cody *(Indian)*, Franco Corsaro *(Man)*, Noble Johnson *(Indian Chief)*, Julian Rivero *(Proprietor)*.

Famed director James Whale attempted to get back in the good graces of the Hollywood studios with GREEN HELL, but it turned out to be a pathetic disaster. Desperate to work again after receiving no offers since directing the financially successful THE MAN IN THE IRON MASK in 1939 (American producers didn't like the homosexual Englishman and avoided using his valuable talents for fear of controversy), Whale grabbed a bad script penned by mediocre screenwriter Frances Marion. The project got off the ground because producer David Lewis, a friend of Whale and Marion, set things into motion. Everyone knew the script was terrible, but Whale convinced them that he could salvage it. Unfortunately, while the film is stunningly shot, the story and dialog are wretched. Fairbanks, Price, Hale, Howard, and Sanders play archaeologists determined to hack their way through the South American jungles to find hidden Inca treasures. Price is killed by poison darts (forever thankful that his participation in this debacle ended earlier than the others—he stated that GREEN HELL is one of the most unintentionally funny films ever made) and when native guide McDonald returns from town with supplies, he is accompanied by Price's widow, Bennett. The introduction of a woman into this all-male expedition causes some trouble, especially involving Fairbanks and Sanders between whom she is romantically vacillating. She finally decides on Fairbanks, but he too becomes a pin-cushion for poison darts and it looks as if he also will die. Miraculously, Fairbanks recovers in time for the climactic showdown between his men and the native hordes. GREEN HELL was given a lavish production by Universal which allowed a massive indoor jungle set to be built on a soundstage. An Inca Temple 125 feet high and 225 feet wide was constructed and it covered 45,000 square feet. Having spent so much money on what turned out to be a critical and financial disaster, Universal used the temple set again, this time as an Egyptian temple for THE MUMMY'S HAND (1940). Sadly, GREEN HELL rang the death-knell for Whale's film career. He would go on to begin production of THEY DARE NOT LOVE for Columbia in 1941, but after Whale and the cast clashed almost daily, the director was fired and replaced by Charles Vidor. A brilliant film stylist, Whale will always be remembered for the horror movies FRANKENSTEIN (1931), THE BRIDE OF FRANKENSTEIN (1935), THE OLD DARK HOUSE (1932), and THE INVISIBLE MAN (1933).

p, Harry Edington; d, James Whale; w, Frances Marion; ph, Karl Freund; ed, Ted J. Kent.

Adventure **(PR:A MPAA:NR)**

GREEN HELMET, THE*½ (1961, Brit.) 89m MGM bw

Bill Travers *(Rafferty)*, Ed Begley *(Bartell)*, Sidney James *(Richie Launder)*, Nancy Walters *(Diane)*, Ursula Jeans *(Mrs. Rafferty)*, Megs Jenkins *(Kitty Launder)*, Sean Kelly *(Taz Rafferty)*, Tutte Lemkow *(Carlo Zaraga)*, Gordon Tanner *(Hastrow)*, Ferdy Mayne *(Rossano)*, Peter Colingwood *(Charlie)*, Ronald Curram *(George)*, Diane Clare *(Pamela)*, Harold Kasket *(Lupi)*, Lyn Cole *(Jackie)*, Glyn Houston *(Pit Manager)*, Jack Brabham *(Himself)*, Roy Salvadori, Lucky Casner, John Coundley, Steve Ouvaroff, Mike Salmon *(Themselves)*.

Predictable car racing film revolves around aging racer Travers, who is losing his nerve after several bad crashes. He takes a job racing for a big tire company, owned by wealthy American Begley, as part of a promotional hype. In the meantime, he falls in love with Begley's daughter, Walters, who begs him to quit racing. But hoping to prove himself still capable, Travers enters a 1,000 mile Italian event, during which his car hits an oily patch and kills his navigator, James. This time a sense of duty rises above his fears and Travers goes on to win the big race. The dull script is saved by realistic race scenes which were actually shot from inside the cockpit of cars to give the feeling of real speed.

p, Charles Francis Vetter; d, Michael Forlong; w, Jon Cleary; ph, Geoffrey Faithfull; m, Ken Jones; ed, Frank Clarke; art d, Alan Withy; cos, Ivy Baker; spec eff, Tom Howard; makeup, Sydney Turner.

Action/Drama **(PR:A MPAA:NR)**

GREEN ICE*½ (1981, Brit.) 115m ITC c

Ryan O'Neal *(Wiley)*, Anne Archer *(Holbrook)*, Omar Sharif *(Argenti)*, Domingo Ambriz *(Miguel)*, John Larroquette *(Claude)*, Philip Stone *(Kellerman)*, Michael Sheard *(Jaap)*, Manuel Ojeda, Tara Fellner, Sandra Kerns, Raul Martinez, Enrique Novi, Miguel Angel Fuentes, Deloy White.

This unconvincing film stars Ryan O'Neal as a naive electronic engineer who hooks up with phony sophisticate Archer while in Mexico. The two travel south to Colombia where they team up with a left-wing terrorist and plan a giant emerald heist. Their problems just begin when they run into Sharif, who controls the illegal emerald empire. The credibility of GREEN ICE is stretched to the limits, especially when the trio uses hot-air balloons to steal the jewels and then land on top of a skyscraper undetected.

p, Jack Wiener; d, Ernest Day; w, Edward Anhalt, Ray Hassett, Anthony Simmons, Robert de Laurentis (based on the book by Gerald Browne); ph, Gilbert Taylor (Eastmancolor); m, Bill Wyman; ed, John Jympson; art d, Alan Tomkins, Leslie Tomkins, Pamela Carlton; cos, Yvonne Blake; spec eff, Martin Gutteridge.

Crime **Cas.** **(PR:C MPAA:NR)**

GREEN LIGHT½** (1937) 85m COS-FN/WB bw

Errol Flynn *(Dr. Newell Paige)*, Anita Louise *(Phyllis Dexter)*, Margaret Lindsay *(Frances Ogilvie)*, Sir Cedric Hardwicke *(Dean Harcourt)*, Walter Abel *(Dr. John Stafford)*, Henry O'Neill *(Dr. Endicott)*, Spring Byington *(Mrs. Dexter)*, Erin O'Brien-Moore *(Pat Arlen)*, Henry Kolker *(Dr. Lane)*, Pierre Watkin *(Dr. Booth)*, Granville Bates *(Sheriff)*, Russell Simpson *(Sheep Man)*, Myrtle Stedman, Shirley Lloyd *(Nurses)*, Wade Boteler *(Traffic Cop)*, Jim Pierce *(Harcourt's Chauffeur)*, Jim Thorpe *(Indian)*, Milton Kibbee *(Other Man)*.

The credibility of this plot is hard to swallow as we see Flynn cast as a young surgeon who sacrifices his career to protect the reputation of an elderly doctor played by O'Neill. During an operation, O'Neill was responsible for a surgical slip which proved fatal to his patient. The victim's daughter, Louise, had been romantically involved with Flynn, but now she suspects him of being responsible for her mother's death. A nurse who was on duty at the time tells Louise the truth. In the meantime, Flynn nobly becomes involved in risky experimental research which causes him to contract a dreaded illness. Our hero not only survives, but goes on to prove the effectiveness of a new serum and renews affections with his lady love. Overly idealistic story was the inspiration of Lutheran minister-turned-novelist Douglas.

p, Hal B. Wallis; d, Frank Borzage; w, Milton Krims (based on the novel by Lloyd C. Douglas); ph, Byron Haskin; m, Max Steiner; ed, James Gibbons; art d, Max Parker; cos, Orry-Kelly; spec eff, Fred Jackman, Jr., H.F. Koenekamp, Willard Van Enger.

Drama **(PR:A MPAA:NR)**

GREEN MAN, THE**** (1957, Brit.) 80m Grenadier/Distributors Corporation of America bw

Alastair Sim *(Hawkins)*, George Cole *(William Blake)*, Jill Adams *(Ann Vincent)*, Avril Angers *(Marigold)*, Terry-Thomas *(Boughtflower)*, John Chandos *(McKecknie)*, Dora Bryan *(Lily)*, Colin Gordon *(Reginald)*, Eileen Moore *(Joan Wood)*, Raymond Huntley *(Sir Gregory Upshoot)*, Cyril Chamberlain *(Sgt. Bassett)*, Doris Yorke *(Mrs. Bostock)*, Arthur Brough *(Landlord)*, Marie Burke *(Felicity)*, Vivienne Wood *(Annabel)*, Peter Bull, Willoughby Goddard, Arthur Lowe, Michael Ripper, Leslie Weston, Terence Alexander, Lucy Griffiths.

This hilarious comedy stars Sim as a professional assassin who has long been dormant. He is reactivated to do away with pompous Huntley, a politician. Sim tracks his quarry to a decrepit seaside resort called The Green Man and here waits to spring his trap. Sim is unctuous and arch in his disguise as a simple (if not simple-minded) clockmaker, putting up with a bevy of dowagers at the crusty resort, doting upon their teas, talks, and string quartet. Meanwhile he has planted a bomb to be exploded just when Huntley arrives, but it seems as if the victim never will appear as Sim plays out his impossible impersonation. Vacuum salesman Cole, a bumbler of the first rank, stumbles upon the plot and conducts a wild search for the killer at the inn, never for a moment suspecting the meek-mannered Sim. At the last minute he unearths the bomb and, seconds before it explodes, throws it out of a window and literally undoes Sim. Terry-Thomas is also very funny in this magnificent farce. One of the many priceless scenes is a throw-away where Sim is about to order a meal in the inn's uninviting dining room. He eyeballs a truculent waiter who stares back at him from a service counter where he is cleaning his nails with a fork. When Sim brusquely calls over the waiter, the servant contemptuously throws the fork back into the serving tray. The look of disgust on Sim's face is worth the whole movie. Love interest is provided by Adams, who begins with Huntley and ends on the unlikely arm of salesman Cole. Pure and wonderful entertainment.

p, Sidney Gilliat, Frank Launder; d, Robert Day; w, Gilliat, Launder (based on their play, "Meet a Body"); ph, Gerald Gibbs; m, Cedric Thorpe Davie; ed, Bernard Gribble.

Comedy **(PR:A MPAA:NR)**

GREEN MANSIONS** (1959) 104m MGM c

Audrey Hepburn *(Rima)*, Anthony Perkins *(Abel)*, Lee J. Cobb *(Nuflo)*, Sessue Hayakawa *(Runi)*, Henry Silva *(Kua-Ko)*, Nehemiah Persoff *(Don Panta)*, Michael Pate *(Priest)*, Estelle Hemsley *(Cla-Cla)*, Bill Saito, Yoneo Iguchi *(Native Guides)*.

GREEN MANSIONS is a film that will confuse those who haven't read the W. H. Hudson novel and disappoint those who have. Hepburn plays Rima, the bird girl, and Perkins is Abel, the man who finds her in the jungles of Venezuela and falls in love with her. Perkins is in hiding after a political uprising in which his father has been killed. Talk of gold in the area catches his ear as he searches for money to avenge his father's murder. Hepburn, who can communicate with nature, is seen by the Indians as an evil spirit, and the chief's son, Silva, wants to kill her. She is killed when the Indians trap her atop a tall, hollow tree, and set it on fire, but her foster-grandfather, Cobb, leads Perkins to the hidden gold—and maybe, maybe not, Perkins finds Rima alive in a jungle clearing. Hepburn was director Mel Ferrer's wife at the time the movie was produced.

p, Edmund Grainger; d, Mel Ferrer; w, Dorothy Kingsley (based on the novel by William Henry Hudson); ph, Joseph Ruttenberg (CinemaScope, Metrocolor); m, Hector Villa-Lobos, Bronislau Kaper; ed, Ferris Webster; art d, William A. Horning, Preston Ames; set d, Henry Grace, Jerry Wunderlich; cos, Dorothy Jeakins; ch, Katharine Dunham; spec eff, A. Arnold Gillespie, Lee LeBlanc, Robert R. Hoag.

Adventure/Romance **(PR:A MPAA:NR)**

GREEN MARE, THE½** (1961, Fr./Ital.) GAU-S.O.P.A.C.-Zebra-Productions Raimbourg-Star Presse/Zenith International c (LA JUMENT VERTE; LA GIUMENTA VERDA; AKA: BEDROOM VENDETTA)

Bourvil *(Honore Haudoin)*, Sandra Milo *(Marguerite Maloret)*, Francis Blanche *(Ferdinand Haudoin)*, Yves Robert *(Zephe Maloret)*, Valerie Lagrange *(Juliette Haudoin)*, Mireille Perrey *(Madame Houdoin, Honore's Mother)*, Carette *(Philibert, the Mayor)*, Guy Bertil *(Toucheur)*, Marie Mergey *(Adelaide)*, Nicole Mirel *(Aline)*, Georges Wilson *(Honore's Father, "Old Haudoin")*, Amedde *(Ernest)*, Martine Havet *(Clotilde)*, Achille Zavatta *(Deodat, the Mailman)*, Marie Dea *(Anais Maloret)*, Claude Sainlouis *(Noel Maloret)*.

A horse dealer has unusual luck when one of his mares gives birth to a green colt. The family become quite wealthy and when the mare finally dies, its portrait is hung in a place of honor. Soon after, the horse dealer dies, leaving his estate to his sons, Bourvil and Blanche. Robert, a neighbor of the family, jealous of the family's wealth, betrays Bourvil to the Prussians and to save her son his mother is forced to submit to a Prussian officer, not knowing her son and his friend Bertil are hiding beneath the bed. Bourvil keeps this a secret, plotting revenge all the while, and 15 years later decides to seduce Robert's daughter. His brother, however, has nominated the traitor Robert for mayor. Bourvil is further enraged when he discovers that Robert's family may know all about his mother's disgrace. When his daughter Lagrange falls in love with Robert's son, Sainlouis, Bourvil can take it no longer. He forces Sainlouis beneath his bed and there he reenacts the disgrace inflicted upon himself and his mother with Sainlouis's mother as (willing) victim. Very French. (In French; English subtitles.)

p&d, Claude Autant-Lara; w, Jean Aurenche, Pierre Bost (based on a story by Marcel Ayme); ph, Jacques Natteau (Franscope, Eastmancolor); m, Rene Clorec; ed, Madeleine Gug; art d, Max Douy; cos, Rosine Delamare; English titles, Rose Sokol.

Comedy/Drama (PR:O MPAA:NR)

GREEN PACK, THE½** (1934, Brit.) 72m BL bw

John Stuart *(Larry Dean)*, Aileen Marson *(Joan Thurston)*, Hugh Miller *(Martin Creet)*, Garry Marsh *(Tubby Storman)*, Michael Shepley *(Mark Elliott)*, J.H. Roberts *(Dr. Thurston)*, Antony Holles *(Inspector Aguilar)*, Percy Walsh *(Monty Carr)*.

Three young men talk a rich man into covering their costs for a trip to Africa after some hidden gold. While they are gone, their backer traps the fiancee of one of the young men into a gambling debt she cannot pay. To save her father, who has also been lured by the backer, she becomes the rich man's mistress. The expedition returns, successful, but the backer reneges on his agreement and the three decide he must be killed. They decide on the killer by drawing cards, thus the title. The double-dealer is killed and the ending reveals who did it—but the coroner's verdict is suicide.

p, Herbert Smith; d, T. Hayes Hunter; w, John Hunter (based on the play by Edgar Wallace); ph, Alex Bryce.

Crime (PR:C MPAA:NR)

GREEN PASTURES*½** (1936) 93m WB bw

Rex Ingram *(De Lawd, Adam/Hezdrel)*, Oscar Polk *(Gabriel)*, Eddie Anderson *(Noah)*, Frank Wilson *(Moses)*, George Reed *(Mr. Deshee)*, Abraham Gleaves *(Archangel)*, Myrtle Anderson *(Eve)*, Al Stokes *(Cain)*, Edna M. Harris *(Zeba)*, James Fuller *(Cain the Sixth)*, George Randol *(High Priest)*, Ida Forsythe *(Noah's Wife)*, Ray Martin *(Shem)*, Charles Andrews *(Flatfoot)*, Dudley Dickerson *(Ham)*, Jimmy Burress *(Jopeth)*, William Cumby *(Abraham/Head Magician/King of Babylon)*, George Reed *(Isaac)*, Ivory Williams *(Jacob)*, David Bethea *(Aaron)*, Ernest Whitman *(Pharaoh)*, Reginald Federson *(Joshua)*, Slim Thompson *(M.C.)*, Clinton Rosamond *(Prophet)*, Hall Johnson Choir.

Based on the 1930 Pulitzer Prize play that ran more than 5 years in 39 states, this is The Gospel According To Marc (Connelly, that is). Using a series of brief sketches by Roark Bradford, Connelly and co-screenwriter Gibney fashioned an interesting—though somewhat racist by today's standards—account of the Bible, using an all black cast. It took a lot of guts on the part of the brothers Warner to make this movie in the face of planned boycotts by many southern theater owners. The film takes place in a Sunday School and the teacher begins telling biblical stories from the Old Testament. As he speaks, all of the characters come to life, portrayed by notable black actors of the period. On the stage, De Lawd was played by Richard Berry Harrison but he passed away before the film was shot and his role was essayed by Ingram, who also played Adam and Hezdrel. All of the dialog is done in black colloquialisms, with many references to "seegars" and fishfries and expressions like "Gangway for de Lawd God Jehovah." We see the tales of Joshua at Jericho, Abraham, Isaac and Jacob, Noah, Adam and Eve, Moses and even Gabriel (whom De Lawd God refers to as "Gabe"). In many ways, this is one of the best biblical films ever done. Mostly because it doesn't preach, just entertains, and in doing that, the lessons are learned with a minimum of effort. One of the best elements of the movie is the music by the Hall Johnson Choir, who function as sort of a Greek Chorus to the action, singing tunes like "When The Saints Go Marching In," "Let My People Go," "Joshua Fit De Battle Of Jericho," and many more.

p, Henry Blanke; d, Marc Connelly, William Keighley; w, Connelly, Sheridan Gibney (from the play by Connelly, suggested by Roark Bradford's *Ol' Man Adam an' His Chillun*); ph, Hal Mohr; m, various spirituals, arranged and conducted by Hall Johnson; art d, Allen Saalburg, Stanley Fleischer.

Biblical Drama Cas. (PR:AA MPAA:NR)

GREEN PROMISE, THE** (1949) 92m RKO bw (GB: RAGING WATERS)

Marguerite Chapman *(Deborah Matthews)*, Walter Brennan *(Mr. Matthews)*, Robert Paige *(David Barkley)*, Natalie Wood *(Susan Matthews)*, Ted Donaldson *(Phineas Matthews)*, Connie Marshall *(Abigail Matthews)*, Robert Ellis *(Buzz Wexford)*, Jeanne LaDuke *(Jessie Wexford)*, Irving Bacon *(Julius Larkins)*, Milburn Stone *(Rev. Benton)*, Geraldine Wall *(Mrs. Wexford)*.

Brennan is a crusty, old-fashioned farmer trying to raise his four children without a mother. Through his stubbornness, he has ruined one farm and is well on the way to ruining another. While turning away all help and shunning modern methods, he tries to break up his eldest daughter's romance and stop little Wood from her dream of joining the local 4-H and raising sweet little lambs. But lo and behold, Brennan is laid up and Chapman must take over running the farm. With her in charge, everything starts running smoothly, Brennan's hard edges melt, and by the end they're all one big happy farm family. Ho-hum yokel hokum.

p, Robert Paige, Monty F. Collins; d, William D. Russell; w, Collins, ph, John L. Russell; ed, Richard Farrell.

Drama (PR:A MPAA:NR)

GREEN ROOM, THE*½** (1979, Fr.) 94m Les Films Du Carrosse-UA/New World c (LA CHAMBRE VERTE)

Francois Truffaut *(Julien Davenne)*, Nathalie Baye *(Cecilia Mandel)*, Jean Daste *(Bernard Humbert)*, Jean-Pierre Moulin *(Gerard Mazet)*, Antoine Vitez *(Bishop's secretary)*, Jane Lobre *(Mazet's second wife)*, Monique Dury *(Monique, editorial secretary)*, Laurence Ragon *(Julie Davenne)*, Marcel Berbert *(Dr. Jardine)*, Christian Lentretian *(Orator in cemetery)*, Patrick Maleon *(Georges)*, Annie Miller, Marie Jadoul, Jean-Pierre Ducos, Guy D'Ablon, Alphonse Simon, Henri Bienvenu, Thi Loan N'Guyen, Anna Paniez.

Francois Truffaut's testimony to obsession is perhaps the most unheralded film of his career. Truffaut himself plays Julien Davenne, a secretive man who excels at writing obituaries for a fading magazine. He is obsessed with death, believing that the dead are not given the love and attention they deserve. The reason for his reverence is two-fold—the guilt of his returning from WW I unharmed while everyone he knew was killed or injured, and the sudden death of his newlywed wife. In her memory, he constructs a shrine in what was her bedroom. One day at an auction he tries to find a ring of his wife's and ends up meeting Baye, an old acquaintance. He begins running into her on a steady basis at the cemetery, though they rarely make contact. A fire nearly destroys Truffaut's shrine to his wife, causing him to take more extreme steps. He commissions a wax figure of his wife, but it looks horrendous and he has it destroyed. While wandering through the cemetery he discovers an old chapel in need of restoration. After receiving permission from the church, he constructs an elaborate temple for the dead, containing photos of those he knew and a candle for each. In an act of love he asks Baye to help him oversee the temple. He tells her about the people in the photos and offers her the opportunity of lighting candles for the dead in her own life. She tells him that there is only one. On a visit to her apartment, Truffaut sees a number of photos of Paul Massigny, a boyhood friend who destroyed Truffaut's faith in life and taught him suspicion. Angrily, Truffaut runs out of the apartment and refuses to see Baye, or anyone, for months. His health deteriorates and he gives up the will to live. She writes him a letter which explains that the only way he'll ever love her is if she is dead. This shakes Truffaut and he meets her at the temple. Within moments, Truffaut falls to his knees amid the forest of lit candles and dies. Baye lights her only candle—for Truffaut. On the surface, THE GREEN ROOM is an excessively depressing and strange portrait of a man who values death over life, but underneath it becomes the study of a man driven by his obsessions, overflowing with exalted energy—Julien Davenne is obsessed with the dead, as Truffaut was obsessed with the cinema.

d, Francois Truffaut; w, Truffaut, Jean Gruault (based on themes in the writings of Henry James); ph, Nestor Almendros (Eastmancolor); m, Maurice Jaubert; ed, Martine Barraque-Curie; art d, Jean-Pierre Kohut Svelko.

Drama Cas. (PR:C-O MPAA:PG)

GREEN SCARF, THE** (1954, Brit.) 96m BL bw

Michael Redgrave *(Deliot)*, Ann Todd *(Solange)*, Leo Genn *(Rodelec)*, Kieron Moore *(Jacques)*, Richard O'Sullivan *(Child Jacques)*, Jane Lamb *(Child Solange)*, Michael Medwin *(Teral)*, Jane Griffiths *(Danielle)*, Ella Milne *(Louise)*, Jane Henderson *(Mme. Vauthier)*, George Merritt *(Advocate General)*, Peter Burton *(Purser)*, Tristan Rawson *(Prison Governor)*, Phil Brown *(John Bell)*, Anthony Nicholls *(Goirin)*, Walter Horsburgh *(Interpreter)*, Evelyn Roberts *(President of the Court)*, Neil Wilson *(Inspector)*, Michael Golden *(Warder)*, Launce Maraschal *(Sen. Bell)*, Terence Alexander *(Wireless Operator)*, Henry Caine *(Ship's Captain)*.

A murder mystery in which the prime suspect is a blind, deaf and mute man. Moore is the handicapped fellow, who despite his problems has written a successful novel. He returns from America after a lecture tour, only to be arrested for murder. He confesses his guilt as his wife, Todd, acts as interpreter for him. Redgrave takes on the case and the drama builds during the courtroom hearing as Redgrave establishes the man's innocence. Moore them refuses to testify to protect his wife, who it turns out was having an affair with the dead man, which was the reason Moore confessed—he thought she had done it. But she didn't, see—the real killer was actually . . .

p, Bertram Ostrer, Albert Fennell; d, George Moore O'Ferrall; w, Gordon Wellesley (from the novel *The Brute* by Guy Des Cars); ph, Jack Hildyard; m, Brian Easdale; ed Sid Stone; md, Easdale; art d, Wilfred Shingleton.

Mystery (PR:A MPAA:NR)

GREEN SLIME, THE* (1969) U.S./Jap. 90m MGM c (GAMMA SANGO UCHU DAISAKUSEN; AKA: BATTLE BEYOND THE STARS, DEATH AND THE GREEN SLIME)

Robert Horton *(Jack Rankin)*, Richard Jaeckel *(Vince Elliott)*, Luciana Paluzzi *(Lisa Benson)*, Bud Widom *(Jonathan Thompson)*, Ted Gunther *(Dr. Halvorsen)*, Robert Dunham *(Capt. Martin)*, David Yorston *(Lt. Curtis)*, William Ross *(Ferguson)*, Gary Randolf *(Cordier)*, Richard Hylland *(Michael)*, Strong Ilimaiti *(Doctor)*, Arthur Stark *(Barnett)*, Lynne Frederickson *(Secretary)*, David Sentman *(Officer)*, Clarence

Howard *(Patient)*, Hans Jorgseeberger, Bob Morris *(Soldiers)*, Jack Morris, Carl Bengs, Tom Scott *(Rocket Pilots)*, Don Plante, Enver Altenbay, Gunther Greve, Eugene Vince, George Uruf *(Technicians)*, Linda Hardisty, Kathy Horan, Ann Ault, Susan Skersick, Helen Kirkpatrick, Linda Miller, Patricia Elliot, Linda Malson *(Nurses)*, Tom Conrad *(Sergeant)*.

Bargain-basement production with pretensions of being a science fiction thriller. An Asteroid hurtling toward earth must be intercepted. Horton and Jaeckel, after fighting for command of a space ship, destroy the asteroid and take aboard some green slime. The slime has a nasty habit of clinging to the backs of crew members uniforms and proliferating into serpentine monsters that go on a murderous rampage. The only solution is to blow up the ship. Jaeckel is on board when the ship is obliterated and his girl friend winds up with Horton.

p, Ivan Reiner, Walter H. Manley; d, Kinji Fukasaku; w, Charles Sinclair, William Finger, Tom Rowe; ph, Yoshikazu Yamasawa (unidentified color); m, Toshiaki Tsushima; ed, Osamu Tanaka; cos, Miami; spec eff, Akira Watanabe.

Horror/Science Fiction **(PR:C MPAA:G)**

GREEN TREE, THE½** (1965, Ital.) 75m Rol Film-Salesians of Saint John Bosco/Don Bosco Films and Filmstrips bw

Robert Gho *(Mickey Magone)*, Natale Peretti *(Don Bosco)*, P. Terreno *(Theresa)*, A. Caravaggi *(Sara)*, P. Dutrelli *(Giovanni)*, V. Vaglini *(Christini)*, A. Giordenngo *(Gigio)*, Ignazio Dolce *(Ciccio)*.

A sort of Italian BOYS TOWN. During the 1850s Gho's father is jailed. Left to his own devices, Gho quickly becomes the leader of a gang of punks. After getting into serious trouble, he is sent to Peretti's home for boys. There he learns about God and he eventually returns to his old friends to teach them his new ways. Apparently this is based on a true story and produced by the home where the actual events took place. Filmed in 16mm.

p&d, Joseph Roland; w, Joseph Berrutti, Roland; ph, A. Grasso, Joseph Sacchi; m, Happy Ruggero.

Religious Drama **(PR:A MPAA:NR)**

GREEN YEARS, THE** (1946) 127m MGM bw

Charles Coburn *(Alexander Gow)*, Tom Drake *(Robert Shannon)*, Beverly Tyler *(Alison Keith)*, Hume Cronyn *(Papa Leckie)*, Gladys Cooper *(Grandma Leckie)*, Dean Stockwell *(Robert Shannon as a child)*, Selena Royle *(Mama Leckie)*, Jessica Tandy *(Kate Leckie)*, Richard Haydn *(Jason Reid)*, Andy Clyde *(Saddler Boag)*, Norman Lloyd *(Adam Leckie)*, Robert North *(Murdoch Leckie)*, Wallace Ford *(Jamie Nigg)*, Eilene Janssen *(Alison Keith as a Child)*, Hank Daniels *(Gavin Blair)*, Richard Lyon *(Gavin Blair as a Child)*, Henry O'Neill *(Canon Roche)*, Henry Stephenson *(Blakely)*, Norma Varden *(Mrs. Bosomley)*.

Faithful and convincing filmization of A.J. Cronin's *The Green Years* traces a young boy's growth to manhood in Scotland. Coburn is the lad's great-grandfather, who has a fondness for the local brew and is forever getting into trouble despite his likability. Stockwell as the youth observes all this and is mesmerized. Drake plays the boy at an older age as he experiences the joy of falling in love and going to school. He wants to go to college but feels guilty because the tuition would come from the insurance money inherited from the deceased Coburn.

p, Leon Gordon; d, Victor Saville; w, Robert Ardrey, Sonya Levien (based on the novel by A.J. Cronin); ph, George Folsey; m, Herbert Stothart; ed, Robert J. Kern; art d, Cedric Gibbons, Hans Peters; spec eff, A. Arnold Gillespie, Donald Jahraus.

Drama **(PR:A MPAA:NR)**

GREEN-EYED BLONDE, THE*½ (1957) 76m Arwin/WB bw

Susan Oliver *(Greeneyes)*, Linda Plowman *(Betsy Abel)*, Beverly Long *(Ouisie)*, Norma Jean Nilsson *(Cuckoo)*, Tommie Moore *(Trixie)*, Carla Merey *(Joyce)*, Sallie Brophy *(Margaret Wilson)*, Jean Innes *(Mrs. Nichols)*, Olive Blakeney *(Miss Vandingham)*, Anne Barton *(Sally Abel)*, Tom Greenway *(Ed)*, Margaret Brayton *(Mrs. Adams)*, Juanita Moore *(Miss Randall)*, Raymond Foster *(Cliff Munster)*, Betty Lou Gerson *(Mrs. Ferguson)*, Stafford Repp *(Bill Prell)*, Evelyn Scott *(Helen)*, Roy Glenn *(Mr. Budlong)*.

Set in a girls' reformatory prison, THE GREEN-EYED BLONDE, tells the story of several of the inmates who hide the illegitimate baby of one of the interned girls. The infant causes the trouble-making young women to join together as a family unit. When the guards find the baby they take it away, much to the dismay of the prisoners, who tear up the reformatory. During the rioting, Oliver breaks out and joins up with her boyfriend, and the pair are killed when their car crashes during a police chase.

p, Martin Melcher; d, Bernard Girard; w, Sally Stubblefield (based on a story by Stubblefield); ph, Edward Fitzgerald; m, Leith Stevens; ed, Thomas Reilly; art d, Art Loel; m/l, "The Green-Eyed Blonde," Joe Lubin (sung by The Four Grads).

Drama **(PR:C MPAA:NR)**

GREENE MURDER CASE, THE*** (1929) 68m PAR bw

William Powell *(Philo Vance)*, Florence Eldridge *(Sibella Greene)*, Ullrich Haupt *(Dr. Arthur Von Blon)*, Jean Arthur *(Ada Greene)*, Eugene Pallette *(Sgt. Heath)*, E. H. Calvert *(District Attorney John F. X. Markham)*, Gertrude Norman *(Mrs. Tobias Greene)*, Lowell Drew *(Chester Greene)*, Morgan Farley *(Rex Greene)*, Brandon Hurst *(Sproot)*, Augusta Burmeister *(Gertrude Mannheim)*, Marcia Harriss *(Hemming)*, Mildred Golden *(Barton)*, Mrs. Mildred Buckland *(Nurse)*, Helena Phillips *(Police Nurse)*, Shep Camp *(Medical Examiner)*, Charles E. Evans *(Lawyer Canon)*.

The second sound film based on S. S. Van Dine's Philo Vance novels (the first, THE CANARY MURDER CASE, was shot silent and then dubbed for sound), is even better than its predecessor. Powell returns as the dashing and suave psychologist/detective, this time to investigate the murder of a New York millionaire. When the nine suspects Powell has rounded up begin to die off as well, the amateur detective must do a bit of digging to discover that sweet and innocent Miss Arthur is actually the cold-blooded killer. Arthur turns in a superb performance as the crafty and very evil murderess whose pleasant, likable demeanor is transformed into a horribly rotten reality when she desperately tries to eliminate Eldridge before Powell can stop her. The production is top-notch in all respects and the climactic chase sequence is quite thrilling.

p, B. P. Schulberg; d, Frank Tuttle; w, Louise Long, Bartlett Cormack (based on the novel by S. S. Van Dine); ph, Henry Gerrard; ed, Verna Willis.

Mystery **(PR:A MPAA:NR)**

GREENGAGE SUMMER, THE(SEE: LOSS OF INNOCENCE, 1961, Brit.)

GREENWICH VILLAGE** (1944) 83m FOX c

Carmen Miranda *(Princess Querida)*, Don Ameche *(Kenneth Harvey)*, William Bendix *(Danny O'Mara)*, Vivian Blaine *(Bonnie Watson)*, Felix Bressart *(Moger)*, Tony and Sally De Marco *(Themselves)*, B.S. Pully *(Brophy)*, Four Step Brothers *(Specialty)*, Emil Rameau *(Kovesky)*, Frank Orth *(Cadway)*, Torben Meyer *(Butler)*, Herbert Evers *(Young Man)*, Hal K. Dawson *(Cashier)*, William B. Davidson *(Dance Director)*, Eddie Dunn *(Set Designer)*, Sherry Hall *(Assistant Set Designer)*, Paul Hurst *(Milkman)*, Tom Dugan *(Bootlegger)*, Billy Wayne *(Ballyhoo Man)*, Oliver Prickett *(Ambers)*, The Revuers *(Judy Holiday, Betty Comden, Adolphe Green, Alvin Hammer—Themselves)*, Banda Da Lua *(Themselves)* Charles Arnt, Charles Williams.

One of the few Twentieth Century Fox Technicolor musicals to flop during the WW II years. Miranda had her first top billing in this silly presentation which takes place in New York City during the early 1920s. Ameche is a composer who tries to spark interest in his piano concerto. Bendix, a speakeasy owner, is raising money to stage a Broadway show, and he successfully adapts Ameche's concerto into an uptown musical. In her screen debut, Blaine plays a speakeasy singer that Ameche falls for. The film is replete with singing, and dancing numbers by Tony and Sally Demarco's ballroom steps as well as the Four Step Brother's jazz dancing. Songs include: "It Goes to Your Toes," "Give Me a Band and a Bandana," "It's All For Art, Art's Sake," "I'm Down To My Last Dream," "Oh Brother," "I Have To See You Privately," "This Is Our Lucky Day," "You Make Me So Mad," "Never Before," "I've Been Smiling In My Sleep," "Tell Me It's You," "That Thing They Talk About," "Whispering," "Swinging Down The Lane," "When You Wore A Tulip," "I'm Just Wild About Harry."

p, William LeBaron; d, Walter Lang; w, Earl Baldwin, Walter Bullock (based on a story by Fred Hazlitt Brennan, adapted by Michael Fessier and Ernest B. Pagano); ph, Leon Shamroy, Harry Jackson (Technicolor); m, Emil Newman, Charles Henderson; ed, Robert Simpson; songs Leo Robin, Nacio Herb Brown; art d, James Basevi, Joseph C. Wright; spec eff, Fred Sersen.

Musical **(PR:A MPAA:NR)**

GREENWICH VILLAGE STORY½** (1963) 95m Lion Int. bw (AKA: BIRTHPLACE OF THE HOOTENANNY; THEY LOVE AS THEY PLEASE)

Robert Hogan *(Brian)*, Melinda Plank *(Genie)*, Tani Seitz *(Anne)*, Sunja Svendsen *(Claudine)*, James Cresson *(George)*, Aaron Banks *(Franko)*, John G. Avildsen *(Alvie)*, John Brent *(Poet)*, Charles Gosset *(Judge)*, Jim McKernan *(Kimmie)*.

Hogan and Plank are a Bohemian couple living together sans preacher in the Village. He is an ambitious novelist trying to be the next Jack Kerouac; she is a young ballerina. He promises to marry her if the novel is a success. When the novel is uniformly panned by the critics, Hogan takes off for a weekend fling with Seitz, an admiring debutante. Unbeknownst to Hogan, Plank is already pregnant with his child, and she dies having an abortion. The film ends with Hogan realizing his mistakes and crying in grief.

p,d&w, Jack O'Connell; ph, Baird Bryant; ed, Jean Begley, Carl Lerner.

Drama **(PR:C MPAA:NR)**

GREENWOOD TREE, THE zero (1930, Brit.) 60m BIP bw

Marguerite Allan *(Fancy)*, John Batten *(Dick)*, Nigel Barrie *(Shinar)*, Billy Shine *(Leaf)*, Robert Abel *(Penny)*, Maud Gill *(Old Maid)*, Wilfred Shine *(Paison)*.

Based on a Thomas Hardy novel, and set in the period in which he lived, this antique of a film is filled with many of the author's stock characters, complete with villainous glued-on mustaches or other literary gadgets. In an effort to produce Hardy literally, the film produces unintentional laughter.

d, Harry Lachman; w, (based on the work of Thomas Hardy); ph, Claude Friese Greene.

Drama **(PR:A MPAA:NR)**

GREGORY'S GIRL*** (1982, Brit.) 91m Lake Film Prod./Goldwyn c

Gordon John Sinclair *(Gregory)*, Dee Hepburn *(Dorothy)*, Jake D'Arcy *(Phil Menzies)*, Clare Grogan *(Susan)*, Robert Buchanan *(Andy)*, William Greenlees *(Steve)*, Alan Love *(Eric)*, Caroline Guthrie *(Carol)*, Carol Macartney *(Margo)*, Douglas Sannachan *(Billy)*, Allison Forster *(Madeline)*, Chic Murray *(Headmaster)*, Alex Norton *(Alec)*, John Bett *(Alistair)*, Graham Thompson *(Charlie)*.

A funny and touching juvenile romance from Scottish director Forsyth, whose next film, LOCAL HERO, was even better. Sinclair stars as a teenage soccer goalie who develops a crush on Hepburn, the new girl on the team. Sinclair successfully portrays the uneasy quandary most adolescent boys go through when suffering from painful shyness coupled with the outrageous hormonal imbalance that drives them to do ridiculous things to get the attention of a pretty girl. While the plot is a straight, simple romance, the true charm of the film comes from its quirky characterizations and the lively, insightful sense of humor. GREGORY'S GIRL is a refreshing change of pace from the popular American teenage comedies that wallow in unfunny, raunchy, hubba-hubba sexual humor attempted by characters with nothing but sex, drugs, booze, and troublemaking on their minds.

p, Clive Parsons, Davina Belling; d&w, Bill Forsyth; ph, Michael Coulter (Kay Labs color); m, Colin Tully; ed, John Gow; art d, Adrienne Atkinson.

Romance/Comedy   **Cas.**   **(PR:C MPAA:PG)**

GREH**   (1962, Ger./Yugo.) 88m Saphir-Triglav/Globe-John Alexander bw
(AM ANFANG WAR ES SUNDE;
AKA: THE BEGINNING WAS SIN)

Ruth Niehaus (Rosalie), Viktor Staal (Jacob Bauer), Hansi Knotecks (Anna), Peter Carsten (Marko), Laya Raki (Gypsy Dancer), Petr Unkel, Franz Muxeneder, Edith Schultze-Westrum.

Staal is a farmer, married to an apparently infertile woman. His maid, Niehaus, has been raped by farmhand Carsten and is pregnant. After Carsten refuses to marry her, Niehaus goes to her mother's home to give birth. After having a son, she returns to Staal's farm, only to learn the wealthy farmer's wife has passed away. The two marry but Niehaus keeps her child a secret. Staal grows angry when she can't have a child but during a violent argument Niehaus reveals the truth about her bastard son. Staal, humbled by the fact that he's the sterile one, adopts the child as his own.

p, Peter Bamberger; d&w, Franz Cap (based on the story "Histoire d'Une Fille de Ferme" by Guy de Maupassant); ph, Bruno Stephan; m, Bojan Adamic; ed, Hilde Grebner, Klaus Eckstein; art d, Mirko Lippo.

Drama   **(PR:O MPAA:NR)**

GRENDEL GRENDEL GRENDEL**   (1981, Aus.) 90m Victorian Film
Corp. c

Peter Ustinov, Keith Michell, Arthur Dignam, Ed Rosser, Bobby Bright, Ric Stone, Julie McKenna, Ernie Bourne, Allison Bird, Barry Hill (Principal Voices).

An animated film based on John Gardner's novel Grendel, which adapts the classic Beowulf legend and attempts—unsuccessfully—to translate its philosophy to a children's audience. Basically a fable about man's destruction of himself and all life around him, the film gets bogged down in intellectual ramblings that would confuse a child and bore an adult. In addition, the musical numbers (which seem to be a concession to the kiddie trade) are overlong and uninspired, dragging the pace of the film to a near halt. The animation however, is lovely, and colored in soft pastels.

p, Phillip Adams, Alexander Stitt; d&w, Stitt (based on the novel Grendel by John Gardner); m, Bruce Smeaton; prod d, Stitt; m/l, Stitt; animation d, Frank Hellard; animators, Hellard, Anne Joiliffe, Gus Mclaren, Ralph Peverill, David Atkinson, Stitt.

Animated Adventure   **Cas.**   **(PR:AAA MPAA:NR)**

GREY FOX, THE****   (1983, Can.) 92m Mercury/UA c

Richard Farnsworth (Bill Miner), Jackie Burroughs (Kate Flynn), Wayne Robson (Shorty), Ken Pogue (Jack Budd), Timothy Webber (Fernie), Gary Reineke (Detective Seavey), David Peterson (Louis Colquhoun), Don MacKay (Al Sims), Samantha Langevin (Jenny), Tom Heaton (Tom), James McLarty, George Dawson (Accomplices), Ray Michal (Gunsmith), Stephan E. Miller (Danny Young), David L. Crowley (Oregon Engineer), Jack Leaf (Shopkeeper), Isaac Hislop (Town Boy), Sean Sullivan (Newspaper Editor), Bill Murdock (Mission Engineer), David McCulley, Jack Ackroyd, David Raines (Firemen), Gary Chalk, Nicolas Rice (Mail Clerks), Frank Turner (Hotel Clerk), Bill Meilen (Ducks Engineer), Paul Jolicoeur (Conductor), Mel Tuck (Baggage Clerk), Peter Jobin (Sgt. Wilson), Anthony Holland (Judge), Jon York (Prison Guard), Lisa Westman (Farm Girl), John Owen (Piano Player).

This is a great example of what can be done with a small budget and a terrific idea. Farnsworth plays real-life train robber Bill Miner, released after being in prison for 30 years. He finds the old West that he knew has disappeared, but knowing no other trade, he goes back to train robbing. Farnsworth, an ex-stunt man and character actor, suggested for the part by Francis Ford Coppola, is dignified in his first starring role. Borsos' direction is fine, and this too was his first feature, after a career as a documentary film maker. The marvelous photography is by Tidy, who also did the moody lensing on the often overlooked film THE DUELISTS. A class job all the way.

p, Peter O'Brian; d, Philip Borsos; w, John Hunter; ph, Frank Tidy; m, Michael Conway Baker, The Chieftans; ed, Frank Irvine; art d, Bill Brodie.

Western   **Cas.**   **(PR:C MPAA:PG)**

GREYFRIARS BOBBY*½   (1961, Brit.) 91m BV c

Donald Crisp (John Brown), Laurence Naismith (Mr. Traill), Alexander Mackenzie (Old Jock), Kay Walsh (Mrs. Brown), Andrew Cruickshank (Lord Provost), Vincent Winter (Tammy), Moultrie Kelsall (Magistrate), Gordon Jackson (Farmer), Rosalie Crutchley (Farmer's Wife), Freda Jackson (Old Woman Caretaker), Jameson Clark (Constable), Duncan Macrae (Constable Maclean), Joan Buck (Allie), Jennifer Nevinson (Farmer's Daughter), Joyce Carey (1st Lady), Jack Lambert (Doctor), Bruce Seton, Hamish Wilson, Sean Keir.

A typically well done Disney dog picture guaranteed to melt the heart of any animal lover. Set in Edinburgh at the turn of the century, the film follows the adventures of a cute little Skye terrier named Bobby. When his elderly master dies, the loyal dog refuses to leave the grave. Eventually Bobby is persuaded to venture into town and play with the local children, but at night he runs back to the cemetery to the grave of his master. Word of the dog's odd habits spreads throughout Edinburgh and in the end Bobby is made a Freeman of the city. True story.

p, Walt Disney; d, Don Chaffey; w, Robert Westerby (from the story by Eleanor Atkinson); ph, Paul Beeson; m, Francis Chagrin; ed, Peter Tanner; set d, Vernon Dixon; cos, Margaret Bolland; dog trainer, John Darlys.

Children's Drama   **(PR:AAA MPAA:NR)**

GREYHOUND LIMITED, THE**   (1929) 68m WB bw

Monte Blue (Monte Jones), Grant Withers (Bill Williams), Edna Murphy (Edna), Lucy Beaumont (Mrs. Williams), Lew Harvey, Ernie Shields.

Silent actor Blue chugs his way through one of his first sound films playing a railroad engineer. Blue and his buddy Withers, a fireman, are two rough-and-tumble types who are inseparable until Withers is suddenly smitten by Murphy, a little tart who's obviously up to no good in Blue's eyes. Crammed into this saga is a quickie murder mystery that sees Withers arrested for a murder he didn't commit and about to swing for it, when Blue swallows his pride and finds the real killer.

d, Howard Bretherton; w, Anthony Coldeway (based on a story by A. Howson, Joseph Jackson).

Drama   **(PR:A MPAA:NR)**

GRIDIRON FLASH*½   (1935) 62m Radio bw
(GB: THE LUCK OF THE GAME)

Eddie Quillan, Betty Furness, Grant Mitchell, Edgar Kennedy, Grady Sutton, Joseph Sauers, Allen Wood, Margaret Dumont, Lucien Littlefield.

Mitchell is the coach of a college team who sees Quillan, doing time for a bank robbery, playing on a prison team and offers him a chance at parole if he plays football for his team. Quillan jumps at the chance because he wants to pull a few jobs and get away from the college. Mitchell tells his niece, Furness, to make a play for Quillan so he won't leave. It works, but after several misunderstandings with the law, Quillan barely makes it back for the final game of the season—in which he scores the winning touchdown in the final minute of play.

d&w, Glenn Tryon (based on a story by Nicholas Barrows, Earle Snell); ph, John W. Boyle; m, Max Steiner; ed, George Crone.

Sport/Drama   **(PR:A MPAA:NR)**

GRIEF STREET*½   (1931) 64m Chesterfield bw

Barbara Kent (Jean Royce), John Holland (Jim Ryan), Dorothy Christy (Mrs. Merle), Crauford Kent (Alvin Merle), Lillian Rich (Pamela Gregory), James Burtis (Jardin), Larry Steers (Ralph Burns), Lloyd Whitlock (Frank Murray), Lafe McKee (Michael), Creighton Hale, Ray Largay, Arthur Brennan.

A Broadway mystery thriller starring Holland as an overly hard-boiled reporter investigating the murder of a famous New York actor found choked to death in his dressing room. Holland is beset with other problems when the heroine, Kent, is shot and then soon after another corpse surfaces before he can finally drag the killer in and dump him at the feet of dim-witted police sergeant Burtis.

d, Richard Thorpe; w, Arthur Hoerl; ph, M. A. Anderson; ed, Thorpe.

Mystery   **(PR:A MPAA:NR)**

GRIGSBY   (SEE: LAST GRENADE, THE, 1970, Brit.)

GRIM REAPER, THE*½   (1981, Ital.) 81m c
(AKA: ANTHROPOPHAGOUS)

Tisa Farrow, Saverio Vallane, Vanessa Steiger, George Eastman, Zora Kerova, Mark Bodin, Bob Larsen, Mark Logan, Rubina Rey.

Low-budget Italian shocker which stars Mia's sister Tisa (she makes a lot of these turkeys—see ZOMBIE) as an American student vacationing in the Greek isles. Tisa watches in horror as all the nice student tourists she's traveling with are killed and eaten by a nut case with bad skin who somehow thinks he's getting revenge for the deaths of his wife and child during a shipwreck, even though he's the guy who killed them. The effects are gory, the creep's make-up laughable, and the whole thing silly.

p, Oscar Santaniello; d, Joe D'Amato; w, Lewis Montefiore, Aristide Massaccesi; ph, Enrico Birbichi; ed, Ornella Michell.

Horror   **Cas.**   **(PR:O MPAA:R)**

GRINGO**   (1963, Span./Ital.) 95m Tecisa Film/Jolly Film c (DUELLO NEL TEXAS; AKA: GUNFIGHT AT RED SANDS)

Richard Harrison, Giacomo Rossi Stuart, Mikaela, Sara Lezana, Daniel Martin.

Harrison is a soldier in the Mexican revolution who leaves the fighting to take on a battle of his own, seeking revenge on his foster father. This mildly interesting film introduced some ideas to the "Spaghetti Western" that were later expanded by Leone in his films with Eastwood; for example, the avenging stranger (who became Eastwood's "Man with No Name"). Preview of things soon to come.

p, Albert Band [Alfredo Antonini]; d, Ricardo Blasco; w, Band, Blasco; ph, Jack Dalmas [Massimo Dallamano].

Western   **(PR:O MPAA:NR)**

GRIP OF THE STRANGLER   (SEE: HAUNTED STRANGLER, THE, 1958, Brit.)

GRISSLY'S MILLIONS**   (1945) 71m REP bw

Paul Kelly (Joe Simmons), Virginia Grey (Katherine Palmor Bentley), Don Douglas (Ellison Hayes), Elisabeth Risdon (Leona Palmor), Robert H. Barrat (Grissly Morgan Palmor), Clem Bevans (Young Tom), Eily Malyon (Mattie), Adele Mara (Maribelle), Francis Pierlot (Dr. Benny), Addison Richards (Henry Adams), Paul Fix (Lewis Bentley), Byron Foulger (Fred Palmor), Joan Blair (Mrs. Fred Palmor), Grady Sutton (Robert Palmor, Jr.), Frank Jaquet (Robert Palmor, Sr.), Will Wright (John Frey), Louis Mason (The Gatekeeper), Tom London (Policeman Ralph).

Barrat is an aged millionaire near his death, his relatives circling him like vultures waiting for what they think they will receive from the old man's estate. He finally dies, and leaves all of his wealth to his favorite granddaughter, Grey. This sets the rest of the relatives in motion to get rid of Grey. Kelly, a detective, has trailed Grey's estranged husband to the house, but he disappears within the confines.

Kelly stays to protect Grey from her vicious relations and romance blooms between the two.

p, Walter H. Goetz; d, John English; w, Muriel Roy Bolton; ph, William Bradford; ed, Harry Keller; md, Morton Scott; art d, Gano Chittenden; spec eff, Howard Lydecker, Theodore Lydecker.

Mystery (PR:A MPAA:NR)

GRISSOM GANG, THE* (1971) 127m ABC Pictures, Associates and Aldrich/CINERAMA c

Kim Darby (*Barbara Blandish*), Scott Wilson (*Slim Grissom*), Tony Musante (*Eddie Hagen*), Robert Lansing (*Dave Fenner*), Irene Dailey (*Ma Grissom*), Connie Stevens (*Anna Borg*), Wesley Addy (*John P. Blandish*), Joey Faye (*Woppy*), Don Keefer (*Doc*), Dotts Johnson (*Johnny Hutchins*), Mort Marshall (*Heinie*), Michael Baseleon (*Connor*), Ralph Waite (*Mace*), Hal Baylor (*Chief McLaine*), Matt Clark (*Bailey*), Alvin Hammer (*Sam*), Dave Willock (*Rocky*), Alex Wilson (*Jerry McGowan*), Elliott Street (*Station Boy*), John Steadman (*Old Man*), Raymond Guth (*Farmer*).

If you like Robert Aldrich pictures, then you *may* like this one, another example of his extreme indulgence but it does have some saving graces. Despite its over two hours running time, it doesn't stop for a second. Set in the early Thirties, the Grissoms are a Ma Barker-type gang who kidnap heiress Darby. Dailey is the Mother, a notorious sadist. The gang attempts to recover the ransom loot but screws things up royally. Further, Darby and Wilson, Dailey's moronic oaf of a son, seem to have more going for them than the usual captive-captor relationship. Many scenes may have been intended as comedy relief to the bloodbath sequences, but they fall flat. Aldrich had a way of blending the macabre and humor (THE FRISCO KID, TOO LATE THE HERO, WHATEVER HAPPENED TO BABY JANE?) but we're not sure what he meant by this one. It's a dumb plot with mean people but it should delight the blood and guts crowd, the kind of people who love RAMBO. Good camera work by Biroc, sharp editing by veteran Luciano and lots of money spent on the period sets. Weird supporting characters who tend to pull our attention away, rather than focus it. It's a remake of NO ORCHIDS FOR MISS BLANDISH, which was one of the worst gangster films ever made when it escaped in 1948 (U.S. release, 1951). THE GRISSOM GANG is slightly better, but not much. The song "I Can't Give You Anything But Love, Baby" (m, Jimmy McHugh; l, Dorothy Fields) is sung by Rudy Vallee. Mood music.

p&d, Robert Aldrich; w, Leon Griffiths (based on the novel *No Orchids For Miss Blandish* by James Hadley Chase); ph, Joseph Biroc (Metrocolor); m, Gerald Fried; ed, Michael Luciano; art d, James Vance; cos, Norma Koch; ch, Alex Romero.

Crime Drama/Comedy Cas. (PR:C-O MPAA:R)

GRITOS EN LA NOCHE (SEE: AWFUL DR. ORLOFF, THE, 1964, Span./Fr.)

GRIZZLY*½ (1976) 90m Film Ventures Intl. c (AKA: KILLER GRIZZLY)

Christopher George (*The Ranger*), Richard Jaeckel (*The Naturalist*), Andrew Prine (*The Helicopter Pilot*), Joan McCall (*The Photographer*), Joseph Dorsey (*The Park Supervisor*), Maryann Hearn (*A Victim*), Charles Kissinger (*Doctor*), Kermit Echols (*Corwin*).

Film Ventures International (FVI) specialized in turning out cheap imitations based on big block-busters. When THE EXORCIST came out, FVI followed it with BEYOND THE DOOR and as JAWS was a number one money-grosser, they came out with this film, replacing the shark with a 15-foot bear. The meager plot follows the bear as he lumbers about slicing up tourists, and not just to get their picnic baskets. He is pursued by heroic forest ranger, George, and a naturalist, Jaeckel. The bear manages to stay one paw ahead of the search team for most of the film, poking his muzzle out only long enough to chew up Jaeckel and Prine, before he is blown to pieces by George. George, Jaeckel and Prine would star in another nature-gone-mad movie the next year, DAY OF THE ANIMALS.

p&w, David Sheldon, Harvey Flaxman; d, William Girdler; ph, William Anderson (Todd-AO, Movielab Color); m, Robert O. Ragland; spec eff, Phil Corey.

Adventure Cas. (PR:C MPAA:PG)

GROOM WORE SPURS, THE* (1951) 81m UNIV bw

Ginger Rogers (*Abigail Furnival*), Jack Carson (*Ben Castle*), Joan Davis (*Alice Dean*), Stanley Ridges (*Harry Kallen*), James Brown (*Steve Hall*), John Litel (*District Attorney*), Victor Sen Yung (*Ignacio*), Mira McKinney (*Mrs. Forbes*), Gordon Nelson (*Ricky*), George Meader (*Bellboy*), Kemp Niver (*Killer*), Robert B. Williams (*Jake Harris*), Franklyn Farnum (*Reverend*), Kate Drain Lawson (*Witness*), Richard Whorf (*Himself*), Ross Hunter.

Carson, a Hollywood cowboy tough-guy who is actually a marshmallow off-screen with a penchant for girls and gambling, gets himself in trouble on a trip to Las Vegas and is forced to call on lady lawyer Rogers to bail him out. She falls for him and after several breakups winds up as his wife, making a man out of him instead of the phony he was.

p, Howard Welsch; d, Richard Whorf; w, Robert Carson, Robert Libbott, Frank Burt (based on the novel *Legal Bride* by Carson); ph, Peverell Marley; m, Arthur Lange, Charles Maxwell; prod d, Ben Hersh; ed, Otto Ludwig; md, Emil Newman; art d, Perry Ferguson; set d, Julia Heron; cos, Jacie and Eloise Jensson; hair stylist, Louise Miehle; makeup, Frank Westmore.

Comedy (PR:A MPAA:NR)

GROOVE TUBE, THE* (1974) 75m Levitt-Pickman c

Buzzy Linhart, Richmond Baier (*The Hitchhiker*), Ken Shapiro (*Koko the Clown, Kramp TV Kitchen, The Dealer, Newscaster, Sex Olympics, "Four Leaf Clover," "Just You, Just Me"*), Paul Norman, Victoria Medlin (*Mouth Appeal*), Chevy Chase, Jennifer Wells (*Geritan*), Ken Shapiro, Richard Belzer (*The Dealers*), Bill Kemmill, Alex Stephens (*Butz Beer*), Richard Belzer (*President*), Ken Shapiro,

Chevy Chase (*Four Leaf Clover*), Christy Nazareth, Peter William Blaxill, Dennis Helfand, Frederick Stuthman, Lincoln Harrice, Berkeley Harris, William Paxton, Bill Bailey, Lane Sarasohn, Mary Mendham, Bill Bailey.

A sometimes humorous satire of modern television that leaves no aspect of TV programming unscathed. It hits everything from commercials to kiddie programming and shows television to be an insult to viewers. Made up of dozens of sketches and vignettes, THE GROOVE TUBE, was a legitimate theater venture that ran off-Broadway and toured other U.S. cities for five years. Chevy Chase made his first feature film debut before he was on SATURDAY NIGHT LIVE. This film was first rated X, but was later trimmed to an R rating.

p&d, Ken Shapiro; w, Shapiro, Lane Sarasohn; ph, Bob Bailin; animation, Linda Taylor, Pat O'Neill.

Comedy Cas. (PR:O MPAA:NR)

GROUCH, THE*½ (1961, Gr.) 107m Finos/Greek Motion Pictures bw (HO GROUSOUZES: AKA: THE OLD GROUCHY)

Orestis Makris (*Grouch*), Daphne Skouras (*Girl*), Georgia Vassiliadou (*Housekeeper*), Mimi Fotopoulos (*Gossip*), Dinos Iliopoulos (*Friend*).

Makris is an old, bad-tempered cafe owner who lightens up and wears a smile when he is left to care for an abandoned child. When the mother returns to the cafe she and the grouch become the subject of some vicious local gossip but survive the insults and, by the upbeat finale, win them over. An overlong picture which tries too hard to gain sympathy for the main characters and paints the locals in a nasty light.

d&w, George Tzavellas.

Drama (PR:A MPAA:NR)

GROUND ZERO zero (1973) 86m Flocker Enterprises c

Ron Casteel, Melvin Belli, Augie Triebach, Kim Friese, John Waugh, Yvonne D'Angiers, Hal Stein, Dominic Guzzo, Anthony Curcio, Mike Maurantonio, Lia Belli, Charles Granata, David Button, Vincent Turturici, Ernest Arata, Mike Loring, Larry Higgins, Gary Adams, Leo Hutchinson, Norman Nelson, Gerald French, Henry Eslick, John Dunn, Gary Ellis, David Flocker.

A demented gang of terrorists stash a 40-megaton nuclear bomb on San Francisco's Golden Gate Bridge and hold the entire West Coast hostage. Super-Agent Casteel pokes around, however, and saves the world from destruction. Pretty bad, but surprisingly entertaining for one or two brief moments.

p&d, James T. Flocker; w, Samuel Newman; ph, David P. Flocker; m, Phil Comer, Mark Comer, Frank Vierra, Mike Sedlak, Delano Damron; ed, David E. Jackson.

Action/Drama (PR:O MPAA:NR)

GROUNDS FOR MARRIAGE* (1950) 89m MGM bw

Van Johnson (*Dr. Lincoln I. Bartlett*), Kathryn Grayson (*Ina Massine*), Paula Raymond (*Agnes Oglethorpe Young*), Barry Sullivan (*Chris Bartlett*), Lewis Stone (*Dr. Carlton R. Young*), Reginald Owen (*Mr. Delacorte*), Richard Hageman (*Dr. Englestaat*), Theresa Harris (*Stella*), Guy Rennie (*Cab Driver*), Richard Atckison ("*Rodolpho,*" in "*La Boheme*"), Firehouse Five Plus Two (*Themselves*), Milton Cross (*Narrator*).

A fine musical comedy teaming Johnson and Grayson as a divorced couple. Johnson is an ear, throat and nose specialist who is engaged to the daughter of his associate, Stone. Grayson, is an opera singer who is bent on retrieving her ex-husband from his pretty fiancee. "Hymn to the Sun" from the opera La Boheme, a funny dream sequence using music from Carmen, and a hot jazz number by the Firehouse Five Plus Two comprise the best of the musical numbers.

p, Samuel Marx; d, Robert Z. Leonard; w, Allen Rivkin, Laura Kerr, (based on a story by Samuel Marx); ph, John Alton; m, Bronislau Kaper; ed, Frederick Y. Smith; art d, Cedric Gibbons, Paul Groese.

Musical/Comedy (PR:A MPAA:NR)

GROUNDSTAR CONSPIRACY, THE½** (1972, Can.) 95m UNIV c

George Peppard (*Tuxan*), Michael Sarrazin (*Welles*), Christine Belford (*Nicole*), Cliff Potts (*Mosely*), James Olson (*Stanton*), Tim O'Connor (*Gossage*), James McEachin (*Bender*), Alan Oppenheimer (*Hackett*), Roger Dressler (*Kitchen*), Ty Haller (*Henshaw*), Anna Hagen (*Dr. Plover*), Hagen Beggs (*Dr. Hager*), John Destry Adams (*Zabrinski*), Milos Zatovic (*Dr. Zahl*), Don Granberry (*Technician*), Robin Coller (*Secretary*), Bob Meneray (*M.P. Sergeant*), Martin Moore, John Mitchell, Richard Sergeant (*M.P.s*), Ed Collier (*Nicole's Doctor*), Don Vance, William Nunn, Peter Lavender, Barry Cahill (*Reporters*).

Decent spy thriller with some sci-fi overtones, based on the L.P. Davies novel, *The Alien*. The film opens as a top secret American space project hidden away in Vancouver, British Columbia, explodes, killing all the scientists—save Sarrazin who is severely disfigured. Surmising that the explosion was set to cover the theft of top secret documents, the government sends in agent Peppard to investigate. Peppard suspects Sarrazin as a foreign agent and doesn't buy it when the injured scientist pleads memory loss. Sarrazin has indeed lost his memory and he wanders about in search of his identity, while Peppard looks for the terrorist spies. The direction by Johnson is handled well, and Sarrazin (a notoriously spotty actor) turns in what many consider to be his best performance.

p, Trevor Wallace; d, Lamont Johnson; w, Matthew Howard (based on the novel *The Alien* by L.P. Davies); ph, Michael Reed (Panavision, Technicolor); m, Paul Hoffert; ed, Edward M. Abroms; art d, Cam Porteous; cos, Eise Ilse Richter; spec eff, Herbert Ewing.

Espionage (PR:C MPAA:PG)

GROUP, THE* (1966) 150m UA c

Candice Bergen (*Lakey Eastlake*), Joan Hackett (*Dottie Renfrew*), Elizabeth Hartman (*Priss Hartshorn*), Shirley Knight (*Polly Andrews*), Joanna Pettet (*Kay*

Strong), Mary-Robin Redd *(Pokey Prothero)*, Jessica Walter *(Libby MacAusland)*, Kathleen Widdoes *(Helena Davison)*, James Broderick *(Dr. Ridgeley)*, James Congdon *(Sloan Crockett)*, Larry Hagman *(Harald Peterson)*, Hal Holbrook *(Gus Leroy)*, Richard Mulligan *(Dick Brown)*, Robert Emhardt *(Mr. Andrews)*, Carrie Nye *(Norine)*, Philippa Bevans *(Mrs. Hartshorn)*, Leta Bonynge *(Mrs. Prothero)*, Marion Brash *(Radio Man's Wife)*, Sarah Burton *(Mrs. Davison)*, Flora Campbell *(Mrs. MacAusland)*, Bruno di Cosmi *(Nils)*, Leora Dana *(Mrs. Renfrew)*, Bill Fletcher *(Bill the Actor)*, George Gaynes *(Brook Latham)*, Martha Greenhouse *(Mrs. Bergler)*, Russell Hardie *(Mr. Davison)*, Vince Harding *(Mr. Eastlake)*, Doreen Lang *(Nurse Swenson)*, Chet London *(Radio Man)*, Baruch Lumet *(Mr. Schneider)*, John O'Leary *(Putnam Blake)*, Hildy Parks *(Nurse Catherine)*, Lidia Prochnicka *(The Baroness)*, Polly Rowles *(Mrs. Andrews)*, Douglas Rutherford *(Mr. Prothero)*, Truman Smith *(Mr. Bergler)*, Loretta White *(Mrs. Eastlake)*, Ed Holmes *(Mr. MacAusland)*, Richard Graham *(Rev. Garland)*, Arthur Anderson *(Pokey's Husband)*, Clay Johns *(Phil)*.

Based on a huge blockbuster novel by Mary McCarthy, THE GROUP was made in New York with an all New York cast comprised mostly of stage actors. Several young players made their debuts in the movie and went on to large success. Others faded away and were hardly heard from again. It's the middle of the Depression and eight young women (a tough number of major characters to sustain in a film, though not that difficult in a book), graduate from college and look forward to life after education. Bergen, who seems to be the most dominant of the octet, goes off to spend a while in Europe. Hackett, a prim and proper Beacon Hill type, takes up with seedy artist Mulligan but that affair dies almost immediately and she returns to Boston to marry the man her parents have chosen for her. Hartman wants to work for FDR's poverty program but is forced to forego that when the program is shunted aside by Congress. That option gone, she marries Congdon and has two stillbirths before delivering a healthy child by her pediatrician husband. Pettet marries playwright Hagman and discovers to her dismay that he has a penchant for wine and women (the song is never established). That marriage is soon on the rocks. Knight goes to work in a hospital and has an affair with a man who can't bear to leave his wife *or* his analyst. She eventually winds up with psychiatrist James Broderick and, it is assumed, lives happily. Widdoes, the wealthiest member of "The Group," wants to teach but her super-rich parents cannot see their daughter actually *working* for a living so she spends her life collecting art and traveling. Walter becomes a darling of the New York literary set but finds her life is empty and her sex life nil (there are those who wondered if this character wasn't actually based on the author). Redd marries and has two sets of twins. All of this has taken several years and it is now 1939. Bergen returns to the U.S. to avoid the war. The group decides to have a reunion and when they all go to greet her they see that her companion, Prochnika, is *very* masculine. Now they realize that Bergen is a lesbian. At a gala honoring Knight's engagement to Broderick, they hear the radio announce Hitler's moves on the Lowlands. Pettet, by this time, is totally around the bend mentally due to her marriage breakup with Hagman. She hears airplanes outside and becomes hysterical, fearing them to be German planes which have come to attack the U.S. She leans out the apartment window and falls several stories to her death. The seven remaining members meet one last time for the funeral. Bergen verbally assaults Hagman and the film is over. Most authors will tell you that it is virtually impossible to keep this many stories going at once. Something has to suffer. In this case, it was the audience. Director Lumet cast his father in a small role as Schneider but lest you think that's nepotism, the elder Lumet was a distinguished actor on the Yiddish stage long before his son ever got involved with movies. Robert Emhardt (as Knight's somewhat mad father) is superb, and a radiant Carrie Nye scores well as Norine. Odd that Nye didn't have a larger career but she evidently was content to become the wife of witty Dick Cavett. Poorly edited, well-photographed, and far too much story. Still, it has a fascination about it that lingers long after the film has faded out.

p, Sidney Buchman; d, Sidney Lumet; w, Buchman (based on the novel by Mary McCarthy); ph, Boris Kaufman (DeLuxe Color); m, Charles Gross; ed, Ralph Rosenbloom; prod d, Gene Callahan; md, Robert De Cormier; set d, Jack Wright, Jr.; cos, Anna Hill Johnstone.

Drama **Cas.** **(PR:O MPAA:NR)**

GROUPIE GIRL (SEE: I AM A GROUPIE, 1970, Brit.)

GROVE, THE (SEE: NAKED ZOO, THE, 1970)

GROWN-UP CHILDREN½** (1963, USSR) 75m Mosfilm/Artkino bw (VZROSLYYE DETI)

Aleksey Gribov *(Anatoliy Kuzmich Korolyov)*, Zoya Fyodorova *(Tatyana Ivanova Korolyova)*, Liliya Aleshnikova *(Lyusya)*, Aleksandr Demyanenko *(Igor)*, Vsevolod Sanayev *(Vasiliy Vasilyevich)*, A. Tutyshkin *(Boris Vladimirovich)*, Grigoriy Bortnikov, N. Grabbe, Leva Rodionov, M. Khatuntseva, K. Khudyakov.

Gribov is a retiring factory worker who settles into his new apartment with his wife, Fyodorova. Their daughter plans to marry a coworker but the parents cannot bear to think of her moving away. They invite her and her new husband to move in with them, and at first this arrangement works beautifully—until the young couple's friends begin to drive the older folks crazy. The daughter then has a baby and she and her husband plan to put it into a nursery, but the sedate grandparents will not allow it. After an argument, the parents go on vacation and the daughter and her husband, thinking it over, decide to move out on their own, now appreciative of what the older folks have done for them. Simple story line, heavy on the message, and shy of the comedy the producers had aimed for.

p&d, Villen Azarov; w, Valentina Spirina (based on a story by M. Rooz); ph, Sergey Zaytsev, Vladimir Meybom; m, Aleksandr Flyarkovskiy; ed, R. Novikova; md, Yu. Silantyev; art d, S. Ushakov; cos, V. Perelyotov; spec eff, I. Felitsyn, N. Zvonaryov; makeup, S. Kalinin.

Comedy **(PR:A MPAA:NR)**

GRUESOME TWOSOME zero (1968) 72m Mayflower c

Elizabeth Davis, Chris Martell, Gretchen Welles, Rodney Bedell.

A 72-minute bout with nausea about a crazy kid who scalps women for his mom's wig shop. Garbage like this is a great argument for film censorship.

p&d, Herschell Gordon Lewis; w, Louise Downe; m, Larry Wellington.

Horror **(PR:O MPAA:NR)**

GRUMPY½** (1930) 74m PAR bw (AKA: CASCARRABIAS)

Cyril Maude *("Grumpy" Bullivant)*, Phillips Holmes *(Ernest Heron)*, Paul Cavanagh *(Jarvis)*, Frances Dade *(Virginia)*, Halliwell Hobbes *(Ruddock)*, Doris Luray *(Susan)*, Olaf Hytten *(Keble)*, Paul Lukas *(Berci)*, Robert Bolder *(Merridew)*, Colin Kenny *(Dawson)*.

An early George Cukor sound film about the title character, Maude, who is a senile, bombastic, yet lovable old grouch. GRUMPY is a remake of a play brought to Broadway in 1913, with Maude appearing in over 1,400 performances. In 1923 a silent version was made starring Theodore Roberts.

d, George Cukor, Cyril Gardner; w, Doris Anderson (based on a play by Horace Hodges, Thomas Wigney Percyval); ph, David Abel.

Drama **(PR:A MPAA:NR)**

GUADALAJARA*½ (1943, Mex.) 103m Azteca bw

Pedro Armendariz *(Pedro)*, Chaflan *(Melitan)*, Esperanza Baur *(Hortensia)*, Joaquin Pardave *(Piledonio)*, Jorge Velez *(Jorge)*, Emma Roldan *(Mrs. Severo)*, Rosita Lepe *(Esther)*, Lorenzo Barcalata *(Lencho)*, Trio Calaveros, Trio Ascencio Del Rio.

Tedious Mexican musical detailing the near-tragic romances of two sets of lovers who are almost forced into loveless marriages by their short-sighted parents. Armendariz is the noble ranchhand who falls deeply in love with his boss' daughter, Baur, who returns his affection but who has been promised to another man, Velez. However, Velez truly loves Lepe, and after much singing, dancing, and boredom, everything is ironed out and the couples have a double wedding with the partner of their choice. Songs include "Quesera," "El Mariachi," "Jalisco Nunca Piere," and "Guadalajara." (In Spanish; English subtitles.)

d&w, Chano Urueta (based on a story by Ernesto Cortazar); English titles by J.A. Cordero.

Musical/Drama **(PR:A MPAA:NR)**

GUADALCANAL DIARY**** (1943) 93m FOX bw

Preston Foster *(Father Donnelly)*, Lloyd Nolan *(Hook Malone)*, William Bendix *(Taxi Potts)*, Richard Conte *(Capt. Davis)*, Anthony Quinn *(Jesus "Soose" Alvarez)*, Richard Jaeckel *(Pvt. Johnny Anderson)*, Roy Roberts *(Capt. Cross)*, Minor Watson *(Col. Grayson)*, Ralph Byrd *(Ned Rowman)*, Lionel Stander *(Butch)*, Reed Hadley *(Correspondent)*, John Archer *(Lt. Thurmond)*, Eddie Acuff *(Tex)*, Robert Rose *(Sammy)*, Miles Mander *(Weatherby)*, Harry Carter *(Dispatch Officer)*, Jack Luden *(Major)*, Louis Hart *(Lieutenant)*, Tom Dawson *(Captain)*, Selmer Jackson *(Col. Thompson)*, Allen Jung *(Japanese Officer)*, Paul Fung *(Japanese Prisoner)*, Warren Ashe *(Col. Morton)*, Walter Fenner *(Col. Roper)*, Larry Thompson *(Chaplain)*, David Peters, Martin Black, Charles Lang, George Holmes, Bob Ford, Russell Hoyt (Marines).

A hard-hitting and moving WW II action film, GUADALCANAL DIARY drew its based-on-reality story from Richard Tregaskis' best-selling book, and superbly documents the first significant U.S. counterattacks in the Pacific when the Marines invaded the Solomon Islands. One group of Marines is shown as they hit the beaches in August 1942 and their stories are meshed, a cross-section of Americans from all walks of life. Bendix is the tough, dim-witted ex-cab driver with a heart of gold. Conte is the courageous and considerate officer who loses his buddy Roberts. Foster is the company chaplain who provides spiritual guidance with plenty of grit. Nolan is the old pro sergeant, a regular army veteran who looks out for the likes of recruit Jaeckel (in his film debut). Stander is the company clown and Quinn the rugged hero who seeks revenge for the slaughter of his platoon, misled into believing that the Japanese on a nearby island were ready to surrender by a prisoner used as a decoy. In one devastating scene Quinn's platoon is shown pinned down on the beachhead, then chopped to pieces by a powerful ambushing Japanese force. Only Quinn survives, stripping and racing into the ocean to make a swim for it, turning back in anguish to see the hordes of enemy troops pour onto the beach, bayoneting the American bodies. The film takes the recruits through camp, en route to their first engagement, and through the hell that was Guadalcanal. They are shown digging in, repelling counterattacks, and dealing with the myriad snipers who pick off their numbers one by one, until making a massive attack to sweep the island clean of Japanese, driving the last fanatical enemy troops into the sea and destroying them. It's not a pretty picture but one that told in painful detail the day-to-day survival of the downtrodden but stout-hearted Marines. The humor and dedication of the Marines is in full force here from scene to scene. When three Japanese prisoners are brought into camp, they bow and scrape, repeating the word "arigato" ("thank you") over and over again, grateful for being spared. Stander takes one look at them and, misinterpreting their cries, tells them: "We ain't got no avocados!" When Jaeckel proudly discovers a single hair on his 17-year-old chin and announces the fact to his buddies, Bendix yanks it out to display it to his fellow Marines. The Japanese are shown to be insidious, devious creatures who snipe from holes in the ground hidden by underbrush or perch in palm trees, firing sneakily from behind branches, never as standup fighters, making them all the more despicable. Yet this profile proved to be powerfully effective as a propaganda view and was in keeping with Hollywood's early efforts to depict a treacherous enemy when the war was less than a year old. GUADALCANAL DIARY joined the ranks of such stellar WW II films as WAKE ISLAND and BATAAN, but here the U.S. troops won out, where the other films depicted major American defeats. This movie, at least, offered audiences the uplifting possibility of winning the war. Seiler's direction is as quick and relentless as the chatter of a machine gun and all the cast members render believable and telling portraits. Filmed at Camp Pendleton, California.

p, Byron Foy; d, Lewis Seiler; w, Lamar Trotti, Jerry Cady (based on the novel by Richard Tregaskis); ph, Charles Clarke; m, David Buttolph; ed, Fred Allen; md, Emil Newman; art d, James Basevi, Leland Fuller; spec eff, Fred Sersen.

War Drama (PR:C MPAA:NR)

GUARD THAT GIRL*½ (1935) 67m COL bw

Robert Allen (Larry), Florence Rice (Helen), Ward Bond (Budge), Wyrley Birch (Scranton), Barbara Kent (Jeanne), Arthur Hohl (Reynolds), Elisabeth Risdon (Aunt Catherine), Nana Bryant (Sarah), Thurston Hall (Dr. Silas Hudson), Bert Roach (Ellwood), Lobo the Dog.

Dull murder mystery which sees detective Allen investigating the attempted killing of heiress Kent by bow and arrow. While any number of her odd relations could be the killer, Allen and his wonder dog Lobo eventually come up with the family lawyer who committed the crime because he had embezzled money from the family estate.

d&w, Lambert Hillyer; ph, Benjamin Kline; ed, Al Clark.

Mystery (PR:A MPAA:NR)

GUARDIAN OF THE WILDERNESS** (1977) 112m Sunn Classic c

Denver Pyle (Galen Clark), John Dehner (John Muir), Ken Berry (Zachary Moore), Cheryl Miller (Kathleen Clark), Don Shanks (Indian Friend, Teneiya), Cliff Osmond (McCollough, Lumber Foreman), Jack Kruschen (Madden, Surveyor), Prentiss Rowe (Roredes, Surveyor), Brett Palmer, Melissa Jones (Grandchildren), Ford Rainey (Abraham Lincoln).

Another in the seemingly endless series of Sunn Classic wilderness tales, this one is based on the life of Galen Clark, a man who helped to pass legislation to save the Sequoia Forest of Yosemite, in the 1860s. Clark, played by Pyle, is a miner who in his later years contracts black lung disease. He sets out for the wilderness and fresh air, and encounters Dehner, a naturalist, who joins him. Pyle finds a great forest of sequoias and settles down in a nearby valley, where he builds a cabin. Lumber companies try to come in and cut down the huge trees, but Pyle and Dehner fight them off. Dehner goes to Sacramento to get legislation passed that will save the trees. The lumber lobby appears to have won, but Pyle takes his plea to the top and President Lincoln signs a bill saving the forest.

p, Charles E. Sellier; d, David O'Malley; w, Casey Conlon; ph, Henning Schellerup; m, Robert Summers; ed, Sharon Miller; art d, Paul Staheli; spec eff, Doug Hubbard.

Children's Biography (PR:AAA MPAA:NR)

GUARDSMAN, THE**** (1931) 89m MGM bw

Alfred Lunt (The Actor), Lynn Fontanne (The Actress), Roland Young (The Critic), ZaSu Pitts (Liesl), Maude Eburne (Mama), Herman Bing (A Creditor), Ann Dvorak (A Fan).

The clever marital comedy penned by French playwright Molnar was never better performed than by the most illustrious stars of American theater, Lunt and Fontanne, who had made the play a Broadway hit in 1924. This bubbling sex farce begins when Lunt watches Fontanne dreamily playing Chopin on the piano and then going off into a private reverie, suggesting to him that her mind is on another. He quickly builds the assumption that Fontanne is seeing someone else and determines to resolve the vexing doubt by a dangerous charade. He impersonates his imagined rival—a Russian guardsman with mustache and broad accent—and seduces his wife who turns the tables on him the next morning by telling him "I knew it was you all along." Or is this merely a clever way of preserving her marriage? No one ever knew for sure, leaving the husband on edge for an eternity. A delicate play at best, it took the supreme talents of Lunt and Fontanne to make it work convincingly. This would be the only talking film the couple made in their long and famed careers, although Hollywood had successfully wooed them into silents. (They had appeared together in MGM's SECOND YOUTH, 1924, and Lunt alone had been in BACKBONE, 1923, RAGGED EDGE, 1923, LOVERS IN QUARANTINE, 1925, and SALLY OF THE SAWDUST, 1925; she had appeared solo in THE MAN WHO FOUND HIMSELF, 1925.) MGM's Irving Thalberg, ever the aesthetic young man trying to uplift America's filmic tastes, managed to convince the famous pair to leave Broadway for THE GUARDSMAN. It took a lot of convincing. The Lunts looked down their thespian noses at Hollywood, considering movies a primitive art form. When Thalberg and his wife Norma Shearer, the reigning MGM queen, met with the Lunts in New York, Fontanne took it upon herself to instruct Shearer in acting methods, reportedly stating to her: "I have something to tell you. I recently saw you in one of your comedies, and I would like to give you some advice: you must not laugh at your lines after you deliver them!" The pair received $60,000 to make THE GUARDSMAN and when this sum was mentioned to the grand actress, Fontanne remarked: "Alfred and I were prepared to work for less but nobody asked us." The Lunts ignored Hollywood society and affronted Louis B. Mayer by constantly calling him "Mr. Meyers," despite the many corrections politely offered. For director Franklin, working with these Broadway luminaries proved instructional. He was later to state: "I went to school on THE GUARDSMAN. What I learned from this experience—by being with the Lunts for several weeks—I couldn't have picked up in a lifetime." He was also in for a few surprises. In one scene, where Fontanne is required to take a bath, Franklin cleverly designed the set so only her back would show to crew and cast. Yet, when the cameras rolled, Fontanne brazenly turned about to display bare breasts and a wide smile, later explaining that she was distracted by a phone ringing offstage. The Lunts did not do retakes. When asked to do so by Franklin, Lunt rolled his eyes so that the take was unusable. "It always happens when I'm fatigued," he half-heartedly explained. The film was a smashing critical success but the public did not respond well to the sophisticated comedy. Both stars were nominated for Oscars, Lunt losing out to

Fredric March for DR. JEKYLL AND MR. HYDE and Wallace Beery in THE CHAMP (the only time two Oscars were awarded in the Best Actor category), and she to Helen Hayes for THE SIN OF MADELON CLAUDET. THE GUARDSMAN story would be remade as a musical entitled THE CHOCOLATE SOLDIER in 1941 with Nelson Eddy and Rise Stevens but this film marked the last movie appearance by the Lunts, except for cameo roles in STAGE DOOR CANTEEN (1943). The illustrious stars could not wait to get back to Broadway after completing the film, despite the fact that MGM ballyhooed their meteoric careers and offered them a fortune. In one press release the studio crowed: "Idols of the American stage at last in Talkies . . . It is the privilege of MGM to bring the aristocrats of the American stage to you in the talkie of their greatest stage success." Several studios offered them great sums to the Lunts to stay on in Hollywood. Universal studio head Carl Laemmle told them he would pay the stars $250,000 to appear in TRISTAN AND ISOLDE but they didn't even respond. Thalberg and MGM would not be outdone and offered Lunt and Fontanne a cool $1 million for two films, ELIZABETH THE QUEEN and REUNION IN VIENNA. They turned that down, too, Fontanne later telling the press: "We would just be their puppets. This we didn't do in the theater and we couldn't do in the films." To the Lunts the movies were merely cloudy mirrors of their own live theater reputations, reflections they did not appreciate. After viewing THE GUARDSMAN (according to Samuel Marx, writing in Mayer and Thalberg, The Make-Believe Saints), Fontanne remarked to Lunt: "You're wonderful, Alfred. You're manly, dashing, and glamorous. Your makeup is perfect, except in one short scene where the lips aren't straight. But I look frightful. I'm old, haggard, my costumes don't fit. My shape is ghastly. I photograph like a witch." Lunt's response to this temperamental outburst became legend. Moving a finger across his mouth, he replied: "So the lips weren't straight."

p, Irving Thalberg (uncredited), Albert Lewin; d, Sidney Franklin; w, Ernst Vajda, Claudine West (based on the play by Ferenc Molnar); ph, Norbert Brodine; ed, Conrad A. Nervig.

Comedy (PR:A MPAA:NR)

GUDRUN (SEE: SUDDENLY, A WOMAN, 1963, Den.)

GUERRE SECRET (SEE: DIRTY GAME, THE, 1965)

GUERRILLA GIRL zero (1953) 80m UA bw

Helmut Dantine (Demetri Alexander), Marianna (Zaira), Irene Champlin (Nina), Ray Julian (Vanda), Michael Vale (Danov), Gerald Lee (Spiro), Charlotte Paul (Lakme), Dora Weissman (Toula).

A trite film about a Greek couple and how their relationship is torn apart by WW II and the political events afterwards. Dantine is a Greek officer who flees Athens, leaving his fiancee, Champlin, behind when the Germans march in. He meets a gypsy girl, Marianna, with whom he has an affair. After the Nazi defeat, Dantine returns to Athens and becomes a Greek official. He is soon put on the death list of revolutionary forces attempting to turn Greece into a Communist country. His former lover, Marianna, is a member of the Communist revolutionaries and when she discovers that Dantine is on the death list, she tries to warn him. Both are shot and killed and the leaden script mercifully comes to an end.

p&d, John Christian; w, John Byrne, Ben Parker; ph, Charles Wecker, George Stoetzel, Sidney Zucker; m, Bernard Bossick; ed, Christian.

War (PR:C MPAA:NR)

GUESS WHAT!?! (SEE: GUESS WHAT WE LEARNED IN SCHOOL TODAY, 1970)

GUESS WHAT HAPPENED TO COUNT DRACULA* (1970) 80m Merrick International c

Des Roberts (Count Dracula), Claudia Barron (Angelica), John Landon (Guy), Robert Branche (Dr. Harris), Frank Donato (Imp), Sharon Beverly (Vamp), Damu King (Hunch), Jim Settler (Runt), Jeff Cady (Larry), John King III (Gil), James Young-El (Macumba Initiate), Angela Carnon (Nurse), Yvonne Gaudry (Gypsy).

Wretched film features Roberts as a love-lorn Dracula. Landon, in a variation on the Faust theme, offers his girl-pal Barron to the vampire in exchange for stardom. Lots of orgies, drugs, and a discotheque up the time. Some of the disco scenes were filmed at Hollywood's famed Magic Castle disco. Though this garbage was rated PG, rumor has it that an R rated version exists. Supposedly this contains juicier orgy sequences, including a homosexual free-for-all. It certainly couldn't be any worse.

p, Leo Rivers; d&w, Laurence Merrick; ph, Robert Caramico (Movielab); m, Des Roberts; ed, George Watters; md, Roberts; art d, Michael Minor; cos, Berman's; ch, Lou Claudio; makeup, Rick Sagliani.

Horror (PR:O MPAA:PG)

GUESS WHAT WE LEARNED IN SCHOOL TODAY? zero (1970) Cannon Group 96m c

Richard Carballo (Roger), Devin Goldenberg (Robbie), Zachary Haines (Lance), Jane MacLeod (Rita), Yvonne McCall (Lily), Rosella Olson (Eve), Diane Moore (Lydia), Robert Emery (Al), Stanton Edgehill (Billie).

Awful satire on the sexual hangups of rich, white suburbanites, starring Carballo as an uptight, conservative police detective attempting to squash perversion in his community. The film is manipulative and strikes at its targets (hypocrisy, sexual repression, etc.) by creating unrealistic stereotypes that drain the impact of the piece because it is just too ridiculous. Directed by John G. Avildsen who would later direct the first installment in the canonization of Sylvester Stallone, ROCKY.

p, David Gil; d, John G. Avildsen; w, Eugene Price Avildsen (based on a story by Price); ph, Avildsen (DeLuxe Color); m, Harper MacKay, Joan Andre Gil; ed, Avildsen; m/l, "Guess What We Learned at School Today?" Moose Charlap,

Joan Andre Gil, "What's Happened to My Baby?" MacKay (sung by Sandy Stewart).

Comedy   (PR:O MPAA:R)

GUESS WHO'S COMING TO DINNER**½   (1967) 108m COL c

Spencer Tracy (*Matt Drayton*), Sidney Poitier (*John Prentice*), Katharine Hepburn (*Christina Drayton*), Katharine Houghton (*Joey Drayton*), Cecil Kellaway (*Monsignor Ryan*), Roy E. Glenn, Sr. (*Mr. Prentice*), Beah Richards (*Mrs. Prentice*), Isabell Sanford (*Tillie*), Virginia Christine (*Hilary St. George*), Alexandra Hay (*Car Hop*), Barbara Randolph (*Dorothy*), Tom Heaton (*Peter*), D'Urville Martin (*Frankie*), Grace Gaynor (*Judith*), Skip Martin (*Delivery Boy*), John Hudkins (*Cab Driver*).

Controversial in its day but really a lame melodrama, this film was the last in which Tracy and Hepburn were to appear as a team, a less-than-sterling production to cap their dual efforts together on film. Houghton arrives home after a Hawaiian vacation to announce to parents Tracy and Hepburn that she is about to wed a brilliant research physician, Poitier, who happens to be black. This creates for the upper-middle-class family considerable social turmoil. Poitier tells the parents that unless they give their unreserved consent he will not marry their daughter, thereby putting the responsibility for the interracial marriage squarely upon their shoulders. After some soul-searching and breaking with friends who oppose such horrible miscegenation, the parents back up the young couple. Not much here, really, and the script is unimaginative and hortatory, a Kramer crusade that backfires. Tracy looks tired (almost fed up with making movies) in this draggy production where the social message is blatant and hackneyed. Tracy died shortly after completing his scenes and was used as a martyr to movies in promoting this tepid film. He was nominated for an Oscar but only Hepburn received the award for Best Actress, stating at the ceremonies that "I'm sure that mine is for the two of us." Houghton is instantly forgettable and Poitier walks about woodenly spouting cliches. It's all so predictable and has no memorable scenes. An Oscar also went to William Rose for the screenplay.

p&d, Stanley Kramer; w, William Rose; ph, Sam Leavitt (Technicolor); m, Frank De Vol; ed, Robert C. Jones; prod d, Robert Clatworthy; set d, Frank Tuttle; cos, Jean Louis, Joe King; spec eff, Gesa Gaspar; m/l, "The Glory of Love," Billy Hill, sung by Jacqueline Fontaine; makeup, Ben Lane, Joseph Di Bella.

Drama   (PR:C MPAA:NR)

GUEST, THE***   (1963, Brit.) 105m Caretaker/Janus bw (GB: THE CARETAKER)

Alan Bates (*Mick*), Donald Pleasence (*Davis*), Robert Shaw (*Aston*).

Elizabeth Taylor, Peter Sellers, Richard Burton, Noel Coward, and 10 others each put up about $15,000 to make this movie. The stars and creative team all went on deferment and everyone had a piece of the action. We wonder if they ever got a farthing. Pinter is the most highly stylized author around today (with the exception of Samuel Beckett) and if you don't like pauses, pregnant or otherwise, you might hate this movie. The plot is deceptive. Pleasence is a tramp who is invited to stay in a house owned by Alan Bates. But he is asked to the house by Bates' brother, Robert Shaw. For the remainder of the film, the two brothers use Pleasence as a volleyball, tossing him back and forth between them (verbally) and confusing the already addled tramp. Both men want Pleasence to be their caretaker and, in the end, the tramp is tossed out. And that's it! Critics have offered all sorts of hidden meanings to the play while Pinter has always maintained his silence, preferring instead to play his little game and let you attempt to figure out what the hell he meant by it all. If they'd edited out all the pauses that Pinter specifically indicates in his scripts, the dialog in this might have added up to under an hour. Pinter is infuriating but endlessly fascinating; sort of like a rattlesnake with a typewriter.

p, Michael Birkett; d, Clive Donner; w, Harold Pinter (based on his play "The Caretaker"); ph, Nicholas Roeg; m, Ron Grainer; ed, Fergus McDonell; art d, Reece Pemberton.

Drama   (PR:C MPAA:NR)

GUEST AT STEENKAMPSKRAAL, THE*½ (1977, South Africa) 105m Guest Productions c

Athol Fugard (*Eugene Marais*), Marius Weyers (*Dr. Visser*), Gordon Vorster (*Oom Doors*), Wilma Stockenstrom (*Tant Corrie*), James Borthwick (*Doorsie*), Emile Aucamp (*Louis*), Susan MacLennan (*Little Corrie*), Trix Pienaar (*Brenda*), Dan Poho (*Stuurie*).

A plodding, tedious effort that wastes source material filled with potential. Famed playwright Fugard plays a famed scientist whose real-life work on baboons and the study of primate consciousness made a significant impact on the field of evolution. However, the man was hopelessly addicted to morphine, and this film portrays his struggle to break the drug's grip. What that boils down to is Fugard looking sullen, and doing a lot of pacing. Eventually he is able to come to terms with both himself and the family Fugard is staying with, but by that point the story has lost what little interest it ever had. Psychological probing is never present, replaced by a tedium that the filmmakers apparently felt was significant. Though the acting isn't bad, the cast is highly limited by the material, resulting in a mediocre drama.

p, Gerald Berman; d, Ross Devenish; w, Athol Fugard; ph, Rod Stewart; ed, Lionel Selwyn; prod d, Jeni Halliday.

Drama   (PR:O MPAA:NR)

GUEST HOUSE, THE*½   (SEE: IN OLD CHEYENNE, 1931)

GUEST IN THE HOUSE**   (1944) 117m UA bw

Anne Baxter (*Evelyn Heath*), Ralph Bellamy (*Douglas Proctor*), Aline MacMahon (*Aunt Martha*), Ruth Warrick (*Ann Proctor*), Scott McKay (*Dan Proctor*), Jerome

Cowan (*Mr. Hackett*), Marie McDonald (*Miriam*), Percy Kilbride (*John the Butler*), Margaret Hamilton (*Hilda the Maid*), Connie Laird (*Lee Proctor*).

A good cast helps this sometimes unbelievable suspense film from falling on its face. Mentally unbalanced Baxter, with a cardiac condition, is taken into the home of her doctor, McKay. She becomes infatuated with McKay's married older brother, Bellamy. Although she pretends to want to marry McKay and he her, she does her best to disrupt the household in the hopes of destroying Bellamy's marriage. MacMahon, the aunt of the two brothers, foils Baxter's plot.

p, Hunt Stromberg; d, John Brahm; w, Ketti Frings (based on a stage play by Hagar Wilde and Dale Eunson); ph, Lee Garmes; m, Werner Janssen; ed, James Newcom, Walter Hanneman; prod d, Nicolai Remisoff.

Drama   Cas.   (PR:A MPAA:NR)

GUEST OF HONOR*   (1934, Brit.) 53m WB-FN bw

Henry Kendall (*Lord Strathpeffer*), Miki Hood (*Marjorie*), Edward Chapman (*Montague Tidmarsh*), Margaret Yarde (*Emma Tidmarsh*), Eve Gray (*Cissie Poffley*), Joan Playfair (*Mrs. Bodfish*), Hay Plumb (*Mr. Bodfish*), Helen Ferrers (*Mrs. Gilwattle*), Cecil Humphreys (*Mr. Gilwattle*), Louis Goodrich (*Butler*), Florence Woodgate, Bruce Gordon.

Kendall is a dapper lord who pretends to be a professional dinner guest in a plot to uncover a blackmailer's scheme. A weak, stagey comedy that was completely forgotten by 1935.

p, Irving Asher; d, George King; w, W. Scott Darling (based on the play "The Man From Blankleys" by F. Anstey).

Comedy   (PR:A MPAA:NR)

GUEST WIFE**½   (1945) 90m UA bw

Claudette Colbert (*Mary*), Don Ameche (*Joe*), Richard Foran (*Chris*), Charles Dingle (*Worth*), Grant Mitchell (*Detective*), Wilma Francis (*Susy*), Chester Clute (*Urban Nichols*), Irving Bacon (*Nosey Character*), Hal K. Dawson (*Dennis*), Ed Fielding (*Arnold*).

Ameche is a renowned newspaper correspondent who, for nebulous reasons, needs a wife to fool his publisher. He borrows Colbert from her husband, Foran. The expected complications arise, including the trio staying in the same house, while Colbert and Ameche are forced to share the same bedroom to carry out the deception. Production is adequate but the trite situations the story is hung on forespeak its doom as an audience titillator.

p, Jack H. Skirball; d, Sam Wood; w, Bruce Manning, John Klorer; ph, Joseph Valentine; m, Daniele Amfitheatrof; ed, William M. Morgan; art d, Lionel Banks.

Comedy   (PR:A MPAA:NR)

GUESTS ARE COMING**½(1965, Pol.) 110m Film Polski/Mitchell Kowal Films bw (JADA, GOSCIE, JADA; JADA GOSCIE)

1st Episode: Paul Glass (*Peter*), Kazimierz Opalinski (*Uncle Konstanty*), Zenon Burzynski (*Son*), Sylwia Zakrzewska (*Daughter-in-Law*), Wanda Koczewska (*Blonde Woman*), Maryla Butorowicz (*Madzia*); 2nd Episode: Mitchell Kowal (*Mike O'Rawiec*), Wladyslaw Hancza (*Village Priest*), The Gorals (*Highlanders*), Zofia Merle (*Maryna*), Marian Jastrzebski (*Bialas*); 3rd Episode: Zygmunt Zintel (*Harry Kwasnicki*), Ryszard Pietruski (*Truck Driver*).

A three-episode film, with each story involving the adventures of an American in Poland. The first has Glass as a girl-crazy young man on a business trip who visits his uncle, Opalinski, to whom his father was sending money. But Opalinski is in a rest home and the money is going for an apartment for his son and daughter-in-law. For look's sake he moves in with them during the visit, fooling his stupid son and selfish daughter-in-law, and scoring a moral and personal victory for himself. Episode two finds Kowal as an Indiana widower. He goes to the small Polish town of his father's birth, looking for a wife. The local mothers, all anxious to marry off their daughters to this sauve American, treat him like a king. But he goes on a drunken binge and winds up marrying a barmaid who is the town's floozy. The last story involves an American businessman who wants to buy earth from famous battlefields to sell to Polish-Americans back in Chicago. He is told that such a product is to be found all over Poland, as the country has been fought over for so long. The foolish man is sold a good deal of dirt by the Poles, who are only too eager to please. He loads his product aboard a ship bound for America and sails home. Charming in its own way. (In Polish; English subtitles.)

p&d, Gerard Zalewski, Jan Rutkiewicz, Romuald Drobaczynski; w, Jan Jozef Szczepanski; ph, Stanislaw Loth; m, Stefan Kisielewski; English titles, Mitchell Kowal.

Comedy   (PR:A MPAA:NR)

GUEULE D'ANGE

(SEE: PLEASURES AND VICES, 1962, Fr.)

GUIDE, THE**½   (1965, U.S./India) 120m Stratton/Navketan c (AKA: SURVIVAL)

Dev Anand (*Raju*), Waheeda Rehman (*Rosie*), Kishore Sahu (*Marco*), Leela Chitnis (*Mother*), Anwar Hussein (*Gaffur*), K.N. Singh (*Velan*), Levy Aaron (*Dilip*), Rashid Khan (*Joseph*), Dilip Dutt (*Mani*), Iftikhar (*Inspector*), John Voyantiz (*British Correspondent*), Krishna Dhawan (*Defense Lawyer*), Hazel (*Velan's Sister*), Satya Dev Duby (*Velan's Brother*), J.S. Kashyap (*Old Man*), Sheila Burghart (*TV Reporter*), Jagirdar, Ullas, Praveen Paul, Purnima.

Anand is a cocky young man employed as a tour guide in an Indian village. He is hired by Sahu, an older archeologist, to show his wife Rehman around the area's ruins. Anand seduces the woman and offers to help her return to a dancing career. Her husband leaves her and she becomes the younger man's mistress. But when she becomes famous, she leaves Anand and he eventually is jailed for forgery. After his release he wanders the deserted ruins and is mistaken by villagers as a spiritual leader. He plays the part for them, and vows to end a drought by fasting.

But the dream catches up with him and in spite of Rehman's pleas he ends up a martyr to his own twisted thinking. Story was famous novelist Pearl S. Buck's only screenplay.

p&d, Tad Danielewski; w, Danielewski, Pearl S. Buck (based on the novel by R.K. Narayen); ph, Fali Mistry (Eastmancolor); m, S.D. Burman; art d, Ram Yedekar; ch, Hiralil.

Drama (PR:A MPAA:NR)

GUIDE FOR THE MARRIED MAN, A*** (1967) 89m FOX c

Walter Matthau (*Paul Manning*), Robert Morse (*Ed Stander*), Inger Stevens (*Ruth Manning*), Sue Anne Langdon (*Mrs. Irma Johnson*), Jackie Russell (*Miss Harris*), Claire Kelly (*Harriet Stander*), Linda Harrison (*Miss Stardust*), Elaine Devry (*Jocelyn Montgomery*), Jason Wingreen (*Mr. Johnson*), Heather Carroll (*Mrs. Miller*), Robert Patten (*Mr. Miller*), Eddie Quillan (*Cologne Salesman*), Dale Van Sickel (*Stunt Driver*), Mickey Deems (*Waiter*), Aline Towne (*Mrs. Mousey Man*), Chanin Hale (*Miss Crenshaw*), Eve Brent (*Joe X's Blowzy Blonde*), Marvin Brody (*Taxi Driver*), Majel Barrett (*Mrs. Fredy*), Marian Mason (*Mrs. Rance G.*), Tommy Farrell (*Rance G's Hanger-on*), Fred Holliday, Pat Becker, Dee Carroll, Ray Montgomery, Jackie Joseph (*Party Guests*), Heather Young (*Girl With Megaphone*), Evelyn King (*Female Plaintiff*), Nancy De Carl (*Woman With Baby*), Warrene Ott (*Woman With Gun*), Michael Romanoff (*Maitre D'Hotel*), Karen Arthur (*Lady Dinner Partner*), Damian London (*Lone Male Diner*), Julie Tate (*Woman in Bed*), George Neise (*Man in Bed*), Tim Herbert (*Shoe Clerk*), Patricia Sides (*Mau Mau Dancer*), Pat McCaffrie (*Motel Clerk*), Jimmy Cross (*Mr. Brown*), Virginia Wood (*Bubbles*), Sharyn Hillyer (*Girl in Bed*), Lucille Ball, Jack Benny, Polly Bergen, Joey Bishop, Sid Caesar, Art Carney, Wally Cox, Jayne Mansfield, Hal March, Louis Nye, Carl Reiner, Phil Silvers, Terry-Thomas, Ben Blue, Ann Morgan Guilbert, Jeffrey Hunter, Marty Ingels, Sam Jaffe (*Technical Advisors*).

A pretty clever sex spoof—well directed by song-and-dance man Kelly—profiles Matthau, a normally contented married man, being guided into sinful infidelity by rake and ne'er-do-well Morse. It's all froth and is best summed up in one of the captions flashed upon the screen, a quote from Oscar Wilde reading: "The one charm of marriage is that it makes a life of deception absolutely necessary for both parties." Morse entices Matthau into trysting with others, particularly one of his clients, luscious, raven-haired, voluptuous divorcee Devry, by relating anecdotal stories of dos and don'ts when cheating on the wife. Spouse Stevens, a shapely dish, is oblivious to Matthau's bumbling plans and goes about being the sweet, sexy, and perfect wife, victimized by his extramarital deceits. Matthau has eyes for Langdon's body, she being the married next-door lady cavorting every day before him down the street in a skirt so tight her curvaceous body threatens to burst through at any moment. A series of vignettes, recited by Morse as examples of proper and improper cheating, parades a host of stars in often hilarious incidents. Jack Benny gets rid of one unwanted mistress by tightwad machinations, telling the lady that business reversals demand he sell off furs and jewels, as well as lamps, ashtrays, and other curios in the apartment he has provided for her. She immediately suggests they discontinue their relationship and Benny smugly goes to a window to peer down at another lovely lass waiting for him in a convertible. Art Carney appears in cameo with Lucille Ball; he is a construction worker complaining so bitterly about her cooking that she tells him to go elsewhere for his vittles. He does, transforming himself into Mr. First Nighter, dining with a luscious female, then returning with hard hat in hand to wife Ball to apologize. Others appearing in a seemingly endless string of funny vignettes include Jayne Mansfield (in her second-to-last film before her accidental death; she would make one more movie, SINGLE ROOM FURNISHED), Sid Caesar, Wally Cox, Hal March, Louis Nye, Carl Reiner (in a great spoof of a dallying movie star), Phil Silvers, Terry-Thomas, Ben Blue, and Joey Bishop. Matthau, after having learned everything he thinks he needs to know about assignations, picks up Devry and takes her to a motel. The maneater quickly strips to revealing underwear, plops on a bed, and motions the nervous Matthau to her. He stammers that he is married and she caustically states: "Congratulations." Just then there is a riotous noise in the courtyard and Matthau peeks through the window to see, horrified, his best friend and sex counsel, Morse, being caught with Langdon in bed. He pulls the half-clad Devry outside to his car and speeds to a parking lot, dumping her, and racing home where he collapses in relief while a celestial chorus chimes: "There's No Place Like Home." He vows never to stray again. It's all very funny and Kelly does a marvelous job of intercutting the vignettes (many of which are produced on a grand scale) with the main story. A bevy of gorgeous females populates the film, typified in the male perspective as mindless sex objects who bounce, jiggle, and sway through one masculine fantasy after another.

p, Frank McCarthy; d, Gene Kelly; w, Frank Tarloff (based on his book); ph, Joseph MacDonald (Panavision, DeLuxe Color); m, Johnny Williams; ed, Dorothy Spencer; art d, Jack Martin Smith, William Glasgow; set d, Walter M. Scott, Raphael Bretton; cos, Moss Mabry; spec eff, L. B. Abbott, Art Cruickshank, Emil Kosa, Jr.; m/l, title song, Williams, Leslie Bricusse, sung by The Turtles; makeup, Ben Nye.

Comedy (PR:C MPAA:NR)

GUILT* (1930, Brit.) 66m Reginald Fogwell/PAR bw

James Carew (*James Barrett*), Anne Grey (*Anne Barrett*), Harold Huth (*Tony Carleton*), James Fenton (*Roy*), Rex Curtis (*Jack*), Anne Smiley (*Phyllis*), Ernest Lester (*Jennings*).

A predictable romantic melodrama about Grey's affair with an actor and her attempts to pass it off as part of her playwright husband's new play. Weak performances are matched by poor technical quality.

p,d&w, Reginald Fogwell.

Drama (PR:A MPAA:NR)

GUILT**½ (1967, Swed.) 90m Svensk Filmindustri/Crown International bw
(TILLSAMMANS MED GUNILL MANDAG KVALL OCH TISDAG;

TILLSAMMANS MED GUNILLA; AKA: WITH GUNILLA MONDAY EVENING AND TUESDAY)

Sven Bertil Taube (*Hans*), Helena Brodin (*Gunilla*), Tina Hedstrom (*Inga*), Marrit Ohlsson (*1st Woman*), Inga-Lill Ahstrom (*2nd Woman*).

While out driving on a winter night Taube hits a pedestrian, killing him. He and Brodin drive off and try to come up with an excuse for the accident. Their conversation ambles to his dissatisfaction with her in bed, to the carelessness of the victim, and to a myriad of other topics. His neurosis proves too much for her and when she sees her chance, Brodin runs off. But Taube finds her and persuades her to stay with him. They find a newspaper and read about the hit-and-run accident. Knowing their futures are changed, they drive home. As they arrive a police car pulls up next to the pair. Another grim one from the land of the long nights.

d&w, Lars Gorling; ph, Lars Goran Bjorne; m, Ulf Bjorlin; ed, Ulla Ryghe; set d, Rolf Bowan; spec eff, Evald Andersson.

Psycho-Drama (PR:O MPAA:NR)

GUILT IS MY SHADOW** (1950, Brit.) 84m ABP bw

Elizabeth Sellars (*Linda*), Patrick Holt (*Kit*), Peter Reynolds (*Jamie*), Lana Morris (*Betty*), Laurence O'Madden (*Tom*), Esme Cannon (*Peggy*), Wensley Pithey (*Tillingham*), Avice Landone (*Eva*), Aubrey Woods (*Doctor*), Willoughby Gray (*Detective*).

A young wife, Sellars, accidentally kills her good-for-nothing husband in a fight. A farmer she is in love with helps her hide the body, but she is ultimately eaten away by her all-consuming guilty conscience, which drives her to confess. No picture for lovers, but plenty of meat for the grisly-minded.

p, Ivan Foxwell; d, Roy Kellino; w, Foxwell, Kellino, John Gilling (based on the novel *You're Best Alone* by Peter Curtis); ph, William McLeod; m, Hans May; ed, George Clark.

Crime (PR:O MPAA:NR)

GUILT IS NOT MINE**½ (1968, Ital.) 90m Zeus-Electron/Hoffberg bw
(L'INGIUSTA CONDANNA; QUELLI CHE NON MUOIONO)

Rossano Brazzi (*Carlo Rocchi*), Gaby Andre (*Anna Valli*), Sergio Tofano (*Prof. Valli*), Elvy Lissiak (*Barbara Soldani*), Umberto Sacripante (*Vittorio Gori*), Mino Doro, Fedele Gentile, Ubaldo Lay, Amedeo Trilli, Gianna Segale, Guido Riccioli, Nanda Primavera.

Brazzi is a young Italian doctor in 1889. He meets Andre, the daughter of Tofano, a prominent medical professor who disapproves of their romance and talks Brazzi into leaving Rome. Brazzi leaves for Obetello where he comes on a radical, though highly effective, treatment for malaria. Lissiak is his sexually frustrated neighbor who blames him for the malaria epidemic after he ignores her advances. He goes on trial and is sentenced for using unorthodox methods. His punishment is four years behind bars and he is no longer allowed to practice medicine. In prison, Brazzi becomes an orderly, inoculating himself against malaria with his own methods. He proves himself innocent and is released to resume his career and marry Andre.

d, Giuseppe Masini; w, Masini, Siro Angeli, R. Gentili, Luigi Giacosi (based on a story by Masini); ph, Augusto Tiezzi; m, Carlo Innocenzi.

Drama (PR:A MPAA:NR)

GUILT OF JANET AMES, THE**½

(1947) 81m COL bw

Rosalind Russell (*Janet Ames*), Melvyn Douglas (*Smithfield Cobb*), Sid Caesar (*Sammy Weaver*), Betsy Blair (*Katie*), Nina Foch (*Susie Pierson*), Charles Cane (*Walker*), Harry Von Zell (*Carter*), Bruce Harper (*Junior*), Arthur Space (*Nelson*), Richard Benedict (*Joe Burton*), Frank Orth (*Danny*), Ray Walker (*Sidney*), Doreen McCann (*Emmy Merino*), Hugh Beaumont (*Frank Merino*), Thomas Jackson (*Police Sergeant*), Edwin Cooper (*Surgeon*), Emory Parnell (*Susie's Father*), Victoria Horne, Wanda Perry, Eve March, Kathleen O'Malley (*Nurses*), Pat Lane, Fred Howard (*Doctors*), Steve Benton (*Ambulance Attendant*), Doris Colleen (*Student Nurse*), William Trenk (*Headwaiter*), George Riley (*Policeman*), John Farrell (*Janitor*), Bill Wallace (*Orderly*), John Berkes (*Customer*), William Challee (*Ambulance Surgeon*), William Forrest (*Doctor Morton*), Isabelle Withers (*Marian*), Denver Pyle (*Masher*).

Russell is a widow of a soldier who was killed during WW II when he threw himself on a live grenade to save his five fellow soldiers. A couple of years later, Russell goes in search of the five men to see if any of them were deserving of her husband's heroics. When she is slightly injured in an accident, Russell goes into a case of hysterical paralysis which makes her unable to walk. Douglas, one of the soldiers saved by her husband and suffering from a good case of guilts himself, tries to talk Russell out of her fixation. Under his hypnosis, Russell goes on a mental journey in which she talks to all the ex-soldiers involved with her husband's death. It enables her to come to grips with their demise, and she turns around and uses the same process on Douglas to help him overcome his guilt.

d, Henry Levin; w, Louella MacFarlane, Allen Rivkin, Devery Freeman (based on the story by Lenore Coffee); ph, Joseph Walker; m, George Duning; ed, Charles Nelson; md, Morris W. Stoloff; art d, Steven Goosson, Walter Holscher; set d, George Montgomery, Frank Tuttle; m/l, Allan Roberts, Doris Fisher.

Drama (PR:A MPAA:NR)

GUILTY?*½ (1930) 67m COL bw

Virginia Valli, John Holland, John St. Polis, Lydia Knott, Erville Alderson, Richard Carlyle, Robert Haines, Clarence Muse, Eddie Clayton, Frank Fanning, Ed Cecil, Gertrude Howard.

A slow film that tells the story of a man who has committed suicide as related by 10 people who knew him. The suicide victim is a man who had served a prison sentence, and decided to do away with himself so that his daughter may marry the son of a judge and not be shamed by him.

d, George B. Seitz; w, Dorothy Howell (based on the story "Black Sheep" by Howell); ph, Ted Tetzlaff; ed, Leon Barsha.

Drama   **(PR:A MPAA:NR)**

GUILTY, THE**   (1947) 71m MON bw

Bonita Granville (*Estelle Mitchell/Linda Mitchell*), Don Castle (*Mike Carr*), Wally Carsell (*Johnny Dixon*), Regis Toomey (*Detective Heller*), John Litel (*Alex Tremholt*), Ruth Robinson (*Mrs. Mitchell*), Thomas Jackson (*Tim McGinnis*), Oliver Blake (*Jake*), Caroline Andrews (*The Whistler*).

Castle enters a bar in his old neighborhood in search of the woman he can't forget. In flashback he tells the bartender why he left her and why he now returns: After leaving her boyfriend Carsell's apartment, Castle's girl friend's twin sister seemingly disappears. The police discover her body stuffed into an incinerator. All the evidence points to Carsell, but Castle investigates on his own. He discovers that Litel really murdered the girl, believing her to be the sister he loved but could not have. The film switches back to real time and Granville (a dual role for her), as the surviving sister, enters the bar. They kiss and Castle feels something is missing. He returns to the crime scene and is arrested for the murder. It turns out he had been having an affair with both sisters and killed the one he had been with first when she had threatened his new romance. Both acting and photography are a disservice to a highly suspenseful plot.

p, Jack Wrather; d, John Reinhardt; w, Robert R. Presnell, Sr. (based on the short story "Two Men in a Furnished Room" by Cornell Woolrich); ph, Henry Sharp; m, Rudy Schrager; ed, Jodie Caplan; md, David Chudnow; art d, Oscar Yerge.

Crime/Mystery   **(PR:C MPAA:NR)**

GUILTY?***   (1956, Brit.) 93m Gibraltar bw

John Justin (*Nap Rumbold*), Barbara Laage (*Jacqueline Delbois*), Donald Wolfit (*Judge*), Stephen Murray (*Summers*), Norman Wooland (*Pelton*), Andree Debar (*Vicki Martin*), Frank Villard (*Pierre Lemaire*), Betty Stockfeld (*Mrs. Roper*), Sidney Tafler (*Camino*), Leslie Perrins (*Poynter*), Kynaston Reeves (*Col. Wright*), Russell Napier (*Inspector Hobson*).

Frenchwoman Debar is up for the murder of a man she had every reason to kill. She had sheltered him from the Nazis during WW II, was soon betrayed by him, and as a result was sent to a concentration camp while pregnant with his child. Though it appears to be an open and shut case, she denies having stabbed him in his London hotel room. Two journalists, Justin and Villard, take up her cause and find themselves caught in the middle of a ring of international counterfeiters, who hold the answers to the mystery. Lively addition to the thriller genre.

p, Charles A. Leeds; d, Edmond T. Greville; w, Maurice J. Wilson, Ernest Dudley (based on the novel *Death Has Deep Roots* by Michael Gilbert); ph, Stan Pavey.

Crime   **(PR:A MPAA:NR)**

GUILTY AS CHARGED   (SEE: GUILTY AS HELL, 1932)

GUILTY AS HELL**½   (1932) 82m PAR bw

Edmund Lowe (*Russell Kirk*), Victor McLaglen (*Detective McKinley*), Richard Arlen (*Frank Marsh*), Ralph Ince (*Jack Reed*), Adrienne Ames (*Vera Marsh*), Henry Stephenson (*Dr. Tindall*), Elizabeth Patterson (*Mrs. Ward*), Noel Francis (*Julia Reed*), Arnold Lucy (*Dr. Sully*), Willard Robertson (*Sgt. Alcock*), Fred Kelsey (*Detective Duffy*), Earl Pingree (*Detective Brown*), Lillian Harmer (*Mrs. Alvin*), Gordon Westcott (*Dr. Goodman*), Claire Dodd (*Mrs. Tindall*), William B. Davidson (*Governor*), Richard Tucker (*District Attorney*), Charles Sylber, Harold Berquist, Elsa Peterson, Clifford Dempsey, Oscar Smith.

A good little murder mystery that injects some humor in an oft-told tale. The story concerns a physician, Stephenson, who attempts to commit the perfect murder. Using rubber gloves, he strangles his wife, sets up a solid alibi with Arlen to take the blame, and sits back to let the law take its course. The truth comes out only because young reporter Lowe is interested in the suspect's sister, Ames, and takes a special interest in proving her brother's innocence.

d, Eric Kenton; w, Arthur Kober, Frank Partos (based on the play "Riddle Me This" by Daniel Rubin); ph, Karl Struss.

Crime   **(PR:A MPAA:NR)**

GUILTY BYSTANDER**   (1950) 91m Laurel/FC bw

Zachary Scott (*Max Thursday*), Faye Emerson (*Georgia*), Mary Boland (*Smitty*), Sam Levene (*Capt. Tonetti*), J. Edward Bromberg (*Varkas*), Kay Medford (*Angel*), Jed Prouty (*Dr. Elder*), Harry Landers (*Bert*), Dennis Harrison (*Mace*), Elliot Sullivan (*Stitch*), Garney Wilson (*Harvey*), Ray Julian (*Johnny*).

A below-par crime thriller which has Scott as a policeman thrown off the force, turning to the bottle, and becoming a detective in a sleazy hotel. He comes out of his drunken binge when his ex-wife comes to him for help. Their son has been kidnaped and he goes on the trail of the abductors. Scott gets mixed up with a gang of smugglers, but finds his son and brings the crooks to justice. He starts his life anew.

p, Rex Carlton; d, Joseph Lerner; w, Don Ettlinger (based on the novel by Wade Miller); ph, Gerald Hirschfeld; m, Dimitri Tiomkin; ed, Geraldine Lerner; prod d, Leo Kerz; art d, Leo Kerz.

Crime   **(PR:C MPAA:NR)**

GUILTY GENERATION, THE***   (1931) 82m COL bw

Leo Carrillo (*Mike Palermo*), Constance Cummings (*Maria Palermo*), Robert Young (*Marco Ricca*), Boris Karloff (*Tony Ricca*), Leslie Fenton (*Joe*), Jimmy Wilcox (*Don*), Elliott Roth (*Benedicto*), Phil Tead (*Skid*), Frederick Howard (*Bradley*), Eddie Roland (*Willie*), W. J. O'Brien (*Victor*), Ruth Warren (*Publicity Woman*).

THE GUILTY GENERATION places the love story of "Romeo and Juliet" into a 1930s gangster setting. The story has two rival gangster families headed by Karloff on one side and Carrillo on the other. The two had been partners at one time, but their split set into motion a war which has been slowly killing off both families. Carrillo's daughter, Cummings, renounces her father's activities and falls in love with Karloff's son, Young. Fearful that Carrillo will kill Young, Cummings keeps their love a secret. The two lovers wed hastily as the bloodshed mounts, but it is not until after the ceremony that Carrillo learns the true identity of Young. Carrillo is set on killing Young to avenge the death of his own son, but is prevented by his aged mother who shoots him dead.

p, Harry Cohn; d, Rowland V. Lee; w, Jack Cunningham (based on the play by Joe Milward, J. Kirby Hawkes); ph, Byron Haskin; ed, Otis Garrett.

Crime   **(PR:A MPAA:NR)**

GUILTY HANDS**½   (1931) 60m MGM bw

Lionel Barrymore (*Richard Grant*), Kay Francis (*Marjorie West*), Madge Evans (*Barbara Grant*), William Bakewell (*Tommy Osgood*), C. Aubrey Smith (*Rev. Hastings*), Polly Moran (*Aunt Maggie*), Alan Mowbray (*Gordon Rich*), Forrester Harvey (*Spencer Wilson*), Charles Crockett (*H.G. Smith*), Henry Barrows (*Harvey Scott*).

Barrymore is a highly experienced district attorney who attempts to use his vast courtroom knowledge to pull off a perfect murder. He kills his daughter's lover, Mowbray, and decides to make it look like Francis faked Mowbray's suicide by placing a gun in his hand after killing him. Barrymore sets up Mowbray's body, puts the gun in his hand, and proceeds to make a brilliant address to an imaginary jury about Francis' guilt. A weird twist ending makes sure that Barrymore pays for his crime, as the stiffening fingers on Mowbray's hand pull the trigger of the gun, firing a bullet into Barrymore's body.

d, W. S. Van Dyke II; w, Bayard Veiller; ph, Merritt B. Gerstad; ed, Anne Bauchens.

Crime   **(PR:C MPAA:NR)**

GUILTY MELODY*½   (1936, Brit.) 68m Franco-London/ABF bw

Gitta Alpar (*Mme. Marguerite Salvini*), Nils Asther (*Galloni*), John Loder (*Richard Carter*), Ethel Griffies (*Lady Rochester*), Coral Brown (*Cecile*), Arty Ash (*Inspector Bartle*), Robert English (*Chief Inspector*), Don Alcaide (*Duke of Mantua*), F. Rendell (*Rigoletto*), C. Buckton (*Police Inspector*).

GUILTY MELODY unsuccessfully combines a musical with an espionage film. Alpar is a Hungarian opera star innocently involved in a nasty spy caper while having a love affair with a British intelligence officer. She sings excerpts from many different operas. Pretty tedious.

p, F. Deutschmeister; d, Richard Potter; w, G. F. Salmony (based on a novel by Hans Rehfisch); ph, Jan Stallich, Jeff Seaholme; m, Nicolaus Brodszky.

Spy/Musical   **(PR:A MPAA:NR)**

GUILTY OF TREASON**½   (1950) 86m EL bw

Charles Bickford (*Cardinal Mindszenty*), Paul Kelly (*Tom Kelly*), Bonita Granville (*Stephanie Varna*), Richard Derr (*Col. Melnikov*), Barry Kroeger (*Timar*), Elizabeth Risdon (*Mother Mindszenty*), Roland Winters (*Commissar Belou*), John Banner (*Sandor Deste*), Alfred Linder (*Jeno*).

A 1950s anti-Communist propaganda film that shows the terrors of life behind the Iron Curtain through the real-life trial and conviction of Cardinal Mindszenty of Hungary. The story traces Mindszenty, played by Bickford, and details his conflicts with the Communist Hungarian regime after WW II, and his ultimate imprisonment as an enemy of the state. At his trial it is revealed that Bickford's controversial confession was attained through torture, hypnosis, and drugs. A truly believable reconstruction of an ignominious incident in Communist history.

p, Jack Wrather, Robert Golden; d, Felix Feist; w, Emmet Lavery (based on the book *As We See Russia* by members of the Overseas Press Club of America); ph, Jack Russell; m, Emil Newman; ed, Walter Thompson.

Drama   **(PR:C MPAA:NR)**

GUILTY PARENTS*½   (1934) 53m Jay Dee Kay bw

Jean Lacy (*Helen Mason*), Glen Boles (*Jimmy*), Donald Keith (*Billy*), John St. Polis (*Defense Attorney*), Lynton Brent (*Alfred Brent*), Robert Frazer (*District Attorney*), Gertrude Astor (*Marie*), Isabel Lamal (*Mrs. Mason*), Alisa Aristi (*Betty*), Leon Holmes (*Bob*).

A film that attempted to address the issue of sexual ignorance of teenagers in the 1930s, but was a misguided effort to pull in moviegoers looking for exploitation. The trite story deals with a young girl whose virtue is threatened by a shallow man. She kills him, is dragged into court, and is charged with the crime. Her defense counsel blames her narrow-minded mother for her daughter's misdeeds. An unfortunate ending has the girl jumping out of a window to her death before the jury announces a verdict of not guilty.

d&w, Jack Townley; ph, Robert Doran; ed, Ethel Davey.

Crime   **(PR:C MPAA:NR)**

GUILTY TRAILS**   (1938) 57m UNIV bw

Bob Baker (*Bob*), Marjorie Reynolds (*Jackie*), Hal Taliaferro (*Sundown*), Georgia O'Dell (*Martha*), Jack Rockwell (*Brad*), Carleton Young (*Steve*), Forrest Taylor (*Lawson*), Glenn Strange (*Sheriff*), Murdock McQuarrie (*Judge*), Jack Kirk (*Stage Driver*).

An average western starring Baker as a sheriff who outwits a crooked banker. Taylor, a ranch owner, has paid off a $10,000 loan to banker Rockwell, thereby gaining total ownership of his ranch. Rockwell fakes a holdup, kills Taylor, and makes it look as though Baker did it. To top it off, Rockwell steals the paid-off bank loan note, which puts the ranch $10,000 in the hole again. Taylor's heir, whom no one has seen, turns out to be a girl. Baker goes to work for her in straightening out the mess.

d, George Waggner; w, Joseph West; ph, Gus Peterson; m, Frank Sanucci; ed, Carl Pierson; m/l, Fleming Allen, "Ring Around the Moon Tonight" (sung by Bob Baker).

Western (PR:A MPAA:NR)

GUINEA PIG, THE (SEE: OUTSIDER, THE, 1949, Brit.)

GUINGUETTE** (1959, Fr.) 105m Franco London-Gibe/GAU bw

Zizi Jeanmaire (Guinguette), Jean-Claude Pascal (Marco), Maria-Christina Gajoni (Maryse), Paul Meurisse (Vicomte), Maria Megey (Julie), Raymond Bussieres (Chauffeur), Henri Vilbert (Client), Paul Descombies (Inspector).

Reformed hooker Jeanmaire opens up a small nightclub in the French countryside. She gets involved with Pascal but sixteen-year-old Gajoni, doing a bad Brigitte Bardot impersonation, tries to steal him away by any means she can. Noted ballet dancer Jeanmaire carries her role well but is hampered by too many subplots which ultimately make this otherwise well-produced film too long.

d, Jean Delannoy; w, Henri Jeanson, Dominique Daudre, Delannoy; ph, Pierre Montazel; ed, Henri Taverna.

Drama (PR:C MPAA:NR)

GULLIVER'S TRAVELS**½ (1939) 75m PAR c

Lanny Ross (Singing Voice of the Prince), Jessica Dragonette (Singing Voice of the Princess).

With the success of Walt Disney's SNOW WHITE AND THE SEVEN DWARFS in 1937, the Fleisher brothers of POPEYE and BETTY BOOP fame decided to try their hands at a full-length animated feature. They used Jonathan Swift's famed satire for a source, trimming the original story to its bare bones. What was left was the story of Gulliver being shipwrecked on the island of Lilliput, where the inhabitants are only a few inches tall. Before the giant man's arrival King Little of Lilliput and King Bombo of Blefuscu are preparing for the marriage of their respective offspring: Prince David and Princess Glory. But a feud develops when they cannot decide on which country's anthem is to be sung at the royal wedding. When Gulliver washes up on the beach of Little's kingdom, the little people tie him down. But he easily escapes, and rather than terrorize the Lilliputians, he befriends them. Of course he settles the feud between the two kings and everyone lives happily ever after. GULLIVER'S TRAVELS has its share of problems. Without Swift's biting satire, the story is simplistic and a little dull. Characterizations are minimal at best, and Gulliver can never quite get over his charm for the little people. The love story is baldly flat; we don't even hear the prince and princess until the film's end, and that's just for a duo. But artistically the film is interesting to watch. While no SNOW WHITE ("We can do better than that with our second-string animators," Disney is reported to have said) it has some fine animation within. The opening storm sequence is excellent. Gulliver was rotoscoped (animated from live footage) and the technique worked well, making the giant remarkably realistic and a nice contrast to the little people. One character, Gabby, was quite a lively little fellow, and the Fleishers went on to do a series with him. One song "It's a Hap-Hap-Happy Day" by Sammy Timberg, Winston Sharples, and Al Neiburg, also achieved some immortality from the Fleishers, who used it as background music in many of their later shorts. This is by no means a classic film, but interesting enough for technique and historical value. Of course, the kids will love it. Other songs: "Bluebirds in the Moonlight," "All's Well," "We're All Together Again," "Forever," "Faithful," "Faithful Forever" (Ralph Rainger, Leo Robin).

p, Max Fleisher; d, Dave Fleisher; w, Dan Gordon, Ted Pierce, Izzy Sparber, Edmond Seward (based on a story by Seward from the novel by Jonathan Swift); ph, Charles Schettler; m, Victor Young; animation d, Seymour Kneitel, Willard Bowsky, Tom Palmer, Grim Natwick, William Hanning, Roland Crandall, Tom Johnson, Robert Leffingwell, Frank Kelling, Winfield Hoskins, Orestes Calpini.

Animated Fantasy **Cas.** (PR:AAA MPAA:NR)

GULLIVER'S TRAVELS*½ (1977, Brit., Bel.) 80m Valeness-Belvision/Sunn Classic c

Richard Harris (Gulliver), Catherine Schell (Girl), Norman Shelley (Father), Meredith Edwards (Uncle), Voices of Michael Bates, Denis Bryer, Julian Glover, Stephen Jack, Bessie Love, Murray Melvin, Nancy Nevinson, Robert Rietty, Norman Shelley, Valdek Sheybal, Roger Snowden, Bernard Spear, Graham Stark.

Shoddy remake of the 1939 Fleischer Brothers feature, this simplifies Swift's satire even more than the original film. The difference between the two films is that this one incorporates live action footage with animation. Harris is unconvincing as Gulliver, reducing his portrayal to smiles and wrinkled brows. The animation is okay but nothing special, and certainly not as good as the original. The story is cutesified beyond belief. Swift's message about the insanity of war is told in simple black-and-white with no gray shade in between. This film had some financial problems as well, being put on hold half-way through production due to lack of funds. Eventually, the money was scraped up and the film was completed. "Gulliver" was put to animation previous to both this and the Fleischers by the Soviet Union in 1935. Using wax dolls, the story (called THE NEW GULLIVER) was standard Soviet propaganda with Gulliver uniting the Lilliputian workers.

p, Raymon LeBlanc, Derek Horne; d, Peter Hunt; w, Don Black (based on the novel by Jonathan Swift); ph, Alan Hume (Eastmancolor); m, Michel LeGrand; ed, Ron Pope, Robert Richardson; prod d, Michael Stringer; animators, Nic Broca, Marcel Colbrant, Vivian Miessen, Jose Abel, Louis-Michel Carpentier, Michel Leoup, Maddy Grogniet; m/l, LeGrand and Black; cos, Anthony Mendelson.

Animation/Live Action
Fantasy **Cas.** (PR:AAA MPAA:G)

GULLIVER'S TRAVELS BEYOND THE MOON** (1966, Jap.) 85m Toei/CD c

(GULLIVER NO UCHU RYOKO; GARIBAH NO UCHU RYOKO)

A full-length animated feature produced in Japan. A homeless young lad is hit by a car and knocked unconscious. While asleep he dreams he is with Dr. Gulliver, along with a toy-soldier colonel, a crow, and a dog on a trip to planet Hope. Pulled off course, they discover a princess, who explains that Hope is being held in thrall by robots gone mad. The boy and Dr. Gulliver accidentally discover that the robots melt when hit by water; Hope is freed thanks to some fancy water-pistol action. The boy wakes up and continues on his way, this time with a feeling of satisfaction and good feelings about the future. The animation is not bad, sort of like early Disney, though the story has none of the master's charm. This is one of the first science-fiction Japanese animated features and also one of the only ones exported to America. It's very loosely based on the famous Swift tale, though pretty much in name only.

p, Hiroshi Okawa; d, Yoshio Kuroda; w, Shinichi Sekizawa (based on the character in the novel by Jonathan Swift); animation d, Hideo Furusawa; m/l, "The Earth Song," "I Wanna Be Like Gulliver," " That's the Way it Goes," "Keep Your Hopes High," Milton and Anne DeLugg.

Animated Science Fiction
Fantasy (PR:AAA MPAA:NR)

GUMBALL RALLY, THE*½ (1976) 106m First Artists/WB c

Michael Sarrazin (Bannon), Norman Burton (Roscoe), Gary Busey (Gibson), John Durren (Preston), Susan Flannery (Alice), Harvey Jason (Lapchick), Steven Keats (Kandinsky), Tim McIntire (Smith), Joanne Nail (Jane), J. Pat O'Malley (Barney), Tricia O'Neil (Angie), Lazaro Perez (Jose), Nicholas Pryor (Graves), Vaughn Taylor (Andy), Wally Taylor (Avila), Raul Julia (Franco).

One of many coast-to-coast car race films and indistinguishable from the others. The standard stock characters line up their various autos in New York and head for California in a mad dash. Lots of car crashes are used when there's nothing else to say in the story—and that means a lot of car crashes. Burton's the cop trying to stop the race. It's a one-joke film that's stretched out well beyond its welcome. Producer/director Bail was a stunt coordinator before turning to direction.

p&d, Chuck Bail; w, Leon Capetanos (based on a story by Bail and Capetanos); ph, Richard C. Glouner (Panavision, Technicolor); m, Dominic Frontiere; ed, Gordon Scott, Stuart H. Pappe, Maury Winetrobe; art d, Walter Simonds; set d, Morrie Hoffman; stunt coordinator, Eddy Donno.

Action/Comedy **Cas.** (PR:A MPAA:PG)

GUMBO YA-YA (SEE: GIRLS! GIRLS! GIRLS!, 1962)

GUMSHOE*** (1972, Brit.) 88m Memorial Enterprises/COL c

Albert Finney (Eddie Ginley), Billie Whitelaw (Ellen), Frank Finlay (William), Janice Rule (Mrs. Blankerscoon), Carolyn Seymour (Alison Wyatt), Fulton Mackay (Straker), George Innes (Bookshop Proprietor), George Silver (Jacob De Fries), Billy Dean (Tommy), Wendy Richard (Anne Scott), Maureen Lipman (Naomi), Neville Smith (Arthur), Oscar James (Azinge), Joey Kenyon (Joey), Bert King (Mal), Chris Cunningham (Clifford), Ken Jones (Labor Exchange Clerk), Tom Kempinski (Psychiatrist), Harry Hutchinson (Kleptomaniac), Sammy Sharples (Sammy), Ernie Mac and The Saturated Seven, Jason Kane, The Jacksons, Vicki Day, Scott Christian (Club Artists).

An offbeat but interesting film where Finney, a versatile and fascinating actor, satirizes the detective films of the past, particularly the hardboiled private eyes created by Dashiell Hammett and Raymond Chandler. Finney is a bingo caller in a seedy Liverpool nightclub who envisions himself a tough detective a la Humphrey Bogart. On his thirty-first birthday, he places an ad in the paper which reads: "Ginley's the name/Gumshoe's the game/Private Investigation/No divorce work." To his surprise, Finney gets a response from Silver, a mysterious fat man who hands him a package containing a photo of Seymour, a gun, and a thousand pounds in payment, but no instructions. Baffled, Finney explains the situation to Whitelaw, who is unhappily married to his brother Finlay. She urges him to quit his capricious escapade. But Finney plunges on while brother Finlay tries to deflect his sleuthing career, first by offering him a job with his firm which he refuses, then by persuading the nightclub owner where he works to give him a paid vacation. Finney rejects these offers and soon becomes involved with Rule, who wants him to work on a divorce. Through a series of bumbling mishaps, Finney learns that Rule is running guns to Africa, smuggling heroin, and trying to abduct Seymour for political reasons, the latter's father being an African leader Rule and others are trying to depose. Finney watches Rule administer a fatal dose of heroin to her confederate Silver, who is trying to protect Seymour. Finney later learns that it was his sister-in-law Whitelaw who had answered the ad and she explains most of the confused case to him, then begs him to run off with her. He refuses and overcomes his amateur antics by rounding up Rule, Whitelaw, his own brother, and assorted henchmen, while saving the elusive Seymour in the process. GUMSHOE, produced by Finney's own company, is a good spoof of THE MALTESE FALCON and THE BIG SLEEP and is packed with witty—if absurd—dialog and plenty of action, all harking back to the film noir days of the tough detective, made even funnier as Finney struggles through the awkward transition of British commoner to the image of a hard-as-nails American-type sleuth.

p, Michael Medwin; d, Stephen Frears; w, Neville Smith; ph, Chris Menges (Eastmancolor); m, Andrew Lloyd Webber; ed, Fergus McDonell, Charles Rees; prod d, Michael Seymour; art d, Richard Rambaut; set d, Harry Cordwell, Brian Brockwell; cos, Daphine Dare; spec eff, Bowie Films; m/l, "Baby, You're Good for Me," Webber, Tim Rice, sung by Roy Young; makeup, Bob Lawrence.

Satire (PR:C MPAA:PG)

GUN, THE*½ (1978, Ital.) 90m Maratea/CIDIF c (L'ARMA)

Stefano Satta Flores *(Luigi Campagna)*, Claudia Cardinale *(Marta Campagna)*, Benedetta Fantoli *(Rossana Campagna)*.

Insipid film features Flores as a family man losing touch with his wife and teenage daughter. In order to protect what little he has left, he turns to a handgun. The film's smarmy attitudes suggest that this is an okay means of proving manhood and makes up for the inadequacies within the man's character. The vigilantism within the film is confusing and repugnant. This film is little more than a series of cliches strung together. The acting is terrible; Flores is stiff and unnatural. Cardinale tries her best, but just can't overcome the material. Flores and Cardinale co-produced this along with Squittieri as a quickie before the latter's next main feature FATHER OF THE GODFATHERS. This explains the cheapness inherent in this film.

p,d&w, Pasquale Squittierie; ph, Giulio Albonico (Eastmancolor); m, Tullio De Piscopo; ed, Squittieri; art d, Luciana Vedovelli, Renato Ventura.

Drama (PR:O MPAA:NR)

GUN BATTLE AT MONTEREY* (1957) 67m AA bw

Sterling Hayden *(Turner)*, Pamela Duncan *(Maria)*, Ted de Corsia *(Reno)*, Mary Beth Hughes *(Cleo)*, Lee Van Cleef *(Kirby)*, Charles Cane *(Mundy)*, Pat Comiskey *(Frank)*, Byron Foulger *(Carson)*, Mauritz Hugo *(Charley)*, I. Stanford Jolley *(Idwall)*, Fred Sherman, George Baxter, Michael Vallon, John Dalmer.

Hayden is shot in the back by partner de Corsia during a bank holdup. Left for dead, Hayden recovers, with the help of Duncan. He goes out to avenge his betrayal. A predictable film that follows the cliches with close attention: they can be marked off on a checklist. The screenplay gives the males the standard stuff and females hardly anything to do at all. The title is also misleading: no gun battle occurs at Monterey. Technically it's okay for what it is, which isn't much at all.

p, Carl K. Hittleman; d, Hittleman, Sidney A. Franklin, Jr.; w, Jack Leonard, Lawrence Resner; ph, Harry Neumann; m, Robert Wiley Miller; ed, Harry Coswick; md, Miller; art d, David Milton.

Western (PR:C MPAA:NR)

GUN BELT½** (1953) 77m Global/UA c

George Montgomery *(Billy Ringo)*, Tab Hunter *(Chip Ringo)*, Helen Westcott *(Arlene Reach)*, John Dehner *(Matt Ringo)*, William Bishop *(Ike Clinton)*, Douglas Kennedy *(Dixon)*, Jack Elam *(Kolloway)*, Joe Haworth *(Hoke)*, Hugh Sanders *(Frazer)*, Willis Bouchey *(Endicott)*, James Millican *(Wyatt Earp)*, Bruce Cowling *(Virgil Earp)*, Boyd Morgan *(Texas Jack)*, Boyd Stockman *(Turkey Creek)*, William Phillips *(Curly)*, Chuck Roberson *(Oliver)*, Jack Carry *(Mort)*.

Montgomery is a former outlaw, now a rancher. His brother, Dehner, sets him up in a frame for bank robbery, forcing Montgomery to once more take out his old gun belt (hence the film's title). In the process he teaches his nephew Hunter that the outlaw trade is a lot meaner than the ranching life. What could have been a routine B western is made into something better than average by some well-handled direction, in addition to some good acting. Nazarro keeps things moving in good rhythms, building suspense and action nicely. Montgomery and Hunter are both fine in their roles, giving believable performances that go beyond the material. The color photography is also fine: scenery is good to look at and well used. It's not a great picture, but does well within its format.

p, Edward Small; d, Ray Nazarro; w, Richard Schayer, Jack DeWitt (based on a story by Arthur Orloff); ph, W. Howard Greene (Technicolor); m, Irving Gertz; ed, Grant Whytock; art d, Edward L. Ilou.

Western (PR:A MPAA:NR)

GUN BROTHERS½** (1956) 79m Grand/UA bw

Buster Crabbe *(Chad)*, Ann Robinson *(Rose Fargo)*, Neville Brand *(Jubal)*, Michael Ansara *(Shawnee)*, Walter Sande *(Yellowstone)*, Lita Milan *(Meeteetse)*, James Seay *(Blackjack Silk)*, Roy Barcroft *(Sheriff Jergen)*, Slim Pickens *(Moose MacLain)*, Dorothy Ford *(Molly)*.

Former "Flash Gordon" Crabb is the star in one of his last featured roles. Here he returns home from the cavalry in hopes of joining his brother, Brand, a wealthy rancher. Instead, Crabbe discovers that Brand is really the leader of an outlaw gang that specializes in cattle rustling and stage robbery. Brand mistakenly believes that his brother has informed the sheriff about the shady goings-on, but when henchman Ansara forms his own gang the two brothers join forces to fight them off. In the end, Brand repents for his lawlessness by dying. This is a good combination of acting and action within a formula B-Western. Crabbe and Brand carry their respective roles well and have a nice bonding between the two of them. A good supporting group of cowboy regulars, including the ever-popular Pickens, rounds out the cast. Direction is fine for the format, keeping things running at a good pace. The action scenes are particularly well done.

d, Sidney Salkow; w, Gerald Drayson Adams, Richard Schayer (based on a story by Adams); ph, Kenneth Peach; m, Irving Gertz; ed, Arthur Hilton; md, Gertz; art d, Arthur Lonergan.

Western (PR:A MPAA:NR)

GUN CODE*½ (1940) 54m PRC bw

Tim McCoy *(Tim Hammond)*, Inna Gest [Ina Guest] *(Betty Garrett)*, Lou Fulton *(Curly)*, Alden Chase *(James M. Bradley)*, Carleton Young *(Slim Doyle)*, Ted Adams *(Sheriff Kramer)*, Robert Winkler *(Jerry Garrett)*, Dave O'Brien *(Gale)*, George Chesebro *(Bart)*, Jack Richardson *(McClure)*, John Elliott *(Parson Hammond)*.

Short cowboy film stars McCoy as a federal agent assigned to stop a gang of outlaws from creating havoc. The twist here is that the outlaws are "protection" artists, a sort of western Mafia. But the gimmick doesn't work. Everything in this film is hampered by the short running time, with characters and ideas being introduced and then dropped from sight. The terminal gun battle is short and unbelievable. Before becoming a movie cowboy, McCoy had spent some time in Wyoming as an Indian interpreter.

p, Sigmund Neufeld; d, Peter Stewart; w, Joseph O'Donnell; ph, Jack Greenhalgh; ed, Holbrook N. Todd.

Western (PR:A MPAA:NR)

GUN CRAZY** (1949) 87m King Bros./UA bw (AKA: DEADLY IS THE FEMALE)

Peggy Cummins *(Annie Laurie Starr)*, John Dall *(Bart Tare)*, Berry Kroeger *(Packett)*, Morris Carnovsky *(Judge Willoughby)*, Anabel Shaw *(Ruby Tare)*, Harry Lewis *(Clyde Boston)*, Nedrick Young *(Dave Allister)*, Trevor Bardette *(Sheriff Boston)*, Mickey Little *(Bart Tare, Age 7)*, Rusty Tamblyn *(Bart Tare, Age 14)*, Paul Frison *(Clyde Boston, Age 14)*, Dave Bair *(Dave Allister, Age 14)*, Stanley Prager *(Bluey-Bluey)*, Virginia Farmer *(Miss Wynn)*, Anne O'Neal *(Miss Sifert)*, Frances Irwin *(Danceland Singer)*, Don Beddoe *(Man from Chicago)*, Robert Osterloh *(Hampton Policeman)*, Shimen Ruskin *(Taxi Driver)*, Harry Hayden *(Mr. Mallenberg)*.

This much overrated cult film depicts Cummins as a scheming, vicious female patterned after Bonnie Parker, the notorious 1930s outlaw. Dall is an insecure, weak-willed, paranoid WW II veteran who is obsessed with guns and fascinated by the idea that he killed his pet when he was a child. When he meets equally unbalanced Cummins, a carnival markswoman, the two hit it off like Smith & Wesson. Through their love of guns, the pair begin to plan robberies, more out of perverse pleasure than gain, and, with Cummins acting as the real goad, the two embark on a crime spree. They shoot and kill their way through the rest of the film until after a last dance in a diner, being themselves killed by police in a swamp. The lensing is particularly good, with director Lewis using many innovative shots (mounting his camera in the back seat of a car and using a continuous take as the pair alight, rob a bank, and then race out of town). The acting, however, is atrocious. Cummins comes off like a tongue-tied amateur and Dall is swishy and hammy at the same time. Much has been written about this B-film where critics in search of substance have overreached to liken GUN CRAZY to truly substantial films such as YOU ONLY LIVE ONCE (1937), a Fritz Lang classic loosely based on the criminal exploits of Bonnie Parker and Clyde Barrow, and of course, BONNIE AND CLYDE (1967). Contrary to mistaken reviewers and cult-clutching critics, this film really has little to redeem it as a commercial vehicle or an artistic effort. There is nothing subtle or insightful about the characters and the obvious motivation here is to provide cheap thrills and instant shock through the one-dimensional characters who are blatantly berserk. It's sleazier than Monogram's tawdy DILLINGER (1945) and it doesn't pack the punch of any average poverty-row crime production.

p, Frank and Maurice King; d, Joseph H. Lewis; w, McKinlay Kantor, Millard Kaufman (based on the story "Gun Crazy" by Kantor); ph, Russell Harlan; m, Victor Young; ed, Harry Gerstad; prod d, Gordon Wiles; md, Leo Shuken, Sidney Cutner; set d, Raymond Boltz, Jr.; cos, Norma.

Crime Drama (PR:O MPAA:NR)

GUN DUEL IN DURANGO½** (1957) 73m Peerless/UA bw (AKA: DUEL IN DURANGO)

George Montgomery *(Dan)*, Ann Robinson *(Judy)*, Steve Brodie *(Dunston)*, Bobby Clark *(Robbie)*, Frank Ferguson *(Sheriff Howard)*, Donald Barry *(Larry)*, Henry Rowland *(Roy)*, Denver Pyle *(Ranger Captain)*, Mary Treen *(Spinster)*, Al Wyatt *(Jones)*, Red Morgan *(Burt)*, Joe Yrigoyen *(Stacey)*.

Montgomery is the leader of an infamous outlaw gang. Tired of the life he is leading, Montgomery decides to reform and start things anew. He meets ranch owner Robinson who will marry the former outlaw once he proves his intentions are sincere. But his former comrades, led now by Brodie, try to bring Montgomery back to his old ways. Montgomery overcomes their threats and evil doings in a final gunfight and marries Robinson. Pretty routine effort for a Western. The editing is nice and tight, keeping things moving in a good stride. Clark is fine in his supporting role of an orphan befriended by Montgomery.

p, Robert E. Kent; d, Sidney Salkow; w, Louis Stevens; ph, Maury Gertsman; m, Paul Sawtell, Bert Shefter; ed, Robert Golden; art d, William Ross.

Western (PR:A MPAA:NR)

GUN FEVER* (1958) 83m UA bw

Mark Stevens *(Lucas)*, John Lupton *(Simon)*, Larry Storch *(Amigo)*, Jana Davi *(Tanana)*, Aaron Saxon *(Trench)*, Jerry Barclay *(Singer)*, Norman Frederic *(Whitman)*, Clegg Hoyt *(Kane)*, Jean Innes *(Martha)*, Russell Thorson *(Thomas)*, Michael Himm *(Stableman)*, Iron Eyes Cody *(1st Indian Chief)*, Eddie Little *(2nd Indian Chief)*, April Delavanti *(Jerry)*, John Godard *(Lee)*, Vic Smith *(Jack)*, Robert Stevenson *(Norris)*, William Erwin *(Bartender)*, David Bond *(Man)*, George Selk *(Farmer)*.

Stevens is a miner, but he's quick on the draw. With his partner, Lupton, he tracks a renegade who, with a group of Indians, killed his father. In an interesting Oedipal twist, renegade murderer Saxon is the father of Lupton, who disavowed him years before as a result of his retrograde activities. Justice is done; Stevens rides off alone, leaving the wounded Lupton—newly fatherless—in the tender care of Davi. The latter, in her first high-billed role, was a lovely woman whose charms were amply shown in the European release of this double-shot film (one of the first of the western genre to be sexed up for foreign release, heralding a new era); barring a few more quickie westerns, she disappeared from view after this one. Actor Stevens directed and co-wrote this picture.

p, Harry Jackson, Sam Weston; d, Mark Stevens; w, Stevens, Stanley H. Silverman (based on a story by Harry S. Franklin, Julius Evans); ph, Charles Van Enger; m, Paul Dunlap; ed, Lee Gilbert; art d, Bob Kinoshita.

Western (PR:O MPAA:NR)

GUN FIGHT**½** (1961) 67m Zenith/UA bw

James Brown *(Wayne Santley)*, Joan Staley *(Nora Blaine)*, Gregg Palmer *(Brad Santley)*, Ron Soble *(Pawnee)*, Ken Mayer *(Joe Emery)*, Charles Cooper *(Cole Fender)*, Charles Coy *(Sheriff)*, James Parnell *(Moose)*, Connie Buck *(Coheela)*, Kate Murtah *(Molly)*, Andy Albin *(Jonathan)*, Jon Locke *(Saunders)*, Morgan Shaan *(Cory)*, Monte Burkhart *(Hannah)*, David Donaldson *(Prospector)*, John Damler *(Hank)*, Robert Nash *(Vance)*, Jack Kenny *(Jake)*, Frank Watkins *(Roark)*, Frank Eldredge *(Piano Player)*, Gene Coogan *(Bole)*, Bill Koontz *(Krag)*, Boyd Stockman *(Cadiz)*, Bob Woodward *(Mantz)*.

Brown plays a discharged cavalryman who travels to join brother Palmer on the latter's cattle ranch. On the stagecoach to his brother's place, Brown meets Staley, a dancehall girl whom he later rescues from Cooper's advances during a robbery. Upon arriving, Brown discovers that Palmer is no rancher, but a rustler instead. He leaves his crooked sibling, going to work on a trading post and marrying Staley. Soble, one of Palmer's men, convinces his boss that Brown ratted on him to the sheriff. Palmer seeks revenge but learns from his brother that he is part of a frame-up set by Cooper. Palmer decides to join his brother on fur-trapping expeditions, but the disgruntled Soble organizes the old gang to attack the two men. The outlaws are killed, but so is Palmer. Brown and Staley have a baby girl, whom they name after Palmer. Typical Western for its time.

p, Robert E. Kent; d, Edward L. Cahn; w, Gerald Drayson Adams, Richard Schayer (based on a story by Adams); ph, Walter Strenge; m, Paul Sawtell, Bert Shefter; ed, Robert Carlisle; art d, Serge Krizman; cos, Einar Bourman, Sabine Manela; makeup, Harry Thomas.

Western **(PR:C MPAA:NR)**

GUN FOR A COWARD**½** (1957) 88m UNIV c

Fred MacMurray *(Will Keough)*, Jeffrey Hunter *(Bless Keough)*, Janice Rule *(Aud Niven)*, Chill Wills *(Loving)*, Dean Stockwell *(Hade Keough)*, Josephine Hutchinson *(Mrs. Keough)*, Betty Lynn *(Claire)*, Iron Eyes Cody *(Chief)*, Robert Hoy *(Danny)*, Jane Howard *(Marie)*, Marjorie Stapp *(Rose)*, John Larch *(Stringer)*, Paul Birch *(Andy Niven)*, Bob Steele *(Durkee)*, Frances Morris *(Mrs. Anderson)*.

MacMurray is the eldest of three brothers and caretaker of their late father's ranch, in addition to being the paternal figure at large. Hunter is the "coward" of the title, a sensitive, non-violent young man who is convinced that he is to blame for his father's death. Rounding out the trio is Stockwell as the wild-living youngest brother. Rule is the woman who switches her affections from MacMurray to Hunter. Hutchinson is the mother whose overbearing manner induces much of Hunter's guilt. Of course there are the standard gunplay and cattle drives found in this genre but what separates GUN FOR A COWARD from other westerns is the characterizations. Here we get to know the people in the film and with few exceptions, even stock characters are well portrayed. MacMurray is fine as the slighted father figure and Hunter gives an intriguing and entirely natural performance. Stockwell does not live up to the other two, however, looking more like a bad James Dean impersonation than anything else. Still, the interplay between the three is very good, a quality that helps this film rise above some of its standard cowboy elements. Direction is evenly paced, letting the action and story unfold naturally, ever sensitive to the relationships among characters.

p, William Alland; d, Abner Biberman; w, R. Wright Campbell; ph, George Robinson (Cinemascope, Eastmancolor); ed, Edward Curtiss; md, Joseph Gershenson; art d, Alexander Golitzen, Alfred Sweeney; cos, Jay A. Morley, Jr.

Western **(PR:O MPAA:NR)**

GUN FURY**½** (1953) 83m COL c

Rock Hudson *(Ben Warren)*, Donna Reed *(Jennifer Ballard)*, Phil Carey *(Frank Slayton)*, Roberta Haynes *(Estella Morales)*, Leo Gordon *(Jess Burgess)*, Lee Marvin *(Blinky)*, Neville Brand *(Brazos)*, Ray Thomas *(Doc)*, Robert Herron *(Curly Jordan)*, Phil Rawlins *(Jim Morse)*, John Cason *(Westy)*, Forest Lewis, Don Carlos, Pat Hogan, Mel Welles, Post Park.

Hudson and Reed are newlyweds traveling to the West. Carey, in a wonderful performance as a psychotic outlaw, kidnaps Reed; Hudson is forced to pursue the gang. Hudson tries to maintain his composure, but ends up becoming just as crazed as Carey. Though Hudson's change at the denouncement is wholly unbelievable, this isn't too bad a film. Both the script and Walsh's direction are basic but compelling, and Carey just about steals the whole picture. Marvin has a bit part as one of the gang members, turning in a good performance for the small role. Filmed in 3-D.

p, Lewis J. Rachmil; d, Raoul Walsh; w, Irving Wallace, Roy Huggins (based on the novel *Ten Against Caesar* by Kathleen B. George, Robert A. Granger); ph, Lester H. White (Technicolor, 3-d); m, Mischa Bakaleinikoff; ed, James Sweeney, Jerome Thomas; art d, Ross Bellah, James Crowe.

Western **(PR:A MPAA:NR)**

GUN GLORY**½** (1957) 88m MGM c

Stewart Granger *(Tom Early)*, Rhonda Fleming *(Jo)*, Chill Wills *(Preacher)*, Steve Rowland *(Young Tom Early)*, James Gregory *(Grimsell)*, Jacques Aubuchon *(Sam Winscott)*, Arch Johnson *(Gunn)*, William Fawcett *(Martin)*, Carl Pitti *(Joel)*, Lane Bradford *(Ugly)*, Rayford Barnes *(Blondie)*, Ed Mundy *(Ancient)*, Gene Coogan, Michael Dugan, Jack Montgomery *(Farmers)*, Bud Osborne *(Clem)*, May McAvoy *(Woman)*, Steve Widders, Charles Hebert *(Boys)*.

After spending three years as a gunslinger, Granger returns home only to find his wife has died and son Rowland (the real-life son of GUN GLORY's director) has turned against him. When cattleman Gregory threatens to run his herds through the farming valley, the townsfolk, led by preacher Wills and storekeeper Aubuchon, ignore Granger's cautions that Gregory's type only understands violence. When a townsman is killed, the rest finally realize what is happening, but it is too late and the unprepared town nearly falls victim to Gregory and his violent cohorts. All is resolved when outcast Granger blows up a mountain area to halt the drive and kills Gregory in a shoot out. In the end he wins the respect of the town, a new love from his son, and sexy widow Fleming, who has been the only character to have faith in Granger throughout the film. The script is by former ANDY HARDY series writer Ludwig in what certainly is a moral reverse from his previous fare. Rowland is not as strong as he should be in his portrayal of the embittered son, though Granger, minus his British accent, is strong enough to cover. There's a fine use of location and color photography in a routinely, though competently, directed effort. One song, "The Ninety and Nine," is rendered by Burl Ives during the title credits.

p, Nicholas Nayfack; d, Roy Rowland; w, William Ludwig (based on the novel *Man of the West* by Philip Yordan); ph, Harold J. Marzorati (CinemaScope, Metrocolor); m, Jeff Alexander; ed, Frank Santillo; art d, William A. Horning, Merrill Pye; cos, Walter Plunkett.

Western **(PR:A MPAA:NR)**

GUN HAND, THE (SEE: HE RIDES TALL, 1964)

GUN HAWK, THE*½** (1963) 92m AA c

Rory Calhoun *(Blaine Madden)*, Rod Cameron *(Sheriff Corey)*, Ruta Lee *(Marleen)*, Rod Lauren *(Roan)*, Morgan Woodward *(Mitchell)*, Robert J. Wilke *(Johnny Flanders)*, John Litel *(Drunk)*, Rodolfo Hoyos *(Miguel)*, Lane Bradford *(Joe Sully)*, Glenn Stensel *(Luke Sully)*, Joan Connors *(Roan's Woman)*, Ron Whelan *(Blackjack)*, Lee Bradley *(Pancho)*, Jody Daniels, Natividad Vacio, Greg Barton, Frank Gardner, Harry Fleer).

At this point in film history, the screen western was effectively being killed off by television shows such as *Bonanza* and *The Big Valley*, but this didn't stop a few stalwarts from trying their best to keep the genre alive. Here movie cowboy Calhoun is an old gunman who meets Lauren, a wild gunslinger who reminds Calhoun of his younger days. After being wounded in a gunfight, Calhoun returns to Sanctuary, a town populated by outlaws and run by him. The rest of the film consists of Calhoun slowly dying from his wound's infection. Unwilling to die in bed, he bullies Lauren into a duel and dies "with his own kind of dignity," by the much unsettled younger man's gun. Calhoun gives this film his best, but is hampered by a laughable make-up job. The rest is pretty routine. Lauren does a credible job as the confused young man, handling Calhoun's attempts to reform him, and then a complete opposite swing. The latter half of the film just drags on towards the inevitable climax. Calhoun went on to play a retired B-movie cowboy in the 1984 teen exploitation film ANGEL. THE GUN HAWK has a story line oddly redolent of a very superior western of 1950, THE GUNFIGHTER, with Gregory Peck as the aging shootist.

p, Richard Bernstein; d, Edward Ludwig; w, Jo Heims (based on a story by Bernstein, Max Steeber); ph, Paul C. Vogel (DeLuxe Color); m, Jimmy Haskell; ed, Rex Lipton; md, Haskell; art d, Rudi Feld; set d, Clarence Steensen; cos, Roger J. Weinberg; makeup, Beau Hickman; m/l, "A Searcher For Love," Robert Marcucci, Russ Faith.

Western **(PR:C MPAA:NR)**

GUN JUSTICE**½** (1934) 60m UNIV bw

Ken Maynard *(Ken Lance)*, Cecilia Parker *(Ray Harsh)*, Hooper Atchley *(Sam Burkett)*, Walter Miller *(Chris Hogan)*, Jack Rockwell *(Hank Rivers)*, Francis Ford *(Denver)*, Fred McKaye *(Imposter)*, Bill Dyer *(Red Hogan)*, Jack Richardson *(Sheriff)*, Ed Coxen *(Jim Lance)*, Bill Gould *(Jones)*, Sheldon Lewis, Lafe McKee, Ben Corbett, Slim Whitaker, Hank Bell, Blackie Whiteford, Horace B. Carpenter, Bob McKenzie, Frank Ellis, Bud McClure, Roy Bucko, Buck Bucko, Pascale Perry, Jack Ward, Cliff Lyons, "Tarzan".

A group of evil land grabbers plot to take over the ranch of a man they have killed. Nephew Maynard is due to inherit the ranch but since he can't be found, McKaye is hired to pose as the nephew. But Maynard, a state ranger, finally arrives on the scene and avenges his uncle, getting his rightful claim in the process. This typical Western plot rises above others of its type by the excellent portrayal by Maynard. Parker as his fellow legatee cousin/love interest also helps. Though her role has its genre limitations, she does a fine job with what she is given, definitely coming off as honest rather than going through the motions. There is, of course, the standard gunplay and location scenery, but they are given a special look by McCord's camera work. All in all, it's a better than average B. In addition to his starring role, Maynard also served as producer.

p, Ken Maynard; d, Alan James; w, Robert Quigley; ph, Ted McCord.

Western **(PR:A MPAA:NR)**

GUN LAW*½** (1933) 59m Majestic bw

Jack Hoxie, Betty Boyd, J. Frank Glendon, Paul Fix, Mary Carr, Harry Todd, Ben Corbett, Dick Botiller, Edmund Cobb, Robert Burns, Jack Kirk, Horace B. Carpenter.

A villain known as the Sonora Kid forces the law abiding citizens of Arizona to come up with a means to end his rampaging before things get too out of hand. Produced in typical fashion to get a thrill or two out of a bombardment of action.

p, Larry Darmour; d, Lew Collins; w, Collins, Oliver Drake.

Western **(PR:A MPAA:NR)**

GUN LAW***** (1938) 60m RKO bw

George O'Brien *(Tom O'Malley)*, Rita Oehmen *(Ruth Ross)*, Ray Whitley *(Singing Sam McGee)*, Paul Everton *(Mayor Blaine)*, Robert Gleckler *(Flash Arnold)*, Ward Bond *(Pecos)*, Francis MacDonald *(Nevada)*, Edward Pawley *(The Raven)*, Frank O'Connor *(Parson Ross)*, Hank Bell, Paul Fix, Ethan Laidlaw, Lloyd Ingraham, Robert Burns, James Mason, Ken Card, Neal Burns, Ray Jones, Herman Hack, Willie Phelps, Earl Phelps, Norman Phelps.

U.S. Marshal O'Brien, on his way to the town of Gunsight, is ambushed and, by a fluke, relieved of his sidearm by a mysterious outlaw gunslinger known as The Raven—Pawley—who also takes his badge, his horse, and his identifying documents. Trailing the acquisitive outlaw, O'Brien finds him lying near death beside a poisoned water hole. With The Raven nevermore, O'Brien retrieves his own possessions, plus a letter of introduction belonging to the late outlaw which is addressed to Gleckler, a Gunsight outlaw leader. His horse also poisoned, O'Brien solicits a ride from passersby parson O'Connor and his daughter, the lovely Oehmen, returning in their buckboard to Gunsight. Villains Bond and McDonald attempt to prevent O'Connor from holding Sunday services in the town, but O'Brien intervenes and fists fly. By prearrangement, after polishing off the pair, O'Brien meets with "Singing Sam," Whitley, an undercover deputy acting as a singing waiter in the local saloon, owned by Gleckler. Next, visiting the latter, O'Brien introduces himself as the notorious Raven, killer for hire. Assigned by Gleckler to eliminate the U.S. marshal whose arrival is imminent, O'Brien coolly displays his own badge and papers, mute evidence of his having anticipated his task. With this disclosure, the true leader of the outlaw band—the town's mayor, Everton—reveals himself, suggesting that O'Brien impersonate himself to lull the townsfolk into a sense of false security while the gang robs the payroll stagecoach. O'Brien—with his other deputies, who have hidden on the town's outskirts—hastens to the scene of the crime, halts the robbery and captures the criminals, then hurries back to engage the remaining villains in a poker game to protect his imposture. Discovering O'Brien's perfidy, Everton and Gleckler fake a robbery at the local hostelry and plant incriminating evidence in his room. They then race for the bank to procure their stored ill-gotten gains, planning to leave town before their duplicities are discovered. Everton kills Gleckler in order to secure all the spoils for himself. Escaping a pursuing posse, O'Brien arrives at the bank, but is balked in his intentions by villains Bond and McDonald. In a Mack Sennett-style multiple shootout, O'Brien is caught by the posse. As he is about to be hanged, Oehmen arrives with his deputies, and all ends well. A well-made western, unlike many of its precursors. The B-western genre comprises thousands of productions, utilizing only a bare handful of plots. Screenwriter Drake had used this very story line many times before: 1928's WHEN THE LAW RIDES (AKA: WEST OF THE LAW), starring Tom Tyler; GUN LAW (1929), with Jack Hoxie; THE RECKLESS RIDER (1932), starring Lane Chandler; and WEST OF THE DIVIDE (1934), starring John Wayne. This time, it was done properly. O'Brien, who died in 1985, was a fine actor who had appeared in such serious films as F. W. Murnau's SUNRISE (1927). Unlike many cowboy stars of the time, he was entirely credible; audiences were aware that he could handle the fight scenes himself. RKO took its time with this production and with others of its own B films, unlike the work of the "quickie" studios and independent producers. The studio had previously purchased a number of O'Brien starrers for release; this was the first of a series for which RKO was totally responsible, and resulted in an exclusive contract for its star. Songs in this version were "Breezy Whiskers," Ray Whitley; "So Long Old Pinto," Oliver Drake; "Pappy Was a Gun Man," Whitley, Drake.

p, Bert Gilroy; d, David Howard; w, Oliver Drake; ph, Joseph H. August; ed, Frederick Knudtson; md, Roy Webb.

Western (PR:A MPAA:NR)

GUN LAW JUSTICE✫½ (1949) 55m MON bw

Jimmy Wakely, Dub "Cannonball" Taylor, Ray Whitley, Jane Adams, Lee Phelps, Bud Osborne, John James, Edmund Cobb, Myron Healey, Ray Jones, Zon Murray, Tom Chatterton, I. Stanford Jolley, Carol Henry, Bob Curtis, Eddie Majors, Tex Atchinson, George Morrell, Herman Hack, Merrill McCormack.

Singing cowpoke Wakely and his comic sidekick Taylor help a bandit give up the lawless life and follow the trail of the straight and honorable. Sub-standard oater material which barely delivers what's expected.

p, Louis Gray; d, Lambert Hillyer; w, Basil Dickey; ph, Harry Neumann; ed, John Fuller; md, Edward Kay.

Western (PR:A MPAA:NR)

GUN LORDS OF STIRRUP BASIN✫✫ (1937) 55m REP bw

Bob Steele (Dan), Louise Stanley (Gail), Karl Hackett (Bowdre), Ernie Adams (Red), Frank LaRue (Dawson), Frank Ball (Stockton), Steve Clark (Hammond), Lou Meehan (Blackie), Frank Ellis (Horner), Jim Corey, Budd Buster, Lloyd Ingraham, Jack Kirk, Horace Murphy, Milburn Morante, Bobby Nelson, Tex Palmer, Emma Tansey, Horace B. Carpenter, Herman Hack.

Steele is the son of a cattleman and Stanley is the daughter of a homesteader. They're in love but problems arise when Hackett, a shyster lawyer, convinces the cattlemen that they will be left high and dry if the homesteaders are permitted to dam the river. Guns come out but love triumphs. Still, the love story is not center stage; after all, this is a western. There's plenty of two-fisted action, gunplay, and chase sequences, all done better than in most films of this type.

p, A.W. Hackel; d, Sam Newfield; w, George Plympton, Fred Myton (based on a story by Harry F. Olmstead), ph, Bert Longenecker; ed, S. Roy Luby.

Western (PR:A MPAA:NR)

GUN MAN FROM BODIE, THE✫✫ (1941) 62m MON bw (AKA: GUNMAN FROM BODIE)

Buck Jones, Tim McCoy, Raymond Hatton, Christine McIntyre, David O'Brien, Robert Frazer, Frank LaRue, Charles King, Lynton Brent, Max Walzman, Gene Alsace, John Merton, Jerry Sheldon, Jack King, Earl Douglas, Warren Jackson, Billy Carro, Frederick Gee, "Silver."

This is the second film in Monogram's Rough Rider series after ARIZONA BOUND. The semi-complicated plot finds Jones with an orphaned baby on his hands. Seems the child's parents were murdered by rustlers. He takes the infant to McIntyre's ranch, only to discover that she too has suffered at the hands of the rustlers. Along come Jones' pals McCoy and Hatton (who have secretly been working with Jones all along) and together they find out what's really going on and stop the bad guys. A good deal of this film is simply remnants from ARIZONA BOUND. These films were made when Jones and McCoy were getting along in years. Hatton, in the comic "old timer" role, was actually the youngest of the three. The plot of this film is a familiar one, first screened in William Wyler's HELL'S HEROES (1929), and later in many other films, the best-known being

John Ford's THREE GODFATHERS (1948)—itself a remake—starring John Wayne. (See ROUGH RIDERS series, Index.)

p, Scott R. Dunlap; d, Spencer G. Bennet; w, Jess Bowers [Adele Buffington]; ph, Harry Neumann; ed, Carl Pierson; md, Edward Kay.

Western **Cas.** (PR:A MPAA:NR)

GUN MOLL (SEE: JIGSAW, 1949)

GUN PACKER✫✫½ (1938) 51m MON bw

Jack Randall (Jack Dinton), Louise Stanley (Ruth Adams), Charles King (Chance Moore), Barlowe Borland (Prof. Angel), Glenn Strange (Sheriff), Raymond Turner (Pinky), Lloyd Ingraham (Chief Holmes), Lowell Drew (Dad Adams), Ernie Adams (Stage Driver), Forrest Taylor (Express Manager), Curley Dresden, Sherry Tansey, Rusty the Wonder Horse.

This story of an outlaw gang robbing gold-laden stagecoaches and using the booty to salt barren mine shafts so that the unwary can be swindled out of their money on worthless gold mine stock certificates is a cut above most of the independently made B westerns of its time. The lean script offers a straight, unconfusing story line, with no filler material. Hero Randall doesn't sing or simper; he gets the job done with hard riding and fighting, with no nonsense, rounding up the rustlers and winning the affection of the stunning Stanley. An unusual note in a B western of the period is a black featured player, Turner, who does a fine job in his role.

p, Robert Tansey; d, Wallace Fox; w, Robert Emmett; ph, Bert Longenecker.

Western (PR:A MPAA:NR)

GUN PLAY✫✫ (1936) 59m Beacon/FD bw (AKA: LUCKY BOOTS)

[Guinn] "Big Boy" Williams (Bill Williams), Frank Yaconelli (Frank), Marion Shilling (Madge Holt), Wally Wales [Hal Taliaferro] (George Holt), Charles French (Old John Holt), Tom London (Meeker), Roger Williams (Cal), Julian Rivero, Barney Beasley, Dick Botiller, Gordon Griffith, Si Jenks.

Shilling, along with her brother Wales, comes from out East to take over their father's ranch. But some bandidos hear of an old Mexican revolutionary's treasure supposedly buried somewhere on the ranch and begin to harass the pair. Along comes Williams, with sidekick Yaconelli at hand, to save the day. He not only saves the ranch, but wins Shilling's heart as well. It's somewhat comical material that is enhanced by Williams's performance. He was a known character actor who starred in an occasional B feature such as GUN PLAY. Yaconelli was also known for his comedy roles and occasionally upstages the star in this film. The title delivers its promise, with plenty of obligatory action sequences. Slightly better than average product. Wales later changed his name to Hal Taliaferro and became fairly well known as a character actor in features.

p, Arthur Alexander; d, Albert Herman; w, William L. Nolte; ph, William Hyer.

Western (PR:A MPAA:NR)

GUN RANGER, THE✫✫ (1937) 56m REP bw

Bob Steele (Dan Larson), Eleanor Stewart (Molly), John Merton (Kemper), Ernie Adams (Wally), Earl Dwire (Bud), Budd Buster (Carl), Frank Ball (Judge), Horace Murphy (Cook), Lew Meehan, Hal Taliaferro [Wally Wales], Horace B. Carpenter, Jack Kirk, George Morrell, Tex Palmer.

A fairly standard western plot, one later reprised in spades in more urban genres such as the DIRTY HARRY series (see Index). Lawman Steele becomes disgusted with the system when he finds that the outlaws he arrests are being freed by a lax court system. In frustration, he throws his badge aside and takes the law into his own hands. This was one of the last of the Hackel-Steele collaborations, which brought the diminutive actor to the apogee of his popularity; it featured Dwire, Adams, and Stewart, who appeared in so many of his successes, and was directed by Steele's father, Bradbury (one of only two of the Hackel productions released by Republic which Bradbury directed). With the gradual ascendance of the singing cowboy—Republic had signed the actor who was to be its greatest asset, Gene Autry—Steele's career declined following this series, although he attempted to adapt by doing a bit of painfully unmelodic crooning.

p, A.W. Hackel; d, R.N. Bradbury; w, George Plympton (based on a story by Homer Gordon); ph, Bert Longenecker; ed, Roy Claire.

Western (PR:A MPAA:NR)

GUN RIDERS, THE✫✫ (1969) 88m Independent International Pictures c (AKA: FIVE BLOODY GRAVES; LONELY MAN; FIVE BLOODY DAYS TO TOMBSTONE)

Robert Dix (Ben Thompson), Scott Brady (Jim Wade), Jim Davis (Clay Bates), John Carradine (Boone Hawkins), Paula Raymond (Kansas Kelly), John Cardos (Joe Lightfoot/Satago), Tara Ashton (Althea Richards), Kent Osborne (Dave Miller), Vicki Volante (Nora Miller), Denver Dixon (Rawhide), Ray Young (Horace Wiggins), Julie Edwards (Lavinia Wade), Fred Meyers (Driver), Maria Polo (Little Fawn), Gene Raymond (The Voice of Death).

Dix is a deadly man (hence his nickname, "Messenger of Death") who is after Brady and Young for supplying guns to Indian Chief Cardos. Carradine's a lecherous preacher who likes watching prostitutes bathe when he's not busy preaching salvation. Some extreme violence including rape and a man being left on an anthill to die. Is it any wonder this film is narrated by "The Voice of Death?" Cheaply made but somewhat imaginative.

p&d, Al Adamson; w, Robert Dix; ph, Vilmos [William] Zsigmon (Techniscope, Technicolor); ed, William Faris, Peter Perry; set d, Robert Dietz.

Western (PR:O MPAA:GP)

GUN RUNNER✫½ (1949) 56m MON bw

Jimmy Wakely (Jimmy), Dub "Cannonball" Taylor (Cannonball), Noel Neill (Jessica), Mae Clarke (Kate), Kenne Duncan (Nebraska), Marshall Reed (Riley), Carol Henry (Stacey), Bud Osborne (Burt), Steve Clark (Sheriff Harris), Ted Adams

(Danny), Pascale Perry (Allen), Eddie Majors (Joe), Clem Fuller (Tex), Bob Woodward (Sam), Tex Atchinson, Ray Jones, Ray Whitley.

A gang of gun runners is smuggling weapons to some local Indians. It's up to country-and-western singer Wakely to stop them. His old pal Duncan is in cahoots with the smugglers, but when he discovers his long-lost daughter Neill, he gives up the wanton life. Once more, he reunites with Wakely, and together they stop the smugglers. This film was made specifically for the Saturday matinee kiddy crowd and the film aesthetics display this openly. Plot twists are unexplained and poorly motivated and cheap gags such as exploding cigars are employed. The dialog is pretty simplistic, giving the actors little room to do much of anything. Neill would later become a kiddie idol as Lois Lane on the television series SUPERMAN. The gorgeous 39-year-old Clarke—her face received James Cagney's breakfast grapefruit in THE PUBLIC ENEMY (1931)—did make a marvelous menace as the murderous leader of the bad bunch.

p, Louis Gray; d, Lambert Hillyer; w, J. Benton Cheney; ph, Harry Neumann; m, Edward Kay; ed, John Fuller.

Western (PR:A MPAA:NR)

GUN RUNNER, THE (SEE: SANTIAGO, 1956)

GUN RUNNER** (1969) 76m Jabe Films/Grads c
(AKA: THE GUNRUNNERS)

Trent Dolan (Terry Decker), Victoria Carbe (Margarete), John Rico (Vargas), Beach Dickerson (Max Keeler), Carl Steppling, Gilda Hayworth, R.C. Adams, Geretta Taylor, Jerry Petty, Dianne Durrell, Mary Bauer, Julia Blackburn, Mary Jo Bisby, Barbara Peeters, Henry von Seyfried, Melinda Machard, Connie Nelson, Mike Stringer, Sally Blair.

Dickerson is a government agent who is pressured by bureau chiefs to stop a gun running outfit from South America that is giving weapons to a sect of fanatical Texans. He meets drifter Dolan and, using his help, infiltrates the underworld where the gang hangs out. Dolan, dressed as a sailor, meets Carbe, a hooker whose boy friend is one of the men provided guns by Rico. The boy friend introduces Dolan to Rico and the latter gives him a job as a gun inspector. Dolan takes it, but later discovers his government contact stabbed and near death beneath a pier. He is warned that Rico is on to the sting. Dolan runs to Carbe, and the two make love. Later, he helps run the guns ashore, then kills Rico and his gang. He blows up the gun-bearing ship and returns, exhausted, to the beach. There he discovers Carbe and her boy friend murdered. Dickerson is pleased with Dolan's job and offers him more government work. Sick of it all, Dolan declines and wanders off once more. Filmed by Nestor Almendros before he became one of Hollywood's leading cinematographers, though here he used the pseudonym John Nestor.

p, James Tanenbaum; d&w, Richard Compton; ph, John Nestor [Nestor Almendros], Harold Archambault (Eastmancolor); m, Rene DeKnight; ed, Jack Starrett; md, DeKnight; art d, Joel Sussman; m/l, Sallie Blair.

Crime/Action (PR:O MPAA:NR)

GUN RUNNERS, THE**½ (1958) 83m Seven Arts/UA bw (AKA: GUNRUNNERS)

Audie Murphy (Sam Martin), Eddie Albert (Hanagan), Patricia Owens (Lucy Martin), Everett Sloane (Harvey), Gita Hall (Eva), Richard Jaeckel (Buzurki), Paul Birch (Sy Phillips), Jack Elam (Arnold), John Harding (Peterson), Peggy Maley (Blonde), Carlos Romero (Carlos), Edward Colmans (Juan), Steven Peck (Pepito), Lita Leon (Pepita), Ted Jacques (Commander Walsh), John Qualen (Pop), Freddie Roberto (Berenguer).

Audie Murphy stars in this 3rd version of Hemingway's To Have And Have Not (1944 with Bogart and Bacall, and 1950 as THE BREAKING POINT) as a ship's captain in Key West, Florida. When it becomes increasingly difficult to make the payments on his cabin cruiser, Murphy turns to a gunrunning plot organized by Albert which arms Cuban rebels. Torn between his moral opposition to Albert and his desire to pay off his boat, Murphy leans on Sloane, his hard-drinking and likable sidekick, for support. Murphy redeems himself by killing Albert and preventing any further aid to the rebels. An enjoyable adventure picture which considering the talents involved—Siegel, Murphy, Mohr, and Hemingway—should have been even better.

p, Clarence Green; d, Don Siegel; w, Daniel Mainwaring, Paul Monash (based on the novel To Have And Have Not by Ernest Hemingway); ph, Hal Mohr; m, Leith Stevens; ed, Charles Schaeffer; art d, Howard Richmond; m/l, Joe Lubin.

Adventure (PR:A MPAA:NR)

GUN SMOKE*½ (1931) 56m PAR bw

Richard Arlen (Brad Farley), Mary Brian (Sue Vancey), William "Stage" Boyd (Kedge Darvis), Eugene Pallette (Stub Wallack), Charles Winninger (Tack Gillup), Louise Fazenda (Hampsey Dell), Brooks Benedict (Spot Skee), William Arnold (Mugs Maransa), J. Carrol Nash (Mink Gordon), Stanley Mack (Jassy Quinn), Guy Oliver (Posey Meed), James Durkin (J.K. Horton), William V. Mong (Strike Jackson), Dawn O'Day (Horton's Daughter), Willie Fung (Chinese Cook), Imboden Parrish.

Boyd is a gangster on the lam. He and his mob head West to try out their big-city crime styles on the open prairie, only to be foiled by the virtuous cowboy-locals. There is plenty of gunplay but most of it is unimaginatively handled. Despite fine performances by Boyd and Fung GUN SMOKE is a little too preachy and naive in its approach to really catch on.

d, Edward Sloman; w, Grover Jones, William McNutt; ph, Archie Stout.

Western/Crime (PR:A MPAA:NR)

GUN SMOKE* (1936) 57m Willis Kent bw

Buck Coburn (Steve Branning), Marion Shilling (Jean Culverson), Bud Osborne (Haws McGee), Benny Corbett (Shorty), Henry Hall (George Culverson), Roger

Williams (Sam Parsons), Dick Botiller (Felipe), Nelson McDowell (Long Distance Jones), Philo McCullough (Abner Sneed), Lloyd Ingraham (Eli Parker), Tracy Layne (Pecos), Lafe McKee (Sheriff).

Carre and Montana may have concocted the storyline for GUN SMOKE as they filmed it (the script is uncredited), plugging in all the standard western film conventions as they went. Like so many other handsome cowboy heroes Coburn rides to the rescue of an outlaw-bullied rancher and his pretty daughter. En route no innovative additions to the genre are made.

p, Montie Montana; d, Bartlett Carre; ph, Harvey Gould; ed, Roy Claire.

Western (PR:A MPAA:NR)

GUN SMUGGLERS** (1948) 61m RKO bw

Tim Holt (Tim Holt), Richard Martin (Chito), Martha Heyer (Judy), Gary Gray (Danny), Paul Hurst (Hasty), Douglas Fowley (Steve), Robert Warwick (Col. Davis), Don Haggerty (Sheriff Shurlsock), Frank Sully (Clancy), Robert Bray (Dodge), Steve Savage.

Gray is a boy who worships his older brother, an outlaw leader who uses the lad as a decoy during the holdup of an Army wagon train. The outlaws intend to smuggle the stolen guns to an unnamed foreign country, but along comes Holt and funny sidekick Martin to stop the nefarious schemes and save Gray from a life of crime. An okay B western with above-average camera work.

p, Herman Schlom; d, Frank McDonald; w, Norman Houston; ph, J. Roy Hunt; ed, Les Millibrook; art d, Feild Gray.

Western **Cas.** (PR:A MPAA:NR)

GUN STREET* (1962) 67m Harvard/UA bw

James Brown (Sheriff Morton), Jean Willes (Joan Brady), John Clarke (Sam Freed), Med Flory (Willie Driscoll), John Pickard (Dr. Knudson), Peggy Stewart (Mrs. Knudson), Sandra Stone (Pat Bogan), Warren Kemmerling (Frank Bogan), Nesdon Booth (Mayor Phillips), Herb Armstrong (Jeff Baxley), Renny McEvoy (Operator).

Kemmerling is an escaped convict bent on paying back the people responsible for his imprisonment; Brown is the sheriff who must stop him. To complicate matters, they are old friends. Brown chases Kemmerling but when he finally catches up with him, the escapee dies of wounds suffered during his breakout. GUN STREET never delivers on its promise. It builds suspensefully but ultimately lets itself down. The television influence of the film is clearly evident with every major character paralleling the major characters from the program "Gunsmoke." Worst of all is the direction, flat and lifeless.

p, Robert E. Kent; d, Edward L. Cahn; w, Sam C. Freedle; ph, Gilbert Warrenton; m, Richard LaSalle; ed, Kenneth Crane; set d, Harry Reif; cos, Einar Bourman, Sabine Manela; spec eff, Barney Wolff.

Western (PR:C MPAA:NR)

GUN TALK** (1948) 57m MON bw

Johnny Mack Brown (Johnny McVey), Raymond Hutton (Lucky Danvers), Christine McIntyre (Daisy), Douglas Evans (Rod Jackson), Geneva Gray (June), Wheaton Chambers (Herkimer Stone), Frank LaRue (Simpson), Ted Adams (Tim), Carl Mathews (Pepper), Zon Murray (Nolan), Cactus Mack (Marshall Wetherby), Carol Henry (Burke), Bill Hale (Joe), Boyd Stockman (Diggs), Roy Butler (Bartender), Bob McElroy (Pete).

The film starts off quickly and moves along at a brisk pace, running just under an hour. Brown foils a stagecoach robbery, winning the loyalty of mine owner Hatton and the admiration of Gray, who is heading West to visit her sister (McIntyre). Bad guy Chambers and sidekick Evans try to wrest the mine away from Hatton. The acting is typical B western dramatics, though the script does manage to rise above a few of the standard cliches.

p, Barney Sarecky; d, Lambert Hillyer; w, J. Benton Cheney; ph, Harry Neumann; ed, Fred Maguire; md, Edward Kay.

Western (PR:A MPAA:NR)

GUN THAT WON THE WEST, THE** (1955) 69m COL c

Dennis Morgan (Jim Bridger), Paula Raymond (Maxine Gaines), Richard Denning (Jack Gaines), Chris O'Brien (Sgt. Timothy Carnahan), Robert Bice (Chief Red Cloud), Michael Morgan (Afraid of Horses), Roy Gordon (Col. Carrington), Howard Wright (General Pope), Dick Cutting (Edwin M. Stanton), Howard Negley (General Carveth), Kenneth MacDonald (Col. E.M. Still).

A series of forts is being constructed to protect the crews building the railroad in the West, and Morgan and Denning are two cavalry scouts sent to make sure everything goes smoothly in the "hostile" territory. Springfield rifles, which could be called the title character, are brought in to make sure nothing goes awry. There's a good deal of stock Indian footage tacked into the film but no one bothered to see that it matched the shooting stock. Consequently there are a lot of mismatched tints between shots and unmatching grains. Even worse is the racism contained in the film. Unless it's a friendly Indian like Bice, the old Hollywood code "the only good Indian is a dead Indian" is the rule here. The title itself clearly indicates the viewpoint within the film.

p, Sam Katzman; d, William Castle; w, James B. Gordon; ph, Henry Freulich (Technicolor); ed, Al Clark; md, Ross DiMaggio; art d, Paul Palmentola.

Western (PR:C MPAA:NR)

GUN THE MAN DOWN*** (1957) 74m UA bw
(AKA: ARIZONA MISSION)

James Arness (Rem Anderson), Angie Dickinson (Janice), Robert Wilke (Matt Rankin), Emile Meyer (Sheriff Morton), Don Megowan (Ralph Farley), Michael Emmet (Billy Deal), Harry Carey, Jr. (Deputy Lee), Frank Fenton.

Arness, along with partners Wilke and Megowan, stage a robbery but when he's wounded his buddies run out on him, as does girl friend Dickinson. After a year in the pen, he finds his two ex-comrades living in a small border town, but rather than gun down the pair, he plays a waiting game and tries to trap them so they too can have a taste of prison life. They hire Emmet to get rid of Arness and Dickinson tries to warn her former lover. But Wilke discovers her plan and kills her. In the climactic gun battle Arness gets his revenge by killing Emmet. This is a good little western with an intelligent script that never stoops to cliche or easy-outs. Instead characters are well-drawn and the acting is impressive. GUN THE MAN DOWN was the directoral debut of McLaglen, the son of Victor McLaglen.

p, Robert E. Morrison; d, Andrew V. McLaglen; w, Burt Kennedy (based on a story by Sam C. Freedle); ph, William Clothier; m, Henry Vars; ed, Eddie Sutherland; art d, Al Ybarra; cos, Patrick W. Cummings, Neva Rames.

Western **(PR:C MPAA:NR)**

GUN TOWN*½ (1946) 55m UNIV bw

Kirby Grant *(Kip)*, Fuzzy Knight *(Ivory)*, Lyle Talbot *(Lucky Dorgan)*, Claire Carlton *(Belle Townley)*, Louise Currie *("Buckskin" Jane Sawyer)*, Gene Carrick *(Davey Sawyer)*, Dan White *(Joe)*, Ray Bennett *(Nevada)*, Earle Hodgins *(Sheriff)*, Bill Sondholm, George Morrell *(Townsmen)*, Tex Cooper, Merrill McCormack.

Talbot is an outlaw leader who wants to get his hands on Currie's stagecoach line. Carleton is his girl friend, a saloonkeeper and crooner, who helps her boy friend when she's not singing. All appears lost until good guy Grant saves the day and, of course, gets the girl. It's a standard western film that suffers from too much talk and not enough action. The use of stock footage doesn't help much. Talbot is above the material as the villain but still can't help the picture much. Everything else is the same old style.

p&d, Wallace W. Fox; w, William Lively; ph, Maury Gertsman; ed, Ray Snyder; md, Mark Levant; art d, John B. Goodman, Abraham Grossman; m/l, Everett Carter, Milton Rosen.

Western **(PR:A MPAA:NR)**

GUNFIGHT, A*** (1971) 89m Harvest-Thoroughbred-Joel/PAR c

Kirk Douglas *(Will Tenneray)*, Johnny Cash *(Abe Cross)*, Jane Alexander *(Nora Tenneray)*, Raf Vallone *(Francisco Alvarez)*, Karen Black *(Jenny Simms)*, Eric Douglas *(Bud Tenneray)*, Phillip L. Mead *(Kyle)*, John Wallwork *(Toby)*, Dana Elcar *(Marv Green)*, Robert J. Wilke *(Marshal Cater)*, George Le Bow *(Dekker)*, James Cavasos *(Newt Hale)*, Keith Carradine *(Cowboy)*, Paul Lambert *(Ed Fleury)*, Neil Davis *(Canberry)*, David Burleson *(1st Poker Player)*, Dick O'Shea *(2nd Poker Player)*, Douglas Doran *(Teller)*, John Gill *(Foreman)*, Timothy Tuinstra *(Joey)*, R.C. Bishop *(MacIntyre)*, Donna and Paula Dillenschneider *(Saloon Hostesses)*.

A moody, existential western that also serves as an allegory on the fickle nature of fame. Cash is a down-on-his-luck gunfighter stranded in a small town when his snake-bitten horse dies. There he meets Douglas, another gunslinger who earns his wages as a saloon celebrity. They strike up a friendship only to discover that the townspeople are placing bets on who would win a gunfight between the two. Since both need the money, they arrange a showdown with the paid admission to go to the winner. The town is brought to a fevered pitch when Douglas guns down a young cowboy punk out to make a reputation for himself. Finally the big showdown takes place. But it is not Douglas who wins. Cash pulls a fast draw and kills the local favorite. The film ends as Cash prepares to ride off once more. Before he leaves his eyes meet those of Douglas' widow Alexander. We see a dream sequence wherein she imagines what it would be like had the shootout ended with Douglas the winner. Aside from this totally unnecessary ending, A GUNFIGHT is a fine film. The film has the unique distinction of being financed by the Jicarillia Apache tribe of New Mexico. The Apaches had a good deal of money gained from gas, oil and uranium deposits on their reservation and were looking for a good investment. The deal was made in a single day to the tune of $2 million. When told that the film had nothing to do with Indians, the Apaches responded that they were only interested in the investment, not the subject matter.

p, A. Ronald Lubin, Harold Jack Bloom; d, Lamont Johnson; w, Bloom; ph, David M. Walsh (Technicolor); m, Laurence Rosenthal; ed, Bill Mosher; prod d, Tambi Larsen; set d, Darrell Silvera; cos, Mickey Sherard; makeup, Otis Malcolm, Jack Young; m/l, title song, Johnny Cash (sung by Cash).

Western **(PR:O MPAA:GP)**

GUNFIGHT AT ABILENE (SEE: GUNFIGHT IN ABILENE, 1967)

GUNFIGHT AT COMANCHE CREEK** (1964) 90m AA c

Audie Murphy *(Bob Gifford)*, Ben Cooper *(Carter)*, Colleen Miller *(Abbie)*, DeForest Kelley *(Troop)*, Jan Merlin *(Nielson)*, John Hubbard *(Marshal Shearer)*, Damian O'Flynn *(Winton)*, Susan Seaforth *(Janie)*, Adam Williams, Mort Mills, John Milford, Michael T. Mikler, Tom Browne Henry, William Wellman, Jr., Laurie Graham, Tim Graham, Eddie Quillan.

A routine film built around Murphy's talents. It's 1875 and Murphy is a member of the National Detective Agency. He is looking for a group of outlaws who spring convicts from prison, then help the escapees commit more crimes. This raises the price on the cons' heads and the outlaws kill their unwitting victims for the fat rewards. Murphy infiltrates the gang and kills the leader in the end—a standard Murphy tour-de-force. This is a re-make of the 1957 film LAST OF THE BADMEN.

p, Ben Schwalb; d, Frank McDonald; w, Edward Bernds; ph, Joseph F. Biroc (Panavision, DeLuxeColor); m, Marlin Skiles; ed, William Austin; art d, Edward Jewell; set d, Clarence Steensen; cos, Edward Armand; makeup, Wally Westmore.

Western **(PR:A MPAA:NR)**

GUNFIGHT AT DODGE CITY, THE½** (1959) 80m Mirisch/UA c

Joel McCrea *(Bat Masterson)*, Julie Adams *(Pauline)*, John McIntire *(Doc)*, Nancy Gates *(Lily)*, Richard Anderson *(Dave)*, Jim Westerfield *(Rev. Howard)*, Walter Coy *(Ben)*, Don Haggerty *(Regan)*, Wright King *(Billy)*, Harry Lauter *(Ed)*, Myron Healy *(Forbes)*, Mauritz Hugo *(Purley)*, Henry Kulkey *(Bartender)*.

McCrea is Bat Masterson, the famed sheriff of Dodge City, as unlucky with the law as he is with love. Adams is his initial love interest but when she spurns him he contents himself with Gates. McCrea's old outlaw gang shows up determined to bring their comrade back to the fold. They fail, as do the crooked local politicians who take on their sheriff. There are some interesting moments in the film, without many of the cliches usually found in this fare. This film was to be McCrea's last until Sam Peckinpah talked him into one more hurrah for RIDE THE HIGH COUNTRY in 1962.

p, Walter M. Mirisch; d, Joseph M. Newman; w, Daniel B Ullman, Martin M. Goldsmith (based on a story by Ullman); ph, Carl Guthrie (CinemaScope, Deluxe-Color); m, Hans J. Salter ed, Richard V. Heermance; art d, Serge Krizman.

Western **(PR:A MPAA:NR)**

GUNFIGHT AT RED SANDS (SEE: GRINGO, 1963)

GUNFIGHT AT THE O.K. CORRAL***** (1957) 122m PAR c

Burt Lancaster *(Wyatt Earp)*, Kirk Douglas *(John H. "Doc" Holliday)*, Rhonda Fleming *(Laura Denbow)*, Jo Van Fleet *(Kate Fisher)*, John Ireland *(Johnny Ringo)*, Lyle Bettger *(Ike Clanton)*, Frank Faylen *(Cotton Wilson)*, Earl Holliman *(Charles Bassett)*, Ted De Corsia *(Abel Head "Shanghai Pierce")*, Dennis Hopper *(Billy Clanton)*, Whit Bissell *(John P. Clum)*, George Mathews *(John Shanssey)*, John Hudson *(Virgil Earp)*, DeForrest Kelley *(Morgan Earp)*, Martin Milner *(James Earp)*, Kenneth Tobey *(Bat Masterson)*, Lee Van Cleef *(Ed Bailey)*, Joan Camden *(Betty Earp)*, Olive Carey *(Mrs. Clanton)*, Brian Hutton *(Rick)*, Nelson Leigh *(Mayor Kelley)*, Jack Elam *(Tom McLowery)*, Don Castle *(Drunken Cowboy)*, Mickey Simpson *(Frank McLowery)*, Charles Herbert *(Tommy Earp)*, Tony Merrill *(Barber)*, Lee Roberts *(Finn Clanton)*, Frank Carter *(Hotel Clerk)*, Edward Ingram *(Deputy)*, Bing Russell *(Bartender)*, Henry Wills *(Alby)*, Dorothy Abbott *(Girl)*, William S. Meigs *(Wayne)*, John Benson *(Rig Driver)*, Richard J. Reeves *(Foreman)*, John Maxwell *(Merchant)*, Ethan Laidlaw, Frank Hagney, *(Bartenders)*, Henry B. Mendoza *(Cockeyed Frank Loving)*, Roger Creed *(Deputy/Killer/Townsman)*, Tony Joachim *(Old Man)*, Joe Forte, James Davies, Max Power, Courtland Shepard *(Card Players)*, Gregg Martell, Dennis Moore, Len Hendry *(Cowboys)*, Trude Wyler *(Social Hall Guest)*, Morgan Lane, Paul Gary *(Killers)*, Bill Williams *(Stuntman)*, Robert C. Swan *(Shaugnessy Man)*, William N. Bailey.

A landmark western, superbly produced on all levels, this production, more than any other of its era, lifted the concept of the horse opera into major film status. And this story, of course, was the great stuff of legend, the wonderful romance of lore. Strong, resolute, and stoic, Lancaster is the marvelous marshal Wyatt Earp, and his closest friend is Douglas, the deadly gunfighter "Doc" Holliday. The two are shown meeting as Douglas is about to be murdered. Lancaster, looking for outlaws Bettger and Ireland, learns that Van Cleef is waiting for Douglas in Mathews' saloon, planning to kill Douglas as he enters, using a derringer hidden in his boot. Trying to exchange information, Lancaster goes to Douglas and asks him if he knows the whereabouts of Ireland and Bettger, telling him about Van Cleef's hidden derringer, but Douglas tells him nothing about the wanted cattle rustlers. Douglas later kills Van Cleef in the saloon with a knife before he can draw the hidden gun but he is arrested and locked in his room by Faylen, a crooked sheriff, and left to the mercy of a fast-gathering lynch mob. Douglas' prostitute girl friend Van Fleet begs Lancaster to save him. Lancaster knocks out a guard and frees Douglas while Van Fleet starts a fire as a diversion. "Since when did you take to rescuing gamblers in distress?" sneers Douglas. Lancaster tells him that lynch mobs are his business. The indebted gambler flees to Fort Griffith, Texas, with Van Fleet and Lancaster returns to Dodge City, Kansas, where he is town marshal. No sooner is Lancaster sitting in front of his office with Bat Masterson (Tobey) than he sees Fleming, a beautiful female gambler, arrive in town, and learns that Douglas and Van Fleet have checked into the local hotel. Lancaster goes to Douglas who is having a shave in a barbershop and tells him he can stay in town but "no knives, no guns, and no killings." Douglas agrees. Fleming is another matter. Lancaster wants Fleming out of town, telling her she can't gamble in Dodge City—"Women at the tables means trouble." A drunken cowboy (Castle) tries to shoot Earp to protect Fleming's honor but Lancaster backs him down, then arrests Fleming and jails her for disturbing the peace, much to the chagrin of town officials and even his assistant, Holliman. Lancaster later tells Fleming that he'll release her if she does her "gambling south of the dead line." She obstinately refuses and remains behind bars in the jail. When Douglas hears about the jailing of pretty Fleming he bets Mayor "Dog" Kelley (Leigh) $1,000 than he can get Fleming out. Douglas meets with Lancaster at the jail and tells him that the fierce cattle baron, Abel Head "Shanghai Pierce" (De Corsia) is coming to town with a huge herd and an army of cowboys, that he will have Ireland with him and that he has put a price of $1,000 on Lancaster's head—"dead." Lancaster, in exchange for this information, and also at Holliman's request, releases Fleming who returns to the gambling tables with Douglas. Lancaster and Fleming are slowly drawn together and, on their romantic rides through the country, they fall in love. De Corsia and his cowboys show up, start a brawl in a social hall, and Lancaster, with Douglas' help, backs them down. Douglas has a real hate for Ireland who has dallied with his friend Van Fleet; when Ireland goes for his gun, Douglas shoots it out of his hand. By this time Lancaster and Douglas have become close friends; earlier, Lancaster, looking for a deputy when shorthanded, deputizes Douglas who helps him track down three bank robbers who try to ambush them as they lay sleeping on the prairie, but are instead killed by the alert Lancaster and Douglas. Later Douglas learns that Van Fleet has taken up with Ireland and he goes to fetch her, then spurns her when he realizes she's involved with the gunman. Taunting Douglas, Ireland cannot make him break his word to friend Lancaster that he will cause no gunplay. Ireland humiliates Douglas in front of Van Fleet by throwing a drink in his face, but still Douglas will not reach for the gun Ireland has thrown on the table. He clenches his fists, then turns and leaves while Van Fleet lets out a moan of remorse. Meanwhile, Fleming wants Lancaster to quit peacemaking and settle down but he receives word from his brothers, Hudson and Kelley, lawmen in Tombstone, Arizona. They are facing a takeover by the Clanton-McLowery outlaw clan headed by Bettger and ask him to come to their aid. "They're my brothers," he tells Fleming. She explodes and leaves him with the words: "Go—clean up Tombstone. There's a hundred more Tombstones on the frontier waiting for the great Wyatt Earp. Go on —clean them all up!" He tells her he loves her but he rides off to the southwest and destiny, a lone horseman following and overtaking him on the prairie—Douglas. He tells Lancaster that "the decks gone cold" and they go to Tombstone together. In Tombstone Lancaster joins his family, conferring with brothers Kelley, Hudson and the youngest Earp brother, Milner. Kelley complains that Douglas "is the worst killer on the frontier . . . it just don't look good, you coming here with him." Lancaster explains that Douglas saved his life in Dodge City and, as long as Douglas stays out of trouble he should be allowed to stay. They then map out plans to run the Clantons out of the territory. Faylen, the crooked sheriff of Fort Griffith, now working for Bettger, visits Lancaster and offers him $20,000 "against a 6-foot hole in boot hill" if he'll leave the Clantons alone to run their rustled cattle. Lancaster refuses, telling Faylen that he might run for county sheriff, implying that he'll take care of him later. "That don't scare me at all," smirks Faylen. "I got mine. I got a ranch now and $25,000 in the bank and it don't bother my sleep, not one bit." Lancaster states: "It would mine, though." Faylen indicts him for being sanctimonious: "Why don't you get off that pulpit, Wyatt? Ellsworth, Wichita, Dodge City and what have they got you but a life full of misery and a woman that walked out on you . . . and the friendship of a killer." Faylen later reports to his boss Bettger: "He aims to pull the town out from under you, Ike." Bettger forces Lancaster's hand, goes to town with his cowboys, and is faced down by Lancaster, his brothers, and the citizens' committee headed by Bissell. The outlaws, Ireland included, are sent packing, Lancaster telling Bettger that "there's no place in this town for you, Ike." Van Fleet next arrives and once more takes up with Ireland, irking Douglas; both Van Fleet and Ireland shame Douglas in a saloon but the feared gunfighter still won't fight. "It's the way you made your reputation, isn't it?" jeers Ireland to Douglas, "against a bunch of drunks?" Douglas can take it no more and tells the gunman to meet him in the street in five minutes. He goes to his room and gets his gun but Hudson stops him, reminding him that "a killer like you around is the worst thing that can happen" to Lancaster. Douglas, out of the deep friendship he's developed for Lancaster, backs down, swallows his pride, and doesn't meet Ireland. Lancaster later comes to Douglas' room, finds him drinking heavily, and tells him that he hears he is leaving town. "You've got nothing to do with my leaving," Douglas tells him. Lancaster wishes him good luck and adds: "Too bad we won't be in on the finish together." The next day Lancaster delivers a drunken Billy Clanton (Hopper), the youngest of the outlaw clan, to the Clanton ranch. He warns him that "I never saw a gunslinger so tough he lived to celebrate his 35th birthday . . . I learned one rule about gunslingers—there's always a man faster on the draw than you are. The more you use a gun, the sooner you're gonna run into that man. You think I don't know what's inside of you? I had a couple of big brothers. They fought in the Civil War and I was too young to go. I tried to live up to them the same way you're trying to live up to Ike and Finn . . . All gunfighters are lonely. They live in fear. They die without a dime, a woman, or a friend." His words affect Hopper, who promises his mother, Carey: "I won't do it no more, Ma." Then Bettger arrives and is about to shoot Lancaster who is there alone, but he withholds his fire when learning that Lancaster has been appointed U.S. marshal for the whole territory. Bettger once again tries to bribe him but Lancaster says before riding off: "The only thing I want is for you to run that stolen herd back to Mexico!" The Clanton-McLowery clan meets and Bettger decides that they must ambush Lancaster as he makes his nightly rounds of the town. Van Fleet is present with Ireland and she merely shrugs at the suggestion, saying: "It don't make no difference to me." That night Milner takes the place of his exhausted brother, and is shot and killed in his stead. Now, it's a point of the Earp family honor to seek retribution for Milner's death. Douglas tries to dissuade Lancaster from meeting the outlaws but the lawman looks down into the street to Milner's body and says: "To hell with logic! That's my brother lying there!" Next Douglas finds Van Fleet in her hotel room and gets her to admit that the clan has planned to kill the Earps. He is about to attack her when he is overcome with a coughing attack as he suffers from fatal tuberculosis. He collapses and is bedridden. Lancaster meets with his brothers and, after hearing from Hopper that he and his brothers will meet the Earps in a final showdown the next day at the O.K. Corral, goes to get Douglas' help. Lancaster finds the gunfighter comatose. He shakes him, saying: "I need you, Doc, don't let me down." From the shadows, Van Fleet says: "Leave him alone—can't you see he's dying?" Lancaster is alone with his thoughts at dawn, his gunbelt strapped on. He pours a drink and prepares to meet his brothers and the outlaws waiting down the street at the livery stable. At dawn Douglas opens his eyes, crawls from his bed, and throws some water on his face. Van Fleet begs him not to join Lancaster and his brothers. "You can't—you can't even stand up. You'll die for sure if you go out there!" He answers: "If I'm gonna die, at least let me die with the only friend I ever had." The outlaws—six of them—ride into Tombstone and take positions inside the O.K. Corral. Douglas joins Lancaster in his room and the two walk to meet Hudson and Kelley in the street. Solemnly the lawmen walk toward the corral. Faylen, who is with the six outlaws, begs to get out of the upcoming battle. "Ike," he tells Bettger, "I can't take this kind of gunplay anymore." Bettger orders him to stand with them but he later tries to flee and Bettger kills him. Lancaster, Hudson, Kelley, and Douglas march to the corral and are met with shotgun fire. Kelley and Hudson are wounded but return fire as Douglas and Lancaster charge the outlaws. Lancaster shoots out a lantern hanging on a wagon and sets it on fire and Simpson along with it; the outlaw falls screaming from the wagon and his brother, Elam, goes berserk, charging Lancaster who shoots him down. When Lancaster goes to the aid of one of his brothers, Bettger rushes forward to kill him but Lancaster grabs a shotgun and blows off the head of the outlaw leader. Hopper wounds Douglas and is, in turn, wounded twice by Lancaster; he flees while Lancaster chases him into the town. Douglas shoots it out with Ireland, gunning the outlaw down. Lancaster follows Hopper into a photography store where the youthful outlaw has taken refuge. Though wounded, the boy tries to cock his gun to get off one more shot and kill Lancaster, even though the lawman begs: "Don't make me do it." He doesn't have to; just as Hopper is about to gun down Lancaster, Douglas passes the store, sees the threat, and fires a fatal bullet

into Hopper. With the boy dead at his feet, Lancaster drops his gun, then takes the badge from his vest and drops it to the floor. He's through with peacemaking. Lancaster later says goodbye to Douglas in a saloon after telling him to get to a sanitorium for his health, adding: "I just want you to know that I could never have made it without you." Douglas smiles and walks to a poker table, ready to play out his hand while Lancaster rides from Tombstone, apparently going to join Fleming. As he rides from the now legendary town, he looks back at Boot Hill where the bodies of those he has faced now lie, waiting for fame. This truly is a classic western, one that revitalized the genre so completely that its big budget and tremendous box office success overshadowed the continued making of B-westerns which all but vanished in the 1960s. Sturges' masterful direction is careful yet exciting as he takes Lancaster and Douglas through their adventures, all based on actual facts. Those facts were well researched and poignantly scripted by Uris, although some details are awry. The fight at the O.K. Corral on October 26, 1881, the most famous gun battle of the Old West, took place at noon and lasted from two to three minutes with about 30 to 50 shots being fired between the Earp brothers and Holliday and the outlaws, who numbered five— the McLowery brothers, Ike and Billie Clanton, and Billy Clairborne. Tom and Frank McLowery were killed, along with Billie Clanton, Ike and Clairborne fleeing. The battle on screen takes about six minutes, but is fairly accurate as to events. This most famous of all western gun battles was filmed many times before and after GUNFIGHT AT THE O.K. CORRAL, first in FRONTIER MARSHAL (1939), then in John Ford's magnificent MY DARLING CLEMENTINE (1946), again in Sturges' impressive sequel to this film, HOUR OF THE GUN (1967), and in the introspective DOC (1971). But in capturing this one legendary event, none matched the Sturges film which perceptively explored the strange friendship between lawman and gunfighter much the same way such masculine relationships were examined in WHAT PRICE GLORY? (1952), BOOMTOWN (1940), and even in the oddball MIDNIGHT COWBOY (1969). The film certainly nods in the direction of HIGH NOON, from the appearance of the three killers riding over the horizon at the beginning to Lancaster's discarding his badge as did Cooper in HIGH NOON at the solemn finish. Also, Frankie Laine, who had sung the theme song throughout HIGH NOON, does the same here, warbling a plaintive and haunting melody composed by Tiomkin and Washington. The film was beautifully photographed by Lang and made on location in and about Tucson, Phoenix, and Tombstone. It gleaned almost $5 million in its initial U.S. and Canadian release.

p, Hal B. Wallis; d, John Sturges; w, Leon Uris (based on magazine article "The Killer" by George Scullin); ph, Charles Lang, Jr. (VistaVision, Technicolor); m, Dmitri Tiomkin; ed, Warren Low; md, Tiomkin; art d, Hal Pereira, Walter Tyler; cos, Edith Head; spec eff, John P. Fulton; m/l, title song, Tiomkin, Ned Washington, sung by Frankie Laine.

Western Cas. **(PR:C MPAA:NR)**

GUNFIGHT IN ABILENE**½ (1967) 86m UNIV c

Bobby Darin (Cal Wayne), Emily Banks (Amy Martin), Leslie Nielsen (Grant Evers), Donnelly Rhodes (Joe Slade), Don Galloway (Ward Kent), Michael Sarrazin (Cord Decker), Barbara Werle (Leann), Johnny Seven (Loop), William Phipps (Frank Norton), William Mims (Ed Scovie), Robert Sorrells (Nelson), Don Dubbins (Scrague), James McCallion (Smokey Staub), Bryan O'Byrne (Frobisher), Frank McGrath (Ned Martin).

Pop star Darin (who also wrote the film score) is an ex-Confederate officer who has accidentally killed a friend. He wants to avoid all violence, but Nielsen, a cattle baron and brother of the man Darin killed, appoints him sheriff. This remake of the 1956 film SHOWDOWN AT ABILENE is okay for what it is, but it was panned in the U.S. and Hale, a veteran TV director making his feature film debut, retreated to his old medium.

p, Howard Christie; d, William Hale; w, Berne Giler, John D.F. Black (based on the novel Gun Shy by Clarence Upson Young); ph, Maury Gertsman (Techniscope, Technicolor); m, Bobby Darin; ed, Gene Palmer; art d, Alexander Golitzen, William D. DeCinces; set d, John McCarthy, John Austin; cos, Helen Colvig; makeup, Bud Westmore; m/l, "Amy," Darin (sung by Darin).

Western **(PR:C MPAA:NR)**

GUNFIGHTER, THE***** (1950) 84m FOX bw

Gregory Peck (Jimmy Ringo), Helen Westcott (Peggy Walsh), Millard Mitchell (Sheriff Mark Strett), Jean Parker (Molly), Karl Malden (Mac), Skip Homeier (Hunt Bromley), Anthony Ross (Charlie), Verna Felton (Mrs. Pennyfeather), Ellen Corby (Mrs. Devlin), Richard Jaeckel (Eddie), Alan Hale, Jr. (1st Brother), David Clarke (2nd Brother), John Pickard (3rd Brother), B. G. Norman (Jimmie), Angela Clarke (Mac's Wife), Cliff Clark (Jerry Marlowe), Jean Inness (Alice Marlowe), Eddie Ehrhart (Archie), Albert Morin (Pablo), Kenneth Tobey (Swede), Michael Branden (Johnny), Eddie Parkes (Barber), Ferris Taylor (Grocer), Hank Patterson (Jake), Mae Marsh (Mrs. O'Brien), Credda Zajac (Mrs. Cooper), Anne Whitfield (Carrie Lou), Kim Spalding (Clerk), Harry Shannon (Bartender), Houseley Stevenson (Barlow), James Millican (Pete), William Vedder (Minister), Ed Mundy (Street Loafer).

An arresting, superbly produced downbeat western, THE GUNFIGHTER, photographed in stark black and white, gave an unusual first view of the Old West—grim, dirty, and decidedly desperate. Peck is an alienated gunfighter feeling his age and looking backward more than forward. He enters a saloon one night where his notorious reputation has, as usual, preceded him. Loud-mouthed punk Jaeckel picks a fight with him, calling Peck names. Peck tries to beg off, asking anyone in the bar to talk the brash and foolish youth out of going for his gun. But Jaeckel reaches and Peck beats him, shooting and killing the aspiring gunslinger. The seasoned gunfighter is told that, even though he was justified in defending himself, the reasons for the shooting won't matter to Jaeckel's three older brothers. Peck leaves hastily and takes a room in a nearby town, this community being his destination anyway. He has come to see his small son, Norman, along with estranged wife Westcott, the local schoolteacher. First, Peck goes to the local bar where bartender-owner Malden fawns over him, proud that the "great Jimmy Ringo" has deigned to patronize his saloon. The local sheriff, Mitchell, an old friend of Peck's and, unknown to the community, once a member of his outlaw band, meets with him and promises him that he'll ask his wife for permission to bring Peck's son to see him. Meanwhile, Jaeckel's three brothers are shown relentlessly riding toward the grim, clapboard community where Peck waits to see his son. When Homeier, another young swaggering gunslinger yearning for a reputation, hears that Peck is in town, he begins to make remarks about how he thinks Peck "ain't so tough," and deriding the gunfighter's abilities. Parker, an aging saloon girl and widow of one of Peck's gang, also goes to Westcott to plead with her to see Peck. Meanwhile, since Peck is drawing crowds, Mitchell assigns deputy Ross to guard him in the saloon. The deputy spots a glinting flash from a rifle barrel in a second story room across the street from the bar and Clark, an old man, is found waiting to squeeze off a shot at Peck. When Peck questions Clark he finds that the old man's son has been murdered by a gunfighter in a town he, Peck, has never visited. Clark is locked up but Homeier continues to strut and make boasts about how he is faster on the draw than Peck. Westcott finally relents and allows her son to see his father on the proviso he never learns his true identity. Peck has a brief and poignant meeting with Norman and later makes a pact with Westcott. They agree that if he can stay out of trouble for a year, she will rejoin him and Norman will be told the truth about his father. Peck is about to leave town when the three vengeance-seeking brothers are rooted out from hiding by Mitchell where they have lain in ambush to shoot Peck. The now hopeful gunfighter mounts his horse and is immediately shot in the back by Homeier who also has been hiding, waiting to kill "the greatest gunfighter of them all," so he will wear Peck's mantle. The mortally wounded Peck, surrounded by friends, looks up at the smug Homeier and tells him to "go on being a big, tough gunny!" The implication is clear; Homeier himself will be killed by another reputation-seeking gunfighter. Mitchell grabs the smirking Homeier and drags him into a barn where he knocks him down and then kicks him in the face before running him out of town. Peck dies in the arms of his son and wife, who join him unabashedly at the last moment. It's a tough tale with little humor but one scene provides a comedic interlude. Busybody and social gadfly Felton, who has appointed herself head of a group of respectable crusaders, visits the jail while Peck is there alone, waiting for Mitchell to return. They loudly complain to him about the presence of the notorious gunfighter lounging about the saloon down the street. He agrees that the gunfighter (himself) is notorious but his reputation may have been wrongly earned. The tittering ladies then thank the "nice young man" and leave. But, for the most part, this is a grim portrait of a man whose era has fled and whose time has run out and he knows it. Peck is dazzling as the doomed and haunted gunfighter, a man desperately trying to escape his own past and identity and knowing all along that he will fail, that there is no happiness, love, or future ahead, only a bullet. Mitchell is wonderful as the strong and compassionate sheriff, and Parker is memorable as the faded saloon hall lady. Homeier is about as hateful as any badman has ever been. King's direction is a standout, carefully drawn but taut as an overwound clock, while Miller's lensing is effectively glaring and envelopes every pebble and rusty nail as it documents Peck's inexorable trail to death. The film was really a pioneer in transforming the cliched western into a psychological study and this preceded HIGH NOON by two years. The film itself almost wound up as a John Wayne vehicle; the Duke wanted badly to essay the aging gunman tired of living in the saddle and his hand upon his holster (which he would later do well in THE SHOOTIST). Columbia's Harry Cohn originally encouraged director Andre De Toth and scriptwriter William Bowers to complete the screenplay for his studio. But then De Toth got involved with making MAN IN THE SADDLE (1951) and Cohn dropped the project. Wayne was still interested and offered Bowers $10,000 for the script, but the writer declined the offer, telling Wayne that he thought the story was worth a lot more. "You said you wrote it for me," Wayne reportedly told Bowers. "Don't you have any artistic integrity?" Bowers shrugged and said: "No." Then the writer took the script to Darryl Zanuck at Fox who liked it but had his reservations; the film was offbeat, unlike any western ever filmed. Zanuck consulted with writer-producer Johnson who had always wanted to make a class western in the style of STAGECOACH (1939) or THE OX-BOW INCIDENT (1943) and he convinced Zanuck to go ahead. The studio paid Bowers a reported $70,000 for the story and Wayne ever after accused the writer of selling one of the best western stories out from under him. Johnson reworked the script and handed it to Peck in 1949. The brilliant young actor had just completed the classic war film TWELVE O'CLOCK HIGH (1949) and was so impressed with it that he took the script to director King. After reading it, King agreed to direct. King's attention to historic detail was legendary and he immediately sank into heavy research, reading books and yellowed periodicals about the old gunfighters. Historians were consulted and Peck's draw was developed—the old crossover method. The actor was given the guns worn by George O'Brien in Fox's RIDERS OF THE PURPLE SAGE (1931) and he not only practiced his draw each day, but got used to the heavy gunbelt by strapping on the guns each night and wearing them about his home before going to sleep. King insisted that every prop be authentic and great expense was lavished on genuine 1870s coins and even an 1870 slot machine. King had Peck cut his hair in the style of the old westerners, a "soup bowl" cut, round in back, and sport a long, heavy mustache. The dark mustache upset Zanuck. When viewing the finished film he said: "You can't show Peck with a mustache like that! It will ruin him! He looks just terrible! You don't take the best-looking man in the whole world and put him in a funny hat and a funny mustache." Studio president Spyros Skouras also disliked the mustache and he sided with Zanuck, both of them asking production people how much it would cost to reshoot the scenes with Peck in them, without the mustache. "What should I tell him? (Zanuck)" the chief production man asked director King, after stating the cost would be about $175,000. King, who wanted the mustache left in, asked the man to lie: "Why don't you tell him $300,000?" He did and Zanuck thought that too excessive in getting the hairs off Peck's upper lip. The mustache stayed. Yet Zanuck later complained: "I would have given $25,000 of my own money to get that mustache off Peck." He then said: "The picture's a Rembrandt but I don't know if it's box office." It wasn't, even though critics raved about the film. Mogul Skouras blamed the film's failure on Johnson for years to come, introducing the talented writer to others by saying: "Nunnally's the man who put a mustache on Gregory Peck . . . You know you cost that picture a million dollars." Much of the film harkens back to the earliest westerns. The hardscrabble buildings of the town, the roughhewn streets, and the bland clothes are reminiscent of the gritty William S. Hart westerns of the silent era and Mitchell, as the raw boned sheriff with his long, flowing mustache and blank stare, amazingly resembles George K. Barnes who aims his pistol directly at the camera and fires in the legendary THE GREAT TRAIN ROBBERY of 1903. King, who was later to brilliantly direct Peck in the dynamic western THE BRAVADOS (1958), had everything his own way on this masterpiece and it shows in every frame. The only change he made was at Zanuck's request. The studio boss watched the film's end and was so worked up at Homeier's ruthless murder of Peck that he exploded. Originally, Homeier was merely collared by Mitchell, but Zanuck wanted revenge, actually yelling at the screen: "Take that son-of-a------ out and kick the hell out of him!" He turned to King and said: "Henry, you've got to do something. You can't just let him get away with arrest." The final scene was reshot, with Mitchell "kicking the hell" out of Homeier's face.

p, Nunnally Johnson; d, Henry King; w, William Bowers, William Sellers, (uncredited) Johnson (based on a story by Bowers, Andre De Toth); ph, Arthur Miller; m, Alfred Newman; ed Barbara McLean; art d, Lyle Wheeler, Richard Irvine.

Western **(PR:C MPAA:NR)**

GUNFIGHTERS, THE*½ (1947) 87m COL c

Randolph Scott *(Brazos Kane)*, Barbara Britton *(Bess Banner)*, Dorothy Hart *(Jane Banner)*, Bruce Cabot *(Bard Macky)*, Charley Grapewin *(Inskip)*, Steven Geray *(Jose)*, Forrest Tucker *(Hen Orcutt)*, Charles Kemper *(Sheriff Klacaden)*, Grant Withers *(Deputy Bill Yount)*, John Miles *(Johnny O'Neil)*, Griff Barnett *(Banner)*.

After killing a friend in a duel, fast-gun Scott retires from the shooting business and becomes a cowhand. When a friend is killed by an unscrupulous cattle baron, Scott is forced to pick up his gun once more. To complicate matters the baron's two daughters serve as dual romantic interests: nice girl Hart, bad girl Britton. The film ends with Scott emerging victorious from a gun battle with Barnett, his hirelings, and a corrupt sheriff. THE GUNFIGHTERS is hampered by a poor editing job and a confusing script. Despite its weaknesses it was successful enough to convince Scott and producer Brown to form their own production company. Joined by director Budd Boetticher later on, they went on to produce several medium sized Westerns that met with some success in the fifties, including THE TALL T and RIDE LONESOME.

p, Harry Joe Brown; d, George Waggner; w, Alan LeMay (based on the novel *Twin Sombreros* by Zane Grey); ph, Fred H. Jackman, Jr. (Cinecolor); m, Rudy Schrager; ed, Harvey Manger; art d, George Van Marter.

Western **(PR:A MPAA:NR)**

GUNFIGHTERS OF ABILENE*½ (1960) 66m Vogue/UA

Buster Crabbe *(Kip)*, Barton MacLane *(Seth)*, Judith Ames *(Alice)*, Arthur Space *(Rigley)*, Eugenia Paul *(Raquel)*, Russell Thorson *(Wilkinson)*, Kenneth MacDonald *(Harker)*, Richard Cutting *(Hendricks)*, Richard Devon *(Ruger)*, Lee Farr *(Jud)*, Jan Arvan *(Miguel)*, Hank Patterson *(Andy Ferris)*, Reed Howes *(Durwood)*, Boyd "Red" Morgan *(Gene)*.

MacLane is an evil landowner who has lynched Crabbe's brother for siding against him in a feud with some ranchers. MacLane has framed the brother for robbery with the lynching as a result. To complicate matters, Ames is MacLane's daughter and the fiancee of the dead man. Along comes Crabbe to avenge his brother's death, killing everyone who was involved and taking up with Ames where his brother left off. The story suffered from its similarities to countless TV westerns of the time. Crabbe gives a vigorous performance, with MacLane filling the bad guy role nicely.

p, Robert E. Kent; d, Edward L. Cahn; w, Orville H. Hampton; ph, Maury Gertsman; m, Paul Dunlap; ed, Edward Mann; art d, William Glasgow.

Western **(PR:A MPAA:NR)**

GUNFIGHTERS OF CASA GRANDE**

(1965, U.S./Span.) 92m Gregor-Tecisa/MGM c
(LOS PISTOLEROS DE CASA GRANDE)

Alex Nicol *(Joe Daylight)*, Jorge Mistral *("The Traveler")*, Dick Bentley *(Doc)*, Steve Rowland *(The Kid)*, Phil Posner *(Henri)*, Mercedes Alonso *(Maria)*, Diana Lorys *(Gitana)*, Maria Granada *(Pacesita)*, Roberto Rey *(Don Castellar)*, Aldo Sambrell *(Rojo)*, Antonio Fuentes *(Carlos)*, Agel Solano *(Don Ariola)*, Jose Manuel Martin *(Don Luis)*, Jim Gillen *(Sheriff)*, Mike Ekiss *(Deputy)*, Simon Arriaga *(Carvajal)*, Fernando Villena *(Mario)*, Emilio Rodriguez *(Francisco)*, Ana Maria Custodio *(Senora Durano)*, Mario De Barros *(Rio)*, Ivan Tubau *(Pecos)*, Jose Mayens *(Manuel)*, Mike Brendel *(Bartender)*, Maria Jose Collado *(Waitress)*.

Nicol, a gringo desperado, wins a Mexican ranch in a poker game and plans to take its cattle across the Rio Grande to profit off the post-Civil War Americans' desperate need for beef. Some Mexicans go in with him on the deal, but he has no intention of paying them off. After surviving a bandito-attack, Nicol has it out with partner Mistral with six shooters. The story behind the making of this film is interesting. Made in Spain, it was shot and produced by Welch almost immediately after completion of SON OF A GUNFIGHTER. Rowland is the director's son; he was often cast by his old man. In addition to being MGM's last CinemaScope film, GUNFIGHTERS OF CASA GRANDE was also the last script for Chase, author of RED RIVER (1948).

p, Lester Welch; d, Roy Rowland; w, Borden and Patricia Chase, Clarke Reynolds (based on a story by the Chases); ph, Jose F. Aguayo, Manuel Merino (Cinemascope, Metrocolor); m, Johnny Douglas; ed, George A. Lee; md, Douglas;

art d, Francisco Canet; cos, Flora Salamero; makeup, Emilio Puyol; m/l, "Ride Pistoleros," "Gunslingers of Casa Grande," Robert Mellin.
Western **(PR:C MPAA:NR)**

GUNFIRE*½ (1950) 59m Lippert bw

Don Barry *(Fenton/Frank James)*, Robert Lowery *(Kelly)*, Wally Vernon *(Clem)*, Pamela Blake *(Cynthy)*, Claude Stroud *(Mundy)*, Leonard Penn *(Simons)*, Gaylord Pendleton *(Charlie Ford)*, Tommy Farrell *(Lerner)*, Dean Reisner *(Cashier)*, Paul Jordan *(James' Son)*, Steve Conti *(Riley)*, Roger Anderson *(Bob Ford)*, Gil Fallman *(Bank President)*, Kathleen Magginetti *(James' Daughter)*, Bill Bailey *(Officer)*, Barbara Woodell *(Mrs. James)*, Jane Adrian *(Flo)*.

Barry plays both retired outlaw James and bad guy look-alike Fenton. The latter pulls off a series of crimes, correctly assuming everyone will think he is the infamous outlaw. Lowery, a lawman who believes in the ex-robber's innocence, allows James to tail the gang on one front, while he also pursues them. The film ends with a climactic chase. A lot of characters are packed into a relatively short time frame and the film suffers from it and a tendency toward too much talk.

p&d, William Berke; w, Berke, Victor West; ph, Ernest W. Miller; ed, Carl Pierson; md, Albert Glasser; art d, Fred Preble.
Western **(PR:A MPAA:NR)**

GUNFIRE AT INDIAN GAP*½ (1957) 70m Ventura/REP bw

Vera Hruba Ralston *(Cheel)*, Anthony George *(Juan Morales)*, George Macready *(Pike/Mr. Jefferson)*, Barry Kelly *(Sheriff Daniel Harris)*, John Doucette *(Leder)*, George Keymas *(Scully)*, Chubby Johnson *(Samuel)*, Glenn Strange *(Matt)*, Daniel White *(Moran)*, Steve Warren *(Ed Stewart)*, Chuck Hicks *(Deputy)*, Sarah Selby *(Mrs. Moran)*.

A stagecoach driving through Indian territory is protected by sheriff Kelly, who keeps himself hidden away on top of the coach. Lousy oater that just about spelled the end for Ralston's career, taking her husband's studio with her in her downfall.

p, Rudy Ralston; d, Joe Kane; w, Barry Shipman; ph, Jack Marta (Naturama); ed, Fred Knudtson; md, Gerald Roberts; art d, Ralph Oberg; cos, Alexis Davidoff.
Western **(PR:A MPAA:NR)**

GUNG HO!*** (1943) 88m UNIV bw

Randolph Scott *(Col. Thorwald)*, Grace McDonald *(Kathleen Corrigan)*, Alan Curtis *(John Harbison)*, Noah Beery, Jr. *(Kurt Richter)*, J. Carroll Naish *(Lt. Cristoforos)*, David Bruce *(Larry O'Ryan)*, Peter Coe *(Kozzarowski)*, Bob Mitchum *(Pigiron)*, Richard Lane *(Capt. Dunphy)*, Rod Cameron *(Rube Tedrow)*, Sam Levene *(Transport)*, Milburn Stone *(Comdr. Blade)*, Harold Landon *(Frankie Montana)*, John James *(Buddy Andrews)*, Louis Jean Heydt *(Lt. Roland Browning)*, Walter Sande *(Gunner McBride)*, Harry Strang *(Sgt. Jim Corrigan)*, Irving Bacon *(Waiter)*, Joe Hayworth *(Singing Marine)*, Carl Varnell *(Marine on Sub)*, Robert Kent *(Sub-Officer)*, Chet Huntley *(Narrator)*.

"Makin Taken" was an important newspaper headline in August, 1942, signifying the recapture of an essential Pacific island by a hardened group of Marines under the command of Col. Evans Carlson. This lightning raid was well captioned by GUNG HO! (Chinese for "working together"). Scott is the fictional Carlson of "Carlson's Raiders," who organizes the special battalion and sees his men through rigorous training until they are tough jungle fighters. The men embark and sail to their destination, then take the island over fierce and fanatical resistance. This film is exceptional in its final action sequences where the enemy is overcome, brisk and often bloody sequences not for the squeamish. Scott is forceful and often inspiring and the supporting cast is outstanding with Naish as a tough lieutenant (his role based on Capt. W.S. LeFrancois, who was on the Makin raid and chronicled the film story), Levene as a wise old sergeant, Sande as another old line veteran noncom, and tough bruisers Coe, Cameron, Curtis, and Mitchum as stalwart fighters. Mitchum, at one point during the raid, is wounded in the throat so that he cannot speak. "A Marine who can't talk can't squawk," quips Naish who walks away as a Japanese soldier playing dead comes to life and is about to shoot him. Unable to warn his officer, Mitchum struggles to sitting position and hurls a knife into the enemy's back, saving Naish. A minor and somewhat awkwardly presented romance between McDonald and two half brothers, Beery, Jr. and Bruce, who both seek her favors, provides the only female interest in the early part of the film, which is otherwise dominated by males. The raid itself is spectacularly handled by director Enright and Fulton's special effects are top notch.

p, Walter Wanger; d, Ray Enright; w. Lucien Hubbard (based on the story by Capt. W.S. LeFrancois); ph, Milton Krasner; m, Frank Skinner; ed, Milton Carruth; md, H.J. Salter; art d, John B. Goodman, Alexander Golitzen; spec eff, John P. Fulton; cos, Vera West.
War Drama **Cas.** **(PR:C MPAA:NR)**

GUNGA DIN***** (1939) 117m RKO bw

Cary Grant *(Sgt. Cutter)*, Victor McLaglen *(Sgt. MacChesney)*, Douglas Fairbanks, Jr. *(Sgt. Ballantine)*, Sam Jaffe *(Gunga Din)*, Eduardo Ciannelli *(Guru)*, Joan Fontaine *(Emmy Stebbins)*, Montagu Love *(Col. Weed)*, Robert Coote *(Higginbotham)*, Abner Biberman *(Chota)*, Lumsden Hare *(Maj. Mitchell)*, Cecil Kellaway *(Mr. Stebbins)*, Reginald Sheffield *(Journalist)*, Ann Evers, Audrey Manners, Fay McKenzie *(Girls at Party)*, Roland Varno *(Lt. Markham)*, Charles Bennett *(Telegraph Operator)*, Les Sketchley *(Corporal)*, Frank Levya *(Native Merchant)*, George DuCount, Jamiel Hasson, George Regas *(Thug Chieftains)*, Bryant Fryer *(Scotch Sergeant)*, Lal Chand Mehra *(Jadoo)*, Clive Morgan *(Lancer Captain)*, Olin Francis *(Fulad)*.

Here is a film that has everything: humor, suspense, spectacle, action—and what action—permeate every frame of GUNGA DIN, one of RKO's finest productions, and costliest. Based on a superb story by Hecht and MacArthur and the moving Rudyard Kipling poem, this rousing adventure opens when the telegraph lines from a remote mountainous British outpost are cut. British army colonel Love orders Coote to round up his most reliable frontier veterans, sergeants Grant, McLaglen, and Fairbanks, for a mission to the silent outpost. Coote finds the three brawling with a horde of Scottish soldiers and orders them to report to Love. They are then sent to the outpost with a small contingent of Indian troops and water-carriers (bhistis), one of whom is Jaffe, a water carrier whose only ambition in life is to become a soldier like the three brawling cockney sergeants who command him. In the small town, the three sergeants and their men find nothing. The place is deserted and McLaglen orders that the lines be repaired. The sergeants begin looking about the town, inspecting the empty Indian huts. In one, Fairbanks finds a lone Indian, Biberman, who explains that a band of Dacoits raided the town and herded off everyone as slaves. Yet Fairbanks goes into a back room and finds another group of burly, surly men in turbans and loincloths. He rousts them outside where Grant and McLaglen question Biberman, the apparent leader, whom Fairbanks calls "young Toad Face." Biberman becomes defiant, then begins a plaintive wailing prayer to "Kali," an Indian mother goddess. This brings forth a full-scale raid on the town by waves of mounted Indian fighters who shoot several Indian constabulary troops. The three British sergeants lead their men over the rooftops, fighting waves of attackers, hurling dynamite at the enemy, until they leap to the river and escape. The tattered band returns to base and the sergeants deliver a pickax to Love who compares it to an ancient weapon hanging on his office wall, along with other relics of long past wars. "A Thugee pickax," he gasps. Love then explains to the sergeants and others present that the Thugs were the worst killer sect in India, one which had supposedly been exterminated decades earlier, and that, at one time, there were 30,000 of these fanatical killers who murdered as part of practicing their religion, and worshipped the Goddess Kali. It means, Love concludes, that the worst killer cult in India is back and must be dealt with. Meanwhile, the sergeants attend to their special interests. Fairbanks goes to his fiancee, Fontaine, promising her that he will marry her and return to England where he will enter the tea business, just as soon as his enlistment is up, which is very shortly. McLaglen finds that his favorite elephant Annie is sick and gives her some powerful medicine which restores her to health. Grant finds Jaffe behind a house, imitating the soldiers drilling on the parade field, and instructs him in the proper form. Jaffe holds a bugle in his hands, hoping some day to become a regimental bugler. The capricious Grant gives him one command after another, then yells so the entire regiment will hear: "Dismissed!" which causes the hundreds of soldiers on the field to quit their drilling. Grant quickly marches from the scene. At a regimental ball that night McLaglen and Grant learn that the stuffy Coote will replace their pal Fairbanks and they quickly get him drunk on spiked punch so that he will be too sick to go on the next mission, and Fairbanks, despite Fontaine's pleas, winds up going with his friends. While on duty at an outpost Grant gets drunk and McLaglen locks him in the guardhouse, but Jaffe brings the elephant Annie to the rescue and the great beast knocks down the entire building, Grant and Jaffe fleeing on the back of the thundering pachyderm. McLaglen, incensed, follows with Fairbanks to find his beloved elephant. In their wild flight, Grant and Jaffe come upon an ancient temple with a shining dome of gold which sends Grant into paroxysms of joy. They enter the temple but soon see a long line of torch-bearing Thugs arriving and hide behind the massive pillars inside the temple. The great hall fills up with hundreds of religious fanatics at an initiation ceremony which is conducted by the high guru of the cult, Ciannelli. He instructs them how to use strangling cords and pickaxes on their victims, then screams: "Kill for the love of Thugeee! Kill for the love of Kali! Kill! Kill! Kill!" The intrepid Grant tells Jaffe he must warn the British and sends him off while he creates a diversion, marching boldly through the ranks of the surprised Thugs to approach the throne upon which Ciannelli sits, shouting: "You're all under arrest." Jaffe flees into the night as Grant lectures the guru's son, Biberman. "You shall grovel before my son!" hisses Ciannelli. "See here," retorts Grant, "I'm a soldier of her majesty the queen—I grovel before no one!" Thugs grab Grant and Ciannelli sneers: "Take him to the tower and teach him the error of false pride!" Biberman brings McLaglen and Fairbanks to the temple and they are quickly made prisoners and thrown into the tower torture room. Both Fairbanks and McLaglen berate Grant, who is tied to a pillar, for getting them into the predicament until they discover that his back is slashed with whipmarks. As Grant upbraids his friends for falling so easily into the trap, they cut him down and later Ciannelli visits them, threatening to have McLaglen thrown into a pit of slithering poisonous snakes. McLaglen appears to break, saying he will tell Ciannelli the disposition of the British troops, that the information is in a pocket of Fairbank's tunic. The paper is withdrawn and McLaglen pretends to read it, then closes the cell door, locking it so that Ciannelli is his prisoner. He laughs uproariously at having the paper, the signed reenlistment slip which will keep Fairbanks in the service. Now trapped in the torture tower, Ciannelli's presence serves as protection to the sergeants and Jaffe. They climb a stairway to an open porchway where Grant fixes his eyes upon the golden dome, and Fairbanks and McLaglen hold Ciannelli prisoner. Thugee snipers meanwhile keep up a continuous fire on the area so that the sergeants must lie low. Ciannelli then points out the military traps he has set, knowing that if two soldiers come to rescue one, more will follow to rescue the three. He indicates how he has placed his mountain troops in advantageous positions, how cavalry will ride down from ambush upon the sure-to-come British troops. Ciannelli next illustrates how he will spread his killer cult throughout India, then the world. "You're mad," Grant tells him. "Yes, and Caesar was mad," spits the guru. "Hannibal was mad and Napoleon was surely the maddest of the lot!" He then tells them that if they can die for England he can die for India. Ciannelli breaks away and dashes back into the torture room where he hurls himself into the snakepit so he can no longer be used as a shield by the sergeants. The Thugs open fire on the sergeants and climb to the porchway where they overpower McLaglen and Fairbanks, binding and gagging them, and bayoneting Grant and Jaffe. The British troops under Love march toward the trap while McLaglen and Fairbanks watch helplessly as Biberman's captives. The advance guard of Scottish troops are overpowered by Thugs as the main body of British troops march forward. Jaffe, though sorely wounded, climbs painfully to the top of the temple dome with a bugle and, just at the critical moment, alerts the British troops by blowing the danger signal. He is shot and killed, falling from the dome. The British troops take positions and quickly destroy the Thugs, the Indian constabulary cavalry sweeping the Thuggee fighters into a rout and surrender. The day won, Grant, McLaglen, and Fairbanks are later present when Love pays tribute to the slain Jaffe, who is posthumously made a corporal in the British army; Love then reads the last moving stanza of Kipling's classic poem in honor of "Gunga Din." This film was the most expensive RKO production to date, then a staggering $1,915,000, and it did not earn back its investment until constant re-releases made it a money-maker and one of America's all-time favorite action films. Of course, great liberties were taken with history and the actual nature of the killer-cult Thuggee, along with endorsing the imperialistic stance of the British empire. But the performances by all the principals are so delightful, including Jaffe's essaying the part of the slavish but loyal Gunga Din, that all the little sins can be forgiven. It's pure adventure and, as such, is wonderful, directed with care and zeal by Stevens. The story and dialog are replete with wit and humor. Outside of a 15-minute silent sketch dealing with the Kipling poem, produced by the Powers Studio in 1911, no one had ever undertaken a feature-length production of this tale, although Kipling's stories were brought to the screen with WEE WILLIE WINKIE and CAPTAINS COURAGEOUS in 1937. MGM in the late 1920s thought to put GUNGA DIN on film but the script got bogged down in a welter of writers and producers. Then MGM production boss Irving Thalberg abandoned plans for the film after not being able to negotiate the rights with the author. When CLIVE OF INDIA (1935) and THE LIVES OF A BENGAL LANCER (1935) proved to be big box office draws, independent producer Edward Small purchased the rights to film "Gunga Din" in 1936 from Kipling's widow for 5,000 pounds. He hired future Nobel Prize winner William Faulkner to work on the script at $750 a week but this inventive writer got too enmeshed with plot lines and variations on a story that had several endings. RKO acquired the property and slated Howard Hawks to direct, but Hawks later left that studio. Hawks, however, had brought in Ben Hecht and Charles MacArthur to rework Faulkner's story and they essentially applied the concepts they had explored in their hit play, "The Front Page," especially the struggle by McLaglen to keep Fairbanks in the service and out of the manipulative clutches of Fontaine (as reporter Hildy Johnson was kept on in the news business by his scheming editor, Walter Burns). When Hawks got bogged down on one of his masterpieces of zany comedy, BRINGING UP BABY (1938), RKO executives felt that the 35-year-old Stevens could get GUNGA DIN on film faster and assigned him the production; he proved that he was as slow as Hawks would have been. Stevens insisted that much of the film be shot on location near Lone Pine, California, in the middle of the high Sierras, to give the film the atmosphere of northern India. The temperatures soared to 115 degrees, making the task hard on cast, crew, and the hundreds of horses being put through their paces. More exteriors were shot near Chatsworth and Lake Sherwood and the interiors and the temple shots were accomplished at RKO's sound stages. Although Warner Bros. stalwart Erich Wolfgang Korngold was approached to write the score for the film, the chore finally went to Newman and he turned in a smash piece of memorable music, particularly the water carrier theme (which some later insisted Korngold did). Many actors were initially projected for the lead roles, including Roger Livesey, who had been so effective in DRUMS (1938), and Robert Montgomery, Spencer Tracy, Clark Gable and Franchot Tone. Everybody agreed, however, when the film was released, that the Grant-McLaglen-Fairbanks combination was unbeatable, and that Jaffe as Gunga Din was superb. Stevens also had Kipling himself shown in a few scenes as a visiting journalist, played by Reginald Sheffield, who composes "Gunga Din" after the battle and is present while Love reads it over Jaffe's body. Kipling's widow, Caroline, saw the film and agreed with critics that her husband's appearance was a sop to the production, that Kipling's presence was merely a foolish filler and she demanded Sheffield's role be eliminated. It was—one scene in a tent where Sheffield composes the poem, and where he is standing with McLaglen and Fairbanks at the end. In this final scene Sheffield was simply matted out with an optical printer. In re-releases of the film several scenes have been cut so that most prints shown today run about 94 minutes. When the film was originally released it was banned in India where the local press dubbed it "Scandalously Anti-Indian." Well, it was certainly anti-Thugee. The film was loosely remade in 1951 with Stewart Granger and David Niven as SOLDIERS THREE and, again in 1961 as SERGEANTS THREE with Dean Martin, Frank Sinatra, and Sammy Davis, Jr. In this last and poorly made version, really an awkward, amateurish spoof of "Gunga Din," legal trouble arose since no permission to use the story line was obtained by Essex Productions from RKO. Before United Artists released SERGEANTS THREE, Essex fended off a plagiarism suit by purchasing the rights. GUNGA DIN remains one of the all-time great adventure films, even more popular today with film enthusiasts than at the time of its initial release. No one tires of the nonstop action, the incredible heroics and the poignant sacrifice of "good old, grinnin' gruntin' " Sam Jaffe, nor the immortal last lines spoken by the honey-voiced Love: " . . . though I've belted you and flayed you/By the living God that made you/You're a better man than I am, Gunga Din."

p, Pandro S. Berman; d, George Stevens; w, Joel Sayre, Fred Guiol (based on the story by Ben Hecht, Charles MacArthur, William Faulkner (uncredited), suggested by the poem by Rudyard Kipling); ph, John H. August; m, Alfred Newman; ed, Henry Berman, John Lockert; art d, Van Nest Polglase, Perry Ferguson; set d, Darrell Silvera; cos, Edward Stevenson; spec eff, Vernon L. Walker.

Adventure **Cas.** **(PR:C MPAA:NR)**

GUNMAN FROM BODIE (SEE: GUN MAN FROM BODIE, 1941)

GUNMAN HAS ESCAPED, A**

(1948, Brit.) 58m Condor/Monarch bw

John Harvey *(Eddie)*, Jane Arden *(Jane)*, John Fitzgerald *(Sinclair)*, Robert Cartland *(Bill Grant)*, Frank Hawkins *(Mr. Cranston)*, Hope Carr *(Mrs. Cranston)*, Maria Charles *(Goldie)*, Ernest Brightmore *(Johnson)*, Manville Tarrant *(Alf)*, Patrick Westwood *(Red)*, George Self *(Spike)*, Dennis Lehrer *(Mike)*, Melville Crawford *(Inspector Fenton)*, Hatton Duprez *(Detective)*, Peter Gordon *(Customer)*, Tony Casey *(Pedestrian)*, Dennis Spence *(Barrow Boy)*.

Hard-hitting crime drama in which three jewel thieves are forced to flee London after killing a man. Taking refuge on a farm, tensions begin mounting and soon the men take to the road again, with one's suspicions leading him to gun down his two cohorts. Though little has been developed beyond the basic plot, the action is delivered in a manner that never lets up until the anticlimactic end in which the lone survivor takes his own life.

p, Harry Goodman, Richard Grey; d, Grey; w, John Gilling, Joyce Cairns; ph, Cedric Williams; ed, Ray Pitt, Cynthia R. Henry; art d, Victor Hembrow.

Crime **(PR:C MPAA:NR)**

GUNMAN'S CODE* (1946) 57m UNIV bw

Kirby Grant, Fuzzy Knight, Jane Adams, Danny Morton, Bernard Thomas, Karl Hackett, Charles Miller, Frank McCarroll, Jack Montgomery, Artie Ortego, Dan White.

Once Wells Fargo agent Grant sets his sights on the culprits who have been playing a particular stageline, nothing can stand in his way as he brings them to justice. Pretty uneventful.

p&d, Wallace Fox; w, William Lively, Sherman Lowe (based on the story by Arthur St. Clair); ph, Maurice Gertsman; ed, Pat Kelly; art d, Jack Otterson, Frank Richards.

Western **(PR:A MPAA:NR)**

GUNMAN'S WALK*** (1958) 95m COL c

Van Heflin *(Lee Hackett)*, Tab Hunter *(Ed Hackett)*, Kathryn Grant *(Clee Chouard)*, James Darren *(Davy Hackett)*, Mickey Shaughnessy *(Will Motely)*, Robert F. Simon *(Harry Brill)*, Edward Platt *(Purcell Avery)*, Ray Teal *(Jensen Sieverts)*, Paul Birch *(Bob Selkirk)*, Michael Granger *(Curley)*, Chief Blue Eagle *(Black Horse)*, Bert Convy *(Paul Chouard)*, Paul E. Burns *(Cook)*, Paul Bryar *(Bartender)*, Everett Glass *(Rev. Arthur Stotheby)*, Dorothy Adams *(Mrs. Stotheby)*.

Complex and interesting film features Heflin as a patriarch who has brought law and order to the West with his guns. Hunter is the son who wants to top his old man's reputation. Darren is the other son, a gentler man who wants no part of violent business. Grant is a half-breed Indian girl who suffers from racial prejudice. As Hunter grows more ruthless in his task, Heflin realizes what must be done and finally guns down his boy. The film is direct, moving intensely towards its inevitable climax. One of GUNMAN'S WALK's best features is its direct exposure of the racial discrimination aimed at native Americans. Here was a film that honestly portrayed how the white men treated Indians instead of the usual stereotyping westerns were guilty of and in the process provided a timely allegory for American society in the 1950s.

p, Fred Kohlmar; d, Phil Karlson; w, Frank Nugent (based on a story by Rick Hardman); ph, Charles Lawton Jr. (Cinemascope, Technicolor); m, George Duning; ed, Jerome Thomas; md, Morris Stoloff; art d, Robert Peterson; set d, Frank A. Tuttle.

Western **(PR:C MPAA:NR)**

GUNMEN FROM LAREDO*½ (1959) 67m COL c

Robert Knapp *(Gil Reardon)*, Jana Davi *(Rosita)*, Walter Coy *(Ben)*, Paul Birch *(Matt Crawford)*, Don C. Harvey *(Dave Marlow)*, Clarence Straight *(Frank Bass)*, Jerry Barclay *(Jordan Keefer)*, Ron Hayes *(Walt Keefer)*, Charles Horvath *(Coloradas)*, Jean Moorhead *(Katy Reardon)*, X. Brands *(Delgados)*, Harry Antrim *(Judge Parker)*.

Coy's a bad bar owner who's murdered Knapp's wife. He sends the rancher to the pokey on false testimony. Davi is an Indian girl who knows the truth and helps spring Knapp so he can claim revenge. In a STAGECOACH-inspired ending, Birch, a marshall, lets Knapp and Davi ride off after he has captured the escapee. Well acted; slow to start, but once it gets going, its pace doesn't flag. Perhaps a little more violent than necessary, however.

p&d, Wallace MacDonald; w, Clark E. Reynolds; ph, Irving Lippman (Columbia Color); ed, Al Clark; art d, Carl Anderson.

Western **(PR:O MPAA:NR)**

GUNMEN OF ABILENE** (1950) 60m REP bw

Allan "Rocky" Lane *(Himself)*, Black Jack *(His Stallion)*, Eddy Waller *(Nugget Clark)*, Roy Barcroft *(Brink Fallon)*, Donna Hamilton *(Mary Clark)*, Peter Brocco *(Henry Turner)*, Selmer Jackson *(Dr. Johnson)*, Duncan Richardson *(Dickie)*, Arthur Walsh *(Tim Johnson)*, Don Harvey *(Todd)*, Don Dillaway *(Bill Harper)*, George Chesebro *(Martin)*, Steve Clark *(Wells)*.

Bad guys discover a gold mine beneath a town and try to drive out the good citizens so they can stake their ill-gotten claim. Lane is a U.S. Marshall who is supposed to take over for the incompetent sheriff, but he prefers to remain undercover, wearing only a deputy's badge. Of course he stops the bad guys with the usual amount of action, fighting, horse-riding, gunplay, and romance. It's all aimed right at the heart of the kiddie matinee audience.

p, Gordon Kay; d, Fred C. Brannon; w, M. Coates Webster; ph, Ellis W. Carter; m, Stanley Wilson; ed, Irving M. Schoenberg; art d, Frank Arrigo.

Western **(PR:A MPAA:NR)**

GUNMEN OF THE RIO GRANDE** (1965, Fr./Ital./Span.) Llama-West-Flora-Pathe/AA c (SEIDA A RIO BRAVO; DUEL A RIO BRAVO; DESAFIO EN RIO BRAVO; EL SHERIFF DEL O.K. CORRAL; JENNIE LEES HA UNA NUOVA PISTOLA)

Guy Madison *(Wyatt Earp/Laramie)*, Madeleine Lebeau *(Jennie Lee)*, Gerard Tichy *(Zack Williams)*, Fernando Sancho *(Pancho Bogan)*, Carolyn Davys *(Clementine Hewitt)*, Olivier Hussenot *(Judge)*, Massimo Serato *(Leo)*, Beny Deus, Dario Michaelis, E. Marn, H. Morrow, Xan Das Bolas, Alvaro de Luna, Juan Majan, Natividad Zaro.

Madison plays famed sheriff Earp who disguises himself as a drifter to help Lebeau, a French-born saloonkeeper who is trying to keep Tichy from stealing

Davys' silver mines. Tichy hires Sancho, a Mexican bandito, to hijack a wagon full of supplies bound for the mine. Madison incites Serato, a normally lazy sheriff, and the two stop this plan. Tichy kills Sancho, afraid that the Mexican will expose him. He finally meets Madison, no longer in disguise, and they duel it out. Naturally the bad guy gets what's coming to him. Filmed on location in Almeria, Spain.

p, Ike Zingarmann [Italo Zingarelli]; d, Tulio Demicheli; w, Gene Luotto, Giovanni Simonelli, Italo Zingarelli, Natividad Azro, Guy Lionel, Tuilio Demicheli (based on a story by Chen Morrison); ph, Guglielmo Mancori, Mario Capriotti (Totalscope, Eastmancolor); m & md, Angelo Francesco Lavagnino; art d, Angelo de Amicio, Luis Arguello, A. Dea; set d, Alessandro Sarandrea, Mario Amari.

Western **(PR:C MPAA:NR)**

GUNN½** (1967) 84m PAR c

Craig Stevens *(Peter Gunn)*, Laura Devon *(Edie)*, Edward Asner *(Jacoby)*, Albert Paulsen *(Fusco)*, Sherry Jackson *(Samantha)*, Helen Traubel *(Mother)*, M.T. Marshall *(Daisy Jane)*, J. Pat O'Malley *(Tinker)*, Dick Crockett *(Leo Gracey)*, Charles Dierkof *(Lazlo Joyce)*, Jerry Douglas *(Corwin)*, Ken Wales *(Capt. Brady)*, Gary Lasdun *(Harry Ross)*, George Murdock *(Archie)*, Frank Kreig *(Barney)*, Regis Toomey *("The Bishop")*, Mike Angel *(Rasputin)*, Tom Palmer *(Priest)*, Lincoln Demyan *(Julio Scarlotti)*, Chanin Hale *(Scarlotti's Mistress)*, Ed Peck *(Lt. Ashford)*, Jean Carson *(Waitress)*, Alan Opeenheimer, Wayne Heffley, Carol Wayne.

Fairly decent adaptation of the television series "Peter Gunn" which enjoyed three years of success in the early 1960s. Stevens recreates his TV role for the big screen in this episodic adventure. The basic plot finds Stevens investigating a murder of a criminal kingpin. Paulsen, pretender to the throne, is the suspect and Marshall is a madame who wants Stevens to prove him guilty. But Paulsen turns the tables, convincing Stevens of his innocence. Bullets fly, a bomb explodes, and O'Malley, an alcoholic bum helping out with the investigation, is poisoned before Stevens arrives at the mystery's surprising conclusion. The madame is behind the murder and behind the madame's clothes is a transvestite who had hoped to frame Paulsen.

p, Owen Crump; d, Blake Edwards; w, Edwards, William Peter Blatty (based on a story and characters created by Edwards); ph, Philip Lathrop (Technicolor); m, Henry Mancini; ed, Peter Zinner; prod d, Fernando Carrere; art d, Fernando Carrere; set d, Reg Allen, Jack Stevens; cos, Jack Bear; spec eff, Paul K. Lerpac; m/l, "I Like the Look," Mancini, Leslie Bricusse, "Dreamsville," Ray Evans, Jay Livingston (both songs sung by Laura Devon).

Crime **(PR:C MPAA:NR)**

GUNNING FOR JUSTICE*½ (1948) 55m MON bw

Johnny Mack Brown, Raymond Hatton, Max Terhune, Evelyn Finley, I. Stanford Jolley, House Peters, Jr., Bill Potter, Ted Adams, Bud Osborne, Dan White, Bob Woodward, Carol Henry, Boyd Stockman, Dee Cooper, Artie Ortego.

Brown, Hatton, and Terhune team up to help Finley secure the gold her war prisoner uncle had hidden. Much of the plot revolves around a makeshift map the uncle created while in a prison camp, something Jolley and Peters have their hands on. They try to turn the heroic trio against Finley, but they fail and the three see that justice is done. Standard saddle action.

p, Barney Sarecky; d, Ray Taylor; w, J. Benton Cheney; ph, Harry Neumann; ed, John Fuller; md, Edward Kay.

Western **(PR:A MPAA:NR)**

GUNPLAY* (1951) 60m RKO bw

Tim Holt *(Tim)*, Joan Dixon *(Terry)*, Harper Carter *(Chip)*, Mauritz Hugo *(Landry)*, Robert Bice *(Sam)*, Marshall Reed *(Dobbs)*, Jack Hill *(Sheriff)*, Robert Wilke *(Winslow)*, Leo McMahon *(Zeke)*, Richard Martin *(Chito Rafferty)*, Cornelius O'Keefe.

One of Holt's worst films with a completely misleading title. This may be one of the few westerns to have an under-abundance of gunplay. A mysterious murder makes an orphan out of 11-year-old Carter. Holt and Martin seek out the killer and get the boy his inheritance. Everything in this film is lifeless, from the direction to Holt's unbelievably lame performance. But the film wasn't the only lifeless item; total box office receipts amounted to $145,000 nationwide.

p, Herman Schlom; d, Lesley Selander; w, Ed Earl Repp; ph, J. Roy Hunt; ed, Douglas Biggs; md, Constantin Bakaleinikoff; art d, Albert S. D'Agostino, Feild Gray.

Western **Cas.** **(PR:A MPAA:NR)**

GUNPOINT! (SEE: AT GUNPOINT, 1955)

GUNPOINT** (1966) 86m UNIV c

Audie Murphy *(Chad Lucas)*, Joan Staley *(Uvalde)* Warren Stevens *(Nate Harlan)*, Edgar Buchanan *(Bull)*, Denver Pyle *(Cap Hold)*, Royal Dano *(Ode)*, Nick Dennis *(Nicos)*, William Bramley *(Hoag)*, Kelly Thordsen *(Ab)*, David Macklin *(Mark Emerson)*, Morgan Woodward *(Drago)*, Robert Pine *(Mitch)*, Mike Ragan *(Zack)*, John Hoyt *(Mayor Osborne)*, Ford Rainey *(Emerson)*, Roy Barcroft *(Dr. Beardsley)*.

Murphy's the tightlipped sheriff of a small Colorado town. He's leading a posse to catch bad guy Woodward and company. They've robbed a train and kidnaped dance hall girl Staley. Buchanan is fine comic support. The best thing going in this film is the art direction. Locations, sets, and color are blended nicely. Otherwise it's typical Murphy action.

p, Gordon Kay; d, Earl Bellamy; w, Mary and Willard Willingham; ph, William Marguilies (Technicolor); m, Hans J. Salter; ed, Russell F. Schoengarth; md, Joseph Gershenson; art d, Alexander Golitzen, Henry Bumstead; set d, John McCarthy, Oliver Emert.

Western **(PR:A MPAA:NR)**

GUNRUNNERS, THE (SEE: GUN RUNNER, 1969)

GUNS** (1980, Fr.) 95m Quasar/SND c

Patrick Bauchau *(Tony)*, Juliet Berto *(Margot)*, Peggy Frankston *(Lil)*, Hermine Karaghuez *(Katrin)*, Beatrice Lord *(Marie)*, Stephane Fey *(Destrez)*, Robert Kramer *(Robin)*.

A hodgepodge group of people are secretly gun runners to an oil-rich Arab nation. The guns are going for a clandestine government operation to secure continued oil shipments. Very mysterious and slow-moving film with occasional insights.

p, Helen Vager; d&w, Robert Kramer; ph, Richard Kopans, Eric Pittard, Claude Michaud, Louis Bihi (Eastmancolor); ed, Valeria Sarmiento, Claudio Martinez.

Drama **(PR:O MPAA:NR)**

GUNS A'BLAZING (SEE: LAW AND ORDER, 1932)

GUNS AND GUITARS*½ (1936) 58m REP bw

Gene Autry *(Gene)*, Dorothy Dix *(Marjorie)*, Smiley Burnette *(Frog)*, Tom London *(Conner)*, Charles King *(Sam)*, J.P. McGowen *(Morgan)*, Earl Hodgins *(Professor)*, Frankie Marvin *(Shorty)*, Eugene Jackson *(Eightball)*, Jack Rockwell *(Sheriff)*, Ken Cooper *(Deputy)*, Tracy Layne, Wes Warner, Jim Corey, Frank Stravenger *(Henchmen)*, Harrison Greene *(Dr. Schaefer)*, Pascale Perry *(Hall)*, Bob Burns *(Jenkins)*, Jack Don, Jack Kirk, Audry Davis, Al Taylor, George Morrell, Sherry Tansey, Jack Evans, George Plues, Denver Dixon, "Champion."

Autry is framed for the murder of the local sheriff but clears his name, gets elected sheriff, and jails the bad guy who set him up in the first place. Considering this film lasts only an hour, it takes a relatively long time (30 minutes) to get to the meat of the story. But once it gets going there's plenty of action for the ardent western fan. Autry sings "Ridin' All Day" as well as the title song, with Burnette throwing in a few lyrics of his own. (See GENE AUTRY series, Index.)

p, Nat Levine; d, Joseph Kane; w, Dorrell and Stuart McGowan; ph, Ernest Miller; ed, Lester Orlebeck.

Western **Cas.** **(PR:A MPAA:NR)**

GUNS AND THE FURY, THE*½ (1983) 103m A&Z/Bordeaux c

Peter Graves, Cameron Mitchell, Michael Ansara, Albert Salmi, Barry Stokes, Derren Nesbitt, Shaun Curry, Ben Feitelson, Monique Vermeer.

A mindless adventure which casts Graves and Mitchell as a pair of tough-guy oilmen just after the turn of the century in Persia. The natives aren't too fond of their imperialistic ways and take up arms against the cocky Americans. Graves and Mitchell are left to try their luck at fighting off the combined forces of Arabs, Bengal Lancers, and Cossacks. Pretty lame, but good for a laugh.

p&d, Tony M. Zarindast; w, Donald P. Fredette; ph, Elly Zarindast, Tony M. Zarindast (Technicolor); m, Jack Wheaton; ed, Michael Billingsley; art d, Nahid Heusser.

Adventure **(PR:O MPAA:NR)**

GUNS AT BATASI*** (1964, Brit.) 102m FOX bw

Richard Attenborough *(Regimental Sergeant Major Lauderdale)*, Jack Hawkins *(Col. John Deal)*, Flora Robson *(Miss Barker-Wise)*, John Leyton *(Pvt. Charlie Wilkes)*, Mia Farrow *(Karen Ericksson)*, Cecil Parker *(Fletcher)*, Errol John *(Lt. Boniface)*, Graham Stark *(Sgt. "Dodger" Brown)*, Earl Cameron *(Capt. Abraham)*, Percy Herbert *(Sgt. Ben Parkin)*, David Lodge *(Sgt. "Muscles" Dunn)*, Bernard Horsfall *(Sgt. "Schoolie" Prideaux)*, John Meillon *(Sgt. "Aussie" Drake ["Digger"])*, Horace James *(Cpl. Abou)*, Patrick Holt *(Captain)*, Richard Bidlake *(Lieutenant)*, Alan Browning *(Adjutant)*, Joseph Layode *(Archibong Shaw)*, Ric Hutton *(Russell)*, Bloke Modisane.

Attenborough is excellent as a stalwart British soldier stationed in colonial Africa. When the country is declared independent Attenborough and his troops must maintain order. But trouble arrives in the form of John, an African officer who leads a group that opposes the British-approved government. The military and political mismatch theme works nicely and the cast is uniformly excellent. Farrow made her screen debut as the film's love interest.

p, George Brown; d, John Guillermin; w, Robert Holles, C.M. Pennington-Richards, Leo Marks, Marshall Pugh (based on the novel *Siege of Battersea* by Holles), ph, Douglas Slocombe (CinemaScope); m, John Addison; ed, Max Benedict; md, Addison; art d, Maurice Carter.

Drama **Cas.** **(PR:C MPAA:NR)**

GUNS FOR SAN SEBASTIAN** (1968, U.S./Fr./Mex./Ital.) 100m Cipra-Ernesto Enriquez-Filmes Cinematographica/MGM c (LA BATAILLE DE SAN SEBASTIAN; LOS CANONES DE SAN SEBASTIAN; I CANNONI DI SAN SEBASTIAN)

Anthony Quinn *(Leon Alastray)*, Anjanette Comer *(Kinita)*, Charles Bronson *(Teclo)*, Sam Jaffe *(Father Joseph)*, Silvia Pinal *(Felcia)*, Jorge Martinez De Hoyos *(Cayetano)*, Jaime Fernandez *(Golden Lance)*, Rosa Furman *(Agueda)*, Jorge Russek *(Pedro)*, Leon Askin *(Vicar General)*, Ivan Desny *(Col. Calleja)*, Fernand Gravey *(Governor)*, Pedro Armendariz, Jr. *(Father Lucas)*, Aurora Clavel *(Magdalena)*, Julio Aldama *(Diego)*, Ferrusquilla *(Luis)*, Pancho Cordova *(Kino)*, Enrique Lucero *(Renaldo)*, Chano Urueta *(Miguel)*, Noe Murayama *(Capt. Lopez)*, Guillermo Hernandez *(Timoteo)*, Francisco Reiguera *(Bishop)*, Carlos Berriochea *(Pablo)*, Armando Acosta *(Pascual)*, Guy Fox, Rico Lopez *(Villagers)*.

Quinn is really the only reason to see this otherwise slow-moving film. He's a rebel on the run in 1746 Mexico; taken in by Jaffe, a Franciscan priest. When Jaffe is banished to the hinterlands for giving this illegal sanctuary, Quinn disguises himself as a monk and goes with him. They come upon a seemingly empty village but Jaffe is killed by a sniper. Bronson, a local half-breed, mistakes Quinn for a real priest. He tells Quinn that the villagers have been driven from the town by the Yaqui Indians and will continue to be tormented until they give up their faith. But the village leaders refuse and make a reluctant Quinn the new town padre. He supervises the building of a dam. The Indians attempt to sabotage the project, but Quinn has acquired guns through a former mistress, now the governor's wife. The townsfolk fight off the Indians, killing Bronson and the chief. A passing army troop recognizes Quinn and orders his arrest but he escapes, accompanied by Comer, who has known the truth of Quinn's identity since his arrival. Similar to THE SEVEN SAMURAI or THE MAGNIFICENT SEVEN with the good outlaw defending a village, GUNS FOR SAN SEBASTIAN is nowhere near the caliber of these two predecessors.

p, Jacques Bar; d, Henri Verneuil; w, James R. Webb (based on the novel A Wall for San Sebastian by William Barby Flaherty); ph, Armand Thirard (Franscope, Metrocolor); m, Ennio Morricone; ed, Francoise Bonnot; art d, Robert Clavel, Roberto Silva; spec eff, J. McMillan Johnson, Lee Zavits.

Western   **(PR:O MPAA:NR)**

GUNS, GIRLS AND GANGSTERS*½

(1958) 70m Imperial/UA bw

Mamie Van Doren (Vi Victor), Gerald Mohr (Chuck Wheeler), Lee Van Cleef (Mike Bennett), Grant Richards (Joe Darren), Elaine Edwards (Ann Thomas), John Baer (Steve Thomas), Carlo Fiore (Tom Abbott), Paul Fix (Lou Largo), W. Beal Wong (Mr. Wong).

Van Doren lends her voluptuous blonde self to this crime tale about an intricately planned armored car heist. She's a Las Vegas nightclub singer who has a fling while her gangster husband is behind bars. His cellmate is freed and engineers the robbery of the car, which is traveling from Vegas to California with $2 million in winnings. Van Cleef breaks out of prison, pursues the gang, and takes back his wife, while everyone else involved dies. Van Doren's only reason to watch and it's surely not for her acting or singing. One of six films directed by Cahn in 1958.

p, Robert E. Kent; d, Edward L. Cahn; w, Kent; ph, Kenneth Peach; m, Buddy Bregman; ed, Fred Feitshans; art d, William Glasgow.

Crime   **(PR:C MPAA:NR)**

GUNS IN THE AFTERNOON (SEE: RIDE THE HIGH COUNTRY, 1962)

GUNS IN THE DARK**

(1937) 56m REP bw

Johnny Mack Brown, Claire Rochelle, Dick Curtis, Julian Madison, Ted Adams, Sherry Tansey, Slim Whitaker, Lew Meehan, Tex Palmer, Francis Walker, Frank Ellis, Budd Buster, Oscar Gahan, Merrill McCormack, Dick Cramer, Steve Clark, Syd Saylor, Jack C. Smith, Roger Williams, Jim Corey, Chick Hannon,

Brown stars in this familiar oater tale as a gunslinger who swears off guns when he mistakenly believes that he killed his best buddy. All turns out well by the finale, however, for the likable Johnny Mack.

p, A.W. Hackel; d, Sam Newfield; w, Charles Francis Royal (based on a story by E.B. Mann); ph, Bert Longenecker; ed, S. Roy Luby.

Western   **Cas.**   **(PR:A MPAA:NR)**

GUNS IN THE HEATHER**

(1968, Brit.) 90m BV c
(AKA: SPY BUSTERS)

Glenn Corbett (Tom Evans), Alfred Burke (Kersner), Kurt Russell (Rich Evans), Patrick Dawson (Sean O'Connor), Patrick Barr (Lord Boyne), Hugh McDermott (Carleton), Patrick Westwood (Levick), Eddie Byrne (Bailey), Godfrey Quigley (Meister), Kevin Stoney (Ernhardt) Shay Gorman (Headmaster), Niall Toibin (Kettering), Ernst Walder (Vollos), Robert Bernal, Vincent Dowling, John Horton, J.G. Devlin, Nicola Davies, Gerry Alexander, Eamon Morrissey, Declan Mulholland, Mary Larkin, Paul Farrell.

An American exhange student studying in Ireland (Russell) discovers that his brother is a secret agent and helps him save a defecting scientist from Communist agents. Average Disney fare that was shown theatrically in Europe before being cut up for showing on U.S. TV's "Wonderful World Of Disney."

p, Ron Miller; d, Robert Butler; w, Herman Groves, Charles Frend (based on a novel by Lockhart Amerman); ph, Michael Reed (Technicolor); m, Buddy Baker; ed, Peter Boita; art d, Albert Witherick.

Crime   **(PR:AA MPAA:NR)**

GUNS OF A STRANGER*

(1973) 91m UNIV c

Marty Robbins, Chill Wills, Dovie Beams, Steve Tackett, William Foster, Shug Fisher, Tom Hartman, Charley Aldridge, Ronny Robbins, Melody Hinkle.

A dumbfoundlingly empty singing cowboy picture which casts country star Robbins as a drifter who saves Beam's ranch from malicious outlaws while strumming his guitar. This picture tried to emulate the programmers of the 1930s and 1940s and actually succeeds quite well—it's incredibly corny, poorly acted, patently scripted, and filled with unmemorable tunes. Considering it was made in 1973, however, it has no excuse for being old-fashioned.

p&d, Robert Hinkle; w, Charles W. Aldridge; ph, (Technicolor).

Western   **(PR:A MPAA:G)**

GUNS OF DARKNESS**

(1962, Brit.) 102m ABF-Cavalcade Concorde/WB bw

Leslie Caron (Claire Jordan), David Niven (Tom Jordan), James Robertson Justice (Hugo Bryant), David Opatoshu (President Rivera), Derek Godfrey (Hernandez), Richard Pearson (Bastian), Eleanor Summerfield (Mrs. Bastian), Ian Hunter (Dr. Swann), Sandor Eles (Lt. Gomez), Steven Scott (Gabriel), Tutte Lemkow (Gabriel's Cousin), Dorita Sensier (Nightclub Singer), Ali Nagi (Indian Boy), Barry Shawzin (General Zoreno), Peter Allenby (Sergeant), John Carson (1st Officer).

Niven is an Englishman living in the South American nation of Tibulacion with his shrewish wife Caron. He encounters Opatoshu, the deposed president of the country, who has been wounded in the overthrow of his government. Niven ministers to the former leader and tries to smuggle him across the border. There is

trouble along the way and Niven is forced to deal with the moral consequences of killing a man. Too many implausibilities to really work.

p, Thomas Clyde; d, Anthony Asquith; w, John Mortimer (based on the novel Act of Mercy by Francis Clifford); ph, Robert Krasker; m, Benjamin Frankel; ed, Frederick Wilson; md, Frankel; art d, John Howell; cos, Anthony Mendleson; makeup, Jim Hydes

Drama   **(PR:C MPAA:NR)**

GUNS OF DIABLO*½

(1964) 79m MGM c

Charles Bronson (Linc Murdock), Susan Oliver (Maria), Kurt Russell (Jaimie McPheeters), Jan Merlin (Rance Macklin), John Fiedler (Ives), Douglas Fowley (Knudson), Rayford Barnes (Dan Macklin), Robert Carricart (Mendez), Ron Hagerthy (Carey Macklin), Russ Conway (Dr. McPheeters), Byron K. Foulger (Hickey), Marguerita Cordova (Florrie), Mike de Anda (Bryce).

This film is an expanded version of an episode from "The Travels of Jaimie McPheeters," a television series about a wagon train in 1849 told from a youngster's point of view. Bronson and Russell are up against some bad guys who run the town where the pair have gone for supplies. Bronson runs into an old girl friend, the enticing Oliver, who is now married to his enemy Merlin. Bronson had long ago broken Merlin's arm and now the man wants revenge. Merlin has Bronson jailed but Oliver frees him. Bronson, along with Russell and Fowley, an elderly townsman, shoot it out with the gang. The bad guys are killed but so is Fowley, who gives Russell a map just before dying. The map supposedly leads the way to a gold mine and the man and boy, along with Oliver, set out to find it. It's all highly simplistic and Bronson gives his two stock expressions and not much else.

p, Boris Ingster; d, Boris Sagal; w, Berne Giler (based on the novel The Travels of Jaimie McPheeters by Robert Lewis Taylor); ph, John M. Nickolaus; m, Walter Scharf, Harry Sukman, Leigh Harline; ed, Harry Coswick; art d, George W. Davis, Addison Hehr; set d, Henry Grace, Jack Mills.

Western   **(PR:C MPAA:NR)**

GUNS OF FORT PETTICOAT, THE**

(1957) 81m COL c

Audie Murphy (Lt. Frank Hewitt), Kathryn Grant (Ann Martin), Hope Emerson (Hannah Lacey), Jeff Donnell (Mary Wheeler), Jeanette Nolan (Cora Melavan), Sean McClory (Kettle), Ernestine Wade (Hetty), Peggy Maley (Lucy Conover), Isobel Elsom (Mrs. Ogden), Patricia Livingston (Stella Leatham), Kim Charney (Bax), Ray Teal (Salt Pork), Nestor Paiva (Tortilla), James Griffith (Kipper), Charles Horvath (Indian Chief), Ainslie Pryor (Col. Chivington), Dorothy Crider (Jane Gibbons), Madge Meredith (Hazel McCasslin).

Disgusted with a stupid officer's command to massacre the Indians of Sand Creek, Murphy rebels and heads home to Texas. He knows the Indians will want revenge and the women left behind will need protection. His fellow Texans think he's a traitor, but Murphy pays them no heed as he molds the women into a crackfire unit, using an old mission as a base (hence the title). There's one wiseacre in the group, Grant, and she and Murphy fall for each other. In the end Murphy and his ladies defeat the Indians, and Murphy is found not guilty in a court-martial hearing. His C.O., however, is charged for the massacre. A neat twist with its female brigade. This film was Murphy's first independent production, although uncredited.

p, Harry Joe Brown; d, George Marshall; w, Walter Doniger (based on a story by C. William Harrison), ph, Ray Rennahan (Technicolor); ed, Al Clark; md, Mischa Bakaleinikoff; art d, George Brooks.

Western   **(PR:A MPAA:NR)**

GUNS OF HATE**

(1948) 61m RKO bw (AKA: GUNS OF WRATH)

Tim Holt (Bob), Nan Leslie (Judy), Richard Martin (Chito), Steve Brodie (Morgan), Myrna Dell (Dixie), Tony Barrett (Wyatt), Jim Nolan (Sheriff), Jason Robards (Ben Jason), Robert Bray (Rocky), Marilyn Mercer (Mabel).

Holt and Martin are falsely accused of murdering Robards. It turns out the dead man had just discovered a gold mine and was killed by Brodie and Barrett, who framed Holt and Martin to cover the crime. The heroes break out of the pokey and go after the bad guys. Holt has a fun time with this, even if his shooting is a little off now and then. The two villains are fine in their roles. Bit player Mercer had been elevated from the studio messenger department for this film.

p, Herman Schlom, Sid Rogell; d, Lesley Selander; w, Norman Houston, Ed Earl Repp; ph, George E. Diskant; ed, Desmond Marquette; art d, Feild Gray.

Western   **(PR:A MPAA:NR)**

GUNS OF NAVARONE, THE***½

(1961) 157m
Open Road Films/COL c

Gregory Peck (Capt. Mallory), David Niven (Cpl. Miller), Anthony Quinn (Col. Andrea Stavros), Stanley Baker (CPO Brown), Anthony Quayle (Maj. Franklin), Irene Papas (Maria), Gia Scala (Anna), James Darren (Pvt. Pappadimos), James Robertson Justice (Jensen), Richard Harris (Barnsby), Bryan Forbes (Cohn), Allan Cuthbertson (Baker), Michael Trubshawe (Weaver), Percy Herbert (Grogan), George Mikell (Sessler), Walter Gotell (Muesel), Tutte Lemkow (Nikolai), Albert Lieven (Commandant), Norman Wooland (Group Captain), Cleo Scouloudi (Bride), Nicholas Papakonstantinou (Patrol Boat Captain), Christopher Rhodes (German Gunnery Officer).

This WW II spectacle could only be born in a Hollywood dream tank but it's nevertheless great adventure, despite its cliched story, hackneyed characters, and triumph-over-impossible-odds finale. British intelligence learns that two enormous guns have been installed on the Aegean island of Navarone. The long-range field pieces are capable of destroying any British fleets trying to sail to Kheros, near Turkey, where a large British force is facing annihilation unless it is evacuated. It becomes the job of Peck and a handful of men to land secretly on Navarone and somehow dismantle the guns. A savage storm smashes the fishing smack carrying the commandos and they are tossed onto the crags of Navarone with nominal leader Quayle seriously injured. Peck takes over the leadership of the group which includes killers Darren and Baker, explosives expert Niven, and tough Greek patriot Quinn. Papas, a resistance leader, meets the group, along with Scala, a beautiful Greek girl reportedly tortured by the Germans who is now unable to speak. The group is nearly captured several times but manages to escape. Niven finally pieces their bad luck together and it all points to Scala who turns out to be the traitor. She is executed by Papas and the group goes about its business of destroying the guns before a British fleet risks coming within their range. While Quinn, Darren, and Baker create a diversion, Niven and Peck manage to get into the huge gun cave, barricade it against German intervention, and plant bombs before lowering themselves down the cliff to the water where they swim to a boat Papas has waiting. Just as the British fleet arrives the guns open fire but the secret explosive Niven plants goes off and destroys not only the mammoth guns but the mountain in which they have been emplaced, sending the huge cannon tumbling into the sea. Only Peck, Niven, Quinn, and Papas survive to fight another day. There are a few subplots in this florid spectacle—Niven's dislike for Peck's dispassionate procedures, Quinn's dislike for Peck for an old disservice—but the destruction of the guns is the relentless theme and it's handled well by director Thompson with strong cast support and excellent production values that make it all lavish, rich, and often breathtaking, even though the mission is impossible for any realistic mind to grasp. The film deservedly won an Oscar for Special Effects. Filmed on the Greek island of Rhodes. Sequel: FORCE 10 FROM NAVARONE.

p, Carl Foreman; d, J. Lee Thompson; w, Foreman (based on the novel *Guns of Navarone* by Alistair MacLean); ph, Oswald Morris (CinemaScope, Eastmancolor); m, Dmitri Tiomkin; ed, Alan Osbiston; md, Tiomkin; prod d, Geoffrey Drake; art d, Drake; set d, Maurice Fowler; cos, Monty Berman, Olga Lehman; spec eff, Bill Warrington, Wally Veevers; m/l, Paul Francis Webster, Alfred Perry; makeup, George Frost, Wally Schneiderman.

Adventure/War Drama Cas. (PR:C MPAA:NR)

GUNS OF THE BLACK WITCH** (1961, Fr./Ital.) 81m Romana Film-S.N.C./AIP c (IL TERRORE DEI MARE; LA TERREUR DES MERS)

Don Megowan *(Jean)*, Silvana Pampanini *(Delores)*, Emma Danieli *(Elisa)*, Livio Lorenzon *(Guzman)*, Germano Longo *(Michel)*, Loris Gizzi *(Governor)*, Philippe Hersent *(Jean's Stepfather)*, Anna Alberti *(Elisa's Maid)*, Corrado Annicelli, Franco Lamonte, Giovanni Baghino, Nando Angelini, Cesare Lancia, Tullio Altamura, Pasquale De Filippo, Doro Corra, Francesco De Leone.

Lorenzon is a Spanish tyrant who attacks and butchers the people of an island in the Caribbean after they refuse to pay him tribute. Megowan and Longo manage to escape from their island home. They become pirates, commanding a ship called the "Black Witch." They return to avenge the wrongdoings, but Megowan is hurt and Longo is taken prisoner. Danieli, the governor's daughter finds Megowan and nurses him back to health; his captured comrade decides to join up with the enemy. The latter is joined by Pampanini—a woman who wants revenge on Megowan for ignoring her advances—but she is killed, along with the traitorous Longo and Lorenzon, when they try to stop the pirates. Megowan and Danieli are left at the end to continue their romance. The Italian version of this was directed by Domenico Paolella.

p, Fortunato Misiano, Salvatore Billitteri; d, Lee Kresel; w, Luciano Martino, Ugo Guerra; ph, Carlo Bellero (Totalscope, Eastmancolor); m, Michele Cozzoli; ed, Lina D'Amico, Iolanda Benvenuti; set d, Alfredo Montori; cos, Peruzzi; makeup, Massimo Giustini.

Adventure (PR:C MPAA:NR)

GUNS OF THE LAW*½ (1944) 56m PRC bw

Dave O'Brien, Jim Newill, Guy Wilkerson, Jack Ingram, Robert Kortman, Robert Barron, Frank McCarral.

The Texas Rangers go to town on a shifty lawyer who tries to cheat a family out of a fortune when he hears news that an oil company is interested in their property and doesn't inform them. The Rangers, however, bring the folks the good news, putting the lawyer and the gang he's in cahoots with behind bars. (See TEXAS RANGERS series, Index.)

p, Arthur Alexander; d&w, Elmer Clifton; ph, Edward Kull; ed, Charles Henkel, Jr.

Western (PR:A MPAA:NR)

GUNS OF THE MAGNIFICENT SEVEN** (1969) 95m Mirisch/UA c

George Kennedy *(Chris)*, James Whitmore *(Levi Morgan)*, Monte Markham *(Keno)*, Bernie Casey *(Cassie)*, Joe Don Baker *(Slater)*, Scott Thomas *(P.J.)*, Reni Santoni *(Max)*, Michael Ansara *(Colonel Diego)*, Wende Wagner *(Tina)*, Frank Silvera *(Lobero)*, Fernando Rey *(Quintero)*, Tony Davis *(Emiliano Zapata)*, Luis Rivera *(Lt. Presna)*, Sancho Garcia *(Miguel)*, Jorge Rigaud *(Gabriel)*, Ramon Serrano *(Cesar)*, Vincente Sangiovanni *(Manuel)*.

The third rehash of Akira Kurosawa's fine THE SEVEN SAMURAI (1954), the others—THE MAGNIFICENT SEVEN (1960), RETURN OF THE SEVEN (1966)—like this one, being westerns. Kennedy plays the role enacted by Yul Brynner in the first two of the American versions, and handles the part quite capably. With six of the original seven having been variously wiped out, Kennedy recruits another sextet to assist him in his knight-errantry. This time, Kennedy is approached by Santoni, a youthful lieutenant of rebel Quintero—Rey—who, before his internment in jail, had given the lad his patrimony—$600—to help the disparate rebel groups win their battle against tyrannical *presidente* Porfirio Diaz and his evil henchman, Ansara. Rather than purchase arms with the money, as urged by sympathetic *bandido* chieftain Silvera, Ansara seeks out the legendary Kennedy, who uses the money to recruit his roster of killers. Joined by Wagner, the mandatory love interest for consumptive killer Thomas, and by Davis—the youthful Emiliano Zapata, who makes up the seventh team member—the septet heads for the prison to free Rey. Rebuffed by the disgruntled Silvera when they seek his assistance, the unlucky seven free a group of political prisoners which includes Davis' father, and organize a training camp to make killers of the *campesinos*. Assailing the prison fort, the grossly outnumbered group is losing the battle when—at the crucial moment—the repentant Silvera arrives with his band of bandits to save the day. Plenty of action for aficionados of the series, and well-filmed on location in Spain.

p, Vincent M. Fennelly; d, Paul Wendkos; w, Herman Hoffman; ph, Antonio Macasoli (DeLuxe Color); m, Elmer Bernstein; ed, Walter Hannemann; md, Bernstein; art d, Jose Maria Tapiador; set d, Rafael Salazar; cos, Eric Seelig; spec eff, Alex Weldon; makeup, Ramon de Diego.

Western (PR:C MPAA:G)

GUNS OF THE PECOS*½ (1937) 55m FN/WB bw

Dick Foran *(Steve Ainslee)*, Anne Nagel *(Alice Burton)*, Gordon Hart *(Maj. Burton)*, Joseph Crehan *(Capt. Norris)*, Eddie Acuff *(Jeff Carter)*, Robert Middlemass *(Judge Blake)*, Gaby Fay [Fay Holden], *(Aunt Carrie)*, Gordon [Bill] Elliott *(Wellman)*, Milton Kibbee *(Carlos)*, Monte Montague, Bud Osborne, Cliff Saum, Henry Othro, Bob Burns, Douglas Wood, Glenn Strange, Gene Alsace, Bob Woodward, Frank McCarroll, Jack Kirk, Ray Jones, "Smoke."

Problems in the Pecos with rustlers trying to put a move on the cattlemen. But along comes good-guy ranger Foran who saves the day and gets about ten minutes worth of singing in to boot. Nagel is the romantic interest who goes from hating the hero to loving him in just 36 hours, which was no record for the B-westerns by any means! Songs "When a Cowboy Takes a Wife" and "The Prairie Is My Home" by Foran's usual tunesmiths M. K. Jerome and Jack Scholl seem to sum up our hero's philosophy nicely.

p, Bryan Foy; d, Noel Smith; w, Harold Buckley (based on the story "Lone Star Ranger" by Anthony Coldeway); ph, Ted McCord; ed, Frank Dewar.

Western Cas. (PR:A MPAA:NR)

GUNS OF THE TIMBERLAND** (1960) 91m Jaguar/WB c (AKA: STAMPEDE)

Alan Ladd *(Jim Hadley)*, Jeanne Crain *(Laura Riley)*, Gilbert Roland *(Monty Walker)*, Frankie Avalon *(Bert Harvey)*, Lyle Bettger *(Clay Bell)*, Noah Beery, Jr. *(Blackie)*, Verna Felton *(Aunt Sarah)*, Alana Ladd *(Jane Peterson)*, Regis Toomey *(Sheriff Taylor)*, Johnny Seven *(Vince)*, George Selk *(Amos Stearnes)*, Paul E. Burns *(Bill Burroughs)*, Henry Kulky *(Logger)*.

Ladd is the leader of a logging team in search of timber. They come upon some fresh forest land but the local ranchers, led by Crain, implore the lumberjacks not to cut down their forest. Without it, their homes will be buried in mudslides after the first heavy rain. Of course, a romance is hinted at, but not before the townspeople and the loggers take turns dynamiting each other. When Crain's ward Avalon is almost killed, Ladd sees the error of his way. But his partner, Roland, does not, and they have it out. Roland is killed; Ladd leaves town with his new fiancee Crain. A weak film (though a climactic forest fire has some good photography) that quickly becomes routine while trying hard not to. Teen idol Avalon gets a couple of songs, undoubtedly to help pump up the box office. Ladd was fairly dependent on the bottle at this point in his life and it really shows here. His features are bloated and his performance is colorless. Crain is the best thing in the film. Producer Spelling later broke into television scoring big hits with such shows as "Charlie's Angels," "The Love Boat," and "Dynasty." Ladd's daughter, 16-year-old Alana, had her first romantic screen role here opposite Avalon. Songs include "Gee Whiz Willikers Golly Gee," "The Faithful Kind," Mack David, Jerry Livingston, "Cry Timber," Sy Miller.

p, Aaron Spelling; d, Robert D. Webb; w, Spelling, Joseph Petracca (based on the novel by Louis L'Amour); ph, John Seitz (Technicolor); m, David Buttolph; ed, Tom McAdoo; art d, John Beckman.

Western (PR:A MPAA:NR)

GUNS OF THE TREES* (1964) 85m NACG bw

Adolfas Mekas *(Gregory)*, Frances Stillman *(Barbara)*, Ben Carruthers *(Ben)*, Argus Spear Juillard *(Argus)*, Frank Kuenstler *(Frank)*, Leonard Hicks *(Leonard)*, Sudie Bond *(Sudie)*, Louis Brigante *(Luis)*.

One of Mekas' underground films from the early sixties about a suicidal girl who turns to a priest for help. She also seeks out a tortured intellectual and two loving, married friends. It's told symbolically, taking stabs at the various icons of popular American life but, as with many independent films of this nature, there is a tendency to be preachy. Characters are somewhat stereotyped and not fully drawn out. Mekas does have a good camera sense though, and uses it well, incorporating New York's lower east side to its best possible advantage. Poetry on the sound track is read by famous beat writer Allan Ginsberg and Stuart Perkoff. Director Mekas' brother Adolfas, who plays the intellectual, was a known underground filmmaker in his own right. The two brothers often collaborated and contributed to each other's films.

d,w,ph,d&ed, Jonas Mekas (additional ph, Sheldon Rocklin).

Experimental Drama (PR:O MPAA:NR)

GUNS OF WYOMING (SEE: CATTLE KING, 1963)

GUNS, SIN AND BATHTUB GIN (SEE: LADY IN RED, THE, 1979)

GUNSIGHT RIDGE** (1957) 85m UA bw

Joel McCrea *(Mike)*, Mark Stevens *(Velvet)*, Joan Weldon *(Molly)*, Darlene Fields *(Rosa)*, Addison Richards *(Sheriff Jones)*, Carolyn Craig *(Girl)*, Robert Griffin *(Babcock)*, Slim Pickens *(Hank Moss)*, I. Stanford Jolley *(Daggett)*, George Chandler *(Gus Withers)*, Herb Vigran *(Justice)*, Cindy Robbins *(Bride)*, Jody McCrea *(Groom)*, Martin Garralaga *(Ramon)*.

An old story, with Joel McCrea as an undercover agent investigating trouble in the old West. Stevens is an outlaw who is also disguised, fronting as a mine owner. Stevens kills the suspicious sheriff, Richards, and McCrea takes over the job. He exposes Stevens and wins Weldon, Richards' daughter, in the process. All routine material, though the dual casting of McCrea and Stevens was unusual. Both had scored much success solo in films and apparently someone decided that the two of them would mean better box office. The photography is really good for this sort of picture, though the simplistic direction really doesn't use the visuals as it could have.

p, Robert Bassler; d, Francis D. Lyon; w, Talbot and Elizabeth Jennings; ph, Ernest Laszlo; m, David Raksin; ed, Ellsworth Hoagland, Robert Golden.

Western (PR:A MPAA:NR)

GUNSLINGER**** (1956) 77m ARC c

John Ireland (Cane Miro), Beverly Garland (Rose Hood), Allison Hayes (Erica Page), Martin Kingsley (Gideon Polk), Jonathan Haze (Jack Hays), Chris Alcaide (Joshua Tate), Richard Miller (Jimmy Tonto), Bruno Ve Sota (Zebelon Tabb), Margaret Campbell (Felicity Polk), William Schallert (Scott Hood), Aaron Saxon (Nate Signo), Chris Miller (Tessie-Belle).

Garland's a lady marshal, taking over the job after her husband's been rubbed out. Ireland is a gunman hired by evil woman saloonkeeper Hayes to reunite Garland with her late husband. The problem is that he falls for the woman he has to kill. Torn between love and duty, she chooses the latter and kills Ireland. It's a strange little Corman film, made before he went wholeheartedly for horror films, and this too has a semi-sense of the strange. The plot twists and setups are certainly different from those of most B westerns and the whole thing has actors tramping around in ankle-deep mud. The acting and direction unfortunately don't quite pull this off, though cast and crew certainly try their best.

p&d, Roger Corman; w, Charles B. Griffith, Mark Hanna; ph, Fred West (Pathe Color); m, Ronald Stein; ed, Charles Gross.

Western (PR:C MPAA:NR)

GUNSLINGERS*½ (1950) 55m MON bw

Whip Wilson (Whip), Andy Clyde (Winks), Reno Browne (Libby), Sarah Padden (Rawhide Rose), Bill Kennedy (Ace Larabee), Dennis Moore (Brad Brasser), George Chesebro (Jeff Nugent), Steve Clark (Lou Cramer), Frank McCarroll (Parsons), Carol Henry (Steve), George De Normand (Pete), Hank Bell (Hollister), Riley Hill (Tim Cramer), Carl Mathews (Kerner), Reed Howes (Stoner).

Another horse opera that consists of simple cliches and no real sense of intelligence. The railroad is being built through a frontier town. A group of outlaws tries some land grabbing to profit from the iron horse. Of course you know what happens next. Though the camera work is all right for the film, the rest of the production values are standard or less. Too bad the film isn't as exciting as the leading man's name.

p&d, Wallace Fox; w, Adele Buffington; ph, Harry Neumann; m, Edward Kay.

Western (PR:A MPAA:NR)

GUNSMOKE***½ (1953) 78m UNIV c

Audie Murphy (Reb Kittredge), Susan Cabot (Rita Saxon), Paul Kelly (Dan Saxon), Mary Castle (Cora DuFrayne), Charles Drake (Johnny Lake), Jack Kelly (Curly Mather), Jesse White (Professor), William Reynolds (Brazos), Chubby Johnson (Doc Farrell), Bill Radovich (Bartender), Donald Randolph (Matt Telford), James F. Stone (Shay), Jimmy Van Horn (Clay), Clem Fuller (Two Dot).

Typical western action designed for two-fisted war hero Murphy. He's a gun-for-hire considering taking a job from Rancher Randolph. Randolph wants to control the area, but Kelly is in the way of his plans. Kelly tricks Murphy in a card game, and the gunman switches alliances. Drake is hired by Randolph to kill the traitor, but in the end, the two gunmen look after each other and Randolph is shot. The story goes a little too far out too often, but ends up being completely predictable in spite of itself. The acting jobs are fine for the genre, but nothing is terribly different or fresh in characterizations. There's a nice use of Technicolor photography, though, which uses the scenery well, and is highly complimentary of Cabot. Songs sung by saloon cutie Castle include—remember Marlene Dietrich in DESTRY RIDES AGAIN (1939)?—"See What the Boys In the Back Room Will Have," Frederick Hollander, Frank Loesser; "True Love," Frederick Herbert, Arnold Hughes.

p, Aaron Rosenberg; d, Nathan Juran; w, D.D. Beauchamp (based on the novel Roughshod by Norman A. Fox); ph, Charles P. Boyle (Technicolor); ed, Ted Kent; art d, Alexander Golitzen, Robert F. Boyle.

Western (PR:A MPAA:NR)

GUNSMOKE IN TUCSON**** (1958) 80m AA c

Mark Stevens (Chip Coburn), Forrest Tucker (John Brazos), Gale Robbins (Lou Crenshaw), Vaughn Taylor (Ben Jorden), John Ward (Slick Kirby), Kevin Hagen (Clem Haney), Bill Henry (Sheriff Blane), Paul Engle (Young Chip), Anthony Sydes (Young Brazos), John Cliff (Cass), Gail Kobe (Katy Porter), George Keymas (Hondo), Zon Murray (Bragg), Richard Reeves (Notches).

Feuding cattlemen and farmers provide an action-packed backdrop for this oater about two brothers—Stevens and Tucker—who live on opposite sides of the law. Stevens is an outlaw who heads up the Blue Chip gang, while Tucker is a tough lawman. Stevens plans to let the cattlemen and farmers battle it out, then come in and take their land. Instead, with some encouragement from Tucker, he takes up arms with the farmers and redeems himself. It looks impressive but underneath the CinemaScope and DeLuxe Color it's just another oater.

p, Herbert Kaufman; d, Thomas Carr; w, Paul Leslie Peil, Robert Joseph (based on a story by Peil); ph, William Whitley (CinemaScope, DeLuxe Color); m, Sid Cutner; ed, George White; md, Emil Cadkin; art d, Jack Senter; m/l, "I Need A Man," Bebe Blake, Jack Hoffman, Emil Cadkin.

Western (PR:A MPAA:NR)

GUNSMOKE MESA**** (1944) 59m PRC bw

Jim Newill (Jim Steele), Dave "Tex" O'Brien (Tex Wyatt), Guy Wilkerson (Panhandle Perkins), Patti McCarty (Joan Royal), Jack Ingram (Henry Black), Kermit Maynard (Sam Sneed), Robert Barron (Bill Moore), Dick Alexander (Frank Lear), Michael Vallon (Judge Plymouth), Roy Brent (Deputy Mace Page), Jack Rockwell (Sheriff Horner).

One of the films in the TEXAS RANGERS series—next to PRC's BILLY THE KID series with Bob Steele, the most popular of their many "filler" series made to complement the main features shown in the movie houses of the forties. Here Rangers O'Brien, Newill, and Wilkerson are after bad guy Ingram. Seems he's killed his cousin and cousin's wife, taking guardianship of both their baby and gold mine. His henchmen want to do away with the kid, but the Rangers save the day and bring everyone to justice. Lots of gunplay, galloping, and of course a few cowboy tunes. Direction is okay for the fare and some nice shots in an otherwise typical effort.

p, Arthur Alexander; d, Harry Fraser; w, Elmer Clifton; ph, Ira Morgan, ed, Charles Henkel, Jr.; md, Lee Zahler; m/l, Aleth Hansen.

Western **Cas.** (PR:A MPAA:NR)

GUNSMOKE RANCH* (1937) 56m REP bw

Robert Livingston (Stony Brooke), Ray Corrigan (Tucson Smith), Max Terhune (Lullaby Joslin), Kenneth Harlan (Flagg), Julia Thayer (Marion), Sammy McKim (Jimmy), Oscar [Lou Fulton] and Elmer [Ed Platt] (Themselves), Burr Caruth (Warren), Allen Connor (Reggie), Yakima Canutt (Spider), Horace Carpenter (Larkin), Jane Keckley (Mathilda), Bob Walker (Williams), Jack Ingram (Jed), Loren Riebe (Hank), Jack Kirk (Sheriff), Vinegar Roan (Zeke), Wes Warner (Old Man), Jack Padjan (Duke), Fred Toones, John Merton, Bob McKenzie, Edward Piel, Sr., Fred Burns.

One from the THREE MESQUITEERS series used to fill the double bills. Here the trio (Livingston, Corrigan, Terhune) stop a land thief trying to take advantage of refugees during a flood of the Mississippi and Ohio Valleys. It's about as interesting as it sounds, with some painfully unfunny "humor" provided by the hillbilly vaudeville team of Oscar and Elmer.

p, Sol C. Siegel; d, Joseph Kane; w, Oliver Drake; ph, Gus Peterson; ed, Russell Schoengarth.

Western **Cas.** (PR:A MPAA:NR)

GUNSMOKE TRAIL**** (1938) 57m Concord-Conn/MON bw

Jack Randall, Louise Stanley, Al "Fuzzy" St. John, John Merton, Henry Rocquemore, Ted Adams, Al Bridge, Hal Price, Harry Strang, Kit Guard, Jack Ingram, Slim Whitaker, Art Dillard, Carleton Young, Sherry Tansey, George Morrell, Oscar Gahan, Blackjack Ward, Glenn Strange.

Randall and comic sidekick St. John come to the aid of Stanley. Merton is passing as her uncle, trying to get some land she owns. Of course, Randall saves the day. This film did not feature any singing by the star, which definitely is an asset. It's typical B western formula notable for its introduction of St. John to the sagebrush. He had been a Sennet comic in the 1920s, playing alongside Arbuckle and Chaplin, and even achieving some minor success with a comedy series of his own. After sound was introduced, St. John floundered in the movie business until he began doing B westerns.

p, Maurice Conn; d, Sam Newfield; w, Fred Myton (based on a story by Robert Emmett); ph, Glen Glenn.

Western **Cas.** (PR:A MPAA:NR)

GURU, THE**½ (1969, U.S./India) 112m Arcadia Films-Merchant-Ivory/FOX c

Michael York (Tom Pickle), Saeed Jaffrey (Murad), Utpal Dutt (Ustad Zafar Khan), Rita Tushingham (Jenny), Madhur Jaffrey (Begum Sahiba), Usha Katrak (Lady Reporter), Fred Ohringer (Howard), Nargis Cowasji (Society Hostess), Leela Naidu (Girl at Party), Marcus Murch (Snide Guest), Zohra Seghal (Mustani), Aparna Sen (Ghazala), Barry Foster (Chris), Dorothy Strelsin (Tourist), Ismail Merchant (Master of Ceremonies), Rafi Ameer (Arnold D'Mello), Soni Aurora (Miss Teen Queen), Nana Palsikar (Guru's Guru), Nadira (Courtesan), Pincho Kapoor (Murderer), Shri Agarwal (Doctor), Prayag Raaj (Classical Singer).

York is a rock star off to India to learn the sitar and find a life more peaceful than the harried London pop scene. Dutt is the sitar master/guru who works with York, slightly bemused and annoyed with the new arrival. Tushingham is a young hippie who comes along and stays. She can't play the sitar, but the guru is impressed with her eagerness and sincerity. Complicating matters are the master's two wives, Madhur Jaffrey and Sen. They are both competing for his affections and both jealous of one another. He is seemingly ignorant of their behavior. Eventually, Jaffrey's rage carries over to Tushingham. The film is really a mixed bag. It keeps hinting at great spiritual understandings, but never quite delivers what it promises. The East-versus-West conflicts are nicely handled, however. The frenzied life style of York and the peacefulness that Dutt exudes are an interesting comparison. The murky background of the guru's two wives is a nice counterbalance as well, making Dutt more than just a cliched spiritual master. Tushingham is refreshing as the hippie girl, giving the role the right amount of energy and verve. The Indian locations are marvelously photographed and well-used by the director. There is some problem with pacing, it tends to slow down in spots, and the film gets a little dull. Re-recorded sound also hampers the film, especially in long shots. Though an obvious temptation must have been to do a pseudo-biographical film of the Beatles' visit to the Maharishi, the parallels between the real event and the story of THE GURU are inconsequential at best. An interesting, if imperfect, film. Songs include "Tom's Boat Song," Ustad Imrat Hussein Khan, Ruth Prawler Jhabvala; "Where Did You Come From?" Mark London, Don Black.

p, Ismail Merchant; d, James Ivory; w, Ivory, Ruth Prawer Jhabvala; ph, Subrata Mitra (Deluxe Color); m, Ustad Vilayat Khan; ed, Prabhakan Supare; art d, Bansi Chandragupta, Didi Contractor.

Drama (PR:C MPAA:G)

GURU, THE MAD MONK*(1971) 62m Maipix/Nova International c (AKA: GARU, THE MAD MONK)

Neil Flanagan (Father Guru), Judy Israel (Prisoner), Paul Lieber (Jailer), Jacqueline Webb (Vampire), Jack Spenser (Hunchback), Jeremy Brooks (Priest), Frank Engels (Bishop), Julia Willis, Ron Keith.

Medieval gothic horror, if such a category exists, features Flanagan as a crazed chaplain at an island prison. He sends Lieber off grave robbing while he kills assorted vampires, hunchbacks, and his lesbian mistress. Dull and tedious. Despite its setting this was filmed, oddly enough, at Saint Peter's Church in New York City.

p,d&w, Andy Milligan (based on a story by M.A. Isaacs); ph, Milligan; art d, Lillian Greneker; set d, James Fox.

Horror (PR:O MPAA:NR)

GUS** (1976) 96m BV c

Ed Asner (Hank Cooper), Don Knotts (Coach Venner), Gary Grimes (Andy Petrovic), Tim Conway (Crankcase), Liberty Williams (Debbie Kovac), Dick Van Patten (Cal Wilson), Ronnie Schell (Joe Barnsdale), Bob Crane (Pepper), Johnny Unitas (Himself), Dick Butkus (Rob Cargil), Harold Gould (Charles Gwynn), Tom Bosley (Spinner), Dick Enberg (Atoms Announcer), George Putnam (TV Interviewer), Stu Nahan (L.A. Sportscaster).

Typical Walt Disney Productions nonsense. Asner is the owner of the worst football team around until he imports a Yugoslavian soccer player to serve as the field goal kicker. The catch is that the star player is a mule. Grimes is a jealous player, while Gould, Bosley, and Conway are the bad guys trying to stop the team. Would you believe Knotts as a head coach? It's all predictable fluff, but nice in its own way. There is some trouble in matching stock footage within the film, and the special effects were sub-level Disney. But, gosh, that mule is good!

p, Ron Miller; d, Vincent McEveety; w, Arthur Alsberg, Don Nelson (based on a story by Ted Key); ph, Frank Phillips (Technicolor); m, Robert F. Brunner; ed, Robert Stafford; art d, John B. Mansbridge, Al Roelofs; set d, Frank R. McKelvy; spec eff, Eustace Lyatt, Art Cruickshank, Danny Lee; stunts, Buddy Joe Hooker.

Comedy/Fantasy Cas. (PR:AAA MPAA:G)

GUSARSKAYA BALLADA (SEE: BALLAD OF A HUSSAR, THE, 1963, USSR)

GUTS IN THE SUN* (1959, Fr.) 105m Lodice-Zodiaque-Globe/Fernand Rivers bw (LES TRIPES AU SOLEIL)

Jacques Robert (Bob), Toto Bissainthe (Bessie), Gregoire Aslan (Stanley), Douta Seck (Vance), Millie Vitale (Prostie), Anne Carrere (Tourist), Roger Blin (Guide).

A confusing allegory about racism in a small town. It starts with a group of tourists on a guided tour of the area. They are treated to dancing in the street to the music of local buskers, as well as prostitutes who ply their trade in open windows. When a local white man falls for a black girl, racial tensions explode, and some whites start a riot. But the couple's fathers discover a new source of water for the town and all ends peacefully. The film was too talky, never quite sure whether it was social statement, satire, or a combination of the two. Though well produced, with an upbeat jazz score, there's not much to recommend here. The film was banned in its native France.

d, Claude-Bernard Aubert; w, Aubert, Claude Accursi; ph, Jean Isnard; ed, Gabriel Rognier.

Drama (PR:O MPAA:NR)

GUTTER GIRLS**½ (1964, Brit.) 88m Animated Motion Pictures-Tekli British/Topaz Film Corp. bw (GB: THE YELLOW TEDDYBEARS; AKA: THRILL SEEKERS)

Jacqueline Ellis (Anne Mason), Annette Whiteley (Linda), Georgina Patterson (Pat), Anne Kettle (Sally), Margaret Vieler (Marsha), Noel Dyson (Muriel Donaghue), Victor Brooks (George Donaghue), Richard Bebb (Frank Lang), Ann Castle (Eileen Lang), Douglas Sheldon (Mike Griffin), Lesley Dudley (Joan), Iain Gregory (Kinky), Jill Adams (June Wilson), John Bonney (Paul), Lucette Marimar (Susie), John Glynne Jones (Benny Wintle), Valli Newby (Kim), Norman Mitchell (Larry), Earle Green (Cliff), Harriette Johns (Lady Gregg), Ruth Kettlewell (Mrs. Seymour), Hilary Mason (Miss Fletch), Micheline Patton (Mrs. Broome), Raymond Huntley (Harry Halburton), Shirley Cameron (Gloria), Julie Martin (Liz), Bernadette Milnes (Sheila), Caron Gardner (Carol), Paula Gordon (Paula), Irene Richardson (Girl in Laboratory), Sheila Houston (A Teacher), The Embers (Musical Group).

A group of girls at boarding school takes to wearing yellow teddy bear pins to show the world that they've lost their virginity. Whiteley, a 16-year-old who's been ignored by her parents all her life, soon is wearing one of the pins but unfortunately becomes pregnant by Gregory, a window washer-cum-pop singer who is one of her lovers. She is helped by a prostitute who arranges an abortion, but Whiteley must go into the trade herself in order to raise the money. When her father finds out, he blames Ellis, the school's biology teacher. She knows about the teddy bear club and is the only adult who will talk with the girls about sex. She resigns after being reprimanded by the school board, but not before she emotionally states her case. Meanwhile Whiteley, unable to bear the thought of going back to her parents, runs away to London. Based on a true occurrence, the film is a bit preachy.

p&d, Robert Hartford-Davis; w, Derek Ford, Donald Ford; ph, Peter Newbrook; m, Malcolm Mitchell; ed, Teddy Darvas; md, Mitchell; art d, Bernard Sarron; cos, Jackie Cummins; makeup, Jimmy Evans.

Drama (PR:O MPAA:NR)

GUV'NOR, THE (SEE: MISTER HOBO, 1936, Brit.)

GUY, A GAL AND A PAL, A*½ (1945) 62m COL bw

Ross Hunter (Jimmy Jones), Lynn Merrick (Helen Carter), Ted Donaldson (Butch), George Meeker (Granville Breckenridge), Jack Norton (Norton), Will Stanton (Barclay), Sam McDaniel (Porter), Alan Bridge (Mayor), Mary McLeod (Annette Perry), Mary Forbes (Mrs. Breckenridge), Russell Hicks (General), Nella Walker (General's Wife).

Girl meets boy and boy in this quick little number. Does Merrick want marine Hunter or civilian Meeker? Ultimately it's the marine (after all this is the end of WW II and our boys in uniform never lose!). It's a simple little film with adequate production values and reasonable enough acting, though the whole thing is simplistic nonsense at best.

p, Wallace MacDonald; d, Oscar Boetticher, Jr.; w, Monte Brice (based on a story by Gerald Drayson Adams); ph, Glen Gano; ed, Otto Meyer; art d, Hilyard Brown.

Romance (PR:A MPAA:NR)

GUY CALLED CAESAR, A*½ (1962, Brit.) 62m Luckwell/COL bw

Conrad Phillips (Tony), George Moon (Maurice), Philip O'Flynn (Tex), Maureen Toal (Lena), Desmond Perry (Harry), Peter Maycock (Ron).

A typical crime story about a policeman who goes undercover and hooks up with a gang of jewel thieves. He breaks up their ring of lawlessness while falling in love with the daughter of the gang chieftain.

p, Bill Luckwell, Umesh Mallik; d, Frank Marshall; w, Mallick, Tom Burdon (based on a story by Mallick).

Crime (PR:A MPAA:NR)

GUY COULD CHANGE , A*½ (1946) 65m REP bw

Allan "Rocky" Lane (Mike Hogan), Jane Frazee (Barbara Adams), Twinkle Watts (Nancy Hogan), Bobby [Robert] Blake (Alan Schroeder), Wallace Ford (Bill Conley), Adele Mara (Bernice), Mary Treen (Grace Conley), Joseph Crehan (McCarthy), Eddie Quillan (George Cummings), Gerald Mohr (Eddy Raymond), George Chandler (Gus), William Haade (Hank Krane), Betty Shaw (Information Girl).

After losing his wife in childbirth, Lane is forced to bring up his daughter alone. But his job on a big newspaper keeps him busy and he ignores daughter Watts. He meets Frazee, who shames him into taking care of his daughter. Dad and little girl make up and are about to make Frazee number three in the family when a convict, who went to the pen because of Frazee's testimony, breaks out. He wants revenge of course, and follows Frazee with the intention of murder. But dad saves the day, and they all end up happy. The plot goes from point-to-point fairly quickly without any excess to clutter up the film. That's just as well, because A GUY COULD CHANGE is pretty bad. The script is poorly written and Lane keeps the same expression throughout the entire film. You can't tell if he's acting or just bored. Worst of all is eight-year-old Watts. She's the standard precocious kid who uses every trick in the book. After a while you may want the killer to succeed. This picture was a bit of a switch for Lane, whose deadpan face was seen mostly in westerns at the time. Little Bobby Blake, who played the Indian boy in many a western, later became a superstar.

p&d, William K. Howard; w, Al Martin (based on a story by F. Hugh Herbert); ph, John Alton; ed, Harry Keller; md, Richard Cherwin; art d, Hilyard Brown.

Drama (PR:A MPAA:NR)

GUY NAMED JOE, A**** (1943) 120m MGM bw

Spencer Tracy (Pete Sandidge), Irene Dunne (Dorinda Durston), Van Johnson (Ted Randall), Ward Bond (Al Yackey), James Gleason (Col. "Nails" Kilpatrick), Lionel Barrymore (The General), Barry Nelson (Dick Rumney), Esther Williams (Ellen Bright), Henry O'Neill (Col. Sykes), Don Defore ("Powerhouse" James J. Rourke), Charles Smith (Sanderson), Addison Richards (Maj. Corbett), Mary Elliott (Dance Hall Girl), Earl Schenck (Col. Hendricks), Maurice Murphy (Capt. Robertson), Gertrude Hoffman (Old Woman), Mark Daniels (Lieutenant), William Bishop (Ray), Eve Whitney ("Powerhouses' " Girl), Kay Williams (Girl at Bar), Walter Sande (Mess Sergeant), Gibson Gowland (Bartender), John Whitney, Kirk Alyn (Officers in Heaven), James Millican (Orderly), Ernest Severn (Davy), Edward Hardwicke (George), Raymond Severn (Cyril), Yvonne Severn (Elizabeth), Christopher Severn (Peter), John Frederick (Lt. Ridley), Frank Faylen, Phillip Van Zandt (Majors), Blake Edwards, Marshall Reed, Robert Lowell, Michael Owen, Stephen Barclay, Neyle Morrow (Fliers), Irving Bacon (Corporal), Peter Cookson (Sgt. Hanson), Matt Willis (Lt. Hunter), Jacqueline White (Helen), Bill Arthur, John Bogen, Herbert Gunn, Harold S. Landon, Bob Sully, Johnny Dunn, James Martin, Richard Woodruff, Ken Scott, Louis Hart, Fred Beckner (Cadets), Craig Flannagan, Melvin Nix, Earl Kent, Michael Owen (U.S. Lieutenants), Joan Thorsen, Leatrice Gilbert, Mary Ganley (Girls in Chinese Restaurant), Charles King III (Lt. Collins, Radio Operator), Eddie Borden (Taxi Driver), Arthur Space (San Francisco Airport Captain), Alan Wilson (Sergeant in Jeep), Leslie Vincent (Sentry), Elizabeth Valentine (Washerwoman's Child), Arthur Stenning, George Kirby (Fishermen), Mary McLeod, Aileen Haley (Hostesses), Oliver Cross (American Major), Wyndham Standing (English Colonel), Violet Seton (Bartender's Wife), Becky Bohannon (English Girl), Harold S. Landon (Cadet), Jean Prescott (Mother), Simon Oliver (Boy), Richard Graham (Crew Member), James Warren (Irish Guard), George Atkinson (Waiter), Howard Davies (Bartender), Carlie Taylor (English Captain), Jack Saunders (American Captain), Stanley Orr (English Captain), William Bishop (Ray), Allen Wood (Tough Corporal), Eddie Coke (Corporal), Carey Harrison (American Major in Red Lion Inn), Dora Baker (Scrub Woman), Clarence Straight (Flight Sergeant), Verno Downing (English Liaison Officer), William Manning (Co-Pilot), Jesse Tai Sing (Headwaitress), Martin Ashe (Sergeant in Chinese Restaurant).

A delightful, often tear-jerking fantasy, this film was one of the most popular movies during WW II, combining the considerable talents of Tracy, Dunne, and Johnson in a big-scaled production. Tracy is a wise-guy bomber pilot who is constantly taking risks and ignoring orders. He loves Dunne but he loves his dare devil adventures more and, on one mission, he is mortally wounded, crash diving his plane into a German aircraft carrier and sinking it. Following his death Tracy finds himself on cloud nine where he runs into Nelson, an old Air Corps pal. As they walk along through the mist Tracy remembers that Nelson was killed and then discovers to his consternation that he, too, is dead and has gone to the Great Beyond. Tracy is taken by Nelson to see "The General," a one-time Air Corps great, Barrymore, and is assigned to be the guardian angel for a new pilot, Johnson, shepherding him through flying school, pilot training, and to his new post in the Pacific. But in following Johnson about, he finds the young man attracted to —of all people—his old girl friend, Dunne. She, however, is still devoted to the memory of Tracy, an emotional bond Tracy has no intention of severing. In fact, he works against the future of the brash Johnson so much that he is called on the carpet and shown the errors of his ways by Barrymore. He returns to the Pacific island where Johnson is stationed and Dunne, an experienced flier herself, is also posted. She learns that Johnson is assigned to a dangerous mission, from which he is not expected to return, and Dunne takes off in his place. In the plane with her is the ectoplasmic Tracy, guiding her as her invisible co-pilot, talking her through a precarious bomb run. Dunne's plane skirts the anti-aircraft fire and manages to dump its bombs squarely on the target; she flies back to Johnson. When she lands, Johnson begins to run toward her and she toward him. Dunne has now decided, with a spiritual nudge from Tracy, to accept Johnson's love. Before he turns his back on the world, Tracy smiles at the sight of Dunne and Johnson embracing, murmuring: "That's my girl . . . and that's my boy." He saunters across the airstrip, his job done, and vanishes. Entertaining, witty, sad, and funny, this is a film that goes in many directions at the same time with its romantic fantasy line and grim war outlook. But Trumbo's script is wry, with the best lines going to smart-talking Tracy. The direction is swift and expert under Fleming's firm hand and Gillespie's special effects are outstanding. (There are some blatant errors, however. Tracy is shown sinking a German aircraft carrier when Germany had no aircraft carriers during WW II.) One of the most inspirational scenes in the film is where Tracy talks to a group of British children about what it's like to fly above the clouds, delivering in that wonderful prosaic style inimitably his, a poetic description of the Wild Blue Yonder. In another ending not used in the film, Dunne dies during the bombing mission and joins Tracy in the Hereafter and Johnson winds up with Williams (this was the future aquatic star's second film after her debut in ANDY HARDY'S DOUBLE LIFE, 1942). This ending was thought by MGM moguls to be too depressing and was discarded. Many involved with this film had produced ghosts for other films. Producer Riskin had overseen HERE COMES MR. JORDAN, 1941, for Columbia and writer Trumbo had scripted THE REMARKABLE ANDREW, 1942, for Paramount. When Dunne heard that she would be playing in her first MGM film since doing THE SECRET OF MADAME BLANCHE in 1933, she was so overjoyed that she agreed to be second-billed to Tracy, with whom she wanted to work. But Tracy took an inexplicable dislike to Dunne, whom he considered too much of a prudish lady, and he and drinking buddy Fleming unmercifully teased her to tears. This was at a time when Tracy was drinking heavily, although his imbibing did not interfere with the production. Johnson had gotten his part in the film largely due to Tracy's insistence. The older actor had seen Johnson in a few bit parts and believed he was star material. After a few weeks of shooting Johnson accompanied Keenan Wynn and his wife to a movie preview of a Tracy film, KEEPER OF THE FLAME, 1942. Another car ran a red light and crashed into Johnson's car, sending the young actor through the windshield. He was hospitalized in serious condition, his skull torn open. A metal plate was later inserted into his crushed forehead and livid scars would be visible ever after. The accident caused the production to shut down and MGM mogul Louis B. Mayer began to think of bringing a contract player into A GUY NAMED JOE to replace Johnson, talking about either John Hodiak or Peter Lawford. When Tracy heard this he told Mayer that if Johnson was replaced, he, Spencer Tracy, would walk off the production. Mayer backed down and held off the production until Johnson recovered and was able to finish his scenes. Part of this deal, however, meant that Tracy and friend Fleming had to treat Dunne with respect. Both did. Johnson was forever grateful to Tracy for his efforts on his behalf. The Johnson accident worked another type of hardship on Dunne. Because of the film's delay she had to begin filming THE WHITE CLIFFS OF DOVER, 1944, and also complete A GUY NAMED JOE. She was later quoted as saying: "I always lived the characters I played and to have to be those two entirely different women at the same time was unbearable. And yet I think A GUY NAMED JOE is one of the finest pictures I ever made." So did the public, returning more than $4 million to MGM coffers from its initial release; the film ranked in the top ten films of 1943-1944. Oddly, there is no character in the film named "Joe." One of the characters in the film states: "In the Army Air Corps, any fellow who is a right fellow is called 'Joe.'" Songs include "I'll Get By as Long as I Have You" (Roy Turk, Fred Ahlert) and "I'll See You in My Dreams" (Isham Jones, Gus Kahn).

p, Everett Riskin; d, Victor Fleming; w, Dalton Trumbo (based on a story by Chandler Sprague, David Boehm, Frederick H. Brennan); ph, George Folsey, Karl Freund; m, Herbert Stothart; ed, Frank Sullivan; art d, Cedric Gibbons, Lyle Wheeler; set d, Edwin B. Willis, Ralph Hurst; spec eff, Arnold Gillespie, Donald Jahraus, Warren Newcombe; cos, Irene; makeup, Jack Dawn.

War Drama/Romance/Fantasy **(PR:A MPAA:NR)**

GUY WHO CAME BACK, THE½** (1951) 91m FOX bw

Paul Douglas *(Harry Joplin)*, Joan Bennett *(Kath)*, Linda Darnell *(Dee)*, Don De Fore *(Gordon Towne)*, Billy Gray *(Willy)*, Zero Mostel *(Boots Mullins)*, Edmon Ryan *(Joe Demarcus)*, Ruth McDevitt *(Grandma)*, Walter Burke *(O'Hara)*, Henry Kulky *(Wizard)*, Dick Ryan *(Station Master)*, Robert B. Williams *(Paymaster)*, Ted Pearson *(Tom)*, Mack Williams *(Captain of Waiters)*, Garnett Marks *(Waiter)*, Shirley Tegge *(Hat Check Girl)*, Charles Conrad *(Clerk)*, Grandon Rhodes *(Capt. Shallock)*, John H. Hamilton *(Admiral)*, John Close *(Tufano)*, Tom Hanlon *(Announcer)*, Harry Seymour *(Piano Player)*, Lillian West *(Woman)*, Jack Davis, J. Anthony Hughes, Rodney Bell *(Men)*, John Smith, Warren Farlow, Wayne Farlow, Donald Gordon, Whitey Haupt, Tommie Menzies, Pat Mitchell *(Boys)*, Thomas Browne Henry *(Doctor)*, Emile Meyer *(Police Guard)*, Harry Harvey *(Doctor)*, Hal Baylor *(Navy Man)*, Mike Marienthal, Gayle Pace *(Spotters)*, Stanley Pinto *(Referee)*, Robert Foulk *(Flight Manager)*.

Douglas is a pro football player who is dissatisfied and disillusioned that his playing days are over. Bennett is his long-suffering wife who takes a job to make ends meet. Slowly, they lose touch with each other; Bennett has an affair with Darnell. But she soon realizes that Douglas cannot divorce his wife. She seeks out Bennett and together they try to get Douglas back into football. Since good players are being lost to the war effort, the team will take anything it can get. But Douglas sees that he's no longer the same man he once was. He resigns himself to life as a coach after achieving a little taste of his old glory at an All Star-vs.-Navy game. Flashbacks, telling how Douglas and Bennett met, confuse things at the start, but otherwise it's not too bad a film. The characterizations are good, with Bennett and Darnell playing well off one another. Douglas does a fine job in humanizing his character, giving a sadly humorous performance. He's quite good in a wrestling scene, a job taken to make some extra money. The direction is a little plodding, but this is overcome by the performers. Don't miss a brief appearance by Mostel in a semi-parody of Toots Shor.

p, Julian Blaustein; d, Joseph Newman; w, Allan Scott (based on the story "The Man Who Sank the Navy" by William Fay); ph, Joseph La Shelle; m, Leigh Harline; ed, William B. Murphy; md, Lionel Newman; art d, Lyle Wheeler, Chester Gore; m/l, "Keep Your Eye On the Ball," Ken Darby.

Drama **(PR:A MPAA:NR)**

GUYANA, CULT OF THE DAMNED zero (1980, Mex./Span./Panama) 90m Conacine-Izaro-Care/UNIV c
(AKA: GUYANA, CRIME OF THE CENTURY)

Stuart Whitman *(Rev. James Johnson)*, Gene Barry *(Congressman Lee O'Brien)*, John Ireland *(David Cole)*, Joseph Cotten *(Richard Gable)*, Bradford Dillman *(Dr. Gary Shaw)*, Jennifer Ashley *(Anna Kazan)*, Yvonne De Carlo *(Susan Ames)*, Nadiuska *(Leslie)*, Tony Young *(Ron)*, Erika Carlsson *(Marilyn)*, Robert Doqui *(Oliver)*, Hugo Stiglitz *(Cliff)*, Carlos East *(Mike)*.

Mean, ugly, and boring exploitation of the real-life 1978 tragedy in Guyana. Whitman is Rev. Johnson (a not-too-subtle name change!), who leads his followers into the Guyana jungles. When his cult is investigated by congressman Barry, he has everyone drink cyanide-laced Kool-Aid. It's all pretty sleazy and offers no insight to the real horrors. Names are changed only slightly to avoid lawsuits. This is the same company that brought out SURVIVE! an exploitation film about a plane that crashed in the Andes, forcing its survivors into cannibalism. This particular subject later had a more intelligent production created for television called *Guyana Tragedy: The Story of Jim Jones*. As for this film, it later was doubled with another cheapie: AMIN—THE RISE AND FALL. Some considerable talents are in this one (De Carlo, Cotten, music by Riddle), which might cause one to pause and think about what goes on in the film business.

p&d, Rene Cardona, Jr.; w, Cardona and Carlos Valdemar; ph, Leopoldo Villasenor (C.F.I. Color); m, Nelson Riddle, Bob Summers, George S. Price; ed, Earl Watson.

Drama **(PR:O MPAA:R)**

GUYS AND DOLLS*½** (1955) 150m Goldwyn/MGM c

Marlon Brando *(Guy Masterson)*, Jean Simmons *(Sarah Brown)*, Frank Sinatra *(Nathan Detroit)*, Vivian Blaine *(Miss Adelaide)*, Robert Keith *(Lt. Brannigan)*, Stubby Kaye *(Nicely-Nicely Johnson)*, B.S. Pully *(Big Jule)*, Sheldon Leonard *(Harry the Horse)*, Regis Toomey *(Arvide Abernathy)*, Johnny Silver *(Benny Southstreet)*, Dan Dayton *(Rusty Charlie)*, George E. Stone *(Society Max)*, Kathryn Givney *(Gen. Cartwright)*, Veda Ann Borg *(Laverne)*, Mary Alan Hokanson *(Agatha)*, Joe McTurk *(Angie the Ox)*, Kay Kuter *(Calvin)*, Stapleton Kent *(Mission Member)*, Renee Renor *(Cuban Singer)*, John Indrisano *(Liverlips Louis)*, Earle Hodgins *(Pitchman)*, Barry Tyler *(Waiter)*, Matt Murphy *(The Champ)*, Julian Rivero *(Havana Waiter)*, Larri Thomas, Jann Darlyn, June Kirby, Madelyn Darrow, Barbara Brent *(Goldwyn Girls of 1955)*, Harry Wilson, Earle Hodgins, Harry Tyler, Major Sam Harris, Franklyn Farnum, Frank Richards.

GUYS AND DOLLS was a great play that was made into just a good movie by some very talented people. Much of the play's charm came from the stylized depiction of Broadway and the characters that inhabited Runyon's unique world, but when it was put on the screen, it failed to have the same impact. The problem was the casting. Marlon Brando takes second place to no one when it comes to heavy drama, but this required a light touch, something that Brando has never been able to show—witness BEDTIME STORY. Sinatra was equally miscast as Nathan Detroit, and he appeared to walk through the role and had none of the edge that Sam Levene gave it on Broadway. Goldwyn had paid a fortune for the rights and was not about to give the unknowns who starred on the stage a chance at the movie. The only holdovers were Blaine, Silver, Kaye, Pully and a few of the dancers. Sinatra is proprietor of the "oldest established permanent floating crap game in New York." (In truth, there were two brothers who actually did that, and one of them was named Meyer Boston, so it must be presumed that Runyon did base the character of Nathan Detroit on the Boston gamesman.) The town is loaded with high-stakes players, but Sinatra is unable to find a suitable place for the game. The heat is on from Keith, a detective, and Sinatra sees that he is going to lose a fortune if he doesn't find a location. He can get the Biltmore garage for a grand (this place also existed and was used for that very reason), but "we ain't got a grand on hand." All the while, Sinatra's girl friend, Blaine, works at a local nightspot and wishes he would get out of the dice business, settle down, and marry her after their 14-year courtship. In order to raise the needed thousand, he attempts a sucker bet on Brando, a very high roller (hence the name "Sky" Masterson, because the sky is the limit when he bets). The bet is that Masterson can take Simmons, a sort of Salvation Army worker, to Havana. This would appear an impossibility, as this Mission doll is straight as an arrow and lives to reform sinners. She and her uncle, Toomey, are having a hard time getting the locals to join in their crusade that works out of a storefront mission. Brando doesn't really need the thousand he'd get from Sinatra (who doesn't have it anyhow), but he hates to lose any sort of bet, so he goes after Simmons. He appeals to her knowing full well her Save-A-Soul mission is foundering; he promises to deliver some serious sinners to her next midnight meeting if she will have dinner with him. She agrees, then learns that their meal will be in Cuba! Once there, she succumbs to the ambiance, the rum, the music; he can have her if he wants her, but he is seduced by her naivete and does not attempt to take her to bed. Now, he returns her to NYC and must acquire the sinners he has promised. In a rousing scene in the sewer—where Sinatra has arranged the big game—he bets a thousand dollars a sinner and wins. The midnight meeting takes place and the chief of the mission is there. Now Keith arrives and tells the Save-A-Soul people that their store had been used earlier as a site for the game. Simmons saves their tails by telling the cop he's wrong and the picture ends as Sinatra and Blaine are married in a double ceremony with Brando and Simmons. It's a huge wedding in a stylistic set of Times Square. Based on two stories by Runyon told by his never-identified narrator, Burrows and Swerling united both short tales into what must be the quintessential American musical. Loesser's score is deceptively simple, but each tune is a smashing example of how to write for the stage. A few tunes were cut from the original score and some new ones were written for the film. One excellent song was a touching tune by Simmon's uncle called "More I Cannot Wish You." Another was a paean of praise to the late-night life entitled "My Time Of Day," which is only heard as background music with no lyrics. Sinatra received an extra song with "Adelaide," and Brando got to do "A Woman In Love," but did very little with it. Mankiewicz had never directed a musical before and was an odd choice, but he came through as well as he could, given the casting. The dialog was true to Runyon—one never heard a contraction emerge from any of their mouths. "Do not" for "don't" and "should not" for shouldn't." It was a manner of speech invented by Runyon and it lent a patina of originality to all his stories, although it was hardly accurate. The young woman who played the Simmons role on Broadway was Isabel Bigley and she retired shortly thereafter to marry a very successful agent. Robert Alda had a lengthy career in films (RHAPSODY IN BLUE, etc.) but never with the success he had in the play. He is the father of TV star Alan Alda. The songs include: "Guys And Dolls," "Fugue For Tinhorns," "Follow The Fold," "Sue Me," "Take Back Your Mink," "If I Were A Bell," "Luck Be A Lady," "Pet Me, Poppa" (which replaced the smash "A Bushel And A Peck"), "Sit Down, You're Rockin' The Boat," "I'll Know," "A Woman In Love," "The Oldest Established," "Adelaide's Lament," "Adelaide." One of the best tunes in the play was also replaced; "I've Never Been In Love Before," probably because Brando's reedy baritone couldn't hit the notes. The picture and the literary rights cost almost six million dollars and failed to return the triple gross necessary to make it a hit. Despite all its flaws, GUYS AND DOLLS is still great fun to see, but one wonders how much better it would have been if Goldwyn cast it with less of an eye toward insurance and more of an eye to the original material. Gene Kelly was originally selected to play Sky, but MGM wouldn't release him, a crying shame.

p, Sam Goldwyn; d&w, Joseph L. Mankiewicz (from the musical book by Abe Burrows, Jo Swerling, suggested by two short stories of Damon Runyon); ph, Harry Stradling, Sr. (CinemaScope, Eastmancolor); ed, Daniel Mandell; prod d, Oliver Smith; md, Jay Blackton; art d, Joseph Wright; set d, Howard Bristol; cos, Irene Sharaff; m/l Frank Loesser; ch, Michael Kidd.

Musical/Comedy **Cas.** **(PR:A MPAA:NR)**

GYPSY½** (1937, Brit.) 77m FN-WB bw

Roland Young *(Alan Brooks)*, Chili Bouchier *(Hassina)*, Hugh Williams *(Brazil)*, Frederick Burtwell *(Pim)*, Glen Alyn *(Lilli)*, Brian Buchel *(Vicot)*, Andrea Malandrinos *(Hunyadi)*, Victor Fairley *(Strauss)*, Emilio Colombo's Tzigane Band.

Bouchier is a young gypsy girl engaged to a circus lion tamer. He leaves Hungary for England and marriage to another. Not knowing the latter, she follows him. When she finds his bookings have been changed and she has missed him, Bouchier faints. She is picked up by Young, to whom she tells her story. He tries to locate the lion tamer but she hears her former love has been killed. Bouchier and Young marry, but then she discovers her lion tamer is not dead. Feeling bound by duty she goes to him, but discovers him married, so she returns to Young. This all sounds like fluff, but it really works, thanks to the skill of the performers. Bouchier is fine as the gypsy girl, with an accent so convincing it's hard to believe she's British in real life. Young is clever in his role and Burtwell, as his very proper butler, is terrific without being the least bit of a cartoon. Some tight cutting interferes a little with the dialog, but overall it's not a bad film.

p, Irving Asher; d, Roy William Neill; w, Brock Williams, Terence Rattigan (based on Lady Eleanor Smith's novel *Tzigane*).

Romance **(PR:A MPAA:NR)**

GYPSY**** (1962) 149m WB c

Rosalind Russell *(Rose)*, Natalie Wood *(Louise "Gypsy")*, Karl Malden *(Herbie Sommers)*, Paul Wallace *(Tulsa No. 2)*, Betty Bruce *(Tessie Tura)*, Parley Baer *(Mr. Kringelein)*, Harry Shannon *(Grandpa)*, Suzanne Cupito *("Baby" June)*, Ann Jilliann *("Dainty" June)*, Diane Pace *("Baby" Louise)*, Faith Dane *(Mazeppa)*, Roxanne Arlen *(Electra)*, Jean Willes *(Betty Cratchitt)*, George Petrie *(George)*, Ben Lessy *(Mervyn Goldstone)*, Guy Raymond *(Patsy)*, Louis Quinn *(Cigar)*, Jack Benny *(Himself)*, Bert Michaels, Dick Foster, Jim Hubbard, Jeff Parker, Mike Cody, Bo Wagner *(Farmboys)*, Terry Hope, Shirley Chandler, Francie Karath, Paula Martin, Dee Ann Johnston, Renee Aubry *(Hollywood Blondes)*, Trudi Ames *(Hawaiian Girl)*, Harvey Korman *(Phil)*, James Millhollin *(Mr. Beckman)*, William Fawcett *(Mr. Willis)*, Danny Lockin *(Yonkers)*, Ian Tucker *(Angie)*, Lois Roberts *(Agnes)*, Dina Claire *(Dolores)*.

Gypsy was a smash hit on Broadway and the same group who did it for the stage provided the work for the screen. It starred Ethel Merman, a human dynamo, on the Great White Way but the filmmakers tempered her character somewhat by casting Russell in the role. Although the name of the film, play, and book is GYPSY, it should have been called ROSE because that's who the star is. Spigelgass' screenplay filled in the warmth and wit that the exigencies of the stage prohibited. The story, in case you somehow have missed this milestone work, is as follows: Russell, an aggressive, abrasive stage mother with two daughters to support, has vowed to make each of them into the star that she never was. They are doing a "kiddie" act in vaudeville but those days are rapidly fading. She meets Malden, an agent who somehow falls in love with her. Daughter Jillian (June Havoc in real life) is the star and delights the audiences with her "Dainty June" act until she is too old to carry it off. The others in the act are some fill-in boys who work for room and whatever board that Russell can work out. Jillian eventually decides to make it on her own and leaves the act, causing Russell no end of grief. Not only has a daughter left, a meal ticket is also gone. Russell decides that all is not lost and begins to work on a reluctant Wood, trying to make her into a star. They sink further and further into the morass of cheap dates and lowlife theatres until they are stranded in a fifth-rate vaudeville house that has just turned into a burlesque palace. Wood is just going to sing, that's all, but when one of the strippers is arrested for shoplifting, Wood steps into the breach and does a unique strip act. She hardly takes off *anything* and is a sensational smash. Wood goes from a sweet, shy, and demure young thing to a star on the burlesque stage in a quick montage. Russell tags along but there is soon friction when Wood decides to assert herself and step away from the influence of the woman who has pushed her all these years. The two have a terrible argument in Wood's dressing room, then Russell walks out on the empty stage and sings her heart out to an invisible audience. Wood hears her plea, follows Russell on stage, they embrace, and the film ends. The adaptation was a cross between film and stage, as many of the cinematic effects came right from the Broadway version. There are a few dull spots but they are piffle compared to the great moments in this movie. A score that stands up well today (probably will for the next several centuries) includes "Small World," "All I Need Is The Girl," "You'll Never Get Away From Me," "Let Me Entertain You," "Some People," "Everything's Coming Up Roses," "You Gotta Have A Gimmick," and more. Sondheim's lyrics and Styne's music were never better. Super second banana work from Quinn (he was Roscoe on TV's "77 Sunset Strip"), Baer, Raymond and Lessy. Liza Kirk did some of the singing for Russell but all of the others were actual. June Havoc (born Hovick, as was Louise) went on to have a good career in A and B movies and currently teaches acting. In such a long film, there was barely any time to show Gypsy's relationship with men or any other personal story. Judicious editing might have helped, as well as just a little more deepening of both girls' feelings toward Russell, a woman who could have come off as a banshee and a hoyden had it not been for the intelligent softening of the character by the creators and the multi-dimensional playing by Russell. Although Robert Tucker was credited with the choreography, praise must be given to Jerome Robbins who did the original show on stage, and much of whose work is in evidence. It's a "feeling good" movie from start to finish and although you may not love Russell for the way she went about things, you must admit that she got things done and made both her daughters into stars. Other songs: "Baby Jane and the Newsboys," "Mr. Goldstone, I Love You," "Little Lamb," "Dainty June and Her Farmboys," "Rose's Turn," "If Mama Was Married" [cut from release print], "Broadway, Broadway" (Jule Styne, Stephen Sondheim).

p&d, Mervyn LeRoy; w, Leonard Spigelgass (based on the musical play by Arthur Laurents and the book *Gypsy, A Memoir* by Gypsy Rose Lee [Rose Louise Hovick]; ph, Harry Stradling, Sr. (Technirama, Technicolor); ed, Phillip W. Anderson; md, Frank Perkins; art d, John Beckman; set d, Ralph S. Hurst; cos, Orry-Kelly, Howard Shoup, Bill Gaskin; ch, Robert Tucker; makeup, Gordon Bau.

Musical/Biography **Cas.** **(PR:C MPAA:NR)**

GYPSY AND THE GENTLEMAN, THE*½ (1958, Brit.) 107m Rank Films c

Melina Mercouri *(Belle)*, Keith Mitchell *(Sir Paul Deverill)*, Patrick McGoohan *(Jess)*, June Laverick *(Sarah Deverill)*, Lyndon Brook *(John Patterson)*, Flora Robson *(Mrs. Haggard)*, Clare Austin *(Vanessa)*, Helen Haye *(Lady Ayrton)*, Newton Blick *(Ruddock)*, Mervyn Johns *(Brook)*, John Salew *(Duffin)*, Catherine Feller *(Hattie)*, Laurence Naismith *(Forrester)*, Louis Aquilina *(Coco)*, Nigel Green *(The Game Pup)*, Laurence "Larry" Taylor *(Cropped Harry)*, Gladys Boot *(Mrs. Mortimer)*, Edna Morris *(Mrs. Piggot)*, David Hart *(Will)*.

About to enter into a marriage he wants no part of, rich nobleman Mitchell takes up with gypsy Mercouri. They marry but she soon discovers he is no rich man. Rather, he is deeply in debt. Mercouri doesn't care for this at all and lets him have it. She gives a marvelous performance, lively and extremely sexy. It's a good thing because the dialog is pretty lame. Yet Mercouri is able to get past it without much trouble. Laverick is Mitchell's sister, long suffering for her brother's philandering ways. The color and photography are magnificent, as are costumes. Losey goes for emotional values with his direction, a wise choice considering the weaknesses in the script and the emotional power of Mercouri.

p, Maurice Cowan; d, Joseph Losey; w, Janet Green (based on the novel *Darkness I Leave You* by Nina Warner Hooke); ph, Jack Hildyard (Eastmancolor); m, Hans May; ed, Reginald Beck; prod d, Richard MacDonald, Ralph Brinton; md, May; art d, Brinton; set d, Vernon Dixon; cos, Julie Harris.

Drama **(PR:O MPAA:NR)**

GYPSY COLT½** (1954) 72m MGM c

Donna Corcoran *(Meg MacWade)*, Ward Bond *(Frank MacWade)*, Frances Dee *(Em MacWade)*, Lee Van Cleef *(Hank)*, Larry Keating *(Wade Y. Gerald)*, Bobby Hyatt *(Phil Gerald)*, Nacho Galindo *(Pancho)*, Rodolfo Hoyos Jr. *(Rodolfo)*, Bobby Dominguez *(Pedro)*, Joe Dominguez *(Tony)*, Jester Hairston *(Carl)*, Peggy Maley *(Pat)*.

This low-budget film aimed specifically at the family market stars Corcoran as the daughter of Bond and Dee. Gypsy is her prize horse; she rides him everywhere. But a drought is on in their small western town and Bond must sell the girl's beloved friend to a racing stable located 500 miles away. The horse misses his friend, breaks loose, and runs back to his mistress, meeting her at the schoolhouse steps at the usual time. Along comes a timely rain and all is resolved happily. The acting is fine, with Corcoran naturally stealing the show. There's nice photography and the color is used well. Great for the kids.

GYPSY FURY—   **1138**

p, William Grady Jr., Sidney Franklin; d, Andrew Marton; w, Martin Berkeley (based on a story by Eric Knight); ph, Harold Lipstein (Ansco Color); m, Rudolph G. Kopp; ed, Conrad A. Nervig.

Family Drama   **(PR:AAA MPAA:NR)**

GYPSY FURY**   (1950, Fr.) 100m Terra/Discina-MON bw
                                    (AKA: SINGOALLA; THE SAGA OF SINGOALLA;
                                                   THE WIND IS MY LOVER)

Viveca Lindfors (Singoalla), Michel Auclair (Erland), Louis Seignier (Priest), Henri Nassiet (Gypsy Chief), Marie-Helene Daste (Elfrid), Johnny Chambot (Sorgban), Christopher Kent, Romney Brent, Lauritz Falk, Rauzena, Edvin Adolphson, Naima Wifstrand, Marta Dorff, Vibeke Falk.

While on a hunt medieval nobleman Auclair happens upon Lindfors, a fiery gypsy. He falls for her, and countless love scenes and the usual ending follow. The film is hampered by hokey plot twists, caricature acting by the principals, and heavy-handed direction. GYPSY FURY was filmed in three versions: Swedish, French and English. Lindfors had the lead in each of them.

p, Lorens Marmstedt, Alf Jorgensen; d, Christian-Jaque; w, Christian-Jaque, Pierre Very (based on the novel The Wind Is My Lover by Viktor Rydberg); [Engish version: d&w, Romney Brent]; ph, Christian Matras; m, Hugo Alfven, Charles Wildman; ed, Jean Desagneaux; md, Desormier; art d, Bjorn Thulin; set d, Robert Gys.

Drama   **(PR:C MPAA:NR)**

GYPSY GIRL**½   (1966, Brit.) 102m RANK/CD c
                                               (GB: SKY WEST AND CROOKED)

Hayley Mills (Brydie White), Ian McShane (Roibin), Laurence Naismith (Edwin Dacres), Geoffrey Bayldon (Philip Moss), Annette Crosbie (Mrs. White), Norman Bird (Cheeseman), Hamilton Dyce (Bill Slim), Pauline Jameson (Mrs. Moss), Rachel Thomas (Grandma), Judith Furse (Mrs. Rigby), Anne Blake (Mrs. Potts), June Ellis (Mrs. Cheeseman), Jack Bligh (Fred Strong), Len Jones (Dusty Miller), Roland Starling (Harry), Jessica Hobbs (Cathy), Gerald Lawson (Jabal Jones), Jacqueline Pearce (Cammellia), Alan Lake (Camlo), Hira Talfrey (Blossom), Cyril Chamberlain (Hubberd), Susan Chatham (Suzie), Robin Crewe (Chalky), Lola Payne (Biddie), Nicola Street (Nell), Stephen Salt (Jakey), Joyce Mayhead (Emm).

Mills is a young girl who is severely traumatized after seeing a playmate killed by the shotgun left lying around by Naismith, the dead boy's father. It is now seven years later and Mills is a 17-year-old outcast. Her mother is an alcoholic and ignores her, while Naismith blames her for his son's death. Nearly everyone in the village ignores her and she finds comfort and happiness only beside her friend's grave. One day she sees a youngster burying a dead mole and decides to do likewise with two of her recently deceased pets. The local children see her and follow suit. Later she meets McShane, a boy traveling through town in a gypsy caravan. Her mother disapproves of the boy and on a drunken binge strikes her daughter. Mills runs to the graveyard where she encounters Naismith, who is drunk and threatens her with his gun. She runs once more, falls into a river, and is saved by McShane. He takes her to the gypsy camp for safety. However, her disappearance prompts a stroke that kills her mother. Soon Mills is found by some villagers, who want her put in an orphanage. But the local vicar defies the villagers by letting Mills ride off with the caravan. Interesting in many ways, with an ominous feel to it.

p, Jack Hanbury; d, John Mills; w, Mary Hayley Bell, John Prebble (based on a story by Bell); ph, Arthur Ibbetson (Eastmancolor); m, Malcolm Arnold; ed, Gordon Hales; md, Arnold; art d, Carmen Dillon; set d, Patrick McLoughlin; cos, Yvonne Caffin; make-up, Harry Frampton.

Drama   **(PR:C MPAA:NR)**

GYPSY MELODY**½   (1936, Brit.) 73m British Artistic/Wardour bw

Lupe Velez (Mila), Alfred Rode (Capt. Eric Danilo), Jerry Verno (Mme. Beatrice), Fred Duprez (Herbert P. Melon), Wyn Weaver (Grand Duke), Margaret Yarde (Grand Duchess), Raymond Lovell (Court Chamberlain), Monti de Lyle (Marco), Louis Darnley (Hotel Manager), Hector Abbass (Biergarten Manager), G. de Joncourt (Dr. Ipstein).

The fiery Velez is a gypsy who ventures to London with her love Rode, a musician who is also the captain of the guard. He has escaped from prison after being jailed for dueling with a high official. After organizing a gypsy band in a little cafe, the rogue is spotted by an American promoter who promises to make him a big musical star. Duprez gives a fine comic performance. The main reason this film was made was to capitalize on the fame of Rode, a bandleader who had appeared in Shubert revues on Broadway. A well-told story.

p, Leon Hepner, Emil E. Reinert; d, Edmond T. Greville; w, Irving LeRoy, Dan Weilden (based on the French film JUANITA, story by Alfred Rode); ph, Claude Friese-Greene; m/l, Bruce Siever.

Drama   **(PR:A MPAA:NR)**

GYPSY MOTHS, THE***   (1969) 106m MGM c

Burt Lancaster (Mike Rettig), Deborah Kerr (Elizabeth Brandon), Gene Hackman (Joe Browdy), Scott Wilson (Malcolm Webson), William Windom (V. John Brandon), Bonnie Bedelia (Annie Burke), Sheree North (Waitress), Carl Reindel (Pilot), Ford Rainey (Stand Owner), John Napier (Dick Donford).

A thoughtful and moody film from director Frankenheimer featuring Lancaster, Hackman, and Wilson as professional skydivers who arrive in a small town in Kansas to perform their dangerous trade for the locals. The youngest member of the troupe, Wilson, has an aunt and uncle (Kerr and Windom) who live in town and the daredevils are invited to stay with them. Kerr, the victim of a cold, loveless marriage, is drawn to the fatalistic Lancaster and he to her. That night the skydivers go out on the town for a bout of drinking. Hackman takes up with stripper North, while the young Wilson wanders off with pretty college girl Bedelia. Tired and disgusted with their evening routine, Lancaster returns to the house where Kerr is waiting for him. The passion the couple feel for each other surfaces and they make love in the living room under the watchful eye of Windom who makes no move to interrupt. The next morning Lancaster begs Kerr to leave town with him, but, afraid to abandon her secure existence, she refuses. Soon it is time for the air show and the crowd pays $2.50 each for the chance to watch men plummet through the sky and, perhaps, to their death. Lancaster is slated to perform the extremely risky "Cape Jump." Calmly he prepares for the jump and with a strangely serene look on his face leaps out of the plane. Hackman and Wilson immediately sense something is wrong as Lancaster falls lower and lower without making a move toward the ripcord on his parachute. With a near-smile on his face Lancaster plummets headlong into the ground, and to his death. On the ground, Wilson inspects Lancaster's chute and finds nothing wrong with it. Hackman arranges for Lancaster's funeral, but because they have little money the two remaining daredevils must put on another show to pay for the burial. Wilson decides the show will only last as long as one jump, and he will perform the same stunt that killed Lancaster. The next day a huge crowd gathers in anticipation of another death. Wilson successfully performs the jump and then tells Hackman he's retiring. Hackman understands and decides to head out to Hollywood and see if he can land a job as a stuntman. The friends part, leaving Kerr and Windom to their pathetic marriage and the small Kansas town far behind. Frankenheimer's film is an existential drama filled with characters constantly challenging the purposeless-ness of their lives. Lancaster and Hackman are older and more pessimistic than the younger Wilson and they seem to accept the hand life has dealt them. To rebel against their existence, these men willingly face death on a daily basis, living for the brief moment of exhilaration when they control their own destinies by deciding whether or not to pull the ripcord. When Lancaster dies, Wilson finally realizes the life he has pursued is filled with self-loathing and self-imposed loneliness, so he decides to subject himself to one last brush with death before abandoning his nihilistic existence and live. THE GYPSY MOTHS is a fascinating psychological melodrama punctuated with some visually amazing skydiving sequences, which gave those audience members bored or frustrated with the characters something to sit up and pay attention to.

p, Hal Landers, Bobby Roberts; d, John Frankenheimer; w, William Hanley (based on the novel by James Drought); ph, Philip Lathrop (Metrocolor); m, Elmer Bernstein; ed, Henry Berman; art d, George W. Davis, Gary Odell; set d, Henry Grace, Jack Mills; cos, Bill Thomas; makeup, William Tuttle.

Drama/Adventure   **(PR:O MPAA:R)**

GYPSY WILDCAT**   (1944) 77m UNIV c

Maria Montez, (Carla), Jon Hall (Michael), Leo Carrillo (Anube), Gale Sondergaard (Rhoda), Peter Coe (Tonio), Nigel Bruce (High Sheriff), Douglas Dumbrille (Baron Tovar), Curt Bois (Valdi), Harry Cording (Captain Marver), Billy Newell, Howard Mitchell, John Elliott, Clyde Fillmore (Reformers), Ralph Dunn, Harry Strang, Edgar Dearing, Eddie Dunn, Charles McAvoy (Cops), Walter Clinton (Minstrel Man), John Pearson (Minstrel Dancer), William Desmond (Barfly), Joe Kirk (Sign Man), Harry Semels (Drunk), Larry Steers (Van Damm, the Theater Patron Who Gets Garter), Brooks Benedict (Tammany Hall Representative), Howard Hickman, Snub Pollard, Charles K. French (Lambs Club Members), Jac George (Violinist).

This poor attempt at swashbuckling action revolves around a group of gypsies wrongly imprisoned for the murder of a count. Dumbrille portrays the wicked baron who actually commits the crime and then pins it on the gypsies. Hall is the baron's messenger who knows the gypsies are innocent and sets out to prove it. He notices gypsy dancer Montez wearing a pendant with the dead man's coat of arms, and discovers she is really the count's long lost sister and rightful heir to the throne. When Hall accuses Dumbrille of the crime, he is thrown into the dungeon with the gypsies. But they join forces, overpower the guards, and escape. Montez, who had already promised to marry the baron in return for the freedom of her people, is then abducted by Dumbrille. But Hall returns to save the day, killing the baron and winning the heart of Montez. Montez and Hall had been successful in films set in the tropics and Near East, but Universal's attempt to place them in a European setting didn't work out.

p, George Waggner; d, Roy William Neill; w, James Hogan, Gene Lewis, James M. Cain (based on a story by Hogan, Ralph Stock); ph, George Robinson, W. Howard Greene (Technicolor); m, Edward Ward; ed, Russell Schoengarth; md, Ward; art d, John B. Goodman, Martin Obzina; spec eff, John Fulton; ch, Lester Horton; m/l, "Gypsy Song Of Freedom" Ward, Waggner.

Adventure   **(PR:A MPAA:NR)**